2007

Our Sunday Visitor's

CATHOLIC ALMANAC

Matthew Bunson, D.Min.
General Editor

OUR SUNDAY VISITOR'S CATHOLIC ALMANAC
2007 EDITION

STAFF

Greg Erlandson
Editor-in-Chief

Dr. Matthew E. Bunson, D.Min.
General Editor

Murray W. Hubley
Production Editor

Cathy Dee
Web Editor

Contributors to the 2006 Edition
Dr. John Borelli
Barbara Fraze
Dr. Eugene Fisher
Brother Jeffrey Gros, F.S.C.
Rev. Ronald Roberson, C.S.P.
Rev. C. Eugene Morris
Russell Shaw
Rev. Francis Tiso

Jane Cavolina, Editorial Consultant
Carrie Bannister, Assistant

ACKNOWLEDGMENTS: Catholic News Service, for coverage of news and documentary texts; *The Documents of Vatican II*, ed. W. M. Abbott (Herder and Herder, America Press: New York 1966), for quotations of Council documents; *Annuario Pontificio* (2006); *Statistical Yearbook of the Church* (2006); *L'Osservatore Romano* (English editions); *The Official Catholic Directory* — Excerpts of statistical data and other material, reprinted with permission of *The Official Catholic Directory*, © 2006 by Reed Reference Publishing, a division of Reed Publishing (USA) Inc. Trademark used under license from Reed Publishing (Nederland) B.V.; *The Papal Encyclicals*, 5 vols., ed. C. Carlen (Pierian Press, Ann Arbor, MI); *Newsletter of the U.S. Bishops' Committee on the Liturgy*, Kathleen Bullock, Associate for Operations, The United States Catholic Mission Assoc. (3029 Fourth St. N.E., Washington, DC 20017), for U.S. overseas-mission compilations and statistics; *Catholic Press Directory* (2006); *Annuaire Directiore*, Canadian Conference of Catholic Bishops, for latest available Canadian Catholic statistics; Rev. Thomas J. Reese, S.J., for names of dioceses for which U.S. bishops were ordained; other sources as credited in particular entries. Special thanks are owed to His Excellency Most Reverend John P. Foley, President of the Pontifical Council for Social Communications; Bruce Egnew, Associate General Secretary, USCCB; Secretariat for Pro-Life Activities, USCCB; Rev. Mr. William Kokesch, Dir.-Communications Service, Canadian Conference of Catholic Bishops; Msgr. Michael Servinsky; and Rev. Jorge Francisco Vázquez Moreno, adjunct secretary of the *Conferencia del Episcopado Mexicano*.

2007 Catholic Almanac

Copyright © 2006 Our Sunday Visitor Publishing Division, Our Sunday Visitor, Inc.
Published annually by Our Sunday Visitor Publishing Division, Our Sunday Visitor, Inc., 200 Noll Plaza, Huntington, IN 46750
ISBN: 978-1-59276-230-9
ID: T281
Library of Congress Catalog Card No. 73-641001
International Standard Serial Number (ISSN) 0069-1208

Editorial Note: Comments, corrections, and suggestions should be addressed to the editorial offices of the *Catholic Almanac*: 200 Noll Plaza, Huntington, IN 46750; (260) 356-8400; E-mail: almanac@osv.com.

Visit us online at www.CatholicAlmanac.com, and at the Our Sunday Visitor web site at www.OSV.com.

CONTENTS

Year In Review September 2005 to August 2006

SEPTEMBER 2005

VATICAN

Pope Urges Condemnation — On Sept. 1, Pope Benedict XVI appealed to Iraqi Christians and Muslims to condemn jointly the violence in their country, after Wednesday's tragic stampede that left more than 900 Shiite pilgrims dead. The Holy Father sent a telegram to Abp. Fernando Filoni, apostolic nuncio in Iraq, urging "all believers in the one God to unite to deplore all sorts of violence and to cooperate in the return to concord of the afflicted Iraqi land." Pope Benedict XVI entrusted to "divine mercy all those who perished in such a tragic way and assured them of his prayers so that at last an atmosphere of reconciliation and mutual trust will be established in that country."

Dei Verbum Anniversary — More than 400 participants, including some 100 bishops, are scheduled to meet in Rome for an international Bible congress on the theme "Sacred Scripture in the Life of the Church." The congress will mark the 40th anniversary of the Second Vatican Council's constitution on divine revelation, Dei Verbum. Card. Walter Kasper, president of the Pontifical Council for Promoting Christian Unity, explained that the constitution "led to a growing awareness of the significance of Holy Scripture, promoted the biblical pastoral ministry, and gave new impetus to the scientific study of the Bible." The event will be held in the Aurelia Convention Center, Rome, and will be attended also by biblical scholars.

Papal Agenda — The coming activities proposed for Pope Benedict XVI were announced on Sept. 2 by the Vatican and include apostolic trips. The Holy Father has received an invitation to visit the Holy Land both from the Israeli government and the Palestinian National Authority. Patriarch Bartholomew I invited Benedict XVI to visit Istanbul, Turkey, on the occasion of the feast of St. Andrew, Nov. 30. In regard to other trips, the Holy Father engaged in "a period of reflection" during the summer, according to the Irish prime minister. The World Meeting of the Family, convoked by Pope John Paul II and confirmed by Pope Benedict XVI, was scheduled for Valencia, Spain, in July 2006. The Holy Father expressed his intention to attend. He might travel to Latin America in 2007 for the general conference of the Latin American bishops' council. The location of the meeting has not yet been announced. Pope Benedict XVI is also preparing the Synod of Bishops, which will close the Year of the Eucharist. Some 250 bishops from around the world were expected to attend the Oct. 2-23 event at the Vatican. He has made some modifications to the synodal methodology to allow for greater participation and has also convoked a second synod of African bishops. It is also possible that the Holy Father will convoke a consistory to elevate new cardinals, as the number of cardinals is now below the norm of 120. He will have to replace some heads of Holy See dicasteries, as well, as several have reached the normal retirement age of 75. Vatican sources have also confirmed that during his summer break, the Holy Father worked on a book that he had begun while he was still a cardinal. He will preside over his first canonization on Oct. 23 in St. Peter's Square.

Mexican Martyrs — A group of 13 martyrs who died during the 1920s religious persecution in Mexico will be beatified Nov. 20 in Guadalajara, it was announced on Sept. 2 by the archbishop of the diocese. Card. Juan Sandoval Íñiguez also stated that Card. José Saraiva Martins, prefect of the Congregation for Sainthood Causes, will preside over the Mass. In July 2004, in the presence of Pope John Paul II, the Holy See published the decrees of martyrdom of the 13. Among the future blessed are Fr. José Trinidad Rangel Montaño, of the Diocese of Leon; Spanish-born Fr. Andrés Solá Molist, Claretian missionary; and layman and celibate Leonardo Pérez Larios. All three were killed "out of hatred for the faith" on Apr. 25, 1927, in Rancho de San Joaquín.

Also to be beatified are Fr. Darío Acosta Zurita of the Diocese of Veracruz, killed in Veracruz on July 25, 1931, three months after his ordination, and Anacleto González Flores, layman, lawyer and father of a family, and seven other martyred companions. All were killed in 1927-1928. Like Anacleto, three of them were members of Catholic Action of Mexican Youth. Also scheduled for beatification is José Luis Sánchez del Río, a 14-year-old killed on Feb. 10, 1928. These martyrs endured their torments during a particularly hostile era in which the Mexican government unleashed restrictions and punishments on the faithful.

Peace for Iraq — In an address to the people of Iraq on Sept. 4, Pope Benedict XVI urged reconciliation in Iraq, in the wake of one of the country's bloodiest weeks. The Holy Father announced: "May the Almighty touch the hearts of all, so that at last a climate of reconciliation and reciprocal trust will be established in that tormented country," the Holy Father said, after reciting the midday Angelus with pilgrims gathered at the papal summer residence, Castel Gandolfo, south of Rome.

Mexican Prelates — On Sept. 4, Pope Benedict XVI received Mexican bishops making their ad limina, or five-yearly visit to the Holy See. These bishops described their meeting as an introduction to the shepherd of the universal Church, who demonstrated genuine knowledge of and concern about their dioceses. "It was a wonderful meeting, because of the affability, closeness and simplicity of the Holy Father," said Bp. Braulio Rafael León Villegas of Ciudad Guzman. Bp. Gonzalo Galván Castillo of Autlan said that the Holy Father's affability is very much part of his nature. He described Benedict XVI as "a Pope who opens his heart to us, who is kind, delicate and attentive." Bp. Javier Navarro Rodríguez, of San Juan de los Lagos, said that Pope Benedict XVI commended the ministry of priests and vocations to the Blessed Virgin Mary. Bp. Navarro also said that the Holy Father is concerned about the preservation of family values and the sanctity of marriage. "The Holy Father greatly encouraged us to continue working with families," he added. "He knows that the seed of vocations is there, and nothing concerns him as much as religious vocations."

Royal Invitation — King Juan Carlos of Spain invited Pope Benedict XVI to visit his country, during the first audience the Pope granted him and his wife, Queen Sofia, it was announced on Sept. 5. The private audience took place in the papal summer residence of Castel Gandolfo, south of Rome. "I have invited the Pope to come to Spain, on the occasion of the World Meeting of Families in Valencia," said King Juan Carlos to journalists gathered in the small town. The Spanish monarchs were in the Apostolic Palace of Castel Gandolfo for about a half-hour. King Juan Carlos said that it "was an honor to have seen" the Holy Father, as he "is very kind, very open and very sharp." Sofia was dressed in white, a privilege of Spanish queens.

Cable-Car Disaster — On Sept. 6, Pope Benedict XVI expressed his grief over a cable-car accident in the Alps in the ski resort town of Soelden, near Innsbruck, Austria, that killed nine people, including six children. In a telegram sent in the Pope's name to Bp. Manfred Scheuer of Innsbruck, Vatican Secretary of State Card. Angelo Sodano expressed the Holy Father's spiritual closeness to the victims' relatives, especially those of the children who died. Pope Benedict XVI, who is praying for the dead and for the speedy recovery of the injured, sent his apostolic blessing.

Bethlehem Mayor — On Sept. 7, Pope Benedict XVI greeted Victor Batarseh, the mayor of Bethlehem, at the end of a general audience in St. Peter's Square. Batarseh, 70, of Christian origin, replaced Hanna Nasser. Although allied to Hamas, the Islamic militant group, Batarseh announced after his election that he would preserve "the Christian identity of Jesus' city." On Sunday, the Italian newspaper *Il Corriere della Sera* published statements by Fr. Pierbattista Pizzaballa, Franciscan Custodian of the Holy Land, in which he lamented the traumas Palestinian Christians endure at the hands of "Muslim extremists in these regions."

World Leaders — On Sept. 7, Pope Benedict XVI had a private meeting with Irish President Mary McAleese after the general audience in St. Peter's Square. The meeting took place in one of the Vatican offices. President McAleese was accompanied by her husband and her entourage. The Vatican did not reveal details of their conversation.

Also, the Holy Father privately greeted Prime Minister Jacques Sylla of Madagascar, who was accompanied by a small entourage, in a Vatican office.

Balkan Leader — Pope Benedict XVI received in audience Svetozar Marovic, the president of Serbia and Montenegro, who arrived with his wife and entourage at Castel Gandolfo on Sept. 9. The Vatican gave no details of today's meeting. Before leaving for Rome, Marovic met Thursday with the head of the Serbian Orthodox Church, Patriarch Pavle, and the spiritual leader of Serbia's Catholic minority, Abp. Stanislav Hocevar Beograd. President Marovic tried to organize a visit of Pope John Paul II to the Balkans, but that visit never took place reportedly because of the opposition of the Serbian Orthodox Patriarch Pavle. Some 65 percent of Serbia and Montenegro's 10 million inhabitants are Orthodox. Muslims constitute 19 percent of the population, and Catholics constitute five percent.

Sign of the Cross — At Castel Gandolfo, on Sept. 11, Pope Benedict XVI announced that the sign of the cross should not be a routine gesture, but the pronouncement of a visible "yes" to the love of Christ who died for us. Before praying the midday Angelus with several thousand pilgrims gathered today at the papal summer residence, the Holy Father reflected on the significance of the liturgical feast of the Exaltation of the Holy Cross, celebrated Sept. 14. He clarified "the profound and indissoluble bond that unites the Eucharistic celebration with the mystery of the cross."

Armenian Eparchy — On Sept. 12, Pope Benedict XVI raised the Armenian Catholic Exarchate of the United States and Canada to an eparchy. (Dioceses in Eastern Catholic churches are called eparchies.) Bp. Manuel Batakian, head of the exarchate since 2001, was appointed the first eparch. There are some 25,000 Armenian Catholics in the United States and about 10,000 in Canada. The Church has two parishes in Canada, in Toronto and Montreal, and seven in the United States — two in California and one each in Michigan, Pennsylvania, New Jersey, New York and Massachusetts. The new eparchy, which has its headquarters in New York, will be called Our Lady of Nareg in New York for Armenian Catholics. The village of Nareg in Armenia was the site of a famous monastery and home to one of Armenia's most noted theologians and saints, St. Gregory of Nareg.

Prayer Chain — It was announced on Sept. 13 that the postulator of John Paul II's cause of beatification has launched a "prayer chain" for the needs and suffering of the world through the intercession of the deceased pope. Prayer intentions may be sent daily, through the cause's official Web page, www.JohnPaulIIBeatification.org. To join the chain, one must register on the web page. Msgr. Slawomir Oder, the postulator, explains in a message that he is "convinced that in the world there are numerous people who want to form part of this chain of prayer, so that at all times of the day and night, in all corners of the earth, prayers are raised to God to support brothers in the faith and their needs." The web page has a section in which participants can recount their personal experiences of meetings with John Paul II.

Rabbis' Invitation — On Sept. 15, it was reported that the two chief rabbis of Israel, Shlomo Moshe Amar and Yona Metzger, have invited Pope Benedict XVI to visit Jerusalem. The invitation came during a private audience today at the papal summer residence of Castel Gandolfo. The Holy Father warmly welcomed the rabbis, and described their visit as a "further step toward the process of building deeper religious relations between Christians and Jews." The rabbis supported the invitation made previously in a letter from Prime Minister Ariel Sharon to the Bishop of Rome to visit the Holy Land.

Malawi President — On Sept. 22, Pope Benedict XVI received President Bingu Wa Mutharika of Malawi at the papal summer residence. Mutharika was accompanied by his wife and entourage at the audience with the Holy Father. About 80 percent of the southern African nation is Christian.

Hans Küng Visit — On Sept. 26, Pope Benedict XVI had a private conversation with dissident Swiss theologian Hans Küng on subjects the latter has been researching in recent times. The private meeting took place Saturday in the papal summer residence, and was described by a Vatican official as "unfolding in a friendly atmosphere." Küng, 77, was suspended in 1979 from teaching theology in Catholic faculties by the Congregation for the Doctrine of the Faith, before Card. Joseph Ratzinger became its prefect.

The theologians have known each other since 1957, when Joseph Ratzinger published a review of Küng's doctoral thesis.

Beatifications — On Sept. 29, the Vatican formally announced that Pope Benedict XVI would not preside at beatifications but only over canonization ceremonies. The Holy Father instituted this ruling at the beginning of his pontificate. Beatifications, "which are still a pontifical act, will be celebrated by a representative of the Holy Father, who normally will be the prefect of the Congregation for Saints' Causes," said Card. Jose Saraiva Martins. "The rite of beatification will take place in the diocese which promoted the cause of the new blessed or in another suitable location," including the Vatican, with the approval of the Secretariat of State.

General Audiences

Aug. 10 Address on Psalm 130(131) (Sept. 5)
Commentary on Canticle in Colossians 1 (Sept. 7)
Commentary on Psalm 131(132):1-10 (Sept. 14)
Commentary on Psalm 131(132)11-18 (Sept. 21)
Commentary on Psalm 134(135) (Sept. 28)

NATIONAL

Hurricane's Toll — On Sept. 1, it was announced that bishops in Louisiana and Mississippi expect that their dioceses will face tragic devastation from Hurricane Katrina. The U.S. bishops' conference advised bishops in Louisiana, Mississippi, Tennessee, Kentucky and Alabama on Tuesday that reports indicate massive destruction and also informed them that conference president Bp. William Skylstad had called for a national collection and prayers in churches for those afflicted by the disastrous hurricane.

The bishops reporting to the USCCB indicated how much their particular dioceses had been affected by the terrible storm. Abp. Alfred C. Hughes of New Orleans, who had to evacuate to Baton Rouge during the hurricane, reported from a parish there. He said that, assisted by Louisiana State Police, he has been going to visit shelters in the Baton Rouge area, which has taken in 100,000 stricken people from the New Orleans area. Bp. Thomas Rodi of Biloxi, Mississippi, stated that 20 percent of the diocese's churches and a third of its schools had been destroyed.

Catechism Compendium — It was announced on Sept 1 that an English-language version of the new *Compendium of the Catechism of the Catholic Church*, a 200-page synthesis of the 1992 Catechism, will be published this fall. A commission headed by then Card. Joseph Ratzinger, now Benedict XVI, prepared the work, which contains almost 600 questions and brief answers about the essential contents of the faith. Like the 1992 Catechism, the Compendium is structured in four parts. While the text does contain some direct quotes from the Catechism used in a sidebar fashion, the questions and answers themselves are original text.

Jesuit Anniversary — The 200th anniversary of the restoration of the Jesuits in the United States was reported on Sept. 1. Jesuits from the Maryland province celebrated the anniversary during a Mass at St. Ignatius Church in Port Tobacco, the church where three priests professed their vows as Jesuits on Aug. 18, 1805. "We come together today not only to honor the restoration of the society in the United States and the profession of vows of our forebears, but also to re-found the Society today," said Jesuit Fr. Timothy Brown, provincial of the Jesuits' Maryland province and principal celebrant and homilist at the Mass.

Marriage Encounter — It was reported on Sept. 1 that Worldwide Marriage Encounter, which offers weekend programs to help couples renew their marriages, is now also offering its program in weekday sessions to accommodate couples who find it difficult to get away for a weekend. Called Worldwide Marriage Encounter Experience, the sessions provide couples an opportunity to benefit from talks by married couples and clergy in a nonresidential setting. The new programs will provide opportunities for more couples to experience the revitalizing effects of the Marriage Encounter apostolate.

New Orleans Archdiocese — The Archdiocese of New Orleans launched a satellite office in Baton Rouge to make key decisions about restoring social services and rebuilding schools and churches that were devastated by Hurricane Katrina, it was reported on Sept. 1. Abp. Alfred C. Hughes met with archdiocesan officials to organize both immediate short-term responses and a long-term response. Abp. Hughes stated: "Obviously, we face extreme devastation, the likes of which we have not felt in this country apart from the Civil War." The archbishop said he plans to meet daily with a small group of key archdiocesan personnel over the next months to update information and to promote the welfare of the people.

National Prayer Day — President George W. Bush declared Sept. 16 a "national day of prayer and remembrance" for the victims of Hurricane Katrina, it was reported on Sept. 8. "A vast coastline of towns and communities has been decimated. Many lives have been lost, and hundreds of thousands of our fellow Americans are suffering great hardship," President Bush said in a proclamation announcing the prayer day. "To honor the memory of those who lost their lives, to provide comfort and strength to the families of the victims, and to help ease the burden of the survivors, I call upon all Americans to pray to almighty God and to perform acts of service," he said. "Our nation is united in compassion for the victims, and in resolve to overcome the tremendous loss that has come to America. We will strive together in this effort, and we will prevail through perseverance and prayer."

Hurricane Task Force — On Sept. 15 it was announced that the U.S. bishops will appoint a task force to address the aftermath of Hurricane Katrina. Abp. Joseph Fiorenza of Galveston-Houston has been named the chairman. Bp. William Skylstad, president of the episcopal conference, reported on the task force, declaring: "For us as Catholic bishops, Katrina is more than a terrible natural disaster and human catastrophe. It is a test of our faith, our hope and our love." He added: "Faith in Jesus Christ insists life conquers death, resurrection follows crucifixion, recovery comes from suffering and hope overcomes despair. This is a time to live out the Gospel, turn our love into care for others, move our words into action, and practice the solidarity we proclaim."

Dioceses Respond — Catholic dioceses in the nation have already responded to the needs of Katrina victims, raising money to help victims, sending volunteers to the hurricane-ravaged area, and taking in storm evacuees at shelters, schools and homes. In Washington, the U.S. bishops' Office for Priestly Life and Ministry announced that it was coordinating offers by priests around the United States who volunteered to help address pastoral needs in areas hit by the hurricane. Some dioceses across the country are offering liturgical items such as chalices and processional crosses to replace those destroyed by Hurricane Katrina. In the Diocese of Spokane, Bp. William S. Skylstad announced that he planned to assign one priest to work for four to six weeks in the stricken regions. The Archdiocese of Dubuque announced that two priests will be made available to work outside the archdiocese, and the Archdiocese of Milwaukee said it could assign up to 12 priests. The Diocese of Orange already has been in contact with the Archdiocese of Galveston-Houston, offering to assist in aiding the Vietnamese community there.

Intelligent Design — On Sept. 16, Bp. Donald W. Wuerl of Pittsburgh stated that the theory of intelligent design is a rational explanation of the origin of life based on observation and not a "religious tenet superimposed on the facts." Intelligent design holds that science can prove that an unnamed intelligent force is responsible for creation. Bp. Wuerl's views, printed in the diocesan paper, came at a time when a federal court in Pennsylvania was preparing to examine whether teaching intelligent design is introducing a religious creed into a local public school system. The article did not take a stand on the issue of teaching intelligent design as science in public schools. The column appeared shortly before the scheduled start of a federal court civil trial in Harrisburg challenging the policy of the Dover public school board requiring that ninth-grade students hear about intelligent design along with evolution. Plaintiffs complain that the teaching of intelligent design is an introduction of religion in the public schools, a constitutional violation. Dover is a small town in the Harrisburg Diocese.

INTERNATIONAL

Irish Seminary — It was reported on Sept. 1 that for the first time in many years, numbers are up at Ireland's national seminary, St. Patrick's College in Maynooth. Nineteen first-year seminarians began their studies for the priesthood, bringing the total number of seminarians at St. Patrick's at the start of the new academic year to 75, compared with 63 last year. Church officials say the small increase is good news for a country that has seen vocations shrink from thousands to dozens. Seminaries have been closed in the past, but the rise in vocations offers hope for the faith in Ireland.

German Bishops — On Sept. 2 it was announced that German bishops are urging Catholics in their country to vote this month with a conviction to defend life and the family, and solidarity with the poor. A pastoral letter issued by the episcopal conference highlighted the "present-day challenges that are important for the future" of Germany.

The letter is to be read in all Catholic parishes, and describes the need for Germany to create "a society that likes children." The state must "protect the dignity of the person regardless of whether that person is strong or weak, healthy or sick, born or unborn," or "an invalid," said the bishops.

Help Wanted — On Sept. 2 it was reported that the British government put out a "want ad" in some major newspapers looking for "a high caliber individual" to fill a vacancy at its Embassy to the Vatican. The vacancy was not in some low-ranked level of the embassy but was for the ambassadorial position itself, marking the first time Great Britain sought an ambassador among the general public rather than from its diplomatic corps. The Vatican did not respond to this extraordinary method of recruiting a responsible representative of Great Britain to the Holy See. It was also announced that the embassy and the ambassador's residence were going to relocate into the same compound as the British Embassy to Italy. The relocation, a cost-saving move, was criticized in British newspapers.

Priest and Seminarian Arrested — On Sept. 5 it was reported that a Catholic priest and seminarian were arrested in the Chinese province of Hebei for their work among the people and evangelization. Police vans were mobilized for this arrest by the Security Bureau of Qing Yuan Xian province, Hebei.

Fr. Pang Yongxing, 32, and the recently graduated seminarian Ma Yongjiang were arrested. Both are members of the "underground" Church, which recognizes the authority of the Pope but is not officially approved by the Communist government of Beijing and normally harassed or imprisoned by the authorities. Fr. Pang had been arrested previously, in 2001. On that occasion he was sent to a labor camp for three years.

Islamic Arson — A Muslim mob was reported on Sept. 6 to have set fire to Christian buildings in the Christian village of Taybeh, West Bank, in order to avenge a Muslim family's honor. More than a dozen homes and businesses were burned by the mob from a neighboring Muslim village, who blamed a Greek Orthodox man for getting a Muslim woman pregnant. The woman, who had worked for the Greek Orthodox man and his family, had been killed earlier by her brothers for dishonoring the family, after she confessed her activities.

Vicar General's Murder — On Sept. 6, the Catholic bishops' conference of India condemned the "brutal killing" of the vicar general of the Diocese of Tezpur and appealed to the authorities to investigate the crime. The episcopate said Catholics in the northeastern state of Assam were shocked at last Friday night's killing of 65-year-old Msgr. Mathew Nellickal, who began his work as vicar general two months ago. Previously, he had been a parish priest, headmaster, and rector of Muktidata, a minor seminary of the diocese. His body was discovered Saturday morning in a storeroom next to his bedroom in the bishop's residence. He had deep gashes on his temple and face.

Pakistani Court — On Sept. 7 it was reported that the Pakistani Supreme Court struck down a law that called for a religious supervisor, the "*mohtasib*," to monitor citizens' adherence to Islamic values. Catholic Abp. Lawrence Saldanha of Lahore praised the action, saying: "We heartily welcome the Supreme Court's decision to annul the Hasba Bill, a law against the freedom of the people." He added: "This type of law goes against human nature and should always be condemned," the archbishop added.

Ethiopian Web Site — The Catholic Church in Ethiopia has launched its own Web site, www.ecs.org.et, it was reported on Sept. 9. The site was officially launched by Abp. Berhaneyesus Souraphiel of Addis Ababa, in the Ethiopian Catholic Secretariat. It includes profiles of Ethiopia's 10 dioceses and summaries of the 169 country's parishes. Almost half of the country's 73 million inhabitants are Muslim. Orthodox Christians represent about 35 percent of the population. Catholics account for less than one percent, though the Church has an active network of institutions.

Ethiopian University — It was reported on Sept. 28 that Church and government representatives have signed an agreement for the establishment of an international Catholic university in Addis Ababa, the Ethiopian capital, according to the Ethiopian Catholic Secretariat. The agreement was signed by Genet Zewde, the Ethiopian minister of education, Abp. Berhaneyesus Souraphiel of Addis Ababa, Foreign Minister Seyoum Mesfin, and the apostolic nuncio in the country, Abp. Ramiro Moliner Inglés. The archbishop of Addis Ababa emphasized that the university will belong to all Ethiopians. He also recalled the cooperation between the Church and the government's Ministry of Education. According to the prelate, the Church has five colleges in Ethiopia. Almost half of Ethiopia's 73 million inhabitants are Muslim. Orthodox Christians represent about 35 percent of the population. The Catholic Church has been present in Ethiopia since the beginning of Christianity.

OCTOBER 2005

VATICAN

Synod of Bishops — On Oct. 2, Pope Benedict XVI was joined by 250 participants of the Synod of Bishops on the Eucharist in St. Peter's Basilica for the Inaugural Mass, a ceremony that included multicultural displays. During the Mass, the Holy Father said the Eucharist was the true way to build justice in society and to create peace in human hearts. He encouraged the synod not only to pronounce "beautiful things" about the Eucharist, but also to experience its power and communicate it to the world. Pope Benedict XVI, in his sermon, explained the Eucharist as the place where "God comes to meet us . . . God is waiting for us. He wants to be loved by us. Shouldn't this appeal touch our hearts?" he said.

Paulines Praised — On Oct. 4, Pope Benedict XVI praised the St. Paul Society and encouraged members to proclaim the Gospel through the media, in line with their charism. In an audience in the Clementine Hall of the Apostolic Palace, the Holy Father expressed his appreciation for the services provided by St. Paul's Society, headed by its superior general, Fr. Silvio Sassi, inviting them to follow the example and teachings of their founder, Blessed Giacomo Alberione. "Your vanguard apostolate, in a broad and complex field, offers many opportunities and entails, at the same time, not a few problems," the Holy Father declared. "It is an activity that calls for preparation, specific competencies and constant updating, if you are to respond effectively to the challenges of the present-day world, perceived increasingly as 'global village,' " he added. The Pauline family, which was founded by Blessed Giacomo Alberione and has 18,000 members, is made up of a men's religious congregation — St. Paul's Society — and four congregations of women — the Daughters of St. Paul, Disciples of the Divine Master, Sisters of Jesus Good Shepherd, and Sisters of Mary Queen of Apostles. In addition, it has four affiliated institutes — Jesus Priest, St. Gabriel Archangel, Mary Most Holy Annunciation and Holy Family — and the Association of Pauline Cooperators.

Cardinal von Galen — On Oct. 9, Pope Benedict XVI presented newly beatified Card. Clemens August von Galen, a German bishop who defied Nazism, as a model for believers. Card. von Galen was beatified in St. Peter's Basilica, and in his address at the midday Angelus, the Holy Father explained that the new blessed left a profound message for the world: "Faith cannot be reduced to a private sentiment, which, perhaps, is hidden when it becomes something uncomfortable; rather, it implies coherence and witness in the public realm in favor of man, justice and truth." At the end of the celebration, thousands of German pilgrims watched Pope Benedict XVI go to the Altar of the Confession to venerate the cardinal's relics and to pay homage to his "heroic courage to defend the rights of God, of the Church and of man, which the National Socialist regime was violating in a grave and systematic way, in the name of an aberrant neo-pagan ideology." Card. von Galen risked his own liberty and life in protesting against the horrors of the Third Reich during Hitler's period of dominance.

Asian Quake — Pope Benedict XVI, on Oct. 9, assured his prayers for the victims and their loved ones and made an appeal for solidarity among all nations to aid those affected by the deadly earthquake that hit Pakistan, India and Afghanistan. "It was with deep sadness that I learned of yesterday's earthquake in South Asia, which caused such great damage and loss of life in Pakistan, India and Afghanistan," the Pope said in English after reciting the Angelus today with crowds gathered in St. Peter's Square. The Holy Father commended "to God's loving mercy all those who have died" and expressed his "deepest sympathy to the many thousands who are injured or bereaved."

Hans Urs von Balthasar — In a message for the centenary of his birth, Pope Benedict XVI praised his friend, Swiss theologian Hans Urs von Balthasar (1905-1988), on Oct. 10. "Theology, as and how he conceived it, had to be combined with spirituality; only in this way, in fact, could it be profound and effective," said the Holy Father in his message addressed to the international congress entitled "Love Alone Is Credible." The congress was organized at the Lateran University in Rome to pay tribute to von Balthasar, one of the most important Catholic intellectuals and writers of the 20th century. He wrote more than 100 books and hundreds of articles. In 1972 von Balthasar formed *Communio*, an international Catholic review, with Jean Danielou, Henri de Lubac and Joseph Ratzinger (Benedict XVI). From 1961-1987 he produced his most important work, a trilogy published in 15 volumes: *The Glory of the Lord, Theo-Drama*, and *Theo-Logic*. After many years of illness and exhaustion, Balthasar died on June 26, 1988, one day before he was to be made a cardinal by Pope John Paul II.

God's Revolution — On Oct. 11, Pope Benedict XVI's first book as pope went on sale in Italy. The Vatican joined with other publishers in an 18-nation release of the work, a collection of his speeches made during August events in Cologne, Germany. The book also outlines the projects that he has designated for his pontificate. The English edition, published by Ignatius Press, was expected to be ready for release in the United States and Canada by the end of October. The 129-page volume "deals with the questions of Christian faith and the destiny of humanity, of the state of Israel, Islam, the legacy and the future of the church and society," it was explained in a press release. The work is a collection of talks that Pope Benedict XVI gave during the Aug. 18-21 events in Cologne, including World Youth Day and meetings with representatives of Germany's Jewish and Muslim communities. The texts include the complete remarks of the Holy Father.

"Positive Secularity" — Pope Benedict XVI, in a letter to the president of the Italian Senate on Oct. 17, called for a "positive secularity" in the world, which would omit hostility between religion and the state. The Holy Father said that such "positive secularity" guarantees "to each citizen the right to live his own religious faith with genuine freedom, including in the public realm." Pope Benedict XVI addressed his letter to Marcello Pera, who is also honorary president of the Magna Carta Foundation. He added: "It will be necessary to work for a cultural and spiritual renewal of Italy and the European continent so that secularity is not interpreted as hostility against religion."

His remarks accentuate the current apprehension of religious leaders about the obvious antipathy to religion demonstrated in EU documents and programs.

Papal Audience — It was reported on Oct. 17 that Pope Benedict XVI met with the bishops of Ethiopia and Eritrea at the Ethiopian College. The gathering marked the 75th anniversary of the inauguration of the Ethiopian College, a seminary located inside the Vatican walls. Ethiopian candidates for the priesthood moved into the Vatican in 1919 at the invitation of Pope Benedict XV. The current building, with its Eastern-rite chapel and iconostasis, opened in 1930 under Pope Pius XI. "The location of the college here inside Vatican City is an eloquent sign of the close bonds of communion linking the church in your countries with the see of Rome," the Holy Father announced.

Pope Popular — It was reported on Oct. 17 that Pope Benedict XVI's public appearances are drawing huge crowds of pilgrims to the Vatican — even more than those of his beloved predecessor, Pope John Paul II. According to Vatican statistics, more than 1 million people have attended the pope's weekly general audience or his Sunday blessing since his election in Apr. That is more than twice the number of pilgrims who attended the same events in 2004 that were presided over by an infirm Pope John Paul. Observers cited a "new pope" effect, saying people want a personal look at Pope Benedict. For some pilgrims and visitors, the Vatican offers the opportunity for closeness to two pontiffs, the living Pope Benedict XVI and the tomb of Pope John Paul II.

The "Lily of Quito" — On Oct. 20, Pope Benedict XVI blessed a statue of St. Mariana de Jesús Paredes y Flores, called the "Lily of Quito." St. Mariana is Ecuador's first canonized woman saint. The statue, placed in a niche on the outside of St. Peter's Basilica, was made by Ecuadorian sculptor Mario Tapia. St. Mariana de Jesús Paredes y Flores was born in Quito and orphaned from childhood. She consecrated her virginity to God and, unable to enter a convent, began to live an ascetic life at home, dedicated to prayer, until she entered the Franciscan Third Order and performed charitable works as a Tertiary. She died in 1645, beatified in 1853, and canonized in 1950.

Canonizations Held — On Oct. 23, Pope Benedict XVI canonized the first saints of his pontificate. The ceremony also signaled the close of the Year of the Eucharist and the Synod of Bishops and celebrated World Mission Sunday. Those prelates attending the synod and tens of thousands of visitors and pilgrims participated in the canonization ceremonies. During the ceremonies, the Holy Father announced in Italian, Polish, Ukrainian and Spanish: "The saint is he who is so fascinated by the beauty of God and by his perfect truth to be progressively transformed by it." Those canonized at the ceremony were: Gaetano Catanoso (1879-1963) of Italy, priest of the Archdiocese of Reggio Calabria-Bova, and founder of the Congregation of the Daughters of St. Veronica, Missionaries of the Holy Face; Felice de Nicosia (1715-1787) of Italy, a Capuchin religious; Alberto Hurtado Cruchaga (1901-1952) of Chile, a Jesuit evangelizer; Jozef Bilczewski (1860-1923) of Poland, archbishop of Lviv of the Latins; and Zygmunt Gorazdowski (1845-1920) of Poland, diocesan priest

of the Lviv Archdiocese. The Holy Father commented: "In different situations and with different charisms, they loved the Lord with all their heart and the neighbor as themselves to thus become 'an example to all believers.'"

U.S. Bishops' Audience — On Oct. 24, Pope Benedict XVI met with top officials of the U.S. Conference of Catholic Bishops. Bp. William S. Skylstad of Spokane, Washington, USCCB president, Card. Francis E. George of Chicago, conference vice president, and Msgr. William P. Fay, USCCB general secretary, were at the meeting. The conference leaders also met with Vatican officials. The meetings, introduced by Pope John Paul II during his pontificate, allow the conference leadership to present issues for Vatican consideration, to learn Vatican views on issues facing the U.S. bishops, and to listen to Vatican concerns and requests.

Martyr Beatification — It was announced on Oct. 27 that María de los Ángeles Ginard Martí, a martyr who died amid the religious persecution unleashed by the Spanish Civil War, was to be beatified. Card. José Saraiva Martins, prefect of the Congregation for Sainthood Causes, will preside at the beatification Mass in St. Peter's Basilica. At Pope Benedict XVI's request, the cardinal will read the apostolic letter with which the Pope will inscribe among the blessed of the Church the Servant of God, "virgin and martyr," and seven other martyrs of the Spanish Civil War. Killed by a group of republican militiamen who previously had destroyed the congregation's convent in the Dehesa de la Villa, in the Spanish capital, her remains were found in a common grave. They now rest in the cemetery of the congregation's present convent in Madrid. The diocesan phase of her process of canonization opened in Madrid in Apr. 1987. On Apr. 19, 2004, Pope John Paul II approved the publication of the decree on martyrdom for her beatification.

"Heroic Witnesses" — Seven Spanish priests and a nun martyred in 1936 were beatified in St. Peter's Basilica during a Mass celebrated by Portuguese Card. Jose Saraiva Martins, prefect of the Congregation for Saints' Causes on Oct. 29. Pope Benedict XVI called the newly beatified priests and nun "heroic witnesses" of faith and prayed before the relics of the eight Spaniards after the ceremonies, praising their faithfulness unto death. The seven priests from the Diocese of Urgell were Frs. Jose Tapies Sirvant, Pascual Araguas, Silestre Arnau Pascuet, Jose Boher Foix, Francisco Castells Brenuy, Pedro Martret Moles and Jose Perot Juanmarti. Sr. Maria de los Angeles Ginard Marti was a member of a religious order dedicated to eucharistic adoration.

General Audiences

Commentary on Second Part of Psalm 134(135) (Oct. 5)

Commentary on Psalm 121(122) (Oct. 12)
Commentary on Psalm 129(130) (Oct. 19)
Comment on Philippians 2:6-11 (Oct. 26)

NATIONAL

New Orleans — It was reported on Oct. 3 that the Archdiocese of New Orleans announced an anticipated deficit of $40 million by the end of the year, the result of Hurricane Katrina. Drastically reduced parish collections and the loss of income from federal grants that are used to sustain many Catholic Charities programs will affect the operating costs of the archdiocese. Millions more could be needed to repair or rebuild facilities damaged by the hurricane, depending on whether insurers assess the damage as flood-related or wind-related. Church cleansings and repairs will add other expenses in the coming months. (See also News in Depth.)

Archbishop Online — It was reported on Oct. 3 that Abp. Alfred C. Hughes has invited the Catholics of New Orleans to access the archdiocesan Web site, www.archno.org, to receive information. The web site asks all present and former faithful of all the parishes of the Archdiocese of New Orleans to fill out a form in order to carry out a census of the local Church. Catholics gathered at St. Louis Cathedral for the first Sunday Mass celebrated in the landmark since the hurricane.

Family Affair — St. Michael the Archangel Church in La Bajada, New Mexico, was reported on Oct. 3 as the site of a special Mass. The church has been cared for over the decades by one family. The ancestors of Eloy Montoya, Sr., were colonial settlers from Spain, homesteading 400 years ago in an untamed wilderness territory. They helped build San Miguel Church in La Bajada in the 1600s, and for generation after generation family members have been caretakers of the church. A special Mass was concelebrated by Franciscan Frs. Cecil J. Kleber and Wayne Gibbeaut to honor the saint and the devotion of the family.

Orange Diocese — It was reported on Oct. 3 that less than a year after the Diocese of Orange settled clergy sex-abuse lawsuits with 90 plaintiffs for $100 million, the diocese has repaid 70 percent of its half of the debt without affecting the funds of Catholic schools and parishes. Liability insurers paid the other half of the settlement total. The diocese retired $35 million in debt this summer with funds drawn from the diocesan general fund and reductions in the diocesan investment portfolio. Diocesan officials said the remaining $15 million is expected to be repaid by next June.

EWTN's 25th Year — A family-style gathering at the Colorado Convention Center in Denver marked the beginning of a yearlong celebration of EWTN's 25th year, it was reported on Oct. 3. Mother Angelica started her evangelization work by establishing the Eternal Word Television Network, and her labors were praised by Deacon Bill Steltemeier, chairman of the Alabama-based network. The Denver conference, one of several being held in cities around the country, featured prayers, opportunities for eucharistic adoration, and seminars with some of the network's hosts.

Blue Army Shrine — It was reported on Oct. 3 that more than 3,000 people united in prayer at the National Blue Army Shrine of the Immaculate Heart of Mary in the New Jersey town of Washington on Oct. 2, Respect Life Sunday and Worldwide Fatima Sanctity of Life Day. Thousands more at other U.S. sites and in Switzerland, India, Mexico, Puerto Rico, Australia and other countries observed the day of prayer for respect toward life. At the shrine, worshippers prayed the rosary, celebrated Mass and witnessed the dedication of the shrine's new statue, Mary Mother of the Life Within. An identical statue was dedicated the same day at the Marian shrine in Fatima, Portugal.

Ambassador to Vatican — On Oct. 7, the United States Senate confirmed Francis Rooney, a businessman with ties in Oklahoma and Florida, as the U.S. Ambassador to the Vatican. Rooney is chief executive officer of Rooney Holdings, which includes insurance and construction companies. He also has been active in charitable and community organizations including the Knights of Malta, the American Red Cross and the United Way. The post of Vatican ambassador has been vacant since Jim Nicholson became secretary of Veterans Affairs in Jan.

Vocational Campaign — It was reported on Oct. 14 that the U.S. Bishops' Committee on Vocations is launching a new campaign to attract men to the priesthood. The committee made public the "Priestly Life and Vocation Summit: Fishers of Men" program. It is designed to encourage priests to reflect on the many positive reasons they pursued their vocations and to share those reasons, on the diocesan level, with other men with an invitation to the priesthood. "At the basis of the Fishers of Men program is the conviction that there is a close connection between priests regenerating their appreciation of their own priestly vocation and the creation of an environment in which men are actively invited to respond to God's call to the priesthood," said Bp. Blase Cupich of Rapid City, the chairman of the bishops' Committee on Vocations. "Its purpose is twofold," he said, "to renew in us priests and bishops an awareness of how treasured the gift of priesthood is and what it means in each of our lives; and to encourage us all, inspired by this renewal, to urge other men to consider the vocation which we have received as a gift." A resource kit prepared by the Vocations Secretariat, which includes everything a diocese needs to implement the program, has been sent to all 195 dioceses in the United States. The kit includes a trailer for a "Fishers of Men" video, produced by Grassroots Film, which can be incorporated into the summit program.

Black Catholics — On Oct. 14, African Americans from around the country gathered for a Mass at Holy Comforter-St. Cyprian Parish in Washington, D.C., as part of the Millions More events. Aux. Bp. Martin D. Holley celebrated the Mass, which was attended by some 220 people, including a large delegation from the Archdiocese of Detroit, who made a special pilgrimage to Washington to attend the Millions More Movement gathering that weekend. The multiracial and multicultural group from Detroit included Precious Blood Fr. Clarence Williams, director of black Catholic ministry in the archdiocese, and Alejandro Torres-Antonio, coordinator of urban youth ministry, along with representatives of eight parishes in the Detroit area.

"The Mary Page" — It was announced on Oct. 18 that "The Mary Page" on the internet attracted 1 million visitors in 10 years. The Web site at www.udayton.edu/mary offers information about the Blessed Mother through the vast collection of the Marian Library/International Marian Research Institute at the Marianist-run University of Dayton. "People from Finland to Brazil to Korea e-mail questions," said Marianist Fr. Johann Roten, director of the institute. "Interest in Mary today is increasing, compared to the late 1960s and early 1970s when not much was heard or said about Mary." Fr. Roten and a staff of eight scholars routinely answer questions about apparitions and popular images of Mary.

Relics of Mexican Martyrs — It was reported on

Oct. 24 that the relics of the Mexican martyrs have begun a 10-month pilgrimage through Mexico and the United States. The six martyrs were priests and members of the Knights of Columbus who were killed for the faith in Mexico in the 1920s and 1930s. They were among the 25 Mexican martyrs canonized by Pope John Paul II in 2000. The relics will travel to more than 50 cities and towns in Mexico before coming to the United States in mid-Mar. The pilgrimage will conclude in Aug. in Orlando, Florida, during the Knights' annual convention. "This pilgrimage coincides with the (fraternal) order's centennial in Mexico and recalls the ultimate sacrifice made by these Knights for their faith," said Carl A. Anderson, supreme knight. The relics are those of Sts. Luis Batis Sainz, Jose Maria Robles Hurtado, Mateo Correa Megallanes, Miguel de la Mora de la Mora, Rodrigo Aguilar Aleman, and Pedro de Jesus Maldonado Lucero.

INTERNATIONAL

Suicide Bombings — On Oct. 2, religious leaders in Bali condemned the Oct. 1 suicide bombings that killed at least 26 people and injured more than 120 others on the island, which is famed as a center of tourism and Indonesian Hindu culture. "We must strongly condemn the bombing that has hit Bali again. The action of the bombers was uncivilized, and regrettably it has happened in Indonesia, a civilized nation," Bp. Benyamin Bria of Denpasar announced.

Rwanda Pilgrim-Site — On Oct. 6 it was announced that Aid to the Church in Need is supporting a film project on Kibeho, Rwanda, Africa's only pilgrim-site where Church-approved Marian apparitions have taken place. "It may be compared with Guadalupe, Lourdes and Fatima," said Christine du Coudray, head of Aid to the Church in Need's Africa department, upon her return from a visit to Rwanda. "Our Lady of Sorrows appeared here from 1981 to 1983 and the visionaries, now in their 40s, are still alive," she explained.

Same-Sex Marriage — On Oct. 7, it was announced that the Plenary Assembly of the Council of European Bishops' Conferences (CCEE) warned that same-sex marriage, now legal in Spain, is a boomerang that will rebound on future generations. Pope Benedict XVI had sent a message to the assembly through Card. Angelo Sodano, Vatican secretary of state, exhorting the presidents of Europe's 34 episcopal conferences "not to be afraid of facing up to the present-day pastoral challenges, being in a position to listen to the concrete conditions of man's personal and social life, ready to proclaim the Gospel of hope to all." The bishops declared that the Spanish legislation is not progressive or modern but the result of "the culture characterized by secularism" that has thrown into disorder even countries with deep Catholic and missionary traditions.

Euthanasia Law — Catholic and Anglican leaders in Britain are united in condemning a new attempt to legalize euthanasia for the terminally ill, it was reported on Oct 10. Card. Cormac Murphy-O'Connor of Westminster and Abp. Rowan Williams of Canterbury, leader of the worldwide Anglican Communion, spoke out against euthanasia on the eve of a debate in the House of Lords. Card. Cormac Murphy-O'Connor said he hoped politicians would argue against the bill: "If this law is passed, it seems to me that the duty of the law to act on behalf of the people would be broken, because the law is there to protect life, and a right to die can become a duty to die."

Cuba Needs Church — On Oct. 16, Fidel Castro was reported as wanting help from the Church to fight the "plague of abortion" in his country. Card. Tarcisio Bertone, archbishop of Genoa, who visited Castro in Cuba, made the report. "The spread of abortion, as Fidel Castro emphasized, is among the causes of the country's demographic crisis," the cardinal said. "And it is also a consequence of the plague of sexual tourism. The Church can make its contribution in the area of abortion and low birthrates in a country where openness is total," Card. Bertone said. He also said that Castro broached the subject of a papal visit.

Miracle for Newman Cause — On Oct. 17, Catholic officials announced that the cure of a Boston deacon could be the miracle that paves the way for the beatification of a 19th-century English cardinal. The unnamed deacon from Boston is said to have made a complete recovery from a crippling spinal condition after praying to Card. John Henry Newman, whose cause was opened in 1958 in Birmingham, England. Fr. Paul Chavasse, the postulator of Card. Newman's cause, made the claims at Rome's English College.

Tijuana Priest Shot — On Oct. 24, Fr. Luis Velasquez Romero of Tijuana was shot and killed by unknown assailants. Fr. Romero was handcuffed in his car and shot six times with a pistol. Police were "provisionally" treating the murder as related to organized crime. However, police were unaware of Fr. Velasquez having received any threats. He was famous in Tijuana for his outspoken sermons that often criticized local politicians and criminal activities in the area. Fr. Velasquez was slain in Plaza Zapato, a bar and nightclub complex.

Quake Refugees — Families from the epicenter of the recent earthquake in Pakistan and India were reported on Oct. 17 to have found refuge in a Catholic church in the town of Abbottabad, Pakistan. The families were originally part of a small Christian community in the town of Muzaffarabad. Fr. Inayat-Patras, pastor of St. Peter Canisius Parish, arranged for their refuge. "This small community is the 'poorest of the poor'… they are in very low paid jobs, working for the municipality of Muzaffarabad, as cleaners and road sweepers," he said. "When the earthquake struck, I was very concerned for them and I heard news of their plight through a catechist member of the church." Fr. Inayat-Patras asked Caritas Pakistan to visit the families and to listen to their requests so that they could receive aid. Their homes in Muzaffarabad have been destroyed by the earthquake. The families, an estimated 80 individuals including children, are occupying the parish's school classrooms and outbuildings. Caritas Pakistan has been delivering tents to families that have been left without adequate shelter as winter approaches. Fr. Inayat-Patras said that the Church is working to respond to the needs of the entire affected community, regardless of creed.

NOVEMBER 2005

VATICAN

Death Without Fear — On Nov. 1, Pope Benedict XVI urged Christians to "think of the mystery of death without fear." He counseled also: "New life, received through baptism, is not subject to the corruption and power of death." The Holy Father stated that Christians can cultivate a fearless acceptance of death, recognizing that it is a necessary juncture leading from one's journey on earth to one's final destination in heaven. He gave his counsel on death while observing the feast of All Saints and anticipating the Nov. 2 feast of All Souls, days of offering prayers for departed loved ones. "Death is a gateway from the earthly pilgrimage to the home of heaven, where the Father welcomes all his children of every nation, race, people and tongue," he said.

U.N. Future Challenges — On Nov. 4, the Vatican's permanent observer to the United Nations, Abp. Celestino Migliore, addressed the U.N. General Assembly's Commission on Sustainable Development. "My delegation believes that development plans and poverty reduction strategies must be integrated into environmental sustainability," he announced. "Without environmental stewardship, development will have no sound foundation, and without development, there will be no means of investment, rendering environmental protection impossible," continued the apostolic nuncio. Abp. Migliore reminded the General Assembly that "human beings are at the center of concerns for sustainable development," referring to the 1992 Rio de Janeiro Declaration on the Environment and Development.

Vatican Radio — On Nov. 5, Pope Benedict XVI named Jesuit Fr. Federico Lombardi, the program director of Vatican Radio for the past 15 years, as the radio's new general director. Fr. Lombardi, 63, was born in northern Italy near Turin. After he became a Jesuit priest in 1972, he worked for the influential Jesuit-run magazine, *La Civiltà Cattolica*, and served as superior of the Italian province of the Jesuits. He was named program director of Vatican Radio in 1991 and general director of the Vatican television station, CTV, in 2001.

"Mamma Rosa" Beatified — On Nov. 6, Eurosia Fabris, an Italian woman who raised 11 children, was beatified and held up as a model of sainthood for all mothers. Known simply as "Mamma Rosa" throughout her adult life, she was beatified in the northern Italian city of Vicenza. Card. Jose Maria Saraiva Martins, head of the Congregation for Saints' Causes, read the documentation of beatification from Pope Benedict XVI at the ceremony. "Mamma Rosa" was born in 1866, and as a young woman was known for her deep sense of faith. She taught religious education and sewing to children in her parish. At 18, she began caring for two babies whose mother had died. After marrying, she had nine children of her own; three of them became priests. After a life dedicated to homemaking and charity work, she died in 1932. Abp. Cesare Nosiglia of Vicenza, celebrated the Mass, announced: "Mamma Rosa should be seen as a model of holiness for everyone."

Ecumenical Advances — On Nov. 7, Pope Benedict XVI welcomed Rev. Mark Hanson, bishop president of the Lutheran World Federation (LWF), and his delegation to the Vatican. The Holy Father discussed the progress made in the ecumenical dialogue between Catholics and Lutherans, and mentioned the forthcoming joint document on "The Apostolicity of the Church." The private audience, which was also attended by the LWF general secretary, the Rev. Dr. Ishmael Noko, was the first meeting of an LWF delegation with Pope Benedict XVI. "The International Lutheran Roman-Catholic Commission on Unity will soon complete its fourth phase of dialogue and publish its findings in a document on the Apostolicity of the Church," the Holy Father announced during the meeting. "We are all aware that our fraternal dialogue is challenged not just by the need to verify the reception of these shared formulations of doctrine in our respective communions, but even more so today by a general climate of uncertainty regarding Christian truths and ethical principles which formerly went unquestioned," he added.

Vatican Photogallery — It was reported on Nov. 7 that photographs capturing some of the key moments of Benedict XVI's pontificate are now posted on the Vatican's web page. The new Photogallery, which presents pictures of the Holy Father, can be accessed in the "News" section of the main page. One photo shows him imparting an apostolic blessing during his first appearance as Pontiff on Apr. 19. The photographic gallery will be updated as events take place. Photographs from the Holy See's Web page and many others are available on printed paper as well as in digital format, through the photographic service of *L'Osservatore Romano*. To request photos presented on the web page, the code must be indicated in a message sent to photo@ossrom.va.

Assisi Shrine — On Nov. 9, Pope Benedict XVI issued a *motu proprio* concerning the Basilica of St. Francis and St. Mary of the Angels in Assisi, Italy. The document concerns measures to be taken to meet modern needs. Pastoral activities conducted there by the Conventual Friars will be under the jurisdiction of the Bishop of Assisi-Nocera Umbra-Gualdo Tadino, and a cardinal will serve as the papal legate to the basilicas. Any ministerial activities conducted within these shrines must be approved by the local bishop, and the cardinal will have the task of assuring the close bonds of communion between the shrines dedicated to the memory of St. Francis of Assisi. The Holy Father urged the "Sons of St. Francis" to accept this *motu proprio* with "generous willingness."

President of Iran — On Nov. 10, President Jalal Talabani of Iraq was received by Pope Benedict XVI and told the Holy Father that the Iraqi Constitution guarantees the rights and freedom of the nation's Christians. The meeting between the two men took place in an atmosphere that those present described as "very cordial," and started with a private audience of about 20 minutes followed by a public session, during which gifts were exchanged and the members of the delegations were introduced. The Vatican did not publish any official statement on the issues addressed in the audience. After his meeting with the Pope, Talabani met with Vatican Secretary of State Card. Angelo Sodano and spoke to Vatican officials.

Jordan Attacks — On Nov. 10, Pope Benedict XVI sent a message of sympathy to King Abdullah II of Jordan concerning terrorist attacks on three hotels in

Amman, which left at least 56 dead and 115 wounded. In a telegram sent by Card. Angelo Sodano, Vatican secretary of state, on behalf of Pope Benedict XVI, the Holy Father expressed his "heartfelt condolences to Your Majesty, to the families of the deceased and to the entire nation."

English Mass Translation — On Nov. 10, Pope Benedict XVI wrote to members of the Vox Clara Committee, a Vatican-appointed commission of English-speaking bishops, and expressed his hopes that a new English translation of the Mass prayers would be completed soon. The committee was established in 2001 to help the Congregation for Divine Worship and the Sacraments evaluate current English translations of liturgical texts submitted to the Vatican for approval. The International Commission on English in the Liturgy, a body established by English-speaking bishops' conferences, is translating the Latin text into English.

Memorial Mass — On Nov. 11, Pope Benedict XVI offered a memorial Mass for the cardinals and bishops who had died in the previous 12 months. This ceremony is an ongoing November tradition at the Vatican. After praying for the deceased, the Holy Father expressed his personal sense of unity with the "unique community" of the College of Cardinals. He entered that august body 28 years ago and served as dean of the College for more than two years. Pope Benedict XVI named the five cardinals for whom the Mass was celebrated: Cards. Juan Aramburu of Buenos Aires, Argentina; Jan Schotte, general secretary of the Synod of Bishops; Corrado Bafile, former prefect of the Congregation for Saints' Causes; Jaime Sin of Manila, Philippines; and Giuseppe Caprio, a former Vatican diplomat and head of Vatican finances. The bishops around the world who died during the previous year were not mentioned by name but memorialized in the ceremony.

Three Beatified — On Nov. 13, three beatifications were held in St. Peter's Basilica, as Charles de Foucauld (1858-1916), the apostle to the Tuaregs in the Sahara; Maria Pia Pastena (1881-1951), founder of the Sisters of the Holy Face; and Maria Crocifissa Curcio (1877-1957), founder of the Congregation of Carmelite Missionary Religious of St. Thérèse of the Child Jesus were raised to the altars of the Church. The three were beatified at a Mass presided over in the Holy Father's name by Card. José Saraiva Martins, prefect of the Congregation for Sainthood Causes. After the Mass, Pope Benedict XVI came down to the basilica to venerate their relics. He greeted the pilgrims who filled the basilica, among whom were Tuaregs from the desert, with their blue robes and white turbans. The beatification Mass was concelebrated by 65 cardinals and bishops, including Card. Polycarp Pengo, archbishop of Dar es Salaam, Tanzania; Abp. André Vingt-Trois of Paris; Abp. Vincent Landel of Rabat, Morocco; and Bishop Maroun Lahham of Tunis, Tunisia. Blessed Charles de Foucauld is venerated in the Saharan world.

Iraqi Kurdish Leader — Pope Benedict XVI received in audience the president of the Iraqi autonomous region of Kurdistan, Masoud Barzani, on Nov. 14. Since the Gulf War, the Kurds, who represent one-sixth of Iraq's 26 million inhabitants, have enjoyed considerable autonomy in three northern provinces. A series of meetings have been held in the Vatican concerning Iraq's new status. The Kurds are considered a vital element of the Iraqi future.

Austrian Chancellor — Austrian Chancellor Wolfgang Schüssel and his entourage were received in an audience on Nov. 14 by Pope Benedict XVI. The Vatican did not comment on the meeting. Austria will assume the presidency of the European Union on Jan. 1, when the United Kingdom's mandate ends.

Modern Culture — On Nov. 17 the Vatican reported that Pope Benedict XVI sent a message to the annual joint session of the major pontifical academies, including the academies for sciences, social sciences, life, fine arts and archaeology, in which he echoed a key theme of his pontificate. The Holy Father stated that modern culture tends to promote selfishness and self-centeredness, leaving people in a state of "prolonged adolescence." He explained that this aspect of modern culture must be understood because it is a way of life marked by subjectivism, extreme individualism, and relativism, which "pushes people to make themselves the ultimate measure" of things. In too many instances, the Holy Father advised, the individual ego has become "the only criterion to evaluate one's reality and one's choices."

"Pro Orantibus" Day — On Nov. 20, Pope Benedict XVI celebrated the eve of "Pro Orantibus" Day, which is dedicated to prayer for men and women religious of the contemplative life. The day is observed every year on the feast of the Presentation of Virgin Mary in the temple and draws the faithful to understand the sacrifices made by those in the cloister who spend their nights and days in atonement and prayer. The Holy Father appealed to Catholics everywhere to give both spiritual and material support to such individuals, who have been called to a unique vocation by God and have consecrated their lives to Him in prayer. He announced: "On behalf of the whole Church, I express gratitude to those who consecrate their lives to prayer in the cloister, offering an eloquent testimony of the primacy of God and of his kingdom." The message was delivered in St. Peter's Square, after the recitation of the midday Angelus by the Holy Father and countless pilgrims. He added: "I invite all to be close to them with our spiritual and material support."

Greetings for Beatifications — On Nov. 20, Pope Benedict XVI sent greetings to Mexico on the occasion of the beatification of 13 martyrs of the 1920s religious persecution in that country. Card. José Saraiva Martins, prefect of the Vatican Congregation for Sainthood Causes, presided over the beatification Mass today in the Jalisco Stadium of Guadalajara. "On this solemnity of Jesus Christ, King of the Universe, whom they invoked in the supreme moment of surrendering their lives," the Holy Father said, "they are for us a permanent example and stimulation to give a coherent testimony of our own faith in present-day society."

Italian Prime Minister — On Nov. 20, Pope Benedict XVI received Italian Prime Minister Silvio Berlusconi in private audience for the first time. After the audience with the Pope the Italian head of government then met with Card. Angelo Sodano, Vatican secretary of state. The Vatican described the meeting, saying: "In the course of the cordial conversations, there was an exchange of opinions on the bilateral problems between the state and Church in Italy, and the common will was reaffirmed of collaboration between the two parties, in keeping with the Lateran Pacts."

Vatican Document — On Nov. 22, the Italian text of a Vatican document was issued, concerning the priestly ordination of men who are active homosexuals, who have "deeply rooted" homosexual tendencies, or who support the "gay culture." The document was released by an Italian news agency a week before it was expected to be released by the Vatican. A Vatican spokesman did not confirm or deny the authenticity of the text;

church sources said the content was accurate. The document did not define what it meant by "deeply rooted" homosexual tendencies, but contrasted them with the "transitory problems" of adolescence. Such transitory tendencies must be clearly overcome at least three years before ordination as a deacon, it said. It did not explain what was meant by "overcome" and did not say that celibacy or chastity was the criteria for measuring suitability of such candidates for the priesthood.

Renewal in Advent — On Nov. 27, Pope Benedict XVI celebrated the first Sunday of Advent by addressing pilgrims in St. Peter's Square from his study window. The Holy Father appealed for the building of a "new earth," a theme of the Second Vatican Council. He described Advent as an "extremely evocative time from the religious point of view, as it is full of hope and spiritual expectation." He added, "Every time the Christian community prepares to remember the birth of the Redeemer, it feels a tremor of joy, which is communicated, in a certain measure, to the whole society. In Advent," the Holy Father continued, "the Christian population relives a double movement of the spirit: On one hand, it raises its gaze to the final goal of its pilgrimage in history, which is the glorious return of the Lord Jesus; on the other, recalling his birth in Bethlehem with emotion, it bends down before the crib." The Pope explained, "The hope of Christians is directed to the future, but always remains well rooted in the past. Christians must awaken in their hearts the hope of being able, with the help of God, to renew the world." He also commented on the pastoral constitution *Gaudium et Spes* on the Church in the modern world, which states that the expectation of heaven must not lead the faithful to neglect their commitment to transform the earth.

Papal Portrait — A mosaic of Pope Benedict XVI will be added to those of the popes in the Basilica of St. Paul's Outside the Walls, it was announced on Nov. 27. The Pro Music and Sacred Art Foundation presented the artwork to Benedict XVI at the end of the last general audience. The mosaic will face the altar. The artist, Ulisse Sartini, told Vatican Radio that when making the portrait he "concentrated on the face and the eyes, trying to capture his look, always smiling."

General Audiences

Commentary on Psalm 111(112) (Nov. 2)
Commentary on Psalm 135(136):1-9 (Nov. 9)
Commentary on Psalm 135(136):10-26 (Nov. 16)
Comment on Ephesians 1:3-10 (Nov. 23)
Commentary on Psalm 136(137) (Nov. 30)

NATIONAL

Carroll Poem — It was reported on Nov. 1 that a poem written by Charles Carroll of Carrolton, one of the Founding Fathers of the U.S., was discovered in an English Catholic high school. Charles Carroll, a cousin of America's first Catholic bishop, John Carroll, was a signer of the 1776 Declaration of Independence. He wrote the poem in Latin in 1754 when he was in his final year of high school in Saint-Omer, France. It was composed to greet an unnamed visiting dignitary to the Jesuit high school in Saint-Omer, and it bears Carroll's signature. The poem was found in the archives of Stonyhurst College in Clitheroe, England.

Catholic Youth Conference — The 2005 National Catholic Youth Conference was reported on Nov. 1 as attracting more than 16,500 Catholic teenagers to the Georgia Dome in Atlanta. The closing Mass of the conference was attended by more than 120 priests and deacons and 15 bishops, including the main celebrant, Abp. Wilton D. Gregory of Atlanta. During the conference, guest speakers, workshops and presentations to enrich their faith offered young Catholics the opportunity to experience Catholic community events with other enthusiastic worshippers.

Catholic Medical Association — The Catholic Medical Association's 74th annual educational conference in Portland was reported on Nov. 2 as attracting Catholic doctors from 43 states and Canada. The participants discussed the relationship of spirituality to physical health and medicine during the conference, whose theme was: "The Biological and Spiritual Development of the Child." One of the presentations discussed the development of the mind and brain in children, which begins in the womb. Other aspects of spiritual and intellectual growth were also presented.

Maryland Bishops — The Catholic bishops of Maryland issued a strongly worded pastoral letter on marriage that urged Catholics to fight against the ongoing assaults on families, it was reported on Nov. 5. The bishops called on the faithful throughout the state to stand up and defend traditional marriage against the media propaganda that belittles that traditional lifestyle. The pastoral letter opposed continuing attempts by state legislators to legally recognize same-sex relationships and endow them with the status, rights and privileges of marriage. Maryland's bishops announced that it is "clear that the preservation of marriage as the union of one man and one woman requires legislation that provides the strongest possible support for marriage and families."

Mariners Day — On Nov. 14, the U.S. Catholic bishops declared May 22 of each year as a Day of Remembrance and Prayer for Mariners and People of the Sea. Catholics across the nation were urged to participate in various commemorative and prayer services. The date coincides with the annual National Maritime Day celebrated by the U.S. government for the past 62 years. The Maritime Administration of the U.S. Department of Transportation had contacted the U.S. Conference of Catholic Bishops to encourage prayers for mariners on the annual federal observance. National Maritime Day was established in 1933 to honor "the courage, vision and achievements" of those who serve in the U.S. Merchant Marine, a service that distinguished itself during the two world wars and in other times of crisis.

Canonization Cause — On Nov. 15, the U.S. Catholic bishops agreed to support the canonization cause of a Spanish friar, Fray Bartolome de las Casas, who battled endlessly against the enslavement of New World native peoples by the Spanish conquistadors. The bishops were in session in the fall general meeting in Washington and studied the request to support the cause, which was issued to the American bishops by the bishops' conference of Spain and sought collegial action. The matter had been referred earlier to the U.S. bishops' Committee on Doctrine, which said that the bishops could act on the request if they chose. Fray Bartolome de las Casas, a Dominican, was the first bishop of Chiapas, Mexico, in the 16th century and an outspoken critic of the barbarities committed by Spanish conquerors against indigenous peoples. He continued leading the struggle for humane treatment despite threats and confrontations with the local conquistadors, until the Spanish monarchy removed him for political expediency.

INTERNATIONAL

Christians in India — It was reported on Nov. 1 that three nuns were dragged off a bus and beaten by Hindu activists in India's Rajasthan state. Two of their companions escaped, but the nuns taken from the bus were attacked with sticks. A small group of Hindus instituted the assault at the sight of the nuns in habit. Earlier, Bp. Joseph Pathalil of Udaipur was stopped in his vehicle by Hindu extremists while on his way to Catholic ceremonies in the village of Kushalgarh, some distance from Udaipur. A police unit, which was escorting the bishop because of local Hindu animosity, chased the protesters away during the attack, but the Hindu fanatics stoned the bishop's vehicle on his return journey to his diocese.

Chaldean Synod — A special Synod of the Chaldean Church was announced on Nov. 3, with Chaldean bishops from Iraq and other Chaldean dioceses in the world gathering in the Vatican. The future of Iraq's Christians in the newly established democracy and liturgical reform are expected to play prominent roles on the agenda of the Synod. Chaldean Abp. Louis Sako of Kirkuk said that urgent matters include setting up a "direct line" for the Church to make proposals "with courage" to the government; studying the problem of migration; and countering the "growing proselytism of evangelical churches in Iraq." Patriarch Emmanuel III Delly said the "new evangelicals" who arrived after the war seem more committed to collecting money from rich foreign donors rather than spreading the Gospel. Chaldeans in Iraq, inheriting a unique heritage of faith and service from ancient eras in world history, number 550,000; another 150,000 are in eight dioceses around the world. The changes in Iraq and the continued violence haved endangered the Chaldean Catholics, prompting migration from the homeland.

AsiaNews Celebrates — It was announced on Nov. 4 that AsiaNews, an Internet news agency reporting on the Church in China and surrounding countries, is celebrating its second anniversary. AsiaNews is an agency of the Pontifical Institute for Foreign Missions and has developed rapid growth in readership and firm collaboration with other news organizations. Fr. Bernardo Cervellera, director of AsiaNews, said in a statement that the organization's web site receives a monthly total of 250,000 visitors. He reported that the news agency works on a daily basis with many organizations, including Catholic World News, ZENIT, International Christian Network, and Christians Today.

Romanians Honor Pope — It was reported on Nov. 6 that the University of Cluj, in Romania, conferred an honorary doctorate on Benedict XVI "as sign of recognition of his theological and philosophical work." The Holy Father is revered across many parts of the world because of his scholarship and intellect, as well as his faith. Andrei Marga, president of the Academic Council of the Romanian university, cited as reasons for the degree the contribution of Card. Joseph Ratzinger's thought to affirming "the values of the Christian world and the Judeo-Christian tradition." The conferring of the doctorate was considered as early as 2004, well before Card. Ratzinger was elected Pope following the death of Pope John Paul II.

Holy Land's Oldest Church — The Israel Antiquities Authority was reported on Nov. 6 as announcing that it has uncovered what may be the Holy Land's oldest church. The ruins of the Christian house of worship were discovered during construction at a prison in Megiddo, Israel. The find signifies an "important contribution to the study of the development of early Christianity into a recognized religion," it was announced. Two well-preserved mosaic tile floors, containing three Greek inscriptions, were discovered during the exploratory excavation, which was carried out as required by Israeli law before any construction can be conducted. Rather than crosses, the mosaics are decorated with the figures of two fish, early symbols of Christianity. The authorities have dated the structure to the third or fourth century. There is some debate about the site being the oldest church in the Holy Land.

Missionaries' Deaths — On Nov. 17 it was reported that two Missionaries of the Poor were slain in Jamaica. Bro. Marco Laspuna, 22, and Bro. Suresh Barwa, 31, were shot to death in Kingston, the capital. Catholics are hated in some areas of the island.

Fr. Richard Ho Lung, a convert and founder of the congregation, stated: "Was it an accident? We do not know — the detectives are carefully attending to all options." Fr. Ho linked the killings to concerns over a breakdown of law and order in the West Indies nation. The funerals of the missionaries, however, brought countless mourners to the funerals, as the deaths of the two brothers symbolize the decaying Jamaican social scene.

Hanoi Ordinations — On Nov. 30 it was reported that thousands of Vietnamese attended the ceremonies conducted by Card. Crescenzio Sepe, the prefect of the Congregation for the Evangelization of Peoples, for the ordination of 57 new priests. Addressing the ordinands and the vast number of faithful in the Hanoi Cathedral complex, he announced: "You have received the Lord's call to be priests and the privilege of continuing with him his saving mission on this earth," Card. Sepe was on a pastoral visit to this country at the invitation of the Vietnamese bishops' conference. He expressed Pope Benedict XVI's greetings to the thousands of pilgrims who filled the cathedral; its square was not sufficient to accommodate the additional thousands of faithful who came from more distant localities to attend the historic event. Card. Sepe was also scheduled to visit the Archdioceses of Hue and Ho Chi Minh City, as well as Vietnamese Prime Minister Phan Van Kai and members of the Religious Affairs Commission. A high percentage of Vietnamese Catholics — 80 percent to 90 percent — practice their faith and are served by three archdioceses and 23 dioceses, and by 39 bishops, 2,212 diocesan priests and 521 religious priests. In addition, there are 1,778 men religious, 11,443 women religious, 1,395 lay missionaries and 50,605 catechists involved in the work of the local Church.

Mexican Martyrs Beatified — On Nov. 20, 13 Catholic martyrs of Mexico were beatified before tens of thousands in Guadalajara's Jalisco Stadium. "They are a permanent example, a stimulus for defending the faith and having faith in current society," Pope Benedict XVI said in a video message projected on screens in the stadium. Card. Jose Saraiva Martins, prefect of the Vatican Congregation for Saints' Causes, presided over the Mass for an estimated 55,000 of the faithful, who celebrated the occasion with hymns and prayers. Eight of the martyrs were from Jalisco state, and veneration of the martyrs is especially widespread there. Card. Juan Sandoval Iniguez of Guadalajara also was present at the Mass, which moved the martyrs a step closer to sainthood. Of the 13 martyrs, three were priests and 10 laymen, including a 14-year-old, José Sánchez del Río.

DECEMBER 2005

VATICAN

Pope Receives Ambassadors — On Dec. 1, Pope Benedict XVI received the credentials of 11 new ambassadors to the Holy See. He spoke of the need for world peace as he welcomed representatives from Tanzania, Nepal, Finland, Saint Lucia, El Salvador, Denmark, South Africa, Algeria, Eritrea, Togo and Andorra. "This morning, I would like to make a new appeal to all leaders of nations and all human beings of good will to unite to halt violence, which disfigures humanity and mortgages the growth of peoples and the hope of many populations," the Holy Father said, speaking in French.

St. Lucia Ambassador — Pope Benedict XVI, on Dec. 2, received the letters of credence of Gilbert Ramez Chagoury, the new ambassador of the Caribbean island nation of St. Lucia. The island has a population of 166,000, mostly Catholics. The Holy Father made reference to trade and the use of drugs in the region during the ceremony, announcing: "I encourage your government in the efforts it is making to address this scourge and assure you that they have the full support of the Catholic faithful."

"Patrimony of Humanity" — On Dec. 4, Pope Benedict XVI addressed participants of a conference of presidents of the episcopal commissions in Latin America for the family and for life. The Pontifical Council for the Family organized the conference. "Children have the right to be born and to grow within a family based on marriage," the Holy Father announced in Spanish, inviting the ecclesial community to "present in all its richness the extraordinary value of marriage that, as a natural institution, is the 'patrimony of humanity.' " The Pope continued, "Truly, children are the greatest wealth and most appreciated good of the family. That is why it is necessary to help all persons to become aware of the intrinsic evil of the crime of abortion that, in attempting against a human life in its beginning, is also an aggression against society itself."

Liturgical Music — On Dec. 5, Pope Benedict XVI sent a message to participants of a day of study organized today by the Vatican on the topic of "Sacred Music: A Liturgical and Pastoral Challenge." The Holy Father appealed for greater attention to sacred liturgical music, in the message addressed to the prefect of the Congregation for Divine Worship and the Sacraments, Card. Francis Arinze. "Echoing the call of my beloved predecessor, I would like to encourage those who cultivate sacred music to continue this journey," he said. Card. Arinze announced: "Sacred music must be in accord with the grandeur of the liturgical act that celebrates the mysteries of Christ; it must be characterized by a sense of prayer, beauty and dignity." He added: "In no way must it give way to shallowness, superficiality or theatricality."

Prince Albert — Pope Benedict XVI received Prince Albert II in audience on Dec. 5, only weeks after he was enthroned as the new sovereign of Monaco. The meeting took place in the papal library and included the prince's entourage of six people. Prince Albert also visited the tomb of Pope John Paul II in the Vatican Grottoes after meeting with Card. Angelo Sodano, Vatican secretary of state.

Culture of Disbelief — On Dec. 5 it was reported that Pope Benedict XVI condemned the modern culture of disbelief during his remarks at his Sunday blessing. The Holy Father noted that 40 years ago the Second Vatican council issued its Declaration on Religious Freedom, *Dignitatis Humanae*, which declared that religious freedom is a right that stems from the dignity of each person. He counseled that every person, as a spiritual being, has the right and duty to seek the truth and that religious freedom must be given to each individual and community.

Entry Permit — It was reported on Dec. 5 that Pope Benedict XVI received the Palestinian Prime Minister Mahmoud Abbas and discussed the Middle East peace process and the difficulties Palestinian Christians face in the territories. At the end of the private audience the Holy Father was presented with a special entry permit for the West Bank town of Bethlehem. The document was a gift from the people of Bethlehem and declared the Pope an honorary citizen of the town where Jesus was born.

Methodist Delegation — The Pontifical Council for Promoting Christian Unity announced on Dec. 7 that an executive-level delegation of the World Methodist Council was in Rome to meet with Pope Benedict XVI and Vatican officials. The Methodists were there "to renew the commitment and further relations with the Catholic Church" and "to continue with theological dialogue," the Pontifical Council statement declared. The delegation was headed by the Methodist Council's president, Bishop Sunday Mbang of the Methodist Church of Nigeria, and included the secretary-general, the Reverend George Freeman of the United States. The World Methodist Council embraces 76 Methodist communions; it meets in general assembly every five years.

Vatican Council II — On Dec. 8, Pope Benedict XVI celebrated the 40th anniversary of the close of Vatican Council II, describing the 1960s gathering as "the greatest ecclesial event of the 20th century." Pope John XXIII inaugurated the ecumenical council in the name of Mary on Oct. 11, 1962. And in the name of the Immaculate Virgin, Pope Paul VI closed it on Dec. 8, 1965, recalled Benedict XVI in his homily on the solemnity of the Immaculate Conception. After the Mass, when he prayed the midday Angelus with the thousands of people gathered in St. Peter's Square, the Holy Father declared: "Mary has watched with maternal care over the pontificates of my venerated predecessors, each of whom guided Peter's bark on the route of authentic conciliar renewal, working incessantly for the faithful interpretation and execution of the Second Vatican Council."

Olympic Flame — On Dec. 8, Swiss Guard, 24-year-old Anton Kappler carried the Olympic flame to St. Peter's Square for a papal blessing. Pope Benedict XVI declared: "I am happy to bless the Olympic flame that today will go from Rome along its route to Turin, site of the next Winter Olympic Games." The Holy Father, appearing at the window of his papal apartment, waved to the crowds in the square below. The flame, which arrived in Rome from Athens, Greece, was to be carried by 10,001 torchbearers across Italy and neighboring countries on a 7,020-mile, 64-day relay.

Christmas Commercialism — On Dec. 11, Pope Benedict XVI announced that the contemporary Christmas season is being spoiled by "commercial pollution" as he greeted pilgrims from his apartment window. Later he blessed the Nativity figurines of baby Jesus held up by thousands of Italian children in St. Peter's Square. The custom of putting up Nativity scenes in the home is a simple and effective way of bringing back the real meaning of Christmas, the Holy Father counseled, adding: "In modern society, this time of year unfortunately suffers a type of commercial 'pollution' that risks altering its authentic spirit, which is characterized by reflection, solemnity and a joy that is not external but personal."

Romanian Catholic Church — On Dec. 16, it was announced that Pope Benedict XVI has elevated the status of the Romanian Catholic Church to that of a major archbishopric. Raising the Eastern-rite church's status and granting it greater autonomy, the pope made the Romanian Catholic Church the fourth major archbishopric in the Catholic Church. A major archbishop has authority similar to that of the Eastern Catholic patriarchs and the key decisions of their churches, including the election of bishops in their home territories, is made by their synods of bishops.

Catholic Political Identity — Receiving a group of Polish bishops in audience on Dec. 18, Pope Benedict XVI stated that the Church must help Catholic politicians recognize their Christian identity and act accordingly. Citing Vatican Council II's constitution *Gaudium et Spes*, the Holy Father announced: "Those who are suited or can become suited should prepare themselves for the difficult, but at the same time, the very noble art of politics, and should seek to practice this art without regard for their own interests or for material advantages." He added: "It is a matter of helping them, in a particular manner, to be aware of their Christian identity and of the universal moral values that are based in the nature of man, in such a way that, in virtue of a correct conscience, they commit themselves to applying [the values] to civil law, to build a coexistence that respects man in all his dimensions."

Christmas Trees — On Dec. 18, Pope Benedict XVI met with the Austrian delegation that donated the fir tree for St. Peter's Square and declared that the Christmas tree is a sign of the "brilliant light" of Jesus. The 100-foot fir is from the forests of Eferding. "At Christmas the joyful announcement of the birth of the Redeemer resounds in all parts of the globe: The hoped-for Messiah was made man and dwelt among us," the Holy Father told his guests in the Hall of Blessings in the Apostolic Palace. "With his luminous presence," he continued, "Jesus has dissipated the shadows of error and sin and has brought to humanity the joy of divine blind love, of which the Christmas tree is a sign and a reminder." He added: "To believe in Christ means to let yourself be encompassed by the light of his truth that gives full meaning, value and sense to our existence, given that precisely to reveal to us the mystery of his Father and of his love, he also reveals man fully to himself and shows to him his lofty vocation."

Camauro Popular — On Dec. 21, Pope Benedict XVI wore a red hat with white trim at his general audience, reminding the delighted pilgrims of Father Christmas. The hat was the traditional camauro, a fur-trimmed cap that popes used to wear against the cold. The 15,000 pilgrims present in St. Peter's Square cheered and applauded enthusiastically on seeing the red-hatted Holy Father arrive in a white jeep. Camauros date originally to the 12th century but were seldom used until Pope John XXIII appeared in one.

Vatican II Misinterpretations — On Dec. 22, Pope Benedict XVI analyzed the problems following Vatican Council II, stating that a crisis developed, not owing to the conciliar documents, but rather to their interpretation. He made an analysis of the legacy left by the Vatican Council II when he met with his aides in the Roman Curia to express his Christmas greetings.

The Holy Father stated that the reception of the Council's messages took place according to two interpretations, which "confronted each other and have had disputes between them." He defined the first interpretation as the "hermeneutics of discontinuity and rupture between the pre-conciliar and post-conciliar Church." According to this interpretation, what is important about the Council is not its texts but the spirit of renewal brought to the Church. The other interpretation is "the hermeneutics of reform," which was proposed by the popes who opened and closed the Council, John XXIII and Paul VI. According to this view, the objective of the Council and of every reform in the Church is "to transmit the doctrine purely and fully, without diminutions or distortions," conscious that "our duty not only consists in guarding this precious treasure, as though we were concerned only with antiquity, but in dedicating ourselves with a firm will and without fear to the work that our age calls for," the pope said. "Today we can look back with gratitude to the Second Vatican Council," he added. "If we read and receive it, guided by an appropriate hermeneutic, it can be and will be increasingly a great force for the always necessary renewal of the Church."

Papal Christmas — It was announced on Dec. 23 that some 122 TV stations from 74 countries planned to broadcast Pope Benedict XVI's first Christmas Midnight Mass in St. Peter's Basilica. In addition, 111 television channels from 68 countries will broadcast his Christmas day message and blessing *Urbi et Orbi* (to the city of Rome and the world) which he will impart from St. Peter's Square. Among these channels are Sri Lanka TV Corporation, Jordan Radio and Television, and the Israel Broadcasting Authority, as well as numerous national television networks of Africa.

Flame of Peace — On Dec. 25, hours before Midnight Mass on Christmas Eve, Pope Benedict XVI lit a symbolic flame of peace from the window of his study. With this gesture, the Pope concluded the Vigil of Prayer of Peace and Life, which was presided over by Card. Edmund Szoka, president of the Governorate of Vatican City, to unveil the Nativity scene near the obelisk in St. Peter's Square. The Nativity scene has 17 natural-size figures, some of which were made by Vincent Palotti in 1842 for the crèche in the Roman Church of Sant'Andrea della Valle. The nearby 100-foot Christmas tree is a gift to the Pope from Austria.

Christmas Midnight Mass — On Dec. 25, Pope Benedict XVI celebrated his first Christmas Eve Midnight Mass as Pope. "God is so great that he can become small," the Holy Father told the faithful in St. Peter's Basilica. "God is so powerful that he can make himself vulnerable and come to us as a defenseless child, so that we can love him." Addressing about 9,000 faithful, he explained that God "is so good that he can give up his divine splendor and come down to a stable, so that we might find him, so that his goodness might touch us, give itself to us and continue to work through us." He said, "This is Christmas. God has become one of us, so that we can be with him and become like him. On this night," the Holy Father added, "let us pray in a special way for the birthplace of our Redeemer and for the men and women who live and suffer there. We wish to pray for peace in the Holy Land: Look, O Lord, upon this corner of the earth, your homeland, which is so very dear to you! Let your light shine upon it! Let it know peace!"

Christmas Message — In his first Christmas message on Dec. 25, Pope Benedict XVI prayed that the light of the Child Jesus might encourage humanity to build a more just world order. Some 40,000 people gathered in St. Peter's Square, as millions of television viewers worldwide shared in the message as the Holy Father announced: "Men and women of today, humanity come of age yet often still so frail in mind and will, let the Child of Bethlehem take you by the hand! Do not fear; put your trust in him!" The Holy Father added, "The life-giving power of his light is an incentive for building a new world order based on just ethical and economic relationships," praying as well that the love of God, incarnated at Christmas may "guide every people on earth and strengthen their common consciousness of being a 'family' called to foster relationships of trust and mutual support." The Holy Father also announced: "A united humanity will be able to confront the many troubling problems of the present time: from the menace of terrorism to the humiliating poverty in which millions of human beings live, from the proliferation of weapons to the pandemics and the environmental destruction which threatens the future of our planet." He then counseled: "Men and women in our technological age risk becoming victims of their own intellectual and technical achievements, ending up in spiritual barrenness and emptiness of heart. That is why it is so important for us to open our minds and hearts to the Birth of Christ, this event of salvation which can give new hope to the life of each human being." After delivering his message, he imparted his tradition blessing *Urbi et Orbi* (to the city Rome and the world) from the balcony of St. Peter's Basilica, in 33 languages.

3 Million Pilgrims — On Dec. 26, it was announced by the Prefecture of the Pontifical Household that in the first eight months of his pontificate, Pope Benedict XVI drew nearly 3 million pilgrims to public events. According to Vatican statistics, more than 2.8 million people attended the weekly general audiences, the Sunday blessings, special papal audiences or liturgical celebrations at which the Holy Father presided. Some 810,000 people attended Pope Benedict XVI's 32 general audiences in 2005. Since his Apr. 19 election, the Holy Father has held special audiences with more than 250,000 people.

Pueri Cantores — On Dec. 28, thousands of young choir singers from around the world sang for Pope Benedict XVI, chanting "Be-ne-de-tto" when he appeared in the Vatican's audience hall. Some 5,000 young singers, their family members, friends and choirmasters from 15 different countries were taking part in the Dec. 28-Jan. 1 International Congress of *Pueri Cantores* in Rome. Of the 88 children's choir groups attending the papal audience and the congress, 10 different choirs came from the United States. Most choir members ranged from eight years old to high school age.

General Audiences
Commentary on Psalm 137(138) (Dec. 7)
Commentary on Psalm 138(139):1-12 (Dec. 14)
Pre-Christmas Reflection (Dec. 21)

NATIONAL
Katrina Victims — It was reported on Dec. 2 that at St. Luke the Evangelist Church in Slidell, Louisiana, 100 people arrive in the pre-dawn hours twice a week to sign a notebook and wait their turn to speak to parish volunteers and staff members of Catholic Charities in the Archdiocese of New Orleans. The people explain their needs and express their desperation in the wake of Hurricane Katrina. Parish workers move to get the victims of the hurricane information and to help them file applications with the Federal Emergency Management Agency. The parish program also helps with housing, counseling and other necessities.

No Church Inquiry — It was reported on Dec. 2 that the Diocese of Sacramento has no plans to investigate an alleged apparition in which a statue of the Virgin Mary outside a Catholic church has been reported to weep blood. The statue has drawn hundreds of visitors to Vietnamese Catholic Martyrs Church in Sacramento. An inquiry involving field investigators and lab analysts could be initiated later, it was announced.

Canonization Cause Opened — It was reported on Dec 5 that Bp. William K. Weigand of the Diocese of Sacramento Diocese began the initial diocesan portion of the process that could lead to the canonization of the late Sacramento Aux. Bp. Alphonse Gallegos. The Diocese of Sacramento is beginning the process for Bp. Gallegos at the request of his religious order, the Augustinian Recollects. Bp. Gallegos's family members and supporters, as well as members of his religious order, were among those attending a Dec. 4 Mass in the Cathedral. Bp. Gallegos lived in the Sacramento area from 1979 until his death in an automobile accident near Yuba City Oct. 6, 1991. From 1979 to 1981, he served as the first director of the Division of Hispanic Affairs of the California Catholic Conference. He was ordained an auxiliary bishop by Bp. Francis A. Quinn on Nov. 4, 1981, and was the first Hispanic bishop in the California state capital since 1861.

Bishops Debate — It was reported on Dec. 4 that members of the U.S. Conference of Catholic Bishops have conducted a debate on whether the Vatican document restricting admittance of homosexuals to seminaries is a total ban on gays. "It bans anyone with a same-sex orientation," said Bp. John M. D'Arcy of Fort Wayne-South Bend, Ind. Other bishops have said it does not prohibit candidates for the priesthood who are sexually and emotionally mature and can make a faithful commitment to living a celibate life. Bishops who hold this position add that this is something that has to be determined in each individual case. (See also News in Depth.)

Shrine Welcomes Christmas — On Dec. 5, it was reported that the National Shrine of Our Lady of La Salette in Attleboro, Massachusetts, has again presented its annual Christmas display of more than 250,000 lights. "It's a work of love and it makes us joyful," La Salette Bro. Bob Russell, director of the shrine, said of its annual Festival of Lights. The theme for 2005 is "We Are the Light of the World." The Festival of Lights began on Thanksgiving night.

Historic Convent — It was reported on Dec. 6 that the *Clarion Herald*, the newspaper of the Archdiocese of New Orleans, has relocated from its temporary offices in the Baton Rouge Diocese to the Old Ursuline Convent in New Orleans' French Quarter, the oldest existing building in the Mississippi River Valley. The convent, which for decades has housed the archives of the New Orleans Archdiocese, was completed in 1752 and is the oldest surviving example of French colonial period architecture in the United States. Because of insurmountable delays in mail delivery in the New Orleans area, the *Clarion Herald*'s 10-member staff has personally delivered 45,000 copies of each issue to Catholic churches operating again in the Archdiocese of New Orleans.

Arizona Bishops — On Dec. 12, the Catholic bishops of Arizona issued a pastoral letter calling for immigration reform and asking Catholics to respond to the mounting crisis with compassion, education, hospitality and prayer. "We . . . are deeply saddened by the death and suffering we see on our border," the bishops announced in the letter. The 4,000-word document, titled "You Welcomed Me," treats current debates on the issue, federal immigration policies, and the cultural and economic impact on the state as a result of immigration.

Papal Nuncio — Pope Benedict XVI appointed a new papal nuncio to the United States, it as reported on Dec. 18. Abp. Pietro Sambi, apostolic nuncio to Israel, has been appointed to succeed Abp. Gabriel Montalvo, 75, who has held the post since 1998. Abp. Sambi was born in Sogliano sul Rubicone, Italy, incardinated in the Diocese of San Marino-Montefeltro, and ordained a priest in Mar. 1964. He has a doctorate in sacred theology and in canon law. Abp. Sambi speaks Italian, English, French and Spanish. A nuncio represents the Holy Father to both the hierarchy and Church of a particular nation and to that nation's civil government.

Schism and Heresy Trial — A church tribunal in the San Bernardino Diocese was reported on Dec. 27 as having reviewed evidence to determine whether the Rev. Ned Reidy, a former Catholic priest who now pastors his own church, is guilty of heresy and schism. Reidy was automatically excommunicated when he left the Catholic Church, but he was never laicized. He remains a priest, although no longer in good standing. The church tribunal that conducted the trial has not issued a verdict, but the process clarified Reidy's status in the church, since he continues to live and exercise ministry in the area where he used to be a Catholic pastor.

INTERNATIONAL

Fair of Families Planned — It was announced on Dec. 1 that the first International Fair of Families will take place July 1-7, in Valencia, Spain, as part of the 5th World Meeting of Families. The fair is expected to receive more than 100,000 visitors throughout the week. The 5th World Meeting of Families, called by Pope Benedict XVI for Valencia, is expecting 1.5 million people to attend, according to organizers. The event has already registered more than a thousand volunteers.

Christians Evicted — It was reported on Dec. 1 that hundreds of Christian families in Pakistan were evicted from their homes to make way for Muslims left destitute by the Kashmir earthquake. Catholic Bishop Anthony Lobo of Islamabad-Rawalpindi, Pakistan, said the Pakistani government has evicted Christians to solve the problem of how to house some 3 million people left homeless by the disaster. The bishop stated: "In one district near Joharabad, all the people are being thrown out—all of them are Christians. We are the most vulnerable people, we are very poor and we are easy targets."

Nuns Beaten in China — On Dec. 5, the Holy See's missionary news agency Fides expressed alarm over the beatings of nuns in Xian, China, and the subsequent news blackout. The 16 nuns, members of the Congregation of Franciscan Missionaries of the Sacred Heart, were insulted and beaten by some 40 men when they tried to halt the demolition of a Catholic school. No Chinese newspaper reported the news. Chinese officials blocked Catholic web sites as well. The Holy See protested the attack in a communiqué issued by Vatican spokesman Joaquín Navarro Valls.

Cardinal's Killer — On Dec. 11, a Mexican court sentenced a former police commander to 40 years in prison in the 1993 shooting death of Card. Juan Jesús Posadas Ocampo at the Guadalajara airport. The court in Jalisco said Humberto Rodríguez Banuelos was part of a gang of gunmen that shot the cardinal while he was sitting in his car. Six others also were killed in the attack. Church figures have long disputed the official version of the slaying, arguing that the cardinal was killed because he knew about relationships between drug dealers and government officials. This sentencing settled the matter.

Romanian Cathedral — On Dec. 11 it was reported that the Romanian cathedral of Oradea, St. Nicholas Cathedral, has been returned to Eastern-rite Catholics after having been the property of the Orthodox for 60 years. "All of us who attended have written a page of history. We celebrated together with patriarchs, metropolitans, Catholic and Orthodox bishops, for the greater glory of God," said Greek-Catholic Bp. Virgil Bercea of Oradea Mare. The building of the cathedral was begun by Greek-Catholic Bp. Ignavie Darabant and completed by Bp. Samuil Vulcan, of the same rite, in 1810. During the Communist regime, the cathedral and other real estate and properties of the Greek-Catholics were expropriated by the state and turned over to the Orthodox Church, Romania's state church.

Solidarity With Gypsies — It was reported on Dec. 18 that Bp. Patrick O'Donoghue of Lancaster, England, told Catholic schools and parishes in England and Wales to stand in solidarity with Gypsies and other travelers who are increasingly threatened by discrimination and eviction. The bishop urged Catholics to find ways to support such people "in their struggle to obtain adequate accommodation and a decent life for their families." Speaking on behalf of the Catholic Bishops' Conference of England and Wales, he said a special ministry to Gypsies and travelers was not enough. "Every Catholic parish and school must, in the spirit of a welcoming community, find ways of reaching out to Gypsies and travelers in their area," he said. Bp. O'Donoghue heads the Catholic programs for ministry to Gypsies and travelers.

Peace Lamps — On Dec. 24 it was reported that peace lamps are being used symbolically to promote prayers for peace in the Holy Land. Small peace lamps are being placed in churches around the world as the focus of the campaign during the Christmas season. Some are the classic oil lamp and some are in the shape of a dove. The lamps are fashioned out of ceramics in a small West Bank factory. The peace project, conceived and planned by Fr. Raed Abusahlia of Redeemer Catholic Church in Taybeh, is aimed at uniting all Christians around the world in prayer for the peace of the Holy Land. Also involved in organizing the campaign was the Growing Peace Together Association in Florence, Italy, with the blessing of both Card. Ennio Antonelli of Florence and Latin-rite Patriarch Michel Sabbah of Jerusalem.

JANUARY 2006

VATICAN

Papal Intention — It was announced on Jan. 1 that Pope Benedict XVI will pray especially throughout the month that migrants "be recognized as persons created in the image and likeness of God and welcomed with respect and charity." The Apostleship of Prayer announced the Holy Father's missionary intention for January. He will remember the 200 million people "who live and work in a country which is not the one in which they were born. This is a sign of the times and a phenomenon which transforms whole countries." Pope Benedict XVI also prays every month for a general intention, which for the month of January is that all Christians may "grow in unity and love in order to build reconciliation and peace among all peoples of the earth."

Key Threats to Peace — On Jan. 1, Pope Benedict XVI celebrated the solemnity of Mary the Mother of God and the World Day of Peace in St. Peter's Basilica, addressing thousands of the faithful who had gathered there. The Holy Father announced: "In the face of the situations of injustice and violence that continue to oppress different areas of the earth, in the face of the new and more insidious threats against peace — terrorism, nihilism and fanatic fundamentalism — it is more necessary than ever to work together for peace." He also appealed for a "thrust of courage and confidence in God and in man to opt for undertaking the way of peace." The Mass in St. Peter's Basilica and the recitation of the Angelus afterward in St. Peter's Square featured people from around the world dressed in their native costumes. Many carried peace banners. Attending the concelebrated Mass were ambassadors of 172 countries that maintain diplomatic relations with the Holy See, in addition to representatives of the Russian Federation, the Palestine Liberation Organization and the Order of Malta. Participants also came from Mexico, Peru, Pakistan, Vietnam and Democratic Republic of Congo.

Papal Essay — It was reported on Jan. 1 that an essay by Pope Benedict XVI on "Europe and Its Discontents" was published in the Jan. issue of the U.S.-based journal *First Things*. Originally written before his election to the papacy, the essay identifies "Europe" as a cultural identity, not simply a geographical concept. Its civilization, the Holy Father declares, extends to all of the continents, especially North America. He also warns that at a time when European civilization is the thoroughly dominant cultural force in the world today, its emphasis on techno-secular progress appears to have weakened the appreciation of its historical value system, culture and faith. Pope Benedict XVI also commented on the low birthrates in the West that indicate that the "vital energy" of Europe has been lost. The Holy Father states that Christianity is the antidote to a Europe that is beset by materialism, secularism and multiculturalism, a Europe that no longer appreciates its roots and with little interest or energy left to preserve its heritage.

Catholics Slain in 2005 — It was announced on Jan. 1 that a bishop, 20 priests, two men religious, two women religious and a layman were added to the list of pastoral mission personnel who met violent death last year according to the "Martyrology of the Contemporary Church," published by the Congregation for the Evangelization of Peoples. The largest number of victims was registered as having died in the Americas, with the loss of eight priests, two women religious and two men religious. Colombia, with four priests and one nun killed, is listed as the nation where social conflicts are most acute and where the Church pays a heavy price for its commitment to social justice. Two more priests were killed in

Mexico, and a Sister of Notre Dame de Namur was slain in Brazil. Another religious died in Kingston, Jamaica. The report also stated: "Africa was bathed with the blood of a bishop, six priests and a layman." Four priests lost their lives in Asia while evangelizing, and three in India and one in Indonesia.

Feast of Epiphany — On Jan. 6, Pope Benedict XVI addressed 50,000 pilgrims gathered in St. Peter's Square to pray the Angelus on the feast of the Epiphany. He urged the faithful to experience "an authentic epiphany," which means that all must first open their hearts to Christ. The Holy Father extended to the whole Church the message: "Open your hearts wide to God, let yourselves be astonished by Christ!" He added: "Open the doors of your freedom to his merciful love! Show Christ your joys and sorrows, allowing him to illuminate your minds with his light and touch your hearts with his grace." The Feast of the Epiphany is popular in Europe, commemorating the visit of the Three Kings to the Christ-child.

Eastern Christians — On Jan. 6, Pope Benedict XVI greeted the Eastern Churches who were preparing to celebrate Christmas, and called for all to pray for full Christian unity. Among the Oriental Churches celebrating Christmas according to the Julian calendar, the one with the largest membership is the Russian Orthodox Church. The Holy Father expressed his "most cordial good wishes for peace and goodness in the Lord" to these brethren. He also called for prayer "with fervor for full Christian unity so that their testimony will become the leaven of communion for the whole world."

Papal Apartment — Pope Benedict XVI, who inherited the papal apartment on the top floor of the Apostolic Palace when he was elected to the papacy, was reported on Jan. 8 as pleased at the changes made by workmen. The apartment, about 10 rooms in all, underwent a three-month renovation this fall after having been the residence of Pope John Paul II for so many years. Electrical wiring was replaced, new pipes were installed, the kitchen was refurbished and a custom-fitted private library was put in place. "I can only admire the things you've done, like these beautiful floors," the Holy Father told the more than 200 architects, engineers and workers involved in the remodeling project. "I really like my new library, with that antique ceiling," he said. "For me it's like being surrounded by friends, now that there are books on the shelf."

Pope Baptizes Infants — On Jan 8, Pope Benedict XVI baptized 10 newborn babies in the Sistine Chapel, an annual event in the Vatican. The Holy Father addressed pilgrims in St. Peter's Square afterwards, explaining that the "baptism of children expresses and realizes the mystery of the new birth of divine life in Christ." He also expressed the hope that Christians will "discover the joy and beauty of their baptism, that, lived with faith, is an ever present reality; it continually renews us in the image of the new man, in holiness of thoughts and deeds."

Reformed Churches — Pope Benedict XVI received the representatives of the World Alliance of Reformed Churches in a private audience on Jan. 8. "I pray that our meeting today will itself bear fruit in a renewed commitment to work for the unity of all Christians," the Holy Father said during the audience. "The way before us calls for wisdom, humility, patient study and exchange." The delegation of the Reformed Churches was made up of five representatives, including Dr.

Clifton Kirkpatrick, the president of the alliance, from the U.S. Other members of the delegation included Setri Nyomi, secretary-general of the alliance; Sabine Hofmeister, moderator of the Reformed Synod of Denmark; Maria Bonafede, moderator of the Waldensian Church; and Odair Pedroso Mateus, the alliance's executive secretary for theology and ecumenical engagement. Dr. Kirkpatrick told the Holy Father: "We are eager to be partners with you in this important ministry of Christian unity." The delegation also met with the Pontifical Council for Promoting Christian Unity and the Council for Justice and Peace. The World Alliance of Reformed Churches is a fellowship of more than 75 million Reformed Christians in 218 churches in 107 countries.

Vatican Secret Archives — It was announced on Jan. 10 that the Vatican Secret Archives may now be visited on the Internet. After selecting a preferred language on the Holy See's site (http://www.vatican.va/), one may examine documents such as the 14th-century Parchment of Chinon, which records the absolution of Pope Clement V of the leading members of the Templar Order. Also accessible are the proceedings of the trial against Galileo Galilei. The archives include about 52 miles of shelves. The oldest document dates to the eighth century; the archives have an almost uninterrupted documentation starting from 1198. Normally, the archives are used primarily by the Pope and the Roman Curia and were reserved for their use.

Beslan Massacre — On Jan. 11, Pope Benedict XVI met with 29 children from the Russian school of Beslan who survived the 2004 siege by Chechen rebels that left more than 300 dead. The audience took place in a room near the main auditorium of Paul VI Hall. The Holy Father had photographs taken with the children, and asked them their names. The young survivors of the Beslan massacre are in Italy for a few days, thanks to the hospitality given them by the Italian Civil Protection Service, which has been in contact with them since the tragedy. "These children have suffered a most violent trauma," Benedict XVI said to those who were acting as hosts for the children. "We must help them to be able to forget the tragedy so that they will be witnesses of peace for the future of humanity."

Papal Ad-libs — It was reported on Jan. 11 that Pope Benedict XVI ad-libs during public gatherings and events and at times puts down his prepared text and continues with extemporaneous remarks, delivering impromptu talks or sermons that easily clarify Scripture, the patristic writings, or modern social problems. While many are astonished at this ability, one longtime Vatican observer commented: "Even in his spontaneous talks, the flow of argument and the citing of sources is impressive. It's as if he can reference 2,000 years of Christian thought in his head."

Crime-Free Transition — On Jan. 12, it was reported that during the period of papal transition in Apr. 2005, for two weeks the Vatican was virtually crime-free. A Vatican judge reported that from the day of Pope John Paul II's death Apr. 2 to his funeral Apr. 8 and the first seven days of Pope Benedict XVI's pontificate, starting with his election Apr. 19, the 108-acre Vatican City State was without crime. Nicola Picardi, promoter of justice for the Tribunal of Vatican City State, said no crimes were reported and no charges were brought to the Vatican's court during those two weeks, a fact he called extraordinary, considering that at least 6 million people visited the Vatican during this period.

Courageous, Caring Priests — On Jan. 20, Pope Benedict XVI addressed members of the Almo Capranic College, a Roman diocesan seminary, and announced that today's world needs courageous, caring priests who are not afraid to bring God's love to all people everywhere. In order to respond to the expectations of modern society and to take part in the enormous task of evangelization, the Holy Father said: "Prepared and courageous priests are needed, who without ambition and fear, but convinced of Gospel truth, make proclaiming Christ their first concern."

Media Threat — In his first message for World Communications Day, Pope Benedict XVI said on Jan. 24 that the media is capable of undervaluing religious belief in the coverage of world events. "Daily we are reminded that immediacy of communication does not necessarily translate into the building of cooperation and communion in society," the Holy Father stated, and added: "...certain tendencies within the media engender a kind of monoculture that dims creative genius, deflates the subtlety of complex thought and undervalues the specificity of cultural practices and the particularity of religious belief." The Holy Father also expressed the hope the media do not end up becoming, paradoxically, a means of a lack of communication. The theme of the message for World Communications Day was "The Media: A Network for Communication, Communion and Cooperation."

Pope Blesses Lambs — It was reported on Jan. 24 that Pope Benedict XVI blessed two live lambs on the feast of St. Agnes. The lambs will provide the wool used to knit the palliums he will distribute to newly appointed archbishops in the Church. A pallium is a circular wool band with pendants, worn over the shoulders, and is a liturgical insignia of honor and jurisdiction, worn by the Pope and metropolitan archbishops in their churches and in those of their provinces. The pallium traditionally symbolizes the lost sheep that is found again, carried on the shoulders of the Good Shepherd. The insignia also represents the Lamb crucified for the salvation of humanity. The two lambs blessed by the Holy Father were provided by the religious of the Order of Lateran Canons Regular, who serve in the Basilica of St. Agnes Outside the Walls. They were raised in the Trappist monastery of Three Fountains (*Tre Fontane*), on the outskirts of Rome.

***Deus Caritas Est* Published** — On Jan. 25, the first encyclical of Pope Benedict XVI was published. *Deus Caritas Est* ("God Is Love") provides a clear analysis of human love and serves as a dual response to the question of the Church's commandments and regulations and their effect on such love. The encyclical answers the question in two parts. The first reflects on the origins of love and its different manifestations; the second addresses the way in which the Church, as institution, must function as the commandment of love. Pope Benedict XVI begins his commentary by clarifying the Church's condemnation of *eros*, the love of attraction that has been reduced to mere sex in this era. and its promotion of *agape*, unconditional love, which involves both the physical and the spiritual aspects of human nature. (*See under* **News in Depth**.)

Marriage Tribunals — On Jan. 28, Pope Benedict XVI, meeting with members of the Roman Rota, the court that deals mainly with marriage cases, urged marriage tribunal personnel to act as quickly as possible while fully following Church law in such cases. "For more than a few of the faithful," the Holy Father said, "ecclesiastical sentences in this area, in fact, have an impact on the possibility or not of receiving Communion." The Holy Father, acutely aware of problems existing for the laity in this regard, urged the members of the marriage tribunal to respect the stress and anxieties involved and to provide prompt resolutions according to Church law.

GENERAL AUDIENCE
Commentary on 2nd Part of Psalm 138(139) (Jan. 7)
Commentary on Psalm 143(144):1-8 (Jan. 11)
Jan. 4 Commentary on Colossians 1:3,12-20 (Jan. 13)
Start of Week of Prayer for Christian Unity (Jan. 18)
Commentary on Psalm 143(144):9-15 (Jan. 26)

NATIONAL
Trapped Miners — Bishop Michael J. Bransfield of Wheeling-Charleston was reported on Jan. 3 as expressing his deep concern for the miners trapped at the Sago Coal Mine in Upshur County near Buckhannon, West Virginia. Rescue efforts were under way for the miners who were trapped 260 feet below ground as their families waited at the nearby Sago Baptist Church. Bishop Bransfield stated: "This tragedy is being felt at all ends of our state and this is a time when we must come together as one in prayer."

Voucher Program — On Jan. 5, the Florida Supreme Court struck down the state's school voucher program in a 5-2 ruling. The ruling declared that the Opportunity Scholarship program violates the state's constitution that guarantees all Florida students a "uniform, efficient, safe, secure and high-quality system of free public schools." The voucher program, enacted by the Florida Legislature in 1999, has provided tuition vouchers to children in failing public schools that allow them to transfer to the school of their choice, including private or parochial schools.

Abortion Views — It was announced on Jan. 5 that a national survey of high school seniors reported that many of them have a strong moral opposition to abortion and favor restrictions on "a woman's right to choose" an abortion. Most seniors regard abortion as morally wrong and would significantly limit when a woman could have an abortion. The survey, however, also showed that almost 75 percent of the respondents supported legal recognition for gay couples with 54 percent of the respondents supporting gay marriage and 20 percent favoring gay civil unions. The survey of 1,000 public and private school seniors was conducted by Hamilton College in Clinton, New York, and the polling firm of Zogby International.

Education Dialogue — On Jan. 10, in Washington, D.C., the U.S. bishops' Committee on Education approved a set of questions to guide local dialogues nationwide between diocesan bishops and the presidents of Catholic colleges and universities in their dioceses. The dialogues are to be conducted by May 3, the date on which "The Application of 'Ex Corde Ecclesiae' for the United States" took effect five years ago. "Ex Corde Ecclesiae," "from the heart of the church," is Pope John Paul II's 1990 apostolic constitution on Catholic higher education. This papal document set norms to regulate the Catholic mission and to insure the identity of Catholic colleges and universities worldwide. National bishops' conferences were charged with the implementation of the norms.

Marymount Closing — Marymount College in Tarrytown, New York, will close in June 2007, nearly five years after consolidating with Fordham University in New York, it was reported on Jan. 14. John N. Tognino, chairman of the Fordham board of trustees, announced the closing, saying: "This was a very difficult decision because we know how deeply our students valued the supportive environment of an all-women's college and how many alumnae have flourished and excelled because of the strengths they developed at Marymount." The Religious of the Sacred Heart of Mary founded the college in 1907.

Extension Katrina Grants — The Catholic Church Extension Society was reported on Jan. 13, as providing $5 million in rebuilding grants to six Gulf Coast dioceses that suffered severe damage from hurricanes Katrina and Rita last year. The dioceses of Biloxi, Mississippi, and Beaumont, Texas, and four Louisiana dioceses (New Orleans, Lafayette, Lake Charles and Houma-Thibodaux) are being aided in the repairing and rebuilding of damaged Catholic properties. Extension, a century-old Chicago-based funding agency for U.S. home missions, provided $460,000 in emergency relief funds immediately after the devastating storms hit the Gulf Coast in Aug. and Sept. 2005. In addition, since Sept. it has coordinated a Parish Partnership Program. More than 100 parishes registered to participate in the program.

Boston Parishes — On Jan. 14, the Archdiocese of Boston announced that the Vatican's Congregation for Clergy has denied the appeals of 10 parishes that were closed in the process of archdiocesan reconfiguration. Abp. Sean P. O'Malley stated: "We appreciate the disappointment that this news brings to those who submitted the appeals and all who are saddened by the parish closings." He added: "This has been a difficult time for our Catholic community. We wish to express our gratitude to the many priests, deacons, religious and parishioners who have generously accepted the need for change in light of our limited resources." The archdiocese cited "declining numbers of clergy, changing Catholic demographics and significant financial pressures" as the causes of the reconfiguration process that began in Jan. 2004.

Rosary Across America — On Jan. 23, the New York-based National Black Catholic Apostolate for Life held its second annual "Black Catholic Rosary Across America for Life" to mark the 33rd year since the Supreme Court legalized abortion virtually on demand. Black Catholics and people of life were invited to pray the rosary for life to end abortion and all acts of violence against human life, said Franciscan Father James Goode, the founder and president. "By praying the "Black Catholic Rosary Across America for Life," we as black Catholics are committed through the intercession of Mary, the mother of life, to impact our community with the message of life and change lives and attitudes," Father Goode announced.

Pro-Life Celebrations — Gathering near the U. S. Capitol and at the Basilica of the National Shrine of the Immaculate Conception in Washington, D.C., on Jan. 22 and 23, a rally and a Mass attracted thousands of pro-lifers and many young people, who braved severe weather conditions at the outdoor rally. More than 6,000 people, many of them high school and college students, attended the Mass celebrated by Card. William H. Keeler at the shrine. The Mass was part of the National Prayer Vigil for Life on the anniversary of the 1973 *Roe v. Wade* decision legalizing abortion on demand. "We gather in this sacred space to bear witness yet again to the terrible cloud that has darkened our nation since the Supreme Court declared 33 years ago today that the life of a human being, a life created in God's image, may be ended before its birth," the Cardinal announced. "We come together to pray that this darkest of clouds might at last be lifted. We come together again to pray for the triumph of life."

Minor Basilica — On Jan. 25, Bishop Thomas G. Wenski of the Diocese of Orlando celebrated a special Mass honoring the news that Pope Benedict XVI designated St. Paul's Catholic Church in Daytona Beach, Florida, as a minor basilica. Such a designation is bestowed upon churches of historical and spiritual importance. The papal honor makes St. Paul's the 60th church in the United States to be so designated. It is the second church in Florida to receive the honor, after the Cathedral-Basilica of St. Augustine, designated in 1976. It is also the first basilica designated by Pope Benedict. Fr. Robert E. Webster, pastor of the new basilica, stated: "It is a great honor for the parish community and the diocese. The fact that a church is designated as a minor basilica is a great example not only of architecture, but a great example of what the liturgical and spiritual life of any parish community should be."

INTERNATIONAL

Christian Market Bombed — On Jan. 1, a bomb exploded in a crowded Christian market selling pork in Palu, the capital of the Central Sulawesi province of eastern Indonesia, killing seven people and wounding 53. Eastern Indonesia has large pockets of Christians, who eat pork, which is restricted in the Muslim diet. Authorities tightened security, especially in places of worship, and closed the town gates to prevent any more violence.

Standards for Indecency — It was reported on Jan. 3 that recent Canadian Supreme Court rulings that replaced the community-standards test for indecency with a harm-based model will make it harder to get convictions based on moral issues. The rulings legalized commercial clubs that feature group sex and spouse-swapping, or "swinging." Peter Lauwers, a constitutional lawyer, said this change will make prosecutors reluctant to charge people for activities such as bestiality or polygamy because it will be almost impossible to get a conviction using the new standards. "It's a watershed decision and the implications will take years to sort out, not only in this area— for common bawdy houses—but for all the moral issues in the criminal code."

Franciscans of Assisi — On Jan. 10, Minister General Friar Joachim Guernek lamented what he said are lies against the Franciscans of Assisi, following papal measures to organize the city's holy sites. On Nov. 9, Pope Benedict XVI entrusted the pastoral activity of the city's basilicas to the bishop of the local diocese and appointed a Cardinal supervisor. The Holy Father's letter, issued on his own initiative, also streamlined the autonomy that both the Friars Minor and Conventuals have had since 1969, when Pope Paul VI published a similar document. Fr. Giermek wrote: "Authentic lies have been published by some individuals who, despite the fact they knew the truth, have however reproached (to give an example) the friars for having authorized or allowed ritual abuses during the religious ceremonies of some delegations."

Sister Lucia's Remains — On Jan. 12 it was announced that the mortal remains of Sr. Lucia, one of the three who witnessed apparitions of Our Lady in 1917, will be moved from the Carmelite convent of Coimbra, where she died, to the Shrine of Fatima. The news was confirmed by the Roman Society for Pilgrimages, an institution dependent on the Holy See, which is organizing pilgrimages to the Portuguese shrine for the occasion. On Feb. 19, there will be a procession to the Chapel of the Apparitions, followed by Mass, and the transfer of the remains to the basilica. Sr. Lucia's remains will rest beside her two cousins, Blessed Francisco and Blessed Jacinta, who witnessed the Virgin Mary's apparitions with her. Sr. Lucia died at age 97 last Feb. 13.

Defend Values — On the feast of Glasgow, Scotland's patron, St. Mungo, Jan. 13, Abp. Mario Conti of Glasgow is calling on Catholics to resist what he calls "indirect assaults" on traditional values. "Today the assault is indirect; the attack is on the moral order which is the heritage of all Christians, and which enshrines values shared by those of other faiths within our midst," the archbishop declared in a homily that echoed the concern shared by all eight Catholic bishops of Scotland about recent changes in legislation surrounding marriage and family life. Concerned at the way in which the institution of marriage is being undermined, Abp. Conti stated: "Recent legislation to introduce civil partnerships dangerously weakens the uniqueness of marriage as a time-honored, legally recognized and protected social reality and a fiscally privileged entity. It also implicitly places homosexual acts on a plane of moral equivalence to marital love."

Pope Pius XII — On Jan. 17, Rabbi David Dalin, a U.S. Jewish leader, stated that the title "Righteous among the Nations" should be conferred on Pope Pius XII for his efforts to defend the Jews during World War II. A professor of history and political science at Ave Maria University in Florida, Rabbi Dalin makes his case in his book, *The Myth of Hitler's Pope*, published by Regnery. The work shows that in many incidents Pope Pius XII saved Jews from Nazi persecution. Rabbi Dalin quotes authoritative studies by Jewish authors, including Martin Gilbert, one of the most respected living Jewish historians. Gilbert is the official biographer of Winston Churchill and author of more than 70 books on World War II and the Shoah. Gilbert recounts all that the Catholic Church did in defense of the Jews, and to oppose racism and Nazism, and affirms that "Pius XII should be praised and not censured." Rabbi Dalin proposes that Pius XII, for his actions in favor of Jews, be conferred the highest Jewish recognition for a gentile.

Pope John Paul II Cause — It was reported on Jan. 31 that the healing of a French nun suffering from Parkinson's disease could be the miracle needed for the beatification of Pope John Paul II. Msgr. Slawomir Oder, postulator of the cause, chose the case of the French nun from among the many apparently miraculous healings people from around the world have reported. The case involves a French religious who had been diagnosed with Parkinson's when she was "very young; it was a precocious onset." Pope John Paul II had suffered from Parkinson's, a progressive disease that attacks the nervous system.

FEBRUARY 2006

VATICAN

Beatification of Mafia Victim — On Feb. 1, Pope Benedict XVI met with Card. Salvatore De Giorgi, the archbishop of Palermo, to discuss the beatification of a diocesan priest who was murdered by the Sicilian Mafia on Sept. 15, 1993, outside his church, on his 56th birthday. Fr. Puglisi was "guilty" of being concerned for the children of Palermo's Brancaccio neighborhood. His concern conflicted with Mafia interests and cost him his life. A film has been made of the priest's life.

World's Religious — On Feb. 2, Pope Benedict XVI thanked the members of the world's religious orders, describing their total dedication to Christ as a strong sign of faith in modern society. The pope, joined by several thousand men and women religious, celebrated a Mass to mark World Day for Consecrated Life, which was observed in Rome on Feb. 2, the feast of the Presentation of the Lord. The Holy Father concelebrated the Mass with priests of 17 religious orders. In his homily, he declared that this World Day is "a stimulus to promote in the whole People of God knowledge and esteem for those totally consecrated to God." "Their complete surrender in the hands of Christ and of his Church is a strong and clear proclamation of the presence of God in a language that is comprehensible also for our contemporaries," the Holy Father added.

Consecrated Women — On Feb. 2, the10th World Day of Consecrated Life, the Vatican's Congregation for the Evangelization of Peoples paid particular homage to consecrated women, whose contribution it sees as crucial for spreading the Gospel. Anticipating the occasion, the Congregation for the Evangelization of Peoples had recently published, through its Fides news agency, a lengthy report to highlight "the precious contribution offered by the consecrated woman." "The 'weight' of the contribution of feminine consecrated life in the evangelizing and pastoral activity of the Church is of such solidity that Pope John Paul II affirmed that 'the future of the new evangelization is unthinkable without a renewed contribution from women, especially consecrated women," the Vatican said.

Pope Visits Parish — On Feb. 5, Pope Benedict XVI visited the Vatican parish of St. Anne, celebrating Mass in the parish. During the homily he commented on the painting over the church's altar, which depicts St. Anne explaining the Scriptures to her daughter, the Virgin Mary. "Women are also the first bearers of the Gospel's Word of God; they are authentic evangelists," he explained in reference to the work carried out by so many mothers, grandmothers and women committed to various professions or to service in parish communities. The Holy Father was welcomed by his vicar general for Vatican City, Abp. Angelo Comastri, and by the parish priest, Fr. Gioele Schiavella. The territory of the Parish of St. Anne covers more than 10 acres of Vatican City State.

Congo Bishops — On Feb. 6, receiving in audience a group of bishops from Congo, who were concluding their five-yearly visit to the Holy See, Pope Benedict XVI stated that the commitment to promote peace is part of the Church's evangelizing mission and consists of proclaiming that "God is love." The Holy Father also received each of the bishops in a personal audience. Such meetings enabled the Congolese prelates to report directly on the crisis their communities have endured since 1998, when war erupted. Speaking in French, Benedict XVI urged the bishops to invite all Congolese Catholics, "along with the country's inhabitants, to mobilize to work for peace and reconciliation." He suggested as well that the bishops allow themselves to be mobilized by "the imperative of charity."

Apostle of the Untouchables — On Feb. 8 Pope Benedict XVI stated that a ceremony set for the beatification of Fr. Augustine Thevarparampil, Apostle of India's "untouchables," will be held in the priest's native village of Ramapuram this spring. The ceremony will be held in the church of Ramapuram, where "Kunjachan"—or "little priest," as he was popularly known—was born on Apr. 1, 1891. The village belongs to the Eparchy of Palai, in the southern state of Kerala, where the future blessed was a priest, beginning in 1921. The greater part of his priestly ministry was carried out in his own parish, St. Augustine's Church in Ramapuram. He died on Oct. 16, 1973, at age 82. He is buried in the Palai cathedral, in the Diocese of Ramapuram; his place of burialimmediately became a center of pilgrimage. Fr. Thevarparampil baptized more than 5,000 Dalits, or "untouchables."

Friars Minor — On Feb. 8, it was reported that Pope Benedict XVI received in audience Fr. José Rodríguez Carballo, minister general of the Friars Minor, as the order celebrates its eighth centenary. In a statement, the minister general said that the Holy Father showed particular interest in the celebration, "which he judged to be very appropriate for the achievement of a real renewal of the order." "The Holy Father asked me about some particular situations, to which I responded with total frankness and sincerity, and about which the Holy Father showed great understanding," continued the Franciscan superior. "I confess that I had the feeling of being before a father who knows our charism very well; he knows us as an order and loves us," he added. The Friars Minor have some 16,000 religious, in 110 countries.

Serving the Truth — In an address to the Vatican's Congregation of the Faith on Feb. 10, Pope Benedict XVI announced that the Church's service to the truth of faith is a service of profound joy. The Holy Father spoke to 100 participants in the plenary assembly of the Congregation for the Doctrine of the Faith, in which he recalled "with some emotion," his experience as prefect of the congregation for more than 20 years. "If the truth of the faith is placed with simplicity and decision at the center of Christian existence, man's life is vivified by a love that knows no pauses or limits, as I recalled in my recent encyclical letter '*Deus Caritas Est*,'" the Holy Father said. "Jesus is the polar star of human freedom: Without him, it loses its direction, as without knowledge of the truth freedom degenerates, is isolated and is reduced to sterile free will. With him, freedom recovers its reason for being, recognizes itself as being made for good and is expressed in charitable actions and behavior," he said.

First Lady — On Feb.9, Pope Benedict XVI met with U.S. First Lady Laura Bush and expressed his hopes that her trip to the Winter Olympics in Turin, Italy, would be peaceful. He also spoke of his concern about violent protests taking place in many Islamic countries. Laura Bush and one of her 24-year-old twin daughters, Barbara Bush, met the pope at the Vatican during a brief stop in Rome. After the meeting, she told reporters that "his hope and certainly our hope (is) for peace and tolerance" and for everyone to treat others with respect."

Vatican Parking — A new 240-space underground parking garage was opened on Feb. 10 when U.S. Card. Edmund C. Szoka formally blessed a new breach in the Vatican walls, opening a gate to the garage. The cardinal, president of the commission governing Vatican City State, said the work on the walls involved not only destruction, but also the restoration of a segment built during the 1559-1565 pontificate of Pope Pius IV. The ceremony included the unveiling of a new gate inscribed in Latin with the year, the name of Pope Benedict XVI and the fact that it is the first year of his pontificate. The new bronze-covered steel gate was sculpted by Gino Giannetti.

Caring for the Mentally Ill — Pope Benedict XVI stated on Feb. 10 that Catholics can receive special indulgences for caring for people who are ill or suffer from mental illness. He authorized the indulgences to encourage the faithful to show "Christian compassion and social solidarity toward the ill, especially toward those affected by mental illness," said U.S. Card. J. Francis Stafford, head of the Apostolic Penitentiary, the Vatican tribunal that regulates indulgences. The Vatican published the cardinal's statement announcing the indulgences and outlining the requirements for receiving them. The 14th World Day of the Sick, to take place in Adelaide, Australia, on Feb. 11, focused this year on mental health and the importance of offering proper care and support for people who suffer from mental illness.

Liturgical Abuses — The Vatican's top liturgy official was reported on Feb. 10 as saying that he expects Pope Benedict XVI to move against liturgical abuse with firm teaching and a gentle manner, recognizing that such mistakes often reflect ignorance, not ill will. At the same time, the pope wants to offer reconciliation to followers of the late French Abp. Marcel Lefebvre—but not at the cost of "disowning" the Second Vatican Council, said Card. Francis Arinze, the head of the Congregation for Divine Worship and the Sacraments. Card. Arinze spoke about the direction of the new papacy in an interview with Catholic News Service in early Feb. He said he expected important moves under Pope Benedict to improve liturgy. "I do not expect an aggressive correction of abuses. I don't think the pope is going to use the ecclesiastical hammer," Card. Arinze said. "Pope Benedict has very clear doctrine and convictions. What many people may not know is that he is not rough. He is gentlemanly, in the sense of what the prophet Isaiah said: 'A bruised reed he will not break,'" he said.

Olympic Games — On Feb. 12, Pope Benedict XVI expressed his hope that the Winter Olympics, which opened Friday in Turin, will foster "peace among peoples." After praying the midday Angelus from the window of his study today, the Pope greeted "the organizers and officials of the International Olympic Committee and all athletes who have come from all parts of the world." He added: "I hope this beautiful sports competition will be characterized by the Olympic values of loyalty, joy and fraternity, thus offering a contribution to peace among peoples."

Vatican Radio — Pope Benedict XVI noted the station's 75th anniversary, on Feb. 12. The Holy Father recalled that it was Pope Pius XI who asked radio pioneer Guglielmo Marconi (1874-1937) to build the Vatican's broadcasting station. "With radio, and later

television, the message of the Gospel and the words of popes have reached all peoples more rapidly and easily," he added. Pope Benedict was scheduled to visit the radio's installations Mar. 3. Fr. Federico Lombardi, director general of Vatican Radio, said that the station broadcasts programs in 40 languages and has 400 employees. The management of Vatican Radio is entrusted by the Holy See to the Society of Jesus.

Meeting With Curia — On Feb. 13, Pope Benedict XVI presided over his first official meeting with officials of the Roman Curia. Held in the Bologna Hall of the Apostolic Palace, the meeting was attended by cardinals and heads of the Holy See's dicasteries. Reportedly, one of the topics on the agenda was the Holy See's relationship with the Society of St. Pius X, founded by Abp. Marcel Lefebvre. The Holy Father received the group's superior, Bp. Bernard Fellay, at the papal summer residence of Castel Gandolfo in Aug. 2005. A statement issued by the Vatican explained that the desire "to arrive at perfect communion" was evident.

Lebanese Prime Minister — Pope Benedict XVI received Lebanese Prime Minister Fouad Siniora on Feb.16, and discussed "the common commitment to working to educate the populations in reconciliation and peace, respect for human rights and, particularly, religious freedom." The statement released after the meeting reported that "special consideration was reserved to the situation of Christians" in Lebanon and "to the contribution they intend to make to the progress of the country," the statement said. The prime minister also met with Card. Angelo Sodano, Vatican secretary of state.

Cuban Message — It was reported on Feb. 16 that Card. Renato Martino, president of the Pontifical Council for Justice and Peace, traveled to Cuba with a message for Cubans from Pope Benedict XVI. Card. Martino arrived in Havana to attend the celebration by the Cuban bishops' conference marking the 20th anniversary of the Cuban National Ecclesial Conference, the first meeting of bishops permitted after the 1959 revolution. The Holy Father's message, addressed to Card. Jaime Ortega Alamino of Havana, stated the hope that "Cuba would open itself to the world and the world would open itself to Cuba."

Mudslide Victims — On Feb. 19, Pope Benedict XVI spoke of those suffering from the deadly mudslide in the Philippines when he greeted English-speaking pilgrims, after reciting the Angelus with the faithful in St. Peter's Square. "In a special way our hearts turn to all those suffering the devastating consequences of the landslide in the Philippines," the Holy Father said. "I ask you to join me in praying for the victims, their loved ones and all those affected," he exhorted the pilgrims. "May the grieving families experience the consolation of the Lord's presence and rescue workers be assured of our concern and support." The entire village of Guinsaugon, near the city of St. Bernard, on Leyte island, was buried under mud on Friday morning, Feb. 17. Other villages suffered serious damages from the landslide. Authorities have confirmed 72 deaths. Another 1,800 people are missing and presumed dead.

Priestly Vocations — On Feb. 18, the Vatican press office released statistics concerning the number of priests in the world, in connection with the presentation of the 2006 edition of the Vatican yearbook, the *Annuario Pontificio*, which catalogs the church's pastoral presence diocese-by-diocese. The number of priests and seminarians in the world continues to increase, but the situation varies widely from continent to continent, the Vatican said. The most positive signs come from Asia and Africa, while Europe has shown a marked decline in priestly vocations. In its statement, the press office referred to data on church population, priests and seminarians through 2004, the last year for which statistics are available. It said the number of priests in the world was 405,891 at the end of 2004, an increase of 441 from 2003. About two-thirds were diocesan priests and one-third members of religious orders.

African Bishops — Pope Benedict XVI met on Feb. 20 with the bishops of Senegal, Mauritania, Guinea Bissau and Cape Verde at the end of their *ad limina* visits, which heads of dioceses make every five years. The Holy Father praised Catholics in the West African countries for giving witness to the fact that "love for one's neighbor, rooted in the love of God, is an essential part of the Christian life." He also announced: "Christianity must not be reduced to mere human wisdom or confused with social service, because it is rather a spiritual service." At the same time, he said, "for the disciples of Christ, the exercise of charity cannot be a means of proselytism, because love is gratuitous."

New Cardinals — On Feb.22, Pope Benedict XVI announced the creation of fifteen cardinals, including two from the United States. U.S. Archbishops William J. Levada, head of the Vatican's doctrinal congregation, and Sean P. O'Malley of Boston were to be installed with the other cardinals at a special consistory Mar. 24. The Holy Father said he would also convene the entire College of Cardinals for a day of reflection and prayer Mar. 23 and would celebrate Mass with the cardinals Mar. 25, the feast of the Annunciation of the Lord. It will be the first gathering of the College of Cardinals since they elected Pope Benedict last Apr. The U. S. contingent of cardinals now numbers fifteen.

Bosnian bishops — Pope Benedict XVI on Feb. 24 received four bishops from Bosnia-Herzegovina who were on their *ad limina* visits to the Vatican and assured them that he understood their work was difficult in a nation still recovering from its brutal ethnic-based war. "Certainly the difficulties are numerous, but the faith in divine providence on your part and on the part of your priests and faithful is great," the Holy Father said. "After these sad years of the recent war, you today, as workers for peace, are called to strengthen communion and spread mercy, understanding and forgiveness in the name of Christ," both among Christians and the whole of Bosnian society.

Albanian President — On Feb. 24, Pope Benedict XVI received Alfred Moisiu, the president of Albania, in a private audience. Moisiu, 76, a former general, was elected by Parliament to occupy the highest state office in June 2002. Vatican Radio reported that Moisiu, "of Orthodox Christian faith, has always been a promoter of dialogue and peaceful coexistence among the country's different religious confessions." The Albanian president took part in the ceremony of beatification of Mother Teresa of Calcutta on Oct. 19, 2003, and proposed with enthusiasm that that day be

proclaimed a national holiday in Albania to celebrate the Albanian blessed, a petition which was accepted by the Tirana Parliament.

GENERAL AUDIENCE
Commentary on Psalm 144(145) (Feb. 2)
Commentary on Psalm 144(145):14-21 (Feb. 8)
Commentary on the Magnificat (Feb. 15)
On Feast of Chair of St. Peter, Announcement of Consistory for 15 New Cardinals (Feb. 22)

INTERNATIONAL
Hindu Mob Attacks Bishop — It was reported on Feb. 1 that Bp. Thomas Dabre of Vasai, India, and other church officials were attacked when they visited Ghosali, a remote village in western India, to bless a church hostel. A mob of about 200 Hindus shouted slogans, pelted stones and damaged the new building and three church vehicles. The mob shouted "Christians go back" and "foreign dogs get out." Bp. Dabre said: "This was well planned. It arose from the same tactic of anti-Christian propaganda" by Hindu fundamentalist groups.

Glasgow Churches — Abp. Mario Conti announced on Feb. 1 that he will ask authorities for assistance in protecting his clergy, after a spate of six incidents over 12 days. "I am horrified at the level of intimidation my priests are having to face," said the archbishop of Glasgow in a statement. In the latest incident, Fr. Tommy Holloran, 75, was threatened and robbed after someone broke into his residence. Other incidents at parishes involved break-ins or vandalism to priests' cars. Church officials believe that the area's drug problem was a likely motive for the break-in.

Jesuits' Superior Resigns — It was reported on Feb. 2 that Fr. Hans Kolvenbach, superior general of the Jesuits, has announced his intention to resign from his office, adding that he will convoke a general congregation to elect his successor. In a letter to the members of the Society of Jesus, Fr. Kolvenbach officially convoked the order's 35th General Congregation, to open Jan. 5, 2008, in the General Curia of Rome. The letter said: "During the Congregation of Procurators of 2003 and during the recent meeting of Major Superiors of the Society of Jesus, it became increasingly clear that the Society has reached a situation foreseen by St. Ignatius in the Constitutions (680): in which there are 'very difficult things touching upon the whole body of the Society,' 'for more service to God our Lord.' It is a situation that requires a General Congregation." As of Jan. 1, 2005, the Jesuits numbered 19,850, including 13,966 priests.

Priest Shot in Turkish Church — An Italian priest was shot dead in his church in the Turkish Black Sea city of Trabzon, it was reported on Feb. 5. The state Anatolian news agency identified the murdered priest as Fr. Andrea Santoro, 60, reported to have been in Turkey for about five years. Anatolian quoted Trabzon Governor Huseyin Yavuzdemir as saying: "We condemn this attack against a man of religion."

Muslims Murder Philippine Christians — On Feb. 5, it was reported that Muslim extremists killed six Christians in cold blood in the small town of Patikul on Sulu Island, in the Sulu Archipelago of the Philippines. The attackers are suspected Abu Sayyaf guerrillas, a fundamentalist group close to al-Qaida. Brig. Gen.

Alexander Aleo, a spokesman for the Philippine military, confirmed the information, stating that a 9-month-old girl was among the dead. Abu Sayyaf, formed in 1991, is the most feared guerrilla group operating in the southern Philippines.

Priest Killed in Burundi — Pope Benedict XVI called for an end to violence in Burundi on Feb. 7, after learning of the killing of a priest on the outskirts of the capital, Bujumbura. The priest died Saturday after apparently being caught up in a gunfight between rebels and the army. The Holy See published the telegram sent to Abp. Paul Gallagher, apostolic nuncio in Bujumbura, after he learned of the death of Jesuit Fr. Elie Koma, 59, in which the pope expressed "his profound sorrow... to all the members of his family and to his brother Jesuits," offering "a fervent prayer to the Lord of Life for the dead and for all those in mourning." The telegram was sent by Vatican Secretary of State Card. Angelo Sodano. Fr. Koma was in charge of the newly built Jesuit church in Kamenge, one of the poorest neighborhoods of Bujumbura. About 65 percent of Burundi's 6 million inhabitants are Catholics. Of the rest of the population, 23 percent profess indigenous beliefs, and 10 percent Islam. A small percentage is Protestant.

Angola Murder — On Feb. 10 the Vatican Congregation for the Evangelization of Peoples expressed its sadness over the murder of Portuguese missionary Fr. José Afonso, 80. The priest of the Congregation of the Holy Spirit "was shot seven times at close range in the face," a church source stated. He had just gone to bed when about 15 armed men broke into his room and shot him dead without even giving him time to get out of bed. Card. Crescenzio Sepe, prefect of the Congregation for the Evangelization of Peoples, and Abp. Robert Sarah, the dicastery's secretary, sent a telegram of sympathy to Abp. José de Queirós Alves of Huambo and to Fr. Jean Paul Hoch, superior general of the Congregation of the Holy Spirit. Police think the motive was robbery.

Desecrations in Mexico — It was announced on Feb. 13 that incidents involving desecration have prompted the Diocese of La Paz, in Baja California, to close 200 chapels and churches to visitors until Mar. and bells will be silenced. Masses will be still allowed during this time, Bishop Miguel Ángel Alba Díaz said in a communiqué issue over the weekend. The statement came in the wake of desecrations at the Cathedral of La Paz, the Shrine of Guadalupe and two parishes of the municipality of Comondu. The theft of sacred objects and those of worship, as well sacred art, is taking place in La Paz in broad daylight. The tabernacle of the cathedral was stolen, as well as a chalice and the Blessed Sacrament.

Libyan Arsons — It was reported on Feb. 23 that a Catholic church and a convent in Benghazi, Libya, were plundered and burned just days after anti-Italian protests in Libya turned violent. The attacks against the two religious properties forced the apostolic vicar of Benghazi, the rest of his Franciscan community, and the religious men and women who lived and worked in the diocese to be evacuated to the Libyan capital, Tripoli. Bp. Sylvester Magro of Benghazi told Vatican Radio that "everything has gone up in smoke." Everything inside the church and friary was destroyed; "everything that could be set on fire was set on fire," he said. Demonstrators were condemning a recent incident in which an Italian government minister had unbuttoned his shirt on Italian television to display a T-shirt bearing an image of one of the Danish cartoons that have sparked condemnations and demonstrations in many Muslim communities.

NATIONAL

Spokane Diocese — It was reported on Feb. 1 that the Diocese of Spokane is offering a $45.7 million settlement to 75 abuse victims. The settlement, which must be approved by a bankruptcy court and the plaintiffs "is not the end, but the beginning of the end," according to Spokane Bp. William S. Skylstad, president of the U.S. Conference of Catholic Bishops. He said that he hoped that with the announcement of the proposed settlement "we can together begin to take the first small steps toward reconciliation and forgiveness. I also apologize for the fact that this day has been so long in coming." The bishop also addressed all the Catholics in his diocese, telling them it is "imperative that we resolve this tragic chapter in the history of our church and that we do so now."

Inactive Catholics — A project called Mission Chicago 2006 was announced on Feb. 16 by Card. Francis George. The project is a year-long series of Masses, prayer novenas, discussions and other events to revitalize Catholics in the Chicago Archdiocese. The mission began with a three-day Catholic Festival of Faith in suburban Rosemont, and continued with six revival talks at parishes from Feb. 23 to Apr. 9. The talks, or "special missions," will be led by Fr. Robert Barron, a theology professor from the University of St. Mary of the Lake in Mundelein, Illinois, and include "What's Missing in My Life?"; "The Drama of Conversion"; "Christ, the Center of Your Life"; "The Church and the Eucharist"; "The Power of the Cross"; and "Your Life is Not About You."

Bishop Criticizes Production — Bp. John M. D'Arcy, of Fort Wayne-South Bend, was reported on Feb. 19 as criticizing the production of *The Vagina Monologues* at Notre Dame. Bp. D'Arcy said the play "distorts the beautiful gift of human sexuality." "I regret the sponsorship of this play by Notre Dame again this year, and pray it will be the last time," he added. The bishop said the play "reduces sexuality to a particular organ of a woman's body separate from the person of the woman, from her soul and her spirit. It alienates woman from man whom God has entrusted to her as friend and companion. It separates sexuality and the human body from love."

New Orleans — It was reported on Feb. 25 that a new TV ministry is in operation at St. Luke the Evangelist Parish in Slidell, Louisiana. The parish offers a closed-circuit video feed to bring Mass to about 100 people who cannot fit inside its 550-seat worship space, in a community room adjacent to the main church. The room has folding chairs and glass doors that people can use to enter the church to receive Communion. A sound system and television provide the liturgy live. Slidell is north of New Orleans and near the north shore of Lake Pontchartrain. Like most other north shore parishes, St. Luke has experienced a 22 percent increase in Mass attendance as displaced residents from various parts of New Orleans have migrated north to find temporary or permanent homes.

MARCH 2006

VATICAN

Bible Meditation — On Mar. 1, Ash Wednesday, Pope Benedict XVI urged meditation on the word of God, declaring: "Lent stimulates us to allow our lives to be penetrated by the word of God and in that way to know the fundamental truth about who we are, where we come from, where we are going and what is the path we must follow in our lives." "Remember that you are dust and to dust you will return" and "Turn away from sin and be faithful to the Gospel" are part of the Ash Wednesday ritual, and the Holy Father said that the first is a reminder that people have fallen and have limits, and "is meant to urge us to place all our hope in God alone." The admonition to "convert and believe in the Gospel," he said, "places firm and faithful adhesion to the Gospel at the foundation of personal and communal renewal."

Gypsy Pastoral Guidelines — It was announced on Mar. 1 that the Holy See has published an evangelization document particularly geared for the benefit of nomadic people. "The Guidelines for the Pastoral Care of Gypsies" was presented to the press by Card. Stephen Fumio Hamao, president of the Pontifical Council for Migrants and Travelers. "These guidelines are a sign that the Church has a particular concern for Gypsies," the cardinal said. "They are the receiver of a special pastoral action in appreciation of their culture that, like all others, must pass through the paschal mystery of death and resurrection." In 1988 John Paul II established the Pontifical Council for Migrants and Travelers.

Assisi Churches — Pope Benedict XVI on Mar. 1 was reported as having appointed Card. Attilio Nicora papal legate for the basilicas of St. Francis and St. Mary of the Angels in Assisi, Italy. In 2005, the Holy Father introduced new norms for the two basilicas: a papal legate as a sign of the link of the Apostolic See with Assisi, and the jurisdiction of the local bishop over the two major Franciscan churches to harmonize their activities with the diocesan pastoral program. The first basilica, which houses the remains of St. Francis, is entrusted to the Conventual Franciscans. The second basilica, which contains the Portiuncula chapel, is entrusted to the Franciscan Order of the Friars Minor. The cardinal does not have jurisdiction over these Franciscan sites. But, "he will be able to impart the papal blessing in the celebrations over which he will preside on the occasion of major liturgical solemnities," according to a papal letter.

Papal iPod Nano — It was reported on Mar. 3 that Vatican Radio employees presented Pope Benedict XVI with a specially loaded iPod nano, containing special Vatican Radio programming and classical music. To honor the Holy Father's first visit to the radio's broadcasting headquarters, the radio's technical staff decided on the gift. Now that Vatican Radio offers podcasts in eight different languages, the pope has the technological capability to plug in and import the radio's audio files. Pope Benedict XVI's visited the programming and broadcasting hub of "the pope's radio" to mark its 75th anniversary. The Holy Father greeted the staff and praised the evangelizing ministry conducted by the vast network across the world.

Lenten Address — On Mar. 5, Pope Benedict XVI gave his first Lenten Angelus address, announcing: "To fulfill our life in freedom it is necessary to surmount the test that freedom itself implies, that is, temptation." From the window of his study, the Holy Father said, "Only if liberated from falsehood and sin, can the human person, thanks to the obedience of faith that opens him to truth, find the full meaning of his existence and have peace, love and joy," addressing the thousands of pilgrims who gathered in St. Peter's Square to pray the Angelus at midday. He assured all of his prayers that "for all Christians, Lent will be an occasion of conversion and of a more courageous impulse to holiness."

Papal Retreat — Pope Benedict XVI and members of the Roman Curia began Spiritual Exercises on Mar. 5, a weeklong retreat during which the Holy Father will refrain from all audiences. Card. Marco Cé, retired patriarch of Venice, Italy, will preach the retreat on the theme "Walking with Jesus toward Easter, Led by the Evangelist Mark." In his Angelus address the Holy Father said that these spiritual exercises "will help me and my collaborators of the Roman Curia enter with greater awareness in this characteristic Lenten climate... a favorable time for a careful revision of life in recollection, prayer and penance." Card. Cé will preach three meditations each day. There will also be daily recitation of the Liturgy of the Hours, adoration and benediction.

Rosary Teleconnect — On Mar. 12, European and African Students united via a satellite connection to pray the rosary with Pope Benedict XVI. The Holy Father was heard by thousands of university students of Rome, gathered in Paul VI Hall, and by students in Bonn, Germany; Dublin, Ireland; Fribourg, Switzerland; Madrid, Spain; Munich, Germany; Salamanca, Spain; St. Petersburg, Russia; Sofia, Bulgaria; Abidjan, Ivory Coast; Antananarivo, Madagascar; Owerri, Nigeria; and Nairobi, Kenya. The pope and those gathered in Rome could also see the young people of the various countries who were leading the mysteries of the rosary. He said the event was "a beautiful gesture of the communion of the Catholic Church."

Pontifical Councils — It was announced on Mar. 12 that Pope Benedict XVI had merged the leadership of four pontifical councils under two cardinals, a move that he did not say is permanent. The Holy Father appointed Card. Paul Poupard, 75, who is already head of the Pontifical Council for Culture, also to lead the Council for Interreligious Dialogue. The former head of the interreligious council, Abp. Michael Fitzgerald, was named in Feb. 2006 as the Holy See's new ambassador to Egypt and the 22-member Arab League. Pope Benedict XVI accepted the resignation of the president of the Pontifical Council for Migrants and Travelers, Card. Stephen Fumio Hamao, 76, for reasons of age, and "for the time being has united the executive of this council with that of the Pontifical Council for Justice and Peace." He named Card. Renato Martino, 73, as president of both councils.

Egyptian Leader — Pope Benedict XVI and Egyptian President Hosni Mubarak held a private, 20-minute meeting in the Vatican on Mar. 13. The Holy Father and the president assessed ongoing relations between the Holy See and Cairo, as well as the situation in Iran and Iraq. The meeting, which took place in the Pope's private library, was described by Vatican sources as cordial. After the audience, there was the customary exchange of gifts. President Mubarak gave the Holy Father a silver case with Benedict XVI's name engraved in Arabic, and the Holy Father gave the Egyptian president and his entourage rosaries and medals of his pontificate. Some estimates state that about 94 percent of Egypt's 77.5 million inhabitants are Muslims, mostly Sunnis. Most of the rest are Coptic Christians. Baptized Catholics number about 300,000. Coptic Catholics, whose patriarch is Card. Stephanos II Gatas, operate about 170 highly-esteemed schools, in which the majority of pupils are Muslim.

Cooperation Affirmed — On Mar. 17, the Vatican disclosed copies of letters between Pope Benedict XVI and Russian Orthodox Patriarch Alexy II of Moscow that display a mutual understanding and affirm the importance of Catholics and Orthodox cooperating to keep Gospel values alive in increasingly secularized societies. Pope Benedict XVI sent a brief letter on the occasion of Patriarch Alexy's 77th birthday and his name day, Feb. 23. The letter was given to the patriarch by Card. Roger Etchegaray, former president of the Pontifical Council for Justice and Peace, who was invited to Moscow to take part in the Patriarch's birthday festivities. In addition to offering his prayers and best wishes, the Holy Father expressed his hopes for improved relations between the Catholic and Russian Orthodox churches.

Cameroon Bishops — On Mar. 18, Pope Benedict XVI received a group of Catholic bishops from Cameroon. "The church is called to become more and more a home and school of communion," the Holy Father announced to the bishops on their *ad limina* visit to the Vatican, which heads of dioceses make every five years. He encouraged the bishops to continue demonstrating "how the Catholic Church takes to heart the promotion of the well-being and dignity of all the people of Cameroon, without exceptions, and the fulfillment of their profound aspirations to unity, peace, justice and fraternity." The bishops met with other Vatican officials and agencies during their stay in Rome.

Mass for Workers — On Mar. 19, Pope Benedict XVI presided over a Mass dedicated to workers in St. Peter's Basilica. The Holy Father's homily highlighted the feast of St. Joseph, patron of workers, which will be celebrated this year on Monday, because the usual feast day, Mar. 19, coincides with a Sunday of Lent. Card. Camillo Ruini, the Holy Father's vicar for Rome and president of the Italian episcopal conference, concelebrated the Mass with other bishops. In keeping with his concern for the recognition of the worth of individual human beings, Pope Benedict XVI said that work must "always be organized and develop in full respect of human dignity and at the service of the common good. At the same time," he added, "it is indispensable that man not allow himself to be subjected to work, that he not idolize it, intending to find in it the ultimate and definitive meaning of life."

Cause of John Paul II — It was reported on Mar. 19 that the cause for the beatification and canonization of Pope John Paul II now had an official voice that will offer information to the faithful. A monthly publication called *Totus Tuus* and designed to offer documentation, analysis and information on the process that could lead the beloved Polish pope to the honor of the altars of the Church. *Totus Tuus*, "All Yours," refers to Pope John Paul II's personal motto, with which he entrusted his life to the Blessed Virgin Mary. The newsletter can be requested via the web site of the Diocese of Rome: www.vicariatusurbis.org.

Armenian Christians — On Mar. 20, Pope Benedict XVI encouraged Armenian Orthodox and Catholics, who trace their origins back to St. Gregory the Illuminator, to work to restore their unity in one community united with the pope. Meeting with members of the synod of the Armenian Catholic Church and with Armenian Catholic pilgrims, the Holy Father declared: "I encourage this new-found fraternity and collaboration, hoping that from it there would arise new initiatives for a common path toward full unity." Patriarch Nerses Bedros XIX Tarmouni of Beirut, the Armenian Catholic patriarch, led the group and spoke with the Holy Father about their mutual concerns.

Monte Cassino — On Mar. 21, Pope Benedict XVI conveyed greetings to the Benedictine monks of Monte Cassino as they celebrated the day for their founder, St. Benedict, the Holy Father's namesake. Card. Paul Poupard, president of the Pontifical Councils for Culture and for Interreligious Dialogue, conveyed Benedict XVI's greetings to the monks of the historic monastery 55 miles south of Rome. The Holy Father "has asked me to express to you his closeness in prayer, his spiritual participation in this celebration and his profound and continuous interest in the destiny of Europe and of the peoples who comprise it," the cardinal said during a Mass. St. Benedict (c. 480-543) was proclaimed patron of Europe in 1964 by Pope Paul VI. Monte Cassino has long symbolized the monastic life and has played significant roles in many historical eras, including World War II.

Vatican Visitors — It was reported on Mar. 21 that in Apr. 2005, the city of Rome saw record numbers of crowds as millions of people from all over the world arrived at the Vatican for the funeral of Pope John Paul II in St. Peter's Basilica. Vast numbers of the faithful returned for the conclave of cardinals and the subsequent election of Pope Benedict XVI. According to Vatican attendance records, the crowds have just continued to come to in the Vatican. In the first eight months of his pontificate, Pope Benedict XVI drew nearly three million pilgrims to public events. According to the Prefecture of the Pontifical Household, more than 2.8 million people attended the weekly general audiences given by the Holy Father, the Sunday blessings, special papal audiences or liturgical celebrations at which Pope Benedict XVI presided. Also, the number of visitors going through the doors of the Vatican Museums in 2005 broke all records.

Pope Creates Cardinals — Pope Benedict XVI created 15 new cardinals from 11 countries on Mar. 24 in a ceremony full of traditions and spiritual symbols. The main elements in the ceremonies surrounding the creation of new cardinals are the red hat, church and ring. The Holy Father prayed that the red garments they were given would inspire them to an even more "passionate love for Christ, for his church and for all humanity." The Holy Father told the new cardinals they would be called upon to work closely with him "and this will mean for you a more intense participation in the mystery of the cross as you share in the sufferings of Christ." U.S. Card. William J. Levada, the prefect of the Congregation for the Doctrine of the Faith, was the first to receive his red hat. As the top-ranking member of the new group, the former archbishop of San Francisco addressed the Holy Father on behalf of the new cardinals. In accepting their new status, Card. Levada said, the cardinals renew their commitment to "total love and unconditional fidelity to Christ the Lord and to the Christian people." One by one, the new cardinals knelt before Pope Benedict XVI so that he could place the four-cornered red hat, or biretta, on their heads. Each cardinal was given a scroll testifying to his membership in the College of Cardinals and containing the name of his titular church in Rome. By receiving the "title" to a Rome church, each cardinal formally becomes part of the clergy of the Eternal City, Rome. This serves as an important link between the modern tradition of the College of Cardinals electing a pope to the early church practice of Rome's clergy electing their bishop. The cardinals' new status and relationship with the pope were to be sealed with a ring at a Mass celebrated on Mar. 25. (*See under* News in Depth.)

John Paul II Film — It was announced on Mar. 31 that Pope Benedict XVI and six thousand guests viewed the made-for-TV movie, *Karol: A Pope Who Remained Man.* This second part of the two-part film was shown in Paul VI Hall, and was applauded by the viewers. After viewing the movie the Holy Father announced: "Once again we heard the opening appeal of his pontificate, which sounded out so often through the years. 'Open the doors to Christ! Do not be afraid!' " Pope Benedict XVI added: "May our beloved Pope accompany us from on high and obtain for us from the Lord the grace to be always faithful, like him, on our mission."

GENERAL AUDIENCE
On Ash Wednesday (Mar. 3)
Church, Presence of Christ Among Men (Mar. 15)
Apostles as Envoys of Christ (Mar. 22)
The Gift of "Communion" (Mar. 29)

INTERNATIONAL
God is Creator — In a statement released on Mar. 1 a dialogue commission sponsored by the Vatican and the Chief Rabbinate of Israel stated that because God is the creator of human life, people cannot "decide its value or extent" as if they owned it. The learned members of the dialogue commission discussed the modern issues related to human life and technology, particularly concerning the Catholic and Jewish positions on euthanasia. "We affirm the principles of our respective traditions that God is the creator and lord of all life and that human life is sacred," the statement declared. Members of the dialogue specifically condemned "active euthanasia" as an "illegitimate human arrogation of an exclusive divine authority to determine the time of a person's death."

Ukrainian Martyrs — It was reported on Mar. 1 that a memorial to the Ukrainian Martyrs of the Gulag was unveiled recently in the Karaganda region of Kazakhstan. The monument, located in Mamin cemetery in the village of Dolinka, symbolizes the suffering of many victims of Communist persecution and especially honors Blessed Oleksiy Zarytskyi, one of 27 martyrs beatified in June 2001. Blessed Oleksiy died in the Dolinka prison hospital on Oct. 30, 1963. A chapel dedicated to Blessed Oleksiy was opened in 2001, at the Church of the Protection of the Mother of God in Karaganda, a diocese the size of Italy. A former Soviet republic, Kazakhstan has 17 million inhabitants. The majority are Muslims or Orthodox. It has some 360,000 Catholics.

Blasts in Basilica — On Mar. 5, an attack on the Basilica of the Annunciation in Nazareth by an Israeli family elicited an official apology from the authorities of Israel. An Israeli man, together with his wife and daughter, set off explosives with firecrackers and gas canisters in the lower part of the basilica Friday afternoon while the faithful were praying the Stations of the Cross in the upper section. The attackers were seized immediately and locked in the guard room. The incident, however, drew thousands of people representing various religions, who came to the basilica from Nazareth and surrounding villages with the intention of protecting it with their own lives. The crowd remained late into the night. That same night, Israeli authorities formally apologized to Abp. Giovanni Lajolo, Vatican secretary for relations with states, to Latin Patriarch Michel Sabbah of Jerusalem, and to Fr. Pierbattista Pizzaballa, the Custos of the Holy Land. The Latin Patriarchate, the Custos of the Holy Land and the leaders of Churches in Galilee published a communiqué Saturday expressing appreciation for the apology. The message also praised the people who had come to the basilica and displayed courage and fortitude in protecting the house of worship.

Priest Attacked in Turkey — It was reported on Mar. 12 that another priest in the southern Turkish city of Mersin has been attacked. A young man with a knife entered the parish of Capuchin Fr. Hanri Leylek, saying that he wanted to speak with a priest. The Turk insulted the priest and then threatened him with a large knife. The priest was able to repel the aggressor, and that same evening the police arrested a suspect. Bp. Luigi Padovese, the apostolic vicar of Anatolia, reported that this was the second time in two months that an attempt was made to kill a Catholic clergyman in the parish of Mersin, where 700 Catholics reside.

Vietnam Seminaries — Some 250 seminarians are in the theological training center of the Archdiocese of Thanh-Pho Ho Chi Minh, it was reported on Mar. 12 by the archbishop, Card. Jean-Baptiste Pham Minh Mân. As a result of the number of vocations, there is a genuine need for larger facilities and additional trained teachers. The archdiocese (formerly known as Saigon) receives candidates from six southern dioceses, and the government has stipulated that they allow all applicants to be admitted. In Hanoi, St. Joseph's Major Seminary supplies priests to eight northern dioceses. Currently, it has 235 students. About 6 million of Vietnam's 83 million inhabitants are Catholic. The Vietnamese government has demonstrated willingness in recent months to cooperate to some extent with the Catholic Church.

Russian Catholics Pray With Pope — On Mar. 13 it was reported that Catholics in Russia joined Pope Benedict XVI in praying the rosary last Saturday when

32   MARCH 2006

a dozen European and African cities were linked via satellite with the Vatican. A Marian vigil attended by university students was held at the Vatican, and the Church of St. Ekaterina in St. Petersburg was the venue where the connection took place. Some 600 people gathered for the event. St. Petersburg was chosen to lead the fifth mystery of the rosary. The participation of the Russians of St. Petersburg provided them with a sense of unity and solidarity with the Universal Church and offered a rare glimpse of Russian faithful to the other Catholics involved in the satellite program.

Nun Slain — It was reported on Mar. 15 that a member of the Daughters of the Sacred Heart was fatally stabbed in her convent near Ambon, in the Molucca Islands. The 33-year-old sister found an intruder in the convent at Jalan Pattimura, who then attacked her with a knife. Religion was not the reason for the crime, according to local authorities; the nun's murderer is thought to have been a thief. Previously, Ambon was the scene of interreligious clashes between resident Protestant Christians and immigrant Muslims in which as many as 15,000 people were killed. The Catholic Church acted as a mediator to promote reconciliation during the crisis.

Priest Murdered in India — It was reported on Mar. 18 that Fr. Eusebio Ferrão, a beloved parish priest in the state of Goa, India, was brutally murdered. He suffered 27 stab wounds on the back and chest, inflicted after his death by strangulation and smothering. Abp. Filipe do Rosario Ferrão of Goa and Daman, who is not related to the priest, arrived at the parish that morning to lead a prayer service. He described the murder as "the first of its kind in peaceful Goa in recent times." The Archdiocese of Goa said it is "deeply pained and anguished at the cold-blooded murder" of Fr. Ferrão.

Opus Dei — The worldwide Catholic Personal Prelature depicted in vicious fashion in *The Da Vinci Code* has now unveiled a web site in 22 languages to serve the vast number of people interested in the activities of the group. More than three million visited the web site in 2005 to learn about Opus Dei and to find information about the Church. Opus Dei also offered details about the novel's historical inaccuracies. "*The Da Vinci Code* has definitely increased the numbers of visitors to our web site," Peter Bancroft of the Opus Dei communications office in New York stated. The press room section of the site offers contact information for Opus Dei press offices around the world, as well as backgrounders, press releases and other pertinent data.

NATIONAL

Same-Sex Couples' Adoptions — It was reported on Mar. 1 that the bishops of the four Massachusetts dioceses believe that forcing Catholic agencies in Massachusetts to facilitate adoptions by same-sex couples in violation of church teaching prohibiting the practice would present "a serious pastoral problem" and threaten religious freedom. "We are asking the commonwealth to respect the constitutional guarantee of religious freedom and allow the Catholic Church to continue serving children in need of adoption without violating the tenets of our faith," the four said in a Feb. 28 statement. On the same day, Massachusetts Gov. Mitt Romney indicated through a spokesman that he would be open to discussions about exempting Catholic social service agencies from the state's anti-discrimination policy in the matter of adoptions by same-sex couples.

Notre Dame — On Mar. 5, the president of the University of Notre Dame gave permission for continued performances on campus of *The Vagina Monologues*, a controversial play that explicitly discusses women's sexuality. Holy Cross Fr. John I. Jenkins favored the inclusion of panel discussions after future performances, in which Catholic teachings on human sexuality are presented as part of a discussion of the issues in the play. The permission for future performances drew immediate criticism from Bp. John M. D'Arcy of Fort Wayne-South Bend, who said he was "deeply saddened by the decision." He had previously asked that performances be ended as inappropriate for a Catholic university.

Sexual Abuse Claim — On Mar. 8, Bp. William S. Skylstad of Spokane, president of the U.S. Conference of Catholic Bishops, denied a woman's claim that he sexually abused her more than 40 years ago when she was a minor. Bp. Skylstad categorically denies the accusation, stating: "I have kept the promise of celibacy that I made when I was ordained a deacon 47 years ago." Bp. Skylstad added: "I hope that the Spokane community will join me in praying for all those who have come forward to report sexual abuse. Please pray for me as well." Abp. Pietro Sambi, papal nuncio to the United States, has been advised of the accusation. Bp. Skylstad, 72, has been a priest since 1960 and a bishop since 1977. He has headed the Spokane Diocese since 1990.

Vocations Film — On Mar. 14, it was reported that *Fishers of Men*, an 18-minute film aimed at promoting priestly vocations, will be premiered this week by the U.S. bishops' conference. The film is part of a wider project, Priestly Life and Vocation Summit, and is intended to renew priests' sense of fulfillment in their vocation and to encourage them to invite other men to pursue the priesthood. The project was developed by the bishops' Committee on Vocations and was produced by Grassroots Films of New York. The video is accompanied by questions for discussion among priests who view the film together at their diocesan vocation summit. The *Fishers of Men* trailer can be viewed at www.usccb.org/vocations.

Vatican Laicizes Boston Clerics — It was announced on Mar. 17 that seven priests and one deacon of the Boston Archdiocese accused of sexually abusing minors have been laicized by the Vatican. Among the priests removed from the clerical state was Msgr. Frederick Ryan, a former archdiocesan vice chancellor and regional vicar. The Vatican decision means that the men will no longer receive financial support from the archdiocese and may no longer perform public ministry, with the exception that those who are priests may offer absolution to the dying. The deacon who was laicized is Joseph Crowley.

APRIL 2006

VATICAN

Scientific Progress — Pope Benedict XVI, on Apr. 1, addressed participants of a Vatican international conference on higher education, saying that scientific and technological progress must never come at the cost of the life and dignity of people, The seminar was sponsored by the Vatican's Congregation for Catholic Education and focused on the theme of "The Cultural Heritage and Academic Values of the European University and the General Interest in European Higher Education." The Holy Father announced that universities and other institutions of higher learning can play a key role in sustaining the ideals and values that uphold and protect humanity while still pursuing scientific advancements.

John Paul II's Death — On Apr. 2, some 100,000 people gathered at St. Peter's Square to commemorate the first anniversary of the death of Pope John Paul II. The gathering commemorated the praying of the rosary that ended last Apr. 2 with the announcement: "Our Holy Father has returned to the Father's House." Pope Benedict XVI appeared at the window of his study at 9:37 p.m., the precise time of John Paul II's death, to announce: "He continues to be present in our minds and in our hearts. He continues to communicate to us his love for God and his love for men." The Holy Father added: "His illness, faced with courage, made everyone pay more attention to human pain, to all physical and spiritual pain; he gave suffering dignity and value, demonstrating that man's worth is not in his efficiency or his appearance, but in himself, because he has been created and loved by God."

John Paul II — At a Mass to mark the first anniversary of his death, celebrated on Mar. 3, Pope Benedict XVI presented Pope John Paul II, "as a 'rock' in the faith." Addressing a crowd of people in St. Peter's Square, the Holy Father announced: "Whoever had the possibility to see him up close could almost touch with his hand that pure and solid faith that, though it impressed the circle of his collaborators, did not fail to spread, during his long pontificate, his beneficial influence throughout the Church, with a crescendo that reached its summit in the last months and days of his life." He described the faith of Pope John Paul II as "a convinced, strong, authentic faith, free of fears and compromises, which affected the hearts of many people, thanks also to the numerous apostolic pilgrimages to all parts of the world, and especially thanks to that last 'journey,' his agony and death. The deceased Pontiff, whom God endowed with many human and spiritual gifts, passing through the crucible of apostolic fatigues and illness, appeared ever more as a 'rock' in the faith."

Catholics' Role — On Apr. 3, Pope Benedict XVI received the bishops of the Ivory Coast who were ending their *ad limina*, five-yearly visit to Rome. The Holy Father announced: "In your diocesan churches, in the face of political or ethnic tensions, bishops, priests and consecrated persons must always be models of fraternity and charity, and contribute with their word and attitudes to building a unified and reconciled society." He counseled also: "The re-establishment of authentic peace" in their West African country "will only be possible if forgiveness is generously granted and reconciliation realized effectively between affected persons and groups." He told them, "The path to peace is long and difficult, but never impossible," and stressed that Catholics "have the responsibility to contribute to the establishment of harmonious and fraternal relations between individuals and communities."

Eucharistic Congress Ark — It was reported on Apr. 4 that Pope Benedict XVI planned to bless the Eucharistic Congress ark before it tours Canada. The ark was created to inspire, excite and prepare Canadian Catholics for the 2008 International Eucharistic Congress, and was to travel first to Rome, then to dioceses around Canada, it was announced by Quebec Card. Marc Ouellet. The "Ark of the New Covenant" is a chest covered with iconic images related to the Eucharist and will be blessed in Rome by Pope Benedict XVI when the Quebec bishops visit in early May. Up to 20,000 people, mostly from North America, were expected to gather in Quebec City June 15-22, 2008, to celebrate the Eucharistic Congress as part of the celebrations of the 400th anniversary of the founding of the city.

Palm Sunday — Pope Benedict XVI led tens of thousands of people in St. Peter's Square in the celebration of Palm Sunday on Apr. 9. Addressing the faithful, the Holy Father spoke of the happiness brought by Christ dying on the cross, as opposed to the ephemeral promises of power made by the modern society, obsessed with wealth. "There was a time—and it has not been totally surmounted—in which Christianity was rejected precisely because of the cross," the Holy Father said during his homily. The Holy Father said that Jesus bequeaths a message on Palm Sunday that contradicts the world. "We do not attain life by seizing it, but by giving it." Benedict XVI stressed that, "Love is the giving of ourselves and, for this reason, it is the path of authentic life symbolized by the cross." The day's Mass began with the blessing of palms and olive branches carried by the faithful.

Opus Dei Conference — Pope Benedict XVI met with 5,000 university students attending an Opus Dei-sponsored conference on Apr. 10. He encouraged them to deepen their friendship with Christ so they can share their faith. The UNIV 2006 Conference brought students from some 200 universities in 32 countries to Rome for a week of study and exchanges on faith and modern life, focusing especially on the mass media. The Holy Father told the students that it was obvious that the mass media do not always promote "personal relations, sincere dialogue and friendship among people," and they do not always help people cultivate their relationships with God. He urged: "Keep Jesus as one of your dearest friends, rather your best friend. Then you will see how friendship with him will lead to you opening yourselves to others."

Way of the Cross — On Apr. 14, Pope Benedict XVI led the first Way of the Cross of his pontificate. Thousands of copies of the meditations and prayers used in the ceremonies were given to pilgrims and tourists at the Colosseum in the past, and, for the first time, this year the Vatican publishing house also sent 103,000 copies of the booklets to bookstores throughout Italy. Germany's Herder publishing house simultaneously released a German translation of the text. In addition, the Vatican posted the original Italian text Apr. 11 on its Web site, www.vatican.va, along with translations in English, French, German, Polish, Portuguese and Spanish.

Easter Appeal — On Easter Sunday, Apr. 16, Pope Benedict XVI made an Easter plea for peace in the name of the resurrection of Jesus, particularly in Africa, the Middle East and Latin America. After celebrating Easter Mass today, and before imparting the blessing *Urbi et Orbi* (to the city of Rome and the world), the Holy Father read a message for "this modern age marked by anxiety and uncertainty," saying: "Jesus is risen, and he gives us peace; he himself is peace. For this reason the Church repeats insistently: 'Christ is risen—"Christós anésti.' " Let the people of the third millennium not be afraid to open their hearts to him. His Gospel totally quenches the thirst for peace and happiness that is found in every human heart. Christ is now alive and he walks with us. What an immense mystery of love!" Some 100,000 people were gathered in St. Peter's Square to hear the message. Hundreds of millions more, in 65 countries, followed the event on radio or television. After reading his message, Benedict XVI wished the world a happy Easter in 63 languages, including Arabic, Hebrew and Chinese.

Divine Mercy — On Apr. 23, Pope Benedict XVI called devotion to Divine Mercy "an integral dimension of a Christian's faith and prayer." During celebration of Divine Mercy Sunday, the Holy Father prayed the Regina Caeli with more than 50,000 individuals gathered in St. Peter's Square. St. Faustina Kowalski promoted the devotion, which was supported by Pope John Paul II. Pope Benedict XVI commented on the day's Gospel, which narrates the apparition of the risen Christ to the apostles gathered in the Upper Room, announcing: Christ "showed the disciples the signs of the crucifixion, very visible and tangible also in his glorious body. Those sacred wounds, in the hands, the feet and the side, are an inexhaustible source of faith, hope and love in which each one can drink, especially souls most thirsty for divine mercy." Some of the faithful in the square also carried images inspired by a vision St. Faustina had of Christ. The images carry the inscription "Jesus, I trust in you."

Bishops From Ghana — The Catholic bishops of Ghana were received by Pope Benedict XVI on Apr. 24. He announced that he shares their concern about prevalent indigenous forms of matrimony that go against the sacrament of marriage in that nation. "For the Christian, traditional forms of marriage can never be a substitute for sacramental marriage," the Pope said in his address to the bishops, who were concluding their five-yearly visit to Rome. The Holy Father explained to the bishops that it is the "Church's task to assist Christian families to live faithfully and generously as true 'domestic churches.'"

Rome's Welcome — On Apr. 25, Pope Benedict XVI was honored by Rome with a concert, celebrating the 2,759th anniversary of the city's founding and the Holy Father's first anniversary in the papacy. Among those who received the pope were the president of Italy, Carlo Azeglio Ciampi; the vicar general for the Diocese of Rome, Card. Camillo Ruini; and Mayor Walter Veltroni. The Holy Father told the assembled Romans that the memory of the city's foundation "is a propitious occasion to understand better Rome's vocation to be a beacon of civilization and spirituality for the entire world." He added: "A year ago, following the death of the beloved and unforgettable John Paul II, the Catholic community of Rome was entrusted — surprisingly, I must say — by divine Providence to my pastoral care." He also marveled at how "generous, open and hospitable" Romans are and described their "singular human and spiritual warmth," which he said he was able to experience since the day of his election, Apr. 19, 2005.

Moral Mandates — On Apr. 27, Pope Benedict XVI stated that the Ten Commandments and other biblical moral mandates were not designed to limit human freedom, but to help people behave in ways that will lead to their full freedom and happiness. The Holy Father addressed members of the Pontifical Biblical Commission, which is continuing its work on a document about the relationship between the Bible and morality. "The law of God does not diminish or, even less, eliminate human freedom, but on the contrary guarantees and promotes it." He added that many people today think that the only way to reach happiness and fulfillment is by relying own their own reason and pursuing their own desires. "This erroneous conviction is based on a presumed conflict between human freedom and every form of law," he said.

Canonization Decrees — On Apr. 28, Pope Benedict XVI approved the promulgation of decrees of recognition of miracles or martyrdom for the canonization of four and the beatification of a large number of candidates. The approval was given to Card. José Saraiva Martins, prefect of the Congregation for Sainthood Causes, to proceed in these Causes. A miracle was approved for the Cause of Blessed Teodora Guérin, née Anna Teresa Guérin, French founder of the Congregation of the Sisters of Providence of St. Mary of the Woods in the United States (1798-1856). Miracles were also approved for the Causes of Blessed Filippo Smaldone, Italian, diocesan priest, founder of the Congregation of the Salesian Sisters of the Sacred Heart (1848-1923); Blessed Rafael Guízar Valencia, Mexican, bishop of Veracruz, Mexico (1878-1938); and Blessed Rosa Venerini, Italian, founder of the Congregation delle Maestre Pie Venerini (1656-1728). Other candidates, including martyrs, were also determined worthy of beatification and will be so honored at future ceremonies.

Bosnia Pact — It was reported on Apr. 28 that an agreement signed between the Holy See and Bosnia-Herzegovina has regulated the juridical position of the Catholic Church in that country. The agreement was signed in the Presidential Palace of Sarajevo, and regulates "the juridical framework of reciprocal relations taking into account the respective independence and autonomy of the state and the Church and of their willingness for mutual collaboration." The terms of the concordat include: the juridical position of the Catholic Church in civil society, its freedom and independence in apostolic activity and the regulation of the realms of its own competence; freedom of worship and action in the cultural, educational, pastoral and charitable fields and in the media are included, as well as the management of Catholic schools; spiritual assistance to the armed forces, and in prisons and hospitals; and the organization of health and charitable Catholic structures.

Pope Pius XII — On Apr. 28, it was reported that the 50th anniversary of the death of Pope Pius XII is coming up in two years, and supporters of his sainthood cause are growing a little impatient as they see their numbers disappear. The generation of church people who lived and worked with Pope Pius is quietly passing from the scene, but some of them gathered recently at Rome's Pontifical Lateran University to hear new evidence of Pope Pius's virtues and to denounce the attacks being made on his conduct during World War II. Card. Fiorenzo Angelini announced at this meeting: "Pius XII must be declared a saint! Admiration isn't enough—people need to get moving! Too much time has already passed."

GENERAL AUDIENCE
The Service to Communion (Apr. 5)
On the Easter Triduum (Apr. 12)
Role of Church Tradition (Apr. 26)
Apr. 19 Address on 1st Anniversary of Pontificate (Apr. 27)

INTERNATIONAL

Ukrainian Milestone — It was announced on Apr. 2 that the Ukrainian Catholic University celebrated the licensing of theology as an academic discipline by Ukraine's Ministry of Education. The Ukraine had been the only country in Central and Eastern Europe where theology was not licensed. The theology program gained recognition at a session of the National Accreditation Committee early in Mar. Ukrainian President Viktor Yushchenko supported the idea of the accreditation of theology in Ukraine. Also important was the support of other schools, in particular Lviv National University, the National University of the Kyiv Mohyla Academy, Krok University, and Chernihiv National University.

Respect for Women — A congress held at the European University in Rome ended with a "Manifesto for Respect of Women in the Media," it was reported on Apr. 2. The international congress, entitled "Women and the Media," was organized by the Athenaeum Regina University's Institute of Higher Studies. The Manifesto demonstrated their concerns and conclusions relating to the dignity of femininity: the problems of the feminine world, the co-responsibility of women in the development and edification of society, and the active presence of women in public life. The members of the congress stated that they committed themselves to responsibly providing information and sensitization by detecting, documenting and speaking out against situations and practices that limit freedom and violate the rights of women and girls.

Executions Postponed — On Apr. 2 it was announced in Jakarta, Indonesia that the executions of three Indonesian Catholics condemned to death for their purported role in the violence in Poso in 2000 have been postponed. PADMA, a group of lawyers defending the Catholics, had been protesting in order to block the executions. Bishop Joseph Suwatan of Manado also relayed a message of support from Pope Benedict XVI to the three prisoners. Brigadier General Oegroseno, head of the central Sulawesi police, said the execution should take place "in the coming days," but would not comment on the postponement.

Beijing Contact with Vatican — On Apr. 3, the Chinese government publicly admitted that contacts exist between China and the Vatican on the question of diplomatic relations. "The contact between us has been continuing all along but it is hard to set a timetable," Ye Xiaowen, director of the State Administration for Religious Affairs, said. Ye's statements came a few days after Abp. Giovanni Lajolo, the Vatican's secretary for relations with states, said "the time is ripe" to re-establish diplomatic relations with Beijing. For over 15 years, China has been demanding that, as pre-conditions, the Vatican break its ties with Taiwan and refrain from "interfering" in the country's internal affairs. At least 80 percent of bishops in the official Church are in communion with the Holy See and those who are not, including the archbishop of Beijing, are rejected by the faithful and marginalized.

Russians Remember John Paul II — It was reported on Apr. 3 that an ecumenical meeting was held in Moscow Catholic Cathedral to honor Pope John Paul II on the first anniversary of his death. The Catholic Cathedral of Moscow welcomed hundreds of faithful for the event. On hand were representatives of various confessions and religions, as well as Catholic priests of the Eastern rite and diplomats from several countries. Images of the life of John Paul II adorned the interior of the church. "God sent us the man our time needed," exclaimed Abp. Tadeusz Kondrusiewicz of the Archdiocese of the Mother of God in Moscow. His words were echoed by the vice spokesman of the Council of the Russian Federation, Aleksander Torshin, who called John Paul II "a great man." "Our task now is to remember his advice more often," Torshin said. "Not only did John Paul II love Russia, but he understood its complexity, the complexity of forming a new civil society." Rabbi Zinobi Kogan, president of the Congress of Jewish Religious Organizations and Groups, said that John Paul II "was a great spiritual leader of the 20th century who saved the dialogue between Jews and Christians, [and the] understanding between them, and inspired us to work for the improvement of our world." He added: "April 2 will always remain as John Paul II Day."

Substitution of Civilizations — The vice president of the European Parliament, Mario Mauro, warned that within 10 years there will be no "clash of civilizations" but rather a substitution of civilizations in Europe. Mauro addressed the first Convention of Catholics and Public Life, organized in Barcelona by the Catholic Associations of Propagandists and the Abat Oliva CEU University on Apr. 4. "The object of relativism is to deny the truth," the speaker said. In this context, Mauro announced, Pope Benedict XVI insists that "truth exists" and that there are truths on which there can be no discussion, such as life, the family and education, and he stated that political dialogue must recognize the content of truth. Otherwise, relativism becomes an ideology, since it is a totalitarian theory in which power is everything. "When the Christian roots of Europe are attacked, it is thought that one offends the memory of our Fathers," he said, "but what we really offend is the future of our children." Mauro fears that a "substitution of civilizations" looms, and he stated that the first battle that must be won is the battle to have truth recognized.

Franciscans at Assisi — It was reported on Apr. 4 that Pope Benedict XVI has continued to rein in the activities of the Franciscan friars of Assisi, who previously had sponsored a series of interreligious prayer meetings, peace marches and conferences on social justice. Participants in these events included Buddhist monks and Muslim imams, activists and politicians. Former Iraqi Deputy Prime Minister Tariq Aziz, a Christian, lit a candle of peace in Assisi shortly before the United States invaded his country in 2003. Pope Benedict issued a one-page document seven months after his election that gave the local bishop and the Italian bishops' conference control over all pastoral activities of Franciscans in Assisi. Later he named a papal delegate to keep closer ties with the friars.

Ambassador Baptized — On Apr. 17, at a Mass in Rome, Taiwan Ambassador to the Vatican, Tou Chouseng, was baptized Catholic. He explained that he was so impressed by seeing "an inner peace and happiness" in the Catholics that he met while living and working in Rome that he decided to convert to Catholicism. The Church of St. Eugenio in Rome, where he was baptized, is administered by the personal prelature of Opus Dei, and Spanish Bishop Javier Echevarria Rodriguez, head of Opus Dei, presided over the Mass and baptism.

Bolivian President — It was reported on Apr. 30 that Bolivian President Evo Morales, that nation's first indigenous president, said the church plays a critical role in supporting the revolutionary changes he seeks for South America's poorest country. "The participation of the church is important in the transformations we're fighting for." He added: "I am a Christian. I understand Christ as a man who struggled against injustice, who gave his life for humanity. Christ struggled for justice and life. Whatever the church, its mission should be applying Christianity, which means working for justice and equality and community." Morales has vowed to end corruption and inefficiency.

NATIONAL

U.S. Catholicism — Abp. Pietro Sambi, the new papal nuncio to the United States, stated on Apr. 3 that he is impressed by the vitality of U.S. Catholicism. The nuncio, who arrived in the U. S. on Feb. 24, said that he was impressed at reports from U.S. bishops on the "hundreds and hundreds of adult persons" who came to their cathedrals on the first Sunday of Lent to begin the final stages of preparation to be baptized or enter into full communion with the Church at Easter. He is also impressed by the level of weekly Mass attendance among U.S. Catholics and by their generosity toward others.

New Orleans Cathedral — It was announced on Apr. 3 that New Orleans Abp. Alfred Hughes would celebrate an Easter Sunday Mass from the city's Cathedral of St. Louis, available for broadcasting by ABC-TV stations nationwide, to demonstrate the fact that the historic cathedral survived the devastation of Hurricane Katrina. The hour-long liturgical special is being produced by WLAE-TV in New Orleans in cooperation with the U.S. bishops' Catholic Communication Campaign (CCC). Abp. Hughes is scheduled to be the homilist for the Mass. The Cathedral of St. Louis, which was established in 1718, had recently completed an extensive renovation when Hurricane Katrina hit New Orleans last August. Located on Jackson Square in the French Quarter, the cathedral did not sustain major structural damage from the storm and flooding, although a new organ was destroyed.

Immigration Debate — It was reported on Apr. 3 that rallies and boycotts have been chosen by pro-immigration advocates as the preferred method by which the immigration debate can be conducted. Los Angeles Card. Roger M. Mahony also called for Apr. 5 to be observed as a special day of prayer and fasting for just and humane immigration reform. He encouraged all Catholics to attend Mass or set aside time on Apr. 5 to pray for legislators, for humane immigration laws, and for those people who will be most affected by such laws.

Marriage Amendment — The president of the U.S. bishops' conference was reported on Apr. 4 as asking prelates and the people in their dioceses to become involved in the effort to support a federal constitutional marriage amendment. Bishop William Skylstad, in a letter to all U.S. Catholic prelates, informed the faithful that the Knights of Columbus have initiated a national postcard campaign to promote support for the Protection of Marriage Amendment. The amendment defines marriage as consisting only of a union between a man and a woman. "Today there is a growing sense shared by many people, including a wide range of religious leaders, that a Marriage Protection Amendment is the only federal-level action that ultimately will protect and preserve the institution of marriage," Bishop Skylstad said.

"Gospel of Judas" — On Apr. 6, a Gnostic writing, the Gospel of Judas, was put on display Apr. 6 at the National Geographic Society in Washington. The National Geographic Society posted a copy of it on the society's web site, releasing English translations of portions of the text. The Gospel of Judas was mentioned in a book written by St. Irenaeus, bishop of Lyon, France, in 180 A.D., condemning heresies. Jesuit Fr. Gerald O'Collins, a longtime professor of Christology at Rome's Pontifical Gregorian University, said the text, like the gospels of Mary Magdalene and Philip, "does not merit the name 'Gospel.'" He also said that the Gospel of Judas was unimportant to most Christians when it was written hundreds of years ago and it is unimportant today. While including events supposedly related to the life of Jesus, the Gospel of Judas and the others really are texts "attempting to bolster the importance" of the personalities they are named after, not of Jesus, the priest said.

Entering the Church — It was reported on Apr. 10 that thousands of Americans were prepared to enter the Catholic Church on Holy Saturday through the Rite of Christian Initiation of Adults. The Archdiocese of Denver stated that 700 people will be baptized and 1,400 will come into full communion there. The Archdiocese for Military Services reported 425 baptismal candidates and 515 people coming into full communion. According to early figures from the 2006 *Official Catholic Directory*, last year 80,521 adults were baptized in the Catholic Church and 73,296 came into full communion. In addition, there were 940,194 infant baptisms. The conversions are a response to John Paul II's death and the search for spiritual fulfillment. The Rite of Christian Initiation of Adults is an ancient ceremony that was reinstituted in the Church following the Second Vatican Council.

Support for Immigrants — It was reported on Apr. 10 that hundreds of people joined rallies, marches and prayer services in support of immigrants, calling for changes in immigration law and policies. In several cities, Catholic bishops gave speeches and led prayers. Many participants were encouraged to join the activities at their churches. Crowds estimated to be as large as 500,000 in Dallas and in Washington, D.C., blocked city streets. The events were part of the National Day of Action for Immigrant Justice.

Diaconate Convention — It was reported on Apr. 25 that the National Association of Diaconate Directors gathered in Denver and heard an address by Abp. Charles J. Chaput. The archbishop said that deacons were originally chosen because the Twelve Apostles needed helpers. "These assistants were not asked to do something fundamentally different from what the apostles were doing," he announced in a keynote speech during the convention. "They were called to do the works of practical service that belonged integrally to the apostolic ministry, the duties the apostles could not always fulfill." Deacons serve the church through ministry of the liturgy, of the word (Scripture) and of charity. Deacons can officiate at baptisms, weddings, wakes and funerals, and they can assist the priest at Mass by preaching and distributing Communion.

MAY 2006

VATICAN

Beatified Priests — It was reported on May 1 that thousands of the faithful gathered at a parish church in southern India and in the square in front of the cathedral in Milan, Italy, for the beatification of three priests. Pope Benedict XVI signed the beatification decrees but did not preside over the ceremonies. Fr. Augustine Thevarparampil was beatified at St. Augustine Parish in Ramapuram, India, and Frs. Luigi Biraghi and Luigi Monza were beatified in Milan. Card. Varkey Vithayathil, head of India's Syro-Malabar Catholic Church, presided over the beatification of Fr. Thevarparampil, and Card. Dionigi Tettamanzi of Milan presided over the Mass for the beatification of the two Italian priests. The new ceremonies are being held in the hometowns of the beatified in order to inspire people and involve them in the process.

Saint Candidates — Pope Benedict XVI was reported as recommending in a message to the Congregation for Saints' Causes that saint candidates be carefully chosen as models for modern men and women. The Congregation members met to discuss a new instruction for the initial diocesan stages of the sainthood process and were looking at possible changes in the formal criteria for determining martyrdom and miracles. The Holy Father announced that from the moment of his election a year ago, he had put into effect changes that met the "widespread hope" that the difference between beatification and canonization would be underlined and that local churches would be more involved in the entire process. Models of holiness, he said, must be chosen with care in this era of secularism and material expectations.

Europe's Soul — On May 3, Pope Benedict XVI expressed his hope that Catholic and Russian Orthodox representatives would work together to "Give a Soul to Europe." The Holy Father sent this greeting to participants in a meeting organized by the Vatican and the Russian Orthodox Church's Moscow Patriarchate. The May 3-5 meeting in Vienna, Austria, was titled, "Give a Soul to Europe: The Mission and Responsibility of the Churches." Card. Paul Poupard, head of the pontifical councils for Culture and for Interreligious Dialogue, and Russian Orthodox Patriarch Alexy II of Moscow proposed the event marking the first time a Vatican office and the Moscow Patriarchate jointly organized a meeting on culture in Europe. The cultural efforts were inspired by the obvious secular tone of EU documents and the apparent disregard for the Christian bases of the past.

Beatifications Planned — It was announced on May 3 that three women religious and a priest would be beatified in May and June in the Netherlands, Italy, Portugal and Brazil, according to the rites approved by Benedict XVI. The beatification of Maria Teresa of St. Joseph (Anna Maria Tauscher van den Bosch), founder of the Carmelite Sisters of the Divine Heart of Jesus, was scheduled to be held in the Dutch town of Roermond. Maria of the Passion of Our Lord Jesus Christ (Maria Grazia Tarallo, 1866-1912), of the Congregation of Crucified Sisters Adorers of the Eucharist, was scheduled for Naples. Mother Rita Beloved of Jesus (Rita Lopes de Almeida, 1848-1913), Portuguese founder of the Institute of Sisters of Jesus, Mary and Joseph, was also scheduled to be beatified in her homeland. Fr. Eustaquio Van Lieshout (1890-1943), a Dutch priest of the Congregation of the Sacred Hearts of Jesus and Mary, who died in Brazil, was scheduled to be beatified in that country.

European Chief — On May 5, Pope Benedict XVI received Jos Manuel Barroso, the president of the European Commission, in an audience in his private library. During the discussions, President Barroso focused on the current state of the European Union, the challenges awaiting it, and its future prospects. Particular attention was given to the contribution that Christians can make and have made in the evolution of European culture over the centuries. President Barroso said later in an interview on the Vatican Radio that "many of the founding fathers of Europe were Catholics and today, despite the fact that the institutions are secular, the truth is that we have had to acknowledge the contribution that Christian thought has always made to the European idea." The Vatican has protested the disregard shown to the Christian heritage of Europe in EU documents.

Papal Foundation — On May 5, Pope Benedict XVI received and personally thanked members of the Papal Foundation for their help in his charitable endeavors performed "in the name of Christ to developing countries." The Papal Foundation conducts fundraising efforts to provide the pope with the financial means necessary for projects designed to alleviate suffering across the world. The Holy Father, demonstrating his regard for these continued efforts, told the assembled: "I assure you that your love of the Church and your dedication to the practice of Christian charity is much appreciated." He added: "While we prepare to celebrate the great effusion of the Holy Spirit at Pentecost, I encourage you to continue in your generous commitment so that the flame of divine love continues to burn with force in the hearts of believers and everywhere." Card. John Krol, then the retired archbishop of Philadelphia, established the U.S.-based apal Foundation in 1990.

World Day of Vocations — During the ordination Mass of 15 priests in St. Peter's Basilica on May 7, Pope Benedict XVI announced that the priesthood is not "a career" or a way in which "to seek a position through the Church: to be served rather than to serve." The ordinations were part of the celebrations of World Day of Prayer for Vocations, The Holy Father also cautioned that to be a priest is "not to desire to become personally someone, but to live for the other, for Christ and, in this way, through him and with him, to live for the men he seeks, whom he wishes to lead on the path of life." He said also that one "enters the priesthood through the sacrament, that is, through giving oneself to Christ, so that he can dispose of me, so that I serve him and follow his call, even if it is opposed to my desires for self-fulfillment and esteem."

Swiss Guards Anniversary — On May 7, Pope Benedict XVI celebrated a Mass commemorating the arrival in Rome 500 years ago of the first 150 Swiss Guards, requested by Pope Julius II, and he personally thanked the Swiss Guards for 500 years of service and invited them to continue their mission with "courage and fidelity." The 147 guards killed while defending Pope Clement VII during the Sack of Rome, May 6, 1527, were also commemorated. The Holy Father delivered his homily in Italian, French and German, the three official languages of Switzerland, stating that the purpose of the meeting was "to render honor to the Swiss Guard corps." Pope Benedict XVI thanked the Guard on behalf of all of the pontiffs "who, in the course of the centuries, have been faithfully served by your corps." The Mass was part of a series of events. A group of retired Swiss Guards conducted a marathon of over 400 miles to reenact the 500-year-old response to Pope Julius's request. Colorful and ceremonial, the Swiss Guard has adapted to the needs of the modern world and is trained to handle terror attacks and other assaults on the pope or the Vatican.

Royal Family — It was reported on May 7 that Luxembourg's royal family was received in audience by Pope Benedict XVI. Henri, Grand Duke of Luxembourg, and Maria Teresa, Grand Duchess of Luxembourg, met privately with the Holy Father, praying with him in Latin, and then the couple's five children joined their parents in the papal library for prayer with the Holy Father. Pope Benedict remarked on the unusual coincidence that he, the Grand Duke, and 14-year-old Prince Sebastian all celebrate their birthdays Apr. 16.

Directory Published — On May 6, the Pontifical Council for the Laity announced the publication of a directory of new Church movements and ecclesial communities. The work presents descriptions, histories and other data of 122 "Associations of the Faithful." Abp. Stanislaw Rylko, president of the Council for the Laity, explained the directory's purpose, stating: "In our increasingly secularized world, in which the faith of many is sorely tested, and is frequently stifled and dies, the movements and the new ecclesial communities, which are bearers of unexpected and powerful newness, are the response given by the Holy Spirit to this critical challenge." Pope Benedict XVI has convoked the second meeting of these new ecclesial realities in the Vatican on the eve of the feast of Pentecost in keeping with the recognition of their value in this era. Pope John Paul II inaugurated the gathering during his pontificate. Some 300,000 members from around the world are expected to take part in this celebration with the Holy Father.

Quebec Bishops — On May 11, Pope Benedict XVI met with the bishops of Quebec at the end of their *ad limina* visits to the Vatican. The bishops formally invited Pope Benedict to Canada to preside over the 2008 International Eucharistic Congress in Quebec. Quebec Card. Marc Ouellet told reporters later that the audience was not the place to finalize arrangements, but he was confident that the Holy Father's answer would be positive. The Holy Father said he would use the visits to offer his "reflection on significant themes for the mission of the church in Canadian society, which is marked by pluralism, subjectivism and a growing secularism." He also blessed the "Ark of the New Covenant," an icon-covered chest that was constructed and designed to travel across Canada in preparation for the Congress. A nine-year-old Quebec boy sang for the Holy Father during the audience. Jeremy Gabriel, who was born with Treacher Collins syndrome, a genetic disease causing facial disfiguration and deafness, has become a well-known singer in Quebec after various surgeries allowed him to hear. Card. Ouellet said Jeremy sang beautifully, clearly and with great precision.

Venezuelan President — On May 11, Pope Benedict XVI met with Venezuelan President Hugo Chavez and expressed his concern over the nature of reforms under way in Venezuela. The Holy Father focused on some of the Vatican's concerns during the audience and in a letter that he handed to the president at the end of their talk. Protection of life, the nation's educational reforms, the programs of Venezuelan public schools and moves to eliminate religious instruction from the curriculum were all concerns expressed by the Holy Father to President Chavez.

Bulgarian Ambassador — Pope Benedict XVI received Bulgaria's new ambassador to the Vatican, Valentin Vassilev Bozhilov on May 13, welcoming him and accepting his documentation. The Holy Father announced that if European young people are encouraged and supported, they can help renew Europe with their idealism and spiritual values. He also described the modern world's societies as "too exclusively centered on consuming material goods and on the individualistic search for well-being." The Holy Father asked Ambassador Bozhilov to encourage Bulgarians, for the good of Europe, to hold tight to their spiritual and cultural values as their country prepares to enter the European Union in 2007.

Legionaries' Founder — On May 19, the Holy See announced that the Vatican, in a decision approved by Pope Benedict XVI, has decreed that Fr. Marcial Maciel Degollado, the founder of the Legionaries of Christ, who was accused of sexually abusing minors enrolled in the Legionaries, should no longer exercise his priestly ministry publicly. The Holy See stated that it would not begin a canonical process against the founder because of his advanced age and poor health, but called the priest to a life reserved entirely to prayer and penance, renouncing any public ministry.

Pope in Warsaw — On May 25, Pope Benedict XVI arrived in Warsaw, Poland, homeland of Pope John Paul II. "I have come to follow in the footsteps of his life, from his boyhood until his departure for the memorable conclave of 1978," the Holy Father announced. Three thousand people greeted the Holy Father when he landed, and church bells rang throughout the country to greet him. Pope Benedict delivered an address at the airport, alternating passages in Polish and Italian. He left the airport in an open car to go to Warsaw Cathedral, and he was greeted by crowds enthusiastically expressing their affection, as they did during John Paul II's trips.

Religious Order Reforms — On May 22, Pope Benedict XVI addressed a gathering of 1,500 superiors of women's and men's religious orders serving throughout the world. He announced that reforms undertaken by religious orders, while positive and designed to aid in evangelization, are threatened in some instances by too many adaptations to a modern, materialistic culture. The Holy Father announced: "To belong to the Lord: This is the mission of the men and women who have chosen to follow the chaste, poor and obedient Christ so that the world would believe and be saved." He added: "The Lord wants men and women who are free, not bound, able to abandon everything to follow him and who find everything only in him."

Ecclesial Realities — On May 30, it was announced that Pope Benedict XVI will meet with 300,000 members of ecclesial movements and new communities at the Vatican on the eve of Pentecost. A similar gathering was convoked by Pope John Paul II on May 30, 1998. Most of those who will attend the meeting are from Italy, but it is expected that about 30,000 people will come from other European countries: 5,000 from Latin America; 450 from Africa; 300 from Asia; and more than 100 from Oceania. Some 300 representatives of movements will attend a congress in Rocca di Papa, near Rome, to reflect on the theme "The Beauty of Being Christians and the Joy of Communicating It." The three main addresses will be delivered by Card. Christoph Schnborn of Vienna; Card. Marc Ouellet of Quebec; and Card. Angelo Scola of Venice. Prayer vigils are scheduled on Friday that will be led by the movements in the various churches and basilicas of Rome.

GENERAL AUDIENCES

More on Apostolic Tradition (May 3)
On Apostolic Succession (May 10)
Profile of St. Peter (May 17)
On Peter, the Apostle (May 24)
Reflections on Benedict XVI's Trip to Poland (May 31)

INTERNATIONAL

Chinese Ordination — It was reported on May 1 that China stands by its decision to name its own bishops, ignoring the Holy See's wishes and conducting the episcopal ordination of Fr. Ma Yinglin as the bishop of Kunming, in Yunnan province. Leaders of the official state-approved Church attended the ceremony, as well as government officials. Chinese religious authorities have been reported as planning to ordain Fr. Liu Xinhong, a Church administrator in Anhui province, as bishop also. Card. Joseph Zen of Hong Kong called on Beijing in recent days to postpone Fr. Ma's ordination, warning that the ordination could cause a setback in negotiations between the Holy See and China's Foreign Ministry over the possible restoration of diplomatic relations. Some activity in this regard was considered a hopeful sign.

Russian Catholics — Catholics in Russia were reported on May 5 as planning to unite their prayers with Armenian Catholics for the 113 passengers of an Armenian jetliner that crashed into the Black Sea. An Armenian Airbus A-320 went down near Sochi, Russia, with the tragic loss of all on board. The majority of the passengers were Armenians. Abp. Tadeusz Kondrusiewicz of the Archdiocese of the Mother of God in Moscow expressed his profound sympathy to the Armenian and Russian community. Armenia was the first country to adopt Christianity as its official religion in the early

Palestinian Refugees — Lebanon's Maronite Catholic bishops were reported on May 5 as urging the international community to help bear the responsibility of Palestinian refugees in their desperate plight. The prelates also expressed concern about recent Syrian military incursions into Lebanon, considered provocative. A statement presented after a meeting of the bishops stated: "The Palestinian question is still a cause of worry to the Palestinians and the world, especially the countries where Palestinians took refuge." The bishops added: "The international community cannot wash its hands of this problem. The international community must bear its responsibility until it finds the awaited solutions."

Scottish Tribute — It was announced on May 9 that a statue commemorating Pope John Paul II would be unveiled at the Carfin Grotto in Scotland. Bishop Joseph Devine of Motherwell was scheduled to bless the statue on May 13, the 25th anniversary of the assassination attempt on John Paul II, and will be joined by Abp. Szczepan Wesoly, the retired prelate for Polish migrs. The statue was commissioned by the pastoral planning team of St. Francis Xavier's Parish, Carfin. The pontificate of Pope John Paul II is considered global in scope, recognized by people of all faiths.

Catholic Teen Killed — On May 10, the murder of a Catholic teenager at the hands of a Protestant gang was reported as shocking residents of Down and Connor, the second largest diocese in Northern Ireland. "A tragic murder where the victim is a very young boy, killed just because he was a Catholic," said Fr. John McManus, a Church spokesman in the diocese, commenting on the death of Michael McIlveen, a 15-year-old from Ballymena, County Antrim, who was beaten to death with baseball bats. According to the *Belfast Telegraph*, five people are being questioned by police in connection with the murder.

Da Vinci Code — On May 16, some 900 journalists in Cannes, France, previewed the movie *The Da Vinci Code* and laughed when one character told another that she was the last living descendant of Jesus Christ. The derisive laughter was accompanied by critical comments from reporters after the preview. The film follows faithfully most of the book's controversial religious elements, but has been called boring by critics. *The Da Vinci Code* also depicts the Personal Prelature, Opus Dei, as a sinister association bent on murder. Directed by Ron Howard and starring Tom Hanks, who was panned for his performance, the film depicts the novel's story of the American "symbologist" Langdon, who follows a trail that reveals that Christ was not necessarily divine, that he was married to Mary Magdalene, and that their descendants survive today.

Priests Slain — On May 19, the Catholic prison chaplain, the body of Fr. Jude Kibor of the Diocese of Eldoret, in Kenya, was found, with indications that he was strangled to death. Serving the parish of Majengo, Fr. Kibor was on his way to celebrate Mass at the local prison when he was apparently abducted. Witnesses heard Fr. Kibor's cries for help from a car, and others saw three men dump the body in the bush. Another priest, Fr. Gagalo Boru, was slain in April in the northern Diocese of Isolo. Bishop Luigi Locati was killed in the same diocese in July 2005.

NATIONAL

Immigration Rallies — On May 1, supporters of immigration reform staged their second day of major activities in less than a month. Marches, rallies, boycotts and prayerful gatherings were part of the sponsors' efforts to inform their fellow citizens of their concerns. Leading Church figures also took part in the local demonstrations in some dioceses across the nation. In Philadelphia, Card. Justin Rigali celebrated a Mass at the Cathedral Basilica of Saints Peter and Paul, in which he emphasized the U.S. history of welcoming immigrants and the need to embrace the immigrants present in America at this time. The May 1 events followed Apr. 10's rallies and marches, which also drew hundreds of thousands of people in cities and towns large and small. An immigration bill has been debated in Washington.

The New Priests — Data concerning the year's candidates for ordination to the priesthood, collected by the U.S. bishops' Secretariat for Vocations and Priestly

Formation, have been analyzed by the Center for Applied Research in the Apostolate, and the conclusions drawn from this data were made public on May 1. The information indicates that the ordination class of 2006 is better educated, older and more likely to be foreign-born than those in the past. Many had successful careers in the secular world before recognizing a call to a priestly vocation. Nearly 80 percent of the candidates for ordination to the priesthood had a bachelor's degree before entering the seminary and 30 percent had earned a graduate degree as well. The average age of the class of 2006 is 37, with 22 percent under 40 and four percent over 60. Almost a third of the men were born outside of the United States. The data is based on survey responses from 233 seminarians from 98 of the 195 U.S. dioceses and 24 of the more than 200 religious orders of men.

Hawaii Abortions — On May 2, it was reported that the Governor of Hawaii, Linda Lingle, has signed into law a bill that will permit all abortions in the state to be performed on an outpatient basis, and offers other wider latitudes concerning abortion procedures. She signed the bill despite public opposition from Catholic and family rights leaders in the island state. The law also removes a requirement that abortions not be performed on women who have lived in Hawaii for less than 90 days. Bp. Clarence Silva of Honolulu and the board of directors of the Hawaii Catholic Conference urged a veto of the legislation, saying it "jeopardizes the health and safety of women in Hawaii by statutorily authorizing all abortions to be done in an outpatient setting rather than in a hospital." Other religious and family life leaders opposed the bill and urged the governor not to sign it because of its moral and social implications for islanders.

Notre Dame Decision — It was reported on May 2 that prominent University of Notre Dame faculty members have criticized the decision of the university's president, Fr. John J. Jenkins, to allow future performances on campus of *The Vagina Monologues*. Some students and faculty were reported as celebrating the decision as a victory for academic freedom. Other students and faculty, however, have made known their deep concern, and expressed their belief that Fr. Jenkins' policy will damage the university's Catholic character.

Lost Angels — It was announced on May 4 that two long-lost angel statues will return to the sanctuary of the National Shrine of the Basilica of the Assumption of the Blessed Virgin Mary in Baltimore. The figures, twin sculptures made of basswood, will flank the altar in adoration of the Blessed Sacrament, where they were originally displayed. The angels are believed to have been crafted in the early 1800s and were removed from the basilica in the 1940s. Originally, there were four angels but two remain missing.

Pro-Life Gains — The U.S. bishops' conference announced on May 8 that polls show that support for the court decision allowing abortions in the United States is losing support steadily. A recent Harris poll, reported on the bishops' web site, demonstrates that support has dropped below 50 percent for the first time in 30 years. It also showed that 44 percent of Americans said they would support a law in their own state, such as the one in South Dakota, banning all abortions except to save the mother's life. In March, a Zogby poll found a majority support new abortion regulations such as informed consent laws for women and parental notification laws, with 69 percent favoring such measures for girls under 17 years old.

Black Catholics — It was reported on May 8 that the National Black Catholic Apostolate for Life has designated June as abortion and all acts of violence awareness month. Franciscan Fr. Jim Goode, president of the New York-based apostolate for Black Catholics, stated: "We will witness the sacredness of life in all our churches, institutions, national black Catholic conferences, summer family reunions, festivals, church trips and neighborhood gatherings." He added: "Wherever our people will assemble during the month of June and throughout the summer months," a representative of the National Black Catholic Apostolate for Life "will be there praying, proclaiming and mobilizing African-Americans to choose life and help others choose life." The organization has remained faithful to the pro-life agenda over the decades.

Relics of Mexican Martyrs — It was reported on May 10 that a silver cross containing relics of six of the 25 Mexican martyrs was on display in Denver, May 5-7. The martyrs were canonized by Pope John Paul II in 2000. The reliquary will continue visiting dioceses in the United States and will end its tour of the nation in Orlando, Florida. The relics have been traveling under the auspices of the Knights of Columbus. Six of the martyrs, Sts. Pedro de Jesus Maldonado, Luis Batis Sainz, Jose Maria Robles Hurtado, Mateo Correa Megallanes, Miguel del la Mora de la Mora and Rodrigo Aguilar Aleman, were priests and members of the Knights of Columbus, who died during the persecution of the church in Mexico in the 1920s and 1930s. The tour of their relics was sponsored by the Knights of Columbus to foster awareness of all those who sacrificed their lives for the Catholic faith during the Mexican persecution.

Knights Donation — It was reported on May 14 that the Catholic University of America has received an $8 million gift from the Knights of Columbus. The grant was made in order to allow the university to renovate a vacant building, Keane Hall, which will house the John Paul II Institute for Studies on Marriage and Family and to provide space for university classrooms and other academic activity. The renovated structure will be renamed McGivney Hall to honor Fr. Michael J. McGivney, founder of the New Haven, Connecticut-based Catholic men's fraternal organization. The Knights of Columbus have long supported and sustained the academic achievements of the Catholic University of America.

Sisters of Bon Secours — A new web site, designed to commemorate the 125th anniversary of the Sisters of Bon Secours, was reported on May 16. The anniversary honors the founding of the international order and will provide details about the pioneering missionary labors of the Sisters and their modern vocations. The Web site is www.bonsecoursvocations.org, and provides a history of this first religious order to offer home health care in the U.S. In the early eras of the nation, Americans depended upon the European religious who answered the calls of bishops and offered their services to remote wilderness areas and to urban centers.

JUNE 2006

VATICAN

Patrons of Vatican Museums — On June 1, Pope Benedict XVI received the Patrons of the Arts in the Vatican Museum in a special audience. The Patrons of the Arts have been in existence since 1983, when a major exhibition from the Vatican went to the United States. Their donations are used to fund conservation projects, buy equipment for the museums' restoration laboratories, help with capital improvements, and occasionally to assist in the acquisition of artworks. The Holy Father thanked them for their help, which has made possible the conservation and restoration of the Vatican Museums, which assist "the Church's evangelizing mission." "In every age," he said, "Christians have sought to give expression to faith's vision of the beauty and order of God's creation, the nobility of our vocation as men and women made in his image and likeness, and the promise of a cosmos redeemed and transfigured by the grace of Christ... The artistic treasures which surround us are not simply impressive monuments of a distant past," Benedict XVI observed. "Rather, for the hundreds of thousands of visitors who contemplate them year after year, they stand as a perennial witness to the Church's unchanging faith in the Triune God who, in the memorable phrase of St. Augustine, is himself 'Beauty ever ancient, ever new.'" Some 15,000 visitors tour the Vatican Museums daily. The museums are not supported directly by the Holy See, which means there is little money for restoration or modernization. Patrons come from all religious backgrounds and are grouped into chapters throughout North America and Europe.

Interreligious Dialogue — It was announced on June 1 that Pope Benedict XVI will pray especially for the fruits of interreligious dialogue and the spread of the Gospel. He will particularly pray "that pastors and Christian faithful will consider interreligious dialogue and the work of inculturation of the Gospel as a daily service to contribute to the cause of the evangelization of peoples." The Holy Father's general prayer intention for the month is: "That Christian families may welcome with love every child that comes into existence and surround with affection the sick and elderly in need of care and attention."

Vatican's Diplomats — On June 2, Pope Benedict XVI met with students and staff members of the Pontifical Ecclesiastical Academy, marking the 300th anniversary of training Vatican diplomats in its current location in Rome. He advised these students that the priests who represent the Vatican as diplomats around the world must be men of prayer, open to the riches found in other cultures and firm advocates of Catholic doctrine. "Only if you are faithful to your vocation can you render a valid service to the Apostolic See," he said. The priest-diplomats must have a deep background in theology, but also a deep knowledge of and adherence to "the perennial doctrine of the church" and the policy directives of the Vatican.

World Mission Sunday — On June 2, the message of Pope Benedict XVI for World Mission Sunday was published by the Vatican. The Holy Father announced that missionary activity is tied to love for God and service, and that love for God and service to the needy are defining elements of the church's missionary activity around the world. He also stated that Christians are asked to make the world "burn" with divine love. "Isn't this the mission of the church in every age?" he asked. The Holy Father also stressed the fact that missionary work represents an essential and permanent task for every Christian.

British Prime Minister — On June 3, British Prime Minister Tony Blair was received by Pope Benedict XVI, who urged him to keep dialogue open with "moderate Islam." The Holy Father talked with Prime Minister Blair and then greeted Blair's wife, Cherie, and two of their four children. This was the first meeting between Pope Benedict XVI and the British leader. Vatican and British sources said afterward that the private talks covered a wide range of issues, including the true role of religion in politics and in society, the growing threat of global terrorism, and developments in the Middle East and Northern Ireland.

Pentecost Mass — On June 4, Pope Benedict XVI celebrated a Mass in St. Peter's Square with more than 350,000 of the faithful on the feast of Pentecost. The majority of people attending the Mass were part of a gathering of over 400,000 that had filled St. Peter's Square and the broad boulevard leading to it the previous evening for a papal vigil with members of lay movements and communities. At the vigil and Mass, the Holy Father greeted the lay people and urged them to work with one another and with the church to bring God's love to the world and to show modern men and women the beauty of a life lived for others. He expressed the hope that the Church's "pastors will be careful not to extinguish the Spirit" manifested in new movements and ecclesial communities. "And you will not fail to take your gifts to the whole community," the Holy Father said. He added: "One who has found what is true, beautiful and good in his life — the only treasure, the precious pearl! — runs everywhere to share it, in the family, at work, in all the environments of his life."

Vatican Security — It was reported on June 5 that Camillo Cibin, the man responsible for overseeing the security of six popes, has retired. Benedict XVI accepted the resignation of the director of Civil Security and Protection of Vatican City State and inspector general of the Vatican Police Corps for reasons of age. Cibin, who is 80, joined the Vatican security service 58 years ago. He was at the side of Pope John Paul II during his 104 international apostolic trips, as well as his trips around Italy and his summer holidays. Cibin was also in Manila, in the Philippines, when Pope Paul VI suffered an attempt on his life in 1970, at the hands of a mentally unstable person who tried to kill him with a steel blade. On May 13, 1981, the day of the attack on John Paul II in St. Peter's Square, Cibin jumped over the barrier to immobilize Mehmet Ali Agca, while other security officers cleared the way for the jeep that carried the wounded pontiff to the hospital. Pope John Paul II always thanked Cibin for his protection when, a year later, on May 12, 1982, in the Fatima Shrine, he was attacked by a disturbed man with a bayonet.

Women Bishops — On June 6, Card. Walter Kasper, president of the Pontifical Council for Promoting Christian Unity warned the Church of England that a move to ordain women as bishops would destroy any chance of full unity with the Catholic and Orthodox churches. His remarks came in a speech to a private meeting of the Church of England bishops in Market Bosworth, England. Card. Kasper also stated that if the Church of England adopted such a policy the "shared partaking of the one Lord's table, which we long for so earnestly, would disappear into the far and ultimately unreachable distance." He added: "Instead of moving toward one another, we would simply coexist alongside each other." The Cardinal said decisions made by the Church of England gave a "strong indication of the direction in which the communion as a whole was heading."

Corpus Christi Procession — On the feast of Corpus Christi, June 16, Pope Benedict XVI, continuing a tradition that Pope John Paul II reinstated in 1979, celebrated the Mass of the feast of Corpus Christi at the Basilica of St. John Lateran, and led the Eucharistic procession along Via Merulana to the Basilica of St. Mary Major. The Holy Father, in his homily, prayed to the Eucharistic Christ: "Guide us on the paths of our history! Show anew the just path to the Church and her shepherds!" He added: "Look at suffering humanity, which wanders uncertain amid so many questions; look at the physical and psychic hunger that torments it! Give men bread for the body and soul! Give them work! Give them light! Give them yourself! Purify us and sanctify us all! Make us understand that only through participation in your Passion, through the 'yes' of the cross, of denial, of the purifications that you impose on us, our lives can mature and reach their authentic fulfillment." The Eucharistic procession took place by candlelight after Mass. The Holy Father boarded a small white vehicle to kneel in adoration before the Blessed Sacrament, which was exposed in a large monstrance.

Costa Rican President — On June 16, Pope Benedict XVI received the president of Costa Rica, Óscar Arias Sánchez, winner of the 1987 Nobel Peace Prize, in a private audience. The president asked for papal support in seeking peace. "We will need much support in this task," said the Costa Rican president after the meeting. After the audience, Arias Sánchez visited St. Peter's Basilica, and prayed for a few minutes before the tomb of Pope John Paul II in the Vatican Grottoes.

St. Peter's Square — On June 20, workers in St. Peter's Square placed heavy red granite pillars into place on the border between the Vatican and Italy. The pillars are part of an "urban decoration" scheme meant to replace a fence composed of flimsy metal barricades. The barricades, usually found around potholes in Rome, have been replaced with easily removable, zinc-covered iron fence segments. Rather than being flat across the top, the slats of each segment have a design that blends with the lines of the low chains suspended between the original granite pillars.

Regensburg's New Son — On June 21 it was announced that Pope Benedict XVI has been made an honorary citizen of the city of Regensburg, Germany. A delegation from Regensburg, headed by Mayor Hans Schaidinger and diocesan Bishop Gerhard Ludwig Müller, met with the Holy Father in a room in Paul VI Hall, and gave him a document bestowing the honor. The pope expressed thanks to the city, in whose university he was a professor of dogmatic theology and the history of dogma, beginning in 1969. Eventually, he became vice president of the university. "Regensburg is one of the oldest cities of Germany, but it is also a young city, full of vitality," the Holy Father announced. He also presented the city as "an example of resistance in the dark periods of history."

Bishops of Latvia, Estonia and Lithuania — On June 23, Pope Benedict XVI received the bishops of Latvia, Estonia and Lithuania, urging them to defend life and the family. He also noted that a society without authentic values faces a "tyranny of instability." The bishops were received at the close of their *ad limina*, or five-yearly visit to the Vatican. The Holy Father also displayed concern for the "lack of care in the transmission of authentic values to children… the precariousness of work… social mobility that weakens the bonds between generations… [and] young people's growing sense of inner emptiness… A modernity that is not rooted in authentic human values is destined to be dominated by the tyranny of instability and the loss of points of reference." He added: "For this reason, every ecclesial community, with its own faith and supported by the grace of God, is called to be a point of reference and to dialogue with the society in which it is integrated."

Filipino President — Pope Benedict XVI, on June 26, received Philippine President Gloria Macapagal-Arroyo, who gave the Holy Father a copy of the law she recently signed outlawing the death penalty in the Philippines. She also presented him with a statue of Our Lady of Guidance. The Holy Father was complimentary about the passage of the new law and blessed her rosary. President Arroyo faces impeachment and political charges in Manilla that she has condoned political killings and violated the constitution to silence dissent. She and her supporters deny the charges.

Sainthood Causes — On June 26, Pope Benedict XVI advanced the sainthood causes of 149 Spanish martyrs, an Italian martyr killed in Africa, seven founders of religious orders, three women religious, and two 19th-century laypeople. Decrees were promulgated by the Holy Father in the presence of Card. Jose Saraiva Martins, head of the Congregation for Saints' Causes. The Spanish martyrs were slain during the country's 1936-1939 civil war, and the Italian missionary of the Servants of the Poor, Fr. Francesco Spoto, died in 1964 during the civil war in what was then called the Belgian Congo.

Sacred Music — On June 26, Pope Benedict XVI called for an updating of sacred music that he termed "sacred polyphony." The Holy Father stated that the so-called "Roman school" is a legacy that must be carefully conserved, maintained alive and made known. He said also that such updating will be of "benefit not only to scholars and enthusiasts, but to the ecclesial community as a whole, for which it represents an inestimable spiritual, artistic and cultural heritage." After a concert in the Sistine Chapel, the Holy Father advised: "An authentic updating of sacred music cannot occur except in line with the great tradition of the past, of Gregorian Chant, and of sacred polyphony."

Papal Car Fleet — It was announced on June 30 that the fleet of papal automobiles now includes a top-of-the-line, eight-cylinder sport utility vehicle. At the end of the pope's weekly general audience, representatives of the Volvo automobile firm presented the Holy Father with a set of keys to one of their latest XC90 models, which had been outfitted especially for him. The blue SUV has a six-speed automatic transmission and 311-horsepower engine plus state-of-the-art safety features. The XC90 features a patented Roll Over Protection System, Roll Stability Control, and a whiplash protection seating system, all designed to reduce damage to passengers and the vehicle in case of an accident. Other standard features in the seven-passenger vehicle are ergonomically-designed seats, reading lamps, an eight-speaker CD player, 12-volt power outlets and 12 beverage holders.

GENERAL AUDIENCE

Peter, the Rock (June 7)
St. Andrew, the First Called (June 14)
James the Greater (June 21)
James the Less (June 28)

INTERNATIONAL

Amnesty International — It was reported on June 1 that Amnesty International has moved a step closer to adopting a formal policy in favor of abortion after its Canadian section voted to abandon its neutral position on the issue. Most delegates at the annual general meeting in Winnipeg, Manitoba, wanted to change Amnesty International's current neutral position. A decision on the further question of whether a woman's "right to physical and mental integrity includes her right to terminate her pregnancy" will be made at the next International Council Meeting in Aug. 2007 in Mexico.

Human Embryos — On June 2, the Catholic bishops of Europe announced that research is destructive, that does not respect life, and that requires the destruction of human embryos is "not compatible with human dignity." The prelates made this statement following the adoption of the budget for research and technology development for 2007-2013 by the Industry, Research and Energy Committee of the European Union, which allows for funding for research on embryonic stem cells. "We reiterate our objection to EU-funding of research implying the destruction of human embryos," said the communiqué of the Executive Committee of the Commission of the Bishops' Conferences of the European Community.

Insurance Discount — It was reported on June 5 that five health insurance companies in Switzerland give discounts to women who refuse abortions and in vitro fertilization, as well as prenatal diagnosis. The companies since 2004 have had an agreement with the anti-abortion association Swiss Aid for Mother and Child, according to the news service of the Jérôme Lejeune Foundation. The companies offer eligible women rate reductions of 10 percent to 40 percent, and thousands of people have signed these special contracts.

Japanese Martyrs Cause — The Cause of the 188 Japanese martyrs of the 17th century is proceeding in Rome, it was reported on June 10. The Japanese martyrs were decapitated, burned at the stake or scalded to death in the boiling water of a volcanic hot spring, said the promoter of the cause. Augustinian Fr. Fernando Rojo said the historical and theological commissions of the Congregation for Saints' Causes have issued opinions in favor of beatification, a step toward sainthood. The 188 martyrs include four Jesuit priests, other priests, brothers and nuns, lay men and women. They were killed in different cities between 1603 and 1639 after the Japanese government outlawed Christianity. In official terms, the martyrs' cause is referred to as that of Jesuit Fr. Petro Kassui Kibe and 187 Companions.

Pardon for Krakow Priests — On June 19, Card. Stanislaw Dziwisz asked, "in the name of the Church of Krakow," for pardon from those who believe they were mistreated because of some priests' behavior during the Communist era. The archbishop's petition for pardon refers to some priests accused of having collaborated with the Communist regime's security services. The cardinal also asked all those who felt offended by the conduct of some priests not to lose confidence in the Church. The "spy priests," as they are called in the newspapers, includes a priest who directed the Polish pilgrims' center in Rome for 20 years, and accompanied groups of pilgrims in audiences with the Pope, and some 28 other collaborationist priests of the Krakow Archdiocese. Card. Dziwiswz has established an ad hoc "Memory and Vigilant" commission, which is analyzing the cases of diocesan priests who reportedly collaborated with the Secret Services of the Communist regime.

Dutch Missionary Beatified — It was reported on June 19 that Dutch-born Fr. Eustaquio Van Lieshout was beatified in Brazil, and presented as a model of contemplation as well as apostolic action and dedication to souls. Some 70,000 attended the beatification of this missionary of the Sacred Hearts of Jesus and Mary. During the beatification Mass, Card. José Saraiva Martins, prefect of the Congregation for Sainthood Causes, read, at Benedict XVI's behest, the apostolic letter with which the Pope inscribed the servant of God, Fr. Van Lieshout, in the list of the blessed. Some 50 bishops and 60 priests attended the ceremony, in addition to the crowd that gathered in Belo Horizonte's Mineiro stadium. Also present were some 30 members of the new blessed's family, who traveled for the occasion from the Netherlands.

Nuns Detained — On June 25 Indian police detained Catholic nuns of Blessed Mother Teresa of Calcutta's congregation and accused them of trying to convert people to Christianity. Four Missionaries of Charity visited a government-run hospital in the southern state of Andhra Pradesh. The nuns were on a regular visit to Ruia hospital in the town of Tirupati, a popular Hindu pilgrimage center. Christian leaders say police acted at the request of a fanatical Hindu group. About 50 people, some with video cameras, approached the four nuns and accused them of trying to convert patients. The crowd swelled to about 300 and the police arrested the nuns, keeping them in jail overnight. The nuns have been visiting the hospital regularly for the past 20 years and provide medicine to poor patients who cannot afford it.

Apostolic Nuncio — On June 27, Israel President Moshe Katzav received the new apostolic nuncio to Israel and Cyprus, Abp. Antonio Franco. On this occasion, President Katzav again extended an invitation to Pope Benedict XVI to visit the Holy Land. Abp. Franco will also serve as the apostolic delegate in Jerusalem and Palestine. According to Abp. Franco, the Israeli president said that "he hoped that there would be greater knowledge and appreciation of the Second Vatican Council's declaration *Nostra Aetate*," which marked a decisive change in relations between Catholic and Jews. Abp. Franco also said that the Holy See launched an appeal to the international community to help the Palestinian population, which is going through serious difficulties. "We hope an answer will be given!" The papal nuncio also confirmed the exodus of Christians from the Holy Land, explaining that it is a phenomenon caused by "many reasons" which "has lasted for a long time."

NATIONAL

Papal Blessings — On June 1 it was announced that Pope Benedict XVI sends his blessings and prayers to the people of New Orleans. Abp. Alfred C. Hughes relayed the papal message after a private audience that day. Abp. Hughes met with the Holy Father to express gratitude personally for his support during the Katrina crisis. The Abp., who was in Rome to attend meetings of the Vox Clara commission, said the private audience also gave him a chance to give the Holy Father a detailed assessment of the damage to the Archdiocese of New Orleans and the recovery now in operation.

Healthy Marriage Initiative — It was reported on June 1 that Catholic and Protestant leaders held a press conference to praise the Healthy Marriage Initiative, President George W. Bush's program that was passed by Congress on May 16. Some $100 million in new funds are now available to programs that strengthen marriage in America. The press conference was hosted by Marriage Savers, a nonprofit organization that aims to reduce the nation's growing divorce rate. "Marriage is the community's responsibility," said Bishop Joseph E. Kurtz of Knoxville, Tennessee, chairman of the U.S. Conference of Catholic Bishops' Committee on Marriage and Family Life. "Good marriages cannot exist in a vacuum. We need to take action."

Marriage Amendment — Card. Justin Rigali of the Archdiocese of Philadelphia was reported on June 5 as announcing that the vote on the Marriage Protection Amendment was "an opportunity which should not be squandered." Card. Rigali attended an event in Washington, D.C., on that day and supported President Bush's position. The president stated that an amendment was the only way to "take this issue out of the hands of over-reaching judges and put it back where it belongs — in the hands of the American people." He noted that 45 states have passed laws or constitutional amendments defining marriage as only between a man and a woman. Two days after religious leaders and the president renewed their support for it, the bill failed in a procedural vote in the Senate. What is known as a cloture vote to end debate and bring the bill to the floor fell 11 votes short of the 60 needed to get past cloture; the tally was 49-48.

Bishop Skylstad — It was reported on June 7 that Bp. William Skylstad, of Spokane, the president of the USCCB, answered questions at a news conference and announced that an investigation that he ordered produced no evidence to support an unnamed woman's allegation that he sexually abused her 40 years ago when she was a minor. The woman's claim was filed at the end of 2005 and is among the clergy child sex abuse claims made against the Diocese of Spokane after it filed for bankruptcy protection in Nov. 2004. The news conference was called to announce a proposed settlement with one of the diocese's insurers, Oregon Auto Insurance Co.

Vatican Not Immune — On June 7, it was reported that a federal judge in Portland, Oregon, ruled that the Holy See is not entitled to sovereign immunity from a clergy sex abuse lawsuit that named it as a defendant. U.S. District Judge Michael W. Mosman denied the Vatican immunity because there was enough of a connection between the Vatican and the priest accused of the molestation for the priest to be considered a Vatican employee under Oregon law. The Vatican appealed the ruling by Judge Mosman to the 9th U.S. Circuit Court of Appeals.

"Rosary Priest" Recording — On June 10 it was reported that Family Theater Productions, founded by Holy Cross Fr. Patrick Peyton, "the rosary priest," and part of Holy Cross Family Ministries in North Easton, Massachusetts, has announced the production of a self-playing digital audio book that contains information on how to pray the mysteries of the rosary. The luminous mysteries, which Pope John Paul II added to the traditional rosary prayers in 2002, are also included. In the audio book, *Pray the Rosary With Servant of God Father Patrick Peyton, CSC,* the joyful, sorrowful and glorious mysteries are recited by Fr. Peyton. The "Pray the Rosary" Playaway system is available from Holy Cross Family Ministries by phone at: (800) 299-7729, or online at: www.hcfmstore.org.

Order of Mass — On June 15, the U.S. Conference of Catholic Bishops approved a new English translation of the Order of Mass and adopted several U.S. adaptations during their meeting in Los Angeles. The bishops voted 1723-29. The new translation of the main constant parts of the Mass are scheduled to be introduced to American Catholics in a year or two, pending Vatican approval of the translation. When the American bishops receive Vatican confirmation of a new Roman Missal in English, the new Order of Mass will be implemented. (See also under Liturgy and Sacraments.)

Partisan Politics in the Church — On June 15, Card. Theodore E. McCarrick sharply warned the U.S. bishops that partisan politics in the Church is a severe threat. He said that, "the intense polarization and bitter battles of partisan politics may be seeping into (the) broader ecclesial life of our Catholic people and maybe even of our (bishops') conference." Card. McCarrick commented on the situation after making his final report on the work of the bishops' Task Force on Catholic Bishops and Catholic Politicians. He headed that task force for the past three years. Card. McCarrick added: "We are called to teach the truth, to correct errors and to call one another to greater faithfulness. However, there should be no place in the body of Christ for the brutality of partisan politics, the impugning of motives, or turning differences in pastoral judgment into fundamental disagreements on principle."

New Nuncio — On June 15 the new papal nuncio to the United States, Abp. Pietro Sambi, in his first address, stressed the importance of evangelization in the nation. He also counseled the bishops not to be disheartened by the clergy sexual abuse scandals. Abp. Sambi made his brief remarks on the first day of the bishops' three-day spring meeting in Los Angeles. Serving as the Vatican representative to Israel and the Palestinian territories before being assigned to the U. S. in Feb., Abp. Sambi described the U.S. bishops as "a people of great experience, great holiness and also great suffering."

JULY 2006

Vatican

Renewing Faith — During the Angelus on July 2, Pope Benedict XVI addressed the pilgrims in St. Peter's Square, telling them that the necessary response to today's secularized communities is for adults to renew and deepen their faith in Christ. Catholics, he told them, must be authentic examples and teachers of Christian living for future generations. The Holy Father stressed the importance of the Fifth World Meeting of Families, being held in Valencia, Spain. He urged all the world's families to be "authentic communities of love and life in which the flame of faith may be handed down from generation to generation." In the same address, the Holy Father made an appeal for an end to "the blind violence" bloodying Iraq and the Holy Land, and called on world leaders to begin making "a serious and credible commitment to peace" and justice. The Holy Father continued to follow "with growing concern" the latest tragedies unfolding in the Middle East.

Canonizations Scheduled — It was reported on July 2 that Blessed Mother Theodore Guerin, the 19th-century founder of a religious order and numerous schools in Indiana, will be canonized by Pope Benedict XVI on Oct. 15, along with a 20th-century Mexican bishop and two Italian religious founders. The Holy Father and cardinals in Rome met at the Vatican for an ordinary public consistory, which formally concludes the sainthood processes. The final miracles needed for the canonizations of the four candidates were approved prior to the consistory. Born in France's northern province of Brittany Oct. 2, 1798, Mother Theodore Guerin traveled to the United States as a missionary in 1840, promoting education in the young United States and founding the Sisters of Providence of St. Mary-of-the-Woods.

Religious Summit — On July 2, Pope Benedict XVI expressed his support of a three-day international meeting of religious leaders in Moscow, a precedent-setting gathering that included a Vatican delegation led by Card. Walter Kasper, president of the Pontifical Council for Promoting Christian Unity and Card. Paul Poupard, president of the Pontifical Council for Culture. Other members of the delegation include Card. Theodore McCarrick, retired archbishop of Washington, D.C.; Abp. Diarmuid Martin of Dublin, Ireland; and Bp. Joseph Werth, president of the Russian episcopal conference. This gathering preceded the G-8 summit of industrial leaders, the secular powers of the modern world, in St. Petersburg. "This significant meeting of so many exponents of the world's religions indicates the common desire to promote dialogue between civilizations and the pursuit of a more just and peaceful world order," the Holy Father announced as part of his endorsement of the event. He added: "Thanks to the sincere commitment of all, areas will be found for effective collaboration to address the present-day challenges in reciprocal respect and understanding." The Interreligious Council in Russia organized the meeting at the request of Alexy II, patriarch of Moscow. The summit also has the support of Russian President Vladimir Putin.

Pius XI Archives — Pope Benedict XVI was reported on July 2 as having authorized the opening of the Vatican archives for the pontificate of Pope Pius XI, covering the years 1922–1939. The archive includes materials from this period cover the dramatic events leading to World War II, including the rise to power of Mussolini, Hitler and Stalin. The Holy See announced also that researchers will be able to consult all the documents of the period safeguarded in the different series of archives of the Holy See, primarily in the Vatican Secret Archives and the Archive of the Second Section of the Secretariat of State (formerly the Congregation of Extraordinary Ecclesiastical Affairs).

Vatican-China Talks — On July 4, it was announced that Chinese church leaders had welcomed a Vatican delegation's visit to Beijing to discuss relations with Chinese government officials. Abp. Claudio Celli, secretary of the Administration of the Patrimony of the Holy See, and Msgr. Gianfranco Rota Graziosi of the Vatican Secretariat of State were in Beijing for "informal talks" with the Chinese officials. The Vatican delegates met with Chinese government officials and visited eastern China's Shandong province. No official word about the subject of the discussions was made available by the Vatican or the Chinese government.

Uruguayan Ambassador — On July 3, Pope Benedict XVI received Uruguay's new ambassador to the Holy See, Mario Juan Bosco Cayota Zappettini. The Holy Father's address during the ceremony defended marriage and the family. "The highest values, rooted in people's hearts and the social fabric," he announced, "are the soul of nations, making them strong in adversity, generous in loyal collaboration and hopeful in the building of a better future full of life, in which all without exception have the opportunity to develop the human being's full dignity."

Poznan Uprising — On July 3, Pope Benedict XVI sent a message on the 50th anniversary of the workers' revolt in Poznan, Poland, the first anti-Stalinist insurrection in a Soviet bloc country. On June 28, 1956, about 100,000 workers protested on the city's streets against the reduction of their salaries, after the bureaucracy refused to negotiate. The demonstration was suppressed brutally, with 58 protesters killed and 700 arrested. The papal message was read by Abp. Stanislaw Gadecki of Poznan. The Holy Father expressed the hope that "the memory of the heroes of the Poznan insurrection will inspire all Poles to build" society "on eternal Christian values, on truth and authentic justice."

Agents of Peace — Pope Benedict XVI received the bishops of Croatia on July 6, urging them to be promoters of reconciliation and peace. The bishops were ending their five-yearly visit to the Holy See when they met with the Holy Father. "Your country, unfortunately, still experiences the consequences of the recent conflict, whose negative effects are felt not only in the economy, but also in its inhabitants' spirit," he told them, referring to the conflicts caused by the disintegration of former Yugoslavia. "Proclaim reconciliation always and be agents of peace among the citizens of your homeland, encouraging them to undertake the path of Christian reconciliation: forgiveness liberates first of all the one who has the courage to grant it," the Holy Father added. Some eighty percent of Croatia's population of over 4.5 million is Catholic.

Holy Grail — It was announced on July 7 that when Pope Benedict XVI is in Valencia he will venerate the chalice that is traditionally considered the one Christ used at the Last Supper. Revered as a "sacred icon," the holy chalice safeguarded in the cathedral of Valencia is considered authentic by some scholars because of reasonable archaeological and historical evidence. The oldest written historical document describing the holy chalice lists it as a donation from the monks of St. John of the Rock for the King of Aragon, Don Martin I the Human, and is dated Sept. 26, 1399. Ancient tradition traces the movement of the chalice from Jerusalem to Rome with St. Peter. The chalice was sent to Spain around 258 by St. Lawrence after the martyrdom of Pope Sixtus. The cup remained in Spain until the Muslim invasion, when the faithful saved it by hiding it in the mountain area. In the year 1071, it was sent to the Monastery of St. John of the Rock, where it remained for more than three centuries. Pope John Paul II, on a visit to Valencia on Nov. 8, 1982, venerated the relic in his chapel, and celebrated Mass with it.

World Meeting of Families — On July 9, Pope Benedict XVI addressed over one million people attending the vigil of the Fifth World Meeting of Families in Valencia, Spain. "To promote the values of marriage does not stand in the way of fully experiencing the happiness that man and woman encounter in their mutual love," he announced. "Christian faith and ethics are not meant to stifle love, but to make it healthier, stronger and more truly free…," he continued. "Human love needs to be purified and to mature if it is to be fully human and the principle of a true and lasting joy." The Holy Father also met Spanish President José Luis Rodríguez Zapatero for the first time at the archbishop's residence in Valencia. He celebrated the closing Mass with 50 cardinals, 450 bishops and 3,000 priests. The king and queen of Spain and the royal family occupied a reserved place during the Eucharistic celebration. At the Mass, the Pontiff used the holy chalice that is venerated in Valencia's Cathedral. The Holy Father ended the celebration with the recitation of the Angelus, in which he announced that the Sixth World Meeting of Families will be held in 2009 in Mexico City. (*See under* **News in Depth.**)

Siberian Accident — On July 9, Pope Benedict sent word of his grief at the news of the Irkutsk, Siberia, air accident that killed 122, including children planning to vacation in Baikal. In a telegram of condolence, the Holy Father said that his grief is that much deeper knowing that many of the victims and wounded were children. He also expressed his hope for the "speedy healing of the wounded" and "invoked the comforting blessings of God" for all those affected by the tragedy.

Papal Welcome — On July 11, some 200 people of Les Combes, Italy, welcomed Pope Benedict XVI when he arrived for his Alpine vacation in the town. The welcome ceremony took place at Aosta's St. Christophe airport where Bp. Giuseppe Anfossi of Aosta and local government officials were on hand when the papal plane landed. After thanking the people for the welcome, the Holy Father was driven to a chalet outside Les Combes where he was scheduled to stay until July 28. The stay in the chalet was be a period of rest. After his stay in the Aosta Valley, the Holy Father will go to the papal summer residence of Castel Gandolfo, some 19 miles south of Rome, where he will remain until the end of Sept.

Vatican Finances — It was announced on July 12 that the Holy See's consolidated financial statement for the fiscal year 2005 closed with a profit of 9.7 million euro ($12.3 million), the largest gain in eight years. The year 2004 had closed with a surplus of 3.08 million euro. The Holy See's consolidated financial statement includes the Administration of the Patrimony of the Holy See, which provides for all the administrative operations of the offices and entities of the Roman Curia, the Congregation for the Evangelization of Peoples, the Apostolic Camera, Vatican Radio, the Vatican Television Center, the Vatican Printing Press, *L'Osservatore Romano* and the Vatican Publishing House. In addition to the Holy See's consolidated financial statement, the definitive statement of Vatican City State for 2005 listed a positive result of 29.6 million euro.

Peter's Pence Increase — It was reported on July 12 that donations for the Holy Father's apostolic and charitable mission increased 14.95 percent from 2004 to 2005, to nearly $60 million. Card. Sergio Sebastiani, president of the Prefecture for the Economic Affairs of the Holy See, announced the figure. The Peter's Pence collection is taken up in particular churches, especially on the Solemnity of Sts. Peter and Paul, and from contributions of Institutes of Consecrated Life and Foundations, as well as donations from private individuals. Pope Benedict XVI allocated these resources to charitable endeavors to help the populations of several countries hit by disasters such as floods, famine, war and illnesses. The Holy Father also used these funds to support numerous initiatives of Third World ecclesial communities and assistance to the poorest local churches. The origin of Peter's Pence dates back to the end of the eighth century, when the Anglo Saxons converted to Christianity and as a sign of union with the Bishop of Rome decided to send contributions to the Holy Father on a regular basis. "Denarius Sancti Petri" (Peter's Pence) soon spread throughout Europe, a custom that was regulated by Pope Pius IX in the encyclical *Saepe Venerabilis* of Aug. 5, 1871.

St. Bernards — On July 18, Pope Benedict XVI walked across the Italian border to Switzerland to visit the St. Bernard kennel of an Augustinian monastery. The Holy Father also called at a convent of Benedictine nuns at St.-Oyen, Italy. "We had a lovely meeting with the Benedictine sisters and we prayed together," he told reporters. "Then we went to the Great St. Bernard Pass where we prayed vespers with the monks and with the people before having a nice encounter in the refectory." The St. Bernard kennels are world-famous, and have been open for more than three centuries, raising Saint Bernard dogs and training for mountain rescues.

Castel Gandolfo — On July 28, Pope Benedict XVI left the Italian Alps where he was vacationing, and went south to the papal summer residence in Castel Gandolfo, near Rome. The Holy Father traveled by plane today from Aosta to the Roman airport of Ciampino, and then on to Castel Gandolfo. The Vatican press office announced that "beginning on Sunday, July 30, Benedict XVI will pray the Angelus from his summer residence at Castel Gandolfo. General audiences will be held regularly from Wednesday, Aug. 2."

St. Martha's Feast — On July 29, a rosary was recited in the Vatican Gardens on the feast of St. Martha in an event open to the public. The traditional torchlight procession wound through the gardens and the "*Salve Regina*" was sung before the image of the Blessed Virgin of Mercy. Pope John Paul II placed this image in the Vatican Gardens eleven years ago. Entry to the Vatican Gardens was through the Arch of Bells from St. Peter's Square.

Cease-Fire — On July 30, Pope Benedict XVI, addressing pilgrims in a gathering at Castel Gandolfo at the midday Angelus, begged the world to arrange a Mideast cease-fire, hours after Israeli missiles caused such a large loss of life in a southern Lebanon village. "In the name of God I appeal to all those responsible for the spiral of violence, so that they may immediately put down their weapons on all sides." He added: "I ask government leaders and international organizations not to spare any effort to obtain this necessary halt to hostilities and so to be able to begin to build, through dialogue, a lasting and stable concord for all the people of the Middle East." The Holy Father also stated: "I appeal to all people of good to continue and to intensify the shipment of humanitarian help to those populations so tested and needy." The Holy Father made this plea on the 19th day of hostilities between Hezbollah and Israel in southern Lebanon. Some 140 missiles were fired by Hezbollah into Israel on this day.

General Audiences

John, Son of Zebedee (July 5)

International

Convocation — On July 1, it was reported that Catholics of Asian and Pacific Island heritage from all over America had gathered in Arlington, Virginia, for the first National Asian and Pacific Catholic Convocation. Religious and lay leaders, diocesan ministry directors and others met to share diversity and faith. "We meet at a hopeful moment in this world," said Aux. Bp. Dominic M. Luong of Orange, California, "a time when more people have a chance to claim the freedom God intended for us all. It's also a time of great challenge." Bishop Luong is the nation's first Catholic bishop of Vietnamese origin.

Priest Stabbed — It was reported on July 3 that a French missionary, Fr. Pierre Brunissen, 76, was assaulted and stabbed in the Turkish city of Samsun after having suffered threats, insults and vandalism. He was hospitalized after the attack by an apparently unstable man but was in stable condition. Fr. Brunissen was due to return to France within a few weeks, having completed his service after 15 years in Turkey. The Christian community of Samsun is composed mostly of foreigners, people from former Soviet republics and some Japanese.

Mumbai Attacks — The bomb blasts in Mumbai, India, on July 11 were deplored by the Catholic Bishops' Conference of India. The blasts claimed more than 130 lives and injured more than 200 people. "It is a blatant act of aggression on harmless people, and this must be countered with courage and determination by all concerned," the bishops said in a statement. "We appeal to all the affected people to maintain calm and equanimity at this hour of sorrow and grief so that the nefarious designs of the anti-social elements can be

defeated." The seven bomb blasts were considered well-coordinated terrorist attacks. Five minor blasts in Srinagar, the capital of the Indian state of Jammu and Kashmir, killed eight people.

Franciscan Community — A Franciscan community will be canonically established on Jordan's Mount Nebo, it was announced on July 12. The decision was confirmed by Franciscan Fr. Pierbattista Pizzaballa, Custos of the Holy Land. The Patriarch Moses saw the Holy Land from the summit of Mount Nebo but was not able to enter it. The founding community is composed of three brothers from Australia, Italy and Syria, who will live a life of contemplation and prayer while offering hospitality for pilgrims. In 1932, the Custody of the Holy Land acquired the lands of Mount Nebo.

Middle East — On July 18, Card. Renato Raffaele Martino, the president of the Pontifical Council for Justice and Peace, called on the United Nations to promote dialogue and peace in the Middle East. He urged the international community and the United Nations in particular to promote dialogue and peace in the region. Card. Martino said: "The situation is complex and difficult to decipher, so much so as to threaten the peace and security not only of the region, but of the whole world." He added: "At the same time, however, and with determination, in such a scenario of violence and cruel opposition, both the terrorist acts of some, as well as the military reprisals of others must be repudiated, given that both constitute a violation of law and of the most basic principles of justice." Card. Martino was the Holy See's permanent observer to the United Nations for more than 25 years.

Nazareth Empty — On July 30 it was reported that the holy city of Nazareth, where pilgrims visit the Basilica of the Annunciation, has been deserted. The basilica has been a popular destination but over the years Nazareth has become a target of the Hezbollah-Israel war and rocket attacks. Two rockets fell on Nazareth on July 19, killing two children. However, the Franciscan superior of the basilica, Fr. Ricardo Bustos, said that he did not believe that another attack will take place and that he had not taken any special precautions to protect the basilica.

National

Assisted suicide — It was reported on July 1 that the California state Senate Judiciary Committee rejected a long-dormant bill that would have allowed terminally ill patients to obtain life-ending drugs. Democratic Senator Joseph Dunn, who chairs the committee, cast the deciding vote. Dunn explained: "In this society, more often than not, public policy decisions are driven unfortunately by money concerns, not by policy concerns." Supporters of the measure, written by Assemblywoman Patty Berg and Assemblyman Lloyd Levine, both Democrats, declared defeat after being unable to gather the three votes needed from the five-member Judiciary Committee to move it forward.

Bishops' Photos — It was reported on July 3 that the annual membership directory of U.S. Catholic bishops is now available, which includes photographs of the approximately 400 U.S. bishops, along with biographical information, mailing addresses, office phone and fax numbers, and, where available, e-mail addresses. The directory costs $19.95 per copy, plus $3.50 postage and handling for the first four copies. It can be ordered from the USCCB Department of

Communications by e-mail to mburroughs@usccb.org, with "Photo Directory" in the subject line, or by phone at (202) 541-3200.

Milwaukee Bankruptcy — It was reported on July 6 that Abp. Timothy M. Dolan warned that filing for bankruptcy protection is a possibility for the Milwaukee Archdiocese if a California court awards significant damages in upcoming sex abuse civil suits naming two former archdiocesan priests. Abp. Dolan also stated that diocesan ministries "could be seriously curtailed if the resolution of these cases results in staggering financial consequences against us." Three other U.S. dioceses already have filed for bankruptcy. The archbishop added: "Bankruptcy is a significant and soul-searching decision, with wide-ranging consequences, and something which is usually looked at as only a last resort." He brought Catholics in the archdiocese up to date on the situation in an article and column appearing in the archdiocesan newspaper.

Original Cornerstone — On July 7, it was reported that the original cornerstone of the present-day Basilica of the National Shrine of the Assumption of the Blessed Virgin Mary was recovered in time for the re-enactment of the first dedication of the cathedral on July 7, 1806. On that day, a small group led by Bishop John Carroll, America's first bishop, participated in the solemn dedication of the cornerstone of the Baltimore church. Now, with $32 million in renovations on the historic landmark coming to a close, the Basilica Historic Trust, the private, nonprofit organization entrusted with the care of the cathedral, once again honored the vision of Bishop Carroll.

Extension Grant — It was reported on July 29 that the Catholic Extension has given the U.S. Archdiocese for the Military Services a grant of $100,000 to support its young adult ministry initiative, "Catholics Seeking Christ." The grant will fund peer leader courses in the military and will provide resource materials for 40 base parishes. Abp. Edwin F. O'Brien, head of the military archdiocese, said: " 'Catholics Seeking Christ' is a program that encourages single young adults to gather in small groups of six to 10 people for six weeks to discuss the big questions about faith." The program has been under way for about a year. The military archdiocese serves about 1.4 million Catholics around the world.

Same-Sex Marriage Ban — On July 26 it was reported that the Washington Supreme Court upheld the state's ban on same-sex marriage. This ruling leaves Massachusetts as the only U.S. state to allow same-sex couples to wed. In a 5-4 decision, the Washington state court said lawmakers have the power to restrict marriage to a man and a woman, and it left intact the state's 1998 Defense of Marriage Act. Earlier in July, New York's high court dealt homosexual couples a similar blow when it upheld a state law against same-sex marriage.

Cardinal George — On July 26, Card. Francis E. George of Chicago announced that he had bladder cancer and would undergo an operation. "I am informed that I can expect to make a full recovery from this cancer and the surgery to remove it," the cardinal said in his statement. "I ask my fellow priests, the religious, all Catholics in the archdiocese and other friends and colleagues to pray for me. I trust that the Lord will give me the strength and grace I need during these next

days and weeks." The operation was performed on July 27 at Loyola University Medical Center. On the same day, however, the Cardinal returned to the operating room late in the night to repair a small blood vessel in his pelvis that was bleeding. A notice from his medical team, issued on July 28, stated: "Although the episode of postoperative bleeding represents a complication ... it is not an unusual occurrence and is not expected to have a significant impact on Card. George's recovery." It was also reported that after the bleeding was stopped, the cardinal's condition stabilized. He tolerated the second operation well and was listed as resting comfortably.

Polarization in the Church — Bp. Edward K. Braxton of the Diocese of Belleville in Illinois was reported on July 28 as issuing a pastoral letter concerning the growing polarization in the church since the end of the Second Vatican Council, which he believes has rapidly eroded the "common meaning" of faith that unites Catholics as a community. Other prelates in the United States have spoken of this as well. Bp. Braxton discussed the decline of common meaning that is corroding Catholic identity and "is shaking our communal self-understanding, which leads to the dangers of divisions, quarrels and fragmentations." Although a vast majority of Catholics accept Church teachings and the leadership of Church officials, there are small groups with polarized views regarding the value of the structures, nature and teachings of the church, he advised in his pastoral.

Lily of the Mohawks — Abp. Charles J. Chaput of Denver was reported on July 29 as describing Blessed Kateri Tekakwitha as a model for carrying out Christian responsibility in the world. He made this comment at the 67th annual Tekakwitha Conference held at John F. Kennedy High School in Burien, Wash. During the conference, Blessed Kateri was also called a beacon of hope. Blessed Kateri, known as the Lily of the Mohawks, died in 1680.She was the first American Indian to be beatified and her cause for canonization is pending. More than 1,000 American Indians from 23 Tekakwitha Circles in the United States and Canada registered for the three-day conference. Devotion to the Lily of the Mohawks also inspired Roger Zarembinski of Lino Lakes, Minn., to work on a pastel chalk drawing of Blessed Kateri that depicted her standing, a birch cross held to her heart with one hand and a rosary extendied in the other. Zarembinski made the panel for the newly-built St. Anthony mission church on the Fort Berthold Indian Reservation near Mandaree, N.D.

Manuscript Discovered — It was announced on July 26 that an early Christian manuscript, called by specialists from the National Museum of Ireland the "Irish equivalent to the Dead Sea Scrolls," was found in an Irish bog. Fragments of an ancient church manuscript were found in the earth in Ireland's southern Midlands. The find appears to be a Psalter dating from the early Middle Ages. "It is impossible to say how the manuscript ended up in the bog. It may have been lost in transit or dumped after a raid, possibly more than 1,000 to 1,200 years ago," museum specialists said in a July 26 statement. So far only one page of the vellum is legible, identified as Psalm 83, which refers to God's lamentation when the people of Israel are at war.

AUGUST 2006

VATICAN

Mideast Cease-fire — On Aug. 2, Pope Benedict XVI again appealed for an immediate cease-fire in the Middle East, saying nothing could justify the shedding the blood of so many children. The Holy Father asked the faithful attending an audience at the Vatican to "to pray for the dear and martyred region of the Middle East." "With a heart filled with affliction," he said, "once again I renew a pressing appeal for an immediate cessation of all hostilities and all violence." The appeal came the morning after Israel began a major ground invasion into southern Lebanon.

Altar Servers — Pope Benedict XVI's Aug. 2 audience in St. Peter's Square was mainly for 42,000 European altar servers. Some 35,000 altar boys and altar girls from Germany were among the faithful. "Because most of the servers gathered in this square today are German-speakers, I will address them first in my mother tongue," the Holy Father announced. He delivered his speech in German, and then offered greetings in 12 other languages. Including the altar servers, about 55,000 people gathered in St. Peter's Square for the audience.

Pope Paul VI — On Aug. 6, Pope Benedict XVI marked the 28th anniversary of the death of Pope Paul VI, calling him a gift of God to the Catholic Church. Addressing visitors at his summer villa in Castel Gandolfo, the Holy Father announced: "We remember him on this anniversary with hearts grateful to God, who gave him as a gift to the Church in the very important years of the (Second Vatican) Council and following the council." Pope Paul VI was elected to succeed Pope John XXIII in 1963, and he presided over the last sessions of the Second Vatican Council. He died Aug. 6, 1978, at Castel Gandolfo.

Mideast Peace — On Aug. 9, Pope Benedict XVI again urged all sides to lay down their weapons and end the "tragic conflict." The Holy Father encouraged the efforts of UN diplomats and urged them to find a cessation of hostilities and a just and lasting solution to the conflict. Citing a speech by Pope John Paul II, he said peace is possible when reason and good will are made to prevail, along with trust in others, the implementation of prior commitments and cooperation between responsible partners.

Executions postponed — It was reported on Aug. 11 that after an appeal by Pope Benedict XVI, Indonesian officials issued a stay of execution for three Catholics, but said they would be executed after Aug. 20. The three were sentenced to death after being convicted in 2001 of murdering 200 Muslims in May-June 2000 in the Poso area, in Central Sulawesi. The Christian-Muslim confrontations took place from Dec. 1998 to Dec. 2001, killing hundreds of people, with estimates ranging as high as 2,000. Hours before the postponement was announced, the Vatican released the text of a telegram sent to Yudhoyono and signed by Cardinal Angelo Sodano, Vatican secretary of state. In the pope's name, Cardinal Sodano asked Yudhoyono to intervene "on humanitarian grounds."

Cardinal to Lebanon — On Aug. 11 it was announced that Pope Benedict XVI was sending a personal envoy to Lebanon and had asked Catholics in Lebanon and Israel to offer special prayers for peace at Masses Aug. 15, the feast of the Assumption of the Blessed Virgin Mary. The Holy Father asked French Cardinal Roger Etchegaray, retired president of the Pontifical Council for Justice and Peace, to assure Lebanon's "martyred population and all those in the region who are suffering" of his closeness in prayer and his solidarity with them. The Vatican stated: "The visit will have an essentially religious character and will include, if possible, because of the fighting, the celebration of Mass Aug. 15 at the Shrine of Our Lady of Lebanon in Harissa, north of Beirut."

Papal Interview — On Aug. 13, a lengthy TV and radio interview by Pope Benedict XVI was broadcast. Recorded at Castel Gandolfo, the papal retreat, the Holy Father explained some of the priorities of his papacy, saying he was convinced the church needs to frame its moral teachings in a positive way and shed the image of an institution that always says "no." He also addressed a wide range of topics, including ecumenical cooperation, the role of women in the church, and the unifying function of the papacy, offering as well his insights on the burdens of being pope. "It really is tiring," he said, but also commented on the enjoyment of talking to the many people who come to visit him. He also added that he enjoyed the continual encounters with bishops, politicians and other personalities "who want to talk to me personally."

General Audiences

On Being an Apostle (Aug. 18)
On the Assumption (Aug. 17)

International

Japan's Constitution — It was reported on Aug. 2 that the Catholic bishops of Japan strongly oppose efforts under way to change their nation's constitutional renunciation of warfare. The bishops urge the nation to maintain the commitment to nonaggression that Japan has upheld as part of its constitution for the past 60 years. Article 9 in the Japanese constitution states in part: "the Japanese people forever renounce war as a sovereign right of the nation and the threat of the use of force as a means of settling international disputes. . . . The right of belligerency of the state will not be recognized." The bishops warn against the close collaboration of U.S. armed forces in Japan with the Japanese Self-Defense Force and other measures established by a U.S.-Japanese agreement last October that threaten to draw the Self-Defense Force out of its traditional limited posture. Japan now embraces into a new posture as combatants in the U.S. global war on terrorists.

Chinese Seminar — It was reported on Aug. 2 that a seminar on the work of social agencies was held to mark the first-ever registration on the national level of a Catholic nonprofit organization with China's Ministry of Civil Affairs. The director of the nonprofit Jinde Charities, Father John Baptist Zhang Shijiang of Xingtai Diocese, told the seminar the legal identity provided by the registration gives it tax-exempt status and allows it to open bank accounts. Jinde Charities, based in Shijiazhuang, the capital of Hebei province, was registered with the government in mid-April. The seminar on social charities in Shijiazhuang and three separate formation programs — for university students, priests and church workers who minister to the elderly — was held to mark the registration in mid-July.

Iraqi Christians — It was reported on Aug. 2 that half of all Iraqi Christians have fled their country since the 2003 U.S.-led invasion. Before the invasion there were about 1.2 million Christians in the predominantly Shiite Muslim state. Since then the overall number has dropped to about 600,000. An estimated 75 percent of Christians have fled from Baghdad to escape the almost daily outbreaks of sectarian violence. The Chaldean Catholics make up the country's most numerous Christian denomination. Many Chaldeajns sought new lives in the neighboring countries of Syria, Jordan and Turkey. About 97 percent of the country's total 27 million Iraqis are Shiite and Sunni Muslims; Christians make up the majority of the remaining three percent.

Africa's Great Lakes — On Aug. 4 it was reported that the Catholic Peacebuilding Network, or CPN, met in Bujumbura, Burundi at the Third International Conference of the Catholic Peacebuilding Network to discuss ways to promote peace and prevent the outbreak of war and conflict. "The holding of this CPN conference is a chance, or rather a grace, a gift from God for our sub-region, so often misdirected by repetitive and interminable wars," said Bishop Jean Ntagwarara of Bubanza, president of the Burundi bishops' conference. The Great Lakes region includes Burundi, Rwanda, Uganda and the Democratic Republic of Congo, among others. Congo recently held what appeared to be successful elections for the first time in more than four decades. The Catholic Church took a leading role in educating the Congolese and in promoting the elections. The Burundian church has been working for reconciliation and peace. In Rwanda, the church has engaged in similar efforts in the aftermath of the 1994 genocide, where the country's Hutu majority slaughtered nearly one million Tutsi and moderate Hutus.

Iraqi First Communion — On Aug. 4, some 80 children of Holy Spirit Parish in Mosul, Iraq, received their first Communion, as the sounds of renewed violence echoed around the church. The pastor, Father Ragheed Ganni, explained that the day was marked by "immense joy" but then by "terrible panic" over renewed fighting in their neighborhood. The priest said the celebration began at 7:30 a.m. and the church was filled with the faithful. "Suddenly we heard explosions and shots close to the church," he said. "Although people are used to it and remained reasonably calm, they started to wonder whether they were going to make it back to their homes or not. ... I turned the subject into a joke and said to them, 'Do not panic, these are fireworks. The city is celebrating with us.'"

National

World Youth Day 2008 — It was reported on Aug. 2 that the first international World Youth Day to be held in Australia will take place July 15-20, 2008 in Sydney. Auxiliary Bishop Anthony C. Fisher of Sydney, coordinator of World Youth Day 2008, announced that Sydney expects about 25,000 U.S. young people to attend. Young Catholics will be able to experience the pre-World Youth Day activities known as Days in the Dioceses, in which pilgrims stay with families or parishes throughout the host country. These will include Days in the Dioceses in Australia or New Zealand.

Women Excommunicated — On Aug. 1, eight women participated in a riverboat ceremony near Pittsburgh that they said constituted ordination to the priesthood. Another four women said that they were ordained to the diaconate. A July 31 statement by the Pittsburgh Diocese called the ceremony "an invalid ritual" because of church teaching that only men can be ordained to the priesthood and diaconate. It also said those "attempting to confer holy orders were removing themselves from the Church." Catholics in the diocese have been asked to pray for the reconciliation of these women with the church and that the church was ready to welcome them back.

Cardinal George — On Aug. 1 it was announced by doctors treating Cardinal Francis F. George of the Archdiocese of Chicago that his cancer had not spread. Jesuit Father Myles Sheehan, Cardinal George's personal physician, reported: "Given what we knew entering into the cardinal's surgery on Thursday, we are happy to report the best possible outcome. The tumor was contained within the bladder and ureters without evidence of going into the lymph nodes or metastasizing." Cardinal George underwent a five-hour operation to remove his bladder, prostate gland and sections of his ureters on July 27 at the medical center in Maywood. Dr. Robert Flanigan, who performed the surgery, put the five-year prognosis for recovery at Cardinal George's stage of cancer at 70 to 80 percent.

Knights of Columbus — On Aug. 1, Bp. Thomas G. Wenski of Orlando addressed the 124th annual convention of the Knights of Columbus, urging the Knights and their families to preserve the vision of founder Father Michael J. McGivney. "The Knights of Columbus, as a fraternal organization of Catholic men, has fostered since the time of its founding — a faith that is unafraid and strong," he said. "And this faith has helped the Knights in this country — but also in the Philippines and in Mexico and in the other countries into which the Knights have expanded, to face with courage and with humble strength, the enemies of the Gospel that have always challenged the Church." This year's convention marked the first official participation of Knights from Poland, where the organization established councils after last year's convention in Chicago. Bishop Wenski also applauded the Knights for working with the U.S. bishops on important public policy issues in the United States.

Catholic Daughters of the Americas — It was reported on Aug. 4 that the Catholic Daughters of the Americas gathered for their biennial national convention in Minneapolis, attracting nearly 900 members from local and state courts (chapters) in the United States and several other countries attended the meeting. Claudia R. Bosch of Dickinson, N.D., first vice national regent and convention chairman, was elected national regent for the next two years. She succeeds M. Joan McKenna of Boston in that post.

Holy Family Sisters — It was announced on Aug. 5 that the Sisters of the Holy Family of New Orleans have pledged to continue their work for the poor there. Some 100 members of the congregation recommitted themselves to work among the poorest of the poor at their quadrennial general chapter in New Orleans in July. Seven of the nine institutions — orphanages, schools and homes for the aged and infirm — operated by the Sisters of the Holy Family in New Orleans were completely destroyed by Hurricane Katrina last year, with losses estimated at more than $18 million.

Young Adults — The third National Catholic Young Adult Conference was held in San Francisco, Aug. 4-6 at the University of San Francisco. The conference offered programs of education, faith-sharing and recreation for young adults from across the country, as well as those who work in young adult ministry. "We try to cover the basic questions related to faith in a relevant and entertaining way," said Father Dwyer, director of the Paulist Young Adult Ministries and publisher of BustedHalo.com, an online magazine for people in their 20s and 30s, explained.

DEATHS — AUGUST 2005 TO AUGUST 2006

Adams, Victorine Q., 93, Jan. 8, 2006, the first African-American woman to serve on the Baltimore City Council; organized the Colored Women's Democratic Campaign Committee in 1946 and began the Junior Registration Corps to promote voting; elected to the Maryland House of Delegates in the 1960s and served for 16 years on the Baltimore City Council; her funeral was attended by many leading political leaders of MD.

Baumiller, Fr. Robert, S.J., 75, July 13, 2006, noted Jesuit biologist; born in Baltimore, he joined the Jesuits in 1953 and was ordained a priest in 1965; prior to his theological studies he earned a degree in philosophy and a doctorate in biology from St. Louis University and did postdoctoral work in biology at the University of Wisconsin; he taught obstetrics and gynecology at Georgetown University in Washington from 1968-74 and biology in the graduate school and pediatrics in the medical school from 1975-91; he was also a member of the U.S. government's National Advisory Committee on Genetic Testing, a senior research fellow at Georgetown's Kennedy Institute of Ethics from its founding in 1971, dean of the college of health sciences at the University of Detroit Mercy in Michigan 1991-95, and from 1995 until his death associate dean of health programs and professor of biology and philosophy at Xavier University in Cincinnati.

Broderick, Bp. Edwin B., 89, July 2, 2006, bishop of Albany from 1969-76 and executive director of Catholic Relief Services, 1976-82; born on Jan. 16, 1917, in New York, N.Y., he studied at St. Joseph's Seminary in Yonkers, N.Y., and Fordham Univ. in New York City; ordained a priest for New York on May 30, 1942; he served as the archdiocese's first full-time director of radio and television and founded the Catholic Apostolate of Radio, TV and Advertising; he served as rector of St. Joseph's Seminary from 1964-67; consecrated titular bishop of Tizica and auxiliary of New York on Apr. 21, 1967; named bishop of Albany in 1969, he promoted the reforms of Vatican II and was a supporter of ecumenical and interfaith dialogue; he also served on the Attica Commission that called for correctional reforms after a bloody prisoner riot in 1971 at the New York state prison in Attica.

Caprio, Card. Giuseppe, 90, Oct. 15, 2005, Italian Cardinal and long-term figure in the Roman Curia; born on Nov. 15, 1914 in Lapio, Italy, he was ordained on Dec. 17, 1938, and entered the diplomatic service of the Holy See, serving in diplomatic missions in China (1947-51, when Vatican diplomats were expelled by communists), Belgium (1951-54), and South Vietnam (1954-56); he was internuncio in China with residence at Taiwan, 1959-67; ordained the titular archbishop of Apollonia, Dec. 17, 1961, he was named pro-nuncio in India, 1967-69, secretary (1969-77) and then president (1979-81) of APSA with oversight over Vatican finances; substitute secretary of state from 1977-79; he was made a Cardinal deacon on June 30, 1979, and transferred to the order of cardinal priests in Nov. 1990; served as president of Prefecture of Economic Affairs of the Holy See, 1981-90, and Grand Master of the Equestrian Order of the Holy Sepulchre from 1988-95.

Crowley, Patricia C., 92, Nov. 23, 2005 a co-founder of the Christian Family Movement; born in Chicago, she graduated from Trinity College in Washington in 1936 and the next year married Patrick Crowley; she and her husband had six children; in 1949 they helped to establish the Christian Family Movement; she also served on the boards of several organizations and received the Pro Ecclesia et Pontifice Cross from Pope Pius XII in 1957, and awards from Mundelein College, in 1962, and the University of Notre Dame, in 1966.

Deedy, Jr., John G., 82, Mar. 28, 2006, Catholic journalist and author; born in Worcester, Mass., on Aug. 17, 1923, he started his journalism career in 1940 and later graduated from the College of the Holy Cross, with additional studies in Ireland and France; worked as a freelance writer for British and American publications; founding editor of *The Catholic Free Press*, Worcester diocesan newspaper, 1951-59, editor of the *Pittsburgh Catholic*, 1959-67, and managing editor of *Commonweal*, 1967-78; in 1954, he received the Pro Ecclesia et Pontifice Cross; author or editor of 23 books, including the award-winning *The Catholic Fact Book* and *The Catholic Church in the Twentieth Century*.

Duss, Mother Benedict, 94, Oct. 2, 2005, retired abbess of the Abbey of Regina Laudis; born Vera Duss on Nov. 21, 1910, in Pittsburgh, she went with her family to France when she was three and later graduated with a medical degree from the University of Paris; in 1936, she entered the Benedictine Abbey of Notre Dame de Jouarre, outside Paris, where she took the name Sister Benedict; during World War II, she fled the abbey; in 1944, she received permission from Pope Pius XII to start a contemplative order in the U.S.; in 1946, she went to New York and founded the Regina Laudis Monastery in Bethlehem, NY (its founding was the inspiration for the 1948 movie, *Come to the Stable*); the monastery was raised to the status of an abbey and Mother Benedict became abbess; she retired in 1994; among her many achievements was the extensive study and use of Gregorian Chant.

Early, William Tracy, 71, Dec. 16, 2005, longtime and respected reporter for the Catholic News Service; ordained a Baptist minister in 1957 after studies at Baylor University in Waco, Texas, and Southeastern Baptist Theological Seminary in Wake Forest, N.C.; served as a U.S. Army chaplain and then earned a doctorate in theology from the Union Theological Seminary in N.Y. in 1963; was pastor of Urbanna Baptist Church in Va.; became a freelance writer in 1969 and began working with CNS soon after; served as CNS NY correspondent and was respected as one of the finest religion reporters in the country.

Fitzpatrick, Bp. John J., 87. July 15, 2006, bishop of Brownsville, from 1971-1991; born on Oct. 12, 1918, in Trenton, Canada; he was raised in Buffalo, N.Y., studied in Rome, and was ordained a priest for the Buffalo diocese on Dec. 13, 1942; in 1948 he transferred to the St. Augustine diocese in Fla. and served as an assistant pastor, executive editor of the diocesan newspaper, *The Florida Catholic*, and director of St. Augustine's Mission of *Nombre de Dios* (Name of God); he was ordained titular bp. of Cenae and auxiliary bishop of Miami on Aug. 28, 1968; transferred to Brownsville on May 28, 1971, he was noted for his commitment to lay ministry and the cause of immigrants; he retired on Nov. 30, 1991.

Garmendia, Bp. Francisco, 81, Nov. 16, Auxiliary Bishop of New York and the first Hispanic bishop named to the NY Archdiocese; born on Nov. 6, 1924, Lozcano, Spain, he was ordained a priest on June 29,

1947, in Spain for the Canons Regular of the Lateran and was sent to labor in Argentina; in 1964, he was sent by the order to work with the Spanish-speaking population in the Archdiocese of NY; he became a naturalized citizen; ordained titular bishop of Limisa and aux. bishop of New York on June 29, 1977, he served as Vicar for Spanish pastoral development in New York archdiocese; he resigned on Oct. 31, 2001.

Gibeau, Dawn Mignonne, 67, Dec. 29, 2005, noted Catholic journalist; she began her career in the Catholic press in 1961 at *The Catholic Spirit* (then *The Catholic Bulletin*), the archdiocesan newspaper of St. Paul and Minneapolis; worked for the *National Catholic Reporter* from 1972 to 2000 and served as managing editor and an international correspondent, with travels to Europe, Africa, Asia and South America; returned to *The Catholic Spirit* in 2000; retired in 2002.

Heindl, Fr. Elmer W., 96, July 17, 2006, noted and decorated World War II Army chaplain; born in Rochester, N.Y., on June 14, 1910, he was ordained a priest on June 6, 1936; he became a chaplain in the U.S. Army in 1942 and was sent to the Pacific Theater, where he was one of only 19 World War II chaplains to earn a Distinguished Service Cross, the nation's second-highest combat medal, a Silver Star Medal, a Bronze Star Medal and an honorary Purple Heart; he reached the rank of lieutenant colonel, earned the Legion of Merit medal, and in 2005 received the Distinguished Service Award of the Combat Infantrymen's Association.

Hellwig, Monika K., 75, Sept. 30, 2005, theologian and author; born in Germany on Dec. 10, 1929, she grew up in England and studied at the University of Liverpool, majoring in social sciences; in 1956, after moving to the U. S., she earned a master's degree in theology from The Catholic University of America in 1956 and later a doctorate; from 1956 to 1962 she taught at St. Therese's Junior College in Philadelphia; from 1963 to 1966, she worked at the Vatican and served on the English language desk at the Pius XII International Center in Rocca di Papa in Rome; she began teaching at Georgetown in 1967 and was a professor at Boston College, the University of Notre Dame, Princeton Theological Seminary and elsewhere; she took part in the U.S. Catholic-Presbyterian dialogue from 1982-85; president of the Catholic Theological Society of America, she received over 30 honorary degrees and such prestigious awards as the John Courtney Murray Award, the Catholic Theological Society of America's highest honor and The Catholic University of America Alumni Association Award for Outstanding Achievement in the Field of Religion.

Kavanagh, Fr. Aidan, O.S.B., 77, July 9, 2006, noted liturgical theologian and author; born Joseph Michael Suttle in Mexia, Texas, on April 20, 1929, he took the surname of his foster father, Joseph Kavanaugh; he entered the Benedictines in 1951 and took Aidan as his religious name; he took his first vows in 1952 and was ordained a priest in 1957; he went on to earn a doctorate in 1964 from the theology faculty of Trier, Germany, and became one of the Church's leading liturgists; he taught at St. Meinrad School of Theology in the 1960s, founded the University of Notre Dame's doctoral program in liturgical studies, and from 1974 until his retirement was a professor of liturgy at Yale University's Divinity School; he authored a number of important books on the liturgy.

Lawler, Thomas Comerford, 84, Nov. 20, 2005, co-author of the best-selling adult catechism *The Teaching of Christ*; born Dec. 19, 1920, in Cumberland, Md., he served in the Army from 1942-46 and then worked for the Central Intelligence Agency from 1951 to 1977; appointed in 1977 to serve as the first director of the Arlington diocese's newly established Religious Education Department; he also served on the board of Catholic Charities for the Richmond Diocese and was president of the Federation of Catholic Parent-Teacher Organizations of Northern Virginia; he received the Pro Ecclesia et Pontifice Cross in 2001; with then Pittsburgh Bishop Donald W. Wuerl (now Archbishop of Washington) and his brother, the late Capuchin Fr. Ronald Lawler, he helped create *The Teaching of Christ*, a phenomenally successful adult catechism.

Li Du'an, Bp. Anthony, 79, May 25, 2006, Chinese bishop of Xi'an; born to a Catholic family on June 13, 1927, he entered Xi'an minor seminary in 1938 and was ordained a priest in 1951; arrested and imprisoned in 1954 by Communist authorities, he was released but endured decades of state oppression; named bishop of Xi'an in Apr. 1987; worked to promote reconciliation between the government-approved Chinese Catholic Patriotic Association and the underground Catholic Church in the People's Republic.

Long, Fr. John F., 80, Sept. 20, 2005, Jesuit priest and one of the great leaders in modern ecumenism; born in Brooklyn, N.Y., on Apr. 5, 1925, he entered the Jesuits in 1941 and studied at Woodstock College, then studied Russian language and history at Georgetown University and Fordham University; ordained a priest of the Slavo-Byzantine rite in 1956, he was one of several Jesuits being prepared for service in Soviet Union in the event of its collapse; from 1958 to 1961, studied at the Pontifical Oriental Institute in Rome; named to the staff in 1963 of the Secretariat for Christian Unity to assist with Catholic-Orthodox relations; helped to draft the Second Vatican Council's Decree *Nostra Aetate*, on Religious Liberty; from 1967 to 1987, he took part in meetings with the Russian Orthodox Church, visited the Soviet Union 16 times, and assisted the writing of Pope John Paul II's apostolic letter marking the 1,000th anniversary of the baptism of King Vladimir of Rus-Kiev; took part in the International Commission between the Catholic Church and the Coptic Orthodox Church as well as five Catholic-Oriental Orthodox consultations between 1971 and 1988 sponsored by the Pro Oriente Foundation; from 1964 to 1980 taught at the Rome Center of Loyola University of Chicago; served on many committees for Catholic-Orthodox Dialogue until his death.

Macchi, Abp. Pasquale, 82, Apr. 5, 2006, retired archbishop of Loreto, Italy, and long-time personal secretary to Pope Paul VI; born in Varese, near Milan, on Nov. 9, 1923, he was ordained a priest on June 15, 1946; served for 24 years as secretary to Pope Paul VI, starting when the future pope was named archbishop of Milan in 1954; defended the pope during a famous attack in Manila in 1970; ordained archbishop of Loreto on Jan. 6, 1989; retired in 1996.

Maloney, Bp. Charles G., 93, Apr. 30, 2006, Auxiliary Bishop of Louisville from 1955 to 1988; born on Sept. 9, 1912, in Louisville, Ky., he studied St. Joseph's College in Rensselaer, Ind, and the North American College in Rome; ord. a priest for Louisville on Dec. 8, 1937; studied canon law at The Catholic University of America and held a variety of archdiocesan offices; ordained titular bishop of Capsa and aux. bishop of Louisville on Feb. 2, 1955; participated in Vatican II and was active in the deliberations on religious liberty; retired on Jan. 8, 1988; transferred to Bardstown, 1995, when it was reestablished as a titular see.

Marcinkus, Abp. Paul C., 84, Feb. 20, 2006, long-time head of the Vatican Bank; born on Jan. 15, 1922, in Cicero, Ill., he was ordained a priest for Chicago on May 3, 1947; after parish and chancery assignments, he was sent to Rome in 1950 for advanced studies in canon law; entered the Vatican diplomatic service in 1952; served in the Vatican nunciature in Bolivia, then to the apostolic delegation in Canada; returned to Rome in 1959 as an official of the Vatican Secretariat of State; ordained titular bishop of Orta on Jan. 6, 1969; secretary (1968-71) and president (1971-89) of Institute for Works of Religion (the Vatican Bank); appointed titular archbishop on Sept. 26, 1981; head of the Pontifical Commission for the State of Vatican City, 1981-90; served as advance leader for papal travels from 1964 to 1982; became involved in the Italian banking scandals of the 1980s and in 1987 took up residence in the Vatican hours before Italian police tried to serve an arrest warrant at his Rome residence on charges of complicity in the $1.2 billion fraudulent bankruptcy in 1982 of the Banco Ambrosiano, Italy's largest independent bank, though the charges were later dropped; retired in 1990 and moved back to the U.S.

McCarthy, Eugene J., 89, Dec. 10, 2005, U.S. Democratic Senator from Minnesota, best known for his 1968 presidential run as an anti-Vietnam War candidate; born on Mar. 29, 1916, in Watkins, Minn., he studied at St. John's Preparatory School in Collegeville and St. John's University and then taught at public high schools in N.D. and Minn. from 1935-40, and earned a master's degree from the University of Minn. in 1938; he entered the novitiate at St. John's in 1943 but did not remain as he enlisted in the Army that year; he entered politics in 1949 when he was elected to the House of Representatives as a member of Minn.'s Democratic-Farmer-Labor Party; elected to the Senate in 1958, he became a leader of the anti-War movement and ran against Pres. Lyndon B. Johnson in 1968 before losing the Democratic nomination that year to Vice Pres. Hubert H. Humphrey; he retired from the Senate in 1970 but ran again for the Democratic nomination for president in 1972 and as an independent in 1976, 1988, and 1992.

McAuliffe, Bp. Michael F., 85, Jan. 9, 2006, Bishop of Jefferson City from 1969-1997; born on Nov. 22, 1920, in Kansas City, Mo.; after studies at St. Louis Preparatory Seminary and Catholic University of America, he was ordained a priest on May 31, 1945, for the diocese of Kansas City-St. Joseph; appointed bishop of Jefferson City on Aug. 18, 1969; served as chair of the U.S. bishops' Ad Hoc Committee on Women in Church and Society from 1974 to 1982 and was key in the eventual bishops' pastoral letter to women of 1992; retired in June 1997.

McManus, Msgr. Frederick R., 82, Nov. 27, 2005, a noted canon lawyer, teacher, and important leader in liturgical renewal; born on Feb. 8, 1923, in Lynn, Mass., he was ordained a priest of the Boston Archdiocese in 1947; he earned a doctorate in canon law at The Catholic University of America in 1954; after teaching at the Boston archdiocesan seminary, he was named to the faculty of canon law at Catholic University in 1958 (he also served as editor of *The Jurist* until 2000); he served as a professor of canon law at Catholic University from 1958 until his retirement in 1993 and was a consultant to the Vatican's Pontifical Commission for the Revision of the Code of Canon Law from 1967 until the new code was published in 1983; chair of the canon law school from 1967-74, university vice provost and dean of graduate studies from 1974-83, and academic vice president from 1983-85; noted for his expertise in the liturgy, he served as president of the Liturgical Conference in the United States 1959-62 and 1964-65, was appointed to the Second Vatican Council's Liturgy Commission, and was a key figure in the drafting of the council's Constitution on the Sacred Liturgy

(*Sacrosanctum Concilium*); he went on to be a leader in liturgical renewal in the U.S., including the establishment of the International Committee on English in the Liturgy (ICEL) and was its treasurer and a member of its Advisory Committee from 1964 to 2000; in 1995, the Federation of Diocesan Liturgical Commissions began the annual Msgr. Frederick R. McManus Award for achievements in pastoral liturgy; received several honorary doctorates and the papal Benemerenti Medal in 1984.

Mealey, Margaret, 94, Jan. 5, 2006, director of National Council of Catholic Women from 1949 to 1977; born in San Francisco, she graduated cum laude from the College of the Holy Names (now Holy Names University) in Oakland and later attended the University of Calif. at Berkeley; worked in the USO-National Catholic Community Services and was named executive director of the NCCW in 1949, serving until her retirement in 1977; appointed by Pope Paul VI to the Pontifical Commission (now Council) for the Laity and served as the commission's delegate to meetings of the World Union of Catholic Women's Organizations; was a member of President John F. Kennedy's Commission on the Status of Women, and was named by Presidents Lyndon B. Johnson, Richard M. Nixon and Gerald R. Ford to citizens' advisory councils on women; received the Pro Ecclesia et Pontifice Cross from Pope Pius XII in 1954; the Magnificat Medal from Mundelein College in Chicago in 1960; the Christian Excellence Medal from Marymount College in Arlington, Va., in 1963; and the Jesus-Marie Medal from Fort Wright College of the Holy Names in Spokane, Wash., in 1964.

Patterson, Floyd, 71, May 11, 2006, one-time heavyweight boxing champion; born Jan. 4, 1935, into a poor family in Waco, N.C., he was the youngest of 11 children; the family moved to Brooklyn, N.Y., and he sank into delinquency; sent to the Wiltwyck School for Boys, a reform school in upstate N.Y., which he credited with turning his life around; was baptized a Catholic on Mar. 31, 1956; won the Gold medal in the 1952 Helsinki Olympics as a Middleweight at the age of 17; turned pro and had a historic record of 55 wins, 8 losses and 1 draw, with 40 wins by knockout; became world champion in 1956 to become the youngest world heavyweight champion in history at 21; defended and recovered the title several times; retired form the ring in 1972 at the age of 37; became a member of the International Boxing Hall Of Fame; beloved for his chivalry and fair play in the ring, he also served as an usher and eucharistic minister in his parish.

Paul, Bp. John J., 87, Mar. 5, 2006, Bishop of La Crosse from 1983 to 1995; born on Aug. 17, 1918, in La Crosse, Wis.; educated at Loras College, St. Mary's Seminary in Baltimore, and Marquette University, he was ordained a priest on Jan. 24, 1943; rector of Holy Cross Seminary in La Crosse, 1955-66; named a monsignor in 1956; ord. titular bishop of Lambaesis and aux. bishop of La Crosse on Aug. 4, 1977; appointed bishop of La Crosse, Oct. 18, 1983, installed on Dec. 5, 1983; retired on Dec. 10, 1994; as bishop, he presided over a diocesan synod in 1986 and the promulgation in 1987 of that synod's decrees, "The Bishop with His People."

Philbrick, Richard, 85, Jan. 25, 2006, longtime religion and education editor for the *Chicago Tribune* and book review editor for Catholic News Service; born in Salem, Mass., graduated from the University of Chicago and then from the U.S. Merchant Marine Academy at Kings Point,

N.Y.; served in the Merchant Marine during World War II; worked as a religion reporter, was a member of the Religion Newswriters Association and served as its president from 1960 to 1962.

Pospishil, Msgr. Victor J., 91, Feb. 16, 2006, noted expert on canon law and the Eastern Churches; born in Vienna, Austria (at the time capital of the Austro-Hungarian empire), he studied at the Theological Academy and Seminary in Djakovo, Croatia, and was ordained a priest June 16, 1940; after World War II he studied liturgy and canon law at the Pontifical Oriental Institute in Rome and earned a doctorate from the Pontifical Gregorian University in Rome; immigrated to the U.S. in 1950; taught at Manhattan College in N.Y., 1960-70; authored a number of books on Eastern Catholic Church Law; received the 1995 Role of Law Award from the Canon Law Society of America.

Primatesta, Card. Raúl Francisco, 87, May 1, 2006, Argentinean Cardinal and archbishop of Cordoba from 1965-98; born on Apr. 14, 1919, in Capilla del Senor, Argentina; ordained a priest on Oct. 25, 1942, he was sent to Rome for studies and earned degrees in theology from the Pontifical Gregorian University and in Scripture from the Pontifical Biblical Institute; taught at minor and major seminaries of La Plata and contributed to several theology reviews before being ordained titular bishop of Tanais and auxiliary of La Plata on Aug. 15, 1957; named bishop of San Rafael in 1961, he was named archbishop of Cordoba in 1965; appointed a cardinal on Mar. 5, 1973, with the titular church of Blessed Mary Sorrowful Virgin; his long time as archbishop was marked by his efforts to solve Argentina's massive political and social problems.

Rice, Msgr. Charles Owen, 96, Nov. 13, 2005, noted "labor priest" of the Pittsburgh diocese; born in N.Y. in 1908, he studied at Duquesne University and then St. Vincent Seminary in Pittsburgh; ordained in 1934, he founded the Catholic Radical Alliance and St. Joseph's House of Hospitality in 1937 and became active in labor rights; his involvement with labor continued for the rest of his life; he also wrote a column for the diocesan paper, *Pittsburgh Catholic,* for over 50 years and hosted a radio program on two local AM stations for over twenty years.

Ryle, Msgr. Edward, 75, Dec. 28, 2005, head of the Arizona Catholic Conference and social justice advocate; born in Chicago, Ill., he was ordained in 1965 for the diocese of Tucson; head of Catholic Charities for the diocese in the 1960s; taught in the National Catholic School of Social Service at The Catholic University of America in Washington, D.C., and served as dean of the Graduate School of Social Work at Marywood University in Scranton, Pa., from 1977 to 1984; named head of the Arizona Catholic conference; retired in 2003; was a noted advocate for social justice and ecumenical relations.

Scheffczyk, Card. Leo, 85, Dec. 8, German cardinal and highly-respected theologian and expert in Mariology; born on Feb. 21, 1920, in Beuthen Silesia, modern Poland, he was ordained a priest in Freising, Germany, on June 29, 1947, and earned a doctorate in theology in Munich in 1957; he taught at Tübingen University, and then in 1965 returned to the Catholic theological faculty at the Ludwig Maximilian University of Münich, where he taught theology until his retirement in 1985; he edited the *Munich Journal of Theology* from 1966 to 1985 and authored over 80 books, 500 articles and 400 reviews and dictionary entries; he was named a cardinal on Feb. 21, 2001, at the age of 80, with the deaconry St.

Francis Xavier in Garbatella.

Schmidt, Bp. Firmin M., 86, Aug. 4, 2005, missionary and the first bishop of Mendi, Papua New Guinea, from 1966 to 1995; born on Oct. 12, 1918, in Catherine, Kan.; educated at The Catholic University of America, he was ordained a priest on June 2, 1946; after completing his doctoral studies he taught at the Capuchin College in Washington, D.C., until sent to the missions in 1959; appointed prefect apostolic of Mendi, Papua New Guinea, on Apr. 3, 1959, he was ordained titular bishop of Conana and first vicar apostolic of Mendi on Dec.15, 1965; became first bishop of Mendi when vicariate apostolic was raised to a diocese, Nov. 15, 1966; retired on Feb. 22, 1995; his time was bishop was marked by the steady growth of the Church in his region.

Spark, Muriel, 88, Apr. 13, 2006, Catholic novelist and author of *The Prime of Miss Jean Brodie*; born Muriel Sarah Camberg in Edinburgh, Scotland, in 1918, she was the daughter of a Jewish father and an Anglican mother; married Sydney Oswald Spark at the age of 19; after her divorce from her husband, she moved to London in 1944 and worked in the political intelligence department of the British Foreign Office; joined the Church in 1954, she credited the faith with influencing her writing; authored some thirty books, starting with *The Comforters* (1957); her last novel, *The Finishing School,* was published in 2005.

Sullivan, Bp. James S., 76, June 12, 2006, bishop of Fargo form 1985-2002; born on July 23, 1929, in Kalamazoo, Mich., he studied at Sacred Heart Seminary in Detroit and St. John Provincial Seminary in Plymouth, Mich., and was ordained a priest for Lansing on June 4, 1955; consecrated titular bishop of Siccessi and auxiliary of Lansing on Sept. 21, 1972, he was appointed bishop of Fargo on Apr. 2, 1985 and installed on May 30, 1985; as bishop, he was noted for his work in the Pro-Life Movement and gave a memorable address at the World Youth Day in Denver in 1993; he retired on March 19, 2002.

Taofinu'u, Card. Pio, 82, Jan. 20, 2006, the first Polynesian cardinal and a noted Catholic leader in the Pacific; born on Dec. 9, 1923, on Falealupo, Western Samoa; ordained a priest on Dec. 8, 1954 and joined the Society of Mary, 1955; appointed by Pope Paul VI as the first bishop from Polynesia at the age of 44, he was consecrated bishop of Apia (Samoa and Tokelau) on May 29, 1968; appointed a cardinal on Mar. 5, 1973, with the titular church of St. Humphrey; became Archbishop of Samoa-Apia and Tokelau, Sept. 10, 1982 (title of see changed to Samoa-Apia, June 26, 1992); served as a co-president of the Synod of Bishops for Oceania at the Vatican in 1998; retired on Nov. 16, 2002.

Thering, Sr. Rose, O.P., 85, May 6, 2006, Dominican nun and leader in Catholic-Jewish relations; born on Aug. 9, 1920, she joined the Sisters of St. Dominic at the age of 16 and graduated from Dominican College in Racine, Wis.; went on to earn a doctorate form St. Louis University and researched a ground-breaking dissertation on U.S. Catholic teaching materials relative to ethnic groups and other faiths, in particular Jews and Judaism; dedicated most of her life to fighting anti-Semitism; established the Menorah Studies Program at Seton Hall in 1968; a documentary on her life, *Sister Rose's Passion,* won the best documentary short award at the Tribeca Film Festival in NY in 2004 and was nominated for an Academy Award; received more than 80 humanitarian awards for her pioneering work.

Willebrands, Card. Johannes, 97, Aug. 2, 2006, Archbishop of Utrecht, Cardinal, and one of the leaders of the ecumenical movement in the 20th century; born on Sept. 4,

1909, in Bovenkarspel, The Netherlands; he was ord. a priest on May 26, 1934 and studied in Rome before serving as a faculty member and rector of the Seminary of Warmond, 1940-1960; he was then secretary of the Secretariat for Christian Unity, 1960-69, and attended the Second Vatican Council as a *peritus*; ordained titular bp. of Mauriana, on June 28, 1964; he was named cardinal on Apr. 28, 1969, with the titular church St. Sebastian alle Catacombe and served as president of the Council for Christian Unity, 1969-89; in 1975 he was appointed abp. of Utrecht, serving until 1983; he resigned the presidency of the secretariat and was named president emeritus on December 12, 1989; he was decorated with the cross of the Order of Oranje Nassau and granted several honorary doctorates by universities in Europe and the United States.

Wilson, August, 60, Oct. 2, 2005, African-American playwright; born on Apr. 27, 1945, he was one of six children born to Frederick August Kittel, an immigrant German baker, and Daisy Wilson, an African-American woman; raised a Catholic in Pittsburgh's Hill District, he largely educated himself, served in the Army, and began writing in 1965; that same year, he co-founded the Black Horizon Theater; he authored ten major plays on African-American life and won several Pulitzer Prizes, including for *Fences*, and seven New York Drama Critics Circle Awards.

Wycislo, Bp. Aloysius John, 97, Oct. 11, 2005, Bishop of Green Bay from 1968 to 1983; born on June 17, 1908, in Chicago, IL, he studied at St. Mary's Seminary and The Catholic University of America in Washington, D.C., and was ordained a priest on Apr. 4, 1934; he served as an assistant pastor and youth ministry leader from 1934 to 1940 and assistant director of Chicago archdiocesan Catholic Charities in 1939; after earning a master's degree in social work from Catholic University in 1942, he worked for the U.S. Bishops War Relief Services (later renamed Catholic Relief Services) and played a key role in organizing the care of refugees in post-war Europe; director of the National Catholic Resettlement Council, he was also a Vatican observer to the United Nations from 1954 to 1956; ordained titular bishop of Stadia on Dec. 21, 1960, he served as auxiliary bishop of Chicago until his appointment as bishop of Green Bay; installed on Apr. 16, 1968, he retired on May 10, 1983; he took part in the Second Vatican Council and was a friend of Karol Wojtyla, the future Pope John Paul II; he devoted himself to the implementation of the council, established one of the first permanent diaconate programs in the country, and launched a successful catechetical program.

Zens, Clarence M. "Clancy," 87, Nov. 16, 2005, first managing editor of the Washington Archdiocese's *Catholic Standard*; a graduate of Marquette University's College of Journalism, he worked for the National Catholic Welfare Conference News Service, predecessor of Catholic News Service, from 1948 to 1951, when he took over the *Catholic Standard*; from 1961 to 1985, he worked for the U.S. Department of Commerce, editing the *International Trade* magazine; he was a member of the National Press Club for nearly 50 years.

Archbishop Gabriel Montalvo (1930-2006)

Abp. Gabriel Montalvo, who served as the papal nuncio to the United States from 1998 to 2006, died on Aug. 2, 2006 in Rome in a hospice run by the Sisters of Mercy of Alma, Mich. He was 76.

An accomplished and deeply respected Vatican diplomat, Abp. Montalvo served as the Holy See's representative to the U.S. during one of the most tumultuous periods in American Catholic history, including the crisis caused by the sex-abuse scandal and also the aftermath of the 9-11 attacks on the World Trade Center and America's war on terror. He was also, by virtue of his role as papal representative, a key voice in the appointments of bishops that will shape the American Church for many years into the future.

He was born in Bogota, Colombia, on Jan. 27, 1930. Ordained to the priesthood on Jan. 18, 1953, he earned a doctorate in canon law from the Pontifical Lateran University and entered the Vatican diplomatic corps in 1957. He served Vatican embassies in Bolivia, Argentina, and El Salvador before being summoned to Rome in 1964 to work in the Vatican's Secretariat of State. Over the next years, he focused on the Catholic Church in Eastern Europe.

On June 30, 1974, he was ordained titular archbishop of Celene and was sent by Pope Paul VI as nuncio to Honduras and Nicaragua. In 1980, he was named pro-nuncio to Algeria and Tunisia and apostolic delegate in Libya. In 1982, he was appointed by Pope John Paul II as an assistant mediator in Argentina and Chile's dispute over the Beagle Channel, and through the Vatican's efforts, a possible war was averted. In 1986, he was transferred to serve as pro-nuncio to Yugoslavia. To these duties were added those of nuncio to Belarus in 1993. A mere two weeks later, the archbishop received a third post – as president of the Pontifical Ecclesiastical Academy, where Vatican diplomats are trained. In 1994, a new nuncio was named to Belarus, but Abp. Montalvo continued to serve as nuncio to Belgrade until 1996.

On Dec. 7, 1998, Abp. Montalvo was appointed the nuncio to the United States and permanent observer to the Organization of American States and assumed his duties in Washington in January 1999. On Dec. 17, 2005, Abp. Sambi was named nuncio to the United States, and Abp. Montalvo retired to Rome.

John Zierten (1931-2005)

John A. Zierten, a photographer who served on the staff of Our Sunday Visitor for over thirty years, died on Sept. 11, 2005, at the age of 75 in Cincinnati after a long illness. Greg Erlandson, president of Our Sunday Visitor Publishing, said of the professional photographer, "John had a passion for his craft and a love of adventure that made him one of the best field photographers in the Catholic press for many years."

Born on May 20, 1931, in the Panama Canal Zone, Zierten served as a 1st Marine Division photographer during the Korean War and continued his love for photography when working for Our Sunday Visitor. His award-winning photos were some of the most vivid ever published in Our Sunday Visitor and were seen my readers all over the world when carried by the National Catholic News Service, now the Catholic News Service.

Zierten was also distinguished by his many global travels to photograph important stories and events, such as the tragic plight of refugees. While at Our Sunday Visitor, he traveled to Asia, Africa, Central and Latin America and throughout the United States. In 1969, he received the George Washington Honor Medal Award for photography from the Freedom Foundation, based in Valley Forge, Pa. In addition, he won numerous Catholic Press Association awards.

Renowned for his stories about military service and fishing, he was also a Huntington, Ind., city council member and sheriff's deputy reservist, as well as husband, father, and grandfather of 10 grandchildren.

News In Depth

POPE BENEDICT XVI, 2005-2006

DEUS CARITAS EST

On Dec. 25, 2005, Pope Benedict XVI issued the first encyclical of his pontificate and chose as his central theme *Deus Caritas Est* ("God is Love"). The 16,000-word encyclical seeks to provide a deep reflection on the true meaning of love and the ways that love is expressed in *eros* and *agape* and their intrinsic relationship to Christ.

The pontiff begins with the declaration in the First Letter of John, "God is love, and he who abides in love abides in God, and God abides in him" (1 Jn 4:16). Like the first encyclical of Pope John Paul II, *Redemptor Hominis*, *Deus Caritas Est* is expected to set the tone for much of Benedict's pontificate.

Structure Pope Benedict discusses the two-fold purpose of the encyclical when he writes:

"In a world where the name of God is sometimes associated with vengeance or even a duty of hatred and violence, this message is both timely and significant. I wanted here — at the beginning of my Pontificate — to clarify some essential facts concerning the love which God mysteriously and gratuitously offers to man, together with the intrinsic link between that Love and the reality of human love. The second part is more concrete, since it treats the ecclesial exercise of the commandment of love of neighbor. The argument has vast implications, but a lengthy treatment would go beyond the scope of the present Encyclical. I wish to emphasize some basic elements, so as to call forth in the world renewed energy and commitment in the human response to God's love."

Part One In Part One, Pope Benedict discusses the Unity of Love in Creation and Salvation History. He notes that God's love for us is fundamental for our lives and raises important questions regarding both who God is and who we are. He then immediately notes the limitations and challenges of language, observing that in today's world, the term "love" is frequently misused and has attached different meanings to it. Despite the multiple meanings, however, one use stands out especially: the love between man and woman. If that is the epitome of love, then can it be asked of other kinds of love: "Are all these forms of love basically one, so that love, in its many and varied manifestations, is ultimately a single reality, or are we merely using the same word to designate totally different realities?"

Benedict proceeds to study the two forms of love, *eros* and *agape*. Most often, as he notes, love is understood as representing *eros*, the erotic love between a man and a woman. The

Church has offered a striking vision of self-sacrificial love that is expressed in the term *agape*: "The tendency to avoid the word *eros*, together with the new vision of love expressed through the word *agape*, clearly point to something new and distinct about the Christian understanding of love." *Agape* has been viewed negatively in the period since the Enlightenment, and Christianity has been blamed for poisoning the traditional understanding of *eros* with all of the Church's commandments and prohibitions. Hence, in the modern world, *eros* itself has been raised to an exalted place, and the human body as a result has been debased and has become a commodity, "a mere 'thing' to be bought and sold." In truth, *eros* brings a man and a woman to marriage, an exclusive, monogamous, and permanent bond.

The radicalized distinctions between *agape* and *eros* — descending love and ascending love — might seem to detach Christianity from the "vital relations fundamental to human existence." In truth, Benedict teaches that *eros* and *agape* cannot be completely separated. The two, in fact, "in their different aspects, find a proper unity in the one reality of love." The unity rests profoundly in a personal relationship with God and a deeper understanding of the sacrificial love of Jesus Christ. "By contemplating the pierced side of Christ (cf. 19:37), we can understand the starting-point of this Encyclical Letter: 'God is love' (1 Jn 4:8). It is there that this truth can be contemplated. It is from there that our definition of love must begin. In this contemplation the Christian discovers the path along which his life and love must move."

The pope then proceeds to the unbreakable bond between love of God and love of neighbor. "One is so closely connected to the other that to say that we love God becomes a lie if we are closed to our neighbor or hate him altogether. Saint John's words should rather be interpreted to mean that love of neighbor is a path that leads to the encounter with God, and that closing our eyes to our neighbor also blinds us to God."

Part Two The second half of the encyclical concerns itself with The Practice of Love by the Church as a "Community of Love." It stresses two key elements, namely that the Church's charitable activity is a manifestation of Trinitarian love and that such activity must never be motivated by political or ideological objectives.

Returning to the principle of love of neighbor, grounded in the love of God, the pontiff writes that it is first and foremost a responsibility for each individual member of the faithful, but it is also a responsibility for the entire ecclesial community at every level.

The Church must practice love, and love must be organized if it is to be an ordered service to the community. Pope Benedict gives a history of the Church's charitable labors and defines more accurately the relationship between the necessary commitment to justice and the ministry of charity. He cites two keys: The just ordering of society and the State is a central responsibility of politics and Love — *caritas* — will always prove necessary, even in the most just society.

The building of a just social and civil order is a political task, and while the Church contributes to this through social doctrine, she "cannot and must not take upon herself the political battle to bring about the most just society possible. She cannot and must not replace the State." At the same time, however, the Church cannot stand on the sidelines in the fight for true justice. Likewise, while a just society must be the achievement of politics and not of the Church, the promotion of justice must be a great concern to the Church "through efforts to bring about openness of mind and will to the demands of the common good."

Even in the just society, love is still necessary, for there is no ordering of the State so just that the service of love can be eliminated. The State is simply incapable of providing for all needs and fully resolving every problem. There will always be suffering, loneliness, and situations of material need. A State that regulates and controls everything is not needed, rather one that acknowledges and supports those initiatives "arising from the different social forces." The Church is certainly one of those living forces.

In assessing the multiple structures of charitable service in the social context of the present day, the pope also notes the distinctiveness of the Church's charitable activity. In keeping with the example of the Good Samaritan, Christian charity is first a response to the immediate needs of the hungry, the poor and sick, prisoners, etc. Consequently, the pope writes, charity workers need both professional training and a "formation of the heart" so that they might lead others to an encounter with God in Christ. In addition, "Christian charitable activity must be independent of parties and ideologies. It is not a means of changing the world ideologically, and it is not at the service of worldly stratagems, but it is a way of making present here and now the love which man always needs." Nor, Pope Benedict urges, must charity be used as a means of proselytism. "Love is free; it is not practiced as a way of achieving other ends. But this does not mean that charitable activity must somehow leave God and Christ aside. For it is always concerned with the whole man."

Finally, the pope turns his attention to those responsible for the Church's charitable activity. He remarks that in conformity with the episcopal structure of the Church, the bishops, the successors to the Apostles, carry the primary responsibility for the Church's program of charity. For those who have the practical responsibility of charitable labors, they must be free of inspiration by ideology and "be guided by the faith which works through love (cf. Gal 5:6)." Equally, the pope calls for a reaffirmation of the importance of "prayer in the face of the activism and the growing secularism of many Christians engaged in charitable work."

In his conclusion, Pope Benedict presents several examples of saints who were clear models for the life of charity. He offers Sts. Martin of Tours, Anthony the Abbot, Francis of Assisi, Ignatius of Loyola, John of God, Camillus of Lellis, Vincent de Paul, Louise de Marillac, Giuseppe B. Cottolengo, John Bosco, Luigi Orione, Teresa of Calcutta, and especially Mary, Mother of the Lord.

NEW MEMBERS OF THE COLLEGE OF CARDINALS

Pope Benedict XVI made his first significant mark upon the future election of his successor when he announced the creation of 15 new cardinals on Feb. 22, 2006. The new members of the College of Cardinals, including the two Americans—Archbishops William J. Levada, prefect of the Congregation for the Doctrine of the Faith, and Sean P. O'Malley of Boston—were from 11 countries and include three officials of the Vatican, nine heads of dioceses or archdioceses around the world, and three older clerics over the age of 80 who were honored for their long service to the Church.

In naming the 15 cardinals, Pope Benedict clearly decided to adhere to the maximum number of 120 electors set by Pope Paul VI in 1973. Pope John Paul II set aside the limit on several occasions during his pontificate. Archbishop Levada, former archbishop of Portland and San Francisco, was picked last May to succeed the newly-elected pope as head of the Vatican's office for doctrine. Two other notable appointments are Archbishop Stanislaw Dziwisz of Krakow and the Salesian Bishop Joseph Zen Ze-kiun of Hong Kong. Cardinal-designate Dziwisz was the longtime personal secretary of Pope John Paul II, and Cardinal-designate Zen has been a vocal critic of the Communist Chinese government's record on human rights and religious freedom. The cardinals were installed officially at a special consistory on Mar. 24.

The New Princes of the Church

Archbishop William Levada, 69, prefect of the Congregation for the Doctrine of the Faith.

Archbishop Franc Rodé, 71, prefect of the Congregation for Institutes of Consecrated Life and Societies of Apostolic Life.

Archbishop Agostino Vallini, 65, prefect of the Apostolic Signature, the Church's supreme court.

Archbishop Sean Patrick O'Malley, OFM Cap., 61, of Boston, Mass.

Archbishop Jean-Pierre Ricard, 61, of Bordeaux, France.

Archbishop Antonio Cañizares Llovera, 60, of Todedo, Spain.

Archbishop Stanislaw Dziwisz, 66, former secretary of Pope John Paul II, of Krakow, Poland.

Archbishop Carlo Caffarra, 67, of Bologna, Italy.

Archbishop Gaudencio Rosales, 73, of Manila, Philippines.

Archbishop Cheong Jin-Suk, 74, of Seoul, South Korea.

Archbishop Jorge Liberato Urosa Savino, 63, of Caracas, Venezuela.

Bishop Joseph Zen Ze-kiun, S.V.D., 74, of Hong Kong.

Archbishop emeritus Peter Poreku Dery, 87, of Tamale, Ghana.

Archbishop Andrea Cordero Lanza Di Montezemolo, 80, archpriest of the Basilica of St. Paul Outside the Walls and retired apostolate delegate in Jerusalem and apostolic nuncio in Italy.

Jesuit Father Albert Vanhoye, 82, theologian and biblical expert.

Pope Benedict XVI's Homily

Following are excerpts from Pope Benedict's homily at the Ordinary Public Consistory for the Creation of Cardinals on Mar. 24:On this vigil of the Solemnity of the Annunciation of the Lord, the penitential mood of Lent makes way for the feast: today, the College of Cardinals is to gain 15 new members. To you in particular, my dear Brothers, whom I have had the joy of raising to the cardinalate, I address a most sincere and cordial greeting, and I thank Cardinal William Joseph Levada for the sentiments and good wishes that he has expressed to me in the name of all of you. I am also pleased to greet the other cardinals present, the venerable Patriarchs, the Bishops, the priests, the men and women religious and the many lay faithful, especially family members who have come here to honor the new cardinals in prayer and Christian joy. With special gratitude I welcome the distinguished civil and governmental authorities, representing various nations and institutions. The Ordinary Public Consistory is an event that manifests most eloquently the universal nature of the Church, which has spread to every corner of the world in order to proclaim to all people the Good News of Christ our Savior. The beloved Pope John Paul II celebrated nine Consistories in all, thus contributing effectively to the renewal of the College of Cardinals along the lines established by the Second Vatican Council and the Servant of God Pope Paul VI. If it is true that down the centuries the College of Cardinals has changed in many ways, nevertheless the substance and essential nature of this important ecclesial body remain unaltered. Its ancient roots, its historical development and its composition today make it truly a kind of "Senate," called to cooperate closely with the Successor of Peter in accomplishing the tasks connected with his universal apostolic ministry. The Word of God, which has just been proclaimed to us, takes us back in time. With the Evangelist Mark we return to the very origin of the Church and specifically to the origin of the Petrine ministry. With the eyes of our hearts we see the Lord Jesus once again, to whose praise and glory this act in which we are engaged is totally directed and dedicated. The words he speaks to us recall to our minds the definition of the Roman Pontiff so dear to the heart of Saint Gregory the Great: "*Servus servorum Dei*." When Jesus explains to the twelve Apostles that their authority will have to be exercised quite differently from that of "the rulers of the Gentiles," he expresses it in terms of service: "Whoever would be great among you must be your servant (äéÜëïïù), and whoever would be first among you must be slave of all" (here Jesus uses a stronger word—äïöëïù: Mk 10:43-44). Total and generous availability to serve others is the distinctive mark of those in positions of authority in the Church, because it was thus for the Son of Man, who came "not to be served but to serve, and to give his life as a ransom for

many" (Mk 10:45). Although he was God, or one might even say driven by his divinity, he assumed the form of a servant—"*formam servi*"—as is wonderfully expressed in the hymn to Christ contained in the Letter to the Philippians (cf. 2:6-7).The first "servant of the servants of God" is therefore Jesus. After him, and united with him, come the Apostles; and among these, in a particular way, Peter, to whom the Lord entrusted the responsibility of guiding his flock. The Pope must be the first to make himself the servant of all. Clear testimony to this is found in the first reading of today's liturgy, which puts before us Peter's exhortation to the "presbyters" and elders of the community (cf. 1 Pt 5:1). It is an exhortation given with the authority that comes to the Apostle from the fact that he is a witness of the sufferings of Christ, the Good Shepherd. We sense that Peter's words come from his personal experience of service to God's flock, but first and foremost they are derived from direct experience of Jesus' own behavior: the way he served to the point of self-sacrifice, the way he humbled himself even unto death, death on a cross, trusting in the Father alone, who subsequently raised him on high. Peter, like Paul, was utterly "conquered" by Christ—"*comprehensus sum a Christo Iesu*" (cf. Phil 3:12)—and like Paul he can exhort the elders with full authority because it is no longer he who lives, but Christ lives in him—"*vivo autem iam non ego, vivit vero in me Christus*" (Gal. 2:20).Yes, venerable and dear Brothers, these words of the Prince of the Apostles apply particularly to those who are called to wear the cardinalatial scarlet: "I exhort the elders among you, as a fellow elder and a witness of the sufferings of Christ as well as a partaker in the glory that is to be revealed" (1 Pt 5:1). These words, in their essential structure, recall the Paschal Mystery, specially present in our hearts during these days of Lent. Saint Peter applies them to himself as a "fellow elder" (óôìñáóâyôâñïï), indicating that the elder in the Church, the presbyter, through experience accumulated over the years and through trials faced and overcome, must be particularly "in tune" with the inner dynamic of the Paschal Mystery. How many times, dear Brothers who have just received the cardinalatial dignity, have you found in these words matter for meditation and a source of spiritual inspiration to follow in the footsteps of the crucified and risen Lord! The demands that your new responsibility places upon you will confirm these words in a new and exacting way. More closely linked to the Successor of Peter, you will be called to work together with him in accomplishing his particular ecclesial service, and this will mean for you a more intense participation in the mystery of the Cross as you share in the sufferings of Christ. All of us are truly witnesses of his sufferings today, in the world and also in the Church, and hence we also have a share in his glory. And so you will be able to draw more abundantly upon the sources of grace and to disseminate their life-giving fruits more effectively to those around you. Venerable and dear Brothers, I want to sum up the meaning of this new call that you have received in the word which I placed at the heart of my first Encyclical: *caritas*. This matches well the color of your cardinalatial robes. May the scarlet that you now wear always express the *caritas Christi*, inspiring you to a passionate love for Christ, for his Church and for all humanity. You now have an additional motive to seek to rekindle in yourselves those same sentiments that led the incarnate Son of God to pour out his blood in atonement for the sins of the whole world. I am counting on you, venerable Brothers, I am counting on the entire College into which you are being incorporated, to proclaim to the world that "*Deus caritas est*," and to do so above all through the witness of sincere communion among Christians: "By this," said Jesus, "all people will know that you are my disciples, if you have love for one another" (Jn 13:35). I am counting on you, dear Brother Cardinals, to ensure that the principle of love will spread far and wide, and will give new life to the Church at every level of her hierarchy, in every group of the faithful, in every religious Institute, in every spiritual, apostolic or humanitarian initiative. I am counting on you to see to it that our common endeavor to fix our gaze on Christ's open Heart will hasten and secure our path towards the full unity of Christians. I am counting on you to see to it that the Church's solicitude for the poor and needy challenges the world with a powerful statement on the civilization of love. All this I see symbolized in the scarlet with which you are now invested. May it truly be a symbol of ardent Christian love shining forth in your lives. I entrust this my prayer into the maternal hands of the Holy Virgin of Nazareth, source of the life-blood which the Son of God was to pour out on the Cross as the supreme expression of his love. In the mystery of the Annunciation which we are about to celebrate, it is revealed to us that the divine Word was made flesh through the action of the Holy Spirit and came to dwell among us. Through Mary's intercession, may the Spirit of truth and love be poured out abundantly upon the new Cardinals and upon us all, so that as we become ever more fully conformed to Christ, we may dedicate ourselves tirelessly to building up the Church and to spreading the Gospel in the world.

Cardinals' Oath on Receiving the Biretta

Below is a translation of the oath of fidelity and obedience to the Pope and his Successors, pronounced by the Cardinals at the time they receive the biretta, or cardinal's hat:

"I [name and surname], Cardinal of the Holy Roman Church, promise and swear to be faithful henceforth and forever, while I live, to Christ and his Gospel, being constantly obedient to the Holy Roman Apostolic Church, to Blessed Peter in the person of the Supreme Pontiff Benedict XVI, and of his canonically elected Successors; to maintain communion with the Catholic Church always, in word and deed; not to reveal to any one what is confided to me in secret, nor to divulge what may bring harm or dishonor to Holy Church; to carry out with great diligence and faithfulness those tasks to which I am called by my service to the Church, in accord with the norms of the law.

So help me Almighty God." *[Translation by Zenit.]*

500TH ANNIVERSARY OF THE SWISS GUARD

On May 6, 2006, Pope Benedict XVI celebrated a Mass in honor of the 500th anniversary of the founding of the Swiss Guard, the traditional bodyguard of the popes.

The *Guardia Svizzera Pontificia*, the Swiss Guards are recruited from the Catholic Swiss cantons and were first established by Pope Julius II (r. 1503–1513) around 1505. Also called the *Cohors Helvetica*, the Swiss Guard was created as the result of an agreement reached by Julius with the cantons of Zurich and Lucerne in which he contracted several hundred well-trained soldiers to serve as a guard. The first troops arrived in Rome on Jan. 21, 1506, marching to St. Peter's Square through the Porta del Popolo under their first commanding officers, Peter Hertenstein and Gaspar de Silinon.

There they received the pope's blessing. The anniversary of the occasion is celebrated every year. The design of the uniform given to the Swiss Guard was traditionally ascribed to Michelangelo, although some scholars have argued that the Swiss entered into papal service wearing their distinctive uniform. Today, the blue-and-gold-striped uniform, with fluffy beret and high ruffled collar, is known the world over. Recruitment of the guard is generally limited to Catholics from Switzerland. If found acceptable for service, the potential guardsman signs up for two years, although he is able to leave at any time after giving notice of three months. After 18 years, a guardsman is eligible for a pension equal to half pay; this increases to full pay after 30 years. The guard has a barracks just inside St. Anne's Gate and its own chapel. The whole corps is commanded by a colonel and three other officers. There is also a chaplain, over 20 other noncommissioned officers, two drummers, and some 70 guardsmen who carry halberds, the tall axe-tipped poles used especially for crowd control on hot Roman summer days. The guardsmen are also trained to use more modern weapons that are kept at easy-to-reach spots, although in the event of a major breach of the peace, the Vatican will rely on the gendarmerie, or more properly, the Vigilanza, assisted by Italian police. The Swiss Guard's presence around the pontiff is ubiquitous, however, and a squad travels with him wherever he goes. That the guardsmen have historically been willing to die in the service of the pope was proven in 1527 when the troops of Emperor Charles V sacked Rome and St. Peter's. The guard put up a valiant defense of the Vatican to protect Pope Clement VII, and nearly 150 were killed in a brutal fight in St. Peter's Square, buying time for Clement to escape over the loggia to the safety of Castel Sant'Angelo. The dead included the guard commander and his wife, who were tortured and put to death in their quarters. Among the imperial troops were good Catholic mercenaries. May 6 is still commemorated every year, in honor of the fallen guardsmen. Also on that day new members are given their oath and entered into the corps.

Following are excerpts from the pope's homily for the Mass:

This year we are commemorating several significant events that occurred in 1506, exactly 500 years ago: the rediscovery of the sculptural group of the Laocoön that led to the establishment of the Vatican Museums; the laying of the foundation stone of this building, St. Peter's Basilica, rebuilt on the site of Constantine's Basilica; and the birth of the Pontifical Swiss Guard. Today, it is especially the latter event that we wish to recall. Indeed, on Jan. 22, 500 years ago, the first 150 Swiss Guards arrived in Rome at the express request of Pope Julius II and entered his service in the Apostolic Palace. That chosen corps was very soon required to show its faithfulness to the Pontiff: in 1527, Rome was invaded and sacked, and on May 6, 147 Swiss Guards were killed because they were defending Pope Clement VII, while the remaining 42 escorted him safely to Castel Sant'Angelo. Why should we commemorate today these events that happened so long ago, in a Rome and a Europe so different from the situation today? First of all, to pay honor to the Swiss Guard Corps, whose role ever since has always been reconfirmed, even in 1970 when the Servant of God Paul VI disbanded all the other military corps of the Vatican. However, at the same time and above all, let us call to mind these historic events so as to draw a lesson from them in the light of God's Word.

To this end, the biblical readings of today's liturgy are helpful, and the Risen Christ, whom we celebrate with special joy during this Easter Season, opens our minds to understanding the Scriptures (cf. Lk 24:45), so that we may recognize God's plan and do his will. The First Reading is taken from the Book of Wisdom, traditionally attributed to the great King Solomon. This entire book is a hymn of praise to Divine Wisdom, presented as the most valuable treasure that man can desire and discover, the greatest good on which all other goods depend. For wisdom, it is worth giving up every other thing; for wisdom alone gives life its full meaning, a meaning that overcomes death itself because it puts people in authentic communion with God. Wisdom, the text says, "makes them friends of God" (Wis 7:27).

On the one hand, it highlights the "formative" aspect, in other words, the fact that Wisdom forms people, making them grow from within towards the full stature of their maturity; and it contextually affirms that this fullness of life consists in friendship with God, in an intimate harmony with his being and his will.

The interior place in which Divine Wisdom operates is what the Bible calls "the heart," the person's spiritual center. Thus, the Response of the Responsorial Psalm had us pray: "Give us, O God, wisdom of heart."

Psalm 90[89] then recalls that this wisdom is granted to those who learn how to "number [their] days" (cf. v. 12), that is, to recognize that all the rest of life is fleeting, short-lived and transient; and that sinful human beings cannot and must not hide from God, but must recognize themselves for what they are: creatures in need of mercy and grace. Those who accept this truth and are prepared to accept wisdom, receive it as a gift. For wisdom, then, it is worth giving up all other things. This theme, to "leave" in order to "find," is the center of the Gospel passage we have just heard, taken from chapter 19 of St. Matthew. After the episode of the "rich young man" who did not have the courage to detach himself from his "many riches" in order to follow Jesus (cf. Mt. 19:22), the Apostle Peter asked the Lord what instead would be the reward of those disciples of his who left everything in order to follow him (cf. Mt. 19:27). Christ's answer reveals the immense greatness of his heart: he promised the Twelve that they would share in his authority over the new Israel; then he assured them all that "everyone who has left" their earthly goods for his sake would "receive a hun-

dredfold, and inherit eternal life" (Mt. 19:29). The person who chooses Jesus finds the greatest treasure, the pearl of great value (cf. Mt 13:44-46) that gives value to all the rest, for Jesus is Divine Wisdom incarnate (cf. Jn 1:14), who came into the world so that humanity might have life in abundance (cf. Jn 10:10). And the person who accepts Christ's superior goodness and beauty and truth, in which the whole fullness of God dwells (cf. Col 2:9), enters with him into his Kingdom where the value judgments of this world decay and, indeed, are overturned.

We find one of the most beautiful definitions of the Kingdom of God in the Second Reading. It is a text that belongs to the exhortational part of the Letter to the Romans. The Apostle Paul, after urging Christians always to allow themselves to be guided by love and not to be objects of scandal for those who are weak in faith, recalls that the Kingdom of God is "righteousness and peace and joy in the Holy Spirit" (Rom 14:17). And he adds: "He who thus serves Christ is acceptable to God and approved by men. Let us then pursue what makes for peace and for mutual upbuilding" (Rom 14:18-19). "What makes for peace" is a concise and complete expression of biblical wisdom in the light of the revelation of Christ and his mystery of salvation.

The person who has recognized Christ as Wisdom Incarnate, and for his sake has left everything else, becomes a "peacemaker," both in the Christian community and in the world. In other words, he becomes a seed of the Kingdom of God that is already present and growing towards its full manifestation. Therefore, in the perspective of the two words, "Wisdom-Christ," the Word of God offers us a complete vision of man in history: fascinated by wisdom, he seeks it and finds it in Christ, leaving everything for him and receiving in exchange the priceless gift of the Kingdom of God; and clothed in temperance, prudence, justice and strength — the "cardinal" virtues — he lives the witness of charity in the Church. One might wonder whether this perception of the human being can also constitute an ideal of life for the people of our time, especially for the young. That this is possible is shown by countless personal and community testimonies of Christian life, which still constitute the wealth of the People of God, pilgrims through history.

Among the many expressions of the lay presence in the Catholic Church, there is also the very special one of the Pontifical Swiss Guards. These young men, motivated by love for Christ and for the Church, put themselves at the service of the Successor of Peter. For some of them, membership in this Guard Corps is limited to a brief period; for others, it extends until it becomes the choice of their entire life. For some of them, and I say so with deep satisfaction, service at the Vatican has led to the development of the response to a priestly or religious vocation.

However, for them all, being a Swiss Guard means adhering to Christ and the Church without reserve, and being prepared to die for them.

A Swiss Guard's active service may come to an end, but inside he always remains a Swiss Guard. This is what 80 former Swiss Guards desired to testify. From Apr. 7 to May 4 they accomplished an extraordinary feat, marching from Switzerland to Rome, following the route of the Via Francigena as closely as possible.

I would like to renew my greeting to each one of them and to all the Swiss Guards. I also remember the authorities who have come from Switzerland for the occasion, and the other civil and military authorities, the chaplains who enliven the Guards' daily service with the Gospel and the Eucharist, as well as their many relatives and friends. Dear friends, I offer this Eucharist, the highest spiritual point of your celebration, especially for you and for the deceased members of your Corps. Nourish yourselves on the Eucharistic Bread and be first and foremost men of prayer, so that

Divine Wisdom may make you genuine friends of God and servants of his Kingdom of love and peace. The service offered by your long ranks winding through these 500 years acquires fullness of meaning and value in the Sacrifice of Christ.

As I make myself in spirit the interpreter of the Pontiffs whom your Corps has served faithfully down the centuries, I express well-deserved and heartfelt gratitude, while looking to the future, I invite you to march on, *acriter and fideliter,* with courage and fidelity.

PAPAL TRIPS 2006

POLAND, May 25-28, 2006

On the second foreign apostolic trip of his pontificate, Pope Benedict XVI visited Poland from May 25–28, 2006. The trip was especially significant as it marked the journey of to Poland of the successor of Pope John Paul II, a beloved and revered figure of the Polish people. The pontiff visited Auschwitz, the infamous Nazi concentration camp where millions died during World War II and the Holocaust.

Program

Welcome ceremony at the International Airport of Okecie — Warsaw, May 25, 2006
Meeting with the clergy in the Cathedral of St. John in Warsaw — May 25, 2006
Ecumenical meeting in the Lutheran Church of the Most Holy Trinity in Warsaw — May 25, 2006
Holy Mass at Pilsudski Square in Warsaw — May 26, 2006
Meeting with the men and women religious, seminarians, representatives of movements and consecrated life at the Shrine of Jasna Góra — May 26, 2006
Greeting by the Holy Father "From the Window" to Young People at the Archbishop's Palace Kraków — May 26, 2006
Meeting with the faithful at Rynek Square in Wadowice — May 27, 2006
Visit to the Shrine of Our Lady of Kalwaria in Kalwaria Zebrzydowska — May 27, 2006
Meeting with the sick — Visit to the Shrine of Divine Mercy — Kraków-Lagiewniki, May 27, 2006
Meeting with youth at Blonie Park in Krakow — May 27, 2006
Greeting by the Holy Father after the meeting with young people, Kraków-Blonie — May 27, 2006
Holy Mass at Blonie Park in Krakow — May 28, 2006
Recital of the Regina Cæli, Krakow — May 28, 2006
Prayer to commemorate the victims of the concentration camp of Auschwitz-Birkenau — May 28, 2006
Farewell ceremony at the Airport of Balice, Krakow— May 28, 2006

Excerpts from Addresses and Homilies
(*Complete texts of papal addresses, remarks and homilies can be found at* www.vatican.va.)

Welcome Ceremony at the International Airport of Okėcie — Address (Warsaw, May 25, 2006)
I am happy to stand in your midst today on the soil of the Republic of Poland. I have very much wanted to make this visit to the native land and people of my

beloved predecessor, the Servant of God, John Paul II. I have come to follow in the footsteps of his life, from his boyhood until his departure for the memorable conclave of 1978. Along this journey I would like to meet and come to know the generations of believers who offered him to the service of God and the Church, as well as those who were born and matured for the Lord under his pastoral guidance as priest, bishop and pope. Our journey together will be inspired by the motto: "Stand firm in your faith." I mention this from the outset, in order to stress that this is no mere sentimental journey, although it is certainly that, too, but rather a journey of faith, a part of the mission entrusted to me by the Lord in the person of the Apostle Peter, who was called to confirm his brothers and sisters in the faith (cf. Lk 22:32). I too wish to draw from the abundant fountain of your faith, which has flowed continuously for over a millennium. "Stand firm in your faith" — this is the motto of my Apostolic Visit. I would hope that these days will serve to strengthen all of us in faith — the members of the Church in Poland and myself as well. And for those who do not have the gift of faith, but whose hearts are full of good will, may my visit be a time of fraternity, goodness and hope. May these enduring values of humanity lay a firm foundation for building a better world, one in which everyone can enjoy material prosperity and spiritual joy. This is my prayer for all the Polish people. Once again I thank His Excellency the president and the bishops of Poland for their invitation. I cordially embrace Polish people everywhere and I ask them to accompany me in prayer along this journey of faith.

Meeting with the Clergy in the Cathedral of St. John — Address (Warsaw, May 25, 2006)
I am meeting you today in the great cathedral of Warsaw, every stone of which speaks of the tragic history of your capital and your country. How many trials you have endured in the recent past! We call to mind heroic witnesses to the faith, who gave their lives to God and to their fellow human beings, both canonized saints and ordinary people who persevered in rectitude, authenticity and goodness, never giving way to despair. In this cathedral I recall particularly the Servant of God Cardinal Stefan Wyszyński, whom you call "the Primate of the Millennium." Abandoning himself to Christ and to his Mother, he knew how to serve the Church faithfully, despite the tragic and prolonged trials that surrounded him. Let us remember with appreciation and gratitude those who did not let themselves be overwhelmed by the forces of darkness, and let us learn from them the courage to be consistent and constant in our adherence to the Gospel of Christ. Today I am

meeting you, priests called by Christ to serve him in the new millennium.... The greatness of Christ's priesthood can make us tremble. We can be tempted to cry out with Peter: "Lord, depart from me, for I am a sinful man" (Lk 5:8), because we find it hard to believe that Christ called us specifically. Could he not have chosen someone else, more capable, more holy? But Jesus has looked lovingly upon each one of us, and in this gaze of his we may have confidence. Let us not be consumed with haste, as if time dedicated to Christ in silent prayer were time wasted. On the contrary, it is precisely then that the most wonderful fruits of pastoral service come to birth. There is no need to be discouraged on account of the fact that prayer requires effort, or because of the impression that Jesus remains silent. He is indeed silent, but he is at work. . . . The faithful expect only one thing from priests: that they be specialists in promoting the encounter between man and God. The priest is not asked to be an expert in economics, construction or politics. He is expected to be an expert in the spiritual life. With this end in view, when a young priest takes his first steps, he needs to be able to refer to an experienced teacher who will help him not to lose his way among the many ideas put forward by the culture of the moment. In the face of the temptations of relativism or the permissive society, there is absolutely no need for the priest to know all the latest, changing currents of thought; what the faithful expect from him is that he be a witness to the eternal wisdom contained in the revealed word. Solicitude for the quality of personal prayer and for good theological formation bear fruit in life. Living under the influence of totalitarianism may have given rise to an unconscious tendency to hide under an external mask, and in consequence to become somewhat hypocritical. Clearly this does not promote authentic fraternal relations and may lead to an exaggerated concentration on oneself. In reality, we grow in affective maturity when our hearts adhere to God. Christ needs priests who are mature, virile, capable of cultivating an authentic spiritual paternity. For this to happen, priests need to be honest with themselves, open with their spiritual director and trusting in divine mercy....Stand firm in your faith! To you too I entrust this motto of my pilgrimage. Be authentic in your life and your ministry. Gazing upon Christ, live a modest life, in solidarity with the faithful to whom you have been sent. Serve everyone, be accessible in the parishes and in the confessionals, accompany the new movements and associations, support families, do not forget the link with young people, remember the poor and the abandoned. If you live by faith, the Holy Spirit will suggest to you what you must say and how you must serve. You will always be able to count on the help of her who goes before the Church in faith. I exhort you to call upon her always in words that you know well: "We are close to you, we remember you, we watch." My Blessing upon all of you!

Ecumenical Meeting in the Lutheran Church of the Most Holy Trinity — Address
(Warsaw, May 25, 2006)

We note much progress in the field of ecumenism and yet we always await something more. Allow me to draw attention to two questions for today, in somewhat greater detail. The first concerns the charitable service of the Churches. There are many brothers and sisters who expect from us the gift of love, of trust, of witness, of spiritual and concrete material help. I referred to this problem in my first encyclical, Deus Caritas Est, in which I said: "Love of neighbor, grounded in the love of God, is first and foremost a responsibility for each individual member of the faithful, but it is also a responsibility for the entire ecclesial community at every level: from the local community to the particular Church and to the Church universal in its entirety. As a community, the Church must practise love" (no. 20). We cannot forget the essential idea that from the outset constituted the very firm foundation for the disciples' unity: "within the community of believers there can never be room for a poverty that denies anyone what is needed for a dignified life" (no. 20). This idea is always current, even if in the course of the centuries the forms of fraternal aid have changed; accepting contemporary charitable challenges depends in large measure on our mutual co-operation. I rejoice that this problem finds a vast resonance in the world in the form of numerous ecumenical initiatives. I note with appreciation that in the community of the Catholic Church and in other churches and ecclesial communities, various new forms of charitable activity have spread and old ones have reappeared with renewed vigor. They are forms which often combine evangelization and works of charity (no. 20, 30b). It seems that, despite all the differences that need to be overcome in the sphere of interdenominational dialogue, it is legitimate to attribute charitable engagement to the ecumenical community of Christ's disciples in search of full unity. We can all enter into cooperation in favor of the needy, exploiting this network of reciprocal relations, the fruit of dialogue between ourselves and of joint action. In the spirit of the gospel commandment we must assume this devoted solicitude towards those in need, whoever they may be. In this regard, I wrote in my encyclical that "the building of a better world requires Christians to speak with a united voice in working to inculcate 'respect for the rights and needs of everyone, especially the poor, the lowly and the defenseless' " (no. 30b). To all those who are taking part in our encounter today I express the wish that the practice of fraternal caritas will bring us ever closer to one another and will render our witness in favor of Christ more credible before the world. The second question to which I want to refer concerns married life and family life. We know that among Christian communities, called to witness to love, the family occupies a special place. In today's world, in which international and intercultural relations are multiplying, it happens increasingly often that young people from different traditions, different religions, or different Christian denominations, decide to start a family. For the young people themselves and for those dear to them, it is often a difficult decision that brings with it various dangers concerning both perseverance in the faith and the future structuring of the family, the creation of an atmosphere of unity in the family and of suitable conditions for the spiritual growth of the children. Nevertheless, thanks to the spread of ecumenical dialogue on a larger scale, the decision can lead to the formation of a practical laboratory of unity. For this to happen there is a need for mutual good will, understanding and maturity in faith of both parties, and also of the communities from which they come.

Holy Mass at Pilsudski Square — Homily
(Warsaw, May 26, 2006)

Dear brothers and sisters in Christ our Lord, "Together with you I wish to sing a hymn of praise to divine Providence, which enables me to be here as a pilgrim." Twenty-seven years ago, my beloved predecessor Pope John Paul II began his homily in Warsaw with these words. I make them my own, and I thank the Lord who has enabled me to come here today to this historic Square. Here, on the eve of Pentecost, Pope John Paul II uttered the significant words of the prayer: "Let your Spirit descend, and renew the face of the earth," and he added, "The face of this land." This very place witnessed the solemn funeral ceremony of the great Primate of Poland, Cardinal Stefan Wyszyński, whose 25th anniversary occurs during these days. God united these two men not only through the same faith, hope and love, but also through the same human vicissitudes, which linked each of them so strongly to the history of this people and of the Church that lives in their midst. At the beginning of his pontificate, Pope John Paul II wrote to Cardinal Wyszyński: "This Polish Pope would not be on the Chair of Peter today, beginning a new Pontificate, full of the fear of God, but also full of trust, had it not been for your faith, which did not bend in the face of imprisonment and suffering, your heroic hope, your trusting to the end in the Mother of the Church; had it not been for Jasna Góra and this whole period of the history of the Church in our homeland, linked to your service as Bishop and Primate" (Letter of Pope John Paul II to the Polish People, Oct. 23, 1978). How can we not thank God today for all that was accomplished in your native land and in the whole world during the Pontificate of John Paul II? Before our eyes, changes occurred in entire political, economic and social systems. People in various countries regained their freedom and their sense of dignity. "Let us not forget the great works of God" (cf. Ps 78:7). I thank you too for your presence and for your prayer. I thank the Cardinal Primate for the words that he addressed to me. I greet all the Bishops here present. I am glad that the President and the Authorities of national and local government could be here. I embrace with my heart all the Polish people both at home and abroad…Christ says: "If you love me…" Faith does not just mean accepting a certain number of abstract truths about the mysteries of God, of man, of life and death, of future realities. Faith consists in an intimate relationship with Christ, a relationship based on love of him who loved us first (cf. 1 Jn 4:11), even to the total offering of himself. "God shows his love for us in that while we were yet sinners Christ died for us" (Rom 5:8). What other response can we give to a love so great, if not that of a heart that is open and ready to love? But what does it mean to love Christ? It means trusting him even in times of trial, following him faithfully even on the Via Crucis, in the hope that soon the morning of the Resurrection will come. Entrusting ourselves to Christ, we lose nothing, we gain everything. In his hands our life acquires its true meaning. Love for Christ expresses itself in the will to harmonize our own life with the thoughts and sentiments of his Heart. This is achieved through interior union based on the grace of the Sacraments, strengthened by continuous prayer, praise, thanksgiving and penance. We have to listen attentively to the inspirations that he evokes through his Word, through the people we meet, through the situations of daily life. To love him is to remain in dialogue with him, in order to know his will and to put it into effect promptly. Yet living one's personal faith as a love-relationship with Christ also means being ready to renounce everything that constitutes a denial of his love. That is why Jesus said to the Apostles: "If you love me, you will keep my commandments." But what are Christ's commandments? When the Lord Jesus was teaching the crowds, he did not fail to confirm the law, which the Creator had inscribed on men's hearts and had then formulated on the tablets of the Decalogue. "Think not that I have come to abolish the law and the prophets; I have come not to abolish them but to fulfill them. For truly, I say to you, till heaven and earth pass away, not an iota, not a dot, will pass from the law until all is accomplished" (Mt 5:17-18). But Jesus showed us with a new clarity the unifying centre of the divine laws revealed on Sinai, namely love of God and love of neighbor: "To love [God] with all the heart, and with all the understanding, and with all the strength, and to love one's neighbor as oneself, is much more than all whole burnt offerings and sacrifices" (Mk 12:33). Indeed, in his life and in his Paschal Mystery Jesus brought the entire law to completion. Uniting himself with us through the gift of the Holy Spirit, he carries with us and in us the "yoke" of the law, which thereby becomes a "light burden" (Mt 11:30). In this spirit, Jesus formulated his list of the inner qualities of those who seek to live their faith deeply: Blessed are the poor in spirit, those who weep, the meek, those who hunger and thirst for justice, the merciful, the pure in heart, the peacemakers, those who are persecuted for righteousness' sake… (cf. Mt 5:3-12).

Meeting with the Men and Women religious, seminarians, representatives of movements and consecrated life at the Shrine of Jasna Góra — Address
(May 26, 2006)

"Faith is contact with the mystery of God," to quote Pope John Paul II (Redemptoris Mater, 17), because "to believe means 'to abandon oneself' to the truth of the word of the living God, knowing and humbly recognizing 'how unsearchable are his judgments and how inscrutable his ways' " (ibid., 14). Faith is the gift, given to us in Baptism, which makes our encounter with God possible. God is hidden in mystery; to claim to understand him would mean to want to confine him within our thinking and knowing and consequently to lose him irremediably. With faith, however, we can open up a way through concepts, even theological concepts, and can "touch" the living God. And God, once touched, immediately gives us his power. When we abandon ourselves to the living God, when in humility of mind we have recourse to him, a kind of hidden stream of divine life pervades us. How important it is to believe in the power of faith, in its capacity to establish a close bond with the living God! We must give great attention to the development of our faith, so that it truly pervades all our attitudes, thoughts, actions and intentions. Faith has a place, not only in our state of soul and religious experiences, but above all in thought and action, in everyday work, in the struggle against ourselves, in community life and in the apostolate, because it ensures that our life is pervaded by the power of God himself. Faith can always bring us back to God even when our sin leads us astray. In the Upper Room the Apostles did not know what awaited them.

They were afraid and worried about their own future. They continued to marvel at the death and resurrection of Jesus and were in anguish at being left on their own after his ascension into Heaven. Mary, "she who believed in the fulfillment of the Lord's words" (cf. Lk 1:45), assiduous in prayer alongside the Apostles, taught perseverance in the faith. By her own attitude she convinced them that the Holy Spirit, in his wisdom, knew well the path on which he was leading them, and that consequently they could place their confidence in God, giving themselves to him unreservedly, with their talents, their limitations and their future. Many of you here present have experienced this secret call of the Holy Spirit and have responded with complete generosity of heart. The love of Jesus "poured into your hearts through the Holy Spirit who has been given to you" (cf. Rom 5:5), has shown you the way of the consecrated life. It was not you who looked for it. It was Jesus who called you, inviting you to a more profound union with him. In the sacrament of Holy Baptism you renounced Satan and his works and received the necessary graces for a Christian life and for holiness. From that moment the grace of faith has blossomed within you and has enabled you to be united with God. At the moment of your religious profession or promises, faith led you to a total adherence to the mystery of the Heart of Jesus, whose treasures you have discovered. You then renounced such good things as disposing freely of your life, having a family, acquiring possessions, so as to be free to give yourselves without reserve to Christ and to his Kingdom. Do you remember your enthusiasm when you began the pilgrimage of the consecrated life, trusting in the grace of God? Try not to lose this first fervor, and let Mary lead you to an ever fuller adherence. Dear men and women religious, dear consecrated persons! Whatever the mission entrusted to you, whatever cloistered or apostolic service you are engaged in, maintain in your hearts the primacy of your consecrated life. Let it renew your faith. The consecrated life, lived in faith, unites you closely to God, calls forth charisms and confers an extraordinary fruitfulness to your service…When the Apostles, filled with the Holy Spirit, went out to the whole world proclaiming the Gospel, one of them, John, the Apostle of love, took Mary into his home (cf. Jn 19:27). It was precisely because of his profound bond with Jesus and with Mary, that he could so effectively insist on the truth that "God is love" (1 Jn 4:8, 16). These were the words that I placed at the beginning of the first encyclical of my Pontificate: Deus caritas est! This is the most important, most central truth about God. To all for whom it is difficult to believe in God, I say again today: "God is love." Dear friends, be witnesses to this truth. You will surely be so if you place yourselves in the school of Mary. Beside her you will experience for yourselves that God is love, and you will transmit this message to the world with the richness and the variety that the Holy Spirit will know how to enkindle.

Greeting by the Holy Father "From the Window" to Young People at the Archbishop's Palace (Kraków, May 26, 2006)

Following the practice which arose during Pope John Paul II's visits to Kraków, you have gathered in front of the Archbishop's residence to greet the Pope. Thank you for being here and for your warm welcome. I know that on the second of every month, at the hour of my beloved Predecessor's death, you come together here to commemorate him and to pray for his elevation to the honors of the altars. This prayer supports those working on his Cause, and enriches your hearts with every grace. During his last visit to Poland, John Paul II said to you with regard to the passing of time: "We cannot remedy it. There is only one remedy. It is the Lord Jesus.'I am the resurrection and the life' means — notwithstanding old age, notwithstanding death — youthfulness is found in God. This is my wish for you: for all the young of Kraków, of Poland, and of the world" (Aug. 17, 2002). This was his faith, his firm conviction, his witness. And today, despite death, he — youthful in God — is among us. He invites us to reinvigorate the grace of faith, to be renewed in the Spirit and to "put on the new nature, created after the likeness of God, in the uprightness and holiness of the truth" (Eph 4:24). I thank you once again for wishing to be with me this evening. Please pass on my greetings and blessing to the members of your families and to your friends. Thank you!

Meeting with the Faithful at Rynek Square — Address (Wadowice, May 27, 2006)

I am filled with emotion in the birthplace of my great Predecessor, the Servant of God John Paul II, in this town of his childhood and young adult life. Indeed, I could not leave out Wadowice as I make this pilgrimage in Poland following in his footsteps I wished to stop precisely here, in the place where his faith began and matured, to pray together with all of you that he may soon be elevated to the glory of the altars. Johann Wolfgang von Goethe, the great German poet, said: "He who wishes to understand a poet, should visit his native land." This is also true for those who wish to understand the life and ministry of John Paul II; it is necessary to come to the city of his birth. He himself confessed that here, in Wadowice, "everything began: life, studies, the theatre and the priesthood" (Wadowice, June 16, 1999). John Paul II, returning to his beginnings, often referred to a sign: that of the baptismal font, to which he himself gave special veneration in the Church of Wadowice. In 1979, during his first pilgrimage in Poland he stated: "In this baptismal font, on June 20, 1920, I was given the grace to become a son of God, together with faith in my Redeemer, and I was welcomed into the community of the Church. I have already solemnly kissed this baptismal font in the year of the millennium of the Baptism of Poland, when I was Archbishop of Kraków. I kissed it again on the 50th anniversary of my baptism, when I was a cardinal, and today I kiss this baptismal font for the third time, as I come from Rome as the Successor of St. Peter" (Wadowice, June 7, 1979). It seems that in these words of John Paul II is contained the key to understanding the consistency of his faith, the radicalism of his Christian life and the desire for sanctity that he continuously manifested. Here is the profound awareness of divine grace, the unconditional love of God for man, that by means of water and the Holy Spirit places the Catechumen among the multitude of his children, who are redeemed by the Blood of Christ. The way of an authentically Christian life equals faithfulness to the promises of holy Baptism. The watchword of this pilgrimage: "Stand firm in your faith," finds in this place its concrete dimension that can be expressed with the exhortation: "Stand firm in the observance of your baptismal promises." A witness of just such a faith — f whom this place speaks in a very special way — is the Servant of God John Paul II. My great Predecessor indicated the Basilica of Wadowice, his home parish, as a place of particular importance for the development of his spiritual life and the priestly vocation that was manifesting itself within him. He once stated: "In this church I made my first Confession and received my first Holy Communion. Here I was an altar boy. Here I gave thanks to God for the gift of the priesthood and, as Archbishop of Kraków, I celebrated the 25th anniversary of my ordination to the priesthood. God alone, the giver of every grace, knows what goodness and what manifold graces I received from this church and from this parish community. To him, the Triune God, I give glory today at the doors of this church" (Wadowice, June 16, 1999). The church is a sign of the communion of believers united by the presence of God who dwells in their midst. This community is the Church Pope John Paul II loved. His love for the Church was born in the parish of Wadowice. In it he experienced the sacramental life, evangelization and the formation of a mature faith. For this reason, as a priest, as a bishop and as Pope, he treated parochial communities with such great care. In the spirit of that same solicitude, during the visit ad limina Apostolorum, I asked the Polish Bishops to do everything possible to ensure that the Polish parish would truly be an "ecclesial community" and a "family of the Church."In conclusion, let me recall once again a characteristic of the faith and spirituality of John Paul II, which is united to this place. He himself remembered many times the deep attachment of the inhabitants of Wadowice to the local image of Our Lady of Perpetual Help and the custom of daily prayer in front of her by the school children. This memory helps us arrive at the source of the conviction that nourished John Paul II — the conviction regarding the exceptional place that the Mother of God had in his life, a conviction that he himself, filled with devotion, expressed in the motto "Totus tuus." Until the last moments of his earthly pilgrimage he remained faithful to this dedication.

Meeting with Youth at Blonie Park — Address (Krakow, May 27, 2006)

Dear Young Friends, My friends, in the heart of every man there is the desire for a house. Even more so in the young person's heart there is a great longing for a proper house, a stable house, one to which he cannot only return with joy, but where every guest who arrives can be joyfully welcomed. There is a yearning for a house where the daily bread is love, pardon and understanding. It is a place where the truth is the source out of which flows peace of heart. There is a longing for a house you can be proud of, where you need not be ashamed and where you never fear its loss. These longings are simply the desire for a full, happy and successful life. Do not be afraid of this desire! Do not run away from this desire! Do not be discouraged at the sight of crumbling houses, frustrated desires and faded longings. God the Creator, who inspires in young hearts an immense yearning for happiness, will not abandon you in the difficult construction of the house called life. My friends, this brings about a question: "How do we build this house?" Without doubt, this is a question that you have already faced many times and that you will face many times more. Every day you must look into your heart and ask: "How do I build that house called life?" Jesus, whose words we just heard in the passage from the evangelist Matthew,

encourages us to build on the rock. In fact, it is only in this way that the house will not crumble. But what does it mean to build a house on the rock? Building on the rock means, first of all, to build on Christ and with Christ. Jesus says: "Every one then who hears these words of mine and does them will be like a wise man who built his house upon the rock" (Mt 7:24). These are not just the empty words of some person or another; these are the words of Jesus. We are not listening to any person: we are listening to Jesus. We are not asked to commit to just anything; we are asked to commit ourselves to the words of Jesus. To build on Christ and with Christ means to build on a foundation that is called "crucified love." It means to build with Someone who, knowing us better than we know ourselves, says to us: "You are precious in my eyes and honored, and I love you" (Is 43:4). It means to build with Someone, who is always faithful, even when we are lacking in faith, because he cannot deny himself (cf. 2 Tm 2:13) . . .To build on the rock means to build on Christ and with Christ, who is the rock. In the First Letter to the Corinthians, St. Paul, speaking of the journey of the chosen people through the desert, explains that all "drank from the supernatural rock, which followed them, and the rock was Christ" (1 Cor 10:4). The fathers of the Chosen People certainly did not know that the rock was Christ. They were not aware of being accompanied by him who in the fullness of time would become incarnate and take on a human body. . . My friends, what does it mean to build on the rock? Building on the rock also means building on Someone who was rejected. St. Peter speaks to the faithful of Christ as a "living stone rejected by men but in God's sight chosen and precious" (1 Pt 2:4). The undeniable fact of the election of Jesus by God does not conceal the mystery of evil, whereby man is able to reject Him who has loved to the very end. This rejection of Jesus by man, which St. Peter mentions, extends throughout human history, even to our own time. . . Dear friends, what does it mean to build on the rock? Building on the rock means being aware that there will be misfortunes. Christ says: "The rain fell and the floods came, and the winds blew and beat upon the house..." (Mt 7:25). These natural phenomena are not only an image of the many misfortunes of the human lot, but they also indicate that such misfortunes are normally to be expected. Christ does not promise that a downpour will never inundate a house under construction, he does not promise that a devastating wave will never sweep away that which is most dear to us, he does not promise that strong winds will never carry away what we have built, sometimes with enormous sacrifice... My friends, allow me to ask again: what does it mean to build on the rock? It means to build wisely. It is not without reason that Jesus compares those who hear his words and put them into practice to a wise man who has built his house on the rock. It is foolish, in fact, to build on sand, when you can do so on rock and therefore have a house that is capable of withstanding every storm... My friends, once again: what does it mean to build on the rock? Building on the rock also means to build on Peter and with Peter. In fact the Lord said to him: "You are Peter, and on this rock I will build my Church, and the powers of death shall not prevail against it" (Mt 16:18). If Christ, the Rock, the living and precious stone, calls his Apostle "rock," it means that he wants Peter, and together with him the entire Church, to be a visible sign of the one Savior and Lord. Here, in Kraków, the beloved city of my Predecessor John Paul II, no one is astonished by the words "to build with Peter and on Peter." For this reason I say to you: do not be afraid to build your life on the Church and with the Church.

Holy Mass at Blonie Park — Homily (Krakow, May 28, 2006)

"Men of Galilee, why do you stand looking up to heaven?" (Acts 1:11).Brothers and Sisters, today in Blonie Park in Kraków we hear once again this question from the Acts of the Apostles. This time it is directed to all of us: "Why do you stand looking up to heaven?" The answer to this question involves the fundamental truth about the life and destiny of every man and woman. The question has to do with our attitude to two basic realities which shape every human life: earth and heaven. First, the earth: "Why do you stand?" Why are you here on earth? Our answer is that we are here on earth because our Maker has put us here as the crowning work of his creation. Almighty God, in his ineffable plan of love, created the universe, bringing it forth from nothing. Then, at the completion of this work, he bestowed life on men and women, creating them in his own image and likeness (cf. Gen 1:26-27). He gave them the dignity of being children of God and the gift of immortality. We know that man went astray, misused the gift of freedom and said "No" to God, thus condemning himself to a life marked by evil, sin, suffering and death. But we also know that God was not resigned to this situation, but entered directly into humanity's history, which then became a history of salvation. "We stand" on the earth, we are rooted in the earth and we grow from it. Here we do good in the many areas of everyday life, in the material and spiritual realms, in our relationships with other people, in our efforts to build up the human community and in culture. Here too we experience the weariness of those who make their way towards a goal by long and winding paths, amid hesitations, tensions, uncertainties, in the conviction that the journey will one day come to an end. That is when the question arises: Is this all there is? Is this earth on which "we stand" our final destiny? And so we need to turn to the second part of the biblical question: "Why do you stand looking up to heaven?" We have read that, just as the Apostles were asking the Risen Lord about the restoration of Israel's earthly kingdom, "He was lifted up and a cloud took him out of their sight." And "they looked up to heaven as he went" (cf. Acts 1:9-10). They looked up to heaven because they looked to Jesus Christ, the Crucified and Risen One, raised up on high. We do not know whether at that precise moment they realized that a magnificent, infinite horizon was opening up before their eyes: the ultimate goal of our earthly pilgrimage. Perhaps they only realized this at Pentecost, in the light of the Holy Spirit. But for us, at a distance of two thousand years, the meaning of that event is quite clear. Here on earth, we are called to look up to heaven, to turn our minds and hearts to the inexpressible mystery of God. We are called to look towards this divine reality, to which we have been directed from our creation. For there we find life's ultimate meaning... Faith is a deeply personal and human act, an act which has two aspects. To believe means first to accept as true what our mind cannot fully comprehend. We have to accept what God reveals to us about himself, about ourselves, about everything around us, including the things that are invisible, inexpressible and beyond our imagination. This act of accepting revealed truth broadens the horizon of our knowledge and draws us to the mystery in which our lives are immersed. Letting our reason be limited in this way is not something easy to do. Here we see the second aspect of faith: it is trust in a person, no ordinary person, but Jesus Christ himself. What we believe is important, but even more important is the One in whom we believe...Today we heard the words of Jesus: "You shall receive power when the Holy Spirit has come upon you; and you shall be my witnesses in Jerusalem and in all Judaea and Samaria, and to the end of the earth" (Acts 1:8). Centuries ago these words reached Poland. They challenged, and continue to challenge all those who say they belong to Christ, who consider his to be the greatest cause. We need to be witnesses of Jesus, who lives in the Church and in human hearts. He has given us a mission. On the day he ascended to heaven, he said to his Apostles: "Go into all the world and preach the Gospel to the whole creation ... And they went forth and preached everywhere, while the Lord worked with them and confirmed the message by the signs that attended it" (Mk 16:15, 20). Dear brothers and sisters! When Karol Wojty3a was elected to the See of Peter in order to serve the universal Church, your land became a place of special witness to faith in Jesus Christ. You were called to give this witness before the whole world. This vocation of yours is always needed, and it is perhaps even more urgent than ever, now that the Servant of God has passed from this life. Do not deprive the world of this witness!

Prayer to Commemorate the Victims of the Concentration Camp of Auschwitz-Birkenau (May 28, 2006)

To speak in this place of horror, in this place where unprecedented mass crimes were committed against God and man, is almost impossible — and it is particularly difficult and troubling for a Christian, for a Pope from Germany. In a place like this, words fail; in the end, there can only be a dread silence — a silence which is itself a heartfelt cry to God: Why, Lord, did you remain silent? How could you tolerate all this? In silence, then, we bow our heads before the endless line of those who suffered and were put to death here; yet our silence becomes in turn a plea for forgiveness and reconciliation, a plea to the living God never to let this happen again. Twenty-seven years ago, on June 7, 1979, Pope John Paul II stood in this place. He said: "I come here today as a pilgrim. As you know, I have been here many times. So many times! And many times I have gone down to Maximilian Kolbe's death cell, paused before the wall of death, and walked amid the ruins of the Birkenau ovens. It was impossible for me not to come here as pope." Pope John Paul came here as a son of that people which, along with the Jewish people, suffered most in this place and, in general, throughout the war. "Six million Poles lost their lives during the Second World War: a fifth of the nation," he reminded us. Here, too, he solemnly called for respect for human rights and the rights of nations, as his predecessors John XXIII and Paul VI had done before him, and added: "The one who speaks these words is... the son of a nation which in its history has suffered greatly from others. He says this, not to accuse, but to remember. He speaks in the name of all those nations whose rights are being violated and disregarded..." Pope John Paul II came here as a son of the Polish people. I come here today as a son of the German people. For this very reason, I can and must echo his words: I could not fail to come here. I had to come. It is a duty before the truth and the just due of all who suffered here, a duty before God, for me to come here as the successor of Pope John Paul II and as a son of the German people — a son of that people over which a ring of criminals rose to power by false promises of future greatness and the recovery of the nation's honor, prominence and prosperity, but also through terror and intimidation, with the result that our people was used and abused as an instrument of their thirst for destruction and power. Yes, I could not fail to come here... We cannot peer into God's mysterious plan — we see only piecemeal, and we would be wrong to set ourselves up as judges of God and history. Then we would not be defending man, but only contributing to his downfall. No—when all is said and done, we must continue to cry out humbly yet insistently to God: Rouse yourself! Do not forget mankind, your creature! And our cry to God must also be a cry that pierces our very heart, a cry that awakens within us God's hidden presence — so that his power, the power he has planted in our hearts, will not be buried or choked within us by the mire of selfishness, pusillanimity, indifference or opportunism. Let us cry out to God, with all our hearts, at the present hour, when new misfortunes befall us, when all the forces of darkness seem to issue anew from human hearts: whether it is the abuse of God's name as a means of justifying senseless violence against innocent persons, or the cynicism which refuses to acknowledge God and ridicules faith in him. Let us cry out to God, that he may draw men and women to conversion and help them to see that violence does not bring peace, but only generates more violence — a morass of devastation in which everyone is ultimately the loser. The God in whom we believe is a God of reason — a reason, to be sure, which is not a kind of cold mathematics of the universe, but is one with love and with goodness. We make our prayer to God and we appeal to humanity, that this reason, the logic of love and the recognition of the power of reconciliation and peace, may prevail over the threats arising from irrationalism or from a spurious and godless reason... By God's grace, together with the purification of memory demanded by this place of horror, a number of initiatives have sprung up with the aim of imposing a limit upon evil and confirming goodness. Just now I was able to bless the Centre for Dialogue and Prayer. In the immediate neighborhood the Carmelite nuns carry on their life of hiddenness, knowing that they are united in a special way to the mystery of Christ's Cross and reminding us of the faith of Christians, which declares that God himself descended into the hell of suffering and suffers with us. In Oœwiêcim is the Centre of St. Maximilian Kolbe, and the International Centre for Education about Auschwitz and the Holocaust. There is also the International House for Meetings of Young People. Near one of the old Prayer Houses is the Jewish Centre. Finally the Academy for Human Rights is presently being established. So there is hope that this place of horror will gradually become a place for constructive thinking, and that remembrance will foster resistance to evil and the triumph of love. At Auschwitz-Birkenau humanity walked through a "valley of darkness." And so, here in this place, I would like to end with a prayer of trust — with one of the Psalms of Israel which is also a prayer of Christians:

"The Lord is my shepherd, I shall not want. He makes me lie down in green pastures; he leads me beside still waters; he restores my soul. He leads me in right paths for his name's sake. Even though I walk through the valley of the shadow of death, I fear no evil; for you are with me; your rod and your staff — they comfort me ... I shall dwell in the house of the Lord my whole life long" (Ps 23:1-4, 6).

Farewell Ceremony at the Airport of Balice — Address (Krakow, May 28, 2006)

When taking leave of his homeland for the last time four years ago, my beloved predecessor Pope John Paul II exhorted the Polish nation always to be guided by sentiments of mercy, fraternal solidarity, and dedication to the common good, and he expressed the firm conviction that in this way she would not only find her proper place within a United Europe, but would also enrich this continent and the whole world with her tradition. Today, as your presence in the family of European States is being constantly consolidated, I wish with my whole heart to repeat those words of hope. I ask you to remain faithful custodians of the Christian deposit, and to transmit it to future generations. Dear Polish people! I want to confide in you that this pilgrimage, during which I have visited places particularly dear to the great John Paul II, has brought me even closer to you, his compatriots. I thank you for the prayer with which you have surrounded me from the moment of my election. During my meetings with you, at audiences in the Vatican, I have often felt a bond of intense prayer and spontaneous sympathy. I would like you to continue to remember me in your prayers, asking the Lord to increase my strength in the service of the universal Church.

VALENCIA, SPAIN, July 8-9

On July 8-9, Pope Benedict XVI traveled to Valencia, Spain, on the third foreign apostolic journey of his pontificate. The purpose of the visit was to participate in the Fifth World Meeting of Families.

Program

Welcome ceremony at the Airport of Manises, Valencia — July 8, 2006

Message to the Spanish Bishops during the visit to the Cathedral and the Basilica of the "Virgen de los Desamparados" — July 8, 2006

Recital of the Angelus in "Plaza de la Virgen" — July 8, 2006

Festive encounter and testimonials at the conclusion of the Fifth World Meeting of Families in the "City of Arts and Sciences" — July 8, 2006

Holy Mass in the "City of Arts and Sciences" — July 9, 2006

Recital of the Angelus in "City of Arts and Sciences" — July 9, 2006

Farewell ceremony at the Airport of Manises — July 9, 2006.

Excerpts from Addresses and Homilies

(*Complete texts of papal addresses, remarks and homilies can be found at www.vatican.va.*)

Welcome Ceremony at the Airport of Manises — Address (Valencia, July 8, 2006)

With great joy I come today to Valencia, to the noble

and much-loved land of Spain, which has given me so many grateful memories from my earlier visits for congresses and meetings... My reason for this long-awaited visit is to take part in the Fifth World Meeting of Families, whose theme is "The Transmission of Faith in the Family." I wish to set forth the central role, for the Church and for society, proper to the family based on marriage. The family is a unique institution in God's plan, and the Church cannot fail to proclaim and promote its fundamental importance, so that it can live out its vocation with a constant sense of responsibility and joy.

My venerable predecessor, a great friend of Spain, the beloved John Paul II, convoked this Meeting. Prompted by the same pastoral solicitude, tomorrow I will have the privilege of concluding it with the celebration of Holy Mass in the City of Arts and Sciences.

In union with all taking part, I will implore from the Lord, through the intercession of our Most Holy Mother and the Apostle Saint James, plentiful graces for the families of Spain and of the whole world.

Message to the Spanish Bishops during the Visit to the Cathedral and the Basilica of the "Virgen de los Desamparados" — Address (Valencia, July 8, 2006)

With heartfelt joy I give thanks to the Lord that I have been able to come to Spain as Pope, in order to take part in the World Meeting of Families in Valencia. I greet you with affection, my brother bishops of this beloved country, and I thank you for your presence here and for the hard work put into the preparation and celebration of this visit.

In times and situations of difficulty, recall those words of the Letter to the Hebrews: "Let us run with perseverance the race that is set before us, looking to Jesus, the pioneer and perfecter of our faith, who for the sake of the joy that was set before him, endured the cross, disregarding the shame... so that you may not grow weary or lose heart" (Heb 12:1-3). Proclaim that Jesus is "the Christ, the Son of the living God" (Mt16:16), "the one who has the words of eternal life" (cf. Jn 6:68), and you will not tire of giving reason for your hope (cf. 1 Pt 3:15).

Prompted by your pastoral solicitude and the spirit of full communion in the proclamation of the Gospel, you have guided the Christian conscience of the faithful about different aspects of the situation confronting them, which occasionally disturb ecclesial life and the faith of the simple. You have also made the Eucharist a central theme of your pastoral plan, with the aim of "revitalizing the Christian life from its very heart, since when we enter into the Eucharistic mystery we encounter the heart of God" (no. 5). Certainly in the Eucharist there takes place "the central act of transformation capable of truly renewing the world" (Homily in Marienfeld, Cologne, Aug. 21, 2005).

Festive Encounter and Testimonials at the Conclusion of the Fifth World Meeting of Families in the "City of Arts and Sciences" — Address (Valencia, July 8, 2006)

United by the same faith in Christ, we have gathered here from so many parts of the world as a community which, with gratitude and joy, bears witness that human beings were created in the image and likeness of God for love, and that complete human fulfillment only comes about when we make a sincere gift of ourselves to others.

The family is the privileged setting where every person learns to give and receive love. That is why the Church constantly wishes to demonstrate her pastoral concern for this reality, so basic for the human person. This is what she teaches in her Magisterium: "God, who is love and who created man and woman for love, has called them to love. By creating man and woman he called them to an intimate communion of life and love in marriage. 'So they are no longer two but one flesh'" (Mt 19:6) (Catechism of the Catholic Church, Compendium, 337).

This is the truth that the Church tirelessly proclaims to the world. My beloved predecessor Pope John Paul II said that man has been made "in the image and likeness of God not only by his being human, but also by the communion of the persons that man and woman have formed since the beginning. They become the image of God, not so much in their aloneness as in their communion" (Catechesis, Nov. 14, 1979).

That is why I confirmed the calling of this Fifth World Meeting of Families in Spain, and specifically here in Valencia, a city rich in tradition and proud of the Christian faith lived and nurtured in so many of its families. The family is an intermediate institution between individuals and society, and nothing can completely take its place. The family is itself based primarily on a deep interpersonal relationship between husband and wife, sustained by affection and mutual understanding. To enable this, it receives abundant help from God in the sacrament of matrimony, which brings with it a true vocation to holiness. Would that our children might experience more the harmony and affection between their parents, rather than disagreements and discord, since the love between father and mother is a source of great security for children and its teaches them the beauty of a faithful and lasting love. The family is a necessary good for peoples, an indispensable foundation for society and a great and lifelong treasure for couples. It is a unique good for children, who are meant to be the fruit of the love, of the total and generous self-giving of their parents. To proclaim the whole truth about the family, based on marriage as a domestic Church and a sanctuary of life, is a great responsibility incumbent upon all... The challenges of present-day society, marked by the centrifugal forces generated especially in urban settings, make it necessary to ensure that families do not feel alone. A small family can encounter difficult obstacles when it is isolated from relatives and friends...Together with passing on the faith and the love of God, one of the greatest responsibilities of families is that of training free and responsible persons. For this reason the parents need gradually to give their children greater freedom, while remaining for some time the guardians of that freedom. If children see that their parents — and, more generally, all the adults around them — live life with joy and enthusiasm, despite all difficulties, they will themselves develop that profound "joy of life" which can help them to overcome wisely the inevitable obstacles and problems which are part of life. Furthermore, when families are not closed in on themselves, children come to learn that every person is worthy of love, and that there is a basic, universal brotherhood which embraces every human being.

Holy Mass in the "City of Arts and Sciences" — Homily (Valencia, July 9, 2006)

In this Holy Mass which it is my great joy to celebrate, together with many of my Brothers in the Episcopate and a great number of priests, I give thanks to the Lord for all of you, the joyful throng of beloved families gathered in this place, and the many others who in distant lands are following this celebration by radio and television. I greet all of you with an affectionate embrace. Both Esther and Paul, as we have just heard in today's readings, testify that the family is called to work for the handing on of the faith. Esther admits: "Ever since I was born, I have heard in the tribe of my family that you, O Lord, took Israel out of all the nations" (Est 14:5). Paul follows the tradition of his Jewish ancestors by worshiping God with a pure conscience. He praises the sincere faith of Timothy and speaks to him about "a faith that lived first in your grandmother Lois and your mother Eunice, and now, I am sure, lives in you" (2 Tm 1:15). In these biblical testimonies, the family includes not only parents and children, but also grandparents and ancestors. The family thus appears to us as a community of generations and the guarantee of a patrimony of traditions. None of us gave ourselves life or single-handedly learned how to live. All of us received from others both life itself and its basic truths, and we have been called to attain perfection in relationship and loving communion with others. The family, founded on indissoluble marriage between a man and a woman, is the expression of this relational, filial and communal aspect of life. It is the setting where men and women are enabled to be born with dignity, and to grow and develop in an integral manner. Once children are born, through their relationship with their parents, they begin to share in a family tradition with even older roots. Together with the gift of life, they receive a whole patrimony of experience. Parents have the right and the inalienable duty to transmit this heritage to their children: to help them find their own identity, to initiate them to the life of society, to foster the responsible exercise of their moral freedom and their ability to love on the basis of their having been loved and, above all, to enable them to encounter God. At the origin of every man and woman, and thus in all human fatherhood and motherhood, we find God the Creator. For this reason, married couples must accept the child born to them, not simply as theirs alone, but also as a child of God, loved for his or her own sake and called to be a son or daughter of God. What is more: each generation, all parenthood and every family has its origin in God, who is Father, Son and Holy Spirit.

Esther's father had passed on to her, along with the memory of her forebears and her people, the memory of a God who is the origin of all and to whom all are called to answer. The memory of God the Father, who chose a people for himself and who acts in history for our salvation. The memory of this Father sheds light on our deepest human identity: where we come from, who

we are, and how great is our dignity.

Certainly we come from our parents and we are their children, but we also come from God who has created us in his image and called us to be his children. Consequently, at the origin of every human being there is not something haphazard or chance, but a loving plan of God. This was revealed to us by Jesus Christ, the true Son of God and a perfect man. He knew whence he came and whence all of us have come: from the love of his Father and our Father. Faith, then, is not merely a cultural heritage, but the constant working of the grace of God who calls and our human freedom, which can respond or not to his call. Even if no one can answer for another person, Christian parents are still called to give a credible witness of their Christian faith and hope. The need to ensure that God's call and the good news of Christ will reach their children with the utmost clarity and authenticity...The Christian family passes on the faith when parents teach their children to pray and when they pray with them (cf. *Familiaris Consortio*, 60); when they lead them to the sacraments and gradually introduce them to the life of the Church; when all join in reading the Bible, letting the light of faith shine on their family life and praising God as our Father... And so the Second Vatican Council teaches that "Christian married couples and parents, following their own way, should support one another in grace all through life with faithful love, and should train their children, lovingly received from God, in Christian doctrine and evangelical virtues. Because in this way they present to all an example of unfailing and generous love, they build up the brotherhood of charity, and they stand as witnesses and co-operators of the fruitfulness of Mother Church, as a sign of and a share in that love with which Christ loved his Bride and gave himself for her" (*Lumen Gentium*, 41). Let us return for a moment to the first reading of this Mass, drawn from the Book of Esther. The Church at prayer has seen in this humble queen interceding with all her heart for her suffering people, a prefigurement of Mary, whom her Son has given to us all as our Mother; a prefigurement of the Mother who protects by her love God's family on its earthly pilgrimage. Mary is the image and model of all mothers, of their great mission to be guardians of life, of their mission to be teachers of the art of living and of the art of loving. The Christian family — father, mother and children — is called, then, to do all these things not as a task imposed from without, but rather as a gift of the sacramental grace of marriage poured out upon the spouses. If they remain open to the Spirit and implore his help, he will not fail to bestow on them the love of God the Father made manifest and incarnate in Christ.

VATICAN DOCUMENTS AND ANNOUNCEMENTS

PATRIARCH OF THE WEST

On Mar. 22, 2006, the Pontifical Council for Promoting Christian Unity issued a statement regarding the decision by Pope Benedict XVI to cease using the title "Patriarch of the West."

In the immediate aftermath of the publication of the *2006 Annuario Pontificio*, there was widespread discussion as to the absence in the Vatican annual in the

list of papal titles. Patriarch of the West appeared in the list included in the *Annuario Pontificio*, starting in the 19th century.

Statement by the Pontifical Council

The statement notes that it is not intended to discuss the complete question of the history of the title Patriarch in all of its many aspects, but it does seek to affirm several significant points regarding the title.

First, the document stresses the point that the ancient patriarchates of the East, established by the Councils of Constantinople (381) and Chalcedon (451) concerned a most clearly delineated territory, while that of the See of the Bishop of Rome remained vague. In the East, in the imperial ecclesiastical system of Emperor Justinian (527-565) there was a system of four Eastern patriarchates (Constantinople, Alexandria, Antioch, and Jerusalem) while parallel to them the pope was considered as patriarch of the West. Conversely, Rome privileged the idea of three Petrine Episcopal sees: Rome, Alexandria, and Antioch. Without using the title "Patriarch of the West," the Fourth Council of Constantinople (869-870), the Fourth Lateran Council (1215), and the Council of Florence (1439) considered the pope to be the be the first of the five patriarchs. The title of "Patriarch of the West" was adopted in the course of the year 642 by Pope Theodore I. Henceforth the title was used only rarely and without having especially clear signification. Development followed in the 16th and 17th centuries with the multiplication of the titles of the pope. The title appeared for the first time in the *Annuario Pontificio* in 1863. The term "West" refers to a cultural context that means more than Western Europe. Rather, it extends to the United States, as well as Australia and New Zealand, as well as other cultural contexts. Naturally, one significant aspect of the term "West" is that it does not describe an ecclesiastical territory and is not used as the definition of a patriarchal territory. If one were to give the term "West" a usage that is applicable to juridical ecclesiastical language, it would describe the special relationship between the Bishop of Rome and the Latin Church and would express the particular jurisdiction of the Bishop of Rome over the Latin Church. By consequence, the title "Patriarch of the West," with its vague origins, became obsolete in the evolution of history. According to the Pontifical Commission, this is especially true in the wake of the Second Vatican Council for through it the Church found a canonical disposition for the Latin Church appropriate to actual necessities by means of the Episcopal Conferences and their international meetings. Dropping the title "Patriarch of the West" does not in any way change the reality of the recognition of the ancient patriarchal Churches, stated with particular solemnity by the Second Vatican Council (*Lumen Gentium*, 23). The suppression of the title is an expression of historical realism and theology, and at the same time it should not be seen as a hindrance to ecumenical dialogue but should actually be viewed positively within the field of wider dialogue.

The Orthodox Response

In response to the decision, the bishops of the Ecumenical Orthodox Patriarchate of Constantinople issued a statement of concern. The statement of June 8, 2006, declared concern on the part of the Orthodox that dropping "Patriarch of the West" while retaining the titles "Vicar of Jesus Christ" and "Supreme Pontiff of the Universal Church" can be interpreted as making a claim to "a universal jurisdiction of the bishop of Rome over the entire church, which is something the Orthodox have never accepted." The Orthodox statement went on to emphasize the importance to the Orthodox of the geographical limits of each ecclesiastical jurisdiction and their key role in the structures of the Church form the first eras Christianity. In keeping with this, it noted as well the Orthodox understanding of the Church as "a unity of full local churches" rather than a series of divided local units for the purpose of governance. Moreover, the often shaky progress of international Catholic-Orthodox theological dialogue may be set back by the decision. As a major topic is papal primacy, the dropping of the title "Patriarch of the West" could become an issue owing to the absence of what the Orthodox see as a lack of prior consultation.

The Title Patriarch

The title of Patriarch traces its origin to the Eastern Church and is the title of a bishop who, second only to the pope, has the highest rank in the hierarchy of jurisdiction. He is the incumbent of one of the traditional major sees of Christendom and is subject only to the pope. A patriarch of the Eastern Church is the head of the faithful belonging to his rite throughout the world. The patriarchal sees are so called because of their special status and dignity in the history of the Church. The Council of Nicaea (325) recognized three patriarchs — the Bishops of Alexandria and Antioch in the East, and of Rome in the West. The First Council of Constantinople (381) added the bishop of Constantinople to the list of patriarchs and gave him rank second only to that of the pope, the bishop of Rome and patriarch of the West; this action was seconded by the Council of Chalcedon (451) and was given full recognition by the Fourth Lateran Council (1215). The Council of Chalcedon also acknowledged patriarchal rights of the bishop of Jerusalem.

Currently, there are a number of patriarchs for Eastern rite Catholics, including for Alexandria, Antioch, of Babylonia, and Sis, or Cilicia, for the Armenians; the latter should be called, more properly, Katholikos — that is, a prelate delegated for a universality of causes. These patriarchs are elected by bishops of their churches; they receive approval and the pallium, symbol of their office, from the pope.

The Orthodox Churches, of course, have their own patriarchs.

Latin Rite patriarchates were established for Antioch, Jerusalem, Alexandria and Constantinople during the Crusades; afterwards, they became patriarchates in name only. Jerusalem, however, was reconstituted as a patriarchate by Pius IX, in virtue of the bull *Nulla Celebrior* of July 23, 1847. In 1964, the Latin titular patriarchates of Constantinople, Alexandria and Antioch, long a bone of contention in relations with Eastern Churches, were abolished. The titular patriarchs (in name only) of the Latin Rite are Lisbon, Venice, the East Indies (archbishop of Goa and Damao, India), and Jerusalem. The patriarchate of the West Indies has been vacant since 1963.

As of Aug. 15, 2006, the patriarchs in the Church were: Antonios Naguib, of Alexandria, for the Copts; Ignace Pierre VIII Abdel-Ahad, of Antioch, for the Syrians; Gregory III Laham, of Antioch, for the Greek Melkites (the patriarch also has personal titles of Alexandria and Jerusalem for the Greek Melkites); Cardinal Nasrallah Pierre Sfeir, of Antioch, for the Maronites; Nerses Bedros XIX Tarmouni, of Cilicia, for the Armenians; Emmanuel III Delly, of Babylon, for the Chaldeans. (For biographical information on the patriarchs, see **Eastern Catholics**.)

The titular patriarchs (in name only) of the Latin Rite were: Cardinal José da Cruz Policarpo of Lisbon; Cardinal Angelo Scola of Venice; Archbishop Filipe Neri António do Rosário Ferrão of the East Indies (archbishop of Goa and Damao, India); and

Archbishop Michel Sabbah of Jerusalem (coadjutor, Archbishop Fouad Twal). **CA**

CRITERIA FOR CAUSES OF CANONIZATION

On Sept. 29, 2005, Cardinal José Saraiva Martins, C.M.F., the Prefect for the Congregation of the Causes of Saints, and Archbishop Edward Nowak, Secretary of the same Congregation, issued a communiqué implementing a number of new measures for the Criteria for Causes of Canonization. Following is the text of the communiqué: Having heard the conclusions of the study of the theological reasons for the rites of Beatification and Canonization and their pastoral requirements, and after receiving the approval of the Holy Father Benedict XVI, this Congregation for the Causes of Saints informs [the faithful] of the following new measures: 1. While it should be understood that the Holy Father will preside at a Canonization, which attributes the devotion of the whole Church to the Blessed, a Beatification, nonetheless a Pontifical act, will be celebrated by a representative of the Holy Father who will normally be the Prefect of the Congregation for the Causes of Saints. 2. The rite of Beatification will take place in the Diocese that has promoted the Cause of the new Blessed, or in any other place deemed suitable. 3. At the request of the Bishops and Promoters of the Cause, after having heard the opinion of the Secretariat of State, the rite of Beatification may take place in Rome. 4. Lastly, the same rite will take place during the Eucharistic celebration unless special liturgical reasons suggest that it take place during the celebration of the Word or of the Liturgy of the Hours."

Canonization Process

The process of canonization—the accepted procedure by which the Church determines whether a person is eligible for beatification and canonization — is deliberately a very lengthy one. The process requires the careful study of the life of a candidate, his or her writings, the eyewitness testimony of those who knew them, and the meticulous examination of any miracles attributed to their intercession. To make clear the process of canonization, Pope John Paul II issued the apostolic constitution *Divinus Perfectionis Magister* on Jan. 25, 1983. Several key points in the process are noteworthy:

- To begin a cause, it is necessary for at least five years to have passed since the death of the candidate. This is to permit greater balance and objectivity in making an evaluation of the case and to let the emotions towards the candidate dissipate.
- The bishop of the diocese in which the person whose cause is being considered died has responsibility for starting the investigation. The bishop requests from the Holy See formal permission (called a *nulla osta*) to launch the formal investigation. Once granted, the bishop forms a diocesan tribunal to investigate the candidate's Christian virtues and determine whether they were heroic. All documents are then gathered together and the candidate is given the title of Servant of God. Overseeing this phase is a postulator.
- The title Servant of God is a declaration that the Church's proper authorities have determined preliminarily that a candidate led a life of demonstrable holiness. If, at a later date, the Congregation for the Causes of Saints and the Pope concur that a person

led a life of heroic virtue, he or she will be named venerable.
- Upon completion of the diocesan investigation, all documents are submitted to the Congregation for the Causes of Saints in Rome. The officials of the congregation then assemble the official summary of the documentation, a *positio*, that demonstrates the heroic exercise of virtue by the candidate. Nine theologians then review the *positio* and give their vote for or against the cause proceeding. If the majority of the theologians approve, the cause is passed on for examination by cardinals and bishops who are members of the congregation. If they also approve, the prefect of the congregation sends all materials related to the cause to the Holy Father, who gives his approval and authorizes the congregation to draft the relative decree.
- A miracle must then be attributed to the Servant of God and proven through appropriate canonical investigation. Once confirmed, the candidate may be beatified and receives the title of Blessed.
- A second miracle is required for canonization. The miracle must be attributed to the intercession of the Blessed and must have occurred after his beatification. Once canonized, the Blessed received the title of Saint. **CA**

HOLY SEE FINANCES

On July 4, 2006, the 40th meeting of the Council of Cardinals for the Study of the Organizational and Economic Problems of the Holy See, chaired by Cardinal Angelo Sodano, was held in the Vatican City State to make public the 2005 Consolidated Financial Statement of the Holy See and that of the Vatican City State Governorate.

In the press conference, Cardinal Sodano explained that the consolidated financial statement contained the income and the expenses of the various pontifical administrations, including the Administration of the Patrimony of the Holy See (APSA, the department that provides for all the administrative operations of the Offices and the Entities of the Roman Curia), the Congregation for the Evangelization of Peoples, the Apostolic Camera, Vatican Radio, the Vatican Television Center, the Vatican Printing Press — *L'Osservatore Romano*, and the Vatican Publishing House.

The primary news in the report was that both the Holy See and Vatican City ended the year with a profit of 9.7 ($12.46) million, the most significant profit in the last eight years and a profit of about 6.6 ($8.48) million, compared to the previous fiscal year. The report then focused on the specific areas of activity: institutional, financial, real estate, media institutions connected with the Holy See, and other incomes and expenses.

In the area of institutional activity, meaning all of the dicasteries of the Roman Curia: the Secretariat of State, the Pontifical Representations, the Roman Congregations, Pontifical Councils, the Synod of Bishops and the various Offices, in 2005 the donations that were provided from Episcopal Conferences, dioceses, religious Institutes, faithful and various Entities, in addition to other slight revenues, decreased from 73.3 million in 2004 to 73.9 million in 2005. The costs of the sector rose from 101.6 million in 2004 to 121.3

million and reflected especially the cost for personnel due to the fixed, up-to-date costs charged to each Administration of the Holy See to cover the potential debt toward all the active personnel and those who retired after Jan. 1, 1993. In addition, there were the costs for "maintenance and repairs" to the building in Piazza di Spagna, headquarters of the Congregation for the Evangelization of Peoples. The costs thus increased from 4 million in 2004 to 10.5 million. Other costs included the extraordinary maintenance of the buildings of the Congregation for the Doctrine of the Faith and those along the Via della Conciliazione. Further, slight increases in costs were noted for the pontifical representations around the world, from 18.3 million in the 2004 fiscal year to 19.6 million in 2005. The net financial statement for institutional activity was a deficit of 36.9 million, an increase from 2004 in which the institutional deficit was 23.2 million.

Financial Activity included all financial activities of the consolidated administrations, especially those of APSA Extraordinary Section (Administration of the Patrimony of the Apostolic See). In 2005 this area

ended with a profit of 43.3 million against 6.1 million in 2004.The Real Estate concerns of the Holy See and Vatican City State ended the year with a net gain of 22.2 million, lower than that of 2004 which had been 24.9 million. Total costs amounted to about 28.9 million, while revenues reached 51 million. Media Institutions connected with the Holy See — i.e., Vatican Radio, the Vatican Printing Press — *L'Osservatore Romano*, the Vatican Television Center and the Vatican Publishing House—marked a net deficit of 11.8 million. The primary areas of the deficit were due to Vatican Radio (about 23.5 million) and of *L'Osservatore Romano* (4.6 million). The Vatican Printing Press enjoyed a surplus of 653 thousand; the Vatican Television Centre had a profit of 650 thousand; the Vatican Publishing House had a surplus of 934 thousand and with a rise of 3.8 million in the volume of the activity (from 8.3 million to 12.1 million).

Finally, the area of other income and expenses showed a negative result of 7 million. The deficit reflected chiefly the costs for the sede vacante in 2005.

CA

SPECIAL REPORTS: INTERNATIONAL NEWS 2005-2006

SYNOD OF BISHOPS

The 11th Ordinary General Assembly of the Synod of Bishops was held in Rome from Oct. 2–23. The topic of the Synod was "The Eucharist: Source and Summit of the Life and Mission of the Church."

The 11th Ordinary General Assembly of the Synod of Bishops took place on the 40th anniversary of its establishment, on Sept. 15, 1965, by the Servant of God Pope Paul VI with the *motu proprio Apostolica Sollicitudo*.The gathering brought together bishops from all over the world and was held under the leadership of Pope Benedict XVI. In all, there were 256 Synodal Fathers from 118 nations, the largest number of participants in a synodal assembly (247 Synodal Fathers took part in the synod of 2001). Of the 256 Synodal participants, 177 were elected, 39 participate *ex officio*, and 40 were appointed by the Holy Father. There were 55 cardinals, eight patriarchs, 82 archbishops, 123 bishops, 36 presidents of episcopal conferences and 12 religious. Members came from every continent where the Church is present: there were 50 from Africa, 59 from America, 44 from Asia, 95 from Europe and eight from Oceania. In addition, there were 32 experts and 27 auditors. The languages of the Synod were Latin, Italian, French, Spanish, English and German. In a noted development, the Chinese government denied passports to four Chinese bishops who had been invited to attend the Synod.

The president-delegates were Cardinal Francis Arinze, prefect of the Congregation for Divine Worship; Cardinal Juan Sandoval Íñiguez of Guadalajara, Mexico; and Cardinal Telesphore Placidus Toppo of Ranchi, India. The reporter general was Cardinal Angelo Scola of Venice; the secretary general was Archbishop Roland Minnerath of Dijon, France. Among those named by Pope Benedict to the Synod are: Cardinal Georges Cottier, theologian to the Pontifical Household; Cardinal Marc Ouellet of Quebec, Canada; Cardinal George Pell of Sydney, Australia; Cardinal Edmund Szoka, president of the Vatican city-state; Archbishop Cyrille Salim Bustros of Newton, Massachusetts (Melkite); Archbishop Stefan Soroka of Philadelphia, Pennsylvania

(Ukrainian); Bishop Javier Echevarria Rodriguez, the prelate of Opus Dei; Father Julian Carron, the president of Communion and Liberation; and Father Peter-Hans Kolvenbach superior general of the Society of Jesus.

The work of the Synod proceeded in 23 General Congregations and seven sessions for the Working Groups. Several changes and innovations were introduced in order to make the work of the participants more streamlined and to improve the collegial atmosphere of the gathering. These included reducing the time allotted for interventions from eight to six minutes for each participant, as well as the number of the sessions of the Working Groups. The Synod also used electronic voting for decisions of minor matters *ad experimentum*.

Topics and Issues

On Oct. 22, at the conclusion of the Synod, the Synodal Fathers gave to Pope Benedict a list of 50 recommendations based on the discussions, interventions, and meetings. Pope Benedict XVI allowed the provisional and unofficial Italian-language text to be published in the Holy See Press Office Bulletin. Normally, the text is confidential and is not published. The most discussed topics by the end of the Synod were the Eucharist and issues of declining vocations, the growing priest shortage, and priestly celibacy.

Regarding the Eucharist, the Synod: gave a firm endorsement to the liturgical reforms called for by the Second Vatican Council by declaring that they benefited the Church; noted the recent trend toward renewed interest in Eucharistic adoration and gave encouragement to pastors to promote the practice; warned against violating the dignity and sacred character of liturgical celebrations through the use of non-liturgical texts; called on pastors to reaffirm the importance of Sunday Mass; urged Catholics to be aware of the relationship between the Eucharist and the Sacrament of Penance; declared that the reception of Communion should never be considered automatic and that Catholics ought to be reminded of the need to be in a state of grace before receiving Communion; reiterated that Catholics who have divorced and civilly remarried without an annulment cannot be admitted to holy Communion, even while such Catholics must be given welcome at Mass and other activities within the Church; pointed to the lack of eucharistic coherence (*coerenza eucaristica*) when laws are promoted that go against the integral good of man, against justice, and the natural law; stressed that non-Catholics attending Mass should be informed that while they are not allowed to receive Communion it should not be considered sign of disrespect, even as the Synod restated Church teaching on shared Communion with non-Catholic Christians as generally not possible; further, ecumenical concelebration of the Eucharist is not permitted, although exceptions should be permitted under precise conditions.

On the issue of vocations and priestly celibacy, the Synod: affirmed the inestimable gift of ecclesiastical celibacy; decided not to go down the road of possibly using *viri probati* (older, married men) as a possible solution to the problem to declining numbers of priestly vocations; called for new efforts at fostering vocations; urged an equitable distribution of priests and for priests to be willing to serve where they are needed; the bishops also went to some effort to thank the world's priests for their selfless service, even at the cost of great sacrifice and personal risk.

In speaking of the Synod's statements regarding clerical celibacy, Cardinal George Pell of Sydney observed to reporters, "I think it is significant that there has been a massive restatement of the tradition in the Latin Church of mandatory celibacy for priests." The Synod marked as well the climax of the Year of the Eucharist that was convened by Pope John Paul II. The bishops in attendance said that they hoped the special year might be "a point of departure for a new evangelization of our globalized humanity that begins with the Eucharist." Pope Benedict XVI formally closed the synod on Oct. 23 with a Mass in St. Peter's Square. In his homily, the pontiff tied together the various themes and issues when he said:

The Synodal work allowed us to deepen the salient aspects of this mystery, given tot he Church from the beginning. Contemplation of the Eucharist must urge all members of the Church, in the first place the priests, ministers of the Eucharist, to revive their commitment of faith. The celibacy that the priests received as a precious gift and the sign of the undivided love toward God and the neighbor is founded upon the Eucharistic Mystery, celebrated and adored. Eucharistic spirituality must also be the interior motor of any activity for the lay persons, and no dichotomy is admissible between faith and life in their mission of Christian animation of the world. While the Year of the Eucharist is coming to an end, how can we not give thanks to God for the many gifts given to the Church during this time? And how can we not take up, once again, the invitation by the beloved Pope John Paul II to "start again from Christ?" Just as the disciples of Emmaus who, hearts warmed by the Word of the Risen and illuminated by His living presence recognized in the breaking of the bread, without pause returned to Jerusalem and became the proclaimers of Christ's resurrection, we too must take up the path again, animated by the fervent desire to witness the mystery of this love that gives hope to the world.

Message of the Synod of Bishops to the People of God

On Oct. 21, 2005, during the Twentieth General Congregation of the Synod, the Synodal participants approved a Message of the Synod of Bishops to the People of God as part of the conclusion of the 11th Ordinary General Assembly of the Synod of Bishops. Following are excerpts from the Message:

Called to Rome by Pope John Paul II, of venerable memory, and confirmed by His Holiness Benedict XVI, we have come from the five continents of the world to pray and reflect together on The Eucharist, Source and Summit of the Life and Mission of the Church. The goal of the Synod was to offer proposals to the Holy Father that might help him to update and deepen the Eucharistic life of the Church. We have been able to experience what the Holy Eucharist has been from the very beginning: one faith and one Church, nourished by one bread of life, in visible communion with the successor of Peter.

The fraternal sharing among the Bishops, the auditors, and also the ecumenical representatives, has renewed our conviction that the Holy Eucharist animates and transforms the life of the particular Churches of the East and West, as well as the many human activities in the very different circumstances in which we live. We have sensed a profound joy in experiencing the unity of our Eucharistic faith in the midst of the widespread diversity of rites, cultures and pastoral situations. The presence of so many Brother bishops has allowed us to experience, in a more direct way, the richness of our different liturgical traditions that makes the depths of the unique Eucharistic mystery shine forth.

We invite you, dear Christian brothers and sisters of every confession, to pray more fervently that the day of reconciliation, and the full visible unity of the Church might come in the celebration of the Holy Eucharist in conformity with the prayer of Jesus on the eve of his death: "That all may be one. As you, Father, are in me and I am in you, that they may be one in us, so that the world will believe that you sent me" (Jn 17:21)....

The meeting of the Synod has been an intense time of sharing and witnessing to the life of the Church in the different continents. We have been made aware of extreme situations and suffering generated by wars, hunger, different forms of terrorism and injustice, which touch the daily life of hundreds of millions of human beings. The explosive violence in the Middle East and in Africa has reminded us that the African continent has been forgotten by the public opinion of the world. Natural disasters, which seem to have multiplied, force us to look upon nature with greater respect and to strengthen our solidarity with those suffering peoples....

The Eucharist is the gift of love, love of the Father who sent his only Son so that the world might be saved (see Jn 3:16-17); the love of Christ who loved us to the end (see Jn 13:1); the love of God poured into our hearts by the Holy Spirit (see Rom 5:5), who cries out in us "Abba, Father!" (Gal 4:6). In celebrating the Holy Sacrifice, therefore, we joyfully announce the salvation of the world in proclaiming the victorious death of the Lord until he comes. In our communion with his Body, we receive the «pledge» of our own resurrection...

Forty years after the Second Vatican Council we wanted to examine to what extent the mysteries of the faith are adequately expressed and celebrated in our liturgical assemblies. The Synod reaffirms that the Second Vatican Council provided the necessary basis for an authentic liturgical renewal. It is necessary now to cultivate the positive fruits of this reform, and to correct abuses that have crept into liturgical practice. We are convinced that respect for the sacred character of the liturgy is transmitted by genuine fidelity to liturgical norms of legitimate authority. No one should consider himself master of the Church's liturgy. Living faith that recognizes the presence of the Lord is the first condition for beautiful liturgical celebrations, which give a genuine «Amen» to the glory of God. Lights in the Eucharistic life of the Church…. Nevertheless, the lack of priests to celebrate the Sunday Eucharist worries us a great deal and invites us to pray and more actively promote priestly vocations. Some priests, undergoing great difficulty, are forced to celebrate many times and to move from one place to another to best meet the needs of the faithful. They truly deserve our deep appreciation and solidarity. Our thanks goes also to those many missionaries whose enthusiasm for the proclamation of the Good News enables us to remain faithful today to the commandment of the Lord to go into the whole world and to baptize in his name (see Mt 28:19).

On the other hand, we are worried because the absence of the priest makes it impossible to celebrate Mass, to celebrate the Day of the Lord. Various forms of celebration already exist in different continents that suffer from a lack of priests. Yet, the practice of "spiritual communion," dear to the Catholic tradition, can and should be better promoted and explained so that the faithful may be helped both to communicate sacramentally in a better way and to bring genuine consolation to those who, for various reasons, cannot receive the Body and Blood of Christ in communion. We believe that this practice should help people who are alone, especially the handicapped, the aged, those imprisoned and refugees. We know the sadness of those who do not have access to sacramental communion because of their family situations that do not conform to the commandment of the Lord (see Mt 19:3-9). Some divorced and remarried people sadly accept their inability to take sacramental communion and they make an offering of it to God. Others are not able to understand this restriction, and live with an internal frustration. We reaffirm that, while we do not endorse their choice (cf. CCC 2384), they are not excluded from the life of the Church. We ask that they participate in Sunday Mass and devote themselves assiduously to listening to the Word of God so that it might nourish their life of faith, of love and of conversion. We wish to tell them how close we are to them in prayer and pastoral concern. Together, let us ask the Lord to obey his will faithfully… Dear Priests, we have thought of you a great deal over these days. We recognize your generosity and your challenges. You bear, in communion with us, the burden of the daily pastoral service of the People of God. You proclaim the Word of God, and you take care to introduce the faithful to the Eucharistic mystery. What a grace your ministry is! We pray with you and for you so that, together, we will remain faithful to the love of the Lord. We ask you to be, with us and following the example of the Holy Father Pope Benedict XVI, "humble workers in the vineyard of the Lord," following a consistent priestly life. May the peace of Christ that you give to repentant sinners and to the Eucharistic gatherings, flow down upon you and on the communities that live from your witness…

At the end of this Synod we experience that Peace full of hope that the disciples of Emmaus, with burning hearts, received from the Risen Lord. They arose and returned in haste to Jerusalem, to share their joy with their brothers and sisters in the faith. We hope that you will go joyfully to meet him in the Holy Eucharist, and that you will experience the truth of his words: "And I am with you until the end of the world" (Mt 28:20). CA

HOMOSEXUALITY AND THE PRIESTHOOD

On Nov. 29, 2005, the Congregation for Catholic Education issued a document, "Instruction Concerning the Criteria for the Discernment of Vocations With R`egard to Persons With Homosexual Tendencies in View of Their Admission to the Seminary and to Sacred Orders."

The instruction declares that the Church cannot admit to the seminary or to holy orders those who practice homosexuality, present deep-seated homosexual tendencies or support the so-called 'gay culture.' " Interpretations of the precise extent and meaning of the ban followed the release of the instruction.

The Vatican newspaper, L'Osservatore Romano, published an article written by French Msgr. Tony Anatrella, a psychoanalyst and consultant to the Pontifical Council for the Family. The article supported a total ban on homosexuals because the priest acts in the "person of Christ," and hence the Church calls only "men mature in their masculine identity." Homosexuals are considered unsuitable candidates even if they have never had a gay experience and are fully committed to celibacy because the homosexual tendency "is a counterindication to the call to holy orders."

The instruction itself was accompanied by a cover letter that was obtained by Catholic News Service. The letter stressed that the new norms must be "faithfully observed" and also applied when seminary guidelines and norms were being drafted or revised. The letter in addition noted that, while the text does not apply to those already ordained, priests with homosexual tendencies should not be given educational roles in seminaries.

Reaction among U.S. bishops was varied. Discussions included whether the instruction requires a total ban or if the possibility remains for some men with homosexual tendencies to be accepted into seminaries. A number of bishops expressed the view that it was in effect a total ban. According to Bishop John M. D'Arcy of Fort Wayne-South Bend, Indiana, "It bans anyone with a same-sex orientation." Other bishops suggested that it does not ban the acceptance of candidates for the priesthood who are sexually and emotionally mature and are capable of making a faithful commitment to living a celibate life. Such cases, the bishops argue, must be made on a case-by-case basis. Bishop William S. Skylstad of Spokane, Wash., who is president of the U.S. Conference of Catholic Bishops, stated, for example, "Once it is determined that there is no 'deep-seated' (homosexual) tendency then the decision is up to the local bishop." Attention was paid also to the issue in the document of the difference between a "deep-seated" tendency and a "transitory problem." Bishop Skylstad observed that the document is vague in what it means by a "deep-seated" tendency and a "transitory problem." Further, it is unclear how the document sees the process by which a candidate moves from one condition to the next. Bishop Skylstad suggested that the question is one that would have to be decided upon by the local bishop and the vocations director as part of the assessment of the candidate's qualifications for ordination. Following is the English-language text of the Vatican Letter:

Introduction

In continuity with the teaching of the Second Vatican Council and in particular with the decree *Optatam Totius* (1) on priestly formation, the Congregation for Catholic Education has published various documents with the aim of promoting a suitable, integral formation of future priests by offering guidelines and precise norms regarding its diverse aspects (2). In the meantime, the 1990 Synod of Bishops also reflected on the formation of priests in the circumstances of the present day, with the intention of bringing to completion the doctrine of the council on this theme and making it more explicit and effective in today's world. Following this synod, Pope John Paul II published the post-synodal apostolic exhortation *Pastores Dabo Vobis* (3). In light of this abundant teaching, the present instruction does not intend to dwell on all questions in the area of affectivity and sexuality that require an attentive discernment during the entire period of formation. Rather, it contains norms concerning a specific question made more urgent by the current situation, and that is: whether to admit to the seminary and to holy orders candidates who have deep-seated homosexual tendencies.

1. Affective Maturity and Spiritual Fatherhood

According to the constant tradition of the church, only a baptized person of the male sex validly receives sacred ordination (4). By means of the sacrament of orders, the Holy Spirit configures the candidate to Jesus Christ in a new and specific way: The priest, in fact, sacramentally represents Christ, the head, shepherd and spouse of the church (5). Because of this configuration to Christ, the entire life of the sacred minister must be animated by the gift of his whole person to the church and by an authentic pastoral charity (6). The candidate to the ordained ministry, therefore, must reach affective maturity. Such maturity will allow him to relate correctly to both men and women, developing in him a true sense of spiritual fatherhood toward the church community that will be entrusted to him (7).

2. Homosexuality and the Ordained Ministry

From the time of the Second Vatican Council until today, various documents of the magisterium, and especially the "Catechism of the Catholic Church," have confirmed the teaching of the church on homosexuality. The catechism distinguishes between homosexual acts and homosexual tendencies.

Regarding acts, it teaches that sacred Scripture presents them as grave sins. The tradition has constantly considered them as intrinsically immoral and contrary to the natural law. Consequently, under no circumstance can they be approved.

Deep-seated homosexual tendencies, which are found in a number of men and women, are also objectively disordered and, for those same people, often constitute a trial. Such persons must be accepted with respect and sensitivity. Every sign of unjust discrimination in their regard should be avoided. They are called to fulfill God's will in their lives and to unite to the sacrifice of the Lord's cross the difficulties they

may encounter (8). In the light of such teaching, this dicastery, in accord with the Congregation for Divine Worship and the Discipline of the Sacraments, believes it necessary to state clearly that the church, while profoundly respecting the persons in question (9), cannot admit to the seminary or to holy orders those who practice homosexuality, present deep-seated homosexual tendencies or support the so-called "gay culture" (10).

Such persons, in fact, find themselves in a situation that gravely hinders them from relating correctly to men and women. One must in no way overlook the negative consequences that can derive from the ordination of persons with deep-seated homosexual tendencies.

Different, however, would be the case in which one were dealing with homosexual tendencies that were only the expression of a transitory problem — for example, that of an adolescence not yet superseded. Nevertheless, such tendencies must be clearly overcome at least three years before ordination to the diaconate.

3. Discernment by the Church Concerning the Suitability of Candidates

There are two inseparable elements in every priestly vocation: the free gift of God and the responsible freedom of the man. A vocation is a gift of divine grace received through the church, in the church and for the service of the church. In responding to the call of God, the man offers himself freely to him in love (11). The desire alone to become a priest is not sufficient, and there does not exist a right to receive sacred ordination. It belongs to the church — in her responsibility to define the necessary requirements for receiving the sacraments instituted by Christ — to discern the suitability of him who desires to enter the seminary (12) to accompany him during his years of formation and to call him to holy orders if he is judged to possess the necessary qualities (13). The formation of the future priest must distinctly articulate, in an essentially complementary manner, the four dimensions of formation: human, spiritual, intellectual and pastoral (14). In this context, it is necessary to highlight the particular importance of human formation as the necessary foundation of all formation (15). In order to admit a candidate to ordination to the diaconate, the church must verify, among other things, that the candidate has reached affective maturity (16). The call to orders is the personal responsibility of the bishop (17) or the major superior. Bearing in mind the opinion of those to whom he has entrusted the responsibility of formation, the bishop or major superior, before admitting the candidate to ordination, must arrive at a morally certain judgment on his qualities. In the case of a serious doubt in this regard, he must not admit him to ordination (18). The discernment of a vocation and of the maturity of the candidate is also a serious duty of the rector and of the other persons entrusted with the work of formation in the seminary.

Before every ordination, the rector must express his own judgment on whether the qualities required by the church are present in the candidate (19). In the discernment concerning the suitability for ordination, the spiritual director has an important task. Although he is bound to secrecy, he represents the church in the internal forum. In his discussions with the candidate the spiritual director must especially point out the demands of the church concerning priestly chastity and the affective maturity that is characteristic of the priest as well as help him to discern whether he has the necessary qualities (20). The spiritual director has the obligation to evaluate all the qualities of the candidate's personality and to make sure that he does not present disturbances of a sexual nature, which are incompatible with the priesthood. If a candidate practices homosexuality or presents deep-seated homosexual tendencies, his spiritual director as well as his confessor have the duty to dissuade him in conscience from proceeding toward ordination. It goes without saying that the candidate himself has the primary responsibility for his own formation (21). He must offer himself trustingly to the discernment of the church, of the bishop who calls him to orders, of the rector of the seminary, of his spiritual director and of the other seminary educators to whom the bishop or major superior has entrusted the task of forming future priests. It would be gravely dishonest for a candidate to hide his own homosexuality in order to proceed, despite everything, toward ordination. Such a deceitful attitude does not correspond to the spirit of truth, loyalty and openness that must characterize the personality of him who believes he is called to serve Christ and his church in the ministerial priesthood.

Conclusion

This congregation reaffirms the need for bishops, major superiors and all relevant authorities to carry out an attentive discernment concerning the suitability of candidates for holy orders from the time of admission to the seminary until ordination. This discernment must be done in light of a conception of the ministerial priesthood that is in accordance with the teaching of the church. Let bishops, episcopal conferences and major superiors look to see that the constant norms of this instruction be faithfully observed for the good of the candidates themselves and to guarantee that the church always has suitable priests who are true shepherds according to the heart of Christ.

The supreme pontiff Benedict XVI on Aug. 31, 2005, approved this present instruction and ordered its publication. Rome, Nov. 4, 2005, memorial of St. Charles Borromeo, Cardinal Zenon Grocholewski prefect Archbishop J. Michael Miller, CSB secretary.

NOTES: 1. Vatican Council II, Decree on Priestly Formation *Optatam Totius* (Oct. 28, 1965): *Acta Apostolicae Sedis* 58 (1966), 713-727. 2. Cf. Congregation for Catholic Education, *Ratio Fundamentalis Institutionis Sacerdotalis* (Jan. 6, 1970; 2nd ed., Mar. 19, 1985); "The Study of Philosophy in Seminaries" (Jan. 20, 1972); "A Guide to Formation in Priestly Celibacy" (Apr. 11, 1974); "On the Teaching of Canon Law to Those Preparing to Be Priests" (Apr. 2, 1975); "The Theological Formation of Future Priests" (Feb. 22, 1976); Circular Letter on the Formation of Adult Vocations (July 14, 1976); Instruction on Liturgical Formation in Seminaries (June 3, 1979); Circular Letter Concerning Some of the More Urgent Aspects of Spiritual Formation in Seminaries (Jan. 6, 1980); "Educational Guidance in Human Love: Outlines for Sex Education" (Nov. 1, 1983); "Pastoral Care of People on the Move in the Formation of Future Priests" (Jan. 25, 1986); "Guide

to the Training of Future Priests Concerning the Instruments of Social Communication" (Mar. 19, 1986); Circular Letter Concerning Studies of the Oriental Churches (Jan. 6, 1987); "The Virgin Mary in Intellectual and Spiritual Formation" (Mar. 25, 1988); "Guidelines for the Study and Teaching of the Church's Social Doctrine in the Formation of Priests" (Dec. 30, 1988); Instruction on the Study of the Fathers of the Church in the Formation of Priests (Nov. 10, 1989); "Directives Concerning the Preparation of Seminary Educators" (Nov. 4, 1993); "Directives on the Formation of Seminarians Concerning Problems Related to Marriage and the Family" (Mar. 19, 1995); Instruction to the Episcopal Conferences on the Admission to Seminary of Candidates Coming from Other Seminaries or Religious Families (Oct. 9, 1986, and Mar. 8, 1996); "The Propaedeutic Period" (May 1, 1998); Circular Letters Concerning the Canonical Norms Relating to Irregularities and Impediments Both for Receiving Orders and Exercising Ordained Ministry (July 27, 1992, and Feb. 2, 1999). 3. Pope John Paul II, post-synodal apostolic exhortation *Pastores Dabo Vobis* (Mar. 25, 1992): AAS 84 (1992), 657-864. 4. Cf. Code of Canon Law, Canon 1024, and Code of Canons for the Eastern Churches, Canon 754; Pope John Paul II, apostolic letter "*Ordinatio Sacerdotalis*" on reserving priestly ordination to men alone (May 22, 1994): AAS 86 (1994), 545-548. 5. Cf. Vatican Council II, Decree on the Ministry and Life of Priests *Presbyterorum Ordinis* (Dec. 7, 1965), 2: AAS 58 (1966), 991-993; *Pastores Dabo Vobis*, 16. With regard to the priest's configuration to Christ, bridegroom of the church, *Pastores Dabo Vobis* states that "the priest is called to be the living image of Jesus Christ, the spouse of the church.... In his spiritual life, therefore, he is called to live out Christ's spousal love toward the church, his bride. Therefore, the priest's life ought to radiate this spousal character, which demands that he be a witness to Christ's spousal love" (no. 22). 6. Cf. *Presbyterorum Ordinis*, 14; *Pastores Dabo Vobis*, 23. 7. Cf. Congregation for the Clergy, "Directory on the Ministry and Life of Priests" (Mar. 31, 1994), 58. 8. Cf. *Catechism of the Catholic Church* (typical edition, 1997), 2357-2358. Cf. also the various documents of the Congregation for the Doctrine of the Faith: declaration "*Persona Humana*" on certain questions concerning sexual ethics (Dec. 29, 1975); Letter to the World's Bishops on the Pastoral Care of Homosexual Persons (*Homosexualitatis Problema*) (Oct. 1, 1986); "Some Considerations Concerning the Response to Legislative Proposals on Nondiscrimination of Homosexual Persons" (July 23, 1992); "Considerations Regarding Proposals to Give Legal Recognition to Unions Between Homosexual Persons" (June 3, 2003). With regard to homosexual inclinations, the letter on the pastoral care of homosexuals states that, "though the particular inclination of the homosexual person is not a sin, it is a more or less strong tendency ordered toward an intrinsic moral evil; and thus the inclination itself must be seen as an objective disorder" (no. 3). 9. Cf. Catechism, 2358; Western Canon 208 and Eastern Canon 11. 10. Cf. Congregation for Catholic Education, A memorandum to bishops seeking advice in matters concerning homosexuality and candidates for admission to seminary (July 9, 1985); Congregation for Divine Worship and the Discipline of the Sacraments, Letter (May 16, 2002): *Notitiae* 38 (2002), 586. 11. Cf. *Pastores Dabo Vobis*, 35-36. 12. Cf. Canon 241.1: "A diocesan bishop is to admit to a major seminary only those who are judged qualified to dedicate themselves permanently to the sacred ministries; he is to consider their human, moral, spiritual and intellectual qualities, their physical and psychic health, and their correct intention"; cf. Eastern Canon 342.1. 13. Cf. *Optatam Totius*, 6. Cf. also Canon 1029. "Only those are to be promoted to orders who, in the prudent judgment of their own bishop or of the competent major superior, all things considered, have integral faith, are moved by the right intention, have the requisite knowledge, possess a good reputation and are endowed with integral morals and proven virtues and the other physical and psychic qualities in keeping with the order to be received"; cf. Eastern Canon 758. Not to call to orders those who do not have the necessary qualities is not an unjust discrimination: cf. Congregation for the Doctrine of the Faith, "Some Considerations Concerning the Response to Legislative Proposals on Nondiscrimination of Homosexual Persons." 14. Cf. *Pastores Dabo Vobis*, 43-59. 15. Cf. ibid., 43: "The priest, who is called to be a 'living image' of Jesus Christ, head and shepherd of the church, should seek to reflect in himself, as far as possible, the human perfection which shines forth in the incarnate Son of God and which is reflected with particular liveliness in his attitudes toward others." 16. Cf. ibid., 44 and 50. Cf. also: Congregation for Divine Worship and Discipline of the Sacraments, Circular Letter to the Diocesan Bishops and Other Ordinaries With Canonical Faculties to Admit to Sacred Orders Concerning Scrutinies Regarding the Suitability of Candidates for Orders (Nov. 10, 1997): *Notitiae* 33 (1997), 507-518, particularly Enclosure V. 17. Cf. Congregation for Bishops, Directory for the Pastoral Ministry of Bishops *Apostolorum Successores* (Feb. 22, 2004), 88. 18. Cf. Canon 1052.3: "If... the bishop doubts for specific reasons whether a candidate is suitable to receive orders, he is not to promote him." Cf. also Eastern Canon 770. 19. Cf. Canon 1051: "The following prescripts regarding the investigation about the qualities required in the one to be ordained are to be observed: ... there is to be a testimonial of the rector of the seminary or house of formation about the qualities required to receive the order, that is, about the sound doctrine of the candidate, his genuine piety, good morals and aptitude to exercise the ministry, as well as, after a properly executed inquiry, about his state of physical and psychic health" 20. Cf. *Pastores Dabo Vobis*, 50 and 66. Cf. also *Ratio Fundamentalis Institutionis Sacerdotalis*, 48. 21. Cf. *Pastores Dabo Vobis*, 69. **CA**

SPECIAL REPORTS: NATIONAL NEWS 2005-2006

THE SEX-ABUSE SCANDAL IN THE U.S. CHURCH

By Russell Shaw

The clergy sex abuse scandal continued to have serious legal and financial repercussions for the Church in 2006.

A new report showed that although the number of allegations of child abuse by Catholic clergy in the United States fell in 2005, financial costs of abuse to the Church rose sharply.

The 783 allegations came from 777 persons claiming they were abused by 532 clergy, mostly diocesan priests. In 2004, 1,083 people made 1,092 allegations involving 756 clergymen.

The $467 million cost of sex abuse to dioceses, eparchies and religious orders in 2005 was $309 million greater than the year before. That brought to more than $1.5 billion the known cost of sex abuse to the Church since 1950. Insurance has covered the greater part, but in many places dioceses also have had to sell property and eliminate jobs.

Most of the money has been paid in settlements to abuse victims. In 2005, settlements totaled $400 million; lawyers' fees, $41 million; victims' therapy, $8 million; and other victim support programs, $13.7 million.

The figures were contained in the annual report on compliance with the "Charter for the Protection of Children and Young People" adopted by the U.S. bishops in 2002. The bishops revised the charter in 2005, and the Vatican's Congregation for Bishops approved the revision in 2006 for an indefinite period of time.

The compliance report was released in Washington March 30 by the bishops' Office for Child and Youth Protection, the U.S. Conference of Catholic Bishops, and the National Review Board that monitors the charter's implementation. It was based on audits of dioceses and eparchies by the Gavin Group of Boston, with supplemental information collected by the Center for Applied Research in the Apostolate.

In a separate report released at the same time, the John Jay College of Criminal Justice, New York, said that even if more cases of clergy sex abuse come to light in the future, most are likely to involve incidents alleged to have occurred "years before." Of the 783 allegations in 2005, nine concerned incidents alleged to have occurred that year while more than half concerned events said have happened before 1980.

The John Jay College's initial study of clergy sex abuse, released in 2004, said 4,392 Catholic clergy in the U.S., almost all priests, had been accused of abuse by 10,667 persons in the years from 1950 to 2002, with 75 percent of the incidents between 1960 and 1984. The totals of abusers and abused have continued to rise as additional allegations have been made.

Corresponding to the profile of sex abuse by Catholic clergy in the 2004 study, in 81 percent of the incidents reported in 2005 the alleged victims were male. About half said they were in the 10-14 age range when the abuse began.

The charter compliance report found nine out of 10 participating dioceses and eparchies in full compliance. Twenty-one were in partial compliance because they had not completed sex abuse training, and five because they had not completed background checks of Church personnel.

A study released April 19 by the Center for Applied Research in the Apostolate found little change from

2001 to 2005 in the percentage of Catholics contributing money to their parishes in the previous year (76 percent in 2002 and 74 percent in 2005) and attending Mass at least weekly (33 percent), or in the percentage of self-identified Catholics in the total population (23 percent). But giving to diocesan appeals fell from 38 percent in 2002 to 29 percent in 2005. The findings were based on national telephone surveys.

Three American dioceses — Portland, Ore., Spokane, Wash., and Tucson, Ariz. — have sought Chapter 11 bankruptcy protection since the costs of the sex abuse scandal began to escalate.

In June, a U.S. district judge overturned a U.S. bankruptcy judge's ruling that the Bishop of Spokane owns parish assets and these could be sold to pay abuse victims' claims against the diocese. Bishop William S. Skylstad welcomed the decision, but the diocese's financial situation remained precarious.

When a settlement finally is reached, Bishop Skylstad said in July, diocesan resources will be "exhausted" and the diocese may have to turn to parishioners for help. Earlier, the bankruptcy court rejected a $45.7 million settlement proposed by the diocese for 75 claimants because it did not provide for others who had come forward — said to number 60 or 70 — or might do so in the future.

In Portland, a U.S. district judge ruled, also in June, that the Holy See may not enjoy sovereign immunity from a clergy abuse suit in which it is accused of knowingly allowing a known abuser-priest from Ireland to be assigned there. The decision has been appealed to the 9th U.S. Circuit Court of Appeals.

Writing to Portland Catholics a month earlier, Archbishop John G. Vlazny announced a $1 million cutback at the archdiocesan pastoral center; the figure later rose to $1.9 million. The archdiocese cut $2 million and 20 jobs in 2003.

The Archdiocese of Boston, possibly the nation's hardest hit by the abuse scandal, on April 19 issued financial reports showing a $46 million deficit in the 18-month period ending June 30, 2005. Observers praised the comprehensiveness and detail of the reports, calling them a model for other dioceses, but Cardinal Sean P. O'Malley, O.F.M. Cap., of Boston said the archdiocese was in "dire" financial straits.

Contributions to the annual Catholic Appeal fell from $15.6 million in 2001 to $11.6 million in 2005, while abuse-related costs of abuse to the archdiocese totaled $150.8 million up to June 30 of last year. In March 2006 the archdiocese announced settlements with another 88 persons; settlements with 554 claimants totaling $85 million were reached in 2003.

In several parts of the country, 2006 also brought continuing conflicts involving state legislators and Church authorities over proposals to extend the statute of limitations in sex abuse cases.

In Colorado Archbishop Charles Chaput, O.F.M. Cap., of Denver led opposition by the bishops of the state to extending the statute of limitations in civil suits. That proposal failed to pass the state legislature, but legislation supported by the bishops — to extend the statute of limitation in criminal cases — was adopted April 12 and signed into law.

Archbishop Chaput and the other bishops objected that the proposed extension in civil suits would apply to church-related institutions while leaving exempt public schools, where much child sex abuse is said to occur. Similar conflicts flared up during the year in other states including Massachusetts, New Hampshire, Ohio, and Maryland. The issue is likely to continue to be raised in various parts of the country for some time to come.

Already, a moratorium on the statute of limitations enacted by the California legislature has allowed hundreds of new claimants to come forward. In a potentially significant development, the U.S. Supreme Court on April 17 rejected the Archdiocese of Los Angeles' appeal from lower court rulings requiring it to provide prosecutors with documents from the personnel files of two former priests.

The Archdiocese of Chicago in March released two reports critical of its handling sex abuse cases, including two priests who were monitored but not immediately removed from ministry after allegations against them surfaced. Cardinal Francis George accepted responsibility for the lapses. **CA**

CATHOLICS AND THE SUPREME COURT

The retirement of Justice Sandra Day O'Connor on July 1, 2005, and the death of Chief Justice William Rehnquist on Sept. 3, 2005, marked the opening of two vacancies on the United States Supreme Court. The two seats were filled by Pres. George W. Bush with two Catholics, John Roberts, 50, and Samuel A. Alito, Jr., 55.

With their subsequent confirmations, the Supreme Court now has a majority of Catholic Justices, with five: Roberts, Alito, Clarence Thomas, Anthony Kennedy, and Antonin Scalia. Roberts and Alito are the 10th and 11th Catholics ever to serve on the court. Roberts is the third Catholic to hold the post of chief justice. The first Catholic on the Supreme Court was also the first Catholic chief justice — Justice Roger B. Taney (chief from 1836–1864). The second chief justice was Edward Douglas White (associate justice from 1894–1910 and chief justice from 1910–21). Judge Alito is the second Italian-American to be appointed to the Supreme Court.

Chief Justice John Roberts

Pres. Bush nominated John Roberts, a judge of the federal appeals court for the District of Columbia, on July 19 after the announcement of Sandra Day O'Connor's retirement. The nomination was subsequently changed following the death of Chief Justice Rehnquist so that Roberts could replace Rehnquist as head of the court. He is the seventeenth chief justice.

Roberts was born on Jan. 27, 1955, in Buffalo, N.Y. His family moved to Long Beach, Ind., when he was two years old, and he was raised in a devout Catholic environment. He graduated from Harvard University summa cum laude in 1976 and then attended Harvard Law School, where he served as managing editor of the Harvard Law Review and graduated magna cum laude in 1979.

After graduating from law school, Roberts served as a law clerk for Judge Henry Friendly on the Second Circuit Court of Appeals. He then served from 1980–1981 as a law clerk to then-Associate Justice William Rehnquist on the U.S. Supreme Court. He held several positions in the Reagan White House, including Special Assistant to U.S. Attorney General William French Smith and Associate Counsel to the President under White House Counsel Fred Fielding.

Roberts entered private law practice in 1986 but returned to the government to serve in the first Bush administration as Principal Deputy Solicitor General from 1989–1993. In 1992, Pres. George H.W. Bush nominated him to the U.S. Court of Appeals for the District of Columbia Circuit; no Senate vote was held, however, and Roberts' nomination expired after the 1992 election. Roberts returned to private practice and was also an adjunct faculty member at the Georgetown University Law Center. Pres. George W. Bush nominated Roberts to the Court of Appeals for the District of Columbia Circuit on May 9, 2001; the nomination, like 29 others, failed to make it out of the Democrat-controlled U.S. Senate Judiciary Committee. He was re-nominated on Jan. 7, 2003, and was approved by the Senate under unanimous consent. His nomination first as Associate Justice and then Chief Justice was approved on Sept. 22 by the Senate Judiciary Committee. Roberts was then confirmed by the full Senate on Sept. 29, by a vote of 78–22. At the age of 50, Roberts is the third-youngest man to become Chief Justice (John Jay was appointed at age 44 in 1789 and John Marshall was appointed at age 45 in 1801).

Associate Justice Samuel A. Alito, Jr.

Alito was nominated by Pres. Bush on Oct. 31, 2005, as a replacement for nominee Harriet Miers to succeed Justice O'Connor. Miers withdrew her acceptance of the nomination on Oct. 27 after encountering widespread opposition from many within the conservative movement and also the Republican Party.

Samuel Anthony Alito, Jr., was born Apr. 1, 1950, in Trenton, N.J., and was raised a Catholic. He graduated from Princeton University's Woodrow Wilson School of Public and International Affairs in 1972 and earned a law degree from the Yale Law School in 1975, where he served as editor on the Yale Law Journal. After graduating from Yale Law School, he served on active duty in the Armed Forces from Sept.–Dec. 1975, while attending the Officer Basic Course for Signal Corps officers at Fort Gordon, Ga. He spent his remaining time in the Army in the inactive Reserves and had the rank of captain when he received an Honorable Discharge in 1980. From 1976–77, Alito worked as a law clerk for Leonard I. Garth of the Third Circuit Court and from 1977-81 as Assistant United States Attorney, for the District of New Jersey. He subsequently served as Deputy Assistant to Attorney General Edwin Meese in the Reagan Administration and United States Attorney for the District of New Jersey. From 1990–2006, he was a judge on the United States Court of Appeals for the Third Circuit Court of Appeals. He was also an adjunct professor of Law at Seton Hall University School of Law in Newark, N.J., from 1999 to 2004. In 1995, Judge Alito was presented with that law school's St. Thomas More Medal. Charged with being an extremist conservative, Alito's nomination was opposed by most of the Democrats in the Senate. Major opposition was never mounted, and despite what proved partisan and at times unpleasant questioning by some Democrats on the Judiciary Committee, Alito was confirmed by a vote of 58–42. No serious effort was undertaken to filibuster the nomination, but the close vote was an indication of the severely polarized political state of affairs in the Senate and the country at large.

Implications

The consensus opinion among legal experts is that the presence of Chief Justice Roberts and Associate Justice Alito has increased the conservative strength on the Supreme Court. Justice O'Connor was considered a moderate swing vote on the Court, and Alito, her replacement, is seen as a strong and reliable Constitutionalist. Chief Justice Rehnquist was one of the more conservative judicial voices on the Court, with Justices Thomas and Scalia, and so Chief Justice Roberts is seen as a consistent successor.

Nevertheless, both Justices in the past have demonstrated a fair and balanced approach to the law in their decisions. During his confirmation hearings prior to his nomination to the highest court, then Judge Roberts stated, for example, that Roe v. Wade is the settled law of the land, and added, "It's a little more than settled. It was reaffirmed in the face of a challenge that it should be overruled in the Casey decision. Accordingly, it's the settled law of the land. There's nothing in my personal views that would prevent me from fully and faithfully applying that precedent, as well as Casey." (The 1992 Planned Parenthood v. Casey case upheld the rights of states to impose restrictions on abortion.)

Judge Alito, meanwhile, expressed his opinion in Planned Parenthood v. Casey that it was constitutional to require wives to notify their husbands before having an abortion, a provision that was struck down in 1992 by the Court even as it upheld most of the Pennsylvania law. The late Chief Justice William Rehnquist quoted Alito in his dissent against striking down the spousal notification portion of the law. In 2000, Alito joined in a ruling that struck down a New Jersey partial-birth abortion law as unconstitutional. The two new Justices will certainly have the opportunity to shape the Court for many years to come.

The confirmation of the two new Justices marked the first time that Catholics have enjoyed a majority on the Court, with five members of the nine. The Catholicism of both nominees did not become a significant topic in the confirmation process, although it was noted that the questions at times pointed to a double standard regarding Catholic nominees, most so regarding socio-political issues such as abortion and homosexuality. Still, the Catholicism of Roberts was raised in a way that concerned some commentators, such as the statement on the American Prospect's Web page that "Rome must be smiling" over the nomination. Such statements suggested that Catholicism become an issue for disqualifying a nominee in a way that other faiths would not. Significant opposition to Robert's nomination collapsed in the weeks before the Senate confirmation hearings, largely because of the errors and misstatements in an advertisement by the abortion-rights activist group NARAL Pro-Choice America against the nomination. **CA**

HURRICANE KATRINA

In late Aug. 2005, Hurricane Katrina, the most destructive storm in American history, struck the Gulf Coast of the United States. The sixth-strongest Atlantic hurricane ever recorded and the third strongest to make landfall, Katrina brought severe devastation to the coastlines of Alabama, Mississippi, and Louisiana, in particular the cities of Mobile, Biloxi, and Gulfport.

The most well-known area of damage occurred in New Orleans, where the images of massive flooding and the suffering of tens of thousands of inhabitants of the city were broadcast around the world. For the

Catholic Church along the Gulf Coast, Katrina brought colossal damage to churches, schools, convents, and hospitals and an enormous financial loss that will take many years from which to recover fully. At the same time, Hurricane Katrina revealed the boundless charity of Americans, the goodwill of people all over the world, and the tireless labors of Catholic aid workers and volunteers in assisting the needs of those whose lives were destroyed along with their homes.

The hurricane formed in the Caribbean and then crossed Florida as a Category 1 hurricane. It then grew in strength over the Gulf of Mexico; fortunately, it weakened to a Category 3 storm on Aug. 29 as it made landfall in southeast Louisiana. The severity of Katrina was such that the levees separating Lake Pontchartrain and Lake Borgne from New Orleans collapsed beneath the surge. The resulting flood inundated approximately 80 percent of the city and some of the surrounding parishes. The cost of the damage across the Gulf was measured in the billions, but far more tragic was the loss of life. Katrina caused the deaths of 1,836 people. It was the deadliest U.S. hurricane since 1928 Okeechobee Hurricane.

The staggering damage caused by Katrina was estimated at $75 billion, but this did not include the long-term economic effects, the money needed for reconstruction (over $100 billion has already been sought by the Bush Administration), the severe displacement of victims across the country, and the painful process of renewal by the cities of Biloxi and especially the famed and beloved City of New Orleans. Almost the entire city was uninhabitable for two months. Even by early Nov., when most of the city's wards were reopened to residents, many areas still lacked basic services, especially electricity.

The Catholic Church and Katrina

Hurricane Katrina brought unparalleled devastation to the dioceses of Louisiana and Mississippi. Bishop Thomas J. Rodi of Biloxi, Mississippi, estimated immediately after the storm that 20 percent of the diocese's churches and a third of its schools had been destroyed. He added that every rectory, school, convent and diocesan building sustained damage to some degree. Archbishop Alfred C. Hughes of New Orleans reported that his archdiocese faced even greater levels of destruction as the floods and subsequent problems in the evacuated city took their toll.

A preliminary report on Church-owned properties in the archdiocese that had suffered wind or flood damage placed the damage at an estimated $84 million, about $70 million more than the insurance carried by the archdiocese. Of the approximately 1,200 buildings in the 142 parishes and nine missions of the Archdiocese of New Orleans, 387 were flooded by storm surge or the result of levee breaches and more than 864 received major wind damage

Less destruction was reported by the dioceses of Shreveport and Baton Rouge, which were far enough north to have escaped the storm. They set out to assist the thousands of displaced people. In a statement of the severity of the problems in the archdiocese of New Orleans, Archbishop Alfred C. Hughes was able to celebrate Mass in St. Louis Cathedral in the famed French Quarter only on Oct. 2.

The response of the Church around the country and the world was immediate. Church facilities in the Gulf area and nationwide launched into assisting both emergency and long-term needs through shelters, food, medicine and schools for the thousands displaced by the hurricane. Millions of Catholics responded with assistance, food, money, and even their own homes. Notable work was undertaken by Catholic Charities, St. Vincent DePaul Societies, Catholic schools, Catholic hospitals, parishes, retreat centers, and even average families. Supplementing the charitably work were collections and special fundraisers.

The U.S. bishops subsequently appointed a task force under Archbishop Joseph A. Fiorenza, then archbishop of Galveston-Houston, to address the needs in the aftermath of Hurricane Katrina. In the announcement of the task force on Sept. 14, 2005, Bishop William Skylstad of Spokane, Washington, president of the United States Conference of Catholic Bishops, stated:

"Our hearts and prayers go out once again to all those whose lives, homes and families have been damaged or destroyed by Katrina. Within the Catholic community, many of our people have lost everything and our Church has lost parishes and schools, hospitals and charitable ministries, and many of the structures which help us preach the Gospel, educate the young and serve the vulnerable. The loss of these institutions affects not only our Church, but is a significant loss for the entire community. As powerful as the winds and water of Katrina have been, our ongoing care and help, our practice of charity and search for justice must become more powerful. The hurricane and the flood came and went in a matter of hours and days. Our support, compassion, and commitment to help make things right must last far longer — not days, but months and years."

Over the next months, the tireless efforts of Catholics and Catholic organizations continued, often without any credit or publicity. In a letter of Dec. 6, 2005, Archbishop Hughes of New Orleans expressed his thanks to American Catholics for their "outpouring of love and concern" for the Church in New Orleans and neighboring dioceses. He noted that dioceses, parishes, lay organizations, corporations, individuals and even young schoolchildren contributed thousands of hours of volunteer time and funds in excess of $12 million to rebuild parishes and schools. The bishop projected that by year's end, the archdiocese would face a multimillion dollar deficit as well as enormous damage to property.

On Feb. 6, 2006, the Archdiocese of New Orleans issued a pastoral plan to implement the enormous task of rebuilding in the wake of Katrina. The plan called for the closing of seven parishes and delays in reopening 23 others until enough parishioners have returned to the area. In addition, the plan calls for establishing six centralized elementary schools, in place of the pre-storm pattern of having individual parish elementary schools.

The plan seeks to create 14 "cluster" parishes in the affected areas. These will facilitate pastoral care to parishes that have yet to reopen, a process that will be particularly attentive to the many communities of African-American, Asian and Hispanic Catholics.

Archbishop Hughes estimated that the archdiocese might benefit from a return of upwards of 60 percent of its pre-Katrina population over the next two years. Before the storm, the there were approximately a half-million Catholics in 142 parishes in the archdiocese. If the estimate of returnees is correct, the Catholic population will be about 295,000. The archbishop also noted that the archdiocese had projected a $40 million deficit in operations by the end of Dec. 2005. However, insurance reimbursements, employee layoffs, and the return to relatively normal operations in outlying parishes had reduced that deficit to $4.5 million.

Disaster Relief

For those who would like to make contributions to the multi-year task of rebuilding the following agencies and collections are available:

Catholic Charities: online at: http://www.catholic-charitiesusa.org/news/katrina.cfm; phone: 800-919-9338; mail: Catholic Charities USA — Hurricane Katrina, P.O. Box 25168, Alexandria, VA 22313-9788.

St. Vincent de Paul Society: online: www.svdpusa.org;mail: The National Council, Society of St. Vincent de Paul, 58 Progress Pkwy, St. Louis, MO 63043-3706.

Knights of Columbus: mail: Knights of Columbus Charities USA Inc., Gift Processing Center, P.O. Box 9028, Pittsfield, MA 01202-9028, Attn: Hurricane Katrina Relief. Donors in Canada should make checks payable to Knights of Columbus Canada Charities Inc. and send them to: Knights of Columbus Charities Canada Inc., Gift Processing Center, P.O. Box 7252 Station A, Toronto, Ontario, Canada M5W 1X9, Attn: Hurricane Katrina Relief.

Catholic Extension Society: online: www.catholicextension.org; mail: Catholic Extension, Hurricane Emergency Relief, 150 S. Wacker Drive, 20th Floor, Chicago, IL 60606.

(Readers are also encouraged to visit www.osv.com to read Our Sunday Visitor's series of articles on Katrina and its aftermath.) **CA**

LIFE ISSUES 2005-2006

Partial-Birth Abortion

On Feb. 21, 2006, the United States Supreme Court announced that it would review *Gonzales v. Carhart*, the partial-birth abortion ruling by the Eighth Circuit Court of Appeals that struck down the partial-birth abortion ban as unconstitutional. Deirdre A. McQuade, spokesperson for the United States Conference of Catholic Bishops' Secretariat for Pro-Life Activities, issued the following statement:

"We welcome the news that the Supreme Court will take a new look at partial-birth abortion.... Abortion advocates once said the procedure was rare, and used only on women whose lives were in danger or whose unborn children were dying or severely disabled. But Ron Fitzsimmons, then Executive Director of the National Coalition of Abortion Providers, admitted in 1997 that partial-birth abortions are 'primarily done on healthy women and healthy fetuses.' The Alan Guttmacher Institute estimates that 2,200 abortions were performed in 2000 using this grotesque method. Partial-birth abortion is not necessary for women's physical or emotional health. Extensive testimony reveals that there is no maternal health reason why such a gruesome and inhumane procedure must be performed. We are hopeful that the federal ban on partial-birth abortion will be upheld."

Abortion

On Jan. 19, 2006, the U.S. Supreme Court voted by 9–0 decision to return the *Ayotte v. Planned Parenthood of Northern New England* back to the district court that had invalidated what had been New Hampshire's parental notification law. Deirdre A. McQuade, spokesperson for the United States Conference of Catholic Bishops' Secretariat for Pro-Life Activities issued the following statement: "In Ayotte, the Supreme Court returns the challenge to New Hampshire's parental notification law back to the district court without answering major questions posed in the case. The lower court, appropriately, was told it should not have preemptively invalidated an entire abortion regulation on the basis of a potentially unconstitutional application to a small number of hypothetical cases. We welcome this development and hope it will end the disposition of lower courts to enjoin the enforcement of reasonable, commonsense abortion regulations for years while challenges are appealed.... But the Court missed an opportunity to address the substantive legal questions raised in Ayotte and we are left with more questions than answers — especially with regard to the so-called health exception first established 33 years ago in *Doe v. Bolton*.... This case concerns the validity of a New Hampshire law that lets parents participate in life-shaping decisions of their children. That law reflects the common sense principle that caring parents know best what their children need. But neither the lower courts nor state legislatures have been given the guidance necessary to address these issues. And that is unfortunate."

Assisted Suicide

On Oct. 5, the United States Supreme Court, under new Chief Justice John Roberts, heard oral arguments in *Gonzales v. Oregon*. The case pertains to the 2001 directive by U.S. Attorney General John Ashcroft that deliberately prescribing lethal overdoses for patients who wish to commit suicide is not to be considered a "legitimate medical purpose" for federally controlled drugs under the Controlled Substances Act. The State of Oregon sued against the so-called Ashcroft directive; its decision was based on the fact that Oregon is the only state with a law allowing physician-assisted suicide for the terminally ill. Moreover, all of the assisted suicides in Oregon used federally controlled drugs (barbiturates) to cause death. The Ashcroft directive replaced a 1998 decision by the then Clinton-run Justice Department and then U.S. Attorney General Janet Reno that removed penalties for assisting the suicides of certain patients. As a result, the State of Oregon effectively and unilaterally amended federal drug laws, thereby creating assisted suicide as what it termed "legitimate medical practice" within the confines of Oregon. Realistically, however, the Federal Controlled Substances Act (CSA) does not stipulate that an individual state may transform assisted suicide into a legitimate medical practice by dropping its own state penalties for a form of manslaughter. Moreover, the CSA was crafted in such a way so as to prevent the use of federally regulated drugs for lethal overdoses. The Act, further, contained provisions that ensured that narcotics and other dangerous drugs are to be used solely for a "legitimate medical purpose" and must not be used against the interests of "public health and safety."

RU-486

On May 11, 2006, the U.S. Food and Drug Administration (FDA) convened a public workshop in Atlanta in response to the increasing number of death among women after using the abortion drug RU-486, also known as Mifeprex. The gathering was co-sponsored by the Centers for Disease Control (CDC) and the National Institutes of Health.

Thus far, five American women have died from infections after undergoing RU-486 abortions, and another died from an undiagnosed ruptured ectopic pregnancy. In addition, over 800 other women have suffered serious or life-threatening adverse health effects, and women in Canada, Sweden and the United Kingdom have also died after taking RU-486.

In reply to the obvious dangers being posed to the health of women as a result of the use of RU-486, a bill has been introduced, called Holly's Law. The RU-486 Suspension and Review Act of 2005 (H.R.1079), "Holly's Law" is named after Holly Patterson, a young California woman who died from septic shock after undergoing an RU-486 abortion. The measure was introduced Mr. Roscoe Bartlett, a Maryland Republican, in Nov. 2003.

The bill provides for the temporary suspension of the Food and Drug Administration (FDA) approval of RU-486 and for a review by the Comptroller General limited to the agency's adherence to applicable regulations in its process of approving the drug. As the Secretariat for Pro-Life Activities of the USCCB noted in its support of the bill:

"More than 800 Adverse Event reports to FDA chronicle fatalities, near-fatalities, hospitalizations of up to a week, heart attacks, ruptured ectopic pregnancies, failed and incomplete abortions, serious-to-lethal infections, women who lost consciousness at home and required sutures to close head wounds, and hemorrhaging so extreme some women required replacement of half to all their blood volume. These cases may represent only a fraction of complications because the FDA doesn't mandate reporting by providers. Dr. Michael Greene calculates the risk of death from infection following RU-486 abortions as tenfold the mortality rate from all causes in surgical abortions in early pregnancy (*New England Journal of Medicine*, Dec. 2005)...

"Documents record 235 emergency surgeries due to this affliction. Women have had heart attacks, and others needed stitches to close head wounds sustained when they lost consciousness. Give up? This 'affliction' is RU-486, a little white pill that was supposed to make abortion safe, effective and available in doctors' offices all over the country — but it has failed, spectacularly, on all counts. "Dr. Michael Greene, while he defends RU-486 in a recent medical journal, also notes that it causes 10 times more deaths, from infection *alone*, than occur in early surgical abortions. He doesn't include deaths from ruptured ectopic pregnancy, hemorrhaging and heart attack. The risk may be far worse. His calculation is based on reported deaths from infection divided by total RU-486 abortions. But no one's sure of either number. The FDA estimates it is notified of only 1–10 percent of adverse events, so there may be unreported deaths and thousands more women injured. We don't even know how many RU-486 abortions have occurred; the distributor cites a figure that is three times the number of packets, regardless of whether they've been used."

UNITED STATES CONFERENCE OF CATHOLIC BISHOPS

MEETINGS OF U.S. BISHOPS 2005-2006

WASHINGTON, D.C., Nov. 14–17, 2005

The Bishops of the United States Catholic Conference gathered in Washington, D.C. for their Nov. 14–17 fall general meeting. The bishops departed from custom by holding most of their sessions in the form of executive sessions (meaning they were not open to the public).

Agenda

The bishops acted on the following issues:

By a vote of 237-4 they reaffirmed opposition to the use of the death penalty.

By a vote of 190-49 they approved new guidelines for the development of lay ecclesial ministry in U.S. parishes.

By a vote of 203-17 they adopted a revised Lectionary for Masses with Children; the lectionary was then sent to the Vatican for confirmation.

By a vote of 222-2 they approved a proposal to request Vatican approval regarding current dollar levels and financial controls in the disposal of Church property.

By a voice vote, they authorized the rewriting of the 1982 manual for preaching to reflect "current liturgical understanding and practice."

Approved May 22 as a Day of Remembrance and Prayer for Mariners and People of the Sea.

Approved a $131.2 million budget the USCCB for 2006; the budget could incur approximately $1.8 million in deficit spending. The bishops also approved efforts to curb spending until the bishops are able to complete plans for streamlining the conference.

In other matters, the bishops:

Unanimously accepted revised guidelines regarding bishops emeritus; the retired bishops have stated a preference not to be referred to as "retired."

Marked the 40th anniversary of the Second Vatican Council's declaration on non-Christian religions (*Nostra Aetate*) by celebrating Mass together at the Basilica of the National Shrine of the Immaculate Conception and attending a concert with members of other faiths.

Received a report from Cardinal William H. Keeler of Baltimore regarding the great risks to children from pornography because of technological advancements.

Gave their support for the canonization cause of Fray Bartolome de las Casas, a Spanish friar opposed the enslavement of native peoples by the Spanish Colonial government.

Received an update on the development of the Church in Africa.

Received an invitation from Cardinal Marc Ouellet of Quebec to attend the International Eucharistic Congress in Quebec in 2008.

Elected a new chairman of their Committee for the Protection of Children and Young People, seven other committee chairs, and two board members of the Catholic Legal Immigration Network; they also chose Msgr. David J. Malloy, USCCB associate general secretary since 2001, to succeed Msgr. William P. Fay as USCCB general secretary.

LOS ANGELES, June 15–17, 2006

The Bishops of the United States Catholic Conference gathered in Los Angeles for their June 15–17 meeting. The bishops held most of their sessions in the form of executive sessions (only the first day was open to media and observers). The primary topics of discussions at the meeting were: the approval of a new translation of the Order of Mass and plans to reorganize and downsize the existing structures of the U.S. Conference of Catholic Bishops.

Agenda

The bishops acted on the following issues:

Approved by a vote of 173–29 a new English translation of the Order of Mass and adopted by a vote of 184–8 several U.S. adaptations. (*See under* **Liturgy-Sacraments** *for details.*)

Approved a proposed plan to downsize the current committee structure of the USCCB.

Approved an extension of the annual national collection for retired religious until 2017.

Approved a 2007 assessment on dioceses, equal to the 2006 assessment, to help fund USCCB operations.

Viewed a new 18-minute DVD on priests and priestly vocations, "Fishers of Men." Heard a report on the work of Catholic Relief Services.

Heard a report on post-hurricane relief in the South.

Heard a report on the on-going issue of Catholics in political life.

U.S. BISHOPS' LABOR DAY STATEMENT

The following letter, "A Labor Day Reflection on Immigration and Work," was issued on Sept. 4, 2006, by Most Rev. Nicholas DiMarzio, Ph.D., D.D., Bishop of Brooklyn and chairman of the Domestic Policy Committee of the United States Conference of Catholic Bishops:

Each year as summer draws to a close many of us gather on Labor Day with family, friends and neighbors to take a rest from our work. As a nation, we set this day aside to pay tribute to the workers who create our nation's wealth and strength. Our Catholic faith reminds us of the inherent dignity and value of our work, through which, no matter how large or small the task, we participate in God's creation, support our families, and contribute to the common good. Each Labor Day we celebrate and share our values on work and workers and remember the importance and the contributions of the labor movement to society.

Labor Day 2006 is a time when our nation and our Church are struggling with the difficult and important issue of immigration. Men, women and children come here seeking work and a better life for their families, hoping to be welcomed as neighbors and contributors to our communities. They come as skilled and unskilled workers, agricultural laborers, or to study or join family already here. They come, in part, because U.S. employers need their labor and our economy depends upon them. Many come through official legal channels. Many others do not.

These realities and our inadequate immigration system have led to a necessary, but sadly divisive, debate on how our nation should respond. Unfortunately, the debate sometimes has not brought out the best in us. People of good will can and do disagree over how to improve our immigration laws. Regrettably, this disagreement sometimes disintegrates into polarization, partisanship and now paralysis. We must get beyond the anger and fear, stereotypes and slogans that too often dominate this essential discussion.

Immigration is not a new reality. We are a nation and a Church built by immigrants. However, immigration raises continuing questions with new urgency. Who is an American? Who is our "neighbor?" What are the impacts of immigration on our national economy? How much is too much—or not enough—immigration? How are individual workers and families affected-both native born workers and those newly arrived? How are we to address the reality that over 10 million people are here without legal documentation, but, with few exceptions, leading lives that share our values of work, family and community? How can we stand with some American workers who feel left behind or pushed aside? How are we to protect our borders against those who would do us harm?

We all bring our own perspectives, biases, even prejudices to this discussion. I hope as we approach Labor Day, each of us might try to see these difficult questions through the eyes and experiences of someone very different from ourselves.

. . . I believe we must and we can find reasonable and responsible ways to welcome those seeking a new life and opportunity. I believe we can help newcomers without legal status to come out from the shadows and contribute more fully to our communities. When we do this, I believe we can also increase the security of our nation and the vitality of our Church.

The Catholic Church has a long history of involvement with immigrants. . . . The Church's mission in assisting and standing with immigrants flows from our belief that every person is created in God's image. Indeed, in His own life and work, Jesus called upon us to "welcome the stranger," for "what you do for the least of my brethren, you do unto me" (Mt cf. 25:35, 40). This is why the Catholic community has a broad and growing Catholic Campaign for Immigration Reform that we hope will contribute to a constructive debate on immigration. (*www.justiceforimmigrants.org*)

Immigration touches many aspects of national life, but in this Labor Day statement, I want to focus on those aspects that touch on work. The challenge of immigration today is not just at the borders, but in our labor markets. Right now, more than 12 percent of U.S. residents and some 15 percent of workers were born in another country, up from about five percent in 1960. Recent census data reveals that many newcomers are settling in parts of the country that until recently saw little immigrant activity. . . . And local communities can feel overwhelmed by the growing presence of people in their midst with different languages and different ways.

The simple fact is many parts of our nation's economy have become dependent on immigrant workers. Agriculture relies heavily on seasonal workers to pick our crops. . . . Immigrant workers are increasingly moving from fields to factories: working in meat and poultry processing plants, and large hog and cattle operations. . . . Our country's hotel and restaurant industries to a great extent rely on foreign born workers; they bus the tables, make the beds and clean up after us. The fact is we have come to depend more and more on international migration to fill our workforce. Without them our economy would have huge gaps.

Our immigration laws have failed to keep up with the demand for labor, so the need is filled by those who come into the country without legal sanction. Over 80 percent of those who have come here illegally are working part-time or full-time, contributing to the common good of our country through the work they perform and the taxes they pay.

. . . According to a study by the Pew Hispanic Center, it appears that overall increases in immigration do not result in increases in unemployment among native born workers.

What draws so many to our country? Many immigrants come because they want to live out the values we celebrate this Labor Day—hard work, providing a decent living for one's family, contributing to the community, a life of dignity and opportunity gained through hard work.

These are also values of our faith. Catholic teaching on work insists that human beings share in God's creation through their work. In Catholic social teaching, work is for the person, not the person for work. Work is the ordinary means by which individuals support themselves and their families and contribute to the common good. Catholic teaching supports the right of workers to decent and fair wages, health care, and time off. This is why our bishops' Conference has traditionally supported the minimum wage and why we urge, once again, that our leaders move beyond their current partisan and ideological conflicts to enact a long over due increase in the minimum wage. Workers, also have a right to organize to protect their rights, to have a voice in the workplace and to be represented by trade unions. These basic human and economic rights are not invalidated or relinquished when one crosses a border.

The increasing international movement of goods, services, money, and people require new economic norms, ethical restraints and wise laws to regulate and address their moral and human dimensions. We need to recognize that growing globalization brings with it benefits, lost jobs, falling living standards, and inhumane working conditions. A role of the Church, as a universal community of faith and an international institution, is to raise up the dignity and value of workers. That is why the U.S. bishops support policies that will help people to remain in their own countries, as well as policies to address the impact of immigration in our own nation.

Men and women come to America because they cannot find in their own countries the economic, political and social conditions they need to support their families, live in dignity and achieve a decent life. The bishops and others are working to develop and advocate policies on global trade, international aid and debt relief that will reduce poverty and empower the poor, foster long-term economic development, protect human dignity in underdeveloped nations, and includes effective protections for workers in the U.S. and other countries. People should be able to provide a decent life for their families in their own countries.

Still, people come from all over the world seeking opportu-nity in the United States, and many come outside of the structures of our immigration laws. While the Church does not condone law-breaking, their presence here is a reality. . . . That is why a comprehensive approach to immigration reform must include a pathway to earned legalization for the millions of those working in our country without legal status. Justice and prudence demand that we treat them with dignity and find a reasonable way for their contributions and presence to be recognized within the law.

Our Conference has also come to support a carefully designed and closely monitored, temporary worker program that ensures workers are not exploited and protects the rights of both foreign-born and U.S. workers. Everyone working in our country should have a safe workplace, wages and employment benefits to support their families, and the protection of our labor laws, including the right to organize and have a voice. Free trade unions have long played an essential and important role in protecting workers' dignity and rights. We welcome the newly announced AFL-CIO partnership with day laborers. The labor movement's effort to bring order and recognition to street corners inhabited by men, mostly immigrants, seeking a day's work is an important step forward.

For the Catholic Church, immigration is not a political issue, but a fundamental human and moral issue. We bring to this discussion our faith, our moral principles and our long experience. Through the decades, immigrants have built our communities of faith and they are still bringing new life to our church. Immigrants are not numbers for us. They are our brothers and sisters; they are our "neighbors."

In his powerful encyclical *Deus Caritas Est*, Pope Benedict XVI reminds us that Jesus calls us to expand who we see as our neighbor. The Holy Father, citing the parable of the Good Samaritan, says that "neighbor" can no longer be limited to the closely-knit community of a single country or people. This limit is now abolished. Anyone who needs me, and whom I can help, is my neighbor. . . . 'As you did it to one of the least of these my brethren, you did it to me' (Mt 25:40). Love of God and love of neighbor have become one: in the least of the brethren we find Jesus himself, and in Jesus we find God. (para. 15).

Who is our neighbor is not dependent on where they were born or what documents they possess.

The immigration debate this Labor Day challenges us to consider again who we are as a nation, how our economy treats all workers, how we welcome the "strangers" among us. As Catholics, we should join this discussion and bring our belief in the sacredness of human life, the inherent dignity of the human person and the value of work. We cannot simply retreat behind walls at our borders or in our hearts and minds. As believers, we are called to build bridges between the native born and newcomer, between legitimate concerns about security and national traditions of welcome, from fear and frustration to hope and action for a better tomorrow.

Today, and years ago when my grandparents came from Italy, immigration is a human story of people yearning for work and longing for freedom. Immigrants come seeking to provide a decent living for their families, dreaming of a better life for their children, hoping to make a contribution. These are the deeply held American values we celebrate on Labor Day. The principles of our faith and the traditions of our nation call us to welcome those who share these values and hopes. They add vitality and energy, diversity and hope to our communities and our country. Together, we can build a better nation, a stronger economy and a more faithful Church.

Doctrine of the Catholic Church

THE CATECHISM OF THE CATHOLIC CHURCH

By Russell Shaw

"The *Catechism of the Catholic Church* . . . is a statement of the Church's faith and of Catholic doctrine, attested to or illumined by Sacred Scripture, the Apostolic Tradition, and the Church's Magisterium. I declare it to be a sure norm for teaching the faith and thus a valid and legitimate instrument for ecclesial communion."

Thus Pope John Paul II in the Apostolic Constitution *Fidei Depositum* ("The Deposit of Faith") formally presented the first official catechism or compendium of doctrine for the universal Church to have been published since the 16th century.

Fidei Depositum is dated Oct. 11, 1992, the 30th anniversary of the opening of the Second Vatican Council (1962-65), and that date is significant. The predecessor of the *Catechism of the Catholic Church* is the Roman Catechism or Catechism of the Council of Trent, which was published by Pope St. Pius V in 1566 following the great reforming council held from 1545 to 1563. As the Roman Catechism sets forth the doctrine of the Church in light of the Council of Trent, so the *Catechism of the Catholic Church* sets forth the Church's teaching against the background of Vatican Council II.

History of the Catechism

In development since 1986, the definitive text of the *Catechism of the Catholic Church* was officially approved by Pope John Paul on June 25, 1992, with Dec. 8 the date of formal promulgation.

Nine separate drafts of the *Catechism* were prepared. The document was written in French. In Nov. 1989, the commission of cardinals sent a draft text to all the bishops of the world asking for their comments and suggestions. Although this consultation produced a reaction generally favorable to the text, more than 24,000 individual amendments were submitted by the bishops, and these were reviewed by the commission, and helped to shape the further revision of the document.

The pope in *Fidei Depositum* described the *Catechism* as "a sure and authentic reference text" both for the teaching of Catholic doctrine and particularly for the preparation of local catechisms; he said the *Catechism* was presented to "all the Church's pastors and the Christian faithful" with these ends in view. Other purposes mentioned included helping Catholics to deepen their knowledge of the faith, supporting ecumenical efforts by "showing carefully the content and wondrous harmony of the Catholic faith," and providing authoritative answers to anyone who wishes to know "what the Catholic Church believes."

Structure and Contents of the Catechism

The *Catechism* adopts the four-fold division of the *Roman Catechism*. The four parts or "pillars" deal with the Creed; the Sacred Liturgy, with special emphasis on the sacraments; the Christian way of life, analyzed according to the Ten Commandments; and prayer, considered in the framework of the petitions of the Our Father.

Describing this organizational scheme, Pope John Paul said: "The four parts are related one to another: the Christian mystery is the object of faith (first part); it is celebrated and communicated in liturgical actions (second part); it is present to enlighten and sustain the children of God in their actions (third part); it is the basis of our prayer, the privileged expression of which is the Our Father, and it represents the object of our supplication, our praise and our intercession (fourth part)."

The Pope also stressed the Christocentric nature of Christian faith as it is presented in the *Catechism*. "In reading the *Catechism of the Catholic Church* we can perceive the wonderful unity of the mystery of God, his saving will, as well as the central place of Jesus Christ, the only-begotten Son of God, sent by the Father, made man in the womb of the Blessed Virgin Mary by the power of the Holy Spirit, to be our Savior. Having died and risen, Christ is always present in his Church, especially in the sacraments; he is the source of our faith, the model of Christian conduct, and the Teacher of our prayer."

The text of the *Catechism of the Catholic Church*, with extensive cross-references and sectional summaries, consists of 2,865 numbered paragraphs. Passages in large print set out its more substantive contents, while passages in small print provide background information and explanations; there are numerous cross-references in the margins directing readers to other passages that treat the same theme or related themes. Among the features of the *Catechism* are the "In Brief" sections found throughout, which sum up the teaching of the preceding unit.

Outline of the Catechism

Prologue (1-25). The nature of catechesis is described, along with the aim of the present *Catechism* and its intended readership, its structure, its use, and the desirability of adaptations for different cultures, age groups, etc.

Part One: The Profession of Faith (26-1065)

Section One discusses the nature of faith. "Faith is man's response to God, who reveals himself and gives himself to man, at the same time bringing man a super-abundant light as he searches for the ultimate meaning of his life. Thus we shall consider first that search (Chapter One), then the divine Revelation by which God comes to meet man (Chapter Two), and finally the response of faith (Chapter Three)" (26). The topics discussed include knowledge of God; Divine Revelation and its transmission; Sacred Scripture; and faith as the human response to God. "We do not believe in formulas, but in those realities they express, which faith allows us to touch. . . . All the same, we do approach these realities with the help of formulations of the faith which permit us to express the faith and to hand it on, to celebrate it in community, to assimilate and live on it more and more" (170).

Section Two deals with the profession of Christian faith, with the treatment organized according to the articles of the Creed. The Creed used is the Apostles' Creed; its "great authority," says the *Catechism*, quoting St. Ambrose, arises from its being "the Creed of the Roman Church, the See of Peter, the first of the apostles" (194). Among the doctrines covered in the three chapters of this section are the Trinity, creation, the angels, the creation of man, original sin, the Incarnation, the virgin birth, redemption, the Resurrection of Christ, the work of the Holy Spirit, the Church, the hierarchical constitution of the Church, the communion of saints, the Virgin Mary as Mother of Christ and Mother of the Church, the resurrection of the dead, judgment, heaven, and hell. "[T]he Creed's final 'Amen' repeats and confirms its first words: 'I believe.' To believe is to say 'Amen' to God's words, promises and commandments; to entrust oneself completely to him who is the 'Amen' of infinite love and perfect faithfulness. The Christian's everyday life will then be the 'Amen' to the 'I believe' of our baptismal profession of faith" (1064).

Part Two: The Celebration of the Christian Mystery (1066-1690)

Section One considers the sacramental economy. It explains that in this present "age of the Church," begun on Pentecost, "Christ now lives and acts in his Church, in a new way appropriate to this new age. He acts through the sacraments in what the common Tradition of the East and the West calls 'the sacramental economy' . . . the communication (or 'dispensation') of the fruits of Christ's Paschal Mystery in the celebration of the Church's 'sacramental' liturgy" (1076). Topics treated here are the Paschal Mystery and its sacramental celebration.

Section Two covers the seven sacraments of the Church. "Christ instituted the sacraments of the new law. . . . The seven sacraments touch all the stages and all the important moments of Christian life: they give birth and increase, healing and mission to the Christian's life of faith. There is thus a certain resemblance between the stages of natural life and the stages of the spiritual life" (1210). The presentation is organized in four chapters. These are: the sacraments of Christian initiation (Baptism, Confirmation, the Eucharist) in chapter one; the sacraments of healing (Penance and Reconciliation, the Anointing of the Sick) in chapter two; the "sacraments at the service of communion" (Holy Orders and Matrimony) in chapter three; and sacramentals and Christian funerals in chapter four.

Part Three: Life in Christ (1691-2557)

Section One is entitled "Man's Vocation: Life in the Spirit." Its three chapters discuss the dignity of the human person, the human community, and "God's Salvation: Law and Grace" (the moral law, grace and justification, the Church as teacher of moral truth). "Catechesis has to reveal in all clarity the joy and the demands of the way of Christ. . . . The first and last point of reference of this catechesis will always be Jesus Christ himself, who is 'they way, and the truth, and the life' " (1697-1698).

Section Two reflects on the contents of Christian moral life. The treatment is organized according to the Ten Commandments, with a chapter devoted to each commandment and its concrete applications. While the commandments admit of what is traditionally called light matter (venial sin), nevertheless, the text says: "Since they express man's fundamental duties toward God and toward his neighbor, the Ten Commandments reveal, in their primordial content, grave obligations. They are fundamentally immutable, and they oblige always and everywhere. No one can dispense from them. The Ten Commandments are engraved by God in the human heart" (2072).

Part Four: Christian Prayer (2558-2865)

Section One considers prayer in Christian life, underlining the relationship of this topic to the rest of the Catechism: "The Church professes this mystery [of faith] in the Apostles' Creed (Part One) and celebrates it in the sacramental liturgy (Part Two), so that the life of the faithful may be conformed to Christ in the Holy Spirit to the glory of God the Father (Part Three). This mystery, then, requires that the faithful believe in it, that they celebrate it, and that they live from it in a vital and personal relationship with the living and true God. This relationship is prayer" (2558). The section then discusses the "revelation of prayer" in the Old Testament and now in the age of the Church, the tradition of prayer, and the life of prayer (kinds of prayer, problems and perseverance in prayer).

Section Two presents an extended reflection on the Our Father, considered as the model of prayer. Quoting Tertullian, the *Catechism* says: "The Lord's Prayer 'is truly the summary of the whole Gospel.' Since the Lord . . . after handing over the practice of prayer, said elsewhere, 'Ask and you will receive,' and since everyone has petitions which are peculiar to his circumstances, the regular and appropriate prayer [the Lord's Prayer] is said first, as the foundation of further desires" (2761).

Reception of the Catechism

Following the publication of the Catechism of the Catholic Church, Pope John Paul established an Interdicasterial Commission for the Catechism, under the chairmanship of Cardinal Ratzinger, responsible for overseeing translations of the volume and reviewing and approving suggested changes in the text. The commission approved the English translation of the Catechism in Feb. 1994, and it was published on June 22 of that year — in the United States, under the auspices of the National Conference of Catholic Bishops (now the United States Conference of Catholic Bishops).

Pope John Paul presented the *editio typica* or normative Latin version of the *Catechism* in a formal ceremony on Sept. 8, 1997.

The following day, Cardinal Ratzinger presented the editio typica at a Vatican news conference. At the same time, he also introduced more than a hundred changes that had been approved for incorporation into the text. Most of the changes were of a minor, editorial nature. The most important was in paragraphs 2265-2267 of the Catechism, where the treatment of capital punishment had been strengthened to reflect the

discussion of the same topic in Pope John Paul's 1995 encyclical letter Evangelium Vitae ("The Gospel of Life").

In the United States, the National Conference of Catholic Bishops in 1994 established an Ad Hoc Committee to Oversee the Use of the Catechism. It has an office and staff at NCCB headquarters in Washington, DC. The committee reviews and approves materials that seek to make substantial direct use of the text of the *Catechism of the Catholic Church*, and also reviews catechetical series for their conformity with the *Catechism*. In addition, the committee was mandated to conduct a feasibility study of a national catechism or catechetical series for the United States.

DOGMATIC CONSTITUTION ON THE CHURCH — *LUMEN GENTIUM*

Following are excerpts from the first two chapters of the "Dogmatic Constitution on the Church" (*Lumen Gentium*) promulgated by the Second Vatican Council. They describe the relation of the Catholic Church to the Kingdom of God, the nature and foundation of the Church, the People of God, the necessity of membership and participation in the Church for salvation. Additional subjects in the constitution are treated in other Almanac entries.

I. MYSTERY OF THE CHURCH

By her relationship with Christ, the Church is a kind of sacrament or sign of intimate union with God, and of the unity of all mankind (No. 1).

He (the eternal Father) planned to assemble in the holy Church all those who would believe in Christ. Already from the beginning of the world the foreshadowing of the Church took place. She was prepared for in a remarkable way throughout the history of the people of Israel and by means of the Old Covenant. Established in the present era of time, the Church was made manifest by the outpouring of the Spirit. At the end of time she will achieve her glorious fulfillment. Then all just men from the time of Adam, "from Abel, the just one, to the last of the elect," will be gathered together with the Father in the universal Church (No. 2).

When the work which the Father had given the Son to do on earth (cf. Jn 17:4) was accomplished, the Holy Spirit was sent on the day of Pentecost in order that he might forever sanctify the Church, and thus all believers would have access to the Father through Christ in the one Spirit (cf. Eph 2:18).

The Spirit dwells in the Church and in the hearts of the faithful as in a temple (cf. 1 Cor 3:16; 6:19).... The Spirit guides the Church into the fullness of truth (cf. Jn 16:13) and gives her a unity of fellowship and service. He furnishes and directs her with various gifts, both hierarchical and charismatic, and adorns her with the fruits of His grace (cf. Eph 4:11-12; 1 Cor 12:4; Gal 5:22). By the power of the Gospel he makes the Church grow, perpetually renews her, and leads her to perfect union with her Spouse (No. 4).

Foundation of the Church

The mystery of the holy Church is manifest in her very foundation, for the Lord Jesus inaugurated her by preaching the Good News, that is, the coming of God's Kingdom, which, for centuries had been promised in the Scriptures.... In Christ's word, in his works, and in his presence this Kingdom reveals itself to men.

The miracles of Jesus also confirm that the Kingdom has already arrived on earth.

Before all things, however, the Kingdom is clearly visible in the very Person of Christ, Son of God and Son of Man.

When Jesus rose up again after suffering death on the cross for mankind, he manifested that he had been appointed Lord, Messiah, and Priest forever (cf. Acts 2:36; Heb 5:6; 7:17-21), and he poured out on his disciples the Spirit promised by the Father (cf. Acts 2:33). The Church, consequently, equipped with the gifts of her Founder and faithfully guarding his precepts receives the mission to proclaim and to establish among all peoples the Kingdom of Christ and of God. She becomes on earth the initial budding forth of that Kingdom. While she slowly grows, the Church strains toward the consummation of the Kingdom and, with all her strength, hopes and desires to be united in glory with her King (No. 5).

Figures of the Church

In the Old Testament the revelation of the Kingdom had often been conveyed by figures of speech. In the same way the inner nature of the Church was now to be made known to us through various images.

The Church is a sheepfold... a flock... a tract of land to be cultivated, the field of God... his choice vineyard... the true vine is Christ... the edifice of God... the house of God... the holy temple (whose members are) living stones... this holy city... a bride... our Mother... the spotless spouse of the spotless Lamb... an exile (No. 6).

In the human nature which he united to himself, the Son of God redeemed man and transformed him into a new creation (cf. Gal 6:15; 2 Cor 5:17) by overcoming death through his own death and resurrection. By communicating his Spirit to his brothers, called together from all peoples, Christ made them mystically into his own body.

In that body, the life of Christ is poured into the believers, who, through the sacraments, are united in a hidden and real way to Christ who suffered and was glorified. Through baptism we are formed in the likeness of Christ.

Truly partaking of the body of the Lord in the breaking of the eucharistic bread, we are taken up into communion with him and with one another (No. 7).

One Body in Christ

As all the members of the human body, though they are many, form one body, so also are the faithful in Christ (cf. 1 Cor 12:12). Also, in the building up of Christ's body there is a flourishing variety of members and functions. There is only one Spirit who distributes his different gifts for the welfare of the Church (cf. 1 Cor 12:1-11). Among these gifts stands out the grace given to the apostles. To their authority, the Spirit himself subjected even those who were endowed with charisms (cf. 1 Cor 14). The head of this body is Christ (No. 7).

Mystical Body of Christ

Christ, the one Mediator, established and ceaselessly sustains here on earth his holy Church, the community of faith, hope, and charity, as a visible structure. Through her he communicates truth and grace to all. But the society furnished with hierarchical agencies and the Mystical Body of Christ are not to be considered as two realities, nor are the visible assembly and the spiritual community, nor the earthly Church and the Church enriched with heavenly things. Rather they form one interlocked reality which is comprised of a divine and a human element. For this reason, this reality is compared to the mystery of the incarnate Word. Just as the assumed nature inseparably united to the divine Word serves him as a living instrument of salvation, so, in a similar way, does the communal structure of the Church serve Christ's Spirit, who vivifies it by way of building up the body (cf. Eph 4:16).

This is the unique Church of Christ which in the Creed we avow as one, holy, catholic, and apostolic. After his Resurrection our Savior handed her over to Peter to be shepherded (Jn 21:17), commissioning him and the other apostles to propagate and govern her (cf. Mt 28:18, ff.). Her he erected for all ages as "the pillar and mainstay of the truth" (1 Tm 3:15). This Church, constituted and organized in the world as a society, subsists in the Catholic Church, which is governed by the successor of Peter and by the bishops in union with that successor, although many elements of sanctification and of truth can be found outside of her visible structure. These elements, however, as gifts properly belonging to the Church of Christ, possess an inner dynamism toward Catholic unity.

The Church, embracing sinners in her bosom, is at the same time holy and always in need of being purified, and incessantly pursues the path of penance and renewal.

The Church, "like a pilgrim in a foreign land, presses forward, announcing the cross and death of the Lord until he comes" (cf. 1 Cor 11:26) (No. 8).

II. THE PEOPLE OF GOD

At all times and among every people, God has given welcome to whosoever fears him and does what is right (cf. Acts 10:35). It has pleased God, however, to make men holy and save them not merely as individuals without any mutual bonds, but by making them into a single people, a people which acknowledges him in truth and serves him in holiness. He therefore chose the race of Israel as a people unto himself. With it he set up a covenant. Step by step he taught this people by manifesting in its history both himself and the decree of his will, and by making it holy unto himself. All these things, however, were done by way of preparation and as a figure of that new and perfect covenant which was to be ratified in Christ.

Christ instituted this New Covenant, that is to say, the New Testament, in his blood (cf. 1 Cor 11:25), by calling together a people made up of Jew and Gentile, making them one, not according to the flesh but in the Spirit.

This was to be the new People of God... reborn... through the Word of the living God (cf. 1 Pt 1:23). from water and the Holy Spirit (cf. Jn 3:5-6)... "a chosen race, a royal priesthood, a holy nation, a purchased people. You who in times past were not a people, but are now the People of God" (1 Pt 2:9-10).

That messianic people has for its head Christ. Its law is the new commandment to love as Christ loved us (cf. Jn 13:34). Its goal is the Kingdom of God, which has been begun by God himself on earth, and which is to be further extended until it is brought to perfection by him at the end of time.

This messianic people, although it does not actually include all men, and may more than once look like a small flock, is nonetheless a lasting and sure seed of unity, hope, and salvation for the whole human race. Established by Christ as a fellowship of life, charity, and truth, it is also used by him as an instrument for the redemption of all, and is sent forth into the whole world as the light of the world and the salt of the earth (cf. Mt 5:13-16).

Israel according to the flesh... was already called the Church of God (Neh 13:1; cf. Nm. 20:4; Dt. 23:1, ff.). Likewise the new Israel... is also called the Church of Christ (cf. Mt 16:18). For he has bought it for himself with his blood (cf. Acts 20:28), has filled it with his Spirit, and provided it with those means which befit it as a visible and social unity. God has gathered together as one all those who in faith look upon Jesus as the author of salvation and the source of unity and peace, and has established them as the Church, that for each and all she may be the visible sacrament of this saving unity (No. 9).

Priesthood

The baptized, by regeneration and the anointing of the Holy Spirit, are consecrated into a holy priesthood. [All members of the Church participate in the priesthood of Christ, through the common priesthood of the faithful. (*See* **Priesthood of the Laity**.)]

Though they differ from one another in essence and not only in degree, the common priesthood of the faithful and the ministerial or hierarchical priesthood are nonetheless interrelated. Each of them in its own special way is a participation in the one priesthood of Christ (No. 10).

It is through the sacraments and the exercise of the virtues that the sacred nature and organic structure of the priestly community is brought into operation (No. 11). (*See* **Role of the Sacraments**.)

Prophetic Office

The holy People of God shares also in Christ's prophetic office. It spreads abroad a living witness to him, especially by means of a life of faith and charity and by offering to God a sacrifice of praise.... The body of the faithful as a whole, anointed as they are by the Holy One (cf. Jn 2:20, 27), cannot err in matters of belief. Thanks to a supernatural sense of faith which characterizes the People as a whole, it manifests this unerring quality when, "from the bishops down to the last member of the laity," it shows universal agreement in matters of faith and morals.

God's People accepts not the word of men but the very Word of God (cf. 1 Thes 2:13). It clings without fail to the faith once delivered to the saints (cf. Jude 3), penetrates it more deeply by accurate insights, and applies it more thoroughly to life. All this it does under the lead of a sacred teaching authority to which it loyally defers.

It is not only through the sacraments and Church ministries that the same Holy Spirit sanctifies and leads the People of God.... He distributes special graces among the faithful of every rank. By these gifts he makes them fit and ready to undertake the various tasks or offices advantageous for the renewal and upbuilding of the Church. These charismatic gifts ... are to be received with thanksgiving and consolation, for they are exceedingly suitable and useful for the needs of the Church.

Judgment as to their genuineness and proper use belongs to those who preside over the Church, and to whose special competence it belongs... to test all things and hold fast to that which is good (cf. 1 Thes 5:12; 19-21) (No. 12).

All Are Called

All men are called to belong to the new People of God. Wherefore this People, while remaining one and unique, is to be spread throughout the whole world and must exist in all ages, so that the purpose of God's will may be fulfilled. In the beginning God made human nature one. After his children were scattered, he decreed that they should at length be united again (cf. Jn 11:52). It was for this reason that God sent his Son.... that he might be Teacher, King, and Priest of all, the Head of the new and universal People of the sons of God. For this God finally sent his Son's Spirit as Lord and Lifegiver. He it is who, on behalf of the whole Church and each and every one of those who believe, is the principle of their coming together and remaining together in the teaching of the apostles and in fellowship, in the breaking of bread and in prayers (cf. Acts 2:42) (No. 13).

One People of God

It follows that among all the nations of earth there is but one People of God, which takes its citizens from every race, making them citizens of a Kingdom which is of a heavenly and not an earthly nature. For all the faithful scattered throughout the world are in communion with each other in the Holy Spirit.... the Church or People of God foster(s) and take(s) to herself, insofar as they are good, the ability, resources and customs of each people. Taking them to herself, she purifies, strengthens, and ennobles them.... This characteristic of universality which adorns the People of God is a gift from the Lord himself. By reason of it, the Catholic Church strives energetically and constantly to bring all humanity with all its riches back to Christ its Head in the unity of his Spirit.

In virtue of this catholicity each individual part of the Church contributes through its special gifts to the good of the other parts and of the whole Church. Thus through the common sharing of gifts. The whole and each of the parts receive increase.

All men are called to be part of this catholic unity of the People of God. And there belong to it or are related to it in various ways, the Catholic faithful as well as all who believe in Christ, and indeed the whole of mankind. For all men are called to salvation by the grace of God (No. 13).

The Catholic Church

This sacred Synod turns its attention first to the Catholic faithful. Basing itself upon sacred Scripture and tradition, it teaches that the Church is necessary for salvation. For Christ, made present to us in his Body, which is the Church, is the one Mediator and the unique Way of salvation. In explicit terms he himself affirmed the necessity of faith and baptism (cf. Mk 16:16; Jn 3:5) and thereby affirmed also the necessity of the Church, for through baptism as through a door men enter the Church. Whosoever, therefore, knowing that the Catholic Church was made necessary by God through Jesus Christ, would refuse to enter her or to remain in her could not be saved.

They are fully incorporated into the society of the Church who, possessing the Spirit of Christ, accept her entire system and all the means of salvation given to her, and through union with her visible structure are joined to Christ, who rules her through the Supreme Pontiff and the bishops. This joining is effected by the bonds of professed faith, of the sacraments, of ecclesiastical government, and of communion. He is not saved, however, who, though he is part of the body of the Church, does not persevere in charity. He remains indeed in the bosom of the Church, but only in a "bodily" manner and not "in his heart."

Catechumens who, moved by the Holy Spirit, seek with explicit intention to be incorporated into the Church, are by that very intention joined to her. Mother Church already embraces them as her own (No. 14).

Other Christians, The Unbaptized

The Church recognizes that in many ways she is linked with those who, being baptized, are honored with the name of Christian, though they do not profess the faith in its entirety or do not preserve unity of communion with the successor of Peter.

We can say that in some real way they are joined with us in the Holy Spirit, for to them also he gives his gifts and graces, and is thereby operative among them with his sanctifying power (No. 15).

Finally, those who have not yet received the Gospel are related in various ways to the People of God. In the first place there is the people to whom the covenants and the promises were given and from whom Christ was born according to the flesh (cf. Rom 9:4-5). On account of their fathers, this people remains most dear to God, for God does not repent of the gifts he makes nor of the calls he issues (cf. Rom 11:28-29).

But the plan of salvation also includes those who acknowledge the Creator. In the first place among these are the Moslems. Nor is God himself far distant from those who in shadows and images seek the unknown God.

Those also can attain to everlasting salvation who through no fault of their own do not know the Gospel of Christ or his Church, yet sincerely seek God and, moved by grace, strive by their deeds to do his will as it is known to them through the dictates of conscience. Nor does divine Providence deny the help necessary for salvation to those who, without blame on their part, have not yet arrived at an explicit knowledge of God, but who strive to live a good life, thanks to his grace. Whatever goodness or truth is found among them is looked upon by the Church as a preparation for the Gospel. She regards such qualities as given by him who enlightens all men so that they may finally have life. (No. l6).

THE POPE, TEACHING AUTHORITY, COLLEGIALITY

The Roman Pontiff—the successor of St. Peter as the bishop of Rome and head of the Church on earth —has full and supreme authority over the universal Church in matters pertaining to faith and morals (teaching authority), discipline and government (jurisdictional authority).

The primacy of the pope is real and supreme power. It is not merely a prerogative of honor—that is, of his being regarded as the first among equals. Neither does primacy imply that the pope is just the presiding officer of the collective body of bishops. The pope is the head of the Church.

Catholic belief in the primacy of the pope was stated in detail in the dogmatic constitution on the Church, *Pastor Aeternus*, approved in 1870 by the fourth session of the First Vatican Council. Some elaboration of the doctrine was made in the Dogmatic Constitution on the Church which was approved and promulgated by the Second Vatican Council Nov. 21, 1964. The entire body of teaching on the subject is based on Scripture and tradition and the centuries-long experience of the Church.

Infallibility

The essential points of doctrine concerning infallibility in the Church and the infallibility of the pope were stated by the Second Vatican Council in the Dogmatic Constitution on the Church, as follows:

"This infallibility with which the divine Redeemer willed his Church to be endowed in defining a doctrine of faith and morals extends as far as extends the deposit of divine revelation, which must be religiously guarded and faithfully expounded. This is the infallibility which the Roman Pontiff, the head of the college of bishops, enjoys in virtue of his office, when, as the supreme shepherd and teacher of all the faithful who confirms his brethren in their faith (cf. Lk 22:32), he proclaims by a definitive act some doctrine of faith or morals. Therefore his definitions, of themselves, are not from the consent of the Church, are justly styled irreformable, for they are pronounced with the assistance of the Holy Spirit, an assistance promised to him in blessed Peter. Therefore they need no approval of others, nor do they allow an appeal to any other judgment. For then the Roman Pontiff is not pronouncing judgment as a private person. Rather, as the supreme teacher of the universal Church, as one in whom the charism of the infallibility of the Church herself is individually present, he is expounding or defending a doctrine of Catholic faith.

"The infallibility promised to the Church resides also in the body of bishops when that body exercises supreme teaching authority with the successor of Peter. To the resultant definitions the assent of the Church can never be wanting, on account of the activity of that same Holy Spirit, whereby the whole flock of Christ is preserved and progresses in unity of faith.

"But when either the Roman Pontiff or the body of bishops together with him defines a judgment, they pronounce it in accord with revelation itself. All are obliged to maintain and be ruled by this revelation, which, as written or preserved by tradition, is transmitted in its entirety through the legitimate succession of bishops and especially through the care of the Roman Pontiff himself.

"Under the guiding light of the Spirit of truth, revelation is thus religiously preserved and faithfully expounded in the Church. The Roman Pontiff and the bishops, in view of their office and of the importance of the matter, strive painstakingly and by appropriate means to inquire properly into that revelation and to give apt expression to its contents. But they do not allow that there could be any new public revelation pertaining to the divine deposit of faith" (No. 25).

Authentic Teaching

The pope rarely speaks *ex cathedra*—that is, "from the chair" of St. Peter—for the purpose of making an infallible pronouncement. More often and in various ways he states authentic teaching in line with Scripture, tradition, the living experience of the Church, and the whole analogy of faith. Of such teaching, the Second Vatican Council said in its Dogmatic Constitution on the Church (No. 25):

"Religious submission of will and of mind must be shown in a special way to the authentic teaching authority of the Roman Pontiff, even when he is not speaking *ex cathedra*. That is, it must be shown in such a way that his supreme magisterium is acknowledged with reverence, the judgments made by him are sincerely adhered to, according to his manifest mind and will. His mind and will in the matter may be known chiefly either from the character of the documents, from his frequent repetition of the same doctrine, or from his manner of speaking."

Bishops "are authentic teachers, that is, teachers endowed with the authority of Christ, who preach to the people committed to them the faith they must believe and put into practice. By the light of the Holy Spirit they make that faith clear, bringing forth from the treasury of revelation new things and old (cf. Mt 13:52), making faith bear fruit and vigilantly warding off any errors which threaten their flock (cf. 2 Tm 4:1-4).

"Bishops, teaching in communion with the Roman Pontiff, are to be respected by all as witnesses to divine and Catholic truth. In matters of faith and morals, the bishops speak in the name of Christ and the faithful are to accept their teaching and adhere to it with a religious assent of soul."

Magisterium—Teaching Authority

Responsibility for teaching doctrine and judging orthodoxy belongs to the official teaching authority of the Church.

This authority is personalized in the pope, the successor of St. Peter as head of the Church, and in the bishops together and in union with the pope, as it was originally committed to Peter and to the whole college of apostles under his leadership. They are the official teachers of the Church.

Others have auxiliary relationships with the magisterium: theologians, in the study and clarification of doctrine; teachers—priests, religious, lay persons— who cooperate with the pope and bishops in spreading knowledge of religious truth; the faithful, who by their sense of faith and personal witness contribute to the development of doctrine and the establishment of its relevance to life in the Church and the world.

The magisterium, Pope Paul VI noted in an address at a general audience Jan. 11, 1967, "is a subordinate and faithful echo and secure interpreter of the divine word." It does not reveal new truths, "nor is it superior to sacred Scripture." Its competence extends to the limits of divine revelation manifested in Scripture and tradition and the living experience of the Church, with respect to matters of faith and morals and related subjects. Official teaching in these areas is infallible when it is formally defined, for belief and acceptance by all members of the Church, by the pope, acting in the capacity of supreme shepherd of the flock of Christ; also, when doctrine is proposed and taught with moral unanimity of bishops with the pope in a solemn collegial manner, as in an ecumenical council, and/or in the ordinary course of events. Even when not infallibly defined, official teaching in the areas of faith and morals is authoritative and requires religious assent.

The teachings of the magisterium have been documented in creeds, formulas of faith, decrees and enactments of ecumenical and particular councils, various kinds of doctrinal statements, encyclical letters and other teaching instruments. They have also been incorporated into the liturgy, with the result that the law of prayer is said to be a law of belief.

Collegiality

The bishops of the Church, in union with the pope, have supreme teaching and pastoral authority over the whole Church in addition to the authority of office they have for their own dioceses.

This collegial authority is exercised in a solemn manner in an ecumenical council and can be exercised in other ways as well, "provided that the head of the college calls them to collegiate action, or at least so approves or freely accepts the united action of the dispersed bishops that it is made a true collegiate act."

This doctrine is grounded on the fact that: "Just as, by the Lord's will, St. Peter and the other apostles constituted one apostolic college, so in a similar way the Roman Pontiff as the successor of Peter, and the bishops as the successors of the apostles are joined together."

Doctrine on collegiality was stated by the Second Vatican Council in the Dogmatic Constitution on the Church (Nos. 22 and 23).

(For coverage of the *Role of Mary in the Mystery of Christ and the Church*, Chapter VIII, *Lumen Gentium*, see the section on the **Blessed Virgin Mary**.)

REVELATION

Following are excerpts from the "Dogmatic Constitution on Divine Revelation" (*Dei Verbum*) promulgated by the Second Vatican Council. They describe the nature and process of divine revelation, inspiration and interpretation of Scripture, the Old and New Testaments, and the role of Scripture in the life of the Church.

I. REVELATION ITSELF

God chose to reveal himself and to make known to us the hidden purpose of his will (cf. Eph 1:9) by which through Christ, the Word made flesh, man has access to the Father in the Holy Spirit and comes to share in the divine nature (cf. Eph 2:18; 2 Pt 1:4). Through this revelation, therefore, the invisible God (cf. Col 1:15; 1 Tm 1:17). speaks to men as friends (cf. Ex 33:11; Jn 15:14-15) and lives among them (cf. Bar. 3:38) so that he may invite and take them into fellowship with himself. This plan of revelation is realized by deeds and words having an inner unity: the deeds wrought by God in the history of salvation manifest and confirm the teaching and realities signified by the words, while the words proclaim the deeds and clarify the mystery contained in them. By this revelation then, the deepest truth about God and the salvation of man is made clear to us in Christ, who is the Mediator and at the same time the fullness of all revelation (No. 2).

God from the start manifested himself to our first parents. Then after their fall his promise of redemption aroused in them the hope of being saved (cf. Gn 3:15), and from that time on he ceaselessly kept the human race in his care, in order to give eternal life to those who perseveringly do good in search of salvation (cf. Rom 2:6-7). He called Abraham in order to make of him a great nation (cf. Gn 12:2). Through the patriarchs, and after them through Moses and the prophets, he taught this nation to acknowledge himself as the one living and true God and to wait for the Savior promised by him. In this manner he prepared the way for the Gospel down through the centuries (No. 3).

Revelation in Christ

Then, after speaking in many places and varied ways through the prophets, God "last of all in these days has spoken to us by his Son" (Heb 1:1-2). Jesus perfected revelation by fulfilling it through his whole work of making himself present and manifesting himself: through his words and deeds, his signs and wonders, but especially through his death and glorious resurrection from the dead and final sending of the Spirit of truth. Moreover, he confirmed with divine testimony what revelation proclaimed: that God is with us to free us from the darkness of sin and death, and to raise us up to life eternal.

The Christian dispensation, therefore, as the new and definitive covenant, will never pass away, and we now await no further new public revelation before the glorious manifestation of our Lord Jesus Christ (cf. 1 Tm 6:14; Ti 2:13) (No. 4).

II. TRANSMISSION OF REVELATION

God has seen to it that what he had revealed for the salvation of all nations would abide perpetually in its full integrity and be handed on to all generations. Therefore Christ the Lord, in whom the full revelation of the supreme God is brought to completion (cf. 2 Cor 1:20; 3:16; 4:6), commissioned the apostles to preach to all men that Gospel which is the source of all saving truth and moral teaching, and thus to impart to them divine gifts. This Gospel had been promised in former times through the prophets, and Christ himself fulfilled it and promulgated it with his own lips. This commission was faithfully fulfilled by the apostles who, by their oral preaching, by example, and by ordinances, handed on what they had received from Christ or what they had learned through the prompting of the Holy Spirit. The commission was fulfilled, too, by those apostles and apostolic men who under the inspiration of the same Holy Spirit committed the message of salvation to writing (No. 7).

Tradition

But in order to keep the Gospel forever whole and alive within the Church, the apostles left bishops as their successors, "handing over their own teaching role" to them. This sacred tradition, therefore, and sacred Scripture of both the Old and the New Testament are like a mirror in which the pilgrim Church on earth looks at God (No. 7).

The apostolic preaching, which is expressed in a special way in the inspired books, was to be preserved by a continuous succession of preachers until the end of time. Therefore the apostles, handing on what they themselves had received, warn the faithful to hold fast to the traditions which they have learned. Now what was handed on by the apostles includes everything which contributes to the holiness of life, and the increase in faith of the People of God; and so the Church, in her teaching, life, and worship, perpetuates and hands on to all generations all that she herself is, all that she believes (No. 8).

Development of Doctrine

This tradition which comes from the apostles develops in the Church with the help of the Holy Spirit. For there is a growth in the understanding of the realities and the words which have been handed down. This happens through the contemplation and study made by believers through the intimate understanding of spiritual things they experience, and through the preaching of those who have received through episcopal succession the sure gift of truth. For, as the centuries succeed one another, the Church constantly moves forward toward the fullness of divine truth until the words of God reach their complete fulfillment in her.

The words of the holy Fathers witness to the living presence of this tradition, whose wealth is poured into the practice and life of the believing and praying Church. Through the same tradition the Church's full canon of the sacred books is known, and the sacred writings themselves are more profoundly understood and unceasingly made active in her; ... and the Holy Spirit, through whom the living voice of the Gospel resounds in the Church, and through her, in the world, leads unto all truth those who believe and makes the word of Christ dwell abundantly in them (cf. Col 3:16) (No. 8).

Tradition and Scripture

Hence there exist a close connection and communication between sacred tradition and sacred Scripture. For both of them, flowing from the same divine wellspring, in a certain way merge into a unity and tend toward the same end. For sacred Scripture is the word of God inasmuch as it is consigned to writing under the inspiration of the divine Spirit. To the successors of the apostles, sacred tradition hands on in its full purity

God's word, which was entrusted to the apostles by Christ the Lord and the Holy Spirit. Thus, led by the light of the Spirit of truth, these successors can in their preaching preserve this word of God faithfully, explain it, and make it more widely known. Consequently, it is not from sacred Scripture alone that the Church draws her certainty about every thing which has been revealed. Therefore both sacred tradition and sacred Scripture are to be accepted and venerated with the same sense of devotion and reverence (No. 9).

Sacred tradition and sacred Scripture form one sacred deposit of the word of God, which is committed to the Church (No. 10).

Teaching Authority of Church

The task of authentically interpreting the word of God, whether written or handed on, has been entrusted exclusively to the living teaching office of the Church, whose authority is exercised in the name of Jesus Christ. This teaching office is not above the word of God, but serves it, teaching only what has been handed on ... it draws from this one deposit of faith everything which it presents for belief as divinely revealed.

It is clear, therefore, that sacred tradition, sacred Scripture, and the teaching authority of the Church ... are so linked and joined together that one cannot stand without the others, and that all together and each in its own way under the action of the one Holy Spirit contribute effectively to the salvation of souls (No. 10).

III. INSPIRATION, INTERPRETATION

Those revealed realities contained and presented in sacred Scripture have been committed to writing under the inspiration of the Holy Spirit. Holy Mother Church, relying on the belief of the apostles, holds that the books of both the Old and New Testament in their entirety, with all their parts, are sacred and canonical because, having been written under the inspiration of the Holy Spirit (cf. Jn 20:31; 2 Tm 3:16; 2 Pt 1:19-21, 3:15-16) they have God as their author and have been handed on as such to the Church herself. In composing the sacred books, God chose men and, while employed by him, they made use of their powers and abilities, so that, with him acting in them and through them, they, as true authors, consigned to writing everything and only those things which he wanted (No. 11).

Inerrancy

Therefore, since everything asserted by the inspired authors or sacred writers must be held to be asserted by the Holy Spirit, it follows that the books of Scripture must be acknowledged as teaching firmly, faithfully, and without error that truth which God wanted put into the sacred writings for the sake of our salvation. Therefore "all Scripture is inspired by God and useful for teaching, for reproving, for correcting, for instruction in justice; that the man of God may be perfect, equipped for every good work" (2 Tm 3:16-17) (No. 11).

Literary Forms

However, since God speaks in sacred Scripture through men in human fashion, the interpreter of sacred Scripture, in order to see clearly what God wanted to communicate to us, should carefully investigate what meaning the sacred writers really intended, and what God wanted to manifest by means of their words.

The interpreter must investigate what meaning the sacred writer intended to express and actually expressed in particular circumstances as he used contemporary literary forms in accordance with the situation of his own time and culture. For the correct understanding of what the sacred author wanted to assert, due attention must be paid to the customary and characteristic styles of perceiving, speaking, and narrating which prevailed at the time of the sacred writer, and to the customs men normally followed at that period in their everyday dealings with one another (No. 12).

Analogy of Faith

No less serious attention must be given to the content and unity of the whole of Scripture, if the meaning of the sacred texts is to be correctly brought to light. The living tradition of the whole Church must be taken into account along with the harmony which exists between elements of the faith. All of what has been said about the way of interpreting Scripture is subject finally to the judgment of the Church, which carries out the divine commission and ministry of guarding and interpreting the word of God (No. 12).

IV. THE OLD TESTAMENT

In carefully planning and preparing the salvation of the whole human race, the God of supreme love, by a special dispensation, chose for himself a people to whom he might entrust his promises. First he entered into a covenant with Abraham (cf. Gn 15:18) and, through Moses, with the people of Israel (cf. Ex 24:8). To this people which he had acquired for himself, he so manifested himself through words and deeds as the one true and living God that Israel came to know by experience the ways of God with men. The plan of salvation, foretold by the sacred authors, recounted and explained by them, is found as the true word of God in the books of the Old Testament: these books, therefore, written under divine inspiration, remain permanently valuable (No. 14).

Principal Purpose

The principal purpose to which the plan of the Old Covenant was directed was to prepare for the coming both of Christ, the universal Redeemer, and of the messianic Kingdom. Now the books of the Old Testament, in accordance with the state of mankind before the time of salvation established by Christ, reveal to all men the knowledge of God and of man and the ways in which God deals with men. These books show us true divine pedagogy (No. 15).

The books of the Old Testament with all their parts, caught up into the proclamation of the Gospel, acquire and show forth their full meaning in the New Testament (cf. Mt 5:17; Lk 24:27; Rom 16:25-26; 2 Cor 3:14-16) and in turn shed light on it and explain it (No. 16).

V. THE NEW TESTAMENT

The word of God is set forth and shows its power in a most excellent way in the writings of the New Testament. For when the fullness of time arrived (cf. Gal. 4:4), the Word was made flesh and dwelt among us in the fullness of grace and truth (cf. Jn 12:32). This mystery had not been manifested to other generations as it was now revealed to his holy apostles and prophets in the Holy Spirit (cf. Eph 3:4-6), so that they might preach the Gospel, stir up faith in Jesus, Christ and Lord, and gather the Church together. To these

realities, the writings of the New Testament stand as a perpetual and divine witness (No. 17).

The Gospels and Other Writings

The Gospels have a special preeminence for they are the principal witness of the life and teaching of the incarnate Word, our Savior.

The Church has always and everywhere held and continues to hold that the four Gospels are of apostolic origin. For what the apostles preached afterwards they themselves and apostolic men, under the inspiration of the divine Spirit, handed on to us in writing: the foundation of faith, namely, the fourfold Gospel, according to Matthew, Mark, Luke, and John (No. 18).

The four Gospels... whose historical character the Church unhesitatingly asserts, faithfully hand on what Jesus Christ, while living among men, really did and taught for their eternal salvation until the day he was taken up into heaven (see Acts 1:1-2). Indeed, after the ascension of the Lord the apostles handed on to their hearers what he had said and done. The sacred authors wrote the four Gospels, selecting some things from the many which had been handed on by word of mouth or in writing, reducing some of them to a synthesis, explicating some things in view of the situation of their churches, and preserving the form of proclamation but always in such fashion that they told us the honest truth about Jesus. For their intention in writing was that we might know "the truth" concerning those matters about which we have been instructed (cf. Lk 1:2-4) (No. 19).

Besides the four Gospels, the canon of the New Testament also contains the Epistles of St. Paul and other apostolic writings, composed under the inspiration of the Holy Spirit. In these writings those matters which concern Christ the Lord are confirmed, his true teaching is more and more fully stated, the saving power of the divine work of Christ is preached, the story is told of the beginnings of the Church and her marvelous growth, and her glorious fulfillment is foretold (No. 20).

SCRIPTURE IN CHURCH LIFE

The Church has always venerated the divine Scriptures just as she venerates the body of the Lord. She has always regarded the Scriptures together with sacred tradition as the supreme rule of faith, and will ever do so. For, inspired by God and committed once and for all to writing, they impart the word of God himself without change, and make the voice of the Holy Spirit resound in the words of the prophets and apostles. Therefore, like the Christian religion itself, all the preaching of the Church must be nourished and ruled by sacred Scripture (No. 21).

Easy access to sacred Scripture should be provided for all the Christian faithful. That is why the Church from the very beginning accepted as her own that very ancient Greek translation of the Old Testament which is named after seventy men (the Septuagint); and she has always given a place of honor to other translations, Eastern and Latin, especially the one known as the Vulgate. But since the word of God should be available at all times, the Church with maternal concern sees to it that suitable and correct translations are made into different languages, especially from the original texts of the sacred books. And if, given the opportunity and the approval of Church authority, these translations are produced in cooperation with the separated brethren as well, all Christians will be able to use them (No. 22).

Biblical Studies, Theology

The constitution encouraged the development and progress of biblical studies "under the watchful care of the sacred teaching office of the Church."

It also noted: "Sacred theology rests on the written word of God, together with sacred tradition, as its primary and perpetual foundation," and that "the study of the sacred page is, as it were, the soul of sacred theology" (Nos. 23, 24).

(*See separate article,* **Interpretation of the Bible.**)

THE BIBLE

The Canon of the Bible is the Church's official list of sacred writings. These works, written by men under the inspiration of the Holy Spirit, contain divine revelation and, in conjunction with the tradition and teaching authority of the Church, constitute the rule of Catholic faith. The Canon was fixed and determined by the tradition and teaching authority of the Church.

THE CATHOLIC CANON

The Old Testament Canon of 46 books is as follows.
• **The Pentateuch,** the first five books: Genesis (Gn), Exodus (Ex), Leviticus (Lv), Numbers (Nm), Deuteronomy (Dt).
• **Historical Books**: Joshua (Jos), Judges (Jgs), Ruth (Ru) 1 and 2 Samuel (Sm), 1 and 2 Kings (Kgs), 1 and 2 Chronicles (Chr), Ezra (Ezr), Nehemiah (Neh), Tobit (Tb), Judith (Jdt), Esther (Est), 1 and 2 Maccabees (Mc).
• **Wisdom Books**: Job (Jb), Psalms (Ps), Proverbs (Prv), Ecclesiastes (Eccl), Song of Songs (Song), Wisdom (Wis), Sirach (Sir).
• **The Prophets**: Isaiah (Is), Jeremiah (Jer), Lamentations (Lam), Baruch (Bar), Ezekiel (Ez), Daniel (Dn), Hosea (Hos), Joel (Jl), Amos (Am), Obadiah (Ob), Jonah (Jon), Micah (Mi), Nahum (Na), Habakkuk (Hb), Zephaniah (Zep), Haggai (Hg), Zechariah (Zec) Malachi (Mal).

The New Testament Canon of 27 books is as follows.
• **The Gospels**: Matthew (Mt), Mark (Mk), Luke (Lk), John (Jn).
• **The Acts of the Apostles** (Acts).
• **The Pauline Letters**: Romans (Rom), 1 and 2 Corinthians (Cor), Galatians (Gal), Ephesians (Eph), Philippians (Phil), Colossians (Col), 1 and 2 Thessalonians (Thes) 1 and 2 Timothy (Tm), Titus (Ti), Philemon (Phlm), Hebrews (Heb).
• **The Catholic Letters**: James (Jas), 1 and 2 Peter (Pt), 1, 2, and 3 John (Jn), Jude (Jude).
• **Revelation** (Rv).

Developments

The Canon of th Old Testament was firm by the fifth century despite some questioning by scholars. It was stated by a council held at Rome in 382, by African councils held in Hippo in 393 and in Carthage in 397 and 419, and by Innocent I in 405.

All of the New Testament books were generally known and most of them were acknowledged as inspired by the end of the second century. The Muratorian Fragment, dating from about 200, listed most of the books recognized as canonical in later decrees. Prior to the end of the fourth century, however, there was controversy over the inspired character of several works — the Letter to the Hebrews, James, Jude, 2 Peter, 2 and 3 John and Revelation. Controversy ended in the fourth century and these books, along with those about which there was no

dispute, were enumerated in the canon stated by the councils of Hippo and Carthage and affirmed by Innocent I in 405.

The Canon of the Bible was solemnly defined by the Council of Trent in the dogmatic decree *De Canonicis Scripturis,* Apr. 8, 1546.

HEBREW AND OTHER CANONS

The Hebrew Canon of sacred writings was fixed by tradition and the consensus of rabbis, probably by about 100 A.D. by the Synod or Council of Jamnia and certainly by the end of the second or early in the third century. It consists of the following works in three categories.
• **The Law** (Torah): the five books of Moses: Genesis, Exodus, Leviticus, Numbers, Deuteronomy.
• **The Prophets**: former prophets — Joshua, Judges, 1 and 2 Samuel, 1 and 2 Kings; latter prophets — Isaiah, Jeremiah, Ezekiel; and 12 minor prophets (Hosea, Joel, Amos, Obadiah, Jonah, Micah, Nahum, Habakkuk, Zephaniah, Haggai, Zechariah, Malachi).
• **The Writings**: 1 and 2 Chronicles, Ezra, Nehemiah, Job, Psalms, Proverbs, Ecclesiastes, Song of Songs, Ruth, Esther, Daniel.

This Canon, embodying the tradition and practice of the Palestine community, did not include a number of works contained in the Alexandrian version of sacred writings translated into Greek between 250 and 100 B.C. and in use by Greek-speaking Jews of the Dispersion (outside Palestine). The rejected works, called apocrypha and not regarded as sacred, are: Tobit, Judith, Wisdom, Sirach, Baruch, 1 and 2 Maccabees, the last six chapters of Esther and three passages of Daniel (3:24-90; 13; 14). These books have also been rejected from the Protestant Canon, although they are included in Bibles under the heading "Apocrypha."

The aforementioned books are held to be inspired and sacred by the Catholic Church. In Catholic usage, they are called deuterocanonical because they were under discussion for some time before questions about their canonicity were settled. Books regarded as canonical with little or no debate were called protocanonical. The status of both categories of books is the same in the Catholic Bible.

The Protestant Canon of the Old Testament is the same as the Hebrew.

The Old Testament Canon of some separated Eastern churches differs from the Catholic Canon. Christians are in agreement on the Canon of the New Testament.

Languages

Hebrew, Aramaic and Greek were the original languages of the Bible. Most of the Old Testament books were written in Hebrew. Portions of Daniel, Ezra, Jeremiah, Esther, and probably the books of Tobit and

Judith were written in Aramaic. The Book of Wisdom, 2 Maccabees and all the books of the New Testament were written in Greek.

Manuscripts and Versions

The original writings of the inspired authors have been lost. The Bible has been transmitted through ancient copies called manuscripts and through translations or versions.

Authoritative Greek manuscripts include the Sinaitic and Vatican manuscripts of the fourth century and the Alexandrine of the fifth century A.D. The Septuagint and Vulgate translations are in a class by themselves.

The Septuagint version, a Greek translation of the Old Testament for Greek-speaking Jews, was begun about 250 and completed about 100 B.C. The work of several Jewish translators at Alexandria, it differed from the Hebrew Bible in the arrangement of books and included several, later called deuterocanonical, which were not acknowledged as sacred by the community in Palestine.

The Vulgate was a Latin version of the Old and New Testaments produced from the original languages by St. Jerome from about 383 to 404. It became the most widely used Latin text for centuries and was regarded as basic long before the Council of Trent designated it as authentic and suitable for use in public reading, controversy, preaching and teaching. Because of its authoritative character, it became the basis for many translations into other languages. A critical revision was completed by a pontifical commission in 1977.

Hebrew and Aramaic manuscripts of great antiquity and value have figured more significantly than before in recent scriptural work by Catholic scholars, especially since their use was strongly encouraged, if not mandated, in 1943 by Pius XII in the encyclical *Divino Afflante Spiritu*.

The English translation of the Bible in general use among Catholics until well into the 20th century was the Douay-Rheims, so-called because of the places where it was prepared and published, the New Testament at Rheims in 1582 and the Old Testament at Douay in 1609. The translation was made from the Vulgate text. As revised and issued by Bishop Richard Challoner in 1749 and 1750, it became the standard Catholic English version for about 200 years.

A revision of the Challoner New Testament, made on the basis of the Vulgate text by scholars of the Catholic Biblical Association of America, was published in 1941 in the United States under the sponsorship of the Episcopal Committee of the Confraternity of Christian Doctrine.

New American Bible

A new translation of the entire Bible, the first ever made directly into English from the original languages under Catholic auspices, was projected in 1944 and completed in the fall of 1970 with publication of the *New American Bible*. The Episcopal Committee of the Confraternity of Christian Doctrine sponsored the NAB. The translators were members of the Catholic Biblical Association of America and scholars of other faiths. The typical edition was produced by St. Anthony Guild Press, Paterson, NJ.

The *Jerusalem Bible*, published by Doubleday & Co., Inc., is an English translation of a French version based on the original languages.

Biblical translations approved for liturgical use by the National Conference of Catholic Bishops and the Holy See are the *New American Bible* (1970 edition), the *Revised Standard Version — Catholic Edition*, and the *Jerusalem Bible* (1966).

The Protestant counterpart of the *Douay-Rheims Bible* was the *King James Bible*, called the *Authorized Version* in England. Originally published in 1611 and in general use for more than three centuries, its several revisions include the *Revised Standard Version* and the *New Revised Standard Version*.

Biblical Federation

In Nov. 1966, Pope Paul VI commissioned the Secretariat for Promoting Christian Unity to start work for the widest possible distribution of the Bible and to coordinate endeavors toward the production of Catholic-Protestant Bibles in all languages.

The World Catholic Federation for the Biblical Apostolate, established in 1969, sponsors a program designed to create greater awareness among Catholics of the Bible and its use in everyday life.

The U. S. Center for the Catholic Biblical Apostolate is related to the Secretariat for Pastoral Research and Practices, United States Conference of Catholic Bishops, 3211 Fourth St. N.E., Washington, DC, 20017.

APOCRYPHA

In Catholic usage, Apocrypha are books which have some resemblance to the canonical books in subject matter and title but which have not been recognized as canonical by the Church. They are characterized by a false claim to divine authority; extravagant accounts of events and miracles alleged to be supplemental revelation; material favoring heresy (especially in New Testament apocrypha); minimal, if any, historical value. Among examples of this type of literature itemized by J. McKenzie, S.J., in *Dictionary of the Bible* are: the Books of Adam and Eve, Martyrdom of Isaiah, Testament of the Patriarchs, Assumption of Moses, Sibylline Oracles, Gospel of James, Gospel of Thomas, Arabic Gospel of the Infancy, History of Joseph the Carpenter, Acts of John, Acts of Paul, Acts of Peter, Acts of Andrew, and numerous epistles.

Books of this type are called "pseudepigrapha" by Protestants.

In Protestant usage, some books of the Catholic Bible (deuterocanonical) are called apocrypha because their inspired character is rejected.

DEAD SEA SCROLLS

The Qumran Scrolls, popularly called the Dead Sea Scrolls, are a collection of manuscripts, all but one of them in Hebrew, found since 1947 in caves in the Desert of Juda west of the Dead Sea.

Among the findings were a complete text of Isaiah dating from the second century, B.C., more or less extensive fragments of other Old Testament texts (including the deuterocanonical Tobit), and a commentary on Habakkuk. Until the discovery of these materials, the oldest known Hebrew manuscripts were from the 10th century A.D.

Also found were messianic and apocalyptic texts, and other writings describing the beliefs and practices of the Essenes, a rigoristic Jewish sect.

The scrolls, dating from about the first century

before and after Christ, are important sources of information about Hebrew literature, Jewish history during the period between the Old and New Testaments, and the history of Old Testament texts. They established the fact that the Hebrew text of the Old Testament was

fixed before the beginning of the Christian era and have had definite effects in recent critical studies and translations of the Old Testament. Together with other scrolls found at Masada, they are still the subject of intensive study.

BOOKS OF THE BIBLE

OLD TESTAMENT BOOKS

Pentateuch

The Pentateuch is the collective title of the first five books of the Bible. Substantially, they identify the Israelites as Yahweh's Chosen People, cover their history from Egypt to the threshold of the Promised Land, contain the Mosaic Law and Covenant, and disclose the promise of salvation to come. Principal themes concern the divine promise of salvation, Yahweh's fidelity and the Covenant. Work on the composition of the Pentateuch was completed in the sixth century.

Genesis: The book of origins, according to its title in the Septuagint. In two parts, covers: religious prehistory, including accounts of the origin of the world and man, the original state of innocence and the fall, the promise of salvation, patriarchs before and after the deluge, the Tower of Babel narrative, genealogies (first 11 chapters); the covenant with Abraham and patriarchal history from Abraham to Joseph (balance of the 50 chapters). Significant are the themes of Yahweh's universal sovereignty and mercy.

Exodus: Named with the Greek word for departure, is a religious epic which describes the oppression of the 12 tribes in Egypt and their departure, liberation or passover therefrom under the leadership of Moses; Yahweh's establishment of the covenant with them, making them his chosen people, through the mediation of Moses at Mt. Sinai; instructions concerning the tabernacle, the sanctuary and Ark of the Covenant; the institution of the priesthood. The book is significant because of its theology of liberation and redemption. In Christian interpretation, the Exodus is a figure of baptism.

Leviticus: Mainly legislative in theme and purpose, contains laws regarding sacrifices, ceremonies of ordination and the priesthood of Aaron, legal purity, the holiness code, atonement, the redemption of offerings and other subjects. Summarily, Levitical laws provided directives for all aspects of religious observance and for the manner in which the Israelites were to conduct themselves with respect to Yahweh and each other. Leviticus was the liturgical handbook of the priesthood.

Numbers: Taking its name from censuses recounted at the beginning and near the end, is a continuation of Exodus. It combines narrative of the Israelites' desert pilgrimage from Sinai to the border of Canaan with laws related to and expansive of those in Leviticus.

Deuteronomy: The concluding book of the Pentateuch, recapitulates, in the form of a testament of Moses, the Law and much of the desert history of the Israelites; enjoins fidelity to the Law as the key to good or bad fortune for the people; gives an account of the commissioning of Joshua as the successor of Moses. Notable themes concern the election of Israel by Yahweh, observance of the Law, prohibitions against the worship of foreign gods, worship of and

confidence in Yahweh, the power of Yahweh in nature. The Deuteronomic Code or motif, embodying all of these elements, was the norm for interpreting Israelite history.

Joshua, Judges, Ruth

Joshua: Records the fulfillment of Yahweh's promise to the Israelites in their conquest, occupation and division of Canaan under the leadership of Joshua. It also contains an account of the return of Transjordanian Israelites and of a renewal of the Covenant. It was redacted in final form probably in the sixth century or later.

Judges: Records the actions of charismatic leaders, called judges, of the tribes of Israel between the death of Joshua and the time of Samuel, and a crisis of idolatry among the people. The basic themes are sin and punishment, repentance and deliverance; its purpose was in line with the Deuteronomic motif, that the fortunes of the Israelites were related to their observance or non-observance of the Law and the Covenant. It was redacted in final form probably in the sixth century.

Ruth: Named for the Gentile (Moabite) woman who, through marriage with Boaz, became an Israelite and an ancestress of David (her son, Obed, became his grandfather). Themes are filial piety, faith and trust in Yahweh, the universality of messianic salvation. Dates ranging from c. 950 to the seventh century have been assigned to the origin of the book, whose author is unknown.

Historical Books

These books, while they contain a great deal of factual material, are unique in their preoccupation with presenting and interpreting it, in the Deuteronomic manner, in primary relation to the Covenant on which the nation of Israel was founded and in accordance with which community and personal life were judged.

The books are: Samuel 1 and 2, from the end of Judges (c. 1020) to the end of David's reign (c. 961); Kings 1 and 2, from the last days of David to the start of the Babylonian exile and the destruction of the Temple (587); Chronicles 1 and 2, from the reign of Saul (c. 1020-1000) to the return of the people from the exile (538); Ezra and Nehemiah, covering the reorganization of the Jewish community after the exile (458-397); Maccabees 1 and 2, recounting the struggle against attempted suppression of Judaism (168-142).

Three of the books listed below—Tobit, Judith, and Esther—are categorized as religious novels.

Samuel 1 and 2: A single work in concept and contents, containing episodic history of the last two Judges, Eli and Samuel, the establishment and rule of the monarchy under Saul and David, and the political consequences of David's rule. The royal messianic dynasty of David was the subject of Nathan's oracle in 2 Sm. 7. The books were edited in final form probably late in the seventh century or during the exile.

Kings 1 and 2: Cover the last days of David and the career of Solomon, including the building of the Temple and the history of the kingdom during his reign; stories of the prophets Elijah and Elisha; the history of the divided kingdom to the fall of Israel in the North (721) and the fall of Judah in the South (587), the destruction of Jerusalem and the Temple. They reflect the Deuteronomic motif in attributing the downfall of the people to corruption of belief and practice in public and private life. They were completed probably in the sixth century.

Chronicles 1 and 2: A collection of historical traditions interpreted in such a way as to present an ideal picture of one people governed by divine law and united in one Temple worship of the one true God. Contents include genealogical tables from Adam to David, the careers of David and Solomon, coverage of the kingdom of Judah to the exile, and the decree of Cyrus permitting the return of the people and rebuilding of Jerusalem. Both are related to and were written about 400 by the same author, the Chronicler, who composed Ezra and Nehemiah.

Ezra and Nehemiah: A running account of the return of the people to their homeland after the exile and of practical efforts, under the leadership of Ezra and Nehemiah, to restore and reorganize the religious and political community on the basis of Israelite traditions, divine worship and observance of the Law. Events of great significance were the building of the second Temple, the building of a wall around Jerusalem and the proclamation of the Law by Ezra. This restored community was the start of Judaism. Both are related to and were written about 400 by the same author, the Chronicler, who composed Chronicles 1 and 2.

Tobit: Written in the literary form of a novel and having greater resemblance to wisdom than to historical literature, narrates the personal history of Tobit, a devout and charitable Jew in exile, and persons connected with him, viz., his son Tobiah, his kinsman Raguel and Raguel's daughter Sarah. Its purpose was to teach people how to be good Jews. One of its principal themes is patience under trial, with trust in divine Providence which is symbolized by the presence and action of the angel Raphael. It was written about 200.

Judith: Recounts, in the literary form of a historical novel or romance, the preservation of the Israelites from conquest and ruin through the action of Judith. The essential themes are trust in God for deliverance from danger and emphasis on observance of the Law. It was written probably during the Maccabean period.

Esther: Relates, in the literary form of a historical novel or romance, the manner in which Jews in Persia were saved from annihilation through the central role played by Esther, the Jewish wife of Ahasuerus; a fact commemorated by the Jewish feast of Purim. Like Judith, it has trust in Divine Providence as its theme and indicates that God's saving will is sometimes realized by persons acting in unlikely ways. It may have been written near the end of the fourth century.

Maccabees 1 and 2: While related to some extent because of common subject matter, are quite different from each other.

The first book recounts the background and events of the 40-year (175-135) struggle for religious and political freedom led by Judas Maccabaeus and his brothers against the Hellenist Seleucid kings and some Hellenophiles among the Jews. Victory was symbolized by the rededication of the Temple. Against the background of opposition between Jews and Gentiles, the author equated the survival of belief in the one true God with survival of the Jewish people, thus identifying religion with patriotism. It was written probably near the year 100.

The second book supplements the first to some extent, covering and giving a theological interpretation to events from 180 to 162. It explains the feast of the dedication of the Temple, a key event in the survival of Judaism which is commemorated in the feast of Hanukkah; stresses the primacy of God's action in the struggle for survival; and indicates belief in an afterlife and the resurrection of the body. It was completed probably about 124.

Wisdom Books

With the exceptions of Psalms and the Song of Songs, the titles listed under this heading are called "wisdom books" because their purpose was to formulate the fruits of human experience in the context of meditation on sacred Scripture and to present them as an aid toward understanding the problems of life. Hebrew wisdom literature was distinctive from pagan literature of the same type, but it had limitations; these were overcome in the New Testament, which added the dimensions of the New Covenant to those of the Old. Solomon was regarded as the archetype of the wise man.

Job: A dramatic, didactic poem consisting mainly of several dialogues between Job and his friends concerning the mystery involved in the coexistence of the just God, evil and the suffering of the just. It describes an innocent man's experience of suffering and conveys the truth that faith in and submission to God rather than complete understanding, which is impossible, make the experience bearable; also, that the justice of God cannot be defended by affirming that it is realized in this world. Of unknown authorship, it was composed between the seventh and fifth centuries.

Psalms: A collection of 150 religious songs or lyrics reflecting Israelite belief and piety dating from the time of the monarchy to the post-Exilic period, a span of well over 500 years. The psalms, which are a compendium of Old Testament theology, were used in the temple liturgy and for other occasions. They were of several types suitable for the king, hymns, lamentations, expressions of confidence and thanksgiving, prophecy, historical meditation and reflection, and the statement of wisdom. About one-half of them are attributed to David; many were composed by unknown authors.

Proverbs: The oldest book of the wisdom type in the Bible, consisting of collections of sayings attributed to Solomon and other persons regarding a wide variety of subjects including wisdom and its nature, rules of conduct, duties with respect to one's neighbor, the conduct of daily affairs. It reveals many details of Hebrew life. Its nucleus dates from the period before the exile. The extant form of the book dates probably from the end of the fifth century.

Ecclesiastes: A treatise about many subjects whose unifying theme is the vanity of strictly human efforts and accomplishments with respect to the achievement of lasting happiness; the only things which are not vain are fear of the Lord and observance of his commandments. The pessimistic tone of the book is due to the absence of a concept of afterlife. It was written by an unknown author probably in the third century.

Song of Songs: A collection of love lyrics reflecting various themes, including the love of God for Israel and the celebration of ideal love and fidelity between man and woman. It was written by an unknown author after the exile.

Wisdom: Deals with many subjects including the reward of justice; praise of wisdom, a gift of Yahweh proceeding from belief in him and the practice of his Law; the part played by him in the history of his people, especially in their liberation from Egypt; the folly and shame of idolatry. Its contents are taken from the whole sacred literature of the Jews and represent a distillation of its wisdom based on the law, beliefs and traditions of Israel. The last of the Old Testament books, it was written in the early part of the first century before Christ by a member of the Jewish community at Alexandria.

Sirach: Resembling Proverbs, is a collection of sayings handed on by a grandfather to his grandson. It contains a variety of moral instruction and eulogies of patriarchs and other figures in Israelite history. Its moral maxims apply to individuals, the family and community, relations with God, friendship, education, wealth, the Law, divine worship. Its theme is that true wisdom consists in the Law. (It was formerly called Ecclesiasticus, the Church Book, because of its extensive use by the Church for moral instruction.) It was written in Hebrew between 200 and 175, during a period of strong Hellenistic influence, and was translated into Greek after 132.

The Prophets

These books and the prophecies they contain "express judgments of the people's moral conduct, on the basis of the Mosaic alliance between God and Israel. They teach sublime truths and lofty morals. They contain exhortations, threats, announcements of punishment, promises of deliverance. In the affairs of men, their prime concern is the interests of God, especially in what pertains to the Chosen People through whom the Messiah is to come; hence their denunciations of idolatry and of that externalism in worship which exclude the interior spirit of religion. They are concerned also with the universal nature of the moral law, with personal responsibility, with the person and office of the Messiah, and with the conduct of foreign nations" (*The Holy Bible*, Prophetic Books, CCD Edition, 1961; preface). There are four major (Isaiah, Jeremiah, Ezekiel, Daniel) and twelve minor prophets (distinguished by the length of books), Lamentations and Baruch. Earlier prophets, mentioned in historical books, include Samuel, Gad, Nathan, Elijah, and Elisha.

Before the exile, prophets were the intermediaries through whom God communicated revelation to the people. Afterwards, prophecy lapsed and the written word of the Law served this purpose.

Isaiah: Named for the greatest of the prophets whose career spanned the reigns of three Hebrew kings from 742 to the beginning of the seventh century, in a period of moral breakdown in Judah and threats of invasion by foreign enemies. It is an anthology of poems and oracles credited to him and a number of followers deeply influenced by him. Of special importance are the prophecies concerning Immanuel (6 to 12), including the prophecy of the virgin birth (7:14). Chapters 40 to 55, called Deutero-Isaiah, are attributed to an anonymous poet toward the end of the exile; this portion contains the Songs of the Servant. The concluding part of the book (56-66) contains oracles by later disciples. One of many themes in Isaiah concerned the saving mission of the remnant of Israel in the divine plan of salvation.

Jeremiah: Combines history, biography and prophecy in a setting of crisis caused by internal and external factors, viz., idolatry and general infidelity to the Law among the Israelites and external threats from the Assyrians, Egyptians and Babylonians. Jeremiah prophesied the promise of a new covenant as well as the destruction of Jerusalem and the Temple. His career began in 626 and ended some years after the beginning of the exile. The book, the longest in the Bible, was edited in final form after the exile.

Lamentations: A collection of five laments or elegies over the fall of Jerusalem and the fate of the people in exile, written by an unknown eyewitness. They convey the message that Yahweh struck the people because of their sins and reflect confidence in his love and power to restore his converted people.

Baruch: Against the background of the already-begun exile, it consists of an introduction and several parts: an exile's prayer of confession and petition for forgiveness and the restoration of Israel; a poem praising wisdom and the Law of Moses; a lament in which Jerusalem, personified, bewails the fate of her people and consoles them with the hope of blessings to come; and a polemic against idolatry. Although ascribed to Baruch, Jeremiah's secretary, it was written by several authors, probably in the second century.

Ezekiel: Named for the priest-prophet who prophesied in Babylon from 593 to 571, during the first phase of the exile. To prepare his fellow early exiles for the impending fall of Jerusalem, he reproached the Israelites for past sins and predicted woes to come upon them. After the destruction of the city, the burden of his message was hope and promise of restoration. Ezekiel had great influence on the religion of Israel after the exile.

Daniel: The protagonist is a young Jew, taken early to Babylon where he lived until about 538, who figured in a series of edifying stories which originated in Israelite tradition. The stories, whose characters are not purely legendary but rest on historical tradition, recount the trials and triumphs of Daniel and his three companions, and other episodes including those concerning Susannah, Bel, and the Dragon. The book is more apocalyptic than prophetic: it envisions Israel in glory to come and conveys the message that men of faith can resist temptation and overcome adversity. It states the prophetic themes of right conduct, divine control of men and events, and the final triumph of the kingdom. It was written by an unknown author in the 160s to give moral support to Jews during the persecutions of the Maccabean period.

Hosea: Consists of a prophetic parallel between Hosea's marriage and Yahweh's relations with his people. As the prophet was married to a faithless wife whom he would not give up, Yahweh was bound in Covenant with an idolatrous and unjust Israel whom he would not desert but would chastise for purification. Hosea belonged to the Northern Kingdom of Israel and began his career about the middle of the eighth century. He inaugurated the tradition of describing Yahweh's relation to Israel in terms of marriage.

Joel: Is apocalyptic and eschatological regarding divine judgment, the Day of the Lord, which is symbolized by a ravaging invasion of locusts, the judgment of the nations in the Valley of Josaphat and the outpouring of the Spirit in the messianic era to come. Its message is that God will vindicate and save Israel, in view of the prayer and repentance of the people, and will punish their enemies. It was composed about 400.

Amos: Consists of an indictment against foreign enemies of Israel; a strong denunciation of the people of Israel, whose infidelity, idolatry and injustice made them subject to divine judgment and punishment; and a messianic oracle regarding Israel's restoration. Amos prophesied in the Northern Kingdom of Israel, at Bethel, in the first half of the eighth century; chronologically, he was the first of the canonical prophets.

Obadiah: A 21-verse prophecy, the shortest and one of the sternest in the Bible, against the Edomites, invaders of southern Judah and enemies of those returning from the exile to their homeland. It was probably composed in the fifth century.

Jonah: A parable of divine mercy with the theme that Yahweh wills the salvation of all, not just a few, men who respond to his call. Its protagonist is a disobedient prophet; forced by circumstances beyond his control to preach penance among Gentiles, he is highly successful in his mission but baffled by the divine concern for those who do not belong to the Chosen People. It was written after the exile, probably in the fifth century.

Micah: Attacks the injustice and corruption of priests, false prophets, officials and people; announces judgment and punishment to come; foretells the restoration of Israel; refers to the saving remnant of Israel. Micah was a contemporary of Isaiah.

Nahum: Concerns the destruction of Nineveh in 612 and the overthrow of the Assyrian Empire by the Babylonians.

Habakkuk: Dating from about 605–597, concerns sufferings to be inflicted by oppressors on the people of Judah because of their infidelity to the Lord. It also sounds a note of confidence in the Lord, the Savior, and declares that the just will not perish.

Zephaniah: Exercising his ministry in the second half of the seventh century, during a time of widespread idolatry, superstition and religious degradation, he prophesied impending judgment and punishment for Jerusalem and its people. He prophesied too that a holy remnant of the people (*anawim*, mentioned also by Amos) would be spared. Zephaniah was a forerunner of Jeremiah.

Haggai: One of the first prophets after the exile, Haggai in 520 encouraged the returning exiles to reestablish their community and to complete the second Temple (dedicated in 515), for which he envisioned greater glory, in a messianic sense, than that enjoyed by the original Temple of Solomon.

Zechariah: A contemporary of Haggai, he prophesied in the same vein. A second part of the book, called Deutero-Zechariah and composed by one or more unknown authors, relates a vision of the coming of the Prince of Peace, the Messiah of the Poor.

Malachi: Written by an anonymous author, presents a picture of life in the post-Exilic community between 516 and the initiation of reforms by Ezra and Nehemiah about 432. Blame for the troubles of the community is placed mainly on priests for failure to carry out ritual worship and to instruct the people in the proper manner; other factors were religious indifference and the influence of doubters who were scandalized at the prosperity of the wicked. The vision of a universal sacrifice to be offered to Yahweh (1:11) is interpreted in Catholic theology as a prophecy of the sacrifice of the Mass. Malachi was the last of the minor prophets.

DATES OF THE OLD TESTAMENT

c.1800–c.1600 B.C.: Period of the patriarchs (Abraham, Isaac, Jacob).

c.1600: Israelites in Egypt.

c.1250: Exodus of Israelites from Egypt.

c.1210: Entrance of Israelites into Canaan.

c.1210–c.1020: Period of the Judges.

c.1020–c.1000: Reign of Saul, first king.

c.1000–c.961: Reign of David.

c.961–922: Reign of Solomon. Temple built during his reign.

922: Division of the Kingdom into Israel (North) and Judah (South).

721: Conquest of Israel by Assyrians.

587–538: Conquest of Judah by Babylonians.

Babylonian Captivity and Exile: Destruction of Jerusalem and the Temple, 587. Captivity ended with the return of exiles, following the decree of Cyrus permitting the rebuilding of Jerusalem.

515: Dedication of the second Temple.

458–397: Restoration and reform of the Jewish religious and political community; building of the Jerusalem wall, 439. Leaders in the movement were Ezra and Nehemiah.

168–142: Period of the Maccabees; war against Syrians.

142: Independence granted to Jews by Demetrius II of Syria.

135–37: Period of the Hasmonean dynasty.

63: Beginning of Roman rule.

37–4: Period of Herod the Great.

NEW TESTAMENT BOOKS

Gospels

The term "Gospel" is derived from the Anglo-Saxon *god-spell* and the Greek *euangelion*, meaning good news, good tidings. In Christian use, it means the good news of salvation proclaimed by Christ and the Church, and handed on in written form in the Gospels of Matthew, Mark, Luke and John.

The initial proclamation of the coming of the kingdom of God was made by Jesus in and through his Person, teachings and actions, and especially through his Passion, death and resurrection. This proclamation became the center of Christian faith and the core of the oral Gospel tradition with which the Church spread the good news by apostolic preaching for some 30 years before it was committed to writing by the Evangelists.

Nature of the Gospels

The historical truth of the Gospels was the subject of an instruction issued by the Pontifical Commission for Biblical Studies Apr. 21, 1964.

• The sacred writers selected from the material at their disposal (the oral Gospel tradition, some written collections of sayings and deeds of Jesus, eyewitness accounts) those things which were particularly suitable to the various conditions (liturgical, catechetical, missionary) of the faithful and the aims they had in mind, and they narrated these things in such a way as to correspond with those circumstances and their aims.

• The life and teaching of Jesus were not simply reported in a biographical manner for the purpose of preserving their memory but were "preached" so as to offer the Church the basis of doctrine concerning faith and morals.

• In their works, the Evangelists presented the true sayings of Jesus and the events of his life in the light of the better understanding they had following their enlightenment by the Holy Spirit. They did not transform Christ into a "mythical" Person, nor did they distort his teaching. Passion narratives are the core of all the Gospels, covering the suffering, death and resurrection of Jesus as central events in bringing about and establishing the New Covenant. Leading up to them are accounts of the mission of John the Baptizer and the ministry of Jesus, especially in Galilee and finally in Jerusalem before the Passion. The infancy of Jesus is covered by Luke and Matthew with narratives inspired in part by appropriate Old Testament citations.

Matthew, Mark and Luke, while different in various respects, have so many similarities that they are called Synoptic; their relationships are the subject of the Synoptic Problem.

Matthew: Written probably between 80 and 100 for Jewish Christians with clear reference to Jewish background and identification of Jesus as the divine Messiah, the fulfillment of the Old Testament. Distinctive are the use of Old Testament citations regarding the Person, activity and teaching of Jesus, and the presentation of doctrine in sermons and discourses.

Mark: Most likely the first of the Gospels, dating from about 70. Written for Gentile Christians, it is noted for the realism and wealth of concrete details with which it reveals Jesus as Son of God and Savior more by his actions and miracles than by his discourses. Theologically, it is less refined than the other Gospels.

Luke: Written about 75 for Gentile Christians. It is noted for the universality of its address, the insight it provides into the Christian way of life, the place it gives to women, the manner in which it emphasizes Jesus' friendship with sinners and compassion for the suffering.

John: Edited and arranged in final form probably between 90 and 100, this is the most sublime and theological of the Gospels, and is different from the Synoptics in plan and treatment. Combining accounts of signs with longer discourses and reflections, it progressively reveals the Person and mission of Jesus— as Word, Way, Truth, Life, Light—in line with the purpose, "to help you believe that Jesus is the Messiah, the Son of God, so that through this faith you may have life in his name" (Jn 20:31). There are questions about the authorship but no doubt about the Johannine authority and tradition behind the Gospel.

Acts of the Apostles

Written by Luke about 75 as a supplement to his Gospel. It describes the origin and spread of Christian communities through the action of the Holy Spirit from the resurrection of Christ to the time when Paul was placed in custody in Rome in the early 60s.

Letters (Epistles)

These letters, many of which antedated the Gospels, were written in response to existential needs of the early Christian communities for doctrinal and moral instruction, disciplinary action, practical advice, and exhortation to true Christian living.

Pauline Letters

These letters, which comprise approximately one-fourth of the New Testament, are primary and monumental sources of the development of Christian theology. Several of them may not have had Paul as their actual author, but evidence of the Pauline tradition behind them is strong. The letters to the Colossians, Philippians, Ephesians and Philemon have been called the "Captivity Letters" because of a tradition that they were written while Paul was under house arrest or another form of detention.

Romans: Written about 57, probably from Corinth, on the central significance of Christ and faith in him for salvation, and the relationship of Christianity to Judaism; the condition of mankind without Christ; justification and the Christian life; duties of Christians.

Corinthians 1: Written near the beginning of 57 from Ephesus to counteract factionalism and disorders, it covers community dissension, moral irregularities, marriage and celibacy, conduct at religious gatherings, the Eucharist, spiritual gifts (charisms) and their function in the Church, charity, the resurrection of the body.

Corinthians 2: Written later in the same year as 1 Cor., concerning Paul's defense of his apostolic ministry, and an appeal for a collection to aid poor Christians in Jerusalem.

Galatians: Written probably between 54 and 55 to counteract Judaizing opinions and efforts to undermine his authority, it asserts the divine origin of Paul's authority and doctrine, states that justification is not through Mosaic Law but through faith in Christ, insists on the practice of evangelical virtues, especially charity.

Ephesians: Written probably between 61 and 63, mainly on the Church as the Mystical Body of Christ.

Philippians: Written between 56 and 57 or 61 and 63 to warn the Philippians against enemies of their faith, to urge them to be faithful to their vocation and unity of belief, and to thank them for their kindness to him while he was being held in detention.

Colossians: Written probably while he was under house arrest in Rome from 61 to 63, to counteract the influence of self-appointed teachers who were watering down doctrine concerning Christ. It includes two highly important Christological passages, a warning against false teachers, and an instruction on the ideal Christian life.

Thessalonians 1 and 2: Written within a short time of each other probably in 51 from Corinth, mainly on doctrine concerning the *Parousia*, the second coming of Christ.

Timothy 1 and 2, Titus: Written between 65 and 67, or perhaps in the 70s, giving pastoral counsels to Timothy and Titus, who were in charge of churches in Ephesus and Crete, respectively. 1 Tm emphasizes pastoral responsibility for preserving unity of doctrine; 2 Tm describes Paul's imprisonment in Rome.

Philemon: A private letter written between 61 and 63 to a wealthy Colossian concerning a slave, Onesimus, who had escaped from him; Paul appealed for kind treatment of the man.

Hebrews: Dating from sometime between 70 and 96, a complex theological treatise on Christology, the priesthood and sacrifice of Christ, the New Covenant, and the pattern for Christian living. Critical opinion is divided as to whether it was addressed to Judaeo or Gentile Christians.

Catholic Letters

These seven letters have been called "catholic" because it was thought for some time, not altogether correctly, that they were not addressed to particular communities.

James: Written sometime before 62 in the spirit of Hebrew wisdom literature and the moralism of Tobit. An exhortation to practical Christian living, it is also noteworthy for the doctrine it states on good works and its citation regarding anointing of the sick.

Peter 1 and 2: The first letter may have been written between 64 and 67 or between 90 and 95; the second may date from 100 to 125. Addressed to Christians in Asia Minor, both are exhortations to perseverance in the life of faith despite trials and difficulties arising from pagan influences, isolation from other Christians and false teaching.

John 1: Written sometime in the 90s and addressed to Asian churches, its message is that God is made known to us in the Son and that fellowship with the Father is attained by living in the light, justice and love of the Son.

John 2: Written sometime in the 90s and addressed to a church in Asia, it commends the people for standing firm in the faith and urges them to perseverance.

John 3: Written sometime in the 90s, it appears to represent an effort to settle a jurisdictional dispute in one of the churches.

Jude: Written probably about 80, it is a brief treatise against erroneous teachings and practices opposed to law, authority and true Christian freedom.

Revelation

Written in the 90s along the lines of Johannine thought, it is a symbolic and apocalyptic treatment of things to come and of the struggle between the Church and evil combined with warning but hope and assurance to the Church regarding the coming of the Lord in glory.

INTERPRETATION OF THE BIBLE

According to the Dogmatic Constitution on Divine Revelation (*Dei Verbum*) issued by the Second Vatican Council, "the interpreter of Sacred Scripture, in order to see clearly what God wanted to communicate to us, should carefully investigate what meaning the sacred writers really intended, and what God wanted to manifest by means of their words" (No. 12).

Hermeneutics, Exegesis

This careful investigation proceeds in accordance with the rules of hermeneutics, the normative science of biblical interpretation and explanation. Hermeneutics in practice is called exegesis.

The principles of hermeneutics are derived from various disciplines and many factors which have to be considered in explaining the Bible and its parts. These include: the original languages and languages of translation of the sacred texts, through philology and linguistics; the quality of texts, through textual criticism; literary forms and genres, through literary and form criticism; cultural, historical, geographical, and other conditions which influenced the writers, through related studies; facts and truths of salvation history; the truths and analogy of faith.

Distinctive to biblical hermeneutics, which differs in important respects from literary interpretation in general, is the premise that the Bible, though written by human authors, is the work of divine inspiration in which God reveals his plan for the salvation of men through historical events and persons, and especially through the Person and mission of Christ.

Textual, Form Criticism

Textual criticism is the study of biblical texts, which have been transmitted in copies several times removed from the original manuscripts, for the purpose of establishing the real state of the original texts. This purpose is served by comparison of existing copies; by application to the texts of the disciplines of philology and linguistics; by examination of related works of antiquity; by study of biblical citations in works of the Fathers of the Church and other authors; and by other means of literary study.

Since about 1920, the sayings of Christ have been a particular object of New Testament study, the purpose being to analyze the forms of expression used by the Evangelists in order to ascertain the words actually spoken by him.

Literary Criticism

Literary criticism aims to determine the origin and kinds of literary composition, called forms or genres, employed by the inspired authors. Such determinations are necessary for decision regarding the nature and purpose and, consequently, the meaning of biblical passages. Underlying these studies is the principle that the manner of writing was conditioned by the intention of the authors, the meaning they wanted to convey, and the then-contemporary literary style, mode or medium best adapted to carry their message — e.g., true history, quasi-historical narrative, poems, prayers, hymns, psalms, aphorisms, allegories, discourses. Understanding these media is necessary for the valid interpretation of their message.

Literal Sense

The key to all valid interpretation is the literal sense of biblical passages. Regarding this matter and the relevance to it of the studies and procedures described above, Pius XII wrote the following in the encyclical *Divino Afflante Spiritu*:

"What the literal sense of a passage is, is not always as obvious in the speeches and writings of ancient authors of the East as it is in the works of our own time. For what they wished to express is not to be determined by the rules of grammar and philology alone nor solely by the context; the interpreter must, as it were, go back wholly in spirit to those remote centuries of the East and with the aid of history, archeology, ethnology, and other sciences accurately determine what modes of writing, so to speak, the authors of that ancient period would be likely to use and in fact did use. In explaining the Sacred Scripture and in demonstrating and proving its immunity from all error [the Catholic interpreter] should make a prudent use of this means, determine to what extent the manner of expression or literary mode adopted by the sacred writer may lead to a correct and genuine interpretation; and let him be convinced that this part of his office cannot be neglected without serious detriment to Catholic exegesis."

The literal sense of the Bible is the meaning in the mind of and intended by the inspired writer of a book or passage of the Bible. This is determined by the application to texts of the rules of hermeneutics. It is not to be confused with word-for-word literalism.

Typological Sense

The typological sense is the meaning which a passage has not only in itself but also in reference to something else of which it is a type or foreshadowing. A clear example is the account of the Exodus of the Israelites: in its literal sense, it narrates the liberation of the Israelites from death and oppression in Egypt; in its typical sense, it foreshadowed the liberation of men from sin through the redemptive death and resurrection of Christ. The typical sense of this and other passages emerged in the working out of God's plan of salvation history. It did not have to be in the mind of the author of the original passage.

Accommodated Senses

Accommodated, allegorical, and consequent senses are figurative and adaptive meanings given to books and passages of the Bible for moral and other purposes. Such interpretations involve the danger of stretching the literal sense beyond proper proportions. Hermeneutical principles require that interpretations like these respect the integrity of the literal sense of the passages in question.

In the Catholic view, the final word on questions of biblical interpretation belongs to the teaching authority of the Church. In other views, generally derived from basic principles stated by Martin Luther, John Calvin and other reformers, the primacy belongs to individual judgment acting in response to the inner testimony of the Holy Spirit, the edifying nature of biblical subject matter, the sublimity and simplicity of the message of salvation, the intensity with which Christ is proclaimed.

Biblical Studies

The first center for biblical studies, in some strict sense of the term, was the School of Alexandria, founded in the latter half of the second century. It was noted for allegorical exegesis. Literal interpretation was a hallmark of the School of Antioch.

St. Jerome, who produced the Vulgate, and St. Augustine, author of numerous commentaries, were the most important figures in biblical studies during the patristic period. By the time of the latter's death, the Old and New Testament canons had been stabilized. For some centuries afterwards, there was little or no progress in scriptural studies, although commentaries were written, collections were made of scriptural excerpts from the writings of the Fathers of the Church, and the systematic reading of Scripture became established as a feature of monastic life.

Advances were made in the 12th and 13th centuries with the introduction of new principles and methods of scriptural analysis stemming from renewed interest in Hebraic studies and the application of dialectics.

By the time of the Reformation, the Bible had become the first book set in movable type, and more than 100 vernacular editions were in use throughout Europe.

The Council of Trent

In the wake of the Reformation, the Council of Trent formally defined the Canon of the Bible; it also reasserted the authoritative role of tradition and the teaching authority of the Church as well as Scripture with respect to the rule of faith. In the heated atmosphere of the 16th and 17th centuries, the Bible was turned into a polemical weapon; Protestants used it to defend their doctrines, and Catholics countered with citations in support of the dogmas of the Church. One result of this state of affairs was a lack of substantial progress in biblical studies during the period.

Rationalists from the 18th century on and later Modernists denied the reality of the supernatural and doctrine concerning inspiration of the Bible, which they generally regarded as a strictly human production expressive of the religious sense and experience of mankind. In their hands, the tools of positive critical research became weapons for biblical subversion. The defensive Catholic reaction to their work had the temporary effect of alienating scholars of the Church from solid advances in archeology, philology, history, textual and literary criticism.

Catholic Developments

Major influences in bringing about a change in Catholic attitude toward use of these disciplines in biblical studies were two papal encyclicals and two institutes of special study, the École Biblique, founded in Jerusalem in 1890, and the Pontifical Biblical Institute established in Rome in 1909. The encyclical Providentissimus Deus, issued by Leo XIII in 1893, marked an important breakthrough; in addition to defending the concept of divine inspiration and the formal inspiration of the Scriptures, it encouraged the study of allied and ancillary sciences and techniques for a more fruitful understanding of the sacred writings. The encyclical Divino Afflante Spiritu, issued by Pope Pius XII 50 years later, gave encouragement for the use of various forms of criticism as tools of biblical research. A significant addition to documents on the subject is "The Interpretation of the Bible in the Church," published by the Pontifical Biblical Commission in Nov. 1993. It presents an overview of approaches to the Bible and probes the question: "Which hermeneutical theory best enables a proper grasp of the profound reality of which Scripture speaks and its meaningful expression for people today?"

The documents encouraged the work of scholars and stimulated wide communication of the fruits of their study.

Great changes in the climate and direction of biblical studies have occurred in recent years. One of them has been an increase in cooperative effort among Catholic, Protestant, Orthodox, and Jewish scholars. Their common investigation of the Dead Sea Scrolls is well-known. Also productive has been the collaboration of Catholics and Protestants in turning out various editions of the Bible.

The development and results of biblical studies in this century have directly and significantly affected all phases of the contemporary renewal movement in the Church. Their influence on theology, liturgy, catechetics, and preaching indicate the importance of their function in the life of the Church.

APOSTLES AND EVANGELISTS

The Apostles were the men selected, trained, and commissioned by Christ to preach the Gospel, to baptize, and to establish, direct and care for his Church as servants of God and stewards of his mysteries. They were the first bishops of the Church.

St. Matthew's Gospel lists the Apostles in this order: Peter, Andrew, James the Greater, John, Philip, Bartholomew, Thomas, Matthew, James the Less, Jude, Simon, and Judas Iscariot. Matthias was elected to fill the place of Judas. Paul became an Apostle by a special call from Christ. Barnabas was called an Apostle.

Two of the Evangelists, John and Matthew, were Apostles. The other two, Luke and Mark, were closely associated with the apostolic college.

Andrew: Born in Bethsaida, brother of Peter, disciple of John the Baptist, a fisherman, the first Apostle called; according to legend, preached the Gospel in northern Greece, Epirus and Scythia, and was martyred at Patras about 70; in art, is represented with an X-shaped cross, called St. Andrew's Cross; is honored as the patron of Russia and Scotland; Nov. 30.

Barnabas: Originally called Joseph but named Barnabas by the Apostles, among whom he is ranked because of his collaboration with Paul; a Jew of the Diaspora, born in Cyprus; a cousin of Mark and member of the Christian community at Jerusalem, influenced the Apostles to accept Paul, with whom he became a pioneer missionary outside Palestine and Syria, to Antioch, Cyprus, and southern Asia Minor; legend says he was martyred in Cyprus during the Neronian persecution; June 11.

Bartholomew (Nathaniel): A friend of Philip; according to various traditions, preached the Gospel in Ethiopia, India, Persia, and Armenia, where he was martyred by being flayed and beheaded; in art, is depicted holding a knife, an instrument of his death; Aug. 24 (Roman Rite), Aug. 25 (Byzantine Rite).

James the Greater: A Galilean, son of Zebedee, brother of John (with whom he was called a "Son of Thunder"), a fisherman; with Peter and John, witnessed the raising of Jairus's daughter to life, the transfiguration, the agony of Jesus in the Garden of Gethsemane; first of the Apostles to die, by the sword in 44 during the rule of Herod Agrippa; there is doubt about a journey that legend says he made to Spain and also about the authenticity of relics said to be his at Santiago de Compostela; in art, is depicted carrying a pilgrim's bell; July 25 (Roman Rite), Apr. 30 (Byzantine Rite).

James the Less: Son of Alphaeus, called "Less" because he was younger in age or shorter in stature than James the Greater; one of the Catholic Epistles bears his name; was stoned to death in 62 or thrown from the top of the temple in Jerusalem and clubbed to death in 66; in art, is depicted with a club or heavy staff; May 3 (Roman Rite), Oct. 9 (Byzantine Rite).

John: A Galilean, son of Zebedee, brother of James the Greater (with whom he was called a "Son of Thunder"), a fisherman, probably a disciple of John the Baptist, one of the Evangelists, called the "Beloved Disciple"; with Peter and James the Greater, witnessed the raising of Jairus's daughter to life, the transfiguration, the agony of Jesus in the Garden of Gethsemane; Mary was commended to his special care by Christ; the fourth Gospel, three Catholic Epistles, and Revelation bear his name; according to various accounts, lived at Ephesus in Asia Minor for some time and died a natural death about 100; in art, is represented by an eagle, symbolic of the sublimity of the contents of his Gospel; Dec. 27 (Roman Rite), May 8 (Byzantine Rite).

Jude Thaddeus: One of the Catholic Epistles, the shortest, bears his name; various traditions say he preached the Gospel in Mesopotamia, Persia, and elsewhere, and was martyred; in art, is depicted with a halberd, the instrument of his death; Oct. 28 (Roman Rite), June 19 (Byzantine Rite).

Luke: A Greek convert to the Christian community, called "our most dear physician" by Paul, of whom he was a missionary companion; author of the third Gospel and Acts of the Apostles; the place — Achaia, Bithynia, Egypt — and circumstances of his death are not certain; in art, is depicted as a man, a writer, or an ox (because his Gospel starts at the scene of temple sacrifice); Oct. 18.

Mark: A cousin of Barnabas and member of the first Christian community at Jerusalem; a missionary companion of Paul and Barnabas, then of Peter; author of the Gospel that bears his name; according to legend, founded the Church at Alexandria, was bishop there and was martyred in the streets of the city; in art, is depicted with his Gospel and a winged lion, symbolic of the voice of John the Baptist crying in the wilderness, at the beginning of his Gospel; Apr. 25.

Matthew: A Galilean, called Levi by Luke and John and the son of Alphaeus by Mark, a tax collector, one of the Evangelists; according to various accounts, preached the Gospel in Judea, Ethiopia, Persia, and Parthia, and was martyred; in art, is depicted with a spear, the instrument of his death, and as a winged man in his role as Evangelist; Sept. 21 (Roman Rite), Nov. 16 (Byzantine Rite).

Matthias: A disciple of Jesus whom the faithful 11 Apostles chose to replace Judas before the Resurrection; uncertain traditions report that he preached the Gospel in Palestine, Cappadocia, or Ethiopia; in art, is represented with a cross and a halberd, the instruments of his death as a martyr; May 14 (Roman Rite), Aug. 9 (Byzantine Rite).

Paul: Born at Tarsus, of the tribe of Benjamin, a Roman citizen; participated in the persecution of Christians until the time of his miraculous conversion on the way to Damascus; called by Christ, who revealed himself to him in a special way; became the Apostle of the Gentiles, among whom he did most of his preaching in the course of three major missionary journeys through areas north of Palestine, Cyprus, Asia Minor, and Greece; 14 epistles bear his name; two years of imprisonment at Rome, following initial arrest in Jerusalem and confinement at Caesarea, ended with martyrdom, by beheading, outside the walls of the city in 64 or 67 during the Neronian persecution; in art, is depicted in various ways with St. Peter, with a sword, in the scene of his conversion; June 29 (with St. Peter), Jan. 25 (Conversion).

Peter: Simon, son of Jonah, born in Bethsaida, brother of Andrew, a fisherman; called Cephas or Peter by Christ, who made him the chief of the Apostles and head of the Church as his vicar; named first in the listings of Apostles in the Synoptic Gospels and the Acts of the Apostles; with James the Greater and John, witnessed the raising of Jairus's daughter to life, the transfiguration, the agony of Jesus in the Garden of Gethsemane; was the first to preach the Gospel in and around Jerusalem and was the leader of the first Christian community there; established a local church in Antioch; presided over the Council of Jerusalem in 51; wrote two Catholic Epistles to the Christians in Asia Minor; established his see in Rome where he spent his last years and was martyred by crucifixion in 64 or 65 during the Neronian persecution; in art, is depicted carrying two keys, symbolic of his primacy in the Church; June 29 (with St. Paul), Feb. 22 (Chair of Peter).

Philip: Born in Bethsaida; according to legend, preached the Gospel in Phrygia where he suffered martyrdom by crucifixion; May 3 (Roman Rite), Nov. 14 (Byzantine Rite).

Simon: Called the Cananean or the Zealot; according to legend, preached in various places in the Middle East and suffered martyrdom by being sawed in two; in art, is depicted with a saw, the instrument of his death, or a book, symbolic of his zeal for the Law; Oct. 28 (Roman Rite), May 10 (Byzantine Rite).

Thomas (Didymus): Notable for his initial incredulity regarding the Resurrection and his subsequent forthright confession of the divinity of Christ risen from the dead; according to legend, preached the Gospel in places from the Caspian Sea to the Persian Gulf and eventually reached India where he was martyred near Madras; Thomas Christians trace their origin to him; in art, is depicted kneeling before the risen Christ, or with a carpenter's rule and square; July 3 (Roman Rite), Oct. 6 (Byzantine Rite).

Judas: The Gospels record only a few facts about Judas, the Apostle who betrayed Christ. The only non-Galilean among the Apostles, he was from Carioth, a town in southern Judah. He was keeper of the purse in the apostolic band. He was called a petty thief by John. He voiced dismay at the waste of money, which he said might have been spent for the poor, in connection with the anointing incident at Bethany. He took the initiative in arranging the betrayal of Christ. Afterwards, he confessed that he had betrayed an innocent man and cast into the Temple the money he had received for that action. Of his death, Matthew says that he hanged himself; the Acts of the Apostles states that he swelled up and burst open; both reports deal more with the meaning than the manner of his death — the misery of the death of a sinner.

The consensus of speculation over the reason why Judas acted as he did in betraying Christ focuses on disillusionment and unwillingness to accept the concept of a suffering Messiah and his own personal suffering as an Apostle.

APOSTOLIC FATHERS, FATHERS, DOCTORS OF THE CHURCH

The writers listed below were outstanding and authoritative witnesses to authentic Christian belief and practice, and played significant roles in giving them expression.

Apostolic Fathers

The Apostolic Fathers were Christian writers of the first and second centuries whose writings echo genuine apostolic teaching. Chief in importance are: St. Clement (d. c. 97), bishop of Rome and third successor of St. Peter in the papacy; St. Ignatius (50-c. 107), bishop of Antioch and second successor of St. Peter in that see, reputed to be a disciple of St. John; St. Polycarp (69-155), bishop of Smyrna and a disciple of St. John. The authors of the Didache and the Epistle of Barnabas are also numbered among the Apostolic Fathers.

Other early ecclesiastical writers included: St. Justin, martyr (100-165), of Asia Minor and Rome, a layman and apologist; St. Irenaeus (130-202), bishop of Lyons, who opposed Gnosticism; and St. Cyprian (210-258), bishop of Carthage, who opposed Novatianism.

Fathers and Doctors

The Fathers of the Church were theologians and writers of the first eight centuries who were outstanding for sanctity and learning. They were such authoritative witnesses to the belief and teaching of the Church that

their unanimous acceptance of doctrines as divinely revealed has been regarded as evidence that such doctrines were so received by the Church in line with apostolic tradition and Sacred Scripture. Their unanimous rejection of doctrines branded them as heretical. Their writings, however, were not necessarily free of error in all respects.

The greatest of these Fathers were: Sts. Ambrose, Augustine, Jerome, and Gregory the Great in the West; Sts. John Chrysostom, Basil the Great, Gregory of Nazianzus, and Athanasius in the East.

The Doctors of the Church were ecclesiastical writers of eminent learning and sanctity who have been given this title because of the great advantage the Church has derived from their work. Their writings, however, were not necessarily free of error in all respects.

Albert the Great, St. (c. 1200-1280): Born in Swabia, Germany; Dominican; bishop of Regensburg (1260-1262); wrote extensively on logic, natural sciences, ethics, metaphysics, Scripture, systematic theology; contributed to development of Scholasticism; teacher of St. Thomas Aquinas; canonized and proclaimed doctor, 1931; named patron of natural scientists, 1941; called *Doctor Universalis, Doctor Expertus;* Nov. 15.

Alphonsus Liguori, St. (1696-1787): Born near Naples, Italy; bishop of Saint Agatha of the Goths (1762-1775); founder of the Redemptorists; in addition to his principal work, *Theologiae Moralis*, wrote on prayer, the spiritual life, and doctrinal subjects in response to controversy; canonized, 1839; proclaimed doctor, 1871; named patron of confessors and moralists, 1950; Aug. 1.

Ambrose, St. (c. 340-397): Born in Trier, Germany; bishop of Milan (374-397); one of the strongest opponents of Arianism in the West; his homilies and other writings — on faith, the Holy Spirit, the Incarnation, the sacraments, and other subjects — were pastoral and practical; influenced the development of a liturgy at Milan which was named for him; Father and Doctor of the Church; Dec. 7.

Anselm, St. (1033-1109): Born in Aosta, Piedmont, Italy; Benedictine; archbishop of Canterbury (1093-1109); in addition to his principal work, *Cur Deus Homo*, on the atonement and reconciliation of man with God through Christ, wrote about the existence and attributes of God and defended the *Filioque* explanation of the procession of the Holy Spirit from the Father and the Son; proclaimed doctor, 1720; called Father of Scholasticism; Apr. 21.

Anthony of Padua, St. (1195-1231): Born in Lisbon, Portugal; first theologian of the Franciscan Order; preacher; canonized, 1232; proclaimed doctor, 1946; called Evangelical Doctor; June 13.

Athanasius, St. (c. 297-373): Born in Alexandria, Egypt; bishop of Alexandria (328-373); participant in the Council of Nicaea I while still a deacon; dominant opponent of Arians, whose errors regarding Christ he refuted in *Apology Against the Arians*, *Discourses against the Arians*, and other works; Father and Doctor of the Church; called Father of Orthodoxy; May 2.

Augustine, St. (354-430): Born in Tagaste, North Africa; bishop of Hippo (395-430) after conversion from Manichaeism; works include the autobiographical and mystical *Confessions*, *City of God*, treatises on the Trinity, grace, passages of the Bible, and doctrines called into question and denied by Manichaeans, Pelagians, and Donatists; had strong and lasting influence on Christian theology and philosophy; Father and Doctor of the Church; called Doctor of Grace; Aug. 28.

Basil the Great, St. (c. 329-379): Born in Caesarea, Cappadocia, Asia Minor; bishop of Caesarea (370-379); wrote three books, *Contra Eunomium*, in refutation of Arian errors, a treatise on the Holy Spirit, many homilies, and several rules for monastic life, on which he had lasting influence; Father and Doctor of the Church; called Father of Monasticism in the East; Jan. 2.

Bede the Venerable, St. (c. 673-735): Born in Northumberland, England; Benedictine; in addition to his principal work, *Ecclesiastical History* of the *English Nation* (covering the period 597-731), wrote scriptural commentaries; regarded as probably the most learned man in Western Europe of his time; called Father of English History; May 25.

Bernard of Clairvaux, St. (c. 1090-1153): Born near Dijon, France; abbot; monastic reformer, called the second founder of the Cistercian Order; mystical theologian with great influence on devotional life; opponent of the rationalism brought forward by Abélard and others; canonized, 1174; proclaimed doctor, 1830; called Mellifluous Doctor because of his eloquence; Aug. 20.

Bonaventure, St. (c. 1217-1274): Born near Viterbo, Italy; Franciscan; bishop of Albano (1273-1274); cardinal; wrote *Itinerarium Mentis in Deum*, *De Reductione Artium ad Theologiam*, *Breviloquium*, scriptural commentaries, additional mystical works affecting devotional life, and a life of St. Francis of Assisi; canonized, 1482; proclaimed doctor, 1588; called Seraphic Doctor; July 15.

Catherine of Siena, St. (c. 1347-1380): Born in Siena, Italy; member of the Third Order of St. Dominic; mystic; authored a long series of letters, mainly concerning spiritual instruction and encouragement, to associates, and *Dialogue*, a spiritual testament in four treatises; was active in support of a crusade against the Turks and efforts to end war between papal forces and the Florentine allies; had great influence in inducing Gregory XI to return himself and the Curia to Rome in 1377, to end the Avignon period of the papacy; canonized, 1461; proclaimed the second woman doctor, Oct. 4, 1970; named a co-patroness of Europe, with St. Edith Stein and St. Bridget of Sweden, on Oct. 1, 1999; Apr. 29.

Cyril of Alexandria, St. (c. 376-444): Born in Egypt; bishop of Alexandria (412-444); wrote treatises on the Trinity, the Incarnation, and other subjects, mostly in refutation of Nestorian errors; made key contributions to the development of Christology; presided at the Council of Ephesus, 431; proclaimed doctor, 1882; June 27.

Cyril of Jerusalem, St. (c. 315-386): Bishop of Jerusalem from 350; vigorous opponent of Arianism; principal work, *Catecheses*, a pre-baptismal explanation of the creed of Jerusalem; proclaimed doctor, 1882; Mar. 18.

Ephraem, St. (c. 306-373): Born in Nisibis, Mesopotamia; counteracted the spread of Gnostic and Arian errors with poems and hymns of his own composition; wrote also on the Eucharist and Mary; proclaimed doctor, 1920; called Deacon of Edessa and Harp of the Holy Spirit; June 9.

Francis of Sales, St. (1567-1622): Born in Savoy; bishop of Geneva (1602-1622); spiritual writer with strong influence on devotional life through treatises such as *Introduction to a Devout Life* and *The Love of God*; canonized, 1665; proclaimed doctor, 1877; patron of Catholic writers and the Catholic press; Jan. 24.

Gregory Nazianzen, St. (c. 330-c. 390): Born in Arianzus, Cappadocia, Asia Minor; bishop of Constantinople (381-390); vigorous opponent of Arianism; in addition to five theological discourses on the Nicene Creed and the Trinity for which he is best known, wrote letters and poetry; Father and Doctor of the Church; called the Christian Demosthenes because of his eloquence and, in the Eastern Church, the Theologian; Jan. 2.

Gregory I, the Great, St. (c. 540-604): Born in Rome; pope (590-604); wrote many scriptural commentaries, a compendium of theology in the *Book of Morals* based on Job, *Dialogues*, concerning the lives of saints, the immortality of the soul, death, purgatory, heaven and hell, and fourteen books of letters; enforced papal supremacy and established the position of the pope vis-á-vis the emperor; worked for clerical and monastic reform and the observance of clerical celibacy; Father and Doctor of the Church; Sept. 3.

Hilary of Poitiers, St. (c. 315-368): Born in Poitiers,

France; bishop of Poitiers (c. 353-368); wrote *De Synodis*, with the Arian controversy in mind, and *De Trinitate*, the first lengthy study of the doctrine in Latin; introduced Eastern theology to the West; contributed to the development of hymnology; proclaimed doctor, 1851; called the Athanasius of the West because of his vigorous defense of the divinity of Christ against Arians; Jan. 13.

Isidore of Seville, St. (c. 560-636): Born in Cartagena, Spain; bishop of Seville (c. 600-636); in addition to his principal work, *Etymologiae*, an encyclopedia of the knowledge of his day, wrote on theological and historical subjects; regarded as the most learned man of his time; proclaimed doctor, 1722; Apr. 4.

Jerome, St. (c. 343-420): Born in Stridon, Dalmatia; translated the Old Testament from Hebrew into Latin and revised the existing Latin translation of the New Testament to produce the Vulgate version of the Bible; wrote scriptural commentaries and treatises on matters of controversy; regarded as Father and Doctor of the Church from the eighth century; called Father of Biblical Science; Sept. 30.

John Chrysostom, St. (c. 347-407): Born in Antioch, Asia Minor; archbishop of Constantinople (398-407); wrote homilies, scriptural commentaries, and letters of wide influence, in addition to a classical treatise on the priesthood; proclaimed doctor by the Council of Chalcedon, 451; called the greatest of the Greek Fathers; named patron of preachers, 1909; called Golden-Mouthed because of his eloquence; Sept. 13.

John Damascene, St. (c. 675-c. 749): Born in Damascus, Syria; monk; wrote *Fountain of Wisdom*, a three-part work including a history of heresies and an exposition of the Christian faith, three discourses against the Iconoclasts, homilies on Mary, biblical commentaries, and treatises on moral subjects; proclaimed doctor, 1890; called Golden Speaker because of his eloquence; Dec. 4.

John of the Cross, St. (1542-1591): Born in Old Castile, Spain; Carmelite; founder of Discalced Carmelites; one of the greatest mystical theologians; wrote *The Ascent of Mt. Carmel, The Dark Night of the Soul, The Spiritual Canticle, The Living Flame of Love*; canonized, 1726; proclaimed doctor, 1926; called Doctor of Mystical Theology; Dec. 14.

Lawrence of Brindisi, St. (1559-1619): Born in Brindisi, Italy; Franciscan (Capuchin); vigorous preacher of strong influence in the post-Reformation period; 15 tomes of collected works include scriptural commentaries, sermons, homilies and doctrinal writings; canonized, 1881; proclaimed doctor, 1959; July 21.

Leo I, the Great, St. (c. 400-461): Born in Tuscany, Italy; pope (440-461); wrote the *Tome of Leo*, to explain doctrine concerning the two natures and one Person of Christ, against the background of the Nestorian and Monophysite heresies; other works included sermons, letters, and writings against the errors of Manichaeism and Pelagianism; was instrumental in dissuading Attila from sacking Rome in 452; proclaimed doctor, 1574; Nov. 10.

Peter Canisius, St. (1521-1597): Born in Nijmegen,

Holland; Jesuit; wrote popular expositions of the Catholic faith in several catechisms which were widely circulated in 20 editions in his lifetime alone; was one of the moving figures in the Counter-Reformation period, especially in southern and western Germany; canonized and proclaimed doctor, 1925; Dec. 21.

Peter Chrysologus, St. (c. 400-450): Born in Imola, Italy; served as archbishop of Ravenna (c. 433-450); his sermons and writings, many of which were designed to counteract Monophysitism, were pastoral and practical; proclaimed doctor, 1729; July 30.

Peter Damian, St. (1007-1072): Born in Ravenna, Italy; Benedictine; cardinal; his writings and sermons, many of which concerned ecclesiastical and clerical reform, were pastoral and practical; proclaimed doctor, 1828; Feb. 21.

Robert Bellarmine, St. (1542-1621): Born in Tuscany, Italy; Jesuit; archbishop of Capua (1602-1605); wrote *Controversies*, a three-volume exposition of doctrine under attack during and after the Reformation, two catechisms, and the spiritual work *The Art of Dying Well*; was an authority on ecclesiology and Church-state relations; canonized, 1930; proclaimed doctor, 1931; Sept. 17.

Teresa of Jesus (Ávila), St. (1515-1582): Born in Ávila, Spain; entered the Carmelite Order, 1535; in the early 1560s, initiated a primitive Carmelite reform which greatly influenced men and women religious, especially in Spain; wrote extensively on spiritual and mystical subjects; principal works included her *Autobiography, Way of Perfection, The Interior Castle, Meditations on the Canticle, The Foundations, Visitation of the Discalced Nuns*; canonized, 1622; proclaimed first woman doctor, Sept. 27, 1970; Oct. 15.

Thérèse of Lisieux, St. (1873-1897): Born in Alençon, Normandy, France; entered the Carmelites at Lisieux in 1888, lived for only nine more years, dying on Sept. 30, 1897, from tuberculosis. Trusting completely in God, a path she described as the "little way," she lived a seemingly ordinary life of a nun, but her spiritual advancement was such that her superiors instructed her to write an autobiography in 1895 (The Story of a Soul). One of the most popular and respected saints throughout the 20th century, she was canonized on May 17, 1925. Pope John Paul II declared her the third woman doctor on Oct. 20, 1997, in the letter *Divini amoris scientia*; her relics also toured the United States, attracting huge crowds; Oct. 1.

Thomas Aquinas, St. (1225-1274): Born near Naples, Italy; Dominican; teacher and writer on virtually the whole range of philosophy and theology; principal works were *Summa contra Gentiles*, a manual and systematic defense of Christian doctrine, and *Summa Theologiae*, a new (at that time) exposition of theology on philosophical principles; canonized, 1323; proclaimed doctor, 1567; called *Doctor Communis, Doctor Angelicus*, the Great Synthesizer because of the way in which he related faith and reason, theology and philosophy (especially that of Aristotle), and systematized the presentation of Christian doctrine; named patron of Catholic schools and education, 1880; Jan. 28.

CREEDS

Creeds are formal and official statements of Christian doctrine. As summaries of the principal truths of faith, they are standards of orthodoxy and are useful for instructional purposes, for actual profession of the faith, and for expression of the faith in the liturgy.

The classical creeds are the Apostles' Creed and the Creed of Nicaea-Constantinople. Two others are the Athanasian Creed and the Creed of Pius IV.

Apostles' Creed

Text: *I believe in God, the Father almighty, Creator of heaven and earth.*

And in Jesus Christ, his only Son, our Lord; who was conceived by the Holy Spirit, born of the Virgin Mary, suffered under Pontius Pilate, was crucified, died, and was buried. He descended into hell; the third day he arose again from the dead; he ascended into heaven, sits at the right hand of God, the Father almighty; from thence he shall come to judge the living and the dead.

I believe in the Holy Spirit, the holy Catholic Church, the communion of saints, the forgiveness of sins, the resurrection of the body, and life everlasting. Amen.

Background: The Apostles' Creed reflects the teaching of the Apostles but is not of apostolic origin. It probably originated in the second century as a rudimentary formula of faith professed by catechumens before the reception of baptism. Baptismal creeds in fourth-century use at Rome and elsewhere in the West closely resembled the present text, which was quoted in a handbook of Christian doctrine written between 710 and 724. This text was in wide use throughout the West by the ninth century. The Apostles' Creed is common to all Christian confessional churches in the West, but is not used in Eastern Churches.

Nicene Creed

The following translation of the Latin text of the Creed was prepared by the International Committee on English in the Liturgy.

Text: *We believe in one God, the Father, the Almighty, maker of heaven and earth, of all that is seen and unseen.*

We believe in one Lord, Jesus Christ, the only Son of God, eternally begotten of the Father, God from God, Light from Light, true God from true God, begotten, not made, one in Being with the Father. Through him all things were made. For us men and for our salvation he came down from heaven: by the power of the Holy Spirit he was born of the Virgin Mary, and became man. For our sake he was crucified under Pontius Pilate; he suffered, died, and was buried. On the third day he rose again in fulfillment of the Scriptures; he ascended into heaven and is seated at the right hand of the Father. He will come again in glory to judge the living and the dead, and his kingdom will have no end.

We believe in the Holy Spirit, the Lord, the giver of life, who proceeds from the Father and the Son. With the Father and the Son he is worshipped and glorified. He has spoken through the prophets.

We believe in one holy catholic and apostolic Church. We acknowledge one baptism for the forgiveness of sins. We look for the resurrection of the dead, and the life of the world to come. Amen.

Background: The Nicene Creed (Creed of Nicaea-Constantinople) consists of elements of doctrine contained in an early baptismal creed of Jerusalem and enactments of the Council of Nicaea (325) and the Council of Constantinople (381).

Its strong trinitarian content reflects the doctrinal errors, especially of Arianism, it served to counteract. Theologically, it is much more sophisticated than the Apostles' Creed.

Since late in the fifth century, the Nicene Creed has been the only creed in liturgical use in the Eastern Churches. The Western Church adopted it for liturgical use by the end of the eighth century.

The Athanasian Creed

The Athanasian Creed, which has a unique structure, is a two-part summary of doctrine concerning the Trinity and the Incarnation-Redemption bracketed at the beginning and end with the statement that belief in the cited truths is necessary for salvation; it also contains a number of anathemas or condemnatory clauses regarding doctrinal errors. Although attributed to St. Athanasius, it was probably written after his death, between 381 and 428, and may have been authored by St. Ambrose. It is not accepted in the East; in the West, it formerly had place in the Roman-Rite Liturgy of the Hours and in the liturgy for the Solemnity of the Holy Trinity.

Creed of Pius IV

The Creed of Pius IV, also called the Profession of Faith of the Council of Trent, was promulgated in the bull *Injunctum Nobis*, Nov. 13, 1564. It is a summary of doctrine defined by the council concerning Scripture and tradition, original sin and justification, the Mass and sacraments, veneration of the saints, indulgences, and the primacy of the See of Rome. It was slightly modified in 1887 to include doctrinal formulations of the First Vatican Council.

CHRISTIAN MORALITY

By Fr. Alfred McBride, O.Praem.

"Incorporated into Christ by Baptism, Christians are 'dead to sin and alive in Christ Jesus. . .'" (Rom 6:11).

CHRISTIAN MORALITY IS LIFE IN CHRIST

The third part of the *Catechism* focuses on Christian morality. After the Creed as faith professed, and sacraments as faith celebrated, the *Catechism* turns our attention to the faith lived. It deals with this issue in two major sections. The first section establishes the context for Christian morality. The second section analyzes the Ten Commandments. This approach preserves the *Catechism's* resolute insistence on the primacy of God's initiative through Revelation, salvation, and grace followed by our human response in faith, celebration, and Christian witness. Hence morality does not begin with the rules but with the call to life in Christ and the Holy Spirit. Covenant love comes first, then the response of Christian affection in the life of the commandments. This saves us both from legalism and from piety without practical witness.

The following excerpt from the *Catechism of the Catholic Church* sets the vision for the Christian moral life.

Life In Christ

1691 "Christian, recognize your dignity and, now that you share in God's own nature, do not return to your former base condition by sinning. Remember who is your head and of whose body you are a member. Never forget that you have been rescued from the power of darkness and brought into the light of the Kingdom of God."[1]

1692 The Symbol of the faith confesses the greatness of God's gifts to man in his work of creation, and even more in redemption and sanctification. What faith confesses, the sacraments communicate: by the sacraments of rebirth, Christians have become "children of God,"[2] "partakers of the divine nature."[3] Coming to see in the faith their new dignity, Christians are called to lead henceforth a life "worthy of the gospel of Christ."[4] They are made capable of doing so by the grace of Christ and the gifts of his Spirit, which they receive through the sacraments and through prayer.

1693 Christ Jesus always did what was pleasing to the Father,[5] and always lived in perfect communion with him. Likewise Christ's disciples are invited to live in the sight of the Father "who sees in secret,"[6] in order to become "perfect as your heavenly Father is perfect."[7]

1694 Incorporated into Christ by Baptism, Christians are "dead to sin and alive to God in Christ Jesus" and so participate in the life of the Risen Lord.[8] Following Christ and united with him,[9] Christians can strive to be "imitators of God as beloved children, and walk in love"[10] by conforming their thoughts, words and actions to the "mind... which is yours in Christ Jesus,"[11] and by following his example.[12]

1695 "Justified in the name of the Lord Jesus Christ and in the Spirit of our God," [13] "sanctified... [and] called to be saints,"[14] Christians have become the temple of the Holy Spirit.[15] This "Spirit of the Son" teaches them to pray to the Father[16] and, having

become their life, prompts them to act so as to bear "the fruit of the Spirit"[17] by charity in action. Healing the wounds of sin, the Holy Spirit renews us interiorly through a spiritual transformation.[18] He enlightens and strengthens us to live as "children of light" through "all that is good and right and true."[19]

1696 The way of Christ "leads to life"; a contrary way "leads to destruction."[20] The Gospel parable of the two ways remains ever present in the catechesis of the Church; it shows the importance of moral decisions for our salvation: "There are two ways, the one of life, the other of death; but between the two, there is a great difference."[21]

1697 Catechesis has to reveal in all clarity the joy and the demands of the way of Christ.[22] Catechesis for the "newness of life"[23] in him should be:

• a catechesis of the Holy Spirit, the interior Master of life according to Christ, a gentle guest and friend who inspires, guides, corrects, and strengthens this life;

• a catechesis of grace, for it is by grace that we are saved and again it is by grace that our works can bear fruit for eternal life;

• a catechesis of the beatitudes, for the way of Christ is summed up in the beatitudes, the only path that leads to the eternal beatitude for which the human heart longs;

• a catechesis of sin and forgiveness, for unless man acknowledges that he is a sinner he cannot know the truth about himself, which is a condition for acting justly; and without the offer of forgiveness he would not be able to bear this truth;

• a catechesis of the human virtues which causes one to grasp the beauty and attraction of right dispositions towards goodness;

• a catechesis of the Christian virtues of faith, hope, and charity, generously inspired by the example of the saints; a catechesis of the twofold commandment of charity set forth in the Decalogue;

• an ecclesial catechesis, for it is through the manifold exchanges of "spiritual goods" in the "communion of saints" that Christian life can grow, develop, and be communicated.

1698 The first and last point of reference of this catechesis will always be Jesus Christ himself, who is "the way, and the truth, and the life."[24] It is by looking to him in faith that Christ's faithful can hope that he himself fulfills his promises in them, and that, by loving him with the same love with which he has loved them, they may perform works in keeping with their dignity: "I ask you to consider that our Lord Jesus Christ is your true head, and that you are one of his members. He belongs to you as the head belongs to its members; all that is his is yours: his spirit, his heart, his body and soul, and all his faculties. You must make use of all these as of your own, to serve, praise, love, and glorify God. You belong to him, as members belong to their head. And so he longs for you to use all that is in you, as if it were his own, for the service and glory of the Father."[25] "For to me, to live is Christ."[26]

Footnotes

[1] St. Leo the Great, Sermon 22 in nat. Dom 3: PL 54, 192C. [2] Jn 1:12; 1 Jn 3:1. [3] 2 Pt 1:4. [4] Phil 1:27. [5] Cf. Jn 8:29. [6] Mt 6:6. [7] Mt 5:48. [8] Rom 6:11 and cf. 6:5; cf. Col 2:12. [9] Cf. Jn 15:5. [10] Eph 5:1-2. [11] Phil 2:5. [12] Cf. Jn 13:12-16. [13] 1 Cor 6:11. [14] 1 Cor 1:2. [15] Cf. 1 Cor 6:19. [16] Cf. Gal 4:6. [17] Gal 5:22, 25. [18] Cf. Eph 4:23. [19] Eph 5:8, 9. [20] Mt 7:13; cf. Dt 30: 15-20. [21] Didache 1, 1: SCh 248, 140. [22] Cf. John Paul II, CT 29. [23] Rom 6:4. [24] Jn. 14:6. [25] St. John Eudes, Tract. de admirabili corde Jesu, 1, 5. [26] Phil 1:21.

THE TEN COMMANDMENTS

Any discussions of the commandments should begin with the scene at Sinai where God gave them to us. Read Ex 19:3-6; 20:1-17. The first event is a covenant experience. God tells Moses how much he has loved the Israelites, is delivering them from slavery by "raising them up on eagles' wings," and is bringing them to freedom. God then offers them a binding covenant of love. He will be their only God and they will be his chosen people. It's like a marriage experience, an exchange of vows between God and Israel.

The next section shows God telling them how to live out the love they have pledged. He gives them the Ten Commandments as the means to live the covenant, to express the love they have promised. The Catechism points out that the Ten Commandments are privileged expressions of the natural law, made known to us by reason as well as Divine Revelation. We are obliged in obedience to observe these laws of love, both in serious and light matters. Love is in the details as well as the large matters. We must remember that what God has commanded, he makes possible by his grace.

Jesus set the tone for understanding the importance of the commandments. When a rich young man came to him and asked him what he should do to enter eternal life, Jesus replied, "if you wish to enter into life, keep the commandments" (Mt 19:17). In another case, someone asked him which were the greatest commandments, Jesus replied, "you shall love the Lord, your God, with all your heart, with all your soul, and with all your mind. This is the greatest and first commandment. The second is like it: You shall love your neighbor as yourself" (Mt 22:37-39). The first three commandments deal with Christ's call to God with all our being. The last seven commandments show us how to love our neighbors as we love ourselves.

The following excerpt from the Catechism of the Catholic Church shows how Jesus taught the importance of the Ten Commandments.

"Teacher, what must I do. . .?"

2052 "Teacher, what good deed must I do, to have eternal life?" To the young man who asked this question, Jesus answers first by invoking the necessity to recognize God as the "One there is who is good," as the supreme Good and the source of all good. Then Jesus tells him: "If you would enter life, keep the commandments." And he cites for his questioner the precepts that concern love of neighbor: "You shall not kill, You shall not commit adultery, You shall not steal, You shall not bear false witness, Honor your father and your mother." Finally Jesus sums up these commandments positively: "You shall love your neighbor as yourself."[1]

2053 To this first reply Jesus adds a second: "If you would be perfect, go, sell what you possess and give to the poor, and you will have treasure in heaven; and come, follow me."[2] This reply does not do away with the first: following Jesus Christ involves keeping the Commandments. The Law has not been abolished,[3] but rather man is invited to rediscover it in the person of his Master who is its perfect fulfillment. In the three synoptic Gospels, Jesus' call to the rich young man to follow him, in the obedience of a disciple and in the observance of the Commandments, is joined to the call to poverty and chastity.[4] The evangelical counsels are inseparable from the Commandments.

2054 Jesus acknowledged the Ten Commandments, but he also showed the power of the Spirit at work in their letter. He preached a "righteousness [which] exceeds that of the scribes and Pharisees"[5] as well as that of the Gentiles.[6] He unfolded all the demands of the Commandments. "You have heard that it was said to the men of old, 'You shall not kill.' ... But I say to you that every one who is angry with his brother shall be liable to judgment."[7]

2055 When someone asks him, "Which commandment in the Law is the greatest?"[8] Jesus replies: "You shall love the Lord your God with all your heart, and with all your soul, and with all your mind. This is the greatest and first commandment. And a second is like it: You shall love your neighbor as yourself. On these two commandments hang all the Law and the prophets."[9] The Decalogue must be interpreted in light of this twofold yet single commandment of love, he fullness of the Law: "The commandments: 'You shall not commit adultery, You shall not kill, You shall not steal, You shall not covet,' and any other commandment, are summed up in this sentence: 'You shall love your neighbor as yourself.' Love does no wrong to a neighbor; therefore love is the fulfilling of the law."[10]

Footnotes

[1] Mt 19:16-19. [2] Mt 19:21. [3] Cf. Mt 5:17. [4] Cf. Mt 19:6-12, 21, 23-29. [5] Mt 5:20. [6] Cf. Mt 5:46-47. [7] Mt 5:21-22. [8] Mt 22:36. [9] Mt 22:37-40; cf. Dt 6:5; Lv 19:18. [10] Rom 13:9-10.

In the traditional Catholic enumeration and according to Dt 5:6-21, the Commandments are:

1. "I, the Lord, am your God You shall not have other gods besides me. You shall not carve idols."
2. "You shall not take the name of the Lord, your God, in vain."
3. "Take care to keep holy the Sabbath day."
4. "Honor your father and your mother."
5. "You shall not kill."
6. "You shall not commit adultery."
7. "You shall not steal."
8. "You shall not bear dishonest witness against your neighbor."
9. "You shall not covet your neighbor's wife."
10. "You shall not desire your neighbor's house or field, nor his male or female slave, nor his ox or ass, nor anything that belongs to him" (summarily, his goods).

Another version of the Commandments, substantially the same, is given in Ex 20:1-17.

The traditional enumeration of the Commandments in Protestant usage differs from the above. Thus: two commandments are made of the first, as above; the third and fourth are equivalent to the second and third, as above, and so on; and the 10th includes the ninth and 10th, as above.

Love of God and Neighbor

The first three of the commandments deal directly with man's relations with God, viz., acknowledgment of one true God and the rejection of false gods and idols; honor due to God and his name; observance of the Sabbath as the Lord 's Day.

The rest cover interpersonal relationships, viz., the obedience due to parents and, logically, to other persons in authority, and the obligations of parents to children and of persons in authority to those under their care; respect for life and physical integrity; fidelity in marriage, and chastity; justice and rights; truth; internal respect for faithfulness in marriage, chastity, and the goods of others.

Perfection in Christian Life

The moral obligations of the Ten Commandments are complemented by others flowing from the twofold law of love, the whole substance and pattern of Christ's teaching, and everything implied in full and active

membership and participation in the community of salvation formed by Christ in his Church. Some of these matters are covered in other sections of the *Almanac* under appropriate headings.

Precepts of the Church

The purpose of the precepts of the Church, according to the *Catechism of the Catholic Church*, is "to guarantee to the faithful the indispensable minimum in the spirit of prayer and moral effort, in the growth and love of God and neighbor" (No. 2041).

1. Attendance at Mass on Sundays and holy days of obligation. (Observance of Sundays and holy days of obligation involves refraining from work that hinders the worship due to God.)

2. Confession of sins at least once a year. (Not required by the precept in the absence of serious sin.)

3. Reception of the Eucharist at least during the Easter season (in the U.S., from the first Sunday of Lent to Trinity Sunday).

4. Keep holy the holy days of obligation.

5. Observance of specified days of fasting and abstinence.

There is also an obligation to provide for the material needs of the Church.

CATHOLIC MORAL TEACHINGS OF POPE JOHN PAUL II

On Aug. 6, 1993, Pope John Paul II published his tenth encyclical, Veritatis Splendor *("The Splendor of the Truth") regarding the fundamental truths of the Church's moral teachings. On Mar. 25, 1995, he published his eleventh encyclical,* Evangelium Vitae *("The Gospel of Life"), concerning the value and inviolability of human life. The following material is adapted from* The Encyclicals of John Paul II, *with the kind permission of Most Rev. J. Michael Miller, C.S.B.*

Veritatis Splendor
("The Splendor of the Truth")

On Aug. 6, 1993, John Paul II signed his tenth encyclical, *Veritatis Splendor*, regarding certain fundamental truths of the Church's moral teaching.[1] Undoubtedly it is the pope's most complex and most discussed document. Since its publication, the encyclical has generated a great deal of comment in the media and among theologians. This is not surprising, since *Veritatis Splendor* is the first-ever papal document on the theological and philosophical foundations of Catholic moral teaching. In this encyclical the pope affirms that divine revelation contains "a specific and determined moral content, universally valid and permanent" (§37.1), which the Magisterium has the competence to interpret and teach.

Six years before, in the apostolic letter *Spiritus Domini* (1987), John Paul had publicly announced his intention to publish a document that would treat "more fully and more deeply the issues regarding the very foundations of moral theology" (§5.1). For several reasons the encyclical's preparation took longer than was first anticipated. First, the pope widely consulted bishops and theologians throughout the world, and various drafts were drawn up. Second, he thought that it was fitting for the encyclical "to be preceded by the Catechism of the Catholic Church, which contains a

complete and systematic exposition of Christian moral teaching" (§5.3). The Catechism, published in 1992, gives a full presentation of the Church's moral doctrine, including that on particular questions, and expounds it in a positive way. *Veritatis Splendor*, on the other hand, limits itself to dealing with the fundamental principles underlying all moral teaching.

But why does John Paul think that an encyclical on moral issues will serve the Church and the world on the threshold of the third millennium? According to him, reflection on the ethical implications of Christian faith, lived from the beginning as the "way" (Acts 22:4), belongs to the full proclamation of the Gospel. Moreover, he is convinced that society is in the throes of a "crisis of truth" (§32.2). This crisis has the "most serious implications for the moral life of the faithful and for communion in the Church, as well as for a just and fraternal social life" (§5.2).

The deChristianization of many cultures involves not only a loss of faith but also "a decline or obscuring of the moral sense" (§106.2). This new moral situation brings with it "the confusion between good and evil, which makes it impossible to build up and to preserve the moral order" (§93.1). The ethical bewilderment of some Catholics has led to "the spread of numerous doubts and objections of a human and psychological, social and cultural, religious and even properly theological nature, with regard to the Church's moral teachings" (§4.2). In an increasingly secular world, believers are "making judgments and decisions [that] often appear extraneous or even contrary to those of the Gospel" (§88.2). Moreover, dissent from Catholic moral teaching often entails "an overall and systematic calling into question of traditional moral doctrine" (§4.2). Thus, as a service to the ethical and spiritual welfare of individuals and cultures, John Paul addresses the basic moral principles handed down by the

Christian Tradition.

In order to meet his goal, the pope responds in a constructive way to the contemporary moral crisis by proclaiming "the splendor of the truth." When he announced the forthcoming publication of *Veritatis Splendor*, he described the encyclical's purpose: "It reaffirms the dignity of the human person, created in God's image, and proposes anew the genuine concept of human freedom, showing its essential and constitutive relationship with the truth in accordance with Christ's words: 'The truth will make you free!' (Jn 8:32)."[2] On another occasion, John Paul said that he intended the encyclical to be "a proclamation of truth and a hymn to freedom: values felt strongly by contemporary man and deeply respected by the Church."[3] His primary aim, then, is not to censure specific dissident moral opinions but to proclaim that Christ is "the true and final answer to the problem of morality" (§85).

John Paul sets several specific objectives for the encyclical. First, he wishes "to reflect on the whole of the Church's moral teaching, with the precise goal of recalling certain fundamental truths of Catholic doctrine which, in the present circumstances, risk being distorted or denied" (§4.2, cf. §30.1). Second, he aims to show the faithful "the inviting splendor of that truth which is Jesus Christ himself" (§83.2). Christ alone is the answer to humanity's questions, "the only response fully capable of satisfying the desire of the human heart" (§7.1). Third, if the present crisis is to be successfully resolved, the magisterium must authoritatively discern "interpretations of Christian morality which are not consistent with 'sound teaching' (2 Tm 4:3)" (§29.4, cf. §27.4). This pastoral discernment of the pope and bishops is necessary as a way of assuring "the right of the faithful to receive Catholic doctrine in its purity and integrity" (§113.2).

The pope addresses *Veritatis Splendor* specifically to his brother bishops. He intends them to be the first, but not exclusive, recipients of the encyclical. John Paul reminds them of their responsibility to safeguard and find "ever new ways of speaking with love and mercy" about "the path of the moral life" (§3.1,2).

John Paul II's training in ethics and moral theology is clearly evident in *Veritatis Splendor*. The encyclical's exposition is sometimes highly technical, especially in its analyses and responses to opinions contrary to Church teaching. While some commentators have voiced disagreement about the accuracy of the pope's descriptions of the ethical positions with which he disagrees, they respect his desire to be fair-minded. As we shall see, whenever John Paul deals with an opinion he disagrees with, he first takes great pains to point out what is positive in the view. Only after doing this does he then examine its weaknesses. When unmasking theological and philosophical ideas incompatible with revealed truth, he scrupulously avoids imposing "any particular theological system, still less a philosophical one" (§29.4).

Throughout the encyclical the pope repeatedly draws inspiration from the Bible. Chapter one, structured around the encounter of Jesus with the rich young man (Mt 19:16-21), establishes a biblical foundation for fundamental moral principles. In this chapter the pope wishes to apply the theological method proposed by the Second Vatican Council: "Sacred Scripture remains the living and fruitful source of the Church's moral doctrine" (§28.2, cf. §5.3). Chapter two, on the other hand, uses Scripture chiefly to corroborate positions advanced on the basis of the natural moral law. The beginning of chapter three returns to a more biblical approach; it discusses discipleship in terms of the Paschal Mystery and of martyrdom as the supreme expression of following Christ.

More so than in his other encyclicals, in *Veritatis Splendor* John Paul relies considerably on the teaching of St. Thomas Aquinas, referring to him directly at least 20 times, and on the teaching of St. Augustine, citing him 16 times. The pope also mines extensively the documents of Vatican II, especially *Gaudium et Spes*, which he cites more than 25 times. Except for one reference to St. Alphonsus Liguori and a single direct citation of John Henry Newman, the pope mentions no moral philosopher or theologian after the Middle Ages.

Footnotes

1. *Acta Apostolicae Sedis*, 85 (1993), 1133-1228. 2. Angelus, Oct. 3, 1993, *L'Osservatore Romano*, 40 (1993), 1. 3. Angelus, Oct. 17, 1993, *L'Osservatore Romano*, 42 (1993), 1.

Evangelium Vitae ("The Gospel of Life")

"The Gospel of life is at the heart of Jesus' message" (§1.1). With these words Pope John Paul II begins his eleventh encyclical, *Evangelium Vitae*, published on March 25, 1995.[1] He aptly chose the feast of the Annunciation, which celebrates Mary's welcoming of the Son of God who took flesh in her womb, to issue a document dedicated to the value and inviolability of human life. By taking up the cause of the "great multitude of weak and defenseless human beings" (§5.4), especially unborn children and those at the end of life, the pope continues the defense of human dignity dealt with in his three social encyclicals. *Evangelium Vitae* is an anguished and vigorous response to "scientifically and systematically programmed threats" against life (§17.2), assaults which have repercussions on Church teaching, touching upon "the core of her faith in the redemptive Incarnation of the Son of God" (§3.1).

For Pope John Paul II, the cause of life is the cause of the Gospel entrusted to the Church, which is duty-bound to raise her voice in the defense of life. His encyclical is a "pressing appeal addressed to each and every person, in the name of God: respect, protect, love and serve life, every human life!" (§5.5).

Preparations for the encyclical began in Apr. 1991, when the pope called a special meeting in Rome of the College of Cardinals to discuss current threats to human life. After their deliberations, the cardinals asked him "to reaffirm with the authority of the Successor of Peter the value of human life and its inviolability" (§5.1). As a first response to their request, the pope wrote a personal letter to every bishop, seeking contributions to the planned document. They replied with valuable suggestions, and he incorporated many of their proposals into the encyclical. *Evangelium Vitae*, then, is the fruit of genuine episcopal collegiality. By taking an active part in its preparation, the bishops "bore witness to their unanimous desire to share in the doctrinal and pastoral mission of the Church with regard to the Gospel of life" (§5.2).

Unlike *Veritatis Splendor*, which was directed primarily to bishops, John Paul intends *Evangelium Vitae* to be read also by the lay faithful, indeed by all people of good will. Concern for the sacredness of human life is not just a matter for Catholics. "The value at stake," writes the pope, "is one which every human being can grasp by the light of reason" (§101.2). The essential truths of the Gospel of life "are written in the heart of every man and woman," echoing in every human conscience "from the time of creation itself" (§29.3). He insists that anyone who is sincerely open to truth and goodness can discover "the sacred value of human life from its very beginning until its end, and can affirm the right of every human being to have this primary good respected to the highest degree" (§2.2).

The encyclical's style is typically Wojtylan. It intersperses rigorous analysis with prayers and exhortations. As can be seen from the more than three hundred biblical quotations and references, Scripture accompanies the pope's presentation from start to finish, giving *Evangelium Vitae* an inspirational tone and familiar style. He also relies heavily on the Church Fathers. The eighteen patristic quotations that appear in the encyclical reinforce the truths that God is the origin of life, that human beings share in divine life, and that Jesus gave his life so that others might live. As is customary, John Paul frequently cites the documents of the

Second Vatican Council — here, more than 25 times. He also makes use of the Catechism of the Catholic Church, citing it on 10 occasions.

Of particular significance in *Evangelium Vitae* are the pope's three authoritative doctrinal pronouncements: on the direct and voluntary killing of innocent human life (cf. §57.4), on abortion (cf. §62.3), and on euthanasia (cf. §65.3). In each of these formal statements John Paul recalls, through his ordinary magisterium, that a specific proposition is taught infallibly by the ordinary and universal Magisterium of the College of Bishops in communion with the Successor of Peter. He does not, therefore, call upon the charism which belongs to the Petrine ministry to teach infallibly, as this was defined at the First Vatican Council (1870). Rather, the pope "confirms" or "declares" (as in the case of abortion) a doctrine already taught by the bishops as belonging to the Catholic faith. Thus, there is nothing "new" in the Pope's affirmations, but merely the reiteration of teaching about which a consensus exists in the Episcopal College.

Footnotes

1. *Acta Apostolicae Sedis*, 87 (1995), 401-522.

CATHOLIC SOCIAL DOCTRINE

Nature of the Doctrine

Writing in *Christianity and Social Progress*, Pope John XXIII made the following statement about the nature and scope of the Church's social doctrine as stated in the encyclicals in particular and related writings in general:

"What the Catholic Church teaches and declares regarding the social life and relationships of men is beyond question for all time valid.

"The cardinal point of this teaching is that individual men are necessarily the foundation, cause, and end of all social institutions insofar as they are social by nature, and raised to an order of existence that transcends and subdues nature.

"Beginning with this very basic principle whereby the dignity of the human person is affirmed and defended, Holy Church — especially during the last century and with the assistance of learned priests and laymen, specialists in the field — has arrived at clear social teachings whereby the mutual relationships of men are ordered. Taking general norms into account, these principles are in accord with the nature of things and the changed conditions of man's social life, or with the special genius of our day. Moreover, these norms can be approved by all."

Background

While social concerns have always been a part of the Church's teachings, Catholic social doctrine has been the subject of much consideration since the end of the last century and has been formulated in a progressive manner in a number of authoritative documents starting with the encyclical *Rerum Novarum* ("On Capital and Labor") issued by Leo XIII in 1891. Owing to its significance, the encyclical was called by Pope John XXIII the *magna carta* of Catholic social doctrine.

Other outstanding examples are the encyclicals: *Quadragesimo Anno* ("On Reconstruction of the Social Order") by Pius XI in 1931; *Mater et Magistra* ("Christianity and Social Progress") and *Pacem in Terris* ("Peace on Earth"), by John XXIII in 1961 and 1963, respectively; *Populorum Progressio* ("Development of Peoples"), by Paul VI in 1967; *Laborem Exercens* ("On Human Work"), *Sollicitudo Rei Socialis* ("On Social Concerns") and *Centesimus Annus* ("The 100th Year") by John Paul II in 1981, 1987, and 1991, respectively. Among many other accomplishments of ideological importance in the social field, Pius XII made a distinctive contribution with his formulation of a plan for world peace and order in Christmas messages from 1939 to 1941, and in other documents.

Of particular significance to the contemporary application of social doctrine are the document *Gaudium et Spes* (Pastoral Constitution on the Church in the Modern World) issued by the Second Vatican Council and Pope John Paul II's encyclical letters, *Laborem Exercens* ("On Human Work"), *Sollicitudo Rei Socialis* ("On Social Concerns"), and *Centesimus Annus* ("The 100th Year").

These documents represent the most serious attempts in modern times to systematize the social implications of divine revelation as well as the socially relevant writings of the Fathers and Doctors of the Church. Their contents are theological penetrations into social life, with particular reference to human rights, the needs of the poor and those in underdeveloped countries, and humane conditions of life, freedom, justice and peace. In some respects, they read like juridical documents; essentially, however, they are Gospel-oriented and pastoral in intention.

Gaudium et Spes

Gaudium et Spes ("Pastoral Constitution on the

Church in the Modern World") was the last document issued by Vatican Council II (Dec. 7, 1965). The document has as its purpose to search out the signs of God's presence and meaning in and through the events of this time in human history. Accordingly, it deals with the situation of men in present circumstances of profound change, challenge and crisis on all levels of life. It is evenly divided into two main parts: the Church's teaching on humanity in the modern era and urgent problems of the times.

Part One

The first part begins: "The joys and the hopes, the griefs and the anxieties of this age" (No. 1)—a clear indication that the Council Fathers were aware both of the positive nature of the modern world and its many dangers and travails. Further, the council places great emphasis throughout on the human existence, a stress that was quite innovative in its presentation: "According to the almost unanimous opinion of believers and unbelievers alike, all things on earth should be related to man as their center and crown" (No. 12). Having developed an analysis of humanity, the document then offered a thorough summary of traditional Church teaching on human life, complete with discussion of sin, the union of body and soul, and the moral conscience.

There is, as well, a genuinely realistic appraisal of contemporary society, noting the pervasiveness of atheism, adding that its spread can be attributed in part to the fault and carelessness of those within the Church whose actions and failures "must be said to conceal rather than reveal the authentic face of God and religion" (No. 19). Toward the fuller understanding of the place of the Church in the modern world, *Gaudium et Spes* emphasizes the harmony that should exist between the Catholic faith and scientific progress because "earthly matters and the concerns of faith derive from the same God" (No. 36). This does not mean, however, that there ought to be no qualifying elements or restraints to science; the Council Fathers add to this positive statement the provision that such research, "within every branch of learning," must be "carried out in a genuinely scientific manner and in accord with moral norms" (No. 36). Finally, the first part makes an ecumenical gesture, noting that the Church "holds in high esteem the things which other Christian Churches or ecclesial communities have done..." (No. 40).

Part Two

Part Two offers the practical application of the Church's teaching and message enunciated in Part One. Most pressing is the council's concern for the family, and its treatment of family life and marriage is the most detailed and extensive in the history of the councils of the Church. This leads to study of the deeply troubling presence of contraception. The council reiterates Church instruction in an affirmation of opposition to contraception that would receive even fuller expression in three years in the encyclical *Humanae Vitae*. In the matter of abortion, the document states clearly: "... from the moment of its conception life must be guarded with the greatest care, while abortion and infanticide are unspeakable crimes" (No. 51). In its study of culture, in which the council reminds all humanity that culture and civilization are creations of man, it points out his responsibility over it and his duty to seek that which is above, which entails an "obligation to work with all men in constructing a more human world" (No. 57). Here we have a powerful preface or introduction to the next concerns voiced in *Gaudium et Spes*: the questions of economic life, political systems, and war. In building upon earlier social encyclicals, *Gaudium et Spes* discusses economics as vital to human progress and social development, striking the important balance (developed so masterfully in the later writings of Pope John Paul II) between the rights of an individual to possess goods and the obligation to aid the poor (Nos. 63-72). While declaring the autonomous and independent nature of the Church and politics, the Council Fathers do acknowledge: "There are, indeed, close links between earthly affairs and those aspects of man's condition which transcend this world. The Church herself employs the things of time to the degree that her own proper mission demands" (No. 76). The document goes on to state that "the arms race is an utterly treacherous trap for humanity" (No. 81) and "It is our clear duty, then, to strain every muscle as we work for the time when all war can be completely outlawed by international consent" (No. 82).

SOCIAL DOCTRINE UNDER POPE JOHN PAUL II

Background

Throughout his pontificate, Pope John Paul II has traveled the globe speaking out on all matters of the Church's social teachings and has written a number of important encyclicals that are reflective not only of the Church's traditions of social doctrine but that seek to utilize the teachings of the faith to offer specific points of reflection and solutions to the many pressing problems of the late 20th century. Rooted in Christian anthropology and Tradition, Scripture, and Magisterium, John Paul's writings have encompassed economic ethics, the rights and dignity of the worker, the primacy of the human person, the place of the family in society and the Church, and the integrative teachings of the Church in the areas of moral and pastoral theology.

The three main expressions of his social teachings have been the encyclicals: *Laborem Exercens* (1981); *Sollicitudo Rei Socialis* (1987); and *Centesimus Annus* (1991).

SOCIAL ENCYCLICALS OF POPE JOHN PAUL II

The following material is adapted from The Encyclicals of John Paul II, *with the kind permission of the Most Rev. J. Michael Miller, C.S.B.*

Laborem Exercens

Fascinated as he is by commemorative events, Pope John Paul II marked the 90th anniversary of Leo XIII's *Rerum Novarum* (1891) by publishing his first social encyclical, *Laborem Exercens*, on Sept. 14, 1981.[1] Before him, Pius XI in *Quadragesimo Anno* (1931), John XXIII in *Mater et Magistra* (1961), and Paul VI in *Octogesima Adveniens* (1971) had observed the anniversary of Leo's ground-breaking encyclical with documents of their own.

Laborem Exercens is a very personal document. The encyclical has solid roots in the pope's own experience as a worker. It reflects his familiarity with various worlds of work: in mines and factories, in artistic and literary production, in scholarship and pastoral ministry. More particularly, *Laborem Exercens* has its origins in the long debate carried on by the Archbishop of Kracow with Marxist intellectuals. The topics chosen, which include the struggle between capital and labor, ownership of the means of production, and solidarity, as well as the terminology of the encyclical, bear ample witness to this background of controversy. Here, however, he is less concerned with economic systems than with the human person as a "worker." Furthermore, John Paul intended his letter to encourage the Solidarity union movement, which in the early 1980s was the primary motor for effecting social and political change in a Poland under a totalitarian regime.

The style of encyclical is distinctively Wojtylan. It reveals the pope's preference for combining a phenomenological description of experience with philosophical-theological meditation. While he cites the Second Vatican Council's *Gaudium et Spes*, John Paul never directly quotes from any previous social encyclical, not even from *Rerum Novarum*. The encyclical's footnotes are almost entirely biblical, indicating that its primary inspiration is Sacred Scripture. As in his two previous encyclicals, *Redemptor Hominis* (1979) and *Dives in Misericordia* (1980), the pope relies heavily upon the plastic and descriptive language of the Bible, especially from the opening chapters of Genesis, to develop his theme. The encyclical unfolds the meaning of the human vocation to work in light of the biblical text on "subduing the earth" (cf. Gn 1:28). This call to exercise dominion is to be carried out by those created "in the image of God" (Gn 1:27) through their work, which the pope qualifies as "one of the characteristics that distinguish man from the rest of creatures" (preface).

Unlike earlier social encyclicals which dealt with a wide range of different questions, *Laborem Exercens* is sharply focused. John Paul chooses a very specific theme—the dignity and role of human work—and explores its many ramifications: "Through work man must earn his daily bread and contribute to the continual advance of science and technology and, above all, to elevating unceasingly the cultural and moral level of the society within which he lives in community with those who belong to the same family" (preface). At the present moment, he believes, the world is faced with important choices. It is "on the eve of new developments in technological, economic, and political conditions which, according to many experts, will influence the world of work and production no less than the industrial revolution of the last century" (§1.3).

A crisis in the meaning of human work is a crucial factor contributing to society's current plight. "Work, as human issue, is at the very center of the 'social question' " (§2.1). Moreover, the pope adds, "human work is a key, probably the essential key, to the whole social question" (§3.2). It is a problem with ramifications which extend beyond the so-called "working class"; the dimensions of the crisis are universal. Therefore he does not confine his encyclical to a reflection on the work only of industrial or agricultural workers. Instead, he extends it to encompass the work done by every sector of society: management, white-collar workers, scientists, intellectuals, artists, women in the home. "Each and every individual, to the proper extent and in an incalculable number of ways, takes part in the giant process whereby man 'subdues the earth' through his work" (§4.4). To use a favorite expression of the pope's, the world's "workbench" includes all those who labor for their daily bread — all men and women.

As in his two previous encyclicals, John Paul takes up the "way" of the human person, this time with regard to his fundamental activity of work. *Laborem Exercens* is yet another chapter in the pope's book on Christian anthropology. Moreover, since work is a great gift and good for humanity, his tone throughout the encyclical is constructive and exhortatory.

Footnote

1. *Acta Apostolicae Sedis*, 73 (1981), 577-647.

Sollicitudo Rei Socialis

Although signed on Dec. 30, 1987, Pope John Paul II's encyclical "on social concern" was not officially published until Feb. 19, 1988.[1] Like *Laborem Exercens* (1981), this second social encyclical commemorates a previous papal document. *Sollicitudo Rei Socialis* marks the twentieth anniversary of Paul VI's *Populorum Progressio* (1967). But more than merely recalling the relevance and doctrine of Pope Paul's encyclical, it highlights new themes and responds to the problems of development in the Third World which had emerged in the intervening 20 years.

John Paul writes as a teacher, explaining why the proclamation of the Church's social doctrine belongs to her evangelizing mission. He also writes as an informed witness to the increasing injustice and poverty in the world. Lastly, he writes as a defender of human dignity and inalienable rights, and of every person's transcendent vocation to communion with the Triune God.

In some ways *Sollicitudo Rei Socialis* echoes *Laborem Exercens* (1981). John Paul's use of Sacred Scripture, for example, is similar in that he frequently quotes from the opening chapters of Genesis. The differences between the two social encyclicals, however, are noteworthy. Whereas in *Laborem Exercens* (1981) the pope never directly cites *Rerum Novarum* (1891), the encyclical of Leo XIII which it commemorates, throughout *Sollicitudo Rei Socialis* John Paul quotes or refers to *Populorum Progressio* more than forty times. It is his constant point of reference. Second, to support his presentation, the pope marshals statements taken from earlier writings and discourses of his own pontificate, as well as the social teaching of the Second Vatican Council expressed in *Gaudium et Spes*. Third, more than in any other encyclical, John Paul makes use of documents published by the Roman Curia. Especially notable are his six references to the Instruction on Christian Freedom and Liberation (1986) issued by the Congregation for the Doctrine of the Faith. He also cites two publications of the Pontifical Commission "Iustitia et Pax": *At the Service of the Human Community: An Ethical Approach to the International Debt Question* (1986) and *The Church and the Housing Problem* (1987).

While *Sollicitudo Rei Socialis* perceptively analyzes the economic, political, social, and cultural dimensions of world development, its perspective is primarily ethical and theological. John Paul rereads *Populorum Progressio* through a moral-spiritual lens. His main concern is to form the consciences of individual men and women, to help them in their task of promoting authentic development "in the light of faith and of the Church's Tradition" (§41.7).

Footnote
1. *Acta Apostolicae Sedis*, 80 (1988), 513-586.

Centesimus Annus

Pope John Paul II issued his ninth encyclical, *Centesimus Annus*, on May 1, 1991.[1] Not surprisingly, the pope chose to mark the centenary of Leo XIII's *Rerum Novarum* (1891) with a document of his own. In the four years since the signing of *Sollicitudo Rei Socialis* (1987) the Berlin Wall had collapsed, and in the light of this event John Paul offers his "rereading" of *Rerum Novarum*. His purpose is twofold. He wishes to recall Leo's contribution to the development of the Church's social teaching and to honor the popes who drew upon the encyclical's "vital energies" in their social teaching.

Centesimus Annus has some interesting peculiarities. First, among all John Paul's encyclicals, it relies the least on citing Sacred Scripture. Its few biblical references are primarily exhortatory or illustrative. For his

sources the pope depends mostly on *Rerum Novarum* and on the social encyclicals of his predecessors, as well as on earlier documents and discourses of his own Magisterium. Second, much of the encyclical's content is conditioned by current geopolitical affairs. Indeed, the encyclical reads as if the pope had *Rerum Novarum* in one hand and a diary of the 1989 events sweeping eastern Europe in the other.

Despite the opinions of some commentators, John Paul's primary interest is not to pass judgment on either failed socialism or contemporary capitalism. Above all, in keeping with his desire to articulate a Christian anthropology, he recalls the need for Catholic social doctrine to have a "correct view of the human person and of his unique value" (§11.3). Without such a view, he believes, it is impossible to solve today's social, economic, and political problems. The Church's distinctive contribution to meeting these challenges is her vision of the transcendent dignity of the human person created in God's image and redeemed by Christ's blood.

The pope's rereading of Leo XIII encompasses three time frames: "looking back" at *Rerum Novarum* itself, "looking around" at the contemporary situation, and "looking to the future" (§3.1). In looking back, John Paul confirms the enduring principles of Leo's encyclical, principles that belong to the Church's doctrinal inheritance. His "pastoral solicitude" also impels the pope to analyze recent political events from the perspective of the Gospel "in order to discern the new requirements of evangelization" (§3.5).

Even more clearly than in his two previous social encyclicals, *Laborem Exercens* (1981) and *Sollicitudo Rei Socialis* (1987), John Paul clearly distinguishes the authentic doctrine contained in the Church's social teaching from the analysis of contingent historical events. This analysis, he states, "is not meant to pass definitive judgments, since this does not fall per se within the Magisterium's specific domain" (§3.5). Whatever comes within the doctrinal sphere, however, "pertains to the Church's evangelizing mission and is an essential part of the Christian message" (§5.5).

Footnote
1. *Acta Apostolicae Sedis*, 83 (1991), 793-867.

SOCIO-ECONOMIC STATEMENTS BY U.S. BISHOPS

Over a period of nearly 80 years, the bishops of the United States have issued a great number of socio-economic statements reflecting papal documents in a U.S. context.

One such statement, entitled "Economic Justice for All: Social Teaching and the U.S. Economy" was issued in Nov., 1986. Its contents are related in various ways with the subsequently issued encyclical letter, Centesimus Annus. Principles drawn from the bishops' document are given in the following excerpt entitled "A Catholic Framework for Economic Life." Another significant statement, entitled "The Harvest of Justice Is Sown in Peace" (1993) follows.

A Catholic Framework for Economic Life

As followers of Jesus Christ and participants in a powerful economy, Catholics in the United States, are called to work for greater economic justice in the face

of persistent poverty, growing income gaps and increasing discussion of economic issues in the United States and around the world. We urge Catholics to use the following ethical framework for economic life as principles for reflection, criteria for judgment and directions for action. These principles are drawn directly from Catholic teaching on economic life.

1. The economy exists for the person, not the person for the economy.

2. All economic life should be shaped by moral principles. Economic choices and institutions must be judged by how they protect or undermine the life and dignity of the human person, support the family and serve the common good.

3. A fundamental moral measure of an economy is how the poor and vulnerable are faring.

4. All people have a right to life and to secure the basic necessities of life (e.g., food, clothing, shelter,

education, health care, safe environment, economic security).

5. All people have the right to economic initiative, to productive work, to just wages and benefits, to decent working conditions as well as to organize and join unions or other associations.

6. All people, to the extent they are able, have a corresponding duty to work, a responsibility to provide for the needs of their families and an obligation to contribute to the broader society.

7. In economic life, free markets have both clear advantages and limits; government has essential responsibilities and limitations; voluntary groups have irreplaceable roles, but cannot substitute for the proper working of the market and the just policies of the state.

8. Society has a moral obligation, including governmental action where necessary, to assure opportunity, meet basic human needs and pursue justice in economic life.

9. Workers, owners, managers, stockholders and consumers are moral agents in economic life. By our choices, initiative, creativity and investment, we enhance or diminish economic opportunity, community life and social justice.

10. The global economy has moral dimensions and human consequences. Decisions on investment, trade, aid and development should protect human life and promote human rights, especially for those most in need wherever they might live on this globe.

The Harvest of Justice Is Sown in Peace

The National Conference of Catholic Bishops, at a meeting Nov. 17, 1993, issued a statement entitled "The Harvest of Justice Is Sown in Peace," marking the 10th anniversary of their earlier pastoral letter, "The Challenge of Peace: God's Promise and Our Response."

The Challenge of Peace

"The challenge of peace today is different, but no less urgent" than in 1983, and the threat of global nuclear war "may seem more remote than at any time in the nuclear age." Questions of peace and war, however, cannot be addressed "without acknowledging that the nuclear question remains of vital political and moral significance."

The statement outlines an agenda for action to guide future advocacy efforts of the bishops' national conference. It also urges that the cause of peace be reflected constantly in liturgical prayers of petition, preaching and Catholic education at all levels.

Confronting the temptation to isolationism in U.S. foreign policy is among "the major challenges peacemakers face in this new era."

Factors in a vision for peace include a commitment to the universal common good and recognition of the imperative of human solidarity.

Nonviolent revolutions in some countries "challenge us to find ways to take into full account the power of organized, active nonviolence."

With respect to just war criteria, the statement says that "important work needs to be done in refining, clarifying and applying the just war tradition to the choices facing our decision-makers in this still violent and dangerous world."

Subjects of concern include humanitarian intervention, deterrence, conscientious objection and the development of peoples.

Presumption against Force

"Our conference's approach, as outlined in 'The Challenge of Peace,' can be summarized in this way:

"1) In situations of conflict our constant commitment ought to be, as far as possible, to strive for justice through nonviolent means.

"2) But when sustained attempts at nonviolent action fail to protect the innocent against fundamental injustice, then legitimate political authorities are permitted as a last resort to employ limited force to rescue the innocent and establish justice."

Lethal Force

"Whether lethal force may be used is governed by the following criteria:

• "Just cause: Force may be used only to correct a grave, public evil, i.e., aggression or massive violation of the basic rights of whole populations.

• "Comparative justice: While there may be rights and wrongs on all sides of a conflict, to override the presumption against the use of force, the injustice suffered by one party must significantly outweigh that suffered by the other.

• "Legitimate authority: Only duly constituted public authorities may use deadly force or wage war.

• "Right intention: Force may be used only in a truly just cause and solely for that purpose.

• "Probability of Success: Arms may not be used in a futile cause or in a case where disproportionate measures are required to achieve success.

• "Proportionality: The overall destruction expected from the use of force must be outweighed by the good to be achieved.

• "Last Resort: Force may be used only after all peaceful alternatives have been seriously tried and exhausted.

"These criteria [of just war], taken as a whole, must be satisfied in order to override the strong presumption against the use of force."

Just War

"The just-war tradition seeks also to curb the violence of war through restraint on armed combat between the contending parties by imposing the following moral standards for the conduct of armed conflict:

• "Noncombatant Immunity: Civilians may not be the object of direct attack, and military personnel must take due care to avoid and minimize indirect harm to civilians.

• "Proportionality: In the conduct of hostilities, efforts must be made to attain military objectives with no more force than is militarily necessary and to avoid disproportionate collateral damage to civilian life and property.

• "Right Intention: Even in the midst of conflict, the aim of political and military leaders must be peace with justice so that acts of vengeance and indiscriminate violence, whether by individuals, military units or governments, are forbidden."

Structures for Justice and Peace

Quoting an address given by Pope John Paul in Aug. 1993 in Denver, the statement said:

" 'The international community ought to establish more effective structures for maintaining and promoting justice and peace. This implies that a concept of strategic interest should evolve which is based on the full development of peoples — out of poverty and toward a more dignified existence, out of injustice and exploitation toward fuller respect for the human person and the defense of universal rights.'

"As we consider a new vision of the international community, five areas deserve special attention: (1) strengthening global institutions; (2) securing human rights; (3) promoting human development; (4) restraining nationalism and eliminating religious violence; and (5) building cooperative security."

Humanitarian Intervention

"Pope John Paul, citing the 'conscience of humanity and international humanitarian law,' has been outspoken in urging that 'humanitarian intervention be obligatory where the survival of populations and entire eth-

nic groups is seriously compromised. This is a duty for nations and the international community.' He elaborated on this right and duty of humanitarian intervention in his 1993 annual address to the diplomatic corps (accredited to the Holy See):

" 'Once the possibilities afforded by diplomatic negotiations and the procedures provided for by international agreements and organizations have been put into effect, and that [sic], nevertheless, populations are succumbing to the attacks of an unjust aggressor, states no longer have a 'right to indifference.' It seems clear that their duty is to disarm this aggressor if all other means have proved ineffective. The principles of the sovereignty of states and of noninterference in their internal affairs — which retain all their value — cannot constitute a screen behind which torture and murder may be carried out.' "

THE BLESSED VIRGIN MARY

ROLE OF MARY IN THE MYSTERY OF CHRIST AND THE CHURCH

The following excerpts are from Chapter VIII of the Second Vatican Council's "Constitution on the Church," Lumen Gentium.

I. Preface

Wishing in his supreme goodness and wisdom to effect the redemption of the world, "when the fullness of time came, God sent his Son, born of a woman, that we might receive the adoption of sons" (Gal 4:4-5). "He for us men, and for our salvation, came down from heaven, and was incarnate by the Holy Spirit from the Virgin Mary." This divine mystery of salvation is revealed to us and continued in the Church, which the Lord established as his own body. In this Church, adhering to Christ the head and having communion with all his saints, the faithful must also venerate the memory "above all of the glorious and perpetual Virgin Mary. Mother of our God and Lord Jesus Christ." (52)

At the message of the angel, the Virgin Mary received the Word of God in her heart and in her body, and gave Life to the world. Hence, she is acknowledged and honored as being truly the Mother of God and Mother of the Redeemer. Redeemed in an especially sublime manner by reason of the merits of her Son, and united to him by a close and indissoluble tie, she is endowed with the supreme office and dignity of being the Mother of the Son of God. As a result, she is also the favorite daughter of the Father and the temple of the Holy Spirit. Because of this gift of sublime grace, she far surpasses all other creatures, both in heaven and on earth.

At the same time, however, because she belongs to the offspring of Adam, she is one with all human beings in their need for salvation. Indeed, she is "clearly the Mother of the members of Christ since she cooperated out of love so that there might be born in the Church the faithful, who are members of Christ their head. Therefore, she is also hailed as a pre-eminent and altogether singular member of the Church, and as the Church's model and excellent exemplar in faith and

charity. Taught by the Holy Spirit, the Catholic Church honors her with filial affection and piety as a most beloved Mother. (53)

This sacred synod intends to describe with diligence the role of the Blessed Virgin in the mystery of the Incarnate Word and the Mystical Body. It also wishes to describe the duties of redeemed mankind toward the Mother of God, who is the Mother of Christ and Mother of men, particularly of the faithful.

The synod does not, however, have it in mind to give a complete doctrine on Mary, nor does it wish to decide those questions which have not yet been fully illuminated by the work of theologians. (54)

II. The Role of the Blessed Virgin in the Economy of Salvation

The Father of mercies willed that the consent of the predestined Mother should precede the Incarnation so that, just as a woman contributed to death, so also a woman should contribute to life. This contrast was verified in outstanding fashion by the Mother of Jesus. She gave to the world that very Life which renews all things, and she was enriched by God with gifts befitting such a role.

It is no wonder, then, that the usage prevailed among the holy Fathers whereby they called the Mother of God entirely holy and free from all stain of sin, fashioned by the Holy Spirit into a kind of new substance and new creature. Adorned from the first instant of her conception with the splendors of an entirely unique holiness, the Virgin of Nazareth is, on God's command, greeted by an angel messenger as "full of grace" (cf. Lk 1:28). To the heavenly messenger she replies: "Behold the handmaid of the Lord; be it done to me according to thy word" (Lk 1:38).

By thus consenting to the divine utterance, Mary, a daughter of Adam, became the Mother of Jesus. Embracing God's saving will with a full heart and impeded by no sin, she devoted herself totally as a handmaid of the Lord to the person and work of her Son. In subordination to him and along with him, by the grace of almighty God she served the mystery of redemption.

Rightly, therefore, the holy Fathers see her as used by God not merely in a passive way but as cooperating in the work of human salvation through free faith and obedience. (56)

This union of the Mother with the Son in the work of salvation was manifested from the time of Christ's virginal conception up to his death. It is shown first of all when Mary, arising in haste to go to visit Elizabeth, was greeted by her as blessed because of her belief in the promise of salvation, while the precursor leaped for joy in the womb of his mother (cf. Lk 1:41-45). This association was shown also at the birth of our Lord, who did not diminish his Mother's virginal integrity but sanctified it, when the Mother of God joyfully showed her first-born Son to the shepherds and the Magi.

When she presented him to the Lord in the Temple, making the offering of the poor, she heard Simeon foretelling at the same time that her Son would be a sign of contradiction and that a sword would pierce the Mother's soul, that out of many hearts thoughts might be revealed (cf. Lk 2:34-35). When the Child Jesus was lost and they had sought him sorrowing, his parents found him in the temple, taken up with things which were his Father's business. They did not understand the reply of the Son. But his Mother, to be sure, kept all these things to be pondered over in her heart (cf. Lk 2:41-51). (57)

In the public life of Jesus, Mary made significant appearances. This was so even at the very beginning, when she was moved with pity at the marriage feast of Cana, and her intercession brought about the beginning of the miracles by Jesus the Messiah (Cf. Jn 2:1-11). In the course of her Son's preaching, she received his praise when, in extolling a kingdom beyond the calculations and bonds of flesh and blood, he declared blessed (cf. Mk 3:35 par.; Lk 11:27-28) those who heard and kept the word of the Lord as she was faithfully doing (cf. Lk 2:19, 51).

Thus, the Blessed Virgin advanced in her pilgrimage of faith and loyally persevered in her union with her Son unto the cross. There she stood, in keeping with the divine plan (cf. Jn 19:25), suffering grievously with her only-begotten Son. There she united herself with a maternal heart to his sacrifice, and lovingly consented to the immolation of this Victim whom she herself had brought forth. Finally, the same Christ Jesus dying on the cross gave her as a mother to his disciple. This he did when he said: "Woman, behold your son" (Jn 19:26-27). (58)

But since it pleased God not to manifest solemnly the mystery of the salvation of the human race until he poured forth the Spirit promised by Christ, we see the apostles before the day of Pentecost "continuing with one mind in prayer with the women and Mary, the Mother of Jesus, and with his brethren" (Acts 1:14). We see Mary prayerfully imploring the gift of the Spirit, who had already overshadowed her in the Annunciation.

Finally, preserved free from all guilt of original sin, the Immaculate Virgin was taken up body and soul into heavenly glory upon the completion of her earthly sojourn. She was exalted by the Lord as Queen of all, in order that she might be the more thoroughly conformed to her Son, the Lord of lords (cf. Rv 19:16) and the conqueror of sin and death. (59)

III. The Blessed Virgin and the Church

We have but one Mediator, as we know from the words of the Apostle: "For there is one God, and one Mediator between God and men, himself man, Christ Jesus, who gave himself as a ransom for all" (1 Tm 2:5-6). The maternal duty of Mary toward men in no way obscures or diminishes this unique mediation of Christ, but rather shows its power. For all the saving influences of the Blessed Virgin on men originate, not from some inner necessity, but from the divine pleasure. They flow forth from the superabundance of the merits of Christ, rest on his mediation, depend entirely on it, and draw all their power from it. In no way do they impede the immediate union of the faithful with Christ. Rather, they foster this union. (60)

In an utterly singular way, she (Mary) cooperated by her obedience, faith, hope and burning charity in the Savior's work of restoring supernatural life to souls. For this reason she is a mother to us in the order of grace. (61)

This maternity of Mary in the order of grace began with the consent which she gave in faith at the Annunciation and which she sustained without wavering beneath the cross. This maternity will last without interruption until the eternal fulfillment of all the elect. For, taken up to heaven, she did not lay aside this saving role, but by her manifold acts of intercession continues to win for us gifts of eternal salvation.

By her maternal charity, Mary cares for the brethren of her Son who still journey on earth surrounded by dangers and difficulties until they are led to their happy fatherland. Therefore, the Blessed Virgin is invoked by the Church under the titles of Advocate, Auxiliatrix, Adjutrix and Mediatrix. These, however, are to be so understood that they neither take away nor add anything to the dignity and efficacy of Christ the one Mediator.

For no creature could ever be classed with the Incarnate Word and Redeemer. But, just as the priesthood of Christ is shared in various ways both by sacred ministers and by the faithful; and as the one goodness of God is in reality communicated diversely to his creatures: so also the unique mediation of the Redeemer does not exclude but rather gives rise among creatures to a manifold cooperation which is but a sharing in this unique source.

The Church does not hesitate to profess this subordinate role of Mary. She experiences it continuously and commends it to the hearts of the faithful so that, encouraged by this maternal help, they may more closely adhere to the Mediator and Redeemer. (62)

Through the gift and role of divine maternity, Mary is united with her Son, the Redeemer, and with his singular graces and offices. By these, the Blessed Virgin is also intimately united with the Church. As St. Ambrose taught, the Mother of God is a model of the Church in the matter of faith, hope and charity, and perfect union with Christ. For in the mystery of the Church, herself rightly called Mother and Virgin, the Blessed Virgin stands out in eminent and singular fashion as exemplar of both virginity and motherhood. (63)

In the most holy Virgin, the Church has already reached that perfection whereby she exists without spot or wrinkle (cf. Eph 5:27). Yet, the followers of Christ still strive to increase in holiness by conquering sin. And so they raise their eyes to Mary who shines forth to the whole community of the elect as a model of the virtues. Devotedly meditating on her and contemplating her in the light of the Word made man, the Church with reverence enters more intimately into the supreme mystery of the Incarnation and becomes ever increasingly like her Spouse. (64)

The Church in her apostolic work looks to her who brought forth Christ, conceived by the Holy Spirit and born of the Virgin, so that through the Church Christ may be born and grow in the hearts of the faithful also. The Virgin Mary in her own life lived as an example of that maternal love by which all should be fittingly animated who cooperate in the apostolic mission of the Church on behalf of the rebirth of men. (65)

IV. Devotion to the Blessed Virgin in the Church

Mary was involved in the mystery of Christ. As the most holy Mother of God she was, after her Son, exalted by divine grace above all angels and men. Hence, the Church appropriately honors her with special reverence. Indeed, from most ancient times the Blessed Virgin has been venerated under the title of "God-bearer." In all perils and needs, the faithful; have fled prayerfully to her protection. Especially after the Council of Ephesus the cult of the people of God toward Mary wonderfully increased in veneration and love, in invocation and imitation, according to her own prophetic words: "All generations shall call me blessed; because he who is mighty has done great things for me" (Lk 1:48).

As it has always existed in the Church, this cult (of Mary) is altogether special, Still, it differs essentially from the cult of adoration which is offered to the Incarnate Word, as well as to the Father and the Holy Spirit. Yet, devotion to Mary is most favorable to this supreme cult. The Church has endorsed many forms of piety toward the Mother of God, provided that they were within the limits of sound and orthodox doctrine. These forms have varied according to the circumstances of time and place, and have reflected the diversity of native characteristics and temperament among the faithful. While honoring Christ's Mother, these devotions cause her Son to be rightly known, loved and glorified, and all his commands observed. Through him all things have their beginning (cf. Col 1: 15-16) and in him "it has pleased (the eternal Father) that all his fullness should dwell" (Col 1:19). (66)

This most holy synod deliberately teaches this Catholic doctrine. At the same time, it admonishes all the sons of the Church that the cult, especially the liturgical cult, of the Blessed Virgin, be generously fostered. It charges that practices and exercises of devotion toward her be treasured as recommended by the teaching authority of the Church in the course of centuries.

This synod earnestly exhorts theologians and preachers of the divine word that, in treating of the unique dignity of the Mother of God, they carefully and equally avoid the falsity of exaggeration on the one hand and the excess of narrow-mindedness on the other.

Let the faithful remember, moreover, that true devotion consists neither in fruitless and passing emotion, nor in a certain vain credulity. Rather, it proceeds from the true faith, by which we are led to know the excellence of the Mother of God, and are moved to a filial love toward our Mother and to the imitation of her virtues. (67)

REDEMPTORIS MATER

Redemptoris Mater (Mother of the Redeemer), Pope John Paul II's sixth encyclical letter, is a "reflection on the role of Mary in the mystery of Christ and on her active and exemplary presence in the life of the Church." The letter was published Mar. 25, 1987.

Central to consideration of Mary is the fact that she is the Mother of God (*Theotokos*), since by the power of the Holy Spirit she conceived in her virginal womb and brought into the world Jesus Christ, the Son of God, who is of one being with the Father and the Holy Spirit.

Mary was preserved from original sin in view of her calling to be the Mother of Jesus. She was gifted in grace beyond measure. She fulfilled her role in a unique pilgrimage of faith. She is the Mother of the Church and the spiritual mother of all people.

The following excerpts are from the English text provided by the Vatican and circulated by the CNS Documentary Service, *Origins*, Apr. 9, 1987 (Vol. 16, No. 43). Subheads have been added. Quotations are from pertinent documents of the Second Vatican Council.

Mary's Presence in the Church

Mary, through the same faith which made her blessed, especially from the moment of the Annunciation, is present in the Church's mission, present in the Church's work of introducing into the world the kingdom of her Son.

This presence of Mary finds as many different expressions in our day just as it did throughout the Church's history. It also has a wide field of action: through the faith and piety of individual believers; through the traditions of Christian families or "domestic churches," of parish and missionary communities, religious institutes and dioceses; through the radiance and attraction of the great shrines where not only individuals or local groups, but sometimes whole nations and societies, even whole continents, seek to meet the Mother of the Lord, the one who is blessed because she believed, is the first among believers, and therefore became the Mother of Emmanuel.

This is the message of the land of Palestine, the spiritual homeland of all Christians, because it was the homeland of the Savior of the world and of his Mother.

This is the message of the many churches in Rome and throughout the world which have been raised up in the course of the centuries by the faith of Christians. This is the message of centers like Guadalupe, Lourdes, Fátima and others situated in the various countries. Among them, how could I fail to mention the one in my own native land, Jasna Gora? One could perhaps speak of a specific "geography" of faith and Marian devotion which includes all of these special places of pilgrimage where the people of God seek to meet the Mother of God in order to find, within the radius of the maternal presence of her "who believed," a strengthening of their own faith.

Mary and Ecumenism

"In all of Christ's disciples the Spirit arouses the desire to be peacefully united, in the manner determined by Christ, as one flock under one shepherd." The journey of the Church, especially in our own time, is marked by the sign of ecumenism: Christians are seeking ways to restore that unity which Christ implored from the Father for his disciples on the day before his passion.

Christians must deepen in themselves and each of their communities that "obedience of faith" of which Mary is the first and brightest example.

Christians know that their unity will be truly rediscovered only if it is based on the unity of their faith. They must resolve considerable discrepancies of doctrine concerning the mystery and ministry of the Church, and sometimes also concerning the role of Mary in the work of salvation.

Mary, who is still the model of this pilgrimage, is to lead them to the unity which is willed by their one Lord, and which is so much desired by those who are attentively listening to what "the Spirit is saying to the churches" today.

A Hopeful Sign

Meanwhile, it is a hopeful sign that these churches and ecclesial communities are finding agreement with the Catholic Church on fundamental points of Christian belief, including matters relating to the Virgin Mary. For they recognize her as the Mother of the Lord and hold that this forms part of our faith in Christ, true God and true man. They look to her who at the foot of the cross accepted as her son the Beloved Disciple (John), the one who in his turn accepted her as his Mother.

On the other hand, I wish to emphasize how profoundly the Catholic Church, the Orthodox Church and the ancient churches of the East feel united by love and praise of the Theotokos. Not only "basic dogmas of the Christian faith concerning the Trinity and God's Word made flesh of the Virgin Mary were defined in ecumenical councils held in the East," but also in their liturgical worship "the Eastern Christians pay high tribute, in very beautiful hymns, to Mary ever-Virgin. God's most holy Mother."

The churches which profess the doctrine of Ephesus proclaim the Virgin as "true Mother of God" since "our Lord Jesus Christ, born of the Father before time began according to his divinity, in the last days he himself, for our sake and for our salvation, was begotten of Mary the Virgin Mother of God according to his humanity." The Greek Fathers and the Byzantine tradition, contemplating the Virgin in the light of the Word made flesh, have sought to penetrate the depth of that bond which unites Mary, as the Mother of God, to Christ and the Church. The Virgin is a permanent presence in the whole reality of the salvific mystery.

Marian Mediation

The Church knows and teaches with St. Paul that there is only one mediator: "For there is one God, and there is one mediator between God and men, the man Christ Jesus, who gave himself as a ransom for all" (1 Tm 2:5-6). "The maternal role of Mary toward people in no way obscures or diminishes the unique mediation of Christ, but rather shows its power." It is mediation in Christ.

The Church knows and teaches that "all the saving influences of the Blessed Virgin on mankind originate from the divine pleasure. They flow forth from the superabundance of the merits of Christ, rest on his mediation, depend entirely on it and draw all their power from it. In no way do they impede the immediate union of the faithful with Christ. Rather, they foster this union." This saving influence is sustained by the Holy Spirit, who, just as he overshadowed the Virgin Mary when he began in her the divine motherhood, in a similar way constantly sustains her solicitude for the brothers and sisters of her Son.

Mediation and Motherhood

In effect, Mary's mediation is intimately linked with her motherhood. It possesses a specifically maternal character, which distinguishes it from the mediation of the other creatures who in various and always subordinate ways share in the one mediation of Christ, although her own mediation is also a shared mediation. In fact, while it is true that "no creature could ever be classed with the Incarnate Word and Redeemer," at the same time "the unique mediation of the Redeemer does not exclude but rather gives rise among creatures a manifold cooperation which is but a sharing in this unique source." Thus "the one goodness of God is in reality communicated diversely to his creatures."

Subordinate Mediation

The teaching of Vatican II presents the truth of Mary's mediation as "a sharing in the one unique source that is the mediation of Christ himself." Thus we read: "The Church does not hesitate to profess this subordinate role of Mary. She experiences it continuously and commends it to the hearts of the faithful so that, encouraged by this maternal help, they may more closely adhere to the Mediator and Redeemer."

This role is at the same time special and extraordinary. It flows from her divine motherhood and can be understood and lived in faith only on the basis of the full truth of this motherhood. Since by virtue of divine election Mary is the earthly Mother of the Father's consubstantial Son and his "generous companion" in the work of redemption, "she is a Mother to us in the order of grace." This role constitutes a real dimension of her presence in the saving mystery of Christ and the Church.

Mary is honored in the Church "with special reverence. Indeed, from most ancient times the Blessed Virgin Mary has been venerated under the title of 'God-bearer.' In all perils and needs, the faithful have fled prayerfully to her protection." This cult is altogether special; it bears in itself and expresses the profound link which exists between the Mother of Christ and the Church. As Virgin and Mother, Mary remains for the Church a "permanent model." It can therefore be said that, especially under this aspect, namely, as a model or rather as a "figure," Mary, present in the mystery of Christ, remains constantly present also in the mystery of the Church. For the Church too is "called mother and virgin," and these names have a profound biblical and theological justification.

Mary and Women

This Marian dimension of Christian life takes on special importance in relation to women and their status. In fact, femininity has a unique relationship with the Mother of the Redeemer, a subject which can be studied in greater depth elsewhere.... The figure of Mary of Nazareth sheds light on womanhood as such by the very fact that God, in the sublime event of the incarnation of his Son, entrusted himself to the ministry, the free and active ministry, of a woman.

... Women, by looking to Mary, find in her the secret of living their femininity with dignity and of achieving their own true advancement. In the light of Mary, the Church sees in the face of women the reflection of a beauty that mirrors the loftiest sentiments of which the human heart is capable: the self-offering totality of love; the strength that is capable of bearing the greatest sorrows; limitless fidelity and tireless devotion to work; the ability to combine penetrating intuition with words of support and encouragement.

APPARITIONS OF THE BLESSED VIRGIN MARY

Seven of the best-known apparitions are described.

Banneux, near Liège, Belgium: Mary appeared eight times between Jan. 15 and Mar. 2, 1933, to an 11-year-old peasant girl, Mariette Beco, in a garden behind the family cottage in Banneux. She called herself the Virgin of the Poor, and has since been venerated as Our Lady of the Poor, the Sick, and the Indifferent. A small chapel was blessed Aug. 15, 1933. Approval of devotion to Our Lady of Banneux was given in 1949 by Bishop Louis J. Kerkhofs of Liège, and a statue of that title was solemnly crowned in 1956.

Beauraing, Belgium: Mary appeared 33 times between Nov. 29, 1932, and Jan. 3, 1933, to five children in the garden of a convent school in Beauraing. A chapel was erected on the spot. Reserved approval of devotion to Our Lady of Beauraing was given Feb. 2, 1943, and final approbation July 2, 1949, by Bishop Charue of Namur (d. 1977).

Fátima, Portugal: Mary appeared six times between May 13 and Oct. 13, 1917, to three children (Lucia dos Santos, 10, who is now a Carmelite nun; Francisco Marto, 9, who died in 1919; and his sister Jacinta, 7, who died in 1920; Jacinta and Francisco were beatified by Pope John Paul II in 2000) in a field called Cova da Iria near Fátima. She recommended frequent recitation of the Rosary; urged works of mortification for the conversion of sinners; called for devotion to herself under the title of her Immaculate Heart; asked that the people of Russia be consecrated to her under this title, and that the faithful make a Communion of reparation on the first Saturday of each month. The apparitions were declared worthy of belief in Oct. 1930, and devotion to Our Lady of Fátima was authorized under the title of Our Lady of the Rosary. In Oct. 1942, Pius XII consecrated the world to Mary under the title of her Immaculate Heart. Ten years later, in the first apostolic letter addressed directly to the peoples of Russia, he consecrated them in a special manner to Mary. For more on the Third Secret of Fátima, see below.

Guadalupe, Mexico: Mary appeared four times in 1531 to an Indian, Juan Diego (declared Blessed in 1990), on Tepeyac hill outside of Mexico City, and instructed him to tell Bishop Zumarraga of her wish that a church be built there. The bishop complied with the request about two years later, after being convinced of the genuineness of the apparition by the evidence of a miraculously painted life-size figure of the Virgin on the mantle of the Indian. The mantle bearing the picture has been preserved and is enshrined in the Basilica of Our Lady of Guadalupe. The shrine church, originally dedicated in 1709 and subsequently enlarged, has the title of basilica. Benedict XIV, in a 1754 decree, authorized a Mass and Office under the title of Our Lady of Guadalupe for celebration on Dec. 12, and named Mary the patroness of New Spain. Our Lady of Guadalupe was designated patroness of Latin America by St. Pius X in 1910 and of the Americas by Pius XII in 1945.

La Salette, France: Mary appeared as a sorrowing and weeping figure Sept. 19, 1846, to two peasant children, Melanie Matthieu, 15, and Maximin Giraud, 11, at La Salette. The message she confided to them, regarding the necessity of penance, was communicated to Pius IX in 1851 and has since been known as the "secret" of La Salette. Bishop de Bruillard of Grenoble declared in 1851 that the apparition was credible, and devotion to Mary under the title of Our Lady of La Salette was authorized. A Mass and Office with this title were authorized in 1942. The shrine church was given the title of minor basilica in 1879.

Lourdes, France: Mary, identifying herself as the Immaculate Conception, appeared 18 times between Feb. 11 and July 16, 1858, to 14-year-old Bernadette Soubirous (canonized in 1933) at the grotto of Massabielle near Lourdes. Her message concerned the necessity of prayer and penance for the conversion of peoples. Mary's request that a chapel be built at the grotto and spring was fulfilled in 1862. Devotion under the title of Our Lady of Lourdes was authorized, and a Feb. 11 feast commemorating the apparitions was instituted by Leo XIII. St. Pius X extended this feast throughout the Church in 1907. The Church of Notre Dame was made a basilica in 1870, and the Church of the Rosary was built later. The underground Church of St. Pius X, with a capacity of 20,000 persons, was consecrated Mar. 25, 1958. Plans were announced in 1994 for renovation and reconstruction of the Lourdes sanctuary.

Our Lady of the Miraculous Medal, France: Mary appeared three times in 1830 to Catherine Labouré (canonized in 1947) in the chapel of the motherhouse of the Daughters of Charity of St. Vincent de Paul, Rue de Bac, Paris. She commissioned Catherine to have made the medal of the Immaculate Conception, now known as the Miraculous Medal, and to spread devotion to her under this title. In 1832, the medal was struck.

THE THIRD SECRET OF FÁTIMA

Courtesy Vatican Information Service.

On June 26, 2000, the Holy See Press Office issued the document "The Message Of Fátima," which had been prepared by the Congregation for the Doctrine of the Faith and carried the signatures of Cardinal Joseph Ratzinger and Archbishop Tarcisio Bertone, S.D.B., respectively prefect and secretary of the congregation.

The document, which is over 40 pages long, was published in English, French, Italian, Spanish, German, Portuguese and Polish. It was made up of an introduction by Archbishop Bertone; the first and second parts of the "secret" of Fátima in Sr. Lucia's original text dated Aug. 31, 1941, and addressed to the bishop of Leiria-Fátima, and a translation; the photostatic reproduction of the original manuscript of the third part of the "secret" and a translation; John Paul II's letter to Sr. Lucia dated Apr. 19, 2000, and a translation; a summary of Sr. Lucia's conversation with Archbishop Bertone and Bishop Serafim de Sousa Ferreira e Silva of Leiria-Fátima which took place on Apr. 27, 2000, in the Carmel Monastery of St. Teresa of Coimbra, Portugal; the words of Cardinal Secretary of State Angelo Sodano at the end of the beatification of Jacinta and Francisco on May 13, 2000; and a theological commentary by Cardinal Ratzinger.

In his introduction, Archbishop Bertone affirms that "Fátima is undoubtedly the most prophetic of modern apparitions.... In 1917 no one could have imagined all this: the three 'pastorinhos' of Fátima see, listen and remember, and Lucia, the surviving witness, commits it all to paper when ordered to do so by the Bishop of Leiria and with Our Lady's permission."

He continues: "The third part of the 'secret' was written … on Jan. 3, 1944. There is only one manuscript, which is here reproduced photostatically. The sealed envelope was initially in the custody of the Bishop of Leiria. To ensure better protection for the 'secret' the envelope was placed in the secret archives of the Holy Office on Apr. 4, 1957. The Bishop of Leiria informed Sr. Lucia of this."

The secretary of the Congregation for the Doctrine of the Faith indicates that "according to the records of the Archives,

the Commissary of the Holy Office, Fr. Pierre Paul Philippe, O.P., with the agreement of Cardinal Alfredo Ottaviani, brought the envelope containing the third part of the 'secret of Fátima' to Pope John XXIII on Aug. 17, 1959. 'After some hesitation,' His Holiness said: 'We shall wait. I shall pray. I shall let you know what I decide.' In fact Pope John XXIII decided to return the sealed envelope to the Holy Office and not to reveal the third part of the 'secret.' Paul VI read the contents with the Substitute, Archbishop Angelo Dell'Acqua, on Mar. 27, 1965, and returned the envelope to the Archives of the Holy Office, deciding not to publish the text. John Paul II, for his part, asked for the envelope containing the third part of the 'secret' following the assassination attempt on May 13, 1981," and this was given to Archbishop Eduardo Martinez Somalo, Substitute of the Secretariat of State, on July 18 of the same year. On August 11 it was returned to the Archives of the Holy Office.

"As is well known," added Archbishop Bertone, "Pope John Paul II immediately thought of consecrating the world to the Immaculate Heart of Mary and he himself composed a prayer for what he called an 'Act of Entrustment' which was to be celebrated in the Basilica of St. Mary Major on June 7, 1981.

"In order to respond more fully to the requests of 'Our Lady,' the Holy Father desired to make more explicit during the Holy Year of the Redemption the Act of Entrustment of June 7, 1981, which had been repeated in Fátima on May 13, 1982.

"Sr. Lucia," continued the archbishop, "personally confirmed that this solemn and universal act of consecration corresponded to what Our Lady wished. Hence any further discussion or request is without basis."

Sr. Lucia had already hinted at the interpretation of the third part of the "secret" in a letter to the Holy Father dated May 12, 1982. That letter is also published in the document.

Finally, Archbishop Tarcisio Bertone indicates that "the decision of His Holiness Pope John Paul II to make public the third part of the 'secret' of Fátima brings to an end a period of history marked by tragic human lust for power and evil, yet pervaded by the merciful love of God and the watchful care of the Mother of Jesus and of the Church."

TRANSLATION OF THE THIRD SECRET OF FÁTIMA

On June 26, 2000, the Holy See issued the complete translation of the original Portuguese text of the third part of the secret of Fátima, revealed to the three shepherd children at Cova da Iria-Fátima on July 13, 1917, and committed to paper by Sr. Lucia on Jan. 3, 1944:

"I write in obedience to you, my God, who command me to do so through his Excellency the Bishop of Leiria and through your Most Holy Mother and mine.

"After the two parts which I have already explained, at the left of Our Lady and a little above, we saw an Angel with a flaming sword in his left hand; flashing, it gave out flames that looked as though they would set the world on fire; but they died out in contact with the splendor that Our Lady radiated towards him from her right hand: pointing to the earth with his right hand, the Angel cried out in a loud voice: 'Penance, Penance, Penance!' And we saw in an immense light that is God: 'something similar to how people appear in

a mirror when they pass in front of it' a Bishop dressed in White 'we had the impression that it was the Holy Father.' Other Bishops, Priests, men and women Religious going up a steep mountain, at the top of which there was a big Cross of rough-hewn trunks as of a cork-tree with the bark; before reaching there the Holy Father passed through a big city half in ruins and half trembling with halting step, afflicted with pain and sorrow, he prayed for the souls of the corpses he met on his way; having reached the top of the mountain, on his knees at the foot of the big Cross he was killed by a group of soldiers who fired bullets and arrows at him, and in the same way there died one after another the Bishops, Priests, men and women Religious, and various lay people of different ranks and positions. Beneath the two arms of the Cross there were two Angels each with a crystal aspersorium in his hand, in which they gathered up the blood of the Martyrs and with it sprinkled the souls that were making their way to God."

EVENTS AT MEDJUGORJE

The alleged apparitions of the Blessed Virgin Mary to six young people of Medjugorje, Bosnia-Herzogovina, have been the source of interest and controversy since they were first reported in June 1981, initially in the neighboring hillside field, subsequently in the village church of St. James and even in places far removed from Medjugorje.

Reports say the alleged visionaries have seen, heard, and even touched Mary during visions, and that they have variously received several or all of 10 secret messages related to coming world events and urging a quest for peace through penance and personal conversion. An investigative commission appointed by former local Bishop Pavao Zanic of Mostar-Duvno reported in Mar. 1984 that the authenticity of the apparitions had not been verified. He called the apparitions a case of "collective hallucination" exploited by local Franciscan priests at odds with him over control of a parish.

Former Archbishop Frane Franic of Split-Makarska, on the other hand, said in Dec. 1985: "Speaking as a believer and not as a bishop, my personal conviction is that the events at Medjugorje are of supernatural inspiration." He based his conviction on the observations of spiritual benefits related to the reported events, such as the spiritual development of the six young people, the increases in Mass attendance and sacramental practice at the scene of the apparitions, and the incidence of reconciliation among people.

On Jan. 29, 1987, the bishops of Yugoslavia declared: "On the basis of research conducted so far, one cannot affirm that supernatural apparitions are involved" at Medjugorje. Currently, the events at Medjugorje are under on-going investigation by the Holy See to determine their authenticity. Nevertheless, the site of Medjugorje remains a popular destination for Catholic pilgrims from Europe and the United States.

THE CODE OF CANON LAW

Canon Law is the term that denotes the body of laws governing the Catholic Church. The name is derived from the Greek word *kanon* (rule, i.e., rule of practical direction), which, from the fourth century, was used to denote the ordinances and regulations promulgated by the various Church councils that were convened to discuss problems or important topics. The actual term "canon law" (*ius canonicum*) came into use in the 1100s and was intended to differentiate ecclesiastical law from civil law (*ius civile*).

History of Canon Law

In a practical sense, the laws and regulations began to take shape as early as apostolic times and were evident in their nascent form in the Didache, the Didscalia and the Apostolic Tradition. Owing to the persecution of the Church, however, there was little effort to gather laws together, and certainly less time was devoted to systematizing them.

The fourth century brought the Church freedom from persecution and the resulting rapid growth in membership that was a concomitant of the favors bestowed upon the faith by the rulers of the Roman Empire. New laws were naturally needed and desired. Local regulations were soon established through the decrees of the councils, although these most often had only a local authority and adherence. The general (or ecumenical) councils made laws for the whole Church, and the custom developed of carrying on the decrees of previous assemblies by having them read before the start of a new council. Collections of these laws or canons were then undertaken, but these did not bear the weight of being an official code as they were gathered under private authority.

The earliest efforts at collecting Church laws were centered around the private compilation of the decrees of the Eastern councils to which were added those of the Western Church. The councils of the African Church also made lasting contributions, the most significant coming out of the Seventeenth Council of Carthage (419), which accepted the book of canons later adopted into the canon law of both the Eastern and Western Churches. An official Code of Canon Law was recognized in the seventh century under the Isidorian Collection. Other important influences were the writings of monks in England and Ireland. The monks compiled lists of sins and various offenses to which confessors applied the proper fines or penances. The resulting books were called Penitentials, and they offer scholars an invaluable glimpse into the state of Church law in early medieval England and the development of moral theology.

The Carolingian Reforms of the Church under Charlemagne facilitated the enactment of much legislation that was beneficial to the faith, but it also signaled a long period of secular interference in ecclesiastical affairs. Two by-products of this lay intrusion were the creation of the forged but interesting False Decretals (collections of false canons and decrees of the popes used to falsify the Church's position) and the application of legal arguments by Churchmen that could protect the Church from abuse. Efforts at revitalization would become heightened under the Gregorian Reform, in particular with the reign of Pope St. Gregory VII (1073-1085). From that time, throughout the Middle Ages, laws from the Church would be centered in and produced by the papacy, assisted in running the administration of the Church by the Roman Curia.

Gradually, legal experts collected the decrees of popes, enactments of councils, and sources of older, ancient canons. To these were added glosses, or commentaries, to assist in the teaching of the details of the subject. Still, the study of canon law was severely handicapped by the sheer number of collections, the contradiction between many points of law, and the inability to find specific laws because of the chronological arrangements of the material. Thus can be seen the major significance of the *Decretum* of Gratian, published around 1148 in Bologna. Compiled by the legal expert Gratian, the *Decretum* (in full, *Concordantia discordantum canonum*) was not a formal collection of canons but sought to provide a juridical system for its readers. Toward this end, though, Gratian examined (and excerpted) virtually every canon ever published. The *Decretum* was quickly adopted as the textbook of canon law, despite the fact that it was a private collection and not codified.

Over the next centuries, the popes added to the body of laws by giving rulings to those questions posed to them by bishops from around the Church. These decretal letters were then brought together and, for purposes of comprehensiveness, added to the *Decretum Gratiani*. The most important of these was the *Liber extra*, the collection made by St. Raymond Peñafort for Pope Gregory IX. This received official approval and was to be a vital source for the *Corpus Juris Canonici*. Other remarkable contributors to canon law in the late Middle Ages were Zenzelinus de Cassanis, Jean Chappuis, Guido de Baysio, John the Teuton (or Joannes Teutonicus), Stephen of Tournai, and most of all, Joannes Andreae (d. 1348).

Considerable activity was initiated by the Council of Trent (1545-1563), which sought to reform and reinvigorate the Church in the wake of the Protestant Reformation. The same century brought the formation in 1588 of the Sacred Congregation of the Curia by Pope Sixtus V (r. 1585-1590), which became the main means of implementing new laws and examining facets of established ones.

The final decision to codify the laws of the Church was made by Pope St. Pius X who, in 1903, issued *Arduum*, the *motu proprio* ordering the complete reform and codification of all canon law. It was completed and promulgated in 1917 as the *Codex Juris Canonici*, the first official guide to the laws of the Catholic Church. A new Code of Canon Law was issued by Pope John Paul II in 1983, the final result of a call for a new code dating back to Pope John XXIII (r. 1958-1963) and continued by Pope Paul VI (r. 1963-1978).

The 1983 Code of Canon Law

Pope John Paul II promulgated a revised Code of Canon Law for the Latin Rite on Jan. 25, 1983, with the apostolic constitution *Sacrae Disciplinae Legis* ("Of the Sacred Discipline of Law") and ordered it into effect as of the following Nov. 27. Promulgation of the Code marked the completion of the last major reform in the Church stemming from the Second Vatican Council.

The 1983 Code of Canon Law replaced the one which had been in effect since 1918. The new Code incorporates into law the insights of Vatican Council II. These 1,752 canons focus on the People of God and the threefold ministries of sanctifying, teaching, and governance. Also included are general norms, temporalities, sanctions and procedures.

Guiding Principles

When Pope John XXIII announced on Jan. 25, 1959, that he was going to convoke the Second Vatican Council, he also called for a revision of the existing Code of Canon Law. His successor, Paul VI, appointed a commission for this purpose in 1963 and subsequently enlarged it. The commission, which began its work after the conclusion of the Council in 1965, was directed by the 1967 Synod of Bishops to direct its efforts in line with 10 guiding principles. The bishops said the revised Code should:

• be juridical in character, not just a set of broad moral principles;

• be intended primarily for the external forum (regarding determinable fact, as opposed to the internal forum of conscience);

• be clearly pastoral in spirit;

• incorporate most of the faculties bishops need in their ministry;

• provide for subsidiarity or decentralization;

• be sensitive to human rights;

• state clear procedures for administrative processes and tribunals;

• be based on the principle of territoriality;

• reduce the number of penalties for infraction of law;

• have a new structure.

The commission carried out its mandate with the collegial collaboration of bishops all over the world and in consultation and correspondence with individuals and experts in canon law, theology, and related disciplines. The group finished its work in 1981 and turned its final draft over to Pope John Paul II at its final plenary meeting in October of that year.

Features

The revised code is shorter (1,752 canons) than the one it replaced (2,414 canons) and has a number of important features:

It is more pastoral and flexible, as well as more theologically oriented than the former Code. It gives greater emphasis than its predecessor to a number of significant facets and concepts in church life.

In the apostolic constitution with which he promulgated the Code, Pope John Paul II called attention to its nature and some of its features, as follows:

Prime Legislative Document

"Since this is so, it seems clear enough that the Code in no way has its scope to substitute for faith, grace, the charisms, and especially charity in the life of the Church of the faithful. On the contrary, its end is rather to create such order in ecclesial society that, assigning primacy to love, grace and charisms, it at the same time renders more active their organic developments in the life both of the ecclesial society and of the individuals belonging to it. Inasmuch as it is the Church's prime legislative document, based on the juridical and legislative heritage of revelation and tradition, the Code must be regarded as the necessary instrument whereby due order is preserved in both individual and social life and in the Church's activity. Therefore, besides containing the fundamental elements of the hierarchical and organic structure of the Church, laid down by her divine Founder and founded on apostolic or at any rate most ancient tradition, and besides outstanding norms concerning the carrying out of the task mandated to the Church herself, the Code must also define a certain number of rules and norms of action."

Suits the Nature of the Church

"The instrument the Code is fully suits the Church's nature, for the Church is presented, especially through the magisterium of the Second Vatican Council, in her universal scope, and especially through the Council's ecclesiological teaching. In a certain sense, indeed, this new Code may be considered as a great effort to transfer that same ecclesiological or conciliar doctrine into canonical language. And, if it is impossible for the image of the Church described by the Council's teaching to be perfectly converted into canonical language, the Code nonetheless must always be referred to that very image, as the primary pattern whose outline the Code ought to express as well as it can by its own nature.

"From this derive a number of fundamental norms by which the whole of the new Code is ruled, of course within the limits proper to it as well as the limits of the very language befitting the material.

"It may rather be rightly affirmed that from this comes that note whereby the Code is regarded as a complement to the magisterium expounded by the Second Vatican Council.

"The following elements are most especially to be noted among those expressing a true and genuine image of the Church: the doctrine whereby the Church is proposed as the People of God and the hierarchical authority is propounded as service; in addition, the doctrine which shows the Church to be a 'communion' and from that lays down the mutual relationships which ought to exist between the particular and universal Church and between collegiality and primacy; likewise, the doctrine whereby all members of the People of God, each in the manner proper to him, share in Christ's threefold office of priest, prophet and king; to this doctrine is also connected that regarding the duties and rights of the Christian faithful, particularly the laity; then there is the effort which the Church has to make for ecumenism."

Code Necessary for the Church

"Indeed, the Code of Canon Law is extremely necessary for the Church … The Church needs it for her hierarchichal and organic structure to be visible: so that exercise of the offices and tasks divinely entrusted to her, especially her sacred power and administration of the sacraments, should be rightly ordered; so that mutual relations of the Christian faithful may be carried out according to justice based on charity, with the rights of all being safeguarded and defined; so that we may then prepare and perform our common tasks, and that these, undertaken in order to live a Christian life more perfectly, may be fortified by means of the canonical laws.

"Thus, canonical laws need to be observed because of their very nature. Hence it is of the greatest importance that the norms be carefully expounded on the basis of solid juridical, canonical and theological foundations."

BOOKS OF THE CODE

Book I, General Norms (Canons 1-203): Canons in this book cover Church laws, in general, custom and law, general decrees and instructions, administrative acts, statutes, physical and juridical persons, juridical acts, the power of governing, ecclesiastical offices, prescription (statutes of limitations), the reckoning of time.

Book II, The People of God (Canons 204-746): Canons in Part I cover the obligations and rights of all the faithful, the obligations and rights of lay persons, sacred ministers and clerics, personal prelatures and associations of the faithful.

Canons in Part II cover the hierarchic constitution of the Church under the headings: the supreme authority of the Church and the college of bishops, diocesan churches and the authority constituted in them, councils of diocesan churches and the internal order of diocesan churches.

Canons in Part III cover institutes of consecrated life and societies of apostolic life.

Book III: The Teaching Office of the Church (Canons 747-833): Canons under this heading cover: the ministry of the divine word, the missionary action of the Church, Catholic education, the instruments of social communication and books in particular, and the profession of faith.

Book IV, The Sanctifying Office of the Church (Canons 834-1252): Canons under this heading cover each of the seven sacraments – baptism, confirmation, the Eucharist, penance, anointing of the sick, holy orders and matrimony; other acts of divine worship including sacramentals, the Liturgy of the Hours, ecclesiastical burial; the veneration of saints, sacred images and relics, vows and oaths.

Book V, Temporal Goods of the Church (Canons 1254-1310): Canons under this heading cover: the acquisition and administration of goods, contracts, the alienation of goods, wills and pious foundations.

Book VI, Sanctions in the Church (Canons 1311-1399): Canons in Part I cover crimes and penalties in general: the punishment of crimes in general, penal law and penal precept, persons subject to penal sanctions, penalties and other punishments, the application and cessation of penalties.

Canons in Part II cover penalties for particular crimes: crimes against religion and the unity of the Church; crimes against the authority of the Church and the liberty of the Church; the usurpation of Church offices and crimes in exercising office; false accusation of a confessor; crimes against special obligations; crimes against human life and liberty; a general norm regarding the punishment of external violations of divine law not specifically covered in the Code.

Book VII, Procedures (Canons 1400-1752): Judicial proceedings are the principal subjects of canons under this heading: tribunals and their personnel, parties to proceedings, details regarding litigation and the manner in which it is conducted, special proceedings – with emphasis on matrimonial cases.

Glossary

A

Abbacy Nullius: A non-diocesan territory whose people are under the pastoral care of an abbot acting in general in the manner of a bishop.

Abbess: The female superior of a monastic community of nuns; e.g., Benedictines, Poor Clares, some others. Elected by members of the community, an abbess has general authority over her community but no sacramental jurisdiction.

Abbey: *See* Monastery.

Abbot: The male superior of a monastic community of men religious; e.g., Benedictines, Cistercians, some others. Elected by members of the community, an abbot has ordinary jurisdiction and general authority over his community. Eastern Rite equivalents of an abbot are a hegumen and an archimandrite. A regular abbot is the head of an abbey or monastery. An abbot general or archabbot is the head of a congregation consisting of several monasteries. An abbot primate is the head of the modern Benedictine Confederation.

Abiogenesis: The term used to describe the spontaneous generation of living matter from non-living matter.

Ablution: A term derived from Latin, meaning washing or cleansing, and referring to the cleansing of the hands of a priest celebrating Mass, after the offering of gifts; and to the cleansing of the chalice with water and wine after Communion.

Abnegation: The spiritual practice of self-denial (or mortification), in order to atone for past sins or in order to join oneself to the passion of Christ. Mortification can be undertaken through fasting, abstinence, or refraining from legitimate pleasure.

Abortion: Abortion is not only "the ejection of an immature fetus" from the womb, but is "also the killing of the same fetus in whatever way at whatever time from the moment of conception it may be procured." (This clarification of Canon 1398, reported in the Dec. 5, 1988, edition of *L'Osservatore Romano*, was issued by the Pontifical Council for the Interpretation of Legislative Texts — in view of scientific developments regarding ways and means of procuring abortion.) Accidental expulsion, as in cases of miscarriage, is without moral fault. Direct abortion, in which a fetus is intentionally removed from the womb, constitutes a direct attack on an innocent human being, a violation of the Fifth Commandment. A person who procures a completed abortion is automatically excommunicated (Canon 1398 of the *Code of Canon Law*); also excommunicated are all persons involved in a deliberate and successful effort to bring about an abortion. Direct abortion is not justifiable for

any reason, e.g.: therapeutic, for the physical and/or psychological welfare of the mother; preventive, to avoid the birth of a defective or unwanted child; social, in the interests of family and/or community. Indirect abortion, which occurs when a fetus is expelled during medical or other treatment of the mother for a reason other than procuring expulsion, is permissible under the principle of double effect for a proportionately serious reason; e.g., when a medical or surgical procedure is necessary to save the life of the mother. Such a procedure should not be confused with the purportedly "medical" procedure of the partial-birth abortion, a particularly cruel form of abortion.

Abrogation: The Abolition or elimination of a law by some official action. In Canon Law, abrogation occurs through a direct decree of the Holy See or by the enactment of a later or subsequent law contrary to the former law.

Absolute: (1) A term in philosophy, first introduced at the end of the 18th century and used by Scholasticism, that signifies the "perfect being" (i.e., God), who relies upon no one for existence. Modern philosophical thought has added two new concepts: a) the Absolute is the sum of all being; b) the Absolute has no relationship with any other things; the Absolute is thus unknowable. These concepts are agnostic and contrary to Catholicism, which holds that God is the cause of all being (and hence not the sum) and is knowable by his creatures, at least in part. (2) Certain truths, revealed by God, which are unchanging.

Absolution, Sacramental: The act by which bishops and priests, acting as agents of Christ and ministers of the Church, grant forgiveness of sins in the sacrament of penance. The essential formula of absolution is: " I absolve you from your sins; in the name of the Father, and of the Son, and of the Holy Spirit. Amen." The power to absolve is given with ordination to the priesthood and episcopate. Priests exercise this power in virtue of authorization (faculties) granted by a bishop, a religious superior or canon law. Authorization can be limited or restricted regarding certain sins and penalties or censures. In cases of necessity, and also in cases of the absence of their own confessors, Eastern and Latin Rite Catholics may ask for and receive sacramental absolution from an Eastern or Latin Rite priest; so may Polish National Catholics, according to a Vatican decision issued in May, 1993. Any priest can absolve a person in danger of death; in the absence of a priest with the usual faculties, this includes a laicized priest or a priest under censure. (*See* additional entry under **Sacraments**.)

Abstinence: 1. The deliberate deprivation by a person of meat or of foods prepared with meat on those days prescribed by the Church as penitential (Ash Wednesday, Good Friday, and all Fridays of the year which are not solemnities — in the United States, not all Fridays of the year but only the Fridays of Lent). Those 14 years of age and above are bound by the discipline. (2) Sexual abstinence is the willing refrain from sexual intercourse; total abstinence is observed in obedience to the Sixth Commandment by single persons and couples whose marriages are not recognized by the Church as valid; periodic abstinence or periodic continence is observed by a married couple for regulating conception by natural means or for ascetical motives.

Adoration: The highest act and purpose of religious worship, which is directed in love and reverence to God alone in acknowledgment of his infinite perfection and goodness, and of his total dominion over creatures. Adoration, which is also called latria, consists of internal and external elements, private and social prayer, liturgical acts and ceremonies, and especially sacrifice.

Adultery: Marital infidelity. Sexual intercourse between a married person and another to whom one is not married, a violation of the obligations of the marital covenant, chastity and justice; any sin of impurity (thought, desire, word, action) involving a married person who is not one's husband or wife has the nature of adultery.

Advent Wreath: A wreath of laurel, spruce, or similar foliage with four candles which are lighted successively in the weeks of Advent to symbolize the approaching celebration of the birth of Christ, the Light of the World, at Christmas. The wreath originated among German Protestants.

Agape: A Greek word, meaning love, love feast, designating the meal of fellowship eaten at some gatherings of early Christians. Although held in some places in connection with the Mass, the agape was not part of the Mass, nor was it of universal institution and observance. It was infrequently observed by the fifth century and disappeared altogether between the sixth and eighth centuries.

Age of Reason: (1) The time of life when one begins to distinguish between right and wrong, to understand an obligation and take on moral responsibility; seven years of age is the presumption in church law. (2) Historically, the 18th century period of Enlightenment in England and France, the age of the Encyclopedists and Deists. According to a basic thesis of the Enlightenment, human experience and reason are the only sources of certain knowledge of truth; consequently, faith and revelation are discounted as valid sources of knowledge, and the reality of supernatural truth is called into doubt and/or denied.

Aggiornamento: An Italian word having the general meaning of bringing up to date, renewal, revitalization, descriptive of the processes of spiritual renewal and institutional reform and change in the Church; fostered by the Second Vatican Council.

Agnosticism: A theory which holds that a person cannot have certain knowledge of immaterial reality, especially the existence of God and things pertaining to him. Immanuel Kant, one of the philosophical fathers of agnosticism, stood for the position that God, as well as the human soul, is unknowable on specula-

tive grounds; nevertheless, he found practical imperatives for acknowledging God's existence, a view shared by many agnostics. The First Vatican Council declared that the existence of God and some of his attributes can be known with certainty by human reason, even without divine revelation. The word agnosticism was first used, in the sense given here, by T. H. Huxley in 1869.

Agnus Dei: A Latin phrase, meaning Lamb of God. (1) A title given to Christ, the Lamb (victim) of the Sacrifice of the New Law (on Calvary and in Mass). (2) A prayer said at Mass before the reception of Holy Communion. (3) A sacramental. It is a round paschal-candle fragment blessed by the pope. On one side it bears the impression of a lamb, symbolic of Christ. On the reverse side, there may be any one of a number of impressions; e.g., the figure of a saint, the name and coat of arms of the reigning pope. The *agnus dei* may have originated at Rome in the fifth century. The first definite mention of it dates from about 820.

Akathist Hymn: The most profound and famous expression of Marian devotion in churches of the Byzantine Rite. It consists of 24 sections, 12 of which relate to the Gospel of the Infancy and 12 to the mysteries of the Incarnation and the virginal motherhood of Mary. In liturgical usage, it is sung in part in Byzantine churches on the first four Saturdays of Lent and in toto on the fifth Saturday; it is also recited in private devotion. It is of unknown origin prior to 626, when its popularity increased as a hymn of thanksgiving after the successful defense and liberation of Constantinople, which had been under siege by Persians and Avars. Akathist means "without sitting," indicating that the hymn is recited or sung while standing. Pope John Paul, in a decree dated May 25, 1991, granted a plenary indulgence to the faithful of any rite who recite the hymn in a church or oratory, as a family, in a religious community or in a pious association — in conjunction with the usual conditions of freedom from attachment to sin, reception of the sacraments of penance and the Eucharist, and prayers for the intention of the pope (e.g., an Our Father, the Apostles' Creed and an aspiration). A partial indulgence can be gained for recitation of the hymn in other circumstances.

Alleluia: An exclamation of joy derived from Hebrew, "All hail to him who is, praise God," with various use in the liturgy and other expressions of worship.

Allocution: A formal type of papal address, as distinguished from an ordinary sermon or statement of views.

Alms: An act, gift or service of compassion, motivated by love of God and neighbor, for the help of persons in need; an obligation of charity, which is measurable by the ability of one person to give assistance and by the degree of another's need. Almsgiving, along with prayer and fasting, is regarded as a work of penance as well as an exercise of charity. (*See* Mercy, Works of.)

Alpha and Omega: The first and last letters of the Greek alphabet, used to symbolize the eternity of God (Rv 1:8) and the divinity and eternity of Christ, the beginning and end of all things (Rv 21:6; 22:13). Use of the letters as a monogram of Christ originated in the fourth century or earlier.

Amen: A Hebrew word meaning truly, it is true. In

the Gospels, Christ used the word to add a note of authority to his statements. In other New Testament writings, as in Hebrew usage, it was the concluding word to doxologies. As the concluding word of prayers, it expresses assent to and acceptance of God's will.

Anamnesis: A prayer recalling the saving mysteries of the death and resurrection of Jesus, following the consecration at Mass in the Latin Rite.

Anaphora: A Greek term for the Canon or Eucharistic Prayer of the Mass.

Anathema: A Greek word with the root meaning of cursed or separated and the adapted meaning of excommunication, used in church documents, especially the canons of ecumenical councils, for the condemnation of heretical doctrines and of practices opposed to proper discipline.

Anchorite: A kind of hermit living in complete isolation and devoting himself exclusively to exercises of religion and severe penance according to a rule and way of life of his own devising. In early Christian times, anchorites were the forerunners of the monastic life. The closest contemporary approach to the life of an anchorite is that of Carthusian and Camaldolese hermits.

Angels: Purely spiritual beings with intelligence and free will whose name indicates their mission as servants and messengers of God. They were created before the creation of the visible universe. Good angels enjoy the perfect good of the beatific vision. They can intercede for persons. The doctrine of guardian angels, although not explicitly defined as a matter of faith, is rooted in long-standing tradition. No authoritative declaration has ever been issued regarding choirs or various categories of angels: seraphim, cherubim, thrones, dominations, principalities, powers, virtues, archangels and angels. Archangels commemorated in the liturgy are: Michael, leader of the angelic host and protector of the synagogue; Raphael, guide of Tobiah and healer of his father; Gabriel, angel of the Incarnation. Fallen angels, the chief of whom is called the Devil or Satan, rejected the love of God and were therefore banished from heaven to hell. They can tempt persons to commit sin.

Angelus: A devotion which commemorates the Incarnation of Christ. It consists of three versicles, three Hail Marys and a special prayer, and recalls the announcement to Mary by the Archangel Gabriel that she was chosen to be the Mother of Christ, her acceptance of the divine will, and the Incarnation (Lk 1:26-38). The Angelus is recited in the morning, at noon and in the evening. The practice of reciting the Hail Mary in honor of the Incarnation was introduced by the Franciscans in 1263. The *Regina Caeli*, commemorating the joy of Mary at Christ's Resurrection, replaces the Angelus during the Easter season.

Anger (Wrath): Passionate displeasure arising from some kind of offense suffered at the hands of another person, frustration or other cause, combined with a tendency to strike back at the cause of the displeasure; a violation of the Fifth Commandment and one of the capital sins if the displeasure is out of proportion to the cause and/or if the retaliation is unjust.

Anglican Orders: Holy orders conferred according to the rite of the Anglican Church, which Leo XIII declared null and void in the bull *Apostolicae Curae*, Sept. 13, 1896. The orders were declared null because they were conferred according to a rite that was substantially defective in form and intent, and because of a break in apostolic succession that occurred when Matthew Parker became head of the Anglican hierarchy in 1559. In making his declaration, Pope Leo cited earlier arguments against validity made by Julius III in 1553 and 1554 and by Paul IV in 1555. He also noted related directives requiring absolute ordination, according to the Catholic ritual, of convert ministers who had been ordained according to the Anglican Ordinal.

Anglican Use Parishes: In line with Vatican-approved developments since 1980, several Anglican use parishes have been established in the United States with the right to continue using some elements of Anglican usage in their liturgical celebrations. A Vatican document dated Mar. 31, 1981, said: "In June, 1980, the Holy See, through the Congregation for the Doctrine of the Faith, agreed to the request presented by the bishops of the United States of America in behalf of some clergy and laity formerly or actually belonging to the Episcopal (Anglican) Church for full communion with the Catholic Church. The Holy See's response to the initiative of these Episcopalians includes the possibility of a 'pastoral provision' which will provide, for those who desire it, a common identity reflecting certain elements of their own heritage."

Animals: Creatures of God, they are entrusted to human stewardship for appropriate care, use for human needs, as pets, for reasonable experimentation for the good of people. They should not be subject to cruel treatment.

Annulment: A decree issued by an appropriate Church authority or tribunal that a sacrament or ecclesiastical act is invalid and therefore lacking in all legal or canonical consequences.

Antichrist: The "deceitful one," the "antichrist" (2 Jn 7), adversary of Christ and the kingdom of God, especially in the end time before the second coming of Christ. The term is also used in reference to anti-Christian persons and forces in the world.

Antiphon: (1) A short verse or text, generally from Scripture, recited in the Liturgy of the Hours before and after psalms and canticles. (2) Any verse sung or recited by one part of a choir or congregation in response to the other part, as in antiphonal or alternate chanting.

Anti-Semitism: A prejudice against Jews, and often accompanied by persecution. The prejudice has existed historically from the time of the ancient Persian Empire and survives even to the present day. It has been condemned consistently by the Church as being in opposition to scriptural principles and Christian charity.

Apologetics: The science and art of developing and presenting the case for the reasonableness of the Christian faith, by a wide variety of means including facts of experience, history, science, philosophy. The constant objective of apologetics, as well as of the total process of pre-evangelization, is preparation for response to God in faith; its ways and means, however, are subject to change in accordance with the various needs of people and different sets of circumstances.

Apostasy: (1) The total and obstinate repudiation of

the Christian faith. An apostate automatically incurs a penalty of excommunication. (2) Apostasy from orders is the unlawful withdrawal from or rejection of the obligations of the clerical state by a man who has received major orders. An apostate from orders is subject to a canonical penalty. (3) Apostasy from the religious life occurs when a Religious with perpetual vows unlawfully leaves the community with the intention of not returning, or actually remains outside the community without permission. An apostate from religious life is subject to a canonical penalty.

Apostolate: The ministry or work of an apostle. In Catholic usage, the word is an umbrella-like term covering all kinds and areas of work and endeavor for the service of God and the Church and the good of people. Thus, the apostolate of bishops is to carry on the mission of the Apostles as pastors of the People of God: of priests, to preach the word of God and to carry out the sacramental and pastoral ministry for which they are ordained; of religious, to follow and do the work of Christ in conformity with the evangelical counsels and their rule of life; of lay persons, as individuals and/or in groups, to give witness to Christ and build up the kingdom of God through practice of their faith, professional competence and the performance of good works in the concrete circumstances of daily life. Apostolic works are not limited to those done within the Church or by specifically Catholic groups, although some apostolates are officially assigned to certain persons or groups and are under the direction of church authorities. Apostolate derives from the commitment and obligation of baptism, confirmation, holy orders, matrimony, the duties of one's state in life, etc.

Apostolic Succession: Bishops of the Church, who form a collective body or college, are successors to the Apostles by ordination and divine right; as such they carry on the mission entrusted by Christ to the Apostles as guardians and teachers of the deposit of faith, principal pastors and spiritual authorities of the faithful. The doctrine of apostolic succession is based on New Testament evidence and the constant teaching of the Church, reflected as early as the end of the first century in a letter of Pope St. Clement to the Corinthians. A significant facet of the doctrine is the role of the pope as the successor of St. Peter, the vicar of Christ and head of the college of bishops. The doctrine of apostolic succession means more than continuity of apostolic faith and doctrine; its basic requisite is ordination by the laying on of hands in apostolic succession.

Archives: Documentary records, and the place where they are kept, of the spiritual and temporal government and affairs of the Church, a diocese, church agencies like the departments of the Roman Curia, bodies like religious institutes, and individual parishes. The collection, cataloguing, preserving, and use of these records are governed by norms stated in canon law and particular regulations. The strictest secrecy is always in effect for confidential records concerning matters of conscience, and documents of this kind are destroyed as soon as circumstances permit.

Ark of the Covenant: The sacred chest of the Israelites in which were placed and carried the tablets of stone inscribed with the Ten Commandments, the basic moral precepts of the Old Covenant (Ex 25: 10-22; 37:1-9). The Ark was also a symbol of God's presence. The Ark was probably destroyed with the Temple in 586 B.C.

Asceticism: The practice of self-discipline. In the spiritual life, asceticism — by personal prayer, meditation, self-denial, works of mortification, and outgoing interpersonal works — is motivated by love of God and contributes to growth in holiness.

Ashes: Religious significance has been associated with their use as symbolic of penance since Old Testament times. Thus, ashes of palm blessed on the previous Sunday of the Passion are placed on the foreheads of the faithful on Ash Wednesday to remind them to do works of penance, especially during the season of Lent, and that they are dust and unto dust will return. Ashes are a sacramental.

Aspergillum: A vessel or device used for sprinkling holy water. The ordinary type is a metallic rod with a bulbous tip which absorbs the water and discharges it at the motion of the user's hand.

Aspersory: A portable metallic vessel, similar to a pail, for carrying holy water.

Aspiration (Ejaculation): Short exclamatory prayer; e.g., My Jesus, mercy.

Atheism: Denial of the existence of God, finding expression in a system of thought (speculative atheism) or a manner of acting (practical atheism) as though there were no God. The Second Vatican Council, in its Pastoral Constitution on the Church in the Modern World (*Gaudium et Spes*, Nos. 19 to 21), noted that a profession of atheism may represent an explicit denial of God, the rejection of a wrong notion of God, an affirmation of man rather than of God, an extreme protest against evil. It said that such a profession might result from acceptance of such propositions as: there is no absolute truth; man can assert nothing, absolutely nothing, about God; everything can be explained by scientific reasoning alone; the whole question of God is devoid of meaning.

Atonement: The redemptive activity of Christ, who reconciled man with God through his Incarnation and entire life, and especially by his suffering and Resurrection. The word also applies to prayer and good works by which persons join themselves with and take part in Christ's work of reconciliation and reparation for sin.

Attributes of God: Perfections of God. God possesses — and is — all the perfections of being, without limitation. Because he is infinite, all of these perfections are one, perfectly united in him. Because of the limited power of human intelligence, divine perfections — such as omnipotence, truth, love, etc. — are viewed separately, as distinct characteristics, even though they are not actually distinct in God.

Authority, Ecclesiastical: The authority exercised by the Church, and particularly by the pope and the bishops; it is delegated by Jesus Christ to St. Peter. This authority extends to all those matters entrusted to the Apostles by Christ, including teaching of the Faith, the liturgy and sacraments, moral guidance, and the administration of discipline.

Avarice (Covetousness): A disorderly and unreasonable attachment to and desire for material things; called a capital sin because it involves preoccupation with material things to the neglect of spiritual goods and obligations of justice and charity.

Ave Maria: See Hail Mary.

B

Baldacchino: A canopy over an altar.

Baptism: *See* Sacraments.

Beatification: A preliminary step toward canonization of a saint. It begins with an investigation of the candidate's life, writings and heroic practice of virtue, and, except in the case of martyrs, the certification of one miracle worked by God through his or her intercession. If the findings of the investigation so indicate, the pope decrees that the Servant of God may be called Blessed and may be honored locally or in a limited way in the liturgy. Additional procedures lead to canonization (see separate entry).

Beatific Vision: The intuitive, immediate and direct vision and experience of God enjoyed in the light of glory by all the blessed in heaven. The vision is a supernatural mystery.

Beatitude: A literary form of the Old and New Testaments in which blessings are promised to persons for various reasons. Beatitudes are mentioned 26 times in the Psalms, and in other books of the Old Testament. The best known Beatitudes — identifying blessedness with participation in the kingdom of God and his righteousness, and descriptive of the qualities of Christian perfection — are those recounted in Mt 5:3-12 and Lk 6:20-23. The Beatitudes are of central importance in the teaching of Jesus.

Benedictus: The canticle or hymn of Zechariah at the circumcision of St. John the Baptist (Lk 1:68-79). It is an expression of praise and thanks to God for sending John as a precursor of the Messiah. The Benedictus is recited in the Liturgy of the Hours as part of the Morning Prayer.

Biglietto: A papal document of notification of appointment to the cardinalate.

Biretta: A stiff, square hat with three ridges on top worn by clerics in church and on other occasions.

Blasphemy: Any internal or external expression of hatred, reproach, insult, defiance or contempt with respect to God and the use of his name, principally, and to the Church, saints and sacred things, secondarily; a serious sin, directly opposed to the second commandment. Blasphemy against the Spirit is the deliberate refusal to accept divine mercy, rejection of forgiveness of sins and of the promise of salvation. The sin that is unforgivable because a person refuses to seek or accept forgiveness.

Blessing: Invocation of God's favor, by official ministers of the Church or by private individuals. Blessings are recounted in the Old and New Testaments, and are common in the Christian tradition. Many types of blessings are listed in the Book of Blessings of the Roman Ritual. Private blessings, as well as those of an official kind, are efficacious. Blessings are imparted with the Sign of the Cross and appropriate prayer.

Bride of Christ: A metaphorical title that denotes the intimate union that Christ enjoys with his Church; the title is mentioned specifically in the NT (2 Cor 11:2).

Brief, Apostolic: A papal letter, less formal than a bull, signed for the pope by a secretary and impressed with the seal of the Fisherman's Ring. Simple apostolic letters of this kind are issued for beatifications and with respect to other matters.

Bull, Apostolic: Apostolic letter, a solemn form of papal document, beginning with the name and title of the pope (e.g., John Paul II, Servant of the Servants of God), dealing with an important subject, sealed with a *bulla* or red-ink imprint of the device on the *bulla*. Bulls are issued to confer the titles of bishops and cardinals, to promulgate canonizations, to proclaim Holy Years and for other purposes. A collection of bulls is called a *bullarium*.

Burial, Ecclesiastical: Interment with ecclesiastical rites, a right of the Christian faithful. The Church recommends burial of the bodies of the dead, but cremation is permissible if it does not involve reasons against church teaching. Ecclesiastical burial is in order for catechumens; for unbaptized children whose parents intended to have them baptized before death; and even, in the absence of their own ministers, for baptized non-Catholics unless it would be considered against their will.

Burse, Financial: A special fund maintained by a diocese, religious institute, or private foundation usually endowed by a private benefactor; it often has the purpose of making possible the education of candidates for the priesthood.

C

Calumny (Slander): Harming the name and good reputation of a person by lies; a violation of obligations of justice and truth. Restitution is due for calumny.

Calvary: A knoll about 15 feet high just outside the western wall of Jerusalem where Christ was crucified, so called from the Latin *calvaria* (skull) which described its shape.

Canon: A Greek word meaning rule, norm, standard, measure. (1) The word designates the Canon of Sacred Scripture, which is the list of books recognized by the Church as inspired by the Holy Spirit. (2) The term also designates the canons (Eucharistic Prayers, anaphoras) of the Mass, the core of the eucharistic liturgy. (3) Certain dignitaries of the Church have the title of Canon, and some religious are known as Canons. (*See* Bible.)

Canonization: An infallible declaration by the pope that a person, who died as a martyr and/or practiced Christian virtue to a heroic degree, is now in heaven and is worthy of honor and imitation by all the faithful. Such a declaration is preceded by the process of beatification and another detailed investigation concerning the person's reputation for holiness, writings, and (except in the case of martyrs) a miracle ascribed to his or her intercession after death. The pope can dispense from some of the formalities ordinarily required in canonization procedures (equivalent canonization), as Pope John XXIII did in the canonization of St. Gregory Barbarigo on May 26, 1960. A saint is worthy of honor in liturgical worship throughout the universal Church. From its earliest years the Church has venerated saints. Public official honor always required the approval of the bishop of the place. Martyrs were the first to be honored. St. Martin of Tours, who died in 397, was an early non-martyr venerated as a saint. The earliest canonization by a pope with positive documentation was that of St. Ulrich (Uldaric) of Augsburg by John XV in 993. Alexander III reserved the process of canonization to the Holy See in 1171. In 1588 Sixtus V established the Sacred Congregation of Rites for the principal purpose of handling causes for beatification and canonization: this function is now the work of the Congregation for the Causes of Saints. The official listing of saints and blessed is contained in the Roman Martyrology (revised, updated, and published in 2002 by the Congregation for Divine Worship and the Discipline of the Sacraments) and related decrees issued after its last publication. Butler's unofficial *Lives of the Saints* (1956 and recently updated) contains 2,565 entries. The Church regards all persons in heaven as saints, not just those who have been officially canonized. (*See* Beatification, Saints, Canonizations by Leo XIII and His Successors.)

Canon Law: *See under* Canon Law.

Canticle: A scriptural chant or prayer differing from the psalms. Three of the canticles prescribed for use in the Liturgy of the Hours are: the *Magnificat*, the Canticle of Mary (Lk 1:46-55); the *Benedictus*, the Canticle of Zechariah (Lk 1:68-79); and the *Nunc Dimittis*, the Canticle of Simeon (Lk 2:29-32).

Capital Punishment: Punishment for crime by means of the death penalty. The political community, which has authority to provide for the common good, has the right to defend itself and its members against unjust aggression and may in extreme cases punish with the death penalty persons found guilty before the law of serious crimes against individuals and a just social order. Such punishment is essentially vindictive. Its value as a crime deterrent is a matter of perennial debate. The prudential judgment as to whether or not there should be capital punishment belongs to the civic community. The U.S. Supreme Court, in a series of decisions dating from June 29, 1972, ruled against the constitutionality of statutes on capital punishment except in specific cases and with appropriate consideration, with respect to sentence, of mitigating circumstances of the crime. Pope John Paul II, in his encyclical *Evangelium Vitae* ("The Gospel of Life"), wrote: "There is a growing tendency, both in the Church and in civil society, to demand that it (capital punishment) be applied in a very limited way or even that it be abolished completely." Quoting the *Catechism of the Catholic Church*, the pope wrote: " 'If bloodless means are sufficient to defend human lives against an aggressor and to protect public order and the safety of persons, public authority must limit itself to such means, because they better correspond to the concrete conditions of the common good and are more in conformity to the dignity of the human person.' "

Capital Sins: Sins which give rise to other sins: pride, avarice, lust, wrath (anger), gluttony, envy, sloth.

Cardinal Virtues: The four principal moral virtues are prudence, justice, temperance and fortitude.

Casuistry: In moral theology, the application of moral principles to specific cases. Casuistry can be of assistance because it takes the abstract and makes it practical in a particular situation. It has definite limitations and does not replace the conscience in the decision-making process; additionally, it must be aligned with the cardinal virtue of prudence.

Catacombs: Underground Christian cemeteries in various cities of the Roman Empire and Italy, especially in the vicinity of Rome; the burial sites of many martyrs and other Christians.

Catechesis: The whole complex of church efforts to make disciples of Christ, involving doctrinal instruction and spiritual formation through practice of the faith.

Catechism: A systematic presentation of the fundamentals of Catholic doctrine regarding faith and morals. Sources are Sacred Scripture, tradition, the magisterium (teaching authority of the Church), the writings of Fathers and Doctors of the Church, liturgy. The new *Catechism of the Catholic Church*, published Oct. 11, 1992, consists of four principal sections: the profession of faith, (the Creed), the sacraments of faith, the life of faith (the Commandments) and the prayer of the believer (the Lord's Prayer). The 16th century Council of Trent mandated publication of the *Roman Catechism*. Catechisms such as these two are useful sources for other catechisms serving particular needs of the faithful and persons seeking admission to the Catholic Church.

Catechumen: A person preparing in a program (catechumenate) of instruction and spiritual formation for baptism and reception into the Church. The Church has a special relationship with catechumens. It invites them to lead the life of the Gospel, introduces them to the celebration of the sacred rites, and grants them various prerogatives that are proper to the faithful (one of which is the right to ecclesiastical burial). (*See* Rite of Christian Initiation of Adults, under Baptism.)

Cathedra: A Greek word for chair, designating the chair or seat of a bishop in the principal church of his diocese, which is therefore called a cathedral.

Cathedraticum: The tax paid to a bishop by all churches and benefices subject to him for the support of episcopal administration and for works of charity.

Catholic: A Greek word, meaning universal, first used in the title Catholic Church in a letter written by St. Ignatius of Antioch about 107 to the Christians of Smyrna.

Celebret: A Latin word, meaning "Let him celebrate," the name of a letter of recommendation issued by a bishop or other superior stating that a priest is in good standing and therefore eligible to celebrate Mass or perform other priestly functions.

Celibacy: The unmarried state of life, required in the Roman Church of candidates for holy orders and of men already ordained to holy orders, for the practice of perfect chastity and total dedication to the service of people in the ministry of the Church. Celibacy is enjoined as a condition for ordination by church discipline and law, not by dogmatic necessity. In the Roman Church, a consensus in favor of celibacy developed in the early centuries while the clergy included both celibates and men who had been married once. The first local legislation on the subject was enacted by a local council held in Elvira, Spain, about 306; it forbade bishops, priests, deacons and other ministers to have wives. Similar enactments were passed by other local councils from that time on, and by the 12th century particular laws regarded marriage by clerics in major orders to be not only unlawful but also null and void. The latter view was translated by the Second Lateran Council in 1139 into what seems to be the first written universal law making holy orders an invalidating impediment to marriage. In 1563 the Council of Trent ruled definitely on the matter and established the discipline in force in the Roman Church. Some exceptions to this discipline have been made in recent years. A number of married Protestant and Episcopalian (Anglican) clergymen who became converts and were subsequently ordained to the priesthood have been permitted to continue in marriage. Married men over the age of 35 can be ordained to the permanent diaconate. Eastern Church discipline on celibacy differs from that of the Roman Church. In line with legislation enacted by the Synod of Trullo in 692 and still in force, candidates for holy orders may marry before becoming deacons and may continue in marriage thereafter, but marriage after ordination is forbidden. Bishops of Eastern Catholic Churches in the U.S., however, do not ordain married candidates for the priesthood. Bishops of Eastern Catholic Churches are unmarried.

Cenacle: The upper room in Jerusalem where Christ ate the Las Supper with his Apostles.

Censer: A metal vessel with a perforated cover and suspended by chains, in which incense is burned. It is used at some Masses, Benediction of the Blessed Sacrament and other liturgical functions.

Censorship of Books: An exercise of vigilance by the Church for safeguarding authentic religious teaching. Pertinent legislation in a decree issued by the Congregation for the Doctrine of the Faith Apr. 9, 1975, is embodied in the Code of Canon Law (Book III, Title IV). The legislation deals with requirements for pre-publication review and clearance of various types of writings on religious subjects. Permission to publish works of a religious character, together with the apparatus of reviewing them beforehand, falls under the authority of the bishop of the place where the writer lives or where the works are published. Clearance for publication is usually indicated by the terms *Nihil obstat* ("Nothing stands in the way") issued by the censor and *Imprimatur* ("Let it be printed") authorized by the bishop. The clearing of works for publication does not necessarily imply approval of an author's viewpoint or his manner of handling a subject.

Censures: Sanctions imposed by the Church on baptized Roman Catholics 18 years of age or older for committing certain serious offenses and for being or remaining obstinate therein: (1) excommunication (exclusion from the community of the faithful, barring a person from sacramental and other participation in the goods and offices of the community of the Church), (2) suspension (prohibition of a cleric to exercise orders) and (3) interdict (deprivation of the sacraments and liturgical activities). The intended purposes of censures are to correct and punish offenders; to deter persons from committing sins which, more seriously and openly than others, threaten the common good of the Church and its members; and to provide for the making of reparation for harm done to the community of the Church. Censures may be incurred automatically (*ipso facto*) on the commission of certain offenses for which fixed penalties have been laid down in church law (*latae sententiae*); or they may be inflicted by sentence of a judge (*ferendae sententiae*). Automatic excommunication is incurred for the offenses of abortion, apostasy, heresy and schism. Obstinacy in crime — also called contumacy, disregard of a penalty, defiance of church authority — is presumed by law in the commission of offenses for which automatic censures are decreed. The presence and degree of contumacy in other cases, for which judicial sentence is required, is subject to determination by a judge. Absolution can be obtained from any censure, provided the person repents and desists from obstinacy. Absolution may be reserved to the pope, the bishop of a place, or the major superior of an exempt clerical religious institute. In danger of death, any priest can absolve from all censures; in other cases, faculties to absolve from reserved censures can be exercised by competent authorities or given to other priests. The penal law of the Church is contained in Book VI of the Code of Canon Law.

Ceremonies, Master of: One who directs the proceedings of a rite or ceremony during the function.

Chamberlain (*Camerlengo*): (1) the Chamberlain of the Holy Roman Church is a cardinal with special responsibilities, especially during the time between the death of one pope and the election of his successor; among other things, he safeguards and administers the goods and revenues of the Holy See and heads particular congregations of cardinals for special purposes. (*See also* **Papal Election.**) (2) the Chamberlain of the College of Cardinals has charge of the property and revenues of the College and keeps the record of business transacted in consistories. (3) the Chamberlain of the Roman Clergy is the president of the secular clergy of Rome.

Chancellor: Notary of a diocese, who draws up written documents in the government of the diocese; takes care of, arranges and indexes diocesan archives, records of dispensations and ecclesiastical trials.

Chancery: (1) A branch of church administration that handles written documents used in the government of a diocese. (2) The administrative office of a diocese, a bishop's office.

Chant: A type of sacred singing. It is either recitative in nature with a short two-to-six tones for an accentus, or melodic in one of three styles (syllabic, neumatic, or melismatic).

Chapel: A building or part of another building used for divine worship; a portion of a church set aside for the celebration of Mass or for some special devotion.

Chaplain: A priest — or, in some instances, a properly qualified religious or lay person — serving the pastoral needs of particular groups of people and institutions, such as hospitals, schools, correctional facilities, religious communities, the armed forces, etc.

Chaplet: A term, meaning little crown, applied to a rosary or, more commonly, to a small string of beads used for devotional purposes; e.g., the Infant of Prague chaplet.

Chapter: A general meeting of delegates of religious orders for elections and the handling of other important affairs of their communities.

Charismatic Renewal: A movement which originated with a handful of Duquesne University students and faculty members in the 1966-67 academic year and spread from there to Notre Dame, Michigan State University, the University of Michigan, other campuses and cities throughout the U.S., and to well over 125 other countries. Scriptural keys to the renewal are: Christ's promise to send the Holy Spirit upon the Apostles; the description, in the Acts of the Apostles, of the effects of the coming of the Holy Spirit upon the Apostles on Pentecost; St. Paul's explanation, in the Letter to the Romans and 1 Corinthians, of the charismatic gifts (for the good of the Church and persons) the Holy Spirit would bestow on Christians; New Testament evidence concerning the effects of charismatic gifts in and through the early Church. The personal key to the renewal is baptism in the Holy Spirit. This is not a new sacrament but the personally experienced actualization of grace already sacramentally received, principally in baptism and confirmation. The experience of baptism in the Holy Spirit is often accompanied by the reception of one or more charismatic gifts. A characteristic form of the renewal is the weekly prayer meeting, a gathering which includes periods of spontaneous prayer, singing, sharing of experience and testimony, fellowship and teaching. (*See* also Index.)

Charisms: Gifts or graces given by God to persons for the good of others and the Church. Examples are special gifts for apostolic work, prophecy, healing, discernment of spirits, the life of evangelical poverty, here-and-now witness to faith in various circumstances of life. The Second Vatican Council made the following statement about charisms in the Dogmatic Constitution on the Church (No. 12): "It is not only through the sacraments and Church ministries that the same Holy Spirit sanctifies and leads the People of God and enriches it with virtues. Allotting his gifts 'to everyone according as he will' (1 Cor 12:11), he distributes special graces among the faithful of every rank. By these gifts he makes them fit and ready to undertake the various tasks or offices advantageous for the renewal and upbuilding of the Church, according to the words of the Apostle: 'The manifestation of the Spirit is given to everyone for profit' (1 Cor 12:7). These charismatic gifts, whether they be the most outstanding or the more simple and widely diffused, are to be received with thanksgiving and consolation, for they are exceedingly suitable and useful for the needs of the Church. Still, extraordinary gifts are not to be rashly sought after, nor are the fruits of apostolic labor to be presumptuously expected from them. In any case, judgment as to their genuineness and proper use belongs to those who preside over the Church, and to whose special competence it belongs, not indeed to extinguish the Spirit, but to test all things and hold fast to that which is good" (cf. 1 Thes 5:12; 19-21).

Charity: Love of God above all things for his own sake, and love of one's neighbor as oneself because and as an expression of one's love for God; the greatest of the three theological virtues. The term is sometimes also used to designate sanctifying grace.

Chastity: Properly ordered behavior with respect to sex. In marriage, the exercise of the procreative power is integrated with the norms and purposes of marriage. Outside of marriage, the rule is self-denial of the voluntary exercise and enjoyment of the procreative faculty in thought, word or action. The vow of chastity, which reinforces the virtue of chastity with the virtue of religion, is one of the three vows professed publicly by members of institutes of consecrated life.

Chirograph or Autograph Letter: A letter written by a pope himself, in his own handwriting.

Chrism: A mixture of olive or other vegetable oil and balsam (or balm), that is consecrated by a bishop for use in liturgical anointings: Baptism, Confirmation, Holy Orders, the blessing of an altar.

Christ: The title of Jesus, derived from the Greek translation *Christos* of the Hebrew term Messiah, meaning the Anointed of God, the Savior and Deliverer of his people. Christian use of the title is a confession of belief that Jesus is the Savior.

Christianity: The sum total of things related to belief in Christ — the Christian religion, Christian churches, Christians themselves, society based on and expressive of Christian beliefs, culture reflecting Christian values.

Christians: The name first applied about the year 43 to followers of Christ at Antioch, the capital of Syria. It was used by the pagans as a contemptuous term. The word applies to persons who profess belief in the divinity and teachings of Christ and who give witness to him in life.

Circumcision: A ceremonial practice symbolic of initiation and participation in the covenant between God and Abraham.

Circumincession: The indwelling of each divine Person of the Holy Trinity in the others.

Clergy: Men ordained to holy orders and commissioned for sacred ministries and assigned to pastoral and other duties for the service of the people and the Church. (1) Diocesan or secular clergy are committed to pastoral ministry in parishes and in other capacities in a particular church (diocese) under the direction of their bishop, to whom they are bound by a promise of obedience. (2) Regular clergy belong to religious institutes (orders, congregations, societies — institutes of consecrated life) and are so called because they observe the rule (*regula*, in Latin) of their respective institutes. They are committed to the ways of life and apostolates of their institutes. In ordinary pastoral ministry, they are under the direction of local bishops as well as their own superiors.

Clericalism: A term generally used in a derogatory sense to mean action, influence and interference by the Church and the clergy in matters with which they allegedly should not be concerned. Anticlericalism is a reaction of antipathy, hostility, distrust and opposition to the Church and clergy arising from real and/or alleged faults of the clergy, overextension of the role of the laity, or for other reasons.

Cloister: Part of a monastery, convent or other house of religious reserved for use by members of the institute. Houses of contemplative Religious have a strict enclosure.

Code: A digest of rules or regulations, such as the Code of Canon Law.

Code of Canon Law: *See under* **Canon Law**.

Collegiality: A term in use especially since the Second Vatican Council to describe the authority exercised by the College of Bishops. The bishops of the Church, in union with and subordinate to the pope — who has full, supreme and universal power over the Church which he can always exercise independently — have supreme teaching and pastoral authority over the whole Church. In addition to their proper authority of office for the good of the faithful in their respective dioceses or other jurisdictions, the bishops have authority to act for the good of the universal Church. This collegial authority is exercised in a solemn manner in an ecumenical council and can also be exercised in other ways sanctioned by the pope. Doctrine on collegiality was set forth by the Second Vatican Council in *Lumen Gentium* (the Dogmatic Constitution on the Church). (*See separate entry.*) By extension, the concept of collegiality is applied to other forms of participation and co-responsibility by members of a community.

Communicatio in Sacris: The reception of the

Church's sacraments by non-members or the reception by Catholics of sacraments in non-Catholic Churches.

Communion of Saints: "The communion of all the faithful of Christ, those who are pilgrims on earth, the dead who are being purified, and the blessed in heaven, all together forming one Church; in this communion, the merciful love of God and his saints is always (attentive) to our prayers" (Paul VI, *Creed of the People of God*).

Communism: The substantive principles of modern communism, a theory and system of economics and social organization, were stated about the middle of the 19th century by Karl Marx, author of *The Communist Manifesto* and, with Friedrich Engels, *Das Kapital*. The elements of communist theory include: radical materialism; dialectical determinism; the inevitability of class struggle and conflict, which is to be furthered for the ultimate establishment of a worldwide, classless society; common ownership of productive and other goods; the subordination of all persons and institutions to the dictatorship of the collective; denial of the rights, dignity and liberty of persons; militant atheism and hostility to religion, utilitarian morality. Communism in theory and practice has been the subject of many papal documents and statements. Pius IX condemned it in 1846. Leo XIII dealt with it at length in the encyclical letter *Quod Apostolici Muneris* in 1878 and *Rerum Novarum* in 1891. Pius XI wrote on the same subject in the encyclicals *Quadragesimo Anno* in 1931 and *Divini Redemptoris* in 1937. These writings have been updated and developed in new directions by Pius XII, John XXIII, Paul VI and John Paul II.

Compline: The night prayer of the Church that completes the daily cursus (course) of the Liturgy of the Hours (Divine Office).

Concelebration: The liturgical act in which several priests, led by one member of the group, offer Mass together, all consecrating the bread and wine. Concelebration has always been common in churches of Eastern Rite. In the Roman Rite, it was long restricted, taking place only at the ordination of bishops and the ordination of priests. The Constitution on the Sacred Liturgy issued by the Second Vatican Council set new norms for concelebration, which is now relatively common in the Roman Rite.

Concordance, Biblical: An alphabetical verbal index enabling a user knowing one or more words of a scriptural passage to locate the entire text.

Concordat: A church-state treaty with the force of law concerning matters of mutual concern — e.g., rights of the Church, arrangement of ecclesiastical jurisdictions, marriage laws, education. Approximately 150 agreements of this kind have been negotiated since the Concordat of Worms in 1122.

Concupiscence: Any tendency of the sensitive appetite. The term is most frequently used in reference to desires and tendencies for sinful sense pleasure.

Confession: Sacramental confession is the act by which a person tells or confesses his sins to a priest who is authorized to give absolution in the sacrament of penance.

Confessor: A priest who administers the sacrament of penance. The title of confessor, formerly given to a category of male saints, was suppressed with publication of the calendar reform of 1969.

Confraternity: An association whose members practice a particular form of religious devotion and/or are engaged in some kind of apostolic work.

Congregation: (1) The collective name for the people who form a parish. (2) One of the chief administrative departments of the Roman Curia. (3) An unofficial term for a group of men and women who belong to a religious community or institute of consecrated life.

Conscience: Practical judgment concerning the moral goodness or sinfulness of an action (thought, word, desire). In the Catholic view, this judgment is made by reference of the action, its attendant circumstances and the intentions of the person to the requirements of moral law as expressed in the Ten Commandments, the summary law of love for God and neighbor, the life and teaching of Christ, and the authoritative teaching and practice of the Church with respect to the total demands of divine Revelation. A person is obliged: (1) to obey a certain and correct conscience; (2) to obey a certain conscience even if it is inculpably erroneous; (3) not to obey, but to correct, a conscience known to be erroneous or lax; (4) to rectify a scrupulous conscience by following the advice of a confessor and by other measures; (5) to resolve doubts of conscience before acting. It is legitimate to act for solid and probable reasons when a question of moral responsibility admits of argument (*See* Probabiliorism and Probabilism).

Conscience, Examination of: Self-examination to determine one's spiritual state before God, regarding one's sins and faults. It is recommended as a regular practice and is practically necessary in preparing for the sacrament of penance. The particular examen is a regular examination to assist in overcoming specific faults and imperfections.

Consequentialism: A moral theory, closely associated with proportionalism and utilitarianism, that holds that the preferable action is one that brings about the best consequences. Preferred results, rather than the objective truth and intentionality, are the object of actions based on consequentialism. While traditional moral theology acknowledges that consequences are important in determining the rightness of an act, importance is also placed on the intrinsic morality of the act and the agent's intention.

Consistory: An assembly of cardinals presided over by the pope.

Constitution: (1) An apostolic or papal constitution is a document in which a pope enacts and promulgates law. (2) A formal and solemn document issued by an ecumenical council on a doctrinal or pastoral subject, with binding force in the whole Church; e.g., the four constitutions issued by the Second Vatican Council on the Church, liturgy, Revelation, and the Church in the modern world. (3) The constitutions of institutes of consecrated life and societies of apostolic life spell out details of and norms drawn from the various rules for the guidance and direction of the life and work of their members.

Consubstantiation: A theory which holds that the Body and Blood of Christ coexist with the substance of bread and wine in the Holy Eucharist. This theory, also called impanation, is incompatible with the doctrine of transubstantiation.

Contraception: Anything done by positive interference to prevent sexual intercourse from resulting in conception. Direct contraception is against the order of nature. Indirect contraception — as a secondary effect of medical treatment or other action having a necessary, good, non-contraceptive purpose — is permissible under the principle of the double effect. The practice of periodic continence is not contraception because it does not involve positive interference with the order of nature. (*See Humanae Vitae*, other entries.)

Contrition: Sorrow for sin coupled with a purpose of amendment. Contrition arising from a supernatural motive is necessary for the forgiveness of sin. (1) Perfect contrition is total sorrow for and renunciation of attachment to sin, arising from the motive of pure love of God. Perfect contrition, which implies the intention of doing all God wants done for the forgiveness of sin (including confession in a reasonable period of time), is sufficient for the forgiveness of serious sin and the remission of all temporal punishment due for sin. (The intention to receive the sacrament of penance is implicit — even if unrealized, as in the case of some persons — in perfect contrition.) (2) Imperfect contrition or attrition is sorrow arising from a quasi-selfish supernatural motive; e.g., the fear of losing heaven, suffering the pains of hell, etc. Imperfect contrition is sufficient for the forgiveness of serious sin when joined with absolution in confession, and sufficient for the forgiveness of venial sin even outside of confession.

Contumely: Personal insult, reviling a person in his presence by accusation of moral faults, by refusal of recognition or due respect; a violation of obligations of justice and charity.

Conversion: In a general sense, the turning away from someone or something and the moving toward another person or thing. In Christian belief, conversion is the embrace of Jesus Christ and a rejection of all that keeps one from God.

Corpus Iuris Canonici: See **Canon Law.**

Council: A formal meeting of Church leaders, summoned by a bishop or appropriate Church leader, with the general purpose of assisting the life of the Church through deliberations, decrees, and promulgations. Different councils include: **diocesan** councils (synod), a gathering of the officials of an individual diocese; **provincial** councils, the meeting of the bishops of a province; **plenary** councils, the assembly of the bishops of a country; and **ecumenical** councils, a gathering of all the bishops in the world under the authority of the Bishop of Rome.

Counsels, Evangelical: Gospel counsels of perfection, especially voluntary poverty, perfect chastity and obedience, which were recommended by Christ to those who would devote themselves exclusively and completely to the immediate service of God. Religious (members of institutes of consecrated life) bind themselves by public vows to observe these counsels in a life of total consecration to God and service to people through various kinds of apostolic works.

Counter-Reformation: The period of approximately 100 years following the Council of Trent (1545-63), which witnessed a reform within the Church to stimulate genuine Catholic life and to counteract effects of the Reformation.

Covenant: A bond of relationship between parties pledged to each other. God-initiated covenants in the Old Testament included those with Noah, Abraham, Moses, Levi, David. The Mosaic (Sinai) covenant made Israel God's Chosen People on terms of fidelity to true faith, true worship, and righteous conduct according to the Decalogue. The New Testament covenant, prefigured in the Old Testament, is the bond people have with God through Christ. All people are called to be parties to this perfect and everlasting covenant, which was mediated and ratified by Christ. The marriage covenant seals the closest possible relationship between a man and a woman.

Creation: The production by God of something out of nothing. The biblical account of creation is contained in the first two chapters of Genesis.

Creator: God, the supreme, self-existing Being, the absolute and infinite First Cause of all things.

Creature: Everything in the realm of being is a creature, except God.

Cremation: The reduction of a human corpse to ashes by means of fire. Cremation is not in line with Catholic tradition and practice, even though it is not opposed to any article of faith. The Congregation for the Doctrine of the Faith, under date of May 8, 1963, circulated among bishops an instruction which upheld the traditional practices of Christian burial but modified anti-cremation legislation. Cremation may be permitted for serious reasons, of a private as well as public nature, provided it does not involve any contempt of the Church or of religion, or any attempt to deny, question, or belittle the doctrine of the resurrection of the body. In a letter dated Mar. 21, 1997, and addressed to Bishop Anthony M. Pilla, president of the National Conference of Catholic Bishops, the Congregation for Divine Worship and the Discipline of the Sacraments granted "a particular permission to the diocesan bishops of the United States of America. By this, local Ordinaries (heads of dioceses) are authorized . . . to permit that the funeral liturgy, including where appropriate the celebration of the Eucharist, be celebrated in the presence of the cremated remains instead of the natural body." Bishop Pilla asked bishops not to use this indult until appropriate texts and ritual directives are approved by the Vatican. (*See* **Burial, Ecclesiastical**).

Crib: Also Crèche, a devotional representation of the birth of Jesus. The custom of erecting cribs is generally attributed to St. Francis of Assisi, who in 1223 obtained from Pope Honorius III permission to use a crib and figures of the Christ Child, Mary, St. Joseph, and others, to represent the mystery of the Nativity.

Crosier: The bishop's staff, symbolic of his pastoral office, responsibility and authority; used at liturgical functions.

Crypt: An underground or partly underground chamber; e.g., the lower part of a church used for worship and/or burial.

Cura Animarum: A Latin phrase, meaning care of souls, designating the pastoral ministry and responsibility of bishops and priests.

Curia: The personnel and offices through which (1) the pope administers the affairs of the universal Church, the Roman Curia (*See p. 253*), or (2) a bishop the affairs of a diocese, diocesan curia. The principal officials of a diocesan curia are the vicar general of the diocese, the chancellor, officials of the diocesan tribunal or court, examiners, consultors, auditors, notaries.

Custos: A religious superior who presides over a

number of convents collectively called a custody. In some institutes of consecrated life a custos may be the deputy of a higher superior.

D

Dean: (1) A priest with supervisory responsibility over a section of a diocese known as a deanery. The post-Vatican II counterpart of a dean is an episcopal vicar. (2) The senior or ranking member of a group.

Decision: A judgment or pronouncement on a cause or suit, given by a church tribunal or official with judicial authority. A decision has the force of law for concerned parties.

Declaration: (1) An ecclesiastical document which presents an interpretation of an existing law. (2) A position paper on a specific subject, e.g., the three declarations issued by the Second Vatican Council on religious freedom, non-Christian religions, and Christian education.

Decree: An edict or ordinance issued by a pope and/or by an ecumenical council, with binding force in the whole Church; by a department of the Roman Curia, with binding force for concerned parties; by a territorial body of bishops, with binding force for persons in the area; by individual bishops, with binding force for concerned parties until revocation or the death of the bishop. The nine decrees issued by the Second Vatican Council were combinations of doctrinal and pastoral statements with executive orders for action and movement toward renewal and reform in the Church.

Dedication of a Church: The ceremony whereby a church is solemnly set apart for the worship of God. The custom of dedicating churches had an antecedent in Old Testament ceremonies for the dedication of the Temple, as in the times of Solomon and the Maccabees. The earliest extant record of the dedication of a Christian church dates from early in the fourth century, when it was done simply by the celebration of Mass. Other ceremonies developed later. A church can be dedicated by a simple blessing or a solemn consecration. The rite of consecration is generally performed by a bishop.

Deposit of the Faith: The body of saving truth, entrusted by Christ to the Apostles and handed on by them to the Church to be preserved and proclaimed. As embodied in Revelation and Tradition the term is very nearly coextensive with objective revelation, in that it embraces the whole of Christ's teaching. But the term of deposit highlights particular features of the apostolic teaching implying that this teaching is an inexhaustible store that rewards and promotes reflection and study so that new insights and deeper penetration might be made into the mystery of the divine economy of salvation. Although our understanding of this teaching can develop, it can never be augmented in its substance; the teaching is a divine trust that cannot be altered, modified, or debased. The term *depositum fidei* first entered official Catholic teaching with the Council of Trent, but its substance is well-attested in the Scriptures and the Fathers.

Despair: Abandonment of hope for salvation arising from the conviction that God will not provide the necessary means for attaining it, that following God's way of life for salvation is impossible, or that one's sins are unforgivable; a serious sin against the Holy Spirit and the theological virtues of hope and faith, involving distrust in the mercy and goodness of God and a denial of the truths that God wills the salvation of all persons and provides sufficient grace for it. Real despair is distinguished from unreasonable fear with respect to the difficulties of attaining salvation, from morbid anxiety over the demands of divine justice, and from feelings of despair.

Detraction: Revelation of true but hidden faults of a person without sufficient and justifying reason; a violation of requirements of justice and charity, involving the obligation to make restitution when this is possible without doing more harm to the good name of the offended party. In some cases, e.g., to prevent evil, secret faults may and should be disclosed.

Devil: (1) Lucifer, Satan, chief of the fallen angels who sinned and were banished from heaven. Still possessing angelic powers, he can cause such diabolical phenomena as possession and obsession, and can tempt men to sin. (2) Any fallen angel.

Devotion: (1) Religious fervor, piety; dedication. (2) The consolation experienced at times during prayer; a reverent manner of praying.

Devotions: Pious practices of members of the Church include not only participation in various acts of the liturgy but also in other acts of worship generally called popular or private devotions. Concerning these, the Second Vatican Council said in the Constitution on the Sacred Liturgy (*Sacrosanctum Concilium*, No. 13): "Popular devotions of the Christian people are warmly commended, provided they accord with the laws and norms of the Church. Such is especially the case with devotions called for by the Apostolic See. Devotions proper to the individual churches also have a special dignity. These devotions should be so drawn up that they harmonize with the liturgical seasons, accord with the sacred liturgy, are in some fashion derived from it, and lead the people to it, since the liturgy by its very nature far surpasses any of them." Devotions of a liturgical type are Exposition of the Blessed Sacrament, recitation of Evening Prayer and Night Prayer of the Liturgy of the Hours. Examples of paraliturgical devotion are a Bible Service or Vigil, and the Angelus, Rosary and Stations of the Cross, which have a strong scriptural basis.

Diocese: A particular church, a fully organized ecclesiastical jurisdiction under the pastoral direction of a bishop as local Ordinary.

Discalced: Of Latin derivation and meaning without shoes, the word is applied to religious orders or congregations whose members go barefoot or wear sandals.

Disciple: A term used sometimes in reference to the Apostles but more often to a larger number of followers (70 or 72) of Christ mentioned in Lk 10:1.

Disciplina Arcani: A Latin phrase, meaning discipline of the secret and referring to a practice of the early Church, especially during the Roman persecutions, to: (1) conceal Christian truths from those who, it was feared, would misinterpret, ridicule and profane the teachings, and persecute Christians for believing them; (2) instruct catechumens in a gradual manner, withholding the teaching of certain doctrines until the catechumens proved themselves of good faith and sufficient understanding.

Dispensation: The relaxation of a law in a particular case. Laws made for the common good sometimes work undue hardship in particular cases. In such cases, where sufficient reasons are present, dispensations may be granted by proper authorities. Bishops, religious superiors and others may dispense from certain laws; the pope can dispense from all ecclesiastical laws. No one has authority to dispense from obligations of the divine law.

Divination: Attempting to foretell future or hidden things by means of things like dreams, necromancy, spiritism, examination of entrails, astrology, augury, omens, palmistry, drawing straws, dice, cards, etc. Practices like these attribute to created things a power which belongs to God alone and are violations of the First Commandment.

Divine Praises: Fourteen praises recited or sung at Benediction of the Blessed Sacrament in reparation for sins of sacrilege, blasphemy and profanity. Some of these praises date from the end of the 18th century: *Blessed be God. / Blessed be his holy Name. / Blessed be Jesus Christ, true God and true Man. / Blessed be the Name of Jesus. / Blessed be his most Sacred Heart. / Blessed be his most Precious Blood. / Blessed be Jesus in the most holy Sacrament of the Altar. / Blessed be the Holy Spirit, the Paraclete. / Blessed be the great Mother of God, Mary most holy. / Blessed be her holy and Immaculate Conception. / Blessed be her glorious Assumption. / Blessed be the name of Mary, Virgin and Mother. / Blessed be St. Joseph, her most chaste Spouse. / Blessed be God in his Angels and in his Saints.*

Double Effect Principle: Actions sometimes have two effects closely related to each other, one good and the other bad, and a difficult moral question can arise: Is it permissible to place an action from which two such results follow? It is permissible to place the action, if: the action is good in itself and is directly productive of the good effect; the circumstances are good; the intention of the person is good; the reason for placing the action is proportionately serious to the seriousness of the indirect bad effect.

Doxology: (1) The lesser doxology, or ascription of glory to the Trinity, is the Glory be to the Father. The first part dates back to the third or fourth century, and came from the form of baptism. The concluding words, As it was in the beginning, etc., are of later origin. (2) The greater doxology, Glory to God in the highest, begins with the words of angelic praise at the birth of Christ recounted in the Infancy Narrative (Lk 2:14). It is often recited at Mass. Of early Eastern origin, it is found in the Apostolic Constitutions in a form much like the present. (3) The formula of praise at the end of the Eucharistic Prayer at Mass, sung or said by the celebrant while he holds aloft the paten containing the consecrated host in one hand and the chalice containing the consecrated wine in the other.

Dulia: A Greek term meaning the veneration or homage, different in nature and degree from that given to God, paid to the saints. It includes honoring the saints and seeking their intercession with God.

Duty: A moral obligation deriving from the binding force of law, the exigencies of one's state in life, and other sources.

E

Easter Controversy: A three-phase controversy over the time for the celebration of Easter. Some early Christians in the Near East, called Quartodecimans, favored the observance of Easter on the 14th day of Nisan, the spring month of the Hebrew calendar, whenever it occurred. Against this practice, Pope St. Victor I, about 190, ordered a Sunday observance of the feast. The Council of Nicaea, in line with usages of the Church at Rome and Alexandria, decreed in 325 that Easter should be observed on the Sunday following the first full moon of spring. Uniformity of practice in the West was not achieved until several centuries later, when the British Isles, in delayed compliance with measures enacted by the Synod of Whitby in 664, accepted the Roman date of observance. Unrelated to the controversy is the fact that some Eastern Christians, in accordance with traditional calendar practices, celebrate Easter at a different time than the Roman and Eastern Churches.

Easter Duty: The serious obligation binding Catholics of Roman Rite, to receive the Eucharist during the Easter season (in the U.S., from the first Sunday of Lent to and including Trinity Sunday).

Easter Water: Holy water blessed with special ceremonies and distributed on the Easter Vigil; used during Easter Week for blessing the faithful and homes.

Ecclesiology: Study of the nature, constitution, members, mission, functions, etc., of the Church.

Ecology: The natural environment of the total range of creation — mineral, vegetable, animal, human — entrusted to people for respect, care and appropriate use as well as conservation and development for the good of present and future generations.

Ecstasy: An extraordinary state of mystical experience in which a person is so absorbed in God that the activity of the exterior senses is suspended.

Economy, Divine: The fulfillment of God's plan of salvation. It was fully developed in his divine mind from eternity, and fully revealed in Jesus Christ. Before the Incarnation it was known only obscurely, but after the ascension of Christ and the coming of the Holy Spirit at Pentecost, it became the substance of apostolic preaching and is preserved in its integrity for each new generation.

Ecumenism: The movement of Christians and their churches toward the unity willed by Christ. The Second Vatican Council called the movement "those activities and enterprises which, according to various needs of the Church and opportune occasions, are started and organized for the fostering of unity among Christians" (Decree on Ecumenism, No. 4). Spiritual ecumenism, i.e., mutual prayer for unity, is the heart of the movement. The movement also involves scholarly and pew-level efforts for the development of mutual understanding and better interfaith relations in general, and collaboration by the churches and their members in the social area. (*See* Index for other entries.)

Elevation: The raising of the host after consecration at Mass for adoration by the faithful. The custom was introduced in the Diocese of Paris about the close of the 12th century to offset an erroneous teaching of the time which held that transubstantiation of the bread did not take place until after the consecration of the wine in the chalice. The elevation of the chalice following the consecration of the wine was introduced in the 15th century.

Encyclical: The highest form of papal teaching document. It is normally addressed to all the bishops and/or to all the faithful.

Envy: Sadness over another's good fortune because it is considered a loss to oneself or a detraction from one's own excellence; one of the seven capital sins, a violation of the obligations of charity.

Epiclesis: An invocation of the Holy Spirit, to bless the offerings consecrated at Mass; before the consecration in the Latin Rite, after the consecration in Eastern usage.

Epikeia: A Greek word meaning reasonableness and designating a moral theory and practice, a mild interpretation of the mind of a legislator who is prudently considered not to wish positive law to bind in certain circumstances.

Episcopate: (1) The office, dignity and sacramental powers bestowed upon a bishop at his ordination. (2) The body of bishops collectively.

Equivocation: (1) The use of words, phrases, or gestures having more than one meaning in order to conceal information which a questioner has no strict right to know. It is permissible to equivocate (have a broad mental reservation) in some circumstances. (2) A lie, i.e., a statement of untruth. Lying is intrinsically wrong. A lie told in joking, evident as such, is not wrong.

Eschatology: Doctrine concerning the last things: death, judgment, heaven and hell, and the final state of perfection of the people and kingdom of God at the end of time.

Eternity: The interminable, perfect possession of life in its totality without beginning or end; an attribute of God, who has no past or future but always is. Man's existence has a beginning but no end and is, accordingly, called immortal.

Ethics: Moral philosophy, the science of the morality of human acts deriving from natural law, the natural end of man, and the powers of human reason. It includes all the spheres of human activity — personal, social, economic, political, etc. Ethics is distinct from but can be related to moral theology, whose primary principles are drawn from divine revelation.

Euthanasia: Mercy killing, the direct causing of death for the purpose of ending human suffering. Euthanasia is murder and is totally illicit, for the natural law forbids the direct taking of one's own life or that of an innocent person. The use of drugs to relieve suffering in serious cases, even when this results in a shortening of life as an indirect and secondary effect, is permissible under conditions of the double-effect principle. It is also permissible for a seriously ill person to refuse to follow — or for other responsible persons to refuse to permit — extraordinary medical procedures even though the refusal might entail shortening of life.

Evangelization: Proclamation of the Gospel, the Good News of salvation in and through Christ, among those who have not yet known or received it; and efforts for the progressive development of the life of faith among those who have already received the Gospel and all that it entails. Evangelization is the primary mission of the Church, in which all members of the Church are called to participate.

Evolution: Scientific theory concerning the development of the physical universe from unorganized matter (inorganic evolution) and, especially, the development of existing forms of vegetable, animal and human life from earlier and more primitive organisms (organic evolution). Various ideas about evolution were advanced for some centuries before scientific evidence in support of the main-line theory of organic evolution, which has several formulations, was discovered and verified in the second half of the 19th century and afterwards. This evidence — from the findings of comparative anatomy and other sciences — confirmed evolution of species and cleared the way to further investigation of questions regarding the processes of its accomplishment. While a number of such questions remain open with respect to human evolution, a point of doctrine not open to question is the immediate creation of the human soul by God. For some time, theologians regarded the theory with hostility, considering it to be in opposition to the account of creation in the early chapters of Genesis and subversive of belief in such doctrines as creation, the early state of man in grace, and the fall of man from grace. This state of affairs and the tension it generated led to considerable controversy regarding an alleged conflict between religion and science.

Gradually, however, the tension was diminished with the development of biblical studies from the latter part of the 19th century onwards, with clarification of the distinctive features of religious truth and scientific truth, and with the refinement of evolutionary concepts. So far as the Genesis account of creation is concerned, the Catholic view is that the writer(s) did not write as a scientist but as the communicator of religious truth in a manner adapted to the understanding of the people of his time. He used anthropomorphic language, the figure of days and other literary devices to state the salvation truths of creation, the fall of man from grace, and the promise of redemption. It was beyond the competency and purpose of the writer(s) to describe creation and related events in a scientific manner.

Excommunication: Severe ecclesiastical penalty imposed by the Church that excludes a member of the faithful from the wider community. Excommunication is today covered in its particulars by Canon 1331 of the new Code of Canon Law, promulgated in 1983. It exists in two contemporary forms, *ferendae sententiae* and *latae sententiae*. The former is a penalty imposed after a formal proceeding presided over by at least three judges. The latter is considered an automatic penalty for certain acts, including the procuring of a successful abortion (Canon 1398), the embrace of heresy (Canon 1364), violation of the Seal of Confession (Canon 1388), and the blasphemous and sacrilegious use of the Eucharist (Canon 1367). A person under the ban of excommunication is unable to take part in all ceremonies of public worship, especially the Eucharist, to receive or celebrate the sacraments, and to discharge any ecclesiastical offices, ministries, or functions. (See Censures).

Ex Opere Operantis: A term in sacramental theology meaning that the effectiveness of sacraments depends on the moral rectitude of the minister or participant. This term was applied to rites of the O.T. in contrast with those of the N.T. when it was first advanced in the thirteenth century.

Ex Opere Operato: A term in sacramental theology meaning that sacraments are effective by means of the sacramental rite itself and not because of the worthiness of the minister or participant.

Exorcism: (1) Driving out evil spirits; a rite in which evil spirits are charged and commanded on the authority of God and with the prayer of the Church to depart from a person or to cease causing harm to a person suffering from diabolical possession or obsession. The sacramental is officially administered by a priest delegated for the purpose by the bishop of the place. Elements of the rite include the Litany of Saints; recitation of the Our Father, one or more creeds, and other prayers; specific prayers of exorcism; the reading of Gospel passages and use of the Sign of the Cross. On Jan. 26, 1999, the Congregation for Divine Worship and the Discipline of the Sacraments published a new rite of exorcism in the Roman Ritual. [See Special Report for additional details.] (2) Exorcisms which do not imply the conditions of either diabolical possession or obsession form part of the ceremony of baptism and are also included in formulas for various blessings; e.g., of water.

Exposition of the Blessed Sacrament: "In churches where the Eucharist is regularly reserved, it is recommended that solemn exposition of the Blessed Sacrament for an extended period of time should take place once a year, even though the period is not strictly continuous. Shorter expositions of the Eucharist (Benediction) are to be arranged in such a way that the blessing with the Eucharist is preceded by a reasonable time for readings of the word of God, songs, prayers and a period for silent prayer." So stated Vatican directives issued in 1973.

F

Faculties: Grants of jurisdiction or authority by the law of the Church or superiors (pope, bishop, religious superior) for exercise of the powers of holy orders; e.g., priests are given faculties to hear confessions, officiate at weddings; bishops are given faculties to grant dispensations, etc.

Faith: In religion, faith has several aspects. Catholic doctrine calls faith the assent of the mind to truths revealed by God, the assent being made with the help of grace and by command of the will on account of the authority and trustworthiness of God revealing. The term faith also refers to the truths that are believed (content of faith) and to the way in which a person, in response to Christ, gives witness to and expresses belief in daily life (living faith). All of these elements, and more, are included in the following statement: " 'The obedience of faith' (Rom 16:26; 1:5; 2 Cor 10:5-6) must be given to God who reveals, an obedience by which man entrusts his whole self freely to God, offering 'the full submission of intellect and will to God who reveals' (First Vatican Council, Dogmatic Constitution on the Catholic Faith, Chap. 3), and freely assenting to the truth revealed by him. If this faith is to be shown, the grace of God and the interior help of the Holy Spirit must precede and assist, moving the heart and turning it to God, opening the eyes of the mind, and giving 'joy and ease to everyone in assenting to the truth and believing it'" (Second Council of Orange, Canon 7) (Second Vatican Council, Constitution on Revelation, *Dei Verbum*, No. 5). Faith is necessary for salvation.

Faith, Rule of: The norm or standard of religious belief. The Catholic doctrine is that belief must be professed in the divinely revealed truths in the Bible and tradition as interpreted and proposed by the infallible teaching authority of the Church.

Fast, Eucharistic: Abstinence from food and drink, except water and medicine, is required for one hour before the reception of the Eucharist. Persons who are advanced in age or suffer from infirmity or illness, together with those who care for them, can receive Holy Communion even if they have not abstained from food and drink for an hour. A priest celebrating two or three Masses on the same day can eat and drink something before the second or third Mass without regard for the hour limit.

Father: A title of priests, who are regarded as spiritual fathers because they are the ordinary ministers of baptism, by which persons are born to supernatural life, and because of their pastoral service to people.

Fear: A mental state caused by the apprehension of present or future danger. Grave fear does not necessarily remove moral responsibility for an act, but may lessen it.

First Friday: A devotion consisting of the reception of Holy Communion on the first Friday of nine consecutive months in honor of the Sacred Heart of Jesus and in reparation for sin. (*See* Sacred Heart, Promises.)

First Saturday: A devotion tracing its origin to the apparitions of the Blessed Virgin Mary at Fátima in 1917. Those practicing the devotion go to confession and, on the first Saturday of five consecutive months, receive Holy Communion, recite five decades of the Rosary, and meditate on the mysteries for 15 minutes.

Fisherman's Ring: A signet ring (termed in Italian the *pescatorio*) engraved with the image of St. Peter fishing from a boat, and encircled with the name of the reigning pope. It is not worn by the pope. It is used to seal briefs, and is destroyed after each pope's death.

Forgiveness of Sin: Catholics believe that sins are forgiven by God through the mediation of Christ in view of the repentance of the sinner and by means of the sacrament of penance. (*See* Penance, Contrition).

Fortitude: Courage to face dangers or hardships for the sake of what is good; one of the four cardinal virtues and one of the seven gifts of the Holy Spirit.

Forty Hours Devotion: A Eucharistic observance consisting of solemn exposition of the Blessed Sacrament coupled with special Masses and forms of prayer, for the purposes of making reparation for sin and praying for God's blessings of grace and peace. The devotion was instituted in 1534 in Milan. St. John Neumann of Philadelphia was the first bishop in the U.S. to prescribe its observance in his diocese. For many years in this country, the observance was held annually on a rotating basis in all parishes of a diocese. Simplified and abbreviated Eucharistic observances have taken the place of the devotion in some places.

Forum: The sphere in which ecclesiastical authority or jurisdiction is exercised. (1) External: Authority is exercised in the external forum to deal with matters affecting the public welfare of the Church and its members. Those who have such authority because of their office (e.g., diocesan bishops) are called ordinaries. (2) Internal: Authority is exercised in the internal forum to deal with matters affecting the private spiritual good of individuals. The sacramental forum is the sphere in which the sacrament of penance is administered; other exercises of jurisdiction in the internal forum take place in the non-sacramental forum.

Freedom, Religious: The Second Vatican Council declared that the right to religious freedom in civil society "means that all men are to be immune from coercion on the part of individuals or of social groups and of any human power, in such wise that in matters religious no one is to be forced to act in a manner contrary to his own beliefs. Nor is anyone to be restrained from acting in accordance with his own beliefs, whether privately or publicly, whether alone or in association with others, within due limits" of requirements for the common good. The foundation of this right in civil society is the "very dignity of the human person" (Declaration on Religious Freedom, *Dignitatis Humanae*, No. 2). The conciliar statement did not deal with the subject of freedom within the Church. It noted the responsibility of the faithful "carefully to attend to the sacred and certain doctrine of the Church" (No. 14).

Freemasons: A fraternal order that originated in London in 1717 with the formation of the first Grand Lodge of Freemasons. From England, the order spread to Europe and elsewhere. Its principles and basic rituals embody a naturalistic religion, active participation in which is incompatible with Christian faith and practice. Grand Orient Freemasonry, developed in Latin countries, is atheistic, irreligious and anticlerical. In some places, Freemasonry has been regarded as subversive of the state; in Catholic quarters, it has been considered hostile to the Church and its doctrine. In the United States, Freemasonry has been widely regarded as a fraternal and philanthropic order. For serious doctrinal and pastoral reasons, Catholics were forbidden to join the Freemasons under penalty of excommunication, according to church law before 1983. Eight different popes in 17 different pronouncements, and at least six different local councils, condemned Freemasonry. The first condemnation was made by Clement XII in 1738. Eastern Orthodox and many Protestant bodies have also opposed the order. In the U.S., there was some easing of the ban against Masonic membership by Catholics in view of a letter written in 1974 by Cardinal Franjo Seper, prefect of the Congregation for the Doctrine of the Faith. The letter was interpreted to mean that Catholics might join Masonic lodges which were not anti-Catholic. This was called erroneous in a declaration issued by the Doctrinal Congregation Feb. 17, 1981. The prohibition against Masonic membership was restated in a declaration issued by the Doctrinal Congregation Nov. 26, 1983, with the approval of Pope John Paul II, as follows. "The Church's negative position on Masonic associations remains unaltered, since their principles have always been regarded as irreconcilable with the Church's doctrine. Hence, joining them remains prohibited by the Church. Catholics enrolled in Masonic associations are involved in serious sin and may not approach Holy Communion. Local ecclesiastical authorities do not have the faculty to pronounce a judgment on the nature of Masonic associations which might include a diminution of the above-mentioned judgment." This latest declaration, like the revised Code of Canon Law, does not include a penalty of excommunication for Catholics who join the Masons. Local bishops are not authorized to grant dispensations from the prohibition. The foregoing strictures against Masonic membership by Catholics were reiterated in a report by the Committee for Pastoral Research and Practice, National Conference of Catholic Bishops, released through Catholic News Service June 7, 1985.

Free Will: The faculty or capability of making a reasonable choice among several alternatives. Freedom of will underlies the possibility and fact of moral responsibility.

Friar: Term applied to members of mendicant orders to distinguish them from members of monastic orders. (*See* Mendicants.)

Fruits of the Holy Spirit: Charity, joy, peace, patience, kindness, goodness, generosity, gentleness, faithfulness, modesty, self-control, chastity.

Fruits of the Mass: The spiritual and temporal blessings that result from the celebration of the Holy Sacrifice of the Mass. The general fruits are shared by all the faithful, living and departed, while the special fruits are applied to the priest who celebrates it, to those for whose intention it is offered, and to all those who participate in its celebration.

Fundamental Option: The orientation of one's life either to God by obedience or against Him through disobedience. Catholic Tradition acknowledges that one free and deliberate act with knowledge renders one at odds with God. A prevalent and vague moral theory today asserts that one act cannot change one's option to God — no matter how grave — unless the action comes from the person's "center." Pope John Paul II cautioned against this ambiguous position in the encyclical *Veritatis Splendor* (1993).

G

Gehenna: Greek form of a Jewish name, Gehinnom, for a valley near Jerusalem, the site of Moloch worship; used as a synonym for hell.

Genuflection: Bending of the knee, a natural sign of adoration or reverence, as when persons genuflect with the right knee in passing before the tabernacle to acknowledge the Eucharistic presence of Christ.

Gethsemani: A Hebrew word meaning oil press, designating the place on the Mount of Olives where Christ prayed and suffered in agony the night before he died.

Gifts of the Holy Spirit: Supernatural habits disposing a person to respond promptly to the inspiration of grace; promised by Christ and communicated through the Holy Spirit, especially in the sacrament of confirmation. They are: wisdom, understanding, counsel, knowledge, fortitude, piety, and fear of the Lord.

Glorified Body: The definitive state of humanity in eternity. The risen Christ calls humanity to the glory of his resurrection; this is a theological premise that presupposes that, like Christ, all of his brothers and sisters will be transformed physically.

Gluttony: An unreasonable appetite for food and drink; one of the seven capital sins.

God: The infinitely perfect Supreme Being, uncaused and absolutely self-sufficient, eternal, the Creator and final end of all things. The one God subsists in three equal Persons, the Father and the Son and the Holy Spirit. God, although transcendent and distinct from the universe, is present and active in the world in realization of his plan for the salvation of human beings, principally through Revelation, the operations of the Holy Spirit, the life and ministry of

Christ, and the continuation of Christ's ministry in the Church. The existence of God is an article of faith, clearly communicated in divine Revelation. Even without this Revelation, however, the Church teaches, in a declaration by the First Vatican Council, that human beings can acquire certain knowledge of the existence of God and some of his attributes. This can be done on the bases of principles of reason and reflection on human experience. Non-revealed arguments or demonstrations for the existence of God have been developed from the principle of causality; the contingency of human beings and the universe; the existence of design, change and movement in the universe; human awareness of moral responsibility; widespread human testimony to the existence of God.

Goods of Marriage: Three blessings — children, faithful companionship, and permanence — that were first enumerated by St. Augustine in a work on marriage.

Grace: A free gift of God to persons (and angels), grace is a created sharing or participation in the life of God. It is given to persons through the merits of Christ and is communicated by the Holy Spirit. It is necessary for salvation. The principal means of grace are the sacraments (especially the Eucharist), prayer and good works. (1) **Sanctifying or habitual grace** makes persons holy and pleasing to God, adopted children of God, members of Christ, temples of the Holy Spirit, heirs of heaven capable of supernaturally meritorious acts. With grace, God gives persons the supernatural virtues and gifts of the Holy Spirit. The sacraments of baptism and penance were instituted to give grace to those who do not have it; the other sacraments, to increase it in those already in the state of grace. The means for growth in holiness, or the increase of grace, are prayer, the sacraments, and good works. Sanctifying grace is lost by the commission of serious sin. Each sacrament confers sanctifying grace for the special purpose of the sacrament; in this context, grace is called sacramental grace. (2) **Actual grace** is a supernatural help of God which enlightens and strengthens a person to do good and to avoid evil. It is not a permanent quality, like sanctifying grace. It is necessary for the performance of supernatural acts. It can be resisted and refused. Persons in the state of serious sin are given actual grace to lead them to repentance.

Grace at Meals: Prayers said before meals, asking a blessing of God, and after meals, giving thanks to God. In addition to traditional prayers for these purposes, many variations suitable for different occasions are possible, at personal option.

Guilt: The condition of an individual who has committed some moral wrong and is liable to receive punishment.

H

Habit: (1) A disposition to do things easily, given with grace (and therefore supernatural) and/or acquired by repetition of similar acts. (2) The garb worn by Religious.

Hagiography: Writings or documents about saints and other holy persons.

Hail Mary: A prayer addressed to the Blessed Virgin Mary; also called the *Ave Maria* (Latin equivalent of Hail Mary) and the Angelic Salutation. In three parts, it consists of the words addressed to Mary by the Archangel Gabriel on the occasion of the Annunciation, in the Infancy Narrative (*Hail Mary, full of grace, the Lord is with you, blessed are you among women*; Lk 1:28); the words addressed to Mary by her cousin Elizabeth on the occasion of the Visitation (*Blessed is the fruit of your womb*; Lk 1-42); a concluding petition (*Holy Mary, Mother of God, pray for us sinners now and at the hour of our death. Amen.*). The first two salutations were joined in Eastern rite formulas by the sixth century, and were similarly used at Rome in the seventh century. Insertion of the name of Jesus at the conclusion of the salutations was probably made by Urban IV about 1262. The present form of the petition was incorporated into the breviary in 1514.

Heaven: The state of those who, having achieved salvation, are in glory with God and enjoy the beatific vision. The phrase, kingdom of heaven, refers to the order or kingdom of God, grace, salvation.

Hell: The state of persons who die in mortal sin, in a condition of self-alienation from God which will last forever.

Heresy: The obstinate post-baptismal denial or doubt by a Catholic of any truth which must be believed as a matter of divine and Catholic faith (Canon 751, of the Code of Canon Law). Formal heresy involves deliberate resistance to the authority of God who communicates revelation through Scripture and tradition and the teaching authority of the Church. Heretics automatically incur the penalty of excommunication (Canon 1364 of the Code of Canon Law). Heresies have been significant not only as disruptions of unity of faith but also as occasions for the clarification and development of doctrine. Heresies from the beginning of the Church to the 13th century are described in Dates and Events in Church History.

Hermeneutics: *See under the section* **Interpretation of the Bible.**

Hermit: *See* **Anchorite.**

Heroic Act of Charity: The completely unselfish offering to God of one's good works and merits for the benefit of the souls in purgatory rather than for oneself. Thus a person may offer to God for the souls in purgatory all the good works he performs during life, all the indulgences he gains, and all the prayers and indulgences that will be offered for him after his death. The act is revocable at will, and is not a vow. Its actual ratification depends on the will of God.

Heroic Virtue: The exemplary practice of the four cardinal virtues and three theological virtues; such virtue is sought in persons considered for sainthood.

Heterodoxy: False doctrine teaching or belief; a departure from truth.

Hierarchy: The hierarchy of order who carry out the sacramental, teaching, and pastoral ministry of the Church; the hierarchy consists of the pope, bishops, priests, and deacons; the pope and the bishops give pastoral governance to the faithful.

Holy Father: A title used for the pope; it is a shortened translation of the Latin title *Beatissimus Pater*, "Most Blessed Father" and refers to his position as the spiritual father of all the Christian faithful.

Holy See: (1) The diocese of the pope, Rome. (2) The pope himself and/or the various officials and bodies of the Church's central administration at Vatican City — the Roman Curia — which act in the name and by authority of the pope.

Holy Spirit: God the Holy Spirit, third Person of the

Holy Trinity, who proceeds from the Father and the Son and with whom he is equal in every respect; inspirer of the prophets and writers of sacred Scripture; promised by Christ to the Apostles as their advocate and strengthener; appeared in the form of a dove at the baptism of Christ and as tongues of fire at his descent upon the Apostles; soul of the Church and guarantor, by his abiding presence and action, of truth in doctrine; communicator of grace to human beings, for which reason he is called the sanctifier.

Holy Water: Water blessed by the Church and used as a sacramental, a practice which originated in apostolic times.

Holy Year: A year during which the pope grants the plenary Jubilee Indulgence to the faithful who fulfill certain conditions. For those who make a pilgrimage to Rome during the year, the conditions are reception of the sacraments of penance and the Eucharist, visits and prayer for the intention of the pope in the basilicas of St. Peter, St. John Lateran, St. Paul and St. Mary Major. For those who do not make a pilgrimage to Rome, the conditions are reception of the sacraments and prayer for the pope during a visit or community celebration in a church designated by the bishop of the locality. Pope Boniface VIII formally proclaimed the first Holy Year on Feb. 22, 1300, and the first three Holy Years were observed in 1300, 1350 and 1390. Subsequent ones were celebrated at 25-year intervals except in 1800 and 1850 when, respectively, the French invasion of Italy and political turmoil made observance impossible. Pope Paul II (1464-1471) set the 25-year timetable. In 1500, Pope Alexander VI prescribed the start and finish ceremonies — the opening and closing of the Holy Doors in the major basilicas on successive Christmas Eves. All but a few of the earlier Holy Years were classified as ordinary. Several — like those of 1933 and 1983-84 to commemorate the 1900th and 1950th anniversaries of the death and resurrection of Christ — were in the extraordinary category. Pope John Paul designated Jubilee Year 2000 to be a Holy Year ending the second and beginning the third millennium of Christianity.

Homosexuality: The condition of a person whose sexual orientation is toward persons of the same rather than the opposite sex. The condition is not sinful in itself. Homosexual acts are seriously sinful in themselves; subjective responsibility for such acts, however, may be conditioned and diminished by compulsion and related factors.

Hope: The theological virtue by which a person firmly trusts in God for the means and attainment salvation.

Hosanna: A Hebrew word, meaning *O Lord, save, we pray.*

Host, The Sacred: The bread under whose appearances Christ is and remains present in a unique manner after the consecration which takes place during Mass. (*See* Transubstantiation.)

Human Dignity: The inherent worth of all human persons as they are made in God's image and likeness and they alone — of all God's creatures on earth — have an immortal soul.

Humanism: A world view centered on man. Types of humanism which exclude the supernatural are related to secularism.

Humility: A virtue which induces a person to evaluate himself or herself at his or her true worth, to recognize his or her dependence on God, and to give glory to God for the good he or she has and can do.

Hyperdulia: The special veneration accorded the Blessed Virgin Mary because of her unique role in the mystery of Redemption, her exceptional gifts of grace from God, and her pre-eminence among the saints. Hyperdulia is not adoration; only God is adored.

Hypostatic Union: The union of the human and divine natures in the one divine Person of Christ.

I

Icons: Byzantine-style paintings or representations of Christ, the Blessed Virgin and other saints, venerated in the Eastern Churches where they take the place of statues.

Idolatry: Worship of any but the true God; a violation of the First Commandment.

IHS: In Greek, the first three letters of the name of Jesus — Iota, Eta, Sigma.

Immaculate Conception: The doctrine that affirms that "the Blessed Virgin Mary was preserved, in the first instant of her conception, by a singular grace and privilege of God omnipotent and because of the merits of Jesus Christ the Savior of the human race, free from all stain of Original Sin," as stated by Pope Pius IX in his declaration of the dogma, Dec. 8, 1854. Thus, Mary was conceived in the state of perfect justice, free from Original Sin and its consequences, in virtue of the redemption achieved by Christ on the cross.

Immortality: The survival and continuing existence of the human soul after death.

Imprimatur: *See* Censorship of Books.

Impurity: Unlawful indulgence in sexual pleasure. (*See* Chastity.)

Imputability: A canonical term for the moral responsibility of a person for an act that he or she has performed.

Incardination: The affiliation of a priest to his diocese. Every secular priest must belong to a certain diocese. Similarly, every priest of a religious community must belong to some jurisdiction of his community; this affiliation, however, is not called incardination.

Incarnation: (1) The coming-into-flesh or taking of human nature by the Second Person of the Trinity. He became human as the Son of Mary, being miraculously conceived by the power of the Holy Spirit, without ceasing to be divine. His divine Person hypostatically unites his divine and human natures. (2) The supernatural mystery coextensive with Christ from the moment of his human conception and continuing through his life on earth; his sufferings and death; his resurrection from the dead and ascension to glory with the Father; his sending, with the Father, of the Holy Spirit upon the Apostles and the Church; and his unending mediation with the Father for the salvation of human beings.

Incense: A granulated substance which, when burnt, emits an aromatic smoke. It symbolizes the zeal with which the faithful should be consumed, the good odor of Christian virtue, the ascent of prayer to God. An incense boat is a small vessel used to hold incense which is to be placed in the censer.

Incest: Sexual intercourse with relatives by blood or marriage; a sin of impurity and also a grave violation of the natural reverence due to relatives. Other sins of impurity desire, etc., concerning relatives have the nature of incest.

Inculturation: The correct and entirely appropriate adaptation of the Catholic liturgy and institutions to the culture, language, and customs of an indigenous or local people among whom the Gospel is first proclaimed. Pope John Paul II, Feb. 15, 1982, at a meeting in Lagos with the bishops of Nigeria proclaimed: "An important aspect of your own evangelizing role is the whole dimension of the inculturation of the Gospel into the lives of your people. The Church truly respects the culture of each people. In offering the Gospel message, the Church does not intend to destroy or to abolish what is good and beautiful. In fact, she recognizes many cultural values and, through the power of the Gospel, purifies and takes into Christian worship certain elements of a people's customs."

Index of Prohibited Books: A list of books which Catholics were formerly forbidden to read, possess or sell, under penalty of excommunication. The books were banned by the Holy See after publication because their treatment of matters of faith and morals and related subjects were judged to be erroneous or serious occasions of doctrinal error. Some books were listed in the Index by name; others were covered under general norms. The Congregation for the Doctrine of the Faith declared June 14, 1966, that the Index and its related penalties of excommunication no longer had the force of law in the Church. Persons are still obliged, however, to take normal precautions against occasions of doctrinal error.

Indifferentism: A theory that any one religion is as true and good — or false — as any other religion, and that it makes no difference, objectively, what religion one professes, if any. The theory is completely subjective, finding its justification entirely in personal choice without reference to or respect for objective validity. It is also self-contradictory, since it regards as equally acceptable — or unacceptable — the beliefs of all religions, which in fact are not only not all the same but are in some cases opposed to each other.

Indulgence: According to The Doctrine and Practice of Indulgences, an apostolic constitution issued by Paul VI Jan. 1, 1967, an indulgence is the remission before God of the temporal punishment due for sins already forgiven as far as their guilt is concerned, which a follower of Christ — with the proper dispositions and under certain determined conditions — acquires through the intervention of the Church. An indulgence is partial or plenary, depending on whether it does away with either part or all of the temporal punishment due for sin. Both types of indulgences can always be applied to the dead by way of suffrage; the actual disposition of indulgences applied to the dead rests with God. Only one plenary indulgence can be gained in a single day. The Apostolic Penitentiary issued a decree Dec. 14, 1985, granting diocesan bishops the right to impart — three times a year on solemn feasts of their choice — the papal blessing with a plenary indulgence to those who cannot be physically present but who follow the sacred rites at which the blessing is imparted by radio or television transmission. In July, 1986, publication was announced of a new and simplified *Enchiridion Indulgentiarum*, in accord with provisions of the revised Code of Canon Law. A revised manual was issued by the Holy See on Sept. 17, 2000.

Indult: A favor or privilege granted by competent ecclesiastical authority, giving permission to do something not allowed by the common law of the Church.

Infallibility: 1) The inability of the Church to err in its teaching, in that she preserves and teaches the deposit of truth as revealed by Christ; 2) The inability of the Roman Pontiff to err when he teaches *ex cathedra* in matters of faith or morals, and indicates that the doctrine is to be believed by all the faithful; and 3) the inability of the college of bishops to err when speaking in union with the pope in matters of faith and morals, agreeing that a doctrine must be held by the universal Church, and the doctrine is promulgated by the Pontiff.

Infused Virtues: The theological virtues of faith, hope, and charity; principles or capabilities of supernatural action, they are given with sanctifying grace by God rather than acquired by repeated acts of a person. They can be increased by practice; they are lost by contrary acts. Natural-acquired moral virtues, like the cardinal virtues of prudence, justice, temperance, and fortitude, can be considered infused in a person whose state of grace gives them supernatural orientation.

Inquisition: A tribunal for dealing with heretics, authorized by Gregory IX in 1231 to search them out, hear and judge them, sentence them to various forms of punishment, and in some cases to hand them over to civil authorities for punishment. The Inquisition was a creature of its time when crimes against faith, which threatened the good of the Christian community, were regarded also as crimes against the state, and when heretical doctrines of such extremists as the Cathari and Albigensians threatened the very fabric of society. The institution, which was responsible for many excesses, was most active in the second half of the 13th century.

Inquisition, Spanish: An institution peculiar to Spain and the colonies in Spanish America. In 1478, at the urging of King Ferdinand, Pope Sixtus IV approved the establishment of the Inquisition for trying charges of heresy brought against Jewish (*Marranos*) and Moorish (*Moriscos*) converts. It acquired jurisdiction over other cases as well, however, and fell into disrepute because of irregularities in its functions, cruelty in its sentences, and the manner in which it served the interests of the Spanish crown more than the accused persons and the good of the Church. Protests by the Holy See failed to curb excesses of the Inquisition, which lingered in Spanish history until early in the 19th century.

I N R I: The first letters of words in the Latin inscription atop the cross on which Christ was crucified: *(I)esus (N)azaraenus, (R)ex (I)udaeorum* — Jesus of Nazareth, King of the Jews.

Insemination, Artificial: The implanting of human semen by some means other than consummation of natural marital intercourse. In view of the principle that procreation should result only from marital intercourse, donor insemination is not permissible.

In Sin: The condition of a person called spiritually dead because he or she does not possess sanctifying grace, the principle of supernatural life, action and merit. Such grace can be regained through repentance.

Instruction: A document containing doctrinal explanations, directive norms, rules, recommendations, admonitions, issued by the pope, a department of the Roman Curia or other competent authority in the

Church. To the extent that they so prescribe, instructions have the force of law.

Intercommunion, Eucharistic Sharing: The common celebration and reception of the Eucharist by members of different Christian churches; a pivotal issue in ecumenical theory and practice. Catholic participation and intercommunion in the Eucharistic liturgy of another church without a valid priesthood and with a variant Eucharistic belief is out of order. Under certain conditions, other Christians may receive the Eucharist in the Catholic Church. (*See* additional Intercommunion entry). Intercommunion is acceptable to some Protestant churches and unacceptable to others.

Interdict: A censure imposed on persons for certain violations of church law. Interdicted persons may not take part in certain liturgical services, administer or receive certain sacraments.

Intinction: A method of administering Holy Communion under the dual appearances of bread and wine, in which the consecrated host is dipped in the consecrated wine before being given to the communicant. The administering of Holy Communion in this manner, which has been traditional in Eastern-Rite liturgies, was authorized in the Roman Rite for various occasions by the Constitution on the Sacred Liturgy promulgated by the Second Vatican Council.

Irenicism: Peace-seeking, conciliation, as opposed to polemics; an important element in ecumenism, provided it furthers pursuit of the Christian unity willed by Christ without degenerating into a peace-at-any-price disregard for religious truth.

Irregularity: A permanent impediment to the lawful reception or exercise of holy orders. The Church instituted irregularities — which include apostasy, heresy, homicide, attempted suicide — out of reverence for the dignity of the sacraments.

J

Jehovah: The English equivalent of the Hebrew *Adonai* ("my Lord") used out of fear and reverence for the Holy Name of Yahweh. *Jehovah* uses the consonants YHWH and the vowels of *Adonai* (a, o, a). Scholars today maintain that *Jehovah* is a false derivation.

Jesus: The name of Jesus, meaning "God saves," expressing the identity and mission of the second Person of the Trinity become man; derived from the Aramaic and Hebrew Yeshua and Joshua, meaning Yahweh is salvation.

Jesus Prayer: A prayer of Eastern origin, dating back to the fifth century: *"Lord Jesus Christ, Son of God, have mercy on me (a sinner)."*

Judgment: (1) **Last or final judgment:** Final judgment by Christ, at the end of the world and the general resurrection. (2) **Particular judgment:** The judgment that takes place immediately after a person's death, followed by entrance into heaven, hell or purgatory.

Jurisdiction: Right, power, authority to rule. Jurisdiction in the Church is of divine institution; has pastoral service for its purpose; includes legislative, judicial and executive authority; can be exercised only by persons with the power of orders. (1) Ordinary jurisdiction is attached to ecclesiastical offices by law; the officeholders, called Ordinaries, have authority over those who are subject to them. (2) Delegated jurisdiction is that which is granted to persons rather than attached to offices. Its extent depends on the terms of the delegation.

Justice: One of the four cardinal virtues by which a person gives to others what is due to them as a matter of right. (*See* Cardinal Virtues.)

Justification: The act by which God makes a person just, and the consequent change in the spiritual status of a person, from sin to grace; the remission of sin and the infusion of sanctifying grace through the merits of Christ and the action of the Holy Spirit.

K

Kenosis: A term from the Greek for "emptying" that denotes Christ's emptying of Himself in his free renunciation of his right to divine status, by reason of the Incarnation, particularly as celebrated in the kenotic hymn (Phil 2:6-11), where it is said that Christ "emptied himself," taking the form of a slave, born in the likeness of man totally integrated with his divinity.

Kerygma: Proclaiming the word of God, in the manner of the Apostles, as here and now effective for salvation. This method of preaching or instruction, centered on Christ and geared to the facts and themes of salvation history, is designed to dispose people to faith in Christ and/or to intensify the experience and practice of that faith in those who have it.

Keys, Power of the: Spiritual authority and jurisdiction in the Church, symbolized by the keys of the kingdom of heaven. Christ promised the keys to St. Peter, as head-to-be of the Church (Mt 16:19), and commissioned him with full pastoral responsibility to feed his lambs and sheep (Jn 21:15-17), The pope, as the successor of St. Peter, has this power in a primary and supreme manner. The bishops of the Church also have the power, in union with and subordinate to the pope. Priests share in it through holy orders and the delegation of authority. Examples of the application of the Power of the Keys are the exercise of teaching and pastoral authority by the pope and bishops, the absolving of sins in the sacrament of penance, the granting of indulgences, the imposing of spiritual penalties on persons who commit certain serious sins.

Kingdom of God: God's sovereign lordship or rule over salvation history, leading to the eschatological goal of eternal life with God.

Koinonia: A term from the Greek word for "community, fellowship, or association" that was used by St. Luke for the fellowship of believers who worshipped together and held all their possessions in common (Acts 2:42-47); it is also used of fellowship with God (1 Jn 1:3, 6), with the Son (1 Cor 1:9), and with the Holy Spirit (2 Cor 13:13; Phil 2:1). St. Paul used *koinonia* to denote the intimate union of the believer with Christ and the community that exists among all the faithful themselves (Rom 15:26; 2 Cor 6:14).

L

Laicization: The process by which a man ordained to holy orders is relieved of the obligations of orders and the ministry and is returned to the status of a lay person.

Languages of the Church: The languages in which the Church's liturgy is celebrated. These include Ge'ez, Syriac, Greek, Arabic, and Old Slavonic in the

Eastern Churches. In the West, there is, of course, Latin and the various vernaculars. The Eastern Rites have always had the vernacular. The first language in church use, for divine worship and the conduct of ecclesiastical affairs, was Aramaic, the language of the first Christians in and around Jerusalem. As the Church spread westward, Greek was adopted and prevailed until the third century when it was supplanted by Latin for official use in the West. In the Western Church, Latin prevailed as the general official language until the promulgation on Dec. 4, 1963, of the Constitution on the Sacred Liturgy (*Sacrosanctum Concilium*) by the second session of the Second Vatican Council. Since that time, vernacular languages have come into use in the Mass, administration of the sacraments, and the Liturgy of the Hours. Latin, however, remains the official language for documents of the Holy See, administrative and procedural matters.

Latria: Greek-rooted Latin term that refers to that form of praise due to God alone.

Law: An ordinance or rule governing the activity of things. (1) **Natural law:** Moral norms corresponding to man's nature by which he orders his conduct toward God, neighbor, society and himself. This law, which is rooted in human nature, is of divine origin, can be known by the use of reason, and binds all persons having the use of reason. The Ten Commandments are declarations and amplifications of natural law. The primary precepts of natural law, to do good and to avoid evil, are universally recognized, despite differences with respect to understanding and application resulting from different philosophies of good and evil. (2) **Divine positive law:** That which has been revealed by God. Among its essentials are the twin precepts of love of God and love of neighbor, and the Ten Commandments. (3) **Ecclesiastical law:** That which is established by the Church for the spiritual welfare of the faithful and the orderly conduct of ecclesiastical affairs. (*See* **Canon Law.**) (4) **Civil law:** That which is established by a socio-political community for the common good.

Liberalism: A multiphased trend of thought and movement favoring liberty, independence and progress in moral, intellectual, religious, social, economic and political life. Traceable to the Renaissance, it developed through the Enlightenment, the rationalism of the 19th century, and modernist- and existentialist-related theories of the 20th century. Evaluations of various kinds of liberalism depend on the validity of their underlying principles. Extremist positions — regarding subjectivism, libertarianism, naturalist denials of the supernatural, and the alienation of individuals and society from God and the Church — were condemned by Gregory XVI in the 1830s, Pius IX in 1864, Leo XIII in 1899, and St. Pius X in 1907. There is, however, nothing objectionable about forms of liberalism patterned according to sound principles of Christian doctrine.

Liberation Theology: Deals with the relevance of Christian faith and salvation — and, therefore, of the mission of the Church — to efforts for the promotion of human rights, social justice and human development. It originated in the religious, social, political and economic environment of Latin America, with its contemporary need for a theory and corresponding action by the Church, in the pattern of its overall mission, for human rights and integral personal and social development. Some versions of liberation theology are at variance with the body of church teaching because of their ideological concept of Christ as liberator, and also because they play down the primary spiritual nature and mission of the Church. Instructions from the Congregation for the Doctrine of the Faith — "On Certain Aspects of the Theology of Liberation" (Sept. 3, 1984) and "On Christian Freedom and Liberation" (Apr. 5, 1986) — contain warnings against translating sociology into theology and advocating violence in social activism.

Life in Outer Space: Whether rational life exists on other bodies in the universe besides earth, is a question for scientific investigation to settle. The possibility can be granted, without prejudice to the body of revealed truth.

Limbo: The limbo of the fathers was the state of rest and natural happiness after death enjoyed by the just of pre-Christian times until they were admitted to heaven following the Ascension of Christ.

Litany: A prayer in the form of responsive petition; e.g., St. Joseph, pray for us, etc. Examples are the litanies of Loreto (Litany of the Blessed Mother), the Holy Name, All Saints, the Sacred Heart, the Precious Blood, St. Joseph, Litany for the Dying.

Logos: A Greek term for "word, speech, or reason." It is most commonly identified with the title given to Jesus in John's Gospel, though not exclusive to that Gospel; In the NT, however, the term reflects more the influence of Hellenistic philosophy: St. Paul uses logos as interchangeable with *sophia*, wisdom (1 Cor 1:24). The *Logos* is the Wisdom of God made manifest in the Son. As a name for the Second Person of the Trinity, the Incarnate Word, the term receives new meaning in the light of the life, death, and resurrection of Jesus Christ.

Loreto, House of: A Marian shrine in Loreto, Italy, consisting of the home of the Holy Family which, according to an old tradition, was transported in a miraculous manner from Nazareth to Dalmatia and finally to Loreto between 1291 and 1294. Investigations conducted shortly after the appearance of the structure in Loreto revealed that its dimensions matched those of the house of the Holy Family missing from its place of enshrinement in a basilica at Nazareth. Among the many popes who regarded it with high honor was John XXIII, who went there on pilgrimage Oct. 4, 1962. The house of the Holy Family is enshrined in the Basilica of Our Lady.

Love: A devotion to a person or object that has been categorized by Greek philosophy into four types: *storge* (one loves persons and things close to him); *philia* (the love of friends); *eros* (sexual love and that of a spiritual nature); *agape* (a self-giving to one in need). Christian charity is love, but not all love is true charity.

Lust: A disorderly desire for sexual pleasure; one of the seven capital sins.

M

Magi: In the Infancy Narrative of St. Matthew's Gospel (2:1-12), three wise men from the East whose visit and homage to the Child Jesus at Bethlehem indicated Christ's manifestation of himself to non-Jewish people. The narrative teaches the universality of salvation. The traditional names of the Magi are Caspar, Melchior and Balthasar.

Magisterium: The Church's teaching authority, instituted by Christ and guided by the Holy Spirit, which seeks to safeguard and explain the truths of the faith. The Magisterium is exercised in two ways. The extraordinary Magisterium is exercised when the pope and ecumenical councils infallibly define a truth of faith or morals that is necessary for one's salvation and that has been constantly taught and held by the Church. Ordinary Magisterium is exercised when the Church infallibly defines truths of the Faith as taught universally and without dissent; which must be taught or the Magisterium would be failing in its duty; is connected with a grave matter of faith or morals; and which is taught authoritatively. Not everything taught by the Magisterium is done so infallibly; however, the exercise of the Magisterium is faithful to Christ and what He taught.

Magnificat: The canticle or hymn of the Virgin Mary on the occasion of her visitation to her cousin Elizabeth (Lk 1:46-55). It is an expression of praise, thanksgiving and acknowledgment of the great blessings given by God to Mary, the Mother of the Second Person of the Blessed Trinity made Man. The *Magnificat* is recited in the Liturgy of the Hours as part of the Evening Prayer.

Martyr: A Greek word, meaning witness, denoting one who voluntarily suffered death for the faith or some Christian virtue.

Martyrology: A catalogue of martyrs and other saints, arranged according to the calendar. The *Roman Martyrology* contains the official list of saints venerated by the Church. Additions to the list are made in beatification and canonization decrees of the Congregation for the Causes of Saints.

Mass for the People: On Sundays and certain feasts throughout the year pastors are required to offer Mass for the faithful entrusted to their care. If they cannot offer the Mass on these days, they must do so at a later date or provide that another priest offer the Mass.

Materialism: Theory that holds that matter is the only reality, and everything in existence is merely a manifestation of matter; there is no such thing as spirit, and the supernatural does not exist. Materialism is incompatible with Christian doctrine.

Meditation: Mental, as distinguished from vocal, prayer, in which thought, affections, and resolutions of the will predominate. There is a meditative element to all forms of prayer, which always involves the raising of the heart and mind to God.

Mendicants: A term derived from Latin and meaning beggars, applied to members of religious orders without property rights; the members, accordingly, worked or begged for their support. The original mendicants were Franciscans and Dominicans in the early 13th century; later, the Carmelites, Augustinians, Servites and others were given the mendicant title and privileges, with respect to exemption from episcopal jurisdiction and wide faculties for preaching and administering the sacrament of penance. The practice of begging is limited at the present time, although it is still allowed with the permission of competent superiors and bishops. Mendicants are supported by free will offerings and income received for spiritual services and other work.

Mercy, Divine: The love and goodness of God, manifested particularly in a time of need.

Mercy, Works of: Works of corporal or spiritual assistance, motivated by love of God and neighbor, to persons in need. (1) **Corporal works:** feeding the hungry, giving drink to the thirsty, clothing the naked, visiting the imprisoned, sheltering the homeless, visiting the sick, burying the dead. (2) **Spiritual works:** counseling the doubtful, instructing the ignorant, admonishing sinners, comforting the afflicted, forgiving offenses, bearing wrongs patiently, praying for the living and the dead.

Merit: In religion, the right to a supernatural reward for good works freely done for a supernatural motive by a person in the state of and with the assistance of grace. The right to such reward is from God, who binds himself to give it. Accordingly, good works, as described above, are meritorious for salvation.

Metanoia: A term from the Greek *metanoein* ("to change one's mind, repent, be converted") that is used in the NT for conversion. It entails the repentance of sin and the subsequent turning toward the Lord. *Metanoia* is fundamental to the Christian life and is necessary for spiritual growth.

Metaphysics: The branch of philosophy (from the Greek *meta* - after + *physika* - physics) dealing with first things, including the nature of being (ontology), the origin and structure of the world (cosmology), and the study of the reality and attributes of God (natural theology). Metaphysics has long been examined by Catholic philosophers, most especially in the writings of St. Augustine and St. Thomas Aquinas.

Millennium: A thousand-year reign of Christ and the just upon earth before the end of the world. This belief of the Millenarians, Chiliasts, and some sects of modern times is based on an erroneous interpretation of Rv 20.

Miracles: Observable events or effects in the physical or moral order of things, with reference to salvation, which cannot be explained by the ordinary operation of laws of nature and which, therefore, are attributed to the direct action of God. They make known, in an unusual way, the concern and intervention of God in human affairs for the salvation of men.

Mission: (1) Strictly, it means being sent to perform a certain work, such as the mission of Christ to redeem mankind, the mission of the Apostles and the Church and its members to perpetuate the prophetic, priestly and royal mission of Christ. (2) A place where: the Gospel has not been proclaimed; the Church has not been firmly established; the Church, although established, is weak. (3) An ecclesiastical territory with the simplest kind of canonical organization, under the jurisdiction of the Congregation for the Evangelization of Peoples. (4) A church or chapel without a resident priest. (5) A special course of sermons and spiritual exercises conducted in parishes for the purpose of renewing and deepening the spiritual life of the faithful and for the conversion of lapsed Catholics.

Modernism: The "synthesis of all heresies," which appeared near the beginning of the 20th century. It undermines the objective validity of religious beliefs and practices which, it contends, are products of the subconscious developed by mankind under the stimulus of a religious sense. It holds that the existence of a personal God cannot be demonstrated, the Bible is not inspired, Christ is not divine, nor did he establish the Church or institute the sacraments. A special danger lies in modernism, which is still influential, because it uses Catholic terms with perverted meanings. St. Pius X condemned 65 propositions of modernism in 1907 in the decree *Lamentabili* and issued the encyclical *Pascendi* to explain and analyze its errors.

Monastery: The dwelling place, as well as the community thereof, of monks belonging to the Benedictine and Benedictine-related orders like the Cistercians and Carthusians; also, the Augustinians and Canons Regular. Distinctive of monasteries are: their separation from the world; the enclosure or cloister; the permanence or stability of attachment characteristic of their members; autonomous government in accordance with a monastic rule, like that of St. Benedict in the West or of St. Basil in the East; the special dedication of its members to the community celebration of the liturgy as well as to work that is suitable to the surrounding area and the needs of its people. Monastic superiors of men have such titles as abbot and prior; of women, abbess and prioress. In most essentials, an abbey is the same as a monastery.

Monk: A member of a monastic order — e.g., the Benedictines, the Benedictine-related Cistercians and Carthusians, and the Basilians, who bind themselves by religious profession to stable attachment to a monastery, the contemplative life and the work of their community. In popular use, the title is wrongly applied to many men religious who really are not monks.

Monotheism: Belief in and worship of one God.

Morality: Conformity or difformity of behavior to standards of right conduct. (*See* **Moral Obligations, Commandments of God, Precepts of the Church, Conscience, Law.**)

Mortification: Acts of self-discipline, including prayer, hardship, austerities and penances undertaken for the sake of progress in virtue.

Motu Proprio: A Latin phrase designating a document issued by a pope on his own initiative. Documents of this kind often concern administrative matters.

Mystagogy: Experience of the mystery of Christ, especially through participation in the liturgy and the sacraments.

Mysteries of Faith: Supernatural truths whose existence cannot be known without revelation by God and whose intrinsic truth, while not contrary to reason, can never be wholly understood even after revelation. These mysteries are above reason, not against reason. Among them are the divine mysteries of the Trinity, Incarnation and Eucharist. Some mysteries — e.g., concerning God's attributes — can be known by reason without revelation, although they cannot be fully understood.

N

Natural Law: *See* **Law**.

Natural Theology: The field of knowledge that relies upon human reason and the observation of nature, instead of revelation, to determine the existence and attributes of God.

Necromancy: Supposed communication with the dead; a form of divination.

Neo-Scholasticism: A movement begun in the late 19th century that had as its aim the restoration of Scholasticism for use in contemporary philosophy and theology. Great emphasis was placed upon the writings of such Scholastic masters as Peter Lombard, St. Albert the Great, St. Anselm, St. Bonaventure, Bl. John Duns Scotus, and especially St. Thomas Aquinas. The movement began at the Catholic University of Louvain, in Belgium, and then found its way into theological centers in Italy, France, and Germany. Particular attention was given to the philosophical and theological works of St. Thomas Aquinas, from which arose a particular school of neo-Thomism; the movement was strongly reinforced by Pope Leo XIII who issued the encyclical *Aeterni Patris* (1879) mandating that Scholasticism, in particular Thomism, be the foundation for all Catholic philosophy and theology taught in Catholic seminaries, universities, and colleges. Neo-Scholasticism was responsible for a true intellectual renaissance in 20th-century Catholic philosophy and theology. Among its foremost modern leaders were Jacques Maritain, Étienne Gilson, M. D. Chenu, Henri de Lubac, and Paul Claudel.

Nihil Obstat: *See* **Censorship of Books**.

Non-Expedit: A Latin expression. It is not expedient (fitting, proper), used to state a prohibition or refusal of permission.

Novena: A term designating public or private devotional practices over a period of nine consecutive days; or, by extension, over a period of nine weeks, in which one day a week is set aside for the devotions.

Novice: A man or woman preparing, in a formal period of trial and formation called a novitiate, for membership in an institute of consecrated life. The novitiate lasts a minimum of 12 and a maximum of 24 months; at its conclusion, the novice professes temporary promises or vows of poverty, chastity and obedience. Norms require that certain periods of time be spent in the house of novitiate; periods of apostolic work are also required, to acquaint the novice with the apostolate(s) of the institute. A novice is not bound by the obligations of the professed members of the institute, is free to leave at any time, and may be discharged at the discretion of competent superiors. The superior of a novice is a master of novices or director of formation.

Nun: (1) Strictly, a member of a religious order of women with solemn vows (*moniales*). (2) In general, all women religious, even those in simple vows who are more properly called sisters.

Nunc Dimittis: The canticle or hymn of Simeon at the sight of Jesus at the Temple on the occasion of his presentation (Lk 2:29-32). It is an expression of joy and thanksgiving for the blessing of having lived to see the Messiah. It is prescribed for use in the Night Prayer of the Liturgy of the Hours.

O

Oath: Calling upon God to witness the truth of a statement. Violating an oath, e.g., by perjury in court, or taking an oath without sufficient reason, is a violation of the honor due to God.

Obedience: Submission to one in authority. General obligations of obedience fall under the Fourth Commandment. The vow of obedience professed by religious is one of the evangelical counsels.

Obsession, Diabolical: The extraordinary state of one who is seriously molested by evil spirits in an external manner. Obsession is more than just temptation.

Occasion of Sin: A person, place, or thing that is a

temptation to sin. An occasion may be either a situation that always leads to sin or one that usually leads to sin.

Octave: A period of eight days given over to the celebration of a major feast such as Easter.

Oils, Holy: The oils blessed by a bishop at the Chrism Mass on Holy Thursday or another suitable day, or by a priest under certain conditions. (1) The oil of catechumens (olive or vegetable oil), used at baptism; also, poured with chrism into the baptismal water blessed in Easter Vigil ceremonies. (2) Oil of the sick (olive or vegetable oil) used in anointing the sick. (3) Chrism (olive or vegetable oil mixed with balm), which is ordinarily consecrated by a bishop, for use at baptism, in confirmation, at the ordination of a priest and bishop, in the dedication of churches and altars.

Ontologism: A philosophical theory (the name is taken from the Greek for being and study) that posits that knowledge of God is immediate and intuitive; it stipulates further that all other human knowledge is dependent upon this. It was condemned in 1861 by Pope Pius IX. (*See also* **Ontology**.)

Ontology: A branch of metaphysics that studies the nature and relations of existence.

Oratory: A chapel.

Ordinariate: An ecclesiastical jurisdiction for special purposes and people. Examples are military ordinariates for armed services personnel (in accord with provisions of the apostolic constitution *Spirituali militum curae*, Apr. 21, 1986) and Eastern-Rite ordinariates in places where Eastern-Rite dioceses do not exist.

Ordination: The consecration of sacred ministers for divine worship and the service of people in things pertaining to God. The power of ordination comes from Christ and the Church, and must be conferred by a minister capable of communicating it.

Organ Transplants: The transplanting of organs from one person to another is permissible provided it is done with the consent of the concerned parties and does not result in the death or essential mutilation of the donor. Advances in methods and technology have increased the range of transplant possibilities in recent years.

Original Sin: The sin of Adam (Gn 2:8-3:24), personal to him and passed on to all persons as a state of privation of grace. Despite this privation and the related wounding of human nature and weakening of natural powers, original sin leaves unchanged all that man himself is by nature. The scriptural basis of the doctrine was stated by St. Paul in 1 Cor 15:21ff., and Rom 5:12-21. Original sin is remitted by baptism and incorporation in Christ, through whom grace is given to persons. Pope John Paul II, while describing original sin during a general audience Oct. 1, 1986, called it "the absence of sanctifying grace in nature which has been diverted from its supernatural end."

O Salutaris Hostia: The first three Latin words, *O Saving Victim*, of a Benediction hymn.

Ostpolitik: Policy adopted by Pope Paul VI in an attempt to improve the situation of Eastern European Catholics through diplomatic negotiations with their governments.

Oxford Movement: A movement in the Church of England from 1833 to about 1845 which had for its objective a threefold defense of the Church as a divine institution, the apostolic succession of its bishops, and the *Book of Common Prayer* as the rule of faith. The movement took its name from Oxford University and involved a number of intellectuals who authored a series of influential Tracts for Our Times. Some of its leading figures — e.g., F. W. Faber, John Henry Newman and Henry Edward Manning — became converts to the Catholic Church. In the Church of England, the movement affected the liturgy, historical and theological scholarship, the status of the ministry, and other areas of ecclesiastical life.

P

Paganism: A term referring to non-revealed religions, i.e., religions other than Christianity, Judaism, and Islam.

Palms: Blessed palms are a sacramental. They are blessed and distributed on the Sunday of the Passion in commemoration of the triumphant entrance of Christ into Jerusalem. Ashes of the burnt palms are used on Ash Wednesday.

Pange Lingua: First Latin words, *Sing, my tongue*, of a hymn in honor of the Holy Eucharist, used particularly on Holy Thursday and in Eucharistic processions.

Pantheism: Theory that all things are part of God, divine, in the sense that God realizes himself as the ultimate reality of matter or spirit through being and/or becoming all things that have been, are, and will be. The theory leads to hopeless confusion of the Creator and the created realm of being, identifies evil with good, and involves many inherent contradictions.

Papal Election: The pope is elected by the College of Cardinals during a secret conclave which begins no sooner than 15 days and no later than 20 days after the death of his predecessor. Cardinals under the age of 80, totaling no more than 120, are eligible to take part in the election by secret ballot. Election is by a two-thirds vote of participating cardinals. New legislation regarding papal elections and church government during a vacancy of the Holy See was promulgated by Pope John Paul Feb. 23, 1996, in the apostolic constitution *Universi Dominici Gregis* ("Shepherd of the Lord's Whole Flock").

Paraclete: A title of the Holy Spirit meaning, in Greek, Advocate, Consoler.

Parental Duties: All duties related to the obligation of parents to provide for the welfare of their children. These obligations fall under the Fourth Commandment.

Parish: A community of the faithful served by a pastor charged with responsibility for providing them with full pastoral service. Most parishes are territorial, embracing all of the faithful in a certain area of a diocese; some are personal or national, for certain classes of people, without strict regard for their places of residence.

Parousia: The coming, or saving presence, of Christ which will mark the completion of salvation history and the coming to perfection of God's kingdom at the end of the world.

Particular Church: A term used since Vatican II that denotes certain divisions of the Universal Church. Examples include dioceses, vicariates, and prelatures.

Paschal Candle: A large candle, symbolic of the risen Christ, blessed and lighted on the Easter Vigil and placed at the altar until Pentecost. It is ornamented with five large grains of incense, representing the wounds of Christ, inserted in the form of a cross; the

Greek letters Alpha and Omega, symbolizing Christ the beginning and end of all things, at the top and bottom of the shaft of the cross; and the figures of the current year of salvation in the quadrants formed by the cross.

Paschal Precept: Church law requiring reception of the Eucharist in the Easter season (*See separate entry*) unless, for a just cause, once-a-year reception takes place at another time.

Passion of Christ: Sufferings of Christ, recorded in the four Gospels.

Pastor: An ordained minister charged with responsibility for the doctrinal, sacramental and related service of people committed to his care; e.g., a bishop for the people in his diocese, a priest for the people of his parish.

Pater Noster: The initial Latin words, *Our Father,* of the Lord's Prayer.

Patriarch: (1) The leaders of the Israelite tribes and heads of prominent families who appear in Genesis from Adam to Joseph. Among the most significant patriarchs of the Old Testament are Abraham, Isaac, and Jacob; the patriarchal narratives in Genesis associated with them constitute the prologue to Israel's salvation history, and the period during which they lived is known as the Age of the Patriarchs. It is noted that the title of patriarch that was used for David (Acts 2:29) was simply one of honor. (2) The head of a branch of the Eastern Church, corresponding to a province of the one-time Roman Empire. There are five official traditional patriarchal sees: Rome, Constantinople, Alexandria, Antioch, and Jerusalem. Presently, the autocephalous churches of the Orthodox Church comprise several of these traditional patriarchates.

Peace, Sign of: A gesture of greeting — e.g., a handshake — exchanged by the ministers and participants at Mass.

Pectoral Cross: A cross worn on a chain about the neck and over the breast by bishops and abbots as a mark of their office.

Penance or Penitence: (1) The spiritual change or conversion of mind and heart by which a person turns away from sin, and all that it implies, toward God, through a personal renewal under the influence of the Holy Spirit. Penance involves sorrow and contrition for sin, together with other internal and external acts of atonement. It serves the purposes of reestablishing in one's life the order of God's love and commandments, and of making satisfaction to God for sin. (2) Penance is a virtue disposing a person to turn to God in sorrow for sin and to carry out works of amendment and atonement. (3) The sacrament of penance and sacramental penance.

People of God: A name for the Church in the sense that it is comprised by a people with Christ as its head, the Holy Spirit as the condition of its unity, the law of love as its rule, and the kingdom of God as its destiny. Although it is a scriptural term, it was given new emphasis by the Second Vatican Council's Dogmatic Constitution on the Church (*Lumen Gentium*).

Perjury: Taking a false oath, lying under oath, a violation of the honor due to God.

Persecution, Religious: A campaign waged against a church or other religious body by persons and governments intent on its destruction. The best known campaigns of this type against the Christian Church were the Roman persecutions which occurred intermittently from about 54 to the promulgation of the Edict of Milan in 313. More Catholics have been persecuted in the 20th century than in any other period in history.

Personal Prelature: *See under* **Opus Dei.**

Peter's Pence: A collection made each year among Catholics for the maintenance of the pope and his works of charity. It was originally a tax of a penny on each house, and was collected on St. Peter's day, whence the name. It originated in England in the 8th century.

Petition: One of the four purposes of prayer. In prayers of petition, persons ask of God the blessings they and others need.

Pharisees: Influential class among the Jews, referred to in the Gospels, noted for their self-righteousness, legalism, strict interpretation of the Law, acceptance of the traditions of the elders as well as the Law of Moses, and beliefs regarding angels and spirits, the resurrection of the dead and judgment. Most of them were laymen, and they were closely allied with the Scribes; their opposite numbers were the Sadducees. The Pharisaic and rabbinical traditions had a lasting influence on Judaism following the destruction of Jerusalem in 70 A.D.

Pious Fund: Property and money originally accumulated by the Jesuits to finance their missionary work in Lower California. When the Jesuits were expelled from the territory in 1767, the fund was appropriated by the Spanish Crown and used to support Dominican and Franciscan missionary work in Upper and Lower California. In 1842 the Mexican government took over administration of the fund, incorporated most of the revenue into the national treasury, and agreed to pay the Church interest of six per cent a year on the capital so incorporated. From 1848 to 1967 the fund was the subject of lengthy negotiations between the U.S. and Mexican governments because of the latter's failure to make payments as agreed. A lump-sum settlement was made in 1967 with payment by Mexico to the U.S. government of more than $700,000, to be turned over to the Archdiocese of San Francisco.

Polytheism: Belief in and worship of many gods or divinities, especially prevalent in pre-Christian religions.

Poor Box: Alms-box; found in churches from the earliest days of Christianity.

Pope: A title from the Italian word *papa* (from Greek *pappas*, father) used for the Bishop of Rome, the Vicar of Christ and successor of St. Peter, who exercises universal governance over the Church.

Portiuncula: (1) Meaning little portion (of land), the Portiuncula was the chapel of Our Lady of the Angels near Assisi, Italy, which the Benedictines gave to St. Francis early in the 13th century. He repaired the chapel and made it the first church of the Franciscan Order. It is now enshrined in the Basilica of St. Mary of the Angels in Assisi. (2) The plenary Portiuncula Indulgence, or Pardon of Assisi, was authorized by Honorius III. Originally, it could be gained for the souls in purgatory only in the chapel of Our Lady of the Angels; by later concessions, it could be gained also in other Franciscan and parish churches. The indulgence (applicable to the souls in purgatory) can be gained from noon of Aug. 1 to midnight of Aug. 2, once each day. The conditions are, in addition to freedom from attachment to sin: reception of the sacraments of penance and the Eucharist on or near the day and a half; a visit to a parish church within the day and a half, during which the Our Father, the Creed and another prayer are offered for the intentions of the pope.

Positivism: The philosophy that teaches that the only reality is that which is perceived by the senses; the only truth is that which is empirically verified. It asserts that ideas about God, morality, or anything else that cannot be scientifically tested are to be rejected as unknowable.

Possession, Diabolical: The extraordinary state of a person who is tormented from within by evil spirits who exercise strong influence over his powers of mind and body. (See also Exorcism.)

Postulant: One of several names used to designate a candidate for membership in a religious institute during the period before novitiate.

Poverty: (1) The quality or state of being poor, in actual destitution and need, or being poor in spirit. In the latter sense, poverty means the state of mind and disposition of persons who regard material things in proper perspective as gifts of God for the support of life and its reasonable enrichment, and for the service of others in need. It means freedom from unreasonable attachment to material things as ends in themselves, even though they may be possessed in small or large measure. (2) One of the evangelical counsels professed as a public vow by members of an institute of consecrated life. It involves the voluntary renunciation of rights of ownership and of independent use and disposal of material goods; or, the right of independent use and disposal, but not of the radical right of ownership. Religious institutes provide their members with necessary and useful goods and services from common resources. The manner in which goods are received and/or handled by religious is determined by poverty of spirit and the rule and constitutions of their institute.

Pragmatism: Theory that the truth of ideas, concepts and values depends on their utility or capacity to serve a useful purpose rather than on their conformity with objective standards; also called utilitarianism.

Prayer: The raising of the mind and heart to God in adoration, thanksgiving, reparation and petition. Prayer, which is always mental because it involves thought and love of God, may be vocal, meditative, private and personal, social, and official. The official prayer of the Church as a worshipping community is called the liturgy.

Precepts: Commands or orders given to individuals or communities in particular cases; they establish law for concerned parties. Preceptive documents are issued by the pope, departments of the Roman Curia and other competent authority in the Church.

Presence of God: A devotional practice of increasing one's awareness of the presence and action of God in daily life.

Presumption: A sin against hope, by which a person striving for salvation (1) either relies too much on his own capabilities or (2) expects God to do things which he cannot do, in keeping with his divine attributes, or does not will to do, according to his divine plan. Presumption is the opposite of despair.

Preternatural Gifts: Exceptional gifts, beyond the exigencies and powers of human nature, enjoyed by Adam in the state of original justice: immunity from suffering and death, superior knowledge, integrity or perfect control of the passions. These gifts were lost as the result of original sin; their loss, however, implied no impairment of the integrity of human nature.

Pride: Unreasonable self-esteem; one of the seven capital sins.

Prie-Dieu: A French phrase, meaning pray God, designating a kneeler or bench suitable for kneeling while at prayer.

Priesthood: (1) The common priesthood of the non-ordained faithful. In virtue of baptism and confirmation, the faithful are a priestly people who participate in the priesthood of Christ through acts of worship, witness to the faith in daily life, and efforts to foster the growth of God's kingdom. (2) The ordained priesthood, in virtue of the sacrament of orders, of bishops, priests and deacons, for service to the common priesthood.

Primary Option: The life-choice of a person for or against God which shapes the basic orientation of moral conduct. A primary option for God does not preclude the possibility of serious sin.

Prior: A superior or an assistant to an abbot in a monastery.

Privilege: A favor, an exemption from the obligation of a law. Privileges of various kinds, with respect to ecclesiastical laws, are granted by the pope, departments of the Roman Curia and other competent authority in the Church.

Probabiliorism: The moral system asserting that the more probable opinion of a varied set of acceptable positions regarding the binding character of a law should be accepted. If the reasons for being free from a law are more probably true, one is freed from the law's obligations. Probabiliorism, however, maintained that if it was probable that the law did not bind, one still had to follow it unless it was more probable that the law did not bind.

Probabilism: A moral system for use in cases of conscience which involve the obligation of doubtful laws. There is a general principle that a doubtful law does not bind. Probabilism, therefore, teaches that it is permissible to follow an opinion favoring liberty, provided the opinion is certainly and solidly probable. Probabilism may not be invoked when there is question of: a certain law or the certain obligation of a law; the certain right of another party; the validity of an action; something which is necessary for salvation.

Pro-Cathedral: A church used as a cathedral.

Promoter of the Faith (Promotor fidei): An official of the Congregation for the Causes of Saints, whose role in beatification and canonization procedures is to establish beyond reasonable doubt the validity of evidence regarding the holiness of prospective saints and miracles attributed to their intercession.

Prophecy: (1) The communication of divine revelation by inspired intermediaries, called prophets, between God and his people. Old Testament prophecy was unique in its origin and because of its ethical and religious content, which included disclosure of the saving will of Yahweh for the people, moral censures and warnings of divine punishment because of sin and violations of the Law and Covenant, in the form of promises, admonitions, reproaches and threats.

Although Moses and other earlier figures are called prophets, the period of prophecy is generally dated from the early years of the monarchy to about 100 years after the Babylonian Exile. From that time on, the written Law and its interpreters supplanted the prophets as guides of the people. Old Testament prophets are cited in the New Testament, with awareness that God spoke through them and that some of their oracles were fulfilled in Christ. John the Baptist is the outstanding prophetic figure in the New Testament. Christ never claimed the title of prophet for himself, although some people thought he was one. There were prophets in the early Church, and St. Paul mentioned the charism of prophecy in 1 Cor 14:1-5. Prophecy disappeared after New Testament times. Revelation is classified as the prophetic book of the New Testament. (2) In contemporary non-scriptural usage, the term is applied to the witness given by persons to the relevance of their beliefs in everyday life and action.

Proportionalism: The moral theory that asserts that an action is judged on whether the evils resulting are proportionate to the goods that result. If the evils outweigh the goods, the act is objectionable; if the opposite is true, the act is permissible. Proportionalism differs from consequentialism in that the former admits that the inherent morality of the act and the agent's intention must also be considered. Proportionalism is rejected by critics as it does not offer an objective criterion for determining when evils are proportionate or disproportionate. It also fails to consider the intrinsic nature of human acts and does nothing to assist Christians to grow in virtue.

Province: (1) A territory comprising one archdiocese called the metropolitan see and one or more dioceses called suffragan sees. The head of the archdiocese, an archbishop, has metropolitan rights and responsibilities over the province. (2) A division of a religious order under the jurisdiction of a provincial superior.

Prudence: Practical wisdom and judgment regarding the choice and use of the best ways and means of doing good; one of the four cardinal virtues.

Punishment Due for Sin: The punishment which is a consequence of sin. It is of two kinds: (1) Eternal punishment is the punishment of hell, to which one becomes subject by the commission of mortal sin. Such punishment is remitted when mortal sin is forgiven. (2) Temporal punishment is a consequence of venial sin and/or forgiven mortal sin; it is not everlasting and may be remitted in this life by means of penance. Temporal punishment unremitted during this life is remitted by suffering in purgatory.

Purgatory: The state or condition of those who have died in the state of grace but with some attachment to sin, and are purified for a time before they are admitted to the glory and happiness of heaven. In this state and period of passive suffering, they are purified of unrepented venial sins, satisfy the demands of divine justice for temporal punishment due for sins, and are thus converted to a state of worthiness of the beatific vision.

Q

Quadragesima: From the Latin for fortieth, the name given to the forty penitential days of Lent.

Quinquennial Report: A report on the current state of a diocese that must be compiled and submitted by a bishop to the Holy See every five years in anticipation of the *ad liminal* visit.

Quinque Viae: From the Latin for the "five ways," the five proofs for the existence of God that were proposed by St. Thomas Aquinas in his *Summa Theologiae* (Part I, question 2, article 3). The five ways are: 1) all the motion in the world points to an unmoved Prime Mover; 2) the subordinate agents in the world imply the First Agent; 3) there must be a Cause Who is not perishable and Whose existence is underived; 4) the limited goodness in the world must be a reflection of Unlimited Goodness; 5) all things tend to become something, and that inclination must have proceeded from some Rational Planner.

R

Racism: A theory which holds that any one or several of the different races of the human family are inherently superior or inferior to any one or several of the others. The teaching denies the essential unity of the human race, the equality and dignity of all persons because of their common possession of the same human nature, and the participation of all in the divine plan of redemption. It is radically opposed to the virtue of justice and the precept of love of neighbor. Differences of superiority and inferiority which do exist are the result of accidental factors operating in a wide variety of circumstances, and are in no way due to essential defects in any one or several of the branches of the one human race. The theory of racism, together with practices related to it, is incompatible with Christian doctrine.

Rash Judgment: Attributing faults to another without sufficient reason; a violation of the obligations of justice and charity.

Rationalism: A theory which makes the mind the measure and arbiter of all things, including religious truth. A product of the Enlightenment, it rejects the supernatural, divine revelation, and authoritative teaching by any church.

Recollection: Meditation, attitude of concentration or awareness of spiritual matters and things pertaining to salvation and the accomplishment of God's will.

Relativism: Theory which holds that all truth, including religious truth, is relative, i.e., not absolute, certain or unchanging; a product of agnosticism, indifferentism, and an unwarranted extension of the notion of truth in positive science. Relativism is based on the tenet that certain knowledge of any and all truth is impossible. Therefore, no religion, philosophy or science can be said to possess the real truth; consequently, all religions, philosophies and sciences may be considered to have as much or as little of truth as any of the others.

Relics: The physical remains and effects of saints, which are considered worthy of veneration inasmuch as they are representative of persons in glory with God. Catholic doctrine proscribes the view that relics are not worthy of veneration. In line with norms laid down by the Council of Trent and subsequent enactments, discipline concerning relics is subject to control by the Congregations for the Causes of Saints and for Divine Worship and the Discipline of the Sacraments.

Religion: The adoration and service of God as expressed in divine worship and in daily life. Religion is concerned with all of the relations existing between God and human beings, and between humans themselves because of the central significance of God. Objectively considered, religion consists of a body of truth that is believed, a code of morality for the guidance of conduct, and a form of divine worship. Subjectively, it is a person's total response, theoretically and practically, to the demands of faith; it is living faith, personal engagement, self-commitment to God. Thus, by creed, code and cult, a person orders and directs his or her life in reference to God and, through what the love and service of God implies, to all people and all things.

Reliquary: A vessel for the preservation and exposition of a relic; sometimes made like a small monstrance.

Reparation: The making of amends to God for sin committed; one of the four ends of prayer and the purpose of penance.

Requiem: A Mass offered for the repose of the soul of one who has died in Christ. Its name is derived from the first word of the Gregorian (Latin) entrance chant (or Introit) at Masses for the dead: *Requiem aeternam dona eis, Domine* ("Eternal rest grant unto them, O Lord"). The revised Rite for Funerals refers to the requiem as the Mass of Christian Burial; however, it would not be uncommon to hear people employ the former usage.

Rescript: A written reply by an ecclesiastical superior regarding a question or request; its provisions bind concerned parties only. Papal dispensations are issued in the form of rescripts.

Reserved Censure: A sin or censure, absolution from which is reserved to religious superiors, bishops, the pope, or confessors having special faculties. Reservations are made because of the serious nature and social effects of certain sins and censures.

Restitution: An act of reparation for an injury done to another. The injury may be caused by taking and/or retaining what belongs to another or by damaging either the property or reputation of another. The intention of making restitution, usually in kind, is required as a condition for the forgiveness of sins of injustice, even though actual restitution is not possible.

Ring: In the Church a ring is worn as part of the insignia of bishops, abbots, et al.; by sisters to denote their consecration to God and the Church. The wedding ring symbolizes the love and union of husband and wife.

Ritual: A book of prayers and ceremonies used in the administration of the sacraments and other ceremonial functions. In the Roman Rite, the standard book of this kind is the Roman Ritual.

Rogito: The official notarial act or document testifying to the burial of a pope.

Rosary: A form of mental and vocal prayer centered on mysteries or events in the lives of Jesus and Mary. Its essential elements are meditation on the mysteries and the recitation of a number of decades of Hail Marys, each beginning with the Lord's Prayer. Introductory prayers may include the Apostles' Creed, an initial Our Father, three Hail Marys and a Glory be to the Father; each decade is customarily concluded with a Glory be to the Father; at the end, it is customary to say the Hail, Holy Queen and a prayer from the liturgy for the feast of the Blessed Virgin Mary of the Rosary. Traditionally, the Mysteries of the Rosary, which are the subject of meditation, are: (1) Joyful — the Annunciation to Mary that she was to be the Mother of Christ, her visit to Elizabeth, the birth of Jesus, the presentation of Jesus in the Temple, the finding of Jesus in the Temple. (2) Sorrowful — Christ's agony in the Garden of Gethsemani, scourging at the pillar, crowning with thorns, carrying of the cross to Calvary, and crucifixion. (3) Glorious — the Resurrection and Ascension of Christ, the descent of the Holy Spirit upon the Apostles, Mary's Assumption into heaven and her crowning as Queen of angels and men.

The complete Rosary, called the Dominican Rosary, consists of 15 decades. In customary practice, only five decades are usually said at one time. Rosary beads are used to aid in counting the prayers without distraction. The Rosary originated through the coalescence of popular devotions to Jesus and Mary from the 12th century onward. Its present form dates from about the 15th century. Carthusians contributed greatly toward its development; Dominicans have been its greatest promoters. The fifteen mysteries were standardized by Pope Pius V in 1569.

In 2002, Pope John Paul II added five new mysteries dedicated to chapters from Jesus' public life. Titled the Mysteries of Light, they are: Christ's baptism in the Jordan River; Christ's self-revelation at the marriage of Cana; Christ's announcement of the kingdom of God with the invitation to conversion; Christ's Transfiguration, when he revealed his glory to his Apostles; and the institution of the Eucharist at the Last Supper as the sacramental expression of the paschal mystery. The pope asked that the Mysteries of Light be recited especially on Thursday.

S

Sabbath: The seventh day of the week, observed by Jews and Sabbatarians as the day for rest and religious observance.

Sacrarium: A basin with a drain leading directly into the ground; standard equipment of a sacristy.

Sacred Heart, Enthronement of the: An acknowledgment of the sovereignty of Jesus Christ over the Christian family, expressed by the installation of an image or picture of the Sacred Heart in a place of honor in the home, accompanied by an act of consecration.

Sacred Heart, Promises: Twelve promises to persons having devotion to the Sacred Heart of Jesus, which were communicated by Christ to St. Margaret Mary Alacoque in a private revelation in 1675.

Sacrilege: Violation of and irreverence toward a person, place or thing that is sacred because of public dedication to God; a sin against the virtue of religion. Personal sacrilege is violence of some kind against a cleric or religious, or a violation of chastity with a cleric or religious. Local sacrilege is the desecration of sacred places. Real sacrilege is irreverence with respect to sacred things, such as the sacraments and sacred vessels.

Sacristy: A utility room where vestments, church furnishings and sacred vessels are kept and where the clergy vest for sacred functions.

Sadducees: The predominantly priestly party among the Jews in the time of Christ, noted for extreme conservatism, acceptance only of the Law of Moses, and rejection of the traditions of the elders. Their opposite numbers were the Pharisees.

Saints, Cult of: The veneration, called *dulia*, of holy persons who have died and are in glory with God in heaven; it includes honoring them and petitioning them for their intercession with God. Liturgical veneration is given only to saints officially recognized by the Church; private veneration may be given to anyone thought to be in heaven. The veneration of saints is essentially different from the adoration given to God alone; by its very nature, however, it terminates in the worship of God. (*See also* **Dulia and Latria.**)

Salvation: The liberation of persons from sin and its effects, reconciliation with God in and through Christ, the attainment of union with God forever in the glory of heaven as the supreme purpose of life and as the God-given reward for fulfillment of his will on earth. Salvation-in-process begins and continues in this life through union with Christ in faith professed and in action; its final term is union with God and the whole community of the saved in the ultimate perfection of God's kingdom. The Church teaches that: God wills the salvation of all men; men are saved in and through Christ; membership in the Church established by Christ, known and understood as the community of salvation, is necessary for salvation; men with this knowledge and understanding who deliberately reject this Church, cannot be saved. The Catholic Church is the Church founded by Christ. (*See below*, **Salvation outside the Church.**)

Salvation History: The facts and the record of God's relations with human beings, in the past, present and future, for the purpose of leading them to live in accordance with his will for the eventual attainment after death of salvation, or everlasting happiness with him in heaven. The essentials of salvation history are: God's love for all human beings and will for their salvation; his intervention and action in the world to express this love and bring about their salvation; the revelation he made of himself and the covenant he established with the Israelites in the Old Testament; the perfecting of this revelation and the new covenant of grace through Christ in the New Testament; the continuing action-for-salvation carried on in and through the Church; the communication of saving grace to people through the merits of Christ and the operations of the Holy Spirit in the here-and-now circumstances of daily life and with the cooperation of people themselves.

Salvation outside the Church: The Second Vatican Council covered this subject summarily in the following manner: "Those also can attain to everlasting salvation who through no fault of their own do not know the Gospel of Christ or his Church, yet sincerely seek God and, moved by grace, strive by their deeds to do his will as it is known to them through the dictates of conscience. Nor does divine Providence deny the help necessary for salvation to those who, without blame on their part, have not yet arrived at an explicit knowledge of God, but who strive to live a good life, thanks to his grace. Whatever good or truth is found among them is looked upon by the Church as a preparation for the Gospel. She regards such qualities as given by him who enlightens all men so that they may finally have life" (Dogmatic Constitution on the Church, *Lumen Gentium*, No. 16).

Sanctifying Grace: *See* **Grace.**

Satanism: Worship of the devil, a blasphemous inversion of the order of worship which is due to God alone.

Scandal: Conduct which is the occasion of sin to another person.

Scapular: (1) A part of the habit of some religious orders like the Benedictines and Dominicans; a nearly shoulder-wide strip of cloth worn over the tunic and reaching almost to the feet in front and behind. Originally a kind of apron, it came to symbolize the cross and yoke of Christ. (2) Scapulars worn by lay persons as a sign of association with religious orders and for devotional purposes are an adaptation of monastic scapulars. Approved by the Church as sacramentals, they consist of two small squares of woolen cloth joined by strings and are worn about the neck. They are given for wearing in a ceremony of investiture or enrollment. There are nearly 20 scapulars for devotional use: the five principal ones are generally understood to include those of Our Lady of Mt Carmel (the brown Carmelite Scapular), the Holy Trinity, Our Lady of the Seven Dolors, the Passion, the Immaculate Conception.

Scapular Medal: A medallion with a representation of the Sacred Heart on one side and of the Blessed Virgin Mary on the other. Authorized by St. Pius X in 1910, it may be worn or carried in place of a scapular by persons already invested with a scapular.

Scapular Promise: According to a legend of the Carmelite Order, the Blessed Virgin Mary appeared to St. Simon Stock in 1251 at Cambridge, England, and declared that wearers of the brown Carmelite Scapular would be the beneficiaries of her special intercession. The scapular tradition has never been the subject of official decision by the Church. Essentially, it expresses belief in the intercession of Mary and the efficacy of sacramentals in the context of truly Christian life.

Schism: Derived from a Greek word meaning separation, the term designates formal and obstinate refusal by a baptized Catholic, called a schismatic, to be in communion with the pope and the Church. The canonical penalty is excommunication. One of the most disastrous schisms in history resulted in the definitive separation of the Church in the East from union with Rome about 1054.

Scholasticism: The term usually applied to the Catholic theology and philosophy which developed in the Middle Ages. (*See also* **Neo-Scholasticism.**)

Scribes: Hebrew intellectuals noted for their knowledge of the Law of Moses, influential from the time of the Exile to about 70 A.D. Many of them were Pharisees. They were the antecedents of rabbis and their traditions, as well as those o the Pharisees, had a lasting influence on Judaism following the destruction of Jerusalem in 70 A.D.

Scruple: A morbid, unreasonable fear and anxiety that one's actions are sinful when they are not, or more seriously sinful than they actually are. Compulsive scrupulosity is quite different from the transient scrupulosity of persons of tender or highly sensitive conscience, or of persons with faulty moral judgment.

Seal of Confession: The obligation of secrecy which must be observed regarding knowledge of things learned in connection with the confession of sin in the sacrament of penance. The seal covers matters whose revelation would make the sacrament burdensome.

Confessors are prohibited, under penalty of excommunication, from making any direct revelation of confessional matter; this prohibition holds, outside of confession, even with respect to the person who made the confession unless the person releases the priest from the obligation. Persons other than confessors are obliged to maintain secrecy, but not under penalty of excommunication. General, non-specific discussion of confessional matter does not violate the seal.

Secularism: A school of thought, a spirit and manner of action which ignores and/or repudiates the validity or influence of supernatural religion with respect to individual and social life.

See: Another name for diocese or archdiocese.

Seminary: A house of study and formation for men, called seminarians, preparing for the priesthood. Traditional seminaries date from the Council of Trent in the middle of the 16th century; before that time, candidates for the priesthood were variously trained in monastic schools, universities under church auspices, and in less formal ways.

Sermon on the Mount: A compilation of sayings of Our Lord in the form of an extended discourse in Matthew's Gospel (5:1 to 7:27) and, in a shorter discourse, in Luke (6:17-49). The passage in Matthew, called the "Constitution of the New Law," summarizes the living spirit of believers in Christ and members of the kingdom of God. Beginning with the Beatitudes and including the Lord's Prayer, it covers the perfect justice of the New Law, the fulfillment of the Old Law in the New Law of Christ, and the integrity of internal attitude and external conduct with respect to love of God and neighbor, justice, chastity, truth, trust and confidence in God.

Seven Last Words of Christ: The Seven Last Words of Christ on the Cross were: (1) *"Father, forgive them; for they do not know what they are doing"* (Lk 23:34); (2) To the penitent thief: *"I assure you: today you will be with me in Paradise"* (Lk 23:24); (3) To Mary and his Apostle John: *"Woman, behold thy son! . . . Behold your mother"* (Jn 19:26); (4) *"Eli Eli, lama sabacthani* [*"My God, my God, why have you forsaken me?"*] (Mt 27:46; cf. Mk 15:34); (5) *"I thirst"* (Jn 19:28); (6) *"It is finished"* (Jn 19:30); (7) *"Father, into thy hands I commend my spirit"*(Lk 23:46).

Shrine, Crowned: A shrine approved by the Holy See as a place of pilgrimage. The approval permits public devotion at the shrine and implies that at least one miracle has resulted from devotion at the shrine. Among the best known crowned shrines are those of the Virgin Mary at Lourdes and Fátima. Shrines with statues crowned by Pope John Paul in 1985 in South America were those of Our Lady of Coromoto, patroness of Venezuela, in Caracas, and Our Lady of Carmen de Paucartambo in Cuzco, Peru.

Shroud of Turin: A strip of brownish linen cloth, 14 feet, three inches in length and three feet, seven inches in width, bearing the front and back imprint of a human body. A tradition dating from the 7th century, which has not been verified beyond doubt, claims that the shroud is the fine linen in which the body of Christ was wrapped for burial. The early history of the shroud is obscure. It was enshrined at Lirey, France, in 1354 and was transferred in 1578 to Turin, Italy, where it has been kept in the cathedral down to the present time. Scientific investigation, which began in 1898, seems to indicate that the markings on the shroud are those of a human body. The shroud, for the first time since 1933, was placed on public view from Aug. 27 to Oct. 8, 1978, and was seen by an estimated 3.3 million people. Scientists conducted intensive studies of it thereafter, finally determining that the material of the shroud dated from between 1260 and 1390. The shroud, which had been the possession of the House of Savoy, was willed to Pope John Paul II in 1983.

Sick Calls: When a person is confined at home by illness or other cause and is unable to go to church for reception of the sacraments, a parish priest should be informed and arrangements made for him to visit the person at home. Such visitations are common in pastoral practice, both for special needs and for providing persons with regular opportunities for receiving the sacraments. If a priest cannot make the visitation, arrangements can be made for a deacon or Eucharistic minister to bring Holy Communion to the homebound or bedridden person.

Sign of the Cross: A sign, ceremonial gesture or movement in the form of a cross by which a person confesses faith in the Holy Trinity and Christ, and intercedes for the blessing of himself or herself, other persons and things. In Roman-Rite practice, a person making the sign touches the fingers of the right hand to forehead, below the breast, left shoulder and right shoulder while saying: *"In the name of the Father, and of the Son, and of the Holy Spirit."* The sign is also made with the thumb on the forehead, the lips, and the breast. For the blessing of persons and objects, a large sign of the cross is made by movement of the right hand. In Eastern-Rite practice, the sign is made with the thumb and first two fingers of the right hand joined together and touching the forehead, below the breast, the right shoulder and the left shoulder; the formula generally used is the doxology, *"O Holy God, O Holy Strong One, O Immortal One."* The Eastern manner of making the sign was general until the first half of the 13th century; by the 17th century, Western practice involved the whole right hand and the reversal of direction from shoulder to shoulder.

Signs of the Times: Contemporary events, trends and features in culture and society, the needs and aspirations of people, all the factors that form the context in and through which the Church has to carry on its saving mission. The Second Vatican Council spoke on numerous occasions about these signs and the relationship between them and a kind of manifestation of God's will, positive or negative, and about subjecting them to judgment and action corresponding to the demands of divine revelation through Scripture, Christ, and the experience, tradition and teaching authority of the Church.

Simony: The deliberate intention and act of selling and/or buying spiritual goods or material things so connected with the spiritual that they cannot be separated therefrom; a violation of the virtue of religion, and a sacrilege, because it wrongfully puts a material price on spiritual things, which cannot be either sold or bought. In church law, actual sale or purchase is subject to censure in some cases. The term is derived from the name of Simon Magus, who attempted to buy from Sts. Peter and John the power to confirm people in the Holy Spirit (Acts 8:4-24).

Sin: (1) Actual sin is the free and deliberate violation of God's law by thought, word or action. (a) Mortal sin — involving serious matter, sufficient reflection and full consent — results in the loss of sanctifying grace and alienation from God, and renders a person incapable of performing meritorious supernatural acts and subject to everlasting punishment. (b) Venial sin — involving less serious matter, reflection and consent — does not have such serious consequences. (2) Original sin is the sin of Adam, with consequences for all human beings. (*See separate entry.*)

Sins against the Holy Spirit: Despair of salvation, presumption of God's mercy, impugning the known truths of faith, envy at another's spiritual good, obstinacy in sin, final impenitence. Those guilty of such sins stubbornly resist the influence of grace and, as long as they do so, cannot be forgiven.

Sins, Occasions of: Circumstances (persons, places, things, etc.) which easily lead to sin. There is an obligation to avoid voluntary proximate occasions of sin, and to take precautions against the dangers of unavoidable occasions.

Sins That Cry to Heaven for Vengeance: Willful murder, sins against nature, oppression of the poor, widows and orphans, defrauding laborers of their wages.

Sister: Any woman religious, in popular speech; strictly, the title applies only to women religious belonging to institutes whose members never professed solemn vows. Most of the institutes whose members are properly called Sisters were established during and since the 19th century. Women religious with solemn vows, or belonging to institutes whose members formerly professed solemn vows, are properly called nuns.

Sisterhood: A generic term referring to the whole institution of the life of women religious in the Church, or to a particular institute of women religious.

Situation Ethics: A subjective, individualistic ethical theory which denies the binding force of ethical principles as universal laws and preceptive norms of moral conduct, and proposes that morality is determined only by situational conditions and considerations and the intention of the person. It has been criticized for ignoring the principles of objective ethics. (*See* also Consequentialism and Proportionalism.)

Slander: Attributing to a person faults which he or she does not have; a violation of the obligations of justice and charity, for which restitution is due.

Sloth (Acedia): One of the seven capital sins; spiritual laziness, involving distaste and disgust for spiritual things; spiritual boredom, which saps the vigor of spiritual life. Physical laziness is a counterpart of spiritual sloth.

Sorcery: A kind of black magic in which evil is invoked by means of diabolical intervention; a violation of the virtue of religion.

Soteriology: The division of theology which treats of the mission and work of Christ as Redeemer.

Species, Sacred: The appearances of bread and wine (color, taste, smell, etc.) which remain after the substance has been changed at the Consecration of the Mass into the Body and Blood of Christ. (*See* Transubstantiation.)

Spiritism: Attempts to communicate with spirits and departed souls by means of seances, table tapping, ouija boards, and other methods; a violation of the virtue of religion. Spiritualistic practices are noted for fakery.

Stational Churches, Days: Churches, especially in Rome, where the clergy and lay people were accustomed to gather with their bishop on certain days for the celebration of the liturgy. The 25 early titular or parish churches of Rome, plus other churches, each had their turn as the site of divine worship in practices which may have started in the third century. The observances were rather well developed toward the latter part of the 4th century, and by the fifth they included a Mass concelebrated by the pope and attendant priests. On some occasions, the stational liturgy was preceded by a procession from another church called a *collecta*. There were 42 Roman stational churches in the 8th century, and 89 stational services were scheduled annually in connection with the liturgical seasons. Stational observances fell into disuse toward the end of the Middle Ages. Some revival was begun by John XXIII in 1959 and continued by Paul VI and John Paul II.

Stations (Way) of the Cross: A form of devotion commemorating the Passion and death of Christ, consisting of a series of meditations (stations): (1) his condemnation to death, (2) taking up of the cross, (3) the first fall on the way to Calvary, (4) meeting his Mother, (5) being assisted by Simon of Cyrene and (6) by the woman Veronica who wiped his face, (7) the second fall, (8) meeting the women of Jerusalem, (9) the third fall, (10) being stripped and (11) nailed to the cross, (12) his death, (13) the removal of his body from the cross and (14) his burial. Depictions of these scenes are mounted in most churches, chapels and in some other places, beneath small crosses. A person making the Way of the Cross passes before these stations, or stopping points, pausing at each for meditation. If the stations are made by a group of people, only the leader has to pass from station to station. A plenary indulgence is granted to the faithful who make the stations, under the usual conditions: freedom from all attachment to sin, reception of the sacraments of penance and the Eucharist, and prayers for the intentions of the pope. Those who are impeded from making the stations in the usual manner can gain the same indulgence if, along with the aforementioned conditions, they spend at least a half hour in spiritual reading and meditation on the passion and death of Christ. The stations originated remotely from the practice of Holy Land pilgrims who visited the actual scenes of incidents in the Passion of Christ. Representations elsewhere of at least some of these scenes were known as early as the 5th century. Later, the stations evolved in connection with and as a consequence of strong devotion to the Passion in the 12th and 13th centuries. Franciscans, who were given custody of the Holy Places in 1342, promoted the devotion widely; one of them, St. Leonard of Port Maurice, became known as the greatest preacher of the Way of the Cross in the 18th century. The general features of the devotion were fixed by Clement XII in 1731.

Statutes: Virtually the same as decrees (*See* separate entry), they almost always designate laws of a particular council or synod rather than pontifical laws.

Stigmata: Marks of the wounds suffered by Christ in his crucifixion, in hands and feet by nails, and side by the piercing of a lance. Some persons, called stigmatists, have been reported as recipients or sufferers of marks like these. The Church, however, has never issued any infallible declaration about their possession by anyone, even in the case of St. Francis of Assisi whose stigmata seem to be the best substantiated and may be commemorated in the Roman-Rite liturgy. Ninety percent of some 300 reputed stigmatists have been women. Judgment regarding the presence, significance, and manner of causation of stigmata would depend, among other things, on irrefutable experimental evidence.

Stipend, Mass: An offering given to a priest for applying the fruits of the Mass according to the intention of the donor. The offering is a contribution to the support of the priest. The disposition of the fruits of the sacrifice, in line with doctrine concerning the Mass in particular and prayer in general, is subject to the will of God. Mass offerings and intentions were the subjects of a decree approved by John Paul II and made public Mar. 22, 1991: (1) Normally, no more than one offering should be accepted for a Mass; the Mass should be offered in accord with the donor's intention; the priest who accepts the offering should celebrate the Mass himself or have another priest do so. (2) Several Mass intentions, for which offerings have been made, can be combined for a "collective" application of a single Mass only if the previous and explicit consent of the donors is obtained. Such Masses are an exception to the general rule.

Stole Fee: An offering given on certain occasions; e.g., at a baptism, wedding, funeral, for the support of the clergy who administer the sacraments and perform other sacred rites.

Stoup: A vessel used to contain holy water.

Suffragan See: Any diocese, except the archdiocese, within a province.

Suicide: The taking of one's own life; a violation of God's dominion over human life. Ecclesiastical burial is denied to persons while in full possession of their faculties; it is permitted in cases of doubt.

Supererogation: Actions which go beyond the obligations of duty and the requirements enjoined by God's law as necessary for salvation. Examples of these works are the profession and observance of the evangelical counsels of poverty, chastity, and obedience, and efforts to practice charity to the highest degree.

Supernatural: Above the natural; that which exceeds and is not due or owed to the essence, exigencies, requirements, powers and merits of created nature. While human beings have no claim on supernatural things and do not need them in order to exist and act on a natural level, they do need them in order to exist and act in the higher order or economy of grace established by God for their salvation. God has freely given them certain things which are beyond the powers and rights of their human nature. Examples of the supernatural are: grace, a kind of participation by human beings in the divine life, by which they become capable of performing acts meritorious for salvation; divine revelation by which God manifests himself to them and makes known truth that is inaccessible to human reason alone; faith, by which they believe divine truth because of the authority of God who reveals it through Sacred Scripture and tradition and the teaching of his Church.

Suspension: A censure by which a cleric is forbidden to exercise some or all of his powers of orders and jurisdiction, or to accept the financial support of his benefices.

Syllabus, The: (1) When not qualified, the term refers to the list of 80 errors accompanying Pope Pius IX's encyclical *Quanta Cura*, issued in 1864. (2) The Syllabus of St. Pius X in the decree *Lamentabili*, issued by the Holy Office July 4, 1907, condemning 65 heretical propositions of modernism. This schedule of errors was followed shortly by that pope's encyclical *Pascendi*, the principal ecclesiastical document against modernism, issued Sept. 8, 1907.

Synod, Diocesan: Meeting of representative persons of a diocese — priests, religious, lay persons — with the bishop, called by him for the purpose of considering and taking action on matters affecting the life and mission of the Church in the diocese. Persons taking part in a synod have consultative status; the bishop alone is the legislator, with power to authorize synodal decrees. According to canon law, every diocese should have a synod every 10 years.

T

Tabernacle: The receptacle in which the Blessed Sacrament is reserved in churches, chapels, and oratories. It is to be immovable, solid, locked, and located in a prominent place.

Te Deum: The opening Latin words, *Thee, God*, of a hymn of praise and thanksgiving prescribed for use in the Office of Readings of the Liturgy of the Hours on many Sundays, solemnities and feasts.

Temperance: Moderation, one of the four cardinal virtues.

Temptation: Any enticement to sin, from any source: the strivings of one's own faculties, the action of the devil, other persons, circumstances of life, etc. Temptation itself is not sin. Temptation can be avoided and overcome with the use of prudence and the help of grace.

Thanksgiving: An expression of gratitude to God for his goodness and the blessings he grants; one of the four ends of prayer.

Theism: A philosophy which admits the existence of God and the possibility of divine revelation; it is generally monotheistic and acknowledges God as transcendent and also active in the world. Because it is a philosophy rather than a system of theology derived from revelation, it does not include specifically Christian doctrines, like those concerning the Trinity, the Incarnation and Redemption.

Theodicy: From the Greek for God (*theos*) and judgment (*dike*), the study of God as he can be known by natural reason, rather than from supernatural revelation. First used by Gottfried Leibnitz (1646-1716), its primary objective is to make God's omnipotence compatible with the existence of evil.

Theological Virtues: The virtues which have God for their direct object: faith, or belief in God's infallible teaching; hope, or confidence in divine assistance; charity, or love of God. They are given to a person with grace in the first instance, through baptism and incorporation in Christ.

Theology: Knowledge of God and religion, deriving from and based on the data of divine Revelation, organized and systematized according to some kind of scientific method. It involves systematic study and presentation of the truths of divine Revelation in Sacred Scripture, tradition, and the teaching of the Church. Theology has been divided under various subject headings. Some of the major fields have been: dogmatic (systematic theology), moral, pastoral, historical, ascetical (the practice of virtue and means of attaining holiness and perfection), sacramental, and mystical (higher states of religious experience). Other subject headings include ecumenism (Christian unity, interfaith relations), ecclesiology (the nature and constitution of the Church), and Mariology (doctrine concerning the Blessed Virgin Mary), etc.

Theotokos: From the Greek for God-bearer, the preeminent title given to the Blessed Mother in the Oriental Church. This title has very ancient roots, stretching as far back as the third century but it did not become official in the Church until the Council of Ephesus in 431.

Thomism: The philosophy based on St. Thomas Aquinas (1224/5-1274), which is mandated to be the dominant philosophy used in Catholic educational institutions. (*See also* **Neo-Scholasticism** and **Scholasticism**.)

Tithing: Contribution of a portion of one's income, originally one-tenth, for purposes of religion and charity. The practice is mentioned 46 times in the Bible. In early Christian times, tithing was adopted in continuance of Old Testament practices of the Jewish people, and the earliest positive church legislation on the subject was enacted in 567. Catholics are bound in conscience to contribute to the support of their church, but the manner in which they do so is not fixed by law. Tithing, which amounts to a pledged contribution of a portion of one's income, has aroused new attention in recent years in the United States.

Titular Sees: Dioceses where the Church once flourished but which now exist only in name or title. Bishops without a territorial or residential diocese of their own; e.g., auxiliary bishops, are given titular sees. There are more than 2,000 titular sees; 16 of them are in the United States.

Transfinalization, Transignification: Terms coined to express the sign value of consecrated bread and wine with respect to the presence and action of Christ in the Eucharistic sacrifice and the spiritually vivifying purpose of the Eucharistic banquet in Holy Communion. The theory behind the terms has strong undertones of existential and "sign" philosophy, and has been criticized for its openness to interpretation at variance with the doctrine of transubstantiation and the abiding presence of Christ under the appearances of bread and wine after the sacrifice of the Mass and Communion have been completed. The terms, if used as substitutes for transubstantiation, are unacceptable; if they presuppose transubstantiation, they are acceptable as clarifications of its meaning.

Transubstantiation: "The way Christ is made present in this sacrament (Holy Eucharist) is none other than by the change of the whole substance of the bread into his Body, and of the whole substance of the wine into his Blood (in the Consecration at Mass), this unique and wonderful change the Catholic Church rightly calls transubstantiation" (encyclical *Mysterium Fidei* of Paul VI, Sept. 3, 1965). The first official use of the term was made by the Fourth Council of the Lateran in 1215. Authoritative teaching on the subject was issued by the Council of Trent.

Treasury of the Church: The superabundant merits of Christ and the saints from which the Church draws to confer spiritual benefits, such as indulgences.

Triduum: A three-day series of public or private devotions.

U-Z

Ultramontanism: The movement found primarily in France during the 19th century that advocated a strong sense of devotion and service to the Holy See. Generally considered a reaction to the anti-papal tendencies of Gallicanism, its name was derived from the Latin for "over the mountains," a reference to the Alps, beyond which rested Rome and the Holy See.

Unction: From the Latin, *ungere*, meaning to anoint or smear, a term used to denote the Sacrament of the Sick (or the Anointing of the Sick); it was more commonly termed Extreme Unction and was given as an anointing to a person just before death.

Universal Law: See **Law**.

Urbi et Orbi: A Latin phrase meaning "To the City and to the World" that is a blessing given by the Holy Father. Normally, the first *Urbi et Orbi* delivered by a pontiff is immediately after his election by the College of Cardinals. This is a blessing accompanied by a short address to the crowds in St. Peter's Square and to the world; frequently, as with Pope John Paul II in 1978, it is delivered in as many languages as possible. The pope also delivers an *Urbi et Orbi* each year at Christmas and at Easter.

Usury: Excessive interest charged for the loan and use of money; a violation of justice.

Vagi: A Latin word meaning wanderers that is used to describe any homeless person with no fixed residence.

Veni Creator Spiritus: A Latin phrase, meaning "Come, Creator Spirit" that is part of a hymn sung to the Holy Spirit. The hymn invokes the presence of the Holy Spirit and was perhaps first composed by Rabanus Maurus (776-856). The hymn is commonly sung as part of the Divine Office, papal elections, episcopal consecrations, ordinations, councils, synods, canonical elections, and confirmations.

Venial Sin: *See under* **Sin**.

Veronica: A word resulting from the combination of a Latin word for true, *vera*, and a Greek word for image, *eikon*, designating a likeness of the face of Christ or the name of a woman said to have given him a cloth on which he caused an imprint of his face to appear. The veneration at Rome of a likeness depicted on cloth dates from about the end of the 10th century; it figured in a popular devotion during the Middle Ages, and in the Holy Face devotion practiced since the 19th century. A faint, indiscernible likeness said to be of this kind is preserved in St. Peter's Basilica. The origin of the likeness is uncertain, and the identity of the woman is unknown. Before the 14th century, there were no known artistic representations of an incident concerning a woman who wiped the face of Christ with a piece of cloth while he was carrying the cross to Calvary.

Vespers: From the Latin for evening, the evening service of the Divine Office, also known as Evening Prayer, or among Anglicans as Evensong.

Viaticum: Holy Communion given to those in danger of death. The word, derived from Latin, means provision for a journey through death to life hereafter.

Vicar Forane: A Latin term meaning "deputy outside" that is applied to the priest given authority by the local bishop over a certain area or region of the diocese.

Vicar General: A priest or bishop appointed by the bishop of a diocese to serve as his deputy, with ordinary executive power, in the administration of the diocese.

Vicar, Judicial: The title given to the chief judge and head of the tribunal of a diocese.

Virginity: Observance of perpetual sexual abstinence. The state of virginity, which is embraced for the love of God by religious with a public vow or by others with a private vow, was singled out for high praise by Christ (Mt 19:10-12) and has always been so regarded by the Church. In the encyclical *Sacra Virginitas*, Pius XII stated: "Holy virginity and that perfect chastity which is consecrated to the service of God is without doubt among the most perfect treasures which the founder of the Church has left in heritage to the society which he established." Paul VI approved in 1970 a rite in which women can consecrate their virginity "to Christ and their brethren" without becoming members of a religious institute. The *Ordo Consecrationis Virginum*, a revision of a rite promulgated by Clement VII in 1596, is traceable to the Roman liturgy of about 50.

Virtue: A habit or established capability for performing good actions. Virtues are natural (acquired and increased by repeating good acts) and/or supernatural (given with grace by God).

Visions: A charism by which a specially chosen individual is able to behold a person or something that is naturally invisible. A vision should not be confused with an illusion or hallucination. Like other charisms, a vision is granted for the good of people; it should be noted, however, that they are not essential for holiness or salvation. Many saints throughout history have beheld visions, among them St. Thomas Aquinas, St. Teresa of Ávila, St. John of the Cross, and St. Francis of Assisi.

Vocation: A call to a way of life. Generally, the term applies to the common call of all persons, from God, to holiness and salvation. Specifically, it refers to particular states of life, each called a vocation, in which response is made to this universal call; viz., marriage, the religious life and/or priesthood, the single state freely chosen or accepted for the accomplishment of God's will. The term also applies to the various occupations in which persons make a living. The Church supports the freedom of each individual in choosing a particular vocation, and reserves the right to pass on the acceptability of candidates for the priesthood and religious life. Signs or indicators of particular vocations are many, including a person's talents and interests, circumstances and obligations, invitations of grace and willingness to respond thereto.

Vow: A promise made to God with sufficient knowledge and freedom, which has as its object a moral good that is possible and better than its voluntary omission. A person who professes a vow binds himself or herself by the virtue of religion to fulfill the promise. The best known examples of vows are those of poverty, chastity and obedience professed by religious (*See* Evangelical Counsels, individual entries). Public vows are made before a competent person, acting as an agent of the Church, who accepts the profession in the name of the Church, thereby giving public recognition to the person's dedication and consecration to God and divine worship. Vows of this kind are either solemn, rendering all contrary acts invalid as well as unlawful; or simple, rendering contrary acts unlawful. Solemn vows are for life; simple vows are for a definite period of time or for life. Vows professed without public recognition by the Church are called private vows. The Church, which has authority to accept and give public recognition to vows, also has authority to dispense persons from their obligations for serious reasons.

Witness, Christian: Practical testimony or evidence given by Christians of their faith in all circumstances of life — by prayer and general conduct, through good example and good works, etc.; being and acting in accordance with Christian belief; actual practice of the Christian faith.

Zeal: The expression of charity that permits one to serve God and others fully with the objective of furthering the Mystical Body of Christ.

Zucchetto: A small skullcap worn by ecclesiastics, most notably prelates and derived from the popular Italian vernacular term *zucca*, meaning a pumpkin, and used as slang for head. The Holy Father wears a white zucchetto made of watered silk; cardinals use scarlet, and bishops use purple. Priests of the monsignorial rank may wear black with purple piping. All others may wear simple black.

The Church Calendar

The calendar of the Roman Church consists of an arrangement throughout the year of a series of liturgical seasons, commemorations of divine mysteries and commemorations of saints for purposes of worship.

The key to the calendar is the central celebration of the Easter Triduum, commemorating the supreme saving act of Jesus in his death and resurrection to which all other observances and acts of worship are related.

The purposes of this calendar were outlined in the Constitution on the Sacred Liturgy (*Sacrosanctum Concilium*, Nos. 102-105) promulgated by the Second Vatican Council.

"Within the cycle of a year ... (the Church) unfolds the whole mystery of Christ, not only from his incarnation and birth until his ascension, but also as reflected in the day of Pentecost, and the expectation of a blessed, hoped-for return of the Lord.

"Recalling thus the mysteries of redemption, the Church opens to the faithful the riches of her Lord's powers and merits, so that these are in some way made present at all times, and the faithful are enabled to lay hold of them and become filled with saving grace (No. 102).

"In celebrating this annual cycle of Christ's mysteries, holy Church honors with special love the Blessed Mary, Mother of God" (No. 103).

"The Church has also included in the annual cycle days devoted to the memory of the martyrs and the other saints (who) sing God's perfect praise in heaven and offer prayers for us. By celebrating the passage of these saints from earth to heaven the Church proclaims the paschal mystery as achieved in the saints who have suffered and been glorified with Christ; she proposes them to the faithful as examples who draw all to the Father through Christ, and through their merits she pleads for God's favors (No. 104).

"In the various seasons of the year and according to her traditional discipline, the Church completes the formation of the faithful by means of pious practices for soul and body, by instruction, prayer, and works of penance and mercy (No. 105)."

The Roman Calendar

Norms for a revised calendar for the Western Church as decreed by the Second Vatican Council were approved by Paul VI in the *motu proprio Mysterii Paschalis* dated Feb. 14, 1969. The revised calendar was promulgated a month later by a decree of the Congregation for Divine Worship and went into effect Jan. 1, 1970, with provisional modifications. Full implementation of all its parts was delayed in 1970 and 1971, pending the completion of work on related liturgical texts. The U.S. bishops ordered the calendar into effect for 1972.

The Seasons

Advent: The liturgical year begins with the first Sunday of Advent, which introduces a season of four weeks or slightly less duration with the theme of expectation of the coming of Christ. During the first two weeks, the final coming of Christ as Lord and Judge at the end of the world is the focus of attention. From Dec. 17 to 24, the emphasis shifts to anticipation of the celebration of his Nativity on the solemnity of Christmas.

Advent has four Sundays. Since the 10th century, the first Sunday has marked the beginning of the liturgical year in the Western Church. In the Middle Ages, a kind of pre-Christmas fast was in vogue during the season.

Christmas Season: The Christmas season begins with the vigil of Christmas and lasts until the Sunday after Jan. 6, inclusive.

The period between the end of the Christmas season and the beginning of Lent belongs to the ordinary time of the year. Of variable length, the pre-Lenten phase of this season includes what were formerly called the Sundays after Epiphany and the suppressed Sundays of Septuagesima, Sexagesima and Quinquagesima.

Lent: The penitential season of Lent begins on Ash Wednesday, which occurs between Feb. 4 and Mar. 11, depending on the date of Easter, and lasts until the Mass of the Lord's Supper (Holy Thursday). It has six Sundays. The sixth Sunday marks the beginning of Holy Week and is known as Passion (formerly called Palm) Sunday.

The origin of Lenten observances dates back to the fourth century or earlier.

Easter Triduum: The Easter Triduum begins with evening Mass of the Lord's Supper and ends with Evening Prayer on Easter Sunday.

Easter Season: The Easter season whose theme is resurrection from sin to the life of grace, lasts for 50 days, from Easter to Pentecost. Easter, the first Sunday after the first full moon following the vernal equinox, occurs between Mar. 22 and Apr. 25. The terminal phase of the Easter season, between the solemnities of the Ascension of the Lord and Pentecost, stresses anticipation of the coming and action of the Holy Spirit.

Ordinary Time: The season of Ordinary Time begins on Monday (or Tuesday if the feast of the Baptism of the Lord is celebrated on that Monday) after the Sunday following Jan. 6 and continues until the day before Ash Wednesday, inclusive. It begins again on the Monday after Pentecost and ends on the Saturday before the first Sunday of Advent. It consists of 33 or 34 weeks. The last Sunday is celebrated as the Solemnity of Christ the King. The overall purpose of the season is to elaborate the themes of salvation history.

The various liturgical seasons are characterized in part by the scriptural readings and Mass prayers assigned to each of them. During Advent, for example, the readings are messianic; during the Easter season, from the Acts of the Apostles, chronicling the Resurrection and the original proclamation of Christ by the Apostles, and from the Gospel of John; during Lent, baptismal and penitential passages. Mass prayers reflect the meaning and purpose of the various seasons.

Commemorations of Saints

The commemorations of saints are celebrated concurrently with the liturgical seasons and feasts of our Lord. Their purpose is to illustrate the paschal mysteries as reflected in the lives of saints, to honor them as heroes of holiness, and to appeal for their intercession.

In line with revised regulations, some former feasts were either abolished or relegated to observance in particular places by local option for one of two reasons: (1) lack of sufficient historical evidence for observance of the feasts; or, (2) lack of universal significance.

The commemoration of a saint, as a general rule, is observed on the day of death (*dies natalis*, day of birth to glory with God in heaven). Exceptions to this rule include the feasts of St. John the Baptist, who is honored on the day of his birth; Sts. Basil the Great and Gregory Nazianzen; and the brother Saints, Cyril and Methodius, who are commemorated in joint feasts. Application of this general rule in the revised calendar resulted in date changes of some observances.

Sundays and Other Holy Days

Sunday is the original Christian feast day and holy day of obligation because of the unusually significant events of salvation history which took place and are commemorated on the first day of the week viz., the Resurrection of Christ, the key event of his life and the fundamental fact of Christianity; and the descent of the Holy Spirit upon the Apostles on Pentecost, the birthday of the Church. The transfer of observance of the Lord's Day from the Sabbath to Sunday was made in apostolic times. The Mass and Liturgy of the Hours (Divine Office) of each Sunday reflect the themes and set the tones of the various liturgical seasons.

Holy days of obligation are special occasions on which Catholics who have reached the age of reason are seriously obliged, as on Sundays, to assist at Mass: they are also to refrain from work and involvement with business that impedes participation in divine worship and the enjoyment of appropriate rest and relaxation.

The holy days of obligation observed in the U.S. are: Christmas, the Nativity of Jesus, Dec. 25; Solemnity of Mary the Mother of God, Jan. 1; Ascension of the Lord; Assumption of Blessed Mary the Virgin, Aug. 15; All Saints' Day, Nov. 1; Immaculate Conception of Blessed Mary the Virgin, Dec. 8.

The precept to attend Mass is abrogated in the U.S.

whenever the Solemnity of Mary, the Assumption, or All Saints falls on a Saturday or Monday (1991 decree of U.S. bishops; approved by Holy See July 4, 1992, and effective Jan. 1, 1993).

In addition to these, there are four other holy days of obligation prescribed in the general law of the Church which are not so observed in the U.S.: Epiphany, Jan. 6; St. Joseph, Mar. 19; Corpus Christi; Sts. Peter and Paul, June 29. The solemnities of Epiphany and Corpus Christi are transferred to a Sunday in countries where they are not observed as holy days of obligation.

Solemnities, Feasts, Memorials

Categories of observances according to dignity and manner of observance are: solemnities, principal days in the calendar (observance begins with Evening Prayer I of the preceding day; some have their own vigil Mass); feasts (celebrated within the limits of the natural day); obligatory memorials (celebrated throughout the Church); optional memorials (observable by choice).

Fixed observances are those that are regularly celebrated on the same calendar day each year.

Movable observances are those that are not observed on the same calendar day each year. Examples of these are Easter (the first Sunday after the first full moon following the vernal equinox), Ascension (40 days after Easter), Pentecost (50 days after Easter), Trinity Sunday (first after Pentecost), Christ the King (last Sunday of the liturgical year).

Weekdays, Days of Prayer

Weekdays are those on which no proper feast or vigil is celebrated in the Mass or Liturgy of the Hours (Divine Office). On such days, the Mass may be that of the preceding Sunday, which expresses the liturgical spirit of the season, an optional memorial, a votive Mass, or a Mass for the dead. weekdays of Advent and Lent are in a special category of their own.

Days of Prayer: Dioceses, at times to be designated by local bishops, should observe "days or periods of prayer for the fruits of the earth, prayer for human rights and equality, prayer for world justice and peace, and penitential observance outside of Lent." So stated the Instruction on Particular Calendars (No. 331) issued by the Congregation for the Sacraments and Divine Worship June 24, 1970.

These days are contemporary equivalents of what were formerly called ember and rogation days.

Ember days originated at Rome about the fifth century, probably as Christian replacements for seasonal festivals of agrarian cults. They were observances of penance, thanksgiving, and petition for divine blessing on the various seasons; they also were occasions of special prayer for clergy to be ordained. These days were observed four times a year.

Rogation days originated in France about the fifth century. They were penitential in character and also occasions of prayer for a bountiful harvest and protection against evil.

Days and Times of Penance

Fridays throughout the year and the season of Lent are penitential times.

Abstinence: Catholics in the U.S., from the age of 14 throughout life, are obliged to abstain from meat on

Ash Wednesday, the Fridays of Lent and Good Friday. The law forbids the use of meat, but not of eggs, the products of milk or condiments made of animal fat. Permissible are soup flavored with meat, meat gravy and sauces. The obligation to abstain from meat is not in force on days celebrated as solemnities (e.g., Christmas, Sacred Heart).

Fasting: Catholics in the U.S., from the day after their 18th birthday to the day after their 59th birthday, are also obliged to fast on Ash Wednesday and Good Friday. The law allows only one full meal a day, but does not prohibit the taking of some food in the morning and evening, observing as far as quantity and quality are concerned approved local custom. The order of meals is optional, i.e., the full meal may be taken in the evening instead of at midday. Also: (1) The combined quantity of food taken at the two lighter meals should not exceed the quantity taken at the full meal; (2) The drinking of ordinary liquids does not break the fast.

Obligation: There is a general obligation to do penance for sins committed and for the remission of punishment resulting from sin. Substantial observance of fasting and abstinence, prescribed for the community of the Church, is a matter of serious obligation; it allows, however, for alternate ways of doing penance (e.g., works of charity, prayer and prayer-related practices, almsgiving).

Readings at Mass

Scriptural readings for Masses on Sundays and holy days are indicated under the appropriate dates in the calendar pages for the year 2006-07. The Year B cycle was prescribed for Sunday Masses in liturgical year 2006, beginning Nov. 27, 2005 to Nov. 26, 2006. The Year C cycle is prescribed for Masses on Sundays in liturgical year 2007, beginning Dec. 3, 2006, to Nov. 25, 2007. The Year Two cycle of weekday readings is prescribed for the year 2006.

Monthly Prayer Intentions

Intentions chosen and recommended by Pope Benedict XVI to the prayers of the faithful and circulated by the Apostleship of Prayer are given for each month of the calendar. Pope John Paul II expressed his desire that all Catholics make these intentions their own "in the certainty of being united with the Holy Father and praying according to his intentions and desires."

Celebrations in U.S. Particular Calendar

The General Norms for the Liturgical Year and the Calendar, issued in 1969 and published along with the General Roman Calendar for the Universal Church, noted that the calendar consists of the General Roman Calendar used by the entire Church and of particular calendars used in particular churches (nations or dioceses) or in families of religious.

The particular calendar for the U.S. contains the following celebrations. **January:** 4, Elizabeth Ann Seton; 5, John Neumann; 6, Bl. André Bessette. **March:** 3, Katharine Drexel. **May:** 10, Bl. Damien DeVeuster; 15, Isidore the Farmer. **July:** 1, Bl. Junípero Serra; 4, Independence Day; 14, Bl. Kateri Tekakwitha. **August:** 18, Jane Frances de Chantal. **September:** 9, Peter Claver. **October:** 6, Bl. Marie-Rose Durocher; 19, Isaac Jogues and John de Brébeuf and Companions; 20, Paul of the Cross. **November:** 13, Frances Xavier Cabrini; 18, Rose Philippine Duchesne; 23, Bl. Miguel Agustín Pro; fourth Thursday, Thanksgiving Day. **December:** 9, Juan Diego; 12, Our Lady of Guadalupe.

TABLE OF MOVABLE FEASTS

Year	Ash Wed.	Easter	Ascension	Pentecost	Weeks of Ordinary Time				First Sunday of Advent
					Before Lent		After Pentct.		
					Week	Ends	Week	Ends	
2006	Mar. 1	Apr. 16	May 25	June 4	8	Feb. 28	9	June 5	Dec. 3
2007	Feb. 21	Apr. 8	May 17	May 27	7	Feb. 20	8	May 28	Dec. 2
2008	Feb. 6	Mar. 23	May 1	May 11	4	Feb. 5	6	May 12	Nov. 30
2009	Feb. 25	Apr. 12	May 21	May 31	7	Feb. 24	9	June 1	Nov. 29
2010	Feb. 17	Apr. 4	May 13	May 23	6	Feb. 16	8	May 24	Nov. 28
2011	Mar. 9	Apr. 24	June 2	June 12	9	Mar. 8	11	June 13	Nov. 27
2012	Feb. 22	Apr. 8	May 17	May 27	7	Feb. 21	8	May 28	Dec. 2
2013	Feb. 13	Mar. 31	May 9	May 19	5	Feb. 12	7	May 20	Dec. 1
2014	Mar. 5	Apr. 20	May 29	June 8	8	Mar. 4	10	June 9	Nov. 30
2015	Feb. 18	Apr. 5	May 14	May 24	6	Feb. 17	8	May 25	Nov. 29
2016	Feb. 10	Mar. 27	May 5	May 15	5	Feb. 9	7	May 16	Nov. 27
2017	Mar. 1	Apr. 16	May 25	June 4	8	Feb. 28	9	June 5	Dec. 3
2018	Feb. 14	Apr. 1	May 10	May 20	6	Feb. 13	7	May 21	Dec. 2
2019	Mar. 6	Apr. 21	May 30	June 9	8	Mar. 5	10	June 1	Dec. 1
2020	Feb. 26	Apr. 12	May 21	May 31	7	Feb. 25	9	June 1	Nov. 29
2021	Feb. 17	Apr. 4	May 13	May 23	6	Feb. 16	8	May 24	Nov. 28
2022	Mar. 2	Apr. 17	May 26	June 5	8	Mar. 1	10	June 6	Nov. 27
2023	Feb. 22	Apr. 9	May 18	May 28	7	Feb. 21	8	May 29	Dec. 3
2024	Feb. 14	Mar. 31	May 9	May 19	6	Feb. 13	7	May 20	Dec. 1
2025	Mar. 5	Apr. 20	May 29	June 8	8	Mar. 4	10	June 9	Nov. 30

2007 CALENDAR

January 2007

General: For all Christians: may they grow in unity and love in order to build reconciliation and peace among all the peoples of the earth.

Missionary: For migrants: may they be recognized as persons created in the image and likeness of God and welcomed with respect and charity.

1 Mon. Octave of Christmas; Solemnity of the Blessed Virgin Mary, Mother of God; Holy Day of Obligation (Nm 6: 22-27; Gal 4:4-7; Lk 2:16-21). [Not a Holy Day of Obligation this year.]

2 Tues. Sts. Basil the Great and Gregory Nazianzus, bishops and doctors of the Church; memorial.

3 Wed. weekday. Most Holy Name of Jesus.

4 Thurs. St. Elizabeth Ann Seton, religious; memorial.

5 Fri. St. John Neumann, bishop; memorial.

6 Sat. weekday. Bl. André Bessette, religious; optional memorial.

7 Sun. Epiphany of Our Lord; solemnity. (Is 60:1-6; Eph 3:2-3a, 5-6; Mt 2:1-12)

8 Mon. Baptism of the Lord; feast (Is 42:1-4, 6-7; Acts 10:34-38; Lk 3:15-16, 21-22).

9 Tues. weekday (First week in ordinary time.)

10 Wed. weekday.

11 Thurs. weekday.

12 Fri. weekday.

13 Sat. weekday. Hilary, bishop-doctor; optional memorial.

14 Sun. Second Sunday in ordinary time (Is 62:1-5; 1 Cor 12:4-11; Jn 2:1-11).

15 Mon. weekday.

16 Tues. weekday.

17 Wed. St. Anthony, abbot; memorial.

18 Thurs. weekday. Week of Prayer for Christian Unity begins.

19 Fri. weekday.

20 Sat. weekday. St. Fabian, pope-martyr; St. Sebastian, martyr; optional memorials.

21 Sun. Third Sunday in ordinary time (Neh 8:2-4a, 5-6, 8-10; 1 Cor 12:12-30; Lk 1:1-4; 4:14-21).

22 Mon. weekday. St. Vincent, deacon, martyr; optional memorial.

23 Tues. weekday.

24 Wed. Francis de Sales, bishop-doctor; memorial.

25 Thurs. Conversion of St. Paul, apostle; feast.

26 Fri. Sts. Timothy and Titus; memorial

27 Sat. weekday. St. Angela Merici, virgin; optional memorial.

28 Sun. Fourth Sunday in ordinary time (Jer 1:4-5, 17-19; 1 Cor 13:4-13; Lk 4:21-30).

29 Mon. weekday.

30 Tue. weekday.

30 Wed. St. John Bosco, priest; memorial.

Observances: The year begins with the Solemnity of the Mother of God, a holy day of obligation, and a papal message for the World Day of Peace, Jan. 1; customary ordination of bishops by the Pope on the Solemnity of the Epiphany, Jan. 6. Week of Prayer for Christian Unity, Jan. 18 -25; National Prayer Vigil for Life and March for Life in Washington, DC, in connection with the 1973 Roe vs. Wade and Dole vs. Bolton pro-abortion decisions of the U.S. Supreme Court, Jan. 21-22. A Day of Penance shall be observed in all dioceses of the U.S. on Jan. 22 for violations to the dignity of the human person.

February 2007

General: That the earth's bounty God gave to all men be used wisely and according to principles of justice and solidarity.

Missionary: That the struggle against diseases and the great epidemics in the Third World find in a spirit of solidarity the ever more generous cooperation of governments.

1 Thurs. weekday.

2 Fri. Presentation of the Lord, feast (Mal 3:1-4; Heb 2:14-18; Lk 2: 22-40.).

3 Sat. weekday. St. Blasé, bishop-martyr; St. Ansgar, bishop; optional memorial

4 Sun. Fifth Sunday in ordinary time (Is 6: 1-2a, 3-8; 1 Cor 15: 1-11; Lk 5: 1-11)

5 Mon. St. Agatha, virgin and martyr; memorial

6 Tue. St. Paul Miki and companions, martyrs; memorial.

7 Wed. weekday.

8 Thurs. weekday. St. Jerome Emiliani, priest; Josephine Bakhita, virgin; optional memorial.

9 Fri. weekday

10 Sat. St. Scholastica, virgin; memorial.

11 Sun. Sixth Sunday in ordinary time. (Jer 17: 5-8; 1 Cor 15: 12, 16-20; Lk 6: 17, 20-26)

12 Mon. weekday.

13 Tues. weekday.

14 Wed. Sts. Cyril, monk and Methodius, bishop; memorial.

15 Thurs. weekday.

16 Fri. weekday.

17 Sat. weekday. Seven Holy Founders of the Order of Servites; optional memorial.

18 Sun. Seventh Sunday in ordinary time. (1 Sam 26: 2, 7-9, 12-13, 22-23; 1 Cor 15: 45-49; Lk 6: 27-38)

19 Mon. weekday.

20 Tue. weekday.

21 Wed. Ash Wednesday (Jl 2:12-18; 2 Cor 5: 20-6:2; Mt 6: 1-6, 16-18.) Fast and abstinence.

22 Thurs. Chair of St. Peter, apostle; feast.

23 Fri. Lenten weekday. St. Polycarp, bishop and martyr; memorial

24 Sat. Lenten weekday.

25 Sun. First Sunday of Lent (Deut 26: 4-10; Rom 10: 8-13; Lk 4:1-13.)

26 Mon. Lenten weekday.

27 Tue. Lenten weekday

28 Wed. Lenten weekday

Observances: The Presentation of the Child Jesus in the Temple, traditional day for the blessings of candles that will be used throughout the year. The Presentation of the Lord is also the World Day for Consecrated Life. Optional memorial of St. Blasé, bishop-martyr, whose intercession is sought against ailments of the throat and other evils. The Sixth Sunday of Ordinary Time (Feb. 11) is also World Day of the Sick, a day of prayer, healing and anointing of those who are ill. The Lenten Season begins with Ash Wednesday (Feb. 21) when ashes are blessed and imposed on the forehead of the faithful to remind them of their obligation to do penance for sins, to seek spiritual renewal by means of prayer, fasting, and good works. Catholics are reminded of the serious obligation to fast and abstain on those appointed days during the Lenten season.

March 2007

General: That the Word of God be more and more listened to, contemplated, loved and lived.

Missionary: That the concern of those in young Churches who train catechists, organizers and lay people at the service of the Gospel be constant.

1 Thurs. Lenten weekday.
2 Fri. Lenten weekday. Abstinence.
3 Sat. Lenten weekday. St. Katherine Drexel, virgin; optional memorial.
4 Sun. Second Sunday of Lent (Gn 15:5-12, 17-18; Phil 3:17-4:1; Lk 9:28b-36.)
5 Mon. Lenten weekday.
6 Tues. Lenten weekday.
7 Weds. Lenten weekday. Sts. Perpetua and Felicity, martyrs; optional memorial.
8 Thurs. Lenten weekday. St. John of God, religious; optional memorial.
9 Fri. Lenten weekday. Abstinence. St. Francis of Rome, religious; optional memorial.
10 Sat. Lenten weekday.
11 Sun. Third Sunday of Lent (Ex 3: 1-8a, 13-15; 1 Cor 10: 1-6, 10-12; Lk 13: 1-9)
12 Mon. Lenten weekday.
13 Tues. Lenten weekday.
14 Weds. Lenten weekday.
15 Thurs. Lenten weekday.
16 Fri. Lenten weekday.
17 Sat. Lenten weekday. Abstinence. St. Patrick, bishop; optional memorial.
18 Sun. Fourth Sunday of Lent. (Jos 5: 9a, 10-12; 2 Cor 5: 17-21; Lk 15: 1-3, 11-32.)
19 Mon. St. Joseph, husband of the Blessed Virgin Mary; solemnity.
20 Tues. Lenten weekday.
21 Weds. Lenten weekday.
22 Thurs. Lenten weekday.
23 Fri. Lenten weekday. St. Toribio, bishop; optional memorial
24 Sat. Lenten weekday.
25 Sun. Fifth Sunday of Lent. (Is 43: 16-21; Phil 3: 8-14; Jn 8: 1-11.)
26 Mon. Annunciation of the Lord; solemnity.
27 Tues. Lenten weekday.
28 Weds. Lenten weekday.
29 Thurs. Lenten weekday.
30 Fri. Lenten weekday. Abstinence
31 Sat. Lenten weekday.

Observances: The Solemnity of St. Joseph, husband of Mary, is observed Mar. 19. The Solemnity of the Annunciation is observed Mar. 25.

April 2007

General: That every Christian, letting himself be enlightened and guided by the Holy Spirit, respond with enthusiasm and fidelity to the universal call for holiness.

Missionary: That the number of priestly and religious vocations grow in North America and in the countries of the Pacific Ocean so as to adequately respond to the pastoral and missionary needs of their populations.

1 Sun. Palm Sunday of the Lord's Passion (Lk 19: 28-40; Is 50: 4-7; Phil 2: 6-11; Lk 22: 14 – 23:56.)
2 Mon. Monday of Holy Week.
3 Tues. Tuesday of Holy Week.
4 Weds. Wednesday of Holy Week.
5 Thurs. Holy Thursday. Chrism Mass in the Morning. The *Easter Triduum* begins with the evening Mass of the Lord's Supper.
6 Fri. Good Friday. The Lord's Passion. Fast and abstinence.
7 Sat. Holy Saturday. Easter Vigil.
8 Sun. Easter Sunday: Resurrection of the Lord; solemnity (Acts 10:34a, 37-43; Col 3:1-4 or 1 Cor 5:6b-8; Jn 20:1-9 or Mt 28:1-10 or [at an afternoon or evening Mass – Lk 24:13-35].)
9 Mon. Easter Monday; solemnity.
10 Tue. Easter Tuesday; solemnity.
11 Weds. Easter Wednesday; solemnity.
12 Thurs. Easter Thursday; solemnity.
13 Fri. Easter Friday; solemnity
14 Sat. Easter Saturday; solemnity
15 Sun. Second Sunday of Easter. Divine Mercy Sunday. (Acts 5: 12-16; Rv 1:9-11a, 12-13, 17-19; Jn 20:19-31.)
16 Mon. Easter Weekday
17 Tues. Easter Weekday
18 Weds. Easter Weekday
19 Thurs. Easter Weekday
20 Fri. Easter Weekday
21 Sat. Easter Weekday. St. Anselm, bishop and doctor; memorial
22 Sun. Third Sunday of Easter. (Acts 5: 27-32; 40b-41; Rev 5: 11-14; Jn 21: 1-19.)
23 Mon. Easter Weekday. St. George, martyr; St. Adalbert, bishop and martyr; optional memorials.
24 Tues. Easter Weekday. St. Fidelis, priest; optional memorial.
25 Weds. St. Mark, evangelist, feast
26 Thurs. Easter Weekday.
27 Fri. Easter Weekday.
28 Sat. Easter Weekday. St. Peter Chanel, priest-martyr; St. Louis Mary de Montfort; optional memorials.
29 Sun. Fourth Sunday of Easter. (Acts 13: 14, 43-52; Rv 7: 9, 14b-17; Jn 10: 27-30.)
30 Mon. Easter Weekday. St. Pius V, pope; optional memorial.

Observances: Holy Week—Passion Sunday also called Palm Sunday begins these most solemn and holy celebrations of the Church Year. It is on this day that the Church blesses and distributes palms commemorating our Lord's triumphal entrance into Jerusalem and it is during this celebration that the Passion is read for the first time during Holy Week. Monday, Tuesday, and Wednesday of Holy Week are preparatory days leading to the *Sacred Triduum*. The Sacred Triduum begins with the Mass of the Lord's Supper on Holy Thursday evening. Good Friday commemorates the Passion of our Lord Jesus. Easter Sunday is the day when the Holy Father delivers the traditional *Urbe et Orbi* address, to Rome and to the World.

May 2007

General: That every Christian, following the example of the Virgin Mary, always heed the signs of the Lord in their lives and let themselves be guided by the Word of God.

Missionary: That the lands of Mission never be found lacking in good and enlightened teachers in the major seminaries and institutes of consecrated life.

1 Tues. St. Joseph, the Worker; memorial
2 Weds. St. Athanasius, bishop-doctor; memorial.
3 Thurs. Sts. Philip and James, apostles; feast.
4 Fri. Easter weekday.
5 Sat. Easter weekday.
6 Sun. Fourth Sunday of Easter (Acts 15: 21-27; Rv 21 1-5a; Jn 13: 31-33a, 34-35.) World Day of Prayer for Vocations
7 Mon. Easter weekday.
8 Tues. Easter weekday.
9 Weds. weekday.
10 Thurs. Easter weekday.
11 Fri. Easter weekday. Bl. Damien Joseph deVeuster of Molokai, priest; optional memorial.
12 Sat. Easter weekday. Sts. Nereus and Achilleus, martyrs; St. Pancras, martyr; optional memorials.
13 Sun. Fifth Sunday of Easter. (Acts 15: 1-2, 22-29; Rv 21: 10-14, 22-23; Jn 14: 23-29.)
14 Mon. Easter weekday.
15 Tues. Easter weekday. St. Isidore the Farmer; optional memorial.
16 Weds. Easter weekday.
17 Thurs. Easter weekday. Ascension of our Lord; solemnity. Holy Day of obligation
18 Fri. Easter weekday. John I, pope and martyr; optional memorial.
19 Sat. Easter weekday.
20 Sun. Seventh Sunday of Easter (Acts 7: 55-60; Rv 22: 12 -14, 16-17, 20; Jn 17: 20-26
21 Mon. Easter weekday.
22 Tues. Easter weekday. St. Rita of Cascia, religious; optional memorial.
23 Weds. Easter weekday.
24 Thurs. Easter weekday.
25 Fri. Easter weekday. St. Bede the Venerable, doctor; St. Gregory VII, pope; St. Mary Magdalene de Pazzi, religious; optional memorials.
26 Sat. Easter weekday. St. Philip Neri, priest; memorial
27 Sun. Pentecost Sunday; solemnity. (Acts 2: 1-11; 1 Cor. 12: 3b-7, 12-13; or Gal 5: 16-25; Jn 20: 19-23 or Jn 15: 26-27; 16: 12 -15.)
28 Mon. weekday.
29 Tues weekday.
30 Weds. weekday.
31 Thurs. Visitation of the Blessed Virgin Mary to Elizabeth; feast.

Observances: The month of May begins with the celebration of St. Joseph the Worker on May 1 reminding society of the dignity of work. Blessed Damien, the Leper priest, is celebrated on May 10. The Solemnity of the Ascension celebrated May 17 (transferred to Sunday in some dioceses) is a Holy Day of Obligation. The Easter Season is completed with the celebration of the Feast of Pentecost (May 27), the celebration of the gift of the Holy Spirit given to the apostles and to the Church. Also, the month of May is traditionally dedicated to our Blessed Mother. Customary Marian devotions include the recitation of the Rosary and the Litany of Loretto, Marian processions.

June 2007

General: That the Lord protect mariners and all those who are involved in activities on the seas.

Missionary: That through its presence and action the Church in North Africa be a witness of God's love for every individual and people.

1 Fri. St. Justin, martyr; memorial.
2 Sat. weekday. Sts. Marcellinus and Peter, martyrs; optional memorial.
3 Sun. Most Holy Trinity; solemnity (Prv 8: 22-31; Rom 5: 1-5; Jn 16: 12 -15.)
4 Mon. weekday. Ninth Week in ordinary time
5 Tues. St. Boniface, bishop and martyr; memorial.
6 Weds. weekday. St. Norbert, bishop; optional memorial
7 Thurs. weekday.
8 Fri. weekday.
9 Sat. weekday. St. Ephrem, deacon and doctor; optional memorial.
10 Sun. The Most Holy Body and Blood of Christ (Corpus Christi); solemnity (Gn 14: 18-20; 1 Cor 11: 23-26; Lk 9: 11b-17.)
11 Mon. St. Barnabas, apostle; memorial
12 Tues. St. Anthony of Padua, priest-doctor; memorial.
13 Weds. weekday. Tenth Week of ordinary time.
14 Thurs. weekday.
15 Fri. Most Sacred Heart of Jesus; solemnity.
16 Sat. Immaculate Heart of Mary; memorial.
17 Sun. Eleventh Sunday in ordinary time. (2 Sam 12: 7-10, 13; Gal 2: 16, 19-21; Lk 7: 36–8: 3.)
18 Mon. weekday.
19 Tues. weekday. St. Romuald, abbot; optional memorial.
20 Weds. weekday.
21 Thurs. St. Aloysius Gonzaga, religious; memorial.
22 Fri. weekday. St. Paulinus of Nola, bishop; Sts. John Fisher, bishop and martyr; Thomas More, martyr; optional memorials.
23 Sat. weekday. Blessed Virgin Mary
24 Sun. Nativity of St. John the Baptist; solemnity. (Is 49:1-6; Acts 13:22-26; Lk 1:57-66, 80.)
25 Mon. weekday. Twelfth Week in ordinary time
26 Tues. weekday.
27 Weds. St. Cyril of Alexandria, bishop and doctor; optional memorial.
28 Thurs. St. Irenaeus, bishop-martyr; memorial.
29 Fri. weekday. Sts. Peter and Paul, apostles; solemnity.
30 Sat. First Martyrs of the Church of Rome; optional memorial.

Observances: The Feast of the Most Holy Trinity is celebrated on June 3. This great feast of the Triune God is followed by the Feast the Body and Blood of Christ (Corpus Christi) celebrated on June 10. It is the customary to gather for a Corpus Christi procession to venerate the Body of Christ at special altars prepared near the Cathedral or parish church. The procession concludes with Benediction of the Blessed Sacrament.

This month is also the celebration of the Most Sacred Heart of Jesus on June 15 followed by the celebration of the Immaculate Hear of Mary. The Feast of the Birth of John the Baptist is celebrated on June 24 followed by the Feast of Sts. Peter and Paul on June 29.

July 2007

General: That every citizen as an individual and in a group actively participate in the life and management of public affairs.

Missionary: That every Christian, conscious of his missionary duty, actively help those involved in the evangelization of peoples.

1 Sun. Thirteenth Sunday in ordinary time. (1 Kgs 19: 16b, 19-21; Gal 5: 1, 13-18; Lk 9:51-62.)

2 Mon. weekday.

3 Tues. weekday. St. Thomas, apostle; feast.

4 Weds. weekday. St. Elizabeth of Portugal; optional memorial. Proper Mass for Independence Day.

5 Thurs. weekday. St. Anthony Maria Zaccaria, priest; optional memorial.

6 Fri. weekday. St. Maria Goretti, virgin and martyr; optional memorial.

7 Sat. weekday. Blessed Virgin Mary

8 Sun. Fourteenth Sunday in ordinary time. (Is 66: 1-14c; Gal 6: 14-18; Lk 10: 1-12, 17-20.)

9 Mon. weekday.

10 Tues. weekday.

11 Weds. St. Benedict, abbot; memorial.

12 Thurs. weekday.

13 Fri. weekday. St. Henry; optional memorial.

14 Sat. Bl. Kateri Tekawitha, virgin; memorial.

15 Sun. Fifteenth Sunday in ordinary time. (Dt 30: 10-14; Col 1: 15-20; Lk 10: 25-37.)

16 Mon. weekday. Our Lady of Mt. Carmel; optional memorial

17 Tues. weekday.

18 Weds. weekday. St. Camillus de Lellis, priest; optional memorial.

19 Thurs. weekday.

20 Fri. weekday. St. Apollinarus, bishop and martyr; optional memorial.

21 Sat. weekday. St. Lawrence of Brandisi, priest-doctor; optional memorial.

22 Sun. Sixteenth Sunday in ordinary time. (Gn 18: 1-10a; Col 1: 24-28; Lk 10: 38-42.)

23 Mon. weekday. St. Bridget of Sweden, religious; optional memorial.

24 Tues. weekday.

25 Weds. James, apostle and martyr; feast.

26 Thurs. Joachim and Anne, parents of the Blessed Virgin Mary; memorial.

27 Fri. weekday.

28 Sat. weekday. Blessed Virgin Mary

29 Sun. Seventeenth Sunday in ordinary time. (Gn 18: 20-32; Col 2: 12-14; Lk 11:1-13.)

30 Mon. weekday. St. Peter Chrysologus, bishop and doctor; optional memorial.

31 Tues. St. Ignatius of Loyola, priest; memorial.

Observances: St. Thomas the apostles is observed on July 3; St. Maria Goretti, July 6; St. Benedict, the founder of western monasticism and patron saint of Europe, July 11; Bl. Kateri Tekawitha, July 14; the feast of St. James is celebrated on July 25 followed by the memorial of the Sts. Joachim and Anne, parents of the Blessed Mother. The month of July concludes with the celebration of the memorial of St. Ignatius of Loyola, founder of the Society of Jesus, the Jesuits.

Independence Day, July 4, is observed with a special Mass for celebration in the United States.

August 2007

General: That all those going through difficult times and trials find in Christ the light and support to discover true happiness.

Missionary: That the Church in China be witness to an always greater internal cohesion and show effective and visible communion with the Successor of Peter.

1 Weds. St. Alphonsus Ligouri, bishop-doctor; memorial.

2 Thurs. weekday. Sts. Eusebius of Vercelli, bishop and Peter Julian Eymard, priest; optional memorials.

3 Fri. weekday.

4 Sat. St. John Mary Vianney, priest; memorial.

5 Sun. Eighteenth Sunday in ordinary time. (Eccl 1:2, 2: 21-23; Col. 3: 1-5, 9-11; Lk 12: 13-21.)

6 Mon Transfiguration of the Lord; feast.

7 Tues. weekday. St. Cajetan, priest; St. Sixtus and Companions, martyrs; optional memorials.

8 Weds. St. Dominic, priest; memorial.

9 Thurs. weekday. St. Teresa Benedicta of the Cross, virgin and martyr; optional memorial.

10 Fri. St. Lawrence, deacon and martyr; memorial.

11 Sat. St. Clare, virgin; memorial.

12 Sun. Nineteenth Sunday in ordinary time (Wis 18: 6-9; Heb 11: 1-2, 8-19; Lk 12:32-48.)

13 Mon. weekday. Sts. Pontian and Hippolytus, martyrs; optional memorial.

14 Tues. St. Maximilian Mary Kolbe, priest and martyr; memorial.

15 Weds. Assumption of the Blessed Virgin Mary; solemnity.

16 Thurs. weekday. St. Stephen of Hungary; optional memorial.

17 Fri. weekday.

18 Sat. weekday. St. Jane Frances de Chantal, religious; optional memorial.

19 Sun. Twentieth Sunday in ordinary time (Jer 38:4-6, 8-10; Heb 12: 1-4; Lk 12:49-53.)

20 Mon. St. Bernard, abbot; memorial.

21 Tues. St. Pius X, pope; memorial.

22 Weds. Queenship of the Blessed Virgin Mary; memorial.

23 Thurs. weekday. St. Rose of Lima, virgin; optional memorial.

24 Fri. St. Bartholomew, apostle; feast.

25 Sat. weekday. Sts. Louis of France and Joseph Calasanz, priest; optional memorials.

26 Sun. Twenty-first Sunday of ordinary time (Is 66: 18-21; Heb 12: 5-7, 11-13; Lk 13: 22-30.)

27 Mon. St. Monica; memorial

28 Tues. St. Augustine, bishop and doctor; memorial.

29 Weds. Martyrdom of St. John the Baptist; memorial.

30 Thurs. weekday.

31 Fri. weekday.

Observances: St. Alphonsus Liguori, doctor of the Church and moral theologian, Aug. 1; St. John Vianney, patron saint of parish priests, Aug. 4; The Feast of the Transfiguration of the Lord, Aug. 6; St. Dominic, founder of the Dominicans, Aug, 8; St. Teresa Benedicta of the Cross, Aug. 9. St. Clare, foundress of the Poor Clares, Aug. 11; St. Maximilian Mary Kolbe, Aug. 14. The Feast of the Assumption of the Blessed Virgin Mary, Aug. 15; The Queenship of the Blessed Virgin Mary, Aug. 22. St. Augustine, Aug. 28 and the Martyrdom of St. John the Baptist, Aug. 29.

September 2007

General: That the ecumenical assembly in Sibiu (Romania) contribute to the growth of unity among Christians for which the Lord prayed at the Last Supper.

Missionary: That when joyfully joining Christ, all missionary men and women know how to overcome the difficulties they encounter in their every day life.

1 Sat. weekday.
2 Sun. Twenty-second Sunday in ordinary time (Sir 3:17-18, 20, 28-29; Heb 12:18-19, 22-24a; Lk 14:1, 7-14.)
3 Mon. Gregory the Great, pope and doctor; memorial. Labor Day. Special Mass for the Blessings of Human Labor.
4 Tues. weekday.
5 Weds. weekday.
6 Thurs. weekday.
7 Fri. weekday.
8 Sat. The Nativity of the Blessed Virgin Mary; feast.
9 Sun. Twenty-third Sunday in ordinary time. (Wis 9:13-18b; Phlm 9-10, 12-17; Lk 14:25-33.)
10 Mon. weekday.
11 Tues. weekday.
12 Weds. weekday. Holy Name of Mary; optional memorial.
13 Thurs. St. John Chrysostom, bishop-doctor; memorial.
14 Fri. Exaltation of the Holy Cross; feast.
15 Sat. Our Lady of Sorrows; memorial.
16 Sun. Twenty-fourth Sunday in ordinary time (Ex 32:7-11, 13-14; 1 Tim 1:12-17; Lk 15:1-32.)
17 Mon. St. Robert Bellarmine, bishop and doctor; memorial.
18 Tues. weekday.
19 Weds. weekday. St. Januarius, bishop-martyr; optional memorial.
20 Thurs. St. Andrew Kim Taegon, priest-martyr, St. Paul Chong Hasang, martyr, and Companions, martyrs; memorial.
21 Fri. St. Matthew, apostle and evangelist; feast.
22 Sat. weekday.
23 Sun. Twenty-fifth Sunday in ordinary time (Am 8:4-7; 1 Tim 2:1-8; Lk 16:1-13.)
24 Mon. weekday.
25 Tues. weekday.
26 Weds. Weekday. Sts. Cosmas and Damian, martyrs; optional memorial.
27 Thurs. St. Vincent de Paul, priest; memorial.
28 Fri. weekday. St. Lawrence Ruiz and companions; martyrs. St. Wenceslaus, martyr; optional memorials.
29 Sat. Sts. Michael, Gabriel, and Raphael, archangels; feast.
30 Sun. Twenty-sixth Sunday in ordinary time. (Am 6:1a, 4-7; 1 Tm 6:11-16; Lk 16:19-31.)

Observances: The Nativity of the Blessed Virgin Mary, Sept. 8; St. John Chrysostom, doctor of the Church, Sept. 13; Exaltation of the Holy Cross, Sept. 14; Our Lady of Sorrows, Sept. 15; St. Matthew, apostle and evangelist Sept. 21; St. Vincent de Paul, founder of the Vincentians and the Daughters of Charity, Sept. 27; Sts. Michael, Gabriel, and Raphael, archangels, Sept. 29.

Labor Day is celebrated Sept. 4 with a special Mass for the blessing of human labor.

October 2007

General: That Christians who live as a minority find the strength and courage to live their faith and persevere in being its witness.

Missionary: That World Missionary Day be a favorable occasion to elicit an ever deeper missionary consciousness in every baptized person.

1 Mon. St. Therese of the Child Jesus, virgin and doctor; memorial.
2 Tues. The Guardian Angels; memorial.
3 Weds. weekday.
4 Thurs. St. Francis of Assisi, religious; memorial.
5 Fri. weekday.
6 Sat. weekday. St. Bruno, priest and Bl. Marie Rose Durocher, virgin; optional memorials.
7 Sun. Twenty-seventh Sunday in ordinary time (Heb 1:2-3; 2:2-4; 2 Tim 1:6-8, 13-14; Lk 17:5-10.)
8 Mon. weekday.
9 Tues. weekday. St. Denis and Companions, martyrs; John Leonardi, priest; optional memorials.
10 Weds. weekday.
11 Thurs. weekday.
12 Fri. weekday.
13 Sat. weekday. Blessed Virgin Mary
14 Sun. Twenty-eighth Sunday in ordinary time (2 Kgs 5:14-17; 2 Tim 2:8-13; Lk 17:11-19.)
15 Mon. St. Teresa of Jesus, virgin and doctor; memorial.
16 Tues. weekday. St. Hedwig, religious; St. Margaret Mary Alacoque, virgin; optional memorials.
17 Weds. St. Ignatius of Antioch, bishop-martyr; memorial.
18 Thurs. St. Luke, evangelist; feast.
19 Fri. St. John de Brebeuf, Isaac Jogues and companions, martyrs; memorial
20 Sat. weekday. St. Paul of the Cross; optional memorial.
21 Sun. Twenty-ninth Sunday in ordinary time. (Ex 17:8-13; 2 Tim 3:14-4:2; Lk 18:1-8.)
22 Mon. weekday.
23 Tues. weekday. St. John of Capistrano, priest; optional memorial
24 Weds. weekday. St. Anthony Mary Claret, bishop; optional memorial.
25 Thurs. weekday.
26 Fri. weekday.
27 Sat. weekday. Blessed Virgin Mary
28 Sun. Thirtieth Sunday in ordinary time. (Sir 35:12-14, 16-18; 2 Tim 4:6-8, 16-18; Lk 18:9-14.)
29 Mon. weekday.
30 Tues. weekday.
31 Weds. weekday.

Observances: St. Therese of the Child Jesus, doctor of the Church, Oct.1; St. Francis of Assisi, founder of the Franciscan Order, Oct. 4; St. Teresa of Jesus, doctor of the Church, reformer of the Carmelite Order, Oct. 15; St. Ignatius of Antioch, Oct. 17; St. Luke, evangelist, Oct. 18. The North American Martyrs, Oct. 19. Sts. Simon and Jude, apostles, Oct. 28.

Respect Life Sunday is celebrated this month calling the nation to a deeper respect for all human life from natural conception to natural death. Mission Sunday is observed during the month, with appeals for prayer and financial support for persons and projects involved in the ministry of evangelization at home and abroad. Vocation Awareness Sunday is also celebrated this month calling to mind the various vocations in the life of the Church with particular attention to priestly and religious vocations.

November 2007

General: That those involved in medical research and in making laws always harbor a profound respect for human life from its beginning to its natural conclusion.

Missionary: That the spirit of reconciliation and peace expand on the Korean peninsula.

1 Thurs. All Saints; solemnity.
2 Fri. Commemoration of All the Faithful Departed. All Souls Day.
3 Sat. weekday. St. Martin de Porres, religious; optional memorial.
4 Sun. Thirty-first Sunday in ordinary time. (Wis 11:22-12: 2; 2 Thes 1:11-22; Lk 19:1-10.)
5 Mon. weekday.
6 Tues. weekday.
7 Weds. weekday.
8 Thurs. weekday.
9 Fri. Dedication of the Basilica of St. John Lateran in Rome; feast
10 Sat. Leo the Great, pope-doctor; memorial.
11 Sun. Thirty-second Sunday in ordinary time (2 Mac. 7:1-2, 9-14; 2 Thes. 2:16-3:5; Lk. 20:27-38.)
12 Mon. St. Josaphat, bishop and martyr; memorial
13 Tues. St. Frances Xavier Cabrini, virgin; memorial.
14 Weds. weekday.
15 Thurs. weekday. St. Albert the Great, bishop-doctor; optional memorial.
16 Fri. weekday. St. Margaret of Scotland, virgin; Gertrude, virgin; optional memorials
17 Sat. St. Elizabeth of Hungary, religious; memorial.
18 Sun. Thirty-third Sunday in ordinary time. (Mal 3:19-20a; 2 Thes 3:7-12; Lk 21:5-19.)
19 Mon. weekday.
20 Tues. weekday.
21 Weds. Presentation of the Blessed Virgin Mary; memorial.
22 Thurs. St. Cecilia, virgin-martyr; memorial. Thanksgiving Day, proper Mass.
23 Fri. weekday. St. Clement, pope; St. Columban, abbot; St. Miguel Pro, priest-martyr; optional memorials
24 Sat. St. Andrew Dung-Lac, priest-martyr and Companions, martyrs; memorials.
25 Sun. Our Lord Jesus Christ the King; solemnity (2 Sm. 5:1-3; Col 1:12-20; Lk. 23:35-43.)
26 Mon. weekday.
27 Tues. weekday.
28 Weds. weekday.
29 Thurs. weekday.
30 Fri. St. Andrew, apostle and martyr; feast.

Observances: All Saints Day, Nov. 1; All Souls Day, Nov. 2; Frances Xavier Cabrini, foundress, first U.S. citizen-saint, Nov. 13; St. Albert the Great, doctor of the Church, Nov. 15; St. Elizabeth of Hungary, Nov. 17. Presentation of the Blessed Virgin Mary, Nov. 21; St. Cecilia, Nov. 22. Thanksgiving Day, Nov. 22; St. Andrew Dung-Lac and companions, the Korean Martyrs, Nov. 24. Christ the King, Nov. 25; The Feast of Saint Andrew, November 30. The annual fall meeting of the bishops of the United States takes place this month in Washington, D.C. Its agenda covers a wide range of topics with particular attention given to doctrinal, pastoral and educational issues that impact the life of the Church in the United States.

December 2007

General: That society promptly take care of those living with AIDS, especially women and children, and may the Church make them feel the love of the Lord.

Missionary: That the Incarnation of the Son of God that the Church solemnly celebrates at Christmas, help the peoples of the Asian continent recognize in Jesus God's Envoy, the one and only Savior of the world.

1 Sat. weekday. Blessed Virgin Mary.
2 Sun. First Sunday of Advent (Is. 2:1-5; Rom. 13:11-14; Mt. 24:37-44.)
3 Mon. St. Francis Xavier, priest; memorial.
4 Tues. Advent weekday. St. John Damascene, priest-doctor; optional memorial.
5 Weds. Advent weekday.
6 Thurs. Advent weekday. St. Nicholas, bishop; optional memorial.
7 Fri. St. Ambrose, bishop and doctor; memorial.
8 Sat. Immaculate Conception of the Blessed Virgin Mary; solemnity (Gn 3:9-15, 20; Eph 1:3-6, 11-12; Lk 1:26-38.) Holy Day of Obligation.
9 Sun. Second Sunday of Advent (Is 11:1-10; Rom 15:4-9; Mt 3:1-12.)
10 Mon. Advent weekday.
11 Tues. Advent weekday. St. Damasus I, pope; optional memorial.
12 Weds. Our Lady of Guadalupe; feast.
13 Thurs. St. Lucy, virgin-martyr; memorial.
14 Fri. St. John of the Cross, priest-doctor; memorial.
15 Sat. Advent weekday.
16 Sun. Third Sunday of Advent (Is. 35:1-6a, 10; Jas. 5:7-10; Mt. 11:2-11.)
17 Mon. Late Advent weekday.
18 Tues. Late Advent weekday.
19 Weds. Late Advent weekday.
20 Thurs. Late Advent weekday.
21 Fri. Late Advent weekday. St. Peter Canisius, priest and doctor; optional memorial.
22 Sat. Late Advent weekday.
23 Sun. Fourth Sunday of Advent. (Is 7:10-14; Rom 1:1-7; Mt. 1:18-24.)
24 Mon. Vigil of Christmas.
25 Tues. Nativity of the Lord, Christmas; solemnity. Holy Day of Obligation. (Vigil Mass – Is 62:1-5; Acts 13:16-17, 22-25; Mt 1:1-25 or 1:18-25. Midnight Mass – Is9:1-6; Ti 2:11-14; Lk 2:1-14. Mass at Dawn – Is 62:11-12; Ti 3:4-7; Lk 2:15 20. Mass during the day – Is 52:7-10; Heb 1:1-6; Jn 1:1-18 or 1:1-5, 9-14.)
26 Weds. St. Stephen, first martyr; feast.
27 Thurs. St. John, apostle-evangelist; feast.
28 Fri. Holy Innocents; feast.
29 Sat. Fifth Day in the Octave of Christmas. St. Thomas Becket, bishop-martyr; optional memorial.
30 Sun. Holy Family of Jesus, Mary, and Joseph (Sir 3:2-7, 12-14; Col 3:12-21; Lk 2:22-40.)
31 Mon. Seventh Day in the Octave of Christmas. St. Sylvester, pope; optional memorial.

Observances: The beginning of the Church Year, the first Sunday of Advent, Dec. 2; Sts. John of Damascus, Ambrose, John of the Cross, Peter Canisius, doctors of the Church; Immaculate Conception, Dec. 8; Our Lady of Guadalupe, Dec. 12; Birth of our Lord, Dec. 25; St. Stephen, proto-martyr, Dec. 26; St. John, apostle-evangelist, Dec. 27; Holy Innocents, Dec. 28; Holy Family, Dec. 30 and St. Sylvester, Dec. 31.

HOLY DAYS AND OTHER OBSERVANCES

The following list includes the six holy days of obligation observed in the U.S. and additional observances of devotional and historical significance. The dignity or rank of observances is indicated by the terms: solemnity (highest in rank); feast; memorial (for universal observance); optional memorial (for celebration by choice).

All Saints, Nov. 1, Holy Day of Obligation, solemnity. Commemorates all the blessed in heaven, and is intended particularly to honor the blessed who have no special feasts. The background of the feast dates to the fourth century when groups of martyrs, and later other saints, were honored on a common day in various places. In 609 or 610, the Pantheon, a pagan temple at Rome, was consecrated as a Christian church for the honor of Our Lady and the martyrs (later all saints). In 835, Gregory IV fixed Nov. 1 as the date of observance.

All Souls, Commemoration of the Faithful Departed, Nov. 2. The dead were prayed for from the earliest days of Christianity. By the sixth century it was customary in Benedictine monasteries to hold a commemoration of deceased members of the order at Pentecost. A common commemoration of all the faithful departed on the day after All Saints was instituted in 998 by St. Odilo, of the Abbey of Cluny, and an observance of this kind was accepted in Rome in the 14th century.

Annunciation of the Lord (formerly, Annunciation of the Blessed Virgin Mary), Mar. 25, solemnity. A feast of the Incarnation which commemorates the announcement by the Archangel Gabriel to the Virgin Mary that she was to become the Mother of Christ (Lk. 1:26-38), and the miraculous conception of Christ by her. The feast was instituted about 430 in the East. The Roman observance dates from the seventh century, when celebration was said to be universal.

Ascension of the Lord, movable observance held 40 days after Easter, holy day of obligation, solemnity. Commemorates the Ascension of Christ into heaven 40 days after his Resurrection from the dead (Mk 16:19; Lk 24:51; Acts 1:2). The feast recalls the completion of Christ's mission on earth for the salvation of all people and his entry into heaven with glorified human nature. The Ascension is a pledge of the final glorification of all who achieve salvation. Documentary evidence of the feast dates from early in the fifth century, but it was observed long before that time in connection with Pentecost and Easter.

Ash Wednesday, movable observance, six and one-half weeks before Easter. It was set as the first day of Lent by Pope St. Gregory the Great (590-604) with the extension of an earlier and shorter penitential season to a total period including 40 weekdays of fasting before Easter. It is a day of fast and abstinence. Ashes, symbolic of penance, are blessed and distributed among the faithful during the day. They are used to mark the forehead with the Sign of the Cross, with the reminder: "Remember you are dust, and to dust you will return," or "Turn away from sin and be faithful to the Gospel."

Assumption, Aug. 15, holy day of obligation, solemnity. Commemorates the taking into heaven of Mary, soul and body, at the end of her life on earth, a truth of faith that was proclaimed a dogma by Pius XII on Nov. 1, 1950. One of the oldest and most solemn feasts of Mary, it has a history dating back to at least the seventh century when its celebration was already established at Jerusalem and Rome.

Baptism of the Lord, movable, usually celebrated on the Sunday after January 6, feast. Recalls the baptism of Christ by John the Baptist (Mk. 1:9-11), an event associated with the liturgy of the Epiphany. This baptism was the occasion for Christ's manifestation of himself at the beginning of his public life.

Birth of Mary, Sept. 8, feast. This is a very old feast which originated in the East and found place in the Roman liturgy in the seventh century.

Candlemas Day, Feb. 2. *See* **Presentation of the Lord.**

Chair of Peter, Feb. 22, feast. The feast, which has been in the Roman calendar since 336, is a liturgical expression of belief in the episcopacy and hierarchy of the Church.

Christmas, Birth of Our Lord Jesus Christ, Dec. 25, holy day of obligation, solemnity. Commemorates the birth of Christ (Lk 2:1-20). This event was originally commemorated in the East on the feast of Epiphany or Theophany. The Christmas feast itself originated in the West; by 354 it was certainly kept on Dec. 25. This date may have been set for the observance to offset pagan ceremonies held at about the same time to commemorate the birth of the sun at the winter solstice. There are texts for three Christmas Masses at midnight, dawn, and during the day.

Christ the King, movable, celebrated on the last Sunday of the liturgical year, solemnity. Commemorates the royal prerogatives of Christ and is equivalent to a declaration of his rights to the homage, service and fidelity of all people in all phases of individual and social life. Pius XI instituted the feast Dec. 11, 1925.

Conversion of St. Paul, Jan. 25, feast. An observance mentioned in some calendars from the 8th and 9th centuries. Pope Innocent III (1198-1216) ordered its observance with great solemnity.

Corpus Christi (The Body and Blood of Christ), movable, celebrated on the Thursday (or Sunday, as in the U.S.) following Trinity Sunday, solemnity. Commemorates the institution of the Holy Eucharist (Mt 26:26-28). The feast originated at Liège in 1246 and was extended throughout the Church in the West by Urban IV in 1264. St. Thomas Aquinas composed the Liturgy of the Hours for the feast.

Cross, The Holy, Sept. 14, feast. Commemorates the finding of the Cross on which Christ was crucified, in 326 through the efforts of St. Helena, mother of Constantine; the consecration of the Basilica of the Holy Sepulcher nearly 10 years later: and the recovery in 628 or 629 by Emperor Heraclius of a major portion of the cross which had been removed by the Persians from its place of veneration at Jerusalem. The feast originated in Jerusalem and spread through the East before being adopted in the West. General adoption followed the building at Rome of the Basilica of the Holy Cross "in Jerusalem," so called because it was the place of enshrinement of a major portion of the cross of crucifixion.

Dedication of St. John Lateran, Nov. 9, feast. Commemorates the first public consecration of a church, that of the Basilica of the Most Holy Savior by Pope St. Sylvester about 324. The church, as well as the Lateran Palace, was the gift of Emperor Constantine. Since the 12th century it has been known as St. John Lateran, in honor of John the Baptist after whom the adjoining baptistery was named. It was rebuilt by Innocent X (1644-55), reconsecrated by Benedict XIII in 1726, and enlarged by Leo XIII (1878-1903). This basilica is regarded as the church of highest dignity in Rome and throughout the Roman rite.

Dedication of St. Mary Major, Aug. 5, optional memorial. Commemorates the rebuilding and dedication by Pope Sixtus III (432-40) of a church in honor of Blessed Mary the Virgin. This is the Basilica of St. Mary Major on the Esquiline Hill in Rome. An earlier building was erected during the pontificate of Liberius (352-66); according to legend, it was located on a site covered by a miraculous fall of snow seen by a nobleman favored with a vision of Mary.

Easter, movable celebration held on the first Sunday after the full moon following the vernal equinox (between Mar. 22 and Apr. 25), solemnity with an octave. Commemorates the Resurrection of Christ from the dead (Mk. 16:1-7). The observance of this mystery, kept since the first days of the Church, extends throughout the Easter season which lasts until the feast of Pentecost, a period of 50 days. Every Sunday in the year is regarded as a "little" Easter. The date of Easter determines the dates of movable feasts, such as Ascension and Pentecost, and the number of weeks before Lent and after Pentecost.

Easter Vigil, called by St. Augustine the "Mother of All Vigils," the night before Easter. Ceremonies are all related to the Resurrection and renewal-in-grace theme of Easter: blessing of the new fire, procession with the Easter Candle, singing of the Easter Proclamation (*Exsultet*), Liturgy of the Word with at least three Old Testament readings, the Litany of Saints, blessing of water, baptism of converts and infants, renewal of baptismal promises, Liturgy of the Eucharist. The vigil ceremonies are held after nightfall on Saturday.

Epiphany of the Lord, Jan. 6 or (in the U.S.) a Sunday between Jan. 2 and 8, solemnity. Commemorates the manifestations of the divinity of Christ. It is one of the oldest Christian feasts, with an Eastern origin traceable to the beginning of the third century and antedating the Western feast of Christmas. Originally, it commemorated the manifestations of Christ's divinity — or Theophany — in his birth, the homage of the Magi, and baptism by John the Baptist. Later, the first two of these commemorations were transferred to Christmas when the Eastern Church adopted that feast between 380 and 430. The central feature of the Eastern observance now is the manifestation or declaration of Christ's divinity in his baptism and at the beginning of his public life. The Epiphany was adopted by the Western Church during the same period in which the Eastern Church accepted Christmas. In the Roman rite, commemoration is made in the Mass of the homage of the wise men from the East (Mt 2:1-12).

Good Friday, the Friday before Easter, the second day of the Easter Triduum. Liturgical elements of the observance are commemoration of the Passion and Death of Christ in the reading of the Passion (accord-

ing to John), special prayers for the Church and people of all ranks, the veneration of the Cross, and a Communion service. The celebration takes place in the afternoon, preferably at 3:00 p.m.

Guardian Angels, Oct. 2, memorial. Commemorates the angels who protect people from spiritual and physical dangers and assist them in doing good. A feast in their honor celebrated in Spain in the 16th century was placed in the Roman calendar in 1615 and Oct. 2 was set as the date of observance. Earlier, guardian angels were honored liturgically in conjunction with the feast of St. Michael.

Holy Family, movable observance on the Sunday after Christmas, feast. Commemorates the Holy Family of Jesus, Mary and Joseph as the model of domestic society, holiness and virtue. The devotional background of the feast was very strong in the 17th century. In the 18th century, in prayers composed for a special Mass, a Canadian bishop likened the Christian family to the Holy Family. Leo XIII consecrated families to the Holy Family. In 1921, Benedict XV extended the Divine Office and Mass of the feast to the whole Church.

Holy Innocents, Dec. 28, feast. Commemorates the infants who suffered death at the hands of Herod's soldiers seeking to kill the child Jesus (Mt. 2:13-18). A feast in their honor has been observed since the fifth century.

Holy Saturday, the day before Easter. The Sacrifice of the Mass is not celebrated, and Holy Communion may be given only as Viaticum. If possible the Easter fast should be observed until the Easter Vigil.

Holy Thursday, the Thursday before Easter. Commemorates the institution of the sacraments of the Eucharist and holy orders, and the washing of the feet of the Apostles by Jesus at the Last Supper. The Mass of the Lord's Supper in the evening marks the beginning of the Easter Triduum. Following the Mass, there is a procession of the Blessed Sacrament to a place of reposition for adoration by the faithful. Usually at an earlier Mass of Chrism, bishops bless oils (of catechumens, chrism, the sick) for use during the year. (For pastoral reasons, diocesan bishops may permit additional Masses, but these should not overshadow the principal Mass of the Lord's Supper.)

Immaculate Conception, Dec. 8, holy day of obligation, solemnity. Commemorates the fact that Mary, in view of her calling to be the Mother of Christ and in virtue of his merits, was preserved from the first moment of her conception from original sin and was filled with grace from the very beginning of her life. She was the only person so preserved from original sin. The present form of the feast dates from Dec. 8, 1854, when Pius IX defined the dogma of the Immaculate Conception An earlier feast of the Conception, which testified to long-existing belief in this truth, was observed in the East by the eighth century, in Ireland in the ninth, and subsequently in European countries. In 1846, Mary was proclaimed patroness of the U.S. under this title.

Immaculate Heart of Mary, Saturday following the second Sunday after Pentecost, memorial. On May 4, 1944, Pius XII ordered this feast observed throughout the Church in order to obtain Mary's intercession for "peace among nations, freedom for the Church, the conversion of sinners, the love of purity and the practice of virtue." Two years earlier, he consecrated the entire human race to Mary under this title. Devotion to Mary under the title of her Most Pure Heart originated during the Middle Ages. It was given great impetus in the 17th century by the preaching of St. John Eudes, who was the first to celebrate a Mass and Divine Office of Mary under this title. A feast, celebrated in various places and on different dates, was authorized in 1799.

Joachim and Ann, July 26, memorial. Commemorates the parents of Mary. A joint feast, celebrated Sept. 9, originated in the East near the end of the sixth century. Devotion to Ann, introduced in the eighth century at Rome, became widespread in Europe in the 14th century; her feast was extended throughout the Latin Church in 1584. A feast of Joachim was introduced in the West in the 15th century.

John the Baptist, Birth of, June 24, solemnity. The precursor of Christ, whose cousin he was, was commemorated universally in the liturgy by the fourth century. He is the only saint, except the Blessed Virgin Mary, whose birthday is observed as a feast. Another feast, on Aug. 29, commemorates his passion and death at the order of Herod (Mk 6:14-29).

Joseph, Mar. 19, solemnity. Joseph is honored as the husband of the Blessed Virgin Mary, the patron and protector of the universal Church and workman. Devotion to him already existed in the eighth century in the East, and in the 11th in the West. Various feasts were celebrated before the 15th century when Mar. 19 was fixed for his commemoration; this feast was extended to the whole Church in 1621 by Gregory XV. In 1955, Pius XII instituted the feast of St. Joseph the Workman for observance May 1; this feast, which may be celebrated by local option, supplanted the Solemnity or Patronage of St. Joseph formerly observed on the third Wednesday after Easter. St. Joseph was proclaimed protector and patron of the universal Church in 1870 by Pius IX.

Michael, Gabriel and Raphael, Archangels, Sept. 29, feast. A feast bearing the title of Dedication of St. Michael the Archangel formerly commemorated on this date the consecration in 530 of a church near Rome in honor of Michael, the first angel given a liturgical feast. For a while, this feast was combined with a commemoration of the Guardian Angels. The separate feasts of Gabriel (Mar. 24) and Raphael (Oct. 24) were suppressed by the calendar in effect since 1970 and this joint feast of the three archangels was instituted.

Octave of Christmas, Jan. 1. See **Solemnity of Mary, Mother of God.**

Our Lady of Guadalupe, Dec. 12, feast (in the U.S.). Commemorates under this title the appearances of the Blessed Virgin Mary in 1531 to an Indian, Juan Diego, on Tepeyac hill outside Mexico City (see Apparitions of the Blessed Virgin Mary). The celebration, observed as a memorial in the U.S., was raised to the rank of feast at the request of the National Conference of Catholic Bishops. Approval was granted in a decree dated Jan. 8, 1988.

Our Lady of Sorrows, Sept. 15, memorial. Recalls the sorrows experienced by Mary in her association with Christ: the prophecy of Simeon (Lk. 2:34-35), the flight into Egypt (Mt. 2:13-21), the three-day separation from Jesus (Lk 2:41-50), and four incidents connected with the Passion — her meeting with Christ on the way to Calvary, the crucifixion, the removal of

Christ's body from the cross, and his burial (Mt 27:31-61; Mk 15:20-47; Lk 23:26-56; Jn 19:17-42). A Mass and Divine Office of the feast were celebrated by the Servites, especially, in the 17th century, and in 1814 Pius VII extended the observance to the whole Church.

Our Lady of the Rosary, Oct. 7, memorial. Commemorates the Virgin Mary through recall of the mysteries of the Rosary which recapitulate events in her life and the life of Christ. The feast was instituted in 1573 to commemorate a Christian victory over invading the forces of the Ottoman Empire at Lepanto in 1571, and was extended throughout the Church by Clement XI in 1716.

Passion Sunday (formerly called Palm Sunday), the Sunday before Easter. Marks the start of Holy Week by recalling the triumphal entry of Christ into Jerusalem at the beginning of the last week of his life (Mt 21:1-9). A procession and other ceremonies commemorating this event were held in Jerusalem from very early Christian times and were adopted in Rome by the ninth century, when the blessing of palm for the occasion was introduced. Full liturgical observance includes the blessing of palm and a procession before the principal Mass of the day. The Passion, by Matthew, Mark or Luke, is read during the Mass.

Pentecost, also called **Whitsunday,** movable celebration held 50 days after Easter, solemnity. Commemorates the descent of the Holy Spirit upon the Apostles, the preaching of Peter and the other Apostles to Jews in Jerusalem, the baptism and aggregation of some 3,000 persons to the Christian community (Acts 2:1-41). It is regarded as the birthday of the Catholic Church. The original observance of the feast antedated the earliest extant documentary evidence from the third century.

Peter and Paul, June 29, solemnity. Commemorates the martyrdoms of Peter by crucifixion and Paul by beheading during the Neronian persecution. This joint commemoration of the chief Apostles dates at least from 258 at Rome.

Presentation of the Lord (formerly called Purification of the Blessed Virgin Mary, also Candlemas), Feb. 2, feast. Commemorates the presentation of Jesus in the Temple — according to prescriptions of Mosaic Law (Lv 12:2-8; Ex 13:2; Lk 2:22-32) — and the purification of Mary 40 days after his birth. In the East, where the feast antedated fourth century testimony regarding its existence, it was observed primarily as a feast of Our Lord; in the West, where it was adopted later, it was regarded more as a feast of Mary until the calendar in effect since 1970. Its date was set for Feb. 2 after the celebration of Christmas was fixed for Dec. 25, late in the fourth century. The blessing of candles, probably in commemoration of Christ who was the Light to enlighten the Gentiles, became common about the 11th century and gave the feast the secondary name of Candlemas.

Queenship of Mary, Aug. 22, memorial. Commemorates the high dignity of Mary as Queen of heaven, angels and men. Universal observance of the memorial was ordered by Pius XII in the encyclical *Ad Caeli Reginam,* Oct. 11, 1954, near the close of a Marian Year observed in connection with the centenary of the proclamation of the dogma of the Immaculate Conception and four years after the proclamation of the dogma of the Assumption. The original date of the memorial was May 31.

Resurrection. See **Easter.**

Sacred Heart of Jesus, movable observance held on the Friday after the second Sunday after Pentecost (Corpus Christi, in the U.S.), solemnity. The object of the devotion is the divine Person of Christ, whose heart is the symbol of his love for all people — for whom he accomplished the work of Redemption. The Mass and Office now used on the feast were prescribed by Pius XI in 1929. Devotion to the Sacred Heart was introduced into the liturgy in the 17th century through the efforts of St. John Eudes who composed an Office and Mass for the feast. It was furthered as the result of the revelations of St. Margaret Mary Alacoque after 1675 and by the work of St. Claude de la Colombière, S.J. In 1765, Clement XIII approved a Mass and Office for the feast, and in 1856 Pius IX extended the observance throughout the Roman rite.

Solemnity of Mary, Mother of God, Jan. 1, holy day of obligation, solemnity. The calendar in effect since 1970, in accord with Eastern tradition, reinstated the Marian character of this commemoration on the octave day of Christmas. The former feast of the Circumcision, dating at least from the first half of the sixth century, marked the initiation of Jesus (Lk 2:21) in Judaism and by analogy focused attention on the initiation of persons in the Christian religion and their incorporation in Christ through baptism. The feast of the Solemnity supplants the former feast of the Maternity of Mary observed on Oct. 11.

Transfiguration of the Lord, Aug. 6, feast. Commemorates the revelation of his divinity by Christ to Peter, James and John on Mt. Tabor (Mt 17:1-9). The feast, which is very old, was extended throughout the universal Church in 1457 by Callistus III.

Trinity, The Holy, movable observance held on the Sunday after Pentecost, solemnity. Commemorates the most sublime mystery of the Christian faith, i.e., that there are Three Divine Persons — Father, Son and Holy Spirit — in one God (Mt 28:18-20). A votive Mass of the Most Holy Trinity dates from the seventh century; an Office was composed in the 10th century; in 1334, John XXII extended the feast to the universal Church.

Visitation, May 31, feast. Commemorates Mary's visit to her cousin Elizabeth after the Annunciation and before the birth of John the Baptist, the precursor of Christ (Lk 1:39-47). The feast had a medieval origin and was observed in the Franciscan Order before being extended throughout the Church by Urban VI in 1389. It is one of the feasts of the Incarnation and is notable for its recall of the *Magnificat,* one of the few New Testament canticles, which acknowledges the unique gifts of God to Mary because of her role in the redemptive work of Christ. The canticle is recited at Evening Prayer in the Liturgy of the Hours.

Liturgical Life
of the Church

The nature and purpose of the liturgy, along with norms for its revision, were the subject matter of *Sacrosanctum Concilium* (the Constitution on the Sacred Liturgy) promulgated by the Second Vatican Council. The principles and guidelines stated in this document, the first issued by the Council, are summarized here and/or are incorporated in other Almanac entries on liturgical subjects.

NATURE AND PURPOSE OF LITURGY

The paragraphs under this and the following subhead are quoted directly from *Sacrosanctum Concilium* (Constitution on the Sacred Liturgy).

"It is through the liturgy, especially the divine Eucharistic Sacrifice, that 'the work of our redemption is exercised.' The liturgy is thus the outstanding means by which the faithful can express in their lives, and manifest to others, the mystery of Christ and the real nature of the true Church" (No. 2).

"The liturgy is considered as an exercise of the priestly office of Jesus Christ. In the liturgy the sanctification of man is manifested by signs perceptible to the senses, and is effected in a way which is proper to each of these signs; in the liturgy full public worship is performed by the Mystical Body of Jesus Christ, that is, by the Head and his members.

"From this it follows that every liturgical celebration, because it is an action of Christ the priest and of his Body the Church, is a sacred action surpassing all others. No other action of the Church can match its claim to efficacy, nor equal the degree of it" (No. 7).

"The liturgy is the summit toward which the activity of the Church is directed; at the same time it is the fountain from which all her power flows. For the goal of apostolic works is that all who are made sons of God by faith and baptism should come together to praise God in the midst of his Church, to take part in her sacrifice, and to eat the Lord's Supper.

"From the liturgy, therefore, and especially from the Eucharist, as from a fountain, grace is channeled into us; and the sanctification of men in Christ and the glorification of God, to which all other activities of the Church are directed as toward their goal, are most powerfully achieved" (No. 10).

Full Participation

"Mother Church earnestly desires that all the faithful be led to that full, conscious, and active participation in liturgical celebrations which is demanded by the very nature of the liturgy. Such participation by the Christian people as 'a chosen race, a royal priesthood, a holy nation, a purchased people' (1 Pt 2:9; cf. 2:4-5),

is their right and duty by reason of their baptism.

"In the restoration and promotion of the sacred liturgy, this full and active participation by all the people is the aim to be considered before all else; for it is the primary and indispensable source from which the faithful are to derive the true Christian spirit" (No. 14).

"In order that the Christian people may more securely derive an abundance of graces from the sacred liturgy, holy Mother Church desires to undertake with great care a general restoration of the liturgy itself. For the liturgy is made up of unchangeable elements divinely instituted, and elements subject to change. The latter not only may but ought to be changed with the passing of time if features have by chance crept in which are less harmonious with the intimate nature of the liturgy, or if existing elements have grown less functional.

"In this restoration, both texts and rites should be drawn up so that they express more clearly the holy things which they signify. Christian people, as far as possible, should be able to understand them with ease and to take part in them fully, actively, and as befits a community" (No. 21).

Norms

Norms regarding the reforms concern the greater use of Scripture; emphasis on the importance of the sermon or homily on biblical and liturgical subjects; use of vernacular languages for prayers of the Mass and for administration of the sacraments; provision for adaptation of rites to cultural patterns.

Approval for reforms of various kinds — in liturgical texts, rites, etc. — depends on the Holy See, regional conferences of bishops and individual bishops, according to provisions of law. No priest has authority to initiate reforms on his own. Reforms may not be introduced just for the sake of innovation, and any that are introduced in the light of present-day circumstances should embody sound tradition.

To assure the desired effect of liturgical reforms, training and instruction are necessary for the clergy, religious and the laity. The functions of diocesan and regional commissions for liturgy, music and art are to set standards and provide leadership for instruction and practical programs in their respective fields.

Most of the constitution's provisions regarding liturgical reforms have to do with the Roman rite. The document clearly respects the equal dignity of all rites, leaving to the Eastern Churches control over their ancient liturgies.

(For coverage of the Mystery of the Eucharist, *see* **The Mass**; other sacraments, *see* separate entries.)

Sacramentals

Sacramentals, instituted by the Church, "are sacred signs which bear a resemblance to the sacraments: they signify effects, particularly of a spiritual kind, which are obtained through the Church's intercession. By them men are disposed to receive the chief effect of the sacraments, and various occasions in life are rendered holy" (No. 60).

"Thus, for well-disposed members of the faithful, the liturgy of the sacraments and sacramentals sanctifies almost every event in their lives; they are given access to the stream of divine grace which flows from the paschal mystery of the passion, death, and resurrection of Christ, the fountain from which all sacraments and sacramentals draw their power. There is hardly any proper use of material things which cannot thus be directed toward the sanctification of men and the praise of God" (No. 61).

Some common sacramentals are priestly blessings, blessed palm, candles, holy water, medals, scapulars, prayers and ceremonies of the Roman Ritual.

Liturgy of the Hours

The Liturgy of the Hours (Divine Office) is the public prayer of the Church for praising God and sanctifying the day. Its daily celebration is required as a sacred obligation by men in holy orders and by men and women religious who have professed solemn vows. Its celebration by others is highly commended and is to be encouraged in the community of the faithful.

"By tradition going back to early Christian times, the Divine Office is arranged so that the whole course of the day and night is made holy by the praises of God. Therefore, when this wonderful song of praise is worthily rendered by priests and others who are deputed for this purpose by Church ordinance, or by the faithful praying together with the priest in an approved form, then it is truly the voice of the bride addressing her bridegroom; it is the very prayer which Christ himself, together with his Body, addresses to the Father" (No. 84).

"Hence all who perform this service are not only fulfilling a duty of the Church, but also are sharing in the greatest honor accorded to Christ's spouse, for by offering these praises to God they are standing before God's throne in the name of the Church their Mother" (No. 85).

Revised Hours

The Liturgy of the Hours, revised since 1965, was the subject of Pope Paul VI's apostolic constitution *Laudis Canticum*, dated Nov. 1, 1970. The master Latin text was published in 1971; its four volumes have been published in authorized English translation since May 1975.

One-volume, partial editions of the Liturgy of the Hours containing Morning and Evening Prayer and other elements, have been published in approved English translation.

The revised Liturgy of the Hours consists of:

• Office of Readings, for reflection on the word of God. The principal parts are three psalms, biblical and non-biblical readings.

• Morning and Evening Prayer, called the "hinges" of the Liturgy of the Hours. The principal parts are a hymn, two psalms, an Old or New Testament canticle,

a brief biblical reading, Zechariah's canticle (the *Benedictus*, morning) or Mary's canticle (the *Magnificat*, evening), responsories, intercessions and a concluding prayer.

• Daytime Prayer. The principal parts are a hymn, three psalms, a biblical reading and one of three concluding prayers corresponding to the time of day.

• Night Prayer. The principal parts are one or two psalms, a brief biblical reading, Simeon's canticle (*Nunc Dimittis*), a concluding prayer and an antiphon in honor of Mary.

In the revised Liturgy of the Hours, the hours are shorter than they had been, with greater textual variety, meditation aids, and provision for intervals of silence and meditation. The psalms are distributed over a four-week period instead of a week; some psalms, entirely or in part, are not included. Additional canticles from the Old and New Testaments are assigned for Morning and Evening Prayer. Additional scriptural texts have been added and variously arranged for greater internal unity, correspondence to readings at Mass, and relevance to events and themes of salvation history. Readings include some of the best material from the Fathers of the Church and other authors, and improved selections on the lives of the saints.

The book used for recitation of the *Office is the Breviary*.

For coverage of the Liturgical Year, see **Church Calendar**.

Sacred Music

"The musical tradition of the universal Church is a treasure of immeasurable value, greater even than that of any other art. The main reason for this pre-eminence is that, as sacred melody united to words, it forms a necessary or integral part of the solemn liturgy.

"Sacred music increases in holiness to the degree that it is intimately linked with liturgical action, winningly expresses prayerfulness, promotes solidarity, and enriches sacred rites with heightened solemnity. The Church indeed approves of all forms of true art, and admits them into divine worship when they show appropriate qualities" (No. 112).

The constitution decreed:

• Vernacular languages for the people's parts of the liturgy, as well as Latin, may be used.

• Participation in sacred song by the whole body of the faithful, and not just by choirs, is to be encouraged and brought about.

• Provisions should be made for proper musical training for clergy, religious and lay persons.

• While Gregorian Chant has a unique dignity and relationship to the Latin liturgy, other kinds of music are acceptable.

• Native musical traditions should be used, especially in mission areas.

• Various instruments compatible with the dignity of worship may be used.

Gregorian Chant: A form and style of chant called Gregorian was the basis and most highly regarded standard of liturgical music for centuries. It originated probably during the formative period of the Roman liturgy and developed in conjunction with Gallican and other forms of chant. Pope St. Gregory I the Great's connection with it is not clear, although it is known that he had great concern for and interest in church music. The earliest extant written versions of Gregorian Chant date from the ninth century. A thousand years later, the Benedictines of Solesmes, France, initiated a revival of chant which gave impetus to the modern liturgical movement.

Sacred Art and Furnishings

"Very rightly the fine arts are considered to rank among the noblest expressions of human genius. This judgment applies especially to religious art and to its highest achievement, which is sacred art. By their very nature both of the latter are related to God's boundless beauty, for this is the reality which these human efforts are trying to express in some way. To the extent that these works aim exclusively at turning men's thoughts to God persuasively and devoutly, they are dedicated to God and to the cause of his greater honor and glory" (No. 122).

The objective of sacred art is "that all things set apart for use in divine worship should be truly worthy, becoming, and beautiful, signs and symbols of heavenly realities. The Church has always reserved to herself the right to pass judgment upon the arts, deciding which of the works of artists are in accordance with faith, piety, and cherished traditional laws, and thereby suited to sacred purposes.

"Sacred furnishings should worthily and beautifully serve the dignity of worship" (No. 122).

According to the constitution:

• Contemporary art, as well as that of the past, shall "be given free scope in the Church, provided that it adorns the sacred buildings and holy rites with due honor and reverence" (No. 123).

• Noble beauty, not sumptuous display, should be sought in art, sacred vestments and ornaments.

• "Let bishops carefully exclude from the house of God and from other sacred places those works of artists which are repugnant to faith, morals, and Christian piety, and which offend true religious sense either by their distortion of forms or by lack of artistic worth, by mediocrity or by pretense.

• "When churches are to be built, let great care be taken that they be suitable for the celebration of liturgical services and for the active participation of the faithful" (No. 124).

• "The practice of placing sacred images in churches so that they may be venerated by the faithful is to be firmly maintained. Nevertheless, their number should be moderate and their relative location should reflect right order. Otherwise they may create confusion among the Christian people and promote a faulty sense of devotion" (No. 125).

• Artists should be trained and inspired in the spirit and for the purposes of the liturgy.

• The norms of sacred art should be revised. "These laws refer especially to the worthy and well-planned construction of sacred buildings, the shape and construction of altars, the nobility, location, and security of the Eucharistic tabernacle, the suitability and dignity of the baptistery, the proper use of sacred images, embellishments, and vestments" (No. 128).

RITES

Rites are the forms and ceremonial observances of liturgical worship coupled with the total expression of the theological, spiritual and disciplinary heritages of particular churches of the East and the West.

Different rites have evolved in the course of church history, giving to liturgical worship and church life in general forms and usages peculiar and proper to the nature of worship and the culture of the faithful in various circumstances of time and place. Thus, there has been development since apostolic times in the prayers and ceremonies of the Mass, in the celebration of the sacraments, sacramentals and the Liturgy of the Hours, and in observances of the liturgical calendar. The principal sources of rites in present use were practices within the patriarchates of Rome (for the West) and Antioch, Alexandria and Constantinople (for the East). Rites are identified as Eastern or Western on the basis of their geographical area of origin in the Roman Empire.

Eastern and Roman Rites

Eastern rites are proper to Eastern Catholic Churches (see separate entry). The principal rites are Byzantine, Alexandrian, Antiochene, Armenian and Chaldean.

The Latin or Roman rite prevails in the Western Church. It was derived from Roman practices and the use of Latin from the third century onward, and has been the rite in general use in the West since the eighth century. Other rites in limited use in the Western Church have been the Ambrosian (in the Archdiocese of Milan), the Mozarabic (in the Archdiocese of Toledo), the Lyonnais, the Braga, and rites peculiar to some religious orders like the Dominicans, Carmelites and Carthusians.

The purpose of the revision of rites in progress since the Second Vatican Council is to renew them, not to eliminate the rites of particular churches or to reduce all rites to uniformity. The Council reaffirmed the equal dignity and preservation of rites as follows.

"It is the mind of the Catholic Church that each individual church or rite retain its traditions whole and entire, while adjusting its way of life to various needs of time and place. Such individual churches, whether of the East or the West, although they differ somewhat among themselves in what are called rites (that is, in liturgy, ecclesiastical discipline and spiritual heritage), are, nevertheless, equally entrusted to the pastoral guidance of the Roman Pontiff, the divinely appointed successor of St. Peter in supreme government over the universal Church. They are, consequently, of equal dignity, so that none of them is superior to the others by reason of rite."

Determination of Rite

Determination of a person's rite is regulated by church law. Through baptism, a child becomes a member of the rite of his or her parents. If the parents are of different rites, the child's rite is decided by mutual consent of the parents; if there is lack of mutual consent, the child is baptized in the rite of the father. A candidate for baptism over the age of 14 can choose to be baptized in any approved rite. Catholics baptized in one rite may receive the sacraments in any of the approved ritual churches; they may transfer to another rite only with the permission of the Holy See and in accordance with other provisions of the Code of Canon Law.

MASS, EUCHARISTIC SACRIFICE AND BANQUET

Declarations of Vatican II

The Second Vatican Council made the following declarations among others with respect to the Mass:

"At the Last Supper, on the night when he was betrayed, our Savior instituted the Eucharistic Sacrifice of his Body and Blood. He did this in order to perpetuate the Sacrifice of the Cross throughout the centuries until he should come again, and so to entrust to his beloved spouse, the Church, a memorial of his death and resurrection: a sacrament of love, a sign of unity, a bond of charity, a paschal banquet in which Christ is consumed, the mind is filled with grace, and a pledge of future glory is given to us" (*Sacrosanctum Concilium*, Constitution on the Sacred Liturgy, No. 47).

"... As often as the Sacrifice of the Cross in which 'Christ, our Passover, has been sacrificed' (1 Cor 5:7) is celebrated on an altar, the work of our redemption is carried on. At the same time, in the sacrament of the Eucharistic bread the unity of all believers who form one body in Christ (cf. 1 Cor 10:17) is both expressed and brought about. All men are called to this union with Christ" (*Lumen Gentium*, Dogmatic Constitution on the Church, No. 3).

"... The ministerial priest, by the sacred power he enjoys, molds and rules the priestly people. Acting in the person of Christ, he brings about the Eucharistic Sacrifice, and offers it to God in the name of all the people. For their part, the faithful join in the offering of the Eucharist by virtue of their royal priesthood" (Ibid., No. 10).

Declarations of Trent

Among its decrees on the Holy Eucharist, the Council of Trent stated the following points of doctrine on the Mass.

1. There is in the Catholic Church a true sacrifice, the Mass instituted by Jesus Christ. It is the sacrifice of his Body and Blood, Soul and Divinity, himself, under the appearances of bread and wine.

2. This Sacrifice is identical with the Sacrifice of the Cross, inasmuch as Christ is the Priest and Victim in both. A difference lies in the manner of offering, which was bloody upon the Cross and is bloodless on the altar.

3. The Mass is a propitiatory Sacrifice, atoning for the sins of the living and dead for whom it is offered.

4. The efficacy of the Mass is derived from the Sacrifice of the Cross, whose superabundant merits it applies to men.

5. Although the Mass is offered to God alone, it may be celebrated in honor and memory of the saints.

6. Christ instituted the Mass at the Last Supper.

7. Christ ordained the Apostles priests, giving them power and the command to consecrate his Body and Blood to perpetuate and renew the Sacrifice.

ORDER OF THE MASS

The Mass consists of two principal divisions called the **Liturgy of the Word**, which features the proclamation of the Word of God, and the **Eucharistic Liturgy**, which focuses on the central act of sacrifice in the Consecration and on the Eucharistic Banquet in Holy Communion. (Formerly, these divisions were called, respectively, the **Mass of the Catechumens** and the **Mass of the Faithful**.) In addition to these principal divisions, there are ancillary introductory and concluding rites.

The following description covers the Mass as celebrated with participation by the people. This Order of the Mass was approved by Pope Paul VI in the apostolic constitution *Missale Romanum* dated Apr. 3, 1969, and promulgated in a decree issued Apr. 6, 1969, by the Congregation for Divine Worship. The assigned effective date was Nov. 30, 1969.

Introductory Rites

Entrance: The introductory rites begin with the singing or recitation of an entrance song consisting of one or more scriptural verses stating the theme of the mystery, season or feast commemorated in the Mass.

Greeting: The priest and people make the Sign of the Cross together. The priest then greets them in one of several alternative ways and they reply in a corresponding manner.

Introductory Remarks: At this point, the priest or another of the ministers may introduce the theme of the Mass.

Penitential Rite: The priest and people together acknowledge their sins as a preliminary step toward worthy celebration of the sacred mysteries.

This rite includes a brief examination of conscience, a general confession of sin and plea for divine mercy in one of several ways, and a prayer for forgiveness by the priest.

Glory to God: A doxology, a hymn of praise to God, sung or said on festive occasions.

Opening Prayer: A prayer of petition offered by the priest on behalf of the worshiping community.

I. Liturgy of the Word

Readings: The featured elements of this liturgy are readings of passages from the Bible. If three readings are in order, the first is usually from the Old Testament, the second from the New Testament (Letters, Acts, Revelation), and the third from one of the Gospels; the final reading is always a selection from a Gospel. The first reading(s) is (are) concluded with the formula, "The Word of the Lord" (effective Feb. 28, 1993; optional before that date), to which the people respond, "Thanks be to God." The Gospel reading is concluded with the formula, "The Gospel of the Lord," (effective as above), to which the people respond, "Praise to you, Lord Jesus Christ." Between the readings, psalm verses are sung or recited. A Gospel acclamation is either sung or omitted.

Homily: An explanation, pertinent to the mystery being celebrated and the special needs of the listeners, of some point in either the readings from sacred Scripture or in another text from the Ordinary or Proper parts of the Mass; it is a proclamation of the Good News for a response of faith.

Creed: The Nicene profession of faith, by priest and people, on certain occasions.

Prayer of the Faithful: Litany-type prayers of petition, with participation by the people. Called general intercessions, they concern needs of the Church, the salvation of the world, public authorities, persons in need, the local community.

II. Eucharistic Liturgy

Presentation and Preparation of Gifts: Presentation to the priest of the gifts of bread and wine, principally, by participating members of the congregation. Preparation of the gifts consists of the prayers and ceremonies with which the priest offers bread and wine as the elements of the sacrifice to take place during the Eucharistic Prayer and of the Lord's Supper to be shared in Holy Communion.

Washing of Hands: After offering the bread and wine, the priest cleanses his fingers with water in a brief ceremony of purification.

Pray, Brothers and Sisters: Prayer that the sacrifice to take place will be acceptable to God. The first part of the prayer is said by the priest; the second, by the people.

Prayer over the Gifts: A prayer of petition offered by the priest on behalf of the worshipping community.

Eucharistic Prayer

Preface: A hymn of praise, introducing the Eucharistic Prayer or Canon, sung or said by the priest following responses by the people. The Order of the Mass contains a variety of prefaces, for use on different occasions.

Holy, Holy, Holy; Blessed is He: Divine praises sung or said by the priest and people.

Eucharistic Prayer (Canon): Its central portion is the Consecration, when the essential act of sacrificial offering takes place with the changing of bread and wine into the Body and Blood of Christ. The various parts of the prayer, which are said by the celebrant only, commemorate principal mysteries of salvation history and include petitions for the Church, the living and dead, and remembrances of saints.

Doxology: A formula of divine praise sung or said by the priest while he holds aloft the chalice containing the consecrated wine in one hand and the paten containing the consecrated host in the other.

Communion Rite

Lord's Prayer: Sung or said by the priest and people.

Prayer for Deliverance from Evil: Called an embolism because it is a development of the final petition of the Lord's Prayer; said by the priest. It concludes with a memorial of the return of the Lord to which the people respond, "For the kingdom, the power, and the glory are yours, now and forever."

Prayer for Peace: Said by the priest, with corresponding responses by the people. The priest can, in accord with local custom, bid the people to exchange a greeting of peace with each other.

Lamb of God (*Agnus Dei*): A prayer for divine mercy sung or said while the priest breaks the consecrated host and places a piece of it into the consecrated wine in the chalice.

Communion: The priest, after saying a preparatory prayer, administers Holy Communion to himself and then to the people, thus completing the sacrifice-banquet of the Mass. (This completion is realized even if the celebrant alone receives the Eucharist.) On giving the Eucharist to each person under both species separately, the priest or eucharistic minister says, "The Body of Christ," "The Blood of Christ." The custom-

ary response is "Amen." If the Eucharist is given by intinction (in which the host is dipped into the consecrated wine), the priest says, "The Body and Blood of Christ."

Communion Song: Scriptural verses or a suitable hymn sung or said during the distribution of Holy Communion. After Holy Communion is received, some moments may be spent in silent meditation or in the chanting of a psalm or hymn of praise.

Prayer after Communion: A prayer of petition offered by the priest on behalf of the worshipping community.

Concluding Rite

Announcements: Brief announcements to the people are in order at this time.

Dismissal: Consists of a final greeting by the priest, a blessing, and a formula of dismissal. This rite is omitted if another liturgical action immediately follows the Mass; e.g., a procession, the blessing of the body during a funeral rite.

Some parts of the Mass are changeable with the liturgical season or feast, and are called the proper of the Mass. Other parts are said to be common because they always remain the same.

Additional Mass Notes

Catholics are seriously obliged to attend Mass in a worthy manner on Sundays and holy days of obligation. Failure to do so without a proportionately serious reason is gravely wrong.

It is the custom for priests to celebrate Mass daily whenever possible. To satisfy the needs of the faithful on Sundays and holy days of obligation, they are authorized to say Mass twice (**bination**) or even three times (**trination**). Bination is also permissible on weekdays to satisfy the needs of the faithful. On Christmas every priest may say three Masses.

The **fruits of the Mass**, which in itself is of infinite value, are: **general**, for all the faithful; **special (ministerial)**, for the intentions or persons specifically intended by the celebrant; **most special (personal)**, for the celebrant himself. On Sundays and certain other days pastors are obliged to offer Mass for their parishioners, or to have another priest do so. If a priest accepts a stipend or offering for a Mass, he is obliged in justice to apply the Mass for the intention of the donor. Mass may be applied for the living and the dead, or for any good intention.

Mass can be celebrated in several ways: e.g., with people present, without their presence (privately), with two or more priests as co-celebrants (concelebration), with greater or less solemnity.

Some of the various types of Masses are: **for the dead** (Funeral Mass or Mass of Christian Burial, Mass for the Dead — formerly called Requiem Mass); **ritual**, in connection with celebration of the sacraments, religious profession, etc.; **nuptial**, for married couples, with or after the wedding ceremony; **votive**, to honor a Person of the Trinity, a saint, or for some special intention.

Places, Altars for Mass

The ordinary place for celebrating the Eucharist is a church or other sacred place, at a fixed or movable altar.

The altar is a table at which the Eucharistic Sacrifice is celebrated.

A fixed altar is attached to the floor of the church. It should be of stone, preferably, and should be consecrated. The Code of Canon Law orders observance of the custom of placing under a fixed altar relics of martyrs or other saints.

A movable altar can be made of any solid and suitable material, and should be blessed or consecrated.

Outside of a sacred place, Mass may be celebrated in an appropriate place at a suitable table covered with a linen cloth and corporal. An altar stone containing the relics of saints, which was formerly prescribed, is not required by regulations in effect since the promulgation Apr. 6, 1969, of *Institutio Generalis Missalis Romani.*

LITURGICAL VESTMENTS

In the early years of the Church, vestments worn by the ministers at liturgical functions were the same as the garments in ordinary popular use. They became distinctive when their form was not altered to correspond with later variations in popular style. Liturgical vestments are symbolic of the sacred ministry and add appropriate decorum to divine worship.

Mass Vestments

Alb: A body-length tunic of white fabric; a vestment common to all ministers of divine worship.

Amice: A rectangular piece of white cloth worn about the neck, tucked into the collar and falling over the shoulders; prescribed for use when the alb does not completely cover the ordinary clothing at the neck.

Chasuble: Originally, a large mantle or cloak covering the body, it is the outer vestment of a priest celebrating Mass or carrying out other sacred actions connected with the Mass.

Chasuble-Alb: A vestment combining the features of the chasuble and alb; for use with a stole by concelebrants and, by way of exception, by celebrants in certain circumstances.

Cincture: A cord which serves the purpose of a belt, holding the alb close to the body.

Dalmatic: The outer vestment worn by a deacon in place of a chasuble.

Stole: A long, band-like vestment worn by a priest about the neck and falling to about the knees. A deacon wears a stole over the left shoulder, crossed and fastened at his right side.

The material, form and ornamentation of the aforementioned and other vestments are subject to variation and adaptation, according to norms and decisions of the Holy See and concerned conferences of bishops. The overriding norm is that they should be appropriate for use in divine worship. The customary ornamented vestments are the chasuble, dalmatic and stole.

The minimal vestments required for a priest celebrating Mass are the alb, stole, and chasuble.

Liturgical Colors

The colors of outer vestments vary with liturgical seasons, feasts and other circumstances. The colors and their use are:

Green: For the season of ordinary time; symbolic of hope and the vitality of the life of faith.

Violet (Purple): For Advent and Lent; may also be used in Masses for the dead; symbolic of penance. (See below, Violet for Advent.)

Red: For the Sunday of the Passion, Good Friday, Pentecost; feasts of the Passion of Our Lord, the Apostles and Evangelists, martyrs; symbolic of the supreme sacrifice of life for the love of God.

Rose: May be used in place of purple on the Third Sunday of Advent (formerly called Gaudete Sunday) and the Fourth Sunday of Lent (formerly called Laetare Sunday); symbolic of anticipatory joy during a time of penance.

White: For the seasons of Christmas and Easter; feasts and commemorations of Our Lord, except those of the Passion; feasts and commemorations of the Blessed Virgin Mary, angels, saints who are not martyrs, All Saints (Nov. 1), St. John the Baptist (June 24), St. John the Evangelist (Dec. 27), the Chair of St. Peter (Feb. 22), the Conversion of St. Paul (Jan. 25). White, symbolic of purity and integrity of the life of faith, may generally be substituted for other colors, and can be used for funeral and other Masses for the dead.

Options are provided regarding the color of vestments used in offices and Masses for the dead. The newsletter of the U.S. Bishops' Committee on the Liturgy, in line with No. 308 of the General Instruction of the Roman Missal, announced in July 1970: "In the dioceses of the U.S., white vestments may be used, in addition to violet (purple) and black, in offices and Masses for the dead."

On more solemn occasions, better than ordinary vestments may be used, even though their color (e.g., gold) does not match the requirements of the day.

Violet for Advent: Violet is the official liturgical color for the season of Advent, according to the September 1988 edition of the newsletter of the U.S. Bishops' Committee on the Liturgy. Blue was being proposed in order to distinguish between the Advent season and the specifically penitential season of Lent. The newsletter said, however, that "the same effect can be achieved by following the official color sequence of the Church, which requires the use of violet for Advent and Lent, while taking advantage of the varying shades which exist for violet. Light blue vestments are not authorized for use in the U.S."

Considerable freedom is permitted in the choice of colors of vestments worn for votive Masses.

Other Vestments

Cappa Magna: Flowing vestment with a train, worn by bishops and cardinals.

Cassock: A non-liturgical, full-length, close-fitting robe for use by priests and other clerics under liturgical vestments and in ordinary use; usually black for priests, purple for bishops and other prelates, red for cardinals, white for the pope. In place of a cassock, priests belonging to religious institutes wear the habit proper to their institute.

Cope: A mantle-like vestment open in front and fastened across the chest; worn by sacred ministers in processions and other ceremonies, as prescribed by appropriate directives.

Habit: The ordinary (non-liturgical) garb of members of religious institutes, analogous to the cassock of diocesan priests; the form of habits varies from institute to institute.

Humeral Veil: A rectangular vestment worn about

the shoulders by a deacon or priest in Eucharistic processions and for other prescribed liturgical ceremonies.

Mitre: A headdress worn at some liturgical functions by bishops, abbots and, in certain cases, other ecclesiastics.

Pallium: A circular band of white wool about two inches wide, with front and back pendants, marked with six crosses, worn about the neck. It is a symbol of the fullness of the episcopal office. Pope Paul VI, in a document issued July 20, 1978, on his own initiative and entitled *Inter Eximia Episcopalis*, restricted its use to the pope and archbishops of metropolitan sees. In 1984, Pope John Paul II decreed that the pallium would ordinarily be conferred by the pope on the solemnity of Sts. Peter and Paul, June 29. The pallium is made from the wool of lambs blessed by the pope on the feast of St. Agnes (Jan. 21).

Rochet: A knee-length, white linen-lace garment of prelates worn under outer vestments.

Surplice: a loose, flowing vestment of white fabric with wide sleeves. For some functions, it is interchangeable with an alb.

Zucchetto: A skullcap worn by bishops and other prelates.

SACRED VESSELS, LINENS

Vessels

Paten and Chalice: The principal sacred vessels required for the celebration of Mass are the paten (plate) and chalice (cup) in which bread and wine, respectively, are offered, consecrated and consumed. Both should be made of solid and noble material which is not easily breakable or corruptible. Gold coating is required of the interior parts of sacred vessels subject to rust. The cup of a chalice should be made of non-absorbent material.

Vessels for containing consecrated hosts (see below) can be made of material other than solid and noble metal — e.g., ivory, more durable woods — provided the substitute material is locally regarded as noble or rather precious and is suitable for sacred use.

Sacred vessels should be blessed, according to prescribed requirements.

Vessels, in addition to the paten, for containing consecrated hosts are:

Ciborium: Used to hold hosts for distribution to the faithful and for reservation in the tabernacle.

Luna, Lunula, Lunette: A small receptacle which holds the sacred host in an upright position in the monstrance.

Monstrance, Ostensorium: A portable receptacle so made that the sacred host, when enclosed therein, may be clearly seen, as at Benediction or during extended exposition of the Blessed Sacrament.

Pyx: A watch-shaped vessel used in carrying the Eucharist to the sick.

Linens

Altar Cloth: A white cloth, usually of linen, covering the table of an altar. One cloth is sufficient. Three were used according to former requirements.

Burse: A square, stiff flat case, open at one end, in which the folded corporal can be placed; the outside is covered with material of the same kind and color as the outer vestments of the celebrant.

Corporal: A square piece of white linen spread on the altar cloth, on which rest the vessels holding the Sacred Species — the consecrated host(s) and wine — during the Eucharistic Liturgy. The corporal is used whenever the Blessed Sacrament is removed from the tabernacle; e.g., during Benediction the vessel containing the Blessed Sacrament rests on a corporal.

Finger Towel: A white rectangular napkin used by the priest to dry his fingers after cleansing them following the offering of gifts at Mass.

Pall: A square piece of stiff material, usually covered with linen, which can be used to cover the chalice at Mass.

Purificator: A white rectangular napkin used for cleansing sacred vessels after the reception of Communion at Mass.

Veil: The chalice intended for use at Mass can be covered with a veil made of the same material as the outer vestments of the celebrant.

THE CHURCH BUILDING

A church is a building set aside and dedicated for purposes of divine worship, the place of assembly for a worshipping community.

A Catholic church is the ordinary place in which the faithful assemble for participation in the Eucharistic Liturgy and other forms of divine worship.

In the early years of Christianity, the first places of assembly for the Eucharistic Liturgy were private homes (Acts 2:46; Rom 16:5; 1 Cor 16:5; Col 4:15) and, sometimes, catacombs. Church building began in the latter half of the second century during lulls in persecution and became widespread after enactment of the Edict of Milan in 313, when it finally became possible for the Church to emerge completely from the underground. The oldest and basic norms regarding church buildings date from about that time.

The essential principle underlying all norms for church building was reformulated by the Second Vatican Council: "When churches are to be built, let great care be taken that they be suitable for the celebration of liturgical services and for the active participation of the faithful" (*Sacrosanctum Concilium*, Constitution on the Sacred Liturgy, No. 124).

This principle was subsequently elaborated in detail by the Congregation for Divine Worship in a document entitled *Institutio Generalis Missalis Romani*, which was approved by Paul VI Apr. 3, 1969, and promulgated by a decree of the congregation dated Apr. 6, 1969. Coverage of the following items reflects the norms stated in Chapter V of the *Institutio*.

Main Features

Sanctuary: The part of the church where the altar of sacrifice is located, the place where the ministers of the liturgy lead the people in prayer, proclaim the word of God and celebrate the Eucharist. It is set off from the body of the church by a distinctive structural feature — e.g., elevation above the main floor — or by ornamentation. (The traditional communion rail, removed in recent years in many churches, served this purpose of demarcation.) The customary location of the sanctuary is at the front of the church; it may, however, be centrally located.

Altar: The main altar of sacrifice and table of the

Lord is the focal feature of the sanctuary and entire church. It stands by itself, so that the ministers can move about it freely, and is so situated that they face the people during the liturgical action. In addition to this main altar, there may also be others; in new churches, these are ideally situated in side chapels or alcoves removed to some degree from the body of the church.

Adornment of the Altar: The altar table is covered with a suitable linen cloth. Required candelabra and a cross are placed upon or near the altar in plain sight of the people and are so arranged that they do not obscure their view of the liturgical action.

Seats of the Ministers: The seats of the ministers should be so arranged that they are part of the seating arrangement of the worshipping congregation and suitably placed for the performance of ministerial functions. The seat of the celebrant or chief concelebrant should be in a presiding position.

Ambo, Pulpit, Lectern: The stand at which scriptural lessons and psalm responses are read, the word of God preached, and the prayer of the faithful offered. It is so placed that the ministers can be easily seen and heard by the people.

Places for the People: Seats and kneeling benches (pews) and other accommodations for the people are so arranged that they can participate in the most appropriate way in the liturgical action and have freedom of movement for the reception of Holy Communion. Reserved seats are out of order.

Place for the Choir: Where it is located depends on the most suitable arrangement for maintaining the unity of the choir with the congregation and for providing its members maximum opportunity for carrying out their proper function and participating fully in the Mass.

Tabernacle: The best place for reserving the Blessed Sacrament is in a chapel suitable for the private devotion of the people. If this is not possible, reservation should be at a side altar or other appropriately adorned place. In either case, the Blessed Sacrament should be kept in a tabernacle, i.e., a safe-like, secure receptacle.

Statues: Images of the Lord, the Blessed Virgin Mary and the saints are legitimately proposed for the veneration of the faithful in churches. Their number and arrangement, however, should be ordered in such a way that they do not distract the people from the central celebration of the Eucharistic Liturgy. There should be only one statue of one and the same saint in a church.

General Adornment and Arrangement of Churches: Churches should be so adorned and fitted out that they serve the direct requirements of divine worship and the needs and reasonable convenience of the people.

Other Items

Ambry: A box containing the holy oils, attached to the wall of the sanctuary in some churches.

Baptistery: The place for administering baptism. Some churches have baptisteries adjoining or near the entrance, a position symbolizing the fact that persons are initiated in the Church and incorporated in Christ through this sacrament. Contemporary liturgical practice favors placement of the baptistery near the sanctuary and altar, or the use of a portable font in the same position, to emphasize the relationship of baptism to the Eucharist, the celebration in sacrifice and banquet of the death and resurrection of Christ.

Candles: Used more for symbolical than illuminative purposes, they represent Christ, the light and life of grace, at liturgical functions. They are made of beeswax. (*See* Index: Paschal Candle.)

Confessional, Reconciliation Room: A booth-like structure for the hearing of confessions, with separate compartments for the priest and penitents and a grating or screen between them. The use of confessionals became general in the Roman rite after the Council of Trent. Since the Second Vatican Council, there has been a trend in the U.S. to replace or supplement confessionals with small reconciliation rooms so arranged that priest and penitent can converse face-to-face.

Crucifix: A cross bearing the figure of the body of Christ, representative of the Sacrifice of the Cross.

Cruets: Vessels containing the wine and water used at Mass. They are placed on a credence table in the sanctuary.

Holy Water Fonts: Receptacles containing holy water, usually at church entrances, for the use of the faithful.

Sanctuary Lamp: A lamp which is kept burning continuously before a tabernacle in which the Blessed Sacrament is reserved, as a sign of the Real Presence of Christ.

LITURGICAL DEVELOPMENTS

The principal developments covered in this article are enactments of the Holy See and actions related to their implementation in the U.S.

Modern Movement

Origins of the modern movement for renewal in the liturgy date back to the 19th century. The key contributing factor was a revival of liturgical and scriptural studies. Of special significance was the work of the Benedictine monks of Solesmes, France, who aroused great interest in the liturgy through the restoration of Gregorian Chant. St. Pius X approved their work in a *motu proprio* of 1903 and gave additional encouragement to liturgical study and development.

St. Pius X did more than any other single pope to promote early first Communion and the practice of frequent Communion, started the research behind a revised breviary, and appointed a group to investigate possible revisions in the Mass.

The movement attracted some attention in the 1920s and '30s but made little progress.

Significant pioneering developments in the U.S. during the '20s, however, were the establishment of the Liturgical Press, the beginning of publication of *Orate Fratres* (now *Worship*), and the inauguration of the League of the Divine Office by the Benedictines at St. John's Abbey, Collegeville, Minn. Later events of influence were the establishment of the Pius X School of Liturgical Music at Manhattanville College of the Sacred Heart and the organization of a summer school of liturgical music at Mary Manse College by the Gregorian Institute of America. The turning point toward real renewal was reached during and after World War II.

Pius XII gave it impetus and direction, principally through

the background teaching in his encyclicals on the Mystical Body (*Mystici Corporis Christi*, 1943), Sacred Liturgy (*Mediator Dei*, 1947), and On Sacred Music (*Musicae sacrae*, 1955), and by means of specific measures affecting the liturgy itself. His work was continued during the pontificates of his successors. The Second Vatican Council, in virtue of *Sacrosanctum Concilium*, the Constitution on the Sacred Liturgy, inaugurated changes of the greatest significance.

Before and After Vatican II

The most significant liturgical changes made in the years immediately preceding the Second Vatican Council were the following:

1. Revision of the rites of Holy Week for universal observance from 1956.
2. Modification of the Eucharistic fast and permission for afternoon and evening Mass, in effect from 1953 and extended in 1957.
3. The Dialogue Mass, introduced in 1958.
4. Use of popular languages in administration of the sacraments.
5. Calendar-missal-breviary reform, in effect from Jan. 1, 1961.
6. Seven-step administration of baptism for adults, approved in 1962.

The Constitution on the Sacred Liturgy, *Sacrosanc-tum Concilium*, approved (2,174 to 4) and promulgated by the Second Vatican Council on Dec. 4, 1963, marked the beginning of a profound renewal in the Church's corporate worship. Implementation of some of its measures was ordered by Paul VI on Jan. 25, 1964, in the *motu proprio Sacram Liturgiam*. On Feb. 29, a special commission, the Consilium for Implementing the Constitution on the Sacred Liturgy, was formed to supervise the execution of the entire program of liturgical reform. Implementation of the program on local and regional levels was left to bishops acting through their own liturgical commissions and in concert with their fellow bishops in national conferences.

Liturgical reform in the U.S. has been carried out under the direction of the Liturgy Committee, National Conference of Catholic Bishops. Its secretariat, established early in 1965, is located at 3211 Fourth St. N.E., Washington, DC 20017.

Stages of Development

Liturgical development after the Second Vatican Council proceeded in several stages. It started with the formulation of guidelines and directives, and with the translation into vernacular languages of virtually unchanged Latin ritual texts. Then came structural changes in the Mass, the sacraments, the calendar, the Divine Office and other phases of the liturgy. These revisions were just about completed with the publication of a new order for the sacrament of penance in February 1974. A continuing phase of development, in progress from the beginning, involves efforts to deepen the liturgical sense of the faithful, to increase their participation in worship and to relate it to full Christian life.

RECENT DEVELOPMENTS

The New English Translation of the Order of the Mass

On June 15, 2006, during their spring meeting in Los Angeles, the Bishops of the United States approved the new English translations of the Order of the Mass and adopted several U.S. adaptations. The new translation was approved

by a vote of 173-29, and the American adaptations comprised of prayers or ritual instructions not contained in the original Latin version were approved by a vote of 184-8.

The new translation will most likely be introduced in a year or two, depending upon the approval of the Vatican, and, according to Bishop Donald Trautman of Erie and chairman of the USCCB Committee on the Liturgy, the U.S. Bishops will probably wait until such time as they have granted approval to the entire new Roman Missal in English and received Vatican approval before implementing the new Order of Mass.

The approved translation included the main parts of the Order of Mass as well as daily prayers, but there are still steps to be taken. For example, the Bishops must still receive and approve the other parts of the Order of Mass, including the prefaces and major elements of the Roman Missal with the prayers for each Sunday or feast throughout the liturgical year. These parts are far from being fully translated.

Liturgists have noted that when the new translation of the texts is fully introduced, Catholics in the U.S. will find that many of the prayers and responses that are now so familiar are suddenly different. Among the most discussed changes will be:

When the priest says "The Lord be with you," the current response, "And also with you" will be replaced by "And with your spirit."

The Nicene Creed, that currently begins with "We believe," will start with, "I believe."

Currently, during the offertory prayer that "our sacrifice will be acceptable," will be replaced by "the sacrifice which is mine and yours will be acceptable."

Where people currently confess, "I have sinned through my own fault," they will instead confess "I have sinned greatly ... through my fault, through my fault, through my most grievous fault."

The Sanctus, that now begins with "Holy, holy, holy Lord, God of power and might" will start instead with "Holy, Holy, Holy is the Lord God of hosts."

On Nov. 14, 2001, the U.S. Bishops, attending the annual fall meeting in Washington, approved revised U.S. adaptations in the liturgy by a vote of 207-7. The adaptations govern matters ranging from liturgical music and church furnishings to posture at Mass and how Communion is to be received.

The bishops had approved a complete set of adaptations at their spring meeting in June 2001, but the Vatican Congregation for Divine Worship and the Sacraments asked for modification of several of those and proposed a new approach that required editorial changes in all of them.

New U.S. Norms for Distribution of Communion Under Both Species

New norms for the distribution and reception of Communion under the outward signs of both bread and wine by Catholics in the U.S. were approved by the U.S. bishops on June 15, 2001, and confirmed by the Holy See on Mar. 22, 2002; they were subsequently published by Bishop Wilton D. Gregory of Belleville, Ill., president of the USCCB.

The norms, which replace the U.S. bishops' 1984 directory titled "This Holy and Living Sacrifice," give specific directives regarding liturgical roles, sacred vessels and the rites to be followed in distributing Communion under both kinds.

The first section of the new norms provides a theological summary of the church's teaching on

Communion under both kinds, while the following section describes the authorized procedures by which such distribution can be accomplished at Mass.

The U.S. adaptations are to be incorporated into the new General Instruction of the Roman Missal and have the same force of law in the U.S. as the rest of the general instruction. The General Instruction of the recently revised Roman Missal permits bishops' conferences to provide norms for the distribution of Communion under both kinds, meaning under the outward signs of both bread and wine.

Included among the norms is an indult — or exception to the general requirement — from the Vatican Congregation for Divine Worship and the Sacraments that provides for the cleansing of sacred vessels by special eucharistic ministers. The indult was promulgated as "particular law" for the dioceses of the U.S. at the same time as the norms and it became effective on Apr. 7, 2002.

However, the Vatican congregation declined to approve an indult authorizing special ministers to assist with the distribution of the consecrated blood to other chalices during the singing of the "Lamb of God."

In the letter confirming the norms, the congregation also made clear that special eucharistic ministers, or indeed any communicant, may assist in the consumption of what remains of the blood after distribution of Communion has been completed.

Texts and Translations

The master texts of all documents on liturgical reform are in Latin. Effective dates of their implementation have depended on the completion and approval of appropriate translations into vernacular languages. English translations were made by the International Committee for English in the Liturgy.

The principal features of liturgical changes and the effective dates of their introduction in the U.S. are covered below under topical headings. (For expanded coverage of various items, especially the sacraments, see additional entries.)

On May 7, 2001, the Congregation for Divine Worship and the Sacraments issued the new instruction, *Liturgiam Authenticam* ("The Authentic Liturgy"). The instruction set stricter rules for the translation of Latin liturgical texts into other languages and bears the subtitle, "On the Use of Vernacular Languages in the Publication of the Books of the Roman Liturgy." The instruction was welcomed by then-NCCB president, Bishop Joseph A. Fiorenza of Galveston-Houston, who said that it reflects long consultations between the Vatican and English-speaking bishops, adding that "It is now our hope and expectation that there will be a much quicker approval of liturgical texts" by the Vatican. The instruction was subsequently debated at the bishops' meeting in November 2001.

General Instruction of the Roman Missal

In spring 2001, Pope John Paul II authorized the publication of an *editio typica tertia* of the *Missale Romanum*. The much anticipated revision included a new edition of the *Institutio Generalis Missalis Romani* (*General Instruction of the Roman Missal*). On Nov. 12, 2002, the Latin Church members of the United States Conference of Catholic Bishops approved a translation of the *Institutio Generalis Missalis Romani* prepared by the International Commission on English in the Liturgy. The translation was confirmed by the Congregation for Divine Worship and the Discipline of the Sacraments on Mar. 17, 2003. This translation of the *General*

Instruction of the Roman Missal is the sole translation of the *Institutio Generalis Missalis Romani, editio typica tertia* for use in the dioceses of the United States of America. Concerning the new edition, Msgr. James P. Moroney, Executive Director of the USCCB Secretariat for the Liturgy, wrote in the Foreword:

"This revised *Institutio Generalis* possesses a unique role among all the documents on the liturgy. Like its preceding editions, it has been published in order to give life to a dream. It was the dream of reformers such as St. Hippolytus, St. Gregory, and St. Leo. It was the dream of Pope Paul VI and clearly remains the vision of Pope John Paul II, who calls us to 'an ever deeper grasp of the liturgy of the Church, celebrated according to the current books and lived above all as a reality in the spiritual order' (*Vicesimus Quintus Annus*, 1988, no. 14). Likewise, this dream is shared by the Bishops' Committee on the Liturgy and the United States Conference of Catholic Bishops that it serves. Finally, it is the vision of the Church itself: the dream of God's people joined to Christ in Baptism and made 'ever more holy by conscious, active, and fruitful participation in the mystery of the Eucharist' (*General Instruction of the Roman Missal*, no. 5)."

Redemptionis Sacramentum

On Apr. 23, 2004, the Congregation for Divine Worship and the Sacraments, in collaboration with the Congregation for the Doctrine of the Faith and at the request of Pope John Paul II issued the instruction "*Redemptionis Sacramentum*: On Certain Matters to Be Observed or to Be Avoided Regarding the Most Holy Eucharist." The instruction states:

"It is not at all the intention here to prepare a compendium of the norms regarding the Most Holy Eucharist, but rather, to take up within this Instruction some elements of liturgical norms that have been previously expounded or laid down and even today remain in force in order to assure a deeper appreciation of the liturgical norms; to establish certain norms by which those earlier ones are explained and complemented; and also to set forth for Bishops, as well as for Priests, Deacons and all the lay Christian faithful, how each should carry them out in accordance with his own responsibilities and the means at his disposal."

The Mass

A new Order of the Mass, supplanting the one authorized by the Council of Trent in the 16th century, was introduced in the U.S. Mar. 22, 1970. It had been approved by Paul VI in the apostolic constitution *Missale Romanum*, dated Apr. 3, 1969.

Preliminary and related to it were the following developments.

Mass in English: Introduced Nov. 29, 1964. In the same year, Psalm 42 was eliminated from the prayers at the foot of the altar.

Incidental Changes: The last Gospel (prologue of John) and vernacular prayers following Mass were eliminated Mar. 7, 1965. At the same time, provision was made for the celebrant to say aloud some prayers formerly said silently.

Rubrics: An instruction entitled *Tres Abhinc Annos*, dated May 4 and effective June 29, 1967, simplified directives for the celebration of Mass, approved the practice of saying the canon aloud, altered the Communion and dismissal rites, permitted purple instead of black vestments in Masses for the dead, discontinued wearing of the maniple, and approved in principle the use of vernacular languages for the canon, ordination rites, and lessons of the Divine Office when read in choir.

Eucharistic Prayers (Canons): The traditional Roman Canon in English was introduced Oct. 22, 1967. Three additional Eucharistic prayers, authorized May 23, 1968, were approved for use in English the following Aug. 15.

The customary Roman Canon, which dates at least from the beginning of the fifth century and has remained substantially unchanged since the seventh century, is the first in the order of listing of the Eucharistic prayers. It can be used at any time, but is the one of choice for most Sundays, some special feasts like Easter and Pentecost, and for feasts of the Apostles and other saints who are commemorated in the canon. Any preface can be used with it.

The second Eucharistic prayer, the shortest and simplest of all, is best suited for use on weekdays and various special circumstances. It has a preface of its own, but others may be used with it. This canon bears a close resemblance to the one framed by St. Hippolytus about 215.

The third Eucharistic prayer is suitable for use on Sundays and feasts as an alternative to the Roman Canon. It can be used with any preface and has a special formula for remembrance of the dead.

The fourth Eucharistic prayer, the most sophisticated of them all, presents a broad synthesis of salvation history. Based on the Eastern tradition of Antioch, it is best suited for use at Masses attended by persons versed in Sacred Scripture. It has an unchangeable preface.

Five additional Eucharistic prayers — three for Masses with children and two for Masses of reconciliation — were approved in 1974 and 1975, respectively, by the Congregation for the Sacraments and Divine Worship.

Use of the Eucharistic Prayers for Various Needs and Occasions, was approved by the U.S. bishops in 1994, confirmed by the appropriate Vatican congregations May 9, 1995, and ratified for use beginning Oct. 1, 1995.

Lectionary: A new compilation of scriptural readings and psalm responsories for Mass was published in 1969. The Lectionary contains a three-year cycle of readings for Sundays and solemn feasts, a two-year weekday cycle, and a one-year cycle for the feasts of saints, in addition to readings for a variety of votive Masses, ritual Masses and Masses for various needs. There are also responsorial psalms to follow the first readings and Gospel or alleluia versicles.

A second edition of the Lectionary, substantially the same as the first, was published in 1981. New features included an expanded introduction, extensive scriptural references and additional readings for a number of solemnities and feasts.

Volume One of a new Lectionary for the Mass was decreed by Bishop Anthony Pilla of Cleveland, then president of the NCCB, as permissible for use as of the first Sunday of Advent, Nov. 29, 1998. The first new Lectionary since 1973, Volume One contains the readings for Sundays, solemnities and feasts of the Lord. Volume Two, containing the readings for weekdays, feasts of saints, and various other occasions, was given final approval on June 19, 1998, by the NCCB but still required confirmation by the Holy See.

Sacramentary (Missal): The Vatican Polyglot Press began distribution in June 1970, of the Latin text of a new Roman Missal, the first revision published in 400 years. The English translation was authorized for optional use beginning July 1, 1974; the mandatory date for use was Dec. 1, 1974.

The **Sacramentary** is the celebrant's Mass book of entrance songs, prayers, prefaces and Eucharistic prayers, including special common sets of texts for various commemorations and intentions — dedication of churches, Mary, the apostles, martyrs, doctors of the Church, virgins, holy men and women, the dead, other categories of holy persons, administration of certain sacraments, special intentions.

Study of the Mass: The Bishops' Committee on the Liturgy, following approval by the National Conference of Catholic Bishops in May 1979, began a study of the function and position of elements of the Mass, including the Gloria, the sign of peace, the penitential rite and the readings. Major phases of the study have been completed, and work is still under way toward completion of the project.

Mass for Special Groups: Reasons and norms for the celebration of Mass at special gatherings of the faithful were the subject of an instruction issued May 15, 1969. Two years earlier, the U.S. Bishops' Liturgy Committee went on record in support of the celebration of Mass in private homes under appropriate conditions.

Sunday Mass on Saturday: The Congregation for the Clergy, under date of Jan. 10, 1970, granted the request that the faithful, where bishops consider it pastorally necessary or useful, may satisfy the precept of participating in Mass in the late afternoon or evening hours of Saturdays and the days before holy days of obligation. This provision is stated in Canon 1248 of the Code of Canon Law.

Bination and Trination: Canon 905 of the Code of Canon Law provides that local ordinaries may permit priests to celebrate Mass twice a day (bination), for a just cause; in cases of pastoral need, they may permit priests to celebrate Mass three times a day (trination) on Sundays and holy days of obligation.

Mass in Latin: According to notices issued by the Congregation for Divine Worship June 1, 1971, and Oct. 28, 1974: (1) Bishops may permit the celebration of Mass in Latin for mixed-language groups; (2) bishops may permit the celebration of one or two Masses in Latin on weekdays or Sundays in any church, irrespective of mixed-language groups involved (1971); (3) priests may celebrate Mass in Latin when people are not present; (4) the approved revised Order of the Mass is to be used in Latin as well as vernacular languages; (5) by way of exception, bishops may permit older and handicapped priests to use the Council of Trent's Order of the Mass in private celebration of the holy Sacrifice. (*See* Permission for **Tridentine Mass.**)

Mass Obligation Waived: The Congregation for Bishops approved July 4, 1992, a resolution of the U.S. bishops to waive the Mass attendance obligation for the holy days of Mary, the Mother of God (Jan. 1), the Assumption of Mary (Aug. 15) and All Saints (Nov. 1) when these solemnities fall on Saturday or Monday.

Inter-Ritual Concelebration: The Apostolic Delegation (now Nunciature) in Washington, D.C., announced in June 1971 that it had received authorization to permit priests of Roman and Eastern rites to celebrate Mass together in the rite of the host church. It was understood that the inter-ritual concelebrations would always be "a manifestation of the unity of the Church and of communion among particular churches."

Ordo of the Sung Mass: In a decree dated June 24

and made public Aug. 24, 1972, the Congregation for Divine Worship issued a new *Ordo of the Sung Mass* — containing Gregorian chants in Latin — to replace the *Graduale Romanum*.

Mass for Children: Late in 1973, the Congregation for Divine Worship issued special guidelines for children's Masses, providing accommodations to the mentality and spiritual growth of pre-adolescents while retaining the principal parts and structures of the Mass. The Directory for Masses with Children was approved by Paul VI Oct. 22 and was dated Nov. 1, 1973. Three Eucharistic prayers for Masses with children were approved by the congregation in 1974; English versions were approved June 5, 1975. Their use, authorized originally for a limited period of experimentation, was extended indefinitely Dec. 15, 1980.

Lectionary for Children: A lectionary for Masses with children, with an announced publication date of September 1993, was authorized for use by choice beginning Nov. 28, 1993. A revised *Lectionary for Masses with Children* was approved by the bishops on Nov. 15, 2006 during their fall general meeting in Washington. The text must also be approved by the Vatican before it can be used in the liturgy in the United States. Assuming approval is given, it will replace the experimental children's Lectionary that has been in use since 1993. The new Lectionary includes stricter rules for its use.

Sacraments

The general use of English in administration of the sacraments was approved for the U.S. Sept. 14, 1964. Structural changes of the rites were subsequently made and introduced in the U.S. as follows.

Pastoral Care of the Sick: Revised rites, covering also administration of the Eucharist to sick persons, were approved Nov. 30, 1972, and published Jan. 18, 1973. The effective date for use of the provisional English prayer formula was Dec. 1, 1974. The mandatory effective date for use of the ritual, Pastoral Care of the Sick in English, was Nov. 27, 1983.

Baptism: New rites for the baptism of infants, approved Mar. 19, 1969, were introduced June 1, 1970.

Rite of Christian Initiation of Adults: Revised rites were issued Jan. 6, 1972, for the Christian initiation of adults — affecting preparation for and reception of baptism, the Eucharist and confirmation; also, for the reception of already baptized adults into full communion with the Church. These rites, which were introduced in the U.S. on the completion of English translation, nullified a seven-step baptismal process approved in 1962. On Mar. 8, 1988, the National Conference of Catholic Bishops was notified that the Congregation for Divine Worship had approved the final English translation of the Rite of Christian Initiation of Adults. The mandatory date for putting the rite into effect was Sept. 1, 1988.

Confirmation: Revised rites, issued Aug. 15, 1971, became mandatory in the U.S. Jan. 1, 1973. The use of a stole by persons being confirmed should be avoided, according to an item in the December 1984 edition of the Newsletter of the Bishops' Committee on the Liturgy. The item said: "The distinction between the universal priesthood of all the baptized and the ministerial priesthood of the ordained is blurred when the distinctive garb (the stole) of ordained ministers is used in this manner."

A decree regarding the proper age for confirmation, approved by the U.S. bishops in June 1993 was ratified by the Congregation for Bishops Feb. 8, 1994. The decree reads: "In accord with prescriptions of canon 891, the National Conference of Catholic Bishops hereby decrees that the sacrament of confirmation in the Latin rite shall be conferred between the age of discretion, which is about the age of seven, and 18 years of age, within the limits determined by the diocesan bishop and with regard for the legitimate exceptions given in canon 891, namely, when there is danger of death or where, in the judgment of the minister, grave cause urges otherwise." The decree became effective July 1, 1994, and continued in effect until July 1, 1999.

Special Ministers of the Eucharist: The designation of lay men and women to serve as special ministers of the Eucharist was authorized by Paul VI in an "Instruction on Facilitating Communion in Particular Circumstances" (*Immensae Caritatis*), dated Jan. 29 and published by the Congregation for Divine Worship Mar. 29, 1973. Provisions concerning them are contained in Canons 230 and 910 of the Code of Canon Law.

Qualified laypersons may serve as special ministers for specific occasions or for extended periods in the absence of a sufficient number of priests and deacons to provide reasonable and appropriate service in the distribution of Holy Communion, during Mass and outside of Mass (to the sick and shut-ins). Appointments of ministers are made by priests with the approval of the appropriate bishop.

The Newsletter of the U.S. Bishops' Committee on the Liturgy stated in its February 1988 edition: "When ordinary ministers (bishops, priests, deacons) are present during a Eucharistic celebration, whether they are participating in it or not, and are not prevented from doing so, they are to assist in the distribution of Communion. Accordingly, if the ordinary ministers are in sufficient number, special ministers of the Eucharist are not allowed to distribute Communion at that Eucharistic celebration." Pope John Paul II approved this decision and ordered it published June 15, 1987.

Holy Orders: Revised ordination rites for deacons, priests and bishops, validated by prior experimental use, were approved in 1970. The sacrament of holy orders underwent further revision in 1972 with the elimination of the Church-instituted orders of porter, reader, exorcist, acolyte and subdeacon, and of the tonsure ceremony symbolic of entrance into the clerical state. The former minor orders of reader and acolyte were changed from orders to ministries.

Matrimony: A revised rite for the celebration of marriage was promulgated by the Congregation for Divine Worship and the Discipline of the Sacraments Mar. 19, 1969, and went into effect June 1, 1970. A second typical edition of the order of celebration, with revisions in accord with provisions of the Code of Canon Law promulgated in 1983, was approved and published in 1990 (*Notitiae*, Vol. 26, No.6). The date for implementation was reported to be dependent on the completion of required translations and appropriate formalities.

Penance: Ritual revision of the sacraments was completed with approval by Pope Paul VI on Dec. 2, 1973, of new directives for the sacrament of penance or reconciliation. The U.S. Bishops' Committee on the Liturgy set Feb. 27, 1977, as the mandatory date for use of the new rite. The committee also declared that it could be used from Mar. 7, 1976, after adequate preparation of priests and people. The Holy See gave authorization in 1968 for the omission of any reference to excommunication or other censures in the formula of absolution unless there was some indication that a censure had actually been incurred by a penitent.

Additional Developments

Music: An instruction on Music in the Liturgy, dated Mar.

5 and effective May 14, 1967, encouraged congregational singing during liturgical celebrations and attempted to clarify the role of choirs and trained singers. More significantly, the instruction indicated that a major development under way in the liturgy was a gradual erasure of the distinctive lines traditionally drawn between the sung liturgy and the spoken liturgy, between what had been called the high Mass and the low Mass.

In the same year, the U.S. Bishops' Liturgy Committee approved the use of contemporary music, as well as guitars and other suitable instruments, in the liturgy. The Holy See authorized in 1968 the use of musical instruments other than the organ in liturgical services, "provided they are played in a manner suitable to worship."

Calendar: A revised liturgical calendar approved by Paul VI Feb. 14 and made public May 9, 1969, went into effect in the U.S. in 1972. Since that time, memorials and feasts of beatified persons and saints have been added.

Communion in Hand: Since 1969, the Holy See has approved the practice of in-hand reception of the Eucharist in regions and countries where it had the approval of the appropriate episcopal conferences. The first grant of approval was to Belgium, in May 1969. Approval was granted the U.S. in June 1977.

Liturgy of the Hours: The background, contents, scope and purposes of the revised Divine Office, called the Liturgy of the Hours, were described by Paul VI in the apostolic constitution *Laudis Canticum*, dated Nov. 1, 1970. A provisional English version, incorporating basic features of the master Latin text, was published in 1971. The four complete volumes of the Hours in English have been published since May 1975. One-volume, partial editions have also been published in approved form. Nov. 27, 1977, was set by the Congregation for Divine Worship and the National Conference of Catholic Bishops as the effective date for exclusive use in liturgical worship of the translation of the Latin text of the Liturgy of the Hours approved by the International Committee on English in the Liturgy.

Holy Week: The English version of revised Holy Week rites went into effect in 1971. They introduced concelebration of Mass, placed new emphasis on commemorating the institution of the priesthood on Holy Thursday, and modified Good Friday prayers for other Christians, Jews and other non-Christians.

The Congregation for Divine Worship released Feb. 20, 1988, a "Circular Letter concerning the Preparation and Celebration of the Easter Feasts." It called the feasts the "summit of the whole liturgical year," and criticized practices which dilute or change appropriate norms for their celebration. Singled out for blame for the abuse or ignorance of norms was the "inadequate formation given to the clergy and the faithful regarding the paschal mystery as the center of the liturgical year and of Christian life." The document set out the appropriate norms for the Lenten season, Holy Week, the Easter Triduum, Easter and the weeks following. It was particularly insistent on the proper celebration of the Easter Vigil, to take place after nightfall on Saturday and before dawn on Sunday.

Oils: The Congregation for Divine Worship issued a directive in 1971 permitting the use of other oils — from plants, seeds or coconuts — instead of the traditional olive oil in admini,stering some of the sacraments. The directive also provided that oils could be blessed at other times than at the usual Mass of Chrism on Holy Thursday, and authorized bishops' conferences to permit priests to bless oils in cases of necessity.

Dancing and Worship: Dancing and worship was the subject of an essay which appeared in a 1975 edition of *Notitiae* (11, pp. 202-205), the official journal of the Congregation for the Sacraments and Divine Worship. The article was called a "qualified and authoritative sketch," and should be considered "an authoritative point of reference for every discussion of the matter."

The principal points of the essay were:
• "The dance has never been made an integral part of the official worship of the Latin Church."
• "If the proposal of the religious dance in the West is really to be made welcome, care will have to be taken that in its regard a place be found outside of the liturgy, in assembly areas which are not strictly liturgical. Moreover, the priests must always be excluded from the dance."

Mass for Deceased Non-Catholic Christians: The Congregation for the Doctrine of the Faith released a decree June 11, 1976, authorizing the celebration of public Mass for deceased non-Catholic Christians under certain conditions: "(1) The public celebration of the Masses must be explicitly requested by the relatives, friends, or subjects of the deceased person for a genuine religious motive. (2) In the Ordinary's judgment, there must be no scandal for the faithful."

Built of Living Stones: Art, Architecture, and Worship: At their November 2001 meeting in Washington, DC, the Bishops approved this document by the U.S. Bishops' Committee on the Liturgy; it replaces the document *Environment and Art in Catholic Worship* issued in March 1978.

Doxology: The bishops' committee called attention in August 1978, to the directive that the Doxology concluding the Eucharistic Prayer is said or sung by the celebrant (concelebrants) alone, to which the people respond, "Amen."

Churches, Altars, Chalices: The Newsletter of the U.S. Bishops' Committee on the Liturgy reported in November 1978, that the Congregation for Divine Worship had given provisional approval of a new English translation for the rite of dedicating churches and altars, and of a new form for the blessing of chalices.

Eucharistic Worship: This was the subject of two documents issued in 1980. *Dominicae Coenae* was a letter addressed by Pope John Paul to bishops throughout the world in connection with the celebration of Holy Thursday; it was dated Feb. 24 and released Mar.18, 1980. It was more doctrinal in content than the "Instruction on Certain Norms concerning Worship of the Eucharistic Mystery" (*Inaestimabile Donum*, "The Priceless Gift"), which was approved by the Pope Apr. 17 and published by the Congregation for the Sacraments and Divine Worship May 23. Its stated purpose was to reaffirm and clarify teaching on liturgical renewal contained in enactments of the Second Vatican Council and in several related implementing documents.

Tridentine Mass: The celebration of Mass according to the 1962 typical (master) edition of the Roman Missal — the so-called Tridentine Mass — was authorized by Pope John Paul II under certain conditions. So stated a letter from the Congregation for Divine Worship, dated Oct. 3, 1984. The letter said the pope wished to be responsive to priests and faithful who remained attached to the so-called Tridentine rite. The principal condition for the celebration was: "There must be unequivocal, even public, evidence that the priest and people petitioning have no ties with those who impugn the lawfulness and doctrinal soundness of the Roman Missal promulgated in 1970 by Pope Paul VI." (This, in particular, with reference to the followers of dissident Archbishop Marcel Lefebvre.)

Six guidelines for celebration of the Tridentine Mass were contained in the letter regarding its "wide and generous" use, for two purposes: to win back Lefebvre followers and to clear up misunderstandings about liberal permission for use of the Tridentine rite. The letter, from the Pontifical Commission *Ecclesia Dei*, said in part:

• The Tridentine Mass can be celebrated in a parish church, so long as it provides a pastoral service and is harmoniously integrated into the parish liturgical schedule.

• When requested, the Mass should be offered on a regular Sunday and holy day basis, "at a central location, at a convenient time" for a trial period of several months, with "adjustment" later if needed.

• Celebrants of the Mass should make it clear that they acknowledge the validity of the postconciliar liturgy.

• Although the commission has the authority to grant use of the Tridentine rite to all groups that request it, the commission "would much prefer that such faculties be granted by the Ordinary himself so that ecclesial communion can be strengthened."

• While the new Lectionary in the vernacular can be used in the Tridentine Mass, as suggested by the Second Vatican Council, it should not be "imposed on congregations that decidedly wish to maintain the former liturgical tradition in its integrity."

• Older and retired priests who have asked permission to celebrate Mass according to the Tridentine rite should be given the chance to do so for groups that request it.

In March 2003, the Vatican Secretariat of State issued new rules allowing the old rite to be used under very strict conditions. These include:

• The Mass cannot be celebrated in the main body of St. Peter's Basilica, but in the Hungarian Chapel in the grotto under the basilica.

• The Mass must be "private," in that the public is not invited and photographs are not allowed, although the priest may have a small group of faithful with him.

• The priest celebrating must show a permission from the Pontifical Commission *Ecclesia Dei*, the Vatican office responsible for the pastoral care of Catholic faithful with a special attachment to the old liturgy.

The ban on the Mass in the main body of the church stemmed from respect for the fact that it was in St. Peter's Basilica that the world's bishops gathered for the Second Vatican Council and ordered the reform of the liturgy.

Spanish: In accord with decrees of the Congregation for Divine Worship, Spanish was approved as a liturgical language in the U.S. (Jan. 19, 1985). The *texto unico* of the Ordinary of the Mass became mandatory in the U.S. Dec. 3, 1989. Spanish translations of Proper-of-the-Mass texts proper to U.S. dioceses were approved Mar. 12, 1990. An approved Spanish version of the Rite for the Christian Initiation of Adults was published in 1991. The Institute of Hispanic Liturgy opened its national office June 1, 1995, on the campus of the Catholic University of America in Washington.

Funeral Rites: A revised Order of Christian Funerals became mandatory in the U.S. Nov. 2, 1989.

Permission for the presence of cremated human remains in the funeral liturgy, including the Eucharist, was granted in 1997 to local bishops in the U.S. by the Congregation for Divine Worship and the Discipline of the Sacraments. Adaptations to existing rites are under study.

Popular Piety and Liturgy: The relation of popular piety to the liturgy was the subject of remarks by Pope John Paul II at a meeting with a group of Italian bishops Apr. 24, 1986. He said, in part:

"An authentic liturgical ministry will never be able to neglect the riches of popular piety, the values proper to the culture of a people, so that such riches might be illuminated, purified and introduced into the liturgy as an offering of the people."

Extended Eucharistic Exposition: In response to queries, the Secretariat of the U.S. Bishops' Committee on the Liturgy issued an advisory stating that liturgical law permits and encourages in parish churches:

• Exposition of the Blessed Sacrament for an extended period of time once a year, with consent of the local Ordinary and only if suitable numbers of the faithful are expected to be present;

• Exposition ordered by the local Ordinary, for a grave and general necessity, for a more extended period of supplication when the faithful assemble in large numbers.

With regard to perpetual exposition, this form is generally permitted only in the case of those religious communities of men or women who have the general practice of perpetual Eucharistic adoration or adoration over extended periods of time.

The Secretariat's advisory appeared in the June-July 1986 edition of the Newsletter of the Bishops' Committee on the Liturgy.

Native American Languages: The Newsletter of the U.S. Bishops' Committee on the Liturgy reported in December 1986, and May 1987, respectively, that the Congregation for Divine Worship had authorized Mass translations in Navajo and Choctaw. Lakota was approved as a liturgical language in 1989.

Communion Guidelines: In 1986 and again in 1996, the U.S. bishops' approved the insertion of advisories in missalettes and similar publications, stating that: (1) The Eucharist is to be received by Catholics only, except in certain specific cases; (2) To receive Communion worthily, a person must be in the state of grace (i.e., free of serious sin) and observe the eucharistic fast (*See* separate entry).

Unauthorized Eucharistic Prayers: The May 1987 Newsletter of the U.S. Bishops' Committee on the Liturgy restated the standing prohibition against the use of any Eucharistic Prayers other than those contained in the Sacramentary. Specifically, the article referred to the 25 unauthorized prayers in a volume entitled Spoken Visions.

Homilist: According to the Pontifical Commission for the Authentic Interpretation of Canon Law, the diocesan bishop cannot dispense from the requirement of Canon 767, par. 1, that the homily in the liturgy be reserved to a priest or deacon. Pope John Paul approved this decision June 20, 1987.

Concerts in Churches: In a letter released Dec. 5, 1987, the Congregation for Divine Worship declared that churches might be used on a limited basis for concerts of sacred or religious music, but not for concerts featuring secular music.

Blessings: A revised *Book of Blessings* was ordered into use beginning Dec. 3, 1989.

Litany of the Blessed Virgin Mary: "Queen of Families," a new invocation, was reported by the U.S. bishops in 1996, for insertion between "Queen of the Rosary" and "Queen of Peace."

Inclusive Language: "Criteria for the Evaluation of Inclusive Language Translations of Scriptural Texts Proposed for Liturgical Use" was issued by the U.S. bishops in November 1990. The criteria distinguish between non-use of vertical inclusiveness in references to God and use of horizontal, gender-inclusive terms (he/she, man/woman and the like) where appropriate in references to persons.

The Sacraments of the Church

The sacraments are actions of Christ and his Church (itself a kind of sacrament) that signify grace, cause it in the act of signifying it, and confer it upon persons properly disposed to receive it. They perpetuate the redemptive activity of Christ, making it present and effective. They infallibly communicate the fruit of that activity — namely grace — to responsive persons with faith. Sacramental actions consist of the union of sensible signs (matter of the sacraments) with the words of the minister (form of the sacraments).

Christ himself instituted the seven sacraments of the New Law by determining their essence and the efficacy of their signs to produce the grace they signify.

Christ is the principal priest or minister of every sacrament; human agents — an ordained priest, baptized persons contracting marriage with each other, any person conferring emergency baptism in a proper manner — are secondary ministers. Sacraments have efficacy from Christ, not from the personal dispositions of their human ministers.

Each sacrament confers sanctifying grace for the special purpose of the sacrament; this is, accordingly, called sacramental grace. It involves a right to actual graces corresponding to the purposes of the respective sacraments.

Baptism, confirmation and the Eucharist are sacraments of initiation; penance (reconciliation) and anointing of the sick, sacraments of healing; order and matrimony, sacraments for service.

While sacraments infallibly produce the grace they signify, recipients benefit from them in proportion to their personal dispositions. One of these is the intention to receive sacraments as sacred signs of God's saving and grace-giving action. The state of grace is also necessary for fruitful reception of the Holy Eucharist, confirmation, matrimony, holy orders and anointing of the sick. Baptism is the sacrament in which grace is given in the first instance and original sin is remitted. Penance is the secondary sacrament of reconciliation, in which persons guilty of serious sin after baptism are reconciled with God and the Church, and in which persons already in the state of grace are strengthened in that state.

Role of Sacraments

The Second Vatican Council prefaced a description of the role of the sacraments with the following statement concerning participation by all the faithful in the priesthood of Christ and the exercise of that priesthood by receiving the sacraments (Dogmatic Constitution on the Church, *Lumen Gentium*, Nos. 10 and 11).

"The baptized by regeneration and the anointing of the Holy Spirit are consecrated into a spiritual house and a holy priesthood. Thus through all those works befitting Christian men they can offer spiritual sacrifice and proclaim the power of him who has called them out of darkness into his marvelous light (cf. 1 Pt 2:4-10).

"Though they differ from one another in essence and not only in degree, the common priesthood of the faithful and the ministerial or hierarchical priesthood (of those ordained to holy orders) are nonetheless interrelated. Each of them in its own special way is a participation in the one priesthood of Christ. The ministerial priest, by the sacred power he enjoys, molds and rules the priestly people. Acting in the Person of Christ, he brings about the Eucharistic Sacrifice, and offers it to God in the name of all the people. For their part, the faithful join in the offering of the Eucharist by virtue of their royal priesthood. They likewise exercise that priesthood by receiving the sacraments, by prayer and thanksgiving, by the witness of a holy life, and by self-denial and active charity.

"It is through the sacraments and the exercise of the virtues that the sacred nature and organic structure of the priestly community is brought into operation."

Baptism: "Incorporated into the Church through baptism, the faithful are consecrated by the baptismal character to the exercise of the cult of the Christian religion. Reborn as sons of God, they must confess before men the faith which they have received from God through the Church."

Confirmation: "Bound more intimately to the Church by the sacrament of confirmation, they are endowed by the Holy Spirit with special strength. Hence they are more strictly obliged to spread and defend the faith both by word and by deed as true witnesses of Christ."

Eucharist: "Taking part in the Eucharistic Sacrifice, which is the fount and apex of the whole Christian life, they offer the divine Victim to God, and offer themselves along with It. Thus, both by the act of oblation and through holy Communion, all perform their proper part in this liturgical service, not, indeed. all in the same way but each in that way which is appropriate to himself. Strengthened anew at the holy table by the Body of Christ, they manifest in a practical way that unity of God's People which is suitably signified and wondrously brought about by this most awesome sacrament."

Penance: "Those who approach the sacrament of penance obtain pardon from the mercy of God for offenses committed against him. They are at the same time reconciled with the Church, which they have wounded by their sins, and which by charity, example, and prayer seeks their conversion."

Anointing of the Sick: "By the sacred anointing of the sick and the prayer of her priests, the whole Church commends those who are ill to the suffering and glorified Lord, asking that he may lighten their suffering and save them (cf. Jas 5:14-16). She exhorts them, moreover, to contribute to the welfare of the whole People of God by associating themselves freely with the passion and death of Christ (cf. Rom 8:17; Col 1:24; 2 Tm 2:11-12; 1 Pt 4:13)."

Holy Orders: "Those of the faithful who are consecrated by holy orders are appointed to feed the Church in Christ's name with the Word and the grace of God."

Matrimony: "Christian spouses, in virtue of the sacrament of matrimony, signify and partake of the mystery of that unity and fruitful love which exists between Christ and his Church (cf. Eph 5:32). The spouses thereby help each other to attain to holiness in their married life and by the rearing and education of their children. And so, in their state and way of life, they have their own special gift among the People of God (cf. 1 Cor 7:7).

"For from the wedlock of Christians there comes the family, in which new citizens of human society are born. By the grace of the Holy Spirit received in baptism these are made children of God, thus perpetuating the People of God through the centuries. The family is, so to speak, the domestic Church. In it parents should, by their word and example, be the first preachers of the faith to their children. They should encourage them in the vocation which is proper to each of them, fostering with special care any religious vocation.

"Fortified by so many and such powerful means of salvation, all the faithful, whatever their condition or state, are called by the Lord, each in his own way, to that perfect holiness whereby the Father himself is perfect."

Baptism

Baptism is the sacrament of spiritual regeneration by which a person is incorporated in Christ and made a member of his Mystical Body, given grace, and cleansed of original sin. Actual sins and the punishment owed for them are remitted also if the person baptized was guilty of such sins (e.g., in the case of a person baptized after reaching the age of reason). The theological virtues of faith, hope and charity are given with grace. The sacrament confers a character on the soul and can be received only once.

The matter is the pouring of water. The form is: "I baptize you in the name of the Father and of the Son and of the Holy Spirit."

The minister of solemn baptism is a bishop, priest or deacon, but in case of emergency anyone, including a non-Catholic, can validly baptize. The minister pours water on the forehead of the person being baptized and says the words of the form while the water is flowing. The water used in solemn baptism is blessed during the rite.

Baptism is conferred in the Roman rite by immersion or infusion (pouring of water), depending on the directive of the appropriate conference of bishops, according to the Code of Canon Law. The Church recognizes as valid baptisms properly performed by non-Catholic ministers. The baptism of infants has always been considered valid and the general practice of infant baptism was well established by the fifth century. Baptism is conferred conditionally when there is doubt about the validity of a previous baptism.

Baptism is necessary for salvation. If a person cannot receive the baptism of water described above, this can be supplied by baptism of blood (martyrdom suffered for the Catholic faith or some Christian virtue) or by baptism of desire (perfect contrition joined with at least the implicit intention of doing whatever God wills that people should do for salvation).

A sponsor is required for the person being baptized. (*See* Godparents, below).

A person must be validly baptized before he or she can receive any of the other sacraments.

Christian Initiation of Infants: Infants should be solemnly baptized as soon after birth as conveniently possible. Anyone may baptize an infant in danger of death. If the child survives, the ceremonies of solemn baptism should be supplied.

The sacrament is ordinarily conferred by a priest or deacon of the parents' parish.

Catholics 16 years of age and over who have received the sacraments of confirmation and the Eucharist and are practicing their faith are eligible to be sponsors or godparents. Only one is required. Two, one of each sex, are permitted. A non-Catholic Christian cannot be a godparent for a Catholic child, but may serve as a witness to the baptism. A Catholic may not be a godparent for a child baptized in a non-Catholic religion, but may be a witness.

"Because of the close communion between the Catholic Church and the Eastern Orthodox churches," states the 1993 *Directory on Ecumenism,* "it is permissible for a just cause for an Eastern faithful to act as godparent together with a Catholic godparent at the baptism of a Catholic infant or adult, so long as there is provision for the Catholic education of the person being baptized and it is clear that the godparent is a suitable one.

"A Catholic is not forbidden to stand as godparent in an Eastern Orthodox Church if he/she is so invited. In this case, the duty of providing for the Christian education binds in the first place the godparent who belongs to the church in which the child is baptized."

The role of godparents in baptismal ceremonies is secondary to the role of the parents. They serve as representatives of the community of faith and with the parents request baptism for the child and perform other ritual functions. Their function after baptism is to serve as proxies for the parents if the parents should be unable or fail to provide for the religious training of the child.

At baptism every child should be given a name with Christian significance, usually the name of a saint, to symbolize newness of life in Christ.

Christian Initiation of Adults: According to the *Ordo Initiationis Christianae Adultorum* ("Rite of the Christian Initiation of Adults") issued by the Congregation for Divine Worship on Jan. 6, 1972, and put into effect in revised form Sept. 1, 1988, adults are prepared for baptism and reception into the Church in several stages:

• An initial period of inquiry, instruction and evangelization.

• The catechumenate, a period of at least a year of

formal instruction and progressive formation in and familiarity with Christian life. It starts with a statement of purpose and includes a rite of election.

• Immediate preparation, called a period of purification and enlightenment, from the beginning of Lent to reception of the sacraments of initiation — baptism, confirmation, Holy Eucharist — during ceremonies of the Easter Vigil. The period is marked by scrutinies, formal giving of the creed and the Lord's Prayer, the choice of a Christian name, and a final statement of intention.

• A mystagogic phase whose objective is greater familiarity with Christian life in the Church through observances of the Easter season and association with the community of the faithful, and through extended formation for about a year.

National Statutes for the Catechumenate were approved by the National Conference of Catholic Bishops Nov. 11, 1986, and were subsequently ratified by the Vatican.

The priest who baptizes a catechumen can also administer the sacrament of confirmation.

A sponsor is required for the person being baptized.

The *Ordo* also provides a simple rite of initiation for adults in danger of death and for cases in which all stages of the initiation process are not necessary, and guidelines for: (1) the preparation of adults for the sacraments of confirmation and Holy Eucharist in cases where they have been baptized but have not received further formation in the Christian life; (2) the formation and initiation of children of catechetical age.

The Church recognizes the right of anyone over the age of seven to request baptism and to receive the sacrament after completing a course of instruction and giving evidence of good will. Practically, in the case of minors in a non-Catholic family or environment, the Church accepts them when other circumstances favor their ability to practice the faith — e.g., well-disposed family situation, the presence of another or several Catholics in the family. Those who are not in such favorable circumstances are prudently advised to defer reception of the sacrament until they attain the maturity necessary for independent practice of the faith.

Reception of Baptized Christians: Procedure for the reception of already baptized Christians into full communion with the Catholic Church is distinguished from the catechumenate, since they have received some Christian formation. Instruction and formation are provided as necessary, however; and conditional baptism is administered if there is reasonable doubt about the validity of the person's previous baptism.

In the rite of reception, the person is invited to join the community of the Church in professing the Nicene Creed and is asked to state: "I believe and profess all that the holy Catholic Church believes, teaches, and proclaims as revealed by God." The priest places his hand on the head of the person, states the formula of admission to full communion, confirms (in the absence of a bishop), gives a sign of peace, and administers Holy Communion during a Eucharistic Liturgy.

Confirmation

Confirmation is the sacrament by which a baptized person, through anointing with chrism and the imposition of hands, is endowed with the fullness of bap-

tismal grace; is united more intimately to the Church; is enriched with the special power of the Holy Spirit; is committed to be an authentic witness to Christ in word and action. The sacrament confers a character on the soul and can be received only once.

According to the apostolic constitution *Divinae Consortium Naturae,* dated Aug. 15, 1971, in conjunction with the *Ordo Confirmationis* ("Rite of Confirmation"): "The sacrament of confirmation is conferred through the anointing with chrism on the forehead, which is done by the imposition of the hand (matter of the sacrament), and through the words: *'N., receive the seal of the Holy Spirit, the Gift of the Father'"* (form of the sacrament). On May 5, 1975, bishops' conferences in English-speaking countries were informed by the Congregation for Divine Worship that Pope Paul VI had approved this English version of the form of the sacrament: *"Be sealed with the gift of the Holy Spirit."*

The ordinary minister of confirmation in the Roman rite is a bishop. Priests may be delegated for the purpose. A pastor can confirm a parishioner in danger of death, and a priest can confirm in ceremonies of Christian initiation and at the reception of a baptized Christian into union with the Church.

Ideally, the sacrament is conferred during the Eucharistic Liturgy. Elements of the rite include renewal of the promises of baptism, which confirmation ratifies and completes, and the laying on of hands by the confirming bishop and priests participating in the ceremony.

"The entire rite," according to the *Ordo*, "has a twofold meaning. The laying of hands upon the candidates, done by the bishop and the concelebrating priests, expresses the biblical gesture by which the gift of the Holy Spirit is invoked. The anointing with chrism and the accompanying words clearly signify the effect of the Holy Spirit. Signed with the perfumed oil by the bishop's hand, the baptized person receives the indelible character, the seal of the Lord, together with the Spirit who is given and who conforms the person more perfectly to Christ and gives him the grace of spreading the Lord's presence among men."

A sponsor is required for the person being confirmed. Eligible is any Catholic 16 years of age or older who has received the sacraments of confirmation and the Eucharist and is practicing the faith. The baptismal sponsor, preferably, can also be the sponsor for confirmation. Parents may present their children for confirmation but cannot be sponsors.

In the Roman rite, it has been customary for children to receive confirmation within a reasonable time after first Communion and confession. There is a trend, however, to defer confirmation until later when its significance for mature Christian living becomes more evident. In the Eastern rites, confirmation is administered at the same time as baptism.

Eucharist

The Holy Eucharist is a sacrifice (see **The Mass**) and the sacrament in which Christ is present and is received under the appearances of bread and wine.

The matter is bread of wheat, unleavened in the Roman rite and leavened in the Eastern rites, and wine of grape. The form consists of the words of consecration said by the priest at Mass: "This is my body. This is the cup of my blood" (according to the traditional usage of the Roman rite).

Only a priest can consecrate bread and wine so they become the body and blood of Christ. After consecration, however, the Eucharist can be administered by deacons and, for various reasons, by religious and lay persons.

Priests celebrating Mass receive the Eucharist under the species of bread and wine. In the Roman rite, others receive under the species of bread only, i.e., the consecrated host, though in some circumstances they may receive under the species of both bread and wine. In Eastern-rite practice, the faithful generally receive a piece of consecrated leavened bread which has been dipped into consecrated wine (i.e., by intinction).

Conditions for receiving the Eucharist, commonly called Holy Communion, are the state of grace, the right intention and observance of the Eucharistic fast.

The faithful of Roman rite are required by a precept of the Church to receive the Eucharist at least once a year, ordinarily during the Easter time.

(See Eucharistic Fast, Mass, Transubstantiation, Viaticum.)

First Communion and Confession: Children are to be prepared for and given opportunity for receiving both sacraments (Eucharist and reconciliation, or penance) on reaching the age of discretion, at which time they become subject to general norms concerning confession and Communion. This, together with a stated preference for first confession before first Communion, was the central theme of a document entitled Sanctus Pontifex and published May 24, 1973, by the Congregation for the Discipline of the Sacraments and the Congregation for the Clergy, with the approval of Pope Paul VI.

What the document prescribed was the observance of practices ordered by St. Pius X in the decree Quam Singulari of Aug. 8, 1910. Its purpose was to counteract pastoral and catechetical experiments virtually denying children the opportunity of receiving both sacraments at the same time. Termination of such experiments was ordered by the end of the 1972-73 school year.

At the time the document was issued, two- or three-year experiments of this kind — routinely deferring reception of the sacrament of penance until after the first reception of Holy Communion — were in effect in more than half of the dioceses of the U.S. They have remained in effect in many places, despite the advisory from the Vatican.

One reason stated in support of such experiments is the view that children are not capable of serious sin at the age of seven or eight, when Communion is generally received for the first time, and therefore prior reception of the sacrament of penance is not necessary. Another reason is the purpose of making the distinctive nature of the two sacraments clearer to children.

The Vatican view reflected convictions that the principle and practice of devotional reception of penance are as valid for children as they are for adults, and that sound catechetical programs can avoid misconceptions about the two sacraments.

A second letter on the same subject and in the same vein was released May 19, 1977, by the aforementioned congregations. It was issued in response to the question:

" 'Whether it is allowed after the declaration of May 24, 1973, to continue to have, as a general rule, the reception of first Communion precede the reception of the sacrament of penance in those parishes in which this practice developed in the past few years.'

"The Sacred Congregations for the Sacraments and Divine Worship and for the Clergy, with the approval of the Supreme Pontiff, reply: Negative, and according to the mind of the declaration.

"The mind of the declaration is that one year after the promulgation of the same declaration, all experiments of receiving first Communion without the sacrament of penance should cease so that the discipline of the Church might be restored, in the spirit of the decree, Quam Singulari."

The two letters from the Vatican congregations have not produced uniformity of practice in this country. Simultaneous preparation for both sacraments is provided in some dioceses where a child has the option of receiving either sacrament first, with the counsel of parents, priests and teachers. Programs in other dioceses are geared first to reception of Communion and later to reception of the Sacrament of Reconciliation.

Commentators on the letters note that: they are disciplinary rather than doctrinal in content; they are subject to pastoral interpretation by bishops; they cannot be interpreted to mean that a person who is not guilty of serious sin must be required to receive the sacrament of penance before (even first) Communion.

Canon 914 of the Code of Canon Law states that sacramental confession should precede first Communion.

Holy Communion under the Forms of Bread and Wine (by separate taking of the consecrated bread and wine or by intinction, the reception of the host dipped in the wine): Such reception is permitted under conditions stated in instructions issued by the Congregation for Divine Worship (May 25, 1967; June 29, 1970), the General Instruction on the Roman Missal (No. 242), and directives of bishops' conferences and individual bishops.

Accordingly, Communion can be administered in this way to: persons being baptized, received into communion with the Church, confirmed, receiving anointing of the sick; couples at their wedding or jubilee; religious at profession or renewal of profession; lay persons receiving an ecclesiastical assignment (e.g., lay missionaries); participants at concelebrated Masses, retreats, pastoral commission meetings, daily Masses and, in the U.S., Masses on Sundays and holy days of obligation.

A communicant has the option of receiving the Eucharist under the form of bread alone or under the forms of bread and wine. (See New U.S. Norms in the Liturgy section.)

Holy Communion More Than Once a Day: A person who has already received the Eucharist may receive it (only) once again on the same day only during a Eucharistic celebration in which the person participates. A person in danger of death who has already received the Eucharist once or twice is urged to receive Communion again as Viaticum. Pope John Paul approved this decision, in accord with Canon 917, and ordered it published July 11, 1984.

Holy Communion and Eucharistic Devotion outside of Mass: These were the subjects of an instruction

(*De Sacra Communione et de Cultu Mysterii Eucharistici extra Missam*) dated June 21 and made public Oct. 18, 1973, by the Congregation for Divine Worship.

Holy Communion can be given outside of Mass to persons unable for a reasonable cause to receive it during Mass on a given day. The ceremonial rite is modeled on the structure of the Mass, consisting of a penitential act, a scriptural reading, the Lord's Prayer, a sign or gesture of peace, giving of the Eucharist, prayer and final blessing. Viaticum and Communion to the sick can be given by extraordinary ministers (authorized lay persons) with appropriate rites.

Forms of devotion outside of Mass are exposition of the Blessed Sacrament (by men or women religious, especially, or lay persons in the absence of a priest; but only a priest can give the blessing), processions and congresses with appropriate rites.

Intercommunion: Church policy on intercommunion was stated in an "Instruction on the Admission of Other Christians to the Eucharist," dated June 1 and made public July 8, 1972, against the background of the Decree on Ecumenism approved by the Second Vatican Council, and the Directory on Ecumenism issued by the Secretariat for Promoting Christian Unity in 1967, 1970 and 1993.

Basic principles related to intercommunion are:

• "There is an indissoluble link between the mystery of the Church and the mystery of the Eucharist, or between ecclesial and Eucharistic communion; the celebration of the Eucharist of itself signifies the fullness of profession of faith and ecclesial communion" (1972 Instruction).

• "Eucharistic communion practiced by those who are not in full ecclesial communion with each other cannot be the expression of that full unity which the Eucharist of its nature signifies and which in this case does not exist; for this reason such communion cannot be regarded as a means to be used to lead to full ecclesial communion" (1972 Instruction).

• The question of reciprocity "arises only with those churches which have preserved the substance of the Eucharist, the sacrament of orders and apostolic succession" (1967 Directory).

• "A Catholic cannot ask for the Eucharist except from a minister who has been validly ordained" (1967 Directory).

The policy distinguishes between separated Eastern Christians and other Christians.

With Separated Eastern Christians (e.g., Orthodox): These may be given the Eucharist (as well as penance and anointing of the sick) at their request. Catholics may receive these same sacraments from priests of separated Eastern churches if they experience genuine spiritual necessity, seek spiritual benefit, and access to a Catholic priest is morally or physically impossible. This policy (of reciprocity) derives from the facts that the separated Eastern churches have apostolic succession through their bishops, valid priests, and sacramental beliefs and practices in accord with those of the Catholic Church.

With Other Christians (e.g., members of Reformation-related churches, others): Admission to the Eucharist in the Catholic Church, according to the Directory on Ecumenism, "is confined to particular cases of those Christians who have a faith in the sacrament in conformity with that of the Church, who experience a serious spiritual need for the Eucharistic sustenance, who for a prolonged period are unable to have recourse to a minister of their own community and who ask for the sacrament of their own accord; all this provided that they have proper dispositions and lead lives worthy of a Christian." The spiritual need is defined as "a need for an increase in spiritual life and a need for a deeper involvement in the mystery of the Church and its unity."

Circumstances under which Communion may be given to other properly disposed Christians are danger of death, imprisonment, persecution, grave spiritual necessity coupled with no chance of recourse to a minister of their own community.

Catholics cannot ask for the Eucharist from ministers of other Christian churches who have not been validly ordained to the priesthood.

Ecclesia de Eucharistia

On Apr. 17, 2002, Holy Thursday, during the Mass of the Lord's Supper, and within the liturgical setting of the beginning of the Paschal Triduum Pope John Paul II issued the fourteenth encyclical letter of his pontificate, *Ecclesia de Eucharistia.* The encyclical was intended to offer a theological reflection on the mystery of the Eucharist in its relationship with the Church.

Specifically, the pope uses the letter to reaffirm the traditional teaching of the Church on the real presence of Christ in the Eucharist, on the need for validly ordained ministers for its celebration, and on the importance of following the Church's liturgical norms.

The encyclical is organized into five chapters and a conclusion, beginning with the declaration: "The Church draws her life from the Eucharist. This truth does not simply express a daily experience of faith, but recapitulates the heart of the mystery of the Church. In a variety of ways she joyfully experiences the constant fulfillment of the promise." The Eucharistic Sacrifice is thus truly "the source and summit of the Christian life," as the Second Vatican Council proclaimed, and contains the Church's entire spiritual wealth: Jesus Christ, who offers himself to the Father for the redemption of the world. In celebrating this "mystery of faith," the Church presents the Paschal Triduum in a contemporary way, for men and women in every age.

Chapter One, "The Mystery of Faith," describes the sacrificial nature of the Eucharist which, through the ministry of the priest, makes sacramentally present at each Mass the body "given up" and the blood "poured out" by Christ for the salvation of the world.

Chapter Two, "The Eucharist Builds the Church," states that the Church "teaches that the celebration of the Eucharist is at the centre of the process of the Church's growth."

Chapter Three, "The Apostolicity of the Eucharist and of the Church," notes that that just as the Church is apostolic so too is the Eucharist in three ways. First, "The Eucharist too has its foundation in the Apostles, not in the sense that it did not originate in Christ himself, but because it was entrusted by Jesus to the Apostles and has been handed down to us by them and by their successors. It is in continuity with the practice of the Apostles, in obedience to the Lord's command, that the Church has celebrated the Eucharist down the centuries." Second, "it is celebrated in conformity with the faith of the Apostles." Third, just as the full reality of Church does not exist without apostolic succession, so there is no true Eucharist without the Bishop.

Chapter Four, "The Eucharist and Ecclesial Communion," teaches that "the culmination of all the sacraments in perfecting our communion with God the Father by identification with his only-begotten Son through the working of the Holy Spirit."

Chapter Five, "The Dignity of the Eucharistic Celebration" is concerned with the truthful celebration of the Eucharist enunciated in the previous chapter.

Chapter Six, "At the School of Mary, 'Woman of the Eucharist,'" offers a reflection on the analogy between the Mother of God, and the Church.

In his conclusion, the pontiff quotes his Apostolic Letter *Novo Millennio Ineunte* in stating, "it is not a matter of inventing a 'new programme'. The programme already exists: it is the plan found in the Gospel and in the living Tradition; it is the same as ever." Clearly, the implementation of this process of a renewed impetus in Christian living passes through the Eucharist. He concludes, "In the humble signs of bread and wine, changed into his body and blood, Christ walks beside us as our strength and our food for the journey, and he enables us to become, for everyone, witnesses of hope." (*See* **Special Reports.**)

Penance

Penance is the sacrament by which sins committed after baptism are forgiven and a person is reconciled with God and the Church.

Individual and integral confession and absolution are the only ordinary means for the forgiveness of serious sin and for reconciliation with God and the Church.

(Other than ordinary means are perfect contrition and general absolution without prior confession, both of which require the intention of subsequent confession and absolution.)

A revised ritual for the sacrament — *Ordo Paenitentiae*, published by the Congregation of Divine Worship Feb. 7, 1974, and made mandatory in the U.S. from the first Sunday of Lent, 1977 — reiterates standard doctrine concerning the sacrament; emphasizes the social (communal and ecclesial) aspects of sin and conversion, with due regard for personal aspects and individual reception of the sacrament; prescribes three forms for celebration of the sacrament; and presents models for community penitential services.

The basic elements of the sacrament are sorrow for sin because of a supernatural motive, confession (of previously unconfessed mortal or grave sins, required; of venial sins also, but not of necessity), and reparation (by means of prayer or other act enjoined by the confessor), all of which comprise the matter of the sacrament; and absolution, which is the form of the sacrament.

The traditional words of absolution — *"I absolve you from your sins in the name of the Father, and of the Son, and of the Holy Spirit"* — remain unchanged at the conclusion of a petition in the new rite that God may grant pardon and peace through the ministry of the Church.

The minister of the sacrament is an authorized priest — i.e., one who, besides having the power of orders to forgive sins, also has faculties of jurisdiction granted by an ecclesiastical superior and/or by canon law.

The sacrament can be celebrated in three ways:

• For individuals, the traditional manner remains acceptable but is enriched with additional elements including: reception of the penitent and making of the Sign of the Cross; an exhortation by the confessor to trust in God; a reading from Scripture; confession of sins; manifestation of repentance; petition for God's forgiveness through the ministry of the Church and the absolution of the priest; praise of God's mercy, and dismissal in peace. Some of these elements are optional.

• For several penitents, in the course of a community celebration including a Liturgy of the Word of God and prayers, individual confession and absolution, and an act of thanksgiving.

• For several penitents, in the course of a community celebration, with general confession and general absolution. In extraordinary cases, reconciliation may be attained by general absolution without prior individual confession as, for example, under these circumstances: (1) danger of death, when there is neither time nor priests available for hearing confessions; (2) grave necessity of a number of penitents who, because of a shortage of confessors, would be deprived of sacramental grace or Communion for a lengthy period of time through no fault of their own. Persons receiving general absolution are obliged to be properly disposed and resolved to make an individual confession of the grave sins from which they have been absolved; this confession should be made as soon as the opportunity to confess presents itself and before any second reception of general absolution.

Norms regarding general absolution, issued by the Congregation for the Doctrine of the Faith in 1972, are not intended to provide a basis for convoking large gatherings of the faithful for the purpose of imparting general absolution, in the absence of extraordinary circumstances. Judgment about circumstances that warrant general absolution belongs principally to the bishop of the place, with due regard for related decisions of appropriate episcopal conferences.

Communal celebrations of the sacrament are not held in connection with Mass.

The place of individual confession, as determined by episcopal conferences in accordance with given norms, can be the traditional confessional or another appropriate setting.

A precept of the Church obliges the faithful guilty of grave sin to confess at least once a year.

The Church favors more frequent reception of the sacrament not only for the reconciliation of persons guilty of serious sins but also for reasons of devotion. Devotional confession — in which venial sins or previously forgiven sins are confessed — serves the purpose of confirming persons in penance and conversion.

Penitential Celebrations: Communal penitential celebrations are designed to emphasize the social dimensions of Christian life — the community aspects and significance of penance and reconciliation.

Elements of such celebrations are community prayer, hymns and songs, scriptural and other readings, examination of conscience, general confession and expression of sorrow for sin, acts of penance and reconciliation, and a form of non-sacramental absolution resembling the one in the penitential rite of the Mass.

If the sacrament is celebrated during the service, there must be individual confession and absolution of sin.

Recent developments: On May 2, 2002, officials of the Roman Curia released a *motu proprio* by Pope John Paul II, *Misericordia Dei* ("Mercy of God, On Certain Aspects of the Celebration of the Sacrament of Penance"). The 15-page document called for a "vigorous revitalization" of the sacrament and asked bishops to adopt stricter observance on Church law's "grave necessity" requirement as a condition for the use of general absolution. It also requested that bishops' conferences submit national norms for general absolution to the Holy See for approval "as soon as possible."

In February 2003, the Bishops' Committee on the Liturgy and the Subcommittee for the Jubilee Year 2000 of the USCCB issued a new booklet, *Celebrating the Sacrament of Penance: Questions and Answers.* The booklet provides answers to some of the frequently asked questions about the Sacrament of Penance, including "Why Do We Need the Sacrament of Penance?" "What Happens in the Sacrament of Penance?" and "What is 'General Absolution'?" The booklet is intended for use in parishes during preparation for the Sacrament of Penance, as a resource for reflection on the sacrament during particular seasons such as Lent, and as a practical tool to aid penitents as they go to confession.

(*See* **Absolution, Confession, Confessional, Confessor, Contrition, Faculties, Forgiveness of Sin, Power of the Keys, Seal of Confession, Sin.**)

Anointing of the Sick

This sacrament, promulgated by St. James the Apostle (Jas 5:13-15), can be administered to the faithful after reaching the age of reason who are in danger because of illness or old age. By the anointing with blessed oil and the prayer of a priest, the sacrament confers on the person comforting grace; the remission of venial sins and inculpably unconfessed mortal sins, together with at least some of the temporal punishment due for sins; and, sometimes, results in an improved state of health.

The matter of this sacrament is the anointing with blessed oil (olive oil, or vegetable oil if necessary) of the forehead and hands; in cases of necessity, a single anointing of another portion of the body suffices. The form is: "Through this holy anointing and his most loving mercy, may the Lord assist you by the grace of the Holy Spirit so that, when you have been freed from your sins, he may save you and in his goodness raise you up."

Anointing of the sick, formerly called extreme unction, may be received more than once, e.g., in new or continuing stages of serious illness. Ideally, the sacrament should be administered while the recipient is conscious and in conjunction with the sacraments of penance and the Eucharist. It should be administered in cases of doubt as to whether the person has reached the age of reason, is dangerously ill or dead.

The sacrament can be administered during a communal celebration in some circumstances, as in a home for the aged.

Holy Orders

Order is the sacrament by which the mission given by Christ to the Apostles continues to be exercised in the Church until the end of time; it is the sacrament of apostolic mission. It has three grades: episcopacy, priesthood and diaconate. The sacrament confers a character on the soul and can be received only once. The minister of the sacrament is a bishop.

Order, like matrimony but in a different way, is a social sacrament. As the Second Vatican Council declared in *Lumen Gentium*, the Dogmatic Constitution on the Church:

"For the nurturing and constant growth of the People of God, Christ the Lord instituted in his Church a variety of ministries, which work for the good of the whole body. For those ministers who are endowed with sacred power are servants of their brethren, so that all who are of the People of God, and therefore enjoy a true Christian dignity, can work toward a common goal freely and in an orderly way, and arrive at salvation" (No. 18).

Bishop: The fullness of the priesthood belongs to those who have received the order of bishop. Bishops, in hierarchical union with the pope and their fellow bishops, are the successors of the Apostles as pastors of the Church: they have individual responsibility for the care of the local churches they serve and collegial responsibility for the care of the universal Church (*see* **Collegiality**). In the ordination or consecration of bishops, the essential form is the imposition of hands by the consecrator(s) and the assigned prayer in the preface of the rite of ordination.

"With their helpers, the priests and deacons, bishops have taken up the service of the community presiding in place of God over the flock whose shepherds they are, as teachers of doctrine, priests of sacred worship, and officers of good order" (No. 20).

Priests: A priest is an ordained minister with the power to celebrate Mass, administer the sacraments, preach and teach the word of God, impart blessings, and perform additional pastoral functions, according to the mandate of his ecclesiastical superior.

Concerning priests, the Second Vatican Council stated in *Lumen Gentium* (No. 28):

"The divinely established ecclesiastical ministry is exercised on different levels by those who from antiquity have been called bishops, priests, and deacons. Although priests do not possess the highest degree of the priesthood, and although they are dependent on the bishops in the exercise of their power, they are nevertheless united with the bishops in sacerdotal dignity. By the power of the sacrament of orders, and in the image of Christ the eternal High Priest (Heb 5:1-10; 7:24; 9:11-28), they are consecrated to preach the Gospel, shepherd the faithful, and celebrate divine worship as true priests of the New Testament.

"Priests, prudent cooperators with the episcopal order as well as its aides and instruments, are called to serve the People of God. They constitute one priesthood with their bishop, although that priesthood is comprised of different functions."

In the ordination of a priest of Roman rite, the essential matter is the imposition of hands on the heads of those being ordained by the ordaining bishop. The essential form is the accompanying prayer in the preface of the ordination ceremony. Other elements in the rite are the presentation of the implements of sacrifice

— the chalice containing the wine and the paten containing a host — with accompanying prayers.

Deacon: There are two kinds of deacons: those who receive the order and remain in it permanently, and those who receive the order while advancing to priesthood. The following quotation — from Vatican II's Dogmatic Constitution on the Church (*Lumen Gentium*, No. 29) — describes the nature and role of the diaconate, with emphasis on the permanent diaconate.

"At a lower level of the hierarchy are deacons, upon whom hands are imposed 'not unto the priesthood, but unto a ministry of service.' For strengthened by sacramental grace, in communion with the bishop and his group of priests, they serve the People of God in the ministry of the liturgy, of the word, and of charity. It is the duty of the deacon, to the extent that he has been authorized by competent authority, to administer baptism solemnly, to be custodian and dispenser of the Eucharist, to assist at and bless marriages in the name of the Church, to bring Viaticum to the dying, to read the sacred Scripture to the faithful, to instruct and exhort the people, to preside at the worship and prayer of the faithful, to administer sacramentals, and to officiate at funeral and burial services. (Deacons are) dedicated to duties of charity and administration.

"The diaconate can in the future be restored as a proper and permanent rank of the hierarchy. It pertains to the competent territorial bodies of bishops, of one kind or another, to decide, with the approval of the Supreme Pontiff, whether and where it is opportune for such deacons to be appointed for the care of souls. With the consent of the Roman Pontiff, this diaconate will be able to be conferred upon men of more mature age, even upon those living in the married state. It may also be conferred upon suitable young men. For them, however, the law of celibacy must remain intact" (No. 29).

The Apostles ordained the first seven deacons (Acts 6:1-6): Stephen, Philip, Prochorus, Nicanor, Timon, Parmenas, Nicholas.

Former Orders, Ministries: With the revision of the sacrament of order which began in 1971, the orders of subdeacon, acolyte, exorcist, lector and porter were abolished because they and their respective functions had fallen into disuse or did not require ordination. The Holy See started revision of the sacrament of order in 1971. By virtue of an indult of Oct. 5 of that year, the bishops of the U.S. were permitted to discontinue ordaining porters and exorcists. Another indult, dated three days later, permitted the use of revised rites for ordaining acolytes and lectors.

To complete the revision, Pope Paul VI abolished Sept. 14, 1972, the orders of porter, exorcist and subdeacon; decreed that laymen, as well as candidates for the diaconate and priesthood, can be installed (rather than ordained) in the ministries (rather than orders) of acolyte and lector; reconfirmed the suppression of tonsure and its replacement with a service of dedication to God and the Church; and stated that a man enters the clerical state on ordination to the diaconate.

The abolished orders were:

• Subdeacon, with specific duties in liturgical worship, especially at Mass. The order, whose first extant mention dates from about the middle of the third century, was regarded as minor until the 13th century;

afterwards, it was called a major order in the West but not in the East.

• Acolyte, to serve in minor capacities in liturgical worship; a function now performed by Mass servers.

• Exorcist, to perform services of exorcism for expelling evil spirits; a function which came to be reserved to specially delegated priests.

• Lector, to read scriptural and other passages during liturgical worship; a function now generally performed by lay persons.

• Porter, to guard the entrance to an assembly of Christians and to ward off undesirables who tried to gain admittance; an order of early origin and utility but of present insignificance.

Permanent Diaconate

Restoration of the permanent diaconate in the Roman rite — making it possible for men to become deacons permanently, without going on to the priesthood — was promulgated by Pope Paul VI June 18, 1967, in a document entitled *Sacrum Diaconatus Ordinem* ("Sacred Order of the Diaconate").

The Pope's action implemented the desire expressed by the Second Vatican Council for reestablishment of the diaconate as an independent order in its own right not only to supply ministers for carrying on the work of the Church but also to complete the hierarchical structure of the Church of Roman rite.

Permanent deacons have been traditional in the Eastern Church. The Western Church, however, since the fourth or fifth century, generally followed the practice of conferring the diaconate only as a sacred order preliminary to the priesthood, and of restricting the ministry of deacons to liturgical functions.

The pope's document, issued on his own initiative, provided:

• Qualified unmarried men 25 years of age or older may be ordained deacons. They cannot marry after ordination.

• Qualified married men 35 years of age or older may be ordained deacons. The consent of the wife of a prospective deacon is required. A married deacon cannot remarry after the death of his wife.

• Preparation for the diaconate includes a course of study and formation over a period of at least three years.

• Candidates who are not members of religious institutes must be affiliated with a diocese. Reestablishment of the diaconate among religious is reserved to the Holy See.

• Deacons will practice their ministry under the direction of a bishop and with the priests with whom they will be associated. (For functions, *see* the description of deacon, under **Holy Orders.**)

Restoration of the permanent diaconate in the U.S. was approved by the Holy See in October 1968. Shortly afterwards the U.S. bishops established a committee for the permanent diaconate, which was chaired by Bishop Edward U. Kmiec of Nashville in 1997. The current head of the committee is Bishop Frederick F. Campbell of Columbus, Ohio. The committee operates through a secretariat, with offices at 3211 Fourth St. N.E., Washington, DC 20017. Deacon John Pistone is executive director.

Status and Functions

The 2006 *Official Catholic Directory* reports that in

the U.S. there were a total of 14,995 permanent deacons (the highest total by far for any single country), a decrease of 32 from the previous year and an increase of 3,468 from 1996. Worldwide, there are currently 32,324 deacons, according to the 2004 edition of the *Annuarium Statisticum Ecclesiæ* (the most recent edition).

Training programs of spiritual, theological and pastoral formation are based on guidelines emanating from the National Conference of Catholic Bishops.

Deacons have various functions, depending on the nature of their assignments. Liturgically, they can officiate at baptisms, weddings, wake services and funerals, can preach and distribute Holy Communion. Some are engaged in religious education work. All are intended to carry out works of charity and pastoral service of one kind or another.

The majority of deacons, the majority of whom are married, continue in their secular work. Their ministry of service is developing in three dimensions: of liturgy, of the word, and of charity. Depending on the individual deacon's abilities and preference, he is assigned by his bishop to either a parochial ministry or to another field of service. Deacons are active in a variety of ministries including those to prison inmates and their families, the sick in hospitals, nursing homes and homes for the aged, alienated youth, the elderly and the poor, and in various areas of legal service to the indigent, of education and campus ministry.

National Association of Diaconate Directors: Membership organization of directors, vicars and other staff personnel of diaconate programs. Established in 1977 to promote effective communication and facilitate the exchange of information and resources of members; to develop professional expertise and promote research, training and self evaluation; to foster accountability and seek ways to promote means of implementing solutions to problems. The association is governed by an executive board of elected officers. Officers include Deacons: Maurice Reed of Green Bay, pres., 1997-98; Peter D'Heilly of St. Paul-Minneapolis, president-elect; Thomas Welch, exec. dir. Office: 1337 W. Ohio St., Chicago, IL 60622.

Ordination of Women

The Catholic Church believes and teaches that, in fidelity to the will of Christ, it cannot ordain women to the priesthood. This position has been set out over the last quarter-century in a series of authoritative documents published by or with the authority of Pope Paul VI and Pope John Paul II.

The first of these, *Inter Insigniores* ("Among the Characteristics"), was issued by the Congregation for the Doctrine of the Faith in October 1976. Its central statement is: "The Sacred Congregation for the Doctrine of the Faith judges it necessary to recall that the Church, in fidelity to the example of the Lord, does not consider herself authorized to admit women to priestly ordination."

In support of this, the document cited the constant tradition of the Church, the fact that Christ called only men to be Apostles and the continuation of this practice by the Apostles themselves, and the sacramental appropriateness of a male priesthood acting *in persona Christi* — in the person of Christ.

In light of continuing discussion, Pope John Paul II returned to the subject in the apostolic letter *Ordinatio Sacerdotalis* ("Priestly Ordination"), issued May 29, 1994: "Wherefore, in order that all doubt may be removed regarding a matter of great importance, a matter which pertains to the Church's divine constitution itself, in virtue of my ministry of confirming the brethren (cf. Lk 22.32) I declare that the Church has no authority whatsoever to confer priestly ordination on women and that this judgment is to be definitively held by all the Church's faithful."

The Congregation for the Doctrine of the Faith followed this on Oct. 28, 1995, with a response, published over the signature of its Prefect, Cardinal Joseph Ratzinger, to a bishop's inquiry concerning how "to be definitively held" should be understood. The response was:

"This teaching requires definitive assent, since, founded on the written Word of God and from the beginning constantly preserved and applied in the Tradition of the Church, it has been set forth infallibly by the ordinary and universal Magisterium (cf. Second Vatican Council, Dogmatic Constitution on the Church *Lumen Gentium*, 25, 2).

Concerning the possible ordination of women to the diaconate, the International Theological Commission in 2002 concluded that the permanent diaconate belongs to the sacrament of orders and thus is limited to men only.

MATRIMONY

Marriage Doctrine

The following excerpts, stating key points of doctrine on marriage, are from *Gaudium et Spes*, (Nos. 48 to 51) promulgated by the Second Vatican Council:

Conjugal Covenant

The intimate partnership of married life and love has been established by the Creator and qualified by his laws. It is rooted in the conjugal covenant of irrevocable personal consent.

God himself is the author of matrimony, endowed as it is with various benefits and purposes. All of these have a very decisive bearing on the continuation of the human race, on the personal development and eternal destiny of the individual members of a family, and on the dignity, stability, peace, and prosperity of the family itself and of human society as a whole. By their very nature, the institution of matrimony itself and conjugal love are ordained for the procreation and education of children, and find in them their ultimate crown.

Thus a man and a woman render mutual help and service to each other through an intimate union of their persons and of their actions. Through this union they experience the meaning of their oneness and attain to it with growing perfection day by day. As a mutual gift of two persons, this intimate union, as well as the good of the children, imposes total fidelity on the spouses and argues for an unbreakable oneness between them (No. 48).

Sacrament of Matrimony

Christ the Lord abundantly blessed this many-faceted love. The Savior of men and the Spouse of the Church comes into the lives of married Christians through the sacrament of matrimony. He abides with them thereafter so that, just as he loved the Church and handed himself over on her behalf, the spouses may love each other with perpetual fidelity through mutual self-bestowal.

Graced with the dignity and office of fatherhood and motherhood, parents will energetically acquit themselves of a duty which devolves primarily on them; namely, education, and especially religious education.

The Christian family, which springs from marriage as a reflection of the loving covenant uniting Christ with the Church, and as a participation in that covenant, will manifest to all men the Savior's living presence in the world, and the genuine nature of the Church (No. 48).

Conjugal Love

The biblical Word of God several times urges the betrothed and the married to nourish and develop their wedlock by pure conjugal love and undivided affection.

This love is an eminently human one since it is directed from one person to another through an affection of the will. It involves the good of the whole person. Therefore it can enrich the expressions of body and mind with a unique dignity, ennobling these expressions as special ingredients and signs of the friendship distinctive of marriage. This love the Lord has judged worthy of special gifts, healing, perfecting, and exalting gifts of grace and of charity.

Such love, merging the human with the divine, leads the spouses to a free and mutual gift of themselves, a gift proving itself by gentle affection and by deed. Such love pervades the whole of their lives. Indeed, by its generous activity it grows better and grows greater. Therefore it far excels mere erotic inclination, which, selfishly pursued, soon enough fades wretchedly away.

This love is uniquely expressed and perfected through the marital act. The actions within marriage by which the couple are united intimately and chastely are noble and worthy ones. Expressed in a manner which is truly human, these actions signify and promote that mutual self-giving by which spouses enrich each other with a joyful and a thankful will.

Sealed by mutual faithfulness and hallowed above all by Christ's sacrament, this love remains steadfastly true in body and in mind, in bright days or dark. It will never be profaned by adultery or divorce. Firmly established by the Lord, the unity of marriage will radiate from the equal personal dignity of wife and husband, a dignity acknowledged by mutual and total love.

The steady fulfillment of the duties of this Christian vocation demands notable virtue. For this reason, strengthened by grace for holiness of life, the couple will painstakingly cultivate and pray for constancy of love, largeheartedness, and the spirit of sacrifice (No. 49).

Fruitfulness of Marriage

Marriage and conjugal love are by their nature ordained toward the begetting and educating of children. Children are really the supreme gift of marriage and contribute very substantially to the welfare of their parents. God himself wished to share with man a certain special participation in his own creative work. Thus he blessed male and female, saying: "Increase and multiply" (Gn 1:28).

Hence, while not making the other purposes of matrimony of less account, the true practice of conjugal love, and the whole meaning of the family life which results from it, have this aim: that the couple be ready with stout hearts to cooperate with the love of the Creator and the Savior, who through them will enlarge and enrich his own family day by day.

Parents should regard as their proper mission the task of transmitting human life and educating those to whom it has been transmitted. They should realize that they are thereby cooperators with the love of God the Creator, and are, so to speak, the interpreters of that love. Thus they will fulfill their task with human and Christian responsibility (No. 50).

Norms of Judgment

They will thoughtfully take into account both their own welfare and that of their children, those already born and those who may be foreseen. For this accounting they will reckon with both the material and the spiritual conditions of the times as well as of their state in life. Finally, they will consult the interests of the family group, of temporal society, and of the Church herself.

The parents themselves should ultimately make this judgment in the sight of God. But in their manner of acting, spouses should be aware that they cannot proceed arbitrarily. They must always be governed according to a conscience dutifully conformed to the divine law itself, and should be submissive toward the Church's teaching office, which authentically interprets that law in the light of the Gospel. That divine law reveals and protects the integral meaning of conjugal love, and impels it toward a truly human fulfillment.

Marriage, to be sure, is not instituted solely for procreation. Rather, its very nature as an unbreakable compact between persons, and the welfare of the children, both demand that the mutual love of the spouses, too, be embodied in a rightly ordered manner, that it grow and ripen. Therefore, marriage persists as a whole manner and communion of life, and maintains its value and indissolubility, even when offspring are lacking — despite, rather often, the very intense desire of the couple (No. 50).

Love and Life

This Council realizes that certain modern conditions often keep couples from arranging their married lives harmoniously, and that they find themselves in circumstances where at least temporarily the size of their families should not be increased. As a result, the faithful exercise of love and the full intimacy of their lives are hard to maintain. But where the intimacy of married life is broken off, it is not rare for its faithfulness to be imperiled and its quality of fruitfulness ruined. For then the upbringing of the children and the courage to accept new ones are both endangered.

To these problems there are those who presume to offer dishonorable solutions. Indeed, they do not recoil from the taking of life. But the Church issues the reminder that a true contradiction cannot exist between the divine laws pertaining to the transmission of life and those pertaining to the fostering of authentic conjugal love.

Church Teaching

For God, the Lord of Life, has conferred on men the surpassing ministry of safeguarding life — a ministry which must be fulfilled in a manner which is worthy of men. Therefore from the moment of its conception life must be guarded with the greatest care, while abortion and infanticide are unspeakable crimes. The sexual characteristics of man and the human faculty of reproduction wonderfully exceed the dispositions of lower forms of life. Hence the acts themselves which are proper to conjugal love and which are exercised in accord with genuine human dignity must be honored with great reverence (No. 51).

Therefore when there is question of harmonizing conjugal love with the responsible transmission of life, the moral aspect of any procedure does not depend solely on the sincere intentions or on an evaluation of motives. It must be determined by objective standards. These, based on the nature of the human person and his acts, preserve the full sense of mutual self-giving and human procreation in the context of true love. Such a goal cannot be achieved unless the virtue of conjugal chastity is sincerely practiced. Relying on these principles, sons of the Church may not undertake methods of regulating procreation which are found blameworthy by the teaching authority of the Church in its unfolding of the divine law.

Everyone should be persuaded that human life and the task of transmitting it are not realities bound up with this world alone. Hence they cannot be measured or perceived only in terms of it, but always have a bearing on the eternal destiny of men (No. 51).

Humanae Vitae

Marriage doctrine and morality were the subjects of the encyclical letter *Humanae Vitae* ("Of Human Life"), issued by Pope Paul VI, July 29, 1968. *Humanae Vitae* was given reaffirmation and its teaching restated and defended by Pope John Paul II in his encyclical *Evangelium Vitae* (*The Gospel of Life*, 1995). Following are a number of key excerpts from *Humanae Vitae*, which was framed in the pattern of traditional teaching and statements by the Second Vatican Council.

Each and every marriage act ("*quilibet matrimonii usus*") must remain open to the transmission of life (No. 11).

Indeed, by its intimate structure, the conjugal act, while most closely uniting husband and wife, capacitates them for the generation of new lives according to laws inscribed in the very being of man and of woman. By safeguarding both these essential aspects, the unitive and the procreative, the conjugal act preserves in its fullness the sense of true mutual love and its ordination toward man's most high calling to parenthood (No. 12).

It is, in fact, justly observed that a conjugal act imposed upon one's partner without regard for his or her condition and lawful desires is not a true act of love, and therefore denies an exigency of right moral order in the relationships between husband and wife. Hence, one who reflects well must also recognize that a reciprocal act of love which jeopardizes the responsibility to transmit life — which God the Creator, according to particular laws, inserted therein — is in contradiction with the design constitutive of marriage and with the will of the Author of life. To use this divine gift, destroying, even if only partially, its meaning and its purpose, is to contradict the nature both of man and of woman and of their most intimate relationship, and therefore it is to contradict also the plan of God and his will (No. 13).

Forbidden Actions

The direct interruption of the generative process already begun, and, above all, directly willed and procured abortion, even if for therapeutic reasons, are to be absolutely excluded as licit means of regulating birth.

Equally to be excluded is direct sterilization, whether perpetual or temporary, whether of the man or of the woman. Similarly excluded is every action which, either in anticipation of the conjugal act, or in its accomplishment, or in the development of its natural consequences, proposes, whether as an end or as a means, to render procreation impossible.

To justify conjugal acts made intentionally infecund, one cannot invoke as valid reasons the lesser evil, or the fact that such acts would constitute a whole together with the fecund acts already performed or to follow later and hence would share in one and the same moral goodness. In truth, if it is sometimes licit to tolerate a lesser evil in order to avoid a greater evil or to promote a greater good, it is not licit, even for the gravest reasons, to do evil so that good may follow therefrom; that is, to make into the object of a positive act of the will something which is intrinsically disorder, and hence unworthy of the human person, even when the intention is to safeguard or promote individual, family or social well-being.

Consequently, it is an error to think that a conjugal act which is deliberately made infecund, and so is intrinsically dishonest, could be made honest and right by the ensemble of a fecund conjugal life (No. 14).

If, then, there are serious motives to space out births, which derive from the physical or psychological conditions of husband and wife, or from external conditions, the Church teaches that it is then licit to take into account the natural rhythms immanent in the generative functions, for the use of marriage in the infecund periods only, and in this way to regulate birth without offending earlier stated principles (No. 16).

Pastoral Concerns

We do not at all intend to hide the sometimes serious difficulties inherent in the life of Christian married persons; for them, as for everyone else, "the gate is narrow and the way is hard that leads to life." But the hope of that life must illuminate their way, as with courage they strive to live with wisdom, justice and piety in this present time, knowing that the figure of this world passes away.

Let married couples then, face up to the efforts needed, supported by the faith and hope which "do not disappoint because God's love has been poured into our hearts through the Holy Spirit, who has been given to us." Let them implore divine assistance by persevering prayer; above all, let them draw from the source of grace and charity in the Eucharist. And, if sin should still keep its hold over them, let them not be discouraged but rather have recourse with humble perseverance to the mercy of God, which is poured forth in the sacrament of penance (No. 25).

Marriage Laws

The Catholic Church claims jurisdiction over its members in matters pertaining to marriage. Church legislation on the subject is stated principally in 111 canons of the Code of Canon Law.

Marriage laws of the Church provide juridical norms in support of the marriage covenant. In 10 chapters, the revised Code covers: pastoral directives for preparing men and women for marriage; impediments in general and in particular; matrimonial consent; form for the celebration of marriage; mixed marriages; secret celebration of marriage; effects of marriage; separation of spouses; and convalidation of marriage.

Catholics are bound by all marriage laws of the Church. Non-Catholics, whether baptized or not, are not considered bound by these ecclesiastical laws except in cases of marriage with a Catholic. Certain natural laws, in the Catholic view, bind all men and women, irrespective of their religious beliefs; accordingly, marriage is prohibited before the time of puberty, without knowledge and free mutual consent, in the case of an already existing valid marriage bond, in the case of antecedent and perpetual impotence.

Formalities

These include, in addition to arrangements for the time and place of the marriage ceremony, doctrinal and moral instruction concerning marriage and the recording of data which verifies in documentary form the eligibility and freedom of the persons to marry. Records of this kind, which are confidential, are preserved in the archives of the church where the marriage takes place.

Premarital instructions are the subject matter of Pre-Cana Conferences.

Marital Consent

Matrimonial consent can be invalidated by an essential defect, substantial error, the strong influence of force and fear, the presence of a condition or intention against the nature of marriage.

Form of Marriage

A Catholic is required, for validity and lawfulness, to contract marriage — with another Catholic or with a non-Catholic — in the presence of a competent priest or deacon and two witnesses.

There are two exceptions to this law. A Roman-rite Catholic (since Mar. 25, 1967) or an Eastern-rite Catholic (since Nov. 21, 1964) can contract marriage validly in the presence of a priest of a separated Eastern-rite Church, provided other requirements of law are complied with. With permission of the competent Roman-rite or Eastern-rite bishop, this form of marriage is lawful, as well as valid. (See Eastern-rite Laws, below.)

With these two exceptions, and aside from cases covered by special permission, the Church does not regard as valid any marriages involving Catholics which take place before non-Catholic ministers of religion or civil officials.

(An excommunication formerly in force against Catholics who celebrated marriage before a non-Catholic minister was abrogated in a decree issued by the Sacred Congregation for the Doctrine of the Faith on Mar. 18, 1966.)

The ordinary place of marriage is the parish of either Catholic party or of the Catholic party in case of a mixed marriage.

Church law regarding the form of marriage does not affect non-Catholics in marriages among themselves. The Church recognizes as valid the marriages of non-Catholics before ministers of religion and civil officials, unless they are rendered null and void on other grounds.

The canonical form is not to be observed in the case of a marriage between a non-Catholic and a baptized Catholic who has left the Church by a formal act.

Impediments

Diriment Impediments to marriage are factors that render a marriage invalid.

• Age, which obtains before completion of the 14th year for a woman and the 16th year for a man

• Impotency, if it is antecedent to the marriage and permanent (this differs from sterility, which is not an impediment)

• The bond of an existing valid marriage

• Disparity of worship, which obtains when one party is a Catholic and the other party is unbaptized

• Sacred orders

• Religious profession of the perpetual vow of chastity

• Abduction, which impedes the freedom of the person abducted

• Crime, variously involving elements of adultery, promise or attempt to marry, conspiracy to murder a husband or wife

• Blood relationship in the direct line (father-daughter, mother-son, etc.) and to the fourth degree inclusive of the collateral line (brother-sister, first cousins)

• Affinity, or relationship resulting from a valid marriage, in any degree of the direct line

•Public honesty, arising from an invalid marriage or from public or notorious concubinage; it renders either party incapable of marrying blood relatives of the other in the first degree of the direct line

• Legal relationship arising from adoption; it renders either party incapable of marrying relatives of the other in the direct line or in the second degree of the collateral line.

Dispensations from impediments: Persons hindered by impediments cannot marry unless they are dispensed therefrom in view of reasons recognized in canon law. Local bishops can dispense from the impediments most often encountered (e.g., disparity of worship) as well as others.

Decision regarding some dispensations is reserved to the Holy See.

Separation

A valid and consummated marriage of baptized persons cannot be dissolved by any human authority or any cause other than the death of one of the persons.

In other circumstances:

1. A valid but unconsummated marriage of baptized persons, or of a baptized and an unbaptized person, can be dissolved:

a. by the solemn religious profession of one of the persons, made with permission of the pope. In such a case, the bond is dissolved at the time of profession, and the other person is free to marry again.

b. by dispensation from the pope, requested for a grave reason by one or both of the persons. If the dispensation is granted, both persons are free to marry again.

Dispensations in these cases are granted for reasons connected with the spiritual welfare of the concerned persons.

2. A legitimate marriage, even consummated, of unbaptized persons can be dissolved in favor of one of them who subsequently receives the sacrament of baptism. This is the Pauline Privilege, so called because it was promulgated by St. Paul (1 Cor. 7:12-15) as a means of protecting the faith of converts. Requisites for granting the privilege are:

a. marriage prior to the baptism of either person;

b. reception of baptism by one person;

c. refusal of the unbaptized person to live in peace with the baptized person and without interfering with his or her freedom to practice the Christian faith. The privilege does not apply if the unbaptized person agrees to these conditions.

3. A legitimate and consummated marriage of a baptized and an unbaptized person can be dissolved by the pope in virtue of the Privilege of Faith, also called the Petrine Privilege.

Civil Divorce

Because of the unity and the indissolubility of marriage, the Church denies that civil divorce can break the bond of a valid marriage, whether the marriage involves two Catholics, a Catholic and a non-Catholic, or non-Catholics with each other.

In view of serious circumstances of marital distress, the Church permits an innocent and aggrieved party, whether wife or husband, to seek and obtain a civil divorce for the purpose of acquiring title and right to the civil effects of divorce, such as separate habitation and maintenance, and the custody of children. Permission for this kind of action should be obtained from proper church authority. The divorce, if obtained, does not break the bond of a valid marriage.

Under other circumstances — as would obtain if a marriage was invalid (see Annulment, below) — civil divorce is permitted for civil effects and as a civil ratification of the fact that the marriage bond really does not exist.

Annulment

This is a decision by a competent church authority — e.g., a bishop, a diocesan marriage tribunal, the Roman Rota — that an apparently valid marriage was actually invalid from the beginning because of the unknown or concealed existence, from the beginning, of a diriment impediment, an essential defect in consent, radical incapability for marriage, or a condition placed by one or both of the parties against the very nature of marriage.

Eastern-rite Laws

Marriage laws of the Eastern Church differ in several respects from the legislation of the Roman rite. The regulations in effect since May 2, 1949, were contained in the *motu proprio Crebre Allatae* issued by Pius XII the previous February.

According to both the Roman Code of Canon Law and the Oriental Code, marriages between Roman-rite Catholics and Eastern-rite Catholics ordinarily take place in the rite of the groom and have canonical effects in that rite.

Regarding the form for the celebration of marriages between Eastern Catholics and baptized Eastern non-Catholics, the Second Vatican Council declared:

"By way of preventing invalid marriages between Eastern Catholics and baptized Eastern non-Catholics, and in the interests of the permanence and sanctity of marriage and of domestic harmony, this sacred Synod decrees that the canonical 'form' for the celebration of such marriages obliges only for lawfulness. For their validity, the presence of a sacred minister suffices, as long as the other requirements of law are honored" (Decree on Eastern Catholic Churches, No. 18).

Marriages taking place in this manner are lawful, as well as valid, with permission of a competent Eastern-rite bishop.

The Rota

The Roman Rota is the ordinary court of appeal for marriage, and some other cases, which are appealed to the Holy See from lower church courts. Appeals are made to the Rota if decisions by diocesan and archdiocesan courts fail to settle the matter in dispute. Pope John Paul II, at annual meetings with Rota personnel, speaks about the importance of the court's actions in providing norms of practice for other tribunals.

MIXED MARRIAGES

"Mixed Marriages" (*Matrimonia Mixta*) was the subject of a letter issued under this title by Pope Paul VI, on Mar. 31, 1970, and also a statement, "Implementation of the Apostolic Letter on Mixed Marriages," approved by the National Conference of Catholic Bishops on Nov. 16, 1970.

One of the key points in the bishops' statement referred to the need for mutual pastoral care by ministers of different faiths for the sacredness of marriage and for appropriate preparation and continuing support of parties to a mixed marriage.

Pastoral experience, which the Catholic Church shares with other religious bodies, confirms the fact that marriages of persons of different beliefs involve special problems related to the continuing religious practice of the concerned persons and to the religious education and formation of their children.

Pastoral measures to minimize these problems include instruction of a non-Catholic party in essentials of the Catholic faith for purposes of understanding. Desirably, some instruction should also be given the Catholic party regarding his or her partner's beliefs.

Requirements

The Catholic party to a mixed marriage is required to declare his (her) intention of continuing practice of the Catholic faith and to promise to do all in his (her) power to share his (her) faith with children born of the marriage by having them baptized and raised as Catholics. No declarations or promises are required of the non-Catholic party, but he (she) must be informed of the declaration and promise made by the Catholic.

Notice of the Catholic's declaration and promise is an essential part of the application made to a bishop for permission to marry a baptized non-Catholic, or a dispensation to marry an unbaptized non-Catholic.

A mixed marriage can take place with a Nuptial Mass. (The bishops' statement added this caution: "To the extent that Eucharistic sharing is not permitted by the general discipline of the Church, this is to be considered when plans are being made to have the mixed marriage at Mass or not.")

The ordinary minister at a mixed marriage is an authorized priest or deacon, and the ordinary place is the parish church of the Catholic party. A non-Catholic minister may not only attend the marriage ceremony but may also address, pray with and bless the couple.

For appropriate pastoral reasons, a bishop can grant a dispensation from the Catholic form of marriage and can permit the marriage to take place in a non-Catholic church with a non-Catholic minister as the officiating minister. A priest may not only attend such a ceremony but may also address, pray with and bless the couple.

"It is not permitted," however, the bishops' statement declared, "to have two religious services or to have a single service in which both the Catholic marriage ritual and a non-Catholic marriage ritual are celebrated jointly or successively."

Pastoral Ministry for Divorced and Remarried

Ministry to divorced and remarried Catholics is a difficult field of pastoral endeavor, situated as it is in circumstances tantamount to the horns of a dilemma.

At Issue

On the one side is firm church teaching on the permanence of marriage and norms against reception of the Eucharist and full participation in the life of the Church by Catholics in irregular unions.

On the other side are men and women with broken unions followed by second and perhaps happier attempts at marriage which the Church does not recognize as valid and which may not be capable of being validated because of the existence of an earlier marriage bond.

Factors involved in these circumstances are those of the Church, upholding its doctrine and practice regarding the permanence of marriage, and those of many men and women in irregular second marriages who desire full participation in the life of the Church.

Sacramental participation is not possible for those whose first marriage was valid, although there is no bar to their attendance at Mass, to sharing in other activities of the Church, or to their efforts to have children baptized and raised in the Catholic faith.

An exception to this rule is the condition of a divorced and remarried couple living in a brother-sister relationship.

There is no ban against sacramental participation by separated or divorced persons who have not attempted a second marriage, provided the usual conditions for reception of the sacraments are in order.

Unverified estimates of the number of U.S. Catholics who are divorced and remarried vary between six and eight million.

Tribunal Action

What can the Church do for them and with them in pastoral ministry, is an old question charged with new urgency because of the rising number of divorced and remarried Catholics.

One way to help is through the agency of marriage tribunals charged with responsibility for investigating and settling questions concerning the validity or invalidity of a prior marriage. There are reasons in canon law justifying the Church in declaring a particular marriage null and void from the beginning, despite the short- or long-term existence of an apparently valid union.

Decrees of nullity (annulments) are not new in the history of the Church. If such a decree is issued, a man or woman is free to validate a second marriage and live in complete union with the Church.

The 2004 *Statistical Yearbook of the Church* (*Annuarium Statisticum Ecclesiae*, the most recent edition) reported in 2004 that U.S. tribunals issued 46,330 annulments (in ordinary and documentary processes). The canonical reasons were: invalid consent (38,831), impotence (5), other impediments (2,281), defect of form (5,111). Worldwide, 61,303 decrees or declarations of nullity were issued in 2004.

On Feb. 8, 2005, Vatican officials issued a new instruction for Church marriage tribunals that was intended clarify Church law, defend the sacrament of marriage, and ensure the efficiency that justice requires. The new handbook for Latin-rite diocesan and interdiocesan tribunals, *Dignitas Connubii* ("The Dignity of Marriage"), details clear procedures for accepting, investigating, assessing, and appealing marriage cases. [For details, *see under News in Depth.*]

Reasons behind Decrees

Pastoral experience reveals that some married persons, a short or long time after contracting an apparently valid marriage, exhibit signs that point back to the existence, at the time of marriage, of latent and serious personal deficiencies which made them incapable of valid consent and sacramental commitment.

Such deficiencies might include gross immaturity and those affecting in a serious way the capacity to love, to have a true interpersonal and conjugal relationship, to fulfill marital obligations, or to accept the faith aspect of marriage.

Psychological and behavioral factors like these have been given greater attention by tribunals in recent years and have provided grounds for numerous decrees of nullity.

Decisions of this type do not indicate any softening of the Church's attitude regarding the permanence of marriage. They affirm, rather, that some persons who have married were really not capable of doing so.

Serious deficiencies in the capacity for real interpersonal relationship in marriage were the reasons behind a landmark decree of nullity issued in 1973 by the Roman Rota, the Vatican high court of appeals in marriage cases. Pope John Paul referred to such deficiencies — the "grave lack of discretionary judgment," incapability of assuming "essential matrimonial rights and obligations," for example — in an address Jan. 26, 1984, to personnel of the Rota.

The tribunal way to a decree of nullity regarding a previous marriage, however, is not open to many persons in second marriages — because grounds are either lacking or, if present, cannot be verified in tribunal process.

Unacceptable Solutions

One unacceptable solution of the problem, called "good conscience procedure," involves administration of the sacraments of penance and the Eucharist to divorced and remarried Catholics unable to obtain a decree of nullity for a first marriage who are living in a subsequent marriage "in good faith."

This procedure, despite the fact that it has no standing or recognition in church law, is being advocated and practiced by some priests and remarried Catholics.

This issue was addressed by the Congregation for the Doctrine of the Faith in a letter to bishops dated Oct. 14, 1994, and published with the approval of Pope John Paul II. The letter said in part:

"Pastoral solutions in this area have been suggested according to which divorced-and-remarried members of the faithful could approach holy Communion in specific cases when they considered themselves authorized according to a judgment of conscience to do so. This would be the case, for example, when they had been abandoned completely unjustly although they sincerely tried to save the previous marriage; or when they are convinced of the nullity of their previous marriage although (they are) unable to demonstrate it in the external forum; or when they have gone through a long period of reflection and penance; or also when for morally valid reasons they cannot satisfy the obligation to separate.

"In some places it has also been proposed that, in order objectively to examine their actual situation, the divorced-and-remarried would have to consult a prudent and experienced priest. This priest, however, would have to respect their eventual decision in conscience to approach holy Communion, without this implying an official authorization.

"In these and similar cases, it would be a matter of a tolerant and benevolent pastoral solution in order to do justice to the different situations of the divorced-and-remarried.

"Even if analogous solutions have been proposed by a few fathers of the Church and in some measure were practiced, nevertheless these never attained the consensus of the fathers and in no way came to constitute the common doctrine of the Church nor to determine her discipline. It falls to the universal magisterium, in fidelity to sacred Scripture and tradition, to teach and to interpret authentically the deposit of faith."

Conditions for Receiving Communion

Practically speaking, "when for serious reasons — for example, for the children's upbringing — a man and a woman cannot satisfy the obligation to separate," they may be admitted to Communion if "they take on themselves the duty to live in complete continence, that is, by abstinence from the acts proper to married couples. In such a case they may receive holy Communion as long as they respect the obligation to avoid giving scandal."

The teaching of the Church on this subject "does not mean that the Church does not take to heart the situation of those faithful who, moreover, are not excluded from ecclesial communion. She is concerned to accompany them pastorally and invite them to share in the life of the Church in the measure that is compatible with the dispositions of divine law, from which the Church has no power to dispense. On the other hand, it is necessary to instruct these faithful so that they do not think their participation in the life of the Church is reduced exclusively to the question of the reception of the Eucharist. The faithful are to be helped to deepen their understanding of the value of sharing in the sacrifice of Christ in the Mass, or spiritual communion, of prayer, of meditation on the word of God, and of works of charity and justice."

The Communion of Saints

SAINTS OF THE CHURCH

Biographical sketches of additional saints and blesseds are found in other *Almanac* entries. See **Index,** under the name of each saint for the apostles, evangelists, Doctors of the Church, and Fathers of the Church. For beatification and canonization procedures, see those entries in the **Glossary.**

An asterisk with a feast date indicates that the saint is listed in the General Roman Calendar or the proper calendar for U.S. dioceses. For rank of observances, see listing in calendar for current year on preceding pages.

Adalbert (956-97): Born in Bohemia; bishop of Prague; Benedictine; missionary in Poland, Prussia and Hungary; martyred by Prussians near Danzig; Apr. 23.*

Adjutor (d. 1131): Norman knight; fought in First Crusade; monk-recluse after his return; Apr. 30.

Agatha (d. c. 250): Sicilian virgin-martyr; her intercession credited in Sicily with stilling eruptions of Mt. Etna; patron of nurses; Feb. 5.*

Agnes (d. c. 304): Roman virgin-martyr; martyred at age of 10 or 12; patron of young girls; Jan. 21.*

Aloysius Gonzaga (1568-91): Italian Jesuit; died while nursing plague-stricken; canonized 1726; patron of youth; June 21.*

Amand (d. c. 676): Apostle of Belgium; b. France; established monasteries throughout Belgium; Feb. 6.

Andre Bessette, Bl. (Bro. Andre) (1845-1937): Canadian Holy Cross Brother; prime mover in building of St. Joseph's Oratory, Montreal; beatified May 23, 1982; Jan. 6* (U.S.).

Andre Grasset de Saint Sauveur, Bl. (1758-92): Canadian priest; martyred in France, Sept. 2, 1792, during the Revolution; one of a group called the Martyrs of Paris who were beatified in 1926; Sept. 2.

Andrew Bobola (1592-1657): Polish Jesuit; joined Jesuits at Vilna; worked for return of Orthodox to union with Rome; martyred; canonized 1938; May 16.

Andrew Corsini (1302-73): Italian Carmelite; bishop of Fiesoli; mediator between quarrelsome Italian states; canonized 1629; Feb. 4.

Andrew Dung-Lac and Companions (d. 18th-19th c.): Martyrs of Vietnam. Total of 117 included 96 Vietnamese, 11 Spanish and 10 French missionaries (8 bishops; 50 priests, including Andrew Dung-Lac; 1 seminarian; 58 lay persons). Canonized June 19, 1988; inscribed in General Roman Calendar, 1989, as a memorial. Nov. 24.*

Andrew Fournet (1752-1834): French priest; cofounder with St. Jeanne Elizabeth Bichier des Anges of the Daughters of the Holy Cross of St. Andrew; canonized 1933; May 13.

Andrew Kim, Paul Chong and Companions (d. between 1839-67): Korean martyrs (103) killed in persecutions of 1839, 1846, 1866, and 1867; among them were Andrew Kim, the first Korean priest, and Paul Chong, lay apostle; canonized May 6, 1984, during Pope John Paul II's visit to Korea. Sept. 20.*

Angela Merici (1474-1540): Italian secular Franciscan; foundress of Company of St. Ursula, 1535, the first teaching order of women Religious in the Church; canonized 1807; Jan. 27.*

Angelico, Bl. (Fra Angelico; John of Faesulis) (1387-1455): Dominican; Florentine painter of early Renaissance; proclaimed blessed by John Paul II, Feb. 3, 1982; patron of artists; Feb. 18.

Anne Marie Javouhey, Bl. (1779-1851): French virgin; foundress of Institute of St. Joseph of Cluny, 1812; beatified 1950; July 15.

Ansgar (801-65): Benedictine monk; b. near Amiens; archbishop of Hamburg; missionary in Denmark, Sweden, Norway, and northern Germany; apostle of Scandinavia; Feb. 3.*

Anthony (c. 251-c. 354): Abbot; Egyptian hermit; patriarch of all monks; established communities for hermits which became models for monastic life, especially in the East; friend and supporter of St. Athanasius in the latter's struggle with the Arians; Jan. 17.*

Anthony Claret (1807-70): Spanish bishop; founder of Missionary Sons of the Immaculate Heart of Mary (Claretians), 1849; archbishop of Santiago, Cuba, 1851-57; canonized 1950; Oct. 24.*

Anthony Gianelli (1789-1846): Italian bishop; founded the Daughters of Our Lady of the Garden, 1829; bishop of Bobbio, 1838; canonized 1951; June 7.

Anthony Zaccaria (1502-39): Italian priest; founder of Barnabites (Clerks Regular of St. Paul), 1530; canonized 1897; July 5.*

Apollonia (d. 249): Deaconess of Alexandria; martyred during persecution of Decius; her patronage of dentists and those suffering from toothaches probably rests on tradition that her teeth were broken by her persecutors; Feb. 9.

Augustine of Canterbury (d. 604 or 605): Italian missionary; apostle of the English; sent by Pope Gregory I with 40 monks to evangelize England; arrived there 597; first archbishop of Canterbury; May 27.*

Bartolomea Capitania (1807-33): Italian foundress with Vincenza Gerosa of the Sisters of Charity of Lovere; canonized 1950; July 26.

Beatrice da Silva Meneses (1424-90): Foundress, b. Portugal; founded Congregation of the Immaculate Conception, 1484, in Spain; canonized 1976; Sept. 1.

Benedict Joseph Labré (1748-83): French layman; pilgrim-beggar; noted for his piety and love of prayer before the Blessed Sacrament; canonized 1883; Apr. 16.

Benedict of Nursia (c. 480-547): Abbot; founder of monasticism in Western Europe; established monastery at Monte Cassino; proclaimed patron of Europe by Paul VI in 1964; July 11.*

Benedict the Black (il Moro) (1526-89): Sicilian Franciscan; born a slave; joined Franciscans as lay brother; appointed guardian and novice master; canonized 1807; Apr. 3.

Bernadette Soubirous (1844-79): French peasant girl favored with series of visions of Blessed Virgin Mary at Lourdes (see Lourdes Apparitions); joined Institute of Sisters of Notre Dame at Nevers, 1866; canonized 1933; Apr. 16.

Bernard of Montjoux (or Menthon) (d. 1081): Augustinian canon; probably born in Italy; founded Alpine hospices near the two passes named for him; patron of mountaineers; May 28.

Bernardine of Feltre, Bl. (1439-94): Italian Franciscan preacher; a founder of montes pietatis; Sept. 28.

Bernardine of Siena (1380-1444): Italian Franciscan; noted preacher and missioner; spread of devotion to Holy Name is attributed to him; represented in art holding to his breast the monogram IHS; canonized 1450; May 20.*

Blase (d. c. 316): Armenian bishop; martyr; the blessing of throats on his feast day derives from tradition that he miraculously saved the life of a boy who had half-swallowed a fish bone; Feb. 3.*

Boniface (Winfrid) (d. 754): English Benedictine; bishop; martyr; apostle of Germany; established monastery at Fulda which became center of missionary work in Germany; archbishop of Mainz; martyred near Dukkum in Holland; June 5.*

Brendan (c. 489-583): Irish abbot; founded monasteries; his patronage of sailors probably rests on a legend that he made a seven-year voyage in search of a fabled paradise; called Brendan the Navigator; May 16.

Bridget (Brigid) (c. 450-525): Irish nun; founded religious community at Kildare, the first in Ireland; patron, with Sts. Patrick and Columba, of Ireland; Feb. 1.

Bridget (Birgitta) (c. 1303-73): Swedish mystic; widow; foundress of Order of Our Savior (Brigittines); canonized 1391; patroness of Sweden; named a co-patroness of Europe, with St. Edith Stein and St. Catherine of Siena, on Oct. 1, 1999; July 23.*

Bruno (1030-1101): German monk; founded Carthusians, 1084, in France; Oct. 6.*

Cabrini, Mother: See Frances Xavier Cabrini.

Cajetan (Gaetano) of Thiene (1480-1547): Italian lawyer; religious reformer; a founder of Oratory of Divine Love, forerunner of the Theatines; canonized 1671; Aug. 7.*

Callistus I (d. 222): Pope, 217-22; martyr; condemned Sabellianism and other heresies; advocated a policy of mercy toward repentant sinners; Oct. 14.*

Camillus de Lellis (1550-1614): Italian priest; founder of Camillians (Ministers of the Sick); canonized 1746; patron of the sick and of nurses; July 14.*

Casimir (1458-84): Polish prince; grand duke of Lithuania; noted for his piety; buried at cathedral in Vilna, Lithuania; canonized 1521; patron of Poland and Lithuania; Mar. 4.*

Cassian of Tangier (d. 298): Roman martyr; an official court stenographer who declared himself a Christian; patron of stenographers; Dec. 3.

Catherine Labouré (1806-76): French Religious; favored with series of visions soon after she joined Sisters of Charity of St. Vincent de Paul in Paris in 1830; first Miraculous Medal (see Index) struck in 1832 in accord with one of the visions; canonized 1947; Nov. 28.

Catherine of Bologna (1413-63): Italian Poor Clare; mystic, writer, artist canonized 1712; patron of artists; May 9.

Cecilia (2nd-3rd c.): Roman virgin-martyr; traditional patroness of musicians; Nov. 22.*

Charles Borromeo (1538-84): Italian cardinal; nephew of Pope Pius IV; cardinal bishop of Milan; influential figure in Church reform in Italy; promoted education of clergy; canonized 1610; Nov. 4.*

Charles Lwanga and Companions (d. between 1885 and 1887): Twenty-two Martyrs of Uganda, many of them pages of King Mwanga of Uganda, who were put to death because they denounced his corrupt lifestyle; canonized 1964; first martyrs of black Africa; June 3.*

Charles of Sezze (1616-70): Italian Franciscan lay brother who served in humble capacities; canonized 1959; Jan. 6.

Christopher (3rd c.): Early Christian martyr inscribed in Roman calendar about 1550; feast relegated to particular calendars because of legendary nature of accounts of his life; traditional patron of travelers; July 25.

Clare (1194-1253): Foundress of Poor Clares; b. at Assisi; was joined in religious life by her sisters, Agnes and Beatrice, and eventually her widowed mother Ortolana; canonized 1255; patroness of television; Aug. 11.*

Claude de la Colombiere (1641-82): French Jesuit; spiritual director of St. Margaret Mary Alacoque; instrumental in spreading devotion to the Sacred Heart; beatified, 1929; canonized May 31, 1992; Feb. 15.

Clement Hofbauer (1751-1820): Redemptorist priest; missionary; born in Moravia; helped spread Redemptorists north of the Alps; canonized 1909; Mar. 15.

Clement I (d. c. 100): Pope, 88-97; third successor of St. Peter; wrote important letter to Church in Corinth settling disputes there; venerated as a martyr; Nov. 23.*

Columba (521-97): Irish monk; founded monasteries in Ireland; missionary in Scotland; established monastery at Iona which became the center for conversion of Picts, Scots, and Northern English; Scotland's most famous saint; patron saint of Ireland (with Sts. Patrick and Brigid); June 9.

Columban (545-615): Irish monk; scholar; founded monasteries in England and Brittany (famous abbey of Luxeuil), forced into exile because of his criticism of Frankish court; spent last years in northern Italy where he founded abbey at Bobbio; Nov. 23.*

Conrad of Parzham (1818-94): Bavarian Capuchin lay brother; served as porter at the Marian shrine of Altotting in Upper Bavaria for 40 years; canonized 1934; Apr. 21.

Contardo Ferrini, Bl. (1859-1902): Italian secular Franciscan; model of the Catholic professor; beatified 1947; patron of universities; Oct. 20.

Cornelius (d. 253): Pope, 251-53; promoted a policy of mercy with respect to readmission of repentant Christians who had fallen away during the persecution of Decius (lapsi); banished from Rome during persecution of Gallus; regarded as a martyr; Sept. 16 (with Cyprian).*

Cosmas and Damian (d. c. 303): Arabian twin brothers, physicians; martyred during Diocletian persecution; patrons of physicians; Sept. 26.*

Crispin and Crispinian (3rd c.): Early Christian martyrs; said to have met their deaths in Gaul; patrons of shoemakers, a trade they pursued; Oct. 25.

Crispin of Viterbo (1668-1750): Capuchin brother; canonized June 20, 1982; May 21.

Cyprian (d. 258): Early ecclesiastical writer; b. Africa; bishop of Carthage, 249-58; supported Pope St. Cornelius concerning the readmission of Christians who had apostatized in time of persecution; erred in his teaching that baptism administered by heretics and schismatics was invalid; wrote *De Unitate*; Sept. 16 (with St. Cornelius).*

Cyril and Methodius (9th c.): Greek missionaries, brothers; venerated as apostles of the Slavs; Cyril (d. 869) and Methodius (d. 885) began their missionary work in Moravia in 863; developed a Slavonic alphabet; used the vernacular in the liturgy, a practice that was eventually approved; declared patrons of Europe with St. Benedict, Dec. 31, 1980; Feb. 14.*

Damasus I (d. 384): Pope, 366-84; opposed Arians and Apollinarians; commissioned St. Jerome to work on Bible translation; developed Roman liturgy; Dec. 11.*

Damian: *See* Cosmas and Damian.

Damien of Molokai, Bl. (d. 1889): The so-called leper priest of Molokai; originally from Belgium, Damien devoted over twenty years to the care of the lepers in Hawaii, ultimately dying from the same disease. He was beatified by Pope John Paul II in 1995.

David (5th or 6th c.): Nothing for certain known of his life; said to have founded monastery at Menevia; patron saint of Wales; Mar. 1.

Denis and Companions (d. 3rd c.): Denis, bishop of Paris, and two companions identified by early writers as Rusticus, a priest, and Eleutherius, a deacon; martyred near Paris; Denis is popularly regarded as the apostle and a patron saint of France; Oct. 9.*

Dismas (1st c.): Name given to repentant thief (Good Thief) to whom Jesus promised salvation (Lk. 23:40-43); regarded as patron of prisoners; Mar. 25 (observed on second Sunday of October in U.S. prison chapels).

Dominic (Dominic de Guzman) (1170-1221): Spanish priest; founded the Order of Preachers (Dominicans), 1215, in France; preached against the Albigensian heresy; a contemporary of St. Francis of Assisi; canonized 1234; Aug. 8.*

Dominic Savio (1842-57): Italian youth; pupil of St. John Bosco; died before his 15th birthday; canonized 1954; patron of choirboys; May 6.

Duns Scotus, John (d. 1308): Scottish Franciscan; theologian; advanced theological arguments for doctrine of the Immaculate Conception; proclaimed blessed; cult solemnly confirmed by John Paul II, Mar. 20, 1993; Nov. 8.

Dunstan (c. 910-88): English monk; archbishop of Canterbury; initiated reforms in religious life; counselor to several kings; considered one of greatest Anglo-Saxon saints; patron of goldsmiths, locksmiths, jewelers (trades in which he is said to have excelled); May 19.

Dymphna (dates unknown): Nothing certain known of her life; according to legend, she was an Irish maiden murdered by her heathen father at Gheel near Antwerp, Belgium, where she had fled to escape his advances; her relics were discovered there in the 13th century; since that time cures of mental illness and epilepsy have been attributed to her intercession; patron of those suffering from mental illness; May 15.

Edith Stein, St. (1891-1942): German Carmelite (Teresa Benedicta of the Cross); born of Jewish parents; author and lecturer; baptized in Catholic Church 1922; arrested with her sister Rosa in 1942 and put to death at Auschwitz; beatified 1987, by Pope John Paul II during his visit to West Germany; was canonized by Pope John Paul II on Oct. 11, 1998, and named a co-patroness of Europe, with St. Bridget of Sweden and St. Catherine of Siena, on Oct. 1, 1999; Aug. 10.

Edmund Campion (1540-81): English Jesuit; convert 1573; martyred at Tyburn; canonized 1970, one of the Forty English and Welsh Martyrs; Dec. 1.

Edward the Confessor (d. 1066): King of England, 1042-66; canonized 1161; Oct. 13.

Eligius (c. 590-660): Bishop; born in Gaul; founded monasteries and convents; bishop of Noyon and Tournai; famous worker in gold and silver; Dec. 1.

Elizabeth Ann Seton (1774-1821): American foundress; convert, 1805; founded Sisters of Charity in the U.S.; beatified 1963; canonized Sept. 14, 1975; the first American-born saint; Jan. 4 (U.S.).*

Elizabeth of Hungary (1207-31): Became secular Franciscan after death of her husband in 1227; devoted life to poor and destitute; a patron of the Secular Franciscan Order; canonized 1235; Nov. 17.*

Elizabeth of Portugal (1271-1336): Queen of Portugal; b. Spain; retired to Poor Clare convent as a secular Franciscan after the death of her husband; canonized 1626; July 4.*

Emily de Rodat (1787-1852): French foundress of the Congregation of the Holy Family of Villefranche; canonized 1950; Sept. 19.

Emily de Vialar (1797-1856): French foundress of the Sisters of St. Joseph of the Apparition; canonized 1951; June 17.

Erasmus (Elmo) (d. 303): Life surrounded by legend; martyred during Diocletian persecution; patron of sailors; June 2.

Ethelbert (552-616): King of Kent, England; baptized by St. Augustine of Canterbury, 597; issued legal code; furthered spread of Christianity; Feb. 26.

Eusebius of Vercelli (283-370): Italian bishop; exiled from his see (Vercelli) for a time because of his opposition to Arianism; considered a martyr because of sufferings he endured; Aug. 2.*

Fabian (d. 250): Pope, 236-50; martyred under Decius; Jan. 20.*

Felicity: *See* Perpetua and Felicity.

Ferdinand III (1198-1252): King of Castile and Leon; waged successful crusade against Muhammadans in Spain; founded university at Salamanca; canonized 1671; May 30.

Fiacre (Fiachra) (d. c. 670): Irish hermit; patron of gardeners; Aug. 30.

Fidelis of Sigmaringen (Mark Rey) (1577-1622): German Capuchin; lawyer before he joined the Capuchins; missionary to Swiss Protestants; stabbed to death by peasants who were told he was an agent of the Austrian emperor; Apr. 24.*

Frances of Rome (1384-1440): Italian model for housewives and widows; happily married for 40 years; after death of her husband in 1436 joined community of Benedictine Oblates she had founded; canonized 1608; patron of motorists; Mar. 9.*

Frances Xavier Cabrini (Mother Cabrini) (1850-1917): American foundress; b. Italy; founded the Missionary Sisters of the Sacred Heart, 1877; settled in the U.S. 1889; became an American citizen at Seattle 1909; worked among Italian immigrants; canonized 1946, the first American citizen so honored; Nov. 13 (U.S.).*

Francis Borgia (1510-72): Spanish Jesuit; joined Jesuits after death of his wife in 1546; became general of the Order, 1565; Oct. 10.

Francis Caracciolo (1563-1608): Italian priest; founder with Father Augustine Adorno of the Clerics Regular Minor (Adorno Fathers); canonized 1807; declared patron of Italian chefs, 1996; June 4.

Francis Fasani (1681-1742): Italian Conventual Franciscan; model of priestly ministry, especially in service to poor and imprisoned; canonized 1986; Nov. 27.

Francis of Assisi (Giovanni di Bernardone) (1181/82-1226): Founder of the Franciscans, 1209; received stigmata 1224; canonized 1228; one of best-known and best-loved saints; patron of Italy, Catholic Action, animals, and ecologists; Oct. 4.*

Francis of Paola (1416-1507): Italian hermit: founder of Minim Friars; Apr. 2.*

Francis Xavier (1506-52): Spanish Jesuit; missionary to Far East; canonized 1602; patron of foreign missions; considered one of greatest Christian missionaries; Dec. 3.*

Francis Xavier Bianchi (1743-1815): Italian Barnabite; acclaimed apostle of Naples because of his work there among the poor and abandoned; canonized 1951; Jan. 31.

Gabriel of the Sorrowful Mother (Francis Possenti) (1838-62): Italian Passionist; died while a scholastic; canonized 1920; Feb. 27.

Gaspar (Caspar) **del Bufalo** (1786-1836): Italian priest; founded Missionaries of the Precious Blood, 1815; canonized 1954; Jan. 2.

Gemma Galgani (1878-1903): Italian laywoman; visionary; subject of extraordinary religious experiences; canonized 1940; Apr. 11.

Genesius (d. c. 300): Roman actor; according to legend, was converted while performing a burlesque of Christian baptism and was subsequently martyred; patron of actors; Aug. 25.

Geneviève (422-500): French nun; a patroness and protectress of Paris; events of her life not authenticated; Jan. 3.

George (d. c. 300): Martyr, probably during Diocletian persecution in Palestine; all other incidents of his life, including story of the dragon, are legendary; patron of England; Apr. 23.*

Gerard Majella (1725-55): Italian Redemptorist lay brother; noted for supernatural occurrences in his life including bilocation and reading of consciences; canonized 1904; patron of mothers; Oct. 16.

Gertrude (1256-1302): German mystic; writer; helped spread devotion to the Sacred Heart; Nov. 16.*

Gregory VII (Hildebrand) (1020?-85): Pope, 1075-85; Benedictine monk; adviser to several popes; as pope, strengthened interior life of Church and fought against lay investiture; driven from Rome by Henry IV; died in exile; canonized 1584; May 25.*

Gregory Barbarigo (1626-97): Italian cardinal; noted for his efforts to bring about reunion of separated Christians; canonized 1960; June 18.

Gregory of Nyssa (c. 335-95): Bishop; theologian; younger brother of St. Basil the Great; Mar. 9.

Gregory Thaumaturgus (c. 213-68): Bishop of Neocaesarea; missionary, famed as wonder worker; Nov. 17.

Gregory the Illuminator (257-332): Martyr; bishop; apostle and patron saint of Armenia; helped free Armenia from the Persians; Sept. 30.

Hedwig (1174-1243): Moravian noblewoman; married duke of Silesia, head of Polish royal family; fostered religious life in country; canonized 1266; Oct. 16.*

Helena (250-330): Empress; mother of Constantine the Great; associated with discovery of the True Cross; Aug. 18.

Henry (972-1024): Bavarian emperor; cooperated with Benedictine abbeys in restoration of ecclesiastical and social discipline; canonized 1146; July 13.*

Herman Joseph (1150-1241): German Premonstratensian; his visions were the subjects of artists; writer; cult approved, 1958; Apr. 7.

Hippolytus (d. c. 236): Roman priest; opposed Pope St. Callistus I in his teaching about the readmission to the Church of repentant Christians who had apostatized during time of persecution; elected antipope; exiled to Sardinia; reconciled before his martyrdom; important ecclesiastical writer; Aug. 13* (with Pontian).

Hugh of Cluny (the Great) (1024-1109): Abbot of Benedictine foundation at Cluny; supported popes in efforts to reform ecclesiastical abuses; canonized 1120; Apr. 29.

Ignatius of Antioch (d. c. 107): Early ecclesiastical writer; martyr; bishop of Antioch in Syria for 40 years; Oct. 17.*

Ignatius of Laconi (1701-81): Italian Capuchin lay brother whose 60 years of religious life were spent in Franciscan simplicity; canonized 1951; May 11.

Ignatius of Loyola (1491-1556): Spanish soldier; renounced military career after recovering from wounds received at siege of Pampeluna (Pamplona) in 1521; founded Society of Jesus (Jesuits), 1534, at Paris; wrote *The Book of Spiritual Exercises*; canonized 1622; July 31.*

Irenaeus of Lyons (130-202): Early ecclesiastical writer; opposed Gnosticism; bishop of Lyons; traditionally regarded as a martyr; June 28.*

Isidore the Farmer (d. 1170): Spanish layman; farmer; canonized 1622; patron of farmers; May 15 (U.S.).*

Jane Frances de Chantal (1572-1641): French widow; foundress, under guidance of St. Francis de Sales, of Order of the Visitation; canonized 1767; Dec. 12* (General Roman Calendar); Aug. 18* (U.S.).

Januarius (Gennaro) (d. 304): Bishop of Benevento; martyred during Diocletian persecution; fame rests on liquefaction of some of his blood preserved in a phial at Naples, an unexplained phenomenon which has occurred regularly several times each year for over 400 years; Sept. 19.*

Jeanne Delanoue (1666-1736): French foundress of Sisters of St. Anne of Providence, 1704; canonized 1982; Aug. 16.

Jeanne (Joan) **de Lestonnac** (1556-1640): French foundress; widowed in 1597; founded the Religious of Notre Dame 1607; canonized 1947; Feb. 2.

Jeanne de Valois (Jeanne of France) (1464-1505): French foundress; deformed daughter of King Louis XI; was married in 1476 to Duke Louis of Orleans who had the marriage annulled when he ascended the throne as Louis XII; Jeanne retired to life of prayer; founded contemplative Annonciades of Bourges, 1504; canonized 1950; Feb. 5.

Jeanne-Elizabeth Bichier des Ages (1773-1838): French Religious; co-founder with St. Andrew Fournet of Daughters of the Cross of St. Andrew, 1807; canonized 1947; Aug. 26.

Jeanne Jugan, Bl. (1792-1879): French Religious; foundress of Little Sisters of the Poor; beatified Oct. 3, 1982; Aug. 30.

Jerome Emiliani (1481-1537): Venetian priest;

founded Somascan Fathers, 1532, for care of orphans; canonized 1767; patron of orphans and abandoned children; Feb. 8.*

Joan Antida Thouret (1765-1826): French Religious; founded, 1799, congregation now known as Sisters of Charity of St. Joan Antida; canonized 1934; Aug. 24.

Joan of Arc (1412-31): French heroine, called The Maid of Orleans, La Pucelle; led French army in 1429 against English invaders besieging Orleans; captured by Burgundians the following year; turned over to ecclesiastical court on charge of heresy, found guilty and burned at the stake; her innocence was declared in 1456; canonized 1920; patroness of France; May 30.

Joaquina de Vedruna de Mas (1783-1854): Spanish foundress; widowed in 1816; after providing for her children, founded the Carmelite Sisters of Charity; canonized 1959; Aug. 28.

John I (d. 526): Pope, 523-26; martyr; May 18.*

John XXIII, Bl.: *see* Popes of the Twentieth Century in Papacy and the Holy See.

John Baptist de la Salle (1651-1719): French priest; founder of Brothers of the Christian Schools, 1680; canonized 1900; patron of teachers; Apr. 7.*

John Berchmans (1599-1621): Belgian Jesuit scholastic; patron of Mass servers; canonized 1888; Aug. 13.

John (Don) Bosco (1815-88): Italian priest; founded Salesians, 1859, for education of boys; co-founder of Daughters of Mary Help of Christians for education of girls; canonized 1934; Jan. 31.*

John Capistran (1386-1456): Italian Franciscan; preacher; papal diplomat; canonized 1690; declared patron of military chaplains, Feb. 10, 1984; Oct. 23.*

John de Ribera (1532-1611): Spanish bishop and statesman; archbishop of Valencia, 1568-1611, and viceroy of that province; canonized 1960; Jan. 6.

John Eudes (1601-80): French priest; founder of Sisters of Our Lady of Charity of Refuge, 1642, and Congregation of Jesus-Mary (Eudists), 1643; canonized 1925; Aug. 19.*

John Fisher (1469-1535): English prelate; theologian; martyr; bishop of Rochester, cardinal; refused to recognize validity of Henry VIII's marriage to Anne Boleyn; upheld supremacy of the pope; beheaded for refusing to acknowledge Henry as head of the Church; canonized 1935; June 22 (with St. Thomas More).*

John Francis Regis (1597-1640): French Jesuit priest; preached missions among poor and unlettered; canonized 1737; patron of social workers, particularly medical social workers, because of his concern for poor and needy and sick in hospitals; July 2.

John Gualbert (d. 1073): Italian priest; founder of Benedictine congregation of Vallombrosians, 1039; canonized 1193; July 12.

John Kanty (Cantius) (1395-1473): Polish theologian; canonized 1767; Dec. 23.*

John Leonardi (1550-1609): Italian priest; worked among prisoners and the sick; founded Clerics Regular of the Mother of God; canonized 1938; Oct. 9.*

John Nepomucene (1345-93): Bohemian priest; regarded as a martyr; canonized 1729; patron of Czechoslovakia; May 16.

John Nepomucene Neumann (1811-60): American prelate; b. Bohemia; ordained in New York 1836; missionary among Germans near Niagara Falls before joining Redemptorists, 1840; bishop of Philadelphia, 1852; first bishop in U.S. to prescribe Forty Hours devotion in his diocese; beatified 1963; canonized June 19, 1977; Jan. 5 (U.S.).*

John of Ávila (1499-1569): Spanish priest; preacher; ascetical writer; spiritual adviser of St. Teresa of Jesus (Ávila); canonized 1970; May 10.

John of Britto (1647-93): Portuguese Jesuit; missionary in India where he was martyred; canonized 1947; Feb. 4.

John of God (1495-1550): Portuguese founder; his work among the sick poor led to foundation of Brothers Hospitallers of St. John of God, 1540, in Spain; canonized 1690; patron of sick, nurses, hospitals; Mar. 8.*

John of Matha (1160-1213): French priest; founder of the Order of Most Holy Trinity, whose original purpose was the ransom of prisoners from the Muslims; Feb. 8.

John Ogilvie (1579-1615): Scottish Jesuit; martyr; canonized 1976, the first canonized Scottish saint since 1250 (Margaret of Scotland); Mar. 10.

John Vianney (Curé of Ars) (1786-1859): French parish priest; noted confessor, spent 16 to 18 hours a day in confessional; canonized 1925; patron of parish priests; Aug. 4.*

Josaphat Kuncevyc (1584-1623): Basilian monk; b. Poland; archbishop of Polotsk, Lithuania; worked for reunion of separated Eastern Christians with Rome; martyred by mob of schismatics; canonized 1867; Nov. 12.*

Josemaria Escrivá de Balaguer (1902-75) Priest and founder of Opus Dei; the society was designed to promote holiness among individuals in the world; beatified in 1992; canonized on Oct. 6, 2002; May 17.

Joseph Benedict Cottolengo (1786-1842): Italian priest; established Little Houses of Divine Providence (*Piccolo Casa*) for care of orphans and the sick; canonized 1934; Apr. 30.

Joseph Cafasso (1811-60): Italian priest; renowned confessor; promoted devotion to Blessed Sacrament; canonized 1947; June 23.

Joseph Calasanz (1556-1648): Spanish priest; founder of Piarists (Order of Pious Schools); canonized 1767; Aug. 25.*

Joseph of Cupertino (1603-63): Italian Franciscan; noted for remarkable incidents of levitation; canonized 1767; Sept. 18.

Joseph Pignatelli (1737-1811): Spanish Jesuit; left Spain when Jesuits were banished in 1767; worked for revival of the Order; named first superior when Jesuits were reestablished in Kingdom of Naples, 1804; canonized 1954; Nov. 28.

Juan Diego (16th c.): Mexican Indian, convert; indigenous name according to tradition Cuauhtlatohuac ("The eagle who speaks"); favored with apparitions of Our Lady (*see* Our Lady of Guadalupe) on Tepeyac hill; beatified 1990; canonized July 30, 2002; Dec. 9* (U.S.).

Julia Billiart (1751-1816): French foundress; founded Sisters of Notre Dame de Namur, 1804; canonized 1969; Apr. 8.

Juliana Falconieri (1270-1341): Italian foundress of the Servite Nuns; the niece of St. Alexis Falconieri; canonized in 1737; June 19.

Justin de Jacobis (1800-60): Italian Vincentian; bishop; missionary in Ethiopia; canonized 1975; July 31.

Justin Martyr (100-65): Early ecclesiastical writer of *Apologies for the Christian Religion, Dialog with the Jew Tryphon*; martyred at Rome; June 1.*

Kateri Tekakwitha, Bl. (1656-80): "Lily of the Mohawks"; Indian maiden born at Ossernenon

(Auriesville), NY; baptized Christian, Easter 1676, by Jesuit missionary Father Jacques de Lambertville; lived life devoted to prayer, penitential practices and care of sick and aged in Christian village of Caughnawaga near Montreal where her relics are now enshrined; beatified June 22, 1980; July 14* (in U.S.).

Katharine Drexel, St. (1858-1955): Philadelphia-born heiress; devoted wealth to founding schools and missions for Indians and Blacks; foundress of Sisters of Blessed Sacrament for Indians and Colored People, 1891; beatified 1988; canonized Oct. 1, 2000; Mar. 3* (U.S.).

Ladislaus (1040-1095): King of Hungary; supported Pope Gregory VII against Henry IV; canonized 1192; June 27.

Lawrence (d. 258): Widely venerated martyr who suffered death, according to a long-standing but unverifiable legend, by fire on a gridiron; Aug. 10.*

Lawrence (Lorenzo) **Ruiz and Companions** (d. 1630s): Martyred in or near the city of Nagasaki, Japan; Lawrence Ruiz, first Filipino saint, and 15 companions (nine Japanese, four Spaniards, one Italian and one Frenchman); canonized 1987; Sept. 28.*

Leonard Murialdo (1828-1900): Italian priest; educator; founder of Pious Society of St. Joseph of Turin, 1873; canonized 1970; Mar. 30.

Leonard of Port Maurice (1676-1751): Italian Franciscan; ascetical writer; preached missions throughout Italy; canonized 1867; patron of parish missions; Nov. 26.

Leopold Mandic (1866-1942): Croatian-born Franciscan priest, noted confessor; spent most of his priestly life in Padua, Italy; canonized 1983; July 30.

Louis IX (1215-70): King of France, 1226-70; participated in Sixth Crusade; patron of Secular Franciscan Order; canonized 1297; Aug. 25.*

Louis de Montfort (1673-1716): French priest; founder of Sisters of Divine Wisdom, 1703, and Missionaries of Company of Mary, 1715; wrote *True Devotion to the Blessed Virgin*; canonized 1947; Apr. 28.*

Louis Zepherin Moreau, Bl. (d. 1901): Canadian bishop; headed St. Hyacinthe, Quebec, diocese, 1876-1901; beatified 1987; May 24.

Louise de Marillac (1591-1660): French foundress, with St. Vincent de Paul, of the Sisters of Charity; canonized 1934; Mar. 15.

Lucy (d. 304): Sicilian maiden; martyred during Diocletian persecution; one of most widely venerated early virgin-martyrs; patron of Syracuse, Sicily; invoked by those suffering from eye diseases; Dec. 13.*

Lucy Filippini (1672-1732): Italian educator, helped improve status of women through education; considered a founder of the Religious Teachers Filippini, 1692; canonized 1930; Mar. 25.

Madeleine Sophie Barat (1779-1865): French foundress of the Society of the Sacred Heart of Jesus; canonized 1925; May 25.

Malachy (1095-1148): Irish bishop; instrumental in establishing first Cistercian house in Ireland, 1142; canonized 1190; Nov. 3 (*See* Prophecies of St. Malachy).

Marcellinus and Peter (d. c. 304): Early Roman martyrs; June 2.*

Margaret Clitherow (1556-86): English martyr; convert shortly after her marriage; one of Forty Martyrs of England and Wales; canonized 1970; Mar. 25.

Margaret Mary Alacoque (1647-90): French Religious; spread devotion to Sacred Heart in accordance with revelations made to her in 1675 (*see*

Sacred Heart); canonized 1920; Oct. 16.*

Margaret of Cortona (1247-97): Secular Franciscan; reformed her life in 1273 following the violent death of her lover; canonized 1728; May 16.

Margaret of Hungary (1242-70): Contemplative; daughter of King Bela IV of Hungary; lived a life of self-imposed penances; canonized 1943; Jan. 18.

Margaret of Scotland (1050-1093): Queen of Scotland; noted for solicitude for the poor and promotion of justice; canonized 1250; Nov. 16.*

Maria Goretti (1890-1902): Italian virgin-martyr; a model of purity; canonized 1950; July 6.*

Mariana Paredes de Jesus (1618-45): South American recluse; Lily of Quito; canonized 1950; May 28.

Marianne Cope, Bl. See *under* Missionaries to the Americas.

Marie-Leonie Paradis, Bl. (1840-1912): Canadian Religious; founded Little Sisters of the Holy Family, 1880; beatified 1984; May 4.

Marie-Rose Durocher, Bl. (1811-49): Canadian Religious; foundress of Sisters of Holy Names of Jesus and Mary; beatified 1982; Oct. 6* (in U.S.).

Martha (1st c.): Sister of Lazarus and Mary of Bethany; Gospel accounts record her concern for homely details; patron of cooks; July 29.*

Martin I (d. 655): Pope, 649-55; banished from Rome by emperor in 653 because of his condemnation of Monothelites; considered a martyr; Apr. 13.*

Martin of Tours (316-97): Bishop of Tours; opposed Arianism and Priscillianism; pioneer of Western monasticism, before St. Benedict; Nov. 11.*

Mary Domenica Mazzarello (1837-81): Italian foundress, with St. John Bosco, of the Daughters of Mary Help of Christians, 1872; canonized 1951; May 14.

Mary Josepha Rossello (1811-81): Italian-born foundress of the Daughters of Our Lady of Mercy; canonized 1949; Dec. 7.

Mary Magdalen Postel (1756-1846): French foundress of the Sisters of Christian Schools of Mercy, 1807; canonized 1925; July 16.

Mary Magdalene (1st c.): Gospels record her as devoted follower of Christ to whom he appeared after the Resurrection; her identification with Mary of Bethany (sister of Martha and Lazarus) and the woman sinner (Lk. 7:36-50) has been questioned; July 22.*

Mary Magdalene dei Pazzi (1566-1607): Italian Carmelite nun; recipient of mystical experiences; canonized 1669; May 25.*

Mary Michaeli Desmaisières (1809-65): Spanish-born foundress of the Institute of the Handmaids of the Blessed Sacrament, 1848; canonized 1934; Aug. 24.

Maximilian Kolbe (1894-1941): Polish Conventual Franciscan; prisoner at Auschwitz who heroically offered his life in place of a fellow prisoner; beatified 1971, canonized 1982; Aug. 14.*

Methodius: *See* Cyril and Methodius.

Miguel Febres Cordero (1854-1910): Ecuadorean Christian Brother; educator; canonized 1984; Feb. 9.

Miguel Pro, Bl. (1891-1927): Mexican Jesuit; joined Jesuits, 1911; forced to flee because of religious persecution; ordained in Belgium, 1925; returned to Mexico, 1926, to minister to people despite government prohibition; unjustly accused of assassination plot against president; arrested and executed; beatified 1988. Nov. 23* (U.S.).

Monica (332-87): Mother of St. Augustine; model of

a patient mother; her feast is observed in the Roman calendar the day before her son's; Aug. 27.*

Nereus and Achilleus (d. c. 100): Early Christian martyrs; soldiers who, according to legend, were baptized by St. Peter; May 12.*

Nicholas of Flüe (1417-87): Swiss layman; at the age of 50, with the consent of his wife and 10 children, he retreated from the world to live as a hermit; called Brother Claus by the Swiss; canonized 1947; Mar. 21.

Nicholas of Myra (4th c.): Bishop of Myra in Asia Minor; one of most popular saints in both East and West; most of the incidents of his life are based on legend; patron of Russia; Dec. 6.*

Nicholas of Tolentino (1245-1305): Italian hermit; famed preacher; canonized 1446; Sept. 10.

Nicholas Tavelic and Companions (Deodatus of Aquitaine, Peter of Narbonne, Stephen of Cuneo) (d. 1391): Franciscan missionaries; martyred by Muslims in the Holy Land: canonized 1970; Nov. 14.

Norbert (1080-1134): German bishop; founded Canons Regular of Premontre (Premonstratensians, Norbertines), 1120; promoted reform of the clergy, devotion to Blessed Sacrament; canonized 1582; June 6.*

Odilia (d. c. 720): Benedictine abbess; according to legend she was born blind, abandoned by her family and adopted by a convent of nuns where her sight was miraculously restored; patroness of blind; Dec. 13.

Oliver Plunket (1629-81): Irish martyr; theologian; archbishop of Armagh and primate of Ireland; beatified 1920; canonized 1975; July 1.

Pancras (d. c. 304): Roman martyr; May 12.*

Paola Frassinetti (1809-82): Italian Religious; foundress, 1834, of Sisters of St. Dorothy; canonized 1984; June 11.

Paschal Baylon (1540-92): Spanish Franciscan lay brother; spent life as door-keeper in various Franciscan friaries; defended doctrine of Real Presence in Blessed Sacrament; canonized 1690; patron of all Eucharistic confraternities and congresses, 1897; May 17.

Patrick (389-461): Famous missionary of Ireland; began missionary work in Ireland about 432; organized the Church there and established it on a lasting foundation; patron of Ireland, with Sts. Bridget and Columba; Mar. 17.*

Paul Miki and Companions (d. 1597): Martyrs of Japan; Paul Miki, Jesuit, and twenty-five other priests and laymen were martyred at Nagasaki; canonized 1862, the first canonized martyrs of the Far East; Feb. 6.*

Paul of the Cross (1694-1775): Italian Religious; founder of the Passionists; canonized 1867; Oct 19* (Oct. 20, U.S.*).

Paulinus of Nola (d. 451): Bishop of Nola (Spain); writer; June 22.*

Peregrine (1260-1347): Italian Servite; invoked against cancer (he was miraculously cured of cancer of the foot after a vision); canonized 1726; May 1.

Perpetua and Felicity (d. 203): Martyrs; Perpetua was a young married woman; Felicity was a slave girl; Mar. 7.*

Peter Chanel (1803-41): French Marist; missionary to Oceania, where he was martyred; canonized 1954; Apr. 28.*

Peter Fourier (1565-1640): French priest; cofounder with Alice LeClercq (Mother Teresa of Jesus) of the Augustinian Canonesses of Our Lady, 1598; canonized 1897; Dec. 9.

Peter Gonzalez (1190-1246): Spanish Dominican; worked among sailors; court chaplain and confessor of King St.

Ferdinand of Castile; patron of sailors; Apr. 14.

Peter Julian Eymard (1811-68): French priest; founder of the Congregation of the Blessed Sacrament (men), 1856, and Servants of the Blessed Sacrament (women), 1864; dedicated to Eucharistic apostolate; canonized 1962; Aug. 2.*

Peter Nolasco (c. 1189-1258): Born in Langueduc area of present-day France; founded the Mercedarians (Order of Our Lady of Mercy), 1218, in Spain; canonized 1628; Jan. 31.

Peter of Alcantara (1499-1562): Spanish Franciscan; mystic; initiated Franciscan reform; confessor of St. Teresa of Jesus (Ávila); canonized 1669; Oct. 22 (in U.S.).

Philip Benizi (1233-85): Italian Servite; noted preacher, peacemaker; canonized 1671; Aug. 23.

Philip Neri (1515-95): Italian Religious; founded Congregation of the Oratory; considered a second apostle of Rome because of his mission activity there; canonized 1622; May 26.*

Philip of Jesus (1517-57): Mexican Franciscan; martyred at Nagasaki, Japan; canonized 1862; patron of Mexico City; Feb. 6.*

Pio, Padre (1887-1968): Pio da Pietrelcina (Francesco Forgione), and Italian Capuchin Franciscan, mystic and stigmatic; assisted souls from all over the world who came to him for counsel and guidance; canonized on June 16, 2002; Sept. 23.

Pius V (1504-72): Pope, 1566-72; enforced decrees of Council of Trent; organized expedition against Turks resulting in victory at Lepanto; canonized 1712; Apr. 30.*

Polycarp (2nd c.): Bishop of Smyrna; ecclesiastical writer; martyr; Feb. 23.*

Pontian (d. c. 235): Pope, 230-35; exiled to Sardinia by the emperor; regarded as a martyr; Aug. 13 (with Hippolytus).*

Rafaela Maria Porras y Ayllon (1850-1925): Spanish Religious; founded the Handmaids of the Sacred Heart, 1877; canonized 1977; Jan. 6.

Raymond Nonnatus (d. 1240): Spanish Mercedarian; cardinal; devoted his life to ransoming captives from the Moors; Aug. 31.

Raymond of Peñafort (1175-1275): Spanish Dominican; confessor of Gregory IX; systematized and codified canon law, in effect until 1917; master general of Dominicans, 1238; canonized 1601; Jan. 7.*

Rita of Cascia (1381-1457): Widow; cloistered Augustinian Religious of Umbria; invoked in impossible and desperate cases; May 22.

Robert Southwell (1561-95): English Jesuit; poet; martyred at Tyburn; canonized 1970, one of the Forty English and Welsh Martyrs; Feb. 21.

Roch (1350-79): French layman; pilgrim; devoted life to care of plague-stricken; widely venerated; invoked against pestilence; Aug. 17.

Romuald (951-1027): Italian monk; founded Camaldolese Benedictines; June 19.*

Rose of Lima (1586-1617): Peruvian Dominican tertiary; first native-born saint of the New World; canonized 1671; Aug. 23.*

Scholastica (d. c. 559): Sister of St. Benedict; regarded as first nun of the Benedictine Order; Feb. 10.*

Sebastian (3rd c.): Roman martyr; traditionally pictured as a handsome youth with arrows; martyred; patron of athletes, archers; Jan. 20.*

Seven Holy Founders of the Servants of Mary

(Buonfiglio Monaldo, Alexis Falconieri, Benedict dell'Antello, Bartholomew Amidei, Ricovero Uguccione, Gerardino Sostegni, John Buonagiunta Monetti): Florentine youths who founded Servites, 1233, in obedience to a vision; canonized 1888; Feb. 17.*

Sharbel Makhlouf (1828-98): Lebanese Maronite monk-hermit; canonized 1977; Dec. 24.

Sixtus II and Companions (d. 258): Sixtus, pope 257-58, and four deacons, martyrs; Aug. 7.*

Stanislaus (1030-79): Polish bishop; martyr; canonized 1253; Apr. 11.*

Stephen (d. c. 33): First Christian martyr; chosen by the Apostles as the first of the seven deacons; stoned to death; Dec. 26.*

Stephen (975-1038): King; apostle of Hungary; welded Magyars into national unity; canonized 1083; Aug. 16.*

Sylvester I (d. 335): Pope 314-35; first ecumenical council held at Nicaea during his pontificate; Dec. 31.*

Tarcisius (d. 3rd c.): Early martyr; according to tradition, was martyred while carrying the Blessed Sacrament to some Christians in prison; patron of first communicants; Aug. 15.

Teresa Margaret Redi (1747-70): Italian Carmelite; lived life of prayer and austere penance; canonized 1934; Mar. 11.

Teresa of Jesus Jornet Ibars (1843-97): Spanish Religious; founded the Little Sisters of the Abandoned Aged, 1873; canonized 1974; Aug. 26.

Teresa, Mother (1910-97): Sister, foundress of the Missionaries of Charity, and Nobel Prize winner; called Mother Teresa of Calcutta; beatified by Pope John Paul II on Oct. 19, 2003; Sept. 5. See News in Depth.

Thérèse Couderc (1805-85): French Religious; foundress of the Religious of Our Lady of the Retreat in the Cenacle, 1827; canonized 1970; Sept. 26.

Thomas Becket (1118-70): English martyr; archbishop of Canterbury; chancellor under Henry II; murdered for upholding rights of the Church; canonized 1173; Dec. 29.*

Thomas More (1478-1535): English martyr; statesman, chancellor under Henry VIII; author of Utopia; opposed Henry's divorce, refused to renounce authority of the papacy; beheaded; canonized 1935; Pope John Paul II declared him patron of politicians on Oct. 31, 2000; June 22 (with St. John Fisher).*

Timothy (d. c. 97): Bishop of Ephesus; disciple and companion of St. Paul; martyr; Jan. 26.*

Titus (d. c. 96): Bishop; companion of St. Paul; recipient of one of Paul's epistles; Jan. 26.*

Titus Brandsma, Bl. (1881-1942): Dutch Carmelite priest; professor, scholar, journalist; denounced Nazi persecution of Jews; arrested by Nazis, Jan. 19, 1942; executed by lethal injection at Dachau, July 26, 1942; beatified 1985; July 26.

Valentine (d. 269): Priest, physician; martyred at Rome; legendary patron of lovers; Feb. 14.

Vicenta Maria Lopez y Vicuna (1847-96): Spanish foundress of the Daughters of Mary Immaculate for domestic service; canonized 1975; Dec. 26.

Vincent (d. 304): Spanish deacon; martyr; Jan. 22.*

Vincent de Paul (1581?-1660): French priest; founder of Congregation of the Mission (Vincentians, Lazarists) and co-founder of Sisters of Charity; declared patron of all charitable organizations and works by Leo XIII; canonized 1737; Sept. 27.*

Vincent Ferrer (1350-1418): Spanish Dominican; famed preacher; Apr. 5.*

Vincent Pallotti (1795-1850): Italian priest; founded Society of the Catholic Apostolate (Pallottines), 1835; Jan. 22.

Vincent Strambi (1745-1824): Italian Passionist; bishop; reformer; canonized 1950; Sept. 25.

Vitus (d.c. 300): Martyr; died in Lucania, southern Italy; regarded as protector of epileptics and those suffering from St. Vitus Dance (chorea); June 15.

Walburga (d. 779): English-born Benedictine Religious; belonged to group of nuns who established convents in Germany at the invitation of St. Boniface; abbess of Heidenheim; Feb. 25.

Wenceslaus (d. 935): Duke of Bohemia; martyr; patron of Bohemia; Sept. 28.*

Zita (1218-78): Italian maid; noted for charity to poor; patron of domestics; Apr. 27.

SAINTS — PATRONS AND INTERCESSORS

A patron is a saint who is venerated as a special intercessor before God. Most patrons have been so designated as the result of popular devotion and long-standing custom. In many cases, the fact of existing patronal devotion is clear despite historical obscurity regarding its origin. The Church has made official designation of relatively few patrons; in such cases, the dates of designation are given in parentheses in the list below. The theological background of the patronage of saints includes the dogmas of the Mystical Body of Christ and the Communion of Saints. Listed are patron saints of occupations and professions, and saints whose intercession is sought for special needs.

Academics: Thomas Aquinas.
Accomodations: Gertrude of Nivelles.
Accountants: Matthew.
Actors: Genesius.
Adopted children: Clotilde; Thomas More.
Advertisers: Bernardine of Siena (May 20, 1960).
Alcoholics: John of God; Monica.
Alpinists: Bernard of Montjoux (or Menthon) (Aug. 20, 1923).
Altar servers: John Berchmans.
Anesthetists: René Goupil.
Animals: Francis of Assisi.
Archaeologists: Damasus.
Archers: Sebastian.
Architects: Thomas, Apostle.
Art: Catherine of Bologna.
Artists: Luke, Catherine of Bologna, Bl. Angelico (Feb. 21, 1984).
Astronauts: Joseph Cupertino.
Astronomers: Dominic.
Athletes: Sebastian.
Authors: Francis de Sales.
Aviators: Our Lady of Loreto (1920), Thérèse of Lisieux, Joseph of Cupertino.
Bakers: Elizabeth of Hungary, Nicholas.
Bankers: Matthew.
Barbers: Cosmas and Damian, Louis.
Barren women: Anthony of Padua, Felicity.
Basket-makers: Anthony, Abbot.
Bees: Ambrose.

Birth: Margaret.
Beggars: Martin of Tours.
Blacksmiths: Dunstan.
Blind: Odilia, Raphael.
Blood banks: Januarius.
Bodily ills: Our Lady of Lourdes.
Bookbinders: Peter Celestine.
Bookkeepers: Matthew.
Booksellers: John of God.
Boy Scouts: George.
Brewers: Augustine of Hippo, Luke, Nicholas of Myra.
Bricklayers: Stephen.
Brides: Nicholas of Myra.
Bridges: John of Nepomucene.
Broadcasters: Gabriel.
Brushmakers: Anthony, Abbot.
Builders: Vincent Ferrer.
Bus drivers: Christopher.
Butchers: Anthony (Abbot), Luke.
Butlers: Adelelm.
Cabdrivers: Fiacre.
Cabinetmakers: Anne.
Cancer patients: Peregrine.
Canonists: Raymond of Peñafort.
Carpenters: Joseph.
Catechists: Viator, Charles Borromeo, Robert Bellarmine.
Catholic Action: Francis of Assisi (1916).
Catholic Press: Francis de Sales.
Chandlers: Ambrose, Bernard of Clairvaux.
Chaplains: John of Capistrano.
Charitable societies: Vincent de Paul (May 12, 1885).
Chastity: Thomas Aquinas.
Childbirth: Raymond Nonnatus; Gerard Majella.
Children: Nicholas of Myra.
Children of Mary: Agnes, Maria Goretti.
Choirboys: Dominic Savio (June 8, 1956), Holy Innocents.
Church: Joseph (Dec. 8, 1870).
Circus people: Julian the Hospitaller.
Clerics: Gabriel of the Sorrowful Mother.
Colleges: Thomas Aquinas.
Comedians: Vitus.
Communications personnel: Bernardine.
Confessors: Alphonsus Liguori (Apr. 26, 1950), John Nepomucene.
Converts: Helena; Vladimir.
Convulsive children: Scholastica.
Cooks: Lawrence, Martha.
Coopers: Nicholas of Myra.
Coppersmiths: Maurus.
Dairy workers: Brigid.
Dancers: Vitus.
Deaf: Francis de Sales.
Dentists: Apollonia.
Desperate situations: Gregory of Neocaesarea, Jude Thaddeus, Rita of Cascia.
Dietitians (in hospitals): Martha.
Diplomats: Gabriel.
Divorce: Helena.
Drug addiction: Maximilian Kolbe.
Dyers: Maurice, Lydia.
Dying: Joseph.
Ecologists: Francis of Assisi (Nov. 29, 1979).
Ecumenists: Cyril and Methodius.
Editors: John Bosco.
Emigrants: Frances Xavier Cabrini (Sept. 8, 1950).

Endurance: Pantaleon.
Engineers: Ferdinand III.
Epilepsy, Motor Diseases: Vitus, Willibrord.
Eucharistic congresses and societies: Paschal Baylon (Nov. 28, 1897).
Expectant mothers: Raymond Nonnatus, Gerard Majella.
Eye diseases: Lucy.
Falsely accused: Raymond Nonnatus.
Farmers: George, Isidore.
Farriers: John the Baptist.
Firemen: Florian.
Fire prevention: Catherine of Siena.
First communicants: Tarcisius.
Fishermen: Andrew.
Florists: Thérèse of Lisieux.
Forest workers: John Gualbert.
Foundlings: Holy Innocents.
Friendship: John the Divine.
Fullers: Anastasius the Fuller, James the Less.
Funeral directors: Joseph of Arimathea, Dismas.
Gardeners: Adelard, Tryphon, Fiacre, Phocas.
Glassworkers: Luke.
Goldsmiths: Dunstan, Anastasius.
Gravediggers: Anthony, Abbot.
Greetings: Valentine.
Grocers: Michael.
Grooms: King Louis IX of France.
Hairdressers: Martin de Porres.
Happy meetings: Raphael.
Hatters: Severus of Ravenna, James the Less.
Headache sufferers: Teresa of Jesus (Ávila).
Heart patients: John of God.
Homeless: Margaret of Cortona; Benedict Joseph Labré.
Horses: Giles; Hippolytus.
Housekeepers: Zita.
Hospital administrators: Basil the Great, Frances X. Cabrini.
Hospitals: Camillus de Lellis and John of God (June 22, 1886), Jude Thaddeus.
Housewives: Anne.
Hunters: Hubert, Eustachius.
Infantrymen: Maurice.
Innkeepers: Amand, Martha, Julian the Hospitaller.
Innocence: Hallvard.
Invalids: Roch.
Janitors: Theobald.
Jewelers: Eligius, Dunstan.
Journalists: Francis de Sales (Apr. 26, 1923).
Jurists: John Capistran.
Laborers: Isidore, James, John Bosco.
Lawyers: Ivo (Yves Helory), Genesius, Thomas More.
Learning: Ambrose.
Librarians: Jerome.
Lighthouse keepers: Venerius (Mar. 10, 1961).
Linguists: Gottschalk.
Locksmiths: Dunstan.
Lost souls: Nicholas of Tolentino.
Lovers: Raphael; Valentine.
Lunatics: Christina.
Maids: Zita.
Marble workers: Clement I.
Mariners: Michael, Nicholas of Tolentino.
Medical record librarians: Raymond of Peñafort.
Medical social workers: John Regis.

Medical technicians: Albert the Great.
Mentally ill: Dymphna.
Merchants: Francis of Assisi, Nicholas of Myra.
Messengers: Gabriel.
Metal workers: Eligius.
Military chaplains: John Capistran (Feb. 10, 1984).
Millers: Arnulph, Victor.
Missions, foreign: Francis Xavier (Mar. 25, 1904), Thérèse of Lisieux (Dec. 14, 1927).
Missions, black: Peter Claver (1896, Leo XIII), Benedict the Black.
Missions, parish: Leonard of Port Maurice (Mar. 17, 1923).
Monks: Benedict of Nursia.
Mothers: Monica.
Motorcyclists: Our Lady of Grace.
Motorists: Christopher, Frances of Rome.
Mountaineers: Bernard of Montjoux (or Menthon).
Musicians: Gregory the Great, Cecilia, Dunstan.
Mystics: John of the Cross.
Notaries: Luke, Mark.
Nuns: Bridget.
Nurses: Camillus de Lellis and John of God (1930, Pius XI), Agatha, Raphael.
Nursing and nursing service: Elizabeth of Hungary, Catherine of Siena.
Orators: John Chrysostom (July 8, 1908).
Organ builders: Cecilia.
Orphans: Jerome Emiliani.
Painters: Luke.
Paratroopers: Michael.
Pawnbrokers: Nicholas.
Plumbers: Vincent Ferrer.
Pharmacists: Cosmas and Damian, James the Greater.
Pharmacists (in hospitals): Gemma Galgani.
Philosophers: Justin.
Physicians: Pantaleon, Cosmas and Damian, Luke, Raphael.
Pilgrims: James the Greater.
Plasterers: Bartholomew.
Poets: David, Cecilia.
Politicians: Thomas More.
Poison sufferers: Benedict.
Policemen: Michael.
Poor: Lawrence, Anthony of Padua.
Poor souls: Nicholas of Tolentino.
Popes: Gregory I the Great.
Porters: Christopher.
Possessed: Bruno, Denis.
Postal employees: Gabriel.
Priests: Jean-Baptiste Vianney (Apr. 23, 1929).
Printers: John of God, Augustine of Hippo, Genesius.
Prisoners: Dismas, Joseph Cafasso.
Protector of crops: Ansovinus.
Public relations: Bernardine of Siena (May 20, 1960).
Public relations (of hospitals): Paul, Apostle.
Publishers: John the Divine.
Race relations: Martin de Porres.
Radiologists: Michael (Jan. 15, 1941).
Radio workers: Gabriel.
Refugees: Alban.
Retreats: Ignatius Loyola (July 25, 1922).
Rheumatism: James the Greater.
Saddlers: Crispin and Crispinian.
Sailors: Cuthbert, Brendan, Eulalia, Christopher, Peter Gonzalez, Erasmus, Nicholas.

Scholars: Bede the Venerable; Brigid.
Schools, Catholic: Thomas Aquinas (Aug. 4, 1880), Joseph Calasanz (Aug. 13, 1948).
Scientists: Albert (Aug. 13, 1948).
Sculptors: Four Crowned Martyrs.
Seamen: Francis of Paola.
Searchers of lost articles: Anthony of Padua.
Secretaries: Genesius.
Secular Franciscans: Louis of France, Elizabeth of Hungary.
Seminarians: Charles Borromeo.
Servants: Martha, Zita.
Shepherds: Drogo.
Shoemakers: Crispin and Crispinian.
Sick: Michael, John of God and Camillus de Lellis (June 22, 1886).
Silversmiths: Andronicus.
Singers: Gregory, Cecilia.
Single mothers: Margaret of Cortona.
Single women: Catherine of Alexandria.
Skaters: Lidwina.
Skiers: Bernard of Montjoux (or Menthon).
Social workers: Louise de Marillac (Feb. 12, 1960).
Soldiers: Hadrian, George, Ignatius, Sebastian, Martin of Tours, Joan of Arc.
Speleologists: Benedict.
Stamp collectors: Gabriel.
Stenographers: Genesius, Cassian.
Stonecutters: Clement.
Stonemasons: Stephen.
Stress: Walter of Portnoise.
Students: Thomas Aquinas.
Surgeons: Cosmas and Damian, Luke.
Swimmers: Adjutor.
Swordsmiths: Maurice.
Tailors: Homobonus.
Tanners: Crispin and Crispinian, Simon.
Tax collectors: Matthew.
Teachers: Gregory the Great, John Baptist de la Salle (May 15, 1950).
Telecommunications workers: Gabriel (Jan. 12, 1951).
Television: Clare of Assisi (Feb. 14, 1958).
Television workers: Gabriel.
Thieves: Dismas.
Theologians: Augustine, Alphonsus Liguori.
Throat ailments: Blase.
Torture victims: Alban; Eustachius; Regina; Vincent; Victor of Marseilles.
Toymakers: Claude.
Travelers: Anthony of Padua, Nicholas of Myra, Christopher, Raphael.
Travel hostesses: Bona (Mar. 2, 1962).
Truck drivers: Christopher.
Universities: Blessed Contardo Ferrini.
Veterinarians: Blaise.
Vocations: Alphonsus.
Whales: Brendan the Voyager.
Watchmen: Peter of Alcantara.
Weavers: Paul the Hermit, Anastasius the Fuller, Anastasia.
Wine merchants: Amand.
Wineries: Morand; Vincent.
Women in labor: Anne.
Workingmen: Joseph.
Writers: Francis de Sales (Apr. 26, 1923), Lucy.
Yachtsmen: Adjutor.

Young girls: Agnes.
Youth: Aloysius Gonzaga (1729, Benedict XIII; 1926, Pius XI), John Berchmans, Gabriel of the Sorrowful Mother.

Patron Saints of Places

Albania: Our Lady of Good Counsel.
Alsace: Odilia.
Americas: Our Lady of Guadalupe, Rose of Lima.
Angola: Immaculate Heart of Mary (Nov. 21, 1984).
Argentina: Our Lady of Lujan.
Armenia: Gregory Illuminator.
Asia Minor: John, Evangelist.
Australia: Our Lady Help of Christians.
Belgium: Joseph.
Bohemia: Wenceslaus, Ludmilla.
Bolivia: Our Lady of Copacabana, "Virgen de la Candelaria."
Borneo: Francis Xavier.
Brazil: Nossa Señora de Aparecida, Immaculate Conception, Peter of Alcantara.
Canada: Joseph, Anne.
Chile: James the Greater, Our Lady of Mt. Carmel.
China: Joseph.
Colombia: Peter Claver, Louis Bertran.
Corsica: Immaculate Conception.
Cuba: Our Lady of Charity.
Czechoslovakia: Wenceslaus, John Nepomucene, Procopius.
Denmark: Ansgar, Canute.
Dominican Republic: Our Lady of High Grace, Dominic.
East Indies: Thomas, Apostle.
Ecuador: Sacred Heart.
El Salvador: Our Lady of Peace (Oct. 10, 1966).
England: George.
Equatorial Guinea: Immaculate Conception (May 25, 1986).
Europe: Benedict (1964); Cyril and Methodius, co-patrons (Dec. 31, 1980); Sts. Catherine of Siena, Bridget of Sweden, and Edith Stein, co-patronesses (Oct. 1, 1999).
Finland: Henry.
France: Our Lady of the Assumption, Joan of Arc, Thérèse (May 3, 1944).
Germany: Boniface, Michael.
Gibraltar: Blessed Virgin Mary, "Our Lady of Europe" (May 31, 1979).
Greece: Nicholas, Andrew.
Holland: Willibrord.
Hungary: Blessed Virgin, "Great Lady of Hungary," Stephen, king.
Iceland: Thorlac (Jan. 14, 1984).
India: Our Lady of Assumption.
Ireland: Patrick, Brigid and Columba.
Italy: Francis of Assisi, Catherine of Siena.
Japan: Peter Baptist.
Korea: Joseph and Mary, Mother of the Church.
Lesotho: Immaculate Heart of Mary.
Lithuania: Casimir, Bl. Cunegunda.
Luxembourg: Willibrord.
Malta: Paul, Our Lady of the Assumption.
Mexico: Our Lady of Guadalupe.
Monaco: Devota.
Moravia: Cyril and Methodius.
New Zealand: Our Lady Help of Christians.

Norway: Olaf.
Papua New Guinea (including northern Solomon Islands): Michael the Archangel (May 31, 1979).
Paraguay: Our Lady of Assumption (July 13, 1951).
Peru: Joseph (Mar. 19, 1957).
Philippines: Sacred Heart of Mary.
Poland: Casimir, Bl. Cunegunda, Stanislaus of Krakow, Our Lady of Czestochowa.
Portugal: Immaculate Conception, Francis Borgia, Anthony of Padua, Vincent of Saragossa, George.
Russia: Andrew, Nicholas of Myra, Thérèse of Lisieux.
Scandinavia: Ansgar.
Scotland: Andrew, Columba.
Silesia: Hedwig.
Slovakia: Our Lady of Sorrows.
South Africa: Our Lady of Assumption (Mar. 15, 1952).
South America: Rose of Lima.
Solomon Islands: Blessed Virgin Mary, Most Holy Name of Mary (Sept. 4, 1991).
Spain: James the Greater, Teresa.
Sri Lanka (Ceylon): Lawrence.
Sweden: Bridget, Eric.
Tanzania: Immaculate Conception (Dec. 8, 1964).
United States: Immaculate Conception (1846).
Uruguay: Blessed Virgin Mary, "La Virgen de los Treinte y Tres" (Nov. 21, 1963).
Venezuela: Our Lady of Coromoto.
Wales: David.
West Indies: Gertrude.

Emblems, Portrayals of Saints

Agatha: Tongs, veil.
Agnes: Lamb.
Ambrose: Bees, dove, ox, pen.
Andrew: Transverse cross.
Anne, Mother of the Blessed Virgin: Door.
Anthony of Padua: Infant Jesus, bread, book, lily.
Augustine of Hippo: Dove, child, shell, pen.
Bartholomew: Knife, flayed and holding his skin.
Benedict: Broken cup, raven, bell, crosier, bush.
Bernard of Clairvaux: Pen, bees, instruments of the Passion.
Bernardine of Siena: Tablet or sun inscribed with IHS.
Blase: Wax, taper, iron comb.
Bonaventure: Communion, ciborium, cardinal's hat.
Boniface: Oak, ax, book, fox, scourge, fountain, raven, sword.
Bridget of Sweden: Book, pilgrim's staff.
Bridget of Kildare: Cross, flame over her head, candle.
Catherine of Ricci: Ring, crown, crucifix.
Catherine of Siena: Stigmata, cross, ring, lily.
Cecilia: Organ.
Charles Borromeo: Communion, coat of arms with word "Humilitas."
Christopher: Giant, torrent, tree, Child Jesus on his shoulders.
Clare of Assisi: Monstrance.
Cosmas and Damian: A phial, box of ointment.
Cyril of Alexandria: Blessed Virgin holding the Child Jesus, pen.
Cyril of Jerusalem: Purse, book.
Dominic: Rosary, star.
Edmund the Martyr: Arrow, sword.
Elizabeth of Hungary: Alms, flowers, bread, the poor, a pitcher.

Francis of Assisi: Wolf, birds, fish, skull, the Stigmata.
Francis Xavier: Crucifix, bell, vessel.
Genevieve: Bread, keys, herd, candle.
George: Dragon.
Gertrude: Crown, taper, lily.
Gervase and Protase: Scourge, club, sword.
Gregory I (the Great): Tiara, crosier, dove.
Helena: Cross.
Ignatius of Loyola: Communion, chasuble, book, apparition of Our Lord.
Isidore: Bees, pen.
James the Greater: Pilgrim's staff, shell, key, sword.
James the Less: Square rule, halberd, club.
Jerome: Lion.
John Berchmans: Rule of St. Ignatius, cross, rosary.
John Chrysostom: Bees, dove, pen.
John of God: Alms, a heart, crown of thorns.
John the Baptist: Lamb, head on platter, skin of an animal.
John the Evangelist: Eagle, chalice, kettle, armor.
Josaphat Kuncevyc: Chalice, crown, winged deacon.
Joseph, Spouse of the Blessed Virgin: Infant Jesus, lily, rod, plane, carpenter's square.
Jude: Sword, square rule, club.
Justin Martyr: Ax, sword.
Lawrence: Cross, book of the Gospels, gridiron.
Leander of Seville: Pen.
Liberius: Pebbles, peacock.
Longinus: In arms at foot of the cross.
Louis IX of France: Crown of thorns, nails.
Lucy: Cord, eyes on a dish.

Luke: Ox, book, brush, palette.
Mark: Lion, book.
Martha: Holy water sprinkler, dragon.
Mary Magdalene: Alabaster box of ointment.
Matilda: Purse, alms.
Matthew: Winged man, purse, lance.
Matthias: Lance.
Maurus: Scales, spade, crutch.
Meinrad: Two ravens.
Michael: Scales, banner, sword, dragon.
Monica: Girdle, tears.
Nicholas: Three purses or balls, anchor or boat, child.
Patrick: Cross, harp, serpent, baptismal font, demons, shamrock.
Paul: Sword, book or scroll.
Peter: Keys, boat, cock.
Philip, Apostle: Column.
Philip Neri: Altar, chasuble, vial.
Rita of Cascia: Rose, crucifix, thorn.
Roch: Angel, dog, bread.
Rose of Lima: Crown of thorns, anchor, city.
Sebastian: Arrows, crown.
Simon Stock: Scapular.
Teresa of Jesus (Ávila): Heart, arrow, book.
Thérèse of Lisieux: Roses entwining a crucifix.
Thomas, Apostle: Lance, ax.
Thomas Aquinas: Chalice, monstrance, dove, ox, person trampled under foot.
Vincent de Paul: Children.
Vincent Ferrer: Pulpit, cardinal's hat, trumpet, captives.

CANONIZATIONS AND BEATIFICATIONS 2005-06

Pope Benedict XVI beatified and canonized the following individuals from Sept. 2005 to Aug. 2006. Included are the dates of the beatifications, as well as relevant biographical information.

Canonizations 2005

Józef Bilczewski (Apr. 26, 1860 – Mar. 20, 1923) A Polish archbishop, he was born in Wilamowice near Kęty, Poland, and was ordained a priest in Krakow in 1864. After receiving a doctorate in theology from the University of Vienna and further studies in Rome and Paris, he became a professor of theology and then rector of the John Casimir University of Leopoli. At the urging of Emperor Franz Joseph of Austria, he was named archbishop of Leopoli in 1900. He was revered for his holiness and intellect and his devotion to the Eucharist and issued a pastoral letter devoted to the Eucharist. He also cared for the many who suffered during World War I across Poland. Pope John Paul II beatified him on June 26, 2001, during his visit to the Ukraine; he was canonized by Pope Benedict XVI on Oct. 23, 2005.

Gaetano Catanoso (Feb. 14, 1879 – Apr. 4, 1963) Italian priest and founder of the Congregation of the Daughters of St Veronica, Missionaries of the Holy Face. Born in Chorio di San Lorenzo, Reggio Calabria, Italy, he was ordained a priest in 1902, and served in a rural parish from 1904 to 1921. Devoted to the Holy Face of Jesus, he founded *The Holy Face Bulletin* and established the Confraternity of the Holy Face in 1920. Transferred to a large parish in 1921, he soon earned a reputation for holiness and for his spiritual gifts. In 1934, he founded the Congregation of the Daughters of St. Veronica,

Missionaries of the Holy Face; it received diocesan approval in 1958. He was beatified by Pope John Paul II on May 4, 1997, and canonized by Pope Benedict XVI on Oct. 23, 2005.

Zygmunt Gorazdowski (Nov. 1, 1845 – Jan. 1, 1920) Ukrainian priest and founder of the Congregation of the Sisters of St Joseph. Born in Sanok, Ukraine, he endured poor health in his youth and went on to receive ordination on July 21, 1871. His heroic service included caring for victims of a cholera outbreak and the spiritual care of his parishioners. In 1884, he founded the Congregation of the Sisters of St. Joseph. Pope John Paul II beatified him on June 26, 2001; canonized by Pope Benedict XVI on Oct. 23, 2005.

Alberto Hurtado Cruchaga (Jan. 22, 1901 – Aug. 18, 1952) Chilean priest and saintly defender of human rights and human dignity. Born in Viña del Mar, Chile, he endured a difficult childhood and entered the Novitiate of the Society of Jesus in 1923. He went on to study in Argentina, Spain, and Belgium and was ordained a priest in 1933; in 1935 obtained a doctorate in pedagogy and psychology. Returning to Chile, he taught for a time and then wrote *Is Chile a Catholic Country?* (1941). He promoted the care of the poor, Catholic Action, the rights of workers, and the needs of poor children through his home, "El Hogar." In 1947, he founded the Chilean Trade Union Association (ASICH) to promote a union movement inspired by the social teaching of the Church. Pope John Paul II beatified him on Oct. 16, 1994, and Pope Benedict XVI canonized him on Oct. 23, 2005.

Felix of Nicosia (Nov. 5, 1715 – May 31, 1787) Italian Capuchin Franciscan and promoter of the Eucharist. Born in Nicosia, Sicily, he desired to enter the Capuchins but faced trials because he was illiterate. Finally admitted to the novitiate in 1743, he soon earned great respect for his holiness and obedience and made his profession on Oct. 10, 1744. He was given the job of collecting alms and had a particular veneration for the Eucharist. He was beatified by Leo XIII on Feb. 12, 1888, and canonized by Pope Benedict XVI on Oct. 23, 2005.

Beatifications 2005

Clemens August von Galen (Mar. 16, 1878 – Mar. 22, 1946) German Cardinal and bishop of Münster, honored as the "Lion of Munster." Born in Dinklage Castle, Oldenburg, Germany, he was the son of Count Ferdinand Heribert and Elisabeth von Spee and a member of a noble family of Westphalia. Raised in the faith, he studied philosophy and theology and was ordained a priest in 1904. After years of parish and devoted priestly service, he was named in 1933 Bishop of Münster by Pope Pius XI. He prophetically chose as his motto, "*Nec laudibus, nec timore*" (Neither praise nor threats will distance me from God). A determined opponent of the Nazi regime of Adolf Hitler, he promoted Pope Pius's famed 1937 encyclical *Mit brennender Sorge* on the Church in Nazi Germany and remained fiercely opposed to Hitler's policies, such as the confiscation of Church property and the programmatic euthanasia carried out by the regime. Surviving the war, he was named a cardinal in Feb. 1946 by Pope Pius XII and returned in triumph to Münster. He was beatified on Oct. 9, 2005.

María De Los Ángeles Ginard Martí (Apr. 3, 1894 – Aug. 26, 1936) Spanish member of the Zealous Sisters of the Eucharist and a martyr. Born at Llucmajor, Majorca, Spain, she was the third of nine children of a strongly Catholic family. To help her family, she took various jobs, even as she dedicated herself to God and helped to insure her siblings' education. Called to the religious life, she was compelled to delay her entry into the convent to help her family. At last, in Nov. 1921, she was able to enter the Zealous Sisters of the Eucharist of Palma on Majorca. There she practiced perpetual adoration and worked in the creation of liturgical vestments. Caught up in the Spanish Civil War, she was arrested on Aug. 25, 1936, and murdered by anti-Church forces. She was beatified on Oct. 29, 2005.

Josep Tàpies and six Companions (d. Aug. 13, 1936) Seven priests of the diocese of Urgel who were martyred during the persecution of the Church in the Spanish Civil War from 1936-1939. They were arrested and shot by anticlerical forces. The seven priests were Fathers Josep Tàpies (b. 1869), Pasqual Araguás i Guárdia (b. 1899), Silvestre Arnau i Pasqüet (b. 1911), Josep Boher i Foix (b. 1887), Francesc Castells i Brenuy (1886), Martret i Moles (1901), and Josep-Joan Perot i Juanmartí (b. 1877). Each had been in dedicated service to the Church in Spain, and as they died they cried out triumphantly, "Viva Cristo Re!" They were beatified on Oct. 29, 2005.

Eurosia Fabris (Sept. 27, 1866 – Jan. 8, 1932) Italian mother and model of charity. Born in Quinto Vicentino, Italy, she grew into the faith and was devoted especially to the Eucharist, the Virgin Mary, and the souls in purgatory. In 1885, she began caring for several young girls who had lost their mother and whose father was away. She subsequently married a man named Carlo Barban in 1886, and the two raised nine children, as well as the poor orphans. Her home was always opened to other children as well. She became a member of the Franciscan Third Order and lived an intense spiritual life while raising her children in the Church. She was beatified on Nov. 6, 2005.

Charles de Foucauld (Brother Charles of Jesus, Sept. 15, 1858 – Dec. 1, 1916) Famed missionary in Africa and martyr. He was born in Strasbourg, France, and was orphaned at the age of six. Raised by his grandfather, he embarked on a military career and lost his faith. After some years, he returned to the Church and pledged his life to God. He then entered the Trappists and served in France, Akbès in Syria, and then near a convent of Poor Clares in Nazareth. Ordained a priest at the age of 43 in 1901, he left for the Sahara Desert to bring the Gospel to Africa. He was killed by a band of marauders. He was beatified on Nov. 13, 2005.

Maria Pia Pastena (Dec. 7, 1881 – June 28, 1951) Italian member of the Institute of the Sisters of Mercy of Verona and a victim soul. Born in Bovolone in the Italian province of Verona, she entered the Institute of the Sisters of Mercy of Verona in 1901 and professed her final vows in October; she took the name Sister Passitea Maria of the Child Jesus. After 19 years of intense labors for the sick and the poor, she received permission in 1927 to enter the Cistercian monastery of Veglie, but soon departed to teach and to promote the new religious institute, the Religious of the Holy Face that received canonical recognition in 1936 and as a Congregation of Pontifical Right in 1947. She was beatified on Nov. 13, 2005.

Maria Crocifissa Curcio (Jan. 30, 1877 – July 4, 1957) Foundress of the Carmelite Missionary Sisters of St. Therese of the Child Jesus. Born in Ispica, Italy, she entered at the age of 13 into the Carmelite Third Order and became deeply familiar with Carmelite Spirituality. Sent to Modica, she assumed care over Carmela Polara dedicated to the assistance of young orphan girls. In 1925, she settled in Santa Marinella and began what became the Congregation of the Carmelite Missionary Sisters of St. Therese of the Child Jesus with the as an institute of diocesan rights. She was beatified on Nov. 13, 2005.

Andrés Solá y Molist, C.M.F. (Oct. 7, 1895 – Apr. 25, 1927) Claretian missionary priest and Mexican martyr. Born in Can Vilarrasa, Spain, he was ordained a priest in Sep. 1922 and the following year was sent to Mexico as a Claretian missionary priest. Arriving at a time when Mexico was in the throes of severe anti-Catholic and anticlerical laws, he went into hiding in the home of Josefina and Jovita Alba in León while he continued to administer the sacraments to the sick despite the threat of death. Informed of a warrant issued for his arrest, he continued to serve his people and was arrested on Apr. 24, 1927, and shot by government soldiers. He was beatified on Nov. 20, 2005, with other Mexican martyrs.

José Trinidad Rangel Montaño (June 4, 1887 – Apr. 25, 1927) Mexican priest and martyr. Born in Dolores Hidalgo, Guanajuato, Mexico, he served with zeal and distinction in the face of severe oppression by the Mexican government. Despite the threat to his life, he served in León and found refuge in the home of Josefina and Jovita Alba where he met Fr. Andrés Solá y Molist, a Claretian missionary and future martyr. Arrested by Mexican anticlerical forces, he was murdered with Fr. Andrés Solá y Molist and Mr. Leonardo Pérez Larios. He was beatified on Nov. 20, 2005, with other Mexican martyrs.

Leonardo Pérez Larios (Nov. 28, 1883 – Apr. 25, 1927) Mexican layman and martyr. Born in Lagos di Moreno, Jalisco, Mexico, he longed to be a priest but could not do so because of his responsibility to care for his two sisters and maintain the family. Arrested at the home of Josefina and Jovita Alba by anticlerical forces, he was thought at first to be a priest. He chose to remain with his companions and was martyred in Rancho de San Joaquín with Fathers José

Trinidad Rangel Montaño and Solá y Molist. He was beatified on Nov. 20, 2005, with other Mexican martyrs.

Ángel Darío Acosta Zurita (Dec. 13, 1908 – July 25, 1931) Mexican priest and martyr. Born in Naolinco, Mexico, he was ordained a priest in 1931 and celebrated his First Mass in the city of Veracruz on May 24. His priestly service was brought to a cruelly short end by the anticlerical laws of Mexico. An anticlerical law was promulgated in the State of Veracruz, and Fr. Darío was murdered by a hail of gunfire exactly three months after his priestly ordination. He was beatified on Nov. 20, 2005, with other Mexican martyrs.

Anacleto González Flores and 8 Companions (d. 1927-1928) A group of Mexican martyrs executed by anticlericalist forces in Mexico. The martyrs were: Anacleto González Flores (b. July 13, 1888), a married man tortured and shot on Apr. 1, 1927, with brothers Jorge Anacleto (Sept. 28, 1899) and Ramón Vargas (Jan. 22, 1905) González, and José Dionisio Luis Padilla Gómez (b. Dec. 9, 1899); José Luciano Ezequiel Huerta Gutiérrez (b. Jan. 6, 1876), a layman shot on Apr. 3, 1927, with his brother Salvador Huerta Gutiérrez (b. Mar. 18, 1880); Miguel Gómez Loza (b. Aug. 11, 1888) shot on Mar. 21, 1928; Luis Magaña Servín (b. Aug. 24, 1902) shot on Feb. 9, 1928; José Sánchez del Río (b. Mar. 28, 1913), executed on Feb. 10, 1928, after horrendous tortures. They were beatified on Nov. 20, 2005.

2006

Luigi Biraghi (Nov. 2, 1801 – Aug. 11, 1879) Italian priest and educator. Born at Vignate, near Milan, he was ordained a priest on May 28, 1825. In 1833 he was named the spiritual director of a major seminary, and in 1841, he was appointed founder of the periodical *L'Amico Cattolico* to promote Christ in modern society. Convinced that the family was the basis of society, he promoted family life and Catholic education. In 1848, he was named canon of the metropolitan church of Milan and in 1855 a head of the Ambrosian Library in Milan. He labored for peace in the politically turbulent city and died with a prayer on his lips. In 1838, he founded the Sisters of St. Marcellina, devoted to the education of young people and to the missions. He was beatified on Apr. 30, 2006, in Milan.

Luigi Monza (June 22, 1898 – Sept. 29, 1954) Founder of the Little Apostles and a remarkable parish priest. Born Cislago near Milan, he dedicated himself to his family for many years and finally received ordination on Sept. 19, 1925. He went on to found the Secular Institute of the Little Apostles of Charity and the Association of Our Family. The Little Apostles were intended to be a community of consecrated women dedicated to emulating the charity of the early Christians, and Our Family to be an institution for the care of handicapped children. He was beatified on Apr. 30, 2006, in Milan.

Agostino Thevarparampil Kunjachan (Apr. 1, 1891 – 1973) An Indian priest from Dalit. He was born at Ramapuram and was ordained a priest in Dec. 1921. After service in pastoral assignments, he visited members of the area of Dalit and foundfertile soil for evangelization. He requested to be assigned there permanently and devoted the next 40 years of his life to the Dalit. He was beatified on Apr. 30, 2006, in Ramapuram, India.

Maria Teresa of Saint Joseph (June 19, 1855 – 1938) Foundress of the Congregation of the Carmelite Sisters of the Divine Heart of Jesus. Born in Sandow, modern Poland, she was raised in a Protestant pastor's family and slowly found her way to the Catholic Church. She entered the Church on Oct. 30, 1888 and dedicated herself to the needs of the poor and the homeless. To accomplish her service to God, she founded in July 1891 the Congregation of the Carmelite Sisters of the Divine Heart of Jesus. Embracing the model of St. Teresa of Ávila, she united contemplative prayer with apostolic labors, and her community was committed to the poor, the helpless and the forgotten. She died at the Mother House of the Carmel in Sittard, Holland. She was beatified on May 13, 2006, in Roermond, The Netherlands.

Maria of the Passion (Sept. 23, 1866 – July 27, 1912) A member of the Sisters Crucified Adorers of the Eucharist and a victim soul, Maria Grazia Tarallo was born in Barra, Naples, Italy, and grew up in a family committed to the faith. She entered the Monastery of the Sisters Crucified Adorers of the Eucharist, in Barra, on June 1, 1891, and received the name Sr. Maria of the Passion by the founder, Servant of God Maria Pia Notari. She served as Novice Mistress and spiritual director to other sisters and worked in the kitchen and laundry. She gave herself to Christ as a victim soul. She was beatified on May 14, 2006.

Rita Amada of Jesus (Mar. 5, 1848 – Jan. 6, 1913) Foundress of the Jesus, Mary, and Joseph Sisters. Born in Ribafeita, Portugal, she displayed from a young age a great love of the Blessed Sacrament, Our Lady, and St. Joseph. This was displayed especially when she promoted the faith in the middle of Portugal's severe persecution of the Church in the 19th century. At the age of 29, she entered the Sisters of Charity in the city of Oporto and went on to establish in 1880 the new congregation of the Jesus, Mary, and Joseph Sisters. She was beatified on May 28, 2006.

Eustáquio von Lieshout (b. Nov. 2, 1890 – Aug. 30, 1943) Priest of the Congregation of the Sacred Heart of Jesus (S.S.C.C.), he was born Humbert in Aarle-Rixtel, in Brabant, Netherlands. He entered the Sacred Hearts Fathers in 1905, made his perpetual profession in March 1918, and was ordained a priest on Aug. 10, 1919. As a pastor in the Netherlands, he was given the honor of the Order of Leopold by the king. In 1925, he went to Brazil with Father Eustaquio and two other Picpus fathers and three brothers to assist missionary work. He gave the rest of his life to the cause of the faith in the most rugged and demanding regions of Brazil and acquired enormous followings wherever he went. He died from a sickness caused by an insect bite. He was beatified on June 15, 2006, in Belo Horizonte, Brazil.

Dates and Events in Catholic History

FIRST CENTURY

c. 33: First Christian Pentecost; descent of the Holy Spirit upon the disciples; preaching of St. Peter in Jerusalem; conversion, baptism and aggregation of some 3,000 persons to the first Christian community.
St. Stephen, deacon, was stoned to death at Jerusalem; he is venerated as the first Christian martyr.

c. 34: St. Paul, formerly Saul the persecutor of Christians, was converted and baptized. After three years of solitude in the desert, he joined the college of the apostles; he made three major missionary journeys and became known as the Apostle to the Gentiles; he was imprisoned twice in Rome and was beheaded there between 64 and 67.

39: Cornelius (the Gentile) and his family were baptized by St. Peter; a significant event signaling the mission of the Church to all peoples.

42: Persecution of Christians in Palestine broke out during the rule of Herod Agrippa; St. James the Greater, the first apostle to die, was beheaded in 44; St. Peter was imprisoned for a short time; many Christians fled to Antioch, marking the beginning of the dispersion of Christians beyond the confines of Palestine. At Antioch, the followers of Christ were called Christians for the first time.

49: Christians at Rome, considered members of a Jewish sect, were adversely affected by a decree of Claudius which forbade Jewish worship there.

51: The Council of Jerusalem, in which all the apostles participated under the presidency of St. Peter, decreed that circumcision, dietary regulations, and various other prescriptions of Mosaic Law were not obligatory for Gentile converts to the Christian community. The crucial decree was issued in opposition to Judaizers who contended that observance of the Mosaic Law in its entirety was necessary for salvation.

64: Persecution broke out at Rome under Nero, the emperor said to have accused Christians of starting the fire which destroyed half of Rome.

64 or 67: Martyrdom of St. Peter at Rome during the Neronian persecution. He established his see and spent his last years there after preaching in and around Jerusalem, establishing a see at Antioch, and presiding at the Council of Jerusalem.

70: Destruction of Jerusalem by Titus.

88-97: Pontificate of St. Clement I, third successor of St. Peter as bishop of Rome, one of the Apostolic Fathers. The First Epistle of Clement to the Corinthians, with which he has been identified, was addressed by the Church of Rome to the Church at Corinth, the scene of irregularities and divisions in the Christian community.

95: Domitian persecuted Christians, principally at Rome.

c. 100: Death of St. John, apostle and evangelist, marking the end of the Age of the Apostles and the first generation of the Church.
By the end of the century, Antioch, Alexandria and Ephesus in the East and Rome in the West were established centers of Christian population and influence.

SECOND CENTURY

c. 107: St. Ignatius of Antioch was martyred at Rome. He was the first writer to use the expression, "the Catholic Church."

112: Emperor Trajan, in a rescript to Pliny the Younger, governor of Bithynia, instructed him not to search out Christians but to punish them if they were publicly denounced and refused to do homage to the Roman gods. This rescript set a pattern for Roman magistrates in dealing with Christians.

117-38: Persecution under Hadrian. Many acts of martyrs date from this period.

c. 125: Spread of Gnosticism, a combination of elements of Platonic philosophy and Eastern mystery religions. Its adherents claimed that its secret-knowledge principle provided a deeper insight into Christian doctrine than divine revelation and faith. One gnostic thesis denied the divinity of Christ; others denied the reality of his humanity, calling it mere appearance (Docetism, Phantasiasm).

c. 144: Excommunication of Marcion, bishop and heretic, who claimed that there was total opposition and no connection at all between the Old Testament and the New Testament, between the God of the Jews and the God of the Christians; and that the Canon (list of inspired writings) of the Bible consisted only of parts of St. Luke's Gospel and 10 letters of St. Paul. Marcionism was checked at Rome by 200 and was condemned by a council held there about 260, but the heresy persisted for several centuries in the East and had some adherents as late as the Middle Ages.

c. 155: St. Polycarp, bishop of Smyrna and disciple of St. John the Evangelist, was martyred.

c. 156: Beginning of Montanism, a form of religious extremism. Its principal tenets were the imminent second coming of Christ, denial of the divine nature of the Church and its power to forgive sin, and excessively rigorous morality. The heresy, preached by Montanus of Phrygia and others, was condemned by Pope St. Zephyrinus (199-217).

161-80: Reign of Marcus Aurelius. His persecution, launched in the wake of natural disasters, was more violent than those of his predecessors.

165: St. Justin, an important early Christian writer, was martyred at Rome.

c. 180: St. Irenaeus, bishop of Lyons and one of the great early theologians, wrote *Adversus Haereses*. He stated that the teaching and tradition of the Roman See was the standard for belief.

196: Easter Controversy, concerning the day of celebration—a Sunday, according to practice in the West, or the 14th of the month of Nisan (in the Hebrew calendar), no matter what day of the week, according to practice in the East. The controversy was not resolved at this time.

The *Didache*, whose extant form dates from the second century, is an important record of Christian belief, practice and governance in the first century.

Latin was introduced as a liturgical language in the West. Other liturgical languages were Aramaic and Greek.

The Catechetical School of Alexandria, founded about the middle of the century, gained increasing influence on doctrinal study and instruction, and interpretation of the Bible.

THIRD CENTURY

202: Persecution under Septimius Severus, who wanted to establish a simple common religion in the Empire.

206: Tertullian, a convert since 197 and the first great ecclesiastical writer in Latin, joined the heretical Montanists; he died in 230.

215: Death of Clement of Alexandria, teacher of Origen and a founding father of the School of Alexandria.

217-35: St. Hippolytus, the first antipope; he was reconciled to the Church while in prison during persecution in 235.

232-54: Origen established the School of Caesarea after being deposed in 231 as head of the School of Alexandria; he died in 254. A scholar and voluminous writer, he was one of the founders of systematic theology and exerted wide influence for many years.

c. 242: Manichaeism originated in Persia: a combination of errors based on the assumption that two supreme principles (good and evil) are operative in creation and life, and that the supreme objective of human endeavor is liberation from evil (matter). The heresy denied the humanity of Christ, the sacramental system, the authority of the Church (and state), and endorsed a moral code which threatened the fabric of society. In the 12th and 13th centuries, it took on the features of Albigensianism and Catharism.

249-51: Persecution under Decius. Many of those who denied the faith (*lapsi*) sought readmission to the Church at the end of the persecution in 251. Pope St. Cornelius agreed with St. Cyprian that *lapsi* were to be readmitted to the Church after satisfying the requirements of appropriate penance. Antipope Novatian, on the other hand, contended that persons who fell away from the Church under persecution and/or those guilty of serious sin after baptism could not be absolved and readmitted to communion with the Church. The heresy was condemned by a Roman synod in 251.

250-300: Neo-Platonism of Plotinus and Porphyry gained followers.

251: Novatian, an antipope, was condemned at Rome.

256: Pope St. Stephen I upheld the validity of baptism properly administered by heretics, in the Rebaptism Controversy.

257: Persecution under Valerian, who attempted to destroy the Church as a social structure.

258: St. Cyprian, bishop of Carthage, was martyred.

c. 260: St. Lucian founded the School of Antioch, a center of influence on biblical studies.

Pope St. Dionysius condemned Sabellianism, a form of modalism (like Monarchianism and Patripassianism). The heresy contended that the Father, Son and Holy Spirit are not distinct divine persons but are only three different modes of being and self-manifestations of the one God. St. Paul of Thebes became a hermit.

261: Gallienus issued an edict of toleration which ended general persecution for nearly 40 years.

c. 292: Diocletian divided the Roman Empire into East and West. The division emphasized political, cultural and other differences between the two parts of the Empire and influenced different developments in the Church in the East and West. The prestige of Rome began to decline.

FOURTH CENTURY

303: Persecution broke out under Diocletian; it was particularly violent in 304.

305: St. Anthony of Heracles established a foundation for hermits near the Red Sea in Egypt.

c. 306: The first local legislation on clerical celibacy was enacted by a council held at Elvira, Spain; bishops, priests, deacons and other ministers were forbidden to have wives.

311: An edict of toleration issued by Galerius at the urging of Constantine the Great and Licinius officially ended persecution in the West; some persecution continued in the East.

313: The Edict of Milan issued by Constantine and Licinius recognized Christianity as a lawful religion in the Roman Empire.

314: A council of Arles condemned Donatism, declaring that baptism properly administered by heretics is valid, in view of the principle that sacraments have their efficacy from Christ, not from the spiritual condition of their human ministers. The heresy was condemned again by a council of Carthage in 411.

318: St. Pachomius established the first foundation of the cenobitic (common) life, as compared with the solitary life of hermits in Upper Egypt.

325: Ecumenical Council of Nicaea (I). Its principal action was the condemnation of Arianism, the most devastating of the early heresies, which denied the divinity of Christ. The heresy was authored by Arius of Alexandria, a priest. Arians and several kinds of Semi-Arians propagandized their tenets widely, established their own hierarchies and churches, and raised havoc in the Church for several centuries. The council contributed to formulation of the Nicene Creed (Creed of Nicaea-Constantinople); fixed the date for the observance of Easter; passed regulations concerning clerical discipline; adopted the civil divisions of the Empire as the model for the jurisdictional organization of the Church.

326: With the support of St. Helena, the True Cross on which Christ was crucified was discovered.

337: Baptism and death of Constantine.

c. 342: Beginning of a 40-year persecution in Persia.

343-44: A council of Sardica reaffirmed doctrine formulated by Nicaea I and declared also that bishops had the right of appeal to the pope as the highest authority in the Church.

361-63: Emperor Julian the Apostate waged an unsuccessful campaign against the Church in an attempt to restore paganism as the religion of the Empire.

c. 365: Persecution of orthodox Christians under Emperor Valens in the East.

c. 376: Beginning of the barbarian invasion in the West.

379: Death of St. Basil, the Father of Monasticism in the East. His writings contributed greatly to the development of rules for the life of Religious.

381: Ecumenical Council of Constantinople (I). It condemned various brands of Arianism as well as Macedonianism, which denied the divinity of the Holy Spirit; contributed to formulation of the Nicene Creed; approved a canon acknowledging Constantinople as the second see after Rome in honor and dignity.

382: The Canon of Sacred Scripture, the official list of the inspired books of the Bible, was contained in the Decree of Pope St. Damasus and published by a regional council of Carthage in 397; the Canon was formally defined by the Council of Trent in the 16th century.

382-c. 406: St. Jerome translated the Old and New Testaments into Latin; his work is called the Vulgate version of the Bible.

396: St. Augustine became bishop of Hippo in North Africa.

FIFTH CENTURY

410: Visigoths under Alaric sacked Rome and the last Roman legions departed Britain. The decline of imperial Rome dates approximately from this time.

430: St. Augustine, bishop of Hippo for 35 years, died. He was a strong defender of orthodox doctrine against Manichaeism, Donatism and Pelagianism. The depth and range of his writings made him a dominant influence in Christian thought for centuries.

431: Ecumenical Council of Ephesus. It condemned Nestorianism, which denied the unity of the divine and human natures in the Person of Christ; defined *Theotokos* (Bearer of God) as the title of Mary, Mother of the Son of God made Man; condemned Pelagianism. The heresy of Pelagianism, proceeding from the assumption that Adam had a natural right to supernatural life, held that man could attain salvation through the efforts of his natural powers and free will; it involved errors concerning the nature of original sin, the meaning of grace and other matters. Related Semi-Pelagianism was condemned by a council of Orange in 529.

432: St. Patrick arrived in Ireland. By the time of his death in 461 most of the country had been converted, monasteries founded and the hierarchy established.

438: The Theodosian Code, a compilation of decrees for the Empire, was issued by Theodosius II; it had great influence on subsequent civil and ecclesiastical law.

451: Ecumenical Council of Chalcedon. Its principal action was the condemnation of Mono-physitism (also called Eutychianism), which denied the humanity of Christ by holding that he had only one, the divine, nature.

452: Pope St. Leo the Great persuaded Attila the Hun to spare Rome.

455: Vandals under Geiseric sacked Rome.

484: Patriarch Acacius of Constantinople was excommunicated for signing the *Henoticon*, a document which capitulated to the Monophysite heresy. The excommunication triggered the Acacian Schism which lasted for 35 years.

494: Pope St. Gelasius I declared in a letter to Emperor Anastasius that the pope had power and authority over the emperor in spiritual matters.

496: Clovis, King of the Franks, was converted and became the defender of Christianity in the West. The Franks became a Catholic people.

SIXTH CENTURY

520: Irish monasteries flourished as centers for spiritual life, missionary training, and scholarly activity.

529: The Second Council of Orange condemned Semi-Pelagianism.

c. 529: St. Benedict founded the Monte Cassino Abbey. Some years before his death in 543 he wrote a monastic rule which exercised tremendous influence on the form and style of religious life. He is called the Father of Monasticism in the West.

533: John II became the first pope to change his name. The practice did not become general until the time of Sergius IV (1009).

533-34: Emperor Justinian promulgated the *Corpus Iuris Civilis* for the Roman world; like the Theodosian Code, it influenced subsequent civil and ecclesiastical law.

c. 545: Death of Dionysius Exiguus who was the first to date history from the birth of Christ, a practice which resulted in use of the B.C. and A.D. abbreviations. His calculations were at least four years late.

553: Ecumenical Council of Constantinople (II). It condemned the Three Chapters, Nestorian-tainted writings of Theodore of Mopsuestia, Theodoret of Cyrus and Ibas of Edessa.

585: St. Columban founded an influential monastic school at Luxeuil.

589: The most important of several councils of Toledo was held. The Visigoths renounced Arianism, and St. Leander began the organization of the Church in Spain.

590-604: Pontificate of Pope St. Gregory I the Great. He set the form and style of the papacy which prevailed throughout the Middle Ages; exerted great influence on doctrine and liturgy; was strong in support of monastic discipline and clerical celibacy; authored writings on many subjects. Gregorian Chant is named in his honor.

596: Pope St. Gregory I sent St. Augustine of Canterbury and 40 monks to do missionary work in England.

597: St. Columba died. He founded an important monastery at Iona, established schools and did notable missionary work in Scotland. By the end of the century, monasteries of nuns were common; Western monasticism was flourishing; monasticism in the East, under the influence of Monophysitism and other factors, was losing its vigor.

SEVENTH CENTURY

613: St. Columban established the influential monastery of Bobbio in northern Italy; he died there in 615.

622: The *Hegira* (flight) of Mohammed from Mecca to Medina signalled the beginning of Islam which, by the end of the century, claimed almost all of the southern Mediterranean area.

628: Heraclius, Eastern Emperor, recovered the True Cross from the Persians.

649: A Lateran council condemned two erroneous formulas (Ecthesis and Type) issued by emperors Heraclius and Constans II as means of reconciling Monophysites with the Church.

664: Actions of the Synod of Whitby advanced the adoption of Roman usages in England, especially regarding the date for the observance of Easter. (*See* Easter Controversy.)

680-81: Ecumenical Council of Constantinople (III). It condemned Monothelitism, which held that Christ had only one will, the divine; censured Pope Honorius I for a letter to Sergius, bishop of Constantinople, in which he made an ambiguous but not infallible statement about the unity of will and/or operation in Christ.

692: Trullan Synod. Eastern-Church discipline on clerical celibacy was settled, permitting marriage before ordination to the diaconate and continuation in marriage afterwards, but prohibiting marriage following the death of the wife thereafter. Anti-Roman canons contributed to East-West alienation. During the century, the monastic influence of Ireland and England increased in Western Europe; schools and learning declined; regulations regarding clerical celibacy became more strict in the East.

EIGHTH CENTURY

711: Muslims began the conquest of Spain.

726: Emperor Leo III, the Isaurian, launched a campaign against the veneration of sacred images and relics; called Iconoclasm (image-breaking), it caused turmoil in the East until about 843.

731: Pope Gregory III and a synod at Rome condemned Iconoclasm, with a declaration that the veneration of sacred images was in accord with Catholic tradition.
Venerable Bede issued his *Ecclesiastical History of the English People.*

732: Charles Martel defeated the Muslims at Poitiers, halting their advance in the West.

744: The Monastery of Fulda was established by St. Sturmi, a disciple of St. Boniface; it was influential in the evangelization of Germany.

754: A council of more than 300 Byzantine bishops endorsed Iconoclast errors. This council and its actions were condemned by the Lateran synod of 769.
Stephen II (III) crowned Pepin ruler of the Franks. Pepin twice invaded Italy, in 754 and 756, to defend the pope against the Lombards. His land grants to the papacy, called the Donation of Pepin, were later

extended by Charlemagne (773) and formed part of the States of the Church.

c. 755: St. Boniface (Winfrid) was martyred. He was called the Apostle of Germany for his missionary work and organization of the hierarchy there.

781: Alcuin was chosen by Charlemagne to organize a palace school, which became a center of intellectual leadership.

787: Ecumenical Council of Nicaea (II). It condemned Iconoclasm, which held that the use of images was idolatry, and Adoptionism, which claimed that Christ was not the Son of God by nature but only by adoption. This was the last council regarded as ecumenical by Orthodox Churches.

792: A council at Ratisbon condemned Adoptionism. The famous *Book of Kells* ("The Great Gospel of Columcille") dates from the early eighth or late seventh century.

NINTH CENTURY

800: Charlemagne was crowned Emperor by Pope Leo III on Christmas Day.
Egbert became king of West Saxons; he unified England and strengthened the See of Canterbury.

813: Emperor Leo V, the Armenian, revived Iconoclasm, which persisted until about 843.

814: Charlemagne died.

843: The Treaty of Verdun split the Frankish kingdom among Charlemagne's three grandsons.

844: A Eucharistic controversy involving the writings of St. Paschasius Radbertus, Ratramnus and Rabanus Maurus occasioned the development of terminology regarding the doctrine of the Real Presence.

846: Muslims invaded Italy and attacked Rome.

847-52: Period of composition of the False Decretals, a collection of forged documents attributed to popes from St. Clement (88-97) to Gregory II (714-731). The Decretals, which strongly supported the autonomy and rights of bishops, were suspect for a long time before being repudiated entirely about 1628.

848: The Council of Mainz condemned Gottschalk for heretical teaching regarding predestination. He was also condemned by the Council of Quierzy in 853.

857: Photius displaced Ignatius as patriarch of Constantinople. This marked the beginning of the Photian Schism, a confused state of East-West relations which has not yet been cleared up by historical research. Photius, a man of exceptional ability, died in 891.

865: St. Ansgar, apostle of Scandinavia, died.

869: St. Cyril died and his brother, St. Methodius (d. 885), was ordained a bishop. The Apostles of the Slavs devised an alphabet and translated the Gospels and liturgy into the Slavonic language.

869-70: Ecumenical Council of Constantinople (IV). It issued a second condemnation of Iconoclasm, condemned and deposed Photius as patriarch of Constantinople and restored Ignatius to the patriarchate. This was the last ecumenical council held in the East. It was first called ecumenical by canonists toward the end of the 11th century.

871-c. 900: Reign of Alfred the Great, the only English king ever anointed by a pope at Rome.

TENTH CENTURY

910: William, duke of Aquitaine, founded the

Benedictine Abbey of Cluny, which became a center of monastic and ecclesiastical reform, especially in France.

915: Pope John X played a leading role in the expulsion of Saracens from central and southern Italy.

955: St. Olga, of the Russian royal family, was baptized.

962: Otto I, the Great, crowned by Pope John XII, revived Charlemagne's kingdom, which became the Holy Roman Empire.

966: Mieszko, first of a royal line in Poland, was baptized; he brought Latin Christianity to Poland.

988: Conversion and baptism of St. Vladimir and the people of Kiev which subsequently became part of Russia.

993: John XV was the first pope to decree the official canonization of a saint — Bishop Ulrich (Uldaric) of Augsburg — for the universal Church.

997: St. Stephen became ruler of Hungary. He assisted in organizing the hierarchy and establishing Latin Christianity in that country.

999-1003: Pontificate of Sylvester II (Gerbert of Aquitaine), a Benedictine monk and the first French pope.

ELEVENTH CENTURY

1009: Beginning of lasting East-West Schism in the Church, marked by dropping of the name of Pope Sergius IV from the Byzantine diptychs (the listing of persons prayed for during the liturgy). The deletion was made by Patriarch Sergius II of Constantinople.

1012: St. Romuald founded the Camaldolese Hermits.

1025: The Council of Arras, and other councils later, condemned the Cathari (Neo-Manichaeans, Albigenses).

1027: The Council of Elne proclaimed the Truce of God as a means of stemming violence; it involved armistice periods of varying length, which were later extended.

1038: St. John Gualbert founded the Vallombrosians.

1043-59: Constantinople patriarchate of Michael Cerularius, the key figure in a controversy concerning the primacy of the papacy. His and the Byzantine synod's refusal to acknowledge this primacy in 1054 widened and hardened the East-West Schism in the Church.

1047: Pope Clement II died; he was the only pope ever buried in Germany.

1049-54: Pontificate of St. Leo IX, who inaugurated a movement of papal, diocesan, monastic and clerical reform.

1054: Start of the Great Schism between the Eastern and Western Churches; it marked the separation of Orthodox Churches from unity with the pope.

1055: Condemnation of the Eucharistic doctrine of Berengarius.

1059: A Lateran council issued new legislation regarding papal elections; voting power was entrusted to the Roman cardinals.

1066: Death of St. Edward the Confessor, king of England from 1042 and restorer of Westminster Abbey.

Defeat, at Hastings, of Harold by William, Duke of Normandy (later William I), who subsequently exerted strong influence on the life-style of the Church in England.

1073-85: Pontificate of St. Gregory VII (Hildebrand).

A strong pope, he carried forward programs of clerical and general ecclesiastical reform and struggled against German King Henry IV and other rulers to end the evils of lay investiture. He introduced the Latin liturgy in Spain and set definite dates for the observance of ember days.

1077: Henry IV, excommunicated and suspended from the exercise of imperial powers by Gregory VII, sought absolution from the pope at Canossa. Henry later repudiated this action and in 1084 forced Gregory to leave Rome.

1079: The Council of Rome condemned Eucharistic errors (denial of the Real Presence of Christ under the appearances of bread and wine) of Berengarius, who retracted.

1084: St. Bruno founded the Carthusians.

1097-99: The first of several Crusades undertaken between this time and 1265. Recovery of the Holy Places and gaining free access to them for Christians were the original purposes, but these were diverted to less worthy objectives in various ways. Results included: a Latin Kingdom of Jerusalem, 1099-1187; a military and political misadventure in the form of a Latin Empire of Constantinople, 1204-1261; acquisition, by treaties, of visiting rights for Christians in the Holy Land. East-West economic and cultural relationships increased during the period. In the religious sphere, actions of the Crusaders had the effect of increasing the alienation of the East from the West.

1098: St. Robert founded the Cistercians.

TWELFTH CENTURY

1108: Beginnings of the influential Abbey and School of St. Victor in France.

1115: St. Bernard established the Abbey of Clairvaux and inaugurated the Cistercian Reform.

1118: Christian forces captured Saragossa, Spain; the beginning of the Muslim decline in that country.

1121: St. Norbert established the original monastery of the Praemonstratensians near Laon, France.

1122: The Concordat of Worms (*Pactum Callixtinum*) was formulated and approved by Pope Callistus II and Emperor Henry V to settle controversy concerning the investiture of prelates. The concordat provided that the emperor could invest prelates with symbols of temporal authority but had no right to invest them with spiritual authority, which came from the Church alone, and that the emperor was not to interfere in papal elections. This was the first concordat in history.

1123: Ecumenical Council of the Lateran (I), the first of its kind in the West. It endorsed provisions of the Concordat of Worms concerning the investiture of prelates and approved reform measures in 25 canons.

1139: Ecumenical Council of the Lateran (II). It adopted measures against a schism organized by antipope Anacletus and approved 30 canons related to discipline and other matters; one of the canons stated that holy orders is an invalidating impediment to marriage.

1140: St. Bernard met Abelard in debate at the Council of Sens. Abelard, whose rationalism in theology was condemned for the first time in 1121, died in 1142 at Cluny.

1148: The Synod of Rheims enacted strict disciplinary decrees for communities of women Religious.

1152: The Synod of Kells reorganized the Church in Ireland.

1160: Gratian, whose *Decretum* became a basic text of canon law, died.

Peter Lombard, compiler of the Four Books of Sentences, a standard theology text for nearly 200 years, died.

1170: St. Thomas Becket, archbishop of Canterbury, who clashed with Henry II over church-state relations, was murdered in his cathedral.

1171: Pope Alexander III reserved the process of canonization of saints to the Holy See.

1179: Ecumenical Council of the Lateran (III). It enacted measures against Waldensianism and Albigensianism (see year 242 regarding Manichaeism), approved reform decrees in 27 canons, provided that popes be elected by a two-thirds vote of the cardinals.

1184: Waldenses and other heretics were excommunicated by Pope Lucius III.

THIRTEENTH CENTURY

1198-1216: Pontificate of Innocent III, during which the papacy reached its medieval peak of authority, influence and prestige in the Church and in relations with civil rulers.

1208: Innocent III called for a crusade, the first in Christendom itself, against the Albigensians; their beliefs and practices threatened the fabric of society in southern France and northern Italy.

1209: Verbal approval was given by Innocent III to a rule of life for the Order of Friars Minor, started by St. Francis of Assisi.

1212: The Second Order of Franciscans, the Poor Clares, was founded.

1215: Ecumenical Council of the Lateran (IV). It ordered annual reception of the sacraments of penance and the Eucharist; defined and made the first official use of the term transubstantiation to explain the change of bread and wine into the body and blood of Christ; adopted additional measures to counteract teachings and practices of the Albigensians and Cathari; approved 70 canons.

1216: Formal papal approval was given to a rule of life for the Order of Preachers, started by St. Dominic. The Portiuncula Indulgence was granted by the Holy See at the request of St. Francis of Assisi.

1221: Rule of the Third Order Secular of St. Francis (Secular Franciscan Order) approved verbally by Honorius III.

1226: Death of St. Francis of Assisi.

1231: Pope Gregory IX authorized establishment of the Papal Inquisition for dealing with heretics. It was a creature of its time, when crimes against faith and heretical doctrines of extremists like the Cathari and Albigenses threatened the good of the Christian community, the welfare of the state and the very fabric of society. The institution, which was responsible for excesses in punishment, was most active in the second half of the century in southern France, Italy and Germany.

1245: Ecumenical Council of Lyons (I). It confirmed the deposition of Emperor Frederick II and approved 22 canons.

1247: Preliminary approval was given by the Holy See to a Carmelite rule of life.

1270: St. Louis IX, king of France, died. Beginning of papal decline.

1274: Ecumenical Council of Lyons (II). It accomplished a temporary reunion of separated Eastern Churches with the Roman Church; issued regulations concerning conclaves for papal elections; approved 31 canons.

Death of St. Thomas Aquinas, Doctor of the Church, of lasting influence.

1280: Pope Nicholas III, who made the Breviary the official prayer book for clergy of the Roman Church, died.

1281: The excommunication of Michael Palaeologus by Pope Martin IV ruptured the union effected with the Eastern Church in 1274.

FOURTEENTH CENTURY

1302: Pope Boniface VIII issued the bull *Unam Sanctam*, concerning the unity of the Church and the temporal power of princes, against the background of a struggle with Philip IV of France; it was the most famous medieval document on the subject.

1309-77: For a period of approximately 70 years, seven popes resided at Avignon because of unsettled conditions in Rome and other reasons; see separate entry.

1311-12: Ecumenical Council of Vienne. It suppressed the Knights Templar and enacted a number of reform decrees.

1321: Dante Alighieri died a year after completing the *Divine Comedy*.

1324: Marsilius of Padua completed *Defensor Pacis*, a work condemned by Pope John XXII as heretical because of its denial of papal primacy and the hierarchical structure of the Church, and for other reasons. It was a charter for conciliarism (an ecumenical council is superior to the pope in authority).

1337-1453: Period of the Hundred Years' War, a dynastic struggle between France and England.

1338: Four years after the death of Pope John XXII, who had opposed Louis IV of Bavaria in a years-long controversy, electoral princes declared at the Diet of Rhense that the emperor did not need papal confirmation of his title and right to rule. Charles IV later (1356) said the same thing in a *Golden Bull*, eliminating papal rights in the election of emperors.

1347-50: The Black Death swept across Europe, killing perhaps one-fourth to one-third of the total population; an estimated 40 per cent of the clergy succumbed.

1374: Petrarch, poet and humanist, died.

1377: Return of the papacy from Avignon to Rome. Beginning of the Western Schism; see separate entry.

FIFTEENTH CENTURY

1409: The Council of Pisa, without canonical authority, tried to end the Western Schism but succeeded only in complicating it by electing a third claimant to the papacy; see Western Schism.

1414-18: Ecumenical Council of Constance. It took successful action to end the Western Schism involving rival claimants to the papacy; rejected the teachings of Wycliff; condemned Hus as a heretic. One decree—passed in the earlier stages of the council but later rejected—asserted the superiority of an ecumenical council over the pope (conciliarism).

1431: St. Joan of Arc was burned at the stake.

1431-45: Ecumenical Council of Florence (also called Basle-Ferrara-Florence). It affirmed the primacy of the pope against the claims of conciliarists that an ecumenical council is superior to the pope. It also formulated and approved decrees of union with several separated Eastern Churches—Greek, Armenian, Jacobite—which failed to gain general or lasting acceptance.

1438: The Pragmatic Sanction of Bourges was enacted by Charles VII and the French Parliament to curtail papal authority over the Church in France, in the spirit of conciliarism. It found expression in Gallicanism and had effects lasting at least until the French Revolution.

1453: The fall of Constantinople to the Turks.

c. 1456: Gutenberg issued the first edition of the Bible printed from movable type, at Mainz, Germany.

1476: Pope Sixtus IV approved observance of the feast of the Immaculate Conception on Dec. 8 throughout the Church.

1478: Pope Sixtus IV, at the urging of King Ferdinand of Spain, approved establishment of the Spanish Inquisition for dealing with Jewish and Moorish converts accused of heresy. The institution, which was peculiar to Spain and its colonies in America, acquired jurisdiction over other cases as well and fell into disrepute because of its procedures, cruelty and the manner in which it served the Spanish crown, rather than the accused and the good of the Church. Protests by the Holy See failed to curb excesses of the Inquisition, which lingered in Spanish history until early in the 19th century.

1492: Columbus discovered the Americas.

1493: Pope Alexander VI issued a Bull of Demarcation which determined spheres of influence for the Spanish and Portuguese in the Americas.

The Renaissance, a humanistic movement which originated in Italy in the 14th century, spread to France, Germany, the Low Countries and England. A transitional period between the medieval world and the modern secular world, it introduced profound changes which affected literature and the other arts, general culture, politics and religion.

SIXTEENTH CENTURY

1512-17: Ecumenical Council of the Lateran (V). It stated the relation and position of the pope with respect to an ecumenical council; acted to counteract the Pragmatic Sanction of Bourges and exaggerated claims of liberty by the Church in France; condemned erroneous teachings concerning the nature of the human soul; stated doctrine concerning indulgences. The council reflected concern for abuses in the Church and the need for reforms but failed to take decisive action in the years immediately preceding the Reformation.

1517: Martin Luther signaled the beginning of the Reformation by posting 95 theses at Wittenberg. Subsequently, he broke completely from doctrinal orthodoxy in discourses and three published works (1519 and 1520); was excommunicated on more than 40 charges of heresy (1521); remained the dominant figure in the Reformation in Germany

until his death in 1546.

1519: Zwingli triggered the Reformation in Zurich and became its leading proponent there until his death in combat in 1531.

1524: Luther's encouragement of German princes in putting down the two-year Peasants' Revolt gained political support for his cause.

1528: The Order of Friars Minor Capuchin was approved as an autonomous division of the Franciscan Order; like the Jesuits, the Capuchins became leaders in the Counter-Reformation.

1530: The Augsburg Confession of Lutheran faith was issued; it was later supplemented by the Smalkaldic Articles, approved in 1537.

1533: Henry VIII divorced Catherine of Aragon, married Anne Boleyn, was excommunicated. In 1534 he decreed the Act of Supremacy, making the sovereign the head of the Church in England, under which Sts. John Fisher and Thomas More were executed in 1535. Despite his rejection of papal primacy and actions against monastic life in England, he generally maintained doctrinal orthodoxy until his death in 1547.

1536: John Calvin, leader of the Reformation in Switzerland until his death in 1564, issued the first edition of Institutes of the Christian Religion, which became the classical text of Reformed (non-Lutheran) theology.

1540: The constitutions of the Society of Jesus (Jesuits), founded by St. Ignatius of Loyola, were approved.

1541: Start of the 11-year career of St. Francis Xavier as a missionary to the East Indies and Japan.

1545-63: Ecumenical Council of Trent. It issued a great number of decrees concerning doctrinal matters opposed by the Reformers, and mobilized the Counter-Reformation. Definitions covered the Canon of the Bible, the rule of faith, the nature of justification, grace, faith, original sin and its effects, the seven sacraments, the sacrificial nature of the Mass, the veneration of saints, use of sacred images, belief in purgatory, the doctrine of indulgences, the jurisdiction of the pope over the whole Church. It initiated many reforms for renewal in the liturgy and general discipline in the Church, the promotion of religious instruction, the education of the clergy through the foundation of seminaries, etc. Trent ranks with Vatican II as the greatest ecumenical council held in the West.

1549: The first Anglican Book of Common Prayer was issued by Edward VI. Revised editions were published in 1552, 1559 and 1662 and later.

1553: Start of the five-year reign of Mary Tudor who tried to counteract actions of Henry VIII against the Roman Church.

1555: Enactment of the Peace of Augsburg, an arrangement of religious territorialism rather than toleration, which recognized the existence of Catholicism and Lutheranism in the German Empire and provided that citizens should adopt the religion of their respective rulers.

1558: Beginning of the reign (to 1603) of Queen Elizabeth I of England and Ireland, during which the Church of England took on its definitive form.

1559: Establishment of the hierarchy of the Church of England, with the consecration of Matthew Parker as archbishop of Canterbury.

1563: The first text of the 39 Articles of the Church of England was issued. Also enacted were a new Act of Supremacy and Oath of Succession to the English throne.

1570: Elizabeth I was excommunicated. Penal measures against Catholics subsequently became more severe.

1571: Defeat of the Turkish armada at Lepanto staved off the invasion of Eastern Europe.

1577: The Formula of Concord, the classical statement of Lutheran faith, was issued; it was, generally, a Lutheran counterpart of the canons of the Council of Trent. In 1580, along with other formulas of doctrine, it was included in the Book of Concord.

1582: The Gregorian Calendar, named for Pope Gregory XIII, was put into effect and was eventually adopted in most countries: England delayed adoption until 1752.

SEVENTEENTH CENTURY

1605: The Gunpowder Plot, an attempt by Catholic fanatics to blow up James I of England and the houses of Parliament, resulted in an anti-Catholic Oath of Allegiance.

1610: Death of Matteo Ricci, outstanding Jesuit missionary to China, pioneer in cultural relations between China and Europe.
Founding of the first community of Visitation Nuns by Sts. Francis de Sales and Jane de Chantal.

1611: Founding of the Oratorians.

1613: Catholics were banned from Scandinavia.

1625: Founding of the Congregation of the Mission (Vincentians) by St. Vincent de Paul. He founded the Sisters of Charity in 1633.

1642: Death of Galileo, scientist, who was censured by the Congregation of the Holy Office for supporting the Copernican theory of the sun-centered planetary system. The case against him was closed in his favor in 1992.
Founding of the Sulpicians by Jacques Olier.

1643: Start of publication of the Bollandist *Acta Sanctorum*, a critical work on lives of the saints.

1648: Provisions in the Peace of Westphalia, ending the Thirty Years' War, extended terms of the Peace of Augsburg (1555) to Calvinists and gave equality to Catholics and Protestants in the 300 states of the Holy Roman Empire.

1649: Oliver Cromwell invaded Ireland and began a severe persecution of the Church there.

1653: Pope Innocent X condemned five propositions of Jansenism, a complex theory which distorted doctrine concerning the relations between divine grace and human freedom. Jansenism was also a rigoristic movement which seriously disturbed the Church in France, the Low Countries and Italy in this and the 18th century.

1673: The Test Act in England barred from public office Catholics who would not deny the doctrine of transubstantiation and receive Communion in the Church of England.

1678: Many English Catholics suffered death as a consequence of the Popish Plot, a false allegation by Titus Oates that Catholics planned to assassinate Charles II, land a French army in the country, burn London, and turn over the government to the Jesuits.

1682: The four Gallican articles, drawn up by Bossuet, asserted political and ecclesiastical immunities of France from papal control. The articles, which rejected the primacy of the pope, were declared null and void by Pope Alexander VIII in 1690.

1689: The Toleration Act granted a measure of freedom of worship to other English dissenters but not to Catholics.

EIGHTEENTH CENTURY

1704: Chinese Rites — involving the Christian adaptation of elements of Confucianism, veneration of ancestors and Chinese terminology in religion — were condemned by Clement XI.

1720: The Passionists were founded by St. Paul of the Cross.

1724: Persecution in China.

1732: The Redemptorists were founded by St. Alphonsus Liguori.

1738: Freemasonry was condemned by Clement XII and Catholics were forbidden to join, under penalty of excommunication; the prohibition was repeated by Benedict XIV in 1751 and by later popes.

1760s: Josephinism, a theory and system of state control of the Church, was initiated in Austria; it remained in force until about 1850.

1764: Febronianism, an unorthodox theory and practice regarding the constitution of the Church and relations between Church and state, was condemned for the first of several times. Proposed by an auxiliary bishop of Trier using the pseudonym Justinus Febronius, it had the effects of minimizing the office of the pope and supporting national churches under state control.

1773: Clement XIV issued a brief of suppression against the Jesuits, following their expulsion from Portugal in 1759, from France in 1764 and from Spain in 1767. Political intrigue and unsubstantiated accusations were principal factors in these developments. The ban, which crippled the society, contained no condemnation of the Jesuit constitutions, particular Jesuits or Jesuit teaching. The society was restored in 1814.

1778: Catholics in England were relieved of some civil disabilities dating back to the time of Henry VIII, by an act which permitted them to acquire, own and inherit property. Additional liberties were restored by the Roman Catholic Relief Act of 1791 and subsequent enactments of Parliament.

1789: Religious freedom in the United States was guaranteed under the First Amendment to the Constitution.
Beginning of the French Revolution which resulted in: the secularization of church property and the Civil Constitution of the Clergy in 1790; the persecution of priests, religious and lay persons loyal to papal authority; invasion of the Papal States by Napoleon in 1796; renewal of persecution from 1797-1799; attempts to dechristianize France and establish a new religion; the occupation of Rome by French troops and the forced removal of Pius VI to France in 1798.
This century is called the age of Enlightenment or Reason because of the predominating rational and scientific approach of its leading philosophers, scientists and writers with respect to religion, ethics and natural law. This

approach downgraded the fact and significance of revealed religion. Also characteristic of the Enlightenment were subjectivism, secularism and optimism regarding human perfectibility.

NINETEENTH CENTURY

1801: Concordat between Napoleon and Pope Pius VII is signed. It is soon violated by the Organic Articles issued by Napoleon in 1802.

1804: Napoleon crowns himself Emperor of the French with Pope Pius in attendance.

1809: Pope Pius VII was made a captive by Napoleon and deported to France where he remained in exile until 1814. During this time he refused to cooperate with Napoleon who sought to bring the Church in France under his own control, and other leading cardinals were imprisoned.

The turbulence in church-state relations in France at the beginning of the century recurred in connection with the Bourbon Restoration, the July Revolution, the second and third Republics, the Second Empire and the Dreyfus case.

1814: The Society of Jesus, suppressed since 1773, was restored.

1817: Reestablishment of the Congregation for the Propagation of the Faith (Propaganda) by Pius VII was an important factor in increasing missionary activity during the century.

1820: Year's-long persecution, during which thousands died for the faith, ended in China. Thereafter, communication with the West remained cut off until about 1834. Vigorous missionary work got under way in 1842.

1822: The Pontifical Society for the Propagation of the Faith, inaugurated in France by Pauline Jaricot for the support of missionary activity, was established.

1829: The Catholic Emancipation Act relieved Catholics in England and Ireland of most of the civil disabilities to which they had been subject from the time of Henry VIII.

1832: Gregory XVI, in the encyclical *Mirari vos*, condemned indifferentism, one of the many ideologies at odds with Christian doctrine which were proposed during the century.

1833: Start of the Oxford Movement which affected the Church of England and resulted in some notable conversions, including that of John Henry Newman in 1845, to the Catholic Church.

Bl. Frederic Ozanam founded the Society of St. Vincent de Paul in France. The society's objectives are works of charity.

1848: *The Communist Manifesto*, a revolutionary document symptomatic of socio-economic crisis, was issued.

1850: The hierarchy was reestablished in England and Nicholas Wiseman made the first archbishop of Westminster. He was succeeded in 1865 by Henry Manning, an Oxford convert and proponent of the rights of labor.

1853: The Catholic hierarchy was reestablished in Holland.

1854: Pius IX proclaimed the dogma of the Immaculate Conception in the bull *Ineffabilis Deus*.

1858: The Blessed Virgin Mary appeared to St. Bernadette at Lourdes, France.

1864: Pius IX issued the encyclical Quanta cura and the Syllabus of Errors in condemnation of some 80 propositions derived from the scientific mentality and rationalism of the century. The subjects in question had deep ramifications in many areas of thought and human endeavor; in religion, they explicitly and/or implicitly rejected divine revelation and the supernatural order.

1867: The first volume of *Das Kapital* was published. Together with the Communist First International, formed in the same year, it had great influence on the subsequent development of communism and socialism.

1869: The Anglican Church was disestablished in Ireland.

1869-70: Ecumenical Council of the Vatican (I). It defined papal primacy and infallibility in a dogmatic constitution on the Church; covered natural religion, revelation, faith, and the relations between faith and reason in a dogmatic constitution on the Catholic faith.

1870-71: Victor Emmanuel II of Sardinia, crowned king of Italy after defeating Austrian and papal forces, marched into Rome in 1870 and expropriated the Papal States after a plebiscite in which Catholics, at the order of Pius IX, did not vote. In 1871, Pius IX refused to accept a Law of Guarantees. Confiscation of church property and hindrance of ecclesiastical administration by the regime followed.

1871: The German Empire, a confederation of 26 states, was formed. Government policy launched a *Kulturkampf* whose May Laws of 1873 were designed to annul papal jurisdiction in Prussia and other states and to place the Church under imperial control. Resistance to the enactments and the persecution they legalized forced the government to modify its anti-Church policy by 1887.

1878: Beginning of the pontificate of Leo XIII, who was pope until his death in 1903. Leo is best known for the encyclical *Rerum novarum*, which greatly influenced the course of Christian social thought and the labor movement. His other accomplishments included promotion of Scholastic philosophy and the impetus he gave to scriptural studies.

1881: The first International Eucharistic Congress was held in Lille, France.

Alexander II of Russia was assassinated. His policies of Russification — as well as those of his two predecessors and a successor during the century — caused great suffering to Catholics, Jews and Protestants in Poland, Lithuania, the Ukraine and Bessarabia.

1882: Charles Darwin died. His theory of evolution by natural selection, one of several scientific highlights of the century, had extensive repercussions in the faith-and-science controversy.

1887: The Catholic University of America was founded in Washington, DC.

1893: The U.S. apostolic delegation was set up in Washington, DC.

TWENTIETH CENTURY

1901: Restrictive measures in France forced the Jesuits, Benedictines, Carmelites and other religious orders to leave the country. Subsequently, 14,000 schools were suppressed; religious orders and congregations were expelled; the concordat was renounced in 1905; church property was confiscated in 1906. For some years the Holy See, refusing to comply with government demands for the control of bishops' appointments, left some ecclesiastical offices vacant.

1903-14: Pontificate of St. Pius X. He initiated the codification of canon law, 1904; removed the ban against participation by Catholics in Italian national elections, 1905; issued decrees calling upon the faithful to receive Holy Communion frequently and daily, and stating that children should begin receiving the Eucharist at the age of seven, 1905 and 1910, respectively; ordered the establishment of the Confraternity of Christian Doctrine in all parishes throughout the world, 1905; condemned Modernism in the decree *Lamentabili* and the encyclical *Pascendi*, 1907.

1908: The United States and England, long under the jurisdiction of the Congregation for the Propagation of the Faith as mission territories, were removed from its control and placed under the common law of the Church.

1910: Laws of separation were enacted in Portugal, marking a point of departure in church-state relations.

1911: The Catholic Foreign Mission Society of America — Maryknoll, the first U.S.-founded society of its type — was established.

1914: Start of World War I, which lasted until 1918.

1914-22: Pontificate of Benedict XV. Much of his pontificate was devoted to seeking ways and means of minimizing the material and spiritual havoc of World War I. In 1917 he offered his services as a mediator to the belligerent nations, but his pleas for settlement of the conflict went unheeded.

1917: The Blessed Virgin Mary appeared to three children at Fatima, Portugal.

A new constitution, embodying repressive laws against the Church, was enacted in Mexico. Its implementation resulted in persecution in the 1920s and 1930s.

Bolsheviks seized power in Russia and set up a communist dictatorship. The event marked the rise of communism in Russian and world affairs. One of its immediate, and lasting, results was persecution of the Church, Jews and other segments of the population.

1918: The Code of Canon Law, in preparation for more than 10 years, went into effect in the Western Church.

1919: Benedict XV stimulated missionary work through the decree *Maximum Illud*, in which he urged the recruiting and training of native clergy in places where the Church was not firmly established.

1920-22: Ireland was partitioned by two enactments of the British government which (1) made the six counties of Northern Ireland part of the United Kingdom in 1920 and (2) gave dominion status to the Irish Free State in 1922. The Irish Free State became an independent republic in 1949.

1922-39: Pontificate of Pius XI. He subscribed to the Lateran Treaty, 1929, which settled the Roman Question created by the confiscation of the Papal States in 1871; issued the encyclical *Casti connubii*, 1930, an authoritative statement on Christian marriage; resisted the efforts of Benito Mussolini to control Catholic Action and the Church, in the encyclical *Non abbiamo bisogno*, 1931; opposed various fascist policies; issued the encyclicals *Quadragesimo anno*, 1931, developing the social doctrine of Leo XIII's *Rerum novarum*, and *Divini Redemptoris*, 1937, calling for social justice and condemning atheistic communism; condemned anti-Semitism, 1937.

1926: The Catholic Relief Act repealed virtually all legal disabilities of Catholics in England.

1931: Leftists proclaimed Spain a republic and proceeded to disestablish the Church, confiscate church property, deny salaries to the clergy, expel the Jesuits and ban teaching of the Catholic faith. These actions were preludes to the civil war of 1936-1939.

1933: Emergence of Adolf Hitler to power in Germany. By 1935 two of his aims were clear, the elimination of the Jews and control of a single national church. Six million Jews were killed in the Holocaust. The Church was subject to repressive measures, which Pius XI protested futilely in the encyclical *Mit brennender sorge* in 1937.

1936-39: Civil war in Spain between the leftist Loyalist and the forces of rightist leader Francisco Franco The Loyalists were defeated and one-man, one-party rule was established. Many priests, religious and lay persons fell victim to Loyalist persecution and atrocities.

1939-45: World War II.

1939-58: Pontificate of Pius XII. He condemned communism, proclaimed the dogma of the Assumption of Mary in 1950, in various documents and other enactments provided ideological background for many of the accomplishments of the Second Vatican Council. (*See* **Twentieth Century Popes.**)

1940: Start of a decade of communist conquest in more than 13 countries, resulting in conditions of persecution for a minimum of 60 million Catholics as well as members of other faiths.

Persecution diminished in Mexico because of non-enforcement of anti-religious laws still on record.

1950: Pius XII proclaimed the dogma of the Assumption of the Blessed Virgin Mary.

1957: The communist regime of China established the Patriotic Association of Chinese Catholics in opposition to the Church in union with the pope.

1958-63: Pontificate of Bl. John XXIII. His principal accomplishment was the convocation of the Second Vatican Council, the twenty-first ecumenical council in the history of the Church. (*See* **Twentieth Century Popes.**)

1962-65: Ecumenical Council of the Vatican (II). It formulated and promulgated 16 documents — two dogmatic and two pastoral constitutions, nine decrees and three declarations — reflecting pastoral orientation toward renewal and reform in the Church, and making explicit dimensions of doctrine and Christian life requiring emphasis for the full development of the Church and the better accomplishment of its mission in the contemporary world.

1963-78: Pontificate of Paul VI. His main purpose and effort was to give direction and provide guidance for the authentic trends of church renewal set in motion by the Second Vatican Council. (*See* **Twentieth Century Popes.**)

1978: The thirty-four-day pontificate of John Paul I. Start of the pontificate of John Paul II; see Index.

1983: The revised Code of Canon Law, embodying reforms enacted by the Second Vatican Council, went into effect in the Church of Roman Rite.

1985: Formal ratification of a Vatican-Italy concordat replacing the Lateran Treaty of 1929.

1989-91: Decline and fall of communist influence and control in Middle and Eastern Europe and the Soviet Union.

1991: The Code of Canon Law for Eastern Churches went into effect.

1992: Approval of the new *Catechism of the Catholic Church.*

The Vatican officially closed the case against Galileo Galilei.

1994: Initiation of celebration preparations of the start of the third Christian millennium in the year 2000.

1997: Pope John Paul II issued an apology for any anti-Semitism by Catholics; a conference on anti-Semitism was also held in Rome and a number of Catholic leaders in Europe issued apologies for historical anti-Semitism.

1998: Pope John Paul II visited Cuba and secured the release of over 300 political prisoners.

The Vatican issued a white paper on Anti-Semitism, entitled: *We Remember: A Reflection on the Shoah.*

Twentieth anniversary of the pontificate of Pope John Paul II; he became the longest reigning pontiff elected in the 20th century.

TWENTY-FIRST CENTURY

2000: The Catholic Church celebrated the Holy Year 2000 and the Jubilee; commencement of the third Christian millennium.

Pope John Paul II issued apology for the sinful actions of the Church's members in the past. Pope John Paul II traveled to the Holy Land in an historic visit.

2001: Pope John Paul II traveled to Greece and Syria. He also named 44 new members to the College of Cardinals in an unprecedented consistory.

On September 11, the World Trade Center was destroyed and the Pentagon attacked by Islamic terrorists who hijacked several planes and used them as weapons of mass destruction. The attacks launched a global war on terror.

2003: Pope John Paul II appealed for a peaceful resolution to the Iraq War. A coalition headed by the U.S. removed Saddam Hussein.

2004: In March, Pope John Paul II became the third longest reigning pontiff in history, surpassing Pope Leo XIII (r. 1878-1903).

2005: Pope John Paul II died on Apr. 2. Cardinal Joseph Ratzinger was elected pope on Apr. 19 and took the name Benedict XVI.

ECUMENICAL COUNCILS

An ecumenical council is an assembly of the college of bishops, with and under the presidency of the pope, which has supreme authority over the Church in matters pertaining to faith, morals, worship and discipline.

The Second Vatican Council stated: "The supreme authority with which this college (of bishops) is empowered over the whole Church is exercised in a solemn way through an ecumenical council. A council is never ecumenical unless it is confirmed or at least accepted as such by the successor of Peter. It is the prerogative of the Roman Pontiff to convoke these councils, to preside over them, and to confirm them" (Dogmatic Constitution on the Church, *Lumen Gentium*, No. 22).

Pope Presides

The pope is the head of an ecumenical council; he presides over it either personally or through legates. Conciliar decrees and other actions have binding force only when confirmed and promulgated by him. If a pope dies during a council, it is suspended until reconvened by another pope. An ecumenical council is not superior to a pope; hence, there is no appeal from a pope to a council.

Collectively, the bishops with the pope represent the whole Church. They do this not as democratic representatives of the faithful in a kind of church parliament, but as the successors of the Apostles with divinely given authority, care and responsibility over the whole Church.

All and only bishops are council participants with deliberative vote. The supreme authority of the Church can invite others and determine the manner of their participation.

Basic legislation concerning ecumenical councils is contained in Canons 337-41 of the Code of Canon Law. Basic doctrinal considerations were stated by the Second Vatican Council in the Dogmatic Constitution on the Church.

Background

Ecumenical councils had their prototype in the Council of Jerusalem in 51, at which the Apostles under the leadership of St. Peter decided that converts to the Christian faith were not obliged to observe all the prescriptions of Old Testament law (Acts 15). As early as the second century, bishops got together in regional meetings, synods or councils to take common action for the doctrinal and pastoral good of their communities of faithful. The expansion of such limited assemblies to ecumenical councils was a logical and historical evolution, given the nature and needs of the Church.

Emperors Involved

Emperors were active in summoning or convoking the first eight councils, especially the first five and the eighth. Among reasons for intervention of this kind were the facts that the emperors regarded themselves as guardians of the faith; that the settlement of religious controversies, which had repercussions in political and social turmoil, served the cause of peace in the state; and that the emperors had at their disposal ways and means of facilitating gatherings of bishops. Imperial actions, however, did not account for the formally ecumenical nature of the councils.

Some councils were attended by relatively few bishops, and the ecumenical character of several was open to question for a time. However, confirmation and de facto recognition of their actions by popes and subsequent councils established them as ecumenical.

Role in History

The councils have played a highly significant role in

the history of the Church by witnessing to and defining truths of revelation, by shaping forms of worship and discipline, and by promoting measures for the ever-necessary reform and renewal of Catholic life. In general, they have represented attempts of the Church to mobilize itself in times of crisis for self-preservation, self-purification and growth.

The first eight ecumenical councils were held in the East; the other 13, in the West. The majority of separated Eastern Churches — e.g., the Orthodox — recognize the ecumenical character of the first seven councils, which formulated a great deal of basic doctrine. Other separated Eastern Churches acknowledge only the first two or first three ecumenical councils.

The 21 Councils

The 21 ecumenical councils in the history of the Church are listed below, with indication of their names or titles (taken from the names of the places where they were held); the dates; the reigning and/or approving popes; the emperors who were instrumental in convoking the eight councils in the East; the number of bishops who attended, when available; the number of sessions. Significant actions of the first 20 councils are indicated under appropriate dates in Dates and Events in Church History.

Nicaea I, 325: St. Sylvester I (Emperor Constantine I); attended by approximately 300 bishops; sessions held between May 20 or June 19 to near the end of August.

Constantinople I, 381: St. Damasus I (Emperor Theodosius I); attended by approximately 150 bishops; sessions held from May to July.

Ephesus, 431: St. Celestine I (Emperor Theodosius II); attended by 150 to 200 bishops; five sessions held between June 22 and July 17.

Chalcedon, 451: St. Leo I (Emperor Marcian); attended by approximately 600 bishops; 17 sessions held between Oct. 8 and Nov. 1.

Constantinople II, 553: Vigilius (Emperor Justinian I); attended by 165 bishops; eight sessions held between May 5 and June 2.

Constantinople III, 680-681: St. Agatho, St. Leo II (Emperor Constantine IV); attended by approximately 170 bishops; 16 sessions held between Nov. 7, 680, and Sept. 6, 681.

Nicaea II, 787: Adrian I (Empress Irene); attended by approximately 300 bishops; eight sessions held between Sept. 24 and Oct. 23.

Constantinople IV, 869-870: Adrian II (Emperor Basil I); attended by 102 bishops; six sessions held between Oct. 5, 869, and Feb. 28, 870.

Lateran I, 1123: Callistus II; attended by approximately 300 bishops; sessions held between Mar. 8 and Apr. 6.

Lateran II, 1139: Innocent II; attended by 900 to 1,000 bishops and abbots; three sessions held in Apr.

Lateran III, 1179: Alexander III; attended by at least 300 bishops; three sessions held between Mar. 5 and 19.

Lateran IV, 1215: Innocent III; sessions held between Nov. 11 and 30.

Lyons I, 1245: Innocent IV; attended by approximately 150 bishops; three sessions held between June 28 and July 17.

Lyons II, 1274: Gregory X; attended by approximately 500 bishops; six sessions held between May 7 and July 17.

Vienne, 1311-1312: Clement V; attended by 132 bishops; three sessions held between Oct. 16, 1311, and May 6, 1312.

Constance, 1414-1418: Gregory XII, Martin V; attended by nearly 200 bishops, plus other prelates and many experts; 45 sessions held between Nov. 5, 1414, and Apr. 22, 1418.

Florence (also called Basel-Ferrara-Florence), 1431-c. 1445: Eugene IV; attended by many Latin-Rite and Eastern-Rite bishops; preliminary sessions were held at Basel and Ferrara before definitive work was accomplished at Florence.

Lateran V, 1512-1517: Julius II, Leo X; 12 sessions held between May 3, 1512, and Mar. 6, 1517.

Trent, 1545-1563: Paul III, Julius III, Pius IV; 25 sessions held between Dec. 13, 1545, and Dec. 4, 1563.

Vatican I, 1869-1870: Pius IX; attended by approximately 800 bishops and other prelates; four public sessions and 89 general meetings held between Dec. 8, 1869, and Sept. 1, 1870.

VATICAN II

The Second Vatican Council, which was forecast by Pope John XXIII Jan. 25, 1959, was held in four sessions in St. Peter's Basilica.

Pope John convoked it and opened the first session, which ran from Oct. 11 to Dec. 8, 1962. Following John's death June 3, 1963, Pope Paul VI reconvened the council for the other three sessions which ran from Sept. 29 to Dec. 4, 1963; Sept. 14 to Nov. 21, 1964; Sept. 14 to Dec. 8, 1965.

A total of 2,860 Fathers participated in council proceedings, and attendance at meetings varied between 2,000 and 2,500. For various reasons, including the denial of exit from Communist-dominated countries, 274 Fathers could not attend.

The council formulated and promulgated 16 documents — two dogmatic and two pastoral constitutions, nine decrees and three declarations — all of which reflect its basic pastoral orientation toward renewal and reform in the Church. Given below are the Latin and English titles of the documents and their dates of promulgation.

Lumen Gentium (Dogmatic Constitution on the Church), Nov. 21, 1964.

Dei Verbum (Dogmatic Constitution on Divine Revelation), Nov. 18, 1965.

Sacrosanctum Concilium (Constitution on the Sacred Liturgy), Dec. 4, 1963.

Gaudium et Spes (Pastoral Constitution on the Church in the Modern World), Dec. 7, 1965.

Christus Dominus (Decree on the Bishops' Pastoral Office in the Church), Oct. 28, 1965.

Ad Gentes (Decree on the Church's Missionary Activity), Dec. 7, 1965.

Unitatis Redintegratio (Decree on Ecumenism), Nov. 21, 1964.

Orientalium Ecclesiarum (Decree on Eastern Catholic Churches), Nov. 21, 1964.

Presbyterorum Ordinis (Decree on the Ministry and Life of Priests), Dec. 7, 1965.

Optatam Totius (Decree on Priestly Formation), Oct. 28, 1965.

Perfectae Caritatis (Decree on the Appropriate Renewal of the Religious Life), Oct. 28, 1965.

Apostolicam Actuositatem (Decree on the

Apostolate of the Laity), Nov. 18, 1965.

Inter Mirifica (Decree on the Instruments of Social Communication), Dec. 4, 1963.

Dignitatis Humanae (Declaration on Religious Freedom), Dec. 7, 1965.

Nostra Aetate (Declaration on the Relationship of the Church to Non-Christian Religions), Oct. 28, 1965.

Gravissimum Educationis (Declaration on Christian Education), Oct. 28, 1965.

The key documents were the four constitutions, which set the ideological basis for all the others. To date, the documents with the most visible effects are those on the liturgy, the Church, the Church in the world, ecumenism, the renewal of religious life, the life and ministry of priests, the lay apostolate.

The main business of the council was to explore and make explicit dimensions of doctrine and Christian life requiring emphasis for the full development of the Church and the better accomplishment of its mission in the contemporary world.

Enactments of the Second Vatican Council have been points of departure for a wide variety of developments in the internal life of the Church and its mission in the world at large. Much effort has been made in the pontificate of Pope John Paul II to provide the interpretation and implementation of the conciliar documents with a more uniform and universal structure.

The Papacy and the Holy See

POPE BENEDICT XVI

Cardinal Joseph Ratzinger of Germany, Prefect of the Congregation for the Doctrine of the Faith since 1981 and one of the great theologians in the Church over the last fifty years, was elected Bishop of Rome and the 264th successor of St. Peter as Supreme Pastor of the Universal Church on Apr. 19, 2005, after four ballots over two days. He chose the name Benedict in honor of Pope Benedict XV, an advocate of peace, and St. Benedict of Nursia, who helped to resurrect civilization in Europe during the Dark Ages. Pope Benedict XVI was invested with the pallium, the symbol of his office, on Apr. 24, 2005, in ceremonies attended by more than 500,000 people in St. Peter's Square.

Early Life

Joseph Aloysius Ratzinger was born on April 16, 1927, while the family was living in a three-story house in the little village of Marktl am Inn, situated in eastern Bavaria. His family moved several times in his early years owing to his father's opposition to the Nazis, and young Joseph was forced to join the Hitler Youth. He was adamantly opposed to the Nazis and made every effort to leave at the first opportunity. In 1939, he entered the minor seminary in Traunstein, his first step toward the priesthood. World War II forced a postponement of his studies, until 1945, when he re-entered the seminary with his brother, Georg. In 1947, he entered the *Herzogliches Georgianum*, a theological institute associated with the University of Munich. Finally, on June 29, 1951, both Joseph and his brother were ordained to the priesthood by Cardinal Faulhaber, in the Cathedral at Freising, on the Feast of Sts. Peter and Paul.

Continuing his theological studies at the University of Munich, he received his doctorate in theology in July 1953, with a thesis entitled *Volk und Haus Gottes in Augustins Lehre von der Kirche* ("The People and House of God in Augustine's Doctrine of the Church"). He fulfilled a requirement for teaching at the university level by completing a book-length treatise, "The Theology of History in St. Bonaventure." On April 15, 1959, he began lectures as a full pro-

fessor of fundamental theology at the University of Bonn. From 1962-1965, he was present during all four sessions of the Vatican II as a *peritus*, or chief theological advisor, to Cardinal Josef Frings of Köln (Cologne), Germany.

In 1963, he began teaching at the University of Münster, taking, in 1966, a second chair in dogmatic theology at University of Tübingen. A wave of student uprisings swept across Europe in 1968, and Marxism quickly became the dominant intellectual system at Tübingen. He found the radicalized environment to be unacceptable, so in 1969 he moved back to Bavaria and took a teaching position at the University of Regensburg. There, he eventually became dean and vice president. He was also a member of the International Theological Commission of the Holy See from 1969 until 1980.

In 1972, together with Hans Urs von Balthasar, Henry De Lubac and others, he launched the Catholic theological journal *Communio*, a quarterly review of Catholic theology and culture. It has been said that this was done in response to the misinterpretation of the Second Vatican Council by various theologians, as represented by the theological journal *Concilium*.

Archbishop and Cardinal

On March 24, 1977, Fr. Ratzinger was appointed Archbishop of Munich and Freising by Pope Paul VI. He was ordained a bishop on May 28, 1977, taking as his Episcopal motto a phrase from 3 John 8, *Cooperatores Veritatis* ("Fellow Worker in the Truth"). On June 27, 1977, he was elevated to Cardinal (Cardinal Priest) by Pope Paul VI, with the titular church of St. Mary of Consolation (in Tiburtina). In 1980, he was named by Pope John Paul II to chair the special Synod on the Laity. Shortly after that, the pope asked him to head the Congregation for Catholic Education. Cardinal Ratzinger declined, feeling he should not leave his post in Munich too soon. On Nov. 25, 1981, he accepted the post of the Prefect for the Congregation for the Doctrine of the Faith, becoming at the same time *ex officio* the president of the Pontifical Biblical Commission, and the International Theological Commission.

Coat of Arms of **Pope Benedict XVI**

Cardinal Ratzinger was president of the Commission for the Preparation of the *Catechism of the Catholic Church*, and after 6 years of work (1986-92) he presented the new *Catechism* to the Holy Father. On April 5, 1993, he was transferred to the order of Cardinal Bishops, with the suburbicarian see of Velletri-Signi. On Nov. 9, 1998, his election as Vice-Dean of the Sacred College of Cardinals was approved by Pope John Paul II, and the Holy Father approved his election as Dean of the College of Cardinals on Nov. 30, 2002, with the title of the suburbicarian See of Ostia added to that of Velletri-Segni.

Besides his prefecture at the Doctrine of the Faith, his curial memberships include: the Second Section of the Secretariat of State, the Congregation of Bishops, of Divine Worship and the Discipline of the Sacraments, of Catholic Education, of Evangelization of Peoples, for the Oriental Churches; and the Pontifical Councils for Christian Unity and for Culture; as well as, the Commissions *Ecclesia Dei*, and for Latin America.

As Dean of the College he was a key figure during the *sede vacante* after the death of Pope John Paul II on April 2, 2005, and delivered the funeral homily for the deceased pontiff.

Pontificate

For details on Pope Benedict XVI's pontificate during 2005-2006, *see under* **Special Reports.**

Foreign Pastoral Visits

2005: Cologne, Germany (World Youth Day), Aug. 18-21.

2006: Poland, May 25-28; Valencia, Spain, July 8-9.

Encyclicals and Other Writings

Cardinal Joseph Ratzinger at the time of his election as Pope Benedict XVI was one of the Church's greatest theologians and was the author of a vast body of writings. Since his election, he has issued several documents, including several *motu proprio* and apostolic letters. His first encyclical, *Deus Caritas Est*, was issued on Dec. 25, 2005. (For details, *see under* **Special Reports.**)

POPE JOHN PAUL II, 1978-2005

Cardinal Karol Wojtyla of Cracow was elected Bishop of Rome and 263rd successor of St. Peter as Supreme Pastor of the Universal Church on Oct. 16, 1978. He chose the name John Paul II in honor of his predecessor, Pope John Paul I, as well as Popes Bl. John XXIII and Paul VI. He was invested with the pallium, symbol of his office, on Oct. 22 in ceremonies attended by more than 250,000 people in St. Peter's Square. He died on Apr. 2, 2005, at 9:37 p.m. in the Apostolic Palace in the Vatican.

From the start, Pope John Paul II labored to keep the Church faithful to its tradition and to the teaching and spirit of Vatican Council II, while positioning it to meet the challenges of the Third Millennium. He was a staunch defender of the sanctity of human life — "from conception to natural death," he often said — and of marriage and the family. Opposition to totalitarianism and support for human rights make this activist, long-reigning pope a major figure on the world political scene.

He was the first non-Italian pope since Adrian VI (1522-23) and the first Polish pope ever. At his election, he was the youngest pope since Pius IX (1846-78). On May 24, 1998, he became the longest-reigning pope elected in the 20th century, surpassing the 19 years, seven months, and seven days of Pius XII (1939-58). (Leo XIII, who died in 1903, was pope for 25 years.) John Paul II's pontificate was also the third longest in the history of the Church. He surpassed Pope Leo XIII (25 years, 5 months), and is behind only Bl. Pius IX (31 years, 7 months, 21 days) and St. Peter (precise dates unknown).

He was the most-traveled pope in history. He covered over 750,000 miles during 104 pastoral visits outside Italy, over 146 within Italy, and 301 to the parishes of Rome. In all, he visited 129 countries and held talks with 1,022 heads of state or government. By the end of his pontificate, the Holy See had diplomatic relations with 174 states, as well as diplomatic relations with the European Union and Sovereign Military Order of Malta, and special relations with the Russian Federation and the PLO.

Certainly he was the pope most prolific in literary output, having issued 14 encyclicals, 14 apostolic exhortations, 11 apostolic constitutions, 45 apostolic letters and 30 *motu proprio*.

John Paul II proclaimed 1,338 Blesseds in 147 ceremonies and had proclaimed 482 Saints in 51 liturgical celebrations; his 17 predecessors from Pope Clement VIII to Pope Paul VI canonized a total of 302 people. He held nine consistories for the creation of cardinals and named a total of 231 cardinals (not including the *in pectore* cardinal. The last consistory was Oct. 2003. The Holy Father presided at 15 synods: the Particular Synod of Bishops of the Netherlands in 1980; six ordinary synods (1980, 1983, 1987, 1990, 1994 and 2001); one extraordinary (1985) and eight special (1980, 1991, 1994, 1995, 1997, two in 1998, and the second synod for Europe in Oct. 1999); the most recent synod was held in Oct. 2001.

Over the years the pope held over 1,161 weekly general audiences and has welcomed over 17 million faithful from every part of the world. Other audiences, including various groups and heads of state and government, total around 1,600. As pontiff, he consecrated 321 bishops and performed over 1,500 baptisms.

He was also the first pope ever to visit a synagogue (Rome, Apr. 1986); the first to visit a mosque (Omayyad Great Mosque of Damascus, May 2001); the first to call for a Day of Pardon (Jubilee Year 2000); and the first to add five new mysteries to the Rosary (Oct. 2002).

Early Life

Karol Josef Wojtyla was born May 18, 1920, in Wadowice, an industrial town near Cracow. His parents were Karol Wojtyla, who had been an adminstrative officer in the Austrian army and was a lieutenant in the Polish army until his retirement in 1927, and Emilia Kaczorowska Wojtyla. His mother died in 1929 of kidney and heart failure. His sister died a few days after birth; his older brother Edmund, a physician, died in 1932, and his father in 1941.

He attended schools in Wadowice and in 1938 enrolled in the faculty of philosophy of the Jagiellonian University in Cracow, where he moved with his father. At the university he was active in the

Studio 38 experimental theater group.

For young Wojtyla, as for countless others, life changed forever on Sept. 1, 1939, when World War II began. Nazi occupation forces closed the Jagiellonian University and the young man had to work in a quarry as a stone cutter and later in a chemical plant to avoid deportation to Germany. In Feb. 1940, he met Jan Tryanowski, a tailor who became his spiritual mentor and introduced him to the writings of St. John of the Cross and St. Teresa of Ávila. He also participated in underground theater groups, including the Rhapsodic Theater of Mieczyslaw Kotlarczyk.

In Oct. 1942, he began studies for the priesthood in the underground seminary maintained by Cardinal Adam Sapieha of Cracow. He was struck by an automobile Feb. 29, 1944, and hospitalized until Mar. 12. In Aug. of that year Cardinal Sapieha transferred him and the other seminarians to the Archbishop's Residence, where they lived and studied until war's end. Ordained a priest by the Cardinal on Nov. 1, 1946, he left Poland Nov. 15 to begin advanced studies in Rome at the Angelicum University (the Pontifical University of St. Thomas Aquinas).

He subsequently earned doctorates in theology and philosophy and was a respected moral theologian and ethicist.

Bishop and Cardinal

On July 4, 1958, Pope Pius XII named him auxiliary bishop to Archbishop Eugeniusz Baziak, Apostolic Administrator of Cracow. His book *Love and Responsibility* was published in 1960. (Earlier, he had published poetry and several plays.) Following Archbishop Baziak's death in 1962, he became Vicar Capitular and then on Jan. 13, 1964, Archbishop of Cracow—the first residential head of the See permitted by the communist authorities since Cardinal Sapieha's death in 1951.

Archbishop Wojtyla attended all four sessions of the Second Vatican Council, from 1962 to 1965, and helped draft Schema XIII, which became *Gaudium et Spes*, the Pastoral Constitution on the Church in the Modern World. He also contributed to *Dignitatis Humanae* (the "Declaration on Religious Freedom") and on the theology of the laity.

Pope Paul VI created him a cardinal in the consistory of June 26, 1967, with the titular Roman church of S. Cesario in Palatio. Although scheduled to attend the first general assembly of the Synod of Bishops in Sept. and Oct. of that year, Cardinal Wojtyla did not go, as a sign of solidarity with Cardinal Stefan Wyszynski of Warsaw, Poland's primate, whom the communist government refused a passport. In Oct. 1969, however, he participated in the first extraordinary assembly of the synod. Earlier that year, with approval of the statutes of the Polish bishops' conference, he became its vice president.

In 1971 he took part in the second general assembly of the synod and was elected to the council of the secretary general. He continued to participate in synod assemblies and to serve on the synod council up to his election as pope. May 8, 1972, saw the opening of the archdiocesan of synod of Cracow, which he had convened and would conclude during his visit to Poland as pope in 1979. Also in 1972 he published *Foundations of Renewal: A Study on the Implementation of the Second Vatican Council.*

Pope Paul died Aug. 6, 1978. Cardinal Wojtyla participated in the conclave that chose Cardinal Albino Luciani of Venice his successor on Aug. 26. When the new pope, who had taken the name John Paul I, died unexpectedly on Sept. 28, Cardinal Wojtyla joined 110 other cardinals in that year's second conclave. He emerged on the second day of voting, Oct. 16, as Pope John Paul II.

Pontificate

Pope John Paul set out the major themes and program of his pontificate in his first encyclical, *Redemptor Hominis* (*The Redeemer of Man*), dated Mar. 4, 1979, and published Mar. 15. "The Redeemer of Man, Jesus Christ, is the center of the universe and of history," he wrote. Throughout his pontificate he emphasized preparation for the year 2000—which he proclaimed a Jubilee Year—and for the Third Millennium of the Christian era, with the aim of fostering a renewed commitment to evangelization among Catholics. He also has produced a significant body of magisterial teaching in such areas as Christian anthropology, sexual morality, and social justice, while working for peace and human rights throughout the world.

His pontificate was uncommonly active and filled with dramatic events. Among the most dramatic are those associated with the fall of communism in Eastern Europe. Many students of that complex event credit John Paul with a central role. His visits to his Polish homeland in 1979 (June 2-10) and 1983 (June 16-23) bolstered Polish Catholicism and kindled Polish resistance to communism, while his determined support for the Solidarity labor movement gave his countrymen a vehicle for their resistance. The result was a growing nonviolent liberation movement leading to the dramatic developments of 1989—the collapse of communist regimes, the emergence of democracy in Poland and other countries, the fall of the Berlin Wall, and, in time, to the breakup of the Soviet Union and the end of the Cold War.

Dramatic in a much different way was the 1981 attempt on the Pope's life. At 5:19 p.m. on May 13, as he greeted crowds in St. Peter's Square before his Wednesday general audience, a Turkish terrorist named Mehmet Ali Agca shot John Paul at close range. Whether the assassin acted alone or at the behest of others—and which others—remain unanswered questions. Following a six-hour operation, John Paul was hospitalized for 77 days at Gemelli Hospital. He visited Ali Agca in the Rebibbia prison on Dec. 27, 1983.

Although he resumed his activities vigorously after his recuperation, the pope's health and strength have declined over the years. In July 1992, he had colon surgery for the removal of a non-cancerous tumor; in Nov. 1993, his shoulder was dislocated in a fall; he suffered a broken femur in another fall in Apr. 1994; and in Oct. 1996, he had an appendectomy. For several years, too, the effects were apparent of what the Vatican acknowledges to be a neurological condition (many observers take the ailment to be Parkinson's disease).

Foreign Pastoral Visits

As noted, his pastoral visits were a striking feature of his pontificate. Many were to nations in the Third World. His 104 trips outside Italy were as follows:
1979 Dominican Republic and Mexico, Jan. 5-Feb. 1;

Poland, June 2-10; Ireland and the United States, Sept. 29-Oct. 7; Turkey, Nov. 28-30.

1980 Africa (Zaire, Congo Republic, Kenya, Ghana, Upper Volta, Ivory Coast), May 2-12; France, May 30-June 2; Brazil (13 cities), June 30-July 12; West Germany, Nov. 15-19.

1981 Philippines, Guam, and Japan, with stopovers in Pakistan and Alaska, Feb. 16-27.

1982 Africa (Nigeria, Benin, Gabon, Equatorial Guinea), Feb. 12-19; Portugal, May 12-15; Great Britain, May 28-June 2; Argentina, June 11-12; Switzerland, June 15; San Marino, Aug. 29; Spain, Oct. 31-Nov. 9.

1983 Central America (Costa Rica, Nicaragua, Panama, El Salvador, Guatemala, Belize, Honduras) and Haiti, Mar. 2-10; Poland, June 16-23; Lourdes, France, Aug. 14-15; Austria, Sept. 10-13.

1984 South Korea, Papua New Guinea, Solomon Islands, Thailand, May 12; Switzerland, June 12-17; Canada, Sept. 9-20; Spain, Dominican Republic, and Puerto Rico, Oct. 10-12.

1985 Venezuela, Ecuador, Peru, Trinidad and Tobago, Jan. 26-Feb. 6; Belgium, the Netherlands, and Luxembourg, May 11-21; Africa (Togo, Ivory Coast, Cameroon, Central African Republic, Zaire, Kenya, and Morocco), Aug. 8-19; Liechtenstein, Sept. 8.

1986 India, Feb. 1-10; Colombia and Saint Lucia, July 1-7; France, Oct. 4-7; Oceania (Australia, New Zealand, Bangladesh, Fiji, Singapore, and Seychelles), Nov. 18-Dec. 1.

1987 Uruguay, Chile, and Argentina, Mar. 31-Apr. 12; West Germany, Apr. 30-May 4; Poland, June 8-14; the United States and Canada, Sept. 10-19.

1988 Uruguay, Bolivia, Peru, and Paraguay, May 7-18; Austria, June 23-27; Africa (Zimbabwe, Botswana, Lesotho, Swaziland, and Mozam-bique), Sept. 10-19; France, Oct. 8-11.

1989 Madagascar, Reunion, Zambia, and Malawi, Apr. 28-May 6; Norway, Iceland, Finland, Denmark, and Sweden, June 1-10; Spain, Aug. 19-21; South Korea, Indonesia, East Timor, and Mauritius, Oct. 6-16.

1990 Africa (Cape Verde, Guinea Bissau, Mali, and Burkna Faso), Jan. 25-Feb. 1; Czechoslovakia, Apr. 21-22; Mexico and Curaçao, May 6-13; Malta, May 25-27; Africa (Tanzania, Burundi, Rwanda, and Ivory Coast), Sept. 1-10.

1991 Portugal, May 10-13; Poland, June 1-9; Poland and Hungary, Aug. 13-20; Brazil, Oct. 12-21.

1992 Africa (Senegal, the Gambia, Guinea), Feb. 10-26; Africa (Angola, São Tome, and Principe), June 4-10; Dominican Republic, Oct. 10-14.

1993 Africa (Benin, Uganda, Sudan), Feb. 2-10; Albania, Apr. 25; Spain, June 12-17; Jamaica, Mexico, Denver (United States), Aug. 9-15; Lithuania, Latvia, Estonia, Sept. 4-10.

1994 Zagreb, Croatia, Sept. 10.

1995 Philippines, Papua New Guinea, Australia, Sri Lanka, Jan. 12-21; Czech Republic and Poland, May 20-22; Belgium, June 3-4; Slovakia, June 30-July 3; Africa (Cameroon, South Africa, Kenya), Sept. 14-20; United Nations and United States, Oct. 4-8.

1996 Central America (Guatemala, Nicaragua, El Salvador), Feb. 5-11; Tunisia, Apr. 17; Slovenia, May 17-19; Germany, June 21-23; Hungary, Sept. 6-

7; France, Sept. 19-22.

1997 Sarajevo, Apr. 12-13; Czech Republic, Apr. 25-27; Lebanon, May 10-11; Poland, May 31-June 10; France, Aug. 21-24; Brazil, Oct. 2-5.

1998 Cuba, Jan. 21-25; Nigeria, Mar. 21-23; Austria, June 19-21; Croatia, Oct. 3-4.

1999 Mexico, Jan. 22-25; St. Louis, United States, Jan. 26-27; Romania, May 2-5; Poland June, 5-17; Slovenia, Sept. 19; India, Nov. 6-7; Georgia, Nov. 8-9.

2000 Egypt and Mount Sinai, Feb. 24-26; Holy Land, Mar. 20-26; Fátima, May 12-13.

2001 Greece, Syria, and Malta, May 4-9; Ukraine, June 23-27; Kazakhstan and Armenia, Sept. 22-27.

2002 Azerbaijan and Bulgaria, May 22-26; Toronto, Canada, July 23-28; Guatemala City, July 29-30; Mexico City, July 31-Aug. 2; Poland, Aug. 16-19.

2003 Spain, May 3-4; Croatia, June 5-9; Bosnia-Herzegovina, June 22; Slovak Republic, Sept. 11-14.

2004 Switzerland, May 5-6; Lourdes, France, Aug. 15-16.

Encyclicals and Other Writings

As noted above, Pope John Paul's first encyclical, *Redemptor Hominis* (1979), set the tone for and in general terms indicated the subject matter of many of the documents to follow. These were infused with the pope's distinctive personalism, which emphasizes the dignity and rights of the human person, most truly understood in the light of Christ, as the norm and goal of human endeavor.

His other encyclical letters were: *Dives in Misericordia* ("On the Mercy of God"), 1980; *Laborem Exercens* ("On Human Work"), 1981; *Slavorum Apostoli* ("The Apostles of the Slavs," honoring Sts. Cyril and Methodius), 1985; *Dominum et Vivificantem* ("Lord and Giver of Life," on the Holy Spirit), 1986; *Redemptoris Mater* ("Mother of the Redeemer"), 1987; *Sollicitudo Rei Socialis* ("On Social Concerns"), 1988; *Redemptoris Missio* ("Mission of the Redeemer") and *Centesimus Annus* ("The Hundredth Year," on the anniversary of Leo XIII's *Rerum Novarum*), both 1991; *Veritatis Splendor* ("The Splendor of Truth"), 1993; *Evangelium Vitae* ("The Gospel of Life") and *Ut Unum Sint* ("That All May Be One"), 1995; *Fides et Ratio* ("Faith and Reason"), 1998; and *Ecclesia de Eucharistia* ("Church of the Eucharist"), 2003.

Among his other publications were: *Catechesi Tradendae*, a post-synodal apostolic exhortation on catechesis, 1979; apostolic letter proclaiming Sts. Cyril and Methodius, together with St. Benedict, patrons of Europe, 1980; post-synodal apostolic exhortation *Familiaris Consortio*, on the family, 1981; apostolic letter *Caritatis Christi*, for the Church in China, 1982; letter for the 500th anniversary of the birth of Martin Luther, 1983; apostolic letter *Salvifici Doloris* ("On the Christian Meaning of Suffering"), apostolic exhortation *Redemptionis Donum*, to men and women religious, apostolic letters *Redemptionis Anno*, on Jerusalem, and *Les Grands Mysteres*, on Lebanon, and post-synodal apostolic exhortation *Reconciliatio et Poenitentia* ("Reconciliation and Penance"), all 1984.

Also: apostolic letter *Dilecti Amici*, on the occasion of the United Nations' International Year of Youth, 1985; apostolic letter *Euntes in Mundum*, for the millennium of Christianity in Kievan Rus', and apostolic letter *Mulieris Dignitatem* ("On the Dignity and Vocation of Women"), all 1988; post-synodal apostolic exhortation *Christifideles Laici* ("The Lay Members of Christ's Faithful People") and apostolic exhortation *Redemptoris Custos* ("On St. Joseph"), 1989; post-synodal apostolic exhortation *Pastores Dabo Vobis* ("I Give You Shepherds"), 1992; "Letter to Families," for the International Year of the Family, "Letter on the International Conference on Population and Development" in Cairo, apostolic letter *Ordinatio Sacerdotalis* ("On Reserving Priestly Ordination to Men Alone"), apostolic letter *Tertio Millennio Adveniente*, on preparation for the Jubilee Year 2000, and "Letter to Children in the Year of the Family," all 1994.

Also: apostolic letter *Orientale Lumen* ("The Light of the East"), on Catholic-Orthodox relations, "Letter to Women," post-synodal apostolic exhortations *Ecclesia in Africa*, *Ecclesia in Asia*, and *Ecclesia in Europa*, and apostolic letter for the fourth centenary of the Union of Brest, all 1995; apostolic constitution *Universi Dominici Gregis* ("On the Vacancy of the Apostolic See and the Election of the Roman Pontiff"), post-synodal apostolic exhortation *Vita Consecrata* ("On the Consecrated Life and Its Mission in the Church and in the World"), and apostolic letter on the 350th anniversary of the Union of Uzhorod, all 1996; post-synodal apostolic exhortation, "A New Hope for Lebanon," 1997; *Incarnationis Mysterium*, Bull of Indiction of the Great Jubilee of the Year 2000, 1998; and the apostolic letter *Misericordia Dei* ("On Certain Aspects of the Celebration of the Sacrament of Penance"), 2002.

In his years as pope he published several books, including Crossing the Threshold of Hope (1994), Gift and Mystery: On the Fiftieth Anniversary of My Priestly Ordination (1996), and Alzatevi, Andiamo (Get Up, Let Us Go, 2004), on the pontiff's 20 years as a bishop in Poland.

Issues and Activities

Doctrinal Concerns: The integrity of Catholic doctrine was a major concern of Pope John Paul. On Nov. 25, 1981, he appointed Archbishop — later, Cardinal and Pope Benedict XVI — Joseph Ratzinger of Munich-Freising, a prominent theologian, Prefect of the Congregation for the Doctrine of the Faith. The congregation under Cardinal Ratzinger has published important documents on bioethics, liberation theology (1984 and 1986), the Church's inability to ordain women as priests, the latter affirming that the teaching on this matter has been "set forth infallibly" (1995), and same-sex unions (2003).

Catechism: One of Pope John Paul's most important initiatives was the *Catechism of the Catholic Church*. The idea for this up-to-date compendium was broached at the extraordinary assembly of the Synod of Bishops held in 1985 to evaluate the implementation of Vatican Council II. The pope approved, and the project went forward under a commission of cardinals headed by Cardinal Ratzinger. Published in 1992 by authorization of John Paul II (the original was in French, with the English translation appearing in 1994 and the authoritative Latin *editio typica* in 1997), this first catechism for the universal Church in four centuries is crucial to the hoped-for renewal of catechesis.

Canon Law: John Paul oversaw the completion of the revision of the Code of Canon Law begun in 1959 at the direction of Pope John XXIII. He promulgated the new code on Jan. 25, 1983; it went into effect on Nov. 27 of that year. In *Sacrae Disciplinae Leges*, the apostolic constitution accompanying the revised code, the pope says it has "one and the same intention" as Vatican Council II — whose convening John XXIII announced at the same time — namely, "the renewal of Christian living."

On Apr. 18, 1990, John Paul promulgated the Code of Canons for the Eastern Churches. Although particular sections of the Eastern code appeared at various times dating back to 1949, this was the first time an integrated code of law for the Eastern Churches had been issued in its entirety.

Ecumenical and Interreligious Relations: Ecumenical and interreligious relations received much attention from Pope John Paul II. Two of his major documents, the encyclical *Ut Unum Sint* and the apostolic letter *Orientale Lumen*, both published in 1995, deal with these matters. He met frequently with representatives of other religious bodies, spoke frequently about the quest for unity, and has called for Catholics and others to pray and work to this end.

Among the important actions in this area were the signings of common declarations with the Ecumenical Patriarch of Constantinople His Holiness Dimitrios (Dec. 7, 1987) and his successor Bartholomew I (June 29, 1995), with the Archbishop of Canterbury and Primate of the Anglican Communion, Dr. Robert Runcie (May 29, 1982, in Canterbury Cathedral and again Oct. 2, 1989, in Rome) and his successor Dr. George Leonard Carey (Dec. 6, 1996), with the Supreme Patriarch and Catholicos of All Armenians, His Holiness Karekin I (Dec. 14, 1996), and with His Holiness Aram I Keshishian, Catholicos of Cilicia of the Armenians (Jan. 26, 1997). On Oct. 5, 1991, for the first time since the Reformation, two Lutheran bishops joined the pope and the Catholic bishops of Stockholm and Helsinki in an ecumenical prayer service in St. Peter's Basilica marking the sixth centenary of the canonization of St. Bridget of Sweden.

Pope John Paul II had Jewish friends since boyhood, and he worked hard to strengthen Catholic-Jewish ties. The Holy See formally initiated diplomatic relations with the State of Israel at the level of apostolic nunciature and embassy on June 15, 1994. In Mar. 1998, the Commission for Religious Relations with the Jews published an important document on the roots of the World War II Jewish Holocaust entitled *We Remember: A Reflection on the Shoah*. In a letter dated Mar. 12 to the commission chairman, Cardinal Edward Idris Cassidy, the Pope expressed "fervent hope" that it would "help to heal the wounds of past misunderstandings and injustices."

On Sunday, Mar. 12, 2000, Pope John Paul II presided over a day of pardon for those sins committed by members of the Church over the centuries. The Holy Father issued a formal apology for the misdeeds of the members of the Church in the past, including a renewed apology for all anti-Semitic actions by Catholics. This apology was given even greater depth by the Holy Father's trip to the Holy Land in Mar. 2000. During his historic visit to Israel, the pope placed a written apology to the Jewish people in the Wailing Wall in Jerusalem. He made further efforts at ecumenical dialogue with the Orthodox Churches during his visits to Greece, Syria, and Ukraine in 2001 and at the Day of Prayer for Peace at Assisi in Jan. 2002.

Women's Concerns: Pope John Paul's insistence that, in fidelity to the will of Christ, the Church is unable to ordain women as priests put him at odds with some feminists, as did his opposition to abortion and contraception. But it is clear from his writings that he was unusually sensitive to women's issues, and he was a strong defender of women's dignity and rights, about which he often had spoken. In 1995 he appointed a woman, Professor Mary Ann Glendon of the Harvard University Law School, head of the Holy See's delegation to the fourth U.N. conference on women, held in Beijing Sept. 4-15, the first time a woman had been named to such a post.

World Affairs: At least since Jan. 1979, when he accepted a request for mediation in a border conflict between Argentina and Chile, John Paul II worked for peace in many parts of the world. He supported efforts to achieve reconciliation between conflicting parties in troubled areas like Lebanon, the Balkans, and the Persian Gulf, where he sought to avert the Gulf War of 1991. He advocated religious liberty and human rights during pastoral visits to many countries, including Cuba and Nigeria in 1998. Among the notable ecumenical and interreligious events of the pontificate was the World Day of Prayer for Peace on Oct. 27, 1986, which he convoked in Assisi and attended along with representatives of numerous other churches and religious groups.

In 1984 the Holy See and the U.S. established diplomatic relations. (The pope has met with Presidents Jimmy Carter, Ronald Reagan, George Bush, Bill Clinton, and George W. Bush.) Relations with Poland were re-established in 1989. Diplomatic relations were established with the Soviet Union in 1990 and with the Russian Federation in 1992. Relations also have been established with other Eastern European countries and countries that were part of the former Soviet Union, with Mexico, and with other nations including Jordan, South Africa, and Libya. Working contacts of a "permanent and official character" were begun with the Palestine Liberation Organization in 1994, leading to the signing of a formal Basic Agreement with the PLO on Feb. 15, 2000. The pope also attempted to prevent the outbreak of hostilities in Iraq in 2003 and welcomed the new sovereign government in 2004.

Administration: Under Pope John Paul II the long-term financial problems of the Holy See were addressed and brought under control. Finances were on the agenda at the first plenary assembly of the College of Cardinals, Nov. 5-9, 1979, and subsequent meetings of that body. A council of cardinals for the study of organizational and economic problems of the Holy See was established in 1981. In 1988, the Holy See's financial report (for 1986) was published for the first time, along with the 1988 budget. In Apr. 1991, a meeting of the presidents of episcopal conferences was held to discuss ways of increasing the Peter's Pence Collection taken in support of the Pope.

A reorganization of responsibilities of Vatican offices was carried out in 1984, and in 1988 an apostolic constitution, *Pastor Bonus*, on reform of the Roman Curia, was issued. A Vatican labor office was instituted in 1989. Pope John Paul established a new Pontifical Academy of Social Sciences in 1994 and Pontifical Academy for Life in 1995. On Apr. 8, 1994, he celebrated Mass in the Sistine Chapel for the unveiling of the Michelangelo frescoes, which had been painstakingly cleaned and restored. The opening presentation of the Holy See's Internet site took place on Mar. 24, 1997.

As Bishop of Rome, John Paul presided over a diocesan synod that concluded May 29, 1993. He also has visited numerous Roman parishes — 301 out of 328 by the time of his passing.

His death on Apr. 2, 2005, came after two months of sharp decline from an infection. He was admitted to Gemelli Clinic, where he had been taken after the assassination attempt in 1981, on Jan. 30. Though released, he never recovered fully, was re-admitted a few weeks later, and eventually needed a tracheotomy to assist his breathing. His voice never returned to normal, and his last two appearances, on Easter Sunday and at his Wednesday audience, proved heartbreaking for those in attendance as he struggled to communicate. His health collapsed completely over the next days, and he journeyed to God at 9:37 p.m. Rome time.

POPES OF THE ROMAN CATHOLIC CHURCH

Information includes the name of the pope, in many cases his name before becoming pope, his birthplace or country of origin, the date of accession to the papacy, and the date of the end of reign that, in all but a few cases, was the date of death. Double dates indicate date of election and date of solemn beginning of ministry as Pastor of the universal Church. *Source:* Annuario Pontificio.

St. Peter (Simon Bar-Jona): Bethsaida in Galilee; d. c. 64 or 67.
St. Linus: Tuscany; 67-76.
St. Anacletus (Cletus): Rome; 76-88.
St. Clement: Rome; 88-97.
St. Evaristus: Greece; 97-105.
St. Alexander I: Rome; 105-115.
St. Sixtus I: Rome; 115-125.
St. Telesphorus: Greece; 125-136.
St. Hyginus: Greece; 136-140.
St. Pius I: Aquileia; 140-155.
St. Anicetus: Syria; 155-166.

St. Soter: Campania; 166-175.
St. Eleutherius: Nicopolis in Epirus; 175-189. Up to the time of St. Eleutherius, the years indicated for the beginning and end of pontificates are not absolutely certain. Also, up to the middle of the 11th century, there are some doubts about the exact days and months given in chronological tables.
St. Victor I: Africa; 189-199.
St. Zephyrinus: Rome; 199-217.
St. Callistus I: Rome; 217-222.
St. Urban I: Rome; 222-230.
St. Pontian: Rome; July 21, 230 to Sept. 28, 235.
St. Anterus: Greece; Nov. 21, 235 to Jan. 3, 236.
St. Fabian: Rome; Jan. 10, 236 to Jan. 20, 250.
St. Cornelius: Rome; Mar. 251 to June 253.
St. Lucius I: Rome; June 25, 253 to Mar. 5, 254.
St. Stephen I: Rome; May 12, 254 to Aug. 2, 257.
St. Sixtus II: Greece; Aug. 30, 257 to Aug. 6, 258.
St. Dionysius: birthplace unknown; July 22, 259 to

Dec. 26, 268.

St. Felix I: Rome; Jan. 5, 269 to Dec. 30, 274.

St. Eutychian: Luni; Jan. 4, 275 to Dec. 7, 283.

St. Caius: Dalmatia; Dec. 17, 283 to Apr. 22, 296.

St. Marcellinus: Rome; June 30, 296 to Oct. 25, 304.

St. Marcellus I: Rome; May 27, 308, or June 26, 308, to Jan. 16, 309.

St. Eusebius: Greece; Apr. 18, 309 to Aug. 17, 309 or 310.

St. Melchiades (Miltiades): Africa; July 2, 311 to Jan. 11, 314.

St. Sylvester I: Rome; Jan. 31, 314 to Dec. 31, 335. (Most popes before St. Sylvester I were martyrs.)

St. Marcus: Rome; Jan. 18, 336 to Oct. 7, 336.

St. Julius I: Rome; Feb. 6, 337 to Apr. 12, 352.

Liberius: Rome; May 17, 352 to Sept. 24, 366.

St. Damasus I: Spain; Oct. 1, 366 to Dec. 11, 384.

St. Siricius: Rome; Dec. 15, or 22 or 29, 384 to Nov. 26, 399.

St. Anastasius I: Rome; Nov. 27, 399 to Dec. 19, 401.

St. Innocent I: Albano; Dec. 22, 401 to Mar. 12, 417.

St. Zosimus: Greece; Mar. 18, 417 to Dec. 26, 418.

St. Boniface I: Rome; Dec. 28 or 29, 418 to Sept. 4, 422.

St. Celestine I: Campania; Sept. 10, 422 to July 27, 432.

St. Sixtus III: Rome; July 31, 432 to Aug. 19, 440.

St. Leo I (the Great): Tuscany; Sept. 29, 440 to Nov. 10, 461.

St. Hilary: Sardinia; Nov. 19, 461 to Feb. 29, 468.

St. Simplicius: Tivoli; Mar. 3, 468 to Mar. 10, 483.

St. Felix III (II): Rome; Mar. 13, 483 to Mar. 1, 492. He should be called Felix II, and his successors of the same name should be numbered accordingly. The discrepancy in the numerical designation of popes named Felix was caused by the erroneous insertion in some lists of the name of St. Felix of Rome, a martyr.

St. Gelasius I: Africa; Mar. 1, 492 to Nov. 21, 496.

Anastasius II: Rome; Nov. 24, 496 to Nov. 19, 498.

St. Symmachus: Sardinia; Nov. 22, 498 to July 19, 514.

St. Hormisdas: Frosinone; July 20, 514 to Aug. 6, 523.

St. John I, Martyr: Tuscany; Aug. 13, 523 to May 18, 526.

St. Felix IV (III): Samnium; July 12, 526 to Sept. 22, 530.

Boniface II: Rome; Sept. 22, 530 to Oct. 17, 532.

John II: Rome; Jan. 2, 533 to May 8, 535.

John II was the first pope to change his name. His given name was Mercury.

St. Agapitus I: Rome; May 13, 535 to Apr. 22, 536.

St. Silverius, Martyr: Campania; June 1 or 8, 536 to Nov. 11, 537 (d. Dec. 2, 537). St. Silverius was violently deposed in Mar. 537, and abdicated Nov. 11, 537. His successor, Vigilius, was not recognized as pope by all the Roman clergy until his abdication.

Vigilius: Rome; Mar. 29, 537 to June 7, 555.

Pelagius I: Rome; Apr. 16, 556 to Mar. 4, 561.

John III: Rome; July 17, 561 to July 13, 574.

Benedict I: Rome; June 2, 575 to July 30, 579.

Pelagius II: Rome; Nov. 26, 579 to Feb. 7, 590.

St. Gregory I (the Great): Rome; Sept. 3, 590 to Mar. 12, 604.

Sabinian: Blera in Tuscany; Sept. 13, 604 to Feb. 22, 606.

Boniface III: Rome; Feb. 19, 607 to Nov. 12, 607.

St. Boniface IV: Abruzzi; Aug. 25, 608 to May 8, 615.

St. Deusdedit (Adeodatus I): Rome; Oct. 19, 615 to Nov. 8, 618.

Boniface V: Naples; Dec. 23, 619 to Oct. 25, 625.

Honorius I: Campania; Oct. 27, 625 to Oct. 12, 638.

Severinus: Rome; May 28, 640 to Aug. 2, 640.

John IV: Dalmatia; Dec. 24, 640 to Oct. 12, 642.

Theodore I: Greece; Nov. 24, 642 to May 14, 649.

St. Martin I, Martyr: Todi; July 649 to Sept. 16, 655 (in exile from June 17, 653).

St. Eugene I: Rome; Aug. 10, 654 to June 2, 657. St. Eugene I was elected during the exile of St. Martin I, who is believed to have endorsed him as pope.

St. Vitalian: Segni; July 30, 657 to Jan. 27, 672.

Adeodatus II: Rome; Apr. 11, 672 to June 17, 676.

Donus: Rome; Nov. 2, 676 to Apr. 11, 678.

St. Agatho: Sicily; June 27, 678 to Jan. 10, 681.

St. Leo II: Sicily; Aug. 17, 682 to July 3, 683.

St. Benedict II: Rome; June 26, 684 to May 8, 685.

John V: Syria; July 23, 685 to Aug. 2, 686.

Conon: birthplace unknown; Oct. 21, 686 to Sept. 21, 687.

St. Sergius I: Syria; Dec. 15, 687 to Sept. 8, 701.

John VI: Greece; Oct. 30, 701 to Jan. 11, 705.

John VII: Greece; Mar. 1, 705 to Oct. 18, 707.

Sisinnius: Syria; Jan. 15, 708 to Feb. 4, 708.

Constantine: Syria; Mar. 25, 708 to Apr. 9, 715.

St. Gregory II: Rome; May 19, 715 to Feb. 11, 731.

St. Gregory III: Syria; Mar. 18, 731 to Nov. 741.

St. Zachary: Greece; Dec. 10, 741 to Mar. 22, 752.

Stephen II (III): Rome; Mar. 26, 752 to Apr. 26, 757. After the death of St. Zachary, a Roman priest named Stephen was elected but died (four days later) before his consecration as bishop of Rome, which would have marked the beginning of his pontificate. Another Stephen was elected to succeed Zachary as Stephen II. (The first pope with this name was St. Stephen I, 254-57.) The ordinal III appears in parentheses after the name of Stephen II because the name of the earlier elected but deceased priest was included in some lists. Other Stephens have double numbers.

St. Paul I: Rome; Apr. (May 29) 757 to June 28, 767.

Stephen III (IV): Sicily; Aug. 1 (7), 768 to Jan. 24, 772.

Adrian I: Rome; Feb. 1 (9), 772 to Dec. 25, 795.

St. Leo III: Rome; Dec. 26 (27), 795 to June 12, 816.

Stephen IV (V): Rome; June 22, 816 to Jan. 24, 817.

St. Paschal I: Rome; Jan. 25, 817 to Feb. 11, 824.

Eugene II: Rome; Feb. (May) 824 to Aug. 827.

Valentine: Rome; Aug. 827 to Sept. 827.

Gregory IV: Rome; 827 to Jan. 844.

Sergius II: Rome; Jan. 844 to Jan. 27, 847.

St. Leo IV: Rome; Jan. (Apr. 10) 847 to July 17, 855.

Benedict III: Rome; July (Sept. 29), 855,to Apr. 17, 858.

St. Nicholas I (the Great): Rome; Apr. 24, 858 to Nov. 13, 867.

Adrian II: Rome; Dec. 14, 867 to Dec. 14, 872.

John VIII: Rome; Dec. 14, 872 to Dec. 16, 882.

Marinus I: Gallese; Dec. 16, 882 to May 15, 884.

St. Adrian III: Rome; May 17, 884 to Sept. 885. Cult confirmed June 2, 1891.

Stephen V (VI): Rome; Sept. 885 to Sept. 14, 891.

Formosus: Bishop of Porto; Oct. 6, 891 to Apr. 4, 896.

Boniface VI: Rome; Apr. 896 to Apr. 896.

Stephen VI (VII): Rome; May 896 to Aug. 897.

Romanus: Gallese; Aug. 897 to Nov. 897.

Theodore II: Rome; Dec. 897 to Dec. 897.

John IX: Tivoli; Jan. 898 to Jan. 900.

Benedict IV: Rome; Jan. (Feb.) 900 to July 903.

Leo V: Ardea; July 903 to Sept. 903.

Sergius III: Rome; Jan. 29, 904 to Apr. 14, 911.

Anastasius III: Rome; Apr. 911 to June 913.

Landus: Sabina; July 913 to Feb. 914.

John X: Tossignano (Imola); Mar. 914 to May 928.

Leo VI: Rome; May 928 to Dec. 928.

Stephen VII (VIII): Rome; Dec. 928 to Feb. 931.

John XI: Rome; Feb. (Mar.) 931 to Dec. 935.

Leo VII: Rome; Jan. 3, 936 to July 13, 939.

Stephen VIII (IX): Rome; July 14, 939 to Oct. 942.

Marinus II: Rome; Oct. 30, 942 to May 946.

Agapius II: Rome; May 10, 946 to Dec. 955.

John XII (Octavius): Tusculum; Dec. 16, 955 to May 14, 964 (date of his death).

Leo VIII: Rome; Dec. 4 (6), 963 to Mar. 1, 965.

Benedict V: Rome; May 22, 964 to July 4, 966. Confusion exists concerning the legitimacy of claims to the pontificate by Leo VIII and Benedict V. John XII was deposed Dec. 4, 963, by a Roman council. If this deposition was invalid, Leo was an antipope. If the deposition of John was valid, Leo was the legitimate pope and Benedict was an antipope.

John XIII: Rome; Oct. 1, 965 to Sept. 6, 972.

Benedict VI: Rome; Jan. 19, 973 to June 974.

Benedict VII: Rome; Oct. 974 to July 10, 983.

John XIV (Peter Campenora): Pavia; Dec. 983 to Aug. 20, 984.

John XV: Rome; Aug. 985 to Mar. 996.

Gregory V (Bruno of Carinthia): Saxony; May 3, 996, to Feb. 18, 999.

Sylvester II (Gerbert): Auvergne; Apr. 2, 999 to May 12, 1003.

John XVII (Siccone): Rome; June 1003 to Dec. 1003.

John XVIII (Phasianus): Rome; Jan. 1004 to July 1009.

Sergius IV (Peter): Rome; July 31, 1009 to May 12, 1012. The custom of changing one's name on election to the papacy is generally considered to date from the time of Sergius IV. Before his time, several popes had changed their names. After his time, it became a regular practice, with few exceptions, e.g., Adrian VI and Marcellus II.

Benedict VIII (Theophylactus): Tusculum; May 18, 1012 to Apr. 9, 1024.

John XIX (Romanus): Tusculum; Apr. (May) 1024 to 1032.

Benedict IX (Theophylactus): Tusculum; 1032 to 1044.

Sylvester III (John): Rome; Jan. 20, 1045 to Feb. 10, 1045.

Sylvester III was an antipope if the forcible removal of Benedict IX in 1044 was not legitimate.

Benedict IX (second time): Apr. 10, 1045 to May 1, 1045.

Gregory VI (John Gratian): Rome; May 5, 1045 to Dec. 20, 1046.

Clement II (Suitger, Lord of Morsleben and Hornburg): Saxony; Dec. 24 (25), 1046 to Oct. 9, 1047. If the resignation of Benedict IX in 1045 and his removal at the Dec. 1046, synod were not legitimate, Gregory VI and Clement II were antipopes.

Benedict IX (third time): Nov. 8, 1047 to July 17, 1048 (d. c. 1055).

Damasus II (Poppo): Bavaria; July 17, 1048 to Aug. 9, 1048.

St. Leo IX (Bruno): Alsace; Feb. 12, 1049 to Apr. 19, 1054.

Victor II (Gebhard): Swabia; Apr. 16, 1055 to July 28, 1057.

Stephen IX (X) (Frederick): Lorraine; Aug. 3, 1057 to Mar. 29, 1058.

Nicholas II (Gerard): Burgundy; Jan. 24, 1059 to July 27, 1061.

Alexander II (Anselmo da Baggio): Milan; Oct. 1, 1061 to Apr. 21, 1073.

St. Gregory VII (Hildebrand): Tuscany; Apr. 22 (June 30), 1073 to May 25, 1085.

Bl. Victor III (Dauferius; Desiderius): Benevento; May 24, 1086 to Sept. 16, 1087. Cult confirmed July 23, 1887.

Bl. Urban II (Otto di Lagery): France; Mar. 12, 1088, to July 29, 1099. Cult confirmed July 14, 1881.

Paschal II (Raniero): Ravenna; Aug. 13 (14), 1099 to Jan. 21, 1118.

Gelasius II (Giovanni Caetani): Gaeta; Jan. 24 (Mar. 10), 1118 to Jan. 28, 1119.

Callistus II (Guido of Burgundy): Burgundy; Feb. 2 (9), 1119 to Dec. 13, 1124.

Honorius II (Lamberto): Fiagnano (Imola); Dec. 15 (21), 1124 to Feb. 13, 1130.

Innocent II (Gregorio Papareschi): Rome; Feb. 14 (23), 1130 to Sept. 24, 1143.

Celestine II (Guido): Citta di Castello; Sept. 26 (Oct. 3), 1143 to Mar. 8, 1144.

Lucius II (Gerardo Caccianemici): Bologna: Mar. 12, 1144 to Feb. 15, 1145.

Bl. Eugene III (Bernardo Paganelli di Montemagno): Pisa; Feb. 15 (18), 1145 to July 8, 1153. Cult confirmed Oct. 3, 1872.

Anastasius IV (Corrado): Rome; July 12, 1153 to Dec, 3, 1154.

Adrian IV (Nicholas Breakspear): England; Dec. 4 (5), 1154 to Sept. 1, 1159.

Alexander III (Rolando Bandinelli): Siena; Sept. 7 (20), 1159 to Aug. 30, 1181.

Lucius III (Ubaldo Allucingoli): Lucca; Sept. 1 (6), 1181 to Sept. 25, 1185.

Urban III (Uberto Crivelli): Milan; Nov. 25 (Dec. 1), 1185 to Oct. 20, 1187.

Gregory VIII (Alberto de Morra): Benevento; Oct. 21 (25), 1187 to Dec. 17, 1187.

Clement III (Paolo Scolari): Rome; Dec. 19 (20), 1187 to Mar. 1191.

Celestine III (Giacinto Bobone): Rome; Mar. 30 (Apr. 14), 1191 to Jan. 8, 1198.

Innocent III (Lotario dei Conti di Segni): Anagni; Jan. 8 (Feb. 22), 1198 to July 16, 1216.

Honorius III (Cencio Savelli): Rome; July 18 (24), 1216 to Mar. 18, 1227.

Gregory IX (Ugolino, Count of Segni): Anagni; Mar. 19 (21), 1227 to Aug. 22, 1241.

Celestine IV (Goffredo Castiglioni): Milan; Oct. 25 (28), 1241 to Nov. 10, 1241.

Innocent IV (Sinibaldo Fieschi): Genoa; June 25 (28), 1243 to Dec. 7, 1254.

Alexander IV (Rinaldo, House of Ienne): Ienne (Rome); Dec. 12 (20), 1254 to May 25, 1261.

Urban IV (Jacques Pantal,on): Troyes; Aug. 29 (Sept. 4), 1261 to Oct. 2, 1264.

Clement IV (Guy Foulques or Guido le Gros): France; Feb. 5 (15), 1265 to Nov. 29, 1268.

Bl. Gregory X (Teobaldo Visconti): Piacenza; Sept. 1, 1271 (Mar. 27, 1272) to Jan. 10, 1276. Cult confirmed Sept. 12, 1713.

Bl. Innocent V (Peter of Tarentaise): Savoy; Jan. 21 (Feb. 22), 1276 to June 22, 1276. Cult confirmed Mar. 13, 1898.

Adrian V (Ottobono Fieschi): Genoa: July 11, 1276 to Aug. 18, 1276.

John XXI (Petrus Juliani or Petrus Hispanus): Portugal; Sept. 8 (20), 1276 to May 20, 1277. There is confusion in the numerical designation of popes named John. The error dates back to the time of John XV.

Nicholas III (Giovanni Gaetano Orsini): Rome; Nov. 25 (Dec. 26), 1277 to Aug. 22, 1280.

Martin IV (Simon de Brie): France; Feb. 22 (Mar. 23), 1281 to Mar. 28, 1285.

The names of Marinus 1 (882-84) and Marinus II (942-46) were construed as Martin. In view of these two pontificates and the earlier reign of St. Martin I (649-55), this pope was called Martin IV.

Honorius IV (Giacomo Savelli): Rome; Apr. 2 (May 20), 1285 to Apr. 3, 1287.

Nicholas IV (Girolamo Masci): Ascoli; Feb. 22, 1288, to Apr. 4, 1292.

St. Celestine V (Pietro del Murrone): Isernia; July 5 (Aug. 29), 1294 to Dec. 13, 1294; d. May 19, 1296. Canonized May 5, 1313.

Boniface VIII (Benedetto Caetani): Anagni; Dec. 24, 1294 (Jan. 23, 1295) to Oct. 11, 1303.

Bl. Benedict XI (Niccolo Boccasini): Treviso; Oct. 22 (27), 1303 to July 7, 1304. Cult confirmed Apr. 24, 1736.

Clen t V (Bertrand de Got): France; June 5 (Nov. 14), 1305 to Apr. 20, 1314. First of Avignon popes.

John XXII (Jacques d'Euse): Cahors; Aug. 7 (Sept. 5), 1316 to Dec. 4, 1334.

Benedict XII (Jacques Fournier): France; Dec. 20, 1334 (Jan. 8, 1335) to Apr. 25, 1342.

Clement VI (Pierre Roger): France; May 7 (19), 1342, to Dec. 6, 1352.

Innocent VI (Etienne Aubert): France; Dec. 18 (30), 1352 to Sept. 12, 1362.

Bl. Urban V (Guillaume de Grimoard): France; Sept. 28 (Nov. 6), 1362 to Dec. 19, 1370. Cult confirmed Mar. 10, 1870.

Gregory XI (Pierre Roger de Beaufort): France; Dec. 30, 1370 (Jan. 5, 1371) to Mar. 26, 1378. Last of Avignon popes.

Urban VI (Bartolomeo Prignano): Naples; Apr. 8 (18), 1378 to Oct. 15, 1389.

Boniface IX (Pietro Tomacelli): Naples; Nov. 2 (9), 1389 to Oct. 1, 1404.

Innocent VII (Cosma Migliorati): Sulmona; Oct. 17 (Nov. 11), 1404 to Nov. 6, 1406.

Gregory XII (Angelo Correr): Venice; Nov. 30 (Dec. 19), 1406 to July 4, 1415, when he voluntarily resigned from the papacy to permit the election of his successor. He died Oct. 18, 1417. (See Western Schism.)

Martin V (Oddone Colonna): Rome; Nov. 11 (21), 1417 to Feb. 20, 1431.

Eugene IV (Gabriele Condulmer): Venice; Mar. 3 (11), 1431 to Feb. 23, 1447.

Nicholas V (Tommaso Parentucelli): Sarzana; Mar. 6 (19), 1447 to Mar. 24, 1455.

Callistus III (Alfonso Borgia): Jativa (Valencia); Apr. 8 (20), 1455 to Aug. 6, 1458.

Pius II (Enea Silvio Piccolomini): Siena; Aug. 19 (Sept. 3), 1458 to Aug. 14, 1464.

Paul II (Pietro Barbo): Venice; Aug. 30 (Sept. 16), 1464 to July 26, 1471.

Sixtus IV (Francesco della Rovere): Savona; Aug. 9 (25), 1471 to Aug. 12, 1484.

Innocent VIII (Giovanni Battista Cibo): Genoa; Aug. 29 (Sept. 12), 1484 to July 25, 1492.

Alexander VI (Rodrigo Borgia): Jativa (Valencia); Aug. 11 (26), 1492 to Aug. 18, 1503.

Pius III (Francesco Todeschini-Piccolomini): Siena; Sept. 22 (Oct. 1, 8), 1503 to Oct. 18, 1503.

Julius II (Giuliano della Rovere): Savona; Oct. 31 (Nov. 26), 1503 to Feb. 21, 1513.

Leo X (Giovanni de' Medici): Florence; Mar. 9 (19), 1513 to Dec. 1, 1521.

Adrian VI (Adrian Florensz): Utrecht; Jan. 9 (Aug. 31), 1522 to Sept. 14, 1523.

Clement VII (Giulio de' Medici): Florence; Nov. 19 (26), 1523 to Sept. 25, 1534.

Paul III (Alessandro Farnese): Rome; Oct. 13 (Nov. 3), 1534 to Nov. 10, 1549.

Julius III (Giovanni Maria Ciocchi del Monte): Rome; Feb. 7 (22), 1550 to Mar. 23, 1555.

Marcellus II (Marcello Cervini): Montepulciano; Apr. 9 (10), 1555 to May 1, 1555.

Paul IV (Gian Pietro Carafa): Naples; May 23 (26), 1555 to Aug. 18, 1559.

Pius IV (Giovan Angelo de' Medici): Milan; Dec. 25, 1559 (Jan. 6, 1560) to Dec. 9, 1565.

St. Pius V (Antonio-Michele Ghislieri): Bosco (Alexandria); Jan. 7 (17), 1566 to May 1, 1572. Canonized May 22, 1712.

Gregory XIII (Ugo Buoncompagni): Bologna; May 13 (25), 1572 to Apr. 10, 1585.

Sixtus V (Felice Peretti): Grottammare (Ripa-transone); Apr. 24 (May 1), 1585 to Aug. 27, 1590.

Urban VII (Giambattista Castagna): Rome; Sept. 15, 1590 to Sept. 27, 1590.

Gregory XIV (Niccolo Sfondrati): Cremona; Dec. 5 (8), 1590 to Oct. 16, 1591.

Innocent IX (Giovanni Antonio Facchinetti): Bologna; Oct. 29 (Nov. 3), 1591 to Dec. 30, 1591.

Clement VIII (Ippolito Aldobrandini): Florence; Jan. 30 (Feb. 9), 1592 to Mar. 3, 1605.

Leo XI (Alessandro de' Medici): Florence; Apr. 1 (10), 1605 to Apr. 27, 1605.

Paul V (Camillo Borghese): Rome; May 16 (29), 1605, to Jan. 28, 1621.

Gregory XV (Alessandro Ludovisi): Bologna; Feb. 9 (14), 1621 to July 8, 1623.

Urban VIII (Maffeo Barberini): Florence; Aug. 6 (Sept. 29), 1623 to July 29, 1644.

Innocent X (Giovanni Battista Pamfili): Rome; Sept. 15 (Oct. 4), 1644 to Jan. 7, 1655.

Alexander VII (Fabio Chigi): Siena; Apr. 7 (18), 1655, to May 22, 1667.

Clement IX (Giulio Rospigliosi): Pistoia; June 20 (26), 1667 to Dec. 9, 1669.

Clement X (Emilio Altieri): Rome; Apr. 29 (May 11),

1670 to July 22, 1676.

Bl. Innocent XI (Benedetto Odescalchi): Como; Sept. 21 (Oct. 4), 1676 to Aug. 12, 1689. Beatified Oct. 7, 1956.

Alexander VIII (Pietro Ottoboni): Venice; Oct. 6 (16), 1689 to Feb. 1, 1691.

Innocent XII (Antonio Pignatelli): Spinazzola (Venosa); July 12 (15), 1691 to Sept. 27, 1700.

Clement XI (Giovanni Francesco Albani): Urbino; Nov. 23, 30 (Dec. 8), 1700 to Mar. 19, 1721.

Innocent XIII (Michelangelo dei Conti): Rome; May 8 (18), 1721 to Mar. 7, 1724.

Benedict XIII (Pietro Francesco Vincenzo Maria Orsini): Gravina (Bari); May 29 (June 4), 1724 to Feb. 21, 1730.

Clement XII (Lorenzo Corsini): Florence; July 12 (16), 1730 to Feb. 6, 1740.

Benedict XIV (Prospero Lambertini): Bologna; Aug. 17 (22), 1740 to May 3, 1758.

Clement XIII (Carlo Rezzonico): Venice; July 6 (16), 1758 to Feb. 2, 1769.

Clement XIV (Giovanni Vincenzo Antonio Lorenzo Ganganelli): Rimini; May 19, 28 (June 4), 1769 to Sept. 22, 1774.

Pius VI (Giovanni Angelo Braschi): Cesena; Feb. 15 (22), 1775 to Aug. 29, 1799.

Pius VII (Barnaba Gregorio Chiaramonti): Cesena; Mar. 14 (21), 1800 to Aug. 20, 1823.

Leo XII (Annibale della Genga): Genga (Fabriano); Sept. 28 (Oct. 5), 1823 to Feb. 10, 1829.

Pius VIII (Francesco Saverio Castiglioni): Cingoli; Mar. 31 (Apr. 5), 1829 to Nov. 30, 1830.

Gregory XVI (Bartolomeo Alberto-Mauro-Cappellari): Belluno; Feb. 2 (6), 1831 to June 1, 1846.

Bl. Pius IX (Giovanni M. Mastai-Ferretti): Senigallia; June 16 (21), 1846 to Feb. 7, 1878.

Leo XIII (Gioacchino Pecci): Carpineto (Anagni); Feb. 20 (Mar. 3), 1878 to July 20, 1903.

St. Pius X (Giuseppe Sarto): Riese (Treviso); Aug. 4 (9), 1903 to Aug. 20, 1914. Canonized May 29, 1954.

Benedict XV (Giacomo della Chiesa): Genoa; Sept. 3 (6), 1914 to Jan. 22, 1922.

Pius XI (Achille Ratti): Desio (Milan); Feb. 6 (12), 1922 to Feb. 10, 1939.

Pius XII (Eugenio Pacelli): Rome; Mar. 2 (12), 1939, to Oct. 9, 1958.

Bl. John XXIII (Angelo Giuseppe Roncalli): Sotto il Monte (Bergamo); Oct. 28 (Nov. 4), 1958 to June 3, 1963.

Paul VI (Giovanni Battista Montini): Concessio (Brescia); June 21 (30), 1963 to Aug. 6, 1978.

John Paul I (Albino Luciani): Forno di Canale (Belluno); Aug. 26 (Sept. 3), 1978 to Sept. 28, 1978.

John Paul II (Karol Wojtyla): Wadowice, Poland; Oct. 16 (22), 1978 to Apr. 2, 2005.

Benedict XVI (Joseph Ratzinger): Marktl Am Inn, Germany; Apr. 19 (24), 2005.

ANTIPOPES

This list of men who claimed or exercised the papal office in an uncanonical manner includes names, birthplaces and dates of alleged reigns. *Source:* Annuario Pontificio.

St. Hippolytus: Rome; 217-235; was reconciled before his death.

Novatian: Rome; 251.

Felix II: Rome; 355 to Nov. 22, 365.

Ursinus: 366-367.

Eulalius: Dec. 27 or 29, 418 to 419.

Lawrence: 498; 501-505.

Dioscorus: Alexandria; Sept. 22, 530 to Oct. 14, 530.

Theodore: ended alleged reign, 687.

Paschal: ended alleged reign, 687.

Constantine: Nepi; June 28 (July 5), 767 to 769.

Philip: July 31, 768; retired to his monastery on the same day.

John: ended alleged reign, Jan. 844.

Anastasius: Aug. 855 to Sept. 855; d. 880.

Christopher: Rome; July or Sept. 903 to Jan. 904.

Boniface VII: Rome; June 974 to July 974; Aug. 984 to July 985.

John XVI: Rossano; Apr. 997 to Feb. 998.

Gregory: ended alleged reign, 1012.

Benedict X: Rome; Apr. 5, 1058 to Jan. 24, 1059.

Honorius II: Verona; Oct. 28, 1061 to 1072.

Clement III: Parma; June 25, 1080 (Mar. 24, 1084) to Sept. 8, 1100.

Theodoric: ended alleged reign, 1100; d. 1102.

Albert: ended alleged reign, 1102.

Sylvester IV: Rome; Nov. 18, 1105 to 1111.

Gregory VIII: France; Mar. 8, 1118 to 1121.

Celestine II: Rome; ended alleged reign, Dec. 1124.

Anacletus II: Rome; Feb. 14 (23), 1130 to Jan. 25, 1138.

Victor IV: Mar. 1138 to May 29, 1138; submitted to Pope Innocent II.

Victor IV: Montecelio; Sept. 7 (Oct. 4), 1159 to Apr. 20, 1164; he did not recognize his predecessor (Victor IV, above).

Paschal III: Apr. 22 (26), 1164 to Sept. 20, 1168.

Callistus III: Arezzo; Sept. 1168 to Aug. 29, 1178; submitted to Pope Alexander III.

Innocent III: Sezze; Sept. 29, 1179 to 1180.

Nicholas V: Corvaro (Rieti); May 12 (22), 1328 to Aug. 25, 1330; d. Oct. 16, 1333.

Four antipopes of the Western Schism:

Clement VII: Sept. 20 (Oct. 31), 1378 to Sept. 16, 1394.

Benedict XIII: Aragon; Sept. 28 (Oct. 11), 1394 to May 23, 1423.

Alexander V: Crete; June 26 (July 7), 1409 to May 3, 1410.

John XXIII: Naples; May 17 (25), 1410 to May 29, 1415 (date of deposition by Council of Constance which ended the Western Schism); d. Nov. 22, 1419.

Felix V: Savoy; Nov. 5, 1439 (July 24, 1440) to Apr. 7, 1449; d. 1451.

AVIGNON PAPACY

Avignon was the residence (1309-77) of a series of French popes (Clement V, John XXII, Benedict XII, Clement VI, Innocent VI, Urban V and Gregory XI). Prominent in the period were power struggles over the mixed interests of Church and state with the rulers of France (Philip IV, John II), Bavaria (Lewis IV), England (Edward III); factionalism of French and Italian churchmen; political as well as ecclesiastical turmoil in Italy, a factor of significance in prolonging the stay of popes in Avignon. Despite some positive achievements, the Avignon papacy was a prologue to the Western Schism that began in 1378.

GREAT WESTERN SCHISM

The Great Western Schism was a confused state of affairs that divided Christendom into two and then three papal obediences from 1378 to 1417.

It occurred some 50 years after Marsilius theorized that a general (not ecumenical) council of bishops and other persons was superior to a pope and nearly 30 years before the Council of Florence stated definitively that no kind of council had such authority.

It was a period of disaster preceding the even more disastrous period of the Reformation.

Urban VI, following the return of the papal residence to Rome after approximately 70 years at Avignon, was elected pope Apr. 8, 1378, and reigned until his death in 1389. He was succeeded by Boniface IX (1389-1404), Innocent VII (1404-1406), and Gregory XII (1406-1415). These four are considered the legitimate popes of the period.

Some of the cardinals who chose Urban pope, dissatisfied with his conduct of the office, declared that his election was invalid. They proceeded to elect Clement VII, who claimed the papacy from 1378 to 1394. He was succeeded by Benedict XIII.

Prelates seeking to end the state of divided papal loyalties convoked the Council of Pisa (1409) which, without authority, found Gregory XII and Benedict XIII guilty in absentia on 30-odd charges of schism and heresy, deposed them, and elected a third claimant to the papacy, Alexander V (1409-1410). He was succeeded by John XXIII (1410-1415).

The schism was ended by the Council of Constance (1414-1418). Although originally called into session in an irregular manner, the council, acquired authority after being convoked by Gregory XII in 1415. In its early irregular phase, it deposed John XXIII whose election to the papacy was uncanonical anyway. After being formally convoked, it accepted the abdication of Gregory in 1415 and dismissed the claims of Benedict XIII two years later, thus clearing the way for the election of Martin V on Nov. 11, 1417. The Council of Constance also rejected the theories of John Wycliff and condemned John Hus as a heretic.

POPES OF THE TWENTIETH CENTURY

LEO XIII

Leo XIII (Gioacchino Vincenzo Pecci) was born May 2, 1810, in Carpineto, Italy. Although all but three years of his life and pontificate were in the 19th century, his influence extended well into the 20th century.

He was educated at the Jesuit college in Viterbo, the Roman College, the Academy of Noble Ecclesiastics, and the University of the Sapienza. He was ordained to the priesthood in 1837.

He served as an apostolic delegate to two States of the Church, Benevento from 1838 to 1841 and Perugia in 1841 and 1842. Ordained titular archbishop of Damietta, he was papal nuncio to Belgium from Jan. 1843 until May 1846; in the post, he had controversial relations with the government over education issues and acquired his first significant experience of industrialized society.

He was archbishop of Perugia from 1846 to 1878. He became a cardinal in 1853 and chamberlain of the Roman Curia in 1877. He was elected to the papacy Feb. 20, 1878. He died July 20, 1903.

Canonizations: He canonized 18 saints and beatified a group of English martyrs.

Church Administration: He established 300 new dioceses and vicariates; restored the hierarchy in Scotland and set up an English, as contrasted with the Portuguese, hierarchy in India; approved the action of the Congregation for the Propagation of the Faith in reorganizing missions in China.

Encyclicals: He issued 86 encyclicals, on subjects ranging from devotional to social. In the former category were *Annum Sacrum*, on the Sacred Heart, in 1899, and 11 letters on Mary and the Rosary.

Social Questions: Much of Leo's influence stemmed from social doctrine stated in numerous encyclicals, concerning liberalism, liberty, the divine origin of authority; socialism, in *Quod Apostolici Muneris*, 1878; the Christian concept of the family, in *Arcanum*, 1880; socialism and economic liberalism, relations between capital and labor, in *Rerum Novarum*, 1891. Two of his social encyclicals were against the African slave trade.

Interfaith Relations: He was unsuccessful in unity overtures made to Orthodox and Slavic Churches. He declared Anglican orders invalid in the apostolic bull *Apostolicae Curae* Sept. 13, 1896.

International Relations: Leo was frustrated in seeking solutions to the Roman Question arising from the seizure of church lands by the Kingdom of Italy in 1870. He also faced anticlerical situations in Belgium and France and in the *Kulturkampf* policies of Bismarck in Germany.

Scholarship: In the encyclical *Aeterni Patris* of Aug. 4, 1879, he ordered a renewal of philosophical and theological studies in seminaries along scholastic, and especially Thomistic, lines, to counteract influential trends of liberalism and Modernism. He issued guidelines for biblical exegesis in *Providentissimus Deus* Nov. 18, 1893, and established the Pontifical Biblical Commission in 1902.

In other actions affecting scholarship and study, he opened the Vatican Archives to scholars in 1883 and established the Vatican Observatory.

United States: He authorized establishment of the apostolic delegation in Washington, DC, Jan. 24, 1893. He refused to issue a condemnation of the Knights of Labor. With a document entitled *Testem Benevolentiae*, he eased resolution of questions concerning what was called an American heresy in 1899.

ST. PIUS X

St. Pius X (Giuseppe Melchiorre Sarto) was born in 1835 in Riese, Italy. Educated at the college of Castelfranco and the seminary at Padua, he was ordained to the priesthood Sept. 18, 1858. He served as a curate in Trombolo for nine years before beginning an eight-year pastorate at Salzano. He was chancellor of the Treviso diocese from Nov. 1875, and bishop of Mantua from 1884 until 1893. He was cardinal-patriarch of Venice from that year until his election to the papacy by the conclave held from July 31 to Aug. 4, 1903.

Aims: Pius's principal objectives as pope were "to restore all things in Christ, in order that Christ may be all and in all," and "to teach (and defend) Christian truth and law."

Canonizations, Encyclicals: He canonized four saints and issued 16 encyclicals. One of the encyclicals was issued in commemoration of the 50th anniversary of the proclamation of the dogma of the Immaculate Conception of Mary.

Catechetics: He introduced a whole new era of religious instruction and formation with the encyclical *Acerbo Nimis* of Apr. 15, 1905, in which he called for vigor in establishing and conducting parochial programs of the Confraternity of Christian Doctrine.

Catholic Action: He outlined the role of official Catholic Action in two encyclicals in 1905 and 1906. Favoring organized action by Catholics themselves, he had serious reservations about interconfessional collaboration.

He stoutly maintained claims to papal rights in the anticlerical climate of Italy. He authorized bishops to relax prohibitions against participation by Catholics in some Italian elections.

Church Administration: With the *motu proprio Arduum Sane* of Mar. 19, 1904, he inaugurated the work that resulted in the Code of Canon Law; the code was completed in 1917 and went into effect in the following year. He reorganized and strengthened the Roman Curia with the apostolic constitution *Sapienti Consilio* of June 29, 1908.

While promoting the expansion of missionary work, he removed from the jurisdiction of the Congregation for the Propagation of the Faith the Church in the United States, Canada, Newfoundland, England, Ireland, Holland and Luxembourg.

International Relations: He ended traditional prerogatives of Catholic governments with respect to papal elections, in 1904. He opposed anti-Church and anticlerical actions in several countries: Bolivia in 1905, because of anti-religious legislation; France in 1906, for its 1901 action in annulling its concordat with the Holy See, and for the 1905 Law of Separation by which it decreed separation of Church and state, ordered the confiscation of church property, and blocked religious education and the activities of religious orders; Portugal in 1911, for the separation of Church and state and repressive measures that resulted in persecution later.

In 1912 he called on the bishops of Brazil to work for the improvement of conditions among Indians.

Liturgy: "The Pope of the Eucharist," he strongly recommended the frequent reception of Holy Communion in a decree dated Dec. 20, 1905; in another decree, *Quam Singulari*, of Aug. 8, 1910, he called for the early reception of the sacrament by children. He initiated measures for liturgical reform with new norms for sacred music and the start of work on revision of the Breviary for recitation of the Divine Office.

Modernism: Pius was a vigorous opponent of "the synthesis of all heresies," which threatened the integrity of doctrine through its influence in philosophy, theology and biblical exegesis. In opposition, he condemned 65 of its propositions as erroneous in the decree *Lamentabili*, July 3, 1907; issued the encyclical *Pascendi* in the same vein, Sept. 8, 1907; backed both of these with censures; and published the Oath against Modernism in Sept. 1910, to be taken by all the clergy. Ecclesiastical studies suffered to some extent from

these actions, necessary as they were at the time.

Pius followed the lead of Leo XIII in promoting the study of scholastic philosophy. He established the Pontifical Biblical Institute May 7, 1909.

His death, Aug. 20, 1914, was hastened by the outbreak of World War I. He was beatified in 1951 and canonized May 29, 1954. His feast is observed Aug. 21.

BENEDICT XV

Benedict XV (Giacomo della Chiesa) was born Nov. 21, 1854, in Pegli, Italy.

He was educated at the Royal University of Genoa and Gregorian University in Rome. He was ordained to the priesthood Dec. 21, 1878.

He served in the papal diplomatic corps from 1882 to 1907, as secretary to the nuncio to Spain from 1882 to 1887, as secretary to the papal secretary of state from 1887, and as undersecretary from 1901.

He was ordained archbishop of Bologna Dec. 22, 1907, and spent four years completing a pastoral visitation there. He was made a cardinal just three months before being elected to the papacy Sept. 3, 1914. He died Jan. 22, 1922. Two key efforts of his pontificate were for peace and the relief of human suffering caused by World War I.

Canonizations: Benedict canonized three saints; one of them was Joan of Arc.

Canon Law: He published the Code of Canon Law, developed by the commission set up by St. Pius X, May 27, 1917; it went into effect the following year.

Curia: He made great changes in the personnel of the Curia. He established the Congregation for the Oriental Churches May 1, 1917, and founded the Pontifical Oriental Institute in Rome later in the year.

Encyclicals: He issued 12 encyclicals. Peace was the theme of three of them. In another, published two years after the cessation of hostilities, he wrote about child victims of the war. He followed the lead of Leo XIII in *Spiritus Paraclitus*, Sept. 15, 1920, on biblical studies.

International Relations: He was largely frustrated on the international level because of the events and attitudes of the war period, but the number of diplomats accredited to the Vatican nearly doubled, from 14 to 26, between the time of his accession to the papacy and his death.

Peace Efforts: Benedict's stance in the war was one of absolute impartiality but not of uninterested neutrality. Because he would not take sides, he was suspected by both the Allies and the Central Powers, and the seven-point peace plan he offered to all belligerents, Aug. 1, 1917, was turned down. The points of the plan were: recognition of the moral force of right; disarmament; acceptance of arbitration in cases of dispute; guarantee of freedom of the seas; renunciation of war indemnities; evacuation and restoration of occupied territories; examination of territorial claims in dispute.

Relief Efforts: Benedict assumed personal charge of Vatican relief efforts during the war. He set up an international missing persons bureau for contacts between prisoners and their families, but was forced to close it because of the suspicion of warring nations that it was a front for espionage operations. He persuaded the Swiss government to admit into the country military victims of tuberculosis.

Roman Question: Benedict prepared the way for the

meetings and negotiations which led to settlement of the question in 1929.

PIUS XI

Pius XI (Ambrogio Damiano Achille Ratti) was born May 31, 1857, in Desio, Italy.

Educated at seminaries in Seviso and Milan, and at the Lombard College, Gregorian University and Academy of St. Thomas in Rome. He was ordained to the priesthood in 1879.

He taught at the major seminary of Milan from 1882 to 1888. Appointed to the staff of the Ambrosian Library in 1888, he remained there until 1911, acquiring a reputation for publishing works on paleography and serving as director from 1907 to 1911. He then moved to the Vatican Library, of which he was prefect from 1914 to 1918. In 1919, he was named apostolic visitor to Poland in Apr. nuncio in June, and was made titular archbishop of Lepanto Oct. 28. He was made archbishop of Milan and cardinal June 13, 1921, before being elected to the papacy Feb. 6, 1922. He died Feb. 10, 1939.

Aims: The objective of his pontificate, as stated in the encyclical *Ubi Arcano*, Dec. 23, 1922, was to establish the reign and peace of Christ in society.

Canonizations: He canonized 34 saints, including the Jesuit Martyrs of North America, and conferred the title of Doctor of the Church on Sts. Peter Canisius, John of the Cross, Robert Bellarmine and Albertus Magnus.

Eastern Churches: He called for better understanding of the Eastern Churches in the encyclical *Rerum Orientalium* of Sept. 8, 1928, and developed facilities for the training of Eastern-Rite priests. He inaugurated steps for the codification of Eastern Church law in 1929. In 1935 he made Syrian Patriarch Tappouni a cardinal.

Encyclicals: His first encyclical, *Ubi Arcano*, in addition to stating the aims of his pontificate, blueprinted Catholic Action and called for its development throughout the Church. In *Quas Primas*, Dec. 11, 1925, he established the feast of Christ the King for universal observance. Subjects of some of his other encyclicals were: Christian education, in *Rappresentanti in Terra*, Dec. 31, 1929; Christian marriage, in *Casti Connubii*, Dec. 31, 1930; social conditions and pressure for social change in line with the teaching in *Rerum Novarum*, in *Quadragesimo Anno*, May 15, 1931; atheistic Communism, in *Divini Redemptoris*, Mar. 19, 1937; the priesthood, in *Ad Catholici Sacerdotii*, Dec. 20, 1935.

Missions: Following the lead of Benedict XV, Pius called for the training of native clergy in the pattern of their own respective cultures, and promoted missionary developments in various ways. He ordained six native bishops for China in 1926, one for Japan in 1927, and others for regions of Asia, China and India in 1933. He placed the first 40 mission dioceses under native bishops, saw the number of native priests increase from about 2,600 to more than 7,000, and the number of Catholics in missionary areas more than double from nine million.

In the apostolic constitution *Deus Scientiarum Dominus* of May 24, 1931, he ordered the introduction of missiology into theology courses.

Interfaith Relations: Pius was negative to the ecumenical movement among Protestants but approved the Malines Conversations, 1921 to 1926, between Anglicans and Catholics.

International Relations: Relations with the Mussolini government deteriorated from 1931 on, as indicated in the encyclical *Non Abbiamo Bisogno*, when the regime took steps to curb liberties and activities of the Church; they turned critical in 1938 with the emergence of racist policies. Relations deteriorated in Germany also from 1933 on, resulting finally in condemnation of the Nazis in the encyclical *Mit Brennender Sorge*, March, 1937. Pius sparked a revival of the Church in France by encouraging Catholics to work within the democratic framework of the Republic rather than foment trouble over restoration of a monarchy. Pius was powerless to influence developments related to the civil war that erupted in Spain in July 1936, sporadic persecution and repression by the Calles regime in Mexico, and systematic persecution of the Church in the Soviet Union. Many of the 10 concordats and two agreements reached with European countries after World War I became casualties of World War II.

Roman Question: Pius negotiated for two and a half years with the Italian government to settle the Roman Question by means of the Lateran Agreement of 1929. The agreement provided independent status for the State of Vatican City; made Catholicism the official religion of Italy, with pastoral and educational freedom and state recognition of Catholic marriages, religious orders and societies; and provided a financial payment to the Vatican for expropriation of the former States of the Church.

PIUS XII

Pius XII (Eugenio Maria Giovanni Pacelli) was born Mar. 2, 1876, in Rome.

Educated at the Gregorian University and the Lateran University, in Rome, he was ordained to the priesthood Apr. 2, 1899.

He entered the Vatican diplomatic service in 1901, worked on the codification of canon law, and was appointed secretary of the Congregation for Ecclesiastical Affairs in 1914. Three years later he was ordained titular archbishop of Sardis and made apostolic nuncio to Bavaria. He was nuncio to Germany from 1920 to 1929, when he was made a cardinal, and took office as papal secretary of state in the following year. His diplomatic negotiations resulted in concordats between the Vatican and Bavaria (1924), Prussia (1929), Baden (1932), Austria and the German Republic (1933). He took part in negotiations that led to settlement of the Roman Question in 1929.

He was elected to the papacy Mar. 2, 1939. He died Oct. 9, 1958, at Castel Gandolfo after the 12th longest pontificate in history.

Canonizations: He canonized 34 saints, including Mother Frances X. Cabrini, the first U.S. citizen-saint.

Cardinals: He raised 56 prelates to the rank of cardinal in two consistories held in 1946 and 1953. There were 57 cardinals at the time of his death.

Church Organization and Missions: He increased the number of dioceses from 1,696 to 2,048. He established native hierarchies in China (1946), Burma (1955) and parts of Africa, and extended the native structure of the Church in India. He ordained the first black bishop for Africa.

Communism: In addition to opposing and condemn-

242   POPES OF THE TWENTIETH CENTURY

ing Communism on numerous occasions, he decreed
in 1949 the penalty of excommunication for all
Catholics holding formal and willing allegiance to the
Communist Party and its policies. During his reign the
Church was persecuted in some 15 countries that fell
under communist domination.

Doctrine and Liturgy: He proclaimed the dogma of
the Assumption of the Blessed Virgin Mary, Nov. 1,
1950 (apostolic constitution, *Munificentissimus Deus*).

In various encyclicals and other enactments, he provided background for the *aggiornamento* introduced
by his successor, John XXIII: by his formulations of
doctrine and practice regarding the Mystical Body of
Christ, the liturgy, sacred music and biblical studies;
by the revision of the Rites of Holy Week; by initiation
of the work which led to the calendar-missal-breviary
reform ordered into effect Jan. 1, 1961; by the first of
several modifications of the Eucharistic fast; by
extending the time of Mass to the evening. He instituted the feasts of Mary, Queen, and of St. Joseph the
Worker, and clarified teaching concerning devotion to
the Sacred Heart.

His 41 encyclicals and nearly 1,000 public addresses
made Pius one of the greatest teaching popes. His concern in all his communications was to deal with specific points at issue and to bring Christian principles to
bear on contemporary world problems.

Peace Efforts: Before the start of World War II, he
tried unsuccessfully to get the contending nations —
Germany and Poland, France and Italy — to settle their
differences peaceably. During the war, he offered his
services to mediate the widened conflict, spoke out
against the horrors of war and the suffering it caused,
mobilized relief work for its victims, proposed a five-
point program for peace in Christmas messages from
1939 to 1942, and secured a generally open status for
the city of Rome. He has been criticized in some quarters for not doing enough to oppose the Holocaust.
This is a matter of historical debate, but it is a fact that
through his direct intercession many thousands of Jews
in Rome and Italy were saved from certain death, and
he resisted wherever possible the threat of Nazism to
human rights. Such were his contributions to assisting
Jews that the rabbi of Rome, Dr. Abraham Zolli, was
converted to Catholicism, and upon his death, Pius was
praised by Golda Meir for his efforts. After the war, he
endorsed the principles and intent of the U.N. and continued efforts for peace.

United States: Pius appointed more than 200 of the
265 American bishops resident in the U.S. and abroad
in 1958, erected 27 dioceses in this country, and raised
seven dioceses to archiepiscopal rank.

BL. JOHN XXIII

John XXIII (Angelo Roncalli) was born Nov. 25,
1881, at Sotto il Monte, Italy.

He was educated at the seminary of the Bergamo diocese and the Pontifical Seminary in Rome, where he
was ordained to the priesthood Aug. 10, 1904.

He spent the first nine or 10 years of his priesthood
as secretary to the bishop of Bergamo and as an
instructor in the seminary there. He served as a medic
and chaplain in the Italian army during World War I.
Afterwards, he resumed duties in his own diocese until
he was called to Rome in 1921 for work with the
Society for the Propagation of the Faith.

He began diplomatic service in 1925 as titular archbishop
of Areopolis and apostolic visitor to Bulgaria. A succession
of offices followed: apostolic delegate to Bulgaria (1931-
1935); titular archbishop of Mesembria, apostolic delegate to
Turkey and Greece, administrator of the Latin vicariate apostolic of Istanbul (1935-1944); apostolic nuncio to France
(1944-1953). On these missions, he was engaged in delicate
negotiations involving Roman, Eastern Rite and Orthodox
relations; the needs of people suffering from the consequences of World War II; and unsettling suspicions arising
from wartime conditions.

He was made a cardinal Jan. 12, 1953, and three days
later was appointed patriarch of Venice, the position he
held until his election to the papacy Oct. 28, 1958. He
died of stomach cancer June 3, 1963.

John was a strong and vigorous pope whose influence far outmeasured both his age and the shortness of
his time in the papacy. He was beatified by Pope John
Paul II on Sept. 3, 2000.

Second Vatican Council: John announced Jan. 25,
1959, his intention of convoking the 21st ecumenical
council in history to renew life in the Church, to
reform its structures and institutions, and to explore
ways and means of promoting unity among Christians.
Through the council, which completed its work two
and a half years after his death, he ushered in a new era
in the history of the Church.

Canon Law: He established a commission Mar. 28,
1963, for revision of the Code of Canon Law. The
revised Code was promulgated in 1983.

Canonizations: He canonized 10 saints and beatified Mother Elizabeth Ann Seton, the first native of
the U.S. ever so honored. He named St. Lawrence of
Brindisi a Doctor of the Church.

Cardinals: He created 52 cardinals in five consistories, raising membership of the College of Cardinals
above the traditional number of 70; at one time in
1962, the membership was 87. He made the college
more international in representation than it had ever
been, appointing the first cardinals from the
Philippines, Japan and Africa. He ordered episcopal
ordination for all cardinals. He relieved the suburban
bishops of Rome of ordinary jurisdiction over their
dioceses so they might devote all their time to business
of the Roman Curia.

Eastern Rites: He made all Eastern Rite patriarchs
members of the Congregation for the Oriental
Churches.

Ecumenism: He assigned to the Second Vatican Council
the task of finding ways and means of promoting unity
among Christians. He established the Vatican Secretariat for
Promoting Christian Unity June 5, 1960. He showed his
desire for more cordial relations with the Orthodox by
sending personal representatives to visit Patriarch
Athenagoras I June 27, 1961; approved a mission of five delegates to the General Assembly of the World Council of
Churches which met in New Delhi, India, in Nov. 1961; and
removed a number of pejorative references to Jews in the
Roman-Rite liturgy for Good Friday.

Encyclicals: Of the eight encyclicals he issued, the
two outstanding ones were *Mater et Magistra*
("Christianity and Social Progress"), in which he reca-
pitulated, updated and extended the social doctrine
stated earlier by Leo XIII and Pius XI; and *Pacem in
Terris* ("Peace on Earth"), the first encyclical ever
addressed to all men of good will as well as to

Catholics, on the natural law principles of peace.

Liturgy: In forwarding liturgical reforms already begun by Pius XII, he ordered a calendar-missal-breviary reform into effect Jan. 1, 1961. He authorized the use of vernacular languages in the administration of the sacraments and approved giving Holy Communion to the sick in afternoon hours. He selected the liturgy as the first topic of major discussion by the Second Vatican Council.

Missions: He issued an encyclical on the missionary activity of the Church; established native hierarchies in Indonesia, Vietnam and Korea; and called on North American superiors of religious institutes to have one-tenth of their members assigned to work in Latin America by 1971.

Peace: John spoke and used his moral influence for peace in 1961 when tension developed over Berlin, in 1962 during the Algerian revolt from France, and later the same year in the Cuban missile crisis. His efforts were singled out for honor by the Balzan Peace Foundation. In 1963, he was posthumously awarded the U.S. Presidential Medal of Freedom.

PAUL VI

Paul VI (Giovanni Battista Montini) was born Sept. 26, 1897, at Concesio in northern Italy. Educated at Brescia, he was ordained to the priesthood May 29, 1920. He pursued additional studies at the Pontifical Academy for Noble Ecclesiastics and the Pontifical Gregorian University. In 1924 he began 30 years of service in the Secretariat of State; as undersecretary from 1937 until 1954, he was closely associated with Pius XII and was heavily engaged in organizing informational and relief services during and after World War II. He declined the offer of the cardinalate by Pope Pius XII.

Ordained archbishop of Milan Dec. 12, 1954, he was inducted into the College of Cardinals Dec. 15, 1958, by Pope John XXIII. Trusted by John, he was a key figure in organizing the first session of Vatican Council II and was elected to the papacy June 21, 1963, two days after the conclave began. He died of a heart attack Aug. 6, 1978.

Second Vatican Council: He reconvened the Second Vatican Council after the death of John XXIII, presided over its second, third and fourth sessions, formally promulgated the 16 documents it produced, and devoted the whole of his pontificate to the task of putting them into effect throughout the Church. The main thrust of his pontificate — in a milieu of cultural and other changes in the Church and the world — was toward institutionalization and control of the authentic trends articulated and set in motion by the council.

Canonizations: He canonized 84 saints. They included groups of 22 Ugandan martyrs and 40 martyrs of England and Wales, as well as two Americans — Elizabeth Ann Bayley Seton and John Nepomucene Neumann.

Cardinals: He created 144 cardinals, and gave the Sacred College a more international complexion than it ever had before. He limited participation in papal elections to 120 cardinals under the age of 80.

Collegiality: He established the Synod of Bishops in 1965 and called it into session five times. He stimulated the formation and operation of regional conferences of bishops, and of consultative bodies on other levels.

Creed and Holy Year: On June 30, 1968, he issued a Creed of the People of God in conjunction with the celebration of a Year of Faith. He proclaimed and led the observance of a Holy Year from Christmas Eve of 1974 to Christmas Eve of 1975.

Diplomacy: He met with many world leaders, including Soviet President Nikolai Podgorny in 1967, Marshal Tito of Yugoslavia in 1971 and President Nicolai Ceausescu of Romania in 1973. He worked constantly to reduce tension between the Church and the intransigent regimes of Eastern European countries by means of a detente type of policy called *Ostpolitik*. He agreed to significant revisions of the Vatican's concordat with Spain and initiated efforts to revise the concordat with Italy. More than 40 countries established diplomatic relations with the Vatican during his pontificate.

Encyclicals: He issued seven encyclicals, three of which are the best known. In *Populorum Progressio* ("Development of Peoples") he appealed to wealthy countries to take "concrete action" to promote human development and to remedy imbalances between richer and poorer nations; this encyclical, coupled with other documents and related actions, launched the Church into a new depth of involvement as a public advocate for human rights and for humanizing social, political and economic policies. In *Sacerdotalis Caelibatus* ("Priestly Celibacy") he reaffirmed the strict observance of priestly celibacy throughout the Western Church. In *Humanae Vitae* ("Of Human Life") he condemned abortion, sterilization and artificial birth control, in line with traditional teaching and in "defense of life, the gift of God, the glory of the family, the strength of the people."

Interfaith Relations: He initiated formal consultation and informal dialogue on international and national levels between Catholics and non-Catholics — Orthodox, Anglicans, Protestants, Jews, Muslims, Buddhists, Hindus, and unbelievers. He and Greek Orthodox Patriarch Athenagoras I of Constantinople nullified in 1965 the mutual excommunications imposed by their respective churches in 1054.

Liturgy: He carried out the most extensive liturgical reform in history, involving a new Order of the Mass effective in 1969, a revised church calendar in 1970, revisions and translations into vernacular languages of all sacramental rites and other liturgical texts.

Ministries: He authorized the restoration of the permanent diaconate in the Roman Rite and the establishment of new ministries of lay persons.

Peace: In 1968, he instituted the annual observance of a World Day of Peace on New Year's Day as a means of addressing a message of peace to all the world's political leaders and the peoples of all nations. The most dramatic of his many appeals for peace and efforts to ease international tensions was his plea for "No more war!" before the U.N., Oct. 4, 1965.

Pilgrimages: A "Pilgrim Pope," he made pastoral visits to the Holy Land and India in 1964, the U.N. and New York City in 1965, Portugal and Turkey in 1967, Colombia in 1968, Switzerland and Uganda in 1969, and Asia, Pacific islands and Australia in 1970. While in Manila in 1970, he was stabbed by a Bolivian artist.

Roman Curia: He reorganized the central administrative organs of the Church in line with provisions of the apostolic constitution, *Regimini Ecclesiae Universae*, streamlining procedures for more effective service and giving the agencies a more international perspective by drawing officials and consultors from all over the world. He also instituted a number of new commissions and other bodies. Coupled with curial reorganization was a simplification of papal ceremonies.

JOHN PAUL I

John Paul I (Albino Luciani) was born Oct. 17, 1912, in Forno di Canale (now Canale d'Agordo) in northern Italy. Educated at the minor seminary in Feltre and the major seminary of the Diocese of Belluno, he was ordained to the priesthood July 7, 1935. He pursued further studies at the Pontifical Gregorian University in Rome and was awarded a doctorate in theology. From 1937 to 1947 he was vice rector of the Belluno seminary, where he taught dogmatic and moral theology, canon law and sacred art. He was appointed vicar general of his diocese in 1947 and served as director of catechetics.

Ordained bishop of Vittorio Veneto Dec. 27, 1958, he attended all sessions of the Second Vatican Council, participated in three assemblies of the Synod of Bishops (1971, 1974 and 1977), and was vice president of the Italian Bishops' Conference from 1972 to 1975.

He was appointed archbishop and patriarch of Venice Dec. 15, 1969, and was inducted into the College of Cardinals Mar. 5, 1973.

He was elected to the papacy Aug. 26, 1978, on the fourth ballot cast by the 111 cardinals participating in the largest and one of the shortest conclaves in history. The quickness of his election was matched by the brevity of his pontificate of 33 days, during which he delivered 19 addresses. He died of a heart attack Sept. 28, 1978.

JOHN PAUL II

See separate entry.

BENEDICT XVI

See separate entry.

PAPAL ENCYCLICALS — BENEDICT XIV (1740) TO BENEDICT XVI

(Source: The Papal Encyclicals [5 vols.], Claudia Carlen, I.H.M.; Pieran Press, Ann Arbor, Mich. Used with permission.)

An encyclical letter is a pastoral letter addressed by a pope to the whole Church. In general, it concerns matters of doctrine, morals or discipline, or significant commemorations. Its formal title consists of the first few words of the official text. Some encyclicals, notably *Pacem in terris* by John XXIII, *Ecclesiam Suam* by Paul VI and several by John Paul II, have been addressed to people of good will in general as well as to bishops and the faithful in communion with the Church.

An encyclical epistle resembles an encyclical letter but is addressed only to part of the Church. The authority of encyclicals was stated by Pius XII in the encyclical *Humani generis* Aug. 12, 1950: "Nor must it be thought that what is contained in encyciosl letters does not of itself demand assent, on the pretext that the popes do not exercise in them the supreme power of their teaching authority. Rather, such teachings belong to the ordinary magisterium, of which it is true to say: 'He who hears you, hears me' (Lk 10:16); for the most part, too, what is expounded and inculcated in encyclical letters already appertains to Catholic doctrine for other reasons."

The Second Vatican Council declared: "Religious submission of will and of mind must be shown in a special way to the authentic teaching authority of the Roman Pontiff, even when he is not speaking ex cathedra. That is, it must be shown in such a way that his supreme magisterium is acknowledged with reverence, the judgments made by him are sincerely adhered to, according to his manifest mind and will. His mind and will in the matter may be known chiefly either from the character of the documents (one of which could be an encyclical), from his frequent repetition of the same doctrine, or from his manner of speaking" (Dogmatic Constitution on the Church, *Lumen Gentium*, No. 25).

The following list contains the titles and indicates the subject matter of encyclical letters and epistles. The latter are generally distinguishable by the limited scope of their titles or contents.

Benedict XIV

(1740-58)

1740: *Ubi primum* (On the duties of bishops), Dec. 3.

1741: *Quanta cura* (Forbidding traffic in alms), June 30.

1743: *Nimiam licentiam* (To the bishops of Poland, on validity of marriages), May 18.

1745: *Vix pervenit* (To the bishops of Italy, on usury and other dishonest profit), Nov. 1.

1748: *Magnae Nobis* (To the bishops of Poland, on marriage impediments and dispensations), June 29.

1749: *Peregrinantes* (To all the faithful, proclaiming a Holy Year for 1750), May 5.

Apostolica Constitutio (On preparation for the Holy Year), June 26.

1751: *A quo primum* (To bishops of Poland, on Jews and Christians living in the same place), June 14.

1754: *Cum Religiosi* (To the bishops of the States of the Church, on catechesis), June 26.

Quod Provinciale (To the bishops of Albania, on Christians using Mohammedan names), Aug. 1.

1755: *Allatae sunt* (To missionaries of the Orient, on the observance of Oriental rites), July 26.

1756: *Ex quo primum* (To bishops of the Greek rite, on the Euchologion), Mar. 1.

Ex omnibus (To the bishops of France, on the apostolic constitution, *Unigenitus*), Oct. 16.

Clement XIII

(1758-69)

1758: *A quo die* (Unity among Christians), Sept. 13.

1759: *Cum primum* (On observing canonical sanctions), Sept. 17.

Appetente Sacro (On the spiritual advantages of fasting), Dec. 20.

1761: *In Dominico agro* (On instruction in the faith), June 14.

1766: *Christianae republicae* (On the dangers of anti-Christian writings), Nov. 25.

1768: *Summa quae* (To the bishops of Poland, on the Church in Poland), Jan. 6.

Clement XIV

(1769-74)

1769: *Decet quam maxime* (To the bishops of Sardinia, on abuses in taxes and benefices), Sept. 21.

Inscrutabili divinae sapientiae (To all Christians, proclaiming a universal jubilee), Dec.12.

Cum summi (Proclaiming a universal jubilee), Dec. 12.

1774: *Salutis nostra* (To all Christians, proclaiming a universal jubilee), Apr. 30.

Pius VI
(1775-99)

1775: *Inscrutabile* (On the problems of the pontificate), Dec. 25.

1791: *Charitas* (To the bishops of France, on the civil oath in France), Apr. 13.

Pius VII
(1800-1823)

1800: *Diu satis* (To the bishops of France, on a return to Gospel principles), May 15.

Leo XII
(1823-29)

1824: *Ubi primum* (To all bishops, on Leo XII's assuming the pontificate), May 5.

Quod hoc ineunte (Proclaiming a universal jubilee), May 24.

1825: *Charitate Christi* (Extending jubilee to the entire Church), Dec. 25.

Pius VIII
(1829-30)

1829: *Traditi humilitati* (On Pius VIII's program for the pontificate), May 24.

Gregory XVI
(1831-46)

1832: *Summo iugiter studio* (To the bishops of Bavaria, on mixed marriages), May 27.

Cum primum (To the bishops of Poland, on civil obedience), June 9.

Mirari vos (On liberalism and religious indifferentism), Aug. 15.

1833: *Quo graviora* (To the bishops of the Rhineland, on the "pragmatic Constitution"), Oct. 4.

1834: *Singulari Nos* (On the errors of Lammenais), June 25.

1835: *Commissum divinitus* (To clergy of Switzerland, on Church and State), May 17.

1840: *Probe nostis* (On the Propagation of the Faith), Sept. 18.

1841: *Quas vestro* (To the bishops of Hungary, on mixed marriages), Apr. 30.

1844: *Inter praecipuas* (On biblical societies), May 8.

Pius IX
(1846-78)

1846: *Qui pluribus* (On faith and religion), Nov. 9.

1847: *Praedecessores Nostros* (On aid for Ireland), Mar. 25.

Ubi primum (To religious superiors, on discipline for religious), June 17.

1849: *Ubi primum* (On the Immaculate Conception), Feb. 2.

Nostis et Nobiscum (To the bishops of Italy, on the Church in the Pontifical States), Dec. 8.

1851: *Exultavit cor Nostrum* (On the effects of jubilee), Nov. 21.

1852: *Nemo certe ignorat* (To the bishops of Ireland, on the discipline for clergy), Mar. 25.

Probe noscitis Venerabiles (To the bishops of Spain, on the discipline for clergy), May 17.

1853: *Inter multiplices* (To the bishops of France, pleading for unity of spirit), Mar. 21.

1854: *Neminem vestrum* (To clergy and faithful of Constantinople, on the persecution of Armenians), Feb. 2.

Optime noscitis (To the bishops of Ireland, on the proposed Catholic university for Ireland), Mar. 20.

Apostolicae Nostrae caritatis (Urging prayers for peace), Aug. 1.

1855: *Optime noscitis* (To the bishops of Austria, on episcopal meetings), Nov. 5.

1856: *Singulari quidem* (To the bishops of Austria, on the Church in Austria), Mar. 17.

1858: *Cum nuper* (To the bishops of the Kingdom of the Two Sicilies, on care for clerics), Jan. 20.

Amantissimi Redemptoris (On priests and the care of souls), May 3.

1859: *Cum sancta mater Ecclesia* (Pleading for public prayer), Apr. 27.

Qui nuper (On Pontifical States), June 18.

1860: *Nullis certe verbis* (On the need for civil sovereignty), Jan. 19.

1862: *Amantissimus* (To bishops of the Oriental rite, on the care of the churches), Apr. 8.

1863: *Quanto conficiamur moerore* (To the bishops of Italy, on promotion of false doctrines), Aug. 10.

Incredibili (To the bishops of Bogota, on persecution in New Granada), Sept. 17.

1864: *Maximae quidem* (To the bishops of Bavaria, on the Church in Bavaria), Aug. 18.

Quanta cura (Conedmning current errors), Dec. 8.

1865: *Meridionali Americae* (To bishops of South America, on the seminary for native clergy), Sept. 30.

1867: *Levate* (On the afflictions of the Church), Oct. 27.

1870: *Respicientes* (Protesting the taking of the Pontifical States), Nov. 1.

1871: *Ubi Nos* (To all bishops, on Pontifical States), May 15.

Beneficia Dei (On the 25th anniversary of his pontificate), June 4.

Saepe Venerabiles Fratres (On thanksgiving for 25 years of pontificate), Aug. 5.

1872: *Quae in Patriarchatu* (To bishops and people of Chaldea, on the Church in Chaldea), Nov. 16.

1873: *Quartus supra* (To bishops and people of the Armenian rite, on the Church in Armenia), Jan. 6.

Etsi multa (On the Church in Italy, Germany and Switzerland), Nov. 21.

1874: *Vix dum a Nobis* (To the bishops of Austria, on the church in Austria), Mar. 7.

Gravibus Ecclesiae (To all bishops and faithful, proclaiming a jubilee for 1875), Dec. 24.

1875: *Quod nunquam* (To the bishops of Prussia, on the Church in Prussia), Feb. 5.

Graves ac diuturnae (To the bishops of Switzerland, on the Church in Switzerland), Mar. 23.

Leo XIII
(1878-1903)

1878: *Inscrutabili Dei consilio* (On the evils of society), Apr. 21.

Quod Apostolici muneris (On socialism), Dec. 28.

1879: *Aeterni Patris* (On the restoration of Christian philosophy), Aug. 4.

1880: *Arcanum* (On Christian marriage), Feb. 10.

Grande munus (On Sts. Cyril and Methodius), Sept. 30.

Sancta Dei civitas (On mission societies), Dec. 3.

1881: *Diuturnum* (On the origin of civil power), June 29.

Licet multa (To the bishops of Belgium, on Catholics in Belgium), Aug. 3.

1882: *Etsi Nos* (To the bishops of Italy, on conditions in Italy), Feb. 15.

Auspicato concessum (On St. Francis of Assisi), Sept. 17.

Cum multa (To the bishops of Spain, on conditions in Spain), Dec. 8.

1883: *Supremi Apostolatus officio* (On devotion to the Rosary), Sept. 1.

1884: *Nobilissima Gallorum gens* (To the bishops of France, on the religious question), Feb. 8.

Humanum genus (On Freemasonry), Apr. 20.

Superiore anno (On the recitation of the Rosary), Aug. 30.

1885: *Immortale Dei* (On the Christian constitution of states), Nov. 1.

Spectata fides (To the bishops of England, on Christian education), Nov. 27.

Quod auctoritate (Proclamation of extraordinary Jubilee), Dec. 22.

1886: *Iampridem* (To the bishops of Prussia, on Catholicism in Germany), Jan. 6.

Quod multum (To the bishops of Hungary, on the liberty of the Church), Aug. 22.

Pergrata (To the bishops of Portugal, on the Church in Portugal), Sept. 14.

1887: *Vieben noto* (To the bishops of Italy, on the Rosary and public life), Sept. 20.

Officio sanctissimo (To the bishops of Bavaria, on the Church in Bavaria), Dec. 22.

1888: *Quod anniversarius* (On his sacerdotal jubilee), Apr. 1.

In plurimis (To the bishops of Brazil, on the abolition of slavery), May 5.

Libertas (On the nature of human liberty), June 20.

Saepe Nos (To the bishops of Ireland, on boycotting in Ireland), June 24.

Paterna caritas (To the Patriarch of Cilicia and the archbishops and bishops of the Armenian people, on reunion with Rome), July 25.

Quam aerumnosa (To the bishops of America, on Italian immigrants), Dec. 10.

Etsi cunctas (To the bishops of Ireland, on the Church in Ireland), Dec. 21.

Exeunte iam anno (On the right ordering of Christian life), Dec. 25.

1889: *Magni Nobis* (To bishops of the United States, on the Catholic University of America), Mar. 7.

Quamquam pluries (On devotion to St. Joseph), Aug. 15.

1890: *Sapientiae Christianae* (On Christians as citizens), Jan. 10.

Dall'alto Dell'Apostolico seggio (To the bishops and people of Italy, on Freemasonry in Italy), Oct. 15.

Catholicae Ecclesiae (On slavery in the missions), Nov. 20.

1891: *In ipso* (To the bishops of Austria, on episcopal reunions in Austria), Mar. 3.

Rerum novarum (On capital and labor), May 15.

Pastoralis (To the bishops of Portugal, on religious union), June 25.

Pastoralis officii (To the bishops of Germany and Austria, on the morality of dueling), Sept. 12.

Octobri mense (On the Rosary), Sept. 22.

1892: *Au milieu des sollicitudes* (To the bishops, clergy and faithful of France, on the Church and State in France), Feb. 16.

Quarto abeunte saeculo (To the bishops of Spain, Italy, and the two Americas, on the Columbus quadricentennial), July 16.

Magnae Dei Matris (On the Rosary), Sept. 8.

Inimica vis (To the bishops of Italy, on Freemasonry), Dec. 8.

Custodi di quella fede (To the Italian people, on Freemasonry), Dec. 8.

1893: *Ad extremas* (On seminaries for native clergy), June 24.

Constanti Hungarorum (To the bishops of Hungary, on the Church in Hungary), Sept. 2.

Laetitiae sanctae (Commending devotion to the Rosary), Sept. 8.

Non mediocri (To the bishops of Spain, on the Spanish College in Rome), Oct. 25.

Providentissimus Deus (On the study of Holy Scripture), Nov. 18.

1894: *Caritatis* (To the bishops of Poland, on the Church in Poland), Mar. 19.

Inter graves (To the bishops of Peru, on the Church in Peru), May 1.

Litteras a vobis (To the bishops of Brazil, on the clergy in Brazil), July 2.

Iucunda semper expectatione (On the Rosary), Sept. 8.

Christi nomen (On the propagation of the Faith and Eastern churches), Dec. 24.

1895: *Longinqua* (To the bishops of the United States, on Catholicism in the United States), Jan. 6.

Permoti Nos (To the bishops of Belgium, on social conditions in Belgium), July 10.

Adiutricem (On the Rosary), Sept. 5.

1896: *Insignes* (To the bishops of Hungary, on the Hungarian millennium), May 1.

Satis cognitum (On the unity of the Church), June 29.

Fidentem piumque animum (On the Rosary), Sept. 20.

1897: *Divinum illud munus* (On the Holy Spirit), May 9.

Militantis Ecclesiae (To the bishops of Austria, Germany, and Switzerland, on St. Peter Canisius), Aug. 1.

Augustissimae Virginis Mariae (On the Confraternity of the Holy Rosary), Sept. 12.

Affari vos (To the bishops of Canada, on the Manitoba school question), Dec. 8.

1898: *Caritatis studium* (To the bishops of Scotland, on the Church in Scotland), July 25.

Spesse volte (To the bishops, priests, and people of Italy, on the suppression of Catholic institutions), Aug. 5.

Quam religiosa (To the bishops of Peru, on civil marriage law), Aug. 16.

Diuturni temporis (On the Rosary), Sept. 5.

Quum diuturnum (To the bishops of Latin America, on Latin American bishops' plenary council), Dec. 25.

1899: *Annum Sacrum* (On consecration to the Sacred Heart), May 25.

Depuis le jour (To the archbishops, bishops, and clergy of France, on the education of clergy), Sept. 8.

Paternae (To the bishops of Brazil, on the education of the clergy), Sept. 18.

1900: *Omnibus compertum* (To the Patriarch and bishops of the Greek-Melkite rite, on unity among the Greek Melkites), July 21.

Tametsi futura prospicientibus (On Jesus Christ the Redeemer), Nov. 1.

1901: *Graves de communi re* (On Christian democracy), Jan. 18.

Gravissimas (To the bishops of Portugal, on religious orders in Portugal), May 16.

Reputantibus (To the bishops of Bohemia and Moravia, on the language question in Bohemia), Aug. 20.

Urbanitatis Veteris (To the bishops of the Latin church in Greece, on the foundation of a seminary in Athens), Nov. 20.

1902: *In amplissimo* (To the bishops of the United States, on the Church in the United States), Apr. 15.

Quod votis (To the bishops of Austria, on the proposed Catholic University), Apr. 30.

Mirae caritatis (On the Holy Eucharist), May 28.

Quae ad Nos (To the bishops of Bohemia and Moravia, on the Church in Bohemia and Moravia), Nov. 22.

Fin dal principio (To the bishops of Italy, on the education of the clergy), Dec. 8.

Dum multa (To the bishops of Ecuador, on marriage legislation), Dec. 24.

St. Pius X

(1903-14)

1903: *E supremi* (On the restoration of all things in Christ), Oct. 4.

1904: *Ad diem illum laetissimum* (On the Immaculate Conception), Feb. 2.

Iucunda sane (On Pope Gregory the Great), Mar. 12.

1905: *Acerbo nimis* (On teaching Christian doctrine), Apr. 15.

Il fermo proposito (To the bishops of Italy, on Catholic Action in Italy), June 11.

1906: *Vehementer Nos* (To the bishops, clergy, and people of France, on the French Law of Separation), Feb. 11.

Tribus circiter (On the Mariavites or Mystic Priests of Poland), Apr. 5.

Pieni l'animo (To the bishops of Italy, on the clergy in Italy), July 28.

Gravissimo officio munere (To the bishops of France, on French associations of worship), Aug. 10.

1907: *Une fois encore* (To the bishops, clergy, and people of France, on the separation of Church and State), Jan. 6.

Pascendi dominici gregis (On the doctrines of the Modernists), Sept. 8.

1909: *Communium rerum* (On St. Anselm of Aosta), Apr. 21.

1910: *Editae saepe* (On St. Charles Borromeo), May 26.

1911: *Iamdudum* (On the Law of Separation in Portugal), May 24.

1912: *Lacrimabili statu* (To the bishops of Latin America, on the Indians of South America), June 7.

Singulari quadam (To the bishops of Germany, on labor organizations), Sept. 24.

Benedict XV

(1914-22)

1914: *Ad beatissimi Apostolorum* (Appeal for peace), Nov. 1.

1917: *Humani generis Redemptionem* (On preaching the Word of God), June 15.

1918: *Quod iam diu* (On the future peace conference), Dec. 1.

1919: *In hac tanta* (To the bishops of Germany, on St. Boniface), May 14.

Paterno iam diu (On children of central Europe), Nov. 24.

1920: *Pacem, Dei munus pulcherrimum* (On peace and Christian reconciliation), May 23.

Spiritus Paraclitus (On St. Jerome), Sept. 15.

Principi Apostolorum Petro (On St. Ephrem the Syrian), Oct. 5.

Annus iam plenus (On children of central Europe), Dec. 1.

1921: *Sacra propediem* (On the Third Order of St. Francis), Jan. 6.

In praeclara summorum (To professors and students of fine arts in Catholic institutions of learning, on Dante), Apr. 30.

Fausto appetente die (On St. Dominic), June 29.

Pius XI

(1922-39)

1922: *Ubi arcano Dei consilio* (On the peace of Christ in the Kingdom of Christ), Dec. 23.

1923: *Rerum omnium perturbationem* (On St. Francis de Sales), Jan. 26.

Studiorum Ducem (On St. Thomas Aquinas), June 29.

Ecclesiam Dei (On St. Josaphat), Nov. 12.

1924: *Maximam gravissimamque* (To the bishops, clergy, and people of France, on French diocesan associations), Jan. 18.

1925: *Quas primas* (On the feast of Christ the King), Dec. 11.

1926: Rerum Ecclesiae (On Catholic missions), Feb. 28.

Rite expiatis (On St. Francis of Assisi), Apr. 30.

Iniquis afflictisque (On the persecution of the Church in Mexico), Nov. 18.

1928: *Mortalium animos* (On religious unity), Jan. 6.

Miserentissimus Redemptor (On reparation to the Sacred Heart), May 8.

Rerum Orientalium (On the promotion of Oriental Studies), Sept. 8.

1929: *Mens Nostra* (On the promotion of Spiritual Exercises), Dec. 20.

Quinquagesimo ante (On his sacerdotal jubilee), Dec. 23.

Rappresentanti in terra (On Christian education), Dec. 31. [Latin text, *Divini illius magistri*, published several months later with minor changes.]

1930: *Ad salutem* (On St. Augustine), Apr. 20.

Casti connubii (On Christian Marriage), Dec. 31.

1931: *Quadragesimo anno* (Commemorating the fortieth anniversary of Leo XIII's *Rerum novarum*, on reconstruction of the soical order), May 15.

Non abbiamo bisogno (On Catholic Action in Italy), June 29.

Nova impendet (On the economic crisis), Oct. 2.

Lux veritatis (On the Council of Ephesus), Dec. 25.

1932: *Caritate Christi compulsi* (On the Sacred Heart), May 3.

Acerba animi (To the bishops of Mexico, on persecution of the Church in Mexico), Sept. 29.

1933: *Dilectissima Nobis* (To the bishops, clergy, and people of Spain, on oppression of the Church in Spain), June 3.

1935: *Ad Catholici sacerdotii* (On the Catholic priesthood), Dec. 20.

1936: *Vigilanti cura* (To the bishops of the United States, on motion pictures), June 29.

1937: *Mit brennender Sorge* (To the bishops of Germany, on the Church and the German Reich), Mar. 14.

Divini Redemptoris (On atheistic communism), Mar. 19.

Nos es muy conocida (To the bishops of Mexico: on the religious situation in Mexico), Mar. 28

Ingravescentibus malis (On the Rosary) Sept. 29.

Pius XII
(1939-58)

1939: *Summi Pontificatus* (On the unity of human society), Oct. 20.

Sertum laetitiae (To the bishops of the United States, on the 150th anniversary of the establishment of the hierarchy in the United States), Nov. 1.

1940: *Saeculo exeunte octavo* (To the bishops of Portugal and its colonies, on the eighth centenary of the independence of Portugal), June 13.

1943: *Mystici Corporis Christi* (On the Mystical Body of Christ), June 29.

Divino afflante Spiritu (On promoting biblical studies, commemorating the fiftieth anniversary of *Providentissimus Deus*), Sept. 30.

1944: *Orientalis Ecclesiae* (On St. Cyril, Patriarch of Alexandria), Apr. 9.

1945: *Communium interpretes dolorum* (To the bishops of the world, appealing for prayers for peace during May), Apr. 15.

Orientales omnes Ecclesias (On the 350th anniversary of the reunion of the Ruthenian Church with the Apostolic See), Dec. 23.

1946: *Quemadmodum* (Pleading for the care of the world's destitute children), Jan. 6.

Deiparae Virginis Mariae (To all the bishops of the world, on the possibility of defining the Assumption of the Blessed Virgin Mary as a dogma of faith), May 1.

1947: *Fulgens radiatur* (On St. Benedict), Mar. 21.

Mediator Dei (On the sacred liturgy), Nov. 20.

Optatissima pax (Prescribing public prayers for social and world peace), Dec. 18.

1948: *Auspicia quaedam* (On public prayers for world peace and solution of problem of Palestine), May 1.

In multiplicibus curis (On prayers for peace in Palestine), Oct. 24.

1949: *Redemptoris nostri cruciatus* (On the holy places in Palestine), Apr. 15.

1950: *Anni Sacri* (On the program for combating atheistic propaganda throughout the world), Mar. 12.

Summi maeroris (On public prayers for peace), July 19.

Humani generis (Concerning some false opinions threatening to undermine the foundations of Catholic doctrine), Aug. 12.

Mirabile illud (On the crusade of prayers for peace), Dec. 6.

1951: *Evangelii praecones* (On the promotion of Catholic missions), June 2.

Sempiternus Rex Christus (On the Council of Chalcedon), Sept. 8.

Ingruentium malorum (On reciting the Rosary), Sept. 15.

1952: *Orientales Ecclesias* (On the persecuted Eastern Church), Dec. 15.

1953: *Doctor Mellifluus* (On St. Bernard of Clairvaux, the last of the fathers), May 24.

Fulgens corona (Proclaiming a Marian Year to commemorate the centenary of the definition of the dogma of the Immaculate Conception), Sept. 8.

1954: *Sacra virginitas* (On consecrated virginity), Mar. 25.

Ecclesiae fastos (To the bishops of Great Britain, Germany, Austria, France, Belgium, and Holland, on St. Boniface), June 5.

Ad Sinarum gentem (To the bishops, clergy, and people of China, on the supranationality of the Church), Oct. 7.

Ad Caeli Reginam (Proclaiming the Queenship of Mary), Oct. 11.

1955: *Musicae sacrae* (On sacred music), Dec. 25.

1956: *Haurietis aquas* (On devotion to the Sacred Heart), May 15.

Luctuosissimi eventus (Urging public prayers for peace and freedom for the people of Hungary), Oct. 28.

Laetamur admodum (Renewing exhortation for prayers for peace for Poland, Hungary, and especially for the Middle East), Nov. 1.

Datis nuperrime (Lamenting the sorrowful events in Hungary and condemning the ruthless use of force), Nov. 5.

1957: *Fidei donum* (On the present condition of the Catholic missions, especially in Africa), Apr. 21.

Invicti athletae (On St. Andrew Bobola), May 16.

Le pelerinage de Lourdes (Warning against materialism on the centenary of the apparitions at Lourdes), July 2.

Miranda prorsus (On the communications field, motion picture, radio, television), Sept. 8.

1958: *Ad Apostolorum Principis* (To the bishops of China, on Communism and the Church in China), June 29.

Meminisse iuvat (On prayers for persecuted Church), July 14.

Bl. John XXIII
(1958-63)

1959: *Ad Petri Cathedram* (On truth, unity, and peace, in a spirit of charity), June 29.

Sacerdotii Nostri primordia (On St. John Vianney), Aug. 1.

Grata recordatio (On the Rosary, prayer for the Church, missions, international and social problems), Sept. 26.

Princeps Pastorum (On the missions, native clergy, lay participation), Nov. 28.

1961: *Mater et Magistra* (On Christianity and social progress), May 15.

Aeterna Dei sapientia (On the fifteenth centenary of the death of Pope St. Leo I, the see of Peter as the center of Christian unity), Nov. 11.

1962: *Paenitentiam agere* (On the need for the practice of interior and exterior penance), July 1.

1963: *Pacem in terris* (On establishing universal peace in truth, justice, charity, and liberty), Apr. 11.

Paul VI
(1963-78)

1964: *Ecclesiam Suam* (On the Church), Aug. 6.

1965: *Mense maio* (On prayers during May for the preservation of peace), Apr. 29.

Mysterium Fidei (On the Holy Eucharist), Sept. 3.

1966: *Christi Matri* (On prayers for peace during Oct.), Sept. 15.

1967: *Populorum progressio* (On the development of peoples), Mar. 26.

Sacerdotalis caelibatus (On the celibacy of the priest), June 24.

1968: *Humanae vitae* (On the regulation of birth), July 25.

John Paul II
(1978-2005)

1979: *Redemptor hominis* (On redemption and dignity of the human race), Mar. 4

1980: *Dives in misericordia* (On the mercy of God), Nov. 30.

1981: *Laborem exercens* (On human work), Sept. 14.

1985: *Slavorum Apostoli* (Commemorating Sts. Cyril and Methodius, on the eleventh centenary of the death of St. Methodius), June 2.

1986: *Dominum et Vivificantem* (On the Holy Spirit in the life of the Church and the world), May 18.

1987: *Redemptoris Mater* (On the role of Mary in the mystery of Christ and her active and exemplary presence in the life of the Church), Mar. 25.

Sollicitudo Rei Socialis (On social concerns, on the 20th anniversary of *Populorum progressio*), Dec. 30.

1991: *Redemptoris missio* (On the permanent validity of the Church's missionary mandate), Jan. 22.

Centesimus annus (Commemorating the centenary of *Rerum novarum* and addressing the social question in a contemporary perspective), May 1.

1993: *Veritatis Splendor* (On fundamental questions on the Church's moral teaching), Aug. 6.

1995: *Evangelium Vitae* (On the value and inviolability of human life), Mar. 25.

Ut Unum Sint (On commitment to ecumenism), May 25.

1998: *Fides et Ratio* (On faith and reason), Oct. 1.

2003: *Ecclesia de Eucharistia* (Church of the Eucharist), April 17.

Benedict XVI (2005-)

2005: *Deus Caritas Est* (God is Love), Dec. 25.

CANONIZATIONS BY LEO XIII AND HIS SUCCESSORS

"Canonization" (*see* **Glossary**) is an infallible declaration by the pope that a person who suffered martyrdom and/or practiced Christian virtue to a heroic degree is in glory with God in heaven and is worthy of public honor by the universal Church and of imitation by the faithful.

Biographies of some of the saints listed below are given elsewhere in the *Almanac; see* **Index**; for biographies of all new saints for 2003-04, *see* **Saints**.

Leo XIII
(1878-1903)

1881: Clare of Montefalco (d. 1308); John Baptist de Rossi (1698-1764); Lawrence of Brindisi (d. 1619).

1883: Benedict J. Labre (1748-83).

1888: Seven Holy Founders of the Servite Order; Peter Claver (1581-1654); John Berchmans (1599-1621); Alphonsus Rodriguez (1531-1617).

1897: Anthony M. Zaccaria (1502-39); Peter Fourier of Our Lady (1565-1640).

1900: John Baptist de La Salle (1651-1719); Rita of Cascia (1381-1457).

St. Pius X
(1903-14)

1904: Alexander Sauli (1534-93); Gerard Majella (1725-55).

1909: Joseph Oriol (1650-1702); Clement M. Hofbauer (1751-1820).

Benedict XV
(1914-22)

1920: Gabriel of the Sorrowful Mother (1838-62); Margaret Mary Alacoque (1647-90); Joan of Arc (1412-31).

Pius XI
(1922-39)

1925: Thérèse of Lisieux (1873-97); Peter Canisius (1521-97); Mary Magdalen Postel (1756-1846); Mary Magdalen Sophie Barat (1779-1865); John Eudes (1601-80); John Baptist Vianney (Curé of Ars) (1786-1859).

1930: Lucy Filippini (1672-1732); Catherine Tomas (1533-74); Jesuit North American Martyrs; Robert Bellarmine (1542-1621); Theophilus of Corte (1676-1740).

1931: Albert the Great (1206-80) (equivalent canonization).

1933: Andrew Fournet (1752-1834); Bernadette Soubirous (1844-79).

1934: Joan Antida Thouret (1765-1826); Mary Michaeli (1809-65); Louise de Marillac (1591-1660); Joseph Benedict Cottolengo (1786-1842); Pompilius M. Pirotti, priest (1710-56); Teresa Margaret Redi (1747-70); John Bosco (1815-88); Conrad of Parzham (1818-94).

1935: John Fisher (1469-1535); Thomas More (1478-1535).

1938: Andrew Bobola (1592-1657); John Leonardi (c. 1550-1609); Salvatore of Horta (1520-67).

Pius XII
(1939-58)

1940: Gemma Galgani (1878-1903); Mary Euphrasia Pelletier (1796-1868).

1943: Margaret of Hungary (d. 1270) (equivalent canonization).

1946: Frances Xavier Cabrini (1850-1917).

1947: Nicholas of Flüe (1417-87); John of Britto (1647-93); Bernard Realini (1530-1616); Joseph Cafasso (1811-60); Michael Garicoits (1797-1863); Jeanne Elizabeth des Ages (1773-1838); Louis Marie Grignon de Montfort (1673-1716); Catherine Labouré (1806-76).

1949: Jeanne de Lestonnac (1556-1640); Maria Josepha Rossello (1811-80).

1950: Emily de Rodat (1787-1852); Anthony Mary Claret (1807-70); Bartolomea Capitanio (1807-33); Vincenza Gerosa (1784-1847); Jeanne de Valois (1461-1504); Vincenzo M. Strambi (1745-1824);

Maria Goretti (1890-1902); Mariana Paredes of Jesus (1618-45).

1951: Maria Domenica Mazzarello (1837-81); Emilie de Vialar (1797-1856); Anthony M. Gianelli (1789-1846); Ignatius of Laconi (1701-81); Francis Xavier Bianchi (1743-1815).

1954: Pope Pius X (1835-1914); Dominic Savio (1842-57); Maria Crocifissa di Rosa (1813-55); Peter Chanel (1803-41); Gaspar del Bufalo (1786-1837); Joseph M. Pignatelli (1737-1811).

1958: Herman Joseph, O. Praem. (1150-1241) (equivalent canonization).

Bl. John XXIII
(1958-63)

1959: Joaquina de Vedruna de Mas (1783-1854); Charles of Sezze (1613-70).

1960: Gregory Barbarigo (1625-97) (equivalent canonization); John de Ribera (1532-1611).

1961: Bertilla Boscardin (1888-1922).

1962: Martin de Porres (1579-1639); Peter Julian Eymard (1811-68); Anthony Pucci, priest (1819-92); Francis Mary of Camporosso (1804-66).

1963: Vincent Pallotti (1795-1850).

Paul VI
(1963-78)

1964: Charles Lwanga and Twenty-one Companions, Martyrs of Uganda (d. between 1885-87).

1967: Benilde Romacon (1805-62).

1969: Julia Billiart (1751-1816).

1970: Maria Della Dolorato Torres Acosta (1826-87); Leonard Murialdo (1828-1900); Therese Couderc (1805-85); John of Ávila (1499-1569); Nicholas Tavelic, Deodatus of Aquitaine, Peter of Narbonne and Stephen of Cuneo, martyrs (d. 1391); Forty English and Welsh Martyrs (d. 16th cent.).

1974: Teresa of Jesus Jornet Ibars (1843-97).

1975: Vicenta Maria Lopez y Vicuna (1847-90); Elizabeth Bayley Seton (1774-1821); John Masias (1585-1645); Oliver Plunket (1629-81); Justin de Jacobis (1800-60); John Baptist of the Conception (1561-1613).

1976: Beatrice da Silva (1424 or 1426-90); John Ogilvie (1579-1615).

1977: Rafaela Maria Porras y Ayllon (1850-1925); John Nepomucene Neumann (1811-60); Sharbel Makhlouf (1828-98).

John Paul II
(1978-2005)

1982: Crispin of Viterbo (1668-1750); Maximilian Kolbe (1894-1941); Marguerite Bourgeoys (1620-1700); Jeanne Delanoue (1666-1736).

1983: Leopold Mandic (1866-1942).

1984: Paola Frassinetti (1809-92); 103 Korean Martyrs (d. between 1839-67); Miguel Febres Cordero (1854-1910).

1986: Francis Anthony Fasani (1681-1742); Giuseppe Maria Tomasi (1649-1713).

1987: Giuseppe Moscati (d. 1927); Lawrence (Lorenzo) Ruiz and Fifteen Companions, Martyrs of Japan (d. 1630s).

1988: Eustochia Calafato (1434-85); 117 Martyrs of Vietnam (96 Vietnamese, 11 Spanish, 10 French, included 8 bishops, 50 priests, 1 seminarian, 58 lay persons); Roque Gonzalez (1576-1628), Alfonso

Rodriguez (1598-1628) and Juan de Castillo (1596-1628), Jesuit martyrs of Paraguay; Rose Philippine Duchesne (1796-1852); Simon de Rojas (1552-1624); Magdalen of Canossa (1774-1835); Maria Rosa Molas y Vollve (d. 1876).

1989: Clelia Barbieri (1847-70); Gaspar Bertoni (1777-1853); Richard Pampuri, religious (1897-1930); Agnes of Bohemia (1211-82); Albert Chmielowski (1845-1916); Mutien-Marie Wiaux (1841-1917).

1990: Marguerite D'Youville (1701-77).

1991: Raphael (Jozef) Kalinowski (1835-1907).

1992: Claude La Colombiere (1641-82); Ezequiel Moreno y Diaz (1848-1905).

1993: Marie of St. Ignatius (Claudine Thevenet) (1774-1837); Teresa "de los Andes" (Juana Fernandez Solar) (1900-20); Enrique de Ossó y Cervelló (1840-96).

1995: Jan Sarkander (1576-1620); Zdislava of Lemberk (d. 1252); Marek Krizin (1588-1619), Stefan Pongracz (1582-1619), Melichar Grodziecky (1584-1619), martyrs of Kosice; Eugene de Mazenod (1782-1861).

1996: Jean-Gabriel Perboyre (1802-40); Juan Grande Roman (1546-1600); Bro. Egidio Maria of St. Joseph (1729-1812).

1997: Hedwig (1371-99); John Dukla, O.F.M. (d. 1484).

1998: Edith Stein (d. 1942).

1999: Marcellin Joseph Benoit Champagnat (1789-1840), Giovanni Calabria (1873-1954); Agostina Livia Pietrantonio (1864-94); Sr. Kunegunda Kinga (1224-92); Cirilo Bertrán and Eight Companion Brothers of the Christian Schools (d. Oct. 9, 1934); Inocencio de la Immaculada (d. Oct. 9, 1934); St. Jaime Hilario Barbal (1889-1937); Benedetto Menni (1841-1914); Tommaso da Cori (1655-1729).

2000: Mary Faustina Kowalska (1905-38); María Josefa of the Heart of Jesus Sancho de Guerra (1842-1912); Cristóbal Magallanes and 24 Companions (d. 1915-28); José Maria de Yermo y Parres (1851-1904); Maria de Jesús Sacramentado Venegas (1868-1959); 120 Martyrs of China (17th-20th centuries); Katherine Drexel (1858-1955); Josephine Bakhita (d. 1947).

2001: Luigi Scrosoppi (1804-84); Agostino Roscelli (1818-1902); Bernardo da Corleone (1605-67); Teresa Eustochio Verzeri (1801-52); Rafqa Petra Choboq Ar-Rayes (1832-1914); Giuseppe Marello (1844-95); Paula Montal Fornés de San José de Calasanz (1799-1889); Léonie Françoise de Sales Aviat (1844-1914); Maria Crescentia Höss (1682-1744).

2002: Alonso de Orozco (1500-91); Ignazio da Santhia (Lorenzo Maurizio Belvisotti) (1686-1770); Umile da Bisignano (Luca Antonio Pirozzo) (1582-1637); Paulina do Coracao Agonizante de Jesus (Amabile Visintainer) (1865-1942); Benedetta Cambiagio Frassinello (1791-1858); Pio da Pietrelcina (Padre Pio,1887-1968); Juan Diego Cuauhlatoatzin (16th century); Pedro de San Jose de Betancur (1619-67); Josemaria Escriva (1902-75).

2003: Pedro Poveda Castroverde (1874-1936); José María Rubio y Peralta (1864-1929); Genoveva Torres Morales (1870-1956); Angela de la Cruz (1846-1932); María Maravillas de Jesus (1891-1974); Jozef Sebastian

Pelczar (1842-1924); Urszula Ledochowska (1865-1939); Maria de Mattias (1805-66); Virginia Centurione Bracelli (1587-1651); Daniel Comboni (1831-1881); Arnold Janssen (1837-1909); Josef Freinademetz (1852-1908).

2004: Gianna Beretta Molla (1922-1962); Nimatullah Kassab al-Hardini (1828-1858); Josep Manyanet Vives (1833-1901); Luigi Orione (1872-1940);

Annibale Di Francia (1851-1927); Paola Elisabetta Cerioli (1816-1865).

Benedict XVI (2005-)

2005: Józef Bilczewski (1860-1923); Gaetano Catanoso (1879-1963); Zygmunt Gorazdowski (1845-1920); Alberto Hurtado Cruchaga (1901-1952); Felix of Nicosia (1715-1787).

BEATIFICATIONS BY POPE JOHN PAUL II, 1979-2004

For biographical details of all those beatified in 2004, please *see under* Saints.

1979: Margarret Ebner (Feb. 24); Francis Coll, O.P., Jacques Laval, S.S.Sp. (Apr. 29); Enrique de Ossó y Cervelló (Oct. 14; canonized June 16, 1993).

1980: José de Anchieta, Peter of St. Joseph Betancurt (canonized July 30, 2002), Francois de Montmorency Laval, Kateri Tekakwitha, Marie Guyart of the Incarnation (June 22); Don Luigi Orione (canonized May 16, 2004), Bartolomea Longo, Maria Anna Sala (Oct. 26).

1981: Sixteen Martyrs of Japan (Lorenzo Ruiz and Companions) (Feb 18; canonized Oct. 18, 1987); Maria Repetto, Alan de Solminihac, Richard Pampuri (canonized Nov. 1, 1989), Claudine Thevenet (canonized Mar. 21, 1993), Aloysius (Luigi) Scrosoppi (canonized June 10, 2001) (Oct. 4).

1982: Peter Donders, C.SS.R., Marie Rose Durocher, Andre Bessette, C.S.C., Maria Angela Astorch, Marie Rivier (May 23); Fra Angelico (equivalent beatification) (July); Jeanne Jugan, Salvatore Lilli and 7 Armenian Companions (Oct. 3); Sr. Angela of the Cross (Nov. 5; canonized May 3, 2003).

1983: Maria Gabriella Sagheddu (Jan. 25); Luigi Versiglia, Callisto Caravario (May 15); Ursula Ledochowska (canonized May 18, 2003) (June 20); Raphael (Jozef) Kalinowski (canonized Nov. 17, 1991), Bro. Albert (Adam Chmielowski), T.O.R. (June 22; canonized Nov. 12, 1989); Giacomo Cusmano, Jeremiah of Valachia, Domingo Iturrate Zubero (Oct. 30); Marie of Jesus Crucified (Marie Bouardy) (Nov. 13).

1984: Fr. William Repin and 98 Companions (Martyrs of Angers during French Revolution), Giovanni Mazzucconi (Feb. 19); Marie Leonie Paradis (Sept. 11); Federico Albert, Clemente Marchisio, Isidore of St. Joseph (Isidore de Loor), Rafaela Ybarra de Villalongo (Sept. 30); José Manyanet y Vives (canonized May 16, 2004), Daniel Brottier, C.S.Sp., Sr. Elizabeth of the Trinity (Elizabeth Catez) (Nov. 25).

1985: Mercedes of Jesus (Feb. 1); Ana de los Angeles Monteagudo (Feb. 2); Pauline von Mallinckrodt, Catherine Troiani (Apr. 14); Benedict Menni (canonized Nov. 21, 1999), Peter Friedhofen (June 23); Anwarite Nangapeta (Aug. 15); Virginae Centurione Bracelli (canonized May 18, 2003) (Sept. 22); Diego Luis de San Vitores, S.J., Jose M. Rubio y Peralta, S.J. (canonized May 4, 2003), Francisco Garate, S.J. (Oct. 6); Titus Brandsma, O.Carm. (Nov. 3); Pio Campidelli, C.P., Marie Teresa of Jesus Gerhardinger, Rafqa Ar-Rayes (canonized June 10, 2001) (Nov. 17).

1986: Alphonsa Mattathupandatu of the Immaculate Conception, Kuriakose Elias Chavara (Feb. 8); Antoine Chevrier (Oct. 4); Teresa Maria of the Cross

Manetti (Oct. 19).

1987: Maria Pilar of St. Francis Borgia, Maria Angeles of St. Joseph, Cardinal Marcellis Spinola y Maestre, Emmanuel Domingo y Sol (Mar. 29); Teresa of Jesus "de los Andes" (canonized March 21, 1993) (Apr. 3); Edith Stein (Teresa Benedicta of the Cross) (May 1; canonized, Oct. 11, 1998); Rupert Meyer, S.J. (May 3); Pierre-Francois Jamet, Cardinal Andrea Carlo Ferrari, Benedicta Cambiagio Frassinello, Louis Moreau (May 10); Carolina Kozka, Michal Kozal (June 10); George Matulaitis (Matulewicz) (June 28); Marcel Callo, Pierino Morosini, Antonia Mesina (Oct. 4); Blandina Marten, Ulricke Nische, Jules Reche (Bro. Arnold) (Nov. 1); 85 Martyrs (d. between 1584-1689) of England, Scotland and Wales (Nov. 22).

1988: Giovanni Calabria (canonized Apr. 18, 1999), Joseph Nascimbeni (Apr. 17); Pietro Bonilli, Kaspar Stangassinger, Francisco Palau y Quer, Savina Petrilli (Apr. 24), Laura Vicuna (Sept. 3); Joseph Gerard (Sept. 11); Miguel Pro, Giuseppe Benedetto Dusmet, Francisco Faa di Bruno, Junipero Serra, Frederick Jansoone, Josefa Naval Girbes (Sept. 25); Bernardo Maria Silvestrelli, Charles Houben, Honoratus Kozminski (Oct. 16); Niels Stensen (Nicolaus Steno) (Oct. 23); Katharine Drexel (canonized Oct. 1, 2000), 3 Missionary Martyrs of Ethiopia (Liberato Weiss, Samuel Marzorati, Michele Pio Fasoli) (Nov. 20).

1989: Martin of Saint Nicholas, Melchior of St. Augustine, Mary of Jesus of the Good Shepherd, Maria Margaret Caiani, Maria of Jesus Siedliska, Maria Catherine of St. Augustine (Apr. 23); Victoria Rasoamanarivo (Apr. 30); Bro. Scubilionis (John Bernard Rousseau) (May 2); Elizabeth Renzi, Antonio Lucci (June 17); Niceforo de Jesus y Maria (Vicente Diez Tejerina) and 25 Companions (martyred in Spain), Lorenzo Salvi, Gertrude Caterina Comensoli, Francisca Ana Cirer Carbonell (Oct. 1); 7 Martyrs from Thailand (Philip Sipong, Sr. Agnes Phila, Sr. Lucia Khambang, Agatha Phutta, Cecilia Butsi, Bibiana Khampai, Maria Phon), Timothy Giaccardo, Mother Maria of Jesus Deluil-Martiny (Oct. 22); Giuseppe Baldo (Oct. 31).

1990:9 Martyrs of Astoria during Spanish Civil War (De la Salle Brothers Cirilo Bertran, Marciano Jose, Julian Alfredo, Victoriano Pio, Benjamin Julian, Augusto Andres, Benito de Jesus, Aniceto Adolfo; and Passionist priest Innocencio Inmaculada; canonized Nov. 21, 1999), Mercedes Prat, Manuel Barbal Cosan (Brother Jaime), Philip Rinaldi, Tommaso da Cori (canonized Nov. 21, 1999) (Apr. 29); Juan Diego (confirmation of Apr. 9 decree; canonized July 31, 2002), 3 Child Martyrs (Cristobal, Antonio and Juan), Fr. Jose Maria de Yermo y Parres (May 6;

canonized May 21, 2001); Pierre Giorgio Frassati (May 20); Hanibal Maria Di Francia (canonized May 16, 2004), Joseph Allamano (Oct. 7); Marthe Aimee LeBouteiller, Louise Therese de Montaignac de Chauvance, Maria Schinina, Elisabeth Vendramini (Nov. 4).

1991: Annunciata Cocchetti, Marie Therese Haze, Clara Bosatta (Apr. 21); Jozef Sebastian Pelczar (June 2; canonized May 18, 2003); Boleslava Lament (June 5); Rafael Chylinski (June 9); Angela Salawa (Aug. 13); Edoardo Giuseppe Rosaz (July 14, Susa, Italy); Pauline of the Heart of Jesus in Agony Visentainer (canonized May 19, 2002) (Oct. 18, Brazil); Adolph Kolping (Oct. 27).

1992: Josephine Bakhita (canonized Oct. 1, 2000), Josemaria Escriva de Balaguer (May 17; canonized Oct. 6, 2000); Francesco Spinelli (June 21, Caravaggio, Italy); 17 Irish Martyrs, Rafael Arnáiz Barón, Nazaria Ignacia March Mesa, Léonie Françoise de Sales Aviat (canonized Nov. 25, 2001), and Maria Josefa Sancho de Guerra (canonized Oct. 1, 2000) (Sept. 27); 122 Martyrs of Spanish Civil War, Narcisa Martillo Morán (Oct. 25); Cristóbal Magellanes and 24 companions, Mexican martyrs (), and Maria de Jesús Sacramentado Venegas (Nov. 22; canonized May 21, 2000).

1993: Dina Belanger (Mar. 20); John Duns Scotus (Mar. 20, cult solemnly recognized); Mary Angela Truszkowska, Ludovico of Casoria, Faustina Kowalska (canonized Apr. 30, 2000), Paula Montal Fornés (canonized Nov. 25, 2001) (Apr. 18); Stanislaus Kazimierczyk (Apr. 18, cult solemnly recognized); Maurice Tornay, Marie-Louise Trichet, Columba Gabriel and Florida Cevoli (May 16); Giuseppe Marello (Sept. 26; canonized Nov. 25, 2001); Eleven Martyrs of Almeria, Spain, during Spanish Civil War (2 bishops, 7 brothers, 1 priest, 1 lay person); Victoria Diez y Bustos de Molina, Maria Francesca (Anna Maria) Rubatto; Pedro Castroverde (canonized May 4, 2003), Maria Crucified (Elisabetta Maria) Satellico (Oct. 10).

1994: Isidore Bakanja, Elizabeth Canori Mora; Dr. Gianna Beretta Molla (Apr. 24; canonized May 16, 2004); Nicolas Roland, Alberto Hurtado Cruchaga, Maria Rafols, Petra of St. Joseph Perez Florida, Josephine Vannini (Oct. 16); Magdalena Caterina Morano (Nov. 5); Hyacinthe Marie Cormier, Marie Poussepin, Agnes de Jesus Galand, Eugenia Joubert, Claudio Granzotto (Nov. 20).

1995: Peter ToRot (Jan. 17); Mother Mary of the Cross MacKillop (Jan. 19); Joseph Vaz (Jan. 21); Rafael Guizar Valencia, Modestino of Jesus and Mary, Genoveva Torres Morales (canonized May 4, 2003), Grimoaldo of the Purification (Jan. 29); Johann Nepomuk von Tschiderer (Apr. 30); Maria Helena Stollenwerk, Maria Alvarado Cordozo, Giuseppina Bonino, Maria Domenica Brun Barbantini, Agostino Roscelli (May 7; canonized June 10, 2001); Damien de Veuster (June 4); 109 Martyrs (64 from French Revolution – Martyrs of La Rochelle – and 45 from Spanish Civil War), Anselm Polanco Fontecha, Felipe Ripoll Morata, and Pietro Casini (Oct. 1); Mary Theresa Scherer, Maria Bernarda Butler and Marguerite Bays (Oct. 29).

1996: Daniel Comboni (canonized Oct. 5, 2003) and Guido Maria Conforti (Mar. 17); Cardinal Alfredo Ildefonso Schuster, O.S.B., Filippo Smaldone and Gennaro Sarnelli (priests) and Candida Maria de Jesus Cipitria y Barriola, Maria Raffaella Cimatti, Maria Antonia Bandres (religious) (May 12), Bernhard Lichtenberg and Karl Leisner (June 23), Wincenty Lewoniuk and 12 companions, Edmund Rice, Maria Ana Mogas Fontcuberta and Marcelina Darowska (Oct 6); Otto Neururer, Jakob Gapp and Catherine Jarrige (Nov. 24).

1997: Bishop Florentino Asensio Barroso, Sr. Maria Encarnacion Rosal of the Sacred Heart, Fr. Gaetano Catanoso, Fr. Enrico Rebuschini and Ceferino Gimenez Malla, first gypsy beatified (May 4); Bernardina Maria Jablonska, Maria Karlowska (June 6); Frédéric Ozanam (Aug. 22); Bartholomew Mary Dal Monte (Sep. 27); Elías del Socorro Nieves, Domenico Lentini, Giovanni Piamarta, Emilie d'Hooghvorst, Maria Teresa Fasce (Oct. 12); John Baptist Scalabrini, Vilmos Apor, María Vicenta of St. Dorothy Chávez Orozco (Nov. 9).

1998: Bishop Vincent Bossilkov, María Sallés, Brigida of Jesus (Mar. 15); Fr. Cyprian Tansi (Mar. 22); Nimatullah al-Hardini (canonized May 16, 2004), 11 Spanish nuns (May 10); Secondo Polla (May 23); Giovanni Maria Boccardo, Teresa Grillo Chavez, Teresa Bracco (May 24); Jakob Kern, Maria Restituta Kafka, and Anton Schwartz (June 21); Giuseppe Tovini (Sept. 20); Cardinal Alojzije Stepinac (Oct. 3); Antônio de Sant'Anna Galvão, Faustino Miguez, Zeferino Agostini, Mother Theodore Guérin (Oct. 25).

1999: Vicente Soler, and six Augustinian Recollect Companions, Manuel Martin Sierra, Nicolas Barre, Anna Schaeffer (Mar. 7); Padre Pio (May 2; canonized June 16, 2002); Fr. Stefan Wincenty Frelichowski (June 7); 108 Polish Martyrs, Regina Protmann, Edmund Bojanowski (June 13); Bishop Anton Slomsek (Sept. 19); Ferdinando Maria Baccilieri, Edward Maria Joannes Poppe, Arcangelo Tadini, Mariano da Roccacasale, Diego Oddi, Nicola da Gesturi (Oct. 3).

2000: André de Soveral, Ambrósio Francisco Ferro and 28 Companions, Nicolas Bunkerd Kitbamrung, Maria Stella Mardosewicz and 10 Companions, PedroCalungsod and Andrew of Phú Yên (Mar. 5); Mariano de Jesus Euse Hoyos, Francis Xavier Seelos, Anna Rosa Gattorno, Maria Elisabetta Hesselblad, Mariam Thresia Chiramel Mankidiyan (Apr. 9); Jacinta and Francisco Marto of Fatima (May 13); Pope Pius IX, Pope John XXIII, Tommaso Reggio, Guillaume-Joseph Chaminade, Columba Marmion (Sept. 3).

2001: José Aparicio Sanz and 232 Companions of the Spanish Civil War (Mar. 11); Manuel Gonzalez Garcia, Marie-Anne Blondin, Caterina Volpicelli, Caterina Cittadini, Carlos Manuel Cecilio Rodriguez Santiago (Apr. 29); George Preca, Ignatius Falzon, Maria Adeodata Pisani (May 9); Abp. Jósef Bilczewski and Fr. Sygmunt Gorazdowski, Ukrainian martyrs (June 27).

2002: Gaetano Errico, Lodovico Pavoni, Luigi Variara, Maria del Transito de Jesus Sacramentado, Artemide Zatti, Maria Romero Meneses (Apr. 14); Kamen Vitchev, Pavel Djidjov, Josaphat Chichkov (May 26); Juan Bautista and Jacinto de Los Angeles (Aug. 1); Zygmunt Szczęsny Feliński, Jan Balicki, Jan Beyzym, Sancja Szymkowiak (Aug. 18); Daudi

Okelo, Jildo Irwa, Andrea Giacinto Longhin, O.F.M. Cap., Marcantonio Durando, Marie de la Passion Hélène Marie de Chappotin de Neuville, Liduina Meneguzzi (Oct. 20).

2003: Pierre Bonhomme, María Dolores Rodríguez Sopeña, María Caridad Brader, Juana María Condesa Lluch, László Batthyány-Strattmann (Mar. 23); Eugenia Ravasco, Giacomo Alberione, Giulia Salzano, Marco d'Aviano, Maria Cristina Brando, Maria Domenica Mantovani (Apr. 27); Maria of Jesus Crucified *Petkovic* (June 6); Ivan Merz (June 22); Vasil' Hopko, Zdenka Schelingová (Sept. 14); Mother Teresa of Calcutta (Oct. 19); Juan Nepomuceno Zegrí y Moreno, Valentin Paquay, Luigi Maria Monti, Bonifacia Rodríguez Castro, Rosalie Rendu (Nov. 9).

2004: Luigi Talamoni, Matilde del Sagrado Corazón Téllez Robles, Piedad de la Cruz Ortiz Real, Maria Candida of the Eucharist (Mar. 21); Augusto Czartoryski, Laura Montoya, María Guadalupe García Zavala, Giulia Nemesia Valle, Eusebia Palomino Yenes, Alexandrina Maria da Costa (Apr. 25); Pere Tarrés i Claret, Alberto Marvelli, Pina Suriano (Sept. 5); Peter Vigne, Joseph-Marie Cassant, Anna Katharina Emmerick, Maria Ludovica De Angelis, Charles of Austria (Oct. 3).

BEATIFICATIONS UNDER POPE BENEDICT XVI (2005-06)

For biographical details of all those beatified in 2005-2006, please *see* under Saints.

2005: Ascension of the Heart of Jesus, Marianne Cope (May 14); Wladyslaw Findysz, Bronislaw Markiewicz, Ignacy Klopotowski (June 19); Cardinal Clemens August von Galen (Oct. 9); Charles de Foucauld, Maria Pia Pastena, Maria Crocifissa Curcio, Eurosia Fabris (Nov. 13); María De Los Ángeles Ginard Martí, Josep Tàpies and six Companions (Oct. 29); Anacleto González Flores and 8 Companions, José Trinidad Rangel, Andrés Solá Molist, Leonardo Pérez, Darío Acosta Zurita (Nov. 20).

2006: Agostino Thevarparampil Kunjachan, Luigi Biraghi, Luigi Monza (Apr. 30); Maria Teresa of Saint Joseph (May 13); Sr. Maria of the Passion (May 14); Rita Amada of Jesus (May 28); Eustáquio von Lieshout (June 15).

ROMAN CURIA

The Roman Curia is the Church's network of central administrative agencies (called dicasteries) serving the Vatican and the local churches, with authority granted by the Pope.

The Curia evolved gradually from advisory assemblies or synods of the Roman clergy with whose assistance the popes directed church affairs during the first 11 centuries. Its original office was the Apostolic Chancery, established in the fourth century to transmit documents. The antecedents of its permanently functioning agencies and offices were special commissions of cardinals and prelates. Its establishment in a form resembling what it is now dates from the second half of the 16th century.

Pope Paul VI initiated a four-year reorganization study in 1963 that resulted in the constitution *Regimini Ecclesiae Universae.* The document was published Aug. 18, 1967, and went into full effect in March 1968. Pope John Paul II, in the apostolic constitution *Pastor Bonus,* published June 28, 1988, and effective Mar. 1, 1989, ordered modifications of the Curia based on the broad outline of Paul VI's reorganization.

In accordance with Pope John Paul II's reform effective Mar. 1, 1989, and later revisions, the Curia consists of the Secretariat of State, nine congregations (governing agencies), three tribunals (judicial agencies), 11 councils (promotional agencies) and three offices (specialized service agencies). All have equal juridical status with authority granted by the pope.

SECRETARIAT OF STATE

The Secretariat of State, *Palazzo Apostolico Vaticano,* Vatican City. Cardinal Tarcisio Bertone, Secretary of State; Most Rev. Leonardo Sandri, Deputy for General Affairs; Dominique Mamberti, Secretary for Relations with States.

The Secretariat of State provides the pope with the closest possible assistance in the care of the universal Church. It consists of two sections:

• The Section for General Affairs assists the pope in expediting daily business of the Holy See. It coordinates curial operations, prepares drafts of documents entrusted to it by the pope, has supervisory duties over the *Acta Apostolicae Sedis, Annuario Pontificio,* the Vatican Press Office and the Central Statistics Office.

• The Section for Relations with States (formerly the Council for Public Affairs of the Church, a separate body) handles diplomatic and other relations with civil governments. Attached to it is a council of Cardinals and Bishops.

Background: Evolved gradually from secretarial offices (dating back to the 15th century) and the Congregation for Extraordinary Ecclesiastical Affairs (dating back to 1793; restructured as the Council for the Public Affairs of the Church by Paul VI in 1967). John Paul II gave it its present form in his June 28, 1988, reform of the Curia.

CONGREGATIONS

Congregation for the Doctrine of the Faith: Piazza del S. Uffizio 11, 00193 Rome, Italy. Cardinal William Levada, prefect; Most Rev. Angelo Amato, S.D.B., secretary.

Has responsibility to safeguard the doctrine of faith and morals. Accordingly, it examines doctrinal questions and promotes studies thereon; evaluates theological opinions and, when necessary and after prior consultation with concerned bishops, reproves those regarded as opposed to principles of the faith; examines books on doctrinal matters and can reprove such works, if the contents so warrant, after giving authors the opportunity to defend themselves. It examines matters pertaining to the Privilege of Faith (Petrine Privilege) in marriage cases, and safeguards the dignity of the sacrament of penance. Attached to the congregation are the Pontifical Biblical Commission and the Theological Commission.

Background: At the beginning of the 13th century, legates of Innocent III were commissioned as the Holy Office of the Inquisition to combat heresy; the same task was entrusted to the Dominican Order by Gregory IX in 1231 and to the Friars Minor by Innocent IV from 1243 to 1254. On July 21, 1542 (apostolic constitution *Licet*), Paul III instituted a permanent congregation of cardinals with supreme and universal competence over matters concerning heretics and those suspected of heresy. Pius IV, St. Pius V and Sixtus V further defined the work of the congregation. St. Pius X changed its name to the Congregation of the Holy Office. Paul VI (*motu proprio Integrae Servandae,* Dec. 7, 1965), began reorganization of the Curia with this body, to which he gave the new title, Congregation for the Doctrine of the Faith. Its orientation is not merely negative, in the condemnation of error, but positive, in the promotion of orthodox doctrine.

Congregation for the Oriental Churches: Palazzo del Bramante, Via della Conciliazione 34, 00193 Rome, Italy. Cardinal Ignace Moussa I Daoud, prefect; Most Rev. Antonio Maria Vegliò, secretary. Members include all patriarchs of the Eastern Catholic Churches and major archbishops.

Has competence in matters concerning the persons and discipline of Eastern Catholic Churches. It has jurisdiction over territories in which the majority of Christians belong to Eastern Churches (i.e., Egypt, the Sinai Peninsula, Eritrea, Northern Ethiopia, Southern Albania, Bulgaria, Cyprus, Greece, Iran, Iraq, Lebanon, Palestine, Syria, Jordan, Turkey, Afghanistan); also, over minority communities of Eastern Church members no matter where they live.

Background: Established by Pius IX Jan. 6, 1862 (apostolic constitution *Romani Pontifices*), and united with the Congregation for the Propagation of the Faith. The congregation was made autonomous by Benedict XV May 1, 1917 (*motu proprio Dei Providentis*), and given wider authority by Pius XI, Mar. 25, 1938 (*motu proprio Sancta Dei Ecclesia*).

Congregation for Divine Worship and the Discipline of the Sacraments: Piazza Pio XII 10, 00193 Rome, Italy. Cardinal Francis Arinze, prefect; Most Rev. Don Albert Malcolm Ranjith Patabendige, secretary.

Supervises everything pertaining to the promotion and regulation of the liturgy, primarily the sacraments, without prejudice to the competencies of the Congregation for the Doctrine of the Faith. Attached to the congregation are special commissions treating causes of nullity of sacred ordinations and dispensations from obligations of sacred ordination of deacons and priests.

Background: Originally two separate congregations: the Congregation for Divine Worship (instituted by Paul VI, May 8, 1969) and the Congregation for the Discipline of the Sacraments (established by St. Pius X, June 29, 1908, to replace the Congregation of Rites instituted by Pope Sixtus V in 1588). They were united by Paul VI, July 11, 1975, as the Congregation for the Sacraments and Divine Worship; reestablished as separate congregations by John Paul II in an autograph letter of Apr. 5, 1984, and reunited anew by the same Pope, June 28, 1988 (apostolic constitution *Pastor Bonus*), as the Congregation for Divine Worship and the Discipline of the Sacraments.

Congregation for the Causes of Saints: Piazza Pio XII 10, 00193 Rome, Italy. Cardinal José Saraiva Martins, C.F.M., prefect; Most Rev. Edward Nowak, secretary.

Handles matters connected with beatification and canonization causes (in accordance with revised procedures decreed in 1983), and the preservation of relics.

Background: Established by Sixtus V in 1588 as the Congregation of Rites; affected by legislation of Pius XI in 1930; title changed and functions defined by Paul VI, 1969 (apostolic constitution *Sacra Rituum Congregatio*). It was restructured and canonization procedures were revised by John Paul II in 1983 (apostolic constitution *Divinus Perfectionis Magister*).

Congregation for Bishops: Piazza Pio XII 10, 00193 Rome, Italy. Cardinal Giovanni Battista Re, prefect; Most Rev. Francesco Monterisi, secretary.

Has functions related in one way or another to bishops and the jurisdictions in which they serve. It supervises the Pontifical Commission for Latin America. Attached to the congregation are a central coordinating office for Military Vicars (established Feb. 2, 1985) and an office for coordinating *ad limina* visits (established June 29, 1988).

Background: Established by Sixtus V Jan. 22, 1588 (apostolic constitution *Immensa*); given an extension of powers by St. Pius X June 20, 1908, and Pius XII Aug. 1, 1952 (apostolic constitution *Exsul Familia*); given present title (was known as Consistorial Congregation) by Paul VI (Aug. 1, 1967); competencies redefined by John Paul II, June 28, 1988.

Congregation for the Evangelization of Peoples: Piazza di Spagna 48, 00187 Rome, Italy. Cardinal Ivan Dias, prefect; Most Rev. Robert Sarah, secretary; Most Rev. Henryk Hoser, S.A.C., adjunct secretary.

Directs and coordinates missionary work throughout the world. Accordingly, it has competence over those matters which concern all the missions established for the spread of Christ's kingdom without prejudice to the competence of other congregations. These include: fostering missionary vocations; assigning missionaries to fields of work; establishing ecclesiastical jurisdictions and proposing candidates to serve them as bishops and in other capacities; encouraging the recruitment and development of indigenous clergy; mobilizing spiritual and financial support for missionary activity.

To promote missionary cooperation, the congregation has a Supreme Council for the Direction of Pontifical Missionary Works composed of the Missionary Union of the Clergy and Religious, the Society for the Propagation of the Faith, the Society of St. Peter the Apostle for Native Clergy, the Society of the Holy Childhood, and the International Center of Missionary Animation.

Background: Originated as a commission of cardinals by St. Pius V and Gregory XII for missions in East and West Indies, Italo-Greeks and for ecclesiastical affairs in Protestant territories of Europe; Clement VIII instituted a Congregation of the Propagation of the Faith in 1599 which ceased to exist after several years. Erected as a stable congregation by Gregory XV June 22, 1622 (apostolic constitution *Inscrutabili Divinae*);

its functions were redefined by John Paul II, June 28, 1988.

Congregation for the Clergy: Piazza Pio XII 3, 00193 Rome, Italy. Cardinal Darío Castrillón Hoyos, prefect; Most Rev. Csaba Ternyák, secretary.

Has three offices with competencies concerning the life, discipline, rights and duties of the clergy; the preaching of the Word, catechetics, norms for religious education of children and adults; preservation and administration of the temporal goods of the Church. Attached to it are the International Council for Catechetics (established in 1973 by Paul VI) and the Institute *Sacrum Ministerium* for the permanent formation of the clergy (established in line with John Paul II's 1992 apostolic exhortation *Pastores Dabo Vobis*).

Background: Established by Pius IV Aug. 2, 1564 (apostolic constitution *Alias Nos*), under the title Congregation of the Cardinals Interpreters of the Council of Trent; affected by legislation of Gregory XIII and Sixtus V; known as Congregation of the Council until Aug. 15, 1967, when Paul VI renamed it the Congregation for the Clergy and redefined its competency; John Paul II gave it added responsibilities June 28, 1988.

Congregation for Institutes of Consecrated Life and Societies of Apostolic Life: Piazza Pio XII 3, 00193 Rome, Italy. Cardinal Franc Rodé, C.M., prefect; Most. Rev. Gianfranco Giardin, O.F.M. Conv., secretary.

Has competence over institutes of Religious, secular institutes, societies of the apostolic life and third (secular) orders. With two sections, the congregation has authority in matters related to the establishment, general direction and suppression of the various institutes; general discipline in line with their rules and constitutions; the movement toward renewal and adaptation of institutes in contemporary circumstances; the setting up and encouragement of councils and conferences of major religious superiors for intercommunication and other purposes.

Background: Founded by Sixtus V May 27, 1586, with the title, Congregation for Consultations of Regulars; confirmed by the apostolic constitution *Immensa* Jan. 22, 1588; made part of the Congregation for Consultations of Bishops and other Prelates in 1601; made autonomous by St. Pius X in 1908 as Congregation of Religious; title changed to Congregation for Religious and Secular Institutes by Paul VI in 1967; given present title by John Paul II, June 28, 1988.

Congregation for Catholic Education (for Seminaries and Institutes of Study): Piazza Pio XII 3, 00193 Rome, Italy. Cardinal Zenon Grocholewski, prefect; Most Rev. Michael Miller, C.S.B., secretary.

Has supervisory competence over institutions and works of Catholic education. It carries on its work through three offices. One office handles matters connected with the direction, discipline and temporal administration of seminaries, and with the education of diocesan clergy, religious and members of secular institutes. A second office oversees Catholic universities, faculties of study and other institutions of higher learning inasmuch as they depend on the authority of the Church; encourages cooperation and mutual assistance among Catholic institutions, and the establishment of Catholic hospices and centers on campuses of non-Catholic institutions. A third office is concerned in various ways with all Catholic schools below the college-university level, with general questions concerning education and studies, and with the cooperation of conferences of bishops and civil authorities in educational matters. The congregation supervises Pontifical Works for Priestly Vocations.

Background: The title (Congregation of Seminaries and Universities) and functions of the congregation were defined by Benedict XV Nov. 4, 1915; Pius XI, in 1931 and 1932, and Pius XII, in 1941 and 1949, extended its functions; Paul VI changed its title to Congregation for Catholic Education in 1967; given its present title by Pope John Paul II, June 28, 1988. Its work had previously been carried on by two other congregations erected by Sixtus V in 1588 and Leo XII in 1824.

INTER-AGENCY CURIA COMMISSIONS

In accordance with provisions of the apostolic constitution *Pastor Bonus*, John Paul II established the following interdepartmental permanent commissions to handle matters when more than one agency of the Curia is involved in activities:

• For matters concerning appointments to local Churches and the setting up and alteration of them and their constitution (Mar. 22, 1989). Members include officials of the Secretariat of State and Congregation for Bishops. President, Cardinal Tarcisio Bertone, Secretary of State.

• For matters concerning members, individually or as a community, of Institutes of Consecrated Life founded or working in mission territories (Mar. 22, 1989). Members include officials of the Congregations for the Evangelization of Peoples and for Institutes of Consecrated Life and Societies of Apostolic Life. President, Cardinal Ivan Dias, prefect of the Congregation for the Evangelization of Peoples.

• For the formation of candidates for Sacred Orders (Mar. 22, 1989). Members include officials of the Congregations for Catholic Education, for Institutes of Consecrated Life and Societies of Apostolic Life, for Evangelization of Peoples, for Oriental Churches. President, Cardinal Zenon Grocholewski, prefect of the Congregation for Catholic Education.

• For promoting a more equitable distribution of priests throughout the world (July 20, 1991). Members include secretaries of congregations for Evangelization of Peoples, for the Clergy, Catholic Education, for the Institutes of Consecrated Life and Societies of Apostolic Life; and vice-president of Commission for Latin America. President, Card. Zenon Grocholewski, Prefect of the Congregation for Catholic Education.

• For the Church in Eastern Europe (Jan. 15, 1993), replacing the Pontifical Commission for Russia which was terminated. The commission is concerned with both Latin and Eastern-rite churches in territories of the former Soviet Union and other nations affected by the historical circumstances resulting from atheistic communism. It is responsible for promoting the apostolic mission of the Church and fostering ecumenical dialogue with the Orthodox and other Churches of the Eastern tradition. Members, under presidency of Cardinal Secretary of State, include the secretary and undersecretary of the Section for Relations with States and secretaries of Congregations for the Oriental Churches, for the Clergy, for Institutes of Consecrated Life and Societies of Apostolic Life, secretary of the Pontifical Council for Promoting Christian Unity.

President, Cardinal Tarcisio Bertone.

TRIBUNALS

Apostolic Penitentiary: Piazza della Cancelleria 1, 00186 Rome, Italy. Cardinal James Francis Stafford, major penitentiary; regent, Rev. P. Gianfranco Girotti, O.F.M. Conv.

Has jurisdiction for the internal forum only (sacramental and non-sacramental). It issues decisions on questions of conscience; grants absolutions, dispensations, commutations, sanations and condonations; has charge of non-doctrinal matters pertaining to indulgences.

Background: Origin dates back to the 12th century; affected by the legislation of many popes; radically reorganized by St. Pius V in 1569; jurisdiction limited to the internal forum by St. Pius X; Benedict XV annexed the Office of Indulgences to it Mar. 25, 1917.

Apostolic Signatura: Piazza della Cancelleria 1, 00186 Rome, Italy. Card. Agostino Vallini, prefect; Most Rev. Velasio De Paolis, C.S., secretary.

The principal concerns of this supreme court of the Church are to resolve questions concerning juridical procedure and to supervise the observance of laws and rights at the highest level. It decides the jurisdictional competence of lower courts and has jurisdiction in cases involving personnel and decisions of the Rota. It is the supreme court of the State of Vatican City.

Background: A permanent office of the Supreme Tribunal of the Apostolic Signatura has existed since the time of Eugene IV in the 15th century; affected by the legislation of many popes; reorganized by St. Pius X in 1908 and made the supreme tribunal of the Church.

Roman Rota: Piazza della Cancelleria 1, 00186 Rome, Italy. Mons. Antoni Stankiewicz, Dean.

The ordinary court of appeal for cases appealed to the Holy See. It is best known for its competence and decisions in cases involving the validity of marriage.

Background: Originated in the Apostolic Chancery; affected by the legislation of many popes; reorganized by St. Pius X in 1908; further revised by Pius XI in 1934; new norms approved and promulgated by John Paul II in 1982 and 1987.

PONTIFICAL COUNCILS

Pontifical Council for the Laity: Piazza S. Calisto 16, 00153 Rome, Italy. Most Rev. Stanislaw Rylko, president; Josef Clemens, secretary; Prof. Guzman Carriquiry, undersecretary.

Its competence covers the apostolate of the laity and their participation in the life and mission of the Church. Members are mostly lay people from different parts of the world and involved in different apostolates.

Background: Established on an experimental basis by Paul VI Jan. 6, 1967; given permanent status Dec. 10, 1976 (*motu proprio Apostolatus Peragendi*).

Pontifical Council for Promoting Christian Unity: Via dell' Erba 1, 00193 Rome, Italy. Cardinal Walter Kasper, president; Most Rev. Brian Farrell, L.C., secretary.

Handles relations with members of other Christian ecclesial communities; deals with the correct interpretation and execution of the principles of ecumenism; initiates or promotes Catholic ecumenical groups and coordinates on national and international levels the efforts of those promoting Christian unity; undertakes dialogue regarding ecumenical questions and activities with churches and ecclesial communities separated from the Apostolic See; sends Catholic observer-representatives to Christian gatherings, and invites to Catholic gatherings observers of other churches; orders into execution conciliar decrees dealing with ecumenical affairs. The **Commission for Religious Relations with the Jews** is attached to the secretariat.

Background: Established by John XXIII June 5, 1960, as a preparatory secretariat of the Second Vatican Council; raised to commission status during the first session of the council in the fall of 1962; status as a secretariat confirmed and functions defined by Paul VI in 1966 and 1967; made a pontifical council by John Paul II, June 28, 1988.

Pontifical Council for the Family: Piazza S. Calisto 16, 00153 Rome, Italy. Cardinal Alfonso López Trujillo, president; Most Rev. Karl Josef Romer, secretary.

Is concerned with promoting the pastoral care of families so they may carry out their educative, evangelizing and apostolic mission and make their influence felt in areas such as defense of human life and responsible procreation according to the teachings of the Church. Members, chosen by the Pope, are married couples and men and women from all parts of the world and representing different cultures. They meet in general assembly at least once a year.

Background: Instituted by John Paul II May 9, 1981, replacing the Committee for the Family established by Paul VI Jan. 11, 1973.

Pontifical Council for Justice and Peace: Piazza S. Calisto 16, 00153 Rome, Italy. Cardinal Renato Raffaele Martino, president; Most Rev. Giampaolo Crepaldi, secretary.

Its primary competence is to promote justice and peace in the world according to the Gospels and social teaching of the Church.

Background: Instituted by Paul VI Jan. 6, 1967, on an experimental basis; reconstituted and made a permanent commission Dec. 10, 1976; its competence was redefined and it was made a pontifical council June 28, 1988, by John Paul II.

Pontifical Council "*Cor Unum*": Piazza S. Calisto 16, 00153 Rome, Italy. Most Rev. Paul Josef Cordes, president; Msgr. Karel Kasteel, secretary.

Its principal aims are to provide informational and coordinating services for Catholic aid and human development organizations and projects on a worldwide scale. Attached to the council are the John Paul II Foundation for the Sahel and "*Populorum Progressio*."

Background: Instituted by Paul VI July 15, 1971.

Pontifical Council for Pastoral Care of Migrants and Itinerant Peoples: Piazza S. Calisto 16, 00153 Rome, Italy. Cardinal Renato Raffaele Martino, president; Most Rev. Agostino Marchetto, secretary.

Is concerned with pastoral assistance to migrants, nomads, tourists, sea, and air travelers.

Background: Instituted by Paul VI and placed under general supervision of Congregation for Bishops, Mar. 19, 1970; made autonomous as a pontifical council and renamed by John Paul II, June 28, 1988.

Pontifical Council for Pastoral Assistance to Health Care Workers: Via della Conciliazione 3, 00193 Rome, Italy. Cardinal Javier Lozano Barragán, president; Most Rev. José Luis Redrado Marchite, O.H., secretary.

Its functions are to stimulate and foster the work of formation, study and action carried out by various international

Catholic organizations in the health care field.

Background: Established in 1985 as a commission by John Paul II; made a council June 28, 1988.

Pontifical Council for the Interpretation of Legislative Texts: Piazza Pio XII 10, 00193 Rome, Italy. Cardinal Julián Herranz, president; Most Rev. Bruno Bertagna, secretary.

Primary function is the authentic interpretation of the universal laws of the Church.

Background: Established by John Paul II, Jan. 2, 1984, as the Pontifical Commission for the Authentic Interpretation of the Code of Canon Law; name changed and given additional functions June 28, 1988. Its competency was extended in 1991 to include interpretation of Code of Canon Law of Oriental Church that was promulgated in 1990.

Pontifical Council for Interreligious Dialogue: Via dell' Erba 1, 00193 Rome, Italy. Cardinal Paul Poupard, president; Most Rev. Pier Luigi Celata, secretary.

Its function is to promote studies and dialogue for the purpose of increasing mutual understanding and respect between Christians and non-Christians. The Commission for Religious Relations with Muslims is attached to the council.

Background: Established by Paul VI May 19, 1964, as the Secretariat for Non-Christians; given present title and functions by John Paul II, June 28, 1988.

Pontifical Council for Culture: Piazza S. Calisto 16, 00153 Rome, Italy. Cardinal Paul Poupard, president; Very Rev. Bernard Ardura, O. Praem., secretary.

Its functions are to foster the Church's and the Holy See's relations with the world of culture and to establish dialogue with those who do not believe in God or who profess no religion provided these are open to sincere cooperation. It consists of two sections: (1) faith and culture; (2) dialogue with cultures. Attached to it is the **Coordinating Council for Pontifical Academies.**

Background: Present council with expanded functions was instituted by John Paul II (*motu proprio* of Mar. 25, 1993) through the merger of the Pontifical Council for Culture (established May 20, 1982, by John Paul II) and the Pontifical Council for Dialogue with Non-Believers (established by Paul VI Apr. 9, 1965, as the secretariat for Non-Believers).

Pontifical Council for Social Communications: Palazzo S. Carlo, 00120 Vatican City. Most Rev. John P. Foley, president; secretary, vacant.

Engaged in matters pertaining to instruments of social communication so that through them the message of salvation and human progress is fostered and carried forward in civil culture and mores.

Background: Instituted on an experimental basis by Pius XII in 1948; reorganized three times in the 1950s; made permanent commission by John XXIII Feb. 22, 1959; established as council and functions restated by John Paul II June 28, 1988.

OFFICES

Apostolic Camera: Palazzo Apostolico, 00120 Vatican City. Cardinal Eduardo Martinez Somalo, chamberlain of the Holy Roman Church; Most Rev. Paolo Sardi, vice-chamberlain.

Administers the temporal goods and rights of the Holy See between the death of one pope and the election of another (*sede vacante*), in accordance with special laws.

Background: Originated in the 11th century; reorganized by Pius XI in 1934; functions redefined (especially of *camerlengo*) by subsequent legislation in 1945, 1962 and 1975.

Administration of the Patrimony of the Apostolic See: Palazzo Apostolico, 00120 Vatican City. Cardinal Attilio Nicora, president; Most Rev. Claudio Maria Celli, secretary.

Handles the estate of the Apostolic See under the direction of papal delegates acting with ordinary or extraordinary authorization.

Background: Some of its functions date back to 1878; established by Paul VI Aug. 15, 1967.

Prefecture for the Economic Affairs of the Holy See: Largo del Colonnato 3, 00193 Rome, Italy. Cardinal Sergio Sebastiani, president; Most Rev. Franco Croci, secretary.

A financial office that coordinates and supervises administration of the temporalities of the Holy See. Membership includes Cardinal Roger M. Mahony and Cardinal Edward Egan.

Background: Established by Paul VI Aug. 15, 1967; functions redefined by John Paul II, June 28, 1988.

OTHER CURIA AGENCIES

Prefecture of the Papal Household: Most Rev. James M. Harvey, prefect.

Oversees the papal chapel — which is at the service of the pope in his capacity as spiritual head of the Church, and the pontifical family — which is at the service of the pope as a sovereign. It arranges papal audiences, has charge of preparing non-liturgical elements of papal ceremonies, makes all necessary arrangements for papal visits and trips outside the Vatican, and settles questions of protocol connected with papal audiences and other formalities.

Background: Established by Paul VI Aug. 15, 1967, under the title Prefecture of the Apostolic Palace; it supplanted the Sacred Congregation for Ceremonies founded by Sixtus V Jan. 22, 1588. The office was updated and reorganized under the present title by Paul VI, Mar. 28, 1968.

Office for Liturgical Celebrations of the Supreme Pontiff: Palazzo Apostolico Vaticano, 00120 Vatican City. Most Rev. Piero Marini, Master of Ceremonies.

Prepares everything necessary for liturgical and other sacred celebrations by the Pope or in his name; directs everything in accordance with prescriptions of liturgical law.

Background: Evolved gradually from the early office of Apostolic Master of Ceremonies; affected by legislation of Pope Paul IV in 1563 and Benedict XV in 1917; restructured by Paul VI in 1967; given its present title (formerly known as Prefecture of Pontifical Ceremonies) and constituted as an autonomous agency of the Roman Curia by John Paul II, June 28, 1988.

Vatican Press Office: Via della Conciliazione 54, 00120 Vatican City. Rev. Federico Lombardi, S.J., director.

Established Feb. 29, 1968, to replace service agencies formerly operated by *L'Osservatore Romano* and an office created for press coverage of the Second Vatican Council. New directives were issued in 1986.

Vatican Information Service (VIS): Via della Conciliazione 54, 00120 Vatican City.

Established Mar. 28, 1990, within the framework but

distinct from the Vatican Press Office. Furnishes information, in English, French and Spanish, on pastoral and magisterial activity of the Pope through use of electronic mail and fax.

Central Statistics Office: Palazzo Apostolico, 00120 Vatican City.

Established by Paul VI Aug. 15, 1967; attached to the Secretariat of State. Compiles, systematizes and analyzes information on the status and condition of the Church.

COMMISSIONS AND COMMITTEES

Listed below are non-curial institutes that assist in the work of the Holy See. Some are attached to curial agencies, as indicated. Other institutes are listed elsewhere in the *Almanac; see* **Index.**

Pontifical Commission for the Cultural Heritage of the Church: Established by John Paul II, June 28, 1988, as Pontifical Commission for Preserving the Church's Patrimony of Art and History and attached to the Congregation for the Clergy; made autonomous and given present title Mar. 25, 1993. Most Rev. Mauro Piacenza, president.

Pontifical Commission for Sacred Archeology: Instituted by Pius IX Jan, 6, 1852. Most Rev. Mauro Piacenza, president.

Pontifical Biblical Commission: Instituted by Leo XIII Oct. 30, 1902; completely restructured by Paul VI June 27, 1971; attached to the Congregation for the Doctrine of the Faith. Cardinal William Levada, president.

Pontifical Commission for Latin America: Instituted by Pius XII Apr. 19, 1958; attached to the Congregation for Bishops July, 1969; restructured by John Paul II in 1988. Cardinal Giovanni Battista Re, president.

Pontifical Commission for the Revision and Emendation of the Vulgate: Established in 1984 by John Paul II to replace the Abbey of St. Jerome instituted by Pius XI in 1933. Rev. Jean Mallet, O.S.B., director.

Pontifical Commission "*Ecclesia Dei*": Established by John Paul II, July 2, 1988, to facilitate the return to full ecclesial communion of priests, seminarians and religious who belonged to the fraternity founded by Marcel Lefebvre. Cardinal Darío Castrillón Hoyos, president.

International Theological Commission: Instituted by Paul VI Apr. 11, 1969, as an advisory adjunct of no more than 30 theologians to the Congregation for the Doctrine of the Faith; definitive statutes promulgated by John Paul II, Aug. 6, 1982. Cardinal William Levada, president; Rev. Luis F. Ladaria, S.J., general secretary.

Commission for Religious Relations with the Jews: Instituted by Paul VI, Oct. 22, 1974, to promote and foster relations of a religious nature between Jews and Christians; attached to the Council for Promoting Christian Unity. Cardinal Walter Kasper, president.

Commission for Religious Relations with Muslims: Instituted by Paul VI, Oct. 22, 1974, to promote, regulate and interpret relations between Catholics and Muslims; attached to the Council for Interreligious Dialogue. Cardinal Paul Poupard, president.

Pontifical Committee for International

Eucharistic Congresses: Instituted, 1879, by Pope Leo XIII; established as a pontifical committee with new statutes by John Paul II, Feb. 11, 1986. Card. Jozef Tomko, president.

Pontifical Committee for Historical Sciences: Instituted by Pius XII Apr. 7, 1954, as a continuation of a commission dating from 1883. Msgr. Walter Brandmüller, president.

Vatican II Archives: Preserves the documents of the Second Vatican Council.

Disciplinary Commission of the Roman Curia: Most Rev. Julián Herranz, president.

Commission for the Protection of the Historical and Artistic Monuments of the Holy See: Instituted by Pius XI in 1923, reorganized by Paul VI in 1963. Cardinal Francesco Marchisano, president.

Institute for Works of Religion: Instituted by Pius XII June 27, 1942, to bank and administer funds for works of religion; replaced an earlier administration established by Leo XIII in 1887; reorganized by John Paul II (chirograph of Mar. 1, 1990). Headed by a commission of cardinals, including Cardinal Angelo Sodano and Cardinal Adam Maida.

Fabric of St. Peter: Administration, care and preservation of Vatican Basilica. Abp. Angelo Comastri, president.

Office of Papal Charities (Apostolic Almoner): Distributes alms and aid to those in need in the name of the pope. Most Rev. Oscar Rizzato, almoner.

Labor Office of the Apostolic See (ULSA - *Ufficio del Lavoro della Sede Apostolica*): Has competence in regard to those who work for the Apostolic See; charged with settling labor issues. Instituted by John Paul II (*motu proprio* of Jan. 1, 1989); functions reaffirmed and definitive text of statutes approved by John Paul II (*motu proprio* of Sept. 30, 1994). Cardinal Francesco Marchisano, president.

INTERNATIONALIZATION

As of May 15, 2006, principal officials of the Roman Curia were from the following countries: Italy (Cards. Antonetti, Bertone, Cacciavillan, Cheli, Fagiolo, Felici, Laghi, Marchisano, Martino, Monduzzi, Nicora, Noè, Pompedda, Ré, Sebastiani, Silvestrini, Sodano, Vallini; Abps. Amato, Celli, Comastri, Crepaldi, Cunial, de Magistris, Lajolo, Marchetto, Marini, Monterisi, Nesti, Pompedda, Salerno, Tamburinno, Veglió; Bps. Bertagna, Pastore); France (Cards. Etchegaray, Poupard, Tauran); United States (Cards. Baum, Levada, Stafford, Szoka, Abps. Foley, Harvey, Miller); Spain (Card. Martinez Somalo, Herranz; Abps. Gil Hellín, Redrado Marchite); Argentina (Card. Mejía); Germany (Card. Kasper, Bp. Cordes); Poland (Card. Grocholewski, Abps. Hoser, Nowak, Rylko); Argentina (Abp. Sandri); Brazil (Abp. Romer); Chile (Card. Medina Estévez); Colombia (Cards. Castrillón Hoyos, Lopez Trujillo); French Guinea (Abp. Sarah); Hungary (Ternyák); Mexico (Card. Lozano Barrágan); Nigeria (Card. Arinze); Portugal (Card. Saraiva Martins); India (Card. Dias), Ireland (Abp. Farrell); Slovakia (Card. Tomko); Slovenia (Card. Rodé); Sri Lanka (Abp. Patabendige Don); Switzerland (Card. Agustoni); Syria (Card. Moussa I Daoud); Ukraine (Abp. Marusyn); Japan (Card. Hamao); Croatia (Abp. Eterovic).

VATICAN CITY STATE

The State of Vatican City (*Stato della Città del Vaticano*) is the territorial seat of the papacy. The smallest sovereign state in the world, it is situated within the city of Rome, embraces an area of 108.7 acres, and includes within its limits the Vatican Palace, museums, art galleries, gardens, libraries, radio station, post office, bank, astronomical observatory, offices, apartments, service facilities, St. Peter's Basilica, and neighboring buildings between the Basilica and Viale Vaticano. The extraterritorial rights of Vatican City extend to more than 10 buildings in Rome, including the major basilicas and office buildings of various congregations of the Roman Curia, and to the papal villas at **Castel Gandolfo** 15 miles southeast of the City of Rome. Castel Gandolfo is the summer residence of the Holy Father.

The government of Vatican City is in the hands of the reigning pope, who has full executive, legislative and judicial power. The administration of affairs, however, is handled by the **Pontifical Commission for the State of Vatican City** under Abp. Giovanni Lajolo. The legal system is based on Canon Law; in cases where this code does not obtain, the laws of the City of Rome apply. The City is an absolutely neutral state and enjoys all the rights and privileges of a sovereign power. The citizens of Vatican City, and they alone, owe allegiance to the pope as a temporal head of state. On Nov. 26, 2000, Pope John Paul II promulgated the new Fundamental Law of the Vatican City State. The new law replaced that first established in 1929 by Pope Pius XI.

Cardinals of the Roman Curia residing outside Vatican City enjoy the privileges of extraterritoriality. The Secretary General for the Governatorate of the Vatican City State is Most Rev. Renato Boccardo.

The normal population is approximately 1,000. While the greater percentage is made up of priests and religious, there are several hundred laypersons living in Vatican City. They are housed in their own apartments in the City and are engaged in secretarial, domestic, trade and service occupations. Approximately 3,400 laypersons are employed by the Vatican.

Services of honor and order are performed by the Swiss Guards, who have been charged with responsibility for the personal safety of popes since 1506. The current Captain of the Swiss Guards is Elmar Theodor Mäder, who was appointed on Nov. 9, 2002. Additional police and ceremonial functions are under the supervision of a special office. These functions were formerly handled by the Papal Gendarmes, the Palatine Guard of Honor, and the Guard of Honor of the Pope (Pontifical Noble Guard); the units were disbanded by Pope Paul VI on Sept. 14, 1970.

The **Basilica of St. Peter**, built between 1506 and 1626, is the largest church in Christendom (with the exception of the Basilica of Our Lady Queen of Peace in Ivory Coast) and the site of most papal ceremonies. The pope's own patriarchal basilica, however, is **St. John Lateran**, whose origins date back to 324.

St. Ann's, staffed by Augustinian Fathers, is the parish church of Vatican City. Its pastor is appointed by the pope, following the recommendation of the prior general of the Augustinians and the archpriest of the Vatican Basilica.

The Church of **Santa Susanna** was designated as the national church for Americans in Rome by Pope Benedict XV Jan. 10, 1922, and entrusted to the Paulist Fathers, who have served there continuously since then except for several years during World War II.

Pastoral care in Vatican City State, which is separate from the diocese of Rome, is entrusted to the archpriest of St. Peter's Basilica, who is also vicar general for Vatican City and the papal villas at Castel Gandolfo (chirograph of Pope John Paul II, Jan. 14, 1991). Cardinal Francesco Marchisano was appointed to the posts in April 2002. In February 2005, Abp. Angelo Comastri was appointed coadjutor Archpriest of St. Peter's Basilica, vicar general for Vatican City, and President of the Fabric of St. Peter.

The **Vatican Library** (00120 Vatican City; Rev. Raffaele Farina, S.D.B., prefect; Dr. Ambrogio Piazzoni, vice-prefect) has among its holdings 150,000 manuscripts, about 1,000,000 printed books, and 7,500 incunabula. The **Vatican Secret Archives** (00120 Vatican City; Rev. Sergio Pagano, prefect), opened to scholars by Leo XIII in 1881, contain central church documents dating back to the time of Innocent III (1198–1216). Cardinal Jean-Louis Tauran is librarian and archivist of the Holy Roman Church.

The independent temporal power of the pope, which is limited to the confines of Vatican City and small areas outside, was for many centuries more extensive than it is now. As late as the 19th century, the pope ruled 16,000 square miles of Papal States across the middle of Italy, with a population of over 3,000,000. In 1870 forces of the Kingdom of Italy occupied these lands that, with the exception of the small areas surrounding the Vatican and Lateran in Rome and the Villas of Castel Gandolfo, became part of the Kingdom by the Italian law of May 13, 1871.

The **Roman Question**, occasioned by this seizure and the voluntary confinement of the pope to the Vatican, was settled with ratification of the Lateran Agreement June 7, 1929, by the Italian government and Vatican City. The agreement recognized Catholicism as the religion of Italy and provided, among other things, a financial indemnity to the Vatican in return for the former Papal States; it became Article 7 of the Italian Constitution, Mar. 26, 1947. The Lateran Agreement was superseded by a new concordat given final approval by the Italian Chamber of Deputies Mar. 20 and formally ratified June 3, 1985.

Papal Flag

The papal flag consists of two equal vertical stripes of yellow and white, charged with the insignia of the papacy on the white stripe — triple crown or tiara over two crossed keys, one of gold and one of silver, tied with a red cord and two tassels. The divisions of the crown represent the teaching, sanctifying and ruling offices of the pope. The keys symbolize his jurisdictional authority.

The papal flag is a national flag inasmuch as it is the standard of the Supreme Pontiff as the sovereign of the state of Vatican City. It is also universally accepted by the faithful as a symbol of the supreme spiritual authority of the Holy Father.

Vatican Radio

The declared purpose of Vatican radio station HVJ is "that the voice of the Supreme Pastor may be heard throughout the world by means of the ether waves, for the glory of Christ and the salvation of souls." Designed by Guglielmo Marconi, the inventor of radio, and supervised by him until his death, the station was inaugurated by Pope Pius XI in 1931. The original purpose has been extended to a wide variety of programming.

Vatican Radio operates on international wave lengths, transmits programs in 37 languages, and serves as a channel of communication between the Vatican, church officials and listeners in general in many parts of the world. The station broadcasts about 400 hours a week throughout the world.

The daily English-language program for North America is broadcast on 6095, 7305, 9600 Khz as well as via satellite INTELSAT 325,5° East (Atlantic) — 4097.75 Mhz — LHCP polarization.

Frequencies, background information and audio files can be obtained at www.radiovaticana.org and www.vatican.va.

The staff of 415 broadcasters and technicians includes 30 Jesuits. Studios and offices are at Palazzo Pio, Piazza Pia, 3, 00193 Rome. The transmitters are situated at Santa Maria di Galeria, a short distance north of Rome. Cardinal Roberto Tucci, S.J., president; Rev. Federico Lombardi, S.J., director-general.

2007 Vatican Stamps and Coins

The Vatican Philatelic and Numismatic Office (00120 Vatican City) published the following list of stamps and coins for 2006:

Stamps

• Automatic postage stamps.
• Pontificate of Pope Benedict XVI.
• Europa 2007.
• General Assembly of the Ordinary Synod of Bishops – The Eucharist.
• The Voyages of Pope John Paul II in the World (2004).
• Great Museums of the World: Louvre and the Vatican Museums.
• Fifth Centenary of the Founding of the Pontifical Swiss Guard.
• Christmas.

Postal Stationery

Aerogram: VII Centenary of the Death of Saint Nicholas of Tolentino (1305- 2005).
Postcards: Start of the Pontificate of Pope Benedict XVI.

Publications

Vaticano 2006

Coins

• Series for the year (2006) of the Pontificate of Benedict XVI; in eight values (1, 2, 5, 10, 20, 50 Eurocent, 1 Euro and 2 Euro). Minting: B.U. and Mirror Proof (with a Silver Medal).
• XX World Youth Day (2 Euro).
• 60th Anniversary of the End of the Second World War (Silver, 5 Euro).
• Year of the Eucharist (Silver, 10 Euro).
• Two Celebrative Gold Coins: Sacrament of Baptism, the Sacrament of Christian Initiation (Gold, 20 and 50 Euro).
• Monetary Division of the Euro 2006.

Papal Audiences

General audiences are scheduled weekly, on Wednesday.

In Vatican City, they are held in the Audience Hall on the south side of St. Peter's Basilica or, weather permitting, in St. Peter's Square. The hall, which was opened in 1971, has a seating capacity of 6,800 and a total capacity of 12,000. Audiences have been held during the summer at Castel Gandolfo when the pope is there on a working vacation.

General audiences last from about 60 to 90 minutes, during which the pope gives a talk and his blessing. A résumé of the talk, which is usually in Italian, is given in several languages. Arrangements for papal audiences are handled by an office of the Prefecture of the Apostolic Household.

American visitors can obtain passes for general audiences by applying to the Bishops' Office for United States Visitors to the Vatican, Casa Santa Maria, Via dell'Umilita, 30, 00187 Rome. Private and group audiences are reserved for dignitaries of various categories and for special occasions.

Publications

Acta Apostolicae Sedis, 00120 Vatican City: The only "official commentary" of the Holy See, was established in 1908 for the publication of activities of the Holy See, laws, decrees and acts of congregations and tribunals of the Roman Curia. The first edition was published in Jan. 1909. St. Pius X made AAS an official organ in 1908. Laws promulgated for the Church ordinarily take effect three months after the date of their publication in this commentary. The publication, mostly in Latin, is printed by the Vatican Press. The immediate predecessor of this organ was Acta Sanctae Sedis, founded in 1865 and given official status by the Congregation for the Propagation of the Faith in 1904.

Activities of the Holy See, an annual documentary volume covering the activities of the pope and of the congregations, commissions, tribunals and offices of the Roman Curia.

Annuario Pontificio, 00120 Vatican City: The yearbook of the Holy See. It is edited by the Central Statistics Office of the Church and is printed in Italian, with some portions in other languages, by the Vatican Press. It covers the worldwide organization of the Church, lists members of the hierarchy, and includes a wide range of statistical information. The publication of a statistical yearbook of the Holy See dates back to 1716, when a volume called *Notizie* appeared. Publication under the present title began in 1860, was suspended in 1870, and resumed again in 1872 under the title *Catholic Hierarchy*. This volume was printed privately at first, but has been issued by the Vatican Press since 1885. The title *Annuario Pontificio* was restored in 1912, and the yearbook was called an "official publication" until 1924.

L'Osservatore Romano, Via del Pellegrino, 00120 Vatican City: The daily newspaper of the Holy See. It began publication July 1, 1861, as an independent enterprise under the ownership and direction of four Catholic laymen headed by Marcantonio Pacelli, vice minister of the interior under Pope Pius IX and a grandfather of the late Pius XII. Leo XIII bought the publication in 1890, making it the "pope's" own newspaper.

The only official material in *L'Osservatore Romano* is what appears under the heading, "*Nostre Informazioni*." This includes notices of appointments by the Holy See, the texts of papal encyclicals and addresses by the Holy Father and others, various types of documents, accounts of decisions and rulings of administrative bodies, and similar items. Additional material includes news and comment on developments in the Church and the world. Italian is the language most used. The editorial board is directed by Prof. Mario Agnes. A staff of about 15 reporters covers Rome news sources. A corps of correspondents provides foreign coverage.

A weekly roundup edition in English was inaugurated in 1968 (Fr. Paul S. Quinter is editor). Other weekly editions are printed in French (1949), Italian (1950), Spanish (1969), Portuguese (1970) and German (1971). The Polish edition (1980) is published monthly. *L'Osservatore della Domenica* is published weekly as a supplement to the Sunday issue of the daily edition.

Statistical Yearbook of the Church (*Annuarium Statisticum Ecclesiae*), issued by the Central Statistics Office of the Church, it contains principal data concerning the presence and work of the Church in the world. The first issue was published in 1972 under the title *Collection of Statistical Tables, 1969*. It is printed in corresponding columns of Italian, French, and Latin. Some of the introductory material is printed in other languages.

Vatican Television Center (*Centro Televisivo Vaticano*, CTV), Palazzo Belvedere, 00120 Vatican City: Instituted by John Paul II Oct. 23, 1983, with the rescript, *Ex Audentia*. Dr. Emilio Rossi is president of the administrative council.

Vatican Press, 00120 Vatican City: The official printing plant of the Vatican. The Vatican press was conceived by Marcellus II and Pius IV but was actually founded by Sixtus V on Apr. 27, 1587, to print the Vulgate and the writings of the Fathers of the Church and other authors. A Polyglot Press was established in 1626 by the Congregation for the Propagation of the Faith to serve the needs of the Oriental Church. St. Pius X merged both presses under the title Vatican Polyglot Press. It was renamed Vatican Press July 1, 1991, by John Paul II following restructuring. The plant has facilities for the printing of a wide variety of material in about 30 languages. Dir., Rev. Elio Torrigiani, S.D.B.

Vatican Publishing House (*Libreria Editrice Vaticana*), Piazza S. Pietro, 00120 Vatican City: Formerly an office of the Vatican Press to assist in the circulation of the liturgical and juridical publications of the Apostolic See, the congregations and later the *Acta Apostolicae Sedis*. In 1926, with the expansion of publishing activities and following the promulgation of the 1917 Code, the office was made an independent entity. An administrative council and editorial commission were instituted in 1983; in 1988 *Pastor Bonus* listed it among institutes joined to the Holy See; new statutes were approved by the Secretariat of State July 1, 1991. President, Msgr. Giuseppe Scotti.

DIPLOMATIC ACTIVITIES OF THE HOLY SEE

REPRESENTATIVES OF THE HOLY SEE

Representatives of the Holy See and their functions were the subject of a document entitled *Sollicitudo Omnium Ecclesiarum* which Pope Paul VI issued on his own initiative under the date of June 24, 1969.

Delegates and Nuncios

Papal representatives "receive from the Roman Pontiff the charge of representing him in a fixed way in the various nations or regions of the world.

"When their legation is only to local churches, they are known as apostolic delegates. When to this legation, of a religious and ecclesial nature, there is added diplomatic legation to states and governments, they receive the title of nuncio, pro-nuncio, and internuncio." An apostolic nuncio has the diplomatic rank of ambassador extraordinary and plenipotentiary. Traditionally, because the diplomatic service of the Holy See has the longest uninterrupted history in the world, a nuncio has precedence among diplomats in the country to which he is accredited and serves as dean of the diplomatic corps on state occasions. Since 1965 pro-nuncios, also of ambassadorial rank, have been assigned to countries in which this prerogative is not recognized. In recent years, the Vatican has phased out the title of pro-nuncio. The title of nuncio (with an asterisk denoting he is not dean of the diplomatic corps) has been given to the majority of appointments of ambassadorial rank. *See* **Other Representatives**.

Service and Liaison

Representatives, while carrying out their general and special duties, are bound to respect the autonomy of local churches and bishops. Their service and liaison responsibilities include the following:

- Nomination of Bishops: To play a key role in compiling, with the advice of ecclesiastics and lay persons, and submitting lists of names of likely candidates to the Holy See with their own recommendations.
- Bishops: To aid and counsel local bishops without interfering in the affairs of their jurisdictions.
- Episcopal Conferences: To maintain close relations with them and to assist them in every possible way. (Papal representatives do not belong to these conferences.)
- Religious Communities of Pontifical Rank: To advise and assist major superiors for the purpose of promoting and consolidating conferences of men and women religious and to coordinate their apostolic activities.
- Church-State Relations: The thrust in this area is toward the development of sound relations with civil governments and collaboration in work for peace and the total good of the whole human family. The mission of a papal representative begins with appointment and assignment by the pope and continues until termination of his mandate. He acts "under the guidance and according to the instructions of the cardinal secretary of state to whom he is directly responsible for the execution of the mandate entrusted to him by the Supreme Pontiff." Normally representatives are required to retire at age 75.

NUNCIOS AND DELEGATES

(*Sources:* Annuario Pontificio, L'Osservatore Romano, Acta Apostolicae Sedis, *Catholic News Service.*) *As of July 30, 2006. Country, rank of legation (corresponding to rank of legate unless otherwise noted), name of legate (archbishop unless otherwise noted) as available. An asterisk indicates a nuncio who is not presently dean of the diplomatic corps.*

Delegate for Papal Legations: Archbishop Carlo M. Viganò, titular archbishop of Ulpiana. The post was established in 1973 to coordinate papal diplomatic efforts throughout the world. The office entails responsibility for "following more closely through timely visits the activities of papal representatives . . . and encouraging their rapport with the central offices" of the Secretariat of State.

Albania: Tirana, Nunciature; Giovanni Bulaitis.*

Algeria: Algiers, Nunciature; Thomas Yeh Sheng-nan* (also nuncio* to Tunisia).

Andorra: Nunciature; Manuel Monteiro de Castro (also nuncio to Spain).

Angola: Luanda, Nunciature; Giovanni Angelo Becciu* (also nuncio* to São Tome and Principe). (Diplomatic relations established in 1997.)

Antigua and Barbuda: Nunciature; Thomas E. Gullickson* (resides in Port of Spain, Trinidad).

Antilles: Apostolic Delegation; Thomas E. Gullickson (resides in Port of Spain, Trinidad).

Arabian Peninsula: Apostolic Delegation; Luigi Gatti (also nuncio in Kuwait and Lebanon; resides in Lebanon).

Argentina: Buenos Aires, Nunciature; Adriano Bernardini.

Armenia: Nunciature; Claudio Gugerotti* (resides in Tbilisi, Georgia; also nuncio* to Georgia and Azerbaijan). (Diplomatic relations established in 1992.)

Australia: Canberra, Nunciature; Ambrose de Paoli.

Austria: Vienna, Nunciature; Edmond Farhat.

Azerbaijan: Nunciature; Claudio Gugerotti* (resides in Tbilisi, Georgia; also nuncio* to Georgia and Armenia). (Diplomatic relations established in 1992.)

Bahamas: Nunciature; Thomas E. Gullickson* (resides in Port of Spain, Trinidad).

Bahrain: Manama; Nunciature; Mounged El-Hachem. (Diplomatic relations established Jan. 12, 2000; also nuncio in Kuwait, Qatar, and Yemen.)

Bangladesh: Dhaka, Nunciature; Paul Tschang In-Nam.*

Barbados: Nunciature; Vacant* (resides in Port of Spain, Trinidad).

Belarus: Nunciature; Martin Vidovic.*

Belgium: Brussels, Nunciature; Karl-Josef Rauber (also nuncio to Luxembourg).

Belize: Nunciature; Luigi Pezzuto* (resides in Port of Spain, Trinidad).

Benin (formerly Dahomey): Nunciature; Michael A. Blume, S.V.D.* (resides in Accra, Ghana).

Bolivia: La Paz, Nunciature; Ivo Scapolo.

Bosnia and Herzegovina: Sarajevo, Nunciature; Alessandro D'Errico.*

Botswana: See South Africa.

Brazil: Brasilia, Nunciature; Lorenzo Baldisseri.

Brunei: See Malaysia and Brunei.

Bulgaria: Sofia, Nunciature (reestablished in 1990);

Giuseppe Leanza.*

Burkina Faso: Ouagadougou, Nunciature; Mario Roberto Cassari* (resides in Abidjan, Côte d'Ivoire; also nuncio* to Niger and Côte d'Ivoire).

Burma: See Myanmar.

Burundi: Bujumbura, Nunciature; Paul Richard Gallagher.*

Cambodia: Nunciature; Vacant* (resides in Bangkok, Thailand). (Diplomatic relations established in 1994.)

Cameroon: Yaounde, Nunciature; Eliseo Antonio Ariotti (also nuncio to Equatorial Guinea).

Canada: Ottawa, Nunciature; Luigi Ventura.*

Cape Verde, Republic of: Nunciature; Giuseppe Pinto* (resides in Dakar, Senegal).

Central African Republic: Bangui, Nunciature; Pierre Nguyên Van Tot* (also nuncio* to Chad).

Chad: Nunciature; Pierre Nguyên Van Tot* (resides in Bangui, Central African Republic).

Chile: Santiago, Nunciature; Aldo Cavalli.

China, Republic of: Taipei (Taiwan), Nunciature; vacant.

Colombia: Bogota, Nunciature; Beniamino Stella.

Comoros: See Madagascar.

Congo (formerly Zaire): Kinshasa-Gombe, Nunciature; Giovanni d'Aniello.*

Congo: Brazzaville, Nunciature; Andrés Carrascosa Coso* (also nuncio* to Gabon).

Costa Rica: San Jose, Nunciature; vacant.

Côte d'Ivoire (Ivory Coast): Abidjan, Nunciature; Mario Roberto Cassari (also nuncio* to Niger and Burkina Faso).

Croatia: Zagreb, Nunciature; Francisco-Javier Lozano.

Cuba: Havana, Nunciature; Luigi Bonazzi.*

Cyprus: Nicosia, Nunciature; Antonio Franco (also nuncio to Israel).

Czech Republic: Prague, Nunciature; Diego Causero.

Denmark: Copenhagen, Nunciature; Giovanni Tonucci* (also nuncio* to Finland, Iceland, Norway and Sweden).

Djibouti: Nunciature (established May 2000); Ramiro Moliner Inglés (resides in Addis Ababa, Ethiopia).

Dominica: Nunciature; Thomas E. Gullickson* (resides in Port-of-Spain, Trinidad).

Dominican Republic: Santo Domingo, Nunciature; Timothy P. Broglio (also serves as Apostolic Delegate to Puerto Rico).

East Timor: Díli, Nunciature; Leopoldo Girelli (also nuncio* to Indonesia). (Diplomatic relations established on May 20, 2002.)

Ecuador: Quito, Nunciature; Giacomo Ottonello.

Egypt: Cairo, Nunciature; Michael Louis Fitzgerald, M.Afr. (also delegate to the Organization of the League of Arab States).*

El Salvador: San Salvador, Nunciature; Luigi Pezzuto.

Equatorial Guinea: Santa Isabel, Nunciature; Eliseo Antonio Ariotti* (resides in Yaounde, Cameroon).

Eritrea: Nunciature; Vacant* (resides in Ethiopia). (Diplomatic relations established in 1995.)

Estonia: Nunciature; Peter Stephan Zurbriggen* (resides in Vilna, Lithuania).

Ethiopia: Addis Ababa, Nunciature; Ramiro Moliner Inglés* (also nuncio* to Eritrea and apostolic delegate to Djibouti).

European Community: Brussels, Belgium, Nunciature; André Dupuy.
Fiji: Nunciature; Charles D. Balvo* (resides in Wellington, New Zealand).
Finland: Helsinki, Nunciature; Giovanni Tonucci* (resides in Denmark).
France: Paris, Nunciature; Fortunato Baldelli.
Gabon: Libreville, Nunciature; Andrés Carrascosa Coso* (resides in Congo).
Gambia: Nunciature; George Antonysamy* (resides in Freetown, Sierra Leone).
Georgia: Tbilisi, Nunciature; Claudio Gugerotti* (also nuncio* to Armenia and Azerbaijan). (Diplomatic relations established in 1992.)
Germany: Bonn, Nunciature; Erwin Josef Ender.
Ghana: Accra, Nunciature; George Kocherry * (also nuncio to Benin and Togo).
Great Britain: London, Nunciature; Faustino Sainz Muñoz* (also papal representative to Gibraltar).
Greece: Athens, Nunciature; Patrick Coveney.*
Grenada: Nunciature; vacant* (resides in Port of Spain, Trinidad).
Guatemala: Guatemala City, Nunciature; Bruno Musarò.
Guinea: Conakry, Nunciature; George Antonysamy* (resides in Freetown, Sierra Leone).
Guinea Bissau: Nunciature; Giuseppe Pinto* (resides at Dakar, Senegal).
Guyana: Nunciature; vacant (resides in Port of Spain, Trinidad).
Haiti: Port-au-Prince, Nunciature; Mario Giordana.
Honduras: Tegucigalpa, Nunciature; Antonio Arcari.
Hungary: Budapest, Nunciature; Juliusz Janusz (also nuncio* to Moldova).
Iceland: Nunciature; Giovanni Tonucci* (resides in Denmark).
India: New Delhi, Nunciature; Pedro López Quintana* (also nuncio* to Nepal).
Indonesia: Jakarta, Nunciature; Leopoldo Girelli (also nuncio to East Timor).*
Iran: Teheran, Nunciature; Angelo Mottola.*
Iraq: Baghdad, Nunciature; Francis Chullikatt* (also nuncio to Jordan).
Ireland: Dublin, Nunciature; Giuseppe Lazzarotto.
Israel: Nunciature; Antonio Franco (also nuncio to Cyprus). (Diplomatic relations established June 1994.)
Italy: Rome, Nunciature; Paolo Romeo (also nuncio to San Marino).
Ivory Coast: See Côte d'Ivoire.
Jamaica: Nunciature; Vacant (resides in Port of Spain, Trinidad).
Japan: Tokyo, Nunciature; Alberto Bottari de Castello*.
Jerusalem and Palestine: Apostolic Delegation (also nuncio to Israel): Antonio Franco.
Jordan: Nunciature; Francis Chullikatt* (also nuncio to Iraq).
Kazakhstan: Almaty, Nunciature; Józef Wesolowski* (also nuncio* to Kyrgyzstan, Tajikistan and Uzbekistan).
Kenya: Nairobi, Nunciature; Alain Lebeaupin.*
Kiribati: Nunciature; Charles D. Balvo* (resides in Wellington, New Zealand).
Korea: Seoul, Nunciature; Emil Paul Tscherrig* (also nuncio* to Mongolia).

Kuwait: Al Kuwait, Nunciature; Mounged El-Hachem* (also nuncio in Qatar, Bahrain, and Yemen).
Kyrgyzstan: Nunciature; Józef Wesolowski * (resides in Kazakhstan; also nuncio* to Kyrgyzstan, Tajikistan and Uzbekistan).
Laos: Apostolic Delegation; vacant (resides in Bangkok, Thailand).
Latvia: Nunciature; Peter Stephan Zurbriggen* (resides in Vilna, Lithuania).
Lebanon: Beirut, Nunciature; Luigi Gatti (also nuncio* to Kuwait and apostolic delegate to Arabian Peninsula).
Lesotho: Maseru, Nunciature; Blasco Francisco Collaço (also nuncio to South Africa, Namibia, and Swaziland; resides in Pretoria, South Africa).
Liberia: Monrovia, Nunciature; George Antonysamy* (resides in Freetown, Sierra Leone).
Libya: Nunciature; Félix del Blanco Prieto* (resides in Malta). (Diplomatic relations established in 1997.)
Liechtenstein: Nunciature; Francesco Canalini (resides in Bern, Switzerland).
Lithuania: Vilnius, Nunciature; Peter Stephan Zurbriggen* (also nuncio to Estonia and Latvia.).
Luxembourg: Nunciature; Karl-Josef Rauber (resides in Brussels, Belgium).
Macedonia: Nunciature; Abril y Castelló Santos* (also nuncio to Slovenia; resides in Slovenia).
Madagascar: Antananarivo, Nunciature; Augustine Kasujja* (also nuncio* to Seychelles, and Mauritius and Apostolic Delegate to Comoros and Reunion).
Malawi: Lilongwe, Nunciature; Nicola Girasoli* (resides in Lusaka, Zambia).
Malaysia and Brunei: Apostolic Delegation: vacant (resides in Bangkok, Thailand).
Mali: Nunciature; Giuseppe Pinto* (resides in Dakar, Senegal).
Malta: La Valletta, Nunciature; Félix del Blanco Prieto (also nuncio* to Libya).
Marshall Islands: Nunciature; Charles D. Balvo* (resides in Wellington, New Zealand).
Mauritania: Nouakchott, Apostolic Delegation; Giuseppe Pinto (resides in Dakar, Senegal).
Mauritius: Port Louis, Nunciature; Augustine Kasujja* (resides in Antananarivo, Madagascar).
Mexico: Mexico City, Nunciature; Giuseppe Bertello.* (Diplomatic relations established in 1992).
Micronesia, Federated States of: Nunciature; Charles D. Balvo* (resides in Wellington, New Zealand).
Moldova: Nunciature; Jean-Claude Périsset* (resides in Bucharest, Romania). (Diplomatic relations established in 1992.)
Mongolia: Nunciature; Emil Paul Tscherrig* (resides in Seoul, South Korea).
Morocco: Rabat, Nunciature; Ali Achour.*
Mozambique: Maputo, nunciature; George Panikulam.* (Diplomatic relations established in 1995.)
Myanmar (formerly Burma): Apostolic Delegation; Vacant (resides in Bangkok, Thailand).
Namibia: Nunciature; Blasco Francisco Collaço* (resides in Pretoria, South Africa).
Nauru: Nunciature; vacant* (resides in Wellington, New Zealand).
Nepal: Nunciature; Pedro López Quintana* (resides in New Delhi, India).

Netherlands: The Hague, Nunciature; François Bacqué.*

New Zealand: Wellington, Nunciature; Charles D. Balvo* (also nuncio* to Fiji, Kiribati, Marshall Islands, Federated States of Micronesia, Tonga, Vanuatu and Western Samoa; Apostolic Delegate to Pacific Islands).

Nicaragua: Managua, Nunciature; Jean-Paul Gobel.

Niger: Niamey, Nunciature; Mario Roberto Cassari* (resides in Abidjan, Côte d'Ivoire; also nuncio* to Burkina Faso and Côte d'Ivoire.)

Nigeria: Lagos, Nunciature; Renzo Fratini.*

Norway: Nunciature; Giovanni Tonucci* (resides in Denmark).

Pacific Islands: Nunciature; Charles D. Balvo (resides in Wellington, New Zealand).

Pakistan: Islamabad, Nunciature; Adolfo Tito Yllana.

Palau, Republic of: Palau, Nunciature; vacant.*

Panama: Panama City, Nunciature; vacant.

Papua New Guinea: Port Moresby; Nunciature; Francisco Padilla* (also nuncio* to Solomon Islands).

Paraguay: Asuncion, Nunciature; Orlando Antonini.

Peru: Lima, Nunciature; Rino Passigato.

Philippines: Manila, Nunciature; Fernando Filoni.

Poland: Warsaw; Nunciature; Hanna Suchoka.

Portugal: Lisbon, Nunciature; Edoardo Rovida.

Puerto Rico: See Dominican Republic.

Qatar: Dawhah, Nunciature; Mounged El-Hachem (Diplomatic relations established in Nov. 2002; also nuncio in Kuwait, Bahrain, and Yemen).

Reunion: See Madagascar.

Romania: Bucharest, Nunciature. Jean-Claude Périsset*

Russia (Federation of): Moscow, Nunciature; Antonio Mennini. (Nuncio appointed Representative of the Holy See to Russian Federation, 1994.)

Rwanda: Kigali, Nunciature. Anselmo Guido Pecorari.

Saint Vincent and the Grenadines: Nunciature; Thomas E. Gullickson, (resides in Port of Spain, Trinidad).

Samoa: Nunciature; Charles D. Balvo* (resides in Wellington, New Zealand).

San Marino: Nunciature; Paolo Romeo.

Santa Lucia: Nunciature; Thomas E. Gullickson* (resides in Port of Spain, Trinidad).

São Tome and Principe: Nunciature; Giovanni Angelo Becciu* (also nuncio* to Angola, where he resides).

Senegal: Dakar, Nunciature; Giuseppe Pinto* (also nuncio* to Cape Verde, Guinea-Bissau and Mali; Apostolic Delegate to Mauritania.)

Seychelles Islands: Nunciature; Augustine Kasujja* (resides in Antananrivo, Madagascar).

Sierra Leone: Freetown, Nunciature (1996); George Antonysamy* (also nuncio* to Gambia, Guinea and Liberia).

Singapore: Nunciature; vacant* (also nuncio to Cambodia and Thailand and apostolic delegate to Laos, Malaysia and Brunei, and Myanmar.)

Slovakia: Nunciature; Henryk Jozef Nowacki.

Slovenia: Ljubljana, Nunciature; Abril y Castelló Santos (also nuncio to Macedonia).

Solomon Islands: Nunciature; Francisco Padilla (resides in Port Moresby, Papua New Guinea).

Somalia: Apostolic Delegation (est. 1992); Vacant (resides in Sudan).

South Africa: Pretoria, Nunciature; Blasco Francisco Collaço.* (also nuncio* to Namibia and Swaziland and apostolic delegate to Botswana.)

Spain: Madrid, Nunciature; Manuel Monteiro de Castro.

Sri Lanka: Colombo, Nunciature; Mario Zenari.*

Sudan: Khartoum, Nunciature; Vacant* (also Apostolic Delegate to Somalia).

Suriname: Nunciature; vacant* (resides in Port of Spain, Trinidad).

Swaziland: Nunciature; Blasco Francisco Collaço* (resides in Pretoria, South Africa).

Sweden: Nunciature; Giovanni Tonucci* (resides in Denmark).

Switzerland: Bern, Nunciature; Francesco Canalini (also nuncio to Liechtenstein).

Syria: (Syrian Arab Republic): Damascus, Nunciature; Giovanni Battista Morandini.*

Tajikistan: Nunciature (1996); Józef Wesolowski* (resides in Kazakhstan; also nuncio* to Kyrgyzstan, Kazakh stan, and Uzbekistan).

Tanzania: Dar-es-Salaam, Nunciature; Joseph Chennoth.*

Thailand: Bangkok, Nunciature; vacant* (also nuncio* to Cambodia and Singapore and Apostolic Delegate to Laos, Malaysia, Brunei, Myanmar).

Togo: Lome, Nunciature; Michael A. Blume, S.V.D.* (resides in Accra, Ghana).

Tonga: Nunciature; Charles D. Balvo* (resides in Wellington, New Zealand).

Trinidad and Tobago: Port of Spain, Trinidad, Nunciature; Thomas E. Gullickson, (also nuncio to Antigua and Barbuda, Bahamas, Barbados, Belize, Dominica, Grenada, Jamaica, Saint Lucia, Saint Vincent and the Grenadines, Suriname and Apostolic Delegate to Antilles).

Tunisia: Tunis, Nunciature; Thomas Yeh Sheng-nan* (resides in Algiers, Algeria).

Turkey: Ankara, Nunciature; Antonio Lucibello.*

Turkmenistan: Nunciature (1996); Antonio Lucibello* (resides in Ankara, Turkey).

Uganda: Kampala, Nunciature; pro-nuncio, Christophe Pierre.

Ukraine: Kiev, Nunciature; Ivan Jurkovic.*

United States of America: Washington, DC, Nunciature; Pietro Sambi.*

Uruguay: Montevideo, Nunciature; Janusz Bolonek.

Uzbekistan: Nunciature; Józef Wesolowski* (resides in Kazakhstan; also nuncio* to Kazakhstan, Kyrgyzstan, and Tajikistan).

Vanuatu: Nunciature; Charles D. Balvo* (resides in Wellington, New Zealand).

Venezuela: Caracas, Nunciature; Giacinto Berloco.

Vietnam: Apostolic Delegation; vacant.

Western Samoa: Nunciature; Charles D. Balvo* (resides in Wellington, New Zealand).

Yemen: San'a, Nunciature; Mounged El-Hachem* (relations established in 1998, also nuncio to Kuwait, Bahrain, and Qatar).

Yugoslavia: Belgrade, Nunciature; Eugenio Sbarbaro.

Zaire: See Congo. Lusaka, Nunciature; Giuseppe Leanza* (also nuncio* to Malawi).

Zambia: Lusaka, Nunciature; Nicola Girasoli* (also nuncio* to Malawi).

Zimbabwe: Harare, Nunciature; Edward Joseph Adams.*

The Current Nuncio to the U.S.

The representative of the Pope to the Church in the United States is Archbishop Pietro Sambi, S.T.D., J.C.D. Archbishop Sambi was born in Sogliano sul Rubicone, Italy on June 27, 1938, and ordained a priest on March 14, 1964. He holds doctorates in sacred theology and in canon law. He began his service in the Diplomatic Corps of the Holy See in Apr. 1969, in Cameroon, and served subsequently in the apostolic nunciatures in Jerusalem in 1971, Cuba in 1974, Algeria in 1978, Nicaragua in 1979, Belgium in 1981, and then in India in 1984, with the rank of counselor. He was ordained as bishop on Nov. 9, 1985 and was named pro-apostolic nuncio in Burundi in Oct. 1985; pro-apostolic nuncio in Indonesia in Nov. 1991; and apostolic nuncio in Israel and Cyprus, and apostolic delegate in Jerusalem and Palestine in June 1998. Archbishop Sambi speaks Italian, English, French and Spanish.

On Dec. 17, 2005, Archbishop Sambi was appointed nuncio to the United States and permanent observer to the Organization of American States, succeeding Archbishop Gabriel Montalvo.

The U.S. Apostolic Nunciature is located at 3339 Massachusetts Ave., N.W., Washington, DC 20008-3687; (202) 333-7121.

A Nuncio represents the Holy Father to both the hierarchy and Church of a particular nation and to that nation's civil government.

From 1893 to 1984, papal representatives to the Church in the U.S. were apostolic delegates (all archbishops): Francesco Satolli (1893-96), Sebastiano Martinelli, O.S.A., (1896-1902), Diomede Falconio, O.F.M. (1902-1911), Giovanni Bonzano (1911-22), Pietro Fumasoni-Biondi (1922-33), Amleto Cicognani (1933-58), Egidio Vagnozzi (1958-67), Luigi Raimondi (1967-73), Jean Jadot (1973-80), and Pio Laghi (1980-90) who was the first to hold the title Pro-Nuncio, beginning in 1984 (*See* Index, U.S.-Vatican Relations). Archbishop (now Cardinal) Agostino Cacciavillan was pro-nuncio and permanent observer to the Organization of American States from 1990 to 1998. Archbishop Gabriel Montalvo was nuncio and permanent observer to the Organization of American States from 1998 to 2005.

Other Representatives

(Sources: Annuario Pontificio; Catholic News Service.)

The Holy See has representatives to or is a regular member of a number of quasi-governmental and international organizations. Most Rev. Ernesto Gallina was appointed delegate to International Governmental Organizations Jan. 12, 1991.

Governmental Organizations: U.N. (Abp. Celestino Migliore, permanent observer); U.N. Office in Geneva and Specialized Institutions (Abp. Silvano Maria Tomasi, permanent observer); International Atomic Energy Agency (Msgr. Leo Boccardi, permanent representative); U.N. Office at Vienna and U.N. Organization for Industrial Development (Msgr. Leo Boccardi, permanent observer); U.N. Food and Agriculture Organization (Msgr. Renato Volante, permanent observer); U.N. Educational, Scientific and Cultural Organization (Msgr. Francesco Follo, permanent observer); World Organization of Commerce (Abp. Silvano Maria Tomasi); Council of Europe (Vito Rallo, special representative with function of permanent observer); Council for Cultural Cooperation of the Council of Europe (vacant, delegate); Organization of American States (Abp. Pietro Sambi, permanent observer, with personal title of apostolic nuncio); Organization for Security and Cooperation in Europe (Msgr. Leo Boccardi, permanent representative); International Institute for the Unification of Private Law (Prof. Giuseppe dalla Torre del Tiempo di Sanguinetto Conte, delegate); International Committee of Military Medicine (Rev. Luc De Maere, delegate); World Organization of Tourism (Msgr. Giovanni Francesco Brugnaro, permanent observer).

Non-Governmental Organizations: International Committee of Historical Sciences (Msgr. Walter Brandmüller); International Committee of the History of Art (Dr. Francesco Buranelli); International Committee of Anthropological and Ethnological Sciences; Committee for the Neutrality of Medicine; International Center of Study for the Preservation and Restoration of Cultural Goods (Dr. Francesco Buranelli); International Council of Monuments and Sites (Msgr. Francesco Follo, delegate); International Alliance on Tourism; World Association of Jurists (Abp. Gabriel Montalvo); International Commission of the Civil State (Msgr. Paul Richard Gallagher); International Astronomical Union; International Institute of Administrative Sciences; International Technical Committee for Prevention and Extinction of Fires; World Medical Association; International Archives Council; World Trade Organization.

DIPLOMATS TO THE HOLY SEE

(*Sources:* Annuario Pontificio, L'Osservatore Romano).

Listed below are countries maintaining diplomatic relations with the Holy See, dates of establishment (in some cases) and names of Ambassadors (as of Aug. 30, 2006).

Albania (1991): Zef Bushati.
Algeria (1972): Idriss Jazaïry.
Andorra (1995): Antoni Morell Mora.
Angola (1997): José Bernardo Domingos Quiosa.
Antigua and Barbuda (1986): vacant.
Argentina: Carlos Luis Custer.
Armenia (1992): Edward Nalbandian.
Australia (1973): Anne Maree Plunkett.
Austria: Helmut Türk.
Azerbaijan (1992): Elchin Oktyabr Oglu Amirbayov.
Bahamas (1979): vacant.
Bahrain (2000): vacant
Bangladesh (1972):Toufiq Ali.
Barbados (1979): Peter Patrick Kenneth Simmons.
Belarus (1992): Vladimir R. Korolev.
Belgium (1835): Benoît Cardon De Lichtbuer.
Belize (1983): vacant.
Benin (formerly Dahomey) (1971): Euloge Hinvi.
Bolivia: Valentin Abecia Baldivieso.
Bosnia and Herzegovina (1992): Miroslav Palameta.
Brazil: Vera Barrouin Machado.
Bulgaria (1990): Valentin Vassilev Bozhilov.
Burkina Faso (1973): Felipe Savadogo.
Burundi (1963): Térence Nsanze.
Cambodia (1994): vacant.
Cameroon (1966): Jean Melaga.
Canada (1969): Donald Smith.
Cape Verde (1976): Domingos Dias Pereira Mascarenhas.
Central African Republic (1975): vacant.
Chad (1988): Moukhtar Wawa Dahab.

Chile: Maximo Pacheco Gómez.
China, Republic of (Taiwan) (1966): Chou-seng Tou.
Colombia: Dr. Guillermo León Escobar-Herrán.
Congo (formerly Zaire) (1963): vacant.
Congo (1977): Henri Marie Joseph Lopes.
Costa Rica: Javier Guerra Laspiur.
Côte d'Ivoire (Ivory Coast) (1971): Kouamé Benjamin Konan.
Croatia (1992): Emilio Marin.
Cuba: Raúl Roa Kourí.
Cyprus (1973): Georgios F. Poulides.
Czech Republic (1929-50, reestablished, 1990, with Czech and Slovak Federative Republic; reaffirmed, 1993): Pavel Jajtner.
Denmark (1982): Sten Erik Malmborg Lilholt.
Djibouti (2000): Barkat Gourad Hamadou.
Dominica (1981): vacant.
Dominican Republic: Carlos Rafael Conrado Marion-Landais Castillo.
East Timor (2002): vacant.
Ecuador: Francisco Salazar Alvarado.
Egypt (1966): Nevine Simaika Halim.
El Salvador: Francisco A. Soler.
Equatorial Guinea (1981): vacant.
Eritrea (1995): Petros Tseggai Asghedom.
Estonia (1991): Priit Kolbre.
Ethiopia (1969): Negash Kebret.
Fiji (1978): Emitat Lausiki Boladuadua.
Finland (1966): Pekka Ojanen.
France: Bernard Kessedjian.
Gabon (1967): Désiré Koumba.
Gambia, The (1978): Gibril Seman Joof.
Georgia (1992): Princess Khétévane Bagration de Moukhrani.
Germany: Gerhard Westdickenberg.
Ghana (1976): Albert Owusu-Sarpong.
Great Britain (1982): Francis Campbell.
Greece (1980): Stavros Lykidis.
Grenada (1979): vacant.
Guatemala: Juan Gavarrete Soberón.
Guinea (1986): El Hadj Aboubacar Dione.
Guinea-Bissau (1986): vacant.
Guyana (Cooperative Republic of): Laleshwar Kumar Narayan Singh.
Haiti: Carl Henri Guiteau.
Honduras: Alejandro Emilio Valladares Lanza.
Hungary (1990): Gábor Erdödy.
Iceland (1976): Hördur H. Bjarnason.
India: Amitava Tripathi.
Indonesia (1965): Bambang Prayitno.
Iran (1966): Mohammad Javad Faridzadeh.
Iraq (1966): Albert Edward Ismail Yelda.
Ireland: Philip McDonagh.
Israel (1994): Oded Ben-Hur.
Italy: Giuseppe Balboni Acqua.
Ivory Coast: See Côte d'Ivoire.
Jamaica (1979): Marcia Gilbert-Roberts.
Japan (1966): Gunkatsu Kano.
Jordan (1994): Dina Kawar.
Kazakhstan (1992): Nurlan Danenov.
Kenya (1965): Raychelle Awuor Omamo.
Kiribati: Diplomatic relations established Apr. 1995.
Korea (1966): Youm Seong.
Kuwait (1969): Ahmad Abdulkarim Al-Ebrahim.
Kyrgyzstan (1992): Apas Dschumagulov
Latvia (1991): Atis Sjanits.

Lebanon (1966): Naji Abi Assi.
Lesotho (1967): Seymour Rehaulele Kikine.
Liberia (1966): vacant.
Libya: (1997): Abdulhafed Gaddur.
Liechtenstein (1985): Nikolaus de Liechtenstein.
Lithuania: Algirdas Saudargas.
Luxembourg (1955): Georges Santer.
Macedonia (1994): Bartolomej Kajtazi.
Madagascar (1967): Jean-Pierre Razafy-Andriamihaingo.
Malawi (1966): Gilton Bazilio Chiwaula.
Mali (1979): Mohamed Salia Sokona.
Malta (1965): Antonio Ganado.
Marshall Islands (1993): vacant.
Mauritius: Mohunlall Goburdhun.
Mexico (personal representative, 1990; diplomatic relations, 1992): Luis Felipe Bravo Mena.
Micronesia, Federated States (1994): vacant.
Moldova (1992): Valeriu Bobuac.
Monaco: Jean- Claude Michel.
Mongolia (1992): Chuluuny Batjargal.
Morocco: Mohammed Sbihi.
Mozambique: Diplomatic relations established Dec. 1995.
Namibia: Diplomatic relations established Sept. 1995.
Nauru (1992): vacant.
Nepal (1983): Madan Kumar Bhattarai.
Netherlands (1967): Monique Patricia Antoinette Frank.
New Zealand (1973): Geoffrey Kenyon Ward.
Nicaragua: Armando Luna Silva.
Niger (1971): Amadou Touré.
Nigeria (1976): Kingsley Sunny Ebenyi.
Norway (1982): Lars Petter Forberg.
Order of Malta (see Index): Alberto Leoncini Bartoli.
Pakistan (1965): Fauzia Mufti Abbas.
Palau, Republic of (1998): vacant.
Panama: Lawrence Edward Chewning Fàbrega.
Papua New Guinea (1977): vacant.
Paraguay: Gerónimo Narváez Torres.
Peru: Pablo Moran Val.
Philippines (1951): Leonida L. Vera.
Poland (1989): Hanna Suchocka.
Portugal: Pedro José Ribeiro de Menezes.
Qatar: (Diplomatic relations established Nov. 2002): Mohamad Jaham Abdulaziz Al-Kawari.
Romania (1920; broken off, 1948; reestablished, 1990): Mihail Dobre.
Rwanda (1964): Joseph Bonesha.
Saint Lucia (1984): Gilbert Ramez Chagoury.
Saint Vincent and the Grenadines (1990): vacant.
San Marino (1986): Giovanni Galassi.
São Tome and Principe (1984): vacant.
Senegal (1966): Félix Oudiane.
Seychelles (1984): vacant.
Sierra Leone: (Diplomatic relations established July 1996): Fode Maclean Dabor.
Singapore (1981): Walter Woon.
Slovak Republic (1993; when it became independent republic): Dr. Marián Servátka.
Slovenia (1992): Dagmar Babcanová.
Solomon Islands (1984): vacant.
South Africa (1994): Dr. Konji Sebati.
Spain: Francisco Vázquez Vázquez.
Sri Lanka (1975): Sarala Manourie Fernando.
Sudan (1972): Abdelbasit Badawi Ali Elsanosi.

Suriname (1994): Edgard Stephanus Ragoenath Amanh.
Swaziland (1992): H.R.H. Prince David M. Dlamini.
Sweden (1982): Fredrik Vahlquist.
Switzerland (1992): Jean-François Kammer, Ambassador with special mission to Holy See.
Syria (Arab Republic) (1966): Siba Nasser.
Tajikistan: Diplomatic relations established June 1996.
Tanzania (1968): Ali Abeid A. Karume.
Thailand (1969): Pradap Pibulsonggram.
Togo (1981): Félix Kodjo Sagbo.
Tonga (1994): vacant.
Trinidad and Tobago (1978): Leari E. Rousseau.
Tunisia (1972): Afif Hendaoui.
Turkey (1966): Osman Durak.
Turkmenistan: Diplomatic relations established July 1996.
Uganda (1966): Tibamanya Mwene Mushanga.
Ukraine (1992): Grygorii Fokovych Khoruzhyi.
United States (1984): L. Francis Rooney, III.
Uruguay: Daniel Pérez del Castillo.

Uzbekistan (1992): vacant.
Vanuatu (1994): Michel Rittié.
Venezuela: Iván Guillermo Rincón Urdaneta.
Western Samoa (1994): vacant.
Yemen: (1998): Yaha Ali Mohamed al-Abiad.
Yugoslavia: Darko Tanaskovic.
Zaire: See Congo.
Zambia (1965): Anderson Kaseba Chibwa.
Zimbabwe (1980): David Douglas Hamadziripi.

Special Representatives

Russia (Federation of) (1989): Vitaly Litvin, Ambassador Extraordinary and Plenipotentiary.
United Nations (Center of Information of UN at the Holy See): Shalini Dewan, director.
Office of the League of Arab States: Mohammad Ali Mohammad.
United Nations High Commission for Refugees: Augustine Mahiga, delegate.
Organization for the Liberation of Palestine: Afif E. Safieh, director.

U.S.-HOLY SEE RELATIONS

The U.S. and the Holy See announced Jan. 10, 1984, the establishment of full diplomatic relations, thus ending a period of 117 years in which there was no formal diplomatic relationship. The announcement followed action by the Congress in Nov. 1983 to end a prohibition on diplomatic relations enacted in 1867.

William A. Wilson, President Reagan's personal representative to the Holy See from 1981, was confirmed as the U.S. ambassador by the Senate, on Mar. 7, 1984. He presented his credentials to Pope John Paul II on Apr. 9, 1984, and served until May 1986, when he resigned. He was succeeded by Frank Shakespeare, 1986-89, and Thomas P. Melady, 1989-93. Raymond L. Flynn, Mayor of Boston, was appointed by Bill Clinton and confirmed by the Senate in July 1993. He served until 1997 when he was succeeded by Corinne Claiborne "Lindy" Boggs. She was succeeded by James Nicholson who served until 2005. On Aug. 1, 2005, Pres. George W. Bush nominated as Nicholson's successor L. Francis Rooney III, an Oklahoma and Florida businessman.

Archbishop (now Cardinal) Pio Laghi, apostolic delegate to the U.S. since 1980, was named first pro-nuncio by the Pope on Mar. 26, 1984. He served until 1990, when he was named prefect of the Congregation for Catholic Education. Archbishop Agostino Cacciavillan was appointed pro-nuncio on June 13, 1990. He served until he was named president of the Administration of the Patrimony of the Apostolic See (APSA) and was succeeded on Dec. 7, 1998, by Archbishop Gabriel Montalvo. Archbishop Montalvo served as nuncio from 1998 to 2005. He was succeeded by Archbishop Pietro Sambi, the current nuncio.

Nature of Relations

The nature of relations was described in nearly identical statements by John Hughes, a State Department spokesman, and the Holy See. Hughes said: "The United States of America and the Holy See, in the desire to further promote the existing mutual friendly relations, have decided by common agreement to establish diplomatic relations between them at the level of embassy on the part of the United States of America, and nunciature on the part of the Holy See, as of today, Jan. 10, 1984."

The Holy See statement said: "The Holy See and the United States of America, desiring to develop the mutual friendly relations already existing, have decided by common accord to establish diplomatic relations at the level of apostolic nunciature on the side of the Holy See and of embassy on the side of the United States beginning today, Jan. 10, 1984."

The establishment of relations was criticized as a violation of the separation-of-church-and-state principle by spokesmen for the National Council of Churches, the National Association of Evangelicals, the Baptist Joint Committee on Public Affairs, Seventh Day Adventists, Americans United for Separation of Church and State, and the American Jewish Congress.

Legal Challenge Dismissed

U.S. District Judge John P. Fullam, ruling May 7, 1985, in Philadelphia, dismissed a legal challenge to U.S.-Holy See relations brought by Americans United for Separation of Church and State. He stated that Americans United and its allies in the challenge lacked legal standing to sue, and that the courts did not have jurisdiction to intervene in foreign policy decisions of the executive branch of the U.S. government. Parties to the suit brought by Americans United were the National Association of Laity, the National Coalition of American Nuns and several Protestant church organizations. Bishop James W. Malone, president of the U.S. Catholic Conference, said in a statement: "This matter has been discussed at length for many years. It is not a religious issue but a public policy question which, happily, has now been settled in this context."

Russell Shaw, a conference spokesman, said the decision to send an ambassador to the Holy See was not a church-state issue and "confers no special privilege or status on the Church."

Earlier Relations

Official relations for trade and diplomatic purposes were maintained by the U.S. and the Papal States while the latter had the character of and acted like other sovereign powers in the international community.

Consular relations developed in the wake of an announcement, made by the papal nuncio in Paris to the American mission there Dec. 15, 1784, that the Papal States had agreed to open several Mediterranean ports to U.S. shipping.

U.S. consular representation in the Papal States began with the appointment of John B. Sartori, a native of Rome, in June 1797. Sartori's successors as consuls were: Felix Cicognani, also a Roman, and Americans George W. Greene, Nicholas Browne, William C. Sanders, Daniel LeRoy, Horatio V. Glentworth, W.J. Stillman, Edwin C. Cushman, David M. Armstrong.

Consular officials of the Papal States who served in the U.S. were: Count Ferdinand Lucchesi, 1826 to 1829, who resided in Washington; John B. Sartori, 1829 to 1841, who resided in Trenton, NJ; Daniel J. Desmond, 1841 to 1850, who resided in Philadelphia; Louis B. Binsse, 1850 to 1895, who resided in New York.

U.S. recognition of the consul of the Papal States did not cease when the states were absorbed into the Kingdom of Italy in 1871, despite pressure from Baron Blanc, the Italian minister. Binsse held the title until his death Mar. 28, 1895. No one was appointed to succeed him.

Diplomatic Relations

The U.S. Senate approved a recommendation, made by President James K. Polk in Dec. 1847 for the establishment of a diplomatic post in the Papal States. Jacob L. Martin, the first charge d'affaires, arrived in Rome Aug. 2, 1848, and presented his credentials to Pius IX Aug. 19. Martin, who died within a month, was succeeded by Lewis Cass, Jr. Cass became minister resident in 1854 and served in that capacity until his retirement in 1858.

John P. Stockton, who later became a U.S. Senator from New Jersey, was minister resident from 1858 to 1861. Rufus King was named to succeed him but, instead, accepted a commission as a brigadier general in the Army. Alexander W. Randall of Wisconsin took the appointment. He was succeeded in Aug. 1862 by Richard M. Blatchford who served until the following year. King was again nominated minister resident and served in that capacity until 1867 when the ministry was ended because of objections from some quarters in the U.S. and failure to appropriate funds for its continuation. J. C. Hooker, a secretary, remained in the Papal States until the end of March, 1868, closing the ministry and performing functions of courtesy.

Personal Envoys

Myron C. Taylor was appointed by President Franklin D. Roosevelt in 1939 to serve as his personal representative to Pope Pius XII and continued serving in that capacity during the presidency of Harry S. Truman until 1951. Henry Cabot Lodge was named to the post by President Richard M. Nixon in 1970, served also during the presidency of Gerald Ford, and represented President Carter at the canonization of St. John Neumann in 1977. Miami attorney David Walters served as the personal envoy of President Jimmy Carter to the Pope from July 1977 until his resignation Aug. 16, 1978. He was succeeded by Robert F. Wagner who served from Oct. 1978 to the end of the Carter presidency in Jan. 1981. William A. Wilson, appointed by President Ronald Reagan in Feb. 1981, served as his personal envoy until 1984 when he was named ambassador to the Holy See.

None of the personal envoys had diplomatic status.

President Harry S. Truman nominated Gen. Mark Clark to be ambassador to the Holy See in 1951, but withdrew the nomination at Clark's request because of controversy over the appointment.

None of Truman's three immediate successors — Dwight D. Eisenhower, John F. Kennedy and Lyndon B. Johnson — had a personal representative to the pope.

PONTIFICAL ACADEMIES

(*Sources:* Annuario Pontificio, *Catholic News Service*.)

The Pontifical Academy of Sciences was constituted in its present form by Pius XI Oct. 28, 1936, in virtue of In Multis Solaciis, a document issued on his own initiative.

The academy is the only supranational body of its kind in the world with a pope - selected, life - long membership of outstanding mathematicians and experimental scientists regardless of creed from many countries. The normal complement of 70 members was increased to 80 in 1985-86 by John Paul II. There are additional honorary and supernumerary members.

The academy traces its origin to the Linceorum Academia (Academy of the Lynxes, its symbol) founded in Rome Aug. 17, 1603. Pius IX reorganized this body and gave it a new name, Pontificia Accademia dei Nuovi Lincei, in 1847. It was taken over by the Italian state in 1870 and called the Accademia Nazionale dei Lincei. Leo XIII reconstituted it with a new charter in 1887. Pius XI designated the Casina di Pope Pius IV in the Vatican Gardens as the site of academy headquarters in 1922 and gave it its present title and status in 1936. In 1940, Pius XII gave the title of Excellency to its members; John XXIII extended the privilege to honorary members in 1961.

Members in U.S.

Scientists in the U.S. who presently hold membership in the Academy are listed below according to year of appointment. Nobel prize-winners are indicated by an asterisk.

Franco Rasetti, professor emeritus of physics at Johns Hopkins University, Baltimore, MD (Oct. 28, 1936); Christian de Duve,* professor of biochemistry at the International Institute of Cellular and Molecular Pathology at Brussels, Belgium, and Rockefeller University, N.Y. (Apr. 10, 1970);

Marshall Warren Nirenberg,* director of Laboratory on genetics and biochemistry at the National Institutes of Health, Bethesda, Md. (June 24, 1974).

George Palade,* professor of cellular biology at University of California, San Diego and Victor Weisskopf, professor of physics at the Massachusetts Institute of Technology, Cambridge, Mass. (Dec. 2, 1975); David Baltimore,* professor of biology at the Massachusetts Institute of Technology, Cambridge, Mass.; Har Gobind Khorana,* professor of biochemistry, and Alexander Rich, professor of biophysics, both at the Massachusetts Institute of Technology, Cambridge, Mass. (Apr. 17, 1978).

Charles Townes,* professor emeritus of physics at the University of California at Berkeley (Jan. 26, 1983); Beatrice Mintz, senior member of the Cancer Research Institute of Philadelphia and Maxine Singer, biochemist, president of Carnegie Institution, Washington, D.C. (June 9, 1986).

Roald Z. Sagdeev, professor of physics at University of Maryland, College Park and Peter Hamilton Raven, professor of biology at the Missouri Botanical Garden of St. Louis, Mo. (Oct. 4, 1990); Luis Angel Caffarelli, professor of mathematics at New York University and Luigi Luca Cavalli-Sforza, professor of genetics at Stanford University (Aug. 2, 1994).

Joshua Lederberg, professor of genetics at Rockefeller University, N.Y. (Mar. 4, 1996); Joseph Edward Murray, professor of plastic surgery at Harvard Medical School, Cambridge, Mass.; Paul Berg, professor of biochemistry at Stanford Univ. and Vera C. Rubin, professor of astronomy at Carnegie Institution of Washington (June 25, 1996); Gary S. Becker,* professor of economics at the University of Chicago (Mar. 3, 1997); Chen-ning Yang,* professor of physics and director of the Institute of Theoretical Physics at the State University of N.Y. at Stony Brook (Apr. 18, 1997); Frank Press, professor of geophysics and director of the Washington Advisory Group (Sept. 3, 1999); Ahmed Zewail, professor of Chemistry and Physics, California Institute of Technology, Pasadena (Sept. 3, 1999); Mario Jose Molina, professor of atmospheric chemistry at the Massachusetts Institute of Technology (Nov. 9, 2000); Günter Blobel,* professor of cellular biology of the Rockefeller University, N.Y. (Sept. 28, 2001); Fotis C. Kafatos, professor of molecular biology at Harvard University (Jan. 23, 2003); Tsung-Dao Lee, professor of Physics at Columbia University in N.Y. (Apr. 14, 2003); William D. Phillips,* professor of physics at the University of Maryland and the National Institute of Standards and Technology, Gaithersburg, Pa. (Oct. 23, 2004); Veerabhadran (Ram) Ramanathan, professor of atmospheric science at the University of California, San Diego, and director of the Center for Atmospheric Science at Scripps Institution of Oceanography, La Jolla (Oct. 23, 2004); Edward Witten, professor of Physics at the Institute for Advanced Study, Princeton, N.J. (June 21, 2006).

There are also two honorary members from the U.S.: Stanley L. Jaki, O.S.B., professor of physics, history and philosophy at Seton Hall University, N.J. (Sept. 5, 1990); Robert J. White, professor of neurosurgery at Case Western Reserve University, Cleveland (Mar. 29, 1994).

Members in Other Countries

Listing includes place and date of selection. Nobel Prize winners are indicated by an asterisk.

Argentina: Antonio M. Battro (Sept. 21, 2002).
Armenia: Rudolf M. Muradian (Oct. 16, 1994).
Austria: Hans Tuppy (Apr. 10, 1970); Walter Thirring (June 9, 1986).
Belgium: Paul Adriaan Jan Janssen (June 25, 1990); Thierry Boon-Falleur (April 9, 2002).
Brazil: Carlos Chagas, former president of the academy (Aug. 18, 1961); Johanna Döbereiner (Apr. 17, 1978); Crodowaldo Pavan (Apr. 17, 1978); Rudolf Muradian (Oct. 16, 1994).
Canada: John Charles Polanyi* (June 9, 1986).

Chile: Héctor Rezzio Croxatto (Dec. 2, 1975); Rafael Vicuna (Nov. 10, 2000).
Congo (formerly Zaire): Felix wa Kalengo Malu (Sept. 26, 1983).
Denmark: Aage Bohr* (Apr. 17, 1978).
France: André Blanc-LaPierre (Apr. 17, 1978); Paul Germain (June 9, 1986); Jacques-Louis Lions (Oct. 4, 1990); Jean-Marie Lehn (May 30, 1996); Claude Cohen-Tannoudji (May 17, 1999); Nicole M. Le Douarin (Sept. 3, 1999); Pierre Jean Léna (Jan. 18, 2001); Yves Quéré (Dec. 20, 2003).
Germany: Rudolf L. Mössbauer* (Apr. 10, 1970); Manfred Eigen* (May 12, 1981); Wolf Joachim Singer (Sept. 18, 1992); Paul Joseph Crutzen (June 25, 1996); Yuri Ivanovich Manin (June 26, 1996); Jürgen Mittelstrass (Sept. 21, 2002); Theodor Wolfgang Hänsch (June 21, 2006).
Ghana: Daniel Adzei Bekoe (Sept. 26, 1983).
Great Britain: Hermann Alexander Brück (Apr. 5, 1955); George Porter* (June 24, 1974); Max Ferdinand Perutz* (May 12, 1981); Stephen William Hawking (Jan. 9, 1986); Martin John Rees (June 25, 1990); Sir Richard Southwood (Sept. 18, 1992); Raymond Hide (June 25, 1996).
India: Mambillikalathil Govind Kumar Menon (May 12, 1981); Chintamani N.R. Rao (June 25, 1990).
Israel: Michael Sela (Dec. 2, 1975).
Italy: Giampietro Puppi (Apr. 17, 1978); Nicola Cabibbo (June 9, 1986), President; Nicola Dallaporta (Oct. 5, 1989), honorary member; Bernardo Maria Colombo (Sept. 18, 1992); Antonino Zichichi (Nov. 9, 2000); Enrico Berti (Sept. 28, 2001).
Japan: Minoru Oda (Sept. 18, 1992); Ryoji Noyori* (Oct. 1, 2002).
Kenya: Thomas R. Odhiambo (May 12, 1981).
Mexico: Marcos Moshinsky (June 9, 1986).
Nigeria: Thomas Adeoye Lambo (June 24, 1974).
Poland: Stanislaw Lojasiewicz (Jan. 28, 1983); Czeslaw Olech (June 9, 1986); Michal Heller (Oct. 4, 1990); Andrzej Szezeklik (Oct. 16, 1994).
Russia: Vladimir Isaakovich Keilis-Borok (Oct. 16, 1994); Sergei Petrovich Novikov (June 25, 1996), also teaches at University of Maryland).
Spain: Manuel Lora-Tamayo (Sept. 24, 1964); Garcia-Bellido, Antonio (June 24, 2003).
Sweden: Sune Bergström* (Dec. 14, 1985); Kai Siegbahn* (Dec. 14, 1985).
Switzerland: Werner Arber* (May 12, 1981); Carlo Rubbia* (Dec. 14, 1985); Albert Eschenmoser (June 9, 1986).
Taiwan: Te-tzu Chang (Apr. 18, 1997).
Vatican City State: Cottier, Rev. George, O.P. (Oct. 28, 1992; honorary member); Rev. Enrico do Rovasenda, O.P. (Nov. 13, 1968), honorary member.
Venezuela: Marcel Roche (Apr. 10, 1970).
Ex officio members: Rev. George V. Coyne, S.J., director of Vatican Observatory (Sept. 2, 1978); Very Rev. Raffaele Farina, S.D.B., prefect of the Vatican Library (May 24, 1997); Very Rev. Sergio B. Pagano, prefect of the Secret Vatican Archives (Jan. 7, 1997). President: Nicola Cabibbo, professor of theoretical physics at University of Rome (app. Apr. 6, 1993). Chancellor: Most Rev. Marcelo Sánchez Sorondo.
Honorary members: Cardinal Carlo Maria Martini, Archbishop emeritus of Milan.

PONTIFICAL ACADEMY OF SOCIAL SCIENCES

Founded by John Paul II (*motu proprio Socialium scientiarum investigationes*), Jan. 1, 1994, to promote the study and the progress of social sciences, to advise the Vatican on social concerns and to foster research aimed at improving society. The number of members is not less than 20 or more than 40. Three of the 30 members of the Academy (as of Jan. 1, 2006) were from the United States: Kenneth J. Arrow of Stanford University, Mary Ann Glendon of Harvard University, and Joseph Stiglitz of Columbia University. President, Mary Ann Glendon; Chancellor, Most Rev. Marcelo Sánchez Sorondo. Address: Casino Pio IV, Vatican Gardens.

PONTIFICAL ACADEMY FOR LIFE

Established by John Paul II (*motu proprio Vitae Mysterium*), Feb. 11, 1994, "to fulfill the specific task of study, information and formation on the principal problems of biomedicine and law relative to the promotion and defense of life, especially in the direct relationship they have with Christian morality and the directives of the Church's magisterium."

Members, appointed by the pope without regard to religion or nationality, represent the various branches of "the biomedical sciences and those that are most closely related to problems concerning the promotion and protection of life." Membership, as of Jan. 1, 2006, included seven from the United States:

Prof. Carl Anderson, Vice-President of the Pontifical John Paul II Institute for Studies of Marriage and the Family; Mrs. Mercedes Arzu-Wilson, founder and president of the Foundations Family of the Americas and founder and director of the Commission at the World Organization for the Family; Dr. Thomas Hilgers, founder and director of the Institute "Paul VI," Omaha, Neb.; Mrs. Christine de Vollmer, president of the World Organization for the Family; Dr. Denis Cavanaugh, professor of obstetrics and gynecology at the University of South Florida College of Medicine; Prof. John M. Finnis, professor of philosophy of law, University of Oxford and the University of Notre Dame; Dr. A.J. Luke Gormally, director emeritus of Linacre Centre for Health Care Ethics in England and research professor at Ave Maria School of Law; Prof. Edmund Pellegrino, director of the Center for Advanced Studies in Ethics at Georgetown University, honorary member. President: Most Rev. Elio Sgreccia, titular bishop of Zama Minor.

Hierarchy of the Catholic Church

ORGANIZATION AND GOVERNMENT

As a structured society, the Catholic Church is organized and governed along lines corresponding mainly to the jurisdictions of the pope and Bishops. The pope is the supreme head of the Church. He has primacy of jurisdiction as well as honor over the entire Church. Bishops, in union with and in subordination to the pope, are the successors of the Apostles for care of the Church and for the continuation of Christ's mission in the world. They serve the people of their own dioceses, or particular churches, with ordinary authority and jurisdiction. They also share, with the pope and each other, common concern and effort for the general welfare of the whole Church.

Bishops of exceptional status are patriarchs of Eastern Catholic Churches who, subject only to the pope, are heads of the faithful belonging to their rites throughout the world.

Subject to the Holy Father and directly responsible to him for the exercise of their ministry of service to people in various jurisdictions or divisions of the Church throughout the world are: resident archbishops and metropolitans (heads of archdioceses), diocesan bishops, vicars and prefects apostolic (heads of vicariates apostolic and prefectures apostolic), certain abbots and prelates, and apostolic administrators. Each of these, within his respective territory and according to the provisions of canon law, has ordinary jurisdiction over pastors (who are responsible for the administration of parishes), priests, religious and lay persons.

Also subject to the Holy Father are titular archbishops and bishops, religious orders and congregations of pontifical right, pontifical institutes and faculties, papal nuncios and apostolic delegates.

Assisting the pope and acting in his name in the central government and administration of the Church are cardinals and other officials of the Roman Curia.

THE HIERARCHY

The ministerial hierarchy is the orderly arrangement of the ranks and orders of the clergy to provide for the spiritual care of the faithful, the government of the Church, and the accomplishment of the Church's total mission in the world.

Persons belong to this hierarchy by virtue of ordination and canonical mission.

The term hierarchy is also used to designate an entire body or group of bishops; for example, the hierarchy of the Church, the hierarchy of the United States.

Hierarchy of Order: Consists of the pope, bishops, priests and deacons. Their purpose, for which they are ordained to holy orders, is to carry out the sacramental and pastoral ministry of the Church.

Hierarchy of Jurisdiction: Consists of the pope and bishops by divine institution, and other church officials by ecclesiastical institution and mandate, who have authority to govern and direct the faithful for spiritual ends.

The Pope

His Holiness the Pope is the Bishop of Rome, Vicar of Jesus Christ, successor of St. Peter, Prince of the Apostles, Supreme Pontiff of the Universal Church, Patriarch of the West, Primate of Italy, Archbishop and Metropolitan of the Roman Province, Sovereign of the State of Vatican City, Servant of the Servants of God.

Cardinals
(See Index)

Patriarchs

Patriarch, a term which had its origin in the Eastern Church, is the title of a bishop who, second only to the pope, has the highest rank in the hierarchy of jurisdiction. He is the incumbent of one of the sees listed below. Subject only to the pope, a patriarch of the Eastern Church is the head of the faithful belonging to his rite throughout the world. The patriarchal sees are so called because of their special status and dignity in the history of the Church.

The Council of Nicaea (325) recognized three patriarchs — the Bishops of Alexandria and Antioch in the East, and of Rome in the West. The First Council of Constantinople (381) added the bishop of Constantinople to the list of patriarchs and gave him rank second only to that of the pope, the bishop of Rome and patriarch of the West; this action was seconded by the Council of Chalcedon (451) and was given full recognition by the Fourth Lateran Council (1215). The Council of Chalcedon also acknowledged patriarchal rights of the bishop of Jerusalem.

Eastern patriarchs are as follows: one of Alexandria, for the Copts; three of Antioch, one each for the Syrians, Maronites and Greek Melkites (the latter also has the personal title of Greek Melkite patriarch of Alexandria and of Jerusalem). The patriarch of Babylonia, for the Chaldeans, and the patriarch of Sis, or Cilicia, for the Armenians, should be called, more properly, *Katholikos* — that is, a prelate delegated for a universality of causes. These patriarchs are elected by bishops of their churches; they receive approval and the pallium, symbol of their office, from the pope.

Latin Rite patriarchates were established for Antioch, Jerusalem, Alexandria and Constantinople during the Crusades; afterwards, they became patriarchates in name only. Jerusalem, however, was reconstituted as a patriarchate by Pius IX, in virtue of the bull *Nulla Celebrior* of July 23, 1847. In 1964, the Latin titular patriarchates of Constantinople, Alexandria and Antioch, long a bone of contention in relations with Eastern Churches, were abolished.

As of Aug. 15, 2006, the patriarchs in the Church were:

Antonios Naguib, of Alexandria, for the Copts; Ignace Pierre VIII Abdel-Ahad, of Antioch, for the Syrians; Gregory III Laham, of Antioch, for the Greek Melkites (the patriarch also has personal titles of Alexandria and Jerusalem for the Greek Melkites); Cardinal Nasrallah Pierre Sfeir, of Antioch, for the Maronites; Nerses Bedros XIX Tarmouni, of Cilicia, for the Armenians; Emmanuel III Delly, of Babylon of the Chaldeans. (For biographical information on the patriarchs, *see* **Eastern Catholics**; *see also* **Special Reports** on the issue of the Pope as the Patriarch of the West.)

The titular patriarchs (in name only) of the Latin Rite were: Cardinal José da Cruz Policarpo of Lisbon; Cardinal Angelo Scola of Venice; Archbishop Filipe Neri António do Rosário Ferrão of the East Indies (archbishop of Goa and Damao, India); and Archbishop Michel Sabbah of Jerusalem (coadjutor, Archbishop Fouad Twal). The patriarchate of the West Indies has been vacant since 1963.

Major Archbishops

A major archbishop has the prerogatives but not the title of a patriarch. As of May 15, 2006, there were four major archbishops: Cardinal Lubomyr Husar of the major archbishopric of Kiev and Halych of the Ukrainian Catholic Church (Ukraine); Cardinal Varkey Vithayathil, C.SS.R. of the major archbishopric of Ernakulam-Angomaly of the Syro-Malabar Church (India); Abp. Cyril Malancharuvil of the major archbishopric of Trivandrum of the Syro-Malankara Catholic Church (India) who was promoted to the rank of major archbishop in Feb. 2005; and Abp. Lucian Muresan of the major archbishopric of Fagaras and Alba Julia for the Romanian Greek Catholic Church (Romania) who was promoted to the rank of major archbishop on Dec. 16, 2005.

Archbishops, Metropolitans

Archbishop: A bishop with the title of an archdiocese.

Coadjutor Archbishop: An assistant archbishop with right of succession.

Metropolitan: Archbishop of the principal see, an archdiocese, in an ecclesiastical province consisting of several dioceses. He has the full powers of bishop in his own archdiocese and limited supervisory jurisdiction and influence over the other (suffragan) dioceses in the province. The pallium, conferred by the pope, is the symbol of his status as a metropolitan.

Titular Archbishop: Has the title of an archdiocese that formerly existed in fact but now exists in title only. He does not have ordinary jurisdiction over an archdiocese. Examples are archbishops in the Roman Curia,

papal nuncios, apostolic delegates.

Archbishop *ad personam*: A title of personal honor and distinction granted to some bishops. They do not have ordinary jurisdiction over an archdiocese.

Primate: A title of honor given to the ranking prelate of some countries or regions.

Bishops

Diocesan Bishop: A bishop in charge of a diocese.

Coadjutor Bishop: An assistant (auxiliary) bishop to a diocesan bishop, with right of succession to the see.

Titular Bishops: A bishop with the title of a diocese that formerly existed in fact but now exists in title only; an assistant (auxiliary) bishop to a diocesan bishop.

Episcopal Vicar: An assistant, who may or may not be a bishop, appointed by a residential bishop as his deputy for a certain part of a diocese, a determined type of apostolic work, or the faithful of a certain rite.

Eparch, Exarch: Titles of bishops of Eastern churches.

Nomination of Bishops: Nominees for episcopal ordination are selected in several ways. Final appointment and/or approval in all cases is subject to decision by the pope.

In the U.S., bishops periodically submit the names of candidates to the archbishop of their province. The names are then considered at a meeting of the bishops of the province, and those receiving a favorable vote are forwarded to the pro-nuncio for transmission to the Holy See. Normally, three names are submitted. Bishops are free to seek the counsel of priests, religious and lay persons with respect to nominees.

Eastern Catholic churches have their own procedures and synodal regulations for nominating and making final selection of candidates for episcopal ordination. Such selection is subject to approval by the pope. The Code of Canon Law concedes no rights or privileges to civil authorities with respect to the election, nomination, presentation or designation of candidates for the episcopate.

Ad Limina Visit: Diocesan bishops and apostolic vicars are obliged to make an ad limina visit ("to the threshold" of the Apostles) every five years to the tombs of Sts. Peter and Paul, have audience with the Holy Father and consult with appropriate Vatican officials. They are required to send a report on conditions in their jurisdiction to the Congregation for bishops approximately six — and not less than three — months in advance of the scheduled visit.

Others with Ordinary Jurisdiction

Ordinary: One who has the jurisdiction of an office: the pope, diocesan bishops, vicars general, prelates of missionary territories, vicars apostolic prefects apostolic, vicars capitular during the vacancy of a see, superiors general, abbots primate and other major superiors of men religious.

Some prelates and abbots, with jurisdiction like that of diocesan bishops, are pastors of the people of God in territories (prelatures and abbacies) not under the jurisdiction of diocesan bishops.

Vicar Apostolic: Usually a titular bishop who has ordinary jurisdiction over a mission territory.

Prefect Apostolic: Has ordinary jurisdiction over a mission territory.

Apostolic Administrator: Usually a bishop appointed to administer an ecclesiastical jurisdiction temporarily. Administrators of lesser rank are also appointed on occasion and have more restricted supervisory duties.

Vicar General: A bishop's deputy for the administration of a diocese; does not have to be a bishop.

Prelates Without Jurisdiction

The title of protonotary apostolic was originally given by the fourth century or earlier to clergy who collected accounts of martyrdom and other church documents, or who served the Church with distinction in other ways. Other titles — e.g., domestic prelate, papal chamberlain, prelate of honor — are titles of clergy in service to the pope and the papal household, or of clergy honored for particular reasons. All prelates without jurisdiction are appointed by the pope, and have designated ceremonial privileges and the title of Rev. Monsignor.

SYNOD OF BISHOPS

The Synod of Bishops was chartered by Pope Paul VI Sept. 15, 1965, in a document he issued on his own initiative under the title *Apostolica Sollicitudo*. Provisions of this *motu proprio* are contained in Canons 342 to 348 of the Code of Canon Law. According to major provisions of the Synod charter:

• The purposes of the Synod are "to encourage close union and valued assistance between the Sovereign Pontiff and the bishops of the entire world; to insure that direct and real information is provided on questions and situations touching upon the internal action of the Church and its necessary activity in the world of today; to facilitate agreement on essential points of doctrine and on methods of procedure in the life of the Church."

• The Synod is a central ecclesiastical institution, permanent by nature.

• The Synod is directly and immediately subject to the pope, who has authority to assign its agenda, to call it into session, and to give its members deliberative as well as advisory authority.

• In addition to a limited number of ex officio members and a few heads of male religious institutes, the majority of the members are elected by and representative of national or regional episcopal conferences. The pope reserved the right to appoint the general secretary, special secretaries and no more than 15 percent of the total membership.

The pope is president of the Synod. The secretary general is Abp. Nikola Eterovic, of Croatia. Address: Palazzo del Bramante, Via della Concilizione 34, 00193 Rome, Italy.

An advisory council of 15 members (12 elected, three appointed by the pope) provides the secretariat with adequate staff for carrying on liaison with episcopal conferences and for preparing the agenda of synodal assemblies. Cardinal William H, Keeler, archbishop of Baltimore, is a member of the secretariat.

Assemblies

1. First Assembly: The first assembly was held from Sept. 29 to Oct. 29, 1967. Its objectives, as stated by Pope Paul VI, were "the preservation and strengthening of the Catholic faith, its integrity, its force, its development, its doctrinal and historical coherence." One result was a recommendation for the establishment of an international commission of theologians to assist the Congregation for the Doctrine of the Faith and to broaden approaches to theological research. Pope Paul set up the commission in 1969.

2. Pope-Bishop Relations: The second assembly, held Oct. 11 to 28, 1969, was extraordinary in character. It opened the way toward greater participation by bishops with the pope and each other in the governance of the Church. Proceedings were oriented to three main points: (1) the nature and implications of collegiality; (2) the relationship of bishops and their conferences to the pope; (3) the relationships of bishops and their conferences to each other.

3. Priesthood and Justice: The ministerial priesthood and justice in the world were the principal topics under discussion at the second ordinary assembly, Sept. 30 to Nov. 6, 1971. In one report, the Synod emphasized the primary and permanent dedication of priests in the Church to the ministry of word, sacrament and pastoral service as a full-time vocation. In another report, the assembly stated: "Action on behalf of justice and participation in the transformation of the world fully appear to us as a constitutive dimension of the preaching of the Gospel; or, in other words, of the Church's mission for the redemption of the human race and its liberation from every oppressive situation."

4. Evangelization: The assembly of Sept. 27 to Oct. 26, 1974, produced a general statement on evangelization of the modern world, covering the need for it and its relationship to efforts for total human liberation from personal and social evil. The assembly observed: "The Church does not remain within merely political, social and economic limits (elements which she must certainly take into account) but leads towards freedom under all its forms—liberation from sin, from individual or collective selfishness—and to full communion with God and with men who are like brothers. In this way the Church, in her evangelical way, promotes the true and complete liberation of all men, groups and peoples."

5. Catechetics: The fourth ordinary assembly, Sept. 30 to Oct. 29, 1977, focused attention on catechetics, with special reference to children and young people. The participants issued a "Message to the People of God," the first synodal statement issued since inception of the body, and also presented a set of 34 related propositions and a number of suggestions to Pope Paul VI.

6. Family: "A Message to Christian Families in the Modern World" and a proposal for a "Charter of Family Rights" were produced by the assembly held Sept. 26 to Oct. 25, 1980. The assembly reaffirmed the indissolubility of marriage and the contents of the encyclical letter *Humanae Vitae* (*see separate entry*), and urged married couples who find it hard to live up to "the difficult but loving demands" of Christ not to be discouraged but to avail themselves of the aid of divine grace. In response to synodal recommendation, Pope John Paul II issued a charter of family rights late in 1983.

7. Reconciliation: Penance and reconciliation in the mission of the Church was the theme of the assembly held Sept. 29 to Oct. 29, 1983. Sixty-three propositions related to this theme were formulated on a wide variety of subjects, including: personal sin and so-called systemic or institutional sin; the nature of serious sin; the diminished sense of sin and of the need of redemption, related to decline in the administration and reception of the sacrament of penance; general absolution; individual and social reconciliation; violence and violations of human rights; reconciliation as the basis of peace and justice in society. In a statement issued Oct. 27, the Synod stressed the need of the world to become increasingly "a reconciled community of peoples," and said that "the Church, as sacrament of reconciliation to the world, has to be an effective sign of God's mercy."

8. Vatican II Review: The second extraordinary assembly was convened Nov. 24 to Dec. 8, 1985, for the purposes of: (1) recalling the Second Vatican Council; (2) evaluating the implementation of its enactments during the 20 years since its conclusion; (3) seeking ways and means of promoting renewal in the Church in accordance with the spirit and letter of the council. At the conclusion of the assembly the bishops issued two documents. (1) In "A Message to the People of God," they noted the need for greater appreciation of the enactments of Vatican II and for greater efforts to put them into effect, so that all members of the Church might discharge their responsibility of proclaiming the good news of salvation. (2) In a "Final Report," the first of its kind published by a synodal assembly, the bishops reflected on lights and shadows since Vatican II, stating that negative developments had come from partial and superficial interpretations of conciliar enactments and from incomplete or ineffective implementation. The report also covered a considerable number of subjects discussed during the assembly, including the mystery of the Church, inculturation, the preferential (but not exclusive) option for the poor, and a suggestion for the development of a new universal catechism of the Catholic faith.

9. Vocation and Mission of the Laity in the Church and in the World 20 years after the Second Vatican Council: The seventh ordinary assembly, Oct. 1 to 30, 1987, said in a "Message to the People of God": "The majority of the Christian laity live out their vocation as followers and disciples of Christ in all spheres of life which we call 'the world': the family, the field of work, the local community and the like. To permeate this day-to-day living with the spirit of Christ has always been the task of the lay faithful; and it should be with still greater force their challenge today. It is in this way that they sanctify the world and collaborate in the realization of the kingdom of God." The assembly produced a set of 54 propositions which were presented to the pope for consideration in the preparation of a document of his own on the theme of the assembly. He responded with the apostolic exhortation, *Christifideles Laici,* "The Christian Faithful Laity," released by the Vatican Jan. 30, 1989.

10. Formation of Priests in Circumstances of the Present Day: The eighth general assembly, Sept. 30 to Oct. 28, 1990, dealt principally with the nature and mission of the priesthood; the identity, multi-faceted

formation and spirituality of priests; and, in a "Message to the People of God," the need on all levels of the Church for the promotion of vocations to the priesthood. Forty-one proposals were presented to the Pope for his consideration in preparing a document of his own on the theme of the assembly. Pope John Paul issued an apostolic exhortation entitled *Pastores Dabo Vobis* ("I Will Give You Shepherds") Apr. 7, 1992.

11. The Consecrated Life and Its Role in the Church and in the World: The ninth general assembly was held Oct. 2 to 29, 1994. Pope John Paul's reflections on the proceedings of the assembly and the recommendations of the bishops were the subjects of his apostolic exhortation entitled *Vita Consecrata* ("Consecrated Life"), issued Mar. 25, 1996. The document dealt with various forms of consecrated life: contemplative institutes, apostolic religious life, secular institutes, societies of apostolic life, mixed institutes and new forms of evangelical life.

12. The Bishop: Servant of the Gospel of Jesus Christ for the Hope of the World: The 10th ordinary general assembly was held from Sept. 30 to Oct. 27, 2001. Pope John Paul II's reflections on the proceedings of the assembly and the recommendations of the Bishops was the subject of the apostolic exhortation *Ecclesia in Europa,* issued on June 28, 2003.

13. The Eucharist: Source and Summit of the Life and Mission of the Church: The 11th ordinary general assembly was held from Oct. 2 to Oct. 23, 2005. Pope Benedict XVI's reflections on the proceedings of the assembly and the recommendations of the Bishops will be the subject of an apostolic exhortation. (*See* Special Reports for details.)

Recent Special Assemblies of the Synod of Bishops: Special Synods have been held for Europe (Nov. 28 to Dec. 14, 1991, on the theme "So that we might be witnesses of Christ who has set us free"); for Africa (Apr. 10 to May 8, 1994, on the theme "The Church in Africa and Her Evangelizing Mission Towards the Year 2000: 'You Shall Be My Witnesses' (Acts 1:8)"); for Lebanon (Nov. 27 to Dec. 14, 1995, on the theme "Christ is Our Hope: Renewed by His Spirit, in Solidarity We Bear Witness to His Love"); the Americas (Nov. 16 to Dec. 12, 1997, on the theme, "Encounter with the Living Jesus Christ: Way to Conversion, Community and Solidarity"); for Asia (Apr. 19 to May 14, 1998, on the theme "Jesus Christ the Savior and His Mission of Love and Service in Asia: '...That They May Have Life, and Have it Abundantly' (Jn 10:10)"); for Oceania (Nov. 12 to Dec. 12, 1998, on the theme "Jesus Christ and the Peoples of Oceania: Walking His Way, Telling His Truth, Living His Life"; and a special assembly for Europe (Oct. 1-23, 1999), on the theme "Jesus Christ, Alive in His Church, Source of Hope for Europe."

COLLEGE OF CARDINALS

Cardinals are chosen by the pope to serve as his principal assistants and advisers in the central administration of church affairs. Collectively, they form the College of Cardinals. Provisions regarding their selection, rank, roles and prerogatives are detailed in Canons 349 to 359 of the Code of Canon Law.

History of the College

The College of Cardinals was constituted in its present form and categories of membership in the 12th century. Before that time the pope had a body of advisers selected from among the bishops of dioceses neighboring Rome, priests and deacons of Rome. The college was given definite form in 1150, and in 1179 the selection of cardinals was reserved exclusively to the pope. Sixtus V fixed the number at 70, in 1586. John XXIII set aside this rule when he increased membership at the 1959 and subsequent consistories. The number was subsequently raised by Paul VI. The number of cardinals entitled to participate in papal elections was limited to 120 by Paul VI in 1973. The limit on the number of cardinals was set aside by Pope John Paul II three times, in 1998, 2001, and 2003. As of Aug. 15, 2006, 119 of the 190 cardinals were eligible to vote.

In 1567 the title of cardinal was reserved to members of the college; previously it had been used by priests attached to parish churches of Rome and by the leading clergy of other notable churches. The Code of Canon Law promulgated in 1918 decreed that all cardinals must be priests. Previously there had been cardinals who were not priests (e.g., Cardinal Giacomo Antonelli, d. 1876, Secretary of State to Pius IX, was a deacon). John XXIII provided in the *motu proprio Cum Gravissima* Apr. 15, 1962, that cardinals would henceforth be bishops; this provision is included in the revised Code of Canon Law.

Age Limits

Pope Paul VI placed age limits on the functions of cardinals in the apostolic letter *Ingravescentem Aetatem*, dated Nov. 21, 1970, and effective Jan. 1, 1971. At 80, they cease to be members of curial departments and offices, and become ineligible to take part in papal elections. They retain membership in the College of Cardinals, however, with relevant rights and privileges.

Three Categories

All cardinals except Eastern patriarchs are aggregated to the clergy of Rome. This aggregation is signified by the assignment to each cardinal, except the patriarchs, of a titular church in Rome. The three categories

of members of the college are cardinal bishops, cardinal priests and cardinal deacons.

Cardinal bishops include the six titular bishops of the suburbicarian sees and Eastern patriarchs. First in rank are the titular bishops of the suburbicarian sees neighboring Rome: Ostia, Palestrina, Porto-Santa Rufina, Albano, Velletri-Segni, Frascati, Sabina-Poggio Mirteto. The dean of the college holds the title of the See of Ostia as well as his other suburbicarian see. These cardinal bishops are engaged in full-time service in the central administration of church affairs in departments of the Roman Curia.

Full recognition is given in the revised Code of Canon Law to the position of Eastern patriarchs as the heads of sees of apostolic origin with ancient liturgies. They are assigned rank among the cardinals in order of seniority, following the suburbicarian titleholders.

Cardinal priests, who were formerly in charge of leading churches in Rome, are bishops whose dioceses are outside Rome.

Cardinal deacons, who were formerly chosen according to regional divisions of Rome, are titular bishops assigned to full-time service in the Roman Curia.

The dean and sub-dean of the college are elected by the cardinal bishops — subject to approval by the pope — from among their number. The dean, or the sub-dean in his absence, presides over the college as the first among equals. Cardinals Angelo Sodano and Roger Etchegeray were elected dean and vice-dean, respectively, on Apr. 30, 2005. The Secretary to the College of Cardinals is Abp. Francesco Monterisi.

Selection and Duties

Cardinals are selected by the pope and are inducted into the college in appropriate ceremonies. Cardinals under the age of 80 elect the pope when the Holy See becomes vacant (*see* Index: **Papal Election**, *see also* below under **Conclave**); and are major administrators of church affairs, serving in one or more departments of the Roman Curia. Cardinals in charge of agencies of the Roman Curia and Vatican City are asked to submit their resignation from office to the pope on reaching the age of 75. All cardinals enjoy a number of special rights and privileges. Their title, while symbolic of high honor, does not signify any extension of the powers of holy orders. They are called princes of the Church.

A cardinal *in pectore (petto)* is one whose selection has been made by the pope but whose name has not been disclosed; he has no title, rights or duties until such disclosure is made, at which time he takes precedence from the time of the secret selection.

BIOGRAPHIES OF CARDINALS

Biographies of the cardinals, as of Sept. 15, 2006, are given below in alphabetical order. For historical notes, order of seniority and geographical distribution of cardinals, see separate entries. An asterisk indicates cardinals ineligible to take part in papal elections.

Agré,* Bernard: b. Mar. 2, 1926, Monga, Côte d'Ivoire; ord., July 20, 1953; headmaster in Dabou; vicar general of

Abidjan archdiocese; app. bp. of Man, June 8, 1968; app. first bp. of Yamoussoukro, Mar. 6, 1992; abp. of Abidjan, 1994-2006; ret. May 2, 2006; pres. of the Episcopal Conferences of Francophone West Africa (CERAO) and chair of the Pan-African Episcopal Committee for Social Communications (CEPACS); cardinal, Feb. 21, 2001; titular church, St. John Chrysostom in Monte Sacro Alto. Abp. emeritus of Abidjan.

Curial membership: Evangelization of Peoples (congregation); Justice and Peace, Family, Social Communications (councils).

Agustoni,* Gilberto: b. July 26, 1922, Schaffhausen, Switzerland; ord., Apr. 20, 1946; called to Rome in 1950 to work under Cardinal Ottaviani in the Congregation for the Holy Office; a Prelate Auditor of the Roman Rota, 1970-86; ord. titular abp. of Caorle Jan. 6, 1987; sec. of the Congregation for the Clergy, 1986-92; pro-prefect of the Apostolic Signatura, 1992-94; cardinal deacon, Nov. 26, 1994; titular church Sts. Urban and Laurence at Prima Porta. Prefect of Supreme Tribunal of Apostolic Signatura, 1994-98. Prefect emeritus of Supreme Tribunal of Apostolic Signatura.

Álvarez Martínez,* Francisco: b. July 14, 1925, Santa Eulalia de Ferroñes Llanera, Spain; ord., June 11, 1950; personal secretary to Abp. Lauzurica y Torralba of Oviedo; chancellor and secretary of archdiocesan curia; chaplain of the university students at Teresian Institute; app. bp. of Tarazona, Apr. 13, 1973; cons., June 3, 1973; bp. of Calahorra and La Calzado-Logroño, Dec. 20, 1976; transferred to Orihuela-Alicante, May 12, 1989; abp. of Toledo, 1995-2002; member of the Standing Committee and the Executive Committee of the Spanish Episcopal Conference; cardinal, Feb. 21, 2001; titular church, St. Mary Regina Pacis in Monte Verde. Abp. emeritus of Toledo.

Ambrozic, Aloysius M.: b. Jan. 27, 1930, Gabrje, Slovenia (emigrated to Austria, 1945, and Canada, 1948); ord., June 4, 1955; taught Scripture, St. Aug.ine's Seminary, 1960-67; taught NT exegesis, Toronto School of Theology, 1970-76; aux. bp. of Toronto, Mar. 26, 1976; co-adjutor of Toronto, May 22, 1986; abp. of Toronto, Mar. 17, 1990; cardinal, Feb. 21, 1998; titular church, Sts. Marcellinus and Peter. Abp. of Toronto.

Curial membership: Oriental Churches, Sacraments, Clergy (congregation); Pastoral Care of Migrants and Itinerant People, Culture (councils).

Amigo Vallejo, O.F.M., Carlos: b. Aug. 23, 1934, Medina de Rioseco, Spain; joined Order of Friars Minor and ord., Aug. 17, 1960; ord. abp. of Tanger, Morocco, Apr. 28, 1974; abp. of Toledo, 1974-84; abp. of Seville, May 22, 1984; cardinal, Oct. 21, 2003; titular church, St. Mary of Monserrat of the Spanish. Abp. of Toledo.

Curial membership: Health Care Workers (council); Latin America (commission).

Angelini,* Fiorenzo: b. Aug. 1, 1916, Rome, Italy; ord., Feb. 3, 1940; master of pontifical ceremonies, 1947-54; ord. bp. (titular see of Messene) July 29, 1956, and head of Rome Vicariate's section for apostolate to health care workers; abp, 1985; pres. of newly established Curia agency for health care workers; cardinal deacon, June 28, 1991, deaconry, Holy Spirit (in Sassio). President of Pontifical Council for Pastoral Assistance to Health Care Workers, 1989-96.

Antonelli, Ennio, b. Nov. 18, 1936, Todi, Italy; ord., Apr. 2, 1960; bp. of Gubbio, Aug. 29, 1982; abp. of Perugia-Città della Pieve, 1988-2001; secretary-general of the Italian Episcopal Conference, 1995; abp. of Florence, Mar. 21, 2001; cardinal, Oct. 21, 2003; titular church, St. Andrew delle Fratte. Abp. of Florence.

Curial membership: Laity, Social Communications (councils).

Antonetti,* Lorenzo: b. July 31, 1922, Romagnano Sesia, Italy; ord., May 26, 1945; entered diplomatic service and served in Lebanon, Venezuela, first section for Extraordinary Affairs of the Secretariat of State, U.S. and France; ord. titular abp. of Roselle, May 12, 1968; apostolic nuncio to Nicaragua and Honduras, 1968-1973, and Zaire, 1973-77;

secretary of the Administration of the Patrimony of the Apostolic See (APSA), 1977-88; apostolic nuncio to France, 1988-95; pro-president Admin. of the Patrimony of the Apostolic See, 1995-1998; pres. Administration of the Patrimony of the Apostolic See (APSA), Feb. 23, 1998; cardinal deacon, Feb. 21, 1998; deaconry, St. Agnes in Agone. President emeritus Administration of the Patrimony of the Apostolic See.

Aponte Martínez,* Luis: b. Aug. 4, 1922, Lajas, Puerto Rico; ord., Apr. 10, 1950; parish priest at Ponce; ord. titular bp. of Lares and aux. of Ponce, Oct. 12, 1960; bp. of Ponce, 1963-64; abp. of San Juan, Nov. 4, 1964-99; cardinal, Mar. 5, 1973; titular church, St. Mary Mother of Providence (in Monte Verde). Abp. emeritus of San Juan.

Arinze, Francis: b. Nov. 1, 1932, Eziowelle, Nigeria; ord., Nov. 23, 1958; ord. titular bp. of Fissiana and aux. bp. of Onitsha, Aug. 29, 1965; abp. of Onitsha, 1967-84; pro-president of Secretariat for Non-Christians (now the Council for Interreligious Dialogue), 1984; cardinal deacon, May 25, 1985; deaconry, St. John (della Pigna); transferred to the order of cardinal priests, Jan. 29, 1996; transferred to the order of cardinal bishops, Apr. 25, 2005, with Suburbicarian See of Veletri-Segni; president of Council for Interreligious Dialogue, 1985-2002; Prefect of the Congregation for Divine Worship and the Discipline of the Sacraments, Oct. 1, 2002.

Curial membership: Doctrine of the Faith, Oriental Churches, Evangelization of Peoples, Causes of Saints (congregations); Laity, Christian Unity, Culture (councils); International Eucharistic Congresses (committee).

Arns,* O.F.M., Paulo Evaristo: b. Sept. 14, 1921, Forquilhinha, Brazil; ord., Nov. 30, 1945; held various teaching posts; director of Sponsa Christi, monthly review for religious, and of the Franciscan publication center in Brazil; ord. titular bp. of Respetta and aux. bp. of São Paulo, July 3, 1966; abp. of São Paulo, Oct. 22, 1970-98; cardinal, Mar. 5, 1973; titular church, St. Anthony of Padua (in Via Tuscolana). Abp. emeritus of São Paulo.

Backis, Audrys Juozas: b. Feb. 1, 1937, Kaunas, Lithuania; ord., Mar. 18, 1961; entered Holy See diplomatic service in 1964 and posted to the Philippines, Costa Rica, Turkey, Nigeria, and the Council for the Public Affairs of the Church; undersecretary to the Council for the Public Affairs of the Church, 1979-88; app. titular abp. of Meta and nuncio to the Netherlands, Aug. 5, 1988; app. abp. of Vilnius Dec. 24, 1991; pres. of the Lithuanian Bishops' Conference; cardinal, Feb. 21, 2001; titular church, Nativity of Our Lord Jesus Christ in Via Gallia. Abp. of Vilnius.

Curial membership: Education (congregation); Social Communication (council); Cultural Heritage of the Church (commission).

Barbarin, Philippe: b. Oct. 17, 1950, Rabat, Morocco; ord., Dec. 17, 1977; from 1994 to 1998, served in Madagascar as pastor and professor in the island's seminary; ord. bp. of Moulins, France, Nov. 22, 1998; abp. of Lyon, July 16, 2002, cardinal, Oct. 21, 2003; titular church, Most Holy Spirit al Monte Pincio. Abp. of Lyon.

Curial membership: Sacraments, Consecrated Life and Societies of Apostolic Life (congregations),

Baum, William Wakefield: b. Nov. 21, 1926, Dallas, TX; moved to Kansas City, MO, at an early age; ord. (Kansas City-St. Joseph diocese), May 12, 1951; executive director of U.S. Bishops' Commission for Ecumenical and Interreligious Affairs, 1964-69; attended Second Vatican Council as peritus (expert adviser); ord. bp. of Springfield-Cape Girardeau, MO, Apr. 6, 1970; abp. of Washington, DC, 1973-80; cardinal, May 24, 1976; titular church, Holy Cross on the Via

Flaminia; prefect of Congregation for Catholic Education (Seminaries and Institutes of Study), 1980-90. Major Penitentiary, 1990-2001; res., Nov. 22, 2001.

Curial membership: Bishops, Oriental Churches, Consecrated Life and Societies of Apostolic Life (congregations).

Bergoglio, S.J., Jorge Mario: b. Dec. 17, 1936, Buenos Aires, Argentina; ord. priest for the Jesuits, Dec. 13, 1969; novice master in the Theological Faculty of San Miguel; Jesuit provincial for Argentina, 1973-79; rector of the Philosophical and Theological Faculty of San Miguel, 1980-86; completed doctoral dissertation in Germany and served as confessor and spiritual director in Córdoba; app. titular bp. of Auca and aux. bp. of Buenos Aires, May 20, 1992; cons., June 27, 1992; app. coadj. abp. of Buenos Aires, June 3, 1997; succeeded as abp. of Buenos Aires, Feb. 28, 1998; also serves as Ordinary for Eastern-rite faithful in Argentina who lack their own ordinary and second vice-pres. of the Argentine Episcopal Conference; cardinal, Feb. 21, 2001; titular church, St. Robert Bellarmine; pres. of Argentine Episcopal Conference for 2005-2008 Abp. of Buenos Aires.

Curial membership: Sacraments, Clergy, Institutes of Consecrated Life and Societies of Apostolic Life (congregations); Family (council); Latin America (commission).

Bertone, S.D.B.,Tarcisio: b. Dec. 2, 1934, Romano Canavese, entered the Society of St. Francis de Sales of St. John Bosco (Salesians); ord., July 1, 1960; prof. of Special Moral Theology, Pontifical Salesian Athenaeum (later Pontifical Salesian University in 1973), 1967-76; prof. of Canon Law, 1976-1991; vice-rector, Pontifical Salesian University of Rome, 1987-1989; ord. abp. of Vercelli, Aug. 1, 1991; sec. of the Cong. for the Doctrine of the Faith, 1995-2002; abp. of Genoa, Dec. 10, 2002; cardinal, Oct. 21, 2003; titular church, St. Mary, Helper in Via Tuscolana; app. Secretary of State, Sept. 15, 2006.

Curial membership: Doctrine of the Faith, Clergy (congregations).

Bevilacqua,* Anthony Joseph: b. June 17, 1923, Brooklyn NY; ord. (Brooklyn diocese), June 11, 1949; ord. titular bp. of Aquae Albae in Byzacena and aux. bp. of Brooklyn, Nov. 24, 1980; bp. of Pittsburgh, Oct. 7, 1983, inst., Dec. 12, 1983; abp. of Philadelphia, Feb. 11, 1988; cardinal, June 28, 1991; titular church, Most Holy Redeemer and St. Alphonsus (on Via Merulana); ret., July 15, 2003. Abp. emeritus of Philadelphia.

Biffi, Giacomo: b. June 13, 1928, Milan, Italy; ord., Dec. 23, 1950; ord. titular bp. of Fidene and aux. of Milan, Jan. 11, 1976; abp. of Bologna, 1984-2003; cardinal, May 25, 1985; titular church, Sts. John the Evangelist and Petronius. Abp. emeritus of Bologna.

Curial membership: Clergy, Catholic Education (congregations).

Bozanic, Josip: b. Mar. 20, 1949, Rijeka, Yugoslavia; ord., June 29, 1975; prof. of canon law and dogmatic theology in the Seminary of Rijeka, 1988-1997; ord. bp. of Krk, Veglia, June 25, 1989; abp. of Zagreb, Croatia, July 5, 1997; pres. of the Croatian Conference of Bishops and vice-pres. of the Council of European Bishops' Conferences; cardinal, Oct. 21, 2003; titular church, St. Jerome of the Croatians. Abp. of Zagreb.

Curial membership: Sacraments (congregation); Laity (council).

Cacciavillan,* Agostino: b. Aug. 14, 1926, Novale de Valdagno (Vicenza), Italy; ord., June 26, 1949; attended Pont. Ecclesiastical Academy; entered Holy See diplomatic service; posted to the Philippines, Spain, Portugal, and Secretariat

of State; pro-nuncio in Kenya and apostolic delegate to Seychelles, 1976; titular abp. of Amiternum, Feb. 28, 1976; nuncio to India, 1981; pro-nuncio to Nepal, 1985; nuncio to United States and permanent observer at the Org. of American States, 1990; pres., Admin. of the Patrimony of the Apostolic See (APSA), 1998-2002; cardinal deacon, Feb. 21, 2001; deaconry, Holy Guardian Angels in Città Giardino. Pres. emeritus Admin. of the Patrimony of the Apostolic See.

Curial membership: Bishops, Causes of Saints, Evangelization of Peoples, Oriental Churches (congregations); Texts, (council); Latin America, Vatican City State (commissions); Signatura (tribunal).

Caffarra, Carlo: b. June 1, 1938 in Samboseto di Busseto, in the province of Parma, Italy; ord., July 2, 1961; studied at the Pontifical Lombard Seminary, Gregorian University, where he earned a doctorate in canon law, and the Pontifical Accademia Alfonsiana, with a diploma for a specialization in Moral Theology; after holding a variety of teaching positions, he was named to the International Theological Commission in 1974; founded in 1981 the John Paul II Pontifical Institute for Studies on Marriage and the Family; consultor to the Cong. for the Doctrine of the Faith, 1983-88; app. Sept. 8, 1995, abp. of Ferrara-Comacchio; app. Dec. 16, 2003, abp. of Bologna; pres. of the Episcopal Conference of Emilia Romagna; cardinal Mar. 24, 2006; titular church, San Giovanni Battista dei Fiorentini. Abp. of Bologna.

Curial membership: Evangelization of People (congregation); Family (council); Pontifical Academy of Life.

Canestri,* Giovanni: b. Sept. 30, 1918, Castelspina, Italy; ord., Apr. 12, 1941; spiritual director of Rome's seminary, 1959; ord. titular bp. of Tenedo and aux. to the cardinal vicar of Rome, July 30, 1961; bp. of Tortona, 1971-75; titular bp. of Monterano (personal title of abp.) and vice regent of Rome, 1975-84; abp. of Cagliari, 1984-87; abp. of Genoa, July 6, 1987-95; cardinal, June 28, 1988; titular church, St. Andrew of the Valley. Abp. emeritus of Genoa.

Cañizares Llovera, Antonio: b. Oct. 10, 1945, Utiel, Spain; after studies in the diocesan seminary of Valencia, he earned a doctorate in theology from the Pontifical University of Salamanca in 1971; ord., June 21, 1970; sec. of the Episcopal Commission for the Doctrine of the Faith, 1985-92; founder and first president of the Spanish Association of Catechists, 1977-89; app. bp. of Ávila, Marh 6, 1992; contributed to the compilation of the Spanish-language edition of the *Catechism of the Catholic Church*; app. abp. of Granada, Dec. 10, 1996; founder and first grand chancellor of the Catholic University, "Santa Teresa de Jesús" in Ávila, 1994-97; app. metropolitan abp. of Toledo and primate of Spain, Oct. 24, 2002; cardinal, Mar. 24, 2006; titular church, di San Pancrazio. Abp. of Toledo.

Curial membership: Doctrine of the Faith.

Carles Gordó,* Ricardo Maria: b. Sept. 24, 1926, Valencia, Spain; ord., June 29, 1951; ord. bp. of Tortosa, Aug. 3, 1969; abp. of Barcelona, 1990-2004; cardinal, Nov. 26, 1994; titular church, St. Mary of Consolation in Tiburtino. Abp. emeritus of Barcelona.

Curial membership: Catholic Education (congregation).

Cassidy,* Edward Idris: b. July 5, 1924, Sydney, Australia; ord., July 23, 1949; entered Vatican diplomatic service in 1955; served in nunciatures in India, Ireland, El Salvador and Argentina; ord. titular bp. of Amantia with personal title of abp., Nov. 15, 1970; pro-nuncio to Republic of China (Taiwan), 1970-79 and pro-nuncio to Bangladesh and apostolic delegate in Burma, 1973-79; pro-nuncio to Lesotho and apostolic delegate to southern Africa, 1979-84; pro-nuncio to the Netherlands, 1984-88; substitute of the Secretary of

State for General Affairs, 1988-89; pres. of Pontifical Council for Promoting Christian Unity, 1989-2001; cardinal deacon, June 28, 1991; deaconry, St. Mary (in via Lata). President emeritus of Pontifical Council for Promoting Christian Unity.

Castillo Lara,* S.D.B., Rosalio José: b. Sept. 4, 1922, San Casimiro, Venezuela; ord., Sept. 4, 1949; ord. titular bp. of Precausa, May 24, 1973; coadj. bp. of Trujillo, 1973-76; abp., May 26, 1982; pro-pres. of Pontifical Commission for Revision of Code of Canon Law, 1982-84; pro-pres. of Commission for Authentic Interpretation of Code of Canon Law, 1984-85; cardinal deacon, May 25, 1985; titular church, Our Lady of Coromoto (in St. John of God); transferred to order of cardinal priests, Jan. 29, 1996; pres. of Administration of Patrimony of the Holy See, 1989-95. President of the Pontifical Commission for the State of Vatican City State, 1990-97.

Castrillón Hoyos, Darío: b. July 4, 1929, Medellín, Colombia; ord., Oct. 26, 1952; served as curate in two parishes; dir. local Cursillo Movement; delegate for Catholic Action; taught canon law at the Free Civil University; gen. sec. of the Colombian Bishops' Conference; coadj. bp. of Pereira, June 2, 1971; bp. of Pereira, 1976-1992; gen. sec. of Latin American Episcopal Council (CELAM), 1983-87; pres. CELAM, 1987-91; abp. of Bucaramanga, 1992-96; pro-prefect Cong. for the Clergy, 1996-98; Pref. Cong. for the Clergy, 1998; cardinal deacon, Feb. 21, 1998; deaconry, Holy Name of Mary on the Forum Traiani. Prefect of the Congregation for the Clergy.

Curial membership: Bishops, Divine Worship and Sacraments, Education, Evangelization of Peoples (congregations); Social Communications, Texts (councils); APSA (office); Latin America (commission).

Cé,* Marco: b. July 8, 1925, Izano, Italy; ord., Mar. 27, 1948; taught sacred scripture and dogmatic theology at seminary in his home diocese of Crema; rector of seminary, 1957; presided over diocesan liturgical commission, preached youth retreats; ord. titular bp. of Vulturia, May 17, 1970; aux. bp. of Bologna, 1970-76; gen. ecclesiastical assistant of Italian Catholic Action, 1976-78; patriarch of Venice, 1978-2001; ret., Jan. 5, 2002; cardinal, June 30, 1979; titular church, St. Mark. Patriarch emeritus of Venice.

Cheli,* Giovanni: b. Oct. 4, 1918, Turin, Italy; ord., June 21, 1942; entered Secretariat of State and diplomatic service; second secretary, apostolic nunciature in Guatemala, 1952-55; first secretary, apostolic nunciature in Madrid, Spain, 1955-62; counselor, nunciature in Rome, 1962-67; Council for Public Affairs of the Church, Vatican City, 1967-73; Permanent Observer of the Holy See to the U.N., 1973-86; ord. titular abp. of Santa Giusta, Sept. 16, 1978; pres. Pontifical Council for the Pastoral Care of Migrants and Itinerant People, 1986-98; cardinal deacon, Feb. 21, 1998; deaconry, Sts. Cosmas and Damian. President emeritus Pontifical Council for the Pastoral Care of Migrants and Itinerant People.

Cheong-Jin-Suk, Nicolas: b. Dec. 7, 1931, Supyo Dong, near Seoul, Korea; raised in the faith, he survived the tumult of the Korean War and then entered the Major Seminary of Song Shin; ord., Mar. 18, 1961; after pastoral service, he was sent to Rome for studies in canon law, and earned a doctorate from the Pontifical Urban University; app. bp. of Cheongju, June 25; member of the Executive Committee of the Korean Episcopal Conference, 1975-99; pres. of the Korean Episcopal Conference, 1996-99; app. abp. of Seoul, Apr. 3, 1998, and administrator of the diocese of P'yong-yang; cardinal, Mar. 24, 2006; titular church, Santa Maria Immacolata di Lourdes a Boccea. Abp. of Seoul.

Curial membership: Family (council).

Cipriani Thorne, Juan Luis: b. Dec. 28, 1943, Lima, Peru; champion basketball player and student in industrial engineering, he joined Opus Dei in 1962; ord. for the prelature Aug. 21, 1977; after a doctorate in theology at the University of Navarre and pastoral work in Lima, he taught moral theology at the Pontifical Faculty of Theology, Lima, and was regional vicar for Peru and vice-chancellor of the University of Piura; app. titular bp. of Turuzi and aux. bp. of Ayacucho, May 23, 1988; cons. July 3, 1988; app. abp. of Ayacucho, May 13, 1995; tried to negotiate a peaceful resolution to the siege of the Japanese ambassador's residence in Lima, Dec. 1996-Apr. 1997 and ministered to Japanese and Peruvian hostages; app. abp. of Lima, Jan. 9, 1999; cardinal, Feb. 21, 2001; titular church St. Camillus de Lellis. Abp. of Lima.

Curial membership: Causes of Saints, Sacraments (congregation); Latin America (commission).

Clancy,* Edward Bede: b. Dec. 13, 1923, Lithgow, New South Wales, Australia; ord., July 23, 1949; ord. titular bp. of Ard Carna and aux. of Sydney, Jan. 19, 1974; abp. of Canberra, 1978-83; abp. of Sydney, Feb. 12, 1983; res., Mar. 26, 2001; cardinal, June 28, 1988; titular church, Holy Mary of Vallicella. Abp. emeritus of Sydney.

Connell,* Desmond: b. Mar. 24, 1926, Phibsboro, Ireland; ord., May 19, 1951; taught at University College Dublin, 1953-72; dean of the faculty of Philosophy and Sociology, 1983; awarded degree of D.Litt. by National University of Dublin, 1981; chaplain to the Poor Clares in Donnybrook and Carmelites in Drumcondra and Blackrock; app. abp. of Dublin, Jan. 21, 1988; cons., Mar. 6, 1988; ret. Apr. 26, 2004; cardinal, Feb. 21. 2001; titular church, St. Sylvester in Capite. Abp. emeritus of Dublin.

Curial membership: Bishops, Doctrine of the Faith (congregations); Laity (council).

Cordero Lanza di Montezemolo,* Andrea: b. Aug. 27, 1925, Turin, Italy; ord., Mar. 13, 1954; entered diplomatic service after studies at the Pontifical Ecclesiastical Academy in 1959; served for 42 years in various diplomatic posts; app. undersecretary and secretary of the Pont. Comm. Justice and Peace; app. nuncio and titular abp. of Anglona, Apr. 5, 1977; nuncio to Papau New Guinea and apostolic delegate to Solomon Islands, 1977; app. apostolic delegate in Jerusalem, Palestine, and Jordan, Apr. 28, 1990; transferred to see of Tuscania, Apr. 13, 1991, and first nuncio to Israel, 1994-98; nuncio to Italy and San Marino, 1998-2001; app. archpriest of the basilica of St. Paul Outside-the-Walls, June 1, 2005; an expert ecclesiastical herald, he assisted the design of the papal coat of arms for Pope Benedict XVI in 2005; cardinal, Mar. 24, 2006; titular church, Diaconia di Santa Maria in Portico.

Corripio Ahumada,* Ernesto: b. June 29, 1919, Tampico, Mexico; ord., Oct. 25, 1942, in Rome, where he remained until almost the end of World War II; taught and held various positions in local seminary of Tampico, 1945-50; ord. titular bp. of Zapara and aux. bp. of Tampico, Mar. 19, 1953; bp. of Tampico, 1956-67; abp. of Antequera, 1967-76; abp. of Puebla de los Angeles, 1976-77; abp. of Mexico City and primate of Mexico, July 19, 1977-1994; cardinal, June 30, 1979; titular church, Mary Immaculate al Tiburtino. Abp. emeritus of Mexico City.

Cottier,* O.P., Georges: b. Apr. 25, 1922; ord., July 2, 1951; theologian of the Papal Household theologian, 1989; secretary general of the International Theological Commission, 1989-2004; cons. Titular abp. of Tullia, Oct. 20, 2003; cardinal, Oct. 21, 2003;

titular church, Sts. Dominic and Sixtus.

Daly,* Cahal Brendan: b. Oct. 1, 1917, Loughguile, Northern Ireland; ord., June 22, 1941; earned advanced degrees in philosophy and theology; 30 years of priestly life dedicated to teaching; attended Second Vatican Council as a theological adviser to members of Irish hierarchy; outspoken critic of violence in Northern Ireland; ord. bp. of Ardagh, July 16, 1967; bp. of Down and Connor, 1982-90; abp. of Armagh and primate of All Ireland, 1990-96; cardinal, June 28, 1991; titular church, St. Patrick. Abp. emeritus of Armagh.

Danneels, Godfried: b. June 4, 1933, Kanegem, Belgium; ord., Aug. 17, 1957; professor of liturgy and sacramental theology at Catholic University of Louvain, 1969-77; ord. bp. of Antwerp, Dec. 18, 1977; app. abp. of Mechelen-Brussel, Dec. 19, 1979; inst., Jan. 4, 1980; cardinal, Feb. 2, 1983; titular church, St. Anastasia. Abp. of Mechelen-Brussel, military ordinary of Belgium.

Curial membership: Secretariat of State (second section); Divine Worship and Sacraments, Education, Evangelization of Peoples, Oriental Churches (congregations).

Darmaatmadja, S.J., Julius Riyadi: b. Dec. 20, 1934, Muntilan, Mageland, Central Java, Indonesia; entered Society of Jesus in 1957; ord., Dec. 18, 1969; ord. abp. of Semarang, June 29, 1983 (transferred to Jakarta, Jan. 11, 1996); cardinal, Nov. 26, 1994; titular church, Sacred Heart of Mary. Abp. of Jakarta, military ordinary of Indonesia.

Curial membership: Evangelization of Peoples (congregation); Interreligious Dialogue, Culture (councils).

de Giorgi, Salvatore: b. Sep. 6, 1930 Vernole, Italy; ord., June 28, 1953; diocesan chaplain to the Teachers' Movement of Catholic Action; dir. Diocesan Pastoral Office; app. titular bp. of Tulana and aux. bp. of Oria, Nov. 21, 1973; bp. of Oria, Mar. 17, 1978; abp. of Foggia, Apr. 4, 1981; abp. of Taranto, Oct. 10, 1987 (res., 1990); general president of Catholic Action, 1990-96; abp. of Palermo, Apr. 4, 1996; president of the Sicilian Episcopal Conference; cardinal, Feb. 21, 1998; titular church, St. Mary in Ara Caeli. Abp. of Palermo.

Curial membership: Clergy, Divine Worship and Sacraments (congregations); Laity, Family (councils).

Dery,* Peter Poreku: b. May 10, 1918, Zemuopare, Ghana; ord., Feb. 11, 1951; served as parish priest and assistant director of Catholic schools in Tamale, Ghana; app. bp. of Wa, Mar. 16, 1960 and introduced liturgical inculturation to the diocese; app. apostolic admin. of Tamale, 1972; app. bp. of Tamale, Nov. 18, 1974; first abp. of Tamale, May 30, 1977; ret. as abp. June 30, 1994; cardinal, Mar. 24, 2006; titular church, Diaconia di Sant'Elena fuori Porta Prenestina. Abp. emeritus of Tamale.

Deskur,* Andrzej Maria: b. Feb. 29, 1924, Sancygniow, Poland; ord., Aug. 20, 1950, in France; assigned to Vatican secretariat of state, 1952; undersecretary and later secretary of Pontifical Commission for Film, Radio and TV (Social Communications), 1954-73; ord. titular bp. of Tene, June 30, 1974; abp., 1980; president of Pontifical Commission for Social Communications, 1974-84; cardinal deacon, May 25, 1985; deaconry, St. Cesario (in Palatio); transferred to order of cardinal priests, Jan. 29, 1996. President emeritus of Council for Social Communications.

Dias, Ivan: b. Apr. 14, 1936, Bandra, India; ord., Dec. 8, 1958; entered the Holy See diplomatic service and was posted to Indonesia, Madagascar, Reunion, the Comorros, Mauritius, and Secretariat of State; app. titular abp. of Rusubisir and pro-nuncio in Ghana, Togo and Benin, May 8, 1982; cons., June 19, 1982; nuncio in Korea, 1987-91; nuncio in Albania, 1991-97; abp. of Bombay, Jan. 22, 1997-May 22, 2006; cons., Mar. 13, 1997; cardinal, Feb. 21, 2001; titu-

lar church, Holy Spirit in Ferratella; app. Prefect of the Cong. for the Evang. of Peoples, May 20, 2006. Prefect of the Cong. for the Evangelization of Peoples.

Curial membership: Doctrine of the Faith, Sacraments, Education (congregations); Culture, Laity (councils); Economic Affairs (office); Cultural Heritage of the Church (commission).

do Nascimento,* Alexandre: b. Mar. 1, 1925, Malanje, Angola; ord., Dec. 20, 1952, in Rome; professor of dogmatic theology in major seminary of Luanda, Angola; editor of *O Apostolada*, Catholic newspaper; forced into exile in Lisbon, Portugal, 1961-71; returned to Angola, 1971; active with student and refugee groups; professor at Pius XII Institute of Social Sciences; ord. bp. of Malanje, Aug. 31, 1975; abp. of Lubango and apostolic administrator of Onjiva, 1977-86; held hostage by Angolan guerrillas, Oct. 15 to Nov. 16, 1982; cardinal, Feb. 2, 1983; titular church, St. Mark in Agro Laurentino. Abp. of Luanda, 1986.

Curial membership: Catholic Education (congregations).

Dulles,* S.J., Avery: b. Aug. 24, 1918, Auburn, NY; the son of U.S. Secretary of State John Foster Dulles; raised a Protestant, he converted to the Catholic faith while a student at Harvard; served in U.S. Navy and then entered the Jesuits; ord. priest for the Jesuits, June 16, 1956; earned a doctorate in theology at the Gregorian University, Rome; taught theology at Woodstock College, 1960-74, and Catholic University of America, 1974-88; visiting professor at numerous other institutions; author of 21 books and over 650 articles; pres. of the Catholic Theological Society of America; member of the International Theological Commission and the U.S. Lutheran/Roman Catholic Dialogue; consultor to the U.S. Bishops' Committee on Doctrine; currently the Laurence J. McGinley Professor of Religion and Society at Fordham University; cardinal deacon, Feb. 21, 2001; deaconry, Most Holy Names of Jesus and Mary in Via Lata.

Dziwisz, Stanislaw: b. Apr. 27, 1939, in Raba Wyzna, Poland; ord., June 23, 1963; secretary to Cardinal Karol Wojtyla, 1966-78; with election of Wojtyla as Pope John Paul II in 1978, he became papal secretary, a post he held until John Paul II's passing in 2005; named a prelate of his holiness in 1985, titular bishop of San Leone e Prefetto and adjunct prefect of the Papal Household on Feb. 7, 1998, and named titular archbishop on Sept. 29, 2003; app. abp. of Cracow, June 3, 2005; cardinal Mar. 24, 2006; titular church, Titolo di Santa Maria del Popolo. Abp. of Cracow.

Curial membership: Education (Congregation); Social Communications (Council).

Egan, Edward Michael: b. Apr. 2, 1932, Oak Park, IL; ord., Dec. 15, 1957, in Rome; sec. to Cardinal Albert Meyer, 1958-60; assistant vice-rector of the North American College, 1960-64; vice-chancellor of the archdiocese of Chicago, 1964-68; co-chancellor for human relations and ecumenism, 1968-72; judge of Roman Rota, 1972-85; ord. titular bp. of Allegheny and aux. bp. of New York, May 22, 1985; app. bp. of Bridgeport, Nov. 5, 1988; abp. of New York, May 11, 2000, inst., June 19, 2000; cardinal, Feb. 21, 2001; titular church, St. John and Paul. Abp. of New York.

Curial membership: Family (council); Signatura (tribunal); Economic Affairs (office); Cultural Heritage (commission).

Erdö, Peter: b. June 25, 1952 Budapest, Hungary; ord., June 18, 1975 and earned doctorates in Theology and Canon Law from the Lateran University, Rome; professor of Theology and Canon Law, at the seminary of Esztergom, 1980-1988; guest professor, in Canon Law, Pontifical Gregorian University, 1986; rector of the Catholic University Péter Pázmány, 1998; ord., Jan. 6, 2000, titular bp. of Puppi and aux. bp. of Szikesfehirvar; abp. of Esztergom-Budapest, Dec. 7, 2002; cardinal, Oct. 21, 2003; titular church, St. Balbina. Abp. of Esztergom-Budapest.

Curial membership: Education (congregation); Legislative Texts (council); Supreme Tribunal of the Apostolic Signatura (tribunal).

Errázuriz Ossa, Francisco Javier: b. Sept. 5, 1933, Santiago, Chile; ord. for the Schönstatt Fathers, July 16, 1961; chaplain to students and professionals of the Schönstatt Movement and regional superior; elected superior general of the Schönstatt Fathers, 1974; app. titular abp. of Hólar and sec. of the Cong. For Institutes of Consecrated Life and Societies of Apostolic Life, Dec. 22, 1990; app. abp. of Valparaiso, Sept. 24, 1996; transferred to archdiocese of Santiago, Apr. 24, 1998; pres. of the Episcopal Conference of Chile and first vice-pres. of CELAM; cardinal, Feb. 21, 2001; titular church, St. Mary of Peace. Abp. of Santiago.

Curial membership: Consecrated Life and Societies of Apostolic Life (congregation); Culture, Family (council); Latin America (commission).

Etchegaray,* Roger: b. Sept. 25, 1922, Espelette, France; ord., July 13, 1947; deputy director, 1961-66, and secretary general, 1966-70, of French Episcopal Conference; ord. titular bp. of Gemelle di Numidia and aux. of Paris, May 27, 1969; abp. of Marseilles, 1970-84; prelate of Mission de France, 1975-82; president of French Episcopal Conference, 1979-81; cardinal, June 30, 1979; titular church, St. Leo I. President of Council Cor Unum, 1984-95; president of Council for Justice and Peace (1984-98) and President of Central Committee for the Jubilee of the Holy Year 2000 (1994-98); transferred to order of cardinal bishops, June 24, 1998 (suburbicarian see of Porto-Santa Rufina); vice-dean of the Sacred College of Cardinals (Apr. 30, 2005).

Etsou-Nzabi-Bamungwabi, C.I.C.M., Frédéric: b. Dec. 3, 1930, Mazalonga, Zaire; ord., July 13, 1958; educ. Catholic Institute of Paris (degree in sociology) and "Lumen Vitae" in Belgium (degree in pastoral theology); ord. titular bp. of Menefessi and coadj. abp. of Mbandaka-Bikora, Nov. 7, 1976; abp. of Mbandaka-Bikora, 1977-1990; abp. of Kinshasa, July 7, 1990; cardinal, June 28, 1991; titular church, St. Lucy (a Piazza d'Armi). Abp. of Kinshasa.

Curial membership: Evangelization of Peoples (congregation); Family, Culture (councils).

Falcão,* José Freire: b. Oct. 23, 1925, Erere, Brazil; ord., June 19, 1949; ord. titular bp. of Vardimissa and coadj. of Limoeiro do Norte, June 17, 1967; bp. of Limoeiro do Norte, Aug. 19, 1967; abp. of Teresina, Nov. 25, 1971; abp. of Brasilia, 1984-2004; res. Jan. 28, 2004; cardinal, June 28, 1988; titlar church, St. Luke (Via Prenestina). Abp. emeritus of Brasilia.

Felici,* Angelo: b. July 26, 1919, Segni, Italy; ord., Apr. 4, 1942; in Vatican diplomatic service from 1945; ord. titular bp. of Cesariana, with personal title of abp., Sept. 24, 1967; nuncio to Netherlands, 1967-76, Portugal, 1976-79, France, 1979-88; cardinal deacon, June 28, 1988; deaconry, Sts. Blaise and Charles in Catinari; promoted to cardinal priest, Jan. 9, 1999. Prefect of Congregation for Causes of Saints, 1988-95. President of Pontifical Commission "Ecclesia Dei," 1995.

Fernandes de Araújo,* Serafim: b. Aug. 13, 1924, Minas Novas, Brazil; ord., Mar. 12, 1949; taught canon law at provincial seminary of Diamantina; titular bp. of Verinopolis and aux. bp. of Belo Horizonte, Jan. 19, 1959; co-adjutor abp. of Belo Horizonte, 1982; abp. Belo Horizonte, 1986-2004; res. Jan. 28, 2004; co-

president of the Fourth General Conference of the Latin American Episcopate, 1992; cardinal, Feb. 21, 1998; titular church, St. Louis Marie Grignion de Montfort. Abp. emeritus of Belo Horizonte.

Furno,* Carlo: b. Dec. 2, 1921, Bairo Canavese, Italy; ord., June 25, 1944; entered diplomatic service of the Holy See in the 1950s; served in Colombia, Ecuador and Jerusalem; worked in Secretariat of State for 11 years and taught at Pontifical Ecclesiastical Academy, 1966-73; ord. titular bp. of Abari with personal title of abp., Sept. 16, 1973; nuncio in Peru, 1973-78, Lebanon, 1978-82, Brazil, 1982-92, Italy, 1992-94; cardinal deacon, Nov. 26, 1994; deaconry, Sacred Heart of Christ the King. Grand Master of the Equestrian Order of the Holy Sepulchre, 1995; pontifical delegate for Patriarchal Basilica of St. Francis in Assisi, 1996. Archpriest emeritus of the patriarchal basilica of Santa Maria Maggiore, Rome, 1998-2004.

Gagnon,* P.S.S., Edouard: b. Jan. 15, 1918, Port Daniel, Que., Canada; ord., Aug. 15, 1940; ord. bp. of St. Paul in Alberta, Mar. 25, 1969 (res., May 3, 1972); rector of Canadian College in Rome, 1972-77; vice president-secretary of Vatican Committee for the Family, 1973-80; titular abp. of Giustiniana Prima, July 7, 1983; pro-president of Pontifical Council for the Family, 1983; cardinal deacon, May 25, 1985; deaconry, St. Elena (fuori Porta Prenestina); transf. to order of cardinal priests, Jan. 29, 1996; titular church St. Marcellus. President of Pontifical Council for the Family, 1985-90; president of Pontifical Committee for International Eucharistic Congresses, 1991-2000.

Gantin,* Bernardin: b. May 8, 1922, Toffo, Dahomey (now Benin); ord., Jan. 14, 1951; ord. titular bp. of Tipasa di Mauritania and aux. bp. of Cotonou, Feb. 3, 1957; abp. of Cotonou, 1960-71; associate secretary (1971-73) and secretary (1973-75) of Congregation for Evangelization of Peoples; vice-president (1975) and president (1976-84) of Pontifical Commission for Justice and Peace; cardinal deacon, June 27, 1977; transferred to order of priests, June 25, 1984; titular church, Sacred Heart of Christ the King; titular bp. of suburbicarian see of Palestrina Sept. 29, 1986, when he entered the order of cardinal bishops, and of Ostia June 5, 1993 (res. Nov. 30, 2002), when he became dean of the college of cardinals. Prefect of Congregation for Bishops, 1984-98; president of commission for Latin America, 1984-98; dean of college of cardinals, 1993-2002.

George, O.M.I., Francis E.: b. Jan. 16, 1937, Chicago, IL; ord., Dec. 21, 1963; provincial of central region of Oblates of Mary Immaculate, 1973-74, vicar general, 1974-86; ord. bp. of Yakima, Sept. 21, 1990; abp. of Portland, OR, Apr. 30, 1996, inst., May 27, 1996; abp. of Chicago, Apr. 8, 1997, inst., May 7, 1997; cardinal, Feb. 21, 1998; titular church, St. Bartholomew on Tiber Island. Abp. of Chicago.

Curial membership: Divine Worship and the Discipline of the Sacraments, Institutes of Consecrated Life and Societies of Apostolic Life, Oriental Churches, Evangelization (congregations); Cor Unum, Culture (council); Cultural Heritage of the Church (commission).

Giordano, Michele: b. Sept. 26, 1930, S. Arcangelo, Italy; ord., July 5, 1953; ord. titular bp. of Lari Castello and aux. of Matera, Feb. 5, 1972; abp. of Matera and Irsina, 1974-87; abp. of Naples, May 9, 1987-May 20, 2006; cardinal, June 28, 1988; titular church, St. Joachim. Abp. emeritus of Naples.

Curial membership: Clergy (congregation); Health

Care Workers (council).

Glemp, Józef: b. Dec. 18, 1929, Inowroclaw, Poland; assigned to forced labor on German farm in Rycerzow during Nazi occupation; ord., May 25, 1956; studied in Rome, 1958-64; received degree in Roman and canon law from Pontifical Lateran University; secretary of primatial major seminary at Gniezno on his return to Poland, 1964; spokesman for secretariat of primate of Poland and chaplain of primate for archdiocese of Gniezno, 1967; ord. bp. of Warmia, Apr. 21, 1979; abp. of Gniezno, 1981-92, with title of abp. of Warsaw and primate of Poland; cardinal, Feb. 2, 1983; titular church, St. Mary in Trastevere. Abp. of Warsaw (Mar. 25, 1992), primate of Poland, ordinary for Eastern-rite faithful in Poland who do not have ordinaries of their own rites. Abp. of Warsaw.

Curial membership: Oriental Churches (congregation); Signatura (tribunal); Culture (council).

González Zumárraga,* Antonio José: b. Mar. 18, 1925, Pujilí (Cotopaxi), Ecuador; ord., June 29, 1951; taught at the Pontifical Catholic University of Ecuador; chancellor of the Curia, 1964; rector of Our Mother of Mercy College; app. titular bp. of Tagarata and aux. bp. of Quito; apostolic admin. of Machala, Mar. 1976; bp. of Machata, Jan. 30, 1978; coadj. abp. of Quito, June 28, 1980; abp. of Quito, June 1, 1985; served two terms as pres. of the Ecuadorean Episcopal Conference; cardinal, Feb. 21, 2001; titular church, St. Mary in Via. Abp. of Quito.

Grocholewski, Zenon: b. Oct. 11, 1939, Bródki, Poland; ord., May 26, 1963; earned a doctorate in canon law; served in the Supreme Tribunal of the Apostolic Signatura, 1972-1999; prefect of the Supreme Tribunal of the Apostolic Signatura; member of the commission studying the 1983 Code of Canon Law; titular bp. of Agropoli, Dec. 21, 1982; titular abp., Dec. 16, 1991; prefect of the Cong. for Catholic Education, Nov. 15, 1999; cardinal deacon, Feb. 21, 2001; titular church, deaconry, St. Nicholas in Carcere. Prefect of the Congregation for Catholic Education.

Curial membership: Bishops, Doctrine of the Faith (congregations); Texts (council).

Gulbinowicz,* Henryk Roman: b. Oct. 17, 1923, Szukiszki, Poland; ord., June 18, 1950; ord. titular bp. of Acci and apostolic administrator of Polish territory in Lithuanian archdiocese of Vilnius (Vilna), Feb. 8, 1970; abp. of Wroclaw, Poland, 1976-2004; cardinal, May 25, 1985; titular church, Immaculate Conception of Mary (a Grottarosa). Abp. of Wroclaw. Abp. emeritus of Wroclaw

Hamao, Stephen Fumio: b. Mar. 9, 1930, Tokyo, Japan; ord., Dec. 21, 1957; ord. titular bp. of Oreto and aux. bp. of Tokyo, Apr. 29, 1970; bp. of Yokohama, 1979-98; abp. and pres. of Pontifical Council for Pastoral Care of Migrants and Itinerants, 1998-2006; cardinal deacon, Oct. 21, 2003; deaconry, St. John Bosco in Via Tuscolana. Pres. emeritus Pontifical Council for Pastoral Care of Migrants and Itinerants.

Curial membership: Evangelization, Causes of Saints (congregations); "Cor Unum," Justice and Peace (council); Eucharistic Congresses (Commission).

Herranz Casado, Julián: b. Mar. 31, 1930, Baena, Spain; joined the personal prelature of Opus Dei and ord., Aug. 7, 1955; earned doctorates in canon law and medicine; Sec. of the Pontifical Commission for the Interpretation of the Code of Canon Law (later Pontifical Council for the Interpretation of the Legislative Texts), 1984; ord. titular bp. of Vertara, Jan. 6, 1991; named abp. and pres. of the Pontifical Council for the Interpretation of the Legislative Texts, Dec. 19, 1994;

president of the Disciplinary Commission of the Roman Curia, Dec. 3, 1999; cardinal deacon, Oct. 21, 2003; titular church, St. Eugene. Pres. of the Pontifical Council for the Interpretation of Legislative Texts.

Curial membership: Bishops, Causes of Saints, Doctrine of the Faith, Evangelization of Peoples (congregations); Apostolic Signatura (Tribunal); Laity (Council); Ecclesia Dei (commission).

Honoré,* Jean: b. Aug. 13, 1920; ord., June 29, 1943; authored doctoral dissertation under the direction of Jean Daniélou at the Institute Catholique, Paris; taught at St. Vincent's College in Rennes and in Saint-Malo; worked for six years at the National Religious Education Centre (CNEC); rector of the Catholic University of Angers; app. bp. of Evreux, Oct. 24, 1972; cons., Dec. 17, 1972; app. abp. of Tours, Aug. 13, 1981; participated in the preparation of the Catechism, following the 1985 Synod of Bishops; res. as abp. of Tours, July 22, 1997; cardinal, Feb. 21, 2001; titular church, St. Mary of Health in Primavalle. Abp. emeritus of Tours.

Hummes, O.F.M., Cláudio: b. Aug. 8, 1934, Montenegro, Brazil; ord. priest for the Franciscans, Aug. 3, 1958; specialist in ecumenism; taught philosophy at the Franciscan seminary in Garibaldi, at the major seminary of Viamão and the Pontifical Catholic University of Porto Alegre; adviser for ecumenical affairs to the National Bishops' Conference of Brazil; Provincial of Rio Grande do Sul, 1972-75; pres. of the Union of Latin American Conferences of Franciscans; app. coadj. bp. of Santo André, Mar. 22, 1975; cons., May 25, 1975; succeeded to see, Dec. 29, 1975; app. abp. of Fortaleza, July 21, 1996; transferred to São Paulo, May 23, 1998; cardinal, Feb. 21, 2001; titular church, St. Anthony of Padua in Via Merulana. Abp. of São Paulo.

Curial membership: Bishops, Doctrine of the Faith, Sacraments (congregation); Cor Unum, Culture, Family, Interreligious Dialogue, Laity (councils); Latin America (commission).

Husar, M.S.U., Lubomyr: b. Feb. 26, 1933, Lviv, Ukraine; family fled to Austria because of the war and then to the U.S.; ord. for the eparchy of Stamford for Ukrainians, U.S., Mar. 30, 1958; entered the Studite Monks after completing a doctorate in theology in Rome; superior of the Studion in Grottaferrata, Italy; ord. bp. Apr. 2, 1977; app. archimandrite of Studite Monks residing outside Ukraine; organized a new Studite monastery in Ternopil, Ukraine, 1994; elected exarch of Kyiv-Vyshorod, 1995; app. aux. bp. to major abp. of Lviv, 1996; elected major abp. of Lviv for Ukrainians, Jan. 25, 2001; title changed to major abp. of Kiev and Halych, Aug. 21, 2005; cardinal, Feb. 21, 2001; titular church, Holy Wisdom in Via Boccea. Major Abp. of Kiev and Halych.

Curial membership: Oriental Churches (congregation); Christian Unity, Culture, Texts (councils).

Innocenti,* Antonio: b. Aug. 23, 1915, Poppi, Italy; ord., July 17, 1938; held curial and diplomatic positions; ord. titular bp. of Eclano with personal title of abp., Feb. 18, 1968; nuncio to Paraguay, 1967-73; secretary of Congregation for Causes of Saints, 1973-75; secretary of Congregation for Sacraments and Divine Worship, 1975-80; nuncio to Spain, 1980-85; cardinal deacon, May 25, 1985; transferred to order of cardinal priests, Jan. 29, 1996; titular church, St. Marie (in Aquiro); prefect of Congregation for the Clergy, 1986-91; president of Pontifical Commission for Preservation of Artistic Patrimony of the Church, 1988-91; president of Pontifical Commission "Ecclesia Dei," 1991-95.

Javierre Ortas,* S.D.B., Antonio María: b. Feb. 21, 1921, Sietamo, Spain; ord., Apr. 24, 1949; leading European writer on ecumenism; ord. titular bp. of Meta with personal title of abp., June 29, 1976; Secretary of Congregation for Catholic Education, 1976-88; cardinal, June 28, 1988; deacon (Santa Maria Liberatrice a Monte Testaccio), promoted to cardinal priest, Jan. 9, 1999 (Santa Maria Liberatrice a Monte Testaccio; raised to presbyteral title); librarian and Archivist of the Holy Roman Church, 1988-92. Prefect of Congregation for Divine Worship and the Sacraments, 1992-96.

Jaworski,* Marian: b. Aug. 21, 1926, Lwów, Poland (modern Lviv, Ukraine); ord., June 25, 1950; taught at the Catholic Theological Academy of Warsaw and Pontifical Theological faculty of Kraków; first rector of the Pontifical Theological Academy, Kraków, 1981-87; app. titular bp. of Lambaesis and apostolic admin. of Lubaczów, May 21, 1984; cons., June 23, 1984; app. abp. of Lviv for Latins, Jan. 16, 1991; pres. of the Ukrainian Episcopal Conference, 1992; cardinal (in pectore), Feb. 21, 1998; titular church, St. Sixtus. Abp. of Lviv for Latins.

Curial membership: Clergy (congregation); Family (council).

Kasper, Walter: b. Mar. 5, 1933, Heidenheim/Brenz, Germany; ord., Apr. 6, 1957; taught theology and was later dean of the theological faculty in Münster and Tübingen; app. bp. of Rottenburg-Stuttgart, Apr. 17, 1989, cons., June 17, 1989; co-chair of the International Commission for Lutheran/Catholic Dialogue, 1994; sec. of the Pontifical Council for Promoting Christian Unity, June 1, 1999; pres. Pontifical Council for Promoting Christian Unity, 2001; cardinal deacon, Feb. 21, 2001; deaconry, All Saints in Via Appia Nuova. President of the Pontifical Council for Promoting Christian Unity.

Curial membership: Doctrine of the Faith, Oriental Churches (congregations); Apostolic Signatura (tribunal); Culture, Legislative Texts (council).

Keeler, William Henry: b. Mar. 4, 1931, San Antonio, TX; ord. (Harrisburg diocese) July 17, 1955; secretary to Bp. Leech at Vatican II, named peritus by Pope John XXIII; ord. titular bp. of Ulcinium and aux. bp. of Harrisburg, Sept. 21, 1979; bp. of Harrisburg, Nov. 10, 1983, inst., Jan. 4, 1984; abp. of Baltimore, Apr. 6, 1989; cardinal, Nov. 26, 1994; titular church, St. Mary of the Angels. Abp. of Baltimore.

Curial membership: Oriental Churches (congregation); Christian Unity (council).

Kim Sou-hwan,* Stephen: b. May 8, 1922, Tae Gu, Korea; ord., Sept. 15, 1951; ord. bp. of Masan, May 31, 1966; abp. of Seoul, Apr. 9, 1968 (res., May 29, 1998); cardinal, Apr. 28, 1969; titular church, St. Felix of Cantalice (Centocelle). Abp. emeritus of Seoul, apostolic administrator emeritus of Pyeong Yang.

Kitbunchu, Michael Michai: b. Jan. 25, 1929, Samphran, Thailand; ord., Dec. 20, 1959, in Rome; rector of metropolitan seminary in Bangkok, 1965-72; ord. abp. of Bangkok, June 3, 1973; cardinal, Feb. 2, 1983, the first from Thailand; titular church, St. Laurence in Panisperna. Abp. of Bangkok.

Curial membership: Evangelization of Peoples (congregation).

Korec,* Ján Chryzostom, S.J.: b. Jan. 22, 1924, Bosany, Slovakia; entered Society of Jesus in 1939; ord., Oct. 1, 1950; ord. bp. secretly, Aug. 24, 1951; sentenced to 12 years in prison in 1960 for helping seminarians with their study and ordaining priests; paroled in 1968; appointed bp. of Nitra, Feb. 6, 1990; ret. June 9, 2005; cardinal, June 28, 1991; titu-

lar church, Sts. Fabian and Venantius (a Villa Forelli). Bp. emeritus of Nitra.

Kozlowiecki,* S.J., Adam: b. Apr. 1, 1911, Huta Komorowska, Poland; ord., June 24, 1937; arrested by Nazi Gestapo with 24 fellow priests in Kraków in 1939 and sent to Auschwitz concentration camp; moved to Dachau six months later where he suffered throughout the war; sent to Rhodesia after the war and taught until 1950; appointed apostolic administrator of prefecture of Lusaka, 1950; appointed bp. and vicar apostolic, Sept. 11, 1955; appointed abp. of Lusaka, 1959; res., 1969, to allow a native African to receive the post; member Congregation for the Evangelization of People, 1970-91; cardinal, Feb. 21, 1998; titular church, St. Andrew on the Quirinal.

Laghi,* Pio: b. May 21, 1922, Castiglione, Italy; ord., Apr. 20, 1946; entered diplomatic service of the Holy See in 1952; served in Nicaragua, the U.S. (as secretary of the apostolic delegation, 1954-61) and India; recalled to Rome and served on Council for Public Affairs of the Church; ord. titular abp. of Mauriana, June 22, 1969; apostolic delegate to Jerusalem and Palestine, 1969-74; nuncio to Argentina, 1974-80; apostolic delegate, 1980-84, and first pro-nuncio, 1984-90, to the U.S.; pro-prefect of Congregation for Catholic Education, 1990-91; cardinal deacon, June 28, 1991; deaconry, St. Mary Auxiliatrix (in Via Tuscolana). Prefect of Congregation for Catholic Education, 1991-99. Grand chancellor of Pontifical Gregorian University. Patron of Sovereign Military Order of Malta, 1993. Protodeacon, 1999-2002.

Law, Bernard F.: b. Nov. 4, 1931, Torreon, Mexico, the son of U.S. Air Force colonel; ord. (Jackson diocese), May 21, 1961; editor of Natchez-Jackson, MS, diocesan paper, 1963-68; director of NCCB Committee on Ecumenical and Interreligious Affairs, 1968-71; ord. bp. of Springfield-Cape Girardeau, MO, Dec. 5, 1973; abp. of Boston, Jan. 11, 1984; cardinal, May 25, 1985; titular church, St. Susanna; res., Dec.13, 2002; archpriest of the patriarchal basilica of Santa Maria Maggiore, Rome, May 27, 2004, Abp. emeritus of Boston.

Curial membership: Bishops, Clergy, Consecrated Life and Societies of Apostolic Life, Divine Worship and Sacraments, Education, Evangelization of Peoples, Oriental Churches; (congregations); Family (council).

Lehmann, Karl: b. May 16, 1936, Sigmaringen, Germany; ord., Oct. 10, 1963; earned doctorates in theology and philosophy; assistant to Fr. Karl Rahner at University of Münster; taught dogmatic theology at the Johannes Gutenberg University, Mainz; member of the Central Committee of German Catholics and the Jaeger-Stählin Ecumenical Circle; taught at the Albert Ludwig University, Freiburg im Breisgau; member of the International Theological Commission; edited the official publication of the documents of the Joint Synod of the Dioceses in the Federal Republic of Germany, Synod of Würzburg, 1971-75; app. bp. of Mainz, June 21, 1983; cons., Oct. 2, 1983; pres. of the German Bishops' Conference; cardinal, Feb. 21, 2001; titular church, St. Leo I. Bp. of Mainz.

Curial membership: Bishops, Oriental Churches (congregations); Christian Unity (council); APSA (office).

Levada, William J.: b. June 15, 1936, Long Beach, CA; studied at St. John's College, Camarillo, California, and the Gregorian Univ. in Rome; ord., Dec. 20, 1961; ord. titular bp. of Capri and aux. bp. of Los Angeles, May 12, 1983; app. abp. of Portland, OR, July 3, 1986; coadj. abp. of San Francisco, Aug. 17, 1995; abp. of San Francisco, Dec. 27, 1995; ret. and app. Prefect for the Congregation for the Doctrine of the Faith, May 13, 2005; cardinal, Mar. 24, 2006;

titular church, Diaconia di Santa Maria in Dominica. Prefect for the Congregation for the Doctrine of the Faith.

Curial Membership: Bishops, Causes of Saints (congregations); Christian Unity (council); Synod of Bishop (special council).

López Rodriguez, Nicolás de Jesús: b. Oct. 31, 1936, Barranca, Dominican Republic; ord. Mar. 18, 1961; sent to Rome for advanced studies at the Angelicum and Gregorian Univ.; served in various diocesan offices after returning to his home diocese of La Vega; ord. first bp. of San Francisco de Macoris, Feb. 25, 1978; abp. of Santo Domingo, Nov. 15, 1981; cardinal, June 28, 1991; titular church, St. Pius X (alla Balduina). Abp. of Santo Domingo and Military Ordinary for Dominican Republic.

Curial membership: Clergy, Institutes of Consecrated Life and Societies of Apostolic Life (congregations); Social Communications (council); Latin America (commission).

López Trujillo, Alfonso: b. Nov. 8, 1935, Villahermosa, Colombia; ord., Nov. 13, 1960, in Rome; returned to Colombia, 1963; taught at major seminary; was pastoral coordinator for 1968 International Eucharistic Congress in Bogota; vicar general of Bogota, 1970-72; ord. titular bp. of Boseta, Mar. 25, 1971; aux. bp. of Bogota, 1971-72; secretary-general of CELAM, 1972-78; helped organize 1979 Puebla Conference in which Pope John Paul II participated; app. coadj. abp. of Medellin, May 22, 1978; abp. of Medellin, June 2, 1979 (res. Jan 9, 1991); president of CELAM, 1979-83; cardinal, Feb. 2, 1983; titular church, St. Prisca; promoted to cardinal bishop, Nov. 17, 2001; suburbicarian see, Frascati. Abp. emeritus of Medellin. President of the Pontifical Council for the Family, 1990.

Curial membership: Bishops, Doctrine of the Faith, Causes of Saints, Evangelization of Peoples (congregations); Latin America (commission).

Lorscheider,* O.F.M., Aloísio: b. Oct. 8, 1924, Estrela, Brazil; received in Franciscan Order, Feb. 1, 1942; ord., Aug. 22, 1948; professor of theology at the Antonianum, Rome, and director of Franciscan international house of studies; ord. bp. of Santo Angelo, Brazil, May 20, 1962; abp. of Fortaleza, 1973-95; president of CELAM, 1975-79; cardinal, May 24, 1976; titular church, S. Pietro (in Montorio); abp. of Aparecida, 1995-2004; res. Jan. 28, 2004. Abp. emeritus of Aparecida.

Lourdusamy,* D. Simon: b. Feb. 5, 1924, Kalleri, India; ord., Dec. 21, 1951; ord. titular bp. of Sozusa and aux. of Bangalore, Aug. 22, 1962; titular abp. of Filippi and coadj. abp. of Bangalore, Nov. 9, 1964; abp. of Bangalore, 1968-71; associate secretary, 1971-73, and secretary, 1973-85, of Congregation for Evangelization of Peoples; cardinal deacon, May 25, 1985; deaconry, St. Mary of Grace; transferred to the order of cardinal priests, Jan. 29, 1996; prefect of Congregation for Oriental Churches, 1985-91.

Lozano Barragán, Javier: b. Jan. 26, 1933, Toluca, Mexico; ord., Oct. 30, 1955; pres. of the Mexican Theological Society and dir. of the Institute of Pastoral Theology of the Episcopal Conference of Latin America (CELAM); ord. titular bishop of Tinisia di Numidia and aux. bp. of Mexico, Aug. 15, 1979; bp. of Zacatecas, 1984-96; pres. of Pontifical Council for Health Care Workers, Oct. 31, 1996; named abp. 1997; cardinal deacon, Oct. 21, 2003, deaconry, St. Michael the Archangel. Pres. of Pontifical Council for Health Care Workers.

Curial membership: Bishops, Causes of Saints, Evangelization (congregations); Eucharistic Congresses,

Latin America (commissions).

Lustiger,* Jean-Marie: b. Sept. 17, 1926, Paris, France, of Polish-Jewish parents who emigrated to France after World War I; taken in by Catholic family in Orleans when his parents were deported during Nazi occupation (his mother died in 1943 at Auschwitz); convert to Catholicism, baptized Aug. 25, 1940; active in Young Christian Students during university days; ord., Apr. 17, 1954; ord. bp. of Orleans, Dec. 8, 1979; abp. of Paris, 1981-2005; cardinal, Feb. 2, 1983; titular church, St. Louis of France. Abp. emeritus of Paris.

Curial membership: Secretariat of State (second section); Bishops, Clergy, Consecrated Life and Societies of Apostolic Life, Oriental Churches, (congregations).

McCarrick, Theodore E.: b. July 7, 1930, New York, NY; ord., May 31, 1958; dean of students Catholic Univ. of America, 1961-63; pres., Catholic Univ. of Puerto Rico, 1965-69; secretary to Cardinal Cooke, 1970; ord. titular bp. of Rusubisir and aux. bp. of New York, June 29, 1977; app. first bp. of Metuchen, NJ, Nov. 19, 1981, inst., Jan. 31, 1982; app. abp. of Newark, June 3, 1986, inst., July 25, 1986; abp. of Washington, Nov. 21, 2000; ins., Jan. 3, 2001; cardinal priest, Feb. 21, 2001; titular church, Sts. Nereus and Achilleus; ret. May 16, 2006. Abp. emeritus of Washington.

Curial membership: Christian Unity, Justice and Peace, Migrants and Itinerant People (councils); APSA (office), Latin America (commission).

Macharski, Franciszek: b. May 20, 1927, Kraków, Poland; ord., Apr. 2, 1950; engaged in pastoral work, 1950-56; continued theological studies in Fribourg, Switzerland, 1956-60; taught pastoral theology at the Faculty of Theology in Kraków; app. rector of archdiocesan seminary at Kraków, 1970; abp. of Kraków, 1979-2005; cardinal, June 30, 1979; titular church, St. John at the Latin Gate. Abp. emeritus of Kraków.

Curial membership: Secretariat of State (second section); Bishops, Clergy, Consecrated Life and Societies of Apostolic Life, Education, Evangelization of Peoples (congregations).

Mahony, Roger M.: b. Feb. 27, 1936, Hollywood, CA; ord., (Fresno diocese) May 1, 1962; ord. titular bp. of Tamascani and aux. bp. of Fresno, Mar. 19,1975; bp. of Stockton, Feb. 15, 1980, inst., Apr. 25, 1980; abp. of Los Angeles, July 16, 1985, inst., Sept. 5, 1985; cardinal, June 28, 1991; titular church, Four Crowned Saints. Abp. of Los Angeles.

Curial membership: Social Communications (council); Economic Affairs (office).

Maida, Adam Joseph: b. Mar. 18, 1930, East Vandergrift, PA; ord., (Pittsburgh diocese) May 26, 1956; ord. bp. of Green Bay, Jan. 25, 1984; app. abp. of Detroit, Apr. 28, 1990, inst., June 12, 1990; cardinal, Nov. 26, 1994; titular church, Sts. Vitalis, Valeria, Gervase and Protase. Abp. of Detroit.

Curial membership: Clergy, Education (congregations); Legislative Texts, Migrants and Itinerant Peoples (council); Institute for Works of Religion (commission).

Majella Agnelo, Geraldo: b. Oct. 19, 1933, Juiz de Fora, Brazil; ord., June 29, 1957; taught at the seminary of Aparecida, Immaculate Conception Seminary, and Pius XI Theological Institute; rector of Our Lady of the Assumption Seminary; bp. of Toledo, May 5, 1978; cons., Aug. 6, 1978; app. abp. of Londrina, Oct. 27, 1982; pres. of the Brazilian Bishops' Liturgical Commission; app. sec. of the Cong. For Divine Worship and the Discipline of Sacraments, Sept. 16, 1991; app. abp. of São Salvador da Bahia, Jan. 13, 1999; cardinal, Feb. 21, 2001; titular church, St. Gregory the Great in Magliana Nuova. Abp. of São Salvador da Bahia.

Curial membership: Pastoral Care of Migrants and Itinerant People (council); Cultural Heritage of the Church (commission).

Marchisano, Francesco, b. June 25, 1929, Racconigi, Italy; ord., June 29, 1952; ord. titular bp. of Populonia, Jan. 6, 1989; sec. of the Pontifical Commission for the Preservation of the Artistic and Cultural Patrimony of the Church, 1988-91; pres. of the Pontifical Commission of Sacred Archeology, 1991; pres. of the Pontifical Commission for the Cultural Patrimony of the Church, 1993-2003; named abp. 1994; archpriest of the Patriarchal Vatican Basilica, vicar general for the State of Vatican City, and president of the Fabric of St. Peter, Apr. 24, 2002; pres. of the Permanent Commission for the Care of the Historical and Artistic Monuments of the Holy See, Mar. 8, 2003; cardinal deacon, Oct. 21, 2003; deaconry, St. Lucy of Gonfalone; pres. of the Labor Office of the Apostolic See, Feb. 5, 2005. Archpriest of the Patriarchal Vatican Basilica, vicar general for the State of Vatican City, and pres. of the Labor Office of the Apostolic See. Pres. emeritus of the Fabric of St. Peter.

Curial membership: Education (congregation); Culture (council); Cultural Heritage of the Church (commission).

Margéot,* Jean: b. Feb. 3, 1916, Quatre-Bornes, Mauritius; ord., Dec. 17, 1938; ord. bp. of Port Louis, 1969-93; cardinal, June 28, 1988; titular church, St. Gabriel the Archangel all'Acqua Traversa. Bp. emeritus of Port Louis.

Martinez Somalo, Eduardo: b. Mar. 31, 1927, Baños de Rio Tobia, Spain; ord., Mar. 19, 1950; ord. titular bp. of Tagora with personal title of abp., Dec. 13, 1975; in secretariat of state from 1956; substitute (assistant) secretary of state, 1979-88; cardinal deacon, June 28, 1988; deaconry, Most Holy Name of Jesus (raised pro hac vice to presbyteral title); promoted to cardinal priest, Jan. 9, 1999; prefect of Congregation for Divine Worship and Sacraments, 1988-92; prefect of Congregation for Institutes of Consecrated Life and Societies of Apostolic Life, 1992-2004; Chamberlain (Camerlengo) of the Holy Roman Church, Apr. 5, 1993; Protodeacon, 1996-99.

Curial membership: Secretariat of State (second section); Bishops, Causes of Saints, Clergy, Divine Worship and Sacraments, Education, Evangelization of Peoples (congregations); Legislative Texts (council); Latin America, Institute for Works of Religion (commissions).

Martini, S.J., Carlo Maria: b. Feb. 15, 1927, Turin, Italy; entered Jesuits, Sept. 25, 1944; ord., July 13, 1952; biblical scholar; seminary professor, Chieri, Italy, 1958-61; professor and later rector, 1969-78, of Pontifical Biblical Institute; rector of Pontifical Gregorian University, 1978-79; author of theological, biblical and spiritual works; abp. of Milan, 1980-2002; cardinal, Feb. 2, 1983; titular church, St. Cecilia. Abp. emeritus of Milan.

Curial membership: Consecrated Life and Societies of Apostolic Life, Education Oriental Churches (congregations); Cultural Heritage of the Church (commission).

Martino, Renato: b. Nov. 23, 1932, Salerno, Italy; ord., June 27, 1957; entered the diplomatic service of the Holy See, July 1, 1962; served in various diplomatic postings, 1962-80; ord. titular abp. of Segerme, Dec. 14, 1980; pronuncio in Thailand and apostolic delegate in Laos, Malaysia and Singapore, 1980-86; permanent observer of the Holy See to the U.N., 1986-2002; pres. of the Pontifical Council Justice and Peace, 2002-2006; cardinal deacon, Oct. 21, 2003, titular

church, St. Francis of Paola ai Monti; Pres. of the Pontifical for Council for Pastoral Care of Migrants and Itinerants, Mar. 11, 2006. Curial membership: Evangelization of Peoples (congregation); "Cor Unum" (council); Vatican City State (commission); Administration of the Patrimony of the Apostolic See (APSA).

Mayer,* O.S.B., Paul Aug.in: b. May 23, 1911, Altötting, Germany; ord., Aug. 25, 1935; rector of St. Anselm's Univ., Rome, 1949-66; secretary of Congregation for Religious and Secular Institutes, 1972-84; ord. titular bp. of Satriano with personal title of abp., Feb. 13, 1972; pro-prefect of Congregations for Sacraments and Divine Worship, 1984; cardinal deacon, May 25, 1985; deaconry, St. Anselm; transferred to order of cardinal priests, Jan. 29, 1996. Prefect of Congregation for Divine Worship and Sacraments, 1985-88; president of Pontifical Commission "Ecclesia Dei," 1988-91.

Medina Estévez, Jorge Arturo: b. Dec. 23, 1926, Santiago, Chile; ord., June 12, 1954; ord. abp., Jan. 6, 1985, Santiago, Chile; appointed pro-Prefect, Congregation for Divine Worship and the Discipline of the Sacraments, 1996-98; prefect of the Congregation for Divine Worship and the Discipline of the Sacraments, 1998-2002; cardinal deacon, Feb. 21, 1998; deaconry, St. Sabas; Protodeacon, 2005. Prefect emeritus of the Congregation for Divine Worship and the Discipline of the Sacraments.

Curial membership: Bishops, Clergy, Doctrine of the Faith (congregations); Family (council); Latin America, Ecclesia Dei (commission).

Meisner, Joachim: b. Dec. 25, 1933, Breslau, Silesia, Germany (present-day Wroclaw, Poland); ord., Dec. 22, 1962; regional director of Caritas; ord. titular bp. of Vina and aux. of apostolic administration of Erfurt-Meiningen, E. Germany, May 17, 1975; bp. of Berlin, 1980-88; cardinal, Feb. 2, 1983; titular church, St. Prudenziana. Abp. of Cologne, Dec. 20, 1988.

Curial membership: Bishops, Clergy, Divine Worship and Sacraments (congregations); Legislative Texts (council); Economic Affairs of Holy See (office).

Mejía,* Jorge María: b. Jan. 31, 1923, Buenos Aires, Argentina; ord., Sept. 22, 1945; prof. of Old Testament studies at Catholic University of Buenos Aires; peritus at Second Vatican Council; sec. of CELAM's Department of Ecumenism, 1967-77; sec. of Pontifical Commission for Religious Relations with Jews, 1977-86; vice-president of the Pontifical Commission Justice and Peace and titular bp. of Apollonia, Apr. 12, 1986; sec. of the Cong. for Bishops and titular abp., Mar. 1994; archivist and Librarian of the Holy Roman Church, 1998-2003; cardinal deacon, Feb. 21, 2001; deaconry, St. Jerome della Carità. Archivist and Librarian emeritus of the Holy Roman Church.

Monduzzi,* Dino: b. Apr. 2, 1922, Brisighella, Italy; ord., July 22, 1945; director of Catholic Action in Calabria and Sardinia; served in Agrarian Reform Agency in Fucino; sec. in the Office of the Maestro di Camera, 1959-67; sec. and regent of the Apostolic Palace, 1967-86; ord. titular bp. of Capri, Jan. 6, 1987; prefect of the Papal Household 1986-1998; cardinal deacon, Feb. 21, 1998; deaconry, St. Sebastian on the Palatine.

Moussa I Daoud, Ignace: b. Sept. 18, 1930, Meskaneh, Syria; ord., Oct. 17, 1954; elected July 2, 1977, bp. of Cairo, Egypt, by Syrian Patriarchal Synod; cons., Sept. 18, 1977; member of the commission for the revision of the Eastern Code of Canon Law and chaired the commission that translated the Code of Canons of the Eastern Churches into

Arabic; promoted abp. of Homs for Syrians, Syria, July 6, 1994; elected patriarch of Antioch for Syrians, Oct. 13, 1998; app. prefect of the Cong. for the Oriental Churches, Nov. 25, 2000; cardinal, Feb. 21, 2001 (as patriarch, he has no titular church). Prefect of the Congregation for the Oriental Churches.

Curial membership: Doctrine of the Faith, Causes of Saints (congregations), Christian Unity, Legislative Texts (councils).

Murphy-O'Connor, Cormac: b. Aug. 24, 1932, Reading, Great Britain; ord., Oct. 28, 1956; dir. of vocations and sec. to the bp.; rector of the Venerable English College, Rome, 1971-77; app. bp. of Arundel and Brighton, Nov. 17, 1977; cons., Dec. 21, 1977; co-chairman of the Anglican-Roman Catholic International Commission (ARCIC), 1982-2000; chairman of several committees of the Bishop's Conference of England and Wales; app. abp. of Westminster, Feb. 15, 2000; cardinal, Feb. 21, 2001; titular church, St. Mary sopra Minerva. Abp. of Westminster.

Curial membership: Sacraments (congregation); Christian Unity, Culture, Family (councils); APSA (office); Cultural Heritage (commission).

Nagy,* Stanislas: b. Sep. 30, 1921, Bieruń Stary, Poland; ord., July 8, 1945; Polish priest of the Sacred Heart of Jesus (Dehonians), Poland; taught with the future Pope John Paul II at Lublin University in Poland; served on Intl. Theological Commission; cons. titular abp. of Hólar, Oct. 13, 2003; cardinal deacon, Oct. 21, 2003; titular church, St. Mary of the Stairs.

Napier, O.F.M., Wilfrid Fox: b. Mar. 8, 1941, Swartberg, South Africa; ord. for the Franciscans, July 25, 1970; app. apostolic admin. of Kokstad, 1978; app. bp. of Kokstad, Nov. 29, 1980; cons., Feb. 28, 1981; deeply involved in the mediation and negotiations surrounding the ending of apartheid in South Africa and subsequent South African politics; pres. of the Southern African Catholic Bishops' Conference, 1987-94; app. abp. of Durban, May 29, 1992; apostolic admin. sede vacante et ad nutum Sanctae Sedis of Umzimkulu, 1994; cardinal, Feb. 21, 2001; titular church, St. Francis of Assisi in Acilia.

Curial membership: Evangelization of Peoples, Institutes of Consecrated Life and Societies of Apostolic Life (congregations).

Nicora, Attilio, b. Mar. 16, 1937, Varese, Italy; ord., June 27, 1964; ord. titular bishop of Fornos minore and aux. bp. of Milan, May 28, 1977; bp. of Verona, 1992-2002; pres. of the Administration of the Patrimony of the Apostolic See (APSA) and abp., Sept. 2002; cardinal deacon, Oct. 21, 2003; deaconry, St. Philip Neri in Eurosia. Pres. of the Administration of the Patrimony of the Apostolic See.

Curial membership: Secretariat of State (second section), Bishops, Evangelization of Peoples (congregation).

Noè,* Virgilio: b. Mar. 30, 1922, Zelata di Bereguardo, Italy; ord., Oct. 1, 1944; master of pontifical ceremonies and undersecretary of Congregation for Sacraments and Divine Worship, 1970-82; ord. titular bp. of Voncario with personal title of abp., Mar. 6, 1982; coadj. Archpriest of St. Peter's Basilica, 1989-2002; vicar general of Vatican City State, 1991-2002; cardinal deacon, June 28, 1991; deaconry, St. John Bosco (in Via Tuscolana). Archpriest emeritus of St. Peter's Basilica, Vicar General emeritus of Vatican City State and President emeritus of the Fabric of St. Peter, 1991.

Obando Bravo, S.D.B.,* Miguel: b. Feb. 2, 1926, La Libertad, Nicaragua; ord., Aug. 10, 1958; ord. titular bp. of Puzia di Bizacena and aux. of Matagalpa, Mar. 31, 1968; abp. emeritus of Managua, 1970-2005; car-

dinal, May 25, 1985; titular church, St. John the Evangelist (a Spinaceta).

Curial membership: Clergy, Consecrated Life and Societies of Apostolic Life, Divine Worship and Sacraments, (congregations).

O'Brien, Keith Michael Patrick: b. Mar. 17, 1938, Ballycastle, Ireland; ord., Apr. 3, 1965; ord. abp. of Saint Andrews and Edinburgh, May 30, 1985; cardinal, Oct. 21, 2003; titular church, Sts. Joachim and Anne at the Tuscolano. Abp. of Saint Andrews and Edinburgh.

Curial membership: Migrants and Itinerant People, Social Communications (councils).

Okogie, Anthony Olubunmi, b. June 16, 1935, Lagos, Nigeria; ord., Dec. 11, 1966; ord. titular bishop of Mascula, June 5, 1971; abp. of Lagos, Apr. 13, 1973; cardinal, Oct. 21, 2003; titular church, Blessed Virgin Mary of Mt. Carmel of Mostacciano. Abp. of Lagos.

Curial membership: Evangelization of Peoples (congregation); Social Communications (council).

O'Malley, Sean P., O.F.M. Cap.: b. June 29, 1944, Lakewood, OH; studied at St. Fidelis Seminary, Capuchin College, and Catholic University, Washington, DC; ord., Aug. 29, 1970; episcopal vicar of priests serving Spanish speaking in Washington archdiocese, 1974-84; executive director of Spanish Catholic Center, Washington, from 1973; ord. coadjutor bp. of St. Thomas, Virgin Islands, Aug. 2, 1984; bp. of St. Thomas, Oct. 16, 1985; app. bp. of Fall River, June 16, 1992; app. bp. of Palm Beach, Sept. 3, 2002; app. abp. of Boston, July 1, 2003; cardinal, Mar. 24, 2006; titular church, Santa Maria della Vittoria. Abp. of Boston.

Curial membership: Clergy; Consecrated Life (Congregation).

Ortega y Alamino, Jaime Lucas: b. Oct. 18, 1936, Jagüey Grande, Cuba; ord., Aug. 2, 1964; detained in work camps (UMAP), 1966-67; parish priest; ord. bp. of Pinar del Rio, Jan. 14, 1979; app. abp. of Havana, Nov. 20, 1981; cardinal, Nov. 26, 1994; titular church, Sts. Aquila and Priscilla. Abp. of Havana.

Curial membership: Clergy (congregation); Health Care Workers (council); Latin America (commission).

Ouellet, Marc P.S.S.: b. June 8, 1944, Lamotte, Canada; ord., May 25, 1968; entered the Society of Priests of Saint-Sulpice, 1972; rector and prof., Major Seminary of Montréal, 1989-1994, and Major Seminary of Edmonton, 1994-1997; prof., John Paul II Institute of Studies on Marriage and the Family, 1997-2001; ord. titular bishop of Agropoli, Mar. 19, 2001; sec. of the Pont. Council for the Promotion of Christian Unity, 2001-2002; abp. of Québec, Nov. 15, 2002; cardinal, Oct. 21, 2003; titular church, St. Mary in Traspontina. Abp. of Quebec.

Curial membership: Sacraments (congregation); Latin America, Eucharistic Congresses (commissions).

Panafieu, Bernard: b. Jan. 26, 1931, Châtellerault, France; ord., Apr. 22, 1956; ord. titular bishop of Tibili June 9, 1974, and aux. bp. of Annecy, 1974-78; abp. of Aix, 1978-94; coadj. abp. of Marseilles, Aug. 24, 1994; abp. of Marseilles, 1995-2006; metropolitan archbishop when Marseille was elevated to that rank, Dec. 16, 2002; cardinal, Oct. 21, 2003; titular church, St. Gregory Barbarigo alle Tre Fontane. Abp. emeritus of Marseilles.

Curial membership: Interreligious Dialogue, Justice and Peace (councils).

Pappalardo,* Salvatore: b. Sept. 23, 1918, Villafranca Sicula, Sicily; ord., Apr. 12, 1941; entered diplomatic service of secretariat of state, 1947; ord. titular abp. of Miletus, Jan. 16, 1966; pro-nuncio in Indonesia, 1966-69; president of

Pontifical Ecclesiastical Academy, 1969-70; abp. of Palermo, 1970-96; cardinal, Mar. 5, 1973; titular church, St. Mary Odigitria of the Sicilians. Abp. emeritus of Palermo.

Paskai, O.F.M., László: b. May 8, 1927, Szeged, Hungary; ord., Mar. 3, 1951; ord. titular bp. of Bavagaliana and apostolic administrator of Veszprem, Apr. 5, 1978; bp. of Veszprem, Mar. 31, 1979; coadj. abp. of Kalocsa, Apr. 5, 1982; abp. of Esztergom (renamed Esztergom-Budapest, 1993), 1987-2002; cardinal, June 28, 1988; titular church, St. Theresa (al Corso d'Italia). Abp. of Esztergom-Budapest.

Curial membership: Consecrated Life and Societies of Apostolic Life, Oriental Churches (congregations).

Pell, George: b. Apr. 8, 1941, Ballarat, Australia; ord., Dec. 16, 1966; episcopal vicar for Education, diocese of Ballarat, 1973-1984; rector of Corpus Christi College, the Provincial Seminary for Victoria and Tasmania, 1985-1987; ord. titular bishop of Scala, May 21, 1987; aux. bp. of Melbourne, 1987-96; abp. of Melbourne, 1996-2001; abp. of Sydney, Mar. 26, 2001; grand prior of the Equestrian Order of the Holy Sepulchre of Jerusalem, Australian Lieutenancy, Southern, 1998; cardinal, Oct. 21, 2003; titular church, St. Mary Dominic Mazzarello. Abp. of Sydney.

Curial membership: Family, Justice and Peace (councils).

Pengo, Polycarp: b. Aug. 5, 1944, Mwayze, Tanzania; ord., Aug. 5, 1971; taught moral theology at the major seminary in Kipalapala, Tanzania, 1977; rector of the major seminary in Segerea, 1978-83; ord. bp. of Nachingwea, Jan. 6, 1984; bp. of Tunduru-Masasi 1986-90; co-adjutor abp. of Dar-es-Salaam, Jan. 22, 1990; abp. of Dar-es-Salaam, July 22,1992, in succession to Laurean Cardinal Rugambwa; cardinal, Feb. 21, 1998; titular church, Our Lady of La Salette. Abp. of Dar-es-Salaam.

Curial membership: Doctrine of the Faith, Evangelization of Peoples (congregation); Culture, Interreligious Dialogue (council).

Pham Dinh Tung,* Paul Joseph: b. June 15, 1919, Binh-Hoa, Vietnam; ord., June 6, 1949; ord. bp. of Bac Ninh, Aug. 15, 1963; apostolic administrator of Hanoi, June 18, 1990; abp. of Hanoi, 1994-2005; cardinal, Nov. 26, 1994; titular church, St. Mary Queen of Peace in Ostia mare. Abp. emeritus of Hanoi.

Pham Minh Man, Jean Baptiste: b. 1934, Ca Mau, Vietnam; ord., May 25, 1965; ord. coadjutor bp. of My Tho, Aug. 11, 1993; abp. of Thàn-Phô Hô Chi Minh (Hô Chi Minh City), Mar. 1, 1998; cardinal, Oct. 21, 2003; titular church, St. Justin. Abp. of Thàn-Phô Hô Chi Minh.

Curial membership: Sacraments, Evangelization of Peoples (congregation).

Pimenta,* Simon Ignatius: b. Mar. 1, 1920, Marol, India; ord., Dec. 21, 1949; ord. titular bp. of Bocconia and aux. of Bombay, June 29, 1971; coadj. abp. of Bombay, Feb. 26, 1977; abp. of Bombay, 1978-96; cardinal, June 28, 1988; titular church, Mary, Queen of the World (a Torre Spaccata). Abp. emeritus of Bombay

Piovanelli,* Silvano: b. Feb. 21, 1924, Ronta di Mugello, Italy; ord., July 13, 1947; ord. titular bp. of Tubune di Mauretania and aux. of Florence, June 24, 1982; abp. of Florence, 1983-2001; cardinal, May 25, 1985; titular church, St. Mary of Graces (Via Trionfale).

Poggi,* Luigi: b. Nov. 25, 1917, Piacenza, Italy; ord., July 28, 1940; studied diplomacy at the Pontifical Ecclesiastical Academy, 1944-46; started work at Secretariat of State; ord. titular bp. of Forontoniana with personal title of abp., May 9, 1965; apostolic delegate for Central Africa, 1965; nuncio in

Peru; recalled to Rome, 1973; negotiated with various Eastern bloc governments to improve situation of the Church; named head of Holy See's delegation for permanent contact with government of Poland, 1974; nuncio in Italy, 1986-92; pro-librarian and pro-archivist of the Holy Roman Church, 1992; cardinal deacon, Nov. 26, 1994; protodeacon, 2002-2005; deaconry, St. Mary in Dominica. Archivist and librarian emeritus of the Holy Roman Church.

Poletto, Severino: b. Mar. 18, 1933, Salgareda (Treviso), Italy; ord., June 29, 1957; pref. of discipline at the diocesan seminary and vocation director; founded the Diocesan Centre for Family Ministry, 1973; coordinated the city mission for the 500th anniversary of the foundation of the diocese of Casale Monferrato; app. coadj. bp. of Fossano, Apr. 3, 1980; cons., May 17, 1980; succeeded to see on Oct. 29, 1980; app. bp. of Asti, Mar. 16, 1989; app. abp. of Turin, June 19, 1999; cardinal, Feb. 21, 2001; titular church, St. Joseph in Via Trionfale. Abp. of Turin.

Curial membership: Clergy (congregation); Economic Affairs of the Holy See (office); Cultural Heritage of the Church (commission).

Policarpo, José Da Cruz: b. Feb. 26, 1936, Alvorninha, Portugal; ord. priest, Aug. 15, 1961; dir. of the seminary in Penafirme, rector of the seminary in Olivais and dean of the Theological Faculty of the Portuguese Catholic University; served two terms as rector of the Portuguese Catholic University, 1988-96; app. titular bp. of Caliabria and aux. bp. of Lisbon, May 26, 1978; cons., June 29, 1978; app. coadj. abp. of Lisbon, Mar. 5, 1997; succeeded as patriarch of Lisbon, Mar. 24, 1998; grand chancellor of the Portuguese Catholic University, pres. of the Portuguese Episcopal Conference; cardinal, Feb. 21, 2001; titular church, St. Anthony in Campo Formio. Patriarch of Lisbon.

Curial membership: Education (congregation); Culture, Laity (councils).

Pompedda, Mario Francesco: b. Apr. 18, 1929, Ozieri (Sardinia), Italy; ord., Dec. 23, 1951, for Vatican clergy; app. to Tribunal of the Roman Rota, 1955, and held a variety of posts, including Defender of the Bond, prelate auditor, 1969, and dean, 1993; pres. of the Appellate Court of Vatican City State; app. titular abp. of Bisarcio, Nov. 29, 1997, and ord. by Holy Father, Jan. 6, 1998; prefect of the Supreme Tribunal of the Apostolic Signatura and pres. of the Court of Cassation of Vatican City State; res. May 27, 2004; cardinal deacon, Feb. 21, 2001; deaconry, Annunciation of the Blessed Virgin Mary in Via Ardeatina. Prefect emeritus of the Supreme Tribunal of the Apostolic Signatura

Curial membership: Doctrine of the Faith, Sacraments (congregation); Texts (council).

Poupard, Paul: b. Aug. 30, 1930, Bouzille, France; ord., Dec. 18, 1954; scholar; author of a number of works; ord. titular bp. of Usula and aux. of Paris, Apr. 6, 1979; title of abp. and pro-president of the Secretariat for Non-Believers, 1980; cardinal deacon, May 25, 1985; transferred to order of cardinal priests, Jan. 29, 1996; titular church, St. Praxedes; president of Pontifical Council for Dialogue with Non-Believers, 1985-93; president of Pontifical Council for Culture, 1988; president of the Pontifical Council for Interreligious Dialogue, 2006.

Curial membership: Divine Worship and Sacraments, Education, Evangelization of Peoples (congregations); Interreligious Dialogue, Laity (council).

Pujats, Janis: b. Nov. 14, 1930, the Rezekne district of Latvia; ord., Mar. 29, 1951; taught art history and liturgy at the Catholic Theological Seminary, Riga; vicar general in the Metropolitan Curia, Riga, 1979-84; declared persona non grata by the KGB, 1984; app. abp. of Riga, May 8, 1991, cons., June 1, 1991; pres. of the Latvian Bishops' Conference; cardinal (in pectore), Feb. 21, 1998, titular church, St. Sylvia. Abp. of Riga.

Curial membership: Causes of Saints (congregation).

Puljic, Vinko: b. Sept. 8, 1945, Prijecani, Bosnia-Herzegovina; ord., June 29, 1970; spiritual director of minor seminary of Zadar, 1978-87; parish priest; app. vice-rector of Sarajevo major seminary, 1990; ord. abp. of Vrhbosna (Sarajevo), Jan. 6, 1991, in Rome; cardinal, Nov. 26, 1994; titular church, St. Clare in Vigna Clara. Abp. of Vrhbosna.

Curial membership: Evangelization of Peoples (congregation); Interreligious Dialogue (council).

Quezada Toruño, Rodolfo: b. Mar. 8, 1932, Ciudad de Guatemala, Guatemala; ord., Sep. 21, 1956; ord. titular bishop of Gadiaufala, May 13, 1972; appointed coadjutor, with right of succession of Zacapa, Apr. 5, 1972; succeeded to the see of Zacapa, Feb. 16, 1980; abp. of Guatemala, June 19, 2001; cardinal, Oct. 21, 2003; titular church, St. Saturnius. Abp. of Guatemala.

Curial membership: Culture (council); Latin America (commission).

Razafindratandra,* Armand Gaétan: b. Aug. 7, 1925, Ambohimalaza, Madagascar; ord., July 27, 1954; ord. bp. of Mahajanga, July 2, 1978; app. abp. of Antananarivo, Feb. 3, 1994; inst., May 15, 1994; cardinal, Nov. 26, 1994; titular church, Sts. Sylvester and Martin ai Monti. Abp. of Antananarivo.

Curial membership: Evangelization of Peoples (congregation).

Re, Giovanni Battista: b. Jan. 30, 1934, Borno (Brescia), Italy; ord., Mar. 3, 1957; earned doctorate in canon law and taught in the Brescia Seminary; entered Holy See diplomatic service, served in Panama and Iran; recalled for service in Secretariat of State; sec. for Cong. for Bishops, 1987; titular abp., Nov. 7, 1987; sostituto for Secretariat of State, 1989; prefect of the Cong. of Bishops and pres. of the Pont. Comm. for Latin America, Sept. 16, 2000; cardinal, Feb. 21, 2001; titular church, Twelve Holy Apostles; transferred to order of cardinal bishops as titular bp. of suburbicarian see of Sabina-Poggio Mirteto. Prefect of the Cong. of Bishops.

Curial membership: Secretariat of State (second section); Doctrine of the Faith (congregation); Vatican City State (commission); APSA (office).

Ricard, Jean-Pierre: b. Sept. 26, 1944, Marseille, France; studied at Institut Catholique in Paris; ord. Oct. 5, 1968; app. titular bp. of Pulcheriopoli and aux. bp. of Grenoble, Apr. 17, 1993; app. coadjutor bp. of Montpellier, July 4, 1996; bp. of Montpellier, Sept. 6, 1996; promoted close relations with the Church in Africa and visited Peru in 1999 to meet a fidei donum priest of the diocese; visited Lebanon in 2000; major supporter of dialogue with the Jews; elected pres. of the Episcopal Conference of France, Nov. 6, 2001; app. abp. of Bordeaux, Dec 21, 2001; in 2003 authored the book, *Sept défis pour l'Eglise* (Seven Challenges for the Church); cardinal, Mar. 24, 2006; titular church, Sant'Agostino. Abp. of Bordeaux.

Curial membership: Doctrine of the Faith (congregation); Ecclesia dei (comisison).

Rigali, Justin Francis: b. Apr. 19, 1935, Los Angeles, CA; educ. St. John's Seminary (Camarillo, CA); ord. priest (Los Angeles*), Apr. 25, 1961; in Vatican diplomatic service from 1964; ord. titular abp. of Bolsena, Sept. 14, 1985, by Pope John Paul II; pres-

ident of the Pontifical Ecclesiastical Academy, 1985-89; secretary of Congregation for Bps., 1989-94, and the College of Cardinals, 1990-94; app. abp. of St. Louis, Jan. 25, 1994, inst., Mar. 16, 1994; app. abp. of Philadelphia, July 15, 2003; cardinal, Oct. 21, 2003; titular church, St. Prisca. Abp. of Philadelphia.

Curial membership: Sacraments (congregation); APSA (office).

Rivera Carrera, Norberto: b. June 6, 1942, La Purísima, Mexico; ord., July 3, 1966; taught dogmatic theology at the major seminary of Mexico City; professor of ecclesiology at Pontifical University of Mexico; bp. of Tehuacán, Nov. 5, 1985; abp. of Mexico City, June 13, 1995; cardinal, Feb. 21, 1998; titular church, St. Francis of Assisi at Ripa Grande. Abp. of Mexico City.

Curial membership: Clergy, Divine Worship and the Discipline of Sacraments (congregation); Family (council); Latin America (commission).

Rodé, Franc, C.M.: b. Sept. 23, 1934, Jarse, Ljubljana, Slovenia; the family left for Austria and then Argentina during World War II; entered the Cong. of the Missions (Vincentians), Mar. 6, 1952, and took his perpetual vows in 1957; studied at the Gregorian University in Rome and the Institut Catholique in Paris; ord., June 29, 1960; returned to Slovenia and after parish ministry, he taught at the Faculty of Theology in Ljubljana; his work in support of Catholic education caused him to be placed under surveillance by state authorities; app. undersecretary of of the Secretariat for Non-Believers and then secretary of the Pont. Council for Culture; app. abp. of Ljubljana, Mar. 5, 1997; app. prefect of the Cong. for the Institutes of Consecrated Life and Societies of Apostolic Life, Feb. 11, 2004; cardinal, Mar. 24, 2006; titular church, Diaconia di San Francesco Saverio alla Garbatella. Prefect of the Cong. for the Institutes of Consecrated Life and Societies of Apostolic Life.

Curial membership: Bishops; Doctrine of the Faith; Sacraments (congregations); Culture (council).

Rodríguez Maradiaga, S.D.B., Oscar Andrés: b. Dec. 29, 1942, Tegucigalpa, Honduras; ord. for the Salesians June 28, 1870; taught in various Salesian colleges in El Salvador, Honduras and Guatemala; prof. at the Salesian Theological Institute, Guatemala, and rector of the Salesian Philosophical Institute, Guatemala; app. titular bp. of Pudentiana and aux. bp. of Tegucigalpa, Oct. 28, 1978; app. abp. of Tegucigalpa, Jan. 8, 1993; pres. of CELAM, 1995-99; pres. of the Episcopal Conference of Honduras; cardinal priest, Feb. 21, 2001; titular church, St. Mary of Hope. Abp. of Tegucigalpa.

Curial membership: Clergy (congregation); Justice and Peace, Social Communication (councils); Latin America (commission).

Rosales, Gaudencio: b. Aug. 10, 1932, Batangas City; ord., Mar. 23, 1958; app. titular bp. of Esco and aux. bp. of Manila, Aug. 12, 1974; app. coadjutor bp. of Malaybalay, June 9, 1982; bp. of Malaybalay, Sept. 14, 1984; app. abp. of Lipa, Dec. 30, 1992; app. abp. of Manila, Sept. 15, 2003; cardinal, Mar. 24, 2006, titular church, Santissimo Nome di Maria a Via Latina. Abp. of Manila.

Curial membership: Interreligious Dialogue; Social Communications (council).

Rouco Varela, Antonio María: b. Aug. 24, 1936, Villalba, Spain; ord., Mar. 28, 1959; taught fundamental theology and canon law at the Mondoñedo seminary; adjunct professor at the Univ. of Munich; taught ecclesiastical law at Pontifical Univ. of Salamanca; vice-rector of Pontifical Univ. of Salamanca; titular bp. of Gergis and aux. bp. of Santiago de Compostela, Sept. 17, 1976; abp. of Santiago de Compostela,

May 9,1984; abp. of Madrid June 29, 1994; cardinal, Feb. 21, 1998, titular church, St. Laurence in Damaso. Abp. of Santiago de Compostela.

Curial membership: Bishops, Clergy, Education (congregations); "Cor Unum," Culture, Texts (councils); Supreme Tribunal of the Apostolic Signatura (tribunal).

Rubiano Sáenz, Pedro: b. Sept. 13, 1932, Cartago, Colombia; ord., July 8, 1956; chaplain to Marco Fidel Suárez Air Force Academy, St. Liberata National College, and Our Lady of Remedies Clinic; app. bp. of Cúcuta, June 2, 1971; cons., June 11, 1971; app. coadj. abp. of Cali, Mar. 26, 1983; abp. of Cali Feb. 7, 1985; apost. admin. of Popayán; pres. of the Episcopal Conference of Colombia; app., Dec. 27, 1994; cardinal priest, Feb. 21, 2001; titular church, Transfiguration of Our Lord Jesus Christ. Abp. of Cali.

Curial membership: Education (congregation); Pastoral Care of Migrants and Itinerant Peoples (council).

Ruini, Camillo: b. Feb. 19, 1931, Sassuolo, Italy; ord., Dec. 8, 1954; taught at seminaries in central Italy; ord. titular bp. of Nepte and aux. bp. of Reggio Emilia and Guastella, June 29, 1983; secretary general of Italian Bishops' Conference, 1986-91; abp. Jan. 17, 1991, and pro-vicar general of the Pope for the Rome diocese; pro-archpriest of Patriarchal Lateran Archbasilica; cardinal, June 28, 1991; titular church, St. Agnes Outside the Wall. Vicar General of the Pope for the Diocese of Rome and Archpriest of Patriarchal Lateran Basilica, July 1, 1991; Grand Chancellor of Pontifical Lateran University; president of the Peregrinatio ad Petri Sedem, 1992-96.

Curial membership: Bishops (congregation); Laity (council); APSA (office).

Saldarini,* Giovanni: b. Dec. 11, 1924, Cantu, Italy; ord., May 31, 1947; respected scripture scholar; taught scripture at Milan archdiocesan seminary, 1952-67; ord. titular bp. of Guadiaba and aux. bp. of Milan, Dec. 7, 1984; abp. of Turin Jan. 31, 1989 (res., June 19, 1999); cardinal, June 28, 1991; titular church, Sacred Heart of Jesus (a Castro Pretorio). Abp. emeritus of Turin.

Sales,* Eugênio de Araújo: b. Nov. 8, 1920, Acari, Brazil; ord., Nov. 21, 1943; ord. titular bp. of Tibica and aux. bp. of Natal, Aug. 15, 1954; abp. of São Salvador, 1968-71; cardinal, Apr. 28, 1969; titular church, St. Gregory VII; abp. of Rio de Janeiro (1971), ordinary for Eastern Rite Catholics in Brazil without ordinaries of their own rites. Abp. emeritus of Rio de Janeiro.

Sánchez,* José T.: b. Mar. 17, 1920, Pandan, Philippines; ord., May 12, 1946; ord. titular bp. of Lesvi and coadj. bp. of Lucena, May 12, 1968; bp. of Lucena, 1976-82; abp. of Nueva Segovia, Jan. 12, 1982 (res. Mar. 22, 1986); secretary of Congregation for Evangelization of Peoples, 1985-91; cardinal deacon, June 28, 1991; deaconry, St. Pius V (a Villa Carpegna); president of Commission for Preservation of Artistic and Historic Patrimony of the Holy See, 1991-93. Prefect of Congr. for the Clergy, 1991-96.

Sandoval Íñiguez, Juan: b. Mar. 28, 1933, Yahualica, Mexico; ord., Oct. 27, 1957; ord. coadj. bp. of Ciudad Juárez, Apr. 30, 1988; bp. of Ciudad Juarez, July 11, 1992; app. abp. of Guadalajara, Apr. 21, 1994; cardinal, Nov. 26, 1994; titular church, Our Lady of Guadalupe and St. Philip the Martyr on Via Aurelia. Abp. of Guadalajara.

Curial membership: Institutes of Consecrated Life and Societies of Apostolic Life, Catholic Education (congregations); Culture, Latin America (commission); Economic Affairs of the Holy See (office);

Works of Religion (commission).

Santos,* O.F.M., Alexandre José Maria dos: b. Mar. 18, 1924, Zavala, Mozambique; ord., July 25, 1953; first Mozambican black priest; ord. abp. of Maputo, Mar. 9, 1975; cardinal, June 28, 1988; titular church, St. Frumentius (ai Prati Fiscali). Abp. emeritus of Maputo.

Saraiva Martins, C.M.F., José: b. Jan. 6, 1932, Gagos do Jarmelo, Portugal; ord. for the Claretians, Mar. 16, 1957; taught at Claretian seminary in Marino, Italy; taught at Claretianum, Rome; taught at the Pontifical Urbanian University and served as rector, 1977-80, 1980-83, 1986-88; sec. of the Cong. for Catholic Education and titular abp. of Thuburnica, May 26, 1988; cons. abp., July 2, 1988; pref. of Cong. for the Causes of Saints, May 30, 1998; cardinal deacon, Feb. 21, 2001; deaconry of Our Lady of the Sacred Heart; pref. of Cong. for the Causes of Saints.

Curial membership: Bishops, Sacraments (congregations); Health Care (council).

Scheid, Eusebio Oscar, b. Dec. 8, 1932, Luzerna, Brazil; ord., July 3, 1960; joined the Congregation of Priests of the Sacred Heart of Jesus (S.C.J.); ord. bp. of São José dos Campos, May 1, 1981; app. abp. of Florianapolis, Jan. 23, 1991; app. abp. of São Sebastião do Rio de Janeiro, July 25, 2001; cardinal, Oct. 21, 2003; titular church, Sts. Boniface and Alexis. Abp. of São Sebastião do Rio de Janeiro.

Curial membership: Social Communications (council); Latin America (commission).

Schönborn, O.P., Christoph: b. Jan. 22, 1945, Skalsko, Bohemia (fled to Austria in Sept. 1945); entered Dominican Order in 1963; ord. 1970; student pastor in Graz University, 1973-75; associate professor of dogma in the University of Fribourg, 1976; professor for theology, 1978; professor for dogmatic theology, 1981-91; member of the Orthodox-Roman Catholic Dialogue Commission of Switzerland, 1980-87; member of the International Theological Commission, 1980-; member of the foundation, "Pro Oriente" since 1984; Secretary for the Draft-Commission of the Catechism of the Catholic Church, 1987-1992; ord. aux. bp. (Sutri) of Vienna, Sept. 29, 1991; co-adjutor of Vienna, Apr. 13, 1995; abp. of Vienna, Sept. 14, 1995; cardinal, Feb. 21, 1998; titular church, Jesus the Divine Worker. Abp. of Vienna.

Curial membership: Doctrine of the Faith, Education, Oriental Churches (congregations); Culture (council); Cultural Heritage of the Church (commission).

Schwery, Henri: b. June 14, 1932, Saint-Leonard, Switzerland; ord., July 7, 1957; director of minor seminary and later rector of the College in Sion; bp. of Sion, 1977-95; cardinal, June 28, 1991; titular church, Protomartyrs (a via Aurelia Antica). Bp. emeritus of Sion.

Curial membership: Causes of Saints (congregation).

Scola, Angelo: b. Nov. 7, 1941, Malgrate, Italy; ord., July 18, 1970; served as professor of theological anthropology at the Pontifical John Paul II Institute for Studies on Marriage and the Family at the Pontifical Lateran University, Rome; and later, professor of Contemporary Christology at the Faculty of Theology, Pontifical Lateran University, Rome; ord. bp. of Grosseto, Sept. 21, 1991; rector of the Pontifical Lateran University, 1995-2002; patriarch of Venice, Jan. 5, 2002; cardinal, Oct. 21, 2003; titular church, the Seven Most Holy Apostles. Patriarch of Venice.

Curial membership: Clergy (congregation); Family (council).

Sebastiani, Sergio: b. Apr. 11, 1931, Montemonaco (Ascoli Piceno), Italy; ord., 1956; studied at Lateran

University and Pontifical Ecclesiastical Academy; entered Holy See diplomatic service and posted to Peru, Brazil, and Chile; recalled to Secretariat of State; app. titular abp. of Caesarea in Mauretania and pro-nuncio in Madagascar and Mauritius and apostolic delegate to Reunion and Comorros; nuncio to Turkey, 1985; sec. to Central Committee for the Great Jubilee of the Year 2000, 1994; pres. Prefecture for the Economic Affairs of the Holy See, Nov. 3, 1997; cardinal, Feb. 21, 2001; titular church, Deaconry of St. Eustace. Pres. of the Prefecture for the Economic Affairs of the Holy See.

Curial membership: Bishops, Causes of Saints, Clergy (congregations); Christian Unity, Interreligious Dialogue (councils); Apostolic Signatura (tribunal).

Sepe, Crescenzio: b. June 2, 1943, Carinaro (Caserta), Italy; ord., Mar. 12, 1967; taught at Lateran and Urbanian Universities; studied at Pontifical Ecclesiastical Academy; entered Holy See diplomatic service and posted to Brazil; recalled to Secretariat of State, 1987; pres. of Commission for Vatican Telecommunications; app. titular abp. of Grado and sec. of the Cong. for the Clergy, Apr. 2, 1992; cons. Apr. 26, 1992; General Secretary of the Central Committee for the Great Jubilee of the Year 2000, 1997-2001; Pref. Cong. for the Evangelization of Peoples, 2001-2006; cardinal deacon, Feb. 21, 2001; deaconry, God the Merciful Father; app. abp. of Naples, May 20, 2006. Abp. of Naples.

Curial membership: Clergy, Doctrine of the Faith (congregation); Christian Unity, Interreligious Dialogue, Legislative Texts, Social Communication (councils); Latin America (commission).

Sfeir,* Nasrallah Pierre: b. May 15, 1920, Reyfoun, in Maronite diocese of Sarba, Lebanon; ord., May 7, 1950; secretary of Maronite patriarchate, 1956-61; taught Arabic literature and philosophy at Marist Fathers College, Jounieh, 1951-61; ord. titular bp. of Tarsus for the Maronites, July 16, 1961; elected Patriarch of Antioch for Maronites, Apr. 19, 1986; granted ecclesial communion by John Paul II May 7, 1986; cardinal, Nov. 26, 1994. Patriarch of Antioch for Maronites.

Curial membership: Oriental Churches (congregation); Health Care (council).

Shan Kuo-hsi,* S.J., Paul: b. Dec. 2, 1923, Puyang, China; ord., Mar. 18, 1955; director of the Chinese section of the Sacred Heart School in Cebu; socius of the novice master in Thu-duc, Vietnam; novice master and rector of Manresa House, Chanhua, Taiwan; rector of St. Ignatius High School, Taipei, Taiwan; bp. of Hualien, Nov. 15, 1979; bp. of Kaohsiung, Taiwan, 1991; cardinal, Feb. 21, 1998; titular church, St. Chrysogonus. Bp. of Kaohsiung.

Shirayanagi, Peter Seiichi: b. June 17, 1928, Hachioji City, Japan; ord., Dec. 21, 1954; ord. titular bp. of Atenia and aux. bp. of Tokyo, May 8, 1966; titular abp. of Castro and coadj. abp. of Tokyo, Nov. 15, 1969; abp. of Tokyo, 1970-2000; cardinal, Nov. 26, 1994; titular church, St. Emerentiana in Tor Fiorenza. Abp. of Tokyo.

Silvestrini,* Achille: b. Oct. 25, 1923, Brisighella, Italy; ord., July 13, 1946; official in Secretariat of State from 1953; ord. titular bp. of Novaliciana with personal title of abp., May 27, 1979; undersec., 1973-79, and sec., 1979-88, of the Council for Public Affairs of the Church (now the second section of the Secretariat of State); cardinal, June 28, 1988; deaconry, St. Benedict Outside St. Paul's Gate, promoted to cardinal priest, Jan. 9, 1999; prefect of Apostolic Signatura, 1988-91. Prefect of Congregation for Oriental Churches,

1991-2001; Grand Chancellor of Pontifical Oriental Institute.

Simonis, Adrianus J.: b. Nov. 26, 1931, Lisse, Netherlands; ord., June 15, 1957; ord. bp. of Rotterdam, Mar. 20, 1971; coadj. abp. of Utrecht, June 27, 1983; abp. of Utrecht, Dec. 3, 1983; cardinal, May 25, 1985; titular church, St. Clement. Abp. of Utrecht.

Curial membership: Consecrated Life and Societies of Apostolic Life, Education (congregations); Christian Unity (council).

Sodano, Angelo: b. Nov. 23, 1927, Isola d'Asti, Italy; ord., Sept. 23, 1950; entered diplomatic service of the Holy See in 1959; served in Ecuador and Uruguay; ord. titular abp. of Nova di Cesare, Jan. 15, 1978; nuncio to Chile, 1978-88; secretary of the Council for Relations with States, 1988-90; pro-Secretary of State, 1990-1991; cardinal, June 28, 1991; titular church, S. Maria Nuova; transferred to order of cardinal bishops, Jan 10, 1994, as titular bp. of suburbicarian see of Albano (while retaining title to S. Maria Nuova); Secretary of State, June 29, 1991-June 22, 2006; vice-dean of the Sacred College of Cardinals, 2002-05; dean of the College of Cardinals (Apr. 30, 2005). Secretary of State emeritus.

Curial membership: Bishops, Doctrine of the Faith, Oriental Churches (congregations); Vatican City State, Institute for Works of Religion (commission).

Spidlik,* Thomas, S.J.: b. Dec. 17, 1919, Boskovice, Czech Republic; Czech theologian and Jesuit; expert in Eastern spirituality; conducted the papal Lenten retreat in 1995; cardinal deacon, Oct. 21, 2003; titular church, St. Agatha of Goti.

Stafford, James Francis: b. July 26, 1932, Baltimore, MD; ord., (Baltimore*) Dec. 15, 1957; ord. titular bp. of Respetta and aux. bp. of Baltimore, Feb. 29, 1976; app. bp. of Memphis, Nov. 17, 1982; app. abp. of Denver, June 3, 1986, inst. July 30, 1986; app. President of Pontifical Council for the Laity, 1996-2003; app. Major Penitentiary of the Apostolic Penitentiary, Oct. 4, 2003; cardinal deacon, Feb. 21, 1998; deaconry, Jesus, the Good Shepherd at Montagnola. Major Penitentiary of the Apostolic Penitentiary.

Curial membership: Bishops, Doctrine of the Faith, Causes of Saints, Evangelization of Peoples (congregations); Texts (council).

Stéphanos II Ghattas, C.M.*: b. Jan. 16, 1920, Sheikh Zein-el-Dine, Egypt; ord., Mar. 25, 1944; taught philosophy and dogmatic theology at the major seminary in Tahta; joined Congregation of the Mission, 1952; worked in Lebanon and served as Vincentian econome and superior in Alexandria; elected by the Coptic Catholic Synod bp. of Thebes-Luxor, May 8, 1967; named apostolic admin. of the patriarchate to substitute for the ailing Patriarch Stéphanos I Sidarous; elected unanimously by the Coptic Catholic Synod patriarch of Alexandria for Copts; changed name from Andraos Ghattas to Stéphanos II in honor of his predecessor; cardinal, Feb. 21, 2001; as a patriarch, he did not receive a titular church. Patriarch of Alexandria for Copts.

Curial membership: Oriental Churches (congregation).

Sterzinsky, Georg Maximilian: b. Feb. 9, 1936, Warlack, Germany; ord., June 29, 1960; vicar general to the apostolic administrator of Erfurt-Meiningen, 1981-89; ord. bp. of Berlin, Sept. 9, 1989; cardinal, June 28, 1991; titular church, St. Joseph (all'Aurelio). Abp. of Berlin.

Curial membership: Catholic Education (congregation); Migrants and Itinerant People (council).

Stickler,* S.D.B., Alfons: b. Aug. 23, 1910,

Neunkirchen, Austria; ord., Mar. 27, 1937; director of the Vatican Library, 1971; ord. titular bp. of Bolsena, Nov. 1, 1983, with personal title of abp.; Pro-Librarian and Pro-Archivist, 1984; cardinal, May 25, 1985; deacon, St. George (in Velabo); transferred to order of cardinal priests, Jan. 29, 1996. Librarian and Archivist of the Holy Roman Church, 1985-88.

Suárez Rivera, Adolfo Antonio: b. Jan. 9, 1927, San Cristobal, Mexico; ord., Mar. 8, 1952; ord. bp. of Tepic, Aug. 15, 1971; bp. of Tlalnepantla, May 8, 1980; app. abp. of Monterrey, Nov. 8, 1983, res., Jan. 25, 2002; cardinal, Nov. 26, 1994; titular church, Our Lady of Guadalupe on Monte Mario. Abp. of Monterrey.

Curial membership: Clergy (congregation).

Swiatek,* Kazimierz: b. Oct. 21, 1914, Walga, in apostolic administration of Estonia; ord., (of Pinsk, Belarus, clergy) Apr. 8, 1939; arrested by KGB Apr. 21, 1941, and imprisoned on death row until June 22, when he escaped during confusion of German invasion and returned to his parish; arrested again by KGB and imprisoned in Minsk until 1945; sentenced to 10 years of hard labor in concentration camps; released June 16, 1954; resumed pastoral work in cathedral parish in Pinsk; ord. abp. of Minsk-Mohilev, Belarus, May 21, 1991, and also appointed apostolic administrator of Pinsk; ret. June 14, 2006; cardinal, Nov. 26, 1994; titular church, St. Gerard Majella. Abp. of Minsk-Mohilev.

Szoka, Edmund C.: b. Sept. 14, 1927, Grand Rapids, MI; ord., (Marquette diocese), June 5, 1954; ord. first bp. of Gaylord, MI, July 20, 1971; abp. of Detroit, 1981-90; cardinal, June 28, 1988; titular church, Sts. Andrew and Gregory (al Monte Celio). President of Prefecture for Economic Affairs of the Holy See, 1990-97. Pres. Pont. Comm. for Vatican City State, 1997-2006. Pres. emeritus of the Pont. Comm. for Vatican City State.

Curial membership: Secretariat of State (second section); Bishops, Causes of Saints, Clergy, Evangelization of Peoples, Consecrated Life and Societies of Apostolic Life (congregations).

Tauran, Jean-Louis: b. Apr. 3, 1943, Bordeaux, France; ord., Sep. 20, 1969; entered the diplomatic service of the Holy See in 1975; app. titular archbishop of Telepte and appointed secretary of the Secretariat of State for the Relations with the States, 1990-2003; Archivist and Librarian of the Holy Roman Church, 2003; cardinal deacon, Oct. 21, 2003; titular church, St. Apollinaris alle Terme Neroniane-Alessandrine. Archivist and Librarian of the Holy Roman Church.

Curial membership: Secretariat of State (second section), Bishops, Doctrine of the Faith, Oriental Churches (Congregations); Supreme Tribunal of the Apostolic Signatura (tribunal); Vatican City State (commission); APSA (office).

Terrazas Sandoval, C.SS.R., Julio: b. Mar. 7, 1936, Vallegrande, Bolivia; ord., for the Redemptorists July 29, 1962; superior of the Redemptorist community in Vallegrande and vicar forane; app. aux. bp. of La Paz and cons., Apr. 15, 1978; transferred to the see of Oruro, Jan. 9, 1982; pres. of the Bolivian Episcopal Conference in 1985 and 1988; app. abp. of Santa Cruz, Feb. 6, 1991; cardinal, Feb. 21, 2001; titular church, St. John Baptist Rossi. Abp. of Santa Cruz.

Curial membership: Laity (council); Latin America (commission).

Tettamanzi, Dionigi: b. Mar. 14, 1934, Renate, Italy; ord., June 28, 1957; taught fundamental theology at the major seminary of Lower Venegono, pastoral theology at the

Priestly Institute of Mary Immaculate and the Lombard Regional Institute of Pastoral Ministry, Milan; rector of the Pontifical Lombard Seminary, Rome; abp. of Ancona-Osimo, July 1,1989 (res., 1991); general secretary of the Italian Episcopal Conference, 1991-95; Vice-President of the Italian Episcopal Conference, May 25, 1995; abp. of Genoa Apr. 20, 1995; cardinal, Feb. 21, 1998; titular church, Sts. Ambrose and Charles; app. abp. of Milan, July 11, 2002. Abp. of Milan.

Curial membership: Clergy, Doctrine of the Faith, Education, Oriental Churches (congregations); Culture (council); Economic Affairs of the Holy See (office).

Tomko,* Jozef: b. Mar. 11, 1924, Udavske, Slovakia; ord., Mar. 12, 1949; ord. titular abp. of Doclea, Sept. 15, 1979; secretary-general of the Synod of Bishops, 1979-85; cardinal deacon, May 25, 1985; transferred to order of cardinal priests, Jan. 29, 1996; titular church, St. Sabina. Prefect of the Congregation for the Evangelization of Peoples, 1985-2001; Grand Chancellor of Pontifical Urban University. President of Pontifical Committee for International Eucharistic Congresses, 2001.

Curial membership: Works of Religion (commission).

Tonini,* Ersilio: b. July 20, 1914, Centovera di San Giorgio Piacentino, Italy; ord., Apr. 18, 1937; vice-rector and later rector of the Piacenza seminary; taught Italian, Latin and Greek; editor of diocesan weekly; ord. bp. of Macerata-Tolentino, June 2, 1969; abp. of Ravenna-Cervia, Nov. 22, 1975-90; cardinal, Nov. 26, 1994; titular church, Most Holy Redeemer in Val Melaina. Abp. of Ravenna-Cervia.

Toppo, Telesphore Placidus: b. Oct. 15, 1939, Chainpur, India, to a tribal family that had converted to Christianity; ord., May 3, 1969; ord. bp. of Dumka, June 8, 1979; abp. of Ranchi, Aug. 7, 1985; supported programs to assist tribes in Jharkhand; cardinal, Oct. 21, 2003; titular church, Sacred Heart of Jesus in Agony at Vitinia. Abp. of Ranchi.

Curial membership: Evangelization of Peoples (congregation); Interreligious Dialogue (council).

Tucci,* S.J., Roberto: b. Apr. 19, 1921, Naples, Italy; ord. for the Jesuits, Aug. 24, 1950; editor of La Civiltà Cattolica; member of the Preparatory Commission on the Apostolate of the Laity for Vatican II and peritus involved in drafting Ad Gentes and Gaudium et Spes; consultor to the Pontifical Council for Social Communications, 1965-89; member of the editorial committee for the Pastoral Instruction Communio et Progressio; vice-pres. of the Italian Catholic Union of the Press, 1961-82; general sec. of the Italian Province of the Jesuits, 1967-69; app. general manager of Vatican Radio, 1973; since 1982, he has been responsible for all papal visits outside Italy; app. chairman of the Administrative Committee of Vatican Radio, 1986; cardinal, Feb. 21, 2001; titular church, Deaconry of St. Ignatius Loyola in Campo Marzio. Chairman of the Administrative Committee of Vatican Radio.

Tumi, Christian Wiyghan: b. Oct. 15, 1930, Kikaikelaki, Cameroon; ord., Apr. 17, 1966; ord. bp. of Yagoua, Jan. 6, 1980; coadj. abp. of Garoua, Nov. 19, 1982; abp. of Garoua, 1984-91; abp. of Douala, Aug. 31, 1991; cardinal, June 28, 1988; titular church, Martyrs of Uganda (a Poggio Ameno). Abp. of Douala.

Curial membership: Divine Worship and Sacraments, Education, Evangelization of Peoples (congregations); Cor Unum (councils).

Turcotte, Jean-Claude: b. June 26, 1936, Montreal, Canada; ord., May 24, 1959; ord. titular bp. of Suas and aux. of Montreal, June 29, 1982; abp. of Montreal, Mar. 17, 1990; cardinal, Nov. 26, 1994; titular church, Our Lady of the Blessed Sacrament and the Holy Canadian Martyrs. Abp. of Montreal.

Curial membership: Causes of Saints (congregation); Social Communications (council).

Turkson, Peter Kodwo Appiah: b. Oct. 11, 1948, Wassaw Nsuta, Ghana; ord., July 20, 1975; abp. of Cape Coast, Jan. 6, 1992; pres. of the Catholic Bishops' Conference and Chancellor of the Catholic University College of Ghana; cardinal priest, Oct. 21, 2003; titular church, St. Liborius. Abp. of Cape Coast.

Curial membership: Christian Unity (council); Cultural Heritage of the Church (commission).

, Urosa Savino, Jorge Liberato: b. Aug. 28, 1942, Caracas, Venezuela; ord., Aug. 15, 1967; earned a doctorate in theology form the Gregorian University in 1971; served as rector of several Venezuelan seminaries, 1974-82 and professor of philosophical anthropology and dogmatic theology; pres. of the organization of Venezuelan Seminries, 1974-77 and vice-pres. of the Organization of Latin American Seminaries, 1976-82; app. titular bishop of Vegesela in Byzacena and aux. bp. of Caracas, July 13, 1982; app. abp. of Valencia in Venezuela, Mar. 17, 1990; app. abp. of Caracas, Sept. 19, 2005; cardinal, Mar. 24, 2006, titular church, Santa Maria ai Monti. Abp. of Caracas.

Curial membership: Justice and Peace (commission); Latin America (commission).

Vachon,* Louis-Albert: b. Feb. 4, 1912, Saint-Frederic-de-Beauce, Que., Canada; ord., June 11, 1938; ord. titular bp. of Mesarfelta and aux. of Quebec, May 14, 1977; abp. of Quebec, 1981-90; cardinal, May 25, 1985; titular church, St. Paul of the Cross (a Corviale). Abp. of Quebec.

Vallini, Agostino: b. Apr. 17, 1940, Poli, Italy; ord., July 19, 1964; after seminary studies, he progressed to the study of canon law at the Pontifical Lateran University, and earned a doctorate in utroque iure; taught in Naples, 1969-71; called back to Rome in 1971 to teach public ecclesiastical law at the lateran, with the task of reorganizing the field in keeping with the Second Vatican Council; rector of the Major Seminary of Naples, 1978; app. titular bp. of Tortibulum and aux. bp. of Naples, Mar. 23, 1989; app. suburbicarian bp. of Albano, Nov. 13, 1999; app. prefect of the Supreme Tribunal of the Apostolic Signatura, May 27, 2004 and elevated to the dignity of archbishop; pres. of the Court of Causation of the Vatican City State; cardinal, Mar. 24, 2006; titular church, Diaconia di San Pier Damiani ai Monti di San Paolo. Prefect of the Supreme Tribunal of the Apostolic Signatura.

Curial membership: Consecrated Life (Congergation); Texts (council); APSA.

Vanhoye,* Albert, S.J.: b. July 24, 1923, Hazebrouck, France; entered the Jesuits, Sept. 11, 1941 and ord., July 24, 1954; earned licentiates in letters, philosophy, and theology, and a doctorate in sacred scripture from the Pontifical Biblical Institute in 1961; professor at the Pontifical Biblical Institute, the Biblicum, in Rome since 1963; dean of the biblical faculty, 1969-75 and rector, 1984-90; taught at the Gregorian University and the Lateran University in Rome; assisted in the preparation of the apostolic constitution, Sapientia Christiana; served as member of the Pontifical Biblical Commission, 1984-2001 and sec. of the commission, 1990-2001; consultor to the Congs. of Catholic Education from 1978 and Doctrine of the Faith from 1990; cardinal, Mar. 24, 2006; titular church, diaconia di Santa Maria della Mercede e Sant'Adriano a Villa Albani.

Vidal, Ricardo J.: b. Feb. 6, 1931, Mogpoc, Philippines; ord., Mar. 17, 1956; ord. titular bp. of Clatterna and coadj. of Melalos, Nov. 30, 1971; abp. of Lipa, 1973-81; coadj. abp. of Cebu, Apr. 13, 1981; abp. of Cebu, Aug. 24, 1982; cardinal, May 25, 1985; titular church, Sts. Peter and Paul (in Via Ostiensi). Abp. of Cebu.

Curial membership: Education, Evangelization of Peoples (congregations); Family, Health Care Workers (councils).

Vithayathil, C.SS.R., Varkey: b. May 29, 1927, North Paravur, India; ord. for the Redemptorists June 12, 1954; taught canon law for 25 years at the Redemptorist major seminary in Bangalore; served as provincial for Redemptorists in India and Sri Lanka, 1978-84; pres. of the Conference of Religious, India, 1984-85; apostolic administrator of the Asirvanum Benedictine Monastery, Bangalore, 1990-96; app. titular abp. of Ohrid and apostolic administrator of the vacant see of Ernakulam-Angamaly for Syro-Malabars; cons. by the pope, Jan. 6, 1997; app. major abp. of Ernakulam-Angamaly for Syro-Malabars, Dec. 18, 1999; cardinal, Feb. 21, 2001; titular church, St. Bernard at the Baths. Major abp. of Ernakulam-Angamaly for Syro-Malabars.

Curial membership: Oriental Churches (congregation); Christian Unity, Texts (council).

Vlk, Miloslav: b. May 17, 1932, Lisnice, Czech Republic; during communist persecution when theological studies were impossible he studied archival science at Charles University and worked in various archives in Bohemia; ord., June 23, 1968, during "Prague Spring"; sent to isolated parishes in Bohemian Forest by State authorities in 1971; state authorization to exercise his priestly ministry was cancelled in 1978; from then until 1986 he worked as a window-washer in Prague, carrying out his priestly ministry secretly among small groups. In 1989, he was permitted to exercise his priestly ministry for a "trial" year; the situation changed with the "velvet revolution"; ord. bp. of Ceske Budejovice, Mar. 31, 1990; abp. of Prague, Mar. 27, 1991; cardinal, Nov. 26, 1994; titular church, Holy Cross in Jerusalem. Abp. of Prague, President of the Council of European Episcopal Conferences, 1993-. Abp. of Prague.

Curial membership: Oriental Churches (congregation); Social Communications (council).

Wamala, Emmanuel: b. Dec. 15, 1926, Kamaggwa, Uganda; ord., Dec. 21, 1957; ord. bp. of Kiyinda-Mityana, Nov. 22, 1981; coadj. abp. of Kampala, June 21, 1988; abp. of Kampala, Feb. 8, 1990; cardinal, Nov. 26, 1994; titular church, St. Hugh. Abp. of Kampala.

Curial membership: Evangelization of Peoples (congregation); Cor Unum (council).

Wetter, Friedrich: b. Feb. 20, 1928, Landau, Germany; ord., Oct. 10, 1953; ord. bp. of Speyer, June 29, 1968; abp. of Munich and Freising, Oct. 28, 1982; cardinal, May 25, 1985; titular church, St. Stephen (al Monte Celio). Abp. of Munich and Freising.

Curial membership: Education, Evangelization of Peoples (congregations).

Williams, Thomas Stafford: b. Mar. 20, 1930, Wellington, New Zealand; ord., Dec. 20, 1959, in Rome; studied in Ireland after ordination, receiving degree in social sciences; served in various pastoral assignments on his return to New Zealand; missionary in Western Samoa to 1976; abp. of Wellington, New Zealand, 1979-2005; cardinal, Feb. 2, 1983; titular church, Jesus the Divine Teacher (at Pineda Sacchetti).

Abp. of Wellington.

Curial membership: Evangelization of Peoples (congregation).

Zen Ze-Kium, Joseph, S.D.B.: b. Jan. 13, 1932, Yang King-pang, Shanghai, China; his parents were converts and survived great hardships during World War II; made his profession in the Salesians on Aug. 16, 1949 and perpetual vows on Aug. 16, 1955; ord. in Turin, Italy on Feb. 11, 1961; taught in several Chinese seminaries from 1989 to 1996; app, coadjutor bp. of Hong Kong, Sept. 13, 1996; bp, of Hong Kong, Sept. 23, 2002; spoke at the 11th Ordinary General Assembly of the Synod of Bishops in Oct. 2005, he spoke of the Church in China; cardinal Marhc 24, 2006; titular church, Santa Maria Madre del Redentore a Tor Bella Monaca. Bp. of Hong Kong.

Curial membership: Evangelization; Sacraments (congregation); Synod of Bishops.

Zubeir Wako, Gabriel: b. Feb. 27, 1941, Mboro, diocese of Wau, Sudan; ord., July 21, 1963; ord. bp. of Wau, Apr. 6, 1975; coadj. abp. of Khartoum, Oct. 30, 1979; abp. of Khartoum, Oct. 10, 1981; cardinal, Oct. 21, 2003; titular church, St. Anthanasius in Via Tiburtina. Abp. of Khartoum.

Curial membership: Evangelization of Peoples (congregation); "Cor Unum" (council).

CATEGORIES OF CARDINALS

(As of Aug. 20, 2006.) Information below includes categories of cardinals listed according to seniority or order of precedence. Seniority or precedence usually depends on order of elevation. It is customary for cardinal deacons to be promoted eventually to the rank of cardinal priest.

Order of Bishops

Titular Bishops of Suburbicarian Sees: Angelo Sodano, dean (June 28, 1991, Albano and Ostia); Roger Etchegaray (June 24, 1998, Porto-Santa Rufina; vice-dean); Bernardin Gantin, (June 27, 1977, Palestrina); Giovanni Battista Re (Oct. 1, 2002, Sabina-Poggio Mirteto); Alfonso López Trujillo (Nov. 17, 2001, Frascati); Francis Arinze (April 25, 2005, Velletri-Segni). Eastern Rite Patriarchs: Nasrallah Pierre Sfeir (Nov. 26, 1994); Ignace Moussa I Daoud (Feb. 21, 2001); Stephanos II Ghattas, (Feb. 21, 2001).

Order of Priests

Stephen Sou-hwan Kim, Eugênio de Araújo Sales, Luis Aponte Martinez, Salvatore Pappalardo, Paulo Evaristo Arns, O.F.M., William W. Baum, Aloisio Lorscheider, Marco Cé, Ernesto Corripio Ahumada, Franciszek Macharski, Michael Michai Kitbunchu, Alexandre do Nascimento, Godfried Danneels, Thomas Stafford Williams, Carlo Maria Martini, Jean-Marie Lustiger, Józef Glemp, Joachim Meisner, Simon D. Lourdusamy, Antonio Innocenti, Miguel Obando Bravo, S.D.B., Paul Augustine Mayer, Ricardo Vidal, Henryk Roman Gulbinowicz, Jozef Tomko, Andrzej Maria Deskur, Paul Poupard, Louis-Albert Vachon, Rosalio José Castillo Lara, S.D.B., Friedrich Wetter, Silvano Piovanelli, Adrianus J. Simonis, Edouard Gagnon, P.S.S., Alfons Stickler, S.D.B., Bernard F. Law, Giacomo Biffi, Eduardo Martinez Somalo, Achille Silvestrini, Angelo Felici, José Freire Falcão, Michele Giordano, Alexandre José Maria dos Santos, O.F.M., Giovanni Canestri, Antonio Maria Javierre Ortas, S.D.B., Simon Ignatius Pimenta, Edward Bede Clancy, Edmund C. Szoka, László Paskai, O.F.M., Christian Wiyghan Tumi, Jean Margéot, Pio Laghi, Edward I. Cassidy, Frédéric Etsou-Nzabi-Bamungwabi, C.I.C.M., Nicolás de Jesús López Rodriguez, José T. Sánchez, Virgilio Noè, Fiorenzo Angelini, Roger Mahony, Anthony J. Bevilacqua, Giovanni Saldarini, Cahal Brendan Daly, Camillo Ruini, Ján Chryzostom Korec, S.J., Henri Schwery, Georg Sterzinsky, Miloslav Vlk, Peter Shirayanagi, Adolfo Antonio Suárez Rivera, Julius Riyadi Darmaatmadja, S.J., Jaime Lucas Ortega y Alamino, Emmanuel Wamala, William Henry Keeler, Jean-Claude Turcotte, Ricardo Maria Carles Gordó, Adam Joseph Maida, Vinko Puljic, Armand Gaétan Razafindratandra, Paul Joseph Pham Dính Tung, Juan Sandoval Íñiguez, Kazimierz Swiàtek, Ersilio Tonino, Salvatore de Giorgi, Serafim Fernandes de Araújo, Antonio Maria Rouco Varela, Aloysius Ambrozic, Dionigi Tettamanzi, Polycarp Pengo, Christoph Schönborn, O.P., Norberto Rivera Carrera, Francis George, O.M.I., Paul Shan Kuo-his, S.J., Adam Kozlowiecki, S.J., Marian Jaworski, Janis Pujats, Antonio Jose Gonzalez Zumarraga, Ivan Dias, Geraldo Majella Agnelo, Pedro Rubiano Sáenz, Theodore E. McCarrick, Desmond Connell, Audrys Juozas Backis, Francisco Javier Errázuriz Ossa, Juan Julio Terrazas Sandoval, C.SS.R., Wilfrid Fox Napier, O.F.M., Oscar Andres Rodríguez Maradiaga, S.D.B., Bernard Agré, Luis Cipriani Thorne, Francisco Álvarez Martínez, Cláudio Hummes, O.F.M., Varkey Vithayathil, C.SS.R., Jorge Mario Bergoglio, S.J., José Da Cruz Policarpo, Severino Poletto, Cormac Murphy-O'Connor, Edward Michael Egan, Lubomyr Husar, Karl Lehmann, Jean Honoré, Angelo Scola, Anthony Olubunmi Okogie, Bernard Panafieu, Gabriel Zubeir Wako, Carlos Amigo Vallejo, Justin Francis Rigali, Keith Michael O'Brien, Eusebio Oscar Scheid, Ennio Antonelli, Tarcisio Bertone, Peter Kodwo Appiah Turkson, Telesphore Placidus Toppo, George Pell, Josip Bozanic, Jean Baptiste Pham Minh Man, Rodolfo Quezada Toruño, Philippe Barbarin, Peter Erdö, Marc Ouellet, P.S.S., Urosa Savino, Rosales, Ricard, Cañizares Llovera, Cheong-Jin-Suk, O'Malley, Dziwisz, Caffara, Zen Ze-Kiun.

Order of Deacons

Luigi Poggi, Carlo Furno, Gilberto Agustoni, Jorge Medina Estévez, Darío Castrillón Hoyos, Lorenzo Antonetti, James Francis Stafford, Giovanni Cheli, Francesco Dino Monduzzi, Agostino Cacciavillan, Sergio Sebastiani, Zenon Grocholewski, José Saraiva Martins, C.M.F., Crescenzio Sepe, Jorge María Mejía, Mario Francesco Pompedda, Walter Kasper, Roberto Tucci, S.J., Avery Dulles, S.J., Jean-Louis Tauran, Renato Martino, Francesco Marchisano, Julián Herranz, Javier Lozano Barragán, Stephen Fumio Hamao, Attilio Nicora, Georges Cottier, O.P., Thomas Spidlik, S.J., Stanislas Nagy, Levada, Rodé, Vallini, Montezemolo, Dery, Vanhoye.

CONSISTORIES

(As of Aug. 15, 2006.) Information below includes dates of consistories at which the current cardinals were created.

They are listed according to seniority. Of these 190 cardinals, 8 were named by Paul VI (consistories of Apr. 28, 1969; Mar. 5, 1973; May 24, 1976; and June 27, 1977); 167 by John Paul II (consistories of June 30, 1979; Feb. 2, 1983; May 25, 1985; June 28, 1988; June 28, 1991; Nov. 26, 1994; Feb. 21, 1998; Feb. 21, 2001; and Oct. 21, 2003); and 15 by Pope

Benedict XVI (Mar. 24, 2006).
Pope Paul VI
1969 (Apr. 28): Stephen Sou-hwan Kim, Eugênio de Araújo Sales.
1973 (Mar. 5): Luis Aponte Martinez, Salvatore Pappalardo, Paulo Evaristo Arns, O.F.M.
1976 (May 24): William W. Baum, Aloisio Lorscheider.
1977 (June 27): Bernardin Gantin,
Pope John Paul II
1979 (June 30): Marco Cé, Ernesto Corripio Ahumada, Roger Etchegaray, Franciszek Macharski.
1983 (Feb. 2): Michael Michai Kitbunchu, Alexandre do Nascimento, Alfonso López Trujillo, Godfried Danneels, Thomas Stafford Williams, Carlo Maria Martini, Jean-Marie Lustiger, Józef Glemp, Joachim Meisner.
1985 (May 25): Simon D. Lourdusamy, Francis A. Arinze, Antonio Innocenti, Miguel Obando Bravo, S.D.B., Paul Augustine Mayer, Ricardo Vidal, Henryk Roman Gulbinowicz, Jozef Tomko, Andrzej Maria Deskur, Paul Poupard, Louis-Albert Vachon, Rosalio José Castillo Lara, S.D.B., Friedrich Wetter, Silvano Piovanelli, Adrianus J. Simonis, Edouard Gagnon, P.S.S., Alfons Stickler, S.D.B., Bernard F. Law, Giacomo Biffi.
1988 (June 28): Eduardo Martinez Somalo, Achille Silvestrini, Angelo Felici, José Freire Falcão, Michele Giordano, Alexandre José Maria dos Santos, O.F.M., Giovanni Canestri, Antonio Maria Javierre Ortas, S.D.B., Simon Ignatius Pimenta, Edward Bede Clancy, Edmund C. Szoka, László Paskai, O.F.M., Christian Wiyghan Tumi, Jean Margéot.
1991 (June 28): Angelo Sodano, Pio Laghi, Edward I. Cassidy, Frédéric Etsou-Nzabi-Bamungwabi, C.I.C.M., Nicolás de Jesús López Rodriguez, José T. Sánchez, Virgilio Noè, Fiorenzo Angelini Roger Mahony, Anthony J. Bevilacqua, Giovanni Saldarini, Cahal Brendan Daly, Camillo Ruini, Ján Chryzostom Korec, S.J., Henri Schwery, Georg Sterzinsky.
1994 (Nov. 26): Nasrallah Pierre Sfeir, Miloslav Vlk, Luigi Poggi, Peter Seiichi Shirayanagi, Carlo Furno, Adolfo Antonio Suárez Rivera, Julius Riyadi Darmaatmadja, S.J., Jaime Lucas Ortega y Alamino, Gilberto Agustoni, Emmanuel Wamala, William Henry Keeler, Jean-Claude Turcotte, Ricardo Maria Carles Gordó, Adam Joseph Maida, Vinko Puljic, Armand Gaétan Razafindratandra, Paul Joseph Pham Dính Tung, Juan Sandoval Íñiguez, Kazimierz Swiàtek, Ersilio Tonino.
1998 (Feb. 21): Jorge Medina Estévez, Darío Castrillón Hoyos, Lorenzo Antonetti, James Francis Stafford, Salvatore de Giorgi, Serafim Fernandes de Araújo, Antonio Maria Rouco Varela, Aloysius Ambrozic, Dionigi Tettamanzi, Polycarp Pengo, Christoph Schönborn, O.P., Norberto Rivera Carrera, Francis George, O.M.I., Paul Shan Kuo-hsi, S.J., Adam Kozlowiecki, S.J., Giovanni Cheli, Dino Monduzzi, Marian Jaworski, Janis Pujats.
2001 (Feb. 21): Giovanni Battista Re, Agostino Cacciavillan, Sergio Sebastiani, Zenon Grocholewski, José Saraiva Martins, C.M.F., Crescenzio Sepe, Jorge María Mejía, Ignace Moussa I Daoud, Mario Francesco Pompedda, Walter Kasper, Antonio Jose Gonzalez Zumarraga, Ivan Dias, Geraldo Majella Agnelo, Pedro Rubiano Sáenz,

Theodore E. McCarrick, Desmond Connell, Audrys Juozas Backis, Francisco Javier Errázuriz Ossa, Juan Julio Terrazas Sandoval, C.SS.R., Wilfrid Fox Napier, O.F.M., Oscar Andres Rodríguez Maradiaga, S.D.B., Bernard Agré, Luis Cipriani Thorne, Francisco Álvarez Martínez, Cláudio Hummes, Varkey Vithayathil, C.SS.R., Jorge Mario Bergoglio, S.J., José Da Cruz Policarpo, Severino Poletto, Cormac Murphy-O'Connor, Edward Michael Egan, Lubomyr Husar, Karl Lehmann, Stephanos II Ghattas, Jean Honoré, O.F.M., Roberto Tucci, S.J., Avery Dulles, S.J.,
2003 (Oct. 21): Jean-Louis Tauran, Renato Martino, Francesco Marchisano, Julián Herranz, Javier Lozano Barragán, Stephen Fumio Hamao, Attilio Nicora, Angelo Scola, Anthony Olubunmi Okogie, Bernard Panafieu, Gabriel Zubeir Wako, Carlos Amigo Vallejo, Justin Francis Rigali, Keith Michael O'Brien, Eusebio Oscar Scheid, Ennio Antonelli, Tarcisio Bertone, Peter Kodwo Appiah Turkson, Telesphore Placidus Toppo, George Pell, Josip Bozanic, Jean Baptiste Pham Minh Man, Rodolfo Quezada Toruño, Philippe Barbarin, Peter Erdő, Marc Ouellet, P.S.S., Georges Cottier, O.P., Stanislas Nagy, Thomas Spidlik, S.J.
Pope Benedict XVI
2006 (Mar. 24): William Levada, Franc Rodé, C.M., Agostino Vallini, Jorge Liberato Urosa Savino, Gaudencio Rosales, Jean-Pierre Ricard, Antonio Cañizares Llovera, Cheong Jin-Suk, Sean Patrick O'Malley, O.F.M.Cap., Stanislaw Dziwisz, Carlo Caffarra, Joseph Zen Ze-Kiun, S.D.B., Andrea Cordero Lanza di Montezemolo, Peter Poreku Dery, Albert Vanhoye, S.J.

DISTRIBUTION OF CARDINALS

As of Aug. 15, 2006, there were 190 cardinals from 68 countries or areas. Listed below are areas, countries, number and last names. Names with asterisks are cardinals ineligible to vote.

Europe — 98

Italy (40): Angelini,* Antonelli, Antonetti,* Bertone, Biffi, Cacciavillan,* Caffarra, Canestri,* Cé,* Cheli,* Cordero Lanza di Montezemolo,* de Giorgi, Felici,* Furno,* Giordano, Innocenti,* Laghi,* Marchisano, Martini, Martino, Monduzzi,* Nicora, Noè,* Pappalardo,* Piovanelli,* Poggi,* Poletto, Pompedda, Re, Ruini, Saldarini,* Scola, Sebastiani, Sepe, Silvestrini,* Sodano, Tettamanzi, Tonini,* Tucci,* Vallini.

France (9): Barbarin, Etchegaray,* Honoré,* Lustiger, Panafieu, Poupard, Ricard, Tauran, Vanhoye.*

Poland (8): Deskur,* Dziwisz, Glemp, Grocholewski, Gulbinowicz,* Kozlowiecki,* Macharski, Nagy.*

Spain (8): Alvarez Martinez,* Cañizares Llovera, Carles Gordó, Herranz, Javierre Ortas,* Martinez Somalo, RoucoVarela, Vallejo.

Germany (6): Kasper, Lehmann, Mayer,* Meisner, Sterzinsky, Wetter.

Switzerland (3): Agustoni,* Cottier,* Schwery.

Austria (2): Schönborn, Stickler.*

Czech Republic (2): Spidlik,* Vlk.

Hungary (2): Erdö, Paskai.

Ireland (2): Connell,* Daly.*

Lithuania (2): Backis, Pujats

Portugal (2): Policarpo, Saraiva Martins
Slovakia (2): Korec,* Tomko.*
Ukraine (2): Husar, Jaworski.
One from each of the following countries: Belarus, Swiatek*; Belgium, Danneels; Bosnia-Herzegovina, Puljic; England, Murphy-O'Connor; Netherlands, Simonis; Scotland, O'Brien; Slovenia, Rodé; Yugoslavia, Bozanic.

Asia — 20

India (5): Dias, Lourdusamy,* Pimenta,* Toppo, Vithayathil.
Philippines (3): Rosales, Sánchez,* Vidal.
Japan (2): Hamao, Shirayanagi.
Korea (2) Cheong Jin-Suk, Kim.*
Vietnam (2): Pham Dinh Tung,* Pham Minh Man.
One from each of the following countries: Hong Kong, Zen Ze-kiun; Indonesia, Darmaatmadja; Lebanon, Sfeir;* Syria, Moussa I Daoud; Taiwan, Shan Kuo-hsi;* Thailand, Kitbunchu.

Oceania — 4

Australia (3): Cassidy,* Clancy,* Pell.
New Zealand (1): Williams.

Africa — 17

Ghana (2): Dery,* Turkson
Nigeria (2): Arinze, Okogie.
One from each of the following countries: Angola, do Nascimento*; Benin, Gantin*; Cameroon, Tumi; Congo (formerly Zaire), Etsou-Nzabi-Bamungwabi; Egypt, Stephanos II Ghattas*; Ivory Coast, Agre*; Madagascar, Razafindratandra*; Mauritius, Margeot*; Mozambique, Santos*; South Africa, Napier; Sudan, Wako; Tanzania, Pengo; Uganda, Wamala.

North America – 26

United States (15): Baum, Bevilacqua,* Dulles,* Egan, George, Keeler, Law, Levada, McCarrick, Mahony, Maida, O'Malley, Rigali, Stafford, Szoka.
Canada (5): Ambrozic, Gagnon,* Ouellet, Turcotte, Vachon.*
Mexico (5): Corripio Ahumada,* Lozano Barragán, Rivera Carrera, Sandoval Iñiguez, Suárez Rivera.
Puerto Rico (1): Aponte Martinez.*

Central and South America – 25

Brazil (8): Arns,* Falcão,* Fernandes de Araújo,* Hummes, Lorscheider,* Majella Agnelo, Sales,* Scheid.
Colombia (3): Castrillón Hoyos, Lopez Trujillo, Rubiano Saenz.
Argentina (2): Bergoglio, Mejia.*
Chile (2): Errazuriz Ossa, Medina Estévez.
Venezuela (2): Castillo Lara,* Urosa Savino
One each from the following countries: Bolivia, Sandoval; Cuba, Ortega y Alamino; Dominican Republic, Lopez Rodriguez; Ecuador, Gonzalez Zumarraga*; Guatemala, Quezada Toruño; Honduras, Rodriguez Maradiaga; Nicaragua, Obando Bravo*; Peru, Cipriani Thorne.

Cardinal Electors: 119

As of Aug. 15, 2006, there were 119 electors from 54 countries: 59 from Europe, 20 from North America, 17 from South America, 8 from Africa, 13 from Asia, and two from Oceania. Of the current cardinal electors, 12 were named by Benedict XVI, 1 by Paul VI, and 106 by John Paul II.

Ineligible to Vote

As of Oct. 1, 2006, 74 of the 190 cardinals were ineligible to take part in a papal election in line with the apostolic letter *Ingravescentem Aetetem* effective Jan. 1, 1971, which limited the functions of cardinals after completion of their 80th year.

Cardinals affected are: Agré, Agustoni, Álvarez Martínez, Angelini, Antonetti, Aponte Martínez, Arns, Bevilacqua, Cacciavillan, Canestri, Carles Gordó, Cassidy, Castillo Lara, Cé, Cheli, Clancy, Connell, Cordero Lanza di Montezemolo, Corripio Ahumada, Cottier, Daly, Dery, Deskur, do Nascimento, Dulles, Etchegaray, Falcão, Felici, Fernandes de Araújo, Furno, Gagnon, Gantin, Gonzalez Zumarraga, Gulbinowicz, Honoré, Innocenti, Javierre Ortas, Jaworski, Kim Sou-hwan, Korec, Kozlowiecki, Laghi, Lorscheider, Lourdusamy, Lustiger, Margéot, Mayer, Mejia, Monduzzi, Nagy, Noè, Obando Bravo, Pappalardo, Pham Dinh Tung, Pimenta, Piovanelli, Poggi, Razafindratandra, Saldarini, Sales, Sánchez, Santos, Sfeir, Shan Kuo-hsi, Silvestrini, Spidlik, Stephanos II Ghattas, Stickler, Swiatek, Tomko, Tonini, Tucci, Vachon, Vanhoye.

Cardinals who complete their 80th year in 2006-2007 and who become ineligible to vote: 2006 — Baum, Medina Estévez, Wamala; 2007 — Macharski, Martinez Somalo, Martini, Paskai, Sodano, Suárez Rivera, Szoka, Vithayathil.

Cardinals of the United States

As of Aug. 15, 2005, the following cardinals were in service, according to their years of elevation (for biographies, *see* College of Cardinals *above*):

1976: William W. Baum (major penitentiary emeritus); 1985: Bernard F. Law (abp. emeritus of Boston); 1988: Edmund C. Szoka (governor of the Vatican City State); 1991: Roger M. Mahony (abp. of Los Angeles), Anthony M. Bevilacqua (abp. emeritus of Philadelphia); 1994: William H. Keeler (abp. of Baltimore), Adam J. Maida (abp. of Detroit); 1998: Francis E. George, O.M.I. (abp. of Chicago), James F. Stafford (Major Penitentiary of the Apostolic Penitentiary); 2001: Edward M. Egan (abp. of New York), Theodore E. McCarrick (abp. emeritus of Washington), Avery Dulles, S.J. (theologian); 2003: Justin F. Rigali (abp. of Philadelphia); 2006: William J. Levada (prefect of the Congregation for the Doctrine of the Faith), Sean P. O'Malley, O.F.M.Cap. (abp. of Boston). Cardinal Lubomyr Husar, M.S.U., major abp. of Lviv for Ukrainians, is also an American citizen.

U.S. Cardinals of the Past (according to year of elevation; for biographical data, *see* American Catholics of the Past at www.catholicalmanac.com):

1875: John McCloskey; 1886: James Gibbns; 1911: John Farley, William O'Connell; 1921: Dennis Dougherty; 1924: Patrick Hayes, George Mundelein; 1946: John Glennon, Edward Mooney, Francis Spellman, Samuel Stritch; 1953: James F. McIntyre; 1958: John O'Hara, C.S.C., Richard Cushing; 1959: Albert Meyer, Aloysius Muench; 1961: Joseph Ritter; 1965: Lawrence J. Shehan; 1967: Francis Brennan, John P. Cody, Patrick A. O'Boyle, John J. Krol; 1969: John J. Wright, Terence J. Cooke, John F. Dearden, John J. Carberry; 1973: Humberto S. Medeiros, Timothy Manning; 1983: Joseph L. Bernardin; 1985: John J. O'Connor; 1988: James A. Hickey. (Myroslav Lubachivsky, major abp. of Lviv of the Ukrainians (Ukraine), was made a cardinal in 1985. He was a citizen of the United States and metropolitan of the Philadelphia Ukrainian Rite Archeparchy, from 1979-81.)

Prelates who became cardinals after returning to their native countries: John Lefebvre de Chevrus, first bp. of Boston (1808-23) and apostolic administrator of New York (1810-15), elevated to the cardinalate, 1836, in France. Ignatius Persico, O.F.M. Cap., bp. of Savannah (1870-72), elevated to the cardinalate, 1893, in Italy; Diomede Falconio, O.F.M. ord. a priest in Buffalo, NY, missionary in U.S., apostolic delegate to the U.S. (1902-11), elevated to cardinalate, 1911, in Italy.

ELECTING THE POPE: THE CONCLAVE

One of the primary duties of the Cardinals of the Catholic Church is the election of the Bishop of Rome who becomes thereby the Supreme Pontiff of the Church. The election is held in what is termed the conclave. The name is derived from the Latin *cum* (with) and *clavis* (key), and implies the fact that the cardinals are locked together in a room until a new pontiff has been chosen. This form of papal election began in 1274 and is considered the third period in the historical evolution of choosing the successor to St. Peter. Central to the full understanding of the conclave is the firm belief that the entire process of election is guided by the Holy Spirit.

In the early Church, new Bishops of Rome were chosen in the manner customarily used in the other dioceses, that is, the clergy, with the people of the diocese, elected or chose the new bishop in the presence of the other bishops in the province. This was a simple method, but it became impractical as the Christian population grew in size and there arose rival claimants and hostility between the upper classes (the patricians) and the lower classes (the plebeians), each of whom had their own candidates. This situation created considerable upheaval in Rome as demonstrated by the riots accompanying the contested elections of Pope St. Damasus I (366-384) and the antipope Ursinus in 366. Such was the violence that the prefect of the city was called in to restore order.

On the basis of these disturbances, the Roman emperors began to involve themselves in the elections by guaranteeing proper procedure and ensuring free voting by the clergy in cases where two claimants had emerged. This intervention launched a long period of secular interference that would continue, to various degrees, until 1903. The so-called barbarian kings often supervised elections until the sixth century when the Byzantines reconquered Italy. The emperors not only demanded tribute from the popes but also retained the right of confirmation, a practice that routinely created long delays, as word would have to be sent to Constantinople (later Ravenna) to request approval. The last pope to seek confirmation from imperial authorities was Gregory III in 731. After this time, the popes sought the protection of the Franks, and in 769, Pope Stephen III convened a synod at Rome that confirmed the decree of 502 (under Symmachus) that laypeople should no longer vote for the popes and that only higher clerics should be considered eligible.

A major reform was achieved in 1059 when Pope Nicholas II decreed that the cardinal bishops should choose the popes, a procedure modified by the Third Lateran Council (1179), which declared an end to distinctions among the three orders of cardinals in terms of voting, and requiring that a candidate receive a two-thirds majority.

The new need of a majority complicated many elections as a two-thirds plurality would often be quite difficult to reach owing to competing international interests among the cardinals. After the death of Pope Clement IV in 1268, for example, three years passed until the 18 cardinals gathered at Viterbo could agree on Pope Gregory X (r. 1271-1276). Gregory introduced changes through the Second Council of Lyons (1272) to speed up elections, inaugurating the system of the conclave. It remained essentially unchanged until 1975. In that year, Pope Paul VI issued the apostolic constitution *Romano Pontifici Eligendo* (Oct. 1) that stipulated various requirements for the conclave. Among these were: only cardinals may be electors; their number is limited to 120, with each cardinal allowed to bring two or three assistants; while not essential for validity, it is the recognized form of election; three forms are acceptable: acclamation (*acclamatio*); compromise (by which certain cardinals are named delegates and are given power to act on behalf of the others); and balloting; if the person chosen is not a bishop, he is to be ordained to the episcopacy immediately (if a bishop, he is pope at once); secrecy is to be carefully observed; all ecumenical councils are immediately adjourned; and, if no one is elected after three days, one day is to be spent in prayer and meditation.

New legislation regarding papal elections and church government during a vacancy of the Holy See was promulgated by Pope John Paul II on Feb. 23, 1996, in the apostolic constitution *Universi Dominici Gregis* ("Shepherd of the Lord's Whole Flock"). Among the changes that were introduced was the call for heightened security in preventing electronic surveillance and the provision that after a set number of unsuccessful ballots, the cardinals may elect the new pope by a simple majority vote. The constitution was used in the conclave of 2005 that elected Cardinal Joseph Ratzinger as Pope Benedict XVI.

The last election not held in the Vatican (the Sistine Chapel) was in 1846 (Pius IX), which took place at the Quirinal Palace. The last pope not a cardinal at the time of his election was Urban VI (1378-1389); the last by compromise was John XXII (r. 1316-1334); and the last by acclamation was Gregory XV (1621-1623).

The Universal Church

THE CHURCH IN COUNTRIES THROUGHOUT THE WORLD

(Principal sources for statistics: Annuarium Statisticum Ecclesiae, Statistical Yearbook of the Church, 2004 — the most recent edition; Annuario Pontificio, 2006; and Agenzia Internazionale FIDES. Figures are as of Jan. 1, 2005, except for cardinals [as of Aug. 30, 2006] and others which are indicated. For 2006 developments, see Index entries for individual countries.)

An asterisk indicates that the country has full diplomatic relations with the Holy See (see Diplomats to the Holy See in the Holy See section).

Abbreviations (in order in which they appear): archd. – archdiocese; dioc. – diocese; ap. ex. – apostolic exarchate; prel. – prelature; abb. – abbacy; v.a. – apostolic vicariate; p.a. – apostolic prefecture; a.a. – apostolic administration; mil. ord. – military ordinariate; card. – cardinal; abp. – archbishops; bp. – bishops (diocesan and titular); priests (dioc. – diocesan or secular priests; rel. – those belonging to religious orders); p.d. – permanent deacons; sem. – major seminarians, diocesan and religious; bros. – brothers; srs. – sisters; bap. – baptisms; Caths. – Catholic population; tot. pop. – total population; (AD) – apostolic delegate (see Index: Papal Representatives).

Afghanistan

Republic in south-central Asia; capital, Kabul. Christianity antedated Muslim conquest in the seventh century but was overcome by it. All inhabitants are subject to the law of Islam. Under Afghan's Taliban regime, religious freedom was severely restricted, and proselytizing was forbidden. In January 2002, Italian and English chaplains celebrated the first public Mass in nearly 10 years in Kabul, at the Italian Embassy.

Albania*

Archd., 2; dioc., 3; a.a., 1; abp., 3; bp., 3; parishes, 118; priests, 135 (49 dioc., 86 rel.); p.d.,1; sem., 24; bros., 16; srs., 424; bap., 3,092; Caths., 506,000 (12.2%); tot. pop., 4,133,000.

Republic in the Balkans, bordering the Adriatic Sea; capital, Tirana. Christianity was introduced in apostolic times. The northern part of the country remained faithful to Rome while the South broke from unity following the schism of 1054. A large percentage of the population was to become Muslim following the invasion (15th century) and long centuries of occupation by the Ottoman Turks. Many Catholics fled to southern Italy, Sicily and Greece. In 1945, at the time of the communist takeover, an estimated 68 percent of the population was Muslim; 19 percent was Orthodox and 13 percent Roman Catholic. The Catholic Church prevailed in the north. During 45 years of communist dictatorship, the Church fell victim, as did all religions, to systematic persecution.

In 1967, the government, declaring it had eliminated all religion in the country, proclaimed itself the first atheist state in the world. The right to practice religion was restored in late 1990. In March 1991, a delegation from the Vatican was allowed to go to Albania; later in the year diplomatic relations were established with the Holy See at the request of the Albanian prime minister. Pope John Paul II made a one-day visit to the country Apr. 25, 1993, during which he ordained four bishops appointed by him in December 1992 to fill long-vacant sees. The first Albanian cardinal was named in November 1994.

Although Catholics are a minority, they are well respected, including for their work in the education and health fields. Albanians welcomed hundreds of thousands of ethnic Albanians from Kosovo during Yugoslav persecution in 1999.

Algeria*

Archd., 1; dioc., 3; abp., 2; bp., 3; parishes, 40; priests, 92 (37 dioc., 55 rel.); p.d., 2; sem., 8; bros., 21; srs., 197; bap., 9; Caths., 4,000 (.01%); tot. pop., 32,379,000.

Republic in northwest Africa; capital, Algiers. Christianity, introduced at an early date, succumbed to Vandal devastation in the fifth century and Muslim conquest in 709, but survived for centuries in small communities into the 12th century. Missionary work was unsuccessful except in service to traders, military personnel and captives along the coast. Church organization was established after the French gained control of the territory in the 1830s. A large number of Catholics were among the estimated million Europeans who left the country after it secured independence from France July 5, 1962. Islam is the state religion.

Armed Islamic militants and guerrillas have caused terror and unrest in Algeria since 1992. Among the more than 80,000 people killed were seven Trappist monks and the Catholic bishop of Oran, all in 1996.

Andorra*

Parishes, 7; priests, 17 (11 dioc., 6 rel.); srs., 11; bap., 369; Caths., 64,000 (94%); tot. pop., 68,000.

Parliamentary state (1993) in the Pyrenees; capital, Andorra la Vella. From 1278-1993, it was a co-principality under the rule of the French head of state and the bishop of Urgel, Spain, who retain their titles. Christianity was introduced at an early date. Catholicism is the state religion. Ecclesiastical jurisdiction is under the Spanish Diocese of Urgel. The constitution calls for freedom of religion, but also guarantees "the Roman Catholic Church free and public exercise of its activities and the preservation of the relations of special cooperation with the state."

Angola*

Archd., 3; dioc., 13; card., 1; abp., 5; bp., 17; parishes, 275; priests, 713 (374 dioc., 339 rel.); sem., 1,267; p.d., 1; bros., 121; srs., 1,874; catechists, 23,127; bap., 195,251; Caths., 7,923,000 (57.1%); tot. pop., 13,866,000.

Republic in southwest Africa; capital, Luanda. Evangelization by Catholic missionaries from Portugal, dating from 1491, reached high points in the 17th and 18th centuries. Independence from Portugal in 1975 and the long civil war that followed (peace accord signed in 1991) left the Church with a heavy loss of personnel resulting from the departure of about half the foreign missionaries and the persecution and martyrdom experienced by the Church during the war. Renewed fighting following elections in late 1992 brought repeated appeals for peace from the nation's bishops and religious in 1993 and 1994.

Despite another peace accord signed by the rebels and the government in late 1994, conditions have remained unsettled. One effect of the fighting was to cut off Church leaders from large groups of the faithful. In an attempt to encourage peace efforts, the Vatican established diplomatic relations with Angola in 1997. Attacks on Church workers, however, continued in 1998 and 1999. In 2000, Church leaders began an active peace movement, holding national and diocesan congresses and beginning a consultation with Angolan political leaders. Government and rebel representatives signed a peace agreement in 2002, after the government killed rebel leader Jonas Savimbi, and the Church offered humanitarian aid and helped to rebuild the country.

Antigua and Barbuda*

Dioc., 1; bp., 1; parishes, 2; priests, 12 (7 dioc., 5 rel.); p.d., 8; sem., 1; srs., 11; bap., 95; Caths., 8,000 (12.5%); tot. pop., 64,000.

Independent (1981) Caribbean island nation; capital, St. John's, Antigua. The Diocese of St. John's-Basseterre includes Antigua and Barbuda, St. Kitts and Nevis, Anguilla, the British Virgin Islands and Montserrat.

Argentina*

Archd., 14; dioc., 50; prel., 3; ap. ex., 3 (for Armenians of Latin America); mil. ord., 1; card., 2; abp., 22; bp., 79; parishes, 2,649; priests, 5,778 (3,753 dioc., 2,025 rel.); p.d., 675; sem., 1,704; bros., 785; srs., 9,214; bap., 552,069; catechists, 97,921; Caths., 35,170,000 (90%); tot. pop., 38,856,000

Republic in southeast South America, bordering on the Atlantic; capital, Buenos Aires. Priests were with the Magellan exploration party and the first Mass in the country was celebrated Apr. 1, 1519. Missionary work began in the 1530s, diocesan organization in the late 1540s, and effective evangelization about 1570. Independence from Spain was proclaimed in 1816. Since its establishment in the country, the Church has

been influenced by Spanish cultural and institutional forces, antagonistic liberalism, government interference and opposition; the latter reached a climax during the last five years of the first presidency of Juan Peron (1946-55).

Widespread human rights violations, including the disappearance of thousands of people, marked the "Dirty War," the period of military rule from 1976 to December 1983, when an elected civilian government took over. In 1996 the Argentine bishops said they did not do enough to stop human rights violations during the "Dirty War." In the late 1990s, the bishops spoke out against government corruption and a severe government economic program, and early in the 21st century — at the invitation of the government — they organized national meetings of civic leaders to seek solutions to the country's crises.

Armenia*

Ord., 1 (for Catholic Armenians of Eastern Europe, with seat in Armenia); parishes, 18; abp., 2; priests, 4 (rel.); sem., 10; bros., 1; srs., 20; bap., 794; Caths., 150,000 (4%); tot. pop., 3,210,000.

Republic in Asia Minor; capital Yerevan. Part of the USSR from 1920 until it declared its sovereignty in September 1991. Ancient Armenia, which also included territory annexed by Turkey in 1920, was Christianized in the fourth century. Diplomatic relations were established with the Holy See on May 23, 1992. Pope John Paul II visited Armenia in late September 2001 to help mark the 1,700th anniversary of Christianity in the nation. The small Catholic community in Armenia has good relations with the predominant Armenian Apostolic Church, an Oriental Orthodox Church.

Australia*

Archd., 7; dioc., 24; mil. ord., 1; card., 3; abp., 10; bp., 52; parishes, 1,388; priests, 3,220 (1,952 dioc., 1,268 rel.); p.d., 56; sem., 266; bros., 1,115; srs., 7,299; catechists, 6,920; bap., 65,405; Caths., 5,568,000 (28%); tot. pop. 20,100,000.

Commonwealth; island continent southeast of Asia; capital, Canberra. The first Catholics in the country were Irish under penal sentence, 1795-1804; the first public Mass was celebrated May 15, 1803. Official organization of the Church dates from 1820. The country was officially removed from mission status in March 1976.

As the 20th century neared its end, the Church in Australia was rocked by allegations of sexual abuse from previous decades. In 1996 the Australian bishops published a plan for dealing with such cases. In 1998 the bishops also apologized to aboriginal children, saying their support of government policy in the 1970s might have contributed to separation of the children from their families.

In an unusual move, in mid-November 1998, just before the Synod of Bishops for Oceania at the Vatican and after the Australian bishops' "ad limina" visits, Vatican officials met with Church leaders from Australia to discuss doctrinal and pastoral issues. In December 1998, the Vatican and representatives of Australian Church leaders signed a document, later endorsed by the Australian bishops' conference, that spoke of a "crisis of faith" in the Catholic Church on the continent. The Australian Church, like many others in the late 20th and early 21st century, struggled with cases of clergy sexual abuse.

Austria*

Archd., 2; dioc., 7; abb., 1; ord., 1; mil. ord., 1; card., 2; abp., 4; bp., 16; parishes, 3,070; priests, 4,381 (2,667 dioc., 1,714 rel.); p.d., 487; sem., 302; bros., 456; srs., 5,372; catechists, 1,936; bap., 54,049; Caths., 5,940,000 (73%); tot. pop., 8,170,000.

Republic in central Europe; capital, Vienna. Christianity was introduced by the end of the third century, strengthened considerably by conversion of the Bavarians from about 600, and firmly established in the second half of the eighth century. Catholicism survived and grew stronger as the principal religion in the country in the post-Reformation period, but suffered from Josephinism in the 18th century. Although liberated from much government harassment in the aftermath of the Revolution of 1848, the Church came under pressure again some 20 years later in the Kulturkampf. The Church faced strong opposition from Socialists after World War I and suffered persecution from 1938 to 1945 during the Nazi regime. Some Church-state matters are regulated by a concordat originally concluded in 1934.

At the turn of the century, the Church in Austria was beset by internal difficulties, including a seminary pornography scandal and the launch of a global movement seeking more lay participation in Church decision-making and changes in Church policy on ordination of women and priestly celibacy. In 1995, Cardinal Hans Hermann Gröer resigned as archbishop of Vienna amid charges of sexual misconduct. His successor, Cardinal Christoph Schönborn, worked to restore a sense of unity to the Church.

Azerbaijan*

Independent republic (1991) on the Caspian Sea; formerly part of the USSR; capital, Baku. Islam is the prevailing religion. Soviet rulers destroyed Baku's one Catholic church in the late 1930s. A small Catholic community of Polish and Armenian origin near the capital is ministered to by two missionaries. Latin-rite Catholics are under the apostolic administration of Caucasus (seat in Georgia), established in December 1993.

Bahamas*

Dioc., 1; bp., 1; parishes, 30; priests, 31 (14 dioc., 17 rel.); p.d., 14; sem., 6; srs., 29; catechists, 235; bap., 402; Caths., 48,000 (15%); tot. pop., 325,000.

Independent (July 10, 1973) island group consisting of some 700 (30 inhabited) small islands southeast of Florida and north of Cuba; capital, Nassau. On Oct. 12, 1492, Columbus landed on one of these islands, where the first Mass was celebrated in the New World. Organization of the Catholic Church in the Bahamas dates from about the middle of the 19th century.

Bahrain*

Parish, 1; priests, 4 (2 dioc., 2 rel.); srs., 15; bap., 183; Caths., 30,000 (4.3%); tot. pop., 690,000. (AD)

Island state in Persian Gulf; capital, Manama. Population is Muslim; Catholics are foreign workers, under ecclesiastical jurisdiction of Arabia apostolic vicariate. Diplomatic relations were established between Bahrain and the Holy See in January 2000.

Bangladesh*

Archd., 1; dioc., 5; abp., 2; bp., 8; parishes, 80; priests, 272 (141 dioc., 131 rel.); sem., 113; bros., 68; srs., 1,079; catechists, 1,508; bap., 6,903; Caths., 291,000 (.20%); tot. pop. 141,124,000.

Formerly the eastern portion of Pakistan. Officially constituted as a separate nation Dec. 16, 1971; capital, Dhaka. Jesuit, Dominican and Augustinian missionaries were in the area in the 16th century. An apostolic vicariate (of Bengali) was established in 1834; the hierarchy was erected in 1950. Islam, the principal religion, was declared the state religion in 1988; freedom of religion is granted. Church-run humanitarian and development agencies have been instrumental in responding to natural disasters, such as flooding. The bishops have emphasized inculturation and Church social doctrine.

Barbados*

Dioc., 1; bp., 2; parishes, 5; priests, 7 (3 dioc., 4 rel.); p.d., 1; srs., 14; bap., 108; sem., 1; Caths., 10,000 (4%); tot. pop., 272,000.

Parliamentary democracy (independent since 1966), easternmost of the Caribbean islands; capital, Bridgetown. About 70 percent of the population are Anglican.

Belarus*

Archd., 1; dioc., 3; card., 1; abp., 1; bp., 4; parishes, 410; priests, 381 (209 dioc., 172 rel.); sem., 182; bros., 11; srs., 355; bap., 6,514; Caths., 1,027,000 (10%); tot. pop., 10,312,000.

Independent republic (1991) in eastern Europe; former Soviet republic (Byelorussia); capital, Minsk. Slow recovery of the Church was reported after years of repression in the Soviet Union, although in the mid-1990s under the authoritarian rule of President Alexander Lukashenka, the Church encountered tensions, especially in refusal of permits for foreign religious workers. In December 2000, the nation's bishops asked forgiveness for the "human weaknesses" of Church members throughout the centuries and said the Church forgave acts of Soviet-era persecution. In October 2002, Belarus adopted one of the most restrictive religion laws in the former Soviet Union, but by April 2003 government officials had granted the Catholic Church full legal status.

Belgium*

Archd., l; dioc., 7; mil. ord., 1; card., 1; abp., 2; bp., 18; parishes, 3,940; priests, 7,228 (4,387 dioc., 2,841 rel.); p.d., 562; sem., 224; bros., 1,026; srs., 13,265; catechists, 8,306; bap., 82,005; Caths., 7,791,000 (76%); tot. pop., 10,350,000.

Constitutional monarchy in northwestern Europe; capital, Brussels. Christianity was introduced about the first quarter of the fourth century and major evangelization was completed about 730. During the rest of the medieval period the Church had firm diocesan and parochial organization, generally vigorous monastic life and influential monastic and cathedral schools. Lutherans and Calvinists made some gains during the Reformation period but there was a strong Catholic restoration in the first half of the 17th century, when the country was under Spanish rule. Jansenism disturbed the Church from about 1640 into the 18th century. Josephinism, imposed by an Austrian regime, hampered the Church late in the same century. Repressive and persecutory measures were enforced during the Napoleonic conquest. Freedom came with separation of Church and state in the wake of the Revolution of 1830, which ended the reign of William I. Thereafter, the Church encountered serious problems with philosophical liberalism and political socialism.

Catholics have long been engaged in strong educational, social and political movements. In 1990, in an unprecedented political maneuver, King Baudouin temporarily gave up his throne, saying his Catholic conscience would not allow him to sign a law legalizing abortion. In the mid- and late-1990s, Church leaders expressed concern that the Church was characterized by indifference toward the papacy and dissent from Church teachings. Therapeutic in vitro fertilization for stable married couples continued at a leading Belgian Catholic hospital despite Vatican objections. The bishops fought a losing battle against the 2002 legalization of euthanasia.

Belize*

Dioc., 1; bp., 2; parishes, 13; priests, 36 (16 dioc., 20 rel.); sem., 3; bros., 3; srs., 64 catechists, 518; bap., 2,615; Caths., 215,000 (76%); tot. pop., 283,000.

Independent (Sept. 21, 1981) republic on eastern coast of Central America; capital, Belmopan. Its history has points in common with Guatemala, where evangelization began in the 16th century. The Church in Belize worked with refugees during the decades of Central American civil wars.

Benin*

Archd., 2; dioc., 8; card., 1; abp., 3; bp., 10; parishes, 223; priests, 548 (436 dioc., 112 rel.); sem., 537; bros., 122; srs., 1,101; catechists, 9,366; bap., 47,091; Caths., 1,833,000 (25%); tot. pop., 7,232,000.

Democratic republic in West Africa, bordering on the Atlantic; capital, Porto Novo. Missionary work was very limited from the 16th to the 18th centuries. Effective evangelization dates from 1861. The hierarchy was established in 1955. In the 1970s, Benin's Marxist-Leninist government nationalized Catholic schools, expelled foreign missionaries and jailed some priests. After the government dropped the one-party system in 1989, Archbishop Isidore de Souza of Cotonou presided over the 1990 national conference that drew up a new constitution and prepared the way for elections. One challenge facing the Church as it entered the 21st century was maintaining peace with people of other faiths.

Bermuda

Dioc., 1; bp., 1; parishes, 6; priests, 6 (2 dioc., 6 rel.); sem., 1; srs., 2; bap., 71; Caths., 9,000 (16%); tot. pop., 67,000. (AD)

British dependency, consisting of 360 islands (20 of them inhabited), nearly 600 miles east of Cape Hatteras; capital, Hamilton. Catholics were not permitted until about 1800. Occasional pastoral care was provided the few Catholics there by visiting priests during the 19th century. Early in the 1900s priests from Nova Scotia began serving the area. An apostolic prefecture was set up in 1953. The first bishop

assumed jurisdiction in 1956, when it was made an apostolic vicariate; diocese established, 1967.

Bhutan

Parish; catechist, 1; bap., 1; Caths., 400 (approx.); tot. pop., 2,311,000.

Kingdom in the Himalayas, northeast of India; capital, Thimphu. Buddhism is the state religion; Christians, including Catholics, are free to worship in private homes but cannot erect religious buildings, proselytize or congregate in public. Jesuits (1963) and Salesians (1965) were invited to the country to direct schools. Salesians were expelled in February 1982, on disputed charges of proselytism. The only Catholic missionary allowed to stay in the country was Canadian Jesuit Father William Mackey, who served Catholics there from 1963 until his death in 1995. Ecclesiastical jurisdiction is under the Darjeeling (India) Diocese, which ordained the first indigenous Bhutanese priest in 1995.

Bolivia*

Archd., 4; dioc., 6; prel., 2; mil. ord., 1; v.a., 5; card., 1; abp., 6; bp., 17; parishes, 596; priests, 1,207 (508 dioc., 699 rel.); p.d., 83; sem., 727; bros., 233; srs., 2,561; catechists, 13,098; bap., 154,089; Caths., 7,686,000 (85%); tot. pop., 8,973,000.

Republic in central South America; capital, Sucre; seat of government, La Paz. Catholicism, the official religion, was introduced in the 1530s, and the first diocese was established in 1552. Effective evangelization among the Indians, slow to start, reached high points in the middle of the 18th and the beginning of the 19th centuries and was resumed about 1840. Independence from Spain was proclaimed in 1825, at the end of a campaign that started in 1809. Church-state relations are regulated by a 1951 concordat with the Holy See. Catholics have worked against social poverty and corruption. Early in the 21st century, amid social and economic turmoil, surveys showed the Catholic Church was seen as the most credible institution in the country.

Bosnia and Herzegovina*

Archd., 1; dioc., 2; card., 1; abp., 1; bp., 3; parishes, 286; priests, 612 (271 dioc., 341 rel.); sem., 104; bros., 15; srs., 564; bap., 5,278; Caths., 467,000 (11%); tot. pop., 3,840,000.

Independent republic (1992) in southeastern Europe; formerly part of Yugoslavia; capital, Sarajevo. During the three years of fighting that erupted after Bosnia-Herzegovina declared its independence, some 450,000 Catholics were driven from their homes; many fled to Croatia or southern Bosnia. Sarajevo Cardinal Vinko Puljic, named a cardinal in 1994, has led the bishops in calls for the safe return of all refugees from the war and acknowledged that in some areas Croatian Catholics were responsible for atrocities. Although the bishops worked to rebuild the Church, they said ethnic discrimination and violence still plagued the nation a decade after the war ended.

Botswana

Dioc., 1; v.a., 1; bp., 2; parishes, 35; priests, 60 (22 dioc., 38 rel.); p.d., 7; sem., 15; bros., 5; srs., 69; catechists, 401; bap., 1,512; Caths., 84,000 (4.6%); tot. pop., 1,834,000.

Republic (independent since 1966) in southern Africa; capital, Gaborone. The first Catholic mission was opened in 1928 near Gaborone; earlier attempts at evangelization dating from 1879 were unsuccessful.

The Church in Botswana gave strong support to tens of thousands of South African refugees from apartheid. As Botswana's diamond industry grew, Church leaders worked to minimize the effects of social changes such as pockets of unemployment and competition for jobs.

Brazil*

Archd., 41; dioc., 211; prel., 13; abb., 1; exarch., 1; mil. ord., 1; card., 8; abp., 61; bp., 342; parishes, 9,359; priests, 17,786 (10,470 dioc., 7,316 rel.); p.d., 1,650; sem., 9,582; bros., 2,754; srs., 33,966; catechists, 492,240; bap., 1,879,141; Caths., 153,440,000 (85%); tot. pop., 181,590,000.

Federal republic in northeastern South America; capital, Brasilia. One of several priests with the discovery party celebrated the first Mass in the country Apr. 26, 1500. Evangelization began some years later, and the first diocese was erected in 1551. During the colonial period, which lasted until 1822, evangelization made some notable progress — especially in the Amazon region between 1680 and 1750 — but was seriously hindered by government policy and the attitude of colonists regarding Amazon Indians the missionaries tried to protect from exploitation and slavery. The Jesuits were suppressed in 1782 and other missionaries expelled as well. Liberal anti-Church influence grew in strength. The government exercised maximum control over the Church. After the proclamation of independence from Portugal in 1822 and throughout the regency, government control was tightened and the Church suffered greatly from dissident actions of ecclesiastical brotherhoods, Masonic anticlericalism and general decline in religious life. Church and state were separated by the constitution of 1891, proclaimed two years after the end of the empire.

The Church carried into the 20th century problems associated with increasingly difficult political, economic and social conditions affecting the majority of the population. Many Afro-Brazilians indiscriminately mixed African-based rites such as candomble with Catholic rituals. In the second half of the 20th century, the bishops became known for their liberal stances on social and some theological issues. In the 1980s, Vatican officials had a series of meetings with Brazilian bishops to discuss liberation theology and other issues. The Brazilian bishops' conference took the lead in advocating for land reform in the country. Members of the Church's Pastoral Land Commission often faced threats, harassment and murder. The Church-founded Indigenous Missionary Council worked for the rights of the country's Indians. Each year, the bishops' Lenten campaign targets a social issue, such as women's rights or economic reform.

Brunei

P.a., 1; parishes, 3; priests, 4 (3 dioc., 1 rel); sem., 1; srs. 2; bap., 189; Caths., 2,200 (0.6%); tot. pop., 355,000.

Independent state (1984) on the northern coast of Borneo; formal name, Brunei Darussalam; capital, Bandar Seri Begawan. Islam is the official religion; other religions are allowed with some restrictions. Most of the Catholics are technicians and skilled workers from other countries who are not permanent residents; under ecclesiastical jurisdiction of Miri Diocese, Malaysia.

Bulgaria*

Dioc., 2; ap. ex., 1; abp., 2; bp., 3; parishes, 56; priests, 54 (18 dioc., 36 rel.); sem., 10; bros., 4; srs., 92; bap., 352; Caths., 77,000 (1%); tot. pop., 8,000,000.

Republic in southeastern Europe on the eastern part of the Balkan peninsula; capital, Sofia. Most of the population is Orthodox. Christianity was introduced before 343 but disappeared with the migration of Slavs into the territory. The baptism of Boris I about 865 ushered in a new period of Christianity, which soon became involved in switches of loyalty between Constantinople and Rome. Through it all the Byzantine, and later Orthodox, element remained stronger and survived under the rule of Ottoman Turks into the 19th century.

In 1947 the constitution of the new republic decreed the separation of Church and state. Catholic schools and institutions were abolished and foreign religious banished in 1948. A year later the apostolic delegate was expelled. Ivan Romanoff, vicar general of Plovdiv, died in prison in 1952. Bishop Eugene Bossilkoff, imprisoned in 1948, was sentenced to death in 1952; his fate remained unknown until 1975, when the Bulgarian government informed the Vatican that he had died in prison shortly after being sentenced. He was beatified in 1998. Although Church leaders were permitted to attend the Second Vatican Council, all Church activity was under surveillance and/or control by the government, which professed to be atheistic. Pastoral and related activities were strictly limited. There was some improvement in Bulgarian-Vatican relations in 1975. In 1979, the Sofia-Plovdiv apostolic vicariate was raised to a diocese, and a bishop was appointed for the vacant see of Nicopoli.

Diplomatic relations with the Holy See were established in 1990. In the late 1990s, the government instituted religion classes in state schools, but Church leaders complained they had no input into the curriculum and that teachers were predominantly Orthodox. In 2002, Pope John Paul II visited Bulgaria, one of several trips to predominantly Orthodox Soviet-bloc countries, and said Catholics and Orthodox should work for closer relations.

Burkina Faso*

Archd., 3; dioc., 10; abps., 2; bp., 14; parishes, 140; priests, 755 (575 dioc., 180 rel.); sem., 415; bros., 212; srs., 1,172; catechists, 10,732; bap., 65,659; Caths., 1,584,000 (11.9%); tot. pop., 13,393,000.

Republic inland in West Africa; capital, Ouagadougou. Missionaries of Africa started the first missions in 1900 and 1901. Their sisters began work in 1911. A minor and a major seminary were established in 1926 and 1942, respectively. The hierarchy was established in 1955. The first indigenous bishop in modern times from West Africa was ordained in 1956 and the first cardinal created in 1965. In 1980 and 1990, Pope John Paul II's visits to the country were used to launch appeals for an end to desertification of sub-Saharan Africa and an end to poverty in the region. In later years, the pope encouraged increased evangelization and interreligious harmony.

Burma (See Myanmar)

Burundi*

Archd., 1; dioc., 6; abp., 2; bp., 8; parishes, 132; priests, 478 (377 dioc., 101 rel.); sem., 492; bros., 197; srs., 1,228; catechists, 5,182; bap., 179,155; Caths., 4,757,000 (67%); tot. pop., 7,068,000.

Republic (1966), near the equator in east-central Africa; capital, Bujumbura. The first permanent Catholic mission station was established late in the 19th century. Large numbers were received into the Church following the ordination of the first Burundian priests in 1925. The first indigenous bishop was appointed in 1959.

In 1972-73, the country was torn by tribal warfare between the Tutsis, the ruling minority, and the Hutus. In 1979, the government began expelling foreign missionaries, and in 1986, seminaries were nationalized. A gradual resumption of Church activity since 1987 has been hampered by continuing ethnic violence, which began in 1993 and left more than 150,000 Burundians dead. The bishops repeatedly have called for peace and for an end to sanctions imposed by the Organization of African Unity in 1996. Missionaries continued to be the target of violent attacks, and the papal nuncio was killed after being shot in an ambush in late December 2003.

Cambodia*

V.a., 1; p.a., 2; bp., 2; parishes, 41 (there were also 18 mission stations without resident priests); priests, 60 (17 dioc., 43 rel.); sem., 8; bros., 9; srs., 75; catechists, 204; baptisms, 515; Caths., 23,000 (.15%); tot. pop., 12,821,000.

Republic in Southeast Asia; capital, Phnom Penh. Evangelization dating from the second half of the 16th century had limited results, more among Vietnamese than Khmers. Thousands of Catholics of Vietnamese origin were forced to flee in 1970 because of Khmer hostility. Most indigenous priests and nuns were killed under the 1975-79 Pol Pot regime. During those years, the Vietnamese invasion in 1979 and the long civil war that followed, foreign missionaries were expelled, local clergy and religious were sent to work the land and a general persecution followed. Religious freedom was re-established in 1990. Diplomatic relations with the Holy See were established in March 1994. Despite a lack of vocations, many Catholics maintain their faith through small Christian communities led by lay catechists. In the 21st century, Church leaders described their congregations as young and vibrant, involved in such things as AIDS ministry.

Cameroon*

Archd., 5; dioc., 18; card., 1; abp., 7; bp., 20; parishes, 741; priests, 1,519 (986 dioc., 533 rel.); p.d., 15; sem., 1,176; bros., 245; srs., 2,040; catechists, 19,426; bap., 94,055; Caths., 4,314,000 (26%); tot. pop., 16,571,000.

Republic in West Africa; capital, Yaounde. Effective evangelization began in 1890, although Catholics had been in the country long before that time. In the 40-year period from 1920 to 1960, the number of Catholics increased from 60,000 to 700,000. The first black priests were ordained in 1935. Twenty years later the first indigenous bishops were ordained and the hierarchy established. The first Cameroonian cardinal (Christian Wiyghan Tumi) was named in 1988. Around that same time, unknown people began persecuting Church personnel. Among those murdered was Archbishop Yves Plumy of Garoua in 1991. Some felt the government did not do enough to investigate.

Canada* (See Catholic Church in Canada; see also Statistics of the Church in Canada)

Cape Verde*

Dioc., 2; bp., 2; parishes, 31; priests, 51 (15 dioc., 36 rel.); sem., 21; bros., 8; srs., 125; catechists, 3,225; bap., 7,108; Caths., 439,000 (93%); tot. pop., 473,000.

Independent (July 5, 1975) island group in the Atlantic 300 miles west of Senegal; formerly a Portuguese overseas province; capital, Praia, São Tiago Island. Evangelization began some years before the establishment of a diocese in 1532. The Church languished from the 17th to the 19th centuries, and for two long periods there was no resident bishop. Portugal's anti-clerical government closed the only minor seminary in 1910. Missionaries returned in the 1940s. Cape Verde has faced massive emigration of youth because of perennial drought and a weak economy.

Central African Republic*

Archd., 1; dioc., 8; abp., 3; bp., 9; parishes, 115; priests, 285 (151 dioc., 134 rel.); sem., 164; bros., 30; srs., 398; catechists, 4,162; bap., 18,970; Caths., 829,000 (20%); tot. pop., 3,912,000.

Former French colony (independent since 1960) in central Africa; capital, Bangui. Effective evangelization dates from 1894. The region was organized as a mission territory in 1909. The first indigenous priest was ordained in 1938. The hierarchy was organized in 1955. Pope John Paul II has urged the country's bishops to give hope to a people ruled by corrupt dictatorships and the military. The Church in the country also has expressed concern about the growing number of sects.

Chad*

Archd., 1; dioc., 6; p.a., 1; abp., 2; bp., 6; parishes, 109; priests, 243 (138 dioc., 105 rel.); sem., 123; bros., 46; srs., 376; catechists, 8,638; bap., 22,091; Caths., 881,000 (9.7%); tot. pop., 9,091,000.

Republic (independent since 1960) in north-central Africa; former French possession; capital, N'Djamena. Evangelization began in 1929, leading to firm organization in 1947 and establishment of the hierarchy in 1955. Many catechists, who often were local community leaders, were killed during Chad's 1982-87 civil war. The Vatican established diplomatic relations with Chad in 1988. After the government established more freedoms in the early 1990s, the Church worked to teach people, including Catholics, that solidarity must extend across religious, ethnic and regional boundaries. Church workers were involved in ministering to hundreds of thousands of refugees displaced during the conflict in the Darfur region of Sudan.

Chile*

Archd., 5; dioc., 18; prel., 2; v.a., 1; mil. ord., 1; card., 2; abp., 9; bp., 38; parishes, 931; priests, 2,359 (1,181 dioc., 1,178 rel.); p.d., 743; sem., 695; bros., 376; srs., 5,144; catechists, 59,789; bap., 144,032; Caths., 11,915,000 (74.6%); tot. pop., 15,960,000.

Republic on the southwest coast of South America; capital, Santiago. Priests were with the Spanish on their entrance into the territory early in the 16th century. The first parish was established in 1547 and the first diocese in 1561. Overall organization of the Church took place later in the century. By 1650, most of the peaceful Indians in the central and northern areas were evangelized. Missionary work was more difficult in the southern region. Church activity was hampered during the campaign for independence, 1810-18, and through the first years of the new government, to 1830. Later, Church activity increased but was hampered by shortages of indigenous personnel and attempts by the government to control Church administration through the patronage system. Separation of Church and state was decreed in the constitution of 1925.

Church-state relations were strained during the regime of Marxist President Salvador Allende (1970-73). In the mid-

1970s, the Archdiocese of Santiago established the Vicariate of Solidarity to counter human-rights abuses under the rule of Gen. Augusto Pinochet. The Chilean bishops issued numerous statements strongly critical of human rights abuses by the military dictator, who remained in power until 1990, when an elected president took office. The Church was praised for its role in educating and registering voters in the 1988 plebiscite that rejected another term for Pinochet. In 1999, when a British court ruled that Pinochet could be extradited from Britain to Spain to face trial for torture and murder, some Chilean bishops said the ruling damaged the Chilean democracy they had fought so hard to get.

China, People's Republic of

Archd., 20; dioc., 92; p.a., 29. No Roman Catholic statistics are available. In 1949 there were between 3,500,000-4,000,000 Catholics, about .7% of the total population; current total is unknown. Tot. pop. 1,306,272,000. **Hong Kong**: Dioc., 1; card., 1; bps., 2; parishes, 52; priests, 296 (63 dioc., 233 rel.); p.d., 9; sem., 21; bros., 66; srs., 557; catechists, 1,335; bap., 3,739; Caths., 348,000 (5.2%); tot. pop., 6,867,000. **Macau**: Dioc., 1; bp., 2; parishes, 8; priests, 78 (24 dioc., 54 rel.); sem., 1; bros., 12; srs., 184; bap., 309; catechists, 117; Caths., 28,000; tot. pop. 465,000.

People's republic in eastern part of Asia; capital, Beijing. Christianity was introduced by Nestorians who had some influence on part of the area from 635 to 845 and again from the 11th century until 1368. John of Monte Corvino started a Franciscan mission in 1294; he was ordained an archbishop about 1307. Missionary activity involving more priests increased for a while thereafter, but the Franciscan mission ended in 1368. Jesuit Matteo Ricci initiated a remarkable period of activity in the 1580s. The Chinese-rites controversy, concerning the adaptation of rituals and other matters related to Chinese traditions and practices, ran throughout the 17th century, ending in a negative decision by mission authorities in Rome. Francis de Capillas, the Dominican protomartyr of China, was killed in 1648. Persecution occurred several times in the 18th century and resulted in the departure of most missionaries from the country.

The Chinese door swung open again in the 1840s, and progress in evangelization increased with an extension of legal and social tolerance. At the turn of the 20th century, however, Christian missionary activity helped provoke the Boxer Rebellion.

Missionary work in the 1900s reached a new high. The hierarchy was instituted by Pope Pius XII, Apr. 11, 1946 (Apostolic Constitution Quotidie Nos). Then followed persecution initiated by communists, before and especially after they established the republic in 1949. The government began a savage persecution as soon as it came into power. Among its results were outlawed missionary work and pastoral activity; the expulsion of more than 5,000 foreign missionaries, 510 of whom were American; the arrest, imprisonment and harassment of Chinese Church officials; the forced closing of more than 4,000 schools, institutions and homes; denial of the free exercise of religion; the detention of hundreds of priests, religious and lay people in jail and their employment in slave labor; the proscription of Catholic movements for "counterrevolutionary activities" and "crimes against the new China."

The government formally established the Chinese Catholic Patriotic Association, independent of the Holy See, in July 1957. Initially, relatively few priests and lay people joined the

organization, which was condemned by Pius XII in 1958. The government formed the nucleus of what it hoped might become the hierarchy of a schismatic Chinese Church in 1958 by "electing" 26 bishops and having them consecrated validly but illicitly between Apr. 13, 1958, and Nov. 15, 1959, without the permission or approval of the Holy See. Additional bishops were subsequently ordained. An underground Church continued to exist and face persecution.

Gradually, and in some regions more than others, the underground and patriotic churches began to mingle. Church leaders say more than 85% of the government-approved bishops in the Patriotic Association have secretly reconciled with the Vatican, and that the Vatican often approves the ordination of government-appointed bishops as long as the ordinations are conducted by the reconciled bishops. Others familiar with the Chinese Church say in some cases bishops of the two churches live in the same residence, although in some regions division remain. After China insisted on ordaining bishops Jan. 6, 2000, the same day the pope ordained bishops at the Vatican, many bishops and clergy of the Patriotic Association began trying to distance themselves from the government.

In the early 21st century, Hong Kong Church leaders were outspoken against and took the lead in some protests about the region's new security law. The Vatican's diplomatic relations with Taiwan remain one of the biggest stumbling blocks to Sino-Vatican ties.

Macau, the former Portuguese-administered territory in Southeast Asia across the Pearl River estuary from Hong Kong, reverted to Chinese control Dec. 20, 1999. Christianity was introduced by the Jesuits in 1557. Diocese was established in 1576. Macau served as a base for missionary work in Japan and China. Portuguese and Chinese Catholics remained somewhat segregated throughout the more than 400 years of Portuguese rule. Bishop Domingos Lam Ka Tseung became the first Chinese bishop of Macau in 1988 and launched a lay formation plan that included Chinese and Portuguese language training. The Church has been prominent in education. A Catholic priest was among three religious leaders named to the committee to prepare for the enclave's return to Chinese rule in December 1999. Church leaders said the transition proceeded smoothly.

Colombia*

Archd., 13; dioc., 51; v.a., 10; mil. ord., 1; card., 3; abp., 20; bp., 94; parishes, 3,831; priests, 8,239 (5,906 dioc., 2,333 rel.); p.d., 298; sem., 4,722; bros., 1,071 srs., 16,972; catechists, 46,744; bap., 677,533; Caths., 39,570,000 (88%); tot. pop., 45,390,000.

Republic in northwest South America; capital, Bogotá. Evangelization began in 1508. The first two dioceses were established in 1534. Vigorous development of the Church was reported by the middle of the 17th century despite obstacles posed by the multiplicity of Indian languages, government interference through patronage rights, rivalry among religious orders and the small number of native American priests among the predominantly Spanish clergy. Some persecution, including the confiscation of property, followed in the wake of the proclamation of independence from Spain in 1819. Guerrilla warfare aimed at Marxist-oriented radical social reform and redistribution of land, along with violence related to drug traffic, has plagued the country since the 1960s, posing problems for the Church, which backed reforms but rejected actions of radical groups. In the late 20th and early 21st centuries, the Church worked as a mediator between the government and guerrillas, but Church leaders suffered threats, attacks, and sometimes death, including from paramilitaries. For example, on Mar. 16, 2002, Abp. Isaias Duarte Cancino of Cali was shot to death for speaking out about the political situation; he was one of at least 10 Church workers killed in 2002.

Comoros

A.a., 1; parishes, 2; missions, 4; priests, 4 (1 dioc., 3 rel.); bros., 1; srs., 8; catechists, 12; bap., 19; Caths., 4,000 (.02%); tot. pop., 790,000. (AD)

Consists of main islands of Grande Comore, Anjouan and Moheli in Indian Ocean off southeast coast of Africa; capital, Moroni, Grande Comore Island. Former French territory; independent (July 6, 1975). The majority of the population is Muslim. An apostolic administration was established in 1975.

Congo, Democratic Republic of *

Archd., 6; dioc., 41; card., 1; abp., 6; bp., 57; parishes, 1,272; priests, 4,612 (2,903 dioc., 1,709 rel.); sem., 2,963; bros., 1,340; srs., 7,577; catechists, 71,180; bap., 421,872; Caths., 30,258,000 (53%); tot. pop., 57,223,000.

Republic in south central Africa; capital, Kinshasa. Christianity was introduced in 1484 and evangelization began about 1490. The first bishop from black Africa was ordained in 1518. Subsequent missionary work was hindered by factors including 18th- and 19th-century anticlericalism. Modern evangelization started in the second half of the 19th century. The hierarchy was established in 1959. In the civil disorders that followed independence in 1960, some missions and other Church installations were abandoned, thousands of people reverted to tribal religions and many priests and religious were killed.

Church-state tensions developed in the late 1980s and 1990s because of the Church's criticism of President Mobutu Sese Seko, who called a 1990 bishops' pastoral letter seditious. In 1992, after troops fired on thousands of protesters and killed 13, the government blamed priests who organized the march. In 1992, Archbishop Laurent Monswengo Pasinya was named president of a council charged with drafting a new constitution and overseeing a transition to democracy, but Mobutu supporters blocked effective change, and the archbishop resigned in 1994. As government and rebel forces battled in the Bukavu region of the country in 1996, Archbishop Christophe Munzihirwa Mwene Ngabo was killed in unclear circumstances. In the ensuing years of civil war, in which neighboring countries became involved, Church personnel worked to meet humanitarian needs and to promote peace through dialogue, but often were targeted for their work. Rebels forced one bishop into exile and house arrest for seven months.

Congo, Republic of *

Archd., 1; dioc., 5; p.a., 1; abp., 2; bp., 6; parishes, 164; priests, 285 (219 dioc., 66 rel.); sem., 288; bros., 44; srs., 344; catechists, 4,822; bap., 28,009; Caths., 2,216,000 (58%); tot. pop., 3,818,000.

Republic (independent since 1960) in west central Africa; former French possession; capital, Brazzaville. Small-scale missionary work with little effect preceded modern evangelization dating from the 1880s. The work of the Church has been affected by political instability, communist influence, tribalism and hostility to foreigners. The hierarchy was established in 1955. In 1992 Bishop Ernest Kombo of Owando was appointed chief organizer of the country's parliamentary elections. In 1994, the Church canceled independence day celebrations after more than 142 Catholics, mostly children, were crushed or suffocated in a rain-induced stampede at a Catholic church in Brazzaville. During renewed violence in the late 1990s, the bishops appealed for peace and stability.

Costa Rica*

Archd., 1; dioc., 7; abp., 3; bp., 10; parishes, 274; priests, 727 (526 dioc., 201 rel.); sem., 173; p.d., 5; bros., 73; srs., 892; catechists, 11,916; bap., 41,492; Caths., 3,628,000 (86%); tot. pop., 4,218,000.

Republic in Central America; capital, San José. Evangelization began about 1520 and proceeded by degrees to real development and organization of the Church in the 17th and 18th centuries. The republic became independent in 1838. Twelve years later Church jurisdiction also became independent with the establishment of a diocese in the present capital.

Côte d'Ivoire (Ivory Coast)*

Archd., 4; dioc., 10; card., 1; abp., 5; bp., 13; parishes, 278; priests, 978 (738 dioc., 240 rel.); p.d., 7; sem., 585; bros., 375; srs., 820; catechists, 13,342; bap., 45,304; Caths., 3,156,000 (17%); tot. pop., 18,550,000.

Republic in western Africa; capital, Abidjan. The Holy Ghost Fathers began systematic evangelization in 1895. The first priests from the area were ordained in 1934. The hierarchy was set up in 1955; the first indigenous cardinal (Bernard Yago) was named in 1983. In 1990 Pope John Paul II consecrated the continent's biggest, most costly and most controversial cathedral in Yamoussoukro. The pope only agreed to accept the cathedral after convincing the country's president to build an adjacent hospital and youth center.

Croatia*

Archd., 4; dioc., 10; mil. ord., 1; abp., 8; bp., 16; parishes, 1,574; priests, 2,342 (1,507 dioc., 835 rel.); p.d., 2; sem., 394; bros., 87; srs., 3,714; catechists, 1,815; bap., 37,291; Caths., 3,839,000 (86%); tot. pop., 4,455,000.

Independent (1991) republic in southeastern Europe; capital Zagreb; formerly a constituent republic of Yugoslavia. Christianity was introduced in the seventh century. On-again, off-again fighting from 1991 to 1995 pitted mostly Catholic Croats against mostly Orthodox Serbs. In 1995, Croatian bishops issued guidelines for rebuilding the nation including suppressing feelings of vengeance toward Serbs. However, in 1996 the head of Croatia's Helsinki human rights committee criticized the bishops for taking a weak stance on Croat abuses after the 1995 Croatian recapture of the Serb-occupied Krajina region. Pope John Paul II's 1998 beatification of Croatian Cardinal Alojzije Stepinac generated controversy among some Serb and Jewish leaders, who considered the cardinal a Nazi sympathizer.

Cuba*

Archd., 3; dioc., 8; card., 1; abp., 3; bp., 8; parishes, 299; priests, 333 (193 dioc., 140 rel.); p.d., 61; sem.,

97; bros., 33; srs., 657; catechists, 4,717; bap., 71,624; Caths. 6,342,000 (56%); tot. pop., 11,240,000.

Republic under Communist dictatorship, south of Florida; capital, Havana. Effective evangelization began about 1514, leading eventually to the predominance of Catholicism on the island. Vocations to the priesthood and religious life were unusually numerous in the 18th century but declined in the 19th. The island became independent of Spain in 1902 following the Spanish-American War.

Fidel Castro took control of the government Jan. 1, 1959. In 1961, after Cuba was officially declared a socialist state, the University of Villanueva was closed, 350 Catholic schools were nationalized and 136 priests expelled. A greater number of foreign priests and religious had already left the country. Freedom of worship and religious instruction were limited to Church premises and no social action was permitted by the Church, which survived under surveillance. A new constitution approved in 1976 guaranteed freedom of conscience but restricted its exercise. Small improvements in Church-state relations occurred in the late 1980s and early 1990s. In December 1997, just before Pope John Paul II's historic visit, the government allowed public celebration of Christmas, banned for 30 years. Although the pope's January 1998 visit was seen as a new dawn for the Church on the islands, Cuban Catholics say change has come slowly. The last several years have witnessed a return of political oppression.

Cyprus*

Archd., 1 (Maronite); abp., 1; parishes, 13; priests, 20 (8 dioc., 12 rel.); sem., 1; bros., 8; srs., 48; bap., 75; Caths., 17,000 (2.2%); tot. pop., 786,000.

Republic in the eastern Mediterranean; capital, Nicosia. Christianity was preached on the island in apostolic times and has a continuous history from the fourth century. Latin and Eastern rites were established but the latter prevailed and became Orthodox after the schism of 1054. Christians have suffered under many governments, particularly during the period of Turkish dominion from late in the 16th to late in the 19th centuries, and from differences between the 80 percent Greek majority and the Turkish minority. About 80 percent of the population are Orthodox.

Czech Republic*

Archd., 2; dioc., 6; ap. ex., 1; card., 2; abp., 2; bp., 16; parishes, 3,097; priests, 1,964 (1,354 dioc., 610 rel.); p.d., 154; sem., 227; bros., 112; srs., 1,998; catechists, 1,194; bap., 23,492; Caths., 3,399,000 (34%); tot. pop., 10,281,000.

Independent state (Jan. 1, 1993); formerly part of Czechoslovakia; capital, Prague. The martyrdom of Prince Wenceslaus in 929 triggered the spread of Christianity. Prague has had a continuous history as a diocese since 973. A parish system was organized about the 13th century in Bohemia and Moravia. Mendicant orders strengthened relations with the Latin rite in the 13th century. In the following century the teachings of John Hus in Bohemia brought trouble to the Church in the forms of schism and heresy and initiated a series of religious wars that continued for decades following his death at the stake in 1415. So many of the faithful joined the Bohemian Brethren that Catholics became a minority.

In the 1560s, a Counter-Reformation got under way and led to a gradual restoration through the thickets of Josephinism, the Enlightenment, liberalism and troubled politics. St. Jan Sarkander, a priest accused of helping an invading Polish army, was killed by Protestants in 1620. (His 1995 canonization caused strains with the Protestant community.)

In 1920, two years after the establishment of the Republic of Czechoslovakia, the schismatic Czechoslovak Church was proclaimed at Prague, resulting in numerous defections from the Catholic Church in the Czech region. Following the accession of the Gottwald regime to power early in 1948, persecution began in the Czech part of Czechoslovakia. A number of theatrical trials of bishops and priests were staged in 1950. Pressure was applied on Eastern Catholics in Slovakia to join the Orthodox Church. Diplomatic relations with the Holy See were terminated in 1950. In the following decade, thousands of priests were arrested and hundreds were deported, and attempts were made to force government-approved "peace priests" on the people. Pope Pius XII granted the Czech Church emergency powers to appoint clergy during the communist persecution.

From January to October 1968, Church-state relations improved to some extent under the Dubcek regime: a number of bishops were reinstated; some priests were still barred from priestly work; the "peace priests" organization was disbanded. The Eastern Catholic Church was re-established. In 1969, rehabilitation trials for priests and religious ended, but there was no wholesale restoration of priests and religious to their proper ways of life and work. Government restrictions continued to hamper the work of priests and nuns. Signatories of the human rights declaration Charter 77 were particular objects of government repression and retribution.

In December 1983, the Czechoslovakian foreign minister met with the pope at Vatican City; it was the first meeting of a high Czech official with a pope since the country had been under communist rule. In 1988, three new bishops were ordained in Czechoslovakia, the first since 1973. The communist government fell in late 1989. In 1990, bishops were appointed to fill vacant sees; diplomatic relations between the Holy See and Czechoslovakia were re-established, and Pope John Paul II visited the country. In 1997 the issue of married Czech priests secretly ordained under communist rule was resolved when they began work in the country's new Eastern Catholic jurisdiction. Under a 1949 communist decree declaring priests Culture Ministry employees, Czech priests were still paid by the state. A Church spokesman said confiscation of Church property under communist rule left priests still financially dependent on the state.

Denmark*

Dioc., 1; bp., 2; parishes, 48; priests, 78 (35 dioc., 43 rel.); p.d., 9; sem., 23; bros., 5; srs., 194; bap., 603; Caths., 37,000 (.6%); tot. pop., 5,413,000.

Includes the Faroe Islands and Greenland. Constitutional monarchy in northwestern Europe; capital, Copenhagen. Christianity was introduced in the ninth century and the first diocese for the area was established in 831. Intensive evangelization and full-scale organization of the Church occurred from the second half of the 10th century and ushered in a period of great development and influence in the 12th and 13th centuries. Decline followed, resulting in almost total loss to the Church during the Reformation, when Lutheranism became the national religion. A few Catholic families practiced the faith secretly until religious freedom was legally assured in the mid-1800s. Since then, immigration has increased the number of Catholics. About 95 percent of the population are Evangelical Lutherans.

Catholicism was introduced in Greenland, a Danish island province northeast of North America, about 1000. The first diocese was established in 1124 and a line of bishops dated from then until 1537. The first known churches in the Western Hemisphere, dating from about the 11th century, were on Greenland. The departure of Scandinavians and spread of the Reformation reduced the Church to nothing. The Moravian Brethren evangelized the Inuit from the 1720s to 1901. By 1930 the Danish Church — Evangelical Lutheran — was in full possession. Since 1930, priests have been in Greenland, which is part of the Copenhagen Diocese.

Djibouti*

Dioc., 1; bp., 2; parishes, 5; priests, 7 (2 dioc., 5 rel.); bros., 6; srs., 24; catechists, 15; sem., 1; bap., 14; Caths., 7,000 (1%); tot. pop., 712,000. (AD)

Independent (1977) republic in East Africa; capital, Djibouti. Christianity in the area, formerly part of Ethiopia, antedated but was overcome by the Arab invasion of 1200. Modern evangelization, begun in the latter part of the 19th century, had meager results. The hierarchy was established in 1955. Formal diplomatic relations with the Holy See were established in May 2000.

Dominica*

Dioc., 1; bp., 1; parishes, 15; priests, 49 (6 dioc., 42 rel.); sem., 10; bros., 11; srs., 21; catechists, 474; bap., 608; Caths., 42,000 (79%); tot. pop., 75,000.

Independent (Nov. 3, 1978) state in Caribbean; capital, Roseau. Evangelization began in 1642.

Dominican Republic*

Archd., 2; dioc., 9; mil. ord., 1; v.a., 1; card., 1; abp., 3; bp., 16; parishes, 566; priests, 910 (461 dioc., 449 rel.); p.d., 367; sem., 678; bros., 159; srs., 2,986; catechists, 40,428; bap., 105,044; Caths., 7,923,000 (90%); tot. pop., 8,870,000.

Caribbean republic on the eastern two-thirds of the island of Hispaniola, bordering on Haiti; capital, Santo Domingo. Evangelization began shortly after discovery by Columbus in 1492 and Church organization, the first in America, was established by 1510. Catholicism is the state religion. Pope John Paul II visited the country in 1992 to mark the quincentennial celebrations of Columbus's discovery. The pope also opened the Fourth General conference of the Latin American Episcopate there. Church leaders worked to end social injustices, including the plight of mistreated sugar cane workers.

East Timor*

Dioc., 2; bp., 2; parishes, 37; priests, 159 (65 dioc., 94 rel.); sem., 141; p.d., 1; bros., 31; srs., 366; catechists, 1,716; bap., 28,418; Caths., 767,000 (93%); tot. pop., 824,000.

Independent (May 2002) state; capital, Dili. The predominantly Catholic former Portuguese colony was invaded by Indonesia in 1975 and annexed the following year. Most countries did not recognize the annexation. The Catholic Church worked to bring peace between the Indonesian government and guerrilla forces seeking independence. Bishop Carlos Filipe

Ximenes Belo, former apostolic administrator of Dili, was a co-winner of the 1996 Nobel Peace Prize for his peace efforts. In 1999, dozens of civilians— including more than two dozen at a Catholic church — were killed during a terror campaign waged by pro-Indonesia paramilitaries in the run-up to an August vote on independence for East Timor. Indonesian troops withdrew, and in August 2001, East Timor held elections for a transitional government. The Church has worked on peace and reconciliation issues and at raising awareness of social issues.

Ecuador*

Archd., 4; dioc., 11; v.a., 7; p.a., 1; mil. ord., 1; card., 1; abp., 7; bp., 31; parishes, 1,215; priests, 1,997 (1,157 dioc., 840 rel.); p.d., 74; sem., 750; bros., 404; srs., 5,451; catechists, 38,870; bap., 235,305; Caths., 11,952,000 (92%); tot. pop., 13,030,000.

Republic on the west coast of South America, includes Galápagos Islands; capital, Quito. Evangelization began in the 1530s. The first diocese was established in 1545. Multi-phased missionary work, spreading from the coastal and mountain regions into the Amazon, made the Church highly influential during the colonial period. The Church was practically enslaved by the constitution enacted in 1824, two years after Ecuador, as part of Colombia, gained independence from Spain. Some change for the better took place later in the century, but from 1891 until the 1930s the Church labored under serious liabilities imposed by liberal governments. Foreign missionaries were barred from the country for some time; the property of religious orders was confiscated; education was taken over by the state; traditional state support was refused; legal standing was denied; attempts to control Church offices were made through insistence on rights of patronage. A period of harmony and independence for the Church began after agreement was reached on Church-state relations in 1937. In 1998, the Church was actively involved in peace talks that ended a border dispute of some 170 years with Peru. As the 20th century came to a close, Ecuador's bishops were working to fight social turmoil and the results of severe economic austerity measures.

Egypt*

Patriarchates, 2 (Alexandria for the Copts and for the Melkites); dioc., 11; v.a., 1; ex., 1; patriarch, 1; card., 1; abp., 3; bp., 16; parishes, 206; priests, 501 (213 dioc., 288 rel.); p.d., 3; sem., 88; bros., 66; srs., 1,308; catechists, 1,986; bap., 2,995; Caths., 311,000 (.42%); tot. pop., 73,437,000.

Arab Republic in northeastern Africa; capital, Cairo. Alexandria was the influential hub of a Christian community established by the end of the second century; it became a patriarchate and the center of the Coptic Church and had great influence on the spread of Christianity in various parts of Africa. Monasticism developed from desert communities of hermits in the third and fourth centuries. Arianism was first preached in Egypt in the 320s. In the fifth century, the Coptic Church went Monophysite through failure to accept doctrine formulated by the Council of Chalcedon in 451 with respect to the two natures of Christ. The country was thoroughly Arabized after 640 and was under the rule of Ottoman Turks from 1517 to 1798.

Islam, the religion of some 90 percent of the population, is the state religion. The tiny Catholic minority has a dialogue with the Muslims, but sometimes each side treats the other warily and with mistrust. Pope John Paul II's visit to Cairo and Mount Sinai in 2000 was considered to have given impetus to interreligious dialogue.

El Salvador*

Archd., 1; dioc., 7; mil. ord., 1; abp., 2; bp., 11; parishes, 405; priests, 731 (487 dioc., 244 rel.); p.d., 3; sem., 598; bros., 84; srs., 1,428; catechists, 14,068; bap., 80,107; Cath., 5,386,000 (77%); tot. pop., 6,760,000.

Republic in Central America; capital, San Salvador. Evangelization affecting the whole territory followed Spanish occupation in the 1520s. The country was administered by the captaincy general of Guatemala until 1821, when independence from Spain was declared and it was annexed to Mexico. El Salvador joined the Central American Federation in 1825, declared independence in 1841 and became a republic formally in 1856.

During the country's 1980-92 civil war, Church leaders worked to achieve social justice. The San Salvador Archdiocese's human rights office, Tutela Legal, documented abuses and political killings and offered legal support to victims, despite Church persecution. Archbishop Oscar Romero of San Salvador, peace advocate and outspoken champion of human rights, was murdered Mar. 24, 1980, while celebrating Mass. Four U.S. Church women were murdered the same year. Six Jesuits and two lay women were assassinated Nov. 16, 1989, at Central American University in El Salvador. Church leaders, particularly Archbishop Romero's successor, Archbishop Arturo Rivera Damas, were active in the peace process. In the 1990s, Church-government relations cooled. Church leaders often urged the U.S. government not to deport the hundreds of thousands of Salvadoran refugees who lived, often illegally, in the United States, and sent money to their families in El Salvador. The situation worsened after the destruction caused by Hurricane Mitch in 1998.

England*

Archd., 4; dioc., 15; ap. ex., 1; mil. ord. (Great Britain), 1; card., 1; abp., 5; bp., 32; parishes, 2,428; priests, 4,558 (3,249 dioc., 1,309 rel.); p.d., 619; sem., 147; bros., 1,751; srs., 5,868; bap., 59,328; Caths., 3,922,317 (8.8%; tot. Catholic pop. for Great Britain: 4,626,694); tot. pop., 44,420,822 (tot. pop. for Great Britain: 49,420,929). Note: England and Wales share a joint Episcopal Conference; see also **Scotland** and **Wales**.

Center of the United Kingdom of Great Britain (England, Scotland, Wales) and Northern Ireland, off the northwestern coast of Europe; capital, London. The arrival of St. Augustine of Canterbury and a band of monks in 597 marked the beginning of evangelization. Real organization of the Church took place some years after the Synod of Whitby, held in 663. Heavy losses were sustained in the wake of the Danish invasion in the 780s, but recovery starting from the time of Alfred the Great and dating especially from the middle of the 10th century led to Christianization of the whole country and close Church-state relations. The Norman Conquest of 1066 opened the Church in England to European influence. The Church began to decline in numbers in the 13th century. In the 14th century, John Wycliff presaged the Protestant Reformation.

Henry VIII, failing in 1529 to gain annulment of his marriage to Catherine of Aragon, refused to acknowledge papal authority over the Church in England, had himself proclaimed its head, suppressed all houses of religious, and persecuted people — Sts. Thomas More and John Fisher, among others — for not subscribing to the Oath of Supremacy and Act of Succession. He held the line on other-than-papal doctrine, however, until his death in 1547. Doctrinal aberrations were introduced during the reign of Edward VI (1547-53), through the Order of Communion, two books of Common Prayer, and the Articles of the Established Church. Mary Tudor's attempted Catholic restoration (1553-58) was a disaster, resulting in the deaths of more than 300 Protestants. Elizabeth (1558-1603) firmed up the established Church with the aid of Matthew Parker, archbishop of Canterbury, with formation of a hierarchy, legal enactments and multiphased persecution. More than 100 priests and 62 lay persons were among the casualties of persecution during the underground Catholic revival that followed the return to England of missionary priests from France and the Lowlands.

Several periods of comparative tolerance ensued after Elizabeth's death. The first of several apostolic vicariates was established in 1685; this form of Church government was maintained until the restoration of the hierarchy and diocesan organization in 1850. The revolution of 1688 and subsequent developments to about 1781 subjected Catholics to a wide variety of penal laws and disabilities in religious, civic and social life. The situation began to improve in 1791, and from 1801 Parliament frequently considered proposals for the repeal of penal laws against Catholics.

The Act of Emancipation restored citizenship rights to Catholics in 1829. Restrictions remained in force for some time afterward, however, on public religious worship and activity. The hierarchy was restored in 1850. Since then the Catholic Church, existing side by side with the established Churches of England and Scotland, has followed a general pattern of growth and development. After the Church of England began ordaining women priests in 1994, more than 200 Anglican priests and four Anglican bishops were received into the Catholic Church, although many said ordination of women was not their primary reason for leaving. In the late 20th and early 21st centuries, the Church was active in the prolife movement and was outspoken on bioethical issues. (See also **Ireland, Northern**)

Equatorial Guinea*

Archd., 1; dioc., 2; abp., 1; bp., 2; parishes, 68; priests, 120 (65 dioc., 55 rel.); p.d. 2; sem., 73; bros., 48; srs., 223; catechists, 1,686; bap., 16,284; Caths., 460,000 (88%); tot. pop., 507,000.

Republic on the west coast of Africa, consisting of Rio Muni on the mainland and the islands of Bioko and Annobon in the Gulf of Guinea: capital, Malabo. Evangelization began in 1841. The country became independent of Spain in 1968. The Church was severely repressed during the 11-year rule of President Macias Nguema. Developments since his overthrow in 1979 indicated some measure of improvement. An ecclesiastical province was established in October 1982.

In the 1990s, bishops worked to educate Catholics about the need for social justice and respect for human rights. In mid-1998, the government expelled three foreign missionaries involved in development programs partially funded by the United States.

Eritrea*

Dioc., 3; bp., 5; parishes, 125; priests, 381 (82 dioc., 299 rel); sem., 187; bros., 121; srs., 702; catechists, 178; bap., 3,245; Caths., 150,000 (3.5%); tot. pop., 4,297,000.

Independent state (May 24, 1993) in northeast Africa; formerly a province of Ethiopia. Christianity was introduced in the fourth century. Population is evenly divided between Christians and Muslims. Catholics form a small minority; most of the population is Orthodox or Muslim. In 1995, two new dioceses were established, but because of three decades of civil war, the dioceses had no facilities and little staffing. In 1998 the government announced plans to take over private schools and health clinics, most of which were run by the Church. Eritrean bishops form an episcopal conference with Ethiopia, and the bishops of the two countries frequently appealed for peace during their governments' border war.

Estonia*

A.a., 1; abp., 1 (nuncio is apostolic administrator); parishes, 8; priests, 9 (6 dioc., 3 rel); sem., 1; srs., 20; bap., 62; Caths., 6,000 (.43%); tot. pop., 1,365,000.

Independent (1991) Baltic republic; capital, Tallinn. (Forcibly absorbed by the USSR in 1940, it regained independence in 1991.) Catholicism was introduced in the 11th and 12th centuries. Jurisdiction over the area was made directly subject to the Holy See in 1215. Lutheran penetration was general in the Reformation period, and Russian Orthodox influence was strong from early in the 18th century until 1917, when independence was attained. The first of several apostolic administrators was appointed in 1924. The small Catholic community was hard-hit during the 1940-91 Soviet occupation (not recognized by the Holy See or the United States). Since its independence, the small Catholic community in Estonia has worked to re-establish Catholic theology and education. In 1999 the Holy See and government of Estonia reached agreement on a number of issues, including guarantees that the Church could name its own bishops and that priests from abroad would be able to continue to work in the country.

Ethiopia*

Archd., 1; dioc., 2; v.a., 5; p.a., 2; abp., 2; bp., 8; parishes, 267; priests, 446 (217 dioc., 229 rel.); p.d., 1; sem., 283; bros., 90; srs., 680; catechists, 2,462; bap., 24,392; Caths., 551,000 (.8%); tot. pop., 71,260,000.

People's republic in northeast Africa; capital, Addis Ababa. The country was evangelized by missionaries from Egypt in the fourth century and had a bishop by about 340. Following the lead of its parent body, the Egyptian (Coptic) Church, the Church in the area suc-

cumbed to the Monophysite heresy in the sixth century. An apostolic delegation was set up in Addis Ababa in 1937 and several jurisdictions were organized, some under Vatican congregations. The northern Church jurisdictions follow the Alexandrian rite, while the southern part of the country is Latin rite. The small Church has good relations with Orthodox and Protestant Churches, all of which face the task of helping people move from a rural society to a more modern society without losing Christian identity. Although the constitution calls for religious freedom, treatment of the churches can vary in different localities. The bishops share an episcopal conference with the Eritrean bishops, and the bishops of the two countries frequently appealed for peace during their governments' border war.

Falkland Islands

P.a., 1; parish, 1; srs., 1; bap., 1; Caths., 200 (approx.) (10%); tot. pop., 2,000 (approx).

British colony off the southern tip of South America; capital, Port Stanley. The islands are called Islas Malvinas by Argentina, which also claims sovereignty.

Fiji*

Archd., 1; abp., 1; parishes, 35; priests, 146 (34 dioc., 92 rel.); p.d., 1; sem., 61; bros., 53; srs., 145; bap., 1,836; catechists, 504; Caths., 92,000 (9%); tot. pop., 982,000.

Independent island group (100 inhabited) in the southwest Pacific; capital, Suva. Marist missionaries began work in 1844 after Methodism had been firmly established. An apostolic prefecture was organized in 1863. The hierarchy was established in 1966.

Finland*

Dioc., 1; bp., 1; parishes, 7; priests, 18 (5 dioc., 13 rel.); p.d., 1; sem., 14; srs., 37; bap., 168; Caths., 9,000 (.01%); tot. pop., 5,230,000.

Republic in northern Europe; capital, Helsinki. Swedes evangelized the country in the 12th century. The Reformation swept the country, resulting in the prohibition of Catholicism in 1595, general reorganization of ecclesiastical life and affairs, and dominance of the Evangelical Lutheran Church. Catholics were given religious liberty in 1781 but missionaries and conversions were forbidden by law. The first Finnish priest since the Reformation was ordained in 1903 in Paris. An apostolic vicariate for Finland was erected in 1920 (made a diocese in 1955). A law on religious liberty, enacted in 1923, banned the foundation of monasteries.

France*

Archd., 23; dioc., 71; prel., 1; ap. ex., 2; mil. ord., 1; card., 9; abp., 37; bp., 142; parishes, 17,955; priests, 22,185 (16,859 dioc., 5,326 rel.); p.d., 1,947; sem., 1,255; bros., 3,030; srs., 41,761; catechists, 69,107; bap., 357,262; Caths., 45,988,000 (77%); tot. pop., 60,051,000.

Republic in Western Europe; capital, Paris. Christianity was known around Lyons by the middle of the second century. By 250 there were 30 dioceses. The hierarchy reached a fair degree of organization by the end of the fourth century. Vandals and Franks subsequently invaded the territory and caused barbarian turmoil and doctrinal problems because of their Arianism. The Frankish nation was converted following the baptism of Clovis about 496. Christianization was complete by some time in the seventh century. From then on the Church, its leaders and people, figured in virtually every important development — religious, cultural, political and social — through the periods of the Carolingians, feudalism, the Middle Ages and monarchies to the end of the 18th century. The University of Paris became one of the intellectual centers of the 13th century. Churchmen and secular rulers were involved with developments surrounding the Avignon residence of the popes and curia from 1309 until near the end of the 14th century and with the disastrous Western Schism that followed.

Strong currents of Gallicanism and conciliarism ran through ecclesiastical and secular circles in France; the former was an ideology and movement to restrict papal control of the Church in the country, the latter sought to make the pope subservient to a general council. Calvinism entered the country about the middle of the 16th century and won a strong body of converts. Jansenism appeared in the next century, to be followed by the highly influential Enlightenment. The Revolution, which started in 1789 and was succeeded by the Napoleonic period, completely changed the status of the Church, taking a toll of numbers by persecution and defection and disenfranchising the Church in practically every way. Throughout the 19th century the Church was caught up in the whirl of imperial and republican developments and was made the victim of official hostility, popular indifference and liberal opposition.

In the 20th century, the Church struggled with problems involving the heritage of the Revolution and its aftermath, the alienation of intellectuals, liberalism, the estrangement of the working classes because of the Church's former identification with the ruling class, and the massive needs of contemporary society. In the 1990s, French bishops fought a racist backlash that resulted from large-scale emigration from Africa.

Gabon*

Archd., 1; dioc., 4; p.a., 1; abp., 1; bp., 4; parishes, 73; priests, 121 (58 dioc., 63 rel.); p.d., 1; sem., 88; bros., 20; srs., 157; catechists, 1,547; bap., 9,723; Caths., 751,000 (55%); tot. pop., 1,351,000.

Republic on the west coast of central Africa; capital Libreville. Sporadic missionary effort took place before 1881 when effective evangelization began. The hierarchy was established in 1955. In 1993, Gabon's president defeated a Catholic priest in presidential elections. In the late 1990s, the government and the Holy See signed an agreement setting out the rights of the Church in society.

Gambia*

Dioc., 1; bp., 1; parishes, 54; priests, 26 (15 dioc., 11 rel.); sem., 3; bros., 12; srs., 49; bap., 1,527; Caths., 42,000 (2%); tot. pop., 1,462,000.

Republic (1970) on the northwestern coast of Africa; capital, Banjul. Christianity was introduced by Portuguese explorers in the 15th century; effective evangelization began in 1822. The country was under the jurisdiction of an apostolic vicariate until 1931. The hierarchy was established in 1957.

Georgia*

A.a., 1; parishes, 28; abp., 1; bp., 1; priests, 29 (15 dioc., 14 rel); sem., 12; brs. 3; srs., 25; bap, 78; Caths., 100,000 (1.9%); tot. pop., 4,291,000.

Independent (1991) state in the Caucasus; former Soviet republic; capital, Tbilisi. Christianity came to the area under Roman influence and, according to tradition, was spread through the efforts of St. Nino (or Christiana), a maiden who was brought as a captive to the country and is venerated as its apostle. The apostolic administration of the Caucasus (with seat in Georgia) was established in December 1993 for Latin-rite Catholics of Armenia, Azerbaijan and Georgia. Chaldean- and Armenian-rite Catholics also are present. Differences between Catholicism and Orthodoxy often are blurred on the parish level. The Catholic Church and the Armenian Orthodox Church have been unable to secure the return of Churches closed during the Soviet period, many of which were later given to the Georgian Orthodox Church. Early in 21st century, many denominations, including Catholics, reported attacks and harassment from Orthodox mobs.

Germany*

Archd., 7; dioc., 20; ap. ex., 1; mil. ord., 1; card., 6; abp., 9; bp., 94; parishes, 12,310; priests, 18,570 (14,165 dioc., 4,407 rel.); p.d., 2,554; sem., 1,204; bros., 1,634; srs., 33,214; catechists, 12,752; bap., 201,041; Caths., 26,032,000 (33.2%); tot. pop., 82,500,000.

Country in northern Europe; capital, Berlin. From 1949-90 it was partitioned into the Communist German Democratic Republic in the East (capital, East Berlin) and the German Federal Republic in the West (capital, Bonn). Christianity was introduced in the third century, if not earlier. Trier, which became a center for missionary activity, had a bishop by 400. Visigoth invaders introduced Arianism in the fifth century but were converted in the seventh century by the East Franks, Celtic and other missionaries. St. Boniface, the apostle of Germany, established real ecclesiastical organization in the eighth century.

Beginning in the Carolingian period, bishops began to act in dual roles as pastors and rulers, a state of affairs that inevitably led to confusion and conflict in Church-state relations and perplexing problems of investiture. The Church developed strength and vitality through the Middle Ages but succumbed to abuses that antedated and prepared the ground for the Reformation. Martin Luther's actions from 1517 made Germany a confessional battleground. Religious strife continued until the conclusion of the Peace of Westphalia at the end of the Thirty Years' War in 1648. Nearly a century earlier the Peace of Augsburg (1555) had been designed, without success, to assure a degree of tranquility by recognizing the legitimacy of different religious confessions in different states, depending on the decisions of princes. The implicit principle that princes should control the churches emerged in practice into the absolutism and Josephinism of subsequent years. St. Peter Canisius and his fellow Jesuits spearheaded a Counter Reformation in the second half of the 16th century. Before the end of the century, however, 70 percent of the population of north and central Germany were Lutheran. Calvinism also had established a strong presence.

The Church suffered some impoverishment as a result of shifting boundaries and the secularization of property shortly after 1800. It came under direct attack in the Kulturkampf of the 1870s but helped to generate the opposition that resulted in a dampening of the campaign of Bismarck against it. Despite action by Catholics on the social front and other developments, discrimination against the Church spilled over into the 20th century and lasted beyond World War I. Catholics in politics struggled with others to pull the country through numerous postwar crises. The dissolution of the Center Party, agreed to by the bishops in 1933 without awareness of the ultimate consequences, contributed in part to the rise of Hitler to supreme power. Church officials protested the Nazi anti-Church and anti-Semitic actions, but to no avail.

After World War II East Germany, compelled to communism under Soviet domination, initiated a program of control and repression of the Church. The regime eliminated religious schools, curtailed freedom for religious instruction and formation, and restricted the religious press. Beginning in the mid-1950s, the communists substituted youth initiation and Communist ceremonies for many sacraments. Bishops were generally forbidden to travel outside the Republic. The number of priests decreased, partly because of reduced seminary enrollments ordered by the East German government.

The official reunification of Germany took place Oct. 3, 1990, and the separate episcopal conferences were merged to form one conference in November. During the 1990s, the united German bishops fought against introduction of the former East Germany's more liberal abortion law. When a high-court decision allowed a woman to obtain an abortion after visiting a state-approved counseling center and obtaining proof she had been counseled, German Church leaders searched for a compromise position, since they ran more than 250 such centers. In 1999, Pope John Paul II asked the German bishops to include a line on the proof-of-counseling certificate that said it could not be used for abortion, but some German states said they would not consider the line valid. Eventually, most of the bishops withdrew their centers from the system. As the 20th century came to an end, German Church leaders also spoke on behalf of immigrants, refugees and asylum seekers and against a surge in racist and anti-Semitic attacks. Early in the 21st century, a change in the country's tax rate and growing unemployment led to a severe budget crisis for many German dioceses.

Ghana*

Archd., 4; dioc., 14; card., 2; abp., 4; bp., 16; parishes, 379; priests, 1,115 (919 dioc., 196 rel.); p.d., 2; sem., 648; bros., 191; srs., 815; catechists, 6,252; bap., 49,827; Caths., 2,652,000 (12%); tot. pop., 21,962,000.

Republic on the western coast of Africa; capital, Accra. Priests visited the country in 1482, 11 years after discovery by the Portuguese, but missionary effort, hindered by the slave trade and other factors, was slight until 1880 when systematic evangelization began. An apostolic prefecture was set up in 1879. The hierarchy was established in 1950.

In 1985, the government shut down the Church's newspaper, The Catholic Standard, for criticizing the government; in 1989 the government ordered religious bodies to register. However, in 1992 the paper resumed publication, and five new dioceses were established in 1995. In 1997 the bishops issued a pastoral letter urging an end to political corruption and ethnic tension.

Gibraltar

Dioc., 1; bp., 2; parishes, 5; priests, 15 (14 dioc., 1 rel.); sem., 1; bros., 2; srs., 8; bap., 325; Caths., 21,000 (72%); tot. pop., 27,000.

British dependency on the tip of the Spanish Peninsula on the Mediterranean. Evangelization took place after the Moors were driven out near the end of the 15th century. The Church was hindered by the British, who acquired the colony in 1713. Most of the Catholics were, and are, Spanish and Italian immigrants and their descendants. An apostolic vicariate was organized in 1817. The diocese was erected in 1910.

Great Britain **(See separate entries for** England, Scotland, Wales, Northern Ireland)

Greece*

Archd., 4; dioc., 4; v.a., 1; ap. ex., 2; abp., 7; bp., 3; parishes, 88; priests, 96 (55 dioc., 41 rel.); p.d., 2; sem., 3; bros., 28; srs., 129; bap., 599; Caths., 128,000 (1%); tot. pop., 11,050,000.

Republic in southeastern Europe on the Balkan Peninsula; capital, Athens. St. Paul preached the Gospel at Athens and Corinth on his second missionary journey and visited the country again on his third tour. Other Apostles may have passed through. Two bishops from Greece attended the First Council of Nicaea. After the division of the Roman Empire, the Church remained Eastern in rite and later broke ties with Rome as a result of the schism of 1054. A Latin-rite jurisdiction was set up during the period of the Latin Empire of Constantinople, 1204-61, but crumbled afterward. Unity efforts of the Council of Florence had poor results and failed to save the Byzantine Empire from conquest by the Ottoman Empire in 1453. The country now has Latin, Byzantine and Armenian rites. The Greek Orthodox Church is predominant. The Catholic Church continues to work to obtain full legal rights. In May 2001, during the first papal visit to Greece since the eighth century, Pope John Paul II apologized for past wrongs against the Orthodox, including the 13th-century sack of Constantinople.

Greenland (Statistics for Greenland are included in Denmark)

Grenada*

Dioc., 1; bp., 2; parishes, 20; priests, 22 (2 dioc., 20 rel.); p.d., 3; sem., 3; bros., 3; srs., 29; catechists, 128; bap., 514; Caths., 56,000 (54%); tot. pop., 103,000.

Independent island state in the West Indies; capital, St. George's.

Guam

Archd., 1; abp., 1; parishes, 24; priests, 43 (31 dioc., 12 rel.); p.d., 20; sem., 22; bro., 1; srs., 107; bap., 1,928; catechists, 471; Caths., 131,000 (80%); tot. pop., 155,000.

Outlying area of U.S. in the southwest Pacific; capital, Agana. The first Mass was offered in the Mariana Islands in 1521. The islands were evangelized by the Jesuits, from 1668, and other missionaries. The first Micronesian bishop was ordained in 1970. The Agana Diocese, which had been a suffragan of San Francisco, was made a metropolitan see in 1984.

Guatemala*

Archd., 2; dioc., 10; prel., 1; v.a., 2; card., 1; abp., 3; bp., 20; parishes, 453; priests, 956 (471 dioc., 485 rel.); p.d., 7; sem., 310; bros., 166; srs., 2,664; catechists, 51,598; bap., 177,277; Caths. 10,066,000 (81%); tot. pop. 12,390,000.

Republic in Central America; capital, Guatemala City. Evangelization dates from the beginning of Spanish occupation in 1524. The first diocese, for all Central American territories administered by the captaincy general of Guatemala, was established in 1534. The country became independent in 1839, following annexation to Mexico in 1821, secession in 1823 and membership in the Central American Federation from 1825. In 1870, a government installed by a liberal revolution repudiated the concordat of 1853 and took active measures against the Church. Separation of Church and state was decreed; religious orders were suppressed and their property seized; priests and religious were exiled; schools were secularized. Full freedom was subsequently granted.

During the nation's 36-year civil war, which ended in 1996, Church officials spoke out against atrocities and illegal drafting of youths and often were persecuted. The Guatemala City archbishop's human rights office, established after decades of war, was one of the few agencies able to document abuses. Bishops participated in the country's peace process, at times withdrawing in an effort to force government and guerrilla leaders back to the table.

After the war, the archbishop's human rights office began an extensive project to help document abuses during the war. Two days after the report was released in April 1998, Auxiliary Bishop Juan Gerardi Conedera of Guatemala City, who headed the project, was murdered. In 2001, a priest who lived with the bishop and three military officers were convicted of involvement in the murder, but said they would appeal the decision. One of the three officers was killed in a Guatemala City prison riot in 2003. Church leaders mobilized to help Guatemalans after mudslides and flooding from Hurricane Stan in 2005 made it the country's worst natural disaster in nearly 30 years.

Guinea*

Archd., 1; dioc., 2; abp. 1; bp., 2; parishes, 61; priests, 108 (89 dioc., 19 rel.); sem., 46; bros., 18; srs., 58; catechists, 604; bap., 1,761; Caths., 233,000 (3%); tot. pop., 8,620,000.

Republic on the west coast of Africa; capital, Conakry. Occasional missionary work followed exploration by the Portuguese about the middle of the 15th century; organized effort dates from 1877. The hierarchy was established in 1955. Following independence from France in 1958, Catholic schools were nationalized, youth organizations banned and missionaries restricted. Foreign missionaries were expelled in 1967. Archbishop Raymond-Marie Tchidimbo of Conakry, sentenced to life imprisonment in 1971 on a charge of

conspiring to overthrow the government, was released in August 1979; he resigned his see. Private schools, suppressed by the government for more than 20 years, again were authorized in 1984.

Guinea-Bissau*

Dioc., 2; bp., 2; parishes, 35; priests, 71 (15 dioc., 56 rel.); sem., 22; bros., 12; srs., 135; bap., 2,576; catechists, 740; Caths., 122,000 (9.2%); tot. pop., 1,335,000.

Independent state on the west coast of Africa; capital, Bissau. Catholicism was introduced in the second half of the 15th century but limited missionary work, hampered by the slave trade, had meager results. Missionary work in the 20th century began in 1933. An apostolic prefecture was made a diocese in 1977. In 1998, Bishop Settimio Ferrazzetta of Bissau worked to mediate a crisis between the government and military leaders.

Guyana*

Dioc., 1; bp., 2; parishes, 24; priests, 35 (5 dioc., 30 rel.); p.d., 1; sem., 3; bros., 4; srs., 45; catechists, 588; bap., 719; Caths., 88,000 (10.2%); tot. pop., 800,000.

Republic on the north coast of South America; capital, Georgetown. In 1899 the Catholic Church and other churches were given equal status with the Church of England and the Church of Scotland. Most of the Catholics are Portuguese. The Georgetown Diocese was established in 1956, 10 years before Guyana became independent of England. The first indigenous bishop was appointed in 1971. Schools were nationalized in 1976. In the late 1970s and in the 1980s, The Catholic Standard newspaper was cited by the Inter-American Press Association as the "sole independent voice" in Guyana.

Haiti*

Archd., 2; dioc., 7; abp., 5; bp., 14; parishes, 317; priests, 713 (439 dioc., 274 rel.); p.d., 3; sem., 401; bros., 323; srs., 1,772; catechists, 5,279; bap., 97,881; Caths., 6,832,000 (81%); tot. pop., 8,419,000.

Caribbean republic on the western third of Hispaniola adjacent to the Dominican Republic; capital, Port-au-Prince. Evangelization followed discovery by Columbus in 1492. Capuchins and Jesuits did most of the missionary work in the 18th century. From 1804, when independence was declared, until 1860, the country was in schism. Relations were regularized by a concordat concluded in 1860, when an archdiocese and four dioceses were established.

In the second half of the 20th century, the Church worked to develop the small nation, considered among the poorest in the Western Hemisphere. In the 1980s and 1990s, priests and religious often were targets of political violence, which resulted in a series of coups. The Church was sometimes seen as the lone voice for the people and, at times, was seen as backing the government. A Salesian priest, Father Jean-Bertrand Aristide, known for his fiery, anti-government sermons, won the December 1990 president election, considered the first genuinely democratic vote in Haitian history. A 1991 military coup forced him into exile for three years and resulted in an international trade embargo against Haiti. Aristide was laicized by the Vatican and married in January 1996. In the late

1990s, the Church continued its service in the social field through programs in basic literacy and operation of schools and health facilities. Early in the 21st century, Church workers often decried worsening poverty and social injustices.

Honduras*

Archd., 1; dioc., 7; card., 1; abp., 2; bp., 8; parishes, 183; priests, 411 (203 dioc., 208 rel.); p.d., 1; sem., 167; bros., 33; srs., 820; catechists, 13,151; bap., 76,863; Caths., 5,727,000 (81%); tot. pop., 7,030,000.

Republic in Central America; capital, Tegucigalpa. Evangelization preceded establishment of the first diocese in the 16th century. Under Spanish rule and after independence from 1823, the Church held a favored position until 1880, when equal legal status was given to all religions. Harassment of priests and nuns working among indigenous peasants and Salvadoran refugees was reported during the years of Central American civil unrest in the late 20th century. In 1998 Hurricane Mitch killed more than 6,000 Hondurans and forced more than 2 million in the country to evacuate their homes. The Church took a lead role in post-hurricane relief and development efforts.

Hungary*

Archd., 4; dioc., 9; abb., 1; ap. ex., 1; mil. ord. 1; card., 2; abp., 5; bp., 21; parishes, 2,240; priests, 2,412 (1,894 dioc., 518 rel.); p.d., 54; sem., 353; bros., 80; srs., 1,368; catechists, 2,859; bap., 46,939; Caths., 6,176,000 (61%); tot. pop., 10,090,000.

Republic in east central Europe; capital, Budapest. The early origins of Christianity in the country, whose territory was subject to a great deal of change, is not known. Magyars accepted Christianity about the end of the 10th century. St. Stephen I promoted its spread and helped to organize some of its historical dioceses. Bishops became influential in politics as well as in the Church.

For centuries the country served as a buffer for the Christian West against barbarians from the East, notably the Mongols in the 13th century. Hussites and Waldensians prepared the way for the Reformation, which struck at almost the same time as the Turks. The Reformation made considerable progress after 1526, resulting in the conversion of large numbers to Lutheranism and Calvinism by the end of the century. Turks repressed the Churches, Protestant as well as Catholic, during a reign of 150 years, but they managed to survive. Domination of the Church was one of the objectives of government policy during the reigns of Maria Theresa and Joseph II in the second half of the 18th century; their Josephinism affected Church-state relations until World War I.

Secularization increased in the second half of the 19th century, which also witnessed the birth of many new Catholic organizations and movements. Catholics were involved in the social chaos and anti-religious atmosphere of the years following World War I, struggling with their compatriots for religious as well as political survival.

After World War II, the communist campaign against the Church started with the disbanding of Catholic organizations in 1946. In 1948, Caritas, the Catholic charitable organization, was taken over, and all Catholic institutions were suppressed. Interference in Church administration and attempts to split the bishops preceded the arrest of Cardinal Jozsef Mindszenty Dec. 26, 1948, and his sentence to life imprisonment in 1949. (He was free for a few days during the unsuccessful uprising of 1956. He then took up residence at the U.S. Embassy in Budapest, where he remained until September 1971, when he was permitted to leave the country. He died in 1975 in Vienna.)

In 1950, religious orders and congregations were suppressed and 10,000 religious were interned. Several dozen priests and monks were assassinated, jailed or deported. About 4,000 priests and religious were confined in jail or concentration camps. The government sponsored a national "Progressive Catholic" Church and captive organizations for priests. Despite a 1964 agreement with the Holy See regarding episcopal appointments, bishops remained subject to government surveillance and harassment.

On Feb. 9, 1990, an accord was signed between the Holy See and Hungary re-establishing diplomatic relations. Pope John Paul II reorganized the ecclesiastical structure of the country in May 1993. In 1997, the Vatican and Hungary signed an agreement that restored some Church property confiscated under communism and provided some sources of funding for Church activities. Hungary's bishops have said social conflicts, political changes and economic strains have put new pressures on the Church.

Iceland*

Dioc., 1; bp., 1; parishes, 4; priests, 12 (6 dioc., 6 rel.); sem., 1; bros., 1; srs., 38; bap., 103; Caths., 6,000 (1.4%); tot. pop., 293,000.

Island republic between Norway and Greenland; capital, Rekjavik. Irish hermits were there in the eighth century. Missionaries subsequently evangelized the island and Christianity was officially accepted about 1000. The first bishop was ordained in 1056. The Black Death had dire effects, and spiritual decline set in during the 15th century. Lutheranism was introduced from Denmark between 1537 and 1552 and made the official religion. Some Catholic missionary work was done in the 19th century. Religious freedom was granted to the few Catholics in 1874. A vicariate was erected in 1929 and was made a diocese in 1968.

India*

Patriarchate, 1 (titular of East Indies); major archbishoprics (Syro-Malabar and Syro-Malankara), 2; archd., 27; dioc., 127; card., 5; patr., 2; abp., 35; bp., 153; parishes, 8,771; priests, 21,931 (12,207 dioc., 9,724 rel.); p.d., 25; sem., 13,216; bros., 3,078; srs., 89,300; catechists, 61,670; bap., 342,715; Caths., 17,663,000 (1.6%); tot. pop. 1,085,600,000.

Republic on the subcontinent of south central Asia; capital, New Delhi. Long-standing tradition credits the Apostle Thomas with the introduction of Christianity in the Kerala area. Evangelization followed the establishment of Portuguese posts and the conquest of Goa in 1510. Jesuits, Franciscans, Dominicans, Augustinians and members of other religious orders figured in the early missionary history. An archdiocese for Goa, with two suffragan sees, was set up in 1558.

Missionaries had some difficulties with the British East India Co., which exercised virtual government control from 1757 to 1858. They also had trouble because of a conflict that developed between policies of the Portuguese government, which pressed its rights of patronage in episcopal and clerical appointments, and the Vatican Congregation for the Propagation of the Faith, which sought greater freedom of action in the same appointments. This struggle resulted in the schism of Goa between 1838 and 1857. In 1886, when the number of Catholics was estimated to be 1 million, the hierarchy for India and Ceylon was restored.

Jesuits contributed greatly to the development of Catholic education from the second half of the 19th century. A large percentage of the Catholic population is located around Goa and Kerala and farther south. The country is predominantly Hindu. Anti-conversion laws in effect in several states have had a restrictive effect on pastoral ministry and social service.

Recent years have seen tensions within the Syro-Malabar rite over liturgy and tradition. In addition, there have been tensions between the Latin-rite and Eastern-rite Catholic churches in India over the care of Catholics outside the traditional boundaries of their rites. In the late 20th and early 21st centuries, Church leaders campaigned for the rights of low-caste Indians. Religious also faced a series of attacks, including murders, by extremist Hindus who claimed they were trying to convert people to Christianity.

Indonesia*

Archd., 10; dioc., 27; mil. ord. 1; card., 1; abp., 13; bps., 32; parishes, 1,147; priests, 3,280 (1,351 dioc., 1,929 rel.); p.d., 12; sem., 2,880; bros., 1,007; srs., 7,388; catechists, 21,801; bap., 190,528; Caths., 6,477,000 (3%); tot. pop., 217,080,000.

Republic in the Malay Archipelago, consisting of some 3,000 islands; capital, Jakarta. Evangelization by the Portuguese began about 1511. St. Francis Xavier spent some 14 months in the area. Christianity was strongly rooted in some parts of the islands by 1600. Islam's rise to dominance began at this time. The Dutch East Indies Co., which gained effective control in the 17th century, banned evangelization by Catholic missionaries for some time, but Dutch secular and religious priests managed to resume the work. A vicariate of Batavia for all the Dutch East Indies was set up in 1841. About 90 percent of the population is Muslim. The hierarchy was established in 1961.

From 1981 to about 1996, Catholics and Protestants clashed more than 40 times over what Catholics perceived as Communion host desecration. At least three Protestants died from beatings by Catholics after the incidents.

In the late 1990s, as the Indonesian economy took a nose-dive, Muslim-Christian violence increased, especially in the Molucca Islands. Church leaders continued to urge calm and dialogue, and at one point a bishop sought U.N. intervention to prevent what he saw as a potential genocide of Christians. A militant Muslim group charged with inciting much of the violence disbanded in late 2002, Church leaders expressed hope for peace. The Church worked for years to help victims of the December 2004 tsunami and subsequent earthquakes and tsunamis, offering its services to people regardless of religious affiliation.

Iran*

Archd., 4; dioc., 2; abp., 4; bp., 1; parishes, 17;

priests, 16 (6 dioc., 10 rel.); p.d., 5; sem., 1; srs., 32; bap., 30; Caths., 25,000 (.02%); tot. pop., 67,480,000.

Islamic republic (Persia until 1935) in southwestern Asia; capital, Teheran. Some of the earliest Christian communities were established in this area outside the Roman Empire. They suffered persecution in the fourth century and were then cut off from the outside world. Nestorianism was generally professed in the late fifth century. Islam became dominant after 640. Some later missionary work was attempted but without success. Religious liberty was granted in 1834, but Catholics were the victims of a massacre in 1918. Islam is the religion of perhaps 98 percent of the population. Catholics belong to the Latin, Armenian and Chaldean rites.

After Iran nationalized many Church-run social institutions in 1980, about 75 Catholic missionaries left the country, by force or by choice. In recent years, however, Iranian authorities have shown more cooperation regarding entry visas for Church personnel. Although freedom of worship is guaranteed in Iran, Church sources said Catholic activities are monitored carefully by authorities. Since Pope John Paul II and Iranian President Mohammed Khatami met in 1999, the Holy See and Iran have had several high-level diplomatic exchanges.

Iraq*

Patriarchate, 1; archd., 9; dioc., 5; ap. ex., 2; patriarch, 1; abp., 8; bp., 8; parishes, 100; priests, 155 (123 dioc., 32 rel.); p.d., 12; sem., 85; bros., 15; srs., 332; catechists, 1,038; bap., 2,849; Caths., 256,000 (1%); tot. pop., 25,733,000.

Republic in southwestern Asia; capital, Baghdad. Some of the earliest Christian communities were established in the area, whose history resembles that of Iran. Catholics belong to the Armenian, Chaldean, Latin and Syrian rites; Chaldeans are most numerous. Islam is the religion of some 90 percent of the population. Iraq's Chaldean Catholic patriarch was outspoken against the international embargo against Iraq, saying it especially hurt children and the sick. In early 2003, Vatican officials met separately with U.S. and Iraqi leaders in an effort to prevent the U.S.-led war; the Vatican embassy in Baghdad remained open throughout the conflict, and Church aid agencies treated wounded. Catholic aid organizations geared up relief efforts after the war but were frustrated by lawlessness and looting. After the war, Catholic leaders were among Christians expressing alarm at the growing number of Christians leaving the country.

Ireland*

Archd., 4; dioc., 22; card., 2; abp., 8; bp., 38; parishes, 1,366; priests, 5,275 (3,141 dioc., 2,134 rel.); p.d., 1; sem., 186; bros., 827; srs., 8,545; bap., 65,746 (preceding figures include Northern Ireland); Caths., 4,958,000 (76%); tot. 6,512,000 (population numbers include Northern Ireland; in Republic of Ireland, Catholics comprise 95% of the population).

Republic in the British Isles; capital, Dublin. St. Patrick, who is venerated as the apostle of Ireland, evangelized parts of the island for some years after the middle of the fifth century. Conversion of the island was not accomplished, however, until the seventh century or later. Celtic monks were the principal missionaries. The Church was organized along monastic lines at first, but a movement developed in the 11th century for the establishment of jurisdiction along episcopal lines. The Church gathered strength during the period from the Norman Conquest of England to the reign of Henry VIII despite a wide variety of rivalries, wars, and other disturbances.

Henry introduced an age of repression of the faith, which continued for many years under several of his successors. The Irish suffered from proscription of the Catholic faith, economic and social disabilities, subjection to absentee landlords and a plantation system designed to keep them from owning property, and actual persecution which took an uncertain toll of lives up until about 1714. Some penal laws remained in force until emancipation in 1829. Nearly 100 years later Ireland was divided in two, making Northern Ireland, consisting of six counties, part of the United Kingdom (1920) and giving dominion status to the Irish Free State, made up of the other 26 counties (1922). This state (Eire, in Gaelic) was proclaimed the Republic of Ireland in 1949. The Catholic Church predominates but religious freedom is guaranteed for all. The Irish Republic and Northern Ireland share a bishops' conference, which has worked for peace in Northern Ireland. Recent years have witnessed a decrease in vocations and growing turmoil over issues such as priestly pedophilia, divorce, and abortion.

Ireland, Northern

Tot. pop., 1,610,000; Catholics comprise more than one third. (Other statistics are included in **Ireland**).

Part of the United Kingdom, it consists of six of the nine counties of Ulster in the northeast corner of Ireland; capital, Belfast. Early history is given under **Ireland**.

Nationalist-unionist tensions fall primarily along Catholic-Protestant lines, with nationalists, mainly Catholics, advocating an end to British rule. Violence and terrorism began in the late 1960s and, by the late 1990s, more than 3,000 people had been killed.

On Apr. 10, 1998, the governments of the Irish Republic and Great Britain and the political parties of Northern Ireland reached an agreement known as the Good Friday agreement. Irish bishops supported it, and it was endorsed by the voters in Ireland and Northern Ireland. However, the agreement or the coalition government established as a result of the agreement were suspended several times, and Northern Ireland's bishops spoke out in support of continuing democratic structures.

For years, Catholics claimed discrimination in the workplace and harassment from the Royal Ulster Constabulary, Northern Ireland's police force that was disbanded and reformed as the Police Service of Northern Ireland. In 2002 some 40 percent of the new force was Catholic, compared to 8 percent in 2001.

Israel*

Patriarchates, 2 (Jerusalem for Latins; patriarchal vicariate for Greek-Melkites); archd., 2; ap.ex., 5; patriarch, 1; abp., 3; bp., 6; parishes, 81; priests, 374 (80 dioc., 294 rel.); p.d., 5; sem., 86; bros., 159; srs., 984; bap., 1,916; Caths., 127,000 (1.7%); tot. pop., 6,847,000.

Parliamentary democracy in the Middle East; capi-

tals, Jerusalem and Tel Aviv (diplomatic). Israel was the birthplace of Christianity, the site of the first Christian communities. Some persecution was suffered in the early Christian era and again during the several hundred years of Roman control. Muslims conquered the territory in the seventh century and, except for the period of the Kingdom of Jerusalem established by Crusaders, remained in control most of the time up until World War I. The Church survived in the area, sometimes just barely, but it did not prosper greatly or show any notable increase in numbers. The British took over the protectorate of the area after World War I.

Partition into Israel for the Jews and Palestine for the Arabs was approved by the United Nations in 1947. War broke out a year later with the proclamation of the Republic of Israel. The Israelis won the war and 50 percent more territory than they had originally been ceded. War broke out again for six days in June 1967, and in October 1973.

Judaism is the faith professed by about 85 percent of the inhabitants; approximately one-third of them are considered observant. Israeli-Holy See relations improved in 1994 with the implementation of full diplomatic relations, and the Church gained legal status in 1997, although some taxation issues remained unresolved.

The Holy See repeatedly has asked for an internationally guaranteed statute to protect the sacred nature of Jerusalem, which is holy to Christians, Muslims and Jews. It has underlined that this means more than access to specific holy places and that the political and religious dimensions of Jerusalem are interrelated. During the Palestinian intifada, the Vatican and Holy Land Church leaders defended Israeli rights to live without the threat of terrorism and the Palestinians' right to a homeland, saying both would only be achieved through a negotiated settlement.

Italy*

Patriarchate, 1 (Venice); archd. 60 (40 are metropolitan sees); dioc., 156; prel., 3; abb., 7; mil. ord. 1; pat., 1 (Venice); card., 40; abp., 167; bps., 275 (hierarchy includes 221 residential, 27 coadjutors or auxiliaries, 127 in Curia offices, remainder in other offices or retired); parishes, 25,655; priests, 51,635 (33,684 dioc., 17,951 rel.); p.d., 3,886; sem., 5,915; bros., 3,553; srs., 102,363; catechists, 202,870; bap., 454,189; Caths., 56,036,000 (97%); tot. pop., 58,170,000.

Republic in southern Europe; capital, Rome. A Christian community was formed early in Rome, probably by the middle of the first century. St. Peter established his see there. He and St. Paul suffered death for the faith in the 60s. The early Christians were persecuted at various times, as in other parts of the empire, but the Church developed in numbers and influence, gradually spreading out from towns and cities in the center and south to rural areas and the north.

Church organization began in the second century. The Church emerged from underground in 313, with the Edict of Milan, and rose to a position of prestige and lasting influence on politics and culture until well into the 19th century. In the 1870s, the Papal States were annexed by the Kingdom of Italy. The 1929 Lateran Pacts included a treaty recognizing the Vatican as an independent state, a financial agreement by which Italy agreed to compensate the Vatican for loss of the papal states, and a concordat regulating Church-state relations. In 1984 the Vatican and Italy signed a revised concordat, reducing some of the Church's privileges and removing Catholicism as the state religion.

The Church strongly opposed Italy's abortion law in 1978 and forced a 1981 referendum on the issue. Abortion remained legal, and the Italian Church has taken a more low-profile stance. The Church has been active in social issues, including helping unprecedented numbers of illegal immigrants in the late 1990s. Church leaders have expressed concern about Italy's low birth rate.

Jamaica*

Archd., 1; dioc., 2; abp., 1; bp., 3; parishes, 65; priests, 83 (51 dioc., 32 rel.); p.d., 33; sem., 14; bros., 123; srs., 163; catechists, 499; bap., 888; Caths., 115,000 (4.3%); tot. pop., 2,664,000.

Republic in the West Indies; capital, Kingston. Franciscans and Dominicans evangelized the island from about 1512 until 1655. Missionary work was interrupted after the English took possession but was resumed by Jesuits about the turn of the 19th century. An apostolic vicariate was organized in 1837. The hierarchy was established in 1967. In the late 1990s, Church leaders spoke out against violence; more than 800 people were murdered in Jamaica in 1997 alone.

Japan*

Archd., 3; dioc., 13; card., 2; abp., 4; bp., 21; parishes, 843; priests, 1,660 (537 dioc., 1,123 rel.); p.d., 14; sem., 159; bros., 222; srs., 6,163; catechists, 1,681; bap., 7,426; Caths., 533,000 (.4%); tot. pop., 127,778,000.

Archipelago in the northwest Pacific; capital, Tokyo. Jesuits began evangelization in the middle of the 16th century and about 300,000 converts, most of them in Kyushu, were reported at the end of the century. The Nagasaki Martyrs were victims of persecution in 1597. Another persecution took some 4,000 lives between 1614 and 1651. Missionaries, banned for two centuries, returned about the middle of the 19th century and found Christian communities still surviving in Nagasaki and other places in Kyushu. A vicariate was organized in 1866. Religious freedom was guaranteed in 1889. The hierarchy was established in 1891. Several Japanese bishops at the 1998 Synod of Bishops for Asia said Catholicism has grown slowly in the region because the Church is too Western.

Since the 1980s, on several occasions Church leaders have apologized and asked forgiveness for the Church's complicity in the nation's aggression during the 1930s and 1940s. At the end of the 20th century, bishops and religious superiors suggested that during the 21st century the Japanese Church focus on pastoral care for migrant workers, concern for the environment and interreligious dialogue.

Jordan*

Archd., 1; ex. pat., 2; abp., 2; bp., 1; parishes, 64; priests, 90 (60 dioc., 30 rel.); sem., 3; bros., 5; srs., 238; bap., 1,157; Caths., 75,000 (1%); tot. pop., 5,632,000.

Constitutional monarchy in the Middle East; capital,

Amman. Christianity there dates from apostolic times. Survival of the faith was threatened many times under the rule of Muslims from 636 and Ottoman Turks from 1517 to 1918, and in the Islamic Emirate of Trans-Jordan from 1918 to 1949. In the years following the creation of Israel, some 500,000 Palestinian refugees, including Christians, moved to Jordan. In the 1990s, Jordan cared for some 130,000 Iraqi refugees, including about 30,000 Chaldean Catholics. Islam is the state religion, but religious freedom is guaranteed for all. The Greek Melkite Archdiocese of Petra and Filadelfia is located in Jordan. Latin-rite Catholics are under the jurisdiction of the Latin Patriarchate of Jerusalem. Jordan established diplomatic relations with the Holy See in 1994.

Kazakhstan*

Archd. 1, dioc., 2; a.a.; 1; abp., 3; bp., 1; parishes, 59; priests, 76 (45 dioc., 31 rel.); sem., 11; bros., 9; srs., 91; bap., 639; Caths., 183,000 (1.2%); tot. pop., 14,960,000.

Independent republic (1991); formerly part of USSR; capital, Astana. About 47 percent of the population is Muslim, and about 44 percent is Orthodox. The Catholic population is mainly of German, Polish and Ukrainian origin, descendants of those deported during the Stalin regime. A Latin-rite apostolic administration was established in 1991. In 1998, the Vatican and the Kazakh government signed an agreement guaranteeing the Church legal rights. Diocesan structure was established in 1999, and the Vatican created the first archdiocese and diocese in 2003. The country had its first priestly ordinations on Kazakh soil in 2006.

Kenya*

Archd. 4; dioc., 20; v.a., 1; mil. ord., 1; abp. 5; bp., 28; parishes, 726; priests, 2,028 (1,194 dioc., 834 rel.); p.d., 1; sem., 1,521; bros., 722; srs., 3,719; catechists, 10,152; bap., 255,199; Caths., 8,349,000 (25%); tot. pop., 33,580,000.

Republic in East Africa on the Indian Ocean; capital, Nairobi. Systematic evangelization by the Holy Ghost Missionaries began in 1889, nearly 40 years after the start of work by Protestant missionaries. The hierarchy was established in 1953. Three metropolitan sees were established in 1990. Kenyan Catholics were in the forefront of ministering to victims of the 1998 explosion at the U.S. Embassy in Nairobi. The Kenyan bishops have been outspoken against ethnic violence, poverty, government corruption and mismanagement, and the need for a constitutional review. In some rural areas, Church workers, including foreign missionaries, were targeted for their work with the poor.

Kiribati*

Dioc., 1; bp., 1; parishes, 24; priests, 29 (20 dioc., 9 rel.); p.d. 1; sem., 13; bros., 13; srs., 96; catechists, 211; bap., 1,808; Caths., 46,000 (54.2%); tot. pop., 84,000.

Former British colony (Gilbert Islands) in Oceania; became independent July 12, 1979; capital, Bairiki on Tarawa. French Missionaries of the Sacred Heart began work in the islands in 1888. A vicariate for the islands was organized in 1897. The hierarchy was established in 1966.

Korea, North

Tot. pop., 22,650,000. No recent Catholic statistics available; there were an estimated 100,000 Catholics reported in 1969.

Northern part of peninsula in eastern Asia; formal name Democratic People's Republic of Korea (May 1, 1948); capital, Pyongyang. See **South Korea** for history before country was divided. After liberation from Japan in 1945, the Soviet regime in the North systematically punished all religions. After the 1950-53 Korean war, Christian worship was not allowed outside of homes until 1988, when the country's one Catholic Church was built in Pyongyang. A 1999 South Korean government report said North Korea clearly restricts religious practices and churches in the North exist only for show.

Korea, South*

Archd., 3; dioc., 12; mil. ord. 1; card., 2; abp., 5; bp., 23; parishes, 1,420; priests, 3,315 (2,761 dioc., 554 rel.); sem., 1,629; bros., 707; srs., 8,463; catechists, 24,219; bap., 138,222; Caths., 4,572,000 (9.4%); tot. pop., 48,217,000.

Southern part of peninsula in eastern Asia; formal name, Republic of Korea (1948); capital, Seoul. Some Catholics may have been in Korea before it became a "hermit kingdom" toward the end of the 16th century and closed its borders to foreigners. The modern introduction to Catholicism came in 1784 through lay converts. A priest arriving in the country in 1794 found 4,000 Catholics there who had never seen a priest. A vicariate was erected in 1831 but was not manned for several years thereafter. There were 15,000 Catholics by 1857. Four persecutions in the 19th century took a terrible toll; several thousand died in the last one, 1866-69. (Pope John Paul II canonized 103 martyrs of this period during his 1984 visit to South Korea.) Freedom of religion was granted in 1883, when Korea opened its borders. During World War II, most foreign priests were arrested and expelled, seminaries were closed and churches were taken over. After liberation from Japan in 1945, the Church in the South had religious freedom. Since the 1950-53 Korean war, the Church in South Korea has flourished. Church leaders in the South have worked at reconciliation with the North and to alleviate famine in the North.

Kuwait*

V.a., 1; pat. ex., 1; abp., 1; bp., 1; parishes, 5; priests, 12 (3 dioc., 9 rel.); p.d., 1; bros., 13; bap., 546; Caths., 159,000 (.7%); tot. pop., 2,390,000.

Constitutional monarchy (sultanate or sheikdom) in southwest Asia bordering on the Persian Gulf. Remote Christian origins probably date to apostolic times. Islam is the predominant and official religion. Catholics are mostly foreign workers; the Church enjoys religious freedom.

Kyrgyzstan*

A.a., 1; parishes, 16; priests, 9 (2 dioc., 7 rel.); sem., 1; bros., 1; srs., 7; bap., 10; Caths., 1,000; tot. pop., 5,070,000.

Independent republic bordering China; former Soviet republic; capital, Bishkek (former name, Frunze). Most of the people are Sunni Muslim. Established diplomatic relations with the Holy See in August 1992;

became apostolic administration in March 2006. The country received its first bishop in July 2006.

Laos

V.a., 4; bp., 3; parishes, 77; priests, 12 (12 dioc.); p.d., 1; sem., 20; srs., 88; catechists, 298; bap., 1,518; Caths., 42,000 (.6%); tot. pop., 5,731,000. (AD)

People's republic in southeast Asia; capital, Vientiane. Systematic evangelization by French missionaries started about 1881; earlier efforts ended in 1688. The first mission was established in 1885; an apostolic vicariate was organized in 1899. Most of the foreign missionaries were expelled following the communist takeover in 1975. Catholic schools remain banned, and the government lets foreign missionaries into the country only as "social workers." A Laotian bishop at the 1998 Synod of Bishops for Asia said religious practice was nearly normal in two of the country's four apostolic vicariates, but elsewhere was more controlled and sometimes difficult. Buddhism is the state religion.

Latvia*

Archd., 1; dioc., 3; bp., 5; parishes, 268; priests, 133 (104 dioc., 29 rel.); p.d., 1; sem., 43; brs., 29; srs., 88; catechist, 282; bap., 5,557; Caths., 429,000 (18%); tot. pop., 2,310,000.

Independent (1991) Baltic republic; capital, Riga. (Forcibly absorbed by the USSR in 1940; it regained independence in 1991). Catholicism was introduced late in the 12th century. Lutheranism became the dominant religion after 1530. Catholics were free to practice their faith during the long period of Russian control and during independence from 1918 to 1940. The relatively small Catholic community in Latvia was repressed during the 1940-91 Soviet takeover, which was not recognized by the Holy See or the United States. After Latvia declared its independence, the Church began to flourish, including among people who described themselves as nonreligious. In the late 1990s, one archbishop urged the Russian government not to interfere in disputes over citizenship for the country's ethnic Russians, who make up about one-third of the country's population.

Lebanon*

Patriarchates, 3; achd., 12 (1 Armenian, 4 Maronite, 7 Greek Melkite); dioc., 8 (1 Chaldean, 6 Maronite); v.a., 1 (Latin); card., 1 (patriarch of the Maronites); patriarchs, 3 (patriarchs of Antioch of the Maronites, Antioch of the Syrians and Cilicia of the Armenians who reside in Lebanon); abp., 24; bp., 18; parishes, 1,083; priests, 1,425 (787 dioc., 638 rel.); p.d., 9; sem., 454; bros., 176; srs., 2,539; catechists, 491; bap., 11,390; Caths., 1,860,000 (52%); tot. pop., 3,698,000.

Republic in the Middle East; capital, Beirut. Christianity, introduced in apostolic times, was firmly established by the end of the fourth century and has remained so despite heavy Muslim influence since early in the seventh century. The country is the center of the Maronite rite. In the 1980s, the country was torn by violence and often heavy fighting among rival political-religious factions drawn along Christian-Muslim lines. Pope John Paul II convened a synod of bishops for Lebanon in 1995 to urge Lebanese to forgive and forget the wounds of the war. Synod members provoked controversy by directly criticizing Israeli occupation of southern Lebanon and Syria's continued deployment of troops in the area. In 1999, Lebanon was the site of a historic meeting of Mideast and North African Church leaders, who discussed the future of the Catholic Church in the Arab world. After Syria withdrew the majority of its troops in 2005, Lebanon's bishops were outspoken in calling for free and fair elections. The bishops also called for an immediate cease-fire after Israel began airstrikes against Islamic militants (Hezbollah) in the country in 2006.

Lesotho*

Archd., 1; dioc., 3; abp., 1; bp., 3; parishes, 86; priests, 138 (68 dioc., 70 rel.); sem., 95; bros., 32; srs., 687; catechists, 1,628; bap., 20,547; Caths., 1,093,000 (51%); tot. pop., 2,151,000.

Constitutional monarchy, an enclave in the southeastern part of South Africa; capital, Maseru. Oblates of Mary Immaculate, the first Catholic missionaries in the area, started evangelization in 1862. Father Joseph Gerard, beatified in 1988, worked 10 years before he made his first conversion. An apostolic prefecture was organized in 1894. The hierarchy was established in 1951. Under the military government of the late 1980s, Lesotho's Catholics pressed for democratic reforms. In the 1990s, they gave special pastoral care to families whose breadwinners had to travel to South Africa to work, often for weeks at a time.

Liberia*

Archd., 1; dioc., 2; abp., 1; bp., 2; parishes, 52; priests, 56 (38 dioc., 18 rel.); sem., 34; bros., 15; srs., 48; catechists, 933; bap. 4,487; Caths., 172,000 (5%); tot. pop., 3,487,000.

Republic in West Africa; capital, Monrovia. Missionary work and influence, dating intermittently from the 16th century, were slight before the Society of African Missions undertook evangelization in 1906. The hierarchy was established in 1982. Fighting within the country, which began in 1989, culminated in 1996 and resulted in the evacuation of most Church workers and the archbishop of Monrovia. The war claimed the lives of 150,000 and made refugees of or displaced another million. Most Church institutions in Monrovia were destroyed. Monrovia Archbishop Michael Francis was among leaders calling for U.S.-led intervention to quell chaos in the country in mid-2003.

Libya*

V.a., 3; p.a., 1; abp., 1; bp., 2; parishes, 6; priests, 14 (3 dioc., 11 rel.); srs., 95; bap., 87; Caths., 104,000 (1.8%); tot. pop., 5,654,000.

Arab state in North Africa; capital, Tripoli. Christianity was probably preached in the area at an early date but was overcome by the spread of Islam from the 630s. Islamization was complete by 1067, and there has been no Christian influence since then. Almost all Catholics are foreign workers. Islam is the state religion. After implementation of a U.N. embargo against the country in 1992, the government removed most limitations on entry of Catholic religious orders, especially health care workers. Libya established diplomatic relations with the Holy See in 1997.

Liechtenstein*

Archd. 1; abp., 1; parishes, 10; priests, 31 (20 dioc., 11 rel); sem., 8; srs., 44; bap., 278; Caths., 26,000 (80%); tot. pop., 34,000.

Constitutional monarchy in central Europe; capital, Vaduz. Christianity in the country dates from the fourth century. The Reformation had hardly any influence in the country. Catholicism is the state religion, but religious freedom for all is guaranteed by law.

Lithuania*

Archd., 2; dioc., 5; mil. ord., 1; card., 2; abp., 1; bp., 12; parishes, 677; priests, 802 (690 dioc., 112 rel.); p.d., 5; sem., 190; bros., 40; srs., 724; catechists, 2,183; bap., 26,180; Caths., 2,701,000 (80%); tot. pop., 3,440,000.

Baltic republic forcibly absorbed and under Soviet domination from 1940; regained independence, 1991; capital, Vilnius. Catholicism was introduced in 1251 and a short-lived diocese was established by 1260. Effective evangelization took place between 1387 and 1417, when Catholicism became the state religion. Efforts of czars to "russify" the Church between 1795 and 1918 were strongly resisted. Concordat relations with the Vatican were established in 1927, nine years after independence from Russia and 13 years before Russia annexed Lithuania. The Russians closed convents and seminaries; in Kaunas, men needed government approval to attend the seminary. Priests were restricted in pastoral ministry and subject to appointment by government officials; no religious services were allowed outside churches; religious press and instruction were banned. Some bishops and hundreds of priests and laity were imprisoned or detained in Siberia between 1945 and 1955. Two bishops — Vincentas Sladkevicius and Julijonas Steponavicius — were forbidden to act as bishops and relegated to remote parishes in 1957 and 1961, respectively. Despite such conditions, a vigorous underground Church flourished in Lithuania.

In the 1980s, government pressure eased, and some bishops were allowed to return to their dioceses. In 1989, Pope John Paul II appointed bishops in all six Lithuanian dioceses. The Church strongly supported the 1990 independence movement, and Lithuanian independence leaders urged young men to desert the Russian army and seek sanctuary in churches. However, communist rule had nearly destroyed the Church's infrastructure. In 2000 the Church and government signed a series of agreements regularizing the Church's position.

Luxembourg*

Archd., 1; abp., 2; parishes, 275; priests, 238 (173 dioc., 65 rel.); p.d., 9; sem., 5; bros., 12; srs., 566; catechism, 460; bap., 2,850; Caths. 394,000 (87%); tot. pop., 455,000.

Constitutional monarchy in Western Europe; capital, Luxembourg. Christianity, introduced in the fifth and sixth centuries, was firmly established by the end of the eighth century. A full-scale parish system was in existence in the ninth century. Monastic influence was strong until the Reformation, which had minimal influence in the country. The Church experienced some adverse influence from the currents of the French Revolution. In recent years, the Church has restructured its adult formation program to involve more lay workers.

Macau (See China, People's Republic of)

Macedonia*

Dioc., 1; bp., 2; parishes, 7; priests, 16 (11 dioc., 5 rel.); sem., 19; srs., 32; bap., 87; Caths., 15,000 (.9%); tot. pop., 2,350,000.

Former Yugoslav Republic of Macedonia; declared independence in 1992; capital, Skopje. The Diocese of Skopje-Prizren includes the Yugoslav province of Kosovo, so the Macedonian Church helped with ethnic Albanians during the period of ethnic cleansing by Serb forces and retaliatory NATO air strikes.

Madagascar*

Archd., 4; dioc., 16; card., 1; abp., 6; bp., 20; parishes, 328; priests, 1,142 (531 dioc., 611 rel.); sem., 879; bros., 414; srs., 4,111; catechists, 19,806; bap., 167,010; Caths., 5,079,000 (28%); tot. pop. 17,941,000.

Republic (Malagasy Republic) off the eastern coast of Africa; capital, Antananarivo. Missionary efforts were generally fruitless from early in the 16th century until the Jesuits were permitted to start open evangelization about 1845. An apostolic prefecture was set up in 1850 and an apostolic vicariate in the North was placed in charge of the Holy Ghost Fathers in 1898. There were 100,000 Catholics by 1900. The first indigenous bishop was ordained in 1936. The hierarchy was established in 1955. In the late 1980s and early 1990s, the Church joined opposition calls for renewal of social institutions. Today, the Church in Madagascar runs hundreds of schools and dozens of orphanages and is active in the island's social justice concerns; some consider it the largest landowner, after the government.

Malawi*

Archd., 1; dioc., 6; abp., 2; bp., 11; parishes, 146; priests, 379 (289 dioc., 90 rel.); sem., 367; bros., 87; srs., 775; catechists, 2,654; bap., 125,132; Caths., 3,342,000 (28%); tot. pop., 11,940,000.

Republic in the interior of East Africa; capital, Lilongwe. Missionary work, begun by Jesuits in the late 16th and early 17th centuries, was generally ineffective until the end of the 19th century. The Missionaries of Africa (White Fathers) arrived in 1889 and later were joined by others. A vicariate was set up in 1897. The hierarchy was established in 1959. In the late 1980s, the Church in Malawi helped hundreds of thousands of refugees from the war in Mozambique. Malawi's churches, especially the Catholic Church, were instrumental in bringing about the downfall of President Hastings Kamuzu Banda, who ruled for 30 years. A 1992 bishops' pastoral letter criticized Banda's rule and the nation's poverty and galvanized Malawians into pro-democracy protests. Banda responded by summoning the country's bishops, seizing copies of the letter and expelling an Irish member of the Malawi hierarchy. Western donors called off aid, and in 1994 Banda was forced to call multi-party elections, which he lost. In 2002, Church officials were outspoken against plans by Banda's successor, President Bakili Muluzi, to seek a third term of office;

Church officials said they were threatened and attacked for that criticism.

Malaysia

Archd., 2; dioc., 6; abp., 5; bp., 7; parishes, 142; priests, 224 (178 dioc., 46 rel.); p.d., 1; sem., 59; bros., 58; srs., 568; catechists, 1,979; bap., 21,676; Caths., 796,000 (3%); tot. pop., 25,580,000. (AD)

Parliamentary democracy in southeast Asia; capital, Kuala Lumpur. Christianity, introduced by Portuguese colonists about 1511, was confined almost exclusively to Malacca until late in the 18th century. The effectiveness of evangelization increased from then on because of the recruitment and training of indigenous clergy. Singapore (see separate entry), founded in 1819, became a center for missionary work. Effective evangelization in Sabah and Sarawak began in the second half of the 19th century. The hierarchy was established in 1973. In accordance with government wishes for Bahasa Malaysia to be the national language, the Church has tried to introduce it into its liturgies. For more than a decade, Church leaders campaigned against the Internal Security Act, which allows renewable 30-day detentions without trial. Proselytizing Muslims is illegal, but the government allows conversions from other religions.

Maldives

Republic, an archipelago 400 miles southwest of India and Ceylon; capital, Male. No serious attempt was ever made to evangelize the area, which is completely Muslim. Population, 290,000.

Mali*

Archd., 1; dioc., 5; abp., 1; bp., 5; parishes, 43; priests, 160 (91 dioc., 69 rel.); sem., 58; bros., 21; srs., 253; catechists, 1,293; bap., 3,597; Caths., 232,000 (.2%); tot. pop., 13,409,000.

Republic, inland in western Africa; capital, Bamako. Catholicism was introduced late in the second half of the 19th century. Missionary work made little progress in the midst of the predominantly Muslim population. A vicariate was set up in 1921. The hierarchy was established in 1955. In recent years, the Church has promoted the role of women in society. Catholics have cordial relations with Muslims.

Malta*

Archd., 1; dioc., 1; abp., 5; bp., 2; parishes, 84; priests, 894 (489 dioc., 405 rel.); sem., 86; bros., 82; srs., 1,148; catechists, 1,230; bap., 3,782; Caths., 407,000 (95%); tot. pop., 427,000.

Republic south of Sicily; capital, Valletta. Early catacombs and inscriptions are evidence of the early introduction of Christianity. St. Paul was shipwrecked on Malta in 60. Saracens controlled the islands from 870 to 1090, a period of difficulty for the Church. The line of bishops extends from 1090 to the present. Church-state conflict developed in recent years over passage of government-sponsored legislation affecting Catholic schools and Church-owned property. An agreement reached in 1985 ended the dispute. An influx of several thousand African migrants early in the 21st century strained Maltese hospitality, and Jesuit priests were targeted with arson because of their advocacy for the groups.

Marshall Islands*

P.a., 1; parishes, 4; priests, 5 (rel.); p.d., 1; sem., 2; brs., 1; srs., 15; bap., 174; Caths., 5,000 (12.5%); tot. pop., 53,000.

Island republic in central Pacific Ocean; capital, Majura. Formerly administered by United States as part of U.N. Trust Territory of the Pacific; independent nation, 1991. An apostolic prefecture was erected May 25, 1993 (formerly part of Carolines-Marshall Diocese), with U.S. Jesuit Rev. James Gould as first apostolic prefect.

Mauritania*

Dioc., 1; bp., 1; parishes, 6; priests, 11 (3 dioc., 8 rel.); brs. 1; srs., 32; sem., 2; bap., 31; Caths., 5,000 (.2%); tot. pop., 2,980,000. (AD)

Islamic republic on the northwest coast of Africa; capital, Nouakchott. With few exceptions, the Catholics in the country are foreign workers. At the 1994 Synod of Bishops for Africa, a bishop from Mauritania reported increasing problems with fundamentalist Muslims, but cautioned Church leaders against generalizing about Muslims.

Mauritius*

Dioc., 1; v.a., 1; card., 1; bp., 2; parishes, 42; priests, 99 (55 dioc., 44 rel.); sem., 10; bros., 30; srs., 257; catechists, 1,026; bap., 2,329; Caths., 314,000 (26%); tot. pop., 1,191,000.

Island republic in the Indian Ocean; capital, Port Louis. Catholicism was introduced by Vincentians in 1722. Port Louis, made a vicariate in 1819 and a diocese in 1847, was a jumping-off point for missionaries to Australia, Madagascar and South Africa. During a 1989 visit to Mauritius, Pope John Paul II warned against sins that accompanied its rapid economic development and booming tourism industry.

Mexico* (See Catholic Church in Mexico; see also Statistics of the Church in Mexico)

Micronesia*

Dioc., 1; bp., 1; parishes, 24; priests, 23 (10 dioc., 13 rel.); p.d., 40; sem., 10; bros., 1; srs., 56; catechists, 528; bap., 1,219; Caths., 59,000 (53%); tot. pop., 109,000.

Federated States of Micronesia (Caroline archipelago) in southwest Pacific; capital, Palikir; former U.N. trust territory under U.S. administration; became independent nation September 1991. Effective evangelization began in the late 1880s. The government established diplomatic relations with the Holy See in 1994.

Moldova*

Dioc., 1; bp., 1; parishes, 11; priests, 24 (10 dioc., 14 rel.); p.d., 1; sem., 11; bros., 3; srs., 40; bap., 54; Caths., 20,000 (.46%); tot. pop., 3,800,000.

Independent republic, former constituent republic of the USSR; capital, Kishinev. The majority of people belong to the Orthodox Church. Catholics are mostly of Polish or German descent.

Monaco*

Archd., 1; abp., 1; parishes, 6; priests, 21 (15 dioc., 6 rel.); p.d., 1; sem., 2; srs., 13; bap., 126; Caths., 29,000 (90%); tot. pop., 32,000.

Constitutional monarchy, an enclave on the Mediterranean coast of France; capital, Monaco. Christianity was introduced before 1000. Catholicism is the official religion but religious freedom is guaranteed for all.

Mongolia*

Bp., 1; parishes, 3; priests, 15 (3 dioc., 12 rel.); sem., 4; bros., 3; srs., 44; bap., 47; Caths., 2,000 (.08%); tot. pop., 2,532,000.

Republic in north central Asia; formerly under communist control; capital, Ulan Bator. Christianity was introduced by Oriental Orthodox. Some Franciscans were in the country in the 13th and 14th centuries, en route to China. Freedom of worship is guaranteed under the new constitution, which went into effect in 1992. The government established relations with the Holy See in 1992 and indicated that missionaries would be welcome to help rebuild the country. The first Catholic parish was established in 1994, and by 1997 the Church had extended its work beyond the capital. In 2003 a missionary from the Philippines became Mongolia's first bishop.

Morocco*

Archd., 2; abp., 5; parishes, 40; priests, 41 (6 dioc., 35 rel.); bros., 15; srs., 234; bap., 44; Caths., 22,000 (.07%); tot. pop., 30,540,000.

Constitutional monarchy in North Africa; capital, Rabat. Christianity was known in the area by the end of the third century. Bishops from Morocco attended a council at Carthage in 484. Catholic life survived under Visigoth and, from 700, Arab rule; later it became subject to influence from the Spanish, Portuguese and French. Islam is the state religion. The hierarchy was established in 1955. Pope John Paul II visited in 1985.

Mozambique*

Archd., 3; dioc., 9; card., 1; abp. 4; bp., 13; parishes, 287; priests, 611 (179 dioc., 432 rel.); p.d., 1; sem., 322; bros., 85; srs., 1,132; catechists, 42,536; bap., 159,097; Caths., 4,976,000 (23%); tot. pop., 19,182,000. (AD)

Republic in southeast Africa; capital, Maputo. Christianity was introduced by Portuguese Jesuits about the middle of the 16th century. Evangelization continued from then until the 18th century, when it went into decline largely because of the Portuguese government's expulsion of the Jesuits. Conditions worsened in the 1830s, improved after 1881, but deteriorated again during the anticlerical period from 1910 to 1925.

Conditions improved in 1940, the year Portugal concluded a new concordat with the Holy See and the hierarchy was established. Missionaries' outspoken criticism of Portuguese policies in Mozambique resulted in Church-state tensions in the years immediately preceding independence. The first two indigenous bishops were ordained March 9, 1975. Two ecclesiastical provinces were established in 1984. Mozambican bishops and members of the Rome-based Sant' Egidio Community were official mediators in the talks that ended 16 years of civil war in 1992. Since then, Church participation has flourished, with high attendance at Mass, a boom in vocations and active catechists at the parish level.

Myanmar

Archd., 3; dioc., 10; abp., 4; bp., 13; parishes, 296; priests, 574 (540 dioc., 34 rel.); sem., 399; bros., 105; srs., 1,488; catechists, 3,224; bap., 19,586; Caths., 623,000 (1.2%); tot. pop., 49,985,000. (AD)

Socialist republic in southeast Asia, formerly Burma; name changed to Myanmar in 1989; capital, Yangon (Rangoon). Christianity was introduced about 1500. Small-scale evangelization had limited results from the middle of the 16th century until the 1850s, when effective organization of the Church began. The hierarchy was established in 1955. Buddhism was declared the state religion in 1961, but the state is now officially secular. In 1965, Church schools and hospitals were nationalized. In 1966, all foreign missionaries who had entered the country for the first time after 1948 were forced to leave when the government refused to renew their work permits. The Church is involved primarily in pastoral and social activities.

Namibia*

Archd., 1; dioc., 1; v.a., 1; abp., 1; bp., 1; parishes, 91; priests, 88 (15 dioc., 73 rel.); p.d., 43; sem., 28; bros., 22; srs., 428; catechists, 1,326; bap., 12,028; Caths., 392,000 (18%); tot. pop., 2,271,000. (AD)

Independent (March 21, 1990) state in southern Africa; capital, Windhoek. The area shares the history of South Africa. The hierarchy was established in 1994. The Church is hindered by a lack of priests.

Nauru*

Parish; priest, 1 (rel); p.d., 2; srs., 3; bap., 95; Caths., 3,000 (37%); tot. pop., 8,000.

Independent republic in western Pacific; capital, Yaren. Forms part of the Tarawa and Nauru Diocese (Kiribati). Established diplomatic relations with the Holy See in 1992.

Nepal*

P.a., 1; parishes, 42; priests, 50 (12 dioc.; 38 rel.); sem., 24; bros., 2; srs., 124; bap., 834; Caths., 7,000 (.2%); tot. pop., 25,148,000.

Constitutional monarchy, the only Hindu kingdom in the world, in central Asia; capital, Katmandu. Little is known of the country before the 15th century. Some Jesuits passed through from 1628 and some sections were evangelized in the 18th century, with minimal results, before the country was closed to foreigners. Conversions from Hinduism, the state religion, are not recognized in law and are punishable by imprisonment.

Netherlands*

Archd., 1; dioc., 6; mil ord., 1; card., 2; abp., 1; bp., 16; parishes, 1,490; priests 3,378 (1,378 dioc., 2,000 rel.); p.d., 324; sem., 188; bros., 1,060; srs., 9,442; bap., 37,288; Caths., 4,923,000 (31%); tot. pop., 16,270,000.

Constitutional monarchy in northwestern Europe; capital, Amsterdam (seat of government, The Hague). Evangelization, begun about the turn of the sixth century by Irish, Anglo-Saxon and Frankish missionaries, resulted in Christianization of the country by 800 and subsequent strong influence on the Lowlands. Invasion by French Calvinists in 572 brought serious losses to the Catholic Church and made the Reformed Church dominant. Catholics suffered a practical persecution of official repression and social handicap in the 17th century. The schism of Utrecht occurred in 1724. Only one-third of the population was Catholic in 1726. The Church had only a skeletal organization from 1702 to 1853, when the hierarchy was re-established.

Despite this upturn, cultural isolation was the experience of Catholics until about 1914. From then on new vigor came into the life of the Church, and a whole new climate of interfaith relations began to develop. Before and for some years following the Second Vatican Council, the thrust and variety of thought and practice in the Dutch Church moved it to the vanguard position of "progressive" renewal. A synod of Dutch bishops held at the Vatican in January 1980 discussed ideological differences among Catholics with the aim of fostering unity and restoring some discipline within the nation's Church. However, even into the 1990s Church leaders spoke of a polarization among Catholics over issues such as sexual morality, ministries for women and priestly celibacy. The bishops also spoke out against permissive laws on euthanasia and assisted suicide.

New Zealand*

Archd., 1; dioc., 5; mil. ord., 1; card., 1; abp., 1; bp., 11; parishes, 271; priests, 512 (319 dioc., 193 rel.); p.d., 9; sem., 27; bros., 181; srs., 978; bap., 7,287; Caths. 468,000 (11%); tot. pop., 4,060,000.

Parliamentary democracy in southwestern Pacific Ocean; capital, Wellington. Protestant missionaries were the first evangelizers. On North Island, Catholic missionaries started work before the establishment of two dioceses in 1848; their work among the Maoris was not organized until about 1881. On South Island, whose first resident priest arrived in 1840, a diocese was established in 1869. These three jurisdictions were joined in a province in 1896. The Marists were the predominant Catholic missionaries in the area. The first Maori bishop was named in 1988. In 1998, Pope John Paul II urged New Zealand's bishops not to allow the Church to fall prey to the practices and values of prevailing culture. However, the president of the bishops' conference used the same occasion to express the bishops' concern to the pope about inconsistency in the way the Vatican exercises its authority.

Nicaragua*

Archd., 1; dioc., 6; v.a., 1; card., 1; abp., 1; bp., 12; parishes, 273; priests, 494 (325 dioc., 169 rel.); p.d., 30; sem., 283; bros., 45; srs., 1,017; catechists, 21,125; bap., 82,872; Caths., 4,785,000 (89%); tot. pop., 5,370,000.

Republic in Central America: capital, Managua. Evangelization began shortly after the Spanish conquest, about 1524, and eight years later the first bishop took over jurisdiction of the Church in the country. Jesuits were leaders in missionary work during the colonial period, which lasted until the 1820s. Evangelization endeavor increased after establishment of the republic in 1838 and extended to the Atlantic coastal area, where Protestant missionaries began work about the middle of the 1900s.

Many Church leaders, clerical and lay, supported the aims but not necessarily all the methods of the revolution, which forced the resignation and flight July 17,

1979, of Anastasio Somoza, whose family had controlled the government since the early 1930s. During the Sandinista period that followed, four priests accepted government posts. Some Nicaraguan Catholics threw their energies behind the Sandinista program of land reform and socialism, forming what some called a "popular church" based on liberation theology, while others strongly opposed the government. Managua Cardinal Miguel Obando Bravo helped mediate ceasefire talks during the war between the Sandinistas and U.S.-backed guerrillas. Land distribution, exacerbated by a wide gap in incomes, continued to be an issue, and in the late 1990s the Nicaraguan bishops continued to call for compromise between the government and former government officials. Despite an influx of aid after Hurricane Mitch in 1998 killed more than 2,500 Nicaraguans and forced 900,000 to evacuate, Church leaders still cited poverty as a major issue.

Niger*

Dioc., 2; bp., 3; parishes, 16; priests, 38 (14 dioc., 24 rel.); sem., 14; bros., 6; srs., 85; catechists, 143; bap., 229; Caths., 16,000 (.1%); tot. pop., 12,307,000.

Republic in west central Africa; capital, Niamey. The first mission was set up in 1831. An apostolic prefecture was organized in 1942, and the first diocese was established in 1961. The country is predominantly Muslim. The Church is active in the fields of health and education.

Nigeria*

Archd., 9; dioc., 40; v.a., 2; card., 2; abp., 11; bp., 44; parishes, 2,178; priests, 4,405 (3,837 dioc., 768 rel.); p.d., 5; sem., 5,127; bros., 534; srs., 4,139; catechists, 32,155; bap., 481,490; Caths., 19,336,000 (14.8%); tot. pop., 129,972,000.

Republic in West Africa; capital, Lagos. The Portuguese introduced Catholicism to the coastal region in the 15th century. Capuchins did some evangelization in the 17th century but systematic missionary work did not get under way along the coast until about 1840. A vicariate for this area was organized in 1870. A prefecture was set up in 1911 for missions in the northern part of the country, where Islam was strongly entrenched. From 1967, when Biafra seceded, until early in 1970 the country was torn by civil war. The hierarchy was established in 1950. Under the 1993-99 rule of Gen. Sani Abacha, Church leaders spoke out on behalf of human rights and democracy. After Abacha announced elections, the bishops said the country needed "new leading actors and fresh vision." As the 21st century began, bishops spoke out against imposition of Islamic law in individual states within the country.

Norway*

Dioc., 1; prel., 2; bp., 3; parishes, 33; priests, 77 (32 dioc., 45 rel.); p.d., 3; sem., 7; bros., 2; srs., 164; bap., 734; Caths., 60,000 (1%); tot. pop., 4,590,000.

Constitutional monarchy in northern Europe; capital, Oslo. Evangelization begun in the ninth century by missionaries from England and Ireland put the Church on a firm footing about the turn of the 11th century. The first diocese was set up in 1153 and development of the Church progressed until the Black Death in 1349 inflicted losses from which it never recovered.

Lutheranism, introduced from outside in 1537 and furthered cautiously, gained general acceptance by about 1600 and was made the state religion. Legal and other measures crippled the Church, forcing priests to flee the country and completely disrupting normal activity. Changes for the better came in the 19th century, with the granting of religious liberty in 1845 and the repeal of many legal disabilities in 1897. Norway was administered as a single apostolic vicariate from 1892 to 1932, when it was divided into three jurisdictions.

Oman

Parishes, 4; priests, 9 (1 dioc., 8 rel.); bap., 166; Caths., 60,000 (2.6%); tot. pop., 2,724,000.

Independent monarchy in eastern corner of Arabian Peninsula; capital, Muscat. Under ecclesiastical jurisdiction of Arabia apostolic vicariate.

Pakistan*

Archd., 2; dioc., 4; p.a., 1; abp., 3; bp., 5; parishes, 114; priests, 269 (145 dioc., 124 rel.); sem., 102; bros., 58; srs., 781; catechists, 630; bap., 20,121; Caths., 1,207,000 (.08%); tot. pop., 150,470,000.

Islamic republic in southwest Asia; capital, Islamabad. Islam, firmly established in the eighth century, is the state religion. Christian evangelization of the native population began about the middle of the 19th century, years after earlier scattered attempts. The hierarchy was established in 1950. A series of death sentences against Christians accused of blasphemy resulted in acquittals during appeal processes, but in 1998 Bishop John Joseph of Faisalabad committed suicide to protest the strict blasphemy laws, which continued to be used as reasons for Christian arrests. In early 2002, the government did away with the system under which religious minorities, such as Catholics, could only vote in elections for members of their religious group. Pakistani Christians, including Catholics, have been the target of several terrorist incidents since the United States attacked Afghanistan in October 2001.

Palau*

Parishes, 3; priests, 5 (2 dioc., 3 rel.); p.d., 1; srs., 6; bap., 316; Caths., 9,000 (42%); tot. pop., 19,000.

Independent (1994) nation in western Pacific; capital, Koror; part of Caroline chain of Islands. Under ecclesiastical jurisdiction of diocese of Caroline Islands, Federated States of Micronesia.

Panama*

Archd., 1; dioc., 5; prel., 1; v.a., 1; abp., 2; bp., 8; parishes, 189; priests, 408 (210 dioc., 198 rel.); p.d., 75; sem., 109; bros., 49; srs., 439; catechists, 3,473; bap., 26,896; Caths., 2,665,000 (89%); tot. pop., 3,170,000.

Republic in Central America; capital, Panama City. Catholicism was introduced by Franciscan missionaries and evangelization started in 1514. The Panama Diocese, oldest in the Americas, was set up at the same time. The Catholic Church has favored status and state aid for missions, charities and parochial schools, but freedom is guaranteed to all religions. In May 1989, Panama's bishops accused the government of thwarting the presidential elections and of attempting to intimidate the Church. The elections' legitimate leader, Guillermo Endara, temporarily sought refuge at the

Vatican Embassy in Panama City. After increasing unrest and violence, on Dec. 24, 1989, the country's dictator, Gen. Manuel Noriega, sought refuge at the Vatican Embassy. Ten days later, after U.S. troops spent days blasting the embassy with loud rock music and after meetings with Church diplomatic officials, Noriega surrendered.

Papua New Guinea*

Archd., 4; dioc., 15; abp., 6; bp., 21; parishes, 310; priests, 522 (193 dioc., 329 rel.); p.d., 7; sem., 425; bros., 193; srs., 848; catechists, 3,624; bap., 33,899; Caths., 1,720,000 (33%); tot. pop., 5,490,000.

Independent (Sept. 16, 1975) republic in southwest Pacific; capital, Port Moresby. Marists began evangelization about 1844 but were handicapped by many factors, including "spheres of influence" laid out for Catholic and Protestant missionaries. An apostolic prefecture was set up in 1896 and placed in charge of the Divine Word Missionaries. The territory suffered greatly during World War II. Hierarchy was established for New Guinea and adjacent islands in 1966. A decade-long war that began in the Bougainville area in the late 1980s left many churches, schools and health centers destroyed. At the end of the century, the Church fought social disintegration marked by violence, poverty and corruption.

Paraguay*

Archd., 1; dioc., 11; v.a., 2; mil. ord. 1; abp., 4; bp., 17; parishes, 386; priests, 1,115 (346 dioc., 769 rel.); p.d., 116; sem., 348; bros., 100; srs., 2,143; bap., 83,071; catechists, 52,397; Caths., 5,444,000 (90%); tot. pop., 6,018,000.

Republic in central South America; capital, Asunción. Catholicism was introduced in 1542, evangelization began almost immediately. A diocese erected in 1547 was occupied for the first time in 1556. On many occasions thereafter, dioceses in the country were left unoccupied because of political and other reasons. Jesuits who came into the country after 1609 devised the reductions system for evangelizing the Indians, teaching them agriculture, husbandry, trades and other arts, and giving them experience in property use and community life. The reductions were communes of Indians only, and had an average population of 3,000-4,000, under the direction of the missionaries. At their peak, some 30 reductions had a population of 100,000. Political officials regarded the reductions with disfavor because politicians did not control them and feared that the Indians trained in them might foment revolt and upset the established colonial system under Spanish control. The reductions lasted until about 1768, when the Jesuits were expelled.

Church-state relations following independence from Spain in 1811 were often tense because of government efforts to control the Church through continued exercise of Spanish patronage rights and by other means. The Church as well as the whole country suffered during the War of the Triple Alliance, 1865-70. After that time, the Church had the same kind of experience in Paraguay as in the rest of Latin America, with forces of liberalism, anticlericalism, massive educational needs, poverty, and a shortage of priests and other personnel. In the 1980s, Church-state tensions increased as Catholic leaders spoke out against President Alfredo

Stroessner's decades of one-man rule. A 1988 papal visit seemed to increase the Church's confidence, as bishops repeatedly spoke out against him. The army general who overthrew Stroessner in 1989 said he did so in part to defend the Catholic Church.

Peru*

Archd., 7; dioc., 18; prel., 11; v.a., 8; mil. ord. 1; card., 1; abp., 11; bp., 59; parishes, 1,445; priests, 2,823 (1,540 dioc., 1,283 rel.); p.d., 62; sem., 2,153; bros., 575; srs., 5,714; catechists, 40,855; bap., 342,522; Caths., 24,285,000 (88%); tot. pop., 27,550,000.

Republic on the west coast of South America; capital, Lima. An effective diocese became operational in 1537, five years after the Spanish conquest. Evangelization, already under way, developed for some time after 1570 but deteriorated before the end of the colonial period in the 1820s. The first American saint of the new world was a Peruvian, Rose of Lima, a Dominican tertiary who died in 1617 and was canonized in 1671.

In the new republic founded after the wars of independence the Church experienced problems of adjustment, government efforts to control it through continuation of the patronage rights of the Spanish crown; suppression of houses of religious and expropriation of Church property; religious indifference and outright hostility. In the 20th century, liberation theology was born in Peru under the leadership of Father Gustavo Gutierrez. In the 1980s and early 1990s, the Maoist Sendero Luminoso guerrillas often targeted Church workers, who also found themselves prone to false charges of terrorism. A Peruvian cardinal was credited with much of the success of an early 1990s government effort to win the surrender of the rebels. When the government initiated a drastic economic program in 1990, Peruvian Church leaders worked to help feed and clothe the poor. In the late '90s, the Church successfully fought a government program of sterilization.

Philippines*

Archd., 16; dioc., 56; prel., 6; v.a., 7; mil. ord. 1; card., 3; abp., 16; bp., 101; parishes, 2,947; priests, 7,866 (5,328 dioc., 2,538 rel.); p.d., 13; sem., 6,728; bros., 840; srs., 12,340; catechists, 108,662; bap., 1,587,913; Caths., 67,112,000 (82%); tot. pop., 82,539,000.

Republic, an archipelago of 7,000 islands off the southeast coast of Asia; capital, Manila. Systematic evangelization was begun in 1564 and resulted in firm establishment of the Church by the 19th century. During the period of Spanish rule, which lasted from the discovery of the islands by Magellan in 1521 to 1898, the Church experienced difficulties with the patronage system under which the Spanish crown tried to control ecclesiastical affairs through episcopal and other appointments. This system ended in 1898 when the United States gained possession of the islands and instituted a policy of separation of Church and state. Anticlericalism flared late in the 19th century. The Aglipayan schism, an attempt to set up a nationalist Church, occurred in 1902.

Church leaders and human rights groups constantly criticized abuses under former president and dictator

Ferdinand Marcos. Church newspapers were among those censored or closed after he declared martial law, and religious and lay people were arrested and held without formal charges for long periods of time. After Marcos declared himself the victor in the 1986 elections and international observers declared his win a fraud, the Philippine bishops' call for a nonviolent struggle for justice was seen as the catalyst for the nation's "people power" revolution. Corazon Aquino, Marcos's successor, took refuge with Carmelite nuns during the revolution. At the turn of the century, Church workers often found themselves unintentional victims of violence spurred by Muslim separatists' fight for autonomy in the southern Philippines. Church social action focused on the poor, overseas workers, ecology and a fight against the death penalty.

Poland*

Archd., 15; dioc., 28; mil. ord., 1; ordinariate, 1; cards., 7; abps., 20; bps., 101; parishes, 10,114; priests, 28,546 (22,221 dioc., 6,325 rel.); p.d., 7; sem., 6,427; bros., 1,522; srs., 23,304; catechists, 14,418; bap., 342,613; Caths., 36,617,000 (96%); tot. pop., 38,214,000.

Republic in Eastern Europe; capital, Warsaw. The first traces of Christianity date from the second half of the ninth century. Its spread was accelerated by the union of the Slavs in the 10th century. The first diocese was set up in 968. The Reformation, supported mainly by city dwellers and the upper classes, peaked from about the middle of the 16th century, resulting in numerous conversions to Lutheranism, the Reformed Church and the Bohemian Brethren. A successful Counter-Reformation, with the Jesuits in a position of leadership, was completed by about 1632. The movement served a nationalist as well as religious purpose; in restoring religious unity to a large degree, it united the country against potential invaders, the Swedes, Russians and Turks. The Counter-Reformation had bad side effects, leading to the repression of Protestants long after it was over and to prejudice against Eastern-rite Catholics. The Church, in the same manner as the entire country, was adversely affected by the partitions of the 18th and 19th centuries. Russification hurt the Eastern- and Latin-rite Catholics.

In the republic established after World War I the Church reorganized itself, continued to serve as a vital force in national life, and enjoyed generally harmonious relations with the state. Progressive growth was strong until 1939, when German and Russian forces invaded and World War II began. In 1945, seven years before the adoption of a Soviet-type of constitution, the communist-controlled government initiated a policy that included a constant program of atheistic propaganda; a strong campaign against the hierarchy and clergy; the imprisonment in 1948 of 700 priests and even more religious; rigid limitation on the activities of the Catholic press and religious movements.

Regular contacts on a working level were initiated by the Vatican and Poland in 1974; regular diplomatic relations were established in 1989. Cardinal Karol Wojtyla of Krakow was elected to the papacy in 1978. Church and papal support was strong for the independent labor movement, Solidarity, which was recognized by the government in August 1980 but outlawed in December 1981, when martial law was imposed (mar-

tial law was suspended in 1982). In May 1989, following recognition of Solidarity and a series of political changes, the Catholic Church was given legal status for the first time since the communists took control of the government in 1944. In 1990, a new constitution was adopted, declaring Poland a democratic state. In 1992, the pope restructured the Church in Poland, adding 13 new dioceses. A new concordat between the Polish government and the Holy See was signed in 1993.

Since the end of communist rule, Poland's Church has struggled with anti-Semitism among some clergy. A dispute over a Carmelite convent outside the former Nazi death camp at Auschwitz resulted in the convent's removal, but several years later the Church was forced to speak against Catholic protesters who posted hundreds of crosses outside the camp. A nearly eight-year national synod process concluded in 1999 with calls for priests to live less luxurious lifestyles and to keep parishes finances open. The Polish Church continued to be a source of missionary priests in more than 90 countries.

Portugal*

Patriarchate (Lisbon), 1; archd., 2; dioc., 17; mil. ord., 1; patriarch, 1; card., 2; abp., 7; bp., 41; parishes, 4,400; priests, 4,010 (2,966 dioc., 1,044 rel.); p.d., 161; sem., 498; bros., 298; srs., 6,026; catechists, 61,835; bap., 86,096; Caths., 9,388,000 (92%); tot. pop., 10,450,000.

Republic in the western part of the Iberian peninsula; capital, Lisbon. Christianity was introduced before the fourth century. From the fifth century to early in the eighth century the Church experienced difficulties from the physical invasion of barbarians and the intellectual invasion of doctrinal errors in the forms of Arianism, Priscillianism and Pelagianism. The Church survived under the rule of Arabs from about 711 and of the Moors until 1249. Ecclesiastical life was fairly vigorous from 1080 to 1185, and monastic influence became strong. A decline set in about 1450. Several decades later Portugal became the jumping-off place for many missionaries to newly discovered colonies. The Reformation had little effect in the country.

In the early 1700s, King John V broke relations with Rome and required royal approval of papal acts. His successor, Joseph I, expelled the Jesuits from Portugal and the colonies. Liberal revolutionaries with anti-Church policies made the 19th century a difficult one for the Church. Similar policies prevailed in Church-state relations in the 20th century until the accession to power of Premier Antonio de Oliveira Salazar in 1928; the hierarchy was seen as closely aligned with him. In 1940 Salazar concluded a concordat with the Holy See that regularized Church-state relations but still left the Church in a subservient condition.

In 1930, after lengthy investigation, the Church authorized devotion to Our Lady of Fátima, who appeared to three Portuguese children in 1917. Pope John Paul II, who credited Our Lady of Fátima with saving his life during a 1981 assassination attempt on her feast day, visited Portugal several times, including in May 2000 to beatify two of the Fátima visionaries. At that time, he had his Secretary of State, Cardinal Angelo Sodano, announce that the so-called third secret of Fátima would be published. The following month, the Vatican published the secret and said the message predicted the struggles of the Church with Nazism and communism and foretold the shooting of Pope John Paul.

Puerto Rico

Archd., 1; dioc., 4; card., 1; abp., 1; bp., 7; parishes, 327; priests, 721 (378 dioc., 343 rel.); p.d., 402; sem., 100; bros., 57; srs., 1,113; catechists, 25,840; bap., 27,604; Caths., 3,059,000 (78%); tot. pop., 3,899,000. (AD)

A U.S. commonwealth, the smallest of the Greater Antilles, 885 miles southeast of the southern coast of Florida; capital, San Juan. Following its discovery by Columbus in 1493, the island was evangelized by Spanish missionaries and remained under Spanish ecclesiastical as well as political control until 1898, when it became a possession of the United States. The original diocese, San Juan, was erected in 1511. The present hierarchy was established in 1960.

Qatar

Parish; priest, 6 (1 dioc., 5 rel.); p.d., 1; bap., 164; Caths., 50,000 (11.8%); tot. pop., 585,000.

Independent state in the Persian Gulf; capital, Doha. Under ecclesiastical jurisdiction of Arabia apostolic vicariate.

Réunion

Dioc., 1; bp., 2; parishes, 56; priests, 115 (61 dioc., 54 rel.); p.d., 14; sem., 13; bros., 17; srs., 319; catechists, 3,410; bap., 11,246; Caths., 620,000 (82.6%); tot. pop., 750,000. (AD)

French overseas department, 450 miles east of Madagascar; capital, Saint-Denis. Catholicism was introduced in 1667 and some intermittent missionary work was done through the rest of the century. An apostolic prefecture was organized in 1712. Vincentians began work there in 1817 and were joined later by Holy Ghost Fathers. In 1998 the bishops joined their counterparts in Guadeloupe, French Guiana and Martinique to call slavery "an immense collective sin."

Romania*

Archd., 3; dioc., 8; ord., 1; ex., 1; abp., 6; bp., 12; parishes, 1,438; priests, 1,828 (1,588 dioc., 240 rel.); p.d., 1; sem., 701; bros., 171; srs., 1,327; catechists, 686; bap., 10,957; Caths., 1,932,000 (8.4%); tot. pop., 21,850,000.

Republic in southeastern Europe; capital, Bucharest. Latin Christianity, introduced in the third century, all but disappeared during the barbarian invasions. The Byzantine rite was introduced by the Bulgars about the beginning of the eighth century and established firm roots. It eventually became Orthodox, but a large number of its adherents returned later to union with Rome.

Communists took over the government following World War II, forced the abdication of Michael I in 1947, and enacted a Soviet type of constitution in 1952. By that time a campaign against religion was already in progress. In 1948 the government denounced a concordat concluded in 1929, nationalized all schools and passed a law on religions that resulted in the disorganization of Church administration. The 1.5 million-member Romanian Byzantine-rite Church, by government decree, was incorporated into the Romanian Orthodox Church, and Catholic properties were given to the Orthodox. Five of the six Latin-rite bishops were immediately disposed of by the government, and the last was sentenced to 18 years' imprisonment in 1951. Religious orders were suppressed in 1949.

Some change for the better in Church-state relations was reported after the middle of the summer of 1964, although restrictions were still in effect. The Eastern Church regained liberty in 1990 with the change of government. The hierarchy was restored and diplomatic relations with the Holy See were re-established. Today, most Latin-rite Catholics are ethnic Hungarians residing in Transylvania.

Pope John Paul II visited Romania May 7-9, 1999, but remained in Bucharest; he split time between visits with Catholics and Orthodox and did not visit Transylvania, despite an invitation from the region's bishops. To facilitate the visit, Eastern Catholics gave up their demands for the return of all former Church properties and agreed to work on committees with Orthodox to discuss each case individually. Church leaders said the historic visit led to a deeper openness and understanding between Catholics and Orthodox.

Russia*

Archd., 2; dioc. 5 (3 for European Russia, 2 for Siberia); ap. ex., 1; abp., 2; bp., 3; parish, 411; priests, 301 (122 dioc., 179 rel.); p.d., 1; sem., 99; bros., 27; srs, 365; bap., 1,366; Caths., 809,000 (.05%); tot. pop., 147,120,000.

Federation in Europe and Asia; capital, Moscow. The Orthodox Church has been predominant in Russian history. It developed from the Byzantine Church before 1064. Some of its members subsequently established communion with Rome as the result of reunion movements, but most remained Orthodox. The government has always retained some kind of general or particular control of this Church.

From the beginning of the Communist government in 1917, all churches of whatever kind became the targets of official campaigns designed to negate their influence on society and/or to eliminate them entirely. An accurate assessment of the situation of the Catholic Church in Russia was difficult to make. Research by a Polish priest, reported in 1998, documented the arrests, trials and fabricated confessions of priests in the 1920s and 1930s. A report by a team of research specialists made public by the Judiciary Committee of the U.S. House of Representatives in 1964 said: "The fate of the Catholic Church in the USSR and countries occupied by the Russians from 1917 to 1959 shows the following: (a) the number killed: 55 bishops; 12,800 priests and monks; 2.5 million Catholic believers; (b) imprisoned or deported: 199 bishops; 32,000 priests and 10 million believers; (c) 15,700 priests were forced to abandon their priesthood and accept other jobs; and (d) a large number of seminaries and religious communities were dissolved." Despite repression, Lithuania and Ukraine remained strongholds of Catholicism.

During his 1985-91 presidency, Soviet President Mikhail Gorbachev met twice with Pope John Paul II — meetings later credited with the return of religious freedom in the Soviet Union. In 1991, the pope established two Latin-rite apostolic administrations in the Russian Republic: one in Moscow and one based in Novosibirsk, Siberia.

Catholic communities in Europe and the United States have been instrumental in helping to rebuild the Church in Russia. Under a 1997 religion law, every religious organization in Russia had to register on a national level, then re-register each parish by the end of 1999 to enjoy full legal benefits such as owning property and publishing religious literature. The apostolic administrations registered with no problems, but after the Russian government rejected the Jesuits' registration application, they were forced to take the matter to the country's constitutional court, which ruled that they qualified.

The Vatican's upgrading of Russia's four apostolic administrations to dioceses in early 2002 provoked new tensions with the Orthodox, who accused the Catholic Church of trying to convert its members. Russian authorities refused to readmit five prominent Church leaders, including one bishop, after they left the country. The Vatican eventually appointed a new bishop for the vacant Russian diocese and transferred the expelled bishop.

Rwanda*

Archd., 1; dioc., 8; abp., 2; bp., 8; parishes, 143; priests, 579 (456 dioc., 123 rel.); p.d., 2; sem., 403; bros., 152; srs., 1,442; catechists, 4,125; bap., 130,855; Caths., 4,167,000 (47%); tot. pop., 8,817,000.

Republic in east central Africa; capital, Kigali. Catholicism was introduced about the turn of the 20th century. The hierarchy was established in 1959. Intertribal warfare between the ruling Hutus (90 percent of the population) and the Tutsis (formerly the ruling aristocracy) plagued the country for a number of years. In April 1994, the deaths of the presidents of Rwanda and Burundi in a suspicious plane crash sparked the outbreak of a ferocious civil war. Among the thousands of victims — mostly Tutsis — were three bishops and about 25 percent of the clergy. Thousands more fled the country.

Although in 1996 Pope John Paul II said that all members of the Church who participated in the genocide must face the consequences, in 1997 the Vatican donated $50,000 to help ensure that certain people — including priests and religious — received fair trials. Two nuns accused of participating in the genocide were sent to prison in Belgium, but a bishop was acquitted after a nine-month trial in Rwanda. The bishop later said Marian apparitions in his diocese in the 1980s foretold the genocide.

Saint Lucia*

Archd., 1; abp., 1; parishes, 22; priests, 28 (14 dioc., 14 rel.); sem., 3; p.d., 9; bros., 6; srs., 47; catechists, 304; bap., 1,336; Caths., 100,000 (63%); tot. pop., 158,000.

Independent (Feb. 22, 1979) island state in West Indies; capital, Castries.

Saint Vincent and the Grenadines*

Dioc., 1; bp., 1; parishes, 6; priests, 10 (5 dioc., 5 rel.); sem., 1; srs., 16; catechists, 63; bap., 107; Caths., 10,000 (9%); tot. pop., 109,000.

Independent state (1979) in West Indies; capital, Kingstown. The Kingstown diocese (St. Vincent) was

established in 1989; it was formerly part of Bridgetown-Kingstown Diocese with see in Barbados. The Vatican established diplomatic relations with St. Vincent and the Grenadines in 1990. The Church is recognized for its role in education and health care.

Samoa, American

Dioc., 1; bp., 1; parishes, 14; priests, 16 (11 dioc., 5 rel.); p.d., 16; sem., 6; srs., 17; bap., 403; Caths., 12,000 (20%); tot. pop., 64,000.

Unincorporated U.S. territory in southwestern Pacific, consisting of six small islands; seat of government, Pago Pago on the Island of Tutuila. Samoa-Pago Pago Diocese established in 1982.

Samoa, Western*

Archd., 1; abp., 1; parishes, 35; priests, 52 (32 dioc., 20 rel.); p.d., 17; sem., 10; bros., 18; srs., 78; catechists, 149; bap., 1,365; Caths., 34,000 (19%); tot. pop., 183,000.

Independent state in the southwestern Pacific; capital, Apia. Catholic missionary work began in 1845. Most of the missions now in operation were established by 1870 when the Catholic population numbered about 5,000. Additional progress was made in missionary work from 1896. The first Samoan priest was ordained in 1892. A diocese was established in 1966; elevated to a metropolitan see in 1982.

San Marino*

Parishes, 12; priests, 29 (12 dioc., 17 rel.); p.d. 1; bros., 2; srs 17; bap., 257; Caths., 28,000 (96%); tot. pop., 29,000.

Republic, a 24-square-mile enclave in northeastern Italy; capital, San Marino. The date of initial evangelization is not known, but a diocese was established by the end of the third century. Ecclesiastically, it forms part of the Diocese of San Marino-Montefeltro in Italy.

São Tome and Principe*

Dioc., 1; bp., 1; parishes, 12; priests, 10 (2 dioc., 8 rel.); sem. 8; bros., 1; srs., 40; catechists, 592; bap., 2,665; Caths., 103,000 (73%); tot. pop., 140,000.

Independent republic (July 12, 1975), consisting of two islands off the western coast of Africa in the Gulf of Guinea; former Portuguese territory; capital, São Tome. Evangelization was begun by the Portuguese who discovered the islands in 1471-72. The São Tome Diocese was established in 1534. In a 1992 visit to São Tome, a major transport center for slaves until the mid-1800s, Pope John Paul II condemned slavery as "a cruel offense" to African dignity.

Saudi Arabia

Parishes, 4; priests, 4 (1 dioc., 3 rel.); p.d., 1; srs., 16.; bap., 444; Caths., 801,000; total pop., 22,100,000.

Monarchy occupying four-fifths of Arabian peninsula; capital, Riyadh. Population is Muslim; all other religions are banned. Christians in the area are workers from other countries. The Church falls under the ecclesiastical jurisdiction of the Arabian apostolic vicariate. In May 1999, Pope John Paul II met with the crown prince of Saudi Arabia at the Vatican.

Scotland*

Archd., 2; dioc., 6; card., 1; abp., 1; bp., 7; parishes,

471; priests, 726 (599 dioc., 127 rel.); p.d., 30; sem., 24; bros., 222; srs., 727; bap., 8,224; Caths., 704,377 (14%); tot. pop., 5,000,107.

Part of the United Kingdom, in the northern British Isles; capital, Edinburgh. St. Ninian's arrival in 397 marked the beginning of Christianity in Scotland. The arrival of St. Columba and his monks in 563 inaugurated a new era of evangelization that reached into remote areas by the end of the sixth century. He was extremely influential in determining the character of the Church, which was tribal, monastic, and in union with Rome. Considerable disruption of Church activity resulted from Scandinavian invasions in the late eighth and ninth centuries. By 1153 the Scottish Church took a turn away from its insularity and was drawn into closer contact with the European community. Anglo-Saxon religious and political relations, complicated by rivalries between princes and ecclesiastical superiors, were not always the happiest.

From shortly after the Norman Conquest of England to 1560 the Church suffered adverse effects from the Hundred Years' War, the Black Death, the Western Schism and other developments. In 1560 Parliament abrogated papal supremacy over the Church in Scotland and committed the country to Protestantism in 1567. The Catholic Church was proscribed, to remain that way for more than 200 years, and the hierarchy was disbanded. Defections made the Church a minority religion from that time on. Presbyterian Church government was ratified in 1690. Priests launched the Scottish Mission in 1653, incorporating themselves as a mission body under an apostolic prefecture and working underground to serve the faithful in much the same way their confreres did in England. Catholics got some relief from legal disabilities in 1793 and more relief later. Many left the country about that time. Some of their numbers were filled subsequently by immigrants from Ireland. About 100 heather priests, trained in clandestine places in the heather country, were ordained by the early 19th century. The hierarchy was restored in 1878. In a 1997 message to celebrations marking 1,600 years of Christianity in Scotland, Pope John Paul II urged Catholics to make new efforts at evangelization and ecumenism.

Senegal*

Archd., 1; dioc., 6; abp., 2; bp., 8; parishes, 120; priests, 401 (285 dioc., 116 rel.); sem., 136; bros., 172; srs., 753; catechists, 2,332; bap., 11,286; Caths., 544,000 (5%); tot. pop., 10,456,000.

Republic in West Africa; capital, Dakar. The country had its first contact with Catholicism through the Portuguese some time after 1460. Some incidental missionary work was done by Jesuits and Capuchins in the 16th and 17th centuries. A vicariate for the area was placed in charge of the Holy Ghost Fathers in 1779. More effective evangelization efforts were accomplished after the Senegambia vicariate was erected in 1863; the hierarchy was established in 1955. During a 1992 trip to the predominantly Muslim country, Pope John Paul II praised the small Catholic community for its contributions, especially in the areas of health care and education.

Serbia and Montenegro*

Archd., 2; dioc., 3; ex., 1; a.a., 1; abp., 5; bp., 5; parishes, 294; priests, 276 (229 dioc., 47 rel.); p.d., 7; sem., 62; bros., 5; srs., 327; bap., 4,273; Caths., 515,000 (5%); tot. pop., 10,738,000.

Federation in southeastern Europe formed in 2003 from the former Yugoslav republics of Serbia and Montenegro; capital, Belgrade.

Christianity was introduced from the seventh to ninth centuries in the regions combined to form Yugoslavia after World War I. Since these regions straddled the original line of demarcation for the Western and Eastern Empires (and churches), and since the Reformation had little lasting effect, the Christians are nearly all either Latin- or Eastern-rite Catholics or Orthodox. Yugoslavia was proclaimed a Socialist republic in 1945, and persecution of the Catholic Church began. In an agreement signed June 25, 1966, the government recognized the Holy See's spiritual jurisdiction over the Church in the country and guaranteed to bishops the possibility of maintaining contact with Rome in ecclesiastical and religious matters. During early 1990s the split of the Yugoslav republic, Catholic leaders joined Orthodox and, in some cases, Muslim leaders in calling for peace.

Seychelles*

Dioc., 1; bp., 1; parishes, 17; priests, 14 (8 dioc., 6 rel.); p.d., 1; sem., 4; bros. 1; srs., 54; catechists, 410; bap., 1,106; Caths., 70,000 (85%); tot. pop., 82,000.

Independent (1976) group of 92 islands in the Indian Ocean; capital, Victoria. Catholicism was introduced in the 18th century. An apostolic vicariate was organized in 1852. All education in the islands was conducted under Catholic auspices until 1954. In 1991, Bishop Felix Paul of Port Victoria said the country's one-party socialist government was an affront to the rights and dignity of its people, but President France-Albert René continued to lead the government into the 21st century. Pope John Paul II warned Seychelles to beware of the dark side of tourism, a main industry in the country.

Sierra Leone*

Archd., 1; dioc., 2; abp., 2; bp., 3; parishes, 60; priests, 129 (78 dioc., 51 rel.); sem., 49; bros., 36; srs., 55; catechists, 512; bap., 6,090; Caths., 196,000 (4%); tot. pop., 5,168,000.

Republic on the west coast of Africa; capital, Freetown. Catholicism was introduced in 1858. Members of the African Missions Society, the first Catholic missionaries in the area, were joined by Holy Ghost Fathers in 1864. Protestant missionaries were active in the area before their Catholic counterparts. Educational work had a major part in Catholic endeavor. The hierarchy was established in 1950. Most of the inhabitants are followers of traditional African religions.

Church leaders suffered at the hands of rebel soldiers in the late 1990s, when a military coup ousted the country's democratically elected government. Although some Church workers fled to neighboring Guinea, some remained. Rebels kidnapped several foreign missionaries and, shortly before West African intervention forces ousted them from power in 1998, rebels forced the archbishop of Freetown to strip naked while they plundered his office. As the war lessened and later ended, the Church worked for reconciliation, to rehabilitate child soldiers and to rebuild damaged Church property.

Singapore*

Archd., 1; abp., 2; parishes, 30; priests, 139 (70 dioc., 69 rel.); sem., 33; bros., 61; srs., 245; catechists, 1,768; bap., 3,784; Caths., 166,000 (3.8%); tot. pop., 4,240,000.

Independent island republic off the southern tip of the Malay Peninsula; capital, Singapore. Christianity was introduced in the area by Portuguese colonists about 1511. Singapore was founded in 1819; the first parish Church was built in 1846. Freedom of religion is generally respected, although in the late 1980s nearly a dozen people involved in Catholic social work were arrested and detained without trial under the Internal Security Act.

Slovakia*

Archd., 2; dioc., 5; ap. ex., 1; card., 2; abp., 3; bp., 19; parishes, 1,493; priests, 2,691 (2,107 dioc., 584 rel.); p.d., 19; sem., 656; bros., 186; srs., 2,917; catechists, 2,322; bap., 39,935; Caths., 3,964,000 (73%); tot. pop., 5,399,000.

Independent state (Jan. 1, 1993); formerly part of Czechoslovakia; capital, Bratislava. Christianity was introduced in Slovakia in the eighth century by Irish and German missionaries, and the area was under the jurisdiction of German bishops. In 863, Sts. Cyril and Methodius began pastoral and missionary work in the region, ministering to the people in their own language. A diocese established at Nitra in 880 had a continuous history (except for one century ending in 1024). The Church in Slovakia was severely tested by the Reformation and political upheavals. After World War I, when it became part of the Republic of Czechoslovakia, it was 75 percent Catholic.

Vigorous persecution of the Church began in Slovakia in 1944, when communists mounted an offensive against bishops, priests and religious. Msgr. Josef Tiso, a Catholic priest who served as president of the Slovak Republic from 1939-45, was tried for "treason" in December 1946 and was executed the following April.

In 1972, the government ordered the removal of nuns from visible but limited apostolates to farms and mental hospitals. In 1973, the government allowed the ordination of three bishops in the Slovak region.

When Slovakia split from Czechoslovakia in 1993, the country slid into economic difficulties. Church-state tensions increased, and the Slovakian government eventually apologized to Bishop Rudolf Balaz of Banska Bystrica, whose house had been raided in a government investigation of stolen art. In an attempt to fight the effects of decades of communism, in 1996 the bishops said all adult Catholics who had not received confirmation must undergo a special two-year catechism course. In 2000, the government and Vatican signed an accord establishing the Church's legal status.

Slovenia*

Archd., 1; dioc., 2; abp., 2; card., 1; bp., 8; parishes, 793; priests, 1,160 (843 dioc., 317 rel.); p.d., 14; sem., 118; bros., 40; srs., 714; catechists, 505; bap., 13,043; Caths., 1,620,000 (82.6%); tot. pop., 1,993,000.

Independent republic (1991) in southeastern Europe; formerly part of Yugoslavia; capital, Ljubljana. Established diplomatic relations with the Holy See in 1992. After independence, Church leaders found themselves in repeated skirmishes with Slovenia's governing coalition over religious education, restitution of Church property and the Church's proper social role.

Solomon Islands*

Archd., 1; dioc., 2; abp., 1; bp., 3; parishes, 27; priests, 67 (38 dioc., 29 rel.); sem., 43; bros., 17; srs., 95; catechists, 1,074; bap., 2,592; Caths., 93,000 (21%); tot. pop., 442,000.

Independent (July 7, 1978) island group in Oceania; capital, Honiara, on Guadalcanal. After violence interrupted the Marists' evangelization of the Southern Solomons, they resumed their work in 1898. An apostolic vicariate was organized in 1912. A similar jurisdiction was set up for the Western Solomons in 1959. World War II caused a great deal of damage to mission installations.

Somalia

Dioc., 1; parish, 1; priests, 4 (1 dioc., 3 rel.), bros., 1; srs., 4; Caths., 100; tot. pop., 6,773,000. (AD)

Republic on the eastern coast of Africa; capital, Mogadishu. The country has been Muslim for centuries. Pastoral activity has been confined to immigrants. Schools and hospitals were nationalized in 1972, resulting in the departure of some foreign missionaries.

South Africa*

Archd., 4; dioc., 21; v.a., 1; mil. ord., 1; card., 1; abp., 5; bp., 29; parishes, 744; priests, 1,130 (480 dioc., 650 rel.); p.d., 224; sem., 600; bros., 178; srs., 2,456; catechists, 13,356; bap., 55,749; Caths., 3,162,000 (7%); tot. pop., 46,590,000.

Republic in the southern part of Africa; capitals, Cape Town (legislative), Pretoria (administrative) and Bloemfontein (judicial). Christianity was introduced by the Portuguese who discovered the Cape of Good Hope in 1488. Boers, who founded Cape Town in 1652, expelled Catholics from the region. There was no Catholic missionary activity from that time until the 19th century. A bishop established residence in 1837, and evangelization got under way thereafter among the Bantus and white immigrants. The hierarchy was established in 1951.

Under South Africa's apartheid regime, the Church found itself the victim of attacks, from the parish level to the headquarters of the bishops' conference in Pretoria. Some Church leaders were detained, tortured and deported, particularly in the 1970s and 1980s. However, in a 1997 statement to South Africa's Truth Commission, the Catholic Church said the complicity of some Catholics with apartheid was in "acts of omission rather than commission." Since the end of apartheid, Catholic leaders have spoken out against an increase in violence and anti-Muslim sentiment and have worked to combat the growing AIDS problem. Reports of clergy sexual abuse became public in 2003.

Spain*

Archd., 14; dioc., 55; mil. ord., 1; card., 9; abp., 25; bp., 93; parishes, 22,599; priests, 26,330 (17,866 dioc.,

8,464 rel.); p.d., 248; sem., 2,259; bros., 4,691; srs., 55,388; catechists, 102,973; bap., 324,901; Caths., 38,470,000 (94%); tot. pop., 41,954,000.

Constitutional monarchy on the Iberian peninsula in southwestern Europe; capital, Madrid. Christians were on the peninsula by 200; some of them suffered martyrdom during persecutions of the third century. A council held in Elvira about 305 enacted the first legislation on clerical celibacy in the West. Vandals invaded the peninsula in the fifth century, bringing with them an Arian brand of Christianity that they retained until their conversion following the baptism of their king, Reccared, in 589.

In the seventh century, Toledo was established as the primatial see. The Visigoth kingdom lasted to the time of the Arab invasion, 711-14. The Church survived under Muslim rule but experienced some doctrinal and disciplinary irregularities as well as harassment. Re-evangelization of most of the peninsula was accomplished by 1248; unification was achieved during the reign of Ferdinand and Isabella. The discoveries of Columbus and other explorers ushered in an era of colonial expansion in which Spain became one of the greatest missionary-sending countries in history. In 1492, in repetition of anti-Semitic actions of 694, the expulsion of unbaptized Jews was decreed, leading to mass baptisms but a questionable number of real conversions in 1502. Activity by the Inquisition followed. Spain was not seriously affected by the Reformation. Ecclesiastical decline set in about 1650.

Anti-Church actions authorized by a constitution enacted in 1812 resulted in the suppression of religious and other encroachments on the leaders, people and goods of the Church. Political, religious and cultural turmoil recurred during the 19th century and into the 20th. A revolutionary republic was proclaimed in 1931, triggering a series of developments that led to civil war from 1936 to 1939. During the conflict, which pitted leftist Loyalists against the forces of Francisco Franco, more than 6,600 priests and religious and an unknown number of lay people were massacred. One-man, one-party rule, established after the civil war and with rigid control policies with respect to personal liberties and social and economic issues, continued for more than 35 years before giving way after the death of Franco to democratic reforms. Since the 1970s, the Catholic Church has not been the established religion; the constitution guarantees freedom for other religions as well. In the late 20th century, Spanish Church leaders fought a growing feeling of indifference among many Catholics. After the March 2004 al-Qaida bombings led to the election of a Socialist government, Spanish Church leaders were appalled by the series of social policy changes being proposed by the new government.

Sri Lanka*

Archd., 1; dioc., 10; abp., 5; bp., 10; parishes, 391; priests, 1,080 (683 dioc., 397 rel.); sem., 445; bros., 180; srs., 2,461; catechists, 9,863; bap., 25,499; Caths., 1,365,000 (7%); tot. pop., 20,372,000.

Independent socialist republic, island southeast of India; capital, Colombo. The Portuguese began evangelizing in the 16th century. In 1638, the Dutch began forcing Portuguese from the coastal areas. The Dutch outlawed Catholicism, banished priests and confiscat-

ed buildings, forcing people to become Calvinists. Blessed Joseph Vaz, an Oratorian priest, is credited with almost single-handedly reviving the Catholic Church toward the end of the 17th century.

Anti-Catholic laws were repealed by the British in 1806. The hierarchy was established in 1886; the country gained independence in 1948. Sri Lankan bishops repeatedly called for reconciliation in the nearly two-decade war between the Liberation Tigers of Tamil Eelam and the Sinhalese-dominated government; a cease-fire was signed in early 2002. In an unusual move in January 1998, Archbishop Nicholas M. Fernando of Colombo, authorized by the Vatican Congregation for the Doctrine of the Faith, lifted the excommunication of a prominent Sri Lankan theologian, Oblate Father Tissa Balasuriya.

Sudan*

Archd., 2; dioc., 7; ap. ex., 1; card., 1; abp., 2; bp., 11; parishes, 217; priests, 379 (264 dioc., 115 rel.); p.d., 4; sem., 246; bros., 70; srs., 311; catechists, 3,562; bap., 45,383; Caths., 4,047,000 (13%); tot. pop., 34,510,000.

Republic in northeastern Africa, the largest country on the continent; capital Khartoum. Christianity was introduced from Egypt and gained acceptance in the sixth century. Under Arab rule, it was eliminated in the northern region. No Christians were in the country in 1600.

Evangelization attempts begun in the 19th century in the south yielded hard-won results. By 1931 there were nearly 40,000 Catholics there, and considerable progress was made by missionaries after that time. In 1957, a year after the republic was established, Catholic schools were nationalized. An act restrictive of religious freedom went into effect in 1962, resulting in the harassment and expulsion of foreign missionaries. By 1964 all but a few Sudanese missionaries had been forced out of the southern region. The northern area, where Islam predominates, is impervious to Christian influence.

Late in 1971 some missionaries were allowed to return to work in the South. The hierarchy was established in 1974. The most recent fighting, which began in 1983, originally pitted the mostly Arab and Muslim North against the mostly black African Christian and animist South, but it has since evolved into a nation-wide conflict fuelled by religion, ethnicity, oil and ideology. The imposition of Islamic penal codes in 1984 was a cause of concern to all Christian Churches. Recent government policies have denied Christians the right to places of worship and authorization to gather for prayer. Bishops from the South have condemned human rights violations — aggravated by famine and war — in their area. They have said they want peace but cannot accept an Islamic state and were hopeful that terms of a 2005 peace agreement would hold. The agreement would allow southerners to vote on independence after a six-year period of power-sharing.

Surinam*

Dioc., 1; bp., 1; parishes, 32; priests, 22 (6 dioc., 16 rel.); sem., 1; bros., 7; srs., 10; bap., 1,090; Caths., 137,000 (23%); tot. pop., 475,000.

Independent (Nov. 25, 1975) state in northern South America; capital, Paramaribo. Catholicism was introduced in 1683. Evangelization began in 1817.

Swaziland*

Dioc., 1; bp., 1; parishes, 15; priests, 24 (12 dioc., 12 rel.); sem., 9; bros., 7; srs., 58; bap., 912; Caths., 55,000 (5.1%); tot. pop., 1,083,000.

Monarchy in southern Africa, almost totally surrounded by South Africa; capital, Mbabane. Missionary work was entrusted to the Servites in 1913. An apostolic prefecture was organized in 1923. The hierarchy was established in 1951. Swaziland established diplomatic relations with the Holy See in 1992. In the 1990s, Swazi Catholics worked to help transform the country to a democracy but to retain the traditions of the people.

Sweden*

Dioc., 1; abp., 1; bp., 3; parishes, 43; priests, 156 (74 dioc., 82 rel.); p.d., 24; sem., 7; bros., 11; srs., 210; catechists, 394; bap., 1,193; Caths., 149,000 (1.6%); tot. pop., 9,011,000.

Constitutional monarchy in northwestern Europe; capital, Stockholm. Christianity was introduced by St. Ansgar, a Frankish monk, in 829-830. The Church became well-established in the 12th century and was a major influence at the end of the Middle Ages. Political and other factors favored the introduction and spread of the Lutheran Church, which became the state religion in 1560. The Augsburg Confession of 1530 was accepted by the government; all relations with Rome were severed; monasteries were suppressed; the very presence of Catholics in the country was forbidden in 1617. A decree of tolerance for foreign Catholics was issued about 1781. Two years later an apostolic vicariate was organized for the country. In 1873 Swedes were given the legal right to leave the Lutheran church and join another Christian church. Membership in the Lutheran church is presumed by law unless notice is given of membership in another church.

Since 1952 Catholics have enjoyed almost complete religious freedom. The hierarchy was re-established in 1953. Hindrances to growth of the Church are the strongly entrenched established church, limited resources, a clergy shortage and the size of the country. In the 1960s, an influx of guest workers increased the number of Catholics, and in the 1970s and 1980s, refugees helped increase Church numbers. In 1998, the pope named the first Swedish bishop in more than 400 years. In the early 21st century, the government worked to give the Church and other minority faiths the right to operate as legal entities, including owning property.

Switzerland*

Dioc., 6; abb., 2; card., 3; abp., 4; bp., 18; parishes, 1,660; priests, 2,970 (1,747 dioc., 1,223 rel.); p.d., 187; sem., 199; bros., 348; srs., 5,590; catechists, 1,923; bap., 30,410; Caths., 3,257,000 (44%); tot. pop., 7,266,000.

Confederation in central Europe; capital, Bern. Christianity was introduced in the fourth century or earlier and was established on a firm footing before the barbarian invasions of the sixth century. Constance, established as a diocese in the seventh century, was a stronghold of the faith against the pagan Alamanni, in particular, who were not converted until some time in the ninth century. During this period of struggle with the barbarians, a number of monasteries of great influence were established.

The Reformation in Switzerland was triggered by Zwingli in 1519 and furthered by him at Zurich until his death in battle against the Catholic cantons in 1531. Calvin set in motion the forces that made Geneva the international capital of the Reformation and transformed it into a theocracy. Catholics mobilized a Counter-Reformation in 1570, six years after Calvin's death. Struggle between Protestant and Catholic cantons was a fact of Swiss life for several hundred years. The Helvetic Constitution enacted at the turn of the 19th century embodied anti-Catholic measures and consequences, among them the dissolution of 130 monasteries. The Church was reorganized later in the century to meet the threats of liberalism, radicalism and the Kulturkampf. In the process, the Church, even though on the defensive, gained the strength and cohesion that characterizes it to the present time. In 1973, constitutional articles banning Jesuits from the country and prohibiting the establishment of convents and monasteries were repealed. In the 1990s, Swiss bishops battled internal divisions and sought forgiveness for any anti-Semitism on behalf of the Church.

Syria*

Patriarchates, 1 (Greek Melkites; patriarchs of Antioch of Maronites and Syrians reside in Lebanon); archd., 12 (1 Armenian, 2 Maronite, 5 Greek Melkite, 4 Syrian); dioc., 3 (Armenian, Chaldean, Maronite); v.a., 1 (Latin); ap.ex., 1; patriarch, 1; card., 1; abp., 17; bp., 4; parishes, 211; priests, 265 (185 dioc., 80 rel.); p.d., 11; sem., 81; bros., 12; srs., 354; catechists, 1,025; bap., 2,639; Caths., 417,000 (2%); tot. pop., 17,980,000.

Arab socialist republic in southwest Asia; capital, Damascus. Christian communities were formed in apostolic times. It is believed that St. Peter established a see at Antioch before going to Rome. Damascus became a center of influence. The area was the place of great men and great events in the early history of the Church. Monasticism developed there in the fourth century; so did the Monophysite and Monothelite heresies to which a portion of the Church succumbed. Byzantine Syrians who remained in communion with Rome were given the name Melkites. Christians of various persuasions — Jacobites, Orthodox and Melkites — were subject to various degrees of harassment from the Arabs who took over in 638 and from the Ottoman Turks who isolated the country and remained in control from 1516 to the end of World War II.

Syrian Catholics are members of the Armenian, Chaldean, Greek-Melkite, Latin, Maronite and Syrian rites. During a visit to Syria in May 2001, Pope John Paul II became the first pontiff in history to enter a mosque. Early in the 21st century, growing instability in neighboring countries, including Iraq, led to an influx of Christians and challenges for the small but flourishing Catholic community.

Taiwan*

Archd., 1; dioc., 7; card., 1; abp., 3; bp., 9; parishes, 448; priests, 705 (235 dioc., 470 rel.); p.d., 1; sem., 84;

bros., 119; srs., 1,083; catechists, 504; bap., 3,417; Caths., 306,000 (1.3%); tot. pop., 22,314,000.

Democratic island state, 100 miles off the southern coast of mainland China; capital, Taipei. Attempts to introduce Christianity in the 17th century were unsuccessful. Evangelization in the 19th century resulted in some 1,300 converts in 1895. Missionary endeavor was hampered by the Japanese, who occupied the island following the Sino-Japanese war of 1894-95. Great progress was made in missionary endeavor among the Chinese who emigrated to the island (seat of the Nationalist Government of the Republic of China) following the Communist takeover of the mainland in 1949. The hierarchy was established in 1952. Many Taiwanese Catholics have worked to form a bridge to Catholics in mainland China. China has said the Vatican's diplomatic relations with Taiwan form the biggest stumbling block to Sino-Vatican relations.

Tajikistan*

Mission, 3; parishes, 2; priests, 5 (5 rel.); srs., 4; bap., 13; Cath., 2,000; tot. pop. 6,570,000.

Independent republic (1992) in Asia; formerly part of the USSR; capital, Dushanbe. The majority of the population is Sunni Muslim. When the Vatican established diplomatic relations in 1996, Church officials estimated most of the country's Catholics had fled. In 1997, the Vatican established a mission in the country.

Tanzania*

Archd., 5; dioc., 25; card., 1; abp., 5; bp., 33; parishes, 853; priests, 2,242 (1,513 dioc., 729 rel.); p.d. 2; sem., 1,191; bros., 854; srs., 7,851; catechists, 12,601; bap., 289,511; Caths., 10,847,000 (29%); tot. pop., 37,671,000.

Republic on and off the eastern coast of Africa; capital, Dar es Salaam. The first Catholic mission in the former Tanganyikan portion of the republic was manned by Holy Ghost Fathers in 1868. The hierarchy was established there in 1953. Zanzibar was the landing place of Augustinians with the Portuguese in 1499. Some evangelization was attempted between then and 1698 when the Arabs expelled all priests from the territory. There was no Catholic missionary activity from then until the 1860s. The Holy Ghost Fathers arrived in 1863 and were entrusted with the mission in 1872. Zanzibar was important as a point of departure for missionaries to Tanganyika, Kenya and other places in East Africa. A vicariate for Zanzibar was set up in 1906.

In the late 20th century the Church in Tanzania saw an increase in vocations and an active Church life. The bishops assisted hundreds of thousands of refugees from Rwanda, Burundi and Mozambique. More recently, Church leaders worked to stem the AIDS pandemic and to improve education.

Thailand*

Archd., 2; dioc., 8; card., 1; abp., 2; bp., 9; parishes, 436; priests, 703 (443 dioc., 260 rel.); sem., 274; bros., 113; srs., 1,442; catechists, 1,735; bap., 5,887; Caths., 928,000 (1.4%); tot. pop., 63,928,000.

Constitutional monarchy in southeast Asia; capital, Bangkok. The first Christians in the region were Portuguese traders who arrived early in the 16th century. A number of missionaries began arriving in the mid-1500s, but pastoral care was confined mostly to the Portuguese until the 1660s, when evangelization began. A seminary was organized in 1665, a vicariate was set up four years later, and a point of departure was established for China. Persecution and death for some of the missionaries ended evangelization efforts in 1688. It was resumed, however, and made progress from 1824 onward. In 1881 missionaries were sent from Siam to neighboring Laos. The hierarchy was established in 1965. Archbishop Michael Michai Kitbunchu was named the first Thai cardinal in 1983. The Church is recognized for its social justice efforts, including work with refugees.

Togo*

Archd., 1; dioc., 6; abp., 1; bp., 6; parishes, 160; priests, 485 (358 dioc., 127 rel.); sem., 324; bros., 210; srs., 764; catechists, 4,795; bap., 32,875; Caths., 1,521,000 (30%); tot. pop., 5,058,000.

Republic on the west coast of Africa; capital, Lome. The first Catholic missionaries in the area, where slave raiders operated for nearly 200 years, were members of the African Missions Society who arrived in 1563. They were followed by Divine Word Missionaries in 1914, when an apostolic prefecture was organized. At that time the Catholic population numbered about 19,000. The African Missionaries returned after their German predecessors were deported following World War I. The first indigenous priest was ordained in 1922. The hierarchy was established in 1955. In the early 1990s, Archbishop Philippe Fanoko Kossi Kpodzro of Lome served as president of the transitional legislative assembly.

Tonga*

Dioc., 1; bp., 1; parishes, 10; priests, 21 (14 dioc., 7 rel.); sem., 27; bros., 7; srs., 43; bap., 458; Caths., 14,000 (14.5%); tot. pop., 94,000.

Polynesian monarchy in the southwestern Pacific, consisting of about 150 islands; capital, Nuku'alofa. Marists started missionary work in 1842, some years after Protestants had begun evangelization. By 1880 the Catholic population numbered about 1,700. A vicariate was organized in 1937. The hierarchy was established in 1966. Tonga established diplomatic relations with the Holy See in 1994.

Trinidad and Tobago*

Archd., 1; abp., 2; bp., 1; parishes, 61; priests, 124 (46 dioc., 78 rel.); sem., 22; bros., 10; srs., 147; catechists, 311; bap., 4,203; Caths., 390,000 (30%); tot. pop., 1,307,000.

Independent nation, consisting of two islands in the Caribbean; capital, Port-of-Spain. The first Catholic Church in Trinidad was built in 1591, years after several missionary ventures had been launched and a number of missionaries killed. Capuchins were there from 1618 until about 1802. Missionary work continued after the British gained control early in the 19th century. Cordial relations have existed between the Church and state, both of which have manifested their desire for the development of indigenous clergy. In 1999, Church leaders protested reinstatement of the death penalty.

Tunisia*

Dioc., 1; abp., 1; parishes, 11; priests, 35 (16 dioc.,

19 rel.); bros., 7; sem., 2; srs., 130; bap., 35; Caths., 20,000 (.02%); tot. pop., 9,937,000.

Republic on the northern coast of Africa; capital, Tunis. Ancient Carthage, now a site outside the capital city of Tunis, hosted early Church councils and was home to Church fathers like St. Augustine. Carthage was devastated by Vandals in the fifth century and invaded by Muslims in the seventh century, after which it had few Christians until the 19th century. An apostolic vicariate was organized in 1843, and the Carthage Archdiocese was established in 1884. The Catholic population in 1892 consisted of most of the approximately 50,000 Europeans in the country. When Tunis became a republic in 1956, most of the Europeans left the country. A 1964 agreement with the Vatican and Holy See suppressed the Archdiocese of Carthage and replaced it with the Territorial Prelature of Tunis. In 1995 the prelature was made a diocese.

Today Tunisia's Catholics are predominantly foreign nationals. The Church's social presence is seen in schools, hospitals and institutions for the disabled.

Turkey*

Archd., 3; v.a., 2; ord., 1; ap. ex., 1; abp., 5; bp., 2; parishes, 48; priests, 65 (13 dioc., 52 rel.); p.d., 4; sem., 5; bros., 11; srs., 95; bap., 97; Caths., 32,000 (.05%); tot. pop., 71,700,000.

Republic in Asia Minor and southeastern Europe; capital, Ankara. Christian communities were established in apostolic times, as attested in the Acts of the Apostles, some of the Letters of St. Paul, and Revelation. The territory was the scene of heresies and ecumenical councils, the place of residence of Fathers of the Church, and the area in which ecclesiastical organization reached the dimensions of more than 450 sees in the middle of the seventh century. The region remained generally Byzantine except for the period of the Latin occupation of Constantinople from 1204 to 1261, but was conquered by the Ottoman Turks in 1453 and remained under their domination until establishment of the republic in 1923. Christians, always a minority, numbered more Orthodox than Catholics; they all were under some restrictions during the Ottoman period. They suffered persecution in the 19th and 20th centuries, the Armenians being the most numerous victims. Turkey is overwhelmingly Muslim. Catholics are tolerated to a degree.

Turkmenistan*

Mission, 1; parish, 1; priests, 2 (rel.); bap., 1; Caths., 1,000; tot. pop., 6,520,000.

Former constituent republic of USSR; independent, 1991; capital, Ashgabat. Almost all the population is Sunni Muslim. The Vatican established diplomatic relations with the country in 1996 and set up a mission in 1997.

Tuvalu

Mission, 1; parish, 1; priest, 2 (rel.); bap., 2; Caths., 100; tot. pop., 11,000.

Independent state (1978) in Oceania, consisting of 9 islands; capital, Funafuti.

Uganda*

Archd., 4; dioc., 15; mil. ord., 1; card., 1; abp., 3; bp., 25; parishes, 441; priests, 1,688 (1,350 dioc., 338 rel.);

p.d., 1; sem., 1,011; bros., 479; srs., 3,059; catechists, 12,491; bap., 329,562; Caths., 11,628,000 (44%); tot. pop., 26,628,000.

Republic in East Africa; capital, Kampala. The Missionaries of Africa (White Fathers) were the first Catholic missionaries, starting in 1879. Persecution broke out from 1885 to 1887, taking a toll of 22 Catholic martyrs, who were canonized in 1964, and a number of Anglican victims. (Pope Paul VI honored all those who died for the faith during a visit to Kampala in 1969.) By 1888, there were more than 8,000 Catholics. Evangelization was resumed in 1894, after being interrupted by war, and proceeded thereafter. The first African bishop was ordained in 1939. The hierarchy was established in 1953.

The Church was suppressed during the erratic regime of President Idi Amin, who was deposed in the spring of 1979. Guerrilla activity in northern and southwestern Uganda has hampered Church workers, and Church leaders have worked for peace. The Church has devoted much of its resources to caring for the many victims of HIV/AIDS in the country.

Ukraine*

Major archbishopric, 1 (Ukrainian); archd., 3 (Metropolitans); dioc., 14; pat. ex., 2; card., 2; abp., 3; bp., 25; parishes, 4,135; priests, 2,897 (2,458 dioc., 439 rel.); p.d., 22; sem., 1,103; bros., 101; srs., 1,134; catechists, 1,785; bap., 31,633; Caths., 4,697,000 (10%); tot. pop., 47,440,000.

Independent republic bordering on the Black Sea; former USSR republic; capital, Kiev. The baptism of Vladimir and his people in 988 marked the beginning of Christianity in the territory of Kievan Rus, which is included in today's Ukraine. The 1596 Union of Brest brought the Ukrainian Byzantine-rite community back into communion with Rome. The Eastern Catholic Church was officially suppressed and underground in the USSR from the late 1940s; all of its bishops were killed or imprisoned and its property seized by the government and given to the Orthodox. Some Catholic priests continued to minister clandestinely under communist rule.

As the Eastern Church regained its legal status under Soviet President Mikhail Gorbachev, serious tensions arose with the Orthodox over ownership of property and the allegiance of priests and lay people. Latin-rite dioceses were re-established in 1991. In the late 1990s, rising inflation and weakening currency, aggravated by the government's and some companies' failure to pay wages, led Ukrainian Church leaders to fight homelessness and hunger. Despite opposition from Ukraine's largest Orthodox Church, Pope John Paul II visited Ukraine in June 2001. He challenged Ukrainians to talk to each other and focus on unity, despite religious, ethnic and political tensions. Despite Russian Orthodox objections, the Ukrainian Catholic Church moved its headquarters from Lviv to Kiev and Halych in 2005.

United Arab Emirates

V.a, 1; bp., 2; parishes, 6; priests, 20 (5 dioc., 15 rel.); srs., 42; bap., 1,550; Caths., 356,000 (10%); tot. pop., 3,480,000.

Independent state along Persian Gulf; capital, Abu Dhabi. The apostolic vicariate of Arabia has its seat in

Abu Dhabi. It includes the states of Bahrain, Oman, Qatar, Saudi Arabia and Yemen (see separate entries) as well as United Arab Emirates.

United States*

(See Catholic Church in the U.S.; see also Chronology of American Catholic History; and Statistics of the Church in the U.S.)

Uruguay*

Archd., 1; dioc., 9; abp., 3; bp., 15; parishes, 227; priests, 481 (210 dioc., 271 rel.); p.d., 82; sem., 90; bros., 102; srs., 1,014; catechists, 5,027; bap., 27,268; Caths., 2,560,000 (75%); tot. pop., 3,400,000.

Republic on the southeast coast of South America; capital, Montevideo. The Spanish established a settlement in 1624 and evangelization followed. Missionaries followed the reduction pattern to reach the Indians, form them in the faith and train them in agriculture, husbandry, other arts, and the experience of managing property and living in community. The constitution of 1830 made Catholicism the religion of the state and subsidized some of its activities, principally the missions to the Indians. Separation of Church and state was provided for in the constitution of 1917. In 1997, despite a court decision halting further investigations, the Church pledged to make one last effort to help search for people who remained missing from the 1973-85 military dictatorship.

Uzbekistan*

A.a, 1; parishes, 5; priests, 9 (9 rel.); bros., 3; sem., 1; srs., 10; bap., 56; Caths. 4,000; tot. pop. 26,210,000.

Former republic of USSR; independent, 1991; capital, Tashkent. The communist government confiscated Catholic properties in 1917 and severely repressed the practice of religion in the country. The country won its independence in 1991. The majority of the population is Sunni Muslim. A small number of Catholics live in Tashkent. The Vatican established a mission in 1997. In 2005 the Church became an apostolic administration and received its first Catholic bishop.

Vanuatu*

Dioc., 1; bp., 1; parishes, 23; priests, 27 (15 dioc., 12 rel.); p.d., 1; sem., 12; bros., 19; srs., 59; catechists, 299; bap., 479; Caths., 32,000 (16%); tot. pop., 211,000.

Independent (July 29, 1980) island group in the southwest Pacific; capital, Vila. Effective, though slow, evangelization by Catholic missionaries began about 1887. An apostolic vicariate was set up in 1904. The hierarchy was established in 1966.

Vatican City State (See separate entry)

Venezuela*

Archd., 9; dioc., 23; ord.; v.a., 4; ap. ex., 2; mil. ord. 1; card., 2; abp., 11; bp., 41; parishes, 1,291; priests, 2,501 (1,531 dioc., 970 rel.); p.d., 164; sem., 1,264; bros., 265; srs., 3,844; catechists, 26,979; bap., 403,376; Caths., 22,606,000 (87%); tot. pop., 26,170,000.

Republic in northern South America; capital, Caracas. Evangelization began in 1513-14 and involved members of a number of religious orders who worked in assigned territories, developing missions into pueblos or villages of Indian converts. Nearly 350 towns originated as missions. The first diocese was established in 1531.

Fifty-four missionaries met death by violence from the start of missionary work until 1817. Missionary work was seriously hindered during the wars of independence in the second decade of the 19th century and continued in decline through the rest of the century as dictator followed dictator in a period of political turbulence. Restoration of the missions got under way in 1922. In the 1990s, the Church worked at reconciliation in the country but condemned government corruption and violent crime. Church leaders also called for respect for human rights. In mid-2005, amid increasing poverty, several surveys found the Catholic Church had the highest respect of any of the nation's institutions.

Vietnam

Archd., 3; dioc., 22; card., 2; abp., 1; bp., 38; parishes, 2,234; priests, 2,862 (2,308 dioc., 554 rel.); p.d., 20; sem., 2,136; bros., 1,885; srs., 11,514; catechists, 50,984; bap., 147,126, Caths., 5,777,000 (6.8%); tot. pop., 81,799,000.

Country in southeast Asia, reunited officially July 2, 1976, as the Socialist Republic of Vietnam; capital, Hanoi.

Catholicism was introduced in 1533, but missionary work was intermittent until 1615, when Jesuits arrived to stay. Two vicariates were organized in 1659. A seminary was set up in 1666, and two Vietnamese priests were ordained two years later. A congregation of native women religious formed in 1670 is still active. Severe persecution broke out in 1698, three times in the 18th century, and again in the 19th. Up to 300,000 people suffered in some way from persecution during the 50 years before 1883, when the French moved in to secure religious liberty for the Catholics. Most of the 117 beatified Martyrs of Vietnam were killed during this 50-year period. After the French were forced out of Vietnam in 1954, the country was partitioned at the 17th parallel. The North became Communist and the Viet Cong, joined by North Vietnamese regular army troops in 1964, fought to gain control of the South. In 1954 there were approximately 1.1 million Catholics in the North and 480,000 in the South. More than 650,000 fled to the South to avoid the government repression. In South Vietnam, the Church continued to develop during the war years.

After the end of the war in 1975, the government exercised control over virtually all aspects of Church life. In the late 1980s, bishops noted some softening of the government's hard line. In the 1990s, the Vatican and Vietnam held intermittent talks on Church-state issues, with sporadic progress reported, but in 1997, the government censored the section of the "Catechism of the Catholic Church" that dealt with human rights. Although at times the Vatican was forced to wait years for government approval of bishops' appointments, in the late 20th and early 21st century, Vatican delegations made regular visits to Vietnam to discuss the appointments and other Church-related issues. Early in the 21st century, the government approved a series of bishops' appointments in northern Vietnam, and Church leaders said they saw a rejuvenation of the faith there.

Virgin Islands (U.S.)

Dioc., 1 (St. Thomas, suffragan of Washington, D.C.); bp., 2; parishes, 8; priests, 20 (14 dioc., 6 rel.); p.d., 30; sem., 6; bros., 4; srs., 18; bap., 234; Caths., 30,000 (29%); tot. pop., 109,000.

Organized unincorporated U.S. territory in Atlantic Ocean; capital, Charlotte Amalie on St. Thomas (one of the three principal islands). The islands were discovered by Columbus in 1493 and named for St. Ursula and her virgin companions. Missionaries began evangelization in the 16th century. A church on St. Croix dates from about 1660; another, on St. Thomas, from 1774. The Baltimore Archdiocese had jurisdiction over the islands from 1804 to 1820, when it was passed on to the first of several places in the Caribbean area. Some trouble arose over a pastoral appointment in the 19th century, resulting in a small schism. The Redemptorists took over pastoral care in 1858; normal conditions have prevailed since.

Wales*

Archd., 1; dioc., 2; abp., 2; bp., 3; parishes, 179; priests, 236 (138 dioc., 98 rel.); p.d., 10; sem., 11; bros., 109; srs., 396; bap, 2,275; Caths., 140,242 (.5%); tot. pop., 2,895,350.

Part of the United Kingdom, on the western part of the island of Great Britain. Celtic missionaries completed evangelization by the end of the sixth century, the climax of what has been called the age of saints. Welsh Christianity received its distinctive Celtic character at this time. Some conflict developed when attempts were made — and proved successful later — to place the Welsh Church under the jurisdiction of Canterbury; the Welsh opted for direct contact with Rome.

The Church made progress despite the depredations of Norsemen in the eighth and ninth centuries. Norman infiltration occurred near the middle of the 12th century, resulting in a century-long effort to establish territorial dioceses and parishes to replace the Celtic organizational plan of monastic centers and satellite churches. The Western Schism produced split views and allegiances. Actions of Henry VIII in breaking away from Rome had serious repercussions. Proscription and penal laws crippled the Church, resulted in heavy defections and touched off a 150-year period of repression. Methodism prevailed by 1750. Modern Catholicism came to Wales with Irish immigrants in the 19th century, when the number of Welsh Catholics was negligible. Catholic emancipation was granted in 1829. The hierarchy was restored in 1850. Wales shares a bishops' conference with England.

Yemen*

Parishes, 4; priests, 5 (rel.); srs., 24; bap., 2; Caths., 4,000; tot. pop., 20,801,000.

Republic on southern coast of Arabian peninsula; capital, Sana. Formerly North Yemen (Arab Republic of Yemen) and South Yemen (People's Republic of Yemen); formally reunited in 1990. Christians perished in the first quarter of the sixth century. Muslims have been in control since the seventh century. The state religion is Islam; the Church is under the ecclesiastical jurisdiction of Arabia apostolic vicariate. In the early 1990s, Salesians reported some harassment of Church workers in the South. In early 1998, three Missionaries of Charity nuns were murdered. The Vatican established diplomatic relations with Yemen in October 1998.

Zambia*

Archd., 2; dioc., 8; abp., 5; bp., 6; parishes, 265; priests, 639 (302 dioc., 337 rel.); p.d., 3; sem., 408; bros., 173; srs., 1,640; catechists, 9,744; bap., 54,317; Caths., 3,532,000 (31%); tot. pop., 11,244,000.

Republic in central Africa; capital, Lusaka. Portuguese priests did some evangelizing in the 16th and 17th centuries but no results of their work remained in the 19th century. Jesuits began work in the South in the 1880s and White Fathers in the North and East in 1895. Evangelization of the western region began for the first time in 1931. The number of Catholics doubled in the 20 years following World War II.

Zambian Catholics have welcomed tens of thousands of refugees from the region. In the 1990s, Zambian Church leaders worked caring for victims of HIV/AIDS and spoke out against foreign debt. In 2003, the bishops urged parishes to set up civic education programs to help with the nation's constitutional review process.

Zimbabwe*

Archd., 2; dioc., 6; abp., 4; bp., 3; parishes, 212; priests, 453 (202 dioc., 251 rel.); p.d., 11; sem., 441; bros., 99; srs., 1,064; catechists, 8,588; bap., 33,401; Caths., 1,312,000 (10%); tot. pop., 13,311,000.

Independent republic (1980) in south central Africa; capital, Harare. Earlier unsuccessful missionary ventures preceded the introduction of Catholicism in 1879. Missionaries began to make progress after 1893. The hierarchy was established in 1955; the first black bishop was ordained in 1973.

In 1969, four years after the government of Ian Smith made a unilateral declaration of independence from England, a new constitution was enacted for the purpose of assuring continued white supremacy over the black majority. Catholic and Protestant prelates in the country protested. The Smith regime was ousted in 1979 after seven years of civil war in which at least 25,000 people were killed.

In 1997, the bishops published a report detailing more than 7,000 cases of killings, torture and human rights abuses by government troops in western Zimbabwe from 1981-87. As the Church entered the 21st century, it was devoting tremendous resources toward palliative care of AIDS victims and work with AIDS orphans. However, the Church was sometimes criticized for not doing enough to prevent the spread of AIDS, which Church and health-care workers said was exacerbated by poverty and cultural beliefs. Some lay Church leaders were outspoken against government-backed campaigns of violence against white landowners and the poor; Bishop Pius Ncube of Bulawayo was targeted for speaking against government abuses.

CATHOLIC WORLD STATISTICS

(Principal sources: Statistical Yearbook of the Church, 2004 (the latest edition); figures are as of Jan. 1, 2005, unless indicated otherwise.)

	Africa	North America	South America	Asia	Europe	Oceania	WORLD TOTALS
Patriarchates[2]	2	-	-	8	2	-	12
Archdioceses	86	87	99	129	176	18	596
Dioceses	389	363	411	334	507	55	2,059
Prelatures	-	7	31	6	6	-	50
Abbacies	-	-	-	-	10	-	10
Exarchates/Ords.	-	-	6	1	17	-	24
Military Ords.	3	4	9	3	14	2	35
Vicariates Apostolic	16	5	37	19	1	-	78
Prefectures	7	-	2	6	-	1	16
Apostolic Admin.	1	-	1	2	4	-	8
Independent Missions	1	2	-	4	1	2	10
Cardinals[3]	17	26	25	20	100	4	192
Patriarchs[2]	-	-	-	8	2	-	10
Archbishops	120	138	156	166	358	24	962[4]
Bishops	521	721	747	493	1,074	98	3,628[4]
Priests	31,259	77,256	44,378	48,222	199,978	4,798	405,891
Diocesan	20,358	51,128	26,628	28,497	139,494	2,728	268,833
Religious	10,901	26,128	17,750	19,725	60,484	2,070	137,058
Perm. Deacons	368	17,114	3,953	148	10,528	213	32,324
Brothers	7,791	9,902	6,685	9,028	19,942	1,682	55,030
Sisters	57,475	132,852	86,149	150,736	329,898	10,076	767,459
Maj. Seminarians	22,791	14,640	22,041	29,220	23,401	951	113,044
Sec. Inst. Mbrs. (Men)	47	40	151	34	399	1	672
Sec. Inst. Mbrs. (Women)	481	1,799	4,053	1,493	20,401	43	28,270
Lay Missionaries	3,926	22,916	144,920	11,920	2,263	522	186,467
Catechists	379,656	850,996	875,238	297,259	522,865	15,131	2,940,798
Parishes	12,212	33,650	22,047	21,584	125,337	2,341	217,171[5]
Kindergartens	11,102	8,306	6,749	12,918	22,809	1,189	63,073
Students	1,014,584	859,048	948,229	1,714,162	1,683,150	92,942	6,312,115
Elem./PrimarySchools	31,130	14,231	10,036	15,502	17,187	3,004	91,090
Students	11,985,1381	829,758	3,443,362	4,964,853	3,176,389	639,042	7,975,541
Secondary Schools	7,968	4,030	6,925	8,676	10,008	670	38,277
Students	3,021,647	1,590,434	2,087,703	4,972,926	3,815,610	379,853	15,868,173
Students, Higher Insts.[6]	55,753	399,559	176,325	954,763	235,740	8,009	1,830,149
Social Service Facilities	15,424	18,534	22,845	20,090	34,836	2,324	114,053
Hospitals	953	1,020	746	1,136	1,221	170	5,246
Dispensaries	4,922	2,894	2,598	3,637	2,677	496	17,224
Leprosariums	236	17	49	341	3	2	648
Homes for Aged/Handic.	638	1,914	1,928	1,835	8,158	454	14,927
Orphanages	1,675	970	1,457	3,104	2,887	70	10,163
Nurseries	1,236	1,280	2,711	3,217	2,396	92	10,932
Matrimonial Advice Ctrs.	1,407	2,971	2,578	1,074	5,531	305	13,866
Social Educ. Ctrs.	2,568	5,689	7,742	4,032	9,818	682	30,531
Other Institutions	1,789	1,779	3,036	1,714	2,145	53	10,516
Baptisms	3,474,749	3,874,415	4,501,862	2,580,416	2,374,087	123,412	16,928,941
Under Age 7	2,244,582	3,599,978	3,893,547	2,182,384	2,296,805	109,429	14,326,725
Over Age 7	1,230,167	274,437	608,315	398,032	77,282	13,983	2,602,216
Marriages	341,184	663,708	596,848	610,383	842,897	23,191	3,078,211
Between Catholics	302,258	589,931	580,112	552,790	776,513	14,659	2,816,263
Mixed Marriages	38,926	73,777	16,736	57,593	66,384	8,532	261,948
Catholic Pop.[7]	148,817,000	233,753,000	315,003,000	113,489,000	278,736,000	8,568,000	1,098,366,000
World Population	876,720,000	511,906,000	368,415,000	3,893,898,000	704,912,000	32,649,000	6,388,500,000

1. Includes Central America. 2. For listing and description, see Index. 3. As of Aug. 30, 2006. 4. Figures for the hierarchy (cardinals, abps. and bps.) includ. 2,697 ordinaries, 593 coadjutors or aux., 272 with offices in the Roman Curia, 17 in other offices, 1,205 ret. 5. 164,856 have parish priests; 48,165 are administered by other priests; 599 are entrusted to perm. deacons; 188 to bros; 773 to women rel.; 1,575 to lay people; 1,015 vacant. 6. There are also approximately 262,141 in univs. for ecclesiastical studies and 2,399,022 other univ. students. 7. Percentages of Catholics in world pop.: Africa, 16.9; North America (Catholics 80,400,000; tot. pop., 327,494,000), 24.5; Central America (Catholics, 153,353,000; tot. pop., 184,412,000), 83.1; South America, 85; Asia, 2.9; Europe, 39.5; Oceania, 26.5; world, 17.2 (Catholic totals do not include those in areas that could not be surveyed, est. to be approx. 9 million).

EPISCOPAL CONFERENCES

(*Principal sources:* Annuario Pontificio *and* Catholic Almanac *survey.*)

Episcopal conferences, organized and operating under general norms and particular statutes approved by the Holy See, are official bodies in and through which the bishops of a given country or territory act together as pastors of the Church.

Listed according to countries or regions are titles and addresses of conferences, telephone numbers (where possible), and names and sees of presidents.

Africa, Northern: *Conference Episcopale Regionale du Nord de l'Afrique* (CERNA), 13 rue Khelifa-Boukhalfa, 16000 Algiers, Algeria; (021) 63-35-62. Abp. Vincent Landel (Rabat).

Africa, Southern: Southern African Catholic Bishops' Conference (SACBC), 140 Visagie St., P.O. Box 941, Pretoria 0001, S. Africa; (021) 65-35-62. Cardinal Wilfrid Napier, O.F.M. (Durban, South Africa).

Albania: *Conferenza Episcopale dell'Albania*, Tirane, Rruga Don Bosco 1, Kulia Postare 2950; (042) 47-159. Abp. Angelo Massafra, O.F.M. (Shkodre, Albania).

Angola and São Tome: *Conferencia Episcopal de Angola e HR Tome* (CEAST), C.P. 3579 Luanda, Angola; (02) 44-36-86. Archbishop Franklin Damiao (Luanda).

Antilles: Antilles Episcopal Conference (AEC), P.O. Box 3086, St. James (Trinidad and Tobago), W.I.; (868) 622-2932. Abp. Lawrence Burke (Nassau).

Arab Countries: *Conférence des Evêques Latins dans les Régions Arabes* (CELRA), Latin Patriarchate, P.O. Box 14152, Jerusalem (Old City); (02) 628-85-54. Patriarch Michel Sabbah (Jerusalem).

Argentina: *Conferencia Episcopal Argentina* (CEA), C1008AAV, Calle Suipacha 1034, 1008 Buenos Aires; (011) 4328-95-70. Card. Jorge Mario Bergoglio, S.J. (Buenos Aires).

Australia: Australian Catholic Bishops' Conference, 63 Currong St., Braddon, A.C.T. 2601; (02) 6201-9845; www.catholic.org.au. Abp. Francis Patrick Carroll (Canberra, Australia).

Austria: *Österreichische Bischofskonferenz*, Wollzeile 2, A-1010 Vienna; 01-516-11-32.80. Cardinal Christoph Schönborn, O.P. (Vienna).

Bangladesh: Catholic Bishops' Conference of Bangladesh (CBCB), P.O. Box 3, Dhaka-1000; (02) 40-88-79. Abp. Paulinus Costa (Dhaka).

Belgium: *Bisschoppenconferentie van België — Conférence Episcopale de Belgique*, Rue Guimard 1, B-1040 Brussels; (02) 509-96-93; www.catho.be, www.kerknet.be. Card. Godfried Danneels (Mechelen-Brussel).

Belarus: *Conferentia Episcoporum Catholicorum*, 220030 Minsk, pl. Swobody 9; (017) 26.61.27. Card. Kazimierz Swiàtek (Minsk-Mohilev).

Benin: *Conférence Episcopale du Bénin*, Cotonou, 01 B.P. 491; 30.01.45. Abp. Nestor Assogba (Dhaka).

Bolivia: *Conferencia Episcopal Boliviana* (CEB), Casilla 2309, Calle Potosi 814, La Paz; (02) 40-67-98. Card. Julio Terrazas Sandoval, C.SS.R. (Santa Cruz de la Sierra).

Bosnia and Herzegovina: *Biskupska Konferencija Bosne i Hercegovine* (B.K. B.i.H.), *Nadbiskupski Ordinariat*, Kaptol 7, 71000 Sarajevo; (071) 47-21-78. Card. Vinko Puljic (Vrhbosna).

Brazil: *Conferência Nacional dos Bispos do Brasil* (CNBB), C.P. 02067, SE/Sul Quadra 801, Conjunto "B," 70259-970 Brasilia, D.F.; (061) 313-8300. Card. Geraldo Majella Agnelo (São Salvador da Bahia).

Bulgaria: *Mejduritual Episcopska Konferenzia vâv Bâlgaria*, Ul. Liulin Planina 5, 1606 Sofia; (0) 540-406. Bp. Christo Proykov (Briula, titular see).

Burkina Faso and Niger: *Conférence des Evêques de Burkina Faso et du Niger*, B.P. 1195, Ouagadougou, Burkina Faso; 30-60-26. Bp. Philippe Ouédraogo (Ouahigouya).

Burma: See **Myanmar.**

Burundi: *Conférence des Evêques catholiques du Burundi* (C.E.CA.B.), B. P. 1390, 5 Blvd. de l'Uprona, Bujumbura; 223-263. Bp. Jean Ntagwarara (Bubanza).

Cameroon: *Conférence Episcopale Nationale du Cameroun* (CENC), BP 1963, Yaoundé; 231-15-92. Bp. Simon-Victor Tonyé Bakot (Yaoundé).

Canada: *See* **Canadian Conference of Catholic Bishops in Catholic Church in Canada.**

Central African Republic: *Conférence Episcopale Centrafricaine* (CECA), B.P. 1518, Bangui; 50-24-84. Bp. François-Xavier Yombandje (Bossangoa).

Chad: *Conférence Episcopale du Tchad*, B.P. 456, N'Djaména; (235) 51-74-44. Bp. Jean-Claude Bouchard, O.M.I. (Pala).

Chile: *Conferencia Episcopal de Chile* (CECH), Casilla 517-V, Correo 21, Cienfuegas 47, Santiago; (02) 671-77-33. Bp. Alejandro Goic Karmelic (Rancagua).

China: Chinese Regional Episcopal Conference, 34 Lane 32, Kuang-Fu South Rd., Taipeh 10552, Taiwan; (02) 578-2355. Card. Paul Shan Kuo-hsi, S.J. (Kaohsiung).

Colombia: *Conferencia Episcopal de Colombia*, Apartado 7448, Carrera 8ª 47, N. 84-85, Santafé de Bogotá D.E.; (91) 311-42-77. Abp. Luis Augusto Catsro Quiroga, I.M.C. (Tunja).

Congo: *Conférence Episcopale du Congo*, B.P. 200, Brazzaville; (83) 06-29. Bp. Ernest Kombo, S.J. (Owando).

Congo, Democratic Republic (formerly Zaire): *Conférence Episcopale du Zaïre* (CEZ), B.P. 3258, Kinshasa-Gombe; 012-33-992. Abp. Laurent Monsengwo Pasinya (Kisangami).

Costa Rica: *Conferencia Episcopal de Costa Rica* (CECOR), Apartado 497, 1000 San Jose; 221-30-53. Bp. José Francisco Ulloa Rojas (Limon).

Côte d'Ivoire: *Conference Episcopale de la Côte d'Ivoire*, B.P. 1287, Abidjan 01. Bp. Laurent Akran Mandjo (Yopougon).

Croatia: *Hrvatska Biskupska Konferencija*, Kaptol 22, HR-10000 Zagreb; 385-01-481-18-93; www.hbk.hr. Card. Josip Bozanic (Zagreb).

Cuba: *Conferencia de Obispos Católicos de Cuba* (COCC), Apartado 594, Calle 26 n. 314 Miramar, 10100 Havana 1; (07) 22-3868. Card. Jaime Lucas Ortega y Alamino (Havana).

Czech Republic: *Ceská Biskupská Konference*, Sekretariat, Thakurova 3, 160 00 Praha (Prague) 6; (02) 33-15-421. Bp. Jan Graubner (Olomouc).

Dominican Republic: *Conferencia del Episcopado*

Dominicano (CED), Apartado 186, Santo Domingo; (809) 685-3141. Bp. Ramon Benito de la Rosa y Carpio (Nuestra Señora de la Altagracia en Higuey).

Ecuador: *Conferencia Episcopal Ecuatoriana,* Apartado 1081, Avenida América 1805 y Lagasca, Quito; (02) 23-82-21. Bp. Nestor Rafael Herrera Heredia (Machala).

El Salvador: *Conferencia Episcopal de El Salvador* (CEDES). 15 Av. Norte 1420, Col. Layco, Apartado 1310, San Salvador; 25-8997. Abp. Fernando Sáenz Lacalle (San Salvador).

Equatorial Guinea: *Conferencia Episcopal de Guinea Ecuatorial,* Apartado 106, Malabo. Abp. Ildefonso Obama Obono (Malabo).

Ethiopia: Ethiopian Episcopal Conference, P.O. Box 21322, Addis Ababa; (01) 55-03-00. Abp. Berhaneyesus Demerew Souraphiel, C.M. (Addis Ababa).

France: *Conférence des Evêques de France,* 106 rue du Bac, 75341 Paris CEDEX 07; 33-01-45-49-69-70; www.cef.fr. Card. Jean-Pierre Ricard (Bordeaux).

Gabon: *Conférence Episcopale du Gabon,* B.P. 2146, Libreville; 72-20-73. Bp. Timothée Modibo-Nzockena (Franceville).

Gambia, Liberia and Sierra Leone: Inter-Territorial Catholic Bishops' Conference of the Gambia, Liberia and Sierra Leone (ITCABIC), Santanno House, P.O. Box 893, Freetown, Sierra Leone; (022) 22-82-40. Bp. George Biguzzi, S.X. (Makeni).

Germany: *Deutsche Bischofskonferenz,* Postfach 2962, Kaiserstrasse 163, D-53019 Bonn; (0049) 228-103-290. Card. Karl Lehmann (Mainz).

Ghana: Ghana Bishops' Conference, National Catholic Secretariat, P.O. Box 9712 Airport, Accra; (021) 500-491. Bp. Lucas Abadamloora (Navrongo-Bolgatanga).

Great Britain: Bishops' Conference of England and Wales, General Secretariat, 39 Eccleston Square, London, SWIV IBX; (020) 7630-8220. Card. Cormac Murphy-O'Connor (Westminster).

Greece: *Conferentia Episcopalis Graeciae,* Odos Homirou 9, 106 72 Athens; (01) 3642-311. Bp. Franghiskos Papamanolis, O.F.M. Cap. (Syros and Milos and Santorini).

Guatemala: *Conferencia Episcopal de Guatemala* (CEG), Apartado 1698, 01901 Ciudad de Guatemala; 543-18-27/8. Card. Rodolfo Quezada Toruño (Guatemala).

Guinea: *Conférence Episcopale de la Guinée,* B.P. 1006 bis, Conkary. Bp. Philippe Kourouma (N'Zerekore).

Guinea-Bissau: See **Senegal.**

Haiti: *Conférence Episcopale de Haïti* (CEH). B.P. 1572, Angle rues Piquant et Lammarre, Port-au-Prince; 222-5194. Bp. Louis Kébreau, S.D.B. (Hinche).

Honduras: *Conferencia Episcopal de Honduras* (CEH), Apartado 847, Blvd. Estadio Suyapa, Tegucigalpa; (504) 32-40-43. Card. Oscar Andrés Rodríguez Maradiaga (Tegucigalpa).

Hungary: *Magyar Katolikus Püspöki Konferencia,* H-1071 Budapest VII, Városligeti fasor 45; 1-342-69-59. Abp. István Seregély (Eger).

India: Catholic Bishops' Conference of India (CBCI), CBCI Centre, Ashok Place, Goldakkhana,

New Delhi-110001; (011) 334-44-70. Bp. Oswald Gracias (Agra). Conference of Catholic Bishops of India–Latin Rite (CCBI - L.R.), Divya Deepti Sadan, Second Floor, P.B. 680, 9-10 Bhai Vir Singh Marg; (011) 336-42-22. Card.. Placidius Telesphore Toppo (Ranchi).

Indian Ocean: *Conférence Episcopale de l'Océan Indien* (CEDOI) (includes Islands of Mauritius, Seychelles, Comore and La Réunion), 13 rue Msgr. Gonin, Port Louis, Mauritius; (230) 208-3068. Bp. Gilbert Aubry (Reunion).

Indonesia: *Konperensi Waligereja Indonesia* (KWI), Jl. Cut Mutiah 10, Tromolpos 3044, Jakarta 10002; (021) 33-64-22. Card. Julius Riyadi Darmaatmadja, S.J. (Jakarta).

Ireland: Irish Episcopal Conference, *"Ara Coeli,"* Armagh BT61 7QY; 028-3752-2045. Abp. Sean B. Brady (Armagh).

Italy: *Conferenza Episcopale Italiana* (CEI), Circonvallazione Aurelia, 50, 00165 Rome; 06-663-981. Card. Camillo Ruini (Vicar General, Rome).

Ivory Coast: See **Côte d'Ivoire.**

Japan: Catholic Bishops' Conference of Japan, Shiomi 2-10-10, Koto-Ku, Tokyo, 135; (03) 56324411. Bp. Augustinus Junichi Nomura (Nagoya).

Kazakstan: Episcopal Conference of Kazakstan, 473003 Astana, 3 Tashenova St., P.O. Box 622; (3172) 37.29.35. Abp. Tomasz Peta (Most Blessed Mary, Astana).

Kenya: Kenya Episcopal Conference (KEC), The Kenya Catholic Secretariat, P.O. Box 13475, Nairobi; (020) 444-3133. Bp. Cornelius Kipng'eno Arap Korir (Eldoret).

Korea: Catholic Bishops' Conference of Korea, Box 16, Seoul 100-600; (02) 466-3417. Bp. Augustine Cheong Myeng-cho (Pusan).

Laos and Cambodia: *Conférence Episcopale du Laos et du Cambodge,* c/o Msgr. Pierre Bach, Paris Foreign Missions, 254 Silom Rd., Bangkok 10500; (02) 234-1714. Bp. Emile Destombes, M.E.P. (Altava).

Latvia: *Latvijas Biskapu Konference,* Maza Pils iela 2/a, LV-1050, Riga; (7) 22-72-66. Card. Janis Pujats (Riga).

Lesotho: Lesotho Catholic Bishops' Conference, Catholic Secretariat, P.O. Box 200, Maseru 100; (0501) 31-25-25. Bp. Evaristus Thatho Bitsoane (Qacha's Nek).

Liberia: Catholic Bishops' Conference of Liberia, 1000 Monrovia 10, P.O. Box 10-2078; 227-245. Bp. Lewis Zeigler (Gbarnga).

Lithuania: *Conferentia Episcopalis Lituaniae,* Sventaragio, 4, 2001 Vilnius; (5) 212-54-55. Abp. Sigitas Tamkevicius (Kaunas).

Madagascar: *Conférence Episcopale de Madagascar,* 102 bis Av. Maréchal Joffre, Antanimena, B. P 667, Antananarivo; (02) 2220-478. Bp. Fulgence Rabeony, S.J. (Toliara).

Malawi: Episcopal Conference of Malawi, Catholic Secretariat of Malawi, P.O. Box 30384, Lilongwe 3; 782-066. Bp. Tarcisius Gervazio Ziyaye (Blantyre).

Malaysia-Singapore-Brunei: Catholic Bishops' Conference of Malaysia, Singapore and Brunei (BCMSB), Xavier Selangor Darul Ehsan, 46000 Petaling Jaya, Malaysia; (03) 758-1371. Abp. Nicholas Chia (Singapore).

Mali: *Conférence Episcopale du Mali,* B.P. 298,

Bamako; 225-499. Bp. Jean-Gabriel Diarra.

Malta: Konferenza Episkopali Maltija, Archbishop's Curia, Floriana; (356) 234317; www.maltachurch.org.mt. Abp. Joseph Mercieca (Malta).

Mexico: See the Conferencia del Episcopado Mexicano (CEM), in the section on the Catholic Church in Mexico.

Mozambique: Conferência Episcopal de Moçambique (CEM), Av. Paulo Samuel Kankhomba 188/RC, C.P. 286; (01) 49-07-66. Bp. Jaime Pedro Gonçalves (Beira).

Myanmar: Myanmar Catholic Bishops' Conference (MCBC), 292 Pyi Rd., P.O. Box 1080, Yangon; (01) 23-71-98. Bp. Bo Charles Maung, S.D.B. (Pathein).

Namibia: Namibian Catholic Bishops' Conference (NCBC). P.O. Box 11525 W., Windhoek; (061) 22-47-98. Vacant.

Netherlands: Nederlandse Bisschoppenconferentie, Postbus 13049, NL-3507 LA, Utrecht; (31)-30-232-69-00; www.omroep.nl/rkk. Card. Adrianus J. Simonis (Utrecht).

New Zealand: New Zealand Catholic Bishops Conference, P.O. Box 1937, Wellington 6015; (04) 496-1747. Bp. Denis George Browne (Hamilton).

Nicaragua: Conferencia Episcopal de Nicaragua (CEN), Apartado Postal 2407, de Ferretería Lang 1 cuadro al Norte y 1 cuadro al Este, Managua; (02) 666-292. Abp. Leopoldo José Brenes Solorzano (Managua).

Niger: See Burkina Faso.

Nigeria: Catholic Bishops Conference of Nigeria, P.O. Box 951, 6 Force Rd., Lagos; (01) 263-58-49. Abp. John Olorunfemi Onaiyekan (Abuja).

Pacific: Conferentia Episcopalis Pacifici (CE PAC), P.O. Box 289, Suva (Fiji); 300-340. Abp. Anthony Apuron, O.F.M. Cap. (Agana).

Pakistan: Pakistan Episcopal Conference, P.O. Box 909, Lahore 54000; (042) 6366-137. Abp. Lawrence J. Saldanha (Lahore).

Panama: Conferencia Episcopal de Panamá (CEP), Apartado 870033, Panama 7; 223-0075. Abp. José Luis Lacunza Maestrojuán, O.A.R. (David).

Papua New Guinea and Solomon Islands: Catholic Bishops' Conference of Papua New Guinea and Solomon Islands, P.O. Box 398, Waigani, N.C.D., Papua New Guinea; 25-9577. Bp. Francesco Sarego, S.V.D. (Goroka).

Paraguay: Conferencia Episcopal Paraguaya (CEP), Alberdi 782, Casilla Correo 1436, Asunción; (021) 490-920. Bp. Izaguirre Gogorza Ignacio, S.C.I. (Encarnacion).

Peru: Conferencia Episcopal Peruana, Apartado 310, Rio de Janeiro 488, Lima 100; (01) 463-10-10. Bp. José Hugo Garaycoa Hawkins (Tacna y Moquega).

Philippines: Catholic Bishops' Conference of the Philippines (CBCP), P.O. Box 3601, 470 General Luna St., 1099 Manila; (02) 527-4054. Abp. Angel N. Lagdameo (Jaro).

Poland: Konferencja Episkopatu Polski, Skwer Kardynala Stefana Wyszynskiego 6, 01-015 Warsaw; (022) 838-92-51. Jozef Michalik (Przemysl of the Latins).

Portugal: Conferência Episcopal Portuguesa, Campo dos Mártires da Pátria, 43-1 Esq., 1100 Lisbon; 21-885-21-23. Abp. Jorge Ferreira da Costa (Braga).

Puerto Rico: Conferencia Episcopal Puertorriqueña (CEP), P.O. Box 40682, Estacion Minillas, San Juan 00940-0682; (787) 728-1650. Abp. Roberto Octavio Gonzalez Nieves, O.F.M. (San Juan de Puerto Rico).

Romania: Conferinte Episcopala România, Via Popa Tatu 58, Bucharest; (01) 311-12-89. Abp. Lucian Muresan (Major Abp. of Fagaras and Alba Julia).

Russian Federation: Conference of Catholic Bishops of the Russian Federation (C.V.C.F.R.), 101031 Moskva, Via Pietrovka, d. 19 str., 5Kv. 35; (095) 923-16-97. Bp. Joseph Werth, S.J. (Transfiguration at Novosibirsk).

Rwanda: Conférence Episcopale du Rwanda (C.Ep.R.), B.P. 357, Kigali; 75439. Abp. Alexis Habiyambere, S.J. (Nyundo).

Scandinavia: Conferentia Episcopalis Scandiae, Trollbärsvägen 16, S-426 55 Västra Frölunda (Sweden); (031) 709-64-87. Bp. Anders Arborelius, O.C.D. (Stockholm).

Scotland: Bishops' Conference of Scotland, 64 Aitken St., Airdrie, ML6; 44-1236-764-061. Card. Keith Michael Patrick O'Brien (St. Andrews and Edinburgh).

Senegal, Mauritania, Cape Verde and Guinea Bissau: Conférence des Evêques du Sénégal, de la Mauritanie, du Cap-Vert et de Guinée-Bissau, B.P. 941, Dakar, Senegal. Bp. Jean-Noël Diouf (Tambacounda).

Serbia and Montenegro: Biskupska konferecija Srbije I Crne Gore, 11000 Beograd, Visegradska 23; (011) 303.22.46. Bp. Stanslav Hocevar, S.D.B. (Beograd).

Sierra Leone: See Gambia, Liberia and Sierra Leone.

Slovakia: Biskupská Konferencia Slovenska, Kapitulská 11, 81521 Bratislava; (07) 733-54-50. Bp. Frantisek Tondra (Spis).

Slovenia: Slovenska Skofovska Konferenca, Ciril-Metodov trg 4, p.p.1990, 1001 Ljubljana; (386) 1-2342612. Bp. Franc Kramberger (Maribor).

Spain: Conferencia Episcopal Española, Apartado 29075, Calle Añastro 1, 28080 Madrid; 91-343-96-15. Bp. Perez Ricardo Blazquez (Bilbao).

Sri Lanka: Catholic Bishops' Conference of Sri Lanka, 19 Balcombe Place, Cotta Rd., Borella, Colombo 8; (01) 95-091; 59-70-62. Bp. Joseph Vianney Fernando (Kandy).

Sudan: Sudan Catholic Bishops' Conference (SCBC), P.O. Box 6011, Khartoum; (011) 225-075-9. Abp. Paulino Lukudu Loro, M.C.C.I. (Juba).

Switzerland: Conférence des Evêques Suisses, Secretariat, C.P. 22, av. Moléson 21, CH-1706 Fribourg; (026) 322-47-94; www.kath.ch. Bp. Amédée Grab, O.S.B. (Chur).

Tanzania: Tanzania Episcopal Conference (TEC), P.O. Box 2133, Mansfield St., Dar-es-Salaam; (022) 51-075. Bp. Severine Niwemugizi (Rulenge).

Thailand: Bishops' Conference of Thailand, 122-6-7 Soi Naaksuwan, Nonsi Road, Yannawa, Bangkok; 02-6815361-8. Card. Michael Michai Kitbunchu (Bangkok).

Togo: Conférence Episcopale du Togo, B.P. 348, Lomé; 21-22-72. Abp. Philippe Fanoko Kossi Kpodzro (Lomé).

Turkey: Turkish Episcopal Conference, Ölçek Sokak

83, Harbiye, 80230 Istanbul; (212) 248-07-75. Bp. Ruggero Franceschini, O.F.M. Cap. (Sicilibba).

Uganda: Uganda Episcopal Conference, P.O. Box 2886, Kampala; (041) 510-398. Abp. Paul K. Bakyenga (Mbarara).

Ukraine: Ukraine Episcopal Conference, 79008 Lviv, Mytropolycha Kuria Latynskoho Obriadu, Pl. Katedralna 1; (0322) 76-94-15. Card. Marian Jaworski (Lviv of Latins).

United States: *See* **National Conference of Catholic Bishops.**

Uruguay: *Conferencia Episcopal Uruguaya* (CEU), Avenida Uruguay 1319, 11100 Montevideo; (02) 900-26-42. Pablo Jaime Galimberti di Vietri (San Jose de Mayo).

Venezuela: *Conferencia Episcopal de Venezuela* (CEV), Apartado 4897, Torre a Madrices, Edificio Juan XXIII, Piso 4, Caracas 1010-A; (0212) 4432-23-65. Abp. Baltazar Porras Cardozo (Mérida).

Vietnam: *Conferenza Episcopale del Viêt Nam*, Nha Trang, Khán Hoà, 22 Tran Phu; (058) 822-842. Bp. Paul Nguyen Van Hòa (Nha Trang).

Yugoslavia: *Biskupska Konferencija Savezne Republike Jugoslavije*, 11000 Beograd, Visegradska 23; (011) 642-280. Abp. Stanislav Hocevar, S.D.B. (Beograd).

Zambia: Zambia Episcopal Conference, P.O. Box 31965, 20201 Lusaka; (01) 212-070. Bp. Telesphore George Mpundu (Mpika).

Zimbabwe: Zimbabwe Catholic Bishops' Conference (ZCBC), Causeway, P.O. Box 8135, Harare; (14) 705-368. Bp. Michael Dixon Bhasera (Masvingo).

Regional Conferences

(*Sources:* Almanac survey; Annuario Pontificio.)

Africa: Symposium of Episcopal Conferences of Africa and Madagascar (SECAM) (*Symposium des Conférences Episcopales d'Afrique et de Madagascar,* SCEAM): Abp. John Olorunfemi Onaiyekan, abp. of Abuja, president. Address: Secretariat, P.O. Box 9156 Airport, Accra, Ghana.

Association of Episcopal Conferences of Central Africa (*Association des Conférences Episcopales de l'Afrique Centrale,* ACEAC): Comprises Burundi, Rwanda and Zaire. Bp. Nicolas Djomo Lolo, bp. of Tshumbe, president. Address: B.P. 20511, Kinshasa, Democratic Republic of Congo.

Association of Episcopal Conferences of the Region of Central Africa (*Association des Conférences Episcopales de la Région de l'Afrique Central,* ACER-AC): Comprises Cameroon, Chad, Congo, Equatorial Guinea, Central African Republic and Gabon. Bp. Farnçois-Xavier Yombandje, bp. of Bossango, president. Address: Secretariat, B.P. 200, Brazzaville, Republic of the Congo.

Association of Episcopal Conferences of Anglophone West Africa (AECAWA): Comprises Gambia, Ghana, Liberia, Nigeria and Sierra Leone. Bp. John Olorunfemi Onaiyekan, abp. of Abuja, president. Address: P.O. Box 11, Santasi, Ghana.

Association of Member Episcopal Conferences in Eastern Africa (AMECEA): Represents Eritrea, Ethiopia, Kenya, Malawi, Sudan, Tanzania, Uganda and Zambia. Affiliate members: Seychelles (1979), Somalia (1994). Bp. Josaphat L. Lebulu, bp. of Arusha, president. Address: P.O. Box 21191, Nairobi, Kenya.

Regional Episcopal Conference of French-Speaking West Africa (*Conférence Episcopale Régionale de l'Afrique de l'Ouest Francophone,* CERAO): Comprises Benin, Burkina Faso, Cape Verde, Côte d'Ivoire, Guinea, Guinea-Bissau, Mali, Mauritania, Niger, Senegal and Togo. Abp. Théodore-Adrien Sarr, abp. of Dakar, president. Address: Secretariat General, B.P.470 CIDEX 1, Abidjan — Côte d'Ivoire.

Inter-Regional Meeting of Bishops of Southern Africa (IMBISA): Bishops of Angola, Botswana, Lesotho, Mozambique, Namibia, São Tome e Principe, South Africa, Swaziland and Zimbabwe. Abp. Joseph Tlhagale Buti, O.M.I., bp. of Johannesburg, president. Address: 88 Broadlands Rd., Avondale, Harare, Zimbabwe.

Asia: Federation of Asian Bishops' Conferences (FABC): Represents 14 Asian episcopal conferences and four independent jurisdictions (Hong Kong, Macau, Nepal, Mongolia) as regular members (excluding the Middle East). Established in 1970; statutes approved experimentally Dec. 6, 1972. Abp. Orlando B. Quevedeo, O.M.B., abp. of Cotabato, secretary general. Address: 16 Caine Road, Hong Kong; 25258021; www.fabc.org.ph.

Oceania: Federation of Catholic Bishops' Conferences of Oceania (FCBCO). Statutes approved Dec. 25, 1997. Bp. Denis George Browne, bp. of Hamilton in New Zealand, president. Address: P.O. Box 1937, 22-30 Hill St., Wellington, New Zealand 6015.

Europe: Council of European Bishops' Conferences (*Consilium Conferentiarum Episcoporum Europae,* CCEE): Reorganized in 1993 in accordance with suggestions made during the 1991 Synod of Bishops on Europe. Bp. Amédé Grab, O.S.B., bp. of Chur, president. Address of secretariat: Gallusstrasse 24, CH-9000 Sankt Gallen, Switzerland; (0041) 71-227-33-74; www.kath.ch/ccee.

Commission of the Episcopates of the European Community (*Commissio Episcopatuum Com-munitatis Europaeae,* COMECE): Established in 1980; represents episcopates of states belonging to European Community. Bp. Josef Homeyer, bp. of Hildesheim, Germany, president. Address of secretariat: 42, Rue Stévin, B-1000 Brussels, Belgium; (02) 230-73-16.

Central and South America: Latin American Bishops' Conference (*Consejo Episcopal Latino-Americano,* CELAM): Established in 1956; statutes approved Nov. 9, 1974. Represents 22 Latin American national bishops' conferences. Card. Francisco Javier Errázuriz Ossa, president. Address of the secretariat: Carrera 5 No. 118-31, Usaquén, Bogotá, Colombia; (91) 612-16-20.

Episcopal Secretariat of Central America and Panama (*Secretariado Episcopal de America Central y Panama,* SEDAC): Statutes approved experimentally Sept. 26, 1970. Bp. José Francisco Ulloa, bp. of Cartago, president. Address of secretary general: Calle 20 y Av Mexico 24-45, Apartado 6386, Panama 5, Panama; 262-7802.

INTERNATIONAL CATHOLIC ORGANIZATIONS

(Principal sources: Sr. Dorothy Farley, Executive Director, ICO Information Center; Pontifical Council for the Laity; Catholic Almanac survey.)

Guidelines

International organizations wanting to call themselves "Catholic" are required to meet standards set by the Vatican's Council for the Laity and to register with and get the approval of the Papal Secretariat of State, according to guidelines dated Dec. 3 and published in Acta Apostolicae Sedis under the date of Dec. 23, 1971.

Among conditions for the right of organizations to "bear the name Catholic" are:

• leaders "will always be Catholics," and candidates for office will be approved by the Secretariat of State

• adherence by the organization to the Catholic Church, its teaching authority and the teachings of the Gospel

• evidence that the organization is really international with a universal outlook and that it fulfills its mission through its own management, meetings and accomplishments.

The guidelines also stated that leaders of the organizations "will take care to maintain necessary reserve as regards taking a stand or engaging in public activity in the field of politics or trade unionism. Abstention in these fields will normally be the best attitude for them to adopt during their term of office."

The guidelines were in line with a provision stated by the Second Vatican Council: "No project may claim the name 'Catholic' unless it has obtained the consent of the lawful Church authority."

They made it clear that all organizations are not obliged to apply for recognition, but that the Church "reserves the right to recognize as linked with her mission and her aims those organizations or movements which see fit to ask for such recognition."

Conference of International Catholic Organizations

A permanent body for collaboration among various organizations the conference seeks to promote the development of international life along the lines of Christian principles. Eleven international Catholic organizations participated in its foundation and first meeting in 1927 at Fribourg, Switzerland. In 1951, the conference established its general secretariat and adopted governing statutes that were approved by the Vatican Secretariat of State in 1953.

The permanent secretariat is located at 37-39 rue de Vermont, CH-1202 Geneva, Switzerland. Other office addresses are: 1 rue Varembe, CH-1211 Geneva 20, Switzerland (International Catholic Center of Geneva); 9, rue Cler, F-75007 Paris, France (International Catholic Center for UNESCO); ICO Information Center, 323 East 47th St., New York, NY 10017.

Charter

According to its charter (adopted in November 1997), the conference "responds to the challenge of Christifideles Laici: Open to the saving power of Christ the frontiers of States, economic and political systems, the vast domains of culture, civilization and development (no. 34)."

In a universal vision of those problems, these organizations have the following responsibilities to their members:

• to make them increasingly aware of the complexities of the situations in which they live and work

• to help them to grow in discernment and critical analysis

• to facilitate the search for solutions to concrete difficulties.

The Conference is open to any organization which is acting and is involved recognizably Catholic in its work in the international world, which accepts the present Charter, respects its principles in practice and adheres to its Statutes. The Conference witnesses to the organized presence of Catholics in the international world.

Fundamental Convictions

• Their desire to announce Jesus Christ to the women and men of our time, and their vocation to serve the world, are indivisible; faith calls for action

• Their wish to contribute to the building of the Kingdom of God is demonstrated by solidarity with all women and men of good will

• Their desire for participation in decision-making in the Church in areas which concern their competence and in which they are involved.

A unique spirituality

In its desire to live fully its faith in Jesus Christ, the Conference stresses:

• The need to be rooted in reality, through a relationship with God lived out in the world

• An experience of community nourished by group sharing and exchange

• Openness to the international dimension, validated by experiences at local level to which it gives meaning

• Adaptation to different human groups and to different sensibilities

• The witness of Christian freedom to initiate, as well as willingness to live in "solid and strong communion" with the Church

• Desire to serve the universal Church through insertion in the local Churches by respecting diverse pastoral programs, but also to participate in major events in the life of the universal Church.

Members

Members of the Conference of International Catholic Organizations are listed below. Information includes name, date and place of establishment (when available), address of general secretariat. Approximately 30 of the organizations have consultative status with other international or regional non-governmental agencies.

Caritas Internationalis (1951, Rome, Italy): Piazza San Calisto 16, I-00153, Rome, Italy. Coordinates and represents its 146 national member organizations (in 194 countries) operating in the fields of development, emergency aid, social action.

Catholic International Education Office (1952): 60, rue des Eburons, B-1000 Brussels, Belgium.

Catholic International Union for Social Service (1925, Milan, Italy): rue de la Poste 111, B-1210

Brussels, Belgium (general secretariat).

Christian Life Community (CVX) (1953): Borgo Santo Spirito 8, C.P. 6139, I-00195 Rome, Italy. First Sodality of Our Lady founded in 1563.

International Ascent, The: 84, rue Charles Michels, F-93206 Saint Denis Cedex, France. Member of ICO.

International Association of Charities (1617, Chatillon les Dombes, France): Rue Joseph Brand, 118, B-1030 Brussels, Belgium.

International Catholic Child Bureau (1948, in Paris): 63, rue de Lausanne, CH-1202 Geneva, Switzerland.

International Catholic Committee of Nurses and Medico-Social Assistants (ICCN) (1933): Square Vergote, 43, B-1040 Brussels, Belgium.

International Catholic Conference of Scouting (1948): Piazza Pasquale Paoli, 18, I-00186 Rome, Italy.

International Catholic Migration Commission (1951): 37-39 rue de Vermont, C.P. 96, CH-1211 Geneva 20, Switzerland. Coordinates activities worldwide on behalf of refugees and migrants, both administering programs directly and supporting the efforts of national affiliated agencies.

International Catholic Organization for Cinema and Audiovisual (1928, The Hague, The Netherlands): Rue du Saphir, 15, B-1040 Brussels, Belgium (general secretariat). Federation of National Catholic film offices.

International Catholic Society for Girls (1897): 37-39, rue de Vermont, CH-1202 Geneva, Switzerland.

International Catholic Union of the Press: 37-39 rue de Vermont, Case Postale 197, CH-1211 Geneva 20 CIC, Switzerland. Coordinates and represents at the international level the activities of Catholics and Catholic federations or associations in the field of press and information. Has seven specialized branches: International Federation of Catholic Journalists; International Federation of Dailies; International Federation of Periodicals; International Federation of Catholic News Agencies; International Catholic Federation of Teachers and Researchers in the Science and Techniques of Information; International Federation of Church Press Associations; and International Federation of Book Publishers.

International Conference of Catholic Guiding (1965): c/o Mlle Francoise Parmentier, rue de la Tour 64, 75016 Paris. Founded by member bodies of interdenominational World Association of Guides and Girl Scouts.

International Coordination of Young Christian Workers (YCYCW): via dei Barbieri 22, I-00186 Rome, Italy.

International Council of Catholic Men (ICCM) (Unum Omnes) (1948): Wahringer Str. 2-4, A.1090 Vienna IX, Austria.

International Federation of Catholic Medical Associations (1954): Palazzo San Calisto, I-00120 Vatican City.

International Federation of Catholic Parochial Youth Communities (1962, Rome, Italy): St. Kariliquai 12, 6000 Lucerne 5, Switzerland.

International Federation of Catholic Pharmacists (1954): Bosdorf 180, 9190 Stekene, Belgium.

International Federation of Rural Adult Catholic Movements (1964, Lisbon, Portugal): Rue Jaumain

15, B-5330 Assesse, Belgium.

International Federation of Catholic Universities (1949): 21, rue d'Assas, F-75270 Paris 06, France.

International Federation of the Catholic Associations of the Blind: Avenue Dailly 90, B-1030 Brussels, Belgium. Coordinates actions of Catholic groups and associations for the blind and develops their apostolate.

International Independent Christian Youth (IICY): 11, rue Martin Bernard, 75013 Paris, France.

International Military Apostolate (1967): Breite Strasse 25, D-53111 Bonn, Germany. Comprised of organizations of military men.

International Movement of Apostolate of Children (1929, France): 24, rue Paul Rivet, F-92350 Le Plessis Robinson, France.

International Movement of Apostolate in the Independent Social Milieux (MIAMSI) (1963): Piazza San Calisto 16, 00153 Rome, Italy.

International Movement of Catholic Agricultural and Rural Youth (1954, Annevoie, Belgium): 53, rue J. Coosemans, B-1030 Brussels, Belgium (permanent secretariat).

International Young Catholic Students (1946, Fribourg, Switzerland; present name, 1954): 171 rue de Rennes, F-75006 Paris, France.

Pax Romana (1921, Fribourg, Switzerland, divided into two branches, 1947): **Pax Romana - IMCS (International Movement of Catholic Students)** (1921): 171, rue de Rennes, F-75006, Paris, France, for undergraduates; **Pax Romana - ICMICA (International Catholic Movement for Intellectual and Cultural Affairs)** (1947): rue du Grand Bureau 15, CH-1227 Geneva, Switzerland, for Catholic intellectuals and professionals.

Society of St. Vincent de Paul (1833, Paris): 5, rue du Pré-aux-Clercs, F-75007 Paris, France.

Unda: International Catholic Association for Radio and Television (1928, Cologne, Germany): rue de l'Orme, 12, B-1040 Brussels, Belgium.

World Movement of Christian Workers (1961): Blvd. du Jubilé 124, 1080 Brussels, Belgium.

World Organization of Former Pupils of Catholic Education (1967, Rome): 48, rue de Richelieu, F-75001 Paris, France.

World Union of Catholic Teachers (1951): Piazza San Calisto 16, 00153 Rome, Italy.

World Union of Catholic Women's Organizations (1910): 18, rue Notre Dame des Champs, F-75006 Paris, France.

Other Catholic Organizations

Apostleship of Prayer (1849): Borgo Santo Spirito 5, I-00193 Rome, Italy. National secretariat in most countries.

Apostolatus Maris (Apostleship of the Sea) (1922, Glasgow, Scotland): Pontifical Council for Migrants and Itinerant People, Piazza San Calisto 16, 00153 Rome, Italy. (See **Index.**)

L'Arche Communities: B.P. 35, 60350 Cuise Lamotte, France.

Associationes Juventutis Salesianae (Associations of Salesian Youth) (1847): Via della Pisana, 1111, 00163 Rome, Italy.

Blue Army of Our Lady of Fatima: P.O. Box 976, Washington, NJ, 07882.

Catholic International Federation for Physical and Sports Education (1911; present name, 1957): 5, rue Cernuschi, 75017 Paris, France.

Christian Fraternity of the Sick and Handicapped: 9, Avenue de la Gare, CH-1630, Bulle, Switzerland.

"Communione e Liberazione" Fraternity (1955, Milan, Italy): Via Marcello Malpighi 2, 00161 Rome, Italy. Catholic renewal movement.

"Focolare Movement" (Work of Mary) (1943, Trent, Italy): Via di Frascati, 306, I-00040 Rocca di Papa (Rome), Italy.

Foi et Lumiere: 8 rue Serret, 75015 Paris, France.

Franciscans International: 345 E. 47th St., New York, NY 10017. A non-governmental organization at the UN.

Inter Cultural Association (ICA, 1937, Belgium) and Association Fraternelle Internationale (AFI): 91, rue de la Servette, CH-1202 Geneva, Switzerland.

International Association of Children of Mary (1847): 67 rue de Sèvres, F-75006 Paris, France.

International Catholic Rural Association (1962, Rome): Piazza San Calisto, 00153 Rome, Italy. International body for agricultural and rural organizations. Invited member of ICO.

International Catholic Union of Esperanto: Via Berni 9, 00185 Rome, Italy.

International Centre for Studies in Religious Education LUMEN VITAE (1934-35, Louvain, Belgium, under name Catechetical Documentary Centre; present name, 1956): 184, rue Washington, B-1050 Brussels, Belgium. Also referred to as Lumen Vitae Centre; concerned with all aspects of religious formation.

International Young Christian Workers (1925, Belgium): 11, rue Plantin, B-1070 Brussels, Belgium. Associate member of ICO.

Legion of Mary (1921, Dublin, Ireland): De Montfort House, North Brunswick St., Dublin, Ireland. (See Index.)

Medicus Mundi Internationalis (1964, Bensberg, Germany FR): P.O. Box 1547, 6501 BM Nijmegen, Netherlands. To promote health and medico-social services, particularly in developing countries; recruit essential health and medical personnel for developing countries; contribute to training of medical and auxiliary personnel; undertake research in the field of health.

NOVALIS, Marriage Preparation Center: University of St. Paul, 1 rue Stewart, Ottawa 2, ON, Canada.

Our Lady's Teams (Equipes Notre-Dame) (1937, France): 49, rue de la Glacière, 75013 Paris, France.

Movement for spiritual formation of couples.

Pax Christi International (1950): rue du Vieux Marché aux grains 21, B-1000 Brussels, Belgium. International Catholic peace movement. Originated in Lourdes, France, in 1948 by French and German Catholics to reconcile enemies from World War II; spread to Italy and Poland and acquired its international title when it merged with the English organization Pax. Associate member of ICO.

Pro Sanctity Movement: Piazza S. Andrea della Valle 3, 00166 Rome, Italy.

St. Joan's International Alliance (1911, in England, as Catholic Women's Suffrage Society): Quai Churchill 19, Boite 061, B-4020 Liège, Belgium. Associate member of ICO.

Salesian Cooperators (1876, Turin, Italy): Salesian Cooperators: Founded by St. John Bosco; for lay men and women and diocesan clergy. A public association of the faithful, members commit themselves to apostolates in the local Church, especially on behalf of the young, in the Salesian spirit and style. Address: 174 Filors Lane, Stony Point, NY 10980-2645; (845) 947-2200.

Secular Franciscan Order (1221, first Rule approved): Via Piemonte, 70, 00187, Rome, Italy.

Secular Fraternity of Charles de Foucauld: Katharinenweg 4, B4700 Eupen, Belgium.

Serra International (1953, in U.S.): 65 E. Wacker Pl. Suite 1210, Chicago, IL 60601.

Unio Internationalis Laicorum in Servitio Ecclesiae (1965, Aachen, Germany): Postfach 990125, Am Kielshof 2, 5000 Cologne, Germany 91. Consists of national and diocesan associations of persons who give professional services to the Church.

Union of Adorers of the Blessed Sacrament (1937): Largo dei Monti Parioli 3, I-00197, Rome, Italy.

World Catholic Federation for the Biblical Apostolate (1969, Rome): Mittelstrasse, 12, P.O. Box 601, D-7000, Stuttgart 1, Germany.

Regional Organizations

European Federation for Catholic Adult Education (1963, Lucerne, Switzerland): Hirschengraben 13, P.B. 2069, CH-6002 Lucerne, Switzerland.

European Forum of National Committees of the Laity (1968): 169, Booterstown Av., Blackrock, Co. Dublin, Ireland.

Movimiento Familiar Cristiano (1949-50, Montevideo and Buenos Aires): Carrera 17 n. 4671, Bogotá, D.E., Colombia. Christian Family Movement of Latin America.

Eastern Catholic Churches

Sources: Rev. Ronald Roberson, C.S.P., Associate Director, Ecumenical and Interreligious Affairs, USCCB.; Annuario Pontificio; Official Catholic Directory.

The Second Vatican Council, in its Decree on Eastern Catholic Churches (Orientalium Ecclesiarum), stated the following points regarding Eastern heritage, patriarchs, sacraments and worship.

Venerable Churches: The Catholic Church holds in high esteem the institutions of the Eastern Churches, their liturgical rites, ecclesiastical traditions, and Christian way of life. For, distinguished as they are by their venerable antiquity, they are bright with that tradition which was handed down from the Apostles through the Fathers, and which forms part of the divinely revealed and undivided heritage of the universal Church (No. 1). That Church, Holy and Catholic, which is the Mystical Body of Christ, is made up of the faithful who are organically united in the Holy Spirit through the same faith, the same sacraments, and the same government and who, combining into various groups held together by a hierarchy, form separate Churches or rites. It is the mind of the Catholic Church that each individual Church or rite retain its traditions whole and entire, while adjusting its way of life to the various needs of time and place (No. 2).

Such individual Churches, whether of the East or of the West, although they differ somewhat among themselves in what are called rites (that is, in liturgy, ecclesiastical discipline, and spiritual heritage) are, nevertheless, equally entrusted to the pastoral guidance of the Roman Pontiff, the divinely appointed successor of St. Peter in supreme government over the universal Church. They are consequently of equal dignity, so that none of them is superior to the others by reason of rite (No. 3).

Eastern Heritage: Each and every Catholic, as also the baptized of every non-Catholic Church or community who enters into the fullness of Catholic communion, should everywhere retain his proper rite, cherish it, and observe it to the best of his ability (No. 4). The Churches of the East, as much as those of the West, fully enjoy the right, and are in duty bound, to rule themselves. Each should do so according to its proper and individual procedures (No. 5). All Eastern rite members should know and be convinced that they can and should always preserve their lawful liturgical rites and their established way of life, and that these should not be altered except by way of an appropriate and organic development (No. 6)

Patriarchs: The institution of the patriarchate has existed in the Church from the earliest times and was recognized by the first ecumenical Synods. By the name Eastern Patriarch is meant the bishop who has jurisdiction over all bishops (including metropolitans), clergy, and people of his own territory or rite, in accordance with the norms of law and without prejudice to the primacy of the Roman Pontiff (No. 7). Though some of the patriarchates of the Eastern Churches are of later origin than others, all are equal in patriarchal dignity. Still the honorary and lawfully established order of precedence among them is to be preserved (No. 8). In keeping with the most ancient tradition of the Church, the Patriarchs of the Eastern Churches are to be accorded exceptional respect, since each presides over his patriarchate as father and head.

This sacred Synod, therefore, decrees that their rights and privileges should be re-established in accord with the ancient traditions of each Church and the decrees of the ecumenical Synods. The rights and privileges in question are those which flourished when East and West were in union, though they should be somewhat adapted to modern conditions.

The Patriarchs with their synods constitute the superior authority for all affairs of the patriarchate, including the right to establish new eparchies and to nominate bishops of their rite within the territorial bounds of the patriarchate, without prejudice to the inalienable right of the Roman Pontiff to intervene in individual cases (No. 9).

What has been said of Patriarchs applies as well, under the norm of law, to major archbishops, who preside over the whole of some individual Church or rite (No. 10).

Sacraments: This sacred Ecumenical Synod endorses and lauds the ancient discipline of the sacraments existing in the Eastern Churches, as also the practices connected with their celebration and administration (No. 12).

With respect to the minister of holy chrism (confirmation), let that practice be fully restored which existed among Easterners in most ancient times. Priests, therefore, can validly confer this sacrament, provided they use chrism blessed by a Patriarch or bishop (No. 13).

In conjunction with baptism or otherwise, all Eastern-Rite priests can confer this sacrament validly on all the faithful of any rite, including the Latin; licitly, however, only if the regulations of both common and particular law are observed. Priests of the Latin rite, to the extent of the faculties they enjoy for administering this sacrament, can confer it also on the faithful of Eastern Churches, without prejudice to rite. They do so licitly if the regulations of both common and particular law are observed (No. 14).

The faithful are bound on Sundays and feast days to attend the divine liturgy or, according to the regulations or custom of their own rite, the celebration of the Divine Praises. That the faithful may be able to satisfy their obligation more easily, it is decreed that this obligation can be fulfilled from the Vespers of the vigil to the end of the Sunday or the feast day (No. 15). Because of the everyday intermingling of the communicants of diverse Eastern Churches in the same Eastern region or territory, the faculty for hearing confession, duly and unrestrictedly granted by his proper bishop to a priest of any rite, is applicable to the entire territory of the grantor, also to the places and the faithful belonging to any other rite in the same territory, unless an Ordinary of the place explicitly decides otherwise with respect to the places pertaining to his rite (No. 16).

This sacred Synod ardently desires that where it has fallen into disuse the office of the permanent diaconate be restored. The legislative authority of each individual church should decide about the subdiaconate and the minor orders (No. 17).

By way of preventing invalid marriages between Eastern Catholics and baptized Eastern non-Catholics, and in the interests of the permanence and sanctity of marriage and of domestic harmony, this sacred Synod decrees that the canonical 'form' for the celebration of such marriages obliges only for lawfulness. For their validity, the presence of a sacred minister suffices, as long as the other requirements of law are honored (No. 18).

Worship: Henceforth, it will be the exclusive right of an ecumenical Synod or the Apostolic See to establish, transfer, or suppress feast days common to all the Eastern Churches. To establish, transfer, or suppress feast days for any of the individual Churches is within the competence not only of the Apostolic See but also of a patriarchal or archiepiscopal synod, provided due consideration is given to the entire region and to other individual Churches (No. 19). Until such time as all Christians desirably concur on a fixed day for the celebration of Easter, and with a view meantime to promoting unity among the Christians of a given area or nation, it is left to the Patriarchs or supreme authorities of a place to reach a unanimous agreement, after ascertaining the views of all concerned, on a single Sunday for the observance of Easter (No. 20). With respect to rules concerning sacred seasons, individual faithful dwelling outside the area or territory of their own rite may conform completely to the established custom of the place where they live. When members of a family belong to different rites, they are all permitted to observe sacred seasons according to the rules of any one of these rites (No. 21). From ancient times the Divine Praises have been held in high esteem among all Eastern Churches. Eastern clerics and religious should celebrate these Praises as the laws and customs of their own traditions require. To the extent they can, the faithful too should follow the example of their forebears by assisting devoutly at the Divine Praises (No. 22).

Restoration of Ancient Practices

An "Instruction for the Application of the Liturgical Prescriptions of the Code of Canons of the Eastern Churches" was published in Italian by the Congregation for Eastern-Rite Churches in Jan. 1996. Msgr. Alan Detscher, executive director of the U.S. bishops' Secretariat for the Liturgy, said it was the first instruction on liturgical renewal of the Eastern Catholic Churches since the Second Vatican Council (1962-65).

JURISDICTIONS AND FAITHFUL OF THE EASTERN CATHOLIC CHURCHES

Introduction

The Church originated in Palestine, whence it spread to other regions of the world where certain places became key centers of Christian life with great influence on the local churches in their respective areas. These centers developed into the ancient patriarchates of Constantinople, Alexandria, Antioch and Jerusalem in the East, and Rome in the West. The main lines of Eastern Church patriarchal organization and usages were drawn before the Roman Empire became two empires, East (Byzantine) and West (Roman), in 292. Other churches with distinctive traditions grew up beyond the boundaries of the Roman Empire in Persia, Armenia, Syria, Egypt, Ethiopia, and India. The "nestorian" church in Persia, known today as the Assyrian Church of the East, broke communion with the rest of the church in the wake of the Council of Ephesus (431) whose teachings it did not accept. The "monophysite" churches of Armenia, Syria, Egypt, Ethiopia, Eritrea and India (known today as the Oriental Orthodox Churches) did not accept the christological teachings of the Council of Chalcedon (451) and so broke away from the church within the Roman Empire. And finally, in the wake of the mutual excommunications of 1054 between the Patriarch of Constantinople and the papal legate, the church within the empire divided into what would become the Catholic Church in the West and the Orthodox Church in the East. This was a lengthy process of estrangement that culminated only in 1204 and the sack of Constantinople by the Latin Crusaders.

In the following centuries, attempts to overcome these divisions took place, most notably at the Second Council of Lyons in 1274 and the Council of Ferrara-Florence in 1438-39. Both failed. Subsequently, the Catholic Church began to send missionaries to work with separated Eastern Christians, and some groups within those churches spontaneously asked to enter into full communion with Rome. Thus began the formation of the Eastern Catholic Churches, which retained most of the liturgical, canonical, spiritual and theological patrimony of their non-Catholic counterparts.

The Code of Canons of the Eastern Churches groups these churches today into four categories: patriarchal, major archiepiscopal, metropolitan, and other churches *sui iuris*. In common usage, an eparchy is equivalent to a diocese in the Latin rite.

STATISTICS

Principal source: 2006 Annuario Pontificio.

The following statistics are the sum of those reported for Eastern Catholic jurisdictions only, and do not include Eastern Catholics under the jurisdiction of Latin bishops. Some of the figures reported are only approximate. The churches are grouped according to their liturgical traditions.

PATRIARCHS

The current Patriarchs of the Eastern Catholic Churches (as of July 15, 2006) are as follows:

Abdel-Ahad, Ignatius Peter VIII: b. June 28, 1930; ord. Oct. 17, 1954; cons. bp. June 21, 1997; Patriarch of Antioch of the Syrians, Feb. 16, 2001; granted "ecclesiastical communion" with Pope John Paul II, Feb. 20, 2001.

Naguib, Antonios: b. Mar. 16, 1935; ord. Oct. 30, 1960; cons. bp. Sept. 9, 1977; Patriarch of Alexandria of the Copts, Mar. 30, 2006; granted "ecclesiastical communion" with Pope Benedict XVI, Apr. 7, 2006.

Delly, Emmanuel III: b. Oct. 6, 1927; cons. Apr. 19, 1963; Patriarch of Babylon of the Chaldeans, Dec. 3, 2003; granted "ecclesiastical communion" with Pope John Paul II, Dec. 3, 2003.

Ghattas, Stéphanos II, C.M.: Patriarch emeritus of Alexandria; for details, see *under* **Cardinals, College of.**

Laham, Gregory III: b. Dec. 15, 1933; ord. Feb. 15, 1959; cons. bp. Nov. 27, 1981; patriarch of Greek Melkites, Nov. 29, 2000; granted "ecclesiastical communion" with Pope John Paul II, Dec. 5, 2000.

Sfeir, Nasrallah Pierre: Patriarch of Antioch of the Maronites; for details, see **Cardinals, College of.**

Tarmouni, Nerses XIX Bedros: b. Jan. 17, 1940, in Cairo, Egypt; ord. Aug. 15, 1965; patriarch of Cilicia of the Armenians, Oct. 7, 1999; granted "ecclesiastical communion" with the Pope John Paul II, Oct. 13, 1999.

ALEXANDRIAN

The liturgical tradition of Egypt, in particular that of the early Greek Patriarchate of Alexandria. In the Egyptian desert monasteries the rite evolved in a distinctive way and eventually became that of the Coptic Orthodox Church. The Greek Patriarchate of Alexandria adopted the Byzantine rite by the 12th century. The Coptic rite, with its Alexandrian origins, spread to Ethiopia in the fourth century where it underwent substantial modifications under strong Syrian influence. The Catholic Churches in this group are:

The Coptic Catholic Church (Patriarchate): Seven eparchies in Egypt; 265,500.

Catholic missionaries were present since the 17th century. The Patriarchate was established first in 1824 and renewed in 1895. Liturgical languages are Coptic and Arabic.

The Ethiopian Catholic Church (Metropolitanate): Three eparchies in Ethiopia and three in Eritrea; 215,615. Catholic missionary activity began in the 19th century, and the present ecclesiastical structure dates from 1961. The liturgical languages are Ge'ez and Amharic.

ANTIOCHIAN

The liturgical tradition of Antioch, one of the great centers of the early Christian world, also known as West Syrian. In Syria it developed under strong influence of Jerusalem, especially the Liturgy of St. James, into the form used by today's Syrian Orthodox and Catholics in the Middle East and in India. The Maronites of Lebanon developed their own liturgical traditions under the influence of both the Antiochian and Chaldean rites.

The Catholic Churches of this group are:

The Syro-Malankara Catholic Church (Major Archbishopric): Five eparchies in India; 408,263. Began in 1930 when two bishops, a priest, a deacon and a layman of the Malankara Orthodox Church were received into full communion with Rome. Raised to Major Archepiscopal status in 2005 and Abp. Cyril Malancharuvil of Trivandrum was promoted to the rank of major archbishop. The liturgical language is Malayalam.

The Maronite Catholic Church (Patriarchate): Ten eparchies in Lebanon, three in Syria, two in the United States, and one each in Cyprus, Egypt, Argentina, Brazil, Australia, the Holy Land, Canada, and Mexico, plus patriarchal exarchates in Jordan and Jerusalem; 3,111,934.

Founded by St. Maron in the fourth century, the Maronites claim to have always been in communion with Rome. They have no counterpart among the separated Eastern churches. The patriarchate dates to the eighth century, and was confirmed by Pope Innocent III in 1216. Liturgical language is Arabic.

The Syrian Catholic Church (Patriarchate): Four eparchies in Syria, two in Iraq, and one each in Lebanon, Egypt, and North America, and patriarchal exarchates in Turkey, Venezuela, and Iraq/Kuwait; 132,283.

Catholic missionary activity among the Syrian Orthodox began in the 17th century, and there has been an uninterrupted series of Catholic patriarchs since 1783. The liturgical languages are Syriac/Aramaic and Arabic.

ARMENIAN

The liturgical tradition of the Armenian Apostolic and Catholic Churches. It contains elements of the Syriac, Jerusalem, and Byzantine rites. From the fifth to the seventh centuries there was strong influence from Syria and Jerusalem. More Byzantine usages were adopted later, and in the Middle Ages elements of the Latin tradition were added.

The Armenian Catholic Church (Patriarchate): Three eparchies in Syria, one each in Lebanon, Iran, Iraq, Egypt, Turkey, Ukraine, France, Argentina and the United States/Canada, and Ordinariates in Greece, Romania, and Eastern Europe (Armenia); 374,283.

Catholic missionaries had been working among the Armenians since the 14th century, and an Armenian Catholic patriarchate was established in Lebanon in 1742. The liturgical language is classical Armenian. His Beatitude Nerses Bedros XIX Tarmouni, canonically elected as patriarch of Cilicia of the Armenians, by the Synod of Bishops of the Armenian Catholic Church was approved by Pope John Paul II on Oct. 18, 1999.

BYZANTINE

The tradition of the Eastern Orthodox and Byzantine Catholic Churches which originated in the Orthodox Patriarchate of Constantinople (Byzantium). Its present form is a synthesis of Constantinopolitan and Palestinian elements that took place in the monasteries between the ninth and 14th centuries. It is by far the most widely used Eastern liturgical tradition. The Catholic Churches of this group are:

Albanians: One apostolic administration in southern Albania, mostly of the Latin rite; 3,400. Very small groups of Albanian Orthodox became Catholic in 1628 and again in 1900; liturgical language is Albanian.

Belarusans (formerly Byelorussian, also known as White Russian): No hierarchy, Apostolic Visitator. Most Belarusan Orthodox became Catholic with the Union of Brest in 1595-6, but this union was short lived. A modest revival has taken place since the end of communism. The liturgical language is Belarusan.

The Bulgarian Catholic Church: One apostolic exarchate in Bulgaria; 10,000. Originated with a group of Bulgarian Orthodox who became Catholic in 1861; liturgical language is Old Slavonic.

Greek Catholics in Former Yugoslavia: One eparchy (Krizevci) located in Zagreb with jurisdiction over Slovenia, Croatia, and Bosnia-Herzegovina; Apostolic Exarchates in Serbia-Montenegro and in Macedonia; 55,847. A bishop for former Serbian Orthodox living in Catholic Croatia was first appointed in 1611; liturgical languages are Old Slavonic and Croatian.

The Greek Catholic Church: Apostolic exarchates in Greece and Turkey; 2,330. Catholic missionaries in Constantinople formed a small group of Byzantine Catholics there in the mid-19th century. Most of them moved to Greece in the 1920s. The liturgical language is Greek.

The Hungarian Catholic Church: One eparchy and one apostolic exarchate in Hungary; 290,000. Descendants of groups of Orthodox in Hungary who became Catholic in the 17th century and after. The liturgical language is Hungarian.

The Italo-Albanian Catholic Church: Two eparchies, one territorial abbey in Italy; 63,298. Descended mostly from Albanian Orthodox who came to southern Italy and Sicily in the 15th century and eventually became Catholic; liturgical languages are Greek and Italian.

The Melkite Greek Catholic Church (Patriarchate): Five eparchies in Syria, seven in Lebanon, one each in Jordan, Israel, Brazil, US, Canada, Mexico, and Australia. Apostolic Exarchates in Venezuela and Argentina, and patriarchal exarchates in Iraq and Kuwait; 1,350,207.

Catholic missionaries began work within the Greek Orthodox Patriarchate of Antioch in the mid-17th century. In 1724 it split into Catholic and Orthodox counterparts, the Catholics becoming known popularly as Melkites. Liturgical languages are Greek and Arabic.

The Romanian Greek Catholic Church (Major Archbishopric): Five eparchies in Romania and one in the US; 759,620. Romanian Orthodox in Transylvania formally entered into union with Rome in 1700; the liturgical language is Romanian. In Dec. 2005, the Romanian Greek Catholic Church was raised to the rank of Major Archbishopric.

Russians: No hierarchy. An apostolic exarchate was established for Russia in 1917 and for Russians in China in 1928, but neither is functioning today. There are now at least five parishes in Russia under the local Latin bishops and 13 in the diaspora.

The Ruthenian Catholic Church (Metropolitanate in the United States): One eparchy in Ukraine, four in the United States, and an apostolic exarchate in the Czech Republic; 596, 992. Originated with the reception of 63 Orthodox priests into the Catholic Church at the Union of Uzhhorod in 1646. Liturgical languages are Old Slavonic and English.

The Slovak Catholic Church: One eparchy and one apostolic exarchate in Slovakia, and one eparchy in Canada; 219,015. Also originated with the Union of Uzhhorod in 1646; eparchy of Presov was established for them in 1818. Liturgical languages are Old Slavonic and Slovak.

The Ukrainian Greek Catholic Church (Major Archbishopric): Nine eparchies and two archepiscopal exarchates in Ukraine, two eparchies in Poland, five eparchies in Canada, four in the United States, one each in Australia, Brazil and Argentina, apostolic exarchates in Great Britain, Germany, and France; 4,287,664. Originated with the Union of Brest between the Orthodox Metropolitanate of Kiev and the Catholic Church in 1595-6. Liturgical languages are Old Slavonic and Ukrainian.

CHALDEAN

Also called East Syrian, the liturgical tradition of the Chaldean Catholic and Syro-Malabar Catholic Churches as well as the Assyrian Church of the East. Descends from the ancient rite of the church of Mesopotamia in the Persian Empire. It is celebrated in the eastern dialect of classical Syriac. The Catholic Churches of this tradition are:

The Chaldean Catholic Church (Patriarchate): Ten eparchies in Iraq, three in Iran, two in the U.S., one each in Lebanon, Egypt, Syria, and Turkey; 351,141. A group of disaffected members of the ("Nestorian") Assyrian Church of the East asked for union with Rome in 1553. In that year Pope Julius III ordained their leader a bishop and named him Patriarch; liturgical languages are Syriac, Arabic.

The Syro-Malabar Catholic Church (Major Archbishopric): 25 eparchies in India, one in the U.S.; 3,758,710. Descended from Thomas Christians of India who became Catholic in the wake of Portuguese colonization; the diocese of Ernakulam-Angamaly was raised to Major Archepiscopal status in 1993; the liturgical language is Malayalam.

EASTERN JURISDICTIONS

For centuries Eastern Churches were identifiable with a limited number of nationality and language groups in certain countries of the Middle East, Eastern Europe, Asia and Africa. The persecution of religion in the former Soviet Union since 1917 and in communist-controlled countries for more than 40 years following World War II — in addition to decimating and destroying the Church in those places — resulted in the emigration of many Eastern Catholics from their homelands. This forced emigration, together with voluntary emigration, has led to the spread of Eastern Churches to many other countries.

Europe

Bishop Krikor Ghabroyan, of the Armenian Eparchy of Sainte-Croix-de-Paris, France, is apostolic visitator for Armenian Catholics in Western Europe who do not have their own bishop. Bishop Youssef Ibrahim Sarraf of Cairo of the Chaldeans is apostolic visitator for Chaldeans in Europe. Bishop Samis Mazloum is apostolic visitator for Maronites in Western and Northern Europe. Archimandrite Jan Sergiusz Gajek is Apostolic Visitator for Greek Catholics in Belarus.

Albania: Byzantine apostolic administration.

Austria: Byzantine ordinariate.

Bulgaria: Bulgarian apostolic exarchate.

Croatia: Eparchy of Krizevci.
Czech Republic: Ruthenian apostolic exarchate.
France: Ukrainian apostolic exarchate. Armenian eparchy (1986). Ordinariate for all other Eastern Catholics.
Germany: Ukrainian apostolic exarchate.
Great Britain: Ukrainian apostolic exarchate.
Greece: Byzantine apostolic exarchate. Armenian ordinariate.
Hungary: Hungarian Byzantine eparchy, apostolic exarchate.
Italy: Two Italo-Albanian eparchies, one abbacy.
Macedonia: One apostolic exarchate.
Poland: Ukrainian metropolitan see (1996), one eparchy. Ordinariate for all other Eastern Catholics.
Romania: Romanian Byzantine metropolitan, four eparchies; Armenian ordinariate.
Russia: Russian apostolic exarchate (for Byzantine Catholics in Moscow).
Serbia and Montenegro: One apostolic exarchate.
Slovakia: Slovak Byzantine eparchy, one apostolic exarchate.
Ukraine: Armenian archeparchy; Ruthenian eparchy; Ukrainian major archbishopric, eight eparchies, two archepiscopal exarchates.

Asia
Armenia: Armenian ordinariate (for Armenians of Eastern Europe).
China: Russian Byzantine apostolic exarchate.
Cyprus: Maronite archeparchy.
India: Syro-Malankara metropolitan see, five eparchies. Syro-Malabar major archbishopric (1993), three metropolitan sees (1995), 18 eparchies.
Iran: Two Chaldean metropolitan sees, one archeparchy, one eparchy; Armenian eparchy.
Iraq: Two Syrian archeparchies; Melkite patriarchal exarchate; Chaldean patriarchate, two metropolitan sees, three archeparchies and five eparchies; Armenian archeparchy.
Israel (including Jerusalem): Syrian patriarchal exarchate; Maronite archeparchy; Melkite archeparchy, patriarchal exarchate; Chaldean patriarchal exarchate; Armenian patriarchal exarchate.
Jordan: Melkite archeparchy.
Kuwait: Melkite patriarchal exarchate; Syrian patriarchate exarchate.
Syria: Two Maronite archeparchies, one eparchy; two Syrian metropolitan and two archeparchal sees; Melkite patriarchate, four metropolitan sees, one archeparchy; Chaldean eparchy; Armenian archeparchy, one eparchy .
Turkey: Syrian patriarchal exarchate; Greek apostolic exarchate; Chaldean archeparchy; Armenian archeparchy.

Oceania
Australia: Ukrainian eparchy; Melkite eparchy (1987); Maronite eparchy.

Africa
Egypt: Coptic patriarchate, five eparchies; Maronite eparchy; Syrian eparchy; Melkite patriarchal dependency; Chaldean eparchy; Armenian eparchy.
Eritrea: Three Ethiopian eparchies.
Ethiopia: Ethiopian metropolitan see, two eparchies.

Sudan: Melkite patriarchal dependency.

North America
Canada: One Ukrainian metropolitan, four eparchies; Slovak eparchy; Melkite eparchy; Armenian eparchy for Canada and the U.S. (New York is see city); Maronite eparchy.
United States: Two Maronite eparchies; Syrian eparchy (1995); one Ukrainian metropolitan see, three eparchies; one Ruthenian metropolitan see, three eparchies; Melkite eparchy; Romanian eparchy; a new Syro-Malabar eparchy based in Chicago; Belarusan apostolic visitator; Armenian eparchy for Canada and U.S. (New York is see city); two Chaldean eparchies; other Eastern Catholics are under the jurisdiction of local Latin bishops. (See Eastern Catholics in the United States.)
Mexico: Melkite eparchy; Maronite eparchy (1995).

South America
Armenian Catholics in Latin America (including Mexico and excluding Argentina) are under the jurisdiction of an apostolic exarchate .
Argentina: Ukrainian eparchy; Maronite eparchy; Armenian eparchy; Melkite apostolic exarchate; ordinariate for all other Eastern Catholics.
Brazil: Maronite eparchy; Melkite eparchy; Ukrainian eparchy; ordinariate for all other Eastern Catholics.
Venezuela: Melkite apostolic exarchate.

Synods, Assemblies
These assemblies are collegial bodies that have pastoral authority over members of the Eastern Catholic Churches. (Canons 102-113, 152-153, 322 of Oriental Code of Canon Law.)
Patriarchal Synods:
Synod of the Coptic Catholic Church: Antonios Naguib, patriarch of Alexandria of the Copts.
Synod of the Greek-Melkite Catholic Church: Gregory III Laham, patriarch of Antioch of the Greek Catholics-Melkites.
Synod of the Syrian Catholic Church: Ignatius Peter VIII, patriarch of Antioch of the Syrians.
Synod of the Maronite Church: Cardinal Nasrallah Pierre Sfeir, patriarch of Antioch of the Maronites.
Synod of the Chaldean Church: Emmanuel III Delly, patriarch of Babylonia of the Chaldeans.
Synod of the Armenian Catholic Church: Nerses Bedros XIX Tarmouni, patriarch of Cilicia of the Armenians.

Major Archiepiscopal Synods:
The Synod of the Ukrainian Greek Catholic Church (raised to major archiepiscopal status Dec. 23, 1963): Cardinal Lubomir Husar, major archbishop of Kiev and Halych, president.
The Synod of the Syro-Malabar Catholic Church (raised to major archiepiscopal status, Jan. 29, 1993): Cardinal Varkey Vithayathil, C.SS.R., major archbishop of Ernakulam-Angamaly of the Syro-Malabars, president.
The Synod of the Syro-Malankara Catholic Church (raised to major archiepiscopal status February 10, 2005): Abp. Cyril Baselios Malancharuvil, O.I.C., of Trivandrum of the Syro-Malankarese, president.

The Synod of the Romanian Greek Catholic Church (raised to major archiepiscopal status December 16, 2005): Abp. Lucian Muresan of Fagaras and Alba Julia, president.

Councils, Assemblies, Conferences

Council of Ethiopian Churches: Most Rev. Berhane-Yesus Demerew Souraphiel, C.M. of Addis Ababa, president.

Council of Ruthenian Churches, U.S.A.: Most Reverend Basil Schott, OFM, Metropolitan of Pittsburgh of the Byzantines, president.

Assembly of the Catholic Hierarchy of Egypt (Dec. 5, 1983): Cardinal Stéphanos II Ghattas, C.M., patriarch of Alexandria of the Copts, president.

Assembly of Catholic Patriarchs and Bishops of Lebanon: Cardinal Nasrallah Pierre Sfeir, patriarch of Antioch of the Maronites, president.

Assembly of Ordinaries of the Syrian Arab Republic: Maximos V Hakim, patriarch of Antioch of the Greek Catholics-Melkites, president.

Assembly of Catholic Ordinaries of the Holy Land (Jan. 27, 1992): Michel Sabbah, patriarch of Jerusalem of the Latins, president.

Interritual Union of the Bishops of Iraq: Emmanuel III Delly, patriarch of Babylonia of the Chaldeans, president.

Iranian Episcopal Conference (Aug. 11, 1977): Most Rev. Vartan Tékéyan, bishop of Ispahan of the Armenians of the Armenians, president.

Episcopal Conference of Turkey (Nov. 30, 1987): Most Rev. Louis A. Pelâtre, A.A., vicar apostolic of Istanbul, president.

EASTERN CATHOLIC CHURCHES IN THE U.S.

Statistics, from the 2006 Annuario Pontificio unless noted otherwise, are membership figures reported by Eastern jurisdictions. Additional Eastern Catholics are included in statistics for Latin dioceses.

Byzantine Tradition

Ukrainians: There were 102,632 reported in four jurisdictions in the U.S.: the metropolitan see of Philadelphia (1924, metropolitan 1958) and the suffragan sees of Stamford, CN (1956), St. Nicholas of Chicago (1961) and St. Josaphat in Parma (1983).

Ruthenians: There were 99,288 reported in four jurisdictions in the US: the metropolitan see of Pittsburgh (est. 1924 at Pittsburgh; metropolitan and transferred to Munhall, 1969; transferred to Pittsburgh, 1977) and the suffragan sees of Passaic, NJ (1963), Parma, OH (1969) and Van Nuys, CA (1981). Hungarian and Croatian Byzantine Catholics in the U.S. are also under the jurisdiction of Ruthenian bishops.

Melkites: There were 27,207 reported under the jurisdiction of the Melkite eparchy of Newton, MA (established as an exarchate, 1965; eparchy, 1976).

Romanians: There were 5,000 reported in 15 Romanian Catholic Byzantine Rite parishes in the U.S., under the jurisdiction of the Romanian eparchy of St. George Martyr, Canton, OH (established as an exarchate, 1982; eparchy, 1987).

Russians: In the United States, there are parishes in New York City (St. Michael) and in El Segundo in the Los Angeles area (St. Andrew). They are under the jurisdiction of local Latin bishops.

Alexandrian Tradition

Copts: Have a Catholic Chapel — Resurrection, in Brooklyn, N.Y., and St. Mary's Coptic Catholic parish, Los Angeles, CA.

Antiochian Tradition

Maronites: There were 75,232 reported in two jurisdictions in the US: the eparchy of St. Maron, Brooklyn (established at Detroit as an exarchate, 1966; eparchy, 1972; transferred to Brooklyn, 1977) and the eparchy of Our Lady of Lebanon of Los Angeles (resident in St. Louis, MO, established Mar. 1, 1994).

Syrians: The eparchy of Our Lady of the Deliverance of Newark with 13,270 faithful was established in 1995 for Syrian Catholics of the U.S. and Canada.

Syro-Malankarese: Have twelve mission parishes in the United States under the direction of Most Rev. Dr. Joseph Mar Thomas, Auxiliary Bishop of Trivandrum and Apostolic visitor for Europe and North America.

Armenian Tradition

An apostolic exarchate for Canada and the United States was established July 3, 1981; raised to status of eparchy on September 12, 2005; 36,000 in the two countries.

Chaldean Tradition

Chaldeans: There were 120,200 reported under the jurisdictions of the eparchy of St. Thomas the Apostle of Detroit (established as an exarchate, 1982; eparchy, 1986) and the eparchy of St. Peter the Apostle of San Diego (established on May 21, 2002).

Syro-Malabarese (Malabar): Have an eparchy based in Chicago with seven parishes around the country. Estimated 100,000 faithful with 26 diocesan priests.

Eastern Catholic Associates

Eastern Catholic Associates is the association of all Eastern Catholic bishops and their equivalents in law in the United States, representing the Armenian, Chaldean, Maronite, Melkite, Syriac, Romanian, Ruthenian and Ukrainian churches. The Syro-Malabar and Russian churches are also represented even though they do not have bishops in the U.S. President: Bishop Robert M. Moskal, Eparch of St. Josaphat, P.O. Box 347180, Parma, OH 44134. The Vice President is Bishop Basil Schott, OFM, metropolitan abp. of Pittsburgh.

The association meets at the same time as the United States Conference of Catholic Bishops in the fall of each year.

BYZANTINE DIVINE LITURGY

The Divine Liturgy in all rites is based on the consecration of bread and wine by the narration-reactualization of the actions of Christ at the Last Supper, and the calling down of the Holy Spirit. Aside from this fundamental usage, there are differences between the Roman (Latin) Rite and Eastern Rites, and among the Eastern Rites themselves. Following is a general description of the Byzantine Divine Liturgy which is in widest use in the Eastern Churches.

In the Byzantine, as in all Eastern Rites, the bread and wine are prepared at the start of the Liturgy. The priest does this in a little niche or at a table in the sanctuary. Taking a round loaf of leavened bread stamped with religious symbols, he cuts out a square host and other particles while reciting verses expressing the symbolism of the action. When the bread and wine are ready, he says a prayer of offering and incenses the oblations, the altar, the icons and the people.

Liturgy of the Catechumens: At the altar a litany for all classes of people is sung by the priest. The congregation answers, "Lord, have mercy." The Little Entrance comes next. In procession, the priest leaves the sanctuary carrying the Book of the Gospels, and then returns. He sings prayers especially selected for the day and the feast. These are followed by the solemn singing of the prayer, "Holy God, Holy Mighty One, Holy Immortal One." The Epistle follows. The Gospel is sung or read by the priest facing the people at the middle door of the sanctuary.

An interruption after the Liturgy of the Catechumens, formerly an instructional period for those learning the faith, is clearly marked. Catechumens, if present, are dismissed with a prayer. Following this are a prayer and litany for the faithful.

Great Entrance: The Great Entrance or solemn Offertory Procession then takes place. The priest first says a long silent prayer for himself, in preparation for the great act to come. Again he incenses the oblations, the altar, the icons and people. He goes to the table on the Gospel side for the veil-covered paten and chalice. When he arrives back at the sanctuary door, he announces the intention of the Mass in the prayer: "May the Lord God remember all of you in his kingdom, now and forever." After another litany, the congregation recites the Nicene Creed.

Consecration: The most solemn portion of the sacrifice is introduced by the preface, which is very much like the preface of the Roman Rite. At the beginning of the last phrase, the priest raises his voice to introduce the singing of the Sanctus. During the singing he reads the introduction to the words of consecration. The words of consecration are sung aloud, and the people sing "Amen" to both consecrations. As the priest raises the Sacred Species in solemn offering, he sings: "Thine of Thine Own we offer unto Thee in behalf of all and for all." A prayer to the Holy Spirit is followed by the commemorations, in which special mention is made of the all-holy, most blessed and glorious Lady, the Mother of God and ever-Virgin Mary. The dead are remembered and then the living.

Holy Communion: A final litany for spiritual gifts precedes the Our Father. The Sacred Body and Blood are elevated with the words, "Holy Things for the Holy." The Host is then broken and commingled with the Precious Blood. The priest recites preparatory prayers for Holy Communion, consumes the Sacred Species, and distributes Holy Communion to the people under the forms of both bread and wine. During this time the choir or congregation sings a communion verse.

The Liturgy closes quickly after this. The consecrated Species of bread and wine are removed to the side table to be consumed later by the priest. A prayer of thanksgiving is recited, a prayer for all the people is said in front of the icon of Christ, a blessing is invoked upon all, and the people are dismissed.

BYZANTINE CALENDAR

The Byzantine calendar has many distinctive features of its own, although it shares common elements with the Roman calendar — e.g., general purpose, commemoration of the mysteries of faith and of the saints, identical dates for some feasts. Among the distinctive things are the following. The liturgical year begins on Sept. 1, the Day of Indiction, in contrast with the Latin or Roman start on the First Sunday of Advent late in November or early in December. The Advent season begins on Dec. 10.

Cycles of the Year

As in the Roman usage, the dating of feasts follows the Gregorian Calendar. Formerly, until well into this century, the Julian Calendar was used. (The Julian Calendar, which is now about 13 days late, is still used by some Eastern Churches.) The year has several cycles, which include proper seasons, the feasts of saints, and series of New Testament readings. All of these elements of worship are contained in liturgical books of the rite. The ecclesiastical calendar, called the *Menologion*, explains the nature of feasts, other observances and matters pertaining to the liturgy for each day of the year. In some cases, its contents include the lives of saints and the history and meaning of feasts.

The Divine Liturgy (Mass) and Divine Office for the proper of the saints, fixed feasts, and the Christmas season are contained in the Menaion. The *Triodion* covers the pre-Lenten season of preparation for Easter; Lent begins two days before the Ash Wednesday observance of the Roman Rite. The *Pentecostarion* contains the liturgical services from Easter to the Sunday of All Saints, the first after Pentecost. The *Evangelion* and *Apostolos* are books in which the Gospels, and Acts of the Apostles and the Epistles, respectively, are arranged according to the order of their reading in the Divine Liturgy and Divine Office throughout the year.

The cyclic progression of liturgical music throughout the year, in successive and repetitive periods of eight weeks, is governed by the *Oktoechos*, the *Book of Eight Tones*.

Sunday Names

Many Sundays are named after the subject of the Gospel read in the Mass of the day or after the name of a feast falling on the day — e.g., Sunday of the Publican and Pharisee, of the Prodigal Son, of the Samaritan Woman, of St. Thomas the Apostle, of the Fore-Fathers (Old Testament Patriarchs).

Other Sundays are named in the same manner as in the Roman calendar e.g., numbered Sundays of Lent and after Pentecost.

Holy Days

The calendar lists about 28 holy days. Many of the major holy days coincide with those of the Roman calendar, but the feast of the Immaculate Conception is observed on Dec. 9 instead of Dec. 8, and the feast of All Saints falls on the Sunday after Pentecost rather than on Nov. 1. Instead of a single All Souls' Day, there are five All Souls' Saturdays. According to regulations in effect in the Byzantine (Ruthenian) Archeparchy of Pittsburgh and its suffragan sees of Passaic, Parma and Van Nuys, holy days are obligatory, solemn and simple, and attendance at the Divine Liturgy is required on five obligatory days —the feasts of the Epiphany, the Ascension, Sts. Peter and Paul, the Assumption of the Blessed Virgin Mary, and Christmas. Although attendance at the liturgy is not obligatory on 15 solemn and seven simple holy days, it is recommended. In the Byzantine (Ukrainian) Archeparchy of Philadelphia and its suffragan sees of St. Josaphat in Parma, St. Nicholas (Chicago) and Stamford, the obligatory feasts are the Epiphany, Annunciation, Ascension, Sts. Peter & Paul, Dormition, and Christmas.

Lent

The first day of Lent — the Monday before Ash Wednesday of the Roman Rite — and Good Friday are days of strict abstinence for persons in the age bracket of obligation. No meat, eggs, or dairy products may be eaten on these days. All persons over the age of 14 must abstain from meat on Fridays during Lent, Holy Saturday, and the vigils of the feasts of Christmas and Epiphany; abstinence is urged, but is not obligatory, on Wednesdays of Lent. The abstinence obligation is not in force on certain "free" or "privileged" Fridays.

Synaxis

An observance without a counterpart in the Roman calendar is the synaxis. This is a commemoration, on the day following a feast, of persons involved with the occasion for the feast — e.g., Sept. 9, the day following the feast of the Nativity of the Blessed Virgin Mary, is the Synaxis of Joachim and Anna, her parents.

Holy Week

In the Byzantine Rite, Lent is liturgically concluded with the Saturday of Lazarus, the day before Palm Sunday, which commemorates the raising of Lazarus from the dead. On the following Monday, Tuesday and Wednesday, the Liturgy of the Presanctified is prescribed.

On Holy Thursday, the Liturgy of St. Basil the Great is celebrated together with Vespers.

The Divine Liturgy is not celebrated on Good Friday. On Holy Saturday, the Liturgy of St. Basil the Great is celebrated along with Vespers.

BYZANTINE FEATURES

Art: Named for the empire in which it developed, Byzantine art is a unique blend of imperial Roman and classic Hellenic culture with Christian inspiration. The art of the Greek Middle Ages, it reached a peak of development in the 10th or 11th century. Characteristic of its products, particularly in mosaic and painting, are majesty, dignity, refinement and grace. Its sacred paintings, called icons, are reverenced highly in all the Eastern Churches of the Byzantine tradition.

Church Building: The classical model of Byzantine church architecture is the Church of the Holy Wisdom (*Hagia Sophia*), built in Constantinople in the first half of the sixth century and still standing. The square structure, extended in some cases in the form of a cross, is topped by a distinctive onion-shaped dome and surmounted by a triple-bar cross. The altar is at the eastern end of building, where the wall bellies out to form an apse. The altar and sanctuary are separated from the body of the church by a fixed or movable screen, the iconostas, to which icons or sacred pictures are attached (see below).

Clergy: The Byzantine Churches have married as well as celibate priests. In places other than the U.S., where married candidates have not been accepted for ordination since about 1929, men already married can be ordained to the diaconate and priesthood and can continue in marriage after ordination. Celibate deacons and priests cannot marry after ordination; neither can a married priest remarry after the death of his wife. Bishops must be unmarried.

Iconostasis: A large screen decorated with sacred pictures or icons that separates the sanctuary from the nave of a church; its equivalent in the Roman Rite, for thus separating the sanctuary from the nave, is an altar rail. An iconostas has three doors through which the sacred ministers enter the sanctuary during the Divine Liturgy: smaller (north and south) Deacons' Doors and a large central Royal Door. The Deacons' Doors usually feature the icons of Sts. Gabriel and Michael; the Royal Door, the icons of the Evangelists—Matthew, Mark, Luke and John. To the right and left of the Royal Door are the icons of Christ the Teacher and of the Blessed Virgin Mary with the Infant Jesus. To the extreme right and left are the icons of the patron of the church and St. John the Baptist (or St. Nicholas of Myra). Immediately above the Royal Door is a picture of the Last Supper. To the right are six icons depicting the major feasts of Christ, and to the left are six icons portraying the major feasts of the Blessed Virgin Mary. Above the picture of the Last Supper is a large icon of Christ the King. Some icon screens also have pictures of the 12 Apostles and the major Old Testament prophets surmounted by a crucifixion scene.

Liturgical Language: In line with Eastern tradition, Byzantine practice has favored the use of the language of the people in the liturgy. Two great advocates of the practice were Sts. Cyril and Methodius, apostles of the Slavs, who devised the Cyrillic alphabet and pioneered the adoption of Slavonic in the liturgy.

Sacraments: Baptism is administered by immersion, and confirmation (Chrismation) is conferred at the same time. The Eucharist is administered by intinction, i.e., by giving the communicant a piece of consecrated leavened bread that has been dipped into the consecrated wine. When giving absolution in the sacrament of penance, the priest holds his stole over the head of the penitent. Distinctive marriage ceremonies include the crowning of the bride and groom. Ceremonies for anointing the sick closely resemble those of the Roman Rite. Holy orders are conferred by a bishop.

Sign of the Cross: The sign of the cross in conjunction with a deep bow expresses reverence for the presence of Christ in the Blessed Sacrament. (*See entry in* **Glossary.**)

VESTMENTS, APPURTENANCES

Antimension: A silk or linen cloth laid on the altar for the Liturgy; it may be decorated with a picture of the burial of Christ and the instruments of his passion; the relics of martyrs are sewn into the front border.

Asteriskos: Made of two curved bands of gold or silver which cross each other to form a double arch; a star depends from the junction, which forms a cross; it is placed over the diskos holding the consecrated bread and is covered with a veil.

Diskos: A shallow plate, which may be elevated on a small stand, corresponding to the Roman-Rite paten.

Eileton: A linen cloth that corresponds to the Roman-Rite corporal.

Epimanikia: Ornamental cuffs; the right cuff symbolizing strength, the left, patience and good will.

Epitrachelion: A stole with ends sewn together, having a loop through which the head is passed; its several crosses symbolize priestly duties.

Lance: A metal knife used for cutting up the bread to be consecrated during the Liturgy.

Phelonion: An ample cape, long in the back and sides and cut away in front; symbolic of the higher gifts of the Holy Spirit.

Poterion: A chalice or cup that holds the wine and Precious Blood.

Spoon: Used in administering Holy Communion by intinction; consecrated leavened bread is dipped into consecrated wine and spooned onto the tongue of the communicant.

Sticharion: A long white garment of linen or silk with wide sleeves and decorated with embroidery; formerly the vestment for clerics in minor orders, acolytes, lectors, chanters, and subdeacons; symbolic of purity.

Veils: Three are used, one to cover the poterion, the second to cover the diskos, and the third to cover both.

Zone: A narrow clasped belt made of the same material as the *epitrachelion*; symbolic of the wisdom of the priest, his strength against enemies of the Church and his willingness to perform holy duties.

CODE OF CANONS OF THE EASTERN CHURCHES

The **Code of Canons of the Eastern Churches** serves as the legal corpus for the Eastern Churches, providing the legal principles for the preservation of the rich heritage of these Churches. The overarching theological structure for the Code was enunciated by the Second Vatican Council in its declaration in *Orientalium Ecclesiarum* (3):

These individual Churches, whether of the East or the West, although they differ somewhat among themselves in rite (to use the current phrase), that is, in liturgy, ecclesiastical discipline, and spiritual heritage, are, nevertheless, each as much as the others, entrusted to the pastoral government of the Roman Pontiff, the divinely appointed successor of St. Peter in primacy over the universal Church. They are consequently of equal dignity, so that none of them is superior to the others as regards rite and they enjoy the same rights and are under the same obligations, also in respect of preaching the Gospel to the whole world (cf. Mk 16:15) under the guidance of the Roman Pontiff.

Background

The creation and promulgation of the Code for the Eastern Churches began during the pontificate of Pope Pius XI (1922-39) when he established a commission of cardinals in 1929 to examine the requirements for a code. This preparatory commission was succeeded in 1935 by a new commission with the task of undertaking the actual composition of the Code. What followed was a gradual process of promulgations. Pope Pius XII (1939-58) issued a series of apostolic letters as different elements of the Eastern Code were completed. This method of promulgation continued until 1972 when Pope Paul VI (1963-78) established the Pontifical Commission for the Revision of the Code of Eastern Canon Law.

The commission approached the initial stages of its work quite deliberately. Extensive consultation was made with canonists as well as many bishops of the Eastern Churches. These efforts culminated in November 1988 with the unanimous vote of the commission's members accepting the draft of the new Code. On Oct. 18, 1990, Pope John Paul II officially promulgated the Code of Canons of the Eastern Churches. The Code became effective on Oct. 1, 1991. As the decree makes clear, in accordance with this universal legislation, each Eastern Catholic Church is to develop its own particular law. This stands in contrast to the Code of Canon Law that applies only to the single Latin Church.

Contents and Structure

The Code of Canons of the Eastern Churches marked a significant milestone in the history of Church law. It represented the long process in the development of Canon Law for the Eastern Churches throughout the 20th century and was an eloquent means of both respecting and preserving the proper discipline of those Churches. It was noted from the start that the Code for the Eastern Catholics was organized differently in comparison with the Code of Canon Law for the Latin Rite. There are different elements to Eastern Law, and the Code presents the independence of these laws from the Latin Rite, save, of course, for those canons that give reference to the Pope. Nevertheless, while safeguarding the centuries' old traditions and heritage of the Eastern Catholic Churches, the differences are not disruptive to the unity of the Church. Rather, the Code is an instrument in moving toward appropriate unity. As the 1996 document, "Applying the Liturgical Prescriptions of the Code of Canons of the Eastern Catholic Churches" (9), by the Congregation for the Eastern Churches states:

The Code of Canons of the Eastern Churches, in can. 28 § 1 which refers to *Lumen Gentium*, no. 23, and *Orientalium Ecclesiarum*, no. 3, elucidates the important areas which articulate the heritage of each of the Churches *sui iuris*: liturgy, theology, spirituality and discipline. It is necessary to note that these particular fields penetrate and condition one another in turn inside a global vision of divine revelation which pervades all life and which culminates in the praise of the most holy Trinity.

The Catholic Church in the United States

CHRONOLOGY OF U.S. CATHOLIC HISTORY

The following are key dates in U.S. Catholic History. Reprinted from *Our Sunday Visitor's Encyclopedia of American Catholic History*.

1492 Christopher Columbus sailed to the New World and reached San Salvador (probably Watlings Island in the Bahamas). He subsequently made three voyages and established a Spanish presence on Santo Domingo (Hispaniola).

1497 John Cabot, a Genoese sailing under the English flag, reached the coasts of Labrador and Newfoundland.

1499 Alonso de Ojeda and Amerigo Vespucci reached Venezuela and explored the South American coast.

1500 Pedro Cabral reached Brazil.

1511 Diocese of Puerto Rico established as suffragan of Seville, Spain. Bishop Alonso Manso, sailing from Spain in 1512, became first bishop to take up residence in New World.

1513 Juan Ponce de León reached Florida and sailed as far north as the Carolinas.

1519 Hernando Cortes began the conquest of Mexico; by the next year, the Aztec Empire had been conquered and the Spanish rule over Mexico was established.

1521 Missionaries accompanying Ponce de León and other explorers probably said first Masses within present limits of U.S.

1526 Lucas Vázquez de Ayllón attempted to establish a colony in South Carolina; it later failed.

1534-36 Jacques Cartier explored the Newfoundland area and sailed up the St. Lawrence River.

1539 Hernando de Soto journeyed through Florida and as far north as Arkansas.

1540 Francisco Coronado set out to find the Seven Cities of Gold, journeying through Texas, Kansas and New Mexico. Franciscans Juan de Padilla and Marcos de Niza accompanied Coronado expedition through the territory. They celebrated the first Mass within territory of 13 original colonies.

c. 1540 Juan de Padilla, the first martyr of the United States, was murdered on the plains of Kansas by local Indians.

1565 City of St. Augustine, oldest in U.S., founded by Pedro Menendez de Aviles, who was accompanied by four secular priests. America's oldest mission, Nombre de Dios, was established. Fr. Martin Francisco Lopez de Mendoza Grajales became the first parish priest of St. Augustine, where the first parish in the U.S. was established.

1602 Carmelite Anthony of the Ascension offered first recorded Mass in Calif. on shore of San Diego Bay.

1608 Samuel de Champlain established the first permanent French colony at Québec.

1606 Bishop Juan de las Cabeyas de Altamirano, O.P., conducted the first episcopal visitation in the U.S.

1609 Henry Hudson entered New York Bay and sailed up the Hudson River. Santa Fe established as a mission in New Mexico. It later served as a headquarters for missionary efforts in the American Southwest.

1611 Pierre Biard, S.J., and Ennémond Massé, S.J., began missionary labors among the Indians of Maine.

1612 First Franciscan province in U.S. erected under title of Santa Elena; it included Georgia, South Carolina and Florida.

1613 Four Jesuits attempted to establish permanent French settlement near mouth of Kennebec River, Maine.

1619 French Franciscans began work among settlers and Indians. They were driven out by English in 1628.

1620 The Mayflower Compact drawn up by the Pilgrims. The chapel of Nombre de Dios was dedicated to Nuestra Senora de la Leche y Buen Parto (Our Nursing Mother of the Happy Delivery) in Florida; oldest shrine to the Blessed Mother in the U.S.

1622 Pope Gregory XV established the Congregation de Propaganda Fide to oversee all mission territories. The Catholics of America remained under its jurisdiction until 1908.

1630 New England made a prefecture apostolic in charge of French Capuchins.

1634 Ark and Dove reached Maryland with the first settlers. Maryland established by Lord Calvert; two Jesuits were among first colonists. First Mass offered on Island of St. Clement in Lower Potomac by Jesuit Fr. Andrew White.

1638 Jean Nicolet discovered the water route to the Mississippi.

1642 Jesuits Isaac Jogues and René Goupil were mutilated by Mohawks; Goupil was killed shortly afterwards. Dutch Calvinists rescued Fr. Jogues. The colony of Virginia outlawed priests and disenfranchised Catholics.

1646 Jesuit Isaac Jogues and John Lalande were martyred by Iroquois at Ossernenon, now Auriesville.

1647 Massachusetts Bay Company enacted an antipriest law.

1649 The General Assembly of Maryland passed an act of religious toleration for the colony.

1653 Jesuits opened a school at Newton Manor, the first school in the American English colonies.

1654 Following the English Civil War and the deposition of King Charles I, the installed Puritan regime in Maryland repealed the act of religious toleration in Maryland.

1656 Church of St. Mary erected on Onondaga Lake, in first French settlement within the state. Kateri Tekakwitha, "Lily of the Mohawks," was born at Ossernenon, now Auriesville (d. in Canada, 1680). She was beatified in 1980.

1660 Jesuit René Menard opened first regular mission in Lake Superior region.

1668 Fr. Marquette founded Sainte Marie Mission at Sault Sainte Marie.

1671 Sieur de Lusson and Claude Allouez, S.J., arrived at Mackinac Island and claimed possession of the western country in the name of France.

1673 Louis Joliet and Jacques Marquette, S.J., began their expedition down the Mississippi River.

1674 Fr. Marquette set up a cabin for saying Mass in what later became the city of Chicago.

1675 Fr. Marquette established Mission of the Immaculate Conception among Kaskaskia Indians, near present site of Utica; transferred to Kaskaskia, 1703.

1678 Franciscan Recollect Louis Hennepin, first white man to describe Niagara Falls, celebrated Mass there.

1680 Louis Hennepin followed the Mississippi to its source. The missions of New Mexico destroyed by a local Indian uprising.

1682 Mission Corpus Christi de Isleta (Ysleta) founded by Franciscans near El Paso, first mission in present-day Texas.

1682 Religious toleration extended to members of all faiths in Pennsylvania.

1683 The New York colony passed the Charter of Liberties providing for religious freedom for believers in Christ.

1687 Eusebio Kino, S.J., launched the missions in Arizona at Pimería Alta.

1688 Maryland became royal colony as a result of the so-called Glorious Revolution in England; Anglican Church became the official religion (1692). Toleration Act repealed; Catholics disenfranchised and persecuted until 1776. Hanging of Ann Glover, an elderly Irish-Catholic widow, who refused to renounce her Catholic religion.

1689 Jesuit Claude Allouez died after 32 years of missionary activity among Indians of midwest; he had evangelized Indians of 20 different tribes. Jesuit Jacques Gravier succeeded Allouez as vicar general of Illinois.

1690 Mission San Francisco de los Tejas founded in east Texas.

1692 The Church of England officially established in Maryland. New Mexico re-subjugated by the Spanish and the missions re-opened.

1697 Religious liberty granted to all except "papists" in South Carolina.

1700 Jesuit Eusebio Kino, who first visited the area in 1692, established mission at San Xavier del Bac,

near Tucson. In 1783, under Franciscan administration, construction was begun of the Mission Church of San Xavier del Bac near the site of the original mission; it is still in use as a parish church. Although the New York Assembly enacted a bill calling for religious toleration for all Christians in 1683, other penal laws were now enforced against Catholics; all priests were ordered out of the province.

1701 Tolerance granted to all except "papists" in New Jersey.

1703 Mission San Francisco de Solano founded on Rio Grande; rebuilt in 1718 as San Antonio de Valero, or the Alamo.

1704 Destruction of Florida's northern missions by English and Indian troops led by Governor James Moore of South Carolina. Franciscans Juan de Parga, Dominic Criodo, Tiburcio de Osorio, Augustine Ponze de León, Marcos Delgado and two Indians, Anthony Enixa and Amador Cuipa Feliciano, were slain by the invaders.

1709 French Jesuit missionaries obliged to give up their central New York missions.

1716 Antonio de Margil, O.F.M., began his missionary labors in Texas.

1718 The Catholics in Maryland officially disenfranchised. City of New Orleans founded by Jean Baptiste Le Moyne de Bienville.

1727 Ursuline Nuns founded convent in New Orleans, oldest convent in what is now U.S.; they conducted a school, hospital and orphan asylum.

1735 Bishop Francis Martinez de Tejadu Diaz de Velasco, auxiliary of Santiago, was the first bishop to take up residence in U.S., at St. Augustine.

1740s The First Great Awakening among Protestants.

1741 Because of an alleged popish plot to burn the city of New York, four whites were hanged and 11 blacks burned at the stake.

1744 Mission church of the Alamo built in San Antonio.

1751 First Catholic settlement founded among Huron Indians near Sandusky, Ohio, by Jesuit Fr. de la Richardie.

1754-63 The French and Indian War (The Seven Years War in Europe), the first world war; the conflict ended with the defeat of France and the loss of their American colonies.

1755 Fifty-six Catholics of Acadia expelled from the American colonies; those landing in Boston were denied the services of a Catholic priest.

1763 The Jesuits banished from the territories of Louisiana and Illinois Spain ceded Florida to England. The English also gained control of all French territories east of the Mississippi following the cessation of the French and Indian War.

1765 The Quartering Act imposed on the colonies by the British as a means of paying the cost of colonial defense. It was followed by the Stamp Act, sparking the rise of the Sons of Liberty and the convening of the Stamp Act Congress.

1767 Jesuits expelled from Spanish territory. Spanish Crown confiscated their property, including the Pious Fund for Missions. Upper California missions entrusted to Franciscans.

1769 Franciscan Junípero Serra, missionary in Mexico for 20 years, began establishment of Franciscan missions in California, in present San Diego. He was beatified in 1988.

1770 The Boston Massacre resulted in the deaths of five colonists in Boston.

1773 The Tea Act sparked the Boston Tea Party. The British responded with the Intolerable Acts in 1774. Charles Carroll of Carrollton published the "First Citizen" letter in defense of the Church and Catholics against Daniel Dulany and the royal colonial government in Maryland.

1774 Elizabeth Bayley Seton, foundress of the American Sisters of Charity, was born in New York City on Aug. 28. She was canonized in 1975. The British Parliament passed the Quebec Act granting the French in the region the right to their own religion, language and customs. The first Continental Congress is convened.

1775-1781 The American Revolution, in which Catholics played a major role. In 1790, newly elected President George Washington wrote to American Catholics to thank them for their instrumental role in the war for American freedom.

1775 The Continental Congress denounced the rampant anti-Catholicism of the colonies to King George III. General Washington discouraged Guy Fawkes Day procession, in which pope was carried in effigy.

1776 Charles Carroll received appointment with Samuel Chase and Benjamin Franklin to a commission of the Continental Congress seeking aid from Canada; Fr. John Carroll accompanied them on their mission. Virginia became the first state to vote for full religious freedom in the new state's bill of rights. Similar provisions were passed by Maryland and Pennsylvania. The Continental Congress passed the Declaration of Independence (Charles Carroll was also the longest surviving signer). The New Jersey State Constitution tacitly excluded Catholics from office.

1777 The New York State Constitution gave religious liberty, but the naturalization law required an oath to renounce allegiance to any foreign ruler, ecclesiastical as well as civil.

1778 Fr. Gibault aided George Rogers Clark in campaign against British in conquest of Northwest Territory.

1780 The Massachusetts State Constitution granted religious liberty, but required a religious test to hold public office and provided for tax to support Protestant teachers of piety, religion and morality.

1781 Expedition from San Gabriel Mission founded present city of Los Angeles, Pueblo "de Nuestra Senora de los Angeles." British General Cornwallis surrendered at Yorktown, ending the Revolutionary War.

1783 The Treaty of Paris ended the American Revolution; Great Britain recognized the independence of the United States.

1784 The Vatican appointed Fr. John Carroll to the post of superior of the American Catholic missions. The State Constitution of New Hampshire included a religious test that barred Catholics from public office; local support was provided for public Protestant teachers of religion.

1787 Daniel Carroll of Maryland and Thomas FitzSimons of Pennsylvania signed the Constitution of the United States.

1788 First public Mass said in Boston on Nov. 2 by Abbé de la Poterie, first resident priest.

1789 Pope Pius VI erected the first United States diocese, Baltimore; John Carroll is named the first bishop.

1790 Catholics given right to vote in South Carolina.

1791 French Sulpicians opened the first seminary in the United States, St. Mary's in Baltimore. Georgetown Academy is established and begins holding classes. Bishop Carroll convoked the first synod of the clergy of the diocese. The Bill of Rights ratified by the Congress. Pierre Charles L'Enfant designed the Federal City of Washington. His plans were not fully implemented until the early 1900s.

1792 James Hoban designed the White House.

1793 Rev. Stephen T. Badin first priest ordained by Bishop Carroll; he soon began missionary work in Kentucky.

1799 Prince Demetrius Gallitzin (Fr. Augustine Smith) arrived in the Allegheny Mountains. He labored there for the next 40 years and established the Church in western Pennsylvania, at Loretto.

1800 Jesuit Leonard Neale became first bishop consecrated in present limits of U.S.

1801 Start of the Second Great Awakening among Protestants.

1802 First mayor of Washington, appointed by President Jefferson, was Catholic Judge Robert Brent.

1803 The Louisiana Purchase resulted in the acquisition by the United States of all French lands from the Mississippi River to the Rocky Mountains for $15 million.

1804-06 President Jefferson sponsored the expedition of Lewis and Clark into the Louisiana Territory.

1806 New York anti-Catholic 1777 Test Oath for naturalization repealed.

1808 Pope Pius VII declared Baltimore the first metropolitan see of the United States, erecting at the same time the new dioceses of Bardstown (KY), Boston, New York, and Philadelphia as suffragans.

1809 Mother Elizabeth Ann Seton established the first native American congregation of sisters, at Emmitsburg, Maryland.

1810 The United States annexed West Florida under the pretext that it was included in the Louisiana Purchase.

1811 Catholic Canadian trappers and traders with John J. Astor expedition founded first American settlement, Astoria. Rev. Guy I. Chabrat becomes first priest ordained west of the Allegheny Mountains.

1812 The War of 1812; it was ended by the Treaty of Ghent in 1814.

1814 St. Joseph's Orphanage, Philadelphia, opened, the first Catholic asylum for children in the United States.

1818 Religious freedom established by new constitution in Connecticut, although the Congregational Church remained, in practice, the state church. Bishop Dubourg arrived at St. Louis, with Vincentians Joseph Rosati and Felix de Andreis. Rose Philippine Duchesne arrived at St. Charles; founded first American convent of the Society of the Sacred Heart. She was beatified in 1940 and canonized in 1988.

1822 Bishop John England founded the United States

Catholic Miscellany, the first Catholic newspaper in the country of a strictly religious nature. The Society for the Propagation of the Faith is founded in France; it sent missionaries throughout the world. Vicariate Apostolic of Mississippi and Alabama established.

1823 President Monroe proposed the Monroe Doctrine of foreign policy. Fr. Gabriel Richard elected delegate to Congress from Michigan territory; he was the first priest elected to the House of Representatives.

1828 New York State Legislature enacted a law upholding sanctity of seal of confession. The first hospital opened west of the Mississippi in St. Louis, staffed by the Sisters of Charity from Emmitsburg, Maryland.

1829 The First Provincial Council of Baltimore convoked. The Oblate Sisters of Providence, the first African-American congregation of women religious in the United States was established in Baltimore.

1831 Xavier University founded.

1833 Fr. Frederic Baraga celebrated first Mass in present Grand Rapids.

1834 First native New Yorker to become a secular priest, Rev. John McCloskey, was ordained. Indian missions in Northwest entrusted to Jesuits by Holy See. A mob of Nativists attacked and burned down the Ursuline Convent at Charlestown, Massachusetts.

1835 Samuel F. B. Morse published *The Foreign Conspiracy Against the Liberties of the United States.*

1836 Texans under Stephen F. Austin declared their independence from Mexico; the Battle of the Alamo in San Antonio resulted in the deaths of 188 Texans, including the commander William B. Travis and perhaps Davy Crockett. Texas soon won its independence and was annexed in 1845. John Nepomucene Neumann arrived from Bohemia and was ordained a priest in Old St. Patrick's Cathedral, New York City. He was canonized in 1977. The infamous work of Maria Monk's Awful Disclosures of the Hotel Dieu Nunnery of Montreal, detailing supposed scandals of Catholic religious, was published. President Jackson nominated Roger Brooke Taney as chief justice of the Supreme Court.

1838 Fathers Blanchet and Demers, "Apostles of the Northwest," sent to territory by Abp. of Québec.

1839 Pope Gregory XVI condemned the slave trade in his decree In Supremo Apostolatus.

1840 Mother Theodore Guérin founded the Sisters of Providence of St.-Mary-of-the-Woods in Indiana.

1842 Fr. Augustine Ravoux began ministrations to French and Indians at Fort Pierre, Vermilion and Prairie du Chien; printed devotional book in Sioux language the following year. Henriette Delille and Juliette Gaudin began the Sisters of the Holy Family in New Orleans, the second African-American community of women religious. University of Notre Dame founded by Holy Cross Fr. Edward Sorin and Brothers of St. Joseph on land given the diocese of Vincennes by Fr. Stephen Badin.

1844 Thirteen persons killed, two churches and a school burned in Know-Nothing riots at Philadelphia. Orestes Brownson received into the Church; he subsequently founded *Brownson's*

Quarterly Review.

1845 Nativists opposed to Catholics and Irish immigration, established the Native American Party. Issac Hecker received into the Church. The potato famine began in Ireland, causing in part the mass migration of Irish to the United States. The St. Vincent de Paul Society founded in the United States.

1846-48 The Mexican-American War was caused by a border dispute between the United States and Mexico. Catholic chaplains were appointed to the army, to minister to Mexican Catholics.

1846 Peter H. Burnett, who became first governor of California in 1849, received into Catholic Church. First Benedictine Abbey in New World founded near Latrobe by Fr. Boniface Wimmer.

1847 The Bishops of the United States requested Pope Pius IX to name the Immaculate Conception patron of the United States.

1848 The first permanent American Trappist foundation established, in Kentucky. Jacob L. Martin named the first American representative to the Vatican.

1852 The First Plenary Council of Baltimore held. Redemptorist John Nepomucene Neumann became fourth bishop of Philadelphia. He was beatified in 1963 and canonized in 1977.

1853 Calling for the exclusion of Catholics and foreigners from office and a 21-year residence requirement, the American Party was founded, known also as the Know-Nothing Party.

1854 Members of the Benedictine Swiss-American congregation established a community at St. Meinrad in southern Indiana.

1855 The German Catholic Central Verein founded. The "Bloody Monday" Riots in Louisville, Kentucky, leave 20 dead.

1857 The Supreme Court issued the Dred Scott Decision; Chief Justice Roger Taney stated that Congress could not exclude slavery from the territories since, according to the Constitution, slaves were property and could be transported anywhere. The American College at Louvain opened.

1858 Jesuit Fr. De Smet accompanied General Harney as chaplain on expedition sent to settle troubles between Mormons and U.S. government. The Paulists, the first native religious community for men, established. Cornerstone of second (present) St. Patrick's Cathedral, New York City, was laid; the cathedral was completed in 1879.

1859 The North American College founded in Rome as a training center for American seminarians.

1860 South Carolina seceded from the Union.

1861-65 The American Civil War. Catholics participated in large numbers on both sides. There were approximately 40 Catholic chaplains in the Union army and 28 in the Confederate army. More than 500 Catholic nuns ministered to the sick and wounded. Over 20 generals in the Union army and 11 generals in the Confederate army were Catholics.

1861 The Confederacy was formed after 11 states seceded from the Union. Jefferson Davis was elected president of the Confederacy.

1865 *Catholic World* founded. A Test Oath law passed by state legislature (called Drake Convention) to crush Catholicism in Missouri. Law declared unconstitutional by Supreme Court in 1866. Rev. H. H.

Spalding, a Protestant missionary, published the Whitman Myth to hinder work of Catholic missionaries in Oregon. President Lincoln was assassinated. The murder sparked anti-Catholicism, including charges that Jesuits orchestrated his death. Congress passed the Thirteenth Amendment abolishing slavery.

1866 The Second Plenary Council of Baltimore.

1867 Reconstruction launched in the South; the presence of Federal troops did not end until 1877. The Ku Klux Klan founded to defeat Reconstruction, oppose Catholicism, and establish white supremacy in the post-war South. The U.S. purchased Alaska for $7.2 million; organized by Secretary of State William Seward, the purchase was called "Seward's Folly."

1869-70 The Fist Vatican Council convoked. Most of the bishops of the United States took part in the deliberations of the council.

1869 The Transcontinental Railroad completed, with the two tracks meeting at Promontory, near Ogden, Utah. The Knights of Labor founded.

1870 The Holy Name Society organized in the U.S.

1873 Blessed Fr. Damien de Veuster of the Sacred Hearts Fathers arrived in Molokai and spent the remainder of his life working among lepers. He was beatified in 1995.

1875 James A. Healy, first bishop of Negro blood consecrated in U.S., became second Bishop of Portland. Archbishop John McCloskey of New York became the first American prelate to be elevated to the College of Cardinals.

1876 George Armstrong Custer killed at the Battle of Little Bighorn (in the Second Sioux War) in Montana. *The American Catholic Quarterly Review* is established. James Gibbons publishes *Faith of Our Fathers.*

1878 Franciscan Sisters of Allegany becomes first native American community to send members to foreign missions.

1880 William R. Grace becomes the first Catholic mayor of New York City.

1882 Knights of Columbus founded by Fr. Michael J. McGivney.

1884 The Third Plenary Council of Baltimore held. John Gilmary Shea began the U.S. Catholic Historical Society.

1886 Abp. Charles J. Seghers, "Apostle of Alaska," was murdered by a guide; he had surveyed southern and northwest Alaska in 1873 and 1877. Archbishop James Gibbons of Baltimore is named the second American cardinal. Augustus Tolton is ordained the first African-American priest for the United States. The Knights of St. John was established.

1887 The American Protective Association (APA) was established to resist the growth of immigration. The Dawes Act was passed, dissolving all Indian tribes and distributing their lands among their former members, who were not permitted to dispose of their property for 25 years.

1889 The Catholic University of America opened. The first African-American Lay Congress was held in Washington, DC; subsequent congresses held in Cincinnati (1890), Philadelphia (1892), Chicago (1893), and Baltimore (1894). Mother Frances Xavier Cabrini arrived in New York City to begin

work among Italian immigrants. She was canonized in 1946. *American Ecclesiastical Review* begun.

1890 Archbishop Ireland delivered an address on public and private schools at the gathering of the National Education Association in St. Paul, Minnesota.

1891 Vicariate Apostolic of Oklahoma and Indian Territory was established. Katharine Drexel founded Sisters of Blessed Sacrament for Indians and Colored Peoples. She was canonized in 2000. The Rosary Society organized.

1893 The Apostolic Delegation under Archbishop Francesco Satolli established in Washington, DC; it became an Apostolic Nunciature in 1984 with the establishment of full diplomatic relations between the U.S. and the Holy See. The first Catholic college for women in the United States, College of Notre Dame of Maryland, was established. *St. Anthony Messenger* launched.

1898 Puerto Rico ceded to U.S. (became self-governing Commonwealth in 1952); inhabitants granted U.S. citizenship in 1917. The United States annexed Hawaii; the monarchy had been overthrown in 1897.

1898 The Spanish-American War.

1899 Pope Leo XIII issued *Testem Benevolentiae.*

1901 President McKinley assassinated.

1904 The National Catholic Education Association (NCEA) founded. First publication of the *Catholic Almanac.*

1905 The Catholic Church Extension Society for home missions established.

1907 The first volume of the *Catholic Encyclopedia* was published by the Catholic University of America.

1908 Pope St. Pius X published Pascendi Domini Gregis against Modernism. Pope Pius issued the bull Sapienti Consilio, by which the Church in the U.S. was removed from mission status and the jurisdiction of the Congregation de Propaganda Fide. First American Missionary Congress held in Chicago.

1909 The Holy Name Society was established. *America Magazine* founded by the Jesuits.

1911 The Catholic Foreign Mission Society of America (Maryknoll) founded. Katharine Drexel founded the Sisters of the Blessed Sacrament.

1912 *Our Sunday Visitor* founded.

1914-18 World War I.

1917 The United States entered the First World War. The National Catholic War Council was founded. Over one million Catholics served in the Armed Forces (over 20% of the total U.S. military).

1919 The Bishops' Program of Social Reconstruction published. The National Catholic Welfare Council was founded. Peter Guilday began the American Catholic Historical Association.

1920 The National Catholic News Service (NC, now the Catholic News Service, CNS) was established.

1924 The Federated Colored Catholics of the United States was established. *Commonweal Magazine* was founded by Michael Williams.

1925 The Supreme Court declares the Oregon school law unconstitutional. The Scopes Trial, also called the Dayton Monkey Trial, took place in Dayton, Ohio.

1926 The Twenty-Eighth International Eucharistic Congress was held in Chicago.

1928 Alfred E. Smith of New York nominated for president by the Democratic Party; he was the first Catholic ever chosen to head a major-party national ticket. He was defeated by Herbert Hoover, in part because of his opposition to Prohibition and his faith.

1929 The stockmarket crash signaled the start of the Great Depression. The Catholic Church devoted enormous resources to alleviating the suffering of those afflicted by the global Depression.

1932 Franklin Delano Roosevelt was elected president, launching the New Deal period (1933-45).

1933 The Catholic Worker Movement was established by Dorothy Day and Peter Maurin.

1934 John LaFarge, S.J., begins the first Catholic Interracial Council in New York.

1937 The Association of Catholic Trade Unionists (ACTU) established.

1939 Myron C. Taylor named personal representative of President Roosevelt to Pope Pius XII.

1939-45 World War II.

1941 Pearl Harbor was attacked by Japan; the U.S. entered World War II. Catholics comprised over 25% of the Armed Forces.

1945 End of World War II. Delegates from 50 nations established the Charter of the United Nations.

1947 The Christian Family Movement was begun by Pat and Patty Crowley. The Supreme Court issued the decision *Everson v. Board of Education* approving the use of public school buses to carry Catholic students to parochial schools.

1948 Protestants and Other Americans for Separation of Church and State (POAU) founded.

1951 President Truman nominates General Mark Clark as Ambassador to Vatican City. The nomination later withdrawn in the face of anti-Catholic protests.

1954 The Sisters Formation Conference was founded. The Supreme Court decided *Brown v. Board of Education of Topeka*; the decision declared that segregation in the public schools was unconstitutional.

1955 John Tracy Ellis published *American Catholics and the Intellectual Life*.

1956 Leadership Conference of Women Religious and Conference of Major Superiors of Men founded.

1957 The Civil Rights Act was passed, the first since 1875.

1958 Christopher Dawson was named the first holder of the Chauney Stillman Chair of Roman Catholic Studies at the Harvard Divinity School.

1959 Pope John XXIII announced his intention to convoke the Second Vatican Council.

1960 John F. Kennedy elected president of the United States; he was the first Catholic president.

1962-65 The Second Vatican Council.

1962 Gustave Weigel, S.J., appointed by the Vatican to be one of the five Catholic observers at the third general assembly of the World Council of Churches at New Delhi. Archbishop Joseph Rummel of New Orleans announced the integration of archdiocesan Catholic schools.

1963 The Catholic University of America prohibited Hans Küng, John Courtney Murray, S.J., Gustave Weigel, S.J., and Godfrey Diekmann, O.S.B., from speaking at the school. Elizabeth Ann Seton, the first American to be so honored, was beatified. President Kennedy assassinated in Dallas.

1964 The Civil Rights Act passed.

1965 Pope Paul VI visited the United Nations, the first pope to visit the U.S. Gommar A. De Pauw organizes the Catholic Traditionalist movement.

1966 The National Conference of Catholic Bishops and the United States Catholic Conference were organized. Harold Perry, S.V.D., became the second African-American to be named a bishop.

1967 The Land O' Lakes Statement issued. The Catholic Charismatic Movement began. The Catholic Committee on Urban Ministry (CCUM) was established.

1968 Pope Paul VI issued *Humanae Vitae*. The National Black Catholic Clergy Caucus, the National Black Sisters' Conference, the National Black Catholic Seminarians Association, and the National Federation of Priests' Council were formed. Catholics United for the Faith established.

1969 The Organization of Priests Associated for Religious, Educational, and Social Rights (PADRES) established. The Campaign for Human Development established.

1970 Patricio Flores, the first modern Latino bishop, ordained.

1971 The Leadership Conference of Women Religious established.

1972 Religious Brothers Conference established.

1973 *Roe v. Wade* decision handed down by the Supreme Court, legalizing abortion.

1975 Pope Paul VI canonized the first American saint, Elizabeth Ann Seton.

1976 The U.S. celebrated the Bicentennial.

1977 Fellowship of Catholic Scholars established.

1979 Pope John Paul II visited the U.S.

1983 The NCCB issued the Challenge of Peace.

1986 The NCCB issued Economic Justice for All. The Vatican and Catholic University of America removed Fr. Charles Curran from teaching theology at the university.

1987 Pope John Paul II visited the U.S. for the second time. The National Black Catholic Congress convoked in Washington, DC.

1991 The U.S. played a major role in the Gulf War.

1992 Council of Major Superiors of Women Religious founded.

1993 World Youth Day held in Denver.

1995 Pope John Paul II visited the United Nations, Baltimore, and New York.

1997 U.S. Bishops took part in a special assembly of the Synod of Bishops on the Church in the Americas.

1999 Pope John Paul II visited St. Louis.

2001 The U.S. attacked on Sept. 11. The NCCB and USSC merged to form the United States Conference of Catholic Bishops (USCCB); Bishop Wilton Gregory of Belleville was elected its first black president of the USCCB.

2002 The pedophilia crisis erupted across the country; the USCCB passed a series of protective norms.

2003 The U.S. launched the Iraq War to topple Saddam Hussein.

2004 Pres. George W. Bush is re-elected. The Democratic nominee, Sen. John Kerry, a Catholic, is the cause of considerable controversy for his pro-abortion position. The issue sparks a national debate over the issue of Catholic politicians and abortion.

U.S. CATHOLIC HISTORY

Courtesy Rev. Clyde Crews, Ph.D.

The starting point of the mainstream of Catholic history in the U.S. was in Baltimore at the end of the Revolutionary War. Long before that time, however, Catholic explorers had traversed much of the country and missionaries had done considerable work among Indians in the Southeast, Northeast and Southwest. (See Index, Chronology of Church in U.S.)

Spanish and French Missions

Missionaries from Spain evangelized Indians in Florida (which included a large area of the Southeast), New Mexico, Texas and California. Franciscan Juan de Padilla, killed in 1542 in what is now central Kansas, was the first of numerous martyrs among the early missionaries. The city of St. Augustine, settled by the Spanish in 1565, was the first permanent settlement in the United States and also the site of the first parish, established the same year with secular Fr. Martin Francisco Lopez de Mendoza Grajales as pastor. Italian Jesuit Eusebio Kino (1645-1711) established Spanish missions in lower California and southern Arizona, where he founded San Xavier del Bac mission in 1700. Bl. Junípero Serra (1713-84), who established nine of the famous chain of 21 Franciscan missions in California, was perhaps the most noted of the Spanish missionaries. He was beatified in 1988.

French missionary efforts originated in Canada and extended to parts of Maine, New York and areas around the Great Lakes and along the Mississippi River as far south as Louisiana. Sts. Isaac Jogues, René Goupil and John de Brébeuf, three of eight Jesuit missionaries of New France martyred between 1642 and 1649 (canonized in 1930), met their deaths near Auriesville, New York. Jesuit explorer Jacques Marquette (1637-75), who founded St. Ignace Mission at the Straits of Mackinac in 1671, left maps and a diary of his exploratory trip down the Mississippi River with Louis Joliet in 1673. Claude Allouez (1622-89), another French Jesuit, worked for 32 years among Indians in the Midwest, baptizing an estimated 10,000. French Catholics founded the colony in Louisiana in 1699. In 1727, Ursuline nuns from France founded a convent in New Orleans, the oldest in the United States.

English Settlements

Catholics were excluded by penal law from English settlements along the Atlantic coast.

The only colony established under Catholic leadership was Maryland, granted to George Calvert (Lord Baltimore) as a proprietary colony in 1632; its first settlement at St. Mary's City was established in 1634 by a contingent of Catholic and Protestant colonists who had arrived from England on the Ark and the Dove. Jesuits Andrew White and John Altham, who later evangelized Indians of the area, accompanied the settlers. The principle of religious freedom on which the colony was founded was enacted into law in 1649 as the Act of Toleration. It was the first such measure passed in the colonies and, except for a four-year period of Puritan control, remained in effect until 1688, when Maryland became a royal colony and the Anglican Church was made the official religion in 1692. Catholics were disenfranchised and persecuted until 1776.

The only other colony where Catholics were assured some degree of freedom was Pennsylvania, founded by the Quaker William Penn in 1681.

One of the earliest permanent Catholic establishments in the English colonies was St. Francis Xavier Mission, Old Bohemia, in northern Maryland, founded by the Jesuits in 1704 to serve Catholics of Delaware, Maryland and southeastern Pennsylvania. Its Bohemia Academy, established in the 1740s, was attended by sons of prominent Catholic families in the area.

Catholics and the Revolution

Despite their small number, which accounted for about one percent of the population, Catholics made significant contributions to the cause for independence from England.

Fr. John Carroll (1735-1815), who would later become the first bishop of the American hierarchy, and his cousin, Charles Carroll (1737-1832), a signer of the Declaration of Independence, were chosen by the Continental Congress to accompany Benjamin Franklin and Samuel Chase to Canada to try to secure that country's neutrality. Fr. Pierre Gibault (1737-1804) gave important aid in preserving the Northwest Territory for the revolutionaries. Thomas FitzSimons (1741-1811) of Philadelphia gave financial support to the Continental Army, served in a number of campaigns and later, with Daniel Carroll of Maryland, became one of the two Catholic signers of the Constitution. John Barry (1745-1803), commander of the *Lexington*, the first ship commissioned by Congress, served valiantly and is considered a founder of the U.S. Navy. There is no record of the number of Catholics who served in Washington's armies, although 38 to 50 percent had Irish surnames.

Casimir Pulaski (1748-79) and Thaddeus Kosciusko (1746-1817) of Poland served the cause of the Revolution. Assisting also were the Catholic nations of France, with a military and naval force, and Spain, with money and the neutrality of its colonies.

Acknowledgment of Catholic aid in the war and the founding of the Republic was made by General Washington in his reply to a letter from prominent Catholics seeking justice and equal rights: "I presume your fellow citizens of all denominations will not forget the patriotic part which you took in the accomplishment of our Revolution and the establishment of our government or the important assistance which they received from a nation [France] in which the Roman Catholic faith is professed."

In 1789, religious freedom was guaranteed under the First Amendment to the Constitution. Discriminatory laws against Catholics remained in force in many of the states, however, until well into the 19th century.

Beginning of Organization

Fr. John Carroll's appointment as superior of the American missions on June 9, 1784, was the first step toward organization of the Church in this country. According to a report he made to Rome the following year, there were 24 priests and approximately 25,000 Catholics, mostly in Maryland and Pennsylvania, in a general population of four million. Many of them had been in the Colonies for several generations. For the most part, however, they were an unknown minority laboring under legal and social handicaps.

Establishment of the Hierarchy

Fr. Carroll was named the first American bishop in 1789 and placed in charge of the Diocese of Baltimore, whose boundaries were coextensive with those of the United States. He was ordained in England on Aug. 15, 1790, and installed in his see the following Dec. 12.

Ten years later, Fr. Leonard Neale became his coadjutor and the first bishop ordained in the U.S. Bishop Carroll became an archbishop in 1808 when Baltimore was designated a metropolitan see and the new dioceses of Boston, New York, Philadelphia and Bardstown (now Louisville) were established. These jurisdictions were later subdivided, and by 1840 there were, in addition to Baltimore, 15 dioceses, 500 priests and 663,000 Catholics in the general population of 17 million.

Priests and First Seminaries

The original number of 24 priests noted in Bishop Carroll's 1785 report was gradually augmented with the arrival of others from France and other countries. Among arrivals from France after the Civil Constitution of the Clergy went into effect in 1790 were Jean Louis Lefebvre de Cheverus and Sulpicians Ambrose Maréchal, Benedict Flaget and William Dubourg, who later became bishops.

The first seminary in the country was St. Mary's, established in 1791 in Baltimore, and placed under the direction of the Sulpicians. French seminarian Stephen T. Badin (1768-1853), who fled to the U.S. in 1792 and became a pioneer missionary in Kentucky, Ohio and Michigan, was the first priest ordained (1793) in the U.S. Demetrius Gallitzin (1770-1840), a Russian prince and convert to Catholicism who did pioneer missionary work in western Pennsylvania, was ordained to the priesthood in 1795; he was the first to receive all his orders in the U.S. By 1815, St. Mary's Seminary had 30 ordained alumni.

Two additional seminaries, Mt. St. Mary's at Emmitsburg, Maryland, and St. Thomas at Bardstown, Kentucky, were established in 1809 and 1811, respectively. These and similar institutions founded later played key roles in the development and growth of the American clergy.

Early Schools

Early educational enterprises included the establishment in 1791 of a school at Georgetown that later became the first Catholic university in the U.S.; the opening of a secondary school for girls, conducted by Visitation Nuns, in 1799 at Georgetown; and the start of a similar school in the first decade of the 19th century at Emmitsburg, Maryland, by St. Elizabeth Ann Seton.

By the 1840s, which saw the beginnings of the present public school system, more than 200 Catholic elementary schools, half of them west of the Alleghenies, were in operation. From this start, the Church subsequently built the greatest private system of education in the world.

Sisterhoods

Institutes of women Religious were largely responsible for the development of educational and charitable institutions. Among them were Ursuline Nuns in Louisiana from 1727 and Visitation Nuns at Georgetown in the 1790s.

The first contemplative foundation in the country was established in 1790 at Fort Tobacco, Maryland, by three American-born Carmelites trained at an English convent in Belgium.

The first community of American origin was the Sisters of Charity of St. Joseph, founded in 1808 at Emmitsburg, Maryland, by Mother Elizabeth Ann Bayley Seton (canonized in 1975). Other early American communities were the Sisters of Loretto and the Sisters of Charity of Nazareth, both founded in 1812 in Kentucky, and the Oblate Sisters of Providence, a black community founded in 1829 in Baltimore by Mother Mary Elizabeth Lange.

Among pioneer U.S. foundresses of European communities were Mother Rose Philippine Duchesne (canonized in 1980), who established the Religious of the Sacred Heart in Missouri in 1818, and Mother Theodore Guérin, who founded the Sisters of Providence of St.-Mary-of-the-Woods in Indiana in 1840.

The number of sisters' communities, most of them branches of European institutes, increased apace with needs for their missions in education, charitable service and spiritual life.

Trusteeism

The initial lack of organization in ecclesiastical affairs, nationalistic feeling among Catholics and the independent action of some priests were factors involved in several early crises.

In Philadelphia, some German Catholics, with the reluctant consent of Bishop Carroll, founded Holy Trinity, the first national parish in the U.S. They refused to accept the pastor appointed by the bishop and elected their own. This and other abuses led to formal schism in 1796, a condition that existed until 1802, when they returned to canonical jurisdiction. Philadelphia was also the scene of the Hogan Schism, which developed in the 1820s when Fr. William Hogan, with the aid of lay trustees, seized control of St. Mary's Cathedral. His movement, for churches and parishes controlled by other than canonical procedures and run in extralegal ways, was nullified by a decision of the Pennsylvania Supreme Court in 1822.

Similar troubles seriously disturbed the peace of the Church in other places, principally New York, Baltimore, Buffalo, Charleston and New Orleans.

Dangers arising from the exploitation of lay control were gradually diminished with the extension and enforcement of canonical procedures and with changes in civil law about the middle of the century.

Anti-Catholicism

Bigotry against Catholics waxed and waned during the 19th century and into the 20th. The first major campaign of this kind, which developed in the wake of the panic of 1819 and lasted for about 25 years, was mounted in 1830 when the number of Catholic immigrants began to increase to a noticeable degree. Nativist anti-Catholicism generated a great deal of violence, represented by loss of life and property in

Charlestown, Massachusetts, in 1834, and in Philadelphia 10 years later. Later bigotry was fomented by the Know-Nothings, in the 1850s; the Ku Klux Klan, from 1866; the American Protective Association, from 1887; and the Guardians of Liberty. Perhaps the last eruption of virulently overt anti-Catholicism occurred during the campaign of Alfred E. Smith for the presidency in 1928. Observers feel the issue was muted to a considerable extent in the political area with the election of John F. Kennedy to the presidency in 1960.

The Catholic periodical press had its beginnings in response to the attacks of bigots. The *U.S. Catholic Miscellany* (1822-61), the first Catholic newspaper in the U.S., was founded by Bishop John England of Charleston to answer critics of the Church. This remained the character of most of the periodicals published in the 19th and into the 20th century.

Growth and Immigration

Between 1830 and 1900, the combined factors of natural increase, immigration and conversion raised the Catholic population to 12 million. A large percentage of the growth figure represented immigrants: some 2.7 million, largely from Ireland, Germany and France, between 1830 and 1880; and another 1.25 million during the 1880s when Eastern and Southern Europeans came in increasing numbers. By the 1860s the Catholic Church, with most of its members concentrated in urban areas, was probably the largest religious body in the country.

The efforts of progressive bishops to hasten the acculturation of Catholic immigrants occasioned a number of controversies, which generally centered around questions concerning national or foreign-language parishes. One of them, called Cahenslyism, arose from complaints that German Catholic immigrants were not being given adequate pastoral care.

Eastern Rite Catholics

The immigration of the 1890s included large numbers of Eastern Rite Catholics with their own liturgies and tradition of a married clergy, but without their own bishops. The treatment of their clergy and people by some of the U.S. (Latin Rite) hierarchy and the prejudices they encountered resulted in the defection of thousands from the Catholic Church.

In 1907, Basilian monk Stephen Ortynsky was ordained the first bishop of Byzantine Rite Catholics in the U.S. Eventually jurisdictions were established for most Byzantine and other Eastern Rite Catholics in the country.

Councils of Baltimore

The bishops of the growing U.S. dioceses met at Baltimore for seven provincial councils between 1829 and 1849.

In 1846, they proclaimed the Blessed Virgin Mary patroness of the United States under the title of the Immaculate Conception, eight years before the dogma was proclaimed in Rome.

After the establishment of the Archdiocese of Oregon City in 1846 and the elevation to metropolitan status of St. Louis, New Orleans, Cincinnati and New York, the first of the three plenary councils of Baltimore was held.

The first plenary assembly was convoked on May 9,

1852, with Abp. Francis P. Kenrick of Baltimore as papal legate. The bishops drew up regulations concerning parochial life, matters of church ritual and ceremonies, the administration of church funds and the teaching of Christian doctrine.

The second plenary council, meeting from Oct. 7 to 21, 1866, under the presidency of Abp. Martin J. Spalding, formulated a condemnation of several current doctrinal errors and established norms affecting the organization of dioceses, the education and conduct of the clergy, the management of ecclesiastical property, parochial duties and general education.

Abp. (later Cardinal) James Gibbons called into session the third plenary council which lasted from Nov. 9 to Dec. 7, 1884. Among highly significant results of actions taken by this assembly were the preparation of the line of Baltimore catechisms that became a basic means of religious instruction in this country; legislation that fixed the pattern of Catholic education by requiring the building of elementary schools in all parishes; the establishment of the Catholic University of America in Washington, DC, in 1889; and the determination of six holy days of obligation for observance in this country.

The enactments of the three plenary councils have had the force of particular law for the Church in the U.S.

The Holy See established the Apostolic Delegation in Washington, DC, on Jan. 24, 1893.

Slavery

In the Civil War period, as before, Catholics reflected attitudes of the general population with respect to the issue of slavery. Some supported it, some opposed it, but none were prominent in the Abolition Movement. Pope Gregory XVI had condemned the slave trade in 1839, but no contemporary pope or American bishop published an official document on slavery itself. The issue did not split Catholics in schism as it did Baptists, Methodists and Presbyterians.

Catholics fought on both sides in the Civil War. Five hundred members of 20 or more sisterhoods served the wounded of both sides.

One hundred thousand of the four million slaves emancipated in 1863 were Catholics; the highest concentrations were in Louisiana, about 60,000, and Maryland, 16,000. Three years later, their pastoral care was one of the subjects covered in nine decrees issued by the Second Plenary Council of Baltimore. The measures had little practical effect with respect to integration of the total Catholic community, predicated as they were on the proposition that individual bishops should handle questions regarding segregation in churches and related matters as best they could in the pattern of local customs.

Long-entrenched segregation practices continued in force through the rest of the 19th century and well into the 20th. The first effective efforts to alter them were initiated by Cardinal Joseph Ritter of St. Louis in 1947, Cardinal (then Abp.) Patrick O'Boyle of Washington in 1948, and Bishop Vincent Waters of Raleigh in 1953.

Friend of Labor

The Church became known during the 19th century

as a friend and ally of labor in seeking justice for the working man. Cardinal Gibbons journeyed to Rome in 1887, for example, to defend and prevent a condemnation of the Knights of Labor by Leo XIII. The encyclical *Rerum Novarum* (1891) was hailed by many American bishops as a confirmation, if not vindication, of their own theories. Catholics have always formed a large percentage of union membership, and some have served unions in positions of leadership.

Americanism

Near the end of the century some controversy developed over what was characterized as Americanism or the phantom heresy. It was alleged that Americans were discounting the importance of contemplative virtues, exalting the practical virtues, and watering down the purity of Catholic doctrine for the sake of facilitating convert work.

The French translation of Fr. Walter Elliott's *Life of Isaac Hecker*, which fired the controversy, was one of many factors that led to the issuance of Leo XIII's Testem Benevolentiae in January 1899, in an attempt to end the matter. It was the first time the orthodoxy of the Church in the U.S. was called into question.

Schism

In the 1890s, serious friction developed between Poles and Irish in Scranton, Buffalo and Chicago, resulting in schism and the establishment of the Polish National Catholic Church. A central figure in the affair was Fr. Francis Hodur, who was excommunicated by Bishop William O'Hara of Scranton in 1898. Nine years later, his ordination by an Old Catholic Abp. of Utrecht gave the new church its first bishop.

Another schism of the period led to formation of the American Carpatho-Russian Orthodox Greek Catholic Church.

Coming of Age

In 1900, there were 12 million Catholics in the total U.S. population of 76 million, 82 dioceses in 14 provinces, and 12,000 priests and members of about 40 communities of men Religious. Many sisterhoods, most of them of European origin and some of American foundation, were engaged in Catholic educational and hospital work, two of their traditional apostolates.

The Church in the U.S. was removed from mission status with promulgation of the apostolic constitution *Sapienti Consilio* by Pope St. Pius X on June 29, 1908.

Before that time, and even into the early 1920s, the Church in this country received financial assistance from mission-aid societies in France, Bavaria and Austria. Already, however, it was making increasing contributions of its own. At the present time, it is one of the major national contributors to the worldwide Society for the Propagation of the Faith.

American foreign missionary personnel increased from 14 or less in 1906 to an all-time high in 1968 of 9,655 priests, brothers, sisters, seminarians, and lay persons. The first missionary seminary in the U.S. was in operation at Techny, Illinois, in 1909, under the auspices of the Society of the Divine Word. Maryknoll, the first American missionary society, was established in 1911 and sent its first priests to China in 1918. Despite these contributions, the Church in the U.S. has not matched the missionary commitment of some other nations.

Bishops' Conference

A highly important apparatus for mobilizing the Church's resources was established in 1917 under the title of the National Catholic War Council. Its name was changed to National Catholic Welfare Conference several years later, but its objectives remained the same: to serve as an advisory and coordinating agency of the American bishops for advancing works of the Church in fields of social significance and impact — education, communications, immigration, social action, legislation, youth and lay organizations.

The forward thrust of the bishops' social thinking was evidenced in a program of social reconstruction they recommended in 1919. By 1945, all but one of their 12 points had been enacted into legislation — including many later social security programs.

The NCWC was renamed the United States Catholic Conference (USCC) in November 1966, when the hierarchy also organized itself as a territorial conference with pastoral-juridical authority under the title, National Conference of Catholic Bishops. The USCC carried on the functions of the former NCWC until July 2001, when it merged with the National Conference of Catholic Bishops to create the USCCB.

Catholic Press

The establishment of the National Catholic News Service (NC) — now the Catholic News Service (CNS) — in 1920 was an important event in the development of the Catholic press, which had its beginnings about 100 years earlier. Early in the 20th century there were 63 weekly newspapers. The 2006 *Catholic Press Directory*, published by the Catholic Press Association, reported a total of 609 periodicals in North America, with a circulation of 26,134,515. The figures included 205 newspapers, with a circulation of 6,611,583; 238 magazines, with a circulation of 14,459,258; 118 newsletters, with a circulation of 3,804,308; and 48 other-language periodicals (newspapers and magazines), with a circulation of 1,259,366.

Lay Organizations

A burst of lay organizational growth occurred from the 1930s onwards with the appearance of Catholic Action types of movements and other groups and associations devoted to special causes, social service and assistance for the poor and needy. Several special apostolates developed under the aegis of the National Catholic Welfare Conference (now the U.S. Catholic Conference); the outstanding one was the Confraternity of Christian Doctrine.

Nineteenth-century organizations of great influence included: The St. Vincent de Paul Society, whose first U.S. office was set up in 1845 in St. Louis; the Catholic Central Union (*Verein*), dating from 1855; the Knights of Columbus, founded in 1882; the Holy Name Society, organized in the U.S. in 1870; the Rosary Society (1891); and scores of chapters of the Sodality of the Blessed Virgin Mary.

Pastoral Concerns

The potential for growth of the Church in this country by immigration was sharply reduced but not entirely curtailed after 1921 with the passage of restrictive federal legislation. As a result, the Catholic population became more stabilized and, to a certain extent and for many reasons, began to acquire an identity of its own.

Some increase from outside has taken place in the past 50 years, however, from Canada, from Central and Eastern European countries, and from Puerto Rico and Latin American countries since World War II. This influx, while not as great as that of the 19th century and early 20th, has enriched the Church here with a sizable body of Eastern Rite Catholics for whom 12 ecclesiastical jurisdictions have been established. It has also created a challenge for pastoral care of millions of Hispanics in urban centers and in agricultural areas where migrant workers are employed.

The Church continues to grapple with serious pastoral problems in rural areas, where about 600 counties have no priests in ministry. The National Catholic Rural Life Conference was established in 1922 in an attempt to make the Catholic presence felt on the land, and the Glenmary Society since its foundation in 1939 has devoted itself to this single apostolate. Religious communities and diocesan priests are similarly engaged.

Other challenges lie in the cities and suburbs, where 75 percent of the Catholic population lives. Conditions peculiar to each segment of the metropolitan area have developed in recent years as the flight to the suburbs has not only altered some traditional aspects of parish life but has also, in combination with many other factors, left behind a complex of special problems in inner city areas.

A Post-War World

In the years after the Second World War, Catholics increasingly assumed a mainline role in American life. This was evidenced especially in the 1960 election of John F. Kennedy as the nation's first Catholic president. Catholic writers and thinkers were making a greater impact in the nation's life. One example of this was Trappist Thomas Merton's runaway best-selling book of 1948, *The Seven Storey Mountain*; another was the early television success of Bishop Fulton Sheen's "Life is Worth Living" series, begun in 1952. Meanwhile, lay leader Dorothy Day, founder of the Catholic Worker movement, continued to challenge American society with her views on pacifism and evangelical poverty.

A Post-Conciliar World

Catholic life in the United States was profoundly affected by the Second Vatican Council (1962-65). In the post-conciliar generation, American Catholicism grew both in numbers and complexity. Lay ministry and participation expanded; extensive liturgical changes (including the use of English) were implemented; and the numbers of priests, vowed religious and seminarians declined.

The Church has taken a high profile in many social issues. This has ranged from opposition to abortion, capital punishments and euthanasia to support for civil rights, economic justice and international peace and cooperation. Meanwhile Catholics have been deeply involved in inter-faith and ecumenical relationships. The bishops have issued landmark pastoral statements, including "The Challenge of Peace" (1983) and "Economic Justice for All" (1986).

In these years after the Council, the Catholics in America have known something of alienation, dissent and polarity. They also found new intensity and maturity. New U.S. saints have been declared by the universal church, such as Elizabeth Ann Seton (1975), John Nepomucene Neumann (1977), and Rose Philippine Duchesne (1988). Especially at the time of visits to America by Pope John Paul II (e.g., in 1979, 1987, 1993, 1995, and 1999), U.S. Catholics have given evidence – in their personal and corporate lives – of the ongoing power of faith, liturgy and the primal call of the Gospel in its many dimensions.

Modern U.S. Catholicism

In the decades after Vatican Council II, the American Church confronted a variety of challenges, including the increasing age of American religious, especially in the Religious Institutes of Women; the decline in vocations; the presence of nominally Catholic organizations that nevertheless work to counter or alter Catholic teaching on such issues as abortion, contraception, papal supremacy, collegiality, women's ordination, clerical celibacy, and homosexuality; the societal decay precipitated by a proliferation of an abortion culture; the weakening of the family structure and the destructive effects of unrestrained materialism and secular humanism; the spread of religious apathy and indifferentism; the needs of Catholic immigrants; and the lamentable state of American education.

The varied difficulties, however, were overshadowed from late 2001 by the sexual scandal involving child molestation by a small number of priests in the country and the resulting legal cases, lawsuits, and media frenzy. While perpetrated by only a few hundred priests over nearly 40 years, the cases of child molestation (the vast majority of cases involved teenage boys) created the most severe scandal faced by the Church in the U.S. in the previous century.

Compounding the legal and financial problems caused by the actions of the priests was the failure on the part of many bishops to recognize the severity of the scandal and the willingness of some bishops to move pedophile priests from one pastoral assignment to another.

At the summer meeting of the USCCB, the American bishops drafted a series of documents to insure the safety of children and to improve oversight of the situation. The bishops approved a Charter for the Protection of Children and Young People and Essential Norms for Diocesan/Eparchial Policies Dealing With Allegations of Sexual Abuse of Minors by Priests, Deacons, or Other Church Personnel. Officials of the Holy See rejected initially certain elements of canonical details of the norms, but the subsequent changes made by the bishops were given full Vatican approval. Nevertheless, the scandal created crushing financial difficulties for many dioceses facing a host of lawsuits, as well as a crisis of confidence among American Catholics.

Even in the face of these problems, there are a number of positive developments that give reason for guarded optimism: the progress in ecumenism; the rise of new religious congregations; the increase in conversions (over 400,000 a year); the marked sophistication of Catholic communications, centered in the USCCB; the Church's active role in social issues (human rights, poverty, health care, race relations, abortion and economic justice); and the greater involvement of the laity

– especially women – in the life of the Church. Today, the membership in the U.S. is approximately 23 percent (67 million) of the U.S. population.

MISSIONARIES TO THE AMERICAS

An asterisk with a feast date indicates that the saint or blessed is listed in the General Roman Calendar or the proper calendar for U.S. dioceses.

Allouez, Claude Jean (1622-89): French Jesuit; missionary in Canada and midwestern U.S.; preached to 20 different tribes of Indians and baptized over 10,000; vicar general of Northwest.

Altham, John (1589-1640): English Jesuit; missionary among Indians in Maryland.

Amadeus of the Heart of Jesus (1846-1920): Provincial Superior of the Ursulines in the United States and missionary in Montana, Wyoming, and Alaska; founded 12 Ursuline missions for the Native Americans.

Anchieta, José de, Bl. (1534-97): Portuguese Jesuit, born Canary Islands; missionary in Brazil; writer; beatified 1980; feast, June 9.

Andreis, Felix de (1778-1820): Italian Vincentian; missionary and educator in western U.S.

Aparicio, Sebastian, Bl. (1502-1600): Franciscan brother, born Spain; settled in Mexico, c. 1533; worked as road builder and farmer before becoming Franciscan at about the age of 70; beatified 1787; feast, Feb. 25.

Badin, Stephen T. (1768-1853): French missioner; came to U.S., 1792, when Sulpician seminary in Paris was closed; ordained 1793, Baltimore, the first priest ordained in U.S.; missionary in Kentucky, Ohio and Michigan; bought land on which Notre Dame University now stands; buried on its campus.

Baraga, Frederic (1797-1868): Slovenian missionary bishop in U.S.; studied at Ljubljana and Vienna, ordained 1823; came to U.S., 1830; missionary to Indians of Upper Michigan; first bishop of Marquette, 1857-1868; wrote Chippewa grammar, dictionary, prayer book and other works.

Bauer, Benedicta (1803-65): Missionary Dominican sister who helped establish convents and schools for German-speaking immigrants in New Jersey, California, Missouri, Washington, and Kansas.

Bertran, Louis, St. (1526-81): Spanish Dominican; missionary in Colombia and Caribbean, 1562-69; canonized 1671; feast, Oct. 9.

Betancur, Pedro de San José, Bl. (1626-67): Secular Franciscan, born Canary Islands; arrived in Guatemala, 1651; established hospital, school and homes for poor; beatified 1980; feast, Apr. 25.

Bourgeoys, Marguerite, St. (1620-1700): French foundress, missionary; settled in Canada, 1653; founded Congregation of Notre Dame, 1658; beatified 1950; canonized 1982; feast, Jan. 12.

Brébeuf, Jean de, St. (1593-1649): French Jesuit; missionary among Huron Indians in Canada; martyred by Iroquois, Mar. 16, 1649; canonized 1930; one of Jesuit North American martyrs; feast, Oct. 19* (U.S.).

Cancer de Barbastro, Louis (1500-49): Spanish Dominican; began missionary work in Middle America, 1533; killed at Tampa Bay, Florida.

Castillo, John de, St. (1596-1628): Spanish Jesuit;

worked in Paraguay Indian mission settlements (reductions); martyred; beatified 1934; canonized 1988; feast, Nov. 16.

Catala, Magin (1761-1830): Spanish Franciscan; worked in California mission of Santa Clara for 36 years.

Chabanel, Noel, St. (1613-49): French Jesuit; missionary among Huron Indians in Canada; murdered by renegade Huron, Dec. 8, 1649; canonized 1930; one of Jesuit North American martyrs; feast, Oct. 19* (U.S.).

Chaumonot, Pierre Joseph (1611-93): French Jesuit; missionary among Indians in Canada.

Clarke, Mary Frances (1803-87): Founder of the Sisters of Charity of the Blessed Virgin Mary; went to Iowa to start schools for children of white farmers and Native Americans; in Iowa Women's Hall of Fame.

Claver, Peter, St. (1581-1654): Spanish Jesuit; missionary among Negroes of South America and West Indies; canonized 1888; patron of Catholic missions among black people; feast, Sept. 9*.

Cope, Marianne, Bl. (1838-1918): German-born immigrant; entered Sisters of St. Francis; led sisters to Hawaii to take over a hospital and then to Molokai to care for lepers, including Bl. Damien de Veuster; she cared for women and young girls with the disease; beatified May 2005.

Daniel, Anthony, St. (1601-48): French Jesuit; missionary among Huron Indians in Canada; martyred by Iroquois, July 4, 1648; canonized 1930; one of Jesuit North American martyrs; feast, Oct. 19* (U.S.).

De Smet, Pierre Jean (1801-73): Belgian-born Jesuit; missionary among Indians of northwestern U.S.; served as intermediary between Indians and U.S. government; wrote on Indian culture.

Duchesne, Rose Philippine, St. (1769-1852): French nun; educator and missionary in the U.S.; established first convent of the Society of the Sacred Heart in the U.S., at St. Charles, Missouri; founded schools for girls; did missionary work among Indians; beatified 1940; canonized 1988; feast, Nov. 18* (U.S.).

Farmer, Ferdinand (family name, Steinmeyer) (1720-86): German Jesuit; missionary in Philadelphia, where he died; one of the first missionaries in New Jersey.

Flaget, Benedict J. (1763-1850): French Sulpician bishop; came to U.S., 1792; missionary and educator in U.S.; first bishop of Bardstown, Kentucky (now Louisville), 1810-32; 1833-50.

Frances Xavier Cabrini: See under **Saints.**

Friess, Caroline (1824-92): Mother Superior of the School Sisters of Notre Dame in America from 1850-92; through her labors, the sisters opened 265 parochial schools in 29 diocese and four institutes of higher education for women.

Gallitzin, Demetrius (1770-1840): Russian prince, born The Hague; convert, 1787; ordained priest at Baltimore, 1795; frontier missionary, known as Fr. Smith; Gallitzin, PA, named for him.

Garnier, Charles, St. (c. 1606-49): French Jesuit;

missionary among Hurons in Canada; martyred by Iroquois, Dec. 7, 1649; canonized 1930; one of Jesuit North American martyrs; feast, Oct. 19* (U.S.).

Gibault, Pierre (1737-1804): Canadian missionary in Illinois and Indiana; aided in securing states of Ohio, Indiana, Illinois, Michigan and Wisconsin for the Americans during Revolution.

Gonzalez, Roch, St. (1576-1628): Paraguayan Jesuit; worked in Paraguay Indian mission settlements (reductions); martyred; beatified 1934; canonized 1988; feast, Nov. 16.

Goupil, René, St. (1607-42): French lay missionary; had studied surgery at Orleans, France; missionary companion of St. Isaac Jogues among the Hurons; martyred, Sept. 29, 1642; canonized 1930; one of Jesuit North American martyrs; feast, Oct. 19* (U.S.).

Gravier, Jacques (1651-1708): French Jesuit; missionary among Indians of Canada and midwestern U.S.

Guérin, St. Theodore (1798-1856): Pioneer educator and Sister of Providence; arrived in U.S. in 1830 and founded St. Mary-of the-Woods in Vincennes, Indiana. Canonized Oct. 15, 2006.

Hennepin, Louis (d. c. 1701): Belgian-born Franciscan missionary and explorer of Great Lakes region and Upper Mississippi, 1675-81, when he returned to Europe.

Ireland, Seraphine (1842-1930): Mother Superior of the Sisters of St. Joseph in the upper Midwest; opened 30 schools, five hospitals, and the College of St. Catherine, the second Catholic college for women in the U.S.

Jesuit North American Martyrs: Isaac Jogues, Anthony Daniel, John de Brébeuf, Gabriel Lalemant, Charles Garnier, Noel Chabanel (Jesuit priests), and René Goupil and John Lalande (lay missionaries) who were martyred between Sept. 29, 1642, and Dec. 9, 1649, in the missions of New France; canonized June 29, 1930; feast, Oct. 19* (U.S.). See separate entries.

Jogues, Isaac, St. (1607-46): French Jesuit; missionary among Indians in Canada; martyred near present site of Auriesville, NY, by Mohawks, Oct. 18, 1646; canonized 1930; one of Jesuit North American Martyrs; feast, Oct. 19* (U.S.).

Kino, Eusebio (1645-1711): Italian Jesuit; missionary and explorer in U.S.; arrived Southwest, 1681; established 25 Indian missions, took part in 14 exploring expeditions in northern Mexico, Arizona, and southern California; helped develop livestock raising and farming in the area. He was selected in 1965 to represent Arizona in Statuary Hall.

Lalande, John, St. (d. 1646): French lay missionary, companion of Isaac Jogues; martyred by Mohawks at Auriesville, NY, Oct. 19, 1646; canonized 1930; one of Jesuit North American Martyrs; feast, Oct. 19* (U.S.).

Lalemant, Gabriel, St. (1610-49): French Jesuit; missionary among the Hurons in Canada; martyred by the Iroquois, Mar. 17, 1649; canonized 1930; one of Jesuit North American Martyrs; feast, Oct. 19* (U.S.).

Lalor, Teresa (d. 1846): Co-founder, with Bp. Neale of Baltimore, of the Visitation Order in the U.S.; helped establish houses in Mobile, Kaskaskia, and Baltimore.

Lamy, Jean Baptiste (1814-88): French prelate; came to U.S. 1839; missionary in Ohio and Kentucky; bishop in Southwest from 1850; first bishop (later Abp.) of Santa Fe, 1850-85. He was nominated in 1951 to represent New Mexico in Statuary Hall.

Las Casas, Bartolome (1474-1566): Spanish Dominican; missionary in Haiti, Jamaica and Venezuela; reformer of abuses against Indians and black people; bishop of Chalapas, Mexico, 1544-47; historian.

Laval, Françoise de Montmorency, Bl. (1623-1708): French-born missionary bishop in Canada; named vicar apostolic of Canada, 1658; first bishop of Québec, 1674; jurisdiction extended over all French-claimed territory in New World; beatified 1980; feast, May 6.

Manogue, Patrick (1831-95): Missionary bishop in U.S., born Ireland; migrated to U.S.; miner in California; studied for priesthood at St. Mary's of the Lake, Chicago, and St. Sulpice, Paris; ordained 1861; missionary among Indians of California and Nevada; coadj. bishop, 1881-84, and bishop, 1884-86, of Grass Valley; first bishop of Sacramento, 1886-95, when see was transferred there.

Margil, Antonio, Ven. (1657-1726): Spanish Franciscan; missionary in Middle America; apostle of Guatemala; established missions in Texas.

Marie of the Incarnation, St. (Marie Guyard Martin) (1599-1672): French widow; joined Ursuline Nuns; arrived in Canada, 1639; first superior of Ursulines in Québec; missionary to Indians; writer; beatified 1980; feast, Apr. 30.

Marquette, Jacques (1637-75): French Jesuit; missionary and explorer in America; sent to New France, 1666; began missionary work among Ottawa Indians on Lake Superior, 1668; accompanied Joliet down the Mississippi to mouth of the Arkansas, 1673, and returned to Lake Michigan by way of Illinois River; made a second trip over the same route; his diary and map are of historical significance. He was selected in 1895 to represent Wisconsin in Statuary Hall.

Massias (Macias), John de, St. (1585-1645): Dominican brother, a native of Spain; entered Dominican Friary at Lima, Peru, 1622; served as doorkeeper until his death; beatified 1837; canonized 1975; feast, Sept. 16.

Mazzuchelli, Samuel C. (1806-64): Italian Dominican; missionary in midwestern U.S.; called builder of the West; writer. A decree advancing his beatification cause was promulgated July 6, 1993.

Membre, Zenobius (1645-87): French Franciscan; missionary among Indians of Illinois; accompanied LaSalle expedition down the Mississippi (1681-82) and Louisiana colonizing expedition (1684) that landed in Texas; murdered by Indians.

Mozcygemba, Leopold (1824-91): Polish Franciscan priest and missionary, the patriarch of American Polonia; labored as a missionary in Texas and 11 other states for nearly 40 years; co-founded the Polish seminary of Sts. Cyril and Methodius in Detroit (1885) and served as confessor at Vatican Council I.

Nerinckx, Charles (1761-1824): Belgian priest; missionary in Kentucky; founded Sisters of Loretto at the Foot of the Cross.

Nobrega, Manoel (1517-70): Portuguese Jesuit; leader of first Jesuit missionaries to Brazil, 1549.

Padilla, Juan de (d. 1542): Spanish Franciscan; missionary among Indians of Mexico and southwestern U.S.; killed by Indians in Kansas; proto-martyr of the U.S.

Palou, Francisco (c. 1722-89): Spanish Franciscan; accompanied Junípero Serra to Mexico, 1749; founded Mission Dolores in San Francisco; wrote history of the Franciscans in California.

Pariseau, Mary Joseph (1833-1902): Canadian Sister of Charity of Providence; missionary in state of Washington from 1856; founded first hospitals in Northwest Territory; artisan and architect. Represents Washington in National Statuary Hall.

Peter of Ghent (d. 1572): Belgian Franciscan brother; missionary in Mexico for 49 years.

Porres, Martin de, St. (1579-1639): Peruvian Dominican oblate; his father was a Spanish soldier and his mother a black freedwoman from Panama; called wonder worker of Peru; beatified 1837; canonized 1962; feast, Nov. 3*.

Quiroga, Vasco de (1470-1565): Spanish missionary in Mexico; founded hospitals; bishop of Michoacan, 1537.

Ravalli, Antonio (1811-84): Italian Jesuit; missionary in far-western U.S., mostly Montana, for 40 years.

Raymbaut, Charles (1602-43): French Jesuit; missionary among Indians of Canada and northern U.S.

Richard, Gabriel (1767-1832): French Sulpician; missionary in Illinois and Michigan; a founder of University of Michigan; elected delegate to Congress from Michigan, 1823; first priest to hold seat in the House of Representatives.

Riepp, Benedicta (1825-62): Founder of the first Benedictine community of nuns in the U.S.; by the time of her death, the order had founded convents in Illinois, Kentucky, Minnesota, and New Jersey.

Rodriguez, Alfonso, St. (1598-1628): Spanish Jesuit; missionary in Paraguay; martyred; beatified 1934; canonized 1988; feast, Nov. 16.

Rosati, Joseph (1789-1843): Italian Vincentian; missionary bishop in U.S. (vicar apostolic of Mississippi and Alabama, 1822; coadj. of Louisiana and the Two Floridas, 1823-26; administrator of New Orleans, 1826-29; first bishop of St. Louis, 1826-1843).

Russell, Mary Baptist (1829-98): Mother Superior of the Sisters of Mercy in San Francisco from 1854-98; founded St. Mary's Hospital in 1857, schools, and homes the aged and former prostitutes.

Sahagun, Bernardino de (c. 1500-90): Spanish Franciscan; missionary in Mexico for over 60 years; expert on Aztec archaeology.

Seelos, Francis X. (1819-67): Redemptorist missionary, born Bavaria; ordained 1844, at Baltimore; missionary in Pittsburgh and New Orleans.

Seghers, Charles J. (1839-86): Belgian missionary bishop in North America; Apostle of Alaska; Abp. of Oregon City (now Portland), 1880-84; murdered by berserk companion while on missionary journey.

Serra, Junípero, Bl. (1713-84): Spanish Franciscan, born Majorca; missionary in America; arrived Mexico, 1749, where he did missionary work for 20 years; began work in Upper California in 1769 and established nine of the 21 Franciscan missions along the Pacific coast; baptized some 6,000 Indians and confirmed almost 5,000; a cultural pioneer of California Represents California in Statuary Hall. He was declared venerable May 9, 1985, and beatified Sept. 25, 1988; feast, July 1* (U.S.).

Solanus, Francis, St. (1549-1610): Spanish Franciscan; missionary in Paraguay, Argentina and Peru; wonder worker of the New World; canonized 1726; feast, July 14.

Sorin, Edward F. (1814-93): French priest; member of Congregation of Holy Cross; sent to U.S. in 1841; founder and first president of the University of Notre Dame; missionary in Indiana and Michigan.

Todadilla, Anthony de (1704-46): Spanish Capuchin; missionary to Indians of Venezuela; killed by Motilones.

Turibius de Mogrovejo, St. (1538-1606): Spanish Abp. of Lima, Peru, c. 1580-1606; canonized 1726; feast, Mar. 23*.

Twelve Apostles of Mexico (early 16th century): Franciscan priests who arrived in Mexico, 1524: Fathers Martin de Valencia (leader), Francisco de Soto, Martin de la Coruna, Juan Suares, Antonio de Ciudad Rodrigo, Toribio de Benevente, Garcia de Cisneros, Luis de Fuensalida, Juan de Ribas, Francisco Ximenes; Brothers Andres de Coroboda, and Juan de Palos.

Valdivia, Luis de (1561-1641): Spanish Jesuit; defender of Indians in Peru and Chile.

Vasques de Espiñosa, Antonio (early 17th century): Spanish Carmelite; missionary and explorer in Mexico, Panama and western coast of South America.

Vieira, Antonio (1608-87): Portuguese Jesuit; preacher; missionary in Peru and Chile; protector of Indians against exploitation by slave owners and traders; considered foremost prose writer of 17th-century Portugal.

Ward, Mary Francis Xavier (1810-84): Established the Sisters of Mercy in U.S.; arrived in Pittsburgh in 1843; founded convents in 10 states to care for the sick and poor and provide education.

White, Andrew (1579-1656): English Jesuit; missionary among Indians in Maryland.

Wimmer, Boniface (1809-87): German Benedictine; missionary among German immigrants in the U.S.

Youville, Marie Marguerite d', St. (1701-71): Canadian widow; foundress of Sisters of Charity (Grey Nuns), 1737, at Montréal: beatified 1959; canonized 1990, first native Canadian saint; feast, Dec. 23.

Zumarraga, Juan de (1468-1548): Spanish Franciscan; missionary; first bishop of Mexico; introduced first printing press in New World, published first book in America, a catechism for Aztec Indians; extended missions in Mexico and Central America; vigorous opponent of exploitation of Indians; approved of devotions at Guadalupe; leading figure in early church history in Mexico.

FRANCISCAN MISSIONS

The 21 Franciscan missions of Upper California were established during the 54-year period from 1769 to 1822. Located along the old El Camino Real, or King's Highway, they extended from San Diego to San Francisco and were the centers of Indian civilization, Christianity and industry in the early history of the state.

Junípero Serra (beatified 1988) was the great pioneer of the missions of Upper California He and his successor as superior of the work, Fermin Lasuen, each directed the establishment of nine missions. One hundred and 46 priests of the Order of Friars Minor, most of them Spaniards, labored in the region from 1769 to 1845; 67 of them died at their posts, two as martyrs. The regular time of mission service was 10 years.

The missions were secularized by the Mexican government in the 1830s but were subsequently restored to the Church by the U.S. government. They are now variously used as the sites of parish churches, a university, houses of study and museums.

The names of the missions and the order of their establishment were as follows:

San Diego de Alcala, San Carlos Borromeo (El Carmelo), San Antonio de Padua, San Gabriel Arcangel, San Luis Obispo de Tolosa, San Francisco de Asis (Dolores), San Juan Capistrano; Santa Clara de Asis, San Buenaventura, Santa Barbara, La Purisima Concepcion de Maria Santisima, Santa Cruz, Nuestra Señora de la Soledad, San José de Guadalupe, San Juan Bautista, San Miguel Arcangel, San Fernando Rey de España, San Luis Rey de Francia, Santa Iñes, San Rafael Arcangel, San Francisco Solano de Sonoma (Sonoma).

Find more material at: www.CatholicAlmanac.com.

CHURCH-STATE RELATIONS IN THE UNITED STATES

CHURCH-STATE DECISIONS OF THE SUPREME COURT

Among sources of this selected listing of U.S. Supreme Court decisions was *The Supreme Court on Church and State*, Joseph Tussman, editor; Oxford University Press, New York, 1962.

Watson v. Jones, 13 Wallace 679 (1872): The Court declared that a member of a religious organization may not appeal to secular courts against a decision made by a church tribunal within the area of its competence.

Reynolds v. United States, 98 US 145 (1879): Davis v. Beason, 133 US 333 (1890); Church of Latter-Day Saints v. United States, 136 US 1 (1890). The Mormon practice of polygamy was at issue in three decisions and was declared unconstitutional.

Bradfield v. Roberts, 175 US 291 (1899): The Court denied that an appropriation of government funds for an institution (Providence Hospital, Washington, DC) run by Roman Catholic sisters violated the No Establishment Clause of the First Amendment.

Pierce v. Society of Sisters, 268 US 510 (1925): The Court denied that a state can require children to attend public schools only. The Court held that the liberty of the Constitution forbids standardization by such compulsion, and that the parochial schools involved had claims to protection under the Fourteenth Amendment.

Cochran v. Board of Education, 281 US 370 (1930): The Court upheld a Louisiana statute providing textbooks at public expense for children attending public or parochial schools. The Court held that the children and state were beneficiaries of the appropriations, with incidental secondary benefit going to the schools.

United States v. MacIntosh, 283 US 605 (1931): The Court denied that anyone can place allegiance to the will of God above his allegiance to the government since such a person could make his own interpretation of God's will the decisive test as to whether he would or would not obey the nation's law. The Court stated that the nation, which has a duty to survive, can require citizens to bear arms in its defense.

Everson v. Board of Education, 330 US 1 (1947): The Court upheld the constitutionality of a New Jersey statute authorizing free school bus transportation for parochial as well as public school students. The Court expressed the opinion that the benefits of public welfare legislation, included under such bus transportation, do not run contrary to the concept of separation of Church and State.

McCollum v. Board of Education, 333 US 203 (1948): The Court declared unconstitutional a program

for releasing children, with parental consent, from public school classes so they could receive religious instruction on public school premises from representatives of their own faiths.

Zorach v. Clauson, 343 US 306 (1952): The Court upheld the constitutionality of a New York statute permitting, on a voluntary basis, the release during school time of students from public school classes for religious instruction given off public school premises.

Torcaso v. Watkins, 367 US 488 (1961): The Court declared unconstitutional a Maryland requirement that one must make a declarati on of belief in the existence of God as part of the oath of office for notaries public.

McGowan v. Maryland, 81 Sp Ct 1101; Two Guys from Harrison v. McGinley, 81 Sp Ct 1135; Gallagher v. Crown Kosher Super Market, 81 Sp Ct 1128; Braunfield v. Brown, 81 Sp Ct 1144 (1961): The Court ruled that Sunday closing laws do not violate the No Establishment of Religion Clause of the First Amendment, even though the laws were religious in their inception and still have some religious overtones. The Court held that, "as presently written and administered, most of them, at least, are of a secular rather than of a religious character, and that presently they bear no relationship to establishment of religion as those words are used in the Constitution of the United States."

Engel v. Vitale, 370 US 42 (1962): The Court declared that the voluntary recitation in public schools of a prayer composed by the New York State Board of Regents is unconstitutional on the ground that it violates the No Establishment of Religion Clause of the First Amendment.

Abington Township School District v. Schempp and Murray v. Curlett, 83 Sp Ct 1560 (1963): The Court ruled that Bible reading and recitation of the Lord's Prayer in public schools, with voluntary participation by students, are unconstitutional on the ground that they violate the No Establishment of Religion Clause of the First Amendment.

Chamberlin v. Dade County, 83 Sp Ct 1864 (1964): The Court reversed a decision of the Florida Supreme Court concerning the constitutionality of prayer and devotional Bible reading in public schools during the school day, as sanctioned by a state statute which specifically related the practices to a sound public purpose.

Board of Education v. Allen, No. 660 (1968): The Court declared constitutional the New York schoolbook-loan law that requires local school boards to purchase books with state funds and lend them to parochial and private school students.

Walz v. Tax Commission of New York (1970): The Court upheld the constitutionality of a New York statute exempting church-owned property from taxation.

Earle v. DiCenso, Robinson v. DiCenso, Lemon v. Kurtzman, Tilton v. Richardson (1971): In Earle v. DiCenso and Robinson v. DiCenso, the Court ruled unconstitutional a 1969 Rhode Island statute that provided salary supplements to teachers of secular subjects in parochial schools; in Lemon v. Kurtzman, the Court ruled unconstitutional a 1968 Pennsylvania statute that authorized the state to purchase services for the teaching of secular subjects in nonpublic schools. The principal argument against constitutionality in these cases was that the statutes and programs at issue entailed excessive entanglement of government with religion. In Tilton v. Richardson, the Court held that this argument did not apply to a prohibitive degree with respect to federal grants, under the Higher Education Facilities Act of 1963, for the construction of facilities for nonreligious purposes by four church-related institutions of higher learning, three of which were Catholic, in Connecticut.

Yoder, Miller and Yutzy (1972): In a case appealed on behalf of Yoder, Miller and Yutzy, the Court ruled that Amish parents were exempt from a Wisconsin statute requiring them to send their children to school until the age of 16. The Court said in its decision that secondary schooling exposed Amish children to attitudes, goals and values contrary to their beliefs, and substantially hindered "the religious development of the Amish child and his integration into the way of life of the Amish faith-community at the crucial adolescent state of development."

Committee for Public Education and Religious Liberty, et al., v. Nyquist, et al., No. 72-694 (1973): The Court ruled that provisions of a 1972 New York statute were unconstitutional on the grounds that they were violative of the No Establishment Clause of the First Amendment and had the "impermissible effect" of advancing the sectarian activities of church-affiliated schools. The programs ruled unconstitutional concerned: (1) maintenance and repair grants, for facilities and equipment, to ensure the health, welfare and safety of students in nonpublic, nonprofit elementary and secondary schools serving a high concentration of students from low income families; (2) tuition reimbursement ($50 per grade school child, $100 per high school student) for parents (with income less than $5,000) of children attending nonpublic elementary or secondary schools; tax deduction from adjusted gross income for parents failing to qualify under the above reimbursement plan, for each child attending a nonpublic school.

Sloan, Treasurer of Pennsylvania, et al., v. Lemon, et al., No. 72-459 (1973): The Court ruled unconstitutional a Pennsylvania Parent Reimbursement Act for Nonpublic Education which provided funds to reimburse parents (to a maximum of $150) for a portion of tuition expenses incurred in sending their children to nonpublic schools. The Court held that there was no significant difference between this and the New York tuition reimbursement program (above), and declared that the Equal Protection Clause of the Fourteenth Amendment cannot be relied upon to sustain a program held to be violative of the No Establishment Clause.

Levitt, et al., v. Committee for Public Education and Religious Liberty, et al., No. 72-269 (1973): The Court ruled unconstitutional the Mandated Services Act of 1970 under which New York provided $28 million ($27 per pupil from first to seventh grade, $45 per pupil from seventh to 12th grade) to reimburse nonpublic schools for testing, recording and reporting services required by the state. The Court declared that the act provided "impermissible aid" to religion in contravention of the No Establishment Clause.

In related decisions handed down June 25, 1973, the Court: (1) affirmed a lower-court decision against the constitutionality of an Ohio tax credit law benefiting parents with children in nonpublic schools; (2) reinstated an injunction against a parent reimbursement program in New Jersey; (3) affirmed South Carolina's right to grant construction loans to church-affiliated colleges, and (4) dismissed an appeal contesting its right to provide loans to students attending church-affiliated colleges (Hunt v. McNair, Durham v. McLeod).

Wheeler v. Barrera (1974): The Court ruled that nonpublic school students in Missouri must share in federal funds for educationally deprived students on a comparable basis with public school students under Title I of the Elementary and Secondary Education Act of 1965.

Norwood v. Harrison 93 S. Ct. 2804 (1974): The Court ruled that public assistance that avoids the prohibitions of the "effect" and "entanglement" tests (and which therefore does not substantially promote the religious mission of sectarian schools) may be confined to the secular functions of such schools.

Wiest v. Mt. Lebanon School District (1974): The Court upheld a lower court ruling that invocation and benediction prayers at public high school commencement ceremonies do not violate the principle of separation of Church and State.

Meek v. Pittenger (1975): The Court ruled unconstitutional portions of a Pennsylvania law providing auxiliary services for students of nonpublic schools; at the same time, it ruled in favor of provisions of the law permitting textbook loans to students of such schools. In denying the constitutionality of auxiliary services, the Court held that they had the "primary effect of establishing religion" and involved "excessive entanglement" of Church and state officials with respect to supervision; objection was also made against providing such services only on the premises of nonpublic schools and only at the request of such schools.

TWA, Inc., v. Hardison, 75-1126; International Association of Machinists and Aero Space Workers v. Hardison, 75-1385 (1977): The Court ruled that federal civil-rights legislation does not require employers to make more than minimal efforts to accommodate employees who want a particular working day off as their religion's Sabbath Day, and that an employer cannot accommodate such an employee by violating seniority systems determined by a union collective bargaining agreement. The Court noted that its ruling was not a constitutional judgment but an interpretation of existing law.

Wolman v. Walter (1977): The Court ruled constitutional portions of an Ohio statute providing tax-paid textbook loans and some auxiliary services (standardized and diagnostic testing, therapeutic and remedial services, off school premises) for nonpublic school students. It decided that other portions of the law, providing state funds for nonpublic school field trips and instructional materials (audio-visual equipment, maps, tape recorders), were unconstitutional.

Byrne v. Public Funds for Public Schools (1979): The Court decided against the constitutionality of a 1976 New Jersey law providing state income tax deductions for tuition paid by parents of students attending parochial and other private schools.

Student Bus Transportation (1979): The Court upheld a Pennsylvania law providing bus transportation at public expense for students to nonpublic schools up to 10 miles away from the boundaries of the public school districts in which they lived.

Reimbursement (1980): The Court upheld the constitutionality of a 1974 New York law providing direct cash payment to nonpublic schools for the costs of state-mandated testing and record-keeping.

Ten Commandments (1980): The Court struck down a 1978 Kentucky law requiring the posting of the Ten Commandments in public school classrooms in the state.

Widmar v. Vincent (1981): The Court ruled that the University of Missouri at Kansas City could not deny student religious groups the use of campus facilities for worship services. The Court also, in Brandon v. Board of Education of Guilderland Schools, declined without comment to hear an appeal for reversal of lower court decisions denying a group of New York high school students the right to meet for prayer on public school property before the beginning of the school day.

Lubbock v. Lubbock Civil Liberties Union (1983): By refusing to hear an appeal in this case, the Court upheld a lower court ruling against a public policy of permitting student religious groups to meet on public school property before and after school hours.

Mueller v. Allen (1983): The Court upheld a Minnesota law allowing parents of students in public and nonpublic (including parochial) schools to take a tax deduction for the expenses of tuition, textbooks and transportation. Maximum allowable deductions were $500 per child in elementary school and $700 per child in grades seven through 12.

Lynch v. Donnelly (1984): The Court ruled 5-to-4 that the First Amendment does not mandate "complete separation of church and state," and that, therefore, the sponsorship of a Christmas nativity scene by the City of Pawtucket, RI, was not unconstitutional. The case involved a scene included in a display of Christmas symbols sponsored by the city in a park owned by a non-profit group. The majority opinion said "the Constitution (does not) require complete separation of church and state; it affirmatively mandates accommodation, not merely tolerance, of all religions and forbids hostility toward any. Anything less" would entail callous indifference not intended by the Constitution. Moreover, "such hostility would bring us into 'war with our national tradition as embodied in the First Amendment's guaranty of the free exercise of religion.' " (The additional quotation was from the 1948 decision in McCollum v. Board of Education.)

Christmas Nativity Scene (1985): The Court upheld a lower court ruling that the Village of Scarsdale, NY, must make public space available for the display of privately sponsored nativity scenes.

Wallace v. Jaffree, No. 83-812 (1985): The Court ruled against the constitutionality of a 1981 Alabama law calling for a public-school moment of silence that specifically included optional prayer.

Grand Rapids v. Ball, No. 83-990, and **Aguilar v. Felton, No. 84-237** (1985): The Court ruled against the constitutionality of programs in Grand Rapids and New York City allowing public school teachers to teach remedial entitlement subjects (under the Elementary and Secondary Education Act of 1965) in private schools, many of which were Catholic.

Bender v. Williamsport Area School District (1986): The Court let stand a lower federal-court decision allowing a public high school Bible study group the same "equal access" to school facilities as that enjoyed by other extracurricular clubs. A similar decision was handed down in 1990 in Board of Education v. Mergens, involving Westside High School in Omaha.

County of Allegheny v. American Civil Liberties Union (1989): The Court ruled (1) that the display of a Christmas nativity scene in the Allegheny County Courthouse in Pittsburgh, PA, violated the principle of separation of church and state because it appeared to be a government-sponsored endorsement of Christian belief; (2) and that the display of a Hanukkah menorah outside the Pittsburgh-Allegheny city-county building was constitutional because of its "particular physical setting" with secular symbols.

Unemployment Division v. Smith (1990): The Court ruled that religious use of the hallucinogenic cactus peyote is not covered by the First Amendment protection of religious freedom.

Lee v. Weisman (1992): The Court banned officially organized prayer at public school graduation ceremonies.

Lamb's Chapel v. Center Moriches Union School District (1993): The Court reversed a ruling by the 3rd U.S. Circuit Court of Appeals, declaring that the school district was wrong in prohibiting the congregation of Lamb's Chapel from using public school meeting space after hours to show a film series addressing family problems from a religious perspective. In view of the variety of organizations permitted to use school property after school hours, said the Court's opinion: "There would have been no realistic danger that the community would think that the district was endorsing religion or any particular creed, and any benefit to religion or to the church would have been no more than incidental."

5th U.S. Circuit Court of Appeals (1993): The Court let stand a ruling by the 5th U.S. Circuit Court of Appeals, permitting students in Texas, Mississippi and Louisiana to include student-organized and student-led prayers in graduation exercises.

Church of Lukumi Babalu Aye v. City of Hialeah (1993): The Court ruled that municipal laws that effectively prohibit a single church from performing its religious rituals are unconstitutional. The ordinances at issue singled out one religion, Santeria, for the purpose of restricting its members from the practice of ritual animal sacrifices.

Zobrest v. Catalina Foothills School District

(1993): The Court ruled that a public school district may provide a sign-language interpreter for a deaf student attending a Catholic school without violating constitutional separation of church and state. The majority opinion said: "Handicapped children, not sectarian schools are the primary beneficiaries of the Disabilities Education Act; to the extent sectarian schools benefit at all from (the act), they are only incidental beneficiaries."

Fairfax County, Va., school district (1994): The Court upheld lower court rulings against a Fairfax County, VA, school district's practice of charging churches more rent than other entities for the use of school buildings.

Board of Education of Kiryas Joel Village School District v. Grumet (1994): The Court ruled in 1994 that a school district created to meet the special education needs of an Hasidic Jewish community violated the Establishment Clause of the Constitution. The Court said the New York Legislature effectively endorsed a particular religion when it established a public school district for the Satmar Hasidic Village of Kiryas Joel.

Agostino v. Felton (1997): The court reversed, 5 to 4, its 1985 Aguilar v. Felton ruling, which had declared it unconstitutional for teachers employed by public school districts to hold Title I remedial programs for low-income students on the property of church-related schools.

Boerne v. Flores (1997): The court ruled, 6 to 3, that the Religious Freedom Restoration Act (1993) was unconstitutional because Congress overstepped its constitutional authority in enacting the law. Congress "has been given the power to 'enforce,' not the power to determine what constitutes a constitutional violation," said the majority opinion.

Mitchell v. Helms (2000): The court ruled, 6 to 3, that a Louisiana parish can distribute money for instructional equipment — including computers, books, maps, and film strip projectors — to private schools as long as it is done in a "secular, neutral and non-ideological" way. The court's decision overturns two previous Supreme Court bans on giving public materials to parochial schools.

Santa Fe Independent School District v. Doe (2000): The court affirmed a lower court ruling that said prayer in public schools must be private and that such prayers at high school football games violate the constitutionally required separation of church and state. At issue in the Santa Fe case was a Texas school policy which permitted students selected by their peers to deliver an inspirational message of their own design at football games and the graduation ceremony. In 1999, the Santa Fe policy was struck down by the U.S. Court of Appeals for the Fifth Circuit. The Court of Appeals held that the policy violated the Establishment Clause of the First Amendment, even though the government played no role in creating the message or selecting the messenger.

Chandler v. Siegelman (2001): The court let stand a lower court ruling that students may participate in group prayers at school functions such as football games or graduations.

The Good News Club v. Milford Central Schools (2001): The court ruled that if the Boy Scouts and 4-H can use a public school as a meeting hall, a children's Bible study class can also.

Brown v. Gilmore (2001): The court declined to hear a challenge to Virginia's mandatory minute of silence in schools.

Children's Health Care is a Legal Duty Inc. v. McMullan (2001): The court turned down an appeal that claimed Medicare and Medicaid payments to church-run health centers violate the constitutional separation of church and state.

Gentala v. Tucson (2001): The court ordered a federal appeals court to take another look at a case that asked whether taxpayers must cover $340 in expenses from a prayer rally in a city park, saying it should be reconsidered in light of the high court's earlier ruling that a Bible club cannot be excluded from meeting at a public school so long as other groups with a moral viewpoint are allowed to gather there.

Cleveland Voucher Program (2002): By a 5-4 ruling, the court upheld the Cleveland voucher program that had been implemented in 1995 to assist the improvement of one of the worst public school systems in the country.

Ten Commandments (2005): By a 5-4 vote, the court prohibited the posting of the Ten Commandments in court houses; at the same time, the court permitted their posting in state houses.

RELIGION IN PUBLIC SCHOOLS

Based on a Catholic News Service article by Carol Zimmermann.

A diverse group of religious and civil rights organizations issued a joint statement Apr. 13, 1995, in an effort to clarify the confusing issue of prayer and religious observances or discussions in public schools. Their six-page statement outlines what is and what is not currently permissible in expressing religious beliefs in public schools.

The statement says, for example: "Students have the right to pray individually or in groups, or to discuss their religious views with their peers so long as they are not disruptive." But, the statement specifies that such prayers or discussions do not include "the right to have a captive audience listen or to compel other students to participate."

Prayer at Graduations

Regarding prayer at graduation ceremonies, the document says school officials may not mandate or organize prayer, but fails to set the record straight about student-led prayer at these services.

"The courts have reached conflicting conclusions under the federal Constitution" in this area, says the statement, recommending that schools consult their lawyers for the rules that apply to them, "until the issue is authoritatively resolved."

Since the Supreme Court's 1992 Lee v. Weisman opinion prohibited school authorities from even arranging for a speaker to present a prayer, lower courts in different states have made various rulings about student-led prayer at commencement exercises.

In Virginia, the state's Attorney General and the Board of Education proposed guidelines in mid-April to allow student-led prayer at graduations, despite a 1994 ruling by a U.S. district judge banning all prayer at graduations.

Religion in the Classroom

"It is both permissible and desirable to teach objectively about the role of religion in the history of the United States and other countries," but public school teachers may not specifically teach religion.

The same rules apply to the recurring controversy surrounding theories of evolution. Teachers may discuss explanations of the beginnings of life, but only within the confines of classes on religion or social studies. Public school teachers are required, according to the statement, to teach only scientific explanations of life's beginnings in science classes. And, just as teachers may not advance a religious view, they should not ridicule a student's religious belief.

Constitutional Protection

The statement says that students' expressions of religious beliefs in reports, homework or artwork are constitutionally protected. Likewise, students have the right to speak to and attempt to persuade their peers on religious topics. "But school officials should intercede to stop student religious speech if it turns into religious harassment aimed at a student or a small group of students."

The statement also says:

• Students have the right to distribute religious literature to their schoolmates, subject to reasonable restrictions for any non-school literature.

• Student religious clubs in secondary schools "must be permitted to meet and to have equal access" to school media for announcing their events.

• Religious messages on T-shirts and the like cannot be singled out for suppression.

• Schools can use discretion about dismissing students for off-site religious instruction.

The 35 organizations that endorsed the statement included the National Association of Evangelicals, the American Jewish Congress, the Christian Legal Society, the National Council of Churches, the Baptist Joint Committee on Public Affairs, the American Muslim Council, the Presbyterian Church (USA) and the American Civil Liberties Union.

Purpose of the Statement

"By making this document available," said Phil Baum, executive director of the American Jewish Congress, "the organizations are attempting to clarify what has become one of the most divisive issues of our time: religion in the public schools."

He said the document attempts to "ensure that the rights of all students are respected in the public schools."

Baum noted that the American Jewish Congress, which initiated the effort to draft the statement, had a long-standing commitment to ensuring that public schools are themselves religiously neutral.

"We believe, however, that it is inconsistent with that historic commitment to ask the public schools to root out private expressions of religious faith."

CHURCH TAX EXEMPTION

The exemption of church-owned property was ruled constitutional by the U.S. Supreme Court May 4, 1970, in the case of Walz v. The Tax Commission of New York.

Suit in the case was brought by Frederick Walz, who

purchased in June 1967, a 22-by-29-foot plot of ground in Staten Island valued at $100 and taxable at $5.24 a year. Shortly after making the purchase, Walz instituted a suit in New York State, contending that the exemption of church property from taxation authorized by state law increased his own tax rate and forced him indirectly to support churches in violation of his constitutional right to freedom of religion under the First Amendment. Three New York courts dismissed the suit, which had been instituted by mail. The Supreme Court, judging that it had probable jurisdiction, then took the case.

In a 7-1 decision affecting Church-state relations in every state in the nation, the Court upheld the New York law under challenge.

For and Against

Chief Justice Warren E. Burger, who wrote the majority opinion, said that Congress from its earliest days had viewed the religion clauses of the Constitution as authorizing statutory real estate tax exemption to religious bodies. He declared: "Nothing in this national attitude toward religious tolerance and two centuries of uninterrupted freedom from taxation has given the remotest sign of leading to an established church or religion, and on the contrary it has operated affirmatively to help guarantee the free exercise of all forms of religious beliefs."

Justice William O. Douglas wrote in dissent that the involvement of government in religion as typified in tax exemption may seem inconsequential but: "It is, I fear, a long step down the establishment path. Perhaps I have been misinformed. But, as I read the Constitution and the philosophy, I gathered that independence was the price of liberty."

Burger rejected Douglas' "establishment" fears. If tax exemption is the first step toward establishment, he said, "the second step has been long in coming."

The basic issue centered on the following question: Is there a contradiction between federal constitutional provisions against the establishment of religion, or the use of public funds for religious purposes, and state statutes exempting church property from taxation? In the Walz decision, the Supreme Court ruled that there is no contradiction.

Legal Background

The U.S. Constitution makes no reference to tax exemption. There was no discussion of the issue in the Constitutional Convention nor in debates on the Bill of Rights.

In the Colonial and post-Revolutionary years, some churches had established status and were state-supported. This changed with enactment of the First Amendment, which laid down no-establishment as the federal norm. This norm was adopted by the states which, however, exempted churches from tax liabilities.

No establishment, no hindrance, was the early American view of Church-State relationships.

This view, reflected in custom law, was not generally formulated in statute law until the second half of the 19th century, although specific tax exemption was provided for churches in Maryland in 1798, in Virginia in 1800, and in North Carolina in 1806.

The first major challenge to church property exemption was initiated by the Liberal League in the 1870s. It reached the point that President Grant included the recommendation in a State of the Union address in 1875, stating that church property should bear its own proportion of taxes. The plea fell on deaf ears in Congress, but there was some support for the idea at state levels. The exemption, however, continued to survive various challenges.

About 36 state constitutions contain either mandatory or permissive provisions for exemption. Statutes provide for exemption in all other states.

There has been considerable litigation challenging this exemption, but most of it focused on whether a particular property satisfied statutory requirements. Few cases before Walz focused on the strictly constitutional question, whether directly under the First Amendment or indirectly under the Fourteenth.

Objections

Objectors to the tax exempt status of churches feel that churches should share, through taxation, in the cost of the ordinary benefits of public services they enjoy, and/or that the amount of "aid" enjoyed through exemption should be proportionate to the amount of social good they do.

According to one opinion, exemption is said to weaken the independence of churches from the political system that benefits them by exemption.

In another view, exemption is said to involve the government in decisions regarding what is and what is not religion.

The Wall of Separation

Thomas Jefferson, in a letter written to the Danbury (Connecticut) Baptist Association Jan. 1, 1802, coined the metaphor, "a wall of separation between Church and State," to express a theory concerning interpretation of the religion clauses of the First Amendment: "Congress shall make no law respecting an establishment of religion or prohibiting the free exercise thereof."

The metaphor was cited for the first time in judicial proceedings in 1879, in the opinion by Chief Justice Waite in Reynolds v. United States. It did not, however, figure substantially in the decision.

Accepted as Rule

In 1947 the wall of separation gained acceptance as a constitutional rule, in the decision handed down in Everson v. Board of Education. Associate Justice Black, in describing the principles involved in the No Establishment Clause, wrote:

"Neither a state nor the Federal Government can set up a church. Neither can pass laws which aid one religion, aid all religions, or prefer one religion over another. Neither can force nor influence a person to go to or to remain away from church against his will or force him to profess a belief or disbelief in any religion. No person can be punished for entertaining or professing religious beliefs or disbeliefs, for church attendance or non-attendance. No tax in any amount, large or small, can be levied to support any religious activities or institutions, whatever they may be called, or whatever form they may adopt to teach or practice religion. Neither a state nor the Federal Government can, openly or secretly, participate in the affairs of any religious organizations or groups and vice versa. In the words of Jefferson, the clause against establishment of religion by law was intended to erect 'a wall of separation between Church and State.'"

Mr. Black's associates agreed with his statement of principles, which were framed without reference to the Freedom of Exercise Clause. They disagreed, however, with respect to application of the principles, as the split decision in the case indicated. Five members of the Court held that the benefits of public welfare legislation — in this case, free bus transportation to school for parochial as well as public school students — did not run contrary to the concept of separation of Church and State embodied in the First Amendment.

(For coverage of the recent Supreme Court decision pertaining to vouchers, see Education.)

CATHOLICS IN THE U.S. GOVERNMENT

CATHOLICS IN PRESIDENTS' CABINETS

From 1789 to 1940, nine Catholics were appointed to cabinet posts by six of 32 presidents. The first was Roger Brooke Taney (later named first Catholic Supreme Court Justice) who was appointed in 1831 by Andrew Jackson. Catholics have been appointed to cabinet posts from the time of Franklin D. Roosevelt to the present. Listed below in chronological order are presidents, Catholic cabinet officials, posts held, dates.

Andrew Jackson: Roger B. Taney, Secretary General, 1831-33, Secretary of Treasury, 1833-34.

Franklin Pierce: James Campbell, Postmaster General, 1853-57.

James Buchanan: John B. Floyd, Secretary of War, 1857-61.

William McKinley: Joseph McKenna, Attorney General, 1897-98.

Theodore Roosevelt: Robert J. Wynne, Postmaster General, 1904-05; Charles Bonaparte, Secretary of Navy, 1905-06, Attorney General, 1906-09.

Franklin D. Roosevelt: James A. Farley, Postmaster General, 1933-40; Frank Murphy, Attorney General,

1939-40; Frank C. Walker, Postmaster General, 1940-45.

Harry S. Truman: Robert E. Hannegan, Postmaster General, 1945-47; J. Howard McGrath, Attorney General, 1949-52; Maurice J. Tobin, Secretary of Labor, 1948-53; James P. McGranery, Attorney General, 1952-53.

Dwight D. Eisenhower: Martin P. Durkin, Secretary of Labor, 1953; James P. Mitchell, Secretary of Labor, 1953-61.

John F. Kennedy: Robert F. Kennedy, Attorney General, 1961-63; Anthony Celebrezze, Secretary of Health, Education and Welfare, 1962-63; John S. Gronouski, Postmaster General, 1963.

Lyndon B. Johnson: Robert F. Kennedy, 1963-64, Anthony Celebrezze, 1963-65, and John S. Gronouski, 1963-65, reappointed to posts held in Kennedy Cabinet; John T. Connor, Secretary of Commerce, 1965-67; Lawrence O'Brien, Postmaster General, 1965-68.

Richard M. Nixon: Walter J. Hickel, Secretary of Interior, 1969-71; John A. Volpe, Secretary of

Transportation, 1969-72; Maurice H. Stans, Secretary of Commerce, 1969-72; Peter J. Brennan, Secretary of Labor, 1973-74; William E. Simon, Secretary of Treasury, 1974.

Gerald R. Ford: Peter J. Brennan, 1974-75, and William E. Simon, 1974-76, reappointed to posts held above.

Jimmy Carter: Joseph Califano, Jr., Secretary of Health, Education and Welfare, 1977-79; Benjamin Civiletti, Attorney General, 1979-81; Moon Landrieu, Secretary of Housing and Urban Development, 1979-81; Edmund S. Muskie, Secretary of State, 1980-81.

Ronald Reagan: Alexander M. Haig, Secretary of State, 1981-82; Raymond J. Donovan, Secretary of Labor, 1981-84; Margaret M. Heckler, Secretary of Health and Human Services, 1983-85; William J. Bennett, Secretary of Education, 1985-88; Ann Dore McLaughlin, Secretary of Labor, 1988-89; Lauro F. Cavazos, Secretary of Education, 1988-89; Nicholas F. Brady, Secretary of Treasury, 1988-89.

George Bush: Lauro F. Cavazos (reappointed), Secretary of Education, 1989-90; Nicholas F. Brady (reappointed), Secretary of Treasury, 1989-93; James D. Watkins, Secretary of Energy, 1989-93; Manuel Lujan, Jr., Secretary of Interior, 1989-93; Edward J. Derwinski, Secretary of Veteran Affairs, 1989-92; Lynn Martin, Secretary of Labor, 1990-93; Edward Madigan, Secretary of Agriculture, 1991-93; William P. Barr, Attorney General, 1991-93.

Bill Clinton: Henry G. Cisneros, Secretary of Housing and Urban Development, 1993-97; Federico F. Peña, Secretary of Transportation, 1993-97; Donna Shalala, Secretary of Health and Human Services, 1993-2001; William M. Daley, Secretary of Commerce, 1997-2000; Andrew Cuomo, Secretary of Housing and Urban Development, 1997-2001; Alexis H. Herman, Secretary of Labor, 1997-2001.

George W. Bush: Paul O'Neill, Secretary of the Treasury, 2001-03; Tommy Thompson, Secretary of Health and Human Services, 2001-05; Mel Martinez, Secretary of Housing and Urban Development, 2001-05; Anthony Principi, Secretary of Veterans Affairs, 2001-.

Cabinet members who became Catholics after leaving their posts were: Thomas Ewing, Secretary of Treasury under William A. Harrison and Secretary of Interior under Zachary Taylor; Luke E. Wright, Secretary of War under Theodore Roosevelt; Albert B. Fall, Secretary of Interior under Warren G. Harding.

Catholics in the 109th Congress

As of the start of the 109th Congress in 2005, there were 152 Catholic members, comprising 29 percent of the total Congressional membership and therefore the largest faith group in that body (Baptists were second, with 65 House members and seven senators). There are presently 128 Catholics in the House and 24 Catholics in the Senate (13 Democrats and 11 Republicans), according to the *Congressional Quarterly*. The number of Catholics in the Senate is distributed essentially the same as it was for the 108th Congress, with 14 Democrats and 10 Republicans. It is noted, however,

that Catholic representatives and senators do not vote as a bloc, nor do many vote consistently in line with the teachings of the Church.

Catholic Supreme Court Justices

Roger B. Taney, Chief Justice 1836-64; app. by Andrew Jackson.

Edward D. White, Associate Justice 1894-1910, app. by Grover Cleveland; Chief Justice 1910-21; app. by William H. Taft.

Joseph McKenna, Associate Justice 1898-1925; app. by William McKinley.

Pierce Butler, Associate Justice 1923-39; app. by Warren G. Harding.

Frank Murphy, Associate Justice 1940-49; app. by Franklin D. Roosevelt.

William Brennan, Associate Justice 1956-90; app. by Dwight D. Eisenhower.

Antonin Scalia, Associate Justice 1986-; app. by Ronald Reagan.

Anthony M. Kennedy, Associate Justice 1988-; app. by Ronald Reagan.

Clarence Thomas, Associate Justice 1991-; app. by George H. W. Bush.

John Roberts, Chief Justice 2005-; app. by George W. Bush.

Samuel Alito, Associate Justice 2005-; app. George W. Bush.

Sherman Minton, Associate Justice from 1949 to 1956; became a Catholic several years before his death in 1965.

Catholics in Statuary Hall

Statues of 13 Catholics deemed worthy of national commemoration are among those enshrined in National Statuary Hall and other places in the U.S. Capitol. The Hall, formerly the chamber of the House of Representatives, was erected by Act of Congress July 2, 1864.

Donating states, names and years of placement are listed.

Arizona: Rev. Eusebio Kino, S. J., missionary, 1965.

California: Rev. Junípero Serra, O. F. M. missionary, 1931. (Beatified 1988.)

Hawaii: Fr. Damien, missionary, 1969. (Beatified 1995.)

Illinois: Gen. James Shields, statesman, 1893.

Louisiana: Edward D. White, Justice of the U.S. Supreme Court (1894-1921), 1955.

Maryland: Charles Carroll, statesman, 1901.

Nevada: Patrick A. McCarran, statesman, 1960.

New Mexico: Dennis Chavez, statesman, 1966. (Abp. Jean B. Lamy, pioneer prelate of Santa Fe, was nominated for Hall honor in 1951.)

North Dakota: John Burke, U.S. treasurer, 1963.

Oregon: Dr. John McLoughlin, pioneer, 1953.

Washington: Mother Mary Joseph Pariseau, pioneer missionary and humanitarian.

West Virginia: John E. Kenna, statesman, 1901.

Wisconsin: Rev. Jacques Marquette, S.J., missionary, explorer, 1895.

United States Hierarchy

U.S. CATHOLIC JURISDICTIONS, HIERARCHY, STATISTICS

The organizational structure of the Catholic Church in the United States consists of 34 provinces with as many archdioceses (metropolitan sees); 152 suffragan sees (dioceses); five Eastern Church jurisdictions immediately subject to the Holy See — the eparchies of St. Maron and Our Lady of Lebanon of Los Angeles (Maronites), Newton (Melkites), St. Thomas Apostle of Detroit (Chaldeans), St. Thomas of Chicago (Syro-Malabars, created on Mar. 13, 2001), St. George Martyr of Canton, Ohio (Romanians), and eparchy for Armenian Catholics in the United States and Canada; and the Military Services Archdiocese. The current number of archdioceses reflects the creation of the archdiocese of Galveston-Houston on Dec. 29, 2004; the current number of suffragan sees reflects the creation of the new diocese of Laredo, Texas, on July 3, 2000, the eparchy of St. Peter the Apostle of San Diego of the Chaldeans on May 21, 2002, and the elevation of the Apostolic Exarchate for Armenian Catholics in the United States and Canada to the rank of eparchy on Sept. 13, 2005. The eparchy of Our Lady of Deliverance of Newark for Syrian-rite Catholics in the U.S. and Canada has its seat in Newark, N.J. The Armenian apostolic eparchy for the United States and Canada has its seat in New York. Each of these jurisdictions is under the direction of an archbishop or bishop, called an ordinary, who has apostolic responsibility and authority for the pastoral service of the people in his care.

The structure includes the territorial episcopal conference known as the United States Conference of Catholic Bishops (USCCB). In and through this body, which is an amalgamation of the National Conference of Catholic Bishops (NCCB) and the United States Catholic Conference (USCC), the bishops exercise their collegiate pastorate over the Church in the entire country (*see* **Index**).

The representative of the Holy See to the Church in the United States is an apostolic nuncio (presently Abp. Pietro Sambi, J.C.D., S.T.D.)

ECCLESIASTICAL PROVINCES

(Sources: The Official Catholic Directory, *Catholic News Service.)*

The 34 ecclesiastical provinces bear the names of archdioceses, i.e., of metropolitan sees.

Anchorage: Archdiocese of Anchorage and suffragan sees of Fairbanks, Juneau. Geographical area: Alaska.

Atlanta: Archdiocese of Atlanta (GA) and suffragan sees of Savannah (GA); Charlotte and Raleigh (NC), Charleston (SC). Geographical area: Georgia, North Carolina, South Carolina.

Baltimore: Archdiocese of Baltimore (MD) and suffragan sees of Wilmington (DE); Arlington and Richmond (VA); Wheeling-Charleston (WV). Geographical area: Maryland (except five counties), Delaware, Virginia, West Virginia.

Boston: Archdiocese of Boston (MA) and suffragan sees of Fall River, Springfield and Worcester (MA); Portland (ME); Manchester (NH); Burlington (VT). Geographical area: Massachusetts, Maine, New Hampshire, Vermont.

Chicago: Archdiocese of Chicago and suffragan sees of Belleville, Joliet, Peoria, Rockford, Springfield. Geographical area: Illinois.

Cincinnati: Archdiocese of Cincinnati and suffragan sees of Cleveland, Columbus, Steubenville, Toledo, Youngstown. Geographical area: Ohio.

Denver: Archdiocese of Denver (CO) and suffragan sees of Colorado Springs and Pueblo (CO); Cheyenne (WY). Geographical area: Colorado, Wyoming.

Detroit: Archdiocese of Detroit and suffragan sees of Gaylord, Grand Rapids, Kalamazoo, Lansing, Marquette, Saginaw. Geographical area: Michigan.

Dubuque: Archdiocese of Dubuque and suffragan sees of Davenport, Des Moines, Sioux City. Geographical area: Iowa.

Galveston-Houston: Archdiocese of Galveston-Houston and suffragan sees of Austin, Beaumont, Brownsville, Corpus Christi, Tyler, and Victoria. Geographical area: Southeast Texas.

Hartford: Archdiocese of Hartford (CT) and suffragan sees of Bridgeport and Norwich (CT); Providence (RI). Geographical area: Connecticut, Rhode Island.

Indianapolis: Archdiocese of Indianapolis and suffragan sees of Evansville, Fort Wayne-South Bend, Gary, Lafayette. Geographical area: Indiana.

Kansas City (KS): Archdiocese of Kansas City and suffragan sees of Dodge City, Salina, Wichita. Geographical area: Kansas.

Los Angeles: Archdiocese of Los Angeles and suffragan sees of Fresno, Monterey, Orange, San Bernardino, San Diego. Geographical area: Southern and Central California.

Louisville: Archdiocese of Louisville (KY) and suffragan sees of Covington, Lexington and Owensboro (KY); Knoxville, Memphis and Nashville (TN). Geographical area: Kentucky, Tennessee.

Miami: Archdiocese of Miami and suffragan sees of Orlando, Palm Beach, Pensacola-Tallahassee, St. Augustine, St. Petersburg, Venice. Geographical area: Florida.

Milwaukee: Archdiocese of Milwaukee and suffragan sees of Green Bay, La Crosse, Madison, Superior. Geographical area: Wisconsin.

Mobile: Archdiocese of Mobile, AL, and suffragan sees of Birmingham (AL); Biloxi and Jackson (MS). Geographical area: Alabama, Mississippi.

Newark: Archdiocese of Newark and suffragan sees of Camden, Metuchen, Paterson, Trenton. Geographical area: New Jersey.

New Orleans: Archdiocese of New Orleans and suffragan sees of Alexandria, Baton Rouge, Houma-Thibodaux, Lafayette, Lake Charles and Shreveport. Geographical area: Louisiana.

New York: Archdiocese of New York and suffragan sees of Albany, Brooklyn, Buffalo, Ogdensburg, Rochester, Rockville Centre, Syracuse. Geographical area: New York.

Oklahoma City: Archdiocese of Oklahoma City (OK) and suffragan sees of Tulsa (OK) and Little Rock (AR). Geographical area: Oklahoma, Arkansas.

Omaha: Archdiocese of Omaha and suffragan sees of Grand Island, Lincoln. Geographical area: Nebraska.

Philadelphia: Archdiocese of Philadelphia and suffragan sees of Allentown, Altoona-Johnstown, Erie, Greensburg, Harrisburg, Pittsburgh, Scranton. Geographical area: Pennsylvania.

Philadelphia (Byzantine, Ukrainians): Metropolitan See of Philadelphia (Byzantine) and Eparchies of St. Josaphat in Parma (OH), St. Nicholas of the Ukrainians in Chicago and Stamford, CT The jurisdic-

tion extends to all Ukrainian Catholics in the U.S. from the ecclesiastical province of Galicia in the Ukraine.

Pittsburgh (Byzantine, Ruthenians): Metropolitan See of Pittsburgh, PA and Eparchies of Passaic (NJ), Parma (OH), Van Nuys (CA).

Portland: Archdiocese of Portland (OR) and suffragan sees of Baker (OR); Boise (ID); Great Falls-Billings and Helena (MT). Geographical area: Oregon, Idaho, Montana.

St. Louis: Archdiocese of St. Louis and suffragan sees of Jefferson City, Kansas City-St. Joseph, Springfield-Cape Girardeau. Geographical area: Missouri.

St. Paul and Minneapolis: Archdiocese of St. Paul and Minneapolis (MN) and suffragan sees of Crookston, Duluth, New Ulm, St. Cloud and Winona (MN); Bismarck and Fargo (ND); Rapid City and Sioux Falls (SD). Geographical area: Minnesota, North Dakota, South Dakota.

San Antonio: Archdiocese of San Antonio (TX) and suffragan sees of Amarillo, Dallas, El Paso, Fort Worth, Laredo, Lubbock, and San Angelo. Geographical area: Texas.

San Francisco: Archdiocese of San Francisco (CA) and suffragan sees of Oakland, Sacramento, San Jose, Santa Rosa and Stockton (CA); Honolulu (HI); Reno (NV); Las Vegas (NV); Salt Lake City (UT). Geographical area: Northern California, Nevada, Utah, Hawaii.

Santa Fe: Archdiocese of Santa Fe (NM) and suffragan sees of Gallup and Las Cruces (NM); Phoenix and Tucson (AZ). Geographical area: New Mexico, Arizona.

Seattle: Archdiocese of Seattle and suffragan sees of Spokane, Yakima. Geographical area: Washington.

Washington: Archdiocese of Washington, D.C., and suffragan see of St. Thomas (VI). Geographical area: District of Columbia, five counties of Maryland, Virgin Islands.

ARCHDIOCESES, DIOCESES, ARCHBISHOPS, BISHOPS

(Sources: *Official Catholic Directory*; Catholic News Service; *L'Osservatore Romano.* As of Aug. 20, 2006.)

Information includes name of diocese, year of foundation (as it appears on the official document erecting the see), present ordinaries (year of installation), auxiliaries and former ordinaries (for biographies, *see* Index).

Archdioceses are indicated by an asterisk.

Albany, NY (1847): Howard J. Hubbard, bishop, 1977.

Former bishops: John McCloskey, 1847-64; John J. Conroy, 1865-77; Francis McNeirny, 1877-94; Thomas M. Burke, 1894-1915; Thomas F. Cusack, 1915-18; Edmund F. Gibbons, 1919-54; William A. Scully, 1954-69; Edwin B. Broderick, 1969-76.

Alexandria, LA (1853): Ronald P. Herzog, bishop, 2004.

Established at Natchitoches, transferred to Alexandria, 1910; title changed to Alexandria-Shreveport, 1977; redesignated Alexandria, 1986, when Shreveport was made a diocese.

Former bishops: Augustus M. Martin, 1853-75; Francis X. Leray, 1877-79, administrator, 1879-83; Anthony Durier, 1885-1904; Cornelius Van de Ven, 1904-32; Daniel F. Desmond, 1933-45; Charles P.

Greco, 1946-73; Lawrence P. Graves, 1973-82; William B. Friend, 1983-86; John C. Favalora, 1986-89; Sam G. Jacobs, 1989-2003.

Allentown, PA (1961): Edward P. Cullen, 1997.

Former bishop: Joseph McShea, 1961-83; Thomas J. Welsh, 1983-97.

Altoona-Johnstown, PA (1901): Joseph V. Adamec, bishop, 1987.

Established as Altoona, name changed, 1957.

Former bishops: Eugene A. Garvey, 1901-20; John J. McCort, 1920-36; Richard T. Guilfoyle, 1936-57; Howard J. Carroll, 1958-60; J. Carroll McCormick, 1960-66; James J. Hogan, 1966-86.

Amarillo, TX (1926): John W. Yanta, bishop, 1997.

Former bishops; Rudolph A. Gerken, 1927-33; Robert E. Lucey, 1934-41; Laurence J. Fitzsimon, 1941-58; John L. Morkovsky, 1958-63; Lawrence M. De Falco, 1963-79; Leroy T. Matthiesen, 1980-97.

Anchorage,* AK (1966): Roger Lawrence Schwietz O.M.I., archbishop, 2001.

Former archbishop: Joseph T. Ryan, 1966-75; Francis T. Hurley, 1976-2001.

Arlington, VA (1974): Paul S. Loverde, bishop, 1999.

Former bishop: Thomas J. Welsh, 1974-83; John R. Keating, 1983-98.

Atlanta,* GA (1956; archdiocese, 1962): Wilton Daniel Gregory, archbishop, 2004.

Former ordinaries: Francis E. Hyland, 1956-61; Paul J. Hallinan, first archbishop, 1962-68; Thomas A. Donnellan, 1968-87; Eugene A. Marino, S.S.J., 1988-90; James P. Lyke, 1991-92; John F. Donoghue, 1993-2004.

Austin, TX (1947): Gregory Michael Aymond, bishop, 2001.

Former bishops: Louis J. Reicher, 1947-71; Vincent M. Harris, 1971-86; John E. McCarthy, 1986-2001.

Baker, OR (1903): Robert Francis Vasa, bishop, 2000.

Established as Baker City, name changed, 1952.

Former bishops: Charles J. O'Reilly, 1903-18; Joseph F. McGrath, 1919-50; Francis P. Leipzig, 1950-71; Thomas J. Connolly, 1971-99.

Baltimore,* MD (1789; archdiocese, 1808): Cardinal William H. Keeler, archbishop, 1989. W. Francis Malooly, Mitchell Thomas Rozanski, Denis James Madden, auxiliaries.

Former ordinaries: John Carroll, 1789-1815, first archbishop; Leonard Neale, 1815-17; Ambrose Marechal, S.S., 1817-28; James Whitfield, 1828-34; Samuel Eccleston, S.S., 1834-51; Francis P. Kenrick, 1851-63; Martin J. Spalding, 1864-72; James R. Bayley, 1872-77; Cardinal James Gibbons, 1877-1921; Michael J. Curley, 1921-47; Francis P. Keough, 1947-61; Cardinal Lawrence J. Shehan, 1961-74; William D. Borders, 1974-89.

Baton Rouge, LA (1961): Robert W. Muench, bishop, 2001.

Former bishops: Robert E. Tracy, 1961-74; Joseph V. Sullivan, 1974-82; Stanley J. Ott, 1983-93; Alfred C. Hughes, 1993-2001.

Beaumont, TX (1966): Curtis J. Guillory, S.V.D., bishop, 2000.

Former bishops: Vincent M. Harris, 1966-71; Warren L. Boudreaux, 1971-77; Bernard J. Ganter, 1977-93; Joseph A. Galante, 1994-2000.

Belleville, IL (1887): Edward Braxton, bishop, 2005.

Former bishops: John Janssen, 1888-1913; Henry Althoff, 1914-47; Albert R. Zuroweste, 1948-76; William M. Cosgrove, 1976-81; John N. Wurm, 1981-84; James P. Keleher, 1984-93; Wilton D. Gregory, 1994-2004.

Biloxi, MS (1977): Thomas John Rodi, bishop, 2001. Former bishop: Joseph Lawson Howze, 1977-2001.

Birmingham, AL (1969): vacant.

Former bishops: Joseph G. Vath, 1969-87; Raymond J. Boland, 1988-93; David E. Foley, 1994-2005.

Bismarck, ND (1909): Paul A. Zipfel, bishop, 1996.

Former bishops: Vincent Wehrle, O.S.B., 1910-39; Vincent J. Ryan, 1940-51; Lambert A. Hoch, 1952-56; Hilary B. Hacker, 1957-82; John F. Kinney, 1982-95.

Boise, ID (1893): Michael P. Driscoll, 1999.

Former bishops: Alphonse J. Glorieux, 1893-1917; Daniel M. Gorman, 1918-27; Edward J. Kelly, 1928-56; James J. Byrne, 1956-62; Sylvester Treinen, 1962-88; Tod David Brown, 1989-98.

Boston,* MA (1808; archdiocese, 1875): Sean O'Malley, O.F.M. Cap., 2003. John P. Boles, Francis Xavier Irwin, Emilio Allué, S.D.B., Walter James Edyvean, auxiliaries.

Former ordinaries: John L. de Cheverus, 1810-23; Benedict J. Fenwick, S.J., 1825-46; John B. Fitzpatrick, 1846-66; John J. Williams, 1866-1907, first archbishop; Cardinal William O'Connell, 1907-44; Cardinal Richard Cushing, 1944-70; Cardinal Humberto Medeiros, 1970-83; Cardinal Bernard F. Law, 1984-2002.

Bridgeport, CT (1953): William Edward Lori, 2001.

Former bishops: Lawrence J. Shehan, 1953-61; Walter W. Curtis, 1961-88; Edward M. Egan, 1988-2000.

Brooklyn, NY (1853): Nicholas A. DiMarzio, 2003. Ignatius Catanello, Octavio Cisneros, Guy Sansaricq, Frank J. Caggiano, auxiliaries.

Former bishops: John Loughlin, 1853-91; Charles E. McDonnell, 1892-1921; Thomas E. Molloy, 1921-56; Bryan J. McEntegart, 1957-68; Francis J. Mugavero, 1968-90; Thomas V. Daily, 1990-2003.

Brownsville, TX (1965): Raymundo J. Peña, bishop, 1995.

Former bishops: Adolph Marx, 1965; Humberto S. Medeiros, 1966-70; John J. Fitzpatrick, 1971-91; Enrique San Pedro, S.J., 1991-94.

Buffalo, NY (1847): Edward U. Kmiec, bishop, 2004. Edward M. Grosz, auxiliary.

Former bishops: John Timon, C.M., 1847-67; Stephen V. Ryan, C.M., 1868-96; James E. Quigley, 1897-1903; Charles H. Colton, 1903-15; Dennis J. Dougherty, 1915-18; William Turner, 1919-36; John A. Duffy, 1937-44; John F. O'Hara, C.S.C., 1945-51; Joseph A. Burke, 1952-62; James McNulty, 1963-72; Edward D. Head, 1973-95 Henry J. Mansell, 1995-2003.

Burlington, VT (1853): Salvatore R. Matano, bishop, 2005.

Former bishops: Louis De Goesbriand, 1853-99; John S. Michaud, 1899-1908; Joseph J. Rice, 1910-38; Matthew F. Brady, 1938-44; Edward F. Ryan, 1944-56; Robert F. Joyce, 1957-71; John A. Marshall, 1972-91; Kenneth A. Angell, bishop, 1992-2005.

Camden, NJ (1937): Joseph Galante, bishop, 2004.

Former bishops: Bartholomew J. Eustace, 1938-56; Justin J. McCarthy, 1957-59; Celestine J. Damiano, 1960-67; George H. Guilfoyle, 1968-89; James T. McHugh, 1989-98; Nicholas A.DiMarzio, 1999-2003.

Charleston, SC (1820): Robert J. Baker, bishop, 1999.

Former bishops: John England, 1820-42; Ignatius W. Reynolds, 1844-55; Patrick N. Lynch, 1858-82; Henry P. Northrop, 1883-1916; William T. Russell, 1917-27; Emmet M. Walsh, 1927-49; John J. Russell, 1950-58; Paul J. Hallinan, 1958-62; Francis F. Reh, 1962-64; Ernest L. Unterkoefler, 1964-90; David B. Thompson, 1990-99.

Charlotte, NC (1971): Peter J. Jugis, bishop, 2003.

Former bishops: Michael J. Begley, 1972-84; John F. Donoghue, 1984-93; William G. Curlin, 1994-2002.

Cheyenne, WY (1887): David Laurin Ricken, bishop, 2001.

Former bishops: Maurice F. Burke, 1887-93; Thomas M. Lenihan, 1897-1901; James J. Keane, 1902-11; Patrick A. McGovern, 1912-51; Hubert M. Newell, 1951-78; Joseph Hart, 1978-2001.

Chicago,* IL (1843; archdiocese, 1880): Cardinal Francis E. George, archbishop, 1997. John R. Manz, Joseph N. Perry, Francis J. Kane, Thomas J. Paprocki,

Gustavo Garcia-Siller, M.Sp.S., George J. Rassas, auxiliaries.

Former ordinaries: William Quarter, 1844-48; James O. Van de Velde, S.J., 1849-53; Anthony O'Regan, 1854-58; James Duggan, 1859-70; Thomas P. Foley, administrator, 1870-79; Patrick A. Feehan, 1880-1902, first archbishop; James E. Quigley, 1903-15; Cardinal George Mundelein, 1915-39; Cardinal Samuel Stritch, 1939-58; Cardinal Albert Meyer, 1958-65; Cardinal John Cody, 1965-82; Cardinal Joseph L. Bernardin, 1982-96.

Cincinnati,* OH (1821; archdiocese, 1850): Daniel E. Pilarczyk, archbishop, 1982. Carl K. Moeddel, auxiliary.

Former ordinaries: Edward D. Fenwick, O.P., 1822-32; John B. Purcell, 1833-83, first archbishop; William H. Elder, 1883-1904; Henry Moeller, 1904-1925; John T. McNicholas, O.P., 1925-50; Karl J. Alter, 1950-69; Paul F. Leibold, 1969-72; Joseph L. Bernardin, 1972-82.

Cleveland, OH (1847): Richard Gerard Lennon, bishop, 2006. A. James Quinn, Roger W. Gries, O.S.B., Martin John Amos, auxiliaries.

Former ordinaries: L. Amadeus Rappe, 1847-70; Richard Gilmour, 1872-91; Ignatius F. Horstmann, 1892-1908; John P. Farrelly, 1909-21; Joseph Schrembs, 1921-45; Edward F. Hoban, 1945-66; Clarence G. Issenmann, 1966-74; James A. Hickey, 1974-80; Anthony M. Pilla, 1980-2006.

Colorado Springs, CO (1983): Michael J. Sheridan, bishop, 2003.

Former ordinaries: Richard C. Hanifen, 1984-2003.

Columbus, OH (1868): Frederick Francis Campbell, bishop, 2004.

Former bishops: Sylvester H. Rosecrans, 1868-78; John A. Watterson, 1880-99; Henry Moeller, 1900-03; James J. Hartley, 1904-44; Michael J. Ready, 1944-57; Clarence Issenmann, 1957-64; John J. Carberry, 1965-68; Clarence E. Elwell, 1968-73; Edward J. Herrmann, 1973-82; James A. Griffin, 1983-2004.

Corpus Christi, TX (1912): Edmond Carmody, bishop, 2000.

Former bishops: Paul J. Nussbaum, C.P., 1913-20; Emmanuel B. Ledvina, 1921-49; Mariano S. Garriga, 1949-65; Thomas J. Drury, 1965-83; Rene H. Gracida, 1983-97. Roberto O. Gonzalez, O.F.M., 1997-99.

Covington, KY (1853): Roger J. Foys, bishop, 2002.

Former bishops: George A. Carrell, S.J., 1853-68; Augustus M. Toebbe, 1870-84; Camillus P. Maes, 1885-1914; Ferdinand Brossart, 1916-23; Francis W. Howard, 1923-44; William T. Mulloy, 1945-59; Richard Ackerman, C.S.Sp., 1960-78; William A. Hughes, 1979-95; Robert W. Muench, 1996-2001.

Crookston, MN (1909): Victor H. Balke, bishop, 1976.

Former bishops: Timothy Corbett, 1910-38; John H. Peschges, 1938-44; Francis J. Schenk, 1945-60; Laurence A. Glenn, 1960-70; Kenneth J. Povish, 1970-75.

Dallas, TX (1890): Charles V. Grahmann, bishop, 1990.

Established 1890, as Dallas, title changed to Dallas-Ft. Worth, 1953; redesignated Dallas, 1969, when Ft. Worth was made a diocese.

Former bishops: Thomas F. Brennan, 1891-92; Edward J. Dunne, 1893-1910; Joseph P. Lynch,

1911-54; Thomas K. Gorman, 1954-69; Thomas Tschoepe, 1969-90.

Davenport, IA (1881): William E. Franklin, bishop, 1993.

Former bishops: John McMullen, 1881-83; Henry Cosgrove, 1884-1906; James Davis, 1906-26; Henry P. Rohlman, 1927-44; Ralph L. Hayes, 1944-66; Gerald F. O'Keefe, 1966-93.

Denver,* CO (1887; archdiocese, 1941): Charles J. Chaput, O.F.M. Cap., archbishop, 1997.

Former ordinaries: Joseph P. Machebeuf, 1887-89; Nicholas C. Matz, 1889-1917; J. Henry Tihen, 1917-31; Urban J. Vehr, 1931-67, first archbishop; James V. Casey, 1967-86; J. Francis Stafford, 1986-96.

Des Moines, IA (1911): Joseph L. Charron, C.PP.S., bishop, 1993.

Former bishops: Austin Dowling, 1912-19; Thomas W. Drumm, 1919-33; Gerald T. Bergan, 1934-48; Edward C. Daly, O.P., 1948-64; George J. Biskup, 1965-67; Maurice J. Dingman, 1968-86; William H. Bullock, 1987-93.

Detroit,* MI (1833; archdiocese, 1937): Cardinal Adam J. Maida, archbishop, 1990. Earl Boyea, John M. Quinn, Francis R. Reiss, auxiliaries.

Former ordinaries: Frederic Rese, 1833-71; Peter P. Lefevere, administrator, 1841-69; Caspar H. Borgess, 1871-88; John S. Foley, 1888-1918; Michael J. Gallagher, 1918-37; Cardinal Edward Mooney, 1937-58, first archbishop; Cardinal John F. Dearden, 1958-80; Cardinal Edmund C. Szoka, 1981-90.

Dodge City, KS (1951): Ronald M. Gilmore, bishop, 1998.

Former bishops: John B. Franz, 1951-59; Marion F. Forst, 1960-76; Eugene J. Gerber, 1976-82; Stanley G. Schlarman, 1983-98.

Dubuque,* IA (1837; archdiocese, 1893): Jerome Hanus, O.S.B., archbishop, 1995.

Former ordinaries: Mathias Loras, 1837-58; Clement Smyth, O.C.S.O., 1858-65; John Hennessy, 1866-1900, first archbishop; John J. Keane, 1900-11; James J. Keane, 1911-29; Francis J. Beckman, 1930-46; Henry P. Rohlman, 1946-54; Leo Binz, 1954-61; James J. Byrne, 1962-83; Daniel W. Kucera, O.S.B., 1984-95.

Duluth, MN (1889): Dennis M. Schnurr, 2001.

Former bishops: James McGolrick, 1889-1918; John T. McNicholas, O.P., 1918-25; Thomas A. Welch, 1926-59; Francis J. Schenk, 1960-69; Paul F. Anderson, 1969-82; Robert H. Brom, 1983-89; Roger L. Schwietz, O.M.I., 1990-2000.

El Paso, TX (1914): Armando X. Ochoa, bishop, 1996.

Former bishops: Anthony J. Schuler, S.J., 1915-42; Sidney M. Metzger, 1942-78; Patrick F. Flores, 1978-79; Raymundo J. Pena, 1980-95.

Erie, PA (1853): Donald W. Trautman, bishop, 1990.

Former bishops: Michael O'Connor, 1853-54; Josue M. Young, 1854-66; Tobias Mullen, 1868-99; John E. Fitzmaurice, 1899-1920; John M. Gannon, 1920-66; John F. Whealon, 1966-69; Alfred M. Watson, 1969-82; Michael J. Murphy, 1982-90.

Evansville, IN (1944): Gerald A. Gettelfinger, bishop, 1989.

Former bishops: Henry J. Grimmelsman, 1944-65; Paul F. Leibold, 1966-69; Francis R. Shea, 1970-89.

Fairbanks, AK (1962): Donald Kettler, bishop, 2002.

Former bishops: Francis D. Gleeson, S.J., 1962-68; Robert L. Whelan, S.J., 1968-85; Michael J. Kaniecki, S.J., 1985-2000.

Fall River, MA (1904): George William Coleman, bishop, 2003.

Former bishops: William Stang, 1904-07; Daniel F. Feehan, 1907-34; James E. Cassidy, 1934-51; James L. Connolly, 1951-70; Daniel A. Cronin, 1970-91; Sean O'Malley, O.F.M. Cap., 1992-2002.

Fargo, ND (1889): Samuel J. Aquila, bishop, 2002. Established at Jamestown, transferred, 1897.

Former bishops: John Shanley, 1889-1909; James O'Reilly, 1910-34; Aloysius J. Muench, 1935-59; Leo F. Dworschak, 1960-70; Justin A. Driscoll, 1970-84; James S. Sullivan, 1985-2002.

Fort Wayne-South Bend, IN (1857): John M. D'Arcy, bishop, 1985.

Established as Fort Wayne, name changed, 1960.

Former bishops: John H. Luers, 1858-71; Joseph Dwenger, C.Pp. S., 1872-93; Joseph Rademacher, 1893-1900; Herman J. Alerding, 1900-24; John F. Noll, 1925-56; Leo A. Pursley, 1957-76; William E. McManus, 1976-85.

Fort Worth, TX (1969): Kevin W. Vann, bishop, 2005.

Former bishop: John J. Cassata, 1969-80; Joseph P. Delaney, 1981-2005.

Fresno, CA (1967): John T. Steinbock, bishop, 1991. Formerly Monterey-Fresno, 1922.

Former bishops (Monterey-Fresno): John J. Cantwell, administrator, 1922-24; John B. MacGinley, first bishop, 1924-32; Philip G. Sher, 1933-53; Aloysius J. Willinger, 1953-67.

Former bishops (Fresno): Timothy Manning, 1967-69; Hugh A. Donohoe, 1969-80; Joseph J. Madera, M.Pp.S., 1980-91.

Gallup, NM (1939): Donald Pelotte, S.S.S., bishop, 1990.

Former bishops: Bernard T. Espelage, O.F.M., 1940-69; Jerome J. Hastrich, 1969-90.

Galveston-Houston, TX* (1847; archdiocese, 2004): Daniel N. DiNardo, archbishop, 2006. Vincent M. Rizzotto, José S. Vasquez, auxiliaries.

Established as Galveston, name changed, 1959.

Former bishops: John M. Odin, C.M., 1847-61; Claude M. Dubuis, 1862-92; Nicholas A. Gallagher, 1892-1918; Christopher E. Byrne, 1918-50; Wendelin J. Nold, 1950-75; John L. Morkovsky, 1975-84; Joseph A. Fiorenza, 1985-2004, first archbishop, 2004-2006.

Gary, IN (1956): Dale J. Melczek, bishop, 1996.

Former bishops: Andrew G. Grutka, 1957-84; Norbert F. Gaughan, 1984-96.

Gaylord, MI (1971): Patrick R. Cooney, bishop, 1989, installed 1990.

Former bishops: Edmund C. Szoka, 1971-81; Robert J. Rose, 1981-89.

Grand Island, NE (1912): William J. Dendinger, bishop, 2004.

Established at Kearney, transferred, 1917.

Former bishops: James A. Duffy, 1913-31; Stanislaus V. Bona, 1932-44; Edward J. Hunkeler, 1945-51; John L. Paschang, 1951-72; John J. Sullivan, 1972-77; Lawrence J. McNamara, 1978-2004.

Grand Rapids, MI (1882): Walter A. Hurley, bishop, 2005.

Former bishops: Henry J. Richter, 1883-1916;

Michael J. Gallagher, 1916-18; Edward D. Kelly, 1919-26; Joseph G. Pinten, 1926-40; Joseph C. Plagens, 1941-43; Francis J. Haas, 1943-53; Allen J. Babcock, 1954-69; Joseph M. Breitenbeck, 1969-89; Robert J. Rose, 1989-2003; Kevin M. Britt, 2003-2004.

Great Falls-Billings, MT (1904): Anthony M. Milone, bishop, 1988.

Established as Great Falls, name changed, 1980.

Former bishops: Mathias C. Lenihan, 1904-30; Edwin V. O'Hara, 1930-39; William J. Condon, 1939-67; Eldon B. Schuster, 1968-77; Thomas J. Murphy, 1978-87.

Green Bay, WI (1868): David A. Zubic, bishop, 2003. Robert F. Morneau, auxiliary.

Former bishops: Joseph Melcher, 1868-73; Francis X. Krautbauer, 1875-85; Frederick X. Katzer, 1886-91; Sebastian G. Messmer, 1892-1903; Joseph J. Fox, 1904-14; Paul P. Rhode, 1915-45; Stanislaus V. Bona, 1945-67; Aloysius J. Wycislo, 1968-83; Adam J. Maida, 1984-90; Robert J. Banks, 1990-2003.

Greensburg, PA (1951): Lawrence E. Brandt, bishop, 2004.

Former bishops: Hugh L. Lamb, 1951-59; Willam G. Connare, 1960-87; Anthony G. Bosco, 1987-2004.

Harrisburg, PA (1868): Kevin C. Rhoades, bishop, 2004.

Former bishops: Jeremiah F. Shanahan, 1868-86; Thomas McGovern, 1888-98; John W. Shanahan, 1899-1916; Philip R. McDevitt, 1916-35; George L. Leech, 1935-71; Joseph T. Daley, 1971-83; William H. Keeler, 1984-89; Nicholas C. Dattilo, 1990-2004.

Hartford,* CT (1843; archdiocese, 1953): Henry J. Mansell, archbishop, 2003. Peter A. Rosazza, Christie A. Macaluso, auxiliaries.

Former ordinaries: William Tyler, 1844-49; Bernard O'Reilly, 1850-56; F. P. MacFarland, 1858-74; Thomas Galberry, O.S.A., 1876-78; Lawrence S. McMahon, 1879-93; Michael Tierney, 1894-1908; John J. Nilan, 1910-34; Maurice F. McAuliffe, 1934-44; Henry J. O'Brien, 1945-68, first archbishop; John F. Whealon, 1969-91; Daniel A. Cronin, 1991-2003.

Helena, MT (1884): George L. Thomas, bishop, 2004.

Former bishops: John B. Brondel, 1884-1903; John P. Carroll, 1904-25; George J. Finnigan, C.S.C., 1927-32; Ralph L. Hayes, 1933-35; Joseph M. Gilmore, 1936-62; Raymond Hunthausen, 1962-75; Elden F. Curtiss, 1976-93; Alexander J. Brunett, 1994-97; Robert C. Morlino, 1999-2003.

Honolulu, HI (1941): Clarence L. Silva, bishop, 2005.

Former bishops: James J. Sweeney, 1941-68; John J. Scanlan, 1968-81; Joseph A. Ferrario, 1982-93; Francis X. DiLorenzo (apostolic administrator, 1993), 1994-2004.

Houma-Thibodaux, LA (1977): Sam G. Jacobs, 2003.

Former bishop: Warren L. Boudreaux, 1977-92; C. Michael Jarrell, 1993-2002.

Indianapolis,* IN (1834; archdiocese, 1944): Daniel M. Buechlein, O.S.B., archbishop, 1992.

Established at Vincennes, transferred, 1898.

Former ordinaries: Simon G. Bruté, 1834-39; Celestine de la Hailandiere, 1839-47; John S. Bazin, 1847-48; Maurice de St. Palais, 1849-77; Francis S.

Chatard, 1878-1918; Joseph Chartrand, 1918-33; Joseph E. Ritter, 1934-46, first archbishop; Paul C. Schulte, 1946-70; George J. Biskup, 1970-79; Edward T. O'Meara, 1980-92.

Jackson, MS (1837): Joseph Latino, bishop, 2003.

Established at Natchez, title changed to Natchez-Jackson, 1956; transferred to Jackson, 1977 (Natchez made titular see).

Former bishops: John J. Chanche, S.S., 1841-52; James Van de Velde, S.J., 1853-55; William H. Elder, 1857-80; Francis A. Janssens, 1881-88; Thomas Heslin, 1889-1911; John E. Gunn, S.M., 1911-24; Richard O. Gerow, 1924-67; Joseph B. Brunini, 1968-84; William R. Houck, 1984-2003.

Jefferson City, MO (1956): John R. Gaydos, bishop, 1997.

Former bishops: Joseph Marling, C.Pp.S., 1956-69; Michael F. McAuliffe, 1969-97.

Joliet, IL (1948): James Peter Sartain, bishop, 2006. Former bishops: Martin D. McNamara, 1949-66; Romeo Blanchette, 1966-79; Joseph L. Imesch, 1979-2006.

Juneau, AK (1951): Michael W. Warfel, bishop, 1996.

Former bishops: Dermot O'Flanagan, 1951-68; Joseph T. Ryan, administrator, 1968-71; Francis T. Hurley, 1971-76, administrator, 1976-79; Michael H. Kenny, 1979-95.

Kalamazoo, MI (1971): James A. Murray, bishop, 1997.

Former bishop: Paul V. Donovan, 1971-94; Alfred J. Markiewicz, 1995-97.

Kansas City,* KS (1877; archdiocese, 1952): Joseph F. Naumann, archbishop, 2005.

Established as vicariate apostolic, 1850, became Diocese of Leavenworth, 1877, transferred to Kansas City, 1947.

Former ordinaries: J. B. Miege, vicar apostolic, 1851-74; Louis M. Fink, O.S.B., vicar apostolic, 1874-77, first bishop, 1877-1904; Thomas F. Lillis, 1904-10; John Ward, 1910-29; Francis Johannes, 1929-37; Paul C. Schulte, 1937-46; George J. Donnelly, 1946-50; Edward Hunkeler, 1951-69, first archbishop; Ignatius J. Strecker, 1969-93; James P. Keleher, 1993-2005.

Kansas City-St. Joseph, MO (Kansas City, 1880, St. Joseph, 1868, united 1956): Robert W. Finn, bishop, 2005.

Former bishops: John J. Hogan, 1880-1913; Thomas F. Lillis, 1913-38; Edwin V. O'Hara, 1939-56; John P. Cody, 1956-61; Charles H. Helmsing, 1962-77; John J. Sullivan, 1977-93; Raymond J. Boland, 1993-2005.

Former bishops (St. Joseph): John J. Hogan, 1868-80, administrator, 1880-93; Maurice F. Burke, 1893-1923; Francis Gilfillan, 1923-33; Charles H. Le Blond, 1933-56.

Knoxville, TN (1988): Joseph E. Kurtz, 1999.

Former bishops: Anthony J. O'Connell, bishop, 1988-98.

La Crosse, WI (1868): Jerome E. Listecki, bishop, 2004.

Former bishops: Michael Heiss, 1868-80; Kilian C. Flasch, 1881-91; James Schwebach, 1892-1921; Alexander J. McGavick, 1921-48; John P. Treacy, 1948-64; Frederick W. Freking, 1965-83; John J. Paul, 1983-94; Raymond L. Burke, 1995-2003.

Lafayette, IN (1944): William L. Higi, bishop, 1984.

Former bishops: John G. Bennett, 1944-57; John J. Carberry, 1957-65; Raymond J. Gallagher, 1965-82; George A. Fulcher, 1983-84.

Lafayette, LA (1918): C. Michael Jarrell, bishop, 2002.

Former bishops: Jules B. Jeanmard, 1918-56; Maurice Schexnayder, 1956-72; Gerard L. Frey, 1973-89; Harry J. Flynn, 1989-94; Edward J. O'Donnell, 1994-2002.

Lake Charles, LA (1980): vacant.

Former bishop: Jude Speyrer, 1980-2000; Edward Braxton, 2000-2005.

Lansing, MI (1937): Carl F. Mengeling, bishop, 1995; installed 1996.

Former bishops: Joseph H. Albers, 1937-65; Alexander Zaleski, 1965-75; Kenneth J. Povish, 1975-95.

Laredo, TX (2000): James A. Tamayo, bishop, 2000.

Las Cruces, NM (1982): Ricardo Ramirez, C.S.B., bishop, 1982.

Las Vegas, NV (1995): Joseph Pepe, 2001.

Formerly Reno-Las Vegas, 1976; made separate diocese 1995.

Former bishops: Daniel F. Walsh, 1995-2000.

Lexington, KY (1988): Ronald William Gainer, bishop, 2002.

Former bishops: James Kendrick Williams, 1988-2002.

Lincoln, NE (1887): Fabian W. Bruskewitz, bishop, 1992.

Former bishops: Thomas Bonacum, 1887-1911; J. Henry Tihen, 1911-17; Charles J. O'Reilly, 1918-23; Francis J. Beckman, 1924-30; Louis B. Kucera, 1930-57; James V. Casey, 1957-67; Glennon P. Flavin, 1967-92.

Little Rock, AR (1843): vacant.

Former bishops: Andrew Byrne, 1844-62; Edward Fitzgerald, 1867-1907; John Morris, 1907-46; Albert L. Fletcher, 1946-72; Andrew J. McDonald, 1972-2000; James Peter Sartain, 2000-2006.

Los Angeles,* CA (1840; archdiocese, 1936): Cardinal Roger M. Mahony, archbishop, 1985. Thomas J. Curry, Gerald E. Wilkerson, Gabino Zavala, Edward William Clark, Oscar Azarcon Solis, Alexander Salazar, auxiliaries.

Founded as diocese of Two Californias, 1840; became Monterey diocese, 1850; Baja California detached from Monterey diocese, 1852; title changed to Monterey-Los Angeles, 1859, Los Angeles-San Diego, 1922; became archdiocese under present title, 1936 (San Diego became separate see).

Former ordinaries: Francisco Garcia Diego y Moreno, O.F.M., 1840-46; Joseph S. Alemany, O.P., 1850-53; Thaddeus Amat, C.M., 1854-78; Francis Mora, 1878-96; George T. Montgomery, 1896-1903; Thomas J. Conaty, 1903-15; John J. Cantwell, 1917-47, first archbishop; Cardinal James McIntyre, 1948-70; Cardinal Timothy Manning, 1970-85.

Louisville,* KY (1808; archdiocese, 1937): Thomas C. Kelly, O.P., archbishop, 1982.

Established at Bardstown, transferred, 1841.

Former ordinaries: Benedict J. Flaget, S.S., 1810-32; John B. David, S.S., 1832-33; Benedict J. Flaget, S.S., 1833-50; Martin J. Spalding, 1850-64; Peter J. Lavialle, 1865-67; William G. McCloskey, 1868-1909;

Denis O'Donaghue, 1910-24; John A. Floersh, 1924-67, first archbishop; Thomas J. McDonough, 1967-81.

Lubbock, TX (1983): Placido Rodriguez, C.M.F., bishop, 1994.

Former bishop: Michael J. Sheehan, 1983-93.

Madison, WI (1946): Robert C. Morlino, bishop, 2003.

Former bishops: William P. O'Connor, 1946-67; Cletus F. O'Donnell, 1967-92; William H. Bullock, 1993-2003.

Manchester, NH (1884): John B. McCormack, bishop, 1998. Francis J. Christian, auxiliary.

Former bishops: Denis M. Bradley, 1884-1903; John B. Delany, 1904-06; George A. Guertin, 1907-32; John B. Peterson, 1932-44; Matthew F. Brady, 1944-59; Ernest J. Primeau, 1960-74; Odore J. Gendron, 1975-90; Leo E. O'Neil, 1990-97.

Marquette, MI (1857): Alexander K. Sample, bishop, 2005.

Founded as Sault Ste. Marie and Marquette; changed to Marquette, 1937.

Former bishops: Frederic Baraga, 1857-68; Ignatius Mrak, 1869-78; John Vertin, 1879-99; Frederick Eis, 1899-1922; Paul J. Nussbaum, C.P., 1922-35; Joseph C. Plagens, 1935-40; Francis Magner, 1941-47; Thomas L. Noa, 1947-68; Charles A. Salatka, 1968-77; Mark F. Schmitt, 1978-92; James H. Garland, 1992-2005.

Memphis, TN (1970): J. Terry Steib, S.V.D., bishop, 1993.

Former bishops: Carroll T. Dozier, 1971-82; J. Francis Stafford, 1982-86; Daniel M. Buechlein, O.S.B.,1987-92.

Metuchen, NJ (1981): Paul G. Bootkoski, bishop, 2002.

Former bishops: Theodore E. McCarrick, 1981-86; Edward T. Hughes, 1987-97; Vincent DePaul Breen, 1997-2002.

Miami,* FL (1958; archdiocese, 1968): John C. Favalora, archbishop, 1994. Felipe de Jesús Estevez, John Gerard Noonan, auxiliaries.

Former ordinaries: Coleman F. Carroll, 1958-77, first archbishop; Edward A. McCarthy, 1977-94.

Milwaukee,* WI (1843; archdiocese, 1875): Timothy M. Dolan, archbishop, 2002. Richard J. Sklba, auxiliary.

Former ordinaries: John M. Henni, 1844-81, first archbishop; Michael Heiss, 1881-90; Frederick X. Katzer, 1891-1903; Sebastian G. Messmer, 1903-30; Samuel A. Stritch, 1930-39; Moses E. Kiley, 1940-53; Albert G. Meyer, 1953-58; William E. Cousins, 1959-77; Rembert G. Weakland, O.S.B., 1977-2002.

Mobile,* AL (1829; archdiocese, 1980): Oscar H. Lipscomb, first archbishop, 1980.

Founded as Mobile, 1829, title changed to Mobile-Birmingham, 1954; redesignated Mobile, 1969.

Former bishops: Michael Portier, 1829-59; John Quinlan, 1859-83; Dominic Manucy, 1884; Jeremiah O'Sullivan, 1885-96; Edward P. Allen, 1897-1926; Thomas J. Toolen, 1927-69; John L. May, 1969-80.

Monterey in California (1967): Sylvester D. Ryan, bishop, 1992.

Formerly Monterey-Fresno, 1922. (Originally established in 1850, see Los Angeles listing.)

Former bishops (Monterey-Fresno): John J.

Cantwell, administrator, 1922-24; John B. MacGinley, first bishop, 1924-32; Philip G. Sher, 1933-53; Aloysius J. Willinger, 1953-67.

Former bishops (Monterey): Harry A. Clinch, 1967-82; Thaddeus A. Shubsda, 1982-91.

Nashville, TN (1837): David R. Choby, bishop, 2005.

Former bishops: Richard P. Miles, O.P., 1838-60; James Whelan, O.P., 1860-64; Patrick A. Feehan, 1865-80; Joseph Rademacher, 1883-93; Thomas S. Byrne, 1894-1923; Alphonse J. Smith, 1924-35; William L. Adrian, 1936-69; Joseph A. Durick, 1969-75; James D. Niedergeses, 1975-92; Edward U. Kmiec, 1992-2004.

Newark,* NJ (1853; archdiocese, 1937): John J. Myers, 2001. Edgar M. da Cunha, Thomas A. Donato, John W. Flesey, auxiliaries.

Former ordinaries: James R. Bayley, 1853-72; Michael A. Corrigan, 1873-80; Winand M. Wigger, 1881-1901; John J. O'Connor, 1901-27; Thomas J. Walsh, 1928-52, first archbishop; Thomas A. Boland, 1953-74; Peter L. Gerety, 1974-86; Theodore E. McCarrick, 1986-2000.

New Orleans,* LA (1793; archdiocese, 1850): Alfred Hughes, 2002. Dominic Carmon, S.V.D., Roger Paul Morin, auxiliaries.

Former ordinaries: Luis Penalver y Cardenas, 1793-1801; John Carroll, administrator, 1805-15; W. Louis Dubourg, S.S., 1815-25; Joseph Rosati, C.M., administrator, 1826-29; Leo De Neckere, C.M., 1829-33; Anthony Blanc, 1835-60, first archbishop; Jean Marie Odin, C.M., 1861-70; Napoleon J. Perche, 1870-83; Francis X. Leray, 1883-87; Francis A. Janssens, 1888-97; Placide L. Chapelle, 1897-1905; James H. Blenk, S.M., 1906-17; John W. Shaw, 1918-34; Joseph F. Rummel, 1935-64; John P. Cody, 1964-65; Philip M. Hannan, 1965-88; Francis B. Schulte, 1988-2002.

Newton, MA (Melkite) (1966; eparchy, 1976): Cyrille Salim Bustros, S.M.S.P., eparch, 2004.

Former ordinaries: Justin Najmy, exarch, 1966-68; Joseph Tawil, exarch, 1969-76, first eparch, 1976-89; Ignatius Ghattas, B.S.O., 1990-92; John A. Elya, B.S.O., 1993-2004.

New Ulm, MN (1957): John Clayton Nienstedt, bishop, 2001.

Former bishop: Alphonse J. Schladweiler, 1958-75; Raymond A. Lucker, 1975-2000.

New York,* NY (1808; archdiocese, 1850): Cardinal Edward M. Egan, archbishop, 2000. Robert A. Brucato, Robert J. Iriondo, Dominick J. Lagonegro, Gerald T. Walsh, Dennis J. Sullivan, auxiliaries.

Former ordinaries: Richard L. Concanen, O.P., 1808-10; John Connolly, O.P., 1814-25; John Dubois, S.S., 1826-42; John J. Hughes, 1842-64, first archbishop; Cardinal John McCloskey, 1864-85; Michael A. Corrigan, 1885-1902; Cardinal John Farley, 1902-18; Cardinal Patrick Hayes, 1919-38; Cardinal Francis Spellman, 1939-67; Cardinal Terence J. Cooke, 1968-83; Cardinal John J. O'Connor, 1984-2000.

Norwich, CT (1953): Michael R. Cote, bishop, 2003.

Former bishops: Bernard J. Flanagan, 1953-59; Vincent J. Hines, 1960-75; Daniel P. Reilly, 1975-94;

Daniel A. Hart, 1995-2003.

Oakland, CA (1962): Allen H. Vigneron, bishop, 2003.

Former bishop: Floyd L. Begin, 1962-77; John S. Cummins, 1977-2003.

Ogdensburg, NY (1872): Robert Joseph Cunningham, bishop, 2004.

Former bishops: Edgar P. Wadhams, 1872-91; Henry Gabriels, 1892-1921; Joseph H. Conroy, 1921-39; Francis J. Monaghan, 1939-42; Bryan J. McEntegart, 1943-53; Walter P. Kellenberg, 1954-57; James J. Navagh, 1957-63; Leo R. Smith, 1963; Thomas A. Donnellan, 1964-68; Stanislaus J. Brzana, 1968-93; Paul S. Loverde, 1993-99; Gerald M. Barbarito, 1999-2003.

Oklahoma City,* OK (1905; archdiocese, 1972): Eusebius J. Beltran, archbishop, 1993.

Former ordinaries: Theophile Meerschaert, 1905-24; Francis C. Kelley, 1924-48; Eugene J. McGuinness, 1948-57; Victor J. Reed, 1958-71; John R. Quinn, 1971-77, first archbishop; Charles A. Salatka, 1977-92.

Omaha,* NE (1885; archdiocese, 1945): Elden F. Curtiss, archbishop, 1993.

Former ordinaries: James O'Gorman, O.C.S.O., 1859-74, vicar apostolic; James O'Connor, vicar apostolic, 1876-85, first bishop, 1885-90; Richard Scannell, 1891-1916; Jeremiah J. Harty, 1916-27; Francis Beckman, administrator, 1926-28; Joseph F. Rummel, 1928-35; James H. Ryan, 1935-47, first archbishop; Gerald T. Bergan, 1948-69; Daniel E. Sheehan, 1969-93.

Orange, CA (1976): Tod D. Brown, bishop, 1998; Jaime Soto, Dominic Mai Luong, auxiliaries.

Former bishop: William R. Johnson, 1976-86; Norman F. McFarland, 1986-98.

Orlando, FL (1968): Thomas G. Wenski, bishop, 2005.

Former bishops: William Borders, 1968-74; Thomas J. Grady, 1974-89; Norbert M. Dorsey, C.P., 1990-2005.

Our Lady of Deliverance of Newark (for Syrian-rite Catholics of the U.S. and Canada, 1995): Joseph Younan, bishop, 1996.

Our Lady of Lebanon of Los Angeles, CA (Maronite) (1994): Robert J. Shaheen, 2000.

Former eparch: John G. Chedid, 1994-2000.

Owensboro, KY (1937): John J. McRaith, bishop, 1982.

Former bishops: Francis R. Cotton, 1938-60; Henry J. Soenneker, 1961-82.

Palm Beach, FL (1984): Gerald Michael Barbarito, 2003.

Former bishop: Thomas V. Daily, 1984-90; J. Keith Symons, 1990-98; Anthony J. O'Connell, 1998-2002; Sean O'Malley, O.F.M. Cap., 2002-2003.

Parma, OH (Byzantine, Ruthenian) (1969): John Kudrick, bishop, 2002.

Former bishops: Emil Mihalik, 1969-84; Andrew Pataki, 1984-95; Basil Schott, O.F.M., 1996-2002.

Passaic, NJ (Byzantine, Ruthenian) (1963): Andrew Pataki, eparch, 1996.

Former bishops: Stephen Kocisko, 1963-68; Michael J. Dudick, 1968-95.

Paterson, NJ (1937): Arthur J. Serratelli, bishop, 2004.

Former bishops: Thomas H. McLaughlin, 1937-47; Thomas A. Boland, 1947-52; James A. McNulty, 1953-63; James J. Navagh, 1963-65; Lawrence B. Casey, 1966-77; Frank J. Rodimer, 1978-2004.

Pensacola-Tallahassee, FL (1975): John H.Ricard, S.S.J., bishop, 1997.

Former bishops: Rene H. Gracida, 1975-83; J. Keith Symons, 1983-90; John M. Smith, 1991-95.

Peoria, IL (1877): Daniel R. Jenky, C.S.C., bishop, 2002.

Former bishops: John L. Spalding, 1877-1908; Edmund M. Dunne, 1909-29; Joseph H. Schlarman, 1930-51; William E. Cousins, 1952-58; John B. Franz, 1959-71; Edward W. O'Rourke, 1971-90; John J. Myers, 1990-2001.

Philadelphia,* PA (1808; archdiocese, 1875): Cardinal Justin F. Rigali, archbishop, 2003. Robert P. Maginnis, Joseph Robert Cistone, Joseph Patrick McFadden, Daniel E. Thomas, auxiliaries.

Former ordinaries: Michael Egan, O.F.M., 1810-14; Henry Conwell, 1820-42; Francis P. Kenrick, 1842-51; John N. Neumann, C.SS.R., 1852-60; James F. Wood, 1860-83, first archbishop; Patrick J. Ryan, 1884-1911; Edmond F. Prendergast, 1911-18; Cardinal Dennis Dougherty, 1918-51; Cardinal John O'Hara, C.S.C., 1951-60; Cardinal John Krol, 1961-88; Cardinal Anthony J. Bevilacqua, 1988-2003.

Philadelphia,* PA (Byzantine, Ukrainian) (1924; metropolitan, 1958): Stephen Soroka, archbishop, 2001. John Bura, auxiliary.

Former ordinaries: Stephen Ortynsky, O.S.B.M., 1907-16; Constantine Bohachevsky, 1924-61; Ambrose Senyshyn, O.S.B.M., 1961-76; Joseph Schmondiuk, 1977-78; Myroslav J. Lubachivsky, 1979-80, apostolic administrator, 1980-81; Stephen Sulyk, 1981-2000.

Phoenix, AZ (1969): Thomas J. Olmsted, bishop, 2003.

Former bishops: Edward A. McCarthy, 1969-76; James S. Rausch, 1977-81; Thomas J. O'Brien, 1982-2003.

Pittsburgh,* PA (Byzantine, Ruthenian) (1924; metropolitan, 1969): Basil Schott, O.F.M., archbishop, 2002.

Former ordinaries: Basil Takach 1924-48; Daniel Ivancho, 1948-54; Nicholas T. Elko, 1955-67; Stephen J. Kocisko, 1968-91, first metropolitan; Thomas V. Dolinay, 1991-93; Judson M. Procyk, 1995-2001.

Pittsburgh, PA (1843): vacant. Paul J. Bradley, auxiliary.

Former bishops: Michael O'Connor, 1843-53, 1854-60; Michael Domenec, C.M., 1860-76; J. Tuigg, 1876-89; Richard Phelan, 1889-1904; J.F. Regis Canevin, 1904-20; Hugh C. Boyle, 1921-50; John F. Dearden, 1950-58; John J. Wright, 1959-69; Vincent M. Leonard, 1969-83; Anthony J. Bevilacqua, 1983-88; Donald W. Wuerl, 1988-2006.

Portland, ME (1853): Richard Joseph Malone, bishop, 2004.

Former bishops: David W. Bacon, 1855-74; James A. Healy, 1875-1900; William H. O'Connell, 1901-06; Louis S. Walsh, 1906-24; John G. Murray, 1925-31; Joseph E. McCarthy, 1932-55; Daniel J. Feeney, 1955-69; Peter L. Gerety, 1969-74; Edward C. O'Leary, 1974-88, Joseph J. Gerry, O.S.B., 1989-2004.

Portland,* OR (1846): John G. Vlazny, archbishop,

1997. Kenneth D. Steiner, auxiliary.

Established as Oregon City, name changed, 1928.

Former ordinaries: Francis N. Blanchet, 1846-80 vicar apostolic, first archbishop; Charles J. Seghers, 1880-84; William H. Gross, C.SS.R., 1885-98; Alexander Christie, 1899-1925; Edward D. Howard, 1926-66; Robert J. Dwyer, 1966-74; Cornelius M. Power, 1974-86; William J. Levada, 1986-95; Francis E. George, 1996-97.

Providence, RI (1872): Thomas J. Tobin, bishop, 2005.

Former bishops: Thomas F. Hendricken, 1872-86; Matthew Harkins, 1887-1921; William A. Hickey, 1921-33; Francis P. Keough, 1934-47; Russell J. McVinney, 1948-71; Louis E. Gelineau, 1972-97; Robert E. Mulvee, 1997-2005.

Pueblo, CO (1941): Arthur N. Tafoya, bishop, 1980. Former bishops: Joseph C. Willging, 1942-59; Charles A. Buswell, 1959-79.

Raleigh, NC (1924): Michael F. Burbidge, bishop, 2006.

Former bishops: William J. Hafey, 1925-37; Eugene J. McGuinness, 1937-44; Vincent S. Waters, 1945-75; F. Joseph Gossman, 1975-2006.

Rapid City, SD (1902): Blase Cupich, bishop, 1998. Established at Lead, transferred, 1930.

Former bishops: John Stariha, 1902-09; Joseph F. Busch, 1910-15; John J. Lawler, 1916-48; William T. McCarty, C.SS.R., 1948-69; Harold J. Dimmerling, 1969-87; Charles J. Chaput, O.F.M., Cap., 1988-97.

Reno, NV (1931): Randolph R. Calvo, bishop, 2005. Established at Reno, 1931; title changed to Reno-Las Vegas, 1976, redesignated Reno, 1995, when Las Vegas was made a separate diocese.

Former bishops (Reno/Reno-Las Vegas): Thomas K. Gorman, 1931-52; Robert J. Dwyer, 1952-66; Joseph Green, 1967-74; Norman F. McFarland, 1976-86; Daniel F. Walsh, 1987-95; Phillip F. Straling, 1995-2005.

Richmond, VA (1820): Francis X. DiLorenzo, 2004. Former bishops: Patrick Kelly, 1820-22; Ambrose Marechal, S.S., administrator, 1822-28; James Whitfield, administrator, 1828-34; Samuel Eccleston, S.S., administrator, 1834-40; Richard V. Whelan, 1841-50; John McGill, 1850-72; James Gibbons, 1872-77; John J. Keane, 1878-88; Augustine Van de Vyver, 1889-1911; Denis J. O'Connell, 1912-26; Andrew J. Brennan, 1926-45; Peter L. Ireton, 1945-58; John J. Russell, 1958-73; Walter F. Sullivan, 1974-2003.

Rochester, NY (1868): Matthew H. Clark, bishop, 1979.

Former bishops: Bernard J. McQuaid, 1868-1909; Thomas F. Hickey, 1909-28; John F. O'Hern, 1929-33; Edward F. Mooney, 1933-37; James E. Kearney, 1937-66; Fulton J. Sheen, 1966-69; Joseph L. Hogan, 1969-78.

Rockford, IL (1908): Thomas G. Doran, bishop, 1994.

Former bishops: Peter J. Muldoon, 1908-27; Edward F. Hoban, 1928-42; John J. Boylan, 1943-53; Raymond P. Hillinger, 1953-56; Loras T. Lane, 1956-68; Arthur J. O'Neill, 1968-94.

Rockville Centre, NY (1957): William Francis Murphy, bishop, 2001. John C. Dunne, Emil A. Wcela, Paul H. Walsh, auxiliaries.

Former bishop: Walter P. Kellenberg, 1957-76; John R. McGann, 1976-2000; James McHugh, 2000.

Sacramento, CA (1886): William K. Weigand, bishop, 1993, installed, 1994. Richard J. Garcia, auxiliary.

Former bishops: Patrick Manogue, 1886-95; Thomas Grace, 1896-1921; Patrick J. Keane, 1922-28; Robert J. Armstrong, 1929-57; Joseph T. McGucken, 1957-62; Alden J. Bell, 1962-79; Francis A. Quinn, 1979-93.

Saginaw, MI (1938): Robert J. Carlson, bishop, 2004.

Former bishops: William F. Murphy, 1938-50; Stephen S. Woznicki, 1950-68; Francis F. Reh, 1969-80; Kenneth E. Untener, 1980-2004.

St. Augustine, FL (1870): Victor Benito Galeone, bishop, 2001.

Former bishops: Augustin Verot, S.S., 1870-76; John Moore, 1877-1901; William J. Kenny, 1902-13; Michael J. Curley, 1914-21; Patrick J. Barry, 1922-40; Joseph P. Hurley, 1940-67; Paul F. Tanner, 1968-79; John J. Snyder, 1979-2000.

St. Cloud, MN (1889): John F. Kinney, bishop, 1995. Former bishops: Otto Zardetti, 1889-94; Martin Marty, O.S.B., 1895-96; James Trobec, 1897-1914; Joseph F. Busch, 1915-53; Peter Bartholome, 1953-68; George H. Speltz, 1968-87; Jerome Hanus, O.S.B.,1987-94.

St. George's in Canton, OH (Byzantine, Romanian) (1982; eparchy, 1987): John Michael Botean, bishop, 1996.

Former bishop: Vasile Louis Puscas, 1983-93.

St. Josaphat in Parma, OH (Byzantine, Ukrainians) (1983): Robert M. Moskal, bishop, 1984.

St. Louis,* MO (1826; archdiocese, 1847): Raymond L. Burke, archbishop, 2003. Robert J. Hermann, auxiliary.

Former ordinaries: Joseph Rosati, C.M., 1827-43; Peter R. Kenrick, 1843-95, first archbishop; John J. Kain, 1895-1903; Cardinal John Glennon, 1903-46; Cardinal Joseph Ritter, 1946-67; Cardinal John J. Carberry, 1968-79; John L. May, 1980-92; Justin F. Rigali, 1994-2003.

St. Maron, Brooklyn, NY (Maronite) (1966; diocese, 1971): Gregory John Mansour, eparch, 2004.

Established at Detroit, transferred to Brooklyn, 1977.

Former eparchs: Francis Zayek, exarch 1966-72, first eparch 1972-97; Hector Y. Doueihi, 1997-2004.

St. Nicholas in Chicago (Byzantine Eparchy of St. Nicholas of the Ukrainians) (1961): Richard Stephen Seminack, 2003.

Former bishops: Jaroslav Gabro, 1961-80; Innocent H. Lotocky, O.S.B.M., 1981-93; Michael Wiwchar, C.SS.R., 1993-2000.

St. Paul and Minneapolis,* MN (1850; archdiocese, 1888): Harry J. Flynn, archbishop, 1995. Richard Edmund Pates, auxiliary.

Former ordinaries: Joseph Crétin, 1851-57; Thomas L. Grace, O.P., 1859-84; John Ireland, 1884-1918, first archbishop; Austin Dowling, 1919-30; John G. Murray, 1931-56; William O. Brady, 1956-61; Leo Binz, 1962-75; John R. Roach, 1975-95.

St. Peter the Apostle of San Diego (Chaldean) (2002, eparchy): Sarhad Jammo, first eparch, 2002.

St. Petersburg, FL (1968): Robert N. Lynch, bishop, 1996.

Former bishops: Charles McLaughlin, 1968-78; W. Thomas Larkin, 1979-88; John C. Favalora, 1989-94.

St. Thomas the Apostle of Detroit (Chaldean) (1982; eparchy, 1985): Ibrahim N. Ibrahim, exarch, 1982; first eparch, 1985.

St. Thomas of the Syro-Malabars of Chicago (Syro-Malabars) (2001, eparchy): Jacob Angadiath, first eparch, 2001.

Salina, KS (1887): Paul S. Coakley, bishop, 2004. Established at Concordia, transferred, 1944.

Former bishops: Richard Scannell, 1887-91; John J. Hennessy, administrator, 1891-98; John F. Cunningham, 1898-1919; Francis J. Tief, 1921-38; Frank A. Thill, 1938-57; Frederick W. Freking, 1957-64; Cyril J. Vogel, 1965-79; Daniel W. Kucera, O.S.B., 1980-84; George K. Fitzsimons, 1984-2004.

Salt Lake City, UT (1891): vacant.

Former bishops: Lawrence Scanlan, 1891-1915; Joseph S. Glass, C.M., 1915-26; John J. Mitty, 1926-32; James E. Kearney, 1932-37; Duane G. Hunt, 1937-60; J. Lennox Federal, 1960-80; William K. Weigand, 1980-93; George H. Niederauer, 1995-2005.

San Angelo, TX (1961): Michael D. Pfeifer, O.M.I., bishop, 1985.

Former bishops: Thomas J. Drury, 1962-65; Thomas Tschoepe, 1966-69; Stephen A. Leven, 1969-79; Joseph A. Fiorenza, 1979-84.

San Antonio,* TX (1874; archdiocese, 1926): José H. Gomez, archbishop, 2004. Patrick J. Zurek, auxiliary.

Former ordinaries: Anthony D. Pellicer, 1874-80; John C. Neraz, 1881-94; John A. Forest, 1895-1911; John W. Shaw, 1911-18; Arthur Jerome Drossaerts, 1918-40, first archbishop; Robert E. Lucey, 1941-69; Francis Furey, 1969-79; Patrick F. Flores, 1979-2004.

San Bernardino, CA (1978): Gerald R. Barnes, bishop, 1995. Rutilio J. Del Riego, auxiliaries.

Former bishop: Phillip F. Straling, 1978-95.

San Diego, CA (1936): Robert H. Brom, bishop, 1990. Gilbert Espinoza Chavez, Salvatore Cordileone, auxiliaries.

Former bishops: Charles F. Buddy, 1936-66; Francis J. Furey, 1966-69; Leo T. Maher, 1969-90.

San Francisco,* CA (1853): George H. Niederauer, archbishop, 2005. John C. Wester, Ignatius Wang, auxiliaries.

Former ordinaries: Joseph S. Alemany, O.P., 1853-84; Patrick W. Riordan, 1884-1914; Edward J. Hanna, 1915-35; John Mitty, 1935-61; Joseph T. McGucken, 1962-77; John R. Quinn, 1977-95; William J. Levada, 1995-2005.

San Jose, CA (1981): Patrick J. McGrath, bishop, 1999.

Former ordinaries: R. Pierre DuMaine, 1981-98.

Santa Fe*, NM (1850; archdiocese, 1875): Michael J. Sheehan, archbishop, 1993.

Former ordinaries: John B. Lamy, 1850-85; first archbishop; John B. Salpointe, 1885-94; Placide L. Chapelle, 1894-97; Peter Bourgade, 1899-1908; John B. Pitaval, 1909-18; Albert T. Daeger, O.F.M., 1919-32; Rudolph A. Gerken, 1933-43; Edwin V. Byrne, 1943-63; James P. Davis, 1964-74; Robert F. Sanchez, 1974-93.

Santa Rosa, CA (1962): Daniel Walsh, 2000.

Former bishops: Leo T. Maher, 1962-69; Mark J. Hurley, 1969-86; John T. Steinbock, 1987-91; G. Patrick Ziemann, 1992-99.

Savannah, GA (1850): John Kevin Boland, bishop,

1995.

Former bishops: Francis X. Gartland, 1850-54; John Barry, 1857-59; Augustin Verot, S.S., 1861-70; Ignatius Persico, O.F.M. Cap., 1870-72; William H. Gross, C.SS.R., 1873-85; Thomas A. Becker, 1886-99; Benjamin J. Keiley, 1900-22; Michael Keyes, S.M., 1922-35; Gerald P. O'Hara, 1935-59; Thomas J. McDonough, 1960-67; Gerard L. Frey, 1967-72; Raymond W. Lessard, 1973-95.

Scranton, PA (1868): Joseph F. Martino, bishop, 2003. John M. Dougherty, auxiliary.

Former bishops: William O'Hara, 1868-99; Michael J. Hoban, 1899-1926; Thomas C. O'Reilly, 1928-38; William J. Hafey, 1938-54; Jerome D. Hannan, 1954-65; J. Carroll McCormick, 1966-83; John J. O'Connor, 1983-84; James C. Timlin, 1984-2003.

Seattle,* WA (1850; archdiocese, 1951): Alexander J. Brunett, archbishop, 1997. Joseph J. Tyson, Eusebio Elizondo, M.Sp.S., auxiliaries.

Established as Nesqually, name changed, 1907.

Former ordinaries; Augustin M. Blanchet, 1850-79; Aegidius Junger, 1879-95; Edward J. O'Dea, 1896-1932; Gerald Shaughnessy, S.M., 1933-50; Thomas A. Connolly, first archbishop, 1950-75; Raymond G. Hunthausen, 1975-91; Thomas J. Murphy, 1991-97.

Shreveport, LA (1986): William B. Friend, bishop, 1986.

Sioux City, IA (1902): Ralph W. Nickless, bishop, 2005.

Former bishops: Philip J. Garrigan, 1902-19; Edmond Heelan, 1919-48; Joseph M. Mueller, 1948-70; Frank H. Greteman, 1970-83; Lawrence D. Soens, 1983-98; Daniel N. DiNardo, 1998-2004.

Sioux Falls, SD (1889): Paul J. Swain, bishop, 2006.

Former bishops: Martin Marty, O.S.B., 1889-94; Thomas O'Gorman, 1896-1921; Bernard J. Mahoney, 1922-39; William O. Brady, 1939-56; Lambert A. Hoch, 1956-78; Paul V. Dudley, 1978-95; Robert J. Carlson, 1995-2004.

Spokane, WA (1913): William S. Skylstad, bishop, 1990.

Former bishops: Augustine F. Schinner, 1914-25; Charles D. White, 1927-55; Bernard J. Topel, 1955-78; Lawrence H. Welsh, 1978-90.

Springfield, IL (1853): George J. Lucas, 1999.

Established at Quincy, transferred to Alton, 1857; transferred to Springfield, 1923.

Former bishops: Henry D. Juncker, 1857-68; Peter J. Baltes, 1870-86; James Ryan, 1888-1923; James A. Griffin, 1924-48; William A. O'Connor, 1949-75; Joseph A. McNicholas, 1975-83; Daniel L. Ryan, bishop, 1984-99.

Springfield, MA (1870): Timothy A. McDonnell, bishop, 2004.

Former bishops: Patrick T. O'Reilly, 1870-92; Thomas D. Beaven, 1892-1920; Thomas M. O'Leary, 1921-49; Christopher J. Weldon, 1950-77; Joseph F. Maguire, 1977-91; John A. Marshall, 1991-94; Thomas L. Dupre, 1995-2004.

Springfield-Cape Girardeau, MO (1956): John J. Leibrecht, bishop, 1984.

Former bishops: Charles Helmsing, 1956-62; Ignatius J. Strecker, 1962-69; William Baum, 1970-73; Bernard F. Law, 1973-84.

Stamford, CT (Byzantine, Ukrainian) (1956): Paul

P. Chomnycky, O.S.B.M., eparch, 2006.

Former eparchs: Ambrose Senyshyn, O.S.B.M., 1956-61; Joseph Schmondiuk, 1961-77; Basil Losten, 1977-2006.

Steubenville, OH (1944): Robert Daniel Conlon, 2002.

Former bishops: John K. Mussio, 1945-77; Albert H. Ottenweller, 1977-92; Gilbert I. Sheldon, 1992-2002.

Stockton, CA (1962): Stephen E. Blaire, bishop, 1999.

Former bishops: Hugh A. Donohoe, 1962-69; Merlin J. Guilfoyle, 1969-79; Roger M. Mahony, 1980-85; Donald W. Montrose, 1986-99.

Superior, WI (1905): Raphael M. Fliss, bishop, 1985.

Former bishops: Augustine F. Schinner, 1905-13; Joseph M. Koudelka, 1913-21; Joseph G. Pinten, 1922-26; Theodore M. Reverman, 1926-41; William P. O'Connor, 1942-46; Albert G. Meyer, 1946-53; Joseph Annabring, 1954-59; George A. Hammes, 1960-85.

Syracuse, NY (1886): James M. Moynihan, bishop, 1995.

Former bishops: Patrick A. Ludden, 1887-1912; John Grimes, 1912-22; Daniel J. Curley, 1923-32; John A. Duffy, 1933-37; Walter A. Foery, 1937-70; David F. Cunningham, 1970-76; Frank J. Harrison, 1976-87; Joseph T. O'Keefe, 1987-95.

Toledo, OH (1910): Leonard P. Blair, bishop, 2003.

Former bishops: Joseph Schrembs, 1911-21; Samuel A. Stritch, 1921-30; Karl J. Alter, 1931-50; George J. Rehring, 1950-67; John A. Donovan, 1967-80; James R. Hoffman, 1980-2003.

Trenton, NJ (1881): John M. Smith, bishop, 1997.

Former bishops: Michael J. O'Farrell, 1881-94; James A. McFaul, 1894-1917; Thomas J. Walsh, 1918-28; John J. McMahon, 1928-32; Moses E. Kiley, 1934-40; William A. Griffin, 1940-50; George W. Ahr, 1950-79; John C. Reiss, 1980 -97.

Tucson, AZ (1897): Gerald F. Kicanas, bishop, 2003.

Former bishops: Peter Bourgade, 1897-99; Henry Granjon, 1900-22; Daniel J. Gercke, 1923-60; Francis J. Green, 1960-81; Manuel D. Moreno, 1982-2003.

Tulsa, OK (1972): Edward J. Slattery, bishop, 1993.

Former bishops: Bernard J. Ganter, 1973-77; Eusebius J. Beltran, 1978-92.

Tyler, TX (1986): Alvaro Corrada del Rio, S.J., 2000.

Former bishop: Charles E. Herzig, 1987-91; Edmond Carmody, 1992-2000.

Van Nuys, CA (Byzantine, Ruthenian) (1981): William C. Skurla, 2002.

Former bishops: Thomas V. Dolinay, 1982-90; George M. Kuzma, 1991-2000.

Venice, FL (1984): John J. Nevins, bishop, 1984; Frank J. Dewane, coadjutor, 2006.

Victoria, TX (1982): David E. Fellhauer, bishop, 1990.

Former bishop: Charles V. Grahmann, 1982-89.

Washington,* DC (1939): Donald W. Wuerl, archbishop, 2005. Kevin J. Farrell, Francisco González Valer, S.F., Martin D. Holley, auxiliaries.

Former ordinaries: Michael J. Curley, 1939-47; Cardinal Patrick O'Boyle, 1948-73; Cardinal William Baum, 1973-80; Cardinal James A. Hickey, 1980-2000; Cardinal Theodore E. McCarrick, 2000-2006.

Wheeling-Charleston, WV (1850): Michael J. Bransfield, bishop, 2004.

Established as Wheeling, name changed, 1974.

Former bishops: Richard V. Whelan, 1850-74; John J. Kain, 1875-93; Patrick J. Donahue, 1894-1922; John J. Swint, 1922-62; Joseph H. Hodges, 1962-85; Francis B. Schulte, 1985-88; Bernard W. Schmitt, 1989-2004.

Wichita, KS (1887): Michael Owen Jackels, bishop, 2005.

Former bishops: John J. Hennessy, 1888-1920; Augustus J. Schwertner, 1921-39; Christian H. Winkelmann, 1940-46; Mark K. Carroll, 1947-67; David M. Maloney, 1967-82; Eugene J. Gerber, 1982-2001; Thomas J. Olmsted, 2001-2003.

Wilmington, DE (1868): Michael A. Saltarelli, bishop, 1995.

Former bishops: Thomas A. Becker, 1868-86; Alfred A. Curtis, 1886-96; John J. Monaghan, 1897-1925; Edmond Fitzmaurice, 1925-60; Michael Hyle, 1960-67; Thomas J. Mardaga, 1968-84; Robert E. Mulvee, 1985-95.

Winona, MN (1889): Bernard J. Harrington, 1998.

Former bishops: Joseph B. Cotter, 1889-1909; Patrick R. Heffron, 1910-27; Francis M. Kelly, 1928-49; Edward A. Fitzgerald, 1949-69; Loras J. Watters, 1969-86; John G. Vlazny, 1987-97.

Worcester, MA (1950): Robert McManus, bishop, 2004.

Former bishops: John J. Wright, 1950-59; Bernard J. Flanagan, 1959-83; Timothy J. Harrington, 1983-94; Daniel P. Reilly, 1994-2004.

Yakima, WA (1951): Carlos A. Sevilla, S.J., bishop, 1996.

Former bishops: Joseph P. Dougherty, 1951-69; Cornelius M. Power, 1969-74; Nicolas E. Walsh, 1974-76; William S. Skylstad, 1977-90; Francis E. George, O.M.I., 1990-96.

Youngstown, OH (1943): vacant.

Former bishops: James A. McFadden, 1943-52; Emmet M. Walsh, 1952-68; James W. Malone, 1968-95; Thomas J. Tobin, 1995-2005.

Apostolic Eparchy for Armenian Catholics in the United States and Canada, New York, NY (1981, eparchy, 2005): Manuel Batakian, exarch, 2000; first eparch, 2005.

Former exarchs: Nerses Mikael Setian, 1981-93; Hovhannes Tertzakian, O.M. Ven., 1995-2000.

Archdiocese for the Military Services, U.S.A., Washington, DC (1957; restructured, 1985): Archbishop Edwin F. O'Brien, military ordinary, 1997. John J. Kaising, Richard Brendan Higgins, Joseph Walter Estabrook, auxiliaries.

Military vicar appointed, 1917; canonically established, 1957, as U.S. Military Vicariate under jurisdiction of New York archbishop; name changed, restructured as independent jurisdiction, 1985.

Former military vicars: Cardinal Patrick Hayes, 1917-38; Cardinal Francis Spellman, 1939-67; Cardinal Terence J. Cooke, 1968-83; Cardinal John J. O'Connor, apostolic administrator, 1984-85.

Former military ordinaries: Archbishop Joseph T. Ryan, 1985-91; Joseph T. Dimino, 1991-97.

(Note: For coverage of **Missionary Bishops,** *see under* **Missionary Activity of the Church in the U.S.**)

CHANCERY OFFICES OF U.S. ARCHDIOCESES AND DIOCESES

A chancery office, under this or another title, is the central administrative office of an archdiocese or diocese. (Archdioceses are indicated by asterisk.)

7417, 71306. (318) 445-2401; www.diocesealex.org.

Allentown, PA: The Chancery Office, P.O. Box F, 18105-1538. (610) 437-0755.

Altoona-Johnstown, PA: The Chancery, 126 Logan Blvd., Hollidaysburg, 16648. (814) 695-5579; www.diocesealtjtn.org.

Amarillo, TX: Pastoral Center, 1800 N. Spring St., P.O. Box 5644, 79117-5644. (806) 383-2243.

Anchorage,* AK: The Chancery Office, 225 Cordova St., 99501. (907) 297-7700; www.archdioceseofanchorage.org.

Arlington, VA: The Chancery Office, Suite 914, 200 N. Glebe Rd., 22203. (703) 841-2500.

Atlanta,* GA: Catholic Center, 680 W. Peachtree St. N.W., 30308. (404) 888-7802; www.archatl.com.

Austin, TX: The Chancery Office, 1600 N. Congress Ave., P.O. Box 13327, 78711. (512) 476-4888; www.austindiocese.org.

Baker, OR: Diocesan Pastoral Office, P.O. Box 5999, Bend, 97708. (541) 388-4004; usersbendnet.com/diocbakr/.

Baltimore,* MD: The Chancery Office, 320 Cathedral St., 21201. (410) 547-5446; www.archbalt.org.

Baton Rouge, LA: Catholic Life Center, P.O. Box 2028, 70821-2028. (225) 387-0561; www.diobr.org.

Beaumont, TX: Diocesan Pastoral Office, 703 Archie St., P.O. Box 3948, 77704-3948. (409) 838-0451.

Belleville, IL: The Chancery, 222 S. Third St., 62220-1985, (618) 277-8181; www.diobelle.org.

Biloxi, MS: Administration Offices, P.O. Box 6489, 39522-6489. (228) 702-2100; www.biloxidiocese.org.

Birmingham, AL: Catholic Life Center, P.O. Box 12047, 35202-2047. (205) 838-8322.

Bismarck, ND: The Chancery Office, 420 Raymond St., Box 1575, 58502-1575. (701) 223-1347.

Boise, ID: The Chancery Office, 303 Federal Way, 83705-5925. (208) 342-1311.

Boston,* MA: The Chancery Office, 2121 Commonwealth Ave., Brighton, 02135. (617) 254-0100; www.rcab.org.

Bridgeport, CT: The Catholic Center, 238 Jewett Ave., 06606-2892. (203) 372-4301.

Brooklyn, NY: The Chancery Office, 75 Greene Ave., P.O. Box C, 11238. (718) 399-5970.

Brownsville, TX: The Catholic Pastoral Center, P.O. Box 2279, 1910 E. Elizabeth St., 78522-2279. (956) 542-2501; www.cdob.org.

Buffalo, NY: The Chancery Office, 795 Main St., 14203. (716) 847-5500; www.buffalodiocese.org.

Burlington, VT: The Chancery Office, P.O. Box 489, Burlington, VT. 05402-0489. (802) 658-6110; www.vermontcatholic.org.

Camden, NJ: Camden Diocesan Center, 631 Market St., P.O. Box 708, 08101. (609) 756-7900.

Charleston, SC: The Chancery Office, 119 Broad St., P.O. Box 818, 29402. (843) 723-3488; www.catholic-doc.org.

Charlotte, NC: The Pastoral Center, P.O. Box 36776, 28236. (704) 370-6299; www.charlottediocese.org.

Cheyenne, WY: The Chancery Office, Box 1468, 82003-0426. (307) 638-1530.

Chicago,* IL: Pastoral Center, P.O. Box 1979,

Albany, NY: Pastoral Center, 40 N. Main Ave., 12203. (518) 453-6611; www.rcda.org.

Alexandria, LA: The Chancery Office, P.O. Box 60690. (312) 751-7999; www.archdiocese-chgo.org.

Cincinnati,* OH: The Chancery Office, 100 E. 8th St. 45202. (513) 421-3131; www.archdiocese-cinti.org.

Cleveland, OH: The Chancery Office, 1027 Superior Ave., 44114. (216) 696-6525; www.cle-dioc.org.

Colorado Springs, CO: The Chancery Office, 29 W. Kiowa, 80903-1498. (719) 636-2345.

Columbus, OH: The Chancery Office, 198 E. Broad St., 43215-3766. (614) 224-2251.

Corpus Christi, TX: The Chancery Office, 620 Lipan St. P.O. Box 2620, 78403-2620. (512) 882-6191; www.diocesecc.org.

Covington, KY: The Catholic Center, P.O. Box 18548, Erlanger, 41018-0548. (859) 283-6200; www.dioofcovky.org.

Crookston, MN: The Chancery Office, 1200 Memorial Dr., P.O. Box 610, 56716. (218) 281-4533; www.crookston.org.

Dallas, TX: The Chancery Office, 3725 Blackburn, P.O. Box 190507, 75219. (214) 528-2240; www.cathdal.org.

Davenport, IA: The Chancery Office, St. Vincent Center, 2706 N. Gaines St., 52804-1998. (319) 324-1911; www.davenportdiocese.org.

Denver,* CO: Catholic Pastoral Center, 1300 South Steele St., 80210. (303) 715-2000; www.archden.org/archden.

Des Moines, IA: The Chancery Office, P.O. Box 1816, 50306. (515) 243-7653; www.dmdiocese.org.

Detroit,* MI: The Chancery Office, 1234 Washington Blvd., 48226. (313) 237-5816.

Dodge City, KS: The Chancery Office, 910 Central Ave., P.O. Box 137, 67801-0137. (316) 227-1500; www.dcdiocese.org.

Dubuque,* IA: The Chancery Office, P.O. Box 479, 52004-0479.   (319)   556-2580; www.archdiocese.dbq.pvt.k12.ia.us.

Duluth, MN: Pastoral Center, 2830 E. 4th St., 55812. (218) 724-9111; www.dioceseduluth.org.

El Paso, TX: The Chancery Office, 499 St. Matthews St., 79907. (915) 595-5000; www.elpasodiocese.org.

Erie, PA: St. Mark Catholic Center, P.O. Box 10397, 16514-0397. (814) 824-1111; www.eriecd.org.

Evansville, IN: The Chancery Office, P.O. Box 4169, 47724-0169. (812) 424-5536; www.evansville-diocese.org.

Fairbanks, AK: The Chancery Office, 1316 Peger Rd., 99709. (907) 474-0753; www.cbna.org.

Fall River, MA: The Chancery Office, Box 2577, 02722. (508) 675-1311.

Fargo, ND: The Chancery Office, 1310 Broadway, Box 1750, 58107. (701) 235-6429; www.fargodiocese.org.

Fort Wayne-South Bend, IN: The Chancery Office, P.O. Box 390, Fort Wayne, 46801. (260) 422-4611; www.diocesefwsb.org.

Fort Worth, TX: Catholic Center, 800 W. Loop 820 South, 76108. (817) 560-3300; www.fwdioc.org.

Fresno, CA: The Chancery Office, 1550 N. Fresno St., 93703-3788. (559) 488-7400.

Gallup, NM: The Chancery Office, 711 S. Puerco Dr., P.O. Box 1338, 87305. (505) 863-4406.

Galveston-Houston, TX: The Chancery Office, P.O. Box 907, 77001. (713) 659-5461.

Gary, IN: The Chancery Office, 9292 Broadway,

Merrillville, 46410. (219) 769-9292; www.chancery@dcgary.org.

Gaylord, MI: Diocesan Pastoral Center, 611 North St., 49735. (517) 732-5147.

Grand Island, NE: The Chancery Office, 311 W. 17th St., P.O. Box 996, 68802. (308) 382-6565.

Grand Rapids, MI: The Chancery Office, 660 Burton St., S.E., 49507. (616) 243-0491; www.dioceseofgrandrapids.org.

Great Falls-Billings, MT: The Chancery Office, P.O. Box 1399, Great Falls, 59401. (406) 727-6683; www.mcn.net/~dioceseofgfb.

Green Bay, WI: The Chancery Office, P.O. Box 23825, 54305-3825. (920) 437-7531; www.gbdioc.org.

Greensburg, PA: The Chancery Office, 723 E. Pittsburgh St., 15601. (724) 837-0901; www.catholicgbg.org.

Harrisburg, PA: The Chancery Office, P.O. Box 2153, 17105-2153. (717) 657-4804; www.hbgdiocese.org.

Hartford,* CT: The Chancery Office, 134 Farmington Ave., 06105-3784. (860) 541-6491; www.archdioceseofhartford.org.

Helena, MT: The Chancery Office, 515 North Ewing, P.O. Box 1729, 59624-1729. (406) 442-5820; www.diocesehelena.org.

Honolulu, HI: The Chancery Office, 1184 Bishop St., 96813. (808) 585-3342; www.catholichawaii.com.

Houma-Thibodaux, LA: The Chancery Office, P.O. Box 505, Schriever, 70395. (504) 868-7720; www.htdiocese.org.

Indianapolis,* IN: The Archbishop Edward T. O'Meara Catholic Center, 1400 N. Meridian St., 46206. (317) 236-1403; www.archindy.org.

Jackson, MS: The Chancery Office, 237 E. Amite St., P.O. Box 2248, 39225-2248. (601) 969-1880; www.jacksondiocese.org.

Jefferson City, MO: Chancery Office, 605 Clark Ave., P.O. Box 417, 65102-0417. (573) 635-9127; www.diojeffcity.org.

Joliet, IL: The Chancery Office, 425 Summit St., 60435. (815) 722-6606.

Juneau, AK: The Chancery Office, 419 6th St., No. 200, 99801. (907) 586-2227; www.juneau-diocese.addr.com.

Kalamazoo, MI: The Chancery Office, 215 N. Westnedge Ave., 49007-3760. (616) 349-8714.

Kansas City,* KS: The Chancery Office, 12615 Parallel Pkwy., 66109. (913) 721-1570; www.archkck.org.

Kansas City-St. Joseph, MO: The Chancery Office, P.O. Box 419037, Kansas City, 64141-6037. (816) 756-1850; www.diocese-kcsj.org.

Knoxville, TN: The Chancery Office, 805 Northshore Dr., P.O. Box 11127, 37939-1127. (865) 584-3307.

La Crosse, WI: The Chancery Office, 3710 East Ave. S., Box 4004, 54602-4004. (608) 788-7700; www.dioceseoflacrosse.com.

Lafayette, IN: The Bishop's Office, P.O. Box 260, 47902-0260. (765) 742-0275; www.diocese-oflafayette.org.

Lafayette, LA: The Chancery Office, 1408 Carmel Ave., 70501. (337) 261-5614; www.dol-louisiana.org.

Lake Charles, LA: The Chancery Office, P.O. Box 3223, 70602. (318) 439-7400; lcdiocese.laol.net.

Lansing, MI: The Chancery Office, 300 W. Ottawa St., 48933-1577. (517) 342-2440.

Laredo, Tx.: Diocesan Pastoral Center, P.O. Box 2247, 78044. (956) 727-2140.

Las Cruces, NM: The Chancery Office, 1280 Med Park Dr., 88005. (505) 523-7577;

www.zianet.com/diocese.

Las Vegas, NV: Chancery Office, P.O. Box 18316, 89114-8316. (702) 735-3500.

Lexington, KY: Catholic Center, 1310 Main St., 40508-2040. (606) 253-1993; www.cdlex.org.

Lincoln, NE: The Chancery Office, P.O. Box 80328, 68501-0328. (402) 488-0921.

Little Rock, AR: The Chancery Office, 2415 N. Tyler St., P.O. Box 7239, 72217. (501) 664-0340.

Los Angeles,* CA: Archdiocesan Catholic Center, 3424 Wilshire Blvd., 90010-2241. (213) 637-7000; www.LA-Archdiocese.org.

Louisville,* KY: Chancery Office, 212 E. College St., P.O. Box 1073, 40201-1073. (502) 585-3291; www.archlou.org.

Lubbock, TX: The Catholic Center, P.O. Box 98700, 79499. (806) 792-3943; www.catholiclubbock.org.

Madison, WI: Bishop O'Connor Catholic Pastoral Center, P.O. Box 44983, 3577 High Point Rd., 53744-4983. (608) 821-3000; www.madisondiocese.org.

Manchester, NH: The Chancery Office, 153 Ash St., P.O. Box 310, 03105-0310. (603) 669-3100; www.diocesemanch.org.

Marquette, MI: The Chancery Office, 444 S. Fourth St., P.O. Box 550, 49855. (906) 225-1141.

Memphis, TN: The Catholic Center, 5825 Shelby Oaks Dr., P.O. Box 341669, 38184-1669. (901) 373-1200; www.cdom.org.

Metuchen, NJ: The Chancery Office, P.O. Box 191, 08840. (732) 283-3800; www.diometuchen.org.

Miami,* FL: The Chancery Office, 9401 Biscayne Blvd., Miami Shores, 33138. (305) 757-6241; www.archdioceseofmiami.org.

Milwaukee,* WI: The Chancery Office, P.O. Box 07912, 53207. (414) 769-3340; www.archmil.org.

Mobile,* AL: The Chancery Office, 400 Government St., P.O. Box 1966, 36633. (334) 434-1585.

Monterey, CA: The Chancery Office, P.O. Box 2048, 93942-2048. (831) 373-4345; www.dioceseofmonterey.org.

Nashville, TN: The Chancery Office, 2400 21st Ave. S., 37212-5387. (615) 383-6393; www.serve.com/DIOCNASH/.

Newark,* NJ: Chancery Office, P.O. Box 9500, 07104-0500. (973) 497-4000; www.rcan.org.

New Orleans,* LA: The Chancery Office, 7887 Walmsley Ave., 70125. (504) 861-9521; www.catholic.org/neworleans/.

Newton, MA (Melkite): The Chancery Office, 158 Pleasant St., Brookline, 02446. (617) 566-4511; www.melkite.org.

New Ulm, MN: Catholic Pastoral Center, 1400 Sixth St. N., 56073-2099. (507) 359-2966; www.dnu.org.

New York,* NY: The Chancery Office, 1011 First Ave., 10022-4134. (212) 371-1000; www.ny-archdiocese.org.

Norwich, CT: The Chancery Office, 201 Broadway, P.O. Box 587, 06360-0587. (860) 887-9294; www.norwichdiocese.org.

Oakland, CA: The Chancery Office, 2900 Lakeshore Ave., 94610. (510) 893-4711.

Ogdensburg, NY: The Chancery Office, 604 Washington St., P.O. Box 369, 13669. (315) 393-2920.

Oklahoma City,* OK: The Chancery Office, P.O. Box 32180, 73123. (405) 721-5651.

Omaha,* NE: The Chancery Office, 100 N. 62nd St., 68132-2795. (402) 558-3100; www.oarch.org.

Orange, CA: The Chancery Office, 2811 E. Villa Real Dr., P.O. Box 14195, 92863-1595. (714) 282-3000; www.rcbo.org.

Orlando, FL: The Chancery Office, P.O. Box 1800, 32802-1800. (407) 246-4800; www.orlandodiocese.org.

Our Lady of Deliverance of Newark, for Syrian rite Catholics of the U.S. and Canada: P.O. Box 8366, Union City, NJ, 07087-8262. (201) 583-1067; www.syriac-catholic.org.

Our Lady of Lebanon of Los Angeles, CA (Maronite): The Chancery Office, P.O. Box 16397, Beverly Hills, 90209. (310) 247-8322; www.eparchyla.org.

Owensboro, KY: The Catholic Pastoral Center, 600 Locust St., 42301-2130. (502) 683-1545; www.owensborodio.org.

Palm Beach, FL: Pastoral Center, P.O. Box 109650, Palm Beach Gardens, 33410-9650. (561) 775-9500; www.diocese.maco.net.

Parma, OH (Byzantine): The Chancery Office, 1900 Carlton Rd., 44134-3129. (216) 741-8773; www.parma.com.

Passaic, NJ (Byzantine): The Chancery Office, 445 Lackawanna Ave., W. Paterson, 07424. (973) 890-7777; members.aol.com/byzruth/index/htm.

Paterson, NJ: Diocesan Pastoral Center, 777 Valley Rd., Clifton, 07013. (973) 777-8818; www.patersondiocese.org.

Pensacola-Tallahassee, FL: Pastoral Center, P.O. Drawer 17329, Pensacola, 32522. (904) 432-1515; www.cfi.net/ptdiocese/pt.html.

Peoria, IL: The Chancery Office, 607 N.E. Madison Ave., P.O. Box 1406, 61655. (309) 671-1550.

Philadelphia,* PA: The Chancery Office, 222 N. 17th St., 19103. (215) 587-4538; www.archdiocese-phl.org.

Philadelphia,* PA (Byzantine): The Chancery Office, 827 N. Franklin St., 19123-2097. (215) 627-0143.

Phoenix, AZ: The Chancery Office, 400 E. Monroe St., 85004-2376. (602) 257-0030; www.catholicsun.org.

Pittsburgh,* PA (Byzantine): The Chancery Office, 66 Riverview Ave. 15214-2253. (412) 231-4000.

Pittsburgh, PA: Pastoral Center, 111 Blvd. of the Allies, 15222-1618. (412) 456-3000; www.diopitt.org.

Portland, ME: The Chancery Office, 510 Ocean Ave., P.O. Box 11559, 04104-7559. (207) 773-6471.

Portland, OR*: Pastoral Center, 2838 E. Burnside St., 97214. (503) 234-5334; www.archdpdx.org/.

Providence, RI: The Chancery Office, One Cathedral Sq., 02903-3695. (401) 278-4500; www.dioceseofprovidence.com.

Pueblo, CO: Catholic Pastoral Center, 1001 N. Grand Ave., 81003-2948. (719) 544-9861; www.pueblo-diocese.com.

Raleigh, NC: Catholic Center, 715 Nazareth St., 27606-2187. (919) 821-9700; www.raldioc.org.

Rapid City, SD: The Chancery Office, 606 Cathedral Dr., P.O. Box 678, 57709. (605) 343-3541.

Reno, NV: Pastoral Center, P.O. Box 1211, 89504-1211. (775) 329-9274; www.catholicreno.com.

Richmond, VA: The Chancery Office, 811 Cathedral Pl., 23220-4801. (804) 359-5661; www.diocric.org.

Rochester, NY: The Pastoral Center, 1150 Buffalo Rd., 14624. (716) 328-3210; www.dor.org.

Rockford, IL: The Chancery Office, 1245 N. Court St., P.O. Box 7044, 61126-7044. (815) 962-3709; www.rockforddiocese.org.

Rockville Centre, NY: The Chancery Office, 50 N. Park Ave., 11570-4184. (516) 678-5800; www.drvc.org.

Sacramento, CA: Pastoral Center, 2110 Broadway, 95818-2541. (916) 733-0100; www.diocese-sacramento.org.

Saginaw, MI: The Chancery Office, 5800 Weiss St., 48603-2799. (517) 799-7910; www.dioceseofsaginaw.org.

St. Augustine, FL: Catholic Center, P.O. Box 24000, Jacksonville, 32241-4000. (904) 262-3200; staugustine.ml.org/diocese.

St. Cloud, MN: The Chancery Office, P.O. Box 1248, 56302. (320) 251-2340; www.stcdio.org.

St. George's in Canton, OH (Byzantine, Romanian): The Chancery Office, 1121 44th St. N.E., 44714-1297. (330) 492-4086; www.RomanianCatholic.org.

St. Josaphat in Parma, OH (Byzantine): The Chancery Office, P.O. Box 347180, 44134-7180. (440) 888-1522.

St. Louis,* MO: The Catholic Center, 4445 Lindell Blvd., 63108-2497. (314) 633-2222; www.archstl.org.

St. Maron of Brooklyn (Maronite): The Pastoral Center, 294 Howard Ave., Staten Island, NY 10301-4409. (718) 815-0436.

St. Nicholas in Chicago (Byzantine): The Chancery Office, 2245 W. Rice St., 60622. (312) 276-5080.

St. Paul and Minneapolis,* MN: The Chancery Office, 226 Summit Ave., St. Paul, 55102-2197. (651) 291-4400; www.mtn.org/archcom/.

St. Peter the Apostle of San Diego (Chaldean): Chancery Office, 1627 Jamacha Way, El Cajon, CA 92019. (619) 579-7913.

St. Petersburg, FL: The Chancery Office, P.O. Box 40200, 33743-0200. (727) 344-1611; www.dioceseofstpete.org.

St. Thomas of Chicago (Syro-Malabar): Diocesan Office, 717 N. Eastland, Elmhurst, IL 60126. (630) 530-8399.

St. Thomas the Apostle of Detroit (Chaldean Catholic Diocese – USA): The Chancery Office, 25603 Berg Rd., Southfield, MI 48034. (248) 351-0440.

Salina, KS: The Chancery Office, P.O. Box 980, 67402-0980. (785) 827-8746.

Salt Lake City, UT: The Chancery Office, 27 C St., 84103-2397. (801) 328-8641; www.utahcatholicdiocese.org.

San Angelo, TX: The Chancery Office, P.O. Box 1829, 76902-1829. (915) 651-7500; www.san-angelodiocese.org.

San Antonio,* TX: The Chancery Office, P.O. Box 28410, 78228-0410. (210) 734-2620; www.archdiosa.org.

San Bernardino, CA: The Chancery Office, 1201 E. Highland Ave., 92404. (909) 475-5300; www.sbdiocese.org.

San Diego, CA: Pastoral Center, P.O. Box 85728, 92186-5728, (619) 490-8200; www.diocese-sdiego.org.

San Francisco,* CA: The Chancery Office, 445 Church St., 94114. (415) 565-3609; www.sfarchdiocese.org.

San Jose, CA: The Chancery Office, 900 Lafayette St., Suite 301, Santa Clara, 95050-4966. (408) 983-

0100; www.dsj.org.

Santa Fe,* NM: Catholic Center, 4000 St. Joseph's Pl. N.W., Albuquerque, 87120. (505) 831-8100.

Santa Rosa, CA: The Chancery Office, P.O. Box 1297, 95402-1297. (707) 545-7610; www.santarosacatholic.org.

Savannah, GA: Catholic Pastoral Center, 601 E. Liberty St., 31401-5196. (912) 238-2320; www.dioceseofsavannah.org.

Scranton, PA: The Chancery Office, 300 Wyoming Ave., 18503-1279. (570) 207-2216; www.dioceseofscranton.org.

Seattle,* WA: The Chancery Office, 910 Marion St., 98104-1299. (206) 382-4560; www.seattlearch.org.

Shreveport, LA: Catholic Center, 3500 Fairfield Ave., 71104. (318) 868-4441; www.dioshpt.org.

Sioux City, IA: The Chancery Office, P.O. Box 3379, 51102-3379. (712) 255-7933; www.scdiocese.org.

Sioux Falls, SD: Catholic Pastoral Center, 523 N. Duluth Ave., 57104-2714. (605) 334-9861; Dioceseof-Sioux-Falls.org.

Spokane, WA: Catholic Pastoral Center, Catholic Diocese of Spokane, P.O. Box 1453, 99210-1453. (509) 358-7300; www.dioceseofspokane.org.

Springfield, IL: Catholic Pastoral Center, 1615 West Washington, P.O. Box 3187, 62708-3187. (217) 698-8500.

Springfield, MA: The Chancery Office, P.O. Box 1730, 01101. (413) 732-3175; www.diospringfield.org.

Springfield-Cape Girardeau, MO: The Catholic Center, 601 S. Jefferson Ave., Springfield, 65806-3143. (417) 866-0841; www.diocspfdcape.org.

Stamford, CT (Byzantine): The Chancery Office, 14 Peveril Rd., 06902-3019. (203) 324-7698.

Steubenville, OH: The Chancery Office, P.O. Box 969, 43952. (740) 282-3631; www.diosteub.org.

Stockton, CA: The Chancery Office, 1125 N. Lincoln St., 95203. (209) 466-0636.

Superior, WI: The Chancery Office, 1201 Hughitt Ave., Box 969, 54880. (715) 392-2937.

Syracuse, NY: The Chancery Office, P.O. Box 511, 13201-0511. (315) 422-7203; wwwsyrdioc.org.

Toledo, OH: The Chancery Office, P.O. Box 985, 43697-0895. (419) 244-6711; www.toledodiocese.org.

Trenton, NJ: Chancery Office, 701 Lawrenceville Rd., P.O. Box 5147, 08638. (609) 406-7400.

Tucson, AZ: The Chancery Office, 192 S. Stone Ave., Box 31, 85702. (520) 792-3410; www.azstarnet.com/~rccdot.

Tulsa, OK: The Chancery Office, P.O. Box 690240, 74169. (918) 294-1904.

Tyler, TX: The Chancery Office, 1015 E.S.E. Loop 323, 75701-9663. (903) 534-1077.

Van Nuys, CA (Byzantine): The Chancery Office, 8131 N. 16th St., Phoenix, AZ 85020. (602) 861-9778; eparchy-of-van-nuys.org.

Venice, FL: The Catholic Center, P.O. Box 2006, 34284. (941) 484-9543; www.dioceseofvenice.org.

Victoria, TX: The Chancery Office, P.O. Box 4070, 77903. (361) 573-0828.

Washington,* DC: Archdiocesan Pastoral Center, P.O. Box 29260, 20017. (301) 853-4500.

Wheeling-Charleston, WV: The Chancery Office, 1300 Byron St., P.O. Box 230, Wheeling, 26003. (304) 233-0880; www.dwc.org.

Wichita, KS: The Chancery Office, 424 N. Broadway, 67202. (316) 269-3900.

Wilmington, DE: The Chancery Office, P.O. Box 2030, 19899-2030. (302) 573-3100; www.cdow.org.

Winona, MN: The Chancery Office, P.O. Box 588, 55987. (507) 454-4643; www.dow.org.

Worcester, MA: The Chancery Office, 49 Elm St., 01609-2597. (508) 791-7171; www.worcesterdiocese.org.

Yakima, WA: The Chancery Office, 5301-A Tieton Dr., 98908. (509) 965-7117.

Youngstown, OH: The Chancery Office, 144 W. Wood St., 44503. (330) 744-8451; www.doy.org.

Military Archdiocese: P.O. Box 4469, Washington, DC 20017-0469; 3311 Toledo Terrace, Suite A201, Hyattsville, MD 20782-4135. (202) 269-9100; www.milarch.org.

Armenian Apostolic Exarchate for the United States and Canada: 110 E. 12th St., New York, NY 10003. (212) 477-2030.

CATHEDRALS, BASILICAS, AND SHRINES IN THE U.S.

CATHEDRALS IN THE UNITED STATES

A cathedral is the principal church in a diocese, the one in which the bishop has his seat (cathedra). He is the actual pastor, although many functions of the church, which usually serves a parish, are the responsibility of a priest serving as the rector. Because of the dignity of a cathedral, the dates of its dedication and its patronal feast are observed throughout a diocese. The pope's cathedral, the Basilica of St. John Lateran, is the highest-ranking church in the world.

(Archdioceses are indicated by asterisk.)

Albany, NY: Immaculate Conception.

Alexandria, LA: St. Francis Xavier.

Allentown, PA: St. Catherine of Siena.

Altoona-Johnstown, PA: Blessed Sacrament (Altoona); St. John Gualbert (Johnstown).

Amarillo, TX: St. Laurence.

Anchorage,* AK: Holy Family.

Arlington, VA: St. Thomas More.

Atlanta,* GA: Christ the King.

Austin, TX: St. Mary (Immaculate Conception).

Baker, OR: St. Francis de Sales.

Baltimore,* MD: Mary Our Queen; Basilica of the National Shrine of the Assumption of the Blessed Virgin Mary (Co-Cathedral).

Baton Rouge, LA: St. Joseph.

Beaumont, TX: St. Anthony (of Padua).

Belleville, IL: St. Peter.

Biloxi, MS: Nativity of the Blessed Virgin Mary.

Birmingham, AL: St. Paul.

Bismarck, ND: Holy Spirit.

Boise, ID: St. John the Evangelist.

Boston,* MA: Holy Cross.

Bridgeport, CT: St. Augustine.
Brooklyn, NY: St. James (Minor Basilica).
Brownsville, TX: Immaculate Conception.
Buffalo, NY: St. Joseph.
Burlington, VT: Immaculate Conception; St. Joseph (Co-Cathedral).
Camden, NJ: Immaculate Conception.
Charleston, SC: St. John the Baptist.
Charlotte, NC: St. Patrick.
Cheyenne, WY: St. Mary.
Chicago,* IL: Holy Name (of Jesus).
Cincinnati,* OH: St. Peter in Chains.
Cleveland, OH: St. John the Evangelist.
Colorado Springs, CO: St. Mary.
Columbus, OH: St. Joseph.
Corpus Christi, TX: Corpus Christi.
Covington, KY: Basilica of the Assumption.
Crookston, MN: Immaculate Conception.
Dallas, TX: Cathedral-Santuario de Guadalupe.
Davenport, IA: Sacred Heart.
Denver,* CO: Immaculate Conception (Minor Basilica).
Des Moines, IA: St. Ambrose.
Detroit,* MI: Most Blessed Sacrament.
Dodge City, KS: Our Lady of Guadalupe.
Dubuque,* IA: St. Raphael.
Duluth, MN: Our Lady of the Rosary.
El Paso, TX: St. Patrick.
Erie, PA: St. Peter.
Evansville, IN: Most Holy Trinity (Pro-Cathedral).
Fairbanks, AK: Sacred Heart.
Fall River, MA: St. Mary of the Assumption.
Fargo, N.D.: St. Mary.
Fort Wayne-S. Bend, IN: Immaculate Conception (Fort Wayne); St. Matthew (South Bend).
Fort Worth, TX: St. Patrick.
Fresno, CA: St. John (the Baptist).
Gallup, NM: Sacred Heart.
Galveston-Houston, TX: St. Mary (Minor Basilica, Galveston); Sacred Heart Co-Cathedral (Houston).
Gary, IN: Holy Angels.
Gaylord, MI: St. Mary, Our Lady of Mt. Carmel.
Grand Island, NE: Nativity of Blessed Virgin Mary.
Grand Rapids, MI: St. Andrew.
Great Falls-Billings, MT: St. Ann (Great Falls); St. Patrick Co-Cathedral (Billings).
Green Bay, WI: St. Francis Xavier.
Greensburg, PA: Blessed Sacrament.
Harrisburg, PA: St. Patrick.
Hartford,* CT: St. Joseph.
Helena, MT: St. Helena.
Honolulu, HI: Our Lady of Peace; St. Theresa of the Child Jesus (Co-Cathedral).
Houma-Thibodaux, LA: St. Francis de Sales (Houma); St. Joseph Co-Cathedral (Thibodaux).
Indianapolis,* IN: Sts. Peter and Paul.
Jackson, MS: St. Peter.
Jefferson City, MO: St. Joseph.
Joliet, IL: St. Raymond Nonnatus.
Juneau, AK: Nativity of the Blessed Virgin Mary.
Kalamazoo, MI: St. Augustine.
Kansas City,* KS: St. Peter the Apostle.
Kansas City-St. Joseph, MO: Immaculate Conception (Kansas City); St. Joseph Co-Cathedral (St. Joseph).
Knoxville, TN: Sacred Heart of Jesus.

La Crosse, WI: St. Joseph the Workman.
Lafayette, IN: St. Mary.
Lafayette, LA: St. John the Evangelist.
Lake Charles, LA: Immaculate Conception.
Lansing, MI: St. Mary.
Laredo, TX: San Augustin.
Las Cruces, NM: Immaculate Heart of Mary.
Las Vegas, NV: Guardian Angel.
Lexington, KY: Christ the King.
Lincoln, NE: Cathedral of the Risen Christ.
Little Rock, AR: St. Andrew.
Los Angeles,* CA: Cathedral of Our Lady of the Angels of Los Angeles (opened in 2002).
Louisville,* KY: Assumption.
Lubbock, TX: Christ the King.
Madison, WI: St. Raphael.
Manchester, NH: St. Joseph.
Marquette, MI: St. Peter.
Memphis, TN: Immaculate Conception.
Metuchen, NJ: St. Francis (of Assisi).
Miami,* FL: St. Mary (Immaculate Conception).
Milwaukee,* WI: St. John.
Mobile,* AL: Immaculate Conception (Minor Basilica).
Monterey, CA: San Carlos Borromeo.
Nashville, TN: Incarnation.
Newark,* NJ: Sacred Heart (Minor Basilica).
New Orleans,* LA: St. Louis. (Minor Basilica)
Newton, MA (Melkite): Our Lady of the Annunciation (Boston).
New Ulm, MN: Holy Trinity.
New York,* NY: St. Patrick.
Norwich, CT: St. Patrick.
Oakland, CA: St. Francis de Sales.
Ogdensburg, NY: St. Mary (Immaculate Conception).
Oklahoma City,* OK: Our Lady of Perpetual Help.
Omaha,* NE: St. Cecilia.
Orange, CA: Holy Family.
Orlando, FL: St. James.
Our Lady of Deliverance of Newark, New Jersey for Syrian Rite Catholics in the U.S. and Canada: Our Lady of Deliverance.
Our Lady of Lebanon of Los Angeles, CA (Maronite): Our Lady of Mt. Lebanon-St. Peter.
Owensboro, KY: St. Stephen.
Palm Beach, FL: St. Ignatius Loyola, Palm Beach Gardens.
Parma, OH (Byzantine): St. John the Baptist.
Passaic, NJ (Byzantine): St. Michael.
Paterson, NJ: St. John the Baptist.
Pensacola-Tallahassee, FL: Sacred Heart (Pensacola); Co-Cathedral of St. Thomas More (Tallahassee).
Peoria, IL: St. Mary.
Philadelphia,* PA: Sts. Peter and Paul (Minor Basilica).
Philadelphia,* PA (Byzantine): Immaculate Conception of Blessed Virgin Mary.
Phoenix, AZ: Sts. Simon and Jude.
Pittsburgh,* PA (Byzantine): St. John the Baptist, Munhall.
Pittsburgh, PA: St. Paul.
Portland, ME: Immaculate Conception.
Portland,* OR: Immaculate Conception.
Providence, RI: Sts. Peter and Paul.
Pueblo, CO: Sacred Heart.

Raleigh, NC: Sacred Heart.
Rapid City, SD: Our Lady of Perpetual Help.
Reno, NV: St. Thomas Aquinas.
Richmond, VA: Sacred Heart.
Rochester, NY: Sacred Heart.
Rockford, IL: St. Peter.
Rockville Centre, NY: St. Agnes.
Sacramento, CA: Blessed Sacrament.
Saginaw, MI: St. Mary.
St. Augustine, FL: St. Augustine (Minor Basilica).
St. Cloud, MN: St. Mary.
St. George's in Canton, OH (Byzantine, Romanian): St. George.
St. Josaphat in Parma, OH (Byzantine): St. Josaphat.
St. Louis,* MO: St. Louis.
St. Maron, Brooklyn, NY (Maronite): Our Lady of Lebanon.
St. Nicholas in Chicago (Byzantine): St. Nicholas.
St. Paul and Minneapolis,* MN: St. Paul (St. Paul); Basilica of St. Mary Co-Cathedral (Minneapolis).
St. Petersburg, FL: St. Jude the Apostle.
St. Thomas the Apostle of Detroit (Chaldean): Our Lady of Chaldeans Cathedral (Mother of God Church), Southfield, MI
St. Thomas of Chicago (Syro-Malabar): Mar Thoma Shleeha Church.
Salina, KS: Sacred Heart.
Salt Lake City, UT: The Madeleine.
San Angelo, TX: Sacred Heart.
San Antonio,* TX: San Fernando.
San Bernardino, CA: Our Lady of the Rosary.
San Diego, CA: St. Joseph.
San Francisco,* CA: St. Mary (Assumption).
San Jose, CA: St. Joseph (Minor Basilica); St. Patrick, Proto-Cathedral.
Santa Fe,* NM: San Francisco de Asis (Minor Basilica).
Santa Rosa, CA: St. Eugene.

Savannah, GA: St. John the Baptist.
Scranton, PA: St. Peter.
Seattle,* WA: St. James.
Shreveport, LA: St. John Berchmans.
Sioux City, IA: Epiphany.
Sioux Falls, SD: St. Joseph.
Spokane, WA: Our Lady of Lourdes.
Springfield, IL: Immaculate Conception.
Springfield, MA: St. Michael.
Springfield-Cape Girardeau, MO: St. Agnes (Springfield): St. Mary (Cape Girardeau).
Stamford, CT (Byzantine): St. Vladimir.
Steubenville, OH: Holy Name.
Stockton, CA: Annunciation.
Superior, WI: Christ the King.
Syracuse, NY: Immaculate Conception.
Toledo, OH: Queen of the Most Holy Rosary.
Trenton, NJ: St. Mary (Assumption).
Tucson, AZ: St. Augustine.
Tulsa, OK: Holy Family.
Tyler, TX: Immaculate Conception.
Van Nuys, CA (Byzantine): St. Mary (Patronage of the Mother of God), Van Nuys; St. Stephen's (Pro-Cathedral), Phoenix, AZ
Venice, FL: Epiphany.
Victoria, TX: Our Lady of Victory.
Washington,* DC: St. Matthew.
Wheeling-Charleston, WV: St. Joseph (Wheeling); Sacred Heart (Charleston).
Wichita, KS: Immaculate Conception.
Wilmington, DE: St. Peter.
Winona, MN: Sacred Heart.
Worcester, MA: St. Paul.
Yakima, WA: St. Paul.
Youngstown, OH: St. Columba.
Apostolic Exarchate for Armenian Catholics in the U.S. and Canada: St. Ann (110 E. 12th St., New York, NY 10003).

BASILICAS IN THE UNITED STATES

Basilica is a title assigned to certain churches because of their antiquity, dignity, historical importance or significance as centers of worship. Major basilicas have the papal altar and holy door, which is opened at the beginning of a Jubilee Year; minor basilicas enjoy certain ceremonial privileges.

Among the major basilicas are the patriarchal basilicas of St. John Lateran, St. Peter, St. Paul Outside the Walls and St. Mary Major in Rome; St. Francis and St. Mary of the Angels in Assisi, Italy. The patriarchal basilica of St. Lawrence, Rome, is a minor basilica. The dates in the listings below indicate when the churches were designated as basilicas.

Minor Basilicas in U.S., Puerto Rico, Guam

Alabama: Mobile, Cathedral of the Immaculate Conception (Mar. 10, 1962).

Arizona: Phoenix, St. Mary's (Immaculate Conception) (Sept. 11, 1985).

California: San Francisco, Mission Dolores (Feb. 8, 1952); Carmel, Old Mission of San Carlos (Feb. 5, 1960); Alameda, St. Joseph (Jan. 21, 1972); San Diego, Mission San Diego de Alcala (Nov. 17, 1975); San Jose, St. Joseph (Jan. 28, 1997).

Colorado: Denver, Cathedral of the Immaculate Conception (Nov. 3, 1979).

District of Columbia: National Shrine of the Immaculate Conception (Oct. 12, 1990).

Florida: St. Augustine, Cathedral of St. Augustine (Dec. 4, 1976).

Illinois: Chicago, Our Lady of Sorrows (May 4, 1956); Queen of All Saints (Mar. 26, 1962).

Indiana: Vincennes, Old Cathedral (Mar. 14, 1970); Notre Dame, Parish Church of Most Sacred Heart, Univ. of Notre Dame (Nov. 23, 1991).

Iowa: Dyersville, St. Francis Xavier (May 11, 1956); Des Moines, St. John the Apostle (Oct. 4, 1989).

Kentucky: Trappist, Our Lady of Gethsemani (May 3, 1949); Covington, Cathedral of Assumption (Dec. 8, 1953).

Louisiana: New Orleans, St. Louis King of France (Dec. 9, 1964).

Maryland: Baltimore, Assumption of the Blessed Virgin Mary (Sept. 1, 1937; designated national shrine, 1993); Emmitsburg, Shrine of St. Elizabeth Ann Seton (Feb. 13, 1991).

Massachusetts: Roxbury, Perpetual Help ("Mission Church") (Sept. 8, 1954); Chicopee, St. Stanislaus (June 25, 1991); Webster, St. Joseph (Oct. 1998).

Michigan: Grand Rapids, St. Adalbert (Aug. 22, 1979).

Minnesota: Minneapolis. St. Mary (Feb. 1, 1926).

Missouri: Conception, Basilica of Immaculate Conception (Sept. 14, 1940); St. Louis, St. Louis King of France (Jan. 27, 1961).

New Jersey: Newark, Cathedral Basilica of the Sacred Heart (Dec. 22, 1995).

New York: Brooklyn, Our Lady of Perpetual Help (Sept. 5, 1969), Cathedral-Basilica of St. James (June 22, 1982); Lackawanna, Our Lady of Victory (1926); Youngstown, Blessed Virgin Mary of the Rosary of Fatima (Oct. 7, 1975).

North Carolina: Asheville, St. Lawrence (Apr. 6, 1993; ceremonies, Sept. 5, 1993); Belmont, Our Lady Help of Christians (July 27, 1998).

North Dakota: Jamestown, St. James (Oct. 26, 1988).

Ohio: Carey, Shrine of Our Lady of Consolation (Oct. 21, 1971).

Pennsylvania: Latrobe, St. Vincent Basilica, Benedictine Archabbey (Aug. 22, 1955); Conewago, Basilica of the Sacred Heart (June 30, 1962); Philadelphia, Sts. Peter and Paul (Sept. 27, 1976); Danville, Sts. Cyril and Methodius (chapel at the motherhouse of the Sisters of Sts. Cyril and Methodius) (June 30, 1989); Loretto, St. Michael the Archangel (September 9, 1996); Scranton, National Shrine of St. Ann (Oct. 18, 1997).

Texas: Galveston, St. Mary Cathedral (Aug. 11, 1979); San Antonio, Basilica of the National Shrine of the Little Flower (Sept. 27, 1931); Basilica of Our Lady of San Juan del Valle-National Shrine (May 2, 1954).

Virginia: Norfolk, St. Mary of the Immaculate Conception (July 9, 1991).

Wisconsin: Milwaukee, St. Josaphat (Mar. 10, 1929).

Puerto Rico: San Juan, Cathedral of San Juan (Jan. 25, 1978).

Guam: Agana, Cathedral of Dulce Nombre de Maria (Sweet Name of Mary) (1985).

BASILICA OF THE NATIONAL SHRINE OF THE IMMACULATE CONCEPTION

The Basilica of the National Shrine of the Immaculate Conception is dedicated to the honor of the Blessed Virgin Mary, declared patroness of the United States under this title in 1846, eight years before the proclamation of the dogma of the Immaculate Conception. The church was designated a minor basilica by Pope John Paul II Oct. 12, 1990. The church is the eighth largest religious building in the world and the largest Catholic church in the Western Hemisphere, with numerous special chapels and with normal seating and standing accommodations for 6,000 people. Open daily, it is adjacent to The Catholic University of America, at Michigan Ave. and Fourth St. NE, Washington, D.C. 20017; (202) 526-8300; www.nationalshrine.com. Rev. Msgr. Walter R. Rossi, rector.

SHRINES AND PLACES OF HISTORIC INTEREST IN THE U.S.

(Principal source: Catholic Almanac *survey.)*

Listed below, according to state, are shrines, other centers of devotion and some places of historic interest with special significance for Catholics. The list is necessarily incomplete because of space limitations.

Information includes, where possible: name and location of shrine or place of interest, date of foundation, sponsoring agency or group, and address for more information.

Alabama: Our Lady of the Angels, Hanceville; Birmingham Diocese. Address: Our Lady of the Angels Monastery, 3222 County Road 548, Hanceville, 35077; (256) 352-6267.

• St. Jude Church of the City of St. Jude, Montgomery (1934; dedicated, 1938); Mobile Archdiocese. Address: 2048 W. Fairview Ave., Montgomery, 36108; (334) 265-1390.

• Shrine of the Most Blessed Trinity, Holy Trinity (1924); Missionary Servants of the Most Blessed Trinity. Address: Holy Trinity, 36859.

Arizona: Chapel of the Holy Cross, Sedona (1956); Phoenix Diocese: P.O. Box 1043, W. Sedona 86339.

• Mission San Xavier del Bac, near Tucson (1692); National Historic Landmark; Franciscan Friars and Tucson Diocese; Address: 1950 W. San Xavier Rd., Tucson, 85746-7409; (520) 294-2624.

• Shrine of St. Joseph of the Mountains, Yarnell (1939); erected by Catholic Action League; currently maintained by Board of Directors. Address: P.O. Box 267, Yarnell, 85362.

California: Mission San Diego de Alcala (July 16, 1769); first of the 21 Franciscan missions of Upper California;

Minor Basilica; National Historic Landmark; San Diego Diocese. Address: 10818 San Diego Mission Rd., San Diego, 92108; (619) 283-7319.

• Carmel Mission Basilica (Mission San Carlos Borromeo del Rio Carmelo), Carmel by the Sea (June 3, 1770); Monterey Diocese. Address: 3080 Rio Rd., Carmel, 93923; (831) 624-1271.

• Old Mission San Luis Obispo de Tolosa, San Luis Obispo (Sept. 1, 1772); Monterey Diocese (Parish Church). Address: Old Mission Church, 751 Palm St., San Luis Obispo, 93401.

• San Gabriel Mission, San Gabriel (Sept. 8, 1771); Los Angeles Archdiocese (Parish Church, staffed by Claretians). Address: 537 W. Mission, San Gabriel, 91776.

• Mission San Francisco de Asis (Oct. 9, 1776) and Mission Dolores Basilica (1860s); San Francisco Archdiocese. Address: 3321 Sixteenth St., San Francisco, 94114.

• Old Mission San Juan Capistrano, San Juan Capistrano (Nov. 1, 1776); Orange Diocese. Address: P.O. Box 697, San Juan Capistrano, 92693; (949) 248-2026; www.missionsjc.com.

• Old Mission Santa Barbara, Santa Barbara (Dec. 4, 1786); National Historic Landmark; Parish Church, staffed by Franciscan Friars. Address: 2201 Laguna St., Santa Barbara, 93105; (805) 682-4713.

• Old Mission San Juan Bautista, San Juan Bautista (June 24, 1797); National Historic Landmark; Monterey Diocese (Parish Church). Address: P.O. Box 400, San Juan Bautista, 95045.

• Mission San Miguel, San Miguel (July 25, 1797);

Parish Church, Monterey diocese; Franciscan Friars. Address: P.O. Box 69, San Miguel, 93451; (805) 467-3256.

• Old Mission Santa Inés, Solvang (1804); Historic Landmark; Los Angeles Archdiocese (Parish Church, staffed by Capuchin Franciscan Friars). Address: P.O. Box 408, Solvang, 93464; (805) 688-4815; www.missionsantaines.org.

Franciscan Friars founded 21 missions in California. (See Index: Franciscan Missions.)

• Shrine of Our Lady of Sorrows, Sycamore (1883); Sacramento Diocese. Address: c/o Our Lady of Lourdes Church, 745 Ware Ave., Colusa, 95932.

Colorado: Mother Cabrini Shrine, Golden; Missionary Sisters of the Sacred Heart. Address: 20189 Cabrini Blvd., Golden, 80401.

Connecticut: Shrine of Our Lady of Lourdes, Litchfield (1958); Montfort Missionaries. Address: P.O. Box 667, Litchfield, 06759.

• Shrine of the Infant of Prague, New Haven (1945); Dominican Friars. Address: P.O. Box 1202, 5 Hillhouse Ave., New Haven, 06505.

District of Columbia: Mount St. Sepulchre, Franciscan Monastery of the Holy Land (1897; church dedicated, 1899); Order of Friars Minor. Address: 1400 Quincy St. NE, Washington, DC 20017.

• Basilica of the National Shrine of the Immaculate Conception. See Index for separate entry.

Florida: Mary, Queen of the Universe Shrine, Orlando (1986, temporary facilities; new shrine dedicated, 1993); Orlando diocese. Address: 8300 Vineland Ave., Orlando, 32821; (407) 239-6600; www.maryqueenoftheuniverse.org.

• Our Lady of La Leche Shrine (Patroness of Mothers and Mothers-to-be) and Mission of Nombre de Dios, St. Augustine (1565); Angelus Crusade Headquarters; St. Augustine Diocese. Address: 30 Ocean Ave., St. Augustine, 32084.

Illinois: Holy Family Log Church, Cahokia (1799; original log church erected 1699); Belleville Diocese (Parish Church). Address: 116 Church St., Cahokia, 62206; (618) 337-4548.

• Marytown/Shrine of St. Maximilian Kolbe and Retreat Center, Libertyville; Our Lady of the Blessed Sacrament Sanctuary of Perpetual Eucharistic Adoration (1930) and Archdiocesan Shrine to St. Maximilian Kolbe (1989), conducted by Conventual Franciscan Friars, 1600 West Park Ave., Libertyville, 60048; (847) 367-7800.

• National Shrine of Our Lady of the Snows, Belleville (1958); Missionary Oblates of Mary Immaculate. Address: 442 S. De Mazenod Dr., Belleville, 62223.

• National Shrine of St. Jude, Chicago (1929); located in Our Lady of Guadalupe Church, founded and staffed by Claretians. Address: 3200 E. 91st St., Chicago, 60617; (312) 236-7782.

• National Shrine of St. Therese and Museum, Darien (1930), at St. Clara's Church, Chicago; new shrine, 1987, after original destroyed by fire); Carmelites of Most Pure Heart of Mary Province. Address: Carmelite Visitor Center, 8501 Bailey Rd., Darien, 60561; (630) 969-3311; www.saint-therese.org.

• Shrine of St. Jude Thaddeus, Chicago (1929) located in St. Pius V Church; staffed by Dominicans, Central Province. Address: 1909 S. Ashland Ave.,

Chicago, 60608; (312) 226-0020; www.op.org/domcentral/places/stjude.

Indiana: Our Lady of Monte Cassino Shrine, St. Meinrad (1870); Benedictines. Address: St. Meinrad Archabbey, Highway 62, St. Meinrad, 47577; (812) 357-6585; www.saintmeinrad.edu/abbey/shrine.

• Old Cathedral (Basilica of St. Francis Xavier), Vincennes (1826, parish records go back to 1749); Evansville Diocese. Minor Basilica, 1970. Address: 205 Church St., Vincennes, 47591; (812) 882-5638.

Iowa: Grotto of the Redemption, West Bend (1912); Sioux City Diocese. Life of Christ in stone. Mailing address: P.O. Box 376, West Bend, 50597; (515) 887-2371; www.aw-cybermail.com/grotto.htm.

Louisiana: National Votive Shrine of Our Lady of Prompt Succor, New Orleans (1810); located in the Chapel of the Ursuline Convent (a National Historic Landmark). Address: 2635 State St., New Orleans, 70118.

• Shrine of St. Ann. Mailing address: 4920 Loveland St., Metaire, 70006; (504) 455-7071.

• Shrine of St. Roch, New Orleans (1876); located in St. Roch's Campo Santo (Cemetery); New Orleans Archdiocese. Address: 1725 St. Roch Ave., New Orleans, 70117.

Maryland: Basilica of the National Shrine of the Assumption of the Blessed Virgin Mary, Baltimore (1806). Mother Church of Roman Catholicism in the U.S. and the first metropolitan cathedral. Designed by Benjamin Henry Latrobe (architect of the Capitol) it is considered one of the finest examples of neoclassical architecture in the world. The church hosted many of the events and personalities central to the growth of Roman Catholicism in the U.S. Address: Cathedral and Mulberry Sts., Baltimore, 21201.

• National Shrine Grotto of Our Lady of Lourdes, Emmitsburg (1809, Grotto of Our Lady; 1875, National Shrine Grotto of Lourdes); public oratory, Archdiocese of Baltimore. Address: Mount St. Mary's College and Seminary, Emmitsburg, 21727; (301) 447-5318; www.msmary.edu/grotto/.

• National Shrine of St. Elizabeth Ann Seton, Emmitsburg. Foundation of Sisters of Charity (1809); first parochial school in America (1810); dedicated as Minor Basilica (1991). Address: 333 South Seton Ave., Emmitsburg, 21727; (301) 447-6606; www.setonshrine.org.

• St. Francis Xavier Shrine, "Old Bohemia," near Warwick (1704); located in Wilmington Diocese; restoration under auspices of Old Bohemia Historical Society, Inc. Address: P.O. Box 61, Warwick, 21912.

• St. Jude Shrine (1873), Archdiocese of Baltimore. Address: 308 N. Paca St., P.O. Box 1455, Baltimore, 21203.

Massachusetts: National Shrine of Our Lady of La Salette, Ipswich (1945); Missionaries of Our Lady of La Salette. Address: 251 Topsfield Rd., Ipswich, 01938.

• Our Lady of Fatima Shrine, Holliston (1950); Xaverian Missionaries. Address: 101 Summer St., Holliston, 01746; (508) 429-2144.

• St. Anthony Shrine, Boston (1947); downtown Service Church with shrine; Boston Archdiocese and Franciscans of Holy Name Province. Address: 100 Arch St., Boston, 02107.

• Saint Clement's Eucharistic Shrine, Boston (1945);

Boston Archdiocese, staffed by Oblates of the Virgin Mary. Address: 1105 Boylston St., Boston, 02215.

• National Shrine of The Divine Mercy, Stockbridge (1960); Congregation of Marians. Address: National Shrine of The Divine Mercy, Eden Hill, Stockbridge, 01262.

Michigan: Cross in the Woods-Parish, Indian River (1947); Gaylord diocese; staffed by Franciscan Friars of Sacred Heart Province, St. Louis. Address: 7078 M-68, Indian River, 49749; (231) 238-8973; www.rc.net/gaylord/crossinwoods.

• Shrine of the Little Flower, Royal Oak (c. 1929, by Father Coughlin); Detroit archdiocese. Address: 2123 Roseland, Royal Oak, 48073.

Minnesota: National Shrine of St. Odilia; St. Cloud Diocese. Address: P.O. Box 500, Onamia, 56359.

Missouri: Memorial Shrine of St. Rose Philippine Duchesne, St. Charles; Religious of the Sacred Heart of Jesus. Address: 619 N. Second St., St. Charles, 63301; (314) 946-6127.

• National Shrine of Our Lady of the Miraculous Medal, Perryville; located in St. Mary of the Barrens Church (1837); Vincentians. Address: 1811 W. St. Joseph St., Perryville, 63775; (573) 547-8343; www.amm.org.

• Old St. Ferdinand's Shrine, Florissant (1819, Sacred Heart Convent; 1821, St. Ferdinand's Church); Friends of Old St. Ferdinand's, Inc. Address: No. 1 Rue St. Francois, Florissant, 63031.

• Shrine of Our Lady of Sorrows, Starkenburg (1888; shrine building, 1910); Jefferson City Diocese. Address: c/o Church of the Risen Savior, 605 Bluff St., Rhineland, 65069; (573) 236-4390.

Nebraska: The Eucharistic Shrine of Christ the King (1973); Lincoln Diocese and Holy Spirit Adoration Sisters. Address: 1040 South Cotner Blvd., Lincoln, 68510; (402) 489-0765.

New Hampshire: Shrine of Our Lady of Grace, Colebrook (1948); Missionary Oblates of Mary Immaculate. Address: R.R. 1, Box 521, Colebrook, 03576-9535; (603) 237-5511.

• Shrine of Our Lady of La Salette, Enfield (1951); Missionaries of Our Lady of La Salette. Address: Rt. 4A, P.O. Box 420, Enfield, 03748.

New Jersey: Blue Army Shrine of the Immaculate Heart of Mary (1978); National Center of the Blue Army of Our Lady of Fatima, USA, Inc. Address: Mountain View Rd. (P.O. Box 976), Washington, 07882-0976; (908) 689-1701; www.bluearmy.com.

• Shrine of St. Joseph, Stirling (1924); Missionary Servants of the Most Holy Trinity. Address: 1050 Long Hill Rd., Stirling, 07980; (908) 647-0208; www.STShrine.org.

New Mexico: St. Augustine Mission, Isleta (1613); Santa Fe Archdiocese. Address: P.O. Box 463, Isleta, Pueblo, 87022.

• Santuario de Nuestro Senor de Esquipulas, Chimayo (1816); Santa Fe archdiocese, Sons of the Holy Family; National Historic Landmark, 1970. Address: Santuario de Chimayo, P.O. Box 235; Chimayo, 87522.

• Shrine of St. Bernadette (2003); Santa Fe archdiocese, St. Bernadette parish. Address: 1800 Martha St., N.E., Albuquerque, 87112-3161; (505) 298-7557; www.shrineofstbernadette.com.

New York: National Shrine of Bl. Kateri Tekakwitha, Fonda (1938); Order of Friars Minor Conventual. Address: P.O. Box 627, Fonda, 12068.

• Marian Shrine (National Shrine of Mary Help of Christians), West Haverstraw (1953); Salesians of St. John Bosco. Address: 174 Filors Lane, Stony Point, NY 10980-2645; (845) 947-2200; www.MarianShrine.org.

• National Shrine Basilica of Our Lady of Fatima, Youngstown (1954); designated a national shrine in 1994; Barnabite Fathers. Address: 1023 Swann Rd., Youngstown, 14174; (716) 754-7489.

• Original Shrine of St. Ann in New York City (1892); located in St. Jean Baptiste Church; Blessed Sacrament Fathers. Address: 184 E. 76th St., NY, 10021; (212) 288-5082.

• Our Lady of Victory National Shrine, Lackawanna (1926); Minor Basilica. Address: 767 Ridge Rd., Lackawanna, 14218.

• Shrine Church of Our Lady of Mt. Carmel, Brooklyn (1887); Brooklyn Diocese (Parish Church). Address: 275 N. 8th St., Brooklyn, 11211; (718) 384-0223.

• Shrine of Our Lady of Martyrs, Auriesville (1885); Society of Jesus. Address: Auriesville, 12016; (518) 853-3033; www.klink.net/~jesuit.

• Shrine of Our Lady of the Island, Eastport (1975); Montfort Missionaries. Address: Box 26, Eastport, 11941; (516) 325-0661.

• Shrine of St. Elizabeth Ann Seton, New York City (1975); located in Our Lady of the Rosary Church. Address: 7 State St., NY, 10004.

• Shrine of St. Frances Xavier Cabrini, New York (1938; new shrine dedicated 1960); Missionary Sisters of the Sacred Heart. Address: 701 Fort Washington Ave., 10040; (212) 923-3536; www.cabrinishrineny.org

Ohio: Basilica and National Shrine of Our Lady of Consolation, Carey (1867); Minor Basilica; Toledo Diocese; staffed by Conventual Franciscan Friars. Address: 315 Clay St., Carey, 43316; (419) 396-7107.

• National Shrine of Our Lady of Lebanon, North Jackson (1965); Eparchy of Our Lady of Lebanon of Los Angeles. Address: 2759 N. Lipkey Rd., North Jackson, 44451; (330) 538-3351; www.national-shrine.org.

• National Shrine and Grotto of Our Lady of Lourdes, Euclid (1926); Sisters of the Most Holy Trinity. Address: 21281 Chardon Rd., Euclid, 44117-2112; (216) 481-8232.

• National Shrine of St. Dymphna, Massillon (1938); Youngstown diocese. Address: 3000 Erie St. S., Massillon, 44648-0004.

• Our Lady of Czestochowa Shrine, Garfield Heights (1939); Sisters of St. Joseph, Third Order of St. Francis. Address: 12215 Granger Rd., Garfield Hts., 44125; (216) 581-3535.

• Our Lady of Fatima, Ironton (1954); Address: Old Rt. 52, Haverhill, OH. Mailing address: St. Joseph Church, P.O. Box 499, Ironton, 45638-0499; (740) 429-2144.

• St. Anthony Shrine, Cincinnati (1888); Franciscan Friars, St. John Baptist Province. Address: 5000 Colerain Ave., Cincinnati, 45223.

• Shrine and Oratory of the Weeping Madonna of Mariapoch, Burton (1956); Social Mission Sisters. Parma Diocese (Byzantine). Address: 17486 Mumford Rd., Burton, 44021.

• Shrine of the Holy Relics (1892); Sisters of the Precious Blood. Address: 2291 St. Johns Rd., Maria

Stein, 45860; (419) 925-4532.

• Sorrowful Mother Shrine, Bellevue (1850); Society of the Precious Blood. Address: 4106 State Rt. 269, Bellevue, 44811; (419) 483-3435.

Oklahoma: National Shrine of the Infant Jesus of Prague, Prague (1949); Oklahoma City Archdiocese. Address: P.O. Box 488, Prague, 74864.

Oregon: The Grotto (National Sanctuary of Our Sorrowful Mother), Portland (1924); Servite Friars. Address: P.O. Box 20008, Portland, 97294; www.the-grotto.com.

Pennsylvania: Basilica of the Sacred Heart of Jesus, Conewago Township (1741; present church, 1787); Minor Basilica; Harrisburg Diocese. Address: 30 Basilica Dr., Hanover, 17331.

• National Shrine Center of Our Lady of Guadalupe, Allentown (1974); located in Immaculate Conception Church; Allentown Diocese. Address: 501 Ridge Ave., Allentown, 18102; (610) 433-4404.

• National Shrine of Our Lady of Czestochowa (1955); Order of St. Paul the Hermit (Pauline Fathers). Address: P.O. Box 2049, Doylestown, 18901.

• National Shrine of St. John Neumann, Philadelphia (1860); Redemptorist Fathers, St. Peter's Church. Address: 1019 N. 5th St., Philadelphia, 19123.

• National Shrine of the Sacred Heart, Harleigh (1975); Scranton Diocese. Address: P.O. Box 500, Harleigh (Hazleton), 18225; (570) 455-1162.

• Old St. Joseph's National Shrine, Philadelphia (1733); Philadelphia Archdiocese (Parish Church). Address: 321 Willings Alley, Philadelphia, 19106; (215) 923-1733; www.oldstjoseph.org.

• St. Ann's Basilica Shrine, Scranton (1902); Passionist Community. Designated a minor basilica Aug. 29, 1996. Address: 1230 St. Ann's St., Scranton, 18504; (570) 347-5691.

• St. Anthony's Chapel, Pittsburgh (1883); Pittsburgh Diocese. Address: 1700 Harpster St., Pittsburgh, 15212.

• Shrine of St. Walburga, Greensburg (1974); Sisters of St. Benedict. Address: 1001 Harvey Ave., Greensburg, 15601; (724) 834-3060.

South Dakota: Fatima Family Shrine, Alexandria; St. Cloud Diocese. Address: St. Mary of Mercy Church, Box 158, Alexandria, 57311.

Texas: Mission Espiritu Santo de Zuniga, Goliad (1749). Victoria Diocese.

• Mission Nuestra Senora de la Purisma Concepcion, San Antonio. San Antonio Archdiocese. Address: 807 Mission Rd., San Antonio,78210.

• Mission San Francisco de la Espada, San Antonio (1731); San Antonio Archdiocese. Address: 10040 Espada Rd., San Antonio, 78214; (210) 627-2064.

• Mission San Jose y San Miguel de Aguayo, San Antonio (1720); San Antonio Archdiocese. Address: 701 E. Pyron Ave., 78214; (210) 922-0543.

• Mission San Juan Capistrano, San Antonio (1731); San Antonio Archdiocese. Address: 9101 Graf Rd., San Antonio,

• National Shrine of Our Lady of San Juan Del Valle, San Juan (1949); Brownsville Diocese; staffed by Oblates of Mary Immaculate. Address: P.O. Box 747, San Juan, 78589; (956) 787-0033.

• Nuestra Senora de la Concepcion del Socorro, Socorro, El Paso (1692).

• Oblate Lourdes Grotto Shrine of the Southwest, Tepeyac de San Antonio, San Antonio Archdiocese. Address: P.O. Box 96, San Antonio, 78291-0096; (210) 342-9864; www.oblatemissions.org.

• Old Mission San Francisco de los Tejas, Weches (1690); San Antonio Archdiocese.

• Presidio La Bahia, Goliad (1749); Victoria Diocese. Address: P.O. Box 57, Goliad, 77963; (361) 645-3752.

• San Elizario Presidio Chapel, El Paso (1789); El Paso Diocese. Address: El Paso Co., San Elceario, P.O. Box 398, 79855.

• Ysleta Mission (Nuestra Senora del Carmen), Ysleta, El Paso (1744). El Paso Diocese.

Vermont: St. Anne's Shrine, Isle La Motte (1666); Burlington Diocese, conducted by Edmundites. Address: West Shore Rd., Isle La Motte, 05463; (802) 928-3362.

Wisconsin: Holy Hill — National Shrine of Mary, Help of Christians (1857); Discalced Carmelite Friars. Address: 1525 Carmel Rd., Hubertus, 53033.

• National Shrine of St. Joseph, De Pere (1889); Norbertine Fathers. Address: 1016 N. Broadway, De Pere, 54115.

• Shrine of Mary, Mother Thrice Admirable Queen and Victress of Schoenstatt (1965), Address: W284 N698 Cherry Lane, Waukesha, 53188-9402; (414) 547-7733.

Biographies of American Bishops

(*Sources:* Catholic Almanac *survey,* The Official Catholic Directory, Annuario Pontificio, *Catholic News Service. As of Aug. 20, 2006. For notable former bishops of the U.S., see* American Catholics of the Past *at www.CatholicAlmanac.com.)*

Information includes: date and place of birth; educational institutions attended; date of ordination to the priesthood with, where applicable, name of archdiocese (*) or diocese in parentheses; date of episcopal ordination; episcopal appointments; date of resignation/retirement.

A

Adamec, Joseph V.: b. Aug. 13, 1935, Bannister, MI; educ. Michigan State Univ. (East Lansing), Nepomucene College and Lateran Univ. (Rome); ord. priest (for Nitra diocese, Slovakia), July 3, 1960; served in Saginaw diocese; ord. bp. of Altoona-Johnstown, May 20, 1987.

Adams, Edward J.: b. Aug. 24, 1944, Philadelphia, PA; educ. St. Charles Borromeo Seminary (Philadelphia), Pontifical Ecclesiastical Academy (Rome); ord. priest (Philadelphia*), May 16, 1970; in Vatican diplomatic service from 1976; ord. titular abp. of Scala, Oct. 23, 1996; papal nuncio to Bangladesh.

Ahern, Patrick V.: b. Mar. 8, 1919, New York, NY; educ. Manhattan College and Cathedral College (New York City), St. Joseph's Seminary (Yonkers, NY), St. Louis Univ. (St. Louis, MO), Notre Dame Univ. (Notre Dame, IN); ord. priest (New York*), Jan. 27, 1945; ord. titular bp. of Naiera and aux. bp. of New York, Mar. 19, 1970; ret., Apr. 26, 1994.

Allué, Emilio S., S.D.B.: b. Feb. 18, 1935, Huesca, Spain; educ. Salesain schools (Huesca, Spain) Don Bosco College/Seminary (Newton, NJ); Salesian Pontifical Univ. (Rome), Fordham Univ. (New York); ord. priest Dec. 22, 1966, in Rome; ord. titular bp. of Croe and aux. bp. of Boston, Sept. 17, 1996.

Amos, Martin J.: b. Dec. 8, 1941, Cleveland; educ. St. Mary Seminary Cleveland; ord. priest (Cleveland), May 25, 1968; app. aux. bp. of Cleveland April 3, 2001, ord., June 7, 2001.

Anderson, Moses B., S.S.E.: b. Sept. 9, 1928, Selma, AL; educ. St. Michael's College (Winooski, VT), St. Edmund Seminary (Burlington, VT), Univ. of Legon (Ghana); ord. priest, May 30, 1958; ord. titular bp. of Vatarba and aux. bp. of Detroit, Jan. 27, 1983; ret. Oct. 24, 2003.

Angadiath, Jacob: b. Oct. 26, 1945, Periappuram, Kerala, India; educ. St. Thomas Apostolic Seminary, Vadavathoor, Kottayam, India, Univ. of Kerala, India, Univ. of Dallas (U.S.); ord. priest (Palai, Kerala) Jan. 5, 1972; Director, Syro-Malabar Catholic Mission, Archdiocese of Chicago, 1999-2001; app. bp. of Eparchy of St. Thomas of Chicago of the Syro-Malabarians and Permanent Apostolic Visitator in Canada, March 13, 2001; inst., July 1, 2001.

Angell, Kenneth A.: b. Aug. 3, 1930, Providence, RI; educ. St. Mary's Seminary (Baltimore, MD); ord. priest (Providence) May 26, 1956; ord. titular bp. of Septimunicia and aux. bp. of Providence, RI, Oct. 7, 1974; bp. of Burlington, Oct. 6, 1992; inst., Nov. 9, 1992; ret. Nov. 9, 2005.

Apuron, Anthony Sablan, O.F.M. Cap.: b. Nov. 1, 1945, Agana, Guam; educ. St. Anthony College and Capuchin Seminary (Hudson, NH), Capuchin Seminary (Garrison, NY), Maryknoll Seminary (New York), Notre Dame Univ. (Notre Dame, IN); ord. priest, Aug. 26, 1972, in Guam; ord. titular bp. of Muzuca in Proconsulari and aux. bp. of Agana, Guam (unicorporated U.S. territory), Feb. 19, 1984; abp. of Agana, Mar. 10, 1986.

Aquila, Samuel J.: b. Sept. 24, 1950, Burbank, CA; educ. St. Thomas Seminary, Denver, San Anselmo (Rome); ord. priest (Denver*), June 5, 1976; rector, St. John Vianney Seminary (Denver), 1999-2001; app. coadjutor bp. of Fargo, June 12, 2001; ord., Aug. 24, 2001; bp. of Fargo, March 19, 2002.

Arias, David, O.A.R.: b. July 22, 1929, Leon, Spain; educ. St. Rita's College (San Sebastian, Spain), Our Lady of Good Counsel Theologate (Granada, Spain), Teresianum Institute (Rome, Italy); ord. priest, May 31, 1952; ord. titular bp. of Badie and aux. bp. of Newark, Apr. 7, 1983; episcopal vicar for Hispanic affairs; ret. May 21, 2004.

Arzube, Juan A.: b. June 1, 1918, Guayaquil, Ecuador; educ. Rensselaer Polytechnic Institute (Troy, NY), St. John's Seminary (Camarillo, CA); ord. priest, (Los Angeles*), May 5, 1954; ord. titular bp. of Civitate and aux. bp. of Los Angeles, Mar. 25, 1971; ret., Sept 7, 1993.

Aymond, Gregory M.: b. Nov. 12, 1949, New Orleans, LA; educ. St. Joseph Seminary College, Notre Dame Seminary (New Orleans, LA); ord. priest (New Orleans*), May 10, 1975; ord. titular bp. of Acolla and aux. bp. of New Orleans, Jan. 10, 1997; co-adjutor bp. of Austin, June 2, 2000, ins., Aug. 3, 2000; bp. of Austin, Jan. 2, 2001.

Azarcon Solis, Oscar: b. Oct. 13, 1953, San Jose, Philippines; educ: Divine Word Seminary, Tagaytay City, Univ. of St. Thomas Seminary, Manila; ord. April 28, 1979 (Cabanatuan, Philippines); incard. Houma-Thibodaux 1992; app. tit. bp. of Urci and aux. bp. of Los Angeles, Dec. 1, 2003; ord. Feb. 10, 2004.

B

Baker, Robert J.: b. June 4, 1944, Fostoria, OH; educ. Pontifical College Josephinum, Columbus, OH, Gregorian Univ., Rome; ord. (St. Augustine), March 21, 1970; app. bp of Charleston, July 13, 1999; ord., Sept. 29, 1999.

Balke, Victor H.: b. Sept. 29, 1931, Meppen, IL; educ. St. Mary of the Lake Seminary (Mundelein, IL), St. Louis Univ. (St. Louis, MO); ord. priest (Springfield, IL), May 24, 1958; ord. bp. of Crookston, Sept. 2, 1976.

Baltakis, Paul Antanas, O.F.M.: b. Jan. 1, 1925, Troskunai, Lithuania; educ. seminaries of the Franciscan Province of St. Joseph (Belgium); ord. priest, Aug. 24, 1952, in Belgium; served in U.S. as director of Lithuanian Cultural Center, New York, and among Lithuanian youth; head of U.S. Lithuanian Franciscan Vicariate, Kennebunkport, ME, from 1979; ord. titular bp. of Egara, Sept. 24, 1984; assigned to pastoral assistance to Lithuanian Catholics living outside Lithuania (resides in Brooklyn).

Balvo, Charles Daniel: b. June 29, 1951, Brooklyn, New York; educ. North American College and Pontifical Gregorian University (Rome) and Catholic University of America (Washington, DC); ord. priest (New York*), June 6, 1976; studied at the Pontifical Ecclesiastical Academy and entered the diplomatic service of the Holy See; served in nunciatures in Africa, South America, and Eastern Europe; ord. titular abp. of Castello, June 29, 2005 and appointed apostolic nuncio to New Zealand, Cook Islands, Fiji, Marshall Islands, Kiribati, Fed. States Micronesia, Nauru, Western Samoa, Tonga, Palau and Vanuatu, and Apostolic Delegate to the Pacific Ocean, Apr. 1, 2005.

Banks, Robert J.: b. Feb. 26, 1928, Winthrop, MA; educ. St. John's Seminary (Brighton, MA), Gregorian Univ., Lateran Univ. (Rome); ord. priest (Boston*), Dec. 20, 1952, in Rome; rector of St. John's Seminary, Brighton, MA, 1971-81; vicar general of Boston archdiocese, 1984; ord. titular bp. of Taraqua and aux. bp. of Boston, Sept. 19, 1985; bp. of Green Bay, Oct. 16, 1990, inst., Dec. 5, 1990; ret. Oct. 10, 2003.

Barbarito, Gerald M.: b. Jan. 4, 1950, Brooklyn, NY; educ. Cathedral College (Douglaston, NY), Immaculate Conception Seminary (Huntington, NY), Catholic University (Washington, DC); ord. priest (Brooklyn), Jan. 31, 1976; ord. titular bp. of Gisipa and aux. bp. of Brooklyn, Aug. 22, 1994; bp. of Ogdensburg, Oct. 27, 1999; inst., Jan. 7, 2000; app. bp. of Palm Beach, July 1, 2003.

Barnes, Gerald R.: b. June 22, 1945, Phoenix, AZ, of Mexican descent; educ. St. Leonard Seminary (Dayton, OH), Assumption-St. John's Seminary (San Antonio, TX); ord. priest (San Antonio*), Dec. 20, 1975; ord. titular bp. of Montefiascone and aux. bp. of San Bernardino, Mar. 18, 1992; bp. of San Bernardino, Dec. 28, 1995.

Batakian, Manuel: b. Nov. 5, 1929, Greece; moved with his family to Lebanon during World War II; educ. philosophy and theology studies in Rome; ord. priest (as a member of the Institute of the Clergy of Bzommar, an Armenian patriarchal religious order), Dec. 8, 1954; patriarchal vicar of the Institute and superior of its motherhouse in Bzommar, 1978-84; pastor of the Armenian Catholic Cathedral, Paris, 1984-90; rector of the Armenian Pontifical College,

Rome, 1990-94; elected auxiliary of the patriarchate, Dec. 8, 1994, ordained bishop, March 12, 1995; trans. Our Lady of Nareg in New York Sept. 12, 2005.

Baum, William W.: (*See* Cardinals, Biographies.)

Beltran, Eusebius J.: b. Aug. 31, 1934, Ashley, PA; educ. St. Charles Seminary (Philadelphia, PA); ord. priest (Atlanta*), May 14, 1960; ord. bp. of Tulsa, Apr. 20, 1978; app. abp. of Oklahoma City, Nov. 24, 1992; inst., Jan 22, 1993.

Bennett, Gordon D., S.J.: b. Oct. 21, 1946, Denver; educ. Mount St. Michael's (Spokane, WA), Jesuit School of Theology (Berkeley, CA), Fordham Univ. (NY); entered Society of Jesus, 1966; ord priest, June 14, 1975; app. titular bp. of Nesqually and aux. bp. of Baltimore, Dec. 23, 1997, ord. Mar 3, 1998; app. bp. of Mandeville (Jamaica), July 6, 2004; ret. Aug. 6, 2006.

Bevilacqua, Anthony J.: (*See* Cardinals, Biographies.)

Blair, Leonard P.: b. Apr. 12, 1949, Detroit; educ. Sacred Heart Seminary, Detroit, MI; Pontifical North American College, Gregorian University, and the Angelicum, Rome; ord. priest (Detroit*), June 26, 1976; at Vatican Secretariat of State, 1986-1991; Secretary to the President of the Prefecture for the Economic Affairs of the Holy See, 1994-1997; app. aux. of Detroit, July 9, 1999, ord., Aug. 24, 1999; app. bp. of Toledo, Oct. 7, 2003.

Blaire, Stephen E.: b. Dec. 22, 1941, Los Angeles, CA; educ. St. John's Seminary (Camarillo, CA); ord. priest (Los Angeles*), Apr. 29, 1967; ord. titular bp. of Lamzella and aux. of Los Angeles, May 31, 1990; app. bp. of Stockton, Jan. 19, 1999, inst., March 16, 1999.

Blume, Michael A., S.V.D.: b. May 30, 1946, South Bend, Ind.; educ. Gregorian Univ. (Rome); ord. priest Dec. 23, 1972 (Divine Word Fathers); Under-Sec. of the Pont. Council for the Pastoral Care of Migrants and Itinerants, April 6, 2000; app. archbishop (nuncio to Benin and Togo) and titular archbishop of Alessano, Alexanum Aug. 24, 2005; cons. Sept. 30, 2005.

Boland, Ernest B., O.P.: b. July 10, 1925, Providence, RI; educ. Providence College (RI), Dominican Houses of Study (Somerset, OH; Washington, DC); ord. priest, June 9, 1955; ord. bp. of Multan, Pakistan, July 25, 1966; res., Oct. 20, 1984.

Boland, J.(John) Kevin: b. Apr. 25, 1935, Cork, Ireland (brother of Bp. Raymond J. Boland); educ. Christian Brothers School (Cork), All Hallows Seminary (Dublin); ord. priest (Savannah), June 14, 1959; ord. bp. of Savannah, Apr. 18, 1995.

Boland, Raymond J.: b. Feb. 8, 1932, Tipperary, Ireland; educ. National Univ. of Ireland and All Hallows Seminary (Dublin); ord. priest (Washington*), June 16, 1957, in Dublin; vicar general and chancellor of Washington archdiocese; ord. bp. of Birmingham, Mar. 25, 1988; app. bp. of Kansas City-St. Joseph, June 22, 1993; ret. May 24, 2005.

Boles, John P.: b. Jan. 21, 1930, Boston, MA; educ. St. John Seminary, Boston College (Boston, MA); ord. priest (Boston*), Feb. 2, 1955; ord. titular bp. of Nova Sparsa and aux. bp. of Boston, May 21, 1992.

Bootkoski, Paul G: b. July 4, 1940, Newark, NJ; educ. Seton Hall Univ. (South Orange, NJ), Immaculate Conception Seminary (Darlington, NJ); ord. priest, (Newark*), May 29, 1966; ord. titular bp. of Zarna and aux. bp. of Newark, Sept. 5, 1997; app.

bp. of Metuchen, Jan. 4, 2002.

Borders, William D.: b. Oct. 9, 1913, Washington, IN; educ. St. Meinrad Seminary (St. Meinrad, IN), Notre Dame Seminary (New Orleans, LA), Notre Dame Univ. (Notre Dame, IN); ord. priest (New Orleans*), May 18, 1940; ord. first bp. of Orlando, June 14, 1968; app. abp. of Baltimore, Apr. 2, 1974, inst., June 26, 1974; ret., Apr. 11, 1989.

Bosco, Anthony G.: b. Aug. 1, 1927, New Castle, PA; educ. St. Vincent Seminary (Latrobe, PA), Lateran Univ. (Rome); ord. priest (Pittsburgh), June 7, 1952; ord. titular bp. of Labicum and aux. of Pittsburgh, June 30, 1970; app. bp. of Greensburg, Apr. 14, 1987, inst., June 30, 1987; ret..

Botean, John Michael: b. July 9, 1955, Canton, OH; educ. St. Fidelis Seminary (Herman, PA), Catholic University of America (Washington, DC), St. Gregory Melkite Seminary (Newton Centre, MA), Catholic Theological Union (Chicago, IL); ord. priest (Romanian rite St. George's in Canton), May 18, 1986; ord. bp. of Saint George's in Canton for Romanians, Aug. 24, 1996.

Boyea, Earl: b. April 10, 1951, Pontiac, Mich.; educ. Sacred Heart Seminary (Detroit), North American College and Pontifical Gregorian University (Rome), Wayne State University (Detroit), Catholic University of America (Washington, DC); ord., May 20, 1978 (Detroit*); rector and president of the Pontifical College *Josephinum* (Columbus, Ohio), 2000-2002; app. titular bp. of Siccenna and aux. bp. of Detroit, July 22, 2002, ord., Sept. 13, 2002.

Boyle, Paul M., C.P.: b. May 28, 1926, Detroit, MI; educ. Passionist houses of study, Lateran Univ. (Rome); professed in Congregation of the Passion July 9, 1946; ord. priest, May 30, 1953; president of Conference of Major Superiors of Men, 1969-74; superior general of Passionists, 1976-88; ord. titular bp. of Canapium and first vicar apostolic of Mandeville, Jamaica, July 9, 1991; ret. Jul. 6, 2004.

Bradley, Paul J.: b. Oct. 18, 1945, Glassport, PA; educ. St. Meinrad Seminary (St. Meinrad, Ind.); ord. priest May 1, 1971 (Pittsburgh); app. aux. bp. of Pittsburgh and tit. bp. of Afufenia Dec. 16, 2004; ord. Feb. 2, 2005.

Brandt, Lawrence E.: b. Mar. 27, 1939, Charleston,WV; educ. Pontifical College Josephinum (Worthington, Ohio), North American College (Rome), University of Innsbruck (Austria), Pontifical Lateran University (Rome); ord. priest (Rapid City), Dec. 19, 1969; after studies in the Pontifical Ecclesiastical Academy, entered into the diplomatic service of the Holy See, 1973 and held posts in Madagascar, Germany, Ecuador and Algeria; incardinated in Erie diocese in 1981; app. bp. of Greensburg of Jan. 2, 2004.

Bransfield, Michael J.: b. Sept. 8, 1943; educ. St. Charles Borromeo Sem. (Wynnewood, PA), The Catholic University of America (Washington); ord. priest May 15, 1971 (Philadelphia); app. bp. of Wheeling-Charleston Dec. 9, 2004; ord. Feb. 22, 2005.

Braxton, Edward K.: b. June 28, 1944, Chicago, IL; educ. Loyola Univ. of Chicago, Univ. of St. Mary of the Lake and Mundelein Seminary (Chicago), Louvain Univ. (Belgium); ord. priest (Chicago*), May 13, 1970; ord. titular bp. of Macomades rusticiana and aux. bp. of St. Louis, May 17, 1995; app. bp. of Lake Charles, Dec. 11, 2000; inst., Feb. 22, 2001; app. bp. of Bellevile, Mar. 16, 2005; inst. June 22, 2005.

Broglio, Timothy M.: b. Dec. 22, 1951, Cleveland, OH; educ. Boston College (Boston, MA), North American College and Gregorian Univ. (Rome); ord. May 19, 1977; graduate of the Pontifical Ecclesiastical Academy; entered the diplomatic corps in 1983; chief of staff to the Vatican Secretary of State; app. titular abp. (Amiternum) and papal nuncio to the Dominican Republic and apostolic delegate to Puerto Rico, Feb. 27, 2001; ord., Mar. 19, 2001.

Brom, Robert H.: b. Sept. 18, 1938, Arcadia, WI; educ. St. Mary's College (Winona, MN), Gregorian Univ. (Rome); ord. priest (Winona), Dec. 18, 1963, in Rome; ord. bp. of Duluth, May 23, 1983; coadjutor bp. of San Diego, May, 1989; bp. of San Diego, July 10, 1990.

Brown, Tod D.: b. Nov. 15, 1936, San Francisco, CA; educ. St. John's Seminary (Camarillo, CA), North American College (Rome); ord. priest (Monterey-Fresno), May 1, 1963; ord. bp. of Boise, Apr. 3, 1989; app. bp. of Orange, June 30, 1998.

Brucato, Robert A.: b. Aug. 14, 1931, New York, NY; educ. Cathedral College (Douglaston, NY), St. Joseph's Seminary (Dunwoodie, NY), Univ. of Our Lady of the Lake (San Antonio, TX); ord. priest (New York*), June 1, 1957; air force chaplain for 22 years; ord. titular bp. of Temuniana and aux. of New York, Aug. 25, 1997.

Brunett, Alexander J.: b. Jan. 17, 1934, Detroit, MI; educ. Gregorian Univ. (Rome), Sacred Heart Seminary, University of Detroit (Detroit, MI), Marquette Univ. (Milwaukee, WI); ord. priest (Detroit*), July 13, 1958; ord. bp. of Helena, July 6, 1994; app. abp. of Seattle, Oct. 28, 1997, inst., Dec. 18, 1997.

Bruskewitz, Fabian W.: b. Sept. 6, 1935, Milwaukee, WI; educ. North American College, Gregorian Univ. (Rome); ord. priest (Milwaukee*), July 17, 1960; ord. bp. of Lincoln, May 13, 1992.

Buechlein, Daniel M., O.S.B.: b. Apr. 20, 1938; educ. St. Meinrad College and Seminary (St. Meinrad, IN), St. Anselm Univ. (Rome); solemn profession as Benedictine monk, Aug. 15, 1963; ord. priest (St. Meinrad Archabbey) May 3, 1964; ord. bp. of Memphis, Mar. 2, 1987; app. abp. of Indianapolis, July 14, 1992; inst., Sept. 9, 1992.

Bukovsky, John, S.V.D.: b. Jan. 18, 1924, Cerova, Slovakia; educ. Slovakia, Divine Word Seminary (Techny, IL), Catholic Univ. (Washington, DC), Univ. of Chicago, Gregorian Univ. (Rome); ord. priest, Dec. 3, 1950; became U.S. citizen, 1958; worked at East European desk of Secretariat of State; ord. titular abp. of Tabalta, Oct. 13, 1990; nuncio to Romania, 1990-94; app. papal representative to Russia, Dec. 20, 1994-99.

Bullock, William H.: b. Apr. 13, 1927, Maple Lake, MN; educ. St. Thomas College and St. Paul Seminary (St. Paul, MN), Notre Dame Univ. (Notre Dame, IN); ord. priest (St. Paul-Minneapolis*), June 7, 1952; ord. titular bp. of Natchez and aux. bp. of St. Paul and Minneapolis, Aug. 12, 1980; app. bp. of Des Moines, Feb. 10, 1987; app. bp. of Madison, WI, Apr. 13, 1993; ret., May 23, 2003.

Bura, John: b. June 12, 1944, Wegeleben, Germany; educ. St. Basil College Seminary (Stamford), St.

Josaphat Ukrainian Catholic Seminary, The Catholic University of America, Washington; ord. priest Feb. 14, 1971 (Philadelphia/Ukrainian); ap. aux. bp. Ukrainian Arch. of Philadelphia and tit. bp. of Limisa Jan. 3, 2006; inst. Feb. 21, 2006.

Burbidge, Michael F.: b. June 16, 1957, Philadelphia; educ. St. Charles Borromeo Seminary; ord. priest (Philadelphia*), May 19, 1984; app. titular bp. of Cluain Iraird and aux. bp. of Philadelphia, June 21, 2002, ord., Sept. 5, 2002; app. bp. of Raleigh, June 8, 2006.

Burke, John J., O.F.M.: b. Mar. 16, 1935, River Edge, NJ; educ. St. Joseph Seminary (Callicoon, NY), St. Bonaventure Univ. (St. Bonaventure, NY), Holy Name College (Washington, DC); solemnly professed in Franciscan Order, Aug. 20, 1958; ord. priest, Feb. 25, 1961; missionary in Brazil from 1964; ord. coadjutor bp. of Miracema do Tocantins, Brazil, Mar. 25, 1995; bp. of Miracema do Tocantins, Feb. 14, 1996.

Burke, Raymond L.: b. June 30, 1948, Richland Center, WI; educ. Holy Cross Seminary (La Crosse, WI), Catholic Univ. (Washington, DC), North American College and Gregorian Univ. (Rome); ord. priest (La Crosse), June 29, 1975; ord. bp. of La Crosse, Jan. 6, 1995, inst., Feb. 22, 1995; app. abp. of St. Louis, Dec. 2, 2003.

Bustros, Cyrille Salim, S.M.S.P.: b. Jan. 26, 1939, Ain-Bourday, Lebanon; educ. Missionaries of St. Paul and Seminary of Sainte-Anne of Jerusalem (Jerusalem), University of Louvain (Louvain, Belgium); ord. June 29, 1962 (Society of the Missionaries of St. Paul); elected abp. of Baalbeck, Lebanon, Oct. 25, 1988; app. eparch of Newton, June 22, 2004.

Buswell, Charles A.: b. Oct. 15, 1913, Homestead, OK; educ. St. Louis Preparatory Seminary (St. Louis, MO), Kenrick Seminary (Webster Groves, MO), American College, Univ. of Louvain (Belgium); ord. priest (Oklahoma City*), July 9, 1939; ord. bp. of Pueblo, Sept. 30, 1959; resigned, Sept. 18, 1979.

C

Caggiano, Frank J.: b. March 29, 1959, Brooklyn; educ. Immaculate Conception Seminary (Huntington, N.Y.), Gregorian Univ. (Rome); ord. priest May 16, 1987 (Brooklyn); appointed aux. bp. of Brooklyn and tit. bp. of Inis Cathaig June 6, 2006; ord. Aug. 22, 2006.

Calvo, Randolph R.: b. Aug. 28, 1950, Agana, Guam; educ. St. Patrick's Seminary and University (Menlo Park, Cal.), Angelicum (Rome); ord. priest May 21, 1977 (San Francisco); app. bp of Reno Dec. 23, 2005; ord. bp. Feb. 17, 2006.

Camacho, Tomas Aguon: b. Sept. 18, 1933, Chalon Kanoa, Saipan; educ. St. Patrick's Seminary (Menlo Park, CA); ord. priest, June 14, 1961; ord. first bp. of Chalan Kanoa, Northern Marianas (U.S. Commonwealth), Jan. 13, 1985.

Campbell, Frederick F.: b. Aug. 5, 1943, Elmira, NY; educ. Ohio State Univ., St. Paul Seminary, St. Paul, MN; ord. priest (St. Paul and Minneapolis*), May 31, 1980; app. titular bp. of Afufenia and aux. bp. of St. Paul and Minneapolis, March 2, 1999, ord., May 14, 1999; app. bp. of Columbus, Oct. 14, 2004; inst. Jan. 13, 2005.

Carlson, Robert J.: b. June 30, 1944, Minneapolis, MN; educ. Nazareth Hall and St. Paul Seminary (St. Paul, MN), Catholic Univ. (Washington, DC): ord. priest (St. Paul-Minneapolis*), May 23, 1970; ord. titular bp. of Avioccala and aux. bp. of St. Paul and Minneapolis, Jan. 11, 1984; app. coadjutor bp. of Sioux Falls, Jan. 13, 1994; succeeded as bp. of Sioux Falls, Mar. 21, 1995; app. bp. of Saginaw, Dec. 29, 2004; inst. Feb. 24, 2005.

Carmody, Edmond: b. Jan. 12, 1934, Ahalena, Kerry, Ireland; educ. St. Brendan's College (Killarney), St. Patrick Seminary (Carlow); ord. priest (San Antonio*), June 8, 1957; missionary in Peru 1984-89; ord. titular bp. of Mortlach and aux. bp. of San Antonio, Dec. 15, 1988; app. bp. of Tyler, 1992-2000; app. bp. of Corpus Christi, Feb. 3, 2000; inst., March 17, 2000.

Carmon, Dominic, S.V.D.: b. Dec. 13, 1930, Opelousas, LA; entered Society of Divine Word, 1946; ord. priest, Feb. 2, 1960; missionary in Papua-New Guinea, 1961-68; ord. titular bp. of Rusicade and aux. bp. of New Orleans, Feb. 11, 1993.

Casey, Luis Morgan: b. June 23, 1935, Portageville, MO; ord. priest (St. Louis*), Apr. 7, 1962; missionary in Bolivia from 1965; ord. titular bp. of Mibiarca and aux. of La Paz, Jan. 28, 1984; vicar apostolic of Pando, Bolivia, Jan. 18, 1988, and apostolic administrator (1995) of La Paz.

Catanello, Ignatius A.: b. July 23, 1938, Brooklyn, NY; educ. Cathedral Preparatory Seminary and St. Francis College (Brooklyn, NY), Catholic Univ. (Washington, DC); St. John's University (Jamaica, NY), New York University; ord. priest (Brooklyn), May 28, 1966; ord. titular bp. of Deulto and aux. bp. of Brooklyn, Aug. 22, 1994.

Chaput, Charles J., O.F.M. Cap.: b. Sept. 26, 1944, Concordia, KS; educ. St. Fidelis College (Herman, PA), Capuchin College and Catholic Univ. (Washington, DC), Univ. of San Francisco; solemn vows as Capuchin, July 14, 1968; ord. priest, Aug. 29, 1970; ord. bp. of Rapid City, SD, July 26, 1988, the second priest of Native American ancestry (member of Prairie Band Potawatomi Tribe) ordained a bp. in the U.S.; app abp. of Denver, inst., Apr. 7, 1997.

Charron, Joseph L., C.PP.S.: b. Dec. 30, 1939, Redfield, SD; educ. St. John's Seminary (Collegeville, MN); ord. priest, June 3, 1967; ord. titular bp. of Bencenna and aux. bp. of St. Paul and Minneapolis, Jan. 25, 1990; app. bp. of Des Moines, Nov. 12, 1993.

Chavez, Gilbert Espinoza: b. May 9, 1932, Ontario, CA; educ. St. Francis Seminary (El Cajon, CA), Immaculate Heart Seminary (San Diego), Univ. of CA; ord. priest (San Diego) Mar. 19, 1960; ord. titular bp. of Magarmel and aux. of San Diego, June 21, 1974.

Chedid, John: b. July 4, 1923, Eddid, Lebanon; educ. seminaries in Lebanon and Pontifical Urban College (Rome); ord. priest, Dec. 21, 1951, in Rome; ord. titular bp. of Callinico and aux. bp. of St. Maron of Brooklyn for the Maronites, Jan. 25, 1981; app. first bp. of Eparchy of Our Lady of Lebanon of Los Angeles for the Maronites, Mar. 1, 1994; res., Dec. 5, 2000.

Choby, David R.: b. Jan. 17, 1947, Nashville, TN; educ. St. Ambrose College (Davenport, Iowa), The Catholic University of America (Washington), and the Angelicum (Rome); ord. priest Sept. 6, 1974 (Nashville); app. bp of Nashville Dec. 20, 2005; ord.

bp. Feb. 27, 2006.

Chomnycky, Paul P.: b. April 5, 2002, Vancouver, B.C; educ. University of British Columbia (Vancouver), Pont. St. Anselm Univ., Pont. Gregorian University (Rome); ord. Oct. 1, 1988 (Basilians); app. bp for Ukrainian Catholics living in Great Britain April 5, 2002; ord. bp. June 11, 2002; trans. Ukrainian Diocese of Stamford Jan. 3, 2006; inst. Feb. 20, 2006.

Christian, Francis J.: b. Oct. 8, 1942, Peterborough, NH; educ. St. Anselm College (Manchester, NH), St. Paul Seminary (Ottawa), American College in Louvain (Belgium); ord. priest (Manchester), June 29, 1968; ord titular bp. of Quincy and aux. of Manchester, May 14, 1996.

Cisneros, Octavio: b. July 19, 1945, Cuba; educ.: Immaculate Conception Sem. (Huntington, N.Y.); ord. priest Mary 29, 1971; appointed aux. bp. of Brooklyn and tit. bp. of Eanach Duin June 6, 2006; ord. Aug. 22, 2006.

Cistone, Joseph R.: b. May 18, 1949, Philadelphia, PA; educ. St. Charles Borromeo Seminary (Overbrook, PA); ord. priest (Philadelphia*), May 17, 1975; app. titular bp. of Case mediane and aux. bp. of Philadelphia, June 8, 2004; ord. July 28, 2004.

Clark, Edward W.: b. Nov. 30, 1946, Minneapolis; educ. Our Lady Queen of Angels Seminary (San Fernando, CA), St. John's Seminary College (Camarillo, CA), Gregorian University (Rome); ord. priest (Los Angeles*), May 9, 1972; President/Rector, St. John's Seminary College (Camarillo, CA), 1994-2001; app. titular bp. of Gardar and aux. bp. of Los Angeles, Jan. 16, 2001, ord., Mar. 26, 2001.

Clark, Matthew H.: b. July 15, 1937, Troy, NY; educ. St. Bernard's Seminary (Rochester, NY), Gregorian Univ. (Rome); ord. priest (Albany) Dec. 19, 1962; ord. bp. of Rochester, May 27, 1979; inst., June 26, 1979.

Coakley, Paul S.: b. June 3, 1955, Norfolk, VA; educ. University of Kansas (Lawrence), St. Pius X Seminary (Erlanger, KY), Mount St. Mary's Seminary (Emmitsburg, MD); ord. Priest May 21, 1983 (Wichita); app. bp. of Salina Oct. 21, 2004; ord. Dec. 28, 2004.

Coleman, George W.: b. Feb. 1, 1939, Fall River, MA; educ. Holy Cross College (Worcester, MA), Fall River, Saint John's Seminary (Boston, MA), North American College and Gregorian Univ. (Rome), Brown University (Providence, RI); ord. priest, Dec. 16, 1964; app. bp. of Fall River, April 30, 2003; ord. bp., July 22, 2003.

Conlon, Robert D.: b. Dec. 4, 1948, Cincinnati; educ. Mount St. Mary's Seminary of the West, University of St. Paul, Ottawa; ord. priest (Cincinnati*), Jan. 15, 1977; app. bp. of Steubenville, May 31, 2002.

Connolly, Thomas J.: b. July 18, 1922, Tonopah, NV; educ. St. Patrick's Seminary (Menlo Park, CA), Catholic Univ. (Washington, DC), Lateran Univ. (Rome); ord. priest (Reno-Las Vegas), Apr. 8, 1947; ord. bp. of Baker, June 30, 1971; res., Nov. 19, 1999.

Connors, Ronald G., C.SS.R.: b. Nov. 1, 1915, Brooklyn, NY; ord. priest, June 22, 1941; ord. titular bp. of Equizetum and coadjutor bp. of San Juan de la Maguana, Dominican Republic, July 20, 1976; succeeded as bp. of San Juan de la Maguana, July 20, 1977; ret., Feb. 20, 1991.

Cooney, Patrick R.: b. Mar. 10, 1934, Detroit, MI; educ. Sacred Heart Seminary (Detroit), Gregorian Univ. (Rome), Notre Dame Univ. (Notre Dame, IN); ord. priest (Detroit*), Dec. 20, 1959; ord. titular bp. of Hodelm and aux. bp. of Detroit, Jan. 27, 1983; app. bp. of Gaylord, Nov. 6, 1989; inst., Jan. 28, 1990.

Cordileone, Salvatore: b. June 5, 1956, San Diego, Calif.; educ. Saint Francis Seminary (San Diego), University of San Diego (San Diego), North American College (Rome), Pontifical Gregorian University (Rome); ord. July 9, 1982; official of the Supreme Tribunal of the Apostolic Signatura in Roma, 1995-2002 and vice-director of Villa Stritch in Rome; app. titular bp. of Natchez and aux. bp. of San Diego, July 5, 2002, ord., Aug. 21, 2002.

Corrada del Rio, Alvaro, S.J.: b. May 13, 1942, Santurce, Puerto Rico; entered Society of Jesus, 1960, at novitiate of St. Andrew-on-Hudson (Poughkeepsie, NY); educ. Jesuit seminaries, Fordham Univ. (New York), Institut Catholique (Paris); ord. priest, July 6, 1974, in Puerto Rico; pastoral coordinator of Northeast Catholic Hispanic Center, New York, 1982-85; ord. titular bp. of Rusticiana and aux. bp. of Washington, DC, Aug. 4, 1985; app. apostolic administrator of Caguas, Puerto Rico, Aug. 5, 1997 (retained his title as aux. bp. of Washington); app. bp. of Tyler, Dec. 5, 2000; inst., Jan. 30, 2001.

Coscia, Benedict Dominic, O.F.M.: b. Aug. 10, 1922, Brooklyn, NY; educ. St. Francis College (Brooklyn, NY), Holy Name College (Washington, DC); ord. priest June 11, 1949; ord. bp. of Jatai, Brazil, Sept. 21, 1961.

Costello, Thomas J.: b. Feb. 23, 1929, Camden, NY; educ. Niagara Univ. (Niagara Falls, NY), St. Bernard's Seminary (Rochester, NY), Catholic Univ. (Washington, DC); ord. priest (Syracuse), June 5, 1954; ord. titular bp. of Perdices and aux. bp. of Syracuse, Mar. 13, 1978; ret. March 23, 2004.

Cote, Michael R.: b. June 19, 1949, Sanford, ME; educ. Our Lady of Lourdes Seminary (Cassadaga, NY), St. Mary's Seminary College (Baltimore, MD); Gregorian Univ. (Rome), Catholic Univ. (Washington, DC); ord. priest (Portland, ME), June 29, 1975, by Pope Paul VI in Rome; secretary, 1989-94 at apostolic nunciature, Washington; ord. titular bp. of Cebarades and aux. of Portland, ME, July 27, 1995; app. bp. of Norwich, March 11, 2003; inst., May 13, 2003.

Cotey, Arnold R., S.D.S.: b. June 15, 1921, Milwaukee, WI; educ. Divine Savior Seminary (Lanham, MD), Marquette Univ. (Milwaukee, WI); ord. priest, June 7, 1949; ord. first bp. of Nachingwea (now Lindi), Tanzania, Oct. 20, 1963; ret., Nov. 11, 1983.

Cronin, Daniel A.: b. Nov. 14, 1927, Newton, MA; educ. St. John's Seminary (Boston, MA), North American College and Gregorian Univ. (Rome); ord. priest (Boston*), Dec. 20, 1952; attaché apostolic nunciature (Addis Ababa), 1957-61; served in papal Secretariat of State, 1961-68; ord. titular bp. of Egnatia and aux. bp. of Boston, Sept. 12, 1968; bp. of Fall River, Dec. 16, 1970; abp. of Hartford, Dec. 10, 1991; ret. Oct. 23, 2003.

Cullen, Edward P.: b. Mar. 15, 1933, Philadelphia, PA; educ. St. Charles Borromeo Seminary (Overbrook, PA), Univ. of Pennsylvania and LaSalle Univ. (Philadelphia), Harvard Graduate School of

Business; ord. priest (Philadelphia*), May 19, 1962; ord. titular bp. of Paria in Proconsolare and aux. of Philadelphia, Feb. 8, 1994; app. bp. of Allentown, Dec. 16, 1997, inst., Feb. 9, 1998.

Cummins, John S.: b. Mar. 3, 1928, Oakland, CA; educ. St. Patrick's Seminary (Menlo Park, CA), Catholic Univ. (Washington, DC), Univ. of CA; ord. priest (San Francisco*), Jan. 24, 1953; executive director of the CA Catholic Conference 1971-76; ord. titular bp. of Lambaesis and aux. bp. of Sacramento, May 16, 1974; app. bp. of Oakland, inst., June 30, 1977; ret. Oct. 1, 2003.

Cunningham, Robert J.: b. June 18, 1943, Buffalo, N.Y.; educ. St. John Vianney Seminary (East Aurora, N.Y.), Catholic University of America (Washington, D.C.); ord. May 24, 1969 (Buffalo); bp. of Ogdensburg March 9, 2004; ord. May 18, 2004.

Cupich, Blase: b. Mar. 19, 1949, Omaha, NE; educ. College of St. Thomas (St. Paul, MN), Gregorian Univ. (Rome), Catholic University of America (Washington, DC); ord. priest (Omaha*), Aug. 16, 1975; service at the apostolic nunciature, Washington, DC, 1981-87; rector, Pontifical College Josephinum (Columbus, OH), 1989-97; app. bp. of Rapid City, SD, July 7, 1998; ord., Sept. 21, 1998.

Curlin, William G.: b. Aug. 30, 1927, Portsmouth, VA; educ. Georgetown Univ. (Washington, DC), St. Mary's Seminary (Baltimore, MD); ord. priest (Washington*), May 25, 1957; ord. titular bp. of Rosemarkie and aux. bp. of Washington, Dec. 20, 1988; app. bp. of Charlotte, Feb. 22, 1994, ret., Sept. 16, 2002.

Curry, Thomas J.: b. Jan. 17, 1943, Drumgoon, Ireland; educ. Patrician College (Ballyfin), All Hallows Seminary (Dublin); ord. priest (Los Angeles*), June 17, 1967; ord. titular bp. of Ceanannus Mór and aux. of Los Angeles, Mar. 19, 1994.

Curtiss, Elden F.: b. June 16, 1932, Baker, OR; educ. St. Edward Seminary College and St. Thomas Seminary (Kenmore, WA); ord. priest (Baker), May 24, 1958; ord. bp. of Helena, MT, Apr. 28, 1976; app. abp. of Omaha, NE, May 4, 1993.

D

Da Cunha, Edgar M., S.D.V.: b. Aug. 21, 1953, Riachão do Jacuípe Bahia, Brazil; educ. Catholic University of Salvador (Brazil), Immaculate Conception Seminary (Newark, NJ); professed perpetual vows, Feb. 11, 1979, and ord., priest March 27, 1982; app. titular bp. of Ucres and aux. of Newark, June 27, 2003.

Daily, Thomas V.: b. Sept. 23, 1927, Belmont, MA; educ. Boston College, St. John's Seminary (Brighton, MA); ord. priest (Boston*), Jan. 10, 1952; missionary in Peru for five years as a member of the Society of St. James the Apostle; ord. titular bp. of Bladia and aux. bp. of Boston, Feb. 11, 1975; app. first bp. of Palm Beach, FL, July 17, 1984; app. bp. of Brooklyn, Feb. 20, 1990; inst., Apr. 18, 1990; ret., Aug. 1, 2003.

Daly, James: b. Aug. 14, 1921, New York, NY; educ. Cathedral College (Brooklyn, NY), Immaculate Conception Seminary (Huntington, L.I.); ord. priest (Brooklyn), May 22, 1948; ord. titular bp. of Castra Nova and aux. bp. of Rockville Centre, May 9, 1977; ret., July 1, 1996.

D'Antonio, Nicholas, O.F.M.: b. July 10, 1916, Rochester, NY; educ. St. Anthony's Friary (Catskill, NY); ord. priest, June 7, 1942; ord. titular bp. of Giufi Salaria and prelate of Olancho, Honduras, July 25, 1966; resigned, 1977; vicar general of New Orleans archdiocese and episcopal vicar for Spanish Speaking, 1977-91.

D'Arcy, John M.: b. Aug. 18, 1932, Brighton, MA; educ. St. John's Seminary (Brighton, MA), Angelicum Univ. (Rome); ord. priest (Boston*), Feb. 2, 1957; spiritual director of St. John's Seminary; ord. titular bp. of Mediana and aux. bp. of Boston, Feb. 11, 1975; app. bp. of Fort Wayne-South Bend, Feb. 26, 1985, inst., May 1, 1985.

Del Riego, Rutilio: b. Sept. 21, 1940, Valdesandinas (Leon), Spain; educ. Diocesan Laborer Priests seminary (Salamanca, Spain), Catholic Univ. of America; ord. priest June 5, 1965, (Diocesan Laborer Priests); app. aux. bp. San Bernardino and tit. bp. of Daimlaig July 26, 2005; ord. Sept. 20, 2005.

Dendinger, William J.: b. May 20, 1939, Omaha; educ. Conception College Seminary (Conception, Missouri), Aquinas Institute (Iowa); ord. priest May 29, 1965; U.S. Air Force chaplain, 1970-2002, achieving the rank of Major General; app. bp. of Grand Island Oct. 14, 2004; ord. Dec. 13, 2004.

De Palma, Joseph A., S.C.J.: b. Sept. 4, 1913, Walton, NY; ord. priest, May 20, 1944; superior general of Congregation of Priests of the Sacred Heart, 1959-67; ord. first bp. of De Aar, South Africa, July 19, 1967; ret., Nov. 18, 1987.

De Paoli, Ambrose: b. Aug. 19, 1934, Jeannette, PA, moved to Miami at age of nine; educ. St. Joseph Seminary (Bloomfield, CT), St. Mary of the West Seminary (Cincinnati, OH), North American College and Lateran Univ. (Rome); ord. priest (Miami*), Dec. 18, 1960, in Rome; served in diplomatic posts in Canada, Turkey, Africa and Venezuela; ord. titular abp. of Lares, Nov. 20, 1983, in Miami; apostolic pro-nuncio to Sri Lanka, 1983-88; apostolic delegate in southern Africa and pro-nuncio to Lesotho, 1988; first apostolic nuncio to South Africa, 1994; apostolic nuncio to Australia, 2004.

De Simone, Louis A.: b. Feb. 21, 1922, Philadelphia, PA; educ. Villanova Univ. (Villanova, PA), St. Charles Borromeo Seminary (Overbrook, PA); ord. priest (Philadelphia*), May 10, 1952; ord. titular bp. of Cillium and aux. bp. of Philadelphia, Aug. 12, 1981; ret., Apr. 5, 1997.

DeWane, Frank J.: b. March 9, 1950, Green Bay, Wis.; educ. Univ. of Wisconsin (Oshkosh), American Univ., George Washington Univ. (Washington, DC), North American College, Pont. Gregorian Univ., Angelicum (Rome); ord. priest July 16, 1988 (Green Bay); app. coadj. bp. of Venice April 25, 2006; ord. bp. July 25, 2006.

Di Lorenzo, Francis X.: b. Apr. 15, 1942, Philadelphia, PA; educ. St. Charles Borromeo Seminary (Philadelphia), Univ. of St. Thomas (Rome); ord. priest (Philadelphia*), May 18, 1968; ord. titular bp. of Tigia and aux. bp. of Scranton, Mar. 8, 1988; app. apostolic administrator of Honolulu, Oct. 12, 1993; bp. of Honolulu, Nov. 29, 1994; app. bp. of Richmond, Mar. 31, 2004.

DiMarzio, Nicholas: b. June 16, 1944, Newark, NJ; educ. Seton Hall University (South Orange, NJ),

Immaculate Conception Seminary (Darlington, NJ), Catholic Univ. (Washington, DC), Fordham Univ. (New York), Rutgers Univ. (New Brunswick, NJ); ord. priest (Newark*), May 30, 1970; ord. titular bp. of Mauriana and aux. bp. of Newark, Oct. 31, 1996, app. Bishop of Camden, June 8, 1999, inst., July 22, 1999; app. bp. of Brooklyn, Aug. 1, 2003.

Dimino, Joseph T.: b. Jan. 7, 1923, New York, NY; educ. Cathedral College (Douglaston, NY), St. Joseph's Seminary (Yonkers, NY), Catholic Univ. (Washington, DC); ord. priest (New York*), June 4, 1949; ord. titular bp. of Carini and aux. bp. of the Military Services archdiocese, May 10, 1983; app. ordinary of Military Services archdiocese, May 14, 1991; ret., Aug. 12, 1997.

DiNardo, Daniel N.: b. May 23, 1949, Steubenville, OH; educ. Catholic Univ. of America (Washington, DC) North American College, (Rome), Gregorian Univ. (Rome); ord. priest (Pittsburgh), July 16, 1977; app. coadjutor Bp. of Sioux City, Aug. 19, 1997, ord., Oct. 7, 1997, bp. of Sioux City, Nov. 28, 1998; app. coadjutor bp. of Galveston-Houston, Jan. 16, 2004; inst. March 26, 2004; app. coadjutor abp. of Galveston-Houston, Dec. 29, 2004; abp. of Galveston-Houston, Feb. 28, 2006.

Dion, George E., O.M.I.: b. Sept. 25, 1911, Central Falls, RI; educ. Holy Cross College (Worcester, MA), Oblate Juniorate (Colebrook, NH), Oblate Scholasticates (Natick, MA, and Ottawa, Ont.); ord. priest, June 24, 1936; ord. titular bp. of Arpaia and vicar apostolic of Jolo, Philippines Apr. 23, 1980; ret., Oct. 11, 1991; titular bp. of Arpaia.

Dolan, Timothy M.: b. Feb. 6, 1950, St. Louis; educ. St. Louis Preparatory Seminary, Cardinal Glennon College, North American College, Pontifical Univ. of St. Thomas (Rome), Catholic University of America (Washington, DC); ord. priest (St. Louis*), June 19, 1976; served on staff of apostolic nunciature (Washington, DC); rector, North American College (Rome), 1994-2001; app. titular bp. of Natchez and aux. bp. of St. Louis, June 19, 2001; ord., Aug. 15, 2001; app. abp. of Milwaukee, June 25, 2002; inst., Aug. 28, 2002.

Donato, Thomas A.: b. Oct. 1, 1940, Jersey City, NJ; educ. Seton Hall Univ. (South Orange, NJ), Immaculate Conception Seminary (Darlington, NJ); ord. priest (Newark*), May 29, 1965; app. aux. bp. of Newark and tit. bp of Jamestown, May 21, 2004; ord. Aug. 4, 2004.

Donnelly, Robert William: b. Mar. 22, 1931, Toledo, OH; educ. St. Meinrad Seminary College (St. Meinrad, IN), Mount St. Mary's in the West Seminary (Norwood, OH); ord. priest (Toledo), May 25, 1957; ord. titular bp. of Garba and aux. bp. of Toledo, May 3, 1984; ret. May 30, 2006.

Donoghue, John F.: b. Aug. 9, 1928, Washington, DC; educ. St. Mary's Seminary (Baltimore, MD); Catholic Univ. (Washington, DC); ord. priest (Washington*), June 4, 1955; chancellor and vicar general of Washington archdiocese, 1973-84; ord. bp. of Charlotte, Dec. 18, 1984; app. abp. of Atlanta, June 22, 1993; inst., Aug. 19, 1993; ret. Dec. 9, 2004.

Donovan, Paul V.: b. Sept. 1, 1924, Bernard, IA; educ. St. Gregory's Seminary (Cincinnati, OH), Mt. St. Mary's Seminary (Norwood, OH), Lateran Univ. (Rome); ord. priest (Lansing), May 20, 1950; ord. first

bp. of Kalamazoo, July 21, 1971; ret., Nov. 22, 1994.

Doran, Thomas George: b. Feb. 20, 1936, Rockford, IL; educ. Loras College (Dubuque, IA), Gregorian Univ. (Rome), Rockford College (Rockford, IL); ord. priest (Rockford), Dec. 20, 1961; ord. bp. of Rockford, June 24, 1994.

Dorsey, Norbert M., C.P.: b. Dec. 14, 1929, Springfield, MA; educ. Passionist seminaries (eastern U.S. province), Pontifical Institute of Sacred Music and Gregorian Univ. (Rome, Italy); professed in Passionists, Aug. 15, 1949; ord. priest, Apr. 28, 1956; assistant general of Passionists, 1976-86; ord. titular bp. of Mactaris and aux. bp. of Miami, Mar. 19, 1986; app. bp. of Orlando, Mar. 20, 1990, inst., May 25, 1990; ret. Nov. 13, 2004.

Doueihi, Stephen Hector: b. June 25, 1927, Zghorta, Lebanon; educ. University of St. Joseph (Beirut, Lebanon), Propaganda Fide, Gregorian Univ. and Institute of Oriental Study (Rome); ord. priest, Aug. 14, 1955; came to U.S. in 1973; ord. eparch of Eparchy of St. Maron of Brooklyn, Jan 11, 1997; ret. January 10, 2004.

Dougherty, John Martin: b. Apr. 29, 1932, Scranton, PA; educ. St. Charles College (Catonsville, MD), St. Mary's Seminary (Baltimore), Univ. of Notre Dame (South Bend); ord. priest (Scranton), June 15, 1957; ord. titular bp. of Sufetula and aux. bp. of Scranton, Mar. 7, 1995.

Driscoll, Michael P.: b. Aug. 8, 1939, Long Beach, CA; educ. St. John Seminary (Camarillo, CA), Univ. of Southern CA; ord. priest (Los Angeles*), May 1, 1965; ord. titular bp. of Massita and aux. bp. of Orange, Mar. 6, 1990; app. bp. of Boise, Jan. 19, 1999, inst., Mar. 18, 1999.

Dudick, Michael J.: b. Feb. 24, 1916, St. Clair, PA; educ. St. Procopius College and Seminary (Lisle, IL); ord. priest (Passaic, Byzantine Rite), Nov. 13, 1945; ord. bp. of Byzantine Eparchy of Passaic, Oct. 24, 1968; ret., Nov. 6, 1995.

Dudley, Paul V.: b. Nov. 27, 1926, Northfield, MN; educ. Nazareth College and St. Paul Seminary (St. Paul, MN); ord. priest (St. Paul-Minneapolis*), June 2, 1951; ord. titular bp. of Ursona and aux. bp. of St. Paul and Minneapolis, Jan. 25, 1977; app. bp. of Sioux Falls, inst., Dec. 13, 1978; ret., Mar. 21, 1995.

Duffy, Paul, O.M.I.: b. July 25, 1932, Norwood, MA; educ Oblate houses of study in Canada and Washington, DC; ord. priest, 1962; missionary in Zambia from 1984; app. first bp. of Mongu, Zambia, July 1, 1997.

Duhart, Clarence James, C.SS.R.: b. Mar. 23, 1912, New Orleans, LA; ord. priest, June 29, 1937; ord. bp. of Udon Thani, Thailand, Apr. 21, 1966; resigned, Oct. 2, 1975.

DuMaine, (Roland) Pierre: b. Aug. 2, 1931, Paducah, KY; educ. St. Joseph's College (Mountain View, CA), St. Patrick's College and Seminary (Menlo Park, CA), Univ. of CA (Berkeley), Catholic Univ. (Washington, DC); ord. priest (San Francisco), June 15, 1957; ord. titular bp. of Sarda and aux. bp. of San Francisco, June 29, 1978; app. first bp. of San Jose, Jan. 27, 1981; inst., Mar. 18, 1981; res., Nov. 27, 1999.

Dunne, John C.: b. Oct. 30, 1937, Brooklyn, NY; educ. Cathedral College (Brooklyn, NY). Immaculate Conception Seminary (Huntington, NY), Manhattan College (New York); ord. priest (Rockville Centre),

June 1, 1963; ord. titular bp. of Abercorn and aux. bp. of Rockville Centre, Dec. 13, 1988. Vicar for Central Vicariate.

Dupre, Thomas L.: b. Nov. 10, 1933, South Hadley Falls, MA; educ. College de Montreal, Assumption College (Worcester, MA), Catholic Univ. (Washington, DC), ord. priest (Springfield, MA), May 23, 1959; ord. titular bp. of Hodelm and aux. bp. of Springfield, MA, May 31, 1990; bp. of Springfield, Mar. 14, 1995; res. Feb.11, 2004.

Durning, Dennis V., C.S.Sp.: b. May 18, 1923, Germantown, PA; educ. St. Mary's Seminary (Ferndale, CT); ord. priest, June 3, 1949; ord. first bp. of Arusha, Tanzania, May 28, 1963; resigned, Mar. 6, 1989.

E

Edyvean, Walter J.: b. Oct. 18, 1938, Medford, MA; educ. Boston College, St. John's Seminary (Brighton, MA), the North American College and the Gregorian Univ. (Rome); ord. priest (Boston*), Dec. 16, 1964; served on staff of Congregation for Catholic Education, 1990-2001; app. titular bp. of Elie and aux. bp. of Boston, June 29, 2001, ord., Sept. 14, 2001

Egan, Edward M.: (*See* Cardinals, Biographies.)

Elizondo, Eusebio: b. Aug. 8, 1954, Victoria, Mexico; educ. Missionaries of the Holy Spirit seminary, (Jalisco, Mexico), Gregorian University (Rome); ord. priest (Missionaries of Holy Spirit) Aug. 18, 1984; app. auxiliary bishop of Seattle and titular bishop of Acolla May 12, 2005; ord. bp. June 6, 2005.

Elya, John A., B.S.O.: b. Sept. 16, 1928, Maghdouche, Lebanon; educ. diocesan monastery (Sidon, Lebanon), Gregorian Univ. (Rome, Italy); professed as member of Basilian Salvatorian Order, 1949; ord. priest, Feb. 17, 1952, in Rome; came to U.S., 1958; ord. titular bp. of Abilene of Syria and aux. bp. of Melkite diocese of Newton, MA, June 29, 1986; app. bp. of Newton (Melkites), Nov. 25, 1993, res. Jun. 22, 2004.

Estabrook, Joseph W.: b. May 19, 1944, Kingston, New York; educ. St. Bonaventure University and Christ the King Seminary (St. Bonaventure, NY), Jesuit School of Theology (Berkeley, CA); ord. priest (Albany), May 30, 1969; entered the Archdiocese for the Military Services as a Marine Corps chaplain, 1977; app. titular bp. of Flenucleta and aux. bp. of the Archdiocese for the Military Ordinariate, May 7, 2004.

Estevez, Felipe de Jesus: b. Feb. 5, 1946, Betancourt, Cuba; educ: Grand Seminary, Montreal, Gregorian Univ., Rome; ord. May 30, 1970 (Matanzas, Cuba); incard. Miami Feb. 1979; app. aux. bp. of Miami and tit. bp. of Kearney Nov. 21, 2003; ord. Jan. 7, 2004.

F

Farrell, Kevin J.: b. Dublin, Ireland, Sept. 2, 1947; educ. University of Salamanca (Spain), Gregorian University and University of St. Thomas Aquinas (Rome), University of Notre Dame (South Bend, IN); ord. priest (of the Legionaries of Christ), Dec. 24, 1978; incardinated into Archdiocese of Washington, 1984; app. titular bp. of Rusuccuru and aux. bp. of Washington, Dec. 28, 2001.

Favalora, John C.: b. Dec. 5, 1935, New Orleans, LA; educ. St. Joseph Seminary (St. Benedict, LA),

Notre Dame Seminary (New Orleans, LA), Gregorian Univ. (Rome), Catholic Univ. of America (Washington, DC), Xavier Univ. and Tulane Univ. (New Orleans); ord. priest (New Orleans*), Dec. 20, 1961; ord. bp. of Alexandria, LA, July 29, 1986; bp. of St. Petersburg, Mar. 14, 1989; app. abp. of Miami, inst., Dec. 20, 1994.

Fellhauer, David E.: b. Aug. 19, 1939, Kansas City, MO; educ. Pontifical College Josephinum (Worthington, OH), St. Paul Univ. (Ottawa); ord. priest (Dallas), May 29, 1965; ord. bp. of Victoria, May 28, 1990.

Fernandez, Gilberto: b. Feb. 13, 1935, Havana, Cuba; educ. El Buen Pastor Seminary (Havana); ord. priest (Havana*), May 15, 1959; came to US, 1967; app. titular bp. of Irina and aux. of Miami, June 24, 1997; ret., Dec. 10, 2002.

Finn, Robert W.: b. April 2, 1953, St. Louis; educ. Kenrick-Glennon Seminary (St. Louis), North American College and Angelicum University (Rome); ord. July 7, 1979 (St. Louis); coad. bp. Kansas City-St. Joseph, Mo., March 9, 2004; ord. May 3, 2004; bp. of Kansas City-St. Joseph, Mo., May 24, 2005.

Fiorenza, Joseph A.: b. Jan. 25, 1931, Beaumont, TX; educ. St. Mary's Seminary (LaPorte, TX); ord. priest (Galveston-Houston), May 29, 1954; ord. bp. of San Angelo, Oct. 25, 1979; app. bp. of Galveston-Houston, Dec. 18, 1984, inst., Feb. 18, 1985; vice president, NCCB/USCC, 1995-1998, President, 1998-2001; app. first abp. of Galveston-Houston, Dec. 29, 2004; ret. Feb. 28, 2006.

Fitzsimons, George K.: b. Sept. 4, 1928, Kansas City, MO; educ. Rockhurst College (Kansas City, MO), Immaculate Conception Seminary (Conception, MO); ord. priest (Kansas City-St. Joseph), Mar. 18, 1961; ord. titular bp. of Pertusa and aux. bp. of Kansas City-St. Joseph, July 3, 1975; app. bp. of Salina, Mar. 28, 1984, inst., May 29, 1984.

Flanagan, Thomas Joseph: b: Oct. 23, 1930, Rathmore, Ireland; educ. St. Patrick's College, Thurles, Ireland; ord priest (San Antonio*), June 10, 1956; app. titular bp. of Bavagaliana and aux. bp. of San Antonio, Jan. 5, 1998, ord., Feb. 16, 1998; ret. Dec. 15, 2005.

Flesey, John W.: b. Aug. 6, 1942, Jersey City (NJ); educ. St. Peter's College (Jersey City), Immaculate Conception Seminary (South Orange, NJ), Catholic University of America (Washington, D.C.), Iona College (New Rochelle, NY), Pontifical Gregorian University, Pontifical University of St. Thomas Aquinas (Rome); ord. priest (Newark*), May 31, 1969; dean of the School of Theology, Seton Hall Univ.; app. aux. bp. of Newark and tit. bp. of Allegheny May 21, 2004; ord. Aug. 4, 2004.

Fliss, Raphael M.: b. Oct. 25, 1930, Milwaukee, WI; educ. St. Francis Seminary (Milwaukee, WI), Catholic University (Washington, DC), Pontifical Lateran Univ. (Rome); ord. priest (Milwaukee*), May 26, 1956; ord. coadjutor bp. of Superior with right of succession, Dec. 20, 1979; bp. of Superior, June 27, 1985.

Flores, Patrick F.: b. July 26, 1929, Ganado, TX; educ. St. Mary's Seminary (Houston, TX); ord. priest (Galveston-Houston), May 26, 1956; ord. titular bp. of Itolica and aux. bp. of San Antonio, May 5, 1970 (first Mexican-American bp.); app. bp. of El Paso, Apr. 4, 1978, inst., May 29, 1978; app. abp. of San Antonio,

1979; inst., Oct. 13, 1979; ret. Dec. 29, 2004.

Flynn, Harry J.: b. May 2, 1933, Schenectady, NY; educ. Siena College (Loudonville, NY), Mt. St. Mary's College (Emmitsburg, MD); ord. priest (Albany), May 28, 1960; ord. coadjutor bp. of Lafayette, LA, June 24, 1986; bp. of Lafayette, LA, May 15, 1989; app. coadjutor abp. of St. Paul and Minneapolis, Feb. 24, 1994, inst., Apr. 27, 1994; abp. of St. Paul and Minneapolis, Sept. 8, 1995.

Foley, David E.: b. Feb. 3, 1930, Worcester, MA; educ. St. Charles College (Catonsville, MD), St. Mary's Seminary (Baltimore, MD); ord. priest (Washington*), May 26, 1952; ord. titular bp. of Octaba and aux. bp. of Richmond, June 27, 1986; app. bp. of Birmingham, Mar. 22, 1994; ret. May 10, 2005.

Foley, John Patrick: b. Nov. 11, 1935, Sharon Hill, PA; educ. St. Joseph's Preparatory School (Philadelphia, PA), St. Joseph's College (now University) (Philadelphia, PA), St. Charles Borromeo Seminary (Overbrook, PA), St. Thomas Univ. (Rome), Columbia School of Journalism (New York); ord. priest (Philadelphia*), May 19, 1962; assistant editor (1967-70) and editor (1970-84) of *The Catholic Standard and Times*, Philadelphia archdiocesan paper; ord. titular abp. of Neapolis in Proconsulari, May 8, 1984, in Philadelphia; app. president of the Pontifical Council for Social Communications, Apr. 5, 1984.

Forst, Marion F.: b. Sept. 3, 1910, St. Louis, MO; educ. St. Louis Preparatory Seminary (St. Louis, MO), Kenrick Seminary (Webster Groves, MO); ord. priest (St. Louis*), June 10, 1934; ord. bp. of Dodge City, Mar. 24, 1960; app. titular bp. of Scala and aux. bp. of Kansas City, KS, Oct. 16, 1976; ret., Dec. 23, 1986; titular bp. of Leavenworth.

Foys, Roger J.: b. July 27, 1945, Chicago; educ. University of Steubenville, St. John Vianney Seminary, (Bloomingdale, OH), the Catholic University of America, Washington, DC; ord. priest (Steubenville), May 16, 1973; Knight Commander of the Equestrian Order of the Holy Sepulchre of Jerusalem, 1986; app. bp. of Covington, May 31, 2002.

Franklin, William Edwin: b. May 3, 1930, Parnell, IA; educ. Loras College and Mt. St. Bernard Seminry (Dubuque, IA); ord. priest (Dubuque*), Feb. 4, 1956; ord. titular bp. of Surista and aux. bp. of Dubuque, Apr. 1, 1987; app. bp. of Davenport, Nov. 12, 1993, inst., Jan. 20, 1994.

Franzetta, Benedict C.: b. Aug. 1, 1921, East Liverpool, OH; educ. St. Charles College (Catonsville, MD), St. Mary Seminary (Cleveland, OH); ord. priest (Youngstown), Apr. 29, 1950; ord. titular bp. of Oderzo and aux. bp. of Youngstown, Sept. 4, 1980; ret., Sept. 4, 1996.

Frey, Gerard L.: b. May 10, 1914, New Orleans, LA; educ. Notre Dame Seminary (New Orleans, LA); ord. priest (New Orleans*), Apr. 2, 1938; ord. bp. of Savannah, Aug. 8, 1967; app. bp. of Lafayette, LA, Nov. 7, 1972, inst., Jan, 7, 1973; ret., May 15, 1989.

Friend, William B.: b. Oct. 22, 1931, Miami, FL; educ. St. Mary's College (St. Mary, KY), Mt. St. Mary Seminary (Emmitsburg, MD), Catholic Univ. (Washington, DC), Notre Dame Univ. (Notre Dame, IN); ord. priest (Mobile*), May 7, 1959; ord. titular bp. of Pomaria and aux. bp. of Alexandria-Shreveport, LA, Oct. 30, 1979; app. bp. of Alexandria-Shreveport, Nov. 17, 1982, inst., Jan 11, 1983; app. first bp. of Shreveport, June, 1986; inst., July 30, 1986.

G

Gainer, Ronald W.: b. Aug. 24, 1947, Pottsville, PA; educ. St. Charles Borromeo Seminary (Philadelphia), Gregorian Univ. (Rome); ord. priest (Allentown), May 19, 1973; app. bp. of Lexington, KY, ord. bp., Feb. 22, 2003.

Galante, Joseph A.: b. July 2, 1938, Philadelphia, PA; educ. St. Joseph Preparatory School, St. Charles Seminary (Philadelphia, PA); Lateran Univ., Angelicum, North American College (Rome); ord. priest (Philadelphia*), May 16, 1964; on loan to diocese of Brownsville, TX, 1968-72, where he served in various diocesan posts; returned to Philadelphia, 1972; assistant vicar (1972-79) and vicar (1979-87) for religious; undersecretary of Congregation for Institutes of Consecrated Life and Societies of Apostolic Life (Rome), 1987-92; ord. titular bp. of Equilium and aux. bp. of San Antonio, Dec. 11, 1992; app. bp. of Beaumont, Apr. 5, 1994; app. co-adjutor bp. of Dallas, Nov. 23, 1999; app. bp. of Camden, March 23, 2004.

Galeone, Victor Benito: b. Sept. 13, 1935, Philadelphia; educ. St. Charles College (Baltimore), North American College, Pontifical Gregorian University (Rome), ord. priest (Baltimore*), Dec. 18, 1960; served as missionary in Peru, 1970-75, 1978-85; app. bp. of St. Augustine, June 25, 2001, ord., Aug. 21, 2001.

Garcia, Richard J.: b. Apr. 24, 1947, San Francisco; educ. St. Patrick's Seminary (Menlo Park, CA); ord priest (San Francisco*), May 13, 1973; app. Titular bp. of Bapara and aux. bp. of Sacramento, Nov. 25, 1997, ord., Jan. 28, 1998.

Garcia-Siller, Gustavo, M.Sp.S.: b. Dec. 21, 1956, San Luis Potosi, Mexico, educ. St. John's Seminary (Camarillo, Calif.), Western Jesuit University (Guadalajara, Mexico), Gregorian University (Rome); ord. priest, June 22, 1984; app. aux. bp of Chicago and titular bp. of Esco, Jan. 24, 2003; ord., March 19, 2003.

Garland, James H.: b. Dec. 13, 1931, Wilmington, OH; educ. Wilmington College (OH), Ohio State Univ. (Columbus, OH); Mt. St. Mary's Seminary (Cincinnati, OH), Catholic Univ. (Washington, DC); ord. priest (Cincinnati*), Aug. 15, 1959; ord. titular bp. of Garriana and aux. bp. of Cincinnati, July 25, 1984; app. bp. of Marquette, Oct. 6, 1992; inst., Nov. 11, 1992; ret. Dec. 13, 2005.

Garmo, George: b. Dec. 8, 1921, Telkaif, Iraq; educ. St. Peter Chaldean Patriarchal Seminary (Mossul, Iraq), Pontifical Urban Univ. (Rome); ord. priest, Dec. 8, 1945; pastor of Chaldean parish in Detroit archdiocese, 1960-64, 1966-80; ord. abp. of Chaldean archdiocese of Mosul, Iraq, Sept. 14, 1980.

Gaydos, John R.: b. Aug. 14, 1943, St. Louis, MO; educ Cardinal Glennon College (St. Louis, MO), North American College, Gregorian Univ. (Rome); ord. priest (St. Louis*), Dec. 20, 1968; ord. bp. of Jefferson City, Aug. 27, 1997.

Gelineau, Louis E.: b. May 3, 1928, Burlington, VT; educ. St. Michael's College (Winooski, VT), St. Paul's Univ. Seminary (Ottawa), Catholic Univ. (Washington, DC); ord. priest (Burlington), June 5, 1954; ord. bp. of Providence, RI, Jan. 26, 1972; ret., June 11, 1997.

Gendron, Odore J.: b. Sept. 13, 1921, Manchester,

NH; educ. St. Charles Borromeo Seminary (Sherbrooke, QC), Univ. of Ottawa, St. Paul Univ. Seminary (Ottawa, Ont., Canada); ord. priest (Manchester), May 31, 1947; ord. bp. of Manchester, Feb. 3, 1975; res., June 12, 1990.

George, Cardinal Francis E., O.M.I.: (*See Cardinals, Biographies*).

Gerber, Eugene J.: b. Apr. 30, 1931, Kingman, KS; educ. St. Thomas Seminary (Denver, CO), Wichita State Univ.; Catholic Univ. (Washington, DC), Angelicum (Rome); ord. priest (Wichita), May 19, 1959; ord. bp. of Dodge City, Dec. 14, 1976; app. bp. of Wichita, Nov. 17, 1982, inst., Feb. 9, 1983; res. Oct. 4, 2001.

Gerety, Peter L.: b. July 19, 1912, Shelton, CT; educ. Sulpician Seminary (Paris, France); ord. priest, (Hartford*), June 29, 1939; ord. titular bp. of Crepedula and coadjutor bp. of Portland, ME, with right of succession, June 1, 1966; app. apostolic administrator of Portland, 1967; bp. of Portland, ME, Sept. 15, 1969; app. abp. of Newark, Apr. 2, 1974; inst., June 28, 1974; ret., June 3, 1986.

Gerry, Joseph J., O.S.B.: b. Sept. 12, 1928, Millinocket, ME; educ. St. Anselm Abbey Seminary (Manchester, NH), Univ. of Toronto (Canada), Fordham Univ. (New York); ord. priest, June 12, 1954; abbot of St. Anselm Abbey, Manchester, NH, 1972; ord. titular bp. of Praecausa and aux. of Manchester, Apr. 21, 1986; bp. of Portland, ME, Dec. 27, 1988, inst., Feb. 21, 1989; ret. Feb. 10, 2004.

Gettelfinger, Gerald A.: b. Oct. 20, 1935, Ramsey, IN; educ. St. Meinrad Seminary (St. Meinrad, IN), Butler Univ. (Indianapolis, IN); ord. priest (Indianapolis*), May 7, 1961; ord. bp. of Evansville, Apr. 11, 1989.

Gilbert, Edward J., C.SS.R.: b. Dec. 26, 1936, Brooklyn, NY; educ. Mt. St. Alphonsus Seminary (Esopus, NY), Catholic Univ. (Washington, DC); ord. priest (Redemptorists, Baltimore Province), June 21, 1964; ord. bp. of Roseau, Dominica, Sept. 7, 1994.

Gilmore, Ronald W.: b. Apr. 23, 1942, Wichita, KS; educ. University Seminary (Ottawa), St. Paul University (Ottawa); ord. priest (Wichita), June 7, 1969; app. Bp. of Dodge City, May 11, 1998, ord., July 16, 1998.

Goedert, Raymond E.: b. Oct. 15, 1927, Oak Park, IL; educ. Quigley Preparatory Seminary (Chicago, IL), St. Mary of the Lake Seminary and Loyola Univ. (Chicago, IL), Gregorian Univ. (Rome); ord. priest (Chicago*), May 1, 1952; ord. titular bp. of Tamazeni and aux. bp. of Chicago, Aug. 29, 1991; ret., Jan. 24, 2003.

Gomez, José H.: b. Dec. 26, 1951, Monterrey, Mexico (became U.S. citizen 1995); educ. National University, Mexico, University of Navarre (Spain); ord. priest of the Prelature of Opus Dei, Aug. 15, 1978; Vicar of Opus Dei for State of Texas, 1999-2001; app. titular bp. of Belali and aux. bp of Denver, Jan. 23, 2001, ord., Mar. 26, 2001; app. abp. of San Antonio, Dec. 29, 2004; inst. Feb. 15, 2005.

Gonzalez, Roberto O., O.F.M., b. June 2, 1950, Elizabeth, NJ; educ. St. Joseph Seminary (Callicoon, NY), Siena College (Loudonville, NY), Washington Theological Union (Silver Spring, MD), Fordham Univ. (New York, NY); solemnly professed in Franciscan Order, 1976; ord. priest, May 8, 1977; ord.

titular bp. of Ursona and aux. bp. of Boston, Oct. 3, 1988; app. coadjutor bp. of Corpus Christi, May 16, 1995; bishop of Corpus Christi, Apr. 1, 1997; app. abp. of San Juan de Puerto Rico, Mar. 26, 1999, inst., May 8, 1999.

Gonzalez Valer, S.F., Francisco: b. Arcos de Jalon, Spain, May 22, 1939; educ. Missionary Seminary of the Holy Family, Barcelona (Spain), Catholic University of America (Washington, DC); ord. priest (of the Congregation of the Sons of the Holy Family), May 1, 1964; Episcopal Vicar for Hispanic Catholics, Archdiocese of Washington, 1997; app. titular bp. of Lamfua and aux. bp. of Washington, Dec. 28, 2001.

Gorman, John R.: b. Dec. 11, 1925, Chicago, IL; educ, St. Mary of the Lake Seminary (Mundelein, IL), Loyola Univ. (Chicago, IL); ord. priest (Chicago*), May 1, 1956; ord. titular bp. of Catula and aux. bp. of Chicago, Apr. 11, 1988; ret., Jan. 24, 2003.

Gossman, F. Joseph: b. Apr. 1, 1930, Baltimore, MD; educ. St. Charles College (Catonsville, MD), St. Mary's Seminary (Baltimore, MD), North American College (Rome), Catholic Univ. (Washington, DC); ord. priest (Baltimore*), Dec. 17, 1955; ord. titular bp. of Agunto and aux. bp. of Baltimore, Sept. 11, 1968; app. bp. of Raleigh, Apr. 8, 1975; ret. June 8, 2006.

Gracida, Rene H.: b. June 9, 1923, New Orleans, LA; educ. Rice Univ. and Univ. of Houston (Houston, TX), Univ. of Fribourg (Switzerland); ord. priest (Miami*), May 23, 1959; ord. titular bp. of Masuccaba and aux. bp. of Miami, Jan. 25, 1972; app. first bp. of Pensacola-Tallahassee, Oct. 1, 1975, inst., Nov. 6, 1975; app. bp. of Corpus Christi, May 24, 1983, inst., July 11, 1983; ret., Apr. 1, 1997.

Grahmann, Charles V.: b. July 15, 1931, Halletsville, TX; educ. The Assumption-St. John's Seminary (San Antonio, TX); ord. priest (San Antonio*), Mar. 17, 1956; ord. titular bp. of Equilium and aux. bp. of San Antonio, Aug. 20, 1981; app. first bp. of Victoria, TX, Apr. 13, 1982; app. coadjutor bp. of Dallas, Dec. 9, 1989; bp. of Dallas, July 14, 1990.

Gregory, Wilton D.: b. Dec. 7, 1947, Chicago, IL; educ. Quigley Preparatory Seminary South, Niles College of Loyola Univ. (Chicago, IL), St. Mary of the Lake Seminary (Mundelein, IL), Pontifical Liturgical Institute, Sant'Anselmo (Rome); ord. priest, (Chicago*), May 9, 1973; ord. titular bp. of Oliva and aux. bp. of Chicago, Dec. 13, 1983; app. bp. of Belleville, Dec. 29, 1993; inst., Feb. 10, 1994 vice president, NCCB/USCC, 1998-2001; president, USCCB, 2001-2004; app. abp. of Atlanta, Dec. 9, 2004; inst. Jan. 17, 2005.

Gries, Roger W., O.S.B.: b. Mar. 26, 1937, Cleveland; educ. St. John Univ., (Collegeville, MN), St. Joseph's Seminary, Cleveland, Loyola Univ., Chicago; ord. priest (Order of St. Benedict), May 16, 1963; Abbot, St. Andrew Abbey, Cleveland, 1981-2001; app. aux. bp. of Cleveland, April 3, 2001, ord., June 7, 2001.

Griffin, James A.: b. June 13, 1934, Fairview Park, OH; educ. St. Charles College (Baltimore, MD), Borromeo College (Wicklife, OH); St Mary Seminary (Cleveland, OH); Lateran Univ. (Rome); Cleveland State Univ.; ord. priest (Cleveland), May 28, 1960; ord. titular bp. of Holar and aux. bp. of Cleveland, Aug. 1, 1979; app. bp. of Columbus, Feb. 8, 1983.

Grosz, Edward M.: b. Feb. 16, 1945, Buffalo, NY;

educ. St. John Vianney Seminary (East Aurora, NY), Notre Dame Univ. (Notre Dame, IN); ord. priest (Buffalo), May 29, 1971; ord. titular bp. of Morosbisdus and aux. bp. of Buffalo, Feb. 2, 1990.

Guillory, Curtis J., S.V.D.: b. Sept. 1, 1943, Mallet, LA; educ. Divine Word College (Epworth, IA), Chicago Theological Union (Chicago), Creighton Univ. (Omaha, NE); ord. priest, Dec. 16, 1972; ord. titular bp. of Stagno and aux. bp. of Galveston-Houston, Feb. 19, 1988; bp. of Beaumont, June 2, 2000, inst., July 28, 2000.

Gullickson, Thomas E.: b. Aug. 14, 1950, Sioux Falls, SD; educ. North American College and Pontifical Gregorian University (Rome, Italy); ord. priest, June 27, 1976 (Sioux Falls); after studies in the Pontifical Ecclesiastical Academy, he entered the diplomatic service of the Holy See in 1985 and served in the nunciatures in Rwanda, Austria, Czechoslovakia, Jerusalem, and Germany; app. titular abp. of Bomarzo, Oct. 2, 2004; cons. Nov. 11, 2004; Apostolic Nuncio to Trinidad and Tobago, Bahamas, Dominica, Saint Kitts and Nevis, Santa Lucia, San Vincenzo and Grenadine.

Gumbleton, Thomas J.: b. Jan. 26, 1930, Detroit, MI; educ. St. John Provincial Seminary (Detroit, MI), Pontifical Lateran Univ. (Rome); ord. priest (Detroit*), June 2, 1956; ord. titular bp. of Ululi and aux. bp. of Detroit, May 1, 1968; ret. Feb. 2, 2006.

H

Hanifen, Richard C.: b. June 15, 1931, Denver, CO; educ. Regis College and St. Thomas Seminary (Denver, CO), Catholic Univ. (Washington, DC), Lateran Univ. (Rome); ord. priest (Denver*), June 6, 1959; ord. titular bp. of Abercorn and aux. bp. of Denver, Sept. 20, 1974; app. first bp. of Colorado Springs, Nov. 10, 1983; inst., Jan. 30, 1984; ret., Jan. 30, 2003.

Hannan, Philip M.: b. May 20, 1913, Washington, DC; educ. St. Charles College (Catonsville, MD), Catholic Univ. (Washington, DC), North American College (Rome); ord. priest (Washington*), Dec. 8, 1939; ord. titular bp. of Hieropolis and aux. bp. of Washington, DC, Aug. 28, 1956; app. abp. of New Orleans, inst., Oct. 13, 1965; ret., Dec. 6, 1988.

Hanus, Jerome George, O.S.B.: b. May 25, 1940, Brainard, NE; educ. Conception Seminary (Conception, MO), St. Anselm Univ. (Rome), Princeton Theological Seminary (Princeton, NJ); ord. priest (Conception Abbey, MO), July 30, 1966; abbot of Conception Abbey, 1977-87; president of Swiss American Benedictine Congregation, 1984-87; ord. bp. of St. Cloud, Aug. 24, 1987; app. coadjutor abp. of Dubuque, Aug. 23, 1994; abp. of Dubuque, Oct. 16, 1995.

Harrington, Bernard J.: b. Sept. 6, 1933, Detroit, MI; educ. Sacred Heart Seminary (Detroit), St. John's Provincial Seminary (Plymouth, MI), Catholic Univ. of America (Washington, DC), University of Detroit; ord. priest (Detroit*), June 6, 1959; ord. titular bp. of Uzali and aux. bp. of Detroit, Jan. 6, 1994; app. Bp. of Winona, Nov. 5, 1998, inst., Jan. 6, 1999.

Hart, Daniel A.: b. Aug. 24, 1927, Lawrence, MA; educ. St. John's Seminary (Brighton, MA); ord. priest (Boston*), Feb. 2, 1953; ord. titular bp. of Tepelta and aux. bp. of Boston, Oct. 18, 1976; bp. of Norwich, Sept. 12, 1995; ret. March 11, 2003.

Hart, Joseph: b. Sept. 26, 1931, Kansas City, MO; educ. St. John Seminary (Kansas City, MO), St. Meinrad Seminary (Indianapolis, IN); ord. priest (Kansas City-St. Joseph), May 1, 1956; ord. titular bp. of Thimida Regia and aux. bp. of Cheyenne, WY, Aug. 31, 1976; app. bp. of Cheyenne, inst., June 12, 1978; ret., Sept. 26, 2001.

Harvey, James M.: b. Oct. 20, 1949, Milwaukee, WI; educ. De Sales Preparatory Seminary and St. Francis De Sales College, Milwaukee, North American College and Gregorian Univ. (Rome); ord. priest (Milwaukee*), June 29, 1975; entered Vatican diplomatic service, 1980; Apostolic Nunciature, Dominican Republic, 1980-82; transferred to the Vatican Secretariat of State, 1982; named assessor of the Secretariat, 1997; named titular bp. of Memphis and prefect of the papal household, Feb. 7, 1998; ordained bp., Mar. 19, 1998; named titular abp. Sept. 29, 2003.

Heim, Capistran F., O.F.M.: b. Jan. 21, 1934, Catskill, NY; educ. Franciscan Houses of Study; ord. priest, Dec. 18, 1965; missionary in Brazil; ord. first bp. of prelature of Itaituba, Brazil, Sept. 17, 1988; inst., Oct. 2, 1988.

Hermann, Robert J.: b. Aug. 12, 1934, Weingarten, Mo.; educ. Cardinal Glennon College (Shrewsbury, MO.), St. Louis Univ.; ord. priest (St. Louis), March 30, 1963; aux. bp. St. Louis and tit. bp. of Zerta, Oct. 16, 2002; ord., Dec. 12, 2002.

Hermes, Herbert, O.S.B.: b. May 25, 1933, Scott City, KS; ord. priest (St. Benedict Abbey, Atchison, KS), May 26, 1960; missionary in Brazil; ord. bp. of territorial prelature of Cristalandia, Brazil, Sept. 2, 1990.

Herzog, Ronald P.: b. April 22, 1942, Akron, OH; educ. St. Joseph Seminary (St. Benedict, LA), Pontifical College Josephinum (Worthington, OH); ord. priest June 1, 1968 (Natchez-Jackson, MS; now Biloxi); app. bp. of Alexandria Nov. 4, 2004; ord. Jan. 5, 2005.

Higgins Richard B.: b. Feb. 22, 1944, Longford, Ireland; educ. Pontifical Lateran Univ. (Rome); ord. priest (Sacramento), Mar. 9, 1968; entered the Air Force as a chaplain, 1974; app. titular bp. of Case Calane and aux. bp. of the Archdiocese for the Military Services, May 7, 2004.

Higi, William L.: b. Aug. 29, 1933, Anderson, IN; educ. Our Lady of the Lakes Preparatory Seminary (Wawasee, IN), Mt. St. Mary of the West Seminary and Xavier Univ. (Cincinnati, OH); ord. priest, (Lafayette, IN) May 30, 1959; ord. bp. of Lafayette, IN, June 6, 1984.

Holley, Martin D.: b. Dec. 31, 1954, Pensacola, FL; educ. Alabama State University (Montgomery, AL), Catholic University of America (Washington, DC), Saint Vincent de Paul Regional Seminary (Boynton Beach); ord. priest (Pensacola-Tallahassee), May 8, 1987; app. titular bp. of Rusibisir and aux. bp. of Washington, May 18, 2004; ord. July 2, 2004.

Houck, William Russell: b. June 26, 1926, Mobile, AL; educ. St. Bernard Junior College (Cullman, AL), St. Mary's Seminary College and St. Mary's Seminary (Baltimore, MD), Catholic Univ. (Washington, DC); ord. priest (Mobile*), May 19, 1951; ord. titular bp. of Alessano and aux. bp. of Jackson, MS, May 27, 1979, by Pope John Paul II; app. bp. of Jackson, Apr. 11,

1984, inst., June 5, 1984; ret., Jan. 3, 2003.

Howze, Joseph Lawson: b. Aug. 30, 1923, Daphne, AL; convert to Catholicism, 1948; educ. St. Bonaventure Univ. (St. Bonaventure, NY); ord. priest (Raleigh), May 7, 1959; ord. titular bp. of Massita and aux. bp. of Natchez-Jackson, Jan. 28, 1973; app. first bp. of Biloxi, Mar. 8, 1977; inst., June 6, 1977; res. May 15, 2001.

Hubbard, Howard J.: b. Oct. 31, 1938, Troy, NY; educ. St. Joseph's Seminary (Dunwoodie, NY); North American College and Gregorian Univ. (Rome), Catholic Univ. (Washington, DC); ord. priest (Albany), Dec. 18, 1963; ord. bp. of Albany, Mar. 27, 1977.

Hughes, Alfred C.: b. Dec. 2, 1932, Boston, MA; educ. St. John Seminary (Brighton, MA), Gregorian Univ. (Rome); ord. priest (Boston*), Dec. 15, 1957, in Rome; ord. titular bp. of Maximiana in Byzacena and aux. bp. of Boston, Sept. 14, 1981; app. bp. of Baton Rouge, Sept. 7, 1993; co-adj. abp. of New Orleans, Feb. 16, 2001; abp. of New Orleans, Jan. 3, 2002.

Hughes, Edward T.: b. Nov. 13, 1920, Lansdowne, PA; educ. St. Charles Seminary, Univ. of Pennsylvania (Philadelphia); ord. priest (Philadelphia*), May 31, 1947; ord. titular bp. of Segia and aux. bp. of Philadelphia, July 21, 1976; app. bp. of Metuchen, Dec. 11, 1986, inst., Feb. 5, 1987; ret., July 8, 1997.

Hughes, William A.: b. Sept. 23, 1921, Youngstown, OH; educ. St. Charles College (Catonsville, MD), St. Mary's Seminary (Cleveland, OH), Notre Dame Univ. (Notre Dame, IN); ord. priest (Youngstown), Apr. 6, 1946; ord. titular bp. of Inis Cathaig and aux. bp. of Youngstown, Sept. 12, 1974; app. bp. of Covington, inst., May 8, 1979; ret., July 4, 1995.

Hunthausen, Raymond G.: b. Aug. 21, 1921, Anaconda, MT; educ. Carroll College (Helena, MT), St. Edward's Seminary (Kenmore, WA), St. Louis Univ. (St. Louis, MO), Catholic Univ. (Washington, DC), Fordham Univ. (New York City), Notre Dame Univ. (Notre Dame, IN); ord. priest (Helena), June 1, 1946; ord. bp. of Helena, Aug. 30, 1962; app. abp. of Seattle, Feb. 25, 1975; ret., Aug. 21, 1991.

Hurley, Francis T.: b. Jan. 12, 1927, San Francisco, CA; educ. St. Patrick's Seminary (Menlo Park, CA), Catholic Univ. (Washington, DC); ord. priest (San Francisco*), June 16, 1951; assigned to NCWC in Washington, DC, 1957; assistant (1958) and later (1968) associate secretary of NCCB and USCC; ord. titular bp. of Daimlaig and aux. bp. of Juneau, AK, Mar. 19, 1970; app. bp. of Juneau, July 20, 1971, inst., Sept. 8, 1971; app. abp. of Anchorage, May 4, 1976, inst., July 8, 1976; res., March 3, 2001.

Hurley, Walter A.: b. May 30, 1937, Fredericton, New Brunswick; educ. Sacred Heart Seminary, St. John Provincial Seminary, The Catholic University of America; ord. priest, June 5, 1965 (Detroit); app. aux. bp. of Detroit and titular bishop of Cunavia, July 7, 2003; app. bp. of Grand Rapids, June 21, 2005; inst. Aug. 5, 2005.

I-J

Ibrahim, Ibrahim N.: b. Oct. 1, 1937, Telkaif, Mosul, Iraq.; educ. Patriarchal Seminary (Mosul, Iraq), St. Sulpice Seminary (Paris, France); ord. priest, Dec. 30, 1962, in Baghdad, Iraq; ord. titular bp. of Anbar and apostolic exarch for Chaldean Catholics in the United States, Mar. 8, 1982, in Baghdad; inst., in Detroit, Apr. 18, 1982; app. first eparch, Aug. 3, 1985, when exarchate was raised to eparchy of St. Thomas Apostle of Detroit.

Imesch, Joseph L.: b. June 21, 1931, Detroit, MI; educ. Sacred Heart Seminary (Detroit, MI), North American College, Gregorian Univ. (Rome); ord. priest (Detroit*), Dec. 16, 1956; ord. titular bp. of Pomaria and aux. bp. of Detroit, Apr. 3, 1973; app. bp. of Joliet, June 30, 1979; ret. May 16, 2006.

Iriondo, Robert J.: b. Dec. 19, 1938, Legazti, Spain; educ. Collegio San Vittore and Pontifical Gregorian University, Rome; ord. priest (of the Canons Regular of the Lateran), Dec. 22, 1962; incardinated into Archdiocese of New York, 1996; Vicar for Hispanics, 1997; ord. titular bp. of Alton and aux. of New York, Dec. 12, 2001.

Irwin, Francis X.: b. Jan 9, 1934, Medford, MA; educ. Boston College High School, Boston College, St. John's Seminary (Brighton, MA), Boston College School of Social Service; ord. priest (Boston*), Feb. 2, 1960; ord. titular bp. of Ubaza and aux. bp. of Boston, Sept. 17, 1996.

Jackels, Michael O.: b. April 13, 1954, Rapid City, S.D.; educ. University of Nebraska-Lincoln, St. Pius X Seminary (Erlanger, KY), Mount St. Mary's (Emmitburg, MD); ord. priest May 30, 1981 (Lincoln, NE); app. bp. of Wichita Jan. 29, 2005; ord. April 4, 2005.

Jacobs, Sam Gallip: b. Mar. 4, 1938, Greenwood, MS; educ. Immaculata Seminary (Lafayette, LA), Catholic Univ. (Washington, DC); ord. priest (Lafayette), June 6, 1964; became priest of Lake Charles diocese, 1980, when that see was established; ord. bp. of Alexandria, LA, Aug. 24, 1989; app. bp. of Houma-Thibodaux, Aug. 1, 2003.

Jakubowski, Thad J.: b. Apr. 5, 1924, Chicago, IL; educ. Mundelein Seminary, St. Mary of the Lake Univ., Loyola Univ. (Chicago); ord priest (Chicago*), May 3, 1950; ord. titular bp. of Plestia and aux. bp. of Chicago, Apr. 11, 1988; ret., Jan. 24, 2003.

Jammo, Sarhad: b. March 14, 1941, Baghdad, Iraq; educ. Patriarchal Seminary of Mosul, Urban College of the Propaganda Fide Pontifical Oriental Institute (Rome); ord. priest (Baghdad*), Dec. 19, 1964; rector, Chaldean Seminary, Baghdad; after service in Iraq, transferred in 1977 to the Eparchy of Saint Thomas the Apostle of Detroit for Chaldeans; app. first eparch of the eparchy of St. Peter the Apostle of San Diego (Chaldean), May 21, 2002.

Jarrell, C. Michael: b. May 15, 1940, Opelousas, LA; educ. Immaculata Minor Seminary (Lafayette, LA); Catholic Univ. (Washington, DC); ord. priest (Lafayette, LA), June 3, 1967; ord. bp. of Houma-Thibodaux, Mar. 4, 1993; app. bp. of Lafayette, Nov. 8, 2002.

Jenky, Daniel R.: b. Mar. 3, 1947, Chicago; educ. University of Notre Dame; ord. priest, Apr. 6, 1974; Religious Superior of the Holy Cross religious at Notre Dame, 1985-1990; app.Titular Bp. of Amanzia and Aux. of Fort Wayne-South Bend, Oct. 21, 1997, ord., Dec. 16, 1997, bp. of Peoria, Feb. 12, 2002, inst. Apr. 10, 2002.

Jugis, Peter J.: b. March 3, 1957, Charlotte, NC; educ. University of North Carolina at Charlotte, North American College and Gregorian Univ. (Rome), Catholic University of America (Washington, DC);

ord. priest, June 12, 1983; app. bp. of Charlotte, Aug. 1, 2003; ord. Oct. 24, 2003.

K

Kaffer, Roger L.: b. Aug. 14, 1927, Joliet, IL; educ. Quigley Preparatory Seminary (Chicago, IL), St. Mary of the Lake Seminary (Mundelein, IL), Gregorian Univ. (Rome); ord. priest (Joliet), May 1, 1954; ord. titular bp. of Dusa and aux. bp. of Joliet, June 26, 1985; res., Aug. 15, 2002, ret., Sept. 1, 2002.

Kaising, John. J.: b. March 3, 1936, Cincinnati; educ. Seminary of Cincinnati, Xavier University; ord. priest (Cincinnati*), Dec. 22, 1962; military chaplain in the Army 1970-1998, exec. assist. to the Chief of Chaplains of the Army, 1994-1998; app. titular bp. of Orreacelia and aux. bp. of the Archdiocese for the Military Services, Feb. 21, 2000, ord., April 11, 2000.

Kalisz, Raymond P., S.V.D.: b. Sept. 25, 1927, Melvindale, MI; educ. St. Mary's Seminary (Techny, IL); ord. priest, Aug. 15, 1954; ord. bp. of Wewak, Papua New Guinea, Aug. 15, 1980; ret. Aug. 14, 2002.

Kane, Francis Joseph: b. Oct. 30, 1942, Chicago, IL; educ. Quigley Preparatory Seminary (Chicago, IL), Niles College Seminary (Chicago, IL), Saint Mary of the Lake Seminary (Chicago, IL); ord. priest, May 14, 1969 (Chicago*); app. aux. bp. of Chicago and titular bp. of Sault Sainte Marie in Michigan Jan. 24, 2003; ord., March 19, 2003.

Keeler, Cardinal William Henry: (*See* **Cardinals, Biographies.**)

Keleher, James P.: b. July 31, 1931, Chicago, IL; educ. Quigley Preparatory Seminary (Chicago, IL), St. Mary of the Lake Seminary (Mundelein, IL); ord. priest (Chicago*), Apr. 12, 1958; ord. bp. of Belleville, Dec. 11, 1984; app. abp. of Kansas City, KS, June 28, 1993; ret. Jan. 15, 2005.

Kelly, Thomas C., O.P.: b. July 14, 1931, Rochester, NY; educ. Providence College (Providence, RI), Immaculate Conception College (Washington, DC), Angelicum (Rome); professed in Dominicans, Aug. 26, 1952; secretary, apostolic delegation, Washington, DC, 1965-71; associate general secretary, 1971-77, and general secretary, 1977-81, NCCB/USCC; ord. titular bp. of Tusurus and aux. bp. of Washington, DC, Aug. 15, 1977; app. abp. of Louisville, Dec. 28, 1981, inst., Feb. 18, 1982.

Kettler, Donald J.: b. Nov. 26, 1944, Minneapolis: educ. St. John's Seminary Collegeville, Minnesota; ord. priest (Sioux Falls), May 29, 1970; app. bp. of Fairbanks, Alaska, June 7, 2002, ord., Aug. 22, 2002.

Kicanas, Gerald F.: b. Aug. 18, 1941, Chicago, IL; educ. Quigley Preparatory Seminary, St. Mary of the Lake Seminary and Loyola University in Chicago; ord. priest (Chicago*), Apr. 27, 1967; ord. titular bp. of Bela and aux. of Chicago, Mar. 20, 1995; app. coadj. bp. of Tucson, Oct. 30, 2001; inst. as coadj. bp. of Tuscon, Jan. 17, 2002; bp. of Tucson, March 7, 2003.

Kinney, John F.: b. June 11, 1937, Oelwein, IA; educ. Nazareth Hall and St. Paul Seminaries (St. Paul, MN); Pontifical Lateran University (Rome); ord. priest (St. Paul-Minneapolis*), Feb. 2, 1963; ord. titular bp. of Caorle and aux. bp. of St. Paul and Minneapolis, Jan. 25, 1977; app. bp. of Bismarck June 30, 1982; app. bp. of St. Cloud, May 9, 1995.

Kmiec, Edward U.: b. June 4, 1936, Trenton, NJ; educ. St. Charles College (Catonsville, MD), St. Mary's Seminary (Baltimore, MD), Gregorian Univ. (Rome); ord. priest (Trenton), Dec. 20, 1961; ord. titular bp. of Simidicca and aux. bp. of Trenton, Nov. 3, 1982; app. bp. of Nashville, Oct. 13, 1992; inst., Dec. 3, 1992; app. bp. Of Buffalo, Aug. 12, 2004.

Kucera, Daniel W., O.S.B.: b. May 7, 1923, Chicago, IL; educ. St. Procopius College (Lisle, IL), Catholic Univ. (Washington, DC); professed in Order of St. Benedict, June 16, 1944; ord. priest, May 26, 1949; abbot, St. Procopius Abbey, 1964-71; pres. Illinois Benedictine College, 1959-65 and 1971-76; ord. titular bp. of Natchez and aux. bp. of Joliet, July 21, 1977; app. bp. of Salina, Mar. 5, 1980; app. abp. of Dubuque, inst., Feb. 23, 1984; ret., Oct. 16, 1995.

Kuchmiak, Michael, C.SsR.: b. Feb. 5, 1923, Obertyn, Horodenka, Western Ukraine; left during World War II; educ. St. Josaphat Ukrainian Seminary (Rome, Italy), St. Mary's Seminary (Meadowvale, Ont., Canada); ord. priest, May 13, 1956; in the U.S. from 1967; ord. titular bp. of Agathopolis and aux. bp. of Ukrainian metropolitan of Philadelphia, Apr. 27, 1988; exarch of apostolic exarchate for Ukrainian Catholics in Great Britain, June 24, 1989.

Kudrick, John M.: b. Dec. 23, 1947, Lloydell, PA; educ. Third Order Regular of St. Francis, 1967; ord. priest, May 3, 1975; granted bi-ritual faculties for service in the Byzantine Rite, 1978; app. bp. of Parma, May 3, 2002.

Kupfer, William F., M.M.: b. Jan. 28, 1909, Brooklyn, NY; educ. Cathedral College (Brooklyn, NY), Maryknoll Seminary (Maryknoll, NY); ord. priest, June 11, 1933; missionary in China; app. prefect apostolic of Taichung, Taiwan, 1951; ord. first bp. of Taichung, July 25, 1962; ret., Sept. 3, 1986.

Kurtz, Joseph E.: b. Aug. 18, 1946, Shenandoah, PA.; educ. St. Charles Borromeo Seminary, Philadelphia, Marywood College, Scranton; ord. priest (Allentown), Mar. 18, 1972; app. bishop of Knoxville, Oct. 26, 1999, ord., Dec. 8, 1999.

Kurtz, Robert, C.R.: b. July 25, 1939, Chicago, IL; ord. priest, Mar. 11, 1967; ord. bp. of Hamilton, Bermuda, Sept. 15, 1995.

Kuzma, George M.: b. July 24, 1925, Windber, PA; educ. St. Francis Seminary (Loretto, PA), St. Procopius College (Lisle, IL), Sts. Cyril and Methodius Byzantine Catholic Seminary, Duquesne Univ. (Pittsburgh, PA); ord. priest (Pittsburgh*, Byzantine Rite), May 5, 1955; ord. titular bp. of Telmisso and aux. bp. of Byzantine eparchy of Passaic, 1987; app. bp. of Byzantine diocese of Van Nuys, CA, Oct. 23, 1990, inst., Jan. 15, 1991; res., Dec. 5, 2000.

L

Lagonegro, Dominick J.: b. Mar. 6, 1943, White Plains, NY; educ. Cathedral College, (Douglaston), St. Joseph Seminary, Yonkers; ord. priest (New York*), May 31, 1969; ord. titular bp. of Modrus and aux. of New York, Dec. 12, 2001.

Lambert, Francis, S.M.: b. Feb. 7, 1921, Lawrence, MA; educ. Marist Seminary (Framingham, MA); ord. priest, June 29, 1946; served in Marist missions in Oceania; provincial of Marist Oceania province, 1971; ord. bp. of Port Vila, Vanuatu (New Hebrides), Mar. 20, 1977; ret., Nov. 30, 1996.

Larkin, W. Thomas: b. Mar. 31, 1923, Mt. Morris, NY; educ. St. Andrew Seminary and St. Bernard

Seminary (Rochester, NY); Angelicum Univ. (Rome); ord. priest (St. Augustine), May 15, 1947; ord. bp. of St. Petersburg, May 27, 1979; ret., Nov. 29, 1988.

Latino, Joseph: b. Oct. 21, 1937, New Orleans, LA; educ. Saint Joseph College Seminary (Covington, LA), Notre Dame Seminary (New Orleans, LA); ord. priest, May 25, 1963; app. bp. Jackson, Jan. 3, 2003; ord., March 7, 2003.

Law, Bernard F.: (*See* **Cardinals, Biographies.**)

Leibrecht, John J.: b. Aug. 30, 1930, Overland, MO; educ. Catholic Univ. (Washington, DC); ord. priest (St. Louis*), Mar. 17, 1956; superintendent of schools of St. Louis archdiocese, 1962-1981; ord. bp. of Springfield-Cape Girardeau, MO, Dec. 12, 1984.

Lennon, Richard G.: b. Mar. 26, 1947, Arlington, (MA); educ. St. John's Seminary, Brighton; ord. priest (Boston*), May 19, 1973; rector, St. John's Seminary 1999-2001; app. titular bp. of Sufes and aux. bp. of Boston, June 29, 2001, ord., Sept. 14, 2001; apost. admin. of Boston, 2002-03; app. bp. of Cleveland, Apr. 4, 2006.

Lessard, Raymond W.: b. Dec. 21, 1930, Grafton, N.D.; educ. St. Paul Seminary (St. Paul, MN), North American College (Rome); ord. priest (Fargo), Dec. 16, 1956; served on staff of the Congregation for Bps. in the Roman Curia, 1964-73; ord. bp. of Savannah, Apr. 27, 1973; ret., Feb. 7, 1995.

Levada, William J.: (*See* **Cardinals, Biographies**).

Lipscomb, Oscar H.: b. Sept. 21, 1931, Mobile, AL; educ. McGill Institute, St. Bernard College (Cullman, AL), North American College and Gregorian Univ. (Rome), Catholic Univ. (Washington, DC); ord. priest (Mobile*), July 15, 1956; ord. first abp. of Mobile, Nov. 16, 1980.

Listecki, Jerome E.: b. March 12, 1949, Chicago; educ. Loyola University and St. Mary of the Lake Seminary, Mundelein, IL, De Paul University College of Law, University of St. Thomas Aquinas and Pontifical Gregorian University, Rome; ord. priest (Chicago*), June 1, 1975, app. titular bp. of Nara and aux bp. of Chicago, Nov. 7, 2000, ord., Jan. 8, 2001; app. bp. of La Crosse, Dec. 29, 2004; inst. Mar. 1, 2005.

Lohmuller, Martin N.: b. Aug. 21, 1919, Philadelphia, PA; educ. St. Charles Borromeo Seminary (Philadelphia, PA), Catholic Univ. (Washington, DC); ord. priest (Philadelphia*), June 3, 1944; ord. titular bp. of Ramsbury and aux. bp. of Philadelphia, Apr. 2, 1970; ret., Oct. 11, 1994.

Lori, William E.: b. May 6, 1951, Louisville, KY; educ. St. Pius X College (Covington, KY), Mount St. Mary's Seminary (Emmitsburg, MD), Catholic Univ. (Washington, DC); ord. priest (Washington*), May 14, 1977; ord. titular bp. of Bulla and aux. bp. of Washington, DC, Apr. 20, 1995; app. bp. of Bridgeport, Jan. 23, 2001; inst., Mar. 19, 2001.

Losten, Basil: b. May 11, 1930, Chesapeake City, MD; educ. St. Basil's College (Stamford, CT), Catholic University (Washington, DC); ord. priest (Philadelphia* Ukrainian Byzantine), June 10, 1957; ord. titular bp. of Arcadiopolis in Asia and aux. bp. of Ukrainian archeparchy of Philadelphia, May 25, 1971; app. apostolic administrator of archeparchy, 1976; app. bp. of Ukrainian eparchy of Stamford, Sept. 20, 1977; ret. Jan. 3, 2006.

Lotocky, Innocent Hilarius, O.S.B.M.: b. Nov. 3,

1915, Petlykiwci, Ukraine; educ. seminaries in Ukraine, Czechoslovakia and Austria; ord. priest, Nov. 24, 1940; ord. bp. of St. Nicholas of Chicago for the Ukrainians, Mar. 1, 1981; ret., July 15, 1993.

Loverde, Paul S.: b. Sept. 3, 1940, Framingham, MA; educ. St. Thomas Seminary (Bloomfield, CT), St. Bernard Seminary (Rochester, NY), Gregorian Univ. (Rome), Catholic Univ. (Washington, DC); ord. priest (Norwich), Dec. 18, 1965; ord. titular bp. of Ottabia and aux. bp. of Hartford, Apr. 12, 1988; app. bp. of Ogdensburg, Nov. 11, 1993; inst., Jan. 17, 1994; app. bp. of Arlington, Jan. 25, 1999, inst., Mar. 25, 1999.

Lucas, George J.: b. June 12, 1949, St. Louis, MO; educ. Major Seminary of St. Louis, Univ. of St. Louis; ord. priest (St. Louis*), May 24, 1975; rector, Kenrick-Glennon Seminary, 1995-1999; app. bishop of Springfield in Illinois, Oct. 19, 1999, ord., Dec. 14, 1999.

Luong, Dominic Dinh Mai: b: Dec. 20, 1940, Minh Cuong, Vietnam; educ. seminary (Buffalo, N.Y.), and St. Bernard Seminary (Rochester, N.Y.), Canisius College (Buffalo); ord. priest in Buffalo for Diocese of Danang, Vietnam, May 21, 1966; incardinated into New Orleans 1986; named aux. bp. of Orange, CA, and titular bp. of Cebarades, April 25, 2003; ord., June 11, 2003.

Lynch, Robert N.: b. May 27, 1941, Charleston, WV; educ. Pontifical College Josephinum (Columbus, OH); John XXIII National Seminary (Weston, MA); ord. priest (Miami*), May 13, 1978; associate general secretary (1984-89) and general secretary (1989-95) of the NCCB/USCC; app. bp. of St. Petersburg, Dec. 5, 1995; ord. and inst., Jan. 26, 1996; app. apostolic administrator of Palm Beach (while continuing as bp. of St. Petersburg), June 2, 1998.

Lyne, Timothy J.: b. Mar. 21, 1919, Chicago, IL; educ. Quigley Preparatory Seminary, St. Mary of the Lake Seminary (Mundelein, IL); ord. priest (Chicago*), May 1, 1943; ord. titular bp. of Vamalla and aux. bp. of Chicago, Dec. 13, 1983; ret., Jan. 24, 1995.

M

Macaluso, Christie Albert: b. June 12, 1945, Hartford, CT; educ. St. Thomas Seminary (Bloomfield, CT), St. Mary's Seminary (Baltimore, Md), Trinity College (Hartford, CT), New York University; ord. priest (Hartford*), May 21, 1971; ord. titular bp. of Grass Valley and aux. bp. of Hartford, June 10, 1997.

McCarrick, Theodore E.: (*See* **Cardinals, Biographies.**)

McCarthy, James F.: b. July 9, 1942, Mount Kisco, NY; educ. Cathedral College and St. Joseph's Seminary, New York; ord. priest (New York*), June 1, 1968; app. titular bp. of Veronna and aux. bp. of New York, May 11, 1999, inst., June 29, 1999; res., June 12, 2002.

McCarthy, John E.: b. June 21, 1930, Houston, TX; educ. Univ. of St. Thomas (Houston, TX); ord. priest (Galveston-Houston), May 26, 1956; assistant director Social Action Dept. USCC, 1967-69; executive director Texas Catholic Conference; ord. titular bp. of Pedena and aux. bp. of Galveston-Houston, Mar. 14, 1979; app. bp. of Austin, Dec. 19, 1985, inst., Feb. 25, 1986; res., Jan. 2, 2001.

McCormack, John B.: b Aug. 12, 1935, Winthrop, MA; educ. St. John Seminary College and St. John Seminary Theologate (Boston, MA); ord. priest (Boston*), Feb. 2, 1960; ord. titular bp. of Cerbali and aux. bp. of Boston, Dec. 27, 1995; app. bp. of Manchester, NH, July 21, 1998, inst., Sept. 22, 1998.

McCormack, William J.: b. Jan. 24, 1924, New York, NY; educ. Christ the King Seminary, St. Bonaventure Univ. (St. Bonaventure, NY); ord. priest (New York*), Feb. 21, 1959; national director of Society for the Propagation of the Faith, 1980; ord. titular bp. of Nicives and aux. bp. of New York, Jan. 6, 1987; res., Oct. 31, 2001.

McDonald, Andrew J.: b. Oct. 24, 1923, Savannah, GA; educ. St. Mary's Seminary (Baltimore, MD), Catholic Univ. (Washington, DC), Lateran Univ. (Rome); ord. priest (Savannah), May 8, 1948; ord. bp. of Little Rock, Sept. 5, 1972; res., Jan. 4, 2000.

McDonnell, Charles J.: b. July 7, 1928, Brooklyn, NY; educ. Seton Hall Univ. (South Orange, NJ), Immaculate Conception Seminary (Darlington, NJ), Long Island Univ. (Brooklyn, NY); ord. priest (Newark*), May 29, 1954; U.S. Army Chaplain, 1965-89; ret., from active duty with rank of Brigadier General; ord. titular bp. of Pocofelto and aux. bp. of Newark, May 12, 1994; ret. May 21, 2004.

McDonnell, Timothy A.: b. Dec. 23, 1937, New York City; educ. St. Joseph Seminary, Yonkers, Iona College, New Rochelle; ord. priest (New York*), June 1, 1963; ord. titular bp. of Semina and aux. bp. of New York, Dec. 12, 2001; app. bp. of Springfield in Massachusetts, Mar. 9, 2004.

McDowell, John B.: b. July 17, 1921, New Castle, PA; educ. St. Vincent College, St. Vincent Theological Seminary (Latrobe, PA), Catholic Univ. (Washington, DC); ord. priest (Pittsburgh), Nov. 4, 1945; superintendent of schools, Pittsburgh diocese, 1955-70; ord. titular bp. of Tamazuca, and aux. bp. of Pittsburgh, Sept. 8, 1966; ret., Sept. 9, 1996.

McFadden, Joseph P.: b. May 22, 1947, Philadelphia, PA; Saint Charles Borromeo Seminary (Overbrook, PA); ord. priest (Philadelphia*), May 16, 1981; app. titular bp. of Orreomargo and aux. bp. of Philadelphia, June 8, 2004; ord. July 28, 2004.

McFarland, Norman F.: b. Feb. 21, 1922, Martinez, CA; educ. St. Patrick's Seminary (Menlo Park, CA), Catholic Univ. (Washington, DC); ord. priest (San Francisco*), June 15, 1946; ord. titular bp. of Bida and aux. bp. of San Francisco, Sept. 8, 1970; apostolic adminstrator of Reno, 1974; app. bp. of Reno, Feb. 10, 1976, inst., Mar. 31, 1976; title of see changed to Reno-Las Vegas; app. bp. of Orange, CA, Dec. 29, 1986; inst., Mar. 31, 1976; res., June 30, 1998.

McGarry, Urban, T.O.R.: b. Nov. 11, 1911, Warren, PA; ord. priest, Oct. 3, 1942, in India; prefect apostolic of Bhagalpur, Aug. 7, 1956; ord. first bp. of Bhagalpur, India, May 10, 1965; res., Nov. 30, 1987.

McGrath, Patrick J.: b. July 11, 1945, Dublin, Ire.; educ. St. John's College Seminary (Waterford), Lateran Univ. (Rome, Italy); ord. priest in Ireland, June 7, 1970; came to U.S. same year and became San Francisco archdiocesan priest; ord. titular bp. of Allegheny and aux. bp. of San Francisco, Jan. 25, 1989; app. coadj. bp. of San Jose, June 30, 1998; bp. of San Jose, Nov. 29, 1999.

McKinney, Joseph C.: b. Sept. 10, 1928, Grand Rapids, MI: educ. St. Joseph's Seminary (Grand Rapids, MI), Seminaire de Philosophie (Montreal, Canada), Urban Univ. (Rome, Italy); ord. priest (Grand Rapids), Dec. 20, 1953; ord. titular bp. of Lentini and aux. bp. of Grand Rapids, Sept. 26, 1968; res., Oct. 2, 2001.

McLaughlin, Bernard J.: b. Nov. 19, 1912, Buffalo, NY; educ. Urban Univ. (Rome, Italy); ord. priest (Buffalo), Dec. 21, 1935, at Rome; ord. titular bp. of Mottola and aux. bp. of Buffalo, Jan. 6, 1969; res., Jan. 5, 1988.

McManus, Robert J.: b. July 5, 1951, Warwick, RI; educ. Our Lady of Providence Seminary, Catholic Univ. (Washington, DC), Seminary of Toronto, Canada, Pontifical Gregorian Univ. (Rome); ord. priest (Providence), May 27, 1978; diocesan Vicar for Education and Rector of Our Lady of Providence; app. titular bp. of Allegheny and aux. of Providence, Dec. 1, 1998, ord., Feb. 22, 1999; app. bp. of Worcester, Mar. 9, 2004.

McNabb, John C., O.S.A.: b. Dec. 11, 1925, Beloit, WI; educ. Villanova Univ. (Villanova, PA), Augustinian College and Catholic Univ. (Washington, DC), De Paul Univ. (Chicago, IL); ord. priest, May 24, 1952; ord. titular bp. of Saia Maggiore, June 17, 1967 (resigned titular see, Dec. 27, 1977); prelate of Chulucanas, Peru, 1967; first bp. of Chulucanas, Dec. 12, 1988; ret. Oct. 28, 2000).

McNaughton, William J., M.M.: b. Dec. 7, 1926, Lawrence, MA; educ. Maryknoll Seminary (Maryknoll, NY); ord. priest, June 13, 1953; ord. titular bp. of Thuburbo Minus and vicar apostolic of Inchon, Korea, Aug. 24, 1961; first bp. of Inchon, Mar. 10, 1962, when vicariate was raised to diocese; ret. Apr. 25, 2002.

McRaith, John Jeremiah: b. Dec. 6, 1934, Hutchinson, MN; educ. St. John Preparatory School (Collegeville, MN), Loras College, St. Bernard Seminary (Dubuque, IA); ord. priest (New Ulm), Feb. 21, 1960; exec. dir. of Catholic Rural Life Conference, 1971-78; ord. bp. of Owensboro, KY, Dec. 15, 1982.

Madden, Denis J.: b. March 8, 1940, Carbondale, Pa.; educ. Univ. of Notre Dame, Univ. of Maryland; ord. priest April 1, 1967 (Benedictines); inc. Baltimore Nov. 4, 1976; app. aux. bp. of Baltimore and tit. bp. of Baia, May 10, 2005; ord. bp. Aug. 24, 2005.

Madera, Joseph J., M.Sp.S.: b. Nov. 27, 1927, San Francisco, CA; educ. Domus Studiorum of the Missionaries of the Holy Spirit (Coyoacan, D.F. Mexico); ord. priest, June 15, 1957; ord. coadjutor bp. of Fresno, Mar. 4, 1980; bp. of Fresno, July 1, 1980; app. titular bp. of Orte and aux. of Military Services archdiocese, June 30, 1991; ret. Sept. 15, 2004.

Maginnis, Robert P.: b. Dec. 22, 1933, Philadelphia, PA; educ. St. Charles Borromeo Seminary (Overbrook, PA); ord. priest (Philadelphia*), May 13, 1961; ord. titular bp. of Siminina and aux. bp. of Philadelphia, Mar. 11, 1996.

Maguire, Joseph F.: b. Sept. 4, 1919, Boston, MA; educ. Boston College, St. John's Seminary (Boston, MA); ord. priest (Boston*), June 29, 1945; ord. titular bp. of Macteris and aux. bp. of Boston, Feb. 2, 1972; app. coadjutor bp. of Springfield, MA, Apr. 13, 1976; succeeded as bp. of Springfield, MA, Oct. 15, 1977; ret., Dec. 27, 1991.

Mahony, Roger M.: (*See* **Cardinals, Biographies**.)

Maida, Adam J.: (See Cardinals, Biographies.)

Malone, Richard J.: b. March 19, 1946, Salem, MA; educ. St. John's Seminary, Brighton, Boston University, ord. priest (Boston*), May 20, 1972; app. titular bp. of Aptuca and aux. bp. of Boston, Jan. 27, 2000, ord., March 1, 2000; app. bp. of Portland, ME, Feb. 10, 2004.

Malooly, William Francis: b. Jan. 18, 1944, Baltimore; educ. St. Charles Minor Seminary, St. Mary's Seminary (Baltimore); ord priest (Baltimore*), May 7, 1970, app. titular bp. of Flumenzer and aux. bp. of Baltimore, Dec. 12, 2000, ord., March 1, 2001.

Manning, Elias (James), O.F.M. Conv.: b. Apr. 14, 1938, Troy, NY; educ. Sao José Seminary (Rio de Janeiro, Brazil); ord. priest, Oct. 30, 1965, in New York; ord. bp. of Valenca, Brazil, May 13, 1990.

Manning, Thomas R., O.F.M.: b. Aug. 29, 1922, Baltimore, MD; educ. Duns Scotus College (Southfield, MI), Holy Name College (Washington, DC); ord. priest, June 5, 1948; ord. titular bp. of Arsamosata, July 14, 1959 (res. titular see, Dec. 30, 1977); prelate of Coroico, Bolivia, July 14, 1959; became first bp., 1983, when prelature was raised to diocese; ret., Oct. 9, 1996.

Mansell, Henry J.: b. Oct. 10, 1937, New York, NY; educ. Cathedral College, St. Joseph's Seminary and College (New York); North American College, Gregorian Univ. (Rome); ord. priest (New York*), Dec. 19, 1962; ord. titular bp. of Marazane and aux. bp. of New York, Jan. 6, 1993, by John Paul II in Vatican City; app. bp. of Buffalo, Apr. 18, 1995; inst., June 12, 1995; app. abp. of Hartford, Oct. 20, 2003.

Mansour, Gregory John: b. Nov. 11, 1955, Flint, MI; educ. University of Michigan (Kalamazoo, MI), Catholic Univ, of America (Washington, DC), North American Colege and Pontifical Gregorian Univ. (Rome); ord. priest (Eparchy of Saint Maron of Brooklyn), Sept. 18, 1982; app. bp. of the Eparchy of St. Maron, Brooklyn, NY, January 10, 2004.

Manz, John R.: b. Nov. 14, 1945, Chicago, IL; educ. Niles College Seminary (Niles, IL), Univ. of St. Mary of the Lake-Mundelein Seminary (Chicago); ord. priest (Chicago*), May 12, 1971; ord. titular bp. of Mulia and aux. bp. of Chicago, Mar. 5, 1996.

Marconi, Dominic A.: b. Mar. 13, 1927, Newark, NJ; educ. Seton Hall Univ. (S. Orange, NJ), Immaculate Conception Seminary (Darlington, NJ), Catholic Univ. (Washington, DC); ord. priest (Newark*), May 30, 1953; ord. titular bp. of Bure and aux. bp. of Newark, June 25, 1976; res., July 1, 2002.

Martino, Joseph F.: b. May 1, 1946, Philadelphia, PA; educ. St. Charles Borromeo Seminary (Overbrook, PA), Gregorian Univ. (Rome); ord. priest (Philadelphia*), Dec. 18, 1970; ord. titular bp. of Cellae in Mauretania and aux. bp. of Philadelphia, Mar. 11, 1996; app. bp. of Scranton, July 25, 2003.

Matano, Salvatore R.: b. Sept. 15, 1946, Providence, RI; educ. Our Lady of Providence Seminary College (Warwick, RI), Gregorian University (Rome); ord. priest Dec. 17, 1971 (Providence); served on staff of apostolic nunciature (Washington, DC); app. coadjutor bp. of Burlington March 3, 2005; ord. April 19, 2005; bp. of Burlington, Nov. 9, 2005.

Matthiesen, Leroy Theodore: b. June 11, 1921, Olfen, TX; educ. Josephinum College (Columbus,

OH), Catholic Univ. (Washington, DC), Register School of Journalism; ord. priest (Amarillo), Mar. 10, 1946; ord. bp. of Amarillo, May 30, 1980; ret., Jan. 21, 1997.

Melczek, Dale J.: b. Nov. 9, 1938, Detroit, MI; educ. St. Mary's College (Orchard Lake, MI), St. John's Provincial Seminary (Plymouth, MI), Univ. of Detroit; ord. priest (Detroit*), June 6, 1964; ord. titular bp. of Trau and aux. bp. of Detroit, Jan. 27, 1983; apostolic administrator of Gary, Aug. 19, 1992; coadjutor bp. of Gary, Oct. 28, 1995; bp. of Gary, June 1, 1996.

Mengeling, Carl F.: b. Oct. 22, 1930, Hammond, IN; educ. St. Meinrad College and Seminary (St. Meinrad, IN), Alphonsianum Univ. (Rome); ord. priest (Gary), May 25, 1957; ord. bp. of Lansing, Jan. 25, 1996.

Mestice, Anthony F.: b. Dec. 6, 1923, New York, NY; educ. St. Joseph Seminary (Yonkers, NY); ord. priest (New York*), June 4, 1949; ord. titular bp. of Villa Nova and aux. bp. of New York, Apr. 27, 1973; ret., Oct. 31, 2001.

Michaels, James E., S.S.C.: b. May 30, 1926, Chicago, IL; educ. Columban Seminary (St. Columban, NE), Gregorian Univ. (Rome); ord. priest, Dec. 21, 1951; ord. titular bp. of Verbe and aux. bp. of Kwang Ju, Korea, Apr. 14, 1966; app. aux. bp. of Wheeling, Apr. 3, 1973 (title of see changed to Wheeling-Charleston, 1974); res., Sept. 22, 1987.

Miller, J. Michael, C.S.B.: b. July 9, 1946, Ottawa, Canada; educ. St. Michael's College, Univ. of Toronto (Toronto, Canada), Gregorian Univ. (Rome); ord. priest (Congregation of St. Basil), June 29, 1975, Congregation of St. Basil; official in Secretariat of State, Rome, 1992-97; pres. of Univ. of St. Thomas Aquinas, Houston, Texas, 1997-2004; 2004; app.titular abp. of Vertara and sec. of the Cong. for Catholic Education, Rome, Nov. 25, 2003.

Milone, Anthony M.: b. Sept. 24, 1932, Omaha, NE; educ. North American College (Rome); ord. priest (Omaha*), Dec. 15, 1957, in Rome; ord. titular bp. of Plestia and aux. bp. of Omaha, Jan. 6, 1982; app. bp. of Great Falls-Billings, Dec. 14, 1987, inst., Feb. 23, 1988; ret. July 12, 2006.

Minder, John, O.S.F.S.: b. Nov. 1, 1923, Philadelphia, PA; educ. Catholic Univ. (Washington, DC); ord. priest, June 3, 1950; ord. bp. of Keimos (renamed Keimos-Upington, 1985), South Africa, Jan. 10, 1968; ret. June 5, 2000.

Moeddel, Carl K.: b. Dec. 28, 1937, Cincinnati, OH; educ. Athenaeum of Ohio, Mt. St. Mary's Seminary (Cincinnati); ord. priest (Cincinnati*), Aug. 15, 1962; ord. titular bp. of Bistue and aux. bp. of Cincinnati, Aug. 24, 1993.

Montrose, Donald W.: b. May 13, 1923, Denver, CO; educ. St. John's Seminary (Camarillo, CA); ord. priest (Los Angeles*), May 7, 1949; ord. titular bp. of Forum Novum and aux. bp. of Los Angeles, May 12, 1983; app. bp. of Stockton, Dec. 17, 1985, inst., Feb. 20, 1986; res., Jan. 19, 1999.

Moreno, Manuel D.: b. Nov. 27, 1930, Placentia, CA; educ. Univ. of CA (Los Angeles), Our Lady Queen of Angels (San Fernando, CA), St. John's Seminary (Camarillo, CA); ord. priest (Los Angeles*), Apr. 25, 1961; ord. titular bp. of Tanagra and aux. bp. of Los Angeles, Feb. 19, 1977; bp. of Tucson, Jan. 12, 1982, inst., Mar. 11, 1982; res., March 7, 2003.

Morin, Roger Paul: b. March 7, 1941, Lowell, MA;

educ. Notre Dame Seminary (New Orleans, LA), Tulane University (New Orleans, LA); ord. priest, April 15, 1971 (New Orleans*); app. aux. bp. of New Orleans and titular bishop of Aulona, Feb. 11, 2003; ord., April 22, 2003.

Morlino, Robert C.: b. Dec. 31, 1946, Scranton, PA; educ. Fordham Univ., University of Notre Dame, Weston School of Theology, Cambridge, MA, Gregorian University, Rome; ord. priest for the Society of Jesus, Maryland Province, June 1, 1974, incardinated into the Diocese of Kalamazoo, MI, Oct. 26, 1983, app. bp. of Helena, July 6, 1999, inst,. Sept. 21, 1999; app. bp. of Madison, May 23, 2003.

Morneau, Robert F.: b. Sept. 10, 1938, New London, WI; educ. St. Norbert's College (De Pere, WI), Sacred Heart Seminary (Oneida, WI), Catholic Univ. (Washington, DC); ord. priest (Green Bay), May 28, 1966; ord. titular bp. of Massa Lubrense and aux. bp. of Green Bay, Feb. 22, 1979.

Moskal, Robert M.: b. Oct. 24, 1937, Carnegie, PA; educ. St. Basil Minor Seminary (Stamford, CT), St. Josaphat Seminary and Catholic Univ. (Washington, DC); ord. priest (Philadelphia*, Byzantine Ukrainian), Mar. 25, 1963; ord. titular bp. of Agatopoli and aux. bp. of the Ukrainian archeparchy of Philadelphia, Oct. 13, 1981; app. first bp. of St. Josaphat in Parma, Dec. 5, 1983.

Moynihan, James M.: b. July 16, 1932, Rochester, NY; educ. St. Bernard's Seminary (Rochester, NY), North American College and Gregorian Univ. (Rome); ord. priest (Rochester), Dec. 15, 1957, in Rome; ord. bp. of Syracuse, May 29, 1995.

Muench Robert W.: b. Dec. 28, 1942, Louisville, KY; educ. St. Joseph Seminary and Notre Dame Seminary (New Orleans, LA), Catholic Univ. (Washington, DC); ord. priest (New Orleans*), June 18, 1968; ord. titular bp. of Mactaris and aux. bp. of New Orleans, June 29, 1990; app. bp. of Covington Jan., 1996; inst., Mar. 19, 1996; app. bp. of Baton Rouge, Dec. 15, 2001.

Mulvee, Robert E.: b. Feb. 15, 1930, Boston, MA; educ. St. Thomas Seminary (Bloomfield, CT), University Seminary (Ottawa, ON), American College (Louvain, Belgium), Lateran Univ. (Rome); ord. priest (Manchester), June 30, 1957; ord. titular bp. of Summa and aux. bp. of Manchester, NH, Apr. 14, 1977; app. bp. of Wilmington, Del., Feb. 19, 1985; app. coadjutor bp. of Providence, Feb. 9, 1995; bp. of Providence, June 11, 1997; ret. Mar. 31, 2005.

Mundo, Miguel P.: b. July 25, 1937, New York, NY; educ. Fordham Univ. (Bronx, NY), St. Jerome's College (Kitchener, ON), St Francis Seminary (Loretto, PA); ord. priest (Camden), May 19, 1962; missionary in Brazil from 1963; ord. titular bp. of Blanda Julia and aux. bp. of Jatai, Brazil, June 2, 1978.

Murphy, Michael J.: b. July 1, 1915, Cleveland, OH; educ. Niagara Univ. (Niagara Falls, NY); North American College (Rome), Catholic Univ. (Washington, DC); ord. priest (Cleveland), Feb. 28, 1942; ord. titular bp. of Ariendela and aux. bp. of Cleveland, June 11, 1976; app. coadjutor bp. of Erie, Nov. 20, 1978; bp. of Erie, July 16, 1982; ret., June 12, 1990.

Murphy, William F.: b. May 14, 1940, Boston MA; educ. Boston Latin School (Boston), Harvard College, St. John's Seminary (Boston), Gregorian Univ.

(Rome); ord. priest (Boston*), Dec. 16, 1964; ord. titular bp. of Saia Maggiore and aux. bp. of Boston, Dec. 27, 1995; app. bp. of Rockville Centre, June 25, 2001, ord., Sept. 5, 2001.

Murray, James A.: b. July 5, 1932, Jackson, MI; educ. Sacred Heart Seminary Detroit, St. John Provincial Seminary (Plymouth, MI), Catholic Univ. of America; ord. priest (Lansing), June 7, 1958; app. bp. of Kalamazoo, Nov. 18, 1997, ord., Jan. 27, 1998.

Murry, George V., S.J.: b. Dec. 28, 1948, Camden, NJ; educ. St. Joseph's College (Philadelphia, PA), St. Thomas Seminary (Bloomfield, CT), St. Mary Seminary (Baltimore, MD), Jesuit School of Theology (Berkeley, CA), George Washington Univ. (Washington, DC); entered Jesuits 1972; ord. priest, June 9, 1979; ord. titular bp. of Fuerteventura and aux. bp. of Chicago, Mar. 20, 1995; app. co-adjutor of St. Thomas in the Virgin Islands, May 5, 1998; bp. of St. Thomas in the Virgin Islands, June 30, 1999.

Myers, John Joseph: b. July 26, 1941, Ottawa, IL; educ. Loras College (Dubuque, IA), North American College and Gregorian Univ. (Rome), Catholic Univ. of America (Washington, DC); ord. priest (Peoria), Dec. 17, 1966, in Rome; ord. coadjutor bp. of Peoria, Sept. 3, 1987; bp. of Peoria, Jan. 23, 1990; app. abp. of Newark, July 24, 2001.

N

Naumann, Joseph F.: b. June 4, 1949, St. Louis, MO; educ. Cardinal Glennon Seminary College and Kenrick Seminary (St. Louis, MO); ord. priest (St. Louis*), 1975; app. titular bp. of Caput Cilla and aux. bp. of St. Louis, July 9, 1997; app. coadjutor abp. of Kansas City, January 7, 2004; abp. of Kansas City, Jan. 15, 2005.

Nevins, John J.: b. Jan. 19, 1932, New Rochelle, NY; educ. Iona College (New Rochelle, NY), Catholic Univ. (Washington, DC); ord. priest (Miami*), June 6, 1959; ord. titular bp. of Rusticana and aux. bp. of Miami, Mar. 24, 1979; app. first bp. of Venice, FL, July 17, 1984; inst., Oct. 25, 1984.

Newman, William C.: b. Aug. 16, 1928, Baltimore, MD; educ. St. Mary Seminary (Baltimore, MD), Catholic Univ. (Washington, DC), Loyola College (Baltimore, MD); ord. priest (Baltimore*), May 29, 1954; ord. titular bp. of Numluli and aux. bp. of Baltimore, July 2, 1984; ret. Aug. 28, 2003.

Nickless, R. Walker: b. May 28, 1947, Denver; educ. St. Thomas Seminary, University of Denver, Gregorian Univ. (Rome); ord. priest Aug. 4, 1973 (Denver); app. bp. of Sioux City, Iowa, Nov. 10, 2005; ord. bp. Jan. 20, 2006.

Niederauer, George H.: b. June 14, 1936, Los Angeles, CA; educ. St. John's Seminary (Camarillo, CA), Catholic Univ. (Washington, DC), Loyola Univ. of Los Angeles, Univ. of Southern CA, Loretta Heights College (Denver, CO); ord. priest (Los Angeles*), Apr. 30, 1962; app. bp. of Salt Lake City, Nov. 3, 1994, ord., Jan. 25, 1995; app. Abp. of San Francisco, Dec. 15, 2005.

Niedergeses, James D.: b. Feb. 2, 1917, Lawrenceburg, TN; educ. St. Bernard College (St. Bernard, AL), St. Ambrose College (Davenport, IA), Mt. St. Mary Seminary of the West and Athenaeum (Cincinnati, OH); ord. priest (Nashville), May 20, 1944; ord. bp. of Nashville, May 20, 1975; ret., Oct. 13, 1992.

Nienstedt, John C.: b. Mar. 18, 1947, Detroit, MI; educ. Sacred Heart Seminary (Detroit), North American College, Gregorian Univ., Alphonsianum (Rome); ord. priest

(Detroit*), July 27, 1974; served in Vatican Secretariat of State, 1980-86; rector of Sacred Heart Seminary (Detroit), 1988-94; pastor of the Shrine of the Little Flower (Royal Oak, MI), 1994; ord. titular bp. of Alton and aux. bp. of Detroit, July 9, 1996; app. bp. of New Ulm, June 12, 2001, inst., Aug. 6, 2001.

Noonan, John G.: b. Feb. 26, 1951, Limerick, Ireland; educ. St. John Vianney College Seminary (Miami), St. Vincent de Paul Seminary (Boynton Beach, Fla.); app. aux. bp. Miami June 21, 2005; ord. bp. Aug. 24, 2005.

Novak, Alfred, C.SS.R.: b. June 2, 1930, Dwight, NE; educ. Immaculate Conception Seminary (Oconomowoc, WI); ord. priest, July 2, 1956; ord. titular bp. of Vardimissa and aux. bp. of Sao Paulo, Brazil, May 25, 1979; bp. of Paranagua, Brazil, Mar. 14, 1989.

O

O'Brien, Edwin F.: b. Apr. 8, 1939, Bronx, NY; educ. St. Joseph's Seminary (Yonkers, NY), Angelicum (Rome); ord. priest (New York*), May 29, 1965; ord. titular bp. of Tizica and aux. bp. of New York, Mar. 25, 1996; app. coadjutor abp. for Military Services Archdiocese, Apr. 8, 1997; abp. of Military Services Archdiocese, Aug. 12, 1997.

O'Brien, Thomas Joseph: b. Nov. 29, 1935, Indianapolis, IN; educ. St. Meinrad High School Seminary, St. Meinrad College Seminary (St. Meinrad, IN); ord. priest (Tucson), May 7, 1961; ord. bp. of Phoenix, Jan. 6, 1982; res., June 18, 2003.

Ochoa, Armando: b. Apr. 3, 1943, Oxnard, CA; educ. Ventura College (Ventura, CA), St. John's College and St. John's Seminary (Camarillo, CA); ord. priest (Los Angeles*), May 23, 1970; ord. titular bp. of Sitifi and aux. bp. of Los Angeles, Feb. 23, 1987; app. bp. of El Paso, Apr. 1, 1996; inst., June 26, 1996.

O'Connell, Anthony J.: b. May 10, 1938, Lisheen, Co. Clare, Ireland; came to U.S. at age 20; educ. Mt. St. Joseph College (Cork), Mungret College (Limerick), Kenrick Seminary (St. Louis); ord. priest (Jefferson City), Mar. 30, 1963; ord. First Bp. of Knoxville, TN, Sept. 8, 1988; app. bp. of Palm Beach, Nov. 12, 1998, inst., Jan. 14, 1999; res., March 8, 2002.

O'Donnell, Edward J.: b. July 4, 1931, St. Louis, MO; educ. St. Louis Preparatory Seminary and Kenrick Seminary (St. Louis, MO); ord. priest (St. Louis*), Apr. 6, 1957; ord. titular bp. of Britania and aux. bp. of St. Louis, Feb. 10, 1984; app. bp. of Lafayette, LA, inst., Dec. 16, 1994; ret. Nov. 8, 2002.

Olivier, Leonard J., S.V.D.: b. Oct. 12, 1923, Lake Charles, LA; educ. St. Augustine Major Seminary (Bay St. Louis, MS), Catholic Univ. (Washington, DC), Loyola Univ. (New Orleans, LA); ord. priest, June 29, 1951; ord. titular bp. of Leges in Numidia and aux. bp. of Washington, Dec. 20, 1988; ret. May 18, 2004.

Olmsted, Thomas J.: b. Jan. 21, 1947, Oketo, Kansas; educ. St. Thomas Seminary (Denver), North American College and Pontifical Gregorian University (Rome); ord. priest (Lincoln), July 2, 1973; served in Vatican Secretariat of State, 1979-1988; Dean of Formation, Pontifical College Josephinum, Columbus, OH, 1993, President and Rector, Pontifical College, Josephinum, 1997; app. coadjutor bp. of Wichita, Feb. 16, 1999, ord., Apr. 20, 1999; bp. of Wichita, Oct. 4, 2001; app. bp. of Phoenix, November 25, 2003.

O'Malley, Sean, O.F.M.Cap.: (*See* **Cardinals' Biographies**).

O'Neill, Arthur J.: b. Dec. 14, 1917, East Dubuque, IL; educ. Loras Collge (Dubuque, IA), St. Mary's Seminary (Baltimore, MD); ord. priest (Rockford), Mar. 27, 1943; ord. bp. of Rockford, Oct. 11, 1968; ret., Apr. 19, 1994.

Ottenweller, Albert H.: b. Apr. 5, 1916, Stanford, MT; educ. St. Joseph's Seminary (Rensselaer, IN), Catholic Univ. (Washington, DC); ord. priest (Toledo), June 19, 1943; ord. titular bp. of Perdices and aux. bp. of Toledo, May 29, 1974; app. bp. of Steubenville, OH, Oct. 11, 1977, inst., Nov. 22, 1977; ret., Jan. 28, 1992.

P

Paprocki, Thomas J.: b. Aug. 5, 1952, Chicago, IL; educ. Niles College of Loyola (Chicago, IL), Saint Mary of the Lake Seminary (Chicago, IL), DePaul University College of Law (Chicago, IL), Gregorian University (Rome); ord. priest, May 10, 1978 (Chicago); app. aux. bp. of Chicago and titular bishop of Vulturara, Jan. 24, 2003; ord., March 19, 2003.

Paska, Walter: b. Nov. 29, 1923, Elizabeth, NJ; educ. St. Charles Seminary (Catonsville, MD), Catholic Univ. (Washington, DC), Fordham Univ. (New York); ord. priest (Philadelphia of Ukrainians*), June 2, 1947; ord. titular bp. of Tigilava and aux. of Ukrainian archdiocese of Philadelphia, Mar. 19, 1992; res., Nov. 29, 2000.

Pataki, Andrew: b. Aug. 30, 1927, Palmerton, PA; educ. St. Vincent College (Latrobe, PA), St. Procopius College, St. Procopius Seminary (Lisle, IL), Sts. Cyril and Methodius Byzantine Catholic Seminary (Pittsburgh, PA), Gregorian Univ. and Oriental Pontifical Institute (Rome, Italy); ord. priest (Pittsburgh,* Ruthenian Byzantine), Feb. 24, 1952; ord. titular bp. of Telmisso and aux. bp. of Byzantine diocese of Passaic, Aug. 23, 1983; app. bp. of Ruthenian Byzantine diocese of Parma, July 3, 1984; app. bp. of Ruthenian Byzantine diocese of Passaic, Nov. 6, 1995; inst., Feb. 8, 1996.

Pates, Richard E.: b. Feb. 12, 1943, St. Paul; educ. St. Paul Seminary, North American College (Rome); ord. priest (St. Paul and Minneapolis*), Dec. 20, 1968; staff, Apostolic Nunciature, Washington, 1975-81; app. titular bp. of Suacia and aux. bp. of St. Paul and Minneapolis, Dec. 22, 2000, ord., March 26, 2001.

Pearce, George H., S.M.: b. Jan. 9, 1921, Brighton, MA; educ. Marist College and Seminary (Framington, MA); ord. priest, Feb. 2, 1947; ord. titular bp. of Attalea in Pamphylia and vicar apostolic of the Samoa and Tokelau Islands, June 29, 1956; title changed to bp. of Apia, June 21, 1966; app. abp. of Suva, Fiji Islands, June 22, 1967; res., Apr. 10, 1976.

Pelotte, Donald E., S.S.S.: b. Apr. 13, 1945, Waterville, ME; educ. Eymard Seminary and Junior College (Hyde Park, NY), John Carroll Univ. (Cleveland, OH), Fordham Univ. (Bronx, NY); ord. priest, Sept. 2, 1972; ord. coadjutor bp. of Gallup, May 6, 1986 (first priest of Native American ancestry to be named U.S. bp.); bp. of Gallup, Mar. 20, 1990.

Peña, Raymundo J.: b. Feb. 19, 1934, Robstown, TX; educ. Assumption Seminary (San Antonio, TX); ord. priest (Corpus Christi), May 25, 1957; ord. titular bp. of Trisipa and aux. bp. of San Antonio, Dec. 13, 1976; app. bp. of El Paso, Apr. 29, 1980; app. bp. of Brownsville, May 23, 1995.

Pepe, Joseph A.: b. June 18, 1942, Philadelphia; educ. St. Charles Borromeo Seminary, University of St. Thomas

(Rome); ord. priest (Philadelphia*), May 16, 1970; app. bp. of Las Vegas, April 6, 2001, ord., May 31, 2001.

Perry, Joseph N.: b. Apr. 18, 1948, Chicago, IL; educ. Capuchin Seminary of St. Lawrence, (Milwaukee), St. Mary Capuchin Seminary, Crown Point, (Indiana), St. Francis Seminary (Milwaukee), Catholic Univ. of America (Washington, DC); ord. priest (Milwaukee*), May 24, 1975; app. titular bp. of Lead and aux. bp. of Chicago, May 5, 1998; ord., June 29, 1998.

Pevec, A. Edward: b. Apr. 16, 1925, Cleveland, OH; educ. St. Mary's Seminary, John Carroll Univ. (Cleveland, OH); ord. priest (Cleveland), Apr. 29, 1950; ord. titular bp. of Mercia and aux. bp. of Cleveland, July 2, 1982; res., Apr. 3, 2001.

Pfeifer, Michael, O.M.I.: b. May 18, 1937, Alamo, TX; educ. Oblate school of theology (San Antonio, TX); ord. priest, Dec. 21, 1964; provincial of southern province of Oblates of Mary Immaculate, 1981; ord. bp. of San Angelo, July 26, 1985.

Pilarczyk, Daniel E.: b. Aug. 12, 1934, Dayton, OH; educ. St. Gregory's Seminary (Cincinnati, OH), Urban Univ. (Rome), Xavier Univ. and Univ. of Cincinnati (Cincinnati, OH); ord. priest (Cincinnati*), Dec. 20, 1959; ord. titular bp. of Hodelm and aux. bp. of Cincinnati, Dec. 20, 1974; app. abp. of Cincinnati, Oct. 30, 1982; inst., Dec. 20, 1982; president of NCCB/USCC, 1989-92.

Pilla, Anthony M.: b. Nov. 12, 1932, Cleveland, OH; educ. St. Gregory College Seminary (Cincinnati, OH), Borromeo College Seminary (Wickliffe, OH), St. Mary Seminary and John Carroll Univ. (Cleveland, OH); ord. priest (Cleveland), May 23, 1959; ord. titular bp. of Scardona and aux. bp. of Cleveland, Aug. 1, 1979; app. apostolic administrator of Cleveland, 1980; bp. of Cleveland, Nov. 13, 1980. President of NCCB/USCC, 1995-98; res. Apr. 4, 2006.

Popp, Bernard F.: b. Dec. 6, 1917, Nada, TX; educ. St. John's Seminary and St. Mary's Univ. (San Antonio, TX); ord. priest (San Antonio*), Feb. 24, 1943; ord. titular bp. of Capsus and aux. bp. of San Antonio, July 25, 1983; ret., Mar. 23, 1993.

Potocnak, Joseph J., S.C.J.: b. May 13, 1933, Berwick, PA; educ. Dehon Seminary (Great Barrington, MA), Kilroe Seminary (Honesdale, PA), Sacred Heart (Hales Corners, WI); ord. priest, Sept 21, 1966; missionary in South Africa from 1973; ord. bp. of De Aar, South Africa, May 1, 1992.

Puscas, Vasile Louis: b. Sept. 13, 1915, Aurora, IL; educ. Quigley Preparatory Seminary (Chicago, IL), seminary in Oradea-Mare (Romania), Propaganda Fide Seminary (Rome), Illinois Benedictine College (Lisle, IL); ord. priest (Erie), May 14, 1942; ord. titular bp. of Leuce and first exarch of apostolic exarchate for Byzantine Romanians in the U.S., June 26, 1983 (seat of the exarchate, Canton, OH); app. first eparch, Apr. 11, 1987, when exarchate was raised to eparchy of St. George's in Canton; ret., July 15, 1993.

Q

Quinn, Alexander James: b. Apr. 8, 1932, Cleveland, OH; educ. St. Charles College (Catonsville, MD), St. Mary Seminary (Cleveland, OH), Lateran Univ. (Rome), Cleveland State Univ.; ord. priest (Cleveland), May 24, 1958; ord. titular bp. of Socia and aux. bp. of Cleveland, Dec. 5, 1983.

Quinn, Francis A.: b. Sept. 11, 1921, Los Angeles, CA; educ. St. Joseph's College (Mountain View, CA), St. Patrick's

Seminary (Menlo Park, CA), Catholic Univ. (Washington, DC); Univ. of CA (Berkeley); ord. priest (San Francisco*), June 15, 1946; ord. titular bp. of Numana and aux. bp. of San Francisco, June 29, 1978; app. bp. of Sacramento, Dec. 18, 1979; ret., Nov. 30, 1993.

Quinn, John M.: b. Dec. 17, 1945, Detroit; educ. Sacred Heart Seminary, St. John Provincial Seminary, University of Detroit and the Catholic University of America (Washington, D.C.); ord. priest, March 17, 1972; app. aux. bp. of Detroit and titular bishop of Ressiana, July 7, 2003.

Quinn, John R.: b. Mar. 28, 1929, Riverside, CA; educ. St. Francis Seminary (El Cajon, CA), North American College (Rome); ord. priest (San Diego), July 19, 1953; ord. titular bp. of Thisiduo and aux. bp. of San Diego, Dec. 12, 1967; bp. of Oklahoma City and Tulsa, Nov. 30, 1971; first abp. of Oklahoma City, Dec. 19, 1972; app. abp. of San Francisco, Feb. 22, 1977, inst., Apr. 26, 1977; president NCCB/USCC, 1977-80; res., see Dec. 27, 1995.

R

Ramirez, Ricardo, C.S.B.: b. Sept. 12, 1936, Bay City, TX; educ. Univ. of St. Thomas (Houston, TX), Univ. of Detroit (Detroit, MI), St. Basil's Seminary (Toronto, ON), Seminario Concilium (Mexico City, Mexico), East Asian Pastoral Institute (Manila, Philippines); ord. priest, Dec. 10, 1966; ord titular bp. of Vatarba and aux. of San Antonio, Dec. 6, 1981; app. first bp. of Las Cruces, NM, Aug. 17, 1982; inst., Oct. 18, 1982.

Rassas, George J.: b. Baltimore May 26, 1942; educ. University of St. Mary of the Lake (Mundelein, Ill.), Loyola University (Chicago); ord. priest May 2, 1968 (Chicago); app. aux. bp. Chicago and tit. bp. of Reperi Dec. 1, 2005; ord. bp. Feb. 2, 2006.

Raya, Joseph M.: b. July 20, 1917, Zahle, Lebanon; educ. St. Louis College (Paris, France), St. Anne's Seminary (Jerusalem); ord. priest, July 20, 1941; came to U.S., 1949, became U.S. citizen; ord. abp. of Acre, Israel, of the Melkites, Oct. 20, 1968; res., Aug. 20, 1974; assigned titular metropolitan see of Scytopolis (resides in Canada).

Reichert, Stephen J., O.F.M. Cap.: b. May 14, 1943, Leoville, KS; educ. Capuchin minor seminary (Victoria, KS), St. Fidelis College (Hermann, PA), Capuchin College (Washington, DC); ord. priest, Sept. 27, 1969; missionary in Papua New Guinea since 1970; ord. bp. of Mendi, Papua New Guinea, May 7, 1995.

Reilly, Daniel P.: b. May 12, 1928, Providence, RI; educ. Our Lady of Providence Seminary (Warwick, RI), St. Brieuc Major Seminary (Cotes du Nord, France); ord. priest (Providence), May 30, 1953; ord. bp. of Norwich, Aug. 6, 1975; app. bp. of Worcester, Oct. 27, 1994, inst., Nov. 8, 1994; ret. Mar. 9, 2004.

Reiss, Francis R.: b. Nov. 11, 1940, Detroit; educ. Sacred Heart Seminary, St. John Provincial Seminary, University of Detroit, Gregorian University; ord. priest, June 4, 1966; app. aux. bp. of Detroit and titular bishop of Remesiana, July 7, 2003.

Reiss, John C.: b. May 13, 1922, Red Bank, NJ; educ. Catholic Univ. (Washington, DC), Immaculate Conception Seminary (Darlington, NJ); ord. priest (Trenton), May 31, 1947; ord. titular bp. of Simidicca and aux. bp. of Trenton, Dec. 12, 1967; app. bp. of Trenton, Mar. 11, 1980; ret., July 1, 1997.

Rhoades, Kevin C.: b. Nov. 26, 1957, Mahanoy City, PA; educ. Mount St. Mary's College (Emmitsburg,

MD), St. Charles Borromeo Seminary (Wynnewood, PA); Gregorian University (Rome); ord. priest July 9, 1983 (Harrisburg); app. bp. of Harrisburg Oct. 14, 2004; ord. Dec. 9, 2004.

Riashi, Georges, B.C.O.: b. Nov. 25, 1933, Kaa-el-Rim, Lebanon; ord. priest, Apr. 4, 1965; parish priest of Our Lady of Redemption Parish, Warren, MI (Newton Greek-Catholic Melkite eparchy); U.S. citizen; ord. first bp. of eparchy of St. Michael's of Sydney (Australia) for Greek-Catholic Melkites, July 19, 1987; app. abp. of archeparchy of Tripoli of Lebanon for Greek-Melkites, Aug. 5, 1995.

Ricard, John H., S.S.J.: b. Feb. 29, 1940, Baton Rouge, LA; educ. St. Joseph's Seminary (Washington, DC), Tulane Univ. (New Orleans, LA); ord. priest, May 25, 1968; ord. titular bp. of Rucuma and aux. of Baltimore, July 2, 1984; urban vicar, Baltimore; app. bp. of Pensacola-Tallahassee, Jan 21, 1997.

Ricken, David L.: b. Nov. 9, 1952, Dodge City, Kansas; educ. Conception Seminary College, MO, Univ. of Louvain (Belgium), Pontifical Gregorian Univ., Rome; ord. priest (Pueblo), Sept. 12, 1980; official of the Congregation for the Clergy, 1996-1999; app. Coadjutor Bishop of Cheyenne, Dec. 14, 1999, ord. bp. by Pope John Paul II at the Vatican, Jan. 6, 2000; bp. of Cheyenne, Sept. 26, 2001.

Rigali, Justin F.: (*See* Cardinals, Biographies.)

Rizzotto, Vincent M.: b. Sept. 9, 1931, Houston; educ. St. Mary Seminary (Houston), the Catholic University of America (Washington, D.C.), ord. priest, (Galveston, now Galveston-Houston) May 26, 1956; Vicar General of Galveston-Houston, 1994; app. titular bp. of Lamasba and aux. bp. of Galveston-Houston June 22, 2001, ord., July 31, 2001.

Rodi, Thomas J: b. March 27, 1949, New Orleans; educ. Georgetown University (Washington, D.C.), Tulane University School of Law (New Orleans), Notre Dame Seminary (New Orleans); ord. priest, (New Orleans*), May 20, 1978; app. bp. of Biloxi, May 15, 2001, ord., July 2, 2001.

Rodimer, Frank J.: b. Oct. 25, 1927, Rockaway, NJ; educ. Seton Hall Prep (South Orange, NJ), St. Charles College (Catonsville, MD), St. Mary's Seminary (Baltimore, MD), Immaculate Conception Seminary (Darlington, NJ), Catholic Univ. (Washington, DC); ord. priest (Paterson), May 19, 1951; ord. bp. of Paterson, Feb. 28, 1978; ret. June 1, 2004.

Rodriguez, Miguel, C.SS.R.: b. Apr. 18, 1931, Mayaguez, P.R.; educ. St. Mary's Minor Seminary (North East, PA), Mt. St. Alphonsus Major Seminary (Esopus, NY); ord. priest, June 22, 1958; ord. bp. of Arecibo, P.R., Mar. 23, 1974; res., Mar. 20, 1990.

Rodriguez, Placido, C.M.F.: b. Oct. 11, 1940, Celaya, Guanajuato, Mexico; educ. Claretian Novitate (Los Angeles, CA), Claretville Seminary College (Calabasas, CA), Catholic Univ. (Washington, DC), Loyola Univ. (Chicago, IL); ord. priest, May 23, 1968; ord. titular bp. of Fuerteventura and aux. bp. of Chicago, Dec. 13, 1983; app. bp. of Lubbock, TX, Apr. 5, 1994.

Roman, Agustin A.: b. May 5, 1928, San Antonio de los Banos, Havana, Cuba; educ. San Alberto Magno Seminary (Matanzas, Cuba), Missions Etrangeres (Montreal, Canada), Barry College (Miami, FL); ord. priest, July 5, 1959, Cuba; vicar for Spanish speaking in Miami archdiocese, 1976; ord. titular bp. of Sertei and aux. bp. of Miami, Mar. 24, 1979; ret., June 7, 2003.

Roque, Francis X.: b. Oct. 9, 1928, Providence RI; educ. St. John's Seminary (Brighton, MA); ord. priest, (Providence) Sept. 19, 1953; became chaplain in U.S. Army 1961; ord. titular bp. of Military Services archdiocese, May 10, 1983; ret. Sept. 15, 2004.

Rosazza, Peter Anthony: b. Feb. 13, 1935, New Haven, CT; educ. St. Thomas Seminary (Bloomfield, CT), Dartmouth College (Hanover, NH), St. Bernard's Seminary (Rochester, NY), St. Sulpice (Issy, France); ord. priest (Hartford*), June 29, 1961; ord. titular bp. of Oppido Nuovo and aux. bp. of Hartford, June 24, 1978.

Rose, Robert John: b. Feb. 28, 1930, Grand Rapids, MI; educ. St. Joseph's Seminary (Grand Rapids, MI), Seminaire de Philosophie (Montreal, Canada), Urban University (Rome), Univ. of Michigan (Ann Arbor); ord. priest (Grand Rapids), Dec. 21, 1955; ord. bp. of Gaylord, Dec. 6, 1981; app. bp. of Grand Rapids, inst., Aug. 30, 1989; ret. Oct. 13, 2003.

Rozanski, Mitchell Thomas: b. Aug. 6, 1958, Baltimore, MD; educ. Catholic University of America (Washington, DC); ord. priest (Baltimore*), Nov. 24, 1984; app. titular bp. of Walla Walla and aux. bp. of Baltimore, July 2, 2004; ord. Aug. 24, 2004.

Rueger, George E.: b. Sept. 3, 1933, Framingham, Mass; educ. Holy Cross College (Worcester, MA), St. John's Seminary (Brighton), Harvard University (Cambridge, MA); ord. priest (Worcester), Jan. 6, 1958; ord. titular bp. of Maronana and aux. bp. of Worcester, Feb. 25, 1987; ret. Jan. 25, 2005.

Ryan, Daniel L.: b. Sept. 28, 1930, Mankato, MN; educ. St. Procopius Seminary (Lisle, IL), Lateran Univ. (Rome); ord. priest (Joliet), May 3, 1956; ord. titular bp. of Surista and aux. bp. of Joliet, Sept. 30, 1981; app. bp. of Springfield, IL, Nov. 22, 1983, inst., Jan. 18, 1984; res. Oct. 19, 1999.

Ryan, Sylvester D.: b. May 3, 1930, Catalina Is., CA; educ. St. John's Seminary (Camarillo, CA); ord. priest (Los Angeles*), May 3, 1957; ord. titular bp. of Remesiana and aux. bp. of Los Angeles, May 31, 1990; app. bp. of Monterey, Jan. 28, 1992.

S

Salazar, Alexander: b. Nov. 28, 1949, San Jose, Costa Rica; educ. California State Univ. and Immaculate Heart College (Los Angeles), St. John's Seminary (Camarillo, CA); ord. priest June 16, 1984; appointed auxiliary bishop of Los Angeles and titular bishop of Nesqually Sept. 7, 2004; ord. Nov. 4, 2004.

Saltarelli, Michael A.: b. Jan. 17, 1932, Jersey City, NJ; educ. Seton Hall College and Immaculate Conception Seminary (S. Orange, NJ); ord. priest (Newark*), May 28, 1960; ord. titular bp. of Mesarfelta and aux. bp. of Newark, July 30, 1990; app. bp. of Wilmington, Nov. 21, 1995; inst., Jan. 23, 1996.

Sample, Alexander K.: b. Nov. 7, 1960, Kalispell, Mont.; educ. Michigan Technological University (Houghton), St. Thomas College (St. Paul, Minn.), Pontifical College Josephinum (Columbus, Ohio), Angelicum (Rome); ord. priest June 1, 1990 (Marquette); app. bp of Marquette Dec. 13, 2005; ord. bp. Jan. 25, 2006.

Samra, Nicholas J.: b. Aug. 15, 1944, Paterson, NJ; educ. St. Anselm College (Manchester, NH), St. Basil Seminary (Methuen, MA), St. John Seminary (Brighton, MA); ord. priest (Newton), May 10, 1970; ord. titular bp. of Gerasa and aux. bp. of Melkite diocese of Newton, July 6, 1989; res. Jan. 11, 2005.

Sanchez, Robert F.: b. Mar. 20, 1934, Socorro, NM; educ. Immaculate Heart Seminary (Santa Fe, NM), Gregorian Univ. (Rome), Catholic Univ. (Washington, DC); ord. priest (Santa Fe*), Dec 20, 1959; ord. abp. of Santa Fe, NM, July 25, 1974; res., Apr. 6, 1993.

Sansaricq, Guy A.: b. Oct. 6, 1934, Jeremie, Haiti; educ. St. Paul College (Ottawa); ord. priest June 29, 1960 (Les Cayes, Haiti); incard. Brooklyn 1991; appointed aux. bp. of Brooklyn and tit. bp. of Glenndalocha June 6, 2006; ord. Aug. 22, 2006.

Sartain, James P.: b. June 6, 1952, Memphis, TN; educ. St. Meinrad Seminary, (Indiana), North American College, (Rome), Pontifical University of St. Thomas (the Angelicum), Pontifical Institute of St. Anselm (Rome); ord. priest (Memphis), July 15, 1978; app. bp. of Little Rock, Jan. 4, 2000, ord., March 6, 2000; app. bp. of Joliet, May 16, 2006.

Sartoris, Joseph M.: b. July 1, 1927, Los Angeles, CA; educ. St. John's Seminary (Camarillo, CA); ord. priest (Los Angeles*), May 30, 1953; ord. titular bp. of Oliva and aux. bp. of Los Angeles, Mar. 19, 1994; ret., Dec. 31, 2002.

Scarpone Caporale, Gerald, O.F.M.: b. Oct. 1, 1928, Watertown, MA; ord. priest, June 24, 1956; ord. coadjutor bp. of Comayagua, Honduras, Feb. 21, 1979; succeeded as bp. of Comayagua, May 30, 1979.

Schlarman, Stanley Gerard: b. July 27, 1933, Belleville, IL; educ. St. Henry Prep Seminary (Belleville, IL), Gregorian Univ. (Rome), St. Louis Univ. (St. Louis, MO); ord. priest (Belleville), July 13, 1958, Rome; ord. titular bp. of Capri and aux. bp. of Belleville, May 14, 1979; app. bp. of Dodge City, Mar. 1, 1983; res., May 12, 1998.

Schleck, Charles A., C.S.C.: b. July 5, 1925, Milwaukee, WI; educ. Univ. of Notre Dame (IN), Pontifical Univ. of St. Thomas (Rome); ord. priest, Dec. 22, 1951; ord. titular abp. of Africa (Mehdia), Apr. 1, 1995; adjunct secretary of Congregation for Evangelization of Peoples; president of the superior council of the Pontifical Mission Societies.

Schmitt, Bernard W.: b. Aug. 17, 1928, Wheeling, WV; educ. St. Joseph College (Catonsville, MD), St. Mary's Seminary (Baltimore), Ohio Univ. (Athens, OH); ord. priest (Wheeling-Charleston), May 28, 1955; ord. titular bp. of Walla Walla and bp. of Wheeling-Charleston, Aug. 1, 1988; bp. of Wheeling-Charleston, Mar. 29, 1989; ret. Dec. 9, 2004.

Schmitt, Mark F.: b. Feb. 14, 1923, Algoma, WI; educ. Salvatorian Seminary (St. Nazianz, WI), St. John's Seminary (Collegeville, MN); ord. priest (Green Bay), May 22, 1948; ord. titular bp. of Ceanannus Mor and aux. bp. of Green Bay, June 24, 1970; app. bp. of Marquette, Mar. 21, 1978, inst., May 8, 1978; ret., Oct. 6, 1992.

Schmitz Simon, Paul, O.F.M. Cap.: b. Dec. 4, 1943, Fond du Lac, WI; ord. priest, Sept. 3, 1970; missionary in Nicaragua from 1970; superior of vice province of Capuchins in Central America (headquartered in Managua), 1982-84; ord. titular bp. of Elepla and aux. of the vicariate apostolic of Bluefields, Nicaragua, Sept. 17, 1984; app. bp. of vicariate apostolic of Bluefields, Aug. 17, 1994.

Schnurr, Dennis M.: b. June 21, 1948, Sheldon, Iowa; educ. Loras College (Dubuque), Gregorian University (Rome), Catholic University of America (Washington, DC); ord. priest (Sioux City), July 20, 1974; Staff, Apostolic Nunciature, Washington, DC, 1985-1989; Associate General Secretary, National Conference of Catholic Bishops/United States Catholic Conference (NCCB/USCC), 1989-1995;

National Executive Director, World Youth Day 1993, Denver, 1991-1993; General Secretary, NCCB/USCC, 1995-2001; app. bp. of Duluth, Jan. 18, 2001, ord., Apr. 2, 2001.

Schoenherr, Walter J.: b. Feb. 28, 1920, Detroit, MI; educ. Sacred Heart Seminary (Detroit, MI), Mt. St. Mary Seminary (Norwood, OH); ord. priest (Detroit*), Oct. 27, 1945; ord. titular bp. of Timidana and aux. bp. of Detroit, May 1, 1968; ret., Mar. 7, 1995.

Schott, Basil, O.F.M.: b. July 21, 1939, Freeland, PA; entered Byzantine Franciscans, professed Aug. 4, 1959; educ. Immaculate Conception College (Troy, NY), St. Mary's Seminary (Norwalk, CT) and Post Graduate Center (New York, NY); ord. priest, Aug. 29, 1965; ord. bp. of Byzantine eparchy of Parma, July 11, 1996; app. metropolitan abp. of Pittsburgh (Byzantine Ruthenian), May 3, 2002.

Schulte, Francis B.: b. Dec. 23, 1926, Philadelphia, PA; educ. St. Charles Borromeo Seminary (Overbrook, PA); ord. priest (Philadelphia*), May 10, 1952; ord. titular bp. of Afufenia and aux. bp. of Philadelphia, Aug. 12, 1981; app. bp. of Wheeling-Charleston, June 4, 1985; abp. of New Orleans, Dec. 6, 1988, inst., Feb. 14, 1989; ret., Jan. 3, 2002.

Schwietz, Roger L., O.M.I.: b. July 3, 1940, St. Paul, MN; educ. Univ. of Ottawa (Canada), Gregorian Univ. (Rome); ord. priest, Dec. 20, 1967; ord. bp. of Duluth Feb. 2, 1990; bp. of Duluth, 1990-2000; coadj. abp. of Anchorage, Jan. 18, 2000; abp. of Anchorage, March 3, 2001.

Seminack, Richard: b. March 3, 1942, Philadelphia; educ. St. Basil Seminary (Stamford, Conn.), St. Josaphat Major Seminary and Catholic University of America (Washington), Oriental Institute (Rome); ord. priest, May 25, 1967 (archeparchy of Philadelphia); incard. Eparchy of St. Josaphat (Parma) 1983; app. bp. of St. Nicholas of Chicago for Ukrainians, March 25, 2003; ord., June 4, 2003.

Serratelli, Arthur J.: b. April 18, 1944, Newark, NJ; educ. Seton Preparatory School (NJ), Seton Hall University (NJ), North American College and Gregorian University (Rome), Pontifical Biblical Institute (Rome); ord. priest (Newark*), Dec. 20, 1968; prof. of Sacred Scripture, Immaculate Conception Seminary; rector of the College Seminary, Seton Hall University; prelate of honor, 1998; app. titular bp. of Enera and aux. bp. of Newark, July 3, 2000; app. bp. of Paterson, June 1, 2004.

Sevilla, Carlos A., S.J.: b. Aug. 9, 1935, San Francisco, CA; entered Jesuits Aug. 14, 1953; educ. Gonzaga Univ. (Spokane, WA), Santa Clara Univ. (Santa Clara, CA), Jesuitenkolleg (Innsbruck, Austria), Catholic Institute of Paris (France); ord. priest, June 3, 1966; ord. titular bp. of Mina and aux. bp. of San Francisco, Jan. 25, 1989; bp. of Yakima, Dec. 31, 1996.

Shaheen, Robert J.: b. June 3, 1937, Danbury, Conn.; ord., May 2, 1964; elected eparch of Our Lady of Lebanon of Los Angeles of the Maronites (U.S.A.), Dec. 5, 2000.

Sheehan, Michael J.: b. July 9, 1939, Wichita, KS; educ. Assumption Seminary (San Antonio, TX), Gregorian Univ. and Lateran Univ. (Rome); ord. priest (Dallas), July 12, 1964; ord. first bp. of Lubbock, TX, June 17, 1983; apostolic administrator of Santa Fe, Apr. 6, 1993; app. abp. of Santa Fe, Aug. 17, 1993.

Sheldon, Gilbert I.: b. Sept. 20, 1926, Cleveland, OH; educ. John Carroll Univ. and St. Mary Seminary (Cleveland, OH); ord. priest (Cleveland), Feb. 28, 1953; ord. titular bp. of Taparura and aux. bp. of Cleveland, June 11, 1976; app. bp. of Steubenville,

Jan. 28, 1992, ret., May 31, 2002.

Sheridan, Michael J.: b. Mar. 4, 1945, St. Louis, MO; educ. Glennon College, Kenrick Seminary (St. Louis, MO), Angelicum (Rome); ord. priest (St. Louis*), 1971; app. titular bp. of Thibiuca and aux. bp. of St. Louis, July 9, 1997; coadjutor bp. of Colorado Springs, Dec. 4, 2001; bp. of Colorado Springs, Jan. 30, 2003.

Sheridan, Patrick J.: b. Mar. 10, 1922, New York, NY; educ. St. Joseph's Seminary (Yonkers, NY), University of Chicago; ord. priest (New York*), Mar. 1, 1947; ord. titular bp. of Curzola and aux. bp. of New York, Dec. 12, 1990; res., Jan.15, 2001.

Silva, Clarence: b. Aug. 6, 1949, Honolulu; educ. St. Patrick Seminary (Menlo Park, Calif.); ord. priest May 2, 1975 (Oakland); app. bp. of Honolulu May 17, 2005; ord. bp. July 21, 2005.

Sklba, Richard J.: b. Sept. 11, 1935, Racine, WI; educ. Old St. Francis Minor Seminary (Milwaukee, WI), North American College, Gregorian Univ., Pontifical Biblical Institute, Angelicum (Rome); ord. priest (Milwaukee*), Dec. 20, 1959; ord. titular bp. of Castra and aux. bp. of Milwaukee, Dec. 19, 1979.

Skurla, William C.: b. June 1, 1956, Duluth; educ. Columbia Univ., New York, Mary Immaculate Seminary, Northhampton, PA; ord. priest (Franciscan), 1987; incardinated into Eparchy of Van Nuys, 1996; app. bp. of Van Nuys Byzantine Catholic Eparchy in California, Feb. 19, 2002.

Skylstad, William S.: b. Mar. 2, 1934, Omak, WA; educ. Pontifical College Josephinum (Worthington, OH), Washington State Univ. (Pullman, WA), Gonzaga Univ. (Spokane, WA); ord. priest (Spokane), May 21, 1960; ord. bp. of Yakima, May 12, 1977; app. bp. of Spokane, Apr. 17, 1990; vice-pres. of USCCB, 2001-.

Slattery, Edward J.: b. Aug. 11, 1940, Chicago, IL; educ. Quigley Preparatory, St. Mary of the Lake Seminary (Mundelein, IL), Loyola Univ. (Chicago); ord. priest (Chicago*), Apr. 26, 1966; vice president, 1971-76, and president, 1976-94, of the Catholic Church Extension Society; ord. bp. of Tulsa, Jan. 6, 1994.

Smith, John M.: b. June 23, 1935, Orange, NJ; educ. Immaculate Conception Seminary (Darlington, NJ), Seton Hall Univ. (South Orange, NJ), Catholic Univ. (Washington, DC); ord. priest (Newark*), May 27, 1961; ord. titular bp. of Tre Taverne and aux. bp. of Newark, Jan. 25, 1988; app. bp. of Pensacola-Tallahassee, FL, June 25, 1991; app. coadjutor bp. of Trenton, Nov. 21, 1995; bp. of Trenton, July 1, 1997.

Snyder, John J.: b. Oct. 25, 1925, New York, NY; educ. Cathedral College (Brooklyn, NY), Immaculate Conception Seminary (Huntington, NY); ord. priest (Brooklyn), June 9, 1951; ord. titular bp. of Forlimpopli and aux. bp. of Brooklyn, Feb. 2, 1973; app. bp. of St. Aug.ine, inst., Dec. 5, 1979; res., Dec. 11, 2000.

Soens, Lawrence D.: b. Aug. 26, 1926, Iowa City, IA; educ. Loras College (Dubuque, IA), St. Ambrose College (Davenport, IA), Kenrick Seminary (St. Louis, MO), Univ. of Iowa; ord. priest (Davenport), May 6, 1950; ord. bp. of Sioux City, Aug. 17, 1983, res., Nov. 28, 1998.

Soroka, Stephen: b. Nov. 13, 1951, Winnipeg, Manitoba; educ. Univ. of Manitoba, Ukrainian Seminary, Washington, DC, Catholic Univ. of America, ordained (Ukrainian Archdiocese of Winnipeg*), June 13, 1982; Chancellor and financial administrator of the Winnipeg archdiocese, 1994, auxiliary bishop, Winnipeg, 1996; metropolitan abp. of Philadelphia for the Ukrainians, Nov. 29, 2000; inst., Feb. 27, 2001.

Soto, Jaime: b. Dec. 31, 1955, Inglewood, CA; educ. St. John's Seminary, Camarillo, CA, Columbia University School of Social Work, New York; ord. priest (Orange), June 12, 1982; Episcopal Vicar for Hispanic Ministry, 1989; app. titular bp. of Segia and aux. bp. of Orange, Mar. 23, 2000, ord., May 31, 2000.

Sowada, Alphonse A., O.S.C.: b. June 23, 1933, Avon, MN; educ. Holy Cross Scholasticate (Fort Wayne, IN), Catholic Univ. (Washington, DC); ord. priest, May 31, 1958; missionary in Indonesia from 1958; ord. bp. of Agats, Indonesia, Nov. 23, 1969.

Speyrer, Jude: b. Apr. 14, 1929, Leonville, LA; educ. St. Joseph Seminary (Covington, LA), Notre Dame Seminary (New Orleans, LA), Gregorian Univ. (Rome), Univ. of Fribourg (Switzerland); ord. priest (Lafayette, LA), July 25, 1953; ord. first bp. of Lake Charles, LA, Apr. 25, 1980; res., Dec. 11, 2000.

Stafford, James Francis: (*See* **Cardinals, Biographies**).

Steib, J. (James) Terry, S.V.D.: b. May 17, 1940, Vacherie, LA; educ. Divine Word seminaries (Bay St. Louis, MS, Conesus, NY, Techny, IL), Xavier Univ. (New Orleans, LA); ord. priest, Jan. 6, 1967; ord. titular bp. of Fallaba and aux. bp. of St. Louis, Feb. 10, 1984; app. bp. of Memphis, Mar. 24, 1993.

Steinbock, John T.: b. July 16, 1937, Los Angeles, CA; educ. Los Angeles archdiocesan seminaries; ord. priest (Los Angeles*), May 1, 1963; ord. titular bp. of Midila and aux. bp. of Orange, CA, July 14, 1984; app. bp. of Santa Rosa, Jan. 27, 1987; app. bp. of Fresno, Oct. 15, 1991.

Steiner, Kenneth Donald: b. Nov. 25, 1936, David City, NE; educ. Mt. Angel Seminary (St. Benedict, OR), St. Thomas Seminary (Seattle, Wash); ord. priest (Portland,* OR), May 19, 1962; ord. titular bp. of Avensa and aux. bp. of Portland, OR, Mar. 2, 1978.

Straling, Phillip F.: b. Apr. 25, 1933, San Bernardino, CA; educ. Immaculate Heart Seminary, St. Francis Seminary, Univ. of San Diego and San Diego State University (San Diego, CA), North American College (Rome); ord. priest (San Diego), Mar. 19, 1959; ord. first bp. of San Bernardino, Nov. 6, 1978; app. first bp. of Reno, Mar. 21, 1995, when Reno-Las Vegas diocese was made two separate dioceses; res. Jun. 21, 2005.

Sullivan, Dennis J.: b. Mar. 17, 1945, New York, NY; educ. Iona College (New Rochelle, NY), St. Joseph Seminary (Dunwoodie, NY); ord. May 29, 1971; app. titular bp. of Enera and aux. bp. of New York, June 28, 2004; ord. Sept. 21, 2004.

Sullivan, Joseph M.: b. Mar. 23, 1930, Brooklyn, NY; educ. Immaculate Conception Seminary (Huntington, NY), Fordham Univ. (New York); ord. priest (Brooklyn), June 2, 1956; ord. titular bp. of Suliana and aux. bp. of Brooklyn, Nov. 24, 1980; ret. May 12, 2005.

Sullivan, Walter F.: b. June 10, 1928, Washington, DC; educ. St. Mary's Seminary (Baltimore, MD), Catholic Univ. (Washington, DC); ord. priest (Richmond), May 9, 1953; ord. titular bp. of Selsea and aux. bp. of Richmond, VA, Dec. 1, 1970; app. bp. of Richmond, June 4, 1974; ret. Sept. 16, 2003.

Sulyk, Stephen: b. Oct. 2, 1924, Balnycia, Western Ukraine; migrated to U.S. 1948; educ. Ukrainian Catholic Seminary of the Holy Spirit (Hirschberg, Germany), St. Josaphat's Seminary and Catholic Univ. (Washington, DC); ord. priest (Philadelphia,* Byzantine), June 14, 1952; ord. abp. of the Ukrainian archeparchy of Philadelphia, Mar. 1, 1981; res., Nov. 29, 2000.

Symons, J. Keith: b. Oct. 14, 1932, Champion, MI; educ. St. Thomas Seminary (Bloomfield, CT), St. Mary Seminary (Baltimore, MD); ord. priest (St. Augustine), May 18, 1958; ord. titular bp. of Siguitanus and aux. bp. of St. Petersburg, Mar. 19, 1981; app. bp. of Pensacola-Tallahassee, Oct. 4, 1983, inst., Nov. 8, 1983; app. bp. of Palm Beach, June 12, 1990; res., June 2, 1998.

Szoka, Edmund C.: (See Cardinals, Biographies.)

T

Tafoya, Arthur N.: b. Mar. 2, 1933, Alameda, NM; educ. St. Thomas Seminary (Denver, CO), Conception Seminary (Conception, MO); ord. priest (Santa Fe*), May 12, 1962; ord. bp. of Pueblo, Sept. 10, 1980.

Tamayo, James A.: b. Oct. 23, 1949, Brownsville, TX; educ. Del Mar College (Corpus Christi, TX), Univ. of St. Thomas and Univ. of St. Thomas School of Theology (Houston); ord. priest (Corpus Christi), June 11, 1976; ord. titular bp. of Ita and aux. bp. of Galveston-Houston, Mar. 10, 1993; app. first bp. of Laredo, TX, July 3, 2000, ins., Aug. 9, 2000.

Thomas, Daniel E.: b. June 11, 1959, Philadelphia; educ. St. Charles Borromeo Sem. (Philadelphia), Gregorian Univ. (Rome); ord. priest May 18, 1985 (Philadelphia); appointed aux. bp. of Philadelphia and tit. bp. of Bardstown June 8, 2006; ord. July 26, 2006.

Thomas, Elliott G.: b. July 15, 1926, Pittsburgh, PA; educ. Howard Univ. (Washington, DC), Gannon Univ. (Erie, PA), St. Vincent de Paul Seminary (Boynton Beach, FL); ord. priest (St. Thomas, Virgin Islands), June 6, 1986; ord. bp. of St. Thomas in the Virgin Islands, Dec. 12, 1993; res., June 30, 1999.

Thomas, George L.: b. May 19, 1950, Anaconda, MT, educ. St. Thomas Seminary, Seattle, Univ. of Washington, Seattle; ord. priest (Seattle*), May 22, 1976; chancellor and vicar general, 1988-1999, diocesan administrator of Seattle, 1996-1997; app. titular bp. of Vagrauta and aux. bp. of Seattle, Nov. 19, 1999, inst., Jan. 28, 2000; app. bp. of Helena, March 23, 2004.

Thompson, David B.: b. May 29, 1923, Philadelphia, PA; educ. St. Charles Seminary (Overbrook, PA), Catholic Univ. (Washington, DC); ord. priest (Philadelphia*), May 27, 1950; ord. coadjutor bp. of Charleston, May 24, 1989; bp. of Charleston, Feb. 22, 1990; res., July 13, 1999

Timlin, James C.: b. Aug. 5, 1927, Scranton, PA; educ. St. Charles College (Catonville, MD), St. Mary's Seminary (Baltimore, MD), North American College (Rome); ord. priest (Scranton), July 16, 1951; ord. titular bp. of Gunugo and aux. bp. of Scranton, Sept. 21, 1976; app. bp. of Scranton, Apr. 24, 1984; ret., July 25, 2003.

Tobin, Thomas J.: b. Apr. 1, 1948, Pittsburgh, PA; educ. St. Mark Seminary High School, Gannon Univ. (Erie, PA), St. Francis College (Loretto, PA), North American College (Rome); ord. priest (Pittsburgh), July 21, 1973; ord. titular bp. of Novica and aux. bp. of Pittsburgh, Dec. 27, 1992; app. bp. of Youngstown Dec. 5, 1995; inst., Feb. 2, 1996; app. bp. of Providence, Mar. 31, 2005; inst. May 31, 2005.

Trautman, Donald W.: b. June 24, 1936, Buffalo, NY; educ. Our Lady of Angels Seminary (Niagara Falls, NY), Theology Faculty (Innsbruck, Austria), Pontifical Biblical Institute (Rome), Catholic Univ. (Washington, DC); ord. priest (Buffalo), Apr. 7, 1962, in Innsbruck; ord. titular bp. of Sassura and aux. of Buffalo, Apr. 16, 1985; app. bp. of Erie, June 12, 1990.

Tschoepe, Thomas: b. Dec. 17, 1915, Pilot Point, TX; educ. Pontifical College Josephinum (Worth-ington, OH); ord. priest (Dallas), May 30, 1943; ord. bp. of San Angelo, TX, Mar. 9, 1966; app. bp. of Dallas, TX, Aug. 27, 1969; ret., July 14, 1990.

Turley Murphy, Daniel T. , O.S.A.: b. Jan. 25, 1943, Chicago, IL; ord. priest, Dec. 21, 1961; ord. coadjutor bp. of Chulucanas, Peru, Aug. 17, 1996.

Tyson, Joseph J.: b. Oct. 16, 1957, Moses Lake, Wash.; educ. University of Washington, The Catholic University of America; ord. priest June 10, 1989 (Seattle); app. auxiliary bishop of Seattle and titular bishop of Migirpa May 12, 2005; ord. bp. June 6, 2005.

U-V

Valero, René A.: b. Aug. 15, 1930, New York, NY; educ. Cathedral College, Immaculate Conception Seminary (Huntington, NY), Fordham Univ. (New York); ord. priest (Brooklyn), June 2, 1956; ord. titular bp. of Turris Vicus and aux. bp. of Brooklyn, Nov. 24, 1980; ret. Oct. 27, 2005.

Vann, Kevin W.: b. May 10, 1951, Springfield, Ill.; educ. Milikin Univ. (Decatur, Ill.), Immaculate Conception Seminary (Springfield), Kenrick Seminary (St. Louis), Univ. of St. Thomas Aquinas (Rome); ord. May 30, 1981 (Springfield); app. coadjutor bp. Forth Worth May 17, 2005; ord. bp. July 13, 2005.

Vasa, Robert F.: b. May 7, 1951, Lincoln, NE, educ. St. Thomas Seminary, Denver, Holy Trinity Seminary, Dallas, Pontifical Gregorian Univ. (Rome, Italy); ord. priest (Lincoln), May 22,1976; Vicar General and Moderator of the Curia, 1996; app. bp. of Baker, OR Nov. 19, 1999, inst., Jan. 26, 2000.

Vasquez, José S.: b. July 9, 1957, Stamford, Texas; educ. St. Mary Seminary, Houston, University of St. Thomas, North American College and Pontifical Gregorian University (Rome); ord. priest (San Angelo), June 30, 1984; app. titular bp. of Cova and aux. of Galveston-Houston, Nov. 30, 2001, ord., Jan. 23, 2002.

Veigle, Adrian J.M., T.O.R.: b. Sept. 15, 1912, Lilly, PA; educ. St. Francis College (Loretto, PA), Pennsylvania State College; ord. priest, May 22, 1937; ord. titular bp. of Gigthi, June 9, 1966 (res., titular see May 26, 1978); prelate of Borba, Brazil, 1966; ret., July 6, 1988.

Vigneron, Allen H.: b. Oct. 21, 1948, Detroit, MI; educ. Sacred Heart Seminary (Detroit, MI), North American College, Gregorian Univ. (Rome), Catholic Univ.(Washington, DC); ord. priest (Detroit*), July 26, 1975; served in Vatican Secretariat of State, 1991-94; rector of Sacred Heart Seminary (Detroit), 1994; ord. titular bp. of Sault Sainte Marie and aux. bp. of Detroit, July 9, 1996; app. coadjutor bp. of Oakland, Jan. 10, 2003; bp. of Oakland Oct. 1, 2003.

Vlazny, John G.: b. Feb. 22, 1937, Chicago, IL; educ. Quigley Preparatory Seminary (Chicago, IL), St. Mary of the Lake Seminary (Mundelein, IL), Gregorian Univ. (Rome), Univ. of Michigan, Loyola Univ. (Chicago, IL); ord. priest (Chicago*), Dec. 20, 1961; ord. titular bp. of Stagno and aux. bp. of Chicago, Dec. 13, 1983; app. bp. of Winona, MN, May 19, 1987; app. abp. of Portland in Oregon, Oct. 28, 1997, inst., Dec. 19, 1997.

W

Walsh, Daniel Francis: b. Oct. 2, 1937, San Francisco, CA; educ. St. Joseph Seminary (Mountain View, CA), St. Patrick Seminary (Menlo Park, CA) Catholic Univ. (Washington, DC); ord. priest (San Francisco*), Mar. 30,

1963; ord. titular bp. of Tigia and aux. bp. of San Francisco, Sept. 24, 1981; app. bp. of Reno-Las Vegas, June 9, 1987; app. first bp. of Las Vegas, Mar. 21, 1995, when the Reno-Las Vegas diocese was made two separate dioceses; app. bp. Santa Rosa, Apr. 11, 2000.

Walsh, Gerald T.: b. Apr. 25, 1942, New York, NY; educ. Iona College (New Rochelle, NY), Saint Joseph Seminary (Dunwoodie, NY), Fordham University (New York, NY); ord. May 27, 1967; app. titular bp. of Altiburo and aux. bp. of New York, June 28, 2004; ord. Sept. 21, 2004.

Walsh, Paul H.: b. Aug. 17, 1937, Brooklyn; educ. Providence College (R.I.), St. Stephen's College (Dover, MA), Dominican House of Studies (Washington); ord. Dominican, June 9, 1966; incard. Rockville Centre Dec. 13, 1984; app. aux. bp. of Rockville Centre and titular bishop of Abtugni, April 3, 2003; ord. bp., May 29, 2003.

Wang, Ignatius: b. Feb. 27, 1934, Beijing, China; educ. Urbanian Univ. and Gregorian Univ. (Rome); ord. priest (for apostolic vicariate in southern China) July 4, 1959; unable to return home, he served in the Antilles and transferred to San Francisco in 1974; auxiliary bishop of San Francisco and titular bishop of Sitipa, Dec. 13, 2002; ord., Jan. 30, 2003.

Ward, John J.: b. Sept. 28, 1920, Los Angeles, CA; educ. St. John's Seminary (Camarillo, CA), Catholic Univ. (Washington, DC); ord. priest (Los Angeles*), May 4, 1946; ord. titular bp. of Bria and aux. of Los Angeles, Dec. 12, 1963; ret., May 7, 1996; titular bp. of CA.

Warfel, Michael William: b. Sept 16, 1948, Elkhart, IN; educ. Indiana Univ, St. Gregory's College Seminary, Mt. St. Mary's Seminary of the West (Cincinnati, OH); ord. priest, Apr. 26, 1980; ord. bp. of Juneau, Dec. 17, 1996.

Watters, Loras J.: b. Oct. 14, 1915, Dubuque, IA; educ. Loras College (Dubuque, IA), Gregorian Univ. (Rome), Catholic Univ. (Washington, DC); ord. priest (Dubuque*), June 7, 1941; ord. titular bp. of Fidoloma and aux. bp. of Dubuque, Aug. 26, 1965; bp. of Winona, inst., Mar. 13, 1969; ret., Oct. 14, 1986.

Watty Urquidi, Ricardo, M.Sp.S.: b. July 16, 1938, San Diego, CA; ord. priest, June 8, 1968; ord. titular bp. of Macomedes and aux. bp. of Mexico City, July 19, 1980; app. first bp. of Nuevo Laredo, Mexico, Nov. 6, 1989.

Wcela, Emil A.: b. May 1, 1931, Bohemia, NY; educ. St. Francis College (Brooklyn, NY), Immaculate Conception Seminary (Huntington, NY), Catholic Univ. (Washington, DC), Pontifical Biblical Institute (Rome, Italy); ord. priest (Brooklyn), June 2, 1956; ord. titular bp. of Filaca and aux. bp. of Rockville Centre, Dec. 13, 1988.

Weakland, Rembert G., O.S.B.: b. Apr. 2, 1927, Patton, PA; joined Benedictines, 1945; ord. priest, June 24, 1951; abbot-primate of Benedictine Confederation, 1967-77; ord. abp. of Milwaukee, Nov. 8, 1977; res., May 24, 2002.

Weigand, William K.: b. May 23, 1937, Bend, OR; educ. Mt. Angel Seminary (St. Benedict, OR), St. Edward's Seminary and St. Thomas Seminary (Kenmore, WA); ord. priest (Boise), May 25, 1963; ord. bp. of Salt Lake City, Nov. 17, 1980; app. bp. of Sacramento, Nov. 30, 1993, inst., Jan. 27, 1994.

Weitzel, John Quinn, M.M.: b. May 10, 1928, Chicago, IL; educ. Maryknoll Seminary (Maryknoll, NY); ord. priest, Nov. 5, 1955; missionary to Samoa, 1979; ord. bp. of Samoa-Pago Pago, American Samoa, Oct. 29, 1986.

Welsh, Thomas J.: b. Dec. 20, 1921, Weatherly, PA; educ. St. Charles Borromeo Seminary (Philadelphia, PA), Catholic Univ. (Washington, DC); ord. priest (Philadelphia*), May 30, 1946; ord. titular bp. of Scattery Island and aux. bp. of Philadelphia, Apr. 2, 1970; app. first bp. of Arlington, VA, June 4, 1974; app. bp. of Allentown, Feb. 8, 1983, inst., Mar. 21, 1983; ret.,: Dec. 16, 1997.

Wenski, Thomas G.: b. Oct. 18, 1950, West Palm Beach, FL; educ. St. John Vianney College Seminary, St. Vincent de Paul Regional Seminary, Fordham Univ.; ord. priest (Miami*), May 15, 1976; director of Miami Haitian Apostolate; app. titular bp. of Kearney and aux. of Miami, June 24, 1997; app. coadjutor bp. of Orlando, July 1, 2003; bp. of Orlando, Nov. 13, 2004.

Wester, John Charles: b. Nov. 5, 1950, San Francisco; educ.St. John's Seminary, Camarillo, CA, St. Patrick's Seminary, Menlo Park, CA, Univ. of San Francisco; ord. priest (San Francisco*), May 15, 1976; app. titular bp. of Lamiggiga and aux. bp. of San Francisco, June 30, 1998.

Wilkerson, Gerald E.: b. Oct. 21, 1939, Des Moines, IA; educ. St. John's Seminary (Camarillo, CA); ord. priest (Los Angeles*), Jan. 5, 1965; app. Titular Bp. of Vincennes and aux. bp. of Los Angeles, Nov. 5, 1997, ord., Jan. 21, 1998.

Williams, James Kendrick: b. Sept. 5, 1936, Athertonville, KY; educ. St. Mary's College (St. Mary's, KY), St. Maur's School of Theology (South Union, KY); ord. priest (Louisville*), May 25, 1963; ord. titular bp. of Catula and aux. bp. of Covington, June 19, 1984; first bp. of Lexington, KY, inst., Mar. 2, 1988; res., June 11, 2002.

Winter, William J.: b. May 20, 1930, Pittsburgh, PA; educ. St. Vincent College and Seminary (Latrobe, PA), Gregorian Univ. (Rome, Italy); ord. priest (Pittsburgh), Dec. 17, 1955; ord. titular bp. of Uthina and aux. bp. of Pittsburgh, Feb. 13, 1989; ret. May 20, 2005.

Wirz, George O.: b. Jan. 17, 1929, Monroe, WI; educ. St. Francis Seminary and Marquette Univ. (Milwaukee, WI); Cath. Univ. (Washington, DC); ord. priest (Madison), May 31, 1952; ord. titular bp. of Municipa and aux. bp. of Madison, Mar. 9, 1978; ret. Feb. 10, 2004.

Wiwchar, Michael, C.SS.R.: b. May 9, 1932, Komarno, Manitoba, Can.; educ. Redemptorist Seminary (Windsor, Ontario); made solemn vows as Redemptorist, 1956; ord. priest, June 28, 1959; pastor St. John the Baptist Parish, Newark, NJ 1990-93; ord. bp. of St. Nicholas of Chicago for the Ukrainians, Sept. 28, 1993; bp. of Saskatoon of Ukrainians, Nov. 29, 2000.

Wuerl, Donald W.: b. Nov. 12, 1940, Pittsburgh, PA; educ. Catholic Univ. (Washington, DC), North American College, Angelicum (Rome); ord. priest (Pittsburgh), Dec. 17, 1966, in Rome; ord. titular bp. of Rosemarkie Jan. 6, 1986, in Rome; aux. bp. of Seattle, 1986-87; app. bp. of Pittsburgh, Feb. 11, 1988, inst., Mar. 25, 1988; app. Abp. of Washington, May 16, 2006.

Y-Z

Yanta, John W.: b. Oct. 2, 1931, Runge, TX; educ. St. John's Preparatory Seminary and Assumption Seminary (San Antonio); ord. priest (San Antonio*), Mar. 17, 1956; ord. titular bp. of Naratcata and aux. bp. of San Antonio, Dec. 30, 1994; app. bp. of Amarillo, Jan. 21,1997, inst., Mar. 17, 1997.

Younan, Joseph: b. Nov. 15, 1944, Hassakeh, Syria; educ. Our Lady of Deliverance Seminary (Charfet, Lebanon), Pontifical College of the Propagation of the Faith (Rome); ord. priest, Sept. 12, 1971; came to U.S., 1986; served Syrian

Catholics in U.S.; ord. first bp. Our Lady of Deliverance of Newark for Syrian Catholics in the U.S. and Canada, Jan. 7, 1996, in Kamisly, Syria.

Zavala, Gabino: b. Sept. 7, 1951, Guerrero, Mexico; became U.S. citizen, 1976; educ. St. John's Seminary (Los Angeles), Catholic Univ. (Washington, DC); ord. priest (Los Angeles*), May 28, 1977; ord. titular bp. of Tamascani and aux. bp. of Los Angeles, Mar. 19, 1994.

Zayek, Francis: b. Oct. 18, 1920, Manzanillo, Cuba; ord. priest, Mar. 17, 1946; ord. titular bp. of Callinicum and aux. bp. for Maronites in Brazil, Aug. 5, 1962; named apostolic exarch for Maronites in U.S., with headquarters in Detroit; inst., June 11, 1966; first eparch of St. Maron of Detroit, Mar. 25, 1972; see transferred to Brooklyn, June 27, 1977; given personal title of abp., Dec. 22, 1982; ret., Nov. 23, 1996.

Ziemann, G. Patrick: b. Sept. 13, 1941, Pasadena, CA; educ. St. John's College Seminary and St. John's Seminary (Camarillo, CA), Mt. St. Mary's College (Los Angeles, CA); ord. priest (Los Angeles*), Apr. 29, 1967; ord. titular bp. of Obba and aux. bp. of Los Angeles, Feb. 23, 1987; app. bp. of Santa Rosa, July 14, 1992; res., July 22, 1999.

Zipfel, Paul A.: b. Sept. 22, 1935, St. Louis, MO; educ. Cardinal Glennon College, Kenrick Seminary (St. Louis, MO), Catholic Univ. (Washington, DC); St. Louis Univ. (St. Louis, MO); ord. priest (St. Louis*), Mar. 18, 1961; ord. titular bp. of Walla Walla and aux. bp. of St. Louis, June 29, 1989; app. bp. of Bismarck, Dec. 31, 1996.

Zubic, David A.: b. Sept. 4, 1949, Sewickley, PA; educ. St. Paul Seminary-Duquesne Univ. (Pittsburgh), St. Mary's Seminary (Baltimore), Duquesne Univ. (Pittsburgh); ord. priest (Pittsburgh), May 3, 1975; ord. titular bp. of Jamestown and aux. of Pittsburgh, Apr. 6, 1997; app. bp. of Green Bay, Oct. 10, 2003.

Zurek, Patrick J.: b. Aug. 17, 1948, Wallis, TX; educ. Univ.of St. Thomas (Houston), Angelicum and Alphonsian Academy (Rome); ord priest (Austin), June 29, 1975; app. titular bp. of Tamugadi and aux. bp. of San Antonio, Jan. 5, 1998, ord., Feb. 16, 1998.

BISHOP-BROTHERS

(The asterisk indicates brothers who were bishops at the same time.)

There have been 10 pairs of brother-bishops in the history of the U.S. hierarchy.

Living: Francis T. Hurley,* abp. of Anchorage and Mark J. Hurley,* bp. emeritus of Santa Rosa (deceased). Raymond J. Boland,* bp. emeritus of Kansas City-St. Joseph, MO and John Kevin Boland,* bp. of Savannah.

Deceased: Francis Blanchet* of Oregon City (Portland) and Augustine Blanchet* of Walla Walla; John S. Foley of Detroit and Thomas P. Foley of Chicago; Francis P. Kenrick,* apostolic administrator of Philadelphia, bp. of Philadelphia and Baltimore, and Peter R. Kenrick* of St. Louis; Matthias C. Lenihan of Great Falls and Thomas M. Lenihan of Cheyenne; James O'Connor, vicar apostolic of Nebraska and bp. of Omaha, and Michael O'Connor of Pittsburgh and Erie; Jeremiah F. and John W. Shanahan, both of Harrisburg; Sylvester J. Espelage, O.F.M.* of Wuchang, China, who died 10 days after the ordination of his brother, Bernard T. Espelage, O.F.M.* of Gallup; Coleman F. Carroll* of Miami and Howard Carroll* of Altoona-Johnstown.

U.S. BISHOPS OVERSEAS

Cardinal William W. Baum, major penitentiary emeritus; Cardinal Edmund C. Szoka, President emeritus, Pontifical Commission for Vatican City State; Cardinal James Francis Stafford, major penitentiary; Card. William Levada, prefect of the Congregation for the Doctrine of the Faith; Abp. John P. Foley, president of Pontifical Commission for Social Communications; Abp. James M. Harvey, prefect of the Papal Household; Abp. Ambrose de Paoli, apostolic nuncio to Japan; Abp. Charles A. Schleck, C.S.C., former adjunct secretary of the Congregation for the Evangelization of Peoples; Abp. Edward Joseph Adams, nuncio in Bangladesh; Abp. Timothy P. Broglio, apostolic nuncio to the Dominican Republic and apostolic delegate to Puerto Rico; Abp. Thomas E. Gullickson, apostolic nuncio to Trinidad and Tobago, Bahamas, Dominica, Saint Kitts and Nevis, Santa Lucia, San Vincenzo and Grenadine; Abp. Charles Daniel Balvo, apostolic nuncio to the Pacific Islands (Oceania), Abp. Michael A. Blume, apostolic nuncio to Benin and Togo, Abp. George Riashi, B.C.O., abp. of archeparchy of Tripoli of Lebanon (Lebanon) for Greek-Catholic Melkites; Abp. John Bukovsky, S.V.D. (naturalized U.S. citizen), former papal representative to Russia;

Bp. Michael R. Kuchmiak, exarch of apostolic exarchate emeritus of Great Britain for Ukrainian Catholics; Bp. Joseph Pelletier, M.S., bp. of Morondava, Madagascar; Bp. Paul Simon Schmitz, O.F.M.Cap., bp. of Bluefields, Nicaragua; Bp. Ambrose Ravasi, I.M.C., bp. of Marsabit, Kenya; Bp. Caesar Mazzolari, M.C.C.J., bp. of Rumbek, Kenya; Bp. George Biguzzi, S.X., bp. of Makeni, Sierra Leone; Bp. John B. Minder, O.S.F.S., bp. of Keimoes-Upington, South Africa; Bp. Joseph J. Potocnak, S.C.J., bp. of De Aar, South Africa; Bp. Paul Duffy, O.M.I., bp. of Mongu, Zambia; Bp. Henry Howaniec, O.F.M., apostolic admin. of Almaty, Kazakstan; Bp. William J. McNaughton, M.M. bp. of Inchon., Korea; Bp. Gerald Scarpone Caporale, O.F.M., bp. of: Comayagua, Honduras; Bp. Thomas Maurus Muldoon, O.F.M., bp. of Juticalpa, Honduras; Bp. Gordon D. Bennett, S.J., bp. of Mandeville, Jamaica; Bp. Edward J. Gilbert, C.SS.R., bp. of Port of Spain, Trinidad and Tobago; Bp. George Murry, S.J., bp. of St. Thomas, Virgin Islands; Bp. Robert Kurtz, C.R., bp. of Hamilton, Bermuda; Bp. Ricardo Watty Urquidi, M.Sp.S., bp. of Nuevo Laredo, Mexico; Bp. John Quinn Weitzel, M.M., bp. of Samoa-Pago Pago, American Samoa; Bp. Stephen J. Reichert, O.F.M.Cap., bp. of Mendi, Papua New Guinea; Bp. Raymond P. Kalisz, S.V.D., bp. of Wewak Papua New Guinea; Bp. Christopher Cardone, O.P., Gizo, Solomon Islands; Bp. Luis Morgan Casey, vicar apostolic of Pando, Bolivia; Bp. Herbert Hermes, O.S.B., prelate of Cristalandia, Brazil; Bp. Capistran Heim, O.F.M., prelate of Itaituba, Brazil; Bp. John J. Burke, O.F.M., bp. of Miracema do Tocantins Brazil; Bp. Alfred Novak, C.Ss.R., bp. of Paranagua, Brazil; Bp. Elias James Manning, O.F.M. Conv., bp. of Valença, Brazil; Bp. John C. McNabb, O.S.A., bp. of Chulucanas, Peru; Bp. Daniel Thomas Turley Murphy, O.S.A., coadjutor bp. of Chulucanas, Peru; Bp. Michael La Fay Bardi, O.Carm. prelate of Sicuani, Peru. (*See* **Missionary Bishops.**)

RETIRED/RESIGNED U.S. PRELATES

Information, as of Aug. 20, 2006, includes name of the prelate and see held at the time of retirement or resignation; abps. are indicated by an asterisk. Most of the prelates listed below resigned their sees because of age in accordance with church law. See **Index: Biographies, U.S. Bishops.**

Forms of address of retired residential prelates

(unless they have a titular see): Abp. or Bp. Emeritus of (last see held); Former Abp. or Bp. of (last see held).

Patrick V. Ahern (New York, aux.), Moses B. Anderson (Detroit, aux.), Kenneth A. Angell (Burlington), Juan Arzube (Los Angeles, aux.), Robert J. Banks (Green Bay), Gordon D. Bennett (Mandeville, Jamaica), Cardinal Anthony J. Bevilacqua* (Philadelphia), Ernest B. Boland, O.P. (Multan, Pakistan), Raymond J. Boland (Kansas-City-St. Joseph), William D. Borders* (Baltimore), Anthony G. Bosco (Greensburg), Paul M. Boyle, C.P. (Mandeville, Jamaica), Joseph M. Breitenbeck (Grand Rapids), William H. Bullock (Madison), Charles A. Buswell (Pueblo).

John Chedid (Our Lady of Lebanon), John W. Comber, M.M. (Foratiano, titular see), Thomas Connolly (Baker), Ronald G. Connors, C.SS.R. (San Juan de la Maguana, Dominican Republic), Thomas J. Costello (Syracuse, aux.), Arnold R. Cotey, S.D.S. (Nachingwea, now Lindi, Tanzania), Daniel A. Cronin* (Hartford), John Stephen Cummins (Oakland), William G. Curlin (Charlotte), James J. Daly (Rockville Centre, aux.), Thomas V. Daily (Brooklyn), Nicholas D'Antonio, O.F.M. (Olancho, Honduras).

Joseph A. DePalma, S.C.J. (DeAar, South Africa), Louis A. DeSimone (Philadelphia, aux.), Joseph T. Dimino* (Military Services archdiocese), George Dion, O.M.I. (titular see, Arpaia), Robert W. Donnelly (Toledo, aux.), John F. Donoghue* (Atlanta), Paul V. Donovan (Kalamazoo), Norbert M. Dorsey, C.P. (Orlando), Stephen Hector Doueihi (St. Maron of Brooklyn), Michael J. Dudick (Passaic, Byzantine rite), Paul V. Dudley (Sioux Falls), Roland Pierre DuMaine (San Jose), Thomas L. Dupre (Springfield), Dennis V. Durning, C.S.Sp. (Arusha, Tanzania), John Elya (Newton), J. Lennox Federal (Salt Lake City), Gilberto Fernandez (Miami, aux.), Joseph A. Fiorenza* (Galveston-Houston), Thomas J. Flanagan (San Antonio, aux.), Patrick F. Flores* (San Antonio), David E. Foley (Birmingham), Marion F. Forst (Dodge City), Benedict C. Franzetta (Youngstown, aux.), Gerard L. Frey (Lafayette, LA).

James H. Garland (Marquette), Louis E. Gelineau (Providence), Odore Gendron (Manchester), Peter L. Gerety* (Newark), Joseph J. Gerry, O.S.B. (Portland, ME), Raymond E. Goedert (Chicago, aux.), John R. Gorman (Chicago, aux.), F. Joseph Gossman (Raleigh), Rene H. Gracida (Corpus Christi), Thomas J. Gumbleton (Detroit, aux.), Richard C. Hanifen (Colorado Springs), Philip M. Hannan* (New Orleans), Daniel A. Hart (Norwich), Edward D. Head (Buffalo), Joseph Hart (Cheyenne).

Joseph L. Hogan (Rochester), William Russell Houck (Jackson), Joseph Lawson Howze (Biloxi), Edward T. Hughes (Metuchen), William A. Hughes (Covington), Raymond G. Hunthausen* (Seattle), Joseph L. Imesch (Joliet), Thad J. Jakubowski (Chicago, aux.) Roger L. Kaffer (Joliet, aux.), Raymond Kalisz, S.V.D. (Wewak), James P. Keleher* (Kansas City), Daniel W. Kucera, O.S.B.* (Dubuque), William F. Kupfer, M.M. (Taichung, Taiwan), George Kuzma (Van Nuys), Francis Lambert, S.M. (Port Vila, Vanuatu), W. Thomas Larkin (St. Petersburg), Bernard Cardinal Law* (Boston), Raymond W. Lessard (Savannah), Martin N. Lohmuller (Philadelphia, aux.), Basil Losten (Stamford), Innocent Hilarius Lotocky, O.S.B.M. (St. Nicholas of Chicago for Ukrainians), Timothy J. Lyne

(Chicago, aux.).

Cardinal Theodore McCarrick* (Washington, D.C.), James F. McCarthy (New York, aux.) John McCarthy (Austin), William J. McCormack (New York, aux.), Andrew McDonald (Little Rock), Charles J. McDonnell (Newark, aux.), John B. McDowell (Pittsburgh, aux.), Norman McFarland (Orange, CA), Urban McGarry, T.O.R. (Bhagalpur, India), Bernard J. McLaughlin (Buffalo, aux.), John C. McNabb, O.S.A. (Chulucanas), William J. McNaughton (Inchon), Joseph Madera (Military Archdiocese, aux.), Joseph F. Maguire (Springfield, MA), Thomas R. Manning, O.F.M. (Coroico, Bolivia), Dominic Anthony Marconi (Newark, aux.), Leroy T. Matthiesen (Amarillo), Anthony F. Mestice (New York, aux.), James E. Michaels (Wheeling-Charleston, aux.), Anthony M. Milone (Great Falls-Billings), John B. Minder (Keimos-Upington), Donald W. Montrose (Stockton), Manuel D. Moreno (Tucson), Robert E. Mulvee (Providence), Michael J. Murphy (Erie), William C. Newman (Baltimore, aux.), James D. Niedergeses (Nashville), Thomas Joseph O'Brien (Phoenix), Anthony J. O'Connell (Palm Beach), Edward J. O'Donnell (Lafayette, LA), Leonard James Olivier, S.V.D. (Washington, aux.), Arthur J. O'Neill (Rockford).

Albert H. Ottenweller (Steubenville), Walter Paska (Philadelphia, Ukrainians, aux.), George H. Pearce, S.M.* (Suva, Fiji Islands), Edward Pevec (Cleveland, aux.), Anthony M. Pilla (Cleveland), Bernard F. Popp (San Antonio, aux.), Vasile Louis Puscas (St. George's in Canton of the Romanians), Francis A. Quinn (Sacramento), John R. Quinn* (San Francisco), Joseph M. Raya* (Acre), Daniel P. Reilly (Worcester), John C. Reiss (Trenton), Agustin Roman (Miami, aux.), Francis X. Roque (Military Archdiocese, aux.), Robert John Rose (Grand Rapids), George E. Rueger (Worcester, aux.), Daniel Ryan (Springfield, IL).

Nicholas J. Samra (Melkite eparchy of Newton, aux.), Robert F. Sanchez* (Santa Fe), Joseph Sartoris (Los Angeles, aux.), Stanley G. Schlarman (Dodge City), Bernard W. Schmitt (Wheeling-Charleston), Mark Schmitt (Marquette), Walter J. Schoenherr (Detroit, aux.), Francis B. Schulte* (New Orleans), Daniel E. Sheehan* (Omaha), Gilbert I. Sheldon (Steubenville), Patrick Sheridan (New York, aux.), John Snyder (St. Augustine), Jude Speyrer (Lake Charles), Philip Straling (Reno), Joseph M. Sullivan (Brooklyn, aux.), Walter Francis Sullivan (Richmond), Stephen Sulyk* (Philadelphia, Ukrainians).

Elliott Thomas (Virgin Islands), David B. Thompson (Charleston), Thomas Tschoepe (Dallas), James C. Timlin (Scranton), René A. Valero (Brooklyn, aux.), Adrian Veigle, T.O.R. (Borba, Brazil, Prelate), John J. Ward (Los Angeles, aux.), Loras J. Watters (Winona), Rembert G. Weakland, O.S.B.* (Milwaukee), Thomas J. Welsh (Allentown), James Kendrick Williams (Lexington), George O. Wirz (Madison, aux.), Francis Zayek (St. Maron of Brooklyn); G. Patrick Ziemann (Santa Rosa).

American Bishops of the Past: For coverage of the deceased bishops who served in the United States, please visit www.CatholicAlmanac.com.

The United States Conference of Catholic Bishops

When the Bishops merged their two national organizations into the United States Conference of Catholic Bishops (USCCB) on July 1, 2001, it marked the latest chapter in the evolution of the bishops' national structure, which was established 82 years ago in the aftermath of the First World War. Like its immediate predecessors — the National Conference of Catholic Bishops (NCCB) and United States Catholic Conference (USCC) – the USCCB is an organization staffed by lay people, priests, and members of religious orders, but whose members are the bishops of the United States, and it is the bishops who direct its activities.

The concept of the Bishops acting together on matters of mutual interest can be traced back to 1919 when, in their first national meeting since 1884, they agreed to meet annually and to form the National Catholic Welfare Council (NCWC) to serve as their organized voice on the national scene. The word "Council" was replaced by the word "Conference" in 1922.

In 1966, following the Second Vatican Council, NCWC was reorganized into two parallel conferences. The National Conference of Catholic Bishops – sometimes referred to as the canonical arm – would deal with matters connected to the internal life of the Church, such as liturgy and priestly life and ministry. The U.S. Catholic Conference – in effect the civil arm – would represent the bishops as they related to the "secular" world, in areas such as social concerns, education, communications and public affairs.During the period from 1992 to 1996, a Conference committee on mission and structure, headed by the late Cardinal Joseph L. Bernardin of Chicago, led the bishops in extensive consultation on restructuring. A primary purpose of this undertaking was to provide more of the nation's approximately 300 bishops with an opportunity to be directly involved in the work of the Conference, which operates primarily through a committee structure.

In 1997 the bishops voted to combine NCCB-USCC into one conference, to be called the U.S. Conference of Catholic Bishops. They decided that in the future only bishops would be voting members of committees, but non-bishops could serve on some committees as consultants or advisers. A new committee on statutes and bylaws, headed by Archbishop Daniel E. Pilarczyk of Cincinnati, which was formed to lead the rest of the reorganization process, completed its work last year. The new statutes and bylaws were subsequently approved by the Holy See.

It is unlikely that persons outside the Bishops' Conference will notice any immediate difference in the new structure. Many of the same concerns that motivated the Bishops in 1919 – like the welfare of immigrants, communicating through the Catholic press, and defending the legal rights of the Church – are still pressing today, as evidenced in the departments which carry out these functions, though many others have been added as well. In a May 23, 2001, letter sent to organizations which have dealings with the Conference, its General Secretary, Monsignor William P. Fay, said the renaming "will not affect any change in the activities or programs of the Conference but simply how the Conference is identified."

Mission Statement

The United States Conference of Catholic Bishops is a permanent institute composed of Catholic Bishops of the United States of America in and through which the bishops exercise in a communal or collegial manner the pastoral mission entrusted to them by the Lord Jesus of sanctification, teaching, and leadership, especially by devising forms and methods of the apostolate suitably adapted to the circumstances of the times. Such exercise is intended to offer appropriate assistance to each bishop in fulfilling his particular ministry in the local Church, to effect a commonality of ministry addressed to the people of the United States of America, and to foster and express communion with the Church in other nations within the Church universal, under the leadership of its chief pastor, the pope.

Administration

The principal officers of the conference are: Bishop William S. Skylstad, president; Cardinal Francis E. George, OMI, vice president; Archbishop James P. Keleher, treasurer; Archbishop Michael J. Sheehan, secretary; Msgr. David J. Malloy, general secretary. Headquarters of the conferences are located at 3211 Fourth St. N.E., Washington, DC 20017; (202) 541-3000; www.usccb.org.

USCCB REGIONS

I. Maine, Vermont, New Hampshire, Massachusetts, Rhode Island, Connecticut. II. New York. III. New Jersey, Pennsylvania. IV. Delaware, District of Columbia, Maryland, Virgin Islands, Virginia, West Virginia, Military Archdiocese. V. Alabama, Kentucky, Louisiana, Mississippi, Tennessee. VI. Michigan, Ohio. VII. Illinois, Indiana, Wisconsin. VIII. Minnesota, North Dakota, South Dakota. IX. Iowa, Kansas, Missouri, Nebraska. X. Arkansas, Oklahoma,

Texas. XI. California, Hawaii, Nevada. XII. Idaho, Montana, Alaska, Washington, Oregon. XIII. Utah, Arizona, New Mexico, Colorado, Wyoming, including El Paso. XIV. Florida, Georgia, North Carolina, South Carolina.

PASTORAL COUNCIL

The conference, one of many similar territorial conferences envisioned in the conciliar Decree on the Pastoral Office of Bishops in the Church (No. 38), is "a council in which the bishops of a given nation or territory [in this case, the United States] jointly exercise their pastoral office to promote the greater good which the Church offers mankind, especially through the forms and methods of the apostolate fittingly adapted to the circumstances of the age."

Its decisions, "provided they have been approved legitimately and by the votes of at least two-thirds of the prelates who have a deliberative vote in the conference, and have been recognized by the Apostolic See, are to have juridically binding force only in those cases prescribed by the common law or determined by a special mandate of the Apostolic See, given either spontaneously or in response to a petition of the conference itself."

All bishops who serve the Church in the U.S., its territories and possessions, have membership and voting rights in the USCCB. Retired bishops cannot be elected to conference offices nor can they vote on matters that by law are binding by two-thirds of the membership. Only diocesan bishops can vote on diocesan quotas, assessments or special collections.

OFFICERS, COMMITTEES

The conference operates through a number of bishops' committees with functions in specific areas of work and concern. Their basic assignments are to prepare materials on the basis of which the bishops, assembled as a conference, make decisions, and to put suitable action plans into effect.

The officers, with several other bishops, hold positions on executive-level committees — Administrative, Executive, the Committee on Budget and Finance, the Committee on Personnel, and the Committee on Priorities and Plans. They also, with other bishops, serve on the USCCB Administrative Committee.

Standing Committees

The standing committees and their chairmen (Cardinals, Archbishops, and Bishops) are as follows (names in parentheses are chairmen elect):
American College, Louvain: Edward K. Braxton
African-American Catholics: Joseph N. Perry
Boundaries of Dioceses and Provinces: William S. Skylstad
Canonical Affairs: Thomas G. Doran (John J. Myers)
Catechesis: Daniel M. Buechlein, O.S.B. (Donald W. Wuerl)
Communications: Gerald F. Kicanas (George H. Niederauer)
Church in Latin America: John R. Manz
Catholic Campaign for Human Development: Howard J. Hubbard
Consecrated Life: Jerome G. Hanus, O.S.B. (J. Terry Steib)
Diaconate: Frederick F. Campbell

Doctrine: Arthur J. Serratelli (William E. Lori)
Domestic Policy: Nicholas A. DiMarzio
Ecumenical and Interreligious Affairs: Stephen E. Blaire
Education: Robert J. McManus
Evangelization: Edward J. Slattery
Hispanic Affairs: James A. Tamayo
Home Missions: J. Peter Sartain (Michael W. Warfel)
International Policy: John H. Ricard, S.S.J. (Thomas G. Wenski)
Laity: David A. Zubik
Latin America: John R. Manz (Jaime Soto)
Liturgy: Donald W. Trautman
Marriage and Family Life: Joseph E. Kurtz
Migration: Gerald R. Barnes
North American College, Rome: Edwin F. O'Brien
Pastoral Practices: Jerome E. Listecki
Priestly Formation: John C. Nienstedt (Thomas J. Olmsted)
Priestly Life and Ministry: Timothy M. Dolan (Robert J. Carlson)
Pro-Life Activities: William Cardinal Keeler (Justin Cardinal Rigali)
Protection of Children & Young People: Gregory M. Aymond
Relationship between Eastern and Latin Catholic Churches: Basil Schott (Stefan Soroka)
Science and Human Values: Francis X. DiLorenzo (John C. Dunne)
Selection of Bishops: William S. Skylstad
Vocations: Blase J. Cupich
Women in Society and in the Church: Joseph A. Pepe
World Mission: Daniel F. Walsh

Ad Hoc Committees

Aid to the Church in Central and Eastern Europe: Justin Cardinal Rigali
Bishops' Life and Ministry: Robert H. Brom
Catholic Charismatic Renewal: Thomas J. Flanagan
Catholic Health Care Issues and the Church: Henry J. Mansell
Church in Africa: John H. Ricard
Concilliation and Arbitration: Adam Cardinal Maida
Diocesan Audits: Daniel F. Walsh
Economic Concerns of the Holy See: John G. Vlazny
Native American Catholics: Charles J. Chaput, OFM Cap.
Nomination of Conference Offices: Michael J. Sheehan
Oversee the Use of The Catechism of the Catholic Church: Alfred C. Hughes
Review of Scripture Translations: Arthur J. Serratelli
Shrines: James P. Keleher
Spanish Language Bible: Jose H. Gomez
Special Assembly 2007: Dennis M. Schnurr
Stewardship: Robert J. Baker

STATE CATHOLIC CONFERENCES

These conferences are agencies of bishops and dioceses in the various states. Their general purposes are to develop and sponsor cooperative programs designed to cope with pastoral and common-welfare needs, and to represent the dioceses before governmental bodies, the public, and in private sectors. Their membership consists of representatives from the dioceses in the states — bishops, clergy and lay persons in various capacities.

The National Association of State Catholic Conference Directors maintains liaison with the general secretariat of the United States Conference of Catholic Bishops. President: Robert J. Castagna, executive director of Oregon Catholic Conference.

Alaska Catholic Conference, 415 6th St., Ste. 300, Juneau. AK 99801; (907) 586-2404; Exec. Dir., Chip Wagoner.

Arizona Catholic Conference, 400 E. Monroe St., Phoenix, AZ 85004-2376; (602) 354-2391; Exec. Dir., Ron Johnson.

California Catholic Conference, 1119 K St., 2nd Floor, Sacramento, CA 95814; (916) 443-4851; Exec. Dir., Edward Dolejsi.

Colorado Catholic Conference, 1535 Logan St., Denver, CO 80203; (303) 894-8808; Exec. Dir. Timothy Dore.

Connecticut Catholic Conference, 134 Farmington Ave., Hartford, CT 06105; (860) 524-7882; Exec. Dir., Dr. Marie T. Hilliard, Ph.D., R.N.

Florida Catholic Conference, 201 W. Park Ave., Tallahassee, FL 32301; (850) 222-3803; Exec. Dir., Dr. D. Michael McCarron, Ph.D.

Georgia Catholic Conference, Office Bldg., 3200 Deans Bridge Rd., Augusta, GA 30906; (706) 798-1719; Exec. Dir., Francis J. Mulcahy, Esq.

Hawaii Catholic Conference, Stephen Diocesan Center, 6301 Pali Hwy., Kaneohe, HI 96744; (808) 585-3341; Exec. Dir., Deacon Walter Yoshimitsu.

Illinois, Catholic Conference of, 65 E. Wacker Pl., Ste. 1620, Chicago, IL 60601; (312) 368-1066. 108 E. Cook, Springfield, IL 62701; (217) 528-9200; Exec. Dir., Robert Gilligan.

Indiana Catholic Conference, 1400 N. Meridian St., P.O. Box 1410, Indianapolis, IN 46206; (317) 236-1455; Exec. Dir., Glenn Tebbe.

Iowa Catholic Conference, 530-42nd St., Des Moines, IA 50312-2707; (515) 243-6256; Exec. Dir., Sara Eide.

Kansas Catholic Conference, 6301 Antioch, Merriam, KS 66202; (913) 722-6633; Exec. Dir., Michael P. Farmer.

Kentucky, Catholic Conference of, 1042 Burlington Lane, Frankfort, KY 40601; (502) 875-4345; Exec. Dir., Edward Monahan.

Louisiana Catholic Conference, 3423 Hundred Oaks Ave., Baton Rouge, LA 70808; (225) 344-7120; Exec. Dir., Daniel J. Loar.

Maryland Catholic Conference, 188 Duke of Gloucester St., Annapolis, MD 21401; (410) 269-1155; Exec. Dir., Richard J. Dowling, Esq.

Massachusetts Catholic Conference, 150 Staniford St., West End Pl., Boston, MA 02114-2511; (617) 367-6060; Exec. Dir., Edward F. Saunders.

Michigan Catholic Conference, 510 N. Capitol Ave., Lansing, MI 48933; (517) 372-9310; President and CEO, Sr. Monica Kostielney, R.S.M.

Minnesota Catholic Conference, 475 University Ave. W., St. Paul, MN 55103; (651) 227-8777; Exec. Dir., Christopher Leifeld.

Missouri Catholic Conference, P.O. Box 1022, 600 Clark Ave., Jefferson City, MO 65102; (573) 635-7239; Exec. Dir., Deacon Lawrence A. Weber.

Montana Catholic Conference, P.O. Box 1708, Helena, MT 59624; (406) 442-5761; www.mt.net/~mcc; Exec. Dir., Vacant.

Nebraska Catholic Conference, 215 Centennial Mall South, Suite 410, Lincoln, NE 68508-1890; (402) 477-7517; Exec. Dir., James R. Cunningham.

Nevada Catholic Conference, 290 South Arlington Ave., Ste. 200, Reno, NV 89501-1713; (775) 322-7412; Exec. Dir., Judge Robert Payant.

New Jersey Catholic Conference, 211 N. Warren St., Trenton, NJ 08618; (609) 599-2110; Exec. Dir., William F. Bolan, Jr., J.D.

New York State Catholic Conference, 465 State St., Albany, NY 12203; (518) 434-6195; www.nyscatholicconference.org; Interim Exec. Dir., Richard E. Barnes.

North Dakota Catholic Conference, 227 West Broadway, Suite No. 2, Bismarck, ND 58501; (701) 223-2519; www.ndcatholic.org; Exec. Dir., Christopher T. Dodson.

Ohio, Catholic Conference of, 9 E. Long St., Suite 201, Columbus, OH 43215; (614) 224-7147; Exec. Dir., Timothy V. Luckhaupt.

Oregon Catholic Conference, 2838 E. Burnside, Portland, OR 97214; (503) 233-8387; General Counsel and Exec. Dir., Robert J. Castagna.

Pennsylvania Catholic Conference, 223 North St., Box 2835, Harrisburg, PA 17105; (717) 238-9613; (717) 238-9613; Exec. Dir., Dr. Robert J. O'Hara, Jr.

Texas Catholic Conference, 1625 Rutherford Lane, Bldg. D, Austin, TX 78754; (512) 339-9882; Exec. Dir., Bro. Richard Daly, C.S.C.

Washington State Catholic Conference, 508 2nd Ave. West, Seattle, WA 98119-3928; (206) 301-0556; Exec. Dir., Sr. Sharon Park, O.P.

West Virginia State Catholic Conference, P.O. Box 230, Wheeling, WV 26003; (304) 233-0880; Dir., Very Rev. John R. Gallagher.

Wisconsin Catholic Conference, 30 W. Mifflin St., Suite 302, Madison, WI 53703; (608) 257-0004; Exec. Dir., John A. Huebscher.

Background

The National Conference of Catholic Bishops (NCCB), was established by action of the U.S. hierarchy Nov. 14, 1966, as a strictly ecclesiastical body with defined juridical authority over the Church in this country. It was set up with the approval of the Holy See and in line with directives from the Second Vatican Council. Its constitution was formally ratified during the November 1967 meeting of the U.S. hierarchy. The NCCB was a development from the Annual Meeting of the Bishops of the United States, whose pastoral character was originally approved by Pope Benedict XV, Apr. 10, 1919.

The USCC, as of Jan. 1, 1967, took over the general organization and operations of the former National Catholic Welfare Conference, Inc., whose origins dated back to the National Catholic War Council of 1917. The council underwent some change after World War I and was established on a permanent basis on Sept. 24, 1919, as the National Catholic Welfare Council to serve as a central agency for organizing and coordinating the efforts of U.S. Catholics in carrying out the social mission of the Church in this country. In 1923, its name was changed to National Catholic Welfare Conference, Inc., and clarification was made of its nature as a service agency of the bishops and the Church rather than as a conference of bishops with real juridical authority in ecclesiastical affairs.

The Official Catholic Directory stated that the USCC assisted "the bishops in their service to the Church in this country by uniting the people of God where voluntary collective action on a broad interdiocesan level is needed. The USCC provided an organizational structure and the resources needed to insure coordination, cooperation, and assistance in the public, educational and social concerns of the Church at the national, regional, state and, as appropriate, diocesan levels."

CATHOLIC RELIEF SERVICES

Catholic Relief Services is the official overseas aid and development agency of U.S. Catholics; it is a separately incorporated organization of the U.S. Conference of Catholic Bishops.

CRS was founded in 1943 by the bishops of the United States to help civilians in Europe and North Africa caught in the disruption and devastation of World War II. As conditions in Europe improved in the late 1940s and early 1950s, the works conducted by CRS spread to other continents and areas — Asia, Africa and Latin America.

Although best known for its record of disaster response, compassionate aid to refugees and commitment to reconstruction and rehabilitation, CRS places primary focus on long-term development projects designed to help people to help themselves and to determine their own future. Administrative funding for CRS comes largely from the American Bishops' Overseas Appeal (ABOA). Major support is derived from private, individual donors and through programs such as Operation Rice Bowl and the new Global Village Project.

Kenneth F. Hackett is Executive Director. CRS headquarters are located at 209 W. Fayette St., Baltimore, MD 21201; (410) 625-2220.

Hispanic, African-American, and Native-American Catholics

HISPANIC CATHOLICS IN THE UNITED STATES

The nation's Hispanic population totaled 35.3 million in 2000, according to figures reported by the U.S. Census Bureau. It is estimated that 73 percent of the Hispanics were baptized Catholics. It was estimated that perhaps 100,000 Catholic Hispanics a year were being lost, principally to fundamentalist and pentecostal sects.

Pastoral Patterns

Pastoral ministry to Hispanics varies, depending on cultural differences and the availability of personnel to carry it out. The pattern in cities with large numbers of Spanish-speaking people is built around special and bilingual churches, centers or other agencies where pastoral and additional forms of service are provided in a manner suited to the needs, language and culture of the people. Services in some places are extensive and include legal advice, job placement, language instruction, recreational and social assistance, specialized counseling, and replacement services. In many places, however, even where there are special ministries, the needs are generally greater than the means available to meet them.

Some urban dwellers have been absorbed into established parishes and routines of church life and activity. Many Spanish-speaking communities remain in need of special ministries. An itinerant form of ministry best meets the needs of the thousands of Hispanic migrant workers who follow the crops.

Pastoral ministry to Hispanics was the central concern of three national meetings, Encuentros, held in 1972, 1977 and 1985.

The third National Encuentro in 1985 produced a master pastoral plan for ministry which the National Conference of Catholic Bishops approved in 1987. Its four keys are collaborative ministry; evangelization; a missionary option regarding the poor, the marginalized, the family, women and youth; and the formation of lay leadership. A National Encuentro was held in 2000. In 2002, the Secretariat published *Encuentro and Mission: A New Pastoral Framework for Hispanic Ministry.*

The U.S. bishops, at their annual meeting in Nov. 1983,

approved and subsequently published a pastoral letter on Hispanic Ministry under the title, "The Hispanic Presence: Challenge and Commitment." (For text, see pp. 46-49 of the *1985 Catholic Almanac.*)

Bishops

As of Aug. 1, 2006, there were 33 (24 active) bishops of Hispanic origin in the United States; all were named since 1970 (*for biographies, see* Index). Eleven were heads of archdioceses or dioceses: Archbishop José H. Gomez (San Antonio); Bishops Raymundo J Peña (Brownsville), James A. Tamayo (Laredo), Ricardo Ramirez, C.S.B. (Las Cruces), Alvaro Corrada del Rio, S.J. (Tyler), Arthur N. Tafoya (Pueblo), Placido Rodriguez, C.M.F. (Lubbock), Gerald R. Barnes (San Bernardino), Armando Ochoa (El Paso), Carlos A. Sevilla, S.J. (Yakima), and Victor Benito Galeone (St. Augustine).

Thirteen were auxiliary bishops: Gabino Zavala (Los Angeles), Gilbert Espinoza Chavez (San Diego), Joseph J. Madera (Military Services), Rene Valero (Brooklyn), David Arias, O.A.R. (Newark), Edgar M. Da Cunha, S.D.V. (Newark), Dominick J. Lagonegro (New York), Emilio Simeon Allué (Boston), Richard J. Garcia (Sacramento), Francisco Gonzalez Valer, S.F. (Washington, D.C.), José S. Vasquez (Galveston-Houston), Felipe de Jesus Estevez (Miami), and Gustavo Garcia-Siller, M.SpS. (Chicago). Resigned/retired prelates: Archbishop Robert F. Sanchez (Santa Fe), Archbishop Patrick F. Flores (San Antonio), Bishop Juan Arzube (Los Angeles), Bishop Rene H. Gracida (Corpus Christi), Bishop Manuel D. Moreno (Tucson), Bishop Francisco Garmendia (New York), Bishop Agustin Roman (Miami), Bishop Gilberto Fernandez (Miami). Bishop Roberto O. Gonzalez, O.F.M. (Corpus Christi), was appointed archbishop of San Juan de Puerto Rico on Mar. 26, 1999, by Pope John Paul II.

Hispanic priests and nuns in the U.S. number about 1,600 and 2,900, respectively, according to an estimate made in June 1988 by Father Gary Riebe Estrella, S.V.D., director of a Hispanic vocational recruitment program and recent estimates by the U.S. Census.

Secretariat for Hispanic Affairs

The national secretariat was established by the U.S.

Catholic Conference for service promoting and coordinating pastoral ministry to the Spanish-speaking. Its basic orientation is toward integral evangelization, combining religious ministry with development efforts in programs geared to the culture and needs of Hispanics. Its concerns are urban and migrant Spanish-speaking people; communications and publications in line with secretariat purposes and the service of people; bilingual and bicultural religious and general education; liaison for and representation of Hispanics with church, civic and governmental agencies.

The Secretariat states that its mission is:

"To assist the Catholic Church in its efforts to serve the large Catholic Hispanic/Latino population in the United States and in the New Evangelization as we approach the Great Jubilee of the Year 2000.

"To coordinate Hispanic ministry efforts in the Catholic Church through regional and diocesan offices, pastoral institutes, secular and ecclesial organizations, and apostolic movements.

"To promote the implementation of the National Pastoral Plan for Hispanic Ministry, Ecclesia in America, Many Faces in God's House: A Catholic Vision for the Third Millennium, and other church documents, as well as the development of small ecclesial communities.

"To integrate the Hispanic presence into the life of the Catholic Church and society."

The secretariat publishes a newsletter, En Marcha, available to interested parties.

Ronaldo M. Cruz is executive director of the national office at 3211 Fourth St. N.E., Washington, DC, 20017, (202) 541-3000, www.usccb.org.

The secretariat works in collaboration with regional and diocesan offices and pastoral institutes throughout the country.

The Northeast Regional Office, officially the Northeast Hispanic Catholic Center, was established in 1976 under the auspices of the bishops in 12 states from Maine to Virginia. It has established the Conference of Diocesan Directors of the Hispanic Apostolate, the Association of Hispanic Deacons, a Regional Youth Task Force and a Regional Committee of Diocesan Coordinators of Religious Educators for the Hispanics. The office is the official publishing house for the Hispanic Lectionary approved by the National Conference of Catholic Bishops for the United States. The center has liturgical, evangelization and youth ministry departments and an office of cultural affairs. Rudy Vargas IV is executive director. The center is located at 1011 First Ave., New York, NY 10022, (212) 751-7045.

The Southeast Regional Office serves 26 dioceses in Tennessee, North and South Carolina, Florida, Georgia, Mississippi, Alabama and Louisiana. Father Mario Vizcaíno, Sch. P., is director of the region and institute. The office is located at 7700 S.W. 56 St., Miami, FL 33155, (305) 279-2333. The Southeast Pastoral Institute serves as the educational arm of the regional office by providing formation programs for the development of leadership skills focused on ministry among Hispanics, at the Miami site and in the various dioceses of the region.

The Midwest Regional Office serves dioceses in the following states: Michigan, Ohio, Indiana, Illinois, and Wisconsin. Luis Beteta is director. The office is located at 660 Burton Street, S.E., Grand Rapids, MI 49507, (616) 243-0491, ext. 557.

In the southwest, the Mexican American Cultural Center serves as convener of diocesan directors and representatives of Hispanic ministry in Arkansas, Oklahoma and Texas.

The North Central region covers dioceses in the following states: Iowa, Kansas, Missouri, Nebraska, North Dakota, South Dakota, and Minnesota. Bro. Dale Mooney, FSC, is coordinator. The office is reached at P.O. Box 419037, Kansas City, MO 64141-6037, (816) 756-1850.

The South West region covers dioceses in the following states: Oklahoma, Texas, and Arkansas. Sr. María Elena González is director. The office is contacted at: Mexican American Cultural Center, 3115 W. Ashby, San Antonio, TX 78228, (210) 732-2156.

The Mountain States region covers dioceses in the following states: Arizona, Colorado, New Mexico, Utah, and Wyoming. Mrs. Mar Muñoz-Visoso is coordinator. The office is located at 1300 South Steel Street, Denver, CO 80210, (303) 295-9470.

The Far West region covers dioceses in the following states: California, Nevada and Hawaii. Anibal (Al) Hernandez is director. The office is located at 1119 K Street, 2nd Floor, Sacramento, CA 95814-3904, (916) 313-4014.

The North West region covers dioceses in the following states: Alaska, Idaho, Montana, Oregon, and Washington. Mrs. Jane Villanueva is director. The office address is 5301-B Tieton Drive, Yakima, WA 98908, (509) 965-7110.

The National Pastoral Plan for Hispanic Ministry

The National Pastoral Plan for Hispanic Ministry was approved by the NCCB in November 1987. This plan is addressed to the entire Church in the United States. It focuses on the pastoral needs of the Hispanic Catholic, but it challenges all Catholics as members of the Body of Christ.

General Objective: To live and promote by means of a Pastoral de Conjunto, a model of Church that is: communitarian, evangelizing, and missionary, incarnate in the reality of the Hispanic people and open to the diversity of cultures, a promoter and example of justice . . . that develops leadership through integral education . . . that is leaven for the Kingdom of God in society.

Specific Dimensions: Pastoral de Conjunto: To develop a Pastoral de Conjunto, which through pastoral agents and structures, manifests communion in integration, coordination in servicing, and communication of the Church's pastoral action, in keeping with the general objective of this plan. Evangelization: To recognize, develop, accompany and support small ecclesial communities and other church groups (e.g., Cursillos de Cristiandad, Movimiento Familiar Cristiano, RENEW, Charismatic Movement, prayer groups, etc.) which in union with the bishop are effective instruments of evangelization for the Hispanic people. These small ecclesial communities and other groups within the parish framework promote experiences of faith and conversion, prayer life, missionary outreach and evangelization, interpersonal relations and fraternal love, and prophetic questioning and actions for justice. They are a prophetic challenge for the renewal of our Church and humanization of our society. Missionary Option: To promote faith and effective participation in Church and societal structures on the part of priority groups (the poor, women, families, youth) so that they may be agents of their own destiny (self-determination) and capable of progressing and becoming organized. Formation: To provide leadership formation adapted to the Hispanic culture in the United States that will help people to live and promote a style of Church that will be leaven of the Kingdom of God in society.

National Hispanic Priests Association

The National Association of Hispanic Priests of the U.S.A. (ANSH — La Asociación Nacional de Sacerdotes Hispanos, EE. UU.) was established in September 1989 with a representation of about 2,400 Hispanic priests residing and ministering in the U.S. The association came into its present form after a 20-year process of organization by different groups of Hispanic priests around the country. By 1985, the first National Convention of Hispanic Priests was organized in New York City, and in 1989 the Association was established in Miami, FL, as a non-profit corporation for priestly fraternity and support for Hispanic priests in the United States. Among the multiple objectives are: to help members develop their priestly identity in the United States and encourage a genuine spirituality; to provide a national forum of Hispanic priests to help solve the problems that arise in the Hispanic community; to promote vocations to the priesthood among Hispanics; to pray and ask for more Hispanic bishops in the U.S., for the growing needs of the Catholic Hispanic community; and to cooperate with the bishops and the laity in implementing the National Pastoral Plan for Hispanic Ministry. The Association publishes a quarterly newsletter and holds an annual national convention. The president is Rev. José H. Gomez, S.T.D., 2472 Bolsover, Suite 442, Houston, TX 77005, (713) 528-6517.

National Catholic Council for Hispanic Ministry (NCCHM)

The council is a volunteer federation of Roman Catholic organizations, agencies and movements committed to the development of Hispanics/Latinos in Church and society. It was established June 17, 1990, at a gathering at Mundelein College, Chicago; its by-laws were adopted in January 1991 at Mercy Center, Burlingame, CA. The council convokes a national gathering every three years called *Raices y Alas* (Roots and Wings). With funding from foundations NCCHM has designed and piloted a leadership development program that links contemporary understandings of leadership with experiences and insights from faith and Hispanic cultures. NCCHM has 53 member organizations. It publishes *Puentes*, a newsletter. Exec. Dir., Armando A. Contreras, 3131 E. Camelback Rd., Ste. 200, Phoenix, AZ 85016, (602) 266-8623.

Mexican American Cultural Center

This national center, specializing in pastoral studies and language education, was founded in 1972 to provide programs focused on ministry among Hispanics and personnel working with Hispanics in the U.S. Courses — developed according to the see-judge-act methodology — include culture, faith development, Scripture, theology, and praxis; some are offered in Spanish, others in English. Intensive language classes are offered in Spanish, with emphasis on pastoral usage.

The center also conducts workshops for the development of leadership skills and for a better understanding of Hispanic communities. Faculty members serve as resource personnel for pastoral centers, dioceses and parishes throughout the U.S. The center offers master's degree programs in pastoral ministry in cooperation with Incarnate Word College, Boston College, the Oblate School of Theology, St. Mary's University and Loyola University, and other educational institutions.

The center is a distribution agency for the circulation of bilingual pastoral materials in the U.S. and Latin America. Sr. Maria Elena Gonzalez, R.S.M., is president of the center, which is located at 3019 W. French Place, San Antonio, TX 78228.

Institute of Hispanic Liturgy

Spanish-speaking communities in the U.S. are served by the Institute of Hispanic Liturgy, a national organization of liturgists, musicians, artists and pastoral agents, funded in part by the U.S. bishops. The institute promotes the study of liturgical texts, art, music and popular religiosity in an effort to develop liturgical spirituality among Hispanics. It works closely with the U.S. Bishops' Committee on the Liturgy, and has published liturgical materials. Rev. Heliodoro Lucatero, is the president; Sr. Doris Mary Turek, S.S.N.D., is executive director. Address: P.O. Box 29387, Washington, DC, 20017, (202) 319-6450.

Statistics

(*Courtesy, Secretariat for Hispanic Affairs, USCCB.*)
The official 2000 Census estimates a population of 35.3 million Hispanics, or about 12.5 percent of the total population. Since 1990, the Hispanic population has increased 58 percent.

The nation's Hispanic Catholic population (not including Puerto Rico) has increased by 71 percent since 1960. The total Hispanic Catholic population as a percentage of the U.S. Catholic population is 39 percent. Of these Hispanic Catholics, 64 percent attend church services regularly.

According to the most recent statistics based on the 2000 Census, there are 4,000 U.S. parishes with Hispanic ministry; 20.6 percent of U.S. parishes have a majority Hispanic presence. There are approximately 2,900 Hispanic priests and 25 active Hispanic bishops.

The 10 metropolitan areas with the largest Hispanic populations are: Los Angeles, New York, Chicago, Miami, Houston, Riverside-San Bernardino, Orange County, Phoenix, San Antonio, and Dallas. Seven states in 2000 had more than one million Hispanic residents: Arizona, California, Florida, Illinois, New Jersey, New York, and Texas. Approximately one half of the Hispanic population lived in just two states: California and Texas. In New Mexico, Hispanics made up 42 percent of the state's total population, the highest for any state.

Current U.S. Census figures reveal that the Hispanic population increased by 13 million between 1990 and 2000. Hispanics also accounted for 40 percent of the nation's increase in population over the decade. The Hispanic population more than tripled between 1990 and 2000 in Alabama, Arkansas, Georgia, Nevada, North Carolina, South Carolina, and Tennessee.

Data demonstrate that the Hispanic population in the U.S. is young. In 2000, 35.7 percent of Hispanics were less than 18 years old, compared with 23.5 percent of non-Hispanic whites. Only 5.3 percent of Hispanics are older than 65.

The poverty rate in the general population in 1999 was 7.7 percent among non-Hispanic whites; the poverty rate among Hispanics was 21.2 percent or 7.2 million people. This is a record low matching that of the 1970s.

It is projected that in 2020, the Hispanic population will be approximately 52.7 million; by 2040, the population will be about 80.2 million; by 2050 the population will be 96.5 million, comprising approximately 24.5 percent of the U.S. population.

AFRICAN-AMERICAN CATHOLICS IN THE UNITED STATES

Secretariat for African-American Catholics

(Courtesy, Secretariat for African-American Catholics, USCCB.)

The Secretariat for African-American Catholics is the officially recognized voice of the African-American Catholic community as it articulates the needs and aspirations regarding ministry, evangelization, social justice issues, and worship.

The USCCB Secretariat for African-American Catholics supports the Bishops' Committee for African-American Catholics through identification and communication of the socio-cultural dimension of the African-American Community. The vastness of this dimension encompasses historical, social and cultural elements at work within African-American communities. The Secretariat's role is consultative. It is often the voice of conscience, as we, a people of faith, grow toward a truly universal church.

The Secretariat for African-American Catholics serves as the chief advisor to the National Conference of Catholic Bishops and the United States Catholic Conference in fulfilling its ministry to African-American Catholics in the United States. The Secretariat has as its function the coordination of responses regarding ministry, evangelization, and worship in the African-American Community on the national level. The work of the Secretariat is guided by the Bishop's Committee on African-American Catholics whose primary mission is to encourage the development and assist in the implementation of pastoral programs relating to evangelization and incorporation into the local church of racial, ethnic, cultural and language groups within the National Conference of Catholic Bishops.

It also serves as a liaison to the National Black Catholic Clergy Caucus, the National Black Catholic Seminarians Association, the National Black Catholic Sisters' Conference, the National Association of Black Catholic Administrators, Knights of St. Peter Claver and Ladies Auxiliary, the National Black Catholic Congress, and the National Black Catholic Theological Society. The Secretariat for African-American Catholics is under the executive direction of Beverly Carroll. The committee and secretariat have offices at 3211 Fourth St. N.E., Washington, DC, 20017, (202) 541-3000, www.usccb.org/saac.

USCCB Committee

The Committee on African-American Catholics, established by the National Conference of Catholic Bishops in 1987, is chaired by Bishop Joseph N. Perry, aux. bp. of Chicago. The purpose of the committee is to assist the bishops in their evangelization efforts to the African-American community by initiating, encouraging and supporting programs that recognize and respect African-American genius and values. Priorities of the committee include implementation of the National Black Catholic Pastoral Plan of 1987, inculturation of liturgy and ministry, and increasing lay leadership and vocations.

The Secretariat for African-American Catholics was established as a service agency to the committee.

National Office for Black Catholics

The National Office for Black Catholics, organized in July 1970, is a central agency with the general purposes of promoting active and full participation by black Catholics in the Church and of making more effective the presence and ministry of the Church in the black community.

Its operations are in support of the aspirations and calls of black Catholics for a number of objectives, including the following:

• representation and voice for blacks among bishops and others with leadership and decision-making positions in the Church

• promoting vocations to the priesthood and religious life

• sponsoring programs of evangelization, pastoral ministry, education and liturgy on a national level

• recognition of the black heritage in liturgy, community life, theology and education.

Walter T. Hubbard is executive director of the NOBC. The NOBC office is located at 3025 Fourth St. N.E., Washington, DC, 20017, (202) 635-1778.

National Black Catholic Clergy Caucus

The National Black Catholic Clergy Caucus, founded in 1968 in Detroit, is a fraternity of several hundred black priests, permanent deacons and brothers pledged to mutual support in their vocations and ministries.

The Caucus develops programs of spiritual, theological, educational and ministerial growth for its members, to counteract the effects of institutionalized racism within the Church and American society. A bimonthly newsletter is published. The NBCCC office is located at 440 W. 36th St., New York, NY 10018, (212) 868-1847, fax (212) 563-0787. Other peer and support groups are the National Black Sisters' Conference and the National Black Catholic Seminarians Association.

National Black Catholic Congress

The National Black Catholic Congress, Inc., was formed in 1985 exclusively to assist in the development of the Roman Catholic Church in the African-American community and to devise effective means of evangelization of African-American peoples in the

United States. Its fundamental purpose is the formation and development of concrete approaches toward
the evangelization of African-Americans through revitalization of African-American Catholic life.

The Congress is under the sponsorship of the African-
American Roman Catholic bishops of the United States, the
National Black Catholic Clergy Caucus, the National Black
Sisters' Conference, the National Association of Black
Catholic Administrators and the Knights of Peter Claver and
Ladies Auxiliary. The Congress is also in consultation with
African-American clergy and vowed religious communities
of women. The Congress sponsors "Pastoring in African-
American Parishes," an annual workshop first held in 1988,
and an African-American Catholic Ministries Program, a
week-long curriculum presented twice a year, usually in
January and June.

The National Black Catholic Congress sponsored the seventh assembly of African-American Catholics and those serving in African-American communities, July 9–12, 1992, in
New Orleans. The most recent National Congress convened
in Baltimore, Aug. 27 to 31, 1997. The Congress is sponsoring construction of "Our Mother of Africa Chapel" at the
Basilica of the National Shrine of the Immaculate Conception
in Washington, DC. The office of the Congress is located at
the Archdiocese of Baltimore Catholic Center, 320 Cathedral
St., 3rd Floor, Baltimore, MD 21201, (410) 547-8496,
www.nbccongress.org. The executive director is Valerie E.
Washington.

Josephite Pastoral Center

The Josephite Pastoral Center was established in
September 1968 as an educational and pastoral service
agency for the Josephites in their mission work, specifically in the black community, subsequently to all
those who minister in the African-American community. St. Joseph's Society of the Sacred Heart, the sponsoring body, has about 134 priests and 11 brothers in
64 mostly southern parishes in 17 dioceses. Address:
Josephite Pastoral Center 1200 Varnum St. N.E.,
Washington, DC, 20017, (202) 526-9270.

African-American Evangelization

The National Black Catholic Pastoral Plan adopted
by the National Black Catholic Congress in May 1987
was approved and recommended for implementation
by the National Conference of Catholic Bishops in
November 1989.

Following is an account of several points in the bishops' statement, based on coverage by the CNS
Documentary Service, Origins, Dec. 28, 1989 (Vol.
19, No. 30).

"Evangelization," wrote the bishops, "would not be complete if it did not take account of the unceasing interplay of
the Gospel and of man's concrete life, both personal and

social. Evangelization involves an explicit message, adapted
to the different situations constantly being realized, about the
rights and duties of every human being, about family life,
without which personal growth and development are hardly
possible, about life in society, about international life, peace,
justice and development — a message especially energetic
today about liberation."

Three Areas

The pastoral plan "embraces three broad areas: 1) the
Catholic identity of African-American Catholics; 2)
ministry and leadership within the African-American
community; and 3) the responsibility of this community to reach out to the broader society. Within these
areas are such issues as culture, family, youth, spirituality, liturgy, ministry, lay leadership, parishes, education, social action and community development."

Reflecting a recommendation of the plan, the bishops
encourage African-American Catholics to "discover
their past" since "possession of one's history is the
first step in an appreciation of one's culture."

Bishops

There were 13 (8 active) black bishops as of Sept. 1, 2006.
Six were heads of dioceses: Abp. Wilton D. Gregory (Atlanta,
president of the USCCB, 2001-2004); Bishops Curtis J.
Guillory, S.V.D. (Beaumont), George V. Murry, S.J. (St.
Thomas, Virgin Islands), John H. Ricard, S.S.J. (Pensacola-
Tallahassee), Edward K. Braxton (Belleville), J. Terry Steib,
S.V.D. (Memphis). Three were auxiliary bishops: Dominic
Carmon, S.V.D. (New Orleans), Joseph N. Perry (Chicago),
and Martin D. Holley (Washington). Elliott G. Thomas, of St.
Thomas, Virgin Islands (res., June 30, 1999), Joseph L.
Howze of Biloxi (res., May 15, 2001), Moses Anderson,
S.S.E. Detroit aux. (ret., Oct. 24, 2003), and Leonard J.
Olivier, S.V.D. Washington aux. (ret., May 18, 2004), are
retired. Bp. Gordon D. Bennett was named Bp. of Mandeville
on July 6, 2004; he retired on Aug. 8, 2006.

African-American Bishops of the Past: James August Healy
(1830-1900); Joseph A. Francis, S.V.D. (1923-1997); Eugene
A. Marino, S.S.J. (1934-2000); Raymond Rodly Caeser,
S.V.D. (1932-1987); James Lyke, O.F.M. (1939-1992); Carl
A. Fisher, S.S.J. (1945-1993); Emerson J. Moore (1938-
1995); Harold R. Perry, S.V.D. (1916-1991).

Statistics

The Secretariat for African-American Catholics reports that
there are presently approximately 2.3 million African-
American Catholics in the United States out of 36 million
total African-Americans. They are served by 798 parishes and
75 African-American pastors. There are approximately 225
African-American priests, 400 African-American sisters, 75
African-American brothers, 437 African-American deacons,
and 26 African-American seminarians.

NATIVE-AMERICAN CATHOLICS IN THE UNITED STATES

The Kateri Tekakwitha Conference is so named in honor of Blessed Kateri Tekakwitha, "Lily of the Mohawks," who was born in 1656 at Ossernenon (Auriesville), NY, in 1656, baptized in 1676, lived near Montreal, died in 1680, and was beatified in 1980.

The conference was established in 1939 as a missionary-priest advisory group in the Diocese of Fargo. It was a missionary-priest support group from 1946 to 1977. Since 1977 it has been a gathering of Catholic Native peoples and the men and women — clerical, religious and lay persons — who minister to Native Catholic communities.

The primary focus of conference concern and activity is evangelization, with specific emphasis on development of Native ministry and leadership. Other priorities include catechesis, liturgy, family life, social justice ministry, chemical dependency, youth ministry, spirituality and Native Catholic dialogue. Conferences and local Kateri Circles serve as occasions for the exchange of ideas, prayer and mutual support. Since 1980, the national center has promoted and registered 130 Kateri Circles in the U.S. and Canada. Publications include a quarterly newsletter.

The conference has a board of 12 directors, the majority of whom are Native people. Archbishop Charles Chaput, O.F.M. Cap., is the episcopal moderator. Address: Tekakwitha Conference National Center, P.O. Box 6768, Great Falls, MT 59406, (406) 727-0147.

STATISTICS

On June 19, 2003, the United States Conference of Catholic Bishops issued a report, "Native American Catholics at the Millennium," on the current state of Native American Catholics in the United States. There are 4.1 million people who identify themselves as Native American. Of these, 493,615 Native Americans, or 12 percent of the total population, are considered Catholic.

Bishops

There are presently two Native American bishops in active service in the United States. They are: Archbishop Charles J. Chaput, O.F.M. Cap., of Denver and Bishop Donald Pelotte, S.S.S., of Gallup.

MISSIONARY ACTIVITY OF THE U.S. CHURCH

Sources: U.S. Catholic Mission Handbook 2004: Mission Inventory 2002-2003 *(the most recent issue),* reproduced with permission of the United States Catholic Mission Council, 3029 Fourth St. N.E., Washington, DC.

OVERSEAS MISSIONS

Field Distribution, 2002-2003

Africa: 691 (373 men; 318 women). Largest numbers in Kenya, 186; Tanzania, 92; South Africa, 59; Zambia, 53; Uganda, 53; Ghana, 50; Nigeria, 39.

Asia: 737 (495 men; 242 women). Largest numbers in Philippines, 166; Japan, 139; Taiwan, 99; China PRC-Hong Kong SAR, 82; India, 60; Korea, 43; Thailand, 42. (Those present in China were there for professional services.)

Caribbean: 347 (178 men; 169 women). Largest numbers in Puerto Rico, 96; Dominican Republic 52; Haiti, 51; Belize, 46; Jamaica, 41.

Eurasia (Kazakhstan, Russia, Siberia): 13 (12 men; 1 women). Largest group, Russia, 10.

Europe: 179 (91 men; 88 women). Largest numbers in Italy, 64; Ireland, 27; England, 15; France, 11; Germany, 11; Spain, 8.

Latin America: 1,238 (632 men; 606 women). Largest numbers in Peru, 237; Mexico, 202; Brazil, 198; Guatemala, 118; Bolivia, 105; Chile, 98.

Middle East: 39 (35 men; 4 women). Largest numbers in Israel, 27; Jordan, 5; Lebanon, 4.

North America (Canada and United States): 3,117 (855 men; 2,262 women). Largest number in the United States, 3,060.

Oceania: 160 (99 men; 61 women). Largest numbers in Papua New Guinea, 61; Micronesia, 37; Australia, 13; Marshall Island, 11; Guam, 10.

TOTAL: 6,521 (2,770 men; 3,751 women).

Missionary Personnel, 2002-2003

Bishops: See below.
Religious Priests: 70 mission-sending groups had 1,833 priests in overseas assignments. Listed below are those with 15 or more members abroad.

Jesuits, 332; Maryknoll Fathers and Brothers, 266; Franciscans (O.F.M.), 136; Oblates of Mary Immaculate, 134; Society of Divine Word, 91; Redemptorists, 84; Franciscans (O.F.M. Cap), 54; Holy Cross Fathers, 50; Dominicans, 44; Columbans, 38; Vincentians, 36; Oblates of St. Francis de Sales, 29; Legionaries of Christ, 25; Passionists, 23; Comboni Missionaries, 19; Carmelites, 18; LaSalette Fathers, 17; Marianists, 17; Congregation of Sacred Heart, 16; Spiritans, 15; Xaverian Missionaries, 15.

Diocesan Priests: There were 121 priests from 54 dioceses. The majority were in Latin American countries.

Religious Brothers: 46 mission-sending groups had 361 brothers in overseas assignments. Those with 15 or more members:

Christian Brothers (Brothers of the Christian Schools), 38; Marianists, 29; Holy Cross Brothers, 29; Franciscans (O.F.M.), 29; Christian Brothers, 26; Maryknoll Priests and Brothers, 24.

Religious Sisters: 174 mission-sending communities of women Religious had 2,804 sisters in overseas missions. Those with 15 or more members:

Maryknoll Mission Sisters, 270; School Sisters of Notre Dame, 150; Dominicans,114; Franciscan Missionaries of Mary, 124; Blessed Sacrament Sisters, 110; Missionaries of Charity, 78; Sisters of Mercy (various communities), 75; Sisters of Notre Dame de Namur, 67; Society of the Sacred Heart, 63; Medical Mission Sisters, 57; Congregation of Sisters of St. Agnes, 53; Marist Missionary Sisters, 48; Providence Sisters, 46; Daughters of Charity, 45; Sisters of Charity of the BVM, 44; Presentation Sisters, 41; Ursulines, 41; St. Joseph Sisters, 40; Franciscan Sisters, 40; Holy Cross, Cong. of Sisters, 40; Sisters of St. Joseph of Carondelet, 36; Cong. of St. Joseph, 29; Medical Missionaries of Mary, 28; Franciscan Sisters of Atonement, 27; Sacred Heart of Jesus Sisters, 27; IHM Sisters of Immaculata, 26; School Sisters of St. Francis, 23; Franciscan Sisters of Little Falls, 22; Benedictine Sisters, 22; Little Sisters of the Poor, 20; Mission Sisters of the Immaculate Heart of Mary, 20; Apostles of the

Sacred Heart, 19; Immaculate Heart of Mary Sisters of Monroe, 18; Franciscan Sisters of Charity, 17.

Lay Persons: 101 mission-sending groups had 1,368 members in overseas missions. Those with 15 or more members:

Jesuit Volunteer Corps, 364; Maryknoll Mission Associates, 124; Our Lady of the Most Holy Trinity, 54; Catholic Medical Mission Board, 51; Holy Cross Assoc., 44; Mercy Corps, 33; Jesuit Volunteers International, 29; Vincentian Service Corps, 22; Salesian Lay Missionaries, 20.

Seminarians: There were 8 from 4 groups.

Jesuits, 4; Holy Cross Fathers, 2; Glenmary Home Missioners, 1; Dominicans, 1.

MISSIONARY BISHOPS

The following is a list of missionary bishops in active service around the world. This last does not include retired bishops.

Africa

Kenya: Marsabit (diocese), Ambrose Ravasi, I.M.C.; Rumbek (diocese), Caesar Mazzolari, M.C.C.J.

Madagascar: Morondava (diocese), Donald Pelletier, M.S.

Sierra Leone: Makeni (diocese), George Biguzzi, S.X.

South Africa: De Aar (diocese), Joseph J. Potocnak, S.C.J.

Zambia: Mongu (diocese), Paul Duffy, O.M.I.

Asia

Kazakhstan: Almaty (diocese), Henry Howaniec, O.F.M.

Central America, West Indies

Honduras: Comayagua (diocese), Gerald Scarpone Caporale, O.F.M.; Juticalpa (diocese), Thomas Maurus Muldoon, O.F.M.

Jamaica: Mandeville (diocese), Paul M. Boyle, C.P.

Nicaragua: Bluefields (vicariate apostolic), Paul Simon Schmitz, O.F.M.Cap.

Trinidad and Tobago: Port of Spain (archdiocese), Edward J. Gilbert, C.SS.R.

Virgin Islands: St. Thomas (diocese), George Murry, S.J.

North America

Bermuda: Hamilton (diocese), Robert Kurtz, C.R.

Mexico: Nuevo Laredo (diocese), Ricardo Watty Urquidi, M.Sp.S., first bishop.

Oceania

American Samoa: Samoa-Pago Pago (diocese), John Quinn Weitzel, M.M.

Papua New Guinea: Mendi (diocese), Stephen J. Reichert, O.F.M.Cap.

Solomon Islands: Gizo (diocese), Christopher Cardone, O.P., aux. bp.

South America

Bolivia: Pando (vicariate apostolic), Luis Morgan Casey.

Brazil: Cristalandia (prelacy), Herbert Hermes, O.S.B.; Itaituba (prelacy), Capistran Heim, O.F.M.; Miracema do Tocantins (prelacy), John J. Burke, O.F.M.; Paranagua (diocese), Alfred Novak, C.Ss.R.; Valença (diocese), Elias James Manning, O.F.M. Conv.

Peru: Chulucanas (diocese), Daniel Thomas Turley Murphy, O.S.A.; Sicuani (prelacy), Michael La Fay Bardi, O.Carm.

U.S. CATHOLIC MISSION ASSOCIATION

This is a voluntary association of individuals and organizations for whom the missionary presence of the universal Church is of central importance. It is a non-profit religious, educational and charitable organization which exists to promote global missions. Its primary emphasis is on cross-cultural evangelization and the promotion of international justice and peace. The association is also responsible for gathering and publishing annual statistical data on U.S. missionary personnel overseas. President: Joseph Nangle, O.F.M.; Executive Director, Sr. Rosanne Rustemeyer, S.S.N.D. Address: 3029 Fourth St. N.E., Washington, DC, 20017, (202) 832-3112, www.uscatholicmission.org.

Mission Statement

In its 1996-97 handbook, the association included the following in a mission statement.

"In the Church, our understanding of the mission of

evangelization is evolving to embrace dialogue, community building, struggles for justice, efforts to model justice and faith in our lifestyles, activities and structures, in addition to the teaching/preaching/witnessing role traditionally at the heart of the mission enterprise. Still, the contemporary 'identity-confusion' about 'mission' stands forth as a major challenge for USCMA as we move toward the 21st century.

"The larger context of mission is the Spirit moving in the Signs of our Times: the liberation movements, the women's movements, the economy movements, the rising awareness and celebration of cultural diversity, the search for ways to live peacefully and creatively with great pluralism, rapid technological change, the emergence of the global economy, the steady increase in poverty and injustice, the realigning of the global political order – and the many ripples radiating out from each of these."

HOME MISSIONS

The expression "home missions" is applied to places in the U.S. where the local church does not have its own resources, human and otherwise. These areas share the name "missions" with their counterparts in foreign lands because they too need outside help to provide the personnel and means for making the Church present and active there in carrying out its mission for the salvation of people.

Dioceses in the southeast, the southwest, and the far west are most urgently in need of outside help to carry on the work of the Church. Millions of people live in counties in which there are no resident priests. Many others live in rural areas beyond the reach and influence of a Catholic center. According to recent statistics compiled by the Glenmary Research Center, there are more than 500 priestless counties in the United States.

Mission Workers

A number of forces are at work to meet the pastoral needs of these missionary areas and to establish permanent churches and operating institutions where they are required. In many dioceses, one or more missions and stations are attended from established parishes and are gradually growing to independent status. Priests, brothers and sisters belonging to scores of religious institutes are engaged full-time in the home missions. Lay persons, some of them in affiliation with special groups and movements, are also involved.

The Society for the Propagation of the Faith, which conducts an annual collection for mission support in all parishes of the U.S., allocates 40 percent of this sum for disbursement to home missions through the American Board of Catholic Missions.

Various mission-aid societies frequently undertake projects on behalf of the home missions.

The Glenmary Home Missioners, founded by Fr. W. Howard Bishop in 1939, is the only home mission society established for the sole purpose of carrying out the pastoral ministry in small towns and rural districts of the U.S. Glenmary serves in many areas where at least 20 percent of the people live in poverty and less than one percent are Catholic. With 61 priests and 19 professed brothers as of January 1998 the Glenmary Missioners had missions in the archdioceses of Atlanta and Cincinnati, and in the dioceses of Birmingham, Charlotte, Covington, Jackson, Lexington, Little Rock, Nashville, Owensboro, Richmond, Savannah, Tulsa, Tyler and Wheeling-Charleston. National headquarters are located at 4119 Glenmary Trace, Fairfield, OH. The mailing address is P.O. Box 465618, Cincinnati, OH 45246, (513) 874-8900.

Organizations

Black and Indian Mission Office (The Commission for Catholic Missions among the Colored People and the Indians): Organized officially in 1885 by decree of the Third Plenary Council of Baltimore. Provides financial support for religious works among Blacks and Native Americans in 133 archdioceses and dioceses through funds raised by an annual collection in all parishes of the U.S. on the first Sunday of Lent, the designated Sunday. In 2005, $9,137,462 was raised; disbursements amounted to $8,700,000 for African-American missions and for Native American evangelization programs.

Bureau of Catholic Indian Missions (1874): Established as the representative of Catholic Indian missions before the federal government and the public; made permanent organization in 1884 by Third Plenary Council of Baltimore. After a remarkable history of rendering important services to the Indian people, the bureau continues to represent the Catholic Church in the U.S. in her apostolate to the American Indian. Concerns are evangelization, catechesis, liturgy, family life, education, advocacy. Address: 2021 H St. NW, Washington, DC 20006-4207, (202) 331-8542.

Catholic Negro-American Mission Board (1907): Supports priests and sisters in southern states and provides monthly support to sisters and lay teachers in the poorest black schools.

Board of Directors of the three organizations above are: Card. Anthony Bevilacqua, president; Cardinal William Keeler; Msgr. Paul A. Lenz, secretary-treasurer; Patricia L. O'Rourke, D.St.G.G., assistant secretary/treasurer. Address: 2021 H St. NW, Washington, DC 20006-4207, (202) 331-8542.

The Catholic Church Extension Society (1905): Established with papal approval for the purpose of preserving and extending the Church in rural and isolated parts of the U.S. and its dependencies through the collection and disbursement of funds for home mission work. Since the time of its founding, more than $300 million has been received and distributed for this purpose. The Society celebrated its 100th anniversary in 2005. Works of the society are supervised by a 14-member board of governors: Cardinal Francis George of Chicago, chancellor; Bishop William R. Houck, president; three archbishops, three bishops and six lay people, Headquarters: 150 S. Wacker Dr., 20th Floor, Chicago, IL 60601, (312) 236-7240.

National Catholic Rural Life Conference: Founded in 1923 through the efforts of Bp. Edwin V. O'Hara. Applies the Gospel message to rural issues through focus on rural parishes and the provision of services including distribution of educational materials development of prayer and worship resources, advocacy for strong rural communities. Bp. David Ricken, president; Bro. David G. Andrews, C.S.C., exec. dir. National headquarters: 4625 Beaver Ave., Des Moines, IA 50310, (515) 270-2634, www.ncrlc.com.

BISHOPS' COMMITTEE ON THE HOME MISSIONS

Established in 1924, the Committee on the Home Missions of the U.S. Conference of Catholic Bishops provides financial support for missionary activities that strengthen and extend the presence of the Church in the United States and its island territories in the Caribbean and the Pacific. Funding for mission dioceses and national organizations engaged in home mission work is provided through the annual Catholic Home Missions Appeal, which is nationally scheduled on the last weekend of April. For 2004-2005, a record $12 million has been allocated to 90 mission dioceses and 21 mission organizations thanks to the faithfulness and sustained generosity of Catholics. Since 1924, close to $300 million has been collected and disbursed for home missions. The committee's work is supervised by seven bishops and a small national staff. Bp. Peter J. Sartain (Little Rock, Ark.), chairperson; Dr. David M. Byers, exec. dir. National headquarters: U. S. Conference of Catholic Bishops, 3211 4th NE, Washington, DC, 20017-1194, (202) 541-3450, www.usccb.org.

U.S. Catholic Statistics

U.S. STATISTICAL SUMMARY

(Principal sources: The Official Catholic Directory, 2006, Almanac *survey comparisons, where given, are with figures reported in the previous edition of the* Directory. *Totals below do not include statistics for Outlying Areas of U.S. unless otherwise noted. These are given in tables on the preceding pages and elsewhere in the* Catholic Almanac; see **Index.***)*

Catholic Population: 69,135,254; increase, 1,314,421. Percent of total population: 23%.

Jurisdictions: 34 archdioceses (includes 33 metropolitan sees and the Military Archdiocese), 152 dioceses (includes St. Thomas, Virgin Islands, and the eparchy of Our Lady of Deliverance of Newark for Syrians of the U.S. and Canada), 1 apostolic exarchate (New York-based Armenian exarchate for U.S. and Canada). The current number of dioceses reflects the elevation of the diocese of Galveston-Houston to an archdiocese on Dec. 29, 2004, and the creation on July 3, 2000, of the new diocese of Laredo. There are also the eparchies of St. Maron and Our Lady of Lebanon of Los Angeles (Maronites), Newton (Melkites), St. Thomas Apostle of Detroit (Chaldeans), St. George Martyr of Canton, Ohio (Romanians), St. Thomas of Chicago (Syro-Malabars) which was created on March 13, 2001, and the Eparchy of St. Peter the Apostle of San Diego which was created on May 21, 2002. The eparchy of Our Lady of Deliverance of Newark has its seat in Newark, NJ. The Armenian apostolic exarchate for the United States and Canada has its seat in New York. Vacant jurisdictions (as of Aug. 15, 2006): Birmingham, Great Falls-Billing, Lake Charles, Little Rock, Pittsburgh, Salt Lake City, Sioux Falls, Youngstown.

Cardinals: 16 (8 head archiepiscopal sees in U.S.; 2 are Roman Curia officials; five are retired, including Puerto Rico, one is a theologian). As of July 10, 2006.

Archbishops: 36. Diocesan, in U.S., 28 (does not include 7 cardinals and military archbishop); retired, 16; there are also 10 archbishops serving outside U.S. As of Aug. 11, 2006.

Bishops: 419. Diocesan, in U.S. (and Virgin Islands), 152; coadjutors, 1; auxiliaries, 79; retired, 151; there are also 25 bishops serving outside U.S. As of Aug. 11, 2006.

Priests: 42,178; decrease, 1,244. Diocesan, 28,538 (decrease, 348); religious order priests (does not include those assigned overseas), 13,640 (decrease, 880). There were 438 newly ordained priests; decrease, 29.

Permanent Deacons: 14,995; decrease, 32.

Brothers: 5,252; decrease, 265.

Sisters: 67,773; decrease, 2,190.

Seminarians: 5,642. Diocesan seminarians, 3,929; religious order seminarians, 1,713.

Receptions into Church: 1,097,765. Includes 943,264 infant baptisms; 80,817 adult baptisms and 73,684 already baptized persons received into full communion with the Church.

First Communions: 832,643.

Confirmations: 630,448.

Marriages: 212,456.

Deaths: 452,832.

Parishes: 18,992.

Seminaries, Diocesan: 73.

Religious Seminaries: 131.

Colleges and Universities: 231. Students, 763,757.

High Schools: 1,354. Students, 679,506.

Elementary Schools: 6,511. Students, 1,762,401

Non-Residential Schools for Handicapped: 79. Students, 5,745.

Teachers: 172,785 (priests, 1,494; brothers, 1,149; scholastics, 56; sisters, 6,414; laity, 163,672).

Public School Students in Religious Instruction Programs: 4,216,226. High school students, 729,421; elementary school students, 3,486,805.

Hospitals: 573; patients treated, 84,723,272.

Health Care Centers: 392; patients treated, 6,054,544.

Specialized Homes: 1,503; patients assisted, 687,519.

Residential Care of Children (Orphanages): 1,023; children assisted, 77,926.

Day Care and Extended Day Care Centers: 968; children assisted, 119,786.

Special Centers for Social Services: 2,801; assisted annually, 27,393,912.

PERCENTAGE OF CATHOLICS IN TOTAL POPULATION IN U.S.

(Source: The Official Catholic Directory, 2006; figures are as of Jan. 1, 2006. Total general population figures at the end of the table are U.S. Census Bureau estimates for Jan. 1 of the respective years. Archdioceses are indicated by an asterisk; for dioceses marked +, see Dioceses with Interstate Lines; #indicates statistics for New Orleans reflect 2005 totals.)

State Diocese	Catholic Pop.	Total Pop.	Cath. Pct.	State Diocese	Catholic Pop.	Total Pop.	Cath. Pct.
Alabama	153,939	4,488,386	3.4	Illinois, cont.			
*Mobile	67,434	1,669,324	4	Springfield	158,741	1,142,843	13.8
Birmingham	86,505	2,819,062	3	Indiana	767,349	6,206,265	12.3
Alaska	55,643	634,610	8.7	*Indianapolis	232,273	2,430,606	9.6
*Anchorage	32,170	401,610	8.0	Evansville	87,821	497,433	17.6
Fairbanks	18,000	160,000	11.2	Ft.Wayne-S.Bend	156,509	1,247,850	12.8
Juneau	5,473	73,000	7.4	Gary	185,550	778,463	24
Arizona	908,123	5,782,835	15.7	Lafayette	105,196	1,251,913	8.4
Phoenix	551,721	4,208,723	13.1	Iowa	494,698	2,886,494	17.1
Tucson	356,402	1,574,112	23	*Dubuque	210,173	927,161	22.6
Arkansas				Davenport	105,650	744,990	14.1
Little Rock	107,524	2,752,629	3.9	Des Moines	91,347	742,190	12
California	10,906,992	37,759,158	28.8	Sioux City	87,528	472,153	18.5
*Los Angeles	4,448,763	11,012,763	40.3	Kansas	406,916	2,683,594	15.1
*San Francisco	420,397	1,689,491	24.8	*Kansas City	196,391	1,193,425	16.0
Fresno	581,000	2,584,894	23	Dodge City	43,682	222,502	19.6
Monterey	195,000	976,071	19.9	Salina	46,316	314,779	14.7
Oakland	468,718	4,464,379	10.4	Wichita	120,527	952,888	12.6
Orange	1,130,464	2,900,000	39.0	Kentucky	387,062	3,974,602	9.7
Sacramento	541,321	3,381,449	16.0	*Louisville	196,858	1,180,143	16.6
San Bernardino	1,146,960	3,823,202	30	Covington	89,755	464,629	19.3
San Diego	950,743	3,098,942	30.6	Lexington	48,070	1,492,784	30
San Jose	650,000	1,682,585	38.6	Owensboro	52,379	837,046	6.4
Santa Rosa	159,763	881,492	17.7	Louisiana	816,260	3,124,648	26.1
Stockton	212,663	1,263,890	16.8	*New Orleans	490,898	1,361,488	36.0
Colorado	666,213	4,509,034	14.7	Alexandria	48,050	388,903	12.3
*Denver	384,611	3,012,180	12.7	Baton Rouge	212,224	870,624	23.3
Colo. Springs	166,602	876,854	19	Houma-			
Pueblo	115,000	620,000	18.5	Thibodaux	120,671	202,000	59.7
Connecticut	1,357,992	3,503,604	38.7	Lafayette	317,226	568,154	54.2
*Hartford	668,231	1,910,542	35	Lake Charles	77,934	277,849	28
Bridgeport	460,298	903,291	50.9	Shreveport	40,155	817,118	5
Norwich+	229,463	689,771	33.2	Maine			
Delaware+				Portland	193,228	1,274,923	15.1
Wilmington	230,000	1,215,156	18.3	Maryland			
District of Columbia				*Baltimore	517,679	3,055,407	16.9
*Washington+	575,824	2,617,382	21.9	Massachusetts	2,736,216	6,407,058	42.7
Florida	2,265,450	17,738,582	12.7	*Boston	1,845,846	3,974,846	46.4
*Miami	752,025	4,196,741	18	Fall River	347,385	831,965	41.7
Orlando	369,151	3,736,180	9.8	Springfield	234,616	820,759	28
Palm Beach	276,003	2,068,981	13.3	Worcester	308,369	779,488	39.5
Pensacola-				Michigan	2,064,103	10,028,273	20.5
Tallahassee	65,209	1,320,827	4.9	*Detroit	1,286,985	4,441,551	28.9
St. Augustine	162,964	1,821,166	9.0	Gaylord	70,327	514,001	13.6
St. Petersburg	415,412	2,769,418	15.0	Grand Rapids	162,670	1,283,717	12.6
Venice	223,686	1,825,269	12.2	Kalamazoo	109,348	954,564	11.4
Georgia	441,749	8,656,981	5.1	Lansing	230,981	1,801,941	12.8
*Atlanta	368,100	5,856,981	6.3	Marquette	67,400	308,357	21.8
Savannah	73,649	2,800,000	2.8	Saginaw	136,392	724,142	19.2
Hawaii				Minnesota	1,093,533	5,065,397	21.5
Honolulu	143,240	1,262,840	11.3	*St. Paul and			
Idaho				Minneapolis	646,313	3,001,500	21.5
Boise	148,100	1,417,800	10.4	Crookston	35,780	250,941	14.2
Illinois	3,867,102	12,954,363	63.0	Duluth	68,037	432,904	15.7
*Chicago	2,348,000	6,021,000	39	New Ulm	68,087	285,453	24.1
Belleville	100,100	848,743	12	St. Cloud	144,036	537,030	26.8
Joliet	655,051	1,808,308	36	Winona	131,280	557,684	23.5
Peoria	174,008	1,748,316	9.9	Mississippi	117,942	2,925,399	4.0
Rockford	431,202	1,385,153	31.1	Biloxi	67,244	813,806	8.2

State Diocese	Catholic Pop.	Total Pop.	Cath. Pct.
Mississippi, cont.			
Jackson	50,698	2,111,593	2.4
Missouri	835,581	5,654,252	14.7
*St. Louis	555,750	2,118,721	26.2
Jefferson City	85,150	860,700	9.8
Kansas City- St. Joseph	130,465	1,448,752	9.0
Springfield- C. Girardeau	64,216	1,226,079	5.2
Montana	110,409	911,091	12.1
Great Falls- Billings	51,629	391,360	13.2
Helena	58,780	519,731	11.3
Nebraska	375,808	1,753,984	21.4
*Omaha	225,936	881,782	25.6
Grand Island	55,884	301,328	18.5
Lincoln	93,988	570,874	16.4
Nevada	661,300	2,383,670	27.7
Las Vegas	539,953	1,700,000	31
Reno	121,347	683,670	17.7
New Hampshire			
Manchester	314,471	1,299,500	24
New Jersey	3,605,265	8,764,790	41.1
*Newark	1,319,558	2,835,594	46.5
Camden	459,118	1,347,648	34
Metuchen	603,214	1,436,225	42.0
Paterson	425,411	1,140,818	37.2
Trenton	797,964	2,004,505	39.8
New Mexico	494,449	2,306,838	21.4
*Santa Fe	302,455	1,336,638	22.6
Gallup	59,348	471,892	12.5
Las Cruces	132,646	498,308	26.5
New York	7,433,366	19,727,130	37.6
*New York	2,542,432	5,649,849	45
Albany	400,000	1,300,000	30.7
Brooklyn	1,556,575	4,712,506	33
Buffalo	694,992	1,570,179	44.2
Ogdensburg	120,085	490,107	25
Rochester	341,772	1,504,019	22.7
Rockville Ctr.	1,431,774	3,325,583	43
Syracuse	345,736	1,174,887	29.4
North Carolina	336,738	8,649,894	3.9
Charlotte	150,431	4,506,384	3.3
Raleigh	186,307	4,143,510	4.4
North Dakota	145,789	638,820	22.2
Bismarck	62,898	258,999	24.2
Fargo	82,891	379,821	22
Ohio	2,128,619	11,487,971	18.5
*Cincinnati	498,493	2,960,898	16.8
Cleveland	797,898	2,852,022	28
Columbus	252,103	2,447,972	10.2
Steubenville	40,001	516,405	7.7
Toledo	306,532	1,489,769	21
Youngstown	233,592	1,220,905	19.1
Oklahoma	160,878	3,451,634	4.6
*Oklahoma City	105,416	1,891,634	5.5
Tulsa	55,462	1,560,000	3.5
Oregon	432,170	3,543,350	12.1
*Portland	396,523	3,103,850	12.8
Baker	35,647	439,500	8.1
Pennsylvania	3,614,694	12,271,636	29.4
*Philadelphia	1,462,388	3,882,573	37.6
Allentown	275,129	1,161,932	23.6
Altoona-J'town	103,694	644,307	16.1

State Diocese	Catholic Pop.	Total Pop.	Cath. Pct.
Pennsylvania, cont.			
Erie	225,575	874,057	25.8
Greensburg	170,486	680,630	25
Harrisburg	247,492	2,027,835	12.2
Pittsburgh	781,811	1,956,597	39.9
Scranton	348,119	1,043,705	33.3
Rhode Island Providence	640,274	1,080,632	59.2
South Carolina Charleston	157,450	4,229,990	3.7
South Dakota	154,435	751,364	20.5
Rapid City	25,729	227,211	11.7
Sioux Falls	128,706	524,153	24.8
Tennessee	190,684	5,900,431	3.2
Knoxville	53,942	2,193,608	2.4
Memphis	67,342	1,516,890	4.3
Nashville	69,400	2,189,933	3.1
Texas	6,742,690	23,089,747	29.2
*Galveston -Houston	1,495,030	5,250,984	28
*San Antonio	673,526	2,068,895	32.5
Amarillo	40,293	415,493	9.6
Austin	500,000	2,309,396	21.6
Beaumont	80,281	603,648	13.2
Brownsville	943,611	1,110,130	85.0
Corpus Christi	388,878	555,540	70
Dallas	955,298	3,473,568	27.5
El Paso+	656,035	811,739	80.8
Fort Worth	450,000	2,922,302	15.3
Laredo	229,141	346,200	66.1
Lubbock	84,780	514,406	16.4
San Angelo	77,630	673,801	12.1
Tyler	61,390	1,824,930	3.3
Victoria	106,797	208,736	51.1
Utah			
Salt Lake City	200,000	2,389,039	8.3
Vermont			
Burlington	118,000	620,000	19.0
Virginia	620,399	7,630,908	8.1
Arlington	400,539	2,646,698	15.1
Richmond	219,860	4,984,210	4.3
Washington	745,614	6,185,248	12
*Seattle	570,800	4,878,300	11.7
Spokane	97,665	715,452	13.6
Yakima	77,149	591,496	13.0
West Virginia Wheeling- Charleston	82,749	1,802,000	4.6
Wisconsin	1,605,155	5,535,190	29
*Milwaukee	674,736	2,271,840	31.1
Green Bay	369,556	998,800	37
La Crosse	206,191	863,610	23
Madison	272,787	957,731	28.4
Superior	81,885	443,209	18.4
Wyoming Cheyenne	49,121	506,529	9.7
East. Churches	543,565	-	-
Military Arch.('99)	1,194,000	-	-
Outlying Areas	3,083,704	4,440,914	69.4
Total 2006	69,135,254	297,838,972	23.2
Total 2005	67,820,833	295,865,704	22.9
Total 1996	60,280,454	268,784,851	22.4

CATHOLIC POPULATION OF THE UNITED STATES

(*Source:* The Official Catholic Directory, 2006; *figures as of Jan. 1, 2006. Archdioceses are indicated by an asterisk; for dioceses marked +, see Dioceses with Interstate Lines.#* indicates as of 2005; ** does not include New Orleans.)

State Diocese	Cath. Pop.	Dioc. Priests	Rel. Priests	Total Priests	Perm. Deac.	Bros.	Sisters	Parishes
Alabama	**153,939**	**186**	**72**	**258**	**116**	**40**	**289**	**131**
*Mobile	67,434	107	34	141	60	24	135	76
Birmingham	86,505	79	38	117	56	16	154	55
Alaska	**55,643**	**41**	**26**	**67**	**55**	**5**	**56**	**77**
*Anchorage	32,170	19	8	27	14	2	34	19
Fairbanks	18,000	11	16	27	38	3	18	47
Juneau	5,473	11	2	13	3	-	4	11
Arizona	**908,123**	**232**	**180**	**412**	**383**	**24**	**446**	**163**
Phoenix	551,721	120	107	227	235	15	218	89
Tucson	356,402	112	73	185	148	9	228	74
Arkansas, Little Rock	**107,524**	**73**	**47**	**120**	**72**	**30**	**234**	**88**
California	**10,906,992**	**1,985**	**1,560**	**3,620**	**816**	**499**	**4,639**	**1,073**
*Los Angeles	4,448,763	533	633	1,166	216	170	1,730	288
*San Francisco	420,397	212	173	385	73	50	825	89
Fresno	581,000	125	33	158	32	-	120	86
Monterey	195,200	78	19	97	5	36	153	46
Oakland	468,718	170	100	270	-	65	368	86
Orange	1,131,464	126	127	253	80	7	337	58
Sacramento	541,321	171	61	232	127	28	186	101
San Bernardino	1,146,960	111	117	228	104	18	157	97
San Diego	950,743	183	83	341	88	23	294	98
San Jose	650,000	134	189	323	6	62	359	49
Santa Rosa	159,763	77	8	85	37	36	49	42
Stockton	212,663	65	17	82	41	4	61	33
Colorado	**666,213**	**289**	**161**	**450**	**232**	**19**	**497**	**207**
*Denver	384,611	172	112	284	171	13	315	120
Colo. Springs	166,602	45	30	75	26	3	110	35
Pueblo	115,000	72	19	91	35	3	72	52
Connecticut	**1,357,992**	**728**	**209**	**937**	**443**	**52**	**1,455**	**378**
*Hartford	668,231	342	111	453	287	32	827	213
Bridgeport	460,298	251	44	295	88	-	390	87
Norwich+	229,463	135	54	189	68	20	238	78
Delaware, Wilmington+	**230,000**	**123**	**88**	**211**	**94**	**34**	**253**	**57**
D.C., *Washington+	**575,824**	**282**	**344**	**626**	**249**	**85**	**629**	**140**
Florida	**2,265,450**	**904**	**406**	**1,310**	**646**	**143**	**1,088**	**463**
*Miami	752,025	264	89	353	150	55	314	111
Orlando	369,151	127	51	178	167	5	107	77
Palm Beach	276,003	112	28	140	50	6	133	49
Pensacola-Tallahassee	65,209	77	14	91	57	6	35	49
St. Augustine	163,964	89	23	112	36	3	116	50
St. Petersburg	415,412	127	131	258	99	47	278	73
Venice	223,686	108	70	178	87	21	105	54
Georgia	**441,749**	**235**	**104**	**339**	**210**	**31**	**198**	**134**
*Atlanta	368,100	160	782	38	174	25	105	82
Savannah	73,649	75	26	101	36	6	93	52
Hawaii, Honolulu	**143,240**	**61**	**72**	**133**	**53**	**50**	**192**	**66**
Idaho, Boise	**148,100**	**78**	**14**	**92**	**68**	**6**	**91**	**51**
Illinois	**3,867,102**	**1,709**	**1,081**	**2,790**	**1,096**	**464**	**4,076**	**1,014**
*Chicago	2,348,000	835	787	1,622	632	322	2,397	366
Belleville	100,100	124	45	169	20	12	166	124
Joliet	655,051	191	111	302	197	70	593	121
Peoria	174,008	249	38	287	110	13	250	163
Rockford	431,202	183	44	227	133	11	226	104
Springfield	158,741	127	56	183	4	36	444	136
Indiana	**767,349**	**545**	**319**	**864**	**98**	**166**	**1,700**	**428**
*Indianapolis	232,273	153	103	256	1	30	700	139
Evansville	87,821	84	7	91	23	2	279	70
Ft. Wayne-South Bend	156,509	89	148	237	19	124	558	84
Gary	185,550	109	45	154	43	8	87	72
Lafayette	105,196	110	16	126	12	2	76	63

State Diocese	Cath. Pop.	Dioc. Priests	Rel. Priests	Total Priests	Perm. Deac.	Bros.	Sisters	Par- ishes
Iowa	494,698	578	44	622	226	24	1,181	476
*Dubuque	210,173	222	30	252	79	20	833	187
Davenport	105,650	114	2	116	44	1	180	84
Des Moines	91,347	89	10	99	65	3	81	82
Sioux City	87,528	153	2	155	38	-	87	123
Kansas	406,916	321	77	398	10	24	1,154	347
*Kansas City	196,391	96	55	151	-	22	588	118
Dodge City	43,682	35	7	42	9	1	99	49
Salina	46,316	64	13	77	-	1	180	88
Wichita	120,527	126	2	128	1	1	287	92
Kentucky	387,062	368	109	477	170	82	1,481	296
*Louisville	196,858	158	60	218	102	70	796	112
Covington	89,755	86	7	93	28	7	346	47
Lexington	48,070	50	25	75	38	31	21	58
Owensboro	52,379	74	17	91	2	2	218	79
Louisiana**	816,260	449	130	579	186	51	622	341
*#New Orleans	490,898	220	195	415	186	103	695	142
Alexandria	48,050	61	14	75	6	4	39	48
Baton Rouge	212,224	72	33	105	39	9	117	68
Houma-Thibodaux	120,671	59	7	66	26	4	30	39
Lafayette	317,226	160	48	208	61	27	364	121
Lake Charles	77,934	61	15	76	33	1	25	38
Shreveport	40,155	36	13	49	21	6	47	27
Maine, Portland	193,228	161	35	196	34	17	340	133
Maryland, *Baltimore	517,679	272	245	517	185	66	1,047	151
Massachusetts	4,865,216	1,383	838	2,221	476	256	3,459	644
*Boston	3,974,846	821	587	1,408	233	162	2,234	303
Fall River	347,385	162	121	283	85	10	212	96
Springfield	234,616	160	36	196	66	8	609	120
Worcester	308,369	240	94	334	92	76	404	125
Michigan	2,064,103	993	313	1,306	375	102	2,803	795
*Detroit	1,286,985	437	217	654	159	88	1,713	303
Gaylord	70,327	66	11	77	17	3	35	81
Grand Rapids	162,670	106	15	121	32	1	249	90
Kalamazoo	109,348	58	10	68	25	1	150	46
Lansing	230,981	147	39	186	92	8	490	95
Marquette	67,400	83	13	96	35	-	56	74
Saginaw	136,392	96	8	104	15	1	110	106
Minnesota	1,093,533	773	238	1,011	327	153	2,227	711
*St.Paul & Minneapolis	646,313	348	106	454	217	63	978	219
Crookston	35,780	46	4	50	15	1	118	67
Duluth	68,037	75	11	86	4	35	130	93
New Ulm	68,087	70	1	71	3	-	69	80
St. Cloud	144,036	121	107	228	48	69	537	137
Winona	131,280	113	9	122	9	20	395	115
Mississippi	117,942	107	47	154	36	21	262	119
Biloxi	67,244	51	17	68	29	8	44	45
Jackson	50,698	56	30	86	7	13	218	74
Missouri	835,581	742	513	1,255	361	222	2,302	439
*St. Louis	555,750	459	353	812	239	125	1,859	191
Jefferson City	85,150	103	7	110	51	2	78	95
Kansas City-St. Joseph	130,465	114	99	213	58	37	273	87
Springfield-Cape Girardeau	64,216	66	54	120	13	58	92	66
Montana	110,409	143	19	162	35	3	105	125
Great Falls-Billings	51,629	65	13	78	7	-	67	66
Helena	58,780	78	6	84	28	3	38	59
Nebraska	375,808	419	102	521	202	26	534	308
*Omaha	225,936	199	92	291	200	26	329	139
Grand Island	55,884	70	-	70	-	-	70	36
Lincoln	93,988	150	10	160	3	2	135	133
Nevada	661,300	64	27	91	23	10	40	53
Las Vegas	539,953	38	16	54	12	5	5	25
Reno	121,347	26	11	37	11	5	35	28
New Hampshire Manchester	314,471	199	57	256	48	19	530	117

State Diocese	Cath. Pop.	Dioc. Priests	Rel. Priests	Total Priests	Perm. Deac.	Bros.	Sisters	Par- ishes
New Jersey	3,605,265	1,699	484	2,187	1,026	256	3,176	690
*Newark	1,319,558	734	186	920	210	111	1,338	232
Camden	459,118	294	44	338	130	18	324	125
Metuchen	603,214	201	46	247	151	22	350	103
Paterson	425,411	244	159	403	206	35	776	111
Trenton	797,964	226	49	278	326	70	388	119
New Mexico	494,449	200	131	331	275	89	393	194
*Santa Fe	302,455	123	71	194	202	69	228	93
Gallup	59,348	43	23	66	31	13	124	56
Las Cruces	132,646	34	37	71	42	7	41	45
New York	7,433,366	2,886	1,460	4,346	1,264	867	8,357	1,611
*New York	2,542,432	687	849	1,536	365	437	3,028	405
Albany	400,000	234	110	344	102	81	815	169
Brooklyn	1,556,575	593	171	764	150	162	1,078	216
Buffalo	694,992	376	152	528	112	48	1,116	264
Ogdensburg	120,085	135	7	142	65	10	146	111
Rochester	341,772	206	64	270	136	33	585	149
Rockville Centre	1,431,774	373	63	436	264	84	1,251	134
Syracuse	345,736	282	44	326	70	12	338	163
North Carolina	336,738	196	114	310	109	16	172	145
Charlotte	150,431	103	65	168	72	9	114	69
Raleigh	186,307	93	49	142	37	7	58	76
North Dakota	145,789	218	33	251	114	21	282	199
Bismarck	62,898	68	26	94	72	21	122	62
Fargo	82,891	150	7	157	42	-	160	137
Ohio	2,128,619	1,340	467	1,807	691	230	3,456	877
*Cincinnati	498,493	286	229	515	149	140	1,056	222
Cleveland	797,898	423	113	536	200	51	1,203	233
Columbus	252,103	177	42	219	87	3	297	106
Steubenville	40,001	100	24	124	5	10	74	70
Toledo	306,532	184	39	223	189	8	620	131
Youngstown	233,592	170	20	190	61	18	206	115
Oklahoma	160,878	167	54	231	128	27	229	148
*Oklahoma City	105,416	94	29	123	71	9	134	70
Tulsa	55,462	73	25	109	57	18	95	78
Oregon	432,170	184	159	343	50	88	462	160
*Portland	396,523	152	155	307	37	87	447	124
Baker	35,647	32	4	36	13	1	15	36
Pennsylvania	3,614,694	2,233	811	3,047	533	193	6,638	1,236
*Philadelphia	1,462,388	649	379	1,028	213	116	3,180	274
Allentown	275,129	213	77	293	87	-	397	151
Altoona-Johnstown	103,694	139	58	197	34	8	80	97
Erie	225,575	208	6	214	41	-	421	125
Greensburg	170,486	132	70	202	-	29	206	101
Harrisburg	247,492	146	34	180	47	-	411	89
Pittsburgh	781,811	416	112	528	47	34	1,326	214
Scranton	348,119	330	75	405	64	6	617	185
Rhode Island								
Providence	640,274	294	127	421	105	103	564	150
South Carolina								
Charleston	157,450	92	44	136	78	26	134	91
South Dakota	154,435	159	49	208	56	16	393	239
Rapid City	25,729	40	19	59	26	5	49	89
Sioux Falls	128,706	119	30	149	30	11	344	150
Tennessee	190,684	164	66	230	128	53	282	137
Knoxville	53,942	53	17	70	24	12	33	44
Memphis	67,342	66	20	86	50	40	72	42
Nashville	69,400	45	29	74	54	1	177	51
Texas	6,742,690	1,257	776	2,033	1,541	216	2,435	1,061
*Galveston-Houston	1,495,030	197	210	407	357	13	523	149
*San Antonio	673,526	150	184	334	320	89	784	139
Amarillo	40,293	48	11	59	51	1	102	41
Austin	500,000	162	52	214	187	48	102	103
Beaumont	80,281	49	24	73	32	2	28	45
Brownsville	943,611	76	41	117	66	18	111	67

State Diocese	Cath. Pop.	Dioc. Priests	Rel. Priests	Total Priests	Perm. Deac.	Bros.	Sisters	Par- ishes
Texas, cont.								
Corpus Christi	388,878	106	30	136	66	7	185	68
Dallas	955,298	96	72	168	157	8	127	67
El Paso	656,035	82	36	118	14	11	155	58
Fort Worth	450,000	64	47	111	75	6	29	89
Laredo	229,141	32	22	54	28	8	81	32
Lubbock	84,780	40	6	46	46	-	24	62
San Angelo	77,630	31	17	48	62	-	21	49
Tyler	61,390	71	15	86	55	4	55	42
Victoria	106,797	53	9	62	25	-	108	50
Utah, Salt Lake City	200,000	53	26	79	53	11	47	47
Vermont, Burlington	118,000	106	43	149	43	13	210	84
Virginia	620,399	317	108	425	139	32	287	213
Arlington	400,539	155	74	229	58	20	140	67
Richmond	219,860	162	34	196	81	12	147	146
Washington	745,614	341	177	518	184	29	736	265
*Seattle	570,800	183	91	274	104	18	450	142
Spokane	97,665	84	74	158	52	7	244	82
Yakima	77,149	74	12	86	28	4	42	41
West Virginia								
Wheeling-Charleston	82,749	116	64	180	48	13	215	112
Wisconsin	1,605,155	964	487	1,451	407	124	3,867	793
*Milwaukee	674,736	387	332	719	166	77	2,327	217
Green Bay	369,556	196	113	309	128	36	593	169
La Crosse	206,191	161	15	176	31	3	447	165
Madison	272,787	152	18	170	24	7	406	135
Superior	81,885	68	9	77	58	1	94	107
Wyoming, Cheyenne+	49,121	49	13	62	19	6	24	36
EASTERN CHURCHES	543,565	596	127	723	161	30	301	563
*Philadelphia	60,200	55	5	60	5	-	77	71
St. Nicholas	10,000	28	13	41	9	-	7	37
Stamford	16,600	39	17	56	8	3	47	51
St. Josaphat (Parma)	10,937	37	2	39	11	-	6	38
*Pittsburgh	59,719	64	9	73	10	3	88	80
Parma	12,371	40	1	41	8	-	9	31
Passaic	21,808	77	12	89	23	1	18	88
Van Nuys	2,863	21	4	25	8	4	3	19
St. Maron (Maronites)	30,000	58	7	65	14	8	2	34
Our Lady of Lebanon (Maronites)	41,232	34	18	52	13	-	6	26
Newton (Melkites)	24,435	50	15	65	44	-	3	35
St. Peter the Apostle of San Diego	40,200	8	-	8	-	-	12	7
St. Thomas Apostle of Detroit (Chaldean)	80,000	12	-	12	-	-	-	8
St. Thomas (Syro-Malabrs)	85,000	41	14	55	-	-	14	8
St. George Martyr (Romanian)	5,000	18	2	20	3	-	-	14
Our Lady of Deliverance (Syrians, U.S.-Canada)	18,200	11	-	11	3	-	-	9
Armenian Ex.(U.S.-Canada)	25,000	3	8	11	2	-	11	7
Military Archd. ('99)[1]	1,194,000	-	-	-	-	-	-	-
Outlying Areas								
Puerto Rico	2,791,518	379	300	679	420	67	1,009	327
Samoa-Pago Pago	14,500	11	5	16	14	-	9	15
Caroline Islands	68,500	14	15	29	40	2	33	27
Chalan Kanoa (N. Mariana Is.)	43,000	14	2	16	-	-	-	11
Guam, *Agana	131,584	40	15	55	20	1	105	24
Marshall Islands	4,602	1	3	4	1	-	9	4
Virgin Islands, St. Thomas	30,000	5	3	8	26	3	18	8
TOTAL 2006	69,135,254	28,538	13,640	42,178	14,995	5,252	67,773	18,992
TOTAL 2005	67,820,833	28,886	14,520	43,422	15,027	5,517	69,963	19,297
TOTAL 1996	60,280,454	32,442	16,629	49,009	11,527	6,357	89,125	19,726

[1]763 diocesan and 155 religious-order chaplains are on loan to the military (*2006 Annuario Pontificio*).

RECEPTIONS INTO THE CHURCH IN THE UNITED STATES

(Source: The Official Catholic Directory, 2006; figures as of Jan. 1, 2006. Archdioceses are indicated by an asterisk; for dioceses marked +, see Dioceses with Interstate Lines. Information includes infant and adult baptisms and those received into full communion. # as of 2005; ** does not include New Orleans.)

State Diocese	Infant Baptisms	Adult Bapts.	Rec'd into Full Com.	State Diocese	Infant Baptisms	Adult Bapts.	Rec'd into Full Com.
Alabama	3,352	355	710	Indiana, cont.			
*Mobile	1,133	152	291	Lafayette	2,079	305	395
Birmingham	2,219	203	419	Iowa	8,058	564	1,170
Alaska	772	75	86	*Dubuque	2,923	113	325
*Anchorage	510	48	60	Davenport	1,579	211	192
Fairbanks	200	7	14	Des Moines	1,960	137	438
Juneau	62	20	12	Sioux City	1,596	103	215
Arizona	16,470	5,049	1,649	Kansas	8,454	756	1,370
Phoenix	9,798	4,734	910	*Kansas City	3,985	299	561
Tucson	6,672	315	739	Dodge City	990	62	168
Arkansas, Lit. Rock	2,608	304	472	Salina	926	65	161
California	190,145	7,525	8,793	Wichita	2,553	330	480
*Los Angeles	82,083	2,395	1,980	Kentucky	5,601	1,018	897
*San Francisco	5,209	250	406	*Louisville	2,544	280	436
Fresno	19,395	524	1,287	Covington	1,443	220	142
Monterey	5,970	169	147	Lexington	655	360	86
Oakland	10,331	542	695	Owensboro	959	158	233
Orange	16,008	695	653	Louisiana	**11,182	610	1,766
Sacramento	11,168	556	1,063	*#New Orleans	5,845	524	505
San Bernardino	10,483	797	1,078	Alexandria	660	98	129
San Diego	11,100	787	554	Baton Rouge	2,437	184	365
San Jose	8,869	396	369	Houma-Thibodaux	1,489	60	145
Santa Rosa	3,521	159	185	Lafayette	4,856	123	488
Stockton	6,008	255	376	Lake Charles	1,262	85	521
Colorado	15,080	1,778	633	Shreveport	478	60	118
*Denver	11,254	1,244	-	Maine, Portland	2,145	237	226
Colorado Springs	1,526	324	233	Maryland,*Baltimore	7,820	580	831
Pueblo	2,300	210	400	Massachusetts	29,861	3,763	1,057
Connecticut	15,628	478	801	*Boston	18,834	3,419	348
*Hartford	8,177	195	414	Fall River	4,192	80	96
Bridgeport	5,008	138	127	Springfield	2,993	127	382
Norwich+	2,443	145	260	Worcester	3,842	137	231
Delaware, Wilm.+	2,717	206	304	Michigan	23,331	2,465	3,338
D.C., *Washington+	5,420	2,269	750	*Detroit	12,606	1,034	1,748
Florida	38,503	2,791	3,309	Gaylord	818	87	171
*Miami	15,803	750	651	Grand Rapids	2,936	287	-
Orlando	6,693	438	658	Kalamazoo	1,491	374	358
Palm Beach	4,796	352	274	Lansing	3,347	472	714
Pensacola-				Marquette	680	43	128
Tallahassee	877	181	180	Saginaw	1,453	168	219
St. Augustine	2,113	285	501	Minnesota	16,207	792	1,740
St. Petersburg	4,668	606	572	*St. Paul and			
Venice	3,553	179	473	Minneapolis	10,147	432	1,049
Georgia	12,874	1,023	1,803	Crookston	565	14	70
*Atlanta	11,143	825	1,529	Duluth	859	74	109
Savannah	1,731	198	274	New Ulm	964	56	123
Hawaii, Honolulu	2,974	241	223	St. Cloud	2,180	113	214
Idaho, Boise	2,841	266	226	Winona	1,492	103	175
Illinois	62,133	3,087	3,530	Mississippi	1,782	598	549
*Chicago	39,602	1,710	1,500	Biloxi	832	454	220
Belleville	1,183	180	259	Jackson	950	144	329
Joliet	9,753	292	513	Missouri	9,933	3,389	3,731
Peoria	2,855	424	463	*St. Louis	5,838	1,615	-
Rockford	6,660	212	416	Jefferson City	1,334	204	293
Springfield	2,080	269	379	Ks. City-St. Joe	2,099	1,039	3,138
Indiana	12,458	1,569	1,821	Springfield-			
*Indianapolis	4,364	680	675	Cape Girardeau	662	531	300
Evansville	1,224	90	193	Montana	1,375	596	195
Ft. Wayne-S. Bend	2,851	355	365	Great Falls-Billings	831	84	90
Gary	1,940	139	193	Helena	544	512	105

State Diocese	Infant Baptisms	Adult Bapts.	Rec'd into Full Com.	State Diocese	Infant Baptisms	Adult Bapts.	Rec'd into Full Com.
Nebraska	6,596	629	843	Tennessee, cont.			
*Omaha	4,170	368	533	Memphis	1,426	136	237
Grand Island	1,014	129	150	Nashville	1,571	224	345
Lincoln	1,412	132	160	Texas	88,220	10,294	6,871
Nevada	6,942	598	454	*Galv.-Houston	21,687	2,036	973
Las Vegas	5,364	415	327	*San Antonio	10,963	652	678
Reno	1,578	183	127	Amarillo	1,340	84	111
New Hampshire				Austin	7,300	509	845
Manchester	3,282	133	355	Beaumont	1,374	86	229
New Jersey	47,254	2,000	8,453	Brownsville	3,989	4,380	635
*Newark	16,967	532	564	Corpus Christi	3,349	187	345
Camden	6,559	534	544	Dallas	16,860	792	718
Metuchen	5,895	122	350	El Paso	5,046	244	283
Paterson	8,058	156	215	Fort Worth	6,524	421	588
Trenton	9,775	656	780	Laredo	2,964	137	765
New Mexico	8,700	754	1,499	Lubbock	1,564	214	200
*Santa Fe	5,899	345	1,284	San Angelo	1,783	245	162
Gallup	753	218	134	Tyler	2,075	226	254
Las Cruces	2,048	191	81	Victoria	1,402	81	76
New York	87,484	3,826	3,531	Utah, Salt Lake City	3,528	364	377
*New York	29,461	913	1,129	Vermont, Burlington	1,256	87	90
Albany	4,350	300	175	Virginia	11,499	1,309	729
Brooklyn	19,143	761	606	Arlington	7,609	784	361
Buffalo	5,338	436	407	Richmond	3,890	525	368
Ogdensburg	1,316	324	91	Washington	11,666	1,573	945
Rochester	3,699	240	273	*Seattle	6,949	1,094	589
Rockville Centre	19,830	623	319	Spokane	1,511	369	-
Syracuse	4,347	229	531	Yakima	3,206	110	356
North Carolina	10,286	749	1,192	West Virginia			
Charlotte	4,616	258	548	Wheeling-Chas.	968	276	269
Raleigh	5,670	491	644	Wisconsin	19,784	925	1,517
North Dakota	2,082	106	302	*Milwaukee	8,686	349	549
Bismarck	873	58	111	Green Bay	4,307	167	229
Fargo	1,209	48	191	La Crosse	2,482	115	281
Ohio	25,329	3,467	3,264	Madison	3,325	77	269
*Cincinnati	6,806	756	861	Superior	984	217	189
Cleveland	8,679	844	693	Wyoming, Chey.+	901	129	182
Columbus	3,738	467	645	Eastern Churches	3,823	151	320
Steubenville	534	175	101	*Philadelphia	224	15	29
Toledo	3,181	1,004	565	St. Nicholas	201	4	-
Youngstown	2,391	221	399	Stamford	140	1	-
Oklahoma	3,894	444	898	St. Josaphat (Parma)	75	9	-
*Okla. City	2,340	301	593	*Pittsburgh	202	19	53
Tulsa	1,554	143	305	Parma	106	11	35
Oregon	6,524	740	591	Passaic	225	6	24
*Portland	5,618	600	547	Van Nuys	60	5	13
Baker	906	140	44	St. Maron (Maronites)	408	24	60
Pennsylvania	36,882	2,948	2,378	Our Lady of Lebanon			
*Philadelphia	15,187	1,153	513	(Maronites)	352	19	77
Allentown	3,602	134	-	Newton (Melkites)	332	19	16
Altoona-Johnstn.	1,289	108	103	St. Peter the Apostle	303	6	-
Erie	1,724	190	108	St. Thomas Apostle of			
Greensburg	1,609	112	220	Detroit(Chaldeans)	871	-	-
Harrisburg	2,966	401	446	St. Thomas (Syro-Mal.)	123	1	7
Pittsburgh	6,738	292	738	St. George Martyr			
Scranton	3,767	558	250	(Romanian)	29	3	-
Rhode Island				Our Lady of Deliverance (Syrians,			
Providence	4,874	201	260	U.S.-Can.)	54	6	6
South Carolina				Arme. Ex. (U.S.-Can.)	118	3	-
Charleston	2,247	1,023	518	Military Archd.	3,573	862	380
South Dakota	2,270	123	304	Outlying Areas	29,778	4,225	3,620
Rapid City	694	41	84				
Sioux Falls	1,576	82	220	Total 2006	943,264	80,817	73,684
Tennessee	4,020	496	890	Total 2005	977,578	73,405	81,720
Knoxville	1,023	136	308				

The Catholic Church in Canada

Background

The first date in the remote background of the Catholic history of Canada is July 7, 1534, when a priest in the exploration company of Jacques Cartier celebrated Mass on the Gaspe Peninsula.

Successful colonization and the significant beginnings of the Catholic history of the country date from the foundation of Québec in 1608 by Samuel de Champlain and French settlers. Montréal was established in 1642.

The earliest missionaries were Franciscan Récollets (Recollects) and Jesuits who arrived in 1615 and 1625, respectively. They provided some pastoral care for the settlers but worked mainly among the 100,000 Indians — Algonquins, Hurons and Iroquois — in the interior and in the Lake Ontario region. Eight of the Jesuit missionaries, killed in the 1640s, were canonized in 1930. (*See* Index: **Jesuit North American Martyrs.**) Sulpician Fathers, who arrived in Canada late in the 1640s, played a part in the great missionary period, which ended about 1700.

Kateri Tekakwitha, "Lily of the Mohawks," who was baptized in 1676 and died in 1680, was declared "Blessed" on June 22, 1980.

The communities of women religious with the longest histories in Canada are the Canonesses of St. Augustine and the Ursulines, since 1639; and the Hospitallers of St. Joseph, since 1642. Communities of Canadian origin are the Congregation of Notre Dame, founded by St. Marguerite Bourgeoys in 1658, and the Grey Nuns, formed by St. Marie Marguerite d'Youville in 1737.

Mother Marie (Guyard) of the Incarnation, an Ursuline nun, was one of the first three women missionaries to New France; called "Mother of the Church in Canada," she was declared "Blessed" on June 22, 1980.

Start of Church Organization

Ecclesiastical organization began with the appointment in 1658 of François De Montmorency-Laval, "Father of the Church in Canada," as vicar apostolic of New France. He was the first bishop of Québec from 1674 to 1688, with jurisdiction over all French-claimed territory in North America. He was declared "Blessed" on June 22, 1980.

In 1713, the French Canadian population numbered 18,000. In the same year, the Treaty of Utrecht ceded Acadia, Newfoundland and the Hudson Bay Territory to England. The Acadians were scattered among the American colonies in 1755.

The English acquired possession of Canada and its 70,000 French-speaking inhabitants by virtue of the Treaty of Paris in 1763. Anglo-French and Anglican-Catholic differences and tensions developed. The pro-British government at first refused to recognize the titles of church officials, hindered the clergy in their work and tried to install a non-Catholic educational system. Laws were passed that guaranteed religious liberties to Catholics (Québec Act of 1774, Constitutional Act of 1791, legislation approved by Queen Victoria in 1851), but it took some time before actual respect for these liberties matched the legal enactments. The initial moderation of government antipathy toward the Church was caused partly by the loyalty of Catholics to the Crown during the American Revolution and the War of 1812.

Growth

The 15 years following the passage in 1840 of the Act of Union, which joined Upper and Lower Canada, were significant. New communities of men and women religious joined those already in the country. The Oblates of Mary Immaculate, missionaries par excellence in Canada, advanced the penetration of the West that had been started in 1818 by Abbé Provencher. New jurisdictions were established, and Québec became a metropolitan see in 1844. The first Council of Québec was held in 1851. The established Catholic school system enjoyed a period of growth.

Laval University was inaugurated in 1854 and canonically established in 1876.

Abp. Elzear-Alexandre Taschereau of Québec was named Canada's first cardinal in 1886.

The apostolic delegation to Canada was set up in 1899. It became a nunciature October 16, 1969, with the establishment of diplomatic relations with the Vatican. The present Apostolic Nuncio is Abp. Luigi Ventura, appointed on June 22, 2001.

Early in this century, Canada had eight ecclesiastical provinces, 23 dioceses, three vicariates apostolic, 3,500 priests, 2 million Catholics, about 30 communities of men religious, and 70 or more communities of women religious. The Church in Canada was phased out of mission status and removed from the jurisdiction of the Congregation for the Propagation of the Faith in 1908.

Diverse Population

The greatest concentration of Catholics is in the eastern portion of the country. In the northern and western portions, outside metropolitan centers, there are some of the most difficult parish and mission areas in the world. Bilingual (English-French) differences in the general population are reflected in the Church; for example, in the parallel structures of the Canadian Conference of Catholic Bishops, which was established in 1943. Québec is the center of French cultural influence. Many language groups are represented among Catholics, who include more than 257,000 members of Eastern Rites in one metropolitan see, seven eparchies and an apostolic exarchate.

Education, a past source of friction between the Church and the government, is administered by the civil provinces in a variety of arrangements authorized by the Canadian Constitution. Denominational schools have tax support in one way in Québec and Newfoundland, and in another way in Alberta, Ontario and Saskatchewan. Several provinces provide tax support only for public schools, making private financing necessary for separate church-related schools.

ECCLESIASTICAL JURISDICTIONS OF CANADA

Provinces

Names of ecclesiastical provinces and metropolitan sees in bold face; suffragan sees in parentheses.

Edmonton (Calgary, St. Paul).

Gatineau-Hull (Amos, Mont-Laurier, Rouyn Noranda).

Grouard-McLennan (Mackenzie-Ft. Smith, Prince George, Whitehorse).

Halifax (Antigonish, Charlottetown, Yarmouth).

Keewatin-LePas (Churchill-Hudson Bay, Labrador-Schefferville, Moosonee).

Kingston (Alexandria-Cornwall, Peterborough, Sault Ste. Marie).

Moncton (Bathurst, Edmundston, St. John).

Montréal (Joliette, St. Jean-Longueuil, St. Jerome, Valleyfield).

Ottawa (Hearst, Pembroke, Timmins).

Québec (Chicoutimi, Ste.-Anne-de-la-Pocatiere, Trois Rivieres).

Regina (Prince Albert, Saskatoon, Abbey of St. Peter).

Rimouski (Baie-Comeau, Gaspe).

St. Boniface (no suffragan).

St. John's (Grand Falls, St. George).

Sherbrooke (Nicolet, St. Hyacinthe).

Toronto (Hamilton, London, St. Catharines, Thunder Bay).

Vancouver (Kamloops, Nelson, Victoria).

Winnipeg-Ukrainian (Edmonton, New Westminster, Saskatoon, Toronto).

Jurisdictions immediately subject to the Holy See: Roman-Rite Archdiocese of Winnipeg, Byzantine Eparchy of Sts. Cyril and Methodius for Slovaks, Byzantine Eparchy of St. Sauveur de Montréal for Greek Melkites; Antiochene Eparchy of St. Maron of Montréal for Maronites.

JURISDICTIONS, HIERARCHY

(Principal sources: Information office, Canadian Conference of Catholic Bishops; Rev. Mr. William Kokesch, Dir., Communications Service, Canadian Conference of Catholic Bishops; Annuaire, Conférence des Évêques Catholiques du Canada; Catholic Almanac survey; Annuario Pontificio; L'Osservatore Romano; Catholic News Service. As of June 1, 2006.)

Information includes names of archdioceses (indicated by asterisk) and dioceses, date of foundation, present ordinaries and auxiliaries; addresses of chancery office/bishop's residence; cathedral.

Alexandria-Cornwall, ON (1890 as Alexandria; name changed to Alexandria-Cornwall, 1976): Paul-André Durocher, bishop, 2002.

Diocesan Center: 220, chemin Montréal, C.P. 1388, Cornwall, ON K6H 5V4; (613) 933-1138; www.alexandria cornwall.ca/. Cathedral: St. Finnans (Alexandria); Nativity Co-Cathedral (Cornwall).

Amos, QC (1938): Eugène Tremblay, bishop, 2004.

Bishop's Residence: 450, rue Principale Nord, Amos, QC J9T 2M1; (819) 732-6515; www.dioceseamos.org. Cathedral: St. Teresa of Ávila.

Antigonish, NS (Arichat, 1844; transferred, 1886): Raymond J. Lahey, bishop, 2003.

Chancery Office: 168 Hawthorne St., P.O. Box 1330, Antigonish, NS B2G 2L7; (902) 863-3335; www.antigonish diocese.com/title.htm. Cathedral: St. Ninian.

Baie-Comeau, QC (p.a., 1882; v.a., 1905; diocese Gulf of St. Lawrence, 1945; name changed to Hauterive, 1960; president title, 1986): Pierre Morissette, bishop, 1990.

Bishop's Residence: 639, rue de Bretagne, Baie-Comeau, QC G5C 1X2; (418) 589-5744; www.diocese-bc.org. Cathedral: Paroisse St. Jean-Eudes.

Bathurst, NB (Chatham, 1860; transferred, 1938): Valéry Vienneau, bishop, 2002.

Bishop's Residence: 645, avenue Murray, C.P. 460, Bathurst, NB E2A 3Z4; (506) 546-1420; www.diocese bathurst.com. Cathedral: Sacred Heart of Jesus.

Calgary, AB (1912): Frederick Henry, bishop, 1997.

Address: Room 290, The Iona Building, 120 17 Ave. SW, Calgary, AB T2S 2T2; (403) 218-5526; www.rcdiocese-cal-gary.ab.ca. Cathedral: St. Mary.

Charlottetown, PEI (1829): Joseph Vernon Fougere, bishop, 1992.

Bishop's Residence: P.O. Box 907, Charlottetown, PEI C1A 7L9; (902) 368-8005; www.dioceseofchar-lottetown/com. Cathedral: St. Dunstan's.

Chicoutimi, QC (1878): André Rivest, bishop, 2004. Roch Pedneault, aux.

Bishop's Residence: 602, Racine Est, Chicoutimi, QC G7H 6J6; (418) 543-0783; www.evechedechicoutimi.qc.ca. Cathedral: St. Francois-Xavier.

Churchill-Hudson Bay, MB (p.a., 1925; v.a. Hudson Bay, 1931; diocese of Churchill, 1967; present title, 1968): Reynald Rouleau, O.M.I., bishop, 1987.

Diocesan Office: P.O. Box 10, Churchill, MB R0B 0E0; (204) 675-2252. Cathedral: Holy Canadian Martyrs.

Edmonton,* AB (St. Albert, 1871; archdiocese, transferred Edmonton, 1912): Thomas C. Collins, archbishop, 1999.

Archdiocese Office: 8421-101 Avenue, Edmonton, Alta. T6A 0L1; (780) 469-1010; www.edmonton-catholic-church.com. Cathedral: Basilica of St. Joseph.

Edmonton, AB (Ukrainian Byzantine) (ap. ex. of western Canada, 1948; eparchy, 1956): vacant.

Eparch's Residence: 9645 108th Ave., Edmonton, Alta. T5H 1A3; (780) 424-5496. Cathedral: St. Josaphat.

Edmundston, NB (1944): François Thibodeau, C.J.M., bishop, 1994.

Diocesan Center: 60, rue Bouchard, Edmundston,

NB E3V 3K1; (506) 735-5578; www.diocese-edmunston.ca. Cathedral: Immaculate Conception.

Gaspé, QC (1922): Jean Gagnon, bishop, 2002.
Bishop's House: 172, rue Jacques-Cartier, Gaspé, QC G4X 1M9; (418) 368-2274; www.gaspesie.net/diocesegaspe. Cathedral: Christ the King.

Gatineau-Hull,* QC (1963, as Hull; name changed, 1982; archdiocese, 1990): Roger Ébacher, bishop, 1988; first archbishop, Oct. 31, 1990.
Diocesan Center: 180 Boulevard Mont-Bleu, Hull, QC J8Z 3J5; (819) 771-8391; www.diocesegatineau hull.qc.ca.

Grand Falls, NL (Harbour Grace, 1856; present title, 1964): Martin W. Currie, bishop, 2000.
Chancery Office: 8A Church Rd., P.O. Box 771, Grand Falls-Windsor, NL A2A 2M4; (709) 489-2778; www.rcdiocesegrandfalls.net/. Cathedral: Immaculate Conception.

Grouard-McLennan,* AB (v.a. Athabaska-Mackenzie, 1862; Grouard, 1927; archdiocese Grouard-McLennan, 1967); Arthé Guimond, archbishop, 2000.
Archbishop's Residence: 210-1 Street West, C.P. 388, McLennan, AB T0H 2L0; (780) 324-3820. Cathedral: St. Jean-Baptiste (McLennan).

Halifax,* NS (1842; archdiocese, 1852): Terrence Prendergast, S.J., archbishop, 1998. Claude Champagne, auxiliary.
Chancery Office: 1531 Grafton St., P.O. Box 1527, Halifax, NS B3J 2Y3; (902) 429-9800; www.catholic halifax.org.

Hamilton, ON (1856): Anthony Tonnos, bishop, 1984. Matthew Ustrzycki, Gerard Paul Bergie, auxiliaries.
Chancery Office: 700 King St. West, Hamilton, ON L8P 1C7; (905) 528-7988; www.hamiltondiocese.com/. Cathedral: Christ the King.

Hearst, ON (p.a., 1918; v.a., 1920; diocese, 1938): vacant.
Bishop's Residence: 76 7e rue, C.P. 1330, Hearst, ON P0L 1N0; (705) 362-4903; www.hearstdiocese.com. Cathedral: Notre Dame of the Assumption.

Joliette, QC (1904): Gilles Lussier, bishop, 1991.
Bishop's Residence: 2 rue Saint-Charles-Borromée Nord, C.P. 470, Joliette, QC J6E 6H6; (450) 753-7596; www.diocesedejoliette.org. Cathedral: St. Charles Borromeo.

Kamloops, BC (1945): David Monroe, bishop, 2002.
Bishop's Residence: 635-A Tranquille Rd., Kamloops, BC V2B 3H5; (250) 376-3351. Cathedral: Sacred Heart.

Keewatin-Le Pas,* MB (v.a., 1910; archdiocese, 1967): Sylvain Lavoie, O.M.I., archbishop, 2006.
Archbishop's Residence: 76 1st St. W., P.O. Box 270, The Pas, MB R9A 1K4; (204) 623-6152. Cathedral: Our Lady of the Sacred Heart.

Kingston,* ON (1826; archdiocese, 1889): Anthony Meagher, archbishop, 2002.
Chancery Office: 390 Palace Rd., Kingston, ON K7L 4T3; (613) 548-4461; www.romancatholic.kingston.on.ca. Cathedral: St. Mary of the Immaculate Conception.

Labrador City-Schefferville, QC (v.a. Labrador, 1946; diocese, 1967): Douglas Crosby, O.M.I., bishop, 1997.
Bishop's Residence: Sutton House, 320 avenue Elizabeth,

C.P. 545, Labrador City, Labrador, NL A2V 2L3; (709) 944-2046; www.labdiocese.com. Cathedral: Our Lady of Perpetual Help.

London, ON (1855; transferred Sandwich, 1859; London, 1869): Ronald P. Fabbro, C.S.B., bishop, 2002. Robert Anthony Daniels, auxiliary.
Bishop's Residence: 1070 Waterloo St., London, ON N6A 3Y2; (519) 433-0658; www.rcec.london.on.ca. Cathedral: St. Peter's Cathedral Basilica.

Mackenzie-Fort Smith, NT (v.a. Mackenzie, 1902; diocese Mackenzie-Fort Smith, 1967): Denis Croteau, O.M.I., bishop, 1986.
Diocesan Office: 5117 - 52nd St., Yellowknife, NT X1A 1T7; (867) 920-2129. Cathedral: St. Joseph (Ft. Smith).

Moncton,* NB (1936):André Richard, C.S.C., archbishop, 2002.
Archbishop's Residence: 452, rue Amirault, Dieppe, NB E1A 1G3; (506) 857-9531. Cathedral: Our Lady of the Assumption.

Mont-Laurier, QC (1913): Vital Massé, bishop, 2001.
Bishop's Residence: 435, rue de la Madone, Mont-Laurier, QC J9L 1S1; (819) 623-5530. Cathedral: Notre Dame de Fourvières.

Montréal,* QC (1836; archdiocese, 1886): Card. Jean-Claude Turcotte, archbishop, 1990. Anthony Mancini, Lionel Gendron, P.S.S., André Gazaille, auxiliaries.
Archbishop's Residence: 2000, rue Sherbrooke Ouest, Montréal, QC H3H 1G4; (514) 931-7311; www.diocesemontreal.org. Cathedral: Basilica of Mary Queen of the World and Saint James.

Montréal, QC (Sauveur de Montréal, Eparchy of Greek Melkites) (ap. ex. 1980; eparchy, 1984): Ibrahim M. Ibrahim, 2003.
Address: 34 rue Maplewood, Montréal, QC H2V 2MI; (514) 272-6430.

Montréal, QC (St. Maron of Montréal, Maronites) (1982): Joseph Khoury, eparch, 1996.
Chancery Office: 12 475 rue Grenet, Montréal, QC H4J 2K4; (514) 331-2807. Cathedral: St. Maron.

Moosonee, ON (v.a. James Bay, 1938; diocese Moosonee, 1967): Vincent Cadieux, O.M.I., bishop, 1992.
Bishop's Residence: 2 Bay Rd., C.P. 40, Moosonee, ON P0L 1Y0; (705) 336-2908. Cathedral: Christ the King.

Nelson, BC (1936): Eugene J. Cooney, bishop, 1996.
Bishop's Residence: 402 West Richards St., Nelson, BC VIL 3K3; (250) 354-6921; www.diocese.nelson.bc.ca/. Cathedral: Mary Immaculate.

New Westminster, BC (Ukrainian Byzantine) (1974): Severian Stephen Yakymyshyn, O.S.B.M., eparch, 1995.
Eparch's address: 502 5th Ave., New Westminster, BC V3L 1S2; (604) 524-8824; www.vcn.bc.ca/ucep-nw.

Nicolet, QC (1885): Raymond Saint-Gelais, bishop, 1989.
Bishop's Residence: 49, rue Mgr Brunault, Nicolet, QC J3T 1X7; (819) 293-4696. Cathedral: St. Jean-Baptiste.

Ottawa,* ON (Bytown, 1847, name changed, 1854; archdiocese, 1886): Marcel A.J. Gervais, archbishop, 1989.

Archbishop's Residence: 1247 Place Kilborn, Ottawa, ON K1H 6K9; (613) 738-5025; www.ecclesia-ottawa.org. Cathedral: Basilica of Notre Dame-of-Ottawa.

Pembroke, ON (v.a. 1882; diocese, 1898): Richard Smith, bishop, 2002.

Bishop's Residence: 188 Renfrew St., P.O. Box 7, Pembroke, ON K8A 6X1; (613) 732-7933; www.diocesepembroke.org. Cathedral: St. Columbkille.

Peterborough, ON (1882): Nicola De Angelis, C.F.I.C., bishop, 2002.

Bishop's Residence: 350 Hunter St. West, P.O. Box 175, Peterborough, ON K9J 6Y8; (705) 745-5123; www.peterboroughdiocese.org. Cathedral: St. Peter-in-Chains.

Prince Albert, SK (v.a., 1890; diocese, 1907): Blaise Morand, bishop, 1983.

Address: 1415 4th Ave. West, Prince Albert, SK S6V 5H1; (306) 922-4747; www.padiocese.sk.ca. Cathedral: Sacred Heart.

Prince George, BC (p.a., 1908; v.a. Yukon and Prince Rupert, 1944; diocese Prince George, 1967): Gerald Wiesner, O.M.I., bishop, 1993.

Chancery Office: 6500 Southbridge Ave., P.O. Box 7000, Prince George, BC V2N 3Z2; (250) 964-4424; www.pgdiocese.bc.ca. Cathedral: Sacred Heart.

Québec,* QC (v.a., 1658; diocese, 1674; archdiocese, 1819; metropolitan, 1844; primatial see, 1956): Cardinal Marc Ouellet, P.S.S., archbishop, 2002. Jean Pierre Blais, Pierre-André Fournier, Gilles Lemay, auxiliaries.

Chancery Office: 1073, boul. René-Lévesque ouest, Québec, QC G1S 4R5; (418) 688-1211; www.diocesequebec.qc.ca/. Cathedral: Notre-Dame- de-Québec (Basilica).

Regina,* SK (1910; archdiocese, 1915): Daniel Bohan, archbishop, 2005.

Chancery Office: 445 Broad St. North, Regina, SK S4R 2X8; (306) 352-1651; www.archregina.sk.ca. Cathedral: Our Lady of the Most Holy Rosary.

Rimouski,* QC (1867; archdiocese, 1946): Bertrand Blanchet, archbishop, 1992.

Archbishop's Residence: 34, rue de l'Évêché Ouest, C.P. 730, Rimouski, QC G5L 7C7; (418) 723-3320; www.dioceserimouski.com.

Rouyn-Noranda, QC (1973): Dorylas Moreau, bishop, 2001.

Bishop's Residence: 515, avenue Cuddihy, C.P. 1060, Rouyn-Noranda, QC J9X 4C5; (819) 764-4660; www.dioc-cath-rouyn-noranda.org. Cathedral: St. Michael the Archangel.

Saint-Boniface,* MB (1847; archdiocese, 1871): Émilius Goulet, P.S.S.

Archbishop's Residence: 151, avenue de la Cathédrale, Saint-Boniface, MB R2H 0H6; (204) 237-9851. Cathedral: Basilica of St. Boniface.

St. Catharine's, ON (1958): James M. Wingle, bishop, 2001.

Bishop's Residence: P.O. Box 875, St. Catharines, ON L2R 6Y3; (905) 684-0154; www.roman catholic.niagara.on.ca. Cathedral: St. Catherine of Alexandria.

St. George's, NL (p.a., 1870; v.a., 1890; diocese, 1904): Douglas Crosby, O.M.I., bishop, 2003 (also bp. of Labrador City-Schefferville).

Bishop's Residence: 13 Mount Bernard, Corner Brook, NL

A2H 6K6; (709) 639-7073; www.rcchurch.com. Cathedral: Most Holy Redeemer and Immaculate Conception.

Saint-Hyacinthe, QC (1852): François Lapierre, P.M.E., bishop, 1998.

Bishop's Residence: 1900, rue Girouard Ouest, C.P. 190, Saint-Hyacinthe, QC J2S 7B4; (450) 773-8581; www.diocese-st-hyacinthe.qc.ca. Cathedral: St. Hyacinthe the Confessor.

Saint-Jean-Longueuil, QC (1933 as St.-Jean-de-Québec; named changed, 1982): Jacques Berthelet, C.S.V., bishop, 1996. Louis Dicaire, auxiliary.

Bishop's Residence: 740, boulevard Sainte-Foy, C.P. 40, Longueuil, QC J4K 4X8; (450) 679-1100; www.diocese-st-jean-longueuil.org. Cathedral: St. John the Evangelist.

St. Jérôme, QC (1951): Gilles Cazabon, O.M.I., bishop, 1998; Donald Lapointe, auxiliary.

Bishop's Residence: 355, Place du Curé Labelle, Saint-Jerome, QC J7Z 5A9; (450) 432-9742; www.diocese-st jerome.qc.ca. Cathedral: St. Jerome.

Saint John, NB (1842): Joseph Faber MacDonald, bishop, 1998.

Chancery Office: 1 Bayard Dr., Saint John, NB E2L 3L5; (506) 653-6800; www.dioceseofsaintjohn.org. Cathedral: Immaculate Conception.

St. John's,* NL (p.a., 1784; v.a., 1796; diocese, 1847; archdiocese, 1904): Brendan Michael O'Brien, archbishop, 2000.

Chancery Office: P.O. Box 37, St. John's, NL. A1C 5N5; (709) 726-3660; www.stjohnsarchdiocese.nf.ca. Cathedral: St. John the Baptist.

St. Paul in AB (1948): Joseph Luc André Bouchard, bishop, 2001.

Bishop's Residence: 4410, 51e avenue, Saint Paul, AB T0A 3A2; (780) 645-3277. Cathedral: St. Paul.

Sainte-Anne-de-la-Pocatière, QC (1951): Clément Fecteau, bishop, 1996.

Bishop's Residence: 1200, 4e avenue, C.P. 430, La Pocatière, QC G0R 1Z0; (418) 856-1811. Cathedral: St. Anne.

Saskatoon, SK (1933): Albert LeGatt, 2001.

Chancery Office: 100-5th Ave. North, Saskatoon, SK S7K 2N7; (306) 242-1500; www.saskatoonrcdiocese.com. Cathedral: St. Paul.

Saskatoon, SK (Ukrainian Byzantine) (ap. ex., 1951; diocese, 1956): Michael Wiwchar, C.Ss.R., 2000.

Address: 866 Saskatchewan Crescent East, Saskatoon, SK S7N 0L4; (306) 653-0138.

Sault Ste. Marie, ON (1904): Jean-Louis Plouffe, bishop, 1990; Robert Harris, auxiliary.

Chancery Office: 30, chemin Ste. Anne, Sudbury, ON P3C 5E1, (705) 674-2727; www.isys.ca/cath-com.htm. Cathedral: Pro-Cathedral of the Assumption, North Bay.

Sherbrooke,* QC (1874; archdiocese, 1951); André Gaumond, archbishop, 1996.

Archbishop's Residence: 130, rue de la Cathédrale, C.P. 430, Sherbrooke, QC J1H 5K1; (819) 563-9934; www.diosher.org. Cathedral: St. Michel.

Thunder Bay, ON (Ft. William, 1952; transferred, 1970): Frederick J. Colli, bishop, 1999.

Bishop's Office: 1222 Reaume St., P.O. Box 10400, Thunder Bay, ON P7B 6T8; (807) 343-9313; www.dotb.ca. Cathedral: St. Patrick.

Timmins, ON (v.a. Temiskaming, 1908; diocese

Haileybury, 1915; present title, 1938): Paul Marchand, S.M.M., bishop, 1999.

Address: 65, Ave. Jubilee Est, Timmins, ON P4N 5W4; www.nt.net/~dioctims/. Cathedral: St. Anthony of Padua.

Toronto,* ON (1841; archdiocese, 1870): Cardinal Aloysius M. Ambrozic, archbishop, 1990. John A. Boissonneau, Richard Grecco, Peter Joseph Hundt, auxiliaries.

Chancery Office: Catholic Pastoral Centre, 1155 Yonge St., Toronto, ON M4T 1W2; (416) 934-0606; www.archtoronto.org. Cathedral: St. Michael.

Toronto, ON (Eparchy for Slovakian Byzantine) (1980): John Pazak, C.Ss.R., 2000.

Eparch's Residence: 223 Carlton Rd., Unionville, ON L3R 3M2; (905) 477-4867.

Toronto, ON (Eparchy for Ukrainian Byzantine) (ap. ex., 1948; eparchy, 1956): Isidore Borecky (exarch 1948-56), first eparch, 1956. Stephen Victor Chmilar eparch, 2003.

Chancery Office: 3100-A Weston Rd., Weston, ON M9M 2S7; (416) 746-0154; www.ucet.ca. Cathedral: St. Josaphat.

Trois-Rivières, QC (1852): Martin Veillette, bishop, 1996.

Bishop's Residence: 362, rue Bonaventure, C.P. 879, Trois-Rivières, QC G9A 5J9; (819) 374-9847; www.diocese-tr.qc.ca/. Cathedral: The Assumption.

Valleyfield, QC (1892): Luc Cyr, bishop, 2001.

Bishop's Residence: 11, rue de l'Eglise, Salaberry-de-Valleyfield, QC J6T 1J5; (450) 373-8122; www.rocler.qc.ca/diocese-valleyfield/. Cathedral: St. Cecilia.

Vancouver,* BC (v.a. British Columbia, 1863; diocese New Westminster, 1890; archdiocese Vancouver, 1908): Raymond Roussin, S.M., archbishop, 2004.

Chancery Office: 150 Robson St., Vancouver, BC V6B 2A7; (604) 683-0281; www.rcav.bc.ca. Cathedral: Holy Rosary.

Victoria, BC (diocese Vancouver Is., 1846; archdiocese, 1903; diocese Victoria, 1908): Richard Gagnon, 2004.

Chancery Office: Diocesan Pastoral Centre, #1-4044 Nelthorpe St., Victoria, BC V8X 2A1; (250) 479-1331; www.rcdvictoria.org. Cathedral: St. Andrew.

Whitehorse, YT (v.a., 1944; diocese 1967): Gary Gordon, bishop, 2006.

Chancery Office: 5119 5th Ave., Whitehorse, YT Y1A 1L5; (867) 667-2052. Cathedral: Sacred Heart.

Winnipeg,* MB (1915): V. James Weisberger, archbishop, 2000.

Chancery Office: Catholic Centre, 1495 Pembina Highway, Winnipeg, MB R3T 2C6; (204) 452-2227; www.archwinnipeg.ca. Cathedral: St. Mary.

Winnipeg,* MB (Ukrainian Byzantine) (Ordinariate of Canada, 1912; ap. ex. Central Canada, 1948; ap. ex. Manitoba, 1951; archeparchy Winnipeg, 1956):

Lawrence Huculak, O.S.B.M., archeparch, 1993; David Motiuk, auxiliary.

Archeparchy Office: 233 Scotia St., Winnipeg, MB R2V 1V7; (204) 338-7801; www.archeparchy.ca. Cathedral: Sts. Vladimir and Olga.

Yarmouth, NS (1953): vacant.

Address: C.P. 278, Yarmouth, NS B5A 4B2; (902) 742-7163; www.dioceseyarmouth.org. Cathedral: St. Ambrose.

Military Ordinariate of Canada (1951):Donald J. Thériault, bishop, 1998.

Address: Canadian Forces Support Unit (Ottawa), Uplands Site – Bldg. 469, Ottawa, ON K1A 0K2; (613) 990-7824.

An Apostolic Exarchate for Armenian-Rite Catholics in Canada and the United States was established in July 1981 with headquarters in New York City (110 E. 12th St., New York, NY 10003); (212) 477-2030. Manuel Batakian, exarch, 1995.

The Eparchy of Our Lady of Deliverance of Newark for Syrian-rite Catholics in the United States and Canada was established Nov. 6, 1995. Address: 502 Palisade Ave., Union City, NJ 08087-5213; (201) 583-1067; www.Syriac-Catholic.org. Joseph Younan, bishop.

Hungarian Emigrants throughout the world, resides in Canada: Most Rev. Attila Mikloshazy, S.J., titular bishop of Cast'el Minore. Address: 2661 Kingston Rd., Scarborough, ON M1M 1M3; (416) 261-7207.

Note: The diocese of Gravelbourg, in Saskatchewan, was dissolved in September 1998 as part of a reorganization of Canadian dioceses. The regions under the jurisdiction of Gravelbourg were integrated into the neighboring dioceses of Regina and Saskatoon. The Territorial Abbacy of St. Peter, Muenster, SK, was also dissolved.

Dioceses with Interprovincial Lines

The following dioceses, indicated by + in the table, have interprovincial lines.

Churchill-Hudson Bay includes part of Northwest Territories.

Keewatin-LePas includes part of Manitoba and Saskatchewan provinces.

Labrador City-Schefferville includes the Labrador region of Newfoundland and the northern part of Québec province.

Mackenzie-Fort Smith, Northwest Territories, includes part of Alberta and Saskatchewan provinces.

Moosonee, Ontario, includes part of Québec province.

Pembroke, Ontario, includes one county of Québec province.

Whitehorse, Yukon Territory, includes part of British Columbia.

CANADIAN CONFERENCE OF CATHOLIC BISHOPS

The Canadian Conference of Catholic Bishops was established Oct. 12, 1943, as a permanent voluntary association of the bishops of Canada, was given official approval by the Holy See in 1948, and acquired the status of an episcopal conference after the Second Vatican Council.

The CCCB acts in two ways: (1) as a strictly ecclesiastical body through which the bishops act together with pastoral authority and responsibility for the Church throughout the country; (2) as an operational secretariat through which the bishops act on a wider scale for the good of the Church and society.

At the top of the CCCB organizational table are the president, an executive committee, a permanent council and a plenary assembly. The membership consists of all the bishops of Canada.

Departments and Offices

The CCCB's work is planned and coordinated by the Programmes and Priorities Committee composed of the six chairmen of the national episcopal commissions and the two general secretaries. It is chaired by the vice-president of the CCCB.

The CCCB's 12 episcopal commissions undertake study and projects in special areas of pastoral work. Six serve nationally (social affairs; canon law/inter-rite; relations with associations of clergy, consecrated life and laity; evangelization of peoples; ecumenism; theology); three relate to French sectors (*communications sociale, éducation Chrétienne, liturgie*); and three relate to corresponding English sectors (social communications, Christian education, liturgy).

The general secretariat consists of a general secretary and assistants and directors of public relations. The current general secretary is Msgr. Mario Paquette, P.H.

Administrative services for purchasing, archives and library, accounting, personnel, publications, printing and distribution are supervised by directors who relate to the general secretaries.

Various advisory councils and committees with mixed memberships of lay persons, religious, priests and bishops also serve the CCCB on a variety of topics.

Operations

Meetings for the transaction of business are held at least once a year by the plenary assembly, six times a year by the executive committee, and four times a year by the permanent council.

Archbishop André Gaumond of Sherbrooke is president of the CCCB and Archbishop James Weisberger of Winnipeg is vice president, for the 2005-2007 term.

The Conference headquarters is located at 2500 Don Reid Dr., Ottawa K1N 2J2, Canada; (613) 241-9461; www.cccb.ca.

CANADIAN SHRINES

Our Lady of the Cape (Cap de la Madeleine), Queen of the Most Holy Rosary: The Three Rivers, Québec, parish church, built in 1714 and considered the oldest stone church on the North American continent preserved in its original state, was rededicated June 22, 1888, as a shrine of the Queen of the Most Holy Rosary. The site increased in importance as a pilgrimage and devotional center, and in 1904 St. Pius X decreed the crowning of a statue of the Blessed Virgin which had been donated 50 years earlier to commemorate the dogma of the Immaculate Conception. In 1909, the First Plenary Council of Québec declared the church a shrine of national pilgrimage. In 1964, the church at the shrine was given the status and title of minor basilica.

St. Anne de Beaupre: The devotional history of this shrine in Québec began with the reported cure of a cripple, Louis Guimont, on Mar. 16, 1658, the starting date of construction work on a small chapel of St. Anne. The original building was successively enlarged and replaced by a stone church, which was given the rank of minor basilica in 1888. The present structure, a Romanesque-Gothic basilica, houses the shrine proper in its north transept, including an eight-foot-high oaken statue and a relic of St. Anne, a portion of her forearm.

St. Joseph's Oratory: The massive oratory basilica standing on the western side of Mount Royal and overlooking the city of Montréal had its origin in a primitive chapel erected there by Blessed André Bessette, C.S.C., in 1904. Eleven years later, a large crypt was built to accommodate an increasing number of pilgrims, and in 1924 construction work was begun on the large church. A belfry, housing a 60-bell carillon and standing on the site of the original chapel, was dedicated May 15, 1955, as the first major event of the jubilee year observed after the oratory was given the rank of minor basilica.

Martyrs' Shrine: A shrine commemorating several of the Jesuit Martyrs of North America who were killed between 1642 and 1649 in the Ontario and northern New York area is located on the former site of old Fort Sainte Marie. Before its location was fixed near Midland, ON, in 1925, a small chapel had been erected in 1907 at old Mission St. Ignace to mark the martyrdom of Fathers Jean de Brebeuf and Gabriel Lalemant. This sanctuary has a U.S. counterpart in the Shrine of the North American Martyrs near Auriesville, NY, under the care of the Jesuits.

Others

In Québec City: Basilica of Notre Dame (1650), once the cathedral of a diocese stretching from Canada to Mexico; Notre Dame des Victoires (1690); the Ursuline Convent (1720), on du Parloir St.

Near Montréal: Hermitage of St. Anthony, La Bouchette; Ste. Anne de Micmacs, Restigouche; Chapel of Atonement, Pointe aux Trembles; Our Lady of Lourdes, Rigaud; St. Benoît du Lac, near Magog.

In Montréal: Notre Dame Basilica (1829).

Near Montréal: Chapel of St. Marie Marguerite d'Youville, foundress of the Grey Nuns; Notre Dame de Lourdes, at Rigaud.

STATISTICAL SUMMARY OF THE CATHOLIC CHURCH IN CANADA

(Principal source: 2006 Directory of the Canadian Conference of Catholic Bishops; *figures as of Jan. 2006.)* Catholic population statistics are those reported in the 2001 Canadian Census. Archdioceses are indicated by an asterisk. For dioceses marked +, see Canadian Dioceses with Interprovincial Lines.

Canada's 10 civil provinces and two territories are divided into 18 ecclesiastical provinces consisting of 18 metropolitan sees (archdioceses) and 45 suffragan sees; there are also eight Oriental Rite dioceses, one archdiocese and three eparchies immediately subject to the Holy See, and the Military Ordinariate.

This table presents a regional breakdown of Catholic statistics. In some cases, the totals are approximate because diocesan boundaries fall within several civil provinces.

Civil Province Diocese	Cath. Pop.	Dioc. Priests	Rel. Priests	Total Priests	Perm. Deacs.	Brothers	Sisters	Lay Assts.	Parishes[1]
Newfoundland	191,885	103	22	125	-	11	286	14	221
St. John's*	111,605	41	12	52	-	10	211	2	71
Grand Falls	35,850	32	1	33	-	-	26	5	72
Labrador-Schefferville+	12,370	2	8	10	-	1	21	2	23
St. George's	32,060	28	1	29	-	-	28	5	55
Prince Edward Island									
Charlottetown	63,240	51	1	52	-	-	128	1	58
Nova Scotia	327,945	215	34	249	29	5	565	44	238
Halifax*	161,115	63	21	84	28	1	251	25	75
Antigonish	129,730	131	8	139	1	4	297	15	123
Yarmouth	37,100	21	5	26	-	-	17	4	40
New Brunswick	385,985	263	52	315	3	28	711	123	245
Moncton*	110,895	49	26	75	1	21	291	84	60
Bathurst	107,655	52	7	59	-	6	192	7	62
Edmundston	52,035	32	10	42	-	-	102	12	32
St. John	115,400	70	9	79	2	1	126	20	91
Québec	5,922,385	2,476	1,582	4,058	406	1,252	13,271	1,117	1,654
Gatineau-Hull*	234,725	47	32	79	-	8	205	61	61
Montréal*	1,499,425	507	681	1,188	100	284	4,643	123	253
Québec*	917,045	461	320	781	90	235	3,282	185	224
Rimouski*	143,640	110	13	123	10	33	634	16	114
Sherbrooke*	245,495	194	99	293	20	78	976	51	115
Amos	95,030	23	14	37	-	8	95	45	61
Baie Comeau	86,800	41	11	52	8	5	59	20	44
Chicoutimi	263,950	162	25	187	40	34	542	64	70
Gaspé	85,840	53	5	58	4	1	150	12	65
Joliette	201,735	81	52	133	6	92	215	45	56
Mont Laurier	77,340	40	7	47	-	4	62	15	56
Montréal, St. Maron (Maronites)	4,100	9	7	16	1	-	5	-	14
Montréal, St. Sauveur (Greek-Melkites)	9,200	6	8	14	1	-	-	-	8
Nicolet	184,625	138	23	161	24	90	398	43	81
Rouyn-Noranda	56,380	24	8	32	-	1	81	17	40
Ste-Anne-de-la-Pocatière	87,700	100	-	100	7	-	164	16	58
St.-Hyacinthe	336,445	135	65	200	32	173	692	106	100
St.-Jean-Long	553,470	92	36	128	2	98	310	111	53
St. Jérôme	407,065	84	89	173	18	24	161	85	50
Trois Rivières	232,985	102	69	171	30	64	515	56	70
Valleyfield	199,390	67	18	85	13	20	82	46	61
Ontario	3,575,065	850	938	1,788	422	149	2,989	264	1,253
Kingston*	116,845	79	10	89	18	-	183	-	71
Ottawa*	392,635	142	175	317	70	54	825	18	111
Toronto*	1,626,465	385	485	833	111	55	660	61	227
Alexandria-Corn	55,570	39	9	48	17	4	24	2	31
Hamilton	559,290	134	88	222	5	11	290	51	150

Civil Province Diocese	Cath. Pop.	Dioc. Priests	Rel. Priests	Total Priests	Perm. Deacs.	Bro-thers	Sis-ters	Lay Assts.	Par-ishes[1]
Ontario, cont.									
Hearst	31,790	30	-	30	3	-	6	18	28
London	444,310	147	69	216	16	6	473	85	165
Moosonee+	3,830	-	3	3	1	1	4	1	18
Pembroke+	67,870	69	2	71	7	3	165	7	64
Peterborough	99,785	103	7	110	11	-	65	2	75
St. Catharine's	153,565	54	35	89	4	4	39	10	46
Sault Ste. Marie	206,405	91	26	117	103	4	195	2	113
Thunder Bay	73,780	26	15	41	29	-	18	-	42
Timmins	50,605	19	3	22	7	5	15	6	29
Toronto (Ukr.)	42,330	89	9	98	19	2	27	1	76
Toronto (Slovaks)	10,000	3	2	5	1	-	-	-	7
Manitoba	346,180	191	03	294	57	16	487	32	386
Keewatin-Le Pas*+	37,380	5	11	16	-	1	8	13	48
St. Boniface*	113,495	88	48	136	25	13	329	9	98
Winnipeg*	158,095	65	22	87	18	2	122	3	93
Winnipeg (Ukrainians)*	29,760	33	15	48	14	-	26	-	130
Churchill-Hud. Bay+	6,115	-	7	7	-	-	2	7	17
Saskatchewan+	301,335	181	86	267	6	24	437	23	448
Regina*#	126,980	93	17	110	2	7	108	5	167
Prince-Albert	55,450	23	9	32	1	1	90	9	87
Saskatoon#	86,645	43	50	93	-	14	221	9	105
Saskatoon (Ukrainians)	17,550	22	10	32	3	2	18	-	89
Alberta	665,870	211	171	382	38	30	540	71	434
Edmonton*	333,545	75	87	162	2	19	360	52	137
Grouard-McL*	44,470	7	19	28	2	-	23	11	66
Calgary	320,425	87	42	129	26	10	104	-	85
Edmonton (Ukrainians)	28,845	26	16	42	6	1	35	3	87
St. Paul	56,655	16	7	23	2	-	18	5	59
British Columbia	600,175	187	129	316	6	33	264	248	316
Vancouver*	402,310	88	93	181	1	22	130	-	92
Kamloops	51,435	14	7	21	1	3	15	-	79
Nelson	67,025	32	4	36	-	-	20	-	53
New Westminster (Ukrainians)	7,780	12	2	14	2	-	2	-	13
Prince Geo	49,500	12	7	19	1	4	16	248	38
Victoria	94,465	29	16	45	1	4	81	-	41
Yukon Territory									
Whitehorse+	8,150	5	7	12	-	-	7	8	20
Northwest Territories									
MacKenzie-Ft. Smith+	20,110	5	5	10	2	1	13	20	40
Military Ordinariate	43,007	36*	2**	37	1	-	-	38	24**
TOTALS	12,987,637[2]	4,774	3,132	7,906	970	1,549	19,698	2,003	5,337

1. Denotes both parishes and missions.
2. Catholics comprise about 43 percent of the total population. According to the 2004 *Annuarium Statisticum Ecclesiae* (the most recent edition), there were 122,275 baptisms and 28,048 marriages.
* The Canadian Military Ordinariate does not incardinate clerics.
** Not included in the total.

The Catholic Church in Mexico

BACKGROUND

Start of Church Organization

The history of the Catholic Church in Mexico began in 1519 with the capture of Mexico's native civilization, the Aztec Empire, by the Spanish *conquistadores* under Hernándo Cortés. The Spanish army besieged the Aztec capital of Tenochtitlan, massacred most of the inhabitants, strangled the Aztec emperor Montezuma, and crushed the rest of the empire. Mexico City became the chief city of New Spain and the cultural and religious center of colonial Mexico; it was declared a diocese in 1530.

The record of Colonial Spanish treatment of the native peoples of Mexico is a grim one. The Indians suffered exploitation, slavery, and rapid depletion of their population from disease; they were forced to labor in inhuman conditions in mines and endured servitude in the *encomienda* system.

In sharp contrast to the treatment of the natives by the government was the effort to evangelize Mexico by the religious orders, who followed the command of Pope Alexander VI in the 1494 Treaty of Tordesillas to convert all peoples who would be encountered in the coming age of exploration. A papal bull, dated Apr. 25, 1521, gave the Franciscans the permission of the Holy See to preach in New Spain. They were joined by the Dominicans and, later, by the Jesuits. The missionary orders soon distinguished themselves by their resistance to the brutal enslavement of the Indians, their mastery of native languages, and their willingness to endure enormous hardships in bringing the faith to the distant corners of Mexico.

As the Church became more established, however, the missionary priests and friars came increasingly into conflict with the secular clergy, who desired full control over ecclesiastical affairs, resented the extensive powers of religious orders, and normally identified closely with the interests of the crown. The government thus decreed that the missionaries were to have 10 years in which to convert the Indians, after which control would pass to the diocesan clergy. This was protested by the missionary orders, and the conflict was resolved in favor of the diocesan priests in 1640 thanks to the efforts of Bp. Juan de Palafox de Mendoza of Puebla.

The alliance of the secular clergy with the government was a reflection of the control enjoyed by the Spanish Crown over the Church in Mexico. The Holy See had granted to the kings of Spain royal patronage over the Church in Mexico, and the practice of *Patronato Real* meant that the king nominated all Church officials in New Spain and held authority over the Church's temporal concerns. A major element in this policy was the forced conversion of the local peoples. Coerced into adopting the faith, many Indians were insincere or hesitant to embrace the faith. To insure the full embrace of the faith, Spanish authorities received permission from King Philip II in 1569 to introduce the Inquisition to Mexico. Indians who had survived the mines, diseases, and brutality of the colonial rulers were now subjected to tribunals to test their faith. This practice was eventually ended when authorities decided that the natives were not culpable because of limited intelligence. Nevertheless, the close identification of the diocesan clergy with the interests and policies of the Spanish crown created a hostility toward the Church in Mexico by the lower classes that endures today.

On the positive side, the Church did much through its missionaries to save many Indians from death and enslavement and to preserve vital portions of Mesoamerican culture, art, and history. Friars also traveled to northern Mexico and beyond, bringing the faith into California, Texas, and New Mexico.

The native peoples were given a profound encouragement to embrace the Catholic faith in 1531 by the appearance of Our Lady of Guadalupe to the farmer Juan Diego (beatified in 1990 by Pope John Paul II) on the Tepeyac hill just outside of Mexico City. The shrine built in her honor remains the most important religious site in Mexico. Enshrined within it is the mantle brought by Juan Diego to Bishop Zumaragga to convince him of the genuine nature of the apparition. Miraculously emblazoned upon it is the life-size image of the Virgin Mary.

Mexican Independence

The Spanish domination of Mexico endured for nearly three centuries, deteriorating gradually throughout the 1700s as the gulf widened between the Spanish ruling class and the native classes that were joined by the *mestizos* and *creoles* (descendants of Native Americans and Europeans). Unrest broke out into a full-scale rebellion in 1810 with the uprising of many priests led by Fr. Miguel Hidalgo y Costilla and, after his execution, by Fr. José Maria Morelos y Pavón. While suppressed in 1816 by the colonial regime with the support of the upper classes and most of the diocesan clergy, it proved only the first of several revolts, culminating in the 1821 declaration of Mexican independence. By the terms of the independence, the

Church received a special status and had enormous sway in political life.

A republic was proclaimed in 1834 and various liberal regimes came to power. Anticlericalism became commonplace, made even more strident by the lingering hostility over the Church's activities with Spanish colonial government. Much influenced by the ideals of the European revolutions then taking place, the Mexican republican movements were strongly anti-Catholic. For more than a decade, power was in the hands of Antonio López de Santa Anna (also known for his victory at the Alamo) and Valentín Gómez Farías. After the Mexican-American War (1846-1848), the political instability led to the dictatorship of Santa Anna.

Santa Anna was toppled in 1855 by a liberal regime whose anti-Church legislation sparked an armed struggle called the War of the Reform (1858-1861). The laws issued by the government included the *Ley Juárez*, abolishing all ecclesiastical courts, and the *Ley Lerdo*, forcing the Church to sell all of its lands. Deprived of its properties, the Church lost control of education and schools, and Mexico's educational system became often bitterly anti-Catholic.

While the liberal forces won the War of the Reform, the conflict had so debilitated Mexico that the French were able to intervene in 1861 and install their puppet, the Austrian duke Maximilian, on the Mexican throne. As the United States was embroiled in its own civil war from 1861-1865, it was unable to respond to French imperialist ambitions in Mexico. Maximilian initially enjoyed the support of the conservative elements and the Church, but his liberal reforms alienated the mistrustful conservatives and he soon clung to power only with French support. When France finally withdrew its troops in 1867, Maximilian was deposed by republican forces and executed.

Modern Mexico

The fall of Emperor Maximilian signaled a restoration of the anticlerical constitution of 1857 and the elevation of Benito Juárez – the republican leader long recognized by the United States – as president. His successor, Sebastián Lerdo de Tijada, was toppled in 1876 by Porfirio Diáz, who remained dictator for thirty-four years. A civil war ended his regime, and more bloodshed ensued. Finally, a constitution was issued in 1917 that placed severe restrictions on the Church: there could be no criticism of the government, only Mexicans could be clergy, the Church was not permitted to own property, and any privileges were stripped away.

The situation became worse after 1923, when the papal legate was expelled. The administration of Plutarco Calles (1924-1928) launched a wave of persecution that sparked a popular but ultimately unsuccessful uprising called the Cristero Rebellion. Coupled with the repressive measures of local governments, the Calles regime and its successors forced the Church into very difficult circumstances, with only a few priests remaining in the country. The tragedy was deepened by the execution of dozens of priests and nuns by republican forces for assorted and imaginary crimes or for speaking out on behalf of the poor or oppressed Catholics. A number of the executed clergy have been beatified and canonized since the tragedy,

most so during the pontificate of Pope John Paul II. The persecution prompted Pope Pius XI to issue the encyclicals *Iniquis afflictisque* (1926) and *Acerba animi* (1932).

An easing of the situation began in 1940 as the rigid anticlerical laws ceased to be enforced with enthusiasm. A rapprochement was visible in the 1958 elections, when the Church received conciliatory gestures from the ruling Revolutionary Party and its presidential candidate Adolfo López Mateos. The Church continued to exist under numerous legal disabilities and was oppressed in a number of the Mexican states.

Gradual improvement in relations between Mexico and the Holy See led to the exchange in 1990 of personal representatives between the Mexican president and Pope John Paul II. The Holy Father's efforts to build a further diplomatic bridge culminated in the establishment of full diplomatic ties in 1992. This was followed by the final easing of many of the handicaps under which the Church had long suffered.

The faith of the Mexican people is profoundly deep, as was seen in the nearly frenzied greeting given to Pope John Paul II in 1979, 1990, 1993, and 1999. However, social unrest, poverty, economic challenges, the violence of drug cartels, and corruption still plague the country. Church leaders — especially religious orders — have been outspoken in their criticism of government human rights abuses and corruption. During the mid-1990s, the Jesuits said they were the target of a "campaign of intimidation" because of their human rights work.

On May 24, 1993, Card. Juan Jesus Posadas Ocampo of Guadalajara was killed during a supposed shoot-out among rival drug cartels. The murder remained unsolved, although Cardinal Posadas' successor, Card. Juan Sandoval Iñiguez, continued to claim that high-ranking officials, including the Mexican attorney general at the time, lied to protect others involved in a plot. In 2001 Card. Sandoval said he would seek a reopening of the case because he had new evidence contradicting the findings of the official investigation; he also claimed he had been almost fatally poisoned in 1999 during a dinner with federal officials angry with his insistence that the murder was not accidental.

In the 1970s and 1980s, one of Mexico's most prominent proponents of liberation theology was Bp. Samuel Ruiz Garcia of San Cristobal de las Casas. In the early 1990s the Vatican began investigating his views, but because he had the trust of indigenous peasants, in 1994 he was thrown into the role of mediator between the government and the mostly native Zapatista National Liberation Army in Chiapas. He continued that role until 1998, when he resigned after accusing the government of "dismantling any possible means or effort to solve the crisis in Chiapas." Mexico's bishops said at that time that they would provide support to the peace process but would not seek to mediate the conflict.

On July 2, 2000, Vicente Fox Quesada, head of the National Action Party and a practicing Catholic, won the Mexican presidential election, marking the first time since 1929 that the country was not ruled by the Institutional Revolutionary Party. Mexico City Cardinal Norberto Rivera Carrera told reporters the election was "not a miracle, as some have suggested, but it is an extraordinary act." Church officials emphasized that they expected no special privileges from the new government, but the general climate was one of optimism for an improvement in church-state relations.

Within weeks, Fox – with news cameras flashing – received Communion in his hometown parish. However, in July 2001, the Vatican said he failed to have his first marriage annulled before marrying his spokeswoman in a civil ceremony; thus, he would be prohibited from receiving the sacraments. In June 2001, federal and state officials participated in a public Mass at the Basilica of Our Lady of Guadalupe,

breaking a taboo on government officials publicly practicing their religion.

On July 31, 2002, during his fifth pastoral visit to Mexico, Pope John Paul II proclaimed Juan Diego a saint. The pope declared at the canonization: " 'The Guadalupe Event,' as the Mexican Episcopate has pointed out, 'meant the beginning of evangelization with a vitality that surpassed all expectations. Christ's message, through his Mother, took up the central elements of the indigenous culture, purified them and gave them the definitive sense of salvation."

ORGANIZATION

Presently, the Church in Mexico is organized into 14 provinces. There are 14 archdioceses, 68 dioceses (including the 2003 and 2004 creation of a new suffragan diocese of the archdiocese of Oaxaca in 2003, and a suffragan diocese of San Luis Potosi in 2004), 5 prelacies, and 2 eparchs, for the Greek Melkites and Maronites. As of Aug. 15, 2006, there were five Mexican members of the College of Cardinals: Ernesto Corripio Ahumada, Norberto Rivera Carrera, Juan Sandoval Íñiguez, Javier Lozano Barragán, and Adolfo Antonio Suárez Rivera. (For statistical information on the Church in Mexico, see below.)

The current apostolic delegation to Mexico was set up in 1992 as a nunciature with the establishment of renewed formal diplomatic relations with the Vatican. The present Apostolic Nuncio is Archbishop Giuseppe Bertolli, appointed in December 2000.

ECCLESIASTICAL JURISDICTIONS OF MEXICO

Provinces

Names of ecclesiastical provinces and metropolitan sees in bold face: suffragan sees in parentheses.

Acapulco (Ciudad Lázaro Cárdenas, Chilpancingo-Chilapa, Ciudad Altamirano, Tlapa).

Chihuahua (Ciudad Juárez, Cuauhtémoc-Madera, Parral, Tarahumara).

Durango (Culiacán, Mazatlán, Torreón, El Salto,).

Guadalajara (Aguascalientes, Autlán, Ciudad Guzmán, Colima, San Juan de los Lagos, Tepic, Zacatecas; Prelature of Jesús Maria del Nayar).

Hermosillo (Ciudad Obregón, La Paz, Mexicali, Tijuana).

México (Atlacomulco, Cuernavaca, Toluca, Tula, Tulancingo).

Monterrey (Ciudad Valles, Ciudad Victoria, Linares, Matamoros, Nuevo Laredo, Piedras Negras, Saltillo, Tampico, Nuevo Casas Grandes).

Morelia (Apatzingán, Tacámbaro, Zamora).

Oaxaca, Antequera (San Cristóbal de las Casas, Puerto Escondido, Tapachula, Tehuantepec, Tuxtla Gutiérrez, Tuxtepec; Prelacies of Mixes and Huautla).

Puebla de los Angeles (Huajuapan de León, Huejutla, Tehuacán, Tlaxcala).

San Luis Potosi (Celaya, Irapuato, León, Querétaro, Matehuala).

Tlalnepantla (Texcoco, Cuautitlán, Netza-hualcóy-otl, Ecatepec, Valle de Chalco).

Xalapa (Papantla, San Andrés Tuxtla, Coatza-coalcos, Tuxpan, Veracruz, Orizaba, Córdoba).

Yucatán (Campeche, Tabasco, Prelacy of Cancún-Chetumal; Eparchy of Nuestra Señora del Paraiso).

Jurisdictions, Hierarchy

(Principal sources: Information office, Mexican Conference of Catholic Bishops; Catholic Almanac survey; Annuario Pontificio; L'Osservatore Romano; Catholic News Service. As of July 1, 2006. Addresses and phone numbers are provided by the Annuario Pontificio.)

Information includes names of archdioceses (indicated by asterisk) and dioceses, date of foundation, present ordinaries and auxiliaries; addresses of chancery office/bishop's residence.

Acapulco* (1958; promoted to archdiocese, 1983): Felipe Aguirre Franco, archbishop, 2001; Juan Navarro Castellanos, auxiliary.

Diocesan Address: Apartado Postal 201, Quebrada 16, 39850 Acapulco, Guerrero; (748) 2-07-63.

Aguascalientes (1899): Ramón Godinez Flores, bishop, 1998.

Diocesan Address: Apartado 167, Galeana 105 Norte, 20000 Aguascalientes, Aguascalientes; (449) 9-15-32-61.

Apatzingán (1962): Miguel Patiño Velázquez, M.S.F., bishop, 1981.

Diocesan Address: Calle Esteban Vaca Calderón 100, 60600 Apatzingán, Mich.; (453) 5-34-17-87.

Atlacomulco (1984): Constancio Miranda Weckmann, bishop, 1998.

Diocesan Address: Hidalgo Sur 1, Apartado 22, 50450 Atlacomulco, Méx.; (712) 1-22-05-53.

Autlán (1961): Gonzalo Galván Castillo, bishop, 2004.

Diocesan Address: Apartado 8, Hidalgo 74, 48900 Autlán, Jal., Mex.; (317) 3-82-12-28.

Campeche (1895): Ramón Castro Castro, bishop, 2006.

Diocesan Address: Calle 53 # 1-B Entre 8 y 10 Centro Apdo. Postal # 12724000 - Campeche, Camp.; (981) 8-16-25-24.

Cancún-Chetumal, Prelacy of (1970, as Chetumal; name changed in 1996): Pedro Pablo Elizondo Cárdenas, L.C., bishop, 2004.

Diocesan Address: Apartado Postal 165, Othón P. Blanco 150, 77000 Chetumal, Quintana Roo; (983) 2-06-38.

Celaya (1973): Jesús Humberto Velázquez Garay, bishop, 1988.

Diocesan Address: Curia Diocesana, Apartado 207, Manuel Doblado 110, 38000 Celaya, Gto.; (461) 6-12-48-35.

Chihuahua* (1891; promoted to archdiocese, 1958): José Fernández Arteaga, archbishop, 1991.

Diocesan Address: Av. Cuauhtémoc # 1828 Col. Cuauhtémoc, Apartado Postal 7, 31000 Chihuahua, Chihuahua; (614) 4-10-32-02.

Chilpancingo-Chilapa (1863 as Chilpancingo; name changed to Chilpancingo-Chilapa, 1989): Alejo Zavala Castro, bishop, 2005.

Diocesan Address: Abasolo e Hidalgo, Apartado Postal #185, 39000 Chilpancingo, Gro.; (747) 4-71-05-92.

Ciudad Altamirano (1964): José Miguel Ángel Giles Vázquez, bishop, 2004.

Diocesan Address: Juárez 18 Oriente, Centro, Apdo 17, 40680 Ciudad Altamirano, Gro.; (767) 6-72-17-74.

Ciudad Guzmán (1972): Braulio Rafael León Villegas, bishop, 1999.

Diocesan Address: Ramón Corona 26, Apartado 86, 49000 Ciudad Guzman, Jal.; (341) 4-12-19-94.

Ciudad Juárez (1957): Renato Ascencio León, bishop, 1994; José Guadalupe Torres Campos, auxiliary.

Diocesan Address: Apartado Postal 188, 32000 Cuidad Juárez, Chih.; (16) 15-09-22.

Ciudad Lázaro Cárdenas (1985): Salvador Flores Huerta, bishop, 1993.

Diocesan Address: Apartado 500, Andador Ciudad del Carmen #4, Fideicomiso 2° Sector, 60950 Lázaro Cardenas, Mich.; (753) 5-41-64-07.

Ciudad Obregón (1959): Juan Manuel Mancilla Sanchez, bishop, 2005.

Diocesan Address: Apartado 402, Sonora 161 Norte, 85000 Ciudad Obregón, Son.; (644) 4-13-20-98.

Ciudad Valles (1960): Roberto Octavio Balmori Cinta, M.J., bishop, 2002.

Diocesan Address: 16 de Septiembre 726, Apartado 170, 79000 Ciudad Valles, S.L.P.; (138) 2-25-97

Ciudad Victoria (1964): Antonio González Sánchez, bishop, 1995.

Diocesan Address: 15 Hidalgo y Juárez, Centro, Apartado Postal #335, 87000 Ciudad Victoria, Tamps.; (834) 3-12-87-16.

Coatzacoalcos (1984): Rutilo Muñoz Zamora, bishop, 2002.

Diocesan Address: Apartado 513 y 513, Aldama 502, 96400 Coatzacoalcos, Ver.; (921) 2-12-23-99.

Colima (1881): José Luis Amezcua Melgoza, bishop, 2005.

Diocesan Address: Hidalgo 135, Apartado 1, 28000 Colima, Colima; (312) 3-12-02-62.

Cordoba (2000): Eduardo Porfirio Patiño Leal, bishop, 2000.

Diocesan Address: Avenida 11-1300, Esquina con Calle 13, Apartado 154, Zona Centro, 94500 Cordoba, Ver., Mexico; (271) 7-14-91-56.

Cuauhtémoc-Madera (1966): Juan Guillermo López Soto, bishop, 1995.

Diocesan Address: Reforma y 4ª # 479, Apartado Postal 209, 31500 Cuauhtemoc, Chih.; (625) 5-81-57-22.

Cuautitlán (1979): Rodrigo Guillermo Ortiz Mondragón, bishop, 2005.

Diocesan Address: Apartado 14-21, Sor Juana Inés de la Cruz 208, Anexo a Catedral, 54800 Cuautitlán de Romero Rubio; (55) 58-72-19-96.

Cuernavaca (1891): Florencio Olvera Ochoa, bishop, 2002.

Diocesan Address: Apartado 13, Hidalgo #17, 62000 Cuernavaca, Mor.; (777) 3-18-45-90.

Culiacán (1883 as Sinaloa; name changed 1959): Benjamin Jiménez Hernández, bishop, 1993.

Diocesan Address: Apartado Postal 666, Av. Las Palmas #26 Oriente, 80220 Culiacán, Sinaloa; (667) 7-12-32-72.

Durango* (1620, promoted to archdiocese, 1891): Hector González Martínez, archbishop, 2003; Juan de Dios Caballero Reyes, aux.

Diocesan Address: Apartado Postal 116, 34000 Durango, Durango; (618) 8-11-42-42

Ecatepec (1995): Onésimo Cepeda Silva, bishop, 1995.

Diocesan Address: Plaza Principal s/n, San Cristóbal Centro, Apartado Postal 95, 55000 Ecatepec de Morelos; (5) 116-09-76.

El Salto, Prelacy of (1968): Ruy Rendón Leal, bishop, 2005.

Prelature Address: Mons. Francisco Medina s/n, Apartado Postal 58, 34950 El Salto, Durango; (675) 8-76-00-70.

Guadalajara* (1548; promoted to archdiocese, 1863): Cardinal Juan Sandoval Íñiguez, archbishop, 1994; José Trinidad González Rodriguez, Miguel Romano Gómez, Rafael Martínez Sainz, José María De la Torre Martín, José Leopoldo González González, auxiliaries.

Diocesan Address: Arzobispado, Apartado Postal 1-331, Calle Liceo 17, 44100 Guadalajara, Jal.; (33) 36-14-55-04; www.arquidiocesisgdl.org.mx.

Hermosillo* (1779, as Sonora, promoted to an archdiocese, 1963): José Ulises Macias Salcedo, archbishop, 1996.

Diocesan Address: Apartado 1, Dr. Paliza 81, 83260 Hermosillo, Son.; (662) 2-13-21-38.

Huajuapan de Leon (1903): Teodoro Enrique Pino Miranda, 2000.

Diocesan Address: Apartado 43, Anexos de Catedral, 69000 Huajuapan de León, Oax.; (953) 5-32-07-97.

Huautla, Prelacy of (1972): Héctor Luis Morales Sánchez, bishop, 2005.

Diocesan Address: Casa Prelaticia Calle 5 de Feb. # 15, Apartado 2, 68500 Huautla de Jiménez, Oaxaca; (236) 3-78-00-19.

Huejutla (1922): Salvador Martínez Pérez, bishop, 1994.

Diocesan Address: Obispado, Apartado 8, Ave. Corona del Rosal s/n, Col. Tecoluco, 43000 Huejutla, Hgo.; (789) 8-96-01-85.

Irapuato (2004): José de Jesús Martínez Zepeda, first bishop, 2004.

Diocesan Address: N/A.

Jesús María of Nayar, Prelature of (1962): José Antonio Pérez Sánchez, O.F.M., bishop, 1992.

Diocesan Address: Curia Prelaticia de Jesús María, Belén #24, Apartado 33-B, 63150 Tepic, Nayar; (311) 2-13-88-80.

La Paz en la Baja California Sur (1988): Miguel Angel Alba Diáz, 2001.

Diocesan Address: Apartado 25, Revolución y 5 de Mayo, 23000 La Paz, B.C.S.; (112) 2-25-96.

León (1863): José Guadalupe Martin Rábago, bishop, 1995; Juan Frausto Pallares, auxiliary.

Diocesan Address: Pedro Moreno #312, Apartado 108, 37000 León, Gto.; (477) 7-13-27-47; www.diocesisleon.org.mx.

Linares (1962): Ramón Calderón Batres, bishop, 1988.

Diocesan Address: Morelos y Zaragoza s/n,

Apartado 70, 67700 Linares, N.L.; (821) 2-00-54.
Matamoros (1958): Faustino Armendáriz Jiménez, bishop, 2005.
Diocesan Address: Apartado 70, Calle 5 y Morelos, 87351 Matamoros, Tamps.; (88) 13-55-11; www.communion.org.mx.
Matehuala (1997): Rodrigo Aguilar Martínez, bishop, 1997.
Diocesan Address: Rayón #200 Centro, Apartado 40, 78700 Matehuala, S.L.P.; (01) 488-2-51-42.
Mazatlán (1958): Mario Espinosa Contreras, bishop, 2005.
Diocesan Address: Apartado Postal 1, Canizales y Benito Juárez s/n, 82000 Mazatlán, Sin.; (69) 81-33-52.
Mexicali (1966): José Isidro Guerrero Macías, bishop, 1997.
Diocesan Address: Av. Morelos #192, Col. Primera sécción, Apartado 3-547, 21100 Mexicali, B.C. Norte; (686) 5-52-40-09.
México* (1530, promoted to an archdiocese, 1546): Cardinal Norberto Rivera Carrera, archbishop, 1995; Abelardo Alvarado Alcántara, José de Jesús Martinez Zepeda, Marcelino Hernández Rodríguez, Luis Fletes Santana, Felipe Tejeda Garcia, M.Sp.S., Francisco Clavel Gil, Rogelio Esquivel Medina, Jonás Guerrero Corona, Antonio Ortega Franco, C.O., Víctor Sánchez Espinosa, Carlos Briseño Arch, O.A.R., auxiliaries.
Diocesan Address: Curia Arzobispal, Apartado Postal 24-433, Durango 90, Col. Roma, 06700 - México, D. F.; (55) 55-25-11-10; www.arzobispadomexico.org.mx.
Mixes, Prelacy of (1964): Vacant.
Diocesan Address: Casa del Señor Obispo, 70283, Ayutla, Mixes, Oax.; (951) 5-58-20-98.
Monterrey* (1777, as Linares o Nuevo León, promoted to an archdiocese, 1891; name changed 1922): Francisco Robles Ortega, archbishop, 2003; José Lizares Estrada, Gustavo Rodríguez Vega, **Alfonso Cortés Contreras,** auxiliaries.
Diocesan Address: Apartado 7, Zuazua 1110 Sur con Ocampo, 64000 Monterrey, N.L.; (81) 83-45-24-66; www.pixel.com.mx/info-gral/info-nl/religion/catolica/arqui.html.
Morelia* (1536, as Michoacan, promoted to an archdiocese 1863, name changed in 1924): Alberto Suárez Inda, archbishop, 1995; Enrique Díaz Díaz, Octavio Villegas Aguilar, auxiliaries.
Diocesan Address: Apartado 17, 58000 Morelia, Mich.; (443) 3-12-05-23.
Netzahualcóyotl (1979): Carlos Garfias Merlos, bishop, 2003.
Diocesan Address: Apartado 89, 4 Avenida esq. Bellas Artes, Col. Evolución, 57700 Cuidad Netzahualcóyotl; (55) 57-97-61-32.
Nuestra Señora de los Mártires del Libano, Eparchy of (Maronites, 1995): Georges M. Saad Abi Younes, O.L.M., eparch, 2003.
Diocesan address: Ntra. Sra. de Balvarena Correo Mayor # 65, 06060 — México, D. F.; (55) 55-21-20-11.
Nuestra Señora del Paraiso, Eparchy of (Greek Melkites, 1988): vacant.
Diocesan Address: Matías Romero 1014, Dpto. 601, Col. Del Valle, 3100 Mexico, D.F.; (5) 542-0225.
Nuevo Casas Grandes (1977): Gerardo de Jesús Rojas López, bishop, 2004.

Diocesan Address: Apartado Postal 198, Av. Hidalgo #105, 31700 Nuevo Casas Grandes, Chih.; (636) 6-94-05-20.
Nuevo Laredo (1989): Ricardo Watty Urquidi, M.Sp.S., bishop, 1989.
Diocesan Address: Saltillo 206, Apartado Postal #20-B, Col. México, 88280 Nuevo Laredo, Tamps.; (867) 7-15-29-28.
Oaxaca* (Also Antequera, 1535, promoted to archdiocese, 1891): José Luis Chávez Botello, archbishop, 2003; Miguel Ángel Alba Díaz, Oscar Campos Contreras, auxiliaries.
Diocesan Address: Apartado Postal # 31, Garcia Vigil #600, 68000 Oaxaca, Oax.; (951) 6-20-49.
Orizaba (2000): Hipolito Reyes Larios, bishop, 2000. Diocesan Address: Templo de Ntra. Sra. del Carmen, Sur 9 # 142 esq. Oriente 4, Apdo. Postal # 151, 94300 - Orizaba, Ver.; (272) 7-24-17-33.
Papantla (1922): Lorenzo Cárdenas Aregullin, bishop, 1980.
Diocesan Address: Apartado 27, Juárez 1102, 73800 Teziutlán, Pue.; (231) 3-24-30.
Parral (1992): José Andrés Corral Arredondo, bishop, 1992.
Diocesan Address: Apartado Postal 313, Fray Bartolomé de las Casas #13, 33800 Parral, Chih.; (152) 2-03-71.
Piedras Negras (2003): Alonso Gerardo Garza Treviño, first bishop, 2003. Diocesan address: Hidalgo Sur # 404 Centro 26000 - Piedras Negras, Coah.; (878) 7-82-94-80.
Puebla de los Angeles* (1525, as Tlaxcala, renamed in 1903): Rosendo Huesca Pacheco, archbishop, 1977.
Diocesan Address: Apartado 235, Av. 2, Sur N. 305, 72000 Puebla, Pue.; (222) 2-32-62-12.
Puerto Escondido (2003): Eduardo Carmona Ortega, O.R.C., first bishop, 2003.
Diocesan Address: N/A.
Querétaro (1863): Mario de Gasperín Gasperín, bishop, 1989.
Diocesan Address: Apartado Postal 49, Reforma #48, 76000 Querétaro, Qro.; (42) 12-10-33.
Saltillo (1891): Raul Vera López, O.P., bishop, 1999.
Diocesan Address: Hidalgo Sur 166, Apartado 25, 25000 Saltillo, Coah.; (844) 4-12-37-84.
San Andrés Tuxtla (1959): José Trinidad Zapata Ortiz, bishop, 2004.
Diocesan Address: Constitución y Morelos, 95700 San Andrés Tuxtla, Ver.; (294) 9-42-03-74.
San Cristóbal de las Casas (1539, as Chiapas, renamed in 1964): Felipe Arizmendi Esquivel, bishop, 2000.
Diocesan Address: 5 de Feb. y 20 de Nov. # 1 Centro 29200 — San Cristóbal las Casas, Chis; (967) 6-78-00-53; www.laneta.apc.org/curiasc.
San Juan de los Lagos (1972): Javier Navarro Rodríguez, bishop, 1999.
Diocesan Address: Morelos 30, Apartado #1, 47000 San Juan de los Lagos, Jal.; (395) 7-85-05-70; www.redial.com.mx/obispado/index.htm.
San Luis Potosí* (1854, promoted to an archdiocese, 1988): Luis Morales Reyes, archbishop, 1999.
Diocesan Address: Madero # 300, Apartado N. 1, 78000 - San Luis Potosí, S.L.P.; (444) 8-12-45-55.
Tabasco (1880): Benjamin Castillo Plascencia, bishop, 2003.

Diocesan Address: Apartado Postal 97, Fidencia 502, 86000 Villahermosa, Tab.; (93) 12-13-97.

Tacámbaro (1913): Luis Castro Medellín, M.S.F., bishop, 2002.

Diocesan Address: Apartado 4, Professor Enrique Aguilar 49, 61650 Tacámbaro, Mich.; (459) 6-00-44.

Tampico (1870, as Ciudad Victoria o Tamaulipas, renamed in 1958): José Luis Dibildox Martinez, bishop, 2003.

Diocesan Address: Apartado 545, Altamira 116 Oriente, 89000 Tampico, Tamps.; (12) 12-28-02.

Tapachula (1957): Leopoldo González González, bishop, 2005.

Diocesan Address: Apartado 70, Av. Primera Sur 1, 30700 Tapachula, Chiapas; (962) 6-15-03; www.diocesis-tapachula.org.mx.

Tarahumara (1958, as a vicariate apostolic, promoted to diocese, 1993): Rafael Sandoval Sandoval, M.N.M., bishop, 2005.

Diocesan Address: Apartado Postal 11, Av. López Mateos #7, 33190 Guachochi, Chih.; (649) 5-43-02-23.

Tehuacán (1962): Rodrigo Aguilar Martínez, bishop, 2006.

Diocesan Address: Apartado Postal 137, Agustin A. Cacho 107, 75700 Tehuacán, Pue.; (238) 3-83-14-68.

Tehuantepec (1891): Felipe Padilla Cardona, bishop, 2000.

Diocesan Address: Apartado Postal 93, Mina s/n. Anexos de Catedral, 70760 Tehuantepec, Oax.; (971) 7-15-00-60.

Tepic (1891): Alfonso Humberto Robles Cota, bishop, 1981.

Diocesan Address: Apartado 15, Av. de las Flores 10, Fracciónamiento Residencial La Loma, 63137 Tepic, Nay.; (311) 2-14-46-45.

Texcoco (1960): Carlos Aguiar Retes, bishop, 1997; Víctor René Rodríguez Gómez, auxiliary.

Diocesan Address: Apartado Postal 35, Fray Pedro de Gante 2, 56100 Texcoco, Méx.; (595) 4-08-69.

Tijuana (1963): Rafael Romo Muñoz, bishop, 1996.

Diocesan Address: Apartado 226, Calle 10ª y Av. Ocampo # 1049, 22000 Tijuana, B.C.N.; (664) 6-84-84-11 y 12; www.iglesiatijuana.org.

Tlalnepantla* (1964, promoted to archdiocese, 1989): Ricardo Guizar Díaz, archbishop, 1996; Francisco Ramírez Navarro, auxiliary.

Diocesan Address: Apartado 268 y 270, Av. Juárez 42, 54000 Tlalnepantla, Méx.; (55) 55-65-39-44.

Tlapa (1992): Vacant.

Diocesan Address: Anexo Catedral, Centro, 41300 Tlapa de Comonfort, Gro.; (757) 4-76-08-35.

Tlaxcala (1959): Jacinto Guerrero Torres bishop, 2001.

Diocesan Address: Apartado 84, Lardizábal 45, 90000 Tlaxcala, Tlax.; (246) 4-62-32-43.

Toluca (1950): Francisco Javier Chavolla Ramos, bishop, 2003.

Diocesan Address: Apartado 82, Portal Reforma Norte 104, 50000 Toluca, Méx.; (72) 15-25-35; www.diocesistoluca.org.mx.

Torreón (1957): Vacant.

Diocesan Address: Apartado Postal 430, Av. Morelos 46 Poniente, 27000 Torreón, Coah.; (871) 7-12-30-43.

Tula (1961):Vacant.

Diocesan Address: 5 de Mayo, #5, Apartado 31, 42800 Tula de Allende, Hgo.; (773) 7-32-02-75.

Tulancingo (1863): Pedro Aranda Díaz-Muñoz, bishop, 1975.

Diocesan Address: Apartado #14, Plaza de la Constitución, 43600 Tulancingo, Hgo.; (775) 3-10-10.

Tuxpan (1962): Domingo Díaz Martínez, bishop, 2002.

Diocesan Address: Independencia #56, 92870 Tuxpan, Ver.; (783) 4-16-36.

Tuxtepec (1979): José Antonio Fernández Hurtado, bishop, 2005.

Diocesan Address: Bonfil # 597, entre Juárez y Villa Col. Santa Fe Apartado Postal 9, 68320 — Tuxtepec, Oax.; (287) 5-00-42.

Tuxtla Gutiérrez (1964): Rogelio Cabrera López, 2004.

Diocesan Address: Uruguay # 500 A Col. El Retiro Apdo. Postal # 36529040 - Tuxtla Gutiérrez, Chis.; (961) 6-04-06-44; www.chisnet.com.mx/~cosi/obispado.

Valle de Chalco (2003): Luis Artemio Flores Calzada, first bishop, 2003.

Diocesan Address: Calle Colorines 12, Col. Granjas, 56600 Chalco, Mex.

Veracruz (1962): Luis Felipe Gallardo Martín del Campo, S.D.B., bishop, 2006.

Diocesan Address: Insurgentes Veracruzanos #470, Paseo del Malecón, 91700 Veracruz, Ver.; (229) 9-31-24-13.

Xalapa* (1962; originally Veracruz and Xalapa, 1863; promoted to archdiocese, 1951): Sergio Obeso Rivera, archbishop, 1979.

Diocesan Address: Apartado 359, Av. Manuel Avila Camacho #73, 91000 Xalapa, Ver.; (228) 8-12-05-79.

Yucatán* (1561, promoted to archdiocese, 1906): Emilio Carlos Berlie Belaunzarán, archbishop, 1995; José Rafael Palma Capetillo, auxiliary.

Diocesan Address: Calle 58 N. 501, 97000 Mérida, Yuc.; (99) 23-79-83; www.geocities.com/SoHo/207/principa.html.

Zacatecas (1863): Fernando Chávez Ruvalcaba, bishop, 1999.

Diocesan Address: Apartado #1, Miguel Auza #219, 98000 Zacatecas, Zacatecas; (492) 9-22-02-32; www.logicnet.com.mx/obispado.

Zamora (1863): Carlos Suárez Cázares, bishop, 1994.

Diocesan Address: Altos de Catedral (Calle Hidalgo), Apartado Postal #18, 59600 Zamora, Mich.; (351) 5-12-12-08.

CONFERENCIA DEL EPISCOPADO MEXICANO

(Sources: Annuario Pontificio; Pbro. Jorge Fco. Vázquez M., Secretario Adjunto, Conferencia del Episcopado Mexicano; Conferencia del Episcopado Mexicano, Directorio, 2006; translation courtesy Suzanne Lea.)

STRUCTURE

The Mexican Conference of Bishops (CEM, Conferencia del Episcopado Mexicano) is the permanent body of Mexican bishops. The bishops adhere to the guidelines of the conference in specific fulfillment of their pastoral labors. They do this in order to obtain the greatest good for the people that the church can achieve. The conference proposes:

1) To study the problems that occur in pastoral work, and to seek solutions. 2) To initiate, with a common end in mind and a common course of action, the forms and methods of preaching that best suit the needs of the country. 3) In regard to the collective salvific mission of the church: To look for and to teach the best way in which the respective activities of the deacons, priests, religious, and lay person will be most efficient. 4) To facilitate relations with the civil authority and with other organizations in specific cases. 5) To write to the Episcopal commission regarding patrimonial and proprietary matters, and give counsel on determined financial or labor related points.

All those elected to the body of the CEM will have three years of service and will not be reelected to the same position after two three-year sessions have been completed consecutively.

The address of the conference headquarters is: Prolongación Misterios No. 26, Col. Tepeyac Insurgentes, 07020 México, D.F. Tels. (01-55) 5577-5401; www.cem.org.mx.

Permanent Assembly

The Permanent Assembly is the representative arm of the bishops belonging to the CEM. Its function is to ensure the continuation of the works of the conference and the fulfillment of its accords.

The Permanent Assembly is comprised of the Presidential Assembly and the Assembly of Pastoral Regions. It meets four times per year in ordinary session. It meets in extraordinary sessions whenever the majority of its members or those of the Presidential Assembly determine it to be necessary.

A session is valid if two-thirds of the members are present.

Officers

President: Bishop José Guadalupe Martín Rábago of León.

Vice-President: Bishop Alberto Suárez Inda of Morella.

Secretary General: Bishop Carlos Aguiar Retes of Texcoco.

General Treasurer: Bishop Alonso Gerardo Garza Treviño of Piedras Negras.

Vocals: Bishop Rogelio Cabrera López of Tapachula; Ramón Godinez Flores of Aguascalientes.

Commissions, Section One:

Biblical Studies: Bishop Juan Manuel Mancilla Sánchez.

Doctrine: Cardinal Juan Sandoval Iñiguez.

Culture: Cardinal Norberto Rivera Carrera.

Education: Bishop Ramón Godínez Flores.

Evangelization: Bishop Benjamín Castillo Plascencia.

Health Care: Jacinto Guerrero Torres

Liturgy: Bishop Jonás Guerrero Corona.

Missions: Bishop Florencio Olvera Ochoa.

Pastoral Sanctuaries: Bishop Fernando Chávez Ruvalcaba.

Social Communications: Bishop Rodrigo Guillermo Ortiz Mondragón.

Social Justice: Bishop Sergio Obeso Rivera.

Commissions, Section Two:

Clergy: Bishop José Ulises Macías Salcedo.

Consecrated Life: Bishop Felipe Tejeda García, M.Sp.S.

Lay Apostolates: Bishop Ricardo Watty Urquidi, M.Sp.S..

Lay Ministry and Diaconate: Bishop Luis Felipe Gallardo Martín del Campo, S.D.B.

Military Chaplains: Bishop Hilario Chávez Joya.

Priestly Formation: Bishop Benjamin Jiménez Hernández.

Seminaries and Vocations: Bishop Hipólito Reyes Larios.

STATISTICAL SUMMARY OF THE CATHOLIC CHURCH IN MEXICO

(Principal sources: Annuario Pontificio, 2006; Conferencia del Espicopado Mexicano, Directorio, 2006; figures as of January 2006. Catholic population statistics are those reported in the most recent Annuario population estimates. Archdioceses are indicated by an asterisk.)

Includes 14 provinces: 14 archdioceses, 68 dioceses, 5 prelacies, and two eparchies. The Catholic population of Mexico comprises approximately 89 percent of the overall Mexican population of 106,302,412 according to the Conferencia del Episcopado Mexicano, Directorio, 2006 (the most recent edition). In 2004, there were 1,892,779 baptisms and 319,870 marriages. This table presents a provincial breakdown of Catholic statistics. The population totals are approximate because diocesan estimates are often considered unreliable owing to difficulties in adequate assessment of demographics and population distribution.

Province Diocese	Cath. Pop.	Dioc. Priests	Rel. Priests	Total Priests	Perm. Deacs.	Bro- thers	Sis- sters	Par- ishes
Acapulco	5,806,780	330	70	400	20	89	493	226
Acapulco*	2,908,000	92	19	111	20	31	140	78
Chilpancingo-Chilapa	826,000	123	16	139	-	16	170	73
Ciudad Altamirano	876,000	56	5	61	-	5	81	27
Ciudad Lázaro								
Cárdenas	717,780	23	13	36	-	16	63	23
Tlapa	479,000	36	17	53	-	21	39	25
Chihuahua	4,560,647	290	104	394	28	141	671	209
Chihuahua*	1,163,729	86	28	114	-	34	197	63
Ciudad Juárez	2,156,000	83	32	115	13	49	179	67
Cuauhtémoc-Madera	329,509	26	10	36	-	11	71	26
Nuevo Casas Grandes	117,419	52	9	61	-	9	33	22
Parral	515,790	28	8	36	15	12	71	17
Tarahumara	278,200	15	17	32	-	26	120	14
Durango	5,606,267	544	82	626	5	120	1,025	282
Durango*	1,642,200	205	18	223	-	38	434	105
Culiacán	2,287,722	145	5	150	4	10	291	70
El Salto	319,000	22	-	22	1	3	14	15
Mazatlán	721,125	82	8	89	-	9	128	42
Torreón	636,220	90	51	141	-	60	158	50
Guadalajara	12,498,035	2,247	443	2,706	5	1,144	5,262	858
Guadalajara*	6,097,000	1,003	336	1,339	2	906	3,043	409
Aguascalientes	1,581,500	238	59	297	-	92	661	96
Autlán	315,487	98	-	98	2	-	159	47
Ciudad Guzmán	414,285	104	12	116	-	18	132	52
Colima	649,996	125	7	132	-	13	243	52
San Juan los Lagos	941,096	270	18	288	-	72	377	70
Tepic	1,068,671	210	4	214	-	4	268	65
Zacatecas	1,300,000	189	7	196	-	18	362	104
Jesús Maria of Nayar[1]	130,000	10	16	26	1	21	17	15
Hermosillo	6,430,218	542	145	687	15	268	1,099	313
Hermosillo*	985,807	106	8	114	1	12	138	56
Ciudad Obregón	880,000	117	18	135	1	31	144	58
La Paz	484,000	46	19	65	-	19	148	42
Mexicali	1,284,411	107	20	127	1	59	138	51
Tijuana	2,796,000	166	80	246	12	147	531	106
Mexico	15,742,294	1,380	1,169	2,549	115	2,198	5,973	854
Mexico*	7,103,000	664	1,035	1,699	111	1,990	4,745	434
Atlacomulco	888,700	89	9	98	1	9	103	56
Cuernavaca	1,833,954	132	62	194	2	118	457	109
Toluca	2,994,640	257	50	307	-	60	433	131
Tula	982,000	62	11	73	1	11	85	41
Tulancingo	1,940,000	176	2	178	-	10	150	83
Monterrey	11,394,917	835	297	1,429	50	451	1,659	490
Monterrey*	5,223,000	353	177	530	29	268	758	175
Ciudad Valles	890,000	56	14	70	-	17	106	41
Ciudad Victoria	393,000	32	12	43	-	18	89	33
Linares	274,000	36	13	49	17	22	71	34

Province Diocese	Cath. Pop.	Dioc. Priests	Rel. Priests	Total Priests	Perm. Deacs.	Bro- thers	Sis- ters	Par- ishes
Monterrey, cont.								
Matamoros	1,689,975	108	12	120	3	18	90	56
Nuevo Laredo	795,942	42	19	61	-	26	77	35
Saltillo	1,000,000	112	37	149	1	64	317	54
Tampico	1,129,000	96	13	109	-	18	151	62
Morelia	5,049,846	827	150	977	8	334	2,166	398
Morelia*	2,470,000	395	124	519	8	249	1,062	218
Apatzingán	639,000	56	-	56	-	-	132	26
Tacámbaro	322,000	87	1	88	-	1	128	33
Zamora	1,618,846	289	25	314	-	84	844	121
Oaxaca	7,417,033	522	144	666	399	191	1,005	381
Oaxaca*	1,120,000	128	38	166	26	57	211	111
Puerto Escondido	423,000 26	5		31	-	5	9	29
San Cristobal	1,255,665	45	35	80	339	51	219	49
Tapachula	1,439,158	80	8	88	-	8	95	41
Tehuantepec	1,330,000	69	7	76	-	8	120	43
Tuxtepec	670,000	33	10	43	17	10	23	29
Tuxtla Gutiérrez	924,000	119	12	131	-	14	280	55
Huautla[1]	125,210	15	5	20	1	8	5	8
Mixes[1]	130,000	7	24	31	16	30	43	16
Puebla de los Angeles	7,262,387	838	237	1,075	1	320	1,330	445
Puebla de los Angeles*	4,140,413	419	200	619	-	279	750	215
Huajuapan de León	720,000	110	-	110	-	-	166	71
Huejutla	497,300	85	8	93	-	8	60	38
Tehuacán	925,626	87	9	96	-	11	136	57
Tlaxcala	979,048	137	20	157	1	22	218	64
San Luis Potosi	8,483,896	912	416	1,328	10	635	3,719	431
San Luis Potosi*	1,751,800	207	50	257	10	163	862	89
Celaya	1,372,326	164	61	225	-	111	542	64
Irapuato	1,062,000	108	39	147	-	50	168	61
León	2,407,572	216	164	380	-	169	1,008	104
Matehuala	219,148	23	6	29	-	6	39	17
Querétaro	1,671,050	194	96	290	-	136	1,100	96
Tlalnepantla	18,132,633	807	210	1,017	41	371	1,036	533
Tlalnepantla*	3,494,000	256	95	351	14	143	372	192
Cuautitlan	3,750,000	186	56	242	-	156	289	85
Ecatepec	3,400,000	110	17	127	4	21	12	89
Netzahualcóvotl	5,400,000	100	27	127	-	36	94	83
Xalapa	8,776,801	643	68	711	50	97	1,218	392
Xalapa*	1,094,393	133	10	143	-	18	264	68
Coatzacoalcos	891,000	40	5	45	3	12	149	25
Cordoba	644,494	72	4	76	-	4	163	38
Orizaba	498,648	59	13	72	-	20	168	40
Papantla	1,500,000	86	-	86	1	-	139	54
San Andrés Tuxtla	968,266	74	2	76	35	3	108	48
Tuxpan	1,380,000	90	-	90	3	-	19	55
Veracruz	1,800,000	89	34	123	8	40	208	64
Yucatán	4,674,072	347	137	484	34	260	952	237
Yucatán*	1,619,505	168	54	222	25	89	549	100
Campeche	601,600	50	9	59	-	33	118	35
Tabasco	1,343,000	115	16	131	-	79	170	61
Cancún-Chetumal[1]	957,000	7	50	57	3	59	114	37
Nuestra Sra. de los Mártires[2]	148,267	4	3	7	3	-	-	3
Nuestra Sra. del Paraiso		4,700[2]	2	3	5	-	3	1
Totals:	94,964,000[3]	11,064	3,672	14,736	781	6,619	27,606	6,049

Note: 1. Prelacy 2. Eparchy. 3.According to the *Conferencia del Episcopado Mexicano*.

Consecrated Life

INSTITUTES OF CONSECRATED LIFE

Religious institutes and congregations are special societies in the Church — institutes of consecrated life — whose members, called Religious, commit themselves by public vows to observance of the evangelical counsels of poverty, chastity and obedience in a community kind of life in accordance with rules and constitutions approved by church authority.

Secular institutes (covered in their own *Almanac* entries) are also institutes of consecrated life.

The particular goal of each institute and the means of realizing it in practice are stated in the rule and constitutions proper to the institute. Local bishops can give approval for rules and constitutions of institutes of diocesan rank. Pontifical rank belongs to institutes approved by the Holy See. General jurisdiction over all religious is exercised by the Congregation for Institutes of Consecrated Life and Societies of Apostolic Life. General legislation concerning religious is contained in Canons 573 to 709 in Book II, Part III, of the Code of Canon Law.

All institutes of consecrated life are commonly called religious orders, despite the fact that there are differences between orders and congregations. The best known orders include the Benedictines, Trappists, Franciscans, Dominicans, Carmelites and Augustinians, for men; and the Carmelites, Benedictines, Poor Clares, Dominicans of the Second Order and Visitation Nuns, for women. The orders are older than the congregations, which did not appear until the sixteenth century.

Contemplative institutes are oriented to divine worship and service within the confines of their communities, by prayer, penitential practices, other spiritual activities and self-supporting work. Examples are the Trappists and Carthusians, the Carmelite and Poor Clare nuns. Active institutes are geared for pastoral ministry and various kinds of apostolic work. Mixed institutes combine elements of the contemplative and active ways of life. While most institutes of men and women can be classified as active, all of them have contemplative aspects.

Clerical communities of men are those whose membership is predominantly composed of priests.

Non-clerical or lay institutes of men are the various brotherhoods.

"The Consecrated Life and Its Role in the Church and in the World" was the topic of the ninth general assembly of the Synod of Bishops held Oct. 2-29, 1994.

Societies of Apostolic Life

Some of the institutes listed below have a special kind of status because their members, while living a common life characteristic of religious, do not profess the vows of religious. Examples are the Maryknoll Fathers, the Oratorians of St. Philip Neri, the Paulists and Sulpicians. They are called societies of apostolic life and are the subject of Canons 731 to 746 of the Code of Canon Law.

RELIGIOUS INSTITUTES OF MEN IN THE UNITED STATES

Sources: Annuario Pontificio, The Official Catholic Directory; Catholic Almanac *survey. As of June 1, 2006.*

Africa, Missionaries of, M. Afr.: Founded 1868 at Algiers by Cardinal Charles M. Lavigerie; known as White Fathers until 1984. Generalate, Rome, Italy. U.S. headquarters, 1624 21st St. N.W., Washington, DC 20009, (202) 232-5154. Missionary work in Africa.

African Missions, Society of, S.M.A.: Founded 1856, at Lyons, France, by Bishop Melchior de Marion Brésillac. Generalate, Rome, Italy. American province (1941), 23 Bliss Ave., Tenafly, NJ 07670, (201) 567-9085, www.smafathers.com. Missionary work.

Alexian Brothers, C.F.A.: Founded fourteenth century in western Germany and Belgium during the Black Plague. Motherhouse, Aachen, Germany. Generalate, 198 James Blvd., Signal Mountain, TN

37377, (423) 886-0380. Hospital and general health work.

Assumptionists (Augustinians of the Assumption), A.A.: Founded 1845, at Nimes, France, by Rev. Emmanuel d'Alzon; in U.S., 1946. General House, Rome, Italy. U.S. province, 330 Market St., Brighton, MA 02135, (617) 783-0400, www.assumptionists.com. Educational, parochial, ecumenical, retreat, foreign mission work.

Atonement, Franciscan Friars of the, S.A.: Founded as an Anglican Franciscan community in 1898 at Garrison, NY, by Rev. Paul Wattson. Community corporately received into the Catholic Church in 1909. Generalate, St. Paul's Friary, Graymoor, Rte. 9, P.O. Box 300, Garrison, NY 10524, (914) 424-2113. Ecumenical, mission, retreat and charitable works.

Augustinian Recollects, O.A.R.: Founded 1588; in U.S., 1944. General motherhouse, Rome, Italy.

=6

Monastery of St. Cloud (formerly St. Augustine Province, 1944), 29 Ridgeway Ave., W. Orange, NJ 07052-3297, (973) 731-0616, www.augustinianrecollects.org. St. Nicholas of Tolentino Province (U.S. Delegation), St. Nicholas of Tolentino Monastery, 3201 Central Ave., Union City, NJ 07087, (201) 422-7550. Missionary, parochial, education work.

Augustinians (Order of St. Augustine), O.S.A.: Established canonically in 1256 by Pope Alexander IV; in U.S., 1796. General motherhouse, Rome, Italy. St. Thomas Monastery, 800 Lancaster Ave., Villanova, PA 19085-1687, (610) 519-7548, www.augustinians.org., (1796). Our Mother of Good Counsel Province (1941), Tolentine Center, 20300 Governors Hwy., Olympia Fields, IL 60461-1081, (708) 283-6659, www.midweststaugustinians.org. St. Augustine, Province of (1969), 1605 28th St., San Diego, CA 92102-1417, (619) 235-0247.

Barnabites (Clerics Regular of St. Paul), C.R.S.P.: Founded 1530, in Milan, Italy, by St. Anthony M. Zaccaria; approved 1533; in U.S., 1952. Historical motherhouse, Church of St. Barnabas (Milan). Generalate, Rome, Italy. North American province, 981 Swann Rd, P.O. Box 167, Youngstown, NY 14174, (716) 754-7489, www.catholicchurch.org/barnabites. Parochial, educational, mission work.

Basil the Great, Order of St. (Basilian Order of St. Josaphat), O.S.B.M.: General motherhouse, Rome, Italy. U.S. province, 29 Peacock Ln., Locust Valley, NY 11560, (516) 609-3262. Parochial work among Byzantine Ukrainian Rite Catholics.

Basilian Fathers (Congregation of the Priests of St. Basil), C.S.B.: Founded 1822, at Annonay, France. General motherhouse, Toronto, ON, Canada. U.S. address: 1910 W. Alabama, Houston, TX 77098, (713) 522-1736. Educational, parochial work.

Basilian Salvatorian Fathers, B.S.O.: Founded 1684, at Saida, Lebanon, by Eftimios Saifi; in U.S., 1953. General motherhouse, Saida, Lebanon. American headquarters, 30 East St., Methuen, MA 01844. Educational, parochial work among Eastern Rite peoples.

Benedictine Monks (Order of St. Benedict), O.S.B.: Founded 529, in Italy, by St. Benedict of Nursia; in U.S., 1846.

• **American Cassinese Congregation (1855):** Pres., Rt. Rev. Melvin J. Valvano, O.S.B., Newark Abbey, 528 Dr. Martin Luther King Blvd., Newark, NJ 07102, (973) 733-2822. Abbeys and priories belonging to the congregation:

St. Vincent Archabbey, 300 Fraser Purchase Rd., Latrobe, PA 15650, (724) 805-2503, www.benedictine.stvincent.edu. Saint John's Abbey, P.O. Box 2015, Collegeville, MN 56321, (320) 363-2548, www.saintjohnsabbey.org. St. Benedict's Abbey, 1020 North Second St., Atchison, KS 66002, (913) 367-7853, www.benedictine.edu/abbey/index.html. St. Mary's Abbey, 230 Mendham Rd., Morristown, NJ 07960, (973) 538-3231, www.osbmonks.org. Newark Abbey, 528 Dr. Martin Luther King, Jr., Blvd., Newark, NJ 07102, (973) 643-4800. Belmont Abbey, 100 Belmont-Mt. Holly Rd., Belmont, NC 28012, (704) 825-6675, www.bac.edu/monastery. St. Bernard Abbey, Cullman, AL 35055, (256) 734-8291. St. Gregory's Abbey, 1900 W. MacArthur, Shawnee, OK 74804, (405) 878-5491, www.stgregorys.edu. St. Leo Abbey, St. Leo, FL 33574, (352) 588-8626, www.saintleoabbey.org. Assumption Abbey, P.O. Box A, Richardton, ND 58652,

(701) 974-3315. St. Bede Abbey, Peru, IL 61354, (815) 223-3140, www.theramp.net/stbede/index.html. St. Martin's Abbey, 5300 Pacific Ave. S.E., Lacey, WA 98503-1297, (360) 438-4440, www.stmartin.edu. Holy Cross Abbey, P.O. Box 1510, Canon City, CO 81215, (719) 275-8631, www.holycrossabbey.org. St. Anselm's Abbey, 100 St. Anselm Dr., Manchester, NH, 03102, (603) 641-7651, www.anselm.edu. Holy Trinity Priory, P.O. Box 990, Butler, PA 16003, (724) 287-4461. Benedictine Priory, 6502 Seawright Dr., Savannah, GA 31406, (912) 356-3520, www.bcsav.net. Woodside Priory, 302 Portola Rd., Portola Valley, CA 94028, (650) 851-6133. Mary Mother of the Church Abbey, 12829 River Rd., Richmond, VA 23233, (804) 784-3508, www.richmondmonks.org. Abadia de San Antonio Abad, P.O. Box 729, Humacao, PR 00792, (787) 852-1616.

• **Swiss-American Congregation (1870):** Abbeys and priory belonging to the congregation:

St. Meinrad Archabbey, 100 Hill Dr., St. Meinrad, IN 47577-1003, (812) 357-6514, www.saintmeinrad.edu. Conception Abbey, 37114 State Hwy., VV, Conception, MO 64433-0501, (660) 944-3100, www.conceptionabbey.org. Mt. Michael Abbey, 22520 Mt. Michael Rd., Elkhorn, NE 68022-3400, (402) 289-2541, www.mountmichael.org. Subiaco Abbey, Subiaco, AR 72865, (479) 934-1001, www.subi.org. St. Joseph's Abbey, St. Benedict, LA 70457, (504) 892-1800. Mt. Angel Abbey, St. Benedict, OR 97373, (503) 845-3030. Marmion Abbey, 850 Butterfield Rd., Aurora, IL 60502, (630) 897-7215.

St. Benedict's Abbey, 12605 224th Ave., Benet Lake, WI 53102, (888) 482-1044, www.benetlake.org. Glastonbury Abbey, 16 Hull St., Hingham, MA 02043, (781) 749-2155, www.glastonburyabbey.org. Blue Cloud Abbey, Marvin, SD 57251-0098, (605) 398-9200, www.bluecloud.org. Corpus Christi Abbey, 101 South Vista Dr., Sandia, TX 78383, (361) 547-3257, www.geocities.com/Athens/styx/8125/ccabbey.html. Prince of Peace Abbey, 650 Benet Hill Rd., Oceanside, CA 92054, (760) 967-4200, www.princeofpeaceabbey.org. St. Benedict Abbey, 254 Still River Rd., PO Box 22, Still River (Harvard), MA 01467, (978) 456-8017.

• **Congregation of St. Ottilien for Foreign Missions:** St. Paul's Abbey, P.O. Box 7, 289 Rt. 206 South, Newton, NJ 07860, (973) 383-2470. Christ the King Priory, P.O. Box 528, Schuyler, NE 68661, (402) 352-2177, www.benedictinemissionhouse.com

• **Congregation of the Annunciation:** St. Andrew Abbey, P.O. Box 40, Valyermo, CA 93563-0040, (661) 944-2178, www.valyermo.com.

• **English Benedictine Congregation:** St. Anselm's Abbey, 4501 S. Dakota Ave. N.E., Washington, DC 20017, (202) 269-2300. Abbey of St. Gregory the Great, Cory's Lane, Portsmouth, RI 02871-1352, (401) 683-2000. Abbey of St. Mary and St. Louis, 500 S. Mason Rd., St. Louis, MO 63141-8500, (314) 434-3690, www.priory.org, www.stlouisabbey.org.

• **Houses Not in Congregations:** Mount Saviour Monastery, 231 Monastery Rd., Pine City, NY 14871-9787, (607) 734-1688, www.servtech.com/~msaviour; Weston Priory, 58 Priory Hill Rd., Weston, VT 05161-6400, (802) 824-5409, www.westonpriory.org.

Benedictines, Camaldolese Hermits of America, O.S.B. Cam.: Founded 1012, at Camaldoli, near Arezzo, Italy, by St. Romuald; in U.S., 1958. General motherhouse, Arezzo, Italy. U.S. foundation, New Camaldoli Hermitage, 62475 Highway 1, Big Sur, CA 93920, (831) 667-2456, www.contemplation.org.

Benedictines, Olivetan, O.S.B.: General motherhouse,

Siena, Italy. U.S. monasteries: Our Lady of Guadalupe Abbey, P.O. Box 1080, Pecos, NM 87552, (505) 757-6600, www.pecosabbey.org. Holy Trinity Monastery, P.O. Box 298, St. David, AZ 85630-0298, (520) 720-4642, www.holy trinitymonastery.org. Monastery of the Risen Christ, P.O. Box 3931, San Luis Obispo, CA 93403-3931, (805) 544-1810. Benedictine Monastery of Hawaii, P.O. Box 490, Waialua, HI 96791, (808) 637-7887, www.catholichawaii.com/religious/benedictine.

Benedictines, Subiaco Congregation, O.S.B.: Independent priory, 1983. Monastery of Christ in the Desert, Abiquiu, NM 87510, (505) 470-6668, www.christdesert.org. St. Mary's Monastery, P.O. Box 345, Petersham, MA 01366, (978) 724-3350.

Benedictines, Sylvestrine, O.S.B.: Founded 1231, in Italy, by Sylvester Gozzolini. General motherhouse, Rome, Italy. U.S. foundations: 17320 Rosemont Rd., Detroit, MI 48219, (313) 531-0140. 2711 E. Drahner Rd., Oxford, MI 48370, (248) 628-2249, www.bene-dictinemonks.org. 1697 State Highway 3, Clifton, NJ 07012, (201) 778-1177.

Blessed Sacrament, Congregation of the, S.S.S.: Founded 1856, at Paris, France, by St. Pierre Julien Eymard; in U.S., 1900. General motherhouse, Rome, Italy. U.S. province, 5384 Wilson Mills Rd., Cleveland, OH 44143-3092, (440) 442-6311, www.blessedsacra-ment.com. Eucharistic apostolate.

Brigittine Monks (Order of the Most Holy Savior), O.Ss.S.: Monastery of Our Lady of Consolation, 23300 Walker Lane, Amity, OR 97101, (503) 835-8080, www.brigittine.org.

Camaldolese Hermits of the Congregation of Monte Corona, Er. Cam.: Founded 1520, from Camaldoli, Italy, by Bl. Paul Giustiniani; in U.S., 1959; Motherhouse, Frascati (Rome), Italy. U.S. foundation, Holy Family Hermitage, 1501 Fairplay Rd., Bloomingdale, OH 43910-7971, (740) 765-4511.

Camillian Fathers and Brothers (Order of St. Camillus; Order of Servants of the Sick), O.S.Cam.: Founded 1582, at Rome, by St. Camillus de Lellis; in U.S., 1923. General motherhouse, Rome, Italy. North American province, 3345 South 1st St., Milwaukee, WI 53215, (414) 481-3696, www.camil-lians.org.

Carmelites (Order of Our Lady of Mt. Carmel), O. Carm.: General motherhouse, Rome, Italy. Most Pure Heart of Mary Province (1864), 1317 Frontage Rd., Darien, IL 60559, (630) 971-0050. North American Province of St. Elias (1931), P.O. Box 3079, Middletown, NY 10940-0890, (845) 344-2225. Mt. Carmel Hermitage, Pineland, R.R. 1, Box 330 C, Bolivar, PA, 15923, (724) 238-0423. Educational, charitable work.

Carmelites, Order of Discalced, O.C.D.: Established 1562, a Reform Order of Our Lady of Mt. Carmel; in U.S., 1924. Generalate, Rome, Italy. Western Province (1983), 926 E. Highland Ave., P.O. Box 2178, Redlands, CA 92373, (909) 793-0424. Province of St. Thérèse (Oklahoma, 1935), 515 Marylake Dr., Little Rock AR 72206, (501) 888-5827. Immaculate Heart of Mary Province (1947), 1233 S. 45th St., Milwaukee, WI 53214, (414) 672-7212. Our Lady of Mt. Carmel Monastery, 1628 Ridge Rd., Munster, IN 46321, (219) 838-7111. Spiritual direc-tion, retreat, parochial work.

Carmelites of Mary Immaculate, C.M.I.: Founded

1831, in India, by Bl. Kuriakose Elias Chavara and two other Syro-Malabar priests; canonically established, 1855. Generalate, Kerala, India. North American head-quarters, Holy Family Church, 21 Nassau Ave., Brooklyn, NY 11222, (718) 388-4866.

Carthusians, Order of, O. Cart.: Founded 1084, in France, by St. Bruno; in U.S., 1951. General mother-house, St. Pierre de Chartreuse, France. U.S., Charterhouse of the Transfiguration, Carthusian Monastery, 1800 Beartown Rd., Arlington, VT 05250, (802) 362-2550, www.chartreux.org. Cloistered con-templatives; semi-eremitic.

Charity, Brothers of, F.C.: Founded 1807, in Belgium, by Canon Peter J. Triest. General mother-house, Rome, Italy. American District (1963), 7720 Doe Lane, Laverock, PA 19038.

Charity, Servants of (Guanellians), S.C.: Founded 1908, in Italy, by Bl. Luigi Guanella. General mother-house, Rome, Italy. U.S. headquarters, St. Louis School, 16195 Old U.S. 12, Chelsea, MI 48118, (734) 475-8430, www.stlouiscenter.org.

Christ, Society of, S.Ch.: Founded 1932. General Motherhouse, Poznan, Poland; U.S.-Canadian Province, 3000 Eighteen Mile Rd., Sterling Heights, MI 48311.

Christian Brothers, Congregation of, C.F.C. (for-merly Christian Brothers of Ireland): Founded 1802 at Waterford, Ireland, by Bl. Edmund Ignatius Rice; in U.S., 1906. General motherhouse, Rome, Italy. American Province, Eastern U.S. (1916), 33 Pryer Terr., New Rochelle, NY 10804, (914) 712-7580. Brother Rice Province, Western U.S. (1966), 958 Western Ave., Joliet, IL 60435, (815) 723-5464. Educational work.

Christian Instruction, Brothers of (La Mennais Brothers), F.I.C.: Founded 1817, at Ploermel, France, by Abbe Jean Marie de la Mennais and Abbe Gabriel Deshayes. General motherhouse, Rome, Italy. American province, Notre Dame Institute, P.O. Box 159, Alfred, ME 04002, (207) 324-0067, www.ficbrothers.org.

Christian Schools, Brothers of the (Christian Brothers), F.S.C.: Founded 1680, at Reims, France, by St. Jean Baptiste de la Salle. General motherhouse, Rome, Italy. U.S. Conference, 4351 Garden City Dr., Suite 200, Landover, MD 20785, (301) 459-9410, www.cbconf.org. Baltimore Province (1845), Box 29, Adamstown, MD 21710-0029, (301) 874-5188, www.fscbaltimore.org. Brothers of the Christian Schools (Midwest Province) (1995), 7650 S. County Line Rd., Burr Ridge, IL 60527-4718, (630) 323-3725, www.cbmidwest.org. New York Province (1848), 800 Newman Springs Rd., Lincroft, NJ 07738, (732) 842-7420. Long Island-New England Province (1957), Christian Brothers Center, 635 Ocean Rd., Narragansett, RI 02882-1314, (401) 789-0244, www.cbline.org. San Francisco Province (1868), P.O. Box 3720, Napa, CA 94558, (707) 252-0222, www.delasalle.org. Fe Province (1921), De La Salle Christian Brothers, 1522 Carmel Dr., Lafayette, LA 70501, (337) 234-1973. Educational, charitable work.

Cistercians, Order of, O.Cist.: Founded 1098, by St. Robert. Headquarters, Rome, Italy. Our Lady of Spring Bank Abbey, 17304 Havenwood Rd., Sparta, WI 54656-8177, (608) 269-8138. Our Lady of Dallas Abbey, 3550 Cistercian Rd., Irving, TX 75039, (972) 438-2044. Cistercian Monastery of Our Lady of Fatima, 564 Walton Ave., Mt. Laurel, NJ 08054, (856)

235-1330. Cistercian Conventual Priory, St. Mary's Priory, 70 Schuylkill Rd., New Ringgold, PA 17960, (570) 943-2645, www.cistercian.org.

Cistercians of the Strict Observance, Order of (Trappists), O.C.S.O.: Founded 1098, in France, by St. Robert; in U.S., 1848. Generalate, Rome, Italy.

Abbey of Gethsemani (1848), 3642 Monks Rd., KY 40051, (502) 549-3117. Our Lady of New Melleray Abbey (1849), 6632 Melleray Circle, Peosta, IA 52068-7079, (563) 588-2319. Holy Spirit Monastery (1944), 2625 Hwy. 212 S.W., Conyers, GA 30094-4044, (770) 483-8705 (fax), www.trappist.net. Our Lady of Guadalupe Abbey (1947), P.O. Box 97, Lafayette, OR 97127, (503) 852-7174, www.trappistabbey.org. Our Lady of the Holy Trinity Abbey (1947), 1250 South 9500 East, Huntsville, UT 84317, (801) 745-3784, www.xmission.com~hta. Abbey of the Genesee (1951), P.O. Box 900, Piffard, NY 14533, (585) 243-0660, www.geneseeabbey.org. Mepkin Abbey (1949), 1098 Mepkin Abbey Rd., Moncks Corner, SC 29461-4796, (843) 761-8509, www.mepkinabbey.org. Our Lady of the Holy Cross Abbey (1950), 901 Cool Spring Lane, Berryville, VA 22611-2900, (540) 955-5277, www.holycrossabbeyberryville.org. Assumption Abbey (1950), Rt. 5, Box 1056, Ava, MO 65608-9142, (417) 683-5110. Abbey of New Clairvaux (1955), Vina, CA 96092, (530) 839-2161, www.maxinet.com/trappist. St. Benedict's Monastery (1956), 1012 Monastery Rd., Snowmass, CO 81654, (970) 927-3311.

Claretians (Missionary Sons of the Immaculate Heart of Mary), C.M.F.: Founded 1849, at Vich, Spain, by St. Anthony Mary Claret. General headquarters, Rome, Italy. Western Province, 1119 Westchester Pl., Los Angeles, CA 90019-3523, (323) 734-1824. Eastern Province, 400 N. Euclid Ave, Oak Park, IL 60302, (708) 848-2076. Missionary, parochial, educational, retreat work.

Clerics Regular Minor (Adorno Fathers) C.R.M.: Founded 1588, at Naples, Italy, by Ven. Augustine Adorno and St. Francis Caracciolo. General motherhouse, Rome, Italy. U.S. address, 575 Darlington Ave., Ramsey, NJ 07446, (201) 327-7375, members.tripod.com/~adornofathers.

Columban, Missionary Society of St. (St. Columban Foreign Mission Society), S.S.C.: Founded 1918. General headquarters, Dublin, Ireland. U.S. headquarters, P.O. Box 10, St. Columbans, NE 68056, (402) 291-1920, www.columban.org. Foreign mission work.

Comboni Missionaries of the Heart of Jesus (Verona Fathers), M.C.C.J.: Founded 1867, in Italy by Bl. Daniel Comboni; in U.S., 1939. General motherhouse, Rome, Italy. North American headquarters, Comboni Mission Center, 8108 Beechmont Ave., Cincinnati, OH 45255, (513) 474-4997. Mission work in Africa and the Americas.

Consolata Missionaries, I.M.C.: Founded 1901, at Turin, Italy, by Bl. Joseph Allamano. General motherhouse, Rome, Italy. U.S. headquarters, P.O. Box 5550, 2301 Rt. 27, Somerset, NJ 08875, (732) 297-9191.

Crosier Fathers (Canons Regular of the Order of the Holy Cross), O.S.C.: Founded 1210, in Belgium by Bl. Theodore De Celles. Generalate, Rome, Italy. U.S. Province of St. Odilia, 3510 Vivian Ave., Shoreview, MN 55126-3852, (651) 486-7456, www.crosier.org. Mission, retreat, educational work.

Cross, Brothers of the Congregation of Holy, C.S.C.: Founded 1837, in France, by Rev. Basil Moreau; U.S. province, 1841. Generalate, Rome, Italy.

Midwest Province (1841), Box 460, Notre Dame, IN 46556-0460, (219) 631-2912, www.hcc-nd.edu/mwp/. Southwest Province (1956), 1101 St. Edward's Dr., Austin, TX 78704-6512, (512) 442-7856, www.holycross-sw.org. Eastern Province (1956), 85 Overlook Circle, New Rochelle, NY 10804, (914) 632-4468, www.holycrossbrothers.org. Educational, social work, missions.

Cross, Congregation of Holy, C.S.C.: Founded 1837, in France; in U.S., 1841. Generalate, Rome, Italy. Indiana Province (1841), 54515 State Rd. 933, North, P.O. Box 1064, Notre Dame, IN 46556-1064, (574) 631-6196. Eastern Province (1952), 835 Clinton Ave., Bridgeport, CT 06604-2393, (203) 367-7252, www.holycross.org. Southern Province (1968), 2111 Brackenridge St., Austin, TX 78704, (512) 443-3886, www.southerncsc.org. Educational and pastoral work; home missions and retreats; foreign missions; social services and apostolate of the press.

Divine Word, Society of the, S.V.D.: Founded 1875, in Holland, by Bl. Arnold Janssen. General motherhouse, Rome, Italy. North American Province founded 1897 with headquarters in Techny, IL. Province of Bl. Joseph Freinademetz (Chicago Province) (1985, from merger of Eastern and Northern provinces), 1985 Waukegan Rd., Techny, IL 60082, (847) 272-2700. St. Augustine (Southern Province) (1940), 201 Ruella Ave., Bay St. Louis, MS 39520, (228) 467-4322, www.svdsouth.com. St. Therese of the Child Jesus (Western Province) (1964), 2737 Pleasant St., Riverside, CA 92507, (323) 735-8130.

Dominicans (Order of Friars Preachers), O.P.: Founded early 13th century by St. Dominic de Guzman. General headquarters, Santa Sabina, Rome, Italy. Eastern Province of St. Joseph (1805), 869 Lexington Ave., New York, NY 10021-6680, (212) 737-5757, www.op-stjoseph.org. Most Holy Name of Jesus (Western) Province (1912), 5877 Birch Ct., Oakland, CA 94618-1626, (510) 658-8722, www.opwest.org. St. Albert the Great (Central) Province (1939), 1909 S. Ashland Ave., Chicago, IL 60608, (312) 666-3244, www.op.org/domcentral. St. Martin de Porres Province (1979), 1421 N. Causeway Blvd., Suite 200, Metairie, LA 70001-4144, (504) 837-2129, www.opsouth.org. Spanish Province, U.S. foundation (1926), P.O. Box 279, San Diego, TX 78384, (512) 279-3596. Preaching, teaching, missions, research, parishes.

Edmund, Society of St., S.S.E.: Founded 1843, in France, by Fr. Jean Baptiste Muard. General motherhouse, Edmundite Generalate, 270 Winnoski Park, Colchester, VT 05439-0270, (802) 654-3400, www.sse.org. Educational, missionary work.

Eudists (Congregation of Jesus and Mary), C.J.M.: Founded 1643, in France, by St. John Eudes. General motherhouse, Rome, Italy. North American province, 6125 Premiere Ave., Charlesbourg, QC G1H 2V9, Canada, (418) 626-6494; U.S. community, 36 Flohr Ave., W. Seneca, NY 14224, (716) 825-4475, www.eudistes.org. Parochial, educational, pastoral, missionary work.

Francis, Brothers of Poor of St., C.F.P.: Founded 1857. Motherhouse, Aachen, Germany. U.S. province, P.O. Box 35, Wever, IA 52658-0035, (319) 752-4000, www.brothersofthepoorofstfrancis.org. Educational work, especially with poor and neglected youth.

Francis, Third Order Regular of St., T.O.R.: Founded 1221, in Italy; in U.S., 1910. General motherhouse, Rome, Italy. Most Sacred Heart of Jesus Province (1910), 128 Woodshire Dr., Pittsburgh, PA 15215-1714, (412) 781-8333. Immaculate Conception Province (1925), 3811 Emerson Ave. N., Minneapolis, MN 55412, (612) 529-7779, www.franciscanfriarstor.com. Franciscan Commissariat of the Spanish Province (1924), 301 Jefferson Ave., Waco, TX 76701-1419, (254) 752-8434. Educational, parochial, missionary work.

Francis de Sales, Oblates of St., O.S.F.S.: Founded 1871, by Fr. Louis Brisson. General motherhouse, Rome, Italy. Wilmington-Philadelphia Province (1906), 2200 Kentmere Parkway, Wilmington, DE 19806, (302) 656-8529, www.oblates.org. Toledo-Detroit Province (1966), 2056 Parkwood Ave., Toledo, OH 43620, (419) 243-5105. Educational, missionary, parochial work.

Francis Xavier, Brothers of St. (Xaverian Brothers), C.F.X.: Founded 1839, in Belgium, by Theodore J. Ryken. Generalate, 4409 Frederick Ave., Baltimore, MD, 21229, (410) 644-0034. Educational work.

Franciscan Brothers of Brooklyn, O.S.F.: Founded in Ireland; established at Brooklyn, 1858. Generalate, 135 Remsen St., Brooklyn, NY 11201, (718) 858-8217, www.franciscanbros.org. Educational work.

Franciscan Brothers of Christ the King, O.S.F.: Founded 1961. General motherhouse, 7329 E. Eastwood Ave., Indianapolis, IN 46239, (317) 862-9211.

Franciscan Brothers of the Holy Cross, F.F.S.C.: Founded 1862, in Germany. Generalate, Hausen, Linz Rhein, Germany; U.S. region, 2500 St. James Rd., Springfield, IL 62707, (217) 747-5947. Educational work.

Franciscan Brothers of the Third Order Regular, O.S.F.: Generalate, Mountbellew, Ireland. U.S. region, 2117 Spyglass Trail W., Oxnard, CA 93030, (805) 485-5002. Mailing address: 4522 Gainsborough Ave., Los Angeles, CA 90029.

Franciscan Friars of the Immaculate, F.F.I: Founded 1990, Italy. General motherhouse, Benevento, Italy. U.S. addresses, 600 Pleasant St., New Bedford, MA. 02740; 22 School Hill Rd., Baltic, CT 06330, (508) 996-8274.

Franciscan Friars of the Renewal, C.F.R.: Community established under jurisdiction of the archbishop of New York. Central House, St. Crispin Friary, 420 E. 156th St., Bronx, NY 10455, (718) 665-2441, www.franciscanfriars.com.

Franciscan Missionary Brothers of the Sacred Heart of Jesus, O.S.F.: Founded 1927, in the St. Louis archdiocese. Motherhouse, St. Joseph Rd., Eureka, MO 63025, (314) 587-3661. Care of aged, infirm, homeless men and boys.

Franciscans (Order of Friars Minor), O.F.M.: A family of the First Order of St. Francis (of Assisi) founded in 1209 and established as a separate jurisdiction in 1517; in U.S., 1844. General headquarters, Rome, Italy. English-speaking conference: 1615 Vine St., Cincinnati, OH 45210-1200, (513) 721-4700.

Immaculate Conception Province (1855), 125 Thompson St., New York, NY 10012, (212) 674-4388. Sacred Heart Province, Franciscan Missionary Union (1858), 3140 Meramec St., St. Louis, MO 63118-4339, (314) 353-7729. Assumption of the Blessed Virgin Mary Province (1887), P.O. Box 100, 165 East Pulaski St., Pulaski, WI 54162-0100. Holy Name Province (1901), 158 W. 27th St., 6th Floor, New York, NY 10001, (212) 924-1451, www.hnp.org. St. Barbara Province (1915), 1500 34th Ave., Oakland, CA 94601, (510) 536-3722.

Our Lady of Guadalupe Province (1985), 1350 Lakeview Rd. S.W., Albuquerque, NM 87105, (505) 877-5425. Commissariat of the Holy Cross (1912), P.O. Box 608, Lemont, IL 60439-0608, (630) 257-2494. Mt. Alverna Friary, 517 S. Belle Vista Ave., Youngstown, OH 44509, (330) 799-1888. Holy Family Croatian Custody (1926), 4851 S. Drexel Blvd., Chicago, IL 60615-1703, (773) 536-0552.

St. Casimir Lithuanian Vice-Province, P.O. Box 980, Kennebunkport, ME 04046, (207) 967-2011. Holy Gospel Province (Mexico), U.S. foundation, 2400 Marr St., El Paso, TX 79903, (915) 565-2921. Commissariat of the Holy Land, Mt. St. Sepulchre, 1400 Quincy St. N.E., Washington, DC 20017, (202) 269-5430. Holy Dormition Friary, Byzantine Slavonic Rite, P.O. Box 270, Rt. 93, Sybertsville, PA 18251, (570) 788-1212, www.holydorm.com. Academy of American Franciscan History, 1712 Euclid Ave., Berkeley, CA 94709. Preaching, missionary, educational, parochial, charitable work.

Franciscans (Order of Friars Minor Capuchin), O.F.M. Cap.: A family of the First Order of St. Francis (of Assisi) founded in 1209 and established as a separate jurisdiction in 1528. St. Joseph Province/St. Bonaventure Monastery (1857), 1740 Mt. Elliott Ave., Detroit, MI 48207-3427, (313) 579-2100. Province of St. Augustine (1873), 220 37th St., Pittsburgh, PA 15201, (412) 682-6011, www.capuchin.com. St. Mary Province (1952), 30 Gedney Park Dr., White Plains, NY 10605, (914) 761-3008. Province of the Stigmata of St. Francis (1918), P.O. Box 809, Union City, NJ 07087-0809, (201) 865-0611. Western American Capuchin Province, Our Lady of the Angels, 1345 Cortez Ave., Burlingame, CA 94010, (650) 342-1489, www.beafriar.com.

St. Stanislaus Friary (1948), 2 Manor Dr., Oak Ridge, NJ 07438, (973) 697-7757. Province of Mid-America (1977), 3553 Wyandot St., Denver, CO 80211, (303) 477-5436, www.midamcaps.org. Vice-Province of Texas, 604 Bernal Dr., Dallas, TX 75212, (214) 631-1937. St. John the Baptist Vice-Province, P.O. Box 21350, Rio Piedras, Puerto Rico 00928-1350, (787) 764-3090. General motherhouse, Rome, Italy. Missionary, parochial work, chaplaincies.

Franciscans (Order of Friars Minor Conventual), O.F.M. Conv.: A family of the First Order of St. Francis (of Assisi) founded in 1209 and established as a separate jurisdiction in 1517; first U.S. foundation, 1852. General curia, Rome, Italy. Immaculate Conception Province (1852), Immaculate Conception Friary, P.O. Box 629, Rensselaer, NY 12144, (518) 472-1000, www.franciscanseast. St. Anthony of Padua Province (1906), 12300 Folly Quarter Rd., Ellicott City, MD 21042, (410) 531-1400,www.stanthonyprovince.org. St. Bonaventure Province (1939), 6107 Kenmore Ave., Chicago, IL 60660, (773) 274-7681. Our Lady of Consolation Province (1926), 101 St. Anthony Dr., Mt. St. Francis, IN 47146, (812) 923-8444. St. Joseph of Cupertino Province (1981), P.O. Box 820, Arroyo Grande, CA 93421-0820, (805) 489-1012. Missionary, educational, parochial work.

Glenmary Missioners (The Home Missioners of

America): Founded 1939, in U.S.. General headquarters, P.O. Box 465618, Cincinnati, OH 45246, (513) 874-8900, www.glenmary.org. Home mission work.

Good Shepherd, Little Brothers of the, B.G.S.: Founded 1951, by Bro. Mathias Barrett. Foundation House, P.O. Box 389, Albuquerque, NM 87103, (505) 243-4238. General headquarters, Hamilton, ON, Canada. Operate shelters and refuges for aged and homeless; homes for handicapped men and boys, alcoholic rehabilitation center.

Holy Eucharist, Brothers of the, F.S.E.: Founded in U.S., 1957. Generalate, P.O. Box 25, Plaucheville, LA 71362, (318) 922-3630. Teaching, social, clerical, nursing work.

Holy Family, Congregation of the Missionaries of the, M.S.F.: Founded 1895, in Holland, by Rev. John P. Berthier. General motherhouse, Rome, Italy. U.S. provincialate, 3014 Oregon Ave., St. Louis, MO, 63118-1498, (314) 577-6300, www.msf-america.org. Belated vocations for the missions.

Holy Family, Sons of the, S.F.: Founded 1864, at Barcelona, Spain, by Bl. Jose Mañanet y Vives; in U.S., 1920. General motherhouse, Barcelona, Spain. U.S. address, 401 Randolph Rd., P.O. Box 4138, Silver Spring, MD 20914-4138, (301) 622-1184, www.hometown.aol.com/holyfamsem/index.htm.

Holy Ghost Fathers, C.S.Sp.: Founded 1703, in Paris, France, by Claude Francois Poullart des Places; in U.S., 1872. Generalate, Rome, Italy. Eastern Province (1872), 6230 Brush Run Rd., Bethel Park, PA 15102, (412) 831-0302, www.spiritans.org. Western Province (1964), 1700 W. Alabama St., Houston, TX 77098-2808, (713) 522-2882, www.spiritans.org. Missions, education.

Holy Ghost Fathers of Ireland: Founded 1971. U.S. delegates: 4849 37th St., Long Island City, NY 11101 (East); St. Dunstan's Church, 1133 Broadway, Mill Brae, CA 94030 (West).

Holy Spirit, Missionaries of the, M.Sp.S.: Founded 1914, at Mexico City, Mexico, by Felix Rougier. General motherhouse, Mexico City. U.S. headquarters, 9792 Oma Place, Garden Grove, CA 92841, (714) 534-5476, www.msps.org. Missionary work.

Immaculate Heart of Mary, Brothers of the, I.H.M.: Founded 1948, at Steubenville, Ohio, by Bishop John K. Mussio. Villa Maria Generalate, 609 N. 7th St., Steubenville, OH 43952, (740) 283-2462. Educational, charitable work.

Jesuits (Society of Jesus), S.J.: Founded 1534, in France, by St. Ignatius of Loyola; received papal approval, 1540; suppressed in 1773 and revived in 1814 by Pope Pius VII; first U.S. province, 1833. The Jesuits remain the largest single order in the Church. Generalate, Rome, Italy. U.S. national office, Jesuit Conference, 1616 P Street, N.W., Suite 300, Washington, DC 20036-1420, (202) 462-0400, www.jesuit.org. Maryland Province (1833), 5704 Roland Ave., Baltimore, MD 21210, (410) 532-1400, www.mdsj.org. New York Province (1943), 39 East 83rd St., New York, NY 10028, (212) 774-5500, www.nysj.org. Missouri Province (1863), 4511 W. Pine Blvd., St. Louis, MO 63108-2191, (314) 361-7765, www.jesuits-mis.org. New Orleans Province (1907), 500 S. Jefferson Davis Pkwy., New Orleans, LA 70119, (504) 821-0334.

California Province (1909), 300 College Ave., P.O. Box 519, Los Gatos, CA 95031, (408) 884-1600, www.calprov.org. New England Province (1926), 771 Harrison Ave., Boston, MA 02118, (617) 266-7233. Chicago Province (1928), 2050 N. Clark St., Chicago, IL 60614, (773) 975-6363, www.jesuits-chi.org. Oregon Province (1932), 2222 N.W. Hoyt, Portland, OR 97210, (503) 226-6977. Detroit Province (1955), 7303 W. Seven Mile Rd., Detroit, MI 48221-2121, (313) 861-7500, www.jesuitdet.org. Wisconsin Province (1955), PO Box 080288, Milwaukee, WI 53208-0288, (414) 937-6949, www.jesuitwisprov.org. Province of the Antilles (1947), U.S. address, 12725 S.W. 6th St., Miami, FL 33184, (305) 559-9044. Missionary, educational, literary work.

John of God, Brothers of the Hospitaller Order of St., O.H.: Founded 1537, in Spain. General motherhouse, Rome, Italy. American province, 2425 S. Western Ave., Los Angeles, CA 90018, (323) 731-0233, www.hospitallers.org. Nursing and related fields.

Joseph, Congregation of St., C.S.J.: General motherhouse, Rome, Italy. U.S. vice-province, 338 North Grand Ave., San Pedro, CA 90731-2006, (310) 831-5360. Parochial, missionary, educational work.

Joseph, Oblates of St., O.S.J.: Founded 1878, in Italy, by Bl. Joseph Marello; in U.S., 1929. General motherhouse, Rome, Italy. Our Lady of Sorrows Province, 1880 Hwy 315, Pittston, PA 18640, (570) 654-7542. California Province, 544 W. Cliff Dr., Santa Cruz, CA 95060, (831) 457-1868, www.osjoseph.org. Parochial, educational work.

Josephite Fathers, C.J.: General motherhouse, Ghent, Belgium; U.S. foundation, 180 Patterson Rd., Santa Maria, CA 93455, (805) 937-5378.

Josephites (St. Joseph's Society of the Sacred Heart), S.S.J.: Established 1893, in U.S. as American congregation (originally established in U.S., in 1871 by Mill Hill Josephites from England). General motherhouse, 1130 N. Calvert St., Baltimore, MD 21202-3802, (410) 727-3386, www.josephite.com. Evangelization in African-American community.

LaSalette, Missionaries of Our Lady of: Province of Mary, Mother of the Americas, 915 Maple Ave., Hartford, CT 06114-2330, (860) 956-8870. Mary Queen of Our Lady of LaSalette, P.O. Box 777, Twin Lakes, WI 53181.

Lateran, Canons Regular of the, C.R.L.: General House, Rome, Italy. U.S. address: 2317 Washington Ave., Bronx, NY 10458, (212) 295-9600.

Legionaries of Christ, L.C.: Founded 1941, in Mexico, by Rev. Marcial Maciel; in U.S., 1965. General headquarters, Rome, Italy. U.S. headquarters, 393 Derby Ave., Orange, CT 06477, (203) 795-2800; novitiate, 475 Oak Ave., Cheshire, CT 06410, (203) 271-0805, www.legionofchrist.org.

Little Brothers of St. Francis, L.B.S.F.: Founded 1970 in Archdiocese of Boston by Bro. James Curran. General fraternity, 785-789 Parker St., Boston, MA 02120-3021, (617) 442-2556, www.littlebrothersofstfrancis.org. Combine contemplative life with evangelical street ministry.

Mariannhill, Congregation of the Missionaries of, C.M.M.: Trappist monastery, begun in 1882 by Abbot Francis Pfanner in Natal, South Africa, became an independent modern congregation in 1909; in U.S., 1920. Generalate, Rome, Italy. U.S.-Canadian province (1938), Our Lady of Grace Monastery, 23715 Ann

Arbor Trail, Dearborn Hts., MI 48127-1449, (313) 561-2330, www.rc.net/detroit/marianhill. Foreign mission work.

Marians of the Immaculate Conception, Congregation of, M.I.C.: Founded 1673; U.S. foundation, 1913. General motherhouse, Rome, Italy. St. Casimir Province (1913), 6336 S. Kilbourn Ave., Chicago, IL 60629-5588, (773) 582-8191, www.themarians.org. St. Stanislaus Kostka Province (1948), Eden Hill, Stockbridge, MA 01262, (413) 298-1100. Educational, parochial, mission, publication work.

Marist Brothers, F.M.S.: Co-founded 1817, in France, by St. Marcellin Champagnat. Generalate, Rome, Italy. U.S. Province, 1241 Kennedy Blvd., Bayonne, NJ 07002, (201) 823-1115; www.maristbr.com. Educational, social, catechetical work.

Marist Fathers (Society of Mary), S.M.: Founded 1816, at Lyons, France, by Jean Claude Colin; in U.S., 1863. General motherhouse, Rome, Italy. Atlanta Province, P.O. Box 81144, Atlanta, GA 30366-1144, (770) 458-1435, www.maristsociety.org. Boston Province (1924), 27 Isabella St., Boston, MA 02116, (508) 879-7223. Educational, foreign mission, pastoral work.

Maronite Lebanese Missionaries, Congregation of, C.M.L.M.: Founded in Lebanon 1865; established in the U.S., 1991. U.S. foundation, Our Lady of the Cedars Maronite Mission, 11935 Bellfort Village, Houston, TX 77031, (281) 568-6800.

Maronite Monks of Most Holy Trinity Monastery: Founded in 1978 and canonically approved by John Paul II and established in the Eparchy of St. Maron in 1989. A community of contemplative monks dedicated to a life of prayer and Eucharistic Adoration. Most Holy Trinity Monastery, 67 Dugway Road, Petersham, MA 01366-9725, (978) 724-3347, www.maronitemonks.org.

Mary, Society of (Marianist Fathers and Brothers; Brothers of Mary), S.M.: Founded 1817, at Bordeaux, France, by Rev. William-Joseph Chaminade; in U.S., 1849. General motherhouse, Rome, Italy. Marianist Province of the U.S. (Meribah), 240 Emory Rd., Mineola, NY 11501, (516) 292-0200, www.marianists.org. The Marianist provinces of Cincinnati, St. Louis, Pacific, and New York have merged to form one province. Educational work.

Mary Immaculate, Missionary Oblates of, O.M.I.: Founded 1816 in France, by St. Charles Joseph Eugene de Mazenod; in U.S., 1849. General House, Rome, Italy. U.S. Province: 391 Michigan Ave., N.E., Washington, DC, 20017, (202) 529-4505. Southwest Area, 327 Oblate Dr., San Antonio, TX 78216-6602, (210) 349-1475, www.omiusa.org. Parochial, foreign mission, educational work, ministry to marginal.

Maryknoll (Catholic Foreign Mission Society of America), M.M.: Founded 1911, in U.S., by Frs. Thomas F. Price and James A. Walsh. General Center, Maryknoll, NY 10545, (914) 941-7590.

Mercedarians (Order of Our Lady of Mercy), O. de M.: Founded 1218, in Spain, by St. Peter Nolasco. General motherhouse, Rome, Italy. U.S. headquarters, 7758 E. Main Rd., LeRoy, NY, 14482, (716) 768-7110.

Mercy, Brothers of, F.M.M.: Founded 1856, in Germany. General motherhouse, Montabaur, Germany. American headquarters, 4520 Ransom Rd., Clarence, NY 14031, (716) 759-8341. Hospital work.

Mercy, Brothers of Our Lady, Mother of, C.F.M.M.: Founded 1844, in the Netherlands by Abp.

Jan Zwijsen. Generalate, Tilburg, the Netherlands. U.S. region, 7140 Ramsgate Ave., Los Angeles, CA 90045, (310) 338-5954, www.cmmbrothers.nl.

Mercy, Congregation of Priests of (Fathers of Mercy), C.P.M.: Founded 1808, in France, by Rev. Jean Baptiste Rauzan; in U.S., 1839. General mission house, Auburn, KY 42206, (270) 542-4164; www.fathersofmercy.com. Mission work.

Mill Hill Missionaries (St. Joseph's Society for Foreign Missions), M.H.M.: Founded 1866, in England, by Cardinal Vaughan; in U.S., 1951. International headquarters, London, England. American headquarters, 222 W. Hartsdale Ave., Hartsdale, NY 10530, (914) 682-0645.

Minim Fathers, O.M.: General motherhouse, Rome, Italy. North American delegation (1970), 3431 Portola Ave., Los Angeles, CA 90032, (213) 223-1101.

Missionaries of St. Charles, Congregation of the (Scalabrinians), C.S.: Founded 1887, at Piacenza, Italy, by Bl. John Baptist Scalabrini. General motherhouse, Rome, Italy. St. Charles Borromeo Province (1888), 27 Carmine St., New York, NY 10014, (212) 675-3993. St. John Baptist Province (1903), 546 N. East Ave., Oak Park, IL 60302, (708) 386-4430.

Missionaries of the Holy Apostles, M.Ss.A.: Founded 1962, Washington, DC, by Very Rev. Eusebe M. Menard. North American headquarters, 24 Prospect Hill Rd., Cromwell, CT 06416, (860) 632-3039.

Missionarii Franciscani Verbi Aeterni: Franciscan Missionaries of the Eternal Word, 5821 Old Leeds Rd., Irondale, AL 35210, www.mfva.info.

Missionary Servants of Christ, M.S.C.: Founded 1979 in U.S. by Bro. Edwin Baker. Headquarters, P.O. Box 270, 305 S. Lake St., Aurora, IL 60507-0270, (630) 892-2371, www.misacor-usa.org.

Missionhurst-CICM (Congregation of the Immaculate Heart of Mary): Founded 1862, at Scheut, Brussels, Belgium, by Very Rev. Theophile Verbist. General motherhouse, Rome, Italy. U.S. province, 4651 N. 25th St., Arlington, VA 22207, (703) 528-3800, www.missionhurst.org. Home and foreign mission work.

Montfort Missionaries (Missionaries of the Company of Mary), S.M.M.: Founded 1715, by St. Louis Marie Grignon de Montfort; in U.S., 1948. General motherhouse, Rome, Italy. U.S. province, 101-18 104th St., Ozone Park, NY 11416, (718) 849-5885. Mission work.

Mother Co-Redemptrix, Congregation of, C.M.C.: Founded 1953 at Lein-Thuy, Vietnam (North), by Fr. Dominic Mary Tran Dinh Thu; in U.S., 1975. General house, Hochiminhville, Vietnam. U.S. provincial house, 1900 Grand Ave., Carthage, MO 64836, (417) 358-7787, www.dongcong.net. Work among Vietnamese Catholics in U.S.

Oblates of the Virgin Mary, O.M.V.: Founded 1815, in Italy; in U.S., 1976; Generalate, Rome, Italy. U.S. provincialate: 2 Ipswich St., Boston, MA 02215, (617) 536-4141.

Oratorians (Congregation of the Oratory of St. Philip Neri), C.O.: Founded 1575, at Rome, by St. Philip Neri. A confederation of autonomous houses. U.S. addresses: P.O. Box 11586, Rock Hill, SC 29731, (803) 327-2097, www.rockhilloratory.org. P.O. Box 1688, Monterey, CA 93940, (831) 373-0476. 4450

Bayard St., Pittsburgh, PA 15213, (412) 681-3181. P.O. Drawer II, Pharr, TX 78577, (956) 843-8217. 109 Willoughby St., Brooklyn, NY 11201, (718) 788-5693.

Pallottines (Society of the Catholic Apostolate), S.A.C.: Founded 1835, at Rome, by St. Vincent Pallotti. Generalate, Rome, Italy. Immaculate Conception Province (1953), P.O. Box 979, South Orange, NJ 07079, (201) 762-2926. Mother of God Province (1946), 5424 W. Blue Mound Rd., Milwaukee, WI 53208, (414) 259-0688. Irish Province (1909), U.S. address: 3352 4th St., Wyandotte, MI 48192, www.irishpallotines.com. Queen of Apostles Province (1909), 448 E. 116th St., New York, NY 10029, (212) 534-0681. Christ the King Province, 3452 Niagara Falls, Blvd., N. Tonawanda, NY 14120, (716) 694-4313. Charitable, educational, parochial, mission work.

Paraclete, Servants of the, s.P.: Founded 1947, Santa Fe, N.M., archdiocese. Generalate and U.S. motherhouse, 18161 State Hwy. 4, Jemez Springs, NM 87025-0010, (505) 829-3586, www.theservants.org. Devoted to care of priests.

Paris Foreign Missions Society, M.E.P.: Founded 1662, at Paris, France. Headquarters, Paris, France; U.S. establishment, 930 Ashbury St., San Francisco, CA 94117, (415) 664-6747. Mission work and training of native clergy.

Passionists (Congregation of the Passion), C.P.: Founded 1720, in Italy, by St. Paul of the Cross. General motherhouse, Rome, Italy. St. Paul of the Cross Province (Eastern Province) (1852), 80 David St., South River, NJ 08882, (732) 257-7177, www.thepassionists.org. Holy Cross Province (Western Province), 5700 N. Harlem Ave., Chicago, IL 60631, (773) 631-6336.

Patrician Brothers (Brothers of St. Patrick), F.S.P.: Founded 1808, in Ireland, by Bishop Daniel Delaney. U.S. novitiate, 7820 Bolsa Ave., Midway City, CA 92655, (714) 897-8181. Educational work.

Patrick's Missionary Society, St., S.P.S.: Founded 1932, at Wicklow, Ireland, by Msgr. Patrick Whitney; in U.S., 1953. International headquarters, Kiltegan Co., Wicklow, Ireland. U.S. foundations: 70 Edgewater Rd., Cliffside Park, NJ 07010, (201) 943-6575, 19536 Eric Dr., Saratoga, CA 95070, (408) 253-3135, www.spms.org; 1347 W. Granville Ave., Chicago, IL 60660, (773) 973-3737.

Pauline Fathers (Order of St. Paul the First Hermit), O.S.P.P.E.: Founded 1215; established in U.S., 1955. General motherhouse, Czestochowa, Jasna Gora, Poland; U.S. province, P.O. Box 2049, Doylestown, PA 18901, (215) 345-0607.

Pauline Fathers and Brothers (Society of St. Paul for the Apostolate of Communications), S.S.P.: Founded 1914, by Very Rev. James Alberione; in U.S., 1932. Motherhouse, Rome, Italy. New York province (1932), P.O. Box 139, Ellsworth, OH 44416-0139, (330) 533-7427. Social communications work.

Paulists (Missionary Society of St. Paul the Apostle), C.S.P.: Founded 1858, in New York, by Fr. Isaac Thomas Hecker. Motherhouse: 86-11 Midland Pkwy, Jamaica Estates, NY 11432, (718) 291-5995, www.paulist.org. Missionary, ecumenical, pastoral work.

Piarists (Order of the Pious Schools), Sch.P.: Founded 1617, at Rome, Italy, by St. Joseph Calasanctius. General motherhouse, Rome, Italy. U.S. province, 363 Valley Forge Rd., Devon, PA 19333,

(610) 688-7337. New York-Puerto Rico vice-province (Calasanzian Fathers), P.O. Box 34118, Ponce, PR 00734, (787) 840-0610. California vice province, 3940 Perry St., Los Angeles, CA 90063, (323) 261-1386. Educational work.

Pius X, Brothers of St., C.S.P.X.: Founded 1952, at La Crosse, WI, by Bishop John P. Treacy. Motherhouse, P.O. Box 217, De Soto, WI 54624. Education.

Pontifical Institute for Foreign Missions, P.I.M.E.: Founded 1850, in Italy, at request of Pope Pius IX. General motherhouse, Rome, Italy. U.S. province, 17330 Quincy Ave., Detroit, MI 48221, (313) 342-4066, www.pimeusa.org work.

Precious Blood, Society of, C.P.P.S.: Founded 1815, in Italy, by St. Gaspar del Bufalo. General motherhouse, Rome, Italy. Cincinnati Province, 431 E. Second St., Dayton, OH 45402, (937) 228-9263, www.cpps-preciousblood.org. Kansas City Province, P.O. Box 339, Liberty, MO 64069-0339, (816) 781-4344. Pacific Province, 2337 134th Ave. W., San Leandro, CA 94577, (510) 357-4982, www.rc.net/oakland/cpps. Atlantic Province 100 Pelmo Cres., Toronto, ON M9N 2Y1, (416) 614-7096, www.precious-blood.org.

Premonstratensians (Order of the Canons Regular of Premontre; Norbertines), O. Praem.: Founded 1120, at Premontre, France, by St. Norbert; in U.S., 1893. Generalate, Rome, Italy. St. Norbert Abbey, 1016 N. Broadway, DePere, WI 54114, (920) 337-4300, www.snc.edu/norbertines. Daylesford Abbey, 220 S. Valley Rd., Paoli, PA 19301, (610) 647-2530, www.daylesford.org. St. Michael's Abbey, 19292 El Toro Rd., Silverado, CA 92676, (949) 858-0222, www.abbeynews.com. Immaculate Conception Priory (1997), 3600 Philadelphia Pike, Claymont, DE 19703, (302) 792-2791. Educational, parish work.

Priestly Fraternity of St. Peter, F.S.S.P.: Founded and approved Oct. 18, 1988; first foundation in U.S., 1991. U.S. headquarters, St. Peter's House, Griffin Rd., P.O. Box 196, Elmhurst, PA 18416, (570) 842-4000, www.fssp.com. Pastoral and sacramental ministry using the 1962 liturgical books.

Providence, Sons of Divine, F.D.P.: Founded 1893, at Tortona, Italy, by Bl. Luigi Orione; in U.S., 1933. General motherhouse, Rome, Italy. U.S. address, 111 Orient Ave., E. Boston, MA 02128, (617) 569-2100.

Redemptorist Fathers and Brothers (Congregation of the Most Holy Redeemer), C.SS.R.: Founded 1732, in Italy, by St. Alphonsus Mary Liguori. Generalate, Rome, Italy. Baltimore Province (1850), 7509 Shore Rd., Brooklyn, NY 11209, (718) 833-1900. Redemptorist-Denver Province (1875), Box 300399, Denver, CO 80203-0399, (303) 370-0035, www.redemptorists-denver.org. Richmond Vice-Province (1942), 313 Hillman St., P.O. Box 1529, New Smyrna Beach, FL 32170, (904) 427-3094. Mission work.

Resurrectionists (Congregation of the Resurrection), C.R.: Founded 1836, in France, under direction of Bogdan Janski. Motherhouse, Rome, Italy. U.S. Province, 7050 N. Oakley Ave., Chicago, IL 60645-3426, (773) 465-8320, www.resurrectionists.com. Ontario Kentucky Province, U.S. address, 338 N. 25th St., Louisville, KY 40212, (502) 772-3694.

Rogationist Fathers, R.C.J.: Founded by Bl. Annibale (Hannibal) di Francia, 1887. General motherhouse, Rome, Italy. U.S. delegation: 2688 S. Newmark Ave., Sanger, CA 91343, (209) 875-5808. Charitable work.

Rosary, Brothers of Our Lady of the Holy, F.S.R.:

Founded 1956, in U.S. motherhouse and novitiate, 232 Sunnyside Dr., Reno, NV 89503-3510, (775) 747-4441.

Rosminians (Institute of Charity), I.C.: Founded 1828, in Italy, by Antonio Rosmini-Serbati. General motherhouse, Rome, Italy. U.S. address, 2327 W. Heading Ave., Peoria, IL 61604, (309) 676-6341. Charitable work.

Sacred Heart, Brothers of the, S.C.: Founded 1821, in France, by Rev. Andre Coindre. General motherhouse, Rome, Italy. New Orleans Province (1847), 4600 Elysian Fields Ave., New Orleans, LA 70122, (504) 282-5693. New England Province (1945), 159 Earle St., Woonsocket, RI 02895, (401) 769-0313, www.brothersofthesacredheart.org. New York Province (1960), 141-11 123 Ave., South Ozone Park, NY 11436-1426, (718) 322-3309. Educational work.

Sacred Heart, Missionaries of the, M.S.C.: Founded 1854, by Rev. Jules Chevelier. General motherhouse, Rome, Italy. U.S. province, 305 S. Lake St., Aurora, IL 60507-0271, (630) 892-8400.

Sacred Heart of Jesus, Congregation of the (Sacred Heart Fathers and Brothers), S.C.J.: Founded 1877, in France. General motherhouse, Rome, Italy. U.S. provincial office, P.O. Box 289, Hales Corners, WI 53130-0289, (414) 425-6910, www.scj.org. Educational, preaching, mission work.

Sacred Hearts of Jesus and Mary, Congregation of (Picpus Fathers), SS.CC.: Founded 1805, in France, by Fr. Coudrin. General motherhouse, Rome, Italy. Eastern Province (1946), 77 Adams St. (Box 111), Fairhaven, MA 02719, (508) 993-2442, www.sscc.org. Western Province (1970), 2150 Damien Ave., La Verne, CA 91750, (909) 593-5441. Hawaii Province, Box 797, Kaneohe, Oahu, HI 96744, (808) 247-5035. Mission, educational work.

Sacred Hearts of Jesus and Mary, Missionaries of the, M.SS.CC.: Founded 1833, in Naples, Italy, by Cajetan Errico. General motherhouse, Rome, Italy. U.S. headquarters, 2249 Shore Rd., Linwood, NJ 08221, (609) 927-5600.

Salesians of St. John Bosco (Society of St. Francis de Sales), S.D.B.: Founded 1859, by St. John (Don) Bosco. Generalate, Rome, Italy. St. Philip the Apostle Province (1902), 148 Main St., P.O. Box 639, New Rochelle, NY 10802-0639, (914) 636-4225. San Francisco Province (1926), 1100 Franklin St., San Francisco, CA 94109, (415) 441-7144.

Salvatorians (Society of the Divine Savior), S.D.S.: Founded 1881, in Rome, by Fr. Francis Jordan; in U.S., 1896. General headquarters, Rome, Italy. U.S. province, 1735 N. Hi-Mount Blvd., Milwaukee, WI 53208-1720, (414) 258-1735, www.salvatorians.com. Educational, parochial, mission work; campus ministries, chaplaincies.

Scalabrinians: *See* **Missionaries of St. Charles.**

Servites (Order of Friar Servants of Mary), O.S.M.: Founded 1233, at Florence, Italy, by Seven Holy Founders. Generalate, Rome, Italy. United States Province (1967), 3121 W. Jackson Blvd., Chicago, IL 60612, (773) 533-0360. General apostolic ministry.

Somascan Fathers, C.R.S.: Founded 1534, at Somasca, Italy, by St. Jerome Emiliani. General motherhouse, Rome, Italy. U.S. address, Pine Haven Boys Center, River Rd., P.O. Box 162, Suncook, NH 03275, (603) 485-7141, www.somascans.org.

Society of Our Lady of the Most Holy Trinity, S.O.L.T.: Headquarters, Casa San Jose, 109 W. Avenue F, P.O. Box 152, Robstown, TX 78380, (512) 387-2754.

Sons of Mary Missionary Society (Sons of Mary, Health of the Sick), F.M.S.I.: Founded 1952, in the Boston archdiocese, by Rev. Edward F. Garesche, S.J. Headquarters, 567 Salem End Rd., Framingham, MA 01701-5599, (508) 879-2541, www.sonsofmary.com.

Stigmatine Fathers and Brothers (Congregation of the Sacred Stigmata), C.S.S.: Founded 1816, by St. Gaspar Bertoni. General motherhouse, Rome, Italy. North American Province, 554 Lexington St., Waltham, MA 02452-3097, (781) 209-3100, www.stigmatines.com. Parish work.

Sulpicians (Society of Priests of St. Sulpice), S.S.: Founded 1641, in Paris, by Rev. Jean Jacques Olier. General motherhouse, Paris, France; U.S. province, 5408 Roland Ave., Baltimore, MD 21210, (410) 323-5070, www.sulpicians.org. Education of seminarians and priests.

Theatines (Congregation of Clerics Regular), C.R.: Founded 1524, in Rome, by St. Cajetan. General motherhouse, Rome, Italy. U.S. headquarters, 1050 S. Birch St., Denver, CO 80246, (303) 756-5522.

Trappists: *See* **Cistercians of the Strict Observance.**

Trinitarians (Order of the Most Holy Trinity), O.SS.T.: Founded 1198, by St. John of Matha; in U.S., 1911. General motherhouse, Rome, Italy. U.S. headquarters, P.O. Box 5742, Baltimore, MD 21282, (410) 486-5171.

Trinity Missions (Missionary Servants of the Most Holy Trinity), S.T.: Founded 1929, by Fr. Thomas Augustine Judge. Generalate, P.O. Box 7130, Silver Springs, MD 20907-7130, (301) 434-6761, www.trinitymissions.org. Home mission work.

Viatorian Fathers (Clerics of St. Viator), C.S.V.: Founded 1831, in France, by Fr. Louis Joseph Querbes. General motherhouse, Rome, Italy. Province of Chicago (1882), 1212 E. Euclid Ave., Arlington Hts., IL 60004, (847) 398-1353. Educational work.

Vincentians (Congregation of the Mission; Lazarists), C.M.: Founded 1625, in Paris, by St. Vincent de Paul; in U.S., 1818. General motherhouse, Rome, Italy. Eastern Province (1867), 500 E. Chelten Ave., Philadelphia, PA 19144, (215) 848-1985. Midwest Province (1888), 13663 Rider Trail North, Earth City, MO 63045, (314) 344-1184, www.vincentian.org. New England Province (1975), 234 Keeney St., Manchester, CT 06040-7048, (860) 643-2828. American Italian Branch, Our Lady of Pompei Church, 3600 Claremont St., Baltimore, MD 21224, (410) 675-7790. American Spanish Branch (Barcelona, Spain), 118 Congress St., Brooklyn, NY 11201-6045, (718) 624-5670. American Spanish Branch (Zaragoza, Spain), Holy Agony Church, 1834 3rd Ave., New York, NY 10029, (212) 289-5589. Western Province (1975), 420 Date St., Montebello, CA 90640, (323) 721-5486. Southern Province (1975), 3826 Gilbert Ave., Dallas, TX 75219, (214) 526-0234, www.cmsouth.org. Educational work.

Vocationist Fathers (Society of Divine Vocations), S.D.V.: Founded 1920, in Italy; in U.S., 1962. Generalate, Rome, Italy. U.S. headquarters, 90 Brooklake Rd., Florham Park, NJ 07932, (973) 966-6262, www.vocationist.org.

Xaverian Missionary Fathers, S.X.: Founded 1895, by Bl. Guido Conforti, at Parma, Italy. General motherhouse, Rome, Italy. U.S. province, 12 Helene Ct., Wayne, NJ 07470, (973) 942-2975, www.xaviermis- sionaries.org. Foreign mission work.

MEMBERSHIP OF RELIGIOUS INSTITUTES OF MEN

Principal source: Annuario Pontificio. *Statistics as of Jan. 1, 2006, unless indicated otherwise.* Listed below are world membership statistics of institutes of men of pontifical right with 500 or more members; the number of priests is in parentheses. Also listed are institutes with less than 500 members with houses in the U.S.

Jesuits (13,965)	19,850
Salesians (11,072)	16,665
Franciscans (Friars Minor) (10,671)	15,794
Franciscans (Capuchins) (7,080)	11,229
Benedictines (4,344)	7,798
Dominicans (4,488)	6,109
Society of the Divine Word (3,891)	6,070
Brothers of Christian Schools	5,728
Redemptorists (4,092)	5,622
Franciscans (Conventuals) (2,927)	4,595
Oblates of Mary Immaculate (3,270)	4,569
Marist Brothers	4,369
Discalced Carmelites (O.C.D.) (2,627)	4,053
Vincentians (3,123)	4,049
Claretians (2,065)	3,089
Holy Spirit (Holy Ghost), Vincentians Congregation of (2,185)	2,985
Augustinians (2,092)	2,824
Pallottines (1,632)	2,356
Carmelites of the BVM (1,437)	2,327
Priests of the Sacred Heart (1,629)	2,316
Trappists (918)	2,266
Passionists (1,715)	2,261
Combonian Missionaries of the Heart of Jesus (1,317)	2,141
Carmelites (O.Carm.) (1,383)	2,091
Missionaries of the Sacred Heart of Jesus (1,443)	2,044
Legionaries of Christ (642)	1,917
Missionaries of Africa (1,553)	1,881
Holy Cross, Congregation of (756)	1,588
Marianists (461)	1,473
Cistercians (Common Observance) (717)	1,470
Christian Brothers	1,435
Piarists (1,014)	1,404
Hospitallers of St. John of God (142)	1,347
Premonstratensians (952)	1,294
Brothers of Christian Instruction of St. Gabriel (27)	1,280
Brothers of the Sacred Heart (40)	1,249
Salvatorians (825)	1,222
Missionaries of St. Francis de Sales of Annecy (681)	1,216
Augustinians (Recollects) (940)	1,179
Marists (976)	1,172
Ministers of the Sick (Camillians) (687)	1,126
Little Workers of Divine Providence (707)	1,082
Society of St. Paul (557)	1,077
Immaculate Heart of Mary, Congregation of (Missionhurst; Scheut Missionaries) (850)	1,058
Brothers of Christian Instruction of Ploërmel	1,001
Consolata Missionaries (770)	987
Montfort Missionaries (692)	970
Sacred Hearts, Congregation of (Picpus) (760)	970
Society of African Missions (847)	967
LaSalette Missionaries (698)	967
Missionaries of the Holy Family (662)	947
Blessed Sacrament, Congregation of (663)	915
Assumptionists (589)	911
Servants of Mary (650)	902
Franciscans (Third Order Regular) (564)	863
Xaverian Missionaries (663)	854
Scalabrinians (607)	769
Mercedarians (514)	735
Canons Regular of St. Augustine (581)	703
Most Precious Blood (463)	665
Viatorians (273)	645
St. Joseph, Congregation of (474)	630
Oblates of St. Francis de Sales (468)	613
Order of St. Basil the Great (Basilians of St. Josaphat) (310)	609
Missionaries of the Mill Hill (437)	589
Columbans (541)	584
Trinitarians (385)	569
Brothers of Charity (Ghent)	565
Pontifical Institute for Foreign Missions (488)	557
Oratorians (418)	554
Society of Christ (381)	545
Oblates of St. Joseph (339)	542
Maryknollers (449)	534
Order of St. Paul the First Hermit (308)	510
Marian Fathers and Brothers (350)	500
Eudists (387)	496
Somascans (354)	486
Servants of Charity (313)	476
Stigmatine Fathers and Brothers (316)	443
Crosiers (Order of the Holy Cross) (292)	434
Resurrection, Congregation of the (338)	415
Mariannhill Missionaries (210)	411
St. Patrick's Mission Society (324)	405
Rogationists (260)	400
Missionaries of the Holy Spirit (262)	393
Brothers of the Immaculate Conception (115)	383
Barnabites (298)	382
Carthusians (170)	335
Vocationist Fathers (155)	324
Sulpicians (322)	322
Paris Foreign Mission Society (297)	310
Rosminians (209)	308
Priestly Fraternity of St. Peter (169)	270
Little Brothers of Jesus (66)	234
Xaverian Brothers	232
Brothers of St. Patrick	207
Theatines (122)	203

Sons of the Holy Family (134)	197	Clerics Regular Minor (Adorno Fathers)	
Oblates of the Virgin Mary (119)	196	(45)	97
Discalced Augustinians (101)	192	Alexian Brothers (3)	96
Charitable Schools (95)	188	Franciscan Brothers of Brooklyn	91
Minim Fathers (109)	173	Brothers of Our Lady Mother of Mercy (22)	88
Paulists (155)	170	Glenmary Missioners (53)	72
Bethlehem Missionaries (127)	169	Camaldolese Hermits of Monte Corona	
Missionary Servants of the Most Holy		(26)	61
Trinity (89)	134	Clerics Regular of the Mother of God (46)	61
Franciscan Friars of the Atonement (84)	128	Sacerdotal Fraternity, Cong. of the (23)	48
Basilian Salvatorian Fathers (95)	121	Brothers of Mercy	44
Mary Immaculate, Sons of (74)	116	Franciscan Brothers of the Holy Cross (1)	43
Josephites (C.J.) (84)	113	Society of St. Edmund (38)	42
Presentation Brothers	108	Servants of the Holy Paraclete (19)	37
Josephites (St. Joseph's Society of the Sacred		Little Brothers of the Good Shepherd (3)	33
Heart—S.S.J.) (89)	101		

RELIGIOUS INSTITUTES OF WOMEN IN THE UNITED STATES

Sources: The Official Catholic Directory; Catholic Almanac *survey. As of June 1, 2006.*

Adorers of the Blood of Christ, A.S.C.: Founded 1834, in Italy; in U.S., 1870. General motherhouse, Rome, Italy. U.S. provinces: 721 Emerson Rd., #685, St. Louis, MO 63141, (314) 991-5400, Columbia, PA 17512, (717) 285-4536, www.adorers.org. Education, retreats, social services, pastoral ministry.

Africa, Missionary Sisters of Our Lady of (Sisters of Africa), M.S.O.L.A.: Founded 1869, at Algiers, Algeria, by Cardinal Lavigerie; in U.S., 1929. General motherhouse, Rome, Italy. U.S. headquarters, 47 W. Spring St., Winooski, VT 05404-1397, (802) 655-4003, www.smnda.org. Medical, educational, catechetical and social work in Africa.

Agnes, Sisters of St., C.S.A.: Founded 1858, in U.S., by Rev. Caspar Rehrl. General motherhouse, 320 County Rd., Fond du Lac, WI 54935, (920) 907-2321, www.csasisters.org. Education, health care, social services.

Ann, Sisters of St., S.S.A.: Founded 1834, in Italy; in U.S., 1952. General motherhouse, Rome, Italy. U.S. headquarters, Mount St. Ann, Ebensburg, PA 15931, (814) 472-9354.

Anne, Sisters of St., S.S.A.: Founded 1850, at Vaudreuil, QC, Canada; in U.S., 1866. General motherhouse, Lachine, QC, Canada. U.S. address, 720 Boston Post Rd., Marlborough, MA 01752, (508) 597-0204, www.sistersofsaintanne.org. Retreat work, pastoral ministry, religious education.

Anthony, Missionary Servants of St., M.S.S.A.: Founded 1929, in U.S., by Rev. Peter Basque. General motherhouse, 100 Peter Baque Rd., San Antonio, TX 78209, (210) 824-4553. Social work.

Antonine Maronite Sisters: Founded in Beirut, Lebanon. Motherhouse, Couvent Mar-Doumith, Roumieh, El-Metn, B.P. 84, Borumana, Lebanon. U.S. house, 2691 North Lipkey Rd., North Jackson, OH 44451, (330) 538-9822.

Assumption, Little Sisters of the, L.S.A.: Founded 1865, in France; in U.S., 1891. General motherhouse, Paris, France. U.S. provincialate, 100 Gladstone Ave., Walden, NY 12586, (914) 778-0667, www.littlesisters.org. Social work, nursing, family life education.

Assumption, Religious of the, R.A.: Founded 1839, in France; in U.S., 1919. Generalate, Paris, France. North American province, 11 Old English Rd., Worcester, MA 01609, (508) 793-1954.

Assumption of the Blessed Virgin, Sisters of the, S.A.S.V.: Founded 1853, in Canada; in U.S., 1891. General motherhouse, Nicolet, QC, Canada. U.S. province, 316 Lincoln St., Worcester, MA 01605, (508) 856-9450. Education, mission, pastoral ministry.

Augustinian Nuns of Contemplative Life, O.S.A.: Established in Spain in 13th century. U.S. foundation, Convent of Our Mother of Good Counsel, 440 Marley Rd., New Lenox, IL, 60451, (815) 463-9662, www.lampsalight.org.

Augustinian Sisters, Servants of Jesus and Mary, Congregation of, O.S.A.: Generalate, Rome, Italy. U.S. foundation, St. John School, 513 E. Broadway, Brandenburg, KY 40108, (270) 422-2088, www.stjohnonline.org.

Basil the Great, Sisters of the Order of St. (Byzantine Rite), O.S.B.M.: Founded fourth century, in Cappadocia, by St. Basil the Great and his sister, St. Macrina; in U.S., 1911. Generalate, Rome, Italy. U.S. motherhouses: Philadelphia Ukrainian Byzantine Rite, 710 Fox Chase Rd., Philadelphia, PA 19046-4198, (215) 342-4222, www.basilianfoxchase.org. Pittsburgh Ruthenian Byzantine Rite, Mount St. Macrina, P.O. Box 878, Uniontown, PA 15401, (724) 438-8644. Education, health care.

Benedict, Sisters of the Order of St., O.S.B.: Our Lady of Mount Caritas Monastery (founded 1979, Ashford, CT), 54 Seckar Rd., Ashford, CT 06278, (860) 429-7457. Contemplative.

Benedictine Nuns, O.S.B.: St. Scholastica Priory, Box 606, Petersham, MA 01366, (978) 724-3213, www.petershampriory.org. Cloistered.

Benedictine Nuns of the Congregation of Solesmes, O.S.B.: U.S. establishment, 1981, in Burlington diocese. Monastery of the Immaculate Heart of Mary, 4103 Vt. Rte 100, Westfield, VT 05874, (802) 744-6525, www.ihmwestfield.com. Cloistered, papal enclosure.

Benedictine Nuns of the Primitive Observance, O.S.B.: Founded c. 529, in Italy; in U.S., 1948. Abbey of Regina Laudis, Flanders Rd., Bethlehem, CT 06751, (203) 266-7727, www.abbeyofreginalaudis.com. Cloistered.

Benedictine Sisters, O.S.B.: Founded c. 529, in Italy; in U.S., 1852. General motherhouse, Eichstatt, Bavaria, Germany. U.S. addresses: St. Emma

Monastery, motherhouse and novitiate, 1001 Harvey Ave., Greensburg, PA 15601, (724) 834-3060, www.stemma.org. Abbey of St. Walburga, 32109 N. U.S. Highway 287, Virginia Dale, CO 80536, (970) 472-0612, www.walburga.org.

Benedictine Sisters, Missionary, O.S.B.: Founded 1885. Generalate, Rome, Italy. U.S. motherhouse, 300 N. 18th St., Norfolk, NE 68701-3687, (402) 371-3438, www.norfolkosb.org.

Benedictine Sisters, Olivetan, O.S.B.: Founded 1887, in U.S. General motherhouse, Holy Angels Convent, P.O. Drawer 130, Jonesboro, AR 72403-0130, (870) 935-5810, www.olivben.org. Educational, hospital work.

Benedictine Sisters of Perpetual Adoration of Pontifical Jurisdiction, Congregation of the, O.S.B.: Founded in U.S., 1874, from Maria Rickenbach, Switzerland. General motherhouse, 8300 Morganford Rd., St. Louis, MO 63123, (314) 638-6427.

Benedictine Sisters of Pontifical Jurisdiction, O.S.B.: Founded c. 529, in Italy. No general motherhouse in U.S. Three federations:

• **Federation of St. Scholastica** (1922): Pres., Sister Esther Fangman, O.S.B., 3741 Forest Ave., Kansas City, MO 64109, (816) 753-2514. Motherhouses belonging to the federation:
Mount St. Scholastica, 801 S. 8th St., Atchison, KS 66002, (913) 360-6210, www.mountosb.org. Benedictine Sisters of Elk Co., St. Joseph's Monastery, St. Mary's, PA 15857, (814) 834-2267, www.osbnuns.org. Benedictine Sisters of Erie, 6101 E. Lake Rd., Erie, PA 16511, (814) 899-0614, www.eriebenedictines.org. Benedictine Sisters of Chicago, St. Scholastica Priory, 7430 N. Ridge Blvd., Chicago, IL 60645, (773) 764-2413, www.osbchicago.org. Benedictine Sisters of the Sacred Heart, 1910 Maple Ave., Lisle, IL 60532-2164, (630) 725-6000, www.shmlisle.org. Benedictine Sisters of Elizabeth, St. Walburga Monastery, 851 N. Broad St., Elizabeth, NJ 07208-2593, (201) 352-4278, www.catholic-forum.com/bensisnj. Benedictine Sisters of Pittsburgh, 4530 Perrysville Ave., Pittsburgh, PA 15229, (412) 931-2844, www.osbpgh.org.
Red Plains Monastery, 728 Richland Rd. S.W., Piedmont, OK 73078, (405) 373-4565, www.redplainsmonastery.org. St. Joseph's Monastery, 2200 S. Lewis, Tulsa, OK 74114, (918) 742-4989, www.tulsaosb.org. St. Gertrude's Monastery, 14259 Benedictine Lane, Ridgely, MD 21660, (410) 634-2497. St. Walburga Monastery, 2500 Amsterdam Rd., Villa Hills, KY 41017, (859) 331-6324, www.stwalburg.org. Sacred Heart Monastery, P.O. Box 2040, Cullman, AL 35056, (256) 734-4622, www.shmon.org. Benedictine Sisters of Virginia, 9535 Linton Hall Rd., Bristow, VA 20136-1217, (703) 361-0106, www.osbva.org. St. Scholastica Monastery, 416 W. Highland Dr., Boerne, TX 78006, (830) 816-8504, www.boernebenedictines.com. St. Lucy's Priory, 19045 E. Sierra Madre Ave., Glendora, CA 91741, (626) 335-1682. Benedictine Sisters of Florida, Holy Name Monastery, P.O. Box 2450, St. Leo, FL 33574-2450, (352) 588-8320, www.floridabenedictines.com. Benet Hill Monastery, 2555 N. Chelton Rd., Colorado Springs, CO 80909, (719) 633-0655, www.benethillmonastery.org. Queen of Heaven Monastery (Byzantine Rite), 8640 Squires Lane N.E., Warren, OH 44484, (330) 856-1813, www.benedictinebyzantine.org. Queen of Angels Monastery, 23615 N.E. 100th St., Liberty, MO 64068, (816) 750-4618.

• **Federation of St. Gertrude the Great** (1937): Office: St. Benedict of Ferdinand, Indiana, 802 E. 10th

St., Ferdinand, IN 47532, (812) 367-1411, www.thedome.org. Pres., Sister Kathryn Huber, O.S.B. Motherhouses belonging to the federation:
Mother of God Monastery, 110 28th Ave., S.E., Watertown, SD 57201, (605) 882-6633, www.watertownbenedictines.org. Sacred Heart Monastery, 1005 W. 8th St., Yankton, SD 57078-3389, (605) 668-6000, www.yanktonbenedictines.org. Mt. St. Benedict Monastery, 620 E. Summit Ave., Crookston, MN 56716, (218) 281-3441, www.msb.net. Sacred Heart Monastery, P.O. Box 364, Richardton, ND 58652, (701) 974-2121, www.sacredheartmonastery.com. St. Martin Monastery, 2110-C St. Martin's Dr., Rapid City, SD 57702-9660, (605) 343-8011, www.blackhillsbenedictine.com. Monastery of Immaculate Conception, 802 E. 10th St., Ferdinand, IN 47532, (812) 367-2313. Monastery of St. Gertrude, 465 Keuterville Rd., Cottonwood, ID 83522-5183, (208) 962-3224, www.stgertrudes.org.
Monastery of St. Benedict Center, Box 5070, Madison, WI 53705-0070, (608) 836-1631, www.sbcenter.org. Queen of Angels Monastery, 840 S. Main St., Mt. Angel, OR 97362, (503) 845-6141, www.benedictine-srs.org. St. Scholastica Monastery, P.O. Box 3489, Fort Smith, AR 72913-3489, (479) 783-4147, www.scholasticafortsmith.org. Our Lady of Peace Monastery, 3710 W. Broadway, Columbia, MO 65203, (573) 446-2300, www.benedictinesister.org. Queen of Peace Monastery, Box 370, Belcourt, ND 58316, (701) 477-6167. Our Lady of Grace Monastery, 1402 Southern Ave., Beech Grove, IN 46107, (317) 787-3287, www.benedictine.com. Holy Spirit Monastery, 22791 Pico St., Grand Terrace, CA 92324, (909) 783-4446. Spirit of Life Monastery, 10760 W. Glennon Dr., Lakewood, CO 80226, (303) 986-9234. St. Benedict's Monastery 225 Masters Ave., Winnipeg, MB, R4A 2A1, Canada, (204) 338-4601, www.mts.net/~stbens. The Dwelling Place Monastery, 150 Mt. Tabor Rd., Martin, KY 41649, (606) 886-9624.

• **Federation of St. Benedict** (1947): Pres., Sister Colleen Haggerty, O.S.B., St. Benedict Convent, 104 Chapel Lane, St. Joseph, MN 56374-0220, (320) 363-7100, www.sbm.osb.org. Motherhouses in U.S. belonging to the federation:
St. Benedict's Convent, St. Joseph, MN 56374, (320) 363-7100. St. Scholastica Monastery, 1001 Kenwood Ave., Duluth, MN 55811-2300, (218) 723-7001, www.duluthbenedictines.org. St. Bede Monastery, 1190 Priory Rd., Eau Claire, WI 54702, (715) 834-3176, www.saintbede.org. St. Mary Monastery, 2200 88th Ave. W., Rock Island, IL 61201, (309) 283-2101, www.smmsisters.org. Annunciation Monastery, 7520 University Dr., Bismarck, ND 58504, (701) 255-1520, www.annunciationmonastery.org. St. Paul's Monastery, 2675 Larpenteur Ave. E., St. Paul, MN 55109, (651) 777-8181, www.osb.org/spm. St. Placid Priory, 500 College St. N.E., Lacey, WA 98516, (360) 438-1771, www.stplacid.org. Mount Benedict Monastery, 6000 South 1075 East, Ogden, UT 84405-4945, (801) 479-6030, www.mbutah.org.

Bethany, Sisters of, C.V.D.: Founded 1928, in El Salvador; in U.S. 1949. General motherhouse, Santa Tecla, El Salvador. U.S. address: 850 N. Hobart Blvd., Los Angeles, CA 90029, (213) 669-9411.

Bethlemita Sisters, Daughters of the Sacred Heart of Jesus (Beth.): Founded 1861, in Guatemala.

Motherhouse, Bogota, Colombia. U.S. address, St. Joseph Residence, 330 W. Pembroke St., Dallas, TX 75208, (214) 948-3597.

Bon Secours, Congregation of, C.B.S.: Founded 1824, in France; in U.S., 1881. Generalate, Rome, Italy. U.S. provincial house, 1525 Marriottsville Rd., Marriottsville, MD 21104, (410) 442-1333, www.bonsecours.org. Hospital work.

Brigid, Congregation of St., C.S.B.: Founded 1807, in Ireland; in U.S., 1953. U.S. regional house, 5118 Loma Linda Dr., San Antonio, TX 78201, (210) 733-0701, www.brigidine.org.au.

Brigittine Sisters (Order of the Most Holy Savior), O.SS.S.: Founded 1344, at Vadstena, Sweden, by St. Bridget; in U.S., 1957. General motherhouse, Rome, Italy. U.S. address, Vikingsborg, 4 Runkenhage Rd., Darien, CT 06820, (203) 655-1068.

Canossian Daughters of Charity (Fd.C.C.): Founded 1808 in Verona, Italy, by St. Magdalen of Canossa. General motherhouse, Rome, Italy. U.S. provincial house, 5625 Isleta Blvd. S.W., Albuquerque, NM 87105, (505) 873-2854, www.fdcc.org.

Carmel, Congregation of Our Lady of Mount, O. Carm.: Founded 1825, in France; in U.S., 1833. Generalate, P.O. Box 476, Lacombe, LA 70445, (504) 882-7577, www.mountcarmel.home.mindspring.com. Education, social services, pastoral ministry, retreat work.

Carmel, Institute of Our Lady of Mount, O. Carm.: Founded 1854, in Italy; in U.S., 1947. General motherhouse, Rome, Italy. U.S. novitiate, 5 Wheatland St., Peabody, MA 01960, (978) 531-4733. Apostolic work.

Carmelite Community of the Word, C.C.W.: Motherhouse and novitiate, 394 Bem Rd., Gallitzin, PA 16641, (814) 886-4098 (fax).

Carmelite Nuns, Discalced, O.C.D.: Founded 1562, Spain. First foundation in U.S. in 1790, at Charles County, MD; this monastery was moved to Baltimore. Monasteries in U.S. are listed below by state.

Alabama: 716 Dauphin Island Pkwy., Mobile 36606, (334) 471-3991. Arkansas: 7201 W. 32nd St., Little Rock 72204, (501) 565-5121, www.littlerockcarmel.org. California: 215 E. Alhambra Rd., Alhambra 91801, (626) 282-2387, www.carmelites.org/teresacarmel; 27601 Highway 1, Carmel 93923, (831) 624-3043, www.carmelitesistersbythesea.net; 68 Rincon Rd., Kensington 94707; 6981 Teresian Way, Georgetown 95634, (530) 333-1617; 5158 Hawley Blvd., San Diego 92116, (619) 280-5424, www.carmelsandiego.com; 721 Parker Ave., San Francisco 94118; 530 Blackstone Dr., San Rafael 94903, (415) 479-6872; 1000 Lincoln St., Santa Clara 95050-5285, (408) 296-8412, www.members.aol.com/santaclaracarmel.

Colorado: 6138 S. Gallup St., Littleton 80120, (303) 798-4176. Georgia: Coffee Bluff, 11 W. Back St., Savannah 31419, (912) 925-8505, www.savannahcarmel.org. Hawaii: 6301 Pali Hwy., Kaneohe 96744, (808) 261-6542. Illinois: 1101 N. River Rd., Des Plaines 60016, (847) 298-4241. Indiana: 2500 Cold Spring Rd., Indianapolis 46222-2323, (317) 926-5654, www.praythenews.com; 59 Allendale Pl., Terre Haute 47802, (812) 299-1410, www.heartsawake.org. Iowa: 17937 250th St., Eldridge 52748, (319) 285-8387; 2901 S. Cecilia St., Sioux City 51106, (712) 276-1680. Kentucky: 1740 Newburg Rd., Louisville 40205, (502) 451-6796. Louisiana: 1250 Carmel Ave., Lafayette

70501, (337) 232-4651; 73530 River Rd., Covington 70435.

Maryland: 1318 Dulaney Valley Rd., Towson, Baltimore 21286, (410) 823-7415, www.geocities.com/baltimorecarmel; 5678 Mt. Carmel Rd., La Plata, 20646, (301) 934-1654, www.carmelofporttobacco@erols.com.

Massachusetts: 61 Mt. Pleasant Ave., Roxbury, Boston 02119, (617) 442-1411, www.carmelitesofboston.org; 15 Mt. Carmel Rd., Danvers 01923, (978) 774-3008. Michigan: 4300 Mt. Carmel Dr. NE, Ada 49301, (616) 691-8538; 35750 Moravian Dr., Clinton Township 48035, (586) 790-7255, www.rc.net/detroit/carmelite; U.S. 2 Highway, P.O. Box 397, Iron Mountain 49801, (906) 774-0561; 3501 Silver Lake Rd., Traverse City 49684, (231) 946-4960. Minnesota: 8251 De Montreville Trail N., Lake Elmo 55042-9547, (651) 777-3882. Mississippi: 2155 Terry Rd., Jackson 39204, (601) 373-1460.

Missouri: 2201 W. Main St., Jefferson City 65101, (573) 636-3364; 9150 Clayton Rd., Ladue, St. Louis Co. 63124, (314) 993-3494, www.stormpages.com/mtcarmel; 424 E. Monastery Rd., Springfield 65807, (417) 881-2115. Nevada: 1950 La Fond Dr., Reno 89509-3099, (775) 323-3236. New Hampshire: 275 Pleasant St., Concord, 03301-2590, (603) 225-5791. New Jersey: 26 Harmony School Rd., Flemington 08822-2606, www.carmelitehermitage.com/flemingtoncarmel.htm; 189 Madison Ave., Morristown 07960, (973) 538-2886. New Mexico: 49 Mt. Carmel Rd., Santa Fe 87505-0352, (505) 983-7232. New York: c/o Chancery Office, Diocese of Brooklyn, 361 Highland Blvd., Brooklyn 11207, (718) 235-0422; 89 Hiddenbrook Dr., Beacon, 12508, (914) 831-5572; 75 Carmel Rd., Buffalo 14214, (716) 837-6499; 1931 W. Jefferson Rd., Pittsford, NY 14534, (585) 427-7094.

Ohio: 3176 Fairmount Blvd., Cleveland Heights 44118, (216) 321-6568, www.clevelandcarmel.org. Oklahoma: 20000 N. County Line Rd., Piedmont 73078, (405) 348-3947, www.okcarmel.org. Oregon: 87609 Green Hill Rd., Eugene 97402, (541) 345-8649. Pennsylvania: 70 Monastery Rd., Elysburg 17824-9697, (570) 672-2935, www.carmelelysburg.org; 510 E. Gore Rd., Erie 16509-3799, (814) 825-0846; 5206 Center Dr., Latrobe 15650, (724) 539-1056, www.latrobecarmel.org; P.O. Box 57, Loretto 15940-0057, (814) 472-8620; Byzantine Rite, 403 West County Rd., Sugarloaf 18249-9998, (570) 788-1205; 66th and Old York Rd., Philadelphia 19126, (215) 424-6143. Rhode Island: 25 Watson Ave., Barrington 02806, (401) 245-3421. South Dakota: 221 5th St., W., Alexandria, 57311, (605) 239-4382.

Texas: 600 Flowers Ave., Dallas 75211; 5801 Mt. Carmel Dr., Arlington 76017, (817) 468-1781; 1100 Parthenon Pl., Roman Forest, New Caney 77357-3276, (281) 399-0270, www.icansurf.com/ocdnewcaney; 6301 Culebra and St. Joseph Way, San Antonio 78238-4909, (210) 680-1834, www.carmelsanantonio.org. Utah: 5714 Holladay Blvd., Salt Lake City 84121, (801) 277-6075, www.carmelslc.org. Vermont: 94 Main St., Montpelier, 05601, (914) 831-5572. Washington, DC: 2215 N.E. 147th St., Shoreline 98155, (206) 363-7150. Wisconsin: W267 N2517 Meadowbrook Rd., Pewaukee 53072, (262) 691-0336, www.geocities.com/pewaukeecarmel.org; 6100 Pepper Rd., Denmark 54208, (920) 863-5055.

Carmelite Nuns of the Ancient Observance (Calced Carmelites), O. Carm.: Founded 1452, in the Netherlands; in U.S., 1930, from Naples, Italy, convent (founded 1856). U.S. monasteries: Carmelite Monastery of St. Therese and St. Mary Magdalen di Pazzi, 3551 Lanark Rd., Coopersburg, PA 18036. Carmel of Mary, Wahpeton, ND 58075. Our Lady of

Grace Monastery, 6202 CR 339 Via Maria, Christoval, TX 76935 (325) 853-1722. Carmel of the Sacred Heart, 430 Laurel Ave., Hudson, WI 54016, (715) 862-2156, www.pressenter.com/~carmelit. Papal enclosure.

Carmelite Sisters (Corpus Christi), O. Carm.: Founded 1908, in England; in U.S., 1920. General motherhouse, Tunapuna, Trinidad, W.I. U.S. address: Mt. Carmel Home, 412 W. 18th St., Kearney, NE 68845, (308) 237-2287, www.corpuschristicarmelites.org. Home and foreign mission work.

Carmelite Sisters for the Aged and Infirm, O. Carm.: Founded 1929, at New York, by Mother M. Angeline Teresa, O. Carm. Motherhouse, 600 Woods Rd., Avila-on-Hudson, Germantown, NY 12526, (518) 537-5000, www.carmelitesisters.com. Social work, nursing and educating in the field of gerontology.

Carmelite Sisters of Charity, C.a.Ch.: Founded 1826 at Vich, Spain, by St. Joaquina de Vedruna. Generalate, Rome, Italy. U.S. address, 701 Beacon Rd., Silver Spring, MD 20903, (301) 434-6344.

Carmelite Sisters of St. Therese of the Infant Jesus, C.S.T.: Founded 1917, in U.S. General motherhouse, 1300 Classen Dr., Oklahoma City, OK 73103, (405) 232-7926, www.oksister.com. Educational work.

Carmelite Sisters of the Divine Heart of Jesus, Carmel D.C.J.: Founded 1891, in Germany; in U.S., 1912. General motherhouse, Sittard Netherlands. U.S. provincial houses: Northern Province, 1230 Kavanaugh Pl., Milwaukee, WI 53213, (414) 453-4040, www.carmelitedcjnorth.org. Central Province, 10341 Manchester Rd., St. Louis, MO 63122, (314) 965-7616, www.carmelitesdcj.org. South Western Province, 8585 La Mesa Blvd., La Mesa, CA 91941-3901, (619) 466-3163. Social services, mission work.

Carmelite Sisters of the Most Sacred Heart of Los Angeles, O.C.D.: Founded 1904, in Mexico. General motherhouse and novitiate, 920 E. Alhambra Rd., Alhambra, CA 91801-2799, (626) 289-1353, www-carmelgeneralate.homestead.com. Social services, retreat and educational work.

Carmelites, Calced, O. Carm.: Founded 1856 in Naples, Italy. U.S. address: Carmelite Monastery of St. Therese, 3551 Lanark Rd., Coopersburg, PA 18036.

Carmelites of St. Theresa, Congregation of Missionary, C.M.S.T.: Founded 1903, in Mexico. General motherhouse, Mexico City, Mexico. U.S. foundation, 9548 Deer Trail Dr., Houston, TX 77038, (281) 445-5520.

Casimir, Sisters of St., S.S.C.: Founded 1907, in U.S., by Mother Maria Kaupas. General motherhouse, 2601 W. Marquette Rd., Chicago, IL 60629, (773) 776-1324. Education, missions, social services.

Cenacle, Congregation of Our Lady of the Retreat in the, R.C.: Founded 1826, in France; in U.S., 1892. Generalate, Rome, Italy. Eastern Province, Cenacle Rd., Lake Ronkonkoma, NY 11779, (516) 471-6270. Midwestern Province, 513 Fullerton Pkwy., Chicago, IL 60614-6428, (773) 528-6300, www.cenaclesisters.org.

Charity, Daughters of Divine, F.D.C.: Founded 1868, at Vienna, Austria; in U.S., 1913. General motherhouse, Rome, Italy. U.S. province: 205 Major Ave., Staten Island, NY 10305, (718) 720-4377, www.godslovefdc.org. Education, social services.

Charity, Missionaries of, M.C.: Founded 1950, in Calcutta, India, by Mother Teresa; first U.S. foundation, 1971. General motherhouse, 54A, A.J.C. Bose Rd., Calcutta 700016, India. U.S. address, 335 E. 145th St., Bronx, NY 10451, (718) 292-0019. Service of the poor.

Charity, Religious Sisters of, R.S.C.: Founded 1815, in Ireland; in U.S., 1953. Motherhouse, Dublin, Ireland. U.S. headquarters, 206 N. Edgemont St., Los Angeles, CA 90029, (310) 559-0176.

Charity, Sisters of (of Seton Hill), S.C.: Founded 1870, at Altoona, PA, from Cincinnati foundation. Generalate, De Paul Center, 463 Mt. Thor Rd., Greensburg, PA 15601, (724) 836-0406, www.scsh.org. Educational, hospital, social, foreign mission work.

Charity, Sisters of (Grey Nuns of Montréal), S.G.M.: Founded 1737, in Canada, by St. Marie Marguerite d'Youville; in U.S., 1855. General administration, Montréal, QC H2Y 2L7, Canada. U.S. provincial house, 10 Pelham Rd., Ste. 1000, Lexington, MA 02421, (781) 862-4700, www.sqmlex.org.

Charity, Sisters of (of Leavenworth), S.C.L.: Founded 1858, in U.S. Motherhouse, 4200 S. 4th St., Leavenworth, KS 66048, (913) 758-6508, www.scls.org/.

Charity, Sisters of (of Nazareth), S.C.N.: Founded 1812, in U.S. General motherhouse, SCN Center, P.O. Box 172, Nazareth, KY 40048, (502) 348-1561, www.scnazareth.org. Education, health services.

Charity, Sisters of (of St. Augustine), C.S.A.: Founded 1851, at Cleveland, Ohio. Motherhouse, 5232 Broadview Rd., Richfield, OH 44286, (330) 659-5100, www.srsofcharity.org.

Charity, Sisters of Christian, S.C.C.: Founded 1849, in Paderborn, Germany, by Bl. Pauline von Mallinckrodt; in U.S., 1873. Generalate, Rome, Italy. U.S. provinces: Mallinckrodt Convent, 350 Bernardsville Rd., Mendham, NJ 07945, (973) 543-6528, www.scceast.org. 2041 Elmwood Ave., Wilmette, IL 60091-1431, (847) 920-9341, www.sccwilmette.org. Education, health services, other apostolic work.

Charity, Vincentian Sisters of, V.S.C.: Founded 1835, in Austria; in U.S., 1902. General motherhouse, 8200 McKnight Rd., Pittsburgh, PA 15237, (412) 364-3000, www.vincentiansrspgh.org.

Charity, Vincentian Sisters of, V.S.C.: Founded 1928, at Bedford, Ohio. General motherhouse, 1160 Broadway, Bedford, OH 44146, (440) 232-4755.

Charity of Cincinnati, Ohio, Sisters of, S.C.: Founded 1809; became independent community, 1852. General motherhouse, 5900 Delhi Rd., Mt. St. Joseph, OH 45051, (513) 347-5201, www.srcharitycinti.org. Educational, hospital, social work.

Charity of Ottawa, Sisters of (Grey Nuns of the Cross), S.C.O.: Founded 1845, at Ottawa, Canada; in U.S., 1857. General motherhouse, Ottawa, Canada. U.S. provincial house, 559 Fletcher St., Lowell, MA 01854, (978) 453-4993. Educational, hospital work, extended health care.

Charity of Our Lady, Mother of Mercy, Sisters of, S.C.M.M.: Founded 1832, in Holland; in U.S., 1874. General motherhouse, Den Bosch, the Netherlands. U.S. provincialate, 520 Thompson Ave., East Haven, CT 06512, (203) 469-7872.

Charity of Our Lady, Mother of the Church, S.C.M.C: U.S. foundation, 1970. General motherhouse, 520 Thompson Ave., East Haven, CT 06512, (203) 469-7872.

Charity of Our Lady of Mercy, Sisters of, O.L.M.: Founded 1829, in Charleston, SC. Generalate and motherhouse, 424 Fort Johnson Rd., P. O. Box 12410, Charleston, SC 29422, (843) 795-6083. Education, campus ministry, social services.

Charity of Quebec, Sisters of (Grey Nuns), S.C.Q.: Founded 1849, at Quebec; in U.S., 1890. General motherhouse, 2655 Le Pelletier St., Beauport, QC GIC 3X7, Canada. U.S. address, 359 Summer St., New Bedford, MA 02740, (508) 996-6751. Social work.

Charity of St. Elizabeth, Sisters of (Convent Station, N.J.), S.C.: Founded 1859, at Newark, NJ. General motherhouse, P.O. Box 476, Convent Station, NJ 07961-0476, (973) 290-5335. Education, pastoral ministry, social services.

Charity of St. Hyacinthe, Sisters of (Grey Nuns), S.C.S.H.: Founded 1840, at St. Hyacinthe, Canada; in U.S., 1878. General motherhouse, 16470 Avenue Bourdages, SUD, St. Hyacinthe, QC J2T 4J8, Canada. U.S. regional house, 98 Campus Ave., Lewiston, ME 04240, (207) 797-8607.

Charity of St. Joan Antida, Sisters of, S.C.S.J.A.: Founded 1799, in France; in U.S., 1932. General motherhouse, Rome, Italy. U.S. provincial house, 8560 N. 76th Pl., Milwaukee, WI 53223, (414) 354-9233, www.scsja.org.

Charity of St. Louis, Sisters of, S.C.S.L.: Founded 1803, in France; in U.S., 1910. Generalate, Rome, Italy. U.S. provincialate, 4907 S. Catherine St., Plattsburgh, NY 12901, (518) 563-0383.

Charity of St. Vincent de Paul, Daughters of, D.C.: Founded 1633, in France; in U.S., 1809, at Emmitsburg, MD, by St. Elizabeth Ann Seton. General motherhouse, Paris, France. U.S. provinces: 333 South Seton Ave., Emmitsburg, MD 21727, (301) 447-2900, www.daughtersofcharity-emmitsburg.org. 7800 Natural Bridge Rd., St. Louis, MO 63121, (314) 382-2800. 9400 New Harmony Rd., Evansville, IN 47720-8912, (812) 963-3341, www.doc-ecp.org. 96 Menands Rd., Albany, NY 12204, (518) 462-5593, www.dc-northeast.org. 26000 Altamont Rd., Los Altos Hills, CA 94022, (650) 949-8865.

Charity of St. Vincent de Paul, Sisters of, V.Z.: Founded 1845, in Croatia. in U.S., 1955. General motherhouse, Zagreb, Croatia; U.S. foundation, 171 Knox Ave., West Seneca, NY 14224, (716) 825-5859.

Charity of St. Vincent de Paul, Sisters of, Halifax, S.C.: Founded 1856, at Halifax, NS, from Emmitsburg foundation. Generalate, Mt. St. Vincent, Halifax, NS, Canada. U.S. addresses: Commonwealth of Massachusetts, 125 Oakland St., Wellesley Hills, MA 02481-5338, (781) 997-1165, www.schalifax.ca. Boston Province, 26 Phipps St., Quincy, MA 02169, (617) 773-6085. New York Province, 84-32 63rd Ave., Middle Village, NY 11379, (718) 651-1685. Educational, hospital, social work.

Charity of St. Vincent de Paul, Sisters of, New York, SC.: Founded 1817, from Emmitsburg foundation. General motherhouse, Mt. St. Vincent on Hudson, 6301 Riverdale Ave., Bronx, NY 10471, (718) 549-9200, www.scny.org. Educational, hospital work.

Charity of the Blessed Virgin Mary, Sisters of, B.V.M.: Founded 1833, in U.S. by Mary Frances Clarke. General motherhouse, BVM Center, 1100 Carmel Dr., Dubuque, IA 52003, (563) 588-2351, www.bvmcong.com. Education, pastoral ministry, social services.

Charity of the Immaculate Conception of Ivrea, Sisters of, S.C.I.C.: Founded 18th century, in Italy; in U.S., 1961. General motherhouse, Rome, Italy. U.S. address, Immaculate Virgin of Miracles Convent, Box 348, Mt. Pleasant, PA 15666, (724) 887-6753.

Charity of the Incarnate Word, Congregation of the Sisters of, C.C.V.I.: Founded 1869, at San Antonio, TX, by Bishop C. M. Dubuis. Generalate, 3200 McCullough, San Antonio, TX 78212, (210) 734-8310, www.incarnatewordsisters.org.

Charity of the Incarnate Word, Congregation of the Sisters of (Houston, TX), C.C.V.I.: Founded 1866, in U.S., by Bishop C. M. Dubuis. General motherhouse, P.O. Box 230969, Houston, TX 77223, (713) 928-6053. Educational, hospital, social work.

Charity of the Sacred Heart, Daughters of, F.C.S.C.J.: Founded 1823, at La Salle de Vihiers, France; in U.S., 1905. General motherhouse, La Salle de Vihiers, France. U.S. address, Sacred Heart Province, 226 Grove St., P.O. Box 642, Littleton, NH 03561, (603) 444-3970.

Charles Borromeo, Missionary Sisters of St. (Scalabrini Srs.): Founded 1895, in Italy; in U.S., 1941. American novitiate, 3800 Lottsford Vista Rd., Mitchellville, MD 20721, (301) 459-4700.

Child Jesus, Sisters of the Poor, P.C.J.: Founded 1844, at Aix-la-Chapelle, Germany; in U.S., 1924. General motherhouse, Simpelveld, the Netherlands. American provincialate, 4567 Olentangy River Rd., Columbus, OH 43214, (614) 451-3900.

Chretienne, Sisters of Ste., S.S.Ch.: Founded 1807, in France; in U.S., 1903. General motherhouse, Metz, France. U.S. provincial house, 297 Arnold St., Wrentham, MA 02093, (508) 384-8066, www.sister-sofstchretienne.org. Educational, hospital, mission work.

Christ the King, Missionary Sisters of, M.S.C.K.: Founded 1959 in Poland; in U.S., 1978. General motherhouse, Poznan, Poland. U.S. address, 3000 18-Mile Rd., Sterling Heights, MI 48314.

Christ the King, Sister Servants of, S.S.C.K.: Founded 1936, in U.S. General motherhouse, Loretto Convent, N8114 Calvary St., Mt. Calvary, WI 53057, (920) 753-3211. Social services.

Christian Doctrine, Sisters of Our Lady of, R.C.D.: Founded 1910, in New York. Marydell Convent, 110 Larchdale Ave., Nyack, NY 10960, (845) 727-1011.

Christian Education, Religious of, R.C.E.: Founded 1817, in France; in U.S., 1905. General motherhouse, France. U.S. provincial residence, 55 Parkwood Dr., Milton, MA 02186, (617) 696-7732.

Cistercian Nuns, O. Cist.: Headquarters, Rome, Italy. U.S. address, Valley of Our Lady Monastery, E. 11096 Yanke Dr., Prairie du Sac, WI 53578, (608) 643-3520, www.nunocist.org.

Cistercian Nuns of the Strict Observance, Order of, O.C.S.O.: Founded 1125, in France, by St. Stephen Harding; in U.S., 1949. U.S. addresses: Mt. St. Mary's Abbey, 300 Arnold St., Wrentham, MA 02093, (508) 528-1282. HC 1, Box 929, Sonoita, AZ 85637, (520) 455-5595, www.santaritabbey.org. Our Lady of the Redwoods Abbey, 18104 Briceland Thorn Rd., Whitethorn, CA 95589, (707) 986-7419, www.red-woodsabbey.org. Our Lady of the Mississippi Abbey, 8400 Abbey Hill Rd., Dubuque, IA 52003, (563) 582-

2595, www.mississippiabbey.org/. Our Lady of the Angels Monastery, 3365 Monastery Dr., Crozet, VA 22932, (434) 823-1452, www.olamonastery.org.

Clare, Sisters of St., O.S.C.: General motherhouse, Dublin, Ireland. U.S. foundation, St. Francis Convent, 1974 Cherrywood St., Vista, CA 92083, (760) 945-8040.

Claretian Missionary Sisters (Religious of Mary Immaculate), R.M.I.: Founded 1855, in Cuba; in U.S., 1956. Generalate, Rome, Italy. U.S. address, 7080 SW 99 Ave., Miami, FL 33173, (305) 274-5695 (fax), www.claretiansisters.org.

Clergy, Congregation of Our Lady, Help of the, C.L.H.C.: Founded 1961, in U.S. Motherhouse, Maryvale Convent, 2522 June Bug Rd., Vale, NC 28168, (704) 276-2626.

Clergy, Servants of Our Lady Queen of the, S.R.C.: Founded 1929, in Canada; in U.S., 1934. General motherhouse, 57 Jules A. Brillant, Rimouski, QC G5L 1X1 Canada, (418) 724-0508. Domestic work.

Colettines: See Franciscan Poor Clare Nuns.

Columban, Missionary Sisters of St., S.S.C.: Founded 1922, in Ireland; in U.S., 1930. General motherhouse, Wicklow, Ireland. U.S. region, 73 Mapleton St., Brighton, MA 02135, (617) 782-5683.

Comboni Missionary Sisters (Missionary Sisters of Verona), C.M.S.: Founded 1872, in Italy; in U.S., 1950. U.S. address, 5405 Loch-Raven Blvd., Baltimore, MD 21239, (410) 323-1469, www.combonisrs.com.

Consolata Missionary Sisters, M.C.: Founded 1910, in Italy, by Bl. Giuseppe Allamano; in U.S., 1954. General motherhouse, Turin, Italy. U.S. headquarters, 6801 Belmont Rd., P.O. Box 97, Belmont, MI 49306 (616) 361-9609, www.consolatasisters.org.

Cross, Daughters of the, D.C.: Founded 1640, in France; in U.S., 1855. General motherhouse, 411 E. Flournoy-Lucas Rd., Shreveport, LA 71115, (318) 797-0887. Educational work.

Cross, Daughters of, of Liege, F.C.: Founded 1833, in Liege, Belgium; in U.S., 1958. U.S. address, 165 W. Eaton Ave., Tracy, CA 95376.

Cross, Sisters of the Holy, C.S.C.: Founded 1841, at Le Mans, France; established in Canada, 1847; in U.S., 1881. General motherhouse, St. Laurent, Montreal, QC, Canada. U.S. regional office, 377 Island Pond Rd., Manchester, NH 03109, (603) 622-9504. Educational work.

Cross, Sisters of the Holy, Congregation of, C.S.C.: Founded 1841, at Le Mans, France; in U.S., 1843. General motherhouse, 101 Bertrand Hall – Saint Mary's, Notre Dame, IN 46556, (574) 284-5572, www.cscsisters.org. Education, health care, social services, pastoral ministry.

Cross and Passion, Sisters of the (Passionist Sisters), C.P.: Founded 1852; in U.S., 1924. Generalate, Northampton, England. U.S. address: Holy Family Convent, One Wright Lane, N. Kingstown, RI 02852, (401) 294-3554.

Cyril and Methodius, Sisters of Sts., SS.C.M.: Founded 1909, in U.S., by Rev. Matthew Jankola. General motherhouse, Villa Sacred Heart, Danville, PA 17821, (570) 275-4929, www.sscm.org. Education, care of aged.

Disciples of the Lord Jesus Christ, D.L.J.C.:

Founded 1972; canonically erected 1991. P.O. Box 17, Channing, TX 79018, (806) 534-2312, www.dljc.org.

Divine Compassion, Sisters of, R.D.C.: Founded 1886, in U.S. General motherhouse, 52 N. Broadway, White Plains, NY 10603, (914) 949-2950. Education, other ministries.

Divine Love, Daughters of, D.D.L.: Founded 1969, in Nigeria; in U.S., 1990. General house, Enugu, Nigeria. U.S. regional house, 140 North Ave., Highwood, IL 60040, (847) 432-4946.

Divine Spirit, Congregation of the, C.D.S.: Founded 1956, in U.S., by Archbishop John M. Gannon. Motherhouse, 409 W. 6th St., Erie, PA 16507, (330) 453-8137. Education, social services.

Divine Zeal, Daughters of, F.D.Z.: Founded 1887 in Italy by Bl. Hannibal Maria DiFrancia; in U.S., 1951. Generalate, Rome. U.S. headquarters, Hannibal·House Spiritual Center, 1526 Hill Rd., Reading, PA 19602, (610) 375-1738.

Dominicans

Dominican Nuns: Nuns of the Order of Preachers, O.P.: Founded 1206 by St. Dominic at Prouille, France. Cloistered, contemplative. Two branches in the United States:

• Dominican Nuns having Perpetual Adoration: First monastery established 1880, in Newark, NJ, from Oullins, France, foundation (1868). Autonomous monasteries:

Monastery of St. Dominic, 375 13th Ave., Newark, NJ 07103-2124, (973) 622-6622. Corpus Christi Monastery, 1230 Lafayette Ave., Bronx, NY 10474, (718) 328-6996. Blessed Sacrament, 29575 Middlebelt Rd., Farmington Hills, MI 48334-2311, (248) 626-8321, www.opnuns-fh.org. Monastery of the Angels, 1977 Carmen Ave., Los Angeles, CA 90068-4098, (323) 466-2186, www.op-stjoseph.org/nuns/angels/. Corpus Christi Monastery, 215 Oak Grove Ave., Menlo Park, CA 94025-3272, (650) 322-1801, www.op.org/nunsmenlo. Infant Jesus, 1501 Lotus Lane, Lufkin, TX 75904-2699, (936) 634-4233.

Dominican Nuns devoted to the Perpetual Rosary: First monastery established 1891, in Union City, NJ, from Calais, France, foundation (1880). Autonomous monasteries (some also observe Perpetual Adoration):

Dominican Nuns of Perpetual Rosary, 14th and West Sts., Union City, NJ 07087. 217 N. 68th St., Milwaukee, WI 53213, (414) 258-0579, www.dsopr.org. Perpetual Rosary, 1500 Haddon Ave., Camden, NJ 08103. Our Lady of the Rosary, 335 Doat St., Buffalo, NY 14211. Our Lady of the Rosary, 543 Spingfield Ave., Summit, NJ 07901, (908) 273-1228, www.op.org/nunsopsummit. Monastery of the Mother of God, 1430 Riverdale St., W. Springfield, MA 01089-4698, (413) 736-3639, www.op-stjoseph.org/nuns/ws. Dominican Monastery of the Perpetual Rosary, 802 Court St., Syracuse, NY 13208-1766. Monastery of the Immaculate Heart of Mary, 1834 Lititz Pike, Lancaster, PA 17601-6585, (717) 569-2104. Mary the Queen, 1310 W. Church St., Elmira, NY 14905, (607) 734-9506, www.oporg/maryqueen. St. Jude, Marbury, AL 36051-0170, (205) 755-1322, www.stjude monastery.org. Our Lady of Grace Monastery, 11 Race Hill Rd., North Guilford, CT 06437, (203) 345-0599, www.op-stjoseph.org/nuns/olgrace. St. Dominic's Monastery, 4901 16th St. N.W., Washington, DC 20011, (202) 726-2107.

Dominican Sisters of Charity of the Presentation, O.P.: Founded 1696, in France; in U.S., 1906. General motherhouse, Tours, France. U.S. headquarters, 3012

Elm St., Dighton, MA 02715, (508) 669-5425, www.dominicansistersofthepresentation.org. Hospital work.

Dominican Sisters of Hope, O.P.: Formed 1995 through merger of Dominican Sisters of the Most Holy Rosary, Newburgh, NY, Dominican Sisters of the Sick Poor, Ossining, NY, and Dominican Sisters of St. Catherine of Siena, Fall River, MA. General Offices: 299 N. Highland Ave., Ossining, NY 10562, (914) 941-4420, www.ophope.org.

Dominican Sisters of Our Lady of the Rosary and of St. Catherine of Siena (Cabra): Founded 1644 in Ireland. General motherhouse, Cabra, Dublin, Ireland. U.S. regional house, 1930 Robert E. Lee Rd., New Orleans, LA 70122, (504) 288-1593.

Dominican Sisters of the Perpetual Rosary, O.P.: 217 N. 68th St., Milwaukee, WI 53213. Cloistered, contemplative.

Dominican Sisters of the Roman Congregation of St. Dominic, O.P.: Founded 1621, in France; in U.S., 1904. General motherhouse, Rome, Italy. U.S. province, 123 Dumont Ave., Lewiston, ME 04240, (207) 782-3535. Educational work.

Eucharistic Missionaries of St. Dominic, O.P.: Founded 1927, in Louisiana. General motherhouse, 3801 Canal St., Suite 400, New Orleans, LA 70119, (504) 486-1133 (temporary, post-Katrina location: 2645 Bardstown Rd., St. Catharine, KY 40061, 859-336-9303), www.emdsisters.org. Parish work, social services.

Religious Missionaries of St. Dominic, O.P.: General motherhouse, Rome, Italy. U.S. address (Spanish province), 2237 Waldron Rd., Corpus Christi, TX 78418, (361) 939-8102.

Sisters of St. Dominic, O.P.: Names of congregations are given below, followed by the date of foundation, and location of motherhouse. St. Catherine of Siena, 1822. 2645 Bardstown Rd., St. Catharine, KY 40061, (606) 336-9303, www.opkentucky.org. St. Mary of the Springs, 1830. 2320 Airport Dr., Columbus, OH 43219-2098, (614) 416-1038, www.columbusdominicans.org. Most Holy Rosary, 1847. Sinsinawa, WI 53824, (608) 748-4411. Most Holy Name of Jesus, 1850. 1520 Grand Ave., San Rafael, CA 94901, (415) 453-8303, www.sanrafael-op.org. Holy Cross, 1853. 555 Albany Ave., Amityville, NY 11701, (631) 842-6788, www.ami-tyvilleop.org. St. Cecilia, 1860. 801 Dominican Dr., Nashville, TN 37228, (615) 256-5486, www.nashville-dominican.org.

St. Mary, 1860. 7300 St. Charles Ave., New Orleans, LA 70118, (504) 861-8183, www.dominican-sisters.net/stmarys. St. Catherine of Siena, 1862. 5635 Erie St., Racine, WI 53402, (262) 639-4100, www.racinedominicans.org. Sacred Heart Convent, 1873. 1237 W. Monroe St., Springfield, IL 62704, (217) 787-0481, www.springfieldop.org. Sisters of Our Lady of the Rosary, Dominican Convent, 175 Route 340, Sparkill, NY 10976, (845) 359-6400, www.sparkill.org. Dominican Sisters of Mission San Jose, 43326 Mission Blvd., Mission San Jose, CA 94539, (510) 657-2468, www.msjdominicans.org. Most Holy Rosary, 1892. 1257 Siena Heights Dr., Adrian, MI 49221, (517) 266-3570.

Our Lady of the Sacred Heart, 1877. 2025 E. Fulton St., Grand Rapids, MI 49503, (616) 459-2910. St. Dominic,

1878. 496 Western Hwy., Blauvelt, NY 10913, (845) 359-0696, www.opblauvelt.org. St. Catherine de Ricci, 1880. 750 Ashbourne Rd., Elkins Park, PA 19027, (215) 635-6027. Sisters of St. Dominic, 1881. 1 Ryerson Ave., Caldwell, NJ 07006, (973) 403-3331, www.caldwellop.org. Dominican Sisters of Houston, 1882. 6501 Almeda Rd., Houston, TX 77021-2095, (713) 747-3310, www.houstonop.org. Tacoma Dominican Center, 1888. 935 Fawcett Ave., Tacoma, WA 98402, (253) 272-9688. Holy Cross, 1890. P.O. Box 280, Edmonds, WA 98020, (206) 542-3212, www.opedmonds.org.

St. Rose of Lima (Servants of Relief for Incurable Cancer) 1896. 600 Linda Ave., Hawthorne, NY 10532, (914) 769-0114, www.hawthorne-dominicans.org. Dominican Sisters of Great Bend, 1902. 3600 Broadway, Great Bend, KS 67530, (316) 792-1232, www.ksdom.org. Mission Center, 1911. Box 1288, Kenosha, WI 53141, (262) 694-2067. St. Rose of Lima, 1923. 775 Drahner Rd., #204, Oxford, MI 48371, (248) 628-2872, www.op.org/oxford. Immaculate Conception, 1929. 9000 W. 81st St., Justice, IL 60458, (708) 458-3040. Immaculate Heart of Mary, 1929. 1230 W. Market St., Akron, OH 44313-7108, (330) 836-4908, www.akronop.org. Dominican Sisters of Oakford (St. Catherine of Siena), 1889. Motherhouse, Oakford, Natal, South Africa; U.S. regional house, 1965. 980 Woodland Ave., San Leandro, CA 94577, (510) 638-2822.

Dorothy, Institute of the Sisters of St., S.S.D.: Founded 1834, in Italy, by St. Paola Frassinetti; in U.S., 1911. General motherhouse, Rome, Italy. U.S. provincialate, St. Dorothy Convent, 1305 Hylan Blvd., Si, NY, 10305, (718) 987-2604.

Eucharist, Religious of the, R.E.: Founded 1857, in Belgium; in U.S., 1900. General motherhouse, Belgium. U.S. foundation, 2907 Ellicott Terr., N.W., Washington, DC 20008, (202) 966-3111.

Felix, Congregation of the Sisters of St. (Felician Sisters), C.S.S.F.: Founded 1855, in Poland by Bl. Mary Angela Truszkowska; in U.S., 1874. General motherhouse, Rome, Italy. U.S. provinces: 36800 Schoolcraft Rd., Livonia, MI 48150, (734) 591-1730. 600 Doat St., Buffalo, NY 14211, (716) 892-4141. 3800 W. Peterson Ave., Chicago, IL 60659-3116, (773) 463-3020, www.felicianchicago.org. 260 South Main St., Lodi, NJ 07644, (973) 473-7447, www.felician.edu/cssf.htm. 1500 Woodcrest Ave., Coraopolis, PA 15108, (412) 264-2890, www.felicianspa.org. 1315 Enfield St., Enfield, CT 06082, (860) 745-7791. 4210 Meadowlark Lane, S.E., Rio Rancho, NM 87124-1021, (505) 892-8862.

Filippini, Religious Teachers, M.P.F.: Founded 1692, in Italy; in U.S., 1910. General motherhouse, Rome, Italy. U.S. provinces: St. Lucy Filippini Province, Villa Walsh, Morristown, NJ 07960, (973) 538-2886. Queen of Apostles Province, 474 East Rd., Bristol, CT 06010, (860) 584-2138, www.queenofa-postles.com. Educational work.

Francis de Sales, Oblate Sisters of St., O.S.F.S.: Founded 1866, in France; in U.S., 1951. General motherhouse, Troyes, France. U.S. headquarters, Villa Aviat Convent, 399 Childs Rd., MD 21916, (410) 398-3699. Educational, social work.

FRANCISCANS

Bernardine Sisters of the Third Order of St. Francis, O.S.F.: Founded 1457, at Cracow, Poland; in U.S., 1894. Generalate, 403 Allendale Rd., King of Prussia, PA 19406, (610) 337-3864. Educational, hospital, social work.

Capuchin Poor Clares, O.S.C. Cap: U.S. establishment, 1981, Amarillo diocese. Convent of the Blessed Sacrament and Our Lady of Guadalupe, 4201 N.E. 18th St., Amarillo, TX 79107, (806) 383-9877. Cloistered.

Congregation of the Servants of the Holy Child Jesus, O.S.F.: Founded 1855, in Germany; in U.S., 1929. General motherhouse, Würzburg, Germany. American motherhouse, Villa Maria, 641 Somerset St., North Plainfield, NJ 07060-4909, (908) 757-3050.

Congregation of the Third Order of St. Francis of Mary Immaculate, O.S.F.: Founded 1865, in U.S., by Fr. Pamphilus da Magliano, O.F.M. General motherhouse, 520 Plainfield Ave., Joliet, IL 60435, (815) 727-3686. Educational and pastoral work.

Daughters of St. Francis of Assisi, D.S.F.: Founded 1894, in Hungary; in U.S., 1946. Provincial motherhouse, 507 N. Prairie St., Lacon, IL 61540, (309) 246-2175. Nursing, CCD work.

Eucharistic Franciscan Missionary Sisters, E.F.M.S.: Founded 1943, in Mexico. Motherhouse, 943 S. Soto St., Los Angeles, CA 90023, (323) 264-6556.

Franciscan Handmaids of the Most Pure Heart of Mary, F.H.M.: Founded 1916, in U.S. General motherhouse, 15 W. 124th St., New York, NY 10027-5634, (212) 289-5655. Educational, social work.

Franciscan Hospitaller Sisters of the Immaculate Conception, F.H.I.C.: Founded 1876, in Portugal; in U.S., 1960. General motherhouse, Lisbon, Portugal. U.S. novitiate, 300 S. 17th St., San Jose, CA 95112, (408) 998-3407.

Franciscan Missionaries of Mary, F.M.M.: Founded 1877, in India; in U.S., 1904. General motherhouse, Rome, Italy. U.S. provincialate, 3305 Wallace Ave., Bronx, NY 10467, (718) 547-4693, www.fmmusa.org. Mission work.

Franciscan Missionaries of Our Lady, O.S.F.: Founded 1854, at Calais, France; in U.S., 1913. General motherhouse, Desvres, France. U.S. provincial house, 4200 Essen Lane, Baton Rouge, LA 70809, (225) 926-1627. Hospital work.

Franciscan Missionaries of St. Joseph (Mill Hill Sisters), F.M.S.J.: Founded 1883, at Rochdale, Lancashire, England; in U.S., 1952. Generalate, Manchester, England. U.S. headquarters, Franciscan House, 1006 Madison Ave., Albany, NY 12208, (518) 482-1991.

Franciscan Missionary Sisters for Africa, O.S.F.: American foundation, 1953. Generalate, Ireland. U.S. headquarters, 172 Foster St., Brighton, MA 02135, (617) 254-4343.

Franciscan Missionary Sisters of Assisi, F.M.S.A.: First foundation in U.S., 1961. General motherhouse, Assisi, Italy. U.S. address, St. Francis Convent, 1039 Northampton St., Holyoke, MA 01040, (413) 536-0853.

Franciscan Missionary Sisters of Our Lady of Sorrows, O.S.F.: Founded 1939, in China, by Bishop Rafael Palazzi, O.F.M.; in U.S., 1949. 3600 S.W. 170th Ave., Beaverton, OR 97006, (503) 649-7127. Educational, social, domestic, retreat and foreign mission work.

Franciscan Missionary Sisters of the Divine Child, F.M.D.C.: Founded 1927, at Buffalo, NY, by Bishop William Turner. General motherhouse, 6380 Main St., Williamsville, NY 14221, (716) 632-3144. Educational, social work.

Franciscan Missionary Sisters of the Infant Jesus, F.M.I.J.: Founded 1879, in Italy; in U.S., 1961. Generalate, Rome, Italy. U.S. provincialate, 1215 Kresson Rd., Cherry Hill, NJ 08003, (609) 428-8834.

Franciscan Missionary Sisters of the Sacred Heart, F.M.S.C.: Founded 1860, in Italy; in U.S., 1865. Generalate, Rome, Italy. U.S. provincialate, 250 South St., Peekskill, NY 10566-4419, (914) 737-5409. Educational and social welfare apostolates.

Franciscan Poor Clare Nuns (Poor Clares, Order of St. Clare, Poor Clares of St. Colette), P.C., O.S.C., P.C.C.: Founded 1212, at Assisi, Italy, by St. Francis of Assisi; in U.S., 1875. Proto-monastery, Assisi, Italy. Addresses of autonomous motherhouses in U.S. are listed below.

8650 Russell Ave., S., Minneapolis, MN 55431, (952) 881-4766, www.poorclare.com. 3626 N. 65th Ave., Omaha, NE 68104-3299, (402) 558-4916, www.omahapoorclare.org. 720 Henry Clay Ave., New Orleans, LA 70118-5891, (504) 895-2019, www.poorclarenuns.com. 6825 Nurrenbern Rd., Evansville, IN 47712-8518, (812) 425-4396, www.poorclare.org/com. 1310 Dellwood Ave., Memphis, TN 38127-6399, (901) 357-6662, www.poorclare.org/memphis. 920 Centre St., Jamaica Plain, MA 02130-3099, (617) 524-1760, www.stanthonyshrine.org/poorclares. 327 S. Broad St., Trenton, NJ 08608, (609) 392-7673. 1271 Langhorne-Newtown Rd., Langhorne, PA 19047-1297, (215) 968-5775. 4419 N. Hawthorne St., Spokane, WA 99205, (509) 327-4479. 86 Mayflower Ave., New Rochelle, NY, 10801-1615, (914) 632-5227, www.poorclaresny.com. 421 S. 4th St., Sauk Rapids, MN 56379-1898, (612) 251-3556. 3501 Rocky River Dr., Cleveland, OH 44111, (216) 941-820.

1671 Pleasant Valley Rd., Aptos, CA 95001, (831) 761-9659. 2111 S. Main St., Rockford, IL 61102, (815) 963-7343, www.poorclare.org/rockford. 215 E. Los Olivos St., Santa Barbara, CA 93105-3605, (805) 682-7670. 445 River Rd., Andover, MA 01810, (978) 683-7599. 809 E. 19th St., Roswell, NM 88201-7514, (505) 622-0868. 28210 Natoma Rd., Los Altos Hills, CA 94022, (650) 948-2947, www.chcweb.com. 1916 N. Pleasantburg Dr., Greenville, SC 29609-4080, (864) 244-4514. 28 Harpersville Rd., Newport News, VA 23601, (804) 596-5942. 1175 N. 300 W., Kokomo, IN 46901-1799, (765) 457-5743, www.thepoorclares.org. 3900 Sherwood Blvd., Delray Beach, FL 33445, (561) 498-3294. 200 Marycrest Dr., St. Louis, MO 63129, (314) 846-2618. 6029 Estero Blvd., Fort Myers Beach, FL 33931, (239) 463-5599, www.poorclares-fmb.org. 9300 Hwy 105, Brenham, TX 77833, (409) 836-2444, www.franciscanpoorclares.org.

Franciscan Sisters, Daughters of the Sacred Hearts of Jesus and Mary, O.S.F.: Founded 1860, in Germany; in U.S., 1872. Generalate, Rome, Italy. U.S. motherhouse, P.O. Box 667, Wheaton, IL 60189-0667, (630) 462-7422, www.wheatonfranciscan.org. Educational, hospital, foreign mission, social work.

Franciscan Sisters Daughters of Mercy, F.H.M.: Founded 1856, in Spain; in U.S., 1962. General motherhouse, Palma de Mallorca, Spain. U.S. address, 612 N. 3rd St., Waco, TX 76701, (254) 753-5565.

Franciscan Sisters of Allegany, O.S.F.: Founded 1859, at Allegany, NY, by Fr. Pamphilus da Magliano, O.F.M. General motherhouse, P.O. Box W, 115 East Main St., Allegany, NY 14706, (716) 373-0200, www.fsalleg.org. Educational, hospital, foreign mission work.

Franciscan Sisters of Baltimore, O.S.F.: Founded 1868, in England; in U.S., 1881. General motherhouse, 3725 Ellerslie Ave., Baltimore, MD 21218, (410) 235-0139. Educational work; social services.

Franciscan Sisters of Chicago, O.S.F.: Founded 1894, in U.S., by Mother Mary Therese (Josephine Dudzik). General motherhouse, 11500 Theresa Dr., Lemont, IL 60439, (630) 243-3558. Educational work, social services.

Franciscan Sisters of Christian Charity, O.S.F.: Founded 1869, in U.S. Motherhouse, Holy Family Convent, 2409 S. Alverno Rd., Manitowoc, WI 54220, (920) 682-7728, www.fscc-calledtobe.org. Hospital work.

Franciscan Sisters of Little Falls, MN, O.S.F.: Founded 1891, in U.S. General motherhouse, 116 8th Ave., S.E., Little Falls, MN 56345, (320) 632-0612, www.fslf.org. Health, education, social services, pastoral ministry, mission work.

Franciscan Sisters of Mary, F.S.M.: Established, 1987, through unification of the Sisters of St. Mary of the Third Order of St. Francis (founded 1872, St. Louis) and the Sisters of St. Francis of Maryville, MO (founded 1894). Address of general superior: 1100 Bellevue Ave., St. Louis, MO 63117-1883, (314) 768-1833, www.fsmonline.org. Health care, social services.

Franciscan Sisters of Mary Immaculate of the Third Order of St. Francis of Assisi, F.M.I.: Founded 16th century, in Switzerland; in U.S., 1932. General motherhouse, Bogota, Colombia. U.S. provincial house, 4301 N.E. 18th Ave., Amarillo, TX 79107-7220, (806) 383-5769. Education.

Franciscan Sisters of Our Lady of Perpetual Help, O.S.F.: Founded 1901, in U.S., from Joliet, IL, foundation. General motherhouse, 335 South Kirkwood Rd., St. Louis, MO 63122, (314) 965-3700, www.franciscansisters-olph.org. Educational, hospital work.

Franciscan Sisters of Peace, F.S.P.: Established 1986, in U.S., as archdiocesan community, from Franciscan Missionary Sisters of the Sacred Heart. Congregation Center, 20 Ridge St., Haverstraw, NY 10927, (845) 942-2527, www.fspnet.org.

Franciscan Sisters of Ringwood, F.S.R.: Merged with the Sisters of St. Francis of Philadelphia in 2003.

Franciscan Sisters of St. Elizabeth, F.S.S.E.: Founded 1866, at Naples, Italy, by Bl. Ludovico of Casorio; in U.S., 1919. General motherhouse, Rome, Italy. U.S. delegate house, 499 Park Rd., Parsippany, NJ 07054, (973) 539-3797, www.franciscansisters.com. Educational work, social services.

Franciscan Sisters of St. Joseph, F.S.S.J.: Founded 1897, in U.S. General motherhouse, 5286 S. Park Ave., Hamburg, NY 14075, (716) 649-1205, www.franciscansistershamburg.org. Educational, hospital work.

Franciscan Sisters of St. Joseph (of Mexico): U.S. foundation, St. Paul College, 3015 4th St. N.E., Washington, DC 20017, (202) 832-6262.

Franciscan Sisters of the Atonement (Graymoor Sisters), S.A.: Founded 1898, in U.S., as Anglican community; entered Church, 1909. General motherhouse, St. Francis Convent-Graymoor, 41 Old Highland Turnpike, Garrison, NY 10524, (914) 424-3624. Mission work.

Franciscan Sisters of St. Paul, MN, O.S.F.: Founded 1863, at Neuwied, Germany (Franciscan Sisters of the Blessed Virgin Mary of the Holy Angels); in U.S., 1923. General motherhouse, Rhine, Germany. U.S. motherhouse, 1388 Prior Ave. S., St. Paul, MN 55116, (516) 690-1501. Educational, hospital, social work.

Franciscan Sisters of the Immaculate Conception, O.S.F.: Founded in Germany; in U.S., 1928. General motherhouse, Kloster, Bonlanden, Germany. U.S. province, 291 North St., Buffalo, NY 14201, (716) 881-2323.

Franciscan Sisters of the Immaculate Conception, O.S.F.: Founded 1874, in Mexico; in U.S., 1926. U.S. provincial house, 11306 Laurel Canyon Blvd., San Fernando, CA 91340, (818) 365-2582.

Franciscan Sisters of the Immaculate Conception and St. Joseph for the Dying, O.S.F.: Founded 1919, in U.S. General motherhouse, 1249 Joselyn Canyon Rd., Monterey, CA 93940, (408) 372-3579.

Franciscan Sisters of the Poor, S.F.P.: Founded 1845, at Aachen, Germany, by Bl. Frances Schervier; in U.S., 1858. Congregational office, 133 Remsen St., Brooklyn, NY 11201, (718) 643-1919, www.franciscansisters.org. Hospital, social work and foreign missions.

Franciscan Sisters of the Sacred Heart, O.S.F.: Founded 1866, in Germany; in U.S., 1876. General motherhouse, St. Francis Woods, 9201 W. St. Francis Rd., Frankfort, IL 60423-8335, (815) 469-4895, www.fssh.com. Education, health care, other service ministries.

Hospital Sisters of the Third Order of St. Francis, O.S.F.: Founded 1844, in Germany; in U.S., 1875. General motherhouse, Muenster, Germany. U.S. motherhouse, 4849 La Verna Rd., Springfield, IL 62707, (217) 522-3386, www.springfieldfranciscans.org. Hospital work.

Institute of the Franciscan Sisters of the Eucharist, F.S.E.: Founded 1973. Motherhouse, 405 Allen Ave., Meriden, CT 06451, (203) 237-0841, www.fscommunity.org.

Little Franciscans of Mary, P.F.M.: Founded 1889, in U.S. General motherhouse, Baie St. Paul, QC, Canada. U.S. region, 55 Moore Ave., Worcester, MA 01602, (508) 755-0878. Educational, hospital, social work.

Missionary Franciscan Sisters of the Immaculate Conception, M.F.I.C.: Founded 1873, in U.S. General motherhouse, Rome, Italy. U.S. address, 790 Centre St., Newton, MA 02458, (617) 527-1004, www.mficusa.org. Educational work.

Missionary Sisters of the Immaculate Conception of the Mother of God, S.M.I.C.: Founded 1910, in Brazil; in U.S., 1922. U.S. provincialate, P.O. Box 3026, Paterson, NJ 07509, (973) 279-3790, www.smic-missionarysisters.com. Mission, educational, health work, social services.

Mothers of the Helpless, M.D.: Founded 1873, in Spain; in U.S., 1916. General motherhouse, Valencia, Spain. U.S. address, Sacred Heart Residence, 432 W. 20th St., New York, NY 10011, (212) 929-5790.

Poor Clares of Perpetual Adoration, P.C.P.A.: Founded 1854, at Paris, France; in U.S., 1921, at Cleveland, OH. U.S. monasteries: 4200 N. Market Ave., Canton, OH 44714. 2311 Stockham Lane, Portsmouth, OH 45662-3049, (740) 353-4713. 4108 Euclid Ave., Cleveland, OH 44103, (216) 361-0783. 3900 13th St. N.E., Washington, DC 20017, (202) 526-6808. 5817 Old Leeds Rd., Birmingham, AL 35210, (205) 271-2917. 3222 County Rd. 548, Hanceville, AL 35077,

(256) 352-6267, www.olamshrine.com. Contemplative, cloistered, perpetual adoration.

St. Francis Mission Community, O.S.F.: Autonomous province of Franciscan Sisters of Mary Immaculate. 4305 54th St., Lubbock, TX 79413, (806) 793-9859.

School Sisters of St. Francis, O.S.F.: Founded 1874, in U.S. General motherhouse, 1501 S. Layton Blvd., Milwaukee, WI 53215, (414) 384-4105.

School Sisters of St. Francis, (Pittsburgh, PA), O.S.F.: Established 1913, in U.S. Motherhouse, Mt. Assisi Convent, 934 Forest Ave., Pittsburgh, PA 15202-1199, (412) 761-2855, www.franciscansisters-pa.org. Education, health care services and related ministries.

School Sisters of the Third Order of St. Francis (Bethlehem, PA), O.S.F.: Founded in Austria, 1843; in U.S., 1913. General motherhouse, Rome, Italy. U.S. province, 395 Bridle Path Rd., Bethlehem, PA 18017, (610) 866-2597. Educational, mission work.

School Sisters of the Third Order of St. Francis (Panhandle, TX), O.S.F.: Established 1931, in U.S., from Vienna, Austria, foundation (1845). General motherhouse, Vienna, Austria. U.S. center and noviatiate, P.O. Box 906, Panhandle, TX, (806) 537-3182, www.panhandlefranciscans.org. Educational, social work.

Sisters of Mercy of the Holy Cross, S.C.S.C.: Founded 1856, in Switzerland; in U.S. 1912. General motherhouse, Ingenbohl, Switzerland. U.S. provincial residence, 1400 O'Day St., Merrill, WI 54452, (715) 539-1460, www.holycrosssisters.org.

Sisters of Our Lady of Mercy (Mercedarians), S.O.L.M.: General motherhouse, Rome, Italy. U.S. address: Most Precious Blood, 133 27th Ave., Brooklyn, NY 11214.

Sisters of St. Francis (Clinton, IA), O.S.F.: Founded 1868, in U.S. General motherhouse, 588 N. Bluff Blvd., Clinton, IA 57232-3953, (563) 242-7611, www.clintonfranciscans.com. Educational, hospital, social work.

Sisters of St. Francis (Millvale, PA), O.S.F.: Founded 1865, Pittsburgh. General motherhouse, 146 Hawthorne Rd., Millvale P.O., Pittsburgh, PA 15209, (412) 821-2200. Educational, hospital work.

Sisters of St. Francis (Hastings-on-Hudson), O.S.F.: Founded 1893, in New York. General motherhouse, 49 Jackson Ave., Hastings-on-Hudson, NY 10706-3217, (914) 478-3930. Education, parish ministry, social services.

Sisters of St. Francis of Assisi, O.S.F.: Founded 1849, in U.S. General motherhouse, 3221 S. Lake Dr., St. Francis, WI 53235-3799, (414) 744-3150, www.lakeosfs.org. Education, other ministries.

Sisters of St. Francis of Christ the King, O.S.F.: Founded 1864, in Austria; in U.S., 1909. General motherhouse, Rome, Italy. U.S. provincial house, 13900 Main St., Lemont, IL 60439, (630) 257-7495. Educational work, home for aged.

Sisters of St. Francis of Penance and Christian Charity, O.S.F.: Founded 1835, in Holland; in U.S., 1874. General motherhouse, Rome, Italy. U.S. provinces: 4421 Lower River Rd., Stella Niagara, NY 14144-1001, (716) 754-2193, www.franciscans-stella-niagara.org. 2851 W. 52nd Ave., Denver, CO 80221, (303) 458-6270; 3910 Bret Harte Dr., P.O. Box 1028, Redwood City, CA 94064, (650) 369-1725.

Sisters of St. Francis of Philadelphia, O.S.F.: Founded 1855, at Philadelphia, by Mother Mary Francis Bachmann and St. John N. Neumann. General motherhouse, Convent of Our Lady of the Angels, Aston, PA 19014, (610) 558-7701, www.osfphila.org. Education, health care, social services.

Sisters of St. Francis of Savannah, MO, O.S.F.: Founded 1850, in Austria; in U.S., 1922. Provincial house, La Verna Heights, Box 488, 104 E. Park, Savannah, MO 64485-0488, (816) 324-3179. Educational, hospital work.

Sisters of St. Francis of the Congregation of Our Lady of Lourdes, O.S.F.: Founded 1916, in U.S. General motherhouse, 6832 Convent Blvd., Sylvania, OH 43560-2897, (419) 824-3606, www.sistersosf.org. Education, health care, social services, pastoral ministry.

Sisters of St. Francis of the Holy Cross, O.S.F.: Founded 1881, in U.S., by Rev. Edward Daems, O.S.C. General motherhouse, 3025 Bay Settlement Rd., Green Bay, WI 54311, (920) 884-2700, www.gbfranciscans.org. Educational, nursing work, pastoral ministry, foreign missions.

Sisters of St. Francis of the Holy Eucharist, O.S.F.: Founded 1378, in Switzerland; in U.S., 1893. General motherhouse, 2100 N. Noland Rd., Independence, MO 64050, (816) 252-1673. Education, health care, social services, foreign missions.

Sisters of St. Francis of the Holy Family, O.S.F.: U.S. foundation, 1875. Motherhouse, Mt. St. Francis, 3390 Windsor Ave., Dubuque, IA 52001, (563) 583-9786, www.osfdbq.org. Varied apostolates.

Sisters of St. Francis of the Immaculate Conception, O.S.F.: Founded 1890, in U.S. General motherhouse, 2408 W. Heading Ave., West Peoria, IL 61604-5096, (309) 674-6168, www.osfsisterswpeoria.org. Education, care of aging, pastoral ministry.

Sisters of St. Francis of the Immaculate Heart of Mary, O.S.F.: Founded 1241, in Bavaria; in U.S., 1913. General motherhouse, Rome, Italy. U.S. motherhouse, 102 6th St., S.E., Hankinson, ND 58041, (701) 242-7195, www.fargodiocese.org/sfc/index.htm. Education, social services.

Sisters of St. Francis of the Martyr St. George, O.S.F.: Founded 1859, in Germany; in U.S., 1923. General motherhouse, Thuine, Germany. U.S. provincial house, St. Francis Convent, 2120 Central Ave., Alton, IL 62002, (618) 463-2750, www.altonfranciscans.org. Education, social services, foreign mission work.

Sisters of St. Francis of the Perpetual Adoration, O.S.F.: Founded 1863, in Germany; in U.S., 1875. General motherhouse, Olpe, Germany. U.S. provinces: Box 766, Mishawaka, IN 46546-0766, (574) 259-5427, www.ssfpa.org. 7665 Assisi Heights, Colorado Springs, CO 80919, (719) 598-5486, www.stfrancis.org.

Sisters of St. Francis of the Providence of God, O.S.F.: Founded 1922, in U.S., by Msgr. M. L. Krusas. General motherhouse, 3603 McRoberts Rd., Pittsburgh, PA 15234, (412) 885-7407. Education, varied apostolates.

Sisters of St. Joseph of the Third Order of St. Francis, S.S.J.: Founded 1901, in U.S. Administrative office, P.O. Box 305, Stevens Pt., WI 54481-0305, (715) 341-8457, www.ssj-tosf.org. Education, health care, social services.

Sisters of the Infant Jesus, I.J.: Founded 1662, at

Rouen, France; in U.S., 1950. Motherhouse, Paris, France. Generalate, Rome, Italy. U.S. address: 20 Reiner St., Colma, CA 94014.

Sisters of the Sorrowful Mother (Third Order of St. Francis), S.S.M.: Founded 1883, in Italy; in U.S., 1889. General motherhouse, Rome, Italy. U.S. address: 17600 E. 51st St., Broken Arrow, OK 74012, (918) 355-1148, www.ssmfranciscans.org. Educational, hospital work.

Sisters of the Third Franciscan Order, O.S.F.: Founded 1860, at Syracuse, NY. Generalate offices, 2500 Grant Blvd., Syracuse, NY 13208, (315) 425-0115.

Sisters of the Third Order of St. Francis, O.S.F.: Founded 1877, in U.S., by Bishop John L. Spalding. Motherhouse, 1175 St. Francis Lane, E. Peoria, IL 61611-1299, (309) 699-7215. Hospital work.

Sisters of the Third Order of St. Francis (Oldenburg, IN), O.S.F.: Founded 1851, in U.S. General motherhouse, Sisters of St. Francis, P.O. Box 100, Oldenburg, IN 47036-0100, (812) 934-2475, www.oldenburgfranciscans.org. Education, social services, pastoral ministry, foreign missions.

Sisters of the Third Order of St. Francis of Penance and Charity, O.S.F.: Founded 1869, in U.S., by Rev. Joseph Bihn. Motherhouse, 200 St. Francis Ave., Tiffin, OH 44883, (419) 447-0435, www.tiffin-franciscans.org. Education, social services.

Sisters of the Third Order of St. Francis of the Perpetual Adoration, F.S.P.A.: Founded 1849, in U.S. Generalate, 912 Market St., La Crosse, WI 54601, (608) 782-5610, www.fspa.org. Education, health care.

Sisters of the Third Order Regular of St. Francis of the Congregation of Our Lady of Lourdes, O.S.F.: Founded 1877, in U.S. General motherhouse, Assisi Heights, 1001 14th St., NW, Rochester, MN 55901, (507) 282-7441. Education, health care, social services.

Good Shepherd Sisters (Servants of the Immaculate Heart of Mary), S.C.I.M.: Founded 1850, in Canada; in U.S., 1882. General motherhouse, QC, Canada. In U.S., Provincial House, Bay View, 313 Seaside Ave., Saco, Maine 04072, (207) 284-6429. Educational, social work.

Good Shepherd, Sisters of the, R.G.S.: Founded 1835, in France, by St. Mary Euphrasia Pelletier; in U.S., 1843. Generalate, Rome, Italy. U.S. provinces: 2108 Hatmaker St., Cincinnati, OH 45204, (513) 921-5923. 82-31 Doncaster Pl., Jamaica, NY 11432, (718) 380-3270, www.goodshepherdsistersna.org. 504 Hexton Hill Rd., Silver Spring, MD 20904, (301) 384-1169. 7654 Natural Bridge Rd., St. Louis, MO 63121, (314) 381-3400, www.goodshepherdsisters.org. 5100 Hodgson Rd., St. Paul, MN 55126, (651) 484-0221. Active and contemplative (Contemplative Sisters of the Good Shepherd, C.G.S.).

Graymoor Sisters: See Franciscan Sisters of the Atonement.

Grey Nuns of the Sacred Heart, G.N.S.H.: Founded 1921, in U.S. General motherhouse, 1750 Quarry Rd., Yardley, PA 19067-3998, (215) 968-4236, www.greynun.org.

Guadalupan Missionaries of the Holy Spirit, M.G.Sp.S.: Founded 1930 in Mexico by Rev. Felix de Jesus Rougier, M.Sp.S. General motherhouse, Mexico.

U.S. delegation: 2483 S.W. 4th St. Miami, FL 33135-2907, (305) 642-9544.

Guardian Angel, Sisters of the, S.A.C.: Founded 1839, in France. General motherhouse, Madrid, Spain. U.S. foundation, 1245 S. Van Ness, Los Angeles, CA 90019, (213) 732-7881.

Handmaids of the Precious Blood, Congregation of, H.P.B.: Founded 1947, at Jemez Springs, NM. Motherhouse and novitiate, Cor Jesu Monastery, P.O. Box 90, Jemez Springs, NM 87025, (505) 829-3906.

Helpers, Society of, H.H.S.: Founded 1856, in France; in U.S., 1892. General motherhouse, Paris, France. American province, 3206 S. Aberdeen, Chicago, IL 60657, (773) 523-8638.

Hermanas Catequistas Guadalupanas, H.C.G.: Founded 1923, in Mexico; in U.S., 1950. General motherhouse, Mexico. 4110 S. Flores, San Antonio, TX 78214, (210) 533-9344.

Hermanas Josefinas, H.J.: General motherhouse, Mexico. U.S. foundation, Assumption Seminary, 2600 W. Woodlawn Ave., P.O. Box 28240, San Antonio, TX 78284, (210) 734-0039. Domestic work.

Holy Child Jesus, Society of the, S.H.C.J.: Founded 1846, in England; in U.S., 1862. General motherhouse, Rome, Italy. U.S. province, 460 Shadeland Ave., Drexel Hill, PA 19026, (610) 626-1400, www.shcj.org.

Holy Faith, Congregation of the Sisters of the, C.H.F.: Founded 1856, in Ireland; in U.S., 1953. General motherhouse, Dublin, Ireland. U.S. province, 12322 S. Paramount Blvd., Downey, CA 90242, (562) 869-6092.

Holy Family, Congregation of the Sisters of the, S.S.F.: Founded 1842, in Louisiana, by Henriette Delille and Juliette Gaudin. General motherhouse, 6901 Chef Menteur Hwy., New Orleans, LA 70126, (504) 242-8315, www.sistersoftheholyfamily. Hospital work.

Holy Family, Sisters of the, S.H.F.: Founded 1872, in U.S. General motherhouse, P.O. Box 3248, Fremont, CA 94539, (510) 624-4500 www.holyfamilysisters.com. Educational, social work.

Holy Family of Nazareth, Sisters of the, C.S.F.N.: Founded 1875, in Italy; in U.S., 1885. General motherhouse, Rome, Italy. U.S. provinces: Sacred Heart, 310 N. River Rd., Des Plaines, IL 60016-1211, (847) 298-6760. Immaculate Conception BVM, 4001 Grant Ave., Philadelphia, PA 19114, (215) 268-1035, www.phila-csfn.org. St. Joseph, 285 Bellevue Rd., Pittsburgh, PA 15229-2195, (412) 931-4778, www.csfn.org. Immaculate Heart of Mary, Marian Heights, 1428 Monroe Turnpike, Monroe, CT 04648, (203) 268-7646. Bl. Frances Siedliska Provincialate, 1814 Egyptian Way, Box 530959, Grand Prairie, TX 75053, (972) 641-4496, www.csfn.org.

Holy Heart of Mary, Servants of the, S.S.C.M.: Founded 1860, in France; in U.S., 1889. General motherhouse, Montreal, QC, Canada. U.S. province, 15 Elmwood Dr., Kankakee, IL 60901, (815) 937-2380, www.sscm-usa.org. Educational, hospital, social work.

Holy Names of Jesus and Mary, Sisters of the, S.N.J.M.: Founded 1843, in Canada by Bl. Marie Rose Durocher; in U.S., 1859. Generalate, Longueuil, QC, Canada. U.S. addresses: Oregon Province, Box 25, Marylhurst, OR 97036, (503) 675-2449. California Province, P.O. Box 907, Los Gatos, CA 95031, (408) 395-5150, www.holynames.net. New York Province, 1061 New Scotland Rd., Albany, NY 12208, (518)

489-5469, www.snjm.org. Washington Province, 2911 W. Ft. Wright Dr., Spokane, WA 99224, (509) 328-7470, www.snjm.org, www.holynames.net.

Holy Spirit, Community of the, C.H.S.: Founded 1970 in San Diego, CA. 6151 Rancho Mission Rd., No. 205, San Diego, CA 92108, (619) 584-0809.

Holy Spirit, Daughters of the, D.H.S.: Founded 1706, in France; in U.S., 1902. Generalate, Bretagne, France. U.S. motherhouse, 72 Church St., Putnam, CT 06260-1817, (860) 928-0891. Educational work, district nursing, pastoral ministry.

Holy Spirit, Mission Sisters of the, M.S.Sp.: Founded 1932, at Cleveland, OH. Motherhouse, 1030 N. River Rd., Saginaw, MI 48603, (517) 781-0934.

Holy Spirit, Missionary Sisters, Servants of the: Founded 1889, in Holland; in U.S., 1901. Generalate, Rome, Italy. U.S. motherhouse, Convent of the Holy Spirit, P.O. Box 6026, Techny, IL 60082-6026, (847) 441-0126, www.ssps-usa.org. International congregation for the spread of the Gospel ad gentes.

Holy Spirit, Sisters of the, C.S.Sp.: Founded 1890, in Rome, Italy; in U.S. as independent diocesan community, 1929. General motherhouse, 10102 Granger Rd., Garfield Hts., OH 44125. Educational, social, nursing work.

Holy Spirit, Sisters of the, S.H.S.: Founded 1913, in U.S., by Most Rev. J. F. Regis Canevin. General motherhouse, 5246 Clarwin Ave., Ross Township, Pittsburgh, PA 15229-2208, (412) 931-1917. Educational, nursing work, care of aged.

Holy Spirit and Mary Immaculate, Sisters of, S.H.Sp.: Founded 1893, in U.S. Motherhouse, 301 Yucca St., San Antonio, TX 78203, (210) 533-5149. Education, hospital work.

Holy Spirit of Perpetual Adoration, Sister Servants of the, S.Sp.S.deA.P.: Founded 1896, in Holland; in U.S., 1915. Generalate, Bad Driburg, Germany. U.S. novitiate, 2212 Green St., Philadelphia, PA 19130, (215) 567-0123, www.adorationsisters.org.

Holy Union Sisters, S.U.S.C.: Founded 1826, in France; in U.S., 1886. Generalate, Rome, Italy. U.S. provinces: P.O. Box 410, Milton, MA 02186-0006, (617) 696-8765. Box 993, Main St., Groton, MA 01450, (978) 448-6049. Varied ministries.

Home Mission Sisters of America (Glenmary Sisters), G.H.M.S.: Founded 1952, in U.S. Glenmary Center, P.O. Box 22264, Owensboro, KY 42304-2264, (270) 686-8401.

Home Visitors of Mary, Sisters, H.V.M.: Founded 1949, in Detroit, MI. Motherhouse, 121 E. Boston Blvd., Detroit, MI 48202, (313) 869-2160, www.sistershomevisitors.org.

Humility of Mary, Congregation of, C.H.M.: Founded 1854, in France; in U.S., 1864. U.S. address, Humility of Mary Center, Davenport IA, 52804, (319) 323-9466, www.chmiowa.org.

Humility of Mary, Sisters of the, H.M.: Founded 1854, in France; in U.S., 1864. U.S. address, Villa Maria Community Center, Villa Maria, PA 16155, (724) 964-8861, www.humilityofmary.org.

Immaculate Conception, Little Servant Sisters of the, L.S.I.C.: Founded 1850, in Poland; in U.S., 1926. General motherhouse, Poland. U.S. provincial house, 1000 Cropwell Rd., Cherry Hill, NJ 08003, (609) 424-1962. Education, social services, African missions.

Immaculate Conception, Sisters of the, R.C.M.: Founded 1892, in Spain; in U.S., 1962. General moth-

erhouse, Madrid, Spain. U.S. address, 2230 Franklin, San Francisco, CA 94109, (415) 474-0159.

Immaculate Conception, Sisters of the, C.I.C.: Founded 1874, in U.S. General motherhouse, P.O. Box 50426, New Orleans, LA 70185, (504) 486-7426.

Immaculate Conception of the Blessed Virgin Mary, Sisters of the (Lithuanian): Founded 1918, at Mariampole, Lithuania; in U.S., 1936. U.S. headquarters, Immaculate Conception Convent, 600 Liberty Hwy., Putnam, CT 06260, (860) 928-7955.

Immaculate Heart of Mary, Missionary Sisters, I.C.M.: Founded 1897, in India; in U.S., 1919. Generalate, Rome, Italy. U.S. province, 283 E. 15th St., New York, NY 10003, (212) 254-0658. Educational social, foreign mission work.

Immaculate Heart of Mary, Sisters of the, I.H.M.: Founded 1848, in Spain; in U.S., 1878. General motherhouse, Rome, Italy. U.S. province, 3820 Sabino Canyon Rd., Tucson, AZ 85750, (520) 886-4273. Educational work.

Immaculate Heart of Mary, Sisters, Servants of the, I.H.M.: Founded 1845. SSIHM Leadership Council, 610 W. Elm, Monroe, MI 48162, (734) 340-9700, www.sistersihm.org.

Immaculate Heart of Mary, Sisters, Servants of the, I.H.M.: Founded 1845; established in Scranton, PA, 1871. General motherhouse, 2300 Adams Ave., Scranton, PA 18509, (570) 346-5404, www.sistersofihm.org.

Immaculate Heart of Mary, Sisters Servants of the, I.H.M.: Founded 1845; established in West Chester, PA, 1872. General motherhouse, Villa Maria, Immaculata, PA 19345, (610) 647-2160, www.ihmimmaculata.org.

Immaculate Heart of Mary of Wichita, Sisters of, I.H.M.: Established at Wichita, KS. 1979. Address: 605 N. Woodchuck, Wichita, KS 67212, (316) 722-9316, www.sistersofwichita.org.

Incarnate Word, Religious of, C.V.I.: General motherhouse, Mexico City, Mexico. U.S. address, 153 Rainier Ct., Chula Vista, CA 92011, (619) 420-0231.

Incarnate Word and Blessed Sacrament, Congregation of, C.V.I.: Founded 1625, in France; in U.S., 1853. Incarnate Word Convent, 3400 Bradford Pl., Houston, TX 77025, (713) 668-0423.

Incarnate Word and Blessed Sacrament, Congregation of the, I.W.B.S.: Motherhouse, 1101 Northeast Water St., Victoria, TX 77901, (361) 575-2266, www.iwbsvictoria.org.

Incarnate Word and Blessed Sacrament, Congregation of the, I.W.B.S.: Motherhouse, 2930 S. Alameda, Corpus Christi, TX 78404, (361) 882-5413, www.iwbscc.org.

Incarnate Word and Blessed Sacrament, Sisters of the, S.I.W.: Founded 1625, in France; in U.S. 1853. Motherhouse, 6618 Pearl Rd., Parma Heights, Cleveland, OH 44130, (216) 886-6440, www.incarnatewordorder.org.

Infant Jesus, Congregation of the (Nursing Sisters of the Sick Poor), C.I.J.: Founded 1835, in France; in U.S., 1905. General motherhouse, 310 Prospect Park W., Brooklyn, NY 11215, (718) 965-7300.

Institute of the Blessed Virgin Mary (Loretto Sisters), I.B.V.M.: Founded 17th century in Belgium; in U.S., 1954. Motherhouse, Rathfarnham, Dublin, Ireland. U.S. address: 2521 W. Maryland Ave.,

Phoenix, AZ 85017, (602) 242-2544.

Institute of the Blessed Virgin Mary (Loretto Sisters), I.B.V.M.: Founded 1609, in Belgium; in U.S., 1880. Loretto Convent, Box 508, Wheaton, IL 60189, (630) 665-3814. Educational work.

Jesus, Daughters of (Filles de Jesus), F.J.: Founded 1834, in France; in U.S., 1904. General motherhouse, Kermaria, Locmine, France. U.S. address, 4209 3rd Ave. S., Great Falls, MT 59405, (406) 452-7231. Educational, hospital, parish and social work.

Jesus, Little Sisters of, L.S.J.: Founded 1939, in Sahara; in U.S., 1952. General motherhouse, Rome, Italy. U.S. headquarters, 400 N. Streeper St., Baltimore, MD 21224, www.rc.net/org/littlesisters.

Jesus, Society of the Sisters, Faithful Companions of, F.C.J.: Founded 1820, in France; in U.S., 1896. General motherhouse, Kent, England. U.S. province, St. Philomena Convent, Cory's Lane, Portsmouth, RI 02871, (401) 683-2000, www.portsmouthabbey.org.

Jesus and Mary, Little Sisters of, L.S.J.M.: Founded 1974 in U.S. Joseph House, P.O. Box 1755, Salisbury, MD 21802, (410) 742-9590, www.the-josephhouse.org.

Jesus and Mary, Religious of, R.J.M.: Founded 1818, at Lyons, France; in U.S., 1877. General motherhouse, Rome, Italy. U.S. province, 6103 Baltimore Ave., Ste. T-5, Riverdale, MD 20713, (301) 277-2535. Educational work.

Jesus Crucified, Congregation of: Founded 1930, in France; in U.S., 1955. General motherhouse, Brou, France. U.S. foundation: Benedictines of Jesus Crucified, Monastery of the Glorious Cross, 61 Burban Dr., Branford, CT 06405-4003, (203) 315-9964, www.benedictinesjc.org.

Jesus Crucified and the Sorrowful Mother, Poor Sisters of, C.J.C.: Founded 1924, in U.S., by Rev. Alphonsus Maria, C.P. Motherhouse, 261 Thatcher St., Brockton, MA 02402. Education, nursing homes, catechetical centers.

Jesus, Mary and Joseph, Missionary Sisters of, M.J.M.J.: Founded 1942, in Spain; in U.S., 1956. General motherhouse, Madrid, Spain. U.S. regional house, 12940 Leopard St., Corpus Christi, TX 78410, (361) 241-1955.

John the Baptist, Sisters of St., C.S.J.B.: Founded 1878, in Italy; in U.S., 1906. General motherhouse, Rome, Italy. U.S. provincialate, 3308 Campbell Dr., Bronx, NY 10465, (718) 518-7820, www.home.att.net/~baptistines. Education, parish and retreat work; social services.

Joseph, Poor Sisters of St., P.S.S.J.: Founded 1880, in Argentina. General motherhouse, Muniz, Buenos Aires, Argentina. U.S. addresses: Casa Belen, 305 E. 4th St., Bethlehem, PA 78015, (610) 867-4030. Casa Nazareth, 5321 Spruce St., Reading, PA 19602, (610) 378-1947. St. Gabriel Convent, 4319 Sano St., Alexandria, VA 22312, (703) 354-0395 .

Joseph, Religious Daughters of St., F.S.J.: Founded 1875, in Spain. General motherhouse, Spain. U.S. foundation, 319 N. Humphreys Ave., Los Angeles, CA 90022.

Joseph, Servants of St., S.S.J.: Founded 1874, in Spain; in U.S., 1957. General motherhouse, Salamanca, Spain. U.S. address, 203 N. Spring St., Falls Church, VA 22046, (703) 533-8441.

Joseph, Sisters of St., C.S.J. or S.S.J.: Founded 1650, in France; in U.S., 1836, at St. Louis. Independent motherhous-es in U.S.: 637 Cambridge St., Brighton, MA 02135, (617) 783-9090. 1515 W. Ogden Ave., La Grange Park, IL, 60526, (708) 354-9200, www.ministryofhearts.org. 480 S. Batavia St., Orange, CA 92868, (714) 633-8121, www.sistersof-stjosephorange.org. St. Joseph Convent, 1725 Brentwood Rd., Brentwood, NY 11717-5587, (516) 273-4531. 23 Agassiz Circle, Buffalo, NY 14214, (716) 838-4400. 3430 Rocky River Dr., Cleveland, OH 44111, (216) 252-0440, www.csjcleveland.org. 1440 W. Division Rd., Tipton, IN 46072, (765) 675-6203, www.csjtipton.org. Motherhouse and novitiate, Nazareth, MI 49074, (616) 381-6290. 1425 Washington St., Watertown, NY 13601, (315) 782-3460, www.ssjwatertown.org. 1020 State St., Baden, PA 15005-1342, (724) 869-2151, www.stjosephbaden.org. 5031 W. Ridge Rd., Erie, PA 16506, (814) 836-4208, www.ssjerie.org. 150 French Rd., Rochester, NY 14618, (585) 641-8119, www.ssjvolunteers. Mont Marie, 34 Lower Westfield Rd. Holyoke, MA 01040, (413) 536-0853. Pogue Run Rd., Wheeling, WV 26003, (304) 232-8160, www.ssjwhg.org. 3700 E. Lincoln St., Wichita, KS 67218, (316) 686-7171, www.csjwichita.org. 215 Court St., Concordia, KS 66901, (785) 243-2149, www.csjkansas.org.

Joseph, Sisters of St. (Lyons, France), C.S.J.: Founded 1650, in France; in U.S., 1906. General motherhouse, Lyons, France. U.S. provincialate, 93 Halifax St., Winslow, ME 04901, (207) 873-4512, www.e-livingwater.org. Educational, hospital work.

Joseph, Sisters of St., of Peace, C.S.J.P.: Founded 1884, in England; in U.S. 1885. Generalate, 3043 Fourth St., N.E., Washington, DC 20017, (202) 832-5333. Educational, hospital, social service work.

Joseph of Carondelet, Sisters of St., C.S.J.: Founded 1650, in France; in U.S., 1836, at St. Louis, MO. U.S. headquarters, 2311 S. Lindbergh Blvd., St. Louis, MO 63131, (314) 966-4048, www.csjcongregation.org.

Joseph of Chambery, Sisters of St.: Founded 1650, in France; in U.S., 1885. Generalate, Rome, Italy. U.S. provincial house, 27 Park Rd., West Hartford, CT 06119, (860) 233-5126. Educational, hospital, social work.

Joseph of Chestnut Hill, Sisters of St., S.S.J.: Founded 1650; Philadelphia foundation, 1847. Motherhouse, Mt. St. Joseph Convent, 9701 Germantown Ave., Philadelphia, PA 19118, (215) 248-7200, www.ssjphila.org.

Joseph of Cluny, Sisters of St., S.J.C.: Founded 1807, in France. Generalate, Paris, France. U.S. provincial house, Brenton Rd., Newport, RI 02840, (401) 846-4757.

Joseph of Medaille, Sisters of, C.S.J.: Founded 1650, in France; in U.S., 1855. Became an American congregation Nov. 30, 1977. Central office, 1821 Summit Rd., Suite 210, Cincinnati, OH 45237, (513) 761-2888.

Joseph of St. Augustine, Florida, Sisters of St., S.S.J.: General motherhouse, 241 St. George St., P.O. Box 3506, St. Augustine, FL 32085, (904) 824-1752. Educational, hospital, pastoral, social work.

Joseph of St. Mark, Sisters of St., S.J.S.M.: Founded 1845, in France; in U.S., 1937. General motherhouse, 21800 Chardon Rd., Euclid, Cleveland, OH 44117, (216) 531-7426. Nursing homes.

Joseph the Worker, Sisters of St., S.J.W.: General motherhouse, St. William Convent, 1 St. Joseph Lane, Walton, KY 41094, (859) 485-4256.

Lamb of God, Sisters of the, A.D.: Founded 1945, in France; in U.S., 1958. General motherhouse, France. U.S. address, 2063 Wyandotte Ave., Owensboro KY 42301, (502) 281-5450.

Life, Sisters of, S.V. (*Sorer Vitae*): Founded by Cardinal John J. O'Connor, 1991, to protect life. St. Frances de Chantal Convent, 198 Hollywood Ave., Bronx, NY 10465, (718) 863-2264. Our Lady of New York, 1955 Needham Ave., Bronx, NY 10466, (718) 881-8008. Sacred Heart Convent, 450 W. 51st St., New York, NY, (212) 397-1386.

Little Sisters of the Gospel, L.S.G.: Founded 1963 in France by Rev. Rene Voillaume; in U.S., 1972. Box 305, Mott Haven Sta., Bronx, NY 10454, (718) 292-2867.

Little Workers of the Sacred Hearts, P.O.S.C.: Founded 1892, in Italy; in U.S., 1948. General House, Rome, Italy. U.S. address, Our Lady of Grace Convent, 635 Glenbrook Rd., Stamford, CT 06906, (203) 348-5531.

Living Word, Sisters of the, S.L.W.: Founded 1975, in U.S. Motherhouse, Living Word Center, 800 N. Fernandez Ave. B, Arlington Heights, IL 60004-5316, (847) 577-5972, www.slw.org. Education, hospital, parish ministry work.

Loretto at the Foot of the Cross, Sisters of, S.L.: Founded 1812 in U.S., by Rev. Charles Nerinckx. General motherhouse, 300 E. Hampden Ave., Ste. 400, Englewood, CO 80110-2661, (303) 783-0450, www.lorettocommunity.org. Educational work.

Louis, Juilly-Monaghan, Congregation of Sisters of St., S.S.L.: Founded 1842, in France; in U.S., 1949. General motherhouse, Monaghan, Ireland. U.S. regional house, 22300 Mulholland Dr., Woodland Hills, CA 91364, (818) 883-1678. Educational, medical, parish, foreign mission work.

Lovers of the Holy Cross Sisters (Phat Diem), L.H.C.: Founded 1670, in Vietnam; in U.S. 1976. U.S. address, Holy Cross Convent, 14700 South Van Ness Ave., Gardena, CA 90249, (310) 516-0271.

Mantellate Sisters, Servants of Mary, of Blue Island, O.S.M.: Founded 1861, in Italy; in U.S., 1916. Generalate, Rome, Italy. U.S. motherhouse, 13811 S. Western Ave., Blue Island, IL 60406, (708) 385-2103. Educational work.

Mantellate Sisters Servants of Mary, of Plainfield, O.S.M.: Founded 1861 in Italy; in U.S., 1916. 16949 S. Drauden Rd., Plainfield, IL 60544, (815) 436-5796.

Marian Sisters of the Diocese of Lincoln: Founded 1954. Marycrest Motherhouse, 6905 N. 112th St., Waverly, NE 68462-9690, (402) 786-2750.

Marianites of Holy Cross, Congregation of the Sisters, M.S.C.: Founded 1841, in France; in U.S., 1843. Motherhouse, Le Mans, Sarthe, France. North American headquarters, 1011 Gallier St., New Orleans, LA 70117-6111, (504) 945-1620, www.marianites.org.

Marist Sisters, Congregation of Mary, S.M.: Founded 1824, in France. General motherhouse, Rome, Italy. U.S. foundation: 810 Peach, Abilene, TX 79602, (915) 675-5806.

Mary, Company of, O.D.N.: Founded 1607, in France; in U.S., 1926. General motherhouse, Rome, Italy. U.S. motherhouse, 16791 E. Main St., Tustin, CA 92680-4034, (714) 541-3125, www.companyofmary.com.

Mary, Daughters of the Heart of, D.H.M.: Founded 1790, in France; in U.S., 1851. Generalate, Paris, France. U.S. provincialate, 1339 Northampton St., Holyoke, MA 01040, (413) 533-6681, www.dhmna.org. Education, retreat work.

Mary, Missionary Sisters of the Society of (Marist Sisters), S.M.S.M.: Founded 1845, at St. Brieuc, France; in U.S., 1922. General motherhouse, Rome, Italy. U.S. provincial house, 349 Grove St., Waltham, MA 02453, (781) 893-0149. Foreign missions.

Mary, Servants of, O.S.M.: Founded 13th century, in Italy; in U.S., 1893. General motherhouse, England. U.S. provincial motherhouse, 7400 Military Ave., Omaha, NE 68134, (402) 571-2547.

Mary, Servants of (Servite Sisters), O.S.M.: Founded 13th century, in Italy; in U.S., 1912. General motherhouse, Servants of Mary Convent, 1000 College Ave., Ladysmith, WI 54848, (715) 532-3364.

Mary, Sisters of St., of Oregon, S.S.M.O.: Founded 1886, in Oregon, by Bishop William H. Gross, C.Ss.R. General motherhouse, 4440 S.W. 148th Ave., Beaverton, OR 97007, (503) 644-9181, www.ssmo.org. Educational, nursing work.

Mary, Sisters of the Little Company of, L.C.M.: Founded 1877, in England; in U.S., 1893. Generalate, London, England. U.S. provincial house, 9350 S. California Ave., Evergreen Park, IL 60805, (708) 229-5490.

Mary, Sisters Servants of (Trained Nurses), S.M.: Founded 1851, at Madrid, Spain; in U.S., 1914. General motherhouse, Rome, Italy. U.S. motherhouse, 800 N. 18th St., Kansas City, KS 66102, (913) 371-3423. Home nursing.

Mary and Joseph, Daughters of, D.M.J.: Founded 1817, in Belgium; in U.S., 1926. Generalate, Rome, Italy. American provincialate, 5300 Crest Rd., Rancho Palos Verdes, CA 90274, (310) 541-8194.

Mary Help of Christians, Daughters of (Salesian Sisters of St. John Bosco), F.M.A.: Founded 1872, in Italy, by St. John Bosco and St. Mary Dominic Mazzarello; in U.S., 1908. General motherhouse, Rome, Italy. U.S. provinces: 655 Belmont Ave., Haledon, NJ 07508, (937) 790-7963. 6019 Buena Vista St., San Antonio, TX 78237, (210) 432-0090. Education, youth work.

Mary Immaculate, Daughters of (Marianist Sisters), F.M.I.: Founded 1816, in France, by Very Rev. William-Joseph Chaminade. General motherhouse, Rome, Italy. U.S. foundation, 251 W. Ligustrum Dr., San Antonio, TX 78228-4092, (210) 433-5501, www.marianistsisters.org. Educational work.

Mary Immaculate, Religious of, R.M.I.: Founded 1876, in Spain; in U.S., 1954. Generalate, Rome, Italy. U.S. foundation, 719 Augusta St., San Antonio, TX 78215, (210) 226-0025.

Mary Immaculate, Sisters Minor of, S.M.M.I.: Established in U.S., 1989. 138 Brushy Hill Rd., Danbury, CT 06818, (203) 744-8041.

Mary Immaculate, Sisters of, S.M.I.: Founded 1948, in India, by Bishop Louis LaRavoire Morrow; in U.S., 1981. General motherhouse, Bengal, India. U.S. address, 118 Park Rd., Leechburg, PA 15656, (724) 845-2828.

Mary Immaculate, Sisters Servants of, S.S.M.I.: Founded 1878 in Poland. General motherhouse, Mariowka-Opoczynska, Poland; American provincialate, 1220 Tugwell Dr., Catonsville, MD 21228, (410) 747-1353.

Mary Immaculate, Sisters Servants of, S.S.M.I:

Founded 1892, in Ukraine; in U.S., 1935. General motherhouse, Rome, Italy. U.S. address, 9 Emmanuel Dr., P.O. Box 9, Sloatsburg, NY 10974-0009, (845) 753-2840. Educational, hospital work.

Mary of Namur, Sisters of St., S.S.M.N.: Founded 1819, at Namur, Belgium; in U.S., 1863. General motherhouse, Namur, Belgium. U.S. provinces: 241 Lafayette Ave., Buffalo, NY 14213-1453, (716) 884-8221, www.ssmn.org. 909 West Shaw St., Ft. Worth, TX 76110, (817) 923-8393, web2.airmail.net/ssmn.

Mary of Providence, Daughters of St., D.S.M.P.: Founded 1872, at Como, Italy; in U.S., 1913. General motherhouse, Rome, Italy. U.S. provincial house, 4200 N. Austin Ave., Chicago, IL 60634, (773) 545-8300. Special education for mentally handicapped.

Mary of the Immaculate Conception, Daughters of, D.M.: Founded 1904, in U.S., by Msgr. Lucian Bojnowski. General motherhouse, 314 Osgood Ave., New Britain, CT 06053, (860) 225-9406. Educational, hospital work.

Mary Queen, Congregation of, C.M.R.: Founded in Vietnam; established in U.S., 1979. U.S. region, 625 S. Jefferson, Springfield, MO 65806.

Mary Reparatrix, Society of, S.M.R.: Founded 1857, in France; in U.S., 1908. Generalate, Rome, Italy. U.S. province, 225 E. 234th St., Bronx NY 10470.

Maryknoll Sisters, M.M.: Founded in 1912 in U.S. by Mother Mary Joseph. General motherhouse, P.O. Box 311, Maryknoll, NY 10545-0311, (914) 941-7575, www.maryknoll.org.

Medical Mission Sisters (Society of Catholic Medical Missionaries, Inc.), M.M.S.: Founded 1925, in U.S., by Mother Anna Dengel. Generalate, London, England. U.S. headquarters, 8400 Pine Rd., Philadelphia, PA 19111, (215) 742-6100, www.medicalmissionsisters.org. Medical work, health education, especially in mission areas.

Medical Missionaries of Mary, M.M.M.: Founded 1937, in Ireland, by Mother Mary Martin; in U.S., 1950. General motherhouse, Dublin, Ireland. U.S. headquarters, 563 Minneford Ave., City Island, Bronx, NY 10464, (718) 885-0945. Medical aid in missions.

Medical Sisters of St. Joseph, M.S.J.: Founded 1946, in India; first U.S. foundation, 1985. General motherhouse, Kerala, S. India. U.S. address, 3435 E. Funston, Wichita, KS 67218, (316) 689-5360. Health care apostolate.

Mercedarian Sisters of the Blessed Sacrament, H.M.S.S.: Founded 1910, in Mexico; first U.S. foundation, 1926. Regional House, 227 Keller St., San Antonio, TX 78204, (210) 223-5013.

Mercy, Daughters of Our Lady of, D.M.: Founded 1837, in Italy, by St. Mary Joseph Rossello; in U.S., 1919. General motherhouse, Savona, Italy. U.S. motherhouse, Villa Rossello, 1009 Main Rd., Newfield, NJ 08344, (856) 697-2983. Educational, hospital work.

Mercy, Missionary Sisters of Our Lady of, M.O.M.: Founded 1938, in Brazil; in U.S., 1955. General motherhouse, Brazil. U.S. address, 388 Franklin St., Buffalo, NY 14202, (716) 854-5198.

Mercy, Religious Sisters of, R.S.M.: Founded 1973 in U.S. Motherhouse, 1835 Michigan Ave., Alma, MI 48801, (517) 463-6035.

Mercy, Sisters of, of the Americas: Formed in July, 1991, through union of nine provinces and 16 regional communities of Sisters of Mercy which previously were independent motherhouses or houses which formed the Sisters of Mercy of the Union. Mother Mary Catherine McAuley founded the Sisters of Mercy in Dublin, Ireland, in 1831; first established in the U.S., 1843, in Pittsburgh. Administrative office, 8300 Colesville Rd., No. 300, Silver Spring, MD 20910, (301) 587-0423.

Mill Hill Sisters: *See* **Franciscan Missionaries of St. Joseph.**

Minim Daughters of Mary Immaculate, C.F.M.M.: Founded 1886, in Mexico; in U.S., 1926. General motherhouse, Leon, Guanajuato, Mexico. U.S. address, 555 Patagonia Hwy., Nogales, AZ 85621, (520) 287-3377.

Misericordia Sisters, S.M.: Founded 1848, in Canada; in U.S., 1887. General motherhouse, 12435 Ave. Misericorde, Montreal, QC H4J 2G3, Canada. U.S. address, 225 Carol Ave., Pelham, NY 10803. Social work with unwed mothers and their children; hospital work.

Mission Helpers of the Sacred Heart, M.H.S.H.: Founded 1890, in U.S. General motherhouse, 1001 W. Joppa Rd., Baltimore, MD 21204, (410) 823-8585, www.missionhelpers.org. Religious education, evangelization.

Missionary Catechists of the Sacred Hearts of Jesus and Mary (Violetas), M.C.S.H.: Founded 1918, in Mexico; in U.S., 1943. Motherhouse, Tlalpan, Mexico. U.S. address, 805 Liberty St., Victoria, TX 77901, (512) 578-9302.

Missionary Daughters of the Most Pure Virgin Mary, M.D.P.V.M.: Founded in Mexico; in U.S., 1916. 919 N. 9th St., Kingsville, TX 78363, (512) 595-1087.

Mother of God, Missionary Sisters of the, M.S.M.G.: Byzantine, Ukrainian Rite, Stamford. Motherhouse, 711 N. Franklin St., Philadelphia, PA 19123, (215) 627-7808.

Mother of God, Sisters Poor Servants of the, S.M.G.: Founded 1869, in London, England; in U.S., 1947. General motherhouse, Maryfield, Roehampton, London. U.S. address: Maryfield Nursing Home, Greensboro Rd., High Point, NC 27260, (336) 886-2444, www.greensboro.com/mnh. Hospital, educational work.

Nazareth, Poor Sisters of, P.S.N.: Founded in England; U.S. foundation, 1924. General motherhouse, Hammersmith, London, England. U.S. novitiate, 3333 Manning Ave., Los Angeles, CA 90064, (310) 839-2361. Social services, education.

Notre Dame, School Sisters of, S.S.N.D.: Founded 1833, in Germany; in U.S., 1847. General mother-house, Rome, Italy. U.S. provinces: 13105 Watertown Plank Rd., Elm Grove, WI 53122-2291, (262) 782-9850, www.ssnd-milw.org. 6401 N. Charles St., Baltimore, MD 21212, (410) 377-7774, www.ssndba.org. 320 E. Ripa Ave., St. Louis, MO 63125, (314) 633-7000, www.ssnd.org. 170 Good Counsel Dr., Mankato, MN 56001-3138, (507) 389-4210, www.ssnd mankato.org. 345 Belden Hill Rd., Wilton, CT 06897, (203) 762-1220. P.O. Box 227275, Dallas, TX 75222, (214) 330-9152, www.ssnddallas.org. 1431 Euclid Ave., Berwyn, IL 60402, (708) 749-1380.

Notre Dame, Sisters of, S.N.D.: Founded 1850, at Coesfeld, Germany; in U.S., 1874. General mother-house, Rome, Italy. U.S. provinces: 13000 Auburn Rd., Chardon, OH 44024, (440) 286-7101. 1601 Dixie

Highway, Covington, KY 41011, (606) 291-2040. 3837 Secor Rd., Toledo, OH 43623, (419) 474-5485. 1776 Hendrix Ave., Thousand Oaks, CA 91360, (805) 496-3243.

Notre Dame, Sisters of the Congregation of, C.N.D.: Founded 1658, in Canada, by St. Marguerite Bourgeoys; in U.S., 1860. General motherhouse, Montréal, QC, Canada. U.S. province, 223 West Mountain Rd., Ridgefield, CT 06877-3627, (203) 438-3115, www.cnd-m.com. Education.

Notre Dame de Namur, Sisters of, S.N.D.deN.: Founded 1804, in France; in U.S., 1840. General motherhouse, Rome, Italy. U.S. provinces: 351 Broadway, Everett, MA 02149, (617) 387-2500, www.SNDdeN.org. 30 Jeffrey's Neck Rd., Ipswich, MA 01938, (978) 356-2159. 468 Poquonock Ave., Windsor, CT 06095-2473, (860) 688-1832, www.sndden.org. 1531 Greenspring Valley Rd., Stevenson, MD 21153, (410) 486-5599. 305 Cable St., Baltimore, MD 21210, (410) 243-1993, www.sndden.org. 701 E. Columbia Ave., Cincinnati, OH 45215, (513) 761-7636. 1520 Ragston Ave., Belmont, CA 94002-1908, (650) 593-2045. SND Base Communities, 3037 Fourth St. N.E., Washington, DC 20017, (202) 884-9750. Educational work.

Notre Dame de Sion, Congregation of, N.D.S.: Founded 1850, in France; in U.S., 1892. Generalate, Rome, Italy. U.S. province, 3823 Locust St., Kansas City, MO 64109, (816) 531-1374. Creation of better understanding between Christians and Jews.

Notre Dame Sisters: Founded 1853, in Czechoslovakia; in U.S., 1910. General motherhouse, Javornik, Czech Republic. U.S. motherhouse, 3501 State St., Omaha, NE 68112, (402) 455-2994, www.notredamesisters.org. Educational work.

Oblates of the Mother of Orphans, O.M.O: Founded 1945, in Italy. General motherhouse, Milan, Italy. U.S. address, 20 E. 72 St., New York, NY 10021.

Our Lady of Charity, North American Union of Sisters of, Eudist Sisters (Sisters of Our Lady of Charity of the Refuge), N.A.U.-O.L.C.: Founded 1641, in Caen, France, by St. John Eudes; in U.S., 1855. Autonomous houses were federated in 1944 and in March 1979 the North American Union of the Sisters of Our Lady of Charity was established. General motherhouse, 154 Edgington Ln., Wheeling, WV 26003, (304) 242-0042. Primarily devoted to re-education and rehabilitation of women and girls in residential and non-residential settings.

Independent houses: 1125 Malvern Ave., Hot Springs, AR 71901, (501) 623-1393, www.lightofmary.org. 4500 W. Davis St., Dallas, TX 75211, (214) 331-1754.

Our Lady of Sorrows, Sisters of, O.L.S.: Founded 1839, in Italy; in U.S., 1947. General motherhouse, Rome, Italy. U.S. headquarters, 9894 Norris Ferry Rd., Shreveport, LA 71106.

Our Lady of the Holy Rosary, Daughters of, F.M.S.R. (*Filiae Mariae Sacri Rosarii*): Founded 1946, in North Vietnam; foundation in U.S., 1968. General Motherhouse, Saigon, Vietnam. U.S. Province, 1492 Moss St., New Orleans, LA 70119, (504) 486-0039.

Our Lady of Victory Missionary Sisters, O.L.V.M.: Founded 1922, in U.S. Motherhouse, Victory Noll, 1900 W. Park Dr., P.O. Box 109, Huntington, IN 46750, (260) 356-0628, www.olvmorg. Educational, social work.

Pallottine Missionary Sisters (Missionary Sisters of the Catholic Apostolate), S.A.C.: Founded in Rome, 1838; in U.S., 1912. Generalate, Rome, Italy. U.S. provincialate, 15270 Old Halls Ferry Rd., Florissant, MO 63034, (314) 837-7100, www.geocities.com/pallottinerenewal.

Pallottine Sisters of the Catholic Apostolate, C.S.A.C.: Founded 1843, at Rome, Italy; in U.S., 1889. General motherhouse, Rome. U.S. motherhouse, St. Patrick's Villa, Harriman Heights, Harriman, NY 10926, (914) 783-9007. Educational work.

Parish Visitors of Mary Immaculate, P.V.M.I.: Founded 1920, in New York. General motherhouse, Box 658, Monroe, NY 10950, (845) 783-2251. Mission work.

Passion of Jesus Christ, Religious of (Passionist Nuns), C.P.: Founded 1771, in Italy, by St. Paul of the Cross; in U.S., 1910. U.S. convents: 2715 Churchview Ave., Pittsburgh, PA 15227-2141, (412) 881-1155. 631 Griffin Pond Rd., Clarks Summit, PA 18411-8899, (570) 586-2791, www.intiques.net/cpnuns. 8564 Crisp Rd., Whitesville, KY 42378-9729, (270) 233-4571, www.passionistnuns.org. 1151 Donaldson Hwy., Erlanger, KY 41018, (859) 371-8568. 15700 Clayton Rd., Ellisville, MO 63011, (314) 227-5275. Contemplatives.

Passionist Sisters: *See* Cross and Passion, Sisters of the

Paul, Daughters of St. (Missionary Sisters of the Media of Communication), D.S.P.: Founded 1915, at Alba, Piedmont, Italy; in U.S., 1932. General motherhouse, Rome, Italy. U.S. provincial house, 50 St. Paul's Ave., Boston, MA 02130-3491, (617) 522-8911, www.pauline.org. Apostolate of the communications arts.

Paul of Chartres, Sisters of St., S.P.C.: Founded 1696, in France. General House, Rome, Italy. U.S. address, 2920 Third Ave., So., Escanaba, MI 49828; (906) 399-0420.

Perpetual Adoration of Guadalupe, Sisters of, A.P.G.: U.S. foundation, 2403 W. Travis, San Antonio, TX 78207, (210) 227-7785.

Peter Claver, Missionary Sisters of St., S.S.P.C.: Founded 1894 in Austria by Bl. Maria Teresa Ledochowska; in U.S., 1914. General motherhouse, Rome, Italy. U.S. address, 667 Woods Mill Rd. S., Chesterfield, MO 63006, (314) 434-8084.

Pious Disciples of the Divine Master, P.D.D.M.: Founded 1924 in Italy; in U.S., 1948. General motherhouse, Rome, Italy. U.S. headquarters, 60 Sunset Ave., Staten Island, NY 10314, (718) 494-8597.

Pious Schools, Sisters of the, Sch. P.: Founded 1829 in Spain; in U.S., 1954. General motherhouse, Rome, Italy. U.S. headquarters, 17601 Nordhoff St., Northridge, CA 91325, (818) 882-6265.

Poor, Little Sisters of the, L.S.P.: Founded 1839, in France, by Bl. Jeanne Jugan; in U.S., 1868. General motherhouse, St. Pern, France. U.S. provinces: 110-30 221st St., Queens Village, NY 11429, (718) 464-1800. 601 Maiden Choice Lane, Baltimore, MD 21228, (410) 744-9367. 80 W. Northwest Hwy., Palatine, IL 60067, (847) 358-5700. Care of aged.

Poor Clare Missionary Sisters (Misioneras Clarisas), M.C.: Founded in Mexico. General motherhouse, Rome, Italy. U.S. novitiate, 1019 N. Newhope, Santa Ana, CA 92703-1534, (714) 554-8850.

Poor Clare Nuns: *See* Franciscan Poor Clare Nuns.

Poor Handmaids of Jesus Christ (Ancilla Domini Sisters), P.H.J.C.: Founded 1851, in Germany by Bl. Mary Kasper; in U.S., 1868. General motherhouse, Dernbach, Westerwald, Germany. U.S. motherhouse, Ancilla Domini Convent, Donaldson, IN 46513, (219) 936-9936. Educational, hospital work, social services.

Precious Blood, Daughters of Charity of the Most, D.C.P.B.: Founded 1872, at Pagani, Italy; in U.S., 1908. General motherhouse, Rome, Italy. U.S. convent, 1482 North Ave., Bridgeport, CT 06604, (203) 334-7000.

Precious Blood, Missionary Sisters of the, C.P.S.: Founded 1885, at Mariannhill, South Africa; in U.S., 1925. Generalate, Rome, Italy. U.S. novitiate, P.O. Box 97, Reading, PA 19607, (610) 777-1624. Home and foreign mission work.

Precious Blood, Sisters Adorers of the, A.P.B.: Founded 1861, in Canada; in U.S., 1890. General motherhouse, Canada. U.S. autonomous monasteries: 5400 Fort Hamilton Pkwy., Brooklyn, NY 11219, (718) 438-6371, www.sisterspreciousblood.org. 700 Bridge St., Manchester, NH 03104-5495, (603) 623-4264. 166 State St., Portland, ME 04101. 1106 State St., Lafayette, IN 47905, (765) 742-8227, www.members.aol.com/saotproc/index.htm. 400 Pratt St., Watertown, NY 13601, (315) 788-1669. Cloistered, contemplative.

Precious Blood, Sisters of the, C.PP.S.: Founded 1834, in Switzerland; in U.S., 1844. Generalate, 4000 Denlinger Rd., Dayton, OH 45426, (937) 837-3302. Education, health care, other ministries.

Precious Blood, Sisters of the Most, C.PP.S.: Founded 1845, in Steinerberg, Switzerland; in U.S., 1870. General motherhouse, 204 N. Main St., O'Fallon, MO 63366-2203, (636) 240-3420. Education, other ministries.

Presentation, Sisters of Mary of the, S.M.P.: Founded 1829, in France; in U.S., 1903. General motherhouse, Broons, Côtes-du-Nord, France. U.S. address, Maryvale Novitiate, 11550 River Rd., Valley City, ND 58072, (701) 845-2864, www.sistersofmarypresenation.com. Hospital work.

Presentation of Mary, Sisters of the, P.M.: Founded 1796, in France by Bl. Marie Rivier; in U.S., 1873. General motherhouse, Castel Gandolfo, Italy. U.S. provincial houses: 495 Mammoth Rd., Manchester, NH 03104, (603) 669-1080, www.presentationofmary.com. 209 Lawrence St., Methuen, MA 01844, (978) 687-1369, www.presmarymethuen.org.

Presentation of the B.V.M., Sisters of the, P.B.V.M.: Founded 1775, in Ireland; in U.S., 1854, in San Francisco. U.S. motherhouses: 2360 Carter Rd., Dubuque, IA 52001, (563) 588-2008, www.dubuquepresentations.org. 880 Jackson Ave., New Windsor, NY 12553, (845) 564-0513. 281 Masonic Ave, San Francisco, CA 94118, (415) 422-5013, www.presentationsisterssf.org. St. Colman's Convent, Watervliet, NY 12189, (518) 273-4911. 1101 32nd Ave., S., Fargo ND 58103, (701) 237-4857, www.presetnationsistersfargo.org. Presentation Convent, Aberdeen, SD 57401, (605) 229-8419, Leominster, MA 01453. 419 Woodrow Rd., Staten Island, NY 10312, (718) 356-2121.

Presentation of the Blessed Virgin Mary, Sisters of, of Union: Founded in Ireland, 1775; union established in Ireland, 1976; first U.S. vice province, 1979.

Generalate, Kildare, Ireland. U.S. provincialate, 729 W. Wilshire Dr., Phoenix, AZ 85007, (602) 271-9687.

Providence, Daughters of Divine, F.D.P.: Founded 1832, Italy; in U.S., 1964. General motherhouse, Rome, Italy. U.S. address, 74684 Airport Rd., Covington, LA 70435, (985) 809-1736 (fax).

Providence, Missionary Catechists of Divine, M.C.D.P.: Administrative house, 2318 Castroville Rd., San Antonio, TX 78237, (210) 432-0113.

Providence, Oblate Sisters of, O.S.P.: Founded 1829, in U.S., by Mother Mary Elizabeth Lange and Father James Joubert, S.S. First order of black nuns in U.S. General motherhouse, 701 Gun Rd., Baltimore, MD 21227, (410) 242-8500. Educational work.

Providence, Sisters of, S.P.: Founded 1861, in Canada; in U.S., 1873. General motherhouse, Our Lady of Victory Convent, 5 Gamelin St., Holyoke, MA 01040, (413) 536-7511, wwwsisofprov.org.

Providence, Sisters of, S.P.: Founded 1843, in Canada; in U.S., 1854. General motherhouse, Montreal, QC, Canada. U.S. province, Mother Joseph Province, 506 Second Ave., #1200, Seattle, WA 98104, (206) 464-3394, www.sistersofprovidence.net.

Providence, Sisters of (of St. Mary-of-the-Woods), S.P.: Founded 1806, in France; in U.S., 1 Sisters of Providence, St. Mary-of-the-Woods, IN 47876, (812) 535-3131, www.sistersofprovidence.org.

Providence, Sisters of Divine, C.D.P.: Founded 1762, in France; in U.S., 1866. Generalate, 515 SW 24th St., San Antonio, TX 78207, (210) 434-1866. Educational, hospital work.

Providence, Sisters of Divine, C.D.P.: Founded 1851, in Germany; in U.S., 1876. Generalate, Rome, Italy. U.S. provinces: 9000 Babcock Blvd., Allison Park, PA 15101-2793, (412) 931-5241, www.sistersofdivprovidence.org. 3415 Bridgeland Dr., Bridgetown, MO 63044, (314) 209-9181. 363 Bishops Hwy., Kingston, MA 02364, (781) 585-7707. Educational, hospital work.

Providence, Sisters of Divine (of Kentucky), C.D.P.: Founded 1762, in France; in U.S., 1889. General motherhouse, Fenetrange, France. U.S. province, St. Bartholomew Parish, Cincinnati, OH 45231, (513) 728-3146, www.cdpkentucky.org. Education, social services, other ministries.

Redeemer, Oblates of the Most Holy, O.SS.R.: Founded 1864, in Spain. General motherhouse, Spain. U.S. foundation, 60-80 Pond St., Jamaica Plain, MA 02130, (617) 524-1640.

Redeemer, Order of the Most Holy, O.SS.R.: Founded 1731, by Ven. Mother Marie Celeste Crostarosa, with the help of St. Alphonsus Liguori; in U.S., 1957. U.S. addresses: Mother of Perpetual Help Monastery, P.O. Box 220, Esopus, NY 12429, (914) 384-6533. Monastery of St. Alphonsus, 200 Ligouri Dr. Liguori, MO 63057, (636) 464-1093.

Redeemer, Sisters of the Divine, S.D.R.: Founded 1849, in Niederbronn, France; in U.S., 1912. General motherhouse, Rome, Italy. U.S. province, 999 Rock Run Road, Elizabeth, PA 15037, (412) 751-8600. Educational, hospital work; care of the aged.

Redeemer, Sisters of the Holy, C.S.R.: Founded 1849, in Alsace; in U.S., 1924. General motherhouse, Wurzburg, Germany. U.S. provincial house, 521 Moredon Rd., Huntingdon Valley, PA 19006, (215) 914-4100. Personalized medical care in hospitals, homes for aged, private homes; retreat work.

Reparation of the Congregation of Mary, Sisters of, S.R.C.M.: Founded 1903, in U.S. Motherhouse, St. Zita's Villa, Monsey, NY 10952, (845) 356-2011.

Reparation of the Sacred Wounds of Jesus, Sisters of, S.R.: Founded 1959 in U.S. General motherhouse, 2120 S.E. 24th Ave., Portland, OR 97214-5504, (503) 236-4207.

Resurrection, Sisters of the, C.R.: Founded 1891, in Italy; in U.S., 1900. General motherhouse, Rome, Italy. U.S. provinces: 7432 Talcott Ave., Chicago, IL 60631, (773) 792-6363. Mt. St. Joseph, 35 Boltwood Ave., Castleton-on-Hudson, NY 12033, (518) 732-2429, www.resurrectionsisters.org. Education, nursing.

Rita, Sisters of St., O.S.A.: General motherhouse, Wurzburg, Germany. U.S. foundation, St. Monica's Convent, 3920 Green Bay Rd., Racine, WI 53404, (262) 639-5050, www.srsofstrita.org.

Rosary, Congregation of Our Lady of the Holy, R.S.R.: Founded 1874, in Canada; in U.S., 1899. General motherhouse, Rimouski, QC, Canada. U.S. regional house, 20 Thomas St., Portland, ME 04102-3638, (207) 774-3756, www.soeursdusaintrasaire.org. Educational work.

Rosary, Missionary Sisters of the Holy, M.S.H.R.: Founded 1924, in Ireland; in U.S., 1954. Motherhouse, Dublin, Ireland. In U.S., 741 Polo Rd., Bryn Mawr, PA 19010, (610) 520-1974, www.holyrosarymissionary-sisters.org. African missions.

Sacrament, Missionary Sisters of the Most Blessed, M.SS.S.: General motherhouse, Madrid, Spain. U.S. foundation, 1111 Wordin Ave., Bridgeport, CT 06605.

Sacrament, Nuns of the Perpetual Adoration of the Blessed, A.P.: Founded 1807 in Rome, Italy; in U.S., 1925. U.S. monasteries: 145 N. Cotton Ave., El Paso, TX 79901, (915) 533-5323. 771 Ashbury St., San Francisco, CA 94117, (415) 566-2743.

Sacrament, Oblate Sisters of the Blessed, O.S.B.S.: Founded 1935, in U.S. Motherhouse, St. Sylvester Convent, P.O. Box 217, Marty, SD 57361, (605) 384-3305. Care of American Indians.

Sacrament, Servants of the Blessed, S.S.S.: Founded 1858, in France, by St. Pierre Julien Eymard; in U.S., 1947. General motherhouse, Rome, Italy. American provincial house, St. Charles Borromeo Parish, 1818 Coal Pl. SE, Albuquerque, NM 87106, (505) 242-3692. Contemplative.

Sacrament, Sisters of the Blessed, for Indians and Colored People, S.B.S.: Founded 1891, in U.S., by St. Katharine Drexel. General motherhouse, 1663 Bristol Pike, P.O. Box 8502, Bensalem, PA 19020, (215) 244-9900, www.katharinedrexel.org.

Sacrament, Sisters of the Most Holy, M.H.S.: Founded 1851, in France; in U.S., 1872. Generalate, 313 Corona Dr. (P.O. Box 90037), Lafayette, LA 70509, (337) 981-8475.

Sacrament, Sisters Servants of the Blessed, S.J.S.: Founded 1904, in Mexico; in U.S., 1926. General motherhouse, Mexico. U.S. address: 215 Lomita St., El Segundo, CA 90245, (310) 615-0766.

Sacramentine Nuns (Religious of the Order of the Blessed Sacrament and Our Lady), O.S.S.: Founded 1639, in France; in U.S., 1912. U.S. monasteries: 235 Bellvale Lakes Rd., Warwick NY 10990. 2798 US 31

N, P.O. Box 86, Conway, MI 49722, (231) 347-0447. Perpetual adoration of the Holy Eucharist.

Sacred Heart, Daughters of Our Lady of the, F.D.N.S.C.: Founded 1882, in France; in U.S., 1955. General motherhouse, Rome, Italy. U.S. address, 424 E. Browning Rd., Bellmawr, NJ 08031, (609) 931-8973. Educational work.

Sacred Heart, Missionary Sisters of the (Cabrini Sisters), M.S.C.: Founded 1880, in Italy, by St. Frances Xavier Cabrini; in U.S., 1889. General motherhouse, Rome, Italy. U.S. provincial office, 222 E. 19th St., 5B, New York, NY 10003. Educational, health, social and catechetical work.

Sacred Heart, Society Devoted to the, S.D.S.H.: Founded 1940, in Hungary; in U.S., 1956. U.S. motherhouse, 9814 Sylvia Ave., Northridge, CA 91324, (818) 831-9710; www.sacredheartsisters.com. Educational work.

Sacred Heart, Society of the, R.S.C.J.: Founded 1800, in France; in U.S., 1818. Generalate, Rome, Italy. U.S. provincial house, 4389 W. Pine Blvd., St. Louis, MO 63108, (314) 652-1500, www.rscj.org. Educational work.

Sacred Heart of Jesus, Apostles of, A.S.C.J.: Founded 1894, in Italy; in U.S., 1902. General motherhouse, Rome, Italy. U.S. motherhouse, 265 Benham St., Hamden, CT 06514, (203) 248-4225, www.ascjus.org. Educational, social work.

Sacred Heart of Jesus, Handmaids of the, A.C.J.: Founded 1877, in Spain. General motherhouse, Rome, Italy. U.S. province, 1242 S. Broad St., Philadelphia, PA 19146, (214) 468-6368. Educational, retreat work.

Sacred Heart of Jesus, Missionary Sisters of the Most (Hiltrup), M.S.C.: Founded 1899, in Germany; in U.S., 1908. General motherhouse, Rome, Italy. U.S. province, 2811 Moyers Lane, Reading, PA 19605, (610) 929-5944. Education, health care, pastoral ministry.

Sacred Heart of Jesus, Oblate Sisters of the, O.S.H.J.: Founded 1894; in U.S., 1949. General motherhouse, Rome, Italy. U.S. headquarters, 50 Warner Rd., Hubbard, OH 44425, (330) 759-9329, www.oblatesister.com. Educational, social work.

Sacred Heart of Jesus, Servants of the Most, S.S.C.J.: Founded 1894, in Poland; in U.S., 1959. General motherhouse, Cracow, Poland. U.S. address, 866 Cambria St., Cresson, PA 16630, (814) 886-4223, www.nb.net/~sscjusa. Education, health care, social services.

Sacred Heart of Jesus, Sisters of the, S.S.C.J.: Founded 1816, in France; in U.S., 1903. General motherhouse, St. Jacut, Brittany, France. U.S. provincial house, 11931 Radium St., San Antonio, TX 78216, (210) 344-7203. Educational, hospital, domestic work.

Sacred Heart of Jesus and of the Poor, Servants of the (Mexican), S.S.H.J.P.: Founded 1885, in Mexico; in U.S., 1907. General motherhouse, Apartado 92, Puebla, Mexico. U.S. address, 3310 S. Zapata Hwy, Laredo, TX 78046, (956) 723-3343.

Sacred Heart of Jesus and Our Lady of Guadalupe, Missionaries of the, M.S.C.Gpe.: U.S. address, 1212 E. Euclid Ave., Arlington Heights, IL 60004, (708) 398-1350.

Sacred Heart of Jesus for Reparation, Congregation of the Handmaids of the, A.R.: Founded 1918, in Italy; in U.S., 1958. U.S. address, 36 Villa Dr., Steubenville, OH 43953, (740) 282-3801.

Sacred Heart of Mary, Religious of the, R.S.H.M.: Founded 1848, in France; in U.S., 1877. Generalate, Rome, Italy. U.S. provinces; 50 Wilson Park Dr., Tarrytown, NY 10591, (914) 631-8872, www.rshm.org. 441 N. Garfield Ave., Montebello, CA 90640, (323) 887-8821, www.rshm.org.

Sacred Hearts and of Perpetual Adoration, Sisters of the, SS.CC.: Founded 1797, in France; in U.S., 1908. General motherhouse, Rome, Italy. U.S. provinces: 1120 Fifth Ave., Honolulu, Hawaii 96816, (808) 737-5822, www.ssccpicpus.com (Pacific). 35 Huttleston Ave., Fairhaven, MA 02719, (508) 994-9341 (East Coast). Varied ministries.

Sacred Hearts of Jesus and Mary, Sisters of the, S.H.J.M.: Established 1953, in U.S. General motherhouse, Essex, England. U.S. address, 2150 Lake Shore Ave., Oakland CA 94606, (510) 832-2935.

Savior, Company of the, C.S.: Founded 1952, in Spain; in U.S., 1962. General motherhouse, Madrid, Spain. U.S. foundation, 820 Clinton Ave., Bridgeport, CT 06604, (203) 368-1875.

Savior, Sisters of the Divine, S.D.S.: Founded 1888, in Italy; in U.S., 1895. General motherhouse, Rome, Italy. U.S. province, 4311 N. 100th St., Milwaukee, WI 53222, (414) 466-0810, www.salvatoriansisters.org. Educational, hospital work.

Social Service, Sisters of, S.S.S.: Founded in Hungary, 1923, by Sr. Margaret Slachta. U.S. generalate, 296 Summit Ave., Buffalo, NY 14214, (716) 834-0197, www.sistersofsocialservicebuffalo.org. Social work.

Social Service, Sisters of, of Los Angeles, S.S.S.: Founded 1908, in Hungary; in U.S., 1926. General motherhouse, 2303 S. Figueroa Way, Los Angeles, CA 90007, (213) 746-2117.

Teresa of Jesus, Society of St., S.T.J.: Founded 1876, in Spain; in U.S., 1910. General motherhouse, Rome, Italy. U.S. provincial house, 18080 St. Joseph's Way, Covington, LA 70435, (985) 893-1470, www.teresians.org.

Thomas of Villanova, Congregation of Sisters of St., S.S.T.V.: Founded 1661, in France; in U.S., 1948. General motherhouse, Neuilly-sur-Seine, France. U.S. foundation, W. Rocks Rd., Norwalk, CT 06851, (203) 847-2885.

Trinity, Missionary Servants of the Most Blessed, M.S.B.T.: Founded 1912, in U.S., by Very Rev. Thomas A. Judge. General motherhouse, 3501 Solly Ave., Philadelphia, PA 19136, (215) 335-7550, www.msbt.org. Educational, social work, health services.

Trinity, Sisters Oblates to the Blessed, O.B.T.: Founded 1923, in Italy. U.S. novitiate, Beekman Rd., P.O. Box 98, Hopewell Junction, NY 12533, (914) 226-5671.

Trinity, Sisters of the Most Holy, O.Ss.T.: Founded 1198, in Rome; in U.S., 1920. General motherhouse, Rome, Italy. U.S. address, Immaculate Conception Province, 21281 Chardon Rd., Euclid, OH 44117, (216) 481-8232, www.srstrinity.org. Educational work.

Trinity, Society of Our Lady of the Most Holy, S.O.L.T.: Motherhouse, P.O. Box 189 Skidmore, TX 78389, (361) 287-3256.

Ursula of the Blessed Virgin, Society of the Sisters of St., S.U.: Founded 1606, in France; in U.S., 1902. General motherhouse, France. U.S. novitiate, 50 Linnwood Rd., Rhinebeck, NY 12572, (845) 876-2557, www.societyofstursula.org. Educational work.

Ursuline Nuns (Roman Union), O.S.U.: Founded 1535, in Italy; in U.S., 1727. Generalate, Rome, Italy. U.S. provinces: 1338 North Avenue, New Rochelle, NY 10804, (914) 712-0060. 210 Glennon Heights Rd., Crystal City, MO 63019, (636) 937-6206, www.osu-central.org. 639 Angela Dr., Santa Rosa, CA 95401, (707) 545-6811. 45 Lowder St., Dedham, MA 02026, (781) 326-6219.

Ursuline Sisters of Mount Saint Joseph, O.S.U.: Founded 1535, in Italy; in U.S., 1727, in New Orleans. U.S. motherhouses: 20860 St, Rte. 251, St. Martin, OH 45118-9705, (513) 875-2020. 901 E. Miami St., Paola, KS 66071, (913) 557-2349. 3105 Lexington Rd., Louisville, KY 40206, (502) 896-3914, www.ursuineslou.org. 2600 Lander Rd., Cleveland, OH 44124, (440) 449-1200, www.ursuline sisters.org. 8001 Cummings Rd., Maple Mount, KY 42356, (270) 229-4200, www.ursulinesmsj.org. 4045 Indian Rd., Toledo, OH 43606, (419) 536-9587, www.tole-doursulines.org. 4250 Shields Rd., Canfield, OH 44406, (330) 792-7636. 1339 E. McMillan St., Cincinnati, OH 45206, (513) 961-3410.

Ursuline Sisters of the Congregation of Tildonk, Belgium, O.S.U.: Founded 1535, in Italy; Tildonk congregation, 1832; in U.S., 1924. Generalate, Brussels, Belgium. U.S. address, 81-15 Utopia Parkway, Jamaica, NY 11432, (718) 591-0681, www.tressy.tripod.com. Educational, foreign mission work.

Ursuline Sisters of Belleville, O.S.U.: Founded 1535, in Italy; in U.S., 1910; established as diocesan community, 1983. Central house, 1026 N. Douglas Ave., Belleville, IL 62220, (618) 235-3444. Educational work.

Venerini Sisters, Religious, M.P.V.: Founded 1685, in Italy; in U.S., 1909. General motherhouse, Rome, Italy. U.S. provincialate; 23 Edward St., Worcester, MA 01605, (508) 754-1020, www.venerinisisters.org.

Vietnamese Adorers of the Holy Cross, M.T.G.: Founded 1670 in Vietnam; in U.S. 1976. General motherhouse 7408 S.E. Adler St., Portland, OR 97215, (503) 254-3284.

Vincent de Paul, Sisters: *See* Charity of St. Vincent de Paul, Sisters of.

Visitation Nuns, V.H.M.: Founded 1610, in France; in U.S. (Georgetown, DC), 1799. Contemplative, educational work. Two federations in U.S:

• First Federation of North America. Major pontifical enclosure. Pres., Mother Mary Jozefa Kowalewski, Monastery of the Visitation, 2055 Ridgedale Dr., Snellville, GA 30078, (770) 972-1060. Addresses of monasteries belonging to the federation: 2300 Springhill Ave., Mobile, AL 36607, (251) 473-2321. Beach Rd., Tyringham, MA 01264, (413) 243-3995. 12221 Bievenue Rd, Rockville, VA 23146, (804) 749-4885. 5820 City Ave., Philadelphia, PA 19131, (215) 473-5888. 1745 Parkside Blvd., Toledo, OH 43607, (419) 536-1343. 2055 Ridgedale Dr., Snellville, GA 30078-2443, (770) 972-1060.

• Second Federation of North America. Constitutional enclosure. Pres., Sr. Anne Madeleine Godefroy, Monastery of the Visitation, 3020 N. Ballas Rd., St. Louis, MO 63131, (314) 432-5353, www.visitationmonastery.org/stlouis. Addresses of monasteries belonging to the federation: 1500 35th St., Washington, DC 20007, (202) 337-0305. 3020 N. Ballas Rd., St. Louis, MO 63131, (314) 432-5353. 200 E. Second St., Frederick, MD 21701, (301) 622-3322. Mt. de Chantal Monastery of the Visitation, 410 Washington Ave.,

Wheeling, WV 26003, (304) 232-1283. 8902 Ridge Blvd., Brooklyn, NY 11209, (718) 745-5151, www.visitationsisters.org. 2455 Visitation Dr., Mendota Heights, MN 55120, (651) 683-1700.

Visitation of the Congregation of the Immaculate Heart of Mary, Sisters of the, S.V.M.: Founded 1952, in U.S. Motherhouse, 2950 Kaufmann Ave., Dubuque, IA 52001, (563) 588-7256. Educational work, parish ministry.

Vocationist Sisters (Sisters of the Divine Vocations), S.V.D.: Founded 1921, in Italy; in U.S., 1967 General motherhouse, Naples, Italy. U.S. founda-

tion, Perpetual Help Nursery, 172 Broad St., Newark, NJ 07104, (973) 484-3535.

Wisdom, Daughters of, D.W.: Founded 1703, in France, by St. Louis Marie Grignion de Montfort; in U.S., 1904. General motherhouse, Vendee, France. U.S. province, 385 Ocean Ave., Islip, NY 11751, (631) 277-2660, www.daughtersofwisdom.org. Education, health care, parish ministry, social services.

Xaverian Missionary Society of Mary, Inc., X.M.M.: Founded 1945, in Italy; in U.S., 1954. General motherhouse, Parma, Italy. U.S. address, 242 Salisbury St., Worcester, MA 01609, (508) 757-0514.

MEMBERSHIP OF RELIGIOUS INSTITUTES OF WOMEN

Principal source: Annuario Pontificio. *Statistics as of Jan. 1, 2006, unless indicated otherwise.* Listed below are world membership statistics of institutes of women with 500 or more members. Numbers in parentheses reflect the number of houses. For statistical information of institutes in the United States, see **Statistics.**

Salesian Srs. (1,535)	15,110
Calced Carmelites (745)	10,102
Franciscan Missionaries of Mary (833)	7,239
Claretians (683)	6,922
Franciscan Clarist Congr. (683)	6,922
Carmel, Srs. of the Mother of (596)	6,399
Charity of St. Bartholomew of Capitanio (448)	5,153
Charity, Mission of (720)	4,892
Benedictine Nuns (245)	4,732
Mercy of the Americas, Srs. of (2,198)	4,681
Our Lady of Charity of the Good Shepherd (656)	4,647
Ador. of the Bl. Sacrament. (518)	4,442
Holy Cross, Srs. of Mercy of the (456)	4,252
Notre Dame, School Srs. of (581)	4,040
Paul of Chartres, Srs. of St. (542)	3,987
Holy Spirit, Mission Servants of the (414)	3,571
Sacred Heart Congregation. (394)	3,486
Dominicans (216)	3,330
Immaculate Heart of Mary, Mission. Srs. (163)	3,248
Canossian Daught. of Charity (360)	3,151
Sacred Heart of Jesus "Sophie Barat," Society of the (451)	3,055
Charity of St. Joan Antida, Srs. of (377)	3,052
Joseph, Srs. of St. (Cluny) (424)	3,026
Poor, Little Sisters of the (211)	2,957
Dominicans of the Presentation of the Virgin (393)	2,840
Mercy, Srs. of (Ireland) (611)	2,814
Srs. of Mercy, Cong. of the (611)	2,814
Paul, Daught. of St. (246)	2,589
Ancianos Desamparados, Hermanitas de los (211)	2,550
Anne, Srs. of Charity of St. (303)	2,487
Notre Dame, Srs. of (289)	2,405
Ursulines of the Roman Union (256)	2,352
Visitandine Nuns (142)	2,265
Claretian Capuchins (162)	2,246
Holy Family, Srs. of the (Bordeaux) (316)	2,231

Cross, Srs. of the (Swiss) (275) (2005)	2,196
Carmelites of Charity of Vedruna (302)	2,179
Joseph Benedetto, Srs. of St. (130)	2,084
B.V.M., Inst. of the (English) (244)	2,065
Wisdom, Daught. of (298)	2,062
Concezioniste (Franciscan Concessionists) (157)	2,019
Felician Srs. (248)	1,999
Charity, Srs. of, Our Lady of Mercy (115) (2005)	1,989
Joseph, Srs. of St. (Chambéry) (324)	1,966
Holy Family Sisters (206)	1,911
Franciscans of the Penance and Christian Charity (241)	1,882
Carmelites, Scalced (127)	1,842
Mary Our Lady, Company of (209)	1,828
Notre Dame de Namur, Srs. of (270)	1,821
Mission. Carmelites (270)	1,815
Holy Savior, Srs. of the (191)	1,792
Joseph, Srs. of St. (Carondolet) (766)	1,780
Adorers of the Blood of Christ (291)	1,775
Elizabeth, Srs. of St. (232)	1,765
Mary, Minister of the Infirm, Servants of (115)	1,752
Cistercian Nuns (Strict Observance) (71)	1,684
Comboni Missionary Srs. (219)	1,680
Mercy of Australia, Inst. of Srs. (463)	1,660
Teresa of Jesus, Society of St. (219)	1,649
Heart of Mary, Soc. of Daught. of (154)	1,627
Apostolic Carmel, Srs. of (154)	1,601
Dorothy, Srs. of St. (175)	1,577
Franciscan Hospitallers of the Immaculate Conception (176)	1,559
Jesus and Mary, Religious of (198)	1,535
Anne, Daughters of Saint (248)	1,533
Holy Family of Nazareth, Srs. of (155)	1,519
Divine Master, Pious Disciples of (176)	1,473
Benedictines, Missionary (136)	1,454
Divine Providence, Srs. of (St. Maurice) (251)	1,452
Franciscans of George the Martyr (170)	1,430
Sacred Heart of Jesus, Ancelle (204)	1,423
Sacred Heart of Jesus, Apostles of (204)	1,423
Holy Spirit, Daughters of the (199)	1,422
Destitute, Srs. of the (197)	1,413
Holy Names of Jesus and Mary, Srs. of the (161)	1,395

Jesus, Mary, and Joseph, Society of (151)	1,390	Srs. of St. (308)	983
Presentation of Mary, Srs. of the (189)	1,388	Our Lady of Africa, Mission. Srs. of (143)	982
Union of the Srs. of the Presentation (251)	1,388	Servants of Jesus of Charity (95) 977	
Mary Immaculate, Religious of (129)	1,386	Immaculate Conception, Srs. of Charity	
Notre Dame, Srs. of the Cong. of (165)	1,385	(1158)	976
Immaculate Conception,		Mary Help of Christians, Mission. Srs. (146)	966
Little Srs. of the (240)	1,378	Our Lady of the Missions, Srs. of (262)	960
Cross, Srs. of the (187)	1,376	Anne, Srs. of (154) (1999)	956
Jesus, Daught. of (St. Joseph of		Franciscan Srs. of Dillingen (95)	951
Kermaria) (194)	1,359	Anne, Daught. of Saint (Ranchi) (123)	948
Capuchin Tertiaries of the		Ursulines of Tildonk (116)	945
Holy Family (226)	1,359	Precious Blood, Mission. Srs. of the (98)	941
(2003)		Sacred Heart of Mary Virgin Immaculate,	
Charity of Jesus and Mary, Srs. of (177)	1,345	Srs. of the (152)	939
Adorers of the Blessed Sacrament and		Mary, Mother of Mercy, Daught. of (173)	939
Charity (164)	1,336	Benedictine Srs., Fed. of St. Scholastica (22)	936
Our Lady of the Sacred Heart,		Joseph, Srs. of St. (Lyon) (149)	936
Daughters of (201)	1,326	Joseph of the Apparition, Srs. of St. (161)	931
Salesian Missionaries		Sacred Heart of Jesus, Mission. Srs. (148)	930
of Mary Immaculate (160)	1,313	Mary Immaculate / Catherine of Siena (161)	930
Charity, Dtrs. of Divine (168)	1,293	Augustinians (82)	929
Salvatorians (214)	1,291	Our Lady Mother of Mercy (114)	929
Anne, Srs. of Saint (178)	1,284	Holy Family, Little Srs. of the (139)	922
Assumption, Religious of the (173)	1,273	Immaculate Heart of Mary (153)	918
Mercedarians of Charity (163)	1,270	Benedictine Srs., Federation of	
Infirm of St. Francis, Srs. of (122)	1,269	St. Gertrude the Great (17)	911
Fraternity of Little Sisters of Jesus (292)	1,243	Vincent de Paul, Srs. of Charity of (119)	899
Little Flower of Bethany, Srs. of the (148)	1,225	Poor of the Inst. Palazzolo, Srs. of the (114)	896
Teresian Carmelites of Verapoly (140)	1,216	Immaculate, Mission. of (108)	895
School Srs. of St. Francis of Milwaukee		Baptistine Srs., Srs. of St. John the	
(381)	1,211	Baptist (126)	881
Franciscans of Christ, School Srs. (381)	1,211	Cross, Daughters of, of Liege (109)	878
Hospitallers of the Sacred Heart of		Love of God, Sisters of the (116)	876
Jesus (110)	1,201	Immaculate Heart of Mary, Mother of	
Mercy, Srs. of (Verona) (114)	1,175	Christ (126)	872
Franciscans of Christ the King (161)	1,173	Mary, Daught. of (134)	871
Dorothy of Frassinetti, Srs. of St. (164)	1,172	Queen of Apostles (117) 867	
Franciscans of the Family of Mary (142)	1,164	Little Srs. of Mary Immaculate (127) 867	
Franciscans of the		Carmelite Sisters of St. Teresa (115)	863
Immaculate Conception (146)	1,161	Divine Love, Daughters of (143)	856
Charity (Ancelle della) (102)	1,152	Jesus Crucified, Missionary Sisters of	
Jesus, Daught. of (Salamanca) (151)	1,131	(186)	854
Religious Dominicans of the		Clarist Franciscan Mission. (133)	850
Annunciation (143)	1,127	Sacramentine Srs. (107)	840
Claretian (Urban) (867)	1,122	Ursulines of the Sacred Heart of Jesus	
Servants of Mary, Srs. of Our Lady		(100)	840
of Sorrows (148)	1,103	Charity, Little Mission. Srs. of (119)	839
Caritas Srs. of Miyazaki (176)	1,100	Medical Srs. of St. Joseph (73)	837
Joseph, Srs. of St. (Philadelphia) (150)	1,096	Consolata Missionary Sisters (135)	834
Sacred Heart of Jesus,		Our Lady of the Apostles, Missionary	
Daught. of Charity of the (176)	1,094	Sisters of (131)	827
Franciscan Srs. (Pondicherry) (187)	1,076	Camillus, Dtrs. of St. (94) 827	
Elizabethan Francsicans (117)	1,065	Imitation of Christ, Srs. of the (156)	827
Assumption, Little Srs. of the (150)	1,059	Franciscans Third Order Regular (54) 826	
Servants of the Imm. Hrt. Of Mary, Srs.		Mary Immaculate of the B.V.M. (159) 819	
(92)	1,055	Mary Immaculate, Sisters of the B.V.M.	
Joseph, Inst. of Srs. of St. (228)	1,042	(159)	819
Cross and Passion, Srs. of the		Immaculate Conception, Srs. of the (123)	814
(Passionist Srs.) (153)	1,022	Immaculate Conception of the B.V.M. (123)	814
Our Lady of Mercy, Daught. of (164) 1,011		Mary Most Holy of the Word,	
Sacramentines (Perp. Ador. of the Blessed		Daughters of (124)	812
Sacrament) (61)	1,001	Mary Reparatrix, Society of (100)	811
Cistercian Nuns, O. Cist. (63)	998	Franciscan Mission. of Mary, Auxiliatrix	
Dominicans of the Most Holy Rosary (285)...	997	(122)	809
Providence, Srs. of (102)	992	Benedictine Srs. Fed. of St. Benedict (12)	806
Joseph of the Sacred Heart of Jesus,		Scalabrinians (159)	789

ORGANIZATIONS OF RELIGIOUS

Conferences

Conferences of major superiors of religious institutes, dating from the 1950s, are encouraged by the Code of Canon Law (Code 708) "so that joining forces they can work toward the achievement of the purpose of their individual institutes more fully, transact common business and foster suitable coordination and cooperation with conferences of bishops and also with individual bishops." Statutes of the conferences must be approved by the Holy See "by which alone they are erected" (Canon 709). Conferences have been established in 24 countries of Europe, 14 in North and

Central America, 10 in South America, 35 in Africa and 19 in Asia and Oceania.

Listed below are U.S. and international conferences.

Conference of Major Superiors of Men: Founded in 1956; canonically established Sept. 12, 1957. Membership, 269 major superiors representing institutes with a combined membership of approximately 24,000. Pres., Fr. Canice Connors, O.F.M. Conv.; executive director, Rev. Ted Keating, S.M. National office: 8808 Cameron St., Silver Spring, MD 20910, (301) 588-4030, www.cmsm.org.

Leadership Conference of Women Religious: Founded in 1956; canonically established Dec. 12, 1959. Membership, nearly 1,000 (Dec. 31, 1996), representing approximately 400 religious institutes. Pres., Sr. Beatrice Eichten, O.SF; Mary Dacey, S.S.J., vice president/president elect; executive director, Sister Carole Shinnick, SSND. National office: 8808 Cameron St., Silver Spring, MD 20910, (301) 588-4955, www.lcwr.org.

Council of Major Superiors of Women Religious: Canonically erected June 13, 1992. Membership, 141 superiors of 103 religious congregations. Chairperson, Sister Mary Quentin Sheridan, R.S.M. National office: P.O. Box 4467, Washington, DC 20017-0467, (202) 832-2575, www.cmswr.org.

International Union of Superiors General (Women): Established Dec. 8, 1965; approved 1967. General secretary, Sister Rita Burley, A.C.I. Address: Piazza Ponte S. Angelo, 28, 00186, Rome, Italy, 06-684-00-20.

Union of Superiors General (Men): Established in 1957. President, Father Alvaro Echeverria, F.S.C.; general secretary, Bro. Lino Da Campo, F.S.F. Address: Via dei Penitenzieri 19, 00193 Rome, Italy, 06-686-82-29.

Latin American Confederation of Religious (Confederacion Latinoamericana de Religiosos — CLAR): Established in 1959; statutes reformed in 1984. President, Sr. Vilma Esperanza Quintanilla; secretary general, Sr. Dina Maria Orellana Aquilar, R.M. Address: Calle 64 No 10-45, Piso 5°, Apartado Aéreo 56804, Santafé de Bogotá, D.C., Colombia, (91) 31-00-481-21-57-774, www.clar.org.

Union of European Conferences of Major Superiors (UCESM): Established Dec. 25, 1983. Permanent secretary, P. Jesús Maria Lecea Sainz,

Sch.P. Rue de Pascal 4, B-1040, Bruxelles, Belgium, 02-230-86-22.

Other Organizations

Institute on Religious Life (1974). To foster more effective understanding and implementation of teachings of the Church on religious life, promote vocations to religious life and the priesthood, and promote growth in sanctity of all the faithful according to their state in life. Pres., Bishop Thomas Doran. National office, P.O. Box 410007, Chicago, IL 60641, (773) 267-1195, www.religiouslife.com. Publishes *Religious Life* magazine and *Consecrated Life* periodical.

Religious Brothers Conference (1972): To publicize the unique vocations of brothers, to further communication among brothers and provide liaison with various organizations of the Church. Pres., Br. Stephen Synan, F.M.S., 5420 South Cornell, Chicago, IL 60615, (773) 493-2306, www.brothersonline.org.

National Black Sisters' Conference (1968): Black Catholic women religious and associates networking to provide support through prayer, study, solidarity and programs. Address: 101 Q St., N.E., Washington, DC 20002, (202) 529-9250.

National Conference of Vicars for Religious (1967): National organization of diocesan officials concerned with relations between their respective dioceses and religious communities engaged therein. President, Sr. Therese Sullivan, S.P., 9292 Broadway, Merrillville, IN 46410; secretary, Eymard Flood, O.S.C. Address: 2811 East Villareal Dr., P.O. Box 14195, Orange, CA, 92863-1595, (714) 282-3114.

National Religious Vocation Conference (NRVC) (1988, with merger of National Sisters Vocation Conference and National Conference of Religious Vocation Directors.) Service organization of men and women committed to the fostering and discernment of vocations. Executive director, Br. Paul Bednarczyk, C.S.C. Address: 5420 S. Cornell, #105, Chicago, IL 60615, (773) 363-5454, www.nrvc.net.

Religious Formation Conference (1953): Originally the Sister Formation Conference; membership includes women and men Religious and non-canonical groups. Facilitates the ministry of formation, both initial and ongoing, in religious communities. Executive director, Sister Janet Mock, C.S.J. National office: 8820 Cameron St., Silver Spring, MD 20910-4152, (301) 588-4938, www.relforcon.org.

SECULAR INSTITUTES

Sources: Catholic Almanac *survey; United States Conference of Secular Institutes;* Annuario Pontificio.

Secular institutes are societies of men and women living in the world who dedicate themselves to observe the evangelical counsels and to carry on apostolic works suitable to their talents and opportunities in the areas of their everyday life.

"Secular institutes are not religious communities but they carry with them in the world a profession of evangelical counsels which is genuine and complete, and recognized as such by the Church. This profession confers a consecration on men and women, laity and clergy, who reside in the world. For this reason they should chiefly strive for total self-dedication to God, one inspired by perfect charity. These institutes should preserve their proper and particular character, a secu-

lar one, so that they may everywhere measure up successfully to that apostolate which they were designed to exercise, and which is both in the world and, in a sense, of the world" ("Decree on the Appropriate Renewal of Religious Life," No. 11; Second Vatican Council).

Secular institutes are under the jurisdiction of the Congregation for Institutes of Consecrated Life and Societies of Apostolic Life. General legislation concerning them is contained in Canons 710 to 730 of the Code of Canon Law.

A secular institute reaches maturity in several stages. It begins as an association of the faithful, technically called a pious union, with the approval of a local bishop. Once it has proved its viability, he can give it the status of an institute of diocesan right, in accordance with norms and permission emanating from the Congregation for Institutes of Consecrated Life and Societies of Apostolic Life. On issuance of a separate decree from this congregation, an institute of diocesan right becomes an institute of pontifical right.

Secular institutes, which originated in the latter part of the 18th century, were given full recognition and approval by Pius XII Feb. 2, 1947, in the apostolic constitution Provida Mater Ecclesia. On Mar. 25 of the same year a special commission for secular institutes was set up within the Congregation for Religious. Institutes were commended and confirmed by Pius XII in a motu proprio of Mar. 12, 1948, and were the subject of a special instruction issued a week later, Mar. 19, 1948.

The World Conference of Secular Institutes (CMIS) was approved by the Vatican May 23, 1974. Address: Via Tullio Levi-Civita 5, 00146 Rome, Italy; 0039-06-5410292; www.cmis-int.org.

The United States Conference of Secular Institutes (USCSI) was established following the organization of the World Conference of Secular Institutes in Rome. Its membership is open to all canonically erected secular institutes with members living in the United States. The conference was organized to offer secular institutes an opportunity to exchange experiences, to do research in order to help the Church carry out its mission, and to search for ways and means to make known the existence of secular institutes in the U.S. Address: P.O. Box 4556, 12th St. N.E., Washington, DC 20017, (262) 547-7733, www.secularinstitutes.org. Pres., Rev. George F. Hazler.

Institutes in the U.S.

Apostolic Oblates: Founded in Rome, Italy, 1947; established in the U.S., 1962; for women. Approved as a secular institute of pontifical right Dec. 8, 1994. Addresses: 2125 W. Walnut Ave., Fullerton, CA 92833, (714) 871-3610. 6762 Western Ave., Omaha, NE 68132, (402) 553-4418. 730 E. 87th St., Brooklyn, NY 11236-3621, (718) 649-0324, www.prosanctity.org.

Apostolic Sodales: Founded in Rome, Italy, 1992 by Bp. Guglielmo; for priests. Established to promote a spirit of fraternity among diocesan priests gathered around their bishop in docile availability in the two-fold universal vocation — the call to holiness and brotherhood. Address: Rev. Michael F. Murphy, 655 C. Ave. Coronado, CA 92118-2299, (619) 435-3167.

Caritas Christi: Originated in Marseilles, 1937; for women. Established as a secular institute of pontifical right Mar. 19, 1955. Address: P.O. Box 5162, River Forest, IL 60305. International membership.

Catechists of the Heart of Jesus (Ukrainian): Founded in Parana, Brazil, 1940, by Christoforo Myaskiv, OSBM; approved as Secular Institute of Pontifical Right, 1971; for women. Established for religious instruction, to assist clerics in missionary work, to help the Church, and to maintain the Ukrainian rite and culture. Address: 161 Glenbrook Rd., Stamford, CT 06902, (203) 327-6374.

Company of St. Paul: Originated in Milan, Italy, 1920; for lay people and priests. Approved as a secular institute of pontifical right June 30, 1950. Address: Rev. Stuart Sandberg, 52 Davis Ave., White Plains, NY 10605.

Crusaders of St. Mary: Founded 1947 in Madrid, Spain; approved as a secular institute of diocesan right, 1988; for men. Address: 2001 Great Falls St., McLean, VA 22101, (703) 536-3546.

Diocesan Laborer Priests: Founded 1885 in Spain; approved as a secular institute of pontifical right, 1952. The specific aim of the institute is the promotion, sustenance and cultivation of apostolic, religious and priestly vocations. Address: 3706 15th St. N.E., Washington, DC 20017, (202) 832-4217.

Don Bosco Volunteers: Founded 1917 by Bl. Philip Rinaldi; for women. Approved as a secular institute of pontifical right Aug. 5, 1978. Follow spirituality and charism of St. John Bosco. Address: Cathy Sylvester, Don Bosco Volunteers, P.O. Box 588, Hawthorne, NJ 07507, www.secularinstitutes.org/dby.html.

Don Bosco Institute: Founded in Rome on Sept. 12, 1994, by Fr. Egidio Viganó, rector major of the Salesians of Don Bosco, for celibate men. Recognized as public association of the faithful on May 24, 1998, by Cardinal Ignacio Velasco Garcia, Abp. of Caracas, Venezuela. The association, which follows the spirit and charism of St. John Bosco, intends to become established juridically as a secular institute. Address: P.O. Box 639, New Rochelle, NY 10802-0639, (614) 440-0202; www.secularinstitutes.org/a-dbi.htm.

Family of Mary of the Visitation: Founded in Vietnam, 1976. Approved as a Secular Institute of Diocesan Right; intended to promote faith-filled vowed women, to help people protect their faith and to meet social needs. Address: Therese Chan Ngo, P.O. Box 441, Westminster, CA 92684.

Fr. Kolbe Missionaries of the Immaculata: Founded in Bologna, Italy, in 1954, by Fr. Luigi Faccenda, O.F.M. Conv.; for women. Approved as a secular institute of pontifical right Mar. 25, 1992. Live the fullness of baptismal consecration, strive for perfect charity and promote the knowledge and veneration of Mary. Address: 531 E. Merced Ave., West Covina, CA 91790, (626) 917-0040.

Handmaids of Divine Mercy: Founded in Bari, Italy, 1951; for women. Approved as an institute of pontifical right 1972. Address: 2410 Hughes Ave., Bronx, NY 10458, (718) 295-3770.

Holy Family Institute (aggregated to the Society of St. Paul): Founded by Fr. James Alberione in 1963 for married couples who wish to commit themselves to seeking evangelical perfection in marriage; definitively approved by the Holy See, 1993. First Americans professed, 1988. Address: 9531 Akron-Canfield Rd., Box 498, Canfield, OH 44406; www.vocations-holy-family.com.

Institute of Secular Missionaries: Founded in Vitoria, Spain, 1939; for women. Approved as a secular institute, 1955. Address: 2710 Ruberg Ave., Cincinnati, OH 45211. Attn.: E. Dilger.

Institute of the Heart of Jesus (Men): Originated in France Feb. 2, 1791; restored Oct. 29, 1918; for diocesan priests and laity. Received final approval from the Holy See as a secular institute of pontifical right Feb. 2, 1952. U.S. address, Rev. William S. Whelan, Conception Seminary College, Conception, MO 64433, (660) 944-2900.

Institute of the Heart of Jesus (Women): Foundation stems from the Institute of the Heart of Jesus which originated in France Feb. 2, 1791. Established to help lay women live the Gospel radically in the modern world by means of the evangelical counsels, to engage in group discernment and various forms of prayer. Address, Diana Bland, 417 N. Buena Vista St., Burbank, CA 91505-3208.

Jesu Caritas Fraternity: Founded in France, 1952. Approved as a Secular Institute of Diocesan Right, 1996. Established to form members in the contemplative tradition of Brother Charles de Foucauld, bringing God's love especially to his most neglected children; members strive in their daily life to live the Gospel message. Address: Mary D. Christensen, P.O. Box 92, Yonkers, N.Y. 10704.

Mission of Our Lady of Bethany: Founded in France, 1948; for women. Approved as a secular institute of diocesan right, 1965. Addresses: Estelle Nichols, 109 Rollins Rd., Nottingham, NH 03290. P.O. Box 807, Boston, MA 02130.

Missionaries of the Kingship of Christ the King: Under this title are included three distinct and juridically separate institutes founded by Agostino Gemelli, O.F.M. (1878-1959) and Armida Barelli (1882-1952). Two are active in the U.S.

• **Women Missionaries of the Kingship of Christ:** Founded in 1919, in Italy; definitively approved as an institute of pontifical right 1953. U.S. branch established 1950.

• **Men Missionaries of the Kingship of Christ:** Founded 1928, in Italy, as an institute of diocesan right. U.S. branch established 1962.

Addresses: Rev. Dominic Monti, O.F.M., Spiritual Assistant, 10400 Lorain Ave., Silver Spring, MD 20901 (for Men Missionaries). Rev. Dominic Monti, O.F.M., 10400 Lorain Ave., Silver Spring, MD, 20901 (for Women Missionaries), (301) 593-4479, www.simkc.org.

Nuestra Señora de la Altagracia: Founded in Dominican Republic, 1956; approved as a secular institute of diocesan right, 1964; for women. Address: Ms. Christiana Perez, 129 Van Siclen Ave., Brooklyn, NY 11207.

Oblate Missionaries of Mary Immaculate: Founded, 1952; approved as a secular institute of pontifical right 1984; for women. Address: Oblate Missionaries of Mary Immaculate, P.O. Box 764, Lowell, MA 01853, www.ommi-is.org.

Opus Spiritus Sancti: Originated in West Germany, 1952; for diocesan priests and unmarried permanent deacons. Formally acknowledged by Rome as a secular institute of diocesan right, 1977. Address: Rev. James McCormick, 421 E. Bluff St., Carroll, IA 51401-3099, (712) 792-4386.

Schoenstatt Sisters of Mary: Originated in Schoenstatt, Germany, 1926; for women. Established as a secular institute of diocesan right May 20, 1948; of pontifical right Oct. 18, 1948. Addresses: W. 284 N. 404 Cherry Lane, Waukesha, WI 53188, (262) 548-4384, www.schsrsmary.org. House Schoenstatt, 134 Front St., Rockport, TX 78382, (361) 729-2019.

Secular Institute of Pius X: Originated in Manchester, NH, 1940; for priests and laymen. Approved as a secular institute, 1959. Also admits married couples and unmarried men as associate members. Addresses: C.P. 7731, Charlesbourg, QC G1G 5W6, Canada, (418) 626-5882, www.ispx.org.

Secular Institute of Schoenstatt Fathers: Founded in Germany by Fr. Joseph Kentenich in 1965; for priests serving the International Schoenstatt Movement in over 20 countries. Approved as a secular institute of pontifical right, June 24, 1988. Address: W. 284 N. 746 Cherry Road, Waukesha, WI

53188, (262) 548-9061.

Secular Institute of St. Francis de Sales: Founded in Vienna, Austria, 1940; for women. Pontifical right, 1964. Address: Thérèse Keyes, Dir., 87 Gerrish Ave., T2, East Haven, CT 06512, (203) 469-3277, www.secularinstitutes.org/sfs.ht.

Society of Our Lady of the Way: Originated, 1936; for women. Approved as a secular institute of pontifical right Jan. 3, 1953. Address: 2339 N. Catalina, Los Angeles, CA 90027, (323) 661-3315, www.execpc.com/uscsi/index.html.

Voluntas Dei Institute: Originated in Canada, 1958, by Father L. M. Parent; for secular priests and laymen (with married couples as associates). Approved as a secular institute of pontifical right, July 12, 1987. Established in 21 countries. Address: Rev. George Hazler, 615 Palm Ave., Los Altos, CA 94022-3953, (650) 917-4519, www.voluntasdeiusa.org.

The *Annuario Pontificio* lists the following secular institutes of pontifical right that are not established in the U.S.:

For men: Christ the King; Institute of Our Lady of Life; Institute of Prado; Priests of the Sacred Heart of Jesus.

For women: Alliance in Jesus through Mary; Apostles of the Sacred Heart; Catechists of Mary, Virgin and Mother; Company of St. Ursula, Cordimarian Filiation; Daughters of the Nativity of Mary; Daughters of the Queen of the Apostles; Daughters of the Sacred Heart; Evangelical Crusade; Faithful Servants of Jesus; Handmaids of Our Mother of Mercy; Institute of Notre Dame du Travail; Institute of Our Lady of Life; Institute of St. Boniface; Little Apostles of Charity.

Life and Peace in Christ Jesus; Missionaries of Royal Priesthood; Missionaries of the Sick; Oblates of Christ the King; Oblates of the Sacred Heart of Jesus; Servants of Jesus the Priest; Servite Secular Institute; Union of the Daughters of God; Workers of Divine Love; Workers of the Cross; Handmaids of Holy Church; Augustinian Auxiliary Missionaries; Heart of Jesus; Apostolic Missionaries of Charity; Combonian Secular Missionaries; Missionaries of the Gospel; Secular Servants of Jesus Christ Priest; Women of Schoenstatt; Missionaries of Infinite Love.

Associations

Association of Mary Help of Christians: Founded by St. John Bosco in Turin, Italy, in 1869, for men and women. Public association of the faithful. Members encourage participation in the liturgical life of the Church, emphasizing frequent reception of the Eucharist and the Sacrament of Reconciliation. They also live and spread devotion to Mary Help of Christians according to the spirit of St. John Bosco. Address: 148 Main St., P.O. Box 639, New Rochelle, NY 10802, (614) 440-0202.

Caritas: Originated in New Orleans, 1950; for women. Follows guidelines of secular institutes. Small self-supporting groups who live and work with poor and oppressed; in Louisiana and Guatemala. Address: Box 308, Abita Springs, LA 70420, (985) 892-4345.

Daughters of Our Lady of Fatima: Originated in Lansdowne, PA, 1949; for women. Received diocesan approval, Jan. 1952. Address: Fatima House, P.O. Box 116, Bedminster 18910, (215) 795-2947.

Focolare Movement: Founded in Trent, Italy, in 1943, by Chiara Lubich; for men and women. Approved as an association of the faithful, 1962. It is not a secular institute by statute; however, vows are observed by its totally dedicated core membership of 4,000 who live in small communities called Focolare (Italian word for "hearth") centers. There are 17 resident centers in the U.S. and four in Canada. GEN (New Generation) is the youth organization of the movement. An estimated 75,000 are affiliated with the movement in the U.S. and Canada, 2,000,000 worldwide. Publications include Living City, monthly; GEN II and GEN III for young people and children. Five week-long summer conventions, called "Mariapolis" ("City of Mary"), are held annually. Address for information: 204 Cardinal Rd., Hyde Park, NY 12538, (845) 229-0230 (men's or women's branch), www.rc.net/focolare.

Jesus-Caritas Fraternity of Priests: An international association of diocesan priests who strive to combine an active life with a contemplative calling by their membership in small fraternities. U.S. address for information: Rev. Greg Pawloski, St. Patrick's Church, P.O. Box 96, 126 E. 7th St., Imperial, NE 69033-0096, (308) 882-4995, www.rc.net/org/jesuscaritas.

Franciscan Missionaries of Jesus Crucified: Founded in New York in 1987; separate communities for women and men. Approved as an association of the faithful Jan. 7, 1992. To provide an opportunity for persons with disabilities to live a life of total consecration in the pursuit of holiness in the apostolate of service to the Church and to those who suffer in any way. Address: Louise D. Principe, F.M.J.C., 400 Central Ave., Apt. 3D, Albany, NY 12206, (518) 438-5887.

Madonna House Apostolate: Originated in Toronto, Canada, 1930; for priests and lay persons. Public association of the Christian faithful. Address: Madonna House, 2888 Dafoe Rd., Combermere, ON, Canada KOJ ILO, (613) 756-3713, www.madonnahouse.org. Directors General: Jean Fox (women), Albert Osterberger (men), Fr. Robert Pelton (priests). International membership and missions.

Opus Spiritus Sancti: Originated in Germany; for women. An association of the faithful. Address: 1 Fatima Dr., Cumberland, RI 02864, (401) 723-6719.

Pax Christi: Lay institute of men and women dedicated to witnessing to Christ, with special emphasis on service to the poor in Mississippi. Addresses: St. Francis Center, 709 Ave. I, Greenwood, MS 38930. LaVerna House, 2108 Altawoods Blvd., Jackson, MS 39204, (601) 373-4463.

Rural Parish Workers of Christ the King: Founded in 1942; for women. A secular institute of the Archdiocese of St. Louis. Dedicated to the glory of God in service of neighbor, especially in rural areas. Address: 15540 Cannon Mines Rd., Cadet, MO 63630, (636) 586-5171.

Salesian Cooperators: Founded by St. John Bosco in Turin, Italy, in 1876; for lay men and women and diocesan clergy. Public association of the faithful, members commit themselves to apostolates in the local Church, especially on behalf of the young, in the Salesian spirit and style. Address: P.O. Box 639, New Rochelle, NY 10802-0639; (614) 440-0202. Provincial Coordinator: Lucille Hahn.

Teresian Institute: Founded in Spain 1911 by Pedro Poveda. Approved as an association of the faithful of pontifical right, Jan. 11, 1924. Mailing Address: 3400 S. W. 99th Ave., Miami, FL 33165, (305) 553-8567.

THIRD ORDERS

Augustine, Third Order Secular of St.: Founded 13th century; approved Nov. 7, 1400.

Carmelites, Lay (Third Order of Our Lady of Mt. Carmel): Rule for laity approved by Pope Nicholas V, Oct. 7, 1452; new statutes, January 1991. Addresses: 8501 Bailey Rd., Darien, IL 60561. P.O. Box 613, Williamston, MA 01267. P.O. Box 27, Tappan, NY 10983-0027, (845) 359-0535. Approximately 270 communities and 10,000 members in the U.S. and Canada.

Carmelites, The Secular Order of Discalced (formerly the Third Order Secular of the Blessed Virgin Mary of Mt. Carmel and of St. Teresa of Jesus): Rule based on the Carmelite reform established by St. Teresa and St. John of the Cross; approved Mar. 23, 1594. Revised rule approved May 10, 1979. Office of National Secretariat, U.S.A.: P.O. Box 3079, San Jose, CA 95156-3079, (408) 251-1361. Approximately 24,445 members throughout the world; 130 groups/communities and 5,200 members in the U.S. and Canada.

Dominican Laity (formerly known as Third Order of St. Dominic): Founded in the 13th century. Addresses of provincial promoters in the United States: St. Dominic Priory, 3601 Lindell Blvd., St. Louis, MO 63108-3393, (314) 977-2588, www.op.org/domcentral. Eastern Province, 487 Michigan Ave., N.E., Washington, DC, 20017, (202) 529-5300. Priory of St. Martin de Porres, P.O. Box 12927, Raleigh, NC 27605, (919) 833-1893. Western Province, 2005 Berryman St., Berkeley, CA 94709, (510) 526-4811. Midwest Province, 3904 Golfside Dr., Ypsilanti, MI 48197, (734) 434-0195.

Franciscan Order, Secular (SFO): Founded 1209 by St. Francis of Assisi; approved Aug. 30, 1221. Vocation Director, 37430 Stonegate Circle, Clinton Township, MI 48036, (800) FRANCIS, www.NAFRA-SFO.org. International Secretariate, Via Pomponia Grecina, 31, 00145 Rome. Tau USA, quarterly. Approximately 780,000 throughout the world; 18,000 in the U.S.

Mary, Third Order of (Marist Laity): Founded, Dec. 8, 1850; rule approved by the Holy See, 1857. Addresses of provincial directors: Marist Laity Center, 1706 Jackson Ave., New Orleans, LA 70113-1510, (504) 524-5192, www.maristlaity.org. Marist Fathers, 698 Beacon St., Boston, MA 02115, (617) 262-2271. Marist Fathers, 2335 Warring St., Berkeley, CA 94704. Approximately 14,000 in world, 5,600 in U.S.

Mary, Secular Order of Servants of (Servite): Founded 1233; approved 1304. Revised rule approved 1995. Address: National Assistant for the Secular Order, 3121 W. Jackson Blvd., Chicago, IL 60612-2729, (773) 638-5800.

Mercy, Secular Third Order of Our Lady of (Mercedarian): Founded 1219 by St. Peter Nolasco; approved the same year.

Norbert, Third Order of St.: Founded 1122 by St. Norbert; approved by Pope Honorius II in 1126.

Oblates of St. Benedict: Lay persons affiliated with a Benedictine abbey, or monastery, who strive to direct their lives, as circumstances permit, according to the spirit and Rule of St. Benedict.

Trinity, Third Order Secular of the Most: Founded 1198; approved 1219.

Apostolates and Ministries

RIGHTS AND OBLIGATIONS OF ALL THE FAITHFUL

The following rights are listed in Canons 208-223 of the revised Code of Canon Law; additional rights are specified in other canons.
• Because of their baptism and regeneration, there is equality regarding dignity and action for the building up of the Body of Christ.
• They are bound always to preserve communion with the Church.
• According to their condition and circumstances, they should strive to lead a holy life and promote the growth and holiness of the Church.
• They have the right and duty to work for the spread of the divine message of salvation to all peoples of all times and places.
• They are bound to follow with Christian obedience those things which the bishops, as they represent Christ, declare as teachers of the faith or establish as rulers of the Church.
• They have the right to make known their needs, especially their spiritual needs, to pastors of the Church.
• They have the right, and sometimes the duty, of making known to pastors and others of the faithful their opinions about things pertaining to the good of the Church.
• They have the right to receive help from their pastors, from the spiritual goods of the Church and especially from the word of God and the sacraments.
• They have the right to divine worship performed according to prescribed rules of their rite, and to follow their own form of spiritual life in line with the doctrine of the Church.
• They have the right to freely establish and control associations for good and charitable purposes, to foster the Christian vocation in the world, and to hold meetings related to the accomplishment of these purposes.
• They have the right to promote and support apostolic action but may not call it "Catholic" unless they have the consent of competent authority.
• They have a right to a Christian education.
• They have a right to freedom of inquiry in sacred studies, in accordance with the teaching authority of the Church.
• They have a right to freedom in the choice of their state of life.
• No one has the right to harm the good name of another person or to violate his or her right to maintain personal privacy.
• They have the right to vindicate the rights they enjoy in the Church, and to defend themselves in a competent ecclesiastical forum.
• They have the obligation to provide for the needs of the Church, with respect to things pertaining to divine worship, apostolic and charitable works, and the reasonable support of ministers of the Church.
• They have the obligation to promote social justice and to help the poor from their own resources.
• In exercising their rights, the faithful should have regard for the common good of the Church and for the rights and duties of others.
• Church authority has the right to monitor the exercise of rights proper to the faithful, with the common good in view.

RIGHTS AND OBLIGATIONS OF LAY PERSONS

In addition to rights and obligations common to all the faithful and those stated in other canons, lay persons are bound by the obligations and enjoy the rights specified in these canons (224-231).
• Lay persons, like all the faithful, are called by God to the apostolate in virtue of their baptism and confirmation. They have the obligation and right, individually or together in associations, to work for the spread and acceptance of the divine message of salvation among people everywhere; this obligation is more urgent in those circumstances in which people can hear the Gospel and get to know Christ only through them (lay persons).
• They are bound to bring an evangelical spirit to bear on the order of temporal things and to give Christian witness in carrying out their secular pursuits.
• Married couples are obliged to work for the building up of the people of God through their marital and family life.
• Parents have the most serious obligation to provide for the Christian education of their children according to the doctrine handed down by the Church.
• Lay persons have the same civil liberty as other citizens. In the use of this liberty, they should take care that their actions be imbued with an evangelical spirit. They should attend to the doctrine proposed by the magisterium of the Church but should take care that, in questions of opinion, they do not propose their own opinion as the doctrine of the Church.
• Qualified lay persons are eligible to hold and perform the duties of ecclesiastical offices open to them in accord with the provisions of law.

- Properly qualified lay persons can assist pastors of the Church as experts and counselors.
- Lay persons have the obligation and enjoy the right to acquire knowledge of doctrine commensurate with their capacity and condition.
- They have the right to pursue studies in the sacred sciences in pontifical universities or facilities and in institutes of religious sciences, and to obtain academic degrees.
- If qualified, they are eligible to receive from ecclesiastical authority a mandate to teach sacred sciences.
- Laymen can be invested by liturgical rite and in a stable manner in the ministries of lector and acolyte.
- Lay persons, by temporary assignment, can fulfill the office of lector in liturgical actions; likewise, all lay persons can perform the duties of commentator or cantor.
- In cases of necessity and in the absence of the usual ministers, lay persons — even if not lectors or acolytes — can exercise the ministry of the word, lead liturgical prayers, confer baptism and distribute Communion, according to the prescripts of law.
- Lay persons who devote themselves permanently or temporarily to the service of the Church are obliged to acquire the formation necessary for carrying out their duties in a proper manner.
- They have a right to remuneration for their service which is just and adequate to provide for their own needs and those of their families; they also have a right to insurance, social security and health insurance.

(*See* Canon Law *for details on the* Code.)

DIRECTORY OF LAY GROUPS

In Feb. 2004, the U.S. Conference of Catholic Bishops' Secretariat for Family, Laity, Women and Youth released its 2004-2005 *Directory of Lay Movements, Organizations, and Professional Associations* (the most recent edition).

The directory contains listings for more than 100 national lay movements, professional associations, and organizations. Each listing includes a brief description of the group and the name, address, phone number of a contact person, and web/email information if available. The groups listed are national in scope, but not all are solely lay. Some are included because their work affects the life and mission of the laity and/or because their membership has a significant lay component. The secretariat acknowledges that the listing is a partial one and welcomes suggestions for groups to be included in future editions. Copies may be ordered from the USCCB Secretariat for Family, Laity, Women, and Youth, 3211 4th St., N.E., Washington, DC 20017; (202) 541-3040 (phone); (202) 541-3176 (fax).

SPECIAL APOSTOLATES AND GROUPS

Apostleship of the Sea (1920, Glasgow, Scotland; 1947 in U.S.): 3211 Fourth St. N.E., Washington, DC 20017 (national office); (202) 541-3226; www.aos-usa.org. An international Catholic organization for the moral, social and spiritual welfare of seafarers and those involved in the maritime industry. Formally instituted by the Holy See in 1952 (apostolic constitution *Exul Familia*), it is a sector of the Pontifical Council for Migrants and Itinerant Peoples. Its norms were updated by Pope John Paul II in a *motu proprio* dated Jan. 31, 1997. The U.S. unit, an affiliate of the USCCB, serves port chaplains in 63 U.S. ports. Nat. Dir., Rev. Fr. John A. Jamnicky.

Apostleship of the Sea of the United States of America (formerly, National Catholic Conference for Seafarers); affiliated with the Apostleship of the Sea in the U.S.: Apostleship of the Sea, 1500 Jefferson Dr., Pt. Arthur, TX 77642; (409) 985-5111. The membership organization of the Roman Catholic ministry to the people of the sea. Inspired by Pope John Paul II's apostolic letter, *Stella Maris*, AOSUSA brings together chaplains, clergy, religious, laity, and mariners in the common interest of promoting the spiritual and social life of the people of the sea. The people of the sea include fishermen, their families, U.S. and foreign mariners, cadets and trainees and those who have retired from sea service. Pres., Fr. Sinclair Oubre, J.C.L.

Auxiliaries of Our Lady of the Cenacle (1878, France): 18 Sycamore Meadow Rd., Sunderland, MA 01375; www.cenaclesisters.org. An association of consecrated Catholic laywomen, under the direction of the Congregation of Our Lady of the Cenacle. They profess annually the evangelical counsels of celibacy, poverty and obedience and serve God through their own professions and life styles and pursue individual apostolates. Reg. Dir., Dr. Carolyn Jacobs.

Catholic Central Union of America (1855): 3835 Westminster Pl., St. Louis, MO 63108; (314) 371-1653; www.socialjusticereview.org. One of the oldest Catholic lay organizations in the U.S. and the first given an official mandate for Catholic Action by a committee of the American bishops (1936); *Social Justice Review*, bimonthly.

Catholic Medical Mission Board (1928): 10 W. 17th Street, New York, NY 10011-5765; (212) 242-7757; www.cmmb.org. A charitable, non-profit organization dedicated to providing health care supplies and support for the medically disadvantaged in developing and transitional countries. CMMB depends upon the financial generosity of over 25,000 individual donors and through product contributions by major pharmaceutical corporations. In 2003, CMMB delivered more than $125 million in medicines, volunteer medical services and healthcare programming to 50 countries and responded to emergencies across the globe. New programs include Born to Live, an international effort to prevent mother-to-child transmission of HIV, especially in Africa. The CMMB also aided Cambodian mothers and children in a Phnom Phen Clinic under the CMMB's Physicians on a Mission Program; assisted over 3,000 refugee families from Liberia and Sierra Leone in the capital city of Monrovia; helped Dominican fathers and families living in the bateyes of Monte Plata; and gave emergency relief to Afghanistan, Haiti, South Africa, and Iraq. CMMB's medical program includes a placement service for health care specialists who volunteer at Catholic medical facilities in developing countries. Pres., John F. Galbraith.

Catholic Movement for Intellectual and Cultural Affairs: 3025 Fourth St., N.E., Washington, DC, 20017; (202) 269-6672. The U.S. affiliate of *Pax Romana*-ICMICA (*see* International Catholic Organizations); *The Notebook,* quarterly. Pres., Joseph Kirchner.

Catholic Network of Volunteer Service (1963; formerly, International Liaison of Lay Volunteers in Mission): 6930 Carroll Ave., Suite 506, Takoma Park, MD 201912; (301) 270-0900; www.cnvs.org. Membership organization of 235 faith-based volunteer programs, placing persons in all fifty states and 120 countries; *The Response,* annual directory. Exec. Dir., James Lindsay.

Catholic Volunteers in Florida (1983): P.O. Box 536476, Orlando, FL 32853-6476; (407) 382-7071; www.cvif.org. Co-sponsored by the bishops of Florida to promote values of social justice by direct service to farm workers, homeless, hungry, low-income people, single mothers and others in need. Volunteers, 20 years of age and older, serve for a one-year period in urban and rural settings. Exec. Dir., Richard Galentino.

Center for Applied Research in the Apostolate (CARA): 2300 Wisconsin Ave., N.W., Suite 400, Washington, DC 20007; (202) 687-8080; www.cara.georgetown.edu. A nonprofit research center serving the planning needs of the Catholic Church. CARA gathers empirical data for use by bishops, diocesan agencies, parishes, congregations of men and women religious and Catholic organizations. The CARA Report, quarterly; CARA Catholic Ministry Formation Directory, annually. Exec. Dir., Mary E. Bendyna, R.S.M., Ph.D.

Christian Family Movement (CFM) (1947): National office, Box 272, Ames, IA 50010. Originated in Chicago to Christianize family life and create communities conducive to Christian family life. Since 1968, CFM in the U.S. has included couples from all Christian churches.

Christian Life Communities (1971, promulgation of revised norms by Pope Paul VI; originated, 1563, as Sodalities of Our Lady, at the Jesuit College in Rome): 3601 Lindell Blvd., Room 202, St. Louis, MO 63108 (national office); (314) 977-7370; www.clc-usa.org. The world CLC office is in Rome. Small communities of primarily lay persons who come together to form committed individuals for service to the world and the Church.

Cursillo Movement (1949, in Spain; in U.S., 1957): National Cursillo Center, P.O. Box 210226, Dallas, TX 75211. An instrument of Christian renewal designed to form and stimulate persons to engage in evangelizing their everyday environments.

Franciscan Mission Service of North America, an Overseas Lay Ministry Program (1990): P.O. Box 29034, Washington, DC 20017; (202) 832-1762; www.franciscanmissionservice.catholic.edu. Lay missioners work with Franciscan sisters, brothers and priests for a minimum of three years in underdeveloped countries. Co-Dir. Joseph Nangle, O.F.M. and Megeen White.

Grail, The (1921, in the Netherlands, by Rev. Jacques van Ginneken, S.J.; 1940, in U.S.): Grailville, 932 O'Bannonville Rd., Loveland, OH 45140 (U. S. headquarters); (513) 683-2340; www.grailville.org. Duisburger Strasse 442, 45478 Mulheim, Germany, (international secretariat). An international movement of women concerned about the full development of all

peoples, working in education, religious, social, cultural and ecological areas.

Jesuit Volunteer Corps (1956): 18th and Thompson Sts., Philadelphia, PA 19121 (address for information); (215) 232-0300; www.jesuitvolunteers.org. Sponsored by the Society of Jesus in the U.S. Men and women volunteers work throughout the U.S. serving the poor directly and working for structural change.

LAMP Ministries (Lay Apostolic Ministries with the Poor): 2704 Schurz Ave., Bronx, NY 10465; (718) 409-5062; www.lampministries.org. Missionary service of evangelization with the materially poor and homeless in the larger metropolitan New York-New Jersey area. Newsletter, two times a year. Directors, Drs. Tom and Lyn Scheuring.

Lay Mission-Helpers Association (1955): 3435 Wilshire Blvd., #1035, Los Angeles, CA 90010; (213) 368-1870; www.laymissionhelpers.org. Trains and assigns men and women for work in overseas apostolates for periods of two to three years. Approximately 700 members of the association have served in overseas assignments since its founding. Director, Janice England.

The Mission Doctors Association: same address; (213) 637-7499; www.missiondoctors.org. recruits, trains and sends Catholic physicians and their families to mission hospitals and clinics throughout the world for tours of two to three years. Additionally, MDA has a short-term program for volunteer physicians with a term of service of 1-2 months. Program Dir., Elise Frederick.

Legion of Mary (1921, in Dublin, Ireland, by Frank Duff): Maria Center, 326 E. Ripa, St. Louis, MO 63125 (U.S. address); (314) 631-3447. De Montfort House, Dublin 7, Ireland (headquarters). Membership: active Catholics of all ages, under the direction of local bishops and priests, for the work of conversion, conservation and consolation. Pres., Mary T. Budde.

Movimiento Familiar Cristiano-USA **(MFC)** (1969): 700 Waverly, San Antonio, TX 78201; (210) 736-5228. Movement of Catholic Hispanic families united in their efforts to promote the human and Christian virtues of the family so that it may become a force that forms persons, transmits the faith and contributes to the total development of the community. Rev. Clemente Barron, C.P., national spiritual director.

Pax Christi USA (1972): 532 W. 8th St., Erie, PA 16502; (814) 453-4955. Pax Christi (*see* International Catholic Organizations). Founded to establish peacemaking as a priority for the American Catholic Church. *Pax Christi USA,* quarterly.

Schoenstatt Lay Movement (1914): International Schoenstatt Center, W284 N 698 Cherry Lane, Waukesha, WI 53188; (262) 547-7733. Lay movement founded in Germany by Fr. Joseph Kentenich. A Marian and apostolic way of life, Schoenstatt is present on all continents and includes people of all ages and walks of life, men and women, young and old, priests and laity. The Schoenstatt Shrine, dedicated to Mary, Mother Thrice Admirable, Queen and Victress of Schoenstatt, is an integral part of the spirituality of Schoenstatt. There are over 160 shrines around the world, 6 of them in the U.S., in Minnesota, New York, Texas, and Wisconsin.

Volunteer Missionary Movement (1969): 5980 W. Loomis Rd., Milwaukee, WI 53129; (414) 423-8660; www.vmmusa.org. Independent lay international mission organization with origins in the Catholic tradition but ecumenical and open to all Christian denominations. *Bridges*, quarterly. Exec. Dir., Julie Pagenkopf.

Volunteers for Educational and Social Services (VESS): 1625 Rutherford Lane, Bldg. D, Austin, TX 78754; (512) 339-7123. A program of the Texas Catholic Conference. Volunteers offer their services for a year at mission-sites throughout Texas as teachers, social workers, counselors, ESL instructors, immigration and refugee assistants, parish, youth and campus ministers, health care workers and nurses. The experience offers individuals the opportunity to acquire professional experience by ministering to the needs of parishes, agencies and schools that are economically disadvantaged. Dir., Michael G. Guerra.

CATHOLIC YOUTH ORGANIZATIONS

Camp Fire Boys and Girls: 4601 Madison Ave., Kansas City, MO 64112; (816) 756-1950; www.campfireusa.org. The National Committee for Girl Scouts and Camp Fire, a standing committee of the National Federation for Catholic Youth Ministry, cooperates with Camp Fire Boys and Girls.

Catholic Forester Youth Program, Catholic Order of Foresters: Naperville, IL 60566; (800) 552-0145. To develop Christian leadership and promote the moral, intellectual, social and physical growth of its youth members. Membership: youth up to 16 years of age; over 19,046 in 610 local courts in U.S. *Catholic Forester*. High Chief Ranger-Pres., Robert Ciesla.

Catholic Youth Organization (CYO): Name of parish-centered diocesan Catholic youth programs throughout the country. CYO promotes a program of spiritual, social and physical activities. The original CYO was organized in 1930 by Archbishop Bernard Sheil, auxiliary bishop of Chicago.

Columbian Squires (1925): 1 Columbus Plaza, New Haven, CT 06510-3326; (203) 752-4401; www.kofc.org. The official youth organization of the Knights of Columbus. To train and develop leadership through active participation in a well-organized program of spiritual, service, social, cultural and athletic activities. Membership: Catholic young men, 12-18 years old. More than 25,000 in over 1,000 circles (local units) active in the U.S., Canada, Puerto Rico, Philippines, Mexico, the Bahamas, Virgin Islands and Guam. *Squires Newsletter*, monthly.

Girl Scouts: 830 Third Ave., New York, NY 10022. Girls from archdioceses and dioceses in the U.S. and its possessions participate in Girl Scouting through the collaboration of Girl Scouts of the U.S.A., with the National Catholic Committee for Girl Scouts and Camp Fire, a standing committee of the National Federation for Catholic Youth Ministry.

Holy Childhood Association (Pontifical Association of the Holy Childhood) (1843): 266 Fifth Ave., New York, NY 10001; (212) 563-8700; www.worldmissions-catholic

church.org. The official children's mission-awareness society of the Church. Provides mission awareness for elementary-grade students in parochial schools and religious education programs and financial assistance to children in more than 100 developing countries. Publishes *It's Our World*, three times a year, in two grade levels. Nat. Dir., Rev. Francis W. Wright, C.S.Sp.

The National Catholic Committee on Scouting: P.O. Box 152079, Irving, TX 75015-2079; (972) 580-2114; www.catholic-church.org/catholicscouting; www.nccs-bsa.org. Works with the Boy Scouts of America in developing the character and spiritual life of members in units chartered to Catholic and non-Catholic organizations. National Committee Chairman, Robert Runnels of Leawood, KS. Admin. Sec., Barbara Nestel.

National Catholic Forensic League (1952): 21 Nancy Rd., Milford, MA 01757; (508) 473-0431. To develop articulate Catholic leaders through an interdiocesan program of speech and debate activities. Newsletter, quarterly. Membership: 925 schools; membership open to Catholic, private and public schools through the local diocesan league. Exec. Sec.-Treas., Richard Gaudette.

National Catholic Young Adult Ministry Association (1982): P.O. Box 32253, Washington, DC 20007; (888) NCYAMA1; www.ncyama.org. A response to the needs of young adults, an invitation to share their gifts with the larger community and a challenge to live gospel values in the world. A national network for single and married young adults. Exec. Dir., Michelle M. Miller.

National Federation for Catholic Youth Ministry, Inc. (1981): 415 Michigan Ave., N.E., Washington, DC 20017; (202) 636-3825; www.nfcym.org. To foster the development of youth ministry in the United States. Exec. Dir., Robert McCarty.

Young Christian Students: 19646 W. Dunlap Rd., Dennison, IL 62423; (217) 826-5708. A student movement for Christian personal and social change.

CAMPUS MINISTRY

Campus ministry is an expression of the Church's special desire to be present to all who are involved in higher education and to further dialogue between the Church and the academic community. In the words of the U.S. bishops' 1985 pastoral letter entitled "Empowered by the Spirit," this ministry is "the public presence and service through which properly prepared baptized persons are empowered by the Spirit to use their talents and gifts on behalf of the Church in order to be sign and instrument of the Kingdom in the academic world."

Campus ministry, carried on by lay, Religious and ordained ministers, gathers members of the Church on campus to form the faith community, appropriate the faith, form Christian consciences, educate for justice and facilitate religious development.

The dimensions and challenge of this ministry are evident from, among other things, the numbers involved: approximately 550,000 Catholics on more than 230 Catholic college and university campuses; about four million in several thousand non-Catholic private and public institutions; 1,200 or more campus ministers. In many dioceses, the activities of ministers are coordinated by a local diocesan director. Two professional organizations serve the ministry on the national level:

The National Association of Diocesan Directors of Campus Ministry: Ms. Krista Bajoka (contact), 305 Michigan Ave., Detroit, MI 48226; (313) 237-5962.

The Catholic Campus Ministry Association: 1,200 members. 1118 Pendleton St., Suite 300, Cincinnati, OH 45202; (513) 842-0167; www.ccmanet.org. Exec. Dir., Edmund Franchi.

COLLEGE SOCIETIES

Alpha Sigma Nu (1915): Marquette University, Brooks 201, P.O. Box 1881, Milwaukee, WI 53201-1881 (national headquarters); (414) 288-7542; www.alphasigmanu.org. National honor society of the 30 Jesuit institutions of higher education in the U.S. and a chapter at Sogany University in Korea; members chosen on the basis of scholarship, loyalty and service; 1,575 student and 38,000 alumni members. Member, Association of College Honor Societies. Gamma Pi Epsilon (1925) merged with Alpha Sigma Nu in 1973 to form society for men and women. Exec. Dir., Kate Greatner.

Delta Epsilon Sigma (1939): Barry University, 11300 NE Second Ave., Miami Shores, FL 33161; (305) 899-3020; www.des.barry.edu. National scholastic honor society for students, faculty and alumni of colleges and universities with a Catholic tradition. *Delta Epsilon Sigma Journal*, three times a year. Membership: 60,000 in 116 chapters. Sec., Dr. J. Patrick Lee.

Kappa Gamma Pi (1926): KGP National Office, 10215 Chardon Rd., Chardon, OH, 44024-9700; (440) 286-3764; www.kappagammapi.org. A national Catholic college honor society for graduates who, in addition to academic excellence, have shown outstanding leadership in extra-curricular activities. *Kappa Gamma Pi News*, five times a year.

Membership: more than 37,000 in 139 colleges; 20 alumnae chapters in metropolitan areas. Nat. Exec. Sec., Christine Walick.

Phi Kappa Theta: 3901 W. 86th St., Suite 425, Indianapolis, IN 46268. National social fraternity with a Catholic heritage. Merger (1959) of Phi Kappa Fraternity, founded at Brown University in 1889, and Theta Kappa Phi Fraternity, founded at Lehigh University in 1919. *The Temple Magazine*, semi-annually, and newsletters. Membership: 2,800 undergraduate and 50,500 alumni in 63 collegiate and 40 alumni chapters. Exec. Dir., Mark T. McSweeney.

National Catholic Student Coalition (1988); 45 Lovett Ave., Newark, DE 19717; www.catholicstudent.org. National coalition of Catholic campus ministry groups at public and private institutions of higher education. Formed after National Newman Club Federation and the National Federation of Catholic College Students dissolved in the 1960s. The U.S. affiliate of Pax Romana-IMCS (*see* **International Catholic Organizations**). *The Catholic Collegian*, four times a year. Membership: 200 campus groups. Exec. Dir., Jamie Williams; contact, Kim Zitzner.

ASSOCIATIONS, MOVEMENTS, SOCIETIES IN THE U.S.

Principal source: Catholic Almanac *survey.*

Academy of American Franciscan History (1944): 1712 Euclid Ave., Berkeley, CA 94709; (510) 548-1755; www.aafh.org. To encourage the study of the Franciscan Order in the New World. Dir., Dr. Jeffrey M. Burns.

Adoremus-Society for the Renewal of the Sacred Liturgy (1995): P.O. Box 3286, St. Louis, MO 63130; (314) 863-8385; www.adoremus.org. Promotes authentic renewal of Catholic liturgy in accordance with the Second Vatican Council's Constitution of the Sacred Liturgy, *Sacrosanctum Concilium*. Publishes *Adoremus Bulletin*, 10 times a year; editor, Helen Hull Hitchcock.

Aid to the Church in Need (1947): U.S. office, 725 Leonard St., Brooklyn, N.Y. 11222; (718) 609-0939; www.churchinneed.org. Assists the pastoral activities of the church in Third World countries, Eastern Europe and the former Soviet Union. *Mirror*, newsletter, 9 times a year. Pres./Exec. Dir., Joseph Donnelly.

Albanian Catholic Institute "Daniel Dajani, S.J." (1992): University of San Francisco, Xavier Hall, 650 Parker Ave., San Francisco, CA 94118; (415) 422-6966; www.albanian-catholic-institute.org. To assist the rebuilding of the Catholic Church in Albania and to promote the dissemination of knowledge of Albania's national, religious and cultural heritage. Founder, Gjon Sinishta (1930-95), in memory of the martyr Daniel Dajani (d. 1946). Dir., Raymond Frost; Jesuit Community Liaison, Paul Bernardicou, S.J.

American Benedictine Academy (1947): Saint Meinrad Archabbey, Guest House, 100 Hill Dr. Saint Meinrad, IN, 47577; (800) 581-6905. To promote Benedictine values in contemporary culture. Pres., Eugene Hensell, O.S.B.

American Catholic Correctional Chaplains

Association (1952): 701 Lawrenceville Rd., P.O. Box 1547, Trenton, NJ. 08638; (609) 406-7400. Pres., Rev. Robert R. Schulze.

American Catholic Historical Association (1919): The Catholic University of America, Washington, DC 20064; (202) 319-5079; www.research.cua.edu/acha. *The Catholic Historical Review*, quarterly. Sec.-Treas., Dr. Timothy J. Meagher.

American Catholic Philosophical Association (1926): Administration Building, Fordham University, 441 E. Fordham Rd., Bronx, NY, 10458; (718) 817-3295; www.acpa-main.org. *American Catholic Philosophical Quarterly; proceedings*, annually.

American Committee on Italian Migration (1952): 25 Carmine St., New York, NY 10014; (212) 247-5419; www.acimmmigra.org. *ACIM Newsletter* and *ACIM Nuova Via*, 6 times a year.

American Friends of the Vatican Library (1981): 3535 Indian Trail, Orchard Lake, MI 48324; (248) 683-0311. *AMICI*, newsletter. Sponsored by the Catholic Library Association. To assist in supporting the Vatican Library. Pres., Rev. Msgr. Charles G. Kosanke.

American Life League, Inc. (1979), P.O. Box 1350, Stafford, VA 22555; (540) 659-4171; www.all.org. *Celebrate Life*, six times a year, and the *ABAC Quarterly*, for the American Bioethics Advisory Commission. Pres., Judie Brown.

Ancient Order of Hibernians in America, Inc. (1836): 31 Logan St., Auburn, NY 13021. *National Hibernian Digest*, bimonthly. 120,000 members. Nat. Sec., Thomas McNabb.

Apostleship of Prayer (1844, France; 1861, U.S.): 3 Stephen Ave., New Hyde Park, NY 11040. Promotes

Daily Offering and Sacred Heart devotion. Nat. Dir., Rev. John H. Rainaldo, S.J.

Apostolate for Family Consecration (1975): 3375 County Rd. 36, Bloomingdale, OH 43910; (740) 765-5500; www.familyland.org. Pope John Paul II Holy Family Center, known as Catholic Familyland. To transform families and parishes and nourish families through the Catholic faith. Pres., Jerome F. Coniker.

Archconfraternity of Christian Mothers (Christian Mothers) (1881): 220 37th St., Pittsburgh, PA 15201; (412) 683-2400; www.capuchin.com. Over 3,500 branches. Dir., Rev. Bertin Roll, O.F.M. Cap.

Archconfraternity of the Holy Ghost (1912): Holy Ghost Fathers, 6230 Brush Run Rd., Bethel Park, PA 15102; (412) 831-0302; www.spiritans.org (U.S. head-quarters).

Archdiocese for the Military Services Seminary Education Fund (1988): P.O. Box 4469, Washington, D.C., 20017-0469; (202) 269-9100; www.milarch.org.

Association for Spiritual, Ethical, and Religious Values in Counseling (ASERVIC): Dept. of Educational Psychology and Special Education, Southern Illinois University at Carbondale, Carbondale, IL 62901. *Counseling and Values*, 3 times a year. Division of the American Counseling Association.

Association for Social Economics (formerly the Catholic Economic Association) (1941): Marquette University, Milwaukee, WI 53233. *Review of Social Economy*, quarterly. 1,300 members.

Association of Catholic Diocesan Archivists (1979): 711 W. Monroe, Chicago, IL 60661; (312) 831-0711. To work for establishment of an archival program in every American diocese. *ACDA Bulletin*, quarterly. Treas. John J. Treanor.

Association of Marian Helpers (1944): Eden Hill, 2 Prospect Rds., Stockbridge, MA 01263; (413) 298-3691; www.marian.org. *Marian Helpers Bulletin*, quarterly. 900,000 members, mostly in U.S. To promote vocations to Church service and support worldwide apostolates of Marians of the Immaculate Conception. Exec. Dir., Rev. Joseph, M.I.C.

Assumption Guild — Mass Cards: 330 Market St., Brighton, MA 02135; (617) 783-0495; www.masscardsaa.com.

Beginning Experience (1974): International Ministry Center, 1657 Commerce Dr., Suite 2B, South Bend, IN 46628; (574) 283-0279; www.beginningexperience.org. Adult and youth programs to help divorced, widowed and separated start a new beginning in their lives. Pres., Kathleen Murphy.

The Blue Army of Our Lady of Fatima, USA (1947): P.O. Box 976, Washington, NJ 07882-0976; (908) 689-1701; www.bluearmy.com. *Soul*, bimonthly; *Hearts Aflame*, quarterly. U.S. branch of the World Apostolate of Fatima. Promote the Fatima Message. Fatima shrine. Nat. Pres., Most Rev. James S. Sullivan.

Calix Society (1947): 2555 Hazelwood St., St. Paul, MN 55109; www.calixsociety.org. Association of Catholic alcoholics maintaining their sobriety through 12-step program. Sec., Jim Billigmeier.

Canon Law Society of America (1939): Catholic University, Caldwell Hall, 431, Washington, DC 20064; (202) 269-3491; www.clsa.org. To further

research and study in canon law. 1,600 members. Exec. Coord., Arthur J. Espelage, O.F.M.

Cardinal Mindszenty Foundation (CMF) (1958): P.O. Box 11321, St. Louis, MO 63105-0121; (314) 727-6279; www.mindszenty.org. To uphold and defend the Catholic Church, family life and freedom for all under God. *The Mindszenty Report*, monthly. Pres., Eleanor Schlafly.

Catholic Aid Association (1878): 3499 N. Lexington Ave. North, St. Paul, MN 55126; (651) 490-0170; www.catholicaid.com. Fraternal life insurance society. *Catholic Aid News*, monthly. Chairman of the Board, Michael McGovern.

Catholic Alumni Clubs International (1957): P.O. Box 2412, Youngstown, OH 44509. To advance social, cultural and spiritual well-being of members. Membership limited to single Catholics with professional education. 7,500 members in 48 clubs in U.S. Pres., Sue Gentile.

Catholic Answers (1982): 2020 Gillespie Way, El Cajon, CA 92020; (619) 387-7200; www.catholic.com. Apologetics and evangelization organization. *This Rock*, monthly. Founder and dir., Karl Keating.

Catholic Biblical Association of America (1936): The Catholic University of America, Washington, DC 20064; (202) 319-5519; www.cba.cua.edu. *The Catholic Biblical Quarterly, Old Testament Abstracts*, CBQ monograph series. Exec. Sec., Joseph Jensen, O.S.B.

Catholic Book Publishers Association, Inc. (1987): 8404 Jamesport Dr., Rockford, IL 61108; (815) 332-3245; www.cbpa.org. Exec. Dir., Terry Wessels.

Catholic Cemetery Conference (1949): 710 N. River Rd., Des Plaines, IL 60016; (847) 824-8131. Exec. Dir., Sidney Cristol.

Catholic Coalition on Preaching: Madonna University, 36600 Schoolcraft Rd. Livonia, MI 48150-1173; (734) 432-5538. Pres., Rev. Francis Tebbe, O.F.M.

Catholic Committee of Appalachia (1970): P.O. Box 62, Wittensville, KY 41274; (606) 297-8792. Exec. Coord., Sr. Robbie Pentecost, O.S.F.

Catholic Daughters of the Americas (1903): 10 W. 71st St., New York, NY 10023; (212) 877-3041; www.catholicdaughters.org. *Share Magazine*. 125,000 members. Nat. Regent, M. Joan McKenna.

Catholic Death Row Ministry (1990): P.O. Box 1328, Howe, Texas 75459-1328; (903)892-9411.To share the Catholic faith with death row inmates, as well as send them Catholic books, bibles, etc.; also assist victims and families of death row inmates. Founder and director, Michael Denson.

Catholic Familyland (1975): 3375 County Rd. 36, Bloomingdale, OH 43910; (740) 765-5500; www.familyland.org. Canonically named the John Paul II Holy Family Center; functions under the auspices of the Apostolate for Family Consecration. Pres., Jerome F. Coniker.

Catholic Golden Age (1975): P.O. Box 3658, Scranton, PA 18505-0658; (800) 836-5699. *CGA World*, quarterly. For Catholics over 50 years of age.

Catholic Guardian Society (1913): 1011 First Ave., New York, NY 10022; (212) 371-1000. Exec. Dir., John J. Frein.

Catholic Home Bureau (1899): 1011 First Ave., New York, NY 10022; (212) 371-1000; www.catholichomebureau.com. Exec. Dir., Philip Georgini.

Catholic Home Study Service (1936): P.O. Box 363, Perryville, MO 63775-0363; (573) 547-4084; www.amm.org/chss.htm. Provides instruction in the Catholic faith by mail free of charge. Dir., Rev. Oscar Lukefahr, C.M.

Catholic Interracial Council of New York, Inc. (1934): 899 Tenth Ave., New York, NY 10019; (212) 237-8600; www.amm.org/chss.htm. To promote racial and social justice.

Catholic Knights of America (1877): Publication Office, 1850 Dalton St., Cincinnati, OH 45214. Fraternal insurance society. *CK of A Journal*, monthly. 7,800 members.

Catholic Knights of Ohio (1891): 22005 Mastick Rd., Fairview Park, OH 44126; (440) 777-5355. Fraternal insurance society. *The Messenger*, monthly. 8,000 members in Ohio and Kentucky. Mr. Tom Welsh, General Secretary.

Catholic Kolping Society of America (1849): 9 East 8th St., Clifton, NJ 07011-1101. International society concerned with spiritual and educational development of members. *Kolping Banner*, monthly. Nat. Admin., Edward Farkas.

Catholic Lawyers' Guild: Organization usually on a diocesan basis, under different titles.

Catholic League for Religious Assistance to Poland (1943): 6002 W. Berteau Ave., Chicago, IL 60634-1630; (773) 202-7720. Exec. Dir., Most Rev. Thad Jakubowski.

Catholic League for Religious and Civil Rights (1973): 450 Seventh Ave., 34th Floor, New York, NY 10123; (212) 371-3191; www.catholicleague.org. Local chapters throughout U.S. Serves Catholic community as an anti-defamation and civil rights agency. *Catalyst*, league journal. Pres., William A. Donohue, Ph.D.

Catholic Library Association (1921): 100 North St., Suite 224, Pittsfield, MA 01201-5109; (413) 442-2252. www.cathla.org; *Catholic Library World*, *Catholic Periodical and Literature Index*, quarterlies. Exec. Dir., Jean R. Bostley, S.S.J.

Catholic Marketing Network (1955): 111 Ferguson Court, #102, Irving, TX 75062; (800) 506-6333; www.catholicmarketing.com. A trade association founded to encourage the most effective production and distribution of Catholic goods and provide a common forum for mutual interchange of ideas. *Catholic Marketing Network*, quarterly. Exec. Dir., Cherylann Tucker.

Catholic Near East Welfare Association (1926): 1011 First Ave., Suite 1552, New York, NY 10022; (212) 826-1480; www.cnewa.org. A papal agency for humanitarian and pastoral support serving the churches and peoples of the Middle East, Northeast Africa, India and Eastern Europe, with offices in New York, Vatican City, Addis Ababa, Amman, Jerusalem and Beirut. Pres., Cardinal Edward Egan; Sec. Gen., Msgr. Robert L. Stern.

Catholic Order of Foresters (1883): 355 Shuman Blvd., P.O. Box 3012, Naperville, IL 60566; (630) 983-4900; www.catholicforester.com. Fraternal insurance society. *The Catholic Forester*, bimonthly. 136,685 members. High Chief Ranger, Robert Ciesla.

Catholic Press Association of the U.S. and Canada, Inc. (1911): 3555 Veterans Memorial Highway, Unit O, Ronkonkoma, NY 11779; (631) 471-4730; www.catholicpress.org. *The Catholic Journalist*, monthly; *Catholic Press Directory*, annually. Exec. Dir., Vacant.

Catholic Theological Society of America (1946), John Carroll University, 20700 North Park Blvd., University Hgts., OH, 44118; (216) 397-1631; www.jcu.edu/ctsa. *Proceedings*, annually. Exec. Sec., Dolores Christie.

Catholic Union of Texas, The K.J.T. (1889): 214 E. Colorado St., La Grange, TX 78945-0297; (979) 968-5877; www.kjtnet.org. Fraternal and insurance society. *Nasinec*, weekly, and *K. J. T. News*, monthly. 18,226 members. Pres., Elo J. Goerig.

Catholic War Veterans (1935): 441 N. Lee St., Alexandria, VA 22314; (703) 549-3622; www.cwv.org. *Catholic War Veteran*, bimonthly. 500 posts.

Catholic Worker Movement (1933): 36 E. 1st St., New York, NY 10003. Lay apostolate founded by Peter Maurin and Dorothy Day; has Houses of Hospitality in over 60 U.S. cities and several communal farms in various parts of the country. Promotes the practice of the works of mercy, nonviolence, personalism, voluntary poverty. *The Catholic Worker*, 8 times a year.

Catholic Workman (Katolicky Delnik) (1891): 111 West Main St., New Prague, MN 56071; (612) 758-2229. Fraternal and insurance society. *Catholic Workman*, monthly. 16,405 members.

Catholics Against Capital Punishment (1992): P.O. Box 5706, Bethesda, MD 20824-5706; (301) 652-1125; www.cacp.org. Promotes greater awareness of papal and episcopal statements against the death penalty. *CACP News Notes*, bimonthly. Nat. Coord., Frank McNeirney.

Catholics United for the Faith (1968): 827 N. Fourth St., Steubenville, OH 43952; (740) 283-2484; www.cuf.org. 23,000 members worldwide. Lay apostolic group concerned with spiritual and doctrinal formation of members. *Lay Witness*, monthly. Mike Sullivan, Dir. of Communications.

Center of Concern (1971): 1225 Otis St., N.E., Washington, DC 20017; (202) 635-2757; www.coc.org. Exec. Dir., James E. Hug.

Central Association of the Miraculous Medal (1915): 475 E. Chelten Ave., Philadelphia, PA 19144; (800) 523-3674; www.cammonline.org. *Miraculous Medal*, quarterly. Dir., Rev. James O. Kiernan, C.M.

Chaplains' Aid Association, Inc. (1917): 3311 Toledo Terrace, Hyattsville, MD 20780. To receive and administer funds toward education of seminarians to become priest-chaplains in military services.

Christian Foundation for Children and Aging: One Elmwood Ave., Kansas City, KS 66103; (913) 384-6500; www.cfcausa.org. Grassroots movement dedicated to improving through sponsorship the lives of children and aging at Catholic mission sites around the world. Exec. Dir., Paco Wertin.

Christophers, Inc., The (1945): 12 E. 48th St., New York, NY 10017; (212) 759-4050; www.christophers.org. Founded by Rev. James Keller, M.M. The Christophers stimulate personal initiative and responsible action in line with Judeo-Christian principles through broadcast of Christopher radio and TV programs; free distribution of *Christopher News Notes*, ten times a year; publication of a weekly Christopher column in over 200 newspapers; Spanish literature; annual media awards; youth outreach. Pres., Dennis W. Heaney.

Citizens for Educational Freedom (1959): 921 S. Walter Reed Dr., Suite 1, Arlington, VA 22204. Nonsectarian group concerned with parents' right to educational choice by means of tuition tax credits and vouchers. Exec. Dir., Patrick J. Reilly.

Conference of Slovak Clergy (1985): 126 Logan Blvd., Hollidaysburg, PA, 16648; (814) 695-5579. Founded in 1985 and incorporated in 2000, the Conference seeks to associate priests and deacons of Slovak ancestry in the United States and to assist those preparing themselves for priestly ministry in the Church; provides financial assistance to the Slovak Pontifical College of Saints Cyril and Methodius in Rome and scholarships to individual students. Chair., Bishop Joseph V. Adamec.

Confraternity of Bl. Junipero Serra (1989): P.O. Box 7125, Mission Hills, CA 91346. Founded in Monterey (CA) diocese to help promote process of canonization of Bl. Junipero Serra and increase spiritual development of members. 3,500 members in U.S. and foreign countries. Dir., Rev. Thomas L. Davis, Jr.; Spiritual Dir., Rev. Noel F. Moholy, O.F.M.

Confraternity of Catholic Clergy (1976): 4445 W. 64th St., Chicago, IL 60629; (773) 581-8904. Association of priests pledged to pursuit of personal holiness, loyalty to the pope, theological study and adherence to authentic teachings of the Catholic faith. Sec., Rev. L. Dudley Day, O.S.A.

Confraternity of Christian Doctrine, Inc.: 3211 Fourth St., N.E., Washington, DC 20017; (202) 541-3098; www.usccb.org/nab. A distinct entity, separately incorporated and directed by a Board of Trustees from the United States Catholic Conference of Bishops. Its purpose is to foster and promote the teaching of Christ as understood and handed down by the Roman Catholic Church. To this end it licenses use of the Lectionary for Mass and the New American Bible (NAB), the Revised Psalms of the NAB and the Revised New Testament of the NAB, translations made from the original languages in accordance with the papal encyclical *Divino Afflante Spiritu* (1943) of Pope Pius XII.

Confraternity of the Immaculate Conception of Our Lady of Lourdes (1874): Box 561, Notre Dame, IN 46556; (574) 631-6562. Distributors of Lourdes water.

Confraternity of the Most Holy Rosary: *See* Dominican Rosary Apostolate.

Couple to Couple League (1971), P.O. Box 111184, Cincinnati, OH 45211; (513) 471-2000; www.ccli.org. Founded to teach and promote marital chastity through Natural Family Planning. Exec. Dir., Mark Hayden.

Courage (1980): c/o St. John the Baptist Church and Friary, 210 West 31st St., New York, NY 10001; (212) 268-1010; www.couragerc.org. Ministry to men and women who experience same-sex attractions and desire to live Christian chastity in accordance with the teachings of the Catholic Church. Newsletter, 4 times a year. Nat. Dir., Rev. John F. Harvey, O.S.F.S.

CUSA (Catholics United for Spiritual Action, Inc.) — An Apostolate of the Sick or Disabled (1947): 176 W. 8th St., Bayonne, NJ, 07002-1227; (201) 437-0412; www.cusan.org. A group-correspondence apostolate for the disabled and chronically ill. Admin., Ms. Anna Marie Sopko.

Damien-Dutton Society for Leprosy Aid, Inc. (1944): 616 Bedford Ave., Bellmore, NY 11710; (516) 221-5829; www.damienleprosysociety.org. Provides medicine, rehabilitation and research for conquest of leprosy. *Damien Dutton Call*, quarterly. 25,000 members. Pres., Howard E. Crouch; Vice Pres., Elizabeth Campbell.

Daughters of Isabella (1897): P.O. Box 9585, New Haven, CT 06535; www.daughtersofisabella. To unite Catholic women into a fraternal order for spiritual benefits and to promote higher ideals within society. 100,000 members.

Disaster Response Office (1990): Catholic Charities USA, 1731 King St., Suite 200, Alexandria, VA 22314; (703) 549-1390; www.catholiccharitiesusa.org. Promotes and facilitates Catholic disaster response in the U.S. Dir., Jane A. Gallagher.

Dominican Rosary Apostolate (1806): Dominican Province of St. Joseph, 280 N. Grant Ave., Columbus, OH 43215, (614) 240-5915. Contact, Rev. André-Joseph LaCasse, O.P., Promoter of the Rosary, Dominican Province of St. Joseph.

Edith Stein Guild, Inc. (1955): Church of St. John the Baptist, 210 W. 31st St., New York, NY 10001-2876; (212) 567-8230. Assists and encourages Jewish Catholics; fosters among Catholics a better understanding of their Jewish heritage; promotes spread of knowledge of life and writings of St. Edith Stein; fosters better understanding between Jews and Christians and supports the Church's spirit of ecumenism. Pres., Sr. Marie Goldstein, R.S.H.M.

Enthronement of the Sacred Heart in the Home (1907): P.O. Box 111, Fairhaven, MA 02719; (508) 999-2680.

Federation of Diocesan Liturgical Commissions (FDLC) (1969): P.O. Box 29039, Washington, DC 20017; (202) 635-6990; www.fdlc.org. Voluntary association of personnel from diocesan liturgical commissions and worship offices. The main purpose is promotion of the liturgy as the heart of Christian life, especially in the parish community. Exec. Dir., Rev. Michael J. Spillane.

Federation of Seminary Spiritual Directors (1972): Cardinal Muench Seminary, 100 35th Ave., N.E., Fargo, ND 58102; (701) 232-8969. Responsible for priestly spiritual formation in high school and college seminaries, novitiates, theologates and houses of formation in the U.S. and Canada. Pres., Dennis Skonseng.

Fellowship of Catholic Scholars (1977): Ave Maria School of Law, 3475 Plymouth Rd., Ann Arbor, Michigan 48105; (734) 827-8043. Interdisciplinary research and publications of Catholic scholars in accord with the magisterium of the Catholic Church. 1,000 members. Pres., Bernard Dobranski.

First Catholic Slovak Ladies' Association, USA (1892): 24950 Chagrin Blvd., Beachwood, OH 44122; (800) 464-4642; www.fcsla.com. *Fraternally Yours*, monthly. 102,000 members. Fraternal insurance society. Pres., Mary Ann Johanek.

First Catholic Slovak Union (Jednota) (1890): FCSU Corporate Center, 6611 Rockside Rd., Independence, OH 44131; (216) 642-9406; www.fcsu.com. *Jednota*, biweekly. 96,206 members. Nat. Sec., Kenneth A. Arendt.

Foundation for the Family (1986): P.O. Box 111184, Cincinnati, OH 45211; (513) 471-2000; www.ccli.org. Established by Couple to Couple League (*see entry above*) to provide materials for family not relating to Natural Family Planning, Exec. Dir., Mark Hayden.

Foundations and Donors Interested in Catholic Activities, Inc. (FADICA): 1350 Connecticut Ave. N.W., Suite 303, Washington, DC 20036; (202) 223-3550; www.FADICA.org. A consortium of private foundations providing continuing education and research to members to make church-related philanthropy more effective. Pres., Francis J. Butler.

Franciscan Apostolate of the Way of the Cross (1949): P.O. Box 23, Boston, MA 02112; (617) 542-6659. Distributes religious materials to the sick and shut-in. Dir., Rev. Robert Lynch, O.F.M.

Free The Fathers (1983): 845 Oak St. Chattanooga, TN 37403; (423) 756-9660; www.ftf.org. To work for the freedom of bishops and priests imprisoned in China. Pres., John M. Davies.

Friends of the Holy Land, Inc. (1974): 370 Mile Square Rd., Yonkers, NY 10701. To provide spiritual and material support for the Christian communities in the Holy Land. *Friends of the Holy Land,* newsletter. 300 members. Gen. Dir., Ernest F. Russo.

Gabriel Richard Institute (1949): 3641 Estates Dr., Troy, MI 48084; (248) 643-8887. Conducts Christopher Leadership Course. Exec. Dir., Dolores Ammar.

Guard of Honor of the Immaculate Heart of Mary (1932): 135 West 31st St., New York, NY 10001; (212) 736-8500; www.hnp.org. An archconfraternity approved by the Holy See whose members cultivate devotion to the Blessed Virgin Mary, particularly through a daily Guard Hour of Prayer. Dir., Rev. Cassian A. Miles, O.F.M.

Holy Cross Family Ministries (formerly The Family Rosary, Inc.) (1942): 518 Washington St., North Easton, MA, 02356-1200; (508) 238-4095; www.hcfm.org. Founded by Father Patrick Peyton, C.S.C. Encourages family prayer, especially the Rosary. Pres., Rev. John Phalen, C.S.C.

Holy Name Society: P.O. Box 12012, Baltimore, MD 21224; (410) 325-1523; www.holyname society.info. Founded in 1274 by Blessed John Vercelli, master general of the Dominicans, to promote reverence for the Holy Name of Jesus; this is still the principal purpose of the society, which also develops lay apostolic programs in line with directives of the Second Vatican Council. Introduced in the U.S. in 1870-71 by Dominican Father Charles H. McKenna, the society has about 5 million members on diocesan and parochial levels. With approval of the local bishop and pastor, women as well as men may be members.

Holy Name Society, National Association (NAHNS) (1970): P.O. Box 12012, Baltimore, MD 21281; (410) 276-1166; www.members.aol.com/nahns. Association of diocesan and parochial Holy Name Societies. *Holy Name Newsletter,* monthly.

Hungarian Catholic League of America, Inc. (1945): One Cathedral Sq., Providence, RI 02903-3695; (401) 278-4520. Chair., Rev. Msgr. William I. Varsanyi.

International Catholic Stewardship Council (1962): 1275 K St. N.W., Suite 880, Washington, DC 20005-4083; (202) 289-1093; www.catholicsteward-ship.org. A professional association which fosters an environment in which stewardship is understood, accepted and practiced throughout the church. Moderator, Alex R. Carrion.

International Catholic Charismatic Renewal Services: Palazzo della Cancelleria, 00120 Vatican City; 39 06 698 87538; www.iccrs.org. The ICCRS provides leadership and vision to the Catholic Charismatic Renewal throughout the world in harmony with the Pontifical Council for the Laity which has established ICCRS as a Private Association of the Faithful. See **National Catholic Charismatic Renewal Services.**

Italian Catholic Federation (1924): 675 Hegenberger Rd., #230, Oakland, CA 94621; (888) 423-1924; www.icf.org. Fraternal organization of Italian-American Catholics. 19,000 members.

John Carroll Society, The (1951): P.O. Box 50188, Washington, DC 20091; (703) 573-3043; www.johncarroll society.org. Exec. Asst., Mary Ann Dmochowski, Ph.D.

Judean Society, Inc., The (1966): 1075 Space Park Way No. 336, Mountain View, CA 94043.

Knights of Peter Claver (1909), and **Knights of Peter Claver, Ladies Auxiliary** (1926): 1825 Orleans Ave., New Orleans, LA 70116; (504) 821-4225; www.knightsofpeter-claver.com. Fraternal and aid society. *The Claverite,* biannually. National Chaplain, Most Rev. Curtis J. Guillory, S.V.D.

Knights of St. John, International Supreme Commandery (1886): 89 So. Pine Ave., Albany, N.Y. 12208; (518) 453-5675; www.members.tripod.com/ksji/knights/ksji.html. Supreme Sec., Maj. Gen. Joseph Hauser, Jr.

Ladies of Charity of the United States of America (1960): P.O. Box 31697, St. Louis, MO 63131; (314) 344-1184; www.famvin.org/lcusa. International Association founded by St. Vincent de Paul in 1617. 25,000 members in U.S.; 250,000 worldwide.

Latin Liturgy Association (1975): 34 Dumont Ave., Staten Island, NY 10305-1450; (718) 979-6685; www.latinliturgy.com. To promote the use of the Latin language and music in the approved rites of the Church. Quarterly journal. 850 members. Pres., William J. Leininger.

Legatus (1987): 30 Frank Lloyd Wright Dr., P.O. Box 997, Ann Arbor, MI 48106; (734) 930-3854. To apply Church's moral teaching in business and personal lives of members. *Legatus Newsletter,* monthly.

Lithuanian Groups: Ateitininkai, members of **Lithuanian Catholic Federation Ateitis** (1910), 1209 Country Lane, Lemont, IL 60439. *Ateitis,* bimonthly. Pres., Juozas Polikaitis. **Knights of Lithuania** (1913): Roman Catholic educational-fraternal organization. *Vytis,* monthly. Pres., Evelyn Ozelis, 2533 W. 45th St., Chicago, IL 60632.

Lithuanian Catholic Alliance (1886), 71-73 S. Washington St., Wilkes-Barre, PA 18701. Fraternal insurance organization. Pres., Thomas E. Mack.

Lithuanian Roman Catholic Federation of America (1906): 4545 W. 63rd St., Chicago, IL 60629; (312) 585-9500. Umbrella organization for Lithuanian parishes and organizations. *The Observer,* bimonthly. Pres., Saulius Kuprys.

Lithuanian Catholic Religious Aid, Inc. (1961): 64-25 Perry Ave., Maspeth, NY 11378-2441; (718) 326-5202. To assist Catholics in Lithuania. Chairman and Pres., Most Rev. Paul Baltakis, O.F.M.

Lithuanian Roman Catholic Priests' League (1909): P.O. Box 1025, Humarock, MA 02047-1025; (781) 834-4079. Religious-professional association. Pres., Rev. Albert Contons.

Little Flower Mission League (1957), P.O. Box 25, Plaucheville, LA 71362; (318) 922-3630. Sponsored by the Brothers of the Holy Eucharist. Dir., Bro. André M. Lucia, F.S.E.

Little Flower Society (1923): 1313 Frontage Rd. Darien, IL 60561. 200,000 members. Nat. Dir., Rev. Robert E. Colaresi, O. Carm.

Liturgical Conference, The: 415 Michigan Ave., NE, #65, Washington, DC 20017; (202) 832-6520; www.litconf.org. Liturgy, homily service. Education, research and publication programs for renewing and enriching Christian liturgical life. Ecumenical.

Loyal Christian Benefit Association (1890): P.O. Box 13005, Erie, PA 16514; (814) 453-4331; www.icba.com. Fraternal benefit and insurance society. *The Fraternal Leader*, quarterly. Pres., Jackie Sobania-Robison.

Marian Movement of Priests (1972): P.O. Box 8, St. Francis, ME 04774-0008 (U.S.); (207) 398-3375; www.mmp-usa.net. Via Mercalli, 23, 20122 Milan, Italy (international headquarters). Spiritual renewal through consecration to the Immaculate Heart of Mary. 4,000 clergy members, 53,000 religious and laity (U.S.). Nat. Dir., Rev. Albert G. Roux.

Mariological Society of America (1949): Marian Library, Box 1390, University of Dayton, Dayton, OH 45469; (937) 229-4294; msd62.tripod.com. Founded by Rev. Juniper B. Carol, O.F.M., to promote greater appreciation of and scientific research in Marian theology. *Marian Studies*, annually. Sec., Rev. Thomas A. Thompson, S.M.

Marriage Encounter, National: 4704 Jamerson Pl., Orlando, FL 32807. The national office of Worldwide Marriage Encounter is located at 2210 East Highland Ave., #106, San Bernardino, CA 92404; (909) 863-9963. Brings couples together for a weekend program of events directed by a team of several couples and a priest, to develop their abilities to communicate with each other as husband and wife.

Maryheart Crusaders, The (1964): 22 Button St., Meriden, CT 06450; (203) 239-5979; www.maryheart crusaders.org. Pres., Louise D'Angelo.

Men of the Sacred Heart (1964): National Shrine of the Sacred Heart, P.O. Box 500, Harleigh, PA 18225; (570) 455-1162. Promotes enthronement of Sacred Heart.

Militia Immaculate National Center — Marytown (1917): 1600 W. Park Ave., Libertyville, IL 60048; (847) 367-7800; www.consecration.com. Canonically established with international headquarters in Rome. A pious association to promote total consecration to Mary in the spirit of St. Maximilian Kolbe. Pres., Fr. Patrick Greenough, O.F.M. Conv.

Missionary Association of Catholic Women (1916): 3501 S. Lake Dr., P.O. Box 07212, Milwaukee, WI 53207-0912; (414) 769-3406.

Missionary Vehicle Association, Inc. (MIVA America) (1971): 1400 Michigan Ave., N.E., Washington, DC 20017-7234; (202) 635-3444; www.miva.org. To raise funds and distribute them annually as vehicle grants to missionaries working with the poor in Third World countries. Nat. Dir., Rev. Philip De Rea, M.S.C.; Exec. Dir., Rev. Anthony F. Krisak.

Morality in Media, Inc. (1962): 475 Riverside Dr., New York, NY 10115; (212) 870-3222; www.morality-inmedia.org. Interfaith national organization. Works by constitutional means to curb the explosive growth of hard-core pornography and to turn back the tide of grossly offensive, indecent media. A major project is the National Obscenity Law Center which provides legal information for prosecutors and other attorneys. Newsletter, bimonthly. Pres., Robert W. Peters.

National Assembly of Religious Women (NARW): 529 S. Wabash Ave., Suite 404, Chicago, IL 60605; (312) 663-1980. Founded as the National Assembly of Women Religious, 1970; title changed, 1980. A movement of feminist women committed to prophetic tasks of giving witness, raising awareness and engaging in public action and advocacy for justice in church and society.

National Association for Lay Ministry (1977): 5420 S. Cornell Ave., Chicago, IL 60615; (773) 241-6050; www.nalm.org. Acts as advocate and support for lay people who respond to a call to ministry in the Church.

National Association of Catholic Family Life Ministers: 300 College Park, Dayton, OH 45469; (937) 229-3324; www.nacflm.org. Strives to be a voice and advocate for families and family ministry in Church and society. Exec. Dir., David Abele.

National Association of Catholic Home Educators (1993): 6102 Saints Hill Lane, Broad Run, VA 20137; (540) 349-4314; www.nache.com. Promotion of home-schooling. *The Catholic Home Educator*, quarterly.

National Association of Church Personnel Administrators (1971): 100 E. 8th St., Cincinnati, OH 45202; (513) 421-3134; www.nacpa.org. Association for human resource and personnel directors dedicated to promotion and development of just personnel practices for all church employees. Exec. Dir., Sr. Ellen Doyle, O.S.U.

National Association of Diaconate Directors: 1204 N. Church St., Rockford, IL 61103; (815) 965-0075. Exec. Dir., Deacon Thomas C. Welch.

National Association of Diocesan Ecumenical Officers: 7800 Kenrick Rd., St. Louis, MO 63119; (314) 961-4320. Network of Catholics involved in ecumenical and interreligious work. Pres., Vincent A. Heier.

National Association of Pastoral Musicians (1976): 962 Wayne Ave., Suite 210, Silver Spring, MD 20910; (240) 247-3000; www.npm.org. 9,000 members. Dedicated to fostering the art of musical liturgy. *Pastoral Music*, six times a year. Exec. Dir., Dr. J. Michael McMahon.

National Association of Priest Pilots (1964): 481 N. Shore Dr., Apt. 301, Clear Lake, IA 50428-1368; (641) 357-4539. Pres., Rev. Msgr. John Hemann.

National Catholic AIDS Network: P.O. Box 422984, San Francisco, CA 94142; (707) 874-3031; www.ncan.org. Exec. dir., Rev. Rodney DeMartini; Board Pres., Rev. Robert J. Vitillo.

National Catholic Band Association (1953): 3334 N. Normandy, Chicago, IL 60634; (773) 282-9153; www.catholicbands.org.

National Catholic Conference for Interracial Justice (NCCIJ) (1960): 1200 Varnum St. N.E., Washington, DC 20017; (202) 529-6480. Exec. Dir., Rev. Mr. Joseph M. Conrad, Jr.

National Catholic Conference for Seafarers: 4219 Constance St., New Orleans, LA 70115; (504) 891-6677. Association of chaplains and laity serving in the pastoral care of seafarers.

National Catholic Council on Alcoholism and Related Drug Problems, Inc.: 1550 Hendrickson St., Brooklyn, NY 11234-3514; (718) 951-7177. P.O. Box 248, Lafayette, IN 47902-0248; (765) 420-0129; www.nccatoday.com. An affiliate of the USCCB. Committed to assisting members in a greater awareness of alcoholism, other chemical addictions and prevention issues. Exec. Dir., Thomas A. Russell.

National Catholic Development Conference (1968): 86 Front St., Hempstead, NY 11550; (516) 481-6000. Professional association of organizations and individuals engaged in raising funds for Catholic charitable activities. Pres., Sr. Georgette Lehmuth, O.S.F.

National Catholic Ministry to the Bereaved (NCMB) (1990): 28700 Euclid Ave., Wickliffe, OH, 44092-2527; (440) 943-3480; www.griefwork.org. Offers ongoing education, resources and assistance to dioceses, parishes and caregivers in their ministry to the bereaved. Pres., Sr. Maureen O'Brien, O.P.

National Catholic Pharmacists Guild of the United States (1962): 1012 Surrey Hills Dr., St. Louis, MO 63117; (314) 645-0085. *The Catholic Pharmacist.* Co-Pres., Exec. Dir. and Editor, John P. Winkelmann.

National Catholic Society of Foresters (1891): 320 S. School St., Mt. Prospect, IL 60056; (847) 342-4500; www.ncsf@enteract.com. A fraternal insurance society. *National Catholic Forester,* quarterly. Pres. and CEO, Sue Koleczek.

National Catholic Women's Union (1916): 3835 Westminster Pl., St. Louis, MO 63108; (314) 371-1653; www.socialjustice.org. 7,000 members.

National Center for the Laity (1977): P.O. Box 291102, Chicago, IL 60629; (708) 974-5221; wwwcatholic labot.org/ncl.htm. To promote and implement the vision of Vatican II: That the laity are the Church in the modern world as they attend to their occupational, family and neighborhood responsibilities. *Initiatives,* six times a year.

National Center for Urban Ethnic Affairs (1971): P.O. Box 20, Cardinal Station, Washington, DC 20064; (202) 319-6188. Research and action related to the Church's concern for cultural pluralism and urban neighborhoods. An affiliate of the USCCB. Pres., Dr. John A. Kromkowski.

National Christ Child Society Inc. (1887): 6900 Wisconsin Ave. N.W., Suite 604, Bethesda, MD 20815; (800) 814-2149; www.NationalChristChildSoc.org. Founder, Mary V. Merrick. A non-profit Catholic association of volunteers of all denominations dedicated to the service of needy children and youth regardless of race or creed. Approximately 7,000 adult members in 38 chapters in U.S. Exec. Dir., Margaret Saffell.

National Committee of Catholic Laymen, The (1977): 215 Lexington Ave., Fourth Floor, New York, NY 10016; (212) 685-6666. Lobbying and publishing organization representing "orthodox" Catholics who strongly support Pope John Paul II. *Catholic Eye,* monthly; editor, Mrs. Anne Conlon.

National Conference of Catechetical Leadership (formerly, National Conference of Diocesan Directors of Religious Education) (1936): 3021 4th St. N.E., Washington, DC 20017; (202) 636-3826. To promote catechetical ministry at the national diocesan and parish levels. 1,300 members. Exec. Dir., Neil A. Parent.

National Conference of Catholic Airport Chaplains (1986): P.O. Box 66353, Chicago, IL 60666; (773) 686-2636. Provides support and communication for Catholics performing pastoral ministry to airport and airline workers and Catholic travelers; affiliated with Bishops' Committee on Migration, USCCB. Pres., Deacon James A. O'Malley, D.Min.

National Conference of Diocesan Vocation Directors (NCDVD) (1961): P.O. Box 1570, Little River, SC 29566; (843) 280-7191. Professional organization for diocesan vocation personnel providing resources and on-going education in their promoting, assessing and forming of candidates for the diocesan priesthood.

National Council for Catholic Evangelization (1983): 415 Michigan Ave, NE, Suite 90, Washington, DC, 20017; 1-800-786-NCCE; www.catholicevangelization.org. To promote evangelization as the "primary and essential mission of the Church," in accordance with *Evangelii Nuntiandi,* the 1975 apostolic exhortation of Pope Paul VI. Exec. Dir., Sr. Priscilla Lemire, R.J.M.

National Council of Catholic Women (1920): 200 N. Glebe Rd., Suite 703, Arlington, VA 22203; (703) 224-0990; www.nccw.org. A federation of some 7,000 organizations of Catholic women in the U.S. NCCW unites Catholic organizations and individual Catholic women of the U.S., develops their leadership potential, assists them to act upon current issues in the Church and society, provides a medium through which Catholic women may speak and act upon matters of common interest, and relates to other national and international organizations in the solution of present-day problems. It is an affiliate of the World Union of Catholic Women's Organizations. *Catholic Woman,* bimonthly. Exec. Dir., Sheila McCarron.

National Evangelization Teams (NET): 110 Crusader Ave., West St. Paul, MN 55118-4427; (651) 450-6833; www.netusa.org. Trains Catholic young adults to be evangelists to peers and high school/junior high youth through traveling retreat teams.

National Federation of Catholic Physicians' Guilds (1927): P.O. Box 757, Pewaukee, WI 53072; (262) 523-6201; www.cathmed.com. *Linacre Quarterly.* Exec. Dir., Robert H. Herzog.

National Federation of Priests' Councils (1968): 1337 West Ohio, Chicago, IL 60622-6490; (312) 226-3334; www.nfpc.org. To give priests' councils a representative voice in matters of presbyteral, pastoral and ministerial concern to the U.S. and the universal Church. *Touchstone,* quarterly. Pres., Rev. Donald J. Wolf; Exec. Dir., Bro. Bernard Stratman, S.M.

National Institute for the Word of God (1972): 487 Michigan Ave. N.E., Washington, DC 20017; (202) 529-0001; www.niwg.op.org/niwg. For renewed biblical preaching, Bible sharing and evangelization. Dir., Rev. John Burke, O.P.

National Life Center, Inc.: 686 N. Broad St., Woodbury, NJ 08096; (856) 848-1819, (800) 848-LOVE; www.national lifecenter.com. Interdenominational guidance and referral service organization offering pregnant women alternatives to abortion. Pres., Denise F. Cocciolone.

National Organization for Continuing Education of Roman Catholic Clergy, Inc. (1973): 1337 W. Ohio St., Chicago, IL 60622; (312) 226-1890. Membership: 152 dioceses, 66 religious provinces, 46 institutions, 49 individuals in

U.S., 18 associates outside U.S. Pres., Rev. Francis S. Tebbe, O.F.M.

National Pastoral Life Center: 18 Bleecker St., New York, NY 10012-2404; (212) 431-7825; www.nplc.org. *Church,* quarterly. Dir., Msgr. Philip Murnion.

National Service Committee of the Catholic Charismatic Renewal: Charismcenter USA, P.O. Box 628, Locust Grove, VA 22508; (540) 972-0225; www.nsc-hariscenter.org, www.iccrs.org. The mission of the National Service Committee is "to stir into flame the grace of Pentecost within and beyond the Church, to broaden and deepen the understanding that baptism in the Holy Spirit is the Christian inheritance of all, and to strengthen the Catholic Charismatic Renewal." Exec. Dir., Walter Matthews.

NETWORK, A Catholic Social Justice Lobby (1971): 801 Pennsylvania Ave. S.E., Suite 460, Washington, DC 20003; (202) 547-5556; www.networklobby.org. A national Catholic social justice lobby. *NETWORK Connection,* bimonthly. Nat. Coord., Kathy Thornton, R.S.M.

Nocturnal Adoration Society of the United States (1882): 184 E. 76th St., New York, NY 10021; (212) 288-5082. Nat. Dir., Rev. Mario Marzocchi, S.S.S.

North American Academy of Liturgy: c/o CSSR Executive Office, Valparaiso University, Valparaiso, IN 46383. Foster ecumenical and interreligious liturgical research, publication and dialogue on a scholarly level. *Proceedings,* annually. Pres., Alan Barthel.

North American Conference of Separated and Divorced Catholics (1972): P.O. Box 360, Richland, OR 97870; (541) 893-6089; www.nacsdc.com. Exec. Dir., Irene Varley.

North American Forum on the Catechumenate: 3033 Fourth St. NE, Washington, DC 20017; (202) 884-9758; www.naforum.org. An international network committed to the implementation of the Order of Christian Initiation of Adults. Exec. Dir., James Schellman.

Order of the Alhambra (1904): 4200 Leeds Ave., Baltimore, MD 21229; (410) 242-0660; www.OrderAlhambra.org. Fraternal society dedicated to assisting developmentally disabled and handicapped children. 7,000 members in U.S. and Canada. Exec. Dir., Roger J. Reid.

Our Lady's Rosary Makers (1949): 4611 Poplar Level Rd., Louisville, KY 40233; www.olrm.org. To supply missionaries with free rosaries for distribution throughout the world. *News Bulletin,* monthly. Pres., Michael Ford.

Paulist National Catholic Evangelization Association (1977): 3031 Fourth St., N.E., Washington, DC 20017-1102; (202) 832-5022; www.pncea.org. To work with unchurched and alienated Catholics; to develop, test and document contemporary ways in which Catholic parishes and dioceses can evangelize the unchurched and inactive Catholics. Share the Word, bimonthly magazine; *Evangelization Update,* bimonthly newsletter. Dir., Rev. Kenneth Boyack, C.S.P.

Philangeli (Friends of the Angels) (1949 in England; 1956 in U.S.): Viatorian Fathers, 1115 E. Euclid St., Arlington Heights, IL 60004.

Pious Union of Prayer (1898): St. Joseph's Home, P.O. Box 288, Jersey City, NJ 07303; (201) 798-4141. *St. Joseph's Messenger* and *Advocate of the Blind,* quarterly.

Polish Roman Catholic Union of America (1887): 984 N. Milwaukee Ave., Chicago, IL 60622; (773) 728-2600; www.prcua.org. Fraternal benefit society. *Narod Polski,* bimonthly. Sec.-Treas. Josephine Szarowicz.

Pontifical Mission for Palestine (1949): 1011 First Ave., New York, NY 10022-4195; (212) 826-1480; www.cnewa.org. A papal relief and development agency of the Holy See for the Middle East, with offices in New York, Vatican City, Amman, Beirut and Jerusalem. Pres., Msgr. Archim; Robert L. Stern, J.C.D.

Pontifical Missionary Union (1916): 366 Fifth Ave., New York, NY 10001; (212) 563-8700; www.world-missions-catholicchurch.org. To promote mission awareness among clergy, religious, candidates to priestly and religious life, and others engaged in pastoral ministry of the Church. Nat. Dir., Most Rev. William J. McCormack; Nat. Sec., Rev. Eugene LaVerdiere, S.S.S.

Population Research Institute (1989): 1190 Progress Drive, Suite 2D, P.O. Box 1559, Front Royal, VA 22630; (540) 622-5240; www.pop.org. Non-profit research and educational organization dedicated to objectively presenting the truth about population-related issues. *PRI Review,* a bimonthly newsletter, which reports on population news of interest from around the world. Pres., Steven W. Mosher.

Priests' Eucharistic League (1887): 5384 Wilson Mills Rd., Highland Heights, OH 44143. *Emmanuel,* 10 issues a year. Nat. Dir., Very Rev. Norman Pelletier, S.S.S.

Pro Ecclesia Foundation (1970): 350 Fifth Ave., New York, NY 10118. *Pro Ecclesia Magazine.* Pres., Dr. Timothy A. Mitchell.

Pro Maria Committee (1952): 112 Norris Rd. Tyngsboro, MA 01879; (978) 649-1813. Promotes devotion to Our Lady of Beauraing (see **Index**).

Pro Sanctity Movement: Pro Sanctity Spirituality Center, 205 S. Pine Dr., Fullerton, CA 92833; (714) 956-1020. 730 E. 87th St., Brooklyn, NY 11236, (718) 649-0324. 6762 Western Ave., Omaha, NE 68132; (402) 553-4418. 1102 N. 204 St. Elkhorn, NE 68022; (402) 289-2670; www.prosanctity.org. Organized to spread God's call of all persons to holiness.

Project Children (1975): P.O. Box 933, Greenwood Lake, NY 10925; (845) 477-3472; www.interwebinc.com/children. Nonsectarian volunteer group; provides children of Northern Ireland with a six-week summer vacation with host families in the U.S.

The Providence Association of the Ukrainian Catholics in America (Ukrainian Catholic Fraternal Benefit Society) (1912): 817 N. Franklin St., Philadelphia, PA 19123; (215) 627-4984.

Queen of the Americas Guild, Inc. (1979): P.O. Box 851, St. Charles, IL 60174; (630) 584-1822; www.queenoftheamericasguild.org. To build English information center and retreat center near Basilica in Mexico City and spread the message of Guadalupe. 7,000 members. Nat. Coord., Rebecca Nichols.

Raskob Foundation for Catholic Activities, Inc. (1945): P.O. Box 4019, Wilmington, DE 19807-0019; (302) 655-4440; www.rfca.org. Exec. Pres., Frederick Perella, Jr.

Reparation Society of the Immaculate Heart of Mary, Inc. (1946): 100 E. 20th St., Baltimore, MD 21218. *Fatima Findings,* monthly.

Retrouvaille: P.O.Box 25, Kelton, PA 19346. A ministry to hurting marriages, Retrouvaille consists of a weekend experience with follow-up sessions designed to provide couples with ways and means of healing and reconciling. Emphasis is placed on communication, enabling husband and wife to rediscover each other and to examine their lives in a new and positive way. The ministry is neither a retreat nor a sensitivity group, nor does it include group dynamics or discussions. The program is conducted by trained couples and priests, with programs offered under the auspices of diocesan family life agencies. International Coordinating Team, Bill and Peg Swaan.

Sacred Heart League: 6050 Hwy 61 N, P.O. Box 190, Walls, MS 38680. Pres., Rev. Robert Hess, S.C.J.

St. Ansgar's Scandinavian Catholic League (1910): 3 East 28th St., New York, NY 10016; (212) 675-0400. Prayers and financial support for Church in Scandinavia. *St. Ansgar's Bulletin*, annually. 1,000 members. Pres., Astrid M. O'Brien.

St. Anthony's Guild (1924): P.O. 2948, Paterson, NJ 07509-2948; (973) 777-3737. Promotes devotion to St. Anthony of Padua and support for formation programs, infirm friars and ministries of the Franciscans of Holy Name Province. *The Anthonian*, quarterly. Dir., Fr. Joseph Hertel, O.F.M.

St. Bernadette Institute of Sacred Art (1993): P.O. Box 8249, Albuquerque, NM 87198-8249; (505) 265-9126; www.nmia.com/~paulos. To promote, initiate, encourage interest and sustain projects and persons engaged in sacred art.

St. Gregory Foundation for Latin Liturgy (1989): Newman House, 21 Fairview Ave., Mt. Poconi, PA 18344; (570) 839-2185. To promote within the Church in the U.S. the use of the Latin language in the Mass in accordance with the teachings of Vatican II. Founder and Pres., Rev. Peter M.J. Stravinskas, Ph.D., S.T.D.

St. Jude League (1929): 205 W. Monroe St., Chicago, IL 60606; (312) 236-7782; www.stjude-league.org. Promotes devotion to St. Jude; supports work of Claretian Missionaries throughout the world. Dir., Rev. Mark J. Brummel, C.M.F.

St. Margaret of Scotland Guild, Inc. (1938): Graymoor, P.O. Box 300, Garrison, NY 10524-0300; (845) 424-3671. Moderator, Bro. Pius MacIsaac.

St. Martin de Porres Guild (1935): 141 E. 65th St., New York, NY 10021; (212) 744-2410; www.op-stjoseph.org. Dir., Rev. Raymond F. Halligan, O.P.

Serra International (1934): 220 S. State St., Suite 1703, Chicago, IL 60604; (312) 588-0700; www.serrainternational.org. Fosters vocations to the priesthood, and religious life, trains Catholic lay leadership. Formally aggregated to the Pontifical Society for Priestly Vocations, 1951. *Serran*, bimonthly. 21,000 members in 673 clubs in 35 countries. Exec. Dir., John W. Woodward.

Slovak Catholic Federation (1911): 408 North Main St., Taylor, PA 18517-1108; (570) 562-1341; www.slovakcatholicfederation.org. Founded by Rev. Joseph Murgas to promote and coordinate religious activities among Slovak Catholic fraternal societies, religious communities and Slovak ethnic parishes in their effort to address themselves to the special needs of Slovak Catholics in the U.S. and Canada. Pres., Rev. Philip A. Altavilla.

Slovak Catholic Sokol (1905): 205 Madison St., Passaic, NJ 07055; (973) 777-2606; www.slovak-catholicsokol.org. Fraternal benefit society. *Slovak Catholic Falcon*, weekly. 38,000 members.

Society for the Propagation of the Faith (1822): 366 Fifth Ave., New York, NY 10001; (212) 563-8725 (fax); www.propfaith.org. Established in all dioceses. Church's principal instrument for promoting mission awareness and generating financial support for the missions. General fund for ordinary and extraordinary subsidies for all mission dioceses. Is subject to Congregation for the Evangelization of Peoples. *Mission*, four times a year; *Director's Newsletter*, monthly. Nat. Dir., Rev. John Kozar.

Society of St. Monica (1986): 215 Falls Ave., Cuyahoga Falls, OH 44221. Confident, daily prayer for the return of inactive Catholics and Catholics who have left the Church. More than 10,000 members worldwide. Founder and Spir. Dir., Rev. Dennis M. McNeil.

Society of St. Peter Apostle (1889): 366 Fifth Ave., New York, NY 10001; (212) 563-8700; www.world-missions-catholicchurch.org. Church's central fund for support of seminaries, seminarians and novices in all mission dioceses. Nat. Dir., Rev. John Kozar.

Society of the Divine Attributes (1974): 2905 Castlegate Ave., Pittsburgh, PA 15226; (412) 456-3114. Contemplative prayer society. 3,000 members worldwide (lay, clerical and religious). Spir. Dir., Rev. Ronald D. Lawler, O.F.M. Cap.

Spiritual Life Institute of America (1960): Box 219, Crestone, CO 81131; (719) 256-4778; www.spirituallifeinstitute.org. An eremetical movement to foster the contemplative spirit in America. Forefront, seasonal. Founder, Rev. William McNamara, O.C.D. Second foundation: Nova Nada, Primitive Wilderness Hermitage, Kemptville, Nova Scotia, Canada B0W 1Y0. Third foundation, Holy Hill Hermitage, Skreen, Co. Sligo, Ireland.

Support Our Aging Religious (SOAR) (1986): 1400 Spring St., Suite 320, Silver Spring, MD 20910-2755; (301) 589-9811; www.soar-usa.org. Laity-led campaign to raise funds for retired religious. Pres., Timothy P. Hamer.

Theresians of the United States (1961): 1237 W. Monroe, Springfield, IL 62704; (217) 726-5484; www.theresians.org. Spiritual, educational and ministerial organization of Christian women. Exec. Dir., Victoria S. Schmidt. International division: Theresian World Ministry (1971), same address.

United Societies of U.S.A. (1903): 613 Sinclair St., McKeesport, PA 15132. *Prosvita-Enlightenment*, bimonthly newspaper. 3,755 members.

United States Catholic Historical Society (1884): St. Joseph's Seminary, 201 Seminary Ave., Yonkers, NY 10704; (914) 337-8381; www.uschs.com. Exec. Vice-Pres., John T. Gildea.

Western Catholic Union (1877): 510 Maine St., Quincy, IL 62301; (800) 223-4928; www.wculife.com. 19,000 members. A fraternal benefit society. *Western Catholic Union Record*, quarterly. Pres., Mark A. Wiewel.

Women for Faith and Family (1984): P.O. Box 8326, St. Louis, MO 63132; (314) 863-8385; www.wf-f.org. An international movement to promote Catholic teachings especially on all issues involving the family and roles for women. 60,000 signers worldwide of the Affirmation for Catholic Women. Members sign an eight-point statement of fidelity to the Church. *Voices*, quarterly. Dir., Helen Hull Hitchcock.

Young Ladies' Institute (1887): 1111 Gough St., San Francisco, CA 94109-6606; (415) 346-4367. *Voice*

of YLI, bimonthly. 13,000 members. Grand Sec., Frances Ridley.

Young Men's Institute (1883): 1625 "C" Palmetto Ave., Pacifica, CA 94044; (650) 738-3007; www.ymiusa.org. *Institute Journal*, bimonthly. 4,500 members. Grand Sec., Clifford C. Smethurst.

PERSONAL PRELATURE OF THE HOLY SEE: OPUS DEI

Founded in Madrid in 1928 by Msgr. Josemaría Escrivá de Balaguer (beatified in 1992 and canonized in October 2002), Opus Dei has the aim of spreading throughout all sectors of society a profound awareness of the universal call to holiness and apostolate (of Christian witness and action) in the ordinary circumstances of life, and, more specifically, through one's professional work. On Nov. 28, 1982, Pope John Paul II established Opus Dei as a personal prelature with the full title, Prelature of the Holy Cross and Opus Dei. The 2006 edition of the *Annuario Pontificio* reported that the prelature had 1,790 priests (39 newly ordained) and 355 major seminarians. Also, there were 85,214 lay persons – men and women, married and single, of every class and social condition — of about 80 nationalities, as well as 1,790 churches and pastoral centers.

Further, the prelature operates the Pontifical University of the Holy Cross in Rome; it was established in 1985 and received approval as a pontifical institution in 1995. Courses of study include theology, philosophy, canon law, and the recently established School of Social Communications.

In the United States, members of Opus Dei, along with cooperators and friends, conduct apostolic works corporately in major cities in the East and Midwest, Texas and on the West Coast. Elsewhere, corporate works include universities, vocational institutes, training schools for farmers and numerous other apostolic initiatives. Opus Dei information offices are located at: 99 Overlook Cir., New Rochelle, NY 10804; (914) 235-6128 (office of the New York chaplain); and 655 Levering Ave., Los Angeles, CA 90024; (310) 208-0941; www.opusdei.org.

KNIGHTS OF COLUMBUS

The Knights of Columbus, a fraternal benefit society of Catholic men, is a family service organization founded by Fr. Michael J. McGivney and chartered by the General Assembly of Connecticut on Mar. 29, 1882.

Currently, there are over 1.6 million Knights, more than ever before in the Order's history. Together with their families, the Knights are nearly 6 million strong. From the first local council in New Haven, the Order has grown to more than 12,000 councils in the United States, Canada, Mexico, the Philippines, Puerto Rico, Cuba, the Dominican Republic, Panama, the Virgin Islands, Guatemala, Guam and Saipan.

In keeping with their general purpose to be of service to the Church, the Knights and their families are active in many apostolic works and community programs. The Knights cooperate with the U.S. bishops in pro-life activities and are engaged in other apostolic endeavors as well.

According to the 2004 Survey of Fraternal Activity in 2003 the Knights raised and donated over $128.5 million to charity and volunteered more than 60 million hours of service. Of the $128.5 million raised and donated in 2003, $106 million was raised locally and donated directly to charities chosen by K of C units raising the funds; the remaining $22.3 million was given by the Knights of Columbus Supreme Council and its designated charities from its headquarters. The Knights also leapt into action in response to the devastation caused by Hurricane Katrina; by the end of 2005, members had raised

over $3 million. In May 2006, the Knights announced that they will provide an $8 million grant to The Catholic University of America for the renovation of a prominent building on the university's campus.

In 2002 members raised and contributed to charity more than $128.5 million and volunteered more than 60 million hours of service. In 2001, the Knights raised and donated $120 million and 58 million volunteer hours. Twenty years ago, the Knights reported raising and donating to charity $52 million and volunteering 13.4 million hours of service. In the decade of the 1990s, the Knights donated nearly $1 billion to numerous charitable causes and nearly 400 million hours of volunteer service.

The programmatic activities of the Knights remain much the same from one year to the next. The K of C funded the restoration of the Maderno Atrium of St. Peter's Basilica in Rome, named for the architect, Carlo Maderno (1556-1629). The atrium is the big "front porch" through which every visitor to St. Peter's passes. This is one of a series of projects for the restoration of St. Peter's funded by the Knights over the years: renovation of the roof of the Blessed Sacrament Chapel (1993); renovation of the Room of the Architects and Room of the Window Panes (1987-88); restoration of the facade (1985-86); construction of chapels in the grottoes (1981-82).

The Knights of Columbus headquarters address is One Columbus Plaza, New Haven, CT 06510-3326; (203) 752-4350; www.kofc.org. The Grand Knight is Carl Anderson.

Catholic Social Services

Catholic Charities USA (formerly National Conference of Catholic Charities): 1731 King St., Suite 200, Alexandria, VA 22314; (703) 549-1390; www.catholiccharitiesusa.org. Founded in 1910 by Most Rev. Thomas J. Shahan and Rt. Rev. Msgr. William J. Kerby in cooperation with lay leaders of the Society of St. Vincent de Paul to help advance and promote the charitable programs and activities of Catholic community and social service agencies in the United States. As the central and national organization for this purpose, it services a network of more than 1,400 agencies and institutions by consultation, information and assistance in planning and evaluating social service programs under Catholic auspices.

Diocesan member agencies provide shelter, food, counseling, services to children, teen parents and the elderly, and a variety of other services to people in need — without regard to religion, gender, age or national origin. Each year millions of people receive help from Catholic Charities; in 1995 (latest statistics available), more than 10 million turned to Catholic Charities agencies for help. In addition, Catholic Charities is an advocate for persons and families in need.

Catholic Charities USA serves members through national and regional meetings, training programs, literature and social policy advocacy on the national level. It is charged by the U.S. bishops with responding to disasters in this country. Catholic Charities USA's president represents North America before *Caritas Internationalis*, the international conference of Catholic Charities, and thus maintains contact with the Catholic Charities movement throughout the world. Publications include *Charities USA*, a quarterly membership magazine, and a directory of U.S. Catholic Charities agencies and institutions. Pres., Rev. Larry Snyder.

Society of St. Vincent de Paul, Council of the United States (originally called the Conference of Charity): National Council, 58 Progress Parkway, St. Louis, MO 63043; (314) 576-3993; www.svdpuscouncil.org. An association of Catholic lay men and women devoted to personal service to the poor through the spiritual and corporal works of mercy. The first conference was formed at Paris in 1833 by Bl. Frederic Ozanam and his associates.

The first conference in the U.S. was organized in 1845 at St. Louis. There are now approximately 4,400 units of the society in this country, with a membership of more than 60,000. The society operates world wide in more than 130 countries and has more than 800,000 members.

Besides person-to-person assistance, increasing emphasis is being given to stores and rehabilitation workshops of the society through which persons with marginal income can purchase refurbished goods at minimal cost. Handicapped persons are employed in renovating goods and store operations. The society also operates food centers, shelters, criminal justice and other programs. Publications include *The Ozanam News*, a biannual membership magazine, and *The United States Councilor*, a quarterly newsletter. Nat. Pres., Eugene Smith; Exec. Dir., Richard Hennicke.

Catholic Health Association of the United States (CHA): National Headquarters, 4455 Woodson Road, St. Louis, MO 63134; (314) 427-2500; www.chusa.org. Represents more than 1,200 Catholic-sponsored facilities and organizations, works with its members to promote justice and compassion in healthcare, influence public policy, shape a continuum of care through integrated delivery, and strengthen ministry presence and influence in the U.S. healthcare system. CHA supports and strengthens the Catholic health ministry by being a catalyst through research and development (leading edge tools for sustaining a faith-based ministry in price competitive markets), education and facilitation (annual assembly, conferences, and other methods for engaging the ministry), and advocacy (a united ministry voice for public policy). CHA members make up the nation's largest group of not-for-profit healthcare facilities under a single form of sponsorship. Pres., Rev. Michael D. Place, S.T.D.

National Association of Catholic Chaplains: 3501 S. Lake Dr., Milwaukee, WI 53207; (414) 483-4898. Founded in 1965. Membership is over 3,500.

SOCIAL SERVICE ORGANIZATIONS

(See separate article for a listing of facilities for the handicapped.)

The Carroll Center for the Blind (formerly the Catholic Guild for All the Blind): 770 Centre St., Newton, MA 02458; (617) 969-6200; www.carroll.org. The center conducts diagnostic evaluation and rehabilitation programs for blind people over 16 years of age, and provides computer training and other services. Pres., Rachel Rosenbaum.

International Catholic Deaf Association: 8002 S. Sawyer Rd., Darian, IL 60561; TTY (630) 887-9472. Established by deaf adults in Toronto, Canada, in 1949, the association has more than 8,000 members in 130 chapters, mostly in the U.S. It is the only international lay association founded and controlled by deaf Catholic adults. The ICDA publishes *The Deaf Catholic*, bimonthly, sponsors regional conferences, workshops and an annual convention. Pres., Kathleen Kush.

National Apostolate for Inclusion Ministry

(NAfIM): P.O. Box 218, Riverdale, MD, 20738; (301) 699-9500; www.nafim.org. Formerly known as the National Apostolate for Persons with Mental Retardation (NAPMR). Established in 1968 to promote the full participation by persons with mental retardation in the life of the Church. Exec. Dir., Barbara Lampe.

National Catholic Office for the Deaf: 7202 Buchanan St., Landover Hills, MD 20784; (301) 577-1684; www.ncod.org. Formally established in 1971, at Washington, DC, to provide pastoral service to those who teach deaf children and adults, to the parents of deaf children, to pastors of deaf persons, and to organizations of the deaf. Publishes *Vision*, a quarterly magazine. Exec. Dir., Arvilla Rank.

National Catholic Office Partnership on Disability (NCPD): 415 Michigan Ave., N.E., Suite 240, Washington, DC 20017; (202) 529-2933; www.ncpd.org. NCPD's mission is to provide resources and consultation to a national network of diocesan directors who oversee access and inclusion at the parish level; to collaborate with other national Catholic organizations, advocating for inclusion within all their programs and initiatives and to work with Catholic organizations addressing the concerns and needs of those with various disabilities. Established in 1982 as a result of the 1978 Pastoral Statement of the U.S. Catholic Bishops on People with Disabilities., the office continues to press for words and actions which promote meaningful participation and inclusion at all levels of the Church. Exec. Dir., Mary Jane Owen, M.S.W.

Xavier Society for the Blind: 154 E. 23rd St., New York, NY 10010-4595; (212) 473-7800. Founded in 1900 by Rev. Joseph Stadelman, S.J., it is a center for publications for the blind and partially sighted. Exec. Dir., Rev. Alfred E. Caruana, S.J.

OTHER SOCIAL SERVICES

Cancer Hospitals or Homes: The following homes or hospitals specialize in the care of cancer patients. Capacities are in parentheses.

Our Lady of Perpetual Help Home, Servants of Relief for Incurable Cancer, 760 Pollard Blvd., S.W., Atlanta, GA 30315; (404) 688-9515 (52).

Rose Hawthorne Lathrop Home, Servants of Relief for Incurable Cancer, 1600 Bay St., Fall River, MA 02724; (508) 673-2322 (35).

Our Lady of Good Counsel Home, Servants of Relief for Incurable Cancer, 2076 St. Anthony Ave., St. Paul, MN 55104; (651) 646-2797.

Calvary Hospital, Inc., 1740 Eastchester Rd., Bronx, NY 10461; (718) 863-6900 (200). Operated in connection with Catholic Charities, Department of Health and Hospitals, Archdiocese of New York.

St. Rose's Home, Servants of Relief for Incurable Cancer, 71 Jackson St., New York, NY 10002; (212) 677-8132 (60).

Rosary Hill Home, Servants of Relief for Incurable Cancer, 600 Linda Ave., Hawthorne, NY 10532; (914) 769-0114 (72).

Holy Family Home, Servants of Relief for Incurable Cancer, 6753 State Rd., Parma, OH 44134; (440) 845-7700; www.cle-dioc.org (50).

Sacred Heart Free Home for Incurable Cancer, Servants of Relief for Incurable Cancer, 1315 W. Hunting Park Ave., Philadelphia, PA 19140; (215) 329-3222 (45).

Substance Abuse: Facilities for substance abuse (alcohol and other drugs) include:

Daytop Village, Inc., 54 W. 40th St., New York, NY 10018; (212) 354-6000; www.daytop.org. Twenty-eight residential and ambulatory sites in New York, New Jersey, Pennsylvania, Florida, Texas and California. Msgr. William B. O'Brien, president.

Good Shepherd Gracenter, Convent of the Good Shepherd, 1310 Bacon St., San Francisco, CA 94134; (415) 586-2822. Residential program for chemically dependent women.

New Hope Manor, 35 Hillside Rd., Barryville, NY 12719; fax (914) 557-6603. Residential substance abuse treatment center for teen-age girls and women ages 13-40. Residential; half-way house and aftercare program totaling 6 months or more.

St. Joseph's Hospital, L.E. Phillips Libertas Center for the Chemically Dependent, 2661 County Road, Hwy. I, Chippewa Falls, WI 54729; (715) 723-1811 (46). Residential and outpatient. Adult and adolescent programs. Hospital Sisters of the Third Order of St. Francis.

St. Joseph's Hospital (Chippewa Falls, WI) Libertas Center for the Treatment of Chemical Dependency, 1701 Dousman St., Green Bay, WI 54302 (23). Residental and outpatient adolescent programs. Hospital Sisters of the Third Order of St. Francis.

St. Luke's Addiction Recovery Services, 7707 NW 2nd Ave., Miami, FL 33150; (305) 795-0077; www.catholicharitiesadm.org/stluke. A program of Catholic Community Services, Miami. Adult residential and family outpatient recovery services for drug, alcohol addiction and DUI.

Miami Substance Abuse Prevention Programs, 7707 N.W. Second Ave., Miami, FL 33150; (305) 795-0077; www.catholicharitiesadm.org/stluke. Trains parents, youth, priests and teachers as prevention volunteers in the area of substance abuse.

Transitus House, 1830 Wheaton St., Chippewa Falls, WI 54729; (715) 723-1155. Two programs for chemically dependent: adult intensive residential (15 beds, women); adolescent intensive residential (5 beds, girls 15-18 yrs.). Hospital Sisters of the Third Order of St. Francis.

Matt Talbot Inn, 2270 Professor Ave., Cleveland, OH 44113; (216) 781-0288. Two programs: Chemical dependency Residential Treatment/Halfway House (capacity 27) and outpatient treatment/aftercare. Serves male clients 18 years and over.

Sacred Heart Rehabilitation Center, Inc., 2203 St. Antoine, Detroit, MI 48201 (admissions/assessment, outpatient). 400 Stoddard Rd., P.O. Box 41038, Memphis, MI 48041 (12 beds, detoxification; 70 beds residential treatment). 28573 Schoenherr, Warren, MI 48093 (outpatient). All facilities serve male and female clients 18 and over.

Straight and Narrow, Inc., 396 Straight St., Paterson, NJ 07501. Facilities and services include (at various locations): Straight and Narrow Hospital (Mount Carmel Guild), substance abuse, detoxification (20 beds); Alpha House for Drug and Alcohol Rehabilitation (women; 30 beds — 25 adults, 5 children); Dismas House for Drug and Alcohol Rehabilitation (men; 78 beds); The Guild for Drug and Alcohol Rehabilitation (men, 56 beds); juvenile residential units; outpatient services and facility; three halfway houses; counseling services; employment assistance; intoxicated driver's resource center; medical day care center (available to HIV infected persons and persons diagnosed with AIDS); methadone clinic. The National Catholic Council on Alcoholism and Related Drug Problems, Inc., 1550 Hendrickson St., Brooklyn, NY 11234. Offers educational material to those involved in pastoral ministry on ways of dealing with problems related to alcoholism and medication dependency.

Convicts: Priests serve as full- or part-time chaplains in penal and correctional institutions throughout the country. Limited efforts have been made to assist in the rehabilitation of released prisoners in Halfway House establishments.

Dining Rooms: Facilities for homeless: Representative of places where meals are provided, and in some cases lodging and other services as well, are:

St. Anthony Foundation, 121 Golden Gate Ave., San Francisco, CA 94102; (415) 241-2600; www.stanthonyfdn.org. Founded in 1950 by the Franciscan Friars. Multi-program social service agency serving people who are poor and homeless. Dining room serves up to 2,100 meals daily; more than 25 million since its founding. Other services include free clothing and furniture; free medical clinic; residential drug and alcohol rehabilitation programs; employment program; emergency shelter, housing and daytime facility for homeless women; residence for low-income senior women; free hygiene services; case management for seniors; social services.

St. Vincent de Paul Free Dining Room, 675 23rd St., Oakland, CA 94612; (510) 451-7676. Administered by Daughters of Charity of St. Vincent de Paul, under sponsorship of St. Vincent de Paul Society. Hot meals served at lunch time 7 days a week. Also provides counseling, referral/information services.

St. Vincent's Dining Room, P.O. Box 5099, Reno, NV 89513; (775) 329-5363.

St. Vincent Dining Room, 1501 Las Vegas Blvd., Las Vegas, NV 89101. Structured program for 275 men in which job development office works with homeless to enable them to find employment. For non-residents, there is a hot meal every day at noon. Emergency overnight shelter facility for families, women and men.

Good Shepherd Center, Little Brothers of the Good Shepherd, 218 Iron St. S.W., P.O. Box 749, Albuquerque, NM 87103; (505) 243-2527.

Holy Name Center for Homeless Men, Inc., 18 Bleecker St., New York, NY 10012. A shelter for alcoholic, homeless men. Provides social services and aid to transients and those in need. Affiliated with New York Catholic Charities.

St. Francis Inn, 2441 Kensington Ave., Philadelphia, PA 19125. Serves hot meals. Temporary shelter for men. Day center for women. Thrift shop.

St. John's Hospice for Men, staffed by Little Brothers of the Good Shepherd, 1221 Race St., Philadelphia, PA 19107. Hot meals served daily; 36-bed shelter; clothing distribution, showers, mail distribution, drug/alcohol rehabilitation and work programs. Good Shepherd Program of St. John's Hospice, 1225 Race St., Philadelphia, PA 19107. Ten-bed facility for homeless men with AIDS.

Camillus House, Little Brothers of the Good Shepherd, P.O. Box 11829, Miami, FL 33101; (305) 374-1065; www.camillus.org. Free comprehensive services for the poor and home-

less including daily dinner; night lodging for 70; clothing distribution; showers; mail distribution; drug/alcohol rehabilitation program. Forty-eight units of single-room housing for employed formerly homeless women and men who have completed drug and alcohol rehabilitation programs.

Camillus Health Concern, P.O. Box 12408, Miami, FL 33101; (305) 577-4840. Free comprehensive medical and social services for the homeless.

Shelters: Facilities for runaways, the abused, exploited and homeless include:

Anthony House, supported by St. Anthony's Guild (*see* **Index**). 38 E. Roosevelt Ave., Roosevelt, NY 11575 (with St. Vincent de Paul Society — for homeless men). 128 W. 112th St., New York, NY 10026 (emergency food and clothing). 6215 Holly St., P.O. Box 880, Zellwood, FL 32798 (for migrant workers and their families).

Good Shepherd Shelter-Convent of the Good Shepherd. Office, 2561 W. Venice Blvd., Los Angeles, CA 90019; (323) 737-6111. Non-emergency long-term shelter for battered women and their children.

Covenant House, 346 W. 17th St., New York, NY 10011; (212) 727-4973. President, Sister Mary Rose McGeady, D.C. Provides crisis care — food, shelter, clothing, medical treatment, job placement and counseling — for homeless youth without regard to race, creed, color and national origin. Locations: New York, New Jersey (Newark, Atlantic City), Houston, Ft. Lauderdale, New Orleans, Anchorage, Los Angeles, Detroit, Orlando, Washington, DC; Toronto (Canada), Tegucigalpa (Honduras), Guatemala City (Guatemala), Mexico City (Mexico).

Crescent House, 1000 Howard Ave., Suite 1200, New Orleans, LA 70113. Provides temporary shelter, counseling and advocacy for battered women and their children.

The Dwelling Place, 409 W. 40th St., New York, NY 10018; (212) 564-7887. For homeless women 30 years of age and over.

Gift of Hope, Missionaries of Charity, 724 N.W. 17th St., Miami, FL 33136; (305) 326-0032. Shelter for women and children; soup kitchen for men.

House of the Good Shepherd, 1114 W. Grace St., Chicago, IL 60613; (773) 935-3434. For abused women with children.

Mercy Hospice, 334 S. 13th St., Philadelphia, PA 19107; (215) 545-5153. Temporary shelter and relocation assistance for homeless women and children.

Mt. Carmel House, Carmelite Sisters, 471 G Pl., N.W., Washington, DC 20001. For homeless women.

Ozanam Inn, 843 Camp St., New Orleans, LA 70130. Under sponsorship of the St. Vincent de Paul Society. Hospice for homeless men.

St. Christopher Inn, P.O. Box 150, Graymoor, Garrison, NY 10524; (845) 424-3616; www.atonementfriars.org. Temporary shelter (21 days) for alcohol- and drug-free homeless and needy men.

Siena-Francis House, Inc., P.O. Box 217 D.T.S., Omaha, NE 68102. Two units, both at 1702 Nicholas St., Omaha, NE 68101; (402) 341-1821. Siena House (for homeless and abused women or women with children; provides 24-hour assistance and advocacy services); and Francis House (temporary shelter for homeless men). Also at this location: a 50-bed residential substance abuse program.

Unwed Mothers: Residential and care services for unwed mothers are available in many dioceses.

FACILITIES FOR RETIRED AND AGED PERSONS

Sources: Catholic Almanac *survey,* The Official Catholic Directory.

This list covers residence, health care and other facilities for the retired and aged under Catholic auspices. Information includes name, type of facility if not evident from the title, address, and total capacity (in parentheses); unless noted otherwise, facilities are for both men and women. Many facilities for the aged offer intermediate nursing care.

Alabama: Allen Memorial Home (skilled nursing), 735 S. Washington Ave., Mobile 36603; (334) 433-2642 (119).

Cathedral Place Apartments (retirement complex), 351 Conti St., Mobile 36602; (334) 434-1590 (184).

Mercy Medical (acute rehabilitation hospital, skilled and post-acute nursing, hospice, home Health and assisted and independent living), P.O. Box 1090, Daphne 36526; (334) 626-2694 (162). Not restricted to elderly.

Sacred Heart Residence Little Sisters of the Poor, 1655 McGill Ave., Mobile 36604; (251) 476-6335 (84).

Seton Haven (retirement complex), 3721 Wares Ferry Rd., Montgomery 36193; (334) 272-4000 (114).

Arizona: Guadalupe Senior Village, 222 W. Thomas Rd., Ste. 214, Phoenix, 85103; (602) 406-6218.

California: Alexis Apartments of St. Patrick's Parish, 756 Mission St. 94103; 390 Clementina St., San Francisco 94103; (415) 495-3690 (240).

Casa Manana Inn, 3700 N. Sutter St., Stockton 95204; (209) 466-4046 (162). Non-profit housing for low-income elderly over 62.

Cathedral Plaza, 1551 Third Ave., San Diego 92101; (619) 234-0093 (222 apartments).

Guadalupe Plaza, 4142 42nd St., San Diego 92105; (619) 584-2414 (147 apartments).

Jeanne d'Arc Manor, 85 S. Fifth St., San Jose 95112; (408) 288-7421 (145). For low income elderly and handicapped.

La Paz Villas, P.O. Box 1962, Palm Desert 92261; (760) 772-1382 (24 units).

Little Flower Haven (residential care facility for retired), 8585 La Mesa Blvd., La Mesa 91941; (619) 466-3163 (85).

Little Sisters of the Poor, St. Anne's Home, 300 Lake St., San Francisco 94118; (415) 751-6510 (90).

Little Sisters of the Poor, Jeanne Jugan Residence, 2100 South Western Ave., San Pedro 90732; (310) 548-0625 (100).

Madonna Senior Center and Residence, St. Anthony Foundation, 350 Golden Gate Ave., San Francisco 94102; (415) 592-2864; www.stanthonysf.org (37).

Marian Residence (retirement home), 124 S. College Dr., Santa Maria 93454; (805) 922-7731 (32).

Mercy McMahon Terrace (residential care facility), 3865 J St., Sacramento 95816; (916) 733-6510; www.mercysacramento.org (118 units).

Mercy Retirement and Care Center, 3431 Foothill Blvd., Oakland 94601; (510) 534-8540; www.mercyretirementcenter.org (59).

Mother Gertrude Home for Senior Citizens, 11320 Laurel Canyon Blvd., San Fernando 91340; (818) 898-1546 (98).

Nazareth House (residential and skilled care), 2121 N. 1st St., Fresno 93703; (559) 237-2257 (65 residential; 39 skilled nursing).

Nazareth House (residential and skilled nursing), 3333 Manning Ave., Los Angeles 90064; (310) 839-2361 (123).

Nazareth House (retirement home), 245 Nova Albion Way, San Rafael 94903; (415) 479-8282 (151).

Nazareth House Retirement Home, 6333 Rancho Mission Rd., San Diego 92108; (619) 563-0480 (354).

O'Connor Woods, 3400 Wagner Heights Rd., Stockton 95209; (209) 956-3464; www.oconnorwoods.org, (48).

Our Lady of Fatima Villa (skilled nursing facility), 20400 Saratoga-Los Gatos Rd., Saratoga 95070; (408) 741-2950; www.fatimavilla.org; (85).

St. Bernardine Plaza (retirement home), 550 W. 5th St., San Bernardino 92401; (909) 888-0153 (150 units).

St. John of God (retirement and care center), 2468 S. St. Andrew Place, Los Angeles 90018; (323) 731-0641; www.hospitallers.org, (215).

Vigil Light Apartments, 1945 Long Dr., Santa Rosa 95405; (707) 544-2810 (54).

Villa Scalabrini (retirement center and skilled nursing Care), 10631 Vinedale St., Sun Valley 91352; (818) 768-6500; www.villascalabrini.com (130 residence; 58 skilled nursing).

Villa Siena (residence and skilled nursing care), 1855 Miramonte Ave., Mountain View 94040; (650) 961-6484; www.vsiena.org (56, residence; 20, skilled nursing care).

Colorado: Francis Heights, Inc., 2626 Osceola St., Denver 80212; (303) 433-6268 (384 units; 411 residents).

Gardens at St. Elizabeth (congregate housing and assisted living), 2835 W. 32nd Ave., Denver 80211; (303) 964-2005 (320).

Little Sisters of the Poor, 3629 W. 29th Ave., Denver 80211; (303) 433-7221 (70).

Connecticut: Augustana Homes (residence), Simeon Rd., Bethel 06801; (203) 743-2508.

Carmel Ridge, 6454 Main St., Trumbull 06611; (203) 261-2229.

Holy Family Home and Shelter, Inc., 88 Jackson St., P.O. Box 884, Willimantic 06226; (860) 423-7719; www.holyfamilywillimantic.org (155).

Monsignor Bojnowski Manor, Inc. (skilled nursing facility), 50 Pulaski St., New Britain 06053; (860) 229-0336 (60).

Notre Dame Convalescent Home, 76 West Rocks Rd., Norwalk 06851; (203) 847-5893 (60).

St. Joseph Living Center, 14 Club Rd., Windham 06280; (860) 456-1107 (120).

St. Joseph's Manor (health care facility; home for aged), Carmelite Srs. for Aged and Infirm, 6448 Main St., Trumbull 06611; (203) 268-6204; www.stjosephmanor.org; (297).

St. Joseph's Residence, Little Sisters of the Poor, 1365 Enfield St., Enfield 06082; (860) 741-0791 (84).

St. Lucian's Home for the Aged, 532 Burritt St., New

Britain 06053; (860) 223-2123 (42).

St. Mary's Home (residence and health care facility) 2021 Albany Ave., W. Hartford 06117; (860) 570-8200 (26).

Delaware: The Antonian, 1701 W. 10th St., Wilmington 19805; (302) 421-3758 (136 apartments).

Jeanne Jugan Residence, Little Sisters of the Poor, 185 Salem Church Rd., Newark 19713; (302) 368-5886 (80).

Marydale Retirement Village, 135 Jeandell Dr., Newark 19713; (302) 368-2784 (118 apartments).

St. Patrick's House, Inc., 115 E. 14th St., Wilmington 19801; (302) 654-6908 (12).

District of Columbia: Jeanne Jugan Residence-St. Joseph Villa, Little Sisters of the Poor, 4200 Harewood Rd., N.E., Washington 20017; (202) 269-1831; www.lspasa.org (73).

Florida: All Saints Home, 5888 Blanding Blvd., Jacksonville 32244; (904) 772-1220; www.allsaints.org (118).

Casa Calderon, Inc. (retirement apartments), 800 W. Virginia St., Tallahassee 32304; (850) 222-4026 (111).

Haven of Our Lady of Peace (assisted living and nursing home), 5203 N. 9th Ave., Pensacola 32504; (850) 477-0531 (89).

Palmer House, Inc., 1225 S.W. 107th Ave., Miami 33174; (305) 221-9566 (120 apartments).

St. Andrew Towers (retirement apartments), 2700 N.W. 99th Ave., Coral Springs 33065 (432).

St. Catherine Labouré (skilled and intermediate care), 1750 Stockton St., Jacksonville 32204; (904) 308-4700 (239).

St. Dominic Gardens (retirement apartments), 5849 N.W. 7th St., Miami 33126 (149 apartments).

St. Elizabeth Gardens, Inc. (retirement apartments), 801 N.E. 33rd St., Pompano Beach 33064 (150).

St. John's Rehabilitation Hospital and Nursing Center, Inc., 3075 N.W. 35th Ave., Lauderdale Lakes 33311.

Stella Maris House, Inc., 8636 Harding Ave., Miami Beach 33141 (136 apartments).

Illinois: Addolorata Villa (sheltered intermediate, skilled care facility; apartments), 555 McHenry Rd., Wheeling 60090; (847) 808-6168 (100 apartments).

Alvernia Manor (sheltered care), 13950 Main St., Lemont 60439; (630) 257-7721 (50).

Bishop Conway Residence, 1900 N. Karlov Ave., Chicago 60639; (773) 252-9941.

Carlyle Healthcare Center, 501 Clinton St., Carlyle 62231; (618) 594-3112 (131).

Carmelite Carefree Village, 8419 Bailey Rd., Darien 60561; (630) 960-4060 (98).

Cortland Manor Retirement Home, 1900 N. Karlov, Chicago 60639; (773) 235-3670 (48).

Holy Family Nursing and Rehabilitation Center, 2380 Dempster, Des Plaines 60016; (847) 296-3335 (362).

Holy Family Villa (intermediate care facility), 12395 McCarthy Rd., Lemont 60439; (630) 257-7721 (50).

Jugan Terrace, Little Sisters of the Poor, 2300 N. Racine, Chicago 60614; (773) 935-9600 (50 apartments).

Little Sisters of the Poor, St. Joseph's Home for the

Elderly, 80 W. Northwest Hwy., Palatine 60067; (847) 358-5700 (61).

Little Sisters of the Poor Center for the Aging, 2325 N. Lakewood Ave., Chicago 60614; (773) 935-9600 (71).

Marian Heights Apartments (elderly, handicapped), 20 Marian Heights Dr., Alton 62002; (618) 462-0363 (130).

Marian Park, Inc., 26 W. 171 Roosevelt Rd., Wheaton 60187; (630) 665-9100 (470).

Maryhaven, Inc. (skilled and intermediate care facility), 1700 E. Lake Ave., Glenview 60025; (847) 729-1300 (138).

Mayslake Village (retirement apartments), 1801 35th St., Oak Brook 60523; (630) 850-8232; www.mayslake.com (630 apartments).

Mercy Residence at Tolentine Center, 20300 Governors Hwy., Olympia Fields 60461; (708) 748-9500 (48).

Meredith Memorial Home, 16 S. Illinois St., Belleville 62220; (618) 233-8780 (86).

Merkle-Knipprath Countryside (apartments and nursing facility), 1190 E. 2900 N. Rd., Clifton 60927; (815) 694-2306 (130).

Mother Theresa Home (skilled, intermediate and sheltered care), 1270 Franciscan Dr., Lemont 60439; (630) 257-5801; www.franciscancommunities.com. (150).

Nazarethville (intermediate and sheltered care), 300 N. River Rd., Des Plaines 60016; (847) 297-5900; www.nazarethville.com. (83).

Our Lady of Angels Retirement Home, 1201 Wyoming, Joliet 60435; (815) 725-6631; www.olaretirement.org (101).

Our Lady of the Snows, Apartment Community, 9500 West Illinois Highway 15, Belleville 62223; (618) 397-6700 (201).

Our Lady of Victory Nursing Home (intermediate and skilled care), 20 Briarcliff Lane, Bourbonnais 60914; (815) 937-2022 (107).

Pope John Paul Apartments (elderly and handicapped), 1 Pope John Paul Plaza, Springfield 62703; (217) 528-1771; www.dio.org (160).

Provena Cor Mariae Center (assisted living and nursing home), 3330 Maria Linden Dr., Rockford 61107; (815) 877-7416 (146).

Provena St. Anne Center (nursing home), 4405 Highcrest Rd., Rockford 61107; (815) 229-1999 (179).

Provena St. Joseph's Home for the Aged, 659 E. Jefferson St., Freeport 61032; (815) 232-6181 (120).

Provena Villa Franciscan (skilled care), 210 N. Springfield, Joliet 60435; (815) 725-3400; www.provenahealth.com.

Queen of Peace Center, 1910 Maple Ave., Lisle 60532; (630) 852-5360; www.qopc.net (32).

Red Bud Regional Nursing Home (skilled intermediary facility), 350 W. S. First St., Red Bud 62278; (618) 282-3891 (115).

Resurrection Nursing Pavilion (skilled care), 1001 N. Greenwood, Park Ridge 60068; (847) 692-5600 (295).

Resurrection Retirement Community, 7262 W. Peterson Ave., Chicago, 60631; (773) 792-7930; www.reshealth.org (472 apartments).

Rosary Hill Home (women), 9000 W. 81st St., Justice 60458; (708) 458-3040 (48).

St. Andrew Life Center (retirement residence), 7000

N. Newark Ave., Niles 60714; (847) 647-8332 (99).

St. Anne Place (retirement apartments), 4444 Brendenwood Rd., Rockford 61107; (815) 399-6167 (120).

St. Benedict Home, 6930 W. Touhy Ave., Niles 60714; (847) 647-0003. (99).

St. Elizabeth Home (residence), 704 W. Marion St., Joliet 60436; (815) 727-0125 (11). Group living for Senior women.

St. James Manor, 1251 East Richton Rd., Crete 60417; (708) 672-6700 (110).

St. Joseph's Home (sheltered and intermediate care), 3306 S. 6th St. Rd., Springfield 62703; (217) 529-5596 (110).

St. Joseph's Home (sheltered and intermediate care), 2223 W. Heading Ave., Peoria 61604; (309) 673-7425; www.stjhome.org (200).

St. Joseph Home of Chicago, Inc. (skilled care), 2650 N. Ridgeway Ave., Chicago 60647; (773) 235-8600; www.franciscancommunities.com (173).

St. Patrick's Residence, 1400 Brookdale Rd., Naperville 60563-2125; (630) 416-6565; www.stpatricksresidence.org

Villa Scalabrini (sheltered, intermediate and skilled), 480 N. Wolf Rd., Northlake 60164; (708) 562-0040 (259).

Indiana: Albertine Home, 1501 Hoffman St., Hammond 46327; (219) 937-0575 (35).

Our Lady of Holy Cross Care Center (comprehensive nursing), 7520 S. US Hwy 421, San Pierre 46374; (219) 828-4111 (200).

Provena LaVerna Terrace, 517 N. Main St., Avilla 46710; (260) 897-2093 (51).

Provena Sacred Heart Home (comprehensive nursing), 515 N. Main St., Avilla 46710; (219) 897-2841, (133).

Regina Continuing Care Center (intermediate care Facility), 3900 Washington Ave., Evansville 47714; (812) 485-4226; www.stmarys.org (137).

St. Anne Home (Residential and Comprehensive nursing), 1900 Randallia Dr., Ft. Wayne 46805; (219) 484-5555 (254).

St. Anthony Home, Inc., 203 Franciscan Rd., Crown Point 46307; (219) 661-5100 (219).

St. Augustine Home for the Aged, Little Sisters of the Poor, 2345 W. 86th St., Indianapolis 46260; (317) 872-6420 (92).

St. John's Home for the Aged, Little Sisters of the Poor, 1236 Lincoln Ave., Evansville 47714; (812) 464-3607 (70).

St. Paul Hermitage (residential and intermediate care nursing), 501 N. 17th Ave., Beech Grove 46107; (317) 786-2261 (100).

Iowa: The Alverno Health Care Facility (nursing care), 849 13th Ave. N., Clinton 52732; (563) 242-1521; www.alvernohealthcare.com (194).

Bishop Drumm Retirement Center, 5837 Winwood Dr., Johnston 50131; (515) 270-1100 (64).

Hallmar-Mercy Medical Center, 701 Tenth St. S.E., Cedar Rapids 52403; (319) 369-4638 (57).

Holy Spirit Retirement Home (intermediate care), 1701 W. 25th St., Sioux City 51103; (712) 252-2726 (95).

Kahl Home for the Aged and Infirm (skilled and intermediate care facility), 1101 W. 9th St., Davenport 52804; (319) 324-1621 (135).

The Marian Home, 2400 6th Ave. North, Fort Dodge 50501; (515) 576-1138 (110).

St. Anthony Nursing Home (intermediate care), 406 E. Anthony St., Carroll 51401; (712) 792-3581 (79).

St. Francis Continuation Care and Nursing Home Center, Burlington 52601; (319) 752-4564 (170).

Stonehill Adult Center (day care), 3485 Windsor, Dubuque 52001; (319) 557-7180 (35).

Kansas: Catholic Care Center (skilled and intermediate care facility), 6700 E. 45th St, Wichita 67226; (316) 744-2020 (294).

Mt. Joseph Senior Community (intermediate care facility), 1110 W. 11, Concordia 66901; (785) 243-1347 (16 apartments).

St. John Rest Home (nursing facility), 701 Seventh St., Victoria 67671; (785) 735-2208 (90).

St. John's New Horizons, 2225 Canterbury, Hays 67601; (785) 628-8742 (43).

Villa Maria, Inc. (intermediate care facility), 116 S. Central, Mulvane 67110; (316) 777-1129 (99).

Kentucky: Bishop Soenneker Personal Care Home, 9545 Ky. 144, Knottsville, KY 42366; (270) 281-4881 (55).

Carmel Home (residence, adult day care, respite care and nursing care), 2501 Old Hartford Rd., Owensboro 42303; (270) 683-0227 (101).

Carmel Manor (skilled, intermediate and personal care home), 100 Carmel Manor Rd., Ft. Thomas, 41075; (859) 781-5111; (145).

Madonna Manor Nursing Home, 2344 Amsterdam Rd., Villa Hills 41017; (606) 341-3981 (60).

Marian Home, 3105 Lexington Rd., Louisville 40206; (502) 893-0121 (69).

Nazareth Home, 2000 Newburg Rd., Louisville 40205; (502) 459-9681; www.nazhome.org (168).

St. Charles Care Center and Village, 500 Farrell Dr., Covington 41011; (606) 331-3224; www.stcharlescare.org (149). Nursing home; adult day health program. Independent living cottages (44); assisted living (60); independent living apartments (12).

Louisiana: Annunciation Inn, 1220 Spain St., New Orleans 70117; (504) 944-0512 (111).

Bethany M.H.S. Health Care Center (women), P.O. Box 2308, Lafayette 70502; (337) 234-2459. (200).

Château de Notre Dame (residence and nursing home), 2832 Burdette St., New Orleans 70125; (504) 866-2741 (103).

Christopher Inn Apartments, 2110 Royal St., New Orleans 70116; (504) 949-0312 (144).

Christus St. Joseph's Home (nursing home), 2301 Sterlington Rd., Monroe 71211; (318) 323-3426 (150).

Consolata Home (nursing home), 2319 E. Main St., New Iberia 70560; (337) 365-8226 (114).

Haydel Heights Apartments, 4402 Reynes St., New Orleans 70126; (504) 242-4438 (65 units).

Lafon Nursing Home of the Holy Family, 6900 Chef Menteur Hwy., New Orleans 70126; (504) 246-1100 (171).

Metairie Manor, 4929 York St., Metairie 70001; (504) 456-1467 (287).

Nazareth Inn, 9630 Hayne Blvd., New Orleans 70127; (504) 241-9630 (158).

Ollie Steele Burden Manor (nursing home), 4250 Essen Lane, Baton Rouge 70809; (225) 926-0091 (184).

Our Lady of Prompt Succor Home, 954 East Prudhomme St., Opelousas 70570; (337) 948-3634 (80).

Our Lady's Manor, Inc., 402 Monroe St., Alexandria 71301; (318) 473-2560 (114).

Place Dubourg, 201 Rue Dubourg, LaPlace 70068; (504) 652-1981 (115).

Rouquette Lodge, 4300 Hwy 22, Mandeville 70471; (504) 626-5217 (51).

St. John Berchmans Manor, 3400 St. Anthony Ave., New Orleans 70122; (504) 943-9342 (157).

St. Margaret's Daughters Home (nursing home), 6220 Chartres St., New Orleans 70117; (504) 279-6414 (139).

St. Martin Manor, 1501 N. Johnson St., New Orleans 70116; (504) 945-7728 (145).

Villa St. Maurice 500 St. Maurice Ave., New Orleans 70117; (504) 277-8477 (193).

Villa St. Maurice II, 6101 Douglas St., New Orleans 70117; (504) 277-8731 (80).

Village du Lac, Inc., 1404 Carmel Ave., Lafayette 70501; (337) 234-5106 (200).

Wynhoven Apartments and Wynhoven II (residence for senior citizens), 4600-10th St., Marrero; (504) 347-8442 (375).

Maine: Deering Pavilion (apartments for senior citizens), 880 Forest Ave., Portland 04103; (207) 797-8777 (232 units).

Maison Marcotte (independent living community), 100 Campus Ave., Lewiston 04240; (207) 786-0062 (128 apartments).

Mt. St. Joseph Holistic Care Community, Highwood St., Waterville 04901; (207) 873-0705 (138).

St. Andre Health Care Facility, Inc. (nursing facility), 407 Pool St., Biddeford 04005; (207) 282-5171 (96).

St. Joseph's Manor (nursing care facility), 1133 Washington Ave., Portland 04103; (207) 797-0600; www.saintjosephsmanor.org. (200).

St. Marguerite D'Youville Pavilion, 102 Campus Ave., Lewiston 04240; (207) 777-4200 (280).

St. Xavier's Home (apartments), 199 Somerset St., Bangor 04401; (207) 942-4815 (19 units).

Seton Village, Inc., 1 Carver St., Waterville 04901; (207) 873-0178 (140 housing units).

Maryland: Little Sisters of the Poor, St. Martin's Home (for the aged), 601 Maiden Choice Lane, Baltimore 21228; (410) 744-9367 (104).

Sacred Heart Home, 5805 Queens Chapel Rd., Hyattsville 20782; (301) 277-6500; www.sacredhearthome.org (102).

St. Joseph Nursing Home, 1222 Tugwell Dr., Baltimore 21228; (410) 747-0026 (51).

Villa Rosa Nursing Home, 3800 Lottsford Vista Rd., Mitchellville 20721; (301) 459-4700 (100).

Massachusetts: Catholic Memorial Home (nursing home), 2446 Highland Ave., Fall River 02720; (508) 679-0011 (300).

Don Orione Nursing Home, 111 Orient Ave., East Boston 02128; (617) 569-2100 (185).

D'Youville Manor (nursing home), 981 Varnum Ave., Lowell 01854; (978) 454-5681; www.dyouville.com

(203).

Jeanne Jugan Pavilion, 190 Highland Ave., Somerville 02143; (617) 776-4420 (30).

Jeanne Jugan Residence, Little Sisters of the Poor (home for the elderly), 186 Highland Ave., Somerville 02143; (617) 776-4420 (84).

Madonna Manor (nursing home), 85 N. Washington St., N. Attleboro 02760; (508) 699-2740; www.dhfo.org (129).

Marian Manor, for the Aged and Infirm (nursing home), 130 Dorchester St., S. Boston, 02127; (617) 268-3333; www.marianmanor.org (366).

Marian Manor of Taunton (nursing home), 33 Summer St., Taunton 02780; (508) 822-4885 (184).

Maristhill Nursing Home, 66 Newton St., Waltham 02154; (781) 893-0240 (154).

MI Nursing/Restorative Center, 172 Lawrence St., Lawrence 01841; (978) 685-6321 (335).

MI Residential Community, 189 Maple St., Lawrence 01841; (978) 682-7575; www.mihcs.com (35).

Our Lady's Haven (nursing home), 71 Center St., Fairhaven 02719; (508) 999-4561; www.dhfo.org (158).

Sacred Heart Home (nursing home), 359 Summer St., New Bedford 02740; (508) 996-6751; www.dhfo.org (217).

St. Joseph Manor Health Care, Inc., 215 Thatcher St., Brockton 02302; (508) 583-5834 (118).

St. Joseph's Nursing Care Center, 321 Centre St., Dorchester, Boston 02122; (617) 825-6320 (191).

St. Patrick's Manor (nursing home), 863 Central St., Framingham 01701; (508) 879-8000; www.stpatricks-manor.org (460).

Michigan: Bishop Noa Home for Senior Citizens (nursing home and residence), 2900 3rd Ave. S., Escanaba 49829; (906) 786-5810 (123).

Lourdes Nursing Home (skilled facility), 2300 Watkins Lake Rd., Waterford 48328; (248) 674-2241; www.lourdescampus.com (108).

Marycrest Manor (skilled nursing facility), 15475 Middlebelt Rd., Livonia 48154; (313) 427-9175 (55).

Ryan Senior Residences of the Archdiocese of Detroit: Casa Maria, 600 Maple Vista, Imlay City 48444; (810) 724-6300 (84). Kundig Center, 3300 Jeffries Freeway, Detroit 48208; (313) 894-0555 (160). Lourdes Assisted Living Home, Inc. (residence), 2450 Watkins Lake Rd., Waterford 48328; (248) 618-6361; www.lourdescampus.com (6). Marian-Oakland West, 29250 W. Ten Mile Rd., Farmington Hills 48336; (248) 474-7204 (87). Marian Place, 408 W. Front St., Monroe 48161; (734) 241-2414 (53). Marydale Center, 3147 Tenth Ave., Port Huron 48060; (810) 985-9683 (56). Maryhaven, 11350 Reeck Rd., Southgate 48195; (734) 287-2111 (90). Mercy Madonna Villa 17825 Fifteen Mile Rd., Clinton Twp. 48035; (810) 792-0358 (86). Stapleton Center, 9341 Agnes St., Detroit 48214; (313) 822-0397 (59). Villa Marie, 15131 Newburgh Rd., Livonia 48154; (734) 464-9494 (86). St. Ann's Home, (residence and nursing home), 2161 Leonard St. N.W., Grand Rapids 49504; (616) 453-7715; www.stannshome.com (140). St. Catherine House, 1641 Webb Ave., Detroit 48206; (313) 868-4505 (12). St. Elizabeth Briarbank (women, residence), 1315 N. Woodward Ave., Bloomfield Hills 48304; (248) 644-1011 (44).

St. Francis Home (nursing home), 915 N. River Rd., Saginaw 48609; (989) 781-3150 (100).

St. Joseph's Home, 4800 Cadieux Rd., Detroit

48224; (313) 882-3800 (104).

Minnesota: Alverna Apartments, 300 8th Ave. S.E., Little Falls 56345; (320) 632-1246 (68).

Assumption Home, 715 North First St., Cold Spring 56320; (320) 685-4110 (34).

Benedictine Health Center, 935 Kenwood Ave., Duluth, MN 55811; (218) 723-6408; www.benedictine healthcenter.org.

Divine Providence Community Home (skilled nursing care) and Lake Villa Maria Senior Housing, 702 Third Ave. N.W., Sleepy Eye 56085; (507) 794-5333 (58).

Franciscan Health Community, 1925 Norfolk Ave., St. Paul 55116; (651) 696-8400 (223).

John Paul Apartments, 200 8th Ave. N., Cold Spring 56320; (320) 685-4429 (61).

Little Sisters of the Poor, Holy Family Residence (skilled nursing and intermediate care), 330 S. Exchange St., St. Paul 55102; (651) 227-0336 (73). Independent living apartments (32).

Madonna Towers (retirement apartments and nursing home), 4001 19th Ave. N.W., Rochester 55901; (507) 288-3911 (184).

Mary Rondorf Retirement Home of Sacred Heart Parish, Inc., 222 5th St., N.E., Staples 56479; (218) 894-2124 (45). Board and lodging with special services.

Mother of Mercy Nursing Home and Retirement Center, 230 Church Ave., Box 676, Albany 56307; (320) 845-2195 (114).

Regina Nursing Home and Retirement Residence Center, 1175 Nininger Rd., Hastings 55033; (651) 480-6836; www.reginamedical.com. Nursing home (61); retirement home (43); boarding care (32). Admin., Juliane M. Saxon.

Sacred Heart Hospice (skilled nursing home, adult day care, home health care) 1200 Twelfth St. S.W., Austin 55912; (507) 433-1808 (59).

St. Ann's Residence, 330 E. 3rd St., Duluth 55811; (218) 727-8831; www.stanns.com (185).

St. Anne of Winona (skilled nursing home), 1347 W. Broadway, Winona 55987; (507) 454-3621; www.saintannehosp.homestead.com (74).

St. Benedict's Center, 1810 Minnesota Blvd. S.E., St. Cloud 56304; (320) 252-0010; www.centracare.com (198 bed skilled nursing care; adult day care, respite care). Benedict Village (retirement apartments), 2000 15th Ave. S.E., St. Cloud 56304; (320) 252-0010; www.centracare.com. Benedict Homes (Alzheimer residential care) and Benedict Court (assisted living), 1980 15th Ave. S.E., St. Cloud 56304; (320) 252-0010.

St. Benedict's Senior Community (independent and assisted living), 1301 East 7th St., Monticello, MN 55362; (763) 295-4051; www.centracare.com.

St. Elizabeth's Health Care Center, 1200 Grant Blvd., Wabasha 55981; (651) 565-4531; www.stelizabethswabasha.org (106).

St. Elizabeth's Medical Center, 626 Shields Ave., Wabasha, MN 55981; (651) 565-4581; www.stelizabethswabasha.org.

St. Francis Home, 501 Oak St., Breckenridge 56520; (218) 643-7661; www.sfcare.org (124).

St. Mary's Regional Health Center, 1027 Washington Ave., Detroit Lakes 56501; (218) 847-5611 (100).

St. Otto's Care Center (nursing home), 920 S.E. 4th St., Little Falls 56345; (320) 632-9281 (150).

St. William's Nursing Home, P.O. Box 30, Parkers Prairie 56361; (218) 338-4671 (90).

Villa of St. Francis Nursing Home, 1001 Scott Ave., Morris 56267; (320) 589-1133 (128).

Villa St. Vincent (skilled nursing home and residence), 516 Walsh St., Crookston 56716; (218) 281-3424. Skilled nursing home (80); special care unit (24); apartments (27); board and care (34).

Westwood Senior Apartments, 925 Kenwood Ave., Duluth 55811; (218) 733-2238; www.westwoodduluth.org (70).

Mississippi: Notre Dame de la Mer Retirement Apartments, 292 Hwy. 90, Bay St. Louis 39520; (228) 467-2885 (61).

Santa Maria Retirement Apartments, 674 Beach Blvd., Biloxi, 39530; (228) 432-1289 (223).

Villa Maria Retirement Apartments, 921 Porter Ave., Ocean Springs 39564; (228) 875-8811 (225).

Missouri: Cathedral Square Towers, 444 W. 12th St., Kansas City 64105; (816) 471-6555 (167).

Chariton Apartments (retirement apartments), 4249 Michigan Ave., St. Louis 63111; (314) 352-7600 (122 units; 143 residents).

LaVerna Village Nursing Home, 904 Hall Ave., Savannah 64485; (816) 324-3185 (133).

Little Sisters of the Poor (home for aged), 3225 N. Florissant Ave., St. Louis 63107; (314) 421-6022 (114).

Mary, Queen and Mother Center (nursing care), 7601 Watson Rd., St. Louis 63119; (314) 961-8000; www.cardinalcarberry.org (230).

Mother of Good Counsel Home (skilled nursing, women), 6825 Natural Bridge Rd., Northwoods, 63121; (314) 383-4765 (114).

Our Lady of Mercy Country Home, 2205 Hughes Rd., Liberty 64068; (816) 781-7276; www.ourladyofmercy.net (105).

Price Memorial skilled nursing facility, Forby Rd., P.O. Box 476, Eureka 63025; (636) 587-3200 (120).

St. Agnes Home for the Elderly, 10341 Manchester Rd., Kirkwood 63122; (314) 965-7616 (124).

St. Joseph Hill Infirmary, Inc., (nursing care facility, men), St. Joseph Road, Eureka 63025; (636) 587-3661 (120).

St. Joseph's Home (residential and intermediate care), 723 First Capitol Dr., St. Charles 63301; (314) 946-4140; (110).

St. Joseph's Home (residential and intermediate care facility), 1306 W. Main St., Jefferson City 65109; (573) 635-0166 (90).

Nebraska: Madonna Rehabilitation Hospital, 5401 South St., Lincoln 68506; (402) 489-7102; www.madonna.org (252).

Mercy Care Center (skilled nursing facility for chronic, complex and subacute levels of care and rehabilitation), 1870 S. 75th St., Omaha 68124; (402) 343-8500 (246).

Mercy Villa, 1845 S. 72nd St., Omaha 68124; (402) 391-6224.

Mt. Carmel Home, Keens Memorial (nursing home), 412 W. 18th St., Kearney 68847; (308) 237-2287 (75).

New Cassel Retirement Center, 900 N. 90th St., Omaha

68114; (402) 393-2277; www.newcassel.org (165).

St. Joseph's Rehabilitation and Care Center, 401 N. 18th St., Norfolk 68701; (402) 644-7375 (99).

St. Joseph's Retirement Community, 320 E. Decatur St., West Point 68788; (402) 372-3477 (90).

St. Joseph's Villa (nursing home), 927 7th St., David City 68632; (402) 367-3045; www.saintjosephvilla.org (65).

New Hampshire: Mount Carmel Healthcare Center, 235 Myrtle St., Manchester 03104; (603) 627-3811 (120).

St. Ann Home (nursing home), 195 Dover Point Rd., Dover 03820; (603) 742-2612 (54).

St. Francis Home (nursing home), 406 Court St., Laconia 03246; (603) 524-0466 (51).

St. Teresa Healthcare Center (nursing home), 519 Bridge St., Manchester 03104; (603) 668-2373 (5).

St. Vincent de Paul Healthcare Center, 29 Providence Ave., Berlin 03570; (603) 752-1820 (80).

New Jersey: McCarrick Care Center, 15 Dellwood Lane, Somerset 08873; (732) 545-4200 (142).

Mater Dei Nursing Home, 176 Rt. 40, Newfield 08344; (856) 358-2061 (64).

Morris Hall (St. Joseph Skilled Nursing Center, St. Mary Residence), 1 Bishops' Dr., Lawrenceville 08648-2050; (609) 896-0006; www.morrishall.org (100).

Mount St. Andrew Villa (residence), 55 W. Midland Ave., Paramus 07652; (201) 261-5950 (55).

Our Lady's Residence (nursing home), 1100 Clematis Ave., Pleasantville 08232; (609) 646-2450 (236).

St. Ann's Home for the Aged (a skilled and intermediate nursing care home, women), 198 Old Bergen Rd., Jersey City 07305; (201) 433-0950 (106).

St. Francis Health Resort (residence), 122 Diamond Spring Rd., Denville 07834; www.saintfrancisres.com (150).

St. Joseph's Home for the Elderly, Little Sisters of the Poor, 140 Shepherd Lane, Totowa 07512; (973) 942-0300 (134).

St. Joseph's Rest Home for Aged Women, 46 Preakness Ave., Paterson 07522; (973) 956-1921 (35).

St. Joseph's Assisted Living Residence, 1 St. Joseph Terr., Woodbridge, 07095; (732) 634-0004 (60).

St. Joseph's Nursing Home, 3 St. Joseph Terr., Woodbridge, 07095; (732) 750-0077.

St. Mary's Nursing Home, 210 St. Mary's Dr., Cherry Hill 08003; (856) 424-9521 (215). The Manor at St. Mary's, 220 St. Mary's Dr., Cherry Hill 08003; (856) 424-3817 (739).

St. Vincent's Nursing Home, 45 Elm St., Montclair 07042; (973) 754-4800 (220).

Villa Maria (residence and infirmary, women), 641 Somerset St., N. Plainfield 07061; (908) 757-3050 (86).

New Mexico: Good Shepherd Manor (residential care for aged persons), Little Brothers of the Good Shepherd, P.O. Box 10248, Albuquerque 87184; (505) 898-0177 (40).

New York: Bernardine Apartments, 417 Churchill Ave., Syracuse 13205; (315) 469-7786.

Brothers of Mercy Sacred Heart Home (residence) 4520 Ransom Rd., Clarence 14031; (716) 759-2644 (80). Brothers

of Mercy Nursing Home, 10570 Bergtold Rd., Clarence 14031; (716) 759-6985; www.brothersofmercy.org (240).

Brothers of Mercy Housing Co., Inc. (apartments), 10500 Bergtold Rd., Clarence 14031; (716) 759-2122 (110).

Carmel Richmond Nursing Home, 88 Old Town Rd., Staten Island 10304; (718) 979-5000 (300).

Ferncliff Nursing Home, 21 Ferncliff Dr., Rhinebeck 12572; (845) 876-2011 (328).

Franciscan Health System of New York, 2975 Independence Ave., Bronx 10463; (718) 548-1700.

Good Samaritan Nursing Home (skilled nursing), 101 Elm St., Sayville 11782; (631) 244-2400 (100).

The Heritage (apartments with skilled nursing care), 1450 Portland Ave., Rochester 14621; (716) 342-1700; www.stannsrochester.org (237)

Holy Family Home, 1740-84th St., Brooklyn 11214; (718) 232-3666 (200).

Kateri Residence (skilled nursing), 150 Riverside Dr., New York 10024; (212) 769-0744; www.catholichealthcare system.org/kateri (610).

Little Sisters of the Poor, Jeanne Jugan Residence (Skilled Nursing and Health Related; Adult Care), 3200 Baychester Ave., Bronx 10475; (718) 671-2120 (60).

Little Sisters of the Poor, Queen of Peace Residence, 110-30 221st St., Queens Village 11429; (718) 464-1800.

Mary Manning Walsh Home (nursing home), 1339 York Ave., New York 10021; (212) 628-2800 (362).

Mercy Healthcare Center (skilled nursing facility), 114 Wawbeek Ave., Tupper Lake 12986; (518) 359-3355; www.muhc.org (80).

Mt. Loretto Nursing Home, (skilled nursing home), Sisters of the Resurrection, 302 Swart Hill Rd., Amsterdam 12010; (518) 842-6790 (120).

Nazareth Nursing Home (women), 291 W. North St., Buffalo 14201; (716) 881-2323 (125).

Our Lady of Consolation Nursing and Rehabilitation Care Center (skilled nursing) 111 Beach Dr., West Islip 11795; (631) 587-1600; www.olc.chsli.org (450).

Our Lady of Hope Residence (home for the aged), Little Sisters of the Poor, 1 Jeanne Jugan Lane, Latham 12210; (518) 785-4551 (117).

Ozanam Hall of Queens Nursing Home, Inc., 42-41 201 St., Bayside 11361; (718) 423-2000 (432).

Providence Rest , 3304 Waterbury Ave., Bronx 10465; (718) 931-30000; www.chcn.org/providence (242).

Resurrection Nursing Home (skilled nursing facility), Castleton 12033; (518) 732-7617 (80).

St. Ann's Community (skilled nursing facility), 1500 Portland Ave., Rochester 14621; (585) 697-6000; www.stannscommunity.com (354).

St. Cabrini Nursing Home, 115 Broadway, Dobbs Ferry 10522; (914) 693-6800 (304).

St. Clare Manor (nursing home), 543 Locust St., Lockport 14094; (716) 434-4718 (28).

St. Columban's on the Lake (retirement home), 2546 Lake Rd., Silver Creek 14136; (716) 934-4515 (50).

St. Elizabeth Home (adult home), 5539 Broadway, Lancaster 14086; (716) 683-5150 (117).

St. Francis Home (skilled nursing facility), 147 Reist St., Williamsville 14221; (716) 633-5400 (142).

St. Joseph Manor (nursing home), 2211 W. State St., Olean 14760; (716) 372-7810 (22).

St. Joseph Nursing Home, 2535 Genesee St., Utica 13501; (315) 797-1230; www.stjosephnh.org.

St. Joseph's Guest Home, Missionary Sisters of St. Benedict, 350 Cuba Hill Rd., Huntington 11743; (631) 368-9528.

St. Joseph's Home (nursing home), 420 Lafayette St., Ogdensburg 13669; (315) 393-3780; www.stjh.org (117).

St. Joseph's Villa (adult home), 38 Prospect Ave., Catskill 12414; (518) 943-5701.

St. Luke Manor, 17 Wiard St., Batavia 14020; (585) 343-8806 (20).

St. Mary's Manor, 515 Sixth St., Niagara Falls 14301; (716) 285-3236 (165).

St. Patrick's Home for the Aged and Infirm, 66 Van Cortlandt Park S., Bronx NY 10463; (718) 304-1832; www.stpatrickshome.org (264).

St. Teresa Nursing Home, 120 Highland Ave., Middletown 10940; (914) 342-1033 (98).

St. Vincent's Home for the Aged, 319 Washington Ave., Dunkirk 14048; (716) 366-2066 (40).

Terence Cardinal Cooke Health Care Center (skilled nursing), 1249 Fifth Ave., New York 10029; (212) 360-1000 (523).

Teresian House, 200 Washington Ave. Extension, Albany 12203; (518) 456-2000; www.teresianhouse.com (300).

Uihlein Mercy Center (nursing home), 185 Old Military Rd., Lake Placid 12946; (518) 523-2464 (220).

North Carolina: Maryfield Nursing Home, 1315 Greensboro Rd., High Point 27260; (336) 886-2444 (115).

North Dakota: Manor St. Joseph (basic care facility), 404 Fourth Ave., Edgeley 58433; (701) 493-2477 (40).

Marillac Manor Retirement Center, 1016 28th St., Bismarck 58501-3139; (701) 258-8702; www.marillac-manor.org (78 apartments).

St. Anne's Guest Home, 524 N. 17th St., Grand Forks 58203; (701) 746-9401 (86).

St. Vincent's Care Center (nursing facility), 1021 N. 26th St., Bismarck 58501; (701) 223-6888 (101).

Ohio: Archbishop Leibold Home for the Aged, Little Sisters of the Poor, 476 Riddle Rd., Cincinnati 45220; (513) 281-8001 (100).

The Assumption Village, 9800 Market St., North Lima 44452; (330) 549-0740 (120).

Center for Older Adults (nursing care), 10204 Granger Rd., Cleveland 44125; (216) 581-2900; www.jenningscenter.org (150).

Francesca Residence (retirement), 39 N. Portage Path, Akron 44303; (330) 867-6334 (40).

House of Loreto (nursing home), 2812 Harvard Ave. N.W., Canton 44709; (330) 453-8137 (76).

Little Sisters of the Poor, Sacred Heart Home, 4900 Navarre Ave., Oregon 43616; (419) 698-4331 (81).

Little Sisters of the Poor, Sts. Mary and Joseph Home for Aged, 4291 Richmond Rd., Cleveland 44122; (216) 464-1222 (125).

The Maria-Joseph Living Care Center, 4830 Salem Ave., Dayton 45416; (937) 278-2692; www.maria-joseph.org (440).

Mercy Franciscan Terrace, 100 Compton Rd., Cincinnati 45215; (513) 761-9036 (148).

Mercy St. Theresa Center, 7010 Rowan Hill Dr., Cincinnati 45227; (513) 527-0105; www.e-mercy.com (157).

Mercy Siena Retirement Community, 6125 N. Main St., Dayton 45415; (937) 278-8211; www.mercysiena.com; (99).

Mount Alverna (intermediate care nursing facility), 6765 State Rd., Cleveland 44134; (440) 843-7800; www.franciscanservices.com/facilities/ (203).

Mt. St. Joseph (skilled nursing facility, dual certified), 21800 Chardon Rd., Euclid 44117; (216) 531-7426 (100).

Nazareth Towers, 300 E. Rich St., Columbus 43215; (614) 464-4780 (229).

St. Augustine Manor (skilled nursing facility), 7801 Detroit Ave., Cleveland 44102; (216) 634-7400 (248).

St. Francis Health Care Centre, 401 N. Broadway St., Green Springs 44836; (419) 639-2626; www.sfhcc.org (186).

St. Francis Home, Inc. (residence and nursing care), 182 St. Francis Ave., Tiffin 44883; (419) 447-2723 (173).

St. Joseph's Care Center, 2308 Reno Dr., Louisville 44641; (330) 875-5562 (100, nursing home; 40 assisted living).

St. Margaret Hall (rest home and nursing facility), Carmelite Sisters for the Aged and Infirm, 1960 Madison Rd., Cincinnati 45206; (513) 751-5880 (133).

St. Raphael Home (nursing home), 1550 Roxbury Rd., Columbus 43212; (614) 486-0436 (78).

St. Rita's Home (skilled nursing home), 880 Greenlawn Ave., Columbus 43223; (614) 443-9433 (100).

Schroder Manor Retirement Community (residential care, skilled nursing care and independent living units), Franciscan Sisters of the Poor, 1302 Millville Ave., Hamilton 45013; (513) 867-1300 (125).

The Villa Sancta Anna Home for the Aged, Inc., 25000 Chagrin Blvd., Beachwood 44122; (216) 464-9250 (68).

The Village at St. Edward (apartments, nursing care and assisted living), 3131 Smith Rd., Fairlawn 44333; (330) 666-1183; www.vased.org (160).

Oklahoma: St. Ann's Home, 9400 St. Ann's Dr., Oklahoma City 73162; (405) 728-7888 (120).

Westminster Village, Inc. (residence), 1601 Academy, Ponca City 74604; (580) 762-0927 (131).

Oregon: Benedictine Nursing Center, 540 S. Main St., Mt. Angel 97362; (503) 845-6841 (75). Home Health Agency, Outpatient Therapies. Benedictine Institute for Long Term Care. Child Development Center.

Evergreen Court Independent Retirement Living, 451 O'Connell St., North Bend 97459; (541) 751-7658; www.baycrest-village.com.

Maryville Nursing Home, 14645 S.W. Farmington, Beaverton 97007; (503) 643-8626; www.ssmo.org.

Mt. St. Joseph, 3060 S.E. Stark St., Portland 97214; (503) 535-4700 (347).

St. Catherine's Residence and Nursing Center, 3959 Sheridan Ave., North Bend 97459; (541) 756-4151 (200).

Pennsylvania: Antonian Towers, 2405 Hillside Ave., Easton 18042; (610) 258-2033 (50).

Ascension Manor I (senior citizen housing), 911 N. Franklin St., Philadelphia 19123; (215) 922-1116.

Ascension Manor II (senior citizen housing), 970 N. 7th St., Philadelphia 19123; (215) 922-1116.

Benetwood Apartments, Benedictine Sisters of Erie, 641 Troupe Rd., Harborcreek 16421; (814) 899-0088 (80).

Bethlehem Retirement Village, 100 W. Wissahickon Ave., Flourtown 19031; (215) 233-0998.

Christ the King Manor, 1100 W. Long Ave., Du Bois 15801; (814) 371-3180 (160).

D'Youville Manor (residential care facility), 1750 Quarry Rd., Yardley 19067; (215) 579-1750 (49).

Garvey Manor and Our Lady of the Allegheny Residence (nursing home), 128 Logan Blvd., Hollidaysburg 16648-2693; (814) 695-5571; www.garveymanor.org (150).

Grace Mansion (personal care facility), Holy Family Residential Services, 1200 Spring St., Bethlehem; (610) 865-6748; www.hfmanor.com (33).

Holy Family Apartments, 1318 Spring St., Bethlehem 18018; (610) 865-3963; hfmanor.com/html/independent_living.html (50).

Holy Family Home, Little Sisters of the Poor, 5300 Chester Ave., Philadelphia 19143; (215) 729-5153 (105).

Holy Family Manor (skilled and intermediate nursing facility), 1200 Spring St., Bethlehem 18018; (610) 865-5595; www.hfmanor.com (208).

Holy Family Residence (personal care facility), 900 W. Market St., Orwigsburg 17961; (570) 366-2912 (85).

Immaculate Mary Home (nursing care facility), 2990 Holme Ave., Philadelphia 19136; (215) 335-2100 (296).

John XXIII Home (skilled, intermediate and personal care), 2250 Shenango Freeway, Hermitage 16148; (724) 981-3200; www.johnxxiiihome.org (196).

Little Flower Manor (residence, women), 1215 Springfield Rd., Darby 19023; (610) 534-6000 (180).

Little Flower Manor Nursing Home (skilled nursing), 1201 Springfield Rd., Darby 19023; (610) 534-6000 (185).

Little Flower Manor of Diocese of Scranton, (long-term skilled nursing care facility), 200 S. Meade St., Wilkes-Barre 18702; (570) 823-6131.

Little Sisters of the Poor, 1028 Benton Ave., Pittsburgh 15212; (412) 307-1100; www.littlsesistersofthepoor-pittsburgh.org (40).

Little Sisters of the Poor, Holy Family Residence, 2500 Adams Ave., Scranton 18509; (570) 343-4065 (58).

Maria Joseph Manor (skilled nursing, personal care facility and independent living cottages), 875 Montour Blvd., Danville 17821; (570) 275-4221 (135).

Marian Hall Home for the Aged (women), 934 Forest Ave., Pittsburgh 15202; (412) 761-1999 (49).

Marian Manor (intermediate care), 2695 Winchester Dr., Pittsburgh 15220; (412) 563-6866 (194).

Mount Macrina Manor (skilled nursing facility), 520 W. Main St., Uniontown 15401; (724) 437-1400 (141).

Neumann Apartments (low income), 25 N. Nichols St., St. Clair 17970; (570) 429-0699 (25).

Queen of Angels Apartments, 22 Rothermel St., Hyde Park, Reading 19605; (610) 921-3115 (45 units).

Queen of Peace Apartments (low income), 777 Water St., Pottsville 17901; (570) 628-4504 (65).

Redeemer Village II, 1551 Huntingdon Pike, Huntingdon Valley 19006; (215) 947-8168; www.holyredeemer.com (151).

Sacred Heart Manor (nursing home and independent living), 6445 Germantown Ave., Philadelphia 19119;

(215) 438-5268 (171 nursing home; 48 personal care; 48 independent living).

St. Anne's Home and Village, 3952 Columbia Ave., Columbia 17512; (717) 285-5443 (121).

St. Anne Home (nursing facility), 685 Angela Dr., Greensburg 15601; (724) 837-6070 (125).

St. Ignatius Nursing Home, 4401 Haverford Ave., Philadelphia 19104; (215) 349-8800 (176).

St. John Neumann Nursing Home, 10400 Roosevelt Blvd., Philadelphia 19116; (215) 248-7200 (107).

St. Joseph Home for the Aged (Residential and skilled nursing facility), 1182 Holland Rd., Holland 18966; (215) 357-5511 (76).

St. Joseph Nursing and Health Care Center (skilled nursing facility), 5324 Penn Ave., Pittsburgh 15224; (412) 665-5100 (153).

St. Leonard's Home Inc. (personal care facility), 601 N. Montgomery St., Hollidaysburg 16648; (814) 695-9581 (30).

St. Mary of Providence Center, R.D. 2, Box 145, Elverson 19520; (610) 942-4166 (52).

Saint Mary's East, 607 E. 26th St., Erie 16504-2813; (814) 459-0621; www.stmaryshome.org (131).

Saint Mary's at Asbury Ridge, 4855 West Ridge Rd., Erie, PA 16506; (814) 836-5300.

Saint Mary's Manor (residential, personal care, short-term rehabilitation and nursing care), 701 Lansdale Ave., Lansdale 19446; (215) 368-0900; www.smmphl.org (200).

St. Mary's Villa Nursing Home, 675 St. Mary's Villa Rd., Moscow 18444; (570) 842-7621 (176).

Trexler Pavilion (personal care facility), 1220 Prospect Ave., Bethlehem 18018; (610) 868-7776 (30).

Vincentian de Marillac Nursing Home, 5300 Stanton Ave., Pittsburgh 15206; (412) 361-2833 (52).

Vincentian Home (nursing facility), 111 Perrymont Rd., Pittsburgh 15237; (412) 366-5600 (217).

Rhode Island: Jeanne Jugan Residence of the Little Sisters of the Poor, 964 Main St., Pawtucket 02860; (401) 723-4314 (95).

Saint Antoine Residence (skilled nursing facility), 10 Rhodes Ave., North Smithfield 02896; (401) 767-3500; www.stantoine.net (416).

St. Clare Home (nursing facility), 309 Spring St., Newport 02840; (401) 849-3204 (47).

St. Francis House, 167 Blackstone St., Woonsocket 02895; (401) 762-5255 (59).

Scalabrini Villa (convalescent, rest-nursing home). 860 N. Quidnessett Rd., North Kingstown 02852; (401) 884-1802; www.freeyellow.com/members3/scalabrini (175).

South Carolina: Carter-May Home/St. Joseph Residence, 1660 Ingram Rd., Charleston 29407; (843) 556-8314 (15).

South Dakota: Avera Brady Health and Rehabilitation (skilled nursing facility), 500 S. Ohlman St., Mitchell 57301; (605) 966-7701 (83).

Mother Joseph Manor (skilled nursing facility), 1002 N. Jay St., Aberdeen 57401; (605) 622-5850 (81).

Prince of Peace Retirement Community, 4500 Prince of Peace Pl., Sioux Falls 57103; (605) 322-5600 (204).

St. William's Home for the Aged (intermediate care, 60), and Angela Hall (assisted living center for developmentally handicapped women, 22), 901 E. Virgil, Box 432, Milbank 57252; (605) 432-4538.

Tekakwitha Nursing Home (skilled and intermediate care), 6 E. Chestnut St., Sisseton 57262; (605) 698-7693 (101).

Tennessee: Alexian Village of Tennessee, 100 James Blvd., Signal Mountain 37377; (423) 886-0100 (277).

St. Mary Manor, 1771 Highway 45 Bypass, Jackson 38305; (731) 668-5633.

St. Peter Manor (retirement community), 108 N. Auburndale, Memphis 38104; (901) 278-8200.

St. Peter Villa (intermediate and skilled care), 141 N. McLean, Memphis 38104; (901) 276-2021.

Villa Maria Manor, 32 White Bridge Rd., Nashville 37205; (615) 352-3084 (230).

Texas: Casa, Inc., Housing for Elderly and Handicapped, 3201 Sondra Dr., Fort Worth 76107; (817) 332-7276 (200).

Casa Brendan Housing for the Elderly and Handicapped (56 apartments) and Casa II, Inc. (30 apartments), 1300 Hyman St., Stephenville 76401; (254) 965-6964 (83).

John Paul II Nursing Home (intermediate care and personal care), 209 S. 3rd St., Kenedy 78119; (830) 583-9841.

Mother of Perpetual Help Home (intermediate care facility), 519 E. Madison Ave., Brownsville 78520; (956) 546-6745 (38).

Mt. Carmel Home (personal care home), 4130 S. Alameda St., Corpus Christi 78411; (512) 855-6243 (92).

Nuestro Hogar Housing for Elderly and Handicapped, 709 Magnolia St., Arlington 76012; (817) 261-0608 (63).

St. Ann's Nursing Home, P.O. Box 1179, Panhandle 79068; (806) 537-3194 (56).

St. Dominic Residence Hall, 2401 Holcombe Blvd., Houston 77021; (713) 741-8700 (149).

St. Francis Nursing Home (intermediate care facility), 630 W. Woodlawn, San Antonio 78212; (210) 736-3177 (152).

St. Francis Village, Inc. (retired and elderly), 1 Chapel Plaza, Crowley 76036; (817) 292-5786 (420).

San Juan Nursing Home, Inc. (skilled and intermediate care facility), P.O. Box 1238, San Juan 78589; (956) 787-1771 (127).

Villa Maria (home for aged women-men), 920 S. Oregon St., El Paso 79901; (915) 533-5152 (17 units).

Villa Maria, Inc. (apartment complex), 3146 Saratoga Blvd., Corpus Christi 78415; (361) 857-6171 (59).

Utah: Christus Health Utah (Christus St. Joseph Villa and Christus Marian Center), 451 Bishop Federal Lane, Salt Lake City 84115; (801) 487-7557; www.stjosephvilla.com (300).

Vermont: Loretto Home, 59 Meadow St., Rutland 05701; (802) 773-8840 (57).

Michaud Memorial Manor (residential home for elderly), Derby Line 05830; (802) 873-3152 (34).

St. Joseph's Residential Care Home, 243 N. Prospect St., Burlington 05401; (802) 864-0264 (32).

Virginia: Madonna Home (home for aged), 814 W. 37th St., Norfolk 23508; (757) 623-6662 (16).

Marian Manor (assisted living, nursing care), 5345 Marian Lane, Virginia Beach 23462; (757) 456-5018 (100).

Marywood Apartments, 1261 Marywood Lane, Richmond 23229; (804) 740-5567 (126).

McGurk House Apartments, 2425 Tate Springs Rd., Lynchburg 24501; (434) 846-2425 (89).

Our Lady of the Valley Retirement Community, 650 N. Jefferson St., Roanoke 24016; (540) 345-5111.

Russell House Apartments, 900 First Colonial Rd., Virginia Beach 23454; (757) 481-0770 (126).

St. Francis Home, 2511 Wise St., Richmond 23225; (804) 231-1043 (34).

St. Joseph's Home for the Aged, Little Sisters of the Poor, 1503 Michael Rd., Richmond 23229; (804) 288-6245 (72).

St. Mary's Woods (independent and assisted living apartments), 1257 Marywood Lane, Richmond 23229; (804) 741-8624; www.stmaryswood.com (118 apartments).

Seton Manor (apartments), 215 Marcella Rd., Hampton 23666; (757) 827-6512 (112).

Washington: Cathedral Plaza Apartments (retirement apartments), W. 1120 Sprague Ave., Spokane 99204 (150).

Chancery Place (retirement apartments), 910 Marion, Seattle 98104; (206) 343-9415; www.ccsww.org.

The Delaney, W. 242 Riverside Ave., Spokane 99201; (509) 747-5081 (83).

Elbert House, 16000 N.E. 8th St., Bellevue 98008; (206) 747-5111.

Emma McRedmond Manor, 7960-169th N.E., Redmond 98052; (206) 869-2424 (31).

Fahy Garden Apartments, W. 1403-11 Dean Ave., Spokane 99201 (31).

Fahy West Apartments, W. 1523 Dean Ave., Spokane 99201 (55).

The Franciscan (apartments), 15237-21stAve. S.W., Seattle 98166; (206) 431-8001.

Providence Mt. St. Vincent (nursing center and retirement apartments), 4831 35th Ave. S.W., Seattle 98126; (206) 937-3700 (174).

Tumwater Apartments, 5701-6th Ave. S.W., Tumwater 98501; (360) 352-4321.

West Virginia: Welty Home for the Aged, 21 Washington Ave., Wheeling 26003; (304) 242-5233 (46).

Wisconsin: Alexian Village of Milwaukee (retirement community/skilled nursing home), 9301 N. 76th St., Milwaukee 53223; (414) 355-9300; www.alexianvillage.org (327).

Bethany-St. Joseph Health Care Center, 2501 Shelby Rd., La Crosse 54601; (608) 788-5700 (226).

Clement Manor (retirement community and skilled nursing), 3939 S. 92nd St., Greenfield 53228; (414) 321-1800 (162).

Divine Savior Nursing Home, 715 W. Pleasant St., Portage 53901; (608) 742-4131 (124).

Felician Village (independent living), 1700 S. 18th St., Manitowoc 54020; (920) 683-8811 (134 apartments).

Franciscan Care Center, 500 S. Oakwood Rd., Oshkosh, WI 54901; (920) 223-0110.

Franciscan Skemp Healthcare, Mayo Health System: Arcadia Campus Nursing Home, 464 S. St. Joseph

Ave., Arcadia 54612; (608) 323-3341 (75).

McCormick Memorial Home, 212 Iroquois St., Green Bay 54301; (920) 437-0883 (60).

Marian Catholic Home (skilled care nursing home), 3333 W. Highland Blvd., Milwaukee 53208; (414) 344-8100 (215).

Marian Franciscan Center, 9632 W. Appleton Ave., Milwaukee 53225; (414) 461-8850 (310).

Marian Housing Center (independent living), 4105 Spring St., Racine 53405; (262) 633-5807 (40).

Maryhill Manor Nursing Home (skilled nursing facility), 501 Madison Ave., Niagara 54151; (715) 251-3178 (75).

Milwaukee Catholic Home (continuing care retirement community), 2462 N. Prospect Ave., Milwaukee 53211-4462; (414) 224-9700; www.milwaukeecatholichome.org (131).

Nazareth House (skilled nursing facility), 814 Jackson St., Stoughton 53589; (608) 873-6448 (99).

St. Ann Rest Home (intermediate care facility, women), 2020 S. Muskego Ave., Milwaukee 53204; (414) 383-2630 (50).

St. Anne's Home for the Elderly, 3800 N. 92nd St., Milwaukee 53222; (414) 463-7570; www.wahsa.org/st.anne (106).

St. Camillus Campus (continuing care retirement community), 10100 West Blue Mound Road, Wauwatosa 53226; (414) 258-1814; www.stcam.com (386).

St. Elizabeth Nursing Home, 502 St. Lawrence Ave., Janesville 53545; (608) 752-6709 (43).

St. Francis Home (skilled nursing facility), 1416 Cumming Ave., Superior 54880; (715) 394-5591.

St. Francis Home (skilled nursing), 33 Everett St., Fond du Lac 54935; (920) 923-7980 (106).

St. Joseph's Home, 9244 29th Ave., Kenosha 53143; (262) 694-0080; www.stjosephs.com (93).

St. Joseph's Rehabilitation Center, 2902 East Ave. S., La Crosse 54601; (608) 788-9870; www.crsinc.org (80).

St. Joseph's Nursing Home of St. Joseph Community Health Services, Inc. P.O. Box 527, Hillsboro 54634; (608) 489-8000.

St. Joseph Residence, Inc. (nursing home), 107 E. Beckert Rd., New London 54961; (920) 982-5354 (107).

St. Mary's Home for the Aged (skilled nursing, Alzheimer's unit, respite care), 2005 Division St., Manitowoc 54220; (920) 684-7171; www.feliciancommunity.com (266).

St. Mary's Nursing Home, 3515 W. Hadley St., Milwaukee 53210; (414) 873-9250 (88).

St. Monica's Senior Citizens Home, 3920 N. Green Bay Rd., Racine 53404; (262) 639-5050; www.srsofstrita.org (110).

St. Paul Home, Inc. (intermediate and skilled nursing home), 1211 Oakridge Ave., Kaukauna 54130; (920) 766-6020 (129).

Villa Loretto Nursing Home, N8114 Calvary St., Mount Calvary 53057; (920) 753-3211 (52).

Villa St. Francis, Inc., 1910 W. Ohio Ave., Milwaukee 53215; (414) 649-2888 (142).

FACILITIES FOR CHILDREN AND ADULTS WITH DISABILITIES

Sources: Catholic Almanac *survey;* The Official Catholic Directory.

This listing covers facilities and programs with educational and training orientation. Information about other services for the handicapped can generally be obtained from the Catholic Charities Office or its equivalent (c/o Chancery Office) in any diocese. (*See* Index for listing of addresses of chancery offices in the U.S.)

Abbreviation code: b, boys; c, coeducational; d, day; g, girls; r, residential. Other information includes age for admission. The number in parentheses at the end of an entry indicates total capacity or enrollment.

Deaf and Hearing Impaired

California: St. Joseph's Center for Deaf and Hard of Hearing, 3880 Smith St., Union City 94587.

Louisiana: Chinchuba Institute (d,c; birth through 18 yrs.), 1131 Barataria Blvd., Marrero 70072.

Missouri: St. Joseph Institute for the Deaf (r,d,c; birth to 14 years), 1809 Clarkson Rd., Chesterfield, MO 63017; (314) 532-3211 (voice/TDD).

New York: Cleary School for the Deaf (d,c; infancy through 21), 301 Smithtown Blvd., Nesconset, NY 11767-2077; (516) 588-0530; www.clearyschool.org (70).

St. Francis de Sales School for the Deaf (d,c; infant through elementary grades), 260 Eastern Parkway, Brooklyn 11225; (718) 636-4573 (150).

St. Joseph's School for the Deaf (d,c; parent-infant through 14 yrs.), 1000 Hutchinson River Pkwy, Bronx 10465; (718) 828-9000 (140).

Ohio: St. Rita School for the Deaf (r,d,c; birth to 12th grade), 1720 Glendale-Milford Rd., Cincinnati 45215;

(513) 771-7600; www.srsdeaf.org (130).

Pennsylvania: Archbishop Ryan School for Hearing Impaired Children (d,c; parent-infant programs through 8th grade), 233 Mohawk Ave., Norwood, PA 19074; (610) 586-7044 (49).

De Paul Institute (d,c; birth through 21 yrs.), 2904 Castlegate Ave., Pittsburgh 15226; (412) 561-4848 (77).

Emotionally and/or Socially Maladjusted

This listing includes facilities for abused, abandoned and neglected as well as emotionally disturbed children and youth.

Alabama: St. Mary's Home for Children (r,c; referred from agencies), 4350 Moffat Rd., Mobile 36618; (334) 344-7733.

California: Hanna Boys Center (r,b; 10-15 yrs. at intake; school, 4th to 10th grade), Box 100, Sonoma 95476; (707) 996-6767 (107). Treatment center and therapeutic special school for boys with emotional problems, behavior disorders, learning disabilities.

Rancho San Antonio (r,b; 13-17 yrs.), 21000 Plummer St., Chatsworth 91311; (818) 882-6400.

St. Vincent's (r,d,g; 12-17 yrs.), 4200 Calle Real, Santa Barbara 93110-1454; (805) 683-6381.

Colorado: Mt. St. Vincent Home (r,c; 5-13 yrs.), 4159 Lowell Blvd., Denver 80211; (303) 458-7220; www.nahse.org/member/st.vincent.

Connecticut: St. Francis Home for Children (r,d,c; 4-17 yrs.), 651 Prospect St., New Haven 06511; (203) 777-5513. Exec. Dir., Peter Salerno.

Mt. St. John Home and School for Boys (r,b; 11-16 yrs.), 135 Kirtland St., Deep River 06417; (860) 526-

5391; www.mtstjohn.org (77).

Delaware: Our Lady of Grace Home for Children (r,d,c; 6-12 yrs.), 487 E. Chestnut Hill Rd., Newark 19713; (302) 738-4658.

Seton Villa, Siena Hall and Children's Home (r,c; group home; 12-18 yrs,; mothers and their children), c/o 2307 Kentmere Pkwy, Wilmington 19806; (302) 656-2183.

Florida: Boystown of Florida (r,b; 12-16 yrs.; group home), 11400 S.W. 137th Ave., Miami 33186.

Georgia: Village of St. Joseph (r,c; 6-16 yrs.), 1961 Druid Hills Rd., Ste. 205-B, 30329; (404) 321-2900.

Illinois: Guardian Angel Home (d,c; r,b), 1550 Plainfield Rd., Joliet 60435; (815) 729-0930 (35).

Maryville Academy (r,c; 6-18 yrs.), 1150 North River Rd., Des Plaines 60016; (708) 824-6126.

Mission of Our Lady of Mercy, Mercy Home for Boys and Girls (r,d,c; 15-18 yrs.), 1140 W. Jackson Blvd., Chicago 60607; (312) 738-7560; www.mercyhome.org.

Indiana: Gibault School for Boys (r; 10-18 yrs.), 6301 South U.S. Highway 41, Terre Haute 47802; (812) 298-3120.

Hoosier Boys Town (r; 10-18 yrs.), 7403 Cline Ave., Schererville 46375; (219) 322-8614.

Kentucky: Boys' Haven (r; 12-18 yrs.), 2301 Goldsmith Lane, Louisville 40218; (502) 458-1171; www.boyshaven.org.

Louisiana: Hope Haven Center (r,c; 5-18 yrs.), 1101 Barataria Blvd., Marrero 70072; (504) 347-5581.

Maryland: Good Shepherd Center (r,g; 13-18 yrs.), 4100 Maple Ave., Baltimore, 21227; (410) 247-2770; www.goodshepherdcenter.com.

Massachusetts: The Brightside for Families and Children (r,d,c; 6-16 yrs.), 2112 Riverdale St., W. Springfield 01089; (413) 827-4255; www.mercycares.com. Vice-Pres. James Bastien.

McAuley Nazareth Home for Boys (r; 6-13 yrs.), 77 Mulberry St., Leicester 01524; (508) 892-4886 (16). Residential treatment center.

St. Vincent Home (r,c; 5-22 yrs.), 2425 Highland Ave., Fall River 02720; (508) 679-8511.

Michigan: Don Bosco Hall (r,b; 13-17 years.), 10001 Petoskey Ave., Detroit 48204; (313) 834-8677.

Holy Cross Children's Services (r,d,c; 13-17 yrs.), 8759 Clinton-Macon Rd., Clinton 49236; (517) 423-7451; www.hccsnet.org (650). Facilities located throughout the state and northern Ohio.

Vista Maria (r,g; 11-18 yrs.), 20651 W. Warren Ave., Dearborn Heights 48127; (313) 271-6250; www.community.milive.com/cc/girls.

Minnesota: St. Cloud Children's Home (r,c; 8-18 yrs.), RTC Campus, Bld. 4-D, P.O. Box 1006, Fergus Falls, MN 56538; (218) 739-9325. Day Treatment Program (d,c; 7-14 yrs.), same address.

St. Elizabeth Home (r,c; 18 yrs. and older), 306 15th Ave. N., St. Cloud 56301; (320) 252-8350.

Missouri: Child Center of Our Lady (r,d,c; 5-14 yrs.), 7900 Natural Bridge Rd., St. Louis 63121; (314) 383-0200.

Marygrove (r,d,c; 6-21 yrs.) (97); intense treatment unit (r,b; 13-18 yrs) (13); overnight crises care (r,d,c; birth to 18 yrs.) (8), 2705 Mullanphy Lane, Florissant, 63031; (314) 837-1702; www.marygroveonline.org.

St. Joseph's Home for Boys (r,d,b; 6-14 yrs.), 4753 S. Grand Blvd., St. Louis 63111; (314) 481-9121.

Nebraska: Father Flanagan's Boys' Home (r,c; 10-16 yrs.), 14100 Crawford St., Boys Town 68010; (402) 498-1000; www.boystown.org (556). Boys Town National Research Hospital (r,d,c; 1-18 yrs.), 555 N. 30th St., Omaha 68131; (402) 498-6511; www.boystownhospital.org. Center for abused handicapped children, diagnosis of speech, language and hearing problems in children. Boys Town also has various facilities or programs in Brooklyn, NY; Portsmouth, RI; Philadelphia, PA; Washington, DC; Tallahassee, Orlando and Delray Beach, FL; Atlanta, GA; New Orleans, LA; San Antonio, TX; Las Vegas, NV; and southern CA.

New Jersey: Catholic Community Services/Mt. Carmel Guild, 1160 Raymond Blvd., Newark 07102; (973) 596-4084.

Collier High School (d,c; 13-18 yrs.), 160 Conover Rd., Wickatunk 07765; (732) 946-4771; www.collierservices.com.

Collier Group Home, 180 Spring St., Red Bank, NJ 07701; (732) 842-8337.

Mt. St. Joseph Children's Center (r,d,b; 6-14 yrs.), 124 Shepherd Lane, Totowa 07512; (973) 595-5720.

New York: The Astor Home for Children (r,d,c; 5-12 yrs.), 6339 Mill St., P.O. Box 5005, Rhinebeck 12572-5005; (845) 871-1000; www.astorservices.org. Child Guidance Clinics/Day Treatment (Rhinebeck, Poughkeepsie, Beacon, Bronx). Head Start-Day Care (Poughkeepsie, Beacon, Red Hook, Dover, Millerton).

Baker Victory Services, 780 Ridge Rd. Lackawanna 14218; (716) 828-9500; www.ourladyofvictory.org.

Good Shepherd Services (r,d,c), 305 Seventh Ave., New York, NY 10001; (212) 243-7070; www.goodshepherds.org. City-wide residential programs or adolescents (12-21 yrs.); foster care and adoption services (infant-21 yrs.); training institute for human services workers; day treatment program (13-18 yrs.); community-based neighborhood family services in South Brooklyn Community (infant-adult).

LaSalle School (r,d,b; 12-18 yrs.), 391 Western Ave., Albany 12203; (518) 242-4731.

Madonna Heights Services (r,d,g; 12-18 yrs.), 151 Burrs Lane, Dix Hills 11746; (631) 643-8800; www.sco.org (110). Also conducts group homes on Long Island and outpatient programs.

Saint Anne Institute (r,d,g; 12-18 yrs.), 160 N. Main Ave., Albany 12206; (518) 437-6500.

St. Catherine's Center for Children (r,d,c; birth through 12 yrs.), 40 N. Main Ave., Albany 12203; (518) 453-6700; www.st-cath.org.

St. John's of Rockaway Beach (r,b; 9-21 yrs.), 144 Beach 111th St., Rockaway Park 11694; (718) 945-2800. Programs include diagnostic centers and independent living programs.

North Dakota: Home on the Range (r,c; 10-18 yrs.), 16351 I-94, Sentinel Butte 58654; (701) 872-3745; www.gohotr.org (79). Residential and emergency shelter therapeutic programs.

Home on the Range-Red River Victory Ranch (r,b; 10-18 yrs.), P.O. Box 9615, Fargo 58106; (701) 293-6321; www.hotr.org (12). Residential chemical addictions program.

Ohio: St. Vincent Family Centers (d,c; preschool) Outpatient counseling program (c; 2-18 yrs.), 1490 East Main St., Columbus 43205; (614) 252-0731; www.svfc.org.

Marycrest (r,g; 13-18 yrs.), 7800 Brookside Rd., Independence 44131.

Catholic Charities Services/Parmadale (r,c; 12-18 yrs.), 6753 State Rd., Parma 44134; (440) 845-7700.

Rosemont (r,g;d,c; 11-18 yrs.), 2440 Dawnlight Ave., Columbus 43211; (614) 471-2626.

Oregon: St. Mary's Home for Boys (r; 10-18 yrs.), 16535 S.W. Tualatin Valley Highway, Beaverton 97006; (503) 649-5651.

Pennsylvania: Auberle (r,c; 7-18 yrs.), 1101 Hartman St., McKeesport 15132-1500; (412) 673-5800; www.auberle.org (181). Residential treatment for boys; emergency shelter care, foster care, group home for girls and family preservation program.

De LaSalle in Towne (d,b; 14-17 yrs.), 25 S. Van Pelt St., Philadelphia 19103; (215) 567-5500.

De LaSalle Vocational Day Treatment (b; 15-18 yrs.), P.O. Box 344, Bensalem 19020; (215) 464-0344.

Gannondale (r,g; 12-17 yrs.), 4635 E. Lake Rd., Erie 16511; (814) 899-7659.

Harborcreek Youth Services (r,d,c; 10-17 yrs.), 5712 Iroquois Ave., Harborcreek 16421; (814) 899-7664; www.hys-erie.org.

Holy Family Institute (r,d,c; 0-18 yrs.), 8235 Ohio River Blvd., Emsworth 15202; (412) 766-4030; www.hfi-pgh.org.

Lourdesmont Good Shepherd Youth and Family Services (r,g,d,c; 12-17 yrs.), 537 Venard Rd., Clarks Summit 18411; (507) 587-4741; www.lourdesmont.com. Sponsored by the Sisters of the Good Shepherd. John A. Antognoli.

St. Gabriel's Hall (r,b,; 10-18 yrs.), P.O. Box 7280, Audubon 19407; (215) 247-2776.

St. Michael's School (r,b,d,c; 12-17 yrs.), Box 370, Tunkhannock 18657; (570) 388-6155.

Texas: St. Joseph Adolescent and Family Counseling Center (c; 13-17 yrs.), 5415 Maple Ave., #320, Dallas 75235; (214) 631-TEEN.

Washington: Morning Star Boys Ranch (Spokane Boys' Ranch, Inc.) (r,b; 10-18 yrs.), Box 8087, Spokane 99203-0087; (509) 448-1411; www.morningstarboysranch.org. Dir. Joseph M. Weitensteiner.

Wisconsin: North American Union Sisters of Our Lady of Charity Center (r,c; 10-17 yrs.), 154 Edgington Lane, Wheeling, WV 26003-1535; (304) 242-0042.

St. Charles Youth and Family Services (r,d,b; 12-18 yrs.), 151 S. 84th St., Milwaukee 53214; (414) 476-3710; www.stcharlesinc.org.

Wyoming: St. Joseph's Children's Home (r,c; 6-18 yrs.), P.O. Box 1117, Torrington 82240; (307) 532-4197.

Developmentally Challenged

This listing includes facilities for children, youth, and adults with learning disabilities.

Alabama: Father Purcell Memorial Exceptional Children's Center (r,c; birth to 10 yrs.), 2048 W. Fairview Ave., Montgomery 36108; (334) 834-5590; www.mnw.net/fpm.

Father Walter Memorial Child Care Center (r,c; birth-12 yrs.), 2815 Forbes Dr., Montgomery 36110; (334) 262-6421.

California: Child Study Center of St. John's Hospital (d,c; birth-18 yrs.), 1339-20th St., Santa Monica 90404; (310) 829-8921.

St. Madeleine Sophie's Center (d,c; 18 yrs. and older), 2111 E. Madison Ave., El Cajon 92019.

Tierra del Sol Foundation (d,c; 18 yrs. and older), 9919 Sunland Blvd., Sunland 91040; (818) 352-1419. 14547 Gilmore St., Van Nuys 91411; (818) 904-9164.

Connecticut: Gengras Center (d,c; 3-21 yrs.), St. Joseph College, 1678 Asylum Ave., W. Hartford 06117.

Villa Maria Education Center (d,c; 6-14 yrs.), 161 Sky Meadow Dr., Stamford 06903-3400; (203) 322-5886; www.villamariaedcenter.org.

District of Columbia: Lt. Joseph P. Kennedy, Jr., Institute (d,c; 6 weeks to 5 yrs. for Kennedy Institute for Child Development Center; 6-21 yrs. for Kennedy School; 18 yrs. and older for training and employment, therapeutic and residential services). Founded in 1959 for people of all ages with developmental disabilities and their families in the Washington archdiocese. Headquarters: 801 Buchanan St. N.E., Washington 20017; (202) 529-7600; www.kennedyinstitute.org. Other locations in D.C. and Maryland. No enrollment limit.

Florida: L'Arche Harbor House, (c; 20 yrs. and older; community home), 700 Arlington Rd., Jacksonville 32211; (904) 721-5992.

Marian Center Services for Developmentally Handicapped and Mentally Retarded (r,d,c; 2-21 yrs.), 15701 Northwest 37th Ave., Opa Locka 33054; (305) 625-8354; www.mariancenterschool.org. Pre-school, school, workshop residence services.

Morning Star School (d,c; 4-16 yrs.), 725 Mickler Rd., Jacksonville 32211; (904) 421-2144.

Morning Star School (d,c; school age), 954 Leigh Ave., Orlando 32804.

Morning Star School (d,c; 6-14 yrs.), 4661-80th Ave. N., Pinellas Park 33781; (727) 544-6036; www.morningstarschool.org.

Morning Star School (d,c; 6-16 yrs.), 210 E. Linebaugh Ave., Tampa 33612; (813) 935-0232; www.tampa-morningstar.org..

Georgia: St. Mary's Home (r,c), 2170 E. Victory Dr., Savannah 31404; (912) 236-7164.

Illinois: Bartlett Learning Center (r,d,c; 3-21 yrs.), 801 W. Bartlett Rd., Bartlett 60103; (630) 289-4221.

Brother James Court (r, men over 18 yrs.), 2500 St. James Rd., Springfield 62707; (217) 544-4876.

Good Shepherd Manor (men; 18 yrs. and older), Little Brothers of the Good Shepherd, P.O. Box 260, Momence 60954; (815) 472-3700; www.goodshepherdmanor.org. Resident care for developmentally disabled men.

Misericordia Home South (r,c), 2916 W. 47th St., Chicago 60632; (773) 254-9595. For severely and profoundly impaired children.

Misericordia Home — Heart of Mercy Village (r,c; 6-45 yrs.), 6300 North Ridge, Chicago 60660; (773) 973-6300; www.misericordia.com.

Mt. St. Joseph (developmentally disabled women; over age 21), 24955 N. Highway 12, Lake Zurich 60047; (847) 438-5050.

St. Coletta's of Illinois (r,d; 6 to adult), 123rd and Wolf Rd., Palos Park 60464; (708) 448-6520.

St. Mary of Providence (r; women, 18 yrs. and older), 4200 N. Austin Ave., Chicago 60634; (773) 545-8300.

St. Vincent Community Living Facility (r,c; adults, over 18 yrs.) (20), and St. Vincent Supported Living Arrangement (r,c; adults, over 18 yrs.) (20), 659 E. Jefferson St., Freeport 61032; (815) 232-6181.

Springfield Developmental Center (m; 21 yrs. and over), 4595 Laverna Rd., Springfield 62707; (217) 525-8271.

Massachusetts: Cardinal Cushing Centers (d,c; 3-22

yrs.), 85 Washington St., Braintree 02184; (781) 848-6250; www.coletta.org.

Vocational Training

Indiana: Marian Day School (d,c; 6-16 yrs.), 700 Herndon Dr., Evansville 47711; (812) 422-5346.

Kansas: Lakemary Center, Inc. (r,d,c), 100 Lakemary Dr., Paola 66071; (913) 557-4000.

Kentucky: Pitt Academy (d,c), 6010 Preston Hwy., Louisville 40219; (502) 966-6979; www.pitt.com.

Louisiana: Department of Special Education, Archdiocese of New Orleans, St. Michael Special School (d,c; 6-21 yrs.), 1522 Chippewa St., New Orleans 70130.

Holy Angels Residential Facility (r,c; teenage, 14 yrs. and older), 10450 Ellerbe Rd., Shreveport 71106; (318) 797-8500.

Ocean Avenue Community Home, 361 Ocean Ave., Gretna 70053; (504) 361-0674.

Padua Community Services (r,c; birth-25 yrs.), 200 Beta St., Belle Chasse 70037.

St. Jude the Apostle, 1430 Claire Ave., Gretna 70053; (504) 361-8457.

St. Mary's Residential Training School (r,c; 3-22 yrs.), P.O. Drawer 7768, Alexandria 71306; (318) 445-6443.

St. Peter the Fisherman, 62269 Airport Dr., Slidell 70458; (504) 641-4914.

St. Rosalie (r; men 18 and up), 119 Kass St., Gretna 70056; (504) 361-8320.

Sts. Mary and Elizabeth, 720 N. Elm St., Metairie 70003; (504) 738-6959.

Maryland: The Benedictine School for Exceptional Children (r,c; 6-21 yrs.), 14299 Benedictine Lane, Ridgely 21660; (410) 634-2112; www.benschool.com.

Francis X. Gallagher Services (r), 2520 Pot Spring Rd., Timonium 21093.

St. Elizabeth School and Habilitation Center (d,c; 11-21 yrs.), 801 Argonne Dr., Baltimore 21218; (410) 889-5054; www.stelizabeth-school.org.

Massachusetts: Cardinal Cushing School and Training Center (r,d,c; 16-22 yrs.), Hanover 02339 (116 r; 28 d).

Mercy Centre (d,c; 3-22 yrs. and over), 25 West Chester St., Worcester 01605-1136; (508) 852-7165; www.mercycentre.com.

Michigan: Our Lady of Providence Center (r,g; 11-30 yrs.; d,c; 26 yrs. and older), 16115 Beck Rd., Northville 48118; (734) 453-1300.

St. Louis Center and School (r,d,b; 6-18 yrs. child care; 18-36 yrs. adult foster care), 16195 Old U.S. 12, Chelsea 48118-9646; (734) 475-8430; www.stlouiscenter.org.

Minnesota: Mother Teresa Home (r,c; 18 yrs. and older), 101-10th Ave. N., Cold Spring 56320.

St. Francis Home (r,c; 18 yrs. and older), P.O. Box 326, Waite Park 56387; (320) 251-7630.

St. Luke's Home (r; 18 yrs. and older), 411 8th Ave. N., Cold Springs 56320.

Missouri: Department of Special Education, Archdiocese of St. Louis, 4472 Lindell Blvd., St. Louis. 63108; (314) 533-3454. Serves children with developmental disabilities, mental retardation or learning disabilities; services include special ungraded day classes in 8 parish schools.

Good Shepherd Homes (residential for developmentally disabled men; 18 yrs. and up), The Community of the Good Shepherd, 10101 James A. Reed Rd., Kansas City 64134; (816) 767-8090.

St.Mary's Special School (r,c; 5-21 yrs.), 1724 Redman, St. Louis 63138; (314) 261-8533. St. Mary's Supported Living (r,c) (24); supervised homes for adolescents or adults. St. Mary's Early Intervention (d,c) (30); early intervention for toddlers.

Nebraska: Madonna School for Exceptional Children (d,c; 5-21 yrs.), 2537 N. 62nd St., Omaha 68104; (402) 556-1883; www.madonnaschool.org. Children with learning problems.

Villa Marie School and Home for Exceptional Children (r,d,c; 6-18 yrs.), 3700 Sheridan Blvd., Ste. 3, Lincoln 68506; (402) 488-2040.

New Jersey: Archbishop Damiano School (d,c; 3-21 yrs.), 1145 Delsea Dr., Westville Grove 08093.

Catholic Community Services, Archdiocese of Newark, 1160 Raymond Blvd., Newark 07102.

Department of Special Education, Diocese of Camden, 5609 Westfield Ave., Pennsauken, NJ 08110-1836; (609) 488-7123; www.catholicharities.org. Services include: Archbishop Damiano School (above), and full time programs (d,c; 6-21 yrs.) at 4 elementary (96) and 2 high schools (60) and some religious education programs.

Department for Persons with Disabilities, Diocese of Paterson, 1049 Weldon Rd., Oak Ridge, N.J. 07438; (973) 697-4394; www.dpd.org. Services include 8 residential programs for adults, one adult training center, family support services.

Felician School for Exceptional Children (d,c; 5-21 yrs.), 260 S. Main St., Lodi 07644; (973) 777-5355.

McAuley School for Exceptional Children (d,c; 5-21 yrs.), 1633 Rt. 22 at Terrill Rd., Watchung 07060.

Mt. Carmel Guild Special Education School (d,c ; 6-21 yrs.), 60 Kingsland Ave., Kearny 07032; (201) 995-3280.

St. Anthony's Special Education School (d,c), 25 N. 7th St., Belleville 07109; (973) 844-3700.

Sister Georgine School (d,c; 6-17 yrs.), 544 Chestnut Ave., Trenton 08611; (609) 396-5444.

St. Patrick's Special Education School (d,c), 72 Central Ave., Newark 07102.

New York: Baker Victory Services (r), 780 Ridge Rd., Lackawanna, N.Y. 14218; (716) 828-9500; www.baker victoryservices.org. Residential care for handicapped and retarded children; nursery school program for emotionally disturbed pre-school children.

Bishop Patrick V. Ahern High School (d,c; 15-21 yrs.), 100 Merrill Ave., Staten Island 10314.

Cantalician Center for Learning (d,c; birth-21 yrs.), 3233 Main St., Buffalo 14214; (716) 833-5353; www.cantalician.org. Infant and pre-school; elementary and secondary; workshop (426). Three group homes. Rehabilitation, day treatment and senior rehabilitation programs.

Catholic Charities Residential Services, Rockville Centre Diocese, 269 W. Main St., Bay Shore 11706. Residences for developmentally disabled adults (88).

Cobb Memorial School (r,d,c; 5-21 yrs.), 100-300 Mt. Presentation Way, Altamont 12009; (518) 861-6446.

Joan Ann Kennedy Memorial Preschool (d,c; 3-5 yrs.), 26 Sharpe Ave., Staten Island 10302.

L'Arche Syracuse (r; adults), 1232 Teall Ave., Syracuse 13206-3468; (315) 479-8088; www.larchesyracuse.com (12). Homes where assistants and persons with developmental disabilities share life, following the philosophy of Jean Vanier. Member of International L'Arche Federation. Exec. Dir., Frank Woolever.

Maryhaven Center of Hope (r,d,c; school age to adult), 51 Terryville Rd., Port Jefferson 11776; (631) 474-4120; www.maryhaven.org.

Mercy Home for Children (r,c), 243 Prospect Park West, Brooklyn 11215; (718) 832-1075. Residences for adolescents and young adults who are developmentally disabled: Visitation, Warren, Vincent Haire, Santulli and Littlejohn residences (Brooklyn), Kevin Keating Residence (Queens).

Office for Disabled Persons, Catholic Charities, Diocese of Brooklyn, 191 Joralemon St., Brooklyn 11201; (718) 722-6000; www.ccbg.org. Services include: adult day treatment center; community residences for mentally retarded adults; special events for disabled children (from age 3) and adults.

Office for Disabled Persons, Archdiocese of New York, 1011 First Ave., New York 10022; (212) 371-1000. Services include consultation and referral, variety of services for deaf, blind, mentally retarded, mentally ill.

Seton Foundation for Learning (d,c; 5-15 yrs.), 104 Gordon St., Staten Island 10304; (718) 447-1750.

North Carolina: Holy Angels (r,c; birth to adult), 6600 Wilkinson Blvd., P.O. Box 710, Belmont 28012; (704) 825-4161; www.holyangelsnc.org.

North Dakota: Friendship, Inc. (r,d,c; all ages), 3004 11th St. South, Fargo 58103; (701) 235-8217.

Ohio: Julie Billiart School (d,c; 6-12 yrs.), 4982 Clubside Rd., Cleveland 44124; (216) 381-1191; www.juliebilliartschool.org.

Mary Immaculate School (d,c; 6-14 yrs.), 3835 Secor Rd., Toledo 43623; (419) 474-1688; www.maryimmaculatetoledo.org

OLA/St. Joseph Center (d,c; 6-16 yrs.), 2346 W. 14th St., Cleveland 44113; (216) 621-3451.

Rose Mary, The Johanna Graselli Rehabilitation and Education Center (r,c; 5 yrs. and older), 19350 Euclid Ave., Cleveland 44117.

St. John's Villa (r,c; continued care and training, 15 yrs. and over), P.O. Box 457, Carrollton 44615; (330) 627-9789.

Oregon: Providence Montessori School Early Intervention Program (d,c; 3-5 yrs.), 830 N.E. 47th Ave., Portland 97213; (503) 215-2409.

Pennsylvania: Clelian Heights School for Exceptional Children (r,d,c; 5-21 yrs.), R.D. 9, Box 607, Greensburg 15601; (724) 837-8120 (95). Also conducts re-socialization program (r,d,c; young adults).

Divine Providence Village (adults), 686 Old Marple Rd., Springfield 19064; (610) 328-7730. Admin., Sr. Esther Leroux.

Don Guanella Village: Don Guanella School (r,d,b; 6-21 yrs.) and Cardinal Krol Center (r; adults, post-school age), 1797 S. Sproul Rd., Springfield 19602; (610) 543-3380. Admin. Rev. Dennis Weber, S.C.

John Paul II Center for Special Learning (d,c; 3-21 yrs.), 1092 Welsh Rd., Shillington, PA 19607; (610) 777-0605; www.jp2center.org.

McGuire Memorial (r,d,c; 18 mos. to adult.), 2119 Mercer Rd., New Brighton 15066; (724) 843-3400; www.mcguirememorial.org. Exec. Dir., Sr. Mary Thaddeus Markelewicz.

Mercy Special Learning Center (d,c; 3-21 yrs. and early intervention), 830 S. Woodward St., Allentown 18103; (610) 797-8242.

Our Lady of Confidence Day School (d,c; 4-21 yrs.), 10th and Lycoming Sts., Philadelphia 19140.

Queen of the Universe Day Center (d,c; 4-16 yrs.), 2479 Trenton Rd., Levittown 19056; (215) 945-6090; www.qudaycenter.org.

St. Anthony School Programs (d,c; 5-21 yrs.), 2718 Custer Ave., Pittsburgh 15227; (412) 882-1333.

St. Joseph Center for Special Learning (d,c; 4-21 yrs.), 2075 W. Norwegian St., Pottsville 17901; (570) 622-4638; www.pottsville.com/stjosephctr.

St. Joseph's Center (r,d,c; birth-10 yrs.), 2010 Adams Ave., Scranton 18509; (570) 342-8379; www.stjosephcenter.org. Pres., Therese O'Rourke, I.H.M.

St. Katherine Day School (d,c; 4-21 yrs.), 930 Bowman Ave., Wynnewood 19096; (610) 667-3958.

Tennessee: Madonna Learning Center, Inc., for Retarded Children (d,c; 5-16 yrs.), 7007 Poplar Ave., Germantown 38138.

Texas: Notre Dame of Dallas School (d,c; 3-21 yrs.), 2018 Allen St., Dallas 75204; (214) 720-3911.

Virginia: St. Coletta School (d,c; 5-22 yrs.), 207 S. Peyton St., Alexandria, 22314; (703) 683-3686. For developmentally disabled. Services include: occupational, physical and language therapy; vocational program with job search, placement, training and followup services.

St. Mary's Infant Home (r,c; birth to 14 yrs.), 317 Chapel St., Norfolk 23504; (757) 622-2208. For multiple handicapped.

Wisconsin: St Coletta of Wisconsin, W4955 Hwy 18, Jefferson 53549; (920) 674-4330; www.stcolettawi.org. Year-round special education programs for adolescents and adults; pre-vocational and vocational skills training; residential living alternatives. Young adult population. Employment opportunities for those who qualify.

St. Coletta Day School (c; 8-17 yrs.), 1740 N. 55th St., Milwaukee 53208; (414) 453-1850.

Orthopedically/Physically Challenged

Pennsylvania: St. Edmond's Home for Children (r,c; 1-21 yrs.)., 320 S. Roberts Rd., Rosemont 19010; (610) 525-8800.

Virginia: St. Joseph Villa Housing Corp. (adults), 8000 Brook Rd., Richmond 23227; (804) 553-3283.

Visually Challenged

Maine: Educational Services for Blind and Visually Impaired Children (Catholic Charities, Maine), 1066 Kenduskeag Ave., Bangor 04401. 66 Western Ave., Fairfield 04937. 15 Westminster St., Lewiston 04240. P.O. Box 378, Fairfield, ME 04937; (800) 660-5231. Itinerant teachers, instructional materials center.

New Jersey: St. Joseph's School for the Blind (r,d,c; 3-21 yrs.), 257 Baldwin Ave., Jersey City 07306; (201) 653-0578; www.sjsb.net.

New York: Lavelle School for the Blind (d,c; 3-21 yrs.), East 221st St. and Paulding Ave., Bronx 10469; (718) 882-1212. For visually impaired, multiple handicapped.

Pennsylvania: St. Lucy Day School (d,c; pre-K to 8th grade), 130 Hampden Rd., Upper Darby 19082; (610) 352-4550; www.stlucydayschool.org. For children with visual impairments.

HOUSES OF RETREAT AND RENEWAL

There is great variety in retreat and renewal programs, with orientations ranging from the traditional to teen encounters. Central to all of them are celebration of the liturgy and deepening of a person's commitment to faith and witness in life.

Features of many of the forms are as follows.

Traditional Retreats: Centered around conferences and the direction of a retreat master; oriented to the personal needs of the retreatants; including such standard practices as participation in Mass, reception of the sacraments, private and group prayer, silence and meditation, discussions.

Team Retreat: Conducted by a team of several leaders or directors (priests, religious, lay persons) with division of subject matter and activities according to their special skills and the nature and needs of the group.

Closed Retreat: Involving withdrawal for a period of time — overnight, several days, a weekend — from everyday occupations and activities.

Open Retreat: Made without total disengagement from everyday involvements, on a part-time basis.

Private Retreat: By one person, on a kind of do-it-yourself basis with the one-to-one assistance of a director.

Special Groups: With formats and activities geared to particular groups; e.g., members of Alcoholics Anonymous, vocational groups and apostolic groups.

Marriage Encounters: Usually weekend periods of husband-wife reflection and dialogue; introduced into the U.S. from Spain in 1967.

Charismatic Renewal: Featuring elements of the movement of the same name; "Spirit-oriented," communitarian and flexible, with spontaneous and shared prayer, personal testimonies of faith and witness.

Christian Community: Characterized by strong community thrust.

Teens Encounter Christ (TEC), SEARCH: Formats adapted to the mentality and needs of youth, involving experience of Christian faith and commitment in a community setting.

Christian Maturity Seminars: Similar to teen encounters in basic concept but different to suit persons of greater maturity.

RENEW International: Spiritual renewal process involving the entire parish. Office, 1232 George St., Plainfield, NJ 07062; (908) 769-5400. Director, Msgr. Thomas A. Kleissler.

Cursillo: *See separate entry.*

Conference

Retreats International Inc.: National Office, Box 1067, Notre Dame, IN 46556; (574) 247-4443. An organization for promoting retreats in the U.S. was started in 1904 in New York. Its initial efforts and the gradual growth of the movement led to the formation in 1927 of the National Catholic Laymen's Retreat Conference, the forerunner of the men's division of Retreats International. The women's division developed from the National Laywomen's Retreat Movement that was founded in Chicago in 1936. The men's and women's divisions merged July 9, 1977. The services of the organization include an annual summer institute for retreat and pastoral ministry, regional conferences for retreat center leadership and area meetings of directors and key leadership in the retreat movement. The officers are: Episcopal advisor, Auxiliary Bishop Robert Morneau of Green Bay; Pres., Sr. Mary Elizabeth Imler, O.S.F.; Exec. Dir., Anne M. Luther.

Houses of Retreat and Renewal

Principal sources: Catholic Almanac *survey;* The Official Catholic Directory.

Abbreviation code: m, men; w, women; mc, married couples; y, youth. Houses and centers without code generally offer facilities to most groups. An asterisk after an abbreviation indicates that the facility is primarily for the group designated but that special groups are also accommodated. Houses furnish information concerning the types of programs they offer.

Alabama: Blessed Trinity Shrine Retreat and Cenacle, 107 Holy Trinity Rd., Holy Trinity 36856, (334) 855-4474; Visitation Sacred Heart Retreat House, 2300 Spring Hill Ave., Mobile 36607, (334) 473-2321.

Alaska: Holy Spirit Center, 10980 Hillside Dr., Anchorage 99507, (907) 346-2343, home.gci.net/~hsrh.

Arizona: Franciscan Renewal Center, 5802 E. Lincoln Dr., Scottsdale 85253, (480) 948-7460; Holy Trinity Monastery, P.O. Box 298, St. David 85630, Benedictine community, self-directed/Spirit-directed monastic retreat, (520) 720-4642; Mount Claret Retreat Center, 4633 N. 54th St., Phoenix 85018, (602) 840-5066; Our Lady of Solitude House of Prayer, P.O. Box 1140, Black Canyon City 85324, (623) 374-9204; Redemptorist Picture Rocks Retreat House, 7101 W. Picture Rocks Rd., Tucson 85743, (520) 744-3400, www.desertrenewal.org.

Arkansas: Brothers and Sisters of Charity, Little Portion Hermitage, 350 C R 048, Berryville, 72616-8505, (479) 253-7710, www.johnmichaeltalbot.com; Little Portion Retreat and Training Center, Rt. 4, Box 430, Eureka Springs 72632, (501) 253-7379; St. Scholastica Retreat Center, P.O. Box 3489, Ft. Smith 72913, (479) 783-1135, www. scholasticafortsmith.org; Hesychia House of Prayer, 204 St. Scholastica Rd., New Blaine, Shoal Creek, 72851, (501) 938-7375.

California: Angela Center, 535 Angela Dr., Santa Rosa 95403, (707) 528-8578; Christ the King Retreat Center, 6520 Van Maren Lane, Citrus Heights 95621, (916) 725-4720, www.passionist.org; Claretian Retreat Center, 1119 Westchester Pl., Los Angeles 90019, (323) 737-8464; El Carmelo Retreat House, P.O. Box 446, Redlands 92373, (909) 792-1047, www.elcarmelo.org; Heart of Jesus Retreat Center, 2927 S. Greenville St., Santa Ana 92704, (714) 557-4538; Holy Spirit Retreat Center, 4316 Lanai Rd., Encino 91436, (818) 784-4515; Holy Transfiguration Monastery (m*), Monks of Mt. Tabor (Byzantine Ukrainian), 17001 Tomki Rd., P.O. Box 217, Redwood Valley 95470, (707) 485-8959; Jesuit Retreat House, 300 Manresa Way, Los Altos 94022, (650) 948-4491, www.elretiro.org; Madonna of Peace Renewal Center (y), P.O. Box 71, Copperopolis 95228, (209) 785-2157; Marian Retreat Center, 535 Sacramento St., Auburn 95603, (916) 887-2019; Mary and Joseph Retreat Center, 5300 Crest Rd., Rancho Palos Verdes 90275, (310) 377-4867, www.maryjoseph.org.

Marywood Retreat Center, 2811 E. Villa Real Dr.,

Orange 92863-1595, (714) 282-3000, www.rcbo.org; Mater Dolorosa Retreat Center, 700 N. Sunnyside Ave., Sierra Madre 91024, (626) 355-7188, www.passionist.org; Mercy Center, 2300 Adeline Dr., Burlingame 94010, (650) 340-7474, www.mercy-center.org; Mission San Luis Rey Retreat, 4050 Mission Ave., Oceanside, 92057-6402, (760) 757-3659, www.sanluisrey.org; Mount Alverno Retreat and Conference Center, 3910 Bret Harte Dr., Redwood City 94061, (650) 369-0798, www.mountalverno.com; New Camaldoli Hermitage, Big Sur 93920, (831) 667-2456, www.contemplation.com; Our Lady of the Oaks Villa, P.O. Box 128, Applegate 95703, (530) 878-2776. Poverello of Assisi Retreat House, 1519 Woodworth St., San Fernando 91340, (818) 365-1071; Presentation Education and Retreat Center, 19480 Bear Creek Rd., Los Gatos 95033, (408) 354-2346, www.prescenter.org; Prince of Peace Abbey, 650 Benet Hill Rd., Oceanside 92054, (760) 430-1305; Pro Sanctity Spirituality Center, 205 S. Pine St., Fullerton 92633 (for day use); Sacred Heart Retreat House (w*), 920 E. Alhambra Rd., Alhambra 91801, (626) 289-1353; St. Andrew's Abbey Retreat House, P.O. Box 40, Valyermo 93563, (661) 944-2178, www.valyermo.com; St. Anthony Retreat, P.O. Box 249, Three Rivers 93271, (559) 561-4595, www.stanthonyretreat.org; St. Clare's Retreat, 2381 Laurel Glen Rd., Soquel 95073, (831) 423-8093, www.infoteam.com/nonprofit/stclaresretreat/index.html; St. Francis Retreat, P.O. Box 970, San Juan Bautista 95045, (831) 623-4234, www.stfrancisretreat.com; St. Francis Youth Center (y), 2400 E. Lake Ave., Watsonville 95076; St. Joseph's Salesian Youth Center, P.O. Box 1639, 8301 Arroyo Dr., Rosemead 91770, (626) 280-8622, www.stjoescenter.org; St. Mary's Seminary and Retreat House, 1964 Las Canoas Rd., Santa Barbara 93105, (805) 966-4829; San Damiano Retreat, P.O. Box 767, Danville 94526, (925) 837-9141, www.sandamiano.org.

San Miguel Retreat House, P.O. Box 69, San Miguel 93451, (805) 467-3256; Santa Sabina Center, 25 Magnolia Ave., San Rafael 94901, (415) 457-7727; Serra Retreat, 3401 S. Serra Rd., Box 127, Malibu 90265, (310) 456-6631, www.serraretreat.com; Starcross Community, 34500 Annapolis Rd., Annapolis 95412, (707) 886-1919, www.starcross.org; Villa Maria del Mar, Santa Cruz, 2-1918 E. Cliff Dr., Santa Cruz 95062, (831) 475-1236, www.villamariadelmar.org; Villa Maria – House of Prayer (w) 1252 N. Citrus Dr., La Habra 90631, (562) 691-5838.

Colorado: Benet Pines Retreat Center, 15880 Highway 83, Colorado Springs 80921, (719) 495-2574, www.geocities.com; Camp St. Malo Religious Retreat and Conference Center, 10758, Hwy. 7, Allenspark 80510, (303) 747-2892; Sacred Heart Retreat House, Box 185, Sedalia 80135, (303) 688-4198, www.gabrielmedia.org/shjrh; Spiritual Life Institute (individuals only), Nada Hermitage, P.O. Box 219, Crestone 81131, (719) 256-4778, www.spiritual-lifeinstitute.org.

Connecticut: St. Edmund's Retreat, P.O. Box 399, Mystic 06355, (860) 536-0565, www.sse.org/enders; Emmaus Spiritual Life Center, 24 Maple Ave., Uncasville 06382, (860) 848-3427; Holy Family Retreat, 303 Tunxis Rd., Farmington 06107, (860) 521-0440; Immaculata Retreat House, P.O. Box 55, Willimantic 06226, (860) 423-8484, www.immaculateretreat.org; Mercy Center at Madison, P.O. Box 191, 167 Neck Rd., Madison 06443, (203) 245-0401,

www.mercybythesea.org; My Father's House, Box 22, 39 North Moodus Rd., Moodus 06469, (860) 873-1906, www.myfathershouse.com; Our Lady of Calvary Retreat (w*), 31 Colton St., Farmington 06032, (860) 677-8519, www.ourladyofcalvary.com; Trinita Retreat Center, 595 Town Hill Rd., Rt. 219, New Hartford 06057, (860) 379-4329; Villa Maria Retreat House, 161 Sky Meadow Dr., Stamford 06903, (203) 322-5886; Wisdom House Retreat Center, 229 E. Litchfield Rd., 06759, (860) 567-3163, www.wisdomhouse.org.

Delaware: St. Francis Renewal Center, 1901 Prior Rd., Wilmington 19809, (302) 798-1454.

District of Columbia: Washington Retreat House, 4000 Harewood Rd. N.E., Washington 20017, (202) 529-1111.

Florida: Cenacle Retreat House, 1400 S. Dixie Highway, Lantana 33462-5492, (561) 582-2534, www.cenaclesisters.org; Dominican Retreat House, Inc., 7275 S.W. 124th St., Miami 33156-5324, (305) 238-2711; Franciscan Center, 3010 Perry Ave., Tampa 33603, (813) 229-2695, www.slleganyfranciscans.org/franciscancenter.htm; John Paul II Retreat House, 720 N.E. 27th St., Miami 33137, (305) 576-2748, www.acu-adsum.org; Our Lady of Divine Providence, 702 S. Bayview Ave., Clearwater, 33759, (727) 797-7412, www.divineprovidence.org; Our Lady of Perpetual Help Retreat and Spirituality Center, 3989 S. Moon Dr., Venice 34292, (941) 486-0233, www.olph-retreat.org; Saint John Neumann Renewal Center, 685 Miccosukee Rd., Tallahassee 32308, (850) 224-2971; St. Leo Abbey Retreat Center, P.O. Box 2350, St. Leo 33574, (352) 588-2009.

Georgia: Ignatius House, 6700 Riverside Dr. N.W., Atlanta 30328, (404) 255-0503.

Idaho: Nazareth Retreat Center, 4450 N. Five Mile Rd., Boise 83704, (208) 375-2932.

Illinois: Bellarmine Jesuit Retreat House (mc), 175 W. County Line Rd, Barrington 60010, (847) 381-1261, www.bellarminehall.org; Bishop Lane Retreat House, 7708 E. McGregor Rd., Rockford 61102, (815) 965-5011; Cabrini Retreat Center, 9430 Golf Rd., Des Plaines 60016, (847) 297-6530; Carmelite Spiritual Center, 8433 Bailey Rd., Darien 60561, (630) 969-4141; Cenacle Retreat House, 513 Fullerton Parkway, Chicago 60614, (773) 528-6300; Cenacle Retreat House, P.O. Box 797, Warrenville 60555, (630) 393-1231, www.cenacle.org; King's House Retreat and Renewal Center, 700 N. 66th St., Belleville 62223-3949, (618) 397-0584.

La Salle Manor, Christian Brothers Retreat House, 12480 Galena Rd., Plano 60545, (630) 552-3224, www.lasallemanor.org; St. Mary's Retreat House, P.O. Box 608, 14230 Main St., Lemont 60439, (630) 257-5102; Tolentine Center, 20300 Governors Highway, Olympia Fields 60461, (708) 748-9500.

Indiana: Archabbey Guest House, St. Meinrad Archabbey, St. Meinrad 47577, (800) 581-6905; Benedict Inn Retreat and Conference Center, 1402 Southern Ave., Beech Grove 46107, (317) 788-7581, www.benedictinn.org; Bethany Retreat House, 2202 Lituanica Ave., 46312, (219) 398-5047; Fatima Retreat House, 5353 E. 56th St., Indianapolis 46226-1486, (317) 545-7681, www.archindy.org; John XXIII Retreat Center, 407 W. McDonald St., Hartford City 47348, (765) 348-4008, www.netusa1.net/~john23rd; Kordes Retreat Center, 841 E. 14th St., Ferdinand 47532, (812) 367-2777, www.thedome.org/kordes.

Lindenwood, PHJC Ministry Center, P.O. Box 1, Donaldson 46513, (574) 935-1780; Mary's Solitude, St.Mary's, 100 Lourdes Hall, Notre Dame 46556, (219) 284-5599; Mount Saint Francis Retreat Center and Friary, 101 St. Anthony Dr., Mount Saint Francis 47146, (812) 923-8817, www.mountsaintfrancis.org; Our Lady of Fatima Retreat Center, P.O. Box 929, Notre Dame 46556, (574) 631-8289; Sarto Retreat House, 4200 N. Kentucky Ave., Evansville 47724, (812) 424-5536.

Iowa: American Martyrs Retreat House, 2209 N. Union Rd., P.O. Box 605, Cedar Falls 50613-0605, (319) 266-3543, www.americanmartyrs.tripod.com; Emmanuel House of Prayer Country Retreat and Solitude Center, 4427 Kotts Rd. N.E., Iowa City 52240; New Melleray Guest House, 6500 Melleray Circle, Dubuque 52068, (319) 588-2319; Shalom Retreat Center, 1001 Davis Ave., Dubuque 52001, (319) 582-3592, members.aol.com/dbqshalom.

Kansas: Heartland Center for Spirituality, 3600 Broadway, Great Bend 67530, (316) 792-1232; Manna House of Prayer, 323 East 5th St., Box 675, Concordia 66901, (785) 243-4428; Spiritual Life Center, 7100 E. 45th St., N. Wichita 67226, (316) 744-0167, www.feist.com/~spiritlife/index.html.

Kentucky: Bethany Spring, 115 Dee Head Rd., New Haven, 40051, (502) 549-8277; Catherine Spalding Center, P.O. Box 24, Nazareth 40048, (502) 348-1516, www.scnazarethky.org/csc; Flaget Center, 1935 Lewiston Dr., Louisville 40216, (502) 448-8581; Marydale Retreat Center, 945 Donaldson Hwy., Erlanger 41018, (606) 371-4224; Mt. St. Joseph Retreat Center, 8001 Cummings Rd., Maple Mount 42356-9999, (502) 229-0200, www.msjcenter.org; Our Lady of Gethsemani (m,w; private), The Guestmaster, Abbey of Gethsemani, Trappist, 40051; Passionist Nuns, 8564 Crisp Rd, Whitesville 42378, (270) 233-4571.

Louisiana: Abbey Christian Life Center, St. Joseph's Abbey, St. Benedict 70457, (504) 892-3473; Ave Maria Retreat House, 8089 Barataria Blvd., Crown Point, 70072, (504) 689-3837; Cenacle Retreat House (w*), 5500 St. Mary St., P.O. Box 8115, Metairie 70006, (504) 887-1420, www.cenaclesisters.org/metairie.htm; Jesuit Spirituality Center (m,w; directed), P.O. Box C, Grand Coteau 70541-1003, (337) 662-5251, www.jesuitspiritualitycenter.org; Lumen Christi Retreat Center, 100 Lumen Christi Lane, Hwy. 311, Schriever 70395, (504) 868-1523; Magnificat Center of the Holy Spirit, 23629 Faith Rd., Ponchatoula 70454, (504) 362-4356.

Manresa House of Retreats (m), P.O. Box 89, Convent 70723, (225) 562-3596; Maryhill Renewal Center, 600 Maryhill Rd., Pineville 71360, (318) 640-1378, www.diocesealex.org; Our Lady of the Oaks Retreat House, P.O. Box D, 214 Church St., Grand Coteau 70541, (318) 662-5410; Regina Coeli Retreat Center, 17225 Regina Coeli Rd., Covington 70433, (504) 892-4110; Sophie Barat House, 1719 Napoleon Ave., New Orleans 70115, (504) 899-6027.

Maine: Bay View Villa, 187 Bay View Rd., Saco 04072, (207) 286-8762; Marie Joseph Spiritual Center, 10 Evans Rd., Biddeford 04005, (207) 284-5671, www.mariejosephspiritual.org; Mother of the Good Shepherd Monastery by the Sea, 235 Pleasant Ave., Peaks Island 04108, (207) 766-2717; Notre Dame Retreat & Spiritual Center, P.O. Box 159, Alfred 04002, (207) 324-6160; St. Paul Retreat and Cursillo Center, 136 State St., Augusta 04330, (207) 622-6235.

Maryland: Bon Secours Spiritual Center, Marriottsville 21104, (410) 442-1320, www.bonsecours.org/bssc; Christian Brothers Spiritual Center (m,w,y), P.O. Box 29, 2535 Buckeyestown Pike, Adamstown 21710, (301) 874-5180; Loyola on the Potomac Retreat House, Faulkner 20632, (301) 870-3515, www.loyolaretreat.org; Msgr. Clare J. O'Dwyer Retreat House (y*), 15523 York Rd., P.O. Box 310, Sparks 21152, (410) 666-2400; Our Lady of Mattaponi Youth Retreat and Conference Center, 11000 Mattaponi Rd., Upper Marlboro 20772, (301) 952-9074; Seton Retreat Center, 333 S. Seton Ave., Emmitsburg 21727, (301) 447-6021.

Massachusetts: Boston Cenacle Society, 25 Avery St., Dedham 02026; Calvary Retreat Center, 59 South St., P.O. Box 219, Shrewsbury 01545, (508) 842-8821, www.calvaryretreat.org; Campion Renewal Center, 319 Concord Rd., Weston 02193, (781) 788-6810; Community of Teresian Carmelites, 30 Chrome St., 01613, (508) 752-5734; Don Orione Center, P.O. Box 205, Old Groveland Rd., Bradford 01835, (508) 373-0461; Eastern Point Retreat House, Gonzaga Hall, 37 Niles Pond Rd., Gloucester 01930, (978) 283-0013; Espousal Center, 554 Lexington St., Waltham 02452, (781) 209-3120, www.espousal.org; Esther House of Spiritual Renewal, Sisters of St. Anne, 1015 Pleasant St., Worcester 01602-1338.

Franciscan Center — Retreat House, 459 River Rd., Andover 01810, (978) 851-3391, www.franrcent.org; Genesis Spiritual Life Center, 53 Mill St., Westfield 01085, (413) 562-3627; Glastonbury Abbey (Benedictine Monks), 16 Hull St., Hingham 02043, (701) 749-2155, www.glastonburyabbey.org; Holy Cross Fathers Retreat House, 490 Washington St., N. Easton 02356, (508) 238-2051; La Salette Center for Christian Living, 947 Park St., Attleboro 02703, (508) 222-8530, www.lasalette.shrine.tripod.com; Marian Center, 1365 Northampton St., Holyoke 01040-1913, (413) 534-4502 (day and evening programs); Marist House, 518 Pleasant St., 01701, (508) 879-1620; Miramar Retreat Center, P.O. Box M, Duxbury, 02331-0614, (781) 585-2460; Mt. Carmel Christian Life Center, Oblong Rd., Box 613, Williamstown 01267, (413) 458-3164.

Sacred Heart Retreat Center, Salesians of St. John Bosco, P.O. Box 567, Ipswich 01938; St. Benedict Abbey (Benedictine Monks), 252 Still River Rd., P.O. Box 67, Still River 01467, (978) 456-3221; St. Joseph Villa Retreat Center, Sisters of St. Joseph, 339 Jerusalem Rd., Cohasset 02025, (781) 383-6024; St. Joseph's Abbey Retreat House (m) (Trappist Monks), 167 North Spencer Rd., Spencer 01562, (508) 885-8710, www.spencerabbey.org; St. Stephen Priory Spiritual Life Center (Dominican), 20 Glen St., Box 370, Dover 02030, (508) 785-0124, www.ststephenpriory.org.

Michigan: Augustine Center, 2798 U.S. 31 North, Box 84, Conway 49722, (231) 347-3657, www.dioceseof gaylord.org; Capuchin Retreat, 62460 Mt. Vernon, Box 396, Washington 48094, (248) 651-4826; Colombiere Conference and Retreat Center, 9075 Big Lake Rd., Clarkston 48346, (248) 620-2534, www.colombiere.com; Manresa Jesuit Retreat House, 1390 Quarton Rd., Bloomfield Hills 48304, (248) 644-4933; Marygrove Retreat Center, Garden 49835, (906) 644-2771; Queen of Angels Retreat, 3400 S. Washington Rd., P.O. Box 2026, Saginaw 48605, (517) 755-2149, www.rc.net/saginaw/retreat.

St. Francis Retreat Center, 703 E. Main St., De Witt 48820-9499, (517) 669-8321, www.stfrancis.ws; St.

Lazare Retreat House, 18600 W. Spring Lake Rd., P.O. Box 462, Spring Lake 49456, (616) 842-3370; St. Mary's Retreat House (w*), 775 W. Drahner Rd., Oxford 48371, (248) 628-3894, www.op.org/oxford; St. Paul of the Cross Retreat Center (m*), 23333 Schoolcraft, Detroit 48223, (313) 535-9563; Weber Retreat Center, 1257 Siena Hghts. Dr., Adrian 49221, (517) 266-4000.

Minnesota: Benedictine Center, St. Paul's Monastery, 2675 Larpenteur Ave. East, St. Paul 55109, (651) 777-7251, www.osb.org/spm; The Cenacle, 1221 Wayzata Blvd., Wayzata 55391; Center for Spiritual Development, 211 Tenth St. S., P.O. Box 538, Bird Island 55310, (320) 365-3644, www.centerbi.com; Christ the King Retreat Center, 621 First Ave. S., Buffalo 55313, (763) 682-1394; Dunrovin Christian Brothers Retreat Center, 15525 St. Croix Trail North, Marine-on-St. Croix 55047, (651) 433-2486, www.dunrovin.org.

Franciscan Retreats, Conventual Franciscan Friars, 16385 St. Francis Lane, Prior Lake 55372, (952) 447-2182, www.franciscanretreats.net; Holy Spirit Retreat House, 3864 420th Ave., Janesville, 56048, (507) 234-5712; Jesuit Retreat House (m), 8243 DeMontreville Trail North, Lake Elmo 55042, (651) 777-1311; Maryhill (m,w*), 1988 Summit Ave., St. Paul 55105, (651) 696-2970, www.sdhm.net; Villa Maria Center, Villa Maria Center, 29847 County 2 Blvd., Frontenac 55026, (651) 345-4582.

Missouri: Assumption Abbey, Rte. 5, Box 1056, Ava 65608, (417) 683-5110, www.assumptionabbey.org; The Cenacle, 3393 McKelvey Rd., Apt. 211, Bridgeton, 63044-2544, (314) 387-2211; Cordis House, 648 S. Assisi Way, Republic 65738, (417) 732-6684; *Il Ritiro* - The Little Retreat, P.O. Box 38, Eime Rd., Dittmer 63023, (636) 285-3759; La Salle Institute, 2101 Rue de la Salle, Wildwood 63038, (636) 938-5374; Maria Fonte Solitude (private; individual hermitages), P.O. Box 322, High Ridge 63049, (314) 677-3235.

Marianist Retreat and Conference Center, P.O. Box 718, Eureka 63025-0718, (636) 938-5390; Mercy Center, 2039 N. Geyer Rd., St. Louis 63131, (314) 909-4629; Our Lady of Assumption Abbey (m,w), Trappists, Rt. 5, Box 1056, Ava 65608-9142; Pallottine Renewal Center, 15270 Old Halls Ferry Rd., Florissant 63034, (314) 837-7100, members.aol.com/prcrenewal/home.html; Society of Our Mother of Peace (private, individual hermitages), 12494 Hwy. T, Marionville 65705, (417) 744-2011; White House Retreat, 3601 Lindell Blvd., St. Louis 63108, (314) 846-2575, www.whretreat.org; Windridge Solitude, 1932 W. Linda Lane, Lonedell 63060; (636) 629-4449.

Montana: Sacred Heart Retreat Center, 26 Wyoming Ave., P.O. Box 153, Billings 59103, (406) 252-0322; Ursuline Retreat Centre, 2300 Central Ave., Great Falls 59401, (406) 452-8585.

Nebraska: Our Lady of Good Counsel retreat House, R.R. 1, Box 110, 7303 N. 112th St., Waverly 68462, (402) 786-2705.

New Hampshire: Epiphany Monastery, 96 Scobie Rd., P.O. Box 60, New Boston 03070; La Salette Shrine (private and small groups), 410 NH, Route 4A, P.O. Box 420, Enfield 03748, (603) 632-7087.

New Jersey: Bethany Ridge, P.O. Box 241, Little York 08834, (908) 995-9758; Bethlehem Hermitage, 82 Pleasant Hill Rd., Chester 07930-2135, (908) 879-7059; Carmel Retreat House, 1071 Ramapo Valley Rd., Mahwah 07430,

(201) 327-7090, www.carmelretreat.com; Cenacle Retreat House, 411 River Rd., Highland Park 08904, (732) 249-8100, www.cenacle.sisters.org; Emmaus House, 101 Center St., Perth Amboy 08861, (732) 442-7688; Father Judge Apostolic Center (young adults), 1292 Long Hill Rd., Stirling 07980; Felician Retreat House, 35 Windemere Ave., Mt. Arlington 07856, (973) 398-9806; John Paul II Retreat Center, 414 S. 8th St., Vineland 08360; Loyola House of Retreats, 161 James St., Morristown 07960, (973) 539-0740, www.loyola.org.

Marianist Family Retreat Center (families*), 417 Yale Ave., Box 488, Cape May Point 08212-0488; Maris Stella (Retreat and Vacation Center), 7201 Long Beach Blvd., P.O. Box 3135, Harvey Cedars 08008, (609) 361-8863; Mount Paul Retreat Center, 243 Mt. Paul Rd., Oak Ridge 07438, (973) 697-6341; Franciscan Spiritual Center, 474 Sloatsburg Rd., Ringwood 07456-1978, (973) 962-9778; Queen of Peace Retreat House, St. Paul's Abbey, P.O. Box 7, Newton 07860, (973) 383-2470; Sacred Heart Renewal Center, P.O. Box 68, Belvidere 07823, (908) 475-4694; Sacred Heart Retreat Center (y*, m,w), 20 Old Swartswood Rd., Newton 07860, (973) 383-2620; St. Joseph by the Sea Retreat House, 400 Rte. 35 N., South Mantoloking 08738-1309, (732) 892-8494, www.filippiniusa.org.

St. Pius X Spiritual Life Center, P.O. Box 216, Blackwood 08012, (856) 227-1436; San Alfonso Retreat House, P.O. Box 3098, 755 Ocean Ave., Long Beach 07740, (732) 222-2731, www.sanalfonsoretreats.org; Sanctuary of Mary, Pilgrimage Place, Branchville 07826, (973) 875-7625; Stella Maris Retreat House, 981 Ocean Ave., Elberon 07740, (732) 229-0602, www.stellamarisretreatcenter.org; Villa Pauline Retreat House, 350 Bernardsville Rd., Mendham 07945, (973) 543-9058; Vincentian Renewal Center, 75 Mapleton Rd., P.O. Box 757, Plainsboro 08536, (609) 520-9626; Vocationist Fathers Retreat, 90 Brooklake Rd., Florham Park 07932, (973) 966-6262, www.vocationist.org; Xavier Retreat and Conference Center, P.O. Box 211, Convent Station 07961, (973) 290-5100, www.xaviercenter.org.

New Mexico: Holy Cross Retreat, Conventual Franciscan Friars, P.O. Box 158, Mesilla Park 88047, (505) 524-3688, www.zianet.com/franciscan; Immaculate Heart of Mary Retreat and Conference Center, Mt. Carmel Rd., Santa Fe 87501, (505) 988-1975; Madonna Retreat Center, Inc., 4040 St. Joseph Pl., N.W., 87120, (505) 831-8196; Pecos Benedictine Abbey, Pecos 87552, (505) 757-6600, www.pecosabbey.org; Spiritual Renewal Center, 6400 Coors Rd., NW, Albuquerque 87120; (505) 890-4110; www.spiritualretreats.com; Sacred Heart Retreat, P.O. Box 1989, Gallup 87301.

New York: Bethany Spirituality Center, County Road 105, Box 1003, Highland Mills 10930, (845) 460-3061, www.bthanysiritualitycnter.org; Bethlehem Retreat House, Abbey of the Genesee, Piffard 14533; Bishop Molloy Retreat House, 86-45 Edgerton Blvd., Jamaica 11432, (718) 739-1229, www.bishopmolloy.org; Blessed Kateri Retreat House, National Kateri Shrine, P.O. Box 627, Fonda 11432, (518) 853-3646; Cardinal Spellman Retreat House, Passionist Community, 5801 Palisade Ave., Bronx (Riverdale) 10471, (718) 549-6500, www.passionists.org; Cenacle Center for Spiritual Renewal, 310 Cenacle Rd., Ronkonkoma 11779-2203, (631) 588-8366, www.cenaclesisters.org.

Cenacle Retreat House, State Rd., P.O. Box 467,

Bedford Village 10506, (914) 234-3344; Christ the King Retreat and Conference Center, 500 Brookford Rd., Syracuse 13224, (315) 446-2680; Cormaria Retreat House, Sag Harbor, L.I. 11963, (631) 725-4206; Dominican Retreat and Conference Center, 1945 Union St., Niskayuma, (518) 393-4169, www.dslcny.org; Don Bosco Retreat Center, 174 Filors Lane, Stony Point, 10980-2645, (845) 947-2200, www.marianshrine.org; Graymoor Spiritual Life Center, Graymoor, Route 9, P.O. Box 300, Garrison 10524, (845) 424-3671, www.graymoorcenter.org; Jesuit Retreat House, Auriesville, (518) 853-3033; Monastery of the Precious Blood (w), Ft. Hamilton Parkway and 54th St., Brooklyn 11219 (single day retreats); Mount Alvernia Retreat Center, Box 858, Wappingers Falls 12590, (845) 297-5706, www.mtalvernia.org.

Mount Irenaeus Franciscan Mountain Retreat, Holy Peace Friary, P.O. Box 100, West Clarksville, NY 14786, (716) 973-2470; Mount Manresa Retreat House, 239 Fingerboard Rd., Staten Island 10305, (718) 727-3844; Mt. St. Alphonsus Redemptorist Retreat Ministry, P.O. Box 219, Esopus 12429, (845) 384-8000, www.msaretreat.org; Notre Dame Retreat House, Box 342, 5151 Foster Rd., Canandaigua 14424, (585) 394-5700, www.notredameretreathouse.org; Our Lady of Hope Center, 434 River Rd., Newburgh 12550, (914) 568-0780; Regina Maria Retreat House, 77 Brinkerhoff St., Plattsburgh 12901-2701, (518) 561-3421; St. Andrew's House, 257 St. Andrew's Rd., Walden 12586, (845) 778-5941; St. Columban Center, Diocese of Buffalo, 6892 Lake Shore Rd., P.O. Box 816, Derby 14047, (716) 947-4708, www.stcolumbacenter.org.

St. Francis Retreat, 1 Pryer Manor Rd., Larchmont 10538, (914) 235-6839; St. Francis Center for Spirituality, 500 Todt Hill Rd., Staten Island, NY 10304, (718) 981-3131, www.st-francis-center-for-spirituality.org; St. Gabriel's Spiritual Center for Youth (y, mc), 64 Burns Rd., P.O. Box 3015, Shelter Island Heights 11965, (631) 749-3154 (fax); St. Ignatius Retreat House, 251 Searingtown Rd., Manhasset 11030, (516) 621-8300, www.inisfada.net; St. Josaphat's Retreat House, Basilian Monastery, 1 East Beach Rd., Glen Cove 11542, (516) 671-8980; St. Joseph Center (Spanish Center), 275 W. 230th St., Bronx 10463, (718) 796-4340; St. Mary's Villa, 150 Sisters Servants Lane, P.O. Box 9, Sloatsburg 10974-0009, (914) 753-5100; St. Paul Center, 21-35 Crescent St., Astoria 11105, (718) 932-0752; St. Ursula Retreat Center, 186 Middle Rd., Blue Point 11715, (631) 363-2422, www.ursulinesofbluepoint.org; Stella Maris Retreat Center, 130 E. Genesee St., Skaneateles 13152, (315) 685-6836; Tagaste Monastery, 220 Lafayette Ave., Suffern 10901; Trinity Retreat, 1 Pryer Manor Rd., Larchmont 10538, (914) 235-6839.

North Carolina: Avila Retreat Center, 711 Mason Rd., Durham 27712, (919) 477-1285; Madonna House, 424 Rose Ln., Raleigh 27610.

North Dakota: Presentation Prayer Center, 1101 32nd Ave. S., Fargo 58103, (701) 237-4857; Queen of Peace Retreat, 1310 Broadway, Fargo 58102, (701) 293-9286.

Ohio: Bergamo Center for Lifelong Learning, 4400 Shakertown Rd., Dayton 45430, (937) 426-2363, www.bergamocenter.org; Franciscan Renewal Center,

Pilgrim House, 321 Clay St., Carey 43316, (419) 396-7970, www.olcshrine. com; Friarhurst Retreat House, 8136 Wooster Pike, Cincinnati 45227, (513) 561-2270; Jesuit Retreat House, 5629 State Rd., Cleveland 44134-2292, (440) 884-9300, www.jrh-cleveland.org; Loyola of the Lakes, 700 Killinger Rd., Clinton 44216-9653, (330) 896-2315, www.loyolaofthelakes.com; Maria Stein Center, 2365 St. Johns Rd., Maria Stein 45860, (419) 925-7625, www.spiritual center.net; Milford Spiritual Center, 5361 S. Milford Rd., Milford 45150, (513) 248-3500, www.milfordspiritualcenter.org; Our Lady of the Pines, 1250 Tiffin St., Fremont 43420, (419) 332-6522, www.pinesretreat.org.

Sacred Heart Retreat and Renewal Center, 3128 Logan Ave., P.O. Box 6074, Youngstown 44501, (330) 759-9539; St. Joseph Christian Life Center, 18485 Lake Shore Blvd., Cleveland 44119, (216) 531-7370, www.enterthecenter.org; St. Francis Spirituality Center, 200 St. Francis Ave., Tiffin 44883, (419) 443-1485, www.stfrancisspiritualitycenter.org; St. Therese Retreat Center, 5277 E. Broad St., Columbus, OH 43213, (614) 866-1611, www.cathedral-bookshop.com.

Oklahoma: St. Gregory's Abbey, 1900 W. MacArthut, Shawnee 74804, (405) 878-5491, www.sgc.edu.

Oregon: The Jesuit Spirituality Center, 424 S.W. Mill St., Portland 97201, (503) 242-1973; Mount Angel Abbey Retreat House, 1 Abbey Dr., St. Benedict 97373, (503) 845-3027, www.mtangel.edu; Our Lady of Peace Retreat, 3600 S. W. 170th Ave., Beaverton 97006, (503) 649-7127, www.geocities.com/ourladyofpeaceretreat; St. Rita Retreat Center, P.O. Box 310, Gold Hill 97525, (541) 855-1333; Shalom Prayer Center, Benedictine Sisters, 840 S. Main St., Mt. Angel 97362-9527, (503) 845-6773, www.open.org/shalom; St. Benedict Lodge, 56630 North Bank Rd., McKenzie Bridge 97413, (541) 822-3572; Trappist Abbey Guesthouse (m,w), 9200 N.E. Abbey Rd., Lafayette 97127, (503) 852-0107.

Pennsylvania: Avila Retreat Center, 61 E. High St., Union City 16438, (814) 438-7020; Dominican Retreat House, 750 Ashbourne Rd., Elkins Park 19027, (215) 782-8520; Ecclesia Center, 9101 Ridge Rd., Erie 16417, (814) 774-9691; Fatima Renewal Center, 1000 Seminary Rd., Dalton 18414, (570) 563-8500; Fatima House Retreat Center, P.O. Box 116, Bedminster 18910, (215) 579-2947.

Franciscan Spirit and Life Center, 3605 McRoberts Rd., Pittsburgh 15234, (412) 881-9207; Gilmary Diocesan Center, 601 Flaugherty Run Rd., Coraopolis 15108-3899, (412) 264-8400, www.diopitt.org.

Jesuit Center for Spiritual Growth, Box 223, Church Rd., Wernersville 19565, (610) 670-3676, www.jesuitcenter.org; Kearns Spirituality Center, 9000 Babcock Blvd., Allison Park 15101, (412) 366-1124, www.sistersofdivprovidence.org; Mariawald Renewal Center, P.O. Box 97 (1094 Welsh Rd.), Reading 19607, (610) 777-0135, www.home town.aol.com/mariawald/index.html; Martina Spiritual Renewal Center, 5244 Clarwin Ave., Pittsburgh 15229, (412) 931-9766; St. Emma Retreat House, 1001 Harvey Ave., Greensburg 15601-1494, (724) 834-7483, www.stemm.org; St. Francis Center for Renewal, Monocacy Manor, 395 Bridle Path Rd., Bethlehem 18017, (610) 867-8890, www.catholic-church.org/stfrancis-cfn; St. Francis Retreat House, 3918 Chipman Rd., Easton 18045, (610) 258-3053; St. Gabriel's Retreat House, 631 Griffin Pond Rd., Clarks Summit 18411-

8899, (570) 586-4957, www.intiques.com/cpnuns.

St. Joseph's in the Hills, 315 S. Warren Ave., Malvern 19355-0315, (610) 644-0400, www.malvernretreat.com; St. Paul of the Cross Retreat Center, 148 Monastery Ave., Pittsburgh 15203, (412) 381-7676, www.catholic-church.org/stpaulsretreatcenter; Saint Raphaela Center, 616 Coopertown Rd., Haverford 19041, (610) 642-5715; St. Vincent Summer Retreat Program (m,w,mc; summers only), Latrobe 15650, (724) 805-2139; Urban House of Prayer, 1919 Cambridge St., Philadelphia 19130, (215) 236-8328; Villa of Our Lady Retreat Center (w, mc, y), HCR No. 1, Box 41, Mt. Pocono 18344, (570) 839-7217.

Rhode Island: Bethany Renewal Center, 397 Fruit Hill Ave., N. Providence 02911, (401) 353-5860; Father Marot CYO Center (y), 53 Federal St., Woonsocket 02895, (401) 762-3252; Our Lady of Peace Spiritual Life Center, 333 Ocean Rd., Box 507, Narragansett 02882, (401) 884-7676; St. Paul Priory Guest House, 61 Narrangansett Ave., Newport 02840, (401) 847-2423.

South Carolina: Sea of Peace House of Prayer, 59 Palmetto Pointe Rd., Edisto Island 29438, (843) 869-0513; Springbank Retreat for Eco-Spirituality and the Arts, 1345 Springbank Rd., Kingstree 29556, (800) 671-0361, www.springbankspirit.org.

South Dakota: St. Martin's Community Center, 2110C St. Martin's Dr., Rapid City 57702, (605) 343-8011; Sioux Spiritual Center, 20100 Center Rd., Howes, SD 57748, (605) 985-5906.

Tennessee: Carmelites of Mary Immaculate Center of Spirituality, 610 Bluff Rd., Liberty 37095, (615) 536-5177.

Texas: Benedictine Retreat Center, HC#2, Box 6300, Sandia 78383; Bishop DeFalco Retreat Center, 2100 N. Spring, Amarillo 79107-7274, (806) 383-1811, www.bdrc.org; Bishop Rene H. Gracida Retreat Center, 3036 Saratoga Blvd., Corpus Christi 78415, (512) 851-1443; Catholic Renewal Center of North Texas, 4503 Bridge St., Ft. Worth 76103, (817) 429-2920; Cenacle Retreat House, 420 N. Kirkwood, Houston 77079, (281) 497-3131, www.cenacleretreathouse.org; Christian Renewal Center (Centro de Renovacion Cristiana), Oblates of Mary Immaculate, P.O. Box 699, Dickinson 77539, (281) 337-1312, www.retreatcentercrc.org.

Holy Family Retreat Center, 9920 N. Major Dr., Beaumont 77713-7618, (409) 899-5617, www.dioceseofbmt.org/hfrc.htm; Holy Name Retreat Center, 430 Bunker Hill Rd., Houston 77024, (713) 464-0211; Holy Spirit Retreat and Conference Center, 501 Century Dr. S., Laredo 78040, (956) 726-4352, www.stjean.com/laredo/hsrc/holy.htm; Lebh Shomea House of Prayer, La Parra Ranch, P.O. Box 9, Sarita 78385; Montserrat Retreat House, P.O. Box 1390, Lake Dallas 75065, (940) 321-6020, www.montserratretreat.org; Moye Center, 600 London, Castroville 78009, (830) 931-2233, www.moyecenter.org; Oblate Renewal Center, 5700 Blanco Rd., San Antonio 78216, (210) 349-4173.

Omega Retreat Center, 216 W. Highland Dr., Boerne 78006, (830) 816-8471; Our Lady of Mercy Retreat Center, P.O. Box 744, 19th & Division, Slaton 79364, (806) 828-6428; Prayer Town Emmanuel Retreat House, P.O. Box 17, Channing 79018, (806) 534-2312;

San Juan Retreat House (St. Eugene de Mazenod Retreat Center), P.O. Box 747, San Juan 78589, (956) 787-0033.

Utah: Abbey of Our Lady of the Holy Trinity (m), 1250 S 9500 E, Huntsville 84317, (801) 745-3784, www.xmission.com/~hta; Our Lady of the Mountains, 1794 Lake St., Ogden 84401, (801) 392-9231.

Virginia: Benedictine Retreat and Conf. Center, Mary Mother of the Church Abbey, 12829 River Rd., 23233, (804) 784-3508; Dominican Retreat, 7103 Old Dominion Dr., McLean 22101-2799, (703) 356-4243, www.dominicanretreat.org; The Dwelling Place, 601 Holly Grove Ln., Richmond 23235, (804) 323-3360; Holy Family Retreat House, P.O. 3151, 1414 N. Mallory St., Hampton 23663, (757) 722-3997; Madonna House, 828 Campbell Ave., S.W., Roanoke 24016, (540) 343-8464.

Retreat House, Holy Cross Abbey, Rt. 2, Box 3870, Berryville 22611, (540) 955-3124; Shalom House, P.O. Box 196, Montpelier 23192, (804) 883-6149; Tabor Retreat Center, 2125 Langhorne Rd., Lynchburg 24501, (804) 846-6475; The Well, 18047 Quiet Way, Smithfield 23430, (757) 255-2366, www.thewellretreatcenter.org.

Washington: Immaculate Heart Retreat Center, 6910 S. Ben Burr Rd., Spokane 99223, (509) 448-1224, www.ihrc.net; House of the Lord Retreat Center, P.O. Box 1034, Tum Tum 99034, (509) 276-2219; KAIROS House of Prayer, 1714 W. Stearns Rd., Spokane 99208, (509) 466-2187; Palisades Retreat House, 4700 SW Dash Point Rd., #100, Federal Way 98023, (206) 748-7991, www.seattlearch.org/formationandeducation; St. Peter Retreat Center, 15880 Summitview Rd., Cowiche 98923, (509) 678-4935.

West Virginia: Bishop Hodges Pastoral Center, Rt. 1, Box 9D, Huttonsville, 26273, (304) 335-2165; Good Counsel Friary, 493 Tyrone Rd., Morgantown 26508, (304) 594-1714; John XXIII Pastoral Center, 100 Hodges Rd., Charleston 25314, (304) 342-0507; Paul VI Pastoral Center, 667 Stone and Shannon Rd., Wheeling 26003, (304) 277-3300; Priest Field Pastoral Center, Rt. 51, Box 133, Kearneysville 25430, (304) 725-1435; West Virginia Institute for Spirituality, 1414 Virginia St. E., Charleston, WV 25301, (304) 345-0926, www.wvis.ws.

Wisconsin: Archdiocesan Retreat Center, 3501 S. Lake Dr., P.O. Box 07912, Milwaukee 53207, (414) 769-3491, www.archmil.org; The Dwelling Place, 528 N. 31st St., Milwaukee 53208, (414) 933-1100; Franciscan Spirituality Center, 920 Market St., La Crosse 54601, (608) 791-5295, www.fspa.org; Holy Name Retreat House, Chambers Island, mailing address: 1825 Riverside Drive, P.O. Box 23825, Green Bay 54305, (920) 437-7531; Jesuit Retreat House, 4800 Fahrnwald Rd., Oshkosh 54902, (920) 231-9060, www.jesuitretreathouse.org; Marywood Franciscan Spirituality Center (FSPA), 3560 Hwy. 51 N., Arbor Vitae 54568, (715) 385-3750, www.fspa.org.

Monte Alverno Retreat Center, 1000 N. Ballard Rd., Appleton 54911, (920) 733-8526; Mount Carmel Hermitage, 897 U.S. Hwy. 8, 54001, (715) 268-9313; Mount Tabor, 522 2 St., Menasha 54952, (920) 722-8918; Norbertine Center for Spirituality, St. Norbert Abbey, 1016 N. Broadway, De Pere 54115, (920) 337-4315, www.norbertines.org; Redemptorist Retreat Center, 1800 N. Timber Trail Lane, Oconomowoc

53066-4897, (262) 567-6900, www.redemptoristre-treat.org; St. Anthony Retreat Center, 300 E. 4th St., Marathon 54448, (715) 443-2236, www.sarcenter.com.

St. Bede Retreat and Conference Center, 1190 Priory Rd., P.O. Box 66, Eau Claire 54702, (715) 834-8642, www.saintbede.org; Saint Benedict Center (monastery and ecumenical retreat and conference center), P.O. Box 5070, Madison 53705-0070, (608) 836-1631, www.sbcenter.org; St. Clare Center for Spirituality, 7381 Church St., Custer 54423, (715) 592-4099; St. Joseph's Retreat Center, 3035 O'Brien Rd., Bailey's Harbor 54202, (920) 839-2391; St. Vincent Pallotti Center, N6409 Bowers Rd., Elkhorn 53121, (262) 723-2108, (877) 220-3306, www.elknet.net/vpallelk; Schoenstatt Center, W. 284 N. 698 Cherry Lane, Waukesha 53188, (262) 547-7733.

Catholic Education

LEGAL STATUS OF CATHOLIC EDUCATION

The right of private schools to exist and operate in the United States is recognized in law. It was confirmed by the U.S. Supreme Court in 1925 when the tribunal ruled (Pierce v. Society of Sisters, see Church-State Decisions of the Supreme Court) that an Oregon state law requiring all children to attend public schools was unconstitutional.

Private schools are obliged to comply with the education laws in force in the various states regarding such matters as required basic curricula, periods of attendance, and standards for proper accreditation.

The special curricula and standards of private schools are determined by the schools themselves. Thus, in Catholic schools, the curricula include not only the subject matter required by state educational laws but also other fields of study, principally, education in the Catholic faith.

The Supreme Court has ruled that the First Amendment to the U.S. Constitution, in accordance with the No Establishment of Religion Clause of the First Amendment, prohibits direct federal and state aid from public funds to church-affiliated schools. (*See several cases in* **Church-State Decisions of the Supreme Court.**)

Public Aid

This prohibition does not extend to all child-benefit and public-purpose programs of aid to students of non-public elementary and secondary schools.

Statutes authorizing such programs have been ruled constitutional on the grounds that they:
• have a "secular legislative purpose"
• neither inhibit nor advance religion as a "principal or primary effect"
• do not foster "excessive government entanglement with religion."

Aid programs considered constitutional have provided bus transportation, textbook loans, school lunches and health services, and "secular, neutral or non-ideological services, facilities and materials provided in common to all school children," public and non-public.

The first major aid to education program in U.S. history containing provisions benefiting non-public school students was enacted by the 89th Congress and signed into law by President Lyndon B. Johnson on Apr. 11, 1965. The Elementary and Secondary Education Act was designed to avoid the separation of Church and state impasse which had blocked all earlier aid proposals pertaining to non-public, and especially church-affiliated, schools. The objective of the program, under public control, is to serve the public purpose by aiding disadvantaged pupils in non-public as well as public schools.

With respect to college and university education in church-affiliated institutions, the Supreme Court has upheld the constitutionality of statutes providing student loans and, under the Federal Higher Education Facilities Act of 1963, construction loans and grants for secular-purpose facilities.

Catholic schools are exempt from real estate taxation in all of the states. Since Jan. 1, 1959, nonprofit parochial and private schools have also been exempt from several federal excise taxes.

NCEA

The National Catholic Educational Association, founded in 1904, is a voluntary organization of educational institutions and individuals concerned with Catholic education in the U.S. Its objectives are to promote and encourage the principles and ideals of Christian education and formation by suitable service and other activities. The NCEA serves approximately 200,000 Catholic educators at all levels from pre-K through university. Its official publication is *Momentum.* Numerous service publications are issued to members. Bishop Gregory M. Aymond of Austin, chairman of the Board of Directors; Dr. Karen Ristau, president. Address: 1077 30th St. N.W., Washington, DC 20007, (202) 337-6232, www.ncea.org.

EDUCATIONAL VOUCHERS

Although 41 educational voucher programs funded by private philanthropy were operating in the United States by 1998-99, discussion of vouchers as a political, legal, and educational issue primarily concerns publicly-funded plans allowing parents to send their children to the school of their choice. At present there are three educational voucher programs of this kind — in Milwaukee, Cleveland, and the state of Florida.

The Vouchers Debate

Proponents of vouchers argue that they are not merely consistent with parental rights but an appropriate, even necessary, practical means of realizing them. In particular, it is said, they enable low-income parents to exercise a choice about schools. Another pro-vouchers argument is that they create an incentive for self-improvement by public schools that is lacking when they enjoy a near monopoly.

Arguments against vouchers are that they take funds away from public schools and encourage highly motivated parents and competent students to abandon failing public institutions in favor of private ones. Using vouchers at church-related schools also is said to violate the First Amendment ban on an establishment of religion. The chief opponents of education-al vouchers are teacher unions — the National Education Association, the American Federation of Teachers, and their affiliates — and other public school groups, church-state sep-arationists, and some mainline African-American organiza-tions. Phi Delta Kappa/Gallup polls in 1998 and 1999 found 51% of the respondents, including 60% of public school par-ents in the latter year, were in favor of total or partial govern-ment-paid tuition for children in private or church-related schools, although support declined when vouchers were spec-ified.

Recent Developments

On June 27, 2002, the U.S. Supreme Court upheld the Cleveland voucher program in a 5-4 ruling, saying it is "entirely neutral with respect to religion." The majority opinion, written by Chief Justice William Rehnquist, said the program is therefore "a program of true private choice" and does not violate the Establishment Clause of the First Amendment.

Cleveland established the voucher program in 1995 to help address problems in what was considered one of the worst public school systems in the country. The state Legislature created the system after a federal judge declared the schools were being mismanaged and put them under the authority of the state superin-tendent of public instruction. The program provides for vouchers of up to $4,000 annually for children in low-income families to attend other public or private schools or pay for tutors. The vast majority of partici-pants use their vouchers to pay tuition at church-affil-iated schools, nearly all of them Catholic.

The case came to the Supreme Court after the 6th U.S. Circuit Court of Appeals ruled in 2000 that the program was unconstitutional because the vouchers are primarily used at religious schools. The U.S. Conference of Catholic Bishops in a friend-of-the-court brief argued that the program should not be con-sidered unconstitutional because most voucher recipi-ents choose to attend church schools.

Opponents of the program who filed briefs included

the National Association for the Advancement of Colored People, an association of Ohio school boards and several groups of public schools from around the country. Opponents call vouchers a fraud meant to siphon tax money from struggling public schools. The Ohio school boards argued that the state has ignored its responsibility to provide a good education and is mere-ly shifting the burden to religious schools.

Central to the court's reasoning was that children in the Cleveland program have a theoretical choice of attending religious schools, secular private academies, suburban public schools, or charter schools run by par-ents or others outside the education establishment. The fact that only a handful of secular schools and no sub-urban public schools have signed up to accept voucher students is not the fault of the program itself, Ohio authorities say. "We believe that the program chal-lenged here is a program of true private choice," Chief Justice William H. Rehnquist wrote for himself and Justices Sandra Day O'Connor, Antonin Scalia, Anthony M. Kennedy and Clarence Thomas.

The Cleveland program goes too far toward state-sponsored religion, the dissenting justices said. It does not treat religion neutrally, as Rehnquist contended, wrote Justice David H. Souter. The majority is also wrong about the question of whether parents have a true choice among schools, Souter wrote for himself and Justices John Paul Stevens, Ruth Bader Ginsburg and Stephen Breyer. "There is, in any case, no way to interpret the 96.6 percent of current voucher money going to religious schools as reflecting a free and gen-uine choice by the families that apply for vouchers," Souter wrote.

President George W. Bush has been a staunch advo-cate of school vouchers, and emphasized the issue in his campaign for the White House. Congress last year shelved that effort, but Bush resurrected the idea, pro-posing in his 2003 budget to give families up to $2,500 per child in tax credits if they choose a private school rather than a failing neighborhood public school. Following the court's hearing on arguments in Feb. 2002, Education Secretary Rod Paige said he would continue advocating on behalf of both improved public schools and school choice. Republican lawmakers in Congress agreed with Bush's stance. The Bush admin-istration sided with Ohio, arguing that the program is constitutional because parents control where the money goes. In Cleveland, the public money flows to parents, not directly to the church-run schools, the pro-gram's supporters noted.

EX CORDE ECCLESIAE

On Nov. 17, 1999, the Catholic Bishops of the Unites States approved *The Application of Ex Corde Ecclesiae for the United States,* implementing the Apostolic Constitution *Ex Corde Ecclesiae.* This action received the *recognitio* from the Congregation for Bishops on May 3, 2000. Bishop Joseph Fiorenza, President of the National Conference of Catholic Bishops, decreed that the application would have the force of particular law for the United States on May 3, 2001. Guidelines con-cerning the academic *mandatum* in Catholic universi-ties were subsequently issued, based on Canon 812. The following are the first guidelines.

Pope John Paul II's Constitution *Ex Corde Ecclesiae*

of 1990 fostered a productive dialogue between the Bishops of the United States and the leaders of our Catholic colleges and universities. It is anticipated that this recently approved *Application of Ex Corde Ecclesiae for the United States* would further that dia-logue and build a community of trust between bishops and theologians. Both bishops and theologians are engaged in a necessary though complementary service to the Church that requires ongoing and mutually respectful conversation.

Article 4, 4, e, iv of the *Application* states that "a detailed procedure will be developed outlining the process of requesting and granting (or withdrawing) the *mandatum*." These guidelines are intended to explain and serve as a resource for the conferral of the *mandatum*. Only those guidelines herein which repeat a norm of the *Application* have the force of particular law. They were approved for distribution to the members of NCCB by the Conference's general membership.

Nature of the *mandatum*

• The *mandatum* is fundamentally an acknowledgment by Church authority that a Catholic professor of a theological discipline is a teacher within the full communion of the Catholic Church (*Application*: Article 4,4,e,i).

• The *mandatum*, therefore, recognizes the professor's commitment and responsibility to teach authentic Catholic doctrine and to refrain from putting forth as Catholic teaching anything contrary to the Church's magisterium (cf. *Application*: Article 4,4,e, iii).

• The *mandatum* should not be construed as an appointment, authorization, delegation or approbation of one's teaching by Church authorities. Those who have received a *mandatum* teach in their own name in virtue of their baptism and their academic and professional competence, not in the name of the bishop or of the Church's magisterium (*Application*: Article 4,4,e,ii).

Cardinal Newman Society

The Cardinal Newman Society is a national organization established in 1993 and dedicated to the renewal of Catholic identity in Catholic higher education in the United States. CNS has more than 18,000 members nationwide who share a common concern for the future of Catholic higher education and urge fidelity to the magisterium. The society seeks to: promote discussion and understanding of the message of the Catholic Church concerning the nature and value of Catholic higher education; assist college leaders, educators, students, and alumni in their efforts to preserve the religious identity of Catholic institutions of higher learning; and advocate the faithful implementation of *Ex Corde Ecclesiae* by facilitating an active dialogue among members of the Catholic university community. J. Laurence McCarty, Chairman of the Board; Patrick J. Reilly, president. Address: 10562 Associates Court, Manassas, VA 20109; (703) 367-0333; www.cardinalnewmansociety.org.

SUMMARY OF SCHOOL STATISTICS

Status and figures (as of Jan. 1, 2006) reported by The Official Catholic Directory.

Colleges and Universities: 231 (U.S., 226; outlying areas, 5).

College and University Students: 763,757 (U.S., 742,627; outlying areas, 21,130).

High Schools: 1,354 (782 diocesan and parochial; 572 private). U.S., 1,214 (703 diocesan and parochial; 511 private); outlying areas, 140 (79 diocesan and parochial; 61 private).

High School Students: 679,506 (378,153 diocesan and parochial; 301,353 private). U.S., 635,460 (353,855 diocesan and parochial; 281,605 private; outlying areas, 44,046 (24,298 diocesan and parochial; 19,748 private).

Public High School Students Receiving Religious Instruction: 729,421 (U.S., 704,526; outlying areas, 24,895).

Elementary Schools: 6,511 (6,148 diocesan and parochial; 363 private). U.S., 6,358 (6,047 diocesan and parochial; 311 private; outlying areas, 153 (101 diocesan and parochial; 52 private).

Elementary School Students: 1,762,401 (1,674,317 diocesan and parochial; 88,084 private) U.S., 1,718,138 (1,646,369 diocesan and parochial; 71,769 private; outlying areas, 44,263 (27,948 diocesan and parochial; 16,315 private).

Public Elementary School Students Receiving Religious Instruction: 3,486,805 (U.S., 3,421,859; outlying areas, 64,946).

Non-Residential Schools for Handicapped: 79 (U.S.). Students: 5,745 (U.S.).

Teachers: 172,785 U.S., 167,719 (lay persons 158,967; sisters, 6,177; priests, 1,421; brothers, 1,104; scholastics, 50; outlying areas, 5,066 (lay persons, 4,705; sisters, 237; priests, 73; brothers, 45; scholastics, 6).

Seminaries: 204 (73 diocesan; 131 religious). U.S.: 191 (69 diocesan; 122 religious); outlying areas: 13 (4 diocesan; 9 religious).

Seminarians: 5,642 (3,929 diocesan; 1,713 religious). U.S.: 5,549 (3,872 diocesan; 1,677 religious); outlying areas: 93 (57 diocesan; 36 religious).

CATHOLIC SCHOOLS AND STUDENTS IN THE UNITED STATES

(Source: Official Catholic Directory, 2006; *figures as of Jan. 1, 2006. Archdioceses are indicated by an asterisk;* # as of 2005; **does not include New Orleans.)*

State Diocese	Universities/ Colleges	Students	High Schools	Students	Elem. Schools	Students
Alabama	1	1,867	9	3,183	34	9,220
*Mobile	1	1,867	3	1,466	16	4,722
Birmingham	-	-	6	1,717	18	4,498
Alaska	-	-	3	327	5	754
*Anchorage	-	-	1	108	3	408
Fairbanks	-	-	1	219	1	267
Juneau	-	-	-	-	1	79
Arizona	-	-	12	6,907	53	15,479
Phoenix	-	-	6	4,961	28	9,263
Tucson	-	-	6	1,946	22	5,485
Arkansas						
Little Rock	-	-	7	1,847	29	6,049
California	13	45,543	115	76,681	586	165,282
*Los Angeles	5	11,845	50	30,570	225	61,468
*San Francisco	3	11,499	14	8,394	65	18,613
Fresno	-	-	2	1,292	22	5,634
Monterey	-	-	5	1,805	14	3,790
Oakland	3	6,191	9	6,179	47	13,060
Orange	-	-	7	5,982	37	13,739
Sacramento	-	-	7	7,636	45	11,211
San Bernardino	-	-	2	962	30	7,206
San Diego	1	7,611	5	3,949	45	13,612
San Jose	1	8,397	6	6,451	30	10,446
Santa Rosa	-	-	6	1,896	13	2,625
Stockton	-	-	2	1,565	12	3,392
Colorado	1	16,128	8	4,078	51	13,140
*Denver	1	16,128	7	3,703	40	9,981
Colorado Springs	-	-	1	375	7	2,137
Pueblo	-	-	-	-	4	1,022
Connecticut	4	15,025	22	10,956	123	26,981
*Hartford	2	4,250	9	4,858	66	14,521
Bridgeport	2	10,775	8	3,890	34	8,832
Norwich	-	-	5	2,208	23	3,628
Delaware, Wilmington	-	-	8	4,749	30	10,200
District of Columbia *Wash., DC	3	21,979	17	9,835	94	23,044
Florida	4	24,983	36	25,974	188	68,494
*Miami	2	11,614	13	13,033	61	25,164
Orlando	-	-	5	2,817	31	12,092
Palm Beach	-	-	3	2,196	14	5,784
Pensacola-Tallahassee	-	-	2	793	9	2,492
St. Augustine	-	-	4	2,291	29	8,535
St. Petersburg	1	13,019	6	3,283	33	10,247
Venice	1	350	3	1,561	9	3,561
Georgia	-	-	12	4,892	36	12,439
*Atlanta	-	-	7	3,238	20	7,868
Savannah	-	-	5	1,654	16	4,571
Hawaii, Honolulu	1	4,138	7	2,196	28	9,205
Idaho, Boise	-	-	1	672	13	2,570
Illinois	12	60,669	73	45,008	436	129,512
*Chicago	5	46,063	39	28,390	216	73,141
Belleville	-	-	3	1,378	33	5,587
Joliet	3	12,291	8	5,912	56	18,707
Peoria	1	440	8	2,627	43	10,524
Rockford	1	113	8	4,215	41	11,202
Springfield	2	1,762	7	2,486	47	10,351
Indiana	11	28,284	28	12,556	167	45,024
*Indianapolis	2	3,388	10	5,733	60	17,828
Evansville	-	-	4	1,597	24	6,268

State Diocese	Universities/ Colleges	Students	High Schools	Students	Elem. Schools	Students
Indiana, cont.						
Ft. Wayne-S. Bend	5	16,027	9	3,249	40	10,257
Gary	1	1,275	3	1,386	23	6,299
Lafayette	3	7,594	2	591	20	4,372
Iowa	6	7,714	23	7,133	105	23,946
*Dubuque	3	2,310	7	2,617	49	11,283
Davenport	1	3,623	6	1,019	20	3,537
Des Moines	1	656	2	1,405	16	4,873
Sioux City	1	1,125	8	2,092	20	4,253
Kansas	4	7,125	16	6,629	99	23,362
*Kansas City	3	5,022	7	3,512	45	12,224
Dodge City	-	-	-	-	8	1,194
Salina	-	-	5	745	12	1,827
Wichita	1	2,103	4	2,372	34	8,117
Kentucky	5	6,735	23	11,302	103	31,559
*Louisville	3	4,551	9	6,238	43	16,049
Covington	1	1,434	9	3,340	29	8,977
Lexington	-	-	2	916	15	3,477
Owensboro	1	750	3	808	16	3,058
Louisiana**	1	2,083	27	12,696	85	34,654
*New Orleans#	3	11,091	23	16,675	82	32,596
Alexandria	-	-	3	615	8	2,523
Baton Rouge	1	2,083	8	4,748	24	12,778
Houma-Thib.	-	-	3	1,853	10	4,110
Lafayette	-	-	10	4,078	31	11,551
Lake Charles	-	-	1	531	7	2,061
Shreveport	-	-	2	871	5	1,631
Maine, Portland	1	2,268	3	1,127	19	3,696
Maryland, *Baltimore	4	11,800	21	12,021	66	23,475
Massachusetts	12	34,941	51	25,702	185	49,296
*Boston	7	23,400	35	17,360	116	31,719
Fall River	1	2,366	4	2,982	24	5,455
Springfield	1	1,082	4	1,586	21	6,462
Worcester	3	8,093	8	3,774	24	5,660
Michigan	8	27,790	40	16,813	247	64,464
*Detroit	4	22,897	22	10,501	99	38,128
Gaylord	-	-	4	558	16	2,954
Grand Rapids	1	2,318	3	1,786	39	6,649
Kalamazoo	-	-	3	745	20	2,807
Lansing	3	2,575	5	2,342	41	9,215
Marquette	-	-	-	-	9	1,461
Saginaw	-	-	3	881	23	3,250
Minnesota	7	24,663	23	11,504	190	45,637
*St. Paul and Minn.	3	16,256	13	8,639	96	30,500
Crookston	-	-	1	174	9	1,282
Duluth	1	3,015	-	-	12	1,726
New Ulm	-	-	3	459	17	2,515
St. Cloud	2	4,141	2	1,052	31	5,014
Winona	1	1,251	4	1,180	25	4,600
Mississippi	2	25	9	2,810	29	6,905
Biloxi	-	-	5	1,600	14	3,046
Jackson	2	25	4	1,210	15	3,859
Missouri	4	18,890	40	20,886	239	59,124
*St. Louis	2	14,249	28	15,410	145	41,117
Jefferson City	-	-	2	1,126	38	6,356
Kansas City-St. Joseph	2	4,641	7	3,352	33	7,912
Springfield-Cape Girar.	-	-	3	998	23	3,793
Montana	2	2,300	5	870	17	3,136
Great Falls-Billings	1	801	4	555	12	2,230
Helena	1	1,499	2	315	5	906
Nebraska	2	7,667	27	8,055	92	21,050
*Omaha	2	7,667	17	5,826	58	14,763
Grand Island	-	-	4	485	7	970
Lincoln	-	-	6	1,744	27	5,317

State Diocese	Universities/ Colleges	Students	High Schools	Students	Elem. Schools	Students
Nevada	-	-	2	1,523	11	3,985
Las Vegas	-	-	1	930	7	2,905
Reno	-	-	1	593	4	1,080
New Hampshire Manchester	4	4,264	4	2,584	25	5,793
New Jersey	7	23,212	71	39,277	316	87,292
*Newark	4	17,663	36	16,439	113	32,016
Camden	-	-	10	7,642	56	13,207
Metuchen	-	-	6	3,626	42	12,207
Paterson	2	2,623	8	4,516	58	14,235
Trenton	1	3,656	11	7,670	47	17,035
New Mexico	1	2,565	4	2,110	31	5,739
*Santa Fe	1	2,565	2	1,841	18	3,880
Gallup	-	-	2	269	10	1,359
Las Cruces	-	-	-	-	5	500
New York	26	114,367	124	75,692	609	186,351
*New York	10	61,705	55	30,034	229	82,573
Albany	4	6,500	7	2,777	31	6,595
Brooklyn	3	22,119	20	16,710	126	41,765
Buffalo	7	17,256	16	6,005	78	16,928
Ogdensburg	-	-	2	524	16	2,109
Rochester	-	-	7	3,481	42	8,656
Rockville Centre	1	3,300	11	12,784	58	22,629
Syracuse	1	3,487	6	3,377	29	6,096
North Carolina	1	887	4	2,454	49	13,321
Charlotte	1	887	2	1,404	16	5,945
Raleigh	-	-	2	1,050	33	7,376
North Dakota	2	3,238	4	1,560	23	3,888
Bismarck	1	2,758	3	1,265	11	1,983
Fargo	1	480	1	295	12	1,905
Ohio	13	37,040	77	43,146	406	116,344
*Cincinnati	4	19,717	21	15,025	110	35,522
Cleveland	3	6,715	22	13,903	120	41,059
Columbus	2	3,572	11	4,911	44	12,356
Steubenville	1	2,374	3	657	14	2,213
Toledo	2	2,479	14	6,211	76	17,084
Youngstown	1	2,183	6	2,439	42	8,110
Oklahoma	1	779	4	2,389	32	7,340
*Oklahoma City	1	779	2	915	20	4,131
Tulsa	-	-	2	1,474	12	3,209
Oregon	2	5,305	10	5,267	45	9,787
*Portland	2	5,305	10	5,267	42	9,111
Baker	-	-	-	-	3	676
Pennsylvania	26	84,292		8648,393	530	137,208
*Philadelphia	11	38,846	36	28,913	215	70,714
Allentown	2	4,969	9	3,873	52	11,021
Altoona-Johnstown	2	3,981	3	1,153	23	3,523
Erie	2	6,994	7	2,711	36	7,146
Greensburg	2	3,560	2	802	19	3,714
Harrisburg	-	-	7	3,862	43	9,750
Pittsburgh	3	13,603	12	3,855	102	22,070
Scranton	4	12,339	11	3,224	40	9,270
Rhode Island, Providence	2	8,005	12	6,283	53	13,600
South Carolina Charleston	-	-	4	1,757	26	5,991
South Dakota	2	1,893	5	1,386	22	4,618
Rapid City	-	-	2	470	2	940
Sioux Falls	2	1,893	3	916	20	3,678
Tennessee	2	2,622	11	5,572	48	12,996
Knoxville	-	-	2	1,126	8	2,543
Memphis	1	1,729	6	2,593	21	5,844
Nashville	1	893	3	1,853	19	4,609
Texas	9	24,011	50	18,357	233	61,846
*Galveston-Houston	1	3,776	9	4,194	53	14,582
*San Antonio	4	12,508	9	3,261	39	10,776
Amarillo	-	-	1	132	6	700

State Diocese	Universities/ Colleges	Students	High Schools	Students	Elem. Schools	Students
Texas, cont.						
Austin	1	4,651	5	936	16	4,069
Beaumont	-	-	1	465	5	1,259
Brownsville	-	-	2	906	11	3,118
Corpus Christi	1	34	1	235	16	2,737
Dallas	1	2,992	9	4,122	34	10,626
El Paso	-	-	3	1,215	10	3,163
Fort Worth	1	50	4	1,484	15	5,399
Laredo	-	-	1	636	6	1,387
Lubbock	-	-	1	13	2	301
San Angelo	-	-	-	-	3	751
Tyler	-	-	1	220	4	847
Victoria	-	-	3	518	12	2,131
Utah, Salt Lake City	-	-	3	1,746	12	3,347
Vermont, Burlington	2	2,885	2	549	15	2,207
Virginia	4	5,639	18	7,184	67	22,495
Arlington	4	5,639	6	4,282	39	13,175
Richmond	-	-	12	2,902	28	9,320
Washington	3	15,161	13	7,354	81	20,927
*Seattle	2	8,761	9	6,036	60	16,284
Spokane	1	6,400	3	1,103	15	2,935
Yakima	-	-	1	215	6	1,708
West Virginia, Wheeling-Charleston	1	1,699	8	1,660	26	4,899
Wisconsin	9	31,341	28	11,138	322	56,818
*Milwaukee	5	23,754	13	6,774	121	28,456
Green Bay	2	2,966	6	2,105	64	9,501
La Crosse	1	2,167	7	1,653	74	8,717
Madison	1	2,454	2	606	47	7,532
Superior	-	-	-	-	16	2,612
Wyoming, Cheyenne	-	-	1	14	7	802
EASTERN CHURCHES	1	805	3	656	18	2,845
*Philadelphia	1	805	1	394	5	673
St. Nicholas (Chicago)	-	-	1	112	2	459
Stamford	-	-	1	150	2	179
St. Josaphat (Parma)	-	-	-	-	1	126
*Pittsburgh	-	-	-	-	1	183
Parma	-	-	-	-	2	239
Passaic	-	-	-	-	1	124
Van Nuys	-	-	-	-	-	-
St. Maron (Maronites)	-	-	-	-	-	-
Our Lady of Deliverance (Syriacs)	-	-	-	-	-	-
Our Lady of Lebanon (Maronites)	-	-	-	-	1	35
Newton (Melkites)	-	-	-	-	-	-
St. George Martyr (Romanians)	-	-	-	-	-	-
St. Peter the Apostle (Chaldeans)	-	-	-	-	-	-
St. Thomas Apostle of Detroit (Chaldeans)	-	-	-	-	-	-
St. Thomas (Syro-Malabars)	-	-	-	-	-	-
Armenians (Ap. Ex.)	-	-	-	-	4	951
SCHOOLS AND STUDENTS IN OUTLYING AREAS						
American Samoa	-	-	1	150	2	326
Caroline Islands	-	-	4	825	5	1,480
Guam	-	-	3	840	5	1,668
Marshall Islands	-	-	2	275	5	977
Marianas	-	-	1	195	3	513
Puerto Rico	5	21,130	127	41,564	130	38,742
Virgin Islands	-	-	2	197	3	557
TOTAL 2006	231	763,757	1,354	679,506	6,511	1,762,401
TOTAL 2005	234	772,767	1,378	692,767	6,736	1,846,045
TOTAL 1996	237	691,626	1,350	647,613	7,011	2,052,193

CATHOLIC UNIVERSITIES AND COLLEGES IN THE UNITED STATES

(*Sources:* Catholic Almanac *survey;* The Official Catholic Directory.)

Listed below are institutions of higher learning established under Catholic auspices. Some of them are now independent.

Information includes: name of each institution; indication of male (m), female (w), coeducational (c) student body; name of founding group or group with which the institution is affiliated; year of foundation; total number of students, in parentheses.

Albertus Magnus College (c): 700 Prospect St., New Haven, CT 06511; (203) 773-8550; www.albertus.edu. Dominican Sisters; 1925; independent (2,065).

Alvernia College (c): 400 Saint Bernardine St., Reading, PA 19607; (610) 796-8200; www.alvernia.edu. Bernardine Sisters; 1958 (2,457).

Alverno College (w): 3400 S. 43th St., P.O. Box 343922, Milwaukee, WI 53234; (414) 382-6000; www.alverno.edu. School Sisters of St. Francis; 1887; independent (2,000).

Anna Maria College (c): 50 Sunset Lane, Paxton, MA 01612; (508) 849-3300; www.annamaria.edu. Sisters of St. Anne; 1946; independent (1,244).

Aquinas College (c): 1607 Robinson Rd. S.E., Grand Rapids, MI 49506; (616) 459-8281. Sisters of St. Dominic; 1922; independent (2,571).

Aquinas College (c): 4210 Harding Rd., Nashville, TN 37205; (615) 297-7545; www.aquinas-tn.edu. Dominican Sisters; 1961 (506).

Aquinas Institute of Theology (c): 3642 Lindell Boulevard, St. Louis, MO 63108; (314) 977-3869; www.op.org/aquinas. Dominicans, 1961; graduate theology; offers distance learning program in pastoral studies and specializations in preaching (200).

Assumption College (c): 500 Salisbury St., Worcester, MA 01615-0005; (508) 767-7000; www.assumption.edu. Assumptionist Religious; 1904 (2,766).

Ave Maria School of Law (c): 3475 Plymouth Rd., Ann Arbor, MI 48105; (734) 930-4408.

Avila University (c): 11901 Wornall Rd., Kansas City, MO 64145-1698; (816) 942-8400; www.avila.edu. Sisters of St. Joseph of Carondelet; 1916 (2,658).

Barry University (c): 11300 N.E. 2nd Ave., Miami Shores, FL 33161; (305) 899-3000; www.barry.edu. Dominican Sisters (Adrian, MI); 1940 (8,691).

Bellarmine College (c): 2001 Newburg Rd., Louisville, KY 40205; (502) 452-8211; www.bellarmine.edu. Louisville archdiocese; independent (2,323).

Belmont Abbey College (c): 100 Belmont-Mt. Holly Rd., Belmont, NC 28012; (704) 825-6700; www.belmontabbeycollege.edu. Benedictine Fathers; 1876 (883).

Benedictine College (c): 1020 N. Second St., Atchison, KS 66002; (913) 367-5340; www.benedictine.edu. Benedictines; 1859; independent (1,375).

Benedictine University (formerly Illinois Benedictine College) (c): 5700 College Rd., Lisle, IL 60532-0900; (630) 829-600 0; www.ben.edu. Benedictine Monks of St. Procopius Abbey; 1887 (2,809).

Boston College (University status) (c): Chestnut Hill, MA 02167; (617) 552-8000; www.bc.edu. Jesuit Fathers; 1863 (14,297).

Brescia University (c): 717 Frederica St., Owensboro, KY 42301; (270) 685-3131; www.brescia.edu. Ursuline Sisters; 1950 (820).

Briar Cliff College (c): 3303 Rebecca St., Sioux City, IA 51104; (712) 279-5405; www.briarcliff.edu. Sisters of St. Francis of the Holy Family; 1930 (994).

Cabrini College (c): 610 King of Prussia Rd., Radnor, PA 19087; (610) 902-8100; www.cabrini.edu. Missionary Srs. of Sacred Heart; 1957; private (2,669).

Caldwell College (c): 9 Ryerson Ave., Caldwell, NJ 07006; (973) 618-3000; www.caldwell.edu. Dominican Sisters; 1939 (2,270).

Calumet College of St. Joseph (c): 2400 New York Ave., Whiting, IN 46394; (219) 473-7770; www.ccsj.edu. Society of the Precious Blood, 1951 (1,141).

Canisius College (c): 2001 Main St., Buffalo, NY 14208; (716) 883-7000; www.canisius.edu. Jesuit Fathers; 1870; independent (4,995).

Cardinal Stritch University (c): 6801 N. Yates Rd., Milwaukee, WI 53217; (414) 410-4000; www.stritch.edu. Sisters of St. Francis of Assisi; 1937 (5,855).

Carlow College (w): 3333 5th Ave., Pittsburgh, PA 15213; (412) 578-6059; www.carlow.edu. Sisters of Mercy; 1929 (2,199).

Carroll College (c): 1601 N. Benton Ave., Helena, MT 59625; (406) 447-4300. Diocesan; 1909 (1,400).

Catholic Distance University (c): 120 East Colonial Highway, Hamilton, VA 20158-9012; www.cdu.edu. Offers External Degree programs, including Masters degrees in Religious Studies (7,000).

Catholic Theological Union (c): 5401 South Cornell Ave., Chicago, IL 60615; (773) 324-8000; www.ctu.edu (348). Offers Graduate theological programs, including M.Div., M.A., M.A.P.S., and D.Min.

Catholic University of America, The (c): Michigan Ave. & Fourth St., NE, Washington, DC 20064; (202) 319-5000; www.cua.edu. Hierarchy of the United States; 1887. Pontifical University (5,777).

Chaminade University of Honolulu (c): 3140 Waialae Ave., Honolulu, HI 96816; (808) 735-4711; www.chaminade.edu. Marianists; 1955 (2,788).

Chestnut Hill College (w): 9601 Germantown Ave., Philadelphia, PA 19118; (215) 248-7000; www.chc.edu. Sisters of St. Joseph; 1924 (1,645).

Christendom College (c): 134 Christendom Dr., Front Royal, VA 22630; (540) 636-2900. Independent, 1977 (477).

Christian Brothers University (c): 650 E. Parkway S., Memphis, TN 38104; (901) 321-3000. Brothers of the Christian Schools; 1871 (2,027).

Clarke College (c): 1550 Clarke Dr., Dubuque, IA 52001; (563) 588-6300; www.clarke.edu. Sisters of Charity, BVM; 1843; independent (1,126).

Creighton University (c): 2500 California Plaza, Omaha, NE 68178; (402) 280-2700; www.creighton.edu. Jesuit Fathers; 1878; independent (6,297).

Dallas, University of (c): 1845 E. Northgate, Irving, TX 75062; (972) 721-5000. Dallas diocese; 1956; independent (3,518).

Dayton, University of (c): 300 College Park, Dayton, OH 45469-1660; (937) 229-1000; www.udayton.edu. Marianists; 1850 (10,248).

DePaul University (c): One E. Jackson Blvd., Chicago, IL 60604; (312) 362-8000; www.depaul.edu. Vincentians; 1898 (23,174).

De Sales University (c): 2755 Station Ave., Center Valley, PA 18034; (610) 282-1100; www.desales.edu. Oblates of St. Francis de Sales; 1965 (1,339).

Detroit Mercy, University of (c): 4001 W. McNichols Rd., Detroit, MI, 48221; 8200 W. Outer Dr., Detroit MI 48219; (313) 993-1000. Society of Jesus and Sisters of Mercy; 1877; independent (5,843).

Dominican College (c): 470 Western Hwy., Orangeburg, NY 10962; (845) 359-7800; www.dc.edu. Dominican Sisters; 1952; independent (1,700).

Dominican University of California (c): 50 Acacia Ave., San Rafael, CA 94901-2298; (415) 457-4440; www.dominican.edu. Dominican Sisters; 1890; independent (1,578).

Dominican University (formerly Rosary College) (c): 7900 W. Division St., River Forest, IL 60305; (708) 366-2490; www.dom.edu. Sinsinawa Dominican Sisters; 1901 (2,533).

Duquesne University (c): 600 Forbes Ave., Pittsburgh, PA 15282; (412) 396-6000; www.duq.edu. Congregation of the Holy Ghost; 1878 (9,600).

D'Youville College (c): 320 Porter Ave., Buffalo, NY 14201; (716) 881-3200; www.dyc.edu. Grey Nuns of the Sacred Heart; 1908; independent (2,453).

Edgewood College (c): 1000 Edgewood College Dr., Madison, WI 53711; (608) 663-4861. Sinsinawa Dominican Sisters; 1927 (2,258).

Emmanuel College (w): 400 The Fenway, Boston, MA 02115; (617) 735-9715; www.emmanuel.edu. Sisters of Notre Dame de Namur; 1919; independent (1,549).

Fairfield University (c): 1073 North Benson Rd., Fairfield, CT 06430; (203) 254-4000; www.fairfield.edu. Jesuits; 1942 (6,001).

Felician College (c): 262 S. Main St., Lodi, NJ 07644; (201) 559-6000; www.felician.edu. Felician Sisters; 1942; independent (1,400).

Fontbonne University (c): 6800 Wydown Blvd., St. Louis, MO 63105; (314) 862-3456; www.fontbonne.edu. Sisters of St. Joseph of Carondelet; 1917; independent (2,344).

Fordham University (c): Fordham Rd. and Third Ave., New York, NY 10458; (718) 817-3040. Society of Jesus (Jesuits); 1841; independent (13,800).

Franciscan University of Steubenville (c): 1235 University Blvd., Steubenville, OH 43952; (740) 283-3771; www.franuniv.edu. Franciscan TOR Friars; 1946 (2,208). Also offers distance learning programs.

Gannon University (c): 109 University Square, Erie, PA 16541-0001; (814) 871-7000; www.gannon.edu. Diocese of Erie; 1933 (3,404).

Georgetown University (c): 37th and O Sts. N.W., Washington, DC 20057; (202) 687-0100; www.georgetown.edu. Jesuit Fathers; 1789 (12,688).

Georgian Court College (w/c): 900 Lakewood Ave., Lakewood, NJ 08701; (732) 364-2200; www.georgian.edu. Sisters of Mercy; 1908 (3,561).

Gonzaga University (c): E. 502 Boone Ave., Spokane, WA 99258; (509) 328-4220. Jesuit Fathers; 1887 (4,515).

Graduate School of Theology (c): 5890 Birch Ct., Oakland, CA 94618; (510) 652-1651; www.satgtu.org. Affiliate of the Graduate Theological Union.

Great Falls, University of (c): 1301 20th St. S., Great Falls,

MT 59405; (406) 761-8210; www.ugf.edu. Sisters of Providence; 1932; independent (825).

Gwynedd-Mercy College (c): Gwynedd Valley, PA 19437; (215) 646-7300; www.gmc.edu. Sisters of Mercy; 1948; independent (2,198).

Hilbert College (c): 5200 S. Park Ave., Hamburg, NY 14075; (716) 649-7900; www.hilbert.edu. Franciscan Sisters of St. Joseph; 1957; independent (970).

Holy Cross, College of the (c): Worcester, MA 01610; (508) 793-2011; www.holycross.edu. Jesuits; 1843 (2,811).

Holy Family College (c): Grant and Frankford Aves., Philadelphia, PA 19114 and One Campus Dr., Newtown, PA 18940; (215) 637-7700; www.hfc.edu. Sisters of Holy Family of Nazareth; 1954; independent (2,559).

Holy Names College (c): 3500 Mountain Blvd., Oakland, CA 94619; (510) 436-1000; www.hnc.edu. Sisters of the Holy Names of Jesus and Mary; 1868; independent (947).

Immaculata College (w): Immaculata, PA 19345; (610) 647-4400; www.immaculata.edu. Sisters, Servants of the Immaculate Heart of Mary; 1920 (3,062).

Incarnate Word, University of the (c): 4301 Broadway, San Antonio, TX 78209; (210) 829-6000; www.uiw.edu. Sisters of Charity of the Incarnate Word; 1881 (4,264).

Iona College (c): 715 North Ave., New Rochelle, NY 10801; (914) 633-2000; www.iona.edu. Congregation of Christian Brothers; 1940; independent (4,897).

John Carroll University (c): 20700 N. Park Blvd., Cleveland, OH 44118; (216) 397-1886; www.jcu.edu. Jesuits; 1886 (4,294).

King's College (c): 133 North River St., Wilkes-Barre, PA 18711; (570) 208-5900; www.kings.edu. Holy Cross Fathers; 1946 (2,178).

La Roche College (c): 9000 Babcock Blvd., Pittsburgh, PA 15237; (412) 367-9300; www.laroche.edu. Sisters of Divine Providence; 1963 (1,981).

La Salle University (c): 1900 W. Olney Ave., Philadelphia, PA 19141; (215) 951-1000. Christian Brothers; 1863 (5,567).

Le Moyne College (c): 1419 Salt Springs Rd., Syracuse, NY 13214; (315) 445-4100; www.lemoyne.edu. Jesuit Fathers; 1946; independent (approx. 3,129, full-time, part-time, graduate)

Lewis University (c): Romeoville, IL 60446; (815) 838-0500; www.lewisu.edu. Christian Brothers; 1932 (4,348).

Loras College (c): 1450 Alta Vista St., Dubuque, IA 52004; (563) 588-7100. Archdiocese of Dubuque; 1839 (1,736).

Lourdes College (c): 6832 Convent Blvd., Sylvania, OH 43560; (419) 885-3211; www.lourdes.edu. Sisters of St. Francis; 1958 (1,356).

Loyola College (c): 4501 N. Charles St., Baltimore, MD 21210; (410) 617-2000; www.loyola.edu. Jesuits; 1852; combined with Mt. St. Agnes College, 1971 (6,144).

Loyola Marymount University (c): 7900 Loyola Blvd., Los Angeles, CA 90045-2699; (310) 338-2700; www.lmu.edu. Society of Jesus; Religious of Sacred Heart of Mary, Sisters of St. Joseph of Orange, 1911 (6,591).

Loyola University (c): 6363 St. Charles Ave., New Orleans, LA 70118; (504) 865-2011. Jesuit Fathers;

1912 (5,842).

Loyola University Chicago (c): 820 N. Michigan Ave., Chicago, IL 60611; (312) 915-6000; www.luc.edu. Society of Jesus; 1870 (12,604).

Madonna University (c): 36600 Schoolcraft Rd., Livonia, MI 48150; (734) 432-5300. Felician Sisters; 1947 (3,979).

Magdalen College (c): 511 Kearsarge Mountain Rd., Warner, NH 03278; (603) 456-2656; www.magdalen.edu. Magdalen College Corporation; 1973 (81).

Manhattan College (c): Manhattan College Pkwy., Bronx, NY 11201; (718) 862-7200; www.manhattan.edu. De La Salle Christian Brothers; 1835; independent (2,744). Cooperative program with College of Mt. St. Vincent.

Marian College of Fond du Lac (c): 45 S. National Ave., Fond du Lac, WI 54935; (920) 923-7600; www.mariancollege.edu. Sisters of St. Agnes; 1936 (2,558).

Marian College (c): 3200 Cold Spring Rd., Indianapolis, IN 46222; (317) 955-6000; www.marian.edu. Sisters of St. Francis (Oldenburg, IN); 1851; independent (1,425).

Marquette University (c): P.O. Box 1881, Milwaukee, WI 53201-1881; (414) 288-7250; www.marquette.edu. Jesuit Fathers; 1881; independent (10,832).

Mary, University of (c): 7500 University Dr., Bismarck, ND 58504; (701) 255-7500; www.umary.edu. Benedictine Sisters; 1959 (2,546).

Marygrove College (c): 8425 W. McNichols Rd., Detroit, MI 48221; (313) 927-1200. Sisters, Servants of the Immaculate Heart of Mary; 1905; independent (6,459).

Marylhurst College (c): P.O. Box 261, Marylhurst, OR 97036-0261; (503) 636-8141; www.marylhurst.edu. Sisters of Holy Names of Jesus and Mary; 1893; independent (1,579).

Marymount College (w): Tarrytown, NY 10591; (914) 631-3200; www.marymt.edu. Religious of the Sacred Heart of Mary; 1907; independent (842). Coed in weekend degree programs.

Marymount University (c): 2807 N. Glebe Rd., Arlington, VA 22207; (703) 522-5600; www.marymount.edu. Religious of the Sacred Heart of Mary; 1950; independent (3,672).

Marywood College (c): Scranton, PA 18509; (570) 348-6211; www.marywood.edu. Sisters, Servants of the Immaculate Heart of Mary; 1915; independent (3,087).

Mercy College of Health Sciences (c): 928-6th Ave., Des Moines, IA 50309-1239; (515) 643-3180; www.mchs.edu. Sisters of Mercy of the Americas (552).

Mercyhurst College (c): 501 E. 38th St., Erie, PA 16546; (814) 824-2000; www.mercyhurst.edu. Sisters of Mercy; 1926 (3,404).

Merrimack College (c): North Andover, MA 01845; (978) 837-5000; www.merrimack.edu. Augustinians;1947 (2,108).

Misericordia (College Misericordia) (c): 301 Lake St., Dallas, PA 18612-1098; (570) 674-6400; www.miseri.edu. Religious Sisters of Mercy of the Union; 1924 (1,983).

Molloy College (c): 1000 Hempstead Ave., P.O. Box 5002, Rockville Centre, NY 11570-5002; (516) 678-5000. Dominican Sisters; 1955; independent (2,500).

Mount Aloysius College (c): 7373 Admiral Peary Hwy., Cresson, PA 16630; (814) 886-4131; www.mtaloy.edu. Sisters of Mercy; 1939 (2,000).

Mount Marty College (c): 1105 W. 8th St., Yankton, SD 57078; (800) 658-4552; www.mtmc.edu. Benedictine Sisters; 1936 (1,168).

Mount Mary College (w): 2900 N. Menomonee River Pkwy., Milwaukee, WI 53222; (414) 258-4810. School Sisters of Notre Dame; 1913 (1,368).

Mount Mercy College (c): 1330 Elmhurst Dr. N.E., Cedar Rapids, IA 52402; (319) 363-8213; www.mtmercy.edu. Sisters of Mercy; 1928; independent (1,432).

Mount St. Clare College (c): 400 N. Bluff Blvd., Clinton, IA 52732; (319) 242-4023; www.clare.edu. Sisters of St. Francis of Clinton, Iowa; 1918 (appr. 497).

Mount St. Joseph, College of (c): 5701 Delhi Rd., Cincinnati, OH 45233-1670; (513) 244-4200; www.msj.edu. Sisters of Charity; 1920 (5,527).

Mount Saint Mary College (c): Newburgh, NY 12550; (914) 561-0800; www.msmc.edu. Dominican Sisters; 1954; independent (2,541).

Mount St. Mary's College (c): Emmitsburg, MD 21727; (301) 447-6122; www.msmary.edu. Founded by Fr. John DuBois, 1808; independent (1,821).

Mount St. Mary's College (w/c): 12001 Chalon Rd., Los Angeles, CA 90049 and 10 Chester Pl., Los Angeles, CA 90007 (Doheny Campus); (310) 954-4010; www.msmc.la.edu. Sisters of St. Joseph of Carondelet; 1925. Coed in music, nursing and graduate programs (1,965).

Mount Saint Vincent, College of (c): 6301 Riverdale Ave., New York, NY 10471; (718) 405-3200; www.cmsv.edu. Sisters of Charity; 1847; independent (1,515). Cooperative program with Manhattan College.

Neumann College (c): One Neumann Dr., Aston, PA 19014; (610) 459-0905; www.neumann.edu. Sisters of St. Francis; 1965; independent (2,221).

Newman University (c): 3100 McCormick Ave., Wichita, KS 67213; (316) 942-4291; www.newmanu.edu. Sisters Adorers of the Blood of Christ; 1933 (1,929).

New Rochelle, College of (w/c): 29 Castle Pl., New Rochelle, NY 10805 (main campus); (914) 654-5000; www.cnr.edu. Ursuline Order; 1904; independent (6,084). Coed in nursing, graduate, new resources divisions.

Niagara University (c): Lewiston Rd. Niagara Univ., NY 14109-2015; (716) 285-1212; www.niagara.edu. Vincentian Fathers and Brothers; 1856 (3,446).

Notre Dame de Namur University (c): 1500 Ralston Ave., Belmont, CA 94002; (650) 593-1601; www.cnd.edu. Sisters of Notre Dame de Namur; 1851; independent (1,799).

Notre Dame, University of (c): (University of Notre Dame du Lac) Notre Dame, IN 46556; (219) 631-5000; www.nd.edu. Congregation of Holy Cross; 1842 (11,054).

Notre Dame College of Ohio (w): 4545 College Rd., Cleveland, OH 44121; (216) 381-1680; www.ndc.edu. Sisters of Notre Dame; 1922 (1,093).

Notre Dame of Maryland, College of (w): 4701 N. Charles St., Baltimore, MD 21210; (410) 435-0100; www.ndm.edu. School Sisters of Notre Dame; 1873 (3,077).

Oblate School of Theology (c): 285 Oblate Dr., San Antonio, TX 78216-6693; (210) 341-1366; www.ost.edu. Oblates of Mary Immaculate; 1903 (264). Graduate theology programs.

Ohio Dominican College (c): 1216 Sunbury Rd., Columbus, OH 43219-2099; (614) 253-2741; www.odc.edu.

Dominican Sisters of St. Mary of the Springs; 1911 (2,300).

Our Lady of Holy Cross College (c): 4123 Woodland Dr., New Orleans, LA 70131; (504) 394-7744; www.olhcc.edu. Congregation of Sisters Marianites of Holy Cross; 1916 (3,994).

Our Lady of the Elms, College of (w): Chicopee, MA 01013; (413) 594-2761; www.elms.edu. Sisters of St. Joseph; 1928 (866).

Our Lady of the Lake College (c): 5345 Brittany Dr., Baton Rouge, LA 70808-4398; (225) 768-1710; www.ololcollege. Independent (1,421).

Our Lady of the Lake University (c): 411 S.W. 24th St., San Antonio, TX 78207; (210) 434-6711; www.ollusa.edu. Sisters of Divine Providence; 1895 (3,324).

Pontifical Catholic University of Puerto Rico (c): 2250 Avenida de las Americas, Ponce, PR 00717-0777; (787) 841-2000; www.pucpr.edu. Hierarchy of Puerto Rico; 1948; Pontifical University (9,912).

Portland, University of (c): 5000 N. Willamette Blvd., Portland, OR 97203; (503) 943-7911; www.up.edu. Holy Cross Fathers; 1901; independent (3,234).

Presentation College (c): Aberdeen, SD 7401; (605) 225-1634. Sisters of the Presentation; 1951 (615).

Providence College (c): 549 River Ave., Providence, RI 02918; (401) 865-1000; www.providence.edu. Dominican Friars; 1917 (5,742, day, evening, and graduate).

Queen of the Holy Rosary College (c): P.O. Box 3908, Mission San Jose, CA 94539; (510) 657-2468. Dominican Sisters of Mission San Jose, independent (200).

Quincy University (c): 1800 College Ave., Quincy, IL 62301; (217) 222-8020; www.quincy.edu. Franciscan Friars; 1860 (1,146).

Regis College (w): 235 Wellesley St., Weston, MA 02493-1571; (781) 768-7000; www.regiscollege.edu. Sisters of St. Joseph; 1927; independent (1,300).

Regis University (c): 3333 Regis Blvd. Denver, CO 80221; (303) 458-4100. Jesuits; 1887 (11,240).

Rivier College (c): Nashua, NH 03060; (603) 888-1311; www.rivier.edu. Sisters of the Presentation of Mary; 1933; independent (2,572).

Rockhurst College (c): 1100 Rockhurst Rd., Kansas City, MO 64110; (816) 501-4000; www.rockhurst.edu. Jesuit Fathers; 1910 (3,536).

Rosemont College of the Holy Child Jesus (w): Rosemont, PA 19010-1699; (610) 526-2984; www.rosemont.edu. Society of the Holy Child Jesus; 1921 (1,210).

Sacred Heart University (c): 5151 Park Ave., Fairfield, CT 06432; (203) 371-7999; www.sacredheart.edu. Diocese of Bridgeport; 1963; independent (6,001).

St. Ambrose University (c): Davenport, IA 52803; (319) 333-6300; www.sau.edu. Diocese of Davenport; 1882 (3,500).

Saint Anselm College (c): Manchester NH 03102-1030; (603) 641-7000; www.anselm.edu. Benedictines; 1889 (1,985).

St. Basil College (m): 195 Glenbrook Rd., Stamford, CT 06902; (203) 324-4578; UkrCathSem@aol.com. The Ukrainian Catholic Diocese of Stamford.

Saint Benedict, College of (w): 37 S. College Ave., St. Joseph, MN 56374; (320) 363-5407; www.csbsju.edu. Benedictine Sisters; 1913 (2,072). Sister college of St. John's University, Collegeville

St. Bonaventure University (c): St. Bonaventure,

NY 14778; (716) 375-2000; www.sbu.edu. Franciscan Friars; 1858; independent (2,719).

St. Catherine, College of (w): St. Paul: 2004 Randolph Ave., St. Paul, MN 55105; (651) 690-6000; Minneapolis; www.stkate.edu. Sisters of St. Joseph of Carondelet; 1905 (4,622).

St. Edward's University (c): 3001 S. Congress Ave., Austin, TX 78704; (512) 448-8400; www.stedwards.edu. Holy Cross Brothers; 1881; independent (4,267).

Saint Elizabeth, College of (w): 2 Convent Rd., Morristown, NJ 07960-6989; (973) 290-4000; www.st-elizabeth.edu. Sisters of Charity; 1899; independent (1,766). Coed in adult undergraduate and graduate programs.

St. Francis College (c): 180 Remsen St., Brooklyn Heights, NY 11201; (718) 489-5200. Franciscan Brothers; 1884; private, independent in the Franciscan tradition (2,505).

St. Francis University (c): P.O. Box 600, Loretto, PA 15940-0600; (814) 472-3000; www.sfcpa.edu. Franciscan Friars; 1847; independent (2,012).

St. Francis, University of (c): 500 N. Wilcox, Joliet, IL 60435; (815) 740-3360; www.stfrancis.edu. Sisters of St. Francis of Mary Immaculate (3,920).

St. Francis, University of (c): 2701 Spring St., Fort Wayne, IN 46808-3994; (219) 434-3100; www.sf.edu. Sisters of St. Francis; 1890 (1,740).

St. Gregory's University (c): 1900 W. MacArthur, Shawnee, OK 74801; (405) 878-5100; www.sgc.edu. Benedictine Monks; 1876 (805).

St. John's University (c): 8000 Utopia Pkwy., Jamaica, NY 11439 (Queens Campus); 300 Howard Ave., Staten Island, NY 10301 (Staten Island Campus); (718) 990-6161; www.stjohns.edu. Vincentians; 1870 (18,523).

St. John's University (m): Collegeville, MN 56321; (320) 363-2011; www.csbsju.edu. Benedictines; 1857 (2,072). All classes and programs are coeducational with College of St. Benedict.

St. Joseph in Vermont, College of (c): 71 Clement Rd., Rutland, VT 05701; (802) 773-5900; www.csj.edu. Sisters of St. Joseph; 1950; independent (482).

Saint Joseph College (w/c): 1678 Asylum Ave., West Hartford, CT 06117-2700; (860) 232-4571; www.sjc.edu. Sisters of Mercy; 1932 (1,965). Women's college in undergraduate liberal arts. Coed in graduate school and Weekend College.

Saint Joseph's College (c): 278 Whites Bridge Rd., Standish, ME 04084-5263; (207) 893-7711; www.sjcme.edu. Sisters of Mercy; 1912 (4,197 total; 1,609 graduate). Offers extensive distance education programs.

Saint Joseph's College (c): P.O. Box 909, Rensselaer, IN 47978; (219) 866-6000; www.stjoe.edu. Society of the Precious Blood; 1891 (1,101).

St. Joseph's College (c): 245 Clinton Ave., Brooklyn, NY 11205; (718) 636-6800 and 155 W. Roe Blvd., Patchogue, NY 11772; (631) 447-3200; www.sjcny.edu. Sisters of St. Joseph; 1916; independent (3,444).

St. Joseph's University (c): 5600 City Ave., Philadelphia, PA 19131; (610) 660-1000; www.sju.edu. Jesuit Fathers; 1851 (6,850).

Saint Leo University (c): P.O. Box 6665, MC 2186, Saint Leo, FL 33574; (352) 588-8200; www.saintleo.edu. Order of St. Benedict; 1889; independent (9,931).

Saint Louis University (c): 221 N. Grand Blvd., St. Louis, MO 63103; (314) 977-2222; www.slu.edu. Society of Jesus; 1818; independent (11,274).

Saint Martin's College (c): 5300 Pacific Ave. SE, Lacey, WA 98503-1297; (360) 438-4311; www.stmartin.edu. Benedictine Monks; 1895 (1,474 main and extension campuses).

Saint Mary, College of (w): 1901 S. 72nd St., Omaha, NE 68124; (402) 399-2400; www.csm.edu. Sisters of Mercy; 1923; independent (981).

Saint Mary College (c): Leavenworth, KS 66048; (913) 682-5151. Sisters of Charity of Leavenworth; 1923 (888).

Saint Mary-of-the-Woods College (w): St. Mary-of-the-Woods, IN 47876; (812) 535-5151; www.smwc.edu. Sisters of Providence; 1840 (1,510).

Saint Mary's College (w): Notre Dame, IN 46556; (219) 284-4556; www.saintmarys.edu. Sisters of the Holy Cross; 1844 (1,473).

Saint Mary's College (c): 3535 Indian Trail, Orchard Lake, MI 48324; (248) 683-0521; www.stmarys-avemaria.edu. 1885 (510).

St. Mary's College (c): Moraga, CA 94575; (510) 631-4000. Brothers of the Christian Schools; 1863 (4,127).

Saint Mary's University of Minnesota (c): 700 Terrace Heights, Winona, MN 55987-1399; (507) 452-4430; www.smumn.edu. Brothers of the Christian Schools; 1912 (1,376).

St. Mary's University of San Antonio (c): One Camino Santa Maria, San Antonio, TX 78228-8607; (210) 436-3011; www.stmarytx.edu. Society of Mary (Marianists). 1852 (4,264).

Saint Meinrad School of Theology (c): 200 Hill Dr., St. Meinrad, IN 47577; (812) 357-6611; www.saint-meinrad.edu. Benedictines (91 full- and part-time lay students.) Graduate-level theological studies.

St. Michael's College (c): Winooski Park, Colchester, VT 05439; (802) 654-2211; www.smcvt.edu. Society of St. Edmund; 1904 (2,630).

St. Norbert College (c): De Pere, WI 54115; (920) 403-3181; www.snc.edu. Norbertine Fathers; 1898; independent (2,045).

Saint Peter's College (c): 2641 Kennedy Blvd., Jersey City, NJ 07306; (201) 915-9000; www.spc.edu. Society of Jesus; 1872; independent (4,201).

Saint Rose, College of (c): 432 Western Ave., Albany, NY 12203; (518) 454-5111. Sisters of St. Joseph of Carondelet; 1920; independent (4,441).

St. Scholastica, The College of (c): 1200 Kenwood Ave., Duluth, MN 55811; (218) 723-6000. Benedictine Sisters; 1912; independent (2,518).

St. Thomas, University of (c): 2115 Summit Ave., St. Paul, MN 55105; (651) 962-5000; www.stthomas.edu. Archdiocese of St. Paul and Minneapolis; 1885 (11,366).

St. Thomas, University of (c): 3800 Montrose Blvd., Houston, TX 77006-4696; (713) 522-7911; www.stthom.edu. Basilian Fathers; 1947 (7,174).

St. Thomas Aquinas College (c): Sparkill, NY 10976; (914) 398-4000; www.stac.edu. Dominican Sisters of Sparkill; 1952; independent, corporate board of trustees (2,200).

St. Thomas University (c): 16400 N.W. 32nd Ave., Miami, FL 33054; (305) 625-6000; www.stu.edu. Archdiocese of Miami; 1962 (3,677).

Saint Vincent College (c): 300 Fraser Purchase Rd., Latrobe, PA 15650-2690; (724) 539-9761; www.benedictine.stvincent.edu/seminary. Benedictine Fathers; 1846 (1,222).

Saint Vincent's College (c): 2800 Main St., Bridgeport, CT 06606; (203) 576-5235; www.stvincentscollege.edu. (345).

St. Xavier University (c): 3700 W. 103rd St., Chicago, IL 60655; (773) 298-3000. Sisters of Mercy; chartered 1847 (4,100).

Salve Regina University (c): Ochre Point Ave., Newport, RI 02840-4192; (401) 847-6650; www.salve.edu. Sisters of Mercy; 1934 (1,542). Offers distance learning programs in graduate studies.

San Diego, University of (c): 5998 Alcala Park, San Diego, CA 92110; (619) 260-4600. San Diego diocese and Religious of the Sacred Heart; 1949; independent (7,062).

San Francisco, University of (c): 2130 Fulton St., San Francisco, CA 94117; (415) 422-5555. Jesuit Fathers; 1855 (8,130).

Santa Clara University (c): 500 El Camino Real, Santa Clara, CA 95053; (408) 554-4000; www.scu.edu. Jesuit Fathers; 1851; independent (7,368).

Santa Fe, College of (c): 1600 St. Michael's Dr., Santa Fe, NM 87505; (505) 473-6011. Brothers of the Christian Schools; 1947 (1,588).

Scranton, University of (c): Scranton, PA 18510; (570) 941-7533; www.uofs.edu. Society of Jesus; 1888; independent (4,728).

Seattle University (c): 900 Broadway, Seattle, WA 98122; (206) 296-6000; www.seattleu.edu. Society of Jesus; 1891 (6,337).

Seton Hall University (c): 400 South Orange Ave., South Orange, NJ 07079; (973) 761-9000. Diocesan Clergy; 1856 (9,760).

Seton Hill College (w): Seton Hill Dr., Greensburg, PA 15601-1599; (724) 834-2200; www.setonhill.edu. Sisters of Charity of Seton Hill; 1883 (1,521).

Siena College (c): 515 Loudon Rd., Loudonville, NY 12211; (518) 783-2300; www.siena.edu. Franciscan Friars; 1937 (3,379).

Siena Heights University (c): 1247 E. Siena Heights Dr., Adrian, MI 49221; (517) 263-0731; www.sienahts.edu. Adrian Dominican Sisters; 1919 (2,124).

Silver Lake College of the Holy Family (c): 2406 S. Alverno Rd., Manitowoc, WI 54220-9319; (920) 684-6691. Franciscan Sisters of Christian Charity; 1935 (2,969).

Spalding University (c): 851 S. 4th Ave., Louisville, KY 40203; (502) 585-9911; www.spalding.edu. Sisters of Charity of Nazareth; 1814; independent (1,670).

Spring Hill College (c): 4000 Dauphin St., Mobile, AL 36608; (334) 380-4000; www.shc.edu. Jesuit Fathers; 1830 (1,050).

Stonehill College (c): North Easton, MA 02357; (508) 565-1000; www.stonehill.edu. Holy Cross Fathers; 1948; independent (2,550).

Thomas Aquinas College (c): 10000 N. Ojai Rd., Santa Paula, CA 93060; (805) 525-4417; www.thomasaquinas.edu. Founded 1971 (331).

Thomas More College (c): 333 Thomas More Pkwy., Crestview Hills, Covington, KY 41017; (859) 341-5800; www.thomasmore.edu. Diocese of Covington; 1921 (1,555).

Trinity College of Vermont (w): 208 Colchester Ave., Burlington, VT 05401; (802) 658-0337; www.trinityvt.edu. Sisters of Mercy; 1925 (200). May be closed.

Trinity College (w): 125 Michigan Ave. NE, Washington, DC 20017; (202) 939-5000. Sisters of

Notre Dame de Namur; 1897 (1,600). Coed graduate school.

Ursuline College (w): 2550 Lander Rd., Pepper Pike, OH 44124; (440) 449-4200; www.ursuline.edu. Ursuline Nuns; 1871 (1,319).

Villanova University (c): Villanova, PA 19085; (610) 519-7499; www.villanova.edu. Order of St. Augustine; 1842 (10,396).

Viterbo College (c): 815 S. 9th, La Crosse, WI 54601; (608) 796-3000; www.viterbo.org. Franciscan Sisters of Perpetual Adoration; 1890 (2,200).

Walsh University (c): 2020 Easton St. N.W., North Canton, Ohio 44720-3396; (330) 490-7090; www.walsh.edu. Brothers of Christian Instruction; 1958 (1,648).

Washington Theological Union (c): 6896 Laurel Street N.W., Washington, DC 20012-2016; (202) 726-8800; www.wtu.edu. Coalition of Religious Seminaries; 1968 (263).

Wheeling Jesuit University (c): 316 Washington Ave., Wheeling, WV 26003-6295; (304) 243-2000; www.wju.edu. Jesuit Fathers; 1954 (1,703).

Xavier University (c): 3800 Victory Pkwy., Cincinnati, OH 45207; (513) 745-3000; www.xu.edu. Jesuit Fathers; 1831 (2,631).

Xavier University of Louisiana (c): 1 Drexel Dr., New Orleans, LA 70125; (504) 486-7411; www.xula.edu. Sisters of Blessed Sacrament; 1925 (3,787).

Catholic Two-Year Colleges

Ancilla Domini College (c): P.O. Box 1, Donaldson, IN 46513; (219) 936-8898; www.ancilla.edu. Poor Handmaids of Jesus Christ Sisters; 1937 (546).

Assumption College for Sisters: Mendham, NJ 07945; (973) 543-6528. Sisters of Christian Charity; 1953 (24).

Chatfield College (c): St. Martin, OH 45118; (937) 875-3344; www.chatfield.edu. Ursulines; 1971 (273).

The College of St. Catherine-Minneapolis (c): 601 25th Ave. S., Minneapolis, MN 55454; (651) 690-7702. Sisters of St. Joseph of Carondelet (918).

Donnelly College (c): 608 N. 18th St., Kansas City, KS 66102; (913) 621-6070; www.donnelly.cc.ks.us. Archdiocesan College; 1949 (645).

Don Bosco Technical Institute (m): 1151 San Gabriel Blvd., Rosemead, CA 91770; (626) 307-6500; www.boscotech.tec.ca.us. Salesians; 1969 (994).

Holy Cross College (c): 54515 State Rd., 933 N., Notre Dame, IN 46556-0308; (219) 239-8400; www.hcc-nd.edu. Brothers of Holy Cross; 1966 (503).

Manor College (c): 700 Fox Chase Road, Jenkintown, PA 19046; (215) 885-2360; www.manor.edu. Sisters of St. Basil the Great; 1947.

Maria College (c): 700 New Scotland Ave., Albany, NY 12208. Sisters of Mercy; 1963 (1,048).

Marymount College Palos Verdes (c): 30800 Palos Verdes Dr., E., Rancho Palos Verdes, CA 90275-6299; (310) 377-5501; www.marymountpv.edu. Religious of the Sacred Heart of Mary; independent (840).

St. Catharine College (c): 2735 Bardstown Rd., St. Catharine, KY 40061; (859) 336-5082. Dominican Sisters; 1931 (742).

Springfield College in Illinois (c): 1500 N. Fifth St., Springfield, IL 62702-2694; (217) 525-1420; www.sci.edu. Ursuline Sisters; 1929 (300).

Trocaire College (c): 360 Choate Ave., Buffalo, NY 14220; (716) 827-2423; www.trocaire.edu. Sisters of Mercy; 1958; independent (780).

Villa Maria College of Buffalo (c): 240 Pine Ridge Rd., Buffalo, NY 14225; (716) 896-0700; www.villa.edu. Felician Sisters 1960; independent (475).

DIOCESAN AND INTERDIOCESAN SEMINARIES

(Sources: Catholic Almanac survey; The Official Catholic Directory; Catholic News Service.)

Information, according to states, includes names of archdioceses and dioceses, and names and addresses of seminaries. Types of seminaries, when not clear from titles, are indicated in most cases. Interdiocesan seminaries are generally conducted by religious orders for candidates for the priesthood from several dioceses. The list does not include houses of study reserved for members of religious communities. Archdioceses are indicated by an asterisk.

California: Los Angeles* — St. John's Seminary (major), 5118 Seminary Rd., Camarillo 93012-2599; (805) 482-2755; www.stjohnsem.edu.

San Diego — St. Francis Seminary (college and pre-theology formation program), 1667 Santa Paula Dr., 92111; (619) 291-7446.

San Francisco* — St. Patrick's Seminary (major), 320 Middlefield Rd., Menlo Park 94025; (650) 325-5621; www.stpatricksseminary.org..

Colorado: Denver* — St. John Vianney Theological Seminary (college and pre-theology formation program), 1300 S. Steele St., 80210; (303) 282-3427.

Connecticut: Hartford* — St. Thomas Seminary (college formation program), 467 Bloomfield Ave.,

Bloomfield 06002-2999; (860) 242-5573.

Norwich — Holy Apostles College and Seminary (adult vocations; minor and major), 33 Prospect Hill Rd., Cromwell 06416; (860) 632-3000; www.holyapostles.edu.

Stamford — Byzantine Rite: Ukrainian Catholic Seminary: St. Basil College Seminary (minor), 195 Glenbrook Rd., Stamford 06902-3099; (203) 324-4578.

District of Columbia: Washington, DC* — Theological College (national, major), The Catholic University of America, 401 Michigan Ave., N.E., 20017; (202) 756-4900; www.theologicalcollege.org.

St. Josaphat's Seminary, 201 Taylor St. N.E., 20017; (202) 529-1177. Major house of formation serving the four Ukrainian Byzantine-rite dioceses in the U.S.

Florida: Miami* — St. John Vianney College Seminary, 2900 S.W. 87th Ave., 33165; (305) 223-4561.

Palm Beach — St. Vincent de Paul Regional Seminary (major), 10701 S. Military Trail, Boynton Beach 33436; (561) 732-4424; www.svdp.edu.

Illinois: Chicago* — Archbishop Quigley Preparatory Seminary (high school), 103 East Chestnut St., Chicago 60611; (312) 787-9343; www.quigley.org. St. Joseph Seminary (college), 6551

N. Sheridan Rd., Chicago 60626; (773) 973-9700; www.stjoseph.luc.edu. University of St. Mary of the Lake Mundelein Seminary (School of Theology), 1000 E. Maple Ave., Mundelein 60060; (847) 566-6401; www.vocations.org.

Indiana: Indianapolis* — Saint Meinrad Seminary, College and School of Theology (interdiocesan), St. Meinrad 47577; (812) 357-6611; www.saintmeinrad.edu.

Iowa: Davenport — St. Ambrose University Seminary (interdiocesn), 518 W. Locust St., 52803; (319) 333-6151; www.davenportdiocese.org.

Dubuque* — Seminary of St. Pius X (interdiocesan), Loras College, 52004-0178; (319) 588-7782.

Louisiana: New Orleans* — Notre Dame Seminary Graduate School of Theology, 2901 S. Carrollton Ave., 70118; (504) 866-7426. St. Joseph Seminary College (interdiocesan), St. Benedict 70457-9999; (504) 892-1800; www.stjosephabbey.org.

Maryland: Baltimore* — Mount St. Mary's Seminary and University, 5400 Roland Ave., 21210; (410) 864-4000; www.stmarys.edu. Mount St. Mary's Seminary, Emmitsburg 21727-7797; (301) 447-5295; www.msmary.edu.

Massachusetts: Boston* — St. John's Seminary, School of Theology, 127 Lake St., Brighton 02135; (617) 254-2610. St. John's Seminary, College of Liberal Arts, 127 Lake St., Brighton 02135; (617) 746-5450. Pope John XXIII National Seminary (for ages 30-60), 558 South Ave., Weston 02943; (781) 899-5500; www.blessedjohnXXIII.org.

Newton — Melkite Greek Catholic: St. Gregory the Theologian Seminary, 3 VFW Parkway, Roslindale, MA 02131; (617) 323-9922. Seminary of St. Basil the Great, 30 East St., 01844; (978) 683-2471.

Michigan: Detroit* — Sacred Heart Major Seminary (college/theologate and institute for ministry), 2701 Chicago Blvd., Detroit 48206; (313) 883-8500. Sts. Cyril and Methodius Seminary, St. Mary's College (theologate and college) independent, primarily serving Polish-American community, 3535 Indian Trail, Orchard Lake 48324; (248) 683-0311.

Grand Rapids — Christopher House, 723 Rosewood Ave., S.E., East Grand Rapids 49506; (616) 243-6538.

Minnesota: St. John's School of Theology and Seminary, St. John's University, P.O. Box 7288, Collegeville 56321-7288; (320) 363-2100; www.csb-sju.edu/sot.

St. Paul and Minneapolis* — St. Paul Seminary School of Divinity, University of St. Thomas, St. Paul 55101; (612) 962-5050; www.stthomas.edu. St. John Vianney Seminary (college residence), 2115 Summit Ave., St. Paul 55105; (651) 962-6825; www.stthomas.edu/sjv.

Winona — Immaculate Heart of Mary Seminary, St. Mary's University, No. 43, 700 Terrace Heights, 55987; (507) 457-7373; www.ihmseminary.org.

Missouri: St. Louis* — Kenrick — Glennon Seminary (St. Louis Roman Catholic Theological Seminary). Kenrick School of Theology and Cardinal Glennon College, 5200 Glennon Dr., 63119; (314) 792-6100.

Nebraska: Seward — St. Gregory the Great Seminary (pre-theology), 1301 280th Rd., 68434; (402) 643-4052, www.stgregoryseminary.org. Our Lady of Guadalupe Seminary, P.O. Box 147, Denton, NE 68339; (402) 797-7700; www.fssp.com.

New Jersey: Newark* — Immaculate Conception Seminary — college seminary; major seminary; graduate school — Seton Hall University, 400 South Orange Ave., South Orange 07079; (973) 761-9575; www.shu.edu. Redemptoris Mater, Archdiocesan Missionary Seminary, 672 Passaic Ave., 07032; (201) 997-3220.

New York: Brooklyn — Cathedral Seminary Residence of the Immaculate Conception (college and pre-theology), 7200 Douglaston Parkway, Douglaston 11362; (718) 229-8001. Cathedral Preparatory Seminary, 56-25 92nd St., Elmhurst 11373; (718) 592-6800. St. Alphonsus Formation Residence, 22-04 Parsons Blvd., 11357-3440; (718) 321-1096.

Buffalo — Christ the King Seminary (interdiocesan theologate), P.O. Box 607, 711 Knox Rd., East Aurora 14052; (716) 652-8900. Pope John Paul II Residence, 217 Winston Rd., 14216; (716) 836-5526.

New York* — St. Joseph's Seminary (major), 201 Seminary Ave., Dunwoodie, Yonkers 10704; (914) 968-6200. St. John Neumann Residence (college and pre-theology), 201 Seminary Ave., Yonkers N.Y., 10704-1896; (914) 964-3025. Cathedral Preparatory Seminary, 946 Boston Post Rd., Rye 10580; (914) 968-6200; www.cathedralprep.com.

Rockville Centre — Seminary of the Immaculate Conception (major), 440 West Neck Rd., Huntington, 11743; (631) 423-2346.

St. Maron Eparchy, Brooklyn — Our Lady of Lebanon Maronite Seminary, 7164 Alaska Ave. N.W., Washington, DC 20012; (202) 723-8831; www.maroniteseminary.org.

North Dakota: Fargo — Cardinal Muench Seminary (interdiocesan high school, college and pre-theology), 100 35th Ave. N.E., Fargo 58102; (701) 232-8969; www.cardinalmuench.org.

Ohio: Cincinnati* — Mt. St. Mary's Seminary of the West (division of the Athenaeum of Ohio), 6616 Beechmont Ave., 45230; (513) 231-2223; www.mtsm.org..

Cleveland — St. Mary Seminary and Graduate School of Theology, 28700 Euclid Ave. Wickliffe 44092; (440) 943-7600. Borromeo Seminary, 28700 Euclid Ave., 44092-2585; (440) 943-7600; www.a-full-life.com.

Columbus — Pontifical College Josephinum (national), theologate and college, 7625 North High St., 43235-1498; (614) 885-5585; www.pcj.edu.

Oregon: Portland* — Mount Angel Seminary (interdiocesan, college, pre-theology program, graduate school of theology), 1 Abbey Dr., St. Benedict 97373; (503) 845-3951. Felix Rougier House of Studies, 585 E. College St., 97362. Jesuit Novitiate of St. Francis Xavier, 3301 S.E. 45th Ave., 97206.

Pennsylvania: Erie — St. Mark Seminary, P.O. Box 10397, Erie 16514; (814) 824-1200.

Greensburg — St. Vincent Seminary (interdiocesan; pre-theology program; theologate; graduate programs in theology; religious education), 300 Fraser Purchase Rd., Latrobe 15650-2690; (724) 539-9761; www.stvincent.edu.

Philadelphia* — Theological Seminary of St. Charles Borromeo (College, pre-theology program, spirituality year program, theologate), 100 East Wynnewood Rd., Wynnewood 19096; (610) 667-3394; www.scs.edu.

Pittsburgh* (Byzantine-Ruthenian) — Byzantine Catholic Seminary of Sts. Cyril and Methodius (college, pre-theology program, theologate), 3605 Perrysville Ave., 15214; (412) 321-8383; www.byzcath.org/seminary.

Pittsburgh — St. Paul Seminary (interdiocesan, college and pre-theology), 2900 Noblestown Rd., 15205; (412) 921-5800; www.diopitt.org.

Scranton — St. Pius X Seminary (college and pre-theology formation; interdiocesan), 1000 Seminary Rd., Dalton 18414; (570) 563-1131. Affiliated with the University of Scranton.

Rhode Island: Providence — Seminary of Our Lady of Providence (House of Formation; college students and pre-theology), 485 Mount Pleasant Ave., 02908; (401) 331-1316; www.catholicpriest.com.

Texas: Dallas — Holy Trinity Seminary (college and pre-theology; English proficiency and academic foundation programs), P.O. Box 140309, Irving 75014; (972) 438-2212.

El Paso — St. Charles Seminary College, P.O. Box 17548, 79917; (915) 591-9821.

Galveston-Houston — St. Mary's Seminary (theologate), 9845 Memorial Dr., Houston 77024; (713) 686-4345.

San Antonio* — Assumption Seminary (theologate and pre-theology, Hispanic ministry emphasis), 2600 W. Woodlawn Ave., 78228; (210) 734-2324.

Washington: Spokane — Bishop White Seminary, College Formation Program, E. 429 Sharp Ave., 99202; (509) 326-3255; www.bishopwhiteseminary.org.

Wisconsin: Milwaukee* — St. Francis Seminary, 3257 S. Lake Dr., St. Francis 53235; (414) 747-6400; www.sfs.edu. College Program, 2497 N. Murray Ave., Milwaukee, 53211; (414) 964-6982. Sacred Heart School of Theology (interdiocesan seminary for sec-ond-career vocations), P.O. Box 429, Hales Corners, 53130-0429; (414) 425-8300.

North American College

Founded by the U.S. Bishops in 1859, the North American College serves as a residence and house of formation for U.S. seminarians and graduate students in Rome. The first ordination of an alumnus took place June 14, 1862. Pontifical status was granted the college by Pope Leo XIII Oct. 25, 1884. Students pursue theological and related studies principally at the Pontifical Gregorian University and at the Pontifical University of St. Thomas Aquinas (the Angelicum). The current rector is Msgr. James F. Checcio, J.C.D., M.B.A. Address: 00120 Città del Vaticano; 011-39-06-684-931; www.pnac.org.

American College of Louvain

Founded by U.S. Bishops in 1857, the American College of Louvain, Belgium, is a seminary for U.S. students. It also serves as a community for English-speaking graduate-student priests and religious priests pursuing studies at the Catholic University of Louvain (Université Catholique de Louvain, founded 1425). The college is administered by an American rector and faculty, and operates under the auspices of a committee of the national Conference of Catholic Bishops. The rector is Rev. Kevin A. Codd, S.T.L. Address: The American College, Catholic University of Louvain, Naamsestraat 100, B-3000, Leuven, Belgium; 32-16-32-00-11; www.acl.be.

PONTIFICAL UNIVERSITIES

(Principal source: Annuario Pontificio.)

These universities, listed according to country of location, have been canonically erected and authorized by the Congregation for Catholic Education to award degrees in stated fields of study. New laws and norms governing ecclesiastical universities and faculties were promulgated in the apostolic constitution Sapientia Christiana, issued Apr. 15, 1979. Phone numbers are listed where possible.

Argentina: Pontifical Catholic University of S. Maria of Buenos Aires (June 16, 1960): Av. Alicia Moreau de Justo 1400, 1107 Buenos Aires.

Belgium: Catholic University of Louvain (founded Dec. 9, 1425; canonically erected, 1834), with autonomous institutions for French- (Louvain) and Flemish-(Leuven) speaking: Place de l'Universite I, B-1348 Louvain-La-Neuve (French); Naamsestraat 22/b, B-3000 Leuven (Flemish).

Brazil: Pontifical Catholic University of Rio de Janeiro (Jan. 20, 1947): Rua Marquês de São Vicente 225, 22451-000 Rio de Janeiro, RJ.

Pontifical Catholic University of Minas Gerais (June 5, 1983): Av. Dom José Gaspar 500, C.P. 2686, 30161-000 Belo Horizonte, MG.; (031) 319-1127.

Pontifical Catholic University of Parana (Aug. 6, 1985): Rua Imaculada Conceição, 1155, Prado Velho, C.P. 670, 80001-000 Curitiba, PR; (041) 223-0922.

Pontifical Catholic University of Rio Grande do Sul (Nov. 1, 1950): Av. Ipiranga 6681, C.P.1429,90001-000 Porto Alegre, RS.

Pontifical Catholic University of São Paulo (Jan. 25, 1947): Rua Monte Alegre 984, 05014-901 São Paulo SP.

Pontifical University of Campinas (Sept. 8, 1956): Rua Marechal Deodoro 1099, 13020-000 Campinas, SP.; (0192) 27-001.

Canada: Laval University (Mar. 15, 1876): Case Postale 460, QC G1K 7P4.

St. Paul University (formerly University of Ottawa) (Feb. 5, 1889): 223 Rue Main, Ottawa, ON K1S 1C4;

University of Sherbrooke (Nov. 21, 1957): Chemin Ste.-Catherine, 2500, boulevard de l'Université, Sherbrooke, QC J1K 12R1.

Chile: Pontifical Catholic University of Chile (June 21, 1888): Avenida Bernardo O'Higgins, 340, Casilla 114D, Santiago.

Catholic University of Valparaíso (Nov. 1, 1961): Avenida Brasil 2950, Casilla 4059, Valparaíso.

Colombia: Bolivarian Pontifical Catholic University (Aug. 16, 1945): Circular 1a, N.70-01, Apartado 56006, Medellín.

Pontifical Xaverian University (July 31, 1937): Carrera 7, N. 40-62, Apartado 56710, Santafé de Bogota D.C.; Apartado 26239, Calle 18, N. 118-250, Cali (Cali campus).

Cuba: Catholic University of St. Thomas of Villanueva (May 4, 1957): Avenida Quenta 16,660, Marianao.

Dominican Republic: Pontifical Catholic University "Mother and Teacher" (Sept. 9, 1987): Apartado 822, Santiago de Los Caballeros.

Ecuador: Pontifical Catholic University of Ecuador (July 16, 1954): Doce de Octubre, N. 1076, Apartado

17-01-2184, Quito.

France: Catholic University of Lille (Nov. 18, 1875): Boulevard Vauban 60, 59016 Lille.

Catholic Faculties of Lyon (Nov. 22, 1875): 25, Rue du Plat, 69288 Lyon 02.

Catholic Institute of Paris (Aug. 11, 1875): 21, Rue d'Assas, 75270 Paris 06.

Catholic Institute of Toulouse (Nov. 15, 1877): Rue de la Fonderie 31, 31068 Toulouse.

Catholic University of the West (Sept. 16, 1875): 3, Place André Leroy, B.P. 808, 49005 Angers; 2-41-81-66-00.

Germany: Catholic University Eichstätt (Apr. 1, 1980): Ostenstrasse 26, D-85072, Eichstätt, Federal Republic of Germany; (08421) 201.

Guatemala: Rafael Landívar University (Oct. 18, 1961): Vista Hermosa III, Zona 16, Guatemala; (02) 69-21-51.

Hungary: Catholic University Pázmány Péter (March 25, 1999): Papnövelde Utea 7, H-1053 Budapest, Hungary; (01) 11-73-701.

Ireland: St. Patrick's College (Mar. 29, 1896): Maynooth, Co. Kildare.

Italy: Catholic University of the Sacred Heart (Dec. 25, 1920): Largo Gemelli 1, 20123 Milan.

Libera University Mary of the Assumption (Oct. 26, 1939): Via della Transpontina 21, 00193 Rome, Italy.

Japan: Jochi Daigaku (Sophia University) (Mar. 29, 1913): Chiyoda-Ku, Kioi-cho 7, Tokyo 102.

Lebanon: St. Joseph University of Beirut (Mar. 25, 1881): Rue de l'Université St.-Joseph, Boite Postale 293, Beyrouth (Beirut), Liban; (01) 42-64-56.

Netherlands: Catholic University of Nijmegen (June 29, 1923): P.B. 9102, Comeniuslaam 4, 6500 HC, Nijmegen.

Panama: University of S. Maria La Antigua (May 27, 1965): Apartado 6-1696, Panama 6.

Paraguay: Catholic University of Our Lady of the Assumption (Feb. 2, 1965): Independencia Nacional y Comuneros, Casilla 1718, Asunción; (021) 44-10-44.

Peru: Pontifical Catholic University of Peru (Sept. 30, 1942): Av. Universitaria, s/n. San Miguel, Apartado 1761, Lima 100.

Philippines: Pontifical University of Santo Tomás (Nov. 20, 1645): España Street, 1008 Manila.

Poland: Catholic University of Lublin (July 25, 1920): Aleje Racùawickie 14, Skr. Poczt. 129, 20-950, Lublin.

Catholic Theological Academy (June 29, 1989): Ul. Dewajtis 5, 01-815, Warsaw.

Pontifical Academy of Theology of Krakow (Dec. 8, 1981): Ul. Kanonicza, 25, 31-002 Kraków; (014) 22-33-31.

Portugal: Portuguese Catholic University (Nov. 1, 1967): Palma de Cima, 1 600 Lisbon.

Puerto Rico: Pontifical Catholic University of Puerto Rico (Aug. 15, 1972): 2250 Ave. Las Américas Suite 523, Ponce, Puerto Rico 00731-6382.

Spain: Catholic University of Navarra (Aug. 6, 1960): Campus Universitario, E-31080 Pamplona.

Pontifical University "Comillas" (Mar. 29, 1904): Campus de Cantoblanco, 28049 Madrid.

Pontifical University of Salamanca (Sept. 25, 1940): Compañía 5, 37002 Salamanca.

University of Deusto (Aug. 10, 1963): Avenida de las Universidades, 28, 48007 Bilbao o Apartado 1, 48080 Bilbao; 94-445-31-00.

Taiwan (China): Fu Jen Catholic University (Nov. 15, 1923, at Peking; reconstituted at Taipeh, Sept. 8, 1961): Hsinchuang, Taipeh Hsien 24205.

United States: The Catholic University of America (Mar. 7, 1889): 620 Michigan Ave. N.E., Washington, DC 20064.

Georgetown University (Mar. 30, 1833): 37th and O Sts. N.W., Washington, DC 20057.

Niagara University (June 21, 1956): Lewiston Rd., Niagara Falls, NY 14109.

Uruguay: Catholic University of Uruguay "Dámaso Antonio Larrañaga" (Jan. 25, 1985): Avda. 8 de Octubre 2738, 11.600 Montevideo.

Venezuela: Catholic University "Andrés Bello" (Sept. 29, 1963): Esquina Jesuitas, Apartado 29068,

WORLD AND U.S. SEMINARY STATISTICS

The *2004 Statistical Yearbook of the Church* (the most recent edition) reports the following comparative statistics for the years 1990 to 2004 of candidates in Philosophy and Theology (major seminarians). World totals are given first; U.S. statistics are given in parentheses.

Year	Total Major Seminarians	Diocesan	Religious
1990	96,155 (5,552)	64,629 (3,676)	31,526 (1,876)
1991	99,668 (5,487)	66,305 (3,777)	33,363 (1,710)
1992	102,000 (5,380)	67,960 (3,645)	34,040 (1,735)
1993	103,709 (5,123)	68,829 (3,505)	34,880 (1,618)
1994	105,075 (5,100)	69,613 (3,526)	35,462 (1,574)
1995	106,346 (4,831)	69,777 (3,234)	36,569 (1,597)
1996	105,870 (4,785)	70,034 (3,268)	35,836 (1,517)
1997	108,517 (4,729)	70,534 (3,311)	37,983 (1,418)
1998	109,171 (4,830)	70,564 (3,436)	38,607 (1,394)
1999	110,021 (5,024)	70,989 (3,428)	39,032(1,596)
2000	110,583 (5,109)	71,756 (3,479)	38,827 (1,630)
2001	112,244 (5,080)	72,241 (3,404)	40,003 (1,676)
2002	113,199 (5,169)	72,977 (3,578)	40,222 (1,591)
2003	112,373 (4,676)	72,266 (3,181)	40,107 (1,495)
2004	113,044 (5,642)	71,841 (3,929)	41,203 (1,713)

Caracas 1021; (02) 442-21-20.

ECCLESIASTICAL FACULTIES

(*Principal source*: Annuario Pontificio.)

These faculties in Catholic seminaries and universities, listed according to country of location, have been canonically erected and authorized by the Congregation for Catholic Education to award degrees in stated fields of study.

Argentina: Faculties of Philosophy and Theology, San Miguel (Sept. 8, 1932).

Australia: Catholic Institute of Sydney, Sydney (Feb. 2, 1954).

Austria: Theological Faculty, Linz (Dec. 25, 1978). International Theological Institute for Family Studies (Oct. 1, 1996).

Brazil: Philosophical and Theological Faculties of the Company of Jesus, Belo Horizonte (July 15, 1941 and Mar. 12, 1949).

Ecclesiastical Faculty of Philosophy "John Paul II," Rio de Janeiro (Aug. 6, 1981).

Cameroon: Catholic Institute of Yaoundé (Nov. 15, 1991).

Canada: College of Immaculate Conception — Montréal Section of Jesuit Faculties in Canada (Sept. 8, 1932). Suspended.

Pontifical Institute of Medieval Studies, Toronto (Oct. 18, 1939).

Dominican Faculty of Theology of Canada, Ottawa (1965; Nov. 15, 1975).

Regis College, Toronto Section of the Jesuit Faculty of Theology in Canada, Toronto (Feb. 17, 1956; Dec. 25, 1977).

Congo (formerly Zaire): Catholic Faculties of Kinshasa, Kinshasa (theology, Apr. 25, 1957; philosophy, Nov. 25, 1987).

Côte d'Ivoire (Ivory Coast): Catholic Institute of West Africa, Abidjan (Aug. 12, 1975).

Croatia: Philosophical Faculty, Zagreb (July 31, 1989).

France: Centre Sèvres, Faculties of Theology and Philosophy of the Jesuits, Paris (Sept. 8, 1932).

Germany: Theological Faculty of the Major Episcopal Seminary, Trier (Sept. 8, 1955).

Theological Faculty, Paderborn (June 11, 1966).

Theological-Philosophical Faculty, Frankfurt (1932; June 7, 1971).

Philosophical Faculty, Munich (1932; Oct. 25, 1971).

Theological Faculty, Fulda (Dec. 22, 1978).

Philosophical-Theological School of Salesians, Benediktbeuern (May 24, 1992).

Philosphical-Theological School, Vallendar (Oct. 7, 1993).

Great Britain: Heythrop College, University of London, London (Nov. 1, 1964). Theology, philosophy.

Hungary: Faculty of Theology (1635), Institute on Canon Law (Nov. 30, 1996), Budapest.

India: *Jnana Deepa Vidyapeeth* (Pontifical Athenaeum), Institute of Philosophy and Religion, Poona (July 27, 1926).

Vidyajyoti, Institute of Religious Studies, Faculty of Theology, Delhi (1932; Dec. 9, 1974).

Satya Nilayam, Institute of Philosophy and Culture. Faculty of Philosophy, Madras (Sept. 8, 1932; Dec. 15, 1976).

Pontifical Institute of Theology and Philosophy at the Pontifical Interritual Seminary of St. Joseph, Alwaye, Kerala (Feb. 24, 1972).

Dharmaram Vidya Kshetram, Pontifical Athenaeum of Theology and Philosophy, Bangalore (theology, Jan. 6, 1976; philosophy, Dec. 8, 1983).

Pontifical Oriental Institute of Religious Studies, Kottayam (July 3, 1982).

Faculty of Theology, Ranchi (Aug. 15, 1982).

St. Peter's Pontifical Institute of Theology, Bangalore (Jan. 6, 1985).

Indonesia: Wedabhakti Pontifical Faculty of Theology, Yogyakarta (Nov. 1, 1984).

Ireland: The Milltown Institute of Theology and Philosophy, Dublin (1932).

Israel: French Biblical and Archeological School, Jerusalem (founded 1890; approved Sept. 17, 1892; canonically approved to confer Doctorate in Biblical Science, June 29, 1983).

Italy: Theological Faculty of Southern Italy, Naples. Two sections: St. Louis Posillipo (Mar. 16, 1918) and St. Thomas Aquinas Capodimonte (Oct. 31, 1941).

Pontifical Theological Faculty of Sardinia, Cagliari, (Aug. 5, 1927).

Interregional Theological Faculty, Milan (Aug. 8, 1935; restructured 1969).

Faculty of Philosophy "Aloisianum," Gallarate (1937; Mar. 20, 1974).

Pontifical Ambrosian Institute of Sacred Music, Milan (Mar. 12, 1940).

Theological Faculty of Sicily, Palermo (Dec. 8, 1980).

Theological Institute Pugliese, Molfetta (June 24, 1992).

Theological Institute Calabro, Catanzaro (Jan. 28, 1993).

Theological Faculty of Central Italy, Florence (Sep. 9, 1997).

Japan: Faculty of Theology, Nagoya (May 25, 1984).

Kenya: Catholic Higher Institute of Eastern Africa, Nairobi (May 2, 1984).

Lebanon: Faculty of Theology, University of the Holy Spirit, Kaslik (May 30, 1982).

Madagascar: Superior Institute of Theology and Philosophy, at the Regional Seminary of Antananarivo, Ambatoroka-Antananarivo (Apr. 21, 1960).

Malta: Faculty of Theology, Tal-Virtù (Nov. 22, 1769), with Institute of Philosophy and Human Studies (Sept. 8, 1984).

Mexico: Theological Faculty of Mexico (June 29, 1982) and Philosophy (Jan. 6, 1986), Institute of Canon Law (Sept. 4, 1995), Mexico City.

Nigeria: Catholic Institute of West Africa, Port Harcourt (May 9, 1994).

Peru: Pontifical and Civil Faculty of Theology, Lima (July 25, 1571).

Poland: Pontifical Theological Faculty, Warsaw (May 3, 1988) with two sections: St. John Baptist (1837, 1920, Nov. 8, 1962) at the Metropolitan Seminary Duchowne, and St. Andrew Bobola – Bobolanum (Sept. 8, 1932).

Philosophical Faculty, Krakow (1932; Sept. 20, 1984).

Theological Faculty, Poznan (1969; pontifical designation, June 2, 1974).

Spain: Theological Faculty, Granada (1940; July 31, 1973).

Theological Faculty of San Esteban, Salamanca

(1947; Oct. 4, 1972).

Theological Faculty of the North, of the Metropolitan Seminary of Burgos and the Diocesan Seminary of Vitoria (Feb. 6, 1967).

Theological Faculty of Catalunya, (Mar. 7, 1968), with the Institutes of Fundamental Theology (Dec. 28, 1984), Liturgy (Aug. 15, 1986) and Philosophy (July 26, 1988), Barcelona.

Theological Faculty "San Vicente Ferrer" (two sections), Valencia (Jan. 23, 1974).

Theological Faculty "San Damaso" (Sept. 19, 1996), Madrid.

Switzerland: Theological Faculty, Lucerne (Dec. 25, 1973).

Theological Faculty, Chur (Jan. 1, 1974).

Theological Faculty, Lugano (Nov. 20, 1993).

United States: St. Mary's Seminary and University, School of Theology, Baltimore (May 1, 1822).

St. Mary of the Lake Faculty of Theology, Mundelein, IL (Sept. 30, 1929).

Weston Jesuit School of Theology, Cambridge, MA (Oct. 18, 1932).

The Jesuit School of Theology, Berkeley, CA (Feb. 2, 1934, as "Alma College," Los Gatos, CA).

Faculty of Philosophy and Letters, St. Louis, MO (Feb. 2, 1934).

St. Michael's Institute, Jesuit School of Philosophy and Letters, Spokane, WA (Feb. 2, 1934).

Pontifical Faculty of Theology of the Immaculate Conception, Dominican House of Studies, Washington, DC (Nov. 15, 1941).

Also located in the United States are:

The Marian Library/International Marian Research Institute (IMRI), U.S. branch of Pontifical Theological Faculty "Marianum," University of Dayton, Dayton, OH 45469 (affil. 1976, inc. 1983).

John Paul II Institute for Studies on Marriage and the Family, U.S. section of Pontifical John Paul II Institute for Studies on Marriage and Family at the Pontifical Lateran University, 487 Michigan Ave. N.E., Washington, DC 20017 (Aug. 22, 1988).

Pontifical College Josephinum (Theologate and College) at Columbus, OH, is a national pontifical seminary. Established Sept. 1, 1888, it is directly under the auspices of the Vatican through the Apostolic Pro-Nuncio to the U.S., who serves as the seminary's chancellor.

Vietnam: Theological Faculty of the Pontifical National Seminary of St. Pius X, Dalat (July 31, 1965). Activities suppressed.

In addition to those listed above, there are other faculties of theology or philosophy in state universities and for members of certain religious orders only. These include:

Austria: Katholisch-Theologische Fakultät (1619), Universitätsstrasse, 1, A-5010 Salzburg, Österreich.

Katholisch-Theologische Fakultät (1365), Dr. Karl-Lueger-Ring, 1, A-1010 Wien, Österreich.

Theologische Fakultät (1586), Karl-Franzens-Universität, Universitätsplatz, 3, A-8010 Graz, Österreich.

Theologische Fakultät (1669), Leopold-Franzens-Universität, Karl-Rahner-Platz 1, A-6020 Innsbruck, Österreich.

Canada: Faculté de Theologie et Institut Supérieur de Science Religieuses (1878), University of Montreal, 3034, Bd. Edouard-Montpetit, C.P. 6128, Montral, QC H3C 3J7, Canada.

Croatia: Facolta di Teologia Cattolica nell'Università Statale de Split (1999), Zrinsko-Frankopanska, 19, 21000 Split, Hrvatska.

Katolicki Bogoslovni Fakultet u Zagrebu (1669), Vlaska 38, 10000 Zagreb, Hrvatska.

Czech Republic: Cyrilometodejska teologicka fakulta (1570), Univerzitni 22, 771-11 Olomouc, Ceska Republika.

Katolicka teologicka fakulta University Karlovy (1347), Thakurova 3, 160 00 Praha 6/Dejvice, Ceska Republika.

France: Faculté de Theologie Catholique (1567), 9, Place de l'Université, 67084 Strasbourg, France.

Germany: Katholisch-Theologische Fakultät, Universität Augsburg (1970), Universitätsstrasse 10, D-86159 Augsburg.

Katholisch-Theologische Fakultät, Universität Bamberg (1972), An der Universität 2, D-96045 Bamberg.

Katholisch-Theologische Fakultät (1965), Universität Ruhr, Universitätsstrasse 150, Postfach 102148, D-44801 Bochum.

Katholisch-Theologische Fakultät Universität Bonn (1818), Am Hof 1, D-53113 Bonn.

Theologische Fakultät (1657), Albert-Ludwigs Universität, Erbprinzstrasse 13, D-79098 Freiburg im Breisgau.

Fachbereich Katholische Theologie (1946), Johannes Gutenberg-Universität, Saarstrasse 21, D-55122, Mainz.

Katholisch-Theologische Fakultät (1472), Ludwig-Maximilians-Universität, Geschw.-Scholl-Platz 1, D-80539, München.

Katholisch-Theologische Fakultät (1780), WestfälischeWilhelms-Universität, Johannisstrasse 8-10, D-48143, Münster.

Katholisch-Theologische Fakultät (1978), Michaeligasse 13, D-94032, Passau.

Fachbereich Katholische Theologie (1962), Universitätsstrasse 31, D-93053 Regensburg.

Katholisch-Theologische Fakultät (1477), Eberhard-Karls-Universität Tübingen, Libermeisterstr., 18, D-72076 Tübingen.

Katholisch-Theologische Fakultät (1402), Bayerische Julius-Maximilians-Universität, Sanderring 2, D-97070 Würzburg.

Lithuania: Katholiku Teologijos Fakultetas (1922), Vilniaus 29, LT-3000 Kaunas, Lietuva.

Poland: Wydzial Teologiczny, Wydzial Prawa Kanonicznego, Wydzial Filozofii Chrzescijanskiej (1999), ul. Dewajtis, 5, 01-815 Warszawa.

Wydzial Teologiczny Uniwersytetu Slaskiego w Katowicach (2000), ul. Wita Stwosza 17 A, 40-042 Katowice.

Wydzial Teologii Uniwersytetu Warminsko-Mazurskiego w Olsztynie (1999), ul. Stanislawa Kard. Hozjusza, 15, 11-041 Olsztyn.

Wydzial Teologiczny (1994), ul. Drzymaly, 1/a, 45-342 Opole.

Wydzial Teologiczny Uniwersytetu Mikolaja Kopernika w. Toruniu (2001), pl. Bl. Ks. S. Frelichowskiego 1, 87-100, Torun.

Slovakia: Rimskokatolicka cyrilo-metodska bohoslovecka fakulta (1919), Archdiocese of

Bratislava-Trnava, Kapitulska 26, 814-58 Bratislava.

Slovenia: Teoloska Fakulteta v. Ljublana (1920), p.p. 2007, 1001 Ljubljana.

Switzerland: Theologische Fakultät (1889), University of Fribourg, Misericorde, CH-1700 Fribourg.

PONTIFICAL UNIVERSITIES AND INSTITUTES IN ROME

(*Source*: Annuario Pontificio.)

Pontifical Gregorian University (*Gregorian*) (1552): Piazza della Pilotta, 4, 00187 Rome. Associated with the university are: **Pontifical Biblical Institute** (May 7, 1909): Via della Pilotta, 25, 00187 Rome; **Pontifical Institute of Oriental Studies** (Oct. 15, 1917): Piazza S. Maria Maggiore, 7, 00185 Rome.

Pontifical Lateran University (1773): Piazza S. Giovanni in Laterano, 4, 00184 Rome. Attached to the university is the **Pontifical Institute of Studies of** Marriage and the Family, erected by Pope John Paul II, Oct 7, 1982; a section of the Institute was established at the Dominican House of Studies, Washington, DC, by a decree dated Aug. 22, 1988; sections were opened in Mexico in 1992 and Valencia, Spain, in 1994.

Pontifical Urbaniana University (1627): Via Urbano VIII, 16, 00165 Rome.

Pontifical University of St. Thomas Aquinas (*Angelicum*) (1580), of the Order of Preachers: Largo Angelicum, 1, 00184 Rome.

Pontifical University *Salesianum* (May 3, 1940; university designation May 24, 1973), of the Salesians of Don Bosco: Piazza dell'Ateneo Salesiano, 1, 00139 Rome. Associated with the university is the **Pontifical Institute of Higher Latin Studies**, known as the Faculty of Christian and Classical Letters (June 4, 1971).

Pontifical University *della Santa Croce* (of the Holy Cross) (Jan. 9, 1985), of the Personal Prelature of Opus Dei: Piazza S. Apollinare, 49, 00186 Rome.

Pontifical University *Antonianum* (of St. Anthony) (May 17, 1933), of the Order of Friars Minor: Via Merulana, 124, 00185 Rome. Pontifical University status granted in 2005.

Pontifical Athenaeum of St. Anselm (1687) of the Benedictines: Piazza Cavalieri di Malta, 5, 00153 Rome.

Pontifical Athenaeum *Regina Apostolorum* (Queen of the Apostles), of the Legionaries of Christ: Via Aurelia Antica, 460, 00165 Rome.

Pontifical Institute of Sacred Music (1911; May 24, 1931): Via di Torre Rossa, 21, 00165 Rome.

Pontifical Institute of Christian Archeology (Dec. 11, 1925): Via Napoleone III, 1, 00185 Rome.

Pontifical Theological Faculty *St. Bonaventure* (Dec. 18, 1587), of the Order of Friars Minor Conventual: Via del Serafico, 1, 00142 Rome.

Pontifical Theological Faculty, Pontifical Institute of Spirituality *Teresianum* (1935), of the Discalced Carmelites: Piazza San Pancrazio, 5-A, 00152 Rome.

Pontifical Theological Faculty *Marianum* (1398), of the Servants of Mary: Viale Trente Aprile, 6, 00153 Rome. Attached to the university is **The Marian Library/International Marian Research Institute** (IMRI): U.S. branch of Pontifical Theological Faculty *Marianum*, University of Dayton, Dayton, OH, 45469 (affil. 1976, inc. 1983).

Pontifical Institute of Arabic and Islamic Studies (1926), of the Missionaries of Africa: Viale di Trastevere, 89, 00153 Rome.

Pontifical Faculty of Educational Science *Auxilium* (June 27, 1970), of the Daughters of Mary, Help of Christians: Via Cremolino, 141, 00166 Rome.

Catholic Communications

CATHOLIC PRESS

Statistics

The *2006 Catholic Press Directory*, published by the Catholic Press Association, reported a total of 609 periodicals in North America, with a circulation of 26,134,515. The figures included 205 newspapers, with a circulation of 6,611,583; 238 magazines, with a circulation of 14,459,258; 118 newsletters, with a circulation of 3,804,308; and 48 other-language periodicals (newspapers and magazines), with a circulation of 1,259,366.

Newspapers in the U.S.

There were 196 newspapers in the United States, with a circulation 6,479,726. Six of these had national circulation totaling 206,600; 163 were diocesan newspapers with a total circulation of 5,981,454; 11 were Eastern Catholic Church publications with a total circulation of 69,256. Eighteen other publications were classified by the CPA as Other Diocesan Newspaper and Other Newspapers, to classify them correctly based on their actual format; they had a total circulation of 247,016.

National papers included: **National Catholic Register,** founded 1900; **Our Sunday Visitor,** founded 1912; **National Catholic Reporter,** founded 1964; **The Wanderer,** founded 1867; **The Adoremus Bulletin,** founded 1995; and the English-language weekly edition of *L'Osservatore Romano,* established in the U.S. in 1998.

The oldest U.S. Catholic newspaper is **The Pilot** of Boston, established in 1829 (under a different title).

Other diocesan newspapers: There were three other diocesan newspapers located outside continental North America (Samoa, U.S. Virgin Islands, West Indies), with a circulation of 23,500.

Magazines in U.S.

The *Catholic Press Directory* reported 224 magazines in the U.S., with a circulation of 13,670,847. In addition, there were 117 newsletters, with a circulation of 3,796,808.

America and **Commonweal** are the only weekly and biweekly magazines, respectively, of general interest.

The monthly magazines with the largest circulation are **Columbia** (1,536,333), the official organ of the Knights of Columbus, **Catholic Digest** (350,000) and **St. Anthony's Messenger** (301,000).

Other-language publications: There were an additional 34 publications (newspapers and magazines) in the U.S. in languages other than English, with a circulation of 1,030,366.

Canadian Statistics

There were nine newspapers in Canada with a circulation of 131,857. These included three national newspapers (**The Catholic Register,** founded 1893; **Restoration,** founded 1947; and **Catholic New Times,** founded 1976) and seven diocesan. There were 14 magazines, with a circulation of 788,411; one newsletter, with a circulation of 7,500; and 14 publications in languages other than English, with a circulation of 229,000.

CATHOLIC NEWSPAPERS, MAGAZINES, AND NEWSLETTERS IN THE U.S.

(Sources: Catholic Press Directory; The Catholic Journalist; Catholic Almanac survey; Catholic News Service.) Abbreviation code: a, annual; bm, bimonthly; m, monthly; q, quarterly; w, weekly; bw, bi-weekly.

Newspapers

Our Sunday Visitor, w; 200 Noll Plaza, Huntington, IN 46750; (260) 356-8400; www.osv.com; national.

Acadiana Catholic, m; 1408 Carmel Ave., Lafayette, LA 70501; (337) 261-5511; Lafayette diocese.

A.D. Times, bw; P.O. Box F, Allentown, PA 18105-1538; (610) 871-5200; Allentown diocese.

Adoremus Bulletin, The, 10 times a year; P.O. Box 3286, St. Louis, MO 63130; (314) 863-8385; www.adoremus.org; national liturgical journal.

Agua Viva, m; 1280 Med Park Dr., Las Cruces, NM 88005-3239; (505) 523-7577; www.dioceseoflascruces.org; Las Cruces diocese.

Alaskan Shepherd, bm; 1312 Peger Rd., Fairbanks, AK 99709; (904) 374-9532; www.cbna.info; Fairbanks diocese.

America (Ukrainian-English), 2 times a week; 817 N. Franklin St., Philadelphia, PA 19123; (215) 627-4519; Providence Association of Ukrainian Catholics in America.

Anchor, The, w; P.O. Box 7, Fall River, MA 02722; (508) 675-7151; Fall River diocese.

Arkansas Catholic, w; P.O. Box 7417, Little Rock, AR 72217; (501) 664-0125; www.arkansas-catholic.org. Little Rock diocese.

Arlington Catholic Herald, w; 200 N. Glebe Rd., Suite 607, Arlington, VA 22203; (703) 841-2590;

www.catholicherald.com; Arlington diocese.

Bayou Catholic, The, w; P.O. Box 505, Schriever, LA 70395; (985) 850-3132; Houma-Thibodaux diocese.

Beacon, The, w; P.O. Box 1887, Clifton, NJ 07015-1887; (973) 279-8845; www.patersondiocese.org; Paterson diocese.

Bishop's Bulletin, m; 523 N. Duluth Ave., Sioux Falls, SD 57104-2714; (605) 988-3791; www.sfcatholic.org; Sioux Falls diocese.

Bolletino, m; 675 Hegenberger Rd., Suite 110, Oakland, CA 94621; (510) 633-9058; www.icf.org; Italian Catholic Federation.

Byzantine Catholic World, bw; 66 Riverview Ave., Pittsburgh, PA 15214; (412) 231-4000; Pittsburgh Byzantine archdiocese.

Catholic Accent, 40 times a year; 725 E. Pittsburgh St., Greensburg, PA 15601; (724) 834-4010; www.dioceseofgreensburg.org; Greensburg diocese.

Catholic Advance, The, w; 424 N. Broadway, Wichita, KS 67202-2377; (316) 269-3965; www.catholicadvance.org; Wichita diocese.

Catholic Advocate, The, w; 171 Clifton Ave., Newark, NJ 07104-9500; (973) 497-4200; www.rcan.org/advocate; Newark archdiocese.

Catholic Aid News, m; 3499 N. Lexington Ave., St. Paul, MN 55126; (651) 490-0170; www.catholicaid.com.

Catholic Anchor, w; 225 Cordova St., Anchorage, AK 99501; (907) 297-7708; Anchorage diocese.

Catholic Calendar, semi-monthly; 411 Iris St., Lake Charles, LA 70601; (337) 439-7426; www.lcdiocese.org; one page in local newspaper semi-monthly; Lake Charles diocese.

Catholic Chronicle, bw; P.O. Box 1866, Toledo, OH 43603-1866; (419) 244-6711; www.catholicchronicle.org; Toledo diocese.

Catholic Commentator, The, bw; P.O. Box 14746, Baton Rouge, LA 70898-4746; (225) 387-0983; www.diobr.com; Baton Rouge diocese.

Catholic Connector, The, m; 660 Burton, SE, Grand Rapids, MI 49507; (616) 243-0491; www.dioceseofgrandrapids.org; Grand Rapids diocese.

Catholic Courier, w; P.O. Box 24379, Rochester, NY 14624-0379; (585) 529-9530; www.catholiccourier.com; Rochester diocese.

Catholic East Texas, bw; 1015 ESE Loop 323, Tyler, TX 75701-9663; (903) 534-1077; Tyler diocese.

Catholic Explorer, w (bw July, Aug.); 402 S. Independence Blvd., Romeoville, IL 60446-2264; (815) 838-6475; www.dioceseofjoliet.org/explorer; Joliet diocese.

Catholic Exponent, bw; P.O. Box 6787, Youngstown, OH 44501-6787; (330) 744-5251; www.doy.org; Youngstown diocese.

Catholic Free Press, w; 51 Elm St., Worcester, MA 01609; (508) 757-6387; www.catholicfreepress.org; Worcester diocese.

Catholic Health World, semi-monthly; 4455 Woodson Rd., St. Louis, MO 63134-3797; (314) 427-2500; www.chausa.org; Catholic Health Association.

Catholic Herald, The Colorado, m; 228 N. Cascade Ave., Colorado Springs, CO 80903; (719) 636-2345; www.coloradocatholicherald.com; Colorado Springs diocese.

Catholic Herald, w; P.O. Box 070913, Milwaukee, WI 53207-0913; (414) 769-3500; www.chnonline.org; Milwaukee archdiocese; also publishes editions for Madison and Superior dioceses.

Catholic Herald: Madison Edition, w; P.O. Box 44985, Madison, WI 53744-4985; (608) 821-3070; www.madisoncatholicherald.org; Madison diocese.

Catholic Herald: Superior Edition, w; P.O. Box 969, Superior, WI 54880; (715) 392-8268; www.catholicherald.org; Superior diocese.

Catholic Herald, bw; 5890 Newman Ct., Sacramento, CA 95819; (916) 452-3344; www.diocese-sacramento.org; Sacramento diocese.

Catholic Islander, m; P.O. Box 301825, St. Thomas, USVI, 00803-1825; (340) 774-3166; www.catholicislander.com; Virgin Islands diocese.

Catholic Journalist, The, m; 3555 Veterans Highway, Unit O, Ronkonkoma, NY 11779; (631) 471-4730; www.catholicpress.org; Catholic Press Association.

Catholic Key, 44 times a year; P.O. Box 419037, Kansas City, MO 64141-6037; (816) 756-1850; www.catholickey.org; Kansas City-St. Joseph diocese.

Catholic Light, bw; 300 Wyoming Ave., Scranton, PA 18503; (570) 207-2229; www.dioceseofscranton.org; Scranton diocese.

Catholic Lighthouse, m; P.O. Box 4070, Victoria, TX 77903; (361) 573-0828; www.victoriadiocese.org; Victoria diocese.

Catholic Messenger, w; P.O. Box 460, Davenport, IA 52805; (563) 323-9959; home.catholicweb.com/cathmessdavdio; Davenport diocese.

Catholic Mirror, The, m; 601 Grand Ave., Des Moines, IA 50309; (515) 244-6234; www.dmdiocese.org; Des Moines diocese.

Catholic Miscellany, The, w; 119 Broad St., Charleston, SC 29401; (843) 724-8375; www.catholic-doc.org; Charleston diocese.

Catholic Missourian, The, w; P.O. Box 104900, Jefferson City, MO 65110-4900; (573) 635-9127; Jefferson City diocese.

Catholic Moment, The, w; P.O. Box 1603, Lafayette, IN 47902; (765) 742-2050; www.thecatholicmoment.org; Lafayette diocese.

Catholic New World, The, w; 640 N. La Salle St., Ste. 390, Chicago, IL 60610; (312) 655-7777; www.catholicnewworld.com; Chicago archdiocese.

Catholic New York, bw; 1011 First Ave., New York, NY 10022; (212) 688-2399; www.cny.org; New York archdiocese.

Catholic News, w; P.O. Box 85, Independence Square, Port-of-Spain, Trinidad, West Indies; (868) 623-6093; www.catholicnews-tt.net.

Catholic News and Herald, The, w; P.O. Box 37267, Charlotte, NC 28237; (704) 370-3333; www.charlottediocese.org; Charlotte diocese.

Catholic Northwest Progress, The, w; 910 Marion St., Seattle, WA 98104; (206) 382-4850; www.seattleearch.org;/progress; Seattle archdiocese.

Catholic Observer, bw; Box 1730, Springfield, MA 01101-1730; (413) 737-4744; www.iobserve.org; Springfield diocese.

Catholic Peace Voice, q.; 532 W. Eighth St., Erie, PA 16502-1343; (814) 453-4955; www.paxchristiusa.org; published by Pax Christi.

Catholic Post, The, w; P.O. Box 1722, Peoria, IL

61656; (309) 673-3603; www.cdop.org/post; Peoria diocese.

Catholic Register, bw; P.O. Box 413, Hollidaysburg, PA 16648; (814) 695-7563; www.cathregaj.org; Altoona-Johnstown diocese.

Catholic Review, w; P.O. Box 777, Baltimore, MD 21203; (443) 524-3150; www.catholicreview.org; Baltimore archdiocese.

Catholic San Francisco, bw; One Peter Yorke Way, San Francisco, CA 94109; (415) 614-5630; www.catholic-sf.org; San Francisco archdiocese.

Catholic Sentinel, w; P.O. Box 18030, Portland, OR 97218-0030; (503) 281-1191; www.sentinel.org; Portland archdiocese, Baker diocese.

Catholic Spirit, The, w; 244 Dayton Ave., Ste. 2, St. Paul, MN 55102-1893; (651) 291-4444; www.the-catholicspirit.com; St. Paul and Minneapolis archdiocese.

Catholic Spirit, The, w; P.O. Box 191, Metuchen, NJ 08840-0969; (732) 562-1990; www.catholicspirit.com; Metuchen diocese.

Catholic Spirit, The, m; P.O. Box 13327, Austin, TX 78711; (512) 476-4888; www.austindiocese.org; Austin diocese.

Catholic Spirit, The, m; P.O. Box 951, Wheeling, WV 26003-0119; (304) 233-0880; www.dwc.org; Wheeling-Charleston diocese.

Catholic Standard, w; P.O. Box 4464, Washington, DC, 20017; (202) 281-2410; www.cathstan.org; Washington archdiocese.

Catholic Standard and Times, w; 222 N. 17th St., Philadelphia, PA 19103; (215) 587-3660; www.cst-phl.com; Philadelphia archdiocese.

Catholic Star Herald, w; 15 North 7th St., Camden, NJ 08102; (856) 756-7900; Camden diocese.

Catholic Sun, The, semi-monthly; P.O. Box 13549, Phoenix, AZ 85002; (602) 354-2139; www.catholic-sun.org; Phoenix diocese.

Catholic Sun, The, w; 421 S. Warren St., Syracuse, NY 13202; (315) 422-8153; www.syrdio.org; Syracuse diocese.

Catholic Telegraph, w; 100 E. 8th St., Cincinnati, OH 45202; (513) 421-3131; www.catholiccincinnati.org; Cincinnati archdiocese.

Catholic Times, w; 197 E. Gay St., Columbus, OH 43215-3229; (614) 224-5195; www.ctonline.org; Columbus diocese.

Catholic Times, The, w; P.O. Box 1405, Saginaw, MI 48605; (810) 659-4670; www.catholictimesmi.org; Lansing diocese.

Catholic Times, The, w; P.O. Box 4004, La Crosse, WI 54602-4004; (608) 788-1524; www.diocese-oflacrosse.com; La Crosse diocese.

Catholic Times, w; P.O. Box 3187, Springfield, IL 62708-3187; (217) 698-8500; www.dio.org/catholic-times; Springfield diocese.

Catholic Transcript, w; 467 Bloomfield Ave., Bloomfield, CT 06002; (860) 286-2828; Hartford archdiocese, Bridgeport and Norwich dioceses.

Catholic Universe Bulletin, bw; 1027 Superior Ave. NE, Cleveland, OH 44114-2556; (216) 696-6525; www.catholicuniversebulletin.org; Cleveland diocese.

Catholic Virginian, bw; Box 26843, Richmond, VA 23220; (804) 359-5654; www.catholicvirginia.org; Richmond diocese.

Catholic Vision, m.; P.O. Box 31, Tucson, AZ 85702; (520) 792-3410; www.catholicvision.org; Tuscon diocese.

Catholic Voice, The, bw; 3014 Lakeshore Ave., Oakland, CA 94610; (510) 893-5339; www.catholicvoiceoakland.org; Oakland diocese.

Catholic Voice, The, bw; P.O. Box 4010, Omaha, NE 68104-0010; (402) 558-6611; www.tcvomaha.com; Omaha archdiocese.

Catholic War Veteran, bm; 441 N. Lee St., Alexandria, VA 22314-2344; (703) 549-3622; www.cwv.org.

Catholic Week, The, w; P.O. Box 349, Mobile, AL 36601; (251) 434-1544; Mobile archdiocese.

Catholic Weekly, The, w; P.O. Box 1405, Saginaw, MI 48605; (989) 793-7661; www.catholicweekly.org; Saginaw diocese.

Catholic Weekly, The, w; P.O. Box 1405, Saginaw, MI 48602; (989) 793-7661; Gaylord diocese.

Catholic Witness, The, bw; P.O. Box 2555, Harrisburg, PA 17105; (717) 657-4804; Harrisburg diocese.

Catholic Workman, m; P.O. Box 47, New Prague, MN 56071; (952) 758-2229; www.catholicworkman.com.

Central Washington Catholic, bm; 5301-A Tieton Dr., Yakima, WA 98908; (509) 965-7117; Yakima diocese.

Chicago Catolico (Spanish), m; 721 N. La Salle St., 4th Floor, Chicago, IL 60610; (312) 655-7880; Chicago archdiocese.

Chronicle of Catholic Life, bm; 1001 North Grand Ave., Pueblo, CO 81003; (719) 685-5202; www.dioceseofpueblo.com; Pueblo diocese.

Church Today, twice a month; P.O. Box 7417, Alexandria, LA 71306-0417; (318) 445-2401; www.diocesealex.org; Alexandria diocese.

Clarion Herald, bw; P.O. Box 53247, New Orleans, LA 70153; (504) 596-3035; www.clarionherald.org; New Orleans archdiocese.

Compass, The, w; P.O. Box 23825, Green Bay, WI 54305-3825; (920) 437-7531; www.thecompass-news.org; Green Bay diocese.

Courier, The, m; 55 W. Sanborn St., P.O. Box 949, Winona, MN 55987-0949; (507) 454-4643; www.dow.org; Winona diocese.

Criterion, The, w; P.O. Box 1717, Indianapolis, IN 46206; (317) 236-1570; www.criteriononline.com; Indianapolis archdiocese.

Cross Roads, bw; 1310 W. Main St., Lexington, KY 40508-2040; (859) 253-1993; Lexington diocese.

Dakota Catholic Action, m (except July); P.O. Box 1137, Bismarck, ND 58502-1137; (701) 222-3035; www.bismarckdiocese.com; Bismarck diocese.

Denver Catholic Register, w; 1300 S. Steele St., Denver, CO 80210-2599; (303) 715-3121; www.arch-den.org; Denver archdiocese.

Dialog, The, w; P.O. Box 2208, Wilmington, DE 19899; (302) 573-3109; www.cdow.org/dialog.html; Wilmington diocese.

East Tennessee Catholic, The, bw; P.O. Box 11127, Knoxville, TN 37939-1127; (865) 584-3307; www.etcatholic.com; Knoxville diocese.

East Texas Catholic, semi-monthly; P.O. Box 3948, Beaumont, TX 77704-3948; (409) 832-3944; Beaumont diocese.

Eastern Catholic Life, bw; 445 Lackawanna Ave., W. Paterson, NJ 07424; (201) 890-7794; Passaic Byzantine eparchy.

Eastern Oklahoma Catholic, bw; Box 690240, Tulsa, OK 74169-0240; (918) 294-1904; www.dioceseoftulsa.org; Tulsa diocese.

Eternal Flame (Armenian-English), 110 E. 12th St., New York, NY 10003; (212) 477-2030; Armenian exarchate.

Evangelist, The, w; 40 N. Main Ave., Albany, NY 12203; (518) 453-6688; www.evangelist.org; Albany diocese.

Fairfield County Catholic, m; 238 Jewett Ave., Bridgeport, CT 06606; (203) 372-4301; www.bridgeportdiocese.org; Bridgeport diocese.

Florida Catholic, The, w; P.O. Box 609512, Orlando, FL 32860-9512; (407) 660-9141; www.thefloridacatholic.org; Orlando diocese; publishes editions for Miami archdiocese and Palm Beach, Pensacola-Tallahassee, St. Petersburg and Venice dioceses.

Florida Catholic: Miami Edition, w; 9401 Biscayne Blvd., Miami, FL 33138; (305) 762-1131; www.thefloridacatholic.org.

Florida Catholic: Palm Beach Edition, w; P.O. Box 109650, Palm Beach Gardens, FL 33410-9650; (561) 775-9528; www.thefloridacatholic.org; Palm Beach diocese.

Florida Catholic: Pensacola-Tallahassee Edition, w; 11 North B St., Pensacola, FL 32501; (850) 435-3500; www.thefloridacatholic.org.

Florida Catholic: St. Petersburg Edition, w; P.O. Box 43022, St. Petersburg, FL 33743; (727) 345-3338.

Florida Catholic: Venice Edition, w; 1000 Pinebrook Rd., Venice, FL 34292; (941) 484-9543; www.thefloridacatholic.org.

Four County Catholic, m; 1595 Norwich New London Turnpike, Uncasville, CT 06382; (860) 848-2237; www.norwichdiocese.org; Norwich diocese.

Georgia Bulletin, w; 680 W. Peachtree St. NW, Atlanta, GA 30308; (404) 877-5500; www.archatl.com; Atlanta archdiocese.

Glasilo KSKJ Amerikanski Slovenec (Slovenian), bw; 708 E. 159th, Cleveland, OH 44110; (216) 541-7243; American Slovenian Catholic Union.

Globe, The, w; P.O. Box 5079, Sioux City, IA 51102; (712) 255-2550; www.catholicglobe.org; Sioux City diocese.

Good News for the Diocese of Kalamazoo, The, m; 215 N. Westnedge, Kalamazoo, MI 49007-3760; (269) 349-8714; www.dioceseofkalamazoo.org; Kalamazoo diocese.

Gulf Pine Catholic, w; P.O. Box 1189, Biloxi, MS 39533-1189; (228) 702-2127; Biloxi diocese.

Harvest, The, 121 23rd St. South, Great Falls, MT 59405; (406) 727-6683; www.dioceseofgfb.org; Great Falls diocese.

Hawaii Catholic Herald, bw; 1184 Bishop St., Honolulu, HI 96813; (808) 533-1791; Honolulu diocese.

Hlas Naroda (Voice of the Nation) (Czech-English), bw; 2340 61st Ave., Cicero, IL 60650; (708) 484-0583.

Horizons, twice a month; 1900 Carlton Rd., Parma, OH 44134-3129; (216) 741-3312; www.parma.org; Parma Byzantine eparchy.

Idaho Catholic Register, twice a month; 303 Federal Way, Boise, ID 83705; (208) 342-1311; www.catholicidaho.org/icr.cfm; Boise diocese.

Inland Register, every 3 weeks; P.O. Box 48, Spokane, WA 99210; (509) 358-7340; www.dioceseofspokane.org; Spokane diocese.

Inside Passage, bw; 415 6th St., Juneau, AK 99801; (907) 586-2227; www.dioceseofjuneau.org; Juneau diocese.

Intermountain Catholic, w; P.O. Box 2489, Salt Lake City, UT 84110-2489; (801) 328-8641; www.icnp.com; Salt Lake City diocese.

Jednota (Slovak-Eng.), w; 6611 Rockside Rd., Independence, OH 44131; (216) 642-9406; First Catholic Slovak Union.

Leaven, The, w; 12615 Parallel Parkway, Kansas City, KS 66109; (913) 721-1570; www.theleaven.com; Kansas City archdiocese.

Long Island Catholic, The, w; P.O. Box 9000, Rockville Centre, NY 11575-9000; (516) 594-1000; www.licatholic.org; Rockville Centre diocese.

L'Osservatore Romano, w; P.O. Box 777, The Cathedral Foundation, Baltimore, MD, 21203; (443) 263-0248; www.catholicreview.org. English edition of the Vatican newspaper.

Maronite Voice, The, m; 4611 Sadler Rd., Glen Allen, VA 23060; (804) 270-7234; www.stmaron.org; Eparchy of St. Maron of Brooklyn.

Message, The, w; P.O. Box 4169, Evansville, IN 47724-0169; (812) 424-5536; Evansville diocese.

Messenger, The, w; 2620 Lebanon Ave., Belleville, IL 62221; (618) 233-8670; www.bellevillemessenger.org; Belleville diocese.

Messenger, The, 45 times a year; P.O. Box 15550, Erlanger, KY 41018; (859) 392-1570; www.covingtondiocese.org; Covington diocese.

Michigan Catholic, The, w; 305 Michigan Ave., 4th Floor, Detroit, MI 48226; (313) 224-8000; Detroit archdiocese.

Mirror, The, w; 601 S. Jefferson Ave., Springfield, MO 65806-3143; (417) 866-0841; www.themirror.org; Springfield-Cape Girardeau diocese.

Mississippi Catholic, w; P.O. Box 2130, Jackson, MS 39225-2130; (601) 969-1880; www.mississippicatholic.com; Jackson diocese.

Monitor, The, w; P.O. Box 5147, Trenton, NJ 08638-0147; (609) 406-7404; www.dioceseoftrenton.org; Trenton diocese.

Montana Catholic, The, 16 times a year; P.O. Box 1729, Helena, MT 59624; (406) 442-5820; www.diocesehelena.org; Helena diocese.

Narod Polski (Polish Nation) (Polish-Eng.) semimonthly; 984 Milwaukee Ave., Chicago, IL 60622-4101; (773) 782-2600; www.prcua.com; Polish Roman Catholic Union of America.

National Catholic Register, w; 432 Washington Ave., North Haven, CT 06473; (203) 230-3800; www.ncregister.com; national.

National Catholic Reporter, w; P.O. Box 419281, Kansas City, MO 64141; (816) 531-0538; www.ncronline.org; national.

National Jesuit News, m; 1616 P St. NW, Suite 300, Washington, DC 20036; (202) 462-0400; www.jesuit.org.

New Earth, The, m; 5201 Bishops Blvd., Ste. A, Fargo, ND 58104; (701) 356-7958; www.fargidiocese.org; Fargo diocese.

New Star, The, every 3 weeks; 2208 W. Chicago Ave., Chicago, IL 60622; (312) 772-1919; St. Nicholas of Chicago Ukrainian diocese.

NC Catholic, bw; 715 Nazareth St., Raleigh, NC 27606; (919) 821-9736; www.nccatholic.org; Raleigh diocese.

North Country Catholic, w; P.O. Box 326, Ogdensburg, NY 13669; (315) 393-2540; www.northcountrycatholic.org; Ogdensburg diocese.

North Texas Catholic, w; 800 West Loop 820 South, Fort Worth, TX 76108; (817) 560-3300; www.fwdioc.org; Fort Worth diocese.

Northern Cross, The, m; 2830 E. 4th St., Duluth, MN 55812; (218) 724-9111; www.dioceseduluth.org; Duluth diocese.

Northern Nevada Catholic, m; 290 S. Arlington Ave., #200, Reno, NV 89501; (775) 826-1010; Reno diocese.

Northwest Indiana Catholic, w; 9292 Broadway, Merrillville, IN 46410-7088; (219) 769-9292; www.nwicatholic.com; Gary diocese.

Northwestern Kansas Register, w; P.O. Box 1038, Salina, KS 67402; (785) 827-8746; www.salinadiocese.org; Salina diocese.

Oblate World, The and Voice of Hope, twice a month; P.O. Box 680, Tewksbury, MA 01876; (978) 851-7258; www.omiusa.org; published by the Missionary Oblates of Mary Immaculate.

Observer, The, m; P.O. Box 2079, Monterey, CA 93942; (831) 373-2919; www.dioceseofmonterey.org; Monterey diocese.

Observer, The, m; 4545 W. 63rd St., Chicago, IL 60629; (312) 585-9500; Lithuanian Roman Catholic Federation of America.

Observer, The, twice a month; P.O. Box 7044, Rockford, IL 61125; (815) 399-4300; www.rockforddiocese.org; Rockford diocese.

One Voice, w; P.O. Box 10822, Birmingham, AL 35202; (205) 838-8305; Birmingham diocese.

Orange County Catholic, m.; P.O. Box 14195, Orange, CA 92863-1595; (714) 282-3022; Orange diocese.

Our Lady's Messenger/Our Lady of the Hills Church, six times a year; 2700 Ashland Rd., Columbia, SC 29210; (803) 772-7400.

Our Northland Diocese, semi-monthly; P.O. Box 610, Crookston, MN 56716; (218) 281-4553; www.crookston.org; Crookston diocese.

People of God, m; 4000 St. Joseph Pl. NW, Albuquerque, NM 87120; (505) 831-8188; Santa Fe archdiocese.

Pilot, The, w; 2121 Commonwealth Ave., Brighton, MA 02135-3193; (617) 746-5889; www.rcab.org; Boston archdiocese.

Pittsburgh Catholic, w; 135 First Ave., Suite 200,

Pittsburgh, PA 15222-1506; (412) 471-1252; www.pittsburghcatholic.org; Pittsburgh diocese.

Prairie Catholic, m; 1400 6th St. North, New Ulm, MN 56073-2099; (507) 359-2966; www.dnu.org; New Ulm diocese.

Praxis Press, 10 times a year; P.O. Box 508, San Jose, CA 95103; (408) 370-4748.

Providence Visitor, The, w; 184 Broad St., Providence, RI 02903; (401) 272-1010; www.providencevisitor.com; Providence diocese.

Record, The, w; Maloney Center, 1200 S. Shelby St., Louisville, KY 40203-2600; (502) 636-0296; Louisville archdiocese.

Rio Grande Catholic, The, m; 499 St. Matthews St., El Paso, TX 79907; (915) 872-8414; www.elpasodiocese.org; El Paso diocese.

Saint Cloud Visitor, The, w; P. O. Box 1068, St. Cloud, MN 56302-1066; (320) 251-3022; www.stclouddiocese.org/visitor; St. Cloud diocese.

St. Louis Review, w; 20 Archbishop May Dr., St. Louis, MO 63119; (314) 792-7500; www.stlouisreview.com; St. Louis archdiocese.

Seasons, q; 5800 Weiss St., Saginaw, MI 48603-2799; (989) 797-6666; www.dioceseofsaginaw.org; Saginaw diocese.

Slovak Catholic Falcon (Slovak-English), w; 205 Madison St., P.O.Box 899, Passaic, NJ 07055; (973) 777-4010; Slovak Catholic Sokol.

Sooner Catholic, The, bw; P.O. Box 32180, Oklahoma City, OK 73123; (405) 721-1810; www.catharchdioceseok.org; Oklahoma City archdiocese.

Sophia, q; 200 E. North Ave., Northlake, IL 60164; (708) 865-7050; Newton Melkite eparchy.

South Plains Catholic, twice a month; P.O. Box 98700, Lubbock, TX 79499-8700; (806) 792-3943; www.catholiclubbock.org; Lubbock diocese.

South Texas Catholic, twice a month; P.O. Box 2620, Corpus Christi, TX 78403-2620; (361) 882-6191; www.goccn.org; Corpus Christi diocese.

Southern Cross, semi-monthly; P.O. Box 81869, San Diego, CA 92138; (858) 490-8266; www.thesoutherncross.org; San Diego diocese.

Southern Cross, The, w; 601 E. Liberty St., Savannah, GA 31401-5196; (912) 201-4100; www.diosav.org; Savannah diocese.

Southern Nebraska Register, w; P.O. Box 80329, Lincoln, NE 68501; (402) 488-0090; Lincoln diocese.

Southwest Catholic, The, m; P.O. 411 Iris St., Lake Charles, LA 70601; (337) 439-7426; www.lcdiocese.org; Lake Charles diocese.

Southwest Kansas Register, bw; P.O. Box 137, Dodge City, KS 67801; (620) 227-1519; www.dcdiocese.org/swkregister; Dodge City diocese.

Sower (Ukrainian and English), bw; 14 Peveril Rd., Stamford, CT 06902; (203) 324-7698; www.thesower@adcus.com; Stamford Ukrainian diocese.

Star of Chaldeans (Arabic and English), bm; 25585 Berg Rd., Southfield, MI 48034; St. Thomas the Apostle Chaldean diocese.

Steubenville Register, bw; P.O. Box 160, Steubenville, OH 43952; (740) 282-3631; www.diosteub.org; Steubenville diocese.

Tablet, The, w; 310 Prospect Park West, Brooklyn, NY 11215-6214; (718) 965-7333; www.dioceseofbrooklyn.org/tablet; Brooklyn diocese.

Tautai, bw; P.O. Box 532, Feiloaimauso Hall, Apia, Samoa; Samoa-Apia archdiocese.

Tennessee Register, The, bw; 2400 21st Ave. S., Nashville, TN 37212; (615) 783-0770; www.dioceseofnashville.org; Nashville diocese.

Texas Catholic, The, bw; P.O. Box 190346, Dallas, TX 75219; (214) 528-8792; www.texascatholic.com; Dallas diocese.

Texas Catholic Herald, The, twice a month; 1700 San Jacinto St., Houston, TX 77001-0907; (713) 659-5461; Galveston-Houston diocese.

Tidings, The, w; 3424 Wilshire Blvd, Los Angeles, CA 90010; (213) 637-7360; www.the-tidings.com; Los Angeles archdiocese.

Today's Catholic, w; P.O. Box 11169, Fort Wayne, IN 46856; (260) 456-2824; www.diocesefwsb.org; Fort Wayne-South Bend diocese.

Today's Catholic, bw; P.O. Box 28410, San Antonio, TX 78228-0410; (210) 734-2620; www.satodayscatholic.org; San Antonio archdiocese.

UNIREA (The Union) (Romanian) 10 times a year; 2654 Glen Ave., Altadena, CA 91001; (626) 797-3851; Romanian diocese of Canton.

U. P. Catholic, The, semi-monthly; P.O. Box 548, Marquette, MI 49855; (906) 227-9131; www.upcatholic.org; Marquette diocese.

Valley Catholic, m; 900 Lafayette St., Suite 301, Santa Clara, CA 95050-4966; (408) 983-0260; www.dsj.org/community/valley.asp; San Jose diocese.

Vermont Catholic Tribune, bw; P.O. Box 489, Burlington, VT 05402; (802) 658-6110; www.vermontcatholic.org; Burlington diocese.

Vida Nueva; 3424 Wilshire Blvd., Los Angeles, CA 90010-2241; (213) 637-7310.

Voice of the Southwest, m; 711 S. Puerco, Gallup, NM 87301; (505) 863-4406; Gallup diocese.

Wanderer, The, w; 201 Ohio St., St. Paul, MN 55107; (651) 224-5733; national.

Way, The (Ukrainian-Eng.), bw; 827 N. Franklin St., Philadelphia, PA 19123; (215) 922-5231; Philadelphia archeparchy.

West Nebraska Register, w; P.O. Box 608, Grand Island, NE 68802; (308) 382-4660; Grand Island diocese.

West River Catholic, m; P.O. Box 678, Rapid City, SD 57709; (605) 343-3541; Rapid City diocese.

West Tennessee Catholic, w; P.O. Box 341669, Memphis, TN 38184-1669; (901) 373-1213; www.cdom.org; Memphis diocese.

West Texas Angelus, m; P.O. Box 1829, San Angelo, TX 76902; (915) 651-7500; www.san-angelo-diocese.org; San Angelo diocese.

West Texas Catholic, bw; P.O. Box 5644, Amarillo, TX 79117-5644; (806) 383-2243; www.amarillodiocese.org; Amarillo diocese.

Western Kentucky Catholic, m; 600 Locust St., Owensboro, KY 42301; (270) 683-1545; Owensboro diocese.

Western New York Catholic, m; 795 Main St., Buffalo, NY 14203-1250; (716) 847-8727; www.wny-catholic.org; Buffalo diocese.

Witness, The, w; P.O. Box 917, Dubuque, IA 52004-0917; (319) 588-0556; Dubuque archdiocese.

Wyoming Catholic Register, m; P.O. Box 227, Cheyenne, WY 82003; (307) 638-1530; www.wyocathregister.org; Cheyenne diocese.

Magazines

Abbey Banner, The, 3 times a year; Saint John's Abbey, Collegeville, MN 56321; (320) 363-3875; www.sja.osb/abbeybanner.

AIM: Liturgy Resources, q; 3708 River Rd., Ste. 400, Franklin Park, IL 60131; (800) 566-6150.

America, w; 106 W. 56th St., New York, NY 10019; (212) 581-4640; www.americamagazine.org; Jesuits of U.S. and Canada.

American Benedictine Review, q; Assumption Abbey, Box A, Richardton, ND 58652; (701) 974-3315.

American Catholic Philosophical Quarterly (formerly The New Scholasticism), Fordham University, Bronx, NY 10458; (718) 817-4081; www.acpamain.org; American Catholic Philosophical Assn.

American Catholic Studies; Villanova University, 800 Lancaster Ave., Villanova, PA 19085; (610) 519-5470.

The Annals of St. Anne de Beaupre, m; P.O. Box 1000, St. Anne de Beaupre, Quebec, GOA 3CO; (418) 827-4538.

Anthonian, The, q; c/o St. Anthony's Guild, Paterson, NJ 07509; (212) 924-1451; www.hnp.org/publications; St. Anthony's Guild.

Apostolate of the Little Flower, bm; P.O. Box 5280, San Antonio, TX 78201-0280; (210) 736-3889; Discalced Carmelite Fathers.

Augustinian Journey, q; P.O. Box 340, Villanova, PA 19085; (610) 527-3330; www.augustinian.org; published by the Province of St. Thomas of Villanova.

Barry Magazine, 2 times a year; 11300 NE 2nd Ave., Miami Shores, FL 33161; (305) 899-3188; Barry University.

Benedictines, m., 44 N. Mill St., Kansas City, KS 66101; (913) 342-0938; www.mountosb.com.

Bible Today, The, bm; Liturgical Press, Collegeville, MN 56321-7500; (320) 363-2218; www.litpress.org.

Bright Ideas; P.O. Box 510817, New Berlin, WI, 53151-0817; (800) 876-4574; www.lpiresourcecenter.com.

Carmelite Digest, q; P.O. Box 2178, Relands, CA 92373-0701; (909) 793-0424; www.carmelitedigest.org.

Carmelite Review, twice a month; 6725 Reed Rd., Houston, TX 77087-6830; (713) 644-8400; www.carmelnet.org/publications.htm; published by the Province of the Most Pure Heart of Mary of the Carmelite Order.

Catechist, The, 7 times a year; 2621 Dryden Rd., Dayton, OH 45439; (937) 293-1415; www.pflaum.com.

Catechumenate: A Journal of Christian Initiation, bm; 1800 N. Hermitage Ave., Chicago, IL 60622-1101; (773) 486-8970; www.ltp.org.

Catholic Answer, The, bm; 200 Noll Plaza, Huntington, IN 46750; (260) 356-8400; www.osv.com; Our Sunday Visitor, Inc.

Catholic Biblical Quarterly; Catholic University of America, Washington, DC 20064; (202) 319-5519;

www.cba.cua.edu; Catholic Biblical Assn.

Catholic Cemetery, The, m; 710 N. River Rd., Des Plaines, IL 60016; (847) 824-8131; National Catholic Cemetery Conference.

Catholic Connection, The, m.; 3500 Fairfield Ave., Shreveport, LA 71104; (318) 868-4441; www.dioshpt.org; diocese of Shreveport.

Catholic Digest, m; 1 Montauk Ave., Ste. 200, New London, CT 06320; (860) 437-3012; www.catholicdigest.org.

Catholic Family News, m.; MPO Box 743, Niagara Falls, NY 14302; (905) 871-6292.

Catholic Historical Review, q; 620 Michigan Ave. N.E., Washington, DC 20064; (202) 319-5079; research.cua.edu/acha.

Catholic Knights of America Journal, m; 1850 Dalton St., Cincinnati, OH 45214; (513) 721-0781; Catholic Knights of America.

Catholic Lawyer, q; St. John's University, 8000 Utopia Parkway, Jamaica, NY 11439; (718) 990-6655; St. Thomas More Institute for Legal Research.

Catholic Library World, q; 100 North St., #224, Pittsfield, MA 01201-5109; (413) 443-2252; www.cathla.org; Catholic Library Association.

Catholic Near East Magazine, bm; 1011 First Ave., New York, NY 10022; (212) 826-1480; www.cnewa.org; Catholic Near East Welfare Assn.

Catholic Outlook, m; 2830 E. 4th St., Duluth, MN 55812; (218) 724-9111; www.dioceseduluth.org; Duluth diocese.

Catholic Pharmacist, q; 1012 Surrey Hills Dr., St. Louis, MO 63117-1438; (314) 645-0085; National Catholic Pharmacists Guild.

Catholic Press Directory, a; 3555 Veterans Highway, Unit O, Ronkonkoma, NY 11779; (631) 471-4730; www.catholicpress.com; Catholic Press Assn.

Catholic Response, m.; 21 Fairview Ave., Mt. Pocono, PA 18344; (570) 839-2185; www.jhcnewman.org.

Catholic Review (Braille, tape, large print), bm; 154 E. 23rd St., New York, NY 10010; (212) 473-7800; Xavier Society for the Blind.

Catholic Southwest: A Journal of History and Culture, a; 1625 Rutherford Lane, Bldg. D, Austin, TX, 78754-5105; (512) 339-9882.

Catholic Woman, bm; 200 N. Glebe Rd., Suite 703, Arlington, VA 22203; (202) 224-0990; www.nccw.org; National Council of Catholic Women.

Catholic Worker, 7 times a year; 36 E. First St., New York, NY 10003; (212) 677-8627; Catholic Worker Movement.

Catholic Workman, bi-monthly, P.O. Box 47, New Prague, MN 56071; (952) 758-2229; www.catholicworkmen.org; official publication of the Catholic Workmen.

Catholic World Report, The, 11 times a year; P.O. Box 1328, Dedham, MA 02027 (editorial office); Ignatius Press.

Celebration, m; 115 E. Armour Blvd., Kansas City, MO 64111; (816) 968-2266; National Catholic Reporter Publishing Co.

Charities USA, q; 1731 King St., Suite 200, Alexandria, VA 22314; (703) 549-1390; www.catholiccharitiesusa.org.

Chesterton Review, The, q; Seton Hall University,

400 South Orange Ave., South Orange, NJ 07079; (973) 275-2430; G.K. Chesterton Society.

Chicago Studies, 3 times a year; 1800 N. Hermitage Ave., Chicago, IL 60622-1101; (800) 933-1800.

Christian Renewal News, q.; P.O. Box 6164, Santa Maria, CA 93456; (805) 524-5890; www.theservants andhandmaids.net; published by The Servants and Handmaids of the Sacred Heart of Jesus.

Christianity and the Arts, q; P.O. Box 118088, Chicago, IL 60611; (312) 642-8606; www.christianarts.net.

Church, q; 18 Bleeker St., New York, NY 10012; (212) 431-7825; www.nplc.org; National Pastoral Life Center.

CMMB Today, q., 10 West 17th St., New York, N.Y. 10011; (212) 242-7757; www.cmmb.org; Catholic Medical Mission Board publication.

CNEWA World, bm; 1011 First Ave., New York, NY 10022; (212) 826-1480; www.cnewa.org; Catholic Near East Welfare.

Columban Mission, 8 times a year; St. Columbans, NE 68056; (402) 291-1920; www.columban.org; Columban Fathers.

Columbia, m; One Columbus Plaza, New Haven, CT 06510; (203) 752-4398; www.kofc.org; Knights of Columbus.

Commonweal, bw; 475 Riverside Dr., Room 405, New York, NY 10115; (212) 662-4200; www.commonwealmagazine.org.

Communio: International Catholic Review, q; P.O. Box 4557, Washington, DC 20017-0557; (202) 526-0251; www.communio-icr.org.

Company, q; P.O. Box 60790, Chicago, IL 60660-0790; (773) 760-9432; www.companymagazine.com; Jesuit magazine.

Consecrated Life, semi-annually; P.O. Box 41007, Chicago, IL 60641; (773) 267-1195; www.religiouslife.com; Institute on Religious Life. English edition of *Informationes*, official publication of Congregation for Institutes of Consecrated Life and Societies of Apostolic Life.

Consolata Missionaries, bm; P.O. Box 5550, Somerset, NJ 08875-5550; (732) 297-9191; www.consolata.org.

Cord, The, m; Franciscan Institute, St. Bonaventure University, St. Bonaventure, NY 14778; (716) 375-2160; franinst@sbu.edu; Franciscan Institute.

Counseling and Values, 3 times a year; College of Educational, Southern Illinois University, Carbondale, IL 62901; (618) 537-7791.

Crescat, 3 times a year; Belmont Abbey, Belmont, NC 28012; (704) 825-6707; Benedictine Monks.

Crisis, 11 times a year; 1814 N St. NW, Washington, DC 20036; (202) 861-7790; www.crisismagazine.com; journal of lay Catholic opinion.

Cross Currents, q; College of New Rochelle, New Rochelle, NY 10805; (914) 235-1439; www.aril.org; interreligious; Assn. for Religion and Intellectual Life.

Crusade Magazine, bm; P.O. Box 341, Hanover, PA 17331; (717) 225-9177; Foundation for a Christian Civilization, Inc.

CUA Magazine, 3 times a year; 620 Michigan Ave. N.E., Washington, DC 20064; (202) 319-5600; www.cua.edu; Catholic University of America.

Darbininkas (The Worker) (Lithuanian), w; 341

Highland Blvd., Brooklyn, NY 11207; (718) 827-1352; Lithuanian Franciscans.

Desert Call, q.; P.O. Box 219, Crestone, CO 81131-0219; (719) 256-4778; www.spirituallifeinstitute.org; published by the Spiritual Life Institute.

Desert Clarion, 10 times a year; 4519 Simmons St., North Las Vegas, NV 89031; (702) 657-0200; Las Vegas diocese.

Diakonia, 3 times a year; University of Scranton, Scranton, PA 18510-4643; (570) 941-6141; www.nyssa.cecs.uofs.edu/diaktoc.html; Center for Eastern Christian Studies.

Divine Word Missionaries, q; P.O. Box 6099, Techny, IL 60082-6099; (847) 272-7600; www.svd-missions.org.

Don Bosco Alive/The Salesian Bulletin; 148 Main Street, New Rochelle, NY 10802-0639; (914) 636-4225; www.salesians.org.

Ecumenical Trends, m (except Aug.); Graymoor, Route 9, P.O. Box 306, Garrison, NY 10524-0306; (845) 424-2109; www.atonementfriars.org; Graymoor Ecumenical Institute.

Eglute (The Little Fir Tree) (Lithuanian), m; 13648 Kikapoo Trail, Lockport, IL 60441; (708) 301-6410; for children ages 5-10.

Emmanuel, 10 times a year; 5384 Wilson Mills Rd., Cleveland, OH 44143; (440) 449-2103; www.blessed-sacrament.com; Congregation of Blessed Sacrament.

Envoy, bm; P.O. Box 585, Granville, OH 43023; (740) 587-2292; www.envoymagazine.com; journal of Catholic apologetics and evangelization.

EWTN Religious Catalogue, two times a year; 5817 Old Leeds Rd., Irondale, AL 35210; 205-271-2900; www.ewtn.com; printed catalogue of select new and favorite "holy reminders" for the Easter and Christmas seasons. Circ. 700,000.

Extension, m; 150 S. Wacker Dr., 20th Floor, Chicago, IL 60606; (312) 236-7240; www.catholic-extension.org; Catholic Church Extension Society.

Faith, 209 Seymour Ave., Lansing, MI 48933-1577; (517) 342-2595; www.faithmag.com.

Faith-Diocese of Erie, 429 E. Grandview Blvd., Erie, PA 16504; (814) 824-1160; www.faitherie.com.

Faith and Family, bm; 432 Washington Ave., North Haven, CT 06473; (203) 230-3800; formerly *Catholic Twin Circle*.

Faith and Reason, q; 134 Christendom Dr., Front Royal, VA 22630; (540) 636-2900.

Family Digest, The, bm; P.O. Box 40137, Fort Wayne, IN 46804 (editorial address); (952) 929-6765.

Family Foundations Magazine, P.O. Box 111184, Cincinnati, OH 45211; (513) 471-2000; www.ccli.org; published by the Couple to Couple League.

Family Friend, q; P.O. Box 11563, Milwaukee, WI 53211; (414) 961-0500; www.cfli.org; Catholic Family Life Insurance.

Fidelity, m; 206 Marquette Ave., South Bend, IN 46617; (219) 289-9786.

F.M.A. Focus, q; P.O. Box 598, Mt. Vernon, NY 10551; (914) 664-5604; Franciscan Mission Associates.

Forum Focus, q.; P.O. Box 542, Hudson, WI 54016-0542; (651) 276-1429; www.wandererforum.org.

Franciscan Studies, a; Franciscan Institute, St.

Bonaventure, NY 14778; (716) 375-2105; www.franinst.sbu.edu; Franciscan Institute.

Franciscan Way, q; 1235 University Blvd., Steubenville, OH 43952; (740) 283-6450; www.fra-nuniv.edu.

Fraternal Leader, q; P.O. Box 13005; Erie, PA 16514-1302; (814) 453-4331; Loyal Christian Benefit Association.

Fraternally Yours (Engish-Slovak), m; 24950 Chagrin Blvd., Beachwood, OH 44122; (216) 464-8015; First Catholic Slovak Ladies Assn.

Fuente de Misericordia, q; Eden Hill, Stockbridge, MA 01263; (413) 298-3691; www.marian.org; Congregation of Marians of the Immaculate Conception.

Glenmary Challenge, The, q; P.O. Box 465618, Cincinnati, OH 45246-5618; (513) 874-8900; www.glenmary.org; Glenmary Home Missioners.

God's Word Today, m; 185 Willow St., Mystic, CT 06355; (860) 536-2611; www.godswordtoday.org; Daily Scripture readings.

Good News, m; P.O. Box 432, Milwaukee, WI 53201-0432; (800) 876-4574; www.execpc.com/~lpi; Liturgical Publications.

Good News for Children, 32 times during school year; 2621 Dryden Rd., Suite 300, Dayton, OH 45439; (937) 293-1415; www.pflaum.com.

Good Shepherd (Dobry Pastier) (Slovak-English), a; 8200 McKnight Rd., Pittsburgh, PA 15237; (412) 364-3000.

Greyfriars Review, 3 times a year; Franciscan Institute, St. Bonventure University, St. Bonaventure, NY 14778; (716) 375-2105; www.franinst.sbu.edu; Franciscan Institute.

Growing with the Gospel, w; Liturgical Publications, P.O. Box 510817, New Berlin, WI, 53151; (800) 950-9952.

Guide to Religious Ministries for Catholic Men and Women, A, a; 210 North Ave., New Rochelle, NY 10801; (914) 632-1220; www.religiousministries.com.

Health Progress, bm; 4455 Woodson Rd., St. Louis, MO 63134-3797; (314) 427-2500; www.chausa.org; Catholic Health Association.

Heart, 4389 West Pine Blvd., St. Louis, MO 63108; (314) 652-1500; www.rscj.org.

Hearts Aflame, q; P.O. Box 976, Washington, NJ 07882; (210) 689-1700; www.ewtn.com/Bluearmy/; for youth ages 13-23.

Homiletic and Pastoral Review, m; P.O. Box 591810, San Francisco, CA 94159-1810; (415) 387-2324.

Horizon, q; 5420 S. Cornell Ave., #105, Chicago, IL 60615-5604; (773) 363-5454.

Horizons, 2 times a year; Villanova University, Villanova, PA 19085; (610) 519-7302; College Theology Society.

Human Development, q; 1353 Boston Post Rd., Suite 11, Madison, CT 06443; (203) 318-1886; www.ctu.edu/cishs.html.

ICSC Resource; 1275 K St. N.W., Suite 980, Washington, DC, 20005-4006; (202) 289-1093; www.catholicstewardship.org; published by International Catholic Stewardship Council.

Immaculata, bm; 1600 W. Park Ave., Libertyville, IL 60048; (847) 367-7800; www.marytown.com.

Immaculate Heart Messenger, q; 1224 County Rd. 548, Hanceville, AL 35077; (800) 721-6279; www.fatimafamily.org.

In a Word, m; 199 Seminary Dr., Bay Saint Louis, MS 39520-4626; (601) 467-1097; www.inaword.com; Society of the Divine Word.

Inside the Vatican, 10 times a year; Rome office: Via della Mura Aurelio 7c, 00165 Rome, Italy; U.S. office: St. Martin de Porres Lay Dominican Community, 3050 Gap Knob Rd., New Hope, KY 40052; (270) 325-5499; www.insidethevatican.com. The only current journal that focuses exclusively on Rome, the impact of the papacy worldwide, and the functioning, travels, and activities of the Holy Father and the Roman Curia.

Jesuit Bulletin, 3 times a year; 3601 Lindell Blvd., St. Louis, MO 63108; (314) 977-7363; www.jesuitsmis.org; Jesuit Seminary Aid Association.

Jesuit Journeys, 3 times a year; 3400 W. Wisconsin Ave., Milwaukee, WI 53208-0288; (414) 937-6949; www.jesuitswisprov.org.

Josephinum Journal of Theology, twice a year; 7625 N. High St., Columbus, OH 43235; (614) 985-2278; www.pcj.edu.

Josephite Harvest, The, q; 1130 N. Calvert St., Baltimore, MD 21202-3802; (410) 727-2233; www.josephite.com; Josephite Missionaries.

Journal of Catholic Legal Studies, St. John's University, 8000 Utopia Parkway, Jamaica, NY 11439; (718) 890-6655.

Jurist, The, semi-annually; Catholic University of America, Washington, DC 20064; (202) 319-5439; Department of Canon Law.

Kinship, q; P.O. Box 22264, Owensboro, KY 42304; (270) 686-8401; www.glenmarysisters.org; Glenmary Sisters.

Knights of St. John International, q; 89 South Pine Ave., Albany, NY 12208; (518) 453-5675; www.members.tripod.com/ksji/knights/ksji.html.

Law Briefs, m; 3211 Fourth St. NE, Washington DC 20017; (202) 541-3300; Office of General Counsel, USCCB.

Lay Witness, m; 827 North Fourth St., Steubenville, OH, 43952; (740) 283-2484; www.cuf.org; Catholics United for the Faith.

Leaflet Missal, 16565 South State St., S. Holland, IL 60473; (708) 331-5485; www.leafletmissal.com.

Leaves, bm; P.O. Box 87, Dearborn, MI 48121-0087; (313) 561-2330; www.rc.net/detroit/marianhill/leaves.htm; Mariannhill Mission Society.

Legatus, ten times a year, 2640 Golden Gate Pkwy, #118, Naples, FL 34105; (239) 435-3852; www.legatus.org. Published by Legatus International.

Liguorian, m; 1 Liguori Dr., Liguori, MO 63057; (636) 464-2500; www.liguorian.org; Redemptorists.

Linacre Quarterly, P.O. Box 757, Pewaukee, WI 53072; (262) 523-6201; www.cathmed.org; Catholic Medical Association (National Federation of Catholic Physicians Guilds).

Liturgia y Cancion (Spanish and English), q; 5536 NE Hassalo, Portland, OR 97213; (800) 548-8749;

Oregon Catholic Press.

Liturgical Catechesis, 6 times a year; 160 E. Virginia St., #290, San Jose, CA 95112; (408) 286-8505; www.rpinet.com/lc.

Liturgy Planner, The, semi-annual; P.O. Box 13071, Portland, OR 97213; (503) 331-2965.

Living City, m; P.O. Box 837, Bronx, NY 10465; (718) 828-2932; www.livingcitymagazine.com; Focolare Movement.

Living Faith: Daily Catholic Devotions, q; 1564 Fencorp Dr., Fenton, MO 63026-2942; (636) 305-9777; www.livingfaith.com.

Living Light, The, q; 3211 Fourth St. NE, Washington, DC 20017; (202) 541-3453; www.usccb.org/education/catechetics/livinglt.htm; Department of Education, USCCB.

Magnificat, m.; Dunwoodie, 201 Seminary Ave., Yonkers, NY 10704; (914) 377-8513; www.magnificat.net.

Marian Helper, q.; Eden Hill, Stockbridge, MA 01263; (413) 298-3691; www.marian.org.

Marriage, bm; 955 Lake Dr., St. Paul, MN 55120; (651) 454-7947; www.marriagemagazine; International Marriage Encounter.

Mary's Shrine, 2 times a year; 400 Michigan Ave. NE, Washington, DC 20017-1566; (202) 526-8300; www.nationalshrine.com; Basilica of National Shrine of the Immaculate Conception.

Maryknoll, m; Maryknoll, NY 10545-0308; (914) 941-7590; www.maryknoll.org; Catholic Foreign Mission Society.

Matrimony, q; 215 Santa Rosa Pl., Santa Barbara, CA 93109; (805) 965-9541; Worldwide Marriage Encounter.

Medjugorje Magazine, q; 317 W. Ogden Ave., Westmont, IL 60559; (630) 968-4684; www.medjugor.com.

Migration World, 5 times a year; 209 Flagg Pl., Staten Island, NY 10304; (718) 351-8800; www.cmsny.org; Center for Migration Studies.

Ministry & Liturgy, m.; 160 E. Virginia St., #290, San Jose, CA 95112; (408) 286-8505; www.rpinet.com.

Miraculous Medal, q; 475 E. Chelten Ave., Philadelphia, PA 19144; (215) 848-1010; www.cammonline.org; Central Association of the Miraculous Medal.

Mission, q; 1663 Bristol Pike, Bensalem, PA 19020-8502; (215) 244-9900; www.katharinedrexel.org; Sisters of the Blessed Sacrament.

Mission, q., 10582 Associates Court, Manassas, VA 20109; (703) 367-0333; www.cardinalnewmansociety.org; Cardinal Newman Society to promote Catholic higher education.

MISSION Magazine, q; 366 Fifth Ave., New York, NY 10001; (212) 563-8700; www.worldmissionscatholicchurch.org; Society for Propagation of the Faith.

Mission Helper, The, q; 1001 W. Joppa Rd., Baltimore, MD 21204-3787; (410) 823-8585; Mission Helpers of the Sacred Heart.

Missionhurst, bm; 4651 N. 25th St., Arlington, VA 22207; (703) 528-3804; www.missionhurst.org.

Modern Schoolman, The, q; St. Louis University, P.O. Box 56907, St. Louis, MO 63156; (314) 997-

3149; St. Louis University Philosophy Department.
Momento Catolico, El; 205 W. Monroe St.,
Chicago, IL, 60606; (312) 236-7782;
www.hmrc.claretianpubs.org.
Momentum, q; Suite 100, 1077 30th St. NW,
Washington, DC 20007-3852; (202) 337-6232;
www.ncea.org; National Catholic Educational
Association.
Mountain Spirit, The, bm; P.O. Box 459, Hagerhill,
KY 41222; (606) 789-9791; www.chrisapp.org;
Christian Appalachian Project.
My Daily Visitor, bm; 200 Noll Plaza, Huntington,
IN 46750; (260) 356-8400; www.osv.com; Our Sunday
Visitor, Inc.
My Friend – The Catholic Magazine for Kids, 10
times a year; 50 St. Paul's Ave., Jamaica Plain, Boston,
MA 02130; (617) 522-8911; www.myfriend-
magazine.org; for children ages 6-12.

National Apostolate for Inclusion Ministry, q; P.O.
Box 218, Riverdale, MD, 20738-0218; (301) 699-
9500; www.nafim.org.
National Catholic Forester, q; 320 S. School St.,
Mt. Prospect, IL 60056; (847) 342-4500;
www.ncsf.com.
National Catholic Rural Life, bi-annual; 4625
Beaver Ave., Des Moines, IA 50310; (515) 270-2634;
www.ncrlc.com.
NC Catholic, 715 Nazareth, Raleigh, NC 27606;
(919) 821-9736; www.nccatholics.org; diocese of
Raleigh.
NETWORK Connection, bm; 801 Pennsylvania
Ave. SE, #460, Washington, DC 20003; (202) 547-
5556; www.networklobby.org; Network.
New Oxford Review, 10 issues a year; 1069 Kains
Ave., Berkeley, CA 94706; (510) 526-5374;
www.newoxfordreview.org.
Notebook, The, q; CMICA-USA, 3049 4 St. NE,
Washington, DC 20017; (202) 269-6672; www.pax-
romana.org; Catholic Movement for Intellectual and
Cultural Affairs.
Notre Dame Magazine, q; University of Notre
Dame, Notre Dame, IN 46556; (574) 631-5335;
www.nd.edu/~mdmag.
Nova-Voice of Ministry, bm; P.O. Box 432,
Milwaukee, WI 53201; (800) 876-4574;
www.execpc.com/~lpi; Liturgical Publications.

Oblates Magazine, six times a year, 9480 North De
Mazenod Dr., Belleville, IL 62223-1160; (618) 398-
4848; www.oblatesusa.org.
Old Testament Abstracts, 3 times a year; 320
Caldwell Hall, Catholic University of America,
Washington, DC 20064; (202) 319-5519.
ONE, bm., 1011 First Ave., New York, NY 10022;
(212) 826-1480; www.cnewa.org. Catholic Near East
Welfare Association.
Origins, 48 times a year; 3211 4th St. NE,
Washington, DC 20017; (202) 541-3284; documentary
service.
Ozanam News, The, twice a year; 58 Progress
Parkway, St. Louis, MO 63043-3706; (314) 576-3993;
www.svdpuscouncil.org; Society of St. Vincent de
Paul.

Palabra Entre Nosotros, La, bm; 9639 Dr. Perry

Rd., Unit 126N, Jamesville, MD, 21754; (301) 831-
1262; www.wau.org.
Parish Liturgy, q; 16565 S. State St., S. Holland, IL
60473; (708) 331-5485; www.parishliturgy.com.
**Partners Magazine: Chicago Province of the
Society of Jesus,** 3 times a year; 2059 N. Sedgwick
St., Chicago, IL 60614; (773) 975-8181; www.jesuits-
chi.org.
Passionists' Compassion, The, q; 526 Monastery
Pl., Union City, NJ 07087; (201) 864-0018;
www.cptryon.org.
Pastoral Life, m; Box 595, Canfield, OH 44406;
(330) 533-5503; www.albahouse.org; Society of St.
Paul.
Pastoral Music, bm; 962 Wayne Ave., Suite 210,
Silver Spring, MD 20910-4433; (240) 247-3000;
www.npm.org; National Association of Pastoral
Musicians.
Pax Romana/CMICA-USA, q; 3049 4th St., NE,
Washington, DC 20017; (202) 269-6672; www.pax-
romana.org.
Philosophy Today, q; De Paul University, 2219 N.
Kenmore Ave., Chicago, IL 60614-3504; (773) 325-
7267; Philosophy Department.
PIME World, m (except July-Aug.); 17330 Quincy
St., Detroit, MI 48221; (313) 342-4066;
www.pimeysa.org; PIME Missionaries.
Poverello, The, 10 times a year; 6832 Convent Blvd.,
Sylvania, OH 43560; (419) 824-3627; www.sistersosf;
Sisters of St. Francis of Sylvania.
Prayers for Worship, q; P.O. Box 510817, New
Berlin, WI 532151-0817; (800) 950-9952;
www.execpc.com/~lpi.
Preach: Enlivening the Pastoral Art, 6 times a year,
3708 River Rd., Ste. 400, Franklin Park, IL 60131;
(800) 566-6150; www.wlpmusic.com; published by
World Library Publications.
Priest, The, m; 200 Noll Plaza, Huntington, IN
46750; (260) 356-8400; www.osv.com; Our Sunday
Visitor, Inc.
Proceedings, a; Fordham University, Adm. Bldg.,
Bronx, NY 10458; (718) 817-4081; www.acpa-
main.org; Journal of the American Catholic
Philosophical Association.
Promise, 32 times a year; 2621 Dryden Rd., Suite
300, Dayton, OH 45439; (937) 293-1415;
www.pflaum.com.

Queen of All Hearts, bm; 26 S. Saxon Ave., Bay
Shore, NY 11706; (631) 665-0726; www.montfortmis-
sionaries.com; Montfort Missionaries.

Reign of the Sacred Heart, q; 6889 S. Lovers Lane,
Hales Corners, WI 53130; (414) 425-3383;
www.poshusa.org.
Religion Teacher's Journal, m (Sept.-May); P.O.
Box 180, Mystic, CT 06355; (860) 536-2611;
www.twentythirdpublications.com.
Religious Life, bm., P.O. Box 410007, Chicago, IL
60641; (773) 267-1195; www.religiouslife.com.
Renascence, q; P.O. Box 1881, Marquette
University, Milwaukee, WI 53201-1881; (414) 288-
6725.
Report on U.S. Catholic Overseas Mission, bi-
annually; 3029 Fourth St. N.E., Washington, DC
20017; (202) 832-3112; www.catholicmission.org;

United States Catholic Mission Association.
Response: Directory of Volunteer Opportunities, a; 6930 Carroll Ave., Suite 506, Takoma Park, MD 20912; (301) 270-0900; www.cnvs.org; Catholic Network of Volunteer Service.

Review for Religious, bm; Room 428, 3601 Lindell Blvd., St. Louis, MO 63108; (314) 977-7363; www.reviewforreligious.org.

Review of Politics, q; Box B, Notre Dame, IN 46556; (574) 631-6623; www.nd.edu/~rop.

Review of Social Economy, q; Marquette University, Milwaukee, WI 53233; (414) 288-5438; Association for Social Economics.

Revista Maryknoll (Spanish-English), m; Maryknoll, NY 10545; (914) 941-7590; www.maryknoll.org; Catholic Foreign Mission Society of America.

RITE, 8 times a year; 1800 North Hermitage Ave., Chicago, IL 60622-1101; (773) 486-8970; www.ltp.org.

Roze Maryi (Polish), m; Eden Hill, Stockbridge, MA 01263; (413) 298-3691; www.marian.org; Marian Helpers Center.

Sacred Music, q; 134 Christendom Dr., c/o K. Poterack, Front Royal, VA 22630; (540) 636-2900.

St. Anthony Messenger, m; 28 W. Liberty St., Cincinnati, OH 45210-1298; (513) 241-5615; www.americancatholic.org; Franciscan Friars.

St. Augustine Catholic, bm (Sept-May); 11625 Old St. Augustine Rd., Jacksonville, FL 32258; (904) 262-3200; www.staugcatholic.org; St. Augustine diocese.

St. Joseph's Messenger and Advocate of the Blind, bi-annual; St. Joseph Home, 537 Pavonia Ave., Jersey City, NJ 07303; (201) 798-4141.

St. Paul's Family Magazine, q; 14780 W. 159th St., Olathe, KS 66062; (913) 780-0405.

Salesian Missions of St. John Bosco, q; 2 Lefevre Lane, New Rochelle, NY 10801-5710; (914) 633-8344; www.salesianmissions.org; Salesians of Don Bosco.

SALT/Sisters of Charity, BVM, q; 1100 Carmel Dr., Dubuque, IA 52001; (563) 588-2351; www.bvmcong.org.

Scalabrinians, q; 209 Flagg Pl., Staten Island, NY 10304; (718) 351-0257.

School Guide, a; 210 North Ave., New Rochelle, NY 10801; (914) 632-7771; www.schoolguides.com.

SCN Journey, bm; SCN Office of Communications, P.O. Box 9, Nazareth, KY 40048; (502) 348-1564; www.scnazarethky.org; Sisters of Charity of Nazareth.

Seeds, 32 times a year; 2621 Dryden Rd., Dayton, OH 45439; (937) 293-1415; www.pflaum.com.

Serenity, q; 601 Maiden Choice Lane, Baltimore, MD 21228; (410) 744-9367; Little Sisters of the Poor.

SerraUSA, The, bm; 65 E. Wacker Pl., #802, Chicago, IL 60601-7203; (312) 201-6549; www.serraus.org; Serra International.

Share Magazine, q; 10 W. 71st St., New York, NY 10023; (212) 877-3041; www.catholicdaughters.com; Catholic Daughters of the Americas.

Share the Word, bm; 3031 Fourth St. NE, Washington, DC 20017-1102; (202) 832-5022; www.sharetheword.net; Paulist Catholic Evangelization Association.

Silent Advocate, q; St. Rita School for the Deaf,

1720 Glendale-Milford Rd., Cincinnati, OH 45215; (513) 771-7600; www.srsdeaf.org.

Social Justice Review, bm; 3835 Westminster Pl., St. Louis, MO 63108-3409; (314) 371-1653; www.socialjusticereview.com; Catholic Central Union of America.

SOUL Magazine, bm; P.O. Box 976, Washington, NJ 07882; (908) 213-2223; www.bluearmy.com; The Blue Army of Our Lady of Fatima, USA, Inc.

Spirit, w; 1884 Randolph Ave., St. Paul, MN 55105; (612) 690-7012; www.goodgroundpress.com; for teens.

Spirit, bi-annually; Seton Hall University, South Orange, NJ 07079; (201) 761-9000.

Spirit & Life, bm; 800 N. Country Club Rd., Tucson, AZ 85716; (520) 325-6401; www.benedictinesisters.org; Benedictine Srs. of Perpetual Adoration.

Spiritual Life, q; 2131 Lincoln Rd. NE, Washington, DC 20002; (800) 832-8489; Discalced Carmelite Friars.

Star, 10 times a year; 22 W. Kiowa, Colorado Springs, CO 80903.

Studies in the Spirituality of Jesuits, 5 times a year; 3601 Lindell Blvd., St. Louis, MO 63108; (314) 977-7257.

Sunday by Sunday, w; 1884 Randolph Ave., St. Paul, MN 55105; (651) 690-7012; www.goodgroundpress.com.

Sword Magazine, 2 times a year; 2097 Town Hall Terrace, #3, Grand Island, NY 14072-1737; (716) 773-0992; Carmelite Fathers.

Take Out, 10 times a year; 200 Noll Plaza, Huntington, IN 46750; (260) 356-8400; www.osv.com; Our Sunday Visitor, Inc.

Theological Studies, q; Marquette University, 100 Coughlin Hall, Milwaukee, WI 53201-1881; (414) 288-3164; www.ts.mu.edu.

Theology Digest, q; P.O. Box 56907, St. Louis, MO 63156-0907; (314) 977-3410; St. Louis University.

This Rock Magazine, 10 times a year; 2020 Gillespie Way, El Cajon, CA 92020; (619) 387-7200; www.catholic.com; Catholic apologetics.

Thomist, The, q; 487 Michigan Ave. NE, Washington, DC 20017; (202) 529-5300; www.thomist.org; Dominican Fathers.

Today's Catholic Teacher, m (Sept.-April); 2621 Dryden Rd., Dayton, OH 45439; (937) 293-1415; www.catholicteacher.com.

Today's Liturgy, q; 5536 NE Hassalo, Portland, OR 97213; (800) 548-8749.

Today's Parish, m (Sept.-May); P.O. Box 180, Mystic, CT 06355; (860) 536-2611; www.twentythirdpublications.com.

Together in the Word, bi-annual; Box 577, Techny, IL 60082-0577; (708) 272-2700; www.divineword.org; Chicago province, Society of Divine Word.

The Tower, w; The Catholic University of America, University Center, 127 Pryzbyla Center, Washington, DC 20064; (202) 319-5778.

Tracings, q; 5 Gamelin St., Holyoke, MA 01040; (413) 536-7511; www.sisofprov.org; Sisters of Providence.

Ultreya Magazine, bm; 4500 W. Davis St., P.O. Box 210226, Dallas, TX 75211; (214) 339-6321; Cursillo

Movement.

L'Union (French and English), q; P.O. Box F, Woonsocket, RI 02895; (401) 769-0520.

Universitas, q; 221 N. Grand, Room 39, St. Louis, MO 63103; (314) 977-2537; www.slu.edu; St. Louis University.

U.S. Catholic, m; 205 W. Monroe St., Chicago, IL 60606; (312) 236-7782; www.uscatholic.org; Claretians.

Venture, 32 times during school year; 2621 Dryden Rd., Suite 300, Dayton, OH 45439; (937) 293-1415; www.pflaum.com; intermediate grades.

Vida Catolica, La, m.; 40 Green St., Lynn, MA 01902; (781) 586-0197; www.la-vida.org/catolica; Boston archdiocese Hispanic community.

Vincentian Heritage, twice a year; 2233 N. Kenmore Ave., Chicago, IL 60614; (773) 325-7348; www.depaul.edu/~vstudies.

Vision, a, 205 W. Monroe St., Chicago, IL 60606; (312) 236-7782; www.visionguide.org; Claretian Publications in conjunction with National Religious Vocation Conference.

Vision, 3 times a year; 7202 Buchanan St., Landover Hills, MD 20784; (301) 577-1684; www.ncod.org; National Catholic Office for the Deaf.

Vision (Spanish-English), P.O. Box 28185, San Antonio, TX 78228; (210) 732-2156; www.maccsa.org; Mexican American Cultural Center.

Visions, 32 times during school year; 2621 Dryden Rd., Suite 300, Dayton, OH 45439; (937) 293-1415; www.pflaum.com; for students in grades 7-9.

Vocations and Prayer, q; 6635 Tobias Ave., Van Nuys, CA 91405; (818) 782-1765; www.rcj.org; Rogationist Fathers.

Voice Crying in the Wilderness, A, q; 4425 Schneider Rd., Filmore, NY 14735; (716) 567-4433; Most Holy Family Monastery.

Waif's Messenger, q; 1140 W. Jackson Blvd., Chicago, IL 60607; (312) 738-9522; Mission of Our Lady of Mercy.

Way of St. Francis, bm; 1500 34th Ave., Oakland, CA 94601; (916) 443-5717; www.sbfranciscans.org; Franciscan Friars of California, Inc.

Wheeling Jesuit University Chronicle, 3 times a year; 316 Washington Ave., Wheeling, WV 26003; (304) 243-2296.

Word Among Us, The, m; 9639 Dr. Perry Rd., No. 126N, Jamesville, MD 21754; (301) 831-1262; www.wau.org.

Word and Witness, P.O. Box 510817, New Berlin, WI, 53151-0817; (800) 950-9952; www.lpiresource-center.com.

World Lithuanian Catholic Directory, P.O. Box 1025, Humarock, MA 02407; (781) 834-4079.

Worship, bm; St. John's Abbey, Collegeville, MN 56321; (612) 363-3883.

Newsletters

ACT, 10 times a year; Box 925, Evansville, IN 47706-0925; (812) 962-5508; www.cfm.org; Christian Family Movement.

Action News, q; Pro-Life Action League, 6160 N. Cicero Ave., Chicago, IL 60646; (773) 777-2900; www.prolifeaction.org.

Annual Report, The, 2021 H St. NW, Washington, DC 20006; (202) 331-8542; Black and Indian Mission Office.

Archdiocesan Bulletin, bm; 827 N. Franklin St., Philadelphia, PA 19123; (215) 627-0143; Philadelphia archeparchy.

Baraga Bulletin, The, q; P.O. Box 550, Marquette, MI 49855; (906) 227-9117; www.dioceseofmarquette.org; Bishop Baraga Association.

Bringing Home the Word, w; 28 W. Liberty St., Cincinnati, OH 45202; (513) 241-5615; www.ameri-cancatholic.org; lectionary-based resource from St. Anthony's Messenger Press.

Brothers' Voice, 5420 South Cornell Ave., #205, Chicago, IL 60615-5604; (773) 493-2306.

Called By Joy, three times a year; 4419 N. Hawthorne St., Spokane, WA 99205; (509) 327-4479; Franciscan Monastery of St. Clare.

Campaign Update, bm; 1513 Sixteenth St. NW, Ste. 400, Washington, DC 20036; (202) 833-4999; www.cathcamp.org; Catholic Campaign for America.

Canticle, The, four times a year, 146 Hawthorne Rd., Pittsburgh, PA 15209; (412) 821-2200; www.millvale-franciscans.org; Sisters of St. Francis of Millvale.

Capuchin Chronicle, q.; P.O. Box 15099, Pittsburgh, PA 15237-0099; (412) 367-2222; www.capuchin.org.

CARA Report, The, bm; Georgetown University, Washington, DC 20057-1203; (202) 687-8080; www.cara.georgetown.edu; Center for Applied Research in the Apostolate.

Caring Community, The, m; 115 E. Armour Blvd., Kansas City, MO 64111; (816) 968-2278; www.ncr-pub.com.

Catalyst, 10 times a year; 450 Seventh Ave., New York, NY, 10123; (212) 371-3191; www.catholi-cleague.org; Catholic League for Civil and Religious Rights.

Catechist's Connection, The, 10 times a year; 115 E. Armour Blvd., Kansas City, MO 64111; (816) 968-2278; www.ncrpub.com.

Catholic Communicator, The, q; 120 East Colonial Hgwy., Hamilton, VA 20158-9012; (540) 338-2700; Catholic Distance University Newsletter.

Catholic Trends, bw; 3211 Fourth St. NE, Washington, DC 20017; (202) 541-3290; Catholic News Service.

Catholic Update, m; 28 W. Liberty St., Cincinnati, OH 45202-6498; (513) 241-5615; www.american-catholic.org.

CCHD News, q; 3211 Fourth St. NE, Washington, DC 20017-1194; (202) 541-3210; www.povertyusa.org; Catholic Campaign for Human Development.

Celebration, Sisters of Charity of Seaton Hill, q; DePaul Center, 463 Mount Thor Rd., Greensburg, PA 15601; (724) 836-0406; www.scsh.org.

C.F.C. Newsletter, 5 times a year; 145 Huguenot Ave., Suite 402, New Rochelle, NY 10801; (914) 712-7580; Christian Brothers.

Christ the King Seminary Newsletter, 3 times a year; 711 Knox Rd., Box 607, E. Aurora, NY 14052; (716) 652-8900.

Christian Response Newsletter, P.O. Box 125, Staples, MN 56479-0125; (218) 894-1165.

Christopher News Notes, 10 times a year; 12 E. 48th St., New York, NY 10017; (212) 759-4050; www.christophers.org; The Christophers.

Clarion, The, 5 times a year; Box 159, Alfred, ME 04002-0159; (207) 324-0067; Brothers of Christian Instruction.

CMSM Bulletin, m; 8808 Cameron St., Silver Spring, MD 20910; (301) 588-4030; www.cmsm.org.

Comboni Mission Newsletter, q; 1318 Nagel Rd., Cincinnati, OH 45255-3194; (513) 474-4997; www.combonimissionaries.org.

Connections, five times a year, 610 W. Elm, Monroe, MI 48161; (734) 240-9745; IHM Sisters.

Context, 22 issues a year; 205 W. Monroe St., Chicago, IL 60606; (312) 236-7782; www.contextonline.org; Claretians.

CPN Newsletter, twice a month; 1318 Nagel Rd., Cincinnati, OH, 45255-3120; (513) 474-4997; www.combonimissionaries.org.

Cross and Feathers (Tekakwitha Conference Newsletter), q; P.O. Box 6768, Great Falls, MT 59406; (406) 727-0147; www.tekconf.org; Tekakwitha Conference.

Crossroads, 8 times a year; 1118 Pendleton St., #300, Cincinnati, OH 45202; (888) 714-6631; www.ccmanet.org; Catholic Campus Ministry Association.

CRUX of the News, w; P.O. Box 758, Latham, NY 12110-0758; (518) 783-0058.

Cycles of Faith, P.O. Box 510817, New Berlin, WI 53201; (800) 950-9952; www.lpiresourcecenter.com.

Damien-Dutton Call, q; 616 Bedford Ave., Bellmore, NY 11710.

Dimensions, m; 86 Front St., Hempstead, NY 11550; (516) 481-6000; www.ncdc.org; National Catholic Development Conference.

Diocesan Dialogue, two times a year; 16565 South State St., South Holland, IL 60473; (708) 331-5485; www.acpress.org.

Diocesan Newsletter, The, m; P.O. Box 2147, Harlingen, TX 78551; (956) 421-4111; www.cdob.org; Brownsville diocese.

Environment and Art Letter, m; 1800 N. Hermitage Ave., Chicago, IL 60622-1101; (773) 486-8970; www.ltp.org; Liturgy Training Publications.

E-Proclaim, 10 times a year; 3211 Fourth St., NE, Washington, DC, 20017-1194; (202) 541-3204; www.usccb.org/ccc.

Ethics and Medics, m; 6399 Drexel Rd., Philadelphia, PA 19151; (215) 877-2660; www.ncbcenter.org; National Catholic Bioethics Center.

Eucharistic Minister, m; 115 E. Armour, Kansas City, MO 64111; (816) 968-2278; www.ncrpub.com.

Every Day Catholic, m; 28 W. Liberty St., Cincinnati, OH 45202-6498; (513) 241-5615; www.everydaycatholic.org; St. Anthony Messenger Press.

EWTN Family Newsletter, 13 times a year; 5817 Leeds Rd., Irondale, AL 35210; (205) 271-2900; www.ewtn.com; Eternal Word Television Network.

EWTN Monthly Programming Guide, 13 times a year for each satellite; 5817 Old Leeds Rd., Irondale, AL 35210; 205-271-2900; www.ewtn.com; EWTN Global Catholic Network, lists monthly programming and schedule for each satellite coverage area, including additional special end-of-year Christmas schedule.

Explorations, q; American Interfaith Institute, 321 Chestnut St., Philadelphia, PA, 19106; (215) 238-5345.

Faith Extra, 26 times a year; P.O. Box 10668, Erie, PA 16514; www.eriecd.org; diocese of Erie.

Family Connection, The, bm; 3753 MacBeth Dr., San Jose, CA 95127; (408) 258-8534.

Father Flood, q; P.O. Box 51087, New Berlin, WI 53151-0817; (800) 950-9952; www.lpiresourcecenter.com; Liturgical Publications.

Fellowship of Catholic Scholars Newsletter Quarterly, P.O. Box 495, Notre Dame, IN 46556; www.catholicscholars.org.

Fonda Tekakwitha News, P.O. Box 627, Fonda, NY 12068; (518) 853-3636; www.katerishrine.com; Order Minor Conventuals.

Food for the Poor, 3 times a year; 550 SW 12th Ave., Deerfield Beach, FL 33442; (954) 427-2222; www.foodforthepoor.org.

FOOTSTEPS: Walking with Edmund, q; 145 Huguenot Ave., Ste. 402; (914) 712-7580; Christian Brothers Foundation.

Forum Focus, q; P.O. Box 542, Hudson, WI 54016; (651) 276-1429; www.focusonfaith.org; The Wanderer Forum Foundation.

Foundations Newsletter for Newly Married Couples, bm; P.O. Box 1632, Portland, ME, 04104-1632; (207) 775-4757.

Franciscan Foundation for the Holy Land, three or four times a year; 910 Oakwood Trail, Indianapolis, IN 46260; (317) 726-1679; www.ffhl.org.

Franciscan World Care, q; P.O. Box 29034, Washington, DC 20017; (202) 832-1762; www.franciscanmissionservice.catholic.edu; Franciscan Mission Service.

Frontline Report, bm; 23 Bliss Ave., Tenafly, NJ 07670; (201) 567-0450; www.smafathers.org; Society of African Missions.

Graymoor Today, m; P.O. Box 301, Garrison, NY 10524-0301; (845) 424-3671; www.atonementfriars.org.

Harmony, 3 times a year; 800 N. Country Club Rd., Tucson, AZ 85716; (520) 325-6401; Benedictine Srs. of Perpetual Adoration.

Healing & Hope, 9480 North De Mazenod Dr., Belleville, IL 62223-1160; (618) 398-4848; www.snows.org.

Heart Beats, 169 Cummins Hwy., Roslindale, MA 02131; (617) 325-3322.

Heart to Heart, twice a year; St. Vincent Archabbey, 300 Fraser Purchase Rd., Latrobe, PA 15650; (724) 805-2601; www.stvincentstore.com; Benedictines of St. Vincent Archabbey.

HLI Reports, m; 4 Family Life, Front Royal, VA 22630; Human Life International.

HN People, bm; 158 W. 27th St., New York, NY 10001; (212) 924-1451; www.hnp.org/publications; Franciscans of Holy Name Province.

HNP Today, w; 158 W. 27th St., New York, NY 10001; (212) 924-1451; www.hnp.org/publications; Franciscans of Holy Name Province.

ICSC Commitment, 1275 K St. NW, Suite 980, Washington, DC 20005-4006; (202) 289-1093; www.catholicstewardship.org.

Immaculate Heart of Mary Shrine Bulletin, 3 times a year; Mountain View Rd., P.O. Box 976, Washington, NJ 07882-0976; (908) 689-1700; www.ewtn.com/bluearmy.

Initiatives, bm; P.O. Box 291102, Chicago, IL 60629; (773) 776-9036; www.centerforlaity.org; National Center for the Laity.

Interchange, Assisi Heights, 1001 14 St., NW, #100, Rochester, MN 55901-2525; (507) 529-3523; www.rochesterfranciscan.org; Rochester Franciscan Sisters.

It's Our World, 4 times during school year; 366 Fifth Ave., New York, NY 10001; (212) 563-8700; www.holychildhoodusa.org; Young Catholics in Mission.

Journey, The, q; 210 W. 31st St., New York, NY 10001-2876; (212) 714-0950; www.capuchin.org; Province of St. Mary of Capuchin Order.

Joyful Noiseletter, The, m; P.O. Box 895, Portage, MI 49081-0895; (616) 324-0990; www.joyfulnoiseletter.com; Fellowship of Merry Christians.

Jubilee, q; 3900 Harewood Rd., NE, Washington, DC 20017; (202) 635-5400; www.jp2cc.org; John Paul II Cultural Center.

Knightline, 18 times a year; 1 Columbus Plaza, New Haven, CT 06510-3326; (203) 772-2130; www.kofc.org; Knights of Columbus Supreme Council.

Laity and Family Life Updates, bm; 20 Archbishop May Dr., St. Louis, MO, 63119; (314) 792-7173; www.stlcatholics.org.

Land of Cotton, q; 2048 W. Fairview Ave., Montgomery, AL 39196; (205) 265-6791; City of St. Jude.

Law Reports, q; 4455 Woodson Rd., St. Louis, MO 63134; (314) 427-2500; Catholic Health Association.

LCWR Update, m; 8808 Cameron St., Silver Spring, MD 20910; (301) 588-4955; www.lcwr.org; Leadership Conference of Women Religious.

Legatus, m; P.O. Box 511, Ann Arbor, MI 48106; (734) 930-3854; www.legatus.org; Legatus.

Let's Talk! (English edition), Hablemos! (Spanish edition), bm; 3031 Fourth St. NE, Washington, DC 20017-1102; (202) 832-5022; www.prisonministry.org; prison ministries of Paulist National Catholic Evangelization Assn.

Letter to the Seven Churches, bm; 1516 Jerome St., Lansing, MI 48912; (517) 372-6222; Catholic Charismatics.

Life at Risk, 10 times a year; 3211 Fourth St. NE, Washington, DC 20017; (202) 541-3070; Pro-Life Activities Committee, USCCB.

Life Insight, m; 3211 Fourth St. NE, Washington, DC 20017; (202) 541-3070; Committee for Pro-Life Activities, USCCB.

Liturgical Images, m; P.O. Box 2225, Hickory, NC 28603; (828) 327-3225.

Loyola World, 22 times a year; 820 North Michigan Ave., Chicago, IL, 60611; (312) 915-6157; www.luc.edu.

Magnificat, three times a year; Star Route 1, Box 226, Eagle Harbor, MI, 49950; (906) 289-4388 (fax); www.societystjohn.com.

Malvern Retreat House, q; P.O. Box 315, Malvern, PA 19355-0315; (610) 644-0400; www.malvernretreat.org; Laymen's Retreat League.

Maronites Today, m; P.O. Box 1891, Austin, TX 78767-1891; (512) 458-3693; www.eparchyla.org; Eparchy of Our Lady of Los Angeles.

Medical Mission Sisters News, q; 8400 Pine Rd., Philadelphia, PA 19111; (215) 742-6100; www.medicalmissionsisters.org.

Messenger of St. Joseph's Union, The, 3 times a year; 108 Bedell St., Staten Island, NY 10309; (718) 984-9296.

Mission, The, three times a year; 90 Cherry Lane, Hicksville, NY 11801-6299; (516) 733-7042; www.catholiccharities.cc; Catholic Charities.

Mission Messenger, The, q; P.O. Box 610, Thoreau, NM, 87323; (505) 862-7847; www.stbonaventuremission.org; St. Bonaventure Indian Mission and School.

Missionaries of Africa Report, q; 1624 21st St. NW, Washington, DC 20009; (202) 232-5154; Society of Missionaries of Africa (White Fathers).

Mission Update, bm; 3029 Fourth St. NE, Washington, DC 20017; (202) 832-3112; www.uscatholicmission.org.

Mountain View, q.; 8501 Bailey Rd., Darien, IL 60561; (630) 969-5050; Lay Carmelite Headquarters.

National Holy Name Newsletter, bm; 53 Laux St., Buffalo, NY 14206-2218; (716) 847-6419; www.members.aol.com/nahns.

NCPD National Update, q; 415 Michigan Ave. NE, #240, Washington, DC 20017; (202) 529-2933; www.ncpd.org; National Catholic Office for Persons with Disabilities.

Neighbors, Committee on Home Missions, q.; 3211 Fourth St. NE, Washington, D.C. 20017; (202) 541-5400; Bishops' Committee on Home Missions.

News and Ideas, q.; 9480 North De Mazenod Dr., Belleville, IL 62223; (618) 398-4848; www.snows.org; Missionary Oblates of Mary Immaculate.

News and Views, q; 3900 Westminster Pl., St. Louis, MO 63108; (314) 533-0320; www.sacredheartprogram.org; Sacred Heart Program.

Newsletter of the Bureau of Catholic Indian Missions, 10 times a year; 2021 H St. NW, Washington, DC 20006; (202) 331-8542.

North Coast Catholic, bi-monthly; P.O. Box 1297, Santa Rosa, CA 95402; (707) 566-3302; www.santarosacatholic.org; Santa Rosa diocese.

Nuestra Parroquia (Spanish-English), m; 205 W. Monroe St., Chicago, IL 60606; (312) 236-7782; www.hmrc.claretianpubs.org; Claretians.

Oblates, six times a year; 9480 North De Mazenod Dr., Belleville, IL 62223-1160; (618) 398-4848; www.snows.org; Missionary Oblates of Mary Immaculate.

Origins, 48 times a year; 3211 Fourth St. NE, Washington, DC 20017; (202) 541-3284; Catholic News Service.

Overview, m; 205 W. Monroe St., 6th Floor,

Chicago, IL 60606; (312) 609-8880; Thomas More Assn.

Paulist, Today, q; 415 W. 59th St., New York, NY 10019; (212) 265-3209; www.paulist.org.

Peace Times, 3-4 times a year; P.O. Box 248, Bellevue, WA 98009-0248; (425) 451-1770.

Pentecost Today, q; P.O. Box 628, Locust Grove, VA 22508-0628; (540) 972-0628; www.nsc-chariscenter.org.

Perspectives, q; 912 Market St., La Crosse, WI 54601; (608) 791-5289; www.fspa.org.

Pilgrim, The, q; 136 Shrine Rd., Auriesville, NY 12016; (518) 853-3033; Shrine of North American Martyrs.

Poverello, q; 220 37th St., Pittsburgh, PA 15201; (412) 682-1300; www.capuchin.com; Capuchin Franciscans.

Priests for Life, bm; P.O. Box 141172, Staten Island, NY 10314; (718) 980-4400; www.priestsforlife.org.

Proclaim, 10 times a year; 3211 Fourth St. NE, Washington, DC 20017-1194; (202) 541-3237; www.usccb.org.

Quarterly, The, q; 209 W. Fayette St., Baltimore, MD 21201; (410) 951-7455; www.catholicrelief.org; Catholic Relief Services.

Religious Life, m (bm, May-Aug.); P.O. Box 41007, Chicago, IL 60641; (312) 267-1195; www.ewtn.com/religious life; Institute on Religious Life.

RSCJ Newsletter, m; 1235 Otis St. NE, Washington, DC 20017-2516; (202) 526-6258; www.rscj.org; Religious of Sacred Heart.

St. Anthony's Newsletter, m; 103 St. Francis Blvd., Mt. St. Francis, IN 47146; (812) 923-5250; Conventual Franciscans.

St. Joseph's Parish Life Quarterly, q; 1382 Highland Ave., Needham, MA 02192; (617) 444-0245.

Sacred Ground, three times a year; 1 Elmwood Ave., Kansas City, KS 66103-3719; (913) 384-6500; www.cfcusa.org; Christian Foundation for Children and Aging.

San Francisco Charismatics, m; 2555 17th Ave., San Francisco, CA 94116; (415) 664-8481; www.sfspirit.com.

SCJ News, 9 times a year; P.O. Box 289, Hales Corners, WI 53130-0289; (414) 427-4266; Sacred Heart Fathers and Brothers.

SCRC Spirit, The, bm; 9795 Cabrini Dr., #105, Burbank, CA, 91504-1739; (818) 771-1361; www.scrc.org.

Spirit & The Bride, The, m; 8300 Morganford Rd., St. Louis, MO 63123; (314) 792-7070; www.stlcharis-matic.org.

Spiritual Book Associates, 8 times a year; Notre Dame, IN 46556-0428; (219) 287-2838; www.spiritu-albookassoc.org.

Squires Newsletter, m; One Columbus Plaza, New Haven, CT 06510-3326; (203) 752-4402; Columbian Squires.

SSpS Mission, q; P.O. Box 6026, Techny, IL 60082-6026; (847) 441-0126; Holy Spirit Missionary Sisters.

Tidings, Washington Theological Union, 3 times a year; 6896 Laurel St. NW, Washington, DC 20012; (202) 726-8800; www.wtu.edu.

Touchstone, q; NFPC Office, 1337 W. Ohio St., Chicago, IL 60622; (312) 226-3334; www.nfpc.org; National Federation of Priests' Councils.

Trinity Missions Report, q; 9001 New Hampshire Ave., Silver Spring, MD 20903; (301) 434-6761.

Triumph of the Past, m.; P.O. Box 29535, Columbus, OH 43229; (614) 261-1300.

Unda USA Newsletter, q; 901 Irving Ave., Dayton, OH 45409-2316; (937) 229-2303; www.undausa.org.

Vision: National Association of Catholic Chaplains, 10 times a year; P.O. Box 070473, Milwaukee, WI 53207-0473; (414) 483-4898; www.nacc.org.

Voices, 2 times a year; 1625 Rutherford Ln., Bldg. D, Austin, TX 78754-5105; (512) 339-7123; Volunteers for Educational and Social Services.

Voices in Mission and Ministry, q.; 1257 E. Siena Heights Dr., Adrian, MI 49221; (517) 266-3400; www.adriansisters.org; Adrian Dominicans.

Woodstock Report, q; Georgetown University, Box 571137, Washington, DC 20057; (202) 687-3532; www.georgetown.edu/centers/woodstock; Woodstock Theological Center.

Word One, 5 times a year; 205 W. Monroe St., Chicago, IL 60606; (312) 236-7782; www.wordone.org; Claretians.

Xaverian Missions Newsletter, bm; 101 Summer St., P.O. Box 5857, Holliston, MA 01746; (508) 429-2144; Xaverian Missionary Fathers.

Your Edmundite Missions Newsletter, bm; 1428 Broad St., Selma, AL 36701; (334) 872-2359; www.edmunditemissions.com; Southern Missions of Society of St. Edmund.

Youth Update, m; 28 W. Liberty St., Cincinnati, OH 45210; (513) 241-5615; www.americancatholic.org.

Zeal Newsletter, 3 times a year; P.O. Box 86, Allegany, NY 14706; (716) 373-1130; Franciscan Sisters of Allegany.

BOOKS

The Catholic Almanac, a; Our Sunday Visitor, Inc., 200 Noll Plaza, Huntington, IN 46750, editorial offices, 2017 Scenic Sunrise Dr., Las Vegas, NV 89117; (702) 254-2678; www.osv.com; first edition, 1904.

The Official Catholic Directory, a; P.J. Kenedy & Sons in association with R.R. Bowker, a Reed Reference Publishing Company, 121 Chanlon Rd., New Providence, NJ 07974; (847) 966-8278; first edition, 1817.

BOOK CLUBS

Catholic Book Club (1928), 106 W. 56th St., New York, NY 10019; (212) 581-4640; www.america-press.org/cbc.htm; sponsors the Campion Award.

Catholic Digest Book Club (1954), 2115 Summit Ave., St. Paul, MN 55105-1081; (651) 962-6748.

Spiritual Book Associates (1934), Ave Maria Press Building, P.O. Box 428, Notre Dame, IN 46556; (219) 287-2838.

Thomas More Book Club (1939), Thomas More Association, 205 W. Monroe St., Sixth Floor, Chicago, IL 60606; (312) 609-8880.

General Publishers

(*Source:* Catholic Press Directory, Almanac *Survey.*)

Our Sunday Visitor Publishing: 200 Noll Plaza, Huntington IN 46750; (800) 348-2440, (260) 356-8400; e-mail: booksed@osv.com.

Abbey Press: One Caring Place, Saint Meinrad, IN 47577; (812) 357-8215; www.carenotes.com.

Abingdon Press: 201 8th Ave. South, Nashville, TN 37202; (615) 749-6347; www.abingdonpress.com.

ACTA Publications: 4848 N. Clark St., Chicago, IL 60640; (773) 271-1030; www.actapublications.com.

Alba House/St. Pauls: 2187 Victory Blvd., Staten Island, NY 10314; (718) 698-2759; www.alba-house.com

Alleluia Press: P.O. Box 103, Allendale, NJ 07401; (201) 327-3513.

American Catholic Press: 16565 South State St., South Holland, IL 60473; (708) 331-5485; www.acpress.org.

AMI Press, The Blue Army of Our Lady of Fatima: Mountain View Rd., Washington, NJ 07882; (908) 213-2223.

Ave Maria Press, Inc.: PO Box 428, Notre Dame IN 46556; (800) 282-1865, (219) 287-2831; e-mail: avemariapress.1@nd.edu.

Angelus Press: 2915 Forest Ave., Kansas City, MO 64109; (816) 753-3150; www.angeluspress.org.

Ave Maria Press: P.O. Box 428, Notre Dame, IN 46556; (219) 287-2831.

Cathedral Foundation Press: P.O. Box 777, Baltimore, MD 21203; (443) 263-0248; www.catholicfoundation.org.

Catholic News Service: 3211 Fourth St. NE, Washington DC 20017; (202) 541-3250; www.catholicnews.com.

Catholic Relief Services: 209 West Fayette St., Baltimore, MD 21201; (410) 625-2220.

Catholic University of America Press: 620 Michigan Ave. NE, Washington, DC 20064; (202) 319-5052; www.cuapress.cua.edu.

The Christophers: 12 East 48th St., New York, NY 10017; (212) 759-4050; www.christophers.org.

Claretian Publications: 205 West Monroe St., Chicago, IL 60606; (800) 328-6515, (312) 236-7782; e-mail: editors@uscatholic.org.

Clarity Publishing, Inc.: PO Box 758, Latham, NY 12110-3510; (518) 783-0058.

Doubleday: 1540 Broadway, New York, NY 10036; (212) 782-9392; www.randomhouse.com.

Eerdmans: 255 Jefferson Ave. SE, Grand Rapids, MI 49503; (616) 459-4591; www.eerdmans.com.

Emmaus Road: 827 N. Fourth St., Steubenville, OH 43952; (740) 283-2880.

Franciscan Mission Associates: PO Box 598, Mount Vernon, NY 10551-0598; (914) 664-5604.

Franciscan Press: Quincy University, 1800 College Ave., Quincy, IL 62301; (217) 228-5670; www.qufranciscanpress.com.

Georgetown University Press: 3240 Prospect St.,

NW, Washington, DC 20007; (202) 687-5889; www.press.georgetown.edu.

Ignatius Press: 2515 McAllister St., San Francisco, CA 94118; (415) 387-2324; www.ignatius.com.

Liguori Publications: One Liguori Dr., Liguori, MO 63057; (636) 464-2500.

Liturgical Press: St. John's Abbey, P.O. Box 7500, Collegeville, MN 56321; (320) 363-2213; www.litpress.org.

Loyola Press: 3441 North Ashland Avenue, Chicago, IL 60657; (800) 621-1008; www.loyolapress.org.

Marquette University Press: 1415 West Wisconisn Ave., Milwaukee, WI 53233; (414) 288-1564; www.marquette.edu/mupress/.

Missionary Oblates of Mary Immaculate: 9480 North De Mazenod Dr., Belleville, IL 62223-1160; (888) 330-6264; e-mail: mami@oblatesusa.org.

National Catholic Bioethics Center (NCBC): 159 Washington St., Boston, MA 02135; (617) 787-1900; e-mail: ChadM@ncbcenter.org.

Notre Dame Press, University of: 310 Flanner Hall, Notre Dame, IN 46556; (219) 631-6346; www.undpress.edu.

Orbis Books: P.O. Box 308, Maryknoll, NY 10545; (914) 941-7636; www.orbisbooks.com.

Pauline Books & Media: 50 St. Paul's Ave., Boston, MA 02130; (617) 522-8911; www.pauline.org.

Paulist National Catholic Evangelization Association: 3031 Fourth St. NE, Washington, DC 20017; (800) 237-5515, (202) 832-5022; e-mail: pncea@pncea.org.

Paulist Press: 997 Macarthur Blvd., Mahwah, NJ 07430; (201) 825-7300; www.paulistpress.com.

Pittsburgh Press, University of: 3400 Forbes Ave., 5th Floor Eureka, Pittsburgh, PA 15260; (412) 383-2456; www.pitt.edu/~press.

Pontifical Mission Societies in the United States: 366 Fifth Ave., New York, NY 10001; (800) 431-2222, (212) 563-8700; e-mail: propfaith@aol.com.

St. Anthony Messenger Press: 28 W Liberty St, Cincinnati, OH 45210; (513) 241-5615; www.americancatholic.org.

St. Joseph's University Press: 5600 City Ave., Philadelphia, PA 19131; (610) 660-3400; www.sju.edu/sjupress.

Scepter: P.O. Box 211, New York, NY 10018; (212) 354-0670; www.scepterpublishers.org.

Servant Publications: 1143 Highland Dr., Suite E, Ann Arbor, MI 48108; (734) 677-6490; www.servantpub.com.

Sophia Institute Press: Box 5284, Manchester, NH 03108; (603) 641-9344; www.sophiainstitute.com.

Twenty-Third Publications: P.O. Box 180, Mystic, CT 06355; (860) 437-3012; www.twentythirdpublications.com.

CANADIAN CATHOLIC PUBLICATIONS

(*Principal source:* 2006 Catholic Press Directory.)

Newspapers

Atlantic Catholic, The, bw; 88 College St., Antigonish, NS B2G 2L7; (902) 863-4370.

B. C. Catholic, The, w; 150 Robson St., Vancouver, BC V6B 2A7; (604) 683-0281; www.bcc.rcav.org.

Casket, The, w; 88 College St., Antigonish, NS B2G 2L7; (902) 863-4370.

Catholic New Times (national), bw; 80 Sackville St., Toronto, ON M5A 3E5; (416) 361-0761; www.catholicnewtimes.org.

Catholic Register, The (national), w; 1155 Younge St., Suite 401, Toronto, ON M4T 1W2; (416) 934-3410; www.catholicregister.org; lay edited.

Catholic Times, 10 times a year; 2005 St. Marc St., Montreal, QC H3H 2G8; (514) 937-2301.

Monitor, The, m; P.O. Box 986, St. John's, NF A1C 5M3; (709) 739-6553; www.stjohnsarchdiocese.nf.ca.

New Freeman, The, w; 1 Bayard Dr., St. John, NB E2L 3L5; (506) 653-6806.

Northwest Ontario Catholic, eight times a year, P.O. Box 10400, Thunder Bay, Ontario P7B 6T8; (807) 343-9313; www.dotb.ca.

Prairie Messenger, w; Box 190, Muenster, SK S0K 2Y0; (306) 682-1772; www.stpeters.sk.ca/prairie_messenger.

Restoration, 10 times a year; 2888 Dafoe Rd., Combemere, ON K0J 1L0; (613) 756-3713; www.madonnahouse.org.

St. Vladimir's College Gazette, q; Box 789, Roblin, MB, R0L 1P0; (204) 937-2173.

Teviskes Ziburiai (The Lights of the Homeland) (Lithuanian), w; 2185 Stavebank Rd., Mississauga, ON L5C 1T3; (905) 275-4672.

Western Catholic Reporter, w.; 8421 101 Ave. NW, Edmonton, AB T6A 0L1; (780) 465-8030; www.wcr.ab.ca.

Magazines, Other Periodicals

L'Almanach Populaire Catholique, a; P.O. Box 1000, St. Anne de Beaupre, QC G0A3C0; (418) 827-4538.

ANNALS of St. Anne de Beaupre, The, m; Box 1000, Ste. Anne de Beaupre, QC G0A 3C0; (418) 827-4538; Basilica of St. Anne.

Apostolat, bm; 8844 Notre-Dame Est, Montréal, QC H1L 3M4; (514) 351-9310; Oblates of Mary Immaculate, CMO (Centre Missionnaire Oblat).

Bread of Life, The, bm; P.O. Box 395, Hamilton, ON L8N 3H8; (905) 529-4496; www.breadoflife.ca.

Canadian Catholic Review, The, St. Joseph's College, University of Alberta, Edmonton, AB T6G 2J5; (403) 492-7681.

Canadian League, The, q; 1-160 Murray Park Rd., Winnipeg, MB R3J 3X5; (204) 927-2310; www.cwl.ca; Catholic Women's League of Canada.

Caravan, q; 90 Parent Ave., Ottawa, ON K1N 7B1; (613) 241-9461; www.cccb.ca; Canadian Conference of Catholic Bishops.

Celebrate! (Novalis), bm; St. Paul University, 223 Main St., Ottawa, ON K1S 1C4; (780) 451-2228.

Companion Magazine, m; 695 Coxwell Ave., Suite 600, Toronto, ON M4C 5R6; (416) 690-5611; www.franciscan.on.ca; Conventual Franciscan Fathers.

Compass — A Jesuit Journal, bm (Jan.-Nov.); Box 400, Stn. F, 50 Charles St. East, Toronto, ON M4Y 2L8; (416) 921-0653; www.io.org/ngvanv/compass/com-phome.html.

CRC Bulletin (French-English), q; 219 Argyle Ave., Ottawa, ON K2P 2H4; (613) 236-0824; www.crcn.ca; Canadian Religious Conference.

L'Église Canadienne (French), 11 times a year; 6255 rue Hutchison, Bureau 103, Montreal, QC H2V 4C7; (514) 278-3020; www.novalis.ca.

Fatima Crusader, q; P.O. Box 602, Fort Erie, ON L2A 4M7; (905) 871-7607; www.fatima.org.

Global Village Voice, The, q; 10 St. Mary St., Suite 420, Toronto, ON M4Y 1P9; (416) 922-1592; Canadian Organization for Development and Peace.

Kateri (English-French), q; P.O. Box 70, Kahnawake, QC J0L 1B0; (450) 638-1546.

Le Messager de Saint Antoine (French), 10 times a year; Lac-Bouchette, QC G0W 1V0; (418) 348-6344.

Messenger of the Sacred Heart, m; 661 Greenwood Ave., Toronto, ON M4J 4B3; (416) 466-1195; Apostleship of Prayer.

Mission Canada, q; 201-1155 Younge St., Toronto, ON M4T 1W2; (416) 934-3424; www.missioncanada.ca.

Missions Étrangères (French), bm; 180 Place Juge-Desnoyers, Laval, QC H7G 1A4; (450) 667-4190; www.smelaval.org.

Nouvel Informateur Catholiqué, Le, semi-monthly; 6550 Rte 125, Rawdon, QC J0K 1S0; (450) 834-8503.

Oratory, bm; 3800 Ch. Queen Mary, Montreal, QC H3V 1H6; (514) 733-8211; www.saint-joseph.org.

Our Family, m; P.O. Box 249, Battleford, SK; S0M 0E0; (306) 937-7771; www.ourfamilymagazine.com; Oblates of Mary Immaculate.

Prêtre et Pasteur (French), m; 4450 St. Hubert St., #500, Montreal, QC H2J 2W9; (514) 525-6210.

Prieres Missionaires, m; Missionaires de la Consolata, 2505 Boulevard Gouin ouest, Montréal, QC H3M 1B5; (514) 334-1910; www.consolata.org.

Relations (French), 10 times a year; 25 Rue Jarry Ouest, Montreal, QC H2P 1S6; (514) 387-2541.

Reveil Missionaire, bm; Missionaire de la Consolata, 2505 Boulevard Gouin ouest, Montréal, QC H3M 1B5; (514) 334-1910; www.consolata.org.

La Revue d'Sainte Anne de Beaupre (French), m; P.O. Box 1000, Ste. Anne de Beaupre, Québec G0A 3C0; (418) 827-4538.

Scarboro Missions, 9 times a year; 2685 Kingston Rd., Scarboro, ON M1M 1M4; (416) 261-7135; www.web.net/~sfms.

Spiritan Missionary News, q; 121 Victoria Park Ave., Toronto, ON M4E 3S2; (416) 698-2003; www.spiritans.com.

Unity, q; 308 Young St., Montréal, QC H3C 2G2; (514) 937-5973.

INTERNATIONAL CATHOLIC PERIODICALS

(Principal source: Catholic Almanac survey. Included are English-language Catholic periodicals published outside the U.S.)

African Ecclesial Review (AFER), bm; Gaba Publications, P.O. Box 4002, Eldoret, Kenya.

Australasian Catholic Record, q; 99 Albert Rd., Strathfield 2135, New South Wales, Australia.

Christ to the World, 5 times a year; Via di Propaganda 1-C, 00187, Rome, Italy.

Christian Orient, q; P.B. 1 Vadavathoor, Kottayam 686010, Kerala, India.

Doctrine and Life, m; Dominican Publications, 42 Parnell Sq., Dublin 1, Ireland.

Downside Review, q; Downside Abbey, Stratton on the Fosse, Bath, BA3 4RH, England.

East Asian Pastoral Review, q; East Asian Pastoral Institute, P.O. Box 221, U.P. Campus, 1101 Quezon City, Philippines.

Furrow, The, m; St. Patrick's College, Maynooth, Ireland.

Heythrop Journal, q; Heythrop College,

Kensington Sq., London W8 5HQ, England (editorial office); published by Blackwell Publishers, 108 Cowley Rd., Oxford, OX4 1JF, England.

Holy Land Magazine, q; P.O. Box 186, 91001 Jerusalem, Israel; illustrated.

Irish Biblical Studies, The, q; Union Theological College, 108 Botanic Ave., Belfast BT7 1JT, N. Ireland.

Irish Journal of Sociology, The, a; St. Patrick's College, Maynooth, Ireland.

Irish Theological Quarterly, q; St. Patrick's College, Maynooth, Ireland.

L'Osservatore Romano, w; Vatican City. (See above under U.S. Newspapers.)

Louvain Studies, q; Peeters Publishers, Bondgenotenlaan 153, B-3000, Leuven, Belgium.

Lumen Vitae (French, with English summaries), q; International Center for Studies in Religious Education, 186, rue Washington, B-1050 Brussels, Belgium.

Mediaeval Studies, a; Pontifical Institute of Mediaeval Studies, 59 Queen's Park Crescent East, Toronto, ON M5S 2C4, Canada.

Month, m; 114 Mount St., London WIY 6AH, England.

Music and Liturgy, bm; The Editor, 33 Brockenhurst Rd., Addiscombe Croydan, Surrey CRO 7DR, England.

New Blackfriars, m; edited by English Dominicans, Blackfriars, Oxford OX1 3LY, England.

Omnis Terra (English Edition), m; Pontifical Missionary Union, Congregation for the Evangelization of Peoples, Via di Propaganda 1/c, 00187 Rome, Italy.

One in Christ, q; Edited at Turvey Abbey, Turvey, Bedfordshire MK43 8DE, England.

Priests & People (formerly The Clergy Review), 11 times a year; Blackfriars, Buckingham Rd., Cambridge CB3 0DD, England.

Recusant History, bi-annual; Catholic Record Society, 12 Melbourne Pl., Wolsingham, Durham DL13 3EH, England.

Religious Life Review, bm; Dominican Publications, 42 Parnell Sq., Dublin 1, Ireland.

Scripture in Church, q; Dominican Publications, 42 Parnell Sq., Dublin 1, Ireland.

Southwark Liturgy Bulletin, q; The Editor, 10 Claremont Rd., Maidstone, Kent ME14 5L2, England.

Spearhead, 5 times a year; Gaba Publications, P.O. Box 4002, Eldoret, Kenya.

Spirituality, bm; Dominican Publications, 42 Parnell Sq., Dublin 1, Ireland.

Tablet, The, w; 1 King St. Cloisters, Clifton Walk, London W60QZ, England; 44(1)-20-8748-8484.

Way, The, q; 114 Mount St., London W1Y6AN, England.

CATHOLIC NEWS AGENCIES

(Sources: International Catholic Union of the Press, Geneva; Catholic Press Association, U.S.)

Argentina: Agencia Informativa Catolica Argentina (AICA), av. Rivadavia, 413, 40 Casilla de Correo Central 2886, 1020 Buenos Aires.

Austria: Katholische Presse-Agentur (Kathpress), Singerstrasse 7/6/2, 1010 Vienna 1.

Belgium: Centre d'Information de Presse (CIP), 35

Chausée de Haecht, 1030 Brussels.

Bolivia: Agencia Noticias Fides, ANF, Casilla 5782, La Paz.

ERBOL, Casilla 5946, La Paz.

Chile: Agencia informativa y de comunicaciones (AIC Chile), Brasil 94, Santiago.

Croatia: Christian Information Service, Marulicev 14, PP 434, 410001 Zagreb.

Germany: Katholische Nachrichten Agentur (KNA), Adenauer Allee 134, 5300 Bonn 1.

Greece: Agence TYPOS, Rue Acharnon 246, Athens 815.

Hong Kong: UCA-News, P.O. Box 69626, Kwun Tong (Hong Kong).

Hungary: Magyar Kurir, Milkszath ter 1, 1088, Budapest.

India: South Asian Religious News (SAR-News), PB 6236, Mazagaon, Bombay 400 010.

Italy: Servizio Informazioni Religiosa (SIR), Via di Porta Cavalleggeri 143, I-00165 Roma.

Centrum Informationis Catolicae (CIC-Roma), via Delmonte de la Farina, 30/4, 00186 Roma.

Peru: ACI-PRENSA, A.P. 040062, Lima.

Switzerland: Katholische Internationale Presse-Agentur (KIPA), Case Postale 1054 CH 1701, Fribourg.

Centre International de Reportages et d'Information Culturelle (CIRIC), Chemin Clochetons 8, P.O. Box 1000, Lausanne.

United States of America: Catholic News Service (CNS), 3211 Fourth St. NE, Washington, DC 20017; (202) 541-3250; www.catholicnews.com.

U.S. PRESS SERVICES

Catholic News Service (CNS), established in 1920 (NC News Service), provides a worldwide daily news report by satellite throughout the U.S. and Canada and by wire and computer links into several foreign countries, and by mail to other clients, serving Catholic periodicals and broadcasters including Vatican Radio in about 40 countries. CNS also provides feature and photo services and a weekly religious education package, "Faith Alive!" It publishes "Origins," a weekly documentary service, and Catholic Trends, a fortnightly newsletter, the weekly TV and Movie Guide and Movie Guide Monthly. CNS maintains a full-time bureau in Rome. It is a division of the United States Catholic Conference, with offices at 3211 Fourth St. NE, Washington, DC 20017; (202) 541-3250; www.catholicnews.com.

EWTNews, 5817 Old Leeds Rd., Irondale, AL 35210; 205-271-2900; www.ewtn.com. Exclusive interviews, investigative reports, live coverage of special events and cultural reporting weekly on the World Over Live newsmagazine. Daily coverage of world news from a Catholic perspective.

Spanish-Language Service: A weekly news summary provided by Catholic News Service, used by a number of Catholic newspapers. Some papers carry features of their own in Spanish.

Religion News Service (RNS) provides coverage of all religions as well as ethics, spirituality and moral issues. Founded in 1934 (as the Religious News Service) by the National Conference of Christian and Jews as an independent agency, RNS became an editorially independent subsidiary of the United Methodist

Reporter, an interfaith publishing company, in 1983. It was acquired by Newhouse News Service in 1994.

RADIO, TELEVISION, THEATER

(The following listings are as of June 1, 2006. Sources, Catholic Almanac survey, William Ryan, Communications, USCCB. Telephone and web addresses are listed as available.)

Radio

Catholic Radio Association: an association comprised primarily of the majority of Catholic radio stations in the United States and Catholic program providers united to advance the apostolate of Catholic radio. The Mission Statement states: "The Catholic Radio Association seeks to bring together Catholic radio apostolates, program providers and the hierarchy of the Catholic Church in order that this means of social communication be used effectively and in obedience to the decrees of the Second Vatican Council and the magisterium of the Church, especially as expressed in the words of Pope John Paul II." The Catholic Radio Association, 2221 S Webster Ave. #131, Green Bay, WI 54301; (920) 532-0147; www.catholicradioassociation.org.

Catholic Family Radio (Catholic Radio Network): 8910 University Center Lane, Suite 130, San Diego, CA 92122-1016; (619) 784-6900; www.catholicfamilyradio.com. Rapidly expanding network founded by Fr. Joseph Fessio and Nick Healy; launched in 1999.

EWTN Global Catholic Radio Network (formerly known as WEWN), 5817 Old Leeds Rd., Irondale, AL 35210; 205-271-2900; www.ewtn.com. The first 24-hour U.S. Catholic radio network, launched in 1996.

Vatican Radio: *See under* **Vatican City State.**

Programs

Catholic Views Broadcasts, Inc.: 10 Audrey Place, Fairfield, NJ 07004; (973) 882-8700. Produces weekly 15-minute program "Views of the News." Also operates Catholic community TV stations in Chicago and Minneapolis.

Christopher Radio Program: 14-minute interview series, "Christopher Closeup" weekly and "Christopher Minutes" daily, on 400 stations. 12 E. 48th St., New York, NY 10017; (212) 759-4050; www.christophers.org.

Father Justin Rosary Hour (radio): P.O. Box 454, Athol Springs, NY 14010; (716) 627-3861; www.franciszkanie.com/rosary.hour. Founded in 1931. Polish Catechetical Radio Network. Rev. Marion M. Tolczyk, O.F.M. Conv., director.

Journeys Thru Rock (radio): Produced in cooperation with the Department of Communication, USCCB. A 15-minute weekly program currently employing a youth-oriented music and commentary format (ABC).

Radio Maria (Italian): Italian Catholic radio station founded in 1992. 352 W. 44th St., New York, NY 10036. Rev. Mariano Cisco, C.S., executive director.

Television and Communications Services

Catholic Familyland: A ministry of the Apostolate for Family Consecration. Established in 1975, FL-TV produces television and video programs and operates in Asia, Latin America, Europe and Africa. Familyland Television Network, 3375 County Rd. 36,

Address: 1101 Connecticut Ave. NW, Suite 350, Washington, DC 20036.

Bloomingdale, OH 43910; (740) 765-5500; www.familyland.org.

Catholic Academy for Communication Arts Professionals: The U.S. affiliate of SIGNIS, a Vatican-approved organization for Catholic communication professionals; membership is open to those professionally involved in Catholic church-related communications and to Catholic communicators working in secular organizations. President: Frank Morock, Catholic Academy for Communication Arts Professionals, Irving Ave., Dayton, OH 45409-2316; (937) 229-2303; www.catholicacademy.org.

Catholic Communication Campaign (CCC): A U.S. Catholic bishops' program that produces, distributes and supports Catholic media projects, including a weekly television talk show, "Personally Speaking," television documentaries and public service messages. Ellen McCloskey, 3211 4th St. NE, Washington, DC 20017; (202) 541-3204; www.usccb.org/ccc.

Catholic Communications Foundation (CCF): A foundation established by the Catholic Fraternal Benefit Societies in 1966 to lend support and assistance to development of the communications apostolate of the Church. The CCF promotes diocesan communications capabilities and funds a scholarship program at the Annual Institute for Religious Communications. 303 W. Lancaster Ave., PMB 333, Wayne, PA 19087.

Christopher TV Series, "Christopher Closeup": Originated in 1952. Half-hour interviews, weekly, on commercial TV and numerous cable outlets. 12 E. 48th St., New York, NY 10017; (212) 759-4050; www.christophers.org.

Clemons Productions, Inc.: Produces "That's the Spirit," a family show for television; "Thoughts for the Week," on the ABC Satellite Network, and "Spirituality for Today" on the internet. Available to dioceses, organizations or channels. P.O. Box 7466, Greenwich, CT 06830; www.spirituality.org.

EWTN Global Catholic Network (EWTN): 5817 Old Leeds Rd., Irondale, AL 35210; 205-271-2900; www.ewtn.com. America's largest religious cable network, features 24 hours of spiritual growth programming for the entire family. Offers documentaries, weekly teaching series and talk shows, including the award-winning "Mother Angelica Live." Nightly live programs include "The Journey Home," "Threshold of Hope," "EWTN Live," "Life on the Rock" and "The World Over." Daily live radio programming includes the popular call-in shows, Open Line. Also features live Church events from around the world and devotional programs such as "The Holy Rosary." Mother M. Angelica, P.C.P.A., Foundress.

Family Theater Productions: Founded by Father Peyton. Videocassettes, films for TV. 7201 Sunset Blvd., Hollywood, CA 90046; (323) 874-6633; www.familytheater.org. Nat. Dir., Rev. Wilfred J. Raymond, C.S.C.

Franciscan Communications: Producer of video and print resources for pastoral ministry; St. Anthony Messenger Press, 28 W. Liberty St., Cincinnati, OH

45210; (513) 241-5615; www.AmericanCatholic.org.

Hispanic Telecommunications Network, Inc. (HTN): Produces "Nuestra Familia," a national weekly Spanish-language TV series; 1405 N. Main, Suite 240, San Antonio, TX 78212.

Mary Productions: Originated in 1950. Offers royalty-free scripts for stage, film, radio and tape production. Audio and video tapes of lives of the saints and historical characters. Traveling theater company; Mary Productions, 212 Oakdale Dr., Tomaso Plaza, Middletown, NJ 07748; (732) 617-8144.

National Interfaith Cable Coalition: A 28-member consortium representing 64 faith groups from Roman Catholic, Jewish, Protestant and Eastern Orthodox traditions; works with faith groups to present programming on the Faith and Values Media; 74 Trinity Place, Suite 1550, New York, NY 10006; (212) 406-4121; www.faithandvalues.com.

Oblate Media and Communication Corporation: Producers, Broadcast syndicators and distributors of Catholic and value-centered video programming. 7315 Manchester Rd., St. Louis, MO 63143.

Passionist Communications, Inc.: Presents Sunday Mass on TV seen in U.S. and available to dioceses and channels; publishes "TV Prayer Guide," semi-annually. P.O. Box 440, Pelham, NY 10803-0440.

Paulist Media Works: Full service audio production in syndication to dioceses, religious communities and church groups; 3055 4th St. NE, Washington, DC 20017; (202) 269-6064. Pres., Sue Donovan.

Paulist Productions: Producers and distributors of the INSIGHT Film Series (available for TV) and educational film series. 17575 Pacific Coast Hwy., Pacific Palisades, CA 90272; (310) 454-0688; www.paulist-productions.org.

Sacred Heart Program, Inc.: Produces and distributes free of charge the weekly "CONTACT" program in 30-, 15-, and 5-minute formats to more than 300 stations in North America; 3900 Westminster Pl., St. Louis, MO 63108; (341) 533-0320; www.sacredheart-program.org/www.contactradio.org. Exec. Dir., Gary Kolarcik.

SIGNIS (World Catholic Association for Communication): A Vatican approved non-governmental organization that includes members from 140 countries and brings together radio, television, cinema, video, media education, Internet, and new technology professionals. SIGNIS was established in November 2001 from the merger between Unda (for radio and television) and OCIC (for cinema and audiovisual); both had been created in 1928. Its varied initiatives cover fields such as the promotion of films or television programs (including juries at festivals such as Cannes, Berlin, Monte Carlo, Venice, etc.), the creation of radio, video, and television studios, production and distribution of programs, training professionals in the field, and supplying specialized equipment. General Secretariat, 15, rue du Saphir, 1030 Brussels, Belgium; 00 32 (0)2 7349708; www.signis.net/.

Telecare: non-profit, state-of-the-art television and production facility of the Diocese of Rockville Centre. Broadcasts seven days a week to almost a million homes served by Cablevision, Telecare works through a partnership with WLNY/Channel 55. Programming includes the popular God Squad program that reaches 12 million viewers in New York, New Jersey and Connecticut every weekday. Rev. Msgr. Thomas Hartman, Director. 1200 Glen Curtiss Blvd., Uniondale, 11553; (516) 538-4108; www.telecaretv.org.

Theater

Catholic Actors' Guild of America, Inc.: Established in 1914 to provide material and spiritual assistance to people in the theater. Has more than 500 members; publishes The Call Board. 1501 Broadway, Suite 510, New York, NY 10036; (212) 398-1868 (fax).

FILM

Best Films of 2005

(Courtesy, U.S. Bishops' Office of Film and Broadcasting, OFB). The U.S. Bishops' Office of Film and Broadcasting (OFB) announced its 2005 Ten Best Films List. The following are the best films, in alphabetical order: "The Chronicles of Narnia: The Lion, the Witch and the Wardrobe"; "Cinderella Man"; "Crash"; "Dear; Frankie; The Greatest Game Ever Played"; "Millions"; "The Ninth Day"; "North Country"; "An Unfinished Life"; "The Upside of Anger."

Honorable Mentions: "Cache"; "The Constant Gardener"; "Daltry Calhoun"; "Good Night, and Good Luck"; "The History of Violence"; "Innocent Voices" ("Voces Inocentes"); "Keane"; "Look at Me"; "Mrs. Palfrey at the Claremont"; "Nine Lives"; "Paradise Now"; "The Prize Winner of Defiance, Ohio"; "Proof"; "Rory O'Shea Was Here"; "Saint Ralph"; "Turtles Can Fly"; "Up and Down"; "Walk the Line"; "The White Countess."

The top 10 best family films of 2005, in alphabetical order: "Because of Winn-Dixie"; "Dreamer: Inspired by a True Story"; "Duma"; "Howl's Moving Castle"; "Little Manhattan"; "March of the Penguins"; "Oliver Twist"; "Pride & Prejudice"; "Wallace & Gromit": "The Curse of the Were-Rabbit"; "Zathura: A Space Adventure."

Honorable Mention: "Tim Burton's Corpse Bride"; "Charlie and the Chocolate Factory"; "Madison."

The Office for Film and Broadcasting (OFB) has the responsibility of reviewing and rating theatrical motion pictures, previewing and evaluating television programming, and providing the Catholic public with information about the role of the entertainment and news media in influencing societal and personal values. The Office is supported by the U.S. Bishops' Catholic Communication Campaign (CCC). Weekly movie reviews, brief capsules, and film classifications of new film releases can be heard on the office's toll-free movieline at 1-800-311-4222, sponsored by the CCC. Movie reviews are available online at www.usccb.org/movies.

Vatican List of the Greatest Films of the 20th Century

On the occasion of the 100th anniversary of cinema in 1995, the Vatican compiled this list of "great films." The 45 movies are divided into three categories:

"Religion," "Values," and "Art."

Religion
"Andrei Rublev" (1969); "Babette's Feast" (1988); "Ben-Hur" (1959); "The Flowers of St. Francis" (1950); "Francesco" (1989); "The Gospel According to St. Matthew" (1966); "La Passion de Notre Seigneur Jesus-Christ" (1905); "A Man for All Seasons" (1966); "The Mission" (1986); "Monsieur Vincent" (1947); "Nazarin" (1958); "Ordet" (1954); "The Passion of Joan of Arc" (1928); "The Sacrifice" (1986); "Thérèse" (1986).

Values
"Au Revoir les Enfants" (1988); "The Bicycle Thief" (1949); "The Burmese Harp" (1956); "Chariots of Fire" (1981); "Decalogue" (1988); "Dersu Uzala" (1978); "Gandhi" (1982); "Intolerance" (1916); "It's a Wonderful Life" (1946); "On the Waterfront" (1954); "Open City" (1945); "Schindler's List" (1993); "The Seventh Seal" (1956); "The Tree of Wooden Clogs" (1978); "Wild Strawberries" (1958).

Art
"Citizen Kane" (1941); "8-1/2" (1963); "Fantasia" (1940); "Grand Illusion" (1937); "La Strada" (1956); "The Lavender Hill Mob" (1951); "The Leopard" (1963); "Little Women" (1933); "Metropolis" (1926); "Modern Times" (1936); "Napoleon" (1927); "Nosferatu" (1922); "Stagecoach" (1939); "2001: A Space Odyssey" (1968); "The Wizard of Oz" (1939).

CATHOLIC INTERNET SITES

Web site addresses change periodically. Find this list online at www.CatholicAlmanac.com. Visit Our Sunday Visitor's web site at www.osv.com.

Holy See Sites
Vatican: www.vatican.va
L'Osservatore Romano: www.vatican.va/news_services/or/or_eng/index.html
Vatican Radio: www.vatican.va/news_services/radio

Catholic Megasites, Directories and Links
Catholic Almanac: www.CatholicAlmanac.com
Catholic Canada: www.catholicanada.com
Catholic Community Forum: www:catholic-forum.com
Catholic Goldmine!: www.catholicgoldmine.com
Catholic Hotlinks: www.cathinsight.com
Catholic Information Center on the Internet: www.catholic.net
Catholic Information Network: www.cin.org
Catholic Internet Directory: www.catholic-church.org
Catholic Internet Yellow Pages: www.monksofadoration.org/directory.html
Catholic Kiosk: www.aquinas-multimedia.com/arch
Catholic.Net Periodicals: www.catholic.net/RCC/Periodicals
Catholic Pages: www.catholic-pages.com
Catholic Press Association: www.catholicpress.org
Catholicity Internet Directory: www.catholicity.com
Catholic Exchange: www.catholicexchange.com
Ecclesia Web Service for Catholics: www.catholic-church.org
El Directorio Catolico en Internet: www.iglesia.org
New Advent: www.newadvent.org
Our Sunday Visitor: www.OSV.com
PetersNet: www.catholicculture.org
RCNet: www.rc.net
St. Jane's: www.stjane.org
The Internet Padre: www.internetpadre.com
Theology Library Search Engines: www.shc.edu/theolibrary/engines.htm

Catholic Internet Service Providers
Catholic Families Network: www.catholicfamilies.net
Catholic Online: www.catholiconline.com
FamiLink (ISP for the family): www.familink.com

Catholic Movements and Organizations
Adoremus: www.adoremus.org
Catholic Charismatic Center: www.garg.com/ccc
Catholic Doctrinal Concordance: www.infpage.com/concordance
Catholic Family and Human Rights Institute: www.c-fam.org
Catholic Health Association USA: www.chausa.org
Catholic League: www.catholicleague.org
Focolare Movement: www.rc.net/focolare
Madonna House: www.madonnahouse.org
Nat'l Bioethics Center: www.ncbcenter.org
Opus Dei: www.opusdei.org
Pax Christi International: www.paxchristi.net
Pax Christi USA: www.paxchristiusa.org
Saints Alive: www.ichrusa.com/saintsalive
Schoenstatt (information): www.catholiclinks.org/schoenstattunitedstates.htm
Seton Home Study School: www.setonhome.org

Catholic Newspapers and Magazines
Catholic Digest: www.catholicdigest.org
Catholic New York Online: www.cny.org
Catholic Worker: www.catholicworker.org
First Things: www.firstthings.com
Houston Catholic Worker: www.cjd.org
Our Sunday Visitor: www.osv.com
The Tablet, U.K.: www.thetablet.co.uk
The Universe, U.K.: www.totalcatholic.com
The Wanderer: www.thewandererpress.com

Religious Orders and Apostolates
Apostolates/Orders: www.catholic-forum.com/links/pages/Religious_Orders
EWTN: www.ewtn.com
RCNet-Apostolates: www.rc.net/org

Colleges and Universities (Links To)
Colleges: www.shc.edu/theolibrary/edu.htm
Assocation of Catholic Colleges and Universities: www.accunet.org

Useful and Informative Sites
Mass Times: www.masstimes.org
Mass in Transit: www.massintransit.com

Christworld: www.christworld.com
Catholic-Pages: www.catholic-pages.com
PetersVoice: www.petersvoice.com
Rosary Center: www.rosary-center.org
Daily E-pistle (e-newsletter) Signup Page: www.catholic-forum.com/e-pistle.html
Grace In Action Stewardship: www.GraceInAction.org

For Kids and Families
Catholic Kids Net: www.catholickidsnet.org
Global Schoolhouse: www.gsn.org

My Friend: www.myfriendmagazine.com
Teaching Catholic Kids: www.TeachingCatholicKids.com
Apostolate for Family Consecration: www.family-land.org
Catholic Family and Human Rights Institute: www.c-fam.org
Catholic Fathers: www.dads.org
Catholic Parent Magazine: www.CatholicParent.com
Natural Family Planning: www.ccli.org
Domestic Church: www.domestic-church.com

DEVELOPMENTS IN COMMUNICATIONS 2005-06

The following are significant developments or documents in the field of Catholic communications in 2005-06.

MESSAGE OF THE HOLY FATHER FOR THE 40th WORLD COMMUNICATIONS DAY

On Jan. 24, 2006, Pope Benedict XVI issued his 2006 message for the 40th World Communications Day, held May 8. The theme was: "The Media: A Network for Communication, Communion and Cooperation."

Dear Brothers and Sisters,

1. In the wake of the fortieth-anniversary of the closing of the Second Vatican Ecumenical Council, I am happy to recall its Decree on the Means of Social Communication, *Inter Mirifica*, which in particular recognized the power of the media to influence the whole of human society. The need to harness that power for the benefit of all mankind has prompted me, in this my first message for World Communications Day, to reflect briefly on the idea of the media as a network facilitating communication, communion, and cooperation.

St. Paul, in his letter to the Ephesians, vividly depicts our human vocation to be "sharers in the divine nature" (*Dei Verbum*, 2): through Christ we have access in one Spirit to the Father; so we are no longer strangers and aliens but citizens with the saints and members of the household of God, growing into a holy temple, a dwelling place for God (cf. Eph 2:18-22). This sublime portrayal of a life of communion engages all aspects of our lives as Christians. The call to be true to the self-communication of God in Christ is in fact a call to recognize his dynamic force within us, which then seeks to spread outwards to others, so that his love can truly become the prevalent measure of the world (cf. Homily for World Youth Day, Cologne, Aug. 21, 2005).

2. Technological advances in the media have in certain respects conquered time and space, making communication between people, even when separated by vast distances, both instantaneous and direct. This development presents an enormous potential for service of the common good and "constitutes a patrimony to safeguard and promote" (*Rapid Development*, 10). Yet, as we all know, our world is far from perfect. Daily we are reminded that immediacy of communication does not necessarily translate into the building of cooperation and communion in society.

To inform the consciences of individuals and help shape their thinking is never a neutral task. Authentic communication demands principled courage and resolve. It requires a determination of those working in the media not to wilt under the weight of so much information nor even to be content with partial or provisional truths. Instead it necessitates both seeking and transmitting what is the ultimate foundation and meaning of human, personal and social existence (cf. *Fides et Ratio*, 5). In this way the media can contribute constructively to the propagation of all that is good and true.

3. The call for today's media to be responsible - to be the protagonist of truth and promoter of the peace that ensues - carries with it a number of challenges. While the various instruments of social communication facilitate the exchange of information, ideas, and mutual understanding among groups, they are also tainted by ambiguity. Alongside the provision of a "great round table" for dialogue, certain tendencies within the media engender a kind of monoculture that dims creative genius, deflates the subtlety of complex thought and undervalues the specificity of cultural practices and the particularity of religious belief. These are distortions that occur when the media industry becomes self-serving or solely profit-driven, losing the sense of accountability to the common good.

Accurate reporting of events, full explanation of matters of public concern, and fair representation of diverse points of view must, then, always be fostered. The need to uphold and support marriage and family life is of particular importance, precisely because it pertains to the foundation of every culture and society (cf. *Apostolicam Actuositatem*, 11). In cooperation with parents, the social communications and entertainment industries can assist in the difficult but sublimely satisfying vocation of bringing up children, through presenting edifying models of human life and love (cf. *Inter Mirifica*, 11). How disheartening and destructive it is to us all when the opposite occurs. Do not our hearts cry out, most especially, when our young people are subjected to debased or false expressions of love which ridicule the God-given dignity of every human person and undermine family interests?

4. To encourage both a constructive presence and a positive perception of the media in society, I wish to reiterate the importance of three steps, identified by my venerable predecessor Pope John Paul II, necessary for their service of the common good: formation, participation, and dialogue (cf. *Rapid Development*, 11).

Formation in the responsible and critical use of the media helps people to use them intelligently and appropriately. The profound impact upon the mind of new vocabulary and of images, which the electronic media in particular so easily introduce into society, cannot be overestimated. Precisely because contemporary media shape popular culture, they themselves must overcome any temptation to manipulate, especially the young, and instead pursue the desire to form and serve. In this way they protect rather than erode the fabric of a civil society worthy of the human person.

Participation in the mass media arises from their nature as a good destined for all people. As a public service, social communication requires a spirit of cooperation and co-responsibility with vigorous accountability of the use of public resources and the performance of roles of public trust (cf. Ethics in Communications, 20), including recourse to regulatory standards and other measures or structures designed to effect this goal.

Finally, the promotion of dialogue through the exchange of learning, the expression of solidarity and the espousal of peace presents a great opportunity for the mass media which must be recognized and exercised. In this way they become influential and appreciated resources for building the civilization of love for which all peoples yearn.

I am confident that serious efforts to promote these three steps will assist the media to develop soundly as a network of communication, communion and cooperation, helping men, women and children, to become more aware of the dignity of the human person, more responsible, and more open to others especially the neediest and the weakest members of society (cf. Redemptor Hominis, 15; Ethics in Communications, 4).

In conclusion, I return to the encouraging words of St. Paul: Christ is our peace. In him we are one (cf. Eph 2:14). Let us together break down the dividing walls of hostility and build up the communion of love according to the designs of the Creator made known through his Son!

From the Vatican, Jan. 24, 2006,
the Feast of St. Francis de Sales.
BENEDICTUS XVI

PONTIFICAL HONORS AND AWARDS

Pontifical Orders

The Pontifical Orders of Knighthood are secular orders of merit whose membership depends directly on the pope.

Supreme Order of Christ (Militia of Our Lord Jesus Christ): The highest of the five pontifical orders of knighthood, the Supreme Order of Christ was approved Mar. 14, 1319, by John XXII as a continuation in Portugal of the suppressed Order of Templars. Members were religious with vows and a rule of life until the order lost its religious character toward the end of the 15th century. Since that time it has existed as an order of merit. Paul VI, in 1966, restricted awards of the order to Christian heads of state.

Order of the Golden Spur (Golden Militia): Although the original founder is not certainly known, this order is one of the oldest knighthoods. Indiscriminate bestowal and inheritance diminished its prestige, however, and in 1841 Gregory XVI replaced it with the Order of St. Sylvester and gave it the title of Golden Militia. In 1905 St. Pius X restored the Order of the Golden Spur in its own right, separating it from the Order of St. Sylvester. Paul VI, in 1966, restricted awards of the order to Christian heads of state.

Order of Pius IX: Founded by Pius IX June 17, 1847, the order is awarded for outstanding services for the Church and society, and may be given to non-Catholics as well as Catholics. The title to nobility formerly attached to membership was abolished by Pius XII in 1939. In 1957 Pius XII instituted the Class of the Grand Collar as the highest category of the order; in 1966, Paul VI restricted this award to heads of state "in solemn circumstances." The other three classes are of Knights of the Grand Cross, Knight Commanders with and without emblem, and Knights. The new class was created to avoid difficulties in presenting papal honors to Christian or non-Christian leaders of high merit.

Order of St. Gregory the Great: First established by Gregory XVI in 1831 to honor citizens of the Papal States, the order is conferred on persons who are distinguished for personal character and reputation, and for notable accomplishment. The order has civil and military divisions, and three classes of knights.

Order of St. Sylvester: Instituted Oct. 31, 1841, by Gregory XVI to absorb the Order of the Golden Spur, this order was divided into two by St. Pius X in 1905, one retaining the name of St. Sylvester and the other assuming the title of Golden Militia. Membership consists of three degrees: Knights of the Grand Cross, Knight Commanders with and without emblem, and Knights.

Papal Medals

Pro Ecclesia et Pontifice: This decoration ("For the Church and the Pontiff") had its origin in 1888 as a token of the golden sacerdotal jubilee of Leo XIII; he bestowed it on those who had assisted in the observance of his jubilee and on persons responsible for the success of the Vatican Exposition. The medal, cruciform in shape, bears the likenesses of Sts. Peter and Paul, the tiara and the papal keys, the words *Pro Ecclesia et Pontifice*, and the name of the present pontiff, all on the same side; it is attached to a ribbon of yellow and white, the papal colors. Originally, the medal was issued in gold, silver or bronze. It is awarded in recognition of service to the Church and the papacy.

Benemerenti: Several medals ("To a well-deserving person") have been conferred by popes for exceptional accomplishment and service. The medals, which are made of gold, silver or bronze, bear the likeness and name of the reigning pope on one side; on the other, a laurel crown and the letter "B." These two medals may be given by the pope to both men and women. Their bestowal does not convey any title or honor of knighthood.

Ecclesiastical Orders

Equestrian Order of the Holy Sepulchre of Jerusalem: The order traces its origin to Godfrey de Bouillon who instituted it in 1099. It took its name from the Basilica of the Holy Sepulchre where its members were knighted. After the fall of the Latin

Kingdom of Jerusalem and the consequent departure of the knights from the Holy Land, national divisions were established in various countries.

The order was re-organized by Pius IX in 1847 when he reestablished the Latin Patriarchate of Jerusalem and placed the order under the jurisdiction of its patriarch. In 1888, Leo XIII confirmed permission to admit women — Ladies of the Holy Sepulchre — to all degrees of rank. Pius X reserved the office of grand master to himself in 1907; Pius XII gave the order a cardinal patron in 1940 and, in 1949, transferred the office of grand master from the pope to the cardinal patron. Pope John XXIII approved updated constitutions in 1962; the latest statutes were approved by Paul VI in 1977.

The purposes of the order are strictly religious and charitable. Members are committed to sustain and aid the charitable, cultural and social works of the Catholic Church in the Holy Land, particularly in the Latin Patriarchate of Jerusalem.

The order is composed of knights and ladies grouped in three classes: class of Knights of the Collar and Ladies of the Collar; Class of Knights (in four grades); Class of Ladies (in four grades). Members are appointed by the cardinal grand master according to procedures outlined in the constitution.

Under the present constitution the order is divided into national lieutenancies, largely autonomous, with international headquarters in Rome. Cardinal Carlo Furno is the grand master of the order.

There are nine lieutenancies of the order in the United States and one in Puerto Rico. Vice Governor General, F. Russell Kendall, 309 Knipp Rd., Houston, TX 77024; (713) 468-5602; www.holysepulchre.net.

Order of Malta: The Sovereign Military Hospitaller Order of St. John of Jerusalem of Rhodes and of Malta traces its origin to a group of men who maintained a Christian hospital in the Holy Land in the 11th century. The group was approved as a religious order — the Hospitallers of St. John — by Paschal II in 1113.

The order, while continuing its service to the poor, principally in hospital work, assumed military duties in the 12th century and included knights, chaplains and sergeants-at-arms among its members. All the knights were professed monks with the vows of poverty, chastity and obedience. Headquarters were located in the Holy Land until the last decade of the 13th century and on Rhodes after 1308 (whence the title, Knights of Rhodes).

After establishing itself on Rhodes, the order became a sovereign power like the sea republics of Italy and the Hanseatic cities of Germany, flying its own flag, coining its own money, floating its own navy, and maintaining diplomatic relations with many nations.

The order was forced to abandon Rhodes in 1522 after the third siege of the island by the Turks under Sultan Suleyman I. Eight years later, the Knights were given the island of Malta, where they remained as a bastion of Christianity until near the end of the 18th century. Headquarters have been located in Rome since 1834.

The title of Grand Master of the Order, in abeyance for some time, was restored by Leo XIII in 1879. A more precise definition of both the religious and the sovereign status of the order was embodied in a new constitution of 1961 and a code issued in 1966.

The four main classifications of members are: Knights of Justice, who are religious with the vows of poverty, chastity and obedience; Knights of Obedience, who make a solemn promise to strive for Christian perfection; Knights of Honor and Devotion and of Grace and Devotion, all of noble lineage; and Knights of Magistral Grace. There are also chaplains, Dames and Donats of the order.

The order, with six grand priories, three sub-priories and 40 national associations, is devoted to hospital and charitable works of all kinds in some 100 countries.

Under the provisions of international law, the order maintains full diplomatic relations with the Holy See — on which, in its double nature, it depends as a religious Order, but of which, as a sovereign Order of Knighthood, it is independent — and 68 countries throughout the world.

The Grand Master, who is the head of the order, has the title of Most Eminent Highness with the rank of Cardinal. He must be of noble lineage and under solemn vows for a minimum period of 10 years, if under 50.

The present Grand Master is Fra' Andrew Willoughby Ninian Bertie, member of the British aristocracy, who was elected for life Apr. 8, 1988, by the Council of State. His election was approved by the pope.

On Dec. 6, 1999, John Paul Reiner, an attorney from Manhattan, was elected the new president of the American Association of the Knights of Malta.

The headquarters of the order is at Via Condotti, 68, Palazzo Malta, 00187 Rome, Italy; (011) 3906-679-8851. U.S. addresses: American Association, 1011 First Ave., New York, NY 10022; Western Association of U.S.A., 465 California St., Suite 524, San Francisco, CA 94104; Federal Association of U.S.A., 1730 M St. N.W., Suite 403, Washington, D.C. 20036; (202) 331-2494; www.smom.org.

Order of St. George: The Sacred Military Constantinian Order of St. George was established by Pope Clement XI in 1718. The purposes of the order are to work for the preaching and defense of the Catholic faith and to promote the spiritual and physical welfare of sick, disabled, homeless and other unfortunate persons. The principal officer is Prince Carlo of Bourbon-Two Sicilies, duke of Calabria. Addresses: Via Sistina 121, 00187 Rome, Italy; Via Duomo 149, 80138 Naples, Italy; American Delegation, 302 Gessner Rd., Houston, TX 77024; (713) 888-0242.

AWARDS 2005-2006

2006 CATHOLIC PRESS ASSOCIATION AWARDS

The winners of the 2006 Catholic Press Awards were announced on Friday, May 26, 2006 at the Loews Vanderbilt Hotel in Nashville, Tenn.

Newspapers — General Excellence

National Newspapers: First Place: *National Catholic Reporter*; Second Place: *National Catholic Register* (Toronto); Third Place: *The Catholic Register*.

Diocesan Newspapers, 40,001+ Circulation: First Place: *The Catholic Spirit*, St. Paul, MN.; Second Place: *The Catholic Advocate*, Newark, NJ; Third Place: *The Catholic Sun*, Phoenix, AZ; Honorable Mention: *Clarion Herald*, New Orleans, LA.

Diocesan Newspapers, 17,001-40,000: First Place: *The Colorado Catholic Herald*, Colorado Springs, CO; Second Place: *The Michigan Catholic*, Detroit, MI.; Third Place: *The Southern Cross*, San Diego, CA.

Diocesan Newspapers, 1-17,000: First Place: *Hawaii Catholic Herald*, Honolulu, HI; Second Place: *Today's Catholic*, Fort Wayne-South Bend, IN; Third Place: *The Catholic Northwest Progress*, Seattle, WA; Honorable Mention: *Catholic East Texas*, Tyler, TX.

Magazines

General Excellence: First Place: *Faith & Family*, North Haven, CT; Second Place: *U.S. Catholic*, Chicago, IL; Third Place: *Faith Magazine*, Lansing, MI.

Mission Magazines: First Place: *One Magazine*, New York, NY; Second Place: *Columban Mission*, St. Columbans, NE; Third Place: *Glenmary Challenge*, Cincinnati, OH.

Religious Order: First Place: *Marian Helper*, Stockbridge, MA; Second Place: *Partners Magazine*, Chicago, IL; Third Place: *Jesuit Journeys*, Milwaukee, WI.

Professional/Special Interest: First Place: *CUA Magazine*, Washington, DC; Second Place: *My Friend - The Catholic Magazine for Kids*, Boston, MA; Third Place: *Church*, New York, NY; Honorable Mention: *Today's Catholic Teacher*, Dayton, OH.

Scholarly: First Place: *American Catholic Studies*, Villanova, PA; Second Place: *National Catholic Bioethics Quarterly*, Philadelphia, PA; Third Place: *Horizons*, Villanova, PA.

Prayer and Spirituality: First Place: *Spiritual Life*, Washington, DC; Second Place: *Magnificat*, Yonkers, NY.

General Excellence (Spanish language publication): First Place: *El Pregonero*, Washington, DC; Second Place: *El Pueblo Católico*, Denver, CO; Third Place: *El Mensajero Católico*, Rochester, NY; Honorable Mention: *New Jersey Católico*, Newark, NJ.

Newsletters

General Interest: First Place: *Everyday Catholic*, Cincinnati, OH; Second Place: *Catholic Update*, Cincinnati, OH; Third Place: *Eucharist: Jesus With Us*, Cincinnati, OH.

Special Interest: First Place: *At Home with Our Faith*, Chicago, IL; Second Place: *Ethics and Medics*, Philadelphia, PA; Third Place: *Focus on Future Church*, Cleveland, OH.

Books

Popular Presentation of the Catholic Faith: First Place: The Crossroad Publishing Company, New York, NY, *Blessed among all Women*, Robert Ellsberg; Second Place, Tie: Servant Books, Cincinnati, OH, *The Untapped Power of the Sacrament of Penance*, Father Christopher J. Walsh; ACTA Publications, Skokie, IL, *Remaining Catholic: Six Good Reasons for Staying in an Imperfect Church*, Father Martin Pable, OFM Cap.; Third Place: St. Anthony Messenger Press, Cincinnati, OH, *Here on the Way to There*, William H. Shannon; Honorable Mention: Orbis Books, Maryknoll, NY, *Amazing Church*, Gregory Baum, Loyola Press, Chicago, IL, *The Catholic Passion*, David Scott, Pauline Books & Media, Boston, MA, *Imagining Faith with Kids*, Mary Margaret Keaton.

Spirituality - Softcover: First Place: Orbis Books, Maryknoll, NY, *Walk in a Relaxed Manner*, Joyce Rupp; Second Place, Tie: Wm. B. Eerdmans, Grand Rapids, MI, *To Follow You, Light of Life*, Bruno Forte, Sorin Books-Ave Maria Press, Notre Dame, IN, *The Circle of Life*, Joyce Rupp, Macrina Wiederkehr; Third Place: ICS Publications, Washington, DC, *Story of a Soul: Study Edition*, St. Thérèse of Lisieux.

Spirituality - Hardcover: First Place: Jossey-Bass, San Francisco, CA, *The Way of the Mystics*, John Michael Talbot, with Steve Rabey; Second Place: The Crossroad Publishing Company, New York, NY, *Blessed Among All Women*, Robert Ellsberg; Third Place: Orbis Books, Maryknoll, NY, *Henri Nouwen: His Life and Vision*, Michael O'Laughlin; Honorable Mention: Orbis Books, Maryknoll, NY, *The Way We Were*, Joan Chittister.

Theology: First Place: Georgetown University Press, Washington, DC, *Theological Bioethics*, Lisa Sowle Cahill; Second Place: Georgetown University Press, Washington, DC, *The Moral Theology of Pope John Paul II*, Charles E. Curran; Third Place, Tie: Baker Publishing Group: Brazos Press, Grand Rapids, MI, *Holy People, Holy Land*, Michael Dauphinais and Matthew Levering Continuum International, New York, NY, *The Future of Christology*, Roger Haight, S.J.

Scripture: First Place: Liturgical Press, Collegeville, MN, *Gospels and Acts: The St. John's Bible*; Second Place - Tie: Loyola Press, Chicago, IL, *The Gospel According to Mark: Meaning and Message*, George Martin; Harvard University Press, Cambridge, MA, *Doubting Thomas*, Glenn W. Most; Third Place: Orbis Books, Maryknoll, NY, *God's Economy: Biblical Studies from Latin America*, Ross Kinsler and Gloria Kinsler. Honorable Mention: Novalis, Ottawa, Canada, *Passionate Visionary: Leadership Lessons from the Apostle Paul*, Richard S. Ascough and Sandy Cotton.

Liturgy: First Place: Continuum International, New York, NY, *A Sense of the Sacred*, R. Kevin Seasoltz, O.S.B.; Second Place: The Crossroad Publishing Company, New York, NY, *Fragments of Real Presence*, Teresa Berger, Ph.D.; Third Place: Orbis Books,

Maryknoll, NY, *eucharist with a small "e",* Miriam Therese Winter; Honorable Mention: Liturgical Press, Collegeville, MN, *Directory on Popular Piety and the Liturgy: Principles and Guidelines,* Peter C. Phan, Liturgical Press, Collegeville, MN, *Translating Tradition: A Chant Historian Read Liturgiam Authenticam,* Peter Jeffery, Obl.S.B., Paulist Press, Mahwah, NJ, *Fulfilled in Our Hearing: History and Method of Christian Preaching,* Guerric DeBona, O.S.B.

Pastoral Ministry: First Place: The Crossroad Publishing Company, New York, NY, *Can Religious Life Be Prophetic?,* Michael H. Crosby, O.F.M. Cap.; Second Place, Tie: Ave Maria Press, Notre Dame, IN, *You Did it for Me,* Kevin E. McKenna, Liturgical Press, Collegeville, MN, *The Sacrament of Anointing of the Sick,* Lizette Larson-Miller; Third Place: Orbis Books, Maryknoll, NY, *Transforming Trauma,* Teresa Rhodes McGee. Honorable Mention: New Beginnings, Wilmington, NC, *My Opportunity for Giving: Stewardship as a Way of Life,* Paul Wilkes, ACTA Publications, Skokie, IL, *The Confirmed Catholic's Companion: A Guide to Abundant Living,* Sr. Kathleen Glavich.

Professional Books: First Place: Liturgical Press, Collegeville, MN, *The Spiritual Wisdom of the Gospels for Christian Preachers and Teachers,* John Shea; Second Place: Ave Maria Press, Notre Dame, IN, *Alter Christus,* John J. Gilchrist; Third Place: Ave Maria Press, Notre Dame, IN, *The Joy of Priesthood,* Father Stephen J. Rossetti; Honorable Mention: The Crossroad Publishing Company, New York, NY, Sacred *Is the Call: Formation and Transformation in Spiritual Direction Programs,* Suzanne M. Buckley; Novalis, Ottawa, Canada, *Magnificence at Work: Living Faith in Business,* John Dalla Costa.

Educational Books: First Place: Harcourt Religion Publishers, Orlando, FL, *Call to Faith Student Edition K-6;* Second Place, Tie: Orbis Books, Maryknoll, NY, *War & the Christian Conscience,* Joseph J. Fahey, Orbis Books; Maryknoll, NY, *When God's People Have HIV/AIDS,* Maria Cimperman; Third Place: Orbis Books, Maryknoll, NY, Trinity, Anne Hunt.

Design and Production: First Place: Liturgical Press, Collegeville, MN, *Illuminating the Word: The Making of the St. John's Bible,* Christopher Calderhead; Second Place, Tie: Archabbey Publications, Latrobe, PA, *The St. Vincent Basilica, One Hundred Years,* Kimberley A. Opatka-Metzgar; Liturgical Press, Collegeville, MN, *Ambrose and the Princess,* Margo Sorenson, Katalin Szegedi; Third Place: Acadian House Publishing, Lafayette, LA, Grand Coteau: *The Holy Land of South Louisiana,* Trent Angers. Honorable Mention: Orbis Books, Maryknoll, NY, *Women of Mercy,* Kathy Coffey and Michael O'Neill McGrath, Pauline Books & Media, Boston, MA, *John Paul II: A Marian Treasury,* Marianne Lorraine Trouvé, F.S.P.

Children's Books: First Place: Paulist Press, Mahwah, NJ, *Child's Guide to the Seven Sacraments,* Elizabeth Ficocelli; Second Place, Tie: Our Sunday Visitor, Huntington, IN, *On That First Christmas Eve,* Carol Schulze Dowgiallo and Robert Dowgiallo; Wm. B. Eerdmans, Grand Rapids, MI, *The Song of Francis and the Animals,* Pat Mora; Third Place: Pauline Books & Media, Boston, MA, *Holy Friends: Thirty Saints*

and *Blesseds of the Americas,* Diana M. Amadeo.

First Time Author of a Book: First Place: ACTA Publications, Skokie, IL, *Running into the Arms of God,* Father Patrick Hannon; Second Place: Loyola Press, Chicago, IL, *Swimming with Scapulars,* Matthew Lickona; Third Place: Servant Books, Cincinnati, OH, *The Untapped Power of the Sacrament of Penance,* Fr. Christopher J. Walsh; Honorable Mention: Orbis Books, Maryknoll, NY, *Black Elk,* Damian Costello; Archabbey Publications, Latrobe, PA, *Renewed Each Morning: Reflections from the Rocking Chair,* Philip M. Kanfush, O.S.B.

Family Life: First Place: The Crossroad Publishing Company, New York, NY, *What Not to Expect: Meditations on the Spirituality of Parenting,* Dr. Keith Frome; Second Place: ACTA Publications, Skokie, IL, *Watching My Friend Die: The Honest Death of Bob Schwartz,* Mark Hare; Third Place, Tie: Sophia Institute Press, Manchester, VT, *The Temperament God Gave You,* Art and Laraine Bennett; Servant Books, Cincinnati, OH, *Stand Up Girl: Take Charge of Your Unexpected Pregnancy,* Becky Fraser with Linda Shands.

History: First Place: Orbis Books, Maryknoll, NY, A History of Christianity in Asia — Vol. II, Samuel Hugh Moffett; Second Place: Novalis, Ottawa, Canada, *Amazing Church,* Gregory Baum; Third Place, Tie: Liturgical Press, Collegeville, MN, *The Collegeville Church History Time-Line,* Joseph F. Kelly; Paulist Press, Mahwah, NJ, *The Catholic Worker Movement,* Mark and Louise Zwick.

Biography: First Place: The Crossroad Publishing Company, New York, NY, *American Apostle of the Family Rosary: The Life of Patrick J. Peyton, CSC,* Richard Gribble, CSC; Second Place: University of Notre Dame, Notre Dame, IN, Jacques and Raïssa Maritain: *Beggers for Heaven,* Jean-Luc Barré; Third Place: Westminster John Knox Press, Louisville, KY, *Reflections over the Long Haul,* Robert McAfee Brown. Honorable Mention: Orbis Books, Maryknoll, NY, *The Cave of the Heart: The Life of Swami Abhishiktananda,* Shirley du Boulay.

Gender Issues: First Place: The Crossroad Publishing Company, New York, NY, *Blessed Among All Women,* Robert Ellsberg; Second Place: Orbis Books, Maryknoll, NY, *Women of Mercy,* Kathy Coffey; Third Place: The Crossroad Publishing Company, New York, NY, *Fragments of Real Presence: Liturgical Traditions in the Hands of Women,* Teresa Berger, Ph.D.

Spanish Language Titles: First Place: Harcourt Religion Publishers, Orlando, FL, *Un Llamado a la Fe;* Second Place: Instituto Fe y Vida and Editorial Verbo Divino, Stockton, CA, *La Biblia Católica Para Jóvenes;* Third Place: Orbis Books, Maryknoll, NY, *Un Solo Mundo, Una Sola Familia,* Linda Unger and David Aquije.

Reference Books: First Place: Georgetown University Press, Washington, DC, *Modern Catholic Social Teaching,* Kenneth R. Himes, Editor; Second Place: Baker Publishing Group: Brazos Press, Grand Rapids, MI, *Dictionary for Theological Interpretation of the Bible,* Kevin J. Vanhoozer, Craig G. Bartholomew, Daniel J. Treier and N.T. Wright; Third Place: Paulist Press, Mahwah, NJ, *How to Read a Church: A Guide to Symbols and Images in Churches* and *Cathedrals*, Richard Taylor. Honorable Mention: Baker Publishing Group: Brazos Press, Grand Rapids, MI, *Acts: The Brazos Theological Commentary on the Bible*, Jaroslav Pelikan.

2006 CHRISTOPHER AWARDS

Christopher Awards recognize the creative writers, producers and directors who have achieved artistic excellence in films, books and television specials. The 2006 awards were presented Mar. 16, 2006, in New York.

Books: *The Death of Innocents: An Eyewitness Account of Wrongful Executions,* by Sister Helen Prejean (Random House/Random House, Inc.); *The Glass Castle: A Memoir,* by Jeannette Walls (Scribner/Simon & Schuster Inc.); *One Soldier's Story: A Memoir,* by Bob Dole (HarperCollins Publishers Inc.); *The Prison Angel: Mother Antonia's Journey from Beverly Hills to a Life of Service in a Mexican Jail,* by Mary Jordan & Kevin Sullivan (The Penguin Press/Penguin Group Inc.); *They Poured Fire on Us from the Sky: The True Story of Three Lost Boys from Sudan,* by Benson Deng, Alephonsion Deng & Benjamin Ajak, with Judy A. Bernstein (PublicAffairs/Perseus Books Group).

Books for Young People: Preschool: *Am I a Color Too?,* by Heidi Cole & Nancy Vogl, illustrated by Gerald Purnell (Illumination Arts Publishing Company, Inc.); Ages 6–8: *I Could Do That! Esther Morris Gets Women the Vote,* by Linda Arms White, illustrated by Nancy Carpenter (Melanie Kroupa Books/Farrar Straus Giroux); Ages 8–10: *Game Day,* by Tiki Barber and Ronde Barber with Robert Burleigh, illustrated by Barry Root (Paula Wiseman Books/Simon & Schuster Books for Young Readers); Ages 10–12: *Friendship According to Humphrey,* by Betty G. Birney (G. P. Putnam's Sons/Penguin Young Readers Group); Young Adult: *Hitch,* by Jeanette Ingold (Harcourt, Inc.).

Films: "Good Night, and Good Luck" (Warner Independent Pictures); "Mad Hot Ballroom" (Paramount Classics); "Millions" (Fox Searchlight Pictures); "An Unfinished Life" (Miramax Films); "The Wild Parrots of Telegraph Hill" (Shadow Distribution).

Television and Cable: "14 Hours" (TNT); "Lackawanna Blues" (HBO); "Paper Clips" (HBO Family); "P.O.V.: The Hobart Shakespeareans" (PBS/WNET New York); "The Power of Good" (CINEMAX); "Slavery and the Making of America Miniseries" (PBS/WNET New York)

Christopher Lifetime Achievement Award: Dave Brubeck.

Christopher Spirit Award: Jeanne Davis Glynn.

Special Award: "American Experience."

Ecumenism and Interreligious Dialogue

ECUMENISM

Sources: Brother Jeffrey Gros, F.S.C. and Rev. Ronald Roberson, C.S.P., associate directors, Secretariat for Ecumenical and Interreligious Affairs, USCCB.

The modern ecumenical movement, with roots in 19th-century scholars and individuals began its institutional life in 1910 among Protestants and Orthodox and led to formation of the World Council of Churches in 1948, developed outside the mainstream of Catholic interest for many years. It has now become for Catholics as well one of the great religious facts of our time.

The *magna carta* of ecumenism for Catholics is a complex of several documents which include, in the first place, *Unitatis Redintegratio*, the "Decree on Ecumenism," promulgated by the Second Vatican Council Nov. 21, 1964. Other enactments underlying and expanding this decree are *Lumen Gentium* ("Dogmatic Constitution on the Church"), *Orientalium Ecclesiarum* ("Decree on Eastern Catholic Churches"), and *Gaudium et Spes* ("Pastoral Constitution on the Church in the Modern World").

The Holy See has more recently brought together Catholic ecumenical priorities in Directory for the Application of Principles and Norms on Ecumenism (1993) and The Ecumenical Dimension in the Formation of Pastoral Workers (1998). These, in addition to Pope John Paul II's encyclical, *Ut Unum Sint* (1995), provide a guide for Catholic ecumenical initiatives. Pope Benedict XVI reiterated this irreversible commitment at his installation, and during his meeting with the ecumenical guests the day following his installation (2005).

POPE BENEDICT XVI

Pope Benedict XVI has reaffirmed the commitment of the Catholic Church to the ecumenical movement, and stated that ecumenism would be the "primacy task" of his pontificate. This is an excerpt from his address to the Cardinals at the end of a Mass he celebrated with them the day after his election, on April 20, 2005:

"Nourished and sustained by the Eucharist, Catholics cannot but feel encouraged to strive for the full unity for which Christ expressed so ardent a hope in the Upper Room. The Successor of Peter knows that he must make himself especially responsible for his Divine Master's supreme aspiration. Indeed, he is entrusted with the task of strengthening his brethren (cf. Lk 22: 32).

With full awareness, therefore, at the beginning of his ministry in the Church of Rome which Peter bathed in his blood, Peter's current Successor takes on as his primary task the duty to work tirelessly to rebuild the full and visible unity of all Christ's followers. This is his ambition, his impelling duty. He is aware that good intentions do not suffice for this. Concrete gestures that enter hearts and stir consciences are essential, inspiring in everyone that inner conversion that is the prerequisite for all ecumenical progress.

Theological dialogue is necessary; the investigation of the historical reasons for the decisions made in the past is also indispensable. But what is most urgently needed is that 'purification of memory', so often recalled by John Paul II, which alone can dispose souls to accept the full truth of Christ. Each one of us must come before him, the supreme Judge of every living person, and render an account to him of all we have done or have failed to do to further the great good of the full and visible unity of all his disciples. The current Successor of Peter is allowing himself to be called in the first person by this requirement and is prepared to do everything in his power to promote the fundamental cause of ecumenism. Following the example of his Predecessors, he is fully determined to encourage every initiative that seems appropriate for promoting contacts and understanding with the representatives of the different Churches and Ecclesial Communities. Indeed, on this occasion he sends them his most cordial greeting in Christ, the one Lord of us all."

VATICAN II DECREE

The following excerpts from *Unitatis Redintegratio* cover the broad theological background and principles and indicate the thrust of the Church's commitment to ecumenism.

Men who believe in Christ and have been properly baptized are brought into a certain, though imperfect, communion with the Catholic Church. Undoubtedly, the differences that exist in varying degrees between them and the Catholic Church — whether in doctrine and sometimes in discipline, or concerning the structure of the Church — do indeed create many and sometimes serious obstacles to full ecclesiastical communion. These the ecumenical movement is striving to overcome (No. 3).

Elements Common to Christians

Moreover some, even very many, of the most significant elements or endowments which together go to build up and give life to the Church herself can exist outside the visible boundaries of the Catholic Church: the written word of God; the life of grace; faith, hope, and charity, along with other interior gifts of the Holy Spirit and visible elements. All of these, which come from Christ and lead back to Him, belong by right to the one Church of Christ (No. 3).

[In a later passage, the decree singled out a number of elements which the Catholic Church and other churches have in common but not in complete agreement: confession of Christ as Lord and God and as mediator between God and man; belief in the Trinity; reverence for Scripture as the revealed word of God; baptism and the Lord's Supper; Christian life and worship; faith in action; concern with moral questions.]

The brethren divided from us also carry out many of the sacred actions of the Christian religion. Undoubtedly, in ways that vary according to the condition of each church or community, these actions can truly engender a life of grace, and can be rightly described as capable of providing access to the community of salvation.

It follows that these separated Churches and Communities, though we believe they suffer from defects already mentioned, have by no means been deprived of significance and importance in the mystery of salvation. For the Spirit of Christ has not refrained from using them as means of salvation which derive their efficacy from the very fullness of grace and truth entrusted to the Catholic Church (No. 3).

Unity Lacking

Nevertheless, our separated brethren, whether considered as individuals or as Communities and Churches, are not blessed with that unity which Jesus Christ wished to bestow on all those whom he has regenerated and vivified into one body and newness of life — that unity which the holy Scriptures and the revered tradition of the Church proclaim. For it is through Christ's Catholic Church alone, which is the all-embracing means of salvation, that the fullness of the means of salvation can be obtained. It was to the apostolic college alone, of which Peter is the head, that we believe our Lord entrusted all the blessings of the New Covenant, in order to establish on earth the one Body of Christ into which all those should be fully incorporated who already belong in any way to God's People (No. 3).

What the Movement Involves

Today, in many parts of the world, under the inspiring grace of the Holy Spirit, multiple efforts are being expended through prayer, word, and action to attain that fullness of unity which Jesus Christ desires. This sacred Synod, therefore, exhorts all the Catholic faithful to recognize the signs of the times and to participate skillfully in the work of ecumenism.

The "ecumenical movement" means those activities and enterprises which, according to various needs of the Church and opportune occasions, are started and organized for the fostering of unity among Christians. These are:

• First, every effort to eliminate words, judgments, and actions which do not respond to the condition of separated brethren with truth and fairness and so make mutual relations between them more difficult.

• Then, "dialogue" between competent experts from different Churches and Communities [scholarly ecumenism].

• In addition, these Communions cooperate more closely in whatever projects a Christian conscience demands for the common good [social ecumenism].

• They also come together for common prayer, where this is permitted [spiritual ecumenism].

• Finally, all are led to examine their own faithfulness to Christ's will for the Church and, wherever necessary, undertake with vigor the task of renewal and reform.

It is evident that the work of preparing and reconciling those individuals who wish for full Catholic communion is of its nature distinct from ecumenical action. But there is no opposition between the two, since both proceed from the wondrous providence of God (No. 4).

Primary Duty of Catholics

In ecumenical work, Catholics must assuredly be concerned for their separated brethren, praying for them, keeping them informed about the Church, making the first approaches toward them. But their primary duty is to make an honest and careful appraisal of whatever needs to be renewed and achieved in the Catholic household itself, in order that its life may bear witness more loyally and luminously to the teachings and ordinances which have been handed down from Christ through the Apostles.

Every Catholic must aim at Christian perfection (cf. Jas 1:4; Rom 12:1-2) and, each according to his station, play his part so that the Church may daily be more purified and renewed, against the day when Christ will present her to himself in all her glory, without spot or wrinkle (cf. Eph 5:27).

Catholics must joyfully acknowledge and esteem the truly Christian endowments from our common heritage which are to be found among our separated brethren.

Nor should we forget that whatever is wrought by the grace of the Holy Spirit in the hearts of our separated brethren can contribute to our own edification. Whatever is truly Christian never conflicts with the genuine interests of the faith; indeed, it can always result in a more ample realization of the very mystery of Christ and the Church (No. 4).

Participation in Worship

Norms concerning participation by Catholics in the worship of other Christian Churches were sketched in this conciliar decree and elaborated in a number of other documents such as: the Decree on Eastern Catholic Churches, promulgated by the Second Vatican Council in 1964; Interim Guidelines for Prayer in Common, issued June 18, 1965, by the U.S. Bishops' Committee for Ecumenical and Interreligious Affairs; a Directory on Ecumenism, published in 1967, 1970 and 1993 by the Pontifical Council for Promoting Christian Unity; additional communications from the U.S. Bishops' Committee, and numerous sets of guidelines issued locally by and for dioceses throughout the U.S.

The norms encourage common prayer services for Christian unity and other intentions. Beyond that, they draw a distinction between separated churches of the Reformation tradition and of the Anglican

Communion, and separated Eastern churches, in view of doctrine and practice the Catholic Church has in common with the separated Eastern churches concerning the apostolic succession of bishops, holy orders, liturgy and other credal matters.

Full participation by Catholics in official Protestant liturgies is prohibited, because it implies profession of the faith expressed in the liturgy. Intercommunion by Catholics at Protestant liturgies is prohibited. Under certain conditions, Protestants may be given Holy

Communion in the Catholic Church (*see* **Intercommunion**). A Catholic may stand as a witness, but not as a sponsor, in baptism, and as a witness in the marriage of separated Christians. Similarly, a Protestant may stand as a witness, but not as a sponsor, in a Catholic baptism, and as a witness in the marriage of Catholics.

The principal norms regarding liturgical participations with separated Eastern Churches are included under Eastern Ecumenism.

DIRECTORY ON ECUMENISM

A Directory for the Application of the Principles and Norms of Ecumenism was approved by Pope John Paul II on Mar. 25, 1993, and published early in June. The Pontifical Council for Promoting Christian Unity said on release of the document that revision of Directories issued in 1967 and 1970 was necessary in view of subsequent developments. These included promulgation of the Code of Canon Law for the Latin Church in 1983 and of the Code of Canons of the Eastern Churches in 1990; publication of the Catechism of the Catholic Church in 1992; additional documents and the results of theological dialogues. In 1998, The Ecumenical Dimension in the Formation of Pastoral Workers was published by the Holy See to give practical and detailed guidance in the implementation of Chapter 3 of the Directory.

The following excerpts are from the text published in the June 16, 1993, English edition of L'Osservatore Romano.

Address and Purpose

"The Directory is addressed to the pastors of the Catholic Church, but it also concerns all the faithful, who are called to pray and work for the unity of Christians, under the direction of their bishops."

"At the same time, it is hoped that the Directory will also be useful to members of churches and ecclesial communities that are not in full communion with the Catholic Church."

"The new edition of the Directory is meant to be an instrument at the service of the whole Church, and especially of those who are directly engaged in ecumenical activity in the Catholic Church. The Directory

intends to motivate, enlighten and guide this activity, and in some particular cases also to give binding directives in accordance with the proper competence of the Pontifical Council for Promoting Christian Unity."

Outline

Principles and norms of the document are covered in five chapters.

"I. The Search for Christian Unity. The ecumenical commitment of the Catholic Church based on the doctrinal principles of the Second Vatican Council.

"II. Organization in the Catholic Church at the Service of Christian Unity. Persons and structures involved in promoting ecumenism at all levels, and the norms that direct their activity.

"III. Ecumenical Formation in the Catholic Church. Categories of people to be formed, those responsible for formation; the aims and methods of formation; its doctrinal and practical aspects.

"IV. Communion in Life and Spiritual Activity among the Baptized. The communion that exists with other Christians on the basis of the sacramental bond of baptism, and the norms for sharing in prayer and other spiritual activities, including, in particular cases, sacramental sharing.

"V. Ecumenical Cooperation, Dialogue and Common Witness. Principles, different forms and norms for cooperation between Christians with a view to dialogue and common witness in the world."

ECUMENICAL AGENCIES

Pontifical Council

The top-level agency for Catholic ecumenical efforts is the Pontifical Council for Promoting Christian Unity (formerly the Secretariat for Promoting Christian Unity), which originated in 1960 as a preparatory commission for the Second Vatican Council. Its purposes are to provide guidance and, where necessary, coordination for ecumenical endeavor by Catholics, and to establish and maintain relations with representatives of other Christian Churches for ecumenical dialogue and action.

The council, under the direction of Card. Walter Kasper (successor to Card. Edward I. Cassidy), has established firm working relations with representative agencies of other churches and the World Council of Churches. It has joined in dialogue with Orthodox Churches, the Anglican Communion, the Lutheran World Federation, the World Alliance of Reformed Churches, the World Methodist Council, Baptist World Alliance, World Evangelical Alliance, the Pentecostals, Mennonites and other religious bodies. In the past several years, staff members and representatives of the council have been involved in one way or another in nearly every significant ecumenical enterprise and meeting held throughout the world.

While the council and its counterparts in other churches have focused primary attention on theological and other related problems of Christian unity, they have also begun, and in increasing measure, to emphasize the responsibilities of the churches for greater unity of witness and effort in areas of humanitarian need.

Bishops' Committee

The U.S. Bishops' Committee for Ecumenical and Interreligious Affairs was established by the American hierarchy in 1964. Its purposes are to maintain relationships with other Christian churches and other religious communities at the national level, to help other offices of the Conference do their work ecumenically, to advise and assist dioceses in developing and applying ecumenical policies, and to maintain liaison with corresponding Vatican offices — the Pontifical Councils for Christian Unity and for Interreligious Dialogue.

This standing committee of the United States Conference of Catholic Bishops is chaired by Bp. Richard Sklba of the Archdiocese of Milwaukee. Operationally, the committee is assisted by a secretariat with Rev. James Massa, executive director; Dr. Eugene J. Fisher, executive secretary for Catholic-Jewish Relations; Rev. Francis Tiso, executive secretary for Interreligious Relations, and the Rev. Ronald Roberson, C.S.P

The committee co-sponsors several national consultations with other churches and confessional families. These bring together Catholic representatives and their counterparts from the Episcopal Church, Evangelical Lutheran Church in America, the Polish National Catholic Church, the United Methodist Church, the Orthodox Churches, the Oriental Orthodox Churches, the Reformed Churches: the United Church of Christ, the Presbyterian Church, Christian Reformed Church and Reformed Church in America. There are dialogues with the National Association of Evangelicals, a regular Pentecostal Catholic dialogue in the context of the Society for Pentecostal Studies, and – until 2001 – a thirty year conversation with the Southern Baptist Convention. (See Ecumenical Dialogues.)

The committee relates with the National Council of Churches of Christ, through membership in the Faith and Order Commission and has sponsored a joint study committee investigating the possibility of Roman Catholic membership in that body in the 1970s. Collaboration in multiple areas of Church life have proved to be more fruitful than membership given the disparity of numbers and diversity of program priorities of the Bishop's Conference and the Council.

The USCCB participates in a new ecumenical entity, Christian Churches Together in the USA. It includes representatives from the five major families of Christian churches in the United States which, in addition to the Catholic Church, include the historic Protestant, Orthodox, Evangelical/Pentecostal, and Racial/Ethnic churches.

Advisory and other services are provided by the committee to ecumenical commissions and agencies in dioceses throughout the country.

Through its Section for Catholic-Jewish Relations, the committee is in contact with several national Jewish agencies and bodies. Issues of mutual interest and shared concern are reviewed for the purpose of furthering deeper understanding between the Catholic and Jewish communities.

Through its Subcommittee on Interreligious Dialogue, the committee co-sponsors dialogues with Muslims, Buddhists and Hindus and other interreligious activities and programs. By the end of 2003, there were three regional dialogues with Muslims and one with Buddhists meeting annually and an annual ecumenical consultation with Hindus.

Offices of the committee are located at 3211 Fourth St. NE, Washington, DC 20017; www.usccb.org/seia.

World Council of Churches

The World Council of Churches is a fellowship of churches which acknowledge "Jesus Christ as Lord and Savior." It is a permanent organization providing constituent members — 330 churches with some 450 million communicants in 100 countries — with opportunities for meeting, consultation and cooperative action with respect to doctrine, worship, practice, social mission, evangelism and missionary work, and other matters of mutual concern.

The WCC was formally established Aug. 23, 1948, in Amsterdam with ratification of a constitution by 147 communions. This action merged two previously existing movements — Life and Work (social mission), Faith and Order (doctrine) — which had initiated practical steps toward founding a fellowship of Christian churches at meetings held in Oxford, Edinburgh and Utrecht in 1937 and 1938. A third movement for cooperative missionary work, which originated about 1910 and, remotely, led to formation of the WCC, was incorporated into the council in 1971 under the title of the International Missionary Council.

Additional general assemblies of the council have been held since the charter meeting of 1948: in Evanston, Ill. (1954), New Delhi, India (1961), Uppsala, Sweden (1968), Nairobi, Kenya (1975), Vancouver, British Columbia, Canada (1983) and Canberra, Australia (1991). The 1998 general assembly was held in Harare, Zimbabwe, with the regular Catholic delegation in attendance, led by Abp. Mario Conti from Glasgow, Scotland. The Ninth General Assembly took place in Porto Alegre, Brazil, from Feb. 14 to 23, 2006. A Catholic delegation headed by Card. Walter Kasper, President of the Pontifical Council for Promoting Christian Unity, was present.

The council continues the work of the International Missionary Council, the Commission on Faith and Order, and the Commission on Church and Society. The work of the council is carried out through four program units: unity and renewal; mission, education and witness; justice, peace and creation; sharing and service.

Liaison between the council and the Vatican has been maintained since 1966 through a joint working group. Roman Catholic membership in the WCC is a question officially on the agenda of this body. The Joint Commission on Society, Development and Peace (SODEPAX) was an agency of the council and the Pontifical Commission for Justice and Peace from 1968 to Dec. 31, 1980, after which another working group was formed. Roman Catholics serve individually as full members of the Commission on Faith and Order and in various capacities on other program committees of the council.

WCC headquarters are located in Geneva, Switzerland. The United States Conference for the World Council of Churches at 475 Riverside Dr., Room 915, New York, NY 10115, provides liaison between the U.S. churches and Geneva, a communications office for secular and church media relations, and a publications office. The WCC also maintains fraternal relations with regional, national and local councils of churches throughout the world. Web site: www.wcc-coe.org/wcc/english.html.

National Council of Churches

The National Council of the Churches of Christ in the U.S.A., the largest ecumenical body in the United States, is an organization of 36 Protestant, Orthodox and Anglican communions, with an aggregate membership of about 50 million in 140,000 congregations.

The NCC, established by the churches in 1950, was structured through the merger of 12 separate cooperative agencies. Presently, the NCC carries on work in behalf of member churches in overseas ministries, Christian education, domestic social action, communications, disaster relief, refugee assistance, rehabilitation and development, biblical translation, international affairs, theological dialogue, interfaith activities, worship and evangelism, and other areas.

Policies of the NCC are determined by a general board of approximately 270 members appointed by the constituent churches. The board meets once a year. NCC president: Bp. Thomas L. Hoyt, Jr., President in 2004-2005. General Secretary: Rev. Dr. Robert W. Edgar. NCC headquarters are located at 475 Riverside Dr., New York, NY 10115; (212) 870-2141; www.ncc-cusa.org.

Christian Churches Together in the USA

In early 2001, discussions began in earnest among church leaders in the United States about the possibility of forming a new ecumenical organization. There was an acute awareness that since the members of the current National Council of Churches (NCC) represent only about one third of the Christians in the United States, a much broader ecumenical witness was needed. Thus in the summer of 2001 letters were sent out to various American church leaders inviting them to attend a meeting at St. Mary's Seminary and University in Baltimore on Sept. 7-8. The letter was signed by Bp. Tod Brown, Card. William Keeler, Rev. Wesley Granberg-Michaelson (General Secretary of the Reformed Church in America), and Rev. Dr. Robert Edgar (NCC General Secretary). The meeting was to explore whether or not the time had come to "create a new, more inclusive ecumenical table and/or body." The most striking result was the unanimous strong desire among the participants for a broader structure of some kind that would include all the major groupings of churches, including the Catholic Church and major Evangelical and Pentecostal groups that do not now belong to the NCC. Subsequent organizational meetings were held in Chicago (April 2002), Pasadena (January 2003), and Navasota, Texas (January 2004). The name chosen for the new entity is "Christian Churches Together in the USA" (CCT).

In November 2004, the Catholic Bishops of the United States took an historic ecumenical step by voting to participate in CCT. Bp. Stephen E. Blaire of Stockton, Calif., chairman of the Committee on Ecumenical and Interreligious Affairs, presented the proposal to the body of bishops and urged its adoption, calling CCT a "fresh and creative initiative to broaden the ecumenical table." The bishops approved the proposal to join CCT by a vote of 151-73, slightly more than a 2-to-1 margin.

From June 1 to 3, 2005, sixty-seven national Christian leaders from five Christian families – Evangelical/Pentecostal, Historic Protestant, Historic Racial/Ethnic, Orthodox and Catholic—met in their fifth and largest CCT organizational meeting at the Jesuit Conference Center in Los Altos, California. The gathering at Los Altos brought together a wider, more diverse circle of Christian church leaders than at any of the previous four meetings.

Thirty-one churches and national Christian organizations have now formally decided to join Christian Churches Together. Twenty additional church leaders attended as observers from denominations that are actively considering joining. Through two and a half days of sharing, prayer and worship, the participants wrestled with difficult and complex issues in a spirit of love and good will. Relationships with the Historic Black Churches were deepened through intensive dialogue and sharing.

It was decided at Los Altos to delay a formal launch planned for September 2005 in order to continue the productive and positive conversation with churches and organizations actively considering joining. Participants enthusiastically reaffirmed their commitment to "grow closer together in Christ in order to strengthen our Christian witness in the world." The Rev. Wesley Granberg-Michaelson was unanimously reelected as moderator to lead an expanded Steering Committee.

Another plenary meeting of CCT took place at Simpsonwood Conference and Retreat Center near Atlanta, Georgia, from Mar. 28 to 31, 2006. At this meeting the new By-laws of CCT were adopted and the new organization formally came into existence. Thirty-four churches and national Christian organizations were represented, thus forming the broadest, most inclusive fellowship of Christian churches and traditions in the USA. The general theme of the meeting was poverty in the United States. The next plenary is scheduled for February 2007.

Churches Uniting in Christ

(Courtesy of Rev. David W.A. Taylor, General Secretary; revised by Rev. James Massa, USCCB)

The Consultation on Church Union, officially begun in 1962, is a venture of American churches seeking a united church "truly catholic, truly evangelical, and truly reformed." The churches engaged in this process, representing 25 million Christians, are the African Methodist Episcopal Church, the African Methodist Episcopal Zion Church, the Christian Church (Disciples of Christ), the Christian Methodist Episcopal Church, the Episcopal Church, the Presbyterian Church (U.S.A); the United Church of Christ, the United Methodist Church and the International Council of Community Churches.

At a plenary assembly of COCU in December 1988, a plan of church unity was unanimously approved for submission to member churches for their action. The plan is contained in a 102-page document entitled "Churches in Covenant Communion: The Church of Christ Uniting." It proposes the formation of a covenant communion of the churches which, while remaining institutionally autonomous, would embrace together eight elements of ecclesial communion: claiming unity in faith, commitment to seek unity with wholeness, mutual recognition of members in one baptism, mutual recognition of each other as churches, mutual recognition and reconciliation of ordained ministries, celebrating the Eucharist together, engaging together in Christ's mission, and the formation together of covenanting councils at each level (national, regional, and local). At its January 1999 plenary in St. Louis, the churches proposed a 2002 decision to take one more step towards full communion as the Churches Uniting in Christ. This new step was celebrated in Memphis, during the week of prayer, in Jan. 2002.

Though the participating churches have achieved broad consensus on matters of faith and sacramental worship, agreement about the mutual recognition of ministry remains elusive. Disagreements about ordained ministry are rooted in the distinctive histories, theologies, and polities of the member churches. In 2006 CUIC plans to examine the historic episcopacy and to assess whether it is a "pathway" or "barrier" to unity. Challenges attendant to these theological problems do not deter the churches in covenant from pursuing common witness on racism.

General Secretary: Rev. Dr. Bertrice Wood. Churches Uniting in Christ, 700 Prospect Avenue East, Cleveland, OH 44115; (216) 736-3295, fax: 216-736-2120; www.eden.edu/cuic/cuic.htm.

Graymoor Institute

The Graymoor Ecumenical and Interreligious Institute is a forum where issues that confront the Christian Churches are addressed, the spiritual dimensions of ecumenism are fostered, and information, documentation and developments within the ecumenical movement are published through *Ecumenical Trends*, a monthly journal.

Director: The Rev. James Lougran. Address: 475 Riverside Dr., Rm. 1960, New York, NY 10115-1999.

INTERNATIONAL BILATERAL COMMISSIONS

Anglican-Roman Catholic International Commission, sponsored by the Pontifical Council for Promoting Christian Unity and the Lambeth Conference, from 1970 to 1981; succeeded by a **Second Anglican-Roman Catholic International Commission**, called into being by the Common Declaration of Pope John Paul and the Archbishop of Canterbury in 1982.

The International Theological Colloquium between Baptists and Catholics, established in 1984 by the Pontifical Council for Promoting Christian Unity and the Commission for Faith and Interchurch Cooperation of the Baptist World Alliance.

The Disciples of Christ-Roman Catholic Dialogue, organized by the Council of Christian Unity of the Christian Church (Disciples of Christ) and the U.S. Bishops' Committee for Ecumenical and Interreligious Affairs, along with participation by the Disciples' Ecumenical Consultative Council and the Unity Council; since 1977.

The Evangelical-Roman Catholic Dialogue on Mission, organized by Evangelicals and the Pontifical Council for Promoting Christian Unity; from 1977. This dialogue is now sponsored by the World Evangelical Alliance, on the evangelical side.

The Lutheran-Roman Catholic Commission on Unity, established by the Pontifical Council for Promoting Christian Unity and the Lutheran World Federation; from 1967.

The Joint International Commission for Theological Dialogue between the Orthodox Church and the Catholic Church, established by the Holy See and 14 autocephalous Orthodox Churches, began its work at a first session held at Patmos/Rhodes in 1980. Subsequent sessions have been held at Munich (1982), Crete (1984), Bari (1987), Valamo (1988), Freising (1990), Balamand (1993), and Emmitsburg, Maryland (2000). Another session is scheduled to take place in Belgrade, Serbia, in September 2006.

Pentecostal-Roman Catholic Conversations, since 1966.

The Reformed-Roman Catholic Conversations, inaugurated in 1970 by the Pontifical Council for Promoting Christian Unity and the World Alliance of Reformed Churches.

The International Joint Commission between the Catholic Church and the Coptic Orthodox Church, since 1974. Established officially in the Common Declaration signed by Pope Paul VI and Coptic Pope Shenouda III in Rome in 1973.

The Joint International Commission between the Roman Catholic Church and the Malankara Orthodox Syrian Church, since 1989.

The Joint Commission between the Catholic Church and the Malankara Jacobite Syrian Orthodox Church, since 1990.

The Assyrian Church of the East-Roman Catholic Dialogue, officially established in the Common Declaration signed by Pope John Paul II and Mar Dinkha IV in November 1994. Has been meeting annually since 1995.

A new Catholic Church-Oriental Orthodox Churches International Joint Commission for Dialogue was planned at a Preparatory Meeting held in Rome in January 2003. The first meeting of the Joint Commission took place in Cairo in January 2004, the second in Rome in January 2005, and the third in Etchmiadzin, Armenia, in January 2006.

Dialogue between the World Evangelical Alliance and the Catholic Church begun in 1990 issued a statement in 2002.

Dialogue with the Mennonite World Conference begun in 1998 produced an agreed statement in 2003.

U.S. ECUMENICAL DIALOGUES

Representatives of the Bishops' Committee for Ecumenical and Interreligious Affairs, National Conference of Catholic Bishops, have met in dialogue with representatives of other churches since the 1960s, for discussion of a wide variety of subjects related to the quest for unity among Christians. Following is a list of dialogue groups and the years in which dialogue began.

Anglican-Roman Catholic Consultation, 1965; North American Orthodox-Catholic Theological Consultation, 1965; Joint Committee of Orthodox and Catholic Bishops, 1981; Lutheran Consultation, 1965; Oriental Orthodox Consultation (with Armenian, Coptic, Ethiopian, Indian Malabar and Syrian Orthodox Churches), 1978; Polish National-Catholic Consultation, 1984; Presbyterian/Reformed Consultation, 1965; Southern Baptist Conversations, 1969; United Methodist Consultation, 1966; Faith and Order National Council of Churches, 1968; National Association of Evangelicals, 2003.

COMMON DECLARATIONS OF POPES, OTHER CHURCH LEADERS

(Source: Secretariat of the Bishops' Committee for Ecumenical and Interreligious Affairs, United States Conference of Catholic Bishops.)

The following Common Declarations, issued by several popes and heads, carry the authority given them by their signators.

Paul VI and Orthodox Ecumenical Patriarch Athenagoras I, First Common Declaration, Dec. 7, 1965: They hoped the differences between the churches would be overcome with the help of the Holy Spirit, and that their "full communion of faith, brotherly concord and sacramental life" would be restored.

Paul VI and Anglican Archbishop Michael Ramsey of Canterbury, Mar. 24, 1966: They stated their intention "to inaugurate between the Roman Catholic Church and the Anglican Communion a serious dialogue which, founded on the Gospels and on the ancient common traditions, may lead to that unity in truth for which Christ prayed."

Paul VI and Patriarch Athenagoras I, Second Common Declaration, Oct. 27, 1967: They wished "to emphasize their conviction that the restoration of full communion (between the churches) is to be found within the framework of the renewal of the Church and of Christians in fidelity to the traditions of the Fathers and to the inspirations of the Holy Spirit who remains always with the Church."

Paul VI and Vasken I, Orthodox Catholicos-Patriarch of All Armenians, May 12, 1970: They called for closer collaboration "in all domains of Christian life. . . . This collaboration must be based on the mutual recognition of the common Christian faith and the sacramental life, on the mutual respect of persons and their churches."

Paul VI and Mar Ignatius Jacob III, Syrian Orthodox Patriarch of Antioch, Oct. 27, 1971: They declared themselves to be "in agreement that there is no difference in the faith they profess concerning the mystery of the Word of God made flesh and become really man, even if over the centuries difficulties have arisen out of the different theological expressions by which this faith was expressed."

Paul VI and Shenouda III, Coptic Orthodox Pope of Alexandria, May 10, 1973: Their common declaration recalls the common elements of the Catholic and Coptic Orthodox faith in the Trinity, the divinity and humanity of Christ, the seven sacraments, the Virgin Mary, the Church founded upon the Apostles, and the Second Coming of Christ. It recognizes that the two churches "are not able to give more perfect witness to this new life in Christ because of existing divisions which have behind them centuries of difficult history" dating back to the year A.D. 451. In spite of these difficulties, they expressed "determination and confidence in the Lord to achieve the fullness and perfection of that unity which is his gift."

Paul VI and Anglican Archbishop Donald Coggan of Canterbury, Apr. 29, 1977: They stated many points on which Anglicans and Roman Catholics hold the faith in common and called for greater cooperation between Anglicans and Roman Catholics.

John Paul II and Orthodox Ecumenical Patriarch Dimitrios I, First Common Declaration, Nov. 30, 1979: "Purification of the collective memory of our churches is an important fruit of the dialogue of charity and an indispensable condition of future progress." They announced the establishment of the Catholic-Orthodox Theological Commission.

John Paul II and Anglican Archbishop Robert Runcie of Canterbury, May 29, 1982: They agreed to establish a new Anglican-Roman Catholic commission with the task of continuing work already begun toward the eventual resolution of doctrinal differences.

John Paul II and Ignatius Zakka I, Syrian Orthodox Patriarch of Antioch, June 23, 1984: They recalled and solemnly reaffirmed the common profession of faith made by their predecessors, Paul VI and Mar Ignatius Jacob III, in 1971. They said: "The confusions and the schisms that occurred between the churches, they realize today, in no way affect or touch the substance of their faith, since these arose only because of differences in terminology and culture, and in the various formulae adopted by different theological schools to express the same matter. Accordingly, we find today no real basis for the sad divisions which arose between us concerning the doctrine of the Incarnation." On the pastoral level, they declared: "It is not rare for our faithful to find access to a priest of their own church materially or morally impossible. Anxious to meet their needs and with their spiritual benefit in mind, we authorize them in such cases to ask for the sacraments of penance, Eucharist and anointing of the sick from lawful priests of either of our two sister churches, when they need them."

John Paul II and Orthodox Ecumenical Patriarch Dimitrios I, Second Common Declaration, Dec. 7, 1987: Dialogue conducted since 1979 indicated that the churches can already profess together as common faith about the mystery of the Church and the connection between faith and the sacraments. They also stated that, "when unity of faith is assured, a certain diversity of expressions does not create obstacles to unity, but enriches the life of the Church and the understanding, always imperfect, of the revealed mystery.

John Paul II and Anglican Archbishop Robert Runcie of Canterbury, Oct. 2, 1989: They said: "We solemnly re-commit ourselves and those we represent to the restoration of visible unity and full ecclesial communion in the confidence that to seek anything less would be to betray our Lord's intention for the unity of his people."

John Paul II and His Holiness Mar Dinkha IV, Catholicos-Patriarch of the Assyrian Church of the East, Nov. 11, 1994: Following is the text of the "Common Christological Declaration" between the Catholic Church and the Assyrian Church of the East, signed Nov. 11, 1994, by Pope John Paul II and His Holiness Mar Dinkha IV, Catholicos-Patriarch of the Assyrian Church of the East. The declaration acknowledges that, despite past differences, both churches profess the same faith in the real union of divine and human natures in the divine Person of Christ. Providing background to the declaration was the Assyrian Church's adherence to the teaching of Nestorius who, in the fifth century, denied the real unity of divine and human natures in the single divine Person of Christ.

Pope John Paul II with Ecumenical Orthodox Patriarch Bartholomew I, June 29, 1995: Pope John Paul and Ecumenical Orthodox Patriarch Bartholomew I, after several days of meetings, signed a common declaration June 29, 1995, declaring: "Our meeting has followed other important events which have seen our Churches declare their desire to relegate the excommunications of the past to oblivion and to set out on the way to establishing full communion. "Our new-found brotherhood in the name of the Lord has led us to frank discussion, a dialogue that seeks understanding and unity. This dialogue — through the Joint International (Catholic-Orthodox) Commission — has proved fruitful and has made substantial progress.

Pope John Paul II with Anglican Archbishop George Carey, Common Ecumenical Declaration, Dec. 5, 1996: The pontiff and archbishop praised the work of the Anglican-Roman Catholic International Commission and stated that "In many parts of the world Anglicans and Catholics attempt to witness together in the face of growing secularism, religious apathy and moral confusion."

Pope John Paul II with Karekin I, Catholicos of All Armenians, Dec. 13, 1996.

Pope John Paul and His Holiness Karekin I, Supreme Patriarch and Catholicos of All Armenians, Dec. 13, 1996, signed a common declaration in which they said in part: "Pope John Paul II and Catholicos Karekin I recognize the deep spiritual communion which already unites them and the bishops and clergy and lay faithful of their churches. It is a communion which finds its roots in the common faith in the holy and life-giving Trinity proclaimed by the Apostles and transmitted down the centuries. . . . They rejoice in the fact that recent developments of ecumenical relations and theological discussions . . . have dispelled many misunderstandings inherited from the controversies and dissensions of the past. Such dialogues and encounters have prepared a healthy situation of mutual understanding and recovery of the deeper spiritual communion based on the common faith in the holy Trinity that they have been given through the Gospel of Christ and in the holy tradition of the Church.

Pope John Paul II with Aram I, Armenian Catholicos of Cilicia, Jan. 25, 1997: The common declaration stated, "the two spiritual leaders stress the vital importance of sincere dialogue. The Catholic Church and the Catholicate of Cilicia also have an immense field of constructive cooperation before them."

Cardinal Edward Cassidy with Bishop Christian Krause, President of the Lutheran World Federation, Oct. 31, 1999: "Joint Declaration on Justification by Faith." (See **Special Section.**)

Pope John Paul II with Karekin II, Catholicos of All Armenians, Nov. 10, 2000, in Rome: His Holiness Pope John Paul II, Bishop of Rome, and His Holiness Karekin II, Supreme Patriarch and Catholicos of All Armenians, give thanks to the Lord and Savior Jesus Christ, for enabling them to meet together on the occasion of the Jubilee of the Year 2000 and on the threshold of the 1700th anniversary of the proclamation of Christianity as the state religion of Armenia.

Pope John Paul II with Christodoulos, Archbishop of Athens, May 4, 2001:

We, Pope John Paul II, Bishop of Rome, and Christodoulos, Archbishop of Athens and All Greece, standing before the bema of the Areopagus, from which Saint Paul, the Great Apostle to the Nations, "called to be an Apostle, set apart for the Gospel of God" (Rom 1:1), preached to the Athenians the One True God, Father, Son and Holy Spirit, and called them unto faith and repentance, do hereby declare:

We give thanks to the Lord for our meeting and communication with one another, here in the illustrious City of Athens, the Primatial See of the Apostolic Orthodox Church of Greece.

We repeat with one voice and one heart the words of the Apostle to the Nations: "I appeal to you, brethren, by the name of our Lord Jesus Christ, that all of you agree and that there be no schisms among you, but that you be united in the same mind and the same judgment"(1 Cor 1:10).

We are anguished to see that wars, massacres, torture and martyrdom constitute a terrible daily reality for millions of our brothers. We commit ourselves to struggle for the prevailing of peace throughout the whole world, for the respect of life and human dignity, and for solidarity towards all who are in need. We are pleased to add our voice to the many voices around the world which have expressed the hope that, on the occasion of the Olympic Games to be held in Greece in 2004, the ancient Greek tradition of the Olympic Truce will be revived, according to which all wars had to stop, and terrorism and violence had to cease.

We follow carefully and with unease what is referred to as globalization. We hope that it will bear good fruit. However, we wish to point out that its fruits will be harmful if what could be termed the "globalization of brotherhood" in Christ is not achieved in all sincerity and efficacy.

We rejoice at the success and progress of the European Union. The union of the European world in one civil entity, without her people losing their national self-awareness, traditions and identity, has been the vision of its pioneers. However, the emerging tendency to transform certain European countries into secular states without any reference to religion constitutes a retraction and a denial of their spiritual legacy. We are called to intensify our efforts so that the unification of Europe may be accomplished. We shall do everything in our power, so that the Christian roots of Europe and its Christian soul may be preserved inviolate.

John Paul II and Karekin II, Catholicos of All Armenians, Sept. 27, 2001, in Etchmiadzin, Armenia:

The celebration of the 1700th anniversary of the proclamation of Christianity as the religion of Armenia has brought us together — John Paul II, Bishop of Rome and Pastor of the Catholic Church, and Karekin II, the Supreme Patriarch and Catholicos of All Armenians — and we thank God for giving us this joyous opportunity to join again in common prayer, in praise of his all-holy Name. Blessed be the Holy Trinity — Father, Son and Holy Spirit — now and forever.

Pope John Paul II and Ecumenical Patriarch Bartholomew I signed a Common Declaration on Environmental Ethics, June 10, 2002: We are gathered here today in the spirit of peace for the good of all human beings and for the care of creation. At this moment in history, at the beginning of the third millennium, we are saddened to see the daily suffering of a great number of people from violence, starvation, poverty and disease. We are also concerned about the negative consequences for humanity and for all creation resulting from the degradation of some basic natural resources such as water, air and land, brought about by an economic and technological progress which does not recognize and take into account its limits. Rome — Venice, June 10, 2002

Pope John Paul II and Patriarch Teoctist of the Romanian Orthodox Church signed a Joint Declaration in Rome on Oct. 12, 2002: "The glory which you have given me I have given to them, that they may be one even as we are one, I in them and you in me, that they may become perfectly one, so that the world may know that you have sent me and have loved them even as you have loved me" (Jn 17:22-23).

In the deep joy of being together again in the city of Rome, close to the tombs of the holy Apostles Peter and Paul, we exchange the kiss of peace under the gaze of the One who watches over his Church and guides our steps; and we meditate anew on these words, which the Evangelist John transmitted to us and which constitute Christ's heartfelt prayer on the eve of his Passion.

Pope John Paul II and Ecumenical Patriarch Bartholomew I signed a Common Declaration on June 29, 2004, during the Patriarch's visit to Rome:
"Be watchful, stand firm in your faith, be courageous, be strong. Let all that you do be done in love" (1 Cor 16: 13-14).

1. In the spirit of faith in Christ and the reciprocal love that unites us, we thank God for this gift of our new meeting that is taking place on the Feast of the Holy Apostles Peter and Paul and witnesses to our firm determination to continue on our way towards full communion with one another in Christ.

2. Many positive steps have marked our common journey, starting above all with the historical event that we are recalling today: the embrace of Pope Paul VI and Patriarch Athenagoras I on the Mount of Olives in Jerusalem, on Jan. 5 - 6, 1964. We, their Successors, are meeting today to commemorate fittingly before God that blessed encounter, now part of the history of the Church, faithfully recalling it and its original intentions.

3. The embrace in Jerusalem of our respective Predecessors of venerable memory visibly expressed a hope that dwells in all hearts, as the Communiqué declared: "With eyes turned to Christ, together with the Father, the Archetype and Author of unity and of peace, they pray God that this encounter may be the sign and prelude of things to come for the glory of God and the enlightenment of his faithful people. After so many centuries of silence, they have now met with the desire to do the Lord's will and to proclaim the ancient truth of his Gospel, entrusted to the Church" (Common Declaration of Pope Paul VI and Patriarch Athenagoras I, Tomos Agapis, Vatican-Phanar, 1971, no. 50, p. 120).

4. Unity and Peace! The hope kindled by that historic encounter has lit up our journey in these last decades. Aware that the Christian world has suffered the tragedy of separation for centuries, our Predecessors and we ourselves have persevered in the "dialogue of charity," our gaze turned to that blessed, shining day on which it will be possible to communicate with the same cup of the precious Blood and the holy Body of the Lord (cf. Patriarch Athenagoras I, Address to Pope Paul VI [Jan. 5, 1964], ibid., no. 48, p. 109). The many ecclesial events that have punctuated these past years have put on firm foundations the commitment to brotherly love: a love which, in learning from past lessons, may be ready to forgive, more inclined to believe in good than in evil and intent first and foremost on complying with the Divine Redeemer and in being attracted and transformed by him (Address of Pope Paul VI to Patriarch Athenagoras I [Jan. 6, 1964], ibid., no. 49, p. 117).

5. Let us thank the Lord for the exemplary gestures of reciprocal love, participation and sharing that he has granted us to make; among them, it is only right to recall the Pope's Visit to the Ecumenical Patriarch Dimitrios in 1979, when the creation of the Joint International Commission for Theological Dialogue between the Catholic Church and all the Orthodox Churches was announced at the Phanar, a further step to sustain the "dialogue of truth" with the "dialogue of charity"; Patriarch Dimitrios' visit to Rome in 1987; our meeting in Rome on the feast of Sts. Peter and Paul in 1995, when we prayed in St. Peter's, despite the painful separation during the celebration of the Eucharistic Liturgy, since we cannot yet drink from the same chalice of the Lord. Then, more recently, there was the meeting at Assisi for the "Day of Prayer for Peace in the World," and the Common Declaration on Environmental Ethics for the Safeguard of Creation, signed on June 10, 2002 [in the context of the Fourth Symposium on Ecology: The Adriatic Sea: a Sea at Risk — Unity of Purpose].

6. Despite our firm determination to journey on towards full communion, it would have been unrealistic not to expect obstacles of various kinds: doctrinal, first of all, but also the result of conditioning by a troubled history. In addition, the new problems which have emerged from the radical changes that have occurred in political and social structures have not failed to make themselves felt in relations between the Christian Churches. With the return to freedom of Christians in Central and Eastern Europe, old fears have also been reawakened, making dialogue difficult. Nonetheless, St. Paul's exhortation to the Corinthians: let all things be done in charity, must always be vibrant within us and between us.

7. The Joint International Commission for Theological Dialogue between the Catholic Church and all the Orthodox Churches, created with so much hope, has marked our progress in recent years. It is still a suitable instrument for studying the ecclesiological and historical problems that are at the root of our difficulties, and for identifying hypothetical solutions to them. It is our duty to persevere in the important commitment to reopen the work as soon as possible. In examining the reciprocal initiatives of the offices of Rome and of Constantinople with this in view, we ask the Lord to sustain our determination, and to convince everyone of how essential it is to pursue the "dialogue of truth."

8. Our meeting in Rome today also enables us to face certain problems and misunderstandings that have recently surfaced. The long experience of the "dialogue of charity" comes to our aid precisely in these circumstances, so that difficulties can be faced serenely without slowing or clouding our progress on the journey we have undertaken toward full communion in Christ.

9. Before a world that is suffering every kind of division and imbalance, today's encounter is intended as a practical and forceful reminder of the importance for Christians and for the Churches to coexist in peace and harmony, in order to witness in agreement to the message of the Gospel in the most credible and convincing way possible.

10. In the special context of Europe, moving in the direction of higher forms of integration and expansion towards the East of the Continent, we thank the Lord for this positive development and express the hope that in this new situation, collaboration between Catholics and Orthodox may grow. There are so many challenges to face together in order to contribute to the good of society: to heal with love the scourge of terrorism, to instill a hope of peace, to help set aright the multitude of grievous conflicts; to restore to the European Continent the awareness of its Christian roots; to build true dialogue with Islam, since indifference and reciprocal ignorance can only give rise to diffidence and even hatred; to nourish an awareness of the sacred nature of human life; to work to ensure that science does not deny the divine spark that every human being receives with the gift of life; to collaborate so that our earth may not be disfigured and that Creation may preserve the beauty with which it has been endowed by God; but above all, to proclaim the Gospel Message with fresh vigor, showing contemporary men and women how the Gospel can help them rediscover themselves and to build a more human world.

11. Let us pray to the Lord to give peace to the Church and to the world, and to imbue our journey towards full communion with the wisdom of his Spirit, "ut unum in Christo simus" [so that we may be one in Christ].

From the Vatican, June 29, 2004

ECUMENICAL STATEMENTS

The ecumenical statements listed below, and others like them, reflect the views of participants in the dialogues which produced them. They have not been formally accepted by the respective churches as formulations of doctrine or points of departure for practical changes in discipline. (For other titles, see U.S. Ecumenical Dialogues, Ecumenical Reports.)

• The "Windsor Statement" on Eucharistic doctrine, published Dec. 31, 1971, by the Anglican-Roman Catholic International Commission of theologians. (For text, see pp. 132-33 of the 1973 *Catholic Almanac.*)

• The "Canterbury Statement" on ministry and ordination, published Dec. 13, 1973, by the same commission. (For excerpts, see pp. 127-30 of the 1975 *Catholic Almanac.*)

• "Papal Primacy/Converging Viewpoints," published Mar. 4, 1974, by the dialogue group sanctioned by the U.S.A. National Convention of the World Lutheran Federation and the U.S. Bishops' Committee for Ecumenical and Interreligious Affairs. (For excerpts, see pp. 130-31 of the 1975 *Catholic Almanac.*)

• An "Agreed Statement on the Purpose of the Church," published Oct. 31, 1975, by the Anglican-Roman Catholic Consultation in the U.S.

• "Christian Unity and Women's Ordination," published Nov. 7, 1975, by the same consultation, in which it was said that the ordination of women (approved in principle by the Anglican Communion but not by the Catholic Church) would "introduce a new element" in dialogue but would not mean the end of consultation nor the abandonment of its declared goal of full communion and organic unity.

• "Holiness and Spirituality of the Ordained Ministry," issued early in 1976 by theologians of the Catholic Church and the United Methodist Church; the first statement resulting from dialogue begun in 1966.

• "Mixed Marriages," published in the spring of 1976 by the Anglican-Roman Catholic Consultation in the U.S.

• "Bishops and Presbyters," published in July 1976, by the Orthodox-Roman Catholic Consultation in the U.S. on the following points of common understanding: (1) Ordination in apostolic succession is required for pastoral office in the Church. (2) Presiding at the Eucharistic Celebration is a task belonging to those ordained to pastoral service. (3) The offices of bishop and presbyter are different realizations of the sacrament of order. (4) Those ordained are claimed permanently for the service of the Church.

• "The Principle of Economy," published by the body named above at the same time, concerning God's plan and activities in human history for salvation.

• "Venice Statement" on authority in the Church, published Jan. 20, 1977, by the Anglican-Roman Catholic International Commission of theologians.

• "Response to the Venice Statement," issued Jan. 4, 1978, by the Anglican-Roman Catholic Consultation in the U.S.A., citing additional questions.

• "An Ecumenical Approach to Marriage," published in January 1978, by representatives of the Catholic Church, the Lutheran World Federation and the World Alliance of Reformed Churches.

• "Teaching Authority and Infallibility in the Church," released in October, 1978, by the Catholic-Lutheran dialogue group in the U.S.

• "The Eucharist," reported early in 1979, in which the Roman Catholic-Lutheran Commission indicated developing convergence of views.

• "The Holy Spirit," issued Feb. 12, 1979, by the International Catholic-Methodist Commission.

• A statement on "Ministry in the Church," published in March, 1981, by the International Roman Catholic-Lutheran Joint Commission, regarding possible mutual recognition of ministries.

• The Final Report of the Anglican-Roman Catholic International Commission, 1982, on the results of 12 years of dialogue.

• "The Mystery of the Church and of the Eucharist in the Light of the Mystery of the Holy Trinity," issued by the Mixed International Commission for Theological Dialogue between the Catholic Church and the Orthodox Church at Munich, Germany, in July 1982.

• The Final Report of the Anglican-Roman Catholic International Commission, 1982, on the results of 12 years of dialogue.

• "Justification by Faith," issued Sept. 30, 1983, by the U.S. Lutheran-Roman Catholic dialogue group, claiming a "fundamental consensus on the Gospel."

• "Images of God: Reflections on Christian Anthropology," released Dec. 22, 1983, by the Anglican-Roman Catholic Dialogue in the United States.

• "The Journeying Together in Christ — The Report of the Polish National Catholic-Roman Catholic Dialogue (1984-89)."

• "Salvation and the Church," issued Jan. 22, 1987, by the Second Anglican-Roman Catholic International Commission.

• "Faith, Sacraments and the Unity of the Church," issued by the Mixed International Commission for Theological Dialogue between the Catholic Church and the Orthodox Churches in June 1987.

• "The Sacrament of Order in the Sacramental Structure of the Church, with Particular Reference to the Importance of Apostolic Succession for the Sanctification and Unity of the People of God," issued by the Mixed International Commission for Theological Dialogue between the Catholic Church and the Orthodox Church in Valamo, Finland, in 1988.

• "The Presence of Christ in Church and World" and "Toward a Common Understanding of the Church" (developed between 1984 and 1990), by the Reformed-Roman Catholic Conversations, under the auspices of the Pontifical Council for Promoting Christian Unity and the World Alliance of Reformed Churches.

• "The Church as Communion," issued by the Second Anglican-Roman Catholic International Commission, 1991.

• "Uniatism, Method of Union of the Past, and the Present Search for Full Communion," issued by the Mixed International Commission for Theological Dialogue between the Catholic Church and the Orthodox Church at Balamand, Lebanon, in 1993.

• "Life in Christ: Morals, Communion and the Church," issued by the Second Anglican-Roman Catholic International Commission, 1994.

• "Common Response to the Aleppo Statement on the Date of Easter/Pacha," issued by the North

American Orthodox- Catholic Theological Consultation in Washington, D.C., Oct. 31, 1998.

• "The Gift of Authority," issued by the Second Anglican-Roman Catholic International Commission, May 12, 1999.

• "Baptism and 'Sacramental Economy,' " issued by the North American Orthodox-Catholic Theological Consultation at Crestwood, New York, in June 1999.

• "Guidelines Concerning the Pastoral Care of Oriental Orthodox Students in Catholic Schools," issued by the Oriental Orthodox-Roman Catholic Theological Consultation in the United States at New Rochelle, N.Y., in June 1999.

• "Joint Declaration of the Catholic Church and the Lutheran World Federation on the Doctrine of Justification," issued July 8, 1999, by the International Roman Catholic-Lutheran Joint Commission.

• "Agreed Report on the Local/Universal Church," issued by the United States Anglican-Roman Catholic Consultation, Nov. 12, 1999.

• "Communion in Mission" and "Action Plan to Implement 'Communion in Mission,' " issued by a special consultation of Anglican and Roman Catholic bishops in Mississauga, Ontario, Canada, May 19, 2000.

• "Sharing the Ministry of Reconciliation: A Statement on the Orthodox-Catholic Dialogue and the Ecumenical Movement," issued June 1, 2000, by the North American Orthodox-Catholic Theological Consultation in Brookline, Mass.

• "Methodist-Catholic Dialogues: Thirty Years of Mission and Witness," issued by the U.S. dialogue in 2001.

• "Doing the Truth in Charity," issued in July 2001 by the World Methodist Council and the Pontifical Council for Promoting Unity's Methodist-Catholic International Commission.

• "Interchurch Families: Resources for Ecumenical Hope," issued by the Catholic/Reformed Dialogue in the United States in 2002.

• Response of the Anglican-Roman Catholic Consultation in the USA to the Anglican-Roman Catholic International Commission's "The Gift of Authority" (Mar. 29, 2003)

• "Called Together to be Peacemakes," Mennonite World Conference Catholic Dialogue 2003.

• "Church, Evangelization, and Koinonia," World Evangelical Alliance – Pontifical Council for Promoting Christian Unity 2003.

• "The Filioque: A Church-Dividing Issue?" issued by the North American Orthodox-Catholic Theological Consultation, October 2003.

• "The Church as Koinonia of Salvation: Its Structures and Ministries," May 2004, Lutheran Catholic Dialogue in the U.S.

• "Mary: Grace and Hope in Christ," Anglican Roman Catholic Commission, 2004.

• "Journey in Faith: Forty Years of Reformed-Catholic Dialogue: 1965-2005," 2005.

• "Through Divine Love: The Church in Each Place and All Places," April 2005, United Methodist Roman Catholic Dialogue in the U.S.

• "Joint Declaration on Unity" by the Polish National Catholic – Roman Catholic Dialogue (May 17, 2006).

See online: www.prounione.urbe.it/dia-int/e_dialogues.html, or www.usccb.org/seia/dialogues.htm

ANGLICAN-ROMAN CATHOLIC FINAL REPORT

The Anglican-Roman Catholic International Commission issued a Final Report in 1982 on 12 years of dialogue on major issues of concern, especially the Eucharist and ordained ministry.

In 1988 the Lambeth Conference called parts of the report on these two subjects "consonant in substance with the faith of Anglicans." In 1991 the Congregation for the Doctrine of the Faith and the Pontifical Council for Promoting Christian Unity called the Report a significant milestone not only in relations between the Catholic Church and the Anglican Communion but in the ecumenical movement as a whole. They said, however, that it was not yet possible to state that substantial agreement had been reached on all the questions studied by the commission, and that important differences still remained with respect to essential matters of Catholic doctrine regarding the Eucharist, ordination and other subjects. Clarifications were requested.

The Anglican-Roman Catholic Commission II responded in 1994, saying that its members were in agreement regarding:

• the substantial and sacramental presence of Christ in the Eucharist;

• the propitiatory nature of the Eucharistic Sacrifice, which can also be applied to the deceased;

• institution of the sacrament of order from Christ;

• the character of priestly ordination, implying configuration to the priesthood of Christ.

In 1994 Card. Edward I. Cassidy, president of the Pontifical Council for Interreligious Dialogue addressed a letter to the Catholic and Anglican co-chairmen of the commission, responding to the clarifications, stating that "no further work" seems to be necessary at this time on Eucharist and ministry. Questions still remained to be answered about a number of subjects, including the authority in the Church, ordination of women, infallibility and Marian doctrine.

JOINT DECLARATION ON JUSTIFICATION

By Russell Shaw

Hailed by Pope John Paul II as a "milestone" on the road to Christian unity, a Lutheran-Catholic Joint Declaration on the Doctrine of Justification was signed Oct. 31, 1999, in Augsburg, Germany, by representatives of the Catholic Church and the Lutheran World Federation.

"This document represents a sound basis for continuing the ecumenical theological research and for addressing the remaining problems with a better founded hope of resolving them in the future," Pope John Paul said the same day in Rome in a talk accompanying the recitation of the Angelus. "It is also a valuable contribution to the purification of historical memory and to our common witness."

The Joint Declaration states a "consensus" shared by the signers regarding the doctrine of justification. The key passage formulating this consensus says:

"In faith we together hold the conviction that justification is the work of the triune God. The Father sent his Son into the world to save sinners. The foundation and presupposition of justification is the incarnation, death, and resurrection of Christ. Justification thus means that Christ himself is our righteousness, in which we share through the Holy Spirit in accord with the will of the Father.

"Together we confess: By grace alone, in faith in Christ's saving work and not because of any merit on our part, we are accepted by God and receive the Holy Spirit, who renews our hearts while equipping and calling us to good works."

The signers of the Joint Declaration were Cardinal Edward I. Cassidy, President of the Vatican's Pontifical Council for Promoting Christian Unity, and Bishop Christian Krause, President of the Lutheran World Federation, which represents 58 million of the world's 61 million Lutherans. Most, but not all, of the churches within the federation have accepted the Joint Declaration.

Both the date and the place of the signing had symbolic significance. October 31 is observed by Protestants as Reformation Day, commemorating Martin Luther's nailing of his Ninety-five Theses on the castle church door in Wittenberg on that date in 1517. The city of Augsburg is associated with the Augsburg Confession, a document authored in 1530 by the Protestant Reformer Philipp Melancthon in an attempt to bring about reconciliation between Lutherans and Catholics.

From a theological perspective, the doctrine of justification was of central importance in the Reformation and in the mutual condemnations exchanged by Catholics and Lutherans in the 16th century via the Council of Trent and the Lutheran Confessions.

The Joint Declaration stresses that the churches "neither take the condemnations lightly nor do they disavow their own past." But, it insists, as a result of ecumenical dialogue during the last 30 years, they have come to "new insights" that transcend the mutual polemics of the Reformation era and make it clear that neither party's understanding of justification, as it is expressed in the Joint Declaration, now merits condemnation by the other, while the differences about the doctrine that continue to exist between them "are acceptable."

The Council for Promoting Christian Unity and the Lutheran World Federation reached basic agreement on the document in June 1998, but further clarifications were required on both sides before official approval was forthcoming. These clarifications are embodied in an "Annex" to the text.

Despite the harmonious tone of the document and the various statements that accompanied its signing, the Joint Declaration has been, and to some extent remains, a controversial document. Some Lutheran bodies, including the Lutheran churches of several countries, have not accepted it. Nor has an unknown number of individual Lutherans, theologians among them.

On the Catholic side, there has been criticism that the document does not go far enough in coming to terms with Lutheranism and, on the other hand, that it goes too far in papering-over serious theological differences. According to the theologian Fr. Avery Dulles, S.J., it is "a bold statement, difficult to defend" to claim that the differing views still held by Catholics and Lutherans on various questions relating to the doctrine of justification really do "escape the condemnations" pronounced by each side on the other in the 16th century.

"But notwithstanding all the theological reservations on both sides," Fr. Dulles added in an October 1999, lecture at Fordham University, New York, reprinted in the magazine *First Things*, the signing of the Joint Declaration "can be a powerful symbolic event."

"It says clearly to a world that hovers on the brink of unbelief that the two churches that split Western Christendom on the issue of justification nearly five centuries ago are still united on truths of the highest import," he said.

The Joint Declaration has been hailed as the fruit of some 30 years of ecumenical dialogue between Lutherans and Catholics. The doctrine of justification was an issue in these conversations from the start. The 1972 report of the international Lutheran-Catholic dialogue included five paragraphs on the topic, and observed that "today. . . a far-reaching consensus is developing." This emerging consensus also was noted in 1980 and 1981 reports by the international dialogue.

The doctrine of justification was considered in reports from national Lutheran-Catholic dialogues in the United States ("Justification by Faith," 1985) and Germany ("The Condemnations of the Reformation Era. Do They Still Divide?" 1986). These reports from national dialogues contributed to a lengthy report developed by the third phase of the international dialogue and published in 1993 as "Church and Justification: Understanding the Church in the Light of the Doctrine of Justification." In 1993, at the request of the Lutheran World Federation and the Council for Promoting Christian Unity, a small Lutheran-Catholic working group was formed to begin work on what became the Joint Declaration.

While the document first of all marks a significant new stage in Lutheran-Catholic relations, it also has broader ecumenical significance, Cardinal Cassidy said in an article published in the Vatican newspaper *L'Osservatore Romano*.

"What has been achieved in this mutual agreement of the Joint Declaration surely is an historic development of particular importance in the history of Western Christianity, and indeed for the whole ecumenical movement as well, since it illustrates that ecumenical progress can be made on questions that are of central importance, and have long been seen as church-dividing issues," he wrote.

Cardinal Cassidy listed "three basic truths" that he said were central to the doctrine of justification and to the Lutheran-Catholic consensus expressed in the Joint Declaration. They are:

"First, justification is a free gift bestowed by the Trinitarian God and centers on the person of Christ who became incarnate, died and rose. In being related to the person of Christ through the work of the Holy Spirit, we enter into a condition of righteousness....

"Second, we receive this salvation in faith. . . . [T]he reality of justification is linked to faith, but not simply as an intellectual assent of the mind. Rather the believer is to give him/herself over to Christ in the renewal of life.

"Third, justification points to the heart of the Gospel message, but must be seen in an organic unity with all the other truths of faith: Trinity, Christology, Ecclesiology and Sacraments."

The Joint Declaration begins with a Preamble that includes this statement of the document's intention: ". . . to show that on the basis of their dialogue the subscribing Lutheran churches and the Roman Catholic Church are now able to articulate a common understanding of our justification by God's grace through faith in Christ. It does not cover all that either church teaches about justification; it does encompass a consensus on basic truths of the doctrine of justification and shows that the remaining differences in its explication are no longer the occasion for doctrinal condemnations."

Following an overview of significant scriptural passages on the doctrine (section one), the document notes that, historically, justification has been an ecumenical problem between the Catholic Church and the Reformation churches and that differences focusing on it were the "principal cause" of their division and mutual condemnations in the 16th century. But in the ecumenical dialogue since the Second Vatican Council (1962-1965), it says, a "notable convergence" has emerged (section two).

The Joint Declaration then states the "consensus" on the basic truths of the doctrine, quoted above (section three). Justification is said to be "more than just one part of Christian doctrine. It stands in an essential relation with all truths of faith, which are to be seen as internally related to each other."

The fourth section of the Declaration ("Explicating the Common Understanding of Justification") is the document's longest section. It identifies, one by one, seven particular questions relating to the doctrine, states the consensus shared by Lutherans and Catholics regarding these seven questions, and then sets out distinctive Catholic and Lutheran perspectives on each.

The seven topics treated in this manner are: "Human Powerlessness and Sin in Relation to Justification," "Justification as Forgiveness of Sins and Making Righteous," "Justification by Faith and through Grace," "The Justified as Sinner," "Law and Gospel," "Assurance of Salvation," and "The Good Works of the Justified."

The Joint Declaration closes by once again underlining the "consensus in basic truths" regarding justification and stating its "significance and scope" (section five):

"In light of this consensus the remaining differences of language, theological elaboration, and emphasis in the understanding described in paras. 18 to 39 [section four] are acceptable. Therefore the Lutheran and Catholic explications of justification are in their difference open to one another and do not destroy the consensus regarding the basic truths.

"Thus the doctrinal condemnations of the 16th century, in so far as they relate to the doctrine of justification, appear in a new light. The teaching of the Lutheran churches presented in this Declaration does not fall under the condemnations from the Council of Trent. The condemnations of the Lutheran Confessions do not apply to the teaching of the Roman Catholic Church presented in this Declaration."

The document lists a number of other questions between Catholics and Lutherans that need clarification: the relationship between the Word of God and church doctrine, ecclesiology, ecclesial authority, church unity, ministry, the sacraments, and the relation between justification and social ethics. "We are confident that the consensus we have reached offers a solid basis for this clarification," it says.

An "Official Common Statement" of the Lutheran World Federation and the Catholic Church, issued at the time of the signing in Augsburg, commits both to continued ecumenical dialogue on outstanding questions regarding justification as well as the matters just mentioned. Such dialogue is necessary, it says, "in order to reach full church communion, a unity in diversity, in which remaining differences would be 'reconciled' and no longer have a divisive force."

In his article in L'Osservatore Romano, Cardinal Cassidy linked the signing of the Joint Declaration to the preparations for the third millennium of Christianity and the Great Jubilee of the Year 2000. In his 1994 Apostolic Letter Tertio Millennio Adveniente ("On the Coming of the Third Millennium"), he pointed out, Pope John Paul spoke of the scandal of Christian division and the need to work for unity in the new millennium. The Lutheran-Catholic accord marks important progress toward this goal, he suggested.

At the same time, the Cardinal acknowledged "the limits of our achievement" as represented in the Joint Declaration: "The declaration brings the Catholic Church and the member churches of the Lutheran World Federation which affirmed it a clear step closer to unity. They have not yet, however, achieved the goal of full, visible unity."

In particular, he said, "Catholics are not able to share the Eucharist with their Lutheran brothers and sisters. . . . Our common participation in the Eucharist awaits the full ecclesial communion which we seek."

Nevertheless, Cardinal Cassidy added, the limitations of what has been accomplished in reaching this agreement should not cause it to be underestimated. "Serious difficulties remain, but they are secondary to what we hold in common. No longer may we look upon our different expressions of faith as being like two huge cannons drawn up in battle line and facing each other. . . . We need, above all, to give thanks to God for this achievement."

THE RELATIONSHIP BETWEEN ANGLICANS AND ROMAN CATHOLICS

By Dr. John Borelli, assistant to the President, Georgetown University.

A special consultation of Roman Catholic and Anglican bishops from thirteen regions around the world met in Mississauga, Ontario, May 14-20, 2000, to review and evaluate the accomplishment of 30 years of dialogue between the two traditions and to reflect on how the special relationship has been developing in various parts of the world. Bishops attended from New Zealand, Canada, England, United States, Ireland, India, Nigeria, Papua New Guinea, Southern Africa, Uganda, Australia, Brazil and the West Indies.

The meeting was convened by Edward Card. Cassidy, then President of the Pontifical Council Promoting Christian Unity, and Abp. George Carey of Canterbury. Also participating were the two recently appointed co-chairman for the Anglican-Roman Catholic International Commission: Bp. Frank T. Griswold, Presiding Bishop of the Episcopal Church (U. S.) and Abp. Alexander J. Brunett, Archbishop of Seattle.

The meeting grew out of the visit of Archbishop Carey with Pope John Paul II in Advent 1996 and was suggested in their Common Declaration of Dec. 5, 1996, "it may be opportune at this stage in our journey to consult further about how the relationship between the Anglican Communion and the Catholic Church is to progress." With consensus yet to be achieved on authority in the church and with the new situation created by ordination of women as priests and bishops in some provinces of the Anglican Communion becoming increasingly evident, a certain amount of risk was involved in calling for a special consultation. The meeting could end in a standoff on certain issues and might even conclude with a simple acknowledgment of past achievements, current good will, and hope that the future will be brighter. These scenarios would be viewed as evidence that the dialogue is deadlocked or, at best, lost in a maze of seemingly endless study of details and differences and no certain direction towards reconciliation. Over three years were spent in preparations for the special consultation. Independent provinces of the Anglican Communion and national conferences of Catholic bishops were asked twice in the course of the planning to advise on agenda and other aspects of the proposed meeting. It was postponed once from May 1999 to May 2000 so that careful reflection and thorough preparation could take place first, and conveniently the meeting did not coincide other developments related to restoration of unity between Anglicans and Catholics.

In the meantime, the Lambeth Conference met in July 1998. The Lambeth Conference is a meeting of Anglican bishops, currently from 36 provinces and other churches in the communion worldwide, and one of its actions in 1998 was to receive "the Virginia Report," prepared by the Inter-Anglican Theological and Doctrinal Commission. This study is a response to the particular need recognized by the Lambeth Conference of 1988 for exploration of the meaning and nature of communion and how the Anglican Communion makes authoritative decisions while maintaining unity and interdependence among the independent provinces. The Lambeth Conference of 1998 recommended the report for study throughout the Communion. Also, in May 1999, the Anglican-Roman Catholic International Commission released its third agreed statement on authority in the Church, "The Gift of Authority," which among other suggestions lists eleven advances points of consensus on authority (See page 102 of the 2000 Catholic Almanac.). In a dramatic gesture of unity, on Jan. 18, 2000, Archbishop Carey assisted Pope John Paul II in opening the holy door at St. Paul-Outside-the-Walls Basilica. Thus there was a certain momentum building up to the Mississauga meeting. The second Anglican Roman Catholic International Commission completed its work with the publication of "Mary: Grace and Hope in Christ" in 2004.

On May 20, 2000, Card. Cassidy and Abp. Carey released two short documents resulting from the meeting and a press release: "Communion in Mission" and "Action Plan to Implement 'Communion in Mission.'" They reported that the bishops had spent a week in prayer together, worship, and reflection. They focused on the relationship between their communions which the Second Vatican Council said "occupies a special place" (Decree on Ecumenism, 13). They also reported how the participants came to see that the relationship is no longer to be viewed in minimal terms but has reached a significant new place. The texts acknowledge unresolved differences and challenges, but they felt that these did not compare with all that Anglicans and Catholics hold in common. They also list the essentials of the faith and common practices to which the faithful hold fast and noted areas of theological convergence that have been achieved. They also express a common vision of full and visible unity.

The strength of the texts resulting from the special consultation lies in the recommendations. First, as a sign of the new stage in relations, they recommend the signing and celebration of a Joint Declaration of Agreement. This may turn out to be something on the scale of the joint declaration between Catholics and Lutherans on the doctrine of justification. To prepare the joint declaration and promote and monitor the reception of theological agreements, they recommend the formation of a Joint Unity Commission. They go into some detail how the bishops at the meeting believed the membership, accountability and mandate of the commission should be defined as well as how the participants themselves and how the Anglican-Roman Catholic International Commission for dialogue might follow up to this meeting.

Some of the specific recommendations have been seen before in previous reports. For example, "the Malta Report" (1968) of the Joint Preparatory Commission, established by Pope Paul VI and Abp. Michael Ramsey of Canterbury to work out the steps towards a formal theological dialogue, made several of recommendations that were repeated, in some way or another, in the Mississauga texts. The Anglican-Roman Catholic Consultation in the U.S. produced a 12-year report in 1977 that contained similar recommendations. Also in 1981, a U.S. Anglican/Roman Catholic Leaders Conference proposed, on a smaller scale, that a Joint Commission be established to deal with specific areas, like pastoral ministry for Anglican-Catholic couples, and other recommendations requiring joint efforts and liaison. At best, these various recommendations were implemented sporadically. The difference with the steps taken at the Mississauga meeting is that accountability and responsibility for the implementation of these excellent recommendations lies with the Holy See's Pontifical Council for Promoting Christian Unity and the Inter-Anglican Standing Commission on Ecumenical Relations, a body established at the Lambeth Conference of 1998. The proposed Joint Unity Commission will report to these two high offices.

Much has been achieved in 35 years of dialogue both on the international commission and on various national Anglican-Roman Catholic commissions, but now a special effort will be made to incorporate these theological agreements into the lives of the churches. Also, in more formal ways, Anglicans and Catholics will be encouraged to spend more time together in prayer, study, consultation, teaching, preparation of educational and liturgical materials, marriage preparation, and common action.

Dialogue Results
International
www.prounione.urbe.it/dia-int/e_dialogues.html.

Lukas Vischer and Harding Meyer Eds., Growth in Agreement Reports and Agreed Statements of Ecumenical Conversations on a World Level (New York: Paulist Press, 1984).

William Rusch, Harding Meyer, Jeffrey Gros, eds., Growth in Agreement II, Geneva: World Council of Churches, 2000.

United States
Jeffrey Gros and Joseph Burgess, Eds., Building Unity (New York: Paulist Press, 1989).

Joseph Burgess, Jeffrey Gros, Eds., Growing Consensus, New York: Paulist Press, 1995.

Jeffrey Gros, Lydia Veliko, eds., Growing Consensus II, Washington: U.S. Conference of Catholic Bishops, 2004; www.usccb.org/seia/dialogues.htm.

THE ORTHODOX CHURCH

This is a group of Eastern churches of the Byzantine tradition that were in full communion with Rome during the first millennium, and which all recognize the Patriarch of Constantinople as the first Orthodox bishop. In spite of the division between Catholics and Orthodox, often symbolized by the mutual excommunications of 1054, the Catholic Church considers itself to be in almost full communion with the Orthodox Churches. According to Vatican II, they "are still joined to us in closest intimacy" in various ways, especially in the priesthood and Eucharist. The Orthodox Churches recognize the first seven ecumenical councils as normative for their faith, along with the Scriptures and other local councils that took place in later centuries.

The Orthodox Churches are organized in approximately 15 autocephalous (independent) churches that correspond in most cases to nations or ethnic groups. The Ecumenical Patriarch of Constantinople (modern Istanbul) has a primacy of honor among the patriarchs, but his actual jurisdiction is limited to his own patriarchate. As the spiritual head of worldwide Orthodoxy, he serves as a point of unity, and has the right to call Pan-Orthodox assemblies.

Top-level relations between the Churches have improved in recent years through the efforts of Ecumenical Patriarch Athenagoras I, Bl. John XXIII,

Paul VI and Patriarch Dimitrios I. Pope Paul met with Athenagoras three times before the latter's death in 1972. The most significant action of both spiritual leaders was their mutual nullification of excommunications imposed by the two Churches on each other in 1054. Development of better relations with the Orthodox has been a priority of John Paul II since the beginning of his pontificate. Both he and Orthodox Ecumenical Patriarch Bartholomew have made known their commitment to better relations, despite contentions between Eastern Catholic and Orthodox Churches over charges of proselytism and rival property claims in places liberated from anti-religious communist control in the recent past.

The largest Orthodox body in the United States is the Greek Orthodox Archdiocese of America consisting of nine dioceses; it has an estimated membership of 1.9 million. The second largest is the Orthodox Church in America, with more than one million members; it was given autocephalous status by the Patriarchate of Moscow May 18, 1970, without the consent of the Patriarchate of Constantinople. An additional 650,000 or more Orthodox belong to smaller national and language jurisdictions. Heads of orthodox jurisdictions in this hemisphere hold membership in the Standing Conference of Canonical Orthodox Bishops in the Americas.

JURISDICTIONS

The Autocephalous Orthodox Churches

Patriarchate of Constantinople (Ecumenical Patriarchate), with jurisdiction in Turkey, Crete, the Dodecanese, and Greeks in the rest of the world outside Greece and Africa. Autonomous churches linked to the Ecumenical Patriarchate exist in Finland and Estonia. Several other jurisdictions of various ethnicities in the diaspora are also directly under the Patriarchate.

Patriarchate of Alexandria, with jurisdiction in Egypt and the rest of Africa; it includes a native African Orthodox Church centered in Kenya and Uganda.

Patriarchate of Antioch, with jurisdiction in Syria, Lebanon, Iraq, Australia, the Americas.

Patriarchate of Jerusalem, with jurisdiction in Israel and Jordan. The autonomous church of Mount Sinai is linked to the Jerusalem Patriarchate.

Russian Orthodox Church, the Patriarchate of Moscow with jurisdiction over most of the former Soviet Union. Autonomous churches in Japan and China are linked to the Moscow Patriarchate, and since the breakup of the Soviet Union, a certain autonomy has been granted to the Orthodox churches in the newly independent republics of Ukraine, Belarus, Estonia, Moldova and Latvia.

The Serbian Orthodox Church, a patriarchate with jurisdiction in all of former Yugoslavia, Western Europe, North America and Australia.

The Romanian Orthodox Church, a patriarchate with jurisdiction in Romania, Western Europe and North America.

The Bulgarian Orthodox Church, a patriarchate with jurisdiction in Bulgaria, Western Europe and North America.

The Georgian Orthodox Church, a patriarchate with jurisdiction in the republic of Georgia.

The Orthodox Church of Cyprus, an archbishopric with jurisdiction in Cyprus.

The Orthodox Church of Greece, an archbishopric with jurisdiction in most of Greece.

The Orthodox Church of Poland, a metropolitanate with jurisdiction in Poland.

The Orthodox Church of Albania, an archbishopric with jurisdiction in Albania.

The Orthodox Church in the Czech and Slovak Republics, a metropolitanate with jurisdiction in the Czech and Slovak Republics. Its autocephalous status was granted by Moscow in 1951 but by Constantinople only in 1998.

The Orthodox Church in America, a metropolitanate with jurisdiction in North America and a few parishes in Latin America and Australia. Its autocephalous status was granted by Moscow in 1970; Constantinople and most other Orthodox churches have not recognized this.

Population

The Center for the Study of Global Christianity estimates that in 2004 there were a total of 216,574,000 Orthodox Christians worldwide. Some Orthodox claim a total membership of as many as 300 million.

Standing Conference of Orthodox Bishops

The Standing Conference of Canonical Orthodox Bishops in the Americas was established in 1960 to achieve cooperation among the various Orthodox jurisdictions in the Americas. Office: 8-10 East 79th St., New York, NY 10021.

Member churches are the: Albanian Orthodox Diocese of America (Ecumenical Patriarchate), American Carpatho-Russian Orthodox Diocese in the U.S.A. (Ecumenical Patriarchate), Antiochian Orthodox Christian Archdiocese of North America, Bulgarian Eastern Orthodox Church, Greek Orthodox Archdiocese of America (Ecumenical Patriarchate), Orthodox Church in America, Romanian Orthodox Archdiocese in America and Canada, Serbian Orthodox Church in the United States and Canada, Ukrainian Orthodox Church in the United States (Ecumenical Patriarchate).

THE ORIENTAL ORTHODOX CHURCHES

(By Johan Bonny)
The Oriental Orthodox Churches were the subject of an article by Johan Bonny in the Italian-language edition of L'Osservatore Romano on. The following is an

approved English-language translation of the article. Thanks are expressed to Fr. Ron Roberson, C.S.P., for his kind assistance in providing the translation.

A FAMILY OF CHURCHES

The Oriental Orthodox family of churches is composed of four different traditions: Coptic, Syriac, Malankara and Armenian. The Coptic tradition, first of all, originated in the ancient Patriarchate of Alexandria. It gave birth to three autocephalous churches, each of them distinct from each other in terms of language, liturgy and culture: The Coptic Orthodox Church in Egypt, the Orthodox Church of Ethiopia and the Orthodox Church of Eritrea. The Syriac tradition originated in the ancient Patriarchate of Antioch. It also gave birth to a number of local churches, including the Syriac Orthodox Church with its patriarchal see in Damascus, Syria. The Malankara tradition, situated in Kerala in southern India, has roots in the great missionary outreach of the east Syriac Church that developed in the first centuries of the Christian era under the patronage of the Apostle Thomas. In the 16th century, following ecclesiastical and social problems due to the presence of new colonial authorities in southern India, a part of this local church entered into canonical communion with the Syriac Orthodox Church while maintaining a certain level of autonomy; this church is usually called the Malankara Syrian Orthodox Church. And finally, the Armenian tradition grew out of the evangelization of the Armenian people around the year 301 through the efforts of St. Gregory the Illuminator. For a number of centuries the Armenian Apostolic Church has included two catholicossates, one with its seat in Etchmiadzin, Armenia, and the other in Antelias, Lebanon.

There is a great diversity among these particular churches, each of them having its own language, its own theological, liturgical and canonical tradition, and its own artistic and cultural patrimony. As churches linked to particular ethnic groups or nations, each of them over the course of the centuries has developed close relations with the people or nation to which it belongs. This is why these churches and their leaders, until these more recent ecumenical times, were unable to develop closer relations, and even less on the official level.

But then, what do these churches have in common? First of all there is a theological factor of the greatest importance: the non-recognition of certain doctrinal formulas of the Council of Chalcedon (451). Certainly this was due to theological disputes, but also and perhaps above all there were political factors related to the marginal position these churches had in relation to the Roman Empire with its center in Constantinople. Some of these communities, such as the Armenian, Syrian and Malankara, were for the most part located outside the borders of the empire. These churches also have in common a certain sensitivity and a certain standpoint, determined by the non-chalcedonian character of their Christology, that places greater emphasis on the divine rather than the human aspect, especially in the areas of spirituality and liturgy. Finally, another element that brings them together in this ecumenical era is the desire to work together more closely in various fields, above all in the Middle East, the cradle and homeland of most of these churches. Alongside the three Orthodox, Catholic and Protestant families that are working for greater integration and collaboration in the region, the fourth family, that of the Oriental Orthodox Churches, does not want to be left behind.

A New Phase of Ecumenical Dialogue

Since the time of the Second Vatican Council, the Catholic Church has been engaged in a bilateral dialogue with each of the Oriental Orthodox Churches. The effectiveness of these bilateral dialogues is shown by the publication of a series of impressive Common Declarations, approved and signed by the highest authorities of the Catholic Church and the Oriental Orthodox Churches. These declarations focus on Christology, the theology of the sacraments, and ecclesiology.

A new initiative has just been taken to integrate this dialogue and its results more thoroughly into the lives of our churches. During a preparatory meeting organized in Rome by the Pontifical Council for Promoting Christian Unity in January 2003, representatives of the East and the West decided to establish a new international commission for dialogue between the Catholic Church and the Oriental Orthodox Churches. The first plenary meeting will take place from Jan. 26 to 31, 2002, in Cairo, at the St. Mark Center of the Coptic Orthodox Church, under the co-presidency of Cardinal Walter Kasper and Metropolitan Anba Bishoy. The Orthodox delegation will be composed of 14 representatives (two from each particular church); the Catholic delegation will include the same number of persons, including bishops and theologians of the Latin and

Eastern traditions. This first meeting will study the results of the various official and unofficial bilateral dialogues that have taken place over the course of the last 30 years between the Catholic Church and the Oriental Orthodox Churches. In this way it should be possible to identify the doctrinal questions that remain open and the best way to deal with them. This new multilateral dialogue could also create a favorable atmosphere for the growth of a common initiative among theologians and pastors of the churches involved, allowing the Catholic Church and the Oriental Orthodox Churches to move forward together along the path toward full communion.

This new prospect should not prevent the theological dialogue between the Catholic Church and the Malankara Church in India from taking its own course. In fact, the two joint dialogue commissions with the Malankara Syrian Orthodox Church and the Malankara Orthodox Syrian Church held their annual meetings in Kottayam in October 2003. The meeting of the latter dialogue was dedicated to the study of various themes related to the history of the Church in Kerala, the ecclesiology of communion and common witness. Moreover, a common declaration was published that rules out all forms of proselytism and offensive publications by any of the various Christian communities of the region. As for common witness, some initiatives were taken with regard to the continuing formation of clergy and religious.

The Assyrian Church of the East

In the context of the Oriental Orthodox Churches mentioned above, the Assyrian Church of the East is a special case. Its origins go back to another doctrinal controversy, one that preceded the Council of Chalcedon (451) by about 20 years, and which concerned the Christological definitions of the Council of Ephesus (431). Along with the Chaldean Catholic Church, the Assyrian Church of the East derives from Christian communities in the ancient territory of Mesopotamia or Babylon which, at the time, were opposed to the definitions of the Council of Ephesus. The bilateral dialogue between the Catholic Church and the Assyrian Church of the East followed its normal course in 2003. From Oct. 28 until Nov. 1, 2003, the ninth annual meeting of this dialogue took place in Rome. The two major themes on the program concerned Christology and ecclesiology. In Christology, the contributions of certain theologians of the ancient Mesopotamian tradition to the development of Christian dogma were examined. In ecclesiology, the discussion centered on the relationship between the local church and the universal church, a key question in the ecumenical debate.

Aleppo and the Middle East

In conclusion, we need to remember the city of Aleppo in Syria, since it was there that the material for the 2004 Week of Prayer for Christian Unity was prepared. Aleppo is a typical example of a Middle Eastern city where almost all the churches and ecclesial communities have lived next to each another for centuries. Situated at the crossroads of the most ancient commercial routes of the Middle East, Aleppo is home to the great Christian traditions: Greek, Syriac, Armenian and Assyro-Chaldean, in their Orthodox or Catholic expressions, as well as several Protestant communities. The bishops and pastors of all these communities meet each month to coordinate their pastoral activity and to give witness to their common commitment to Christian unity. The project of drafting the brochure for this year's Week of Prayer reflects the ecumenical hopes that are held by the churches and ecclesial communities of Aleppo and the entire Middle East. From January 18 to 25, 2004, Christians around the world will join the churches of the Middle East in a common prayer that "the Lord's peace" will overcome our divisions and lead us towards full communion.

EASTERN ECUMENISM

The Second Vatican Council, in *Orientalium Ecclesiarum*, the "Decree on Eastern Catholic Churches," pointed out the special role they have to play "in promoting the unity of all Christians." The document also stated in part as follows.

The Eastern Churches in communion with the Apostolic See of Rome have a special role to play in promoting the unity of all Christians, particularly Easterners, according to the principles of this sacred Synod's Decree on Ecumenism first of all by prayer, then by the example of their lives, by religious fidelity to ancient Eastern traditions, by greater mutual knowledge, by collaboration, and by a brotherly regard for objects and attitudes (No. 24).

If any separated Eastern Christian should, under the guidance of grace of the Holy Spirit, join himself to Catholic unity, no more should be required of him than what a simple profession of the Catholic faith demands. A valid priesthood is preserved among Eastern clerics. Hence, upon joining themselves to the unity of the Catholic Church, Eastern clerics are permitted to exercise the orders they possess, in accordance with the regulations established by the competent authority (No. 25).

Divine Law forbids any common worship (*communicatio in sacris*) that would damage the unity of the Church, or involve formal acceptance of falsehood or the danger of deviation in the faith, of scandal, or of indifferentism. At the same time, pastoral experience clearly shows that with respect to our Eastern brethren there should and can be taken into consideration various circumstances affecting individuals, wherein the unity of the Church is not jeopardized nor are intolerable risks involved, but in which salvation itself and the spiritual profit of souls are urgently at issue.

Hence, in view of special circumstances of time, place, and personage, the Catholic Church has often adopted and now adopts a milder policy, offering to all the means of salvation and an example of charity among Christians through participation in the sacraments and in other sacred functions and objects. With these considerations in mind, and "lest because of the harshness of our judgment we prove an obstacle to those seeking salvation," and in order to promote closer union with the Eastern Churches separated from us, this sacred Synod lays down the following policy:

In view of the principles recalled above, Eastern Christians who are separated in good faith from the

Catholic Church, if they ask of their own accord and have the right dispositions, may be granted the sacraments of penance, the Eucharist, and the anointing of the sick. Furthermore, Catholics may ask for these same sacraments from those non-Catholic ministers whose Churches possess valid sacraments, as often as necessity or a genuine spiritual benefit recommends such a course of action, and when access to a Catholic priest is physically or morally impossible (Nos. 26, 27).

Again, in view of these very same principles, Catholics may for a just cause join with their separated Eastern brethren in sacred functions, things, and places (No. 28). Bishops decide

when and if to follow this policy.

RECENT DOCUMENTS

Two recent documents of importance with respect to relations between the Catholic and separated Eastern Churches are the apostolic letter, *Orientale Lumen*, issued May 5, 1995; and the encyclical, *Ut Unum Sint*, issued May 30, 1995, especially paragraphs 50-63.

In addition, the Pontifical Council for Promoting Christian Unity issued *Guidelines for Admission to the Eucharist between the Chaldean Church and the Assyrian Church of the East* on July 20, 2001, and made public on Oct. 25, 2001.

RELATIONS WITH THE MOSCOW PATRIARCHATE

The following Report on Russian Orthodox-Catholic Church Relations was written by Fr. Jozef M. Maj, S.J., of the Pontifical Council for Promoting Christian Unity and appeared on May 5, 2004, in the English-language edition of L'Osservatore Romano.

A look at the events that unfolded on the scene of interecclesial relations in the course of the year 2003, and particularly on relations between the Holy See and the Patriarchate of Moscow, could lead observers who are awaiting decisive and courageous steps in common witness from the Catholic and Orthodox Churches to think that it is a slow and ascending journey.

Such impressions, nonetheless, can be disproved in a certain way by the announcement made last Jan. 22: "Cardinal Walter Kasper, President of' the Pontifical Council for Promoting Christian Unity, receiving the invitation of the Conference of Catholic Bishops of the Russian Federation, will visit Moscow this Feb. 16 (2004)."

The Cardinal was set to meet Catholic Bishops present in the Russian Federation as well as the Catholic Community at Moscow and, as the announcement revealed, "during this visit, which is animated also by heartfelt respect for the Russian Orthodox Church, he will be received in audience by His Holiness Alexis II, Patriarch of Moscow and All Russia, and will have a meeting with the Metropolitan of Smolensk and Kaliningrad, Kirill, the President of the Department for Ecclesiastical Foreign Relations of the Patriarchate of Moscow, in view of the ecumenical dialogue between the two Churches."

This announcement opens new prospects for all contacts between the Catholic Church and the Russian Orthodox Church and for the quality of their relations internationally and locally.

Spirit of Exchange and Enrichment

These last relations have had a noteworthy force in the course of the past year. The initiatives promoted by the Pontifical Representative in the Russian Federation are especially remembered, thanks to which the climate of such relations has notably improved on the local level and reciprocal trust has grown, an indispensable condition for every further bilateral contact.

In this context the regular meetings of the Pontifical Representative with the Primate of the Russian Orthodox Church, His Holiness Alexis II, are recorded, together with the other institutions of the Patriarchate, such as the Department for Ecclesiastical Foreign Relations, led by the Metropolitan of

Smolensk and Kaliningrad, Kirill.

The Nuncio's visits to Catholic communities spread throughout the territory of this great country are no less important. In the course of such visits, alongside meetings with the civil authorities, there is also among the priorities a visit to the local Orthodox bishop. In many cases such encounters foster the already-existing collaboration or favor the start of other forms of meeting and collaboration between the Orthodox and Catholic communities, aimed at eliminating and overcoming mutual prejudices inherited from the past or that have arisen following misunderstandings and interpretations of events that have affected both Churches.

At the level of contacts between the Holy See and the Patriarchate of I Moscow, we note the regular exchange of epistles between Pope John Paul II: and Patriarch Alexis II, or that of the Pontifical Council for Promoting Christian Unity and the Department for Ecclesiastical Foreign Relations of the Patriarchate of Moscow. The presidents of these bodies, Cardinal Walter Kasper and the Metropolitan Kirill, respectively, have met on two occasions: March 19, 2003, at Geneva and in the first days of September at Aachen in Germany.

The Catholic Committee of Cultural Collaboration has continued to provide monetary support for the educational institutions of the Patriarchate of Moscow stationed in various countries of the Community of the Independent States, and support has been maintained for those institutions that, by preserving their autonomy and maintaining their own Orthodox inspiration through editorial and educational activity and conferences and summer courses on theology, work with the participation of Catholic experts for Orthodoxy in Russia, Belarus and Ukraine and for a meeting and collaboration between Catholics and Orthodox in a spirit of mutual exchange and enrichment.

The Russian Orthodox Church

Throughout 2003, various Catholic organizations continued to offer their fraternal support and help for the Russian Orthodox Church, including such agencies as *Kirche in Not* and *Renovabis*. These agencies' activity cannot be interpreted as an isolated and independent choice; rather, they express the entire solidarity of the Catholic faithful which arises and is nourished from the teaching of the Catholic Church and the Holy Father. Any sort of attempt to deny the intrinsic, ecclesial dimension of the solidarity that the agencies or the

Catholic faithful promote would mean that one is trying to reduce it to a mere act which, noble as it may be, would be left void of its testimonial value to brotherly love, respect and high regard for the Russian Orthodox Church.

The brief overview just presented of relations between the Catholic Church and the Russian Orthodox Church does not desire to close with a statement, but rather, desires to open itself up to those testimonies that the Catholic Church and the Russian Orthodox Church are called to give today to Europe and the World.

The recent address delivered by Pope John Paul II on Jan. 12, 2004 to the Diplomatic Corps accredited to the Holy See offers some ideas that could serve as a point for common reflection and an eventual and more meaningful cooperation with the Patriarchate of Moscow. Obviously, it is not collaboration dictated by any sort of pragmatism; rather, it is that ecumenical commitment which aims at overcoming divisions and permits the respective faithful to live and experience the, numerous bonds of communion by which they are already united between themselves.

Only by this reality will a living witness be able to spring up in a position to extend itself at every level of ecclesial life; a witness that will more convincingly spread those Christian values on which Europe's identity is founded.

The Common Commitment

It is precisely our Continent which is above all in need of a renewal and a common commitment by the Catholic and Orthodox Churches. The Christian identity of Europe and the values that have formed it through the centuries are today having a difficult time finding a place in the area of the important European structures and social life of certain countries.

Although, as the Holy Father affirmed in the aforementioned address, "Everyone may agree to respect the religious sentiment of individuals, but the same cannot be said of the 'religious factor,' that is, the social dimension of religions; here the engagements made in the context of what was formerly known as the 'Conference on Security and Cooperation in Europe' have been forgotten" (Address to the Diplomatic Corps Accredited to the Holy See, Jan. 12, 2004; *L'Osservatore Romano* English edition [ORE], Jan. 21, 2004, p. 3).

Such a tendency, which wishes to ignore "what Christianity has contributed to the culture and institutions of the Continent: the dignity of the human being, freedom, the sense of the universal, schools and universities, social services," addresses in a particular way the Churches regarding their presence and role in affirming Gospel values in today's Europe.

This commitment becomes more urgent in the face of the tendency toward laicism that wishes to reduce the presence of religion to the private sector and to propose life models that are inconsistent with a religious view on life.

Under the various atheistic regimes and ideologies, the Russian Orthodox Church and the Catholic Church, together with other Christian communities, have already undergone long periods of limitations and restrictions accompanied by persecutions, whose devastating consequences on life have been felt up to our day by many societies. Among these consequences, it is enough to mention: signs of social injustice, the break-down of families, and the loss of moral values and propagation of alternative lifestyles that attempt to present as a way of life a modern society free from any bond with natural law.

In the face of these challenges, the Holy Father has said that as Christians: "All together, we can effectively contribute to respect for life, to safeguarding the dignity of the human person and his or her inalienable rights, to social justice and to the preservation of the environment."

Bond Between Unity and Peace

Lastly, in the perspective of common action between the Catholic Church and the Russian Orthodox Church, a concern for world peace cannot be lacking.

Peace always remains an imperative for Christians, and wherever it is threatened, in the Middle East or elsewhere, these same people cannot shrink from their duty to act together by investing all their spiritual forces to achieve it.

But there also exists here interdependence between the unity of Christians tend their commitment to peace. In fact, as the Holy Father notes: "We do not give sufficient importance to the pacifying influence that Christians could have, were they united, on their own community as well as on civil society."

And he adds, "If I say this, it is not only to remind all who claim to be followers of Christ of the pressing need to set out with determination on the road that leads to the unity that Christ desired, but also to point out to the leaders of societies the resources they could find in the Christian heritage as well as among those who practice it."

Unity, therefore, is not an optional accessory; rather, it is an essential quality of the vocation of Christians and their presence in the world. This calling in a certain way conditions the Lord's ardent prayer: "so that the world may believe" (Jn 17:21), and the efficacy of that particular mission which they must complete toward humanity as a whole.

In order for such a mission to proceed, the unique contribution that both the Catholic Church and Russian Orthodox Church can offer must not be lacking.

RECENT DEVELOPMENTS

North American Orthodox-Catholic Theological Consultation Issues Agreed Statement on *Filioque*, a Question that Divided the Two Communions for Many Centuries

(Courtesy, USCCB.) The North American Orthodox-Catholic Theological Consultation concluded a four-year study of the *Filioque* on Oct. 25, when it unanimously adopted an agreed text on this difficult question that has divided the two communions for many centuries. This important development took place at the 65th meeting of the Consultation, held at St. Paul's College in Washington, DC, under the joint chairmanship of Metropolitan Maximos of the Greek Orthodox

Metropolis of Pittsburgh and Abp. Daniel E. Pilarczyk of Cincinnati.

The original version of the Creed most Christian churches accept as the standard expression of their faith dates from the First Council of Constantinople, in 381, and has been used by Orthodox Christians since that time. Towards the end, this Creed states that the Holy Spirit "proceeds from the Father." The word *Filioque* ("and the Son") was later added to the Latin version of this Creed used in the West, so that the phrase as most western Christians know it reads that the Holy Spirit "proceeds from the Father and the Son." This modification appeared in some areas of Western Europe as early as the 6th century but was accepted in Rome only in the 11th century. This change in the wording of the Creed and the underlying variations in understanding the origin and procession of the Holy Spirit within the Trinity have long been considered a church-dividing issue between Catholics and Orthodox. The Consultation had been studying this question since 1999 in the hope of eventually releasing an agreed statement.

Entitled "The Filioque: A Church-Dividing Issue?," the ten-thousand word text has three major sections. The first, "The Holy Spirit in the Scriptures," summarizes references to the Spirit in both the Old and New Testaments. The more lengthy second section, "Historical Considerations," provides an overview of the origins of the two traditions concerning the eternal procession of the Spirit and the slow process by which the *Filioque* was added to the Creed in the West. It also shows how this question concerning Trinitarian theology became entwined with disputes regarding papal jurisdiction and primacy, and reviews recent developments in the Catholic Church which point to a greater awareness of the unique and normative character of the original Greek version of the Creed as an expression of the faith that unites the Orthodox East and Catholic West. The third section, "Theological Reflections," emphasizes our limited ability to speak of the inner life of God, points out that both sides of the debate have often caricatured the positions of the other, and lists areas in which the traditions agree. It then explores the differences that have developed regarding terminology, and identifies both theological and ecclesiological divergences that have arisen over the centuries.

In a final section, the Consultation makes eight recommendations to the members and bishops of the two churches. It recommends that they "enter into a new and earnest dialogue concerning the origin and person of the Holy Spirit." It also proposes that in the future both Catholics and Orthodox "refrain from labeling as heretical the traditions of the other side" on this subject, and that the theologians of both traditions make a clearer distinction between the divinity of the Spirit, and the manner of the Spirit's origin, "which still awaits full and final ecumenical resolution." The text also urges theologians to distinguish, as far as possible, the theological issues concerning the origin of the Holy Spirit from ecclesiological issues, and suggests that attention be paid in the future to the status of councils of both our churches that took place after the seven ecumenical councils of the first millennium. And finally, in view of the fact that the Vatican has affirmed the "normative and irrevocable dogmatic value of the Creed of 381" in its original Greek version, the Consultation recommends that the Catholic Church use the same text (without the *Filioque*) "in making translations of that Creed for catechetical and liturgical use," and declare that the anathema pronounced by the Second Council of Lyons against those who deny that the Spirit proceeds eternally from the Father and the Son is no longer applicable.

The North American Orthodox-Catholic Theological Con- sultation is sponsored jointly by the Standing Conference of Canonical Orthodox Bishops of the Americas (SCOBA), the Bishops' Committee for Ecumenical and Interreligious Affairs of the USCCB, and the Canadian Conference of Catholic Bishops. Since its establishment in 1965, the Con- sultation has now issued 22 agreed statements on various topics. All these texts are now available on the website of the US Catholic Conference at: www.usccb.org/seia/dialogues.htm. The full text of the document is available on the USCCB website at: www.usccb.org/seia/filioque.htm.

Pope John Paul II Returns Icon of the Mother of God of Kazan to the Russian Orthodox Church

In August 2004 Pope John Paul II returned to the Russian Orthodox Church an icon of the Mother of God of Kazan that had hung over his desk in his personal study for eleven years. The icon was believed to have been taken out of Russia at the time of the Bolshevik Revolution, and had been given to the Holy Father by the Blue Army in 1993.

Pope John Paul II Returns Relics of Sts John Chrysostom and Gregory Nazianzen to the Patriarchate of Constantinople

In November 2004 Pope John Paul II returned relics of Sts. John Chrysostom and Gregory Nazianzus to the Ecumenical Patriarchate. Patriarch Bartholomew traveled to Rome to receive the relics in a special service in St Peter's Basilica on Nov. 27.

The Third Meeting of the International Joint Commission for Theological Dialogue between the Catholic Church and the Oriental Orthodox Churches took place in Etchmiadzin, Armenia, Jan. 27 - 30, 2006

Catholic and Oriental Orthodox representatives, delegated by their churches, met under the co-chairmanship of His Eminence Cardinal Walter Kasper, President of the Pontifical Council for Promoting Christian Unity and His Eminence Metropolitan Bishoy of Damiette, General Secretary of the Holy Synod of the Coptic Orthodox Church.

The meeting was held in Holy Etchmiadzin, Armenia, at the Catholicosate of All Armenians, hosted by H.H. Karekin II, the Supreme Patriarch and Catholicos of All Armenians. Delegates were present from the Catholic Church and from the following Oriental Orthodox Churches: the Coptic Orthodox Church, Syrian Orthodox Church, Armenian Apostolic Church (Catholicosate of All Armenians), Armenian Apostolic Church (Holy See of Cilicia), and the Malankara Orthodox Syrian Church. Delegates from the Ethiopian Orthodox Church and the Eritrean Orthodox Church were unable to attend. The meeting was originally scheduled to begin on Jan. 26, but was delayed one day because of severe winter weather.

Each working day began with morning prayers, and the sessions took place in a cordial atmosphere. The Catholic and Oriental Orthodox members held separate meetings at various times during the dialogue.

The members of the international commission were received by H.H. Catholicos Karekin II on Jan. 27. He expressed his pleasure at being able to host this session of the dialogue, and encouraged its work. There was an exchange of gifts between the two co-chairmen and himself. The members were invited to attend a Divine Liturgy presided over by H.H. the Catholicos, and celebrated by His Grace Bishop Yeznik Petrossian, Ecumenical Officer of the Catholicosate of All Armenians, in the Cathedral of Holy Etchmiadzin on Sunday Jan. 29. At the conclusion of the Divine Liturgy, there was a special requiem service for H.H. Baselius Mar Thoma Mathews II, the Catholicos of the Malankara Orthodox Syrian Church, who entered into eternal life on Jan. 26.

In accord with the plan for the dialogue that was adopted at the Preparatory Meeting in 2003, papers were presented during this session by Catholic and Oriental Orthodox members on three topics: "Bishops in Apostolic Succession" (by Fr. Matthew Vellanickal/Fr. Ronald Roberson, CSP, and by Fr. John Panicker), "Primacy and Synodality/Conciliarity" (by Bp. Nareg Alemezian and by Prof. Dietmar Winkler), and "Synods, Local and Ecumenical" (by Abp. George Saliba and by Fr. Frans Bouwen).

After an in-depth discussion of the papers and the progress of the dialogue, the commission decided to further develop its methodology. A drafting committee has been appointed that will study points of consensus and difference found in the papers presented at the dialogue so far, and produce a draft common text on these subjects for examination at the next meeting. The drafting committee will be composed of Catholic members Fr. Frans Bouwen, Fr. Mark Sheridan, Msgr. Johan Bonny, and Prof. Dietmar Winkler, and Oriental Orthodox members Metropolitan Kuriakose Theophilose, Bp. Yeznik Petrossian, Bp. Nareg Alemezian, and Fr. John Panicker. The next meeting will also include one paper from each side on "Mission, Witness Service, and the Problem of Proselytism."

During the course of the meeting the international commission members attended a reception given by H.E. Abp. Claudio Gugerotti, the Apostolic Nuncio to Armenia, a dinner hosted by H.H. the Catholicos, and a buffet dinner hosted by the ambassadors of Egypt and Lebanon and the chargé d'affairs of Syria at the residence of the Egyptian ambassador. In addition, on the evening of Jan. 28, the members attended a presentation of the life and work of Mekhitar of Sebastia, the founder of the Mekhitarist community. On the evening of Jan. 29 the members venerated the relics of St. Gregory the Illuminator at the new cathedral in Yerevan dedicated to him.

The fourth meeting of the International Commission will take place from Jan. 28 (day of arrival) until Feb. 3, 2007 (day of departure). On Jan. 29, the Catholic and Oriental Orthodox members will meet separately. Jan. 30-31 and Feb. 1-2 will be full working days. The meeting will be hosted by the Catholic Church at a location to be determined.

The Roman Catholic-Polish National Catholic Dialogue issued this Joint Declaration on Unity on May 17, 2006, in Fall River, Mass.:

With thankfulness to God, the members of the Roman Catholic-Polish National Catholic dialogue in the United States look back on 22 years of theological and canonical reflection concerning the nature of our division and the possibility of reaching full communion. Because of a new outpouring of the Holy Spirit that affected both our churches following the celebration of the Second Vatican Council (1962-1965) and a similar renewal within the Polish National Catholic Church, our faithful have been rediscovering one another increasingly as brothers and sisters in the Lord. At this time we wish to review the progress that we have achieved over the past two decades, and reaffirm our intention to continue our efforts to achieve that unity for which Christ prayed.

Calls for a dialogue between our churches go back as far as 1966, when the Most Reverend Leon Grochowski, Prime Bishop of the Polish National Catholic Church, courageously proposed such a dialogue to the Roman Catholic Bishop of Scranton. Later, in 1980, His Holiness Pope John Paul II of blessed memory expressed the desire that the conference of bishops of the United States examine the relationship that exists with the Polish National Catholic Church and explore the possibility of dialogue. This resulted in an exchange of correspondence between the leaders of our churches that would culminate in the first meeting of an official dialogue in Passaic, N.J., on Oct. 23, 1984.

In view of the fact that most of the ecumenical dialogues began in the 1960s and 1970s, the establishment of our dialogue was late in coming. This was the result of the particularly painful history of our relationship and the circumstances of the origins of the Polish National Catholic Church among ethnic Polish and other Roman Catholics in the United States at the end of the 19th and the beginning of the 20th century. The disputes of that time, we now realize, were more concerned with matters of church governance than points of doctrine. Nevertheless, the complicated series of events that led to our division caused much hurt and anguish even within families whose members often found themselves on opposite sides of the dispute. The consequences of those events can still be felt among us more than a century later, and must be addressed.

For this purpose, a number of highly symbolic gestures of reconciliation have taken place, perhaps most notably at the Service of Healing that was held in St. Stanislaus Polish National Catholic Cathedral in Scranton, Pa., on Feb. 15, 1992. Leaders of our two churches, including Card. Edward I. Cassidy (President of the Pontifical Council for Promoting Christian Unity), His Grace John F. Swantek, Prime Bishop of the Polish National Catholic Church, and the two co-chairmen of the dialogue, asked for forgiveness, and pledged to work to overcome our divisions definitively. In 1997 Bp. James C. Timlin, then the Roman Catholic Co-Chairman of the dialogue, reiterated this request for forgiveness in a letter he issued on the occasion of the centenary of the organization of the Polish National Catholic Church.

Our dialogue has achieved much. For example, in a

1989 report summarizing the first five years of the dialogue's progress, we affirmed our agreement on the seven sacraments of the Church, in spite of some differences in practice that do not touch upon our basic common faith. The report also examined two areas of divergence — our understandings of the Word of God and the life to come — and discovered that here too there are broad areas of agreement. In sum, our report was able to look back over five years of dialogue and state that "we have thus far discovered no doctrinal obstacle that would impede the further growth of our churches toward that unity which we believe is Christ's will." A second report dealing with developments in our dialogue from 1989 to 2002 was published in 2003.

In view of this progress, concrete steps have been taken. In response to an inquiry from the Archbishop of Baltimore, William Keeler, then President of the National Conference of Catholic Bishops, Edward Cardinal Cassidy, President of the Pontifical Council for Promoting Christian Unity, stated in 1993 that members of the Polish National Catholic Church in the United States and Canada may receive the sacraments of Penance, Holy Communion and Anointing of the Sick from Roman Catholic priests if they ask for them on their own, are properly disposed and not otherwise excluded from the sacraments in line with the provisions of canon 844 §3 of The Code of Canon Law. This was followed in 1996 by a letter from Abp. Oscar H. Lipscomb, the Chairman of the Bishops' Committee for Ecumenical and Interreligious Affairs, to the bishops of the United States spelling out in more detail the conditions under which Polish National Catholics may receive the aforementioned sacraments in the Roman Catholic Church. In 1998 the Polish National Catholic Church issued Guidelines for the Reception by Polish National Catholics of Sacraments in the Roman Catholic Church. Canon 844 §2 of The Code of Canon Law also specifies conditions under which Roman Catholics may receive the sacraments in the Polish National Catholic Church.

In light of these concrete steps towards unity, we have much for which to be thankful. Furthermore, we recognize each other's ecclesial character and sacraments, allow a certain amount of sacramental sharing, and maintain many of the same traditions. These facts bear witness to how much we have rediscovered as our common heritage. Our mutual esteem clearly rules out inappropriate actions such as proselytism among each other's faithful or the re-ordination of clergy who pass from one church to the other.

During our century-long division we have grown apart in ways that at first glance make reconciliation appear to be difficult. The Polish National Catholic Church, which during most of its existence was a member of the Union of Utrecht, has developed a strong sense of autonomy and the desire to preserve its distinctive traditions, including the vital role played by the laity in church governance. Even though the primacy and infallibility of the Bishop of Rome was not an issue at the time of our division, our churches today have different understandings of the Pope's role in the Church. Another complicating factor is the presence of a significant number of former Roman Catholic priests in the ranks of the Polish National Catholic clergy. Such is the legacy of the divisions of the past that remain with us today.

At this point in our relationship, therefore, we the members of the Polish National Catholic-Roman Catholic dialogue wish to reaffirm our resolve to overcome what still divides us, and to state clearly that our goal is full communion between our churches. We wish to emphasize that "full communion" does not imply absorption or uniformity, but a unity that fully recognizes differing traditions that are consistent with our common apostolic faith. It must still be determined if any of our divergent traditions are truly church-dividing, or simply examples of legitimate diversity which, in the words of Pope John Paul II, "is in no way opposed to the Church's unity, but rather enhances her splendor and contributes greatly to the fulfillment of her mission" (Ut Unum Sint, no. 50). We plan to give further consideration to other concrete steps concerning reciprocity in regard to the sacraments, acting as godparents, and the requirement of canonical form for lawfulness only in mixed marriages. We are equally committed to a thorough examination of the theological concepts of primacy and conciliarity. This will include searching for a common understanding of the ministry of the Bishop of Rome in the Church.

As members of a commission authorized to engage in this ecumenical dialogue, our role is not to speak definitively for either of our churches. Nevertheless, we hope to propose new incremental steps that will make concrete the growing unity between us, and we wish our faithful to know of our conviction that a way can be found to overcome this regrettable division that took place among Catholics here in the United States. We know that the goal of unity is nothing less than the will of Christ for us. Therefore we ask the faithful of both our churches to join us in fervent prayer that, with a new outpouring of the Holy Spirit, the barriers between us will fall and we will one day soon find ourselves joined again in that perfect unity that befits the disciples of our Lord Jesus Christ.

REFORMATION CHURCHES

LEADERS AND DOCTRINES OF THE REFORMATION

Some of the leading figures, doctrines and churches of the Reformation are covered below. A companion article covers major Protestant Churches in the U.S.

LEADERS

John Wycliff (c. 1320-1384): English priest and scholar who advanced one of the leading Reformation ideas nearly 200 years before Martin Luther — that the Bible alone is the sufficient rule of faith — but had only an indirect influence on the 16th century Reformers. Supporting belief in an inward and practical religion, he denied the divinely commissioned authority of the pope and bishops of the Church; he also denied the Real Presence of Christ in the Holy Eucharist, and wrote against the sacrament of penance and the doctrine of indulgences. Nearly 20 of his propositions were condemned by Gregory XI in 1377; his writings were proscribed more extensively by the Council of Constance in 1415. His influence was strongest in Bohemia and Central Europe.

John Hus (c. 1369-1415): A Bohemian priest and preacher of reform who authored 30 propositions condemned by the Council of Constance. Excommunicated in 1411 or 1412, he was burned at the stake in 1415. His principal errors concerned the nature of the Church and the origin of papal authority. He spread some of the ideas of Wycliff but did not subscribe to his views regarding faith alone as the condition for justification and salvation, the sole sufficiency of Scripture as the rule of faith, the Real Presence of Christ in the Eucharist, and the sacramental system. In 1457 some of his followers founded the Church of the Brotherhood which later became known as the United Brethren or Moravian Church and is considered the earliest independent Protestant body.

Martin Luther (1483-1546): An Augustinian friar, priest and doctor of theology, the key figure in the Reformation. In 1517, as a special indulgence was being preached in Germany, and in view of needed reforms within the Church, he published at Wittenberg 95 theses concerning matters of Catholic belief and practice. Leo X condemned 41 statements from Luther's writings in 1520. Luther, refusing to recant, was excommunicated the following year. His teachings strongly influenced subsequent Lutheran theology; its statements of faith are found in the Book of Concord (1580).

Luther's doctrines included the following: The sin of Adam, which corrupted human nature radically (but not substantially), has affected every aspect of man's being. Justification, understood as the forgiveness of sins and the state of righteousness, is by grace for Christ's sake through faith. Faith involves not merely intellectual assent but an act of confidence by the will. Good works are indispensably necessary concomitants of faith, but do not merit salvation. Of the sacraments, Luther retained baptism, penance and the Holy Communion as effective vehicles of the grace of the Holy Spirit; he held that in the Holy Communion the consecrated bread and wine are the Body and Blood of Christ. The rule of faith is the divine revelation in the Sacred Scriptures. He rejected purgatory, indulgences and the invocation of the saints, and held that prayers for the dead have no efficacy. Catholics clarified their positions at the Council of Trent. The 1999 Joint Declaration indicates that the condemnations of doctrine by the Council of Trent and the Book of Concord do not apply to present day Catholic and Lutheran teaching respectively.

Ulrich Zwingli (1484-1531): A priest who triggered the Reformation in Switzerland with a series of New Testament lectures in 1519, later disputations and by other actions. He held the Gospel to be the only basis of truth; rejected the Mass (which he suppressed in 1525 at Zurich), penance and other sacraments; denied papal primacy and doctrine concerning purgatory and the invocation of saints; rejected celibacy, monasticism and many traditional practices of piety. His symbolic view of the Eucharist, which was at odds with Catholic doctrine, caused an irreconcilable controversy with Luther and his followers. Zwingli was killed in a battle between the forces of Protestant and Catholic cantons in Switzerland.

John Calvin (1509-64): French leader of the Reformation in Switzerland, whose key tenet was absolute predestination of some persons to heaven and others to hell. He rejected Catholic doctrine in 1533 after becoming convinced of a personal mission to reform the Church. In 1536 he published the first edition of Institutes of the Christian Religion, a systematic exposition of his doctrine which became the classic textbook of Reformed — as distinguished from Lutheran — theology. To Luther's principal theses — regarding Scripture as the sole rule of faith, the radical corruption of human nature, and justification by faith alone — he added absolute predestination, certitude of salvation for the elect, and the incapability of the elect to lose grace. Calvin's Eucharist teaching, while affirming Christ's true presence, was not able to find agreement with that of Luther. However, in our own time, agreement has been reached between Lutherans and Reformed (Calvinists), and considerable progress has been made with Catholics and Orthodox toward a common understanding of Christ's presence in Communion.

CHURCHES AND MOVEMENTS

Adventists: Members of several Christian groups whose doctrines are dominated by belief in a more or less imminent second advent or coming of Christ upon earth for a glorious 1,000-year reign of righteousness. This reign, following victory by the forces of good over evil in a final Battle of Armageddon, will begin with the resurrection of the chosen and will end with the resurrection of all others and the annihilation of the wicked. Thereafter, the just will live forever in a renewed heaven and earth. A sleep of the soul takes place between the time of death and the day of judgment. There is no hell. The Bible, in literalist interpretation, is regarded as the only rule of faith and practice. About six churches have developed in the course of the Adventist movement which originated with William Miller (1782-1849) in the United States. Miller, on the basis of calculations made from the Book of Daniel, predicted that the second advent of Christ would occur between 1843 and 1844. After the prophecy went unfulfilled, divisions occurred in the movement and the Seventh Day Adventists, whose actual formation dates from 1860, emerged as the largest single body. The observance of Saturday instead of Sunday as the Lord's Day dates from 1844.

Anabaptism: Originated in Saxony in the first quarter of the 16th century and spread rapidly through southern Germany. Its doctrine included several key Lutheran tenets but was not regarded with favor by Luther, Calvin or Zwingli. Anabaptists believed that baptism is for adults only and that infant baptism is invalid. Their doctrine of the Inner Light, concerning the direct influence of the Holy Spirit on the believer, implied rejection of Catholic doctrine concerning the sacraments and the nature of the Church. Eighteen articles of faith were formulated in 1632 in Holland. Mennonites are Anabaptists.

Arminianism: A modification of the rigid predestinationism of Calvin, set forth by Jacob Arminius (1560-1609) and formally stated in the Remonstrance of 1610. Arminianism influenced some Calvinist bodies.

Baptists: So called because of their doctrine concerning baptism. They reject infant baptism and consider only baptism by immersion as valid. Leaders in the formation of the church were John Smyth (d. 1612) in England and Roger Williams (d. 1683) in America.

Congregationalists: Evangelical in spirit and seeking a return to forms of the primitive church, they uphold individual freedom in religious matters, do not require the acceptance of a creed as a condition for communion, and regard each congregation as autonomous. Robert Browne influenced the beginnings of Congregationalism.

Disciples: From a 19th century revival movement and desire for the unity of the Christian churches, a network of congregations developed which desired to be called simply "Christian churches." These churches opened their communion and membership to all, celebrated the Eucharist each Sunday and baptized only adults. From this movement the Christian Church/Disciples of Christ, the Churches of Christ and the independent Christian Churches emerged.

Methodists: A group who broke away from the Anglican Communion under the leadership of John Wesley (1703-1791), although some Anglican beliefs were retained. Doctrines include the witness of the Spirit to the individual and personal assurance of salvation. The largest Methodist body in the United States is the United Methodist Church. There are three Black Methodist bodies: African Methodist Episcopal, African Methodist Episcopal Zion, and Christian Methodist Episcopal Churches. There are also several Holiness Churches in the Wesleyan tradition: i.e., Nazarene, Free Methodist, Wesleyan Church.

Pentecostals: Churches that grew up after the 1906 enthusiastic revival, accompanied by the phenomena of speaking in foreign tongues and the experience of baptism in the Holy Spirit. From this revival churches of a Methodist or Baptist theological emphasis emerged, such as the Church of God in Christ or the Assemblies of God. In the mid-20th century, the charismatic experience began to be shared by some members of the classical churches, including Roman Catholic.

Puritans: Congregationalists who sought church reform along Calvinist lines in severe simplicity. (Use of the term was generally discontinued after 1660.)

Presbyterians: Basically Calvinistic, called Presbyterian because church polity centers around assemblies of presbyters or elders. John Knox (c. 1513-1572) established the church in Scotland.

Quakers: Their key belief is in internal divine illumination, the inner light of the living Christ, as the only source of truth and inspiration. George Fox (1624-1691) was one of their leaders in England. Called the Society of Friends, the Quakers are noted for their pacifism.

Unitarianism: A 16th century doctrine which rejected the Trinity and the divinity of Christ in favor of a uni-personal God. It claimed scriptural support for a long time but became generally rationalistic with respect to "revealed" doctrine as well as in ethics and its world-view. One of its principal early proponents was Faustus Socinus (1539-1604), a leader of the Polish Brethren. A variety of communions developed in England in the Reformation and post-Reformation periods.

Universalism: A product of 18th-century liberal Protestantism in England. The doctrine is not Trinitarian and includes a tenet that all men will ultimately be saved.

Anglican Communion: This communion, which regards itself as the same apostolic Church as that which was established by early Christians in England, derived not from Reformation influences but from the renunciation of papal jurisdiction by Henry VIII (1491-1547). His Act of Supremacy in 1534 called Christ's Church an assembly of local churches subject to the prince, who was vested with fullness of authority and jurisdiction. In spite of Henry's denial of papal authority, this Act did not reject substantially other principal articles of faith. Notable changes, proposed and adopted for the reformation of the church, took place in the subsequent reigns of Edward VI and Elizabeth, with respect to such matters as Scripture as the rule of faith, the sacraments, the nature of the Mass, and the constitution of the hierarchy. There are more than 27 provinces in the Anglican Communion. (*See* **Episcopal Church, Anglican Orders, Anglican-Catholic Final Report.**)

MAJOR PROTESTANT CHURCHES IN THE UNITED STATES

There are more than 250 Protestant church bodies in the U.S.

The majority of U.S. Protestants belong to the following denominations: Baptist, Methodist, Lutheran, Presbyterian, Protestant Episcopal, the United Church of Christ, the Christian Church (Disciples of Christ), Evangelicals.

See **Ecumenical Dialogues, Reports** and related entries for coverage of relations between the Catholic Church and other Christian churches.

Baptist Churches

Baptist churches, comprising the largest of all American Protestant denominations, were first established by John Smyth near the beginning of the 17th century in England. The first Baptist church in America was founded at Providence by Roger Williams in 1639.

Largest of the nearly 30 Baptist bodies in the U.S. are:

The Southern Baptist Convention, 901 Commerce St., Suite 750, Nashville, TN 37203, with 15.7 million members.

The National Baptist Convention, U.S.A., Inc., 915 Spain St., Baton Rouge, LA 70802, with 8 million members.

The National Baptist Convention of America, Inc., 1320 Pierre Ave., Shreveport, LA 71103, with 4.5 million members.

The American Baptist Churches in the USA, P.O. Box 851, Valley Forge, PA 19482, with 1.5 million members.

The total number of U.S. Baptists is more than 29 million. The world total is 33 million.

Proper to Baptists is their doctrine on baptism. Called an "ordinance" rather than a sacrament, baptism by immersion is a sign that one has experienced and decided in favor of the salvation offered by Christ. It is administered only to persons who are able to make a responsible decision. Baptism is not administered to infants.

Baptists do not have a formal creed but generally subscribe to two professions of faith formulated in 1689 and 1832 and are in general agreement with classical Protestant theology regarding Scripture as the sole rule of faith, original sin, justification through faith in Christ, and the nature of the Church. Their local churches are autonomous.

Worship services differ in form from one congregation to another. Usual elements are the reading of Scripture, a sermon, hymns, vocal and silent prayer. The Lord's Supper, called an "ordinance," is celebrated at various times.

Christian Church (Disciples of Christ)

The Christian Church (Disciples of Christ) originated early in the 1800s from two movements against rigid denominationalism led by Presbyterians Thomas and Alexander Campbell in western Pennsylvania and Barton W. Stone in Kentucky. The two movements developed separately for about 25 years before being merged in 1832.

The church, which identifies itself with the Protestant mainstream, has nearly one million members in almost 4,000 congregations in the US and Canada. The greatest concentration of members in the U.S. is located roughly along the old frontier line, in an arc sweeping from Ohio and Kentucky through the Midwest and down into Oklahoma and Texas.

The general offices of the church are located at 130 E. Washington St., Indianapolis, IN 46204. The church's persistent concern for Christian unity is based on a conviction expressed in a basic document, Declaration and Address, dating from its founding. The document states: "The church of Christ upon earth is essentially, intentionally and constitutionally one."

The Disciples have no official doctrine or dogma. Their worship practices vary widely from more common informal services to what could almost be described as "high church" services. Membership is granted after a simple statement of belief in Jesus Christ and baptism by immersion; most congregations admit un-immersed transfers from other denominations. The Lord's Supper or Eucharist, generally called Communion, is always open to Christians of all persuasions. Lay men and women routinely preside over the Lord's Supper, which is celebrated each Sunday; they often preach and perform other pastoral functions as well. Distinction between ordained and non-ordained members is blurred somewhat because of the Disciples' emphasis on all members of the church as ministers.

The Christian Church is oriented to congregational government, and has a unique structure in which three sections of polity (general, regional and congregational) operate as equals rather than in a pyramid of authority. At the national or international level, it is governed by a general assembly which has voting representation direct from congregations and regions as well as all ordained and licensed clergy.

Episcopal Church

The Episcopal Church, which includes over 100 dioceses in the United States, Central and South America, and elsewhere overseas, regards itself as part of the same apostolic church which was established by early Christians in England. Established in this country during the colonial period, it became independent of the jurisdiction of the Church of England when a new constitution and Prayer Book were adopted at a general convention held in 1789. It has approximately 2.5 million members worldwide.

Offices of the presiding bishop and the executive council are located at 815 Second Ave., New York, NY 10017.

The presiding bishop is chief pastor and primate; he is elected by the House of Bishops and confirmed by the House of Deputies for a term of nine years.

The Episcopal Church, which is a part of the Anglican Communion, regards the Archbishop of Canterbury as the "First among Equals," though not under his authority.

The Anglican Communion, worldwide, has 70 million members in 36 self-governing churches.

Official statements of belief and practice are found in the Book of Common Prayer. Scripture has primary importance with respect to the rule of faith, and authority is also attached to tradition.

An episcopal system of church government prevails, but presbyters, deacons and lay persons also have an active voice in church affairs. The levels of government are the general convention, and executive council, dioceses, and local parishes. At the parish level, the congregation has the right to select its own rector, with the consent of the bishop.

Liturgical worship is according to the Book of Common Prayer as adopted in 1979, but details of ceremonial practice vary from one congregation to another.

Lutheran Churches

The origin of Lutheranism is generally traced to Oct. 31, 1517, when Martin Luther — Augustinian friar, priest, doctor of theology — tacked "95 theses" to the door of the castle church in Wittenberg, Germany. This call to debate on the subject of indulgences and related concerns has come to symbolize the beginning of the Reformation. Luther and his supporters intended to reform the Church they knew. Though Lutheranism has come to be visible in separate denominations and national churches, at its heart it professes itself to be a confessional movement within the one, holy, catholic and apostolic Church.

The world's 61 million Lutherans form the third largest grouping of Christians, after Roman Catholics and Orthodox. About 57 million of them belong to church bodies which make up the Lutheran World Federation, headquartered in Geneva.

There are about 8.5 million Lutherans in the United States, making them the fourth largest Christian grouping, after Roman Catholics, Baptists and Methodists. Although there are nearly 20 U.S. Lutheran church bodies, all but 100,000 Lutherans belong to either the Evangelical Lutheran Church in America (with 5.2 million members and headquarters at 8765 W. Higgins Rd., Chicago, IL 60631), The Lutheran Church-Missouri Synod (with 2.61 million members and headquarters at 1333 S. Kirkwood Rd., St. Louis, MO 63122), or the Wisconsin Evangelical Lutheran Synod (with 420,000 members and headquarters at 2929 N. Mayfair Rd., Milwaukee, WI 53222).

The Evangelical Lutheran Church in America and the Lutheran Church-Missouri Synod carry out some work together through inter-Lutheran agencies such as

Lutheran World Relief and Lutheran Immigration and Refugee Services; both agencies have offices at 390 Park Ave. South, New York, NY 10010.

The statements of faith which have shaped the confessional life of Lutheranism are found in the Book of Concord. This 1580 collection includes the three ancient ecumenical creeds (Apostles', Nicene and Athanasian), Luther's Large and Small Catechisms (1529), the Augsburg Confession (1530) and the Apology in defense of it (1531), the Smalkald Articles (including the "Treatise on the Power and Primacy of the Pope") (1537), and the Formula of Concord (1577).

The central Lutheran doctrinal proposition is that Christians "receive forgiveness of sins and become righteous before God by grace, for Christ's sake." Baptism and the Lord's Supper (Holy Communion, the Eucharist) are universally celebrated among Lutherans as sacramental means of grace. Lutherans also treasure the Word proclaimed in the reading of the Scriptures, preaching and absolution.

In the ELCA, the bishop is the minister of ordination. Much of Lutheranism continues what it understands as the historic succession of bishops (though without considering the historic episcopate essential for the church). All of Lutheranism is concerned to preserve apostolic succession in life and doctrine. Lutheran churches in Scandinavia and the Baltics, in the US, and in Canada have moved into full communion with their Anglican counterparts.

Lutheran jurisdictions corresponding to dioceses are called districts or synods in North America. There are more than 100 of them; each of them is headed by a bishop or president. The Evangelical Lutheran Church in America moved into full communion with the three Reformed Churches (Presbyterian Church, United Church of Christ and Reformed Church in America) in 1997, and in 2000 into full communion with the Episcopal Church, all of its bishops being ordained by bishops including those in the apostolic succession as understood by Anglicans. It also moved into full communion with the Moravian Church in 1999.

Methodist Churches

John Wesley (1703-1791), an Anglican clergyman, was the founder of Methodism. In 1738, following a period of missionary work in America and strongly influenced by the Moravians, he experienced a new conversion to Christ and shortly thereafter became a leader in a religious awakening in England. By the end of the 18th century, Methodism was strongly rooted also in America.

The United Methodist Church, formed in 1968 by a merger of the Methodist Church and the Evangelical United Brethren Church, is the second largest Protestant denomination in the U.S., with more than nine million members; its principal agencies are located in New York, Evanston, IL, Nashville, TN, Washington, DC, Dayton, OH, and Lake Junaluska, NC (World Methodist Council, P.O. Box 518 28745). The second largest body, with just under two million communicants, is the African Methodist Episcopal Church. Four other major churches in the U.S. are the African Methodist Episcopal Zion, Christian Methodist Episcopal, Free Methodist Church and the Wesleyan Church. The total Methodist membership in the US is about 15.5 million.

Worldwide, there are more than 73 autonomous Methodist/Wesleyan churches in 107 countries, with a membership of more than 33 million. All of them participate in the World Methodist Council, which gives global unity to the witness of Methodist communicants.

Methodism rejects absolute predestination and maintains that Christ offers grace freely to all men, not just to a select elite. Wesley's distinctive doctrine was the "witness of the Spirit" to the individual soul and personal assurance of salvation. He also emphasized the central themes of conversion and holiness. Methodists are in general agreement with classical Protestant theology regarding Scripture as the sole rule of faith, original sin, justification through faith in Christ, the nature of the Church, and the sacraments of baptism and the Lord's Supper. Church polity is structured along episcopal lines in America, with ministers being appointed to local churches by a bishop; churches stemming from British Methodism do not have bishops but vest appointive powers within an appropriate conference. Congregations are free to choose various forms of worship services; typical elements are readings from Scripture, sermons, hymns and prayers.

Presbyterian Churches

Presbyterians are so called because of their tradition of governing the church through a system of representative bodies composed of elders (presbyters).

Presbyterianism is a part of the Reformed Family of Churches that grew out of the theological work of John Calvin following the Lutheran Reformation, to which it is heavily indebted. Countries in which it acquired early strength and influence were Switzerland, France, Holland, Scotland and England.

Presbyterianism spread widely in this country in the latter part of the 18th century and afterwards. Presently, it has approximately 4.5 million communicants in nine bodies.

The two largest Presbyterian bodies in the country — the United Presbyterian Church in the U.S.A. and the Presbyterian Church in the United States — were reunited in June 1983, to form the Presbyterian Church (USA), with a membership of 2.7 million. Its national offices are located at 100 Witherspoon St., Louisville, KY 40202.

These churches, now merged, are closely allied with the Reformed Church in America, the United Church of Christ, the Cumberland Presbyterian Churches, the Korean Presbyterian Church in America and the Associate Reformed Presbyterian Church.

In Presbyterian doctrine, baptism and the Lord's Supper, viewed as seals of the covenant of grace, are regarded as sacraments. Baptism, which is not necessary for salvation, is conferred on infants and adults The Lord's Supper is celebrated as a covenant of the Sacrifice of Christ. In both sacraments, a doctrine of the real presence of Christ is considered the central theological principle.

The Church is twofold, being invisible and also visible; it consists of all of the elect and all those Christians who are united in Christ as their immediate head.

Presbyterians are in general agreement with classical Protestant theology regarding Scripture as the sole rule of faith and practice, salvation by grace, and justification through faith in Christ.

Presbyterian congregations are governed by a session composed of elders elected by the communicant membership. On higher levels there are presbyteries, synods and a general assembly with various degrees of authority over local bodies; all such representative bodies are composed of elected elders and ministers in approximately equal numbers. The church annually elects a moderator who presides at the General Assembly and travels throughout the church to speak to and hear from the members.

Worship services, simple and dignified, include sermons, prayer, reading of the Scriptures and hymns. The Lord's Supper is celebrated at intervals.

Doctrinal developments of the past several years included approval in May 1967 by the General Assembly of the United Presbyterian Church of a contemporary confession of faith to supplement the historic Westminster Confession. A statement entitled "The Declaration of Faith" was approved in 1977 by the Presbyterian Church in the U.S. for teaching and liturgical use.

The reunited church adopted "A Brief Statement of Reformed Faith" in 1991 regarding urgent concerns of the church. The Presbyterian Church, USA, has moved into full communion with the Evangelical Lutheran Church in America in 1997.

United Church of Christ

The 1,501,310-member (in 1994) United Church of Christ was formed in 1957 by a union of the Congregational Christian and the Evangelical and Reformed Churches. The former was originally established by the Pilgrims and the Puritans of the Massachusetts Bay Colony, while the latter was founded in Pennsylvania in the early 1700s by settlers from Central Europe. The denomination had 6,362 congregations throughout the United States in 1988.

It considers itself "a united and uniting church" and keeps itself open to all ecumenical options. Its headquarters are located at 700 Prospect, Cleveland, OH 44115.

Its statement of faith recognizes Jesus Christ as "our crucified and risen Lord (who) shared our common lot, conquering sin and death and reconciling the world to himself." It believes in the life after death, and the fact that God "judges men and nations by his righteous will declared through prophets and apostles."

The United Church further believes that Christ calls its members to share in his baptism "and eat at his table, to join him in his passion and victory." Each local church is free to adopt its own methods of worship and to formulate its own covenants and confessions of faith. Some celebrate communion weekly; others, monthly or on another periodical basis. Like other Calvinistic bodies, it believes that Christ is spiritually present in the sacrament.

The United Church is governed along congregational lines, and each local church is autonomous. However, the actions of its biennial General Synod are taken with great seriousness by congregations. Between synods, a 44-member executive council oversees the work of the church. In 1989 the UCC moved into full communion with the Christian Church (Disciples of Christ) and in 1997 with the Evangelical Lutheran Church in America.

Evangelicalism

Evangelicalism, dating from 1735 in England (the Evangelical Revival) and after 1740 in the United States (the Great Awakening), has had and continues to have widespread influence in Protestant churches. It has been estimated that about 45 millon American Protestants — communicants of both large denominations and small bodies — are evangelicals.

The Bible is their rule of faith and religious practice. Being born again in a life-changing experience through faith in Christ is the promise of salvation. Missionary work for the spread of the Gospel is a normal and necessary activity.

Additional matters of belief and practice are generally of a conservative character. Fundamentalists, numbering perhaps 4.5 million, comprise an extreme right-wing subculture of evangelicalism. They are distinguished mainly by militant biblicism, belief in the absolute inerrancy of the Bible and emphasis on the Second Coming of Christ. Fundamentalism developed early in the 20th century in reaction against liberal theology and secularizing trends in mainstream and other Protestant denominations.

The Holiness or Perfectionist wing of evangelicalism evolved from Methodist efforts to preserve, against a contrary trend, the personal-piety and inner-religion concepts of John Wesley. There are at least 30 Holiness bodies in the U.S.

Pentecostals, probably the most demonstrative of evangelicals, are noted for speaking in tongues and the stress they place on healing, prophecy and personal testimony to the practice and power of evangelical faith. There are strong charismatic movements within many of the historic Protestant churches and Roman Catholicism.

The evangelical communities have national and international ecumenical bodies. Black and white Pentecostal churches belong to the Pentecostal and Charismatic Fellowship of North America. Over forty Pentecostal, Holiness and evangelical churches belong to the U.S. National Association of Evangelicals. Internationally, these national evangelical associations collaborate in the World Evangelical Alliance.

Assemblies of God

Assemblies (Churches) of God form the largest body (more than 2 million members) in the Pentecostal Movement which developed from (1) some Holiness Revival in the Methodist Church after the Civil War and (2) the Apostolic Faith Movement at the beginning of the 20th century. Members share with other Pentecostals belief in the religious experience of conversion and in the baptism by the Holy Spirit that sanctifies. Distinctive is the emphasis placed on the charismatic gifts of the apostolic church, healing and speaking in tongues, which are signs of the "second blessing" of the Holy Spirit.

The Assemblies are conservative and biblicist in theology; are loosely organized in various districts, with democratic procedures; are vigorously evangelistic. The moral code is rigid.

INTERRELIGIOUS DIALOGUE

JUDAISM

Judaism is the religion of the Hebrew Bible and of contemporary Jews. Divinely revealed and with a patriarchal background (Abraham and Sarah, Isaac and Jacob), it originated with the Mosaic Covenant, was identified with the Israelites, and achieved distinctive form and character as the religion of the Torah (Law, "The Teaching") from this Covenant and reforms initiated by Ezra and Nehemiah after the Babylonian Exile.

Judaism does not have a formal creed but its principal points of belief are clear. Basic is belief in one transcendent God who reveals himself through the Torah, the prophets, the life of his people and events of history. The fatherhood of God involves the brotherhood of all humanity. Religious faith and practice are equated with just living according to God's Law. Moral conviction and practice are regarded as more important than precise doctrinal formulation and profession. Formal worship, whose principal act was sacrifice from the Exodus times to A.D. 70, is by prayer, reading and meditating upon the sacred writings, and observance of the Sabbath and festivals.

Judaism has messianic expectations of the complete fulfillment of the Covenant, the coming of God's kingdom, the ingathering of his people, and final judgment and retribution for all. Views differ regarding the manner in which these expectations will be realized — through a person, the community of God's people, an evolution of historical events, an eschatological act of God himself. Individual salvation expectations also differ, depending on views about the nature of immortality, punishment and reward, and related matters.

Sacred Books

The sacred books are the 24 books of the Masoretic Hebrew Text of The Law, the Prophets and the Writings (see The Bible). Together, they contain the basic instruction or norms for just living. In some contexts, the term Law or Torah refers only to the Pentateuch (Genesis, Exodus, Leviticus, Numbers, Deuteronomy); in others, it denotes all the sacred books and/or the whole complex of written and oral tradition.

Also of great authority are two Talmuds, which were composed in Palestine and Babylon in the fourth and fifth centuries A.D., respectively. They consist of the Mishna, a compilation of oral laws, and the Gemara, a collection of rabbinical commentary on the Mishna. Midrash are collections of scriptural comments and moral counsels.

Priests were the principal religious leaders during the period of sacrificial and temple worship. Rabbis were originally teachers; today they share with cantors the function of leaders of prayer. The synagogue is the place of community worship. The family and home are focal points of many aspects of Jewish worship and practice.

Of the various categories of Jews, Orthodox are the most conservative in adherence to strict religious traditions. Others — Reformed, Conservative, Reconstructionist — are liberal in comparison with the Orthodox. They favor greater or less modification of religious practices in accommodation to contemporary culture and living conditions.

Principal events in Jewish life include the circumcision of males, according to prescriptions of the Covenant; the bar and bat mitzvah that marks the coming-of-age of boys and girls in Judaism at age 13; marriage; and observance of the Sabbath and festivals.

Observances of the Sabbath and festivals begin at sundown of the previous calendar day and continue until the following sundown.

Sabbath: Saturday, the weekly day of rest prescribed in the Decalogue.

Sukkoth (Tabernacles): A seven-to-nine-day festival in the month of Tishri (Sept.-Oct.), marked by some Jews with Covenant-renewal and reading of The Law. It originated as an agricultural feast at the end of the harvest and got its name from the temporary shelters used by workers in the fields.

Hanukkah (The Festival of Lights, the Feast of Consecration and of the Maccabees): Commemorates the dedication of the new altar in the Temple at Jerusalem by Judas Maccabeus in 165 B.C. The eight-day festival, during which candles in an eight-branch candelabra are lighted in succession, one each day, occurs near the winter solstice, close to Christmas time.

Pesach (Passover): A seven-day festival commemorating the liberation of the Israelites from Egypt. The narrative of the Exodus, the Haggadah, is read at ceremonial Seder meals on the first and second days of the festival, which begins on the 14th day of Nisan (Mar.-Apr.).

Shavuoth, Pentecost (Feast of Weeks): Observed 50 days after Passover, commemorating the anniversary of the revelation of the Law to Moses.

Purim: A joyous festival observed on the 14th day of Adar (Feb.-Mar.), commemorating the rescue of the Israelites from massacre by the Persians through the intervention of Esther. The festival is preceded by a day of fasting. A gift- and alms-giving custom became associated with it in medieval times.

Rosh Hashana (Feast of Trumpets, New Year): Observed on the first day of Tishri (Sept.-Oct.), the festival focuses attention on the ways of life and the ways of death. It is second in importance only to the most solemn observance of Yom Kippur.

Yom Kippur (Day of Atonement): The highest holy day, observed with strict fasting. It occurs 10 days after Rosh Hashana.

Yom HaShoah (Holocaust Memorial Day): Observed in the week after Passover; increasingly observed with joint Christian-Jewish services of remembrance.

CATHOLIC-JEWISH RELATIONS

The Second Vatican Council, in addition to the *Decree on Ecumenism* (concerning the movement for unity among Christians, stated the mind of the Church on a similar matter in *Nostra Aetate*, a" Declaration on the Relationship of the Church to Non-Christian Religions." This document, as the following excerpts indicate, backgrounds the reasons and directions of the Church's regard for the Jews. (Other portions of the document refer to Hindus, Buddhists and Muslims.)

Spiritual Bond

As this sacred Synod searches into the mystery of the

Church, it recalls the spiritual bond linking the people of the New Covenant with Abraham's stock.

For the Church of Christ acknowledges that, according to the mystery of God's saving design, the beginnings of her faith and her election are already found among the patriarchs, Moses, and the prophets. She professes that all who believe in Christ, Abraham's sons according to faith (cf. Gal 3:7), are included in the same patriarch's call, and likewise that the salvation of the Church was mystically foreshadowed by the Chosen People's exodus from the land of bondage.

The Church, therefore, cannot forget that she received the revelation of the Old Testament through the people with whom God in his inexpressible mercy deigned to establish the Ancient Covenant. Nor can she forget that she draws sustenance from the root of that good olive tree onto which have been grafted the wild olive branches of the Gentiles (cf. Rom 11:17-24). Indeed, the Church believes that by his cross Christ, our Peace, reconciled Jew and Gentile, making them both one in himself (cf. Eph 2:14-16).

The Jews still remain most dear to God because of their fathers, for he does not repent of the gifts he makes nor of the calls he issues (cf. Rom 11:28-29). In company with the prophets and the same Apostle (Paul), the Church awaits that day, known to God alone, on which all peoples will address the Lord in a single voice and "serve him with one accord" (Zeph 3:9; cf. Is 66:23; Ps 65:4; Rom 11:11-32).

Since the spiritual patrimony common to Christians and Jews is thus so great, this sacred Synod wishes to foster and recommend that mutual understanding and respect which is the fruit above all of biblical and theological studies, and of brotherly dialogues.

No Anti-Semitism

True, authorities of the Jews and those who followed their lead pressed for the death of Christ (cf. Jn 19:6); still, what happened in his passion cannot be blamed upon all the Jews then living, without distinction, nor upon the Jews of today. Although the Church is the new People of God, the Jews should not be presented as repudiated or cursed by God, as if such views followed from the holy Scriptures. All should take pains, then, lest in catechetical instruction and in the preaching of God's Word they teach anything out of harmony with the truth of the Gospel and the spirit of Christ.

The Church repudiates all persecutions against any person. Moreover, mindful of her common patrimony with the Jews, and motivated by the Gospel's spiritual love and by no political considerations, she deplores the hatred, persecutions, and displays of anti-Semitism directed against the Jews at any time and from any source (No. 4).

The Church rejects, as foreign to the mind of Christ, any discrimination against men or harassment of them because of their race, color, condition of life, or religion (No. 5).

Bishops' Secretariat

The American hierarchy's first move toward implementation of the Vatican II "Declaration on the Relationship of the Church to Non-Christian Religions" (*Nostra Aetate*) was to establish, in 1965, a Subcommission for Catholic-Jewish Relations in the framework of its Commission for Ecumenical and Interreligious Affairs. Its moderator is Card. William H. Keeler of Baltimore. The Secretariat for Ecumenical and Interreligious Relations is located at 3211 Fourth St. NE, Washington, DC 20017. Its Catholic-Jewish efforts are directed by Dr. Eugene J. Fisher.

According to the key norm of a set of guidelines issued by the secretariat Mar. 16, 1967, and updated Apr. 9, 1985: "The general aim of all Catholic-Jewish meetings (and relations) is to increase our understanding both of Judaism and the Catholic faith, to eliminate sources of tension and misunderstanding, to initiate dialogue or conversations on different levels, to multiply intergroup meetings between Catholics and Jews, and to promote cooperative social action."

Vatican Guidelines

In a document issued Jan. 3, 1975, the Vatican Commission for Religious Relations with the Jews offered a number of suggestions and guidelines for implementing the Christian-Jewish portion of the Second Vatican Council's Declaration on Relations with Non-Christian Religions.

Among "suggestions from experience" were those concerning dialogue, liturgical links between Christian and Jewish worship, the interpretation of biblical texts, teaching and education for the purpose of increasing mutual understanding, and joint social action.

Notes on Preaching and Catechesis

On June 24, 1985, the Vatican Commission for Religious Relations with the Jews promulgated its "Notes on the Correct Way to Present Jews and Judaism in Preaching and Catechesis in the Roman Catholic Church," with the intent of providing "a helpful frame of reference for those who are called upon in the course of their teaching assignments to speak about Jews and Judaism and who wish to do so in keeping with the current teaching of the Church in this area."

The document states emphatically that, since the relationship between the Church and the Jewish people is one "founded on the design of the God of the Covenant," Judaism does not occupy "an occasional and marginal place in catechesis," but an "essential" one that "should be organically integrated" throughout the curriculum on all levels of Catholic education.

The Notes discuss the relationship between the Hebrew Scriptures and the New Testament, focusing especially on typology, which is called "the sign of a problem unresolved." Underlined is the "eschatological dimension," that "the people of God of the Old and the New Testament are tending toward a like end in the future: the coming or return of the Messiah." Jewish witness to God's Kingdom, the Notes declare, challenges Christians to "accept our responsibility to prepare the world for the coming of the Messiah by working together for social justice and reconciliation."

The Notes emphasize the Jewishness of Jesus' teaching, correct misunderstandings concerning the portrayal of Jews in the New Testament and describe the Jewish origins of Christian liturgy. One section addresses the "spiritual fecundity" of Judaism to the present, its continuing "witness — often heroic — of its fidelity to the one God," and mandates the development of Holocaust curricula and a positive approach in Catholic education to the "religious attachment which finds its roots in biblical tradition" between the Jewish people and the Land of Israel, affirming the "existence of the State of Israel" on the basis of "the common principles of international law."

WE REMEMBER: A REFLECTION ON THE SHOAH

On Mar. 16, 1998, the Commission for Religious Relations with the Jews under Card. Edward Idris Cassidy, issued a long-awaited white paper on the Holocaust, entitled "We Remember: Reflections on the Shoah."

The document offered repentance for the failures of many Christians to oppose the policies of Nazi Germany and to resist the extermination of the Jews during the years of the Third Reich. It analyzed the history of anti-Semitism in the Church, while distinguishing between the historical anti-Judaism of Christian teaching over the centuries and the modern, racial ideology of Nazism that climaxed with the Holocaust.

"We Remember" defends Pope Pius XII and his efforts on behalf of the Jews during World War II, and at the same time acknowledges the need for a "call to penitence" by the Church as a whole "for the failures of her sons and daughters in every age." Card. Cassidy, in an address given in May 1998 to the American Jewish Committee responding to criticisms of the text, stated clearly that terms such as "sons and daughters" and "members of the Church" are not restricted to a single category, "but can include popes cardinals, bishops, priests and laity," and he acknowledged that Christian anti-Judaism paved the way for Nazi anti-Semitism, though distinct from it.

We Remember begins with a letter from Pope John Paul II expressing his hope that the document will indeed help to heal the wounds of past misunderstandings and injustices and enable memory to play its necessary part in the process of shaping a future in which the unspeakable iniquity of the Shoah will never again be possible."

The U.S. Conference of Catholic Bishops' Committee for Ecumenical and Interreligious Relations in 1998 published the text of "We Remember" along with the statements of European and American bishops' conferences similarly expressing repentance for Christian sins of omission and commission during the Shoah in a volume entitled, *Catholics Remember the Holocaust.* In 2001 the U.S. Bishops issued *Catholic Teaching on the Shoah: Implementing the Holy See's "We Remember"* urging and giving guidelines for Holocaust education in all Catholic schools, from elementary through college and university education.

PAPAL STATEMENTS

(Courtesy of Dr. Eugene Fisher, associate director of the Bishops' Committee for Ecumenical and Interreligious Affairs.)

Pope John Paul

Pope John Paul was deeply loved and admired by the Jewish people worldwide over his long tenure. The Jewish outpouring of grief and condolence was deep and widespread, and save for that when the beloved Bl. John XXIII died, entirely without precedent. The prayers and statements of Jewish groups can be seen on their websites. Pope John Paul II, in a remarkable series of addresses beginning in 1979, sought to promote and give shape to the development of dialogue between Catholics and Jews.

In a homily delivered June 7, 1979, at Auschwitz, which he called the "Golgotha of the Modern World," he prayed movingly for "the memory of the people whose sons and daughters were intended for total extermination."

In a key address delivered Nov. 17, 1980, to the Jewish community in Mainz, the Pope articulated his vision of the three "dimensions" of the dialogue: (1) "the meeting between the people of God of the Old Covenant and the people of the New Covenant"; (2) the encounter of "mutual esteem between today's Christian churches and today's people of the Covenant concluded with Moses"; (3) the "holy duty" of witnessing to the one God in the world and "jointly to work for peace and justice."

During his historic visit to the Great Synagogue in Rome Apr. 13, 1986, the Holy Father affirmed that God's covenant with the Jewish people is "irrevocable," and stated: "The Jewish religion is not 'extrinsic' to us, but in a certain way is 'intrinsic' to our own religion. With Judaism, therefore, we have a relationship which we do not have with any other religion."

Meeting with the Jewish community in Sydney, Australia, Nov. 26, 1986, the Holy Father termed the 20th century "the century of the Shoah" (Holocaust) and called "sinful" any "acts of discrimination or persecution against Jews."

On June 14, 1987, meeting with the Jewish community of Warsaw, the pope called the Jewish witness to the Shoah (Holocaust) a "saving warning before all of humanity" which reveals "your particular vocation, showing you (Jews) to be still the heirs of that election to which God is faithful."

Meeting with Jewish leaders Sept. 11, 1987, in Miami, the Pope praised the efforts in theological dialogue and educational reform implemented in the U.S. since the Second Vatican Council; affirmed the existence of the State of Israel "according to international law," and urged "common educational programs on the Holocaust so that never again will such a horror be possible. Never again!"

On Apr. 7, 1994, the eve of Yom HaShoah, the Jewish day of prayer commemorating the victims of the Holocaust, Pope John Paul II hosted a memorial concert at the Vatican. It was, he noted, a moment of "common meditation and shared prayer," as the Kaddish, the prayer for the dead, and the Kol Nidre, the prayer for forgiveness and atonement, were recited.

Pope Benedict XVI

Because he had already built up an impressive series of positive reflections on Catholic-Jewish relations over the years, including a book, the election of Cardinal Joseph Ratzinger to the papacy was greeted with joy by all involved in Catho- lic-Jewish relations. In a major article in L'Osservatore Romano in December 2000, for example, Cardinal Ratzinger clarified and synthesized Catholic teaching on Jews and Judaism. With regard to the Shoah, for example, he stated: "Even if the most recent, loathsome experience of the Shoah was perpetrated in the name of an anti-Christian ideology, which tried to strike the Christian faith at its Abrahamic roots in the people of Israel, it cannot be denied that a certain insufficient resistance to this atrocity on the part of Christians can be explained by an inherited anti-Judaism present in the hearts of not a few Christians." The dialogue, he said, "must begin with a prayer to our God, first of all that he might grant to us Christians a greater esteem and love for that people, the people of Israel, to whom belong 'the adoption as sons, the glory, the covenants, the giving of the law, the worship, and the promises; theirs are the patriarchs, and from them comes Christ according to the flesh, he who is over all, God, blessed forever. Amen' (Rom 9:4-5), and this not only in the past, but still today, 'for the gifts and the call of God are irrevocable' (Rom 11:29)."

In his first meeting with the International Jewish Committee for Interreligious Consultations, Benedict reassured many by affirming the direction of his predecessor: "At the very beginning of my Pontificate, I wish to assure you that the Church remains firmly committed, in her catechesis and in every aspect of her life, to implementing this decisive teaching."

Similarly, in his meeting with Jews in the Synagogue in Cologne, Benedict stated that "I make my own the words written by my venerable Predecessor on the occasion of the 60th anniversary of the liberation of Auschwitz and I too say: 'I bow my head before all those who experienced this manifestation of the *mysterium iniquitatis.*' The terrible events of that time must 'never cease to rouse consciences, to resolve conflicts, to inspire the building of peace.'"

In his review of the year 2005 with the Vatican Curia in December of that year, the Pope discussed the proper understanding of the Second Vatican Council. He spoke of the "hermeneutics of continuity and discontinuity" in three key areas: faith and science, Church and State (religious freedom), and "the relationship between the Church and the faith of Israel."

Greeting the chief rabbi of Rome in January 2006, Benedict, in a remarkable formulation, emphasized God's enduring and saving love for the Jewish People: "Your visit brings me great joy, and induces me to

renew with you this song of gratitude for the salvation we have received. The people of Israel have been liberated many times from the hands of their enemies and, in times of anti-Semitism, in the dramatic moments of the Shoah, the hand of the Almighty has supported and guided them. The favor of the God of the Covenant has always accompanied them, giving them the strength to overcome trials. To this divine loving attention your Jewish community, present in the city of Rome for more than 2,000 years, can also render testimony."

While affirming the necessity of Jewish, Christian, Muslim dialogue, Benedict emphasized in meeting with the American Jewish Committee in March 2007 that "Jews and Christians have a rich common patrimony. In many ways this distinguishes our relationship as unique among the religions of the world. The Church can never forget that chosen people with whom God entered into a holy covenant (cf. *Nostra Aetate,* 4)."

In May 2006, Benedict visited Auschwitz. "In a place like this," he said, "words fail; in the end, there can only be a dread silence — a silence which is itself a heartfelt cry to God: Why, Lord, did you remain silent? How could you tolerate all this? In silence, then, we bow our heads before the endless line of those who suffered and were put to death here; yet our silence becomes in turn a plea for forgiveness and reconciliation, a plea to the living God never to let this happen again." Returning to Rome and reflecting on the visit at the General Audience, he stated that "At the death camp of Auschwitz-Birkenau, a place of horror and godless inhumanity, I paid homage to the victims, including over a million Jews and many Poles. . . . May modern humanity not forget Auschwitz and the other 'factories of death' where the Nazi regime attempted to eliminate God in order to take his place. May it not give in to the temptation of racial hatred, which is the origin of the worst forms of anti-Semitism."

MILLENNIUM EVENTS

During 2000 the London Philharmonic conducted by Maestro Gilbert Levine played a special series of concerts of Haydn's "Creation" for interreligious audiences in Baltimore, Paris, Jerusalem and, finally in Rome to celebrate the Holy Father's 80th birthday. In London, the Holy See and the World Union for Progressive Judaism sponsored a theological dialogue, papers of which have been published as *He Kissed Him and They Wept* (London: SCM Press) co-edited by Tony Bayfield, Sydney Brichto and Eugene Fisher. A second theological conference on Revelation and Covenant was held in London in 2003.

Pope John Paul II determined that the year marking the beginning of the third millennium would be a year of repentance by the Church for the sins of its members during the secondnd millennium. On the first Sunday of Lent, during Mass in St. Peter's, he lead the Church in a liturgy of repentance in seven categories of Christian sins, one of which was the mistreatment of Jews and Judaism over the centuries including, especially the Shoah in the 20th century.

A high point of the millennium year was the Pope's pilgrimage to the Holy Land. In Israel, he visited not only Christian holy places, but places central to Jewish memory as well. At Yad VaShem in Jerusalem, Israel's memorial to the six million Jews murdered by Nazi Germany, he prayed for the deceased and embraced Jewish survivors, some of them from

his own home town of Wadowice. The prime minister of Israel, Ehud Barak, spoke movingly for his people and his country in a warm response. At the Western Wall (the Kotel, the last remnant of the ancient Temple of Jerusalem), the Pope not only prayed but inserted into the Wall a written petition just as the humblest of Jews have done ever since the Temple's destruction in 70 C.E. Its wording summarizes one of the major themes of the millennium year and of the remarkable pontificate of Karol Wojtyla. Addressing the "God of our fathers," the Pope prayed in the name of the whole Church: "We are deeply saddened by the behavior of those who in the course of history have caused these children of yours to suffer and, asking your forgiveness, we wish to commit ourselves to genuine brotherhood with the People of the Covenant." The note was reverently taken from the wall for permanent display at Yad VaShem.

Pontifical Biblical Commission

In 2002 the Pontifical Biblical Commission issued "The Jewish People and Their Sacred Scriptures in the Christian Bible," a 205-page volume fulfilling the pope's 1997 mandate to the Commission. The first section of the report stresses, contrary to Marcionism, that the Jewish Scriptures are a fundamental part of the Christian Bible. The second section shows how the New Testament attests "conformity" (continuity) to the Jewish Bible in "fulfilling the Scriptures" but also presents a "newness" ("discontinuity, progression") in the life and certain teachings of Christ (IIA). Still, major "fundamental themes" of revelation are shared by both testaments (IIB). Jewish readings of the Bible, from rabbinic times to the present, maintain their own integrity and validity based upon the integrity and validity of the Jewish Scriptures understood in their own terms.

The third section outlines the historical setting of the New Testament as a document of "post-exilic Judaism" (IIIA) and describes the portrait of Jews in each gospel (IIIB) and of Judaism in the Pauline Letters and other apostolic writings (IIIC). The document concludes with "pastoral orientations" urging Jews and Christians to continued dialogue over the "inexhaustible riches" of our shared sacred texts.

INTERNATIONAL LIAISON COMMITTEE

The International Catholic-Jewish Liaison Committee (ILC) was formed in 1971 and is the official link between the Commission for Religious Relations with the Jewish People and the International Jewish Committee for Interreligious Consultations. The committee meets every 18 months to examine matters of common interest.

Topics under discussion have included: mission and witness (Venice, 1977), religious education (Madrid, 1978), religious liberty and pluralism (Regensburg, 1979), religious commitment (London, 1981), the sanctity of human life in an age of violence (Milan, 1982), youth and faith (Amsterdam, 1984), the Vatican Notes on Preaching and Catechesis (Rome, 1985), the Holocaust (Prague, 1990), education and social action (Baltimore, 1992), family and ecology (Jerusalem, 1994), the Catholic Church and the Shoah (Rome, 1998), theological understandings of one another (New York, 2001), and theology (Buenos Aires, 2004).

Pope John Paul, addressing in Rome a celebration of *Nostra Aetate* (the Second Vatican Council's "Declaration on the Relationship of the Church to Non-Christian Religions") by the Liaison Committee, stated: "What you are celebrating is nothing other than the divine mercy which is guiding Christians and Jews to mutual awareness, respect, cooperation and solidarity. The universal openness of *Nostra Aetate* is anchored in and takes its orientation from a high sense of the absolute singularity of God's choice of a particular people. The Church is fully aware that Sacred Scripture bears witness that the Jewish people, this community of faith and custodian of a tradition thousands of years old, is an intimate part of the mystery of revelation and of salvation."

Family Rights and Obligations

The Liaison Committee, at its May, 1994, meeting in Jerusalem, issued its first joint statement, on the family, in anticipation of the UN Cairo Conference subsequently held in September.

The statement affirmed that "the rights and obligations of the family do not come from the State but exist prior to the State and ultimately have their source in God the Creator. The family is far more than a legal, social or economic unit. For both Jews and Christians, it is a stable community of love and solidarity based on God's covenant."

Caring for God's Creation

During its Mar. 23-26, 1998, meeting in the Vatican, the Liaison Committee issued its second joint statement, on the environment. Drawing deeply on the shared sacred text of Genesis, the Committee affirmed that "concern for the environment has led both Catholics and Jews to reflect on the concrete implications of their belief in God, creator of all things," especially "a recognition of the mutual dependence between the land and the human person." "Care for creation," the document concluded "is also a religious act."

In its April 2001, meeting, the Liaison Committee issued

two statements, one affirming the need to preserve the sacred character of Christian and Jewish holy places, as well as the communities who give witness to them, and one urging review and revision where necessary of curriculum and course materials teaching about each other's traditions especially in institutions of theological education.

Protecting Religious Freedom and Holy Sites

At its May 2001, meeting in New York, the Liaison Committee issued a joint declaration on a subject of increasing concern, not only in the Middle East, but in Asia and Africa as well. With regard to the obligation of states, the document notes: "Government and political authorities bear special responsibility for protecting human and religious rights. Those responsible for law, order, and public security should feel themselves obligated to defend religious minorities and to use available legal remedies against those who commit crimes against religious liberty and the sanctity of holy places. Just as they are prohibited from engaging in anti-religious acts, governments must also be vigilant lest by inaction they effectively tolerate religious hatred or provide impunity for the perpetrators of anti-religious actions."

On Education in Catholic and Jewish Seminaries and Theological Schools

Also in New York, the Liaison Committee issued a statement calling on Catholic and Jewish seminaries to provide understanding of the other. In addition to expanding course work and examining existing courses for the treatment of the other, the statement concluded that "educational institutions in both our communities should make every effort to expose students to living Jewish and Christian communities through guest lecturers, field trips, involvement in local national and international dialogue groups and conferences."

Tzedeq and Tzedaqah

The 18th International Catholic-Jewish Liaison Committee Meeting was held in Buenos Aires, from July 5-8, 2004. This encounter, convened for the first time in Latin America, was devoted to the subject of Tzedeq and Tzedaqah (Justice and Charity). The group renewed its "total rejection of anti-Semitism in all its forms, including anti-Zionism as a more recent manifestation of anti-Semitism," noting that while anti-Zionism can be distinguished from anti-Semitism, it can serve as a "screen" for it and lead to it.

Dialogue with the Chief Rabbinate of Israel

After two meetings, in Jerusalem (June 2002) and Grottaferrata/Rome (February 2003) the respective high ranking delegations convened in Jerusalem to discuss the theme of "The Relevance Of Central Teachings In The Holy Scriptures Which We Share For Contemporary Society And The Education Of Future Generations Accordingly." The Feb.

27, 2003 meeting in Rome issued statements on "The Sanctity of Human Life" and "Family Values." In Jerusalem in June, 2005, the Bi-Lateral Commission discussed "The Relationship between Religious and Civil Authority in the Jewish and Christian Traditions," agreeing on the following principles based upon biblical values:

1. Religious values are crucial for the wellbeing of the individual and society

2. The purpose of civil authority is to serve and provide for the welfare of the people through respecting the life and dignity of every individual

3. While emphasizing the importance of democracy in this regard, at the same time it is essential to legally protect society from extreme individualism, exploitation by vested interest groups and insensitivity to the cultural and moral values of religious tradition

4. Freedom of religion must be guaranteed to both individuals and communities by the religious and civil authorities

5. The relationship between religion and state must be based on reciprocity, mutual respect and cooperation

6. Legislation for the promotion of particular religious values is legitimate when done in harmony with the principles of human rights

We have an ethical obligation to demonstrate religious responsibility in these regards, and especially to educate future generations through engaging media opinion makers as well as through conventional educational channels.

At the February 2006 meeting in Rome, the Commission issued a statement on "human Life and Technology," stating among other principle that "The conviction that we share, that life on earth is but one stage in the soul's existence, must only lead us to a greater respect for the vessel – the human form – in which the soul resides in this world. Accordingly we totally reject the idea that the temporary nature of human existence on earth allows us to instrumentalise it. In this regard we strongly condemn any kind of bloodshed to promote any ideology – especially if this is done in the name of Religion. Such action is nothing less than a desecration of the Divine Name."

Vatican-Israel Accord

On Dec. 30, 1993, a year of dramatic developments in the Middle East was capped by the signing in Jerusalem of a "Fundamental Agreement" between representatives of the Holy See and the State of Israel. The agreement acknowledged in its preamble that the signers were "aware of the unique nature of the relationship between the Catholic Church and the Jewish people, and of the historic process of reconciliation and growth in mutual understanding and friendship between Catholics and Jews." Abp. (later Cardinal) William H. Keeler, president of the National Conference of Catholic Bishops, welcomed the accord together with the Israeli Ambassador to the United States at a ceremony at the NCCB headquarters in Washington. In 1996, the Anti-Defamation League published a set of documents related to the accord, entitled "A Challenge Long Delayed," edited by Eugene Fisher and Rabbi Klenicki.

U.S. DIALOGUE

The National Workshop on Christian-Jewish Relations, begun in 1973 by the NCCB Secretariat, draws more than 1,000 participants from around the world. Recent workshops have been held in Baltimore (1986), Minneapolis (1987), Charleston, SC (1989), Chicago (1990), Pittsburgh (1992), Tulsa (1994), Stamford (1996), and Houston (1999).

In October 1987, the Bishops' Committee for Ecumenical and Interreligious Affairs began a series of twice-yearly consultations with representatives of the Synagogue Council of America. Topics of discussion have included education, human rights, respect for life, the Middle East. The consultation has issued several joint statements: "On Moral Values in Public Education" (1990), "On Stemming the Proliferation of Pornography" (1993), "On Dealing with Holocaust Revisionism" (1994).

Ongoing relationships are maintained by the USCCB Secretariat with such Jewish agencies as the American Jewish Committee, the Anti-Defamation League, B'nai B'rith International, and the National Jewish Council for Public Affairs.

In June, 1988, the Bishops' Committee for Ecumenical and Interreligious Affairs published in Spanish and English Criteria for the Evaluation of Dramatizations of the Passion, providing for the first time Catholic guidelines for passion plays.

In January 1989, the Bishops' Committee for the Liturgy issued guidelines for the homiletic presentation of Judaism under the title, "God's Mercy Endures Forever."

When the Synagogue Council of America dissolved in 1995, the Bishops' Committee for Ecumenical and Interreligious Affairs initiated separate consultations with the new National Council of Synagogues (Reform and Conservative), chaired by Card. William H. Keeler, and the Orthodox Union/ Rabbinical Council, chaired by Card. John J. O'Connor, of blessed memory. The bishops have issued several joint statements with the National Council of Synagogues: "Reflections on the Millennium" (1998), "To End the Death Penalty" (1999), "Children and the Environment" (2001), "Filled with Sadness, Charged with Hope" (2001), and "Reflections on Covenant and Mission" (2002). Joint communiqués on issues of common concern, such as the Middle East and Catholic teaching on the Jews and the death of Jesus, were issued in 2003 and 2004. Bp. William Murphy of the Rockville Center diocese has succeeded Card. O'Connor as co-chair of the dialogue with Orthodox Judaism. This ongoing consultation has also issued joint communiqués and is working on a joint statement on aid for private education.

Recent Developments

In December 1999, the Holy See's Commission and the International Jewish Committee for Interreligious Consultations announced the establishment of a committee of three Catholic and three Jewish scholars to look into the many complex historical and moral issues involving the Church and the Shoah beginning with an analysis of the thousands of archival documents for the period of World War II already made public by the Holy See in its 12-volume *Actes et Documents* (1965-80). The Committee met in New York in December 1999, in London in May of 2000, in Baltimore in July 2000, and finally in Rome in October 2000, where it issued its "Preliminary Report." The report affirmed the objectivity of the original team of four Jesuit scholars who selected the tens of thousands of texts from the Vatican archives for inclusion in the 11 volumes of the *Actes et Documents du Saint Siege Relatives a la Seconde Guerre Mondiale* (Libreria Editrice Vaticana, 1965-80), but also raised numerous questions for further study and documentation. The Joint Commission's Catholic Coordinator, Dr.

Eugene Fisher praised the group's "achievement of so much consensus between Catholic and Jewish scholars on what are the questions that need to be faced today. Such solid consensus could by no means be presumed when the group started its work, so emotional and complex are the issues. . . .The scholarly successors of this group will be forever in their debt" (*Catholic International*, May 2002, p. 68). Card. Jorge Mejia, then Vatican Archivist, announced a major increase in the number of archivists working on preparing the remaining material for scholarly review, a process that already resulted in the release of tens of thousands of documents in 2003.

In 2004, the film, *The Passion of the Christ*, precipitated great controversy in the media. Jews, given the often violent history of Passion Plays, with which *The Passion* has much in common, expressed various concerns. Catholic leaders, whatever their personal feelings on the artistic merits of the movie, were strong in condemning any possible anti-Semitic use of it, pointing teachers and preachers to resources where the full and accurate teaching of the Church can be found, such as the BCEIA's *The Bible, the Jews and the Death of Jesus.*

40th Anniversary of Nostra Aetate

Card. Keeler, Fr. Kennedy, and Dr. Fisher represented the BCEIA at the meeting of representatives of Bishops conferences held at the Pontifical Commission on Religious Relations with the Jews on Oct. 27, in conjunction with its celebration of the 40th anniversary of *Nostra Aetate.* The group reported on current efforts and future hopes for the implementation of the document, especially in the area of education. The celebration that evening featured addresses by Cardinals Kasper and Lustiger, and Rabbi David Rosen, International Interfaith Affairs Director of the American Jewish Committee. Ancillary to the main event were dinners hosted by the Ambassador of Great Britain to the Quirinale and the Ambassador of Israel to the Holy See.

The Nov. 2, 2005, meeting of the ongoing Consultation between representatives of the National Council of Synagogues and the BCEIA was held at St. Mary's Seminary and University, Baltimore. In a public session celebrating the 40th anniversary, Card. Keeler recalled being a *peritus* at the Council. In response to concerns from the Jewish side that the Church might be stepping back from the her commitment to the ongoing nature of God's covenant with the Jews, Card. Keeler responded that we are in a new age and Pope Benedict XVI has reaffirmed John Paul II's teachings and the church's stand on this matter. Prof. Byron Sherwin of Spertus College of Judaica challenged the Jewish community, in the light of the Catholic Church's reappraisal of its theological understanding of Judaism, to reappraise its own historic attitude toward the Church and Christianity, replacing its largely defensive posture with a positive assessment of the spiritual reality and integrity of Christianity from a Jewish point of view.

On Nov. 14, 2005, a concert in celebrating the 40th anniversary of *Nostra Aetate* took place at the Basilica of the Shrine of the Immaculate Conception. A dinner beforehand sponsored by the Pope John Paul II Cultural Center was attended by many bishops and representatives of the Jewish community. The concert, sponsored by the Knights of Columbus, featured the world premiere of American composer Richard Danielpour's "Washington Speaks" with Ted Koppel as Narrator. Maestro Gilbert Levine conducted the Baltimore Symphony and the Morgan State University Choir.

On Dec. 7, 2005, a panel was held at the U.S. Holocaust Memorial Museum in Washington on *Nostra Aetate* featuring members of the Advisory Committee to the BCEIA on Catholic-Jewish relations. On Dec. 19, 2005, Bp. Richard Sklba presented a paper, "New Beginnings: Catholic-Jewish Relations after 40 Years," to a special session of the annual meeting of the National Association of Jewish Studies in Washington, with Jewish and Protestant respondents (*Origins*, Jan. 19, 2006, vol. 35, no. 31, pp. 509-514. Similar events honoring *Nostra Aetate* and reflecting on its ongoing influence took place in dioceses across the country.

ISLAM

(Courtesy of Dr. John Borelli, assistant to the President for interreligious initiatives, Georgetown University and Fr. Francis Tiso of the USCCB Secretariat for Interreligious Dialogue.)

Islam, meaning grateful surrender (to God), as a distinct religion originated with Muhammad and the revelation he is believed to have received in seventh century Arabia. Muslims acknowledge that this revelation, recorded in the *Qu'ran*, is from the one God and do not view Islam as a new religion. They profess that Muhammad was the last in a long series of prophets, most of whom are named in the Hebrew Bible and the New Testament, beginning with Adam and continuing through Noah, Abraham, Moses, Jesus and down to Muhammad.

Muslims believe in the one God, Allah in Arabic, and cognate with the Hebrew Elohim and the ancient Aramaic Elah. According to the *Qu'ran*, God is one and transcendent, Creator and Sustainer of the universe, all-merciful and all-compassionate Ruler and Judge. God possesses numerous other titles, known collectively as the 99 names of God. The profession of faith states: "There is no god but the God and Muhammad is the messenger of God."

The essential duties of Muslims are: to witness the faith by daily recitation of the profession of faith; worship five times a day facing in the direction of the holy city of Mecca; give alms; fast daily from dawn to dusk during the month of Ramadan; make a pilgrimage to Mecca once if possible.

Muslims believe in final judgment, resurrection of the body, heaven and hell. Following divinely revealed moral norms are extremely important to Muslims. Some dietary regulations (e.g. avoiding alcoholic beverages and pork) are in effect. On Fridays, the noon prayer is a congregational (*juma*) prayer which should be said in a mosque. The general themes of prayer are adoration and thanksgiving. Friday prayers are required for men. An imam gives a sermon to the congregation, but unlike Judeo-Christian tradition, the day is not a "day of rest." Muslims do not have an ordained ministry.

The basis of Islamic belief is the *Qu'ran*, the word of God revealed to Muhammad through the angel Gabriel over a period of 23 years. The contents of this sacred book are supplemented by the Sunna, a collection of sacred traditions from the life of the prophet Muhammad, and reinforced by Ijma, the consensus of Islamic scholars of Islamic Law (Shariah) which guarantees them against errors in matters of belief and practice.

Conciliar Statement

The attitude of the Church toward Islam was first stated in the Second Vatican Council's "Constitution on the Church":

"But the plan of salvation also includes those who acknowledge the Creator, in the first place among whom are the Muslims: these profess to hold the faith of Abraham, and together with us they adore the one, merciful God, mankind's judge on the last day" (no. 16). The Council's "Declaration on the Relation of the Church to Non-Christian Religions" (*Nostra Aetate*, no. 3) stated the position in further detail:

"The Church has a high regard for the Muslims. They worship God, who is one, living and subsistent, merciful and almighty, the Creator of heaven and earth, who has also spoken to men. They strive to submit themselves without reserve to the hidden decrees of God, just as Abraham submitted himself to God's plan, to whose faith Muslims eagerly link their own. Although not acknowledging him as God, they venerate Jesus as a prophet, his virgin Mother they also honor, and even at times devoutly invoke. Further, they await the day of judgment and the reward of God following the resurrection of the dead, For this reason, they highly esteem an upright life and worship God, especially by way of prayer, alms-deeds and fasting.

"Over the centuries many quarrels and dissensions have arisen between Christians and Muslims. The sacred Council now pleads with all to forget the past, and urges that a sincere effort be made to achieve mutual understanding; for the benefit of all men, let them together preserve and promote peace, liberty, social justice and moral values."

Dialogue

Pope John Paul II met with Muslim leaders and delegations both in Rome and during his trips abroad. He addressed large gatherings of Muslims in Morocco, Indonesia, Mali and elsewhere. In 1979 on a pastoral visit to Turkey, he suggested to the Catholic community: "My brothers, when I think of this spiritual heritage (Islam) and the value it has for man and for society, its capacity of offering, particularly in the young, guidance for life, filing the gap left by materialism, and giving a reliable foundation to social and juridical organization, I wonder if it is not urgent, precisely today when Christians and Muslims have entered a new period of history, to recognize and develop the spiritual bonds that unite us, in order to preserve and promote together for the benefit of all men, 'peace, liberty, social justice and moral values' as the Council calls upon us to do (*Nostra Aetate*, no. 3). In *Tertio Millennio Adveniente*, he recommended for the year 1999 that "the dialogue with Jews and the Muslims ought to have a pre-eminent place" and "meetings in places of significance for the great monotheistic religions." On Feb. 24, 2000, John Paul II traveled to Egypt as part of his Jubilee Year pilgrimages and was received by Grand Sheik Mohammed Sayyid Tantawi at al-Azhar University, the most influential Islamic university in the world. On pastoral visit to Syria in May 2001, John Paul II spoke of the significant relationship that exists between Muslims and Christians concluding with a citation to his first letter of the new millennium: "I am thinking too of the great cultural influence of Syrian Islam, which under the Umayyad caliphs reached the farthest shores of the Mediterranean. Today, in a world that is increasingly complex and interdependent, there is a need for a new spirit of dialogue and cooperation between Christians and Muslims. Together we

acknowledge the one indivisible God, the Creator of all that exists. Together we must proclaim to the world that the name of the one God is 'a name of peace and a summons to peace' (*Novo Millennio Ineunte*, no. 55)!" On the same trip to Syria, on May 6, 2001, John Paul II made the first papal visit to a mosque when he was received at the Umayyad Mosque in Damascus by the Minister of the Waqf and the Grand Mufti of Syria. On Nov. 18, 2001, John Paul II asked Catholics to fast and pray for peace on Friday, Dec. 14, the last Friday of the Ramadan fast that year. He also announced that he was intending to invite representatives of various world religions to Assisi for a day of prayer on Jan. 24, 2002.

The Pontifical Council for Interreligious Dialogue holds formal dialogues with several Islamic organizations on a regular basis. In the U.S., the Bishops' Committee for Ecumenical and Interreligious Affairs holds regular consultations on relations with Muslims. Dialogue on a national level with the participation of Catholics and Muslims from several U.S. cities was initiated in October 1991. A series of conversations with Muslims on international and domestic issues were co-sponsored with the American Muslim Council. In the late 1990s, the Bishops' Committee initiated a series of regional dialogues with Muslims. In 1996, an annual regional dialogue in the Midwest with the co-sponsorship of the Islamic Society of North America in Indianapolis was initiated. This dialogue concluded several years of discussion on revelation in 2005 with a report, *Revelation: Catholic and Muslim Perspectives*, published by USCCB Publishing. In 1998, an annual dialogue in the Mid-Atlantic region with the co-sponsorship of the Islamic Circle of North America in Queens, New York held its first meeting. The group has been working on a common document on marriage. In 2000, the West Coast Dialogue of Muslims and Catholics began meeting in Orange, Calif., with the co-sponsorship of several Islamic councils. The West Coast Dialogue issued a report in December 2003, *Friends and Not Adversaries, a Catholic-Muslim Spiritual Journey*. All three regional dialogues are co-chaired by bishops and Islamic leaders. Also in 1995 a dialogue between representatives of the ministry of W.D. Mohammed and the United States Conference of Catholic Bishops began. Following a pilgrimage to Rome by Card. William Keeler and Imam Warith Deen Mohammed, the spiritual leader of African-American Muslims in the United States, the relationship between Imam Mohammad's American Society of Muslims and the Catholic Church has been served by the Focolare Movement. For the 1999 Interreligious Assembly hosted by the Pontifical Council for Interreligious Dialogue in Rome in preparation for the great jubilee year 2000, Imam Mohammed was selected as the Muslim spokesperson at the closing ceremony.

On Sept. 14, 2001, following the tragic events in New York, Washington, and Western Pennsylvania, Bp. Tod D. Brown, BCEIA chairman, issued a statement with five Muslims leaders, representing the various organizations who have been partners with the bishops' conference in dialogues, condemning terrorist acts, encouraging unity and cooperation, urging restraint, entreating Muslims and Catholics to join with others in services of prayer.

MESSAGE FOR THE END OF RAMADAN 'ID AL-FITR 1426 A.H./A.D. 2005

This message was issued by Archbishop Michael Fitzgerald, President of the Pontifical Council for Interreligious Dialogue, and was addressed to the Muslim community on the observance of the Muslim

feast of 'Id al-Fitr at the end of Ramadan, the month of fasting.

Continuing of the Path of Dialogue

Dear Friends,

1. As 'Id al-Fitr comes round again, at the close of the month of Ramadan, I wish to offer to all of you, in whatever part of the world you may be, my very best wishes for a Happy Feast.

2. It has become a tradition for the Pontifical Council for Interreligious Dialogue to send a message to our Muslim brothers and sisters on the occasion of the end of Ramadan. The message has usually been signed by the president of the Pontifical Council. In 1991, on account of the first Gulf War, the good-will message was signed by His Holiness Pope John Paul II. He wrote about the need for "a sincere, profound and constant dialogue between believing Catholics and believing Muslims, from which there can arise a strengthened mutual knowledge and trust." These words are surely still relevant today.

3. On April 2 of this year, Pope John Paul II completed his earthly life. Many Muslims around the world, with Catholics and other Christians, followed closely the news of the Pope's last illness and his death, and official delegations of Muslims, political and religious leaders from many countries, attended his funeral in St. Peter's Square. Many had appreciated deeply the Pope's constant efforts on behalf of peace. A Muslim journalist who had had occasion to meet personally with Pope John Paul II wrote: "I am not exaggerating when I say that the death of Pope John Paul II has been a great loss for the Catholic Church and for Christians in general, and also for Christian-Muslim relations in particular. There can be no compensation for this loss other than to follow in his footsteps and to continue in the way that he has traced out with the faith and courage of Assisi in 1986, Assisi where lie the remains of St. Francis, pioneer among Catholics of Christian-Muslim dialogue."

4. It was faith in God and confidence in humanity that impelled the late Pope to engage in dialogue. He constantly reached out to brothers and sisters of all religions with respect and a desire for collaboration, as had been encouraged by the Second Vatican Council in its Declaration *Nostra Aetate* of which the 40th anniversary occurs this year. His commitment in this regard was actually rooted in the Gospel, following the example of the Lord Jesus who showed his love and respect for each person, even for those who did not belong to his own people.

5. Following the teaching of the Vatican Council II and continuing on the path taken by Pope John Paul II, His Holiness Pope Benedict XVI, when receiving the representatives of other religions who attended the celebration for the beginning of his Pontificate, stated: "I am particularly grateful for the presence in our midst of members of the Muslim community, and I express my appreciation for the growth of dialogue between Muslims and Christians, both at the local and international levels. I assure you that the Church wants to continue building bridges of friendship with followers of all religions, in order to seek the true good of every person and of society as a whole." Then, making reference to the conflicts, violence and wars present in our world, the Pope emphasized that it is the duty of every one, especially those who profess to belong to a religious tradition, to work for peace, and that "our efforts to come together and foster dialogue are a valuable contribution to building peace on solid foundations." Pope Benedict XVI concluded by saying: "It is therefore imperative to engage in sincere and authentic dialogue, built on respect for the dignity of every human person, created, as we Christians firmly believe, in the image and likeness of God" (cf. Gen 1: 26-27) (*L'Osservatore Romano*, April 26, 2005).

6. Encouraged by these words of the Pope, it is for us to strengthen our engagement in building up good relations among people of different religions, to promote cultural dialogue and to work together for greater justice and enduring peace. Let us, as Christians and Muslims, show that we can live together in true fraternity, striving always to do the will of Merciful God who created humanity to be one family.

Once more I express to you my warmest greetings.

Archbishop Michael L. Fitzgerald, President

HINDUISM AND BUDDHISM

(Courtesy of Dr. John Borelli and Fr. Francis Tiso.)

In its Declaration on the Relation of the Church to Non-Christian Religions, the Second Vatican Council stated: "In Hinduism men explore the divine mystery and express it both in the limitless riches of myth and the accurately defined insights of philosophy. They seek release from the trials of the present life by ascetical practices, profound meditation and recourse to God in confidence and love" (no. 2).

Catholics, especially in India, have sought good relations with Hindus and have engaged in numerous dialogues and conferences. In papal visits to India, Paul VI in 1964 and John Paul II in 1986 and 1999, popes have addressed words of respect for Indian, particularly Hindu, religious leaders. Pope John Paul II said to Hindus in India in 1986: "Your overwhelming sense of the primacy of religion and of the greatness of the Supreme Being has been a powerful witness against a materialistic and atheistic view of life." In 1987, he said of Hinduism: "I hold in esteem your concern for inner peace and for the peace of the world, based not on purely mechanistic or materialistic political considerations, but on self-purification, unselfishness, love and sympathy for all."

In 1995, the Pontifical Council for Interreligious Dialogue began sending a general message to Hindus on the occasion of Diwali, a feast commemorating the victory of light over darkness. In 1999, John Paul II was in India during the celebration and said these words to the religious leaders of India: "On the occasion of Diwali, the festival of lights, which symbolizes the victory of life over death, good over evil, I express the hope that this meeting will speak to the world of the things that unite us all: our common human origin and destiny, our shared responsibility for people's well-being and progress, our need of the light and strength that we seek in our religious convictions." In the United States, there are a few dialogues between Catholics and Hindus, focusing on common themes of spirituality.

The Second Vatican Council, in its Declaration on the Relation of the Church to Non-Christian Religions, stated: "Buddhism in its multiple forms acknowledges the radical insufficiency of this shifting world. It teaches a path by which men, in a devout and confident spirit, can either reach a state of absolute freedom or attain supreme enlightenment by their own efforts or by higher assistance."

Numerous delegations of Buddhists and leading monks have been received by the popes, and John Paul II has met with Buddhist leaders on many of his trips. Paul VI said to a group of Japanese Buddhists in 1973: "Buddhism is one of the riches of Asia: you teach men to seek truth and peace in the kingdom of the Eternal, beyond the horizon of visible things. You likewise strive to encourage the qualities of goodness, meekness and non-violence." In 1995, while in Sri Lanka, John Paul II said to Buddhists: "I express my highest regard for the followers of Buddhism, . . . with its four great values of loving kindness, compassion, sympathy, and equanimity; with its ten transcendental virtues and the joys of the Sangha [the monastic community] . . . At the 1986 World Day of Prayer for Peace at Assisi, the Dalai Lama, principal teacher of the Gelugpa lineage, was placed immediately to the Holy Father's left. Numerous dialogues and good relations between Catholics and Buddhists exist in many countries.

In 1995, the Pontifical Council for Interreligious Dialogue organized a Buddhist-Christian colloquium hosted by the Fo Kuang Shan Buddhist order in Taiwan. A second colloquium was held in Bangalore, India, in 1998. A third was held in Tokyo in 2002. These grew out of the perceived need for greater ongoing contact between the Pontifical Council and Buddhist leaders and scholars. Each of these meetings has produced a report. Also in 1995, the council began sending a message to Buddhists on the feast of Vesakh, the celebration of Gautama Buddha's birth, enlightenment, and final entry into Nirvana.

A meeting of great significance between Buddhist and Catholic monastics took place at Our Lady of Gethsemani Abbey, Kentucky, in July 1996, which was organized and facilitated by Monastic Interreligious Dialogue, a network formed in 1981 mostly of monasteries of men and women following the rule of St. Benedict. The Gethsemani Encounter, the result of several formal visits and hospitality between Catholic and Buddhist monks and nuns, focused on various aspects of monastic life. There were 25 participants on each side with numerous observers. The Buddhists represented the Theravada, Tibetan, and Zen traditions. A second Gethsemani Encounter took place in April 2002, the proceedings of which have been published as Transforming Suffering: Reflections on Finding Peace in Troubled Times.

In 1998, an ongoing dialogue between Buddhists and Catholics in Los Angeles hosted a retreat dialogue for 50 Catholic and Buddhist participants from different regions of the U.S. The retreat/dialogue was co-planned with the Faiths in the World Committee of the National Association of Diocesan Ecumenical Officers, a network of Catholic diocesan staff responsible for ecumenical and interreligious relations. A second retreat/dialogue, co-planned by the Faiths in the World Committee, met at Graymoor, a spiritual life center at the headquarters of the Society of the Atonement, in Garrison, New York, in 2003. This second retreat/dialogue was a "two monastery dialogue," co-hosted by Graymoor and Chuang Yen Buddhist Monastery in nearby Carmel, N.Y.

In 1996, Cardinal Arinze, in a letter to "Dear Buddhist Friends," wrote: "The pluralistic society in which we live demands more than mere tolerance. Tolerance is usually thought of as putting up with the other or, at best, as a code of public conduct. Yet, this resigned, lukewarm attitude does not create the right atmosphere for true harmonious coexistence. The spirit of our religions challenges us to go beyond this. We are commanded, in fact, to love our neighbors as ourselves." The cardinal wrote in the same vein to Muslims on the occasion of their 1996 celebration of Id al-Fitr.

Formal dialogues continue in the Archdiocese of Los Angeles and formal relations are developing in a few other dioceses. In 1989, the Bishops' Committee for Ecumenical and Interreligious Affairs convened its first national consultation on relations with Buddhists; a second consultation was held in 1990.

After a series of meetings in the San Francisco area, the Bishops' Committee inaugurated a Buddhist-Catholic dialogue in March 2003, following the model of its regional dialogues, with the Dharma Realm Buddhist Association and the San Francisco Zen Center as partners. The theme of the first dialogue was "Walking the Bodhisattva Path/Walking the Christ Path." The Northern California Chan/Zen-Catholic Dialogue met again in March 2004 to discuss the theme "Transformation of Hearts and Minds: Chan/Zen-Catholic Approaches to Precepts." In 2005, the theme was "Practice: Means Toward Transformation," at the San Francisco Zen Center. The theme of the 2006 meeting was "Meeting on the Path." The theme for the 2007 meeting will be "Taking Refuge in the Buddha / Abiding in Christ."

In an effort to further the Bishops' interest in interreligious dialogue, planning for a new outreach to the Sikh community began in 2005. In May 2006 the first meeting of a Sikh-Catholic Consultation comprised of representatives of the World Sikh Council - America Region and the U.S. Conference of Catholic Bishops was held in New York. As a sign of Vatican support for this new initiative, Msgr. Felix Machado, Under Secretary of the Pontifical Council for Interreligious Dialogue, was also present for the meeting. At the consultation, the Sikh and Catholic communities expressed shared concerns over the challenges faced by immigrant communities in the US, the curtailment of religious freedom and human rights in South Asia, and the challenges of secularism to both religious communities.

Subcommittee on Interreligious Dialogue

With an increase in dialogues and other cooperative programs with Muslims, Buddhists, Hindus and others, the U. S. Bishops' Committee for Ecumenical and Interreligious Affairs decided that it would be helpful to its work if a Subcommittee were formed to oversee in greater detail interreligious relations. In December 2000, Bp. Tod D. Brown, BCEIA chairman, announced the formation of the Subcommittee on Interreligious Dialogue. Bp. Joseph J. Gerry, former bishop of the diocese of Portland (Maine), who had served for more than 10 years as Bishop Moderator for Interreligious Relations, was the first chairman of the new Subcommittee. The first meeting was held in March 2001. In 2003, Bp. Brown began serving as chairman of the Subcommittee. In addition to discussing the various dialogues in progress and other items of mutual interest, the members decided to undertake a program of education in interreligious relations for the members of the bishops' conference. In March 2003, the first Institute for Bishops on Islam and Catholic-Muslim Relations was held under the sponsorship of the Subcommittee and with the financial assistance of the Catholic Near East Welfare Association. A second institute for bishops met in 2004, and the third institute took place at Georgetown University in 2005. Since 2005, Bp. William Murphy of Rockville Center has chaired the subcommittee.

MESSAGE FOR THE FEAST OF VESAKH 2006

The Pontifical Council for Interreligious Dialogue issued the following message to the Buddhists of the world on the occasion of 2006 celebration of the Feast of Vesakh.

Buddhists and Christians at the Service of Humanity

Dear Buddhist Friends,

1. On behalf of the Pontifical Council for Interreligious Dialogue I offer to you and to all Buddhist communities around the world my very best wishes for Vesakh. I hope that you may have a joyful feast.

2. As is now customary, I would like to take this occasion to share with you some thoughts which may help to strengthen the relations between our two communities. This year these reflections are based on Pope Benedict XVI's first letter to Catholics throughout the world. This letter, God is Love, or according to its Latin title *Deus Caritas Est* (DCE), examines the nature of love. His Holiness the Pope is convinced that this word, so frequently used and yet so often misunderstood, needs to have its true meaning restored in order to become a beacon of light for everyday life.

3. Pope Benedict speaks about two types of love: first eros, the love between a man and a woman, a love which seeks personal satisfaction; then agape, a love which seeks the good of the other, although that person may not be liked or even not known. For Christians this second type of love is only possible if it is grounded in love for God, in response to God's love for human beings. So love of God and love of one's fellow human beings are inseparable, forming one single commandment. "Love grows through love. Love is 'divine' because it comes from God and unites us to God" (DCE, no. 18).

4. We Christians believe that the perfect manifestation of *agape* is founded on Jesus Christ, the Son of God made man, who spent his whole life spreading the Good News of God's love in both words and deeds. The ultimate expression of this love was when Jesus gave his life for the whole of humanity. Moreover Jesus is the source of *agape*, in particular through the gift of himself in the Eucharist. Drawing from this source, Christians strive to follow in the footsteps of Jesus by showing love for their brothers and sisters, especially for the poor and suffering.

5. Through our dialogue we have come to appreciate the importance that you Buddhists give to love for one's fellow human beings which is expressed in the concept of *metta*, a love without any desire to possess but only to help others. It is understood as a love which is willing to sacrifice self-interest for the benefit of humanity. So *metta*, according to Buddhist teaching, is not confined to benevolent thought, but extends to the performance of charitable deeds, to the service of one and all. It is indeed a universal benevolence. Nor should one forget that other virtue, *karuna*, through which is shown loving compassion for all living beings.

6. In this world where the word love is so often used and misused would it not be useful for Buddhists and Christians to rediscover its original meaning according to their respective traditions and to share their understanding with one another? This would be an encouragement for the followers of both traditions to work together to build up relations based on love and truth, to promote mutual respect, to foster dialogue and to further collaboration in the service of those who are in need.

7. These considerations lead me to a final wish, namely that the feast of Vesakh may be a time when the friendship between Buddhists and Christians is consolidated and collaboration in the spirit of *agape* and *metta* is strengthened. In this spirit I wish you a very Happy Vesakh.

Vatican City, Feb. 14, 2006

MESSAGE FOR THE FEAST OF DIWALI 2005

Archbishop Michael L. Fitzgerald, then president of the Pontifical Council for Interreligious Dialogue sent this message to the Hindu faithful of the world on the occasion of the feast of Diwali.

Hindus and Christians in Solidarity

Dear Hindu Friends,

1. As you celebrate Diwali again this year, I wish every one of you much joy and happiness. May this holiday season bring you refreshment in mind and body and renew you in spirit to continue meeting the difficulties of daily life with courage and hope.

2. It is only natural for us to hope that the joyful character of our religious celebrations may extend to every moment of our existence. Yet we know that, unfortunately, life is not like this. We experience it as a mixture of joys and sorrows, hopes and disappointments, wellbeing and sickness, comfort and grief. Religious feasts, recalling to us the spiritual dimension of life and the search for true meaning, provide us with an opportunity to reflect on the significance of tragic events in our own lives or in those of people around us. This reflection is inspired by the occurrence of the "tsunami," the "killing waves" caused by the earthquake in the Indian Ocean at the end of last year. The forces of nature wreaked great havoc, many lives were lost, countless homes were destroyed, sources of livelihood ruined and families, including many children, were left destitute.

3. Many of you who are receiving this message may, like myself, not have been personally affected by the "tsunami." We have learnt about the suffering of the victims at second hand. We have nevertheless wanted to express our sympathy and show our solidarity. And we have been able to do this together. Through the bonds of friendship forged by dialogue over the years, we Christians have come to discover that you, as Hindus, are greatly concerned about those who are suffering. For your part, you may have come to realize that the Christian faith teaches that every human being is created in the image and likeness of God and is thus deserving of attention and concern. In this context I should like to quote from *Nostra Aetate*, the declaration of the Second Vatican Council on the relation of the Church to non-Christian religions. This document, whose fortieth anniversary we are celebrating this year, states: "We cannot in truthfulness call upon God, who is the Father of all, if we refuse to act in a brotherly way toward certain men, created though they be to God's image. A man's relationship with God the Father and his relationship with his brother men are so linked together that Scripture says: 'He who does not love does not know God' (1 Jn 4:8)" (NA 5).

4. In places affected by the "tsunami," solidarity across religious boundaries has helped to bring hope to many of the victims. Teams of relief workers belonging to different religious traditions have been tireless in working to alleviate immediate suffering and to initiate reconstruction. At a time when aggressive secularism would seem to be on the increase and respect for basic human values often appears to be on the decline, such cooperation among people of different religions can bring about a new respect for religion in today's world.

5. Dear Hindu friends, let us continue to collaborate in finding solutions to the problems we face, whether they be small or great, whether local or international. Diwali celebrates light, goodness, reconciliation, peace, harmony and happiness. I wish you all a very happy feast.

Archbishop Michael L. Fitzgerald, President

INDEX

Our Sunday Visitor ...
Your Source for Discovering the Riches of the Catholic Faith

Our Sunday Visitor has an extensive line of materials for young children, teens, and adults. Our books, Bibles, pamphlets, CD-ROMs, audios, and videos are available in bookstores worldwide.

To receive a FREE full-line catalog or for more information, call **Our Sunday Visitor** at **1-800-348-2440, ext. 3**. Or write **Our Sunday Visitor** / 200 Noll Plaza / Huntington, IN 46750.

Please send me ___ A catalog
Please send me materials on:
___ Apologetics and catechetics
___ Prayer books
___ The family
___ Reference works
___ Heritage and the saints
___ The parish

Name _____
Address _____ Apt._____
City _____ State _____ Zip_____
Telephone (   ) _____
                                                        A69BBBBP

Please send a friend ___ A catalog
Please send a friend materials on:
___ Apologetics and catechetics
___ Prayer books
___ The family
___ Reference works
___ Heritage and the saints
___ The parish

Name _____
Address _____ Apt._____
City _____ State _____ Zip_____
Telephone (   ) _____
                                                        A69BBBBP

OurSundayVisitor

200 Noll Plaza, Huntington, IN 46750
Toll free: **1-800-348-2440**
Website: www.osv.com